UNESCO Study Abroad | Études à l'étranger | Estudios en el extranjero

http://www.unesco.org/studyabroad

English	Table of Contents	Eng-v
Français	Sommaire	Fr-v
Español	Índice	Esp-v

International Scholarships and Courses
Bourses et Cours Internationaux
Becas y Cursos Internacionales

International Organizations

1 **Abdus Salam International Centre for Theoretical Physics [ICTP]**
Strada Costiera 11
34014 Trieste, Italy
Tel: +39-40-224-0111
Fax: +39-40-224-163
Web: http://www.ictp.it
e-mail: sci_info@ictp.it

📖 Theoretical physics

Study Domains: physics, sciences.
Programmes: (a) courses in physics; (b) ICTP Diploma Course.
Description: (a) training in physics of condensed matter, physics of high and intermediate energies; mathematics, physics and energy, physics of the environment, physics of the living state, applied physics; (b) high energy physics, condensed matter physics, mathematics; maximum 10 participants per year in each field.
Open to: (a) applicants from UN, IAEA or UNESCO Member States; (b) nationals of developing countries, which are UN, IAEA or UNESCO Member States.
Academic requirements: (a) at least an MSc with 2 years' experience in physics or mathematics; (b) MSc (or an exceptionally good BSc) in physics or mathematics.
Age limit Max: (b) maximum 28 years of age.
Held: in Italy.
Duration: (a) 1 to 3 weeks; (b) 1 year (September to August).
Fees: tuition free.
Financial assistance: (a) scholarships covering living and/or travel expenses are granted to scientists from developing countries; (b) monthly stipend plus travel expenses where applicable.
Languages: (a) and (b) good knowledge of specialized English.
Applications: (a) to (title of activity), ICTP, at the above address; (b) by 31 December of preceding year, to Diploma Course, ICTP.

🎓 Research grants and postdoctoral fellowships

Study Domains: earth science, mathematics, meteorology, physics.
Scholarships: (a) research grants; (b) research grants; (c) postdoctoral fellowships.
Description: (a) physics of condensed matter; physics and energy; earth and environmental sciences; physics of the living state; physics and technology; (b) condensed matter physics, high energy and astroparticle physics, mathematics, physics of weather and climate, radiopropagation, structure and nonlinear dynamics of the Earth; (c) condensed matter physics, high energy and astroparticle physics, mathematics, physics of weather and climate.
Open to: (a) applicants from all developing countries which are Member States of the UN, IAEA or UNESCO; (c) nationals from UN, IAEA or UNESCO Member States.
Academic requirements: (a) at least an MSc with 2 years' experience; PhD an asset; (b) at least an MSc in physics or mathematics plus 2 years' experience; (c) PhD in physics or mathematics.
Place of study: (a) academic and industrial laboratories in Italy; (b) and (c) at ICTP.
Duration: (a) 1 year (plus 6 to 8 months extension); (b) 1 to 12 months; (c) 1 year (renewable).
Value: (a) round-trip contribution, monthly salary and allowances; amount of stipend depends on qualification and seniority; (b) and (c) monthly stipend, round-trip where applicable, and allowances according to length of visit.
Languages: English. Good knowledge of specialized English required.
Applications: (a) to 'ICTP Programme for Training and Research in Italian Laboratories', ICTP, at the above address; (b) and (c) to the Secretary of (relevant) Research Group, ICTP.

1 **Abdus Salam Centre international de physique théorique [ICTP]**
Strada Costiera 11
34014 Trieste, Italie
Tel: +39-40-224-0111
Fax: +39-40-224-163
Web: http://www.ictp.it
e-mail: sci_info@ictp.it

📖 Physique théorique

Domaines d'étude: physique, sciences.
Programmes: (a) physique; (b) cours conduisant au diplôme du CIPT.
Description: (a) cours dans les domaines suivants: physique de la matière condensée, physique de haute énergie, mathématiques, physique et énergie, physique et environnement, physique de l'état vivant, physique appliquée; (b) Cours conduisant au diplôme du CIPT dans les domaines suivants: physique de haute énergie, physique de la matière condensée, mathématiques; maximum 10 participants par an par programme.
A l'intention de: (a) ressortissants des États membres de l'ONU, l'AIEA ou de l'UNESCO; (b) ressortissants des pays en développement, qui sont États membres de l'ONU, l'AIEA ou de l'UNESCO.
Qualifications requises: (a) candidats titulaires au minimum d'une maîtrise ès sciences en physique ou mathématiques; plus deux années d'expériences professionnelles; (b) candidats titulaires d'une maîtrise ès sciences ou titre équivalent en physique ou mathématiques.
Age Max.: 28 ans.
Organisés: en Italie.
Durée: (a) de 1 à 3 semaines; (b) 1 an, débutant en septembre jusqu'en août.
Frais: scolarité gratuite.
Assistance financière: (a) des bourses couvrant les frais de subsistance et/ou de voyage sont accordées aux scientifiques des pays en développement; (b) allocation mensuelle plus frais de voyage.
Connaissances linguistiques: bonnes connaissances d'anglais technique.
Inscriptions: (a) à (intitulé de l'activité), CIPT, à l'adresse ci-dessus; (b) avant le 31 décembre de l'année précédant les cours du diplôme du CIPT, à l'adresse ci-dessus.

🎓 Bourses de recherche et postdoctorales

Domaines d'étude: mathématiques, météorologie, physique, sciences de la terre.
Bourses: (a), (b) bourses de recherche; (c) bourses postdoctorales.
Description: (a) physique de la matière condensée; physique et énergie; sciences de la terre et de l'environnement; physique de l'état vivant; physique et technologie; (b) physique de la matière condensée, mathématiques, microprocesseurs, communications, radiopropagation; (c) physique de la matière condensée, mathématiques; météorologie.
A l'intention de: (a) ressortissants des pays en développement, membres de l'Organisation des Nations Unies, titulaires au minimum du diplôme «M.Sc.» ou de préférence d'un «Ph.D.», plus 2 années d'expérience professionnelle; (b) ressortissants des pays membres des Nations Unies, de l'Agence internationale de l'énergie atomique ou de l'UNESCO, possédant au minimum un «M.Sc» en physique ou mathématiques et ayant 2 années d'expérience professionnelle; (c) ressortissants des pays membres des Nations Unies, de l'Agence internationale de l'énergie atomique ou de l'UNESCO, titulaires d'un «Ph.D.» en physique ou en mathématiques. Bonne connaissance de l'anglais technique requise (la langue de travail est uniquement l'anglais).
Lieu: (a) laboratoires académiques et industriels en Italie; (b) et (c) au CIPT.
Durée: (a) 1 an (plus 6 à 8 mois de prolongation); (b) de 1 à 12 mois; (c) 1 an (renouvelable).
Valeur: (a) contribution aux frais de voyage, salaire mensuel et allocations. Le montant du traitement dépend de l'ancienneté et des qualifications; (b) et (c) traitement mensuel, frais de voyage si applicable et allocations selon la durée du séjour.

Connaissances linguistiques: anglais.
Candidatures: (a) s'adresser à «Programme CIPT de formation et de recherche en laboratoires italiens», CIPT, à l'adresse ci-dessus; (b) et (c) au Secrétaire du groupe de recherche concerné, au CIPT.

1 Centro Internacional de Física Teórica Abdus Salam [ICTP]

Strada Costiera 11
34014 Trieste, Italia
Tel: +39-40-224-0111
Fax: +39-40-224-163
Web: http://www.ictp.it
e-mail: sci_info@ictp.it

📖 Fisíca teórica

Campos de estudios: ciencias, física.
Programas: (a) Cursos en diversas áreas de la física; (b) cursos conducentes al Diploma del CIFT.
Descripción: (a) física de la materia condensada, física de energías intermedia y alta, matemáticas, física y energía, física del medio ambiente, física del estado vivo, física aplicada; (b) física de la alta energía, física de la materia condensada, física y matemáticas; máximo de 10 participantes por año para cada programa.
Se destina(n): (a) a nacionales de Estados Miembros del NU, IAEA o UNESCO; (b) a nacionales de países en desarrollo (que son miembros del UN, IAEA o UNESCO).
Diplomas requeridos: (a) que tengan por lo menos una maestría en ciencias y 2 años de experiencia en física o en matemáticas; (b) que tengan maestría en ciencias (o excelentes calificaciones de licenciatura) en física o matemáticas.
Edad Max.: (b) menores de 28 años.
Se dicta(n): en Italia.
Duración: (a) de 1 a 3 semanas; (b) 1 año (comienzan en septiembre hasta agosto).
Costo(s): la enseñanza es gratuita.
Asistencia financiera: (a) se conceden becas que cubren los gastos de viaje y/o de mantenimiento a científicos de los países en desarrollo; (b) estipendio mensual más gastos de viaje, cuando corresponda.
Idioma: muy buen nivel de inglés técnico.
Inscripciones: (a) en (título de la actividad), ICTP, en la dirección que figura en el título; (b) antes del 31 de diciembre del año anterior al curso del Diploma del ICTP, en la dirección que figura en el título.

📖 Becas de investigación y de posdoctorado

Campos de estudios: ciencias de la tierra, física, matemáticas, meteorología.
Becas: (a) y (b) becas de investigación; (c) becas de posdoctorado.
Descripción: (a) física de la materia condensada; física y energía; ciencias de la tierra y del medio ambiente; física del estado vivo; física y tecnología; (b) física de la materia condensada, física de energías intermedia y alta, matemáticas, microprocesadores, comunicaciones, radiopropagación; (c) física de energías intermedia y alta, física de la materia condensada, matemáticas.
Se conceden: (a) a nacionales de países en desarrollo, miembros de la Organización de las Naciones Unidas, que posean como mínimo una maestría en ciencias, más 2 años de experiencia profesional; se apreciarán los doctorados; (b) a nacionales de países miembros de las Naciones Unidas, de la Agencia Internacional de la Energía Atómica o de la UNESCO, que posean como mínimo una maestría en física o matemáticas, más 2 años de experiencia profesional; (c) a nacionales de países miembros de las Naciones Unidas, de la Agencia Internacional de la Energía Atómica o de la UNESCO, que posean como mínimo un diploma de doctorado en física o matemáticas. Se requiere un buen conocimiento del inglés especializado.
Lugar: (a) laboratorios académicos e industriales de Italia; (b) y (c) en el CIFT.
Duración: (a) 1 año (renovable por 6 u 8 meses más); (b) de 1 a 12 meses; (c) 1 año (renovable).
Importe: (a) contribución para el viaje de ida y vuelta, salario mensual y estipendio. El monto del estipendio depende de las calificaciones y de la antigüedad; (b) y (c) el monto del salario mensual, de la contribución al pago del viaje de ida y vuelta y del estipendio se establecen en función de la duración de la estadía.

Idioma: inglés.
Solicitudes: dirigirse a: (a) "Programa CIFT de formación e investigación en laboratorios italianos"; (b) y (c) al Secretario del Grupo de Investigación correspondiente. En todos los casos la dirección es la que figura en el título.

2 African Institute for Economic Development and Planning [IDEP]

PO Box 3186
Dakar, Senegal
Tel: +221-823-1020
Fax: +221-822-2964
Web: http://www.unidep.org
e-mail: info@unidep.org

📖 Training programmes in development planning

Study Domains: development studies, international studies, political economy.
Programmes: (a) Master of Arts programme in economic development and planning leading to the degree of M.A. in economic policy and management; (b) sectoral specialization courses; (c) tailor-made economic management training workshops.
Description: (a) provides a solid mastery of analytical and technical skills necessary to handle policy issues in macroeconomic management, structural adjustment, growth and sustained development in African economies; (b) provision of training on planning and management of priority sectors of the African economy and on other key themes in economic development in the following areas: agricultural policy analysis, industrial development, long-term perspective studies (NLTPS), science and technology policy analysis and gender in development; (c) covering policy analysis and strategic management, debt and foreign exchange management, project analysis and management, capital markets and private sector development, economic reform (design, analysis and management), and economic cooperation and integration.
Open to: nationals of African countries with first degree (B.A.) or equivalent in economics or related discipline with a minimum of 2 year's experience in government or an institution dealing with development issues or involved in implementation of economic policies at the national, sectoral or project levels; candidates must be nominated by government agencies or non-governmental developmental agencies.
Duration: (a) 18 months; (b) 3 months each; (c) depends on client's request.
Financial assistance: according to the resolutions of IDEP's Governing Council, UNDP Governing Council and the ECA Conference of Ministers of Development and Planning, fellowships covering allowances and travel expenses can be financed from various bilateral and multilateral sponsoring agencies, e.g. country UNDP-IPF or ACBF funds, World Bank, French Agency for Development, ILO, FAO, CFTC, USAID, IDRC, CIDA, GTZ, etc.; stipends include prorata monthly living allowance, allocation for books, medical and travel expenses and tuition fee.
Applications: to IDEP for further information.

2 Institut africain de développement économique et de planification [IDEP]

BP 3186
Dakar, Sénégal
Tel: +221-823-1020
Fax: +221-822-2964
Web: http://www.unidep.org
e-mail: info@unidep.org

📖 Programme de formation en planification du développement

Domaines d'étude: économie politique, études du développement, études internationales.
Programmes: (a) programme de formation conduisant à la maîtrise en planification du développement économique; (b) programme de spécialisation; (c) ateliers sur mesure consacrés à la gestion de l'économie.
Description: (a) cours de base sur l'analyse des politiques macro-économiques: la gestion et la planification: développement économique et transformations structurelles,

analyse macro-économique et stratégies de mise au point, méthodes quantitatives de la planification et de l'élaboration des politiques économiques, planification économique régionale, planification du développement national, économie internationale, évaluation de projets; (b) cours sur le développement industriel en Afrique: énergie, environnement et développement en Afrique, développement des ressources humaines et planification de la main-d'œuvre en Afrique, agriculture et développement rural en Afrique, participation masculine et féminine au développement; (c) cours couvrant l'analyse politique, les stratégies de gestion, la gestion de la dette et des devises, l'analyse et la gestion de projets de marchés financiers et le développement du secteur privé, la réforme économique (mise au point, analyse, gestion), la coopération économique et l'intégration.
A l'intention de: ressortissants des pays africains, titulaires d'un diplôme universitaire (niveau licence) ou équivalent en économie ou dans toute discipline apparentée, et possédant un minimum de 2 ans d'expérience au service de leur gouvernement ou d'une institution concernée par le développement économique. Les candidats doivent être nommés par leur gouvernement ou par des agences de développement non gouvernementales.
Durée: (a) 18 mois; (b) 3 mois; (c) varie selon la demande du client.
Assistance financière: traitement et allocations financés principalement par le chiffre indicatif des résolutions du Conseil exécutif d'IDEP et de la Conférence des ministres du développement et de la planification de l'ECA; possibilité également d'obtenir une assistance financière par l'intermédiaire des gouvernements, auprès des agences multilatérales et bilatérales d'assistance technique, telles que la Banque mondiale, l'Organisation des Nations Unies pour le développement industriel, le Bureau international du travail, l'Agence des États-Unis pour le développement international, l'Agence (française) pour la coopération culturelle et technique, le Centre (canadien) de recherches pour le développement international, le Fonds du Commonwealth pour la coopération technique, etc. Les bourses couvrent les frais mensuels de subsistance proprement dits, indemnités d'achats de livres, frais médicaux, frais de voyage et frais d'inscription.
Inscriptions: s'adresser à l'IDEP pour de plus amples renseignements.

2 Instituto Africano de Desarrollo Económico y Planeamiento [IDEP]

BP 3186
Dakar, Senegal
Tel: +221-823-1020
Fax: +221-822-2964
Web: http://www.unidep.org
e-mail: info@unidep.org

📖 Programas de formación en planificación del desarrollo

Campos de estudios: economía política, estudios internacionales, estudios sobre el desarrollo.
Programas: (a) programa sobre desarrollo económico y planeamiento; (b) cursos de especialización sectorial; (c) seminarios a medida sobre gestión económica.
Descripción: (a) maestría en políticas económicas y gestión; su objetivo es lograr un completo dominio de los conocimientos analíticos y técnicos para la elaboración de planes de gestión macroeconómica, ajuste estructural, crecimiento y desarrollo sustentable en las economías africanas; (b) cursos en áreas de planeamiento y gestión en sectores prioritarios de la economía africana y en otros temas claves del desarrollo económico, en particular: análisis de políticas agrícolas, desarrollo industrial, estudios de perspectivas a largo plano (NLTPS), análisis de políticas científicas y tecnológicas, rol de hombres y mujeres en el desarrollo; (c) cursos incluyendo análisis de políticas y gestión de estrategias, gestión de la deuda y cambio de moneda extranjera, análisis y gestión de proyectos, mercados de capital y desarrollo del sector privado, reformas económicas (diseño, análisis y gestión), y cooperación económica e integración.
Se destina(n): a nacionales de países africanos con título de licenciado o equivalente en economía o disciplina afín, con un mínimo de 2 años de experiencia en gobierno o en

institución que se ocupe de temas de desarrollo o que intervenga en la implementación de políticas económicas a nivel nacional, sectorial o de proyectos; los candidatos deben ser designados por agencias gubernamentales o agencias no gubernamentales para el desarrollo.
Duración: (a) 18 meses; (b) 3 meses cada uno; (c) según las necesidades del cliente.
Asistencia financiera: de acuerdo a las resoluciones del Consejo de Gobierno del IDEP, del Consejo de Gobierno del UNDP y de la Conferencia ECA de Ministros de Planeamiento y Desarrollo, las becas que cubren asignaciones y gastos de viaje, pueden ser financiadas por diversas agencias patrocinadoras bilaterales y multilaterales, por ejemplo fondos locales de UNDP-IPF o ACBF, Banco Mundial, Agencia francesa para el desarrollo, ILO, FAO, CFTC, USAID, IDRC, CIDA, GTZ, etc.; los estipendios incluyen una asignación mensual de subsistencia, monto para libros, gastos médicos, viaje y gastos de enseñanza.
Inscripciones: solicitar más informaciones a IDEP.

3 Asian Development Bank Office of Cofinancing Operations [ADB]

6 ADB Avenue
Mandaluyong City
1550 Metro Manila, Philippines
Fax: +63-2-636-2456
Web: http://www.adb.org
e-mail: adbjsp@adb.org

🕊 Asian Development Bank-Japan Scholarship Program

Study Domains: development studies, management, natural sciences, technology.
Description: for postgraduate studies in selected institutions in the Asian and Pacific region; the programme is funded by the Government of Japan and administered by the ADB.
Subjects: studies in economics, management, science and technology, and other development-related fields.
Duration: for periods of one to three years.
Applications: for application information see website http://www.adb.org/jsp or contact Office of Cofinancing Operations at the above address; adbjsp@adb.org.

4 Asian Institute of Technology [AIT]

PO Box 4
Klong Luang
12120 Pathumthani, Thailand
Tel: +66-2-516-0110
Fax: +66-2-516-2126
Web: http://www.ait.ac.th
e-mail: webteam@ait.ac.th

📖 Master's and Doctoral Degrees, Diploma and Certificate Programmes

Study Domains: ecology, environment, engineering, management, sciences, technology.
Programmes: Master's and Doctoral Degrees, Diploma and Certificate Programmes; International Caliber Courses offered in four Schools: Advanced Technologies (SAT); Civil Engineering (SCE); School of Environment, Resources and Development (SERD); School of Management (SOM).
Open to: well-qualified nationals from Asian countries and beyond; candidates for Master's degree programmes must have Bachelor's degree or equivalent from a recognized institution in appropriate field of study, undergraduate grades above average, proficiency in English and a certificate of physical fitness; for the doctoral programme, candidates must have a Master's degree or equivalent from a recognized institution, with graduate grades above average.
Duration: (a) 16 to 20 months for Master's programme; 36 months for doctoral programme; (b) variable.
Fees: tuition: approximately US$325 per credit hour; estimated living expenses: US$1,200 per semester.
Financial assistance: assistance to qualified students for minimum terms required for a degree programme, to cover any or all of the following: tuition and fees, bursary, textbooks and travel grants; awards are made on the principle that students must contribute to the cost of their education from their personal resources, as far as possible.

Applications: further information may be obtained from the Chief Admission Officer, at the above address.

☞ AIT Postdoctoral Fellowships

Study Domains: civil engineering, ecology, environment, industrial technology, management, technology.
Scholarships: AIT Postdoctoral Fellowships.
Open to: all Asian nationals, recent doctoral graduates of exceptional promise wishing to undertake further research on a full-time basis.
Duration: 6 months to 1 year.
Value: a stipend of Baht 30,000 per month; round-trip economy airfare from the city of origin to Bangkok; no provision for travel expenses of family members; postdoctoral fellows will be provided office space and access to the library and other academic facilities of AIT.
Applications: by 15 July to the Office of the Provost; email: provost@ait.ac.th.

5   Association of African Universities [AAU]

PO Box 5744
Accra-North, Ghana
Tel: +233-21-774-495 / 761-588
Fax: +233-21-774-821
Web: http://www.aau.org
e-mail: programs@aau.org

☞ Staff Exchange Programme

Study Domains: all major fields.
Scholarships: Staff Exchange Programme.
Subjects: higher education management.
Open to: African university staff.
Place of study: universities in African countries.
Duration: 1 to 3 months.
Value: payment of passage and/or honorarium.
Applications: to the Secretary General; announcements made around July; deadline for application: 2 months after announcement.

5   Association des universités africaines [AUA]

PO Box 5744
Accra-North, Ghana
Tel: +233-21-774-495 / 761-588
Fax: +233-21-774-821
Web: http://www.aau.org
e-mail: programs@aau.org

☞ Programme d'échange de personnel

Domaines d'étude: toutes disciplines principales.
Bourses: Programme d'échange de personnel.
A l'intention de: personnel des universités africaines.
Lieu: universités des pays africains.
Durée: de 1 à 3 mois.
Valeur: paiement des frais de voyage et/ou honoraires.
Candidatures: au Secrétaire général; annonces en juillet; date limite d'envoi: 2 mois après l'annonce.

6   Association of Commonwealth Universities [ACU]

John Foster House
36 Gordon Square
WC1H 0PF London, United Kingdom
Tel: +44-20-7380-6700
Fax: +44-20-7387-2655
Web: http://www.acu.ac.uk
e-mail: info@acu.ac.uk

☞ Association of Commonwealth Universities (ACU) Awards

Study Domains: all major fields, administration, communication, health and hygiene, management of human resources, medicine, nutrition, public relations.
Scholarships: (a) Titular Fellowships (up to 20 annually); (b) ACU/FCO Chevening Scholarships (Human Resource Management) (Public Communication and Public Relations Programme); (c) British Academy/Association of Commonwealth Universities: Grants for International Collaboration; (d) Canada Memorial Foundation Scholarships; (e) CUSAC Bursaries for Undergraduate Exchange; (f) Edward Boyle Memorial Trust Medical Electives Bursaries.
Description: (a) unrestricted (subject to terms of specific Titular awards), but preference for fields in which the needs of developing countries are great; not intended for degree courses; (b) support to full-time study on the MA degree (in either Human Resource Management or Public Communication and Public Relations at the University of Westminster, to (1) improve human resources management in higher education in developing countries, or (2) to provide opportunity to share best practices in public relations, media and external communications. Funded jointly by the ACU, the FCO, the Univ. of Westminster & International Students House London; (c): for advanced research at postdoctoral level or above to support international joint activities involving British scholars in collaboration with Commonwealth partners. Priority given to new programmes with an expectation of continued collaboration or a defined outcome such as planned joint publications; (d) for taught postgraduate studies leading to a university degree; (e) CUSAC is a group of universities from across the Commonwealth committed to increasing opportunities for students from developing CUSAC countries to study abroad through bilateral exchanges; bursaries are awarded yearly for student exchange programmes between CUSAC member institutions; (f) bursaries aim to enable medical students in Britain to gain, during their elective period, practical experience in developing Commonwealth countries (particularly those that are least developed or specially disadvantaged) and to help understaffed hospitals in those countries.
Subjects: (a), (d), (e) all major fields, but preference for fields in which the needs of developing countries are great; (b) management of human resources; communications/public relations; (c) humanities and social sciences; (f) health, hygiene, medicine, nutrition.
Open to: (a) staff of university of ACU membership or of Commonwealth inter-university organization or working in industry, commerce or public service in a Commonwealth country. It is not a postdoctoral or degree-earning scheme. Small-scale conference attendance within a study programme allowed, but applications will not be considered where major conference attendance is primary or sole purpose; (b) (1) candidates currently working in human resources or personnel departments of the Association of Commonwealth Universities (ACU) member universities in developing countries; (2) administrative or related staff currently employed by ACU member universities in developing countries; (c) staff of Association of Commonwealth Universities (ACU) member universities; (d) must be United Kingdom citizen and holder of first degree or equivalent (at least upper second class honours), or undergraduate in final year with proven academic record. Some knowledge of Canada required; (e) candidates enrolled in an undergraduate course at a CUSAC member institution; (f) senior medical students from United Kingdom medical faculties/schools.
Age limit Max: (d) 30 years of age in general.
Other conditions: (b) (1) preference given to candidates who combine a strong record of achievement in their careers and have clear plans for using acquired information on return to their countries; (2) candidates should hold good honours degrees or equivalent, although professional qualifications or substantial work experience may be acceptable. In all cases, award holders must return to their universities on completion of programme.
Place of study: (a) unless otherwise stipulated, in any Commonwealth country other than candidate's own;(b) University of Westminster (www.wmin.ac.uk); (c) in Commonwealth countries; (d): any university or other appropriate institution in Canada subject to approval of Canada Memorial Foundation; (e) at other CUSAC member institutions in other countries where an exchange agreement and preferably a credit transfer arrangement exists; (f) in hospitals or other medical establishments in a developing Commonwealth country.
Duration: (a) maximum of 6 months; (c) one year; (d) normally 1 year; (e) 1 or 2 semesters for credit towards the candidate's qualification at their home university; (f) elective period of student.
Value: (a) up to a maximum of £5,000 for travel, board, insurance, fees other than bench fees; (b) full cost of study, including return airfare, fees and maintenance allowance; (c) up to £5,000 per year for research expenditure, travel and living costs in partner country (or countries); funded jointly

by British Academy and ACU; (d) maintenance allowance, return airfare, approved fees, books, thesis, travel and health insurance allowance; (e) return airfare and a single payment of £500 towards maintenance costs; (f) up to £500 to cover part of the travel, subsistence and local costs of the student.
Languages: English.
Applications: See website http://www.acu.ac.uk for full details regarding ACU awards
(a) to be received in London by 31 August; candidates must be nominated by executive head of university in ACU membership or by chief executive officer of a Commonwealth inter-university organization; (b) directly to ACU by 30 April; (c) by 30 September; only submissions by British partner will be considered. Direct applications to the ACU will neither be taken into account nor acknowledged; (d) directly to ACU by third Friday in October; (e) by 20 May, through home university (check with international office where bursaries are often advertised); see website for further details www.acu.ac.uk/cusac; (f) by 31 January: applications must be requested from and submitted in the first instance to the medical dean of student's medical school and NOT to the ACU.

☞ Commonwealth Scholarship and Fellowship Plan (CSFP)

Study Domains: all major fields, distance education.
Scholarships: (a) Commonwealth Academic Fellowships (up to 70 annually); (b) Commonwealth Professional Fellowships (up to 50 annually); (c) Commonwealth Scholarships and Fellowships; (d) Commonwealth Shared Scholarship Scheme; (e) Scholarships by Distance Learning (up to 100 annually).
Description: (a) for academic staff in developing Commonwealth countries; (b) opportunities for individuals working in key occupations in developing Commonwealth countries to spend a short period of professional updating in the United Kingdom (not intended for those undertaking fulltime study, those seeking assistance for cost of commencing or completing formal academic/professional qualifications, or to develop academic research for its own sake); (c) total of up to 200 awards of varying schemes (Commonwealth Scholarships; Commonwealth Academic Staff Scholarships; Commonwealth Split-Site Doctoral Scholarships), primarily for postgraduate study or research in all subjects; (d) for taught postgraduate courses at Master's level at participating institutions in the UK (150-200 annually); (e) for postgraduate study; offered in partnership with institutions in developing Commonwealth countries.
Open to: (a) open only to Commonwealth citizens or British protected persons who have completed their doctorate no less than five years previous to award. Must be permanently resident in and on the teaching staff of a university institution in a developing Commonwealth country; (b) only to citizens of and residents in, a developing Commonwealth country with at least 5 years' appropriate experience in a profession relevant to the subject of the application. Fellows can be drawn from any sector, but must not hold a full-time academic appointment (the Commission operates a separate competition for academic fellowships); (c) Commonwealth citizens and British protected persons who have completed a first degree or Master's degree, and are permanently resident in Commonwealth countries other than the United Kingdom; (d) students from developing Commonwealth countries, who are not already living in and have not already studied in a developed country, for studies in the United Kingdom. Employees of a government department or parastatal organization are ineligible (except for university employees). Priority given to candidates from least developed countries and to candidates under 30 years of age.
Age limit Max: contact local agency as listed on CSFP website for age limits: http://www.csfp-online.org.
Academic requirements: (a) doctorate or other postgraduate qualification, plus at least 2 years' teaching experience normally required.
Place of study: (a) at university-level institutions; (b) at appropriate host organizations in the United Kingdom; (c) at approved institution of higher learning; (d) at participating institutions in the United Kingdom; (e) selected postgraduate taught countries at UK universities.
Duration: (a) 6 months; (b) normally 3 months, exceptionally 6 months; (c) variable from 2 periods of 6 months, to 36 months, according to scheme; (d) one year; (e) for the duration of the course of study concerned.

Value: (a) maintenance and travel allowances; (b) living costs while in the United Kingdom, return airfares to the United Kingdom, allowance for travel and a contribution towards the costs of the host organization. Other costs may be met subject to individual approval; (c) university fees, scholar's return travel, book allowance, apparatus, approved study travel, personal maintenance (plus allowances, where applicable, for spouses and children; (d) full cost of study, including return airfare, maintenance and thesis allowance.
Applications: See website http://www.csfp-online.org for full details regarding CSFP awards and email address of local agencies.
(a) by nomination of candidate's university; to be received in London by 31 December; (b) to be made by organizations based in the United Kingdom able to host fellows. Each host organization can nominate up to 6 individuals in their application. Applications must contain the details of the programme to be followed in the United Kingdom. (Nominating and host organization expected to be the same wherever possible.) Direct applications from individuals cannot be accepted; nominations should be received by 31 May; (c) variable, see website www.csfp-online.org for details; (e) to participating institutions and NOT to the ACU; closing date: April/May; check with specific institutions for precise closing dates; (e) direct to the United Kingdom provider, by November of year preceding start of course.

☞ Marshall Aid Commemoration Commission (MACC)

Study Domains: all major fields.
Scholarships: (a) Marshall Scholarships; (b) Marshall Sherfield Fellowships.
Description: (a) Marshall Scholarships finance young Americans of high ability to study for a degree in the United Kingdom, at graduate or occasionally undergraduate (40 annually); (b) fellowships for American scientists or engineers to undertake post-doctoral research for a period of one to two academic years at a British university or research institute (2 annually).
Nationality: (a) United States citizens who have obtained first degree from accredited university or college in the United States within the last 3 years with a minimum Grade Point Average (GPA) of 3.7; (b) United States citizens only.
Place of study: (a) United Kingdom (for a British degree); (b) United Kingdom university or research institute.
Duration: (a) for 2 academic years (possibility of 1-year extension in some institutions); (b) one or two years.
Value: (a) tuition, books, travel and living costs; (b) laboratory/research support grant, travel and living costs.
Applications: Online application and details available at: www.marshallscholarship.org.
(a) applications must be submitted and authorized by a designated member of staff at the applicant's educational institution (or employer), usually by early October preceding year of award. Applications to local selection committee in the United States; (b) by early October preceding year of award to local selection committees in the United States.

7 Caribbean Institute for Meteorology and Hydrology [CIMH]
PO Box 130
Bridgetown, Barbados
Tel: +1-246-425-1362
Fax: +1-246-424-4733
Web: http://www.cimh.edu.bb

📖 B.Sc. degree in meteorology and operational hydrology

Study Domains: hydrology, meteorology.
Programmes: B.Sc. degree in meteorology and operational hydrology.
Description: B.Sc. degree in association with the University of the West Indies, and other courses through lectures and practical work in meteorology and operational hydrology: maximum 15 participants.
Open to: forecasters and technicians of all nationalities; Cambridge GCE Ordinary Levels (or equivalent); minimum age: 17.
Duration: 3 years (courses begin in September) for B.Sc.; variable for other courses.

Languages: English.
Applications: by 15 July, to the Principal.

7 Institut météorologique des Caraïbes
BP 130
Bridgetown, Barbade
Tel: +1-246-425-1362
Fax: +1-246-424-4733
Web: http://www.cimh.edu.bb

📖 Cours en météorologie et hydrologie opérationnelle
Domaines d'étude: hydrologie, météorologie.
Programmes: cours en météorologie et hydrologie opérationnelle.
Description: Programme de cours et travaux pratiques conduisant au « B.Sc.» et à d'autres diplômes en météorologie et hydrologie opérationnelle (en anglais); 15 participants au maximum.
A l'intention de: météorologues et techniciens en météorologie de tout pays, titulaires du «Cambridge GCE Ordinary Levels» ou diplôme équivalent; âge minimum: 17 ans.
Durée: 3 ans (débutant en septembre) pour le « B.Sc.»; variable pour les autres diplômes.
Connaissances linguistiques: Anglais.
Inscriptions: avant le 15 juillet, s'adresser au Directeur.

8 College of Europe-Bruges
Dyver 11
8000 Bruges, Belgium
Tel: +32-50-477-111
Fax: +32-50-477-110
Web: http://www.coleurop.be
e-mail: bderyckere@coleurop.be

📖 Graduate Programme / European Studies
Study Domains: administration, economy, European studies, law.
Programmes: Masters Degree of European Studies.
Subjects: 4 departments (economics, human resources development, law, politics and administration).
Nationality: candidates of EU countries.
Academic requirements: university degree in related areas.
Age limit Max: under 30 years of age.
Other conditions: see http://www.coleurop.be/requirements.htm.
Duration: one academic year from mid-September to the end of June.
Financial assistance: The College of Europe does not itself grant scholarships; however, most students are granted scholarships by their government or by another public or private institution. For information regarding these scholarships, contact the selection committee of your country before the closing date set by that committee (see website for further information).
Languages: The two working languages of the College are English and French. A good working knowledge of both is an essential condition for admission.
Applications: candidates must submit a formal application for admission to the selection committee in the candidate's country or region and to the Admissions Office of the College of Europe in Bruges, before the closing date. In cases where there is no local selection committee, applications can be sent directly to the Admissions Office at the above address.

8 Collège d'Europe-Bruges
Dyver 11
8000 Bruges, Belgique
Tel: +32-50-477-111
Fax: +32-50-477-110
Web: http://www.coleurop.be
e-mail: bderyckere@coleurop.be

📖 Études européennes
Domaines d'étude: administration, droit, économie, études européennes.
Description: diplôme d'études européennes approfondies.
Domaines d'études: 4 départements (développement des ressources humaines, droit, économie, et études politiques et administratives).
Nationalité: ressortissants de l'UE.
Qualifications requises: être titulaire d'un diplôme universitaire en droit, économie, sciences politiques, sciences sociales ou relations internationales.
Age Max.: Age maximum: 30 ans.
Autres conditions: consulter www.coleurop.be/requirements.htm.
Durée: une année académique.
Assistance financière: Le Collège d'Europe n'octroie pas de bourses, mais la plupart des étudiants sont boursiers des gouvernements nationaux ou d'institutions privées ou publiques. Pour plus de renseignements concernant ces bourses, contactez le comité de sélection de votre pays (voir le site web).
Connaissances linguistiques: l'enseignement est donné en français et en anglais.
Inscriptions: Les candidats doivent présenter leur candidature auprès du comité de sélection de leur pays ou région, et auprès du Bureau des admissions du Collège d'Europe-Bruges, avant la date limite de dépôt. S'il n'y a pas de comité de sélection local, les candidatures peuvent être envoyées directement au Bureau des admissions, à l'adresse ci-dessus.

8 Colegio de Europa
Dyver 11
8000 Brujas, Bélgica
Tel: +32-50-477-111
Fax: +32-50-477-110
Web: http://www.coleurop.be
e-mail: bderyckere@coleurop.be

📖 Programa de estudios europeos
Campos de estudios: administración, derecho, economía, estudios europeos.
Descripción: programa postuniversitario de estudios europeos.
Materias de estudio: 4 departamentos (desarrollo de recursos humanos, derecho, economía y estudios políticos y administrativos).
Nacionalidad: nacionales de países de la Unión Europea.
Diplomas requeridos: titulación universitaria en áreas afines.
Edad Max.: 30 años.
Duración: 1 año académico.
Asistencia financiera: El Colegio de Europa no otorga becas, pero la mayoría de los estudiantes obtienen becas de sus gobiernos o de instituciones privadas o públicas. Por información relativa a dichas becas, dirigirse al comité de selección de cada país (consultar el sitio web).
Idioma: la enseñanza se imparte en francés y en inglés.
Inscripciones: los candidatos deben presentar la solicitud de admisión al comité de selección del país o región, y a la Oficina de Admisiones del Colegio de Europa- Brujas. Si no existe comité de selección local, la solicitud puede enviarse directamente a la Oficina de Admisiones, en la dirección que figura más arriba.

9 Esperanto Foundation
37, Granville Court
Cheney Lane
OX3 OHS Oxford
Tel: +44-1865-245-509
Web: http://esperanto.org/uk/nojef/

📖 Research Grants
Study Domains: Esperanto.
Description: grants for research into teaching of Esperanto.
Open to: candidates of all nationality.
Other conditions: research results must be published.
Value: variable.
Applications: to above address. See website http://www.mintex.demon.co.uk/espinfo/uk/nojef/stip_en.htm for further information.

10 European Commission [EU]

DG Education and Culture
Unit A2 - Jean Monnet Project
Rue Belliard, 7 (B-7 8/06)
1049 Brussels, Belgium
Tel: +32-2-296-0312
Fax: +32-2-296-3106
Web: http://www.europa.eu.int
e-mail: Belen.Bernaldo-de-Quiros@cec.eu.int

Grants for Young Researchers

Study Domains: European studies.
Open to: young researchers working on European integration, under 35 years of age and seeking to enhance their research by spending a period of time in another country.
Place of study: in a country other than the candidate's own country.
Duration: no longer than 6 months.
Value: flat-rate payment of 1,000€ per month for a maximum of six months. Additional assistance of up to 1,000€ for travelling costs actually incurred may also be paid. A flat-rate contribution not exceeding 1,000€ may also be granted to the host university.
Applications: to the above address; see website: http://europa.eu.int/comm/education/programmes/ajm/calls/index_en.html.

10 Commission européenne [CE]

DG Education et Culture
Unité A2- Action Jean Monnet
Rue Belliard, 7 (B-7 8/06)
1049 Bruxelles, Belgique
Tel: +32-2-296-0312
Fax: +32-2-296-3106
Web: http://www.europa.eu.int
e-mail: Belen.Bernaldo-de-Quiros@cec.eu.int

Bourses pour des jeunes chercheurs

Domaines d'étude: études européennes.
A l'intention de: jeunes chercheurs âgés de moins de 35 ans souhaitant compléter leur recherche sur l'intégration européenne au début de leur carrière.
Lieu: dans un pays autre que celui du candidat.
Durée: 6 mois maximum.
Valeur: les bourses auront un caractère forfaitaire de 1.000€ par mois pour une période maximale de 6 mois. Une aide supplémentaire pour les frais de voyage pourra être accordée sur base de frais réels avec une limite de 1.000€. Une contribution forfaitaire d'un maximum de 1.000€ pourra également être octroyée à l'université d'accueil.
Candidatures: à l'adresse ci-dessus; voir http://europa.eu.int/comm/education/index_fr.html.

10 Comisión Europea [CE]

DG Educación y Cultura
Unidad A2- Acción Jean Monnet
Rue Belliard, 7 (B-7 8/06)
1049 Bruselas, Bélgica
Tel: +32-2-296-0312
Fax: +32-2-296-3106
Web: http://www.europa.eu.int
e-mail: Belen.Bernaldo-de-Quiros@cec.eu.int

Becas para jóvenes investigadores

Campos de estudios: estudios europeos.
Becas: becas a jóvenes investigadores.
Se conceden: a jóvenes investigadores menores de 35 años que trabajan sobre la integración europea y que deseen completar su investigación en otro país durante un cierto período.
Lugar: en otro país que el del candidato.
Duración: 6 meses como máximo.
Importe: las becas tendrán carácter global y ascenderán a 1.000 € por mes durante un período máximo de seis meses. Podrá concederse una ayuda complementaria para los gastos de viaje, que cubrirá únicamente los gastos reales hasta un máximo de 1.000 €. Podrá concederse igualmente una contribución global de 1.000 € a la universidad de acogida.
Solicitudes: en la dirección que figura más arriba; ver el sitio http://europa.eu.int/comm/education/programmes/ajm/call_en.html.

11 European School of Oncology [ESO]

Via Beatrice D'Este, 37
20122 Milan, Italy
Tel: +39-2-4335-9611
Fax: +39-2-4335-9640
e-mail: info@esoncology.org

ESO Oncology Courses

Study Domains: cancerology, medicine, nursing, surgery.
Description: ESO postgraduate advanced residential courses, training courses and special programmes in all aspects of oncology. Since 1993, ESO has developed a specialized annual programme for French-speaking specialized doctors, generalists and nurses.
Open to: graduates in medicine, surgery and related disciplines, and to oncology nurses; good knowledge of English required.
Held: in various countries and in collaboration with leading oncological institutes and organizations.
Financial assistance: some awards and fellowships available.
Languages: instruction in English.
Applications: to ESO Secretariat for all further information.

11 École européenne d'oncologie [ESO]

Via G. Ripamonti 66
20122 Milan, Italie
Tel: +39-2-4335-9611
Fax: +39-2-4335-9640
e-mail: info@esoncology.org

Cours ESO en oncology

Domaines d'étude: cancérologie, chirurgie, études d'infirmière, médecine.
Description: cours de 3ème cycle, et séminaires et programmes spéciaux sur les divers domaines de l'oncologie (en anglais). Depuis 1993, l'ESO a également mis en place un programme spécial, annuel, à l'attention des médecins spécialistes et des infirmières d'expression française.
A l'intention de: diplômés en médecine, chirurgie et disciplines connexes, et infirmières diplômées en oncologie. Une bonne connaissance de l'anglais est requise.
Organisés: dans divers pays, en collaboration avec des institutions et organismes de pointe dans le domaine de l'oncologie.
Assistance financière: quelques bourses d'études peuvent être octroyées.
Connaissances linguistiques: l'enseignement est donné en anglais.
Inscriptions: s'adresser au Secrétariat de l'ESO pour de plus amples renseignements.

11 Escuela Europea de Oncología [ESO]

Via Beatrice D'Este, 37
20122 Milan, Italia
Tel: +39-2-4335-9611
Fax: +39-2-4335-9640
e-mail: info@esoncology.org

Cursos ESO en oncología

Campos de estudios: cancerología, cirugía, enfermería, medicina.
Descripción: cursos de posgrado, seminarios y programas especiales sobre todos los aspectos de la oncología (en inglés). A partir de 1993, la Escuela Europea de Oncología ha establecido un programa anual especial dedicado a médicos especialistas e internistas y a enfermeras de lengua francesa, y un programa en lengua española dirigido a los profesionales de la salud hispanohablantes. Los cursos y seminarios organizados por ESO-Barcelona están destinados a profesionales de la salud relacionados con la oncología, dentro de un contexto multidisciplinario.
Se destina(n): a diplomados en medicina, cirugía y disciplinas afines, y a enfermeras diplomadas en oncología.
Se dicta(n): en diversos países, en colaboración con institutos y organismos especializados en la esfera de la oncología.

Asistencia financiera: existen algunas becas de estudios disponibles.
Idioma: los cursos se dictan en inglés.
Inscripciones: dirigirse a la Secretaría de la ESO para obtener otras informaciones.

12 Food and Agriculture Organization of the United Nations [FAO]
Viale delle Terme di Caracalla
00100 Rome, Italy
Tel: +39-6-57051
Fax: +39-6-5705-3152
Web: http://www.fao.org

📖 FAO-Organized Training Courses
Study Domains: economy, fisheries, forestry, health and hygiene, natural resources, nutrition, statistics.
Programmes: FAO-organized training courses, seminars and workshops.
Description: covers fields such as animal reproduction and health, atomic energy, economic analysis, fisheries, forestry, land and water development, nutrition, plant production and protection, public information, human resources and statistics.
Open to: high-level participants, mainly government officials; technical officers and intermediate-level personnel. Candidates are nominated by governments of FAO Member States at the invitation of FAO; these technical assistance fellowships are granted only to specialists working in projects managed by FAO in developing countries.
Held: in different FAO Member States.
Duration: 2 weeks to 9 months.
Applications: to relevant government department in candidate's country.

🎓 Technical Assistance Fellowships
Study Domains: agriculture, economy, fisheries, forestry, nutrition, statistics.
Subjects: fields of agriculture, fisheries, forestry, nutrition, agricultural economics and statistics.
Open to: only to specialists working in projects managed by FAO in developing countries.
Applications: through FAO country representative.

12 Organisation des Nations Unies pour l'alimentation et l'agriculture [FAO]
Viale delle Terme di Caracalla
00100 Rome, Italie
Tel: +39-6-57051
Fax: +39-6-5705-3152
Web: http://www.fao.org

📖 Cours de formation organisés par la FAO
Domaines d'étude: économie, hygiène et santé, nutrition, pêche, ressources naturelles, statistique, sylviculture.
Programmes: cours de formation, séminaires et groupes de travail.
Description: dans des domaines d'études tels que production et santé animales, énergie atomique, analyse économique, pêches, forêts et produits forestiers, mise en valeur des terres et des eaux, nutrition, production végétale et protection des plantes, information, ressources humaines, statistiques.
A l'intention de: (a) personnel de niveau élevé, principalement fonctionnaires occupant des postes de responsabilité dans les administrations nationales; (b) fonctionnaires techniques et personnel de niveau intermédiaire. Les candidats sont proposés par les gouvernements des États membres de la FAO sur invitation de celle-ci.
Organisés: dans divers États membres de la FAO.
Durée: de 2 semaines à 9 mois.
Inscriptions: au ministère compétent dans le pays du candidat.

🎓 Bourses d'assistance technique
Domaines d'étude: agriculture, économie, nutrition, pêche, statistique, sylviculture.
A l'intention de: uniquement aux spécialistes employés dans des projets gérés par la FAO dans les pays en développement.

Candidatures: par l'intermédiaire du représentant de la FAO dans le pays du candidat.

12 Organización de las Naciones Unidas para la Alimentación y la Agricultura [FAO]
Viale delle Terme di Caracalla
00100 Roma, Italia
Tel: +39-6-57051
Fax: +39-6-5705-3152
Web: http://www.fao.org

📖 Cursos de capacitación organizados por la FAO
Campos de estudios: economía, estadística, higiene y salud, nutrición, pesquería, recursos naturales, silvicultura.
Programas: cursos de capacitación, seminarios y talleres organizados por la FAO.
Descripción: diversas materias, tales como zootecnia y sanidad animal, energía atómica, análisis económico, pesca, montes y productos forestales, fomento de tierras y aguas, nutrición, fitotecnia y protección fitosanitaria, información pública, recursos humanos, estadística.
Duración: de 2 semanas a 9 meses.
Inscripciones: departamento gubernamental competente del país del candidato.

🎓 Becas de asistencia técnica
Campos de estudios: agricultura, economía, estadística, nutrición, pesquería, silvicultura.
Se conceden: sólo a especialistas que trabajan en proyectos administrados por la FAO en países en desarrollo.
Solicitudes: por mediación del Representante de la FAO en el país del candidato.

13 Ford Foundation, International Fellowships Program [IFP]
809 UN Plaza, 9th Floor
10017 New York, NY, United States
Tel: +1-212-984-5558
Fax: +1-212-984-5594
Web: http://www.fordifp.net
e-mail: query@FordIFP.Net

🎓 International Fellowships Program, Graduate Studies
Study Domains: all major fields.
Description: The International Fellowships Program (IFP) provides support for up to three years of formal graduate-level study leading to a Master's or doctoral degree in any academic discipline or field of study that is consistent with the interests and goals of the Ford Foundation. The Foundation currently works in fifteen fields to strengthen democratic values, reduce poverty and injustice, promote international cooperation, and advance human achievement.
Subjects: IFP Fellows may pursue studies in academic disciplines and fields that are consistent with the Ford Foundation's grantmaking goals to strengthen democratic values, reduce poverty and injustice, promote international cooperation, and advance human achievement.
Open to: resident nationals or residents of an eligible IFP country for graduate studies.
Nationality: nationals of countries where the Ford Foundation maintains active overseas programmes: Brazil, Chile, China, Egypt, Ghana, Guatemala, India, Indonesia, Kenya, Mexico, Mozambique, Nigeria, Palestinian A.T., Peru, Philippines, Russia, Senegal, South Africa, Tanzania, Thailand, Uganda, Vietnam. U.S. nationals are not eligible, although Fellows may study in the United States.
Other conditions: Fellows are chosen on the basis of their leadership potential and commitment to community or national service, as well as for academic excellence.
Applications: to be submitted to the appropriate IFP International Partner in the country or region where the applicant resides; IFP International Partners determine application deadlines and selection schedules in their region or country; see website for further information: www.FordIFP.Net.

13 Fondation Ford, Programme international de bourses de recherche [IFP]

809 UN Plaza, 9th Floor
10017 New York, NY, États-Unis
Tel: +1-212-984-5558
Fax: +1-212-984-5594
Web: http://www.fordifp.net
e-mail: query@FordIFP.Net

☞ Programme international de bourses de recherche

Domaines d'étude: toutes disciplines principales.
Description: le Programme international de Bourses de Recherche (IFP) fournit une aide pour des études de troisième cycle d'une durée de trois ans et conduisant à la maîtrise ou au doctorat dans les domaines d'études subventionnés par la Fondation Ford. La Fondation intervient sur quinze domaines d'études pour le renforcement des valeurs démocratiques, la réduction de la pauvreté et l'injustice sociale, la promotion de la coopération internationale et du progrès humain.
Domaines d'études: les candidats peuvent poursuivre des études dans les disciplines ou domaines d'études subventionnés par la Fondation Ford.
A l'intention de: ressortissants ou résidants d'un pays IFP pour des études de troisième cycle.
Nationalité: ressortissants des pays où la Fondation Ford assure des programmes à l'étranger en activité: Afrique du Sud, Brésil, Chili, Chine, Egypte, Ghana, Guatemala, Inde, Indonésie, Kenya, Mexico, Mozambique, Nigeria, Ouganda, Pérou, Philippines, R.U. Tanzanie, Russie, Sénégal, T.A. Palestiniens, Thaïlande, Vietnam. Les ressortissants américains ne sont pas éligibles, mais les candidats sont autorisés à étudier aux États-Unis.
Autres Conditions: les candidats sont choisis en vertu de leurs capacités à diriger, de leur engagement communautaire, ainsi que de l'excellence de leurs études.
Candidatures: les candidatures sont à soumettre au partenaire international IFP du pays où réside le candidat; les partenaires internationaux IFP déterminent les dates limites de candidatures et les programmes de sélection pour chaque région ou pays; pour plus d'informations, veuillez consulter le site internet: www.FordIFP.net.

13 Fundación Ford, Programa Internacional de Becas [IFP]

809 UN Plaza, 9th Floor
10017 New York, NY, Estados Unidos
Tel: +1-212-984-5558
Fax: +1-212-984-5594
Web: http://www.fordifp.net
e-mail: query@FordIFP.Net

☞ Programa Internacional de Becas de Posgrado

Campos de estudios: todas las materias principales.
Descripción: El IFP proporciona becas completas por una duración máxima de 24 meses pra mestría y 36 meses para doctorado en universidades de cualquier parte del mundo. Los becarios serán seleccionados con base en su excelencia académica, su compromiso con el desarrollo social y comunitario y su potencial de liderazgo. Los becarios deberán proseguir sus estudios en cualquier campo que favorezca las metas de la Fundación Ford para el fortalecimiento de valores democráticos, la reducción de la pobreza e injusticia y la promoción de la cooperación internacional y el desarrollo humano.
Materias de estudio: los candidatos pueden proseguir estudios en las disciplinas o ámbitos de estudios subvencionados por la Fundación Ford.
Se conceden: nacionales o residiendo de un país IFP para estudios de tercer ciclo.
Nacionalidad: nacionales de los países donde la Fundación Ford garantiza programas en el extranjero en actividad: Brasil, Chile, China, Egipto, Filipinas, Ghana, Guatemala, la India, Indonesia, Kenya, México, Mozambique, Nigeria, Perú, R.U. Tanzania, Rusia, Senegal, Sudáfrica, Tanzania, Tailandia, T.A. Palestinos, Uganda, Viet Nam. Los nacionales americanos no son seleccionables, pero se autoriza a los candidatos a estudiar en los Estados Unidos.
Otras condiciones: elige a los candidatos en virtud de sus capacidades para dirigir, de su compromiso comunitario, así como de la excelencia de sus estudios.

Solicitudes: las candidaturas deben someterse al socio internacional IFP del país donde reside el candidato; los socios internacionales IFP determinan los plazos de candidaturas y los programas de selección para cada región o país; para más información, quiere consultar el sitio Internet: www.FordIFP.net.

14 European University Institute [EUI]

Academic Service
Via dei Roccettini 9
50016 San Domenico di Fiesole (Fl)
Italy
Tel: +39-055-4685-1
Fax: +39-055-4685-444
Web: http://www.iue.it

☐ Postgraduate, Postdoctoral European Studies

Study Domains: economy, European studies, history, law, political economy, political science, social sciences.
Programmes: studies leading to (a) Doctorate degree in history and civilization, economics, law, political and social sciences; (b) LLM in comparative, European and international law.
Open to: (a) university graduates from European Union (EU) Member States and a limited number of nationals from other countries; meeting specific academic requirements and proficient in at least two official languages of the EU; (b) academics, no age limit or restriction of nationality, with PhD and research experience; presentation of research project must be accepted by the entrance board; good knowledge of English required (special test for EUI students comparable to TOEFL); selection on interview with presentation of research project.
Duration: (a) 2 years minimum; (b) 1 year minimum.
Fees: €10,330 per academic year for independent students.
Languages: instruction is mainly in English or French; good English is required in the Departments of Economics and Political and Social Sciences.
Applications: by 15 January to above address; email: applyres@iue.it.

☞ Postdoctoral Fellowships

Study Domains: European studies, human sciences, international law, law, political science, research, social sciences.
Scholarships: (a) Scholarships granted by the various Member States of the European Community; (b) Jean Monnet Postdoctoral Fellowships; (c) Marie Curie Fellowships for studies in economics, history and civilization, law, political and social science.
Description: (a) for PhD: history and civilization, economics, law, political and social sciences; for LLM: international and European comparative law; (b) comparative research in history, economics, law, political and social sciences with a European perspective; (c) mobility grants for researchers to work in other countries either in Europe or internationally.
Open to: (a) university graduates from EU Member States and a limited number of nationals from other countries, up to 30 at admission (with grades above average); preference with an MA in the disciplines of the institute or other qualifications for PhD study, plus knowledge of 2 foreign languages; (b) academics, no age limit or restriction of nationality, with PhD and research experience; presentation of research project has to be accepted by the entrance board; (c) individual researchers of all ages with at least 4 years' experience or with a Doctorate degree, a to participate in a research team in another country; also, in an effort to enhance networking between researchers, for researchers coming from third countries to train in Europe.
Duration: (a) 1 year, renewable twice; (b) 1 year, renewable once; (c) 1 to 2 years.
Applications: (a), (b) variable; see website for details http://www.iue.it/Servac/Postgraduate/HowApply.shtml; (c) 18 February (variable from year to year), see website http://europa.eu.int/comm/research/fp6/mariecurie-actions/home_en.html.

14 **Institut universitaire européen [IUE]**
Service Académique
Via dei Roccettini, 9
50016 San Domenico di Fiesole (FI)
Italie
Tel: +39-055-4685-1
Fax: +39-055-4685-444
Web: http://www.iue.it

📖 Programme de 3e cycle en études européennes

Domaines d'étude: droit, économie, économie politique, études européennes, sciences politiques, sciences sociales.
Programmes: (a) Doctorat en histoire et civilisation, économie, droit et sciences sociales et politiques; (b) Master (LLM) en droit comparé européen et international.
A l'intention de: (a) diplômés universitaires des États Membres de l'Union européenne (UE) et un nombre limité de ressortissants d'autres pays (voir site Internet pour critères) connaissant au moins 2 des langues officielles de l'UE; (b) ressortissants de tous pays, sans condition d'âge, diplômés supérieurs universitaires, ayant déjà entrepris des recherches; le projet de recherche doit être accepté par un comité, une bonne connaissance de l'anglais est demandée (test spécial équivalent à TOEFL) et la sélection comprend un entretien avec présentation du projet de recherche.
Durée: (a) minimum 2 ans; (b) minimum 1 an.
Frais: 10.330 € par année académique pour les étudiants non subventionnés.
Connaissances linguistiques: enseignement en anglais et en français; un bon niveau d'anglais est nécessaire dans le Département de Sciences économiques et politiques et de Sciences sociales.
Inscriptions: avant le 15 janvier à l'adresse ci-dessus; email: applyres@iue.it.

🎓 Bourses pour recherche et études supérieures en thèmes européens

Domaines d'étude: droit, droit international, études européennes, recherche, sciences humaines, sciences politiques, sciences sociales.
Bourses: (a) bourses octroyées par les gouvernements des différents États membres de la Communauté européenne pour études de 3ème cycle en vue de l'obtention du doctorat de l'Institut; (b) Bourses Jean Monnet pour études postdoctorales; (c) Bourses Marie Curie pour études en économie, histoire et civilisation, droit, sciences politiques et sociales.
Description: (a) au niveau doctorat: thèmes à caractère européen; l'économie, le droit, les sciences politiques et sociales; au niveau LLM: droit international et européen; (b) projets de recherche comparative en histoire, économie, droit, sciences politiques et sociales à caractère européen; (c) bourses de mobilité pour chercheurs pour entreprendre des travaux dans des pays européens et autres.
A l'intention de: (a) ressortissants des États membres de l'Union européenne (UE), titulaires d'une licence, âgés de moins de 30 ans et ayant une bonne connaissance de 2 langues officielles de l'UE; un nombre limité de places disponibles pour les ressortissants des autres pays; (b) candidats de toute nationalité titulaires d'un doctorat ou ayant une expérience équivalente dans la recherche, sans limite d'âge; admission sur présentation des projets de recherche; (c) chercheurs de toute nationalité titulaires d'un doctorat ou ayant au moins 4 ans d'expérience et désirant faire parti d'une équipe de recherche dans un autre pays.
Durée: (a) 1 an renouvelable 2 fois; (b) 1 an renouvelable; (c) 1 à 2 ans.
Candidatures: (a), (b) variable; pour de plus amples renseignements: http://www.iue.it/Servac/Postgraduate/HowApply.shtml; (c) avant le 18 février (variable d'année en année); voir http://europa.eu.int/comm/research/fp6/mariecurie-actions/home_en.html.

14 **Instituto Universitario Europeo [IUE]**
Servicio Académico
Via dei Roccettini, 9
50016 San Domenico di Fiesole (FI)
Italia
Tel: +39-055-4685-1
Fax: +39-055-4685-444
Web: http://www.iue.it

📖 Programa de 3er ciclo en Estudios europeos

Campos de estudios: ciencias políticas, ciencias sociales, derecho, economía, economía política, estudios europeos.
Programas: (a) Doctorado en historia y civilización, economía, derecho, ciencias políticas y sociales: (b) Master (LLM) en derecho comparativo, europeo e internacional.
Se destina(n): (a) graduados universitarios nacionales de los Estados Miembros de la Unión Europea (UE) y un número limitado de nacionales de otros países, con buenos conocimentos de 2 lenguas de la UE; (b) a candidatos de cualquier nacionalidad titulares de un doctorado o que posean experiencia equivalente en investigación; el proyecto de investigación debe ser aceptado por un comité de selección; buen conocimiento de inglés requierodo (test especial equivalente al TOEFL); la selección se efectúa en base a entrevista con presentación del proyecto de investigación.
Duración: (a) mínimo 2 años; (b) mínimo 1 año.
Costo(s): 10.330€ por año académico para los estudiantes no subvencionados.
Idioma: enseñanza en inglés y francés; un buen nivel de inglés es necesario en los Departamentos de Ciencias económicas y políticas y en el de Ciencias sociales.
Inscripciones: antes del 15 de enero en la dirección que figura en el título; email: applyres@iue.it.

🎓 Becas para investigación y estudios en temas europeos

Campos de estudios: ciencias humanas, ciencias políticas, ciencias sociales, derecho, derecho internacional, estudios europeos, investigación.
Becas: (a) becas otorgadas por gobiernos de diferentes Estados Miembros de la Unión Europea, para obtención de doctorado del IUE; (b) Becas Jean Monnet para estudios postdoctorales; (c) Becas Marie Curie para estudios en economía, historia y civilización, derecho, ciencias políticas y sociales.
Descripción: (a) a nivel del doctorado: proyectos de estudios europeos en áreas de historia, economía, derecho, ciencias políticas y sociales; a nivel LLM: derecho comparativo internacional y europeo; (b) investigación comparativa con perspectiva europea en áreas de historia, economía, derecho, ciencias políticas y sociales; (c) becas de movilidad para investigadores, para trabajar en Europa u otros países.
Se conceden: (a) a nacionales de los Estados Miembros de la Unión Europea (UE), de hasta 30 años de edad, titulares de licenciatura, con buenas calificaciones y con buenos conocimientos de 2 lenguas de la UE; (b) a candidatos de cualquier nacionalidad titulares de un doctorado o que posean experiencia equivalente en investigación; el proyecto de investigación debe ser aceptado por un comité de selección; (c) investigadores de toda nacionalidad titulares de un doctorado o con al menos 4 años de experiencia, que deseen participar en un equipo de investigación en otro país que el propio.
Duración: (a) 1 año (renovable hasta dos años); (b) 1 año renovable; (c) 1 a 2 años.
Solicitudes: (a), (b) variable; consultar el sitio web para mayor información: http://www.iue.it/Servac/Postgraduate/HowApply.shtml; (c) variables según el año, consultar el sitio web http://europa.eu.int/comm/research/fp6/mariecurie-actions/home_en.html.

15 Institute for Alternative Development Research

PO Box 870
Sentrum
0104 Oslo 1, Norway
Tel: +47-22-420-438
Fax: +47-22-420-438

📖 Alternative Development Training

Study Domains: development studies.
Description: training for development experts and development analyst/administrators in development alternatives: models and theories (economic, sociological, political science, cultural and ecological approaches): minimum 20 participants.
Open to: candidates of all nationalities with higher university background (graduate to postdoctorate) who are involved in work in the field of development; age 20 to 45 years; English proficiency required.
Duration: 1 month, courses begin in July.
Fees: tuition, US$500 plus room and board for 4 weeks (approximately US$1,100); no financial assistance.
Languages: instruction in English.
Applications: by 31 March (with a curriculum vitae).

15 Institut pour la recherche dans les alternatives du développement

BP 870
Sentrum
0104 Oslo 1, Norvège
Tel: +47-22-420-438
Fax: +47-22-420-438

📖 Alternatives du développement

Domaines d'étude: études du développement.
Programmes: alternatives du développement: modèles et théories (économie, sociologie, sciences politiques, approches culturelles et écologiques), conduisant aux diplôme d'expert en développement, d'administrateur, d'analyste en développement; conflits et paix.
A l'intention de: ressortissants de tout pays, ayant une formation universitaire supérieure (de la maîtrise au post-doctorat), qui effectuent des travaux dans le domaine du développement; âge de 20 à 45 ans; bonne connaissance de l'anglais écrit et parlé requise.
Durée: 1 mois (en juillet).
Frais: enseignement: 500 US$ plus frais de pension et de logement (pour 4 semaines environ) 1.100 US$.
Connaissances linguistiques: langue d'enseignement: anglais.
Inscriptions: avant le 31 mars (accompagnées d'un curriculum vitae).

15 Instituto para la Investigación de Alternativas de Desarrollo

PO Box 870
Sentrum
0104 Oslo 1, Noruega
Tel: +47-22-420-438
Fax: +47-22-420-438

📖 Alternativas de desarrollo

Campos de estudios: estudios sobre el desarrollo.
Descripción: modelos y teorías (economía, sociología, ciencias políticas, conflictos y paz). Cursos en inglés que conducen a los diplomas de experto en desarrollo, administrador y analista en desarrollo; 20 participantes como mínimo.
Se destina(n): a nacionales de cualquier país que tengan una formación universitaria superior (de la maestría al posdoctorado), que efectúen trabajos en el área de desarrollo y tengan entre 20 y 45 años de edad; se exige buen conocimiento del inglés hablado y escrito.
Duración: 1 mes (en julio).
Costo(s): enseñanza: 500 dólares de los Estados Unidos; alojamiento y manutención para (4 semanas aproximadamente): 1.100 dólares Estados Unidos.
Inscripciones: hasta el 31 de marzo (acompañadas de un curriculum vitae).

16 Institute of Nutrition of Central America and Panama [INCAP]

Calzada Roosvelt 6-25 zona 11
Apartado Postal 1188-01901
Guatemala City, Guatemala
Tel: +502-2472-3762
Fax: +502-2473-6529
Web: http://www.incap.ops-oms.org
e-mail: hdelgado@incap.ops-oms.org

📖 Advanced tutorial training in World Hunger Programme priority areas

Study Domains: nutrition.
Programmes: Advanced tutorial training in priority areas of the World Hunger Programme as defined by the United Nations University (UNU).
Open to: citizens of all countries who have completed technological or scientific graduate studies, preferably at the Ph.D. or M.Sc. level, in biological, social or economic areas.
Duration: maximum 12 months.
Financial assistance: possibility of individual scholarship programmes, covering a monthly stipend, plus tuition and round-trip air ticket to Guatemala.
Languages: instruction in English and Spanish.
Applications: for more information, write to Senior Academic Officer, The United Nations University, 53-70, Jingumae 5-chome, Shibuya-ku, Tokyo 150, Japan.

📖 Postgraduate courses

Study Domains: food, health and hygiene, nutrition, technology.
Programmes: (a) programme of studies in food and nutrition leading to postgraduate diplomas (Master's); (b) postgraduate course (Master's) in food and nutrition.
Description: (a) 4 fields of study: alimentary-nutritional process, planning, research and education (20 participants); (b) alimentary-nutritional process, planning, research and education. The objective is to enable professionals who may contribute to improving the food supply and nutritional situation of people to specialize in the fields of food and nutrition (18 participants maximum).
Open to: candidates able to take positive action on questions of food: agronomists, food technicians and engineers, nutritionists, nurses, biologists, educators, sociologists, economists, or any professional working in the social or economic sectors; candidates selected for the course must be able to provide documentary proof that they have financial support.
Duration: 20 months, divided into 2 cycles: basic cycle (3 periods of 4 months each) and the specialized cycle (2 periods of 4 months).
Fees: (a) US$24,000 for 20 months of studies: registration US$8,000, maintenance, US$12,000 (does not apply to participants residing in Guatemala and earning a salary); travelling costs from the country of origin (return air ticket depending on the candidate's nationality: for Central America, the return air fare is about US$800); research fees and books, approx. US$3,000; medical and accident insurance, US$300 (for 20 months); (b) registration, US$110 in the University of San Carlos de Guatemala (annually) and US$20 in INCAP (only payment); tuition, US$400 per month; living costs, approx. US$650; insurance, US$15.
Financial assistance: candidates should seek support in the form of grants from international organizations in their own country, such as the Pan American Health Organization (PAHO), the Organization of American States (OAS), the United Nations Educational, Scientific and Cultural Organization (UNESCO), the Food and Agriculture Organization of the United Nations (FAO), the United States Agency for International Development (USAID), the Inter-American Development Bank (IADB), embassies, foundations, the Central American Bank for Economic Integration (CABEI), and other sources.
Languages: (a) instruction in Spanish: (a) (b) Good knowledge of English required.
Applications: (a) 3 to 6 months before the course; new students are accepted every 2 years; enrolment for the selection course (distance education) and the academic test will take place in each country at the end of April; students for the next course will be selected in May; (b) in May. More information is obtainable from INCAP at the above address.

📖 Training programme and courses in nutrition

Study Domains: nutrition.
Programmes: (a) practical training programme; (a), (b) short-term courses in nutrition and related sciences.
Description: (a) aims to improve the student's necessary skills for management and correct application of various methods and techniques on food and in the nutrition field or in laboratories, and develop ability to locate information sources on technical literature covering the subjects.
Open to: (a) professionals and technicians with a high degree of general basic knowledge and university background in these specific fields and/or good expertise in their speciality; candidates must be recommended by their organization; (b) nationals of any country, preferably Central American candidates, meeting the necessary requirements.
Duration: (a) from 1 to 12 months.
Fees: registration: (a) US$20; tuition: (a) and (b) US$500 per month; stipend: (a) and (b) approx. US$600 per month; health insurance: (a) and (b) US$15 per month; (b) research expenses: US$150.
Financial assistance: limited number of fellowships offered every 2 years to Central American students; enquire at above address.
Languages: instruction in Spanish; basic knowledge of English required.
Applications: at any time.

16 Institut de nutrition d'Amérique centrale et du Panama [INCAP]

Calzada Roosvelt 6-25 zona 11
Apartado Postal 1188-01901
Guatemala, Guatemala
Tel: +502-2472-3762
Fax: +502-2473-6529
Web: http://www.incap.ops-oms.org
e-mail: hdelgado@incap.ops-oms.org

📖 Cours niveau maîtrise

Domaines d'étude: alimentation, hygiène et santé, nutrition, technologie.
Programmes: (a) programme (niveau maîtrise) en alimentation et nutrition; 4 spécialisations: le processus alimentation-nutrition, la planification, la recherche et l'éducation; (b) cours (niveau maîtrise) en alimentation et nutrition dans le domaine de la santé.
Description: (a) 4 spécialisations: le processus alimentation-nutrition, la planification, la recherche et l'éducation; (b) la spécialisation, dans le domaine de l'alimentation et de la nutrition, de professionnels contribuant à améliorer la situation alimentaire et nutritionnelle des populations. Il s'agit également de renforcer la capacité des pays de la sous-région à étudier leur propre évolution, leurs perspectives, et de provoquer des stimulations bénéfiques.
A l'intention de: ressortissants pouvant intervenir dans la problématique alimentaire: agronomes, techniciens et ingénieurs en technologie alimentaire, médecins, nutritionnistes, infirmières, biologistes, éducateurs, sociologues, économistes, ou tout professionnel du secteur social et économique. Pour être admis aux cours, les candidats sélectionnés doivent apporter la preuve qu'ils sont financièrement indépendants.
Durée: 20 mois partagés en 2 cycles: cycle de base (12 mois répartis en 3 périodes de 4 mois) et cycle diversifié (8 mois répartis en 2 périodes de 4 mois) (juin-décembre).
Frais: (a) frais de scolarité, 24.000$US, dont 8.000$US pour les frais d'enregistrement et 12.000$US pour les frais d'entretien (logement, transport local, etc.) (ne s'applique pas aux participants résidant au Guatemala et qui reçoivent un salaire); les frais de voyage du pays d'origine (aller/ retour en avion dépendant du pays du bénéficiaire); les frais de recherche et de livres, 3.000$US; les frais d'assurance maladie et accidents, 300$US; (b) inscription: 110$US pour l'Université de San Carlos de Guatemala et 20 $US pour l'INCAP; frais de scolarité: 400$US par mois; séjour: environ 650$US, couvrant les frais d'entretien; et 15$US pour les frais d'assurance maladie et accidents.
Assistance financière: (a) les intéressés devront demander un soutien financier sous forme de bourses, aux organismes internationaux comme l'Organisation panaméricaine de la santé (OPS), l'Organisation des états américains (OEA), l'Organisation des Nations Unies pour l'éducation, la science et la culture (UNESCO), l'Organisation des Nations Unies

pour l'alimentation et l'agriculture (FAO), l'Agence internationale de développement (AID), la Banque interaméricaine de développement (BID), les ambassades, les fondations, la Banque interaméricaine d'intégration économique (BCIE), ou toute autre source.
Connaissances linguistiques: (a) langue d'enseignement: espagnol; (a) (b) bonne connaissance d'anglais requise.
Inscriptions: (a) 3 à 6 mois précédent le cours. La rentrée s'effectue tous les 2 ans; les inscriptions aux cours de remise à niveau (cours à distance) et l'attestation de passage se font dans chaque pays à la fin avril; la sélection des candidats a lieu courant mai; (b) en mai. S'adresser au Service de la maîtrise en alimentation et nutrition, INCAP, à l'adresse ci-dessus.

📖 Programme de formation avancée

Domaines d'étude: nutrition.
Programmes: programme de formation avancée sous forme de travaux pratiques dans les domaines prioritaires du Programme mondial contre la faim, selon la définition de l'Université des Nation Unies (UNU).
A l'intention de: ressortissants de tout pays, ayant terminé des études supérieures (de préférence aux niveaux du doctorat ou de la maîtrise) en sciences ou technologie dans les domaines de la biologie, sciences sociales ou sciences économiques. Une bonne connaissance de l'anglais ou de l'espagnol, ou mieux, des 2 langues, est exigée.
Durée: maximum 12 mois.
Assistance financière: les bourses pour programmes individuels, comprenant une indemnité mensuelle, plus les frais d'inscription et de voyage aller/retour au Guatemala, sont en cours de négociation avec l'UNU.
Connaissances linguistiques: langues d'enseignement: anglais et espagnol.
Inscriptions: Senior Academic Officer, The United Nations University, 53-70, Jingumae 5-chome, Shibuya-ku, Tokyo 150, Japon.

📖 Programmes de formation en nutrition

Domaines d'étude: nutrition.
Programmes: (a) programme de formation, sous forme de travaux pratiques, (b) cours de courte durée, en nutrition et sciences annexes.
Description: (a) l'objectif est de permettre à l'étudiant d'acquérir les connaissances suffisantes, sur le terrain comme en laboratoire, pour le maniement et l'application correcte des diverses méthodes et techniques d'étude en alimentation et en nutrition; de le guider pour lui faciliter l'accès à l'information en lui indiquant les méthodes de localisation des sources pertinentes concernant toute littérature scientifique disponible; (b) 24 participants maximum.
A l'intention de: (a) professionnels et techniciens de tout pays, possédant une grande expérience et une profonde connaissance du sujet, détenant une formation universitaire ou une pratique approfondie dans le domaine de sa spécialité; sélection sur recommandation des supérieurs hiérarchiques; (b) ressortissants de tout pays, de préférence d'Amérique centrale, remplissant les conditions requises.
Durée: (a) 1 à 12 mois.
Frais: inscription: (a) 20 $US; scolarité: (a) et (b) 500 $US; subsistance: (a) et (b) environ 600 $US par mois; assurance maladie et accidents: (a) et (b) 15 $US par mois; (b) frais de recherche: 15 $US.
Assistance financière: nombre limité de bourses offertes aux étudiants d'Amérique centrale; s'adresser à l'adresse ci-dessus.
Connaissances linguistiques: langue d'enseignement: espagnol; connaissance élémentaire de l'anglais.
Inscriptions: à tout moment.

16 Instituto de Nutrición de Centro América y Panamá [INCAP]

Calzada Roosvelt 6-25 zona 11
Apartado Postal 1188-01901
Ciudad de Guatemala, Guatemala
Tel: +502-2472-3762
Fax: +502-2473-6529
Web: http://www.incap.ops-oms.org
e-mail: hdelgado@incap.ops-oms.org

📖 Adiestramiento tutorial en nutrición

Campos de estudios: nutrición.
Programas: (a) adiestramiento tutorial; (b) cursos de corta duración en nutrición y ciencias afines.
Descripción: (a) el objetivo es proporcionar al estudiante las destrezas necesarias para el manejo y aplicación correcta de diversos métodos y técnicas para estudios de campo y laboratorio en alimentación y nutrición, así como guiarlo en la localización de las fuentes pertinentes de información en la literatura científica disponible; (b) alrededor de 24 participantes.
Se destina(n): (a) profesionales y técnicos que posean un adecuado conocimiento básico general y/o experiencia en el área respectiva y con experiencia académica y/o práctica en el campo de su especialidad; selección sobre recomendaciones de los superiores; (b) a nacionales de cualquier país, preferentemente centroamericanos, que cumplan los requisitos exigidos.
Duración: (a) de 1 a 12 meses.
Costo(s): (en dólares de los Estados Unidos). Inscripción: (a) 20 dólares; enseñanza: (a) y (b) 500 dólares por mes; estadía: (a) y (b) 600 dólares por mes aproximadamente; seguro médico, de enfermedad, accidentes y de vida: (a) y (b) 15 dólares por mes; (b) gastos de investigación: 150 dólares.
Asistencia financiera: numéro limitado de becas ofrecido cada 2 años a candidatos centroamericanos.
Idioma: enseñanza en español; conocimientos básicos de inglés requeridos.
Inscripciones: en cualquier fecha.

📖 Cursos de posgrado

Campos de estudios: alimentación, higiene y salud, nutrición, tecnología.
Programas: (a) programa de estudios sobre alimentación y nutrición conducente a la obtención de una maestría en las cuatro áreas siguientes: proceso alimentario-nutricional, planificación, investigación, educación; (b) curso de posgrado (maestría en alimentación y nutrición en salud).
Descripción: el objetivo, en el campo de la alimentación y la nutrición, es especializar profesionales que contribuyan a mejorar la situación alimentaria y nutricional de la población, actuando sobre la disponibilidad, el acceso, el consumo y la utilización biológica de los alimentos, fortaleciendo la capacidad de los países de la subregión, mediante el estudio de su propia evolución, sus perspectivas y las formas de incidir favorablemente en ellas.
Se destina(n): a profesionales que pueden intervenir en la problemática alimentaria nutricional, incluyendo agrónomos, tecnólogos de alimentos, ingenieros de alimentos, médicos, nutricionistas, enfermeras, biólogos, educadores, sociólogos, economistas, así como otros profesionales del área social y económica; si los participantes seleccionados prueban fehacientemente que cuentan con apoyo financiero, serán admitidos en el programa. Admisión mediante examen de conocimientos básicos y pruebas de aptitud.
Duración: 20 meses divididos en 2 ciclos: ciclo básico o común (12 meses, divídos en 3 cuatrimestres) y ciclo diversificado (8 meses, divídos en 2 cuatrimestres).
Costo(s): en dólares de los Estados Unidos, (a) 24.000 dólares para los 20 meses de duración de los estudios: 8.000 dólares por concepto de matrícula; 12.000 dólares por estipendio (alojamiento, transporte local, etc.) (no se aplica a participantes residentes en Guatemala que obtengan un permiso con goce de salario); pasaje aéreo: ida y vuelta al país de origen (depende del lugar de origen del participante); 3.000 dólares para investigación y libros; 300 dólares por seguro médico y de accidentes; (b) inscripción: 110 dólares en Universidad de San Carlos de Guatemala (anual) y 20 dólares en INCAP (pago único). enseñanza: 400 dólares por mes; estadía: 650 dólares aproximadamente para cubrir los gastos de estipendio; 15 dólares para seguro médico.
Asistencia financiera: los interesados deberán solicitar apoyo en forma de becas a organismos internacionales en su propio país (tales como la OPS, la OEA, la UNESCO, la FAO, la AID, el BID) embajadas u otras fuentes como el BCIE, fundaciones y otros.
Idioma: (a) lengua de enseñanza: español; (a) (b) buen conocimiento de inglés.
Inscripciones: (a) 3 a 6 meses antes del curso; los ingresos son cada 2 años; la incripción para el curso de nivelación (a distancia) y la prueba de rendimiento académico, se efectuarán en cada país a finales del mes de abril; el proceso de selección se llevará a cabo durante el mes de mayo; (b) en mayo. Dirigirse a Maestría en Alimentación y Nutrición, INCAP, en la dirección que figura en el título.

📖 Programa de adiestramiento tutorial avanzado en áreas prioritarias del Programa

Campos de estudios: nutrición.
Programas: programa de adiestramiento tutorial avanzado en áreas prioritarias del Programa Mundial contra el Hambre, definido por la Universidad de las Naciones Unidas (UNU).
Se destina(n): a profesionales de cualquier país que hayan terminado los estudios universitarios y de posgrado, preferiblemente a nivel de doctorado o de maestría en disciplinas científicas o tecnológicas en el campo biológico, social o económico. Los aspirantes deben tener suficientes conocimientos de español o de inglés y preferiblemente de ambos idiomas.
Duración: 12 meses como máximo.
Asistencia financiera: las becas para programas individuales, que incluyen una asignación mensual más gastos de matrícula y de viaje de ida y vuelta, están en proceso de renegociación con la UNU.
Idioma: enseñanza en inglés y español.
Inscripciones: para mayores informaciones dirigirse a Senior Academic Officer, The United Nations University, 53-70, Jingumae 5-chome, Shibuya-ku, Tokyo 150, Japan.

17 Instituto Italo-Latino Americano

Servicio para la Cooperación al Desarrollo
Instituto Italo Latino-Americano
Piazza Benedetto Cairoli, 3
00186 Roma, Italia
Tel: +39-06-68492253
Fax: +39-06-68492 254
Web: http://www.iila.org
e-mail: info@iila.org

🎓 Becas en el sector agro-alimentario

Campos de estudios: agricultura, ciencias agronómicas.
Descripción: pasantías post-universitarias de investigación y/o especialización.
Se conceden: a candidatos con título universitario y que trabajen en instituciones locales públicas o privadas o en ONGs del sector.
Nacionalidad: ciudadanos latinoamericanos de los países miembros del IILA (Argentina, Bolivia, Brasil, Chile, Colombia, Costa Rica, Cuba, Ecuador, El Salvador, Guatemala, Haití, Honduras, Italia, México, Nicaragua, Panamá, Paraguay, Perú, República Dominicana, Uruguay, Venezuela).
Edad Max: los candidatos no podrán tener más de 35 años de edad.
Lugar: en universidades o institutos de investigación italianos.
Duración: 4/6 meses de duración en promedio.

18 Inter-American Housing Union [UNIAPRAVI]

Casilla 18-1366
Bajada Balta, N° 169, 4to. Piso
Lima 18, Peru
Tel: +51-1-444-6605/6611
Fax: +51-1-444-6600
Web: http://www.uniapravi.org.pe
e-mail: uniapravi@uniapravi.org.pe

📖 UNIAPRAVI Training Programmes

Study Domains: finance, vocational training.
Programmes: UNIAPRAVI Training Programmes.
Description: The objectives of the UNIAPRAVI Training Institute are permanent training and human resources development, both at managerial and operational levels, of housing finance institutions and other institutions related to sectoral development.
Open to: nationals of the countries of the American continent who work either at managerial or operational levels in institutions dealing with financial housing and who have the professional qualifications necessary for the course envisaged.
Held: in various countries of the American continent.

Duration: varies according to the course taken and the country of study.
Languages: instruction in Spanish; in exceptional cases in English or Portuguese.
Applications: to the Central Office of UNIAPRAVI at the above address for further information.

18 Union interaméricaine du logement [UNIAPRAVI]
Casilla 18-1366
Bajada Balta, N° 169, 4to. Piso
Lima 18, Pérou
Tel: +51-1-444-6605/6611
Fax: +51-1-444-6600
Web: http://www.uniapravi.org.pe
e-mail: uniapravi@uniapravi.org.pe

Cours de formation UNIAPRAVI

Domaines d'étude: finances, formation professionnelle.
Description: L'Institut de formation de l'UNIAPRAVI a pour objectifs la formation permanente et le développement des ressources humaines, tant au niveau directorial qu'opérationnel, des institutions de financement de l'habitat et des autres institutions qui sont en relation avec le développement sectoriel.
A l'intention de: ressortissants des pays du continent américain, employés, soit au niveau directorial soit opérationnel, par des institutions de financement relatif au logement, et ayant les qualifications nécessaires pour le cours envisagé.
Organisés: dans différents pays du continent américain.
Durée: varie selon le cours et le pays.
Connaissances linguistiques: L'enseignement est donné en espagnol pour la plupart des cours et, exceptionnellement en anglais ou en portugais.
Inscriptions: pour de plus amples renseignements, s'adresser au Bureau central de l'UNIAPRAVI à l'adresse ci-dessus.

18 Unión Interamericana para la Vivienda [UNIAPRAVI]
Casilla 18-1366
Bajada Balta, N° 169, 4to. Piso
Lima 18, Perú
Tel: +51-1-444-6605/6611
Fax: +51-1-444-6600
Web: http://www.uniapravi.org.pe
e-mail: uniapravi@uniapravi.org.pe

Programa de capacitación de UNIAPRAVI

Campos de estudios: finanzas, formación profesional.
Descripción: el Instituto de Capacitación de UNIAPRAVI tiene como objetivo la capacitación permanente y el desarrollo de los recursos humanos, tanto a nivel gerencial como operativo, de las instituciones de financiamiento habitacional y de las otras instituciones que están en relación con el desarrollo sectorial.
Se destina(n): a nacionales de los países del continente americano que trabajen a nivel gerencial o como operativo en entidades de financiamiento para la vivienda y tengan la calificación profesional requerida en la especialidad del curso elegido.
Se dicta(n): en diversos países del continente americano.
Idioma: la enseñanza se imparte en español en la mayoría de los cursos y excepcionalmente en inglés o portugués.
Inscripciones: en la Oficina Central de UNIAPRAVI, la cual puede facilitar información complementaria, en la dirección que figura en el título.

19 Inter-University Centre for Development [CINDA]
Santa Magdalena 75, piso 11
Providencia
Santiago, Chile
Tel: +56-2-234-1128
Fax: +56-2-234-1117
Web: http://www.cinda.cl
e-mail: cinda@reuna.cl

CINDA technical seminars and training courses

Study Domains: education, management, technology.
Programmes: Periodic technical seminars and training courses on technology management, international cooperation and policies, and university administration.
Held: in conjunction with universities, business associations and development agencies in Latin America, Spain and Italy.
Financial assistance: determined on a case-by-case basis.

19 Centre interuniversitaire pour le développement [CINDA]
Santa Magdalena 75, piso 11
Providencia
Santiago, Chili
Tel: +56-2-234-1128
Fax: +56-2-234-1117
Web: http://www.cinda.cl
e-mail: cinda@reuna.cl

Séminaires techniques et cours de formation de CINDA

Domaines d'étude: éducation, gestion, technologie.
Programmes: Séminaires techniques et cours de formation organisés périodiquement dans les domaines de l'administration de la technologie, de la coopération internationale, des politiques de l'enseignement supérieur et de l'administration universitaire.
Organisés: en association avec des universités, des associations patronales et des organismes de développement d'Amérique latine, d'Espagne et d'Italie.
Assistance financière: déterminée ponctuellement.

19 Centro Interuniversitario de Desarrollo [CINDA]
Santa Magdalena 75, piso 11
Providencia
Santiago, Chile
Tel: +56-2-234-1128
Fax: +56-2-234-1117
Web: http://www.cinda.cl
e-mail: cinda@reuna.cl

Seminarios técnicos y cursos de capacitación del CINDA

Campos de estudios: educación, gestión, tecnología.
Descripción: organizados periódicamente en las áreas de gestión tecnológica, cooperación internacional y políticas y gestión universitaria.
Se dicta(n): en forma asociada con universidades, asociaciones empresariales y organismos de desarrollo de América Latina, España e Italia.
Asistencia financiera: se determina en cada oportunidad.

20 International Agency for Research on Cancer - World Health Organization [WHO-IARC]
150, cours Albert-Thomas
69372 Lyon Cedex 08, France
Tel: +33-4-7273-8448
Fax: +33-4-7273-8080
Web: http://www.iarc.fr
e-mail: fel@iarc.fr

IARC specialized short-term courses

Study Domains: cancerology, ecology, environment, short-term programmes.
Description: courses in cancer epidemiology and aspects of environmental carcinogenesis.
Open to: candidates of all nationalities with experience in the proposed field of study.
Held: at IARC or various national institutions.
Duration: 1 to 2 weeks.
Fees: a registration fee may be charged for certain advanced courses held at IARC; other courses and elsewhere, tuition free.
Financial assistance: limited number of fellowships available.
Languages: English, French and Spanish.

Applications: 3 months prior to the date of the course, to Courses' Programme, IARC at the above address.

🖋 Postdoctoral Fellowships for Training in Cancer Research

Study Domains: cancerology, research.
Subjects: epidemiology, biostatistics, environmental and viral carcinogenesis, cancer etiology and prevention, molecular cell biology, molecular genetics, molecular pathology and mechanisms of carcinogenesis.
Open to: junior scientists from low- or medium-resource countries wishing to complete their training in those aspects of cancer research related to the Agency's mission: to coordinate and conduct both epidemiological and laboratory research into the causes of cancer.
Nationality: candidates from any country other than those classified as high-income economies by the World Bank (www.worldbank.org/data/countryclass/countryclass.html).
Age limit Max: Candidates should be under the age of 40 at the time of application.
Other conditions: candidates must provide evidence of their ability to return to their home country and keep working in cancer research.
Candidates already working as a postdoctoral fellow at the Agency at the time of application or who have had any contractual relationship with IARC during the 6 months preceding the deadline for application cannot be considered. Candidates should have spent less than five years abroad (including doctoral studies)and have finished their doctoral degree within five years of the closing date for application.
Place of study: the IARC in Lyon, France working in a research group.
Duration: a period of 2 years, the extension for a second year being subject to satisfactory appraisal.
Value: the annual stipend will be approximately 25,000 Euros, net of tax. The cost of travel for the Fellow, and in certain circumstances for dependants, will be met, a dependant's allowance paid, and health insurance provided. A small grant to start up an independent research programme linked to IARC activities upon return to the home country may be provided to selected IARC postdoctoral Fellows upon successful completion of the fellowship.
Languages: the working languages at IARC are English and French. Candidates must have the ability to read and write English at a level sufficient for scientific communication. If English or French is not the candidate's mother-tongue, they must submit proof of language proficiency.
Applications: more information on the Cancer Research Fellowship Programme at above address. Candidates should contact the host Group of their choice at IARC before application. Details regarding the IARC's research programmes are available from the Agency's web site: http://www.iarc.fr.

20 Centre international de recherche sur le cancer - Organisation mondiale de la santé [OMS-CIRC]

150, cours Albert-Thomas
69372 Lyon Cedex 08, France
Tel: +33-4-7273-8448
Fax: +33-4-7273-8080
Web: http://www.iarc.fr
e-mail: fel@iarc.fr

📖 Cours spécialisés de courte durée

Domaines d'étude: cancérologie, écologie, environnement, programmes de courte durée.
Description: cours en épidémiologie du cancer et des aspects de la cancérogenèse de l'environnement.
A l'intention de: ressortissants de tout pays, ayant de l'expérience dans le domaine étudié.
Organisés: au CIRC ou dans divers instituts nationaux.
Durée: de 1 à 2 semaines.
Frais: frais d'inscription pour certains cours avancés dispensés au CIRC; scolarité gratuite pour les autres cours et pour ceux dispensés dans les instituts nationaux.
Assistance financière: nombre limité de bourses.
Connaissances linguistiques: anglais, français et espagnol.
Inscriptions: 3 mois avant le début du cours; au Service

d'éducation et formation, à l'adresse ci-dessus.

🖋 Bourses pour la formation de chercheurs dans le domaine du cancer

Domaines d'étude: biochimie, biologie, cancérologie, cytologie, immunologie, recherche.
Description: recherche dans les domaines de: épidémiologie, biostatistiques, carcinogenèse virale et liée à l'environnement, étiologie et prévention du cancer, biologie cellulaire, biologie et génétique moléculaires, pathologie moléculaire et mécanismes de carcinogenèse.
A l'intention de: jeunes chercheurs provenant de pays à économies à faible ou moyen revenu, désirant compléter leur formation dans les aspects relatifs à la mission du Centre, la coordination et la conduite de recherche épidémiologique et de laboratoire sur les causes du cancer.
Nationalité: candidats de tous pays sauf ceux que la Banque Mondiale classés comme «économies à haut revenus» (www.worldbank.org/data/countryclass/countryclass.html).
Age Max: âgés de moins de 40 ans au moment de l'inscription.
Autres Conditions: les candidats devront prouver leur capacité à retourner dans leur pays d'origine et à poursuivre la recherche sur le cancer.
Les candidats qui effectuent déjà un travail postdoctoral dans le Centre au moment de l'inscription ou qui ont eu des rapports contractuels avec le Centre dans les 6 mois précédant la date limite des candidatures ne seront pas pris en compte. Les candidats ne doivent pas avoir séjourné plus de 5 ans à l'étranger (études doctorales comprises), et avoir obtenu le doctorat dans les 5 ans précédant la candidature.
Lieu: au CIRC à Lyon, France, au sein d'un groupe de recherche.
Durée: une période de 2 ans, mais la deuxième année est conditionnée à ce que la première soit jugée satisfaisante.
Valeur: un montant de autour de 25.000€, libre d'impôts. Les frais de voyage du candidat (et dans certains cas, des dépendants) seront payés; une allocation pour les dépendants et une assurance médicale seront assurées.
A la fin de la bourse, et en fonction des résultats, certains candidats seront sélectionnés pour obtenir un montant permettant de mettre en place un programme indépendant de recherche, en relation avec les activités du CIRC.
Connaissances linguistiques: les langues de travail du CIRC sont l'anglais et le français. Les candidats doivent être capables de lire et d'écrire en anglais, avec un niveau suffisant pour assurer la communication scientifique. Si la langue maternelle du candidat est autre que l'anglais ou le français, ils devront passer une épreuve qui attestera leurs compétences dans ce domaine.
Candidatures: la date varie selon les années; se renseigner auprès du Programme de bourses d'étude en recherche cancérologique, à l'adresse ci-dessus. Les candidats doivent contacter le groupe hôte du CIRC avant de postuler à la bourse. Des détails concernant les programmes de recherche peuvent être consultés sur le site Internet du CIRC.

20 Organización Mundial de la Salud - Centro Internacional de Investigaciones sobre el Cáncer [OMS-CIIC]

150, cours Albert-Thomas
69372 Lyon Cedex 08, Francia
Tel: +33-4-7273-8448
Fax: +33-4-7273-8080
Web: http://www.iarc.fr
e-mail: fel@iarc.fr

📖 Cursos cortos de especialización en oncología

Campos de estudios: cancerología, ecología, medio ambiente, programas de corta duración.
Descripción: cursos en epidemiología del cáncer y aspectos de la carcinogénesis del medio ambiente; 40 participantes.
Se destina(n): a nacionales de cualquier país que tengan experiencia en la materia estudiada.
Se dicta(n): CIIC o varias instituciones nacionales.
Duración: de 1 a 2 semanas.
Costo(s): gastos de inscripción para ciertos cursos avanzados dispensados en el CIIC; escolaridad gratuita para el resto de los cursos y para aquellos dispensados en institutos nacionales.

Asistencia financiera: número limitado de becas disponible.
Idioma: español, francés e inglés.
Inscripciones: 3 meses antes del inicio del curso; Servicio de Educación y Formación, CIIC, en la dirección que figura en el título.

☛ Becas para formación de investigadores en oncología

Campos de estudios: biología, bioquímica, cancerología, citología, inmunología, investigación.
Descripción: epidemiología, bioestadística, carcinogénesis viral y ligadas al medio ambiente, etiología y prevención del cáncer, biología celular, biología y genética molecular, patología molecular y mecanismos de carcinogénesis.
Se conceden: a jóvenes científicos de países con economías de ingresos bajos y medios que deseen completar su formación en los aspectos del cáncer relacionados con la misión del Centro, o sea coordinar y conducir investigaciones epidemiológicas y de laboratorio sobre las causas del cáncer.
Nacionalidad: quedan excluidos los candidatos provenientes de países clasificados por el Banco Mundial como de economía de altos ingresos (www.bancomundial.org/datos/clasificacion_paises.html).
Edad Max: menos de 40 años en la fecha de postulación.
Otras condiciones: Los candidatos deben proporcionar evidencia de su capacidad de volver a su país de orígen y de mantener el trabajar la investigación de cáncer.
No se tomarán en cuanta las postulaciones de candidatos que ya han efectuado un trabajo postdoctoral en el Centro o que ya hayan tenido contratos con el Centro en los 6 meses que preceden la postulación.
Los candidatos deben pasado menos de cinco años en el extranjero (incluyendo estudios postdoctorales) y haber obtenido el doctorado en los cinco años que preceden la postulación.
Lugar: en el CIIC, Lyon Francia, como integrante de un grupo de investigación.
Duración: 2 años, pero el segundo estó condicionado a que el primero sea juzgado satisfactorio.
Importe: el estipendio anual es de aproximadamente 25.000 euros, libre de impuestos. La beca incluye los gastos de viaje del candidato (y en ciertos casos, de familiares), una asignación para personas a cargo, y un seguro médico.
En algunos casos, y en función de los resultados, algunos becarios pueden recibir un monto de dinero que les permita lanzar una actividad de investigación independiente, pero relacionada con las actividades del CIIC. El monto varía según el costo de la vida en el país de estudio. La beca incluye una indemnización diaria y una pequeña asignación familiar, así como gastos de viaje de ida y vuelta del interesado y en algunas circunstancias, de un adulto a cargo.
Idioma: las lenguas de enseñanza son el inglés y el francés. Los candidatos deben poder leer y escribir en inglés a un nivel apropiado para la comunicación científica. Los postulantes cuya lengua materna no sea uno de los idiomas precitados deberán pasar una prueba de suficiencia.
Solicitudes: la fecha varía según el año; dirigirse a Programa de becas de investigaciones sobre el cáncer, en la dirección que figura en el título. No se debe postular a una beca sin haberse puesto previamente en contacto con el grupo de investigación huésped.
Los detalles sobre los programas de investigación del CIIC pueden ser consultados en el sitio web.

21 International Association for the Exchange of Students for Technical Experience [IAESTE]

General Secretariat
PO Box 102
BT32 4WY Banbridge Northern Ireland, UK
Tel: +44-28-4062 -5485
Fax: +44-28-4062-5485
Web: http://www.iaeste.org
e-mail: general.secretary@iaeste.org

📖 IAESTE Exchange Programmes

Study Domains: agriculture, architecture, engineering, forestry, sciences, technology, vocational training.
Description: on-the-job paid technical experience: engineering and science, with opportunities in architecture, agriculture and forestry.

Open to: nationals of countries participating in IAESTE who are students at universities and technical colleges.
Held: in countries participating in IAESTE (see website for further information).
Duration: 8 to 52+ weeks.
Financial assistance: employers pay a maintenance allowance covering living expenses in the host country; travel, health insurance and incidental expenses not included.
Languages: opportunities mainly in English, French or German or in the language of the host country.
Applications: to the IAESTE Committee in candidate's country (see website).

21 Association internationale pour l'échange d'étudiants de l'enseignement technique [IAESTE]

Secrétariat général
PO Box 102
BT32 4WY Banbridge Northern Ireland, UK
Tel: +44-28-4062 -5485
Fax: +44-28-4062-5485
Web: http://www.iaeste.org
e-mail: general.secretary@iaeste.org

📖 Programme d'échange IAESTE

Domaines d'étude: agriculture, architecture, formation professionnelle, ingénierie, sciences, sylviculture, technologie.
Description: programme de formation technique: stages rémunérés en ingénierie et sciences, éventuellement architecture, agriculture et sylviculture.
A l'intention de: ressortissants des pays membres de l'IAESTE qui poursuivent des études dans les universités ou collèges techniques.
Organisés: dans les pays membres de l'IAESTE (voir site web).
Durée: de 8 à 52+ semaines.
Assistance financière: les employeurs versent une indemnité qui couvre les frais de subsistance dans le pays hôte; les frais de voyage, d'assurance maladie ou les dépenses personnelles ne sont pas compris.
Connaissances linguistiques: principalement anglais, français ou allemand, ou bien la langue du pays hôte.
Inscriptions: au Bureau de l'IAESTE dans le pays du candidat (voir site web).

21 Asociación Internacional de Intercambio de Estudiantes para la Formación Técnica Práctica [IAESTE]

Secretaría General
PO Box 102
BT32 4WY Banbridge Northern Ireland, UK
Tel: +44-28-4062 -5485
Fax: +44-28-4062-5485
Web: http://www.iaeste.org
e-mail: general.secretary@iaeste.org

📖 Programa de intercambio IAESTE

Campos de estudios: agricultura, arquitectura, ciencias, formación profesional, ingeniería, silvicultura, tecnología.
Descripción: programa de formación profesional (prácticas remuneradas) en ingeniería y ciencias, con opciones en arquitectura, agricultura y silvicultura.
Se destina(n): a nacionales de los países miembros de la IAESTE que cursan estudios en universidades y colegios técnicos.
Se dicta(n): en los países miembros de la IAESTE (ver sitio web).
Duración: de 8 a 52+ semanas.
Asistencia financiera: las empresas conceden una subvención para cubrir los gastos de mantenimiento; los gastos de viaje, de seguro de enfermedad y gastos personales corren a cargo de los cursillistas.
Idioma: principalmente en inglés, francés o alemán, o en el idioma del país de estudio.
Inscripciones: Comité de la IAESTE en el país del candidato (ver sitio web).

22 International Astronomical Union [IAU]

Secretariat
98bis, Bd. Arago
75014 Paris, France
Tel: +33-1-4325-8358
Fax: +33-1-4325-2616
Web: http://www.iau.org
e-mail: iau@iap.fr

☞ Travel Grants / Astronomy

Study Domains: astronomy, travel grants.
Scholarships: travel grants to promote the international exchange of astronomers and allow study in countries equipped with better observatories, laboratories, computing facilities, etc. The programme is designed to support both the work of young astronomers and established astronomers whose visits may benefit the country or institution visited.
Open to: candidates must be faculty/staff members, postdoctoral fellows or graduate students at any recognized educational/research institution or observatory. All candidates must have an excellent record of research and must have made permanent and professional commitments to astronomy. All recipients should return to their home institutions or countries upon the completion of their visits. All visits must be formally agreed to by the directors of the home and host institutions involved.
Other conditions: see the website for complete information.
Duration: at least 3 months at a single host institution.
Value: generally for return economy air fare; see website for eligibility conditions.
Applications: at any time, to the IAU Program Group (PG) Exchange of Astronomers; Chairperson: Charles Tolbert, University of Virginia, Department of Astronomy, PO Box 3818, Charlottesville, VA 22903, USA; email: tolbert@virginia.edu.; Vice-Chairperson: John R. Percy, Science Division, University of Toronto, Erindale College, CA - Mississauga ON, L5l 1C6, Canada; tel:+1-905-828-5351; fax: +1-905-828-5328; email: jpercy@credit.erin.utoronto.ca.

22 Union astronomique internationale [UAI]

Secrétariat
98bis, Bd. Arago
75014 Paris, France
Tel: +33-1-4325-8358
Fax: +33-1-4325-2616
Web: http://www.iau.org
e-mail: iau@iap.fr

☞ Subventions de voyage / astronomie

Domaines d'étude: astronomie, subventions de voyage.
Bourses: subventions de voyage destinées à promouvoir l'échange international d'astronomes et les études dans les pays équipés des meilleurs observatoires, laboratoires, ressources informatiques, etc. Le programme vise à soutenir aussi bien le travail de jeunes astronomes que celui d'astronomes confirmés, dont le travail sera amélioré grâce à la visite de ce pays ou institution.
A l'intention de: candidats ayant obtenu diplôme ou doctorat, ou membres du personnel, d'institutions éducatives ou de recherche, ou observatoires. Tous les visiteurs doivent retourner dans leur institution ou pays d'origine après la fin de la visite. Celle-ci doit être approuvée formellement par les directeurs des institutions d'origine et à visiter.
Autres Conditions: consulter le site Internet pour connaître l'ensemble des conditions d'admission.
Durée: séjours d'au moins 3 mois, dans la même institution.
Valeur: en général, valeur du billet de retour en classe économique; consulter le site Internet pour connaître les conditions d'applicabilité.
Candidatures: à tout moment, au Groupe de programme (PG) pour les échanges d'astronomes de l'UAI, au Président: Charles Tolbert, University of Virginia, Department of Astronomy, PO Box 3818, Charlottesville, VA 22903, USA; email: tolbert@virginia.edu.; Vice-Chairperson: John R. Percy, Science Division, University of Toronto, Erindale College, CA - Mississauga ON, L5l 1C6, Canada; tel:+1-905-828-5351; fax:

+1-905-828-5328; email: jpercy@credit.erin.utoronto.ca.

22 Unión Astronómica Internacional [UAI]

Secretaría
98 bis, boulevard Arago
75014 París, Francia
Tel: +33-1-4325-8358
Fax: +33-1-4325-2616
Web: http://www.iau.org
e-mail: iau@iap.fr

☞ Subvenciones de viaje

Campos de estudios: astronomía, subvención de viaje.
Becas: subvenciones de viaje para fomentar el intercambio internacional de astrónomos y permitirles estudiar en países que cuenten con los mejores observatorios, laboratorios, instalaciones informáticas, etc. El programa está destinado a apoyar el trabajo tanto de jóvenes astrónomos como de astrónomos confirmados, trabajo que mejorará gracias a la visita de dichas instituciones o países.
Se conceden: a jóvenes astronónomos o a astrónomos en ejercicio (funcionarios o miembros, estudiantes o doctores, de/en alguna institución reconocida educativa o de investigación, u observatorio).
Todos los beneficiarios deben regresar a la institución o país de origen una vez finalizada la visita. Toda visita debe estar avalada formalmente por los directores de las instituciones de origen y de acogida.
Otras condiciones: consultar el sitio web para conocer el conjunto de condiciones y requerimientos.
Duración: por lo menos 3 meses, en la misma institución.
Importe: en general, valor del billete aéreo de regreso; consultar el sitio web para conocer las condiciones de aplicación.
Solicitudes: al Presidente del Grupo de Programa (PG) para el Intercambio de Astrónomos de la UAI; Chairperson: Charles Tolbert, University of Virginia, Department of Astronomy, PO Box 3818, Charlottesville, VA 22903, USA; email: tolbert@virginia.edu.; Vice-Chairperson: John R. Percy, Science Division, University of Toronto, Erindale College, CA - Mississauga ON, L5l 1C6, Canada; tel:+1-905-828-5351; fax: +1-905-828-5328; email: jpercy@credit.erin.utoronto.ca.

23 International Atomic Energy Agency [IAEA]

Vienna International Centre
Wagramerstrasse 5
PO Box 100
Vienna, Austria
Tel: +43-1-2600
Fax: +43-1-2600-7
Web: http://www.iaea.org

☞ IAEA fellowships

Study Domains: energy, sciences, technology.
Subjects: any scientific or technical field related to the peaceful uses of atomic energy and the use of radioisotopes in agriculture, industry, medicine, research, etc.
Open to: nationals of developing member states of the IAEA, nominated by their governments; candidates must have at least a university degree in science or engineering and language competence as required by host institution/country; usually under 40 years.
Place of study: suitable institution in any country.
Duration: up to 1 year (renewable).
Value: stipend at United Nations Development Programme rates.
Applications: by 1 July, though acceptable throughout the year; endorsed by Ministry having jurisdiction over IAEA matters in candidate's country.

23 Agence internationale de l'énergie atomique [AIEA]

Vienna International Centre
Wagramer Strasse 5
PO Box 100
1400 Vienne, Autriche
Tel: +43-1-2600
Fax: +43-1-2600-7

Web: http://www.iaea.org

✆ Bourses de recherche

Domaines d'étude: énergie, sciences, technologie.
Domaines d'études: tout domaine scientifique ou technique relatif à l'emploi de l'énergie atomique à des fins pacifiques et l'utilisation des radioisotopes en agriculture, médecine, industrie, recherche, etc.
A l'intention de: ressortissants des pays en développement membres de l'AIEA choisis par leur gouvernement et titulaires d'un diplôme universitaire en sciences ou ingénierie. Une bonne connaissance de la langue est exigée par le pays ou l'institution hôte; âge maximum: en général 40 ans.
Lieu: institutions appropriées de n'importe quel pays.
Durée: 1 an maximum (renouvelable).
Valeur: indemnité basée sur le barème du Programme des Nations Unies pour le Développement.
Candidatures: avant le 1er juillet, mais acceptables toute l'année; soutenues par le ministère responsable des affaires relatives à l'énergie atomique dans le pays du candidat.

23 Organismo Internacional de Energía Atómica [OIEA]

Vienna International Centre
Wagramer Strasse 5
PO Box 100
1400 Viena, Austria
Tel: +43-1-2600
Fax: +43-1-2600-7
Web: http://www.iaea.org

✆ Becas de estudio

Campos de estudios: ciencias, energía, tecnología.
Materias de estudio: cualquier disciplina científica o técnica relacionada con los usos pacíficos de la energía atómica y la utilización de radioisótopos en la agricultura, medicina, industria, investigación, etc.
Se conceden: a nacionales de los países en desarrollo miembros del OIEA. Los candidatos deben ser designados por sus gobiernos, poseer un diploma universitario en ciencias o en ingeniería y buenos conocimientos del idioma exigido por el país o el centro de estudios; edad máxima: por lo general 40 años.
Lugar: en instituciones apropiadas de cualquier país.
Duración: 1 año (prorrogable).
Importe: subsidio basado en la escala establecida para las becas del Programa de las Naciones Unidas para el Desarrollo.
Solicitudes: hasta el 1° de julio, pero se aceptan durante todo el año; la petición debe estar refrendada por el ministerio encargado de los asuntos relacionados con la energía atómica en el país del candidato.

24 International Centre for Advanced Communication Studies for Latin America [CIESPAL]

Apartado 17-01-584
Ave. Diego de Almagro 2155 y Andrade Marín
Quito, Ecuador
Tel: +593-2-254-8011
Fax: +593-2-250-2487
Web: http://www.ciespal.net
e-mail: info@ciespal.net

✆ CIESPAL Grants

Study Domains: communication.
Scholarships: grants for the production of television news programmes.
Open to: journalists, cameramen, editors of news-programmes in Latin America and the Caribbean who hold degrees in social communications and/or journalism, have a good knowledge of Spanish and can work in the news service of a television channel.
Place of study: CIESPAL, Ecuador.
Duration: 4 weeks.
Value: US$200 per participant (workshop cost); travelling and boarding costs are covered by the CIESPAL and the FES, as well as pocket money for current expenses.
Applications: by March, June or September, to CIESPAL's Department of Professional Training at the above address.

24 Centre international d'études supérieures de communication pour l'Amérique latine [CIESPAL]

Apartado 17-01-584
Ave. Diego de Almagro 2155 y Andrade Marín
Quito, Équateur
Tel: +593-2-254-8011
Fax: +593-2-250-2487
Web: http://www.ciespal.net
e-mail: info@ciespal.net

✆ Bourses CIESPAL

Domaines d'étude: communication.
Bourses: Bourses de production d'information pour la télévision.
A l'intention de: journalistes, cameramen, producteurs de programmes d'information d'Amérique latine et des Caraïbes; titulaires d'un baccalauréat ou d'un diplôme de communication social et/ou de journalisme; ayant travaillé pour le téléjournal d'une chaîne de télévision; maîtrise de l'espagnol requise.
Lieu: CIESPAL, Équateur.
Durée: 4 semaines.
Valeur: 200 US$ par participant; le CIESPAL et la FES prennent en charge les frais de transport aérien, de logement, de restauration, et allouent un peu d'argent pour les dépenses courantes.
Candidatures: avant mars, juin et septembre, auprès du Département de la formation professionnelle, CIESPAL, à l'adresse ci-dessus.

24 Centro Internacional de Estudios Superiores de Comunicación para América Latina [CIESPAL]

Apartado 17-01-584
Av. Diego de Almagro 2155 y Andrade Marín
Quito, Ecuador
Tel: +593-2-254-8011
Fax: +593-2-250-2487
Web: http://www.ciespal.net
e-mail: info@ciespal.net

✆ Becas del CIESPAL

Campos de estudios: comunicación.
Becas: Becas para la producción de programas informativos para la televisión.
Se conceden: periodistas, camarógrafos, editores de programas informativos de América Latina y el Caribe que sean bachilleres en comunicación social y/o periodistas y que sepan bien el español.
Lugar: CIESPAL, Ecuador.
Duración: 4 semanas.
Importe: 200 dólares de los Estados Unidos de América por cada participante (costo del taller); el CIESPAL y la FES cubren el transporte aéreo, el alojamiento, la alimentación, los materiales y una pequeña cantidad para gastos.
Solicitudes: en marzo, junio y septiembre; dirigirse al Departamento de formación profesional del CIESPAL, en la dirección que figura en el título.

25 International Centre for Research, Cooperation and Exchange in the Caribbean and the Americas [CIRECCA]

BP 393
97258 Fort-de-France Cedex (Martinique) France
Tel: +596-727-506
Fax: +596-616-898
e-mail: cirecca@yahoo.fr

✆ CIRECA Internship Programme

Study Domains: American studies, French, international relations, literature and civilization.
Programmes: CIRECCA internship programme to promote cultural dialogue and development of international exchanges in the Caribbean, Latin America and Quebec (Canada): (a) didactics of French as a foreign language; (b) French and French-language Caribbean literature; (c) history, geography and anthropology of the French Antilles and the

Caribbean area.
Open to: candidates from Latin America, the Caribbean and North America or from the following organisms: French departments (or others interested in organizing an internship on a scientific topic) of universities in Latin America and the Caribbean; Alliances françaises; associations of language professors; adult training centres or research institutions.
Held: on the campus of the Université Antilles-Guyane, Schoelcher, or at CIRECCA.
Applications: to the Director for any further information.

25 Centre international de recherches, d'échanges et de coopération de la Caraïbe et des Amériques [CIRECCA]

BP 393
97258 Fort-de-France Cedex(Martinique) France
Tel: +596-727-506
Fax: +596-616-898
e-mail: cirecca@yahoo.fr

⌑ Stages CIRECCA

Domaines d'étude: études américaines, français, littérature et civilisation, relations internationales.
Programmes: stages organisés par le CIRECCA en vue de favoriser le dialogue des cultures et le développement des échanges internationaux dans les Caraïbes, l'Amérique latine et le Québec (Canada): (a) la didactique du français langue étrangère; (b) les littératures française, francophone, et du monde caribéen; (c) histoire, géographie et anthropologie des Antilles françaises et du monde caribéen.
A l'intention de: ressortissants des pays d'Amérique latine, des Caraïbes et d'Amérique du Nord, ou appartenant aux organismes suivants: départements de français (ou autres, désireux d'organiser des stages scientifiques) des universités latino-américaines et caribéennes; bureaux de l'Alliance française; associations de professeurs de langues; centres de formation permanente ou organismes de recherche.
Organisés: soit au campus de l'Université Antilles-Guyane, Schoelcher, ou au CIRECCA.
Inscriptions: auprès du Directeur, pour tout renseignement complémentaire.

25 Centro Internacional de Investigaciones, Intercambios y Cooperación del Caribe y de las Américas [CIRECCA]

BP 393
97258 Fort-de-France Cedex, (Martinique) France
Tel: +596-727-506
Fax: +596-616-898
e-mail: cirecca@yahoo.fr

⌑ Cursillos CIRECCA

Campos de estudios: estudios americanos, francés, literatura y civilización, relaciones internacionales.
Programas: Cursillos organizados por el CIRECCA para favorecer el diálogo entre culturas y el desarrollo de intercambios internacionales en el Caribe, en las América Latina y Québec (Canadá): (a) didáctica del francés como lengua extranjera; (b) literatura francesa, de lengua francesa del Caribe; (c) historia, geografía y antropología de las Antillas Francesas y del Caribe.
Se destina(n): a nacionales de los países de América Latina, Caribe y América del Norte, o que pertenezcan a alguno de los organismos siguientes: departamentos de francés (u otros que deseen organizar cursillos científicos) de universidades latinoamericanas y caribeñas; oficinas de la Alianza Francesa; asociaciones de profesores de lenguas; centros de capacitación profesional u organismos de investigación.
Se dicta(n): en la Université Antille-Guyane, Schoelcher, o en el CIRECCA.
Inscripciones: Dirigirse al Director, para mayores informaciones.

26 International Centre for the Study of the Preservation and the Restoration of Cultural Property [ICCROM]

Via di San Michele 13
00153 Rome, Italy
Tel: +39-6-585-531
Fax: +39-6-58-553-349
Web: http://www.iccrom.org
e-mail: iccrom@iccrom.org

⌑ ICCROM Conservation Courses

Study Domains: architecture, arts, museology and museography.
Programmes: specialist courses in various conservation subjects.
Description: subjects change each year and are taught in courses, seminars and workshops; recent courses include development of conservation of collections in museums and archives and training of teachers, training of conservator-restorers, living heritage sites, wood conservation technology, conservation of immovable heritage in Africa, architectural records, inventories, information systems, preventive conservation, conservation of archaeological sites.
Open to: preferably nationals of the ICCROM member countries, aged 25 to 50; many courses have their own requirements.
Financial assistance: limited availability.
Languages: English or French.
Applications: deadlines vary. Contact the Centre at the above address for further information.

26 Centre international d'études pour la conservation et la restauration des biens culturels [ICCROM]

Via di San Michele 13
00153 Rome, Italie
Tel: +39-6-585-531
Fax: +39-6-58-553-349
Web: http://www.iccrom.org
e-mail: iccrom@iccrom.org

⌑ Cours de spécialisation en matière de conservation

Domaines d'étude: architecture, arts, muséologie et muséographie.
Programmes: Cours de spécialisation dans les divers domaines.
Description: domaines d'étude changent chaque année; enseignement sous forme de cours, de séminaires et d'ateliers; les nouveaux cours couvrent le développement muséologique et la formation des enseignants dans ce domaine; la formation des conservateurs-restaurateurs; la conservation territoriale urbaine intégrée; la technologie de la conservation du bois; la conservation de la pierre; la conservation du patrimoine immobilier en Afrique; documentation, inventaires, systèmes d'informations et conservation en architecture.
A l'intention de: ressortissants des pays membres de l'ICCROM de préférence, âgés de 25 à 50 ans.
Assistance financière: limitée.
Connaissances linguistiques: enseignement en anglais ou français.
Inscriptions: les dates de clôture sont variables, à l'adresse ci-dessus pour de plus amples renseignements.

26 Centro Internacional de Estudio para la Conservación y Restauración de los Bienes Culturales [ICCROM]

Via di San Michele 13
00153 Roma, Italia
Tel: +39-6-585-531
Fax: +39-6-58-553-349
Web: http://www.iccrom.org
e-mail: iccrom@iccrom.org

Cursos especializados en conservación

Campos de estudios: arquitectura, artes, museología y museografía.

Programas: Cursos especializados sobre diversos temas en conservación.

Descripción: los temas del enseñanza cambian cada año, presentados en cursos, seminarios o talleres. Los cursos recientes abarcan el desarrollo museológico y la formación de docentes en este área; la formación de conservadores-restauradores; la conservación territorial urbana integrada; las tecnologías de conservación de la madera; la conservación de la piedra; la conservación de bienes inmuebles en Africa; la documentación, inventarios, sistemas informáticos y la conservación arquitectónica.

Se destina(n): de preferencia a nacionales de los países miembros del ICCROM, que tengan entre 25 y 50 años de edad.

Asistencia financiera: disponibilidad limitada.

Idioma: enseñanza en inglés o en francés.

Inscripciones: las fechas límites varían; por informes complementarios, dirigirse al Centro en la dirección que figura en el título.

27 International Crops Research Institute for the Semi-Arid Tropics [ICRISAT]

Patancheru PO
502 324 Andhra Pradesh, India
Tel: +91-40-3071-3071
Fax: +91-40-3071-3074/5
Web: http://www.icrisat.org
e-mail: icrisat@cgiar.org

ICRISAT Training Programmes

Study Domains: agriculture, agronomic sciences.

Programmes: international research and training programmes in crop improvement, production agronomy, resource management and socio-economic aspects in the semi-arid tropics.

Open to: in-service scientists, in-service technicians and junior scientists working with National Agricultural Research Systems (NARS), graduate students (for thesis research), university students (short-term project work), all nominated and sponsored by their employer or university, and holding a PhD.

Fees: variable, depending on course and duration.

Financial assistance: through sponsors/donors.

Languages: good knowledge in English and French required.

Applications: to Learning Systems Unit, ICRISAT, at the above address.

27 Institut international de recherche sur les cultures des zones tropicales semi-arides [ICRISAT]

Patancheru PO
502 324 Andhra Pradesh, Inde
Tel: +91-40-3071-3071
Fax: +91-40-3071-3074/5
Web: http://www.icrisat.org
e-mail: icrisat@cgiar.org

Programmes en agronomie

Domaines d'étude: agriculture, sciences agronomiques.

Programmes: programmes internationaux de recherche et de formation pour l'amélioration des récoltes, production dans le domaine de l'agronomie, gestion des ressources et aspects socio-économiques dans les zones tropicales semi-arides.

A l'intention de: scientifiques, techniciens et jeunes techniciens en cours d'emploi travaillant pour la NARS («National Agricultural Research Systems»), étudiants de 3e cycle (faisant de la recherche pour une thèse), étudiants travaillant sur un projet à court terme; tous titulaires d'une maîtrise, nommés et parrainés par leur employeur ou leur université.

Assistance financière: par les sponsors/donateurs.

Connaissances linguistiques: très bonne connaissance de l'anglais et du français exigée.

Inscriptions: s'adresser à «Learning Systems Unit»,

ICRISAT à l'adresse ci-dessus.

27 Instituto Internacional de Investigación de Cultivos para las Zonas Tropicales Semiáridas [ICRISAT]

Patancheru PO
502 324 Andhra Pradesh, India
Tel: +91-40-3071-3071
Fax: +91-40-3071-3074/5
Web: http://www.icrisat.org
e-mail: icrisat@cgiar.org

Programas internacionales de investigación y formación

Campos de estudios: agricultura, ciencias agronómicas.

Descripción: programas sobre mejoramiento de cosechas, producción agrícola, gestión de recursos y aspectos socioeconómicos en zonas tropicales semiáridas.

Se destina(n): a científicos y técnicos en actividad, a jóvenes científicos que trabajen en NARS (National Agricultural Research Systems), a estudiantes diplomados (investigación para tesis), a estudiantes universitarios (para proyectos a corto plazo), todos ellos designados y patrocinados por su empleador o universidad, que estén en posesión de una maestría.

Asistencia financiera: número limitado de becas parciales o completas disponible.

Idioma: se requiere buen conocimiento de inglés y francés.

Inscripciones: dirigirse a "Learning Systems Unit", ICRISAT, en la dirección que figura en el título.

28 International Federation of University Women [IFUW]

8, rue de l'Ancien Port
1201 Geneva, Switzerland
Tel: +41-22-731-2380
Fax: +41-22-738-0440
Web: http://www.ifuw.org
e-mail: info@ifuw.org

IFUW Fellowships and Grants

Study Domains: human sciences, natural sciences, social sciences.

Description: The IFUW offers a limited number of fellowships and grants to women graduates for advanced research, study and training. The competitions are normally held every two years.

Open to: members of national federations/associations affiliated to IFUW and independent members; for work in any branch of learning, in the country of the applicant's choice; awards are for study/research/training at the doctoral or post-doctoral level; a limited number of awards will be given for work at the Masters' level.

Place of study: in an accredited institution or institutions, preferably in a country other than Fellow's country of study or habitual residence.

Applications: to national affiliate of IFUW for IFUW members; to IFUW headquarters in Geneva for IFUW independent members. For more information, to IFUW Liaison Office, American Association of University Women, 111 Sixteenth Street, Washington, D.C. 20036, for United States residents; to IFUW Fellowships at the above address for all others; see website for addresses of national affiliates and further information.

28 Fédération internationale des femmes diplômées des universités [FIFDU]

8, rue de l'Ancien Port
1201 Genève, Suisse
Tel: +41-22-731-2380
Fax: +41-22-738-0440
Web: http://www.ifuw.org
e-mail: info@ifuw.org

Bourses et subventions FIFDU

Domaines d'étude: sciences humaines, sciences naturelles, sciences sociales.

Description: la FIFDU offre un nombre limité de bourses

et subventions à des femmes diplômées, pour études, formation et recherche avancée. Les concours d'admission ont lieu habituellement tous les deux ans.

A l'intention de: membres des fédérations/associations affiliées à la FIFDU et membres indépendants, pour travailler dans tous les domaines de la connaissance, dans le pays choisi par la candidate; les subventions sont pour études ou formation ou recherche avancée (il en existe un nombre limité pour des études au niveau master).

Lieu: dans une ou plusieurs institutions agréées, de préférence dans un pays autre que le pays des études ou de résidence habituelle de la candidate.

Candidatures: pour les membres de la FIFDU, à l'association nationale de la FIFDU dans le pays de la candidate; pour les membres indépendants, au siège de la FIFDU à Genève. Pour de plus amples renseignements: IFUW Liaison Office, American Association of University Women, 111 Sixteenth Street, Washington, DC 20036, pour les ressortissants américains; au Service des bourses de la FIFDU, à l'adresse ci-dessus, pour les autres ressortissants. Le site Internet fournit les adresses des institutions nationales affiliées et d'autres informations complémentaires.

28 Federación Internacional de Mujeres Universitarias [FIMU]

8, rue de l'Ancien Port
1201 Ginebra, Suiza
Tel: +41-22-731-2380
Fax: +41-22-738-0440
Web: http://www.ifuw.org
e-mail: info@ifuw.org

☛ Becas y subvenciones FIMU

Campos de estudios: ciencias humanas, ciencias naturales, ciencias sociales.

Descripción: la FIMU ofrece un número limitado de becas y subvenciones a mujeres graduadas, para investigación superior, estudios y formación. Los concursos se llevan a cabo habitualmente cada dos años.

Se conceden: a miembros de las federaciones/asociaciones afiliadas a la FIMU y a miembros independientes, para trabajar en cualquier área de estudio, en el país elegido por la candidata; las subvenciones son para estudios/investigación/formación a nivel de doctorado o post-doctorado (existe un número limitado para trabajos a nivel de maestría).

Lugar: en una o varias instituciones reconocidas, de preferencia en un país diferente del de estudio o de residencia habitual de la candidata.

Solicitudes: para los miembros de la FIMU, dirigirse a la asociación nacional de la FIMU en el país de la candidata; para los miembros independientes, en la sede de la FIMU en Ginebra. Para mayor información: IFUW Liaison Office, American Association of University Women, 111 Sixteenth Street, Washington, D.C. 20036, para las ciudadanas norteamericanas; Servicio de becas de la FIMU, en la dirección que figura en el título, para candidatas de otros países. Se puede consultar el sitio web para obtener la dirección de las instituciones nacionales afiliadas y por informaciones complementarias.

29 International Institute

44905 Bet Berl, Israel
Tel: +972-9-761-2323
Fax: +972-9-742-1868
Web: http://www.peoples.org.il
e-mail: info@peoples.org.il

📖 Leadership Training Course

Study Domains: development studies, human sciences, international relations, international studies, political economy, social sciences.

Programmes: leadership training course in economic and social aspects of development.

Description: specialized leadership training in fields relevant to trade unions, co-operatives, community groups, women's organizations, youth movements, etc.

Open to: nationals from countries located in each of the Institute's 5 geo-political divisions: Africa; Asia and the Pacific; Eastern and Central Europe (including CIS); Latin America and the Caribbean; Middle East and North Africa; candidates having substantial leadership experience in relevant fields and other appropriate qualifications;.

Duration: 35 courses and seminars per year.

Fees: US$3,000 per month, all inclusive (tuition, room, board, field trips and visits, social and cultural activities, medical insurance, laundry, pocket money).

Financial assistance: scholarships available for some participants in all courses; travel expenses generally not included.

Languages: knowledge of one of the languages of instruction (English, Spanish, French, Russian, Arabic) is essential; occasional courses in Hungarian, Bulgarian, Czech, Romanian, etc.

Applications: to Academic Director, at the above address.

29 Institut International

Bet Berl
44905 Bet Berl, Israël
Tel: +972-9-761-2323
Fax: +972-9-742-1868
Web: http://www.peoples.org.il
e-mail: info@peoples.org.il

📖 Cours de formation de dirigeants

Domaines d'étude: économie politique, études du développement, études internationales, relations internationales, sciences humaines, sciences sociales.

Programmes: cours de formation de dirigeants pour le développement économique et social.

Description: cours spécialisés de formation de dirigeants dans les domaines relatifs aux syndicats, coopératives, groupes communautaires, organisations féministes, mouvements de jeunesse, etc.

A l'intention de: ressortissants des institutions des pays faisant partie des 5 divisions géopolitiques: Afrique, Asie et Pacifique, Europe centrale et orientale (CIS y compris), Amérique latine et Caraïbes, Afrique du Nord et Moyen-Orient; candidats dotés d'une expérience affirmée de dirigeant se rattachant aux domaines concernés et pourvus des qualifications requises.

Durée: 35 cours et séminaires par an.

Frais: 3.000 dollars des États-Unis d'Amérique par mois comprenant les frais d'études, d'hébergement, les visites et les voyages sur le terrain, les activités culturelles, l'assurance maladie et l'argent de poche.

Assistance financière: possibilité de bourses; les frais de voyages ne sont généralement pas compris.

Connaissances linguistiques: connaissance obligatoire d'une des langues d'enseignement (anglais, arabe, espagnol, français, russe); organisations parfois de cours en bulgare, hongrois, tchèque, roumain, etc.

Inscriptions: au Bureau des inscriptions, à l'adresse ci-dessus.

29 Instituto Internacional

44905 Bet Berl, Israel
Tel: +972-9-761-2323
Fax: +972-9-742-1868
Web: http://www.peoples.org.il
e-mail: info@peoples.org.il

📖 Cursos de formación de dirigentes

Campos de estudios: ciencias humanas, ciencias sociales, economía política, estudios internacionales, estudios sobre el desarrollo, relaciones internacionales.

Descripción: cursos especializados de formación de dirigentes en aspectos económicos y sociales del desarrollo: organizaciones gremiales, cooperativas, asociaciones comunitarias, organizaciones de mujeres, movimientos juveniles, etc.

Se destina(n): a nacionales de los países de cada una de las 5 divisiones geopolíticas del Instituto: Africa, Asia y el Pacífico, Europa Central y del Este (incluyendo CIS), América Latina y el Caribe, Africa del Medio Oriente y del Norte. Los candidatos deberán acreditar reconocida experiencia en áreas pertinentes, así como calificaciones apropiadas.

Duración: se dictan 35 cursos y seminarios por año.

Costo(s): 3.000 dólares de los Estados Unidos de América, todo incluido (enseñanza, alojamiento, manutención, desplazamientos y visitas, actividades sociales y culturales, seguro médico, lavandería, gastos menudos).

Asistencia financiera: existen algunas becas para todos los cursos; los gastos de viaje, en general, no están incluidos.

Idioma: es imprescindible conocer uno de los idiomas de enseñanza (inglés, español, francés, ruso, árabe); ocasionalmente, se pueden dictar cursos en húngaro, búlgaro, checo, rumano, etc.
Inscripciones: dirigirse al Director Académico, en la dirección que figura en el título.

30 International Institute of Human Rights [IIDH]

2, Allée René Cassin
67000 Strasbourg, France
Tel: +33-3-8845-8445
Fax: +33-3-8845-8450
Web: http://www.iidh.org
e-mail: administration@iidh.org /
bibliotheque@iidh.org

📖 Annual Teaching Session CiedhU

Study Domains: international law, law.
Programmes: within the framework of the study session, the International Center for University Human Rights Teaching (CiedhU) offers university professors, assistants and researchers, formative seminars in to enable them to develop specialized human rights teaching and research in their academic activity. Exchanges between participants are also encouraged. The CiedhU programme requires regular participation in the Study Session's lectures and courses in addition to participation in a series of specialized seminars organized parallel to the session. A special Participation Certificate will be issued to those who participate in CiedhU program on a regular basis.
Duration: approximately 20 hours of training in human rights teaching methods.
Fees: registration fees for the CiedhU programme: 130€.
Languages: French or English; participants are divided into one of the two language groups; a limited number of places are available in each language group.
Applications: by 31 May.

📖 International and Comparative Law of Human Rights

Study Domains: international law, international relations, law.
Programmes: advanced courses on the international and comparative law of human rights; annual study session leading to a diploma of the IIHR and a certificate of participation.
Open to: advanced students in law, political science, human and social sciences, professors and researchers, members of the legal professions and any other profession related to human rights, national and international civil servants, members of non-governmental organisations; applicants must have completed 4 years of university study or the equivalent at the time of the session, or be in possession of a practical knowledge of human rights through work with a governmental agency, intergovernmental or non-governmental organization or similar experience.
Duration: 4 weeks in July.
Fees: 630€ for registration, plus 230€ for accommodation during the session (price subject to change).
Financial assistance: partial financial help; requests must reach the Institute well in advance of the course.
Languages: Session's official languages: French and English; some fundamental courses are in French, English, Spanish and Arabic.
Applications: by 31 May, see website for application and programme details.

📖 Summer Course on Refugee Law

Study Domains: international law, law.
Programmes: since 1998, the International Institute of Human Rights has organized, in collaboration with the United Nations High Commissioner on Refugees (HCR) a specialized intensive course having refugees as its theme. To promote, by teaching and research, the laws governing the protection of refugees. Under the direction of specialists in this field, the courses give a universal, regional and thematic approach to the problems linked with all forms and expressions of exile.
Held: in Strasbourg, France, during 2 weeks in June.
Duration: 2 weeks.

Fees: 290€ for registration, 135€ for lodging and 100€ for meals (lunch and dinner for class days).
Financial assistance: possibility of limited amount of financial assistance; requests should be sent to IIDH along with registration form.
Languages: French only; written and oral competence required.

30 Institut international des droits de l'homme [IIDH]

2, allée René Cassin
67000 Strasbourg, France
Tel: +33-3-8845-8445
Fax: +33-3-8845-8450
Web: http://www.iidh.org
e-mail: administration@iidh.org /
bibliotheque@iidh.org

📖 Cours d'été sur les réfugiés

Domaines d'étude: droit, droit international.
Description: cours d'été sur les réfugiés coopération avec le Haut-Commissariat des Nations Unies pour les réfugiés sur le thème, Droit et protection universelle et régionale des réfugiés.
Les enseignements sont dispensés par des experts du HCR ainsi que par des spécialistes du monde académique, institutionnel, judiciaire, associatif et médiatique. Cette formation s'adresse à un public de secteurs professionnels variés et vise à promouvoir la recherche, l'enseignement et le développement des bonnes pratiques dans le domaine de la protection internationale des réfugiés. Elle consiste en une approche universelle et une approche régionale de la problématique de l'asile. Des cours magistraux, l'étude de cas pratiques, le traitement de questions d'actualité et un exercice de simulation d'une juridiction sont proposés aux participants. A la fin de la session de deux semaines, un test d'évaluation permet de contrôler les connaissances acquises et un certificat est décerné aux participants l'ayant réussi.
A l'intention de: candidats devraient avoir au moins 4 années d'études universitaires minimum; à titre exceptionnel, justifier d'une expérience approfondie dans le domaine des réfugiés ou des droits de l'homme; maîtrise du français exigée.
Durée: à Strasbourg, France pendant 2 semaines au mois de juin.
Frais: 290€ pour frais d'inscription plus environ 140€ pour frais de logement et 90€-130€ pour les repas (petit déjeuner et/ou déjeuner).
Assistance financière: possibilité de bourses pour couvrir une partie ou l'intégralité des frais de cours; la demande d'assistance financière devrait être envoyé à l'IIDH au même temps que le formulaire d'inscription.
Connaissances linguistiques: cours dispensé uniquement en français; une maîtrise de la langue française, orale et écrite est exigée.

📖 Droit international et droit comparé des droits de l'homme

Domaines d'étude: droit, droit international, relations internationales.
Programmes: étude approfondie du droit international et du droit comparé des droits de l'homme; session annuelle d'enseignement conduisant au diplôme de l'Institut international des droits de l'homme et au certificat de participation.
A l'intention de: étudiants avancés dans le domaine des sciences juridiques, politiques, humaines et sociales, enseignants et chercheurs, membres de professions juridiques et de toute autre profession confrontée aux droits de l'homme, fonctionnaires nationaux et internationaux, membres d'organisations non gouvernementales. Les candidats doivent avoir achevé 4 ans d'études universitaires ou l'équivalent au moment de la session, justifier d'une expérience approfondie dans la pratique des droits de l'homme.
Durée: 4 semaines en juillet.
Frais: 630 € pour l'inscription, plus frais d'hébergement de 230 € pour la durée de la session.
Assistance financière: aide financière partielle possible; demandes à adresser à l'Institut plusieurs mois d'avance.
Connaissances linguistiques: excellente connaissance de l'anglais et du français exigée; langues officielles de la session: français et anglais. Les cours fondamentaux sont en français, anglais, espagnol et arabe.

Inscriptions: avant le 31 mai.

Sessions de formation extérieures CiedhU

Domaines d'étude: droit international, relations internationales.
Description: Séminaires de formation sur les méthodes d'enseignement des droits de l'homme; destinée aux universitaires et chercheurs.
Durée: 20 heures, en parallèle à la session annuelle d'enseignement.
Connaissances linguistiques: cours dispensé en français et en anglais; environ 20 participants par groupe linguistique.

30 Instituto Internacional de Derechos Humanos [IIDH]

2, Allée René Cassin
67000 Estrasburgo, Francia
Tel: +33-3-8845-8445
Fax: +33-3-8845-8450
Web: http://www.iidh.org
e-mail: administration@iidh.org / bibliotheque@iidh.org

Curso de verano sobre los refugiados

Campos de estudios: derecho, derecho internacional.
Descripción: curso de verano sobre los refugiados, organizado en colaboración con el Alto Comisionado de las Naciones Unidas para los Refugiados (ACNUR).
Un acercamiento universal y regional a la problemática del asilo, así como un acercamiento temático a asuntos más específicos y actuales en este campo. Al final del curso, los participantes realizan un examen con el fin de evaluar los conocimientos adquiridos durante el programa y se entrega un certificado de participación a quienes lo aprueben.
Se destina(n): miembros de profesiones jurídicas y otras profesiones vinculadas con el derecho de asilo, funcionarios nacionales e internacionales, miembros de organizaciones no gubernamentales y de organizaciones internacionales, profesores e investigadores, y estudiantes a nivel avanzado en ciencias jurídicas, políticas, humanas y sociales. Los participantes deben haber acabado cuatro años de estudios universitarios o tener un nivel equivalente, además de poseer una cierta experiencia en el campo de los refugiados y/o en el campo de los derechos humanos. Se requiere también un alto dominio del francés, lengua oficial del curso.
Duración: 2 semanas en junio.
Asistencia financiera: el ACNUR concede un número limitado de becas para cubrir parcial o totalmente los gastos del curso; la solicitud de la ayuda financiera debe ir dirigida, junto con el formulario de inscripción, al Instituto internacional de los derechos humanos).
Idioma: francés, único idioma utilizado durante el curso.
Inscripciones: antes del 22 de abril.

Derecho internacional y comparativo en derechos humanos

Campos de estudios: derecho, derecho internacional, relaciones internacionales.
Descripción: sesión anual de enseñanza especializada en derecho internacional y comparado de los derechos humanos. Se entregará un certificado de participación a todos los que superen el examen que tiene lugar al final de la sesión. El Diploma del Instituto internacional de los Derechos Humanos se dirige a aquellos participantes de la sesión anual del instituto que posean amplios conocimientos en derecho internacional y comparado de los derechos humanos y que tengan un título de postgraduado o nivel equivalente (licenciatura, master o cursos de postgrado).
Se destina(n): estudiantes a nivel avanzado en ciencias jurídicas, políticas, humanas y sociales, profesores e investigadores, miembros de profesiones jurídicas y otras profesiones vinculadas con los derechos humanos, funcionarios nacionales e internacionales y miembros de organizaciones gubernamentales y no gubernamentales.
Duración: 1 mes (en julio).
Costo(s): 650€ para gastos de matrícula y 230€ de gastos de alojamiento (sujetos a cambios).
Asistencia financiera: en casos especiales se ofrece una ayuda económico para sufragar parte de los gastos.
Idioma: lenguas oficiales de las sesiones: francés y inglés; los cursos fundamentales se dictan en francés, inglés, español y árabe.

Inscripciones: antes del 31 de mayo.

Sesión de enseñanza CiedhU

Campos de estudios: derecho, derecho internacional, relaciones internacionales.
Descripción: dentro del marco de la sesión de enseñanza, el Centro Internacional para la Enseñanza de los Derechos Humanos en las Universidades (CiedhU) propone, a profesores de universidad, a colaboradores y a investigadores, seminarios de formación que les permitan profundizar en la enseñanza y la investigación especializadas de los derechos humanos en sus actividades académicas e instituciones. Los intercambios establecidos entre los participantes resultan muy productivos. Al final de la sesión se entrega un certificado de participación especial a los participantes que asistan regularmente a los seminarios del CiedhU. Desde 1972, y en paralelo a la sesión anual de enseñanza, el Instituto propone unos seminarios de formación con el fin de profundizar en la enseñanza y la investigación especializadas en derechos humanos.
Se destina(n): profesores de universidad, colaboradores e investigadores universitarios (número de plazas limitado).
Duración: 20 horas de formación en métodos de enseñanza de los derechos humanos, dentro del marco de la sesión anual de enseñanza que se lleva a cabo durante el mes de julio.
Costo(s): 130€ para gastos de matrícula.
Idioma: inglés o francés.
Inscripciones: antes del 31 de mayo.

31 International Maritime Organization [IMO]

4 Albert Embankment
SE1 7SR London, United Kingdom
Tel: +44-0207-587-3156
Fax: +44-0207-587-3259
Web: http://www.imo.org
e-mail: info@imo.org

IMO Fellowships and Training Awards

Study Domains: electricity and electronics, international law, marine science, mechanical engineering, shipbuilding, technology, transport, vocational training.
Scholarships: (a) fellowships; (b) training awards offered under the multi/bilateral programme.
Description: naval architecture, shipbuilding, navigational aids, watchkeeping operations, hydrography, port operations, marine engineering and electronics, marine survey procedures, firefighting, marine pollution control, general maritime administration, maritime safety, maritime law, short courses on compliance with conventions, maritime education, various certificates of competency, technical maritime studies, handling/carriage of dangerous cargo.
Open to: suitably qualified nationals from developing countries which are Member States of IMO, subject to availability of funds.
Place of study: in the World Maritime University in Malmö, Sweden, the IMO International Maritime Law Institute in Malta and the IMO International Maritime Academy in Trieste, Italy, and, for general short-term fellowships, in some countries where suitable facilities exist.
Value: monthly allowance based on UNDP stipend or DSA rates as appropriate, book allowance, insurance coverage, etc.
Applications: from the appropriate government department in candidate's country, through the UNDP Regional/Resident Representative.

31 Organisation maritime internationale [OMI]

4 Albert Embankment
SE1 7SR Londres, Royaume-Uni
Tel: +44-0207-587-3156
Fax: +44-0207-587-3259
Web: http://www.imo.org
e-mail: info@imo.org

Bourses d'études et de formation

Domaines d'étude: construction navale, droit international, électricité et électronique, formation professionnelle, mécanique, sciences de la mer, technologie, transports.

Bourses: (a) bourses d'études; (b) bourses de formation, offertes au titre du programme multi/bilatéral.
Description: architecture navale, construction navale, aides à la navigation, essais de tenue du quart, hydrographie, opérations portuaires, mécanique et électronique marines, procédures d'inspection maritime, lutte contre l'incendie, contrôle de la pollution maritime, administration maritime générale, sécurité maritime, droit maritime, cours de courte durée sur l'observation des conventions, éducation maritime, divers certificats d'aptitude, études techniques maritimes, manutention/transport de cargos dangereux.
A l'intention de: ressortissants qualifiés des pays en développement qui sont États membres de l'Organisation maritime internationale, et soumis à la disponibilité des fonds.
Lieu: Université maritime mondiale à Malmö, Suède, Institut de droit maritime international de l'OMI à Malte, Académie maritime internationale de l'OMI à Trieste, Italie et, pour des bourses d'études générales à court terme, quelques pays offrant des conditions adéquates.
Valeur: allocation mensuelle basée sur l'échelle adoptée par le PNUD ou le taux d'allocation journalière de subsistance selon le cas, plus allocation de livres, assurance, etc.
Candidatures: soumises par le ministère compétent dans le pays du candidat, par l'intermédiaire du représentant régional/résident local du PNUD.

31 Organización Marítima Internacional [OMI]
4 Albert Embankment
SE1 7SR Londres, Reino Unido
Tel: +44-0207-587-3156
Fax: +44-0207-587-3259
Web: http://www.imo.org
e-mail: info@imo.org

📧 Becas de estudio y de formación
Campos de estudios: ciencias del mar, construcción naval, derecho internacional, electricidad y electrónica, formación profesional, mecánica, tecnología, transportes.
Becas: (a) becas de estudio; (b) becas de formación profesional ofrecidas gracias al programa multi/bilateral.
Descripción: arquitectura naval, construcción naval, ayudas a la navegación, operaciones de guardia, hidrografía, operaciones en puertos, ingeniería marítima y electrónica, procedimientos de inspección marítima, lucha contra incendios, control de contaminación marina, administración marítima general, seguridad marítima, derecho marítimo, cursos cortos sobre observación de convenciones, educación marítima, varios certificados de competencia, estudios marítimos técnicos, manipulación y transporte de cargamentos peligrosos.
Se conceden: a nacionales debidamente cualificados de los países en desarrollo que son Estados Miembros de la Organización Marítima Internacional y de acuerdo a la disponibilidad de fondos.
Lugar: Universidad Marítima Mundial (Malmoe, Suecia), Instituto de Derecho Marítimo Internacional de la OMI (Malta), Academia Marítima Internacional de la OMI (Trieste) y, para las becas generales de corta duración en ciertos países donde existen las instalaciones adecuadas.
Importe: asignación mensual basada en la pensión de estudios del PNUD o en el viático diario, según el caso, más asignación para libros, seguro, etc.
Solicitudes: sometidas por debe presentarlas el departamento gubernamental competente del país del candidato a través del Representante Regional/Residente local del PNUD.

32 International Monetary Fund [IMF]
700 - 19th Street, NW
20431 Washington, DC, USA
Tel: +1-202-623-6660
Fax: +1-202-623-6490
Web: http://www.imf/org/institute
e-mail: insfil@imf.org

📧 IMF Institution Courses and Seminars
Study Domains: economic and commercial sciences, finance, international studies, management.
Description: training for member country officials who are employed by central banks, ministries of finance, statistical and other agencies.
Subjects: macroeconomics, financial policies, and statistics, including financial programming and policies, macroeconomic management and financial sector issues, financial markets and new financial instruments, public investment and fiscal policy, performance budgeting, government finance statistics, balance of payments statistics, safeguards assessments of central banks, monetary and exchange operations, anti-money laundering, and monetary and financial law.
Open to:
• Courses in Washington, DC are open to nationals of all IMF member countries (35 to 40 participants per course).
• Courses in the regional centres are open to nationals of IMF member countries in the region, as indicated on each regional centre's website.
Place of study: in the IMF Headquarters in Washington, DC and at 6 regional training centres located in Austria, Brazil, China, Singapore, Tunisia, United Arab Emirates.
Duration: Courses typically last from two to seven weeks in Washington, DC and from one to four weeks in the regional training centres. The course on financial programming and policies, which generally lasts seven weeks in Washington or two weeks in the regional training centres, is also offered online as a distance learning course, in both English and French, so participants unable to attend the longer course may study part-time in their home countries for ten weeks and in Washington for two weeks.
Value: tuition free; travel, accommodation, living allowance and medical and travel insurance are covered by the IMF.
Languages:
• in Washington, courses and seminars are offered in English, French, Spanish and Arabic.
• at the regional centres, courses are offered in Arabic, Chinese, English, French, and Russian, or in English with interpretation into one of these languages.
Applications: the applicant or invitee must be sponsored by his or her employing agency. Some courses are offered through an application process, while participants to other courses are nominated by their country authorities.
Participants are selected on the basis of a number of factors, including their education, experience, current responsibilities, background in economics, previous participation in an IMF Institute courses, previous participation by compatriots, and the country's training needs.
Detailed information can be found on the websites indicated.
• IMF Headquarters in Washington, DC: http://www.imf.org/institute
• Joint Vienna Institute in Austria: http://www.jvi.org
• IMF-Singapore Regional Training Institute in Singapore: http://www-imf.sti.org
• IMF-AMF Regional Training Program in the United Arab Emirates: http://www.amf.org.ae
• Joint Africa Institute in Tunisia
• Joint China-IMF Training Program in China
• Joint Regional Training Center for Latin America in Brazil: http://www.esaf.fazenda.gov.br
Do not apply directly to the IMF.

33 International Ocean Institute [IOI]
PO Box 03
Gzira GZR 01, Malta
Tel: +356-21-346-529
Fax: +356-21-346-502
Web: http://www.ioinst.org
e-mail: ioihq@ioihq.org.mt

📖 IOI Training Programme
Study Domains: ecology, environment, marine biology, marine science, natural resources, oceanography.
Programmes: training programme in management and conservation of marine resources.
Description: special emphasis on the UN Convention on the Law of the Sea; eco-tourism and eco-villages, seabed minerals; 20 to 25 participants for each programme.
Open to: candidates from all countries with a focus on developing countries.
Held: in the centres of the International Ocean Institute in different countries each year: Canada, Costa Rica (Spanish), Senegal (French), India, China, Indonesia, Malta, South

Pacific and Southern Africa.
Fees: US$800 per week per course, plus material costs, excluding air fare.
Financial assistance: International Scholarship Scheme awards; applicants must have government endorsement of nomination to attend course.
Languages: instruction in English, French and Spanish.
Applications: approximately 3 months before course, to IOI Regional Centres, e.g. Director IOI Malta (see website for addresses).

☛ Danielle de St. Jorre Scholarship

Study Domains: marine biology, marine science, oceanography.
Description: to enable women from Small Island Developing States (SIDS) to attend training programmes or University Degree programmes in ocean affairs. Candidates will be selected in consultation with the Alliance of Small Island States (AOSIS).
Open to: women from Small Island Developing States.
Applications: applications should include a CV and statement giving the reason for the application and how scholarship funds will be used; to the Executive Director, IOI at the above address.

34 International Rice Research Institute [IRRI]

DAPO Box 7777
Metro Manila, Philippines
Tel: +63-2-845-0563
Fax: +63-2-891-1292
Web: http://www.training.irri.org
e-mail: IRRI-Training@cgiar.org

☛ Research Fellowships

Study Domains: agriculture.
Scholarships: research training programmes: (a) postdoctoral fellowships; (b) MSc/PhD degree fellowships; (c) apprenticeship type non-degree fellowships.
Subjects: agricultural subjects related to rice.
Open to: candidates with at least a B.Sc. degree who are associated with rice and rice-based cropping systems in developing countries and nominated by their employers; (a few exceptions are made for candidates sponsored by their governments or other appropriate organizations); a few candidates from developed countries are accepted provided they have funds to support training at IRRI and are associated with a collaborative project/institution.
Place of study: at IRRI, Los Baños, Philippines and collaborating institution.
Duration: (a) 1 to 2 years; (b) 2 to 3 years; (c) 6 to 12 months.
Languages: applicants must be proficient in English.
Applications: to the Head of Training Center, IRRI, at the above address for further information.

34 Institut international pour la recherche sur le riz [IRRI]

DAPO Box 7777
1099 Manila, Philippines
Tel: +63-2-845-0563
Fax: +63-2-891-1292
Web: http://www.training.irri.org
e-mail: IRRI-Training@cgiar.org

☛ Bourses de recherches

Domaines d'étude: agriculture.
Bourses: programmes de formation pour la recherche: (a) bourses postdoctorales; (b) bourses pour études de maîtrise ou de doctorat; (c) bourses d'apprentissage.
Domaines d'études: agriculture, en rapport avec le riz.
A l'intention de: candidats titulaires au minimum d'une licence intéressés par les problèmes concernant le riz et les systèmes de récoltes basés sur celui du riz dans des pays en développement, et nommés par les institutions qui les emploient; (quelques exceptions sont faites pour des candidats parrainés par leur gouvernement ou autres organismes agréés). Possibilité d'admission de quelques candidats des pays développés à condition qu'ils disposent des ressources financières nécessaires à leur formation à l'IRRI et qu'ils soient associés à un projet ou une institution collaboratrice.

Lieu: à l'IRRI, Los Baños, Philippines et institutions collaboratrices.
Durée: (a) de 1 à 2 ans; (b) de 2 à 3 ans; (c) de 6 à 12 mois.
Connaissances linguistiques: excellente connaissance de l'anglais requise.
Candidatures: au Chef du Centre de formation, IRRI, à l'adresse ci-dessus pour de plus amples renseignements.

34 Instituto Internacional de Investigación sobre el Arroz [IRRI]

DAPO Box 7777
Metro Manila, Filipinas
Tel: +63-2-845-0563
Fax: +63-2-891-1292
Web: http://www.training.irri.org
e-mail: IRRI-Training@cgiar.org

☛ Becas

Campos de estudios: agricultura.
Becas: programas de formación en investigación: (a) Becas posdoctorales; (b) Becas para estudios de maestría o doctorado; (c) Becas de aprendizaje.
Materias de estudio: todas las áreas de la agricultura en relación con el arroz.
Se conceden: a candidatos titulares al menos de una licencitura o equivalente que estén interesados por los problemas relativos al arroz y los sistemas de recolección basados en el arroz en los países en desarrollo y que sean propuestos por las instituciones que los emplean (se hacen algunas excepciones para candidatos patrocinados por sus gobiernos u otros organismos aprobados). Existen posibilidades de admisión para algunos candidatos de países desarrollados siempre que dispongan de los recursos financieros necesarios para su formación en el IRRI y que estén asociados a un proyecto o a una institución colaboradores.
Lugar: en el IRRI, Los Baños, Filipinas e instituciones interesadas en el tema,.
Duración: (a) de 1 a 2 años; (b) de 2 a 3 años; (c) de 6 a 12 meses.
Idioma: los candidatos deben tener un excelente conocimiento del idioma inglés.
Solicitudes: dirigirse al Jefe del Centro de Formación del IRRI para obtener informaciones más detalladas, en la dirección que figura en el título.

35 International Statistical Education Centre [ISEC]

203 Barrackpore Trunk Road
700 108 Kolkata, India
Tel: +91-33-2575-2520/21/22
Fax: +91-33-2578-1834
Web: http://www.isical.ac.in/
e-mail: isec@isical.ac.in

☐ ISEC Statistical Training Course

Study Domains: statistics.
Programmes: studies leading to a Statistical Training Diploma.
Description: studies in theoretical and applied statistics at various levels.
Open to: selected participants from the following regions.
Nationality: Middle East, South and South-East Asia, the Far East and the Commonwealth countries of Africa and the countries covered by the ITEC/SCAAP and TCS of Colombo Plan Scheme of the Government of India.
Academic requirements: candidates should be graduates with qualification of mathematics at least up to GCE (O) level.
Age limit Max: preferably under 35 years of age.
Held: in Kolkata, Delhi and Bangalore.
Duration: 10 months beginning 1 June.
Fees: tuition: 30,000 Rs.; living costs: 10,000 Rs. per month.
Financial assistance: candidates are often sponsored by governmental or inter-governmental sources (Government of India schemes, Commonwealth, UNDP, UNFPA, ADB, etc.).
Languages: English proficiency required.
Applications: by April to Professor Manoranjan Pal,

Member Secretary, Board of Directors, ISEC at the above address: email: isec@isical.ac.in.

☞ Statistical Training

Study Domains: statistics.
Scholarships: Statistical Training Diploma.
Description: the International Statistical Education Centre is operated jointly by the International Statistical Institute and the Indian Statistical Institute, under the auspices of UNESCO and the Government of India. The main purpose of the Centre is to provide courses in theoretical and applied statistics at various levels to selected participants from the countries of the Middle East, South and South-East Asia, the Far East, and the Commonwealth countries of Africa.
Open to: selected participants from the following regional groups.
Nationality: nationals of countries from the Middle East, South and South-East Asia, the Far East and the Commonwealth countries of Africa and the countries covered by the ITEC/SCAAP and TCS of Colombo Plan Scheme of the Government of India.
Duration: 10 months, beginning in June.
Value: tuition and living expenses: approximately 150,000 Rs. for the 10-month course, not including airfare, medical expenses and other miscellaneous expenses.
Languages: English proficiency required.
Applications: by April to Professor Manoranjan Pal, Member Secretary, Board of Directors, ISEC at the above address: email: isec@isical.ac.in.

36 International Telecommunication Union [ITU]

Place des Nations
1211 Geneva 20, Switzerland
Tel: +41-22-730-5011
Fax: +41-22-733-7256/730 6500
Web: http://www.itu.int

☞ ITU Fellowships

Study Domains: communication, short-term programmes, technology, telecommunications.
Description: fellowships for training in the development, planning, organization, operation and maintenance of telecommunication networks for the economic and social development of the Fellow's country.
Subjects: telephony, telecommunication regulatory issues, spectrum management, radio communication services, rural applications, Internet protocol, satellite and space communications, telecommunication management training.
Open to: nationals of all Member States of the United Nations and affiliated organizations at the request of their government; no age limit, but average 25 to 35 years; candidates should have sound technical background (secondary-school education with accent on mathematics and science followed by specialized training in a telecommunications field to the level of technician, engineer or telecommunications administrator); priority is given to candidates from least developed countries.
Academic requirements: sound technical background (secondary education with stress on mathematics and science followed by specialized training in a telecommunications field to the level of technician, engineer or telecommunications administrator).
Duration: short-term module courses/attachments (1 week to 1 month).
Value: fellowships are financed by the United Nations Development Programme (UNDP) or trust funds allocated to the country of origin of the candidate and renewable at the request of the government concerned, or from ITU's own funds. ITU arranges travel, accommodation and full illness and accident insurance coverage.
Applications: through official telecommunication entity in candidate's country of origin, who will submit the candidature to ITU through appropriate channels. NOTE: Applications received directly from individuals will not be considered nor acknowledged.

36 Union internationale des télécommunications [UIT]

Place des Nations
1211 Genève 20, Suisse
Tel: +41-22-730-5011
Fax: +41-22-733-7256/730 6500
Web: http://www.itu.int

☞ Bourses UIT

Domaines d'étude: communication, programmes de courte durée, technologie, télécommunications.
Description: bourses dans les domaines du développement des réseaux de télécommunication, leur organisation, exploitation et entretien ainsi que les technologies de l'information et communication en vue du développement économique et social du pays du candidat.
A l'intention de: ressortissants des États membres des Nations Unies et des institutions spécialisées, à la demande de leur gouvernement; sans limite d'âge (de 25 à 35 ans en moyenne); les candidats doivent être des techniciens, des ingénieurs ou des administrateurs des télécommunications (études secondaires option mathématiques et sciences, suivies d'études spécialisées dans un domaine des télécommunications); les candidats des pays les moins avancés ont priorité.
Qualifications requises: les candidats doivent être des techniciens, des ingénieurs ou des administrateurs des télécommunications (études secondaires option mathématiques et sciences, suivies d'études spécialisées dans un domaine des télécommunications).
Durée: cours en modules de courte durée (1 semaine à 1 mois).
Valeur: les bourses sont financées par le Programme des Nations Unies pour le développement (PNUD), par les fonds de dépôt alloués dans le pays d'origine du candidat et renouvelables à la demande du gouvernement intéressé ou par l'UIT directement de ses fonds propres; l'UIT s'occupe des voyages, de l'assurance maladie et accidents, ainsi que du logement des boursiers.
Candidatures: devraient être adressées a l'UIT par voie officielle par les autorités avec pouvoir décisionnaire en télécommunications des pays demandeurs; les demandes individuelles adressées à l'IUT ne seront pas considérées.

36 Unión Internacional de Telecomunicaciones [UIT]

Place des Nations
1211 Ginebra 20, Suiza
Tel: +41-22-730-5011
Fax: +41-22-733-7256/730 6500
Web: http://www.itu.int

☞ Becas UIT

Campos de estudios: comunicación, programas de corta duración, tecnología, telecomunicaciones.
Descripción: becas para formar personal que pueda contribuir al desarrollo económico y social de su país en las siguientes esferas: incremento de las redes de telecomunicaciones, organización, explotación y conservación de las mismas, así como tecnologías de información y comunicación.
Materias de estudio: telefonía; reglamentación de telecomunicaciones; gestión del espectro; servicios de radiocomunicaciones; aplicaciones rurales; protocolo Internet; uso de las frecuencias de radio; comunicaciones especiales y satelitales; administración en telecomunicaciones.
Se conceden: a nacionales de los Estados Miembros de las Naciones Unidas y de sus organismos especializados, a solicitud de sus gobiernos; no hay edad límite (en general de 25 a 35 años); tienen prioridad los candidatos de los países menos avanzados.
Diplomas requeridos: Los candidatos deben tener una sólida formación técnica (estudios secundarios completos con especialización en matemáticas y ciencias, así como en una rama de las telecomunicaciones, o ser técnicos, ingenieros o administradores de telecomunicaciones).
Lugar: en países donde pueda obtenerse la formación apropiada, siempre y cuando el idioma de enseñanza no represente un obstáculo para asimilar los conocimientos.
Duración: cursos en módulos de corta duración (de una semana a un mes).

Importe: las becas son financiadas por el Programa de las Naciones Unidas para el Desarrollo (PNUD) o con fondos en fideicomiso asignados al país de origen del candidato; el importe se basa en el de las becas que concede el PNUD. La UIT organiza los trámites de viaje, alojamiento y seguro de enfermedad y accidentes.
Solicitudes: a las autoridades nacionales encargadas de coordinar los programas de cooperación técnica del país de origen del candidato, las que someterán a la UIT las candidaturas a través del Representante Residente del PNUD, a fin de asegurarse de la disponibilidad de fondos. No se tomarán en consideración las solicitudes individuales dirigidas a la UIT.

37 International Union for Vacuum Science, Technique and Applications [IUFVS]
Administrator
3 Grierson Lane
K2W 1A6 Ottawa (Ontario) Canada
Web: http://www.iuvsta.org

☛ M. W. Welch Foundation Scholarship
Study Domains: sciences, technology.
Subjects: research in vacuum science and related techniques and applications.
Open to: all qualified scientists with preference for younger scientists with Bachelor's or preferably Doctor's degree; applications judged by a panel of trustees. Applicant must make arrangements to work in an appropriate laboratory of his/her choice, to carry out the research programme approved by the laboratory.
Place of study: in approved laboratories in various countries different to that of the applicant.
Duration: 1 year (not renewable).
Value: US$15,000 per academic year.
Applications: by 15 April, to the Welch Scholarship Administrator. Application forms and information are available from website http://www.iuvsta.org, under 'Welch Scholarship'.

37 Union internationale pour la science, la technique et les applications du vide [UIPLS]
Administrateur
3 Grierson Lane
K2W 1A6 Ottawa (Ontario) Canada
Web: http://www.iuvsta.org

☛ Bourse Fondation M.W. Welch
Domaines d'étude: sciences, technologie.
Domaines d'études: recherche en sciences du vide, ses techniques et applications.
A l'intention de: tout scientifique qualifié, si possible jeune, ayant au moins une licence; la préférence est donnée aux candidats titulaires d'un doctorat; sélection des candidatures par un jury; le candidat doit obligatoirement travailler dans le laboratoire référencé dans le programme de la bourse et doit organiser les démarches dans ce sens.
Lieu: laboratoires reconnus dans différents pays sauf celui du candidat.
Durée: 1 an (non renouvelable).
Valeur: 15.000US$ par année académique.
Candidatures: avant le 15 avril, au Welch Scholarship Administrator; les formulaires d'inscription se trouvent sur le site Internet http://www.iuvsta.org, sous la rubrique, «Welch Scholarship».

37 Unión Internacional para la Ciencia, la Técnica y las Aplicaciones del Vacío [UIPLC]
Administrator
3 Grierson Lane
K2W 1A6 Ottawa (Ontario), Canada
Web: http://www.iuvsta.org

☛ Beca de la Fundación M. W. Welch
Campos de estudios: ciencias, tecnología.
Materias de estudio: ciencia del vacío, técnicas y aplicaciones.

Se conceden: a todo científico con bachillerato como mínimo; la preferencia se da a jóvenes y poseedores de doctorado. La postulaciones son evaluadas por un jurado. El candidato debe gestionar por su admisión y la aprobación de su proyecto de investigación en un laboratorio de su elección.
Lugar: en laboratorios situados fuera del país de residencia del candidato.
Duración: 1 año académico (no prorrogable).
Importe: 15.000 dólares de los Estados Unidos por año académico.
Solicitudes: antes del 15 de abril; dirigirse al Welch Scholarship Administrator; en el sitio web, http://www.iuvsta.org, enlace "Welch Scholarship", se brinda información en línea y se presentan formularios de inscripción en línea.

38 Latin American and Caribbean Institute for Economic and Social Planning [ILPES]
Edificio Naciones Unidas
Avenida Dag Hammarskjöld 3477, Vitacura
Casilla 1567
Santiago, Chile
Tel: +56-2-210-2000
Fax: +56-2-206-6104
Web: http://www.eclac.cl/ilpes/

⌂ Short-term international courses
Study Domains: economic and commercial sciences, short-term programmes.
Description: courses on tax forecasts; provision and regulation of infrastructure services; economic reforms and strategic site management; financing of social security, preparation and evaluation of public investment projects, management of project execution, logical framework and impact evaluation of projects and programmes, use of socioeconomic indicators in the impact evaluation of projects and programs to combat poverty, management and valuation of natural resources, strategic management of local and regional development. Approximately 30-40 participants in each courses; courses lead to a diploma or to a diploma with honours. (See web site for more information).
Open to: government officials at the central, regional and local levels; staff from universities and academic centres and persons from the private sector; participants come mainly from Latin America and Caribbean countries and must hold a university degree.
Held: normally at ILPES, HQ in Santiago de Chile.
Duration: 1 to 5 weeks for each course.
Fees: according to the length and type of course, tuition US$500-US$1,000; accommodation, US$800-$2,000.
Financial assistance: normally no financial assistance available. Candidates that are accepted by the Selection Committee should cover all costs.
Languages: Instruction in Spanish.
Applications: to ILPES at the above address or through the web site of ILPES.

38 Institut latino-américain et des Caraïbes pour le développement économique et social [ILPES]
Edificio Naciones Unidas
Avenida Dag Hammarskjöld 3477, Vitacura
Casilla 1567
Santiago, Chili
Tel: +56-2-210-2000
Fax: +56-2-206-6104
Web: http://www.eclac.cl/ilpes/

⌂ Cours internationaux de courte durée
Domaines d'étude: programmes de courte durée, sciences économiques et commerciales.
Description: cours de: prévisions fiscales; provision et régulation des services d'infrastructure; réformes économiques et gestion publique stratégique; financement de la sécurité sociale; préparation et évaluation de projets d'investissement publique; gestion de l'exécution de projets; cadre logique et évaluation de l'impact de projets et programmes; usage d'indicateurs socioéconomiques dans l'évaluation de l'impact de projets et programmes pour combattre la pauvreté; gestion et valorisation des ressources

naturelles; gestion stratégique du développement local et régional. Les cours sont sanctionnés par des diplômes avec ou sans mention.
A l'intention de: fonctionnaires de gouvernement du niveau central, régional ou local; personnel d'universités et centres académiques; et personnes du secteur privé. Les participants proviennent principalement des pays de l'Amérique latine et des Caraïbes et doivent posséder un titre universitaire.
Organisés: normalement au siège de l'ILPES à Santiago.
Durée: cours de 1 à 5 semaines.
Frais: inscription (selon la durée et type de cours): 500 à 1.500US$; séjour: 800 à 2.000US$.
Assistance financière: normalement pas d'aide financière; les candidats acceptés par le Comité de Sélection doivent couvrir tous les coûts.
Connaissances linguistiques: enseignement en espagnol.
Inscriptions: à l'adresse ci-dessus ou par Internet.

38   Instituto Latinoamericano y del Caribe de Planificación Económica y Social [ILPES]
Edificio Naciones Unidas
Avenida Dag Hammarskjöld 3477, Vitacura
Casilla 1567
Santiago, Chile
Tel: +56-2-210-2000
Fax: +56-2-206-6104
Web: http://www.eclac.cl/ilpes/

Cursos internacionales de corta duración

Campos de estudios: ciencias económicas y comerciales, programas de corta duración.
Descripción: cursos de estimaciones tributarias; de provisión y regulación de servicios de infraestructura; de reformas económicas y gestión pública estratégica; de financiamiento de la seguridad social; de preparación y evaluación de proyectos de inversión pública; de gestión de la ejecución de proyectos; de marco lógico y evaluación del impacto de proyectos y programas; de uso de indicadores socioeconómicos para la evaluación del impacto de programas de lucha contra la pobreza; de gestión et valoración de los recursos naturales; de gestión estratégica del desarrollo local y regional. 30 a 40 participantes aproximadamente; los cursos otorgan un diploma de aprobación y de aprobación con distinción.
Se destina(n): a funcionarios de gobierno del nivel central, regional y local; docentes de universidades y centros académicos; y personas del sector privado; los participantes provienen principalmente de los países de América Latina y del Caribe y poseen un título universitario.
Se dicta(n): principalmente en el ILPES, Santiago.
Duración: 1-5 semanas cada curso.
Costo(s): en dólares de los Estados Unidos y dependiendo de la duración y tipo de curso, inscripción: 500 a 1.500; estadía: 800 a 2.000.
Asistencia financiera: los cursos normalmente no cuentan con algún tipo de asistencia financiera. Los participantes aceptados por el Comité de Selección deben sufragar la totalidad de los costos involucrados.
Idioma: la instrucción se imparte en español.
Inscripciones: en el ILPES a la dirección que figura arriba o a través del sitio web del ILPES.

39   Latin American Faculty of Social Sciences [FLACSO]
675 este de la Iglesia Santa Teresita, n° 3571
Apdo. Postal 5429
1000 San José, Costa Rica
Tel: +506-234-0082
Fax: +506-234-6696
Web: http://www.flacso.org
e-mail: secretaria@flacso.org

Graduate, Postgraduate Programmes

Study Domains: development studies, international relations, international studies, social sciences.
Programmes: programme of studies leading to (a) certificates; (b) Master's and Doctorate degrees in social sciences and development studies.
Open to: candidates of all countries of Latin America and

the Caribbean possessing a university diploma and passing the entrance examination.
Held: at the headquarters of the FLACSO in Costa Rica and in the Academic Units in Argentina, Brazil, Chile, Costa Rica, Cuba, the Dominican Republic, Ecuador, El Salvador, Guatemala and Mexico.
Financial assistance: some scholarships are offered by the FLACSO; the selection criteria are set by the FLACSO and the funding institutions and are subject to competitive examination. Contact the FLACSO to obtain the list of FLACSO Academic Units offering scholarships for postgraduate studies or consult the website.
Applications: to the above address or to one of the FLACSO Academic Units; see the website for the list of addresses: http://www.flacso.org/unidades.

39   Faculté latino-américaine de sciences sociales [FLACSO]
675 este de la Iglesia Santa Teresita, n° 3571
Apdo. Postal 5429
San José, Costa Rica
Tel: +506-234-0082
Fax: +506-234-6696
Web: http://www.flacso.org
e-mail: secretaria@flacso.org

Programme de 2e et 3e cycles

Domaines d'étude: études du développement, études internationales, relations internationales, sciences sociales.
Programmes: programmes de cours conduisant à des: (a) certificats et (b) diplômes de 2e et 3e cycles en matière de sciences sociales et études sur le développement.
A l'intention de: ressortissants des pays d'Amérique latine et des Caraïbes, titulaires d'un diplôme universitaire et ayant réussi l'examen d'entrée.
Organisés: au siège central de la FLACSO au Costa Rica et dans les unités académiques situées dans les pays suivants: Argentine, Brésil, Chili, Costa Rica, Cuba, Equateur, El Salvador, Guatemala, Mexique et République Dominicaine.
Assistance financière: quelques bourses sont octroyées par la FLACSO et obtenues par concours; les conditions d'octroi dépendent des critères académiques fixés par la FLACSO et des institutions ou organisations qui les financent. Contacter la FLACSO pour obtenir la liste complète des institutions qui offrent des bourses pour les cours du 3e cycle en sciences sociales ou consulter le site Internet.
Inscriptions: à l'adresse ci-dessus ou à une unité académique de la FLACSO; voir site Internet pour la liste des adresses: http://www.flacso.org/unidades.

39   Facultad Latinoamericana de Ciencias Sociales [FLACSO]
675 este de la Iglesia Santa Teresita, n° 3571
Apdo. Postal 5429
1000 San José, Costa Rica
Tel: +506-234-0082
Fax: +506-234-6696
Web: http://www.flacso.org
e-mail: secretaria@flacso.org

Programas de grado y posgrado

Campos de estudios: ciencias sociales, estudios internacionales, estudios sobre el desarrollo, relaciones internacionales.
Programas: estudios conducentes a: (a) certificados; (b) master y doctorado en ciencias sociales y estudios para el desarrollo.
Se destina(n): a candidatos de todos los países de América Latina y el Caribe, con diploma universitario, y que superen proceso de admisión.
Se dicta(n): en la sede central de la FLACSO en Costa Rica, y en unidades académicas en Argentina, Brasil, Costa Rica, Cuba, Chile, Ecuador, El Salvador, Guatemala, México y República Dominicana.
Asistencia financiera: la FLACSO ofrece algunas becas sometidas a concurso; los criterios de selección son establecidos por la FLACSO y la instituciones u organismos que financian las becas. Sírvase ponerse en contacto con la FLACSO para obtener la lista de las unidades académicas que ofrecen becas para estudios de posgrado, o consulte el sitio web.

Inscripciones: en la dirección del título o en las unidades académicas; la lista de direcciones puede consultarse en http://www.flacso.org/unidades.

40 North Atlantic Treaty Organization [NATO]

Academic Affairs Unit (AAU)
Boulevard Léopold III
1110 Brussels, Belgium
Tel: +32-2-707-5014
Fax: +32-2-707-5457
Web: http://www.nato.int
e-mail: Academics@hq.nato.int; natodoc@hq.nato.int

NATO Fellowships Programme

Study Domains: international studies.
Scholarships: NATO Fellowships Programme.
Open to: citizens of the 16 member countries of NATO, university graduates with good knowledge of French or English.
Applications: to the above address.

40 Organisation du traité de l'Atlantique nord [OTAN]

Bureau des Affaires universitaires
Boulevard Léopold III
1110 Bruxelles, Belgique
Tel: +32-2-707-5014
Fax: +32-2-707-5457
Web: http://www.nato.int
e-mail: Academics@hq.nato.int; natodoc@hq.nato.int

Programme de bourses OTAN

Domaines d'étude: études internationales.
Bourses: Programme de bourses OTAN.
A l'intention de: ressortissants des 16 pays membres de l'OTAN, titulaires d'un diplôme universitaire et ayant une bonne connaissance de l'anglais ou du français.
Candidatures: à l'adresse ci-dessus.

41 Organization of American States [OAS]

17th Street & Constitution Ave., NW
20006 Washington DC, USA
Tel: +1-202-458-3000
Web: http://www.oas.org
e-mail: scholarships@oas.org

OAS Fellowships

Study Domains: all major fields, distance education, research, vocational training.
Scholarships: for university studies and/or research leading to graduate and undergraduate degrees and awards for short-term professional development training.
Description: the Inter-American Agency for Cooperation and Development (IACD) of the Organization of American States (OAS) administers one of the hemisphere's largest multinational fellowships and training programmes. Every year, the Agency provides several hundred fellowships for graduate studies and research, fellowships for undergraduate studies at universities through the region and awards for specialized, short-term training at educational institutions and training centres in OAS Member and Observer States. Fellowship and training award programmes are managed by the Division of Human Development of the Department of Information Technology for Human Development, Inter-American Agency for Cooperation and Development. As one of its strategic objectives, the Agency has implemented a multi-focused plan to increase fellowships and training opportunities and to expand access to knowledge through greater use of information technology. The Agency has established the Educational Portal for e-learning. As an element of this portal, the Division of Human Development has launched and currently manages a programme of electronic fellowships (e-fellowships) as a more cost-effective mechanism for expanding fellowship and learning opportunities.
Open to: citizens or permanent residents of the OAS Member States. Studies may be carried out by on-site or by distance education or a combination of both.
Nationality: nationals or permanent residents of the OAS

Member States: Antigua & Barbuda, Argentina, Bahamas, Barbados, Belize, Bolivia, Brazil, Canada, Colombia, Costa Rica, Chile, Dominica, Dominican Republic, Ecuador, El Salvador, Grenada, Guatemala, Guyana, Haiti, Honduras, Jamaica, Mexico, Nicaragua, Panama, Paraguay, Peru, St. Kitts & Nevis, Saint Lucia, St. Vincent & the Grenadines, Suriname, Trinidad & Tobago, United States, Uruguay, and Venezuela.
Applications: variable; for further information or assistance, candidates should contact the National Liaison Office (ONE) of their country of origin, the appropriate Office of the General Secretariat of the OAS or the Educational Portal of the Americas http://www.educoas.org/portal.

41 Organisation des États américains [OEA]

17th Street & Constitution Ave., N.W.
20006 Washington, DC, États-Unis
Tel: +1-202-458-3000
Web: http://www.oas.org
e-mail: scholarships@oas.org

Bourses OEA

Domaines d'étude: toutes disciplines principales, enseignement à distance, formation professionnelle, recherche.
Bourses: pour études et recherche universitaires de niveau maîtrise/master et licence ainsi que pour des programmes de développement professionnel à court terme.
Description: l'Agence interaméricaine pour la coopération et le développement (AICD) de l'Organisation des États Américains (OEA) gère un des plus importants programmes multinationaux de bourses et de formation de l'hémisphère. Chaque année, l'Agence attribue plusieurs centaines de bourses d'études et de recherche de niveau maîtrise/master, de bourses d'études de niveau licence/baccalauréat dans des universités de la région et des bourses spéciales de formation à court terme dans des établissements scolaires et des centres de formation/perfectionnement situés dans les pays membres et pays observateurs de l'OEA. Les bourses d'études et de formation/perfectionnement sont gérées par la Division pour le Développement Humain du Département de Technologie de l'Information pour le Développement Humain de l'AICD. L'Agence a également établi le Portail éducationnel pour l'apprentissage en ligne ou «e-apprentissage». L'un des éléments de ce portail a été le lancement et la gestion par la Division pour le développement humain, d'un programme de bourses électroniques (e-bourses) qui constitue un mécanisme plus rentable pour augmenter les offres de bourses et les chances d'apprentissage.
A l'intention de: aux citoyens ou résidents permanents des États membres de l'OEA. Les études peuvent être présentielles et/ou à distance.
Nationalité: ressortissants ou résidents permanents des États membres de l'OEA: Antigua et Barbuda, l'Argentine, les Bahamas, la Barbade, le Belize, la Bolivie, le Brésil, le Canada, la Colombie, le Costa Rica, le Chili, la Dominique, l'Équateur, les États-Unis, la Grenade, le Guatemala, le Guyana, Haïti, le Honduras, la Jamaïque, le Mexique, le Nicaragua, le Panama, le Paraguay, le Pérou, la République Dominicaine, le Salvador, St. Kitts et Nevis, Sainte Lucie, St. Vincent et les Grenadines, le Suriname, Trinité et Tobago, l'Uruguay et le Venezuela.
Candidatures: les candidats qui désirent obtenir plus d'information ou de l'aide peuvent s'adresser au Bureau National de Liaison (ONE) de leur pays d'origine, au Bureau correspondant du Secrétariat Général de l'OEA ou au Portail Éducationnel des Amériques http://www.educoas.org/portal.

41 Organización de los Estados Americanos [OEA]

17th Street & Constitution Ave., NW,
20006 Washington DC, Estados Unidos
Tel: +1-202-458-3000
Web: http://www.oas.org
e-mail: scholarships@oas.org

Becas OEA

Campos de estudios: todas las materias principales, enseñanza a distancia, formación profesional, investigación.

Descripción: la Agencia Interamericana para la Cooperación y el Desarrollo (AICD) de la Organización de Estados Americanos (OEA) administra uno de los programas de becas y capacitación multinacionales más grandes del hemisferio. Cada año, la Agencia provee cientos de becas para estudios de posgrado e investigación, becas para estudios de grado en universidades de la región y becas para capacitación corta y especializada en instituciones educativas y centros de capacitación en los Estados miembros y Observadores de la OEA. Los programas de becas y capacitación son administrados por la División de Desarrollo Humano del Departamento de Tecnología de la Información para el Desarrollo Humano de la AICD. Como uno de sus objetivos estratégicos, la Agencia ha implementado un plan de múltiples enfoques para incrementar las becas y las oportunidades de capacitación y para expandir el acceso al conocimiento a través de un uso mayor de la tecnología de la información. Para esto, está estableciendo un consorcio de amplia base de universidades para el co-financiamiento de las becas.
Se conceden: a ciudadanos o residentes permanentes de Estados Miembros de la OEA. Las modalidades de estudio pueden ser a distancia, presenciales, o una combinación de ambas.
Nacionalidad: ciudadanos o residentes permanentes de los Estados miembros de la OEA: Antigua y Barbuda, Argentina, Bahamas, Barbados, Belice, Bolivia, Brasil, Canadá, Colombia, Costa Rica, Chile, Dominica, Ecuador, El Salvador, Estados Unidos, Granada, Guatemala, Guyana, Haití, Honduras, Jamaica, México, Nicaragua, Panamá, Paraguay, Perú, República Dominicana, St. Kitts y Nevis, Saint Lucia, St. Vincent y las Granadinas, Suriname, Trinidad y Tobago, Uruguay y Venezuela.
Solicitudes: para obtener mayor información o consulta, los candidatos pueden contactar a la Oficina Nacional de Enlace (ONE) de su país de origen, a la Oficina de la Secretaría General de la OEA correspondiente, o en el Portal Educativo de las Américas: http://www.educoas.org/portal.

42 Pan American Association of Student Loans Institutions [APICE]
Apartado Aéreo 17 388
Cra. 11 No. 77-20 Int.3
Bogotá, Colombia
Tel: +57-2-112-875
Fax: +57-2-103-236
Web: http://www.apice.org.co
e-mail: apice@apice.org.co

Student Loans
Study Domains: administration, business, business administration, computer science, economy, international law, law, marketing, political economy, statistics.
Open to: APICE brings together all the educational student loans organizations of the different countries on the American continent. It maintains an Information Network on Higher Education in America, particularly with regard to Latin America and the Caribbean. This includes study programmes offered at polytechnic, university, postgraduate, advanced and in-service training levels, degrees granted and welfare services offered to students.
Applications: information obtainable at APICE at above address or from documentation centres, libraries or advisory services of member bodies of APICE in the following countries and territories: Argentina, Barbados, Bolivia, Brazil, Chile, Colombia, Costa Rica, Dominican Republic, Ecuador, Honduras, Mexico, Nicaragua, Panama, Peru, Spain, United States and Venezuela.

42 Asociación Panamericana de Instituciones de Crédito Educativo [APICE]
Apartado Aéreo 17 388
Cra. 11 No. 77-20 Int 3
Bogotá, Colombia
Tel: +57-2-112-875
Fax: +57-2-103-236
Web: http://www.apice.org.co
e-mail: apice@apice.org.co

Financiación de la educación superior a través del crédito educativo
Campos de estudios: administración, administración de empresas, derecho, derecho internacional, economía, economía política, estadística, informática, marketing, negocio.
Descripción: la APICE agrupa todas las entidades de crédito educativo del continente americano cuyo objetivo principal es la financiación de la educación superior a través del crédito educativo. Posee una red informativa sobre los estudios universitarios latinoamericanos y en el exterior, en cuyos archivos figuran las instituciones de educación superior existentes en el continente americano, especialmente en América Latina y el Caribe, con todos los detalles relativos a los programas de estudio que ofrecen a nivel técnico universitario, universitario y posuniversitario, así como a nivel de perfeccionamiento y capacitación en servicio, los títulos que otorgan y los servicios de bienestar que brindan a los estudiantes.
En el Centro de Información de APICE, CIAP, se suministra información a los interesados acerca de las instituciones a las que se puede acudir en búsqueda de crédito educativo o de otros sistema de financiación para acceder a la Educación Superior, tales como becas totales o parciales que ofrecen los distintos países y organismos internacionales. APICE asocia actualmente 70 instituciones y/o programas de Crédito Educativo en América.
Solicitudes: los informes se pueden solicitar en la dirección del título, consultando la página web, o en los centros de documentación, bibliotecas o servicios de consulta de los organismos miembros de la APICE en los países y territorios siguientes: Argentina, Bolivia, Brasil, Chile, Colombia, Costa Rica, Ecuador, España, Estados Unidos de América, Honduras, México, Nicaragua, Panamá, Perú, República Dominicana y Venezuela.

43 Programa Alban
Asociación Grupo Santander
Universidade do Porto
Rua de Ceuta 118, 5° s/35
4050-190 Porto, Portugal
Fax: +351-22-2046-159
Web: http://www.programalban.org
e-mail: info@programalban.org

Programa de becas de alto nivel de la Unión Europea para América Latina
Campos de estudios: todas las materias principales.
Descripción: estudios de postgrado, formación o actualización profesional superior en la Unión Europea.
Materias de estudio: en principio, se aceptarán candidaturas de todas las áreas de estudio, excepto las de aprendizaje de idiomas. Ocasionalmente, cada Convocatoria específica podrá indicar áreas prioritarias o cualquier otra especificidad que sea relevante.
Se conceden: a ciudadanos residentes en uno de los 18 países elegibles de América que: (a) hayan completado los estudios universitarios mínimos para ser aceptado para estudios de postgrado (máster o doctorado) en una Institución de Educación Superior de la Unión Europea y que ese proyecto tenga el apoyo de una Institución de Educación Superior elegible para el programa Albán; o bien, que sean profesionaled en una organización reconocida en uno de los países elegibles de América Latina y pretendan obtener formación o actualización profesional superior en la Unión Europea, con el apoyo de esa organización; (b) sean aceptados por una Institución de Educación Superior o por un Centro de Formación Superior en un país de la Unión Europea para realizar allí el proyecto de educación/formación que se proponen llevar a cabo; (c) que describan cómo se reintegrarán como miembro activo de una organización en el país de origen una vez que termine el período de educación/formación en la Unión Europea.
Nacionalidad: ciudadanos latinoamericanos residentes en uno de los 18 siguientes países: Argentina, Bolivia, Brasil, Chile, Colombia, Costa Rica, Cuba, Ecuador, El Salvador, Guatemala, Honduras, México, Nicaragua, Panamá, Paraguay, Perú, Uruguay y Venezuela.
Lugar: Alemania, Austria, Bélgica, Chipre, Dinamarca, Eslovaquia, Eslovenia, España, Estonia, Finlandia, Francia, Grecia, Hungría, Irlanda, Italia, Letonia, Lituania, Luxemburgo, Malta, Países Bajos, Polonia, Portugal, Reino

Unido, República Checa y Suecia.
Duración: las becas pueden tener una duración de un mínimo de 6 meses de trabajo efectivo de educación/formación realizado en la Unión Europea hasta un máximo que dependerá del tipo y duración de los estudios: (a) máster máximo de 24 meses; (b) doctorado máximo de 36 meses, (c)especialización máximo de 18 meses.
Importe: (a) becas de postgrado para llevar a cabo estudios: máximo de 1.500 euros por mes de trabajo realizado; en total, la Comisión Europea puede contribuir con un máximo del 75 % del coste total elegible de los proyectos de educación/formación; (b) becas de especialización para profesionales/cuadros directivos con experiencia: máximo de 2.500 euros por mes de trabajo realizado; en total, la Comisión Europea puede contribuir como máximo con el 50 % del coste elegible del proyecto de especialización.
Solicitudes: preferentemente, la candidatura deberá efectuarse on-line, rellenando y enviando un formulario electrónico propio a través de Internet. También es posible enviar candidaturas en soporte papel.

44   Regional Seismological Centre for South America [CERESIS]

Apartado 14-0363
Lima, Peru
Tel: +51-1-225-6283
Fax: +51-1-224-5144
Web: http://www.ceresis.org
e-mail: giescere@inictel.gob.pe

📖 Virtual Course in Seismology

Study Domains: distance education, earth science, geology.
Programmes: virtual courses on specific aspects of seismology.
Held: distance courses through Internet.
Languages: Spanish.
Applications: see announcements on website http://www.ceresis.org/cursos.

44   Centro Regional de Sismología para América del Sur [CERESIS]

Apartado 14-0363
Lima, Perú
Tel: +51-1-225-6283
Fax: +51-1-224-5144
Web: http://www.ceresis.org
e-mail: giescere@inictel.gob.pe

📖 Cursos virtuales sobre sismología

Campos de estudios: ciencias de la tierra, enseñanza a distancia, geología.
Programas: cursos virtuales sobre aspectos específicos de sismología.
Se dicta(n): cursos a distancia vía Internet.
Idioma: español.
Inscripciones: se anuncian oportunamente en el sitio web: http://www.ceresis.org/cursos.

45   Reuters Foundation [RF]

85 Fleet Street
EC4P 4AJ London, United Kingdom
Tel: +44-20-7542-7015
Fax: +44-20-7542-8599
Web: http://www.foundation.reuters.com

🎓 Reuters Foundation Fellowships

Study Domains: journalism.
Scholarships: (a) Oxford University Fellowship; (b) Fellowships in Medical Journalism; (c) Writing News Programmes; (d) Writing and Producing Television News; (e) Writing Environmental News; (f) Stanford University Digital Vision Fellowship Programme.
Open to: full details of eligibility criteria and application forms are available at website.
Place of study: (a) (b) at Green College, University of Oxford, United Kingdom; (f) Stanford University, California, United States of America; (c) (d) (e) in different countries around the world.
Duration: (a) (b) 3, 6 and 9 months at Oxford; (f) full

academic year at Stanford; (d) (e) 1 and 2 weeks.
Value: full details of financial support offered are available at website.
Applications: (a) (b) by 31 December; (f) by 14 March; (c) (d) (e) variable, refer to website. Applications should be addressed to the Director, at the above address; (http://www.foundation.reuters.com/fellowships).

46   Rotary Foundation of Rotary International [RFORI]

1560 Sherman Avenue
60201 Evanston, IL, United States
Tel: +1-847-866-3000
Fax: +1-847-328-8554
Web: http://www.rotary.org
e-mail: scholarshipinquiries@rotaryintl.org

🎓 Rotary Foundation Ambassadorial Scholarships

Study Domains: all major fields, agriculture, Asian studies, journalism, languages, special education.
Scholarships: Rotary Foundation Ambassadorial Scholarships: (a) Academic Year; (b) Multi-Year; (c) Cultural.
Open to: citizens of a country in which there is a Rotary Club. Scholarships are available to individuals of all ages, provided the candidate has completed at least 2 years of university coursework or equivalent professional experience prior to beginning scholarship studies; (c) applications will be considered for candidates interested in studying Arabic, English, French, German, Hebrew, Italian, Japanese, Korean, Mandarin Chinese, Polish, Portuguese, Russian, Spanish, Swahili and Swedish.
Age limit Max: no age limit.
Academic requirements: candidate should have completed at least 2 years of university coursework or equivalent professional experience prior to beginning scholarship studies.
Other conditions: Spouses or descendants of Rotarians are not eligible.
Place of study: in all countries having Rotary Clubs.
Duration: (a) 1 academic year; (b) 2 or 3 years of degree-oriented study; (c) 3 or 6 months of intensive language study and cultural immersion.
Value: (a) covers round-trip transportation, tuition, fees, room and board expenses and some educational supplies up to US$25,000 or its equivalent; (b) flat grant of US$12,500 or its equivalent per year to be applied toward the costs of a degree programme; (c) covers round-trip transportation, language training expenses and homestay living arrangements, up to US$12,000 and US$19,000 respectively.
Languages: a good knowledge of the language of the host country is required.
Applications: through a Rotary Club near candidate's domicile or place of study. Further information obtainable from the above address.

46   Fondation Rotary de Rotary International [FRDRI]

1560 Sherman Avenue
60201 Evanston, IL, États-Unis
Tel: +1-847-866-3000
Fax: +1-847-328-8554
Web: http://www.rotary.org
e-mail: scholarshipinquiries@rotaryintl.org

🎓 Bourses d'études (Ambassadorial Scholarships)

Domaines d'étude: toutes disciplines principales, agriculture, éducation spéciale, études asiatiques, journalisme, langues.
Bourses: Bourses d'études (Ambassadorial Scholarships) de la Fondation Rotary: (a) 1 année académique; (b) plusieurs années académiques; (c) culturelles.
A l'intention de: ressortissants des pays où il existe un Club Rotary; pas de limite d'âge mais étudiants ayant accompli 2 ans (ou plus) d'études universitaires, ou qui ont une expérience équivalente; une bonne connaissance de la langue du pays d'études est requise; les parents de rotariens ou employés de l'organisation ne sont pas acceptés; (c) les candidatures seront retenues pour l'étude des langues suivantes; allemand, anglais, arabe, coréen, chinois mandarin, espagnol, français, hébreux, italien, japonais, polonais, portugais, russe, souahéli et suédois.

Qualifications requises: étudiants ayant accompli 2 ans (ou plus) d'études universitaires, ou qui ont une expérience équivalente.
Age Max: pas de limite d'âge.
Autres Conditions: les parents de rotariens ou employés de l'organisation ne sont pas acceptés.
Lieu: tous les pays où existent des clubs Rotary.
Durée: (a) 1 année académique; (b) 2 à 3 ans pour des études spécialisées; (c) 3 à 6 mois pour l'étude intensive de langue avec immersion culturelle.
Valeur: (a) 25.000$US; comprend le voyage entre le pays d'origine du candidat et le pays d'études, tous les frais universitaires, la nourriture, le logement et quelques fournitures scolaires; (b) 12.500$US pour le logement ou son équivalent pour couvrir les frais d'étude; (c) 12.000$US à 19.000$US pour financer les cours de formation de langue et les frais d'installation.
Connaissances linguistiques: une bonne connaissance de la langue du pays d'études est requise.
Candidatures: au Club Rotary proche du domicile du candidat ou du lieu des études ou d'emploi. Pour de plus amples renseignements, écrire à l'adresse ci-dessus.

46 Fundación Rotary de Rotary Internacional [FRDRI]

1560 Sherman Avenue
60201 Evanston, IL, Estados Unidos
Tel: +1-847-866-3000
Fax: +1-847-328-8554
Web: http://www.rotary.org
e-mail: scholarshipinquiries@rotaryintl.org

🖝 Becas "Ambasadorial" de la Fundación Rotary para la comprensión internacional

Campos de estudios: todas las materias principales, agricultura, educación especial, estudios ásiaticos, idiomas, periodismo.
Descripción: becas: (a) de año académico; (b) multi-anual; (c) culturales.
Se conceden: a personas de cualquier país donde existe un club Rotary. Los candidatos deben haber completado por lo menos 2 años de estudios universitarios o tener experiencia profesional equivalente. (c) se tendrán en cuenta las postulaciones de candidatos interesados en estudiar alemán, árabe, chino mandarín, coreano, español, francés, hebreo, inglés, italiano, japonés, polaco, portugués, ruso, sueco o swahili.
Edad Max: No hay límite de edad.
Otras condiciones: No se aceptan postulaciones a las becas por parte de cónyuges o descendientes de Rotarios.
Lugar: en países donde existen clubes Rotary.
Duración: (a) 1 año académico; (b) 2 o 3 años para estudios conducentes a título; (c) 3 o 6 meses de estudio intensivo de lengua e inmersión cultural.
Importe: (a) incluye el viaje ida y vuelta entre el país de origen del candidato y el país de estudio, gastos universitarios, comida y alojamiento y algunos materiales escolares; no debe sobrepasar 25.000 dólares de los Estados Unidos o equivalente; (b) anualmente, monto de 12.500 dólares o equivalente para cubrir costos de estudio; (c) incluye viaje como (a), más hasta 12.000 dólares para gastos de estudio del idioma y hasta 19.000 dólares para gastos de instalación.
Idioma: se requiere buen conocimiento de la lengua del país donde se realizan los estudios.
Solicitudes: por mediación del Club Rotary de la ciudad más próxima a la residencia permanente del candidato o al lugar de estudio. Mayor información sobre estas becas puede obtenerse en la dirección que figura en el título.

47 The Hague Academy of International Law

Peace Palace
Carnegieplein 2
2517 KJ The Hague, Netherlands
Tel: +31-70-303-4242
Web: http://www.hagueacademy.nl
e-mail: registration@hagueacademy.nl

📖 Courses in International Law and International Relations

Study Domains: international law, international relations, international studies, law, short-term programmes.
Programmes: Courses in international law and international relations.
Description: courses of the Centre for Studies and Research in International Law and International Relations.
Open to: young academics or young lawyers of any nationality, intellectually mature and good experience (at least 3 years of practical experience in international affairs); capacity for research work and holding an advanced university degree. Participants will be selected by the Curatorium of the Academy on the basis of their scientific qualifications; half of the participants (10-12) will carry out their research work in the French-speaking section and half in the English-speaking section.
Duration: 4 weeks (mid-August to mid-September).
Fees: no tuition fees.
Financial assistance: participants will receive through the Administrative Council an allowance of 35€ per day to cover living expenses, plus half of travelling expenses (up to a maximum of 910€) will be covered.
Languages: instruction in English and French.
Applications: by 1 April, to the Secretariat of the Academy at the above address.

📖 International Law, International Relations

Study Domains: international law, international relations, law, short-term programmes.
Programmes: (a) course in private international law; (b) course in public international law; (c) diploma programme.
Open to: candidates of all nationalities; (a) and (b) having at least 4 years of law studies; fluent English and French; (c) having a university degree with advanced knowledge of international law.
Duration: 3 weeks.
Fees: registration: 240€ for 3 weeks and 440€ for 6 weeks.
Financial assistance: scholarships of the Academy.
Languages: instruction in English or French.
Applications: by 1 March to the Secretariat of the Academy at the above address and by email registration@hagueacademy.nl.

🖝 The Hague Academy Scholarships

Study Domains: international law.
Scholarships: (a) scholarships for Academy courses; (b) doctoral scholarships.
Description: (a) international law; (b) completion of (already advanced) doctoral thesis in private or public international law.
Open to: no citizenship requirements, aged under 40; law studies at least for 4 years (or equivalent qualifications); (b) candidates from developing countries residing in their home country, aged under 45; the scholarship is meant for completion of already advanced doctoral theses (postgraduate level).
Duration: (a) 3 weeks; (b) 2 months.
Value: (a) approximately 900 €, covering registration and living expenses; travel expenses not included; (b) allowance of 35 € per day and partial contribution to travel expenses.
Languages: (a) fluent English or French; (b) adequate knowledge of English or French.
Applications: by 1 March, to the Secretariat of the Academy.

47 Académie de droit international de La Haye

Peace Palace
Carnegieplein 2
2517 KJ La Haye, Pays-Bas
Tel: +31-70-303-4242
Web: http://www.hagueacademy.nl
e-mail: registration@hagueacademy.nl

📖 Droit international et relations internationales

Domaines d'étude: droit, droit international, programmes de courte durée, relations internationales.
Programmes: (a) cours en droit international privé; (b) cours en droit international public; (c) programme pour l'obtention du diplôme.

A l'intention de: ressortissants de tout pays; (a) et (b) ayant au moins 4 ans d'études de droit (ou équivalent) et une bonne maîtrise de l'anglais ou du français; (c) possédant un diplôme universitaire et des connaissances approfondies en droit international.
Durée: 3 semaines.
Frais: inscription: 240€ pour 3 semaines ou 440€ pour 6 semaines.
Assistance financière: bourses de l'Académie.
Inscriptions: avant le 1er mars, auprès du Secrétariat de l'Académie, à l'adresse indiquée ci-dessus et par email: registration@hagueacademy.nl.

📖 Programme de cours en droit international et relations internationales

Domaines d'étude: droit, droit international, programmes de courte durée, relations internationales.
Programmes: programme de cours en droit international et relations internationales.
Description: cours du Centre d'étude et de recherche de droit international et de relations internationales.
A l'intention de: jeunes enseignants ou jeunes juristes de toute nationalité hautement qualifiés et possédant aux moins 3 ans d'expérience pratique dans les affaires internationales; possédant une bonne aptitude à la recherche et un diplôme universitaire élevé. Les participants seront sélectionnés par le Curatorium sur la base de leurs qualifications scientifiques. La moitié des participants (10-12) exécutera la recherche par groupe de langue anglaise ou française.
Durée: 4 semaines (mi-août à mi-septembre).
Frais: participation gratuite.
Assistance financière: les participants recevront du Conseil d'administration une allocation de 35€ par jour pour couvrir l'ensemble des frais de séjour et la moitié de leurs frais de voyage (à hauteur de 910€).
Connaissances linguistiques: enseignement en anglais et en français.
Inscriptions: avant le 1er avril, au Secrétariat de l'Académie, à l'adresse indiquée ci-dessus.

🕊 Bourses de l'Académie de La Haye

Domaines d'étude: droit international.
Bourses: (a) bourses d'études pour les sessions de cours; (b) bourses de doctorat.
Description: (a) droit international public et privé; (b) achèvement d'une thèse de doctorat déjà très avancée.
A l'intention de: (a) ressortissants de tout pays, âgés de moins de 40 ans et ayant au moins 4 ans d'études de droit (ou équivalent); (b) ressortissants des pays en développement, résidant dans leur pays d'origine, âgés de moins de 45 ans; cette bourse est pour l'achèvement d'une thèse de doctorat déjà très avancée.
Durée: (a) 3 semaines; (b) 2 mois.
Valeur: (a) environ 900 € couvrant les droits d'inscription et les frais de séjour; les frais de voyage sont à la charge du candidat; (b) allocation de 35 € par jour, avec indemnisation partielle des frais de voyage.
Connaissances linguistiques: (a) bonne maîtrise de l'anglais ou du français; (b) bonnes connaissances de l'anglais ou du français.
Candidatures: avant le 1er mars; au Secrétariat de l'Académie.

48 UNESCO Institute for Water Education [UNESCO-IHE]
Westvest 7
PO Box 3015
2601 DA Delft - The Netherlands
Tel: +31-15-215-1715
Fax: +31-15-212-2921
Web: http://www.unesco-ihe.org
e-mail: info@unesco-ihe.org

🕊 MSc, PhD, Short courses, Group & tailor made trainings, On-line courses

Study Domains: ecology, environment, engineering, hydraulics, hydrology.
Description: International Masters & PhD programmes in environmental science, water management, municipal water and infrastructure, water science and engineering.
Subjects: coastal engineering and port development;

environmental planning and management; environmental science and technology; groundwater hydrology; hydraulic engineering and river basin development; hydroinformatics; integrated urban engineering; land and water development; limnology and wetland ecosystems; sanitary engineering; surface water hydrology; water quality management; water resources management; water services management; water supply engineering.
Open to: graduates of all nationalities with at least 3 years practical experience and a university degree.
Duration: MSc: 18 months, PhD: 3 to 4 years; see website for other course durations.
Value: variable; see website for funding possibilities and contact the Netherlands diplomatic mission in your country for further information.
Languages: proficiency in English required.
Applications: see website for further information.

49 United Nations Educational, Scientific and Cultural Organization - Fellowships Section [UNESCO-ERC/FEL]
7, place de Fontenoy
75352 Paris 07 SP, France
Tel: +33-1-4568-1507
Fax: +33-1-4568-5503
Web: http://www.unesco.org
e-mail: fellowships@unesco.org

📖 Training courses and seminars

Study Domains: cultural studies, education, information science, natural sciences, social sciences, technology.
Description: (a) International or regional courses in the fields of education, natural and technological sciences, social sciences, cultural activities and communication, financed by UNESCO; (b) International courses and seminars sponsored by UNESCO, programmes of which are announced by the organizing institutions.
Open to: restricted to nationals of UNESCO Member States and Associate Member States; participants must be at graduate level, have professional experience in the relevant field of study and be officially nominated by their governments.
Held: in UNESCO Member States, in co-operation with national bodies and specialized institutions of those countries and with other international organizations.
Financial assistance: a limited number of scholarships awarded, covering a monthly allowance, tuition or registration fees, books and travel expenses.
Applications: candidates are officially nominated by their governments; no individual applications for participation can be considered by the UNESCO Secretariat. UNESCO will however supply information on request.

🕊 Individual Fellowships (technical cooperation)

Study Domains: cultural studies, education, information science, natural sciences, social sciences, technology.
Scholarships: individual fellowships awarded within the framework of operational projects financed by extrabudgetary sources.
Open to: nationals of UNESCO Member States and Associate Members of those countries where economic and social development projects are being carried out; the purpose of these awards is to help national project personnel develop and gain skills and knowledge that will best equip them to achieve the objectives of a project as well as their assigned duties.
Place of study: in UNESCO's Member States as well as in the United Kingdom, the United States and Singapore.
Duration: variable, depending on whether the studies should be directed towards obtaining a diploma, degree or qualification, or have mainly a practical or applied orientation.
Value: individual fellowships: monthly allowance usually at ad hoc rates, plus travel, tuition, termination and book allowances.
Applications: through the national authorities specially designated by UNESCO Member States; direct applications by individuals and private bodies cannot be considered by the UNESCO Secretariat.

☛ Individual Fellowships Programme

Study Domains: communication, cultural studies, development studies, education, human sciences, sciences, short-term programmes, social sciences, technology.
Scholarships: individual fellowships granted under the Organization's regular budget.
Description: for studies in designated priority areas: Basic Education for All; Water resources and their associated ecosystems; Ethics of Science; Protection of cultural Diversity and the encouragement of pluralism and dialogue between cultures; and Promoting equitable access to information and knowledge, especially in the public domain.
Open to: nationals of UNESCO Member States and Associate Members; the purpose of these fellowships is to provide opportunities to further primarily higher education or research generally abroad and to acquire international experience in fields of study for which appropriate facilities are not available in the country of origin; in addition, under UNESCO's Fellowship Programme, each Member State is entitled to submit up to 2 requests, listed in order of priority, for deserving candidates.
Place of study: in UNESCO Member States and in Singapore.
Duration: not exceeding 9 months, (6 months maximum under the UNESCO Fellowship Programme).
Value: monthly allowance based on United Nations stipend scale (or ad hoc rates in the case of UNESCO Fellowship Programme), plus travel, tuition, termination and book allowances (on a case-by-case basis).
Applications: through the national authorities specially designated by UNESCO Member States (usually National Commission for UNESCO or appropriate ministry); direct applications by individuals and private bodies cannot be considered by the UNESCO Secretariat.

☛ Study Grants

Study Domains: cultural studies, education, information science, natural sciences, social sciences, technology.
Scholarships: study grants.
Open to: nationals of Member States of UNESCO who occupy positions of high professional responsibility in their countries; candidates will propose their own programme of visits to UNESCO for approval, and will be required to present a report on their return; all candidates must be nominated by their governments.
Place of study: in several countries or in several places within one country, on observation or consultation visits.
Duration: maximum 2 months.
Value: covers economy travel expenses and daily allowance based on United Nations subsistence rate or ad hoc rates.
Applications: must be presented by the competent national authorities designated by the governments of UNESCO Member States (in general the National Commission for UNESCO or the competent ministry in the field of study chosen); no consideration can be given to applications submitted by individuals or private bodies.

☛ UNESCO Co-Sponsored Fellowships Programme

Study Domains: communication, cultural studies, education, sciences, social sciences, technology.
Scholarships: fellowships donated by Member States and sponsored by UNESCO.
Open to: nationals of UNESCO Member States and Associate Members particularly from developing countries; often, donors of sponsored fellowships designate the Member States to be invited to submit applications; the purpose of these awards, provided in the framework of the UNESCO Co-Sponsored Fellowships Programme, is to offer opportunities to further primarily higher education or research abroad and to acquire international experience in relevant fields of study.
Place of study: in donor/sponsoring country.
Duration: variable, depending on each study programme.
Value: in the main financial responsibilities in the country of study undertaken by the sponsoring country; international travel costs (usually not provided) to be borne by beneficiary or his governmental authorities; UNESCO, whenever possible, will endeavour to cover such international travel expenses, particularly for beneficiaries from least developed countries.

Applications: through the national authorities specially designated by UNESCO Member States (usually National Commission for UNESCO or appropriate ministry); direct applications by individuals and private bodies cannot be considered by the UNESCO Secretariat. Information, on request, can be provided through national authorities only.

49 Organisation des Nations Unies pour l'éducation, la science et la culture Section des Bourses [UNESCO-ERC/FEL]

7, place de Fontenoy
75352 Paris 07 SP, France
Tel: +33-1-4568-1507
Fax: +33-1-4568-5503
Web: http://www.unesco.org
e-mail: fellowships@unesco.org

📖 Cours de formation et séminaires

Domaines d'étude: éducation, études culturelles, sciences de l'information, sciences naturelles, sciences sociales, technologie.
Description: (a) cours internationaux ou régionaux dans les domaines de l'éducation, des sciences naturelles et de la technologie, des sciences sociales, des activités culturelles et de l'information, financés par l'UNESCO; (b) cours et séminaires internationaux patronnés par l'UNESCO, dont les programmes sont annoncés par les institutions qui les organisent.
A l'intention de: ressortissants des États membres et membres associés de l'UNESCO. Les participants doivent être du niveau post-universitaire, avoir une expérience professionnelle dans le domaine en question et être présentés officiellement par leur gouvernement.
Organisés: dans les États membres de l'UNESCO, en coopération avec des organismes nationaux et institutions spécialisées de ces pays, ainsi qu'avec d'autres organisations internationales.
Assistance financière: bourses octroyées en nombre limité; allocation mensuelle, frais de scolarité ou d'inscription et de livres, et frais de voyage.
Inscriptions: les participants étant nommés par leur gouvernement, les demandes d'inscriptions individuelles ne peuvent être prises en considération par le Secrétariat de l'UNESCO.

☛ Bourses co-patronnées par l'UNESCO

Domaines d'étude: communication, éducation, études culturelles, sciences, sciences sociales, technologie.
Bourses: bourses offertes par les États membres et patronnées par l'UNESCO.
A l'intention de: ressortissants des États membres et membres associés de l'UNESCO et plus particulièrement des pays en développement. Les donateurs des bourses patronnées désignent souvent les États membres qui sont invités à présenter des candidatures. Le but de ces bourses offertes dans le cadre de Bourses co-patronnées par l'UNESCO, est de donner au candidat la possibilité de poursuivre ses études au niveau de l'enseignement supérieur ou ses travaux de recherche, à l'étranger, et d'acquérir une expérience internationale dans des domaines pour lesquels des facilités d'études n'existent pas dans son pays d'origine.
Lieu: dans les pays donateurs.
Durée: variable, selon le programme d'études offert.
Valeur: couverture financière dans le pays d'étude assurée par le pays donateur; les frais de voyage sont à la charge du bénéficiaire ou de son gouvernement; l'UNESCO prend en charge chaque fois que possible les frais de voyages internationaux surtout lorsque les bénéficiaires viennent des pays les moins avancés.
Candidatures: doivent être présentées par les autorités nationales désignées par les gouvernements des États membres de l'UNESCO (en général la Commission nationale pour l'UNESCO ou le ministère compétent dans le domaine d'étude choisi). Les candidatures présentées à titre privé ne peuvent être prises en considération. Des informations complémentaires peuvent être communiquées par l'intermédiaire des autorités nationales uniquement.

🐦 Bourses individuelles (coopération technique)

Domaines d'étude: éducation, études culturelles, sciences de l'information, sciences naturelles, sciences sociales, technologie.

Bourses: bourses individuelles dans le cadre de projets de coopération technique, financés par des fonds extrabudgétaires.

A l'intention de: ressortissants des États membres de l'UNESCO et des membres associés; dans ces pays doivent se dérouler des projets de développement sociaux et économiques. Ces bourses contribuent à la formation spécialisée de personnel et leur permettent d'acquérir et de développer de nouveaux savoirs et de nouvelles technologies afin qu'ils puissent mener à bien les objectifs d'un projet ou de toute autre tâche qui leur seront confiés.

Lieu: dans les États membres et membres associés de l'UNESCO, ainsi qu'à Singapour.

Durée: variable, selon que les études soient axées sur l'obtention de diplômes, titres de qualifications, ou s'il s'agit d'une orientation pratique appliquée.

Valeur: allocation mensuelle basée sur l'échelle adoptée par les Nations Unies, plus les frais de voyage et les frais d'études.

Candidatures: par l'intermédiaire des autorités locales désignées par les États membres de l'UNESCO. Les candidatures présentées à titre privé ne peuvent être prises en considération.

🐦 Programme de bourses individuelles

Domaines d'étude: communication, éducation, études culturelles, études du développement, programmes de courte durée, sciences, sciences humaines, sciences sociales, technologie.

Bourses: bourses individuelles octroyées sur le budget régulier de l'Organisation.

Description: pour études dans les domaines afférent aux «Objectifs stratégiques» qui figurent dans la «Stratégie à moyen terme pour 2002-2007 (31 C/4)» et correspondant à la «Priorité principale désignée pour chaque programme majeur» précisé dans le programme et budget approuvé de l'Organisation. Ces priorités désignées sont: l'éducation de base pour tous; ressources en eau et écosystèmes; l'éthique des sciences et des technologies; protection de la diversité culturelle et promotion du pluralisme et du dialogue entre les cultures; promouvoir un accès équitable à l'information et au savoir, en particulier dans le domaine public.

A l'intention de: ressortissants des États membres et membres associés de l'UNESCO. Ces bourses permettent aux bénéficiaires de poursuivre, généralement à l'étranger, des études supérieures principalement, ou des activités de recherche et d'acquérir une expérience internationale dans des domaines pour lesquels des facilités d'étude n'existent pas dans le pays d'origine. Il existe également la possibilité, pour chaque État membre, dans le cadre du programme de bourses de l'UNESCO, de proposer, par ordre préférentiel, 1 à 2 candidatures maximum. Ces candidatures doivent être sélectionnées en fonction des mérites du candidat.

Lieu: dans les États membres de l'UNESCO et à Singapour.

Durée: pas plus de 9 mois (6 mois maximum lorsqu'il s'agit de bourses octroyées dans le cadre du programme de bourses de l'UNESCO).

Valeur: soit une allocation mensuelle basée sur le barème adopté par les Nations Unies (ou des barèmes «ad hoc» lorsqu'il s'agit du programme de bourses de l'UNESCO), plus des frais de voyage, de scolarité et de livres.

Candidatures: doivent être présentées par les autorités nationales désignées par les gouvernements des États membres de l'UNESCO (en général la Commission nationale pour l'UNESCO ou le ministère compétent dans le domaine d'étude choisi). Les candidatures présentées à titre privé ne peuvent être prises en considération.

🐦 Voyages d'études

Domaines d'étude: éducation, études culturelles, sciences de l'information, sciences naturelles, sciences sociales, technologie.

Bourses: allocations pour voyages d'étude.

A l'intention de: ressortissants des États membres de l'UNESCO, qui occupent des postes de haute responsabilité professionnelle dans leur pays. Chaque candidat proposera à l'UNESCO son propre programme de visites pour approbation et présentera un rapport au retour de son voyage d'étude. Tous les candidats doivent être nommés officiellement par leur gouvernement.

Lieu: visites d'observation ou de consultation dans plusieurs pays ou plusieurs endroits d'un même pays.

Durée: 2 mois au maximum.

Valeur: couvre les frais de voyage en classe touriste plus une allocation journalière basée sur le taux de subsistance des Nations Unies.

Candidatures: doivent être présentées par les autorités nationales désignées par les gouvernements des États membres de l'UNESCO (en général la Commission nationale pour l'UNESCO ou le ministère compétent dans le domaine d'étude choisi). Les candidatures présentées à titre privé ou par des organismes privés ne peuvent être prises en considération.

49 Organización de las Naciones Unidas para la Educación, la Ciencia y la Cultura Sección del Programa de Becas [UNESCO-ERC/FEL]

7, place de Fontenoy
75352 París 07 SP, Francia
Tel: +33-1-4568-1507
Fax: +33-1-4568-5503
Web: http://www.unesco.org
e-mail: fellowships@unesco.org

📖 Cursos de formación y seminarios

Campos de estudios: ciencias de la información, ciencias naturales, ciencias sociales, educación, estudios culturales, tecnología.

Descripción: (a) cursos internacionales o regionales en temas relacionados con las siguientes áreas: educación, ciencias naturales y tecnología, ciencias sociales, actividades culturales e información; financiados por la UNESCO; (b) Cursos y seminarios internacionales patrocinados por la UNESCO, cuyos programas anuncian las instituciones que los organizan.

Se destina(n): a nacionales de los Estados Miembros y Miembros Asociados de la UNESCO, que tengan un diploma universitario y experiencia profesional en la materia de estudio elegida; los participantes deben ser presentados oficialmente por sus respectivos gobiernos.

Se dicta(n): en estados miembros de la UNESCO, en cooperación con organismos nacionales e instituciones especializadas del país y con otras organizaciones internacionales.

Asistencia financiera: se concede un número limitado de becas que comprenden una subvención mensual, más gastos de viaje, de matrícula o de inscripción y de libros.

Inscripciones: ya que los participantes son designados por sus gobiernos, la Secretaría de la UNESCO no tomará en consideración las solicitudes enviadas directamente. Sin embargo, la UNESCO responderá a toda solicitud de información.

🐦 Becas co-patrocinadas por la UNESCO

Campos de estudios: ciencias, ciencias sociales, comunicación, educación, estudios culturales, tecnología.

Becas: becas ofrecidas por los Estados Miembros y patrocinadas por la UNESCO.

Se conceden: a nacionales de los Estados Miembros y Miembros Asociados de la UNESCO, especialmente de los países en desarrollo. Los donantes de becas designan, por lo general, los Estados Miembros invitados a presentar solicitudes. La finalidad de estas becas, otorgadas en el marco del Programa de becas de la UNESCO, es ofrecer a los becarios principalmente oportunidades para realizar estudios superiores o trabajos de investigación en el extranjero y para adquirir experiencia internacional en campos de estudio para los cuales no hay facilidades disponibles en el país de origen.

Lugar: en los países donantes.

Duración: variable, según el programa de estudios ofrecido.

Importe: el país donante asegura el financiamiento de los gastos en el país de estudio; los gastos de viaje quedan a cargo del beneficiario o de su gobierno. UNESCO, en la medida de lo posible, se esforzará por cubrir los gastos del viaje internacional, especialmente para los becarios de los países menos avanzados.

Solicitudes: deberán ser presentadas por las autoridades nacionales designadas por los gobiernos de los Estados miembros de la UNESCO (en general, la Comisión nacional de la UNESCO o el ministerio competente en el área de estudios elegida). La Secretaría de la UNESCO no tomará en consideración las solicitudes presentadas directamente por individuos u órganos privados. Sólo se comunicarán informaciones complementarias a través de las autoridades nacionales.

☞ Becas individuales (cooperación técnica)

Campos de estudios: ciencias de la información, ciencias naturales, ciencias sociales, educación, estudios culturales, tecnología.
Becas: becas individuales otorgadas en el marco de proyectos existentes financiados con recursos extrapresupuestarios.
Se conceden: a ciudadanos de los Estados Miembros y de Miembros Asociados de la UNESCO en los que se están llevando a cabo proyectos de desarrollo económico y social. La finalidad de estas becas es ayudar al personal nacional a adquirir habilidades y conocimientos que los dotarán mejor para lograr los objetivos del proyecto y para el desempeño de las responsabilidades que se les han asignado.
Lugar: en los Estados Miembros de la UNESCO y Singapur.
Duración: variable, según que el objetivo de los estudios sea la obtención de un diploma, grado o calificación que tengan una orientación principalmente práctica o aplicada.
Importe: estipendio mensual, generalmente basado en la escala de estipendios de las Naciones Unidas, más viaje, costo de la enseñanza, estipendio final y subsidio para libros.
Solicitudes: a través de las autoridades nacionales especialmente designadas por los Estados Miembros de la UNESCO. No serán consideradas por la Secretaría de la UNESCO las solicitudes presentadas a título individual o por organismos privados.

☞ Programa de becas individuales

Campos de estudios: ciencias, ciencias humanas, ciencias sociales, comunicación, educación, estudios culturales, estudios sobre el desarrollo, programas de corta duración, tecnología.
Becas: becas individuales concedidas con cargo al presupuesto regular de la Organización.
Descripción: para estudios en áreas relativas a los "Objetivos Estratégicos" que aparecen en la Estrategia a Medio Plazo Aprobada para 2002-2007 (31C/4) y correspondiendo a las "Prioridades establecidas para cada Programa Principal" especificadas en los Programa y Presupuesto Aprobados para la Organización, son: educación para todos; recursos y ecosistemas hídricos; ética de la ciencia y la tecnología; protección de la diversidad cultural y fomento del pluralismo y el diálogo entre culturas; promoción del acceso equitativo a la información, en particular a la información de dominio público.
Se conceden: a nacionales de los Estados Miembros y Miembros Asociados de la UNESCO. La finalidad de estas becas es ofrecer oportunidades a los becarios para realizar principalmente estudios superiores o actividades de investigación en el extranjero y adquirir una experiencia internacional en los campos de estudio para los cuales no existen posibilidades en el país de origen. Además, cada Estado Miembro tiene derecho a presentar hasta 2 solicitudes, por orden de mérito de los candidatos.
Lugar: en los Estados Miembros de la UNESCO, y Singapur.
Duración: no más de 9 meses (6 meses máximo cuando se trata del programa de becas de la UNESCO).
Importe: subvención mensual basada, en general, en la escala establecida por las Naciones Unidas (o escalas especiales cuando se trata del programa de becas de la UNESCO), más gastos de viaje, de enseñanza, de libros y material de estudio.
Solicitudes: deben presentarlas las autoridades nacionales designadas por los gobiernos de los Estados miembros de la UNESCO (en general la Comisión Nacional de la UNESCO o el ministerio competente en la materia de estudio elegida). No se tomarán en consideración las solicitudes presentadas a título individual.

☞ Subvenciones para viajes de estudio

Campos de estudios: ciencias de la información, ciencias naturales, ciencias sociales, educación, estudios culturales, tecnología.
Becas: subvenciones para viajes de estudio.
Se conceden: a nacionales de los Estados Miembros de la UNESCO que ocupen altos cargos en sus respectivos países. Cada postulante propondrá a la UNESCO su propio programa de visitas para su aprobación y presentará un informe al regresar de su viaje de estudios. Todos los candidatos deben ser nombrados oficialmente por sus gobiernos.
Lugar: visitas de observación o de consulta a varios países o a diversos lugares de un mismo país.
Duración: 2 meses como máximo.
Importe: cubre los gastos de viaje en clase turista, más un subsidio diario basado en la escala de subsistencia de la Organización de las Naciones Unidas.
Solicitudes: deben presentarlas las autoridades nacionales designadas por los gobiernos de los Estados Miembros de la UNESCO (en general la Comisión nacional de la UNESCO o el ministerio competente en la materia de estudio elegida). No se tendrán en cuenta las solicitudes presentadas a título individual o por órganos privados.

50 United Nations Educational, Scientific and Cultural Organization - Man and the Biosphere Programme (MAB) [UNESCO-MAB]

Division of Ecological and Earth Sciences
1, rue Miollis
75732 Paris Cedex 15, France
Fax: +33-1-4568-5804
Web: http://www.unesco.org/mab/capacity/mys/awar mab2.htm
e-mail: mab.awards@unesco.org

☞ Man and the Biosphere (MAB) Young Scientists Research Grant Awards

Study Domains: biology, development studies, ecology, environment, forestry, human sciences, marine science, natural resources, research, rural development.
Description: for studies in biology, development studies, ecology, environment, forestry, human science, marine sciences, natural resources, research and rural development.
Open to: candidates of Member and non-Member States of UNESCO that have a national MAB Committee, holding a first degree (10 annually).
Age limit Max: 40 years of age.
Place of study: in applicant's country; endorsement of national MAB committee is an obligatory requirement.
Duration: 1 or 2 years, depending upon the objectives of study (not renewable).
Value: maximum US$5,000 (funds cannot be used for international travel).
Applications: by 30 April 2005; applications may be downloaded at http://www.unesco.org/mab/capacity/mys/awarmab2.htm#Application Forms and must be submitted via the MAB National Committee or UNESCO National Commission (in countries without MAB Committees) for endorsement before submission to UNESCO. Only applications in English and French will be accepted.

50 Organisation des Nations Unies pour l'éducation, la science et la culture - Programme sur l'Homme et la biosphère (MAB) [UNESCO-MAB]

Division des Sciences écologiques et de la terre
1, rue Miollis
75732 Paris Cedex 15, France
Fax: +33-1-4568-5804
Web: http://www.unesco.org/mab/capacity/mys/awar mab2.htm
e-mail: mab.awards@unesco.org

☙ **L'Homme et la biosphère (MAB) - bourses de recherche pour jeunes scientifiques**

Domaines d'étude: biologie, développement rural, écologie, environnement, études du développement, recherche, ressources naturelles, sciences de la mer, sciences humaines, sylviculture.
A l'intention de: licenciés des pays membres et non-membres de l'UNESCO où se trouve un Comité national du MAB (10 par an).
Age Max: 40 ans.
Lieu: dans le pays du candidat; approbation obligatoire par le Comité national du MAB de son pays.
Durée: 1 ou 2 ans, selon le domaine choisi (non renouvelable).
Valeur: maximum de 5.000$US (les fonds ne peuvent être utilisés pour le voyage international).
Candidatures: avant le 30 avril 2005. Les formulaires de candidature peuvent être téléchargés du site Internet: http://www.unesco.org/mab/capacity/mys/awarmab.htm# et doivent être soumis au Comité national du MAB ou à la Commission nationale pour l'UNESCO (pour les pays n'ayant pas de Comité MAB) pour soutien avant d'être envoyés à l'UNESCO. Seules les candidatures en français et en anglais seront retenues.

50 Organización de las Naciones Unidas para la Educación, la Ciencia y la Cultura - Programa sobre El Hombre y la Biosfera (MAB) [UNESCO-MAB]

División de Ciencias Ecológicas y de la Tierra
1, rue Miollis
75732 París Cedex 15, Francia
Fax: +33-1-4568-5804
Web: http://www.unesco.org/mab/capacity/mys/awarmab2.htm
e-mail: mab.awards@unesco.org

☙ **El Hombre y la Biosfera (MAB) - Becas de investigación para jóvenes científicos**

Campos de estudios: biología, ciencias del mar, ciencias humanas, desarrollo rural, ecología, medio ambiente, estudios sobre el desarrollo, investigación, recursos naturales, silvicultura.
Se conceden: a licenciados de los países miembros y no miembros de la UNESCO donde haya un comité nacional del MAB (10 por año).
Edad Max: 40 años.
Lugar: en el país del candidato; es imprescindible la aprobación del comité nacional del MAB.
Duración: 1 o 2 años, según el área escogida (no renovable).
Importe: máximo 5.000 dólares de los Estados Unidos (el importe no puede ser utilizado para el viaje internacional).
Solicitudes: hasta el 30 de Abril de 2005. Los formularios de candidatura pueden ser cargados por Internet: http://www.unesco.org/mab/capacity/mys/awarmab2.htm y deben estar sometidos, para sostén, al Comité nacional del MAB o a la Comisión nacional para la UNESCO (para los países que no tienen un Comité MAB) antes de ser enviados a la UNESCO. Solamente candidaturas en francés y en inglés serán aceptadas.

51 United Nations High Commissioner for Refugees DAFI Scholarships [UNHCR]

Case Postale 2500
1211 Genève 2 Dépôt, Switzerland
Tel: +41-22-739-8111

☙ **Albert Einstein German Academic Refugee Initiative Fund (DAFI)**

Study Domains: all major fields.
Description: UNHCR provides, on a limited basis, scholarships for refugees at the tertiary level in universities and polytechnic institutions through the Albert Einstein German Academic Refugee Initiative Fund (DAFI). Funding for this programme is provided by the Federal Government of Germany. DAFI programmes are mostly available in developing countries with a significant refugee population,

mostly in Africa and Asia. There are also a limited number of DAFI scholarships in some countries of Eastern Europe.
Open to: refugees with recognized refugee status, having successfully completed secondary schooling to a high standard in camp-based refugee schools, or in national schools of the country of origin or asylum; with no other means of support for university studies, having chosen a course of study that is likely to lead to employment.
Age limit Max: not over 28 years of age at the beginning of studies.
Duration: 1 academic year, renewable; maximum 4 years.

52 United Nations Statistical Institute for Asia and the Pacific [UN-SIAP]

JETRO-IDE Building
3-2-2 Wakaba, Mihama-ku, Chiba-shi;
261-8787 Chiba, Japan
Tel: +81-43-299-9782
Fax: +81-43-299-9780
Web: http://www.unsiap.or.jp
e-mail: staff@unsiap.or.jp

☙ **Training Courses and Seminars in Statistics**

Study Domains: statistics.
Programmes: (a) Group Training Course (GTC) in Modules on Core Official Statistics; (b) Group Training Course (GTC) in Application of Information and Communications Technology to Statistical Processes; (c) Group Training Course (GTC) in Analysis and Interpretation of Official Statistics; (d) Area Focused Training Course in Collection and Analysis of Official Statistics for Central Asian Countries; (e) Course/Workshop on Sample Design for Household and Establishment Surveys; (f) Research-based regional course; (g) Courses/seminars on selected statistical topics.
Open to: statistical personnel nominated by invited governments of member and associate member countries of the Economic and Social Commission for Asia and the Pacific; applicants should have first degree or equivalent from a recognized institution in statistics, economics, sociology or other appropriate field; knowledge of English required.
Duration: (a) 6 months (courses begin in October); (b) to (d) 2 months; (e) 1 month; (f) 6 weeks; (g) 2 to 3 weeks.
Financial assistance: (a) 30 scholarships; (b) 20; (c) 10; (d) 10; (e) 20; (f) 10 to 20; (g) 10 to 20.
Languages: instruction in English.
Applications: through nominating governments and United Nations Development Programme representatives to whom announcements of courses and seminars are sent.

53 Universal Postal Union - International Bureau [UPU]

Case postale 13
3000 Berne 15, Switzerland
Tel: +41-31-350-3111
Fax: +41-31-350-3110
Web: http://www.upu.int/

☙ **Scholarships for professional study and in-service training**

Study Domains: administration, vocational training.
Scholarships: scholarships for professional study and in-service training.
Description: subjects vary according to training needs of country concerned; cover only postal services with the exception of teacher-training course.
Open to: post-office employees of any nationality with professional experience and who are nominated by administrations or postal companies of member countries of the UPU, especially from developing countries.
Place of study: administrations, postal schools, and specialized institutions in all countries.
Duration: from 1 week to 2 years, according to course chosen.
Value: varies according to place of course; between US$1,500-$17,000.
Applications: according to the conditions communicated to postal administrations.

53 ## Union postale universelle [UPU]

Case postale 13
3000 Berne 15, Suisse
Tel: +41-31-350-3111
Fax: +41-31-350-3110
Web: http://www.upu.int/

🗣 Bourses de formation professionnelle et de perfectionnement

Domaines d'étude: administration, formation professionnelle.
Bourses: bourses de formation professionnelle et de perfectionnement.
Description: sujets varient selon les objectifs de formation des divers pays et ne concernent que les services postaux, à l'exception de la formation pédagogique.
A l'intention de: fonctionnaires postaux de toute nationalité, notamment ceux des pays en développement, ayant une expérience professionnelle et dont les candidatures sont présentées par les administrations ou entreprises postales des pays membres de l'UPU.
Lieu: administrations, écoles postales et instituts spécialisés de tous pays.
Durée: d'une semaine à 2 ans, selon la formation choisie.
Valeur: varie, selon le lieu du stage, de 1.500-17.000$US.
Candidatures: selon les conditions communiquées aux administrations postales.

53 ## Unión Postal Universal [UPU]

Case Postal 13
3000 Berna 15, Suiza
Tel: +41-31-350-3111
Fax: +41-31-350-3110
Web: http://www.upu.int/

🗣 Becas de formación y perfeccionamiento profesional

Campos de estudios: administración, formación profesional.
Descripción: materias diversas; varían según los objetivos de formación de los países. En relación con los servicios postales, con excepción de la formación pedagógica.
Se conceden: a funcionarios de empresas postales de cualquier país, especialmente países en desarrollo, con experiencia profesional, que sean presentados por las administraciones o empresas postales de los países miembros de la UPU.
Lugar: administraciones y escuelas postales o institutos especializados de cualquier país.
Duración: de una semana a 2 años, según los estudios.
Importe: varía según el lugar del curso, entre 1.500 y 17.000 dólares de los Estados Unidos.
Solicitudes: según las condiciones comunicadas a las administraciones postales.

54 ## University Institute of European Studies, International Training Centre of the ILO

Via Maria Vittoria 26
10123 Turin
Tel: +39-11-839-4660
Fax: +39-11-839-4664
Web: http://www.iuse.it
e-mail: nfo@iuse.it

📖 Postgraduate Programmes

Study Domains: international business, international law, international relations.
Programmes: International Trade Law Postgraduate Course: international trade relations, international sale of goods, contract negotiation and drafting, main types of international contracts, arbitration and dispute resolution.
Open to: graduates of any nationality in law, political science, business or economics; knowledge of English essential.
Held: at the ILO Turin Centre.
Duration: 2-1/2 months (April-June).
Financial assistance: a limited number of scholarships are available for foreign students and for Italians not resident in Turin to cover part of the boarding expenses.

Languages: instruction in English.
Applications: application forms may be downloaded at http://lbeurope.iuse.it/info_applic.php; apply by 20 January to L.B.E. Course Secretariat; c/o University Institute of European Studies; Via Maria Vittoria, 26; 10123 Torino, Italy: tel: +39-011-839-4660; fax +39-011-839-4664; email: lbeurope@iuse.it; web: http://lbeurope.iuse.it.

55 ## World Bank Institute [WBI]

1818 'H' Street, NW
MSN J4-402
20433 Washington, DC, USA
Tel: +1-202-473-1000
Fax: +1-202-477-6391
Web: http://www.worldbank.org/wbi/
e-mail: wbi_infoline@worldbank.org

🗣 Fellowships / Scholarships Programmes

Study Domains: development studies.
Scholarships: (a) Joint Japan/ World Bank Graduate Scholarship Program (JJ/WBGSP); (b) Robert S. McNamara Fellowship Program.
Description: (a) postgraduate studies (b) course of studies leading to a Master's degree in public policy.
Open to: nationals of World Bank borrowing countries; (a) candidates must be accepted to graduate studies in a university located in any World Bank member country except the applicant's country and be under 45 or preferably under 35 years of age; (see website for further criteria; (b) mid-career professionals from all World Bank borrowing member countries, including former socialist countries, are eligible to apply to the M.P.P. programme as McNamara Fellows, so long as they meet the M.P.P. programme's normal eligibility requirements.
Place of study: (a) in well-known universities in the World Bank member countries, except scholar's own country; (b) at Princeton University, Princeton, New Jersey, U.S.A.
Duration: one year, renewable for a further year.
Value: full tuition, travel allowance and stipend for living expenses (equivalent to approximately US$7,500).
Applications: (a) Strict eligibility criteria and application procedures must be respected in order to be considered. Further information may be requested from the Joint Japan/World Bank Graduate Scholarship Program at the above address; tel: +1-202-473-6849; fax: +1-202-522-4036; email: jjwbgsp@worldbank.org; on-line application forms may be obtained from http://www.worldbank.org/wbi/scholarships; (b) see Princeton University http://www.wws.princeton.edu/degree/mpp.html).

55 ## Institut de la Banque Mondiale [WBI]

1818 "H" Street, NW
MSN J4-402
20433 Washington, DC, États-Unis
Tel: +1-202-473-1000
Fax: +1-202-477-6391
Web: http://www.worldbank.org/wbi/
e-mail: wbi_infoline@worldbank.org

🗣 Programme de bourses universitaires

Domaines d'étude: études du développement.
Bourses: (a) le Programme de bourses universitaires Japon/Banque mondiale, financé exclusivement par le Japon; (b) le Programme de bourses Robert S. McNamara, cofinancé par la Banque mondiale et l'Université de Princeton.
A l'intention de: (a) aux candidats de tous les pays membres emprunteurs de la Banque mondiale admis dans une université et ayant une preuve de demande à une autre université située dans n'importe quel pays membre de la Banque a l'exception du pays de résidence du/de la candidat(e); ayant moins de 45 ans, et de préférence moins de 35 ans (consultez le site Internet pour d'autres critères et conditions d'admission); (b) pour le Programme McNamara, visitez le site de l'Université de Princeton et avant de déposer votre demande, n'oubliez pas de prendre connaissance des critères d'admissibilité.
Lieu: (a) dans plus de 160 établissements réputés dans au moins 40 pays membres de la Banque mondiale autres que le leur; (b) à l'université de Princeton (États-Unis).
Durée: une année avec possibilité d'être renouvelable pour une deuxième année.

Valeur: frais de scolarité, de voyage et une allocation mensuelle de subsistance (logement et nourriture) couvrant aussi l'achat de livres (environ 7.500$US).
Candidatures: (a) pour plus d'informations sur les critères et conditions d'admission, contacter le Joint Japan/World Bank Graduate Scholarship Program à l'adresse ci-dessus; email: jjwbgsp@worldbank.org; des formulaires d'inscription peuvent être téléchargés à partir du site Internet http://www.worldbank.org/wbi/scholarships; (b) Université de Princeton; voir http://www.wws.princeton.edu/degree/mpp.html.

55 Instituto del Banco Mundial [WBI]

1818 "H" Street, NW
MSN J4-402
20433 Washington, DC, Estados Unidos
Tel: +1-202-473-1000
Fax: +1-202-477-6391
Web: http://www.worldbank.org/wbi/
e-mail: wbi_infoline@worldbank.org

☞ Programas de becas

Campos de estudios: estudios sobre el desarrollo.
Becas: (a) Programa Conjunto del Gobierno de Japón y el Banco Mundial de Becas de Posgrado (JJ/WBGSP); (b) Programa de Becas "Robert S. McNamara".
Descripción: (a) estudios universitarios de posgrado; (b) estudios y/o investigación para obtención de maestría.
Materias de estudio: (a) materias relacionadas con el desarrollo (por ejemplo economía, educación, salud pública, medio ambiente, agricultura, estudios sobre la mujer, atención infantil, etc.); (b) políticas públicas o economía del desarrollo.
Se conceden: (a) a personas de países miembros del Banco Mundial; (b) a candidatos prometedores del sector público de los países en desarrollo, como los bancos centrales y ministerios de hacienda y planificación.
Lugar: (a) en universidades de prestigio (más de 160 en 40 países) por sus investigaciones y actividades docentes sobre el desarrollo de los países miembros del Banco; (b) en la Woodrow Wilson School of Public and International Affairs, Princeton University, Estados Unidos de América.
Duración: 12 meses (no renovable).
Importe: 7.500 dólares de los Estados Unidos e incluye gastos de subsistencia, seguro médico y gastos de investigación.
Solicitudes: por información adicional, consultar el sitio web; para (a) en dicho sitio se pueden realizar solicitudes en línea o descargar archivos PDF para envío posterior, pero también se pueden solicitar ejemplares de los formularios impresos a la Secretaría del JJ/WBGSP; (b) ver sitio web del University of Princeton:
http://www.wws.princeton.edu/degree/mpp.html.

56 World Leisure International Centres of Excellence [WICE]

Gen. Foulkesweg 13
6703 BJ Wageningen, Netherlands
Tel: +31-317-484-414
Fax: +31-317-485-441
Web: http://www.wau.nl/
e-mail: Office@users.wice.wau.nl

☐ M.Sc. Programme in Leisure, Tourism and Environment

Study Domains: recreation and leisure, tourism, hotel and catering management.
Description: a collaborative endeavour of World Leisure and Wageningen University and Research Centre. Worldwide in orientation, the course addresses the complete and multifaceted relationship between leisure (free time) and leisure-related issues (such as tourism, sport, the arts) on the one hand and environmental issues on the other; all this from and in a worldwide perspective.
Open to: Master's degree or Bachelor's degree holders with work experience. Open to candidates of all nationalities, aged 22-40; candidates may have qualifications in the field of leisure or leisure-related fields, e.g. tourism, or socio-cultural science; screening at country level. Limited admission per country and world region.
Held: Wageningen University and Research Centre,

Netherlands.
Duration: one year abroad (course begins 15 August).
Fees: the total costs for Non-EU/EFTA (European Union/European Free Trade Association) students 17,245€ (18 months; internship not needed; residential period 12 months), for EU/EFTA students 16,349€. (24 months; for 18 months part of the tuition fee will be reimbursed).
Financial assistance: assistance very limited.
Languages: Instruction in English. Good knowledge of English required (TOEFL); language training available before start of course.
Applications: by 1 June at the above address. See website http://www.worldleisure.org/studies_training/postgrad.html or http://www.wau.nl/wmsc/mscleis.htm for further information.

56 Association mondiale pour les loisirs, Centre international d'excellence [WICE]

Gen. Foulkesweg 13
6703 BJ Wageningen, Pays-Bas
Tel: +31-317-484-414
Fax: +31-317-485-441
Web: http://www.wau.nl/
e-mail: Office@users.wice.wau.nl

☐ Maîtrise en sciences du loisir et de l'environnement

Domaines d'étude: récréologie et loisirs, tourisme, hôtellerie, restauration.
Description: programme créé par l'Association mondiale pour les loisirs (Canada) et la Faculté agronomique de Wageningen (Pays-Bas) avec une perspective internationale, axée sur la problématique des processus de transitions spontanées ou planifiées en matière des ressources du loisir, ainsi que l'impact des activités du loisir sur différents environnements.
A l'intention de: candidats de toute nationalité, âgés de 20 à 40 ans, de niveau universitaire (maîtrise) ou ayant fait des études supérieures avec expérience professionnelle et qualifications dans le domaine du loisir ou dans les domaines affiliés: tourisme ou sciences socioculturelles. Une sélection préalable est effectuée au niveau national. Entraînement d'anglais avant les cours si nécessaire. Admission limitée par pays ou par région.
Organisés: Université agronomique de Wageningen.
Durée: 1 an (début des cours: 15 août).
Frais: pour les ressortissants non européens (non EU/EFTA): 17.245€ pour les ressortissants européens (EU/EFTA): 16.349€.
Assistance financière: très limitée.
Connaissances linguistiques: langue d'enseignement: anglais. Une bonne maîtrise de cette langue est requise (TOEFL).
Inscriptions: avant le 1er juin, à l'adresse ci-dessus; voir http://www.worldleisure.org/studies_training/postgrad.html pour plus d'information ou http://www.wau.nl/wmsc/mscleis.htm.

57 World Meteorological Organization [WMO]

41, avenue Giuseppe-Motta
CP 2300
1211 Geneva 2, Switzerland
Tel: +41-22-730-8111
Fax: +41-22-730-8047
Web: http://www.wmo.ch

☐ Courses in Meteorology

Study Domains: hydrology, meteorology.
Programmes: courses in various aspects of meteorology and operational hydrology.
Open to: citizens of WMO member countries, with the required qualifications.
Held: at WMO Regional Meteorological Training Centres and at national institutions and universities in more than 90 WMO member countries; for more information, see WMO publication n° 240, Compendium of Meteorological Training Facilities.
Applications: through the Office of Permanent Representative of the candidate's country with WMO, to the Secretary-General, WMO, at the above address.

☛ **WMO Voluntary Cooperation Programme (VCP)**

Study Domains: hydrology, meteorology.
Scholarships: WMO Voluntary Cooperation Programme (VCP); courses in general meteorology, applied meteorology, climatology, operational hydrology.
Open to: applicants from developing countries nominated by their governments; qualifications vary according to the individual requirement.
Place of study: in various countries; at WMO Regional Meteorological Training Centres, universities, national meteorological and hydrological services, firms, institutes, etc.
Duration: from 2 weeks to several years (long-term fellowships awarded initially for 12 months with possibility of extensions subject to satisfactory progress).
Value: normally based on UNDP stipend rates or as provided by Member countries for VCP fellowships.
Applications: submitted by government of candidate's country, through local UNDP office; to the Secretary General, WMO (www.wmo.ch/web/tco/vcp).

57 Organisation météorologique mondiale [OMM]

41, avenue Giuseppe-Motta
CP 2300
1211 Genève 2, Suisse
Tel: +41-22-730-8111
Fax: +41-22-730-8047
Web: http://www.wmo.ch

📖 **Cours de météorologie**

Domaines d'étude: hydrologie, météorologie.
Programmes: cours portant sur divers domaines de la météorologie et de l'hydrologie opérationnelle.
A l'intention de: ressortissants des pays membres de l'OMM, ayant les qualifications requises.
Organisés: dans les centres régionaux de formation météorologique de l'OMM, et dans les institutions nationales et universités de plus de 90 États membres de l'OMM. (Pour toute information complémentaire, consulter la brochure OMM n° 240 - Recueil de renseignements sur les possibilités de formation météorologique).
Inscriptions: par l'intermédiaire du bureau du représentant permanent du pays du candidat auprès de l'OMM, qui transmettra au Secrétaire général de l'OMM, à l'adresse ci-dessus.

☛ **Programme de coopération volontaire (PCV)**

Domaines d'étude: hydrologie, météorologie.
Bourses: bourses de l'OMM: l'OMM fournit environ 300 bourses par an au titre du Programme des Nations Unies pour le développement (PNUD), le Système de fonds en dépôt, et de son propre programme d'assistance, principalement le Programme de coopération volontaire (PCV).
A l'intention de: ressortissants de pays en développement qui doivent être nommés par leur gouvernement. Les qualifications requises varient selon les besoins individuels.
Lieu: divers pays, centres régionaux de formation météorologique de l'OMM, universités, services météorologiques et hydrologiques nationaux, entreprises, instituts, etc.
Durée: de 2 semaines à plusieurs années (pour les bourses de longue durée, l'octroi initial est de 12 mois avec possibilité de prolongation dépendant des progrès satisfaisants).
Valeur: allocations basées généralement sur les taux du PNUD ou les taux établis par les pays membres pour les bourses PCV.
Candidatures: soumises par le gouvernement du pays du requérant, par l'intermédiaire du représentant local du PNUD; Secrétariat général de l'OMM (www.wmo.ch/web/tco/vcp).

57 Organización Meteorológica Mundial [OMM]

41, avenue Giuseppe-Motta
CP 2300
1211 Ginebra 2, Suiza
Tel: +41-22-730-8111
Fax: +41-22-730-8047
Web: http://www.wmo.ch

📖 **Programa de cursos**

Campos de estudios: hidrología, meteorología.
Programas: cursos sobre diversos campos de la meteorología y de la hidrología operacional.
Se destina(n): a nacionales de los países miembros de la OMM que tengan las calificaciones requeridas.
Se dicta(n): en los centros regionales de formación meteorológica de la OMM y en las instituciones y universidades de más de 90 Estados miembros de la OMM. (Para mayores informaciones consúltese la publicación n.° 240 de la OMM, Compendio de Instituciones Docentes en Materia de Meteorología).
Inscripciones: por intermedio del Representante Permanente de la OMM en el país del candidato, quien transmitirá al pedido al Secretario General de la OMM en la dirección que figura en el título.

☛ **Programa de Cooperación Voluntaria (PCV)**

Campos de estudios: hidrología, meteorología.
Becas: Becas de estudio. La OMM otorga unas 300 becas anuales, por intermedio del Programa de las Naciones Unidas para el Desarrollo (PNUD), del Sistema de Fondos Fiduciarios y de sus propios programas de asistencia, principalmente el Programa de Cooperación Voluntaria (PCV).
Materias de estudio: meteorología general, meteorología aplicada, climatología, hidrología operacional.
Se conceden: a nacionales de los países en desarrollo, designados por sus gobiernos. Las calificaciones requeridas varían según las necesidades individuales.
Lugar: en varios países; centros regionales de formación meteorológica de la OMM, universidades, servicios meteorológicos e hidrológicos nacionales, firmas comerciales e institutos, etc.
Duración: de 2 semanas a varios años (para las becas de larga duración el período inicial es de 12 meses con posibilidad de prórroga si el resultado de los estudios es satisfactorio).
Importe: basado, en general, en la asignación fijada por el PNUD o en la proporcionada por los países miembros para las becas del PCV.
Solicitudes: el gobierno del país del candidato deberá someterlas al Secretario General de la OMM por conducto de la oficina local del PNUD; (www.wmo.ch/web/tco/vcp).

58 World Tourism Organization [WTO]

Human Resource Development Programme
Capitán Haya 42
28020 Madrid, Spain
Tel: +34-91-567-8100
Fax: +34-91-571-3733
Web: http://www.world-tourism.org

📖 **WTO Education and Training Programmes**

Study Domains: short-term programmes, tourism, hotel and catering management, vocational training.
Description: (a) WTO.TedQual. A framework of programmes for quality in tourism education. The WTO.TedQual Certification is granted to training and education institutions by means of a quality audit. The TedQual institutions can request membership in the WTO Education Council (Affiliate Members). There are also TedQual Seminars (educating the educators) for Member States; (b) WTO.GTAT. Set of programmes designed to improve the performance of teaching and learning in tourism, including software for examinations and course development, GTAT Courses to improve specific knowledge and/or prepare for exams, GTAT Diagnosis to ascertain strong and weak points in specific subjects, GTAT Exams and GTAT Certification of Proficiency. Postgraduate GTAT 'Master in Hotel Administration' and GTAT.TPS PhD 'Tourism Policy and Strategy' are available in Spanish; (c) WTO.Sbest Initiative. A framework for a range of WTO Programmes aimed at contributing to excellence in tourism destinations through quality training and education. Programmes include WTO.Sbest Training, WTO.Sbest Audit and WTO Tourism Labour Market Observatory.
Open to: (a) see website for complete information: http://www.world-tourism.org/education/menu.html (b) and (c) only to public officials from the tourism administrations of WTO Member States.

Held: at WTO Headquarters, in WTO Member States, at WTO.TedQual Certified education institutions.
Duration: 1 week to 3 years, depending on course.
Financial assistance: partial scholarships available only to tourism officials from WTO Member States.
Applications: only through WTO Member States; direct applications will not be considered nor acknowledged. Information on courses appears on the WTO website and through official communications to WTO Member States.

58 Organisation mondiale du tourisme [OMT]

Capitán Haya 42
28020 Madrid, Espagne
Tel: +34-91-567-8100
Fax: +34-91-571-3733
Web: http://www.world-tourism.org

📖 Programme de formation

Domaines d'étude: formation professionnelle, programmes de courte durée, tourisme, hôtellerie, restauration.
Description: (a) OMT.TedQual. Ensemble de programmes cadre pour la qualité dans la formation en tourisme. La Certification OMT.TedQual est octroyée à des institutions d'enseignement et de formation suite à un audit en qualité. Les institutions OMT.TedQual peuvent demander leur incorporation au Conseil Supérieur OMT (membres affiliés). Il existe aussi des séminaires OMT.TedQual pour la formation des formateurs pour les États membres; (b) OMT.GTAT. Ensemble de programmes destiné à améliorer le rendement de l'enseignement et de l'apprentissage en tourisme; il comprend des logiciels pour le passage d'examens et le développement de cours: cours destinés à améliorer des connaissances spécifiques et à passer/faire passer de examens; diagnostic des points faibles et forts sur des sujets spécifiques; examens et certificats de compétence; cours de 3e cycle «Master en gestion hôtelière»; doctorat en «Politiques et stratégies en tourisme» (disponibles en espagnol); (c) Initiative OMT.Sbest. Ensemble de programmes OMT destinés à contribuer à l'excellence en destinations touristiques à travers la formation à la qualité. Les programmes comprennent Formation OMT.Sbest, Audit OMT.Sbest et Observatoire OMT de Marché de travail en tourisme.
A l'intention de: (a) voir le site web pour plus de renseignements: http://www.world-tourism.org/education/menu.html; (b) et (c) seulement aux fonctionnaires des administrations en tourisme des États membres de l'OMT.
Organisés: au siège central de l'OMT, dans les États membres de l'OMT, dans les institutions de formation OMT.TedQual.
Durée: 1 semaine à 3 ans selon les cours.
Assistance financière: bourses partielles disponibles seulement pour les fonctionnaires en tourisme des États membres.
Inscriptions: uniquement à travers les États membres de l'OMT (les demandes individuelles ne sont pas prises en compte). L'information sur les cours est disponible sur le site web de l'Organisation et à travers des communications officielles aux États membres de l'OMT.

58 Organización Mundial del Turismo [OMT]

Capitán Haya 42
28020 Madrid, España
Tel: +34-91-567-8100
Fax: +34-91-571-3733
Web: http://www.world-tourism.org

📖 Programas de formación

Campos de estudios: formación profesional, programas de corta duración, turismo, hotelería.
Descripción: (a) OMT.TedQual. Programas marco de calidad en la formación en turismo. La Certificación OMT.TedQual se otorga a instituciones de enseñanza y formación luego de una auditoría en calidad. Las instituciones TedQual pueden solicitar su integración al Consejo de Educación OMT (miembros afiliados). Existen también seminarios OMT.TedQual (formación de docentes) para los Estados Miembros; (b) OMT.GTAT. Conjunto de programas destinados a mejorar el rendimiento de la enseñanza y el aprendizaje en turismo, incluyendo software para exámenes y desarrollo de cursos: cursos destinados a mejorar conocimientos específicos y/o preparar exámenes; diagnóstico para detectar puntos fuertes y débiles en temas específicos; exámenes y certificados de competencia; posgrado "Master en administración hotelera", doctorado en "Políticas y estrategias en turismo" (disponibles en español); (c) Iniciativa OMT.Sbest. Conjunto de programas OMTdestinados a contribuir a la excelencia en destinaciones turísticas mediante formación a la calidad. Los programas incluyen Formación OMT.Sbest, Auditoría OMT.Sbest y Observatorio OMT de Mercado de Trabajo en Turismo.
Se destina(n): (a) la información completa se puede encontrar en el sitio web http://www.world-tourism.org/education/menu.html; (b) (c) accesibles sólo a funcionarios públicos de las administraciones de turismo de los Estados miembros de la OMT.
Se dicta(n): en la sede central de la OMT, en Estados Miembros de la OMT, en instituciones de enseñanza con Certificación OMT.TedQual.
Duración: 1 semana a 3 años, según las características de cada curso.
Asistencia financiera: becas parciales disponibles sólo para funcionarios en turismo de los Estados Miembros.
Inscripciones: sólo a través de los Estados Miembros de la OMT (no se aceptan solicitudes directas). La información sobre cursos aparece en el sitio web y a través de comunicaciones oficiales a los Estados Miembros de la OMT.

59 Zonta International [ZI]

557 West Randolph Street
60661-2206 Chicago, IL, United States
Tel: +1-312-930-5848
Fax: +1-312-930-0951
Web: http://www.Zonta.org
e-mail: zontafdtn@zonta.org

🎓 Amelia Earhart Fellowship Awards

Study Domains: aerospace, engineering, sciences.
Scholarships: Amelia Earhart Fellowship Awards.
Description: 35 awards granted annually to women pursuing graduate degrees in aerospace-related sciences and aerospace-related engineering.
Open to: women pursuing a PhD/doctoral degree who demonstrate a superior academic record in the field of aerospace-related sciences and aerospace-related engineering are eligible; defence-related and post-doctoral research programmes are not eligible for the Fellowship; candidates must prove acceptance as full-time graduate student in approved institution; see website for further requirements.
Nationality: women of any nationality are eligible.
Academic requirements: must be registered in an accredited PhD/doctoral programme in a qualifying area of science or engineering closely related to advanced studies in aerospace-related science or aerospace-related engineering. A letter of acceptance or verification of enrolment must be submitted with the application. Must demonstrate a superior academic record at a recognized university or college with accredited courses in aerospace-related studies as verified by transcripts and recommendations. Provide evidence of a well-defined research programme in aerospace-related science or aerospace-related engineering as described in the application essay, research and publications.
Place of study: in any qualified university in any country.
Duration: 1 academic year (renewable for 1 academic year).
Value: US$6,000, renewable.
Applications: all applications, recommendations, transcripts and letter of current standing must be received or postmarked by 15 November to be considered. Incomplete applications or late applications due to postal delays will not be considered. Applications are accepted by fax provided the originals are postmarked within three days after the fax is received.
Consult the web site for detailed admission criteria and application procedure.

59 Zonta International [ZI]
557 West Randolph Street
60661-2206 Chicago, IL, États-Unis
Tel: +1-312-930-5848
Fax: +1-312-930-0951
Web: http://www.Zonta.org
e-mail: zontafdtn@zonta.org

Bourses Amelia Earhart

Domaines d'étude: aérospace, ingénierie, sciences.
Description: 35 bourses octroyées annuellement à des femmes, pour poursuivre des études supérieures en sciences ou ingénierie aérospatiales.
A l'intention de: femmes de toute nationalité, qui poursuivent des études supérieures et qui obtiennent d'excellentes qualifications dans les domaines des sciences ou de l'ingénierie aérospatiales. Les bourses ne s'appliquent ni au domaine de la défense ni à un programme de recherche post-doctorale.
Autres Conditions: Les candidates doivent pouvoir prouver qu'elles sont bien inscrites dans un établissement d'enseignement supérieur accrédité, dans un programme reconnu comme une spécialisation dans les domaine mentionnés. Les candidates devront présenter une lettre d'acceptation de l'établissement concerné, la transcription des notes prouvant l'excellence académique, et des recommandations; en outre, elles devront présenter un plan détaillé du programme de recherche.
Lieu: universités appropriées de n'importe quel pays.
Durée: 1 année académique (renouvelable 1 fois).
Valeur: 6.000$US.
Candidatures: les formulaires de candidature et tous les éléments du dossier doivent être envoyés avant le mois de novembre (la date varie chaque année). Toute documentation incomplète ou arrivée en retard ne sera pas considérée; elle peut être envoyé par fax, mais avec au moins trois jours d'avance supplémentaire (les originaux seront demandés ultérieurement).
Consulter le site Internet pour connaître l'ensemble des conditions de candidature et admission.

59 Zonta International [ZI]
557 West Randolph Street
60661-2206 Chicago, IL, Estados Unidos
Tel: +1-312-930-5848
Fax: +1-312-930-0951
Web: http://www.Zonta.org
e-mail: zontafdtn@zonta.org

Becas Amelia Earhart

Campos de estudios: aeroespacio, ciencias, ingeniería.
Descripción: 35 becas asignadas anualmente a mujeres, para estudios superiores en ciencias aeroespaciales e ingeniería.
Se conceden: a mujeres de cualquier nacionalidad, que sigan estudios superiores y que demuestren excelencia en áreas de ciencias o ingeniería aeroespacial. No se aplican estas becas ni a áreas de defensa ni a investigación post-doctoral.
Otras condiciones: Las candidatas deberán demostrar que se han matriculado en un centro de enseñanza acreditado, en un programa superior (doctorado o especialización) reconocido como conducente a un título en estudios avanzados en las áreas mencionadas. Se exigirán una carta de aceptación en la institución de estudio, la transcripción de notas probando la excelencia académica, y recomendaciones. Se deberá presentar también un programa de investigación bien definido.
Lugar: en universidades apropiadas de cualquier país.
Duración: 1 año académico (renovable por un año más).
Importe: 6.000 dólares de los Estados Unidos.
Solicitudes: los formularios de inscripción y toda otra documentación requerida debe ser enviada antes del mes de noviembre (la fecha exacta varía cada año). Las solicitudes incompletas o atrasadas no serán consideradas. Se puede enviar la documentación por fax (los originales serán requeridos posteriormente) pero con al menos tres días de anticipación adicional.
Consultar el sitio web para conocer requerimientos y modalidades exactas de postulación y admisión.

National Scholarships and Courses
Bourses et Cours Nationaux
Becas y Cursos Nacionales

Albanie

Année universitaire: 1er octobre à 30 juin.
Organisation de l'enseignement supérieur: Organisation
de l'enseignement supérieur:
• Le premier cycle de l'enseignement supérieur comporte en
moyenne 8 à 12 semestres (4 à 6 années) (8 semestres pour la
plupart des formations, 10 semestres en Ingénierie, 12
semestres en Médecine). Le titre de Titull est conféré.
• Le second cycle universitaire: Shkollë pas Universitare
(SHPU) (école post-universitaire):
Études supérieures d'une durée de 2-4 semestres après
l'obtention d'un diplôme de premier cycle et menant au
«Diplômë e Studimeve te Thelluara pas Universitare» ou au
«Kandidat I Shkencave». Les candidats doivent préparer une
thèse.
• Le troisième cycle universitaire: Doktor I Shkencave
(Doctor es Sciences):
Études d'une durée de 6 à 10 semestres après le SHPU
comprenant une étude individuelle et de la Recherche
(conjointement à une activité professionnelle). Le titre de
«Doktor I Shkencave» est conféré. Les critères d'admission
comportent les activités scientifiques, les publications et la
recherche. Le candidat, sous la responsabilité d'un chercheur
en sciences, doit préparer et soutenir sa thèse.
Unité monétaire: lek.
Connaissances linguistiques requises: Une année
d'apprentissage de la langue albanaise auprès de la Faculté de
langue et littérature est obligatoire.
Formalités d'immigration: Elles dépendent des ministères
des affaires étrangères des pays respectifs.
Frais pour une année universitaire: Environ 27.000 lek
pour une année universitaire.
Services d'accueil et d'information:
• Ministère de l'éducation, Nr. 23, Rr. « Durresit », Tirana;
web: http://www.mash.gov.al
• La Section des relations internationales auprès de
l'Université de Tirana; web: http://www.mash.gov.al.
Enseignement à distance: Enseignement supérieur à
temps partiel; cours par correspondance.
Reconnaissance des études et diplômes: S'adresser au
Directeur, Directorate d'Enseignement supérieur; Ministère de
l'éducation et de la science; 23, Rr. Durresit; Tirana; Albanie.

---

60   Ministère de l'éducation

Rr. Durresit 23
Tirana
Tel: +355-42-222-60

🎓 Bourses

Domaines d'étude: toutes disciplines principales.
Bourses: bourses offertes par le Ministère de l'éducation.
A l'intention de: ressortissants de tout pays; les étudiants
étrangers suivront un cours d'albanais durant une année.
Durée: toute la durée des études universitaires.
Candidatures: auprès du Ministère de l'éducation dans le
pays d'origine.

61   Université de Tirana [TU]

Fakulteti i Historisë dhe i Filologjisë
Departamenti i Gjuhësisë
Tirana
Tel: +355-42-28402
Fax: +355-42-39189
Web: http://pages.albaniaonline.net/ut/unitirana_en/de
fault_en.htm
e-mail: rectorut@albaniaonline.net

📖 1er cycle / linguistique

Domaines d'étude: études culturelles, langues, lettres,
linguistique, programmes d'été.
Programmes: Cours de linguistique et d'albanais
conduisant au diplôme de Bachelor of Arts.
Description: cours de langue et de culture albanaises
(niveau débutant et avancé).
A l'intention de: ressortissants de tout pays titulaires d'un
diplôme de fin d'études secondaires; l'admission se fait sur
examen.
Durée: 4 années pour le diplôme de Bachelor of Arts; les
programmes d'été se déroulent sur une base de 25 heures
hebdomadaires; la durée des cours d'albanais varie entre 1
mois et 1 an.

Connaissances linguistiques: albanais; examen d'albanais
pour les étudiants étrangers.
Inscriptions: avant le 15 juillet, auprès du Ministère de
l'éducation, département des relations internationales, Tirana,
Albanie.

Algérie

Année universitaire: octobre à juillet.
Unité monétaire: dinar.
Connaissances linguistiques requises: Bonne
connaissance de la langue arabe pour les étudiants étrangers.
Cours obligatoires de langue arabe pour les spécialités
(filières).
Formalités d'immigration: Les étudiants étrangers doivent
être en possession d'un visa ou protocole d'accord entre les
pays signataires.
Services d'accueil et d'information: Organismes officiels:
• Agence de coopération internationale. Ministère des affaires
étrangères, rue Shakespeare El-Mouradia, Wilaya d'Alger.
Autres services (sur place ou à l'étranger):
• Ambassades d'Algérie; site web: http://www.mesrs.edu.dz.
Reconnaissance des études et diplômes: s'adresser à:
Commission nationale d'Équivalences, Ministère de
l'Enseignement supérieur et de la Recherche scientifique, 11
Chemin Doudou Mokhtar, Ben Aknoun, Alger, Algérie; site
internet: http://www.mesrs.edu.dz /
http://www.mesrs.edu.dz/fr/indexfr.htm.
Services du logement: Office national des oeuvres
universitaires, route de Dely-Brahim, Wilaya d'Alger.
Publications / Sites Web: «Guide: l'étudiant étranger en
Algérie».

---

62   Ministère de l'enseignement supérieur et de la recherche scientifique [MDLS]

11, chemin Doudou Mokhtar
Ben-Aknoun
Alger
Tel: +213-21-911-796
Fax: +213-21-914-601
Web: http://www.mesrs.edu.dz
e-mail: mesrs@ist.cerist.dz

🎓 Bourses

Domaines d'étude: toutes disciplines principales.
Bourses: Bourses de coopération.
A l'intention de: ressortissants de tout pays, titulaires du
baccalauréat, ayant une bonne connaissance de l'arabe et du
français.
Durée: 4 à 5 ans et 7 ans pour les études de médecine.
Candidatures: avant le 15 juillet à l'adresse ci-dessus.

63   Université Abderrahmane Mira de Bejaia [UAMB]

Route de Targua-Ouzemmour
06000 Béjaia
Tel: +213-34-214-261
Fax: +213-34-216-098
Web: http://www.univbej.dz
e-mail: infobej.mail@wissal.dz

📖 1er-2e cycles / toutes disciplines principales

Domaines d'étude: anglais, arabe, biochimie, biologie,
comptabilité, droit, écologie, environnement, économie,
électricité et électronique, finances, français, génie chimique,
génie civil, gestion, hydraulique, informatique, ingénierie,
mathématiques, mécanique, météorologie, physique, sciences
économiques et commerciales, sociologie, statistique.
Programmes: Ingéniorat; Diplôme d'études supérieures
(DES), Licence, Diplôme d'études universitaires appliquées
(DEUA).

64   **Université Abou-Bekr Belkaid, Tlemcen**
Rue Abi-Ayad Abdelkrim
BP 94, FG Pasteur
13000 Tlemcen
Tel: +213-7-200-922/20 23 36
Fax: +213-7-204-189/271-503
Web: http://www.univ-tlemcen.dz

📖 **1er-3e cycles**

Domaines d'étude: toutes disciplines principales.
Programmes: Diplôme d'études universitaires appliquées;
Diplôme d'études supérieures (DES); Diplôme d'ingénieur;
Licence; Diplôme de docteur en médecine; Magister; Doctorat
d'État.
A l'intention de: ressortissants de tout pays titulaires d'un
baccalauréat.
Durée: 3 à 5 ans (débutant en septembre).
Assistance financière: possibilité de bourses sous
conditions d'accords passés entre l'Algérie et le pays d'origine
du candidat.
Connaissances linguistiques: langues d'enseignement:
anglais, français et arabe.
Inscriptions: à l'adresse ci-dessus; autorisation obligatoire
du Ministère de l'enseignement supérieur et de la recherche
scientifique et du Ministère des affaires étrangères.

65   **Université d'Alger [UD]**
2, rue Didouche-Mourad
16000 Alger
Tel: +213-21-646-970
Fax: +213-21-635-303
Web: http://www.univ-alger.dz

📖 **1er-3e cycles**

Domaines d'étude: toutes disciplines principales,
interprétation et traduction.
Programmes: Licence, Magistère, Doctorat d'État,
Diplôme universitaire d'études appliquées.
Description: cours conduisant aux diplômes universitaires
dans les domaines suivants: interprétariat et traduction,
langue et littérature arabes, sciences économiques, sciences de
l'information et communication, sciences politiques et
relations internationales, sciences juridiques et
administratives, langues étrangères, psychologie et sciences
de l'éducation, sociologie, histoire, philosophie,
bibliothéconomie, archéologie, éducation physique et
sportive.
A l'intention de: candidats de tout pays remplissant les
conditions requises.
Inscriptions: pour de plus amples renseignements,
s'adresser au Vice-rectorat chargé de la pédagogie, à l'adresse
ci-dessus.

66   **Université d'Oran Es-Sénia [UD]**
BP1524
El M'Naouar
31100 Es-Senia Oran
Tel: +213-6-419-651/6075
Fax: +213-6-416-021
Web: http://www.univ-oran.dz

📖 **1er-3e cycles**

Domaines d'étude: éducation, orthophonie, psychologie.
Programmes: Magistère, Doctorat d'État, Diplôme de
postgraduation spécialisé (D.P.G.S.).
A l'intention de: ressortissants de tout pays, titulaires du
baccalauréat pour la graduation et de la Licence pour le
Magistère et le Doctorat d'État; admission sur concours;
sélection sur évaluation scientifique pour le Doctorat.
Durée: Licence: 4 ans; Magistère: de 3 à 5 ans; Doctorat
d'État: 4 ans et plus.
Connaissances linguistiques: langues d'enseignement:
arabe, français et anglais.
Inscriptions: en août et septembre, auprès du Directeur de
l'Université d'Oran.

67   **Université de Batna [UDB]**
avenue Chahid Med El-Hadi Boukhlouf
05000 Batna
Tel: +213-33-861-240
Fax: +213-33-861-240
Web: http://www.univ-batna.dz
e-mail: unibat@ist.cerist.dz

📖 **Cours conduisant aux diplômes universitaires**

Domaines d'étude: toutes disciplines principales.
Programmes: Cours dans toutes les disciplines conduisant
aux diplômes universitaires.
A l'intention de: ressortissants de tout pays remplissant les
conditions requises.
Inscriptions: au Vice-rectorat de la pédagogie.

68   **Université de M'Sila [UM]**
BP 166
2800 Ichbilia - M'Sila
Tel: +213-35-550-906
Fax: +213-35-550-404/551-836

📖 **1er, 2e cycles**

Domaines d'étude: agriculture, anglais, bâtiment,
construction, biochimie, biologie, chimie, commerce, dessin
industriel, droit, électricité et électronique, français, génie
civil, gestion, hydraulique, industrie chimique, informatique,
lettres, mathématiques, mécanique, physique, recherche,
sciences agronomiques, sciences appliquées, sciences
économiques et commerciales, sciences politiques, sciences
sociales, technologie, urbanisme.
Programmes: cursus de 1er et 2e cycles dans toutes les
disciplines principales.

69   **Université des sciences et de la technologie Houari Boumédiène [UDSEDLT]**
BP32
El Alia - Bab Ezzouar
16123 Alger
Tel: +213-21-247-950
Fax: +213-21-247-992
Web: http://www.usthb.dz

📖 **Programme d'études universitaires et postuniversitaires**

Domaines d'étude: sciences, technologie.
Programmes: Diplômes d'ingénieur, Diplôme d'études
supérieures, Diplôme d'études supérieures appliquées.
A l'intention de: candidats de tout pays remplissant les
conditions requises.
Durée: de 3 à 5 ans.
Connaissances linguistiques: langues d'enseignement:
arabe et français.
Inscriptions: auprès du Vice-recteur chargé de la
pédagogie.

70   **Université Djillali Liabés de Sidi Bel-Abbés [UDL]**
BP 89
Boulevard Laarbi Ben M'Hidi
22000 Sidi Bel Abbes
Tel: +213-48-543-018
Fax: +213-48-541-152
Web: http://www.univ-sba.dz
e-mail: rectorat@univ-sba.dz

📖 **Programme d'études universitaires**

Domaines d'étude: administration, biologie, chimie,
électricité et électronique, formation professionnelle,
informatique, mathématiques, médecine, physique.
A l'intention de: ressortissants de tout pays, titulaires du
baccalauréat ou titre reconnu équivalent.
Durée: de 3 à 7 ans selon la formation.
Inscriptions: auprès du Vice-rectorat chargé de la
pédagogie à l'adresse ci-dessus, sur autorisation délivrée par
le Ministère de l'enseignement supérieur.

71 Université Mohamed Khider - Biskra
BP 145 RP Biskra
07000 Biskra
Tel: +213-33-746-160
Fax: +213-33-733-207

📖 **1er, 2e cycles**

Domaines d'étude: agriculture, anglais, arabe, architecture, bâtiment, construction, biochimie, biologie, chimie, comptabilité, droit, écologie, environnement, économie, électricité et électronique, français, génie chimique, génie civil, gestion, hydraulique, hydrologie, informatique, marketing, mathématiques, mécanique, métallurgie, physique, psychologie, relations internationales, sciences agronomiques, sciences appliquées, sciences économiques et commerciales, sciences humaines, sciences politiques, sciences sociales, sociologie, statistique.
Programmes: (a) programme de cours conduisant aux diplômes en sciences et technologie; (b) programme de cours conduisant aux diplômes en sciences humaines, sociales et économiques.
Assistance financière: possibilité de bourses sur avis du Ministère de l'enseignement supérieur et de la recherche scientifique.
Connaissances linguistiques: cours dispensés en français.

Andorra

Año académico: septiembre a junio.
Organización de la enseñanza superior: El nuevo plan de estudios se ha elaborado siguiendo las recomendaciones que emanan del Proceso de Boloña: (1) La formación del primer ciclo consta de 180 Créditos Europeos (ECTS), equivalentes a 5.400 horas de formación teórica y práctica; (2) En el cómputo global el 66% de la carga lectiva corresponde a la enseñanza / aprendizaje práctico; (3) Los contenidos académicos están estructurados en áreas de conocimiento, módulos y asignaturas de aprendizaje.
Moneda nacional: Euro (€).
Admisiones para estudiantes del país: Dirigirse a la Universidad de Andorra situada en la Plaza de la Hermandad, Santa Julia de Loria Principado de Andorra; web: http://www.uda.ad o bien al Ministerio de educación, cultura, juventud y deportes.
Admisiones para estudiantes extranjeros: Bachillerato andorrano o equivalente.
Conocimientos lingüísticos: Se exigen como mínimo conocimientos de la lengua catalana.
Formalidades de inmigración: Obtención del permiso de estudiante para lo cual es necesario presentar el pasaporte acompañado de fotocopia, certificado de antecedentes penales del país de origen y del último país de residencia, certificado de cobertura sanitaria (100%) que cubra cualquier tipo de coste médico o sanitario, copia del contrato de alquiler, o certificado del hotel donde se resida, certificado de estado civil, una fotografía reciente tamaño carné (35 x 40 mm) y fotocopia de la matrícula del año en curso.
Servicios de información: Las representaciones diplomáticas del Principado de Andorra siempre están dispuestas a ofrecer la ayuda necesaria.
Enseñanza abierta y a distancia: El Centre d'Estudis Virtuals (Centro de Estudios Virtuales) de la Universidad de Andorra ofrece formaciones de primer y segundo ciclo en áreas de ciencias empresariales, investigación y técnicas de mercado, informática, turismo y multimedia, derecho, filología catalana, humanidades, psicología.
Convalidación de estudios y diplomas: Ministeri d'Educació, Cultura, Joventut i Esports, Àrea de Reconeixement de Titulacions, Av. Rocafort 21-23, Edifici del Molí 4a planta Sant Julià de Lòria. Principat d'Andorra; tel. +376-743300; fax:+376-743313.

72 Universidad de Andorra [UDA]
Plaça de la Germandat, 7
AD600 Sant Julià de Lòria
Tel: +376-743-000
Fax: +376-743-043
Web: http://www.uda.ad
e-mail: uda@uda.ad

📖 **Programas de grado y posgrado**

Campos de estudios: administración de empresas, ciencias de la información, enfermería, finanzas, gestión.

Angola

Année universitaire: octobre à juillet.
Unité monétaire: nouveau kwanza (NKZ).
Admission pour étudiants du pays: Les candidats doivent justifier d'un diplôme de fin d'études secondaires («habilitaçoes literárias») et réussir l'examen d'entrée à l'université.
Connaissances linguistiques requises: Les cours étant donnés en portugais, une bonne connaissance de la langue est indispensable.
Services d'accueil et d'information:
• Ministère de l'éducation, Caixa postal 6451, rua Comandante Gika, Luanda, Angola.
Enseignement à distance: Programme d'enseignement à distance pour la mise à niveau des professeurs offert par l'Instituto Superior de Ciências de Educaçao. Les épreuves se passent à l'université. Les professeurs peuvent aussi suivre les cours d'enseignement à distance afin d'améliorer leurs compétences professionnelles.

73 Instituto universitário livre de Luanda [IULL]
7 Travessa Vasco de Gama
Ingombota
Luanda
Tel: +244-2-395-032
Fax: +244-2-395-032

📖 **1er cycle**

Domaines d'étude: droit, sciences politiques.
Programmes: Licence et Certificat en droit, sciences politiques et administratives.
À l'intention de: titulaires d'un diplôme de fin d'études de l'enseignement secondaire.
Durée: 2 ans pour la licence; 3 ans pour le certificat.
Inscriptions: à l'adresse ci-dessus.

74 Universidade Agostinho Neto
Caixa postal 815-C
Avenida 4 de Fevereiro 7
Luanda
Tel: +244-2-37132

📖 **Programmes de cours conduisant aux diplômes universitaires**

Domaines d'étude: agriculture, architecture, droit, économie, éducation, ingénierie, médecine.
Programmes: programmes de cours conduisant aux diplômes universitaires au sein des facultés des sciences, agriculture (y compris vétérinaire), droit, économie, ingénierie (architecture inclue), éducation et médecine; cours également par correspondance (l'université développe des programmes de coopération avec d'autres universités en Allemagne: Berlin; en Fédération de Russie: Moscou, et au Brésil).
À l'intention de: ressortissants de tout pays, titulaires d'un diplôme de fin d'études secondaires ou équivalent; admission sur examen.
Durée: 1 à 6 ans (débutant en octobre).
Connaissances linguistiques: langue d'enseignement: portugais.

Argentina

Año académico: Marzo a diciembre.
Organización de la enseñanza superior: Grado (4 a 6 años); Posgrado: Especialización (1 año); Master (2 años); Doctorado (2 o 3 años más tiempo de elaboración de tesis).
Moneda nacional: Peso argentino.
Admisiones para estudiantes extranjeros: Para los estudiantes internacionales: bachillerato o certificado de fin de estudios secundarios o equivalente, examen de ingreso aprobado en la universidad o instituto (si corresponde), conocimientos probados y suficientes de idioma español.
Conocimientos lingüísticos: Es indispensable dominar el idioma español. Se está implementando actualmente un examen de evaluación del español como lengua extranjera (ELE).
Formalidades de inmigración: La información pertinente debe solicitarse en la embajada o consulado de Argentina del país de origen del estudiante.
Importe de gastos para un año universita: (datos para un mes) enseñanza: grado en universidad pública gratuito, en universidad privada entre US$ 100 y 300, posgrado entre US$ 100 y 500; libros/materiales de estudio: entre US$ 15 y 50 (incluyendo libros); alojamiento: entre US$ 70 y 200.
Servicios de información:
• Ministerio de Cultura y Educación - Comisión Nacional Argentina para la UNESCO, Pizzurno 935, 2do. Piso, 1020 Buenos Aires. El programa de becas brinda información a los estudiantes extranjeros acerca de los centros docentes argentinos.
• Fundación José María Aragón, Centro de Información sobre Estudios de Posgrado y Becas, Avenida Córdoba 1345, Piso 9°, 1055 Buenos Aires. Atiende las consultas que formulen las universidades u organismos oficiales o privados de cualquier país o que presenten individualmente quienes deseen documentarse sobre becas, cursos internacionales, estudios de postgrado, etc. La información es clasificada por país y por especialidad. Por información se paga un arancel.
• Organización de Universidades de América Latina, Pontificia Universidad Católica Argentina "Santa María de los Buenos Aires", Juncal 1912, Buenos Aires. Agrupa a las universidades católicas de América Latina y mantiene vínculos entre las mismas.
Becas para estudiantes internacionales: Programa Nacional de Becas Universitarias (PNBU), Dirección Nacional de Coordinación Institucional, Evaluación y Programación Presupuestaria. Avda. Santa Fe 1548, 13° piso, (1020) Buenos Aires; tel: +54-11-4129-1800 int 6241/6242; email: dncieypp@me.gov.ar; web: http://www.me.gov.ar/spu/pnbu.
Enseñanza abierta y a distancia: Existen cursos a distancia que abarcan el ciclo básico de la educación superior, pero hay módulos presenciales. Se brindan también cursos a distancia a nivel de posgrados, maestrías, capacitación y perfeccionamiento.
Dirigirse a Lic. Horacio Santangelo, Coordinación de Educación a Distancia, Pizzurno 935, 2° piso, 1020 Buenos Aires; tel.: +54-11-4129-1130. También se puede consultar el sitio http://www.universia.com.ar, enlaces "Buscador de carreras" y "Modalidad".
Convalidación de estudios y diplomas: Lic. José Francisco Martín, Departamento de Convalidaciones, Dirección Nacional de Gestión Universitaria, Avda. Santa Fe 1548, 12° piso; email: dngupriv@me.gov.ar; web: http://www.me.gov.ar.
Servicios de alojamiento para estudiante: Existen residencias universitarias, alojamiento en casas de familia, etc.; pedir información en el Departamento de Bienestar Estudiantil o Departamento de Alumnos en la universidad que corresponda.
Publicaciones / Sitios web:
• Ministerio de Educación, Ciencia y Tecnología, http://www.me.gov.ar;
• Secretaría de Políticas Universitarias, http://www.me.gov.ar/spu; publicaciones de la Secretaría de Políticas Universitarias, http://www.me.gov.ar/publicaciones/publicaciones.html.
• Puede ser de interés consultar el sitio de la Agencia de Evaluación y Acreditación de la Calidad Universitaria (CONEAU) que realiza evaluaciones periódicas sobre las ofertas de grado y posgrado que se dictan en universidades públicas y privadas del país.

Informaciones complementarias:
• Area de Internacionalización de la Educación Superior - Secretaría de Políticas Universitarias - Ministerio de Educación, Ciencia y Tecnología: Pizzurno 935, 1er piso, 1020 Buenos Aires; tel: +54-11-4129-1396/7; fax: +54-11-4129-1399.
• Programa de Formación de Recursos Humanos de Alto Nivel en el Exterior - Dirección Nacional de Cooperación Internacional Universitaria - Ministerio de Educación, Ciencia y Tecnología: Pizzurno 935, 1er piso, 1020 Buenos Aires; tel.: +54-11-4129-1287/8; fax: +54- 11-4129-1187; becas@me.gov.ar.

---

75 Centro de Estudios Superiores Fundación "Embajador Rogelio Tristany" [CES]

Teniente General Perón 1538
1037 Capital Federal
Buenos Aires
Tel: +54-114-371 57 11
Fax: +54-114-476 00 91

📖 **Cursos superiores en diplomacia**

Campos de estudios: relaciones públicas.
Descripción:
(a) Técnico en ceremonial y protocolo;
(b) Licenciado en diplomacia, relaciones públicas y ceremonial.
Se destina(n): a candidatos con estudios secundarios completos.
Duración: (a) 2 cuatrimestres; (b) 4 cuatrimestres.
Inscripciones: en marzo.

76 Centro de Investigación de Tecnología del Cuero [CITEC]

Camino Centenario entre 505 y 506
Casilla de Correos 6
1897 M. B. Gonnet
Buenos Aires
Tel: +54-21-841876
Fax: +54-21-840244
Web: http://www.inti.gov.ar/citec/
e-mail: citec@inti.gov.ar

📖 **Cursos sobre tecnología del cuero**

Campos de estudios: ciencias aplicadas, industria química, tecnología, tecnología industrial.
Descripción:
(a) Curso de introducción a la tecnología del cuero: procesos de ribera, curtido y acabado, control de procesos, análisis y ensayos de cueros; 5 participantes extranjeros;
(b) Períodos de adiestramiento sobre: procesos de fabricación, control de calidad, efluentes de curtiembre.
Se destina(n): a nacionales de cualquier país que dominen el idioma español y tengan un diploma conferido por una facultad de ciencias exactas (química o ingeniería química) o por una escuela técnica industrial secundaria (diploma de técnico químico).
Duración: (a) 30 días (generalmente mes de octubre); (b) 6 meses (empieza en abril).
Inscripciones: hasta el 1° de febrero.

77 Comisión de Intercambio Educativo entre los Estados Unidos de América y la República Argentina (Comisión Fulbright) [CDIE]

Viamonte 1653, 2° piso
1055 Buenos Aires
Tel: +54-114-8143561
Fax: +54-114-8141377
Web: http://www.fulbright.edu.ar/index_spanish.html
e-mail: info@fulbright.com.ar

🎓 **Programa de becas Fulbright**

Campos de estudios: todas las materias principales.
Descripción:
Programa Fulbright para ciudadanos argentinos:
(a) Becas para graduados;

(b) Becas de investigación;
(c) Becas Fulbright/LASPAU (Latin American Scholarship Program of American Universities) para docentes universitarios;
(d) Becas de intercambio de profesores de idioma;
(e) Becas Hubert H. Humphrey;
Programa Fulbright para ciudadanos estadounidenses:
(f) Becas para profesores universitarios;
(g) Becas para investigadores;
(h) Becas para graduados.
Materias de estudio: (a) prioritariamente ciencias sociales, humanidades y ciencias básicas, en especial las disciplinas relacionadas con educación, administración pública, medio ambiente, economía, estudios sobre los Estados Unidos, ciencias exactas y naturales e ingenierías; (b) y (c) como (a) y otras de interés para el país; (e) administración pública, planificación educativa, planeamiento urbano y regional, planificación de recursos (humanos, energéticos, industriales y naturales), agricultura (desarrollo rural, administración agrícola, etc.), salud pública y nutrición, desarrollo económico, periodismo y comunicación, planificación y administración de la tecnología, prevención y tratamiento del abuso de drogas; (f) y (g) prioritariamente ciencias sociales y humanidades; (h) prioritariamente ciencias sociales, humanidades y artes.
Se conceden: (a) a estudiantes graduados que deseen obtener un grado de master; (b) a graduados universitarios; (c) a docentes e investigadores de las universidades argentinas; (d) a profesores argentinos de inglés como lengua extranjera; (e) a administradores, planificadores y dirigentes vinculados a la administración pública o privada de programas de servicios a la comunidad; (f) a profesores universitarios; (g) a investigadores que manifiesten su interés en realizar trabajos sobre temas relacionados con la Argentina; (h) a estudiantes cuya tesis de doctorado o de master tenga como base temas relacionados con la Argentina.
Lugar: (a) a (c) universidades estadounidenses; (d) instituciones educativas estadounidenses, a menudo escuelas secundarias; (f) universidades argentinas que lo soliciten.
Duración: (a) y (c) 1 o 2 años académicos; (b) 3 meses; (d) 4 a 6 meses; (e) 1 año académico; (f) por lo menos un trimestre o cuatrimestre académico; (g) variable, en general 3 meses; (h) 8 meses.
Importe: (a) pasaje de ida a vuelta a los Estados Unidos, arancel y derechos académicos (total o parcial según el caso), suplemento para gastos de manutención, seguro de salud; (b) y (c) como (a) más estipendio mensual para alojamiento; como (b) más viajes internos dentro de los Estados Unidos; (f) a (h) pasaje de ida y vuelta, estipendio para manutención del becario, seguro de salud.
Solicitudes: para mayor información sobre otros requisitos, documentación y condiciones de inscripción, dirigirse a la Asesoría Académica de la Comisión Fulbright, en la dirección que figura en el título.

78 Comité Nacional para el Programa Hidrológico Internacional [CONAPHI]

H. Yrigoyen 250 - 11° piso - Oficina 1109
1310 Buenos Aires
Tel: +54-114-3497585/83
Fax: +54-114-3497596

📖 Curso internacional de hidrología general con aspectos ambientales

Campos de estudios: ecología, medio ambiente, geología, hidrología, ingeniería.
Se destina(n): a nacionales de cualquier país, que tengan un título universitario en ingeniería, geología, meteorología, etc., y conocimientos de español.
Se dicta(n): en Universidades Nacionales del Litoral, La Plata y San Juan (Argentina), cada 2 años.
Duración: 6 meses.
Asistencia financiera: el CONAPHI podrá contribuir con los gastos de matrícula, pasajes y mantenimiento en la medida de lo posible.
Inscripciones: hasta fines de febrero; dirigirse al Director del Curso.

79 Consejo Nacional de Investigaciones Científicas y Técnicas [CONICET]

Avenida Rivadavia 1917
1033 Buenos Aires
Tel: +54-114-953-7230 / 9
Fax: +54-114-953--4345
Web: http://www.conicet.gov.ar

🦋 Becas de investigación científica

Campos de estudios: ciencias, ciencias de la tierra, ingeniería, medicina, tecnología.
Descripción:
(a) Becas externas de doctorado y postdoctorado para investigación científica y tecnológica en todas las disciplinas científicas y tecnológicas (exceptuadas las artísticas)
(b) Becas para graduados universitarios latinoamericanos (materias como (a));
(c) Becas en el marco del convenio TWAS (Third World Academy of Sciences)/CONICET en áreas de ciencias de la vida, ciencias básicas, ciencias de la tierra, ingeniería y medicina..
Se conceden: (a) a personas con residencia habitual en Argentina, con experiencia en el campo de la investigación y máximo grado académico, que conozcan el idioma del país donde deseen realizar los estudios; (b) a graduados universitarios latinoamericanos de hasta 35 años de edad, con título universitario; (c) a titulados universitarios residentes permanentes de países del tercer mundo, que conozcan el idioma castellano o en su defecto el inglés; deberán presentar plan de trabajo detallado, y comprometerse a trabajar en su país el doble de tiempo de la duración de la beca.
Lugar: universidades, centros o institutos de investigación: (a) en el extranjero; (b) y (c) en Argentina.
Duración: (a) a (c) 12 meses (prorrogable en determinados casos por 12 meses como máximo).
Solicitudes: (a) habitualmente hasta marzo de cada año; (b) y (c) en cualquier época del año. En todos los casos dirigirse al Departamento de Becas externas del CONICET.

80 Facultad Tecnológica de Enología y de Industria Frutihortícola "Don Bosco" [UMAZA]

Ruta Provincial n° 50
Rodeo del Medio
5529 Mendoza
Tel: +54-61-495-1084
Fax: +56-61-495-1120
Web: http://www.umaza.edu.ar
e-mail: umaza@umaza.edu.ar

📖 Programas universitarios

Campos de estudios: agricultura, ciencias agronómicas, enología, horticultura, industria alimentaría.
Descripción:
(a) Analista universitario en enología y en industria frutihortícola;
(b) Licenciatura en enología y en industria frutihortícola;
(c) Doctorado en enología;
(d) Doctorado en industria frutihortícola.
Se destina(n): a estudiantes que hayan completado estudios secundarios provenientes de carreras agrotécnicas, técnicas, bachilleratos y equivalentes.
Duración: (a) 3 años; (b) 5 años; (c) y (d) 2 años.
Asistencia financiera: becas posibles sólo en casos excepcionales.
Inscripciones: en diciembre y febrero; dirigirse al Secretario Académico.

81 Fuerza Aérea Argentina Servicio Meteorológico Nacional (SMN) [FAA-SMN]

25 de Mayo 658
1002 Buenos Aires
Tel: +54-114-3124481
Fax: +54-114-113968
Web: http://www.faa.mil.ar

📖 Cursos para formación de profesionales

Campos de estudios: física, meteorología.
Descripción:
(a) Inspector meteorológico: instalación e inspección, cómputos e instrumental; de 8 a 10 participantes por grupo;
(b) Técnico en mantenimiento de instrumental meteorológico: estudios y prácticas en laboratorio y en taller de reparación, armado y desarmado de instrumental meteorológico; de 8 a 10 participantes por grupo.
Ambos cursos son de carácter regular pero su dictado está condicionado a contar con un mínimo de 5 alumnos inscriptos.
Se destina(n): a nacionales de cualquier país que hayan cursado estudios secundarios completos. Para (a) se requiere el título de observador meteorológico con 5 años de experiencia, y para (b) el nivel correspondiente a las escuelas secundarias técnicas industriales.
Duración: 8 meses (comienzan en abril).
Inscripciones: 3 meses antes de la iniciación de los cursos; dirigirse a la Dirección General del Servicio Meteorológico Nacional (Centro Regional de Formación Profesional Meteorológica).

82   Fuerza Aérea Argentina Servicio Meteorológico Nacional (SMN) [FAA]

25 de Mayo 658
1002 Buenos Aires
Tel: +54-114-124481
Fax: +54-114-3113968
Web: http://www.faa.mil.ar

📖 Cursos de posgrado

Campos de estudios: física, meteorología.
Descripción:
(a) Nefoanálisis: formación de personal técnico capacitado para realizar tareas de interpretación de imágenes nubosas obtenidas por satélites meteorológicos y evaluación sinóptica de las mismas. El programa consta de nefoanálisis, laboratorio y meteorología sinóptica; 10 a 15 participantes por grupo;
(b) Meteorología operativa aeronáutica: formación de personal técnico capacitado para realizar tareas operativas en oficinas meteorológicas con fines aeronáuticos. El programa consta de las siguientes asignaturas: meteorología aeronáutica, legislación aeronáutica, ética y expresión oral; 10 a 15 participantes por grupo;
(c) Seminario de meteorología en accidentes de aviación: aplicación de criterios de evaluación del impacto de estados meteorológicos para la prevención de accidentes de aviación;
(d) Especialización en meteorología antártica (instrumental, claves y métodos de observación, climatología, dinámica y sinóptica antárticas; el objetivo es la capacitación de realización de pronósticos meteorológicos aplicados a las actividades marítimas y aéreas en la Antártida).
Se destina(n): (a) y (b) a nacionales de cualquier país que hayan cursado estudios universitarios de licenciatura en ciencias de la atmósfera o bachillerato universitario en ciencias de la atmósfera con orientación sinóptica, clase I o II de la clasificación de la OMM; (c) y (d) como (a), con experiencia operativa no inferior a 3 años.
Duración: (a) 4 meses (agosto a noviembre); (b) 3 meses (abril a junio); (c) una semana en junio; (d) 2 meses (inicio en agosto).
Inscripciones: hasta 3 meses antes del inicio del curso, en la Dirección General del SMN, en la dirección que figura en el título.

83   Instituto Balseiro Centro Atómico Bariloche [IB]

Casilla de Correo 439
Av. Bustillo km 9,500, Bariloche
8400 Río Negro
Tel: +54-2944-445163
Fax: +54-2944-445102
Web: http://www.cab.cnea.gov.ar
e-mail: alumnos@ib.edu.ar

📖 Programa de cursos

Campos de estudios: ciencias, ciencias aplicadas, energía, física, hidrología, ingeniería.
Descripción: (a) Licenciatura en física;

(b) Carrera de ingeniería nuclear;
(c) Doctorado en física;
(d) Doctorado en ciencias de la ingeniería;
(e) Especialización en aplicaciones tecnológicas de la energía.
Se destina(n): a argentinos o extranjeros con residencia definitiva o a latinoamericanos a través de convenios bilaterales; los aspirantes deben: (a) y (b) haber aprobado 2 años de cualquier carrera de ciencias exactas o ingeniería, (c) y (d) poseer título de licenciado en física e ingeniería respectivamente; (e) poseer título universitario (ingeniería, física, química, biología, bioquímica, geología), con promedio superior a 7 y conocimientos de inglés. En todos los casos existe proceso de admisión.
Duración: en años académicos: (a) 3 y medio; (b a (d) 4; (e) 1. Inicios en agosto para (a) y (b), en febrero para (e).
Asistencia financiera: existen programas de becas internacionales para grado y postgrado para estudiantes latinoamericanos.
Inscripciones: (a) y (b) hasta el 15 de mayo; (e) hasta el 15 de noviembre; en todos los casos, dirigirse a la Oficina de Estudiantes.

🎓 Becas para cursos

Campos de estudios: energía, física, ingeniería, tecnología.
Descripción:
(a) Licenciatura en física e ingeniería nuclear (30);
(b) Especialización en aplicaciones tecnológicas de la energía nuclear (10).
Se conceden: a latinoamericanos que cumplan los requisitos de ingreso a cursos.
Duración: (a) 3 años y medio; (b) 4 años.
Solicitudes: (a) hasta el 15 de mayo; (b) hasta el 15 de noviembre. En ambos casos, dirigirse a la Oficina de Estudiantes.

84   Pontificia Universidad Católica Argentina "Santa María de los Buenos Aires" Instituto de Extensión Universitaria [PUCA]

Avenida Dávila 1500
1107 Buenos Aires
Tel: +54-114-8112581
Fax: +54-114-8137416
Web: http://www.uca.edu.ar

🎓 Becas para Curso superior de perfeccionamiento periodístico

Campos de estudios: ciencias políticas, periodismo, sociología.
Descripción: Curso superior de perfeccionamiento periodístico: periodismo de investigación, metodología de la investigación, política argentina, MERCOSUR, Medio Oriente, ética profesional, comunicación institucional, herramientas informáticas aplicadas al periodismo, nuevas tecnologías, sistemas de pre-prensa, fenómenos culturales, entrevista, géneros y estilos periodísticos.
Se conceden: a egresados universitarios o terciarios en periodismo o ciencias de la comunicación, o a egresados de otras disciplinas con interés en el área periodística, que acrediten antecedentes laborales en el periodismo; los extranjeros deben ser presentados por un medio asociado a la Sociedad Interamericana de Prensa donde desarrollen actividad profesional; en todos los casos se debe ser soltero, menor de 32 años y disponer de dedicación full-time.
Lugar: IEU y y distintos sectores de redacción del Diario "El Clarín".
Duración: 6 meses (octubre-marzo), (no prorrogable).
Importe: renta mensual y alojamiento en departamento.
Solicitudes: en mayo de cada año.

85   Pontificia Universidad Católica Argentina Instituto de Comunicación Social, Periodismo y Publicidad [PUCA]

Avenida Alicia Moreau de Justo 1500 PB

1107 Buenos Aires
Tel: +54-114-3490408
Fax: +54-114-3490410
Web: http://www.uca.edu.ar

Curso superior de perfeccionamiento periodístico

Campos de estudios: periodismo.
Descripción: incluye prácticas de redacción en diversos sectores del Diario "El Clarín".
Se destina(n): a solteros, menores de 32 años, periodistas o egresados de periodismo y comunicación cuya selección se basa en antecedentes laborales y académicos; se requieren conocimientos de PC y dedicación full-time.
Duración: de octubre a marzo.
Asistencia financiera: para extranjeros, existen becas consistentes en renta mensual y alojamiento.
Inscripciones: hasta fin de mayo.

86　Universidad Adventista del Plata [UAP]

25 de Mayo 99
3103 Libertador San Martín
Entre Ríos
Tel: +54-343-491-0010
Fax: +54-343-491-0300
Web: http://www.uapar.edu
e-mail: uap@uapar.edu

Carreras de grado y posgrado

Campos de estudios: todas las materias principales, administración, ciencias económicas y comerciales, ciencias sociales, enfermería, higiene y salud, medicina, nutrición, psicología, teología, religión.
Descripción:
(a) Facultad de ciencias de la salud: medicina, enfermería, técnico en nutrición, licenciatura en enfermería, en nutrición, en kinesiología y fisiatría;
(b) Facultad de ciencias económicas y de la administración: contador público, analista administrativo, licenciatura en administración, en sistemas de información, analista de sistemas, secretariado ejecutivo bilingüe, secretariado administrativo;
(c) Facultad de humanidades, educación y ciencias sociales: licenciatura en psicología, en psicopedagogía, en ciencias de la educación, profesorado en ciencias de la educación, para nivel inicial, para la EGB, en educación física, en inglés, licenciatura en educación física, en trabajo social, traductorado en inglés, asistente social, comunicación social;
(d) Facultad de teología: licenciatura en teología, en teología pastoral, profesorado en educación religiosa, magíster en teología, doctorado en teología.

87　Universidad Argentina de la Empresa [UADE]

Lima 717
1073 Buenos Aires
Tel: +54-114-372 5454
Fax: +54-114-383 4309
Web: http://www.uade.edu.ar

Programas de estudios universitarios

Campos de estudios: todas las materias principales, ciencias económicas y comerciales, ciencias sociales, comunicación, derecho, informática, ingeniería, tecnología industrial.
Descripción:
(a) Facultad de ciencias económicas: contador público, licenciatura en administración agropecuaria, en administración de empresas, en comercialización, en comercio internacional, en economía, en finanzas, en recursos humanos, en turismo;
(b) Facultad de ciencias jurídicas, sociales y de la comunicación: abogacía, licenciatura en ciencias de la comunicación, en diseño gráfico, en diseño textil e indumentaria, en gobierno y relaciones internacionales, en lengua inglesa, en publicidad, en relaciones públicas e institucionales, traductorado público en idioma inglés;
(c) Facultad de ingeniería y ciencias exactas: ingeniería electromecánica, en alimentos, en comunicaciones, en informática, industrial, licenciatura en informática, en organización de la producción, en tecnología industrial de los

alimentos.
Se destina(n): a argentinos y extranjeros que hayan terminado los estudios secundarios en Argentina o en los países con los que existan tratados de reciprocidad. Los extranjeros deberán hacer una declaración jurada comprometiéndose a no ejercer la profesión en la República Argentina.
Asistencia financiera: ayudas económicas; por informes, dirigirse a becas@uade.edu.ar.

88　Universidad Atlántida Argentina [UAA]

Diagonal Rivadavia 515
7109 Mar de Ajó
Tel: +54-225-742-0338
Fax: +54-225-742-0338
Web: http://www.atlantida.edu.ar
e-mail: atlantida@atlantida.edu.ar

Programas de estudios universitarios

Campos de estudios: ciencias económicas y comerciales, contabilidad, derecho, informática, ingeniería, psicología, turismo, hotelería.
Descripción:
(a) Facultad de ingeniería: ingeniería en informática, licenciatura en informática, analista de sistemas;
(b) Facultad de derecho y ciencias sociales: abogacía;
(c) Facultad de ciencias económicas: contador público, licenciado en comercialización, en administración, técnico universitario en comercialización, en administración;
(d) Facultad de psicología: licenciado en psicología, en psicopedagogía;
(e) Facultad de humanidades: licenciado en turismo, guía de turismo.
Asistencia financiera: solicitar información sobre el Programa de Cooperación Interuniversitaria (ALE, Becas de Intercambio con España) y becas de la Universidad de Calabria.

89　Universidad Austral [UA]

Avenida Juan de Garay 125
1063 Buenos Aires
Tel: +54-115-921-8000
Fax: +54-115-921-8013
Web: http://www.austral.edu.ar
e-mail: informes@austral.edu.ar

Programas de grado y posgrado

Campos de estudios: todas las materias principales, administración de empresas, ciencias de la información, ciencias económicas y comerciales, derecho, enfermería, ingeniería, medicina, negocio.
Descripción:
(a) Carreras de grado: ingeniería en informática, industrial; abogacía; medicina, enfermería; licenciatura en ciencias de la información, en ciencias empresariales, contador público;
(b) Posgrados: doctorado en derecho, master en derecho administrativo, en derecho de la empresa, en derecho y magistratura judicial, especialización en derecho tributario, en derecho penal, en derecho de la regulación de servicios públicos, master en asesoramiento jurídico de empresas; doctorado en ciencias de la información, master en gestión de la comunicación en las organizaciones; master en asesoramiento jurídico de empresas, en ciencias empresariales; EMBA (Executive Master in Business Administration, part-time), MBA (Master in Business Administration, full-time);
(c) Programas especiales y de investigación.
Se dicta(n): en las sedes Centro, Pilar y Rosario.
Asistencia financiera: becas y créditos universitarios (un año, renovables).
Inscripciones: hasta el 15 de diciembre y 15 de mayo para primer y segundo semestre, respectivamente; dirigirse a Secretaría Académica.

**90   Universidad Blas Pascal
      Instituto "Argentum"
      de Estudios Internacionales
      [UBP]**
Avenida Donato Alvarez 380
5147 Argüello
Córdoba
Tel: +54-351-414-4555
Web: http://www.ubp.edu.ar
e-mail: informes@ubp.edu.ar

📖 Programas culturales y de idioma español

Campos de estudios: español, estudios culturales, idiomas.
Descripción: curso intensivo de español (3 niveles),
cultura argentina y latinoamericana; curso de conversación y
comunicación; curso avanzado de comunicación; cursos
opcionales, actividades culturales y sociales.
Se destina(n): a estudiantes extranjeros.
Duración: programas semestrales de 16 semanas
(comienzan en marzo y en agosto), programas intensivos de 5
semanas (comienzan en junio), cursos anuales de 32 semanas
(comienzan en marzo).
Inscripciones: hasta el 15 de noviembre para los cursos
anuales y los del primer semestre; hasta el 15 de marzo para
los intensivos, hasta el 1° de abril para los del segundo
semestre. Por más informaciones e inscripciones:
Argentum-UBP, P.O. Box 99, Medford, M.A. 02153, Estados
Unidos de América.

91   Universidad de Belgrano [UB]
Zabala 1837
1426 Buenos Aires
Tel: +54-114-788 5400
Fax: +54-114-788 8840
Web: http://www.ub.edu.ar

📖 Cursos de posgrado

Campos de estudios: administración de empresas, ciencias
económicas y comerciales, ciencias políticas, gestión, historia,
informática, ingeniería, medicina, negocio, psicología,
relaciones internacionales.
Descripción: (a) Doctorado en ciencia política;
(b) Doctorado en psicología clínica;
(c) Maestría en relaciones internacionales;
(d) Maestría en política económica internacional;
(e) Master en ingeniería de vehículos automotores (título
conjunto de la UB y Universidad Politécnica de Madrid);
(f) Maestría en administración de empresas (especializaciones
en administración estratégica, marketing internacional,
marketing, finanzas de la empresa, relaciones institucionales,
empresa y medio ambiente, logística empresarial);
(g) Master in Business Administration (título conjunto de la
UB y Ecole Nationale des Ponts et Chaussées de Paris);
(h) Maestría en gestión de recursos humanos;
(i) Maestría en psicología organizacional;
(j) Maestría en agronegocios (diploma conjunto de la UB y
University of Illinois);
(k) Maestría en computación gráfica;
(l) Maestría en ingeniería de software;
(m) Magister en psicología clínica;
(n) Magister en epidemiología.
Se destina(n): (a) a graduados en ciencia política, derecho,
ciencias económicas, relaciones internacionales, sociología,
historia y filosofía; (b) a psicólogos y psiquiatras; (c) a
graduados universitarios en economía, ciencias jurídicas,
ciencias políticas, ciencias sociales, diplomáticos (con rango
de Secretario de Estado o superior); (d) a graduados
universitarios en áreas afines; (e) a titulados académicos
afines con la carrera, preferentemente con experiencia en
ingeniería automotriz; (h) a graduados en derecho, ciencias
económicas y sociales, psicología y ciencias sociales; (i) a
graduados en psicología o administración; (j) a ingenieros
agrónomos, economistas, economistas agrarios, profesionales
de carreras afines; (k) a graduados en computación gráfica; (l)
a graduados universitarios en carreras de grado de sistemas,
computación e informática, o en otras disciplinas que posean
experiencia profesional en software; (m) a psicólogos; (n) a
profesionales universitarios del equipo de salud.
Duración: (a), (b), (g) a (l) 2 años más tesis; (c) y (d) 1
año más tesina; (e) 2 años lectivos sucesivos a tiempo parcial
más proyecto de aplicación; (f) y (l) 2 años más tesina; (m) 2
años más proyecto; (n) 2 años más investigación de campo.

Todos los comienzos son en marzo.
Inscripciones: todos salvo (e) en la Oficina de Informes,
en la dirección que figura en el título; (e) Facultad de
Ingeniería de la UB, Villanueva 1324, 1426 Buenos Aires.

📖 Cursos interdisciplinarios

Campos de estudios: español, estudios americanos,
estudios internacionales.
Descripción:
(a) Programa de estudios argentinos y latinoamericanos:
economía argentina, política, cultura e historia
latinoamericanas; español, literatura, otras;
(b) Programa intensivo de español para extranjeros: idioma
castellano más 2 cursos electivos dentro de la lista de cursos
interdisciplinarios detallados en (a).
Se destina(n): (a) estudiantes de nivel terciario de
cualquier nacionalidad; (b) a extranjeros.
Duración: (a) 6 meses (inicios en marzo y julio); (b) 4 a 6
semanas en julio/agosto, y existen cursos de verano.
Inscripciones: (a) un mes antes del inicio; solicitar
informes a Oficina de Intercambio Internacional; (b) hasta el
1° de junio de cada año.

**92   Universidad de Buenos Aires
      Facultad de Ciencias Exactas y
      Naturales
      Departamento de Ciencias
      de la Atmósfera [UBA]**
Pabellón 2 - Piso 2
Ciudad Universitaria
1428 Buenos Aires
Tel: +54-114-783 3098
Fax: +54-114-782 6528
Web: http://www.uba.ar

📖 Programas de estudio

Campos de estudios: ciencias del mar, meteorología,
oceanografía.
Descripción:
(a) Licenciatura en ciencias de la atmósfera; bachillerato
universitario (título intermedio) en ciencias de la atmósfera,
orientaciones: meteorología sinóptica, climatología,
hidrometeorología y meteorología agrícola; licenciatura en
oceanografía, orientación física;
(b) Maestría en meteorología agrícola; doctorado en ciencias
de la atmósfera.
Se destina(n): a personas de cualquier país que hayan
cursado estudios secundarios completos o tengan un grado de
licenciado en ciencias de la atmósfera o en carrera afín, según
el curso.
Duración: entre 2 y 5 años.
Inscripciones: (a) en octubre del año anterior al del año
lectivo a cursar; (b) todo el año.

**93   Universidad de Buenos Aires
      Facultad de Ingeniería
      Secretaría de Posgrado [UBA]**
Paseo Colón 850 - 3er piso
1063 Buenos Aires
Tel: +54-114-342 7878
Fax: +54-114-331 0172
Web: http://www.uba.ar

📖 Programas de posgrado

Campos de estudios: administración, administración de
empresas, electricidad y electrónica, energía, física, geodesia,
hidrología, higiene y salud, informática, ingeniería.
Descripción: (a) Organización y dirección empresarial;
(b) Administración de sistemas de información;
(c) Aplicaciones tecnológicas de la energía nuclear;
(d) Protección radiológica y seguridad nuclear;
(e) Higiene y seguridad en el trabajo;
(f) Telecomunicaciones: conmutación digital o transmisión
digital;
(g) Ingeniería geodésica-geofísica o ingeniería hidrográfica;
(h) Gas o Explotación de yacimientos (Ingeniería de
reservorios);
(i) Ingeniería sanitaria.
Se destina(n): (a) a egresados universitarios de una carrera
de por lo menos 5 años de duración, en cualquier
especialidad, menores de 40 años; se exigen al menos 3 años

de experiencia profesional, conocimiento aceptable de inglés y manejo de computadora; existen instancias de evaluación de los postulantes; (b) a graduados y profesionales de ingeniería y de ciencias económicas; (c) a graduados en ingeniería y en ciencias exactas; (d) a ingenieros químicos, físicos, bioquímicos y en algunos casos, médicos; (e) a ingenieros de cualquier especialidad (excepto agrónomos) egresados de universidades reconocidas; (f) a graduados que superen examen de ingreso; (g) a agrimensores o ingenieros civiles (condicionados a sus estudios de topografía y geodesia); (h) a titulados en ingeniería civil, hidráulica, química, industrial, electromecánica, construcción o de especialidades afines, que superen proceso de selección.
Duración: (a) 2 años (comienza en marzo); (b) 5 cuatrimestres (comienza en abril); (c) 1 año (comienza en febrero); (d) 1 año (comienza en abril); (e) 1 año (intensivo) o 2 años (regular); (f) 10 meses; (g) 2 años y medio; (h) 2 cuatrimestres (comienzan en abril); (i) 12 meses (intensivo) o 21 meses (normal) (comienza en abril).
Asistencia financiera: (c) y (d) se pueden presentar solicitudes de becas simultáneamente a la inscripción; (h) se fomentará sistema de becas para profesionales jóvenes, de no más de 3 años de graduados, seleccionados por profesionales del Instituto del Gas y del Petróleo de la UBA y representantes del organismo que efectúe el aporte económico para la beca; (i) becas por concurso de antecedentes y evaluación por coloquio ante jurado.
Inscripciones: (a) envío de antecedentes desde el 1° de septiembre hasta el 30 de noviembre; matriculación de los aceptados hasta fin de diciembre; (c) de noviembre a diciembre; (d) e (i) en marzo; (e) de noviembre a febrero; (f) presentación de antecedentes entre noviembre y febrero; (g) en marzo; (h) en febrero y marzo. En todos los casos, se pueden solicitar mayores informaciones a Información General, en la dirección que figura en el título.

94 Universidad de Congreso [UC]
Colón 90
5500 Mendoza
Tel: +54-261-423-0960
Fax: +54-261-423-0960
Web: http://www.ucongreso.edu.ar
e-mail: landama@ucongreso.edu.ar

📖 Programas de grado y posgrado
Campos de estudios: administración, ciencias de la información, ciencias económicas y comerciales, contabilidad, ecología, medio ambiente, economía, educación, gestión, relaciones internacionales, turismo, hotelería.
Descripción:
(a) Carreras de grado en administración, ciencias de la educación, comercialización, comunicación, contaduría pública, economía, gestión ambiental, relaciones internacionales, sistemas de información, turismo;
(b) Posgrado en desarrollo gerencial.
Asistencia financiera: para estudiantes de universidades extranjeras que justifiquen situación económica, se concede 50% del arancel mensual durante 6 meses (renovable según desempeño).
Inscripciones: por convenios internacionales de intercambio y de cooperación educativa en particular, solicitar informes a Coordinación de Relaciones Institucionales, en la dirección del título.

95 Universidad de la Marina Mercante [UMM]
Avenida Rivadavia 2258
1034 Capital Federal
Tel: +54-114-953 9000
Web: http://www.udemm.edu.ar
e-mail: udemm@udemm.edu.ar

📖 Programas universitarios
Campos de estudios: administración, contabilidad, economía, electricidad y electrónica, ingeniería, mecánica, psicología, relaciones públicas, transportes.
Descripción:
(a) Ingeniería: licenciatura en higiene y seguridad, ingeniero en seguridad ambiental, ingeniería industrial, electrónica, mecánica, electromecánica, en máquinas navales, en sistemas;
(b) Administración y economía: administración, administración naviera, comercio internacional, contador público, administración de recursos humanos, transporte y

logística operativa, marketing; relaciones públicas;
(c) Humanidades y ciencias sociales: licenciatura en psicología; curso de especialización a distancia en temas de educación y terapia de niños y jóvenes con discapacidades múltiples.
Inscripciones: hasta el 30 de marzo; para mayores informaciones dirigirse a la UMM.

96 Universidad de Morón [UM]
Cabildo 134
B1708 Morón
Tel: +54-11-5627-2000
Fax: +54-11-5627-4598
Web: http://www.unimoron.edu.ar
e-mail: sec-rectorado@unimoron.edu.ar;coopint@uni moron.edu.ar

🎓 Becas de mérito escolar y becas de asistencia
Campos de estudios: todas las materias principales.
Descripción: becas de mérito escolar (en función de nivel y rendimiento académico) y becas de asistencia (en función de situación social y económica del hogar).
Duración: un año (renovable).
Importe: de 25 a 50 % de los gastos de enseñanza.
Solicitudes: en los primeros diez días del mes de marzo. Dirigirse al Departamento de Becas.

97 Universidad de San Andrés [UDSA]
Casilla de Correo 1983
1000 Buenos Aires
Tel: +54-114-746 2608
Fax: +54-114-746 4090
Web: http://www.udesa.edu.ar

📖 Programas universitarios de intercambio
Campos de estudios: administración, ciencias políticas, contabilidad, economía, finanzas, relaciones internacionales.
Descripción:
(a) Licenciaturas: administración de empresas, economía, ciencias políticas, relaciones internacionales;
(b) Licenciatura en contaduría pública;
(c) Maestría en economía de gobierno.
Se destina(n): a estudiantes de casas de altos estudios con las que la Universidad mantiene contacto (Boston College y University; Columbia University; U.C.L.A.; University of Chicago; European Business School; Georgetown University; Harvard University; Instituto Tecnológico Autónomo de México; Instituto Tecnológico y de Estudios Superiores de Monterrey; Johns Hopkins University; Macalester College; McGill University; M.I.T., Sloan School of Management, New York University; Southwestern University, Los Angeles; Tufts University; Universidad Carlos III; Universidad de Pamplona; Universidad Diego Portales; Université de Montreal; University of Bradford; University of Buckingham; University of Illinois; University of London; Queen Mary's College; University of Manchester; University of North Carolina; University of Oregon; University of Quebec à Montreal; University of St. Andrews; University of Toronto; University of Wisconsin, Oshkosh; York University, Toronto). Existen además convenios con Babson College, Boston, Estados Unidos de América, con la Universidad de Edimburg y con St. Anthony's College, Oxford, Reino Unido, para intercambios de profesores y estudiantes.
Duración: 9 meses (de marzo a diciembre).

98 Universidad del Norte "Santo Tomás de Aquino" [UNSTA]
9 de Julio 165
San Miguel de Tucumán
Tel: +54-381-422-8805
Fax: +54-381-430-7500
Web: http://www.unsta.edu.ar
e-mail: info@unsta.edu.ar

📖 Programas universitarios
Campos de estudios: todas las materias principales, administración, administración de empresas, ciencias políticas, derecho, economía, educación, filosofía, higiene y salud, ingeniería, nutrición, psicología.

Descripción:
(a) Carreras de grado en áreas de economía y administración, derecho y ciencias políticas, ingeniería, ciencias de la educación, filosofía, psicología, ciencias de la salud;
(b) Posgrados: maestría en informática, en periodismo; MBA (master ejecutivo en dirección de empresas).
Duración: (a) de 2 a 5 años; (b) 2 años.
Inscripciones: Dirigirse al Centro de Informaciones Universitarias, antes del 30 de noviembre.

99 Universidad del Salvador Oficina de Programas Internacionales [UDS]
Viamonte 1856
1056 Buenos Aires
Tel: +54-114-814 5026
Fax: +54-114-814 5025
Web: http://www.salvador.edu.ar

📖 **Programas universitarios**

Campos de estudios: todas las materias principales, español.
Descripción:
(a) Programas internacionales de intercambio en todas las materias principales y en áreas específicas con más de 150 universidades del mundo;
(b) Cursos de español.
Se destina(n): (b) a estudiantes universitarios extranjeros con conocimientos del idioma (estudios de mínimo 2 años).
Duración: (a) 4 semanas (fines de febrero y en el mes de julio); (b) comienzan en la primera semana de abril y de agosto.
Inscripciones: (a) por mayor información, dirigirse a la Oficina de Programas Internacionales de Intercambio en la dirección que figura en el título o al Departamento de Ingreso, Avenida Callao 801, Buenos Aires; (b) 4 semanas (fines de febrero y en el mes de julio).

100 Universidad Maimonides [UM]
Hidalgo 775 - Ciudad de Buenos Aires
1405 Buenos Aires
Tel: +54-114-982-8488
Fax: +54-114-982-8188 interno 11
Web: http://www.maimonides.edu
e-mail: informes@maimonides.edu

📖 **Programas de grado y posgrado**

Campos de estudios: todas las materias principales, administración, comunicación, higiene y salud, letras y artes, medicina, medios audio-visuales.
Descripción:
(a) Carreras de grado. Area de ciencias de la salud: ciencias biológicas y ecología, enfermería, bioquímica, farmacia, kinesiología y fisiatría, medicina, nutrición, odontología, prótesis dental, asistencia odontológica, dermatocosmiatría, instrumentación quirúrgica, medicina nuclear; área de humanidades: abogacía, administración, artes musicales, ciencias de la educación, contador público, estrategia contemporánea, gerontología, organización y dirección institucional, psicología; profesorado universitario, recursos humanos, turismo, ciencias y humanidades; área de tecnología: comunicación multimedial, ingeniería en sistemas;
(b) Posgrados. Especializaciones en: cirugía buco máxilo facial, diagnóstico por imágenes con orientaciones, endodoncia, geriatría, homeopatía (e/t), medicina familiar, odontología familiar y comunitaria, odontopediatría, oftalmología, ortodoncia, patología médica, pediatría, periodoncia, prótesis, psiquiatría, reumatología. Posgrados en: psicogerontología, psicoterapia familiar, psicoterapia individual y grupal. Maestrías en: gerenciamiento de servicios de enfermería, investigación clínica (e/t), manejo ambiental, neuropsicología, ciencias de la comunicación, geopolítica (e/t), ciencias políticas (e/t). Doctorados en: administración, medicina, odontología, psicología con orientación en neurociencia cognitiva aplicada (e/t).
Duración: Carreras de Grado: tecnicaturas 2 años, licenciaturas 4 o 5 años. Carreras de posgrado: anuales o bianuales.
Inscripciones: dirigirse a la Secretaría Técnica (e-mail: sectecnica@maimonides.edu.ar).

101 Universidad Nacional de Entre Ríos Facultad de Bromatología [UNER]
25 de Mayo 709
2820 Gualeguaychú
Entre Ríos
Tel: +54-344-626-115
Fax: +54-344-626-345
Web: http://www.fb.uner.edu.ar
e-mail: facbrom@fb.uner.edu.ar

📖 **Programas universitarios**

Campos de estudios: alimentación, higiene y salud, industria alimentaría.
Descripción:
(a) Carrera corta a distancia de técnico en control bromatológico;
(b) Licenciatura en bromatología: materias básicas y de especialidad.
Se destina(n): a personas de cualquier país que hayan completado los estudios secundarios y posean conocimientos suficientes de español.
Duración: (a) 2 años; (b) 5 años; (comienzan en marzo-abril).
Asistencia financiera: (b) becas anuales de estudios, renovables.
Inscripciones: hasta el 31 de marzo.

102 Universidad Nacional de Entre Ríos Facultad de Ciencias Agropecuarias [UNER]
Casilla de Correo 24
3100 Paraná
Entre Ríos
Tel: +54-343-497-5075
Fax: +54-343-497-5096
Web: http://overde.com.ar/agro
e-mail: sedeten@fca.uner.edu.ar

📖 **Programas universitarios**

Campos de estudios: ciencias agronómicas.
Descripción:
(a) Programa en ingeniería agronómica: materias básicas y de especialidad;
(b) Curso de análisis de semillas; 30 participantes.
Diplomas requeridos: (a) a candidatos que hayan cursado estudios secundarios completos; (b) a ingenieros agrónomos.
Duración: (a) 6 años; (b) 15 días.
Inscripciones: (b) hasta el 15 de julio.

103 Universidad Nacional de Entre Ríos Facultad de Ciencias de la Alimentación [UNER]
Monseñor Tavella 1450
3200 Concordia
Entre Ríos
Tel: (54) (345) 4 211 771
Fax: (54) (345) 4 218 035
Web: http://www.fcal.uner.edu.ar
e-mail: decano@fcal.uner.edu.ar

📖 **Programa de estudios**

Campos de estudios: alimentación, biología, bioquímica, industria alimentaría, química, tecnología industrial.
Descripción:
(a) Técnico superior en tecnología de alimentos;
(b) Ingeniería de alimentos.
Se destina(n): a candidatos con estudios secundarios completos.
Duración: (a) 3 años; (b) 6 años.

104 Universidad Nacional de Entre Ríos
Facultad de Ciencias de la Salud [UNER]
8 de Junio 600
3260 Concepción del Uruguay
Entre Ríos
Tel: (54) (344) 2 426 112
Fax: (54) (344) 2 422 181
Web: http://www.fcs.uner.edu.ar/salud
e-mail: extensio@fcs.uner.edu.ar

⌂ **Programa de diplomaturas**

Campos de estudios: anatomía, enfermería, estudios paramédicos, farmacia y farmacología, fisiología, higiene y salud, medicina preventiva, nutrición, obstetricia y ginecología, psiquiatría.
Descripción: Programas conducentes a la obtención de diploma de:
(a) Título intermedio de enfermero;
(b) Licenciado en enfermería;
(c) Instrumentador quirúrgico;
(d) Técnico en salud ambiental;
(e) Obstétrica (diploma binacional válido en la República Argentina y en la República Oriental del Uruguay).
Se destina(n): (a) a (d) a candidatos que cumplan los requisitos necesarios; (e) a postulantes de sexo femenino, con secundaria completa, de nacionalidad uruguaya o argentina.
Se dicta(n): (e) en la Facultad de Ciencias de la Salud (UNER) y Universidad del Norte de la República Oriental del Uruguay.
Duración: (a) 2 años y medio; (b) 1 año y medio; (c) y (d) 2 años; (e) 3 años y medio (inicio en febrero).
Asistencia financiera: existen becas de ayuda al estudiante y de ayuda a la investigación.

105 Universidad Nacional de Entre Ríos
Facultad de Ciencias Económicas [UNER]
Urquiza 552
3100 Paraná, Entre Ríos
Tel: (54) (343) 422 2172
Fax: (54) (343) 423 0433
Web: http://www.fceco.uner.edu.ar
e-mail: decano@fceco.uner.edu.ar

⌂ **Carrera de contador público nacional**

Campos de estudios: ciencias económicas y comerciales.
Se destina(n): a candidatos que hayan cursado estudios secundarios completos y aprueben un examen de ingreso.
Duración: 5 años.

106 Universidad Nacional de Entre Ríos [UNER]
Eva Perón 24
Concepción del Uruguay
Entre Ríos
Tel: (54) (344) 2 427 654
Web: http://www.uner.edu.ar
e-mail: saproy@rect.uner.edu.ar

⌂ **Programas universitarios**

Campos de estudios: todas las materias principales, administración, educación, ingeniería, trabajo social.
Descripción: Programas en sus diversas facultades: ingeniería, ciencias de la educación, trabajo social, ciencias de la administración.

107 Universidad Nacional de la Pampa [UNLPAM]
Coronel Gil 353, 3° piso
Santa Rosa, La Pampa
Tel: (54) (295) 445 1600
Fax: (54) (295) 443 3408
Web: http://www.unlpam.edu.ar
e-mail: secacademica@unlpam.edu.ar

⌂ **Programas universitarios**

Campos de estudios: todas las materias principales, ciencias, ciencias agronómicas, contabilidad, derecho, educación, formación de docentes, informática, ingeniería, medicina veterinaria.
Descripción: (a) Agronomía: ingeniero agrónomo, técnico universitario en administración y planificación agraria; técnico universitario en producción lechera;
(b) Ciencias económicas y jurídicas: contador público nacional (posgrado: especialista en gestión agropecuaria) y abogado;
(c) Ciencias exactas y naturales: profesorados en matemáticas, computación, física, ciencias biológicas, química; licenciaturas en: matemáticas, física, ciencias biológicas (posgrado: doctorado en química), química, geología; ingeniería en recursos naturales y medio ambiente (posgrado: doctorado en física);
(d) Ciencias humanas: profesorados y licenciaturas en historia, geografía, inglés, en ciencias de la educación;
(e) Ciencias veterinarias: médico veterinario (posgrado: especialista en docencia universitaria en ciencias veterinarias); técnico universitario en seguridad de los alimentos de origen animal; (posgrado: especialista en seguridad de los alimentos de origen animal); doctorados: en ganadería ecología, en gestión de la empresa agropecuaria en zonas marginales (convenio internacional entre la UNLPam y la Universidad de Córdoba (España);
(f) Ingeniería: ingeniero electromecánico, ingeniero electromecánico orientación en automatización industrial, analista programador en computación.

108 Universidad Nacional de la Patagonia "San Juan Bosco"
Facultad de Ciencias Económicas [UNDLPJB]
San Martín 330
9100 Trelew, Provincia de Chubut
Tel: (54) 965 31 532
Fax: (54) 965 31 532
Web: http://www.unp.edu.ar/fce

⌂ **Programas de grado y posgrado**

Campos de estudios: administración, administración de empresas, ciencias económicas y comerciales, contabilidad, derecho, economía.
Descripción:
(a) Programas de grado: contador público nacional; licenciatura en administración, en economía, en administración de empresas turísticas; técnico universitario contable, en administración pública, en administración bancaria, en administración ambiental, en administración de cooperativas;
(b) Posgrados: maestría en gestión empresarial, en gerencia pública; en ciencias penales; especialización en tributación en sindicatura concursal; en derecho penal, en turismo en espacios naturales y rurales; curso de infancia, derecho y políticas sociales en América Latina.
Duración: (a) 5 años las licenciaturas, 3 las tecnicaturas; (b) entre 1 año y 2 años y medio.
Inscripciones: en febrero.

109 Universidad Nacional de la Patagonia "San Juan Bosco"
Facultad de Ciencias Naturales [UNDLPJB]
Ciudad Universitaria Km. 4, 2° piso
9005 Comodoro Rivadavia
Provincia de Chubut
Tel: (54) (297) 455 9615/6
Fax: (54) (297) 455 0339
Web: http://www.unp.edu.ar
e-mail: fcn@unpata.edu.ar

⌂ **Programas universitarios**

Campos de estudios: biología, bioquímica, ciencias naturales, ecología, medio ambiente, enfermería, farmacia y farmacología, geología.
Descripción:
(a) Carreras: licenciatura en ciencias biológicas; bioquímica; profesorado en ciencias biológicas; farmacia; geología; enfermería; técnico biólogo universitario; técnico

universitario en saneamiento y protección ambiental; técnico universitario en química;
(b) Cursos de grado y de posgrado en su Departamento de química.
Inscripciones: entre noviembre y marzo.

110 Universidad Nacional de la Patagonia "San Juan Bosco" Facultad de Ingeniería [UNDLPJB]
Belgrano 504, 2° piso
9100 Trelew, Provincia de Chubut
Tel: (54) 965 33305
Fax: (54) 965 32602
Web: http://www.ing.unp.edu.ar

📖 **Programas académicos y de extensión**

Campos de estudios: construcción, electricidad y electrónica, informática, ingeniería, ingeniería civil, ingeniería química, matemáticas, mecánica.
Descripción: programas en sus Departamentos de electrónica, estabilidad y materiales, física, ingeniería forestal, industrias, informática, ingeniería civil orientación construcciones, ingeniería civil orientación hidráulica, matemáticas, mecánica.
Inscripciones: en marzo.

111 Universidad Nacional de La Plata [UNLP]
Avenida 7 N° 776
1900 La Plata
Tel: (54) (221) 427 7028
Fax: (54) (221) 423 6817
Web: http://www.unlp.edu.ar

📖 **Carreras y actividades de extensión universitaria**

Campos de estudios: todas las materias principales.
Descripción: programas en las facultades de: arquitectura y urbanismo, ciencias naturales y museo, bellas artes, ciencias veterinarias, ciencias agrarias y forestales, humanidades y ciencias de la educación, ciencias astronómicas y geofísicas, informática, ciencias económicas, ingeniería, ciencias exactas, odontología, ciencias jurídicas y sociales, periodismo y comunicación social, ciencias médicas, trabajo social.

112 Universidad Nacional de La Rioja [UNLaR]
Avenida Laprida y Vicente Bustos
5300 La Rioja
Tel: +54-3822-457-000
Fax: +54-3822-457-000
Web: http://www.unlar.edu.ar
e-mail: unlar@unlar.edu.ar

🍃 **Ayudas financieras**

Campos de estudios: administración de empresas, ciencias económicas y comerciales.
Becas: becas de mérito académico.
Materias de estudio: estudios empresariales.

113 Universidad Nacional de Mar del Plata [UNMDP]
Diagonal Juan Bautista Alberdi n° 2695
7600 Mar del Plata
Tel: (54) (223) 492 1705
Fax: (54) (223) 492 1711
Web: http://www.mdp.edu.ar
e-mail: info@mdp.edu.ar

📖 **Programas universitarios**

Campos de estudios: todas las materias principales, ciencias, ciencias agronómicas, ciencias económicas y comerciales, ciencias humanas, ciencias sociales, derecho, diseño, higiene y salud, ingeniería, psicología, trabajo social, urbanismo.
Descripción: cursos de grado, pregrado, programas de extensión e investigación en áreas de arquitectura, urbanismo y diseño, ciencias agrarias, ciencias económicas y sociales, ciencias exactas y naturales, ciencias de la salud y servicio social, derecho, humanidades, ingeniería, psicología.

Asistencia financiera: solicitar información sobre becas de investigación, internacionales, internacionales Universia, de ayuda económica.

114 Universidad Nacional de Misiones [UNAM]
Campus Universitario Ruta Nac. 12, Km. 7 ½
Estafeta Postal Miguel Lanús
3304 Posadas, Misiones
Tel: (54) (375) 248 1047
Fax: (54) (375) 248 1047
Web: http://www.unam.edu.ar

📖 **Programas universitarios**

Campos de estudios: artes, artes aplicadas, artes plásticas, artesanía, construcción, tecnología, urbanismo.
Duración: programas de estudio en sus facultades y escuelas de: artes; ciencias económicas; ciencias exactas, químicas y naturales; ciencias forestales; humanidades y ciencias sociales; ingeniería; enfermería.
Inscripciones: dirigirse a la Secretaría de Asuntos Estudiantiles.

115 Universidad Nacional de Rosario [UNR]
Córdoba 1814
2000 Rosario, Santa Fé
Tel: (54) (341) 447 2173
Fax: (54) (341) 447 2173
Web: http://www.unr.edu.ar
e-mail: rrii@sede.unr.edu.ar

📖 **Programas universitarios**

Campos de estudios: todas las materias principales.
Descripción:
(a) Facultad de arquitectura, planeamiento y diseño: arquitectura;
(b) Facultad de ciencias agrarias: ingeniería agronómica; M.Sc. en mejoramiento genético vegetal;
(c) Facultad de ciencias bioquímicas y farmacéuticas: bioquímica; farmacia; licenciatura en química, en biotecnología; profesorado en química; doctorado;
(d) Facultad de ciencias económicas y estadística: contaduría pública; licenciatura en economía, en estadística, en administración de empresas; profesorado de contabilidad, de economía, de estadística; posgrado en contaduría pública especializada en sindicatura concursal, en operaciones del comercio exterior;
(e) Facultad de derecho: abogacía; posgrado en abogacía especializada en derecho de familia; magister en filosofía del derecho privado, magister jurídico en derechos humanos, magister en filosofía del derecho y de los derechos humanos;
(f) Facultad de ciencias exactas, ingeniería y agrimensura: ingeniería civil, industrial, mecánica, en electricidad y en electrónica; agrimensura; licenciatura en física y en matemática; profesorado en matemática; posgrado en ingeniería gerencial, en ingeniería especializada en maquinaria agrícola, en ingeniería sanitaria; master en estructuras, en ingeniería vial; doctorado en física;
(g) Facultad de ciencia política y relaciones internacionales: licenciatura en ciencia política, en relaciones internacionales, en trabajo social, en comunicación social; profesorado de enseñanza media y superior en ciencias políticas, sociales y jurídicas;
(h) Facultad de ciencias veterinarias: medicina veterinaria;
(i) Facultad de humanidades y artes: licenciatura en filosofía, en letras, en ciencias de la educación, en historia, en antropología; profesorado de enseñanza media y superior en filosofía, letras, ciencias de la educación, historia, ciencias sociales; licenciatura en bellas artes, profesorado de portugués;
(j) Facultad de odontología: odontólogo;
(k) Facultad de psicología: psicología y profesorado de enseñanza media y superior en psicología;
(l) Facultad de ciencias médicas: licenciatura en enfermería, en fonoaudiología, en medicina; posgrados en medicina legal, endocrinología;
(m) Instituto Politécnico Superior "Gral. San Martín": cursos de técnico superior en organización industrial, en óptica;
(n) Escuela Superior de Comercio "Lib. Gral. San Martín": caligrafía pública, curso de técnico administrativo en comercio exterior;

(o) Escuela de Artes: profesorado en enseñanza primaria, en enseñanza media y superior; licenciatura en bellas artes;
(p) Escuela de Música: cursos, licenciaturas, profesorados de diversos instrumentos.
(q) Centro de Estudios Interdisciplinarios: master en salud pública.
Se destina(n): a argentinos y a extranjeros titulares de los diplomas requeridos (éstos varían según la especialidad).
Inscripciones: hasta el 5 de marzo de cada año en la Facultad correspondiente. Por más informaciones, dirigirse al Departamento de Relaciones Internacionales de la UNR, en la dirección que figura en el título.

116 Universidad Nacional de Salta [UNDS]

Buenos Aires 177
4400 Salta
Tel: (54) (387) 431 1371
Web: http://www.unsa.edu.ar
e-mail: info@unsa.edu.ar

Carreras de grado y posgrado

Campos de estudios: todas las materias principales.
Descripción:
(a) Facultad de humanidades: profesorado y licenciatura en ciencias de la educación, en filosofía, en historia y letras; licenciatura en antropología;
(b) Facultad de ciencias económicas, jurídicas y sociales: contador público nacional; licenciatura en administración (menciones pública o de empresas); profesorado en ciencias jurídicas; maestría en economía política;
(c) Facultad de ciencias de la salud: enfermería, nutrición; especialista y magister en salud pública, especialista en terapia intensiva;
(d) Facultad de ciencias exactas: licenciatura en física, profesorado y licenciatura en química, profesorado en matemática y física, licenciatura en análisis de sistemas, en matemáticas; doctorado en física;
(e) Facultad de ingeniería: ingeniería industrial, química, en construcciones, en vías de comunicaciones, hidráulica, civil;
(f) Facultad de ciencias naturales: profesorado y licenciatura en ciencias biológicas; geología; ingeniería agronómica; licenciatura en recursos naturales; doctorado en ciencias geológicas;
(g) Sede Regional Orán: enfermería; computador universitario;
(h) Sede Regional Tartagal: técnico universitario en perforaciones; profesorado de letras.
Se destina(n): a nacionales de cualquier país que cumplan las condiciones requeridas.
Costo(s): la enseñanza de carreras de grado es gratuita, en cambio las de posgrado por lo general son aranceladas.
Asistencia financiera: existen diversos tipos de ayudas y becas.
Inscripciones: para mayores informaciones dirigirse a Coordinación de Relaciones Internacionales (e-mail: coreinte@unsa.edu.ar).

117 Universidad Nacional de San Juan [UNSJ]

Avenida José Ignacio de la Roza 391 - Este
5400 San Juan
Tel: (54) (264) 421 4510
Fax: (54) (264) 421 4586
Web: http://www.unsj.edu.ar

Programas universitarios

Campos de estudios: todas las materias principales.
Descripción: (a) Facultad de ingeniería: ingeniería en agrimensura, civil, electrónica, eléctrica, mecánica, electromecánica, de minas, química; curso de especialización en ingeniería de caminos de montaña; maestría y doctorado en ingeniería de sistemas de control; doctorado en ingeniería eléctrica; ciclo básico de bioingeniería (por convenio se completa el ciclo superior en la Universidad Superior de Entre Ríos);
(b) Facultad de ciencias exactas, físicas y naturales: licenciaturas en ciencias geológicas, geofísica, ciencias de la información; doctorado en ciencias geológicas; carrera de programador;
(c) Facultad de filosofía, humanidades y artes: licenciaturas en matemática, geografía, filosofía, historia, ciencias de la

educación, inglés, letras, artes visuales; profesorados en matemática, física, química, historia, geografía, letras, filosofía y pedagogía, lengua y literatura inglesa, artes plásticas, educación musical, órgano, piano, instrumento de cuerda, viento o percusión, canto; maestría en historia; maestría y doctorado en letras;
(d) Facultad de ciencias sociales: licenciaturas en ciencias de la información, ciencias políticas, servicio social, sociología; tecnicaturas universitarias en periodismo, publicidad y propaganda; maestrías en relaciones económicas internacionales y comercio exterior;
(e) Facultad de arquitectura, urbanismo y diseño: arquitectura y urbanismo; maestría en gestión del desarrollo urbano regional.
Se destina(n): a argentinos y a extranjeros (éstos deben saber español) titulares de uno de los siguientes diplomas: bachiller, maestro "normal", perito mercantil o técnico. Para maestrías, doctorados y cursos de especialización existen condiciones de admisión particulares.
Duración: varía según la carrera, 6 años para arquitectura y urbanismo; 5 a 5 años y medio para las ingenierías; entre 3 y 5 años para las licenciaturas y el profesorado (comienzan en marzo).
Costo(s): las carreras de grado son gratuitas y el costo de los posgrados se fija anualmente.
Asistencia financiera: existen becas diversas.
Inscripciones: hasta diciembre del año anterior al de los estudios; en la facultad correspondiente.

118 Universidad Nacional de Tres de Febrero

Av. San Martín 2921
(1678) Caseros
Provincia de Buenos Aires
Web: http://www.untref.edu.ar/sedes.htm
e-mail: info@untref.edu.ar

Becas asistidas

Campos de estudios: todas las materias principales.
Descripción: la Untref participa de manera regular de diversos programas de becas, con dos modalidades, una solo para difusión y otra en forma conjunta con el organismo que las promueve.
Asimismo, la Untref ofrece la posibilidad de que estudiantes y profesores cuenten con postulación asistida en relación con oportunidades internacionales.
Se aplican becas de gobierno y de distintos organismos y fundaciones (Fundación Fulbright, Fundación Carolina, gobierno canadiense, DAAD, British Council, otras).
Solicitudes: dirigirse a Cooperación Internacional.

119 Universidad Nacional del Centro [UNCPBA]

General Pinto 399
7000 Tandil, Buenos Aires
Tel: (54) (293) 422000
Web: http://www.unicen.edu.ar

Programas universitarios

Campos de estudios: todas las materias principales, artes del espectáculo, ciencias, ciencias agronómicas, ciencias económicas y comerciales, ciencias humanas, economía, ingeniería, medicina veterinaria.
Descripción: programas de estudio en sus facultades de: agronomía, ciencias humanas, ingeniería, ciencias económicas, ciencias exactas, ciencias sociales, ciencias veterinarias y escuela superior de teatro.
Inscripciones: solicitar informes en la dirección del título para información sobre cada facultad.

120 Universidad Nacional del Comahue [UNCOMA]

Buenos Aires 1400
8300 Neuquén
Tel: (54) (299) 4 490 300
Web: http://www.uncoma.edu.ar
e-mail: webinfo@uncoma.edu.ar

Programas universitarios

Campos de estudios: todas las materias principales.
Descripción: carreras de pregrado, grado y posgrado en

áreas de economía y administración, ingeniería, turismo, humanidades, servicio social, ciencias de la salud, enfermería, ciencias agrarias, ciencias de la educación, medicina, idiomas, derecho y ciencias sociales, biología marina y pesquera, otras.
Se dicta(n): en sus sedes de Neuquén, Allen, Cinco Saltos, Cipolletti, General Roca, San Carlos de Bariloche, S. M. de los Andes, Viedma, Villa Regina, Zapala, San Antonio Oeste.
Inscripciones: solicitar información sobre unidades académicas y programas respectivos a la dirección del título.

121 Universidad Nacional del Litoral
Facultad de Bioquímica y Ciencias Biológicas
Escuela Superior de Sanidad "Dr. Ramón Carrillo" [UNL]
Ciudad Universitaria, Paraje "El Pozo"
Casilla de Correo 530
3000 Santa Fé
Tel: (54) (42) 455 5512
Web: http://www.unl.edu.ar
e-mail: estudiantiles@unl.edu.ar

📖 **Programas universitarios**

Campos de estudios: administración, ecología, medio ambiente, higiene y salud, informática, medicina, medicina preventiva, radiología, trabajo social.
Descripción:
(a) Carreras: técnico en administración de salud, licenciatura en administración de salud, técnico en saneamiento, terapia ocupacional;
(b) Cursos: técnico en estadística de salud, técnico operador de PC;
(c) Cursos de Posgrado: medicina del trabajo, administración de salud, terapeuta en intervención y estimulación temprana, perito médico laboral, radiofísica sanitaria.
Se destina(n): a argentinos y extranjeros: de (a) a (d) que hayan terminado los estudios secundarios; (e) que hayan terminado los estudios secundarios y se desempeñen en salud; (f) a (i) a profesionales y técnicos del área de la salud; (j) que hayan realizado medicina del trabajo.
Inscripciones: dirigirse a la UNL para mayor información.

122 Universidad Nacional del Sur [UNS]
Avenida Alem 1015
8000 Bahía Blanca
Tel: (54) (291) 459 5039
Web: http://www.unl.edu.ar

📖 **Programas universitarios**

Campos de estudios: todas las materias principales.
Descripción: Carreras de: agrimensura, bioquímica; contador público; ingeniería agronómica, civil, eléctrica, electrónica, industrial, química; licenciatura en administración, en ciencias biológicas, en ciencias de la computación, en ciencias geológicas, en economía, en filosofía, en física, en geografía, en historia, en letras, en matemáticas, en química; profesorado en ciencias agrarias, en ciencias biológicas, en contabilidad, en economía, en filosofía, en geografía, en geología, en historia, en letras, en matemática, en química.
Se destina(n): a quienes hayan finalizado la enseñanza secundaria.
Inscripciones: a partir del mes de noviembre; dirigirse al Departamento de Ingreso.

123 Universidad Nacional del Sur [UNS]
Avenida Colón 80
8000 Bahía Blanca
Tel: (54) (291) 459 5015
Fax: (54) (291) 459 5016
Web: http://www.uns.edu.ar
e-mail: secext@uns.edu.ar

📖 **Programas universitarios**

Campos de estudios: administración de empresas, biología, bioquímica, ciencias económicas y comerciales, geología, historia, ingeniería, letras, matemáticas, química.

Descripción:
(a) Carreras de grado en agronomía, biología, bioquímica y farmacia, ciencias de la administración, ciencias e ingeniería de la computación, derecho, economía, física, geografía, geología, humanidades, ingeniería, matemáticas, química;
(b) Posgrados en ciencias e ingeniería de la computación, derecho, economía, geografía, geología, humanidades, ingeniería, ingeniería eléctrica y de computadoras, matemáticas, química, INIBIBB (Cátedra UNESCO de Biofísica y Neurobiología Molecular).
Asistencia financiera: solicitar información a la Secretaría de Relaciones Institucionales y Extensión Universitaria por becas internacionales (AECI, DAAD, Saint-Exupéry, OEA, ALFA, JICA, LASPAU, Fullbright, otras); a la Secretaría de Ciencia y Tecnología por becas para egresados, para alumnos avanzados, de iniciación a la investigación; a la Secretaría de Asuntos Estudiantiles por becas de estímulo, nacionales, de comedor, transporte, residencias y subsidios.
Inscripciones: solicitar información al Departamento de Graduados.

124 Universidad Notarial Argentina
Fundación del Colegio de Escribanos
de la Provincia de Buenos Aires [UNA]
Avenida 51 N° 435
1900 La Plata
Tel: (54) 219 283
e-mail: uninot@satlink.com

📖 **Programas universitarios**

Campos de estudios: ciencias económicas y comerciales, derecho, derecho internacional, estudios internacionales.
Descripción:
(a) Doctorados en: notariado, derecho registral, derecho internacional privado, filosofía del derecho;
(b) Especializaciones en: asesoramiento de la empresa, derecho penal económico, derecho procesal profundizado, documentación y contratación notarial, especialización en sindicatura concursal; especialización en asesoramiento concursal;
(c) Magister en derecho consular y aduanero;
(d) Cátedras libres: teoría trialista del derecho, orientaciones y tendencias modernas del derecho, derecho bursátil, metodología del derecho, historia general del derecho, enseñanza del derecho;
(e) Congresos, cursos y seminarios.
Se destina(n): a graduados en derecho (escribano o abogado) de cualquier país. En algunos programas también son admitidos los graduados en ciencias económicas, administración, ciencias políticas o filosofía.
Asistencia financiera: becas que comprenden los gastos de matrícula y arancel.

Arménie
Année universitaire: septembre à juin.
Unité monétaire: dram arménie (AMD).
Admission pour étudiants du pays: Pour accéder à l'enseignement supérieur les candidats étrangers doivent justifier d'un certificat de fin d'études secondaires et passer un examen d'entrée.
Connaissances linguistiques requises: Les candidats étrangers doivent avoir une bonne connaissance de l'arménien et du russe.
Formalités d'immigration: Les candidats étrangers doivent posséder un visa et être présentés par les agences compétentes de leur pays d'origine. Ils doivent être recommandés par un comité de sélection.
Services d'accueil et d'information:
• Ministère de l'éducation supérieure et des sciences, 13 Movses Khorenatsi, 375010 Erevan; site internet: http://www.edu.am.
Reconnaissance des études et diplômes: s'adresser au Ministère des affaires étrangères, 10, Baghramian Av., 37019 Erevan, Arménie.

125 American University of Armenia [AUA]

50 Marshal Baghramian Avenue
375 0 Yerevan
Tel: +374-1-51-28-40
Fax: +374-1-51-28-40
Web: http://www.aua.am
e-mail: aordian@aua.am

📖 Graduate Programme

Study Domains: accounting, administration, business, business administration, computer science, engineering, English, finance, information science, international business, international law, international relations, international studies, law, management, marketing, political economy, political science, statistics, teacher education.
Programmes: Master's degrees in business and management, engineering, computer and information science, health sciences, law, teaching English as foreign language.
Open to: candidates having completed a 4-5 year programme of an accredited institution of higher education; admission exam and recommendation required.
Duration: 2 years; courses begin in March.
Fees: current registration: US$45; tuition fees: US$6,000 per annum; living costs, approx. US$500 per month.
Languages: language of instruction: English; candidates must pass the TOEFL test.
Applications: by 15 March to the Admissions Office; tel: +374-1-512-790; fax: +374-1-512-840; email: aarmenian@aua.am.

🐾 Scholarship

Study Domains: all major fields.
Scholarships: The Vartkes and Rita Balian Scholarship.
Open to: for CSI and Armenian citizens to cover a portion of the tuition fee; available on the basis of academic performance.
Duration: one year (from January to December).
Value: approximately US$4,000 per annum for CSI students and US$5,000 for Armenian students.
Applications: by October to the above address.

126 Armenian Agricultural Academy [AAA]

Teryan Street 74
37500 Yerevan
Tel: +374-1-581-912
Fax: +374-1-522-361
Web: http://www.iatp.irex.am
e-mail: armagric@usda.am

📖 Undergraduate, Graduate, Postgraduate

Study Domains: agriculture, cattle breeding, veterinary medicine, veterinary sciences.
Description: Studies in agronomy; farm mechanization and machines; food technology; cattle-breeding; zoo-veterinary sciences.
Languages: Armenian, English and Russian.

🐾 Graduate scholarships

Study Domains: agriculture, agronomic sciences, cattle breeding, veterinary medicine, veterinary sciences.
Scholarships: Norma and Harley Martin Excellence Scholarship.
Open to: to enrolled students who demonstrate academic excellence, self-esteem, and belong to a underprivileged social group.

127 Gavar State University [GSU]

Azatutian Avenue 1
Gavar
Tel: +374-64-21-908

📖 Qualified Specialists' Programme

Study Domains: accounting, biology, computer science, ecology, environment, economy, English, finance, geography, history, law, philology, Russian.
Programmes: Qualified specialists' programme.
Duration: 5 years; courses begin in September.
Languages: language of instruction: Armenian.

128 Université d'État d'Erevan

1, rue Alex Manoogian
37540 Erevan
Tel: +374-1-550-612
Fax: +-374-1-151-087
Web: http://www.ysu.am

📖 1er-3e cycles

Domaines d'étude: toutes disciplines principales.
Programmes: cours dans toutes les disciplines principales, conduisant aux diplômes universitaires du 1er au 3e cycles.
A l'intention de: ressortissant de tout pays, titulaires du certificat de fin d'études secondaires; examen d'admission.
Durée: 8 ans en cas de préparation d'une thèse; l'année scolaire est divisée en 2 semestres: septembre-janvier et février-juin.
Connaissances linguistiques: langues d'enseignement: arménien et russe.
Inscriptions: à l'adresse ci-dessus.

129 Université française en Arménie [FUA]

Aygestan 8,
Yerevan
Tel: +374-1-578-456
Fax: +374-1-578-457
Web: http://www.netarmenie.com/economie/formation/unifrancoarm.php
e-mail: ufa@arminco.com

📖 'Diplômes universitaires'

Domaines d'étude: administration, administration des affaires, affaires, affaires internationales, bibliothéconomie, commerce, communication, comptabilité, criminologie, droit, droit international, économie, éducation permanente, finances, gestion, histoire, industrie et commerce, informatique, langues, marketing, mathématiques, philosophie, relations internationales, sciences économiques et commerciales, sciences politiques, sciences sociales, statistique, théologie, religion.
A l'intention de: les candidats doivent passer un examen et un entretien.
Durée: 5 années; les cours débutent en septembre.
Frais: inscription: 6 US$; frais de scolarité: 700 US$.
Connaissances linguistiques: les cours sont dispensés en français.
Inscriptions: 10 juillet; contacter Mher Shahgeldyan; tél.: +374-1-571-605; fax: +374-1-571-602; email: ufa@arminco.com.

130 Yerevan Brusov State Linguistic University [YSLU]

42 Toumanyan Street
Yerevan
Tel: +374-1-530-552 / 531-771
Fax: +374-1-530-552
Web: http://www.brusov.am
e-mail: assrector@brusov.am

📖 Foreign languages programme

Study Domains: cultural studies, languages, political science.
Programmes: foreign languages programme.
Languages: languages of instruction: Armenian, English and Russian.

131 Yerevan State Medical University [YSMU]

2 Korjun Str.
375025 Yerevan
Tel: +374-1-560-594
Fax: +374-1-529-605
Web: http://www.ysmu.am
e-mail: info@ysmu.am

📖 Graduate and Postgraduate Programmes / Health Sciences

Study Domains: education, health and hygiene, medicine, sciences.
Programmes: Master's degree and PhD in health sciences.
Open to: undergraduate studies: candidates who have

secondary school; postgraduate studies (residency and PhD): candidates holding an MD degree.

Duration: undergraduate studies: 5 years for pharmacy and dentistry; 6 years for general and military medicine; postgraduate studies (residency and PhD): variable according to subject matter (from 2 to 4 years).

Languages: languages of instruction: Armenian, English and Russian.

Applications: July and August. For further information regarding admissions for international students contact tel: +374-1-560-595; fax: +374-1-529-605.

Australia

Academic year: early March to late November.

Organization of higher education system: First level (undergraduate) studies: Associate degree: 2 years of study; Bachelor's degree: minimum 3 years of study (honours 4 years); second level: (postgraduate) graduate certificate: 6 months of study; graduate diploma: 12 months; Master's degree: 1-2 years (e.g. M.B.A.); third level: Doctorate degree: 3 years. The Bachelor's degree is the fundamental university qualification and is the basic qualification for entry to the professions.

Monetary unit: Australian dollar (A$).

International student admission: In general, applicants must be eligible for entry to a tertiary institution of good standing in their home country. Each institution will assess competencies of students for admission to proposed course of studies.

Language: Australian education institutions can only accept students with an appropriate level of English proficiency. Institutions set their own English language requirements and may have different IELTS levels for the proposed level of courses than those required for a student visa. Students should check the entry requirements for each institution. For more information: http://studyinaustralia.gov.au/sia/en/WhatToStudy/EntryRequirements.htm.

Immigration requirements: Entry regulations require that students must have confirmation of enrolment, a student visa and sufficient funds to support themselves. Students must undergo a medical examination as part of their visa application and must have Overseas Students Health Cover for the period covered by their visa.

Estimated expenses for one academic year: Expenses vary according to course of study, institution and location. As an indication, international students need between A$8,000-15,000 a year for living expenses (accommodation, food, transport, clothing and entertainment). Medical insurance costs approximately A$300 per year. Tuition fees vary between courses and institutions: degree courses such as economics or law: A$15,000-19,000 per year; and laboratory-based degree courses such as medicine, science or engineering: A$20,000-23,000 per year. Graduate certificate/diploma courses: A$12,000-21,000 per year; Master's and Doctoral degrees: A$18,000-36,000 per year.

Information services:
• Applicants should contact the Australian Education Centre (AEC), the Australian International Education Foundation (AIEF) office, or Australian Diplomatic Mission in their home country or the Australian institution of their choice; all pertinent information can be found at http://www.studyinaustralia.gov.au
• For visa information: Department of Immigration and Multicultural and Indigenous Affairs: http://www.immi.gov.au.

Scholarships for international students: See www.studyinaustralia.gov.au and search the scholarships database (currently over 460).

Open and distance learning: International students may study via distance education at Australian universities and will receive the same degrees as their on-campus counterparts. Degrees obtained following study in this mode receive the same level of recognition by employers and from other universities as the basis of admission to further study. Open Learning Australia (OLA) is an alternative way of providing higher education. It is owned and operated by a consortium of universities and acts as a broker between students and provider institutions in Australia. It arranges bridging units, vocational education and training/TAFE (Technical and Further Education) units, undergraduate units and

postgraduate units leading to formal qualifications in the Australian Qualifications Framework.

Recognition of studies and qualification: Australian universities are self-accrediting bodies. However, the higher education sector also includes non-university institutions; while some of these are self-accrediting, most of them are not. Programmes and degrees offered by non-university institutions often have an applied focus and are most commonly in fields such as art, business, drama, hospitality, music, religion and theology, and teacher education. Higher education programmes and awards offered by non-self-accrediting institutions are accredited by the relevant State or Territory higher education accreditation authority. The accrediting authorities are listed in the Register of Authorities Empowered by Government to Accredit Post-Compulsory Education and Training Courses and may be found on the Australian Qualifications Framework website at http://www.aqf.edu.au. In addition, professional bodies and associations play a significant role as external arbiters in the quality assurance framework through their accreditation of professional courses in areas such as nursing and medicine, law, accounting, engineering and architecture. These bodies and associations also have an on-going role in monitoring the quality of such courses. The Australian Universities Quality Agency (AUQA) was established by the Commonwealth and State and Territory Ministers responsible for higher education on 7 April 2000 as an independent national quality assurance agency to monitor, audit and report on quality assurance in Australian higher education.

• More than 150,000 students from overseas attend education institutions in Australia each year. The Federal Government recognizes the value of its international education industry and seeks to protect and enhance its reputation and integrity, while also offering protection to overseas students studying in Australia. The Education Services for Overseas Students (ESOS) Act 2000 requires that providers of education and training overseas students be registered on the Commonwealth Register of Institutions and Courses for Overseas Students (CRICOS). The ESOS Act and its National Code provide nationally consistent standards for registration and the subsequent conduct of CRICOS-registered providers. It requires that providers meet quality assurance standards, comply with tuition and financial assurance requirements, and encourage overseas students recruited to study in Australia to comply with the conditions of their visas, and report those who do not. Breaches of the Act and the Code can lead to the imposition of sanctions, including their suspension or cancellation from CRICOS. Further information and the full text of the ESOS Act 2000 can be found at the following website:
http://www.dest.gov.au/esos/ESOSguide/foreword.htm
• Bodies dealing with recognition of foreign credentials: National Office of Overseas Skills Recognition (NOOSR); PO Box 1407; Canberra, ACT 2601; email: noosr@dest.gov.au; web: http://www.dest.gov.au/noosr
• Other information sources on recognition of foreign studies: Individual institutions determine the acceptability of foreign qualifications and studies for the purpose of admission or advanced standing (credit). In general, NOOSR's assessment guidelines and advice inform university decisions where relevant. (NOOSR does not assess academic secondary qualifications.).

Accommodation services: A variety of high standard student accommodation is available to suit different budgets and needs. Students can opt to live in university accommodation or with an Australian family. Shared accommodation with other students is common and popular. Institutions provide students with help in finding accommodation and understanding lease and tenancy conditions. Temporary accommodation can be arranged before leaving home allowing time on arrival to consider where and how to be accommodated in the longer term. Student noticeboards and newspapers often advertise rooms, apartments and houses for rent. Further advice is available from each prospective institution.

Work opportunities: International students studying in Australia on a student visa can apply for permission to work once they commence their course. Applying for a student visa with permission to work can be done electronically or on paper using form 157P. A visa with permission to work enables a student to work up to 20 hours a week on a casual basis during course time and full-time during vacation periods. In some cases family members can also apply for

permission to work up to 20 hours a week throughout the year. In the case of Master's and doctorate students and AusAID or defence-sponsored students, family members can apply for permission to work unlimited hours. Family members of a student who has commenced a Masters or Doctorate course must bring evidence from the education provider that the student has started this course. Under certain circumstances dependants of students are permitted to work.
Publications / Websites: Study in Australia book available from Australian Education Centres (AEC) and diplomatic missions in the students country. For further consult www.studyinaustralia.gov.au, the Australian Government website for international students' enquiries.

---

132 Arts Management
420 Elizabeth Street
2010 Surry Hills, N.S.W.
Tel: +61-2-9310-2466
Fax: +61-2-9310-5334
Web: http://www.artsmanagement.com.au
e-mail: enquiries@artsmanagement.com.au

☛ Marten Bequest Travelling Scholarships
Study Domains: architecture, fine arts, graphic arts, music and musicology, performing arts.
Description: 6 scholarships per year for the fields of literature, poetry, drama, ballet, music, art, and architecture.
Subjects: prose, poetry, acting, ballet, singing, instrumental music, painting, sculpture and architecture.
Open to: all people born in Australia; between the ages of 21 and 35 (17 and 35 for ballet).
Place of study: in any country.
Duration: 24 months.
Value: A$18,000 each.
Applications: by end of October (forms available from August), to the above address.

133 Australian Agency for Overseas Development [AusAID]
GPO Box 887
2601 Canberra, A.C.T.
Fax: +61-2-6206-4880
Web: http://www.ausaid.gov.au
e-mail: infoausaid@ausaid.gov.au

☛ Scholarships
Study Domains: development studies.
Scholarships: AusAID Scholarships.
Description: (a) Australian Development Co-operation Scholarships, formerly John Crawford Scholarship Scheme (JCSS); (b) Australian Sponsored Training Scholarships (ASTAS), formerly Sponsored Student Programme (STP); (c) Commonwealth Scholarship and Fellowship Plan (CSFP).
Subjects: wide variety corresponding to needs of developing countries.
Open to: nationals of developing countries with appropriate academic and/or practical experience relevant to training and sufficiently mature to contribute, on their return, to the development process within their country of citizenship; for (b) and (c), individuals must be nominated by their own governments.
Place of study: in Australia, mainly at Australian tertiary institutions.
Duration: varies according to course undertaken; undergraduate: 3 years; specialist and postgraduate: 2 to 6 years; ad hoc practical courses: 2 to 3 months.
Value: variable between countries and institution of enrolment; generally covers annual tuition fees, an annual stipend (tax exempt) and return airfare.
Applications: Australian Diplomatic Mission in respective countries should be contacted for application information.

134 Australian Catholic University (Victoria) [ACU]
International Education Office
PO Box 968
2059 North Sydney, N.S.W.
Tel: +61-2-9739-2929
Fax: +61-2-6739-2905
Web: http://www.acu.edu.au

📖 Undergraduate, Graduate Programmes
Study Domains: arts, cultural studies, education, mechanical engineering, music and musicology, nursing, social work, theology, religion.
Programmes: programme of courses leading to Bachelor's degree, graduate diploma and Master's degree.
Description: (a) Bachelor's degree in arts, business, education (primary and secondary), information systems, human movement studies, music, nursing, science (environmental science), social science, social work; (b) Graduate diploma in arts, education, nursing, religion studies, religious education, social science; (c) Master's degree in arts, education, human movement studies, nursing, music, social science.
Open to: candidates with Australian Year 12 certificate or equivalent (Bachelor's degree only).
Fees: tuition, A$9,000-$10,500 per year.
Applications: by 31 October, to International Education Office. International Education Office, at the above address; tel: +61 2 9739 2072; fax:+61 2 9739 2001; email: international@acu.edu.au.

135 Australian Federation of University Women [AFUW]
Private Box 8
217 Haken Drive
4067 St. Lucia, Queensland
Web: http://www.afuwqfellowships.com/
e-mail: afuwact@afuw.org.au

☛ Scholarships and Fellowships
Study Domains: all major fields.
Scholarships: AFUW Fellowships and Scholarships for Postgraduate Research or Study.
Description: fellowships awarded to women graduates from more than ten countries, for studies in a wide range of disciplines: marine biology; architecture, law, literature, radiography, mathematics, social work, archaeology, economics, molecular biology, management, music, information technology and performing arts.
Open to: women graduates from more than ten countries.
Applications: to Fellowship Convenors, Queensland Fellowship Fund, C/- Academic Dress Hire Service P.O. Box 6083, St. Lucia, Queensland 4067, Australia.

136 Australian Maritime College [AMC]
PO Box 986
7250 Launceston, Tasmania
Tel: +61-3-6335-4711
Fax: +61-3-6326-6493
Web: http://www.amc.edu.au

📖 Undergraduate, Graduate, Postgraduate Programmes
Study Domains: architecture, communication, engineering, fisheries, management.
Programmes: programme of courses leading to Certificate, Diploma, Graduate certificate, Graduate diploma, Bachelor's degree, Master's degree, Doctorate.
Subjects: courses in nautical studies, marine and maritime engineering, naval architecture, maritime electronics, fisheries technology, radio communications, maritime business, fisheries management.
Open to: candidates of all nationalities having completed Year 12 or equivalent.
Duration: 6 months to 4 years.
Applications: by 31 October, to the Admissions Officer.

137 Australian National University [ANU]

International Education Office
0200 Canberra, A.C.T.
Tel: +61-2-6249-5111
Fax: +61-2-6249-5931
Web: http://www.anu.edu.au

📖 Graduate, Postgraduate, Postdoctoral Programmes / Demography

Study Domains: demography and population studies.
Programmes: programme of courses leading to graduate diploma, Master of Arts (M.A.) and Ph.D.
Description: graduate diploma, Master of Arts in demography by course work and Ph.D. in demography by thesis, technical, social, and economic aspects of demography.
Open to: nationals of all countries holding a university degree.
Duration: Diploma: 1 year; Master's degree: 2 years; Ph.D.: 3 years.
Financial assistance: Australian Government Overseas Scholarships are available (all applicants for these awards must be sponsored by their own governments); ANU Ph.D. scholarships.
Applications: at any time, to the Convenor, Graduate Program in Demography, at the above address.

💰 Scholarships

Study Domains: economic and commercial sciences, economy.
Scholarships: ANU Undergraduate Scholarships.
Description: (a) Faculty of Economics and Commerce Undergraduate Scholarships; (b) General Undergraduate Scholarships.
Open to: (a) undergraduate students in the Faculty of economics and commerce from Hong Kong (China), Malaysia, Singapore and Indonesia; (b) candidates of all nationalities.
Duration: the standard duration of the student's degree.
Value: each scholarship covers tuition fees.
Languages: English language proficiency required; contact the University for admission requirements.
Applications: (a) by 17 December; (b) by 16 December, to the above address.

138 Australian Research Council [ARC]

GPO Box 2702
2601 Canberra, A.C.T.
Tel: +61-2-6287-6600
Fax: +61-2-6287-6600
Web: http://www.arc.gov.au/int_activities/default.htm
e-mail: info@arc.gov.au

💰 Australian Research Council Research Fellowships

Study Domains: research.
Description: Australian fellowships for overseas researchers. Fellowships are available under international agreements for the reciprocal exchange of postdoctoral researchers.
(a) ARC International Fellowships funded under international agreements for the reciprocal exchange of postdoctoral researchers, including the Anglo-Australian Observatory (AAO) Fellowship Agreement (managed by the AAO); (b) ARC International Fellowships to fund overseas researcher/s to work in Australia; (c) ARC International Fellowships to fund Australian researcher/s to work in overseas institutions; and Australia-Israel Fellowships co-funded by the ARC and the Australia-Israel Scientific Exchange Foundation; (d) Overseas fellowships for Australian researchers are also available (under reciprocal agreements) through some granting bodies overseas. There are several fellowships available to Australian researchers.
Open to: candidates of any nationality holding a Ph.D. or equivalent qualification and (a) a written agreement of the proposed institution to host the project, preference given to Australian citizens; (b) at least 2 years' post-doctoral experience at the time of application, an excellent academic record, a written agreement of the proposed institution to host the project and evidence of innovative research, preference given to Australian citizens; (c) international recognition as a leader in research; (d) publications in international refereed journals and an established research programme with 3 to 6 years' post-doctoral research experience preferably at an institution other than where the Ph.D. was obtained, awarded on merit to suitably qualified persons, irrespective of nationality.
Value: variable; generally includes salary and research support grant.
Applications: see website http://www.arc.gov.au/apply_grants/linkage_int_fellow.htm for further information.

💰 Scholarships

139 Australian Vice-Chancellors' Committee [AVC]

PO Box 1142
2601 Canberra, A.C.T.
Tel: +61-2-6285-8200
Fax: +61-2-6285-8211
Web: http://sunset.avcc.edu.au
e-mail: general@avcc.edu.au

💰 Fellowships

Study Domains: all major fields.
Scholarships: postgraduate Fellowships.
Description: (a) Commonwealth Scholarship and Fellowship Plan (CSFP) awards; (b) Australian European Awards Program (AEAP).
Subjects: unrestricted study, for postgraduate study or research.
Open to: (a) graduate students from the United Kingdom (4 awards), Canada (2 awards), and New Zealand (2 awards); (b) graduate students from various European countries: Croatia, Finland, France, Germany, Greece, Hungary, Ireland, Italy, Netherlands, Slovenia and Switzerland.
Place of study: in Australian tertiary institutions.
Duration: (a) 2 to 3 years (possible extension if justified); (b) 12 months (not renewable).
Value: living allowance, plus travel to and from Australia, all compulsory fees and health cover.
Applications: (a) by 30 June for awards tenable 7 months later through CSFP authority in applicant's country; (b) by 31 May for awards tenable 8 months later through the Australian Embassy in applicant's country.

140 Central Queensland University [CQU]

Bruce Highway
CQ Mail Center Rockhampton
4702 Rockhampton, Queensland
Tel: +61-7-4930-9724
Fax: +61-7-4930-2007
Web: http://www.cqu.edu.au
e-mail: international-enquiries@cqu.edu.au.

📖 Undergraduate, Graduate, Postgraduate Programmes

Study Domains: agriculture, audio-visual media, business, communication, computer science, education, engineering, health and hygiene, humanities and arts, information science, law, music and musicology, performing arts, recreation and leisure, sciences, social sciences, technology.
Programmes: programme of courses leading to Bachelor's degree, Master's degree, Graduate diploma, Associate diploma and PhD degree.
Description: (a) Bachelor of Arts: (communications and media studies, humanities and social sciences), applied sciences (biology, chemistry, physics), business (accounting, human resource management, information systems, management and marketing), engineering (civil, electrical, mechanical), teaching, health science; (b) Master of Engineering: business, applied science, arts, education, health administration; (c) Graduate diploma in: management, applied computing, information technology, primary and secondary teaching, information systems management, accounting, taxation, health administration and information systems; (d) Associate diploma in aquatic resource management, biological laboratory techniques, information technology, engineering, industrial instrumentation, applied chemistry, education and school support; (f) Ph.D./Doctoral programmes are available in all faculties.

Subjects: agriculture, environment; business, law; communications, media; Central Queensland Conservatorium of Music (Mackay Campus Only); creative and performing arts; education; engineering, technology; health, recreation; humanities, social sciences; information technology; sciences.
Open to: candidates of all nationalities holding a senior certificate (matriculation) or equivalent qualifications; TOEFL, IELTS or equivalent evidence of English competence required for entry into formal programmes; GPA 2.5 over a minimum of 12 months of university study (or the equivalent) for Study Abroad programmes.
Duration: (a) to (d) formal study: 6 months (semester abroad) to 4 years for some full degree programmes (courses begin in February or July).
Applications: any time prior to commencement of academic year, to the Director, International Education, at the above address. Admission form for full-fee international applicants is available at http://www.international.cqu.edu.au/applying/appforadmissio n.pdf.

🐦 Graduate, Postgraduate Awards

Study Domains: all major fields, business administration.
Scholarships: (a) Master of Business Administration; (b) Vice Chancellors Scholarship; (c) International Postgraduate Research Award (IPRA); (d) International Postgraduate Research Scholarship (IPRS).
Open to: candidates of all nationalities; (b) to new international students.
Academic requirements: (a), (b) good grades and work experience, assessed on a case-by-case basis; (c), (d) Honours 1 or equivalent.
Place of study: (a), (b) at Rockhampton Campus.
Value: (a) 33% tuition reduction, approximately A$9,000 per year; (b) 20% tuition reduction, up to A$2,400 per year: (c) tuition: up to A$18,500, including relocation allowance, research support grant, thesis allowance; (d) tuition fees and overseas health coverage for 2-year Master's and 3-year doctoral programmes.
Applications: (a) January and April; contact r.wallace@cqu.edu.au; (b) January, April and September; contact: n.swanson@cqu.edu.au. (c), (d) December; contact: n.swanson@cqu.edu.au.

141 Charles Sturt University [CSU]

International Division
Locked Bag 669
2678 Wagga Wagga, New South Wales
Tel: +61-2-6338-4200
Fax: +61-2-6338-4838
Web: http://www.csu.edu.au

📖 Graduate, Postgraduate Programmes

Study Domains: administration, agriculture, applied arts, business, education, information science, international business, liberal arts, technology.
Programmes: programme of courses leading to Master's degree, Ph.D. and graduate certificate/diploma.
Description: (a) graduate certificate/diploma in business administration, agricultural studies, information systems; (b) M.B.A. in international business; (c) M.App. Science in agriculture, science and technology, environmental science, information technology; (d) M.Education in education; (e) M.Arts in communication, arts (honours); (f) M.Social Science in social science (honours);
(g) Ph.D. in arts, education, science and agriculture.
Open to: candidates of all nationalities who matriculate to recognized university standards and pass a test of English proficiency; documentary evidence of educational qualifications required; extra help in English language available.
Duration: 1 to 3 years depending on the course; courses begin in late February.
Fees: tuition, A$10,500-$14,500; medical insurance over a 4-years period up to A$1,248; room and board, A$130 per week.
Applications: to the International Office at the above address.

📖 Undergraduate Programmes

Study Domains: administration, agriculture, applied arts, biology, business, education, food industry, information science, liberal arts, nursing.
Programmes: Programme of courses leading to Bachelor's degree; also double degree programme.
Description: (a) Business: accounting, finance, business management, electronic commerce, international business management, human resources management, marketing tourism management; (b) Social Science: criminal justice, psychology; (c) Arts: graphic design, arts, television production, psychology, communication, acting for screen and stage, design for theatre and television, journalism, multimedia, public relations and organizational communication, photography; (d) Education: early childhood, secondary mathematics, primary, human movement, technology and applied studies; (e) Applied science: medical imaging, agriculture, environmental analysis, applied maths, biotechnology, food technology, parks and recreation, nuclear medicine technology, business, ecotourism, equine studies, food science, horticulture (environmental horticulture, production horticulture); (f) Information Technology and spatial information systems science; (g) Nursing; (h) Health Science: occupational therapy; nutrition and dietetics, speech pathology; (i) Medicine; (j) Agriculture; (k) Environmental Science;
(l) Science, (m) Associate Diploma in Jewellery.
Open to: candidates of all nationalities who matriculate to recognized university standards and pass a test of English proficiency; documentary evidence of educational qualifications required.
Duration: 1 to 4 years depending on the course; courses begin in late February or July.
Fees: tuition, A$10,500-$14,500; medical insurance over a 4-year period up to A$1,248; room and board, approx. A$130 per week.
Applications: to the International Office, at the above address.

🐦 Scholarships

Study Domains: agriculture, arts, business, education, health and hygiene, sciences.
Scholarships: Postgraduate Research Scholarships.
Description: (a) International Postgraduate Research Scholarships; (b) Charles Sturt University (CSU) Postgraduate Research Studentships.
Open to: candidates of all nationalities who qualified for a postgraduate research course.
Duration: 1 to 3 years depending on the course; courses begin in late February.
Value: (a) for tuition fees only; (b) scholarship provides a stipend (2002 stipend was A$17,609).
Applications: by 1 November, to the International Office at the above address.

142 Curtin University of Technology

GPO Box U1987
6001 Perth, Western Australia
Tel: +61-8-9266-2000
Fax: +61-8-9266-2255
Web: http://www.curtin.edu.au

📖 Undergraduate, Graduate, Postgraduate Programmes

Study Domains: all major fields, agriculture, education, engineering, humanities and arts, sciences.
Programmes: Programme of courses leading to Bachelor's degree, Master's degree and Ph.D.
Subjects: courses in engineering and science, education and social sciences, humanities, business and administration, health sciences, agribusiness and agriculture, mining.
Open to: candidates of all nationalities, with competency in English (IELTS Overall Band Score of 6.0 or over 550 TOEFL), completion of one year of study, in good academic standing (minimum of 2.75 GPA).
Duration: 2 to 5 years; courses begin in February and July.
Financial assistance: scholarships available for qualified applicants through AusAID.
Applications: by March of the preceding year, to the Director, International Office, at the above address.

Scholarships

Study Domains: all major fields.
Scholarships: Curtin U. of T. Scholarships.
Description: (a) Curtin Overseas Student Scholarship; (b) Curtin University Alumni Singapore Scholarship (only 1 scholarship will be current at any one time); (c) Overseas Postgraduate Research Scholarship.
Subjects: unrestricted study subjects.
Open to: (a) overseas students who have completed 2 full years of study at Curtin University of Technology; the scholarship is awarded for academic excellence; whilst in receipt of this award students may not hold another scholarship or be bonded to an employer without the written permission of the Academic Registrar, Commonwealth Government Subsidized Students are not eligible; (b) open to Singaporean citizens who are about to graduate or have graduated from the Western Australian Institute of Technology/Curtin University of Technology who are seeking full-time postgraduate study at Curtin University; (c) awarded on academic merit and research capacity to suitably qualified overseas graduates eligible to commence a higher degree by research.
Place of study: (a) and (b) Curtin University of Technology; (c) an Australian higher education institution to undertake a full-time Master's degree by research or Ph.D. degree.
Duration: (a) 1 year, full-time study.
Value: (a) overseas student tuition fee is paid; (b) annual stipend will be paid to cover the student's living expenses and tuition fee; (c) overseas student tuition fee paid, no other allowances are covered under this award.
Applications: (a) by November; (b) by August; (c) by September, to the Scholarships Officer, Academic Registrar's Office, at the above address.

143   Deakin University

Geelong
VIC 3 Victoria
Tel: +61-3-5227-1100
Fax: +61-3-5227-2001
Web: http://www.deakin.edu.au
e-mail: vpa@deakin.edu.au

Undergraduate, Graduate, Postgraduate Programmes

Study Domains: all major fields.
Programmes: Programme of courses leading to Bachelor's degree, Graduate certificate, Graduate diploma, Master's degree and Doctor's of philosophy (Ph.D.).
Description: (a) Bachelor's degree in applied science, architecture, arts, building, commerce, education, engineering, law, letters, nursing, science, social work, teaching, technology; (b) Graduate Certificate in engineering, professional writing, quantity surveying, media studies, environmental and heritage interpretation; (c) Graduate Diploma of applied science, aquaculture, children's literature, development studies, education, health education, interpreting and translating management, professional writing, media studies, special education, teaching LOTE, TESOL, women's studies; (d) Master's degree by course work in aquaculture, arts, development studies, education, human nutrition, international trade and investment law, laws; (e) Master's degree by research in applied science, architecture, arts, arts education, commerce, nursing, building, economics; (f) Doctor of philosophy.
Open to: candidates who satisfy overseas students entry and English proficiency requirements; with: (a) VCE or overseas equivalent; (b) and (c) undergraduate degree from a recognized university and/or relevant work experience; (d) undergraduate honours degree from a recognized university plus relevant work experience; (e) undergraduate honours degree from a recognized university; (f) eligibility assessed on inquiry.
Duration: (a) 3 to 5 years; double degree: 4 to 5 years; (b) 6 months; (c) 1 year; (d) and (e) 1 to 3 years; (f) up to 3 years.
Applications: to Deakin International, at the above address.

Scholarships

Study Domains: all major fields.
Scholarships: Postgraduate Scholarships for Research.

Description: any field of study offered by a faculty in the University.
Open to: international students who meet the University's entry requirements; candidates for Master's degree or Ph.D. research must satisfy Deakin's Research Committee that they are competent to undertake a higher degree by research.
Duration: Ph.D., from 2 to 4 years; Master's degree, from 1 to 2 years; Doctor of Education, from 3 to 4 years.
Applications: by 16 October, to the above address.

144   Edith Cowan University [ECU]

Pearson Street
6018 Churchlands, Western Australia
Tel: +61-8-9273-8333
Fax: +61-8-9387-7095
Web: http://www.cowan.edu.au
e-mail: d.earl@cowan.edu.au

Undergraduate, Graduate, Postgraduate Programmes

Study Domains: all major fields.
Programmes: programme of courses leading to Associate diploma, diploma, Bachelor's degree, graduate diploma, postgraduate diploma, Master's degree, Doctorate.
Description: (a) Associate diploma and Associate degree courses in arts, education, social science, science and performing arts; (b) Diploma courses in music and performing arts; (c) Bachelor's degree in science, arts, business and commerce, education, engineering, health science, nursing, psychology, social science, technology; (d) graduate diploma in science, arts, business, education, social science; (e) postgraduate diploma in business, nursing; (f) Master's programmes in science, arts, business and commerce, education, engineering, health science, nursing, social science, music, visual arts, art therapy; (g) doctoral programmes in arts, business and commerce, education, engineering, health and human services, science and technology and interdisciplinary programmes.
Open to: candidates of university entrance level; TOEFL required; intensive English language courses available.
Duration: 2 to 3 years; all courses begin in February.
Applications: by 30 November of the previous year for semester 1 intake or 30 May for semester 2 intake, to the International Students Office at the above address.

145   Flinders University of South Australia

GPO Box 2100
5001 Adelaide, South Australia
Tel: +61-8-8201-3911
Fax: +61-8-8201-3000
Web: http://www.flinders.edu.au/international
e-mail: study.abroad@flinders.edu.au

Undergraduate, Graduate Programmes

Study Domains: all major fields.
Programmes: programme of courses leading to Bachelor's and Master's degrees.
Description: (a) Courses in all major fields; (b) Master's of International Business Administration; (c) Master's of Arts in international relations.
Open to: (a) candidates having completed secondary school at a satisfactory level; undergraduate candidates having completed tertiary qualifications at a satisfactory level; eligible postgraduate candidates; (b) holders of appropriate honours degree with at least 2 years' work experience; (c) holders of a completed degree in political science or international relations.
Applications: to the International Office, at the above address.

Scholarships

Study Domains: all major fields.
Scholarships: Flinders University Scholarships.
Description: (a) Polytechnics of Singapore Scholarship Scheme; (b) International Student Merit Scholarship (Graduate Entry Medical Program - GEMP); (c) Alumni Association Honours Scholarship; (d) International Postgraduate Research Scholarships (IPRS).
Open to: (a) selected graduates of diploma courses from the Singapore Polytechnic, Ngee Ann Polytechnic, Nanyang Polytechnic or the Temasek Polytechnic who are accepted to

undertake an undergraduate degree course offered by the Faculty of Science and Engineering; (b) selected students in the international quota for the Graduate Entry Medical Program (GEMP); (c) international students offered admission to an honours course at Flinders. Awarded to the applicant with the best grade point average in the three years of undergraduate study; (d) for any Master's degree by research or Ph.D. study.
Value: (a) 25% remission on standard international student tuition fee; (b) 50% remission of annual tuition fee: (c) A$10,000 per year; (d) full student tuition fees; and student health coverage for recipient and dependants. This scholarship is provided for up to three years for Ph.D. studies and up to two years for a Master's degree by research studies, subject to satisfactory progress.
Applications: (b) further information and application form is available from the GEMP website; (c) from the Scholarships Office from mid-November; applications must be received by 15 December, the winner is announced in January.

146 Greece (Embassy of) [GO]
9 Turrana Street
2600 Yarralumla, A.C.T.
Tel: +61-62-273-3011

Scholarships
Study Domains: all major fields, cultural studies, Greek, languages.
Scholarships: Greek Language and Culture Scholarships.
Description: (a) Australian-Greek Awards (11-15); unrestricted but of a nature that such opportunities for study would not be available in Australia; (b) Aristotle Scholarships (6); improvement of Greek language skills; (c) Greek Government Scholarship; postgraduate studies or research; (d) State Scholarships Foundation (10); postgraduate studies in Greece leading to a doctoral degree; (e) State Scholarships Foundation (5); modern Greek language.
Open to: (a) Australian citizens with some knowledge of Greek language for training, studying or furthering professional experience in Greece; (b) and (c) all Australian citizens; (d) Australian citizens of Greek origin; (e) teachers, residents of Greek-speaking regions.
Place of study: (a) according to individual awardees' programme; (b) University of Thessaloniki (Greece); (c), (d) and (e) any university in Greece.
Duration: (a) 2 to 6 months; (b) 1 year; (c) 10 months; (d) and (e) 1 year, renewable up to 3 years.
Value: return economy class excursion air fares to Greece; weekly allowance towards living expenses payable to awardees for the period of their approved programme.
Applications: to the Education Attaché, at the above address.

147 Griffith University [GU]
Nathan
4111 Brisbane, Queensland
Tel: +61-7-3875-7340
Fax: +61-7-3875-7507
Web: http://www.gu.edu.au
e-mail: griffith.university@gu.edu.au

Undergraduate, Graduate and Postgraduate Programmes
Study Domains: arts, business, ecology, environment, education, engineering, international studies, law, music and musicology, nursing, tourism, hotel and catering management.
Programmes: Bachelor's degree, Master's degree and Ph.D.
Subjects: humanities and social sciences, business, commerce and management, education, health sciences, science, technology and information technology, engineering, creative, visual and performing arts; intensive English language courses also available.
Duration: 1 semester to 4 years; all courses begin in February or July.
Fees: tuition fees approx. A$9,000 per year; living expenses, approx. A$10,000 per year.
Applications: at any time, to the Admissions Officer, International Centre at the above address.

Scholarships
Study Domains: all major fields, arts, business, ecology, environment, education, engineering, health and hygiene, international studies, law, music and musicology, tourism, hotel and catering management.
Scholarships: Postgraduate Research Scholarships.
Description: approximately 3 scholarships available in the following study areas; business and commerce, engineering and technology, education, health, environment, languages and international studies, law and justice, tourism and leisure, humanities, music and art, science, nursing.
Open to: nationals of all countries, with an honours degree from a recognized tertiary institution, or equivalent.
Duration: M. Phil.: 24 months; Ph.D.: 36 months, renewable for 6 months under exceptional circumstances.
Value: living allowance, relocation and thesis allowance; partial reimbursement of travel costs.
Applications: by 31 October, to the Postgraduate Scholarships Officer.

148 Griffith University, Queensland Conservatorium of Music [GU]
P.O. Box 3428
South Brisbane Business Centre
4101 South Brisbane, Queensland
Tel: +61-7-3875-7340
Fax: +61-7-3875-7507
Web: http://www.gu.edu.au
e-mail: griffith.university@gu.edu.au

Music Study Programmes
Study Domains: music and musicology, performing arts.
Programmes: Graduate Diploma of Music; Bachelor of Music; Bachelor of Arts in Music; Bachelor of Music Performance; Diploma of Music; Master of Music.
Open to: students with suitable level of music performance; theory-audition.
Duration: 1 to 4 years; courses begin in February.
Applications: by the first week of August, to the Registrar; audition forms are available in March.

149 International Programme Tasmania [TAFE]
GPO Box TAFE
7001 Hobart TAS
Tel: +61-3 -6233-5487
Fax: +61-3-6233-4865
Web: http://www.tafe.tas.edu.au

Undergraduate Programmes
Study Domains: all major fields.
Programmes: (a) Associate diplomas in art, banking, applied science, child care, community service, graphic design, horticulture, engineering, electrical engineering, civil engineering, travel and tourism, office administration, mechanical engineering, information technology, agriculture; (b) certificates in travel and tourism, beautician studies, restaurant service, cookery, computing, fashion industry studies, mechanics, commercial studies, racing and breeding practices; (c) Advanced Certificates in developmental disability, sound production, laboratory technology, horticultural technology, engineering, CAD; (d) diplomas in management, marketing and accounting; (e) advanced diplomas in children's services and medical laboratory technology.
Open to: candidates of all nationalities, aged over 16; with 10 to 12 years of educational experience.
Duration: (a) 2 years; (b) 6 months to 1 year; (c) 1 year; (d) and (e) 3 years.
Applications: by 30 January, to TAFE International Education Programme, at the above address.

150 James Cook University of North Queensland [JCU]
Townsville Campus
Angus Smith Drive
4811 Douglas, Townsville, Queenslan
Tel: +61-7-4781 4111
Fax: +61 7 4779 6371
Web: http://www.jcu.edu.au
e-mail: registrar@jcu.edu.au

📖 Undergraduate, Graduate, Postgraduate Programmes

Study Domains: all major fields.
Programmes: a) Associate diploma courses in applied photography and commercial art, museum studies, women's studies, diploma of communications; (b) Bachelor's degree courses in: administration of tourism, administration, accounting, applied science in environmental studies, arts, biomedical sciences, commerce, community welfare, construction management, economics, education, engineering, information technology, journalism, laws, management, music, nursing science, psychology, science, social work, theatre, visual arts; (c) graduate diplomas in accounting, arts, community museum management, computer science, Aboriginal and Islander secondary education, management, material anthropology, Melanesian studies, museum curatorship, public health and tropical medicine, tourism; (d) postgraduate diplomas in commerce, economics, engineering, science; (e) Master's degrees in administration, arts, business administration, commerce, creative arts, economics, education, engineering science, laws, letters, museum studies, public health and tropical medicine, science, social policy, social work; (f) Ph.D. in anthropology, archaeology, psychology, botany, chemistry, biochemistry, chemical engineering, electrical engineering, geology, nursing, physics, physiology, remote sensing, tropical health, tropical marine studies, civil and systems engineering, mechanical engineering, commerce, human geography, computer science, mathematics and statistics, creative arts, history and politics, social work, management, marine biology, material anthropology, museum studies, modern languages, physical geography, tourism, tropical agriculture, biomedical and tropical veterinary science, zoology.
Open to: candidates of any nationality, with at least the equivalent of Australian tertiary entrance requirements; if English is not the native language, proficiency in English must be confirmed via IELTS or TOEFL; minimum scores accepted are IELTS 6.5 (5 minimum in all four sub-tests) or TOEFL 550, with a minimum TWE of 5.0.
Duration: (a) 2 years; (b) 3 to 4 years; (c) to (f) depends on programme.
Fees: approx. A$7,500 per year.
Financial assistance: small number of postgraduate scholarships; applicants requiring financial assistance should approach the Australian Diplomatic Post or Government Scholarship Office.
Applications: full-time international students submit the form by 15 December for the undergraduate programme; or 30 October for the postgraduate programme, to the above address.

151   La Trobe University [LTU]
Plenty Road
3083 Bundoora, Victoria
Tel: +61-3-9479-1111
Fax: +61-3-9479-3090
Web: http://www.latrobe.edu.au
e-mail: study@latrobe.edu.au

🎓 Scholarships

Study Domains: all major fields.
Scholarships: research scholarships: limited number available on a highly competitive basis.
Subjects: agriculture, applied mathematics, archaeology, art history, behavioural health sciences, biochemistry, botany, cinema studies, communication disorders, computer science, economics, education, electronic and communication science, English, French, genetics and human variation, geology, health administration and education, history, human biosciences, inorganic and analytical chemistry, Italian, legal studies, linguistics, mathematics, microbiology, music, nursing, occupational therapy, organic and physical chemistry, orthoptics, philosophy, physics, physiotherapy, podiatry, politics, prosthetics, psychology, pure mathematics, religious studies,   social work, sociology, Spanish, statistics, zoology.
Open to: students from any country holding an honours degree from a recognized university, equivalent to a 4-year degree with first-class honours from an Australian university; candidates proficient in English and able to produce evidence of substantial written work.

Duration: Master's degree: 2 years; Ph.D.: up to 3.5 years, renewable each year subject to satisfactory progress.
Value: stipend plus allowance for each dependent child; thesis allowance; small travel allowance.
Applications: by 30 September for international applicants; by 31 October for New Zealanders; international applications to the International Programmes Office, to the above address.

152   Macquarie University
International office
2109 North Ryde, N.S.W.
Tel: +61-2-9850-7346
Fax: +61-2-9850-9198
Web: http://www.mq.edu.au/international
e-mail: iso@mq.edu.au

📖 Undergraduate, Graduate, Postgraduate Programmes

Study Domains: all major fields.
Programmes: Bachelor's, Master's, Ph.D. degrees (distance courses available).
Open to: candidates of all nationalities with secondary school leaving certificate; English language proficiency for undergraduates: IELTS 6.0; postgraduate IELTS 6.5.
Fees: undergraduate programmes, A$12,000-$18,000; postgraduate programmes, A$6,000-$30,000.
Applications: 2 intakes per year in March and July.

🎓 Scholarships

Study Domains: all major fields.
Scholarships: International Macquarie University Research Scholarship.
Description: areas of research of Macquarie University.
Open to: Ph.D. or Master's degree; strict conditions apply.
Duration: term of Ph.D. study.
Value: 3 levels of funding: A$17,000, A$5,000, A$4,000 per year.
Applications: accepted all year round.

153   Marcus Oldham College
Private Bag 116
Geelong Mail Centre
3221 Victoria
Tel: +61-5-2433-3533
Fax: +61-5-2441-263
Web: http://www.ne.com.au/marcus

📖 Farm Business Management Programme

Study Domains: accounting, agriculture, business, business administration, veterinary sciences.
Programmes: diploma and advanced certificate.
Description: courses in farm business management, horse business management and agribusiness administration.
Open to: candidates 18 and over who have completed the prescribed educational standard in their country and have had at least 1 year of practical experience.
Duration: Diploma in farm business management: 3 years (1 year academic session, 1 year practical session, 1 year final academic session); Advanced certificate in horse business management and advanced certificate in agribusiness administration: 1 year academic sessions with practical sessions included.
Applications: at any time during the year to the Principal at the above address.

154   Monash University
Room B02, Building 3.4
Wellington Road
3168 Clayton, Victoria
Tel: +61-3-9905-4000
Fax: +61-3-9905-4007
Web: http://www.monash.edu.au

📖 Undergraduate, Graduate Programmes

Study Domains: all major fields.
Programmes: Bachelor's and Master's degrees in arts, science, engineering, law, business, economics, education, computing and information science, medicine, tourism.
Open to: students who have a Year 12 school certificate or equivalent or who have partially or fully completed studies for a degree at another recognized institution.

Duration: 3 to 6 years depending on course.
Fees: given on application.
Applications: enquiries should be addressed to the Admissions Officer, Monash International, 5th Floor, 26 Sir John Monash Drive, Caulfield, Victoria 3145.

⚓ Graduate, Postgraduate Scholarships

Study Domains: all major fields.
Scholarships: (a) Monash Graduate Scholarships (approx. 125 per year); (b) Monash Silver Jubilee Postgraduate Scholarship.
Description: unrestricted studies.
Open to: graduates of any university, who hold at least an upper second-class honours Bachelor's degree or the equivalent, or undergraduates completing the final year of a course leading to such a degree.
Duration: up to 2 years for a research Master's degree; up to 3 years with a possibility of an additional 6 months extension for a Ph.D.
Value: annual stipend plus allowances.
Applications: by 31 October, to the Research Training and Support Branch.

155 Monash University, Victorian College of Pharmacy [VCP]

Parkville Campus
381 Royal Parade
3052 Parkville, Victoria
Tel: +61-3-903-9000
Fax: +61-3-990-39581
Web: http://www.vcp.monash.edu.au/index.html

📖 Undergraduate Programme / Pharmacy

Study Domains: pharmacy and pharmacology.
Programmes: Bachelor of Pharmacy.
Open to: students with an equivalent of 3 good (Grade B-A) GCE advanced level passes in chemistry and mathematics and physics or biology.
Duration: 3 years beginning in February.
Applications: by 30 November; write to the above address for an application form.

156 Murdoch University

South Street
6150 Murdoch, Western Australia
Tel: +61-8-9360-2750/6177
Fax: +61-8-9310-5090
Web: http://www.murdoch.edu.au/international
e-mail: internatl@central.murdoch.edu.au

📖 Undergraduate, Graduate, Postgraduate Programmes

Study Domains: all major fields.
Programmes: Bachelor's, Master's and Ph.D.
Description: (a) Bachelor's degree in Aboriginal and Islander studies, Asian studies, Asian and business studies, Australian studies, British and European studies, biological sciences, biotechnology, chemistry, Chinese studies, commerce, communication studies, computer science, divinity, economics, education studies, English and comparative literature, environmental science, general studies, history, information systems, Japanese studies, law, marketing and media, mathematics, mineral science, philosophy, physics, politics, population, resources and technology, primary teacher education, psychology, public administration, secondary teacher education, sociology, Southeast Asian studies, theatre and drama, theological studies, theology and education studies, veterinary biology, applied veterinary medicine, women's studies; (b) Graduate and Postgraduate diplomas in applied mathematics, applied statistics, development studies, education, education studies, environmental science, journalism, mineral science, science (biotechnology and energy studies), theological studies, women's studies, environmental impact assessment, physics, public history, public policy, science and technology policy, social research and evaluation; (c) postgraduate coursework and research degrees in applied psychology, biological and environmental sciences, economics and commerce, development studies, humanities, law, mathematical and physical sciences, social sciences, science and technology policy, public policy, business administration, education, veterinary studies; (d) Study Abroad Programme in all fields.

Open to: nationals of all countries having completed an appropriate school leaving examination or a recognized post-secondary school certificate; proficiency in English essential; (d) completed at least one year at a recognized tertiary institution and been in good academic standing at their host institution or have a GPA of 3. on a 4.0 scale, TOEFL 570 and IELTS 6.5 with no score less than 6 on any individual band; proficiency in English essential.
Duration: (a) 3 to 4 years; (b) 1 year; (c) 2 to 4 years; (d) 6 to 12 months; all courses begin in February and July.
Financial assistance: (a) to (c) applicants from developing countries have scholarship opportunities through the Australian Development Co-operation Scholarships (ADCOS) for undergraduate and postgraduate studies; applicants for postgraduate research degrees are eligible for the Overseas Postgraduate Research Scholarship (OPRS); holders of OPRS may also be awarded by the University a stipend equivalent to the Murdoch University Research Studentship to cover living expenses; applications and enquiries regarding ADCOS should be directed to the nearest Australian diplomatic mission or Australian Education Centre in the applicant's country; information regarding OPRS is also available from the University; (d) none.
Applications: (a) to (c) to the International Office at the above address; (d) 2 months before the start date of each semester to Roselynn Lang, study abroad and exchange co-ordinator.

157 New South Wales Department of Education and Training [TAFENSW]

PO Box 707
827–839 George St
2007 Broadway, N.S.W.
Tel: +61-2-9217-4801/4802
Fax: +61-2-9217-4060/6721
Web: http://www.tafensw.edu.au/international
e-mail: isc@det.nsw.ed.au

📖 Certificate, Diplomas and Advanced Diplomas

Study Domains: all major fields.
Programmes: Certificate I-IV, Diplomas and Advanced Diplomas, Technical and Further Education (TAFE).
Subjects: applied science, art and design, aviation, building and construction, business and office studies, computer studies, engineering, fashion, hospitality, travel and tourism studies, marine and maritime studies, manufacturing, rural studies and tertiary preparation.
Open to: candidates of any country, proficiency in English and academic qualifications required.
Duration: from 6 months to 3 years.
Applications: to International Students' Centre at the above address.

158 Northern Territory University [NTU]

PO Box 40146
Casuarina Campus, Ellengowan Drive
0909 Darwin, Northern Territory
Tel: +61-8-8946-6666
Fax: +61-8-8927-0612
Web: http://www.ntu.edu.au
e-mail: marketing@darwin.ntu.edu.au

📖 Undergraduate, Graduate, Postgraduate Programmes

Study Domains: all major fields, arts, business, education, engineering, information science, law, management, nursing, sciences.
Programmes: (a) Ph.D.; (b) Master's degrees and graduate diplomas; (c) Bachelor's degrees; (d) Associate diplomas; (e) certificates.
Subjects: courses in business, science, arts, education, law, engineering, hospitality management, nursing, and information technology.
Open to: students of any nationality, holding appropriate qualifications.
Duration: (a) and (c) 3 years; (b) 1 to 2 years; (d) 2 years; (e) 1 year; courses begin in late February and mid-July.
Applications: 2 months prior to semester commencement; to International Student Unit, Student Services Section, at the above address.

159   Queensland University of Technology [QUT]

P.O. Box 2434
George Street
4001 Brisbane, Queensland
Tel: +61-7-3864-2111
Fax: +61-7-3864-1510
Web: http://www.qut.edu.au
e-mail: www.international@qut.edu.au

Teacher Certificate, Undergraduate, Graduate, Postgraduate Programmes

Study Domains: all major fields.
Programmes: pre-service teacher education courses in all major fields; Bachelor's degree; postgraduate diploma; Master's degrees; Ph.D. degrees.
Open to: candidates of all nationalities with secondary-school certificate.
Duration: variable; depending on programme.
Applications: in advance for start of academic year; to the above address.

Peace Scholarship Trust

Study Domains: all major fields.
Scholarships: (a) diploma programmes; (b) non-diploma programmes.
Subjects: all disciplines/subjects available.
Open to: candidates from Mexico and Colombia.
Duration: one semester, non-renewable.
Value: (a) for study abroad tuition, A$7,500; (b) 12 weeks English (EAP) tuition, A$5,600.
Applications: to the above address, referring to Peace Scholarship, http://www.idp.com/globalpeace. For more information, please contact eleanor.rivers@idp.com.

160   Royal Melbourne Institute of Technology [RMIT]

International Services
GPO Box 2303U
3001 Melbourne, Victoria
Tel: +61-3-9479-1111
Fax: +61-3-9478-5814
Web: http://www.latrobe.edu.au
e-mail: study@latrobe.edu.au

Undergraduate, Graduate, Postgraduate Programmes

Study Domains: all major fields.
Programmes: certificates, advanced certificates, Associate diplomas, Bachelor's degree, graduate diplomas, Master's degree and Ph.D. degrees.
Subjects: architecture/building construction, applied, biomedical and health sciences, business, art and design, communications, computing, education, ELICOS (English language courses), engineering, marine courses, nursing.
Open to: students from any country; entry requirements depend on course.
Duration: 1 to 5 years depending on course.
Applications: no closing date; students are encouraged to apply early.

Scholarships

Study Domains: all major fields.
Scholarships: RMIT University International Scholarships.
Description: 50 scholarships offered every year for study in all major fields.
Open to: all international students enrolled at RMIT University.
Duration: yearly or for the duration of the course.
Value: partial tuition fee.

161   Southern Cross University [SCU]

PO Box 157
2480 Lismore, N.S.W.
Tel: +61-2-6620-3000
Fax: +61-2-6622-1300
Web: http://www.scu.edu.au

Associate Degree Programmes

Study Domains: applied sciences, business, computer science, law.
Programmes: Associate Degree Programme in: (a) Information technology; (b) Law (paralegal studies); (c) Applied science (resource technology).
Open to: nationals of any country with secondary school leaving certificate.
Duration: 2 years.
Fees: A$246 Union fee, plus: (a) and (b) A$10,000 per year; (c) A$15,000 per year.
Applications: by end of October to the above address.

Graduate Certificate Programmes

Study Domains: accounting, business, business administration, economic and commercial sciences, finance, management, marketing.
Programmes: Graduate Certificate Programmes in: (a) Management: management, business administration, accounting, finance, economics, marketing, business; (b) Organizational development and training; (c) Health science.
Open to: (a) and (b) graduates of any nationality with one year's work experience; (c) candidates of any nationality with a degree in nursing or related area; work experience and appropriate professional qualifications.
Duration: (a) 6 months; (b) 6 months beginning in February; (c) 1 year.
Fees: A$246 Union fee, plus (a) A$6,000; (b) $5,000; (c) $12,000.
Applications: by end of March, July or November; to the above address.

Graduate Diploma Programmes

Study Domains: business, education.
Programmes: Graduate Diploma Programme in: (a) Management; (b) Education (secondary); (c) Education (training and development); (d) Organizational development and training.
Open to: nationals of any country: (a) who are graduates with at least 1 year's work experience; (b) who must have completed a degree with at two-ninths of the course subject related; (c) and (d) hold an approved degree, diploma or equivalent, plus a minimum of 2 years' work experience.
Duration: 1 year.
Fees: A$246 Union fee, plus per year: (a) A$12,000; (b) and (d) A$10,000.
Applications: (a) by end of March, July or November; (b) and (c) by end of October; to the above address.

Master's Degree Programmes

Study Domains: accounting, business administration, education.
Programmes: Master's degree Programme in: (a) Accounting studies; (b) Business administration; (c) Education; (d) Education training and development; (e) Organizational training and development; (f) Health science.
Open to: candidates of any nationality: (a) with a degree in any discipline; (b) who are graduates with at least one year's work experience; (c) with a 4-year qualification, plus relevant work experience in teaching/education; (d) and (e) with a 4-year qualification plus relevant work experience or 3 years' full-time and relevant work experience in training and development; (f) candidates of any nationality with a degree in nursing or related area, appropriate work experience and professional qualification.
Duration: (a) 1 year (12 units); (b) 1 year full-time; (c) and (d) 2 years full-time; (f) 1 to 1-1/2 years; courses begin in February.
Fees: A$246 Union fee, plus: (a) and (b) A$18,000 per year; (c), (d) and (e) A$10,000 per year; (f) A$12,000 per year.
Applications: (a) and (b) by end of March, July or November; (c), (d) and (e) by end of October, to the above address.

Undergraduate, Graduate Programmes

Study Domains: arts, business, finance, law, sciences, tourism, hotel and catering management.
Programmes: (a) Bachelor of Law; (b) Master of Business; (c) Master of Arts; (d) Master of Science; (e) Graduate Certificate in International Tourism Management; (f) Master of International Tourism Management; (g)

Graduate Diploma of International Tourism Management.
Open to: candidates of any country with (a) secondary
school leaving certificate; (b) to (e) relevant Bachelor's
degree; (f) and (g) relevant work experience or Graduate
Certificate or Diploma in International Tourism Management.
Duration: (a) 3 years; (b), (c), and (d) 1 to 2 years; (e) 4
months; (f) 1 year; (g) 8 months.
Fees: A$246 Union fee, plus per year: (a) and (c)
A$10,000; (e) A$6,000; (b) A$15,000; (d) and (f) A$18,000;
(g) A$12,000.
Applications: (a), (f) by 31 October; (e), (g) by March,
July or November; (b), (c) and (d) at any time; to the above
address.

📖 Undergraduate, Graduate Programmes / Tourism

Study Domains: all major fields, business, education,
health and hygiene, law, social sciences, tourism, hotel and
catering management.
Programmes: Associate degree, Certificate, Bachelor's
degree, Master's degrees and studies in international tourism
management and all major fields.
Open to: candidates of any nationality with secondary
school leaving certificate.
Applications: by end of October to the above address.

🐦 Postgraduate Scholarships

Study Domains: arts, business, education, law, sciences.
Scholarships: (a) University Postgraduate Research
Scholarship; (b) University Postgraduate Support Scholarship.
Open to: applicants of any country who hold qualification
of at least the standard of a Bachelor's degree with
second-class honours, or equivalent.
Duration: Master's degree: 1 year; Ph.D.: 3 years; both
with possible 6 months extension.
Value: A$12,000.
Applications: by 31 October, to Postgraduate Studies
Office at the above address.

162   Swinburne University of Technology [SUT]
PO Box 218
3122 Hawthorn
Tel: +61-3-9214-8000
Fax: +61-3-819-5454
Web: http://www.swin.edu.au

📖 Undergraduate, Graduate Programmes

Study Domains: arts, business, business administration,
computer science, engineering, industrial technology,
management, performing arts, social sciences, tourism, hotel
and catering management, visual arts.
Description: Studies in the following fields; Applied and
Industrial Sciences, Business: Innnovation and Management,
Computing and IT, Design, Engineering and Technology,
Film and Television, Health and Human Services, Hospitality
and Tourism, Multimedia, Social Science and Arts, Visual
and Performing Arts.

163   TAFE International Western Australia [TIWA]
Level 7, 190, St. George Terrace
Perth, Western Australia
Tel: +61-8-9320-3777
Fax: +61-8-9320-3717
Web: http://www.tiwa.com.au
e-mail: study@eti.wa.edu.au

📖 Technical and Further Education Programme (TAFE)

Study Domains: all major fields.
Programmes: Programme of courses leading to Certificate
and Diploma.
Description: agriculture, applied science, architecture, arts,
business and management, computing, engineering, fashion,
health and community studies, hospitality and tourism,
maritime studies, media, aquaculture, horticulture, surveying
and cartography, aeronautics.
Open to: candidates of any country; Certificate
programmes require Australian Equivalent of Year 11;
Diploma programmes require Australian Equivalent of Year
12; TOEFL 530 and IELTS of 5.5.

Duration: 1 to 2 years.
Applications: 2 months prior to beginning of programme,
to the above address.

164   TAFE South Australia [TAFESA]
Marketing and International Unit
GPO Box 320
5001 Adelaide, SA
Tel: +61-8-8463-6376
Fax: +61-8-8463-6364
Web: http://www.tafe.sa.edu.au
e-mail: international.tafe@saugov.sa.gov.au

📖 Certificate and Diploma Programmes

Study Domains: all major fields.
Programmes: Programme of courses leading to Certificate
and Diploma.
Description: courses in accounting, administration, arts,
business, computer science, dentistry, education, engineering,
finance, food, horticulture, management, music; veterinary
sciences, vocational training.
Open to: candidates of any nationality.
Duration: from 6 months to 3 years; most courses begin in
February and July.
Fees: A$6,875-$9,000.
Applications: to the International Students Programme
Manager, at the above address.

165   University of Adelaide
5005 Adelaide
Tel: +61-8-8303-4071
Fax: +61-8-8303-3988
Web: http://www.adelaide.edu.au
e-mail: international@adelaide.edu.au

📖 Undergraduate, Graduate, Postgraduate Programmes

Study Domains: all major fields, Asian studies, biology,
ecology, environment, engineering, oenology.
Programmes: Bachelor's, Masters, Ph.D., diploma,
Associate diploma.
Description: agricultural science, design studies,
architecture, arts, commerce, dentistry, dental science,
economics, engineering, health science, law, mathematical
science, medicine, music, science; write for full course
catalogue; humanities students have the opportunity to
undertake an internship with a Member of Parliament, or a
government department.
Open to: candidates of all nationalities with secondary
school leaving certificate; language requirement: IELTS score
of 6.0 (TOEFL of 550).
Financial assistance: several scholarships for graduate
students available; see website for further details:
www.adelaide.edu.au.
Applications: by 1 December, to the above address.

🐦 Scholarships

Study Domains: research.
Scholarships: University of Adelaide Scholarships and
Overseas Postgraduate Research Scholarships.
Description: research in any field towards a Master's or
Ph.D. degree.
Open to: nationals of all countries: candidates would be
expected to hold qualifications equivalent to a first-class
honours degree of an Australian university, to display
competence in the English language and to have successfully
applied for a scholarship for tuition fees (OPRS) from the
Australian Government.
Duration: up to 2 years for a Master's degree, up to 3 years
for Ph.D., with extension up to 3-1/2 years in exceptional
cases.
Value: current stipend of university scholarship with other
allowances as appropriate.
Applications: contact the Director of International
Programs for further information.

166   University of Ballarat

International Office
P.O. Box 663
3353 Ballarat, Victoria
Tel: +61-3-5327-9018
Fax: +61-3-5327-9017
Web: http://www.ballarat.edu.au/international
e-mail: international@ballarat.edu.au

Undergraduate, Graduate, Postgraduate programmes.

Study Domains: all major fields, biology, business, chemistry, computer science, education, engineering, human sciences, management, mathematics, social sciences.
Programmes: Bachelor's degree, Master's degree, Ph.D. degree; engineering, postgraduate diploma.
Description: visual and performing arts, behavioural and social sciences, humanities, business, management, tourism, education, engineering, human movement and sport sciences, information technology, math sciences, nursing, food technology and biological resource management, geology; ELICOS programme is available at the local TAFE College.
Open to: students who have satisfactorily completed Australian Year 12 or its equivalent; TOEFL score of 550 or IELTS score of 6.0.
Duration: Bachelor's degree and Ph.D.: 3 years; Engineering: 4 years; Postgraduate diploma: 1 year; Master's degree: 2 years.
Applications: to the International Programs Office, at the above address.

167   University of Canberra

2600 Canberra
Tel: +61-2-6201-5111
Fax: +61-2-6201-5999
Web: http://www.canberra.edu.au
e-mail: keith.hyde@canberra.edu.au

Undergraduate, Graduate, Postgraduate Programmes

Study Domains: all major fields.
Programmes: (a) Bachelor's degree programmes in: accounting, administration, architecture, banking and finance, communication, education, electronics, engineering, health, human biology, journalism, languages, management, mathematics, media, medical science, nutritional science, physics, resource and environmental science, social sciences, sports; (b) Master's degree and Ph.D. programmes in: accounting, architecture, computing, communication, conservation, counselling, cultural heritage, economics, education, electronics, engineering, information studies, law, librarianship, mathematics, nursing, psychology, statistics; (c) Master of Arts in: information and technological sciences.
Open to: candidates of all nationalities, (a) with secondary school leaving certificate, (b) candidates holding an undergraduate degree and for (c) 18 years of age or older, and two years work experience; proficiency in English necessary for all programmes (IELTS 6.5.).
Duration: (a) and (b) variable; (c) 2 years.

168   University of Melbourne

3010 Victoria
Tel: +61-3-8344-4000
Fax: +61-3-8344-5104
Web: http://www.unimelb.edu.au
e-mail: enquiries-international@unimelb.edu.au

Undergraduate, Graduate and Postgraduate Diploma Programmes

Study Domains: all major fields.
Programmes: Bachelor's, Master's, Ph.D. and Postgraduate Diplomas.
Description: agriculture, forestry, architecture, building, planning and design, environmental studies, arts, history, political science, languages, social work, economics and commerce, accounting, education (including early childhood studies, primary, secondary, special education, education and training), engineering, agricultural, chemical, civil, electrical and electronic, mechanical and manufacturing, computer science, environmental mechatronics, law, medicine, dentistry and health science, physiotherapy, psychology, music, visual and performing arts, science, optometry, information systems and veterinary science.
Open to: candidates of any country; educational qualifications and English language requirements differ according to course and level; see http://www.unimelb.edu.au for further details.
Applications: first semester full-time undergraduate by 20 December; postgraduate (coursework) by 31 October; second semester full-time undergraduate by 31 May; postgraduate (coursework) by 30 April; and postgraduate (research) at any time; to the Admissions Officer, International Office, at the above address.

International Undergraduate Scholarship

Study Domains: all major fields.
Open to: Non-Australian citizens who have received an offer of a full-time undergraduate international fee place at the University of Melbourne.
Value: 25% fee remission for the duration of the course; living expenses not included.
Applications: Students are considered by the faculty at the time of course offers. For more information, please see website.

Undergraduate, Postgraduate Scholarships

Study Domains: all major fields.
Scholarships: undergraduate and postgraduate scholarships; see website below for details and other scholarship opportunities (www.services.unimelb.edu.au/scholarships).
Open to: all international students.
Applications: www.services.unimelb.edu.au/scholarships; for faculty scholarship information see: www.unimelb.edu.au/az/azfaculties.

169   University of New England [UNE]

2351 Armidale, N.S.W.
Tel: +61-2-6773-3192
Fax: +61-2-6773-3325
Web: http://www.une.edu.au/ipo
e-mail: studyabroad@une.edu.au

Undergraduate, Graduate and Postgraduate Programmes

Study Domains: all major fields.
Programmes: Bachelor's degree, Master's degree, Ph.D., Graduate Diplomas and Graduate Certificate Courses.
Open to: candidates of any country with secondary school leaving certificate and with a TOEFL of at least 550 and IELTS of 6.0 (or equivalent).
Duration: 6 months to 4 years; courses begin in February or July.
Applications: by 30 November for February semester; by 30 April for July semester; to the above address. For further information, consult http://www.une.edu.au/ipo/overseas.htm.

Postgraduate, Research and Travelling Scholarships

Study Domains: all major fields, agriculture, biology, cattle breeding, industrial technology, research, textile industry.
Scholarships: Several types of scholarships, please consult website http://study.une.edu.au/pages.php3?p=FISCHOL for scholarship details.
Description: all fields of study; research leading to Master's or Ph.D. degrees; cattle breeding; biology, wool processing; cotton production.
Open to: nationals of all countries; candidates having qualifications equivalent to at least a second-class honours degree in the first division of the University and a sound knowledge of English; must provide evidence of personal finances approximately equivalent to the amount of the scholarship; graduates of the University of New England; preference will be given to applicants under age 25.
Place of study: at the University or at an institution overseas approved by the University of New England; University of New England, University of New South Wales or University of Western Australia.
Duration: up to 2 years for Master's candidates and 3 years for Ph.D. candidates, with a possible extension of 6 months for the latter.

Value: basic yearly allowance, non-taxable, plus certain allowances; yearly stipend for person with dependants, plus a yearly amount towards university fees, and travel grant.
Applications: Variable: by 31 October or by 31 January; to the Administrative Officer, Research Grants and Scholarships. See website for details.

170 University of New South Wales [UNSW]
International Office
2052 Sydney, N.S.W.
Tel: +61-2-9385-3078
Fax: +61-2-9313-7382
Web: http://www.unsw.edu.au

📖 Undergraduate, Graduate and Postgraduate Programmes

Study Domains: all major fields.
Programmes: Bachelor's degree, Master's degree, Ph.D. and Postgraduate Diploma.
Description: applied sciences, arts and social sciences, biological and behavioural sciences, the built environment, commerce and economics, engineering, law, medicine, education, librarianship, sciences and sports science.
Open to: international students with secondary studies equivalent to Year 12 in Australia for undergraduate level; applicants for graduate courses must hold an appropriate Bachelor's degree.
Duration: undergraduate courses: 3 to 4 years; graduate and postgraduate: 1 to 2 years; research degrees: 2 to 4 years; 1 or 2 semester programmes available for international students.
Applications: by December, to the Registrar.

171 University of New South Wales - Centre for Public Health [UNSW]
2052 Sydney, N.S.W.
Tel: +61-2-9385-2500
Fax: +61-2-9385-1520
Web: http://www.unsw.edu.au

📖 Public Health and Clinical Education Programmes

Study Domains: health and hygiene, medicine.
Programmes: (a) Courses leading to Master of Public Health; (b) Master of Clinical Education and Graduate Diploma of Clinical Education.
Open to: (a) and (b) appropriately qualified graduates from any country; (b) also requires active engagement in clinical education.
Duration: (a) 1 year coursework with a 6-month project to be undertaken in student's own country; (b) variable; courses are only available by distance education.
Financial assistance: (a) offered by World Health Organization (apply to Ministry of Health in home country) and by Australian Government through the Australian Agency for International Development; contact nearest Australian Embassy or High Commission for more information.
Applications: by October for session 1; by April for session 2.

172 University of New South Wales - School of Medical Education / WHO Regional Training Centre for Health Development [UNSW]
2052 Sydney, N.S.W.
Tel: +61-2-3985-2500
Fax: +61-2-9385-1520
Web: http://www.unsw.edu.au

📖 Health Personnel Education Degree Programme

Study Domains: education, health and hygiene, research.
Programmes: Master of Health Personnel Education degree course: (a) by coursework, to increase the competence of health personnel educators and administrators with regard to the health care needs of their respective countries; (b) by research, for those who wish to investigate in depth a particular aspect of health manpower development; Ph.D. and graduate diploma enrolment also available.

Open to: appropriately qualified graduates with 2 years' minimum full-time teaching and/or administrative experience; minimum 550 TOEFL.
Held: at the University of New South Wales, Sydney.
Duration: (a) 1 year full-time plus a 6-month project in student's own country; (b) 1-1/2 years; graduate diploma: 1 academic year; courses begin in March or July.
Financial assistance: by World Health Organization (apply to Ministry of Health in home country) and by Australian Government through AusAID; contact nearest Australian Embassy or High Commission for more information.
Applications: by end of October for Session 1; by end of April for Session 2; supported by transcripts of academic record, to the Registrar, at the above address.

173 University of Newcastle
University Drive
2308 Callaghan, New South Wales
Tel: +61-2-4921-5000
Fax: +61-2-4921-6922
Web: http://www.newcastle.edu.au
e-mail: usr@newcastle.edu.au

📖 Undergraduate, Graduate, Postgraduate Programmes

Study Domains: all major fields.
Programmes: (a) Bachelor's degree courses in applied sciences, architecture, arts, building, business, commerce, communication, computer science, economics, education, engineering, environmental science, health science, information science, mathematics, medicine, music, nursing, nutrition, science, social science, surveying, sustainable resource management, food technology, design, visual arts; (b) Graduate Diploma, Master's degree and Ph.D. in arts, business administration, commerce, computer science, computing, education, engineering, environmental science, health science, law, mathematics, medical science, nursing, science, scientific studies, special education; (c) Semester or year study abroad.
Open to: (a) candidates who have completed the equivalent overseas qualifications of the New South Wales Higher School Certificate; (b) candidates holding an undergraduate degree (preferably at honours level) of a recognized university; (c) students enrolled in at least Year 2 of a degree programme; IELTS 6.5 or TOEFL 550 required.
Duration: (a) 3 years, with the exception of engineering and health science: 4 years; architecture and medicine, 5 years; (b) graduate diploma: 1 year; Master's: 1 to 2 years; Ph.D.: 3 years; (c) 1-1/2 years; courses begin in March and July.
Financial assistance: (b) a limited number of postgraduate research scholarships offered for Master's degree and Ph.D. for which application closing date is 31 October.
Applications: contact the International Students Office, at the above address, for further information; (c) 30 December for March; 15 May for July, to the above address.

🐚 University of Newcastle Postgraduate Research Scholarship

Study Domains: all major fields.
Subjects: Areas of research strengths.
Open to: International research candidate enrolling in a research higher degree; competitive selection.
Duration: one year, renewable.
Value: $18,484 including living expenses; also possibility of establishment and thesis allowances.
Applications: Successful research higher degree application; holder of International Postgraduate Research Scholarship; minimum English proficiency requirements; appropriate citizenship. Deadline by September 30. For more information, please contact research@newcastle.edu.au.

174 University of Notre Dame
International Office
PO Box 1225
Fremantle, Perth
Tel: +61-8-9239-5650
Fax: +61-8-9239-5653
Web: http://www.nd.edu.au/index.shtml
e-mail: international@nd.edu.au

📖 Undergraduate, Graduate Programmes

Study Domains: business, law.
Programmes: Bachelor's degree, Master's degree, certificate, diploma, graduate diploma.
Description: (a) social justice studies: minor as part of an undergraduate program, graduate diploma or Master of Leadership Certificate or diploma in Social justice studies; (b) business: the College of Business consists of four schools which reflect the opportunity open to business today in a climate of unprecedented change and rapid globalization and in which environmental issues are becoming increasingly important.
Open to: candidates of all nationalities holding a secondary school leaving certificate with matriculation or recognized foreign equivalent; undergraduate students must have IELTS level 6 with minimum of 6 for writing or Notre Dame Language Proficiency Test.
Duration: (a) 6 to 18 months.
Fees: registration: A$140; tuition (approximately): undergraduate: A$10,920 per year; graduate: A$11,280 per year; Master of Leadership certificate: A$11,280 per year.
Applications: 6 weeks before course commencement.

📌 Ciara Glennon Scholarship

Study Domains: all major fields.
Open to: Nationals of African countries.
Nationality: African nationals.
Academic requirements: Applicants must hold a recognized undergraduate degree with first-class honours, provide a 200-word abstract relating to the area of study, demonstrating how the study will be used to impact on the social/economic environment of a particular African community.
Place of study: University of Notre Dame in Fremantle, Australia.
Duration: 1 to 2 years, non-renewable.
Value: Full tuition and A$5,000 for travel to and accommodation in Australia.
Languages: English.

175 University of Queensland

4072 Brisbane, Queensland
Tel: +61-7-3365-7941
Fax: +61-7-3365-1794
Web: http://www.uq.edu.au/grad-school/scholarships/international.html
e-mail: IEOenquiries@mailbox.uq.edu.au

📖 Undergraduate, Graduate, Postgraduate Programmes

Study Domains: all major fields.
Programmes: (a) Doctor of Philosophy in 63 departments, including humanities, business, social sciences, biological sciences, health sciences, engineering; (b) Master by research: 14 faculties, in the above fields; (c) Master by coursework: more than 75 programmes in specialist areas; (d) postgraduate diplomas: programmes in the same areas as for the Master's; (e) graduate certificates: courses in similar areas; (f) Bachelor's degree: more than 80 programmes in liberal arts and science, business, professional registration and research areas; (g) Associate diplomas in the fields of applied science and business; (h) ELICOS programmes for international students - IELTS test centre; (i) student exchange programmes with international universities and participants in the Junior Year Abroad Scheme.
Open to: suitably qualified applicants at the various course levels but generally limited to those with excellent qualifications and acceptable proficiency in English.
Duration: (a) 3 years; (b) and (c) 2 years; (d) 2 semesters; (e) 1 semester; (f) 3 to 4 years; (i) 1 or 2 semesters; (courses begin in February; in July for some courses).
Applications: at least 3 months before classes start, to the Co-ordinator, International Education Office, at the above address.

📌 Postgraduate Research Scholarships

Study Domains: all major fields, research.
Scholarships: (a) Ernest Singer Postgraduate Research Scholarship; (b) University of Queensland Postgraduate Research Scholarship.
Description: unrestricted subjects.

Open to: (a) graduate with first-class honours or equivalent, acceptable as a full-time internal research Master's or Ph.D. candidate; non-English native language but proficient in English; born in a non-English speaking country, not adopted or raised by a family speaking English as their main language; (b) graduates from any country with first-class honours degree or equivalent; proficiency in English required; must be acceptable for postgraduate research study at the University of Queensland.
Duration: (a) and (b) Master's degree by research: 2 years; Ph.D.: 3 years; may be extended by 6 months for Ph.D. in special circumstances.
Value: living allowance A$17,609 per year plus contribution towards travel expenses.
Applications: by 30 August, to the International Admissions Section, International Education Directorate, at the above address.

176 University of South Australia [UNISA]

PO Box 2471
5001 Adelaide, South Australia
Tel: +61-8-8302-6611
Fax: +61-8-8302-2466
Web: http://www.unisa.edu.au
e-mail: International.office@unisa.edu.au

📖 Certificate, Undergraduate, Graduate, Postgraduate Programmes

Study Domains: all major fields.
Programmes: Diploma, Bachelor's degree, Graduate diploma, Graduate certificate, Master's degree, Professional Doctorate, PhD.
Subjects: Aboriginal Studies; Australian Studies; accounting; architecture; biology; business administration; chemical engineering; communication; computer sciences; economic and commercial sciences; education; English; environmental / conservation management; exercise and sports science; finance; fine arts; geography; history; journalism; music; mathematics; psychology; recreation; sociology, urbanism; visual arts. Most study abroad packages incorporate a field-based component.
Open to: nationals of any country who are currently enrolled in a similar course.
Applications: 3 months before start of semester to Study Abroad Adviser, International Students Office, at the above address.

177 University of Southern Queensland [USQ]

Baker Street, Darling Heights,
4350 Toowoomba, Queensland
Tel: +61-7-4631-2100
Fax: +61-7-4636-1762
Web: http://www.usq.edu.au
e-mail: studadm@usq.edu.au

📖 Preparatory, Undergraduate, Postgraduate Programmes

Study Domains: all major fields.
Programmes: Bachelor's degree, Master's degree, Ph.D., certificate, graduate certificate, graduate diploma, postgraduate diploma; also preparatory courses.
Subjects: arts, business, commerce, education, engineering and surveying, and sciences.
Open to: candidates of all nationalities, over school-leaving age; some courses have a basic English requirement.
Duration: 3 to 4 years.
Fees: tuition fees, A$8,720-$12,600 per year; distance education, A$825-$1,250 per unit.
Applications: 4 weeks prior to semester, to Co-ordinator, Student Liaison, at the above address.

178   University of Tasmania, Hobart [UTAS Hobart]
PO Box 252-51
7001 Hobart, Tasmania
Tel: +61-3-6226-2999
Fax: +61-3-6226-2001
Web: http://www.utas.edu.au

📖 Associate and Undergraduate Programmes

Study Domains: all major fields.
Programmes: (a) Associate diplomas; (b) diplomas; (c) Bachelor's degrees.
Description: (a) applied science in aquaculture, fine art and design; (b) applied science in aquaculture; (c) agricultural science, applied computing, applied science, applied science in medical laboratory science, architecture, arts, commerce, computing, economics, education, environmental design, fine arts, geomatics, laws, nursing, music, pharmacy, science, social work, technology (environmental technology).
Open to: (a) and (b) applicants with 12 years of pre-tertiary education plus a satisfactory result in an examination which meets the admission requirements of a recognized university in the applicant's home country; must be proficient in English; (c) same as for (a) with some programmes requiring additional background subjects.
Duration: (a) 2 years; (b) 3 years; (c) 4 years; courses begin in February.
Financial assistance: Tasmania International Scholarships awarded for academic excellence, assistances with course fees.
Applications: by 30 November, to the International Admissions Officer, at the above address.

🎓 Scholarships

Study Domains: all major fields.
Scholarships: Tasmania International Scholarships (30).
Open to: all nationalities, with a high school or university diploma; IELTS score 6.0 or greater.
Duration: for duration of undergraduate or postgraduate course.
Value: course fees.
Applications: by 30 September of year prior to award.

179   University of Tasmania, Launceston [UTAS Lauceston]
Newnham Drive, Newnham
Locked Bag
7250 Launceston, TAS
Tel: +61-3-6324-3999
Web: http://www.utas.edu.au

📖 Undergraduate, Graduate, Postgraduate Programmes

Study Domains: all major fields, applied sciences, architecture, business, computer science, education, health and hygiene, marine biology.
Programmes: (a) Bachelor of applied computing, applied science, applied medical laboratory science, architecture, arts in environmental design, arts in humanities, arts in visual arts, commerce, education, engineering (transfer course), health science in nursing, social work; (b) diploma of applied science in aquaculture, teaching; (c) Associate diploma of applied science in aquaculture, visual arts; (d) graduate diploma of applied computing, applied science in aquaculture, visual arts; (e) Master of applied science in aquaculture, education.
Open to: candidates of any nationality with: (a), (b) and (c) Australia Year 12 or equivalent (for architecture course a Bachelor's degree in environmental design or equivalent; for health science course a registered nurse qualification); (d) a Bachelor's degree or diploma in related field; (e) honours degree in relevant area; English proficiency required.
Duration: (a) 2, 3 or 4 years depending on the course; (b) 3 years; (c) 2 years; (d) and (e) 1 year; courses begin in February.
Applications: to the Student Administration Officer, at the above address.

180   University of Technology, Sydney [UTS]
PO Box 123
2007 Broadway, N.S.W.
Tel: +61-2-9514-2000
Fax: +61-2-9514-1551
Web: http://www.uts.edu.au
e-mail: vc@uts.edu.au

📖 Undergraduate, Postgraduate Programmes

Study Domains: all major fields.
Programmes: (a) Bachelor's degree at pass and honours standard in: accounting, banking, economics, finance, international business, management and marketing, biomedical science, biotechnology, environmental biology, urban horticulture, chemistry, geology, physics, land economics, tourism, leisure studies, human movement studies, nursing, education, engineering, design, law, mathematics, acupuncture; (b) postgraduate programmes at graduate diploma or Master's level in: business, journalism, mathematics, design, engineering management, nursing, life sciences, law, science, education; (c) higher degrees by research (Master's degree and Ph.D.) offered by all faculties.
Open to: all applicants who are not Australian or permanent residents and who meet entry requirements (secondary school leaving certificate) including the English language proficiency standard.
Duration: (a) 3, 4 and 5 years depending on the course; (b) 1 year; Master's: 1 or 2 years; (c) 2 to 5 years depending on programme.
Applications: by 31 October, for first semester or 30 April for courses with second semester intake; applications and further information available from the Director, International Programmes, at the above address.

181   University of Western Australia [UWA]
Stirling Highway, Nedlands
6907 Western Australia
Tel: +61-8-9380-3838
Fax: +61-8-9382-4071
Web: http://www.uwa.edu.au
e-mail: general.enquiries@uwa.edu.au

📖 Undergraduate, Postgraduate Programmes

Study Domains: all major fields.
Programmes: (a) Bachelor's degree, (b) Master's degree, (c) Ph.D., (d) postgraduate diploma.
Description: courses in agriculture, architecture, arts, commerce, dentistry, economics, education, engineering, law, medicine and science; postgraduate non-clinical medical courses are also offered.
Open to: (a) acceptable qualifications including GCE A-levels; (b) and (c) first or upper second division Honours degree or Master's degree in a relevant discipline; (d) holders of a 3-year Bachelor's degree from a recognized institution. TOEFL of 550 required.
Duration: (a) 3 to 6 years; (b) 2 to 3 years; (c) 2 to 4 years; (d) 1 year.
Applications: by 1 December, to the International Students Office, at the above address.

🎓 AUL Fellowships and Postgraduate Awards

Study Domains: medicine, obstetrics and gynaecology, research.
Scholarships: (a) Gledden Visiting Senior Fellowships (up to 8); (b) Saw Medical Research Fellowships (offered when funds permit); (c) W. A. and M. G. Saw Medical Research Fellowships (offered when funds permit); (d) University Postgraduate Awards (up to 12).
Description: (a) applied science, relating to surveying, engineering, mining or cognate subjects; (b) causation, prevention or cure of disease (if appropriate, with special reference to diabetes mellitus); (c) medical research, in particular the common cold: its cause, prevention and cure; (d) unrestricted.
Open to: (a) graduates of any university with doctoral degrees or qualifications, or equivalent experience, nominated by appropriate departments of the University of Western Australia; (b) and (c) any graduate in medicine, science or arts of any recognized university in the United Kingdom, Australia or any Commonwealth country; any person

qualified for medical practice in Western Australia; (d) overseas candidates possessing a minimum of first-class honours degree and reasonable proficiency in English, who have been awarded a fees scholarship under the Australian Government OPRS or ADCOS programmes.
Place of study: (b) usually at the University of Western Australia, exceptionally another appropriate institution could be approved; (c) at the University of Western Australia or elsewhere.
Duration: (a) maximum 1 year, minimum 1 academic term; (b) and (c) normally 1 year but may be renewed for a second and exceptionally a third year; (d) maximum 2 years for Master's degree; 3 years for Ph.D. with possibility of extension for up to 6 months.
Applications: (a) 31 March; (b) and (c) 30 June; (d) 31 August; forms obtained from the Scholarship Office and returned to the Registrar.

182   University of Western Sydney
UWS International Admissions
Locked Bag 1797
1797 Penrith South DC N.S.W.
Tel: +61-2-9678-7468
Fax: +61-2-9678-7160
Web: http://www.uws.edu.au/international
e-mail: internationalstudy@uws.edu.au

📖 **Undergraduate, Graduate, Postgraduate Programmes**

Study Domains: all major fields, agriculture, building industry, engineering, health and hygiene, horticulture, nutrition, performing arts, tourism, hotel and catering management, visual arts.
Programmes: (a) Bachelor's degree in all faculties, including agriculture and horticulture; arts, humanities, social science and psychology; (b) Master's degree by coursework and research in all faculties, including arts, humanities, social science and psychology, business; (c) PhD research in all faculties, including agriculture and horticulture, arts, humanities, social science and psychology, business; (d) Postgraduate research in all faculties, including agriculture and horticulture, arts, humanities, social science and psychology; business.
Open to: students having satisfactorily completed school-leaving exams or appropriate qualifying degree or programme; adults assessed individually; proficiency in written and spoken English required.
Duration: (a) 3 to 5 years; (b) 1 to 3 years; (c) 2 to 4 years; (d) variable, consult faculties for details.
Fees: (a) A$13,000-$17,000; (b) A$12,000-$19,000; (c) A$17,000-$20,000; (d) A$15,000-$19,000.
Applications: applicants are recommended to apply early, by 15 November for the Autumn Session (February/March start), and by 15 May for courses commencing in the Spring Session (July/August start) to the above address.

183   University of Wollongong [UOW]
Northfields Avenue
2522 Wollongong, N.S.W.
Tel: +61-2-4221-3218
Fax: +61-2-4221-3223
Web: http://www.uow.edu.au
e-mail: uniadvice@uow.edu.au

📖 **Undergraduate, Graduate and Postgraduate Programmes**

Study Domains: all major fields.
Programmes: Bachelor degrees; Graduate Certificates; Graduate Diplomas; Masters; Masters by Research; PhD degrees.
Description: humanities, languages, history, politics, international relations, sociology, communication studies, science & technology studies, economics, accounting, finance, banking, marketing, e-commerce, management, international business, information systems, logistics, journalism, graphic design, visual arts, performance, sound, early childhood teaching, primary
and secondary teaching, physical & health education, engineering medical radiation physics, photonics, nanotechnology, physics, psychology, medical sciences, nutrition and dietetics, nursing, exercise science &

rehabilitation, public health, population health, mathematics, statistics, computer science, information technologies, health informatics, digital multimedia, bioinformatics, environmental and natural resources law, transnational crime prevention, biology, chemistry, geography, geology, medicinal chemistry, environmental science, biotechnology, marine science. Non-award study abroad programmes are also available in most of these areas.
Open to: students from all countries who have completed the academic qualifications required for admission to the particular course, either in Australia or the equivalent overseas qualifications.
Duration: from 6 months (1 session) to 4 years' full time, depending on the course; combined undergraduate degree programme vary from 4-1/2 to 5-1/2 years' of study. Non-award study abroad programmes may be taken for 1 or 2 sessions.
Fees: tuition from A$7,500-$11,000 per session.
Applications: to UniAdvice at the above address.

📨 **Postgraduate Research Awards**

Study Domains: all major fields, research.
Scholarships: (a) University of Wollongong postgraduate research awards; (b) international postgraduate coursework scholarships are currently under review - please refer to http://www.uow.edu.au/prospective/international/scholarships /index.html.
Description: A range of research higher degrees across all faculties - please refer to http://www.uow.edu.au/research/rsc/student/prospective/facul ties/.
Open to: graduates with a Bachelor's degree at the standard of Honours Class II Division 2 or higher, or approved equivalent qualification. Specific qualifications vary from one Faculty to another, and for a Master's by research as compared to a doctoral degree.
Duration: 3 years for PhD, with possible extension for a further 6 months, and 2 years for Master's by research degree.
Applications: by 30 September, to the Office of Research.

184   Winston Churchill Memorial Trust [WCMT]
Churchill House
30 Balmain Crescent
2601 Acton ACT
Tel: +61-2-6247-8333/1800 777 2
Fax: +61-2-6249-8944
Web: http://www.churchilltrust.com.au/
e-mail: churchilltrust@bigpond.com

📨 **Fellowships**

Study Domains: all major fields.
Scholarships: Churchill Fellowships (50 to 55).
Description: unrestricted, mainly non-academic.
Open to: permanent residents of Australia of demonstrated ability, with an overseas study project of value to the community; aged 18 and above.
Place of study: in any country other than Australia.
Duration: averages 12 weeks but variable depending upon the requirements of the project.
Value: economy air fare and overseas living allowance; fees paid where appropriate.
Applications: by the last day of February; application and Referee's report forms from the Chief Executive Officer.

Austria

Academic year: October to June.
Organization of higher education system: The new University Study Act provides for two types of studies: degree programme studies (ordentliche Studien) and university courses (Universitätslehrgänge). The degree programme studies are divided into Bachelor's, Master's, Diploma and Doctoral studies. University courses are for post-secondary education.
The Bachelor's programme requires three to four years of study. The curriculum includes all subjects of examination that are essential for academic or artistic pre-professional education in the relevant subject area. Studies are divided into compulsory subjects, restricted elective fields of concentration (subjects that have to be chosen from a list featured in the curriculum) and elective fields of concentration (subjects to be chosen that are not bound by a list). At least two Bachelor's essays have to be composed within the framework of the courses. The study programme concludes with a Bachelor's examination.
A Master's programme requires one to two years of study. Admission is conditional on a completed Austrian Bachelor's programme or an equivalent post-secondary degree. The main emphasis is on the Master's thesis and studies in related subjects. The study programme concludes with a Master's examination. Admission to the Master's examination is conditional on the acceptance of the Master's thesis.
A doctoral programme usually requires two years of study. Admission is conditional on a completed Austrian diploma or Master's programme or an equivalent post-secondary degree. The main emphasis is on the dissertation and studies in related subjects. The study programme concludes with the acceptance of the dissertation and a doctoral examination. (www.studyguide.at for further university study information).
Monetary unit: Euro (€).
National student admission: Foreign students must have qualifications equivalent to the Austrian 'Matura (Reifezeugnis)', and must give evidence that an institution of higher learning in the awarding country has already accepted them for university study. As admission requirements for certain faculties may vary from one year to another, prospective students should first enquire at the Austrian diplomatic mission in their own country. Applications should be addressed to the Rector's office (Universitätsdirektion) of the university concerned, not later than 1 September for winter term and 1 February for summer term.
International student admission: Definition of foreign student: without Austrian citizenship. Foreign students must possess academic qualifications equivalent to the 'Matura' (Reifezeugnis) and must be eligible for admission to universities in their own country. They must also provide evidence that an institution of higher education in the awarding country would accept them for university studies in the respective field. Applications should be addressed in writing to the Admission Office of the university of one's choice. Deadlines for applications are generally 1 September for winter semester or 1 February for summer semester. Documents in languages other than German or English must be submitted with a certified German translation. If accepted, the university will send a notification of admission 'Zulassungsbescheid'. After arrival in Austria.
Language: German language proficiency required. Proficiency may be proven by submission of secondary school leaving certificate showing German lessons of at least 4 years or by German language diploma or similar documents. In numerous artistic fields of study, this proof need not be produced until after the end of the second semester. The language proficiency requirement may be waived for doctoral studies.
Immigration requirements: Nationals of non-EU/EEA countries (so-called "third country nationals") need an entry or residence permit for entry into and residence in Austria. The type of permit depends on the purpose and length of the stay. See www.oead.ac.at for further information on entry and residence.
Estimated expenses for one academic year: Tuition for students from countries other than those of the European Union/European Economic Area: approximately 730 Euros per semester; student fees and insurance approximately 15 Euros. Tuition exemption and refund is possible for certain students. Books/supplies: 260 Euros/semester; housing: 290 Euros/month.

Information services: Admission offices: http://www.oead.ac.at/_English/Austria/index.html.
Scholarships for international students:
• See data base at www.grants.at for scholarship/fellowship information.
Open and distance learning: Distance higher education: Distance education (Fernstudien) has been provided since 1979 by Interuniversitäres Forschungsinstitut für Fernstudien. This Institute has links with all major Austrian universities and offers special courses for adults seeking employment. The programmes which have been developed so far are courses in applied mathematics, energy counselling, teacher training and psychotherapy. Students may also follow normal degree courses at the Fernuniversität Hagen, which has links with centres in Linz, Bregenz and Vienna for students living in Austria. Some 2,000 students use these facilities. There is a similar study centre at the Open University London located in Vienna. Under the University Studies Act, Austrian universities may set up distance study courses.
Recognition of studies and qualification:
• The Austrian Higher Education Institutions: www.oead.ac.at/_English/Austria/Index.html
• NARIC/Austria: Federal Ministry of Education, Science and Culture; Teinfaltstrasse 8, A-1014 Wien; Austria; email: naric@bmbwk.gv.at; web: http://www.bmbwk.gv.at/naric.
Accommodation services:
• Austrian Youth Hostel Association (AYHA): http://www.oejhv.or.at/
• Austrian National Union of Students, 'Österreichische HochschülerInnenschaft': http://oeh.ac.at/oeh/dieoeh/english.
Work opportunities: Opportunities exist for students from non-EU/EEA countries for a maximum of three months per calendar year. (See www.oead.ac.at/_english/austria/entry/working.html for more complete information.).
Publications / Websites:
• Austrian Exchange Service: www.oead.ac.at
• Federal Ministry for Education, Science and Culture www.bmbwk.gv.at/fremdsprachig/index.xml
• Austrian Foreign Ministry: www.bmaa.gv.at
• Study Guide to Austria's Universities: www.studyguide.at
• The Researcher's Mobility Portal, www.researchinaustria.info.

---

185 Academy of Fine Arts Vienna

Schillerplatz 3
1010 Vienna
Tel: +43-1-58816 0 ext. 135
Fax: +43-1-58816 ext. 158
Web: http://www.akbild.ac.at
e-mail: international@akbild.ac.at

📖 Non-Degree Programmes

Study Domains: architecture, art history, arts, arts and crafts, cultural studies, fine arts, graphic arts, visual arts.
Programmes: Courses in arts and architecture.
Applications: contact the Registrar's Office; refer to website for further details.

186 Afro-Asian Institute - Study Advisory Department [AAI]

Türkenstrasse 3
1090 Vienna
Tel: +43-1-310-5145-211
Fax: +43-1-310-5145-312
Web: http://www.aai-wien.at
e-mail: office@aai-wien.at

🏫 Scholarships

Study Domains: all major fields.
Scholarships: Afro-Asiatic Institute Scholarships.
Subjects: all fields available at the University of Vienna.
Open to: needy applicants from developing countries of Africa and Asia with good study results in Austria; applicants must already have begun their studies in Austria and be regular students or students of the preliminary course; age limit is 35 years (for further information, see website http://www.aai-wien.at/templates/frameset_studentinnenservice_stipendien.htm).
Duration: 1 academic year (renewable).

Applications: in April for the following academic year.

187 Atomic Institute of the Austrian Universities [ATI]
Stadionallee 2
1020 Vienna
Tel: +43-1-58-801-14111
Fax: +43-1-58-801-14199
Web: http://www.ati.ac.at

⌨ Research Programmes
Study Domains: physics.
Programmes: Nuclear Research (see website for further information).
Description: (a) Course in utilization of low-energy accelerator physics (2 MeV), including experiments; application of X-ray physics, including experiments; (b) Practical course on neutron physics: measurements of parameters such as neutron temperature, diffusion length, Fermi age, resonance data and others particularly relevant to reactor physics; TRIGA Mk-II reactor (250 kW) and several radioactive neutron sources available; (c) Course on reactor physics and instrumentation: measurements on reactor kinetics, experiments include detectors and electronics; TRIGA Mk-II reactor (250 kW) available; (d) Practical course on radiation protection: dosimetry of alpha-, beta-, gamma-, x-, and neutron-radiation, radiation shielding, measurement of activity concentration in air and water; (e) Practical course on low-temperature physics: experiments with superconducting materials (conventional and high-temperature superconductors), measurements of temperature and magnetic fields at cryogenic temperatures; (f) Practical course on archaeometry: radiocarbon dating, thermoluminescence dating, neutron activation analysis, X-ray fluorescence analysis of archaeological samples; (g) Radiochemistry: handling and measurement of radioactive materials, application of nuclear techniques in analytical chemistry, environmental chemistry, biochemistry, geochemistry. Approximately 15 to 20 participants per course.
Open to: (a) to (f) nationals of all countries with a B.Sc. or equivalent in physics and allied sciences who have at least a basic knowledge of higher mathematics and for: (a) radiation physics; (b) nuclear and neutron physics; (c) nuclear and reactor physics and electronics; (d) nuclear and radiation physics; (e) solid-state and low-temperature physics; (f) radiation physics methods in archaeometry; (g) nationals with a B.Sc. or equivalent in chemistry, physics, biology or geochemistry.
Duration: (a) and (d) 1 to 4 months; (b) and (e) 2 weeks; (c) 1 to 2 weeks; (f) 5 weeks (course begins in November); (g) 1 month.
Fees: tuition free.
Languages: instruction in German and English, depending on courses.
Applications: to Atominstitut der Oesterreichischen Universitäten, at the above address; for further information see website.

188 Austrian Exchange Service (Österreichischer Austauschdienst) Agency for International Educational and Scientific Co-operation
Bureau for Student Mobility
Alserstrasse 4/1/15/6 u. 7
1090 Vienna
Tel: +43-1-4277-28101
Fax: +43-1-4277-9281
Web: http://www.oead.ac.at/
e-mail: zg@oead.ac.at

☞ Scholarships
Study Domains: all major fields.
Scholarships: North-South Dialogue Scholarship Programme (Austrian Government Scholarships).
Description: most major fields, except medicine; priority given to natural and technical sciences.
Open to: university graduates from non-European developing countries holding an M.A. or equivalent with a guarantee of employment upon return to home country or

official nomination by home country authorities required (see http://www.oead.ac.at/info/Intern/bueros/bap.htm).
Place of study: universities or research institutions in Austria.
Duration: from short term to maximum 3-year period (renewable).
Applications: at any time to the Austrian Embassy in home country; download information brochure, "Study in Austria", http://www.oead.ac.at/_english/austria/index.html; for further information and conditions of grant awarding see website: see website:
http://www.oead.ac.at/_english/projects/eza/North-South-Dialogue.html.

189 Austrian Medical Society of Vienna [AMESO]
Höfergasse 13/1
1090 Vienna
Tel: +43-1-405-4568
Fax: +43-1-408-3811
Web: http://www.ameso.at
e-mail: office@ameso.at

⌨ Certificate and Diploma Courses in Medicine
Study Domains: medicine.
Programmes: (a) Certificate Courses; (b) University of Vienna Diploma Course; (c) Fellowship Courses.
Subjects: anaesthesiology, cardiology, dermatology/venerology, gynaecology, immunology, specialized medicine (chemotherapy, endocrinology, gastroenterology, hematology, nephrology, nuclear medicine, oncology, rheumatology, serology), neonatology, neurology, ophthalmology, orthopaedic surgery, oto-rhino-laryngology, pathology, paediatric cardiology, paediatrics, physical medicine, physiology, psychiatry, radiology, surgery, specialized surgery (abdominal surgery, maxillo-facial surgery, neurosurgery, plastic surgery, thoracic surgery), traumatology, tuberculosis and chest diseases, urology.
Open to: graduates of a recognized medical school or university with at least 2 years speciality residency training in an approved hospital and holding a certificate of proficiency in English from a recognized institution.
Held: at the University of Vienna Medical School and major City of Vienna hospitals.
Languages: English and basic knowledge of German.
Applications: see website for further information.

190 FH. Joanneum University of Applied Sciences
Alte Poststrasse 149
8020 Graz
Tel: +43-316-5453-8800
Fax: +43-316-5453-8801
Web: http://www.fh-joanneum.at
e-mail: info@fh-joanneum.at

⌨ Undergraduate, Graduate Programmes
Study Domains: applied sciences, audio-visual media, aviation, aeronautics, building industry, business, civil engineering, electricity and electronics, engineering, industrial technology, industry and commerce, information science, international business, journalism, technology, telecommunications, tourism, hotel and catering management, urbanism.
Programmes: programmes leading to Magister (FH) and Diplom Ingenieur (FH) in the fields of business and technology, information and design, mobility, social work and public health.
Held: Courses are held in 3 different campuses: Graz, Kapfenberg and Bad Gleichenberg.
Duration: 4 years.
Fees: tuition: 363€ per semester; living costs: approx. 600€ per semester.
Applications: beginning of June.

191 IMC University of Applied Management Sciences - Krems (Fachhochschule Krems)

Piaristengasse 1
3500 Krems
Tel: +43-2732-76335
Fax: +43-2732-76335/4
Web: http://www.imc-krems.ac.at
e-mail: office@imc-krems.ac.at

📖 Graduate Programmes

Study Domains: biochemistry, health and hygiene, management, technology, tourism, hotel and catering management.
Programmes: Master's degrees in (a) Biotechnology Governance; (b) Tourism Management; (c) Export-Oriented Management; (d) Health Care Management; (e) Corporate Governance.
Open to: all nationalities on the basis of admission tests and TOEFL for non-European Union students.
Languages: instruction in English and German.
Applications: by beginning of June for winter semester, to the Admissions Office at the above address.

192 Institute of Limnology of the Austrian Academy of Sciences

Gaisberg 116
5310 Mondsee
Tel: +43-6-232-4079
Fax: +43-6-232-3578
Web: http://www.oeaw.ac.at/ipgl/
e-mail: ipgl.mondsee@oeaw.ac.at

📖 International Postgraduate Training Course

Study Domains: natural resources, zoology.
Programmes: International Postgraduate Training Course in Limnology.
Description: aim of the course is to build up scientific capacity in developing countries for in-house expertise on aquatic ecosystems conservation and management through a sound scientific knowledge base. The IPGL course has been restructured and is part of the sandwich M.Sc. programme in 'Limnology and Wetland Ecosystems'. The network builds up on the exchange of graduate students and staff, collaboration in M.Sc. and Ph.D. training programmes and joint supervision and management of research and development programmes.
Open to: citizens of developing countries holding a degree equivalent to Bachelor's or Master's in science, aquaculture or fisheries, and with knowledge of physics, chemistry and zoology; practical experience preferred; certificate of English proficiency required; candidates should be recommended by authorities in their home country and must state the expected use of the course in their future work.
Financial assistance: the Austrian Federal Government provides each participant with free tuition, maintenance and health insurance; www.oeaw.ac.at/ipgl/fellowship.html for further information.
Applications: by 31 October; application forms available from Austrian diplomatic mission in home country; or Limnologisches Institut, Course Secretariat, at the above address; application forms and information brochure can also be downloaded at: http://www.oeaw.ac.at/ipgl/requirements.html.

193 International University

Mondscheingasse 16
1070 Vienna
Tel: +43-1-718-50-6811
Fax: +43-1-718-50-689
Web: http://www.iuvienna.edu
e-mail: pres@iuvienna.edu

📖 Undergraduate and Graduate Programmes

Study Domains: business administration, economic and commercial sciences, finance, international business, international law, international relations, international studies, law, management.
Programmes: Bachelor's and Master's Degrees in Business Administration and Diplomatic Studies.
Open to: students of all nationalities on the basis of admission examinations and English proficiency of TOEFL 500 for undergraduate and 550 for graduate studies.

Fees: (approximate figures) registration: US$50; undergraduate courses: US$750; graduate courses: US$1,000; dormitory: US$200 per month.
Financial assistance: in the form of tuition waivers; dependent upon grades and financial need; valid for one academic year; contact the President, at the above address for further information.
Applications: 2 weeks before beginning of semester.

194 Management Center Innsbruck [MCI]

Universitätsstrasse 15
602 Innsbruck
Tel: +43-512-56-2070-1000
Fax: +43-512-56-2070-1099
Web: http://www.mci.edu
e-mail: office@mci.edu

📖 Undergraduate, Graduate Programmes

Study Domains: accounting, administration, economic and commercial sciences, engineering, European studies, finance, health and hygiene, industry and commerce, international business, international law, international relations, management, marketing, political economy, public relations, sciences, social sciences, social work, tourism, hotel and catering management, trade.
Programmes: Bachelor's and Master's (FH) degrees in: (a) Tourism Business Studies; (b) Applied Informatics and Management; (c) Management and Law; (d) Social Work; (e) Nonprofit-, Social- & Health Management; (f) Engineering and Environmental Management; (g) Biotechnology; (h) Business and Management; (i) General Management Executive.
Open to: nationals of all countries with university entrance qualification or professional qualification and on the basis of a written examination and interview.
Duration: 4 years.
Fees: approximately 400 € per semester.
Financial assistance: possibility of government scholarships, see http://www.oead.ac.at and http://grantsdb.oead.ac.at.
Languages: German and some English.
Applications: by June to the above address.

195 St. Pölten University of Applied Sciences

Herzogenburger Strasse 68
3100 St. Pölten
Tel: +43-2742-313-228
Fax: +43-2742-313-229
Web: http://www.fh-stpoelten.ac.at
e-mail: office@fh-stpoelten.ac.at

📖 Undergraduate, Graduate Programmes

Study Domains: business administration, communication, computer science, information science, management, social work, technology, telecommunications.
Programmes: Telecommunications and Media; Simulation-based Information Technology (SimCom); Media Management and Social Work courses leading to Dipl.-Ing. (FH) and Mag. (FH) diplomas.
Open to: foreign students who possess an Austrian or equivalent foreign secondary school leaving certificate or have passed a university entrance examination; admission on the basis of written examinations and interview.
Duration: 8 semesters.

196 University Mozarteum

Alpenstrasse 48
5020 Salzburg
Tel: +43-662-6198-0
Fax: +43-662-6198-3033
Web: http://www.moz.ac.at
e-mail: moz@moz.ac.at

📖 Undergraduate, Graduate Programmes

Study Domains: arts and crafts, audio-visual media, design, fine arts, music and musicology, performing arts.
Programmes: Bachelor of Arts (B.A.) and Master of Arts (M.A.) in instrumental study, music pedagogy, composition and conducting, music and dance education, stage design and acting.

Financial assistance: grant possibility of 600 € per month from Auslaender Stipendium, Ministry of Education, Science and Culture; also SOCRATES/ERASMUS programme for European Union citizens.

197 University of Applied Arts in Vienna

Oskar Kokoschka-Platz 2
1010 Vienna
Tel: +43-1-71133
Fax: +43-1-71133-2089
Web: http://www.angewandte.at
e-mail: pr@uni-ak.ac.at

⌂ Graduate, Postgraduate Programmes

Study Domains: applied arts, architecture, fine arts, visual arts.
Programmes: programme of courses leading to Master's degree Ph.D. in Arts and Architecture.
Open to: qualified nationals of all countries; minimum age 17; candidates having the equivalent of Austrian Matura for courses in architecture and art teachers education; for the other courses high school diploma required; entrance examination for all subjects; knowledge of German essential.
Duration: Master's degrees in Arts and Architecture, 10 semesters (courses begin in October); Ph.D., Dr. of Natural Sciences or Dr. of Architecture, an additional 4 semesters.
Financial assistance: information on possible scholarship assistance can be obtained through the Federal Ministry of Science and Research, Minoritenplatz 5, 1014 Vienna.
Applications: to the above address for all further information.

198 University of Applied Sciences, BFI VIENNA

Wohlmutstrasse 22
1020 Vienna
Tel: +43-1-7201-286
Fax: +43-1-7201-286-19
Web: http://www.fh-vie.ac.at
e-mail: info@fh-vie.ac.at

⌂ Graduate Programmes

Study Domains: business administration, economy, finance, information science, transport.
Programmes: Master's degree Programme (Mag. FH) in:
(a) European Economy and Business Management (EWUF);
(b) Banking and Finance (BAFI); (c) Project Management and Information Technology (PIT); (d) Logistic and Transport Management (LOTME).
Description: courses are career-oriented.
Duration: 4 years.
Fees: registration: approximately 400 €.
Languages: (b) German and English.

199 University of Music and Dramatic Arts, Graz [KUG]

Leonhardstrasse 15
Palais Meran
8010 Graz
Tel: +43-316-389-0
Fax: +43-316-389-1101
Web: http://www.kug.ac.at

⌂ Undergraduate, Graduate Programmes

Study Domains: decorative arts, music and musicology, performing arts.
Programmes: courses in musical instruments, voice and drama leading to the Magister / Magistra Artium degrees.
Description: most fields of study organized according to the principle of 'master classes'.
Open to: students of all nationalities with proven artistic ability.
Fees: registration: 14 € per semester; tuition: 370 to 730 € per semester; living costs: approximately 650 € per month.
Financial assistance: possibility through the Austrian Federal Ministry of Education, Science and Culture (BMBWK); for further resources, see website http://www.oead.ac.at.

200 University of Music and Performing Arts, Vienna [MDW]

Anton-von-Webern-Platz 1
1030 Vienna
Tel: +43-1-711-55 - 0
Fax: +43-1-711-55 ext 109
Web: http://www.mdw.ac.at
e-mail: studienabteilung@mdw.ac.at

⌂ Advanced, Postgraduate Programmes

Study Domains: music and musicology, performing arts.
Programmes: advanced and postgraduate studies in music and music education and in performing arts.
Description: music education covers all musical instruments, composition, conducting and voice; performing arts includes theatre, film and television. Scientific emphasis is put on several subjects (i.e. cultural management, music therapy, music sociology, etnomusicology).
Open to: candidates of all nationalities with outstanding musical proficiency and fair knowledge of German. Foreign nationals must prove financial independence in order to receive residence permit.
Duration: variable, according to programme.
Financial assistance: some scholarships offered by the University by the Austrian Exchange Service; http://www.oead.ac.at/_english/austria/grants/index.html.
Applications: directly to the University (department for studies and examination to be admitted to the entrance examination, held mainly in June).

201 University of Salzburg [UOS]

Kapitelgasse 4
5020 Salzburg
Tel: +43-662-8044-0
Fax: +43-662-8044-214
Web: http://www.uni-salzburg.at/
e-mail: uni.service@sbg.ac.at

⌂ Graduate Programmes

Study Domains: all major fields.
Programmes: programmes leading to Master's and Doctorate degrees in many major disciplines.
Open to: candidates of all nationalities holding a high school diploma; minimum age 17; good knowledge of German required.
Duration: 4 to 6 academic years; courses begin in March for Summer term; in October for Winter term.
Financial assistance: exemption from tuition fee possible under special circumstances.
Applications: by 1 February for summer term and 1 September for winter term, to Studien und Prüfungsabteilung (Registration), at the above address.

202 University of Vienna [UOV]

Dr. Karl Lueger Ring 1
1010 Vienna
Tel: +43-1-4277-0
Fax: +43-1-4277-9100
Web: http://www.univie.ac.at
e-mail: michael.thunier@univie.ac.at

⌂ Undergraduate, Graduate Studies

Study Domains: cultural studies, German, international relations, languages, political science, social sciences, summer programmes.
Programmes: courses in: (a) European Studies; (b) Political science, economics, history, law, art, music and literature; (c) German language instruction.
Open to: undergraduates, graduates, professionals, suitably qualified candidates.
Languages: German; some classes taught in English.
Applications: to the above address.

203 Vorarlberg University of Applied Sciences
Achstrasse 1
6850 Dornbirn
Tel: +43-5572-20336
Fax: +43-5572-26507
Web: http://www.fhv.at
e-mail: info@fhv.at

📖 Undergraduate and Graduate Programmes

Study Domains: business, design, engineering, social work.
Programmes: Bachelor and Master Programmes in Business, Media Design, Mechatronics, Computer Science, Social Work and Engineering with Business Administration.
Open to: students must hold a secondary-school certificate and pass the admission test. For further details check http://www.en.fhv.at/edu/enroll/.
Duration: 3 years.
Fees: tuition: approximately 750 €; living costs: approximately 600 to 700 € per month.
Languages: language of instruction: English and German; good knowledge of German required.
Applications: by end April.

204 Webster University Vienna [WUV]
Berchtoldgasse 1
1220 Vienna
Tel: +43-1-269-9293-0
Fax: +43-1-269-9293-13
Web: http://www.webster.ac.at
e-mail: info@webster.ac.at

📖 Undergraduate, Graduate Programmes

Study Domains: art history, arts, history, liberal arts, marketing, philosophy, visual arts.
Programmes: Bachelor of Arts, Bachelor of Science, Master of Arts, Master of Business Administration.
Open to: nationals of all countries; TOEFL test obligatory for non-English speakers.
Duration: 4 years.
Fees: approximately 1,000 € per session.
Financial assistance: 50% tuition waiver for duration of studies for full-time students with good academic performance and proven financial need.
Languages: English.

Azerbaijan

Organization of higher education system: The higher education system in the Azerbaijan Republic consists of the following types of state or private institutions: universities, academies, institutes, colleges and conservatoires. One of the most important reforms is the transition to a multi-level system of higher professional education in compliance with the Law on Education. This reform began in 1993. Institutions have the right to choose their approach to the multi-level education of specialists, determine the contents of this education, and draw up academic plans for these disciplines. Several institutions have started to offer the Master as from 1997. The only restrictions are those imposed by the requirements of state educational standards to maintain a minimum of knowledge. The institutions' right to autonomy is guaranteed by the Law on Education. They have acquired independence in financial and management matters. They can therefore obtain their own financial resources. University level studies:
• University level first stage: Bakalavr (Bachelor): This stage lasts for four years and leads to the Bachelor's Degree or Bakalavr. During this period, students may study the Humanities and Natural Sciences as well as the basis of the chosen speciality. The Diploma of Specialist which used to be awarded after five years is being phased out.
• University level second stage: Magistr (Master): During the second stage, which lasts between one-and-a-half and two years and leads to the Master's Degree or Magistr, students acquire in-depth knowledge and professional training in the Humanities and in Natural Sciences. The Kandidat Nauk (aspirantura) which used to be awarded after three years' postgraduate study is being phased out.

• University level third stage: Doctor: The best graduates of the Master stage are admitted to the doctoral stage. After successful completion of their studies (two or three years), they obtain the Doctoral degree (PhD). The Doktor Nauk, which used to be awarded by thesis after the Kandidat Nauk, is being phased out. (Source: IAU World Higher Education Database, 2005/6).
Monetary unit: manat Azeri.
National student admission: Certificate of General Education and National Entrance examination required for admission to university-level studies.
Language: The languages of instruction are Russian, English and Azeri.
Recognition of studies and qualification: ENIC, Ministry of Education; 49 Khatai Avenue; Baku 370008; Azerbaijan; web: http://edu.gov.az.

205 Azerbaijan State Oil Academy
Azadlig Avenue, 20
370010 Baku
Tel: +994-12-934-557
Fax: +994-12-982-941
Web: http://www.adna.baku.az
e-mail: ihm@adna.baku.az

📖 Undergraduate, Graduate, Postgraduate Programmes

Study Domains: business administration, chemical engineering, chemical industry, chemistry, computer science, earth science, ecology, environment, economy, electricity and electronics, energy, engineering, ethnology, geodesy, geology, hydraulics, hydrology, industrial technology, information science, management, marketing, mathematics, mechanical engineering, technical education, technology.
Programmes: programmes of courses leading to Bachelor's, Master's and Ph.D.
Description: Courses and research work in geological-exploration, gas-oil production, storage and transportation, chemico-technological mechanical engineering, electricity and electronics, energy, manufacturing process automation, economy, international economy, business administration.
Financial assistance: US$500 granted to a limited number of foreign students.
Languages: Azeri, Russian and English.

206 Baki Business University [BBU]
prosp. Zardabi 88a
1122 Baku
Tel: +994-12-431-7577
Web: http://www.bbu.edu.az
e-mail: info@bbu.edu.az

📖 Undergraduate, Graduate Programmes

Study Domains: accounting, business, business administration, humanities and arts, law, management, marketing, mathematics.
Open to: students of all nationalities meeting academic and financial requirements.

207 Baku Asia University
Salamzadeh Street, 28
Baku
Tel: +994-12-305-240
Fax: +994-12-313-699

📖 Undergraduate, Graduate Programmes

Study Domains: administration, Arabic, business, economic and commercial sciences, economy, English, international studies, Japanese, journalism, philology, teacher education, Turkish.
Programmes: Bachelor's and Master's of Science Programmes.
Languages: Azeri, English and Russian.
Applications: by October.

208 Baku State University

Z. Khalilov Str., 23
1073/1 Baku
Tel: +994-12-430-3245
Fax: +994-12-498-3376
Web: http://www.bsu.az/en/en.htm
e-mail: bsu@bsu.az

Undergraduate, Graduate, Postgraduate Programmes

Study Domains: biology, earth science, economy, geology, hydrology, international law, international relations, journalism, law, mathematics, oriental studies, philology, philosophy, physics, psychology, sociology, theology, religion.
Programmes: Bachelor's, Master's and Ph.D. programmes in all disciplines.

209 Western University

Istiglaliyyat Str. 27
37000 Baku
Tel: +994-12-927-724
Fax: +994-12-926-163
Web: http://www.wu.edu.az
e-mail: administration@wu.edu.az

Undergraduate, Graduate Programmes

Study Domains: applied arts, archaeology, art history, business administration, demography and population studies, economic and commercial sciences, education, engineering, European studies, fine arts, folklore, food industry, history, industrial technology, interior design, international relations, languages, linguistics, literature and civilization, mechanical engineering, performing arts, philology, philosophy, political science, psychology, social sciences, visual arts.
Programmes: Bachelor's and Master's programmes in business administration.
Languages: Azeri, Russian and English.

Bahrain

Academic year: September to June.
Organization of higher education system: Institutions of higher education in Bahrain are the following: Arabian Gulf University (www.agu.edu.bh); Gulf University (www.gulfuniversity.net); University College (www.ucb.edu.bh); University of Bahrain (www.uob.edu.bh); College of Health Sciences (www.chs.edu.bh); Gulf College of Hospitality and Tourism.
Monetary unit: Bahraini dinar (B.D.).
International student admission: Admission to some institutions is restricted to citizens of the Gulf States. Students should have qualifications equivalent to Bahrain's secondary school general certificate. Candidates should present a good health certificate as a requirement for admission.
Language: Good knowledge of Arabic and English required for regular college courses.
Immigration requirements: Visas are required for all non-Gulf States nationals. Arab Gulf University (AGU) provides visas for other nationals.
Information services: Ministry of Education, Directorate of Cultural Affairs and Scholarships, PO Box 43, Manama.
Open and distance learning: The Arabian Gulf University (AGU) offers diploma programmes at Master's and postgraduate levels; the University of Bahrain has an Electronic-Learning Centre.
Recognition of studies and qualification: For information regarding recognition of foreign credentials): Ministry of Foreign Affairs; PO Box 547, Manama, Bahrain or the cultural affairs department of embassies of the Gulf States in Bahrain.
Accommodation services: The Arabian Gulf University (AGU) provides student housing which includes undergraduate, postgraduate and married student residence.
Publications / Websites: Bulletins and brochures on Bahraini institutions are published and distributed free of charge in Arabic and English.

210 Arabian Gulf University [AGU]

PO Box 26671
Manama
Tel: +973-239-999
Fax: +973-239-555
Web: http://www.agu.edu.bh
e-mail: info@agu.edu.bh

Undergraduate, Graduate, Postgraduate Programmes

Study Domains: biochemistry, earth science, health and hygiene, hydrology, medicine, sciences, special education.
Programmes: Bachelor's, Master's and Doctorate programmes of courses: medicine and medical sciences; desert and arid zones science programme: hydrogeology and water resources management, desert agriculture, desert environment and resources; technology management programme; biotechnology programme: medical biotechnology, agricultural biotechnology, environmental biotechnology; programme of special education; programme of education for gifted and talented students.
Open to: Gulf States nationals and other Arab nationals who have residence in any of the Gulf States; for College of Medicine, not older than 24 years; holding a secondary-school certificate with a minimum average grade of 85%; entrance examination in mid-September with interview; acceptable level of English required; for postgraduate studies, B.Sc. or B.A. with a 'Very Good' grade average; admission based on Accumulative Grade Point Average (AGPA) and interview.
Languages: Arabic and English.
Applications: by April for graduate programmes; by July for undergraduate programmes; to the above address.

Scholarships

Study Domains: medicine, sciences.
Scholarships: AGU Scholarships.
Description: for studies leading to M.Sc. or M.D. degrees at AGU.
Open to: Gulf Cooperation Council (GCC) students.
Value: up to 5,500 Bahrain dinars.
Languages: Arabic and English.
Applications: to University at above address.

211 College of Health Sciences [COHS]

PO Box 12
Manama
Tel: +973-252-612 /251-360
Fax: +973-242-485
Web: http://www.batelco.com.bh/mhealth/cgi-bin/MoH/chs.htm

Undergraduate Programmes

Study Domains: health and hygiene, sciences.
Programmes: Programmes of courses leading to Bachelor's, Diploma, Associate degree and Certificate.
Description: (a) Bachelor of Science in nursing; (b) Bachelor of Science in laboratory; (c) Diploma in teacher development programme, health science, education; (d) Diploma in health education; (e) Diploma in midwifery, psychiatry, community nursing, cardiac care nursing, post-basic programme; (f) Associate Degree Diploma in nursing, pharmacy, dental hygiene, laboratory, sport therapy, health information, radiography, public health, sterilization techniques, medical equipment; (g) Certificate in medical equipment; (h) Certificate in health care administration.
Open to: candidates of any nationality, 18-22 years of age; for Associate degree programme, holding secondary-school certificate; for B.Sc. Nursing, Associate degree plus 2 years experience; for post-basic diploma, B.Sc. plus 1 year's experience; admission test in English and Science; TOEFL score of 450 required.
Duration: variable according to course.
Languages: instruction in English.
Applications: by 15 June, to the above address.

212 Gulf College of Hospitality and Tourism [HACTC]
PO Box 22088
Muharraq
Tel: +973-320-191
Fax: +973-332-547

☛ **Hotel and Catering Diploma Scholarships**

Study Domains: tourism, hotel and catering management.
Scholarships: Hotel and Catering Diploma Scholarships (4-6).
Description: tourism, hotel and catering management.
Open to: candidates of any nationality, aged 18 and above, with the equivalent of Bahrain's Secondary School General Certificate.
Duration: 2 years.
Value: free board and lodging, and transport.
Languages: good knowledge of Arabic and English essential.
Applications: by September to the Vice-Principal.

213 University of Bahrain [UOB]
Registrar
PO Box 32038
Manama
Tel: +973-449-388
Fax: +973-4449-833
Web: http://www.uob.bh

📖 **Undergraduate, Graduate, Postgraduate Programmes**

Study Domains: all major fields.
Programmes: Bachelor's, Master's and Ph.D. Programmes.
Open to: students with Bahrain Secondary School General Certificate or equivalent as accredited by the Ministry of Education.
Languages: instruction in Arabic, except for the Colleges of Business Studies and Engineering.
Applications: to the above address for more information.

Bangladesh

Academic year: January to December.
Organization of higher education system: Higher education institutions include public and private universities, institutes of technology and colleges. The universities are divided into four categories: general, special, open and affiliating. Chittagong, Dhaka, Rajshahi and Shahjahal University of Science and Technology have affiliated medical colleges. All the other colleges are affiliated with the Bangladesh National University. In affiliating systems, the teaching is carried out in the colleges while curriculum and examinations are controlled by the universities. The President of Bangladesh is the Chancellor of the universities and is responsible for the appointment of Vice-Chancellors. The executive body of each institution is the syndicate which approves accounts and reports. Teaching staff elect deans of faculties, who, along with professors and affiliated colleges representatives, make up the Academic Council. Government grants constitute nearly 95% of the income of the universities. They are provided by the University Grants Commission. Tuition fees provide the other main source of funding. The Association of Universities of Bangladesh coordinates activities of the universities in academic and administrative matters. It also liaises with the government and the UGC concerning administrative and financial affairs. Colleges are administratively and financially under government or private control. Some of the larger and better equipped colleges have been named university colleges. All medical colleges are under the administrative control of the Ministry of Health and Family Planning. Since 1986, the degree-offering engineering colleges at Rajshahi, Chittagong, Khulna and Dhaka have become Bangladesh Institutes of Technology and are autonomous. They are outside the UGC system and have a Council of Institutes with the Minister of Education as its chairman. The Independent University was founded recently and the Institute of Postgraduate Medicine and Research, University of Dhaka, has become the Bangabandhu Sheikh Mujib Medical University. (Source: IAU World Higher Education Database.).

Monetary unit: taka.
National student admission: Access to higher education is based on the higher-secondary-school certificate. Candidates may have to take prescribed options (e.g. for engineering: mathematics, physics and chemistry, etc.) and for degree courses they are chosen on merit, according to the number of places available. Applications should be made in March to the Secretary at the Ministry of Education.
Foreign students admission: Entry regulations: Foreign students must hold a visa. Language requirements: Students should be proficient in English.
Language: The principal languages of instruction are English and Bengali. Foreign students must be proficient in English.
Immigration requirements: Foreign students must hold a visa.
Estimated expenses for one academic year: Grants, scholarships, fellowships and assistantships are available to foreign students.
Information services: Ministry of Education; International Relations, Bangladesh Secretariat, 1, Sonargon Road Palashi-Nilkhet, Dhaka 1000; Bangladesh; email: moel@bdcom.com.
Open and distance learning: The Bangladesh Open University offers both formal programmes leading to degrees, diplomas and certificates and non-formal public awareness programmes for those who have been unable to follow the traditional system. The Bangladesh Institute of Distance Education offers a Bachelor of Education through audio-visual programmes. Bangladesh Agricultural University (BAU) offers extension programmes for villages neighbouring the campus. (Source: IAU World Higher Education Database).
Recognition of studies and qualification:
• Ministry of Education, Science and Technology, Bangladesh Secretariat, 1, Sonargon Road, Palashi-Nilkhet, Dhaka 1205, Bangladesh; email: moel@bdcom.com.
Work opportunities: Students are allowed to work on campus.

214 Ahsanullah University of Science and Technology [AUST]
20, West Testuri Bazar Road, Tejgaon, 1215 Dhaka
Tel: +880-2-91-20248 / 30508
Fax: +880-2-81-13010 / 1852
Web: http://www.aust.edu
e-mail: regr@aust.edu

📖 **Undergraduate, Graduate Programmes**

Study Domains: architecture, business administration, education, engineering.
Programmes: Bachelor's and Master's Programmes of Courses.
Description: (a) B.Sc., Engineering; (b) B.A Business Administration; (c) B.Arch.; (d) M.Education; (e) M.B.A.
Open to: candidates of all nationalities.
Duration: (a) and (b) 4 years: (c) 5 years; (d) 1 year; (e) 2 years.
Fees: tuition: US$1,600 per year; living costs, approx. US$1,600 per year.
Financial assistance: foreign student scholarships offered by the university in the amount of US$600 per academic year; candidates must have good grades at 'A' level in Physics, Chemistry and Mathematics or its equivalent of 12 years of schooling; contact the Registrar at the above address for further information.

☛ **Scholarships**

Study Domains: architecture, business administration, civil engineering, computer science, education, electricity and electronics, textile industry.
Scholarships: Foreign Student Scholarship.
Open to: candidates of all nationalities; candidates must have good grades at A-level in physics, chemistry, and mathematics or its equivalent of 12 years of schooling.
Value: US$600 per academic year.
Applications: by 31 July to the Registrar at the above address.

215 Islamic University of Technology [IUT]

Board Bazar
1704 Gazipur
Tel: +880-2-929-1252
Fax: +880-2-9291260
Web: http://www.iutoic-dhaka.edu/index/index.htm
e-mail: regstrar@iut-dhaka.edu

📖 Undergraduate, Graduate Programmes

Study Domains: computer science, engineering, mechanical engineering, teacher education, technical education, vocational training.
Programmes: undergraduate and graduate programmes.
Open to: male nationals of Organisation of Islamic Conference (OIC) member countries; only male students accepted (in 2003); students must be nominated by their respective governments and must meet the minimum criteria of admission.
Applications: by 12 October to the Registrar at the above address; email: regstrar@iit-dhaka.edu.

🎓 Scholarships

Study Domains: engineering, technology.
Scholarships: IUT/IDB Scholarships.
Subjects: for undergraduate engineering programmes and postgraduate programmes in technical education.
Open to: Organisation of Islamic Conference (OIC) nationals.
Duration: for entire duration of studies, provided results are satisfactory.
Value: full tuition, board and monthly stipend of US$40.
Applications: by 6 October; contact the Registrar at the IUC at the above address, Email: registrar@iut-dhaka.edu.

216 Khulna University

9208 Khulna
Tel: +880-41-720-171 / 721-791
Fax: +880-41-731-244
Web: http://www.ugc.org/khulna_uni.htm
e-mail: ku@bdonline.com

📖 Undergraduate Programmes

Study Domains: agriculture, architecture, computer science, ecology, environment, electricity and electronics, engineering, fisheries, forestry, laboratory techniques, pharmacy and pharmacology, sciences, telecommunications, urbanism.
Programmes: Bachelor's degree programmes.
Open to: candidates of any nationality; higher secondary certificate or equivalent; English proficiency.
Duration: 4 to 5 years.
Languages: English.

217 Southern University Bangladesh

GPO Box 842
4000 Chittagong
Tel: +880-31-626-744
Web: http://www.southern-bd.info
e-mail: southern_u@mail.com

🎓 Undergraduate, Graduate Programmes

Study Domains: architecture, business administration, computer science, development studies, economic and commercial sciences, English, law, social sciences, tourism, hotel and catering management.
Subjects: Faculty of Business: BBA, Bachelor of Tourism & Hospitality Management, MBA, EMBA etc.;
Faculty of Science and Technology: BSc. Computer Science and Information Technology (CSIT), BSc.Computer Science and Engineering (CSE) (up coming), BSc.Arch, MSc.IT, MSc.CSIT, M.Sc. (Comparative World Systems); Faculty of Social Science and Arts: BA. Law, BA. Economics, BA. English, MA. Law, MA. English, Economics and Development.
Open to: all enrolled students based on academic results and financial need.
Duration: 4 academic years; renewable.
Value: tuition waiver.

218 The Peoples University of Bangladesh [PUB]

7116, Block B. Lalmatia
Dhaka
Tel: +880-912-7807
Fax: +880-912-7807
Web: http://www.thepub.edu
e-mail: ve-pubd@bdonline.com

📖 Undergraduate, Graduate Programmes

Study Domains: accounting, business administration, computer science, English, finance, marketing.
Programmes: Bachelor's, Honours and Master's Degree Programmes.
Open to: all nationalities.
Academic requirements: admission examination; English proficiency is required.
Languages: English.
Applications: first week of July and first week of January.

219 United International University [UIU]

House No 83 Road No 8/A, Dhanmondi
1209 Dhaka
Tel: +880-2-912-5912
Fax: +880-2-912-5916
Web: http://uiu.ac.bd
e-mail: info@uiu.ac.bd

🎓 Financial Aid

Study Domains: engineering.
Open to: all students in Bachelor's and Master's programmes, based on academic results.
Value: tuition waiver of 25% to 100%.

220 University of Chittagong [CU]

Chittagong
Tel: +880-31-682-031 to 39 / 714-92
Fax: +880-31-726-310
Web: http://www.ctgu.edu
e-mail: vc-cu@spnet.ctg.com

📖 Undergraduate, Graduate, Postgraduate Programmes

Study Domains: arts, business, law, medicine, sciences, social sciences.
Programmes: programme of courses leading to Bachelor's, Master's and Ph.D. degrees.
Description: Bachelor's, Master's, Doctorate degrees in arts, science, commerce, social science, law and medicine.
Open to: candidates of all nationalities.
Financial assistance: some scholarships available; contact the Registrar-in-Charge for further information at the above address.
Languages: Bengali and English.
Applications: decided by the Admissions Committee; write to the Registrar-in-Charge at the above address for further information.

221 University of Dacca (Dhaka Bishwadibidyalaya) [UOD]

Ramna
1000 Dhaka
Tel: +880-2-966-1900
Fax: +880-2-861-5583
Web: http://www.univdhaka.edu
e-mail: duregstr@bangla.net

📖 Undergraduate, Graduate, Postgraduate Programmes

Study Domains: all major fields.
Programmes: Bachelor's, Master's and Ph.D. programme of studies.
Description: undergraduate, graduate and postgraduate programmes in: accounting, applied chemistry and chemical engineering, applied physics and electronics, Arabic, anthropology, Bengali, biochemistry, botany, business administration, chemistry, computer science, economics, education and research, English, finance and banking, fine arts, geography, geology, history, international relations, Islamic studies, Islamic history and cultures, law, library and information science, linguistics, management, marketing,

mathematics, medicine, microbiology, modern languages, mass communication and journalism, nutrition and food sciences, pharmacy, philosophy, physics, political science, psychology, public administration, Sanskrit and Pali, social welfare, sociology, soil sciences, statistical research and training, statistics, Urdu and Persian, zoology.
Open to: qualified candidates of all countries.
Applications: to the Registrar for all further information.

Barbados

Academic year: September to June.
Organization of higher education system: Barbados is affiliated with the University of the West Indies. The supreme authority of the University is the Council, which comprises representatives of member territories, professors and appointed members. The Senate, composed of teaching members of the University, is responsible for academic decisions. Deans of faculties are elected yearly. The University is autonomous. More than 90 per cent of its resources come from contributing territories. Other higher Institutions include Barbados Community College, Erdiston Teacher's College, and the Samuel Jackman Prescod Polytechnic.
Monetary unit: Barbados dollar (BD$).
National student admission: Foreign students should have qualifications equivalent to the General Certificate of Education with a combination of either 4 passes at Ordinary O-level, or 2 passes at Advanced A-level and 3 at O-level, for admission to the University of the West Indies, or 3 passes at A-level and 1 at O-level.
International student admission: Foreign students should have qualifications equivalent to the General Certificate of Education with a combination of either four passes at Ordinary ('O') level or two passes at Advanced ('A') level and three at 'O' level for admission to the University of the West Indies, or three passes at 'A' level and one at 'O' level.
Language: Knowledge of English is essential for regular university courses.
Immigration requirements: Students require a visa from the Immigration Department of Barbados.
Estimated expenses for one academic year: Full-time tuition: BDS$23,000; books/supplies: BDS$2,500; housing: BDS$3,200.
Information services:
• Ministry of Education, Bridgetown (general information and advice).
Open and distance learning: A distance learning programme is available at the University of the West Indies.
Recognition of studies and qualification: National Accreditation Council of Barbados; email: uwichill@edu.bb.

---

222 Barbados Community College [BCC]
The Eyrie
Howell's Cross Road
St. Michael
Tel: +1-246-426-2858
Fax: +1-246-429-5935
Web: http://www.bcc.edu.bb
e-mail: dbradshaw@bcc.edu.bb

📖 Undergraduate Programmes
Study Domains: applied arts, applied sciences, arts, business, civil engineering, health and hygiene, languages, sciences.
Programmes: Associate degree programmes.
Open to: Caribbean nationals with 4 GCE or CXC O-levels or equivalent.
Duration: 2 years for Associate degree; 4 years for Bachelor of Fine Arts; courses begin 15 September.
Fees: to be advertised.
Financial assistance: offered by international donor organizations: CIDA, PAHO, CFTC.
Applications: by 31 July; by 31 May for health sciences and by 31 March for international students.

223 Barbados Institute of Management and Productivity [BIMAP]
BIMAP Drive
Wildey, St. Michael
Tel: +1-246-431-4200
Fax: +1-246-429-6733
Web: http://www.bimap.com.bb
e-mail: office@bimap.com.bb

📖 Management Training and Executive Development Programme
Study Domains: economy, finance, management, marketing, statistics.
Programmes: Management Training and Executive Development Programme: (a) seminars and regular training in the following subject areas: general management, human resources, production, marketing, accounting (financial and managerial), finance, industrial relations, organization development, quantitative methods, customer relations, economics, statistics, retail and sales management, manager and the environment, business policy, personnel, computer applications in management; 20 participants; (b) general management integrated programme for executives: finance and control, business policy, industrial relations, decision-making, strategy and competitive analysis. BIMAP also organizes tailor-made sessions for individual companies and organizations; seminars, workshops and symposia in special interest topics, advisory services for internal management and small business assistance to would-be owner/managers; (c) diploma in management studies; (d) Entrepreneurial Development Programme: Phase I pre-business workshop; Phase II practical sessions ending with the preparation of a business plan; (e) Entrepreneurial Development Programme Diploma: self-analysis, marketing, budgeting and forecasting, computer applications; (f) small business management training programme: marketing, production, accounting, finance, personnel management.
Open to: (a) and (b) candidates with higher national diploma, Bachelor's degree or equivalent and 5 years experience in management or related fields; age over 25; adult student status may be accorded; (c) candidates with minimum of 5 O-level certificates, higher national diploma, Bachelor's degree, etc.; (d) to (f) candidates of any country, over 21 years old, who are interested in starting a business.
Duration: (a) 3 months (beginning in January, April and September); (b) 15 sessions of 3 hours each or scheduled to meet special needs; (c) 1 to 2 years; (d) 4 months (courses begin in November and March); (e) 1 month; (f) 4 months (courses begin in June, July and August).
Fees: available on request.
Financial assistance: (d) to (f) some fellowships are available.
Languages: instruction in English.
Applications: (a) to (c) by 15 November, 15 February and 15 July; to the Executive Trustee, BIMAP; (d) by January and September; (e) by February and November; (f) by May; to the above address.

Belarus, Republic of
Academic year: September to June.
Organization of higher education system:
• Types of higher education institutions: University type institutions: Universitet (University); Academia (Academy); Institut (Institute); Vysshij Kolledz (Higher College); Non-University type Institutions: Kolledz (College); Technikum (Technical College); Uchilische (Specialized Institution).
• Higher education awards: Bakalavr (4 years' study, corresponds to Bachelor's degree); Specialist's Diploma (1 to 2 years' study beyond Bakalavr, corresponds to Master's degree); Magistr (1 year's study beyond Specialist's); Kandidat Nauk (3 to 4 years' study beyond Specialist's, corresponds to PhD. degree); Doktor Nauk (postgraduate studies - by thesis after Kandidat).
• First and second levels of higher education provided by public (State) and private (non-State) accredited higher education institutions (HEIs). Education in public HEIs is free of charge for students passing the entrance competition. Some paying students are also accepted. Tuition fees are charged for

all private institutions. Higher education is under the authority of the Ministry of Education of the Republic of Belarus, which is responsible for accreditation and licensing of HEIs and for developing and implementing the state educational standards.

There are two levels of higher education: (1) first level leading to the Bakalavr (undergraduate Bachelor's degree); (2) second level consisting of 1-2 years leads to the Specialist's Diploma or Master's degree (graduate level). HEIs are authorized to award the Specialist's Diploma (professional degrees such as for law, engineering) after 1 year of study or Master's degree after 2 years of study beyond the Bachelor's.

• Third level of higher education (postgraduate studies): There are two levels of doctoral degrees for the training of scientific and pedagogical personnel: (1) Kandidat Nauk (candidate of sciences) and (2) Doktor Nauk (doctor of sciences - the highest level).

Kandidat Nauk: postgraduate studies called Aspirantura are available at almost every HEI as well as at many university-level and research institutions. The Aspirantura in Belarus does not lead to a degree but is rather a special level of study in scientific postgraduate education. A Candidate of Science degree is granted on completion of studies in a definite research field, passing an examination, preparation and public defense of a thesis before a jury and validation by a state body. The Candidate of Science degree is equal to a PhD degree and is usually recognized worldwide due to high state requirements and level of research.

There are three forms of study in Aspirantura. (1) Full-time is the quickest and most popular form in Belarus and is the choice of most foreign Aspirantura students. Every native Belarusian full-time student of Aspirantura at a public HEI receives a stipend for 3 years of study and student accommodation, if required. Full-time students must attend classes in philosophy, foreign languages and computer science and other courses necessary for professional development; (2) Extramural students study as long as 4 years without obligatory classes but with a course supervisor. Students have the possibility of attending classes with full-time Aspirantura students; (3) 'Soiskatelstvo' is a special form of extramural study lasting five years and does not require class attendance and little course supervision.

Each HEI appoints a personal supervisor and approves the research topic for every Aspirantura student. Aspirantura studies are generally free of charge within a quota, over which the institution may charge tuition to students at fees of 20-50% over the Bachelor's or Master's level.

• Doktor Nauk: The second and highest level of scientific degree, Doctor of Science, is for studies in a specific field of discipline for students with Candidate of Science degrees. Students prepare their doctoral degree dissertations independently. A special fellowship for students in doctorantura may be accorded by the Academic Council of each HEI upon request. The right to run two-year doctorantura can be given by the State to institutions with common recognized scientific schools. Doctoral degree dissertations are defended before a jury and validated by a state commission.

Doctorantura and Aspirantura may also be offered by other research institutes such as the National Academy of Science and national retraining institutions.

• Reforms: The following higher education reforms are under way (in 2005): (1) diversification of higher education; (2) humanization; (3) decentralization of management, university autonomy; (4) creation of a non-public sector of higher education. There are 45 public HEIs and 12 accredited non-State HEIs in Belarus. All public HEIs receive financial support from the state. There are over 160 non-university level educational institutions (colleges, technikums, uchilisches).

Monetary unit: Belarusian rouble.

National student admission: For national students: The access to higher education in Belarus is limited by the pre-requisite of secondary education certificate (11 years of study at a general school or equal training at a vocational school, technicums or college). Admission to Belarusian HEIs is conducted by competitive examinations. Individuals who are permanent residents of the Republic of Belarus as well as citizens of the Republic of Belarus and Belarusians who live outside Belarus and citizens of the Russian Federation have a right to be admitted and receive free education in Belarusian public HEIs. Equal opportunity exists in the Russian Federation for the citizens of Belarus. There is no

discrimination by race, gender, origin and religious or political orientation. Every public higher educational establishment has a certain number of vacancies financially supported by the state budget. The entrants are admitted to fill these vacancies according to the required number of points gained at the entrance examinations. The number of entrance exams is limited by four.

International student admission: International students must hold a secondary school-leaving certificate or an equivalent qualification to that of general secondary school in Belarus. They must submit a valid passport, a notarized copy of their secondary education qualification, a medical certificate and 6 photos. They are then sent an invitation in order to obtain an entry visa. For postgraduate courses, students must hold a Master's Degree. The rules of admission and instruction are specified in the Regulations concerning Training Foreign Citizens in the Republic of Belarus approved by the decree of the Council of Ministers of the Republic of Belarus of 7 July 1993. Admission documents must be submitted at least two-and-a-half months before classes begin in Belarusian, Russian, English, French or Spanish. Admission requirements for foreign students are established by the higher education institutions if not otherwise provided for by intergovernmental agreements. Foreign students sign a contract with the institution. To adjust secondary school programmes and Russian language study the preparatory course (6 to 10 months) is available. Postgraduate studies (aspirantura) last for three years and require at a Master degree level. Foreign nationals entering establishments of higher education under intergovernmental agreements should not be over 28 years of age, or in the case of postgraduate studies, 35.

Language: The language of instruction is Russian and/or Belarusian. Foreign students who have no command of the language of instruction can follow a one-year course at a preparatory department of the institution where they study the language of instruction and specialization subjects that are relevant for the chosen course. At the end of the year, they must sit for an examination. Successful students obtain a graduation certificate and are admitted to the basic course of study in the chosen speciality. Those who fail are dismissed from the institution and asked to leave the country.

Immigration requirements: Students must hold a visa and have financial guarantees. A medical certificate is required.

Estimated expenses for one academic year: Tuition: Foreign students admitted for study at Belarusian establishments of higher education under intergovernmental agreements receive a monthly grant equal to the grant for the corresponding categories of Belarusian students. One year of tuition fees on a contract basis varies from US$1,500-$4,500 per year, depending on the subject chosen, the form of study, and arrangements for board and lodging. Current registration: US$30; living costs: US$200 per month; housing: US$150-$300 per month.

Information services:

• Authority to whom international students' application should be addressed: Further information on study opportunities for international students in the higher educational establishments of the Republic of Belarus can be obtained from the Ministry of Education of the Republic of Belarus - Head of Division of International Education and Cooperation of the Ministry of Education Ul. Sredlova 7 Minsk Belarus; web: http://www.minedu.unibel.by

• Belarusian diplomatic missions in other countries (for general information and advice for foreign students concerning study in Belarus.

Scholarships for international students: Students in public, and sometimes private, universities are eligible to receive stipends that cover housing and some living expenses in residence halls or private apartments. Over 70% of full-time students attending public HEIs receive stipends with the amount varying according to academic results. A personal stipend may also be accorded by the President of the Republic of Belarus, Council of Ministries or Academic Council of the university.

A special stipend is awarded to students with high academic achievements in training, research work and scientific/technological activities. A special stipend is allocated for successful students from low-income families whose average grades do not allow them to receive a regular stipend. To be among the successful students a student should have no academic debts (low grades) in the qualifying examination and attend all the courses and various pertinent learning events.

For further information contact the Division of International Education and Cooperation of the Ministry of Education, Ul. Sredlova 7, Minsk, Belarus; fax: +375-17-227-17-36; which publishes the Grants Publications on student services and financial aid: Title: Scholarship for Study and Research in Belarus.

Open and distance learning: Distance learning is regarded as ICT utilization for provision of a wide variety of education programmes or parts (blocks) of programmes all: higher professional education, vocational education, school education, lifelong education and upgrading courses.

Recognition of studies and qualification:
• Ministry of Education of the Republic of Belarus, Department of Foreign Relations: 7, Sverdlov Str., Minsk, Republic of Belarus; web: http://www.minedu.unibel.by
• National Centre for Recognition of Higher Education Qualifications (Belarusian ENIC), National Institute for Higher Education: Moskowskaya St., 15, Minsk 220001, Belarus; email: enic@nihe.niks.by; web: http://www.nihe.niks.by.

Accommodation services: Photo ID issued by a public HEI is an evidence of the institution its owner belongs to. That gives the right to a public HEI student use all the public libraries free of charge, take public city transport (but not taxi) in a half of rate over the year and inter city public transport, as train and bus, in a half of rate from 1 September to 30 June. A public HEI student whose permanent address is in different place can apply to university for residence hall room under extremely low cost. Foreign students are provided with a place in a dormitory also. Usually, a dormitory room should be shared with one or two roommates. There are many opportunities for the students to participate in additional sport, tourist or cultural classes and clubs free of charge.

Publications / Websites:
• 'Guide to higher education in Belarus', published by the Belarusian ENIC, National Institute for Higher Education.
• 'Higher Education in Belarus' - National Report of the Republic of Belarus, 2004. Directory of Accredited Higher Education Institutions (in Russian, Belarusian, English). Author: National Institute for Higher Education, 2003, Higher Education in Belarus, Author: S. Vetokhin. Publisher: National Institute of Higher Education, Belarusian ENIC, 2001.
• Student Handbook (3rd edition), Author: Council of Europe, Publisher: Bock Verlag in Germany, 1997.
• Belarusian Association of UNESCO Clubs: Ul. Kabushkina 18, 220118, Minsk, Belarus, tel: +375-17-2642-555.

---

224 Académie de médecine vétérinaire de Vitebsk
Rue Dovator 7/11
210602 Vitebsk
Tel: +375-212-372-044
Fax: +375-212-370-284
Web: http://www.ceebd.co.uk/ceeed/un/be/be032.htm

📖 Cours de médecine vétérinaire
Domaines d'étude: médecine vétérinaire, zoologie.
Programmes: (a) Diplôme de docteur en médecine vétérinaire; (b) Cours d'élevage industriel du bétail; (c) Cours de perfectionnement pour les diplômés (jusqu'à 36 ans).
A l'intention de: ressortissants de tout pays, titulaires d'un diplôme de fin d'études secondaires; admission sur examen d'entrée (biologie, chimie); certificat médical requis.
Durée: 4 ans (débutant le 1er septembre); cours d'été en juillet et août.
Connaissances linguistiques: langue d'enseignement: russe; cours spéciaux de russe si nécessaire.
Inscriptions: avant le 15 juin, à l'adresse ci-dessus pour de plus amples renseignements.

225 Académie de musique Bélarus [ADMB]
Internationalnaya St., 30
220030 Minsk
Tel: +375-17-227-4942
Fax: +375-17-206-5501
Web: http://www.bgam.edu.by/bgam_en
e-mail: international@tut.by

📖 1er, 2e, 3e cycles / musique
Domaines d'étude: musique et musicologie.
Programmes: programme de cours allant du 1er au 3e cycles en musique.
Description: cours dans les domaines suivants: piano, compositeurs et études musicales, chœurs, chant, instruments folkloriques, instruments d'orchestre et chef d'orchestre, chorégraphie.
A l'intention de: ressortissants de tout pays.
Inscriptions: à l'adresse ci-dessus pour de plus amples renseignements.

226 Académie des beaux-arts du Bélarus
81, avenue Skorina
220012 Minsk
Tel: +375-17-232-1542
Fax: +375-17-232-2041

📖 Arts du spectacle
Domaines d'étude: arts décoratifs, arts du spectacle, arts graphiques.
Programmes: Diplôme d'éducation supérieure dans les domaines suivants: arts du spectacle, arts décoratifs, graphiques, plastiques, dessin industriel et histoire de l'art.
Languages: cours dispensés en anglais.
Inscriptions: à l'adresse ci-dessus.

227 Académie polytechnique d'État de Bélarus [APDB]
F. Skorina Avenue, 65
220027 Minsk
Tel: +375-17-232-3842
Fax: +375-17-232-9137

📖 1er, 2e, 3e cycles / ingénierie
Domaines d'étude: toutes disciplines principales, architecture, bâtiment, construction, énergie, mécanique, technologie.
Programmes: Diplôme d'ingénieur, Maîtrise et Doctorat dans toutes les disciplines principales et particulièrement en mécanique et technologie énergétique, énergie, construction civile, travaux publics, architecture, systèmes cybernétiques, construction d'outils.
A l'intention de: ressortissants de tout pays, âgés de 17 à 35 ans, titulaires d'un diplôme de fin d'études secondaires pour les facultés et d'un diplôme d'études supérieures pour la maîtrise et le doctorat; russe obligatoire (cours préparatoires de 6 à 10 mois).
Durée: 5 à 6 ans selon les disciplines.
Connaissances linguistiques: enseignement en russe.
Inscriptions: avant le 1er octobre pour les cours préparatoires et le 1er septembre pour la 1ère année.

228 Institut d'agriculture de Grodno [IDDG]
Tereshkova St., 28
230600 Grodno
Tel: +375-152-77-0168
Fax: +375-152-72-1365
Web: http://www.uni-agro.grodno.by
e-mail: ggay@uni-agro.grodno.by

📖 Programme d'études en agronomie, protection des plantes, génie zoologique
Domaines d'étude: horticulture, sciences agronomiques, zoologie.
Programmes: cours en agronomie, protection des plantes, génie zoologique.
A l'intention de: ressortissants de tout pays, remplissant les conditions requises.
Inscriptions: à l'adresse ci-dessus pour de plus amples renseignements.

229 **Institut d'État de médecine de Gomel [IEMG]**
5, Lange
246000 Gomel
Tel: +375-232-53-4121
Fax: +375-232-53-9831
e-mail: medinstitut@mail.gomel.by

  Médecine

Domaines d'étude: assistance sociale, biophysique, chimie, écologie, environnement, études d'infirmière, génétique, médecine, microbiologie, psychiatrie.
Programmes: Diplôme de médecine.
Durée: 6 ans.
Frais: 1.700 US$ par an et 25 US$ par mois pour les frais de séjour.
Inscriptions: avant le 1er octobre au recteur de l'institut, à l'adresse ci-dessus.

230 **Institut d'État de médecine de Grodno**
80, rue Gorki
230015 Grodno
Tel: +375-152-335-561/ 338-221
Fax: +375-152-335-341
Web: http://grsmu.by/english/index.html
e-mail: ief@grsmu.by

  Médecine

Domaines d'étude: médecine.
Programmes: Diplôme de docteur en médecine (pédiatrie, médecine psychologique); cours de formation et d'administration pour les infirmières chefs.
A l'intention de: ressortissants de tout pays, âgés de 35 ans maximum pour les résidents nationaux, titulaires du diplôme de médecin généraliste; admission sur examen.
Durée: 6 ans; spécialisation: 1 an.
Assistance financière: bourse minimale: 400.000 roubles bélarus.
Connaissances linguistiques: russe.
Inscriptions: avant le 15 juillet, à l'adresse ci-dessus.

231 **Institut polytechnique de Brest**
Moskowskaja 267
224017 Brest
Tel: +375-162-427-457
Fax: +375-162-422-127
Web: http://www.brpi.unibel.by
e-mail: canc@cc.brpi.unibel.by

  Diplôme d'ingénieur

Domaines d'étude: architecture, bâtiment, construction, génie civil, hydraulique, informatique.
Programmes: Cours conduisant au Diplôme d'ingénieur dans les domaines suivants: génie civil, matériaux de construction, génie des transports, architecture, ingénierie hydraulique, informatique.
A l'intention de: ressortissants russes et bélorusses, âgés de 17 à 18 ans, titulaires d'un diplôme de fin d'études secondaires ou techniques; admission directe du 16 au 30 juillet; examen et entretien.
Assistance financière: aide financière accordée au cas par cas.
Connaissances linguistiques: langues d'enseignement: russe et biélorusse.

232 **Institut polytechnique de Gomel**
October Avenue, 48
246746 Gomel
Tel: +375-232-481-600/480-020
Fax: +375-232-479-165
Web: http://www.gpi.gomel.by
e-mail: root@gpi.gomel.by

  Cours conduisant aux diplômes en sciences

Domaines d'étude: électricité et électronique, mécanique, technologie.
Programmes: Cours dans les domaines suivants: mathématiques, informatique, sciences naturelles et ingénierie.

A l'intention de: ressortissants de tout pays, remplissant les conditions requises.
Inscriptions: pour de plus amples renseignements, écrire à l'adresse ci-dessus.

233 **Institut technologique de Moguilev**
3, avenue Chmidt
212027 Moguilev
Tel: +375-222-448-573
Fax: +375-222-443-229
e-mail: mti@mti.belpak.mogilev.by

  1er, 2e cycles / ingénierie

Domaines d'étude: économie, ingénierie, mécanique, technologie.
Programmes: Licence, Diplôme d'ingénieur.
Description: technologie, mécanique, automatisation et économie.
A l'intention de: ressortissants de tout pays, titulaires d'un diplôme de fin d'études secondaires.
Connaissances linguistiques: langues d'enseignement: russe et biélorusse.
Inscriptions: pendant le mois de mai, à l'adresse ci-dessus.

234 **Institut technologique de Vitebsk [VSTU]**
Moscow Prospect 72
210028 Vitebsk
Tel: +375-212-255-026
Fax: +375-212-259-000

  Formations conduisant au diplôme d'ingénieur

Domaines d'étude: économie, mécanique, technologie.
Programmes: formation fondamentale et générale dans les disciplines scientifiques de base conduisant au Diplôme d'ingénieur; formation approfondie d'ingénieur (dès la 3e année); stage pratique en entreprise de 4 à 8 semaines.
A l'intention de: ressortissants de tous pays, titulaires du certificat de fin d'études secondaires générales ou techniques; russe obligatoire (test oral).
Durée: 5 ans.
Frais: inscription: 500 US$ (remboursés lors du départ); frais de scolarité: 1.000 US$-2,000 US$ par an; frais pour soins médicaux: 50 US$; prévoir les frais de logement.
Connaissances linguistiques: langue d'enseignement: russe.
Inscriptions: avant le 1er septembre.

235 **State University of Physical Culture of Belarus [BSAPhC]**
International Relations Department
Masherova Ave.
220020 Minsk
Tel: +375-17-250-3084
Fax: +375-17-250-8008
Web: http://www.bgafk.unibel.by
e-mail: mo@bgafk.unibel.by

  Undergraduate, Graduate, Postgraduate Programmes

Study Domains: health and hygiene, physical education, recreation and leisure, teacher education, tourism, hotel and catering management.
Programmes: Bachelor's, Master's and Ph.D. programmes in physical culture and sports.
Description: courses lead to training of highly qualified coaches in different sports, physical training teachers, physical training instructors in the field of rehabilitation, recreation and fitness, massage therapists, and sports managers; the curriculum includes theoretical, medical, biological, pedagogical and scientific cycles as well as special fitness and massage therapy programmes.
Open to: candidates of all nationalities meeting academic, financial, linguistic and medical requirements.
Fees: undergraduate and graduate programmes: US$1,500-$1,700 per year; postgraduate programmes: US$2,500 per year; preparatory language courses: US$700 per year; dormitory: US$150 per year per person.
Applications: to the above address.

236 Université d'État Bélarus [UDB]
F. Skorina Avenue, 4
220080 Minsk
Tel: +375-172-265-940
Fax: +375-172-265-940
Web: http://www.bsu.unibel.by
e-mail: brus@org.bsu.unibel.by

📖 **2e, 3e cycles / toutes disciplines principales**

Domaines d'étude: biologie, chimie, droit, géographie,
histoire, journalisme, mathématiques, mécanique, philologie,
physique.
Programmes: Maîtrise et Doctorat dans toutes les
disciplines principales: biologie, physique, géographie,
chimie, mécanique et mathématiques, histoire, électronique,
journalisme, philologie, philosophie, économie et droit,
mathématiques appliquées, langue et littérature.
A l'intention de: ressortissants de tout pays, titulaires d'un
diplôme de fin d'études secondaires ou titre reconnu
équivalent; bonne connaissance de la langue russe requise;
admission par sélection (tests
écrits et entretien).
Durée: 5 ans.
Connaissances linguistiques: langues d'enseignement:
russe et biélorusse.
Inscriptions: à l'adresse ci-dessus pour de plus amples
renseignements.

**237 Université d'État
d'informatique et de
radioélectronique [UEIRB]**
6, rue P. Brovki
220013 Minsk
Tel: +375-17-231-0914
Fax: +375-17-231-0914
Web: http://www.bsuir.unibel.by
e-mail: shuam@gwbsuir.unibel.by

📖 **1er, 2e cycles / toutes disciplines principales**

Domaines d'étude: économie, électricité et électronique,
enseignement technique, gestion, informatique, ingénierie,
langues, mathématiques, philosophie, physique,
télécommunications.
Programmes: Diplômes de 1er et 2e cycles.
Description: cours dans les domaines suivants:
informatique, radio-électronique, automation et
télécommunication.
Languages: russe.

**238 Université d'État de Gomel
[UDDG]**
Sovetskaya St., 104
246699 Gomel
Tel: +375-232-567-371
Fax: +375-232-578-111

📖 **Programme pluridisciplinaire**

Domaines d'étude: biologie, droit, écologie,
environnement, économie, géographie, géologie, gestion,
histoire, ingénierie, langues, linguistique, mathématiques,
physique, psychologie.
Programmes: Programme de cours dans les domaines
suivants: histoire et droit, philologie, mathématiques, gestion
de l'entreprise, biologie, économie, physique, géologie et
géographie conduisant aux diplômes de professeurs de
mathématiques, de russe, de physique, d'informatique, de
biologie et de chimie, d'économiste-management, de juriste,
de philologue, de physicien, mathématicien, ingénieur,
physicien et géologue; délivre la maîtrise en psychologie,
écologie et protection de la nature, programmation et moulage
mathématique, fiscalité, institutions et droit d'État, italien,
anglais, français et allemand.
A l'intention de: ressortissants de tout pays, âgés de 17 à
18 ans maximum, titulaires d'un diplôme de fin d'études
secondaires; ceux qui maîtrisent le russe sont admis en 4e
année; admission sur dossier et entretien; les étrangers
peuvent suivre des cours préparatoires de russe (10 mois) ou
des cours accélérés; l'enseignement de l'algèbre, de la logique
mathématique et de la théorie des nombres peut s'effectuer en
anglais pour les cours de 3e cycle.
Durée: 5 ans.

Connaissances linguistiques: langue d'enseignement:
russe.
Inscriptions: à l'adresse ci-dessus pour de plus amples
renseignements.

**239 Université d'État de Grodno Y.
Koupala [UDDG]**
Ozheshko St., 22
230023 Grodno
Tel: +375-152-448-578
Fax: +375-172-108-589
Web: http://www.grsu.by
e-mail: root@grsu.by

📖 **1er, 2e, 3e cycles / toutes disciplines principales**

Domaines d'étude: biologie, droit, éducation, éducation
physique, études culturelles, histoire, ingénierie,
mathématiques, physique.
Programmes: (a) cours de mathématiques, physique,
ingénierie, biologie, pédagogie, philologie et culture bélarus,
histoire, droit, éducation physique; (b) cours de russe, incluant
des cours d'été, des cours de longue et courte durée de
différents niveaux de préparation pour les étudiants étrangers
(débutants et non-débutants).
A l'intention de: (a) ressortissants de tout pays, titulaires
d'un diplôme de fin d'études secondaires.
Durée: (a) 5 ans.
Assistance financière: (b) logement économique à l'hôtel
universitaire ou dans des familles.
Inscriptions: à l'adresse ci-dessus pour de plus amples
renseignements.

240 Université d'État de Moguilev
1, rue Kosmonavtov
212022 Moguilev
Tel: +375-222-261-317
Fax: +375-222-261-383
e-mail: mgpi@mgpi.belpak.mogilev.by

📖 **Formation de maîtres**

Domaines d'étude: formation des enseignants.
Programmes: Formation des maîtres du secondaire en
biologie, chimie, géographie, pédagogie, histoire, philologie,
éducation préscolaire, physique, mathématiques, conduisant
au Certificat universitaire et au PhD; cours d'1 an de russe et
de bélarusse pour étrangers.
Durée: 3 à 5 ans.
Inscriptions: à l'adresse ci-dessus.

**241 Université d'État du transport
du Bélarus**
24, rue Kirov
248653 Gomel
Tel: +375-232-551-168
Fax: +375-232-551-168
e-mail: SWS@gut.belpak.gomel.by

📖 **Programme d'études en transport**

Domaines d'étude: comptabilité, économie, électricité et
électronique, gestion, industrie et commerce, mécanique,
transports.
Programmes: Cours conduisant aux Diplômes
universitaires dans les domaines suivants: transports,
économie, électricité, électronique, comptabilité, gestion et
mécanique.
A l'intention de: ressortissants de tout pays, titulaires d'un
diplôme de fin d'études secondaires ou d'un brevet de
technicien supérieur ou équivalent; admission sur tests et
entretien.
Connaissances linguistiques: langue d'enseignement:
russe.
Inscriptions: à l'adresse ci-dessus.

**242 Université économique d'État
du Bélarus [UEDB]**
Partisan Avenue, 26
220672 Minsk
Tel: +375-172-491-107/303-512
Fax: +375-172-495-106
e-mail: rektor@bseu.minsk.by

1er, 2e cycles / économie

Domaines d'étude: commerce, comptabilité, économie, finances, gestion, relations internationales.
Programmes: Bachelor of Business Administration (B.B.A.) et Master of Arts (M.A.) dans les domaines de la gestion, des relations économiques internationales, de l'économie et des finances, de la banque, de la comptabilité et des statistiques, du commerce.
A l'intention de: ressortissants de tout pays, âgés de 18 à 30 ans, titulaires d'un diplôme de fin d'études secondaires; admission sur entretien; bonne connaissance de la langue russe requise; possibilité d'entrer en année préparatoire pour les étudiants ne connaissant pas le russe.
Durée: 5 ans.
Inscriptions: avant le 30 juin, à l'adresse ci-dessus.

243　Université linguistique d'État de Minsk

21 Zakharov Str.
220662 Minsk
Tel: +375-172-488-143
Fax: +375-172-367-504
Web: http://www.mclu.unibel.by
e-mail: lingva@nsys.unibel.by

1er, 2e cycles / langues, linguistiques

Domaines d'étude: allemand, anglais, espagnol, français, interprétation et traduction, langues, linguistique.
Programmes: Baccalauréat (Master's degree en disciplines humanitaires et professionnelles); Diplôme universitaires, Certificat de cours de langues; Qualification d'interprète.
Description: cours de langues étrangères (anglais, français, allemand, espagnol, russe et japonais); interprétariat (domaine des relations internationales ou relations économiques internationales).
A l'intention de: ressortissants de tout pays, titulaires d'un diplôme de fin d'études secondaires, et ayant une préparation linguistique en russe convenable.
Durée: formation universitaire de 4 ou 5 ans (débutant à la mi-septembre); cours de langue russe de 2 semaines et plus.
Connaissances linguistiques: langue d'enseignement: russe.
Inscriptions: avant le 30 septembre (pour la formation universitaire), à l'adresse ci-dessus pour de plus amples renseignements.

1er, 2e cycles / toutes disciplines principales

Domaines d'étude: toutes disciplines principales, biologie, chimie, géographie, histoire, langues, mathématiques, philologie, physique.
Programmes: (a) Baccalauréat; (b) Magistère; (c) Diplôme de pédagogue.
Description: cours dans les domaines de la biologie, physique, mathématiques, psychologie, chimie, géographie, histoire, philologie, pédagogie, musique, langues étrangères, éducation primaire, disciplines sociales, culture physique, cultures mondiale et nationale.
Durée: (a) 5 ans; (b) 1 ans; (c) 5 ans.
Inscriptions: à l'adresse ci-dessus pour de plus amples renseignements.

Belgique

Academic year: mid-September to mid-July.
Organization of higher education system: Belgium is divided into three language communities; French, Flemish and German (the German community has only a limited offer of higher professional education).
***
• FLEMISH COMMUNITY:
First level degrees: professional or academic Bachelor's degree: 3 years or 180 ECTS study points; second level degrees: Master's degree: 1-2 years or 60-120 ECTS study points; third level: doctorate: variable.
Monetary unit: Euro (€).
International student admission: Secondary school-leaving certificate or equivalent; proof of admission to university education of equivalent level in country of origin. Entrance tests may be required for some disciplines. Applications should be sent directly to the institution of choice. Addresses of recognized higher education institutions can be found at the website of the Ministry of Education (see below). Please note that services of official governmental bodies are free of charge and students should not use fee-charging intermediaries for application to public institutions.
Language:
• Flemish Community: Most undergraduate programmes are taught in Dutch. Many postgraduate programmes are also taught in English, in which case proof of sufficient knowledge of English will be required when applying. Dutch language courses are organized for foreign students. For more information contact Ministerie van de Vlaamse Gemeenschap, Administratie Hoger Ondcerwijs en Wetenschappelijk Onderzoek, Koning Albert II-laan 15, 1210 Brussels (Belgilum), tel. +32-2-553-9802; fax: +32-2-553-9845.
Immigration requirements: A student visa is required for all non-EU/EEA citizens, staying in Belgium for more than three months. The following documents are requested when applying for a visa: valid passport, acceptance by an institution of higher education, proof of sufficient funds, medical certificate, promise of good conduct, promise to leave the Belgian territory after completion of studies.
Estimated expenses for one academic year:
• Flemish Community: tuition: 500€ for regular programmes (considerably higher for non-regular programmes); books/supplies: 500€; housing: 300-400€ per month. An average total for one year including medical and personal costs is estimated at 7,000-7,500€ per year.
Scholarships for international students: (1) Development cooperation: the Flemish University Council offers annually a number of scholarships to students of developing countries for specific programmes. More information at the following website: www.vlir.be; (2) Interuniversity cooperation: a limited number of scholarships are offered in the framework of agreements between Flemish higher education institutions with foreign partners; (3) Cultural agreements: the Flemish Community offers annually a number of postgraduate scholarships in the framework of bilateral agreements with several countries. Selections are organised in the home country by the local Ministry of Education. For information please contact your local Education Authority; (4) EU Community programmes: Flemish higher education institutions participate extensively in EU programmes (ERASMUS, TEMPUS, ERASMUS Mundus, Alban, Asialink…).
More information can be obtained directly at the International Relations Office of the respective Flemish higher education institution.
Open and distance learning: On-line courses and programmes in close cooperation with the Open University of the Netherlands. Language of instruction is Dutch. More information at www.ond.vlaanderen.be/Hogeronderwijs/studenten/ou.htm.
Recognition of studies and qualification: National Academic Recognition Information Centre (NARIC) Flanders: Ministry of the Flemish Community, Administration of Higher Education and Scientific Research; Koning Albert II-Laan 15; 1210 Brussels, Belgium; email: erwin.malfroy@ond.vlaanderen.be.
Accommodation services: Students should contact the International Relations Office of the receiving higher education institution for availability.
Work opportunities: Students should contact the International Relations Office of their institution. Routine formalities for EU/EEA citizens are required. Other nationalities must apply at the local Employment Authority for a C work permit, specifically for student jobs after arrival in Belgium. Students receiving a scholarship are not entitled to apply for such a work permit. In some cases such as specific research projects, Ph.D. students may receive a regular salary from the institution.
Publications / Websites: For further information:
• Ministry of the Flemish Community, Administration of Higher Education and Scientific Research, Koning Albert II-Laan 15; 1210 Brussels, Belgium; tel: +32-2-553-9802; fax: +32-2-553-9845; email: universiteiten@ond.vlaanderen.be; web: www.ond.vlaanderen.be/hogeronderwijs
• Flemish Interuniversity Council; web: www.vlir.be
• Flemish Council of Higher Education Institutions: web: www.vlhora.be
• Many Flemish higher education institutions have their own information brochures for international students which may

be obtained through the respective International Relations Office.

---.

Année universitaire: septembre à juin-juillet.
Organisation de l'enseignement supérieur: La Belgique est un pays fédéral. Il est divisé en 3 communautés linguistiques: Flamande, Français, et Germanophone. L'enseignement relève de la compétence de chaque communauté linguistique.

                    ***
• COMMUNAUTE FRANCAISE:
Les titres universitaires décernés sont les suivants: titre de candidat, délivré après les deux ou trois premières années d'études; titre de licencié, délivré après deux ou trois années d'études supplémentaires; titre de docteur. L'enseignement supérieur de type court conduit au titre de gradué.
Unité monétaire: Euro (€).
Admission pour étudiants du pays: Un examen d'entrée est organisé pour certaines branches; de plus, les établissements d'enseignement supérieur sont libres d'imposer des conditions d'admission en plus des conditions réglementaires fixées dans certains domaines. Les citoyens européens doivent réussir les mêmes examens d'entrée que les étudiants belges. L'accès à l'enseignement universitaire et à l'enseignement supérieur de type long et de niveau universitaire requiert la possession du certificat de fin d'études secondaires et du diplôme d'aptitude à accéder à l'enseignement supérieur, lequel est également délivré par les écoles secondaires. Pour accéder à l'enseignement supérieur de type court, le certificat de fin d'études secondaires suffit le plus souvent, mais le diplôme d'aptitude à accéder à l'enseignement supérieur est également requis pour certaines études.
• Des droits d'inscription (appelés minerval dans la communauté française) sont perçus pour tous les types d'enseignement supérieur. Ce sont les universités et les établissements non universitaires qui en fixent le montant. Les citoyens européens doivent payer la même somme que les étudiants belges. Les étudiants doivent s'inscrire avant le premier mai auprès du «service des inscriptions» de leur établissement. Les inscriptions définitives ont lieu début septembre. Les étudiants sont tenus de se présenter personnellement, munis de leur carte d'identité ou de leur passeport, d'une photo d'identité et des titres requis. L'inscription administrative implique le paiement de droits de scolarité.
Admission pour étudiants internationaux: Les candidats étrangers qui justifient d'un diplôme d'enseignement secondaire complet sont admis à entreprendre des études universitaires à condition d'obtenir l'équivalence de ce titre avec le Diplôme belge d'aptitude permettant d'accéder à l'enseignement supérieur (DAES), sauf pour les universités néerlandophones. L'admission aux études d'ingénieur civil est, en outre, subordonnée à la réussite d'un examen d'entrée portant principalement sur les connaissances en mathématiques. Les étudiants étrangers déjà titulaires d'un diplôme universitaire, qui désirent poursuivre leurs études en Belgique au niveau du 2e ou du 3e cycle doivent demander au préalable l'équivalence de leur titre.
Connaissances linguistiques requises: Bonne connaissance de la langue d'enseignement de l'établissement où l'étudiant est inscrit.
Des cours de langue sont organisés par les universités belges durant les vacances d'été, à l'intention des étudiants étrangers. L'Université libre de Bruxelles organise chaque été des cours de langue et de littérature françaises. Des bourses de vacances peuvent également être obtenues à cet effet dans le cadre des accords culturels. Se renseigner auprès du Commissariat général aux relations internationales de la communauté française, 65, avenue Louise, Bte. 9, 1050 Bruxelles, auprès de l'Administration générale de la coopération au développement (Ministère des affaires étrangères), 5, place du Champ-de-Mars, 1050 Bruxelles.
Formalités d'immigration: Les étudiants étrangers doivent se faire inscrire, dans les huit jours suivant leur arrivée, auprès de l'administration communale du lieu de leur résidence et présenter une attestation d'inscription aux cours en même temps qu'une preuve de leurs moyens de subsistance.
Services d'accueil et d'information:
• Secrétariat, services d'information et services sociaux des établissements d'enseignement.

• Centres d'accueil et maisons internationales, ambassades et consulats belges à l'étranger.
Bourses pour étudiants internationaux: La Communauté française de Belgique offre des bourses d'études aux étudiants de condition peu aisée. Ces bourses sont également disponibles pour les ressortissants turcs et de pays en développement: (voir conditions décrites dans page web: (source: http://www.dgcd.be/fr/dgcd/bourses%5Fetude/).
Reconnaissance des études et diplômes:
• Communauté française: Mme Chantal Kaufmann, NARIC, Ministère de la Communauté française; Cité administrative de l'État; Boulevard Pachéco, 19; boîte 0; 1010 Bruxelles; Belgique; email: chantal.kaufmann@cfwb.be; Internet: http://www.enseignement.be/infosup/.
Publications / Sites Web:
• «Politique d'accueil des étudiants étrangers au sein des institutions universitaires de la communauté française de Belgique», publiée par le Conseil interuniversitaire de la communauté française (CIUF), 5, rue d'Egmont, 1050 Bruxelles; gratuite.
• Des annuaires, brochures, guides et programmes de cours sont publiés par chaque institution.

---

244 **Académie des Beaux-Arts de la ville de Tournai**
14, rue de l'Hôpital Notre Dame
7500 Tournai
Tel: +32-69-841-263
Fax: +32-69-843-253
Web: http://www.actournai.be/
e-mail: academie@online.be

📖 **Programme de cours artistique**

Domaines d'étude: arts, arts décoratifs, arts graphiques, arts plastiques, beaux-arts, français, littérature et civilisation, moyens audio-visuels, philosophie, photographie, stylisme.
Programmes: Programme artistique de niveau universitaire.
A l'intention de: toutes nationalités; sans limite d'âge.
Durée: 4 ans.
Connaissances linguistiques: français.

245 **Belgian-American Educational Foundation, Inc. [BAEF]**
11, rue d'Egmont
1000 Bruxelles
Tel: +32-2-513-5955
Fax: +32-2-672-5381
Web: http://www.baef.be
e-mail: mail@baef.be

🎓 **Bourses 3e cycle**

Domaines d'étude: toutes disciplines principales.
Bourses: bourses d'études, de recherche ou de perfectionnement.
A l'intention de: (a) ressortissants belges, titulaires depuis moins de 4 ans (service militaire non inclus) d'un diplôme universitaire final avec mention « grande distinction » (minimum licence) et ayant une bonne connaissance de l'anglais; (b) ressortissants américains, âgés de préférence de moins de 30 ans et connaissant le français, le néerlandais ou l'allemand (minimum «Master's Degree»).
Lieu: exclusivement en Belgique pour les ressortissants des États-Unis et aux États-Unis pour les ressortissants belges.
Durée: 10 mois.
Valeur: couvre les frais de séjour, voyages, livres, etc. et le minerval.
Candidatures: avant le 31 octobre de l'année précédant celle du départ.

246 **Conseil Interuniversitaire de la Communauté française de Belgique [CIUF]**
5, rue d'Egmont
1000 Bruxelles
Tel: +32-2-504-9291
Fax: +32-2-502-2768
Web: http://www.ciuf.be
e-mail: info@ciuf.be

☛ **Bourses dans le domaine du développement**

Domaines d'étude: affaires internationales, droit.
Bourses: Bourse dans le domaine du développement.
A l'intention de: ressortissants de pays en développement; détenteur d'un diplôme de deuxième cycle; âgés de moins de 45 ans.
Valeur: environ 1.000 € par mois + allocation personnes à charge + frais divers.
Connaissances linguistiques: français.
Candidatures: avant le premier mars.

247 Département des Sciences et Gestion de l'Environnement de l'ULg (anciennement Fondation universitaire luxembourgeoise) [FUL]

185, avenue de Longwy
6700 Arlon
Tel: +32-6-323-0811
Fax: +32-6-323-0897
Web: http://www.ful.ac.be
e-mail: arlon.accueil@ulg.ac.be

📖 **Programmes pluridisciplinaires de 3e cycle**

Domaines d'étude: développement rural, écologie, environnement, énergie, espace, études du développement, géographie, gestion, hydrologie, ingénierie, recherche, ressources naturelles, sciences, sciences appliquées, sciences sociales.
Programmes: programmes pluridisciplinaires de 3e cycle conduisant aux diplômes d'études spécialisées: (a) DES en sciences de l'environnement; (b) DES en gestion intégrée des ressources hydriques; (c) DES en gestion des risques naturels; (d) DES en traitement et gestion des déchets; (e) DEA en sciences de l'environnement; (f) Doctorat en sciences de l'environnement; (g) DEA en développement, environnement et société.
Description: (a) 3 orientations: surveillance de l'environnement, développement durable et gestion de l'environnement, agrométéorologie et développement; (b) 3 orientations: gestion des bassins hydrographiques, technologie de l'eau, gestion des ressources biologiques des eaux continentales; (a), (b), (c), (d) travail professionnalisant en fin d'études; (e) formation par et à la recherche: cours, mémoire et soutenance; (f) formation à et par la recherche; peut être assorti d'un DEA probatoire; (g) formation à et par la recherche, cours, mémoire et soutenance; filières socio-économie de l'environnement, société civile et économie sociale, dynamiques agraires, développement régional.
A l'intention de: ressortissants de tout pays: (a) titulaires d'un diplôme de 2ème cycle universitaire; une bonne connaissance du français est indispensable; la connaissance de l'anglais est recommandée; (b) titulaires d'un diplôme de fin d'études d'au moins 8 semestres, obtenu dans une université ou un établissement assimilé; la connaissance du français et de l'allemand est requise; (c) titulaires d'un diplôme de 2ème cycle universitaire et diplôme complémentaire et/ou expérience professionnelle; connaissance de l'anglais exigée.
Age Max.: sans limite d'age.
Organisés: (a) (e) (f) Arlon; (b) Arlon et Liège; (c) Arlon, Liège et Gembloux (g) Arlon, Liège, Gembloux, Louvain-la-Neuve (selon filière).
Durée: (a) à (f) 1 an; (g) 4 mois.
Frais: inscription environ 720 €; séjour environ 500 € par mois.
Assistance financière: bourses pour certaines formations; s'adresser à la Coopération universitaire au développement (CUD), 72/73, rue de Namur, 1000 Bruxelles; site web: http://cud.ciuf.be/bourses_presentation.htm.
Inscriptions: 31 mai pour non ressortissants de l'Union européenne, 31 août pour ressortissants de l'Union européenne; (e) à (g) début octobre. S'adresser au Service Académique, Fondation Universitaire Luxembourgeoise (FUL).

248 Ecole supérieure des arts plastiques et visuels [ESAPV]

Rue des Soeurs Noires, 4A
7000 Mons
Tel: +32-6-539-4760
Fax: +32-6-539-4761
Web: http://www.esapv.be
e-mail: esapv.mons@esapv.be

📖 **Enseignement artistique**

Domaines d'étude: arts, arts appliqués, arts décoratifs, arts graphiques, arts plastiques, beaux-arts, décoration, dessin industriel.
A l'intention de: ressortissants de toute nationalité.

249 Faculté polytechnique de Mons [FPDM]

9, rue de Houdain
7000 Mons
Tel: +32-65-374-111
Fax: +32-65-374-200
Web: http://www.fpms.ac.be
e-mail: secretu@fpms.ac.be

📖 **Programme d'études technologique du 1er et 2ème cycles**

Domaines d'étude: architecture, chimie, électricité et électronique, gestion, informatique, mécanique, métallurgie.
Programmes: diplômes académiques de 1er et 2e cycles: ingénieur civil en architecture, chimie, électricité, informatique et gestion, mécanique, métallurgie, mines et sciences des matériaux.
A l'intention de: étudiants ayant réussi l'examen d'admission et titulaires d'un diplôme d'enseignement secondaire supérieur (DESS); pour les étudiants ayant effectué leurs études en Belgique, d'un baccalauréat ou diplôme équivalent; connaissance du français obligatoire.
Durée: 5 ans (2 ans de candidature et 3 ans de spécialisation).
Assistance financière: quelques bourses sont offertes, réductions de minerval.
Inscriptions: avant le 30 septembre pour les nouveaux étudiants.

250 Faculté universitaire des sciences agronomiques de Gembloux

2, passage des Déportés
5030 Gembloux
Tel: +32-8-162-2111
Fax: +32-8-161-4544
Web: http://www.fsagx.ac.be
e-mail: fsagx@fsagx.ac.be

📖 **Programme d'études en sciences agronomiques du 1er cycle**

Domaines d'étude: développement rural, écologie, environnement, élevage, horticulture, ressources naturelles, sciences agronomiques, technologie industrielle.
Programmes: programme d'études préparant aux diplômes d'ingénieur chimiste et des bio-industries ou d'ingénieur agronome (11 orientations: agronomie générale des régions tempérées, agronomie des régions tropicales et subtropicales, élevage, eaux et forêts, horticulture, défense des végétaux, génie rural, économie et sociologie rurales, économie et sociologie rurales appliquées aux pays en développement, aménagement des territoires, sciences du sol).
A l'intention de: ressortissants de tout pays, titulaires d'un diplôme donnant accès aux études universitaires (baccalauréat). Possibilité de présenter un examen d'admission.
Durée: 2 à 5 années académiques (débutant mi-septembre).
Assistance financière: diverses bourses offertes par l'Administration générale de la coopération au développement, l'UE, etc. Droits d'inscription réduits pour les étudiants boursiers.
Inscriptions: avant le 15 octobre, au Service des études.

📖 Programme d'études postuniversitaires / sciences agronomiques et ingénierie

Domaines d'étude: agriculture, sciences agronomiques, technologie industrielle.
Programmes: programme d'études postuniversitaires en sciences agronomiques et ingénierie biologique conduisant aux: (a) Doctorat en sciences agronomiques et ingénierie biologique; (b) Diplôme d'études complémentaires en sciences agronomiques; (c) Diplôme d'études approfondies en sciences agronomiques; programmes à la demande en statistique et informatique appliquée; (c) Diplôme d'études spécialisées en phytopharmacie et phytiatrie; en gestion des biotechnologies; en génie sanitaire; en gestion et développement des milieux intertropicaux; (e) Cycles de formation spécialisée; (f) Stages de recherche ou d'enseignement.
A l'intention de: ressortissants de tout pays: (a) et (c) titulaires du diplôme belge d'ingénieur agronome ou d'ingénieur chimiste et des industries agricoles, ou de tout autre diplôme reconnu équivalent; (b) titulaires d'un diplôme universitaire (4 années d'études) ou d'un diplôme de l'enseignement supérieur non universitaire; (d) diplômés de l'enseignement universitaire et souhaitant compléter leur formation ou se spécialiser dans un domaine défini.
Durée: (a) 3 ans minimum; (b), (c) et (d) en général 1 an.
Assistance financière: diverses bourses offertes par l'Administration générale de la coopération au développement, l'Union européenne, la Faculté, etc.
Connaissances linguistiques: langue d'enseignement: français.
Inscriptions: avant le 15 octobre, au Service des études.

🖐 Bourses d'études et de recherche

Domaines d'étude: sciences agronomiques.
Bourses: (a) bourses d'études, offertes par le Fonds Eric Daugimont et Dominique Van Der Rest; (b) bourses de recherche, offertes par la Faculté.
A l'intention de: étudiants de toute nationalité: (a) méritants de la Faculté et en difficulté sociale ou financière particulière; (b) âgés de moins de 32 ans et ayant obtenu leur dernier diplôme avec au moins la mention « distinction ».
Durée: (a) une année (renouvelable); (b) de 6 à 24 mois (renouvelables jusqu'à une durée totale de 48 mois).
Valeur: fixée chaque année par le Conseil d'administration.
Candidatures: (a) au Recteur de la Faculté; (b) par l'intermédiaire des membres du corps enseignant auprès du Conseil de recherche.

251 Facultés universitaires catholiques de Mons [FUCAM]

151, chaussée de Binche
7000 Mons
Tel: +32-6-532-3211
Fax: +32-6-531-5691
Web: http://www.fucam.ac.be
e-mail: international@fucam.ac.be

📖 Programme d'études du 1er, 2ème et 3ème cycles

Domaines d'étude: gestion, informatique, sciences appliquées, sciences économiques et commerciales, sciences politiques.
Programmes: (a) cours de 1er cycle conduisant aux diplômes de candidats en sciences économiques appliquées et en sciences politiques administratives; (b) cours de 2ème cycle conduisant aux diplômes d'ingénieur commercial et de gestion, de licenciés en sciences économiques appliquées, et en sciences politiques et administratives, de licencié et maître en sciences économiques appliquées, d'agrégé de l'enseignement secondaire supérieur pour les sciences économiques appliquées, et menant aux certificats d'études supérieures en informatique appliquée, en aspects humains du management et en gestion des risques et de l'assurance; (c) cours de 3ème cycle conduisant aux diplômes de docteurs en sciences économiques appliquées, et en sciences politiques et administratives.
A l'intention de: ressortissants de tout pays, titulaires soit du diplôme belge d'aptitude à accéder à l'enseignement supérieur, soit du baccalauréat ou titre reconnu équivalent.
Assistance financière: allocations ou prêts d'études

accordés par le Ministère de la communauté française.
Inscriptions: pour de plus amples renseignements, écrire à l'adresse ci-dessus.

252 Facultés universitaires Notre-Dame de la Paix [FUNDP]

61, rue de Bruxelles
5000 Namur
Tel: +32-8-172-5030
Fax: +32-8-172-5037
Web: http://www.fundp.ac.be
e-mail: info.etudes@fundp.ac.be

📖 Programme d'études universitaires

Domaines d'étude: toutes disciplines principales.
Programmes: Programme d'études universitaires: (a) Candidature et doctorat en philosophie et lettres, en droit, en médecine et en sciences vétérinaires; (b) Candidature en sciences politiques, sociales et de la communication, en sciences pharmaceutiques, en sciences géographiques, et en sciences géologiques et minéralogiques; (c) Licence, doctorat et agrégation en sciences mathématiques, physiques, chimiques et biologiques; (d) Licence, maîtrise, doctorat et agrégation en sciences économiques et sociales, et en informatique; (e) Diplôme d'études complémentaires: en culture et civilisation de la Belgique; en écotechnologie des eaux continentales; (f) Diplôme d'études spécialisées: en droit et gestion des technologies de l'information et de la communication; en société, science et technologie (gestion de l'information); en biologie; (g) Diplôme d'études approfondies en physique et chimie des matériaux interfaciaux et systèmes mésoscopiques.
A l'intention de: candidats remplissant les conditions requises.
Inscriptions: avant le 15 juillet, pour les étudiants en sciences vétérinaires; avant le 30 juin pour les étudiants non européens résidant dans leur pays; avant le 15 août, pour les étudiants européens ou séjournant déjà en Belgique.

253 Facultés universitaires Saint-Louis [FUSL]

43, Boulevard du Jardin botanique
1000 Bruxelles
Tel: +32-2-211-7811
Fax: +32-2-211-7997
Web: http://www.fusl.ac.be
e-mail: relext@fusl.ac.be

📖 Études du 1er et 3ème cycles

Domaines d'étude: administration des affaires, communication, droit, économie, études européennes, finances, gestion, histoire, journalisme, langues, lettres, littérature et civilisation, philologie, philosophie, sciences économiques et commerciales, sciences politiques, sciences sociales, sociologie, théologie, religion.
Programmes: Études du 1er cycle en philosophie, histoire, langues et littératures, droit, sciences économiques, sociales et politiques; études du 3ème cycle: DEA en théorie du droit; DES en droit de l'environnement et droit public immobilier; DES en droits de l'homme; DES en analyse interdisciplinaire de la construction européenne; DES en gestion des risques financiers.
Organisés: Facultés universitaires Saint-Louis.
Durée: programmes de 3 ans; (b) programmes de 1 an.
Frais: d'inscription: 739 €.
Connaissances linguistiques: français.
Inscriptions: avant le 30 septembre au Service des inscriptions des Facultés universitaires Saint-Louis à l'adresse ci-dessus.

254 Free University Brussels - Institute of Molecular Biology and Medicine [IBMM]

Aéropole
rue des Professeurs Jeener et Brachet 12
6041 Charleroi - Gosselies
Tel: +32-2-359-0288
Fax: +32-2-359-0289
Web: http://www.ulb.ac.be/ibmm/index.html
e-mail: etudes@ulb.ac.be

📖 Graduate Programmes in Molecular Biology

Study Domains: biology.
Programmes: (a) Inter-university programme leading to a Master of Science in molecular biology; programme designed to train young scientists from developing countries in different fields of molecular biology; (b) course leading to a Master of Science in molecular biology and biotechnology.
Open to: candidates of all nationalities, according to academic merit and relevant work experience, holding (a) minimum of 4-year Bachelor of Science Degree; (b) minimum of 3-year Bachelor of Science degree; TOEFL min. 550.
Duration: 2 academic years.
Financial assistance: a number of scholarships (VUBAROS) for students from developing countries; further information can be obtained from the Belgian embassies and consulates in candidate's home country.
Languages: instruction in English.
Applications: by 1 April to the Faculty of Sciences, VUB, Pleinlaan 2, 1050 Brussels, Belgium.

255   Free University Brussels, Vrije Universiteit Brussel [VUB]

Pleinlaan 2
1050 Brussels
Tel: +32-2-629-2111
Fax: +32-2-629-2282
Web: http://www.vub.ac.be
e-mail: infovub@vub.ac.be

📖 Graduate Programme / Educational Research

Study Domains: education, psychology, research.
Programmes: interfaculty research programme leading to a Master's Degree in Educational Research (GAS).
Open to: nationals of all countries holding a Bachelor's degree of at least 3 years and minimum 3 years teaching experience. Knowledge of Dutch essential; TOEFL min. 550.
Duration: 1 academic year.
Financial assistance: VUBAROS scholarships for candidates from developing countries.
Languages: instruction in Dutch and English.
Applications: by 1 April, to the above address.

📖 Graduate Programmes / Business Administration, Management

Study Domains: business administration, management.
Programmes: Faculty of Economic, Social and Political Sciences: (a) courses leading to postgraduate diploma in management; (b) Master of Business Administration.
Open to: (a) candidates of all nationalities holding a Bachelor's Degree of a minimum of 3 years; (b) Bachelor's or Master's in Economics, Applied Economics, Commerce, Management; GMAT
for non-EU nationals; TOEFL min. 550.
Duration: 1 academic year.
Languages: instruction in English.
Applications: by 1 April to the above address.

📖 Graduate Programmes / International Law

Study Domains: international law, law.
Programmes: programme leading to a Master's in International and Comparative Law.
Open to: nationals of all countries holding a Bachelor of Law degree of a minimum of 3 years, or equivalent. Proficiency in English required.
Duration: 1 academic year.
Financial assistance: VUBAROS Scholarships for candidates from developing countries.
Languages: instruction in English.
Applications: by 15 February to the above address.

📖 Graduate Programmes / Medical and Pharmaceutical Research

Study Domains: medicine, pharmacy and pharmacology, research.
Programmes: Master's and Ph.D. programmes in medical and pharmaceutical research.
Open to: qualified candidates of all countries holding a degree in biology, dentistry, medicine, pharmacy or sciences from a recognized university.
Held: at VUB Medical Campus, Laarbeeklaan 103, 1090

Brussels.
Duration: 2 academic years for Master's degree (courses begin in October); 4 academic years for Ph.D. degree.
Languages: instruction in English.
Applications: by April; request application forms from Registration Office at above address.

📖 Graduate Programmes in Science

Study Domains: computer science, ecology, environment, marine science, sciences.
Programmes: (a) courses leading to a Master of Science in Ecological Marine Management, consisting of lectures and practical training in various disciplines of marine sciences; (b) programme leading to a Master of Science in Computer Science and consisting of a common root with two orientations: artificial intelligence and software technology; (c) Master's degree in applied computer science; (d) postgraduate course in human ecology, organized under the auspices of World Health Organization (WHO) and UNESCO, leading to a Master's Degree in Human Ecology.
Open to: candidates of all nationalities holding for (a) a Bachelor of Science degree of a minimum of 3 years in Engineering or Veterinary Medicine; (b) a Bachelor in Computer Science, Engineering or Mathematics (specialized in computer science) of a minimum of 3 years; (c) a Bachelor of Science or Engineering of a minimum of 4 years; (d) a Bachelor of Science of a minimum of 3 years. TOEFL min. 550.
Held: (a) to (c) at above address; (d) at VUB Medical Campus, Laarbeeklaan 103, 1090 Brussels.
Duration: (a) to (c) 1 academic year; (d) 2 academic years (courses begin in October).
Financial assistance: VUBAROS Scholarships available for candidates from developing countries.
Languages: instruction in English.
Applications: by 1 April, to the above address.

📖 International Postgraduate Training Course in Geology

Study Domains: archaeology, biology, chemistry, civil engineering, geology, natural resources.
Programmes: International Postgraduate Training Course on Fundamental and Applied Quaternary Environmental Geology.
Description: subjects include management training in quaternary environmental geology, prospection, new building materials, natural hazards, engineering geology and mapping, and training in fundamental theoretical quaternary geology studies; paleoclimatology and (bio)stratigraphy of the quaternary era and their applications, palaeomagnetism, placer deposits, new building materials, geochemistry, stable isotopes, geochronology, neotectonics and earthquake management, environmental studies, soil mechanics, oceanography, GIS, remote sensing; stratigraphy and mapping, engineering and prospection, marine geology, applied geomorphology.
Open to: nationals of any country with a university degree in geology, geography, biology, chemistry, agricultural and civil engineering, archaeology, and with some years of practical experience.
Duration: 2 academic years; courses begin in September.
Financial assistance: some scholarships are available from the University, the Belgian Ministry for Development Co-operation and from the European Community.
Languages: instruction in English.
Applications: by 1 May.

📖 Water Resources Engineering

Study Domains: hydrology, natural resources.
Programmes: inter-university programme of the Laboratory of Hydrology in water resources engineering leading to a diploma in water resources engineering and to a M.Sc. degree in water resources engineering: surface water hydrology, groundwater hydrology, irrigation engineering, water quality management, etc..
Open to: nationals of any country with a B.Sc. degree in sciences or engineering from a recognized university; good knowledge of English language required.
Duration: 1 or 2 academic years; courses begin in September.
Languages: instruction in English.
Applications: by 1 February.

256 Ghent University
Department of Educational Affairs
International Relations Office
Onderbergen 4 a-c
9000 Ghent
Fax: +32-9-264-8399
Web: http://www.ugent.be/en

📖 **Undergraduate, Graduate, Postgraduate Programmes**
Study Domains: all major fields.

257 Haute Ecole 'Francisco Ferrer' de la Ville de Bruxelles [IC]
11, place Anneessens
1000 Bruxelles
Tel: +32-2-551-0220
Fax: +32-2-551-0226
Web: http://www.brunette.brucity.be/heff/cooremans/index.html
e-mail: heff.cooremans-interpretation@brunette.brucity.be

📖 **Programme de cours du 1er et 2ème cycles**
Domaines d'étude: comptabilité, gestion, interprétation et traduction, transports.
Programmes: cours dans les domaines suivants: traduction et interprétation, administration et commerce, conduisant à la licence en sciences commerciales et financières ainsi qu'à la licence en sciences administratives; cycles postuniversitaires en commerce extérieur, expertise comptable, finance et gestion de l'environnement.
A l'intention de: ressortissants de tout pays, titulaires d'un diplôme d'aptitude à accéder à l'enseignement supérieur.
Durée: de 4 à 5 ans selon la formation.
Inscriptions: à l'adresse ci-dessus pour de plus amples renseignements.

258 Haute École Charlemagne
6, rue des Rivageois
4000 Liège
Tel: +32-4-254-7611
Fax: +32-4-253-3915
Web: http://www.hecharlemagne.be
e-mail: directeur-president.secretariat@hecharlemagne.be

📖 **Programmes d'études de 1er et 2e cycles**
Domaines d'étude: agriculture, éducation, horticulture, hygiène et santé, sciences agronomiques, tourisme, hôtellerie, restauration, transports.
A l'intention de: ressortissants de toutes nationalités.
Connaissances linguistiques: français.

259 Haute École Mosane de l'Enseignement Supérieur [HEMES]
9, Rue de Harlez
4000 Liège
Tel: +32-4-252-0045
Fax: +32-4-252-0099
Web: http://www.hemes.be

📖 **Programmes d'études professionnelles**
Domaines d'étude: assistance sociale, commerce, comptabilité, éducation physique, études d'infirmière, études paramédicales, formation des enseignants, informatique, ingénierie, marketing, sciences sociales, technologie industrielle.
Programmes: études professionnelles.
Connaissances linguistiques: français.

260 Haute Ecole Robert Schuman, Département Technique [HERS]
Chemin de Weyler, 2
6700 Arlon
Tel: +32-6-323-0000
Fax: +32-6-322-0890
Web: http://www.hers.be

e-mail: secretariat@isiarlon.org

📖 **Cours en ingénierie industriel**
Domaines d'étude: ingénierie, technologie industrielle.
Programmes: cours conduisant: (a) à la candidature d'ingénieur industriel; (b) au diplôme d'ingénieur industriel, section industrie.
A l'intention de: ressortissants de tout pays, titulaires du diplôme secondaire supérieur pour les ressortissants belges ou d'un titre admis en équivalence pour les autres candidats.
Durée: 4 ans (débutant en septembre).
Inscriptions: avant le 1er novembre.

261 Haute École Roi Baudouin [HERB]
63, chaussée du Roeulx
7000 Mons
Tel: +32-6-534-9873
Fax: +32-6-534-0452
Web: http://www.herb.be
e-mail: contact@herb.be

📖 **Enseignement supérieur**
Domaines d'étude: allemand, anglais, anthropologie, biologie, botanique, comptabilité, dessin industriel, économie, économie politique, espagnol, folklore, formation des enseignants, géographie, gestion, histoire, histoire de l'art, informatique, langues, marketing, mathématiques, microbiologie, néerlandais, physique, psychologie, publicité, sciences, sciences économiques et commerciales, sciences sociales, statistique.
Programmes: enseignement supérieur.
Connaissances linguistiques: français.

262 HEC Ecole de Gestion de l'Université de Liège [HEC/ULG]
Rue Louvrex, 14
4000 Liège
Tel: +32-4-232-7211
Fax: +32-4-232-7240
Web: http://www.hec.ulg.ac.be
e-mail: hec@ulg.ac.be

📖 **Études en sciences commerciales**
Domaines d'étude: administration des affaires, affaires internationales, commerce, gestion, relations internationales, sciences économiques et commerciales.
Programmes: programme de cours dans les divers domaines des sciences commerciales et de la gestion, conduisant aux titres de: (a) Candidat en sciences commerciales; (b) Licencié en sciences commerciales; (c) Ingénieur commercial; (d) Agrégé de l'enseignement secondaire supérieur pour les sciences commerciales. Programme de cours dans les domaines de la fiscalité, analyse et contrôle, méthodes quantitatives en finance, gestion intégrée de la production, conduisant à la: (e) Licence spéciale, formation postuniversitaire à horaire décalé en management, logistique intégrée, analyse, contrôle et révisorat, finance approfondie.
A l'intention de: ressortissants de tout pays, âgés de 18 ans au moins, titulaires d'un baccalauréat (avec mention) ou d'un diplôme reconnu équivalent par a Communauté française de Belgique.
Durée: (a) 2 ans; (b) 4 ans; (c) et (d) 5 ans; (e) 1 an (débutant mi-septembre).
Connaissances linguistiques: langue d'enseignement: français; français exigé et bonnes connaissances de l'anglais.
Inscriptions: du 1er juillet au 31 octobre; (e) fin novembre.

263 Hogeschool Gent
Jozef Kluyskensstraat, 2B
9000 Gent
Tel: +32-9-266-0800
Fax: +32-9-266-0801
Web: http://www.hogent.be
e-mail: info@hogent.be

Undergraduate and Graduate Programmes

Study Domains: administration, agriculture, architecture, business, engineering, fine arts, health and hygiene, horticulture, interpretation and translation, music and musicology, social work, teacher education, technology, visual arts.

Description: Professional Bachelor's in business studies, office management, information technology, teacher training, remedial education, social work, health care, technology, agriculture and horticulture, landscape and garden architecture, interior design. Academic Bachelor's with corresponding Master's in business administration, public administration and management, translation studies, engineering sciences, biotechnological sciences, music and drama, audio-visual and fine arts.

Duration: 3 to 5 years.
Languages: Dutch.
Applications: to the above address.

264   Hogeschool West-Vlaanderen
Sint-Marrtems-Latemlaan 2A
8500 Kortrijk
Tel: +32-5-624-1290
Fax: +32-5-624-1292
Web: http://www.howest.be
e-mail: info@howest.be

Hogeschool 1st and 2nd Cycle Programmes

Study Domains: economic and commercial sciences, economy, health and hygiene, paramedical studies, social sciences, social work, teacher education.
Programmes: Hogeschool 1st and 2nd cycle programmes in many fields.

265   Institut catholique des hautes études commerciales [ICHEC]
2, boulevard Brand-Whitlock
1150 Bruxelles
Tel: +32-2-739-3711
Fax: +32-2-739-3803
Web: http://www.ichec.be
e-mail: info@ichec.be

Programmes d'études en Gestion

Domaines d'étude: toutes disciplines principales, gestion.
Programmes: (a) programmes dans le domaine de la gestion, visant à l'obtention de la licence en sciences commerciales et financières/consulaires et ingéniorat commercial; (b) «Master's Degree in Intercultural Management» (MIME): matières interdisciplinaires, management comparatif, stratégies multinationales, dynamique culturelle des organisations.
A l'intention de: ressortissants de tout pays: (a) âgés de moins de 21 ans et titulaires d'un diplôme de fin d'études secondaires dont l'équivalence a été accordée par le Ministère belge de l'éducation nationale; (b) titulaires d'un diplôme universitaire ou titre reconnu équivalent.
Durée: (a) 4 ou 5 années universitaires; (b) 12 mois (débutant en septembre).
Assistance financière: (a) allocations et prêts d'études, accordés par le Ministère de la communauté française; (b) bourses « MIME ».
Connaissances linguistiques: langues d'enseignement: français et anglais pour certains cours.
Inscriptions: (a) avant fin août; (b) avant mai, au Secrétariat du MIME.

266   Prince Leopold Institute of Tropical Medicine [ITM Antwerp]
Nationalestraat 155
2000 Antwerpen
Tel: +32-3-247-6666
Fax: +32-3-216-1431
Web: http://www.itg.be
e-mail: info@itg.be

Master's degree scholarships

Study Domains: health and hygiene, immunology, medicine, preventive medicine.
Description: (a) one year postgraduate Master courses; (b) short courses on tropical medicine.
Subjects: Public health (Master's course); disease control (Master's course and short course); tropical animal health (Master's course); HIV/AIDS care (short course).
Open to: Health professionals with a min of 2 to 5 years relevant experience.
Nationality: candidates of all nationalities.
Age limit Min: none.
Age limit Max: 45.
Academic requirements: University degree or equivalent professional experience.
Place of study: ITM Antwerp.
Duration: 11 months.
Value: registration and tuition fees: 14,000€; approximately 850€ living allowance per month.
Languages: Yearly alternating English - French.
Applications: to be sent to above address before 31 January or 31 March, forms on website www.itg.be.

266   Institut de médecine tropicale Prince Léopold [IMT Anvers]
Nationalestraat 155
2000 Anvers
Tel: +32-3-247-6666
Fax: +32-3-216-1431
Web: http://www.itg.be
e-mail: info@itg.be

Bourses de Maîtrise

Domaines d'étude: hygiène et santé, immunologie, médecine, médecine préventive.
Description: (a) Maîtrise post universitaire d'un an; (b) cours de courte-durée.
Domaines d'études: Santé publique (Maîtrise); contrôle des maladies (Maîtrise et cours de courte-durée); santé animale tropical (Maîtrise); HIV/SIDA (cours de courte-durée).
A l'intention de: Candidats originaires des pays en voie de développement, avec un minimum de 2-5 ans d'expérience professionnelle.
Qualifications requises: Degré universitaire ou expérience professionnelle équivalente.
Age Max: maximum 45 ans.
Lieu: IMT Anvers.
Durée: 11 mois.
Valeur: Bourse: 14.000€ frais d'inscription, divers et 850 €mensualités.
Connaissances linguistiques: anglais / français, années alternant.
Candidatures: avant le 31 janvier ou le 31 mars à l'adresse ci-dessus. Formulaires disponibles par internet www.itg.be.

267   Institut Libre Marie Haps [ILMH]
rue d'Arlon, 11
1040 Bruxelles
Tel: +32-2 -511-9292
Fax: +32-2-511-9837
Web: http://www.ilmh.be
e-mail: information@ilmh.be

Programme de 1er cycle en interprétariat/traduction

Domaines d'étude: interprétation et traduction.
Programmes: Cours conduisant à la licence en interprétariat ou en traduction.
A l'intention de: ressortissants de tout pays, âgés de 18 ans minimum et titulaires d'un diplôme de fin d'études secondaires à condition que celui-ci soit équivalent au diplôme belge d'enseignement secondaire supérieur.
Durée: 4 ans (débutant mi-septembre).
Inscriptions: avant le 15 octobre et sur la base d'un dossier administratif complet.

268 Institut supérieur d'architecture de la communauté française, La Cambre

Place Eugène Flagey, 19
1050 Bruxelles
Tel: +32-2-640-9696
Fax: +32-2-647-4655
Web: http://www.lacambre-archi.be
e-mail: isacf@lacambre-archi.be

📖 **Programme d'études en architecture**

Domaines d'étude: architecture, urbanisme.
Programmes: programmes de cours d'architecture: (a) architecture en histoire, théorie et critique conduisant à un niveau universitaire de type long; les diplômés disposent du libre établissement dans les pays de l'Union européenne; (b) stage international de perfectionnement dans le domaine de l'urbanisme et de l'architecture dans les pays en voie de développement.
A l'intention de: (a) ressortissants de tout pays titulaires d'un diplôme d'accès à l'enseignement supérieur ou d'un certificat équivalent délivré par le Ministère de l'éducation; (b) ressortissants des pays en voie de développement, architectes, urbanistes, ingénieurs, économistes, sociologues, géographes et agronomes; français exigé.
Durée: (a) 5 ans; (b) 15 semaines (débutant en septembre).
Assistance financière: (b) l'Administration générale à la coopération au développement octroie 20 bourses couvrant les frais de transports du pays d'origine du candidat au lieu du stage, les frais de séjour, d'installation, et l'assurance soins médicaux.
Connaissances linguistiques: français.
Inscriptions: (a) 15 octobre; (b) avant le 1er juin; formulaires d'inscription à retirer auprès des organisateurs: tél: +32 2 648 6549.

269 Institut supérieur d'architecture intercommunal

Site de Bruxelles « Victor Horta »
Boulevard du Triomphe, 248
1050 Bruxelles
Tel: +32-2-650-5052
Fax: +32-2-650-5093
Web: http://www.ulb.ac.be/horta
e-mail: dmacola@ulb.ac.be

📖 **Programme d'études du 1er et 2ème cycles en architecture**

Domaines d'étude: architecture.
Programmes: Cours (niveau 1er et 2ème cycles) dans le domaine de l'architecture.
A l'intention de: ressortissants de tout pays, titulaires du baccalauréat ou d'un diplôme reconnu équivalent et résidant en Belgique.
Organisés: également à ISAI-Lambert Lombard à Liège et ISAI à Mons.
Durée: 1er cycle: 2 ans; 2e cycle: 3 ans.
Assistance financière: facilités de paiement et prêts pour les étudiants étrangers du 2e cycle, Fonds social d'aides.
Connaissances linguistiques: langue d'enseignement: français.
Inscriptions: avant le 1er octobre; pour les bourses, avant le 1er septembre.

270 Institut supérieur d'architecture Saint-Luc de Wallonie, Liège

41 Bd de la Constitution
4020 Liège 1
Tel: +32-4-341-8111
Fax: +32-4-331-8113
Web: http://www.saint-luc.org

📖 **Programme d'étude en architecture**

Domaines d'étude: architecture, bâtiment, construction, histoire de l'art, urbanisme.
Programmes: cours universitaires en matières théoriques et formation à la pratique de l'architecture, conduisant au diplôme d'architecte; post formation en architecture, mise en valeur, conservation et restauration du patrimoine

architectural.
A l'intention de: ressortissants de tout pays titulaires d'un diplôme de fin d'études secondaires (baccalauréat).
Durée: 5 ans.
Connaissances linguistiques: langue d'enseignement: français.
Inscriptions: avant mi-octobre.

271 Institut supérieur d'architecture Saint-Luc, Bruxelles

Chaussée de Charleroi, 132-134
1060 Bruxelles
Tel: +32-2-537-3419
Fax: +32-2-539-4069
Web: http://www.st-luc-brussels-archi.be
e-mail: administration@st-luc-brussels-archi.be

📖 **Cours dans le domaine de l'architecture**

Domaines d'étude: architecture.
Programmes: formation supérieure conduisant au diplôme d'architecte de l'Institut.
A l'intention de: ressortissants de tout pays, titulaires d'un diplôme reconnu équivalent au certificat de l'enseignement secondaire supérieur et ayant une bonne connaissance du français.
Durée: Durée: 5 ans.
Connaissances linguistiques: française.
Inscriptions: avant fin octobre.

272 Institut supérieur de la communauté française de traducteurs et interprètes [ISTI]

34, rue Joseph-Hazard
1180 Bruxelles
Tel: +32-2-340-1280
Fax: +32-2-346-2134
Web: http://www.heb.be/isti
e-mail: info@isti.be

📖 **Programme d'études en interprétation et traduction**

Domaines d'étude: toutes disciplines principales, formation professionnelle, interprétation et traduction, linguistique.
Programmes: (a) Formation générale dans les domaines suivants: droit, économie, histoire, linguistique et traductologie, philosophie et psychologie, sciences politiques, etc.; (b) Formation linguistique et culturelle: en français langue de base et deux autres langues; (c) Formation professionnelle: traduction et interprétation pour les deux langues étrangères choisies.
A l'intention de: ressortissants de tout pays, titulaires d'un diplôme de fin d'études secondaires donnant accès à l'université; des cours spéciaux de français sont organisés pour les non-francophones. Une attestation est délivrée en vue de l'obtention de « crédits » dans le pays d'origine.
Durée: 4 ans (débutant en septembre).
Assistance financière: possibilité de bourses; se renseigner auprès de l'Institut à l'adresse ci-dessus.
Inscriptions: d'avril à octobre.

273 Katholieke Hogeschool Mechelen [UCPM]

Zandpoortvest 13
2800 Mechelen
Tel: +32-15-369-100
Fax: +32-15-369-109
Web: http://www.khm.be
e-mail: stijn.coenen@khm.be

📖 **Undergraduate and Professional (Master's) Degree Programmes**

Study Domains: business, communication, information science, interior design, management, nursing, teacher education, tourism, hotel and catering management.
Programmes: Bachelor's degrees in nursing; teacher training; interior design; business: Master's degree in hospitality management.
Description: strategic hospitality management; financial

management; international marketing; management of hospitality operations; human resources management; information technology; international hospital law.
Held: 1 semester in Mechelen and Antwerp and choice of 1 semester in Ireland, France, Germany or Spain.
Duration: 10 months to 1 year; courses begin 17 September.
Fees: tuition: 750 €; living costs: 400-500 €.
Languages: English.

274   Katholieke Hogeschool Sint-Lieven

Gebroeders Desmet str. 1
9000 Gent
Tel: +32-9 -265-8610
Fax: +32-9-265-8640
Web: http://www.kahosl.be
e-mail: info@kahosl.be

Undergraduate and Graduate Programmes

Study Domains: accounting, agriculture, applied sciences, biochemistry, building industry, business administration, chemical engineering, chemistry, civil engineering, computer science, dietetics, early childhood education, ecology, environment, electricity and electronics, food, laboratory techniques, management, marketing, mechanical engineering, nursing, teacher education, telecommunications.
Programmes: studies leading to Bachelor's and Master's degrees.
Open to: candidates holding at least a secondary-school certificate.
Languages: Dutch (test and interview for foreign students).
Applications: by 31 October to the above address.

275   Provinciale Hogeschool Limburg [PHL]

Elfde Liniestraat 24
3500 Hasselt
Tel: +32-1-123-8888
Fax: +32-1-123-8889
Web: http://www.phlimburg.be
e-mail: phl@phhlimburhg.be

University-Level Technical Programmes

Study Domains: agriculture, architecture, arts, business, education, health and hygiene, interior design, interpretation and translation, languages, marketing, nursing, photography, transport, visual arts.
Programmes: (a) programme of studies for foreign students including courses in: history of Belgian architecture and urban development and architectural design; (b) international programme including courses in European law, computer science, advertising, direct marketing, general economics in Belgium, international accountancy, Dutch intensive course, advanced business English; (c) Accountancy and tax management.
Open to: students of any nationality, (a) with studies in architecture or related fields, having completed a minimum of 3 years or 6 semesters of study, before arrival; (b) students with certificate of 1st year 1-cycle higher education, 18-25 years of age; (c) students with 1-cycle higher education in commercial sciences and business studies (3 years), at least 21 years of age; minimum knowledge of Dutch required.
Held: (a) Department of Architecture, Diepenbeek; (c) Department of Commercial Sciences, Hasselt.
Duration: (a) 5 months (February - June); (b) 1 month (October and March); (c) 1 year.
Languages: Instruction in (a) and (b) English; (c) Dutch.
Applications: (a) before end of November of the year previous to enrolment (programmes start beginning of February of each academic year), to the Department of Architecture.

276   Université catholique de Louvain [UCL]

Administration des Relations internationales
Halles universitaires
Place de l'Université, 1
1348 Louvain-la-Neuve
Tel: +32-10-47-3095
Fax: +32-10-47-4075
Web: http://www.ucl.ac.be
e-mail: info@adri.ucl.ac.be

Cours du 1er et 2ème cycles dans toutes disciplines

Domaines d'étude: toutes disciplines principales.
Programmes: (a) cours de 1er et 2ème cycles dans les divers domaines enseignés à l'Université; (b) cours d'été: français (3 niveaux), propédeutiques (sciences et sciences humaines); (c) spécialisations de courte durée (niveau 3ème cycle) préparatoires éventuellement au doctorat.
À l'intention de: ressortissants de tout pays pour le 3ème cycle; limité à quelques nationalités pour le 1er et 2ème cycles. Admission sur dossier ou après la réussite d'un test. Un cours de français, préparant à l'examen de français obligatoire pour l'inscription à l'Université, est organisé aux mois de juillet et août pour les non-francophones.
Durée: de 1 à 5 ans (débutant le 15 septembre); 1 ou 2 mois (juillet, août) pour les cours d'été.
Assistance financière: un certain nombre de bourses est accordé chaque année.
Inscriptions: avant le 15 mai; auprès du Secrétariat des étudiants (étudiants étrangers) de l'Université.
Handicapés: Des aménagements spéciaux sont à la disposition des handicapés moteurs.

Bourse pour études de troisième cycle

Domaines d'étude: toutes disciplines principales, études du développement, sciences.
Description: 20 bourses par an (sur concours). Les bourses de DES sont destinées à des candidats qui souhaitent parfaire leur formation après une période d'engagement professionnel au service du développement de leur pays tandis que les bourses de DEA sont octroyées dans la perspective de favoriser et de renforcer l'enseignement et la recherche universitaire au sein de l'institution d'origine du candidat.
À l'intention de: ressortissants des pays en développement possédant un diplôme universitaire de 2ème cycle obtenu après au moins 4 années d'études supérieures; une bonne connaissance du français et une expérience professionnelle et sociale au service du développement sont requises. Les candidats devront faire état de leurs perspectives de travail futur dans des pays en développement et prendront l'engagement formel de ne pas rester en Belgique ou dans un autre pays industrialisé.
Nationalité: originaire d'un pays en développement.
Qualifications requises: détenteur d'un diplôme de deuxième cycle de l'enseignement universitaire, acquis après au moins quatre années d'études (avec mémoire de fin d'études).
Age Max: âgé de moins de 35 ans (pour la réalisation d'un DEA) ou de moins de 40 ans (pour la réalisation d'un DES).
Autres Conditions: moyenne académique considérée par l'UCL comme équivalente à au moins 14/20 (70%); impossibilité de réaliser valablement son plan d'études dans son propre pays (ou dans la sous-région); avoir exercé une activité professionnelle en relation avec la formation demandée pendant au moins deux ans pour un DES; avoir exercé une activité professionnelle d'enseignement et/ou de recherche dans une institution universitaire d'un pays en développement pendant au moins un an après les études universitaires pour un DEA; pour les spécialisations médicales, donner la preuve de l'inscription, dans le pays d'origine ou dans un autre pays en développement, à un programme de spécialisation dans la discipline médicale pour laquelle une formation complémentaire est demandée et démontrer d'une pratique dans cette discipline pendant au moins deux ans.
Lieu: Université catholique de Louvain.
Durée: de 1 an en général; certaines formations peuvent être de 2 ou 3 ans (débutant le 15 septembre).
Valeur: 850 € par mois + complément familial; frais d'inscription et d'assurance maladie; billet aller/retour du boursier pris en charge par l'UCL.

Candidatures: dossier de candidature complet avant le 31 décembre; formulaire et conditions disponibles sur le site web: www.sco.ucl.ac.be/codev/bcodev.html; email: concours@adri.ucl.ac.be: téléphone: +32 10 47 92 38; fax: +32 10 47 40 75.

☞ Bourses de Doctorat

Domaines d'étude: toutes disciplines principales, études du développement, sciences.
Description: L'Université catholique de Louvain (UCL) organise un concours visant à octroyer une dizaine de bourses de doctorat à des ressortissants de pays en développement. Par ce moyen, l'UCL souhaite à la fois contribuer au renforcement du tissu universitaire des pays en voie de développement mais également identifier les porteurs de nouveaux partenariats entre l'UCL et des institutions d'enseignement supérieur des pays en voie de développement.
A l'intention de: tous candidats.
Nationalité: originaire d'un pays en développement.
Qualifications requises: être admissible directement au doctorat.
Age Max: âgé de moins de 40 ans.
Autres Conditions: avoir exercé une activité professionnelle d'enseignement et/ou de recherche dans une institution universitaire d'un pays en développement pendant au moins un an après les études universitaires et y développer un carrière académique au terme du doctorat. Avoir négocié avec un promoteur UCL un projet de recherche et un calendrier de travail.
Lieu: Université catholique de Louvain et, en cas de doctorat en alternance, dans une Université d'un pays du Sud.
Durée: 48 mois maximum.
Valeur: environ 1300 € par mois + billet aller-retour du boursier.
Candidatures: Le promoteur du candidat doit s'adresser à l'Administration des Relations Internationales (ADRI) de l'UCL pour y obtenir le formulaire de candidature. Le dossiers de candidature complet doit être introduit par le promoteur auprès du Recteur de l'UCL avant le 16 septembre.

277 Université d'Anvers Institut de politique et de gestion du développement [UA]

Campus Ville (CST), Venusstraat 35
2020 Anvers
Tel: +32-3-220-4998
Fax: +32-3-220-4481
Web: http://www.ua.ac.be/main.asp?c=*IPGD
e-mail: dev@ua.ac.be

📖 Cycles postuniversitaire en administration et développement

Domaines d'étude: administration, économie politique, études du développement, finances.
Programmes: Cycle postuniversitaire conduisant à l'obtention: (a) du diplôme en politique de développement (après la 1ère année); (b) du diplôme de Master en gestion et administration publiques (après la 2ème année).
A l'intention de: ressortissants de tout pays, titulaires d'un diplôme universitaire ou d'un diplôme d'une école nationale d'administration.
Durée: (a) 1 an; (b) 2 années universitaires.
Connaissances linguistiques: l'enseignement est donné en français et en anglais.
Inscriptions: dépôt de dossier en avril.

278 Université de Liège [ULG]

9, place du 20 Août
4000 Liège
Tel: +32-4-366-2111
Fax: +32-4-366-5700
Web: http://www.ulg.ac.be
e-mail: admission.horsue@ulg.ac.be

📖 Cours du 1er, 2ème et 3ème cycles

Domaines d'étude: toutes disciplines principales.
Programmes: programme d'études conduisant à la licence, à la maîtrise ou au doctorat, dans toutes les disciplines, sauf les sciences agronomiques.
A l'intention de: ressortissants de tout pays, admis sur dossier, en fonction des diplômes obtenus.
Durée: variable.
Inscriptions: avant le 30 juin; au Service des études, à l'adresse ci-dessus.

☞ Bourses postdoctorales

Domaines d'étude: toutes disciplines principales.
A l'intention de: ressortissants des pays en développement titulaires du titre de docteur à thèse.
Durée: de 10 à 12 mois.
Candidatures: au Recteur de l'Université, en réponse à un appel d'offres lancé chaque année.

279 Université de Mons-Hainaut [UMH]

Service des Inscriptions et Certificats
Campus des sciences humaines
17, place Warocqué
7000 Mons
Tel: +32-65-373-013/12
Web: http://www.umh.ac.be
e-mail: sic@umh.ac.be

📖 Cours de 3ème cycle

Domaines d'étude: économie, économie politique, éducation, interprétation et traduction, médecine, sciences.
Programmes: (a) Les facultés des sciences, de médecine-pharmacie, de psychologie et des sciences de l'éducation, la Faculté Warocqé des sciences économiques et l'Institut de linguistique proposent des cours conduisant respectivement: pour le 1er cycle au diplôme d'études complémentaires (DEC1); pour le 2e cycle au diplôme d'études complémentaires (DEC2) et à la licence; pour le 3e cycle au diplôme d'études approfondies (DEA), au diplôme d'études spécialisées (DES), au doctorat et à l'agrégation de l'enseignement supérieur; (b) l'École d'interprètes internationaux prépare pour le 1er cycle, à la candidature en traduction et pour le 2e cycle, aux licences en traduction et en interprétation; admission sur concours 2 fois par an.
A l'intention de: ressortissants de tout pays remplissant les conditions requises.
Durée: 1 à 2 ans selon le programme choisi.
Assistance financière: permet aux étudiants régulièrement inscrits de bénéficier des avantages liés aux diverses conventions passées avec des organismes européens et internationaux (bourses SOCRATES-ERASMUS, Leonardo, CGRI de la Communauté française).
Inscriptions: de juin à 10 octobre; au Service inscriptions et certificats, 17, place Warocque, 7000 Mons: voir site web pour de plus amples renseignements.

280 Université libre de Bruxelles, Institut d'Études européennes [ULB]

39, avenue F.D.-Roosevelt
1050 Bruxelles
Tel: +32-2-650-3077
Fax: +32-2-650-3068
Web: http://www.ulb.ac.be/facs/iee/index.html
e-mail: iee@admin.ulb.ac.be

📖 Études européennes

Domaines d'étude: études européennes.
Programmes: cursus en droit européen, économie européenne et politique européenne aboutissant à un diplôme d'études spécialisées (DES) ou un diplôme d'études approfondies (DEA). Diplôme complémentaire de deuxième cycle (DEC2) en études européennes.
A l'intention de: ressortissants de tout pays, titulaires d'un diplôme de fin d'études universitaires dont l'équivalence est accordée par le président de l'Institut; une excellente connaissance du français est exigée, ainsi que la connaissance de l'anglais et d'une autre langue de l'Union européenne, plus spécialement l'allemand ou l'italien.
Durée: 1 ou 2 ans; cours débutent en septembre.
Assistance financière: la plupart des gouvernements ont un programme de bourses pour l'étranger. Les intéressés sont invités à se renseigner à ce sujet auprès des autorités nationales compétentes. Le gouvernement belge offre également certaines bourses aux étudiants étrangers par l'intermédiaire de l'Administration générale de la coopération au développement et du Commissariat général aux relations

internationales. Les intéressés sont invités à s'adresser à l'ambassade de Belgique dans leur pays d'origine.
Inscriptions: les formulaires, qui peuvent être obtenus auprès du Secrétariat des affaires étudiantes de l'Institut, devront être retournés avant le 15 avril, à l'adresse ci-dessus.

281 Universiteit Antwerpen
Groenenborgerlaan 171
2020 Antwerpen
Fax: +32-3-265-3622
Web: http://www.ua.ac.be/international
e-mail: international@ua.ac.be

 Undergraduate, Graduate and Postgraduate Programmes

Study Domains: all major fields.
Applications: to above address.

282 Universiteit Gent, Faculty of Bioscience Engineering [RUG]
Coupure links 653
9000 Gent
Tel: +32-9-264-5901
Fax: +32-9-264-6245
Web: http://www.fbw.ugent.be

 Formations postuniversitaires

Domaines d'étude: agriculture, sciences agronomiques.
Programmes: (a) formation continue, complémentaire ou spécialisée de niveau postuniversitaire: cours de développement agricole, sciences et technologies de l'environnement, assainissement de l'environnement, aquaculture, érémologie, sciences de la nutrition et de l'alimentation, sciences et technologies de l'alimentation; (b) formations académiques de niveau postsecondaire pour ingénieur biologiste dans une des spécialisations suivantes: agronomie, chimie, technologie de l'environnement, gestion des terres et des forêts, biotechnologie des cellules et des gènes; possibilité de cours accélérés de néerlandais en juillet-août.
A l'intention de: accès direct pour les titulaires de certains diplômes universitaires; examen d'entrée pour les autres diplômés d'universités ou d'écoles supérieures.
Durée: (b) 5 ans (débutant en octobre).
Assistance financière: possibilité de bourses.

Belize
Organization of higher education system: In Belize, degree courses are offered by the University of Belize, founded in 2000 by the merger of the University College of Belize (originally created in 1986), Belmopan Junior College, Belize School of Nursing, Belize School of Education, and Belize College of Agriculture. The University is directly financed by the Ministry of Education and offers its own Bachelor's Degree courses under the authority of the Government of Belize. Through an extra-mural unit, Belize is also affiliated to the University of the West Indies, which is a regional institution with campuses in Jamaica, Barbados and Trinidad.
Monetary unit: Belize dollars (BZD).
International student admission: Foreign students should have a general certificate of education and good knowledge in English.
Information services: Ministry of Education, Belmopan, Belize, C.A; email: educate@btl.net.
Open and distance learning: Non-formal studies consist of continuing education programmes provided by the Extramural Department of the University of the West Indies (UWI) and by government ministries. UWI programmes help people, particularly teachers, wishing to improve their formal academic and professional qualifications.
Recognition of studies and qualification: Ministry of Education, Youth and Sports; Belmopan; Belize; email: educate@btl.net.

283 University of Belize
PO Box 990
Belize City
Tel: +501-223-0256
Fax: +501-223-0255
Web: http://www.ub.edu.bz

 Undergraduate Programmes

Study Domains: agriculture, business, computer science, education, engineering, health and hygiene, liberal arts, nursing, social work, teacher education, technology, tourism, hotel and catering management.
Programmes: Associate and Bachelor's degree programmes.
Description: courses in the Faculties of Agriculture and Natural Resources, Arts and Science, Business, Education, Engineering and Information Technology, Nursing, Health Science and Social Work.
Languages: must meet English language requirements.

Bénin
Année universitaire: octobre à juillet.
Organisation de l'enseignement supérieur: La République du Bénin dispose aujourd'hui de deux universités publiques: l'Université d'Abomey-Calavi et l'Université de Paraklou; de trois universités privées: l'Université Catholique de l'Afrique de l'Ouest Sesssion du Bénin, l'Université des Sciences et Technoloqies du Bénin, Houdégbé North American University Benin) et cinquante-neuf établissements privés d'enseignement supérieur.
La Direction de l'Enseignement supérieur est la direction technique du MInistère de l'Enseignement supérieur et de la recherche scientifique chargée de la coordination des activités du sous-secteur. Les études supérieures sont organisées en trois cycles.
Dans les universités publiques, des établissements de formation professionnelle coexistent avec des facultés traditionnelles
Université d'Abomey-Calavi: 01BP 526, Cotonou - tél: +229-360-074: fax: +229-360-028.
Université de Parakou: BP 123 Parakou: tél/fax: +229-610-712.
Unité monétaire: franc CFA (FCFA).
Admission pour étudiants du pays: l'inscription des nationaux dans l'une de ces universités nationales est subordonnée à la présentation des titres requis et à la constitution d'un dossier d'inscription. Toute première inscription d'étudiants nationaux ayant un diplôme étranger nécessite une étude préalable du dossier des intéressés par la Commission universitaire d'orientation.
Admission pour étudiants internationaux: L'inscription des étudiants étrangers dans l'une des deux universités nationales du Bénin est subordonnée à l'étude préalable des dossiers des intéressés. Le dossier de pré-inscription est constitué de: une demande adressée à Monsieur le vice-recteur précisant la faculté, la filière et l'année d'étude sollicitée; un document officiel indiquant le programme suivi au cours de la dernière année; deux coupons-réponses postaux; un (des) relevé(s) de notes d'années antérieures; des frais d'étude du dossier (10.000 FCFA).
Les dossiers de candidature doivent parvenir au Rectorat (Direction des Affaires académiques) avant le 31 juillet de l'année en cours pour les facultés classiques et avant le 30 avril pour les établissements de formation professionnelle. Les équivalences universitaires ou les dispenses en vue d'une inscription dans une filière déterminée sont prononcées par le vice-recteur chargé des Affaires académiques après avis technique de la Commission universitaire d'orientation.
Le dossier d'inscription consistera des éléments suivants: une demande manuscrite précisant la faculté, la filière et l'année d'étude sollicitée; une copie légalisée de l'extrait de naissance ou fiche individuelle d'état civil; trois photos d'identité (format bijou, 2,25 x 1,2 cm); l'original du diplôme plus une copie légalisée; un certificat de nationalité (original plus une copie légalisée); l'original et une copie légalisée des attestations de succès pour les étudiants venant d'une autre université; une autorisation d'inscription du vice-recteur.
Connaissances linguistiques requises: Une bonne connaissance de la langue française est indispensable.
Formalités d'immigration: Les étudiants étrangers doivent

remplir les formalités administratives requises pour obtenir le certificat d'hébergement.

Frais pour une année universitaire: Les frais d'inscription et de scolarité (non compris livres/fournitures/logement) varient pour les étudiants nationaux de 6.200 à 501.200 FCFA selon la filière, le cycle et le régime d'étude.
Pour les étudiants internationaux ces frais varient de 206.200 à 1.444.200 FCFA selon la filière et le cycle choisis, ainsi que la zone de provenance de l'étudiant (zone Conseil de l'entente, zone CEDEAO, autres nationalités).

Services d'accueil et d'information: * Direction des affaires académiques (DAA), B.P. 526, Cotonou;
- Service des Etudes et de l'Orientation universitaire (SEOU) pour les échanges internationaux d'étudiants, de l'accueil des étudiants internationaux, etc.;
- Service de la Scolarité et de la statistique de la Direction des affaires académiques pour les demandes d'inscription pour étudiants internationaux;
• Ambassades et/ou Consulats du Bénin dans divers pays.

Bourses pour étudiants internationaux: Il n'existe pas de bourse ni d'assistance financière nationales pour étudiants internationaux.

Enseignement à distance: Il existe un Centre d'éducation à distance à l'Université d'Abomey-Calavi qui offre plusieurs programmes de formation aux étudiants. De même, une section de l'Université virtuelle de l'Afrique opère au Bénin sous la tutelle de l'Université d'Abomey-Calavi.

Reconnaissance des études et diplômes:
• Direction des affaires académiques de l'Université Abomey-Calavi
• Direction de l'enseignement supérieur; 02 BP 1211, Cotonou.

Services du logement: Il n'existe pas de service de logements pour étudiants.

Possibilités d'emploi: Il existe pour les étudiants étrangers la possibilité d'exercer une activité rémunérée dans le secteur privé à condition de justifier des qualifications requises par l'employeur.

Publications / Sites Web: * Guide d'information et d'orientation, « Comment s'inscrire à l'université »; peut être obtenu à la Direction des Affaires académiques des universités.
• Au sein de l'Université d'Abomey-Calavi est installée une structure de l'Agence universitaire de la Francophonie dénommée « Le Campus numérique francophone » (CNF). Le site web du CNF, http://www.bj.refer.org, contient des informations utiles sur l'université.
• « Annales de la Faculté des lettres » (annuelle).

284 Université d'Abomey-Calavi [UAC]
Abomey-Calavi University Campus
BP 526
Cotonou
Tel: +229-360-074
Fax: +229-360-028
e-mail: uac@intnet.bj

1er, 2e, 3e cycles

Domaines d'étude: toutes disciplines principales.
Programmes: DEUG, Licence, Maîtrise, DEA et Doctorat dispensés dans diverses facultés, établissements de formation professionnelle, de formation postuniversitaire et para-universitaire.
Description: (a) Cours dans les domaines des lettres, langues, sciences humaines, sciences et techniques, droit, économie, gestion, administration, agronomie, médecine, éducation physique et sportive, conduisant à la maîtrise, au DEA, au diplôme d'ingénieur, et au doctorat; 20 à 150 participants par classe; (b) Cours de langue française: technique d'expression, grammaire, français spécialisé; maximum 30 participants.
A l'intention de: ressortissants de tout pays, titulaires d'un baccalauréat ou équivalent; pour les étudiants internationaux: sélection sur dossier ou test de sélection.
Durée: de 3 à 7 ans.
Connaissances linguistiques: français essentiel; cours de français auprès du Centre béninois des langues étrangères (CEBELAE).
Inscriptions: avant le 30 novembre, se renseigner auprès

du vice-Recteur chargé des affaires académiques, à l'adresse ci-dessus.

Bermuda

Academic year: September to June.
Monetary unit: Bermudian Dollar (BMD$).
National student admission: For entry to Bermuda College, a high school graduation diploma is required, though most programmes have special entry requirements. Overseas applicants would normally have to provide evidence of up to 5 passes at GCE Ordinary O-levels or equivalent. Orientation is provided for all incoming students and particular problems relating to overseas students are dealt with on an individual basis.
Language: English is essential.
Immigration requirements: Immigration clearance is mandatory. A special questionnaire must be completed and lodged well in advance of intended arrival.
Estimated expenses for one academic year: Tuition: (in Bermudian dollars) $3,300; room and board: $4,000; books: $500.
Information services: Ministry of Education, PO Box HM 1185, Hamilton HM EX.
Scholarships for international students: Government of Bermuda/Commonwealth Fund for Technical Cooperation (CFTC) Scholarships. Enquire at Ministry of Education or Bermuda College.

285 Bermuda College [BC]
PO Box PG 297
Paget PG BX
Tel: +1-441-239-4048
Fax: +1-441-239-4008
Web: http://www.bercol.bm
e-mail: info@bercol.bm

Undergraduate Programmes

Study Domains: arts, business, business administration, design, liberal arts, management, recreation and leisure, tourism, hotel and catering management.
Programmes: Associate degree courses (equivalent to the first 2 years of a 4 year Bachelor's degree) in liberal arts, natural sciences, art and design, business administration, hospitality management, office administration, science (electronics), electronics technology; certificate programmes in general studies, general office skills, front office reception, food industry, motor vehicle maintenance, plumbing, wood trades, telecommunications and electronics, refrigeration and air conditioning.
Open to: candidates holding a secondary-school diploma or equivalent; official copies of transcripts, letters of recommendation and the Computerised Placement Test (CPT) are required; written and spoken English necessary; TOEFL 500 required.
Held: Stonington Campus, College Drive, Paget PG 04.
Duration: 2 academic years; courses begin in August and January; summer courses May and June.
Fees: application fee: (in Bermudan dollars) $25 (late application $50); tuition: $1,640 per year; living expenses: $1,200 per month; non-academic courses (CSC and ECA): $300 per year; incidental fee: $320 per year; differential fee: $2,100 per year; books: $400 per year.
Languages: instruction in English.
Applications: by 3 February and 1 July.

Bolivia

Año académico: Marzo a diciembre.
Moneda nacional: Boliviano (Bs).
Admisiones para estudiantes extranjeros: Título de
bachiller, debidamente legalizado por el cónsul de Bolivia en
el lugar de procedencia del estudiante, o certificado
equivalente; examen de admisión o ingreso requerido por
algunas universidades.
Conocimientos lingüísticos: Es indispensable dominar
suficientemente el idioma español.
Formalidades de inmigración: Visado de estudiante,
concedido por el cónsul de Bolivia en la ciudad de origen del
estudiante.
Importe de gastos para un año universita: Los estudiantes
pueden beneficiarse de albergues y comedores a precios
módicos en algunas universidades; consultorio médico-dental
gratuito; cuidados médicos gratuitos en ciertos casos, o la
mitad de los gastos.
Servicios de información:
• Ministerio de Educación y Cultura, Departamento de
Relaciones Internacionales, Avenida Arce 2408, La Paz
(asesoramiento e información relativa a los centros docentes
bolivianos de enseñanza superior, calificaciones o diplomas
requeridos para la admisión en los mismos, convalidación de
estudios, becas internacionales, etc.).
• Subsecretaría de Juventudes, Plaza Murillo, Palacio
Legislativo, La Paz (organismo oficial encargado de los
intercambios internacionales de estudiantes).
• Comité Ejecutivo de Universidades de Bolivia, avenida
Arce, esquina Pinilla, Casilla postal 4722, La Paz
(información sobre ingreso en las universidades bolivianas,
convalidación y revalidación de títulos académicos, becas
internacionales, intercambio estudiantil y docente,
cooperación científica, técnica y cultural; convenios
internacionales culturales).
• Universidad Mayor de San Andrés, Oficina de Bienestar
Estudiantil, avenida Villazón 1995, La Paz (orientación
universitaria para encontrar alojamiento, etc.).
Convalidación de estudios y diplomas: Secretaría de
Planificación Académica, Acreditación y Evaluación. Comité
Ejecutivo de la Universidad Boliviana (CEUB); Secretario
Nacional; PO Box 4722; Avenida Arce 2606; La Paz, Bolivia;
email: webmaster@ceub.edu.bo; web:
http://www.ceub.edu.bo.

286 Fundación Universitaria "Simon I. Patiño"

Casilla Postal 464
Calle Potosí 1450
Cochabamba
Web: http://www.fundacionpatino.org

❦ Becas de estudio

Campos de estudios: biología, economía, física,
matemáticas, psicología, química, sociología.
Se conceden: a candidatos bolivianos de sexo masculino,
bachilleres con buen expediente académico y necesidades
económicas, de edad entre 17 y 22 años, que escojan entre las
carreras ofrecidas; se requiere un conocimiento mínimo de
inglés o francés.
Lugar: en Ginebra y Lausana (Suiza).
Duración: el tiempo que requieran los estudios.
Importe: cubre los gastos de viaje, de estudio, alojamiento,
manutención y libros, más importe mensual para gastos.
Solicitudes: hasta el 30 de noviembre; las convocatorias
son en el mes de octubre. Solicitar información en la dirección
del título o a Fundación Simón I. Patiño, 8 rue Giovanni
Gambini, 1206 Ginebra, Suiza.

287 Universidad Autónoma "Tomás Frías" [UATF]

Casilla 36
Potosí
Tel: (591) 62 27300
Fax: (591) 62 26663

📖 Programas universitarios

Campos de estudios: todas las materias principales.
Descripción: programas conducentes a los grados de

licenciado o técnico superior en sus distintas Facultades: artes
(artes musicales, plásticas), ciencias agrícolas y pecuarias
(ingeniería agronómica, veterinaria y zootecnia), ciencias
económicas, financieras y administrativas (administración de
empresas, auditoría, economía, contabilidad), ciencias
sociales y humanísticas (lingüística e idiomas, trabajo social,
turismo), ciencias puras (estadística, física, informática,
matemáticas, química), derecho, ingeniería (ingeniería civil,
construcciones civiles, topografía), ingeniería geológica,
ingeniería minera (ingeniería minera, ingeniería de procesos
de materias primas minerales), tecnología (electricidad,
electrónica, mecánica automotriz, mecánica general),
enfermería.
Se destina(n): a bachilleres.
Duración: 10 semestres o de 3 a 5 años según la carrera.
Asistencia financiera: existen becas de alimentación y de
albergue.
Inscripciones: dirigirse a Información Académica, Casilla
54, Potosí.

288 Universidad Privada Boliviana [UPB]

Camino Antiguo a Quillacollo km. 6,5
Cochabamba
Tel: (591) (4) 426 8287
Fax: (591) (4) 426 8288
Web: http://www.upb.edu
e-mail: upb@upb.edu

📖 Programas universitarios

Campos de estudios: administración de empresas,
arquitectura, ciencias económicas y comerciales, derecho,
ingeniería.
Descripción:
(a) Programas de pregrado (licenciaturas) en áreas de
ingeniería, arquitectura, ciencias empresariales, derecho;
(b) Programas de posgrado (maestrías) en administración y
derecho.
Se destina(n): a candidatos que superen examen escrito de
admisión.
Se dicta(n): pregrados: en La Paz y Cochabamba;
posgrados: en La Paz, Cochabamba, Santa Cruz, Oruro y
Tarija.
Duración: año académico de febrero a diciembre.
Inscripciones: por mayores informaciones, dirigirse a
Admisiones y Asuntos Estudiantiles.

289 Universidad Privada del Valle [UPV]

Casilla Postal 4742
Cochabamba
Tel: (591) (4) 428 73 73/74
Fax: (591) (4) 431 50 74
Web: http://www.univalle.edu
e-mail: dirnalcor@univalle.edu

📖 Programas universitarios

Campos de estudios: arquitectura, ciencias económicas y
comerciales, ciencias sociales, electricidad y electrónica,
estudios dentales, farmacia y farmacología, higiene y salud,
informática, ingeniería, medicina.
Descripción:
(a) Carreras profesionales en áreas de ciencias de la salud,
ingeniería, ciencias sociales y administrativas, informática y
electrónica, arquitectura;
(b) Maestrías en: administración de empresas, gerencia de la
innovación, marketing y finanzas, derecho comercial y
tributario, administración de sistemas de información,
informática y gestión, ciencia y tecnología de los alimentos,
análisis clínico y técnicas farmacéuticas, psicología social,
ingeniería estructural;
(c) Diplomados en: e-business y comercio electrónico,
educación superior, derecho procesal y moralidad,
normalización de sistemas administrativos, páginas web,
redes integradas en telecomunicaciones.
Se dicta(n): en las ciudades de Cochabamba, La Paz,
Sucre y Trinidad.
Duración: año académico de febrero a diciembre (2
semestres).
Inscripciones: (b) y (c) por mayor información, dirigirse a
Facultad de Postgrado, Edificio Polifuncional Univalle, Planta
Baja, Av. Ayacucho N° 256, Cochabamba (Bolivia), e-mail:

postgradocba@univalle.edu.

290 Universidad Técnica de Oruro [UTO]
Av. Pagador 6548
Oruro
Tel: (591) 52 74 870
Fax: (591) 52 72 835
Web: http://www.uto.edu.bo
e-mail: fnidec@yahoo.com

☰ Carreras profesionales y posgrados

Campos de estudios: ciencias de la tierra, electricidad y electrónica, geología, ingeniería, mecánica, química, tecnología.
Descripción: áreas de ingeniería de minas, metalúrgica, eléctrica, mecánica, química, geología.
Duración: año académico de febrero a noviembre.
Asistencia financiera: becas de la universidad de trabajo y/o alimentación y/o albergue; solicitar información a Bienestar Estudiantil.
Inscripciones: hasta marzo.

Bosnia and Herzegovina
Academic year: October to July.
Organization of higher education system: The Republic of Bosnia and Herzegovina has four universities, namely Sarajevo, Mostar, Tuzla and Banjaluka. The war in Bosnia-Herzegovina (1992-1995) created an extremely difficult situation for the university system. However, pedagogical academies were founded in Zenica and Bihac in 1993, as well as the Faculty of Philosophy (derived from the former Pedagogical Academy) and the Faculty of Special Education in Tuzla. At the end of 1995, the Faculty of Machine Engineering was established in Bihac from the former Advanced Technical School. The higher education institutions in Zenica and Bihac were considered integral parts of the University of Sarajevo. The newly-created University of Sarajevo of the Republika Srpska consists of faculties of the universities of Sarajevo, Tuzla and Mostar which dissociated themselves from their former universities. The legal framework of higher education is laid down in the 1993 University Act. The governing body of the university is the rector and the university board. The professional body is the university council. There is also a Republic Council for the Development of University Education which has a consultative function and examines issues relating to the development of university education.
• University level first stage: First Degree: Diploma Višeg Obrazovanje (Diploma of Higher Education):
University faculties and academies offer programmes that last for two to three years leading to the Diploma Višeg Obrazovanje with a professional title (eg. Inzenjer, Pravnik) in various scientific and artistic fields. It is not a terminal qualification.
• University level second stage: Second Degree: Diploma Visokog Obrazovanja (Advanced Diploma of Higher Education):
Courses leading to the Diploma Visokog Obrazovanja with a professional title (eg. Diplomirani Inzenjer, Diplomirani Pravnik, Profesor) last for four to six years during which students specialize.
University level third stage: Third Degree: Magistar:
Studies for the Magistar require two years' further study and the defence of a thesis.
• University level fourth stage: Doctorate: The Doctorate (PhD) is the highest scientific degree. It is the result of independent research. Public defence of a doctoral thesis is required for this degree. (Source: IAU World Higher Education Database, 2005/6).
National student admission: Secondary school credential Maturska Svjedodzba for entry to: Universities; and Visoka Škola and entrance examination required for universities.
International student admission: Same requirements as for national students.
Language: Croatian and Serbian.
Open and distance learning: Radio Zid Sarajevo has embarked on a youth radio programme with UNICEF aid. It wishes to expand its work in distance education programmes. The SOROS Foundation, the Free University of Amsterdam and World University Service are setting up Internet equipment in order to improve the exchange of programmes and academic staff between Bosnian and foreign universities.
Recognition of studies and qualification:
• Federal Ministry of Education, Science, Culture and Sports; Obala Maka Dizdara 2; 71000 Sarajevo, Bosnia and Herzegovina; email: fmonks@bih.net.ba; web: http://fbihvlada.gov.ba/index.html
• Recognition of studies pursued in foreign countries: University of Sarajevo; Obala Kulina Bana 7; 71000 Sarajevo; Bosnia and Herzegovina; email: rektorat@unsa.ba; web: http://www.unsa.ba.

291 University of Sarajevo
Obala Kulina Bana 7/11
71 000 Sarajevo
Tel: +387-33-663-392
Fax: +387-33-663-393
Web: http://www.unsa.ba
e-mail: info.rektorat@unsa.ba

☰ Undergraduate, Graduate, Postgraduate Programmes

Study Domains: agriculture, criminology, dentistry, economic and commercial sciences, engineering, fine arts, forestry, health and hygiene, law, liberal arts, medicine, music and musicology, performing arts, pharmacy and pharmacology, political science, sciences, teacher education.
Programmes: undergraduate, graduate and postgraduate studies in all major fields of study.
Open to: candidates of all nationalities with secondary-school certificate and passing entrance examination.
Applications: to above address.

Botswana
Academic year: August to May.
Monetary unit: pula.
National student admission: Candidates must be holders of a Senior secondary school certificate or a G.C.E. O-level.
Language: Students must be proficient in the English language (spoken and written).
Estimated expenses for one academic year:
Approximately 11,500 pula per year, including tuition, laboratory and equipment, medical insurance and examination fees. Room and board: 3,385 pula per year.
Open and distance learning: Distance education is currently being developed at diploma and first degree level.
Recognition of studies and qualification: Ministry of Education; Private Bag 005; Gaborone; Botswana; web: http://www.gov.bw/moe/index.html.
Publications / Websites:
• University of Botswana Calendar and Departmental brochures.

292 University of Botswana [UB]
Director, Academic Services
Private Bag UB 0022
Gaborone
Tel: +267-355-0000
Fax: +267-395-6591
Web: http://www.ub.bw
e-mail: admissions@mopipi.ub.bw

☰ Undergraduate, Graduate Programmes

Study Domains: all major fields.
Programmes: Programme of courses leading to Bachelor's degrees, diplomas, certificates, postgraduate diplomas and Master's degrees in all major fields.
Open to: suitably qualified candidates of all nationalities.
Duration: 1 to 5 years depending on the course; also part-time courses over 2 to 3 years.
Applications: to the Admissions Secretary for undergraduate programmes and to the Graduate Studies Secretary for graduate programmes, at the above address for all further information.

Brésil

Année universitaire: mars à décembre.
Unité monétaire: réal (R$).
Admission pour étudiants du pays: Certificat de fin d'études secondaires reconnu par le Ministère de l'éducation nationale et passage d'un examen de langue portugaise, de géographie et d'histoire du Brésil. Les ressortissants des pays d'Amérique latine et d'Afrique ayant conclu des accords culturels avec le Brésil sont dispensés d'examen d'entrée et de taxes scolaires.
Connaissances linguistiques requises: Les étudiants étrangers doivent avoir une bonne connaissance du portugais.
Services d'accueil et d'information:
• Ministère des relations extérieures, Département de la culture, Esplanada dos Ministérios, Brasilia DF (s'occupe spécialement des étudiants et des professeurs des pays d'Amérique latine et d'Afrique qui vont faire leurs études au Brésil; il peut également renseigner les étudiants de tous les autres pays sur les possibilités d'études et de séjour au Brésil. Dans la mesure du possible, le Département de la culture loge les étudiants étrangers dans des foyers d'étudiants ou leur procure une liste, avec le prix et la catégorie des hôtels et des chambres d'étudiants).
• Services culturels des ambassades et des consulats du Brésil à l'étranger (fournissent les mêmes renseignements que le Ministère des relations extérieures).
• Par l'entremise des ministères des relations extérieures et de l'éducation, le gouvernement brésilien offre chaque année un grand nombre de places à des étudiants des différents pays d'Amérique latine et d'Afrique, pour suivre des cours dans ses universités.
Enseignement à distance: Enseignement professionnel de durée variable, parrainé par des entités privées et/ou en accord avec des institutions publiques. Certificat de fin d'études secondaires exigé, Certificado de Conclusão. Telecurso 2000 (Fundação Roberto Marinho, MEC); cours de mise à niveau pour professeurs.
Reconnaissance des études et diplômes: Bureau de Reconnaissance des diplômes étrangers; Ministère de l'Éducation (Ministério de Educação -MEC), Esplanada dos Ministérios; Bloco L, 3 andar, Sala 219; Brasília DF 70047-903; Brésil; Internet: http://www.mec.gov.br.
Publications / Sites Web:
• Annuaires et guides des universités, offerts par les Services académiques des universités ou facultés.

293 Centre brésilien de recherches physiques [CBDRP]
Rua Dr. Xavier-Sigaud, 150
22290 Rio de Janeiro, R.J.
Tel: +55-21-2141-7000
Fax: +55-21-2141-7400
Web: http://www.cbpf.br

🐝 Bourses d'études
Domaines d'étude: physique.
Bourses: Bourses d'études en vue de l'obtention (a) de la maîtrise et (b) du doctorat.
Description: physique nucléaire, cosmologie et gravitation; physique de rayons cosmiques; physique de hautes énergies; théorie de particules; physique de la matière condensée et physique des molécules et solides.
A l'intention de: ressortissants des pays ayant des relations diplomatiques avec le Brésil; les candidats doivent être titulaires d'un diplôme universitaire.
Durée: (a) 4 ans d'étude et 30 mois de bourses; (b) 6 ans d'étude et 48 mois de bourses.
Candidatures: en juin et novembre.

294 Centro Universitario de Barra Mansa [UBM]
Rua Vereador Pinho de Carvalho, 267 Centro
27330 Barra Mansa
Tel: +55-24-3325-0222
Fax: +55-24-3323-3690
Web: http://www.ubm.br
e-mail: ubm@ubm.br

🐝 Réduction Frais Scolarité
Domaines d'étude: toutes disciplines principales.
Bourses: Bourse pour réduction des frais de scolarité.
Domaines d'études: pour tous domaines d'étude.
A l'intention de: tous les étudiants de l'institution, selon besoin financier et résultats académiques.
Nationalité: ouvert aux ressortissants de tous pays.
Valeur: variable selon les études.
Connaissances linguistiques: portugais.

295 Institut national de recherches d'Amazonie [INDRD]
CP 478
69011 Manaus, AM
Tel: +55-92-3643-3118
Fax: +55-92-3643-3124
Web: http://pg.inpa.gov.br/
e-mail: inpappg@inpa.gov.br

📖 2e, 3e cycles / sciences naturelles
Domaines d'étude: biochimie, biologie, botanique, écologie, environnement, hygiène et santé, météorologie, pêche, ressources naturelles, sciences agronomiques, sylviculture.
Programmes: (a) M.Sc.; (b) Ph.D.
Description: cours dans les domaines suivants: botanique, écologie, biologie des poissons et pêches intérieures, agronomie tropicale, sylviculture tropicale, technologie du bois, technologie des aliments, sciences de la santé, entomologie, limnologie, météorologie, phytochimie et biochimie.
A l'intention de: ressortissants de tout pays, ayant une bonne connaissance du portugais et de l'anglais; les candidats doivent être titulaires: pour (a) du B.Sc. ou avoir une formation universitaire en biologie; pour (b) du M.Sc. dans la discipline choisie.
Durée: 2 ans (prolongation possible pour 1 an au maximum).
Inscriptions: avant le 1er octobre.

296 Universidade federal de Minas Gerais [UFMG]
Av. Antônio Carlos, 6627
Caixa Postal 1621
31270-901 Belo Horizonte, MG
Tel: +55-31-3499-4025
Fax: +55-31-3499-4530
Web: http://www.ufmg.br
e-mail: info@cointer.ufmg.br

📖 Undergraduate Programme
Study Domains: civil engineering, ecology, environment, natural resources.
Programmes: Undergraduate programmes in environmental and resource management; Portuguese for foreign students.

297 Université adventiste du Brésil - São Paulo
Estrada de Itapecerica, 5859
Campus
05858-001 São Paulo
Tel: +55-11-5822-8000
Fax: +55-11-5821-1770
Web: http://www.unasp-sp.edu.br/
e-mail: atendimento@sp.unasp.edu.br

📖 1er cycle
Domaines d'étude: éducation, éducation de la première enfance, hygiène et santé, théologie, religion.
Programmes: Diplôme de 1er cycle de l'enseignement supérieur dans les domaines de l'éducation, de l'hygiène, de la santé, de la petite enfance, de la théologie et de la religion.
A l'intention de: ressortissants de tout pays titulaires d'un diplôme de fin d'études secondaires.
Autres conditions: admission sur examen national.
Durée: de 3 à 5 ans.
Inscriptions: pour postuler à la procédure de sélection nationale contacter: josem@iae-sp.br.

🎓 Bourse

Domaines d'étude: théologie, religion.
Bourses: Bourse de l'Université.
Durée: de 3 à 5 ans.
Valeur: variable; pour information contacter:
dyp@iae-sp.br.

298 Université catholique pontificale de Parana [UCPP]

Rue Imaculada Conceiçao, 1155
Prado Velho - CEP 80.215.901
Curitiba
Tel: +55-41-3271-1515
Web: http://www.pucpr.br
e-mail: webmaster@pucpr.br

📖 1er, 2e, 3e cycles / toutes disciplines principales

Domaines d'étude: affaires, architecture, arts décoratifs,
biologie, dessin industriel, droit, écologie, environnement,
informatique, ingénierie, langues, mathématiques, médecine
vétérinaire, philosophie, sciences sociales, théologie, religion,
tourisme, hôtellerie, restauration, zoologie.
Programmes: Diplômes de 1er, 2e et 3e cycles.
Organisés: campus São Jose dos Pinhais, Londrina et
Toledo.
Durée: de 2 à 6 ans; les cours débutent en février et en
août.
Frais: frais de scolarité: 1er cycle, de R$311 à R$1259 par
mois pendant 12 mois; 2ème cycle, de R$800 à R$2041 par
mois; frais de séjour: environ R$1000 par mois.
Connaissances linguistiques: 1er cycle: portugais; 2e
cycle (niveau Master's): portugais et anglais; 3e cycle (niveau
doctorat): portugais, anglais plus une troisième langue.
Inscriptions: pendant les mois de juillet ou janvier.

🎓 Bourses de 1er, 2e et 3e cycles

Domaines d'étude: toutes disciplines principales.
Bourses: (a) Bourses d'études («Bolsas de Estudo»); (b)
«Bolsas Rotativas»; (c) Fonds de financement éducatif
(«Fundo de Financiamento Educational - FIES»).
A l'intention de: (a) et (b) l'attribution se fait sur critère
académique et sociaux; pour information contacter
nezilda@rla13.pucpr.br; (b) et (c) en plus des réductions sur
les frais universitaires le paiement se fait de manière
échelonnée.
Valeur: (a) de 10% à 50% de réduction sur les frais
mensuels de scolarité pour les étudiants étrangers issus des
universités partenaires; (b) et (c) de 10% à 50% de réduction
sur les frais mensuels de scolarité.
Candidatures: (a) (b) et (c) les candidature se font pendant
les mois d'avril et octobre de chaque année.

299 Université catholique pontificale de Rio Grande do Sul

Avenida Ipiranga 6681, Partenon
90619-900 Porto Alegre, R.S.
Tel: +55-51-3320-3500
Fax: +55-51-339-1564
Web: http://www.pucrs.br

📖 2e, 3e cycles / toutes disciplines principales

Domaines d'étude: assistance sociale, biologie, droit,
éducation, études dentaires, histoire, lettres, philosophie,
psychologie, sociologie.
Programmes: Maîtrise; Doctorat; programmes
postuniversitaires.
Description: (a) cours de spécialisation dans les domaines
suivants: littérature, histoire, éducation, odontologie,
médecine, sciences biologiques (niveau maîtrise et doctorat),
philosophie, psychologie, sociologie, assistance sociale, droit,
génie électrique, théologie, informatique et communication
sociale (niveau maîtrise); (b) cours postuniversitaires dans les
domaines suivants: littérature, psychologie, éducation,
sciences politiques et économiques, communication, droit,
médecine, gériatrie, génie civil, informatique, odontologie,
théologie, assistance sociale et sciences biologiques.
A l'intention de: ressortissants de tout pays, titulaires d'un
diplôme universitaire (d'une maîtrise pour les cours du niveau
du doctorat).
Durée: de 18 à 36 mois pour la maîtrise; de 24 à 48 mois

pour le doctorat.
Inscriptions: entre octobre et novembre; à l'adresse
ci-dessus pour de plus amples renseignements.

300 Université d'État de Campinas - Faculté de génie alimentaire [UNICAMP]

CP 6121
13083-970 Campinas, S.P.
Tel: +55-19-3788-2121
Web: http://www.unicamp.br

📖 2e, 3e cycles / alimentation, agronomie

Domaines d'étude: alimentation, industrie alimentaire,
nutrition.
Programmes: Mastère; Doctorat.
Description: programmes de cours dans les domaines
suivants: sciences, génie et technologie alimentaires: sciences
des aliments (microbiologie, toxicologie, biochimie et
chimie); sciences de la nutrition (génie biochimique,
extraction et purification des composants alimentaires, génie
des procédés industriels alimentaires, propriétés physiques des
matériaux biologiques, réfrigération et congélation, écologie
et environnement, informatique dans les industries
alimentaires); technologies des aliments (développement des
produits et emballages, hygiène, qualité et législation des
aliments, technologie de la viande et du poisson, des céréales,
racines et tubercules, fruits, produits horticoles, boissons,
sucres et produits sucrés, café et cacao, lait et produits laitiers,
huiles et graisses.
A l'intention de: ressortissants de tout pays, titulaires d'un
diplôme universitaire dans le domaine alimentaire ou domaine
voisin; un examen d'entrée est exigé, ainsi qu'une bonne
connaissance de la langue portugaise.
Durée: Mastère: 24 mois maximum; Doctorat: 48 mois
maximum (débutant en mars et en août).
Frais: inscription et scolarité gratuites; frais de séjour 800
US$ par mois au minimum.
Inscriptions: en août et septembre pour les cours débutant
en mars; en avril et mai pour ceux débutant en août, à la
Secretaria de Pós-Graduaçao - FEA, UNICAMP, à l'adresse
ci-dessus (http://www.fea.unicamp.br).

301 Université d'État de Londrina [UEL]

Universidade Estadual de Londrina
Assessoria de relaçoes Internacionais
CP 6001
86051-990 Londrina - PR
Tel: +55-43-3371-4000
Fax: +55-43-3328-4440
Web: http://www.uel.br
e-mail: ariuel@uel.br

📖 1er, 2e, 3e cycles / toutes disciplines principales

Domaines d'étude: affaires, agriculture, assistance sociale,
droit, études dentaires, langues, lettres et arts, médecine,
sciences, sciences sociales.
Programmes: Diplômes de 1er cycle, Maîtrise, Doctorat,
Diplôme professionnel.
A l'intention de: ressortissants de tout pays titulaires d'un
diplôme de l'enseignement supérieur; l'obtention d'un accord
de coopération du gouvernement brésilien est nécessaire.

🎓 Bourses

Domaines d'étude: affaires, agriculture, assistance sociale,
droit, études dentaires, langues, lettres et arts, médecine,
sciences sociales.
Bourses: Bourses du fonds gouvernemental - PEC-G.
A l'intention de: candidats de tout pays diplômés de
l'enseignement supérieur.
Valeur: voir site Internet:
http://www.mec.gov.br/sesu/convgrad.shtm.

302   Université d'État de Maringa [UEM]
Avenida Colombo, 5790
Jardim Universitario Maringá
87020-900 Maringá, Paraná State
Tel: +55-44-3261-4040
Web: http://www.uem.br
e-mail: sec-eci@uem.br

📖 **1er, 2e cycles / toutes disciplines principales**
Domaines d'étude: toutes disciplines principales.
Programmes: Diplômes de 1er cycle, Maîtrise, Diplôme
professionnel.

303   Université de la Vallée de Rio dos Sinos [UVRS]
Avenue Unisinos, 950
CEP 93022-000 Sao Leopoldo, Rio Grande do Su
Tel: +55-51-591-1122
Fax: +55-51-590-8305
Web: http://www.unisinos.br
e-mail: unisinos@unisinos.br

📖 **1er, 2e, 3e cycles / toutes disciplines principales**
Domaines d'étude: toutes disciplines principales.
Programmes: Diplômes de 1er cycle, Certificat de
spécialisation, Maîtrise, Doctorat.
Description: (a) 42 diplômes de 1er cycle dans les
domaines suivants: gestion, sciences, génie civil,
informatique, économie, éducation, génie électronique,
alimentation, administration d'hôpitaux, histoire, gestion de
ressources humaines, gestion internationale, génie mécanique,
études d'infirmière, nutrition, éducation physique,
physiologie, relations publiques, publicité, psychologie,
sciences sociales, services sociaux; (b) 13 diplômes de 2e
cycle dans les domaines suivants: gestion, administration,
biologie, communications, éducation, géologie, histoire, droit,
philosophie; (c) diplômes de 3e cycle en éducation, géologie,
histoire et droit.
Durée: année universitaire: 1er semestre, de février à
juillet; 2e semestre, d'août à décembre.
Assistance financière: pas de possibilité de travail pour les
étudiants étrangers.

304   Université de Ribeirão Prêto [UNAERP]
Avenida Costábile Romano 2201 Ribeirânia
14096 Ribeirão Prêto
Tel: +55-16-603-6987
Fax: +55-16-603-7097
Web: http://www.unaerp.br
e-mail: unaerp@unaerp.br

🎓 **Bourses**
Domaines d'étude: toutes disciplines principales.
A l'intention de: ressortissants de tous pays, après étude de
dossier.
Durée: 6 mois.

305   Université de São Paulo - École supérieure d'agriculture «Luiz de Queiroz» [USP]
Avenida Pádua Dias, 11
CP 9
13418-900 Piracicaba, S.P.
Tel: +55-19-3429-4100
Web: http://www.esalq.usp.br
e-mail: director@esalq.usp.br

📖 **1er, 2e, 3e cycles / ingénierie agronomique**
Domaines d'étude: agriculture, sciences agronomiques.
Programmes: (a) cours d'économie agro-industrielle
(niveau bachelier en économie); (b) cours de génie
agronomique et génie forestier (niveau ingénieur); (c) cours
conduisant aux diplômes de Maîtrise et de Doctorat en
agronomie dans les domaines suivants: sols et nutrition des
plantes, science animale et pâturages, microbiologie agricole,
machines agricoles, irrigation et drainage, génétique et
amélioration des plantes, phytotechnie, statistique et
expérimentation agronomique, phytopathologie,
agrométéorologie; (d) cours conduisant aux diplômes de
Maîtrise et de Doctorat en sciences dans les domaines

suivants: économie appliquée, entomologie, physiologie et
biochimie des plantes, science forestière, science et
technologie des bois, science et technologie des aliments.
A l'intention de: ressortissants de tout pays, titulaires: (a)
d'un diplôme de fin d'études secondaires; (b), (c) et (d) d'un
diplôme universitaire et dont l'activité professionnelle reste en
rapport avec les cours choisis; priorité est donnée aux
personnes travaillant dans les domaines de l'enseignement et
de la recherche; langues d'enseignement: anglais et portugais;
2 lettres de recommandation souhaitées.
Durée: (a) 4 ans, (b) 5 ans, (c) et (d) de 2 à 5 ans.
Inscriptions: avant le 31 septembre.

🎓 **Bourses de 2e et 3e cycles**
Domaines d'étude: agriculture.
Bourses: (a) Bourses d'études (niveau Maîtrise et
Doctorat) offertes conjointement par l'USP et le Ministère des
relations extérieures du pays d'origine du candidat; le nombre
de bourses est fixé avec l'ambassade de chaque pays; (b)
Bourses de projets: nombre illimité mais conditionné par
l'excellence du projet de recherche; (c) Bourses de demande
sociale (CNPQ; CAPES); bourses allouées pour la Maîtrise et
le Doctorat en: agronomie et ses spécialisations,
agrométéorologie, science animale et pâturages, statistique et
expérimentation agronomique, phytopathologie, phytotechnie,
génétique et amélioration des plantes, irrigation et drainage,
machines agricoles, sols et nutrition des plantes,
microbiologie agricole; sciences et technologies des aliments,
des bois; sciences et ses spécialisations en: économie
appliquée, entomologie, sciences forestières, physiologie et
biochimie des plantes.
A l'intention de: professeurs d'université, chercheurs ou
professionnels, ressortissants des pays ayant conclu un accord
de coopération culturelle ou scientifique avec le Brésil et
titulaires d'un diplôme universitaire; pas d'examen de
sélection mais contrôle des connaissances en langues:
portugais et anglais exigés.
Durée: (a) 5 ans, (b) 2 ans pour la Maîtrise et 4 ans pour le
Doctorat.
Valeur: variable voir site web pour de plus amples détails.
Candidatures: par l'intermédiaire de l'ambassade du Brésil
du pays d'origine du candidat.

306   Université de Sorocaba [US]
Rodovia Raposo Tavares
km 92,5
CEP 18023-000 Sorocaba-Sao Paulo
Tel: +55-15-2101-7000
Web: http://www.uniso.br
e-mail: uniso@uniso.br

📖 **1er, 2e, 3e cycles / sciences médico-sociales**
Domaines d'étude: biologie, éducation, hygiène et santé,
sciences sociales.
Programmes: Diplômes de 1er, 2ème et 3ème cycles;
Master.
Description: cinq centres spécialisés: sciences biologiques
et de la santé, communication sociale, sciences humaines,
sciences sociales appliquées, sciences exactes et technologie;
le programme comprend 21 cours de 1er cycle, 11 cours de 2e
et 3e cycles et 1 Master en éducation.
Frais: voir le site Internet: http://www.uniso.br.

307   Université fédérale de Pelotas [UFPEL]
Campus Universitário
CP 354
96010-900 Pelotas, R.S.
Tel: +55-53-3275-7107
Fax: +55-53-3275-9023
Web: http://www.ufpel.tche.br

📖 **1er, 2e, 3e cycles**
Domaines d'étude: architecture, droit, études d'infirmière,
études dentaires, médecine, météorologie, nutrition,
obstétrique et gynécologie, sciences agronomiques, sciences
vétérinaires.
Programmes: (a) cours de Spécialisation dans les
domaines suivants: sciences sociales, sciences politiques,
éducation, éducation physique, médecine, endodontie,
chirurgie bucco-maxillo-faciale, sciences des aliments,
technologie des semences, météorologie, chimie, production
de riz, patrimoine culturel, physique; (b) cours conduisant à

l'obtention d'un Master of science (M.Sc.) dans les domaines
suivants: agronomie, santé animale, science et technologie
agro-industrielle, zootechnie, endodontie, chirurgie
bucco-maxillo-faciale, épidémiologie, culture des fruits de
climat tempéré, amélioration des plantes, production végétale
et technologie des semences, éducation, économie
domestique, physiologie végétale; (c) cours conduisant à
l'obtention d'un Doctorat (Ph.D.) dans les domaines suivants:
biotechnologie, technologie des semences, intégration
régionale, culture des fruits, santé animale, épidémiologie,
zootechnie.
A l'intention de: ressortissants de tout pays remplissant les
conditions requises.
Assistance financière: quelques bourses sont offertes par
diverses institutions; renseignements à l'adresse ci-dessus.
Inscriptions: Pró-Reitoria de Pesquisa e Pós-Graduaçao de
l'UFPEL, à l'adresse ci-dessus.

308   Université fédérale de Rio de Janeiro [UFRJ]

Coordenaçao dos Programas de Pós-Graduaçao de
Engenharia (COPPE)
Ilha do Fundao
Centro de Tecnologia, Bloco G
CP 68501
21945-000 Rio de Janeiro, R.J.
Tel: +55-21-2562-7022
Fax: +55-21-2290-6626
Web: http://www.coppe.ufrj.br
e-mail: diretoria@coppe.ufrj.br

📖 **2e, 3e cycles / sciences, ingénierie**

Domaines d'étude: sciences.
Programmes: Maîtrise et Doctorat en sciences de
l'ingénierie: génie chimique, mécanique, métallurgie, génie
des matériaux, génie civil, ingénierie de production, génie
nucléaire, génie biomédical, génie des systèmes et
informatique, génie électrique, génie des transports et
planification énergétique.
A l'intention de: ressortissants des pays d'Amérique latine,
titulaires d'un diplôme universitaire et autres candidats
étrangers ayant de bonnes connaissances en portugais ou en
espagnol.
Frais: scolarité gratuite.
Assistance financière: quelques bourses offertes par
l'Organisation des États américains, ainsi que par différentes
organisations nationales et internationales.
Inscriptions: auprès du Chef du programme d'études
choisi, COPPE/UFRJ, à l'adresse ci-dessus.

309   Université fédérale de Rio de Janeiro - Musée national [UFRJ]

Departamento de Antropologia
Quinta de Boa Vista
São Cristóvao
20940-040 Rio de Janeiro, R.J.
Tel: +55-21-2568-8262
Fax: +55-21-2568-1352
Web: http://acd.ufrj.br/museu
e-mail: museu@acd.ufrj.br

📖 **2e, 3e cycles**

Domaines d'étude: anthropologie, démographie et études
de populations, ethnologie, sciences sociales.
Programmes: programme de cours conduisant à
l'obtention (a) d'un Master en anthropologie sociale; et (b)
d'un Doctorat dans les domaines suivants: anthropologie
sociale, ethnologie générale et ethnologie du Brésil, sciences
sociales.
A l'intention de: ressortissants de tout pays, titulaires d'une
Licence ou d'un diplôme équivalent.
Durée: (a) 36 mois et (b) 48 mois (débutant en mars et en
août).
Assistance financière: quelques bourses sont octroyées
par le gouvernement brésilien.
Connaissances linguistiques: langues d'enseignement:
portugais, anglais et français.
Inscriptions: avant juin au «Programa de Pós-Graduaçao
em Antropologia Social», à l'adresse ci-dessus.

310   Université fédérale de Rio Grande do Sul - Institut de recherches hydrauliques

Avenida Bento Gonçalves 9 500
CP 15029
91501-970 Porto Alegre, R.S.
Tel: +55-51-3316-6567
Fax: +55-51-3316-7291
Web: http://www.iph.ufrgs.br
e-mail: pos@iph.ufrgs.br

📖 **2e, 3e cycles / génie civil**

Domaines d'étude: génie civil, ressources naturelles.
Programmes: cours en génie civil, ressources en eau et
assainissement, conduisant: (a) au «Master» (M.Sc.); (b) au
Doctorat.
A l'intention de: candidats de tout pays, ayant une bonne
connaissance du portugais ou de l'espagnol et possédant pour
(a) un diplôme universitaire en génie civil, agronomie ou
géologie; pour (b) une Maîtrise en ressources en eau et
assainissement.
Durée: (a) 4 semestres (débutant la 1ère semaine de mars);
(b) huit semestres (débutant la 1ère semaine d'août).
Connaissances linguistiques: L'enseignement est donné
en portugais.
Inscriptions: (a) avant le début du cours pour lequel
l'examen d'entrée a lieu soit en janvier, soit en juillet; (b) la
sélection des candidats se fait en juin.

311   Université fédérale de Santa Maria [UFSM]

Campus Universitário,
RS 509, km 9 - Camobi
97105 - 900 Santa Maria, R.S.
Tel: +55-55-220-8774
Fax: +55-55-220-8001
Web: http://www.ufsm.br
e-mail: sai@adm.ufsm.br

📖 **2e, 3e cycles**

Domaines d'étude: agriculture, chimie, éducation,
éducation physique, électricité et électronique, industrie
alimentaire, philosophie, sciences agronomiques, sciences
vétérinaires, sylviculture.
Programmes: cours conduisant à l'obtention: (a) Master en
science dans les domaines suivants: sylviculture, zootechnie,
sciences vétérinaires, sciences agronomiques, philosophie,
industrie alimentaire, électricité et électronique, chimie,
éducation, éducation physique, ingénierie agricole, ingénierie
de production, études linguistiques et littéraires, éducation
agricole, sciences politiques; (b) Doctorat dans les domaines
suivants: sciences de l'éducation, éducation physique,
physique, ingénierie de production, électricité, chimie.
A l'intention de: ressortissants de tout pays (un certificat
de séjour est exigé pour les non-brésiliens), titulaires d'un
diplôme dans la discipline choisie.
Durée: (a) de 24 à 36 mois; (b) de 36 à 48 mois.
Inscriptions: en septembre et octobre; renseignements sur
le site internet: http://www.ufsm.br.

312   Université Nilton Lins [UNL]

Av. Professeur Nilton Lins No. 3259
Parque das Laranjeiras, Flores
CEP 69058-040 Manaus/AM
Tel: +55-92-3643-2000
Web: http://www.niltonlins.br
e-mail: info@niltonlins.br]

📖 **1er, 2e cycles / toutes disciplines principales**

Domaines d'étude: toutes disciplines principales.
Programmes: Diplômes de 1er et 2e cycles.
Description: institution privée comprenant plus 40
programmes de cours d'enseignement supérieur.
Durée: année académique: de février à décembre.

313 Université São Marcos [USM]

Avenida Nazaré, 900
Ipiranga

Sao Paulo - SP
CEP 04262-100 Sao Paulo
Tel: +55-11-3471-5700
Fax: +55-11-6163-7345
Web: http://www.smarcos.br
e-mail: info@smarcos.br

 1er, 2e, 3e cycles / toutes disciplines principales

Domaines d'étude: toutes disciplines principales,
administration, éducation, lettres, télécommunications.
Programmes: (a) Licence en administration, architecture,
sciences comptables, communication sociale, informatique,
droit, géographie, histoire, ingénierie de l'environnement,
ingénierie des télécommunications, kinésithérapie, gestion des
affaires internationales, hôtellerie, lettres, mathématiques,
pédagogie, psychologie, systèmes d'information, technologie
informatique, technologie des télécommunications, tourisme;
(b) Maîtrise en administration, psychologie, coopération
internationale; (c) Doctorat en éducation, administration et
communication; (d) post-doctorat en administration
financière, marketing, informatique, psychothérapie,
psychopédagogie, administration des affaires.
A l'intention de: ressortissants de tous pays, titulaires d'un
diplôme de niveau secondaire ou équivalent; sur entretien et
résultats scolaires.
Durée: (a) 4 à 5 ans, (b) 2 à 4 ans, (c) 2 à 4 ans, (d) 18 à 24
mois; début des cours en février ou en août.
Frais: R$310 à 753.
Inscriptions: à l'adresse ci-dessus pour de plus amples
détails.

314 University Centre of Vila Velha [UVV]

Rua Commissário José Dantas de Melo, 21 Boa Vista
29102 Vila Velha
Tel: +55-27-3320-2001
Fax: +55-27-3320-2029
Web: http://www.uvv.br
e-mail: uvv@uvv-es.br

Bulgaria

Academic year: September/October to June/July.
Organization of higher education system: The Higher
Education Act of 1995 introduced a new system of academic
and professional degrees.
• University education: The first degree level consists of a
minimum of four years and leads to the Bachelor's degree
after a qualifying examination or defence of a thesis. The
second degree consists of a minimum of five years or one
extra year beyond the Bachelor's degree, requires a state
examination or defence of a thesis and leads to the Master's
degree. The third degree level consists of a minimum of three
years beyond the Master's degree and leads to the Doctor's
degree. Students in higher schools may train for the third
degree in the specialization of the school. Doctoral candidates
are trained according to individual curricula and must prepare
and defend a dissertation. This training is carried out under
the guidance of a scientific supervisor appointed by the
Faculty Council of the higher school training the doctoral
candidate. Students may also train for a doctoral educational
and academic degree in certain scientific research
organizations such as the Bulgarian Academy of Sciences, the
Academy of Agriculture, etc. in the relevant scientific
specialities. The Doctor's degree is conferred to doctoral
candidates who have passed the examinations in the
curriculum and have defended their dissertations under the
requisite conditions and order of the Scientific Degrees and
Scientific Titles Act.
• Post-secondary non-university education or professional
higher education: The institutions or colleges belonging to
this type of higher education award qualifications in the field
of professional higher education. The degree "Specialist in" a
given field is awarded by the colleges after a cursus of
professional studies lasting three years. This degree gives
access to Bachelor's degree studies.

Major institutions of higher education: Sofia University
St. Kliment Ohridski; www.uni-sofia.bg; Paisii Hilendarski
University of Plovdiv
www.uni-plovdiv.bg; St. St. Kiril and Metodii University of
Veliko Turnovo; www. uni-vt.bg;
Konstantin Preslavski University, Shoumen; www.shu-bg.net;
Neophit Rilski South-West University; www.swu.bg;
National Sports Academy; www.nsa.inet.bg; Prof. Pancho
Vladigerov State Academy of Music;
www.art.acad.bg/musicaacademy; Krustyu Sarafov National
Academy of Theatre and Film Arts; www.art.acad.bg/natfiz;
National Academy of Arts, 1, Schipka str., 1040 Sofia,
Bulgaria, tel: +359-2-988-1701; fax: +359-2-987-8064;
Academy of Music and dance Arts; 2 Todor Samodumov str.;
4000 Plovdiv; tel: +359-32-60-442; fax: +359-32-631-668;
Technical University of Sofia; www.tu-sofia.acad.bg;
Technical University of Varna; www.tu-varna.acad.bg;
Technical University of Gabrovo; www.tugab.bg; University
of Forestry; 10, Kliment Ohridski bld.; 1756 Sofia, Bulgaria;
tel: +359-2-962-5997; fax +359-262-2889; St. Ivan Rilski
University of Mining and Geology; Studentski grad; 1700
Sofia; tel: 359-2-687-224; fax: +359-2-962-593; Angel
Kunchev University of Rousse; www.ru.acad.bg; University
of Flavour Industries; www.au-plovdiv.bg; University of
Chemical Technology and Metallurgy; www.uctm.edu;
University of Architecture, Building and Geodesy;
www.uasg.acad.bg; Prof. Dr. Assen Zlatarov University;
www.btu.bg; University of National and World Economy;
www.unwe.acad.bg; Varna University of Economics;
www.ue-varna.bg;
Dimitur A.Tsenov Academy of Economics;
www.uni-svishtov.bg; Medical University - Sofia
www.medun.acad.bg; Medical University - Plovdiv; 15A,
Vassil Aprilov str.; 4002 Plovdiv, Bulgaria; tel: +359-32-
602-207; fax +359-32-602-534; Higher Medical Institute of
Pleven; www.vmi-pl.bg; Medical University of Varna;
Trakia University; www.uni-sz.bg; University of Agriculture;
www.au-plovdiv.bg; Tchernorizetz Hrabur Varna Free
University; www.vfu.bg;
New Bulgarian University; www.nbu.bg; Bourgas Free
University; www.bfu.bg; American University in Bulgaria -
Blagoevgrad; www.aubg.com; Luben Karavelov Higher
Construction Engineering School in Sofia; www.vsu.bg;
Todor kablechkov Higher Transport School in Sofia;
www.vtu.acad.bg; G.S. Rakovski Military Academy in Sofia;
82 Evlogi Georgiev Bld.; 1504 Sofia; tel:
+359-2-944-2366; fax: +359-2-944-2366; Vassil Levski
National Military University in Veliko Tarnovo; Bulgaria
Bld.; 5000 Veliko Tarnovo; tel: +359-62- 618-800, fax:
+359-62- 618-899; N.J. Vaptsarov Higher Marine School in
Varna, 73, Vassil Drumev bld., 9000 Varna; tel:
+359-52-633-017; fax: +359-52-303-163; College of
telecommunications in Sofia; www.hcpt.acad.bg; College of
Librarians Training, 119, Tzarigradsko chaussee Bld., 1784
Sofia, Bulgaria; tel: +359-2-790-166; fax: +359-2-790-081;
International College - Albena, Albena Resort, Campus
Maastricht, 9620 Baltchik, tel: +359-579- 62474; fax
+359-579-62425
College of Agriculture, 78, Dunav Bld., 4000 Plovdiv,
Bulgaria; tel: +359-32-650-551; fax:+359-32-650-355;
College of Management, Trade and Marketing, 126 Tzar
Boris III Bld., 1618 Sofia, Bulgaria; tel: +359-2-955-6424;
European College of Economics and Management, 18
Zadruga str., Krim 1, 4004 Plovdiv, Bulgaria, tel:
+359-32-672-362; fax: +359-32-672-362;
Luben Groys College of Drama, 1, Bulgaria sqr., NDK, floor
5, office 12, 1000 Sofia, Bulgaria;
tel: +359-2-986-2026; fax: +359-2-981-6165; Higher School
of Insurance and Finance, 29, Panajot Volov str., Sofia,
Bulgaria; tel: +359-2-926-7355; fax:+359-2- 926-7112;
Telematika College, 26, Petur Partchevitch str., Stara Zagora:
tel: +359-42-30206; International Higher School of
Economics, 14, Gurko str., 2140 Botevgrad, Bulgaria; tel:
+359-723-7097; fax: +359 723-987-0292.
Monetary unit: Bulgarian lev (BGL).
International student admission:
• Foreign citizens may apply for institutions of higher
educations under the same conditions as Bulgarian citizens if
they are: permanent residents on the territory of the Republic
of Bulgaria;
permanent residents abroad from Bulgarian origin; have
refugee status. Candidates must take a competitive entrance
examination and be accepted within the quota limitations.

International students must have a secondary-school leaving certificate enabling them to be admitted to institutions of higher education in their countries of origin and must pay tuition fees.

• Admission to doctoral studies: applicants are required to submit to the Ministry of Education and Science or to the higher education establishments by 1st September the following documents: application form with concise biographical data, name of higher education institutions and desired fields of study; original and copy of education certificate or diploma; certificate for recognized higher education qualification; a medical certificate issued one month prior to the date of application, subject to consular certification by the respective authorities of the applicant's country; a list of publications, if any; two recent photographs.

•The decision will be notified to the applicants by the Ministry of Education and Science or the respective higher education institutions one month after application.

Foreigners may start their training in higher education institutions and scientific organizations after submitting a certificate for successfully completed language training in compliance with the speciality they have applied for. Foreigners may apply for doctoral studies at the Bulgarian higher education institutions under the existing interstate and intergovernmental programmes for educational, scientific and cultural exchange, or against payment on the part of the applicants.

Foreigners may apply for full- as well as for part-time studies and are accepted on the basis of a documentary competition and in compliance with the additional requirements of the higher education institutions.

Language: All students registering for studies in Bulgaria should have evidence of sufficient knowledge of Bulgarian. Students with insufficient knowledge of Bulgarian should attend preparatory courses in Bulgarian language organized by the Bulgarian institutions of higher education. A certificate is awarded on successful completion of the course.

Immigration requirements: Students wishing to study in the Republic of Bulgaria should apply at the Bulgarian Embassy in his/her country of residence for a 'D' type visa. The applicants must show proof of enrolment at a Bulgarian institution of higher education and address of residence in Bulgaria, or a proof rental payment in the respective settlement in which the higher school is located. The applicants may be required to submit proof of financial resources while in Bulgaria. Students must apply for permanent residency in Bulgaria at the Migration office of the Ministry of the interior before the expiration of their visa.

Estimated expenses for one academic year: The Council of Ministers of the Republc of Bulgaria determines annually the amount of tuition for international students, depending on the scientific area of study. Approximate yearly tuition for bachelor's studies: 1,800-3,000 Euros; Master's studies: 2,200-3,500 Euros; Doctoral studies: 2,200-4,000 Euros; preparatory year for Bulgarian language studies: 1,500-3,000 Euros. Books and supplies: 50 Euros per month. Housing: 25-60 Euros per month in student facilities.

Information services:

• Ministry of Education and Science, Department for undergraduate and postgraduate studies, 2A, Kniaz Dondukov Bld.; 1000 Sofia; Bulgaria; email: m.v.georgieva@minedu.government.bg; web: http://www.minedu.government.bg

• Bulgarian CEEPUS Office, European Integration and Bilateral Coooperation Department, Ministry of Education and Science; 2A Kniaz Dondukov Bld.; 1000 Sofia; Bulgaria; web: http://www.minedu.government.bg

• Bulgarian Students Union, National Student House, Narodno subranie sqr.; web: http://www.studenthouse.bg.

Scholarships for international students: Ministry of Education and Science, Department for Under- and Post-Graduate Studies, 2a, Kniaz Dondukov Bld.,1000 Sofia, Bulgaria; tel: +359-2-921-7553; fax: +359-2-921-7753; email: m.v.georgieva@minedu.government.bg; web: www.minedu.government.bg.

Open and distance learning: None.

Recognition of studies and qualification:

• The National Evaluation and Accreditation Agency (NEAA), established in 1996, is the national quality assessment body in respect of the higher education system in Bulgaria.

• Ministry of Education and Science (MES) is the competent body for the recognition of foreign qualifications concerning higher education. In compliance with the Lisbon Recognition Convention amendments to several acts of the secondary legislation regarding recognition of documents, certifying higher education acquired abroad as well as periods of education completed abroad were promulgated. The procedure for recognition of higher education acquired in a foreign institution of higher education is organized and carried out by the Ministry of Education and Science. The National Information Centre for Academic Recognition and Mobility (NIC) shall support the activities on recognition of higher education. Recognition of a study period of higher education is accomplished by the respective higher school where the student has submitted his/her application forms (www.enic-naric.net - Bulgaria).

• The Higher Attestation Commission (HAC) within the Council of Ministers is an institution conferring the Doctor's educational and academic degree, as well as all other scientific degrees and scientific titles. It consists of a Presidium, Scientific Commissions for the various scientific fields and specialities, appointing scientists of academic rank and Doctors of Sciences.

The Presidium of the Higher Attestation Commission determines which scientific councils in which scientific fields are eligible to handle defence of dissertations; it specifies the criteria for conferring of the scientific degrees in the various fields of science; it provides methodological guidance to the scientific councils; exercises control and unifies the criteria for conferring of academic degrees; authorizes the defence of dissertations abroad, and approves and evaluates and determines the place of the academic degrees obtained abroad in the system of the nationally acquired degrees. The Presidium of the Higher Attestation Commission also issues the diplomas for all scientific degrees, as well as the credentials for scientific titles.

The Scientific Commissions are HAC bodies. They are established for the various scientific fields, groups of scientific fields or scientific lines. The Commissions make their decisions on the basis of the proposals of the scientific councils.

Accommodation services: International students should contact the accommodation office of the relevant institution prior their arrival in Bulgaria. Private accommodations are also available.

Work opportunities: Generally, work opportunities are not available to international students.

Additional information:

• The National Assembly plays a principal role in decision-making on the problems related to the system of higher education. It adopts the legislation concerning the development of the whole system. On the strength of its decisions it is empowered to establish, transform and close down higher education establishments. Furthermore, it has a primary function in the financing of the higher education system. The National Assembly votes annually in the State Budget Act the allocations for each state-funded higher education institution.

• The Council of Ministers exercises the executive power in the Republic of Bulgaria. It sets down the main trends in the national policy in the sphere of higher education and submits proposals to the National Assembly for the establishment, transformation or closing down of educational institutions, and for the amount of allocations for each state-funded higher school. On the basis of proposals from the respective higher education institutions or a proposal submitted by the Minister of Education and Science, the Council of Ministers establishes, transforms or closes down faculties, branch-schools, colleges and institutes within the state-funded higher education institutions, determining along with this the status of these units.

315 Académie d'art musical et chorégraphique

2, rue Tudor Samodumov
4000 Plovdiv
Tel: +359-32-228-311
Fax: +359-32-231-668
e-mail: amti@plov.omega.bg

📖 Études en musique

Domaines d'étude: arts du spectacle, musique et musicologie.
Programmes: Cursus en musique et arts du spectacle.
Description: cours dispensés par la faculté de musique folklorique et chorégraphie et la faculté d'éducation classique.
A l'intention de: ressortissants de tout pays ayant les qualités requises.
Frais: études universitaires: 3.600 US$; études doctorales 3.000 US$; année préparatoire en langue bulgare: 2.000 US$.
Inscriptions: à l'adresse ci-dessus.

316 Académie d'études économiques D.A.Tsenov Svishtov

2, rue Emanuil Chakarov
5250 Svishtov
Tel: +359-631-60907
Web: http://www.uni-svishtov.bg
e-mail: rectorat@uni-svishtov.bg

📖 Cursus de 1er et 2e cycle

Domaines d'étude: affaires, commerce, comptabilité, économie, finances, gestion.
Programmes: Diplômes de 1er et 2e cycles.
Description: cours de comptabilité, finances, gestion et marketing, affaires industrielles et commerciales, gestion sociale, économie agraire.
Frais: études universitaires: 1.800-2.100 US$; études doctorales: 2.500 US$; année préparatoire en langue bulgare: 1.300 US$.
Inscriptions: à l'adresse ci-dessus.

317 Académie nationale d'art scénique et cinématographique Krastyo Sarafov [NATFIZ]

108 A. rue Gueorgui Rakovski
1000 Sofia
Tel: +359-2-987-3424
Fax: +359-2-989-7389
Web: http://natfiz.bitex.com
e-mail: natfiz@bitex.com

📖 1er, 2e cycles / art scénique et cinématographique

Domaines d'étude: arts du spectacle, cinématographie, histoire de l'art, moyens audio-visuels.
Programmes: Cours de 1er et 2e cycles dans les domaines suivants: arts du spectacle, histoire de l'art, théâtre, art dramatique, études cinématographiques, animation, marionnettes, télévision et art de la caméra.
A l'intention de: personnes ayant obtenu le test d'admission (durée: 3 jours); maîtrise du bulgare requise.
Durée: 4 ou 5 ans.
Frais: études universitaires: 4.500 US$; études doctorales: 5000 US$; année préparatoire en langue bulgare: 2.500 US$.
Inscriptions: à l'adresse ci-dessus pour de plus amples renseignements.

318 Académie nationale des arts

1, rue Chipka
1000 Sofia
Tel: +359-2-988-1701
Fax: +359-2-987-8064
Web: http://www.nha-bg.org/
e-mail: art_academy@yahoo.com

📖 1er, 2e cycles / arts appliqués et des beaux-arts

Domaines d'étude: arts appliqués, beaux-arts.
Description: Bachelor's et Master's degrees.
Frais: études universitaires: 3.500 US$; études doctorales: 5.000 US$; année préparatoire en langue bulgare: 2.500 US$.
Inscriptions: à l'adresse ci-dessus.

319 Académie nationale des sports

Studentski grad
1710 Sofia
Tel: +359-2-962-0458
Fax: +359-2-629-007
Web: http://www.nsa.bg/en
e-mail: Cape@bg.net.bg

📖 Programme universitaire en éducation physique

Domaines d'étude: anatomie, éducation physique, formation des enseignants, journalisme.
Programmes: cours dans toutes les disciplines sportives, formation d'enseignants et d'entraîneurs, de journalistes sportifs et de kinésithérapeutes.
Frais: études universitaires: 3.000 US$; études doctorales: 4.500 US$; année préparatoire en langue bulgare: 3.000 US$.
Inscriptions: à l'adresse ci-dessus.

320 American University in Bulgaria [AUBG]

2700 Blagoevgrad
Tel: +359-73-885-218
Fax: +359-73-880-174
Web: http://www.aubg.bg
e-mail: Admission@aubg.bg

📖 Undergraduate Programmes

Study Domains: cultural studies, economy, English, European studies, international studies, literature and civilization.
Programmes: Bachelor of Arts degree in applied economics, English literature and civilization, European studies.
Applications: to the above address.

🎓 Financial Aid

Study Domains: all major fields.
Scholarships: a) Financial Aid; b) Tuition Reduction.
Open to: candidates of all nationalities a) meeting admission criteria; b) requesting financial assistance and submitting required supporting documents.
Duration: 4 academic years (8 terms).
Value: US$2,410 -$12,050.
Applications: by 1 June for fall semester; by 1 November for spring semester.

321 Burgas Free University [BFU]

62, San Stefano Street
PO Box 705
8001 Burgas
Tel: +359-56-900-426
Fax: +359-56-900-520
Web: http://www.bfu.bg/English/bourgas_eng.htm
e-mail: rector@bfu.bg

📖 Undergraduate and Graduate Programmes

Study Domains: accounting, administration, agriculture, business administration, communication, computer science, criminology, economic and commercial sciences, electricity and electronics, human sciences, industrial technology, information science, international business, international law, international relations, journalism, law, management, marketing, social sciences.
Programmes: Bachelor's and Master's degrees in Marketing, Management, Accounting, Finance, Law, Public Administration, Journalism, Public Relations, Social Work, Bulgarian Philology, Computer Science, Computer Systems and Technologies, Communication Engineering and Technologies, Transport Management and Technologies.
Open to: candidates of all nationalities meeting academic, linguistic and financial requirements.
Duration: 4 to 5 years.
Fees: tuition: 1,500 € per semester; estimated living costs:300-400 € per month.
Languages: Bulgarian and English.

322 Nouvelle université Bulgare [NUB/NBU]

21, rue Montevideo
1618 Sofia
Tel: +359-2-811-0482
Fax: +359-2-811-0260
Web: http://www2.nbu.bg/english/index.asp
e-mail: intadm@nbu.bg

📖 1er, 2e, 3e cycles / interdisciplinaire

Domaines d'étude: toutes disciplines principales.
Programmes: Qualification, Spécialités, Licence, Maîtrise, Doctorat; le centre d'enseignement à distance, considéré comme une faculté, propose des cours en français, anglais et allemand du 1er au 3e cycle; cours d'été de sciences cognitives.
A l'intention de: ressortissants de tout pays munis d'une lettre de motivation et de deux lettres de recommandation; bonne maîtrise du bulgare souhaitable (remise à niveau possible dans le département «linguistique et enseignement linguistique»).
Durée: de 1 à 4 ans.
Connaissances linguistiques: langue d'enseignement: bulgare; possibilité d'étudier le bulgare pendant 1 an.
Inscriptions: du 18 au 26 septembre, à l'adresse ci-dessus.

323 Université agricole

12, rue Mendeléev
4000 Plovdiv
Tel: +359-32-633-232
Fax: +359-32-633-157
Web: http://www.au-plovdiv.bg
e-mail: rector@au-plovdiv.bg

📖 1er, 2e, 3e cycles

Domaines d'étude: agriculture, botanique, développement rural, horticulture, industrie alimentaire, sciences agronomiques, sylviculture.
Programmes: Diplômes de 1er, 2e et 3e cycles en agriculture, alimentation, développement rural, environnement, viniculture, horticulture, sylviculture, génie agraire, viticulture, protection des plantes, écologie agraire, agronomie tropicale et subtropicale, économie agraire, agronomie-chimie.
A l'intention de: personnes ayant réussi le test d'admission; maîtrise du bulgare requise.
Durée: 4 à 5 ans.
Frais: études universitaires: 2.600-2.800 US$ par an; études doctorales: 4.800 US$ par an; année préparatoire en langue bulgare: 2.500 US$.
Inscriptions: à l'adresse ci-dessus.

324 Université d'Architecture, de Génie Civil et de Géodésie [UACEG]

1, boulevard Christo Smirnenski
1046 Sofia
Tel: +359-2-963-5245
Fax: +359-2-865-6863
Web: http://www.uacg.bg
e-mail: aceadm@uacg.bg

📖 2e, 3e cycles

Domaines d'étude: architecture, génie civil, géodésie, hydraulique, transports.
Programmes: Master's degree et Doctorat (Ph.D.) en génie civil, architecture, géodésie, génie civil des transports, hydrotechnique, restauration des monuments.
Frais: études universitaires: 3.000-3.200 US$; études doctorales: 1.600 US$; année préparatoire en langue bulgare: 2.000 US$.
Inscriptions: à l'adresse ci-dessus.

325 Université d'économie nationale et mondiale [UNWE]

Cité universitaire Christo Botev
1756 Sofia
Tel: +359-2-963-0043
Fax: +359-2-962-3903
Web: http://www.unwe.acad.bg/
e-mail: Sevdas@unwe.acad.bg

📖 1er, 2e, 3e cycles

Domaines d'étude: toutes disciplines principales, commerce, comptabilité, économie, études internationales, informatique, statistique, tourisme, hôtellerie, restauration.
Programmes: Bachelor's degree, Master's degree et Ph.D. en économie, économie internationale, administration, commerce, comptabilité, gestion, informatique dans l'économie, marketing, statistique, tourisme, relations industrielles, relations internationales, études du travail et de la sécurité sociale, économie industrielle, économie agraire, gestion des activités sociales et culturelles, gestion des entreprises coopératives.
A l'intention de: personnes ayant réussi le test d'admission; connaissance de la langue bulgare requise.
Durée: 4 à 5 ans.
Frais: études universitaires: 2.500-3.000 US$ par an; études doctorales: 3.500 US$ par an; année préparatoire en langue bulgare: 2.500 US$.
Connaissances linguistiques: langues d'enseignement: bulgare, anglais, allemand et français.
Inscriptions: à l'adresse ci-dessus pour de plus amples renseignements.

326 Université d'études économiques de Varna [VUE]

77, boulevard Knjaz Boris I
9002 Varna
Tel: +359-52-660-358
Fax: +359-52-660-358
Web: http://ue-varna.bg/en/
e-mail: int_relations@ue-varna.bg

📖 1er, 2e, 3e cycles / économie

Domaines d'étude: droit, économie, gestion, informatique.
Programmes: Bachelor's degree, Master's degree et Ph.D.; cours d'informatique, gestion, économie mondiale, droit.
Frais: études universitaires: 2.500-3.000 US$ par an; études doctorales 3.500 US$ par an; année préparatoire en langue bulgare: 2.500 US$.
Inscriptions: à l'adresse ci-dessus.

327 Université d'industrie alimentaire [VIHVP]

26, Maritza Boulevard
4002 Plovdiv
Tel: +359-32-643-005
Fax: +359-32-440-102
Web: http://www.vihvp.bg/en/index.htm
e-mail: vihvp@hiffi-plovdiv.acad.bg

📖 1er, 2e, 3e cycles

Domaines d'étude: alimentation, horticulture, industrie alimentaire, oenologie, technologie.
Programmes: Diplômes de 1er, 2e et 3 cycle dans l'alimentation, horticulture, industrie alimentaire, technologie du vin et de la bière, du lait et de la viande.
A l'intention de: personnes ayant réussi le test d'admission; maîtrise du bulgare requise.
Durée: 4 ou 5 ans.
Frais: études universitaires: 2.400-3.000 US$ par an; études doctorales: 4.000 US$ par an; année préparatoire en langue bulgare: 1.900 US$.
Inscriptions: à l'adresse ci-dessus pour de plus amples renseignements.

328 Université de Bourgas - Prof. Dr. Assen Zlatarov

Prof. Jakimov str.1
8010 Bourgas
Tel: +359-56-860-041
Fax: +359-56-880-249
Web: http://www.btu.bg
e-mail: office@btu.bg

📖 1er, 2e, 3e cycles

Domaines d'étude: économie, électricité et électronique, enseignement technique, formation des enseignants, génie chimique, gestion, industrie chimique, industrie et commerce, ingénierie, marketing, mécanique.
Programmes: Diplômes de 1er, 2e et 3e cycle dans les domaines des technologies chimiques organiques et inorganiques, technologies du caoutchouc, traitement des

déchets, économie; filière pédagogique et faculté ouverte.
Frais: études universitaires: 2.000-2.500 US$ par an;
études doctorales: 3.500 US$ par an; année préparatoire en
langue bulgare: 2.000 US$.
Inscriptions: à l'adresse ci-dessus.

329 Université de médecine de Plovdiv
15A, rue Vassil Aprilov
4000 Plovdiv
Tel: +359-32-443-839
Fax: +359-32-442-194
Web: http://www.meduniversity-plovdiv.bg

Études universitaires de médecine
Domaines d'étude: études dentaires, médecine.
Description: études universitaires de médecine, technique
et médecine dentaires.
Frais: études universitaires: 2.900-4.000 US$ par an;
études doctorales: 4.500-6.000 US$ par an; année préparatoire
en langue bulgare: 2.800 US$.
Inscriptions: à l'adresse ci-dessus.

330 Université de médecine de Sofia [MUS]
15, rue Dimitar Nestorov
1431 Sofia
Tel: +359-2-590-052
Fax: +359-2-594-094
Web: http://mu-sofia.bg

Études universitaires de médecine
Domaines d'étude: études dentaires, médecine, pharmacie
et pharmacologie.
Programmes: programmes d'étude en médecine, médecine
dentaire, pharmacie et kinésithérapie.
A l'intention de: personnes ayant réussi le test
d'admission; maîtrise du bulgare requise.
Durée: 5 à 7 ans.
Frais: études universitaires: 3.000-4.950 US$ par an;
études doctorales: 3.000-5.800 US$ par an; année préparatoire
en langue bulgare: 2.500 US$.
Connaissances linguistiques: maîtrise du bulgare requise.
Inscriptions: à l'adresse ci-dessus pour de plus amples
renseignements.

331 Université de médecine de Varna
55, rue Marin Drinov
9002 Varna
Web: http://www.varnamed.org
e-mail: admissions@varnamed.org

Études universitaires de médecine
Domaines d'étude: médecine.
Programmes: études universitaires de médecine.
Frais: études universitaires: 2.600-3.800 US$ par an;
études doctorales: 4.000 US$ par an; année préparatoire en
langue bulgare: 2.400-2.600 US$.
Inscriptions: impérativement par le Bureau Amérique du
nord (North American Office); 55 Town Centre Court, Suite
700; Toronto, ON M1P 4X4 Canada; tél: +1-416-290-6107;
fax: +1-416-296-1259; email: admissions@varnamed.org.

332 Université de Plovdiv-Paissii Hilendarski
24, rue Tzar Assen
4000 Plovdiv
Tel: +359-32-629-094
Fax: +359-32-635-049
Web: http://www.pu.acad.bg/default.htm

1er, 2e cycles
Domaines d'étude: biologie, chimie, droit, éducation,
informatique, lettres, mathématiques, physique.
Programmes: Diplômes de 1er et 2e cycle.
Frais: études universitaires: 3.000 US$ par an; études
doctorales: 5.000 US$ par an; année préparatoire en langue
bulgare: 3.000 US$.
Inscriptions: à l'adresse ci-dessus.

333 Université de Shoumen Konstantin Preslavski
115, rue Studentska
9700 Shoumen
Tel: +359-54-830-350
Fax: +359-54-830-371
e-mail: rector@shu-bg.net

1er et 2e cycles
Domaines d'étude: biologie, éducation de la première
enfance, informatique, lettres et arts, littérature et civilisation,
mathématiques, physique.
Programmes: Diplômes de 1er et 2e cycle en langue et
littérature bulgares, langue et littérature russes, lettres
modernes, pédagogie préscolaire, pédagogie des arts,
mathématiques et informatique, physique, chimie et biologie.
Frais: études universitaires: 2.800 US$ par an; études
doctorales 5.000 US$ par an; année préparatoire en langue
bulgare: 2.000 US$.
Inscriptions: à l'adresse ci-dessus.

334 Université de Sofia St Kliment Ohridski [UDS]
15, Boulevard Tsar Osvoboditel
1504 Sofia
Tel: +359-2-9308
Fax: +359-2-946-0255
Web: http://www.uni-sofia.bg
e-mail: Biolchev@ns.admin.uni-sofia.bg

1er, 2e cycles
Domaines d'étude: toutes disciplines principales.
Programmes: Diplômes de 1er et 2e cycle dans toutes
disciplines principales.
A l'intention de: titulaires d'un diplôme d'études
secondaires; admission sur test; maîtrise du bulgare requise.
Durée: 4 ou 5 ans.
Frais: études universitaires: 3.000 US$ par an; études
doctorales: 5.000 US$ par an; année préparatoire en langue
bulgare: 3.000 US$.
Connaissances linguistiques: études universitaires en
bulgare; cours de langue bulgare en été.
Inscriptions: à l'adresse ci-dessus pour de plus amples
renseignements.

335 Université de technologie chimique et de métallurgie [UCTM]
8, avenue St. Kliment Ohridski
1756 Sofia
Tel: +359-2-681-513
Fax: +359-2-685-488
Web: http://www.uctm.edu
e-mail: rectorat@uctm.edu

1er, 2e, 3e cycles
Domaines d'étude: chimie, génie chimique, industrie
chimique, métallurgie, physique.
Programmes: Bachelor's degree, Master's degree et
Doctorat (Ph.D.) en technologie organique et génie chimique,
technologie inorganique et automatisation industrielle,
métallurgie; filières d'enseignement en langues étrangères
(français, allemand) et études universitaires dans le domaine
de la technologie du cuir, du verre et des matières
synthétiques.
Frais: études universitaires: 2.800-3.400 US$ par an;
études doctorales: 4.000 US$ par an; année préparatoire en
langue bulgare: 2.800 US$.
Inscriptions: à l'adresse ci-dessus.

336 Université de Thrace
Cité universitaire
6000 Stara Zagora
Tel: +359-42-22002
Fax: +359-42-74119
Web: http://www.uni-sz.bg
e-mail: rector@uni-sz.bg

Études de sciences médicales et vétérinaires et agriculture
Domaines d'étude: médecine, médecine vétérinaire,

zoologie.
Programmes: programmes de cours conduisant aux diplômes en éducation, médecine, médecine vétérinaire, zoologie, zoogénie; agriculture et écologie.
A l'intention de: personnes ayant réussi le test d'admission; maîtrise du bulgare requise.
Organisés: à Stara Zagora, Yambol, Sliven, Haskovo.
Durée: 4 à 5 ans, cours débutent au mois de septembre.
Frais: scolarité: 2.000 à 3.600 US$ par an; de séjour: 3.000 US$ par an.
Inscriptions: avant le 20 août à l'adresse ci-dessus pour de plus amples renseignements.

337 Université de Veliko Tarnovo-St. Kiril et Methodi
2, rue Theodosi Tarnovski
5003 Veliko Tarnovo
Tel: +359-62-618-306
Web: http://www.uni-vt.bg
e-mail: Rector@uni-vt.bg

📖 **1er, 2e cycles**

Domaines d'étude: arts, droit, économie, histoire, hygiène et santé, informatique, littérature et civilisation, mathématiques, théologie, religion.
Programmes: cours de lettres, histoire, théologie, pédagogie, droit, sciences économiques, arts, santé publique, mathématiques et informatique, faculté ouverte, cours de langue bulgare en été.
Frais: études universitaires: 2.000 US$ par an; études doctorales 2.000 US$ par an; année préparatoire en langue bulgare: 1.500 US$.
Connaissances linguistiques: cours de langue bulgare en été.
Inscriptions: à l'adresse ci-dessus.

338 Université des forêts et du génie forestier
10, avenue St. Kliment Ohridski
1756 Sofia
Tel: +359-2-91907
Fax: +359-2-862-2830
Web: http://www.ltu.bg

📖 **1er, 2e, 3e cycles**

Domaines d'étude: agriculture, développement rural, écologie, environnement, sciences vétérinaires, sylviculture, technologie.
Programmes: cours universitaires de sylviculture, architecture paysagère, technologie du bois, génie agricole, médecine vétérinaire, écologie et aménagement du territoire.
Frais: études universitaires: 2.000-2.500 US$ par an; études doctorales: 2.500 US$ par an; année préparatoire en langue bulgare: 2.000 US$.
Inscriptions: à l'adresse ci-dessus.

339 Université des mines et de géologie St. Ivan Rilski
Cité universitaire Hristo Botev
1700 Sofia
Tel: +359-2-962-4231
Fax: +359-2-962-4940
Web: http://www.mgu.bg
e-mail: cctq@mgu.bg

📖 **1er, 2e, 3e cycles**

Domaines d'étude: électricité et électronique, génie civil, géologie, mécanique.
Programmes: cours universitaires de génie minier, génie minier électromécanique et prospection géologique; faculté ouverte et filière européenne.
Frais: études universitaires: 2.000-3.000 US$ par an; études doctorales: 3.000 US$ par an; année préparatoire en langue bulgare: 2.000 US$.
Inscriptions: à l'adresse ci-dessus.

340 Université Sud-Ouest Néophyte Rilski [SWU]
66, rue Ivan Mihaylov
2700 Blagoevgrad
Tel: +359-73-831-562
Fax: +359-73-85516
Web: http://www.swu.bg
e-mail: info@aix.swu.bg

📖 **1er, 2e cycles**

Domaines d'étude: arts, droit, économie, éducation de la première enfance, études paramédicales, lettres, philosophie, psychologie.
Description: cours de lettres, philosophie, pédagogie, psychologie et pédagogie préscolaires, droit, arts, sciences économiques, sciences naturelles, mathématiques, pédagogie médicale et filière pédagogique.
Frais: études universitaires: 2.400 US$ par an; études doctorales: 3.000 US$ par an; année préparatoire en langue bulgare: 2.000 US$.
Inscriptions: à l'adresse ci-dessus.

341 Université technique de Gabrovo
4, rue Hadji Dimitar
5300 Gabrovo
Tel: +359-66-821-931
Fax: +359-66-801-155
Web: http://www.tugab.bg
e-mail: rector@tugab.bg

📖 **1er, 2e cycles**

Domaines d'étude: électricité et électronique, gestion, ingénierie, mécanique, technologie industrielle.
Description: programme de cours dans le domaine du génie industriel, génie mécanique, électrotechnique et électronique, gestion industrielle.
Frais: études universitaires: 2.200 US$ par an; études doctorales: 3.000 US$ par an; année préparatoire en langue bulgare: 1.900 US$.
Inscriptions: à l'adresse ci-dessus.

342 Université technique de Rousse-Anguel Kanchev
8, rue Studentska
7017 Rousse
Tel: +359-82-846-143
Fax: +359-82-845-708
Web: http://www.ru.acad.bg
e-mail: rector@ru.acad.bg

📖 **1er, 2e cycles**

Domaines d'étude: affaires, électricité et électronique, gestion, mécanique, technologie, technologie industrielle, transports.
Programmes: cours universitaires de technologie mécanique, mécanisation rurale, électronique, automatique, transports routiers, gestion des affaires, technologie des machines agricoles, génie industriel, kinésithérapie et filière pédagogique.
Frais: études universitaires: 2.000 US$ par an; études doctorales: 2.900 US$ par an; année préparatoire en langue bulgare: 1.800 US$.
Inscriptions: à l'adresse ci-dessus.

343 Université technique de Sofia [UTDS]
8, Kliment Ohridski Street
1000 Sofia
Tel: +359-2-965-2111
Fax: +359-2-868-3215
Web: http://www.tu-sofia.bg
e-mail: rector@tu-sofia.bg

📖 **1er, 2e cycles**

Domaines d'étude: toutes disciplines principales.
Programmes: études universitaires d'économie, électricité, environnement, énergie, formation professionnelle, génie civil, gestion, interprétation et traduction, mécanique, technologie, télécommunication, théologie, transport, filière francophone d'ingénieurs de génie électronique, filière anglophone

des études d'ingénierie, filière germanophone d'ingénieurs mécaniques et de gestion industrielle.
A l'intention de: personnes ayant réussi l'examen d'admission.
Durée: 4-5 ans.
Frais: études universitaires: 3.000 US$ par an; études doctorales: 3.500 US$ par an; année préparatoire en langue bulgare: 2.500 US$.
Connaissances linguistiques: maîtrise du bulgare requise.
Inscriptions: à l'adresse ci-dessus pour de plus amples renseignements.

344 Université technique de Varna

1, rue Studentska Street
9010 Varna
Tel: +359-52-302-444
Fax: +359-52-302-771
Web: http://www.tu-varna.bg
e-mail: fs_centr@ms3.tu-varna.acad.bg

 1er, 2e cycles

Domaines d'étude: construction navale, droit, écologie, environnement, électricité et électronique, informatique, mécanique.
Programmes: Diplômes de 1er et 2e cycle.
Description: études universitaires dans les domaines suivants: construction navale, technologies mécaniques, génie mécanique, électronique, informatique et automatique, écologie, électrotechnique, droit.
A l'intention de: ressortissants de tout pays ayant un diplôme d'études secondaires ou équivalent.
Frais: études universitaires: 2.500 US$ par an; études doctorales: 3.000 US$ par an; année préparatoire en langue bulgare: 2.000 US$.
Inscriptions: à l'adresse ci-dessus.

Burkina Faso

Année universitaire: octobre à juillet.
Organisation de l'enseignement supérieur: L'accès à l'enseignement supérieur se fait selon la série du bac obtenu (littéraire, scientifique, administrative, gestion, technique, informatique). L'enseignement supérieur au Burkina comporte deux parties: (1) une partie académique normale qui permet de préparer les diplômes suivants: bac, Diplôme d'Etudes Universitaires Générales (DEUG) deux ans après le bac, la Licence (3 ans), la Maîtrise (4 ans), le Diplôme D'Etudes Approfondies (DEA), 5 ans d'études, le doctorat, 7-8 ans d'études et le Certificat d'Etudes Spécialisées (CES) 3-4 ans d'études après le doctorat pour les filières de la santé. En deuxième année, on peut également préparer un Diplôme Universitaire de Technologie (DUT) dans les filières techniques, commerciales et administratives; (2) une partie professionnelle qui donne accès aux diplômes professionnels suivants: bac, bac professionnel (pas obligatoire dans le cursus), le Brevet de Technicien Supérieur (BTS), 2 ans après le bac, la licence professionnelle ou l'ingéniorat de travaux, 3 ans, le Master ou le Diplôme d'Etudes Supérieures Spécialisées (DESS), 4 à 5 ans.
Unité monétaire: franc CFA.
Admission pour étudiants du pays: Pour étudiants nationaux: l'accès à l'enseignement supérieur exige le baccalauréat de l'enseignement secondaire; pour certaines filières profesionnalisantes, l'accès se fait sur test.
Admission pour étudiants internationaux: L'accès à l'enseignement supérieur exige la baccalauréat de l'enseignement secondaire ou équivalent et sur la base de la qualité du dossier présenté (aptitudes et age). Les étudiant internationaux bénéficient d'un quota d'admission de 10% des places disponibles dans chaque filière d'études.
Connaissances linguistiques requises: Une bonne connaissance de la langue française est essentielle.
Formalités d'immigration: Les conditions varient selon les rapports entre le Burkina Faso et le pays d'origine de l'étudiant. Voir les ambassades et consulats de Burkina Faso accrédités dans les différents pays.
Frais pour une année universitaire: scolarité: 200.500 à 700.500 FCFA; livres/fournitures scolaires: variable; logement: 48.000 FCFA en cité universitaire + 200 FCFA pour les droits aux oeuvres universitaires (restauration, logement, santé...).

Services d'accueil et d'information:
• Université de Ouagadougou; 03 BP 7021; Ouagadougou 03; Burkina Faso; Internet: www.univ-ouaga.bf
• Université de Bobo Dioulasso; 01 BP 1091; Bobo Dioulasso 01: Burkina Faso.
• les ambassades de chaque pays accréditées au Burkina Faso
•Centre national des Œuvres Universitaires (CENOU); BP 1926; Ouagadougou; Burkina Faso.
• Centre National de l'Information, de l'Orientation Scolaire, Professionnelle et des Bourses (CIOSPB); 01 BP 07; Ouagadougou 01; Burkina Faso; email: ciospb@ciospb.bf; Internet: http://www.ciospb.bf.
Enseignement à distance: Campus numérique de l'université de Ouagadougou, BP 4416, Ouagadougou, Burkina Faso; email: info@bf.auf.org.
Reconnaissance des études et diplômes:
• Commission Nationale des Équivalences des Titres et Diplômes, S/C Direction Générale de l'Enseignement Supérieur et de la Recherche Scientifique (DGESRS); tel: +226-5030-8269
• Ministère des Enseignements Secondaire, Supérieur et de la Recherche Scientifique
• Conseil Africain et Malgache pour l'Enseignement Supérieur (CAMES).
Services du logement: Cités universitaires: CENOU, BP 1926, Ouagadougou, Burkina Faso.
Possibilités d'emploi: En général, il n'y a pas de possibilité d'emploi pour les étudiants internationaux.
Publications / Sites Web:
• «Etudes et formations après la classe de terminale au Burkina Faso»; CIOSPB, 2004; web: www.ciospb.bf
• «La refondation de l'Université de Ouagadougou: guide de l'étudiant»; Université de Ouagadougou, 2001; Internet: http://www.univ-ouaga.bf.

345 Groupe des Ecoles EIER-ETSHER [EIER-ETSHER]

03 BP 7023
Ouagadougou 03
Tel: +226-307116 /17; 302053
Fax: +226-312724
Web: http://www.eier.org
e-mail: dir@eieretsher.org

 Diplômes d'ingénieur

Domaines d'étude: génie civil, hydraulique, hydrologie.
Programmes: cours de techniciens supérieurs: (a) formation polyvalente initiale dans les domaines suivants: génie civil, gestion des eaux et des sols, alimentation en eau, assainissement, conduisant au Diplôme de technicien supérieur de l'hydraulique et de l'équipement rural (équivalent au DUT); (b) formation continue; délivrance d'une Attestation d'assiduité; (c) recherche appliquée et ingénierie (génie civil, topographie, eau potable et assainissement, hydraulique villageoise et irrigation).
A l'intention de: ressortissants de tout pays; (a) âgés de 25 ans maximum, titulaires d'un baccalauréat C, D, E ou F, avec au moins mention «bien», ou étudiants ayant au moins 1 an d'enseignement supérieur scientifique; admission sur concours direct, concours professionnel (âge limite 40 ans) et sur titre (exceptionnellement); (b) techniciens supérieurs ou cadres équivalents; techniciens expérimentés; techniciens opérant dans les PME.
Organisés: (b) centre ETSHER, à Kamboinsé et sur le lieu de travail des stagiaires.
Durée: (a) 2 ans; (b) de 1 à 4 semaines.
Frais: (a) environ 7.500.000 FCFA pour 2 ans (hors voyage); pour les stagiaires: assurance et logement assurés par l'école; bourses de subsistance de 82.000 FCFA par mois offerte par l'école.
Inscriptions: à l'adresse ci-dessus; pour de plus amples renseignements sur EIER: École d'Ingénieurs de l'Équipement Rural: dir@eier.org; sur ETSHER: École des Techniciens Supérieurs de l'Hydraulique et de l'Équipement Rural; dir@etscher.org.

346   Université de Ouagadougou

03 BP 7021
Ouagadougou 03
Tel: +226-307-064 / 65
Fax: +226-307-042
Web: http://www.univ-ouaga.bf
e-mail: dpntic@univ-ouaga.bf

📖 **1er, 2e, 3e cycles**

Domaines d'étude: toutes disciplines principales.
Programmes: Doctorat, Maîtrise, Licence, DEUG, DUT
ou Ingéniorat, dans les divers domaines enseignés à
l'Université: droit et sciences politiques, langues, lettres, arts,
sciences humaines et sociales, sciences économiques et
gestion, science de la santé, sciences et techniques, etc.
A l'intention de: ressortissants de tout pays ayant les
qualifications requises, dans la mesure des places disponibles.
Durée: 4 à 7 ans.
Frais: environ 200.500 FCFA par an, pour les
ressortissants étrangers.
Assistance financière: possibilité de bourses, en fonction
du mérite et de l'âge (moins de 22 ans).
Inscriptions: avant le 15 novembre (1er et 2e cycles),
avant le 28 février (3e cycle); auprès de la Direction des
affaires académiques et scolaires (DAAS), à l'adresse
ci-dessus.

Burundi

Année universitaire: octobre à juin.
Unité monétaire: franc burundais (FBu).
Connaissances linguistiques requises: Une bonne
connaissance du français est exigée.
Formalités d'immigration: Obtention d'un visa d'entrée au
Burundi et d'une carte de séjour.
Frais pour une année universitaire: Inscription: 20.000
FBu; frais d'examen: 250 FBu. Livres: 100 FBu et assurances
sociales: 160 FBu par an. Frais de séjour: 3.600 FBu par mois
pour les étrangers venant étudier dans le cadre de la
coopération bilatérale; 5.400 FBu par mois pour les autres;
frais de transport: 100 FBu par mois.
Services d'accueil et d'information:
• Bureau des bourses d'études et des stages; BP 1990;
Bujumbura; Burundi (pour échanges internationaux
d'étudiants).
• Direction de l'enseignement supérieur; BP 1990;
Bujumbura; Burundi (informations générales sur les
conditions d'admission et les frais universitaires).
• Régie des oeuvres universitaires (ROU); BP 1644;
Bujumbura; Burundi (renseignements sur restauration,
logement, transports).
• Secrétariat du Service académique de l'Université du
Burundi; BP 1550; Bujumbura; Burundi.
• Représentations diplomatiques accréditées au Burundi et
ambassades du Burundi à l'étranger.
Reconnaissance des études et diplômes: Directeur,
Commission Nationale d'Équivalence des Diplômes, Titres
Scolaires et Universitaires; BP 1990; Bujumbura; Burundi.
Publications / Sites Web:
• « Vade-mecum de l'étudiant », disponible à titre gratuit
auprès du Service de recherche de l'Université du Burundi.

347   Université Lumière de Bujumbura

BP 1368
Bujumbura
Tel: +257-23-5549
Fax: +257-22-9275
e-mail: ulbu@cbinf.com

📖 **1er cycle**

Domaines d'étude: administration, administration des
affaires, affaires, bibliothéconomie, communication,
comptabilité, démographie et études de populations, droit,
français, gestion, grec, hébreu, journalisme, latin, linguistique,
marketing, moyens audio-visuels, philosophie, psychologie,
publicité, relations publiques, sciences de l'information,
sociologie, théologie, religion.
Programmes: programme de cours conduisant à la

Licence.
A l'intention de: ressortissants de tout pays titulaires du
diplôme des humanités (ou équivalent).
Durée: 4 années; début des cours en octobre.
Frais: frais d'inscription: 50.000 FBu; frais de scolarité:
10.000 FBu.
Connaissances linguistiques: cours dispensés en français
et en anglais.
Inscriptions: avant la fin du mois d'octobre auprès du
recteur de l'université; pour information contacter Grégoire
Njejimana (coordonnées ci-dessus).

Cambodge

Année universitaire: octobre à juillet.
Unité monétaire: riel.
Connaissances linguistiques requises: Khmer.
Services d'accueil et d'information: Ministère de
l'Éducation nationale, de la Jeunesse et des Sports; 80, Preah
Norodom Blvd; Phnom Penh; Cambodge; tél:
+855-2321-7253 / fax: +855-2321-7250; Internet:
http://www.moeys.gov.kh.

348   Université royale d'agriculture [RUA]

Ministère de l'Agriculture, des Forêts-Chasses et de la
Pêche
District de Dankor
Phnom Penh
Tel: +855-23-219-690
Fax: +855-15-364 138
e-mail: rua@forum.org.kh

📖 **1er-2e cycles**

Domaines d'étude: administration, botanique,
communication, écologie, environnement, médecine
vétérinaire, pêche, sciences agronomiques, sciences de
l'information, sylviculture.
Description: 10 programmes d'études pour le 1er cycle; 7
programmes d'études pour le 2e cycle; programmes de
recherche.
Assistance financière: possibilités d'emplois.
Inscriptions: contacter Dr. Chan Nareth pour de plus
amples renseignements: tel:+855-12-888-626; fax:
+855-23-219-690; email: rua@forum.org.kh.

Cameroun

Année universitaire: octobre à juin-juillet.
Organisation de l'enseignement supérieur: Le système
comprend des facultés et des Grandes Écoles rattachées aux
universités d'État. Il comprend aussi des Institutions Privées
d'Enseignement Supérieur (IPES) qui forment en deux ans au
Brevet de Technicien Supérieur (B.T.S.).
Institutions principales d'enseignement: Il existe six
universités étroitement liées à leur environnement immédiat, à
leur région et au marché de l'emploi: (a) Université de
Yaoundé I: (i) Les facultés des arts, lettres et sciences
humaines; des sciences; de médecine et des sciences
biomédicales; (ii) Les grandes écoles: École normale
supérieure (ENS); École nationale supérieure polytechnique
(ENSP); (b) Université de Yaoundé II: B.P. 1365, Yaoundé;
(i) Les facultés des sciences juridiques et politiques; des
sciences économiques et de gestion; (ii) Les grandes écoles:
École supérieure des sciences et techniques de l'information et
de la communication (ESSTIC); Institut des relations
internationales du Cameroun (IRIC); Institut de formation et
recherche démographique (IFORC); (c) Université de Buéa:
(i) Les facultés des arts, lettres et sciences humaines; des
sciences sociales et de gestion; des sciences; des sciences de
l'éducation; des sciences de la santé, de génie mécanique et de
la technologie; faculté d'agriculture et de médecine
vétérinaire; (ii) Les institutions spécialisées: The Advanced
School of Translators and Interpreters (ASTI); (d) Université
de Douala: (i) Les facultés des lettres et sciences humaines;
des sciences juridiques et politiques; des sciences
économiques et gestion appliquées; des sciences; (ii) Les
grandes écoles: École supérieure des sciences économiques et
commerciales (ESSEC); École normale supérieure de

l'enseignement technique (ENSET); Institut universitaire de technologie (IUT).; (e) Université de Dschang: (i) Les facultés des lettres et sciences humaines; des sciences économiques et de gestion; des sciences juridiques et politiques; d'agronomie et des sciences agricoles; (ii) L'Institut universitaire de technologie Fotso Vicor à Bandjoun; (f) Université de Ngaoundere: (i) Les facultés des arts, lettres et sciences humaines; des sciences juridiques; des sciences économiques et de gestion; des sciences; (ii) Les grandes écoles: École nationale supérieure des sciences agro-alimentaires (ENSAI); Institut universitaire de technologie.

Unité monétaire: franc CFA.

Admission pour étudiants du pays: Étre titulaire d'un diplôme sanctionnant la fin des études secondaires, le Baccalaureat ou le GCE advanced level ou un diplôme équivalent.

Admission pour étudiants internationaux: L'admission en faculté se fait sur étude des dossiers pour les nouveaux bacheliers et sur concours pour les grandes Écoles. L'année universitaire est répartie en deux semestres. Les droits universitaires sont à taux variables pour les étudiants étrangers.

Connaissances linguistiques requises: Les langues d'enseignement sont le français ou l'anglais.

Formalités d'immigration: Voir avec l'ambassade de Cameroun de chaque pays pour les formalités d'entrée et de séjour.

Frais pour une année universitaire: Inscription: 3.300 francs CFA; frais d'examen: 1.000 francs CFA. Scolarité gratuite en faculté.

Services d'accueil et d'information:
• Service culturel de l'ambassade du Cameroun dans le pays du candidat
• Ministère de l'Enseignement supérieur; BP 1457; Yaoundé; Cameroun
• Université de Buéa, BP 63; Buéa; Cameroun
• Université de Ngaounderé; BP 454; Ngaounderé; Cameroun
• Université de Douala; BP 2701; Douala; Cameroun
• Université de Yaoundé I; BP 337; Yaoundé; Cameroun
• Université de Yaoundé II; BP 1850A; Yaoundé; Cameroun
• Université de Dschang; BP 96; Dschang; Cameroun
• Université Catholique d'Afrique Centrale.

Bourses pour étudiants internationaux: Il n'existe pas un programme national de bourses pour les étudiants internationaux.

Enseignement à distance: Campus numérique francophone de Yaoundé.

Reconnaissance des études et diplômes: Ministère de l'Enseignement supérieur; Direction du Développement de l'Enseignement supérieur, Cellule des Systèmes universitaires comparés et des équivalences; BP 1457; Yaoundé; Cameroun.

Services du logement:
• Les étudiants étrangers et les étudiants handicapés physiques sont logés en priorité à la Cité universitaire.

Possibilités d'emploi: Il n'y a pas de possibilités de travail pour les étudiants internationaux.

Publications / Sites Web:
• Ministère de l'Enseignement Supérieur (MINESUP); http://www.minesup.gov.cm
• «Le Guide des Études Supérieures au Cameroun», MINESUP, 2001.

---

349 Campus numérique francophone de Yaoundé

Université de Yaoundé I
Extension de la Faculté des arts, lettres et sciences humaines
BP 8114
Yaoundé
Tel: +237-222-8555
Fax: +237-222-8759
Web: http://spip.cm.refer.org/cnf
e-mail: foad@auf.org

☞ Programmes du 1er et 2e cycles

Domaines d'étude: agriculture, commerce, droit, écologie, environnement, industrie alimentaire, informatique, moyens audio-visuels, sciences agronomiques.

Bourses: Déployé au Cameroun, au coeur de l'Université de Yaoundé 1, le Campus Numérique Francophone de Yaoundé (CNFY) est une implantation locale de l'Agence

universitaire de la Francophonie (AUF) offrant une plate-forme technologique spécialisée dans l'ingénierie pédagogique et dédiée à la production et à la diffusion des savoirs et des informations par les TICE.

Description: L'AUF offre des allocations d'études à distance aux meilleurs candidats sélectionnés. Une importante partie des frais pédagogiques seront ainsi pris en charge, et toute personne désireuse de se former à distance pourra bénéficier d'un prix préférentiel, accordé par les Universités diplômantes.

Lieu: Ces formations sont dispensées pour la plupart entièrement à distance, via les technologies numériques, mais les examens se déroulent de façon classique en salle surveillée. Les diplômes proposés à distance ont la même valeur académique que les diplômes classiques. La majeure partie des formations proposées ici débouchent sur un diplôme d'État.

---

350 Université catholique d'Afrique centrale [UCAC]

11628 Yaoundé
Tel: +237-223-7400
Fax: +237-223-7402
Web: http://www.cm.refer.org/edu/ram3/univers/ucac/ucac.htm
e-mail: ucac.icy-nk@camnet.cm

📖 1er, 2e, 3e cycles / toutes disciplines principales

Domaines d'étude: administration, anatomie, anthropologie, biologie, droit, droit canon, économie, études d'infirmière, finances, gestion, histoire, hygiène et santé, latin, marketing, obstétrique et gynécologie, ophtalmologie, pédiatrie, pharmacie et pharmacologie, philosophie, physiologie, psychiatrie, radiologie, sciences politiques, théologie, religion.

Programmes: programme de cours conduisant aux diplômes de 1er, 2e et 3e cycle.

Description: sciences sociales et gestion: cursus conduisant au DEUSS, au DUT et à la prépa MSTCF; philosophie classique et philosophie de l'éducation: cursus conduisant au DEUG, à la Licence et à la Maîtrise; sciences infirmières: cursus conduisant au DEUST (Diplôme d'études universitaires en sciences infirmières) et au DIA (Diplôme d'infirmier anesthésiste); théologie: cursus conduisant au Bachelor's degree, au Master's degree et au Ph.D.; droit canon: cursus conduisant au Bachelor's degree et au Master's degree.

A l'intention de: titulaires d'un diplôme de fin d'études secondaires (Bac ou équivalent); admission sur dossier et éventuellement entretien.

Frais: inscription: entre 100.000 et 605.000 francs CFA; frais de scolarité: entre 715.000 et 825.000 francs CFA par an; frais de séjour: 1.672.000 francs CFA par an.

Inscriptions: sciences sociales et gestion: avant le 15 mai; théologie: avant le 15 mai; droit canon: avant le 1er octobre; philosophie classique et philosophie de l'éducation: avant le 1er octobre; sciences infirmières: avant le 1er septembre.

☞ Bourse

Domaines d'étude: toutes disciplines principales.
Subjects: Gestion; commerce; finance; philosophy; theologie; sciences sociales.
Duration: 1 année, renouvelable.

---

351 Université de Buéa

BP 63
Buea
Tel: +237-352-2134
Fax: +237-343-2508
Web: http://www.cm.refer.org/edu/ram3/univers/ubuea/fsbu.htm

📖 1er, 2e, 3e cycles

Domaines d'étude: agriculture, arts, éducation, gestion, hygiène et santé, ingénierie, interprétation et traduction, mécanique, sciences, sciences sociales, sciences vétérinaires.

Programmes: programmes d'études de tous niveaux dans les facultés des arts, des sciences, des sciences sociales et de gestion, des sciences de l'éducation, des sciences de la santé, de génie mécanique et de la technologie, agriculture et de médecine vétérinaire.

352 Université de Yaoundé II [UYI]
BP 1365
Yaoundé
Tel: +237-223-6553
Fax: +237-223-6554
Web: http://www.cm.refer.org/edu/ram3/univers/uy2/
uy2.htm

📖 **Formation diplômante en communication**

Domaines d'étude: journalisme, sciences de l'information.
Programmes: programme de cours dispensés par l'École
supérieure des sciences et techniques de l'information et de la
communication (ESSTIC): (a) formation de techniciens de
l'information; (b) formation de journalistes généralistes; (c)
formation de journalistes spécialistes.
A l'intention de: ressortissants de tout pays: (a) titulaires
du baccalauréat (Probatoire) et ayant moins de 32 ans au 1er
janvier de l'année du concours, ou professionnels de la
communication titulaires du BEPC et ayant 3 ans d'expérience
professionnelle; (b) titulaires du baccalauréat et âgés de moins
de 32 ans au 1er janvier de l'année du concours; (c)
professionnels titulaires d'une Licence et possédant 5 ans
d'expérience professionnelle, ou titulaires du Diplôme de
journaliste généraliste et possédant 3 ans d'expérience
professionnelle, ou étudiants titulaires d'une Maîtrise de
l'Université; les étudiants doivent être bénéficiaires d'une
bourse d'études; admission sur dossier.
Durée: (a) et (c) 2 ans; (b) 3 ans (débutant en
octobre-novembre).
Frais: (chiffres approximatifs): inscription: 10.000 francs
CFA; frais de scolarité: 1.000.000 francs CFA par an.
Connaissances linguistiques: bonne maîtrise de l'anglais
ou du français requise.
Inscriptions: avant septembre, s'adresser à l'École pour de
plus amples renseignements
(www.cm.refer.org/edu/ram3/univers/uy2/uy2.htm).

Canada

Academic year: September to May.
Monetary unit: Canadian dollar (C$).
National student admission: As a rule, Canadian
universities treat equivalent diplomas and degrees from other
countries as qualification for entrance (requirements may vary
from province to province). Foreign students should contact
the Office of the Registrar (for undergraduate admission), or
the Office of the Dean of Graduate Studies (for graduate
studies) of the university they wish to attend, preferably 12 to
18 months in advance.
Language: All Canadian universities require evidence of
English or French language proficiency, but not all require a
test. Many offer second-language upgrading courses. A lack
of proficiency in English or French will be taken into account
by the Canadian immigration office in the evaluation of the
application.
Immigration requirements: Students must be in
possession of a valid passport. Before coming to Canada all
students will need the following; (a) a 'Study Permit' for
study programmes of greater than six months' duration,
regardless of the length of stay in Canada (not necessary for
certain students such as diplomats and their children, due to
their residence status in Canada); (b) for students wishing to
study in Quebec, a 'Certificat d'acception du Québec' (CAQ)
from the 'Ministère de l'Immigration et des Communautés
culturelles' (MICC); (c) a letter of acceptance from the school
to be attended; (d) proof of sufficient financial resources for
academic and living expenses; (e) assurance that the student
will return home at the end of studies; (f) to pass a medical
exam if requested; (g) to qualify as a temporary resident in
Canada, including holding a temporary resident visa (required
for citizens of many countries).
Estimated expenses for one academic year: Foreign
student fees differ between provinces, institutions and
programmes from C$4,500 to C$45,000; total living costs are
estimated between C$11,000 to C$18,000 for a single student
and C$15,000 to C$28,000 for a married student with no
children.
Information services:
• Association of Canadian Community Colleges (ACCC)
Suite 200 - 1223 Michael Street North Ottawa, Ontario K1J
7T2, Canada; web: http://www.accc.ca/. The ACCC is the
national, voluntary membership organization created in 1972

to represent colleges and institutes to government, business
and industry, both in Canada and internationally.
• Association of Universities and Colleges of Canada
(AUCC), 360 Albert Street, Suite 600, Ottawa, Ontario K1R
1B1 (general information on programmes for foreign students
wishing to study at Canadian universities; application forms
and details on admission requirements available only from the
universities and colleges); http://www.aucc.ca
• Canadian Bureau for International Education (CBIE), 220
Laurier Avenue W., Suite 1100, Ottawa, Ontario K1P 5Z9
(general information on study, work and exchange in Canada
and abroad; reception service for incoming foreign students
during August and September each year at the airports of
Halifax, Toronto and Vancouver); web: http://www.cbie.ca/
• Canadian Information Centre for International Credentials
(CICIC) 95, St. Clair West, Suite 1106, Toronto, Ontario
M4V 1N6 - General information on postsecondary education
in Canada and the recognition of foreign credentials in
Canada; http://www.cicic.ca/
• General information on studying in Canada, visa
requirements, etc., is available at Canadian embassies, high
commissions and consulates abroad.
Scholarships for international students:
• Some scholarships are offered by the Ministries of Foreign
Affairs and International Trade of Canada. These scholarships
are for graduate and postgraduate students who wish to pursue
their studies in higher education or for research work in a
Canadian university.
• Francophone scholarships: The Canadian International
Development Agency (CIDA) offers scholarships to students
who wish to pursue their university studies in Canada in a
field of study corresponding to a priority in their home
countries. More information can be obtained from Canadian
embassies around the world.
• Canadian Information Centre for International Credentials
(CICIC): Consult its website for a listing of sources of
information on awards, scholarships and exchange
programmes, at http://www.cicic.ca/xchange_en.stm.
Open and distance learning:
• The on-line database of recognized postsecondary
institutions in Canada of the Canadian Information Centre for
International Credentials,
http://www.cicic.ca/postsec/institutions/indexe.stm, allows for
listing institutions offering distance education programmes.
• The Canadian Virtual University (CVU)
(http://www.cvu-uvc.ca/) is a consortium of the following
Canadian leaders in university distance education: Acadia
University, Athabasca University, British Columbia Open
University, Laurentian University, Memorial University of
Newfoundland, Royal Military College, Royal Roads
University, Télé-université du Québec, The University of
Manitoba, University College of Cape Breton, University of
New Brunswick
• Le 'Répertoire de l'enseignement à distance en français du
Réseau d'enseignement francophone à distance du Canada'
(REFAD), à http://mail.village.ca/refad/repertoire_cours.html,
is a database of distance education programmes offered in
French by various Canadian institutions and organizations.
•The education@canada International Gateway to Education
in Canada (http://educationcanada.cmec.ca/), established by
the Council of Ministers of Education, Canada, provides links
to distance education resources at the national and
provincial/territorial levels.
Recognition of studies and qualification: For information
on recognition of foreign credentials:
• Canadian Information Centre for International Credentials
(CICIC), National Coordinator, 95 St Clair Avenue West,
Suite 1106, Toronto, Ontario M4V 1N6; email:
info@cicic.ca; web: http://www.cicic.ca and Information for
students educated abroad applying for admission to Canadian
universities and colleges at
http://www.cicic.ca/factsheets/factsheet1en.stm.
Publications / Websites:
• The DestinEducation website,
http://www.destineducation.ca, offers an overview of life in
Canada and suggestions on how to deal with various
situations, maintained by the Canadian Bureau for
International Education.
• 'Directory of Canadian Universities'
http://www.aucc.ca/publications/auccpubs/directories/dcu/dcu
_e.html.
• 'Canada's Universities: a fact-filled guide for international
students';

http://www.aucc.ca/publications/auccpubs/brochures/reach_e. html (free).
• Second Language Instruction in Canada; http://www.cicic.ca/lang.en.stm, maintained by the Canadian Information Centre for International Credentials (CICIC). Most of the above publications are available for consultations at Canadian missions abroad.

* * *.

Année universitaire: Septembre à mai.
Unité monétaire: Dollar canadien (C$).
Admission pour étudiants internationaux: Dans les établissements d'enseignement supérieur: en règle générale, les universités canadiennes acceptent, comme condition d'admission en première année d'études universitaires, les diplômes équivalents délivrés dans d'autres pays. Les demandes d'inscription doivent être adressées au bureau du Registraire (pour admission à des études du 1er cycle) ou au doyen des études supérieures (pour admission aux études supérieures) de l'université choisie, auprès desquels on peut également obtenir tous les renseignements nécessaires sur les cours offerts, les conditions d'admission, les frais et les dépenses. Il faut prévoir des délais d'au moins 12 à 18 mois dans les formalités.
Connaissances linguistiques requises: Toutes les universités canadiennes exigent des étudiants étrangers une preuve de leurs connaissances linguistiques (soit en anglais soit en français), mais toutes n'imposent pas un examen. Une connaissance insuffisante du français ou de l'anglais entrera en ligne de compte dans l'évaluation faite de la demande par les bureaux d'immigration canadiens.
Formalités d'immigration: Les étudiants doivent être en possession d'un passeport valide. De plus, les étudiants souhaitant étudier au Canada ont besoin: (a) d'un permis d'études si le programme d'études choisi dure plus de six mois, indépendamment de la longueur du séjour au Canada; (b) d'un Certificat d'acceptation du Québec (CAQ) du Ministère de l'Immigration et des Communautés culturelles (MICC) (pour les études au Québec uniquement); (c) d'une lettre d'acceptation de l'établissement d'enseignement choisi; (d) la preuve de ressources financières suffisantes pour les droits de scolarité et frais de séjour; (e) assurance du retour au pays d'origine à la fin des études; (f) de passer un examen médical s'il y a lieu; (g) et d'obtenir le statut de résident temporaire au Canada (ainsi qu'un visa de résidence temporaire pour les ressortissants de nombreux pays). Certains étudiants n'ont pas besoin d'avoir un permis d'études en raison de leur statut au Canada (les diplomates et leurs enfants, par exemple).
Frais pour une année universitaire: Les droits de scolarité pour les étudiants étrangers varient selon les provinces, les institutions et les programmes, de C$4.500 à C$45.000 environ; on estime que le coût de la vie se situe entre C$11.000 et C$18.000 pour un étudiant seul, et entre C$15.000 et C$28.000 pour un étudiant marié sans enfant.
Services d'accueil et d'information:
• Association des collèges communautaires du Canada (ACCC) Suite 200 - 1223 rue Michael Street nord, Ottawa (Ontario) K1J 7T2, Canada; http://www.accc.ca/
• Association des universités et collèges du Canada (AUCC), 350 Albert Street, Suite 600, Ottawa, Ontario K1R 1B1; http://www.aucc.ca (informations d'ordre général à l'intention des étudiants étrangers désireux de poursuivre des études dans les universités canadiennes; des renseignements sur les conditions d'admission ainsi que les formulaires d'inscription ne peuvent être obtenus qu'auprès des universités et collèges).
• Bureau canadien de l'éducation internationale (BCEI), 220 Laurier Avenue W., Suite 1100, Ottawa, Ontario K1P 5Z9 (fournit des renseignements généraux concernant les programmes d'études, le travail et les échanges, au Canada et à l'étranger; chaque année aux mois d'août et septembre, le Bureau met à la disposition des étudiants étrangers un service d'accueil aux aéroports de Halifax, Toronto et Vancouver); web: http://www.cbie.ca.
• Centre d'information canadien sur les diplômes internationaux (CICDI) 95, avenue St. Clair Ouest, bureau 1106 Toronto (Ontario) M4V 1N6 Canada; renseignements sur l'éducation universitaire et postsecondaire et sur la reconnaissance des qualifications et diplômes étrangers au Canada; http://www.cicdi.ca/
• Des informations générales sur les études au Canada, les formalités de visa, etc., peuvent être obtenues auprès des ambassades du Canada, des commissions et des consulats

canadiens à l'étranger.
Bourses pour étudiants internationaux:
• Bourses: Le ministère des Affaires étrangères et du Commerce international du Canada offre quelques bourses. Ces bourses permettent aux étudiants de 2e et de 3e cycles de poursuivre des études avancées ou d'effectuer un projet de recherche dans une université canadienne.
• Bourses de la francophonie: l'Agence canadienne de développement international (ACDI) offre des bourses aux étudiants de pays francophones qui désirent poursuivre leurs études universitaires au Canada, dans un domaine correspondant à une réalité prioritaire dans leur pays d'origine. Renseignements dans les ambassades du Canada du pays du candidat ou du pays le plus près.
• Centre d'information canadien sur les diplômes internationaux (CICDI): Consulter sur son site web la liste de sources d'information sur les bourses et programmes d'échange, http://ww.cicdi.ca/xchange_fr.stm.
Enseignement à distance:
La base de données des établissements postsecondaires canadiens reconnus tenue par le Centre d'information canadien sur les diplômes internationaux (http://www.cicic.ca/postsec/institutions/indexf.stm) permet de lister sélectivement les établissements offrant des programmes de formation à distance.
• L'Université virtuelle canadienne (CVU) (http://www.cvu-uvc.ca/) est un consortium qui regroupe onze chefs de file du domaine de l'enseignement universitaire à distance: Acadia University, Athabasca University, British Columbia Open University, Université Laurentienne, Memorial University of Newfoundland, Collège militaire royal, Royal Roads University, Télé-université du Québec, Université du Manitoba, University College of Cape Breton, Université du Nouveau-Brunswick.
• Le répertoire de l'enseignement à distance en français du Réseau d'enseignement francophone à distance du Canada (REFAD), à http://mail.village.ca/refad/repertoire_cours.html, est une base de données des cours à distance en français de différents établissements et organismes pancanadiens
• Le site education@canada (http://educationcanada.cmec.ca/), portail international de l'éducation au Canada, a été établi par le Conseil des ministres de l'Éducation (Canada) [CMEC]. On y trouvera un répertoire de liens relatifs à la formation à distance au Canada et dans chaque province et territoire.
Reconnaissance des études et diplômes: Information sur la reconnaissance des diplômes internationaux:
• Centre d'Information canadien sur les Diplômes internationaux (CICIC); Coordonnateur national, 95, St Clair Avenue West, Suite 1106, Toronto, Ontario M4V 1N6, Canada; tél: email: info@cicic.ca; Internet: http://www.cicic.ca.
Publications / Sites Web:
• Le site DestinEducation (http://www.destination.ca) offre un aperçu de la vie au Canada et propose des solutions à divers problèmes; tenu par le Bureau canadien de l'éducation internationale.
• « Répertoire des universités canadiennes »; http://www.aucc.ca/publications/auccpubs/directories/dcu/dcu _f.html.
• «Notes aux étudiants étrangers» (gratuit) http://www.aucc.ca/publications/auccpubs/brochures/notes20 03_f.html.
• «Les universités canadiennes: Guide d'information à l'intention des étudiants étrangers» http://www.aucc.ca/publications/auccpubs/brochures/reach_f. html.
•«'L'enseignement des langues secondes au Canada»; http://www.cicic.ca/lang.fr.stm), une ressource en ligne tenue par le Centre d'information canadien sur les diplômes internationaux.
La plupart des publications mentionnées ci-dessus peuvent être consultées dans les missions canadiennes à l'étranger.

353 Acadia University

B0P 1X0 Wolfville, Nova Scotia
Tel: +1-902-585-2201
Fax: +1-902-585-1081
Web: http://www.acadiau.ca
e-mail: ask.acadia@acadiau.ca

📖 Undergraduate and Graduate Degree Programmes

Study Domains: accounting, administration, advertising, anatomy, anthropology, applied sciences, art history, arts, biology, business, business administration, chemistry, civil engineering, classical studies, communication, computer science, continuing education, dietetics, earth science, ecology, environment, economic and commercial sciences, economy, education, engineering, finance, fine arts, food, food industry, geology, history, human sciences, humanities and arts, information science, international business, languages, liberal arts, management, marketing, mathematics, music and musicology, nutrition, performing arts, philosophy, physical education, physics, psychology, recreation and leisure, sciences, social sciences, sociology, statistics, teacher education, technology, theology, religion.
Programmes: (a) Bachelor's degrees in applied science, arts, business administration, computer science, education, food science, nutrition, music, music education, physical education, recreation management, science and theology; (b) Master's degrees in arts, science, education, divinity, religious education and theology; (c) Doctor of Ministry.
Description: non-degree programmes include: continuing education; distance education; EUP and ESL, certificate in applied science. rigorous curriculum incorporating the use of notebook computers into academic work.
Open to: qualified students of all nationalities: (a) candidates wishing to study on a full-time basis but who do not meet general admission requirements may be considered for entry as mature students; TOEFL for students whose first language is not English; extension (correspondence and part-time) programmes offered for credit; special arrangements made for handicapped students; job placement services are also available.
Duration: (a) 4 years; (b) 1 year; (c) 3 years.
Financial assistance: (a) some scholarships and bursaries available; (b) some graduate fellowships, scholarships and assistantships.
Languages: English.
Applications: to the Office of Admissions or online at: www.acadiau.ca.

🐿 Undergraduate Entrance Scholarships

Study Domains: all major fields.
Scholarships: Undergraduate entrance scholarships and grants.
Description: for full-time undergraduate study (excluding Bachelor of Education).
Duration: some scholarships/bursaries are renewable, some are 1 year only.
Value: range from C$500 up to C$22,500 (over 4 years).
Applications: complete admission application by 1 March; complete entrance scholarship form and supporting documents by 15 March; apply to financial aid office by email: financial.aid@acadiau.ca.

354 Algonquin College

1385 Woodroffe Avenue
K2G 1V8 Ottawa, Ontario
Tel: +1-613-727-4723 ext. 5343
Fax: +1-613-727-7665
Web: http://www.algonquincollege.com

📖 Undergraduate Programmes

Study Domains: all major fields, applied arts, business, health and hygiene, technology, trade.
Programmes: degree courses in applied arts, business, health sciences, technology, English as a second language and trades.
Open to: candidates fulfilling the necessary requirements.
Duration: from 1 to 3 years.
Applications: to the above address for further information.

355 Bishop's University

J1M 1Z7 Lennoxville, Quebec
Tel: +1-819-822-9600
Fax: +1-819-822-9661
Web: http://www.ubishops.ca

📖 Undergraduate and Graduate Degree Programmes

Study Domains: arts, business administration, education, sciences.
Programmes: (a) Bachelor's degrees in arts, business administration, and science; (b) Master's degree in education.
Open to: academically qualified students of all nationalities; candidates over 23 years old who do not meet general admission requirements may be considered on a mature student basis; continuing education programmes offered for credit; special facilities granted for students with disabilities; student job placement services also available.
Duration: from 3 to 4 years (depending on educational background).
Fees: see website for further information. Students from outside Canada who choose to major in French pay only Canadian fees.
Financial assistance: some countries have financial agreements with the Province of Quebec; students should contact the Ministry of Education in their home country for details.
Languages: instruction in English.
Applications: (a) by 1 March, to the Admissions Office; International Student Office; (b) by 1 February, to the Graduate School of Education; International Student Office.

356 Brandon University

270-18th Street
R7A 6A9 Brandon, Manitoba
Tel: +1-204-727-7314
Fax: +1-204-727-7471
Web: http://www.brandonu.ca

📖 Undergraduate and Graduate Degree Programmes

Study Domains: all major fields, business administration, liberal arts, nursing, psychiatry, social sciences.
Programmes: (a) Bachelor of Applied Disaster and Emergency Studies; (b) Bachelor of Arts; (c) Bachelor of Business Administration; (d) Bachelor of Education; (e) Bachelor of Fine Arts (f) Bachelor of First Nations and Aboriginal Counselling; (g) Bachelor of General Studies; (h) Bachelor of Music; (i) Bachelor of Nursing; (j) Bachelor of Science; (k) Bachelor of Science in Environmental Science; (l) Bachelor of Science in Psychiatric Nursing; (m) Graduate Diploma and Master's Degree in Education; (n) Graduate Diploma and Master's Degree in Rural Development; (o) Master's Degree in Music.
Description: see website for full details and for all programmes.
Fees: (a) to (l): tuition approximately C$5,500 per year; (m) to (o): tuition approximately C$2,200 per year; living costs (all) C$500-600 per month.

357 Brock University

500 Glenridge Avenue
L2S 3A1 St. Catharines, Ontario
Tel: +1-905-688-5550/4293
Fax: +1-905-688-4283
Web: http://www.brocku.ca
e-mail: liaison@brocku.ca

📖 Undergraduate and Graduate Degree Programmes

Study Domains: business, education, humanities and arts, natural resources, natural sciences, nursing, recreation and leisure, sciences, social sciences, speech therapy, tourism, hotel and catering management.
Programmes: Bachelor's, Master's, Ph.D. degrees in business; education; humanities and arts; natural sciences; nursing; sciences; social sciences; tourism.
Fees: see website for further information.
Languages: English.
Applications: application on-line at: www.brocku.ca.

☞**Scholarships**

Study Domains: education, humanities and arts, natural resources, natural sciences, nursing, social sciences, speech therapy, tourism, hotel and catering management.
Scholarships: various scholarships available, see website at: http://www.brocku.ca; international students' page at: http://www.brocku.ca/international/.

358   Canadian Bureau for International Education [CBIE]
FAC International Scholarship Programs
220 Laurier West, Suite 1550
K1P 5Z9 Ottawa, Ontario
Tel: +1-613-237-4820
Fax: +1-613-237-1073
Web: http://www.scholarships.gc.ca
e-mail: scholarships-bourses@cbie.ca

☞**International Scholarship Programs**

Study Domains: all major fields, research.
Scholarships: Government of Canada Awards to Foreign Nationals.
Description: awards to enable foreign students of high academic standing to undertake graduate studies or post doctoral research in Canadian institutions. Awards may be applied to research or studies in all areas of the arts, the social sciences and humanities, commerce, the natural sciences and engineering. Proposed programs of study must focus on a Canadian subject or include significant Canadian content.
Subjects: all disciplines; graduate studies, research or post-doctoral research.
Open to: candidates must have the equivalent of a Canadian undergraduate degree; artists must have completed basic training and begun their professional career; for fellowships: Ph.D. or equivalent; artists must have made a significant contribution over a number of years; English or French proficiency required; not open to students planning to emigrate to Canada; candidate's programme of study or research must have Canadian content.
Nationality: nationals of Brazil, Chile, Colombia, Cuba, France, Germany, Italy, Japan, Korea, Mexico, the Philippines, Russia.
Place of study: tenable only in Canada in universities, research institutes and institutions of higher learning.
Duration: postdoctoral fellowships: 6 months; research scholarships: 1 year maximum.
Value: scholarships, C$900 per month plus tuition and certain other benefits; fellowships, C$1,200 per month plus certain other benefits.
Applications: interested individuals should obtain information from the Canadian Embassy in their home country; see website http://www.scholarships.gc.ca/Pages/GCA_In/nc_GCAp1_e.h tml for further details.

358   Bureau canadien de l'éducation internationale [BCEI]
Programme de bourses internationale de AEC
220 Laurier Ouest, Bureau 1550
K1P 5Z9 Ottawa, Ontario
Tel: +1-613-237-4820
Fax: +1-613-237-1073
Web: http://www.scholarships.gc.ca
e-mail: scholarships-bourses@cbie.ca

☞**Programmes internationaux de bourses d'études**

Domaines d'étude: toutes disciplines principales, recherche.
Bourses: Bourses du Gouvernement canadien aux ressortissants étrangers.
Description: ces bourses permettent à des étudiants de haut niveau académique d'entreprendre des études supérieures ou des recherches dans des institutions canadiennes. Sont admissibles les candidats dans le domaine des arts, des sciences humaines et sociales, du commerce, des sciences naturelles et du génie, à condition que le sujet proposé présente un contenu canadien substantiel.
A l'intention de: les candidats doivent posséder l'équivalent d'un diplôme universitaire canadien et, s'ils étudient les arts, avoir terminé leur formation de base et commencé leur carrière professionnelle. Bourses de recherche

postdoctorale: les candidats doivent être titulaires de l'équivalent d'un Ph.D. et, s'ils sont artistes, avoir accompli une oeuvre remarquable et être reconnus; une bonne connaissance de l'anglais ou du français est indispensable. Les étudiants ayant l'intention d'émigrer au Canada ne peuvent pas postuler; le programme d'études ou de recherche doit se situer dans un contexte canadien.
Nationalité: ressortissants de: Allemagne, Brésil, Chili, Colombie, Corée, Cuba, France, Italie, Japon, Mexique, les Philippines, et Russie.
Lieu: aux universités, institutions de recherche et établissements d'enseignement supérieur au Canada uniquement.
Durée: bourses postdoctorales: six mois et bourses de recherche: une année maximum.
Valeur: bourses d'études: C$900 par mois, plus la scolarité et certains autres avantages; bourses postdoctorales: C$1.200 par mois plus certains autres avantages.
Candidatures: les candidats intéressés peuvent se procurer une brochure descriptive auprès de l'ambassade du Canada dans leur pays d'origine; voir site Internet http://www.scholarships.gc.ca/Pages/GCA_In/nc_GCAp1_f.h tml pour de plus amples informations.

359   Carleton University
1125 Colonel By Drive
K1S 5B6 Ottawa, Ontario
Tel: +1-613-520-7400
Web: http://www.carleton.ca
e-mail: infocarleton@carleton.ca

📖 **Undergraduate, Graduate and Postgraduate Degree Programmes**

Study Domains: all major fields.
Programmes: (a) Bachelor's degrees in architecture, arts, commerce, computer science, engineering, industrial design, international business, journalism, music, public administration, science and social work; (b) Master's degrees in arts, computer science, engineering, journalism, public administration, science and social work; (c) Doctoral degrees in arts, engineering and science;
(d) Certificate in Public Service Studies (CPSS), Graduate Diploma in Public Administration (DPA), Certificate in English Language and Composition (CELC), Certificate in French Language Studies (CFLS), Certificate in Law Enforcement Studies (CLES), Certificate in French Translation Studies (CFTS), Certificate in Teaching English as a Second Language (CTESL).
Open to: candidates fulfilling the necessary requirements; proficiency in English essential; all visa applicants whose mother tongue is other than English are required to present a minimum TOEFL score of 580 as part of the basic requirements for admission to the University.
Duration: (a) and all certificates: variable; (b) and DPA: 1 year beyond Bachelor's degree; (c) 2 years beyond the Master's degree; (courses begin in May and September).
Financial assistance: some scholarships, bursaries and fellowships available.
Applications: by 1 February for applicants to architecture and social work; by 1 March for applicants to music; and by 1 April for applicants to all other programmes; through the Ontario Universities Application Centre, P.O. Box 1328, 650 Woodlawn Road W., Guelph, Ontario N1H 7P4.

360   Concordia University
1455 de Maisonneuve Boulevard West
H3G 1M8 Montreal, Quebec
Tel: +1-514-848-3800
Fax: +1-514-848-2812
Web: http://www.concordia.ca

📖 **Undergraduate, Graduate and Postgraduate Degree Programmes**

Study Domains: administration, arts, business, computer science, education, engineering, fine arts, sciences, trade.
Programmes: (a) Master's and PhD degrees programmes in arts, science, engineering, commerce and fine arts; (b) Bachelor's degree programmes in arts, education, sciences, commerce, administration, engineering, computer science and fine arts.
Open to: (a) applicants holding the equivalent of a Canadian Bachelor's Degree (Master's Programme) or Master's Degree (Doctoral Programme); qualifying

programmes available for students requiring upgrading; (b) candidates of all nationalities fulfilling the necessary entry requirements; students whose first language is not English must provide evidence of proficiency (TOEFL 550).
Duration: (a) 1 to 3 years; (b) 3 to 4 years; courses begin in September or in January in some cases.
Fees: see website for fee information.
Financial assistance: (a) limited number of fee remissions, teaching and research assistantships and scholarships available.
Applications: (a) to the Graduate Programme Director, specifying Department; (b) by 1 March, to the Undergraduate Admissions Office; at the above address.

361 Concordia University College of Alberta

7128 Ada Boulevard North West
T5B 4E4 Edmonton, Alberta
Tel: +1-780-479-8481
Fax: +1-780-474-1933
Web: http://www.concordia.ab.ca
e-mail: admits@concordia.ab.ca

Undergraduate Entrance Awards

Study Domains: all major fields.
Description: Entrance Scholarship Programme is open to all applicants entering their first year of university studies directly from secondary school.
Open to: students with good secondary school scholastic results.
Duration: 1 academic year.
Value: C$1,000-$2,000.
Applications: by 1 April; applicants must submit with their application form, an interim secondary school transcript of Grades 10, 11 and first semester Grade 12 marks; contact the Financial Aid Advisor at the above address.

362 Dalhousie University, Department of Economics

1236 Henry Street
B3H 3J5 Halifax, Nova Scotia
Tel: +1-902-494-2211
Fax: +1-902-494-2319
Web: http://www.dal.ca
e-mail: admissions@dal.ca

Graduate Programme in Development Economics

Study Domains: development studies, economy.
Programmes: Master's degrees in Development Economics:
(a) the Canadian Studies Programme (Canadian economic development); (b) the International Development Studies Programme (international and bilateral aid, health and environmental issues in third world countries).
Open to: candidates with pass or general B.A., B.Sc. or B. Comm. degree with minimum 2 classes in economics plus classes in introductory mathematics and introductory statistics; competence in English is required; students from developing countries are encouraged to integrate their own country experiences.
Duration: normally 2 years; in special cases, students may qualify for admission to a 1-year programme.
Financial assistance: scholarships available; details directly from the Department of Economics.
Applications: to the above address.

363 Dentistry Canada Fund [DCF]

427 Gilmour Street
K2P 0R5 Ottawa, Ontario
Tel: +1-613-236-4763
Fax: +1-613-236-3935
Web: http://www.dcf-fdc.ca/grants.html
e-mail: information@dcf-fdc.ca

Dentistry Scholarships

Study Domains: dentistry, research.
Scholarships: (a) Frank Popovich Memorial Fund; (b) D. C. F. Grants; (c) D. C. F. Undergraduate Students' Grants; (d) D. C. F. Unrestricted Grants; (e) D. C. F. Grants for Needy Students; (f) D. C. F. Dental Technology Scholarships; (g) D. C. F. Biennial Research Award (even years); (h) Brånemark

Cranio-Maxillofacial Rehabilitation Fund; Nobelpharma Canada Inc.; (i) Dentsply Henry Thornton Award; (j) L. E. MacLachlan Fellowships; (k) Procter and Gamble Research Fellowships.
Open to: (a) any orthodontic students seeking their Master's or Ph.D. in orthodontics and who will be applying their skills as teachers in Canada following their studies; (b) any projects relevant to dentistry that do not fit elsewhere, individuals and associations may apply; (c) and (d) all Canadian Faculties of Dentistry; (e) any undergraduate student currently enrolled in a Canadian faculty of dentistry; (f) first year student of dental technology, Nova Scotia Community College; (g) graduate or postgraduate students in association with a Canadian faculty of dentistry; (h) multi-disciplinary team experienced in Branemark System and affiliated with faculties of dentistry and medicine and their associated teaching hospitals; (i) any student applying for a D.C.F. Teaching/Research Fellowship; (j) prosthodontic and maxillofacial prosthodontic divisions at the Dental Faculties of the University of Toronto, McGill University, Dalhousie University and the University of Western Ontario; (l) all Canadian faculties of dentistry on behalf of an undergraduate dental student.
Applications: (a), (b), (f), (g), (k), (n) and (o) 1 March; (h) 1 December; (m) 1 January; (c) to (e), (i), (j) and (l) no deadline.

364 Huron University College [HUC]

1349 Western Road
N6G 1 London, Ontario
Tel: +1-519-438-7224
Fax: +1-519-438-3938
Web: http://www.huronuc.ca/prospective_students/
e-mail: kknowles@uwo.ca

Undergraduate Programmes

Study Domains: arts, social sciences, theology, religion.
Programmes: Bachelor's degrees in arts, social sciences, theology.
Duration: 3 to 4 years, beginning in September.
Fees: tuition: C$11,000.
Languages: English.

Undergraduate Programmes

Study Domains: arts, social sciences, theology, religion.
Programmes: Bachelor's degrees in arts; social sciences; theology.
Duration: 3 to 4 years beginning in September.
Fees: tuition fees: C$11,000.
Languages: English.

Scholarships

Study Domains: arts, Asian studies, cultural studies, development studies, economic and commercial sciences, history, international studies, languages, liberal arts, literature and civilization, philosophy, political science, psychology, theology, religion.
Scholarships: International Scholarships.
Subjects: arts and social science programmes of study.
Value: maximum C$3,000 per year; work study bursaries available based on financial need.
Applications: to Registrar's office; for bursaries contact the college administrator's office.

Scholarships

Study Domains: arts, Asian studies, cultural studies, development studies, economic and commercial sciences, history, international studies, languages, liberal arts, literature and civilization, philosophy, political science, psychology, theology, religion.
Scholarships: International Scholarships.
Subjects: arts and social science programmes of study.
Duration: 4 years, renewable.
Value: maximum C$5,000 per year; work study bursaries available based on financial need.
Applications: Contact the Dean of arts & social sciences, huron@uwo.ca. For more information, www.huronuc.on.ca.

365 International Council for Canadian Studies - Award Programme (PRA)

Organization of American States
325 Dalhousie Street, Suite 800
K1N 7G2 Ottawa, Ontario
Tel: +1-613-789-7828
Fax: +1-613-789-7830
Web: http://www.scholarships.gc.ca
e-mail: general@iccs-ciec.ca

☞ OAS Graduate Awards

Study Domains: all major fields.
Scholarships: Graduate level awards for advanced study and research (10 per year).
Subjects: all subjects except medicine.
Open to: citizens or permanent residents of an OAS member state who hold a university degree or who have demonstrated ability to pursue advanced studies in the field chosen; candidates must know the language of the study country.
Place of study: in a country which is a member of the Organization of American States (OAS).
Duration: 3 months to 2 years.
Value: round-trip ticket, tuition fees, study materials, health insurance and subsistence allowance which varies from country to country (no benefits provided to the family of the fellowship holder).
Applications: to the above address, or through on-line application forms; see website for further information.

366 King's University College (The)

9125 - 50th Street
T6B 2H3 Edmonton, Alberta
Tel: +1-780-465-8334
Fax: +1-780-465-3534
Web: http://www.kingsu.ca
e-mail: admissions@kingsu.ca

⌑ Undergraduate Programmes

Study Domains: biology, business administration, chemistry, computer science, ecology, environment, education, English, history, liberal arts, music and musicology, philosophy, psychology, sociology, theology, religion.
Programmes: Bachelor's degrees in arts; science; commerce; music and education.
Duration: 3 to 4 years.
Fees: tuition fees per credit: C$230; normal course load is 31 credits per year (C$7,130); student fees: C$325 per year; residence and food services fees vary from C$5,250 to C$6,850 per year. international student fee: C$1,500; international health care plan: C$642.
Financial assistance: scholarships, bursaries and awards are available for all major fields; see: http://www.kingsu.ca.
Languages: English.
Applications: deadline: 15 August for fall term; 1 December for winter term to registrar's office or apply on-line at: www.kingsu.ca.

☞ Scholarships

Study Domains: all major fields.
Scholarships: several scholarships offered, see website at: http://www.kingsu.ca.

367 Kwantlen University College [KUC]

12664 - 72 Avenue
V3W 2M8 Surrey, British Columbia
Tel: +1-604-599-2534
Fax: +1-604-599-2449
Web: http://www.kwantlen.ca
e-mail: inted@kwantlen.ca

⌑ Diploma, Associate and Bachelor's Degrees

Study Domains: administration, applied arts, applied sciences, arts, business administration, computer science, criminology, cultural studies, engineering, interior design, liberal arts, music and musicology, nursing, sciences.
Programmes: (a) Diploma courses in Automation/Robotics engineering Technology; Accounting; Applied Science (Engineering); Business Administration;

Business Management; Computer Information Systems; Criminology; Electronics Engineering Technology; Fashion Design and Technology; Fashion Marketing; Fine Arts; General Business Studies; General Studies; Graphics and Visual Design; Graduate Nurse Upgrading, Interdisciplinary Design Studies; Music; Marketing Management; Public Relations; Science; (b) Associate Degrees in Anthropology; General Studies; Geography; History; Music; Political Science; Science; Sociology; (c) Bachelor's Degrees in Business Administration; Applied Design; Psychology.
Held: courses held at Langley, Richmond and Surrey campuses.
Fees: varies according to programme from C$7,000-$9,000; Music and Science courses from C$10,500-$13,500.
Languages: English.
Applications: by 31 March; contact inted@kwantlen.ca for further details.

368 McGill University [McGill]

845 Sherbrooke Street West, Suite 506
H3A 2T6 Montreal, Quebec
Tel: +1-514-398-4180
Fax: +1-514-398-4768
Web: http://www.mcgill.ca

⌑ Undergraduate, Graduate, Postgraduate Programmes

Study Domains: all major fields.
Programmes: Bachelor's, Master's, Ph.D. degrees in all major fields.
Financial assistance: some financial assistance available in various forms and for certain disciplines; value from C$3,000-$15,000; enquire at above address.
Languages: English and French.

369 McGill University, Department of Agricultural Economics

21,111 Lakeshore Road
H9X 3V9 Ste Anne de Bellevue, Québec
Tel: +1-514-398-7820
Fax: +1-514-398-8130
Web: http://www.agrenv.mcgill.ca/agrecon/
e-mail: agr.econ@mcgill.ca

⌑ Undergraduate, Graduate, Postgraduate Programmes

Study Domains: agriculture, economic and commercial sciences.
Programmes: Bachelor's, Master's, Ph.D. degrees in agricultural economics.
Open to: applicants holding an appropriate degree with a TOEFL score of at least 560.
Duration: B.Sc., 3 years; M.Sc.; 2 years; Ph.D.; 3 years.
Fees: tuition: approx. C$10,000 per year for international students.
Financial assistance: some fellowships and research assistantships are available at graduate level only.
Languages: English.
Applications: by 1 March for September admission, to the above address.

☞ Fellowship

Study Domains: agriculture, economy.
Scholarships: Sir Vincent Meredith Fellowship.
Open to: outstanding students admitted to the graduate programme in agricultural economics; holders of this fellowship may be expected to participate in the teaching programme of the Department.
Duration: 2 years (renewable once on the basis of satisfactory progress).
Value: approximately C$10,000 per year.
Applications: by 1 March, to McGill University MacDonald Campus, at the above address.

369 Université McGill - Département d'économie agraire
21,111 Lakeshore Road
H9X 3V9 Ste Anne de Bellevue, Québec
Tel: +1-514-398-7820
Fax: +1-514-398-8130
Web: http://www.agrenv.mcgill.ca/agrecon/
e-mail: agr.econ@mcgill.ca

✿ Bourse
Domaines d'étude: agriculture, économie.
Bourses: Bourse d'études Sir Vincent Meredith.
A l'intention de: candidat méritant remplissant les conditions requises pour l'admission aux études supérieures en économie agraire; il peut être requis du bénéficiaire qu'il participe au programme d'enseignement du Département.
Durée: 2 ans (renouvelable une fois selon les résultats du candidat).
Valeur: C$10.000 par an environ.
Candidatures: avant le 1er mars; Université McGill Campus MacDonald, à l'adresse ci-dessus.

370 Memorial University of Newfoundland [MUN]
Elizabeth Avenue
A1C 5S7 St. John's, Newfoundland
Tel: +1-709-737-8000
Fax: +1-709-737-4569
Web: http://www.mun.ca
e-mail: newstudents@mun.ca

📖 Undergraduate, Graduate, Postgraduate Programmes
Study Domains: all major fields.
Programmes: (a) Bachelor's degrees in arts, police studies, business administration, commerce (co-operative and non-co-operative), education (primary, elementary, intermediate, secondary, postsecondary and Native and Northern), engineering, fine arts (theatre and visual arts), maritime studies, music, music education, nursing (collaborative and post-RN), physical education (co-operative), pharmacy, recreation (co-operative), science, social work, special education, technology; (b) Master's degrees in applied science in environmental engineering and applied science, applied statistics, arts, business administration, education, engineering, environmental science, marine studies (fisheries resource management), nursing, philosophy (M.Phil.) physical education, science, science (in environmental science), science (in pharmacy), social work and women's studies; (c) Doctor of Medicine; (d) Doctor of philosophy and arts, engineering, medicine, science, and social work; (e) Diploma programmes in adult teacher education, business administration, clinical counselling for addictions, clinical epidemiology research, community and primary health care nursing, community health, Native and Northern education in Labrador (T.E.P.L.), nurse-midwifery, outpost nursing, postsecondary education, social work, and technology education; (f) Continuing Education programmes: certificates in business administration, criminology, library studies, municipal administration, Newfoundland studies, public administration, and records and information management; diploma programme in information technology.
Open to: (a) and (e) candidates having successfully completed secondary studies or equivalent, admission to diploma programmes is considered on an individual basis and may require the completion of specific university courses, work experience, and/or other prerequisites; (b) and (c) candidates with Bachelor's degrees, preferably Honours, with minimum B average or equivalent in field of specialization; (d) candidates with Master's degree or equivalent or Honours Bachelor's degree.
Duration: variable; courses begin in September, January and May.
Languages: English.
Applications: by 1 March for Fall semester, 1 October for Winter semester, 1 February for Spring/Summer semester, to the Registrar.

371 Mount Allison University
65 York Street
E4L IE4 Sackville, New Brunswick
Tel: +1-506-364-2300
Fax: +1-506-364-2272
Web: http://www.mta.ca
e-mail: admissions@mta.ca

📖 Undergraduate, Graduate Programmes
Study Domains: accounting, anthropology, art history, astronomy, biochemistry, biology, biophysics, chemistry, classical studies, computer science, ecology, environment, economy, finance, fine arts, geography, history, languages, management, marine biology, marketing, mathematics, music and musicology, performing arts, philosophy, photography, physics, political science, psychology, sociology, statistics, theology, religion, zoology.
Programmes: Bachelor's, Master's degrees in all major fields.
Held: on-campus and limited courses in Moncton and Miramichi.
Duration: 4 years beginning 1 September.
Fees: registration: C$100; tuition: C$9,960, living costs: C$6,810.
Financial assistance: available based on need.
Languages: English.
Applications: by 15 March; admissions@mta.ca.

372 Natural Sciences and Engineering Research Council of Canada [NSERC]
350 Albert Street
K1A 1H5 Ottawa, Ontario
Tel: +1-613-995-4273
Fax: +1-613-992-5337
Web: http://www.nserc-crsng.gc.ca/
e-mail: tpw@nserc.ca

✿ NSERC Fellowships
Study Domains: engineering, natural sciences, research.
Scholarships: (a) NSERC Fellowships: Bachelor of Arts: research fellowships for small universities and in industry; postgraduate studies: postgraduate fellowships (Ph.D.); supplements to postgraduate fellowships; postgraduate fellowships for studies with relevance for industry; postdoctoral studies: postdoctoral fellowships; fellowships for postdoctoral research in industry.
Subjects: natural sciences and engineering.
Place of study: in Canadian universities.
Duration: 1 year (possibility of renewal for a 2nd year).
Value: variable.
Applications: contact NSERC for application information http://www.nserc.gc.ca/funding/funding_e.asp.

372 Conseil de recherches en sciences naturelles et en génie du Canada [CRSNG]
350 rue Albert
K1A 1H5 Ottawa, Ontario
Tel: +1-613-995-4273
Fax: +1-613-992-5337
Web: http://www.nserc-crsng.gc.ca/
e-mail: tpw@nserc.ca

✿ Bourses CRSNG
Domaines d'étude: ingénierie, recherche, sciences naturelles.
Bourses: Bourses du CRSNG en sciences et en génie: 1er cycle: bourses de recherche dans les petites universités et en milieu industriel; 2e et 3e cycles: bourses d'études supérieures; suppléments aux bourses d'études supérieures; bourses d'études supérieures à incidence industrielle; niveau postdoctoral: bourses postdoctorales; bourses pour les chercheurs-boursiers en milieu industriel.
Lieu: universités canadiennes.
Durée: 1 an (renouvelable une fois).
Valeur: variable.
Candidatures: s'adresser au CRSNG pour de plus amples renseignements http://www.crsng.gc.ca/funding/funding_f.asp.

373 Nipissing University
PO Box 5002
100 College Drive
P1B 8L7 North Bay, Ontario
Tel: +1-705-474-3461
Fax: +1-705-495-1772
Web: http://www.nipissingu.ca
e-mail: liaison@nipissingu.ca

Undergraduate Programmes
Study Domains: accounting, arts, biology, business,
business administration, classical studies, criminology,
development studies, ecology, environment, economic and
commercial sciences, education, English, fine arts, geography,
liberal arts, mathematics, nursing, philosophy, psychology,
sociology, visual arts.
Programmes: Bachelor's degrees in all major fields.
Duration: 3 to 4 years beginning 1 September.
Fees: tuition fees C$8,500; living costs C$8,000.
Languages: English.
Applications: international students apply by 1 June to
Liaison Office at liaison@nipissingu.ca.

Caribbean Student Award
Study Domains: all major fields.
Scholarships: Caribbean Student Award.
Open to: Caribbean students.
Value: C$1,500 per year; renewable.

374 Nova Scotia Agricultural College [NSAC]
PO Box 550
B2N 5E3 Truro, Nova Scotia
Tel: +1-902-893-6722
Fax: +1-902-895-5529
Web: http://www.nsac.ns.ca
e-mail: reg@nsac.ns.ca

Undergraduate and Graduate Degree Programmes
Study Domains: agriculture, agronomic sciences, applied
sciences, biology, botany, business, business administration,
chemistry, ecology, environment, economy, engineering,
fisheries, genetics, horticulture, sciences, veterinary sciences,
zoology.
Programmes: Bachelor's and Master's Degrees in
agriculture; applied sciences; biology; business
administration; chemistry; veterinary sciences.
Description: B.Sc., B.Tech., M.Sc.; 2 and 3 year diploma
programmes also offered in various areas of agriculture and
management.
Fees: tuition fees: C$800 per year; living costs: C$10,000
per year.
Languages: English.
Applications: by 1 April for September admission; apply
to the Office of the Registrar.

Scholarships
Study Domains: all major fields.
Scholarships: International Student Scholarships.
Description: based on academic performance.
Open to: all nationalities.
Duration: renewable for a maximum of 4 years.
Value: C$3,000 per year.
Applications: apply to NSAC Awards office; deadline: 30
June; a number of other scholarships are open to application
from foreign students.

375 Nova Scotia College of Art and Design [NSCAD]
5163 Duke Street
B3J 3J6 Halifax, Nova Scotia
Tel: +1-902-444-9600
Fax: +1-902-425-2420
Web: http://www.nscad.ns.ca

Undergraduate and Graduate Programmes in Arts
Study Domains: arts, design, fine arts, graphic arts.
Programmes: Bachelor of Fine Arts, Bachelor of Design,
Master of Fine Arts, Master of Arts.

Open to: eligible applicants of any nationality; TOEFL
550.
Duration: 4½ years; courses begin in September or
January.
Fees: approximately C$11,250 per academic year;
international student tuition, C$14,440 per year.
Languages: English.
Applications: at the above address.

376 Ontario Institute for Studies in Education University of Toronto [OISE/UT]
252 Bloor Street West
M5S 1V6 Toronto, Ontario
Tel: +1-416-923-6641
Fax: +1-416-926-4725
Web: http://www.oise.utoronto.ca/

Graduate, Postgraduate Programmes
Study Domains: education.
Programmes: graduate and postgraduate level degree
programmes in education offered through various academic
departments.
Open to: students from developing countries with an
appropriate undergraduate degree of high standing for
admission to M.A.; experience also required for admission to
M. Ed., and a relevant Master's degree required for admission
to Doctoral study.
Duration: at least 1 to 2 years for Master's programmes
and 2 to 4 years for Doctoral studies.
Fees: approximately C$4,500 for landed immigrants and
Canadians; C$16,000 for international students.
Financial assistance: over 182 assistantships, with a value
of over C$8,000 (plus 4% vacation pay) for an 8-month
period.
Languages: English.
Applications: by 15 January, to Admissions, Office of
Graduate Studies.

377 Redeemer University College
777 Garner Road East
L9K 1J4 Ancaster, Ontario
Tel: +1-905-648-2131
Fax: +1-905-648-2134
Web: http://www.redeemer.on.ca
e-mail: admis@redeemer.on.ca

Undergraduate Degree Programmes
Study Domains: all major fields, theology, religion.
Programmes: Bachelor of Christian Education.
Duration: 4 years; part-time study also available.
Fees: tuition fees: C$9,854; living costs/residence:
C$4,786.
Financial assistance: differs for each applicant.
Languages: English.
Applications: by 1 July to Office of Admissions or email:
sneven@redeemer.on.ca; requests students to apply early.

Bursary
Study Domains: all major fields.
Scholarships: Redeemer University College Bursary.
Open to: all incoming students with financial need.
Value: up to C$2,350; renewable.
Applications: by late February.

378 Ryerson Polytechnic University
350 Victoria Street
M5B 2K3 Toronto, Ontario
Tel: +1-416-979-5000
Fax: +1-416-979-5292
Web: http://www.ryerson.ca

Undergraduate Programmes
Study Domains: all major fields.
Programmes: (a) Bachelor's degree programmes; (b)
Diploma programmes.
Description: courses in (a) administration and information
management, aerospace engineering, applied chemistry and
biology, applied computer science, applied geography,
architectural science, business management, chemical

engineering, child and youth care, civil engineering, early childhood education, electrical engineering, environmental health, fashion, graphic communications management, health services management, hospitality and tourism management, industrial engineering, interior design, journalism, mechanical engineering, midwifery, nursing, nutrition, consumer and family studies, photographic arts, public administration, radio and television arts, social work, technical production (theatre), and urban and regional planning; (b) landscape architecture and theatre (acting and dance).
Open to: nationals of any country. General requirement for admission is an Ontario secondary school diploma with a minimum average of 60% in six Ontario Academic Courses, or equivalent thereof.
Duration: 4 years with the exception of health services management, midwifery and public administration, which are available through part-time study and the diploma programmes which are of 3-year duration.
Fees: approx. C$25,000 per academic year for tuition, food and accommodation, books and supplies, incidentals, local transportation, field trips and medical insurance (costs are somewhat higher for engineering, architecture, nursing, hospitality, and food/nutrition programmes).
Applications: by 15 March, to the above address for further information.

379 Saint Mary's University
923 Robie Street
B3H 3C3 Halifax, Nova Scotia
Tel: +1-902-420-5415
Fax: +1-902-496-8100
Web: http://www.stmarys.ca
e-mail: admissions@stmarys.ca

📖 Undergraduate and Graduate Degree Programmes
Study Domains: American studies, arts, astronomy, business administration, education, engineering, history, psychology, sciences, summer programmes.
Programmes: (a) Bachelor in arts, commerce, education, science; (b) Diploma in engineering; (c) Master in Education; (d) Master in business administration; (e) Master in Atlantic Canada studies, history; (f) Master in international development studies, applied psychology, astronomy, philosophy.
Duration: (a) 3 to 4 years; (b) 2 to 3 months; (c) to (f) 1 to 2 academic years; Summer courses available.
Fees: vary by student status and programme.
Financial assistance: available to students who have completed their first year of study at St. Mary's University.
Languages: English.
Applications: by April, to the Director of Admissions, at the above address.

380 Saint Paul University
223 Main Street
K1S 1C4 Ottawa, Ontario
Tel: +1-613-236-1393/2838
Fax: +1-613-782-3033
Web: http://www.ustpaul.ca

📖 Undergraduate, Graduate Programmes / Religion
Study Domains: canon law, communication, philosophy, theology, religion.
Programmes: (a) Bachelor's degrees in canon law, philosophy, theology, Christian studies; (b) Master's degrees in mission studies, pastoral studies, canon law, theology, religious education; (c) doctoral degrees in philosophy (canon law, theology); (d) certificate of university studies in social communications, missiology, theology, religious education.
Open to: qualified candidates of all nationalities.
Duration: from 2 to 6 trimesters depending on the course. (Courses begin in September, January, May or July.).
Fees: approximately C$4,000 per term (for foreign students).
Financial assistance: limited number of scholarships available.
Languages: Instruction in English and French.
Applications: by 15 August, 15 December or 15 June, to the Admissions Office, at the above address.

380 Université Saint-Paul
223, rue Main
K1S 1C4 Ottawa, Ontario
Tel: +1-613-236-1393/2838
Fax: +1-613-782-3033
Web: http://www.ustpaul.ca

📖 Programmes d'étude du 1er, 2e et 3e cycles
Domaines d'étude: communication, droit canon, philosophie, théologie, religion.
Programmes: (a) « Baccalauréat » (Bachelor's degree) en études chrétiennes, philosophie, théologie, «Eastern Christian Studies», «Anglican Studies»; (b) Maîtrise ès arts en sciences de la mission, sciences pastorales, droit canonique, théologie, éducation religieuse; (c) Doctorats en philosophie, droit canonique, théologie; (d) Certificats d'études universitaires en communication sociale, animation, sciences de la mission, théologie, éducation religieuse, «Catholic Health Care Leadership», «Eastern Christian Studies».
A l'intention de: candidats qualifiés de tout pays.
Durée: de 2 à 6 trimestres selon le programme choisi (débutant en septembre, janvier, mai ou juillet).
Frais: environ C$4.000 par session pour les étudiants étrangers.
Assistance financière: nombre limité de bourses.
Connaissances linguistiques: l'enseignement est donné en anglais et en français.
Inscriptions: avant le 15 août, le 15 décembre ou le 15 juin; au Bureau des admissions, à l'adresse ci-dessus.

381 Simon Fraser University [SFU]
MBC 1200 - 8888 University Drive
V5A 1S6 Burnaby, British Columbia
Tel: +1-604-291-4232
Fax: +1-604-291-5880
Web: http://www.sfu.ca/international/
e-mail: sfu_international@sfu.ca

📖 Undergraduate, Graduate and Postgraduate Programmes
Study Domains: all major fields.
Programmes: Bachelor's, Master's, Ph.D. degrees in all major fields.

382 St Francis Xavier University [STFX]
PO Box 5000, Station Main
B2G 2W5 Antigonish, Nova Scotia
Tel: +1-902-863-3300
Fax: +1-902-867-2448
Web: http://www.stfx.ca

📖 Undergraduate, Graduate Degree Programmes
Study Domains: all major fields, arts, business administration, education, engineering, music and musicology, nursing, nutrition, physical education, sciences.
Programmes: (a) Bachelor's degrees in arts, business administration, human nutrition, music, nursing, physical education, science; (b) Master's degrees in arts, education, teaching, adult education, teaching and science; (c) diplomas in engineering, jazz studies, adult education; (d) Bachelor's degree in education.
Open to: candidates of all nationalities with high school leaving certificate including 5 final year academic courses; continuing education courses for credit are available; placement and counselling services offered.
Duration: (a) 4 years; (b) 1 year; (c) 2 years; (d) 2 years.
Fees: see website for details.
Financial assistance: some scholarships and bursaries available for students of high academic standing.
Languages: English.
Applications: (a) to (d) by 1 March for scholarship consideration, by 1 May for international students; (d) by 15 March; to the Admissions Officer.

383   St Thomas University [STU]

Fredericton, New Brunswick
Tel: +1-506-452-0352
Fax: +1-506-452-0617
Web: http://www.stthomasu.ca/prospective/internatio
nal
e-mail: admissions@stu.ca

📖 Undergraduate Programmes

Study Domains: anthropology, applied arts, biology,
chemistry, criminology, cultural studies, economic and
commercial sciences, education, gerontology, history,
journalism, languages, liberal arts, mathematics, philosophy.
Programmes: Bachelor's degrees in arts, social work,
education, criminology, journalism, and gerontology.
Duration: 4 years; courses begin in September and April.
Fees: tuition fees: C$7,040 (Arts).
Languages: English.
Applications: by 1 June for International students.

🎓 Scholarships

Study Domains: anthropology, applied arts, biology,
chemistry, criminology, cultural studies, economic and
commercial sciences, education, gerontology, history,
journalism, languages, liberal arts, mathematics, philosophy.
Scholarships: University Scholarships.
Open to: students with excellent academic merit.
Value: from C$14,000 to C$27,000 depending on
scholarship.
Applications: by 15 March to Admissions Office.

384   The University of Winnipeg

515 Portage Avenue
R3B 2E9 Winnipeg, Manitoba
Tel: +1-204-786-7811
Fax: +1-204-786-8656
Web: http://www.uwinnipeg.ca

🎓 Undergraduate Awards

Study Domains: all major fields.
Description: (a) Entrance Scholarship Programme (b)
various scholarship programmes (see website for further
information).
Open to: (a) nationals of all countries based on secondary
school scholastic results.
Duration: (a) 1 year.
Value: (a) C$100-$4,500; (b) research grants.
Applications: before 1 March for the following academic
year in September. Contact Director of Awards and Financial
Aid, at the above address.

385   Trent University

1600 West Bank Drive
K9J7B8 Peterborough, Ontario
Tel: +1-705-748-1011
Fax: +1-705-748-1246
Web: http://www.trentu.ca/tip
e-mail: tip@trentu.ca

📖 Undergraduate and Graduate Degree Programmes

Study Domains: all major fields, anthropology,
astronomy, biochemistry, biology, business administration,
chemistry, classical studies, computer science, criminology,
cultural studies, development studies, ecology, environment,
economy, education, English, finance, French, geography,
German, history, international studies, languages, Latin,
liberal arts, linguistics, literature and civilization, management
of human resources, mathematics, medicine, natural sciences,
philosophy, physics, political economy, political science,
psychology, sciences, social sciences, sociology, teacher
education, women's studies.
Programmes: liberal arts, sciences, social sciences,
business, forensics, nursing, education.
Description: Bachelor's, Master's and Ph.D. degrees in all
major fields.
Open to: students fulfilling the necessary entry
requirements; students whose first language is not English
must provide evidence of competence in this language.
Nationality: open to all nationalities.
Academic requirements: a minimum average 70% (some
programmes require a higher average), plus evidence of
English proficiency (i.e. TOEFL 580). Detailed information

about admission requirements can be found on
www.trentu.ca/tip (under 'Applying to Trent').
Age limit Min: no age limit.
Duration: diplomas: 1 to 2 years; Bachelor's: 3 to 4 years;
Master's: 2 to 3 years; Ph.D: 3 to 5 years.
Fees: undergraduate tuition and ancillary fees: C$12,500;
single room in residence: C$7,500; health insurance: C$530.
Financial assistance: full and partial scholarships and
awards to qualified international students for undergraduate
degree studies.
Languages: English.
Applications: undergraduate: June 1 of each year (direct to
Trent University via www.trentu.ca/tip, under 'Applying to
Trent' or through OUAC via www.ouac.on.ca); graduate:
February 1 (visit www.trentu.ca/graduate for detailed
information).
Handicapped: Special Needs office serves students with
learning and physical disabilities.

🎓 Undergraduate Scholarship Programmes

Study Domains: all major fields.
Scholarships: Trent International Global Citizen
Scholarships and Awards; Trent-United World College
Scholarships.
Description: Trent International Programme offers a
limited number of highly competitive renewable Full and
Tuition scholarships as well as International Awards to
students eligible for admission to an undergraduate degree
programme at Trent, and who are not citizens or permanent
residents of Canada. These scholarships and awards are
tenable for up to four years of an Honours degree and are
available for students entering the University in September.
Subjects: open to students wishing to pursue any
undergraduate degree programme.
Open to: candidates demonstrating high academic
achievement, leadership skills, an excellent record of
extra-curricular activities as well as financial need.
Nationality: to all nationalities.
Age limit Min: preference is given to high school
graduates.
Age limit Max: preference is given to high school
graduates.
Academic requirements: high academic achievement (a
minimum 80% would be required to compete for Full and
Tuition scholarships).
Other conditions: Trent-United World College (UWC)
scholarships are open to UWC graduates.
Place of study: Trent University, Peterborough, Ontario,
Canada.
Duration: 4 years, renewable.
Value: Full scholarships: up to C$22,000 (covers tuition,
room and board, other expenses depending on need); Tuition:
up to C$13,000 (covers tuition); International Awards: up to
C$3,000.
Languages: English.
Applications: Deadline: Trent Global Citizen
Scholarships: 1 March of each year; see www.trentu.ca/tip
(under "Choosing Trent") for application procedures as well
as to download an application form;
Trent-United World College scholarships: 15 February of
each year; for more information and application procedures,
contact your home UWC.

386   Université de Moncton

165, avenue Massey
Centre universitaire de Moncton
E1A 3E9 Moncton, Nouveau Brunswick
Tel: +1-506-858-4113
Fax: +1-506-958-4544
Web: http://www.umoncton.ca
e-mail: recteur@umoncton.ca

📖 Programmes d'études du 1er, 2e, 3e cycles

Domaines d'étude: toutes disciplines principales.
Programmes: (a) programme conduisant au Baccalauréat
dans les disciplines suivantes: éducation, éducation physique,
loisirs, service social, psychologie, sciences sociales, sciences
infirmières, arts, musique, arts visuels, traduction, art
dramatique, administration des affaires, sciences et
informatique appliquée, droit, génie industriel, civil,
électrique et mécanique, sciences forestières, nutrition et
études familiales; (b) diplômes en techniques administratives,
génie général, sciences de la santé, études en sciences

agronomiques, techniques de bureau; (c) programme de Maîtrise en administration des affaires, administration publique, français, histoire, philosophie; sciences (nutrition et études familiales), sciences de l'éducation, sciences et génie, et sciences sociales, services sociaux; (d) programme d'éducation permanente conduisant aux Baccalauréats, Certificats et diplômes de Maîtrise dans certaines disciplines; (e) Programme de doctorat en études françaises.
A l'intention de: ressortissants de tout pays, titulaires d'un certificat d'études secondaires ou diplôme équivalent.
Organisés: aux campus de Moncton, Edmundston et Shippagan, Nouveau Brunswick.
Durée: (a) de 4 à 5 ans selon le domaine; (b) de 2 à 3 ans; (c) de 1 à 2 ans (1½ an à temps partiel pour la maîtrise en philosophie); (e) 3 sessions de résidence; 7 ans pour le dépôt de la thèse.
Frais: variables voir site web pour plus d'informations.
Assistance financière: quelques bourses disponibles après des études d'au moins une année (Baccalauréat) ou quatre mois (Maîtrise) à l'Université de Moncton.
Connaissances linguistiques: l'enseignement est donné en français.
Inscriptions: avant le 1er février, au Service de l'admission du Centre universitaire à l'adresse ci-dessus.

Bourse

Domaines d'étude: toutes disciplines principales.
Bourses: Bourse d'étude de recrutement international.
A l'intention de: étudiants canadiens et étrangers.
Durée: une année non renouvelable.
Valeur: C$1.000 par année.
Candidatures: avant le 1er avril, adressée au Registrariat de l'université (coordonnées ci dessus); pour informations, contacter le service des bourses et de l'aide financière de l'université, tel: +1 506 856 3231 ou +1 506 858 4492, email: aidefin@umoncton.ca.

387 Université de Montréal
CP 6128, succursale Centre ville
H3C 3J7 Montréal, Québec
Tel: +1-514-343-6426
Fax: +1-514-343-2252
Web: http://www.umontreal.ca
e-mail: fes-admission@fes.umontreal.ca

Programmes de cours allant du 2e au 3e cycles

Domaines d'étude: toutes disciplines principales.
Programmes: Microprogramme, Diplôme, Maîtrise, DESS, Doctorat, en fonction des filières.
Description: l'université de Montréal comprend différentes facultés et départements ainsi que l'École des hautes études commerciales (HEC; http://www.hec.ca) et l'École polytechnique (http://www.polymtl.ca).
A l'intention de: pour l'inscription en 2e cycle: titulaires d'un Baccalauréat d'une université canadienne (ou équivalent); pour l'inscription en 3e cycle: titulaires d'une Maîtrise (ou équivalent).
Assistance financière: possibilité d'obtention de bourses gouvernementales dans le cadre d'une Maîtrise ou d'un Doctorat; renseignements auprès de Andrée Maniette, adjointe au doyen; tel: +1 514 343 7125; fax: +1 514 343 2252; email: fes-exoner@fes.umontreal.ca.
Connaissances linguistiques: français.
Inscriptions: avant le 1er février pour les trimestres d'été et d'automne, avant le 1er novembre pour les trimestres d'hiver; les formulaires de demande d'admission peuvent être remplis en ligne ou obtenus au format PDF (http://www.umontreal.ca) ou demandés au Registrariat des facultés, départements ou écoles de l'université de Montréal.

388 Université du Québec
2875, boulevard Laurier
G1V 2M3 Sainte-Foy, Québec
Tel: +1-418-657-4349
Fax: +1-418-657-2132
Web: http://www.uqam.ca

Programme d'études du 1er, 2e et 3e cycles

Domaines d'étude: toutes disciplines principales, administration, arts, hygiène et santé, lettres, sciences, sciences humaines.
Programmes: Programme de cours préparant aux

diplômes universitaires du: (a) 1er cycle dans les domaines de la santé, des sciences pures et appliquées, sciences humaines, arts et lettres, sciences de l'administration; (b) 2e cycle (Maîtrise): droit social et du travail, intervention et travail social, sécurité et hygiène industrielle, kinanthropologie, sexologie, sciences comptables, arts (dramatique, plastique), danse, loisirs, culture et tourisme, développement régional, éducation spécialisée, éthique, études régionales, géographie, gestion (des entreprises, des organisations, des ressources maritimes, gestion et planification du tourisme), informatique de gestion, électronique industrielle, médecine expérimentale génétique, microbiologie appliquée, muséologie, ressources renouvelables, sciences de l'activité physique, sciences de l'atmosphère, sciences expérimentales de la santé, sciences politiques; (c) Doctorat: administration, biophysique, communication, économie, éducation, études en pratiques des arts, études littéraires, études québécoises, études urbaines, génie électrique, génie papetier, histoire, ingénierie, linguistique, mathématiques, océanographie, philosophie, psychologie, ressources minérales, sciences politiques, sciences de la terre, sciences de l'eau, sciences de l'énergie et des matériaux, sciences de l'environnement, sciences des religions, sémiologie, télécommunications, théologie, virologie et immunologie; (d) Diplômes d'études avancées et certificats dans les différentes disciplines offertes par l'université.
A l'intention de: ressortissants de tout pays, titulaires: (a) du Baccalauréat québécois ou équivalent; (c) d'une Maîtrise québécoise ou équivalent.
Organisés: dans les différents campus de l'université: Chicoutimi, Hull, Montréal, Rimouski, Rouyn-Noranda, Trois-Rivières, Sainte-Foy et Laval, dans la province de Québec.
Durée: (a) 18 mois à 2 ans; (c) 3 ans; (d) 1 an (sessions débutant en mai, septembre et janvier).
Frais: variable voir site web pour de plus amples informations.
Assistance financière: des bourses peuvent être octroyées sous certaines conditions; s'adresser, pour de plus amples renseignements, au Ministère de l'éducation nationale ou aux Missions canadiennes du pays du candidat.
Inscriptions: avant le 1er mars et le 1er novembre; au Bureau du registraire de l'un des campus de l'Université; voir site web pour les adresses.

389 Université du Quebec à Rimouski [UQAR]
300 Allée des Ursulines CP 3300
G5L 3A1 Rimouski, Quebec
Tel: +1-418-723-1986
Fax: +1-418-724-1525
Web: http://www.uqar.qc.ca
e-mail: uqar@uqar.qc.ca

1er, 2e et 3e cycles

Domaines d'étude: toutes disciplines principales.
Programmes: programme de cours allant du 1er au 3e cycles dans les disciplines concernées.
A l'intention de: admission en 1er cycle: titulaires d'un diplôme d'études collégiales (correspondant à treize ans de scolarité) ou équivalent; admission en 2e cycle: titulaires du baccalauréat québécois (correspondant à seize ans de scolarité) ou équivalent; admission en 3e cycle: titulaires d'un diplôme de maîtrise ou équivalent, soit le Diplôme d'études approfondies (DEA) en France ou le Master's degree au Royaume-Uni et aux États-Unis. Le candidat étranger doit d'abord obtenir une réponse positive à sa demande d'admission à un programme offert par l'Université du Québec à Rimouski; avec cette réponse positive, il doit soumettre sa demande pour l'obtention d'un Certificat d'acceptation du Québec (CAQ) à un représentant d'Immigration-Québec; renseignements sur le site: htp://www.immq.gouv.qc.ca.
Frais: droits de scolarité, 1er cycle: C$9.200 par an, 2e cycle: C$8.300 par an, 3e cycle: C$7.500 par an; frais de séjour: environ C$11.000 par an.
Assistance financière: quelques bourses d'excellence de 2e et de 3e cycles sont accessibles sur concours aux étudiants de toutes nationalités (voir site web).
Connaissances linguistiques: test en français pour les étudiants étrangers non francophones.
Inscriptions: les demandes d'admission peuvent se faire

sur le site web de l'université ou bien auprès du Service de l'admission, Bureau du registraire université du Québec à Rimouski, 300 allée des Ursulines, C.P. 3300 Rimouski (Québec) G5L 3A1; pour information; tél: +1 418 723 1986 poste 1378; fax: +1 418 724 1525; email: admission@uqar.qc.ca.

☞ Bourse

Domaines d'étude: arts, écologie, environnement, éducation, gestion, ingénierie, sciences sociales.
Domaines d'études: Arts; gestion des affaires; education; ingéniérie; sciences sociales; transport maritime; études environnementales.
Valeur: C$1.000 à $20.000 suivant programmes d'études.
Candidatures: Pour plus d'information, veuillez contacter renaud_thibeault@uqar.qc.ca.

390   Université du Québec à Montréal [UQAM]
Case postale 8888
succursale centre ville
H3C 3P8 Montréal, QC
Tel: +1-514-987-3000/3132
Fax: +1-514-987-8932
Web: http://www.uqam.ca
e-mail: admissions@uqam.ca

📖 Programmes de cours du 1er, 2e et 3e cycles

Domaines d'étude: toutes disciplines principales, arts, droit, éducation, gestion, langues, lettres, sciences, sciences humaines, sciences politiques.
Programmes: (a) 1er cycle: programme court, certificat, baccalauréat, combinaison majeure/mineure, baccalauréat par cumul de certificats; (b) 2e et 3e cycles: programme court, diplôme d'études supérieures spécialisées (DESS), maîtrise, doctorat.
A l'intention de: candidats titulaires d'un diplôme approprié obtenu après au moins treize années de scolarité ou l'équivalent. Les conditions d'admission varient en fonction des programmes (examen, entretien, recommandation, dossier). Consultez le site www.regis.uqam.ca.
Frais: de C$1.363 à C$11.040 en fonction des filières, des cycles d'études et de la nationalité des étudiants.
Assistance financière: se renseigner à l'adresse ci-dessus.
Connaissances linguistiques: test de français pour les étudiants étrangers non francophones.
Inscriptions: avant le 15 février pour une admission en septembre et avant le 15 octobre pour une admission en janvier; les formulaires de demandes d'admission peuvent être obtenus auprès du Registrariat de l'Université, Service de l'admission UQAM Case postale 6190, succursale Centre-ville Montréal (Québec) H3C 4N6; tél: +1-514-987-3132 ou sur le site de l'université: www.uqam.ca.

391   Université du Québec, Institut national de la recherche scientifique [INRS]
490 de la Couronne
G1K 9A9 Québec, Québec
Tel: +1-418-654-2500
Fax: +1-418-654-2525
Web: http://www.inrs.uquebec.ca

☞ Bourse de 2e et 3e cycles

Domaines d'étude: biochimie, biologie, biophysique, hydrologie, hygiène et santé, immunologie, littérature et civilisation, médecine, microbiologie, physique, sciences de la terre, sciences sociales, techniques de laboratoires, urbanisme.
Valeur: C$4,000 par semestre pour les programmes de 2e cycle; C$4,666 par semestre pour les programmes de 3e cycle (PhD).
Candidatures: à contacter le Registrar, 490 de la Couronne, Québec (Québec), Canada G1K 9A9.

392   Université Laval
Cabinet du Recteur, Bureau 1656 Pavillon des Sciences de l'Éducation
G1K 7P4 Québec, Québec
Tel: +1-418-656-2272
Fax: +1-418-656-7917
Web: http://www.ulaval.ca
e-mail: info@vrdri.ulaval.ca

📖 Programme de cours du 1er, 2e et 3e cycle

Domaines d'étude: toutes disciplines principales.
Description: 17 facultés offrant 389 programmes, dont plus de la moitié au premier cycle; plusieurs programmes d'études conduisant à la maîtrise ou doctorat, axés sur la recherche ou orientés vers la pratique professionnelle. Pour plus d'information: www.bip.ulaval.ca (info@vrdri.ulaval.ca).
A l'intention de: ressortissants de tous pays.
Qualifications requises: un baccalauréat d'une université canadienne (ou équivalent) pour les études en 2e cycle; une maîtrise (ou équivalent) pour les études en 3e cycle.
Assistance financière: pour renseignements: www.bbaf.ulaval.ca.
Connaissances linguistiques: français.
Inscriptions: au 1er cycle: avant le 1er février pour les sessions d'été, avant le 1er mars pour les sessions d'automne et avant le 1er septembre pour les sessions d'hiver; aux 2e et 3e cycles: avant le 1er février pour les sessions d'été et d'automne et avant le 1er septembre pour les sessions d'hiver. Les formulaires de demande d'admission peuvent être remplis en ligne ou obtenus au format PDF (http://www.bip.ulaval.ca) ou demandés au Bureau du registraire (www.reg.ulaval.ca/admission).

393   Université Sainte-Anne
Pointe-de-l'Eglise
B0W 1M0 Nouvelle Écosse
Tel: +1-902-769-2114
Fax: +1-902-769-2930
Web: http://www.ustanne.ednet.ns.ca
e-mail: admission@ustanne.ednet.ns.ca

📖 Programme d'études de 1er cycle

Domaines d'étude: administration des affaires, affaires, arts, développement communautaire, économie, éducation, français, sciences.
Programmes: (a) Baccalauréats ès arts, et en administration des affaires; (b) Diplôme en administration; (c) Deux premières années du Baccalauréat ès sciences; (d) Baccalauréat en éducation; (e) session d'immersion française.
A l'intention de: ressortissants de tout pays, titulaires d'un certificat d'études secondaires ou diplôme équivalent; français exigé (possibilité de cours intensifs préparatoires).
Durée: Durée: (a) 3 à 4 ans; (b) 2 ans; (c) 5 semaines ou sessions de 100 jours; de septembre à avril.
Frais: variable; voir site web.
Connaissances linguistiques: enseignement en français.
Inscriptions: au Bureau des admissions, à l'adresse ci-dessus.

394   University of Alberta [U of A]
201 Administration Building
T6G 2 Edmonton, Alberta
Tel: +1-780-492-2692
Fax: +1-780-492-1134
Web: http://www.international.ualberta.ca/
e-mail: international@ualberta.ca

📖 Undergraduate, Graduate, Postgraduate Programmes

Study Domains: all major fields.
Programmes: Bachelor's, Master's, Ph.D. degrees in all major fields.
Financial assistance: possibility of research and teaching assistantships for graduate students.
Languages: English.

☞ Scholarships

Study Domains: all major fields.
Scholarships: (a) University of Alberta United World College Scholarship; (b) Registrar's International Student Scholarship; (c) University of Alberta Sweden America Foundation Scholarship; (d) Academic Excellence.

Open to: (a) Must be studying in Canada on permit; (b) Must be studying in Canada on permit; (c) Swedish citizens studying in Canada; (d) All candidates.
Duration: (a) 4 years, renewable; (b) 1 year, non-renewable; (c) 1 year, non-renewable; (d) 1 year, non-renewable.
Value: (a) C$80,000 covering all expenses; (b) C$2,000 to 7,000; (c) 5 awards at C$4,000 each; (d) C$1000 to 5,000.
Applications: (a) 1 December; email: melissa.casey@ualberta.ca; (b) 1 May, automatically considered with application for admission; email: melissa.casey@ualberta.ca; (c) Students must apply through Sweden America Foundation in Stockholm, Sweden; by 1 March; must be on student study permit to qualify; email: melissa.casey@ualberta.ca; (d) Must submit application and transcript, see website; email: melissa.casey@ualberta.ca.

395 University of British Columbia [UBC]
2329 West Mall
V6T 1Z4 Vancouver, British Columbia
Tel: +1-604-822-3014
Fax: +1-604-822-5055
Web: http://students.ubc.ca/international/
e-mail: international.reception@ubc.ca

📖 Undergraduate, Graduate and Postgraduate Degree Programmes
Study Domains: all major fields.
Programmes: Bachelor's, Master's, Ph.D. degrees in all major fields.
Open to: all eligible candidates; no quota system at the graduate level; recognized Bachelor's degree (or equivalent) with first class average; proficiency in English required.
Duration: Master's degree, 2 years; Ph.D., minimum of 3 years; courses begin in September or January.
Fees: see website for tuition and other fees.
Financial assistance: merit-based.
Languages: English.
Applications: variable deadlines; confirm with the relevant department.

🐣 Fellowships
Study Domains: all major fields.
Scholarships: University Graduate Fellowships in all major fields.
Open to: candidates from all countries accepted into graduate studies; fellowships are competitive and successful applicants normally have first-class standing.
Duration: 1 year (renewable for a second year subject to maintenance of adequate standing, number of renewals appropriate to the circumstances).
Value: partial fellowships (not renewable); full fellowships.
Languages: English.
Applications: contact the Administrator at the above address for additional information.

396 University of Guelph
50 Stone Road East
N1G 2W1 Guelph, Ontario
Tel: +1-519-824-4120
Fax: +1-519-767-1693
Web: http://www.uoguelph.ca

📖 Undergraduate, Graduate, Postgraduate Programmes
Study Domains: all major fields, ecology, environment, geography, natural resources.
Programmes: Bachelor's, Master's, Ph.D. degrees in all major fields; especially environmental Sciences: earth and atmosphere science, ecology, environmental analysis, environmental protection, geography, natural resources management, resource and environmental economics and policy environment.
Open to: nationals of any country.
Duration: 4 years.
Financial assistance: some scholarships available for graduate students.
Applications: by 1 August, to the above address for further information.

🐣 Graduate Scholarships
Study Domains: all major fields.
Scholarships: (a) graduate teaching and graduate service assistantships for postgraduate study; (b) university graduate visa student scholarships; (c) Scholarships, fellowships and other awards.
Subjects: (a) and (b) unrestricted; (c) postgraduate study in agricultural and veterinary sciences, arts, biological science, social sciences and physical sciences.
Open to: candidates of all nationalities who are: (a) graduates of a recognized university or college; (b) eligible for graduate study, with first-class academic record and nominations by academic department; (c) graduates of a recognized university or college with a first-class average in previous study; proficiency in English required.
Duration: (a) and (c) 1 year (renewable); (b) 2 to 3 years.
Value: variable.
Applications: to the above address for further information.

397 University of New Brunswick, Fredericton Campus
PO Box 44000
E3B 5A3 Fredericton, New Brunswick
Tel: +1-506-453-4865
Fax: +1-506-453-5016
Web: http://www.unb.ca/prospective/international/
e-mail: qc2@unb.ca

📖 Undergraduate, Graduate, Postgraduate Programmes
Study Domains: all major fields.
Programmes: (a) Bachelor's degrees in business administration, arts, computer science, data analysis, education, engineering, forestry, law, nursing, physical education and recreation, science, office management and forest engineering; (b) Master's degrees in arts, business administration, computer science, education, engineering, forestry, physical education and recreation, science and public administration; (c) Doctoral degrees in arts, computer science, engineering, forestry and science; (d) Diploma courses in engineering (land information management); (e) Certificate in administration (business or public); (f) Special programmes in fields such as Atlantic studies, bio-psychology, linguistics, theatre production and language certification as well as Year Abroad programmes in certain disciplines; (g) Extension programmes.
Open to: (a), (e), (f), and (g) candidates having successfully completed secondary studies, (for Bachelor of Law, previous Bachelor's degree required); (b) and (c) candidates with honours Bachelor's degree with cumulative grade point average of at least 3.0 or equivalent; (d) candidates with undergraduate degree in related field of study such as engineering or surveying engineering, geography, computer science, urban and regional planning, agriculture and forestry; students whose mother tongue is not English must present proof of English proficiency; candidates over 20 years of age who do not meet normal entrance requirements but have been in the work force for at least two years prior to application may be considered on a mature student basis.
Duration: (a) and (f) normally 4 years; post-graduate Bachelor of education degree, 1½ to 2 years; Bachelor of science, engineering and forest engineering, forestry, 5 years; Bachelor of laws, 3 years; (b) 1 to 2 years; (c) 2 to 3 years; (d) and (e) 1 year; (g) variable.
Fees: see website for details.
Financial assistance: some entrance and undergraduate scholarships, loans, research grants and university fellowships available.
Applications: (a), (e), (f) and (g) by 31 March, to Registrar's Office; (b), (c) and (d) by 1 March, to the Graduate School.

398   University of Northern British Columbia [UNBC]

3333 University Way
Prince George
VZN 4Z9 British Columbia
Tel: +1-250-960-5555
Fax: +1-250-960-5794
Web: http://www.unbc.ca
e-mail: internat@unbc.ca

Undergraduate, Graduate Programmes

Study Domains: accounting, anthropology, arts, biology, business, chemistry, computer science, economy, education, finance, forestry, geography, geology, health and hygiene, history, international business, international studies, languages, liberal arts, marketing, natural resources, nursing, physics, political science, psychology, sciences, social work, tourism, hotel and catering management.
Programmes: certificates, Bachelor's, Master's and Ph.D. degrees in all major fields.
Subjects: certificates in Aboriginal Comm. Resource Planning; First Nations Language; First Nations Public Administration; Metis Studies; Nisga'a Studies; Public Administration; Rural and Northern Nursing; Traditional Environmental knowledge.
Fees: tuition fees: C$253 per credit hour; living costs: C$8,000 to C$10,000.
Financial assistance: not available.
Languages: English.
Applications: deadline to apply for Fall term: 1 April; deadline for Winter term: 3 January.

399   University of Ottawa, School of Graduate Studies and Research

Case postale 450
550 rue Cumberland, Succursale A
K1N 6N5 Ottawa, Ontario
Tel: +1-613-562-5800
Fax: +1-613-562-5103
Web: http://www.uottawa.ca/international/students/
e-mail: eureka@uottawa.ca

Undergraduate, Graduate, Postgraduate Programmes

Study Domains: all major fields, nursing, political science, Russian, speech therapy.
Programmes: degree programmes at all levels and in all major fields especially: (a) Master of Science in Nursing programme; (b) collaborative Master's programme in women's studies; (c) Master of Arts in Russian language and literature; (d) Doctorate of Philosophy in Russian language and literature; (e) collaborative Ph.D. programme in Canadian studies.
Duration: 4 years for Master's degree; 6 years for Ph.D.
Fees: foreign student tuition: approximately C$15,000.
Financial assistance: scholarships, loans and teaching assistantships available; waiver of foreign student differential in some cases.
Languages: instruction in English and French.
Applications: by 1 February, at the above address.

400   University of Regina

AH 431, 3737 Wascana Parkway
S4S 0A2 Regina, Saskatchewan
Tel: +1-306-585-4161
Fax: +1-306-585-4893
Web: http://www.uregina.ca/gradstudies/
e-mail: grad.studies@uregina.ca

Undergraduate, Graduate, Postgraduate Programmes

Study Domains: all major fields.
Programmes: Bachelor's, Master's, Ph.D. degrees in all major fields.
Fees: see website at: http://www.uregina.ca.
Languages: English.
Applications: to the Dean of Graduate Studies and Research.

Graduate Assistantships and Scholarships

Study Domains: administration, cultural studies, education, engineering, fine arts, sciences, social sciences, social work.
Scholarships: (a) Teaching Assistantships; (b) University Graduate Scholarships; (c) Research Assistantships - awarded in Spring/Summer only.
Subjects: administration, education, engineering, fine arts, humanities, health studies, interdisciplinary studies, science, social science, social work.
Open to: students of any country with high academic standing, who have been accepted into a graduate programme at the University of Regina as fully qualified Master's or Ph.D. degree candidates; teaching assistants may also apply for Summer scholarships.
Duration: up to 5 semesters for Master's degree; up to 9 semesters for Ph.D.
Value: (a) Doctoral level: C$4,519; Master's degree level: C$3,965; (b) Doctoral level: C$5,000; Master's degree level: C$4,500; (c) Doctoral level C$4,300; Master's degree level: C$3,800.
Applications: (a) (b) 28 February, 15 June, 15 October; (c) 28 February; to the Dean of Graduate Studies and Research at the above address.

401   University of Saskatchewan [UOS]

105 Administration Place
S7N 5A2 Saskatoon, Saskatchewan
Tel: +1-306-966-4343
Fax: +1-306-966-8670
Web: http://www.usask.ca/registrar
e-mail: registrar@usask.ca

Undergraduate, Graduate, Postgraduate Programmes

Study Domains: all major fields.
Programmes: Bachelor's, Master's, Ph.D. degrees in all major fields.
Financial assistance: some financial assistance for graduate students.
Languages: English.
Applications: see website for further information.

Graduate Scholarships and Teaching Fellowships

Study Domains: agriculture, education, engineering, medicine, nursing, pharmacy and pharmacology, physical education, sciences, social sciences, veterinary medicine.
Scholarships: (a) Graduate Scholarships; (b) Graduate Teaching Fellowships.
Subjects: humanities, social sciences, science, education, agriculture, engineering, pharmacy, medicine, veterinary medicine, nursing and physical education.
Open to: nationals of all countries who will have graduated or expect to graduate from an approved university with a four-year honours Baccalaureate or equivalent, or a Master's degree.
Duration: 1 academic year (renewable on application).
Value: (a) Ph.D., C$15,600; Master's degree, C$12,000; (b) C$11,267.
Applications: by 1 December, to the department in which the student plans to study.

402   University of Sudbury [UOS]

935, Ramsey Lake Road
P3E 2C6 Sudbury, Ontario
Tel: +1-705-673-5661
Fax: +1-705-673-4912
Web: http://www.usudbury.ca
e-mail: registrar@usudbury.ca

Undergraduate Programme

Study Domains: cultural studies, philosophy, theology, religion.
Programmes: general and honours Bachelor of Arts in philosophy, religious studies, native studies, French Canadian folklore.
Open to: qualified students of all nationalities; extension programmes for credit available.
Duration: 3 to 4 years.

Financial assistance: some financial awards available; federated with Laurentian University.
Languages: Instruction in English and French.
Applications: to the Laurentian University: luinternational@laurentian.ca.

402 Université de Sudbury [UDS]
935 Chemin du Lac Ramsey
P3E 2C6 Sudbury, Ontario
Tel: +1-705-673-5661
Fax: +1-705-673-4912
Web: http://www.usudbury.ca
e-mail: registrar@usudbury.ca

📖 Programme d'études de 1er cycle
Domaines d'étude: études culturelles, philosophie, théologie, religion.
Programmes: « Baccalauréat » ès arts, général et spécialisé en philosophie, sciences religieuses (cours en anglais et en français), étude des autochtones (cours en anglais) et folklore canadien français (cours en français).
A l'intention de: étudiants qualifiés, de toute nationalité; des programmes d'éducation permanente sont offerts pour l'obtention de crédits.
Durée: de 3 à 4 ans.
Assistance financière: quelques bourses sont offertes pour les personnes fédérées à l'Université Laurentienne.
Inscriptions: au Registraire à l'Université Laurentienne: luinternational@laurentian.ca.

403 University of Toronto [U of T]
International Office
M5S 1 Toronto, Ontario
Tel: +1-416-978-2564
Fax: +1-416-978-4090
Web: http://www.utoronto.ca

📖 Undergraduate, Graduate, Postgraduate Programmes
Study Domains: all major fields.
Programmes: Bachelor's, Master's, Ph.D. degrees in all major fields.
Languages: English.
Applications: undergraduate admissions: ask@adm.utoronto.ca; also see: www.utoronto.ca/prospectivestudents.html; graduate admissions: graduate.information@utoronto.ca; also see: www.sgs.utoronto.ca.

🎓 Financial aid
Study Domains: arts, sciences.
Duration: 1 year, non renewable.
Value: C$2,000.
Applications: by admission deadline to Registrar's, contact Sally Walker, +1 416 978-2460. Academic excellence required.

404 University of Toronto, School of Graduate Studies
63 Saint George Street
M5S 2Z9 Toronto, Ontario
Tel: +1-416-978-2377
Fax: +1-416-978-4367
Web: http://www.sgs.utoronto.ca/prospective/internati onal
e-mail: graduate.information@utoronto.ca

🎓 Scholarships
Study Domains: all major fields.
Scholarships: (a) University of Toronto Open Scholarships (approx. 2,500); (b) Connaught Scholarships (100).
Subjects: unrestricted, graduate study.
Open to: (a) and (b) nationals of all countries, with an excellent academic record and proficiency in English.
Duration: 1 academic year (renewable for a maximum of 3 years).
Value: (a) C$3,600-$10,000; (b) C$11,000 per year plus tuition fees.
Applications: (a) and (b) by 1 February, to the Chairman of the appropriate graduate department; see website for further information.

405 University of Waterloo [UOW]
200 University Avenue West
N2L 3G1 Waterloo, Ontario
Tel: +1-519-888-4567
Fax: +1-519-725-9971
Web: http://www.international.uwaterloo.ca/prospecti ve.htm
e-mail: dknight@waterloo.ca

📖 Undergraduate, Graduate, Postgraduate Programmes
Study Domains: accounting, anthropology, applied arts, applied sciences, architecture, arts, Asian studies, biochemistry, biology, botany, business, cancerology, chemical engineering, chemistry, civil engineering, classical studies, computer science, development studies, earth science, ecology, environment, economic and commercial sciences, economy, engineering, European studies, finance, fine arts, geography, geology, health and hygiene, history, human sciences, hydrology, industry and commerce, information science, international relations, international studies, languages, liberal arts, linguistics, literature and civilization, mathematics, mechanical engineering, microbiology, music and musicology, natural history, natural resources, natural sciences, philosophy, physics, political science, psychology, recreation and leisure, sciences, social sciences, social work, sociology, statistics, tourism, hotel and catering management, trade, urbanism.
Programmes: Bachelors, Masters, Ph.D. degrees in all major fields.
Open to: candidates of any country, fulfilling the necessary requirements.
Duration: variable according to the course; courses begin in September.
Fees: registration: C$50; tuition fees: C$4,567 per term.
Languages: English.

🎓 Undergraduate Entrance Scholarships; Graduate Studies
Study Domains: all major fields.
Description: varies by department; see website above.
Open to: (a) all entering students may be considered based on specific criteria for each award.
Duration: (a) 1-4 academic years.
Value: (a) C$500-$25,000.
Applications: undergraduate studies: www.findoutmore.uwaterloo.ca/financing; graduate studies: www.grad.uwaterloo.ca/scholarships/aid.asp.; for more information www.askthewarrior.ca.

406 University of Western Ontario [UWO]
1151 Richmond Street
N6A 3K7 London, Ontario
Tel: +1-519-661-3031
Web: http://www.uwo.ca
e-mail: iss@sdc.uwo.ca

📖 Undergraduate, Graduate, Postgraduate Programmes
Study Domains: all major fields.
Programmes: (a) Bachelor's degrees in all major fields; (b) Master's degrees; (c) doctoral degrees; (d) Diplomas/Certificates.
Open to: students of all nationalities fulfilling the necessary requirements; proof of English proficiency needed for non-English first language students; correspondence, evening and other undergraduate extension courses offered for credit; counselling and career placement services available; special arrangements and facilities open to handicapped students.
Duration: (a) and (c) 3 to 4 years; (b) 1 to 2 years (courses begin in Summer, Fall and Winter); (d) variable.
Applications: undergraduates: by 1 June (1 March is the latest date applications will be sent to those applying from out-of-country); graduates: variable (students should contact the department approximately 8 to 9 months prior to anticipated starting date); to the Registrar.

407 University of Western Ontario, Faculty of Information and Media Studies [UWO/FIMS]

North Campus Building, Room 240
N6A 5B7 London, Ontario
Tel: +1-519-661-3542
Fax: +1-519-661-3506
Web: http://www.fims.uwo.ca

Graduate Degree Programme

Study Domains: audio-visual media, information science, journalism, library science.
Programmes: Bachelor's, Master's and PhD programmes in journalism and information and media studies.
Open to: candidates with a 4-year honours degree from a Canadian university or equivalent; TOEFL score of 640 for applicants whose first language is not English.
Duration: 12 months; courses begin in May.
Languages: instruction in English.
Applications: by 15 October, to the Dean for further information.

408 Wilfrid Laurier University [WLU]

75 University Avenue
N2L 3C5 Waterloo, ON
Tel: +1-519-884-0710
Web: http://www.wlu.ca
e-mail: liaison@wlu.ca

Undergraduate, Graduate, Postgraduate Programmes

Study Domains: biology, chemistry, computer science, marketing, mathematics, physics, political science, psychology, social work, sociology.
Programmes: Bachelor's, Master's, Ph.D. degrees in biology; chemistry; computer science; physics; mathematics; also short-term study in non-degree programmes, distance education and Summer courses.
Duration: 3 or 4 years; Summer courses also available.
Financial assistance: no financial assistance available.
Languages: English.
Applications: September, January and May.

409 York University [YorkU]

4700 Keele Street
M3J 1 Toronto, Ontario
Tel: +1-416-736-2100
Fax: +1-416-736-5700
Web: http://www.yorku.ca
e-mail: president@yorku.ca

International Awards

Study Domains: all major fields.
Scholarships: (a) Global Leader of Tomorrow; (b) York University offers over 550 awards and scholarships available to international students. Check the Awards Web Search at www.yorku.ca/osfs for other York University scholarships.
Open to: (a) International high school students with outstanding scholastic record nominated by their high school.
Duration: 4 academic years.
Value: (a) full tuition (C$10,500 in academic year 2004-5).
Applications: (a) applications should be received by 1 April to Global Leadership Committee Office of Admission, York University at the above address; (b) Admissions Office, Student Services Centre, York University at the above address. Consult website www.yorku.ca/osfs for further information.

Chile

Año académico: Marzo a diciembre.
Organización de la enseñanza superior:
El Ministerio de Educación es el encargado de desarrollar e implementar políticas y de asignar recursos públicos para la educación superior; el Consejo superior de educación (CSE), es el encargado de acreditar a las nuevas instituciones de educación superior y el Consejo de Rectores de Universidades Chilenas es el encargado de coordinar las universidades del CruCH.
La educación formal se ofrece en tres tipos de instituciones: universidades, institutos profesionales (IP) y centros de formación técnica. (CFT)
La educación superior técnica no universitaria conduce a Títulos Profesionales (8 semestres) y a títulos de Técnico Superior (4 o 5 semestres).
La educación superior universitaria propone niveles de Licenciatura o Título Profesional (4 a 7 años), Magister (2 años más) y Doctorado (3 o 4 años más).
Moneda nacional: Peso chileno.
Admisiones para estudiantes del país: Se requiere la Licencia de Educación Media. Las Universidades bajo el CruCH (y algunas otras) exigen haber rendido la prueba de Selección Universitaria (PSU). Para algunas universidades se requieren pruebas de selección específica.
Admisiones para estudiantes extranjeros: Certificado de fin de estudios de enseñanza media y prueba de aptitud académica.
Conocimientos lingüísticos: Es indispensable dominar suficientemente el idioma español. Algunas instituciones organizan cursos de español para estudiantes extranjeros que deben perfeccionar sus conocimientos lingüísticos. Los institutos binacionales de cultura organizan cursos de lengua española de orientación y adaptación para los estudiantes extranjeros.
Formalidades de inmigración: Obtención del visado de estudiante-residente cuya validez es de un año (renovable anualmente); debe solicitarse en el consulado de Chile del país de origen del estudiante, previa presentación de un certificado del centro de estudio acreditando que hay plaza vacante; quedan exentos de este requisito los estudiantes españoles y los procedentes de países limítrofes.
Importe de gastos para un año universita: Los costos asociados deben soilicitarse a la institución que ofrezca el programa correspondiente, pues dependen de la institución, el tipo de carrera y la ciudad donde se ubique, entre otros. La matrícula tiene un costo anual que fluctúa entre los 500.000 pesos y 5.000.000 de pesos aproximadamente.
Servicios de información:
(a) Consejo de Rectores de Universidades Chilenas, PO Box 14798, Alameda Bernardo O'Higgins 1371, Santiago; Tel: +56-2-6964286, Fax: +56-2-6988436, email: cruch@entelchile.net; web: http://www.cruch.cl;
(b) Ministerio de Educación, División de Educación Superior, Alameda Bernardo O'Higgins 1371, Santiago; Tel.: +56-2-3904401, Fax: +56-2380333, email: superior@mineduc.cl, web: http://www.mineduc.cl,
(c) Consejo Superior de Educación (CSE), Marchant Perira 844, PRovidencia, Santiago, Tel. +56-23413412, Fax: +56-2-2254616, email: consejos@cse.cl, web: http://www.cse.cl.
Becas para estudiantes internacionales: La Agencia de Cooperación Internacional (www.agci.cl) difunde, entre otras, información sobre la Beca República de Chile, otorgada a estudiantes sudamericanos para estudios de posgrado en Chile.
Enseñanza abierta y a distancia: la Universidad de Chile presenta un listado de cursos (pregrado, postítulo, por facultad/instituto/programa).
Convalidación de estudios y diplomas: el proceso lo realiza la Universidad de Chile, la cual acepta y certifica que una persona posee un título profesional o un grado académico obtenido en el extranjero.
La solicitud se hace en la Prorrectoría de la Universidad de Chile, Oficina de Reconocimiento, Revalidación y Convalidación de Grados y Títulos Profesionales Obtenidos en el Extranjero,
Av. Bernardo O'Higgins 1058, Oficina 120, Santiago. Tel.: +56-2-678-1023, Fax: +56-2-6781032.
Servicios de alojamiento para estudiante: solicitar la información en la institución donde se realizarán los estudios.

Posibilidades de empleo: dependen del tipo de visa obtenido y de las facilidades que otorga la institución educativa.
Publicaciones / Sitios web:
• "Guía Académica" editada por la Comisión Coordinadora del Proceso de Admisión a las Universidades Chilenas, calle Cienfuegos 81, Santiago.
• "Información para estudiantes extranjeros" editada por la Secretaría General del Consejo de Rectores de las Universidades Chilenas, Moneda 673, Santiago.

410 Gobierno de Chile Agencia de Cooperación Internacional (AGCI)

Teatinos 950, Piso 11
Santiago de Chile
Tel: (56 2) 399-0900
Fax: (53 2) 399-0992
Web: http://www.agci.cl
e-mail: agencia@agci.cl

☞ Programa de becas

Campos de estudios: todas las materias principales.
Descripción: La AGCI proporciona información sobre becas:
(a) para chilenos en el extranjero: ofertas vigentes y permanentes (becas que oferta la Cooperación Internacional, otros programas de becas sobre los cuales AGCI registra información, otros instrumentos que facilitan el perfeccionamiento en el exterior);
(b) para extranjeros en Chile: becas de cooperación horizontal;
(c) otras ofertas;
(d) cursos y seminarios.
Se conceden: (b) a profesionales con título universitario que se desempeñen como funcionarios del Estado (Gobierno) del que son nacionales, en Ministerios o servicios públicos, así como a académicos docentes o investigadores de Universidades oficialmente reconocidas por sus respectivos países, y que tenga su domicilio en el país de origen. Ests becas se aplican a candidatos de Costa Rica, El Salvador, Guatemala, Honduras, Nicaragua, Panamá, República Dominicana, Cuba, Belice, Ecuador, Bolivia, Paraguay y Perú.
Duración: (b) por el tiempo que dure la realización del curso para el cual se haya presentado la postulación.
Importe: (b) pasaje de ida y vuelta, asignación mensual, costo total de los estudios universitarios, seguro de salud y accidentes, asignación para gastos de instalación y materiales de estudio.
Solicitudes: (b) Los antecedentes para postular a las becas deben presentarse a la institución gubernamental local nominada como "punto focal" en cada país, y enviar una copia a la Embajada de Chile en el país del postulante; sitio web: http://www.agci.cl/becas_extranjeros.html.

411 Instituto Latinoamericano de Doctrina y Estudios Sociales [ILADES]

Amirante Barroso N° 6
Casilla 14446, Correo 21
Santiago
Tel: (56) (2) 6951778
Fax: (56) (2) 698 6873

☞ Programa de becas

Campos de estudios: ciencias económicas y comerciales, ciencias políticas, ciencias sociales, economía, estudios sobre el desarrollo, sociología, teología, religión.
Descripción:
(a) Becas de estudio en ciencias sociales (10 por año);
(b) Becas de ayuda financiera para estudios de magister en doctrina y ética social.
Materias de estudio: (a) economía, sociología, ciencias políticas, ética, teología; (b) ética social y política, análisis socioeconómico, doctrina social de la Iglesia.
Se conceden: (a) a graduados universitarios en ciencias sociales de América Latina, menores de 35 años; es deseable que conozcan el inglés; (b) a ejecutivos de gobierno y dirigentes políticos, dirigentes de organizaciones sociales y ejecutivos de empresas, sacerdotes, religiosos(as) y agentes de

organizaciones no gubernamentales, agentes pastorales.
Duración: (a) 2 años; (b) 1 año (renovable).
Solicitudes: (a) hasta el último día hábil de noviembre, dirigirse al Departamento de Ciencias Sociales; (b) hasta diciembre, dirigirse al Director del Magister.

412 Instituto Latinoamericano de Doctrina y Estudios Sociales [ILADES]

Almirante Barroso N° 6
Correo 21
Santiago
Tel: (56) (2) 695 1778
Fax: (56) (2) 698 6873

☐ Programas de estudio

Campos de estudios: ciencias humanas, ciencias políticas, ciencias sociales, economía, economía política, estudios sobre el desarrollo, historia del arte, relaciones internacionales, sociología, teología, religión.
Descripción:
(a) Diploma latinoamericano en relaciones internacionales y negociación;
(b) Diploma en doctrina social de la Iglesia y gestión del desarrollo: ciencias humanas, análisis socioeconómico;
(c) Programa de licenciatura en ciencias sociales y doctrina social de la Iglesia (ILADES - Pontificia Universidad Gregoriana de Roma): economía, sociología, ciencias políticas, ética, teología;
(d) Programa de posgrado en economía (ILADES - Georgetown University) conducente al "Master of Arts in Economics" con especializaciones en economía de las políticas sociales, en economía de empresas, en economía general;
(e) Magister en doctrina y ética social: ética social y política, análisis socioeconómico, doctrina social de la Iglesia;
(f) Magister en estudios sociales y políticos latinoamericanos; 3 especialidades: democracia y gobernabilidad, relaciones internacionales, integración regional.
Se destina(n): (a) a graduados universitarios, profesionales vinculados a la problemática, funcionarios de la administración pública y de organizaciones internacionales;
(b) a profesionales, sacerdotes, religiosos(as), dirigentes sociales; (c) a graduados universitarios en ciencias sociales de América Latina; (d) a profesionales menores de 35 años, titulados en ingeniería comercial, industrial, civil, matemáticas, etc.; (e) a ejecutivos de gobierno y dirigentes políticos, dirigentes de organizaciones sociales y ejecutivos de empresas, sacerdotes, religiosos(as) y agentes de organizaciones no gubernamentales, agentes pastorales; (f) a graduados universitarios de diversas disciplinas afines, a profesionales universitarios vinculados al ámbito social, económico o político, nacional o internacional.
Se dicta(n): (a) y (f) por ILADES, Universidad de Deusto (Bilbao, España) y Pontificia Universidad Javeriana (Bogotá, Colombia), con apoyo de la CEPAL.
Duración: (a) 1 año (comienzo en mayo); (b) 9 meses (se inicia en marzo); (c) a (f) 2 años (se inician en marzo y (d) comienza a mediados de agosto).
Asistencia financiera: (c) 10 becas anuales; (d) 15 becas anuales otorgadas por el Banco Interamericano de Desarrollo a alumnos que sigan la mención Políticas Sociales. Comprenden la matrícula por 2 años y monto mensual para manutención; (f) monto anual (renovable).
Inscripciones: (a) en la Coordinación del Diploma; (b) hasta marzo; (c) hasta el último día hábil de noviembre, en el Departamento de Ciencias Sociales; (f) en la Coordinación del Magister.

413 Instituto Nacional de Enfermedades Respiratorias y Cirugía Torácica [INERCyT]

Avenida J. M. Infante 717
Casilla 9634 - Correo Central
Santiago
Tel: (56) (2) 2358888
Fax: (56) (2) 2355833

📖 Programa de cursos y conferencias

Campos de estudios: cirugía, educación física, fisiología, inmunología, medicina.
Descripción:
(a) Curso de asma bronquial;
(b) Curso de fisiología y fisiopatología respiratoria;
(c) Ciclo de conferencias sobre inmunología y pulmón; (en inglés y traducción simultánea en español);
(d) Curso de perfeccionamiento en epidemiología de tuberculosis y administración de programas de control de la tuberculosis;
(e) Curso de avances en terapia intensiva respiratoria (nuevas técnicas en ventilación mecánica por patología).
Se destina(n): a nacionales de cualquier país que: (a) sean graduados en medicina; (b) posean título de médico cirujano o equivalente; (c) sean graduados en medicina o en ciencias biológicas; (d) sean médicos o especialistas en salud pública que tengan intereses o responsabilidades en control de tuberculosis; (e) a chilenos o hispanoamericanos, de edad comprendida entre 25 y 35 años, que sean médicos neumológicos o internistas.
Duración: (a) y (c) 3 días; (b) 1 semana; (d) 10 días; (e) 1 mes en septiembre.
Inscripciones: en el Departamento de Docencia del INERyCT.

414 Pontificia Universidad Católica de Chile Dirección de Intercambio Académico y Relaciones Internacionales [PUCCH]

Avda. Libertador Bernardo O'Higgins 340 Oficina 31
Casilla 114 - D
Santiago
Tel: (56) (2) 686 2415
Fax: (56) (2) 222 3116
Web: http://www.puc.cl/dri

🐦 Programa de becas

Campos de estudios: psicología.
Becas: (a) Becas de Fundación Andes;
(b) Becas de la Fundación Ford;
(c) Programa especial de becas "Presidente de la República";
(d) Becas Fulbright;
(e) Becas Holanda para investigación doctoral y postdoctoral;
(f) Programa de Residencia Rockefeller de Humanidades;
(g) Becas Mutis (España);
(h) Programa Alban de la Unión Europea;
(i) Becas UNESCO/Keizo ObuchiI del Gobierno de Japón;
(j) Programa Delnet de la Organización Internacional del Trabajo;
(k) Becas de la Fundación Internacional Matsumae.
Descripción: (a) Programa de inicio de carrera para jóvenes investigadores: apoyo a jóvenes investigadores en el desarrollo de su propia línea de investigación mediante el financiamiento de proyectos que conduzcan a nuevos conocimientos o aplicaciones;
(b) Programa internacional de becas de la Fundación Ford, Región andina y Cono Sur: ofrece a mujeres y hombres, sin límite de edad, la oportunidad de alcanzar el grado de Maestría o Doctorado, seleccionándolos en base a su capacidad y proyección de liderazgo en sus respectivos campos, así como a su potencial académico y al compromiso para contribuir con el desarrollo de sus grupos de referencia y/o de sus comunidades de origen;
(c) Estudios de posgrado en el extranjero;
(d) Programa para universitarios e investigadores chilenos para la realización de investigaciones avanzadas en universidades o centros de investigación en los Estados Unidos;
(e) Becas de investigación post-doctoral: incluyen dinero para viajes, costos de investigación y salario, conforme a los estándares locales. Becas de investigación para doctorado: la propuesta debe incluir un cronograma de investigación y el/la postulante deberá demostrar que puede completar realistamente su borrador de tesis doctoral en el tiempo señalado. Este tipo de becas normalmente no incluye salario;
(f) El tema de este programa, "Desigualdades persistentes en Latinoamerica" promueve investigación actual sobre el problema central del cómo y el porqué Latinoamerica ha

mantenido a través de muchos siglos, una de las sociedades y culturas mas desiguales del mundo. La desigualdad aborda dimensiones sociales, políticas, históricas, culturales y éticas, que van más allá del enfoque tradicional dado en la ciencias sociales. Estamos a la búsqueda principalmente de académicos latinoamericanos o del Caribe;
(h) Becas para estudios de postgrado, formación especializada superior para profesionales y reciclaje, en la Unión Europea;
(i) Becas para candidatos de los Estados Miembros de la UNESCO que cumplan con los requisitos necesarios, destinadas a promover trabajos de investigación post-universitarios;
(j) Programa orientado a técnicos y gestores del desarrollo local y la descentralización;
(k) Becas para realizar proyectos de investigación en Japón.
Materias de estudio: (a) todas las áreas del conocimiento, excepto medicina humana, salud pública, salud animal y odontología;
(f) cualquier campo (o tema en particular) de las humanidades, ciencias sociales o históricas, para ampliación o innovación en el estudio de las desigualdades;
(i) medio ambiente; diálogo intercultural; tecnologías de la información y la comunicación; solución pacífica de los conflictos.
Duración: (e) Becas de investigación post-doctoral: pueden extenderse, desde un mínimo de tres meses hasta un máximo de dos años. Becas de investigación para doctorado: cubren un período de uno a tres años.
Solicitudes: dirigirse a la Dirección de Intercambio Académico y Asuntos Internacionales que ofrece información sobre becas, intercambio, estudiantes extranjeros, becas permanentes (estudios de postgrado en el extranjero, en América latina, organismos que ofrecen becas).

415 Pontificia Universidad Católica de Chile Facultad de Agronomía e Ingeniería Forestal [PUCDC]

Casilla 306, Correo 22
Santiago
Tel: (56) (2) 6864122
Fax: (56) (2) 6865727
Web: http://www.puc.cl

📖 Programas universitarios

Campos de estudios: agricultura, ciencias agronómicas, ciencias veterinarias, economía, zoología.
Descripción:
(a) Magister en ciencias agropecuarias (producción de cultivos);
(b) Magister en economía agraria;
(c) Magister en producción animal.
Se destina(n): a nacionales de cualquier país: (a) ingenieros agrónomos o con título equivalente, en el área de la producción vegetal; existe evaluación de conocimientos; (b) que posean título profesional o grado académico de licenciado en áreas de agronomía y economía agraria, o a otros profesionales interesados en los problemas económicos y de administración de los sectores silvoagropecuario y agroindustrial, los recursos naturales y el medio ambiente; (c) ingenieros agrónomos, médicos veterinarios, zootecnistas, o profesionales del área de la producción animal, que tengan grado académico equivalente de licenciado o bachiller.
Duración: (a) y (c) 3 semestres más tesis; (b) 2 semestres más tesis de grado; todos comienzan en marzo y en agosto.
Asistencia financiera: (a) existen becas completas (pasajes, asignación mensual, matrícula durante 2 años, seguro médico y otros beneficios) para candidatos de Argentina, Bolivia, Colombia, Ecuador, Paraguay, Perú, Uruguay y Venezuela, por convenio con el Servicio de Intercambio Académico Alemán; (b) como (a) y existen además becas para chilenos; (c) becas de mantención y matrícula para alumnos nacionales y extranjeros, otorgadas por OEA, BID, CIID, AEC y diversos programas de cooperación; se otorga también 1 beca como (a).
Inscripciones: fechas de postulaciones: noviembre y mayo; para solicitud de formularios, envío de postulaciones y mayores informaciones, dirigirse a la Dirección del Programa de Posgrado que figura en la dirección del título, o por e-mail: (a) mcadcv@sas.puc.cl; (b) postagro@sas.puc.cl; (c) admzoo@sas.puc.cl.

**416 Pontificia Universidad Católica de Chile
Facultad de Ciencias Biológicas [PUCCH]**
Avenida Libertador B. O'Higgins 340
Casilla 114-D
Santiago
Fax: (56) (2) 6862369
Web: http://www.puc.cl

☐ **Programas universitarios**

Campos de estudios: biología, bioquímica, botánica, ciencias, ciencias agronómicas, ciencias naturales, ecología, medio ambiente, genética, inmunología, microbiología.
Descripción:
(a) Magister en bioquímica;
(b) Doctorado en ciencias biológicas, con menciones en biología celular y molecular, en ciencias fisiológicas, en ecología.
Se destina(n): (a) a licenciados en bioquímica, o a candidatos con grado o título profesional de contenido equivalente; (b) a licenciados en ciencias biológicas y bioquímica, médicos, agrónomos, veterinarios y en general a graduados o titulados universitarios con formación equivalente y experiencia en investigación.
Duración: (a) 4 semestres; (b) 8 semestres.
Asistencia financiera: (a) becas de matrícula y/o mantención; (b) varias posibilidades de becas.
Inscripciones: antes del 15 de octubre del año anterior para postulaciones al 1er semestre, antes del 1° de junio para postulaciones al segundo semestre; solicitar informes a la Dirección de Posgrado.

**417 Pontificia Universidad Católica de Chile
Facultad de Ciencias Sociales [PUCCH]**
Campus San Joaquín
Vicuña Mackenna 4860
Santiago
Tel: (56) (2) 5525700
Fax: (56) (2) 5533092
Web: http://www.puc.cl

☐ **Programas universitarios**

Campos de estudios: ciencias sociales, psicología, sociología, trabajo social.
Descripción:
(a) Psicólogo y licenciado en psicología;
(b) Asistente social y licenciado en trabajo social;
(c) Sociólogo y licenciado en sociología;
(d) Postítulo en estudios de la familia;
(e) Magister en psicología.
Se destina(n): a nacionales y extranjeros: (a) a (c) que hayan cursado por lo menos los 2 últimos años de la enseñanza en el extranjero o 2 períodos académicos de una misma carrera en universidades chilenas o extranjeras; (d) a licenciados y/o titulados profesionales con experiencia en el área; (e) licenciados en psicología.
Duración: (a) y (c) 10 semestres; (b) 9 semestres; (d) 2 semestres; (e) 4 semestres.
Asistencia financiera: (a) a (c) crédito fiscal universitario; (e) becas de posgrado que representan 30% del arancel de la matrícula.
Inscripciones: (a) a (d) hasta diciembre del año anterior al de los estudios; (e) en diciembre-enero, en la Escuela de Psicología, en la dirección que figura en el título.

**418 Pontificia Universidad Católica de Chile
Facultad de Educación [PUCCH]**
Avenida Jaime Guzmán Errázuriz 3300
Santiago
Tel: (56) (2) 6865043
Web: http://www.puc.cl

☐ **Programas universitarios**

Campos de estudios: administración, educación, educación de la primera infancia, educación especial, formación profesional.

Descripción:
(a) Licenciado en educación y educador de párvulos, y licenciado en educación y profesor de educación general básica;
(b) Licenciado en educación y profesor de educación media en: castellano, inglés, francés, alemán, historia, geografía y educación cívica, filosofía, artes plásticas, matemáticas, matemáticas y física, ciencias naturales y biología, ciencias naturales y química, religión y moral;
(c) Postítulo en administración de organizaciones educativas;
(d) Postítulo en consejería educacional y vocacional, con menciones para la educación básica, para la educación media;
(e) Postítulo en curriculum y evaluación escolar;
(f) Postítulo en educación especial y diferencial;
(g) Magister en ciencias de la educación, con menciones en curriculum y en medición y evaluación institucional;
(h) Magister en diseño de instrucción;
(i) Magister en educación, mención administración educacional;
(j) Magister en educación especial;
(k) Doctorado en ciencias de la educación.
Se destina(n): a nacionales de cualquier país: (a) y (b) que hayan cursado por lo menos los 2 últimos años de la enseñanza media en el extranjero o 2 períodos académicos de una misma carrera en universidades chilenas o extranjeras; de (c) a (k) que tengan el grado de licenciado en educación o un título profesional equivalente.
Duración: (a) 8 semestres; (b) 9 semestres; de (c) a (e) 3 semestres; de (g) a (k) 6 semestres.
Asistencia financiera: (c) a (f) becas de matrícula; (g) a (k) becas.
Inscripciones: hasta noviembre del año anterior al de los estudios, en la Subdirección de Asuntos Estudiantiles de la Facultad de Educación, en la dirección que figura en el título.

**419 Pontificia Universidad Católica de Chile
Facultad de Ingeniería [PUCCH]**
Vicuña Mackenna 4860
Casilla 306 Correo 22
Santiago
Tel: (56) (2) 6864232
Fax: (56) (2) 5524054
Web: http://www.puc.cl

☐ **Programas universitarios**

Campos de estudios: construcción, electricidad y electrónica, gestión, informática, ingeniería, ingeniería civil.
Descripción:
(a) Ingeniería Civil con especialidad en ingeniería: de construcción, estructural, hidráulica, de transporte; de minería o ambiental; civil de industrias con especialidad en ingeniería de computación, eléctrica, mecánica, química, de transporte; licenciatura en ciencias de la ingeniería;
(b) Constructor civil;
(c) Postítulo en gestión informática;
(d) Posgrado (magister y doctorado) en ciencias de la ingeniería;
(e) Postítulo en administración de empresas constructoras, mención en desarrollo immobiliario.
Se destina(n): a nacionales y extranjeros: (a) y (b) que hayan cursado por lo menos los 2 últimos años de la enseñanza media en el extranjero o 2 períodos académicos de una misma carrera en universidades chilenas o extranjeras y que superen prueba de conocimientos en matemáticas; (c) a licenciados o titulados profesionales universitarios y experiencia laboral o estudios universitarios en informática; (d) a licenciados en ciencias de la ingeniería, a ingenieros civiles, o graduados académicos o titulados profesionales universitarios en disciplinas afines; (e) a titulados profesionales universitarios con experiencia de 2 años en empresa constructora.
Duración: (a) 12 semestres; (b) 10 semestres; (c) 4 bimestres; (d) 3 semestres el magister y 7 semestres el doctorado; (e) 6 trimestres repartidos en 19 meses.
Asistencia financiera: existen diversas modalidades de apoyo: premios, becas y préstamos.
Inscripciones: (a) y (b) hasta diciembre; (c) 1° al 15 de diciembre en el Departamento de Ciencias de la Computación; (d) antes del 15 de diciembre o del 15 de mayo

según el semestre, en la Dirección de Posgrado de la Escuela de Ingeniería; (e) hasta el 31 de mayo para el curso que se inicia a fines de junio, en el Centro de Extensión de la PUCCH, Alameda 390, 4°piso, Santiago.

420 Pontificia Universidad Católica de Chile Facultad de Matemáticas [PUCCH]
Vicuña Mackenna 4860
Casilla 306
Santiago
Tel: (56) (2) 5525916
Web: http://www.puc.cl

📖 Programas universitarios

Campos de estudios: ciencias, estadística, informática, matemáticas.
Descripción:
(a) Licenciatura en matemáticas con mención matemática, estadística o computación;
(b) Magister en estadística;
(c) Doctorado en ciencias exactas, mención matemática;
(d) Magister en ciencias exactas, mención matemática.
Se destina(n): a chilenos o extranjeros: (a) que posean una licencia de enseñanza media o secundaria; (b) a licenciados en matemáticas mención estadística, o licenciados en estadística, o titulados equivalentes; (c) y (d) a licenciados en ciencias o equivalente a licenciatura en matemática.
Duración: (a) 10 semestres; (b) y (d) 4 semestres; (c) de 8 a 10 semestres.
Asistencia financiera: (b) becas de matrícula y/o mantención; (c) y (d) becas de matrícula.
Inscripciones: (a) hasta noviembre; (b) julio-octubre, al Jefe de Programa de Magister en Estadística, en la dirección que figura en el título; (c) y (d) Oficina de Coordinación del Posgrado en Matemáticas, en la dirección que figura en el título.

421 Pontificia Universidad Católica de Chile Facultad de Medicina [PUCCH]
Vicuña Mackenna 4686
Santiago
Tel: (56) (2) 6396794
Fax: (56) (2) 6331457
Web: http://www.puc.cl

📖 Programas de postítulos

Campos de estudios: cirugía, enfermería, higiene y salud, inmunología, medicina, neurología, obstetricia y ginecología, pediatría, radiología, urología.
Descripción:
(a) Especialidades básicas: anestesiología, anatomía patológica, cirugía general, laboratorio clínico, medicina nuclear, medicina interna, neurocirugía, neurología, obstetricia y ginecología, pediatría, radiología, traumatología y ortopedia;
(b) Sub-especialidades: cardiología, cirugía cardiovascular, cirugía digestiva, cirugía vascular periférica, endocrinología, enfermedades respiratorias, gastroenterología, hematología, immunología clínica y reumatología, nefrología, urología;
(c) Otros: enfermería del adulto con mención en enfermería oncológica, en cuidados respiratorios, neuroquirúrgica, en nefrourología, en cardiología, geriátrica; en enfermería pediátrica con mención en enfermería del recién nacido de alto riesgo, cardiológica infantil, en cuidados intensivos pediátricos, oncológica infantil; en enfermería médico-quirúrgica en cirugía cardiovascular; en enfermería en salud mental y psiquiatría; en enfermería en obstetricia de alto riesgo.
Se destina(n): (a) y (b) a candidatos que cumplan diversos requisitos relacionados con la especialidad, cuya edad no supere los 30 años para (a) y 35 años para (b); (c) a candidatas con título de enfermera o enfermera matrona según corresponda.
Duración: (a) 3 años (comienzan en mayo); (b) 2 años; (c) entre 2 y 4 semestres.
Asistencia financiera: (a) y (b) becas por la totalidad del programa.
Inscripciones: (a) y (b) en diciembre, en la Secretaría de la

Dirección de Posgrado de la Escuela de Medicina, Lira 44, 2° piso o a la casilla 114-D; los extranjeros deben solicitar previamente la lista de documentos que le serán exigidos para su expediente personal y el formulario de postulación que completará los datos sobre sus antecedentes personales y profesionales; (c) en noviembre, Escuela de Enfermería.

422 Pontificia Universidad Católica de Chile Facultad de Teología [PUCCH]
Avenida Jaime Guzmán Errázuriz 3300
Casilla 316
Santiago
Tel: (56) (2) 256164
Web: http://www.puc.cl

📖 Programas universitarios

Campos de estudios: teología, religión.
Descripción:
(a) Licenciatura en teología;
(b) Doctorado en teología.
Se destina(n): (a) a bachilleres en teología, o en ciertas condiciones, a quienes hayan realizados estudios teológicos en institución de formación sacerdotal; (b) a licenciados en teología.
Duración: (a) 5 semestres; (b) entre 2 y 4 años.
Asistencia financiera: se puede postular a ayudas para elaboración de tesis o memorias.

423 Universidad "Diego Portales" [UDP]
Ejército 233
Santiago
Tel: (56) (2) 671 2190
Fax: (56) (2) 676 2815
Web: http://www.udp.cl
e-mail: rene.lara@udp.cl

📖 Programas universitarios

Campos de estudios: todas las materias principales, arquitectura, ciencias de la información, ciencias económicas y comerciales, ciencias humanas, derecho, educación, ingeniería, medicina.
Descripción: cursos de pregrado y posgrado en sus facultades de arquitectura, diseño y bellas artes, ciencias de la comunicación e información, ciencias humanas y educación, ciencias de la ingeniería, ciencias de la salud, derecho, economía y empresa, humanidades.
Asistencia financiera: diversas posibilidades de becas y estudios en el extranjero, programas de intercambio; solicitar información a la Dirección de Intercambio Estudiantil Internacional en la dirección del título o consultar la página web http://www.udp.cl/rrii/portada.htm.
Inscripciones: dirigirse a Admisiones, Av. Manuel Rodríguez Sur 361, Santiago, o por correo electrónico a admision@udp.cl.

424 Universidad "José Santos Ossa" [UJSO]
Los Inmigrantes 733
Antofagasta
Tel: (56) (5) 535 0011
Fax: (56) (5) 535 0010
Web: http://www.ujso.cl

📖 Carreras y diplomados universitarios

Campos de estudios: administración, comercio, contabilidad, ecología, medio ambiente, educación, educación de la primera infancia, formación de docentes, gestión, psicología, trabajo social.
Descripción: programas en sus escuelas de ciencias sociales, de negocios, de educación, de artes y comunicación:
(a) Carreras: psicología, trabajo social; comercio, contaduría auditoría; educación parvularia, psicopedagogía, pedagogía en historia, en lengua castellana;
(b) Diplomados: administración de empresas, administración y gestión de bodegas, técnicas de gestión aplicadas a asistentes ejecutivas, gestión y administración de recursos humanos, medio ambiente, educación general.
Asistencia financiera: becas internas, becas externas, convenios. Solicitar información a la Dirección de Asuntos Estudiantiles.

Inscripciones: dirigirse al Servicio de Admisiones en la dirección del título o a admision@ujso.cl.

425   Universidad Academia de Humanismo Cristiano [UACH]
Condell 343
Santiago
Tel: (56) 787 80 00
Fax: (56) 787 80 22
Web: http://www.academia.cl
e-mail: cleiva@academia.cl

📖 Programas universitarios

Campos de estudios: educación, estudios sobre el desarrollo, trabajo social.
Descripción:
(a) Magister en desarrollo regional y local;
(b) Maestría en trabajo social;
(c) Maestría en investigación educativa.
Se destina(n): a graduados académicos o titulados profesionales.
Duración: 2 años académcios.

426   Universidad Austral de Chile Instituto de Ciencia y Tecnología de Alimentos [UACH]
Casilla 47
Valdivia
Tel: (56) 63 213911
Web: http://www.uach.cl

📖 Programas universitarios

Campos de estudios: alimentación, industria alimentaría, ingeniería, microbiología, química, tecnología, tecnología industrial.
Descripción:
(a) Cursos teórico-prácticos en las esferas de la química y microbiología de la leche y productos lácteos, tecnologías específicas de productos lácteos y mantención de industrias lecheras;
(b) Programa de especialización para personal de la industria lechera, que comprende cursos teórico-prácticos de química y microbiología de la leche, tecnologías de quesos, yogur, mantequilla, etc., administración, ingeniería y mantención de industrias lecheras;
(c) Magister en ciencia y tecnología de la leche.
Se destina(n): a nacionales de los países de América Latina: (a) seleccionados por los organismos de la industria lechera de su país; (b) cuyas actividades estén relacionadas con la industria lechera (además, cada curso tiene requerimientos específicos); (c) que posean título universitario en agronomía, medicina veterinaria, tecnología de alimentos, ingeniería, ciencias naturales u otras áreas afines.
Se dicta(n): (a) 1 curso por año, en Valdivia; (b) cada semestre; (c) todos los años.
Duración: (a) 5 semanas (empiezan en julio); (b) 1 o 2 semestres (5 cursos cada uno), (empiezan en marzo); (c) 2 años (empiezan en marzo).
Inscripciones: (a) en el Instituto de Ciencia y Tecnología de los Alimentos, 2 meses antes del inicio; (b) 2 semanas antes de la fecha de iniciación de cada curso, en el ICYTAL; (c) hasta diciembre de cada año se reciben las postulaciones para el curso que se inicia en marzo del año siguiente.

427   Universidad Austral de Chile [UACH]
Casilla 567
Valdivia
Tel: (56) 63 221259
Fax: (56) 63 221258
Web: http://www.uach.cl

📖 Programas universitarios

Campos de estudios: todas las materias principales.
Descripción:
(a) Ciencias: magister en ciencias (mención botánica, ecología, genética, inmunología, microbiología, zoología), magister en física;

(b) Ciencias agrarias: magister en ciencias (mención ciencias vegetales, producción animal), magister en ciencia y tecnología de la leche, magister en desarrollo rural;
(c) Ciencias económicas y administrativas: magister en economía y gestión regional, magister en administración de empresas;
(d) Ciencias forestales: magister en ciencias (mención silvicultura), magister en ciencias y tecnología de la madera;
(e) Ciencias de la ingeniería: diplomado en ingeniería;
(f) Ciencias veterinarias: magister en ciencias (mención reproducción animal, salud animal, medicina preventiva veterinaria, patología animal); programa de postítulo en ciencias clínicas veterinarias (mención equinos, pequeños animales, rumiantes);
(g) Filosofía y humanidades: magister en filología; programa de educación continua (licenciatura en educación, especialista en ecología ambiental, cursos para directores de educación general
básica);
(h) Medicina: postítulo de especialista (anatomía patológica, cirugía, hematología, laboratorio clínico, medicina interna, microbiología clínica, nefrología, obstetricia y ginecología, oncología y radioterapia, ortopedia y traumatología, pediatría, psiquiatría adultos, urología); programa de adiestramiento para médicos generales (pediatría, obstetricia, psiquiatría, traumatología infantil para pediatras o cirujanos infantiles, medicina interna, salud pública); programa de especialización para enfermería en salud familiar y comunitaria; magister en ciencias (mención anatomía, inmunología, patología, biología celular); programa de doctorado en ciencias biológicas, área inmunología.
Se destina(n): a nacionales o extranjeros (egresados de la enseñanza media por los programas de pregrados) y graduados o titulados (programas de posgrado).
Duración: variable según la carrera, entre 4 y 7 años.
Inscripciones: pregrado: postulaciones hasta la primera semana de enero; matrículas en la primera de marzo en la dirección que figura en el título.

428   Universidad Bolivariana
Huérfanos 2917
Santiago
Tel: (56) (2) 756 3000
Fax: (56) (2) 681 5689
Web: http://www.ubolivariana.com
e-mail: admision@ubolivariana.com

📖 Programas universitarios

Campos de estudios: antropología, comunicación, derecho, economía, educación, gestión, periodismo, psicología, trabajo social.
Descripción:
(a) Estudios de pregrado: carreras de antropología social, derecho, economía, periodismo, psicología;
(b) Postgrados y formación continua en gestión pública, educación, gerontología social, estudios del comportamiento comunicacional.
Se destina(n): en el caso de extranjeros, a quienes superen examen de ingreso (en diciembre-marzo).
Inscripciones: por mayor información, dirigirse a la Dirección de Admisión.

429   Universidad Católica "Cardenal Raúl Silva Henríquez" [UCSH]
Casilla 8 Correo 2
Santiago
Tel: (56) (2) 460 1100
Fax: (56) (2) 635 4192
Web: http://www.ucsh.cl
e-mail: universidad@ucsh.cl

📖 Carreras universitarias

Campos de estudios: administración, educación, educación especial, educación física, formación de docentes, informática, matemáticas, sociología, teología, religión, trabajo social.
Descripción: programas universitarios en áreas de: auditoría, educación parvularia; ingeniería comercial; ingeniería de ejecución en administración; pedagogía en religión, en educación básica, en educación diferencial, en educación física, en filosofía, en historia y geografía, en

inglés, en matemáticas e informática educativa; sociología; trabajo social.
Inscripciones: por mayor información, dirigirse a Relaciones Institucionales.

430 Universidad Católica de Valparaíso [UCDV]
Avenida Brasil 2950
Casilla 4059
Valparaíso
Tel: (56) 32 273278
Fax: (56) 32 273398
Web: http://www.ucv.cl

📖 **Programas de pregrado**

Campos de estudios: todas las materias principales.
Descripción: conducen a los grados de licenciado (o bachiller en algunos casos) en las siguientes áreas:
(a) Agronomía;
(b) Arquitectura, arte, diseño gráfico, diseño industrial;
(c) Ciencias, biología, ciencias naturales, bioquímica, estadística, física, kinesiología, matemáticas, óptica, química, química industrial;
(d) Contaduría auditoría, ingeniería comercial, servicio social;
(e) Derecho, ciencias jurídicas;
(f) Educación y filosofía: castellano, castellano y comunicación; educación: diferencial, física, general básica, parvularia; filosofía, historia y geografía, historia, geografía y ciencias sociales, inglés, interpretación-traducción inglés español, interpretación musical en instrumento principal, música, psicología;
(g) Ingeniería civil bioquímica, eléctrica, electrónica, industrial, informática, mecánica, química, en metalurgia extractiva; ingeniería de transporte, eléctrica, electrónica, en construcción, mecánica; ingeniería de ejecución en bioprocesos, en electricidad, en electrónica, en informática, en mecánica;
(h) Geografía, ingeniería de alimentos, ingeniería pesquera, oceanografía;
(i) Ciencias religiosas, pedagogía en religión;
(j) Periodismo, comunicación social.
Se destina(n): a nacionales de cualquier país que hayan completado estudios equivalentes a la enseñanza media o que cumplan diversas condiciones.
Duración: los semestres van de marzo a julio y agosto a diciembre.
Asistencia financiera: para los programas de pregrado, existen becas de monto variable hasta el equivalente del valor de la matrícula.
Inscripciones: por más información, dirigirse a la Dirección de Admisión y Registro.

431 Universidad Católica de Valparaíso [UCV]
Avenida Brasil 2950
Casilla 4059
Valparaíso
Tel: (56) (3) 227 3288
Fax: (56) (3) 227 3420
Web: http://www.ucv.cl

📖 **Programas de postgrado**

Campos de estudios: todas las materias principales.
Descripción:
(a) Magister en ciencias biológicas con mención en ecología sistemática; magister en ciencias microbiológicas; magister en ciencias con mención en física; magister en estadística; magister en matemática; magister en enseñanza de las ciencias con mención en didáctica de la matemática; magister en ciencias con mención en química; doctorado en ciencias con mención en química;
(b) Magister en gestión con mención en control;
(c) Magister en educación con mención en curriculum; doctorado y magister en filosofía; magister en historia; magister en lingüística aplicada; doctorado en lingüística; magister en literatura hispánica; doctorado en literatura;
(d) Magister en ciencias de la ingeniería con menciones en ingeniería bioquímica, en ingeniería química o en ingeniería eléctrica;
Programas de postítulo (diplomados):
(e) Ciencias actuariales;

(f) Técnicas de la representación con propósitos educacionales, desarrollo de la comunicación escrita, administración educacional;
(g) Sistemas eléctricos de potencia;
(h) Administración regional y municipal, administración legislativa.
Se destina(n): a graduados o titulados con condiciones variables según el programa.
Duración: los semestres van de marzo a julio y de agosto a diciembre.
Inscripciones: por más información, dirigirse a la Dirección General de Postgrado.

432 Universidad Católica del Maule [UCM]
Avenida San Miguel 3605
Talca
Tel: (56) (7) 120 33 00
Fax: (56) (7) 124 17 67
Web: http://www.ucm.cl

📖 **Programas universitarios**

Campos de estudios: todas las materias principales, ciencias agronómicas, construcción, educación, enfermería, informática, ingeniería, silvicultura, teología, religión, trabajo social.
Descripción:
Estudios en sus facultades de ciencias agrarias y forestales, religiosas y filosóficas, de la ingeniería, de la salud:
(a) Pregrados: licenciatura en agronomía; ingeniería forestal, técnico universitario en programación computacional, ingeniería civil informática, en construcción; pedagogía en religón y filosofía, general básica, en educación física, parvularia, especial y diferencial; licenciatura en enfermería, en kinesiología, en psicología, en trabajo social;
(b) Posgrados: magister en salud pública, en pedagogía universitaria, en educación;
(c) Postítulos: licenciado en trabajo social, ingeniería en educación forestal, informática educativa, educación general básica, prevención de riesgos;
(d) Diplomaturas: cuidados paliativos, estudios teológicos.
Inscripciones: por mayor información, dirigirse al Departamento de Admisión y Registros Académicos.

433 Universidad Católica del Norte [UCN]
Avenida Angamos 610
Antofagasta
Chile
Tel: (56) (5) 535 5000
Fax: (56) (5) 535 5059
Web: http://www.ucn.cl
e-mail: pavicel@ucn.cl

🐟 **Programa de becas**

Campos de estudios: todas las materias principales.
Descripción: (a) Fuentes de becas para estudios de posgrado en el extranjero: Agencia de Cooperación Internacional de Chile - AGCI; Mideplan, Conicyt, Fundación Andes, Fundación Ford, Banco Interamericano de Desarrollo;
(b) Estudios en el extranjero: Alemania (DAAD), Canadá, España, Estados Unidos de América (Comisión Fulbright de los Estados Unidos, Instituto Chileno Norteamericano), Inglaterra (British Council);
(b) Becas para estudios de posgrado en la UCN a través de la Agencia de Cooperación Internacional de Chile (AGCI) y el Consejo Superior de Ciencia y Tecnología.
Materias de estudio: (c) las que se pueden cursar en las facultades de la UCN: arquitectura, construcción e ingeniería civil, economía y administración, humanidades, ingeniería y ciencias geológicas, ciencias del mar, derecho, teología.
Se conceden: (a) y (b) alumnos chilenos de la UCN; (c) a extranjeros.
Solicitudes: por mayor información, dirigirse a Relaciones Institucionales de la UCN, en la dirección del título.

**434 Universidad Católica del Norte
[UCN]**
Avenida Angamos 610
Antofagasta
Tel: (56) (5) 535 5000
Fax: (56) (5) 535 5059
Web: http://www.ucn.cl

Cursos de pregrado y postgrado

Campos de estudios: todas las materias principales,
arquitectura, ciencias, ciencias del mar, ciencias económicas y
comerciales, derecho, educación, ingeniería, medicina,
teología, religión.
Descripción:
(a) Arquitectura, construcción, ingeniería civil; posgrado:
información geográfica;
(b) Ciencias: química y farmacia, física (mención en
astronomía), química (química ambiental en metalurgia
extractiva, analista químico, química), matemáticas
(pedadogía en matemáticas y computación, matemáticas,
estadística); posgrados: magister en ciencias mención en
matemáticas, magister en matemáticas (Cochabamba,
Bolivia);
(c) Ciencias del mar: acuicultura, ingeniería marina,
prevención de riesgos y medioambiente; posgrados en
acuicultura, en ciencias del mar;
(d) Economía y administración: ingeniería comercial,
contador-auditor-contador público; posgrados: magister en
contabilidad y auditoría, en dirección de empresas;
(e) Humanidades: periodismo, psicología;
(f) Ingeniería y ciencias geológicas: geología; ingeniería civil
y de ejecución (computación e informática, industrial,
metalurgia, química), ingeniería civil ambiental; posgrados:
magister en geología económica, en aplicación de ingeniería
ambiental, doctorado en ciencias (mención geología);
(g) Derecho;
(h) Ingeniería comercial;
(i) Medicina (cirugía);
(j) Ciencias religiosas, pedagogía en filosofía y religión.
Se destina(n): a extranjeros que ingresen: (a) por vía
especial en el caso de pregrados, acreditando nivel de estudios
y presentando documentación requerida, (b) cumpliendo los
requisitos de cada programa.
Asistencia financiera: diversas posibilidades de becas,
programas de interacambio y de movilidad.
Inscripciones: dirigirse al Servicio de Admisión (en la
dirección del título o e-mail: admision@ucn.cl).

**435 Universidad de Chile
Facultad de Arquitectura y
Urbanismo
Departamento de Geografía**
Marcoleta 250
Casilla 3387
Santiago
Fax: (56) (2) 798 1486
Web: http://www.uchile.cl

Programa de Magister en geografía

Campos de estudios: desarrollo comunitario, desarrollo
rural, geografía, urbanismo.
Descripción: menciones en recursos territoriales y en
organización urbano regional.
Se destina(n): a chilenos y extranjeros que posean el grado
de licenciado en la disciplina o un título profesional
equivalente.
Duración: 2 años (3 semestres más 1 semestre para la
tesis).
Inscripciones: hasta fines de marzo.

**436 Universidad de Chile
Facultad de Ciencias
Económicas y Administrativas
Escuela de Economía y
Administración para
Graduados**
Diagonal Paraguay 257
Torre 26, oficinas 1801-1806
Casilla 9727
Santiago

Tel: (56) (2) 678 2000
Web: http://www.uchile.cl

Programa de postítulos

Campos de estudios: administración, administración de
empresas, ciencias económicas y comerciales, contabilidad,
economía, finanzas, informática.
Descripción:
(a) Programa de Magister en economía;
(b) Programa de Magister en finanzas;
(c) Programa de Magister en administración (MBA);
(d) Postítulos en Evaluación de proyectos, Auditoría
computacional y Economía y finanzas para abogados; 80
participantes en el MBA; 30 participantes en los otros
programas; para (a) a (c) existe un curso preparatorio.
Duración: (a) y (b) 2 años (comienzan en marzo y julio);
(c) 2 años (comienzan en marzo); (d) 1 año (comienzan en
marzo); curso preparatorio: comienza en marzo y julio.
Asistencia financiera: la Escuela otorga becas parciales a
quienes hayan obtenido excelentes calificaciones durante sus
estudios universitarios.
Inscripciones: (a) a (d) los períodos normales de
postulación para los programas de Magister finalizan el 15 de
diciembre y el 15 de mayo de cada año según el semestre.

**437 Universidad de Chile
Facultad de Ciencias
Físicas y Matemáticas
Departamento de Geofísica**
Blanco Encalada 2085
Casilla 2777
Santiago
Tel: (56) (2) 696 6563
Fax: (56) (2) 696 8686
Web: http://www.uchile.cl

Programa multinacional de geofísica (nivel magister)

Campos de estudios: ciencias de la tierra, física, geología.
Descripción: geofísica aplicada, geofísica de la tierra
sólida y ciencias atmosféricas.
Se destina(n): a estudiantes de los países de América
Latina que tengan el grado de bachiller o licenciado en
ciencias, en geología o en ingeniería.
Duración: de 2 a 3 años (empiezan en marzo y en julio);
los candidatos que no posean una formación básica en
geofísica o en ciencias de la tierra deben seguir un plan de
nivelación.
Asistencia financiera: la Organización de los Estados
Americanos (OEA) puede conceder algunas becas para
estudiantes no chilenos (deben solicitarse directamente en la
Secretaría General de la OEA, Washington, D.C. 20006,
Estados Unidos de América).
Inscripciones: en diciembre o en junio.

**438 Universidad de Chile
Facultad de Ciencias
Físicas y Matemáticas
Escuela de Posgrado**
Beauchef 850
Casilla 2777
Santiago
Web: http://www.uchile.cl

Programas universitarios

Campos de estudios: administración, astronomía, ciencias,
ciencias de la información, física, geología, informática,
ingeniería, metalurgia, química.
Descripción:
(a) Programa de magister en gestión y políticas públicas;
(b) Programa de magister en ciencias con menciones en
astronomía, computación, física, geofísica, geología, química;
(c) Programa de magister en ciencias de la ingeniería con
menciones en ingeniería biomédica, electricidad, industrial,
matemáticas aplicadas, mecánica, sísmica, transporte,
química;
(d) Programa de doctorado en ciencias con menciones en
física, geología, química, computación;
(e) Programa de doctorado en ciencias de la ingeniería con
menciones en ciencias de los materiales, modelación
matemática, química, automática;

(f) Programas de especialización profesional: preparación y evaluación de proyectos para ingenieros y sistemas de información administrativos;
(g) Programa de especialización profesional: contaminación ambiental.
Se destina(n): a nacionales de cualquier país que tengan los diplomas necesarios para poder cursar la disciplina elegida.
Duración: (a) 3 semestres; (b) y (c) de 4 a 6 semestres; (d) y (e) de 6 a 8 semestres; (f) y (g) 2 semestres.
Asistencia financiera: becas semestrales (renovables en casos especiales) que cubren parte del arancel de programa. Solicitudes a comienzo de cada semestre.
Inscripciones: las postulaciones se efectúan en diciembre para los ingresos en marzo y en junio para los ingresos en agosto.

439　Universidad de Chile Facultad de Medicina Escuela de Posgrado
Independencia 1027
Santiago
Fax: (56) (2) 735 7279
Web: http://www.uchile.cl

☛ Becas para realización de estudios sobre neumotisiología
Campos de estudios: cirugía, medicina.
Se conceden: a chilenos e hispanoamericanos, de edad comprendida entre 25 y 35 años, que sean médicos cirujanos con diploma en medicina interna, que conozcan el español y el inglés.
Lugar: Instituto Nacional de Enfermedades respiratorias y cirugía torácica, Santiago.
Duración: 2 años (renovable cada año).
Solicitudes: hasta marzo.

440　Universidad de Chile Facultad de Medicina Escuela de Salud Pública
Avenida Independencia 1027
Casilla 70012, Correo 7
Santiago
Fax: (56) (2) 735 5582
Web: http://www.uchile.cl

⌨ Programas universitarios
Campos de estudios: administración, educación, higiene y salud, medicina, psicología, psiquiatría.
Descripción:
(a) Programa de magister en salud pública, con menciones en administración en salud, educación para la salud, epidemiología, salud ambiental, salud materno-infantil, salud ocupacional y salud mental;
(b) Magister en bioestadística;
Programas patrocinados por la Organización Panamericana de la Salud:
(c) Curso de administración hospitalaria para ejecutivos superiores de hospitales;
(d) Curso de estadísticas de salud y registros médicos: estadística general, estadísticas de salud, estadísticas y registros hospitalarios.
Se destina(n): a nacionales de cualquier país que estén en posesión de un grado de licenciado o un título profesional de nivel equivalente, en las áreas de las ciencias biológicas, sociales, o matemáticas obtenido en instituciones de educación superior nacionales o extranjeras. En el caso de postulantes extranjeros, demostrar un adecuado dominio oral y escrito del idioma castellano; (c) ejecer una profesión en las diferentes especialidades de salud y haber desempeñado funciones de jefatura durante 3 años; (d) tener experiencia profesional en estadísticas de salud y registros médicos; además es necesario haber adquirido una experiencia técnica y saber muy bien el español.
Duración: (a) y (b) 3 semestres; (c) 9 meses (empieza en marzo); (d) 7 meses (empieza en junio).
Inscripciones: hasta el 31 de diciembre.

441　Universidad de Chile Instituto de Estudios Internacionales
Condell 249
Casilla 14187 Suc. 21
Santiago
Web: http://www.uchile.cl

⌨ Programas universitarios
Campos de estudios: ciencias económicas y comerciales, ciencias políticas, derecho internacional, economía, economía política, estudios internacionales, relaciones internacionales.
Descripción:
(a) Programa de Magister en Estudios internacionales;
(b) Curso de especialización en Relaciones internacionales.
Se destina(n): a nacionales de cualquier país que posean el grado de licenciado o un título profesional equivalente, con estudios de una duración mínima de 8 semestres.
Duración: (a) 2 años (comienza en marzo); (b) 1 año (comienza en agosto).
Asistencia financiera: becas parciales de arancel de la Universidad de Chile a partir del segundo semestre; becas de Agencia de Cooperación a estudiantes de ciertos países latinoamericanos; becas OEA a estudiantes de países miembros.
Inscripciones: (a) de diciembre a marzo; alumnos especiales en cualquier momento; (b) de marzo a agosto; alumnos especiales en cualquier momento.

442　Universidad de Chile Instituto Interamericano de Educación Musical [INTEM]
Compañía 1264
Casilla 2100
Santiago de Chile
Tel: (56) (2) 6718056
Fax: (56) (2) 980506
Web: http://www.musicaysonologia.uchile.cl

⌨ Programa de postgrado en educación musical
Campos de estudios: música y musicología.
Se destina(n): a profesores de educación musical, licenciados en música, tecnólogos del sonido, instrumentistas, compositores, intérpretes musicales que podrán orientarse en el campo de la informática aplicada a la música o en la docencia musical.
Duración: 2 semestres (comienzo en abril).
Asistencia financiera: 4 medias becas para latinoamericanos.
Inscripciones: dirigirse a la Secretaría del INTEM.

443　Universidad de la Frontera
Avenida Francisco Salazar 1145
Campus Andrés Bello
Casilla 54-D
Temuco
Tel: (56) 45 252627
Fax: (56) 45 252547
Web: http://www.ufro.cl

⌨ Programas Magister
Campos de estudios: ciencias sociales, comunicación, medicina.
Descripción:
(a) Ciencias de la comunicación;
(b) Ciencias sociales aplicadas (convenio con la Universidad de París XII, Val-de-Marne, Francia);
(c) Epidemiología clínica.
Se destina(n): (a) a profesionales de la comunicación o de otras áreas que tengan intereses o realicentareas afines; (b) a postulantes de 40 años como máximo, titulados profesionales en áreas afines a las ciencias sociales; (c) a profesionales de la salud.
Duración: (a) y (b) 2 años (comienzo de cursos en abril); (c) 1 año en forma flexible, en un período no mayor de 3 años (comienzo de cursos en marzo).
Asistencia financiera: posibilidad de postular a becas: (a) de estudio de la CONICYT; (c) becas de la International Clinical Epidemiology Network.
Inscripciones: dirigirse al Coordinador del Programa Magister que corresponda, a la Casilla 54-D, Temuco: (a) hasta enero; (b) hasta febrero; (c) hasta abril.

444 Universidad de la Serena

Casilla 599
La Serena
Tel: (56) 51 225406
Fax: (56) 51 211473
Web: http://www.userena.cl

📖 Programas Magister

Campos de estudios: bioquímica, ecología, medio
ambiente, geología, industria alimentaría, metalurgia,
microbiología, recursos naturales.
Descripción:
(a) Ciencias biológicas mención ecosistemas áridos
(ecosistemas áridos, ecología cuantitativa, gestión vegetal,
ecología animal, bioquímica vegetal, microbiología del
suelo);
(b) Ciencias geográficas (metodología de la investigación
geográfica, percepción remota, manejo de geosistemas
costeros, climatología árida, planificación territorial);
(c) Ingeniería de recursos minerales (diseño de métodos de
explotación minera, bio e hidrometalurgia, geoquímica y
geología ambiental);
(d) Ciencias mención ingeniería de alimentos
(microestructuras en alimentos, fundamentos de biotecnología
y bioprocesos, análisis instrumental, bioquímica de
alimentos).
Se destina(n): (a) a licenciados en ciencias biológicas o
titulados profesionales equivalentes; existe examen escrito de
admisión; (b) a licenciados en ciencias sociales o áreas afines
a las ciencias
geográficas o titulados profesionales equivalentes; existe
examen escrito de admisión y entrevista; (c) egresados o
titulados de la carrera de ingeniería civil de minas o
relacionados con el campo de la minería, la metalurgia
extractiva o la geología; sólo se evalúan los antecedentes
curriculares del candidato; (d) profesionales de alguna carrera
de área de los alimentos o titulado equivalente; sólo se
evalúan los antecedentes curriculares del postulante.
Duración: 2 años (comienzos en marzo y agosto).
Inscripciones: dirigirse a la Dirección de Estudios de
Posgrado.

445 Universidad de los Andes

San Carlos de Apoquindo 2200
Las Condes, Santiago
Tel: (56) (2) 214 1258
Fax: (56) (2) 214 1749
Web: http://www.uandes.cl
e-mail: ecaceres@andes.cl

📖 Programas universitarios

Campos de estudios: todas las materias principales.
Descripción: (a) Pregrados: administración de servicios,
derecho, enfermería, filosofía, ingeniería civil, ingeniería
comercial, medicina, odontología, pedagogía, periodismo,
psicología;
(b) Postgrados: doctorado en filosofía, en derecho;
c) Diplomados: administración y gestión en salud,
administración y gestión de servicios de enfermería, ciencias
de la familia, fundamentación filosófica, sanitario,
implantología oseointegrada.

446 Universidad de Magallanes [UMAG]

Avenida Bulnes 01855
Casilla 113-D
Punta Arenas
Tel: (56) 61 207176
Fax: (56) 61 219276
Web: http://www.umag.cl

📖 Programas universitarios

Campos de estudios: arqueología, biología, ciencias de la
tierra, ciencias humanas, ciencias sociales, geología, historia,
horticultura, ingeniería, investigación.
Descripción:
(a) Programas universitarios en ingeniería, ciencias y
humanidades, ciencias naturales: perfeccionamiento
académico e investigación, siendo las áreas prioritarias
ciencias del mar, ciencias humanas, ciencias de la tierra,
recursos naturales, energía y medioambiente;
(b) Estudios en: procesos educativos no formales, problemas
de salud infantil, planificación ambiental, sistemas antárticos,

estudio de recursos y productos naturales, estudios físicos de
la alta atmósfera, estudios sobre energía no tradicional;
(c) Programas del Instituto de la Patagonia: conocimiento,
desarrollo cultural, social y económico de la Patagonia y
Región Austral en las áreas de biología, historia, arqueología
y geociencias; existe además un centro dedicado a horticultura
y floricultura.
Se destina(n): a nacionales de cualquier país que hayan
terminado los estudios secundarios y posean el nivel necesario
de español.
Asistencia financiera: no se contemplan becas en dinero
para estudiantes extranjeros, salvo para alumnos destacados
en deportes y actividades culturales, una vez ingresados a la
Universidad.

447 Universidad de Playa Ancha de Ciencias de la Educación

Avenida Playa Ancha 850
Casilla 34-V
Valparaíso
Tel: (56) 32 81106
Fax: (56) 32 85041

📖 Programas universitarios

Campos de estudios: artes, biblioteconomía, ciencias,
ciencias naturales, educación, educación de la primera
infancia, educación especial, idiomas, letras, lingüística.
Descripción: (a) Carreras de pregrado: bibliotecología
(mención análisis de sistemas); dibujante proyectista (conduce
también al título profesional de profesor de dibujo técnico),
educación diferencial (menciones deficiencia mental y
trastornos específicos del aprendizaje), educación parvularia,
estadística y computación, geografía, ingeniería ambiental,
ingeniería civil ambiental, ingeniería civil industrial,
kinesiterapia, licenciatura en arte, pedagogía (en artes
plásticas, en biología y ciencias, en castellano, en educación
física, en educación general básica, en educación musical, en
filosofía, en física y computación, en historia y geografía, en
inglés, en matemáticas y computación, en química y ciencias),
periodismo, tecnología en deportes y recreación (menciones
recreación y actividad física adaptadasalud), traducción
alemán-español y técnico universitario en comercio
internacional, traducción e interpretación inglés español,
traducción alemán-español y técnico universitario en turismo,
traducción francés-español y técnico universitario en
comercio internacional, traducción francés-español y técnico
universitario en turismo (estos 4 últimos cursos conducentes
también al título profesional de profesor de alemán y francés,
respectivamente);
(b) Programas de magister y postítulos: consejero educacional
y vocacional, diplomado en estadística e informática, magister
en administración educacional, magister en educación
ambiental, magister en evaluación educacional, magister en
lingüística,
magister en literatura hispanoamericana, magister en
orientación educacional, postítulo en especialización en
educación diferenciada.
Se destina(n): a nacionales de cualquier país que: (a)
hayan terminado los estudios secundarios o hayan cursado por
lo menos 2 años de educación media, con promedio de notas
igual o superior a 5,0 o equivalente (la licencia de educación
media o equivalente, y el certificado de concentración de
notas donde figure la escala y las calificaciones deben estar
traducidas al español y debidamente validados en Chile; los
postulantes pasarán un concurso en noviembre); (b) posean un
título universitario.
Inscripciones: dirigirse a la Unidad de selección y
admisión de alumnos.

448 Universidad de Talca [UTALCA]

Casilla 747
Talca
Tel: (56) (71) 20 0472
Fax: (56) (71) 21 1473
Web: http://www.utalca.cl

📖 Carreras de pregrado y posgrados

Campos de estudios: todas las materias principales.
Descripción: magister, diplomados y doctorados en áreas
de ciencias agrarias, ciencias de la salud, ciencias
empresariales, ciencias forestales, ciencias jurídicas,

ingeniería, biología vegetal y biotecnología, estudios
humanísticos, educación, matemática y física, química de
recursos naturales.
(a) Pregrados: kinesiología; fonoaudiología; agronomía;
arquitectura; contador público y auditor; derecho; ingeniería
comercial (informática, administración); ingeniería en
industrias de la madera; ingeniería forestal; odontología;
psicología; tecnología médica; ingeniería en bioinformática,
mecánica, en computación, civil industrial;
(b) Magisters: agronegocios internacionales, hortofruticultura;
MBA en negocios internacionales y e-business, MBA
Ejecutivo, política y gestión educacional, educación en
ciencias naturales, gestión ambiental;
(c) Doctorados: productos naturales, ciencias (ingeniería
genética vegetal);
(d) Diplomados: litigación oral y proceso penal, ingeniería
industrial, gestión ambiental.
Se dicta(n): en las ciudades de Talca y de Curicó.
Asistencia financiera: Becas doctorales de la Universidad
de Talca; becas para el Programa Master in International
Agribusiness (Magíster en Ciencias Agrarias mención en
Agronegocios Internacionales); otras becas para programas de
magíster para alumnos extranjeros de América Latina y El
Caribe, México y Canadá, a través de la Agencia de
Cooperación Internacional del Gobierno de Chile (AGCI). Por
mayor información, dirigirse a la Dirección de Posgrado, en la
dirección del título o por correo electrónico a
postgrado@utalca.cl.
Inscripciones: para consultas referentes a admisión de
pregrado o postgrado comuníquese a la dirección del título, o
a admision@utalca.cl o postgrado@utalca.cl
respectivamente. Por informaciones referentes a estudiantes
extranjeros, dirigirse a Dirección de Relaciones
Internacionales.

449   Universidad de Temuco [UT]
Avenida Alemania 281
Temuco
Tel: (56) 215252
Fax: (56) 235673

📖 Programas universitarios

Campos de estudios: arquitectura, ciencias sociales,
derecho, diseño, educación de la primera infancia,
informática, periodismo, psicología.
Descripción:
Programas conducentes a diversos grados y títulos
profesionales:
(a) Ingeniería de ejecución en computación e informática;
(b) Contaduría pública y auditoría;
(c) Servicio social;
(d) Educación parvularia;
(e) Diseño gráfico;
(f) Arquitectura;
(g) Psicología;
(h) Derecho;
(i) Periodismo;
(j) Ingeniería forestal;
(k) Ingeniería comercial.
Duración: (a) y (b) 4 años; (c) a (e) y (h) a (k) 5 años; (f) y
(g) 6 años; (todos los cursos comienzan en marzo).
Asistencia financiera: a partir del segundo año académico,
existen becas consistentes en rebajas del arancel.
Inscripciones: hasta marzo, dirigirse al Encargado de
Admisión y Matrícula.

450   Universidad de Valparaíso [UV]
Errazuriz 2190
Casilla 123-V
Valparaíso
Tel: (56) 32 234182
Fax: (56) 32 215687
Web: http://www.uv.cl

📖 Programas universitarios

Campos de estudios: todas las materias principales.
Descripción:
(a) Carreras de pregrado en las siguientes áreas: arquitectura,
ingeniería en construcción, diseño, licenciatura en
matemáticas, licenciatura en matemáticas y analista
computacional, meteorología, ingeniería en estadística,
ingeniería en computación aplicada, derecho, servicio social,
licenciatura en filosofía, licenciatura en historia, medicina,

enfermería y obstetricia, química y farmacia, psicología,
biología marina, fonoaudiología, odontología, ingeniería
comercial, auditoría;
(b) Postítulos en especialidades odontológicas
(odontopediatría, radiología, endodoncia, periodoncia,
prótesis removible);
(c) Postítulos en especialidades médicas (anestesia, cirugía,
medicina interna, neurología, neurocirugía, oftalmología,
otorrinolaringología, oncología, radioterapia, obstetricia y
ginecología, pediatría, psiquiatría, traumatología y ortopedia,
urología, cardiología);
(d) Posgrados: magister en filosofía, en historia, en gestión de
organizaciones con mención en recursos humanos, marketing
y finanzas, en oceanografía con mención en oceanografía
física, química, biológica, en ciencias médicas con mención
en dislipidemias.
Se destina(n): (a) a quienes hayan completado la
educación media completa o al menos los 2 últimos años de
educación media en su país; (b) a cirujanos dentistas que
puedan acreditar 2 certificados de competencia
(recomendaciones); (c) a médicos o cirujanos que puedan
acreditar 2 certificados de competencia (recomendaciones);
(d) a titulados o licenciados que superen entrevista personal;
en el caso del Magister en ciencias médicas, a médicos cuyos
antecedentes serán evaluados por comisión seleccionada.
Duración: (a) el año académico va de marzo a enero; (b) y
(c) 3 años (comienzan en abril); (d) 2 años (comienza en
abril).
Inscripciones: (b) y (c) hasta fin de octubre, (d) hasta
marzo. En todos los casos, solicitar información a la División
Académica, en la dirección del título, o a Dirección de
Vínculos y Cooperación Internacional, Avenida Errazúriz
1108, Valparaíso.

451   Universidad del Bío-Bío
Casilla 5 C
Concepción
Tel: (56) (4) 126 1259
Fax: (56) (4) 132 2883
Web: http://www.ubiobio.cl/home2.htm
e-mail: ubb@ubiobio.cl

📖 Estudios de pregrado y posgrados

Campos de estudios: todas las materias principales.
Descripción: magister, postítulos y diplomados en sus
facultades de:
(a) Arquitectura: arquitectura, urbanismo, ciencias de la
construcción, comunicación visual y diseño industrial;
(b) Ciencias: matemáticas, física, química, ciencias básicas;
(c) Ciencias empresariales: administración, auditoría,
finanzas, computación e informática;
(d) Ciencias de la salud y de los alimentos: agroindustrias,
nutrición y salud pública, enfermería;
(e) Educación y humanidades: artes y letras, ciencias de la
educación, ciencias sociales;
(f) Ingeniería: ingeniería eléctrica y electrónica, industrial, en
maderas, mecánica, civil.
Asistencia financiera: para estudios en la Universidad:
becas de arancel de matrícula de postgrado (media beca) y
becas de investigación de postgrado; becas para estudios en el
extranjero: diversas posibilidades de postulación; solicitar
información a la Dirección de Graduados.
Inscripciones: por mayor información, dirigirse a la
Dirección de Admisión y Registro Académico.

452   Universidad del Pacífico [UP]
Avenida Las Condes 11121
668001 Las Condes
Santiago
Tel: (56) (2) 366 5315
Fax: (56) (2) 366 5318
Web: http://www.upacifico.cl
e-mail: info@upacifico.cl

📖 Programas universitarios

Campos de estudios: todas las materias principales,
administración de empresas, ciencias económicas y
comerciales, comunicación, diseño, educación, periodismo,
psicología, publicidad, trabajo social.
Descripción:
(a) Carreras de grado, posgrados (magister, diplomados,
seminarios y cursos);
(b) Programa Internacional "Study at Pacifico" (un semestre

académico, en calidad de alumno provisional; se podrán
escoger un máximo de veinte créditos por semestre).
Materias de estudio: (a) negocios y marketing; diseño y
multimedia; comunicaciones; ciencias humanas y educación;
(b) comunicaciones y negocios (se podrán escoger un máximo
de veinte créditos por semestre).
Asistencia financiera: becas y ayudas, programas
internacionales y de intercambio.
Inscripciones: solicitar todas las informaciones referentes
a estudiantes extranjeros a la Dirección de Relaciones
Internacionales.

453 Universidad Internacional Sek [UIS]

Av. José Arrieta 10 000
Peñalolén
Santiago
Tel: (56) (2) 279 2940
Fax: (56) (2) 278 3791
Web: http://www.uisek.cl

⊞ Carreras universitarias

Campos de estudios: administración, ciencias económicas
y comerciales, derecho, educación, historia del arte,
periodismo, psicología, turismo, hotelería.
Descripción: enseñanza en sus facultades de ciencias
jurídicas (derecho, administración judicial); ciencias
económicas y administrativas (ingeniería comercial, contador
auditor); estudios del patrimonio cultural (historia del arte,
planificación y gestión turística, arqueología, restauración y
conservación de bienes culturales, artes visuales); psicología
(periodismo, psicología); ciencias de la educación (educación
básica, educación diferencial).
Asistencia financiera: convenios de colaboración con
universidades de América y Europa y programas de práctica
profesional, estancias cortas e intercambio estudiantil con las
sedes en Ecuador y España. Por mayor información, dirigirse
a la Dirección de Relaciones Internacionales en la dirección
del título o a loreto.ortiz@sekmail.com.
Inscripciones: dirigirse al Servicio de Admisiones,
admision@sekmail.com.

454 Universidad Marítima de Chile [UMARITIMA]

Talasia Esquina Halimeda,
Jardín del Mar, Reñaca
Viña del Mar
Tel: (56) (3) 283 9373
Fax: (56) (3) 283 6917
Web: http://www.umaritima.cl
e-mail: info@umaritima.cl

⊞ Programas universitarios

Campos de estudios: todas las materias principales.
Descripción: (a) Carreras: arquitectura, diseño, derecho,
educación parvularia, historia y geografía, ingeniería civil
industria, ingeniería comercial, marina mercante, transporte
marítimo;
(b) Programas de postgrado: diplomado en historia naval,
diplomado en diseño web, administración de la seguridad
privada, administración de transporte marítimo y puertos,
magister en política integrada; master en dirección general de
empresas; curso especial de formación ingeniero;
(c) Programa académico semestral/anual para extranjeros:
durante un semestre o un año académico, en calidad de
alumno extranjero provisional. Amplia alternativa de
complementar con asignaturas de pregrado de distintas áreas
de su interés (dentro de las cuales se podrán escoger un
máximo de cuatro asignaturas); alternativa de consolidar el
dominio del idioma inglés o español como segunda lengua;
(d) Cursos de verano de español para extranjeros.

455 Universidad Metropolitana de Ciencias de la Educación [UMCE]

Avenida José Pedro Alesandri 774
Nuñoa
Santiago
Tel: (56) (2) 744099
Fax: (56) (2) 239067
Web: http://www.umce.cl

⊞ Programas universitarios

Campos de estudios: educación, educación especial.
Descripción:
(a) Carreras de pregrado y posgrado (licenciatura, magister)
en áreas pedagógicas;
(b) Licenciatura en educación diferencial: deficiencia mental,
trastornos de la audición y del lenguaje, trastornos de la
visión, trastornos del aprendizaje.
Se destina(n): (b) a egresados de la enseñanza media con
práctica profesional y/o seminario de título o memoria.
Duración: (b) 4 años (comienza en marzo).

456 Universidad Técnica "Federico Santa María" Escuela de Graduados [UTFSM]

Avenida de España 1680
Casilla 110-V
Valparaíso
Tel: (56) 32 626692
Fax: (56) 32 626532
Web: http://www.utfsm.cl

⊞ Posgrados y doctorados en áreas técnicas

Campos de estudios: ciencias, construcción, electricidad y
electrónica, física, informática, ingeniería, matemáticas,
mecánica, química.
Descripción:
(a) Cursos de posgrado conducentes a los diplomas de
magister en ingeniería eléctrica (especializaciones en sistemas
de potencia, alta tensión o máquinas eléctricas y
accionamientos), ingeniería electrónica (especializaciones en
control automático, o sistemas computacionales y
telecomunicaciones), ingeniería informática
(especializaciones en ingeniería de software, sistemas de
computación o ingeniería asistida por computador), ingeniería
mecánica (especializaciones en ciencias básicas de la
ingeniería mecánica, energía o producción), ingeniería en
mecánica estructural (especializaciones en diseño
sismoresistente, análisis experimental o análisis de
sensibilidad y confiabilidad), ingeniería química
(especializaciones en automatización de procesos,
procesamiento de minerales o ingeniería ambiental), ciencias
mención matemática (especializaciones en sistemas dinámicos
y ecuaciones diferenciales, análisis numérico y complejo o
estadística), ciencias mención física (especializaciones en
física de partículas o campos o física de materia condensada),
ciencias mención química (especializaciones en medio
ambiente, recursos naturales o modelos clásicos y cuánticos
de la materia);
(b) Cursos de doctorado en: ingeniería mecánica
(especializaciones en procesos energéticos o en producción),
ciencias con mención en física (especializaciones en física de
partículas y campos o física de materia condensada).
Se destina(n): a chilenos y extranjeros que posean un
título o grado académico en ingeniería o ciencias; para
postular deben presentar antecedentes: calificaciones,
curriculum vitae y dos cartas de recomendación; en el caso de
doctorado, se exigirá además el conocimiento de otra lengua
además del español.
Duración: (a) 2 años; (b) 4 años; (comienzan en marzo o
julio).
Inscripciones: hasta el 30 de noviembre para el primer
semestre; hasta el 30 de mayo para el segundo semestre.

China

Academic year: September to July.

Organization of higher education system: According to the Higher Education law of the People's Republic of China adopted in 1998, the national government (State Council) shall provide unified guidance and administration for higher education throughout the country, and the governments of provinces, autonomous regions and municipalities directly under the Central Government shall undertake overall coordination of higher education and administration of the higher education institutions in their own administrative regions. The Ministry of Education under the State Council shall be in charge of the work of higher education throughout the country and have some major universities under its jurisdiction. Out of more than 2,200 institutions of higher learning in China in 2005, 73 are under the supervision of the Ministry of Education and most of the others are under the supervision of provincial governments, autonomous regions and municipalities. Programmes are available for both academic qualification and for non-academic qualification in institutions of higher education. Higher education for academic qualification includes special course education, regular course education (undergraduate) and graduate programmes.

The following qualifications are offered at Chinese higher education institutions: (a) Diploma/Certificate, awarded to students who have satisfactorily completed a special course education of two or three years; (b) Bachelor's degree, awarded to students who have satisfactorily completed regular course education of four to five years; (c) Master's degree, awarded to those who have successfully completed postgraduate programme of two to three years; a major thesis is a substantial part of programme; (d) Doctorate degree, awarded to those who have successfully completed a doctorate programme of three to four years after a Master's degree.

Major institutions of higher education: The '211 project' being implemented in China since the beginning of 2000 is concerned with the strengthening of 100 universities and colleges throughout the country. The major universities and colleges in China are all included in the project; at present about 400 universities and colleges in China have foreign students studying on their campuses.

Monetary unit: yuan (RMB).

National student admission: Higher education institutions that offer special course and undergraduate education may accept secondary-school graduates and candidates with an equivalent level based on an entrance examination. Institutions of higher education that offer graduate programmes may accept candidates with undergraduate diplomas for Master's programmes and candidates with equivalent diplomas through an entrance examination; similarly, these institutions may accept Master's degree candidates for doctorate programmes and other candidates with equivalent diplomas through an entrance examination.

International student admission: Both academic qualification programmes and non-academic qualification programmes in Chinese institutions of higher education are open to foreign students. At present there are foreign students studying in Chinese institutions of higher education for academic qualification programmes such as special course, undergraduate, Master's and doctorate programmes as well as in non-academic qualification programmes such as visiting scholar and senior visiting scholar programmes; as Chinese language students and as short-term students. The institutions of higher education each have their own criteria for admission. Generally candidates for academic qualification programmes are accepted on the basis of entrance examinations or academic credentials and related documents, and students working for non-academic qualifications are accepted on the basis of their academic credentials and related documents.

Language: Chinese is the language of instruction in all higher education institutions. A few programmes such as undergraduate programmes in medicine and some graduate programmes are also taught in English or another foreign language.

Immigration requirements: International students in study programmes of greater than 6 months in length must apply for an 'X' visa and present a visa application form (JW 201 or JW202), the admission notice of the institution concerned and medical report. Students in study programmes of less than 6 months must apply for a 'F' visa. Groups of students on short-term programmes may apply for a group 'F' visa accompanied by the invitation letter of the institution concerned. All international students need a residence permit for stays of longer than 6 months. The residence permit may be obtained from the local public security office.

Estimated expenses for one academic year: Variable, according to level of studies and subjects studied.

Information services:
• Chinese embassies or consulates abroad through the appropriate department of the candidate's own government.
• China Scholarship Council; website: http://www.csc.edu.cn.

Scholarships for international students: Government scholarships are available for foreign students studying in the programs of undergraduate, graduate, Chinese language learning, advanced study programmes. Applications for Chinese government scholarships may be made through the Chinese missions in candidate's home country. The China Scholarship Council (CSC) in China is responsible for handling scholarship application; email: laihua@csc.edu.cn; web: http://www.csc.edu.cn.

Open and distance learning: Non-formal studies are offered by the Central Radio and Television University established in 1979. Its courses are accredited by the State Education Commission. The CRTVU offers numerous three-year courses, including mathematics, physics, engineering and electronics, management and agriculture, and Chinese language. Graduates are granted a diploma. There are also forty-three provincial TV universities which work closely with the CRTVU.

Recognition of studies and qualification:
• Academic Degrees Committee under the State Council directs the work pf conferring academic degrees, including Bachelor's, Master's and Doctorate degrees throughout the country
• The Ministry of Education regulates the work of conferring diploma/certificate by institutions of higher education.
• Academic Degree Committee under the State Council: Fax: +86-10-6609-7148; email: xuboliang@moe.edu.cn; web: http://www.moe.gov.cn.

---

457   Beijing Polytechnic University [BPU]

100 Ping Le Yuan
Chaoyang District
100022 Beijing
Tel: +86-10-6739-2071
Fax: +86-10-6739-2319
Web: http://www.bjpu.edu.cn
e-mail: bpuiec@bjpu.edu.cn

📖 **Undergraduate, Graduate, Postgraduate Programmes**

Study Domains: applied sciences, biochemistry, business administration, chemical engineering, chemistry, civil engineering, computer science, ecology, environment, electricity and electronics, energy, engineering, international business, international law, management, mathematics, mechanical engineering, optics, physics, sciences, statistics, technology, telecommunications.

Programmes: Bachelor's, Master's and Ph.D. degree programmes in engineering sciences, management, humanities and social sciences.

458   Beijing University [BU]

5 Yiheyyuan Road
100871 Beijing
Tel: +86-10-6275-1201
Fax: +86-10-6275-1207
Web: http://www.pku.edu.cn/eabout/index.html

📖 **Undergraduate Programmes and Advanced Courses**

Study Domains: all major fields.

Programmes: undergraduate and advanced courses in the following fields: Chinese language and literature, Chinese history, archaeology, political economics, philosophy, classical studies, world history, religion, world economics, national economy administration, history of the international Communist movement, political science, law, international law, international politics, mathematics, chemistry,

biochemistry, biophysics, meteorology, mechanics; Master's and Ph.D. programmes are also available in some selected fields.
Open to: candidates of any nationality.
Duration: undergraduate: 4 years; advanced: 1 to 2 years.
Applications: to the above address for further information.

459 Beijing University of Chinese Medicine

11, East Bei San Hun Road
Chaoyang District
100029 Beijing
Tel: +86-10-6421-3841
Fax: +86-10-6421-3817
Web: http://www.bjucmp.edu.cn
e-mail: bucmpo@public.bta.net.cn

Undergraduate and Advanced Programmes / Traditional Chinese Medicine

Study Domains: Chinese, medicine, obstetrics and gynaecology, paediatrics, pharmacy and pharmacology.
Programmes: Bachelor's degree and advanced courses in the following fields: traditional Chinese medicine, acupuncture, moxibustion and massage, Chinese pharmacology, internal Chinese medicine (including traditional Chinese gynaecology and paediatrics), acupuncture and moxibustion, Chinese pharmacy, basic theory of traditional Chinese medicine, history of Chinese medicine; Master's and Ph.D. programmes are also available in some selected fields.
Open to: candidates of any nationality.
Duration: undergraduate, 5 years; advanced, 1 to 2 years.
Applications: to the above address for further information.

460 Beijing University of Foreign Studies

2, Xisanhuan Bielu
Haidian District
100081 Beijing
Tel: +86-10-6891-6309
Fax: +86-10-6842-3144
Web: http://www.bfsu.edu.cn/english

Undergraduate and Advanced Studies

Study Domains: Chinese, languages, literature and civilization.
Programmes: Bachelor's degree and advanced studies in Chinese language and literature.
Open to: candidates of any country.
Duration: 1 to 2 years.
Applications: to the above address for further information.

461 Beijing University of Physical Education [BUPE]

East Yuanmingyuan Donglu
Haidian District
100084 Beijing
Tel: +86-10-6298-9341
Fax: +86-10-6298-9472
Web: http://www.bupe.edu.cn
e-mail: bupefso@sina.com

Undergraduate, Graduate, Postgraduate Programmes

Study Domains: physical education.
Programmes: Bachelor of Education, Master of Education, Bachelor of Science, Master of Science, Doctor of Science degree programmes in physical education.
Description: courses in wushu, Chinese language, Qigong, tennis, ball games, swimming, sports medicine, sports administration, athletics, gymnastics, wrestling, judo, fencing, boxing.
Open to: candidates of any country with a high school diploma for undergraduate studies, and undergraduate diploma for graduate studies; applicants under 35 years old; fluent Chinese required.
Duration: undergraduate, 4 years; advanced, 1 to 2 years.
Fees: registration: US$50; advanced studies: US$2,000; undergraduate course (per year): US$2,500, approximately.
Applications: by June or December, to the above address for further information.

462 Beijing University of Science and Technology

30 Xueyuanlu
Haidian District
100083 Beijing
Tel: +86-10-6233-2942
Fax: +86-10-6232-7878
Web: http://www.ustb.edu.cn/waishichu/en/index.asp
e-mail: dfa@ustb.edu.cn

Undergraduate Courses in Science and Technology

Study Domains: energy, metallurgy, technology.
Programmes: undergraduate courses in the following fields: mining engineering, mineral processing, mining machinery, iron and steel-making technology, foundry technology, metallic material and heat treatment, plastic working of metals, metallurgical machinery engineering, computer science, industrial automation, metal physics, physical chemistry of metallurgical processing, corrosions and their protections, heat energy engineering; Master's and Ph.D. programmes are also available in some selected fields.
Open to: candidates of any country.
Duration: 4 years.
Applications: to the above address for further information.

463 Central Academy of Drama

39 Dong Mian Hua Hutong
Dongcheng District
100710 Beijing
Tel: +86-10-6403-5626
Fax: +86-10-6401-6479

Undergraduate and Advanced Courses in Theatre

Study Domains: arts, Chinese, performing arts.
Programmes: undergraduate and advanced courses in history of Chinese theatre, stage design, theatre directing and performing; Master's and Ph.D. programmes are also available in some selected fields; non-degree programmes in Chinese language and culture.
Open to: candidates of any country with secondary-school certificate for undergraduate programme; maximum age 25 years; and appropriate degree for graduate courses.
Duration: undergraduate, 4 to 5 years; advanced, 1 to 2 years.
Applications: to the above address for further information.

464 Central Academy of Fine Arts, The [CAFA]

International Office
No.8, Hua Jia Di Nan Jie, Chaoyang District
100102 Beijing
Tel: +86-10-6477-1019
Fax: +86-10-6477-1136
Web: http://www.cafa.com.cn/asp/mfrmlive.htm
e-mail: tie@bjedu.gov.cn

Undergraduate and Advanced Courses in Applied Arts and Design

Study Domains: arts, arts and crafts, industrial design.
Programmes: undergraduate and advanced courses in the following fields: ceramic design, painting and dyeing and weaving embroidery, industrial design, binding and layout of books, commercial arts, costume design, decorative painting and sculpture, metal technology.
Open to: candidates of any nationality.
Duration: undergraduate: 4 years; advanced: 1 year.
Applications: to the above address for further information.

465 Central China Normal University [CCNU]

152 Luoyu Road
430079 Wuhan Hubei
Tel: +86-27-6786-5209
Fax: +86-27-6786-6427
Web: http://www.ccnu.edu.cn
e-mail: cice@mail.ccnu.edu.cn

📖 Undergraduate, Graduate, Postgraduate Programmes

Study Domains: art history, arts, business administration, Chinese, computer science, early childhood education, ecology, environment, economic and commercial sciences, education, engineering, fine arts, information science, journalism, linguistics, physical education, political economy, sciences, social sciences, special education, teacher education, technical education, telecommunications, vocational training.
Programmes: Bachelor's, Master's and Ph.D. degree programmes in liberal arts, education, teacher education; linguistics and other fields; non-degree programmes in Chinese language and culture.
Open to: candidates of all nationalities: Band 3 of HSK is required for degree programmes; Band 6 of HSK is required for Chinese language and literature programmes.
Fees: registration: US$50; tuition US$1,600-$3,200; living costs: US$4,000.
Languages: instruction in Chinese; some classes taught in English.
Applications: by 15 August for degree programmes; any time for language programmes.

☛ CSC and CCNU Scholarships

Study Domains: all major fields.
Scholarships: CSC and CCNU Scholarships.
Value: for CSC scholarship: see website http://www.csc.edu.cn; for CCNU scholarship: see website http://www.ccnu.edu.cn.

466 Central Conservatory of Music [CCOM]
43 Baojia Street
West City District
100031 Beijing
Tel: +86-10-6642-5598
Fax: +86-10-6641-3138
Web: http://www.ccom.edu.cn

📖 Undergraduate and Advanced Courses in Music

Study Domains: music and musicology.
Programmes: undergraduate and advanced courses in theory and technique of music composition, musicology, conducting, vocal music and operatic singing, orchestral, piano, violin, national musical instruments; Master's and Ph.D. programmes are also available in some selected fields.
Open to: candidates of any country.
Duration: undergraduate, 4 to 5 years; advanced, 1 or 2 years.
Applications: to the above address for further information.

467 Chang'an University [CHD]
710061 Xi'an, Shanxi Province
Tel: +86-29-233-8114
Web: http://www.xahu.edu.cn
e-mail: wschu@xahu.edu.cn

📖 Undergraduate, Graduate Programmes

Study Domains: civil engineering, mechanical engineering, transport.
Programmes: Bachelor's, Master's degrees in bridge engineering, highway and urban road engineering, automotive operating engineering, lifting and transport machinery and construction machinery.
Open to: candidates of any nationality.
Duration: undergraduate: 4 years; Master's: 3 years.
Applications: to the above address for further information.

468 Chengdu University of Science and Technology
24, South Section 1
Yihuan Road,
610065 Chengdu, Sichuan Province
Tel: +86-28-8540-2443
Fax: +86-28-8540-3260
Web: http://www.scu.edu.cn
e-mail: wsc@scu.edu.cn

📖 Undergraduate, Graduate and Advanced Courses

Study Domains: all major fields.

Programmes: Bachelor's, Master's degrees and advanced courses in all major fields.
Open to: candidates of any nationality.
Duration: from 1 to 4 years depending on programme.
Applications: to the Overseas Studies Office of the University, at the above address for further information.

469 China Academy of Art [CAA]
218 Nanshanlu
310002 Hangzhou, Zhejiang Province
Tel: +86-571-8716-4613
Web: http://www.caa.edu.cn

📖 Undergraduate and Advanced Courses in Chinese Fine Arts

Study Domains: fine arts.
Programmes: Undergraduate and advanced courses in figure painting, Chinese style landscape painting and flower and bird painting, calligraphy, oil painting, engraving, design, sculpture, art history and theory; Masters and Ph.D. programmes are also available in some selected fields.
Open to: candidates of any country.
Duration: undergraduate: 4 years; Master's: 3 years; advanced: 2 years.
Applications: to the Foreign Affairs Office at the above address for further information.

470 China Pharmaceutical University [CPU]
No. 24, Tong Jia Xiang
210009 Nanjing, Jiangsu Province
Tel: +86-25-327-1423
Fax: +86-25-321-3611
Web: http://www.cpu.edu.cn
e-mail: guojiaochu@mailbox.cpu.edu.cn

📖 Undergraduate and Advanced Courses in Pharmacy

Study Domains: pharmacy and pharmacology.
Programmes: undergraduate and advanced courses in pharmacy (pharmaceutical analysis), pharmaceutics, Chinese traditional pharmacology, analysis and identification of traditional drugs, chemical-pharmaceutical manufacturing, pharmaceutical chemistry, biological pharmaceutics, Chinese traditional pharmacy, traditional Chinese pharmaceutics; Master's and Ph.D. programmes are also available in some selected fields.
Open to: qualified candidates of any nationality.
Duration: undergraduate, 4 to 5 years; advanced, 1 to 2 years; Master's and doctoral candidates, 3 years.
Applications: to Foreign Affairs Office of the China Pharmaceutical University for further information.

471 China University of Geosciences [CUG]
388 Lumo Road
430074 Wuhan, Hubei Province
Tel: +86-27-8748-2986
Fax: +86-27-8748-1364
Web: http://www.cug.edu.cn
e-mail: wsc@cug.edu.cn

📖 Undergraduate and Advanced Courses in Geosciences

Study Domains: geology, hydrology.
Programmes: undergraduate and advanced courses in the following fields: geology, mineral deposits, hydrogeology and engineering geology, stratigraphy and palaeontology, petrology and mineralogy, geochemistry, petroleum geology, prospecting geophysics, mining engineering.
Open to: candidates of all nationality; undergraduates must be under the age of 25 and hold the equivalent of a Chinese Proficiency Test (HSK); written admission exam for undergraduates; graduate students need recommendations from two full professors.
Duration: undergraduate: 4 years; advanced: 1 year.
Applications: to the above address for further information.

472 China University of Mining and Technology [CUMT]

Jietang Road
221008 Xuzhou, Jiangsu Province
Tel: +86-516-388-5150
Fax: +86-516-388-8682
Web: http://www.cumt.edu.cn
e-mail: maste@cumt.edu.cn

📖 Undergraduate, Graduate Programmes

Study Domains: chemical engineering, chemistry, earth science, energy, engineering, geology, liberal arts, mechanical engineering, sciences, technology.
Programmes: undergraduate and graduate programmes in engineering sciences, geology, mechanics, management and liberal arts.

473 Dalian Maritime University [DLMU]

1 Linghai Road
116026 Dalian, Liaoning Province
Tel: +86-411-8472-7874
Fax: +86-411-8472-7395
Web: http://www.dlmu.edu.cn
e-mail: faodmu@dlmu.edu.cn

📖 Undergraduate Programmes in Marine Sciences

Study Domains: communication, computer science, electricity and electronics, marine biology.
Programmes: undergraduate courses in the following fields: navigation, marine engineering, marine electrical engineering, electronic engineering, communications engineering, computer science, automatic control; Master's and Ph.D. programmes are also available in some selected fields.
Open to: qualified candidates of any country.
Duration: undergraduate: 4 to 5 years; graduate: 2½ to 3 years; advanced: 1 to 2 years.
Applications: to the above address for further information.

474 Donghua University [DHU]

1882 West Yan-An Road
200051 Shanghai
Tel: +86-21-6270-8702
Web: http://www.dhu.edu.cn/englishnew/index.asp

📖 Undergraduate, Graduate, Postgraduate Programmes

Study Domains: technology, textile industry.
Programmes: Bachelor's, Master's and doctorate degrees in textile engineering, knitting technology, dyeing, printing and finishing, chemical fibres, textile materials, industrial automation and fashion design.
Open to: candidates of any country under age 25 for undergraduate students, under 35 for Master's degree, and under 45 for doctorate; Chinese language test required.
Duration: undergraduate, 4 years; Master's, 2½ years.
Languages: instruction in Chinese and English.
Applications: to the above address for further information.

475 East China Normal University [ECNU]

3663 Zhongshan Road North
200062 Shanghai
Tel: +86-21-6223-2013
Fax: +86-21-6257-0590
Web: http://www.ecnu.edu.cn
e-mail: homepage@admin.ecnu.edu.cn

📖 Undergraduate, Graduate and Advanced Courses

Study Domains: all major fields, Chinese.
Programmes: Bachelor's, Master's degrees and advanced courses in all major fields except agriculture and health and welfare; non-degree programme in Chinese language.
Open to: candidates of any nationality; HSK levels needed for degree programmes.
Fees: registration: US$40; tuition: US$2,200-$5,200 per academic year.
Applications: by 30 January and 20 June.

476 East China University of Science and Technology [ECUST]

130 Meilong Road
200237 Shanghai
Tel: +86-21-6425-2769
Fax: +86-21-6425-0735
Web: http://www.ecust.edu.cn
e-mail: IES@ecust.edu.cn

📖 Undergraduate Programmes in Science and Technology

Study Domains: chemistry, technology.
Programmes: undergraduate courses in the following fields: petroleum processing, organic chemical technology, chemical engineering, inorganic chemical engineering, inorganic non-metallic materials (glass, ceramics and enamels), biochemical engineering, fine chemical engineering, polymer material science and engineering; Master's and Ph.D. programmes are also available in some selected fields.
Open to: qualified candidates of any country.
Duration: undergraduate: 4 years; graduate: 3 years; advanced: 1 to 2 years.
Applications: to the above address for further information.

477 Fudan University - International Cultural Exchange School

280 Zhengtong Road
200433 Shanghai
Fax: +86-21-6564-2258
Web: http://www.fudan.edu.cn
e-mail: izumiwoo@fudan.edu.cn

📖 Undergraduate, Graduate and Postgraduate Programmes

Study Domains: Chinese, history, humanities and arts, literature and civilization, medicine, philosophy, sciences, social sciences.
Programmes: Bachelor's, Master's, Ph.D. degrees and advanced courses in humanities; social science; natural science; medicine; Chinese language and culture programmes.
Open to: candidates of any nationality; specific programmes have admission requirements; see website for further information.
Duration: variable, according to programme.
Fees: application: 410 RMB; undergraduate and graduate studies (except medicine): 23,000-30,000 RMB; Ph.D. studies: 30,000-37,000 RMB; general and senior advanced studies: 25,000-37,000 RMB. Medical studies: 42,000-54,000 RMB; short-term students: application fee: 410 RBM; tuition: 2,500-3,500 RMB for two weeks; 700 RMB per person for each additional week.
Financial assistance: some scholarships provided by the China Scholarship Council; email: laihua@csc.edu.cn; website: http://www.csc.edu.cn/en.
Applications: by 15 May for Autumn semester or by 15 December for Spring semester; to the above address for further information.

478 Guangxi University

13, Xiuling Road
530004 Nanning
Tel: +86-771-323-5228
Fax: +86-771-323-7734
Web: http://www.gxu.edu.cn
e-mail: gjc@gxu.edu.cn

📖 Undergraduate, Graduate, Postgraduate Programmes

Study Domains: all major fields, Chinese.
Programmes: undergraduate, graduate and postgraduate programmes in education, humanities and liberal arts, social sciences, business, law, sciences, engineering and agriculture; certificate programmes in Chinese language and culture.
Open to: all candidates; HSK certificate of level C or above.
Fees: registration: US$50; tuition: US$1,800-$2,500 per academic year; US$200 per month.

Applications: by 30 June; courses begin on 25 August.

479 Guangzhou University of Traditional Chinese Medicine

12 Jichanglu
510407 Guangzhou, Guangdong Province
Tel: +86-20-3658-8233
Web: http://www.gzhtcm.edu.cn
e-mail: guoji8@gzhtcm.edu.cn

📖 Undergraduate, Graduate and Advanced Courses

Study Domains: Chinese, medicine.
Programmes: Bachelor's, Master's degrees and advanced courses in traditional Chinese medicine therapeutics, acupuncture and moxibustion.
Open to: candidates of any country.
Duration: undergraduate: 5 years; Master's: 2-1/2 years; advanced: 1 year.
Applications: to the above address for further information.

480 Harbin Normal University

50 Hexing Road
Nan gang District
Harbin
Tel: +86-451-8806-0114
Web: http://www.hrbnu.edu.cn
e-mail: xb@postofficehrbnu.edu.cn

📖 Undergraduate, Graduate, Postgraduate Programmes

Study Domains: education, humanities and arts, languages, sciences, social sciences, summer programmes.
Programmes: (a) general training; advanced training; (b) short-term training; (c) undergraduate training; (d) postgraduate training; (e) PhD programme.
Description: Art College; Foreign Language College; Vocational Technical College; Adult Education College; College of Culture and Arts; Hulan college; A'cheng college; International Cultural Communication Centre.
Other conditions: after acceptance students must apply for entry visa at the Chinese embassy or consulate.
Duration: (a) 6 months to 2 years; (b) 1 to 20 weeks; (c) 4 years; (d) and (e) 3 years.
Fees: tuition: (a) US$1,500; (b) US$350 for 4 weeks; (c) US$1,800; (d) and (e) US$2,500; living costs (lodging): from shared rooms at US$3 each to large single rooms at US$5.50 each.
Applications: apply by 1 March to 20 June for fall term; or 1 October to 20 December for spring term to: foreign students' office, email: hnugjjlc@sina.com or telephone: +86 451 631 5015.

481 HoHai University

1 Xikang Road
Nanjing, Jiangsu Province
210098
Tel: +86-25-378-6179
Fax: +86-25-370-8419
Web: http://www.hhu.edu.cn
e-mail: wboi@hhu.edu.cn

📖 Undergraduate, Graduate and Postgraduate Programmes

Study Domains: architecture, geology, hydrology, industrial technology, natural resources.
Programmes: Bachelor's, Master's, Ph.D. and advanced courses in engineering and science, arts, economics, management and law; studies in civil engineering and water resources; non-degree programmes in Chinese language.
Open to: candidates of any country; 18-45 years of age; no age limit for non-degree programmes.
Duration: undergraduate: 4 years; Master's: 2 to 2-1/2 years; Ph.D.: 3 years; advanced: 1 year.
Fees: registration: $US25; tuition: US$150-$3,500; living costs: US$4 per day per person for a single room.
Languages: Chinese and English.
Applications: to the above address for further information.

🎓 Scholarships

Study Domains: all major fields.
Scholarships: Government scholarships: Foreign Student Scholarship; Distinguished Students' Scholarship; Chinese Culture Research Fellowship; HSK Winner Scholarship; Short-Term Studies Scholarship; more scholarship information from China Scholarship Council, tel: +86 10 6606 3253; fax: +86 10 6606 3255; email: hefenghua@mail.jlu.edu.cn; website: http://www.jlu.edu.cn.
Duration: for normal duration of studies.
Value: variable, for tuition, medical expenses; accommodation. supplies.

482 Huazhong Agricultural University [HAU]

Shizi Shan
43007 Wuhan
Tel: +86-27-8739-6057
Fax: +86-27-8739-6057
Web: http://www.hzau.edu.cn
e-mail: fao@hzau.edu.cn

🎓 Scholarship

Study Domains: biochemistry, biology, sciences.
Scholarships: Chinese Government Scholarship.
Subjects: Biochemistry and molecular biology.
Open to: All candidates with master's degree.
Value: Free tuition; living expenses RMB 1400 per month and free accomodation; email: tao@mail.hzau.edu.cn.

483 Hubei Medical University

39 Donghu Road, Wuchang
430077 Wuhan, Hubei Province
Tel: +86-27-8671-7841
Fax: +86-27-8681-4263
Web: http://www.hubu.edu.cn
e-mail: zqh@hubu.edu.cn

📖 Undergraduate Programmes

Study Domains: dentistry, medicine.
Programmes: Bachelor's degrees in medicine and dentistry; Master's and Ph.D. programmes available in some selected fields.
Open to: candidates of any country.
Duration: 1 to 5 years.
Applications: to the above address for further information.

484 Jiangxi Normal University

437 West Beijing Road
330027 Nanchang, Jiangxi Province
Tel: +86-791-821-0461
Fax: +86-791-821-0463
Web: http://www.jxnu.edu.cn
e-mail: icdept@jxnu.edu.cn

📖 Undergraduate, Graduate Programmes

Study Domains: administration, Chinese, computer science, economic and commercial sciences, education, fine arts, humanities and arts, languages, literature and civilization, mathematics, performing arts, physical education, physics.
Programmes: Bachelor's and Master's degree programmes in all major fields.

485 Jilin University

1505 Linyuan Road
130023 Changchun, Jilin Province
Tel: +86-431-516-6885 / 516-6877
Fax: +86-431-516-6570
Web: http://oic.jlu.edu.cn
e-mail: cie@mail.jlu.edu.cn

📖 Undergraduate, Graduate and Postgraduate Programmes

Study Domains: all major fields, Chinese.
Programmes: Bachelor's, Master's, Ph.D. degrees and advanced Courses in all major fields; non-degree programmes in Chinese language and culture.
Open to: candidates of any nationality.
Duration: variable according to programme chosen; Chinese courses begin in March and September.
Fees: registration: US$50; tuition: variable according to

programme: from US$1,900 to US$4,300; living costs: US$4-$5 per day per person for a double room.
Financial assistance: partial scholarships offered by China Scholarship Council, tel.: +86-10-6606-3253; fax: +86-10-6606-3255; email: hefenghua@mail.jlu.edu.cn; website: http://www.jlu.edu.cn.
Applications: by 1 March for spring session; 1 September for autumn session.

🎓 Jilin University Scholarships

Study Domains: all major fields.
Scholarships: (a) Outstanding International Students; (b) bilateral agreements; (c) Distinguished International Student Scholarship (Chinese Government award).
Description: for doctoral or Master's degree studies.
Open to: international students enrolled at the university.
Value: variable; all self-financed international students will receive free health insurance; (b) 15% tuition reduction and 10-30% reduction for on-campus housing.

486   Jimey University [JMU]

Jimei Schools Village
36102 Xiamen
Tel: +86-592-618-0563
Fax: +86-592-618-0247
Web: http://www.jmu.edu.cn
e-mail: dofaojmu@jmu.edu.cn

📖 Undergraduate, Graduate Programmes

Study Domains: agronomic sciences, business administration, economic and commercial sciences, education, food industry, law, literature and civilization, marine science, mechanical engineering, navigation.
Programmes: 46 Bachelor's degree programmes and 13 associate bachelor's degree programs, covering eight areas: economics, law, pedagogy, literature, natural science, mechanical engineering, agronomy and business administration and 4 Master's degree programs in aquaculture, food science, marine engineering and national economics.
Description: 19 colleges/institutes and 2 independent departments: Navigation Institute, Marine Engineering Institute, Fisheries College, Bio-tech Engineering College, Physical Education College, Finance & Economics College, Teachers Education College, School of Business Administration, Art Education College, Information Technology College, Computer Science College, Mechanical Engineering College, College of Science, Foreign Language College, Engineering Technology College, Professional Maritime Education College, Social Science Department and Chinese Department.

487   Jinan University [JNU]

International Affairs Office
510632 Guangzhou, Guangdong Province
Tel: +86-20-8522-0085
Fax: +86-20-8522-1395
Web: http://www.jnu.edu.cn
e-mail: owsc@jnu.edu.cn

📖 Undergraduate, Graduate, Postgraduate Programmes

Study Domains: all major fields, Chinese.
Programmes: Bachelor's, Master's, Ph.D. degrees in all major fields; postdoctoral research programmes in industrial economy and clinical medicine; non-degree programmes in Chinese language and culture.
Open to: candidates must have equivalent of high school certificate and the HSK test at C level; entrance examination also required.
Held: at main campus and 3 branch campuses.
Fees: tuition fees: US$9,800-$11,800; living costs: US$1,500 per year.
Financial assistance: some financial assistance available, see website or contact the Admissions Office for further information; email: ozsb@jnu.edu.cn.

488   Lanzhou University [LZU]

Foreign Affairs Office
Tianshui Road 298
730000 Lanzhou, Gansu
Tel: +86-931-891-2850
Fax: +86-931-861-7355
Web: http://www.lzu.edu.cn
e-mail: yuyj@lzu.edu.cn

📖 Undergraduate, Graduate and Advanced Studies Programmes

Study Domains: all major fields, Chinese.
Programmes: Bachelor's, Master's, Ph.D. and advanced studies programmes in all major fields except agriculture and health and welfare; non-degree programmes in Chinese language and culture.
Open to: Chinese language test (HSK) at C level; admissions examination required for degree programmes.
Age limit Max: 25 years for bachelor's programmes; 35 years for postgraduate and advanced studies programmes.
Financial assistance: some scholarships can be obtained from the China Scholarship Council (CSB).
Languages: Chinese, English and Japanese.
Applications: mid-August and mid-January to Foreign Officers Office at the above address.

489   Liaoning University

66 Chongshan Zhonglu
Huanggu District
110036 Shenyang, Liaoning Province
Tel: +86-24-8672-5294
Fax: +86-24-8686-2106
Web: http://www.lnu.edu.cn
e-mail: mwang@hstar.lnu.edu.cn

📖 Undergraduate, Graduate, Postgraduate and Advanced Courses

Study Domains: Chinese, economy, history, languages, literature and civilization.
Programmes: Bachelor's, Master's, Ph.D. degrees and advanced courses in Chinese language and literature; history and economy.
Open to: candidates of any nationality.
Duration: 1 to 4 years depending on the course.
Applications: to the above address for further information.

490   Nanjing College of Traditional Chinese Medicine [NJUTCM]

282 Hanzhong Road
210029 Nanjing, Jiangsu Province
Tel: +86-25-8679-8078
Web: http://www.njutcm.edu.cn
e-mail: iec@njutcm.edu.cn

📖 Undergraduate, Graduate, Postgraduate and Advanced Courses

Study Domains: biochemistry, biology, chemistry, computer science, medicine, microbiology, paediatrics, philology, physical education.
Programmes: Bachelor's, Master's, Ph.D. degrees and advanced courses in the following fields: traditional Chinese medicine, acupuncture and moxibustion, internal medicine of TCM, Chinese pharmacology.
Open to: candidates of any country; enquire regarding eligibility requirements.
Duration: undergraduate: 5 years; Master's: 3 years; advanced: 1 to 2 years.
Applications: by 30 June, to the above address for further information.

491   Nanjing Normal University [NNU]

122 Ning Hai Road
210097 Nanjing, Jiangsu Province
Tel: +86-25-359-8530
Web: http://www.njnu.edu.cn
e-mail: njiang@njnu.edu.cn

📖 Undergraduate, Graduate, Postgraduate and Advanced Courses

Study Domains: arts, Chinese, education, languages,

literature and civilization, zoology.
Programmes: Bachelor's, Master's, Ph.D. degrees,
advanced courses and short-term programmes in education;
arts; literature.
Description: modern Chinese language and literature,
ancient and modern Chinese language and literature,
pre-school education, Chinese psychology, ancient Chinese
philosophy, Chinese history, Chinese calligraphy, traditional
Chinese painting, zoology, traditional Chinese arts and crafts,
folk music instruments, Taiji, Chinese martial arts.
Open to: candidates of any country.
Duration: undergraduate: 4 years; Master's: 3 years;
Ph.D.: 2½ years; advanced: 1 or 2 years; short-term
programmes: 1 to 6 months.
Applications: to the above address for further information.

492 Nanjing University
22 Hankou Road
210093 Nanjing, Jiangsu Province
Tel: +86-25-8359-3587
Fax: +86-25-8331-6747
Web: http://www.nju.edu.cn
e-mail: issd@nju.edu.cn

Undergraduate and advanced courses
Study Domains: all major fields, Chinese.
Open to: candidates of any nationality.
Duration: undergraduate: 4 years; Master's and Ph.D.: 3
years; advanced: 1 to 2 years.
Applications: to the above address for further information.

493 Nanjing University, Institute for International Students
22 Hankou Road
210093 Nanjing, Jiangsu Province
Tel: +86-25-359-3587
Fax: +86-25-331-6747
Web: http://www.nju.edu.cn
e-mail: issd@nju.edu.cn

Undergraduate, Graduate, Postgraduate and Advanced Courses
Study Domains: archaeology, arts, astronomy, Chinese,
computer science, economic and commercial sciences,
geology, history, humanities and arts, law, physics.
Programmes: Bachelor's degrees and advanced courses;
Master's and Ph.D. programmes are available in some selected
fields; Chinese language short-term studies.
Description: Chinese language and literature, Chinese
history, Chinese philosophy, Chinese economy, Chinese law,
elementary Chinese, Chinese culture, synoptic and dynamic
meteorology, coastal geomorphology, urban and regional
planning, geomorphology and quaternary environment,
regional and physical geography, structural geology and
geophysics, palaeontology and stratigraphy, radio physics,
nucleus physics, crystal physics, semiconductor physics,
acoustics, history and astronomy and ancient astronomy,
computer application, computer software, Chinese calligraphy
and Chinese painting.
Open to: candidates of any nationality with excellent
academic performance in senior high school, undergraduate or
M.A. programmes; HSK required.
Duration: undergraduate: 4 years; Master's and Ph.D.: 3
years; advanced: 1 to 2 years.
Applications: by 30 April for Autumn semester; to the
above address for further information.

494 Nankai University
94 Weijin Road
300071 Tianjin, Nankai District
Tel: +86-22-2350-8229
Fax: +86-22-2350-2990
Web: http://www.nankai.edu.cn

Undergraduate, Graduate, Postgraduate and Advanced Programmes
Study Domains: all major fields, Chinese.
Programmes: Bachelor's, Master's, Ph.D. degrees and
advanced courses in several fields, including Chinese
language and literature, Chinese history, museology, Socialist
economic theory, price theory, research on 'Capital', Chinese
economic history, history of Chinese economic thought,

history of Chinese management, environmental biology,
environmental chemistry, biochemistry, entomology,
chemistry, electronics, micro-electronics, laser physics and
laser technology, optical information processing and
holography, spectroscopy and laser spectroscopy, organic
chemistry, history of Chinese philosophy.
Open to: candidates of any nationality; under 25 for
undergraduate programmes; under 45 for higher degree
programmes; entrance examinations in mid-May; HSK
required.
Duration: from 1 to 4 years depending on the course.
Applications: to the above address for further information.

495 Northeastern University
Wenhua Road
Heping District
110006 Shenyang, Liaoning Province
Tel: +86-24-2389-3000
Fax: +86-24-2389-2454
Web: http://www.neu.edu.cn

Undergraduate, Graduate, Postgraduate and Advanced Programmes
Study Domains: industrial technology, technology.
Programmes: Bachelor's, Master's, Ph.D. degrees and
advanced courses in mining, mineral processing, ferrous
metallurgy, non-ferrous metallurgy, material science and
engineering, metal forming, thermal engineering, automatic
control, computer science, mechanical engineering, business
administration, physical education and sciences.
Open to: candidates of any nationality.
Duration: 1 to 4 years depending on programme.
Applications: to the above address for further information.

496 Northern Jiaotong University [NJTU]
Foreign Students Office
100044 Beijing
Tel: +86-10-6324-0351
Fax: +86-10-6225-5671
Web: http://www.njtu.edu.cn
e-mail: wsclxsk@center.njtu.edu.cn

Undergraduate, Graduate, Postgraduate Programmes
Study Domains: accounting, administration, architecture,
business, Chinese, communication, computer science,
economic and commercial sciences, electricity and
electronics, engineering, English, finance, industry and
commerce, law, mathematics, mechanical engineering,
technology, telecommunications, transport.
Programmes: Bachelor's, Master's, Ph.D. degrees in all
major fields.
Open to: candidates of any country.
Duration: undergraduate: 4 years; Master's: 2 to 3 years;
Ph.D.: 3 years; advanced: 1 to 2 years.
Applications: to the above address for further information.

497 Northwestern Polytechnical University [NWPU]
127 Youyixilu Road
Xian, Shanxi Pr 710072
Tel: +86-29-849-4379
Fax: +86-29-849-1544
Web: http://www.nwpu.edu.cn;
www.nwpu.edu.cn/en/default.asp
e-mail: fao@nwpu.edu.cn

Undergraduate, Graduate, Postgraduate Programmes
Study Domains: architecture, aviation, aeronautics,
building industry, business administration, chemical
engineering, chemical industry, chemistry, Chinese, computer
science, ecology, environment, economic and commercial
sciences, electricity and electronics, energy, industrial
technology, information science, international business,
languages, mechanical engineering, metallurgy, technology.
Programmes: Bachelor's, Master's and Ph.D. degrees in all
major fields; Chinese language programmes of study.
Applications: see website for further information.

498 Renmin (People's) University of China [RUC]
Foreign Students' Office
175 Haidian Road
100872 Beijing, Haidian District
Tel: +86-10-6251-1132
Fax: +86-10-6251-5241
Web: http://www.ruc.edu.cn
e-mail: rmdxxb@ruc.edu.cn

📖 **Undergraduate and Advanced Courses**

Study Domains: all major fields.
Programmes: undergraduate, advanced and senior advanced courses in all major fields; Master's and Ph.D. programmes are available in some selected fields.
Description: RUC offers 58 bachelor's programmes, 7 second bachelor's programmes, 89 master's programmes, 58 PhD programmes, 8 postdoctoral programmes and 26 adult training programmes. Among them 25 are top-ranking key national programmes in social sciences. RUC was the first university to offer correspondence and online education and its Online Education College is the largest one in China, offering higher education via the Internet.
Open to: candidates of any nationality.
Duration: from 1 to 4 years depending on courses.
Applications: to the above address for further information.

499 Shandong University, College of International Education
27 Shanda Nanlu
250100 Jinan, Shandong Province
Tel: +86-531-891-3623
Fax: +86-531-890-7397
Web: http://www.cie.sdu.edu.cn/eng/index.htm

📖 **Undergraduate, Graduate, Postgraduate and Advanced Programmes**

Study Domains: archaeology, business administration, Chinese, economic and commercial sciences, engineering, history, international relations, literature and civilization, philosophy.
Programmes: Bachelor's, Master's, Ph.D. and advanced courses in Chinese language, literature, history and painting, geography, public education, sciences, foreign languages, industrial and business administration, economics, international political and economic relations, technology engineering, international education, adult education.
Open to: qualified candidates of any nationality.
Duration: undergraduate: 4 years; Master's: 2 or 3 years; Ph.D.: 3 years; advanced: 1 or 2 years.
Applications: to the above address for further information.

500 Shanghai Conservatory of Music
20 Fen Yang Road
200031 Shanghai
Tel: +86-21-6433-0536
Fax: +86-21-6433-0866

📖 **Undergraduate, Graduate, Postgraduate and Advanced Courses**

Study Domains: music and musicology.
Programmes: Bachelor's, Master's, Ph.D. and advanced courses in traditional Chinese instruments; orchestral instruments; piano; theory of Chinese traditional music; vocal music and folksong singing; composition; history of Chinese and Western music.
Open to: candidates of any country.
Duration: undergraduate: 4 to 5 years; Master's: 2 to 3 years; Ph.D.: 2 years; advanced: 1 or 2 years.
Applications: to the above address for further information.

501 Shanghai Second Medical University
280 S. Chongqing Road
20002 Shanghai
Tel: +86-21-6384-6590
Fax: +86-21-6384-2916
Web: http://www.shsmu.edu.cn
e-mail: www@shsmu.edu.cn

📖 **Undergraduate Specialty Medicine Programme**

Study Domains: medicine.
Programmes: specialty medicine undergraduate courses; Master's and PhD programmes are also available in some selected fields.
Open to: candidates of any nationality.
Duration: 6 months to 5 years.
Applications: to the above address for further information.

502 Shanghai University [SHU]
149 Yanchanglu
Shanghai 200072
Tel: +86-21-5670-3060
Fax: +86-21-5670-3029
Web: http://www.shu.edu.cn
e-mail: info@mail.shu.edu.cn

📖 **Undergraduate, Graduate, Postgraduate Programmes**

Study Domains: all major fields.
Programmes: Bachelor's, Master's, Ph.D. degrees in all major fields.
Open to: candidates of any nationality.
Applications: to the above address for further information.

503 Shanghai University of Traditional Chinese Medicine [SHUTCM]
530 Lingling Road
Xu Hui District
200032 Shanghai
Tel: +86-21-6417-4600
Fax: +86-21-6417-8290
Web: http://www.shutcm.edu.cn

📖 **Undergraduate, Graduate, Postgraduate and Advanced Courses**

Study Domains: medicine, pharmacy and pharmacology.
Programmes: Bachelor's, Master's, Ph.D. and advanced courses in traditional Chinese medicine; acupuncture and moxibustion; Chinese pharmacology; Chinese medical massage; internal medicine of traditional Chinese medicine.
Open to: candidates of any country.
Duration: undergraduate: 4 to 7 years; Master's and Ph.D.: 3 years; advanced: 1 or 2 years.
Applications: to the above address for further information.

504 South Central University for Nationalities [SCUEC]
5 Min Yuan Road
430074 Wuhan, Hubei Province
Tel: +86-27-8753-2805
Fax: +86-27-8753-2143
Web: http://www.scuec.edu.cn
e-mail: wifao@scuec.edu.cn

📖 **Undergraduate, Graduate Programmes**

Study Domains: accounting, applied sciences, biochemistry, business, business administration, chemical industry, chemistry, Chinese, communication, computer science, criminology, economic and commercial sciences, electricity and electronics, history, languages, law, management, mathematics, philosophy.
Programmes: Bachelor's, Master's degrees in all major fields.
Open to: candidates of all nationalities; based on their resumés.

505 South China Agricultural University [SCAU]
Wushan Tianhe
510642 Guangzhou, Guangdong Province
Tel: +86-20-8759-2114
Fax: +86-20-8759-2114
Web: http://www.scau.edu.cn
e-mail: scaufao@scut.edu.cn

📖 **Undergraduate and Advanced Courses in Agriculture**

Study Domains: agriculture, agronomic sciences, forestry,

veterinary sciences.
Programmes: Bachelor's degrees and advanced courses in
the following fields: agronomy, genetics and crop breeding,
pomology, agricultural entomology, plant pathology, soil
science and agricultural chemistry, sericulture, forestry,
agricultural mechanization, farm machinery design and
manufacture, veterinary medicine, animal surgery and
husbandry, poultry, husbandry and disease control,
vegetables, diagnosis of virus disease of poultry in lab., crop
nutrition and fertilizer practice, occurrence, taxology and
survey of soil, tropical soil science; Master's and Ph.D.
programmes are available in some selected fields.
Open to: candidates of any country.
Duration: 1 to 4 years.
Applications: to the above address for further information.

506 Southeast University
2 Sipailou
210096 Nanjing, Jiangsu Province
Tel: +86-25-379-2412
Fax: +86-25-361-5736
Web: http://www.seu.edu.cn
e-mail: iso@seu.edu.cn

Undergraduate, Graduate Programmes
Study Domains: architecture, building industry, Chinese,
civil engineering, computer science, technology.
Programmes: Bachelor's, Master's, Ph.D. degrees and
advanced courses in architecture; civil engineering;
technology.
Open to: qualified candidates of any country.
Duration: undergraduate: 4 to 5 years; graduate: 2½ to 3
years; Ph.D.: 3 years; advanced: 1 to 2 years.
Applications: to the above address for further information.

507 Southern Yangtze University [SYTU]
170 Huihe Road
214036 Wuxi, Jiangsu Province
Tel: +86-510-586-1034
Fax: +86-510-580-7976
Web: http://www.sytu.edu.cn
e-mail: lxliu@wxuli.edu.cn.

Undergraduate, Graduate, Postgraduate Programmes
Study Domains: business, chemical engineering, chemical
industry, Chinese, communication, design, education,
engineering, industrial technology, languages, mechanical
engineering, medicine, physical education, sciences,
technology, telecommunications, textile industry.
Programmes: (a) engineering-based multidisciplinary
university offering undergraduate, graduate and postgraduate
programmes in all major fields; (b) Chinese language studies.
Open to: candidates of all nationalities; with relevant
diplomas and degrees: secondary education equivalent to
Chinese senior high school for undergraduate studies;
Bachelor's or Master's degrees for higher studies; maximum
age for graduate studies: 45 years of age; students must pass
HSK Band 4 for studies in Chinese language and prove
English proficiency for courses in English.
Duration: 3 to 4 years, according to studies.
Financial assistance: possibility of financial aid through
the China Scholarship Council (CSC); http://www.csc.edu.cn.
Applications: to the above address.

508 Southwest-China Normal University
Beibei District
40071 Chongqing
Tel: +86-23-6825-2225
Fax: +86-23-6886-3805
Web: http://www.swnu.edu.cn
e-mail: fofflce@swnu.edu.cn

Undergraduate, Graduate, Postgraduate Programmes
Study Domains: all major fields.
Programmes: undergraduate and postgraduate courses
leading to Bachelor's, Master's, Doctorate degrees, general
training students, advanced training of students and short-term
training of students in Chinese language and culture.

Subjects: undergraduate studies: economic management,
law, Chinese language and literature, library science,
psychology, physics, information engineering, education,
preschool education, educational management, history,
mathematics, accounting, chemistry, applied chemistry,
environmental science, biology, geography, economic
geography, education techniques, computer science, computer
applications, music, fine arts, architectural decoration and
physical education; (b) MA or MSc courses: logic,
philosophy, Chinese literature, history and language;
psychology, physics, philosophy, education, mathematics,
zoology, botany, ecology, geography, artificial intelligence,
music, fine arts; (c) Doctorate studies: didactics, general
psychology, ecology, basic mathematics.
Open to: see website for full details.
Applications: to Foreign Student Enrolment at above
address; email: fstudent@swnu.edu.cn.

509 Sun Yat-sen University [ZU]
135 Xingang Xilu
510275 Guangzhou, Guangdong Province
Tel: +86-20-8411-2828
Fax: +86-20-8411-1982
Web: http://www.sysu.edu.cn/en/index.html
e-mail: webmaster@sysu.edu.cn

Undergraduate, Graduate, Postgraduate and Advanced Studies
Study Domains: all major fields.
Programmes: Bachelor's, Master's, Ph.D. degrees and
advanced courses in all major fields.
Open to: candidates of any nationality.
Duration: from 1 to 4 years depending on programme.
Applications: to the above address for further information.

510 Sun Yat-Sen University of Medical Sciences
74 2nd Zhongshan Road
510089 Guangzhou, Guangdong Province
Tel: +86-20-8733-1800
Fax: +86-20-8733-1679
Web: http://www.gzsums.edu.cn
e-mail: XB@gzsums.edu.cn

Undergraduate, Graduate, Postgraduate Programmes
Study Domains: medicine.
Programmes: Bachelor's degree in medicine; Master's and
PhD programmes are also available in some selected fields.
Open to: candidates of any nationality.
Duration: 1 to 5 years.
Applications: to the above address for further information.

511 Tianjin College of Traditional Chinese Medicine
88 Yu Quan Road, Nankai District
300193 Tianjin
Tel: +86-22-2737-4931
Fax: +86-22-2727-0636
e-mail: tjtcm@mail.tjgl.com.cn

Undergraduate, Graduate and Advanced Courses
Study Domains: medicine.
Programmes: Bachelor's, advanced and Master's courses
in traditional Chinese medicine; acupuncture; moxibustion;
non-degree courses in Chinese language.
Open to: candidates of any country.
Duration: 6 months to 5 years.
Languages: instruction in Chinese, Japanese and English.
Applications: to the above address for further information.

512 Tianjin Medical University [TMU]
22 Qixiangtai Road Heping District
30007 Tianjin
Tel: +86-22-2354-2757
Fax: +86-22-2354-2584
Web: http://www.ictmu.com.cn
e-mail: jwc@tijmu.edu.cn

Scholarship

Study Domains: health and hygiene, medicine.
Scholarships: Distinguished International Students Scholarship.
Duration: 1 to 5 years, renewable.
Value: US$2,000; living expenses, US$800-1,400.
Applications: Applicants for Master's degree studies, with Bachelor's degree, under the age of 25; applicants for Doctoral degree studies, with Master's degree, under the age of 40; email: laihua@css.edu.cn.

513 Tianjin University

International Students' Office
300072 Tianjin
Tel: +86-22-2740-6147
Fax: +86-22-2335-0853
Web: http://www.tju.edu.cn
e-mail: iso@tju.edu.cn

Undergraduate, Graduate, Postgraduate Programmes

Study Domains: Chinese, industrial technology, law, liberal arts, management, sciences, technology.
Programmes: Bachelor's degree in engineering, science, liberal arts, management science and law; Master's and Ph.D. programmes available in some selected fields; long- and short-term Chinese language and culture courses.
Open to: candidates of any nationality.
Duration: 6 months to 4 years.
Applications: to the International Office for further information.

514 Tianjin University of Foreign Studies

117 Machang Road, Hexi District
300204 Tianjin
Tel: +86-22-2328-0875
Fax: +86-22-2328-2410
Web: http://www.tjfsu.edu.cn/en/
e-mail: info@tjfsu.edu.cn

Undergraduate Programmes

Study Domains: Chinese.
Programmes: Bachelor's Degree in Chinese language.
Open to: candidates of any nationality.
Duration: 6 months to 4 years.
Applications: to the above address.

515 Tongji University

1239 Siping Road
200092 Shanghai
Tel: +86-21-6598-2200
Fax: +86-21-6958-7933
Web: http://www.tongji.edu.cn
e-mail: yanyujin@mail.tongji.edu.cn

Undergraduate, Graduate, Postgraduate Courses

Study Domains: architecture, economic and commercial sciences, education, engineering, law, liberal arts, management, medicine, philosophy, sciences.
Programmes: Bachelor's, Master's and Ph.D. degrees in all major fields; Chinese language programmes; M.B.A., I.M.B.A.
Subjects: architecture and urban planning, automotive engineering, civil engineering, communication and arts, economics and management, electronics and information engineering, environmental science and engineering, liberal arts and law, life science and technology, material science and engineering, mechanical engineering, medicine, ocean and earth science, sciences, traffic and transportation engineering.
Open to: candidates of any nationality.
Duration: Undergraduates (4 to 5 years); Masters (2-1/2 to 3 years); M.B.A., I.M.B.A. (2 years); Ph.D. (3 years).
Applications: to the International Students Office at the above address for further information; email: istju@mail.tongji.edu.cn; Web: http://www.istju.com.

516 Tsinghua University

1 Qinghua Yuan, Haidian District
100084 Beijing
Tel: +86-10-6278-4857
Fax: +86-10-6277-1134
Web: http://www.tsinghua.edu.cn
e-mail: info@tsinghua.edu.cn

Undergraduate, Graduate, Postgraduate Programmes

Study Domains: business administration, Chinese, computer science, design, economic and commercial sciences, electricity and electronics, engineering, English, industrial technology, industry and commerce, languages, literature and civilization, management, technology.
Programmes: Bachelor's, Master's and PhD degrees in all major fields; Chinese language programme.
Description: courses in architecture, civil engineering, hydraulic and hydropower engineering, environmental engineering, mechanical engineering and automation, measurement technology and instruments, industrial engineering, building environmental and equipment engineering, thermal power engineering, vehicle engineering, electrical engineering and automation, automation, electronic information engineering, computer science and technology, electronic science and technology, engineering mechanics, chemical engineering and technology, polymer materials and engineering, materials science and engineering, applied mathematics, physics, chemistry, biological science, economics, finance, accounting, information management and information systems, law, Chinese language and literature, English, journalism and communication, artistic design, industrial design, advertising, painting, sculpture, biomedical engineering, philosophy, education, history and business administration.
Open to: candidates of any country.
Duration: Bachelor's programmes: 4 years (architecture, 5 years); Master's programmes: 2-1/2 to 3 years; PhD programmes: 3 to 4 years; advanced programmes: 1 semester to 2 years; Chinese language courses: 1 or 2 semesters.
Financial assistance: scholarships offered by the Ministry of Education of China, school exchange scholarships.
Applications: to the above address for further information.

517 Wuhan University [WHU]

Luojia Shan
Wuchang
430072 Wuhan, Hubei Province
Tel: +86-27-8768-2804
Fax: +86-27-8768-2661
Web: http://www.whu.edu.cn

Undergraduate and Advanced Courses

Study Domains: all major fields.
Programmes: Bachelor's degrees and advanced courses in all major fields; Master's and Ph.D. programmes are also available in some selected fields.
Open to: candidates of any country.
Duration: 1 to 4 years.
Applications: to the above address for further information.

518 Wuhan University of Technology [WHUT]

International office
No. 205 Luoshi Road, Wuchang, Wuhan
430070 Wuhan, Hubei Province
Tel: +86-27-8765-8253
Fax: +86-27-8765-8253
Web: http://www.whut.edu.cn
e-mail: radnygh@whut.edu.ch

Undergraduate Courses

Study Domains: engineering, industrial technology, management, marine biology, transport.
Programmes: Bachelor's degrees in shipbuilding engineering, marine machinery, internal combustion engine, heat power machinery and installation, material handling and engineering machinery, industrial electrical automation, management engineering of transport; Master's and Ph.D. programmes are also available in some selected fields.
Open to: candidates of any country.

Duration: 1 to 4 years.
Applications: to the above address for further information.

519 Xi'an Jiaotong University [XJTU]
26 Xianning Xilu
710049 Xi'an, Shaan'xi Province
Tel: +86-29-8266-8830
Fax: +86-29-323-4716
Web: http://www.xjtu.edu.cn
e-mail: oic_admin@mail.xjtu.edu.cn

⌂ Undergraduate, Graduate, Postgraduate and Advanced Programmes

Study Domains: chemical engineering, computer science, electricity and electronics, energy, engineering, humanities and arts, management, mechanical engineering, social sciences.
Programmes: Bachelor's, Master's, Ph.D. degrees and advanced courses in mechanical engineering, material science and engineering, energy and power engineering, electrical engineering, electronics and information engineering, architectural engineering and mechanics, chemical engineering, management, sciences, humanities and social sciences.
Open to: candidates of any country.
Duration: 1 to 4 years.
Applications: to the Foreign Affairs Office at the above address for further information.

520 Xiamen University - Overseas Education College [XMU]
International Students' Office
422 Siming South Road
361005 Xiamen, Fujian Province
Tel: +86-592-218-4792
Fax: +86-592-218-0256
Web: http://www.xmu.edu.cn
e-mail: zzyu@xmu.edu.cn

⌂ Undergraduate, Graduate, Postgraduate and Advanced Courses

Study Domains: accounting, Chinese, finance, history, literature and civilization, marine biology, mathematics, political science, statistics.
Programmes: Bachelor's degrees and advanced courses in ancient and modern Chinese literature, Chinese language and literature, ancient and modern Chinese history, Chinese economic history, finance, political economics, accounting, statistics, marine chemistry and biology, mathematics; Master's and Ph.D. programmes are also available in selected fields.
Open to: candidates of any country, over 16 years of age, with secondary school diploma.
Duration: 1 to 4 years.
Applications: to the above address for further information.

521 Yanshan University [YSU]
438 Hebei Avenue
066004 Qinhuangdao, Hebei Province
Tel: +86-335-805-7070
Fax: +86-335-806-1449
Web: http://www.ysu.edu.cn
e-mail: waiban@ysu.edu.cn

⌂ Undergraduate, Graduate, Postgraduate Programmes

Study Domains: accounting, applied sciences, business administration, Chinese, civil engineering, computer science, economy, information science, international studies, mechanical engineering, technology.
Programmes: Bachelor's, Master's and Ph.D. degrees in business; applied sciences; administration; non-degree programmes in Chinese language and culture.
Open to: Bachelor's programmes: under 25 years; Master's programmes: under 40 years.
Financial assistance: some financial assistance offered: US$80 per month for Master's candidates; US$100 per month for Ph.D. candidates.
Languages: language of instruction: Chinese.

522 Zhejiang Agricultural University [ZJAU]
Huajiachi, Kaixuan Road 268
310029 Hangzhou, Zhejiang Province
Tel: +86-571-604-1733
Fax: +86-571-604-1053
Web: http://www.zjau.edu.cn

⌂ Undergraduate Programmes in Agriculture

Study Domains: agriculture, agronomic sciences.
Programmes: Undergraduate courses in 33 major fields including economy and trade, animal science, engineering, environment and resources, land management, agronomy, plant protection, sericulture and mulberry culture, tea science, horticulture, food science and technology; Master's and Ph.D. programmes are available in some selected fields.
Open to: candidates of any nationality.
Duration: 1 to 4 years.
Languages: instruction in Chinese and English.
Applications: to the above address for further information.

523 Zhejiang University, International College [IC]
PO Box W-99
310027 Hangzhou
Tel: +86-571-8795-1386
Fax: +86-571-8795-1755
Web: http://www.zju.edu.cn
e-mail: zupo@zju.edu.cn

⌂ Undergraduate, Graduate Programmes

Study Domains: agriculture, agronomic sciences, applied sciences, architecture, building industry, business administration, Chinese, electricity and electronics, industrial technology, marketing, sciences, technology.
Programmes: Bachelor's, Master's degrees in agriculture; sericulture and mulberry culture, tea science, horticulture; applied mathematics, architecture, sciences, science and technology, business management, marketing, engineering, computer science, economics and finance; Chinese language and literature, foreign languages; PhD programmes are available in all the science and engineering fields.
Open to: candidates of any country.
Duration: 6 months to 5 years.
Applications: to the above address for further information.

China, Hong Kong

Academic year: September to August (universities mainly; variable dates for polytechnics).
Monetary unit: Hong Kong dollar (HK$).
National student admission: Foreign students who apply for degree/diploma programmes must satisfy the entrance requirements of the university/polytechnic they wish to attend unless exempted (details are given in the calendar of the institution concerned). Those who have completed at least one year of university study at a recognized university outside Hong Kong may apply for exemption to the university concerned. Applications for admission to The Chinese University of Hong Kong (CUHK) should be submitted by February for admissions in September of the same year. CUHK also considers applications for associate students before 1 July or 1 November prior to the teaching term of the year of admission. The City Polytechnic of Hong Kong may grant exemptions to normal conditions of entry to applicants aged 25 years and over by 1 September of the year of admission. With regard to the Hong Kong Polytechnic some qualifications, other than those prescribed in the university entrance requirements, are accepted by departments as equivalent, such as the International Baccalaureate. An orientation programme is organized every year for all new students at the Hong Kong Baptist College. General assistance is available for foreign students at other institutions.
Language: Good knowledge of English is required for all programmes and some working knowledge in Chinese preferred for study in some programmes of the Chinese University of Hong Kong and the Hong Kong Polytechnic; good knowledge of English for the University of Hong Kong. Chinese language courses (both in Cantonese and Mandarin) are offered by the New Asia Yale-in-China Chinese Language Centre at the Chinese University of Hong Kong.

Information services:
• Education Department, Wu Chung House, 213 Queen's Road, East Wanchai, Hong Kong (information and advice concerning study opportunities and facilities).
Registrars of:
• The Chinese University of Hong Kong, Shatin, New Territories, Hong Kong.
• University of Hong Kong, Pokfulam Road, Hong Kong.
• Hong Kong Polytechnic, Yuk Choi Road, Hung Hom, Kowloon, Hong Kong.
• Hong Kong Baptist College, 224 Waterloo Road, Kowloon, Hong Kong.
• Lingnan College, 15 Stubbs Road, Hong Kong.
• Shue Yan College, Braemar Hill, North Point, Hong Kong.
Open and distance learning: Distance higher education is offered at the Open University of Hong Kong, founded in 1989. It offers courses in Arts, Business, and Science and Technology. The minimum time for graduation for an Ordinary Degree is three years and four years for an Honours Degree. The continuing education units of the universities offer correspondence courses, radio and television courses and self-learning courses in the form of tapes, programmed texts and resource materials.
Recognition of studies and qualification: Education and Manpower Bureau; Secretary for Education and Manpower, 9/F Central Government Offices; West Wing; Hong Kong; China - Hong Kong; tel.: +852-2810-2631; fax: +852-2868-5916; email: embinfo@emb.gcn.gov.hk; web: http://www.info.gov.hk/emb/eng.
Accommodation services: Residential facilities are available at all institutions. Similarly special arrangements for the visually handicapped are provided at this institution.
Publications / Websites:
• 'The Chinese University of Hong Kong Calendar' (in English and Chinese), can be found at http://www.cuhk.edu.hk.
• 'Hong Kong Baptist College Catalogue' (in English), published every year by the College; available at HK$25 per copy.
• 'Hong Kong Polytechnic Prospectus' (in English), published by the Polytechnic in July every year; price HK$28 plus postage.
• 'Shue Yan College Calendar' (in English), published every two years by the College.
• 'Lingnan College Prospectus' (in English), published every two years.
• 'University of Hong Kong Prospectuses' for undergraduate and graduate students, obtainable free of charge from the Registrar.

---

524 City University of Hong Kong
83 Tat Chee Avenue
Kowloon, Hong Kong
Tel: +852-2788-9094
Fax: +852-2788-9086
Web: http://www.cityu.edu.hk
e-mail: asjtyu@cityu.edu.hk

📖 **Undergraduate, Graduate and Postgraduate Programmes**

Study Domains: all major fields.
Programmes: Diploma, Higher Diploma, Bachelor's Degree, Postgraduate Certificate, Postgraduate Diploma, Master's Degree, Master of Philosophy, Doctor of Philosophy.
Open to: applicants of all nationalities and ages who fulfil the entrance requirements.
Duration: variable depending on degree sought; part-time study available.
Fees: annual full-time tuition, HK$42,100 per year for degree programmes; HK$31,575 per year for diploma/higher diploma programmes.
Financial assistance: in the form of grants and loans.
Languages: English.
Applications: by 15 March for instruction programmes; all year round for research programmes; to the above address; http://www.cityu.edu.hk/cityu/admissions/index.htm.

525 Hong Kong Polytechnic University [PolyU]
Yuk Choi Road
Hung Hom, Kowloon
Tel: +852-2766-5376
Fax: +852-2333-9974
Web: http://www.polyu.edu.hk
e-mail: oastudy@polyu.edu.hk

📖 **Undergraduate, Graduate and Postgraduate Programmes**

Study Domains: all major fields.
Programmes: Bachelor's, Master's, Ph.D. Programmes as well as higher diploma programmes.
Description: see website for further information.
Open to: candidates with good results in appropriate university entrance examinations.
Duration: 3 to 4 years, depending on programme.
Fees: tuition: US$5,400; living costs: US$6,300.
Languages: English.
Applications: by February; http://www.polyu.edu.hk/~aeco/public/enon_overseas.htm.

📌 **International Student Scholarships**

Study Domains: all major fields.
Scholarships: International Student Scholarships.
Open to: students with outstanding academic achievements.
Duration: 3 academic years.
Value: tuition: HK$42,100; living expenses: HK$47,900.
Applications: end February each year; see website for further information; contact: oafanny@polyu.edu.hk.

526 Hong Kong Shue Yan College [HKSYC]
10 Wai Tsui Crescent
Braemar Hill Road
North Point
Tel: +852-570-7110
Fax: +852-806-8044
Web: http://www.hksyc.edu
e-mail: Info@hksyc.edu

📖 **Undergraduate, Graduate and Postgraduate Programmes**

Study Domains: accounting, business administration, Chinese, economy, English, history, industry and commerce, law, literature and civilization, social work.
Programmes: Co-operative programmes leading to: (a) Bachelor of Laws with the University of Glamorgan (United Kingdom); (b) Bachelor of Accounting with the University of Glamorgan (United Kingdom); (c) Bachelor of Economics with the University of Leicester (United Kingdom); (d) Bachelor of Commerce with the University of Wollongong (Australia); (e) Bachelor of English as a second/foreign language with the University of Stirling (United Kingdom); (f) Professional Diploma and Bachelor of Law with Peking University; (g) Master of Civil Law with Peking University; (h) Master of International Law with Peking University; (i) Master of classical Chinese literature with Peking University; (j) Master of World Economics with Peking University; (k) Master of Economic Law with Peking University; (l) Master of International Economic Law with Peking University; (m) Master of Modern and Contemporary Chinese history; (n) Master of Journalism with the People's University of China; (o) Master of Sociology with the Chinese Academy of Social Sciences; Instruction of (f) to (o) in Chinese; (p) Master of Business Administration with Northeast Louisiana University (United States of America); (q) Master of Social Work with the University of Alabama (United States of America).
Description: candidates of all nationalities who are high school leavers with advanced level qualifications; (f) graduates or currently registered students of tertiary institutes, or candidates who have completed Form Six studies in a registered school or college, or candidates who hold certificates of professional qualification; candidates must be able to read, write and converse in Chinese; (g) to (o) Chinese applicants living in Hong Kong; must hold a relevant university degree or equivalent from Hong Kong approved post-secondary colleges; under 40 years; candidates must be able to read, write and converse in Chinese; (p) candidates

with a Bachelor's degree or equivalent; (q) holders of a Bachelor's degree or equivalent with a TOEFL score of 550 or above.
Open to: see website for eligibility criteria.
Languages: instruction of (p) and (q) in English.
Applications: see website for further information.

527 Hong Kong University of Science and Technology
Clear Water Bay Road
Kowloon
Tel: +852-2358-6000
Fax: +852-2358-0769
Web: http://www.ust.hk
e-mail: ugadmit@ust.hk

Bachelor (Honours) Degree Programme
Study Domains: all major fields.
Programmes: Bachelor (Honours) Degree Programme.
Description: courses in biochemistry, biology, chemistry, mathematics, physics, applied physics, chemical engineering, civil and structural engineering, computer engineering, computer science, electronic engineering, industrial engineering and engineering management, mechanical engineering, business administration, accounting, economics, finance, information and systems management, management of organizations, marketing.
Open to: successful applicants are those who have strong support from their school principals or academic referees, have gained high examination marks over a number of years and over a wide range of subjects, and have been actively involved in extra-curricular activities.
Duration: 3 years.
Fees: application fee: HK$120; tuition: HK$30,750 per year, approximately.
Languages: Instruction in English.
Applications: by 31 December, to Admissions, Registration and Records Office, Room 1376 Academic Building, at the above address.

Scholarship
Study Domains: all major fields.
Duration: 1 year, renewable.
Value: HK$12,250 per month.
Applications: The university awards postgraduate studentships to selected full-time research postgraduates; teaching and/or research duties are required.

528 Lingnan College Hong Kong
Tuen Mun
Tel: +852-2616-8888
Fax: +852-2463-8363
Web: http://www.ln.edu.hk

Master of Philosophy in Humanities, Chinese and Business
Study Domains: business, business administration, Chinese, social sciences.
Programmes: Master of Philosophy in Humanities, Chinese and Business.
Open to: all nationalities; applicants must have relevant first or upper-second class honours degree or equivalent qualification as well as sufficient command of the language in which the programme will be conducted.
Duration: 2 years full-time; 3 years part-time; courses begin in October.
Fees: HK$30,750 per annum, approximately.
Financial assistance: some financial assistance available for full-time students.
Applications: in July-September to the above address.

529 Open University of Hong Kong
30 Good Shepherd Street, Homantin
Kowloon, Hong Kong
Tel: +852-2711-2100
Fax: +852-2711-2100
Web: http://www.ouhk.edu.hk
e-mail: webmaster@ouhk.edu.hk

Undergraduate Programmes
Study Domains: arts, business administration, sciences, social sciences, technology.
Programmes: Undergraduate programmes in language and translation, social sciences, business and administration, accounting, banking and finance, corporate administration, human resource management, international business, logistics and supply chain management, management, marketing, information management, science and technology, computing, Internet technology, applied science (biology and chemistry), communications technology, computer engineering,.

530 University of Hong Kong
Pokfulam Road
Hong Kong
Tel: +852-2859-2111
Fax: +852-2858-2549
Web: http://www.hku.hk
e-mail: afss@reg.hku.hk

Undergraduate and Postgraduate Programme
Study Domains: all major fields.
Programmes: (a) undergraduate programme in most major fields; (b) postgraduate programme in most major fields.
Open to: applicants of all nationalities holding (a) one of the following qualifications: GCE examination; the International Baccalaureate; the Higher School Certificate; one year's successful study at universities, member institutions of the Association of Commonwealth Universities; two years successful study at an accredited institution of higher education in the United States; Bachelor's degrees from some other recognized universities; a number of professional qualifications awarded by professional bodies in the United Kingdom and elsewhere; applicants of 25 years of age and, in very exceptional cases, applicants who do not possess formal educational qualifications; (b) a good first degree from a recognized university is a basic requirement; overseas applicants are required to show evidence that they are able to support themselves financially throughout the course.
Duration: (a) 3 to 5 years depending on the course; courses begin mid-September; duration varies from course to course.
Fees: tuition: approximately HK$42,100 per annum (full-time); application: HK$150.
Languages: instruction in English.
Applications: by the end of February for undergraduate courses, to the Academic Services Enquiry Office at the above address; the closing dates for postgraduate courses vary, contact the University for details.

China, Macao
Monetary unit: Macao Pataca (MOP).
Information services: Gabinete de Apoio ao Ensino Superior (GAES); website: http://www.gaes.gov.mo/p_index.html.
Recognition of studies and qualification: Coordenador do Gabinete de Apoio ao Ensino Superior (GAES); Calçada de St.º Agostinho, n.º19, Edf.; Nam Yue, 13.º a 15.º Andares, Macau; tel: +853-345-403; fax: +853-318-401/ 370-105; email: email:info@gaes.gov.mo; web: http://www.gaes.gov.mo/p_index.html.

531 Macau University of Science and Technology [MUST]
Avenida Wai Long
Taipa
Tel: +853-881-122
Fax: +853-880-022
Web: http://www.must.edu.mo
e-mail: registry@must.edu.mo

Undergraduate, Graduate, Postgraduate Programmes
Study Domains: accounting, administration, business, business administration, computer science, economic and commercial sciences, finance, international business, international law, law, management, marketing, medicine,

pharmacy and pharmacology, telecommunications.
Programmes: Bachelor's, Master's and Ph.D. programmes
in (a) Chinese medicine; (b) law; (c) information technology;
(d) management and administration.
Open to: all candidates meeting academic, financial and
linguistic requirements; entrance test required.
Duration: 4 years for Bachelor's degrees; courses begin in
September.
Fees: HK$40,000 per academic year for Bachelor's
degrees; estimated living expenses: HK$30,000 per year.
Financial assistance: possibility of tuition reductions
varying from 10% to 50 % per semester if on faculty dean's
honour list.

🐾 Dean's Honour List Scholarship

Study Domains: accounting, administration, business,
business administration, computer science, economic and
commercial sciences, finance, international business,
international law, law, management, marketing, medicine,
pharmacy and pharmacology, telecommunications.
Scholarships: Dean's Honour List Scholarship.
Open to: full-time Bachelor's degree students of at the
University and under 25 years of age; must be on Dean's
Honour List of relevant faculty.
Value: tuition deduction of 10-50% per semester.

532   University of Macau [UMAC]
Avenue Padre Tomás Pereira S.J.
Taipa
Tel: +853-831-622
Fax: +853-831-694
Web: http://www.umac.mo
e-mail: registry@umac.mo

📖 Undergraduate, Graduate, Postgraduate Programmes

Study Domains: all major fields.
Programmes: Bachelor's, Master's and Ph.D. degree
programmes.
Open to: candidates of all nationalities meeting academic,
financial and linguistic criteria; admission tests and interview
are required.
Fees: tuition: MOP 32,000 per year; living costs:
dormitory: MOP 850 per month.
Languages: Chinese, Portuguese and English.
Applications: by March.

Colombia

Año académico: Febrero a noviembre.
Organización de la enseñanza superior: Comprende tres
niveles de formación: técnico, tecnológico y profesional.
Las instituciones de educación superior se clasifican, por su
origen, en públicas y privadas,
por su carácter académico, en Instituciones técnicas,
Instituciones tecnológicas, Instituciones universitarias o
Escuelas tecnológicas, y Universidades.
• Las instituciones técnicas ofrecen, a nivel de pregrado,
programas de duración aproximada de 2 años, que conducen
al título de "Técnico Profesional";
• Las instituciones tecnológicas, ofrecen programas de 1 a 3
años de duración aproximadamente, que conducen al título de
"Tecnólogo...";
• Las universidades ofrecen programas profesionales, de
especialización, maestrías y doctorados. Los programas
profesionales, de 4 a 5 años de duración, conducen al título de
"Profesional", aún cuando en la práctica coincide con la
denominación del programa; los programas en Educación
conducen al título de "Licenciado", los de Artes conducen al
título de "Maestro". Los programas de postgrado comprenden
las especializaciones, las maestrías y los doctorados; las
duraciones respectivas son 1 a 2 años, 2 años y 3 a 5 años, y
los dos últimos conducen a los títulos de "Magister" y
"Doctor" respectivamente.
Moneda nacional: Peso colombiano.
Admisiones para estudiantes extranjeros: Para los
estudiantes internacionales: (a) para programas de pregrado,
título de bachiller (si es otorgado en el extranjero debe
solicitar la legalización del diploma ante la Oficina Jurídica
del Ministerio de Educación Nacional, Centro Administrativo
Nacional (ver requisitos en http://www.mineducacion.gov.co),
Examen de Estado o su equivalente presentado en el país de

origen y los demás requisitos que señale cada institución de
educación superior; (b) para estudios de postgrado, además de
los fijados por cada institución de educación superior,
acreditar el título de pregrado (si es obtenido en el exterior, no
se requiere la convalidación).
Conocimientos lingüísticos: Es indispensable dominar el
idioma español. En Colombia se aplican las pruebas del
Instituto Cervantes de España, en el Centro Latinoamericano
de la Pontificia Universidad Javeriana. (ver requisitos en
http://www.javeriana.edu.co).
Formalidades de inmigración: Se requiere visa temporal
de estudiante expedida hasta por un año. Puede ser renovada
por periodos iguales hasta la finalización de los estudios y
obtención del título. Los estudiantes que vayan a permanecer
en el país por más de 180 días, deberán inscribirse en el
registro de extranjeros del Departamento Administrativo de
Seguridad, DAS, en un plazo de sesenta (60) días calendario,
que se cuentan a partir de su ingreso al país, o de la fecha de
expedición de la visa si esta se obtuvo dentro del territorio
nacional. Según la procedencia del estudiante y las
condiciones de salubridad de su país, el Ministerio de
Relaciones Exteriores, por razones de seguridad sanitaria,
podrá exigir un certificado médico. Con visa temporal de
estudiante no está permitido trabajar.
Importe de gastos para un año universita: costos
aproximados para universidades privadas: Pregrado desde
US$350 hasta US$1,750, inscripción: US$20, seguro médico
US$15; Especializaciones: desde US$1.750 hasta US$6.900;
Maestrías: US$2.800 hasta US$10.000; Doctorados: desde
US$800 hasta US$12.300; costos aproximados para
universidades públicas: Pregrado desde US$20 hasta US$700,
inscripción US$10; Especializaciones: desde US$700 hasta
US$2.000; Maestría desde US$1.800 hasta US$2.600;
Doctorados desde US$560 hasta US$2.600; libros/materiales
de estudio: aproximadamente US$400.
Servicios de información:
• Organismos oficiales: Instituto Colombiano de Crédito
Educativo y Estudios Técnicos en el Exterior (ICETEX),
Carrera 3A N° 18-32, Bogotá o enlace "Contáctenos" en
http://www.icetex.gov.co
• Otras entidades de ayuda o asesoramiento: Algunos países
como Japón y España tienen Agencias de Cooperación
Internacional con domicilio en Bogotá, quienes apoyan a sus
nacionales en trámites de becas. Son ellas:
JICA Agencia de Cooperación Internacional del Japón:
Carrera 7ª N° 73 - 55 piso 13; web: www.jica.org.co. AECI
Agencia de Cooperación Internacional de España: Calle 92 N°
12 - 68 Tel: +57-1-636-0207; fax +57-1- 622-0215 /
642-1101.
ACCI Agencia Colombiana de Cooperación Internacional,
Calle 26 N° 13- 19, piso 34; tel: +57-1-243-9669 / 337-5402;
email: acci@dnp.gov.co: web: www.acci.gov.co;
ÁPICE, Asociación Panamericana de Instituciones de Crédito
Educativo, Calle 57 N° 8B- 05 local 46; tel: +57-1-212-6054;
fax: +57-1-212-431; email: apice@apice.org.co; web:
www.apice.org.co.
Becas para estudiantes internacionales: A través del
Instituto Colombiano de Crédito Educativo y Estudios
técnicos en el Exterior, ICETEX, quien otorga becas a
estudiantes extranjeros (consultar http://www.icetex.gov.co).
Enseñanza abierta y a distancia:
• Universidad Nacional Abierta y A distancia, UNAD,
propone aproximadamente 500 programas de educación a
distancia ofrecidos por las diferentes instituciones de
educación superior. La información puede consultarse a través
de la página web del Ministerio de Educación Nacional:
http://www.mineducacion.gov.co.
• Educación Superior/Sistema Nacional de Información de la
Educación Superior, SNIES.
Convalidación de estudios y diplomas: Ministerio de
Educación Nacional; Avenida El Dorado; Centro
Administrativo Nacional; tel.: +57-1-222-800 (ver requisitos
en http://www.mineducacion.gov.co).
Publicaciones / Sitios web:
Ministerio de Educación Nacional,
http://www.mineducacion.gov.co,
Instituto Colombiano de FomentoEducativoSuperior,
http://www.icfes.gov.co,
Instituto Colombiano de Crédito Educativo y Estudios
técnicos en el Exterior, http://www.icetex.gov.co.
Ministerio de Relaciones Exteriores,
http://www.minrelext.gov.co.

533 Colegio Mayor "Nuestra Señora del Rosario" [CMNSR]

Calle 14 N° 6-25
Bogotá
Tel: +57-1-297-0279
Fax: +57-1-341-9060
Web: http://www.urosario.edu.co
e-mail: orelaint@urosario.edu.co

Programas de pregrado y posgrado

Campos de estudios: todas las materias principales, administración, administración de empresas, ciencias económicas y comerciales, ciencias humanas, ciencias políticas, ciencias sociales, comercio, derecho, derecho internacional, economía, empresas internacionales, filosofía, finanzas, higiene y salud, interpretación y traducción, medicina, periodismo, relaciones internacionales, sociología.
Descripción: maestrías y especializaciones en sus facultades de: jurisprudencia; altos estudios en administración de empresas; economía; medicina; rehabilitación y desarrollo humano (fisioterapia, fonoaudiología, terapia ocupacional); ciencias humanas; educación continuada.
Asistencia financiera: sistema interno de becas y becas gubernamentales de reciprocidad del ICETEX.
Inscripciones: dirigirse a la Oficina de Admisiones en la dirección del título o por e-mail: admision@urosario.edu.co.

534 Comisión para Intercambio Educativo entre Estados Unidos de América y Colombia, Comisión Fulbright [CPIEE]

Calle 38 n° 13-37
Apartado aéreo 034240
Santafé de Bogotá
Tel: (57) (1) 287 7831
Fax: (57) (1) 287 3520
Web: http://www.fulbright.edu.co
e-mail: fulbcol@fulbright.edu.co;
asesoria@fulbright.edu.co

Programa de becas

Campos de estudios: todas las materias principales.
Descripción:
(a) Becas de estudio parciales para maestría (5);
(b) Becas para pasantías en investigación (5);
(c) Becas de estudio parciales para posgrado (20).
Materias de estudio: ciencias sociales, humanidades, derecho, comunicaciones, artes, ciencias políticas, ciencias naturales, ciencias básicas, educación, ingeniería, campos profesionales y áreas interdisciplinarias.
Se conceden: a colombianos con alto nivel académico, grado universitario y dominio del inglés, menores de 38 años; (a) y (b) se reservan a profesores universitarios.
Lugar: (c) universidades de los Estados Unidos.
Duración: 1 año académico (prorrogable).
Solicitudes: (a) y (b) desde febrero hasta mayo; (c) desde el 15 de octubre hasta el 28 de febrero.

535 Corporación Universitaria Autónoma de Occidente [CUAO]

Calle 25 N° 115-85
PBX 318 8000
Cali
Tel: (57) (2) 318 80 00
Fax: (57) (2) 555 37 57
Web: http://www.cuao.edu.co
e-mail: buzon@cuao.edu.co

Programas universitarios

Campos de estudios: todas las materias principales, comunicación, economía, finanzas, gestión, informática, ingeniería, marketing, tecnología.
Descripción:
(a) Programas de pregrado;
(b) Programas de posgrado (maestrías, especializaciones) en áreas de gestión ambiental, higiene y seguridad industrial, electromedicina, automatización, telemática, comunicación organizacional; mercadeo, finanzas, economía.

Asistencia financiera: (b) becas de reciprocidad para extranjeros del ICETEX para estudios en ingeniería, comunicación, ciencias económicas, medio ambiente. Pueden incluir matrícula, libros, alojamiento, manutención, seguro médico. Dirigirse a los consulados de Colombia o consultar http://www.icetex.gov.co.
Inscripciones: (b) por mayor información, dirigirse a la Escuela de Posgrados, posgrad@cuao.edu.co.

536 Corporación Universitaria de Ciencia y Desarrollo [CUCD]

Calle 74 N° 15 - 73
Bogotá
Tel: (57) (1) 322 0055
Fax: (57) (1) 217 8195
Web: http://www.uniciencia.edu.co

Programas universitarios

Campos de estudios: todas las materias principales.
Descripción: Programas de grado y especializaciones en todas las áreas principales.
Se dicta(n): en Bogotá, Cali, Restrepo, Sabaneta, Medellín, Bucaramanga, Montería, Pasto.
Inscripciones: por mayor información, consultar el sitio web.

537 Corporación Universitaria de Ciencias Aplicadas y Ambientales [UDCA]

Calle 222 N°54-37
Bogotá
Tel: +571-6684700
Web: http://www.udca.edu.co
e-mail: relint@udca.edu.co

Becas de estudio para estudiantes palestinos

Campos de estudios: ciencias veterinarias, ecología, medio ambiente, ingeniería, medicina.
Materias de estudio: ciencias veterinarias, medicina del deporte, ingeniería del medioambiente.
Nacionalidad: a palestinos.
Otras condiciones: nivel suficiente de idioma español.
Importe: costos totales de enseñanza y gastos administrativos de alojamiento.
Solicitudes: ante el Departamento de Relaciones Internacionales de la UDCA, antes del 31 de enero.

Becas de reciprocidad ICETX-UDCA

Campos de estudios: ciencias veterinarias, ecología, medio ambiente, ingeniería, medicina.
Descripción: becas para estudios de posgrado (especializaciones).
Materias de estudio: ciencias veterinarias, medicina del deporte, ingeniería del medioambiente.
Otras condiciones: nivel suficiente de idioma español.
Solicitudes: hasta mediados de noviembre.

538 Corporación Universitaria del Huila "Corhuila" [CUHC]

Calle 21 n° 6-01
Neiva, Huila
Tel: (578) 875 04 66
Fax: (578) 875 42 89
e-mail: corhuila@coll.telecom.com.co

Programas universitarios

Campos de estudios: todas las materias principales.
Descripción: Títulos profesionales en todas las áreas principales.
Duración: 5 años (comienzos en febrero).
Inscripciones: por mayor información, dirigirse a la Secretaría de Rectoría.

539 Fundación Universitaria Konrad Lorenz [FUKL]

Calle 73 N° 10-45
Bogotá
Tel: (57) (1) 347 23 11/75/90
Fax: (57) (1) 248 02 43
Web: http://www.fukl.edu
e-mail: info@fukl.edu

📖 Programas universitarios

Campos de estudios: administración de empresas, informática, matemáticas, negocio, psicología.
Descripción:
(a) Pregrado: carreras profesionales en psicología, administración de empresas, negocios internacionales, ingeniería de sistemas, matemáticas;
(b) Postgrados: especialización en investigación de operaciones, en psicología del consumidor, en gerencia de recursos humanos, en informática y ciencias de la computación, maestría en psicología clínica;
(c) Diplomados en áreas de matemáticas, psicología, gestión de la información, medición y evaluación aplicada, publicidad y consumo, diagnóstico clínico en psicología;
(d) Educación a distancia: diplomados en análisis del comportamiento del consumidor y en análisis del comportamiento organizacional.
Inscripciones: (a) a (c) se puede diligenciar el formulario de preinscripción y enviarlo por el sistema en línea; se enviarán vía e-mail instrucciones para aplicar a las pruebas y entrevista de admisión en la facultad correspondiente; (d) solicitar información a infoevirtual@fukl.edu.

540   Institución Universitaria Fundación Escuela Colombiana de Rehabilitación [ECR]

Carrera 30 n°152-40
Bogotá
Tel: (57) 627 03 66
Fax: (57) 614 13 90
Web: http://www.ecr.edu.co
e-mail: ecr@ecr.edu.co

📖 Programas universitarios

Campos de estudios: estudios paramédicos, fisiología, higiene y salud, ortofonía, trabajo social.
Descripción: Títulos profesionales en fisioterapia; fonoaudiología; terapia ocupacional.
Duración: 4 años académicos.

541   Instituto Colombiano de Crédito Educativo y Estudios Técnicos en el Exterior [ICETEX]

Carrera 3A n° 18-24
Apartado Aéreo 5735
Santafé de Bogotá, D.C.
Tel: (57) (1) 286 7780
Fax: (57) (1) 284 3510
Web: http://www.icetex.gob.co

🎓 Programa de becas para extranjeros

Campos de estudios: todas las materias principales.
Descripción:
(a) Becas para extranjeros en Colombia. Cursos largos: becas de maestría, especialización e investigación, a ciudadanos extranjeros provenientes de países que a su vez otorgan becas a ciudadanos colombianos, en virtud de la reciprocidad de Convenios existentes;
(b) Programa de Cooperación Horizontal para Becas de Adiestramiento (CHBA): Participación en cursos de corta duración en áreas prioritarias para el desarrollo de su región mediante enseñanza especializada.
Se conceden: (a) a extranjeros provenientes de países que mantengan convenios de reciprocidad con Colombia; (b) a candidatos de los países miembros de la OEA.
Lugar: en centros universitarios colombianos.
Duración: (a) hasta cuatro semestres académicos; (b) hasta 3 meses.
Importe: (a) gastos de instalación, matrícula, sostenimiento, gastos de tesis, seguro de salud, imprevistos y pasaje de regreso en algunos casos, según el convenio; (b) la OEA financia los tiquetes aéreos de los participantes, el ICETEX cubre el sostenimiento, seguro médico, materiales de estudio, transporte interno, imprevistos y viáticos de regreso, y la Universidad concede la matrícula.
Solicitudes: (a) la convocatoria para aplicar a este programa es publicada a través de las distintas Embajadas en Colombia y de nuestras misiones diplomáticas en el exterior; (b) a través de las oficinas de la OEA.

542   Instituto Colombiano de Crédito Educativo y Estudios Técnicos en el Exterior [ICETEX]

Carrera 3A n° 18-24
Apartado Aéreo 5735
Santafé de Bogotá D.C.
Tel: (57) (1) 286 7780
Fax: (57) (1) 284 3510
Web: http://www.icetex.gov.co

🎓 Programa de becas para colombianos

Campos de estudios: todas las materias principales, artes, artes del espectáculo, artes plásticas, bellas artes, francés, inglés, investigación, música y musicología.
Descripción: Becas internacionales y programas especiales para colombianos en el extranjero.
(a) Estudios en universidades extranjeras;
Programas especiales:
(b) Intercampus: pasantía para apoyar a un profesor universitario en la organización de tutorías, seminarios, jornadas o clases prácticas orientadas principalmente a los alumnos de los primeros cursos;
(c) Programa El Dorado: intercambio universitario para realizar presentaciones específicas relativas a su país de origen, participar en jornadas de estudio o en trabajos de investigación en grupo;
(d) Becas para artistas sobresalientes "Carolina Oramas";
(e) Profesores asistentes inglés y francés: intercambio entre Colombia y Francia o Gran Bretaña ("asistencia" al profesor titular del área de inglés o francés).
Materias de estudio: (c) trabajo de investigación en un campo específico dirigido por un tutor; (d) especialidades o cursos de actualización en las diferentes modalidades que comprenden el campo de las bellas artes (pintura, música, teatro, escultura); (e) inglés o francés.
Se conceden: (b) a estudiantes de último año, de postgrado y a profesores universitarios; (c) a docentes y estudiantes universitarios que hayan cursado al menos seis semestres o a estudiantes de postgrado, vinculados con universidades inscritas en el programa y que posean conocimientos satisfactorios de francés; (d) a artistas colombianos de reconocido prestigio que residan en Colombia en el momento de la solicitud; los candidatos deben acreditar su participación en eventos destacados del área en que trabajan; (e) a profesores colombianos.
Lugar: (b) en un departamento de una universidad española adscrita al programa; (c) en universidades francesas adscritas al programa; (d) en instituciones internacionales reconocidas; (e) en universidades o colegios de Francia o Gran Bretaña.
Duración: (b) 1 a 3 meses; (c) 8 a 12 semanas; (e) 1 año.
Importe: (c) alojamiento y alimentación a precios moderados, orientados por la universidad receptora; precio especial en los tiquetes aéreos internacionales y crédito posible del ICETEX para la financiación de éstos, de acuerdo con la disponibilidad presupuestal; (d) crédito reembolsable de hasta 10.000 dólares de los Estados Unidos; (e) la universidad o colegio asignado paga una mensualidad para el sostenimiento, previamente establecido.
Solicitudes: las ofertas de becas internacionales para colombianos se difunden a través de Convocatorias, en donde aparece, el perfil y requisitos que debe cumplir el aspirante, la duración del programa, cubrimiento de la beca, fecha de inicio, etc.; éstas están vigentes por un tiempo determinado de acuerdo al oferente. Estas convocatorias se encuentran para su consulta además en la página web (enlace "Convocatorias") en cada una de las Regionales y Representación del ICETEX en todo el país.

543   Instituto Teológico-Pastoral para América Latina [ITPAL]

Transversal 67, N° 173-71
Apartado Aéreo 253353
Santafé de Bogotá D.C.
Tel: (57) (1) 677 6521
Fax: (57) (1) 677 4004

📖 Curso de actualización teológico-pastoral

Campos de estudios: teología, religión.
Descripción: sistema modular de cursos básicos y cursos

de especialización (7 opciones); cada curso exige un trabajo de síntesis o proyecto de trabajo; 50 participantes.
Se destina(n): a obispos, sacerdotes, religiosos, religiosas, laicos, con secundaria completa como mínimo, que presenten trabajo escrito sobre su experiencia pastoral.
Duración: 10 meses en total (comienza en primera semana de febrero).
Inscripciones: hasta 2 meses antes del inicio del curso o hasta cubrir las plazas.

544 Pontificia Universidad Javeriana [PUJ]

Carrera 7a n° 40-62
Bogotá
Tel: (57) (1) 320 83 20
Fax: (57) (1) 320 83 20/20 26
Web: http://www.javeriana.edu.co
e-mail: contacto@javeriana.edu.co

 Carreras de grado y posgrado

Campos de estudios: todas las materias principales.
Descripción: Maestrías, especializaciones y doctorados en sus facultades de:
(a) Arquitectura y diseño, artes, ciencias, ciencias económicas y administrativas, ciencias jurídicas, ciencias políticas y relaciones internacionales, ciencias sociales, comunicación y lenguaje, derecho canónico, educación, enfermería, estudios ambientales y rurales, filosofía, ingeniería, medicina, odontología, psicología, teología;
(b) Ciencias económicas y administrativas, humanidades y ciencias sociales, ingeniería.
Se dicta(n): (a) en Bogotá, (b) en Cali.

545 Universidad Autónoma de Occidente [UAO]

Calle 25 No. 115-85
Km.2 vía Cali-Jamundi
Cali
Tel: +57(2) 318-8000
Fax: +57(2) 555-3757
Web: http://www.cuao.edu.co
e-mail: buzon@cuao.edu.co

 Créditos educativos

Descripción: la universidad cuenta con un servicio de crédito para matrícula otorgado tanto por entidades externas como directamente por la universidad.
Importe: porcentaje variable de importe de matrícula.
Solicitudes: dirigirse a la Oficina de Asesoría de Crédito Educativo.

546 Universidad Católica de Oriente [UCO]

Sector 3, Carrera 46 n° 40B-50
Rionegro
Tel: (57) 531 66 66
Fax: (57) 531 39 72
Web: http://www.uco.edu.co
e-mail: uco@uco.edu.co

 Programas universitarios

Campos de estudios: todas las materias principales, ciencias agronómicas, ciencias económicas y comerciales, ciencias sociales, contabilidad, derecho, educación, ingeniería, tecnología.
Descripción:
(a) Programas de pregrado en áreas de ciencias agropecuarias, ingeniería, contaduría pública, ciencias sociales, ciencias económicas, educación, derecho;
(b) Especializaciones en las mismas áreas y maestría en biotecnología;
(c) Cursos en su centro de idiomas.
Inscripciones: por mayor información, dirigirse a Admisiones y Registro.

547 Universidad de Antioquia [UDEA]

Calle 67 N° 53-108
Apartado Aéreo 1226
Medellín
Tel: (57) (4) 210 52 10/50 00
Fax: (57) (4) 210 52 12
Web: http://www.udea.edu.co
e-mail: relinter@quimbaya.udea.edu.co

 Progamas de pregrado y posgrado

Campos de estudios: todas las materias principales, ciencias, ciencias aplicadas, ciencias sociales, estudios dentales, ingeniería, medicina.
Descripción: maestrías, doctorados, especializaciones y diplomas en áreas de ciencias básicas y aplicadas, ciencias sociales, ciencias de la salud en sus facultades y escuelas de artes, ciencias agrarias, ciencias económicas, ciencias exactas y naturales, ciencias sociales y humanas, comunicaciones, derecho y ciencias políticas, educación, enfermería, ingeniería, medicina, salud pública, odontología, química farmacéutica, bacteriología, laboratorio clínico, bibliotecología, idiomas, nutrición y dietética.
Se destina(n): a nacionales o extranjeros que superen examen escrito.
Se dicta(n): en Medellín o sedes regionales.
Costo(s): en pregrado: 1.480 dólares por semestre académico.
Asistencia financiera: programa de becas para extranjeros en Colombia del ICETEX para ciertos estudios de posgrado. Solicitar información en las Embajadas de Colombia o en http://www.icetex.edu.co.
Inscripciones: exámenes de admisión en febrero y julio de cada año; por mayor información, dirigirse al Departamento de Admisiones y Registro (http://www.admisiones.udea.edu.co). Por informaciones útiles para estudiantes extranjeros, consultar la página web http://internacional.udea.edu.co.

548 Universidad de Antioquia [UDEA]

Calle 67 N° 53-108
Medellín
Tel: (57) (4) 210 52 10/50 00
Fax: (57) (4) 210 52 12
Web: http://www.udea.edu.co
e-mail: relinter@quimbaya.udea.edu.co

 Programa de extranjeros en Colombia

Campos de estudios: biología, ecología, medio ambiente, estudios dentales, ingeniería, química.
Descripción: maestría en ingeniería ambiental, materiales o química; doctorado en biología; especialización en odontología integral del adulto, énfasis en rehabilitación y ortodoncia.
Se conceden: a nacionales (con título de pregrado y buenas calificaciones) de países que tienen convenios de reciprocidad con Colombia, que conozcan otro idioma además del español.
Duración: 4 semestres, no renovable.
Importe: comprende matrícula, gastos de instalación, alojamiento, manutención, seguro de salud, libros y materiales de estudio, gastos de tesis, imprevistos; pasajes de regreso según convenio.
Solicitudes: la fecha límite de presentación de candidaturas es el 15 de noviembre de cada año; por mayor información, dirigirse a las Embajadas de Colombia, o consultar http://www.icetex.gov.co.

549 Universidad de Córdoba [UC]

Km 3 vía Cereté
Montería
Tel: (57) (4) 786 08 61
Fax: (57) (4) 786 05 70
Web: http://www.unicordoba.edu.co
e-mail: unicor@ns.unicordoba.edu.co

 Programas universitarios

Campos de estudios: todas las materias principales, ciencias, ciencias agronómicas, ciencias humanas, ciencias veterinarias, cría de ganado, educación, enfermería, farmacia y farmacología, higiene y salud, ingeniería.

Descripción: Programas de pregrado y especializaciones de posgrado en ciencias agrícolas, medicina veterinaria y zootecnia, ciencias básicas e ingenierías, educación y ciencias humanas, ciencias de la salud.
Inscripciones: por informes sobre pregrados, dirigirse a Oficina de Registros y Admisiones; por postgrados, al Centro de Educación Continuada.

550 Universidad de La Salle [US]
Carrera 5
59A-44 Bogotá
Tel: +57-1-348-8000 ext.1107-1108
Fax: -57-1-348-8032
Web: http://www.lasalle.edu.co
e-mail: relinter@lasalle.edu.co

📖 Programas profesionales universitarios y postgrados

Campos de estudios: todas las materias principales.
Descripción: (a) Programas de pregrado en áreas de: Ciencias Económicas, Administrativas y Contables; Ciencias Sociales y Humanas; Ingenierías y Arquitectura; Ciencias Agropecuarias; Ciencias de la Salud; (b) Programas de Postgrado: Maestría en Docencia y MBA; Especializaciones: Gerencia de Empresas Agropecuarias; Medicina y Producción Aviar; Gerencia de Proyectos en Ingeniería; Gestión Energética y Ambiental; Gerencia en Diseño y Diagnóstico Organizacional; Pedagogía; Filosofía de la Educación; Planeación, Gestión y Control del Desarrollo Social; Sistemas de Información y Gerencia de Documentos; Gerencia Financiera; Gerencia de Mercadeo; (c) Educación Continua: Diplomados en Áreas de Administración de Empresas, Medicina Veterinaria, Ciencias de la Educación, Trabajo Social, Automatización Industrial.
Asistencia financiera: Becas de reciprocidad para estudiantes extranjeros para estudios de posgrado, otorgados por el ICETEX y la Universidad; convenios bilaterales, créditos bancarios. Para mayores informaciones, dirigirse a relinter@lasalle.edu.co.
Inscripciones: dirigirse a la Oficina de Admisiones y Registro admisiones@lasalle.edu.co.

551 Universidad del Magdalena [UM]
Avenida del Ferrocarril
Carrera 38 No. 22-08
Santa Marta D.T.C.H.
Tel: (57) 430 33 68
Fax: (57) 430 83 58
Web: http://www.unimag.edu.co
e-mail: relinternacional@unimag.edu.co

📖 Carreras en todas las áreas principales

Campos de estudios: todas las materias principales.
Se destina(n): ingreso por examen escrito y entrevista posterior.
Duración: año universitario de febrero a noviembre.
Inscripciones: por mayor información, dirigirse a la Dirección de Relaciones Internacionales.

552 Universidad del Valle
Facultad de Artes Integradas
Escuela de Comunicación
Social [UDV]
Sede Meléndez
Bloque 383 - Piso 4
Santiago de Cali
Tel: (57) 330 2150
Fax: (57) 330 9695
Web: http://www.univalle.edu.co

📖 Posgrados

Campos de estudios: ciencias de la información, ciencias humanas, ciencias sociales, comunicación, estudios culturales.
Descripción: especialización en comunicación y cultura y maestría en comunicación y diseño cultural (énfasis en comunicación y ciudad, en consumo cultural).
Se destina(n): a candidatos provenientes de las distintas disciplinas de las ciencias sociales, humanidades o artes, que profesionalmente se preocupen por cuestiones relativas al diseño de políticas de comunicación y de cultura y que demuestren una inclinación explícita hacia la investigación;

existe proceso de admisión en base a curriculum, examen y entrevista.
Duración: 3 y 4 semestres académicos respectivamente (comienzos en marzo).
Inscripciones: hasta el 15 de enero.

553 Universidad EAFIT [UEAFIT]
Carrera 49 n °7 Sur 50
Medellín
Tel: (57) (4) 261 95 00
Fax: (57) (4) 266 42 84
Web: http://www.eafit.edu.co
e-mail: amaliau@eafit.edu.co

📖 Programas de grado y posgrado

Campos de estudios: todas las materias principales.
Descripción:
(a) Programas de grado en áreas de administración (administración de negocios, contaduría, economía, negocios internacionales), ciencias y humanidades (música, ingeniería matemática), derecho, ingeniería (geología, ingeniería civil, de diseño de producto, mecánica, de procesos, de producción, de sistemas);
(b) Programas de postgrado en las mismas áreas: administración (maestría en administración, en ciencias de la administración, especialización en auditoría de sistemas, en gerencia estratégica de costos, en control organizacional, en economía, en economía de la empresa, en finanzas, en gerencia de la calidad, en gerencia del desarrollo humano, en gerencia de proyectos, en mercadeo, en mercadeo internacional, en negocios internacionales), ciencias y humanidades (maestría en matemáticas aplicadas, especialización en filosofía y psicoanálisis, en lógica y filosofía, en semiótica de la interacción comunicativa, en hermenéutica literaria, en estudios políticos, en estudios urbanos, en administración de riesgos y seguros), derecho (especialización en arbitraje, en responsabilidad civil y seguros), ingeniería (maestrías en ingeniería sismo resistente, en informática; especialización en ingeniería sismo resistente, en gestión de la construcción, en mecánica de suelos y cimentaciones, en ciencias de la tierra y el medio ambiente, en mantenimiento industrial, en diseño mecánico, en producción, en procesos de transformación del plástico y del caucho, en desarrollo de software, en teleinformática, en sistemas de información, en tecnologías de información para la educación).
Inscripciones: por informes sobre becas y convenios u otros datos útiles para estudiantes extranjeros, dirigirse a la Oficina de Relaciones Internacionales (email: international@eafit.edu.co).

554 Universidad Industrial de Santander [UIS]
Apartado Aéreo 678
Bucaramanga
Santander
Tel: (57) (7) 634 40 00
Fax: (57) (7) 632 06 15
Web: http://www.uis.edu.co
e-mail: relext@uis.edu.co

🎓 Programa "Becas de especialización" ICETEX-UIS

Campos de estudios: educación, historia, idiomas, informática, ingeniería.
Descripción: maestrías en pedagogía, en historia, en sistemas e informática, en ingeniería de hidrocarburos, en estudios semiológicos.
Se conceden: a profesionales con diplomas afines con los estudios a realizar, con excelentes calificaciones.
Lugar: en las Escuelas Universitarias de la UIS.
Duración: estudios de la maestría, 24 meses.
Importe: valor de la matrícula, manutención, seguro; en algunos casos, libros.
Solicitudes: las fechas límites de presentación de candidaturas dependen de la fecha de apertura de las programas académicos; solicitar información en los consulados de Colombia en el extranjero.

555 Universidad Metropolitana

Apartado aéreo 50-576
Calle 76 No. 42-78
Barranquilla
Tel: +57-5-368-6572
Fax: +57(95) 358-3378
Web: http://www.unimetro.edu.co
e-mail: unimetro@unimetro.edu.co

☛ Créditos educativos

Campos de estudios: higiene y salud, medicina.
Descripción: créditos educativos otorgados por el
ICETEX.
Materias de estudio: ciencias de la salud (bacteriología,
enfermería, fisioterapia, fonoaudiología, medicina, nutrición y
dietética, odontología, optometría, psicología, terapia
ocupacional, trabajo social).

556 Universidad Pedagógica y Tecnológica de Colombia [UPTC]

Autopista Central del Norte
Campus Universitario
Tunja
Tel: (57) (8) 742 52 52
Fax: (57) (8) 743 62 05
Web: http://www.uptc.edu.co
e-mail: relinter@tuja.uptc.edu.co

☐ Programas universitarios

Campos de estudios: todas las materias principales.
Descripción: Estudios de pregrado y grado en áreas de
ciencias básicas, ciencias agropecuarias, ciencias económicas
y administrativas, ciencias de la educación, ciencias de la
salud, derecho y ciencias sociales, ingeniería, estudios
tecnológicos y a distancia.
Se dicta(n): en las seccionales de Tunja, Duitama,
Sogamoso y Chiquinquirá.
Inscripciones: por mayor información, dirigirse a
Admisiones y Registro Académico.

Comores, Les

Année universitaire: octobre à juin.
Organisation de l'enseignement supérieur: Un premier
cycle de 2 ans conduisant au Diplôme d'études universitaires
générales (DEUG); un deuxième cycle de 1 an conduisant à la
Licence et avec 1 an de plus à la Maîtrise; un troisième cycle
conduisant à un Diplôme.
Unité monétaire: franc CFA.
Admission pour étudiants internationaux: Les étudiants
devraient être titulaires du baccalauréat ou d'un diplôme
équivalent.
Publications / Sites Web:
• Éducation aux Comores:
http://www.comores-online.com/mwezinet/education/index.ht
m.

557 Institut de formation des enseignants et de recherche en éducation [IFERE]

Ngazidja
BP 305
Moroni
Tel: +269-731-233
Fax: +269-731-233

☛ Formation de professeurs

Domaines d'étude: éducation, formation des enseignants,
formation professionnelle, mathématiques, physique,
sciences.
Description: formation de professeurs d'enseignement
général de collège et d'instituteurs: cours de
mathématiques-physique et de sciences expérimentales.
A l'intention de: ressortissants de tout pays, titulaires du
baccalauréat ou d'un diplôme équivalent; admission sur
concours.
Durée: 2 ans.

Valeur: tous les étudiants bénéficient d'une bourse
annuelle de 400.000 francs CFA répartie sur 10 mois et de
20.000 francs CFA de frais de mémoire de fin d'études.
Candidatures: sur concours d'admission tous les ans au
mois de septembre. Écrire à l'adresse ci-dessus pour tout
renseignement complémentaire.

558 Université des Comores

Route de la Corniche
BP 881
Moroni
Tel: +269-734-243
Fax: +269-734-231
Web: http://www.univ-comores.com/

☐ Cours allant du 1er au 3e cycles

Domaines d'étude: toutes disciplines principales.
Description: Programme de cours dispensés à la Faculté
des Lettres et des Sciences humaines; Faculté de droit, des
sciences économiques et des sciences politiques; Faculté des
sciences et des techniques; Faculté Imam Shafioun; école de
médecine et de santé publique; Institut de formation des
enseignants et de recherche en éducation; Institut universitaire
de technologie.

Congo

Année universitaire: octobre à juin.
Organisation de l'enseignement supérieur:
L'enseignement supérieur est assuré par l'Université Marien
Ngouabi et ses multiples instituts et écoles. L'université est
une institution publique rattachée au Ministère de
l'enseignement primaire, secondaire et supérieur. Ses
ressources proviennent de subventions de l'État ainsi que de
ses fonds propres.
Unité monétaire: franc CFA.
Reconnaissance des études et diplômes: Ministère de
l'Enseignement primaire, secondaire & supérieur chargé de la
Recherche scientifique; BP 14557/2078; Brazzaville; Congo;
tél./fax.: +242-81-5265.

559 Université Marien Ngouabi

BP 69
Brazzaville
Tel: +242-810-141/811-828
Fax: +242-814-207
Web: http://www.auf.org/membres/membre.html?id=
COGUMNO
e-mail: unimariengouabi@yahoo.fr

☐ 1er, 2e, 3e cycles

Domaines d'étude: toutes disciplines principales.
Programmes: DEUG, Licence, Maîtrise, DEA, Doctorat
d'État, Doctorat unique, Certificat d'études spécialisées,
Doctorat en médecine.
Description: facultés de droit, sciences, sciences
économiques, sciences de la santé, lettres, sciences humaines;
Institut de développement rural; Institut supérieur de gestion;
École normale supérieure; École supérieure polytechnique;
École nationale d'administration et de magistrature; Institut
supérieur d'éducation physique et sportive.
A l'intention de: titulaires d'un diplôme de fin d'études
secondaires (Bac ou équivalent); admission sur concours pour
les écoles, les instituts et la faculté des sciences de la santé;
pour les autres filière admission sur titres; avoir 23 ans
maximum pour les instituts, les écoles et la faculté des
sciences de la santé.
Frais: frais d'inscription pour les étrangers: 149500 FCFA.
Inscriptions: avant le mois de novembre auprès de
Dorothée Mobonda, directrice des affaires académiques,
direction de la scolarité et des examens (coordonnées de
l'université ci-dessus).

Costa Rica

Año académico: Marzo a noviembre.
Moneda nacional: Colón.
Admisiones para estudiantes extranjeros: Bachillerato o
diploma equivalente; examen de admisión o reconocimiento
de estudios.
Conocimientos lingüísticos: Es indispensable dominar
suficientemente el idioma español. La Universidad de Costa
Rica (UCR) organiza cursos de gramática española y de
redacción para extranjeros.
Formalidades de inmigración: Los estudiantes
costarricenses tienen prioridad en la matrícula cuando se fije
cupo. Se exceptúa a los extranjeros con tres años por lo menos
de residencia en el país y a las personas cubiertas por los
tratados o convenios internacionales, siempre que existan
documentos probatorios de trato recíproco o similar, y a las
personas amparadas por el derecho de asilo y la cortesía
internacional. Para el ingreso a una carrera, los estudiantes
deben ser elegibles y aportar a la Vicerrectoría de Vida
Estudiantil los siguientes documentos: carta de solicitud de
estudio de su caso dirigida al Vicerrector de Vida Estudiantil;
certificado de movimiento migratorio desde su ingreso al país,
extendido por el Centro de Cómputo de la Dirección General
de Migración y Extranjería (este trámite requiere
aproximadamente 15 días en la Oficina de Migración);
original y fotocopia del pasaporte o cédula de residencia;
documento que compruebe trato recíproco o similar en caso
de acogerse a tratados o convenios internacionales;
documento del Ministerio de Relaciones Exteriores que
compruebe el otorgamiento del asilo en caso de acogerse a
ello. Quienes no presenten la documentación completa en el
período establecido, no podrán acogerse a lo dispuesto y no se
tramitarán solicitudes incompletas. Los estudiantes
extranjeros aceptados en una carrera, podrán acogerse al pago
de derechos de matrícula como costarricenses, siempre que
cumplan con los requisitos establecidos, los que se publicarán
en la Guía de Horarios de cada ciclo lectivo.
Servicios de información:
• Ministerio de Educación Pública, San José.
• Instituto Tecnológico de Costa Rica, Apartado postal 159,
Cartago, División de Servicios Estudiantiles y Académicos
(oportunidades educativas; trámites de ingreso;
financiamiento de estudios; servicios de transporte;
alojamiento y alimentación; biblioteca y librería; servicios de
asesoría y asistencia individual en aspectos académicos,
profesionales y psicológicos); Departamento de Cultura y
Deporte, Area de Acción Social (intercambio internacional de
estudiantes).
• Universidad de Costa Rica, Ciudad Universitaria "Rodrigo
Facio", San José, Oficina de Bienestar Estudiantil, Sección de
Servicios Estudiantiles (información académica y
asesoramiento para encontrar alojamiento en casas de familia
y en residencias estudiantiles particulares). Bolsa de Empleo,
Oficina de Bienestar Estudiantil (informaciones sobre
posibilidades de empleo). Sección de Servicios Psicológicos o
Sección de Servicios de Orientación (asesoramiento
académico, orientación profesional, problemas de estudio,
etc.). Oficina de Asuntos Internacionales (intercambios
internacionales de estudiantes).
• Universidad Nacional, Vicerrectoría de Vida Estudiantil,
Heredia (intercambios internacionales de estudiantes);
Departamento de Asistencia Socio-Económica (información
sobre alojamiento y alimentación); Departamento de
Orientación y Atención Psicológica (asesoramiento individual
y colectivo en aspectos educativos, psicológicos y de
orientación profesional).
Enseñanza abierta y a distancia: La Universidad Estatal a
Distancia, San José, es una institución de educación superior
debidamente reconocida que ofrece programas regulares de
grado en ciertas áreas (educación, administración, salud).
Convalidación de estudios y diplomas: Oficina de
Reconocimiento y Equiparación de Grados y Títulos, Oficina
de Planificación de la Educación Superior (OPES); Director,
Office of Planning of Higher Education; Apartado 1174-1200
Pavas, San José, Costa Rica; tel: +506-290-3325; fax:
+506-296-5626; email: conare@conare.ac.cr;
ore@conare.ac.cr; web: http://www.conare.ac.cr.
Publicaciones / Sitios web:
• "Publicación de la Oficina de Registro para Estudiantes
Extranjeros", Universidad de Costa Rica, Ciudad
Universitaria "Rodrigo Facio", San José.
• "Oportunidades Académicas" (en español); fichas

profesiográficas y folletos informativos publicados por el
Departamento de Orientación y Atención Psicológica de la
Universidad Nacional, Heredia.
• "Guía de Hospedaje", Instituto Tecnológico de Costa Rica,
División de Servicios Estudiantiles y Académicos, Apartado
Postal 159, Cartago. Contiene información acerca de las
condiciones, servicios y precios que algunas familias de la
comunidad de Cartago ofrecen a los estudiantes para
hospedarse.

---

560 Instituto Tecnológico de Costa Rica [ITCR]
Apartado Postal 159
7050 Cartago
Tel: (506) 552 5333
Fax: (506) 551 5348
Web: http://www.itcr.ac.cr

📖 **Programas universitarios**

Campos de estudios: todas las materias principales,
administración de empresas, ciencias, ciencias agronómicas,
informática, ingeniería, metalurgia, silvicultura, tecnología
industrial.
Descripción:
(a) Programas universitarios conducentes, según el caso, a los
grados de bachillerato universitario, licenciatura universitaria
o maestría en las áreas de: administración de empresas (varios
énfasis), administración de empresas agropecuarias,
computación, enseñanza de las matemáticas asistida por
computadora, diseño industrial, ingeniería agrícola, forestal,
en ciencias agronómicas, en computación, en construcción, en
electrónica, en metalurgia, en producción industrial, en
mantenimiento industrial, en biotecnología;
(b) Técnicos superiores en: seguridad e higiene ocupacional,
dibujo de arquitectura e ingeniería, supervisión de producción.
Se destina(n): a estudiantes que posean el título de
"Bachiller en educación diversificada" o su equivalente, y que
obtengan en el examen de admisión una calificación igual o
superior a una nota mínima establecida cada año, o bien ser
aceptado por exención de examen. Para los programas de
licenciatura y maestría, los aspirantes deben presentar el
título. Los estudiantes extranjeros deben cumplir con los mismos
requisitos y presentar documentos de sus países de origen
autenticados por las autoridades competentes.
Duración: de 6 a 10 semestres académicos; existen cursos
de verano de 6 semanas de diciembre a enero.
Asistencia financiera: existen becas semestrales
consistentes en la exoneración de los derechos de estudio.
Inscripciones: por mayor información, dirigirse al
Departamento de Admisión y Registro.

561 Universidad Adventista de Centro América [UADCA]
Carretera Itiquís
Apartado Postal 138
Alajuela
Tel: (506) 441 5622
Fax: (506) 441 3465
e-mail: unadeca@sol.racsa.co.cr

📖 **Programas universitarios**

Campos de estudios: administración de empresas,
educación, enfermería, formación profesional, teología,
religión.
Descripción: Títulos oficiales (bachillerato y licenciatura)
en administración de empresas, ciencias de la educación con
varios énfasis (1er y 2do ciclo: ciencias naturales,
computación, español, estudios sociales, inglés, matemáticas,
música, religión, secretariado), enfermería, ciencias de la
educación elemental, secretariado profesional ejecutivo y
ejecutivo bilingüe, teología.

562 Universidad Autónoma de Centro América [UACA]
Apartado Postal 7637
1000 San José
Tel: (506) 234 334 0701
Fax: (506) 234 240 0391
Web: http://www.uaca.ac.cr
e-mail: lauaca@sol.racsa.co.cr

Programas universitarios

Campos de estudios: todas las materias principales.
Descripción: Títulos oficiales (licenciatura, maestría, doctorado) en: administración de centros y servicios de salud, de negocios, industrial, pública; anatomía; arquitectura; bellas artes; ciencias de la educación con varios énfasis; ciencias de la organización e informática; ciencias de la salud; contaduría pública; ciencias de la educación preescolar; derecho; diseño industrial, publicitario; economía; enfermería, filología española; filosofía; finanzas; geografía; historia, historia de la medicina; ingeniería civil, electrónica, en computadoras, industrial; medicina del trabajo; música; periodismo; psicología; recursos humanos; relaciones internacionales y públicas; sistemas de computación; terapia física, ocupacional; turismo.
Se destina(n): a nacionales de cualquier país que tengan el título de bachillerato (o equivalente); deberán haber superado las pruebas de acceso a la Universidad.
Duración: todos los cursos empiezan en enero y duran de 1 a 4 años.

563 Universidad Autónoma Monterrey [UAM]

Apartado postal 3510
1000 San José
Tel: (506) 223 5615
Fax: (506) 222 3062

Programas universitarios

Campos de estudios: administración, administración de empresas, contabilidad, negocio, psicología.
Descripción: Títulos oficiales (bachillerato, licenciatura, maestría) en: administración de negocios con varios énfasis, administración de recursos humanos, administración pública, contaduría pública, psicología.
Se destina(n): a nacionales de cualquier país que tengan el grado de bachillerato.

564 Universidad Braulio Carrillo [UBC]

Apartado postal 5635
1000 San José
Tel: (506) 222 6780
Fax: (506) 222 6775

Programas universitarios

Campos de estudios: ciencias económicas y comerciales, comercio, contabilidad.
Descripción: Títulos oficiales (bachillerato y licenciatura) en administración aduanera con énfasis en legislación y en clasificación; maestría en comercio exterior. Existe coordinación con empresas relacionadas con el área de formación profesional de la Universidad para tener una bolsa de empleo.
Se destina(n): a candidatos de cualquier nacionalidad, con bachillerato en educación media, con promedio de 70 o más.
Duración: 3 años.

565 Universidad Católica de Costa Rica "Anselmo Llorente y Lafuente" [UCALYL]

Apartado Postal 519-2100
Guadalupe de Goicochea
San José
Tel: (506) 225 0650
Fax: (506) 224 7054
Web: http://www.ucatolica.ac.cr
e-mail: ucatolic@sol.racsa.co.cr

Programas universitarios

Campos de estudios: ciencias humanas, educación, filosofía, teología, religión.
Descripción: Títulos oficiales (bachillerato y licenciatura) en administración de empresas, ingeniería de sistemas, psicología, administración educativa, deficiencia visual, educación primaria, educación preescolar, trastornos del lenguaje oral y escrito, educación especial, educación religiosa.
Se destina(n): a quienes hayan concluido la educación

media y presenten certificado de aprobación.
Asistencia financiera: becas que van del 10 al 40% de los costos, según condiciones económicas del estudiante.

566 Universidad Central Costarricense [UCC]

Apartado Postal 1788
1002 San José
Tel: (506) 224 0551
Fax: (506) 224 5068

Programas universitarios

Campos de estudios: administración de empresas, educación, informática, turismo, hotelería.
Descripción: Títulos oficiales (bachillerato y licenciatura) en administración de empresas, ingeniería informática, ciencias de la educación con énfasis en I y II ciclos, turismo.
Se destina(n): a nacionales de cualquier país que hayan terminado la enseñanza secundaria.

567 Universidad de Ciencias Médicas [UCIMED]

Apartado 638-1007
San José
Tel: (506) 296 3944
Fax: (506) 231 4368
Web: http://www.ucimed.com
e-mail: info@ucimed.com

Programas universitarios

Campos de estudios: administración, dermatología, farmacia y farmacología, higiene y salud, medicina, medicina preventiva.
Descripción:
(a) Carreras en medicina y farmacia;
(b) Posgrados: maestrías en administración de centros y servicios de salud, en medicina del trabajo, en morfología humana, especialidad en dermatología.

568 Universidad de Costa Rica Departamento de Español para Extranjeros [UCR]

Ciudad Universitaria "Rodrigo Facio"
2060 San José
Tel: (506) 207 5634
Fax: (506) 207 5089
Web: http://www.ucr.ac.cr

Cursos de español

Campos de estudios: español, idiomas.
Descripción: para principiantes, intermedios y avanzados:
(a) semestrales;
(b) intensivos.
Se destina(n): a ciudadanos extranjeros mayores de 18 años.
Duración: (a) 6 horas semanales (de febrero a junio y de agosto a noviembre); (b) 20 horas semanales (comienzan en julio y en enero); existe fórmula vespertina de 3 horas diarias (comienzos en mayo y setiembre).
Asistencia financiera: convenios con instituciones específicas.
Inscripciones: hasta una semana antes del inicio de los cursos; para mayor información, en particular por alojamiento, dirigirse a la Escuela de Filología, Lingüística y Literatura, en la dirección del título.

569 Universidad de Costa Rica Escuela Centroamericana de Geología [UCR]

Ciudad Universitaria "Rodrigo Facio"
2060 San José
Tel: (506) 225 7941
Fax: (506) 234 2347
Web: http://www.ucr.ac.cr

Programas universitarios en geología

Campos de estudios: ciencias de la tierra, geología, hidrología.
Descripción: Programa de bachillerato, de licenciatura y de posgrado en geología (geofísica e hidrogeología).

Se destina(n): a centroamericanos que hayan concluido los estudios secundarios y aprueben el examen de admisión.
Duración: 4 años y medio para el bachillerato, 5 años para la licenciatura y 2 años más para la maestría (comienzan en marzo).
Asistencia financiera: becas posibles en función de la situación personal.
Inscripciones: en febrero, Oficina de Admisiones.

570 Universidad de Costa Rica Escuela Centroamericana de Geología [UCR]

Ciudad Universitaria "Rodrigo Facio"
2060 San José
Tel: (506) 225 7941
Fax: (506) 234 2347
Web: http://www.ucr.ac.cr

☛ Becas para posgrado en geología

Campos de estudios: ciencias de la tierra, geología, hidrología.
Descripción: manejo de recursos hídricos con especialidad en hidrogeología (5 cada 2 años).
Se conceden: a estudiantes centroamericanos y del Caribe que posean título superior universitario en geología y campos afines y que presenten cartas de recomendación y experiencia profesional.
Duración: 2 años.
Importe: monto mensual.
Solicitudes: hasta setiembre.

571 Universidad de Costa Rica [UCR]

Ciudad Universitaria "Rodrigo Facio"
2060 San José
Tel: (506) 207 5080
Fax: (506) 225 5822
Web: http://www.ucr.ac.cr

☛ Becas del Sistema de Estudios de Posgrado

Campos de estudios: todas las materias principales.
Descripción:
(a) Programas de doctorado académico (4);
(b) Programas de maestría (45);
(c) Especialidades (6).
Se conceden: becas para estudiantes extranjeros (exoneración de matrícula únicamente): reservadas a los provenientes de universidades con las cuales la Universidad de Costa Rica mantiene acuerdos de cooperación académica en los que se especifica tal beneficio; becas para estudiantes costarricenses de pregrado (otorgadas por la Vicerrectoría de Vida Estudiantil) y posgrado (para la capacitación del personal académico y administrativo, de conformidad con normas establecidas por la Institución).
Lugar: cualquier país.
Duración: 2 años (prorrogable por 2 años más).
Solicitudes: en junio, en la Vicerrectoría de Docencia de la Universidad de Costa Rica.

572 Universidad de Costa Rica [UCR]

Ciudad Universitaria "Rodrigo Facio"
2060 San José
Tel: (506) 234 0297
Fax: (506) 234 0452
Web: http://www.ucr.ac.cr

📖 Programas universitarios

Campos de estudios: todas las materias principales.
Descripción:
(a) Estudios de pregrado y grado (diplomas, bachilleratos, licenciaturas);
(b) Estudios de posgrado (maestrías, especialidades, doctorados).
Se destina(n): a nacionales de cualquier país: (a) que hayan terminado la enseñanza secundaria y superen examen de admisión; (b) titulares de un grado con promedio ponderado mínimo de 8. Algunos programas exigen examen de admisión para extranjeros.
Duración: (a) 5 años; (b) entre 2 y 4 años; (todos los comienzos son en febrero).

Inscripciones: de abril a junio; los estudiantes extranjeros deben dirigirse a la Oficina de Asuntos Internacionales y Cooperación Externa.

573 Universidad de Iberoamérica [UNIBE]

Apartado 11870
1000 San José
Tel: (506) 297 1003
Fax: (506) 236 0426
e-mail: unibecr@sol.racsa.co.cr

📖 Programas universitarios

Campos de estudios: enfermería.
Descripción:
(a) Bachillerato y licenciatura en enfermería;
(b) Bachillerato y licenciatura en medicina y cirugía; doctorado profesional;
(c) Bachillerato y licenciatura en farmacia;
(d) Bachillerato en psicología; maestría en psicología clínica.
Se destina(n): a quienes hayan concluido los estudios de educación diversificada; existen examen de admisión y entrevista.
Duración: (a) y (c) 3 años y medio; (b) 5 años; (d) 4 años.
Asistencia financiera: existen becas.
Inscripciones: dirigirse al Departamento de Admisiones.

574 Universidad de La Salle

Apartado 536
1007 Centro Colón
San José
Tel: (506) 231 4598
Fax: (506) 231 7898

📖 Programas universitarios

Campos de estudios: administración, administración de empresas, derecho, educación, educación especial.
Descripción:
(a) Administración de empresas: bachillerato y licenciatura;
(b) Derecho: bachillerato y licenciatura;
(c) Ciencias de la educación: bachillerato y licenciatura (con énfasis en educación de I y II ciclos);
(d) Educación especial (con énfasis en sordos): licenciatura;
(e) Administración educativa: maestría;
(f) Psicopedagogía: maestría.
Se destina(n): (a) a (c) a bachilleres en educación media; (d) a bachilleres en ciencias de la educación con modalidad de educación primaria, secundaria o especial, o con énfasis en trastornos de la comunicación; (e) a bachilleres universitarios en ciencias de la educación, administración educativa, humanidades o equivalente; (f) a bachilleres en ciencias de la educación, orientación educativa o psicología.
Duración: (a) bachillerato 9 cuatrimestres, licenciatura 3 cuatrimestres; (b) bachillerato 10 cuatrimestres, licenciatura 3 cuatrimestres; (c) 8 cuatrimestres; (d) 4 cuatrimestres; (e) y (f) 5 cuatrimestres. Los cuatrimestres son de enero a abril, de mayo a agosto y de septiembre a diciembre.

575 Universidad de San José [USJ]

Apartado postal 7446
1000 San José
Tel: (506) 225 3500
Fax: (506) 382 0107
Web: http://www.usj.edu.cr

📖 Programas universitarios

Campos de estudios: administración de empresas, alimentación, biología marina, derecho, educación, formación de docentes, higiene y salud, nutrición, tecnología.
Descripción: Títulos oficiales (bachillerato y licenciatura) en derecho, administración de empresas, educación en la enseñanza primaria (con énfasis en español, inglés, matemáticas, estudios sociales, ciencias), nutrición, tecnología de alimentos, derecho, homeopatía. Existe servicio de bolsa de trabajo.
Se destina(n): a quienes hayan aprobado estudios secundarios con nota mínima de 80%.
Duración: variable; los 3 cuatrimestres comienzan en enero, mayo y septiembre.
Inscripciones: hasta la primera semana de cada cuatrimestre.

576   Universidad del Diseño [UDI]
Apartado 1775
2050 Montes de Oca
San José
Tel: (506) 234 7290
Fax: (506) 234 9308
e-mail: unidis@sol.racsa.co.cr

 📖 **Programas universitarios**

Campos de estudios: arquitectura, diseño.
Descripción: Bachillerato en arquitectura y licenciatura en arquitectura interior.
Se destina(n): a estudiantes que hayan completado la educación media superior.
Duración: 5 años y medio.
Asistencia financiera: se otorgan becas de asistencia y becas de estímulo.
Inscripciones: en la dirección que figura en el título o en c/o Interlink #205, 7801 NW 37th ST, Miami, FL 38166, USA.

577   Universidad EARTH [EARTH]
Apartado 4442-1000
San José
Tel: +506 713-0000
Fax: +506 713-0001
Web: http://www.earth.ac.cr
e-mail: jzaglul@earth.ac.cr

 🐾 **Becas de asistencia**

Descripción: becas otorgadas a la Universidad para candidatos excepcionales y de escasos recursos económicos. Estas becas proporcionan asistencia total o parcial y pueden ser complementadas con aportes por parte de los estudiantes y, en ciertos casos, con préstamos estudiantiles.

578   Universidad Estatal a Distancia [UEAD]
Apartado Postal 474
2050 Montes de Oca
San José
Tel: (506) 253 2121
Fax: (506) 253 4990
Web: http://www.uned.ac.cr
e-mail: rectoria@arenal.uned.ac.cr

 📖 **Programas a distancia**

Campos de estudios: administración, administración de empresas, ciencias, ciencias agronómicas, ciencias humanas, ciencias naturales, ciencias sociales, criminología, educación, informática, recursos naturales.
Descripción:
Títulos oficiales (diploma, bachillerato, profesorado, licenciatura o maestría según el caso) en sus distintas Escuelas:
(a) Ciencias de la administración: administración de empresas con énfasis en empresas cooperativas y asociativas, en banca y finanzas, en contaduría, en gestión organizacional;
(b) Ciencias sociales y humanidades: estudios generales, estudios universitarios, ciencias criminológicas, ciencias de la educación con concentración en enseñanza del inglés;
(c) Escuela de ciencias de la educación: ciencias de la educación con énfasis en I y II ciclos, en administración educativa, en docencia, en educación cívica, en informática educativa, formación para la educación infantil;
(d) Escuela de ciencias exactas y naturales: administración de servicios de salud, de empresas agropecuarias, producción y comunicación agropecuaria, enseñanza de la matemática, de las ciencias naturales, extensión agrícola, manejo de recursos naturales, informática administrativa.
Se destina(n): a bachilleres en secundaria o a titulados universitarios según el caso.
Costo(s): variable, pero los extranjeros pagan 50% del costo de cada asignatura.
Inscripciones: en enero, mayo o agosto según se trate del 1er., 2do. o 3er. cuatrimestre. Los estudiantes en el extranjero pueden solicitar información en la Dirección General de Asuntos Estudiantiles, Apartado 474, 2050 Costa Rica, Fax (506) 224-0580, o e-mail daes@arenal.uned.ac.cr.

579   Universidad Evangélica de Las Américas [UNELA]
Apartado postal 232-1011
San José
Tel: (506) 233 7298
Fax: (506) 225 0257
Web: http://www.unela.net
e-mail: unela@unela.net

 📖 **Programas universitarios**

Campos de estudios: administración, teología, religión.
Descripción: (a) Bachilleratos, diplomados y licenciaturas en áreas de teología y religión y administración de recursos eclesiásticos;
(b) Maestría en ciencias de la religión con menciones en enseñanza de la religión, en misiología, en misión pastoral, en orientación a la familia, con énfasis en Biblia-teología.
Inscripciones: por mayor información, dirigirse a la Oficina de Admisiones.

580   Universidad Federada de Costa Rica [UFDCR]
Avenida 10 y Calle 30
San José
Tel: (506) 223 2767
Fax: (506) 253 0104

 📖 **Programas universitarios**

Campos de estudios: derecho, educación, educación de la primera infancia, informática, ingeniería, periodismo.
Descripción: Títulos oficiales (bachillerato) en: periodismo, ciencias de la educación con énfasis en preescolar y en I y II ciclos, ciencias de la organización e informática, ingeniería y derecho.

581   Universidad Fidelitas [UF]
Barrio Escalante
Apartado postal 8063
1000 San José
Tel: (506) 253 0262
Fax: (506) 253 9576
Web: http://www.fidelitas.ac.cr

 📖 **Maestría en administración de negocios**

Campos de estudios: administración, contabilidad, educación de la primera infancia, ingeniería, negocio.
Se destina(n): a candidatos de 24 años en adelante, con certificación de estudios; existe selección por entrevista directa y valoración de 2 cartas de recomendación.
Duración: 2 años.

582   Universidad Hispanoamericana [UH]
Barrio Aranjuez
Apartado Postal 408
1002 San José
Tel: (506) 221 1283
Fax: (506) 223 2349

 📖 **Programas universitarios**

Campos de estudios: administración, contabilidad, derecho, educación, electricidad y electrónica, enfermería, finanzas, ingeniería, negocio, turismo, hotelería.
Descripción: Títulos oficiales (bachillerato y licenciatura) en: administración de negocios, banca y finanza, ciencias de la educación en énfasis en I y II ciclos, contaduría pública, enfermería, ingeniería electrónica, turismo.
Se destina(n): a nacionales de cualquier país, que tengan el grado de bachiller o equivalente.

583   Universidad Internacional de las Américas [UIDLA]
Apartado Postal 1447
1002 San José
Tel: (506) 255 344
Fax: (506) 222 3216
Web: http://www.uia.ac.cr

 📖 **Programas universitarios**

Campos de estudios: todas las materias principales.
Descripción: Títulos oficiales (bachillerato, licenciatura,

maestría) en: administración de actividades y empresas turísticas, de empresas con varios énfasis; comercio internacional; contaduría pública; derecho; economía con énfasis en economía internacional; educación especial con énfasis en orientación infantil; ingeniería de sistemas; ingeniería electromecánica, industrial; inglés; medicina y cirugía; publicidad; relaciones internacionales con varios énfasis; riesgo y seguro; turismo.
Se destina(n): a nacionales de cualquier país que tengan el grado de bachiller o equivalente; examen de admisión.
Duración: 1 a 4 años; los cursos empiezan en enero.

584 Universidad Latina de Costa Rica [ULCR]
Apartado postal 1561
2050 Montes de Oca
San José
Tel: (506) 224 1920
Fax: (506) 225 4161
Web: http://www.ulatina.ac.cr

& **Programas universitarios**

Campos de estudios: todas las materias principales.
Descripción: Títulos oficiales (bachillerato, licenciatura, maestría, doctorado) en administración de negocios, ciencias biológicas con énfasis en ecología y desarrollo, ciencias de la educación con varios énfasis, contaduría pública, derecho, historia, economía, educación con varias menciones, ingeniería de sistemas informáticos, publicidad, relaciones internacionales, turismo con varios énfasis.
Se destina(n): a nacionales de cualquier país, egresados del bachillerato o equivalente.
Duración: 3 a 5 años (los cursos empiezan en enero).

585 Universidad Latinoamericana de Ciencia y Tecnología [ULACIT]
Urbanización Tournón
Apartado postal 10235
1000 San José
Tel: (506) 257 5767
Fax: (506) 223 9739
Web: http://www.ulacit.ac.cr
e-mail: info@ulacit.ac.cr

& **Programas universitarios**

Campos de estudios: administración, administración de empresas, ciencias económicas y comerciales, contabilidad, derecho, educación, estudios dentales, informática, ingeniería, turismo, hotelería.
Descripción: Títulos oficiales (bachillerato, licenciatura, maestría, doctorado) en administración de empresas con varios énfasis, administración hotelera, ciencias de la administración y gerencia, ciencias de la educación con énfasis en educación preescolar bilingüe, inglés para la enseñanza, para traducción, ciencias económicas y empresariales, contaduría pública, derecho, ingeniería industrial, ingeniería informática, odontología.
Duración: año académico dividido en cuatrimestres; comienzos en enero, mayo y septiembre. Existen cursos de verano en enero y julio.
Asistencia financiera: existen becas laborales, descuentos especiales por excelencia, y becas de posgrado de la ONU.
Inscripciones: al principio de cada cuatrimestre; dirigirse al Departamento de Admisiones.

586 Universidad Libre de Costa Rica [ULDCR]
Apartado postal 5892
1000 San José
Tel: (506) 221 1283
Fax: (506) 221 8115

& **Programas universitarios**

Campos de estudios: administración, ciencias sociales, documentación, estudios sobre el desarrollo, higiene y salud.
Descripción: Títulos oficiales de bachiller en administración de servicios de salud, desarrollo social, planificación de la salud, registros médicos y sistemas de información.
Se destina(n): a nacionales de cualquier país que cumplan

los requisitos necesarios (bachillerato).

587 Universidad Nacional Escuela de Topografía, Catastro y Geodesia [UN]
Apartado 86
3000 Heredia
Tel: (506) 277 3333
Fax: (506) 237 3703
Web: http://www.una.ac.cr

& **Programa universitario**

Campos de estudios: ciencias de la tierra, geodesia, ingeniería, ingeniería civil.
Descripción: Programa de ingeniero en topografía y geodesia (grado de licenciatura).
Se destina(n): a costarricenses y extranjeros graduados de secundaria o universitarios que tengan el título de técnico o diplomado en topografía y catastro u otro equivalente. Existe examen de admisión.
Duración: 5 años académicos (comienzos en febrero).
Inscripciones: hasta fin de octubre.

588 Universidad Nacional [UN]
Campus Omar Dengo
Apartado 86
3000 Heredia
Tel: (506) 261 0101
Fax: (506) 261 0031
Web: http://www.una.ac.cr

& **Programas universitarios**

Campos de estudios: todas las materias principales.
Descripción: La Universidad ofrece las siguientes carreras, con título de técnico o diplomado, o con grados de diplomado, profesor, bachiller o licenciado según la opción, y algunos doctorados y maestrías:
(a) Facultad de filosofía y letras: enseñanza del español, del inglés o del francés; lingüística y literatura, énfasis en español; lingüística aplicada, énfasis en enseñanza del inglés o del francés; francés; inglés; bibliotecología; teología; estudios latinoamericanos;
(b) Facultad de ciencias exactas y naturales: enseñanza de la matemática; biología marina con énfasis en acuacultura o en manejo de recursos pesqueros; biología tropical; enseñanza de las ciencias; topografía, catastro y geodesia; enseñanza de la computación y la informática; sistemas de información; informática; ingeniero en informática;
(c) Facultad de ciencias de la tierra y el mar: ciencias geográficas (manejo territorial de los recursos naturales y el ambiente, administración y manejo territorial de los recursos territoriales o de los recursos naturales); ciencias agrarias; ciencias forestales; educación ambiental;
(d) Facultad de ciencias de la salud: medicina veterinaria; enseñanza de la educación física; director técnico en fútbol; ciencias del deporte;
(e) Facultad de ciencias sociales: economía; administración con énfasis en gestión de recursos humanos o en gestión financiera; secretariado profesional; enseñanza de los estudios sociales; historia; planificación económico-social; sociología; relaciones internacionales; psicopedagogía;
(f) Centro de investigación, docencia y extensión artística: danza; arte escénico (teatro); artes plásticas; artes aplicadas; enseñanza de las artes plásticas y las artes aplicadas; teoría del arte; música con concentraciones en educación musical, en enseñanza e interpretación del instrumento, en enseñanza y dirección coral, en enseñanza e interpretación del canto;
(g) Centro de investigación y docencia en educación: concentraciones en I y II ciclos, en educación preescolar, en orientación educativa, en administración educativa, en educación para adultos; educación especial, con énfasis en integración;
(h) Sistema de estudios de posgrado: maestría en política económica, en manejo de vida silvestre, en ciencias veterinarias tropicales, en estudios de la mujer, en desarrollo rural, en integración regional, en relaciones internacionales, en historia social, en educación con mención procesos de aprendizaje en inglés, en estudios de cultura centroamericana, en estudios latinoamericanos; especialidad profesional en administración de justicia.
Se destina(n): a nacionales y extranjeros que cumplan los

requisitos necesarios.
Duración: técnico o diplomado: de 2 a 2 años y medio;
profesor: 3 años; bachiller: 4 años; licenciatura: 5 a 6 años;
maestría: 2 a 3 años; doctorado: 3 o 5 años.
Asistencia financiera: sistema de becas por situación
socioeconómica para cubrir el pago de créditos únicamente.
El estudiante deberá aportar los documentos probatorios de su
situación autenticados por el Consulado.
Inscripciones: en septiembre; dirigirse al Departamento de
Registro. Por otras informaciones, dirigirse al Programa de
Intercambio.

589 Universidad Nazarena de las Américas [UNDLA]
Apartado Postal 3977
1000 San José
Tel: (506) 285 0432
Fax: (506) 285 0423

Programas universitarios

Campos de estudios: administración, teología, religión.
Descripción: Títulos oficiales (bachillerato, licenciatura,
maestría) en administración de recursos eclesiásticos con
varios énfasis, ciencias de la religión con énfasis en
Biblia-teología, teología.

590 Universidad Panamericana [UP]
Apartado postal 1106
2050 Montes de Oca
San José
Tel: (506) 221 5600
Fax: (506) 221 0868

Programas universitarios

Campos de estudios: todas las materias principales.
Descripción: Títulos oficiales (bachillerato, licenciatura,
maestría) en: administración agroindustrial; administración de
la producción, de negocios, de recursos humanos;
administración con énfasis en contabilidad y finanzas;
arquitectura; ciencias básicas de la ingeniería; ciencias de la
educación preescolar; comercio internacional; derecho;
dirección empresarial; diseño publicitario; enfermería;
finanzas; ingeniería civil, industrial; inglés; mercadeo;
publicidad; relaciones públicas; sistemas de computación.
Se destina(n): a nacionales de cualquier país que tengan el
grado de Bachillerato o equivalente y que hayan superado el
examen de ingreso.

591 Universidad para la Cooperación Internacional [UPLCI]
Apartado postal 222
4005 San José
Tel: (506) 239 2364
Fax: (506) 239 3107

Programas universitarios

Campos de estudios: ciencias económicas y comerciales,
derecho.
Descripción: Títulos oficiales: licenciatura, maestría en
derecho, ciencias económicas con varios énfasis.

592 Universidad para la Paz [UPLP]
Apartado postal 138
6100 Ciudad Colón
Tel: (506) 249 1511
Fax: (506) 249 1929
Web: http://www.centralplaza.net

Programas universitarios

Campos de estudios: ciencias políticas, comunicación,
derecho, ecología, medio ambiente, educación, estudios
culturales, relaciones internacionales.
Descripción:
(a) Curso "Manejo de conflictos en recursos naturales";
(b) Curso "Manejo de zonas de amortiguamiento de áreas
protegidas";
(c) Programa "Cultura de paz y democracia en América
Central";
(d) Programa Internacional de Estudios indígenas (diploma);
(e) Proyecto "Construcción de consensos y resolución

alternativa de conflictos";
(f) Maestría en "Derechos humanos y educación para la paz
en América Central y el Caribe";
(g) Doctorado en "Comunicación y paz para el siglo XXI".

593 Universidad Veritas [UV]
Zapote
Apartado postal 1380
1000 San José
Tel: (506) 283 4747
Fax: (506) 225 2907
Web: http://www.uveritas.ac.cr
e-mail: info@uveritas.ac.cr

Programas universitarios

Campos de estudios: administración de empresas,
arquitectura, comercio, contabilidad, diseño, diseño industrial,
electricidad y electrónica, informática, ingeniería, marketing.
Descripción:
(a) Facultad de ciencias administrativas: bachillerato en
administración de negocios, en mercadeo; licenciatura en
gerencia general, en contaduría pública, en banca, finanzas y
bolsa, en mercadeo, en recursos humanos; maestría en
administración tecnológica;
(b) Facultad autónoma de odontología: licenciatura en
odontología;
(c) Facultad de arte, diseño y arquitectura: bachillerato y
licenciatura en arquitectura, en diseño publicitario, en diseño
del espacio interno;
(d) Facultad de ingeniería: bachillerato y licenciatura en
ingeniería electrónica;
(e) Departamento de idiomas: inglés y español para
extranjeros.
La UV cuenta con un servicio de bolsa de empleo.
Se destina(n): a bachilleres nacionales y extranjeros, en
este caso que presenten documentos autenticados por
autoridades competentes.
Duración: variable; el año académico consta de 3
cuatrimestres con inicios en enero, mayo y septiembre.
Inscripciones: hasta la primera semana de enero, mayo y
septiembre; dirigirse al Departamento de Admisiones.

Côte d'Ivoire
Année universitaire: octobre à juin.
Organisation de l'enseignement supérieur: Il existe un
enseignement supérieur public et un enseignement supérieur
privé subdivisé en 3 cycles d'enseignement:
• 1er cycle: 2 ans
• 2ème cycle: 4 ans
• 3ème cycle: 5 ans et plus.
Institutions principales d'enseignement:
• Université de Abidjan-Cocody;
http://www.ci.refer.org/ivoir_ct/edu/sup/uni/abi/ (formation et
de recherche, les écoles et les centres de recherche.)
• Université Abobo-Adjamé;
http://www.ci.refer.org/ivoir_ct/edu/sup/uni/abo/ (formation
et de recherche, du Centre de formation continue, de l'École
préparatoire aux sciences de la santé et du Centre de
recherche en écologie - l'Unité Régionale d'Enseignement
Supérieur (URES) de Daloa.).
• Université de Bouaké;
http://www.ci.refer.org/ivoir_ct/edu/sup/uni/bke/ (formation
et de recherche, du Centre de formation continue et du Centre
de recherche pour le développement - l'Unité Régionale
d'Enseignement Supérieur (URES) de Korhogo).
Unité monétaire: franc CFA.
Admission pour étudiants du pays: Les nouveaux
bacheliers doivent fournir des pièces de préinscriptions
(s'adresser au service de scolarité); les étudiants doivent
présenter en plus un certificat de scolarité et les diplômes
attestant de leur niveaux.
Admission pour étudiants internationaux: pour toute
inscription en première année, être titulaire du baccalauréat de
l'année en cours ou d'un diplôme en équivalence; analyse de
dossiers.
Facilité de voyage et autres avantages: tarif forfaitaire
pour le transport urbain.
Connaissances linguistiques requises: La langue
d'enseignement est le français. Des cours, d'une durée de 1 à 3
ans, sont organisés par le Centre d'études françaises de
l'Université nationale à l'intention des étudiants étrangers dont

les connaissances sont insuffisantes.
Formalités d'immigration: Les candidats étrangers
doivent posséder un passeport en cours de validité, avec
éventuellement un visa, et être ou non boursiers de leur
gouvernement ou d'un organisme international. Vaccination
contre la fièvre jaune obligatoire.
Frais pour une année universitaire: 1er et 2ème cycle:
200.000 à 300.000 FCFA.
3ème cycle: 300.000 à 500.000 FCFA.
Services d'accueil et d'information:
• Service de la scolarité, Université d'Abidjan.
• Centre national des oeuvres universitaires.
• Ministère de l'Enseignement Supérieur et de la Recherche
Scientifique (MESRS); BP V 151 Abidjan.
• Direction des enseignements supérieurs, fax:
+225-2022-1252.
• Direction de l'information scientifique et technique; fax:
+225-2022-3409.
Reconnaissance des études et diplômes: Ministère de
l'Enseignement supérieur, B.P. V 151 Abidjan, Côte d'Ivoire;
tél: +225 20 213 316 / +225 20 215 773; fax: +225 20 214
987 / +225 20 212 225; telex: 26138 rectu ci.
Services du logement:
Centre régional des Oeuvres universitaires (CROU)
d'Abidjan.

---

594 Centre des métiers de l'électricité

BP 151
Bingerville
Tel: +225-403-110
Fax: +225-403-462
e-mail: info@cie.ci

📖 **Diplôme de technicien supérieur**

Domaines d'étude: administration, électricité et
électronique, énergie, gestion.
Programmes: formation conduisant au diplôme de
technicien supérieur dans les disciplines concernées.
Description: (a) formation de techniciens supérieurs:
option électrotechnique appliquée; (b) formation de
techniciens supérieurs gestion service public; (c) formation de
techniciens niveau exécution;
(d) formation professionnelle continue du personnel en poste
(exécution, maîtrise et cadre); modules de 8 participants par
session.
A l'intention de: ressortissants des pays africains: (a)
possédant le niveau du baccalauréat scientifique et technique
ou le brevet de technicien option électrotechnique; l'admission
se fait sur concours; (b) titulaires du baccalauréat G2 ou
niveau équivalent; admission sur concours; (c) candidats
possédant le niveau du brevet d'études professionnelles ou de
la classe de première scientifique ou technique; admission sur
concours; (d) ouvert à tout le personnel.
Durée: (a) et (b) 3 ans (débutant en septembre); (c) 1 an;
(d) variable de 1 à 8 semaines.
Frais: (chiffres approximatifs): (a) 8.305.100 FCFA; (b)
7.748.900 FCFA; (c) 3.874.450 FCFA; (d) 216.500 FCFA par
semaine (pour l'exécution) et 230.500 FCFA par semaine
(maîtrise et cadres); ces frais s'entendent en pension complète.
Inscriptions: (a), (b) et (d) avant mai; (c) 1 mois avant le
début des cours.

---

595 École nationale supérieure de statistique et d'économie appliquée [ENSEA]

08 BP 3
08 Abidjan
Tel: +225-22-440-840
Fax: +225-22-443-988
Web: http://www.ensea-ci.org
e-mail: ensea@ensea.ed.ci

📖 **Diplômes d'ingénieur et d'adjoint technique / statistiques**

Domaines d'étude: démographie et études de populations,
économie, informatique, mathématiques, statistique.
Programmes: programme de cours conduisant aux
Diplômes d'ingénieur, d'adjoint technique et d'agent technique
dans le domaine de la statistique appliquée à l'économie.

A l'intention de: ressortissants des pays francophones et
lusophones admis sur concours.
Organisés: en avril et mai de chaque année à la demande
des administrations.
Assistance financière: possibilité d'assistance financière
(bourses nationales ou d'organismes internationaux), d'un
montant variant entre 60.000 FCFA et 100.000 FCFA par
mois.
Connaissances linguistiques: français.
Inscriptions: pour de plus amples renseignements
s'adresser à l'ENSEA ou au Service statistique du pays.

---

596 Institut national polytechnique Félix Houphouët-Boigny [INP-HB]

BP 1093
Yamoussoukro
Tel: +225-30-640-641
Fax: +225-30-640-406
Web: http://www.inphb.edu.ci / www.chez.com/inphb
e-mail: inphb@chez.com

📖 **1er, 2e, 3e cycles / ingénierie**

Domaines d'étude: administration, bâtiment, construction,
comptabilité, études internationales, génie chimique, génie
civil, géodésie, ingénierie, sciences agronomiques,
sylviculture.
Programmes: cours dispensés par les 6 écoles qui
composent l'Institut: (a) l'École supérieure d'agronomie (ESA)
forme des ingénieurs des techniques et de conception dans les
domaines suivants: agronomie, défense des cultures,
zootechnie, agro-économie et foresterie; (b) l'École supérieure
d'industrie (ESI) prépare au DUT et aux diplômes
d'ingénieurs de conception généraliste ou de spécialité) dans
les domaines de: l'informatique, électronique, énergétique,
chimie industrielle et génie alimentaire, génie mécanique,
électrotechnique et maintenance; (c) l'École supérieure de
mines et de géologie (ESMG) délivre les Diplômes de
techniciens supérieurs et d'ingénieurs de conception en mines,
géologie et pétrole; (d) l'École supérieure des travaux publics
(ESTP) prépare aux mêmes diplômes que l'ESMG dans les
filières: bâtiment et urbanisme, infrastructure et transport,
hydraulique et géométrie; (e) l'École supérieure de commerce
et d'administration des entreprises (ESCAE) délivre des DUT
et des diplômes d'ingénieurs en management, commerce et
administration des entreprises, finances et comptabilité,
secrétaire, assistanat de direction et marketing; (f) l'École de
formation continue et de perfectionnement des cadres
(EFCPC) prépare aux BTS, expertise comptable, aux
diplômes d'ingénieurs des techniques et de conception et aux
formations qualifiantes dans les divers domaines industriels
(électricité, mécanique, informatique et chimie), du tertiaire
(commerce, comptabilité et secrétariat), du génie civil, des
mines et géologie, de l'agronomie.
A l'intention de: ressortissants de tout pays, titulaires du
baccalauréat, d'un DUT, DUES, DEUG ou diplômes
équivalents; sélection sur concours ouvert aux élèves de Math
spé.
Frais: (chiffres approximatifs): inscription: 150.000
FCFA; logement: 31.000 FCFA; ESTP, ESMG et ESA:
1.700.000 FCFA; ESI: 1.500.000 FCFA; ESCAE: 1.000.000
FCFA.
Connaissances linguistiques: langue d'enseignement:
français (possibilité de cours préparatoires de mise à niveau).
Inscriptions: à l'adresse ci-dessus; ou à l'antenne à
Abidjan, B.P. V 79 Abidjan; tél: +225 443293 / 444288; fax:
+225 448724; email: abj.inp@ci.refer.org.

---

597 Université Catholique de l'Afrique de l'Ouest-Unité universitaire d'Abidjan [UCAO/UUA]

BP 22
Rue Sainte Marie (Cocody)
08 Abidjan
Tel: +225-22-400-650
Fax: +225-22-441-593
Web: http://www.ucao.fr.fm
e-mail: ucao@aviso.ci

1er, 2e, 3e cycles

Domaines d'étude: anthropologie, communication, développement et production de livres, droit, droit canon, droit international, économie, édition, informatique, journalisme, langues, marketing, moyens audio-visuels, philosophie, publicité, sciences de l'information, sciences humaines, sciences sociales, télécommunications, théologie, religion.

Programmes: programme de cours allant du 1er au 3e cycle dans le domaine de la théologie, de la philosophie, du droit et de la communication.

Frais: faculté de droit: 600.000 FCFA par an.

Croatia

Academic year: October to June.

Organization of higher education system: Higher education in the Republic of Croatia is carried out at six universities in Zagreb, Rijeka, Osijek, Split, Zadar and Dubrovnik with about 80 faculties, art academies, two- and three-year post-secondary schools, and university departments and university courses of study; five polytechnical schools in Zagreb, Karlovac, Rijeka, Požega, six independent public colleges in Zagreb, Cakovec, Križevci, Petrinja and Šibenik, and fifteen certified private colleges. The system of higher education employs a total of 9,570 people. In May 2001 Croatia joined the Bologna Process. The Ministry's Directorate for Higher Education actively cooperates with the relevant bodies of the Council of Europe and follows the work of the Bologna follow-up group.

Monetary unit: Kuna (KN).

National student admission: Secondary school credential (Maturalna Svjedodzba) required for admission to all higher education programmes.

International student admission: Admission requirements: Foreign students need a certified copy of their secondary school leaving certificate and any requested secondary education documents submitted in their English translation. Health requirements: Health visa requested.

Language: Language of instruction is Croatian. Foreign students are requested to complete a 2-semester course in the Croatian language and sit for a final examination.

Recognition of studies and qualification: For information regarding recognition of credentials obtained in foreign countries: ENIC Office, Ministry of Science and Technology, Strosmayerov trag.4, 41000 Zagreb, Croatia; tel.: +385-1-459-4444; fax: +385-1-459-4469; email: email: ured@mzt.hr.

598 University of Rijeka, Hrvatska

Trg brace Mazuranica 10
51000 Rijeka
Tel: +385-51-218-288
Fax: +385-51-216- 671
Web: http://www.uniri.hr
e-mail: ured@uniri.hr

Undergraduate, Graduate Programmes

Study Domains: business, civil engineering, continuing education, early childhood education, economic and commercial sciences, education, engineering, health and hygiene, humanities and arts, languages, law, marine science, medicine, natural sciences, philosophy, sciences, teacher education, tourism, hotel and catering management, transport.

Programmes: Bachelor's, Master's, PhD. degrees.

Description: 10 faculties; 3 teacher training institutes.

University Scholarship

Study Domains: humanities and arts, natural sciences, social sciences.

Subjects: natural sciences; social sciences; humanities.

Open to: student has to be in final year of study; based on an average of marks not less than 3.5.

Duration: 1 year.

Value: 800 KN per month.

Applications: by October to Sanja Fabijanic, email above.

Cuba

Año académico: Setiembre a julio.

Moneda nacional: Peso cubano.

Admisiones para estudiantes extranjeros: Se requiere certificado de bachiller o equivalente de haber cursado 12 grados anteriores a los estudios universitarios.

Conocimientos lingüísticos: Cursos obligatorios de lengua española previstos para estudiantes extranjeros. Se debe presentar constancia de los conocimientos de idioma español o matricularse en cursos introductorios para el aprendizaje de la lengua en Facultades preparatorias organizados a tales fines.

Formalidades de inmigración: Requeridas para los estudiantes extranjeros (visa/autorizaciones, permisos de trabajo, etc.). Se necesita visa de estudiante, denominada D2, que se otorga por las embajadas de Cuba en el exterior y que posibilita posteriormente acogerse a la condición de residente temporal en el país. Certificado de salud debidamente legalizado.

Importe de gastos para un año universita: En el caso de haber obtenido una beca de estudios, tanto los costos de matrícula como los de alojamiento, salud y alimentación corren a cargo del Estado cubano. Algunos países destinan un fondo adicional para ayudar a sufragar los gastos de sus becarios en Cuba. Los estudiantes que deciden pagar por sus estudios deben abonar una cantidad que oscila por año académico entre las siguientes cifras: de 4.000 a 7.000 dólares de los Estados Unidos segun los años. El valor dependerá del tipo de carrera y de la ubicación geográfica de la Universidad cubana que se seleccione. Pueden producirse ajustes a estas tarifas por mutuo acuerdo entre las partes para grupos patrocinados por los gobiernos, firmas, organizaciones no gubernamentales, etc. Este pago incluye la matrícula, el acceso a todas las instalaciones universitarias con fines profesionales, entrega del módulo de libros de texto por semestre, pasantías en instituciones y empresas relacionadas con las áreas de sus conocimientos, posibilidad de vincularse a grupos de investigaciones, clases de preparación física o deportes y de educación artística, expedición de título acreditativo y atención primaria de salud en la propia universidad, entre otros servicios. El pago se realizará en cada universidad, semestral o anualmente. La moneda a utilizar será el dólar norteamericano.

Servicios de información:
• Ministerio de Educación Superior, Calle 23, No. 667 entre D y E, Vedado, Ciudad de la Habana.

Convalidación de estudios y diplomas: Centro para la Convalidación de Estudios y Diplomas, Ministerio de Educación Superior, Centro Nacional de Información, Calle 23 No 565 esquina F. Vedado, Plaza de la Revolución C.P. 10400, Ciudad de La Habana 10400, Cuba; tel: +53-7-552-354; fax: +53-7-33329.

Servicios de alojamiento para estudiante: Todas las universidades cuentan con residencias estudiantiles de diverso tipo para alojar a los estudiantes, desde las más económicas hasta otras con más confort y privacidad. Se brindan además los servicios de alimentación en comedores estudiantiles, restaurantes y cafeterías.

Otros servicios: todas las universidades cuentan con policlínicos y servicios de salud que el Estado cubano garantiza con el mayor nivel para todos los ciudadanos residentes en el país, naturales o extranjeros. Existen campos deportivos con libre acceso para los estudiantes de cada universidad, clubes artísticos, bibliotecas, y otros servicios de mantenimiento, reparación, etc.

Posibilidades de empleo: El sistema educacional en Cuba se basa en el sistema de estudio-trabajo. En todas las universidades, en dependencia de las especialidades que son cursadas, los estudiantes se ponen en contacto con las diferentes empresas, talleres, instalaciones industriales, de servicio, docentes o de investigación vinculadas con el perfil de su especialidad y pasan estancias de trabajo en las mismas. La red de Unidades Docentes de cada universidad garantiza la vinculación del estudio con la práctica productiva y social en general. No existen posibilidades de empleo para estudiantes extranjeros durante los años de estudio en Cuba.

Publicaciones / Sitios web:
• Guía para el estudio de carreras en Cuba.
• Libro sobre las universidades en Cuba (amplia información sobre las carreras, estudios de postgrado, grupos de investigación de las universidades, etc.).

599 Centro Nacional de Investigaciones Científicas [CNDIC]
Avenida 25 esquina 158
Cubanacán, Playa Ciudad Habana
Apartado postal 6990 o 6880
Tel: (53) 7 218066
Fax: (53) 7 330497

☐ **Estudios de posgrado**

Campos de estudios: todas las materias principales, biología, ecología, medio ambiente, física, ingeniería, inglés, medicina, química, tecnología.
Descripción: doctorados, maestrías, talleres, diplomaturas entrenamientos y cursos en las ramas de biomedicina, química, física, corrosión, biotecnología, neurociencias, construcción de equipos médicos, contaminación ambiental y otros;
(a) Entrenamientos: metodología y técnicas farmacológicas para el estudio de productos naturales o de síntesis con propiedades hepatoprotectoras, con propiedades anti-inflamatorias o analgésicas; tecnología de cultivo de microalgas; interpretación moderna de espectros infrarrojos, potencialidad y limitaciones; técnicas generales de microscopía electrónica aplicadas a la biología; psicofisiología; potenciales evocados sensoriales multimodales; técnicas de crioconservación de germoplasta vegetal; técnicas de microscopía electrónica aplicadas al estudio de materiales; técnicas de avanzada para el diagnóstico rápido en microbiología y sus aplicaciones; (5 participantes en cada curso);
(b) Cursos de posgrado: fisiología del sistema nervioso; métodos de análisis de la actividad eléctrica cerebral y modelación neurofísica; reconocimiento de patrones; tratamiento de agua con ozono; ciencia de materiales; selección de los aceros; metalografía práctica; metalurgia física; tratamientos térmicos y superficiales; conservación de productos biológicos por congelación y liofilización; análisis genético para el mejoramiento de las plantas; análisis molecular en la caracterización de las plantas; tecnología para el tratamiento de aguas y aguas residuales; producción de biogas a partir de residuos; idioma inglés; idioma inglés especializado; actualización intensiva en idioma inglés; actualización en idioma inglés; francés básico; actualización intensiva en idioma francés; problemas en filosofía y ciencias; curso-debate: El pensamiento del "Che" y la contemporanidad; epistemología; historia de la filosofía occidental; teoría curricular; historia de la pedagogía en Cuba; (10 participantes por curso).
Se destina(n): a graduados universitarios (las opciones están orientadas a médicos, biólogos, químicos, físicos, ingenieros u otros profesionales), que dominen el español, de edad preferentemente entre 25 a 45 años. Hay proceso de selección.
Duración: (a) entre 2 semanas y 2 meses, fecha variable en el año según el curso; (b) entre 1 y 3 meses, fecha variable según el curso.
Inscripciones: por más información, dirigirse al Departamento de Actividades Científicas y Docentes, en la dirección que figura en el título.

600 Centro Universitario de Guantánamo [CUG]
Carretera Guantánamo-Santiago de Cuba Km. 2
95100 Guantánamo
Tel: (53) 21 325925
Fax: (53) 7 334133

☐ **Programa universitario**

Campos de estudios: agricultura, ciencias agronómicas.
Descripción: Carrera de ingeniero agrónomo (agroecología y agricultura sostenible).
Se destina(n): a bachilleres que superen examen de admisión escrito.
Duración: 10 meses (inicio en septiembre).

601 Instituto Superior de Ciencias Agropecuarias de la Habana "Fructuoso Rodríguez"
San José de las Lajas
Apartado postal 1819
La Habana
Tel: (53) 64 62908
Fax: (53) 64 330942
e-mail: iscah@reduniv.edu.cu

☐ **Estudios de posgrado**

Campos de estudios: ciencias agronómicas.
Descripción: cursos, entrenamientos, especialidades, maestrías y doctorados en sus Facultades de agronomía, medicina veterinaria, mecanización agropecuaria, cultura física y en sus centros de investigación en las áreas de ciencia animal, sanidad agropecuaria, ciencia agrícola, mecanización agropecuaria.

602 Instituto Superior de Cultura Física "Manuel Fajardo" Instituto Nacional de Deportes, Educación Física y Recreación [ISDCFF]
Avenida Santa Catalina 12453
Cerro
12000 Ciudad de la Habana
Tel: (53) 7 810074
Fax: (53) 7 669560

☐ **Programas universitarios**

Campos de estudios: educación física, recreología y tiempo libre.
Descripción:
(a) Maestría "Teoría y metodología del entrenamiento deportivo", mención en un deporte;
(b) Maestría "Didáctica de la educación física contemporánea";
(c) Cursos de verano: educación física, teoría y metodología del entrenamiento deportivo, administración deportiva.
Se destina(n): (a) a graduados universitarios que cumplan con los requisitos del programa de mención; (b) a graduados universitarios en educación física o en educación (pedagogía), que tengan como mínimo 2 años de experiencia laboral. En ambos casos hay selección por entrevista.
Duración: (a) y (b) 2 años (inicio en septiembre); (c) en julio y agosto.
Inscripciones: en junio, en la dirección que figura en el título.

603 Instituto Superior de Diseño Industrial [ISDI]
Belascoaín 710
Centro Habana
10300 Ciudad de la Habana
Tel: (53) 7 781729
Fax: (53) 7 230797

☐ **Cursos y adiestramientos para profesionales**

Campos de estudios: diseño, diseño industrial, formación profesional.
Descripción:
(a) Cursos teórico prácticos: diseño de equipos electromédicos; diseño de información; técnicas creativas para el diseño de la imagen del hombre; diseño de productos; curso básico de gerenciamiento del diseño; gestión de diseño global; diseño, comunicación e identidad visual; conceptos, interfases humanas y productos; proceso de enseñanza-aprendizaje en las carreras de diseño industrial y de comunicación visual;
(b) Cursos teóricos: curso básico de diseño de productos cerámicos; diseño y escultura en Cuba; paradigma de la forma moderna.
Duración: (a) entre 30 y 40 horas; (b) 20 horas.
Inscripciones: para mayor información, dirigirse al Coordinador del curso correspondiente, en la dirección que figura en el título.

604 Instituto Superior del Arte [ISA]

Calle 120 N° 1110
Cubanacán, Playa
12100 Ciudad de la Habana
Tel: (53) 7 214257
Fax: (53) 7 336633
e-mail: isa@reduniv.edu.cu

📖 **Programas universitarios**

Campos de estudios: artes, artes del espectáculo, artes plásticas, comunicación, español, medios audio-visuales, música y musicología.
Descripción: (a) Maestría: desarrollo cultural;
(b) Diplomas: turismo cultural, enseñanza y aprendizaje de la artes plásticas, arte de la percusión cubana, pedagogía y psicología en el arte, realización audiovisual y problemas de la percepción;
(c) Licenciaturas: arte danzario, arte teatral;
(d) Posgrados en distintas áreas en las Facultades de música, de artes escénicas, de arte de los medios de comunicación audiovisual, de artes plásticas, de artes escénicas; posgrado de estudios pedagógicos y psicológicos;
(e) Cursos y cursos teórico-prácticos de la Facultad de música;
(f) Cursos extensivos e intensivos de español para extranjeros.
Se destina(n): a bachilleres, profesionales o graduados superiores según el caso; algunos de los programas tienen selección por entrevista.
Inscripciones: para mayor información, dirigirse a la Oficina de Relaciones Internacionales, en la dirección que figura en el título.

605 Instituto Superior Minero Metalúrgico de Moa [ISMMM]

Las Coloradas s/n
Moa
83320 Holguín
Tel: (53) 24 62414
Fax: (53) 24 62290
e-mail: ismmm@reduniv.edu.cu

📖 **Programas universitarios**

Campos de estudios: ciencias de la tierra, electricidad y electrónica, geología, ingeniería, metalurgia, recursos naturales.
Descripción: Formación profesional, educación continua e investigaciones en sus facultades de ingeniería geológica, de minas, metalúrgica, mecánica y eléctrica.

606 Instituto Superior Pedagógico "Rafael María de Mendive" de Pinar del Río

Calle Los Pinos y Avenida Borrego
Reparto Hermanos Cruz
20200 Pinar del Río
Tel: (53) 82 62443

📖 **Formación de profesores**

Campos de estudios: bioquímica, ecología, medio ambiente, educación, formación de docentes, formación profesional.
Descripción: (a) Carreras de formación de profesores en: historia, plástica, música, educación (primaria, especial, preescolar, laboral), español-literatura, matemáticas-computación, física, química, biología, geografía, economía, agronomía, mecanización de la producción agropecuaria, mecánica;
(b) Cursos de posgrado, entrenamientos y maestrías en el área de perfeccionamiento de la actividad docente en la enseñanza general y politécnica y del diseño curricular;
(c) Diplomas en psicología de la educación, enseñanza de la física y la matemática, análisis de textos y enseñanza de la lengua, metodología de la investigación pedagógica, historia regional, estudio bioquímico de plantas medicinales y aceites esenciales, senderos ecológicos, ecoturismo.

607 Instituto Superior Pedagógico "Oscar Lucero Moya" de Holguín

Avenida Libertadores Km. 3.500
80100 Holguín
Tel: (53) 482145

📖 **Formación de profesores**

Campos de estudios: bioquímica, ecología, medio ambiente, educación, educación de la primera infancia, educación especial, enseñanza técnica, formación de docentes, informática.
Descripción:
(a) Carreras de formación de profesores en historia; plástica; música; educación: primaria, especial, prescolar, laboral; español; literatura; inglés; matemática-computación; física; química; biología; geografía; agronomía; electricidad; construcción de máquinas; construcción civil; mecanización de la producción; agropecuaria; electroenergética; economía; mecánica;
(b) Cursos de posgrado, entrenamientos, maestrías y doctorados, principalmente en las áreas de perfeccionamiento de la actividad docente en la enseñanza general y politécnica y del diseño curricular; perfeccionamiento de las vías de diagnóstico; tratamiento y enseñanza especial; historia de la educación; estudios: locales, socio-religiosos; estudio bioquímico de plantas medicinales y obtención de medicamentos; software educacionales, implementación de programas de educación ambiental en la montaña.

608 Instituto Superior Pedagógico para la Enseñanza Técnica y Profesional "Héctor Pineda Zaldivar"

Calzada de Arday
e/Calle A y Calle 100
Reparto El Trigal, Boyeros
La Habana
Tel: (53) 7 442110
Fax: (53) 7 240345

📖 **Formación de profesores**

Campos de estudios: educación, formación de docentes.
Descripción: carreras de agropecuaria, construcción, eléctrica, mecánica, mecanización y transporte, economía; maestrías en pedagogía profesional.

609 Instituto Superior Politécnico "José Antonio Echeverría" [ESPJAE]

Calle 127 s/n
Marianao 15
13390 Ciudad de la Habana
Tel: (53) 7 202980
Fax: (53) 7 272429
Web: http://www.ispjae.cu

📖 **Programas universitarios**

Campos de estudios: arquitectura, ingeniería, ingeniería civil, ingeniería química, mecánica, tecnología industrial.
Descripción: Carreras y posgrados (cursos, maestrías, entrenamientos, doctorados), en sus Facultades de arquitectura, ingeniería civil, ingeniería eléctrica, ingeniería industrial, ingeniería mecánica, ingeniería química.

610 Instituto Superior Técnico de Holguín [ISTDH]

Avenida 20 Aniversario
Gaveta Postal 52
80100 Holguín
Tel: (53) 24 81851
Fax: (53) 24 61126
e-mail: isth@reduniv.edu.cu

📖 **Programas universitarios**

Campos de estudios: ciencias económicas y comerciales, contabilidad, economía, informática, ingeniería, matemáticas, mecánica, tecnología industrial.
Descripción: Cursos universitarios en su Facultad de ingeniería mecánica (Departamentos de física general, mecánica industrial, mecánica aplicada, explotación de

maquinarias, procesos tecnológicos), y en su Facultad de ciencias económicas e ingeniería industrial (Departamentos de contabilidad, economía, matemáticas y computación, ingeniería industrial); principales áreas de investigación: desarrollo y perfeccionamiento de máquinas para la mecanización cañera; recuperación y construcción de piezas y equipos; perfeccionamiento de la gestión industrial; perfeccionamiento de la enseñanza de las disciplinas y la formación de habilidades específicas.

611 Ministerio de Educación Superior [MDES]
Calle 23 esquina F. Vedado
Habana 4
Ciudad de La Habana
Tel: +53-7-552-354
Fax: +53-7-333-096
Web: http://www.mes.edu.cu
e-mail: ministro@reduniv.edu.cu

☞ Becas de formación completa

Campos de estudios: todas las materias principales.
Se conceden: a nacionales de los países que han firmado convenios con Cuba. Los candidatos deben tener el grado de bachiller; edad: de 18 a 25 años.
Lugar: en los centros cubanos de educación superior de: Pinar del Río, Habana, Ciudad de La Habana, Matanzas, Villa Clara, Camagüey, Moa, Santiago de Cuba.
Duración: 5 años académicos, o 6 años si requieren estudios previos de idioma español en Cuba (no prorrogable).
Importe: cubre los gastos de estudio y de permanencia (no cubre los gastos del viaje de ida y vuelta ni los de vacaciones fuera de Cuba).
Solicitudes: en marzo; las candidaturas deben ser presentadas en los Ministerios de Educación de los países que mantienen convenios con Cuba y enviadas a las embajadas cubanas en dichos países; las becas son otorgadas a los países a través del Departamento de Becas del Ministerio de Relaciones Exteriores de Cuba por conducto de sus sedes diplomáticas en los diferentes países.

☞ Becas para obtención del grado científico de Master

Campos de estudios: biología, ciencias, ciencias agronómicas, ciencias aplicadas, ciencias naturales, ciencias sociales, matemáticas, medicina, tecnología.
Becas: becas de estudio para extranjeros en Cuba para obtención del grado científico de Master en áreas de ciencias pedagógicas, ciencias naturales y exactas, ciencias técnicas, ciencias biomédicas, ciencias agropecuarias, ciencias económicas y ciencias sociales y humanísticas.
Se conceden: a nacionales de los países que han firmado convenios culturales con Cuba. Los candidatos deben reunir los siguientes requisitos: diploma universitario en una disciplina afín a la que desean estudiar, buenos conocimientos de idioma español y 35 años como máximo.
Lugar: en la red de centros de educación superior de la República de Cuba y en centros de investigaciones seleccionados.
Duración: 2 años.
Solicitudes: un año antes del inicio del curso académico (septiembre de cada año) a través del Ministerio de Relaciones Exteriores de la República de Cuba y/o a través de la representación diplomática de Cuba en el país del candidato; las becas son otorgadas a los países que tienen firmado convenios culturales con Cuba, a través del Departamento de Becas del Ministerio de Relaciones Exteriores de la República de Cuba por conducto de sus sedes diplomáticas en los diferentes países.

612 Universidad Central de Las Villas
Carretera a Camajuani Km. 10
Santa Clara, Las Villas
Tel: (53) 422 81178
Fax: (53) 422 81682
Web: http://www.uclv.edu.cu
e-mail: uclv@reduniv.edu.cu

📖 Programas universitarios

Campos de estudios: todas las materias principales.
Descripción: Carreras profesionales, maestrías, doctorados en las áreas de ingeniería industrial, ingeniería mecánica, ingeniería eléctrica, química y tecnología del azúcar, ingeniería civil, arquitectura, física, química, letras, economía, derecho, psicología, cibernética, matemáticas, lenguas, agricultura, medicina veterinaria, marxismo-leninismo, ciencias de la computación, educación física, deporte y recreología.
Se destina(n): a candidatos con secundaria completa o equivalente.
Duración: semestres: de setiembre a enero y de febrero a julio. Licenciatura o título profesional: 5 años; maestría: 2 años; doctorado: 4 años más tesis.

613 Universidad de Camagüey Centro de Posgrado Internacional
Carretera Circunvalación Norte Km. 5.500
74650 Camagüey
Tel: (53) 322 6336
Fax: (53) 322 61126
e-mail: uc@reduniv.edu.cu

📖 Programas de posgrado

Campos de estudios: todas las materias principales.
Descripción:
(a) Cursos de posgrado en áreas específicas de: economía, química, derecho, ciencias agropecuarias, construcciones, electromecánica, ciencias sociales, educación, cultura física;
(b) Diplomados en: computación, gestión de información y uso de nuevas tecnologías, protecciones eléctricas, administración de empresas, administración pública, investigación de operaciones para la toma de decisiones, costo y finanzas, reproducción animal sostenible, desastres naturales, acuicultura, lucha integral contra plagas y enfermedades en la agricultura, ciencias de la educación superior;
(c) Maestrías en: desarrollo regional, contabilidad gerencial, ingeniería eléctrica, termofísica, trabajo social, cultura latinoamericana, enseñanza de la química, enseñanza de la física mediante nuevas tecnologías, producción animal sostenible, conservación de centros históricos y del patrimonio edificado, educación superior, enseñanza de la matemática, fertilidad de suelos;
(d) Doctorados en áreas específicas de: energética, tecnología química, ciencias agropecuarias, veterinaria, ciencias económicas, física, pedagogía;
(e) Cursos de excelencia (actualización de profesionales y académicos en diversas ramas de la ciencia);
(f) Cursos de español (básico, intermedio, perfeccionamiento, entrenamiento).
Se destina(n): a nacionales y extranjeros que cumplan con los requisitos necesarios; se requiere conocimientos de inglés para las maestrías y doctorados.
Duración: (b) entre 200 y 300 horas, con varios ciclos de comienzo en el año; (c) 70 créditos; (e) de 15 a 45 horas, en períodos especiales del año; (f) 120 horas en junio, julio y agosto respectivamente para los cursos básico, intermedio y de perfeccionamiento, 40 horas en Semana Santa el de entrenamiento.
Inscripciones: 15 días antes del comienzo de cada evento.

614 Universidad de Ciego de Avila
Carretera de Morón Km. 9.500
Ciego de Avila
Tel: (53) 33 266211
Fax: (53) 33 301365
Web: http://www.unica.edu.cu
e-mail: relint@rect.unica.cu

📖 Programas universitarios

Campos de estudios: todas las materias principales, ciencias agronómicas, mecánica.
Descripción:
(a) Programas de educación superior en agronomía, ingeniería en mecanización agropecuaria;
(b) Programas universitarios en otras áreas principales.

615 Universidad de Granma [UGR]

Apartado 21
85100 Bayamo
Granma
Tel: (53) 23 92330
Fax: (53) 23 92131

 📖 **Programas universitarios**

Campos de estudios: administración de empresas,
agricultura, ciencias agronómicas, ciencias económicas y
comerciales, contabilidad, cría de ganado, medicina
veterinaria.
Descripción:
(a) Ciencias agrícolas (matemática, física, topografía, biología
agrícola, producción vegetal, mecanización agrícola, de
química); las principales temáticas de investigación son:
alimentación, producción, salud y genética animal;
biotecnología vegetal, agricultura sostenible, plagas y
enfermedades, irrigación y drenaje, biofertilizantes; didáctica
de la educación superior agrícola, planificación estatégica y
administración de empresas; estudios cooperativos, desarrollo
rural y extensionismo agrícola;
(b) Medicina veterinaria (morfofisiología, explotación animal
y sanidad animal);
(c) Contabilidad (computación, contabilidad, finanzas,
dirección y gestión empresarial, ciencias sociales, idiomas).

616 Universidad de La Habana

Calle L y Avenida San Lázaro
10400 Vedado
Habana 4, Ciudad de La Habana
Tel: (53) 7 783231
Fax: (53) 7 335774
e-mail: rector@reduniv.edu.cu

 📖 **Programas universitarios**

Campos de estudios: todas las materias principales.
Descripción: Estudios de pregrado, posgrado e
investigación científica en áreas de de filosofía e historia,
derecho, lenguas extranjeras, artes y letras, comunicación
social, psicología, matemática cibernética, farmacia y
alimentos, biología, química, geografía, economía,
contabilidad y finanzas; áreas específicas: investigaciones
marinas, materiales y reactivos para la electrónica, salud y
bienestar humanos, demografía, botánica, alternativas
políticas, economía internacional, educación superior,
estudios sobre los Estados Unidos, economía cubana, técnicas
de dirección, biomateriales, materiales sintéticos para la
medicina, productos naturales, síntesis orgánica, enzimas y
proteínas, biofertilización, agroindustria azucarera, medio
ambiente.

617 Universidad de Matanzas Estación Experimental de Pastos y Forrajes "Indio Hatuey"

Central España Republicana
44280 Matanzas
Tel: (53) 7 37 7482
Fax: (53) 7 33 3028

 📖 **Programas universitarios**

Campos de estudios: agricultura, ciencias agronómicas,
cría de ganado, silvicultura.
Descripción:
(a) Curso sobre Impacto de los árboles forrajeros en la
ganadería: La experiencia cubana. Temas principales:
agroforestería, usos y ventajas de los sistemas silvopastoriles
y su impacto en el ecosistema; germoplasma arbóreo
forrajero: utilización, corte, acarreo, uso como abono verde,
características alimentarias; producción de leche y carne;
(b) Maestría en pastos y forrajes.
Se destina(n): a ingenieros agrónomos, pecuarios,
forestales, veterinarios y especialidades afines. Para (b) se
requiere además certificación de idioma inglés y 2 años de
experiencia; se exige entrevista con el Comité Académico y
carta de la Dirección Institucional que avale al interesado.
Duración: (a) 1 semana en verano (julio); (b) 2 años
académicos (comienza en enero de años pares).
Inscripciones: (a) principios de julio; (b) septiembre a
noviembre de los años nones.

618 Universidad de Matanzas "Camilo Cienfuegos"

Autopista a Varadero km. 3
44740 Matanzas
Tel: (53) 52 62222
Fax: (53) 52 53101
e-mail: umcc@reduniv.edu.cu

 📖 **Programas universitarios**

Campos de estudios: ciencias, formación profesional,
tecnología.
Descripción: Formaciones profesionales en áreas
científicas y tecnológicas, así como cursos y entrenamientos
de posgrado, especialidades, maestrías y doctorados.

619 Universidad de Oriente [UDO]

Patricio Lumumba s/n
Santiago de Cuba
Tel: (53) 226 31860
Fax: (53) 226 3689
Web: http://www.uo.edu.cu
e-mail: uo@reduniv.edu.cu

 📖 **Programas universitarios**

Campos de estudios: todas las materias principales.
Descripción:
(a) Carreras universitarias en las Facultades de ciencias
naturales y matemáticas, ciencias sociales y humanísticas,
derecho, economía, ingeniería mecánica, ingeniería eléctrica,
ingeniería química, construcciones;
(b) Maestrías, especialidades, cursos de posgrado y doctorado
en las áreas de investigación siguientes: resonancia magnética
nuclear, energética, equipos e informática médica, aplicación
del magnetismo a la industria, la medicina y la agricultura,
economía azucarera, pedagogía de la educación superior,
estudios de comunidades, biotecnología industrial y vegetal,
tratamiento y utilización de residuales, obtención de
productos químicos, arquitectura colonial.
Asistencia financiera: existen becas de Gobierno (se
otorgan por convenios intergubernamentales y se solicitan en
los Ministerios de Relaciones Exteriores de sus respectivos
países); programa MUTIS de la AECI, (España), becas de
investigación, doctorados (sólo para Iberoamericanos).
Inscripciones: por toda información útil para estudiantes
extranjeros, dirigirse a la Dirección de Relaciones
Internacionales, Sede Mella de la Universidad de Oriente,
Avenida de las Américas S/N, Santiago de Cuba 90900, Cuba,
o por e-mail: dri@ri.uo.edu.cu, o consultar la página web
http://www.uo.edu.cu/relaciones_int.html.

620 Universidad de Pinar del Río "Hermanos Saíz"

Calle Martí 270
20100 Pinar del Río
Tel: (53) 78 25479
Fax: (53) 78 25813

 📖 **Programas universitarios**

Campos de estudios: todas las materias principales,
ciencias agronómicas, ciencias económicas y comerciales,
desarrollo comunitario, ecología, medio ambiente, educación,
geología, informática, inglés, silvicultura, tecnología.
Descripción: Carreras universitarias en sus Facultades de
ciencias técnicas, agronomía y forestal, economía, montaña;
posgrados en computación, idioma inglés, información
científico técnica, biomasa vegetal y de montaña, orquídeas,
desarrollo cooperativo, pedagogía, medio ambiente;
especialidades, maestrías y doctorados en las áreas de
geología, forestal, agronomía (cultivo del tabaco) y
pedagogía.

Cyprus

Academic year: September to August.
Organization of higher education system: Higher
education is provided through universities or public and
private tertiary schools, colleges or institutes.
• University level: (1) University of Cyprus; established in
1989 with the main objectives of promoting scholarship and
education through teaching and research and the enhancement
of the cultural social and economic development of Cyprus.
The academic year for undergraduate studies consists of two
semesters. Eight semesters are normally required for
graduation, but in special cases the duration of studies may be
extended to 12 semesters. Postgraduate studies towards M.A,
M.Sc. and Ph.D. degrees is based on course work and
dissertation or thesis. The Masters' degrees require full-time
attendance for a minimum of 3 semesters. The period of study
may be extended subject to approval by the Senate, up to
three academic years in the case of full-time attendance and
four academic years in the case of part-time attendance. Ph.D.
programmes require completion of a minimum of 30 credits at
the graduate level in the relevant study field. Master's degree
holders may be exempted from this requirement. The
minimum years of study for a Ph.D. degree is 4 and maximum
8. (2) Open University of Cyprus: scheduled to open in 2005
and will offer an undergraduate programmes in Greek
civilization, postgraduate programme in management of
health services and a postgraduate programme in education.
(3) Technological University of Cyprus: Scheduled to open in
2007 with the following faculties: technological applications;
health services; administration and finance; earth technologies
and science; applied arts and communication.
• Public tertiary education: There are 8 public tertiary
education institutions offering sub-degree level programmes
in technical engineering, forestry, hotel and catering, nursing
and other vocational programmes as well as one institution
offering postgraduate programmes in management. These
institutions function under the supervision of various
ministries and award their own diplomas. The length of study
in these institutions is usually three years.
• Private tertiary education: There are 22 private tertiary
education schools, colleges and institutes registered with the
Ministry of Education and Culture offering a wide range of
programmes of study: business studies, engineering, social
sciences, languages, education, hotel and tourism,
administration, management, graphic design, computer
science and other programmes. Some of these institutions also
offer programmes of study at a Master's level. The
programme of study normally follows a two-semester system
with compulsory attendance. Programmes may lead to a
Certificate (one year of study), Diploma (two years of study),
Higher Diploma (three years of study) or a Bachelor's degree
(four years of study). Some postgraduate programmes leading
to a Master's degree are also offered and consist of one to two
years of additional study.
It should be noted that the qualifications earned at private
tertiary institutions are not recognized unless the
corresponding programme is educationally accredited.
Monetary unit: Cyprus pound (CP).
National student admission: There is a limited number of
places for international students who wish to study at the
University of Cyprus or at the public schools of higher
education. International students should have a school-leaving
certificate (secondary school apolytirion) awarded after
passing the six grades of secondary education. Entrance
examinations are held for the University of Cyprus and all
public post-secondary non-university institutions. Entrance
requirements for private post-secondary non-university
institutions can only be satisfied by 12 years of schooling or
obtaining a secondary-school certificate after six years of
secondary schooling or its equivalent.
Language: Good knowledge of Greek/Turkish for study at
the University of Cyprus and of English for other institutions
is required. Proof of language proficiency may be required.
Immigration requirements: A visa is required for
nationals of all countries except those from the European
Union.
Estimated expenses for one academic year: tuition:
C£1,500-8,500 (depending on the course); books/supplies:
C£500; housing: C£4,000.
• University of Cyprus: fees for European Union nationals,
C£2,000 per year; other nationals C£4,000 per year.
Postgraduate fees: C£100 per credit for the taught stage;

C£500 per semester during the research stage and C£100 per
semester during the dissertation stage.
• Public tertiary education: tuition fees range from C£1,000 to
C£2,500 per year.
• Private schools of tertiary education: tuition fees range from
C£1,500 to approximately C£3,500 per academic year. For
the Master's level, tuition and fees range from C£4,500 to
C£8,500.
Information services: Information can be obtained from
the institutions of higher education, or the Ministry of
Education and Culture (Department of Higher and Tertiary
Education, Thoukididou and Kimonos, CY 1434, Nicosia,
Cyprus; tel: +357-22-800-616; fax: +357-22-427-560; email:
daae@moec.gov.cy; web: http://www.moec.gov.cy, or
through the Cyprus Government Embassies and high
commissions in various countries.
Open and distance learning: The Open University of
Cyprus is expected to operate in September 2005 and will
offer the following programmes of study: undergraduate
programme in Greek civilization; postgraduate programme in
management of health services; postgraduate programme in
eduction.0.
Recognition of studies and qualification: Cyprus Council
for the Recognition of Higher Education Qualifications
(KYSATS), Ministry of Education and Culture, Kimonos and
Thoukididou street, CY 1434, Nicosia, Cyprus; tel:
+357-22-800-666; fax: +357-22-305-116; email:
kysats@cytanet.com.cy. The KYSATS is responsible for the
recognition of titles or degrees awarded in foreign countries
and serves as the National Recognition Information Center
(NARIC) for Cyprus.
Accommodation services: The Office of Student Affairs
functions in every higher education institution and provides
information on university and private housing for students.
Students may contact the educational institution of their
choice for more information.
Work opportunities: Work opportunities are available for
nationals of European Union countries. Other nationals may
be allowed to work on the various campuses. Students in
certain fields requiring practical experience, such as tourism,
hotel management, etc. are also allowed to work within their
programme of study.
Additional information: International students are advised
to contact directly the educational institution in which they
wish to study and to check the status of accreditation of the
programme of study.
Publications / Websites:
• 'Statistics of Education', published by the Statistical Service
of Cyprus, 2004.
• 'Higher Education in Cyprus', published by the Press and
Information Office, 2000
• 'Department of Higher and Tertiary Education, 1984-2004:
Twenty Years of Development and Contribution', published
by the Ministry of Education and Culture, 2004
• Ministry of Education and Culture: www.moec.gov.cy (in
Greek)
• Cyprus Pedagogical Institute:
http://athena.pi.ac.cy/pedagogical/index.html (in Greek)
• Educational Service Commission: www.eev.gov.cy (in
Greek)
• EURYBASE, the information database on education
systems in Europe: www.eurydice.org.

---

621   Americanos College [AC]
2, Omirou Avenue
PO Box 22425
1521 Nicosia
Tel: +357-22-661-122
Fax: +357-22-665-458/664118
Web: http://www.ac.ac.cy
e-mail: college@ac.ac.cy

📖 Undergraduate Programmes

Study Domains: accounting, business, business
administration, computer science, economic and commercial
sciences, management, marketing, summer programmes,
tourism, hotel and catering management.
Programmes: Bachelor´s degrees and 2-year diplomas in
business administration, management, marketing,
management information systems, computer science, hotel
management and intensive course in English language.

Open to: all applicants regardless of nationality with at least 12 years of schooling and a secondary-school certificate; between 17-26 years of age.
Duration: 2 and 4 years.
Fees: tuition fees US$3,500; living expenses: US$3,000 (for academic year 2002-2003).
Financial assistance: 10-50% tuition reduction, based on academic performance.
Applications: by 31 July for Fall (September) semester, by November for Spring (February) semester and by 30 April for Summer (July) semester.

🎓 Scholarships

Study Domains: business, business administration, management, marketing.
Scholarships: Academic Scholarships.
Description: academic scholarships in business administration; management; marketing; management information systems; computer science; hotel management and intensive course in English language.
Open to: all applicants regardless of nationality with at least 12 years of schooling and a school leaving certificate; between 17-26 years of age.
Duration: 1 academic year.
Value: 10-50% tuition reduction, based on academic performance.
Applications: by 31 July for Fall (September) semester, by 30 November for Spring (February) semester and by 30 April for Summer (July) semester.

622   ARTE Music Academy
PO Box 21207
1504 Nicosia
Tel: +357-22-676-823
Fax: +357-22-665-695
e-mail: artechno@spidernet.com.cy

📖 Diploma Programme / Music

Study Domains: music and musicology.
Programmes: higher diploma in music.
Duration: 3 years.
Fees: C£3,900.
Applications: to the above address.

623   C.D.A. College
PO Box 21972
1515 Nicosia
Tel: +357-22-661-104/663-105
Fax: +357-22-671-387
Web: http://www.cdacollege.ac.cy
e-mail: cdacoll@spidernet.com.cy

📖 Undergraduate Programmes

Study Domains: archaeology, interior design, tourism, hotel and catering management.
Programmes: higher diploma in travel and tourism, interior design and architectural drawing, secretarial studies.
Open to: graduates of secondary school.
Duration: 2 years; courses begin in October.
Fees: C£2,000.
Languages: instruction in English.
Applications: to the above address.

624   C.T.L. College
PO Box 51938
3509 Limassol
Tel: +357-25-736-501
Fax: +357-25-736-629
Web: http://www.ctleuro.ac.cy
e-mail: college@ctleuro.ac.cy

📖 Undergraduate Programmes

Study Domains: accounting, computer science, law, tourism, hotel and catering management.
Programmes: (a) certificate, preparatory (Foundation); (b) Diploma in hotel and catering (cookery and pastry); (c) diploma in hotel and catering (waiting and bar tending); (d) higher diploma in office administration with computers; (e) higher diploma in professional marketing; (f) higher diploma in travel and tourism management; (g) higher diploma in law; (h) higher diploma in professional banking; (i) Bachelor of Arts in professional accounting; (j) Bachelor of Arts in computer administration; (k) Bachelor of Science in computer

science.
Duration: (a) to (c) 1 year; (d) to (g) 2 years; (h) 3 years; (i) to (k) 4 years.
Applications: to the above address.

625   Casa College
PO Box 20545
1660 Nicosia
Tel: +357-22-662-423
Fax: +357-22-497-921
Web: http://www.casacollege.ac.cy
e-mail: casa.college@cytanet.com.cy

📖 Undergraduate Programmes

Study Domains: business administration, tourism, hotel and catering management.
Programmes: diploma in hotel administration and in business studies.
Open to: graduates of secondary school.
Duration: 2 years; courses begin in October.
Fees: C£1,100.
Languages: instruction in English.
Applications: to the above address.

626   College of Tourism and Hotel Management [COTHM]
79 Aglangia Avenue
PO Box 20281
2150 Nicosia
Tel: +357-22-334-271
Fax: +357-22-336-295
Web: http://www.cothm.ac.cy
e-mail: cothm@spidernet.com.cy

📖 Undergraduate Programmes

Study Domains: tourism, hotel and catering management, vocational training.
Programmes: Bachelor of Arts in hotel administration; Diploma in travel and tourism administration.
Open to: candidates of all nationalities, between 17 and 25 years of age, with a high-school certificate or equivalent; TOEFL minimum score 500; entrance examinations required.
Duration: 4 years.
Fees: tuition: US$4,000; living expenses: US$400 per month; registration fee: US$70.
Financial assistance: students with cumulative grade average over 85% may benefit from ACE scholarships consisting of fee reductions ranging from 10 to 100%.
Languages: English.
Applications: (a) 3 months before the commencement of classes; (b) by June to the Admissions Officer.

🎓 ACE Scholarships

Study Domains: tourism, hotel and catering management.
Scholarships: ACE Scholarships in tourism, hotel and catering management.
Open to: all students who have completed at least 1 semester at the school; with a minimum grade average (SPA) of over 85%.
Duration: 1 semester; renewable at the end of each semester depending on cumulative GPA.
Value: between 10% and 100% reduction of tuition fees for 1 semester.
Applications: no application needed.

627   Cyprus College
PO Box 22006
1516 Nicosia
Tel: +357-22-713-000
Fax: +357-22-662-051
Web: http://www.cycollege.ac.cy
e-mail: aelefthe@cycollege.ac.cy

📖 Undergraduate and Graduate Programmes

Study Domains: accounting, applied arts, business, business administration, computer science, economy, finance, management, marketing.
Programmes: (a) certificate, diploma, Bachelor of Arts: accounting, applied arts and science, banking and finance, business administration, computer science, economics, European studies, hotel management, management, management information systems, marketing, office administration, travel and tourism; (b) M.B.A. (areas of

concentration): computer and information science, human resource management, international business, management and organization, Marketing and combined major.
Open to: candidates of any nationality with a minimum of 12 years of schooling for the undergraduate programmes.
Duration: Certificate: 1 year; Diploma: 2 years; Bachelor's degree: 4 years; Master's degree: 2 years.
Fees: US$160 per credit.
Financial assistance: scholarships, assistantships and on-campus work.
Applications: by 31 August for Fall semester (September) and by 20 December for Spring semester (January); to the Office of Admissions.

628 Cyprus College of Accountancy and Business Studies
13 Langada Street, Strovolos
PO Box 5361
1309 Nicosia
Tel: +357-22-420-153

⌖ Undergraduate Programmes

Study Domains: accounting, finance.
Programmes: undergraduate programmes leading to diploma and advanced diploma.
Description: (a) diploma in accounting; (b) advanced diploma in advanced accounting; (c) diploma in accounting and finance; (d) diploma in banking.
Duration: (a) 1 to 2 years; (b) 2 years; (c) 1 year; (d) 3-1/2 years.
Applications: to the above address for more information.

629 Cyprus College of Art
Lemba
8260 Paphos
Tel: +357-26-270-557
Fax: +357-26-264-269

⌖ Undergraduate and Postgraduate Programmes

Study Domains: fine arts.
Programmes: Diploma and Postgraduate courses in fine arts.
Open to: candidates of any nationality, aged over 18; proficiency in English required.
Duration: 1 year; courses begin in November.
Fees: tuition: £1,100 (sterling) per year; living expenses: £200-250 (sterling) per month.
Languages: instruction in English.
Applications: by 5 September, to the Principal, at the above address.

630 Cyprus Forestry College
Prodromos
4841 Limassol
Tel: +357-25-462-064/48
Fax: +357-25-462-646
Web: http://www.pio.gov.cy/forestry
e-mail: forcollege@cytanet.com.cy

⌖ Undergraduate Programmes

Study Domains: forestry.
Programmes: (a) diploma in forestry; (b) higher diploma in forestry: limited number of participants; (c) certificate in forestry: limited number of participants.
Open to: nationals of all countries who have: (a) a two-year Certificate in Forestry (or its equivalent) from a well recognized school or, (b) a two-year Certificate in Agriculture or related field with merit grades in all major subjects from a well recognized school of Natural Resources plus some years practical experience in Forestry or, (c) a General Certificate of Education at O-level (or its equivalent) with passes in at least four subjects including relevant sciences plus three years practical experience in forestry or, (d) such other qualifications as the College deems to be acceptable in lieu of those specified above.
Duration: (a) 2 years; courses begin in October; (b) 6 months; courses begin in January and August; (c) 1 to 2 months depending on study topic.
Fees: including board, lodging, tuition and other allowances, (a) C£15,114 (b) C£5,520; (c) C£925 per month.

Financial assistance: the Cyprus Government awards a number of scholarships to overseas students from Commonwealth countries for studies at the College; also other countries and various international organizations give scholarships to students coming from developing countries.
Languages: instruction in English.
Applications: (a) by 31 May; (b) 3 months before the commencement of classes; (c) 3 months before the commencement of classes; to the Principal Forestry College, Cyprus Forestry College, Prodromos, 4841 Limassol, Cyprus, through the respective governments or funding agencies.

631 Cyprus Institute of Marketing
PO Box 25288
3022 Nicosia
Tel: +357-22-778-475
Fax: +357-22-779-331
Web: http://www.cima.com.cy
e-mail: cima@spidernet.com.cy

⌖ Undergraduate, Graduate, Postgraduate Programmes

Study Domains: business administration, European studies, finance, management, marketing, tourism, hotel and catering management.
Programmes: undergraduate level programme; graduate programme (M.B.A.) and postgraduate diploma.
Description: (a) undergraduate level: business administration, European studies, financial and computer studies, marketing, tourism, shipping, banking; (b) postgraduate diploma in Corporate Management and Strategic Planning: marketing communications, planning and control, case studies, international marketing, public relations, executive skills: 33 participants; (c) M.B.A.: accounting and financial management, management of operations, business statistics, marketing and management, business economics, organizational behaviour, business environment, employee relations, financial markets, business policy and strategy, marketing research, European Community law, the European business environment, organizational information resources, financial management, international marketing, advertising and public relations, operations management and operational research.
Open to: (a) secondary school graduates, with an average of 14 over 20 (or 70%); (b) postgraduate qualifications for practising managers; minimum age 25 years; (c) candidates with a university degree plus 3 years of business experience.
Duration: (a) 3 years; (b) 1 year; (c) 2 years.
Fees: (a) C£2,000 per year; (b) C£2,500; (c) C£3,500.
Languages: instruction in English.
Applications: (a) by September; (b) by August; (c) by July; to the Academic Registrar.

632 Cyprus International Institute of Management
PO Box 20378
21 Akadimias Avenue
Aglandjia
2151 Nicosia
Tel: +357-22-330-052
Fax: +357-22-331-121
Web: http://www.ciim.ac.cy
e-mail: ciim@ciim.ac.cy

⌖ Postgraduate Degree Programmes

Study Domains: business administration, management.
Programmes: Master of Business Administration (M.B.A.); Master of Public Sector Management (M.P.S.M.).
Open to: candidates of any nationality, holding a B.Sc. and 2 years of work experience; proficiency in English required.
Duration: 1 or 2 years; courses begin in September.
Fees: C£10,000.
Financial assistance: a special scholarship of C£4,000 is offered to individuals who are not sponsored by companies.
Applications: by end of July, to the Graduate Course Administrator at the above address.

633   Frederick Institute of Technology [FIT]
Yiannis Frederickou Street 7
Pallouriotissa
PO Box 24729
1303 Nicosia
Tel: +357-22-431-355
Fax: +357-22-438-234
Web: http://www.fit.ac.cy
e-mail: admoff@fit.ac.cy

📖 **Undergraduate Programmes**

Study Domains: advertising, audio-visual media, business, computer science, engineering, graphic arts, interior design, journalism, law, mathematics.
Programmes: (a) B.Sc. in business studies, civil engineering, computer engineering, computer science, electrical engineering, mechanical engineering; (b) higher diploma in aesthetic and beauty care, building technology, business studies, civil engineering, mechanical engineering; (c) B.Ed. in preschool education; (d) certificate in secretarial studies.
Open to: students of all nationalities.
Duration: (a) 4 years; courses begin in October and February; (b) 2 years; courses begin in October, except for mechanical engineering, 4 years; (c) 4 years; courses begin in October); (d) 1 year; courses begin in October.
Fees: registration: US$500; tuition: US$2,500 per semester; living expenses: approx. US$5,200 per academic year.
Financial assistance: possibility of scholarships, based on academic performance.
Languages: (a) and (d) instruction in English; (c) instruction in Greek; (b) all in English except aesthetic and beauty care.
Applications: 4 to 6 weeks before academic year starts to the Registrar's Office at the above address.

🎓 **Institute Scholarships**

Study Domains: business, computer science.
Scholarships: Entrance Scholarship and Continuing Students Scholarship Scheme.
Subjects: business, computer science, secretarial studies, aesthetic and beauty care.
Open to: all students without discriminations as to nationality, sex, age, race: candidates for either a diploma or a Bachelor's degree course should possess a six form secondary school (high school) certificate or equivalent qualifications.
Duration: for duration of course; renewable subject to performance review.
Applications: by 15 August.

634   Global International College
PO Box 24621
1301 Nicosia
Tel: +357-22-661-603
Fax: +357-22-667-078
e-mail: GIC@citanet.com.cy

📖 **Undergraduate Programme / Secretarial Studies**

Study Domains: administration.
Programmes: Diploma in secretarial studies.
Duration: 2 years.
Fees: tuition fees: C£2,000.
Languages: English.
Applications: to the above address.

635   Higher Hotel Institute, Cyprus
Aglantzia Avenue
PO Box 24812
1304 Nicosia
Tel: +357-22-305-001/497-481
Fax: +357-22-314-672
e-mail: hhic@cytanet.com.cy

📖 **Undergraduate Programmes**

Study Domains: tourism, hotel and catering management.
Programmes: Undergraduate courses in Hotel and Catering Management, including culinary arts; front office; housekeeping.
Open to: nationals of any country with secondary education certificate and very good English.

Duration: 1 to 3 years.
Fees: C£2,500 per academic year; subject to change without notice.
Financial assistance: scholarships are offered by the Government of Cyprus and the Commonwealth Fund for Technical Cooperation covering tuition and other relevant education and all sciences expenses.
Applications: by 30 April to the Registrar.

636   Higher Technical Institute [HTI]
PO Box 20423
2152 Nicosia
Tel: +357-22-406-300/305-030
Fax: +357-22-494-952
Web: http://www.hti.ac.cy
e-mail: hit@cytanet.com.cy

📖 **Undergraduate Programmes**

Study Domains: civil engineering, electricity and electronics, mechanical engineering.
Programmes: HTI Diploma in: civil engineering, mechanical engineering, electrical engineering, marine engineering and computer science.
Open to: nationals of any country who have completed approximately 6 years of secondary education (general or technical) aged over 18 years; all candidates must take the Institute's entrance examination in English, science and mathematics; the entrance requirements may be waived for candidates possessing the following qualifications: IGCE (General Certificate of Education of the United Kingdom) A-level pass in either mathematics or physics and an O-level GCE pass in English language, or equivalent qualification; entrance examinations may be taken in Cyprus at the beginning of June or abroad mid-March through mid-April provided the candidates make arrangements with a suitable examination centre or an HTI-approved examination centre where available.
Duration: 3 years; courses begin in September.
Fees: tuition: CY£1,000 per year; living expenses: CY£350-£400 (approx. US$560-640) per month.
Applications: by mid-January to the above address.

637   Intercollege
46 Makedonitissas Avenue
PO Box 24005
1700 Nicosia
Tel: +357-22-841-500/841-555
Fax: +357-22-352-059
Web: http://www.intercollege.ac.cy
e-mail: admission-nic@intercollege.ac.cy

📖 **Undergraduate, Graduate Programmes**

Study Domains: accounting, advertising, business, computer science, law, management, marketing, public relations, tourism, hotel and catering management.
Programmes: certificates, professional diplomas, Bachelor's and Master's degrees.
Description: subjects: accounting, business administration, law, banking, business studies, computer engineering, computer science, hotel management, management, communication and media studies, public relations, secretarial studies, and travel and tourism management; possibility of simultaneously earning degrees/diplomas for American/British universities or M.B.A. of British and European universities.
Open to: candidates of all nationalities with secondary school leaving certificate; aged 18-30 years; language coaching possible; for Master's programme, a Bachelor's degree from an accredited university is required.
Duration: diploma: 2 years; Bachelor's degree: 4 years; MBA: 1 to 2 years; courses begin in October/February/June.
Fees: tuition fees, C£3,270 per year; living costs C£3,790 per year.
Financial assistance: financial assistance available; based on academic merit.
Languages: instruction in English.
Applications: by 15 August, to the Admissions Officer for all further information.

638 Kes College
5, Kallipolis Avenue
1055 Nicosia
Tel: +357-22-875-737
Fax: +357-22-756-562
Web: http://www.kes.ac.cy
e-mail: kes@cytanet.com.cy

📖 Undergraduate Programmes

Study Domains: administration, business, journalism.
Programmes: diploma and higher diploma in beauty
therapy, commercial studies, business, food preparation,
administration, medical representatives, journalism and public
relations.
Open to: candidates of all nationalities who have
completed a 6-year secondary education; proficiency in
Greek or English required.
Duration: 2 to 3 years; courses begin in late September
and late January.
Fees: tuition, C£2,150-2,500 per year; living costs, C£400
per month; foundation course, C£1,300.
Languages: instruction in Greek and English.
Applications: by 10 September (for 1st semester), 10
January (for 2nd semester), to the Registration Officer, at the
above address.

639 Kimon College
PO Box 40646
6306 Larnaca
Tel: +357-24-657-534
Fax: +357-24-651-895
Web: http://www.kimoncollege.com
e-mail: info@kimoncollege.com

📖 Undergraduate Programmes

Study Domains: business, business administration,
computer science, languages, tourism, hotel and catering
management, travel grants, vocational training.
Programmes: (a) Higher Diploma in hotel management,
business administration and computer science; (b) Diploma in
secretarial skill, travel and tourism.
Open to: candidates of any nationality with secondary high
school leaving certificate; for the hotel management diploma,
applicants are preferably between 18-22 and have either A- or
O-levels or a high school diploma; an English test is required
before admission.
Duration: 2 years for Higher diploma studies; 1 year for
Diploma studies; courses begin in October.
Fees: C£1,850 per year for Higher diploma; C£1,450 for
Diploma; registration fee C£50.
Applications: by 31 August, to the above address.

🎓 College Scholarships

Study Domains: business administration, computer
science, languages, marketing, psychology, summer
programmes, tourism, hotel and catering management.
Scholarships: Scholarships for Higher Diploma Studies.
Subjects: business studies, hotel management and
computer studies.
Open to: all foreign students, preferably between the ages
of 18-22, having A- or O-levels or a high-school diploma; an
English test is required before admission.
Duration: 2 years (not renewable).
Value: C£1,850 per academic year, plus help in
accommodation.
Applications: by 31 August.

640 Lynn College of Music and Arts
PO Box 12645
2251 Nicosia
Tel: +357-2-485-513

📖 Undergraduate Programmes

Study Domains: arts, arts and crafts, fine arts, music and
musicology.
Programmes: undergraduate courses leading to diploma,
Associate and Bachelor's degrees.
Description: Diploma, Associate degrees and Bachelor
degrees in fine arts, music, ballet, theatre and drama,
radio/T.V. film; 10 participants.
Open to: all nationalities; programmes have individual
requirements.

Duration: 4 years; courses begin in October.
Fees: C£5,000 per year (fees and accommodation).
Languages: instruction in English.
Applications: by 31 July, to the above address.

**641 Mediterranean Institute of
Management [MIM]**
PO Box 20536
Kallipoleos Avenue
1679 Nicosia
Tel: +357-22-806000
Fax: +357-22-376872
Web: http://www.kepa.gov.cy/eng/mim/mim2.htm
e-mail: kepaky@cytanet.com.cy

📖 Postgraduate Programme

Study Domains: management, marketing.
Programmes: Postgraduate Management Diploma.
Description: specifications in general management,
operations management and marketing management; 35
participants including 15 from abroad.
Open to: candidates of any nationality, with a university
first degree or equivalent in any field, with proven academic
ability and managerial potential; good knowledge of English
required; special consideration will be given to candidates
from Commonwealth and developing countries of Africa,
Asia, Latin America and Europe.
Duration: 1 academic year.
Fees: tuition: C£2,000; living expenses: C£350 to C£400
per month; books: C£450.
Financial assistance: CFTC Scholarships. Information
can be obtained from the MIM Secretary.
Languages: instruction in English.
Applications: by 1 June, to the Secretary of the Institute.

642 P.A. College
PO Box 40763
6307 Larnaca
Tel: +357-24-624-975
Fax: +357-24-628-860
Web: http://www.pacollege.ac.cy
e-mail: prgmdean@pacollege.ac.cy

📖 Tertiary Education Studies

Study Domains: accounting, business administration,
computer science, law, vocational training.
Programmes: tertiary education studies in business
administration, law, banking, accounting, computer studies.
Open to: candidates of all nationalities with secondary
school leaving certificate or GCEs (at least 2 A-levels and 3
O-levels, grades A,B,C).
Duration: 1 to 4 years; courses begin in
September/October.
Fees: tuition fees, C£3,500 per year; living costs, approx.
C£350 per month; books, approx. C£200 per year.
Applications: by 1 September.

643 Philips College
PO Box 28008
1301 Nicosia
Tel: +357-22-424-614
Fax: +357-22-315-225
Web: http://www.philips.ac.cy
e-mail: philips@philips.ac.cy

📖 Undergraduate Programmes

Study Domains: accounting, business, computer science,
early childhood education, education, public relations.
Programmes: (a) B.Sc. in accountancy and finance,
business studies, information technology, public relations; (b)
Higher diploma in pre-elementary and elementary education;
(c) diploma in accounting and finance, business studies,
information technology, public relations.
Open to: candidates of all nationalities with
secondary-school certificate.
Duration: (a) 4 years; (b) 3 years; (c) 2 years.
Fees: tuition fees: C£4,200.
Applications: to the above address for more information.

644   School of Nursing
Nicosia General Hospital
1450 Nicosia
Tel: +357-22-801-751/2
Fax: +357-22-668-295
e-mail: nslibrary@cytanet.com.cy

📖 Undergraduate Programmes
Study Domains: nursing.
Programmes: (a) Registered nurses courses in general nursing or psychiatric nursing; (b) Post-diploma courses in nursing administration, midwifery, intensive care and other specialized fields.
Duration: (a) 3 years and 3 months; (b) 12 months.
Fees: living expenses: C£400 per month.
Financial assistance: tuition: students receive a monthly governmental grant and book allowance.
Languages: instruction in Greek.
Applications: to the above address.

645   Susini College
21 Them. Dervi Street
1066 Nicosia
Tel: +357-22-676-663
Fax: +357-22-670-005
e-mail: susini@spidernet.com.cy

📖 Undergraduate Programmes
Study Domains: vocational training.
Programmes: diploma and higher diploma in aesthetics and beauty therapy; also preparation for the diplomas of CIDESCO international and Susini Esthetique of France.
Open to: candidates of all nationalities with secondary-school certificate; age over 17; a good command of English or Greek required.
Duration: 1 or 2 academic years.
Fees: US$4,500 per year.
Applications: by 30 August, to the Academic Registrar.

646   University of Cyprus [UCY]
75 Kallipoleos Avenue
PO Box 20537
1678 Nicosia
Tel: +357-22-892-000
Fax: +357-22-892-100
Web: http://www.ucy.ac.cy
e-mail: admin@ucy.ac.cy

📖 Undergraduate, Graduate and Postgraduate Programmes
Study Domains: all major fields.
Programmes: Bachelor's, Master's and Ph.D. degrees in all major fields except medicine and engineering.
Open to: candidates of any nationality who pass 3 GCE A-Level courses and O-level Greek or equivalent; secondary-school leavers who pass the university entrance examinations.
Duration: variable, depending on programmes.
Fees: tuition: C£2,000 per semester; living expenses C£300 to C£400 per month.
Languages: instruction in Greek.
Applications: by end of April; to Head, Studies and Student Welfare at the above address.

Czech Republic
Academic year: September to August.
Organization of higher education system: The qualification structure provides for the following levels of degrees and courses: the Bachelor's degree lasting 6 to 8 semesters; the Master's degree, which lasts 2 to 6 semesters. There are exceptions of some disciplines where students enter the Master's study programme immediately after completion of secondary education - e.g. medicine, veterinary medicine, dentistry etc. These exceptions are awarded by accreditation. If a study programme does not follow the Bachelor's/ Master's structure it generally involves 5 to 6 years of studies. Graduates of Bachelor's study programmes are awarded the academic degree of 'bakalár' (i.e. 'Bachelor', abbreviated as 'Bc.', used in front of the name). There is an equivalent academic degree in the field of arts - 'bakalár umeni' (i.e. 'Bachelor of Arts', abbreviated as 'BcA.', used in front of the

name). Graduates of Master's study programmes shall be awarded the following academic degrees: 'Inženýr' (i.e. 'Engineer', abbreviated as 'Ing.', used in front of the name) in the field of economics, technical branches of study, agriculture, forestry and military science; 'Inženýr architekt' (i.e. 'Engineer Architect', abbreviated as 'Ing. arch.', used in front of the name) in the field of architecture; 'Doktor medicíny' (i.e. 'Doctor of Medicine', abbreviated as 'MUDr.', used in front of the name) in the field of medical studies; 'Zubní lékar' (i.e. 'Dentist', abbreviated as 'MDDr.' used in front of the name), 'Doktor veterinární medicíny' (i.e. 'Doctor of Veterinary Medicine', abbreviated as'MVDr.', used in front of the name) in the field of veterinary studies; 'Magistr umeni' (i.e. 'Master of Arts', abbreviated as 'MgA.', used in front of the name) in the field of arts; 'Magistr' (i.e. 'Master', abbreviated as 'Mgr.', used in front of the name) in other fields of study. The holders of the academic degree of 'Magistr' are in a position to pass a rigorous state examination in the same branch of study and defend a dissertation. Upon passing the state examination the following academic degrees are awarded: 'Doktor práv' (i.e. 'Doctor of Law', abbreviated as 'JUDr.', used in front of the name) in the field of law; 'Doktor filozofie' (i.e. 'Doctor of Philosophy', abbreviated as 'PhDr.', used in front of the name) in the field of humanities, pedagogical and social sciences; 'Doktor prírodních ved' (i.e. 'Doctor of Natural Sciences', abbreviated as 'RNDr.', used in front of the name) in the field of natural sciences; 'Doktor farmacie' (i.e. 'Doctor of Pharmacy', abbreviated as 'PharmDr.', used in front of the name) in the field of pharmacy; 'Licenciát teologie' (i.e. 'Licentiate of Theology', abbreviated as 'ThLic.', used in front of the name) or 'Doktor theologie' (i.e. 'Doctor of Theology') in the field of catholic theology. The doctoral studies are taken after completion of a Master's study programme The standard duration of doctoral study is 3 years and leads to the degree of 'Doktor' (i.e. 'Doctor', abbreviated as 'Ph.D.', used after the name), or 'Doktor teologie' (i.e. 'Doctor of theology', abbreviated as 'Th.D.', used after the name) in the field of theology.
Major institutions of higher education: Full database of institutions of higher education can be found at http://www.csvs.cz/_en.
Monetary unit: Czech crown (Kc).
International student admission: Foreign applicants for higher education studies must (a) have a secondary-school-leaving certificate (there are allowed exceptions for candidates for the academies of art) and (b) demonstrate their ability to study at university.
There are no uniform admissions procedures at institutions in the Czech Republic, either for home students, or for foreign ones. Foreign school-leaving certificates must either originate from a country with which the Czech Republic (or former Czechoslovakia) concluded conventions on the equivalence of degrees/diplomas required for university entrance; or must be recognized by regional school authorities responsible for primary and secondary schools. Students holding a degree from a foreign higher education institution and wishing to continue their studies in the Czech Republic must apply directly to the institution concerned, which is then responsible for deciding on the equivalence of the qualifications/ periods of study. Candidates for doctoral studies must have completed Master level studies and must pass a special entrance examination or interview. Students may find a professor who will act as advisor during their studies and preparation of their doctoral thesis. The dean of the faculty is also able to assist students in finding a supervisor. Foreign candidates are admitted to institutions of higher education both on the basis of scholarships offered to other states by the Czech Republic in accordance with intergovernmental agreements and of private agreement with the selected school. In the second case the respective faculty is responsible for verifying that foreign students meet both a) and b) conditions.
Language: In general, entrance examinations are held in the language of instruction of the particular course for which the candidate is applying, usually Czech. Some universities provide foreign students with a one-year intensive Czech language course. Students studying a course in a foreign language (usually English or German) should have some basic knowledge of Czech for everyday use and administrative needs.
Immigration requirements: Foreign students must hold a valid passport and a Czech visa provided by the Czech embassy in the candidate's country. To qualify for the residence permit, students must submit the following

documentation: confirmation of the purpose of the stay (for example, an acceptance letter from the institution), confirmation of sufficient financial resources (for example, a bank confirmation or a letter of notification of scholarship approval), and confirmation of accommodation, confirmation that the applicant does not have a criminal record.

Estimated expenses for one academic year: Generally, students do not pay any tuition fees for studies in accredited study programs (at Bachelor, Master, Doctoral level) provided in the Czech language in public and state higher education institutions if their studies do not exceed the standard length of a study programme by more than one year. If study programs are provided in a foreign language, the institution shall set study fees in Bachelor's, Master's or Doctoral study programs at its own discretion. Tuition fees are required for studies provided by private higher education institutions.

Information services:
• Ministry of Foreign Affairs, Loretánské nám 5, 110 00 Praha 1; tel.: +420-2-2418-1111; fax: +420-2-2431-0017.
• Ministry of Education, Youth and Sports, Karmelitská 7, 118 12 Praha 1;
tel.: +420-2-5719-3244; fax: +420-2-5719-3790; email: stastna@msmt.cz.
• House of International Services of the Ministry of Education, Youth and Sports. Academic Information Agency, Senovázné nám. 26, 110 06 Prague 06; tel: +420-2-2422-9698; fax: +420-2-2422-9697.
• Accreditation Commission of the Czech Republic, Karmelitská 7, 118 12 Praha 1; tel.: +420-2-5719-3457; fax: +420-2-5719-3790; e-mail: vins@msmt.cz.
• Czech Rectors' Conference, Rector's Office of Masaryk University, Zerotinovo nám. 9, 601 77 Brno; tel: +420-5-4949-1122; fax: +420-5-4949-1122; email: fojtikova@muni.cz.
• Council of Higher Education Institutions, José Martího 31, 162 52 Praha 6, Velaslavín; tel/fax: +420-2-2056-0221; email: arvs@ftvs.cuni.cz; web: www.radavs.cz
• Student Chamber at Council of Higher Education Institutions, Masarykova univerzita, Údolní 53, 602 00 Brno; tel: +420-5-4114-6292, tel/fax: +420-5-4114-6-290;
• Centre for Higher Education Studies (CHES), U Luzického semin: 13/90, 118 00 Praha 1; tel: +420-2-5701-1311; fax: +420-2-5701-1323; email: csvs@csvs.cz; web: http://www.csvs.cz;
• Centre for Equivalence of Documents about Education (part of CHES); tel:+420-2-5701-1335; fax: +420-2-5753-1672; email: skuhrova@csvs.cz.
• National Centre for Distance Education (part of CHES), U Luzického semináré 13/90, 118 00 Praha 1; email: csvs@csvs.cz; web: http://www.csvs.cz.

Scholarships for international students:
• The Czech Republic offers some grants and scholarships for foreign students, in most cases on the basis of intergovernmental agreements. These consist essentially of study stays at a Czech institution lasting a maximum of one year for students from countries with which the Czech Republic has concluded a cultural co-operation convention. These are offered through the government authorities of the other contracting party.
• Grants for full university or doctoral studies: the Czech Republic informs the respective governments through their embassies on the availability of such study grants. In general, the amount of grants for foreign students admitted on the basis of intergovernmental academic exchange agreements is stipulated by the agreement.
• Some fellowships for study in the Czech Republic are offered under the UNESCO Co-Sponsored Fellowships Scheme. For more information contact UNESCO Fellowships Section, 7, place de Fontenoy, 75700 Paris, SP07 (France).

Open and distance learning:
• Four distance education centres have been established: DESC at Comensky Academy Prague, Tržište 20, 118 43 Praha 1; DESC at TU Liberec, Hálkova 6, 461 17 Liberec; DESC at TU Brno, Antonínská 1, 602 00 Brno; and DESC at Palacky University Olomouc, Biskupské nám 1, 771 11 Olomouc.
• Some non-governmental educational institutions, such as J. A. Comenius and the Open University Fund, also offer distance education.
• The National Centre for Distance Education (information and co-ordination body) was established in 1995 as a department of the Centre for Higher Education Studies.

Recognition of studies and qualification:
• Regional school authorities are responsible for the recognition of secondary school leaving certificates. Public higher education institutions are competent to recognise higher education diplomas. All higher education institutions are responsible for the recognition of periods of studies.
• The Ministry of Education, Youth and Sports is the competent body for the decision if there is an international agreement on automatic recognition of qualifications and in problematic cases.
The list of competent authorities is available at http://www.naric.cz.
• For professional recognition see www.msmt.cz/uok.
• Information and advice: Centre for Equivalence of Documents about Education, Czech ENIC/NARIC (Stredisko pro ekvivalenci dokladu o studiu); Centre for Higher Education Studies; 118 00 Praha 1; Czech Republic; tel: +420-2-5753-0500; fax: +420-2-5753-1672; email: skuhrova@csvs.cz; web: http://www.csvs.cz.

Publications / Websites:
• 'Higher Education in the Czech Republic. Guide for Foreign Students'; published by the Centre for Higher Education Studies in Prague (in English).

---

647   Academy of Fine Arts [AVU]
International Coordinator
U Akademie 4
170 22 Prague 7
Tel: +420-220-408-217
Fax: +420-233-381-662
Web: http://www.avu.cz/avu/eng/english.htm

📖 Undergraduate, Graduate Programmes

Study Domains: architecture, fine arts.
Programmes: B.A. and M.A. degrees in fine art, architecture and restoration techniques, studio work.
Open to: candidates of any nationality passing the entrance examination.
Duration: Bachelor's degree: 4 years; Master's degree: 2 to 3 years.
Fees: approx. US$5,000 per year.
Languages: instruction in Czech.
Applications: by 30 November, to the above address.

648   Academy of Performing Arts [AMU]
Malostranske namesti 12
118 00 Prague 1
Tel: +420-2-5753-4205
Fax: +420-2-5753-0405
Web: http://www.amu.cz
e-mail: intoffic@famu.cz

📖 Undergraduate, Postgraduate Programmes

Study Domains: arts, cinematography, music and musicology, performing arts, photography, summer programmes.
Programmes: Undergraduate and postgraduate courses in: (a) theatre; (b) film and television; (c) music; also photo arts; summer course in music; short term stays in (a) and (b).
Open to: candidates of all nationalities; entrance examination qualification; minimum knowledge of Czech language required.
Age limit Min: must be over 18 years of age.
Held: (a) theatre faculty: DAMU, Karlova 26, 116-65 Prague 1; (b) film and television: FAMU, Metanovo Nabrezi 2, 116-65 Prague 1; (c) music: HAMU, Malostranske namesti 13, 118-00 Prague.
Duration: 4 to 5 years; short stays of 3 months.
Fees: tuition fees: from US$2,500-$9,000 yearly; 3 months short-term study: US$1,600.
Languages: English and German.
Applications: (a) by 15 November; short stays by 15 May; (b) by 30 November; short stays by 1 April; (c) by 15 December.

649   Academy of Sciences of the Czech Republic - Institute of Microbiology

Vídenská Street 1083
142 20 Prague 4-Krc
Tel: +420-296-442-341
Fax: +420-296-442-201
Web: http://www.biomed.cas.cz
e-mail: mbu@biomed.cas.cz

Postgraduate Programmes

Study Domains: biology.
Programmes: Postgraduate courses on modern problems in biology and microbial technology.
Open to: candidates from Central and Eastern European countries and a limited number of students from other regions, with a graduate degree (M.Sc. or Ph.D.), who have practised in their field for 2 to 3 years; under 35 years of age.
Duration: 11½ months (courses begin in October).
Fees: tuition free.
Financial assistance: possibility of scholarships of an amount of 3,200 crowns per month; free accommodation and free medical care; no travel grants available.
Languages: instruction in English.
Applications: by 31 March, to the above address.

650   Charles University [CUNI]

Ovocny trh 3
116 36 Prague 1
Tel: +420-224-491-111
Fax: +420-224-210-695
Web: http://www.cuni.cz
e-mail: zahran@ruk.cuni.cz

Undergraduate, Postgraduate Programmes

Study Domains: education, languages, law, medicine, natural sciences, pharmacy and pharmacology, philosophy, physical education, social sciences, theology, religion.
Programmes: (a) Postgraduate and undergraduate courses in: philosophy, law, education, social sciences, medicine, pharmacy, natural sciences, mathematics and physics, physical education and sport, theology; (b) Slavonic Studies: Czech language, history and literature (instruction in Czech, English, German, French and Russian); (c) Intensive Czech language courses: language and professional preparation for study at Czech universities; (d) Czech summer courses for foreigners: language course with cultural activities and trips.
Open to: (a) candidates of any nationality fulfilling the necessary requirements; (b) professors, assistant professors, lecturers, tutors, translators, postgraduate or advanced students of Czech and Slavonic Studies having an active knowledge of Czech corresponding to at least 1 year of study; (c) and (d) all candidates.
Duration: (a) 4 to 6 years; (b) 4 weeks in August; (c) 1 year, 1 semester or 6 weeks (courses begin in September); (d) 4 weeks in July.
Fees: (a) vary from US$2,600-$10,000 per year; (b) US$900 covering tuition fees, accommodation, meals, excursions and cultural activities; (c) 1 year course: US$1,910-US$2,630; 1 semester course: US$980; 6 week course: US$380; (d) US$864.
Applications: (a) by 28 February to the Faculty concerned which will provide any further information; (b) by 15 May to the Director of the Institute of Bohemian Studies, Faculty of Arts, Jana Palacha 2, 116 38 Prague; (c) by 31 August for fall courses and 15 January for winter courses; (d) by 30 June; to UJOP UK, Jindrisska 29, 110 00 Prague 1.

651   Czech Technical University in Prague [CVUT]

Ul. Zikova 4
166 35 Prague 6
Fax: +420-224-311-042
Web: http://www.cvut.cz
e-mail: pozar@vc.cvut.cz

Undergraduate, Graduate Programmes

Study Domains: architecture, civil engineering, engineering, mechanical engineering, transport.
Programmes: undergraduate, graduate and postgraduate courses leading to Bachelor's, Master's and Ph.D. degrees.

Description: courses in civil, mechanical, electrical and nuclear engineering, architecture and transportation, science leading to a Bachelor's, Master's or Ph.D. degrees; residences and catering facilities available: unlimited number of participants.
Open to: all candidates having completed secondary school; applicants for Master's degree require a Bachelor's degree; applicants for Doctorate require a Master's degree.
Duration: Bachelor's, 3 to 4 years; M.Sc., 5 years; Ph.D., 3 years; (courses begin in September/October).
Fees: US$5,000 yearly.
Financial assistance: scholarships based on merit.
Languages: instruction in English.
Applications: by May, to the University Registrar at the above address.

652   Czech University of Agriculture of Prague [CZU]

Kamycka 129
165 21 Prague 6
Tel: +420-224-384-077
Fax: +420-220-920-434
Web: http://www.czu.cz
e-mail: kovar@lf.czu.cz

Certificate Programme / Hydrology

Study Domains: hydraulics, hydrology, sciences, statistics.
Programmes: certificate programme in hydrological data for water resources planning; study techniques in collection, processing, and use of hydrological data for water resources, planning and management.
Open to: candidates holding a Bachelor's degree in civil engineering; agricultural forestry; geography; geology; under 40 years of age; 1 year practice, recommendations of employer and of national committee of IHP (if possible).
Duration: 5 weeks' intensive programme beginning 25 May.
Fees: tuition fees: US$300; living costs: US$400.
Applications: apply by 31 March to: michaelkova@lf.czu.cz; kubalkova@lf.czu.cz.

UNESCO-International Hydrology Programme

Study Domains: hydrology.
Scholarships: International Hydrology Programme, UNESCO (IHP-UNESCO).
Duration: 5 weeks every 2nd year.
Value: fellowship for 5 weeks at 6,000 Kc plus accommodation; subsidized food.
Applications: apply by 31 March to: michaelkova@lf.czu.cz; or telephone: +420 2 2438 2147.

653   Institute of Chemical Technology, Prague [VSCHT]

Technicka 5
166 28 Prague 6
Tel: +420-224-353-896
Fax: +420-224-310-449
Web: http://www.vscht.cz
e-mail: ozs@vscht.cz

Undergraduate, Graduate, Postgraduate Programmes

Study Domains: applied sciences, biochemistry, chemical engineering, chemical industry, chemistry, continuing education, ecology, environment, food, food industry, microbiology, teacher education.
Programmes: undergraduate, graduate and postgraduate courses leading to B.Sc.; M.Sc.; Ph.D.
Duration: B.Sc.: 3 years; M.Sc.: 5 years; Ph.D.: 3 years.

654   Institute of Information Theory and Automation [UTIA]

Academy of Science of the Czech Republic
Pod vodárenskou vezé 4
182 08 Prague 8
Tel: +420-266-051-111
Fax: +420-2-8689-0378
Web: http://www.utia.cas.cz
e-mail: utia@utia.cas.cz

📖 **Graduate Programme**

Study Domains: computer science.
Programmes: Graduate Programme leading to Ph.D.
Description: graduate programme in the Central European Graduate School in systems and control theory leading to a Ph.D. degree: systems analysis, modelling, identification, control; 20 to 30 participants.
Open to: candidates of any country, holding an M.Sc. or corresponding degree; fluency in English required.
Held: in a network of universities and academic institutions in the Czech Republic and Hungary.
Duration: 1 to 3 years.
Fees: US$5,000 per year.
Financial assistance: a limited number of fellowships for the best applicants.
Languages: instruction in English.
Applications: by 30 June, to the Graduate School, P.O. Box 18, 182 08 Prague 8.

655 Jan Evangelista Purkyne University in Ustí nad Labem [UJEP]

Horení 13
400 96 Ustí nad Labem
Tel: +420-475-812-069
Fax: +420-472-772-982
Web: http://www.ujep.cz
e-mail: ritschelova@rek.ujep.cz

📖 **Undergraduate, Graduate Programmes**

Study Domains: ecology, environment, economic and commercial sciences, economy, languages.
Programmes: undergraduate and graduate courses leading to Bachelor's degree, 'Inzenyr' and teaching qualification.
Description: programme of courses in environmental sciences, social economics, languages, environmental analysis, landscape, restoration, business economics, human resources, management.
Open to: candidates of any nationality fulfilling the necessary requirements; age limit 45 years.
Duration: 1 to 5 years; courses begin in October.
Fees: US$1,200-$5,000 per year.
Languages: instruction in Czech and English (Czech courses for foreign students).
Applications: by 28 February, to the Director of the Study Department of the UJEP.

656 Janácek Academy of Music and Performing Arts [JAMU]

Beethovenova 2
662 15 Brno
Tel: +420-542-591-111
Fax: +420-542-221-873
Web: http://www.jamu.cz
e-mail: faltus@jamu.cz

📖 **Undergraduate, Graduate, Postgraduate Programmes**

Study Domains: music and musicology, summer programmes.
Programmes: Bachelor's, Master's, Ph.D., special programmes: festival of theatre universities encounter; international music master classes.
Description: (a) Faculty of Theatre: drama education for the deaf, theatre management, stage technology, acting, musical acting, directing, theatre dramaturgy, stage design, dance teaching methodology; (b) Faculty of Music: church music, composition, orchestral conducting, choral conducting, voice, opera direction, piano, organ, harpsichord, violin, violoncello, flute, oboe, clarinet, bassoon, French horn, trumpet, trombone, percussion, music management, theory of music production.
Open to: secondary-school graduates of any nationality; 18 years minimum age.
Held: (a) Mozartova 1; telephone: +420-5-422-10136; email: office.difa@jamu.cz; (b) Komenskeho nam.6, 662 15 Brno; telephone/fax: +420-5-422-180-499.
Duration: Bachelor's degree: 3 years; Master's degree: 2 years; PhD degree: 3 years (only with Czech proficiency); lifelong learning: indefinite.

Fees: lifelong learning tuition fees: US$2,000 per semester.
Applications: apply for music faculty by 15 December; theatre faculty by 30 November; lifelong learning: all year long.

657 Masaryk University of Brno [MUNI]

Zerotinovo nam. 9
601 77 Brno
Tel: +420-542-128-111
Fax: +420-542-128-300
Web: http://www.muni.cz
e-mail: info@muni.cz

📖 **Undergraduate, Graduate Programmes**

Study Domains: all major fields, Slavic studies.
Programmes: programmes of study leading to undergraduate and graduate degrees at the Faculties of Law, Medicine, Science, Arts, Education, Economics and Administration, Informatics, Sports Studies, School of Social Studies; also Summer courses in Czech Language.
Duration: 3 to 6 years, depending on the faculty, form of study and type of degree programme. Generally, Bachelor's degrees take 3 years, Master's degrees 2 years (if following after a Bachelor's degree) or 5 years (from the beginning of study), and Doctorate degrees 3 years.
Fees: see website for full information on fees.
Languages: most instruction at the University is in Czech, but some degree programmes are available in English; a number of individual courses are offered in English and other languages.
Applications: to the above address; see website for further information.

658 Mendel University of Agriculture and Forestry Brno

Ul. Zemedelská 1
613 00 Brno
Tel: +420-545-131-111
Fax: +420-545-211-128
Web: http://www.mendelu.cz
e-mail: info@mendelu.cz

📖 **Undergraduate, Graduate, Postgraduate Programmes**

Study Domains: agronomic sciences, economic and commercial sciences, forestry, horticulture, technology.
Programmes: undergraduate, graduate and postgraduate courses leading to Bachelor's, engineering and Ph.D. degrees available from the Faculties of Agronomy, Horticulture, Economics and Science, and Forestry and Wood Technology.
Open to: candidates of any nationality, meeting academic, financial and linguistic criteria.
Duration: engineering programme, 5 years; Bachelor's and Ph.D. programmes 3 years.
Languages: instruction in Czech.
Applications: by the end of February, to the Dean's Office of the relevant faculty.

659 Moravian Museum [MM]

Zelny'trh 6
659 37 Brno
Tel: +420-542-321-205
Fax: +420-542-212-792
Web: http://www.mzm.cz
e-mail: mzm@mzm.cz

📖 **Graduate Programme**

Study Domains: museology and museography.
Programmes: graduate courses in conservation of museum collections.
Open to: graduates with background in chemistry, art history and museum affairs; entrance interview required.
Duration: 3 years.
Fees: 3,500 Kc. per year.
Languages: instruction in Czech.
Applications: by May, to the Museum Documentation Centre, Moravian Museum.

660 Palacky University, Olomouc [UPOL]

Krizkovskeho 8
77147 Olomouc
Tel: +420-585-631-111
Fax: +420-585-232-035
Web: http://www.upol.cz

📖 **Undergraduate, Graduate, Postgraduate Programmes**

Study Domains: American studies, languages, linguistics, literature and civilization, medicine, philology, Slavic studies, social sciences, summer programmes, teacher education.
Programmes: (a) MUDr. (equivalent to M.D.); (b) certificate; (c) Bachelor's; Master's; (d) Bachelor's; (e) certificate; (f) Bachelor's; Master's.
Description: (a) general medicine; (b) central European studies; (c) foreign language courses; (d) Czech language courses; (e) Summer school of Slavonic studies; (f) teaching English/German as a foreign language.
Open to: candidates of any country; language proficiency in English and/or language of study.
Duration: (a) 6 years; (b) 4 months; (c) 5 years; (d) 3 to 5 months (at any time during the year); (e) summer: 4 weeks; (f) 4 years.
Fees: tuition fees: (a) US$8,000 per year; (b) consult website (c) registration: US$25; tuition: US$5,000; (d) consult website; (e) registration: US$30; tuition: US$600; (f) consult website.
Languages: Czech, English, German, French; depending on programme.
Applications: (a) 31 August; (b) March/October; (c) and (f) 28 February; (d) anytime; (e) 20 June.

661 Silesian University

Na Rybnicku 1
746 01 Opava
Tel: +420-553-684-621
Fax: +420-553-684-621
Web: http://www.slu.cz
e-mail: rektorat@slu.cz

📖 **Undergraduate, Graduate Programmes**

Study Domains: all major fields.
Programmes: programme of undergraduate and graduate courses in all major fields at the School of Business Administration; Faculty of Philosophy and Science and the Mathematical Institute.
Applications: generally by 28 February; applicants are invited to the entrance exams by mail.

662 Technical University of Brno [VUTBR]

Vysoké ucení technické
Antoninska 548/1
601 90 Brno
Tel: +420-541-141-111
Fax: +420-541-211-309
Web: http://www.vutbr.cz
e-mail: vut@vutbr.cz

📖 **Undergraduate, Graduate, Postgraduate Programmes**

Study Domains: architecture, business, civil engineering, electricity and electronics, engineering, technology.
Programmes: undergraduate, graduate and postgraduate courses leading to Bachelor's, Master's and Ph.D. in mechanical, civil and electrical engineering, informatics, architecture, fine arts, rubber and leather technology, chemistry and applied sciences, business and management.
Open to: candidates of any nationality fulfilling the necessary requirements.
Duration: B.Sc.: 3 years; M.Sc.: 5 years; Ph.D.: 3 years; courses begin in October.
Fees: variable, from US$2,000-$6,000 yearly.
Languages: instruction in Czech and English.
Applications: by 28 February, to the respective faculties for further information.

663 Technical University of Liberec [VSLIB]

Halkova 6
461 17 Liberec 1
Tel: +420-485-351-111
Fax: +420-485-353-535
Web: http://www.vslib.cz

📖 **Undergraduate, Graduate Programmes / Engineering**

Study Domains: architecture, economy, education, engineering, mechanical engineering, textile industry.
Programmes: programmes of study leading to undergraduate and graduate degrees in mechanical engineering; textile engineering; mechatronics; architecture; education; economics.
Open to: candidates of all nationalities meeting academic, financial and linguistic criteria.
Applications: through the respective faculties; see website for contact details.

🎓 **Scholarships**

Study Domains: mechanical engineering, textile industry.
Scholarships: University Scholarships.
Subjects: manufacturing systems and design of machines.
Open to: students of any nationality with a secondary school certificate; an average of 75% in mathematics and physics; proficiency in English.
Duration: 1 year.
Value: US$4,000 per year.
Applications: by 31 March to the Dean's office at the above address.

664 Technical University of Ostrava [VSB]

tr. 17 Listopadu 15
708 33 Ostrava-Poruba
Tel: +420-596-991-111
Fax: +420-596-998-507
Web: http://www.vsb.cz

📖 **Undergraduate, Postgraduate Programmes**

Study Domains: chemistry, geology.
Programmes: undergraduate and postgraduate courses.
Description: (a) Certificate course in environmental geochemistry and geochemical prospecting methods under the sponsorship of UNESCO; the course aims at studying various aspects of earth sciences (geochemistry) which are of major importance in prospecting for mineral resources and solving environmental problems in the industrial landscape; (b) Undergraduate and postgraduate courses in mining and geology, metallurgy and material engineering, electrical engineering and informatics and economy.
Open to: graduates from all countries with the necessary qualifications.
Duration: (a) 2 months (courses begin in July); (b) 3 to 5 years (courses begin in September).
Fees: (b) US$2,200-$3,500 per year.
Languages: instruction in: (a) English; (b) Czech, with some courses in English.
Applications: (a) by 30 March, to the above address or through UNESCO National Commissions (for addresses see website http://www.unesco.org/ncp/natcom/); (b) by 30 June.

665 The College of Business Studies [VSO Praha]

Masna 13
110 000 Prague 1
Tel: +420-222-311-397
Web: http://www.vso-praha.cz
e-mail: studijni.oddeleni@vso-praha.cz

📖 **Undergraduate Degree Programmes**

Study Domains: economy, finance, human sciences, languages, marketing, psychology, recreation and leisure, sociology, tourism, hotel and catering management.
Programmes: Bachelor's degrees in all major fields.
Description: economy of travel and tourism; technology of services of travel and tourism; enterprise economy; business law; management; human resources; marketing; finance and accounting;
informatics and information technology; computer technology

in travel; psychology and sociology; sociology; languages: English; German, Spanish, French.
Financial assistance: no financial assistance or scholarships available.

666   Tomas Bata University in Zlin [UTB]

Mostni 5139
760 01 Zlin
Tel: +420-576-032-754
Fax: +420-576-032-121
Web: http://www.utb.cz
e-mail: info@utb.cz

📖 Undergraduate, Graduate, Postgraduate Programmes

Study Domains: accounting, administration, advertising, audio-visual media, business administration, chemical engineering, chemistry, communication, computer science, continuing education, design, ecology, environment, economy, fine arts, graphic arts, international business, management, marketing, photography, public relations.
Programmes: undergraduate, graduate and postgraduate courses leading to Bachelor's, Master's and PhD degrees at the Faculties of Technology Management and Economics, Multimedia Communications.
Subjects: chemistry and materials technology; engineering informatics; process engineering; social pedagogical studies; economics and management; commercial policy and administration; fine arts; media and communications.
Applications: contact the Rector's Office.

667   University of Economics, Prague [VSE]

Nám. Winstona Churchilla 4
130 6 Praha
Tel: +420-224-095-787
Fax: +420-224-095-673
Web: http://www.vse.cz
e-mail: brazdova@vse.cz

📖 Undergraduate, Graduate, Postgraduate Programmes

Study Domains: administration, business, business administration, economic and commercial sciences, economy, European studies, finance, history, information science, international studies, languages, management, political science, statistics.
Programmes: Bachelor's; Master's; PhD; specifically (a) degree in CEMS MIM/ Master's in International Management; (b) Master's degree in International Business in Global Context with an Emphasis on Central Europe; (c) certificate in Central and East European Studies; (d) MA degree Economics of International Trade and European Economic Integration.
Description: (a) courses in management knowledge and education; (b) courses covering business knowledge and skills needed for international business such as intermediate macro- and microeconomics; international management, international business law, international business environment with special focus on Central Europe; international business strategies, international finance courses; international marketing; project management; business communications and negotiations etc.; and minor specialization. 4 leaving state exams and diploma thesis (c) 17 courses on central and eastern European economies, societies and cultures; other faculties include: finance and accounting; international relations; business administration; informatics and statistics; economics and public administration; and management; (d) courses in microeconomics, macroeconomics, open economy macroeconomics, international trade, economics and european integration, EU institutions and policies.
Open to: (a) candidates of CEMS programme in CEMS schools; (b) All candidates with a Bachelor's degree, preferably in business or economic science (c) at least 2 completed semesters of university education with grade point average of 2.5 or higher; (a) and (b) and (c) and (d) English language proficiency; good knowledge of another European language; (d) earned minimum 240 ECTS.
Held: (a) University of Economics, Prague; one semester abroad. (b), and (c) University of Economics, Prague; (d) at 7 partner universities - see http://webhost.ua.ac.be/eitei.

Duration: (a) Master's in international management: one or two sessions of 3-1/2 months, plus Summer courses of 5 weeks; beginning in February and September; Summer school during June-July (b)Four semester Master's Programme starting from September each academic year (c) 15 weeks, beginning in February and September + Summer school during June – July; (d) Term I: September-December, Term II: January-April, Term III: April-June.
Fees: (a) no fees or registration; living costs: 200€ per month; (b) registration: 50€; tuition 3,000€ per semester (c) registration: 25€; tuition fees: 2,500€ (accommodation included); living costs: 700€; (d) fixed by each of the partner universities.
Languages: English.
Applications: (a) apply to: subrtova@vse.cz; (b) apply to: krejcii@vse.cz (c) apply by December for spring session; June for autumn session to: cesp@vse.cz; (d) apply to: klosova@vse.cz, klos@mbox.vol.cz.

🎓 Scholarship

Study Domains: business administration, international business.
Subjects: Business administration; international business.
Open to: All candidates with Bachelor's degree.
Value: 3,000 €.
Applications: By February 2006; contact legova@vse.cz for further details.

668   University of Hradec Králové [UHK]

Víta Nejedlého 573
500 0 Hradec Králové
Tel: +420-49-554-5911
Fax: +420-49-554-5911
Web: http://www.uhk.cz
e-mail: postmaster@uhk.cz

🎓 Scholarship

Study Domains: administration, business, computer science.
Subjects: Computer science; business and administration.
Duration: 3 to 5 years, renewable.
Value: 3,000 € per academic year.
Applications: By end of May; contact tereza.prazakova@uhk.cz for further details.

669   University of Ostrava [OSU]

Dvořákova 7
701 03 Ostrava 1
Tel: +420-596-160-184
Fax: +420-596-113-146
Web: http://www.osu.cz

📖 Undergraduate, Graduate Programmes

Study Domains: all major fields.
Programmes: undergraduate and graduate university courses; distance education degree programme through the Virtual University.
Description: Faculties: arts, teacher education, science, medico-social studies; institutes: arts studies, research and application of fuzzy modelling, regional studies.
Open to: candidates of any country: (a) with English proficiency; (b) graduates from secondary art and/or comprehensive schools.
Duration: B.Sc.: 3 years; M.A.: 5 years; Ph.D.: 3 years; all begin in October.
Fees: US$3,000 per year.
Languages: instruction in English.
Applications: by 28 February to the above address.

670   University of Pardubice [UPCE]

Studentská 95
532 10 Pardubice
Tel: +420-466-036-111
Fax: +420-466-036-361
Web: http://www.upce.cz

📖 Undergraduate, Graduate, Postgraduate Programmes

Study Domains: chemistry.
Programmes: Bachelor's, Master's and Ph.D. courses.

Description: graduate and undergraduate courses leading to B.Sc. and M.Sc. degrees in inorganic, organic, general, analytical and physical chemistry, and technology of chemical manufacturing; language training and Ph.D. programmes also offered.
Open to: students having completed A-levels for undergraduate courses.
Duration: 3 to 5 years.
Fees: US$6,000 per year.
Languages: instruction in English.
Applications: by June at the above address.

671 University of South Bohemia [JCU]

Branisovská 31
370 05 Ceské Budejovice
Tel: +420-387-775-403
Fax: +420-385-300-373
Web: http://www.jcu.cz

📖 Undergraduate, Graduate, Postgraduate Programmes

Study Domains: agriculture, biology, languages, summer programmes.
Programmes: Bachelor's, Master's and Ph.D. programmes; also Summer courses.
Description: (a) Bachelor's, Master's and Ph.D. programmes in biological and agricultural specializations; participants accepted on an individual basis; upgrading programmes in related disciplines (accommodation, language coaching, free access to computers and email communications and close contacts with top biological research in the Czech Academy of Sciences are offered); (b) Czech language courses (Summer course including visits to historical sites in South Bohemia.
Open to: (a) high school graduates for Bachelor's and Master's studies; university graduates for Ph.D. programme; (b) candidates with a basic knowledge of Czech.
Held: (a) at the Faculty of Biological Sciences and the Faculty of Agriculture; (b) at the Pedagogical Faculty.
Duration: (a) 3 to 5 years; courses begin in October; (b) 3 weeks; courses begin in August/September.
Fees: (a) US$2,000-$3,000 per year; (b) US$500 including fees and full board.
Financial assistance: (a) outstanding students may be supported from the research grants of their tutors.
Languages: instruction in: (a) English; (b) Czech, German and English.
Applications: (a) by 15 June to Prof. Milan Straskraba, to the above address; (b) by 30 June to Pae Dr. Bohumila Junkova, CSc, Dukelská 9, 370 01 Ceské Budejovice.

672 University of Veterinary and Pharmaceutical Sciences, Brno [VFU]

Palackého 1-3
612 42 Brno
Tel: +420-541-561-111
Web: http://www.vfu.cz
e-mail: sedlarovac@vfu.cz

📖 Undergraduate, Postgraduate Programmes

Study Domains: ecology, environment, medicine, pharmacy and pharmacology, veterinary sciences.
Programmes: undergraduate and postgraduate courses.
Description: studies in veterinary science, hygiene and medicine, ecological sciences and pharmacy.
Open to: candidates of any nationality fulfilling the necessary requirements.
Fees: tuition: US$5,000 per year.
Languages: instruction in English for Veterinary Medicine and in Czech for Pharmacy.
Applications: by 28 February.

673 University of West Bohemia [ZCU]

Univerzitni 8
306 14 Plzen
Tel: +420-377-631-111
Fax: +420-377-631-112
Web: http://www.zcu.cz
e-mail: info@rek.zcu.cz

📖 Undergraduate, Postgraduate Programmes

Study Domains: engineering, languages, summer programmes.
Programmes: Bachelor's (B.Sc.), Master's (M.Sc.) and Ph.D. courses.
Description: (a) Undergraduate and postgraduate courses in: electrical engineering, mechanical engineering, mathematics, physics leading to a B.Sc., M.Sc., or Ph.D.: 10 to 30 participants; (b) International Summer School: Czech, Russian, English, German and French: 200-300 participants.
Open to: candidates of any nationality having completed secondary school or its equivalent; no age limit.
Duration: (a) 3 to 5 years; (b) 3 weeks; courses begin in mid-July.
Fees: (a) US$3,000 per semester for graduate study; US$3,500 per semester for postgraduate study in the 1st and 2nd year, US$4,000 per semester for postgraduate study in the 3rd year; (b) US$650.
Languages: instruction in English for (a).
Applications: (a) by 30 December for Spring semester or by 31 August for Autumn semester; (b) by 30 April; to the above address.

Denmark

Academic year: September to June.
Organization of higher education system: Denmark has three types of higher education institutions - each with well-defined profiles and qualities. This gives the international students a great variety of study options depending on their interest; be they mainly research-oriented or of a more professional and applied character.
• Universities: The research universities have a commitment to teach and do research at the highest international level. Some are multifaculty institutions covering many disciplines; other institutions are specialized in technical science, agriculture and veterinary science, business, architecture etc. The largest university has around 35,000 students. Some of the smaller ones have around 3-6,000 students. All institutions are located in the larger cities, often with close partnerships to business and research institutions. Qualifications: first level, Bachelor's degree (BA/BSc+ field) is awarded after 3 years of study, normally concentrated on one or two fields of study and a project paper. The programmes qualify students for occupational functions and for postgraduate studies. The Candidatus degree (MA or MSc + field) is normally awarded after 2 years of study following a BA/BSc degree and requires the preparation of a thesis of 1/2-1 year's duration. The programmes qualify students for occupational functions and scientific work. The Ph.D. degree is normally awarded after 3 years of higher education and research following a Candidatus degree and requires the preparation of a thesis.
• University colleges/higher education colleges: These institutions have recently undergone major changes including the merging into units that are more comprehensive. The institutions have a professional focus and combine theoretical studies with applied research and practical application in many different fields. The colleges have around 1-5,000 students. Some are placed in the larger cities, others in more tranquil surroundings in smaller towns. All institutions have a strong regional commitment. Qualifications: 3-4 year professional bachelor degrees. The professional bachelor programmes provide students with knowledge of theory and the application of theory to professional practice. All programmes include periods of practical training and require the submission of a project paper. Most programmes give access to further studies in the same field. Programmes are offered in fields such as business, education, engineering, IT, nursing, social work etc.
• Academies of professional higher education: These colleges are also fairly newly, established by the merging of smaller institutions. They have very strong linkages with the regional

business and industry. 2-year academy profession degree programmes are offered in fields such as business, technology, IT, multimedia, food industry, tourism, etc. They combine theoretical and analytical studies with a practice-oriented approach. The programmes require the submission of a project paper.

Major institutions of higher education: Danish universities and similar institutions with university status offering research-based undergraduate, postgraduate and PhD programmes:
• University of Copenhagen; Postbox 2177, 1017 Kbh. K; web: www.ku.dk; Faculties: health sciences, humanities, law, science, social sciences, theology
• Aarhus University; Ndr. Ringgade 1, 8000 Aarhus C; web: www.au.dk; Faculties: Arts, health sciences, science, social sciences, theology
• University of Southern Denmark; Campusvej 55, 5230 Odense M; web: www.sdu.dk; Faculties: health sciences, humanities, science and engineering, social sciences
• Roskilde University; Faculties: humanities, natural sciences, social sciences; Postbox 260, 4000 Roskilde; web: www.ruc.dk
• Aalborg University; Postbox 159, 9100 Aalborg; web: www.auc.dk; Faculties: engineering and science, humanities, social sciences
• Technical University of Denmark; Bygning 101 A, 2800 Lyngby; web: www.dtu.dk
• The Royal Veterinary and Agricultural University; Bülowsvej 17, 1870 Frederiksberg; web: www.kvl.dk
• The Danish University of Pharmaceutical Sciences; Universitetsparken 2, 2100 Kbh. Ø; web: www.dfh.dk
• Copenhagen Business School; Solbjerg Plads 3, 2000 Frederiksberg; web: www.cbs.dk; Faculties: Business Administration, Modern Languages
• The Aarhus School of Business; Fuglesangs Allé 4, 8210 Århus V; web: www.asb.dk; Faculties: Business Administration, Modern Languages
• The Danish University of Education; Emdrupvej 101, 2400 Kbh. NV; web: www.dpu.dk
• The IT-University of Copenhagen; Glentevej 67, 2400 København NV; web: www.itu.dk
• IT University West; Fuglesangs Allé 20, 8210 Århus V; web: www.it-vest.dk
• The Royal Danish Academy of Fine Arts; School of Architecture; Philip de Langes Allé 10, 1435 Kbh. K; web: www.karch.dk
• Aarhus School of Architecture; Nørreport 20, 8000 Aarhus C; web: www.a-aarhus.dk
• The Royal Danish Academy of Fine Arts; Schools of Visual Arts; Kongens Nytorv 1, 1050 Kbh. K; web: www.kunstakademiet.dk
• The Royal Danish Academy of Fine Arts; School of Conservation; Esplanaden 34, 1263 Kbh. K; web: www.kons.dk
• The Royal School of Library and Information Science; Birketinget 6, 2300 Kbh. S; web: www.db.dk.

Monetary unit: Danish krone (DKK).

National student admission: 12 years of education including one of the following secondary-school leaving examinations or comparable qualifications: studentereksamen (upper secondary-school leaving examination); højere forberedelseseksamen (hf) (higher preparatory examination); højere handelseksamen (hhx), (higher commercial xamination); højere teknisk eksamen (htx) (higher technical examination).
Admission to many study programmes depends also on the fulfilment of specific requirements such as subject combinations, the level of subjects taken, the grades obtained, work experience, etc. For a few study programmes there is a numerus clausus.

International student admission: In general, admission to higher education requires a qualifying examination from one of the Danish academic preparatory upper secondary programmes or qualifications recognized or assessed as being comparable to these. For programmes in Danish, they must also prove sufficient command of Danish as well as English, as many textbooks are in English. Some of the study programmes have additional admission requirements, such as specific subjects or level of subjects, practical work experience, etc.

Language: The national language is Danish, most study programmes are therefore taught in Danish. However, there are around 125 programmes (mostly at master level) taught entirely in English). For the Danish language taught programmes a good command of Danish is essential and non-Danish and non-Nordic applicants have to prove sufficient command of Danish by passing a test. A high proficiency in English is required and must be documented for all study programmes (both the Danish and English language taught programmes).

Immigration requirements: Students should always contact the institution where they have been admitted for detailed information and procedures. Students from EU/EEA countries need a residence permit if they intend to stay in Denmark for more than three months. Applications should be made through the local county authority (Statsamt) in Denmark and require documentation of admission to a Danish higher education institution. EU/EEA citizens do not need a work permit.
Students from outside a Nordic or EU/EEA country need to have a residence permit and maybe also a visa before entering Denmark. Application for the residence permit should be addressed to the Danish Embassy or Consulate in the home country of the student. Applicants must provide proof of admission to a Danish higher education institution and financial resources for their studies and living expenses (currently minimum DKK 4.200 per month). For further information, please contact the host university. Work permits are not granted automatically, but students can apply for one for up to 15 hours work per week during the semesters and full time during the summer holidays (June, July and August). Further information: The Danish Immigration Service: www.udlst.dk.

Estimated expenses for one academic year: Tuition is free for Danish students and for citizens from the EU/EEA. Tuition fees are about to be introduced for students outside the EU/EEA for degree programmes. Expected expenses for tuition: 8.000-15.000 Euros; books/supplies: 400-900 Euros; housing: 275-450 Euros. .

Information services:
• Information on studying in Denmark: Cirius, Fiolstraede 44, DK-1171 Copenhagen K, web: http://www.ciriusonline.dk
• Information on scholarships for students from developing countries: Department for Multilateral Affairs, Danish Ministry of Foreign Affairs, Asiatisk Plads 2, 1448 Copenhagen K
• Denmark International Study Program (DiS), Vestergade 7, 1456 Copenhagen K: web: http://www.disp.dk
• Exchanges between Denmark and United States: Fulbright Commission/Denmark-America Foundation, Fiolstræde 24, 3. sal, 1171 Copenhagen, web: http://www.daf-fulb.dk K
• Student and Youth Accommodation in Denmark: Centralindstillingsudvalget (Students' Residence Committee), H.C. Andersens Boulevard 13, 1553 Copenhagen V; web: http://www.ungdomsboliger.dk
• Students should address requests for information directly to to universities of interest:.

Scholarships for international students: Specific information on possible scholarships are normally available from the individual higher education institution.
• General information about grants and scholarships are available from Cirius Denmark, Fiolstraede 44, 1171 Copenhagen K, Denmark; tel: +45 33 95 70 00; fax: +45 33 95 70 01; e-mail: cirius@ciriusmail.dk; web: www.ciriusonline.dk
• Information on scholarships for students from developing countries: Department for Multilateral Affairs, Danish Ministry of Foreign Affairs, Asiatisk Plads 2, 1448 Copenhagen K, Denmark
• SU-Styrelsen (Danish Students Grants and Loans Agency), Danasvej 30, 1780 Copenhagen K, Denmark; tel: +45 33 26 86 00; fax: +45 33 26 86 11; e-mail su@su.dk; web: www.su.dk.

Open and distance learning: Many adult education programmes comparable to the level of the regular higher education programmes are offered. A few of the programmes may be followed as distance e-learning. Most programmes consist of 2 years of part-time study, equivalent to 1 year of full-time study. Admission requirements are a relevant educational qualification and at least 2 years of professional experience.

Recognition of studies and qualification: Recognition in relation to admission to a study programme is the responsibility of each individual university. General information on recognition procedures and recognition/assessment of foreign qualifications; Centre for Assessment of Foreign Qualifications, Fiolstraede 44, 1171 Copenhagen K, Denmark; web: http://www.cvuu.dk.

Accommodation services: International students should contact the university to which they have been admitted for specific details concerning accommodation.

Work opportunities: Non EU/EEA students are not automatically granted a work permit, but may apply for permission to work a maximum of 15 hours per week during semesters and full-time during summer holidays. It should be noted that job opportunities for non-Danish-speaking students are fairly limited.

Publications / Websites:
• Information on Denmark: www.denmark.dk,Information on studying in Denmark: www.ciriusonline.dk/eng
• Information on assessment of foreign qualifications: www.cvuu.dk;
• Information on working and research-opportunities in Denmark: www.workindenmark.dk
• Information on residence and work permits: www.udlst.dk.

---

674   Aalborg University [AUC]
International Office
Fibigerstraede 2
PO Box 159
DK 9100 Aalborg East
Tel: +45-9635-8080
Fax: +45-9815-4522
Web: http://www.auc.dk
e-mail: ek@auc.dk

📖 **Undergraduate, Graduate, Postgraduate Programmes**

Study Domains: communication, cultural studies, ecology, environment, European studies, international studies, sociology.
Programmes: undergraduate, graduate and postgraduate courses.
Description: (a) European Cultural Studies: intercultural communication, international political economy, British/American literature, programme with emphasis on contemporary European culture, communication, politics and cultural expressions; (b) Sociological Theory and Analysis: training in conducting empirical analysis based on a theoretical and methodological knowledge of features and issues in a modern Scandinavian welfare state: minimum 3 to 4 foreign students in English-taught classes; (c) European studies: international political economy, Western Europe and the European Union (EU), intercultural communication, focus on the structure and process of Western European integration; (d) Communication, Culture and Media: media and cultural studies theory, media and reception, theory and practice, media and visual representation, a theoretical framework of cultural studies and case studies; (e) Environmental Engineering: urban drainage engineering and modelling, urban water, teaching and research in chemistry, biology, hydraulics and environmental engineering; (classes in English if a minimum of 5 to 6 foreign students); (f) Indoor Environmental Engineering: air movement in rooms, courses and a group project; (g) International Development Studies: international political economy, Western Europe and the EU, international technology analysis, insight into international relations and development in a historical perspective; (h) Management in an International Perspective: the programme aims to give students an overall view of management theory and practice in an open market-directed economy.
Open to: (a) students with a minimum of 2 years undergraduate studies in the humanities; (b) students normally enrol in their fourth year; knowledge of the philosophy and methodology of social science equivalent to a second-year level is a prerequisite for foreign students; (c) and (g) candidates with a minimum of 3 years of study in the social sciences; (d) students with 2 to 3 years of undergraduate studies in the humanities, teaching on an advanced undergraduate/ graduate level; (e) candidates holding a B.Sc. in civil or environmental engineering or possibly advanced undergraduate students; (f) students with 3 to 4 years of study in building technology and indoor environmental engineering; (h) students expected to have a minimum of 3 years of study or some formal training and relevant practical experience.

Duration: (a), (c), (d) and (f) 5 months; (b) 5 or 10 months; (e) 1 to 4 semesters; courses begin in September; (g) 1 year; courses begin in February; (h) 5 months, composed of 3 eight-week modules; courses begin in September.
Fees: tuition free for students from co-operating universities and students from EU countries; (h) for students not from co-operating universities or EU countries, US$3,000.
Languages: instruction is given in English.
Applications: (a), (b), (c) and (g) by 1 December; (d), (e), (f) and (h) by 1 July; to the above address.

675   Aarhus School of Architecture
Nørreport 20
8000 Aarhus C
Tel: +45-8936-0000
Fax: +45-8613-0645
Web: http://aarch.dk/
e-mail: aaa@aarch.dk

📖 **Graduate Programmes / Architecture**

Study Domains: architecture, decorative arts, design, industrial design, interior design, urbanism.
Programmes: programme of courses in architecture.
Description: courses in architectural education: building design, planning, urban design, landscape and garden design, restoration and town renewal, furniture and interior design and industrial design; 2 programmes: (a) normal study, (b) guest study.
Open to: (a) candidates holding a school leaving certificate (GCE minimum 5 subjects with 2 on A-level) and proficient in Danish language; (b) candidates with at least 3 years' related studies.
Duration: (a) 5 years; (b) 4 months to 1 academic year; courses start in September or February.
Applications: (a) by 15 March; (b) by 15 May or 15 October, to the above address.

676   Aarhus School of Business [ASB]
Fuglesangs Allé 4
8210 Aarhus V
Tel: +45-8948-6688
Fax: +45-8948-6663
Web: http://www.asb.dk
e-mail: webmaster@asb.dk

📖 **Undergraduate, Graduate, Postgraduate Programmes**

Study Domains: accounting, administration, business, business administration, communication, economic and commercial sciences, economy, finance, industrial relations, industry and commerce, information science, international business, international law, international relations, international studies, interpretation and translation, languages, law, management, political economy, public relations, trade.
Programmes: programme of courses leading to Diploma, Bachelor's, Master's and Ph.D. in business studies.
Open to: candidates of all nationalities with relevant qualifications.
Languages: courses in English; TOEFL minimum 220.
Applications: by 15 March.

677   Cirius
Fiolstraede 44
1171 Copenhagen K
Tel: +45-3392-7000
Fax: +45-3395-7001
Web: http://www.ciriusonline.dk
e-mail: cirius@ciriusmail.dk

🎓 **Scholarships**

Study Domains: all major fields.
Scholarships: Danish government grants for undergraduate and graduate studies in Denmark.
Open to: undergraduate and graduate students from Austria, Belgium, Bulgaria, China, Czech Republic, Egypt, Estonia, Finland, France, Germany, Greece, Hungary, Iceland, Israel, Italy, Japan, Latvia, Lithuania, Netherlands, Poland, Portugal, Romania, Russian Federation, Slovakia, Spain and Turkey.
Place of study: in Denmark.

Duration: approx. 4 to 8 months.
Value: approx. 5,000 DKK per month, plus free tuition; an additional travel allowance may be given to students from Israel, Japan, Turkey and Egypt. See website for participating countries.
Languages: candidates must have a good knowledge of Danish, English or German.
Applications: see website: http://www.ciriusonline.dk for further information.

678 Copenhagen Business School, Centre for Conference Interpretation [CBS]

Solbjerg Plads 3
2000 Frederiksberg
Tel: +45-3815-3815
Fax: +45-3815-3855
Web: http://www.cbs.dk
e-mail: cbs@cbs.dk

📖 Postgraduate Programme

Study Domains: interpretation and translation.
Programmes: postgraduate courses in conference interpreting in Danish, English, French, German, Spanish and Italian.
Open to: candidates with knowledge of Danish, the above languages (or Danish) as mother tongue and with university degree or equivalent; entry is subject to successful completion of entrance test (usually in June).
Duration: 6 month full-time course (courses begin in October).
Fees: information upon request.
Languages: all candidates must have Danish in their language combination.
Applications: usually by 15 May, forms available from the above address.

679 Danish Rectors' Conference [RKS]

Fiolstræde 44, 1. th.
1171 Copenhagen K
Tel: +45-3392-5403
Fax: +45-3392-5075
Web: http://www.rks.dk
e-mail: rks@rks.dk

🎓 Scholarships

Study Domains: all major fields, travel grants.
Scholarships: Danish Government grants for undergraduate and graduate studies in Denmark.
Open to: undergraduate and graduate students from Austria, Belgium, Bulgaria, China, Czech Republic, Egypt, Estonia, Finland, France, Germany, Greece, Hungary, Iceland, Israel, Italy, Japan, Latvia, Lithuania, Netherlands, Poland, Portugal, Romania, Russian Federation, Slovakia, Spain and Turkey.
Place of study: in Denmark.
Duration: approximately 4 to 8 months.
Value: approximately 5,000 DKK per month, plus free tuition; an additional travel allowance may be given to students from Israel, Japan, Turkey and Egypt. See website for participating countries.
Languages: candidates must have a knowledge of Danish, English or German.
Applications: variable according to each country; see website for application information.

680 Denmark-America Foundation & Fulbright Commission

Fiolstraede 24, 3
1171 Copenhagen K
Tel: +45-3312-8223
Fax: +45-3332-5323
Web: http://www.daf-fulb.dk
e-mail: daf-fulb@daf-fulb.dk

🎓 CFEEB scholarships.

Study Domains: American studies.
Scholarships: (a) Denmark-America Foundation awards: scholarships for studies in the United States at the graduate/postgraduate university level; trainee programme; (b) Fulbright Commission: grants to both American and Danish graduate students and scholars for the promotion of American Studies in Denmark and Danish Studies in the United States.
Open to: Danish or American graduate students, lecturers and researchers with good projects and strong references.
Place of study: (a) in the United States; (b) Center for American Studies, Odense University, Denmark.
Duration: (a) from 3 to 9 months.
Value: (a) Master's level: 75,000 DKK; Ph.D. level: approx. 70,000 DKK.
Applications: to above address; see website for full information.

681 Roskilde University [RUC]

PO Box 260
4000 Roskilde
Tel: +45-4674-2000
Fax: +45-4674-3000
Web: http://www.ruc.dk/ruc
e-mail: ruc@ruc.dk

📖 Undergraduate, Graduate, Postgraduate Programmes

Study Domains: all major fields.
Programmes: Bachelor's, Master's and Ph.D. degree programmes.
Open to: candidates of all nationalities with secondary school certificate (or equivalent); foreign applicants without a Danish entrance examination are eligible for admission if they meet both of the following two requirements: have passed the Danish test for international students 'Studieprøven i dansk som andetsprog' (special rules apply for students from Nordic countries and students at International Cultural Studies, see the section about language requirements), and have qualifications recognized or assessed as being comparable to Danish entrance qualifications.
Languages: courses in Danish; some programmes are offered in English.

682 Royal Danish Academy of Music

Niels Brocks Gade 1
1574 Copenhagen V
Tel: +45-3369-2269
Fax: +45-3369-2279
Web: http://www.dkdm.dk
e-mail: dkdm@dkdm.dk

📖 Graduate Programmes / Music

Study Domains: music and musicology.
Programmes: graduate-level courses.
Description: (a) Foreign students as 'special students'; (b) Regular education; (c) Soloist education.
Open to: candidates of any nationality: (a) who will be requested to provide evidence of having studied at an acknowledged foreign music school and to give an audition; (b) and (c) who will pass the normal entrance examination which takes place in February for (b) and in June for (c), and follow studies in Danish.
Duration: (a) at least 3 months with 1 hour a week tuition minimum; (b) 4 to 5 years; (c) maximum 2 years.
Fees: (a) an hourly fee equivalent to a quota-calculation of teacher's salary.
Financial assistance: some scholarships available through the Danish government; contact the Danish embassy in country of origin for scholarship possibilities.
Applications: (b) by 1 December; (c) by 1 February.

683 Royal Danish School of Pharmacy [DFH]

Universitetsparken 2
2100 Kebenhaun
Tel: +45-3530-6000
Fax: +45-3530-6001
Web: http://www.dfuni.dk
e-mail: dfuni@dfuni.dk

📖 Graduate, Postgraduate Programmes

Study Domains: pharmacy and pharmacology.
Programmes: Master's and Ph.D. programmes.
Financial assistance: some scholarships offered in Ph.D.

programmes; see website
http://www.dfh.dk/Mariecurie/mariecurie2.htm).

684 Technical University of Denmark [DTU]

Bygning 101,
Anker Engelundsvej I
2800 Lyngby
Tel: +45-4525-2525
Fax: +45-4588-1799
Web: http://www.dtu.dk
e-mail: dtu@dtu.dk

📖 **Undergraduate, Graduate, Postgraduate Programmes**

Study Domains: chemical industry, civil engineering, mechanical engineering.
Programmes: programme of courses leading to Bachelor's, Master's and Ph.D. degrees.
Description: (a) B.Sc. programme in engineering: including mechanical and production, naval, electrical, chemical and civil engineering; (b) Master's programme in engineering: chemical engineering, electrical engineering, energy, informatics, or applied physics, civil and construction engineering, mechanical engineering, environmental engineering; (c) Doctorate programme: mathematics, physics, chemical engineering, electrical engineering, civil engineering, mechanical engineering, and social sciences, planning and technology.
Open to: (a) and (b) students with upper secondary school leaving examination in mathematics-physics; students who are not familiar with the Danish language must pass a language test before admission, though they may be accepted for their final project or as Ph.D. students.
Duration: (a) 3½ years; (b) 5 years; (c) 3 years.
Applications: by 1 March (for Fall) and 1 October (for Spring) for regular students; 1 August (for Fall) and 1 January (for Spring) for guest students; Open University students, 1 August (for Fall) and 1 December (for Spring).

685 University of Copenhagen [KU]

Fiolstraede 24
PO Box 1143
1010 Copenhagen K
Tel: +45-3532-2918
Fax: +45-3532-3900
Web: http://www.ku.dk/sa/inter
e-mail: inter@adm.ku.dk

📖 **Undergraduate, Graduate, Postgraduate Programmes**

Study Domains: all major fields.
Programmes: Bachelor's, Master's and Ph.D. programmes.
Open to: candidates of all nationalities with relevant qualifications.
Languages: courses in Danish (Danish courses for foreign students); some programmes are available in English.

686 University of Southern Denmark

Campusvej 55
5230 Odense M
Tel: +45-6550-2072
Fax: +45-6615-7500
Web: http://www.sdu.dk/indexE.html
e-mail: int@adm.sdu.dk

📖 **Undergraduate, Graduate Programmes**

Study Domains: biochemistry, biology, business administration, chemical industry, chemistry, computer science, European studies, mechanical engineering, oceanography, physics, tourism, hotel and catering management.
Programmes: Bachelor's and Master's degree programmes.
Open to: candidates of all nationalities meeting academic, linguistic and financial requirements.
Held: campuses at Odense, Kolding, Esbjeg and Soenderborg.
Languages: Danish and English.
Applications: to the above address.

Ecuador

Año académico: Octubre a julio (en la región de la Sierra); mayo a diciembre (en la región de la Costa).
Moneda nacional: dólar de los Estados Unidos.
Admisiones para estudiantes extranjeros: Título de bachiller legalizado por el Ministerio de Educación y Cultura. Para el ingreso en algunas facultades o escuelas es necesario además pasar un examen de admisión, seguir un curso preuniversitario o aprobar un curso de nivelación.
Conocimientos lingüísticos: Es indispensable dominar suficientemente el idioma español. Algunas universidades imparten cursos de español para que los estudiantes extranjeros perfeccionen sus conocimientos de español antes de empezar los estudios superiores.
Formalidades de inmigración: Tramitar el respectivo permiso de residencia en la Dirección General de Inmigración y Extranjería.
Servicios de información:
• Ministerio de Educación y Cultura, Departamento de Asuntos y Convenios Internacionales, Quito (información acerca de las instituciones ecuatorianas de enseñanza superior).
• Instituto Ecuatoriano de Crédito Educativo y Becas (IECE), Manuel Larrea 323 y Juan Pablo Arenas, Quito (administra las becas ofrecidas por diversos países y organismos internacionales a ecuatorianos para que adquieran una especialización en el extranjero; dispone de un servicio de préstamos para ayudar a los ecuatorianos que deseen cursar estudios superiores en el Ecuador o en el extranjero).
• Departamentos de relaciones públicas de las diversas universidades ecuatorianas.
• Secretariado General Permanente del Consejo Nacional de Educación Superior, Santa Prisca 269, Quito.
• Las oficinas de bienestar estudiantil de cada una de las universidades ecuatorianas, así como las escuelas politécnicas nacionales, dan toda clase de indicaciones sobre las posibilidades de encontrar alojamiento.
Enseñanza abierta y a distancia: La Facultad de Educación de la Universidad Técnica Particular de Loja ofrece cursos a distancia de 4 años de duración en áreas de formación de docentes, ciencias sociales, matemáticas, química, biología, física y lengua y literatura inglesas.
Convalidación de estudios y diplomas: Consejo Nacional de Educación Superior (CONESUP), 9 de Octubre 624 y Carrión, Quito, Ecuador; tel: +593-2-569-898 / +593-2-569-894; fax: +593-2-563-685; email: conesup@conesup.org.ec; secretariatecnica@conesup.org.ec; web: http://www.conesup.net.
Publicaciones / Sitios web:
• "Boletín Informativo de la Universidad Central del Ecuador", Editorial Universitaria, avenida América y Alfredo Pérez Guerrero; Ciudadela Universitaria, Apartado 3291, Quito.

687 Pontificia Universidad Católica del Ecuador [PUCE]

Apartado 17-01-2184
Avenida 12 de Octubre y Roca
Quito
Tel: +593-2-520-947
Fax: +593-2-567-117
Web: http://www.puce.edu.ec
e-mail: relint@pude.edu.ec

📖 **Programa de becas**

Campos de estudios: todas las materias principales.
Descripción: (a) Becas de estudios de pre-grado y post-grado (20% y 30% de los estudiantes respectivamente); (b) Apoyos financieros procedente de fundaciones y organizaciones no gubernamentales nacionales y extranjeras para alrededor de 100 estudiantes de pre-grado y post-grado, bajo condiciones y acuerdos especiales; (c) Convenios de intercambio académico con universidades extranjeras.
Materias de estudio: las dictadas en sus Facultades y Escuelas de: arquitectura y diseño; ciencias administrativas; ciencias de la educación; ciencias exactas y naturales; ciencias filosóficas-teológicas; ciencias humanas; economía; enfermería; ingeniería; jurisprudencia; comunicación, lingüística y literatura; medicina; psicología; trabajo social.

Solicitudes: solicitar informes a la Dirección de Extensión y Relaciones Internacionales (DERI).

688 Universidad "San Francisco de Quito" Corporación de Promoción Universitaria [USFQ]

P.O. Box 17 12 841
Cumbayá
Tel: (593) 2 895 723
Fax: (593) 2 890 070
Web: http://www.usfq.edu.ec
e-mail: diego@mail.ustq.edu.ec

📖 Programas universitarios

Campos de estudios: todas las materias principales.
Descripción: licenciaturas y maestrías en todas las materias principales.
Se destina(n): a quienes hayan concluído estudios secundarios en el caso de licenciaturas o a titulados universitarios en el caso de maestrías. Existe selección por entrevista, pruebas escritas y curriculum.
Duración: 4 años las licenciaturas y 2 años las maestrías (los semestres comienzan en septiembre y en enero). Hay cursos de verano a partir de fin de mayo.
Asistencia financiera: becas de estudio y crédito educativo para aspirantes a licenciaturas o maestrías; en algunos casos, hay también asistencia en costos de alojamiento y alimentación.

689 Universidad Andina "Simón Bolívar" Sede Ecuador [UASB]

Toledo N22-80,
Casilla 17-12-569
Quito
Tel: (593) 2 255 6405/6406
Fax: (593) 2 250 8156
Web: http://www.uasb.edu.ec
e-mail: uasb@uasb.edu.ec

📖 Programas superiores

Campos de estudios: ciencias sociales, comunicación, derecho, educación, estudios americanos, estudios culturales, gestión, higiene y salud, historia, letras, relaciones internacionales.
Programas:
(a) Programas internacionales de tercer ciclo: doctorados;
(b) Programas internacionales de posgrado: maestrías (o diplomas superiores);
(c) Programas de especialización superior;
(d) Programas de diploma superior.
Materias de estudio: (a) Historia (realizado mendiante convenio con la Universidad Pablo de Olavide, Sevilla); estudios culturales latinoamericanos; derecho; (b) Estudios latinoamericanos, estudios de la cultura, relaciones internacionales, derecho; (c) Tributación; gestión ambiental; derecho financiero, bursátil y de seguros; derecho y gestión de las telecomunicaciones; derechos humanos; gestión de costos; derecho procesal; educación; derecho administrativo; gerencia educativa; dirección de empresas; adolescencia; gestión local; comunicación; (d) Salud y terapias integrativas.
Duración: (a) variable según el doctorado; (b) para maestría: tres o cuatro trimestres más dos o tres trimestres para preparación de tesis; para diplomados: un año académico a tiempo parcial o dos trimestres a tiempo completo; (c) un año académico a tiempo parcial; (d) tres trimestres.
Asistencia financiera: para candidatos procedentes de la Comunidad Andina exclusivamente: becas parciales o totales; becas completas.
Inscripciones: por mayores informaciones dirigirse a la Secretaría General: e-mail: secretaria@uasb.edu.ec.

📖 Becas de estudio

Campos de estudios: derecho, estudios americanos, estudios culturales, relaciones internacionales.
Descripción: estudios a tiempo completo para realizar doctorados y maestrías en áreas de historia, estudios culturales latinoamericanos, derecho; estudios latinoamericanos (políticas culturales, relaciones internacionales, derechos humanos, migraciones transnacionales), cultura (literatura hispanoamericana, políticas culturales, comunicación,

patrimonio cultural), relaciones internacionales (comercio internacional, integración, negociaciones internacionales, política internacional), derecho (derecho del mercado, derechos humanos, derecho tributario).
Se conceden: exclusivamente a procedentes de la Comunidad Andina (Venezuela, Colombia, Ecuador, Perú y Bolivia).
Importe: medias becas de colegiatura; becas completas de colegiatura (equivalente a 5.000 dólares); becas completas de colegiatura, más gastos de estadía y alimentación durante la fase docente del programa, más seguro médico individual o familiar según corresponda, más monto (equivalente a 200 dólares) por única vez para apoyo en material bibliográfico.
Solicitudes: hasta julio; por mayor información, dirigirse a la Secretaría General, secretaria@uasb.edu.uc.

690 Universidad Autónoma de Quito [UNAQ]

Calle Mercadillo n°129 entre Paéz y 10 de Agosto
Quito
Tel: +593(2) 2221457
Fax: +593(2) 2221458
Web: http://www.unaq.net
e-mail: info@unaq.net

📖 Becas académicas y deportivas

Campos de estudios: todas las materias principales.
Se conceden: a estudiantes con altas calificaciones y según condición económica.
Duración: anual, renovable.
Importe: US$ 1.200.
Solicitudes: 2 meses antes del comienzo del semestre.

691 Universidad Católica de Santiago de Guayaquil [UCSG]

Casilla 09-01-4671
Guayaquil
Tel: (593) 42 209 197/201 349/209 2
Fax: (593) 42 200 071/209 197
Web: http://www.ucsg.edu.ec
e-mail: cvcme@ucsg.edu.ec

📖 Programas universitarios

Campos de estudios: todas las materias principales, español, literatura y civilización.
Descripción:
(a) Carreras de grado en todas las áreas principales;
(b) CCIS Study Abroad Program: curso de español, historia, literatura y cultura ecuatorianas y latinoamericanas.
Se destina(n): (b) estudiantes universitarios que pertenezcan al programa Collage Consortium International Studies.
Duración: (b) 3 meses de septiembre a diciembre; 4 semanas en julio (verano) o enero (invierno).
Inscripciones: (a) solicitar información relativa a estudiantes extranjeros a Relaciones Internacionales; (b) dirigirse a Coordinación Internacional, proinex@ucsg.edu.ec.

692 Universidad del Pacífico [UNPAC]

P.O. Box 17-08-8229
Quito
Tel: (593) 2 444 509/510
Fax: (593) 2 459 593
Web: http://www.upacifico.edu.ec
e-mail: gzuguilanda@upacifico.edu.ec

📖 Programas universitarios

Campos de estudios: todas las materias principales, español, estudios culturales, literatura y civilización.
Programas:
(a) Bachilleratos, maestrías, doctorados en todas las áreas principales;
(b) Programa Study Abroad.
Se dicta(n): (b) en Quito, Guayaquil, Cuenca e Islas Galápagos.
Duración: (b) de 2 semanas a 1 año; hay cursos de verano.
Inscripciones: por mayor información relativa a estudiantes extranjeros, dirigirse al Departamento de Relaciones Internacionales.

693 Universidad Internacional del Ecuador [UIDE]
Km. 3 Av. Simón Bolívar, Collacoto
Quito
Tel: +593-2-2985-600
Fax: +593-2-2985-666
Web: http://www.internacional.edu.ec
e-mail: informa@internacional.edu.ec

📖 Ayudas financieras

Campos de estudios: administración, arquitectura, ciencias, ciencias económicas y comerciales, comunicación, derecho, ecología, medio ambiente, estudios dentales, informática.
Descripción: reducción en los gastos de enseñanza.
Materias de estudio: las dictadas en sus Facultades y Escuelas de: ciencias básicas; ciencias administrativas y económicas; ciencias de la seguridad; ciencias médicas; odontología; ciencias ambientales; comunicación; informática y multimedia; mecánica automotriz; jurisprudencia; arquitectura.
Importe: de 25 a 100%.

694 Universidad Internacional SEK [UIS]
Campus del Monasterio de Guápulo
Quito
Tel: (593) 2 223 688
Fax: (593) 2 223 689
Web: http://www.uisek.edu.ec
e-mail: admision@uisek.edu.ec

📖 Programas universitarios

Campos de estudios: todas las materias principales, administración, ciencias económicas y comerciales, ciencias sociales, comunicación, derecho, ecología, medio ambiente, español, literatura y civilización, matemáticas, periodismo, turismo, hotelería.
Descripción: Programas conducentes a diversos grados según el programa en: derecho, ciencias económicas y administrativas, arquitectura y urbanismo, ingeniería del medio ambiente, administración y dirección de empresas turísticas, periodismo y comunicación audiovisual, comunicación y diseño publicitario.
Se destina(n): para las carreras de pregrado, a quienes hayan finalizado la secundaria, y para los posgrados, a quienes posean el grado académico requerido; existe selección por entrevista.
Duración: 4 a 6 años (de octubre a junio); cursos de verano: en septiembre.
Asistencia financiera: se otorgan becas por aprovechamiento académico a partir del segundo año de la carrera.
Inscripciones: del 1° de abril hasta el 15 de septiembre; dirigirse al Departamento de Admisión y Registro Académico.

695 Universidad Técnica de Ambato [UTA]
Avenida Colombia y Chile
Campus Ingahuyco
Casilla 334
Ambato
Tel: (593) 3 849 454
Fax: (593) 3 849 454
Web: http://www.uta.edu.ec
e-mail: saltosha@uta.edu.ec

📖 Programas universitarias

Campos de estudios: ciencias agronómicas, ciencias humanas, contabilidad, educación, ingeniería.
Descripción: Programas universitarios en áreas de ciencias humanas y de la educación, ciencias de la salud, contabilidad y auditoría, ciencia e ingeniería en alimentos, ingeniería en sistemas, ingeniería civil, ingeniería agronómica.
Duración: año universitario de octubre a agosto.
Inscripciones: por mayores informaciones o solicitudes de ingreso, dirigirse a la Vicerrectoría.

696 Universidad Técnica de Cotopaxi [UTC]
Apartado 05-01-491
Latacunga
Tel: (593) 3 810 296
Fax: (593) 3 810 295
Web: http://www.utc.edu.ec
e-mail: webmaster@utc.edu.ec

📖 Programas universitarios

Campos de estudios: todas las materias principales, español, estudios culturales.
Descripción: (a) Carreras de grado en todas las áreas principales;
(b) "CCIS" Study Abroad Program: cursos de español y cultura ecuatoriana para extranjeros.
Duración: (b) 3 meses en otoño (septiembre a diciembre), 4 semanas en verano (julio) e invierno (enero).
Inscripciones: por toda información relativa a estudiantes extranjeros, dirigirse al Departamento de Relaciones Internacionales.

697 Universidad Técnica Estatal de Quevedo [UTEQ]
Km 1,5 vía a Quito
Casilla 73
Tel: (593) 5 750 320
Fax: (593) 5 753 303
e-mail: rinternacionales_uteq@hotmail.com

📖 Formación de profesionales agropecuarios

Campos de estudios: administración de empresas, ciencias agronómicas, ecología, medio ambiente, horticultura, silvicultura.
Descripción: carreras de ingeniería agronómica, administración de empresas agropecuarias, ingeniería forestal, gestión ambiental, ingeniería zootécnica; horticultura; ciencias empresariales.

698 Universidad Técnica Particular de Loja [UTPL]
Apartado 11-01-608
Loja
Tel: (593) 7 570 275
Fax: (593) 7 563 159
e-mail: utpl@accessinter.net

📖 Programas universitarios presenciales y a distancia

Campos de estudios: todas las materias principales.
Descripción:
(a) Programa en "Modalidad abierta" (estudios a distancia): profesorado y especialidades en física y matemáticas, química y biología, lengua y literatura, pedagogía en ciencias humanas y religiosas, administración y supervisión educativa, contabilidad y administración, historia y geografía, inglés;
(b) Carreras en "Modalidad clásica" (cursos, licenciaturas, doctorado) en las áreas de arquitectura, economía, ingeniería civil, ingeniería en industrias agropecuarias, contabilidad y auditoría, inglés, informática, ciencias de la educación, secretariado, artes plásticas, tecnología geominera, turismo y hotelería.
Se destina(n): a bachilleres de cualquier edad y nacionalidad.
Duración: número variable de ciclos (ciclos en octubre-febrero y abril-agosto).

Egypt

Academic year: October to July.
Monetary unit: Egyptian pound (EGP or E£).
National student admission: Foreign students should have qualifications equivalent to a certificate of secondary education or a university degree.
Language: Knowledge of Arabic is essential for regular university studies. Courses are given in English in the faculties of medicine, veterinary medicine, pharmacology, engineering, commercial sciences, at Helwan University; agriculture, at the Universities of Alexandria and Mushtuhur, at the American University in Cairo. An intensive English language programme is also offered at these institutions.
Immigration requirements: Foreign students must obtain a student visa.
Estimated expenses for one academic year: Registration fees are paid once. Undergraduate studies in theoretical faculties: registration E£1,000; tuition E£1,000; in scientific faculties: registration E£1,500; tuition E£1,500. Diploma, Master's, Doctorate degrees: in theoretical faculties: registration fee E£1,200; tuition: Diploma E£1,000; Master's E£1,200; Doctorate E£2,000; in practical colleges: registration fee E£1,700; tuition fees: Diploma E£1,300; Master's E£1,500; Doctorate E£2,500. Tuition fees can be paid in 2 instalments.
Information services:
• Students' Welfare Department, Ministry of Higher Education, Cairo (general information and advice for foreign students).
Open and distance learning: The Egyptian University for Distance Learning is being established.
Recognition of studies and qualification: Ministry of Higher Education and Scientific Research; 101 Kasr Al-Aini Street; Cairo; Egypt; tel: +20 2 795 2155; fax: +20 2 794 2556; telex: 92312 frcu un; email: mohe@frcu.eun.eg; website: http://www.frcu.eun.eg.
Publications / Websites:
• 'A Guide for the Use of Foreign Students', published by the Students' Welfare Department.
• American University in Cairo Catalogue and Admissions Bulletin; from the university at 866 United Nations Plaza, New York, N.Y. 10017, United States, or P.O. Box 2511, Cairo.

---

699   Ain Shams University [ASU]
Abbassia
11566 Cairo
Tel: +202-482-0230/683-1474
Fax: +202-684-7824
Web: http://net.shams.edu.eg
e-mail: info@asunet.shams.edu.eg

📖 Arabic Language and Culture

Study Domains: Arabic, languages, literature and civilization.
Programmes: (a) Arabic language courses for non-Arabic speakers; (b) Arabic culture and civilization courses.
Open to: students of any age, nationality and level.
Duration: 6 to 12 weeks; courses begin in October, December and May.
Fees: US$300 for 6 weeks.
Languages: instruction in English, French and German.
Applications: to the above address.

📖 Training Course / Computer Science

Study Domains: computer science.
Programmes: integrated training course in computer science at the Scientific Computing Center.
Open to: students with a high school diploma or a Bachelor of Commerce degree or equivalent, or candidates from developing countries who hold a university degree.
Duration: 7 months.
Fees: tuition: approximately US$800.
Financial assistance: 5 scholarships covering 50% of tuition fees.
Applications: to the Director of the Center.

📖 Undergraduate, Graduate Programmes

Study Domains: agriculture, arts, business, dentistry, engineering, languages, law, medicine, nursing, pharmacy and pharmacology, sciences, vocational training, women's studies.

700   Alexandria University - Medical Research Institute [AU]
165, El-Horreya Ave., El-Hadara
Alexandria
Tel: +20-3-426-7942
Fax: +20-3-425-5792
Web: http://www.alex.edu.eg/index.asp

📖 Graduate, Postgraduate Programmes

Study Domains: biology, biophysics, chemistry, genetics, immunology, medicine.
Programmes: (a) courses leading to M.Sc. and Ph.D. degrees in immunology, applied medical chemistry, genetics, biophysics, clinical pathology, tumour and cell biology, radiation science; (b) postgraduate programme for medical research workers.
Open to: candidates of any nationality; (b) holding a Bachelor's degree in medicine, science or pharmacy.
Duration: (b) 1 academic year.
Fees: (b) £1,350 (sterling) per year.
Languages: instruction in English.
Applications: (a) to the Dean's Office at the above address for further information; (b) by 30 September, to the Vice-Dean of the Institute.

🐦 M.Sc. and Ph.D. Programme Scholarships

Study Domains: medicine, research.
Scholarships: M.Sc. and Ph.D. programme scholarships.
Subjects: bacteriology, biology, biophysics, cancerology, chemistry, cytology, genetics, immunology, microbiology, pharmacy and pharmacology, physics, physiology, radiology, research.
Open to: candidates of any country; proficiency in English required.
Duration: 2 to 4 years.
Languages: English.
Applications: to the Vice-Dean of the Institute.

701   American University in Cairo (The) [AUIC]
PO Box 2511
113 Sharia Kasr El Aini
Cairo
Tel: +20-2-794-2964
Fax: +20-2-795-7565
Web: http://www.aucegypt.edu
e-mail: aucegypt@aucnyo.edu

📖 Undergraduate, Graduate Programmes

Study Domains: audio-visual media, communication, journalism.
Programmes: undergraduate and graduate degrees in the Schools of Business, Economics, and Communications, Humanities and Social Sciences, Sciences and Engineering.
Open to: qualified candidates of any nationality.
Duration: 4 years for B.A., 2 years M.A.; courses begin in September.
Financial assistance: some scholarships, fellowships and assistantships available.
Applications: by 30 December, to the Chairman.

702   Cairo University - Statistical Studies and Research Institute [CU]
5 Tharwat Street
PO Box 12613
Orman, Giza, Cairo
Tel: +20-2-572-9584
Fax: +20-2-568-8884
Web: http://www.cu.edu.eg

📖 Graduate, Postgraduate Programmes

Study Domains: computer science, demography and population studies, numismatics, statistics.
Programmes: advanced diploma and M.Sc. in the following fields: statistics, computer and information science (computer science for the M.Sc.), operations research and demography; Ph.D. in statistics.
Open to: candidates who hold university degrees from accredited universities; entrance examination in mathematics; aptitude test required for computer science and operations research candidates.

Duration: 2 years.
Fees: E£1,350-2,250 plus tuition per year.
Languages: instruction in Arabic for Diploma; in English and Arabic for M.Sc. and Ph.D. programmes.
Applications: by June; see http://www.cu.edu.eg/Faculties/SS&RI.asp.

703 Egyptian International Centre for Agriculture [EICFA]

Nadi El Seid Street, Dokki
PO Box 239
Cairo
Web: http://www.agri.gov.eg

⌨ Training Course / Agriculture

Study Domains: agriculture, nutrition, rural development, veterinary sciences.
Programmes: programme of degree courses in agricultural subjects: vegetable production, animal health, poultry production and health, cotton production and technology, integrated pest control, agricultural services, soil amelioration, integrated rural development, project analysis, fish culture development, land and water management.
Open to: candidates holding a B.Sc. and 3 years' experience in the subject matter of the course to be attended.
Duration: 10 weeks.
Fees: US$3,500 per course, includes tuition, full board accommodation, medical care and pocket money allowance.
Languages: instruction in English, French and Spanish.
Applications: to the above address.

704 Helwan University [HU]

Ain Helwan
11795 Cairo
Tel: +20-2-548-1025
Fax: +20-2-555-9491
Web: http://www.helwan.edu.eg
e-mail: info@helwan.edu.eg

⌨ Undergraduate, Postgraduate Programmes

Study Domains: all major fields.
Programmes: undergraduate and postgraduate studies in several faculties.
Open to: all nationalities with relevant qualifications.
Languages: instruction in English, French and Arabic.
Applications: to the above address for more information.

705 Higher Institute of Technology-Benha [BHIT]

Benha 13 512
Tel: +20-13-229-263
Fax: +20-13-230-297
e-mail: ahuzayyin@gmx.net

⌨ Undergraduate, Graduate Programmes

Study Domains: civil engineering, electricity and electronics, mechanical engineering.
Programmes: programme of courses leading to diploma, high diploma, Bachelor's (B.Sc.) and Master's (M.Sc.).
Open to: candidates holding a secondary-school certificate (or equivalent).
Duration: diploma: 3 years; Bachelor's: 5 years; Master's: 2 years following Bachelor's; high diploma: 2 years following Bachelor's.
Fees: tuition: diploma and Bachelor's, E£180 per year; high diploma and Master's, E£10 /credit hour.
Languages: English.
Applications: by August to the above address; for information contact A. M. El Hakim; fax +20 13 230 297; email: hak42@yahoo.com.

706 Minufiya University

PO Box 32511
Gamal Abdel Nasser Street
Shebin Al-Kom, Minufiya
Tel: +20-48-222-4216
Fax: +20-48-222-6454
Web: http://www.menofia.edu.eg
e-mail: menofia@mailer.menofia.edu.eg

⌨ Electrical Engineering

Study Domains: electricity and electronics, engineering.
Programmes: Undergraduate, Graduate and Postgraduate programmes in electrical engineering.
Applications: see website:
http://www.menofia.edu.eg/En/faculty_generalInfo.asp?id=6.

⌨ Undergraduate, Graduate, Postgraduate Programmes

Study Domains: agriculture, arts, biology, business, education, electricity and electronics, engineering, genetics, law, medicine, nursing, physical education, sciences, special education, tourism, hotel and catering management, veterinary medicine.
Programmes: programme of courses leading to Bachelor's, Master's and PhD degrees.
Languages: Arabic and English.

707 October 6 University [O6U]

October 6 City
Plot 1/1
Giza
Tel: +20-2-835-3161
Fax: +20-2-835-5277
Web: http://www.o6u.edu.eg
e-mail: info@o6u.edu.eg

⌨ Undergraduate, Graduate Programmes

Study Domains: all major fields.
Programmes: programme of courses leading to B.S., B.A., B.Pharm. and M.B.B.S.
Open to: candidates of any country and all ages holding a secondary school certificate or equivalent.
Duration: 4 to 5 years; engineering programme: 5 years; medicine: 6 years.
Fees: tuition and registration: US$1,000-$5,000 per annum; living costs: approximately US$2,000-$2,200.
Financial assistance: some scholarships available; for information, contact Nehal Salah Ali.
Languages: Arabic and English (TOEFL, SAT1, IGCSE).
Applications: by September.

El Salvador

Año académico: Enero a diciembre.
Moneda nacional: Colón.
Admisiones para estudiantes extranjeros: Título de bachiller (secundaria) o equivalente obtenido en el extranjero. Examen de ingreso, curso de nivelación.
Formalidades de inmigración: Es necesario tener un permiso de residencia temporal.
Servicios de información: * Dirección Nacional de Educación Superior.
Enseñanza abierta y a distancia: La Universidad Abierta ofrece cursos en economía, ciencias, humanidades, derecho y ciencias sociales.
Convalidación de estudios y diplomas: Dirección Nacional de Educación Superior, Ministerio de Educación, Director Nacional de Educación Superior, Edificio A-3 Plan Maestro, Centro de Gobierno, Alameda Juan Pablo II y Calle Guadalupe, San Salvador, El Salvador. tel: +503-281-1361; fax: +503-281-0273; email: educacionsuperior@mined.gob.sv; web: http://www.mined.gob.sv.
Publicaciones / Sitios web: Existen publicaciones gratuitas que proporcionan información sobre las universidades y los institutos tecnológicos, que se pueden obtener en la Dirección Nacional de Educación Superior.

708 Instituto Tecnológico Centroamericano [ITCA]

Km. 11, Carretera a Sta. Tecla
Apartado postal 133
Nueva San Salvador
Tel: +503-2241-4822
Fax: +503-2241-4700
Web: http://www.itca.edu.sv/
e-mail: fep_itca@di.itca.edu.sv

Carreras técnicas y cursos cortos

Campos de estudios: industria alimentaría, ingeniería, ingeniería civil, mecánica, tecnología, tecnología industrial.
Descripción:
(a) Carreras técnicas en ingeniería civil, arquitectura, electrónica industrial, sistemas de comunicaciones, mantenimiento y servicio de computadoras, mantenimiento de equipo biomédico, electricidad, mecánica general, refrigeración y aire acondicionado, mantenimiento industrial, ingeniería industrial, laboratorio químico, conservación del medio ambiente, automotriz, confección industrial, preparación y servicio de alimentos;
(b) Cursos cortos de especialización en áreas relacionadas a las disciplinas indicadas en (a).
Se destina(n): principalmente a nacionales de los países de América Central que tengan el grado de bachiller y superen un examen de admisión.
Duración: (a) 2 años académicos; (b) variables dependiendo del tipo de curso.

709 Universidad Don Bosco [UDB]
Calle Plan del Pino, Cantón Venecia
Soyapango
Tel: +503-251-5046
Fax: +503-292-3051
Web: http://www.udb.edu.sv
e-mail: atencion.estudiante@udb.edu.sv

Carreras y diplomados universitarios

Campos de estudios: todas las materias principales, ciencias, ciencias económicas y comerciales, comunicación, educación, idiomas, ingeniería, medicina, tecnología, teología, religión.
Descripción: (a) Carreras en sus diversas facultades: ingeniería (ingeniería biomédica, en ciencias de la computación, eléctrica, electrónica, industrial, mecánica, en automatización, en telecomunicaciones); estudios tecnológicos (técnico en ingeniería biomédica, en ingeniería en computación, en ingeniería eléctrica, en ingeniería electrónica, en ingeniería mecánica, en ortesis y prótesis, en diseño gráfico, en producción de radio y televisión, en plásticos); ciencias y humanidades (licenciatura en diseño gráfico, en ciencias de la comunicación, en ciencias de la educación (especialidad parvularia), profesorados, formación pedagógica para profesionales, profesorado en inglés, en teología pastoral); ciencias económicas (licenciatura en administración de empresas, en contaduría pública, en mercadotécnia);
(b) Diplomados: dirección y administración de hospitales salvadoreños, enfermería técnica, ingeniería clínica aplicada, seguridad y vulnerabilidad hospitalaria, microempresa.

710 Universidad Tecnológica de El Salvador [UTEC]
Calle Arce 1120
San Salvador
Tel: +503-2275-8888
Fax: +503-2275-8813
Web: http://www.utec.edu.sv
e-mail: mlduque@utec.edu.sv

Programas universitarios

Campos de estudios: antropología, arqueología, ciencias económicas y comerciales, derecho, historia, informática, ingeniería, inglés, periodismo, psicología, relaciones públicas.
Descripción: Carreras en sus facultades de:
(a) Ciencias sociales: técnico en periodismo, licenciatura en relaciones públicas y comunicaciones, en psicología, en idioma inglés, en antropología, en arqueología, en historia;
(b) Ingeniería: ingeniería industrial, en sistemas y computación;
(c) Economía: licenciatura en administración de empresas, en contaduría pública, en mercadotecnia, en informática;
(d) Facultad de jurisprudencia: licenciatura en ciencias jurídicas.
Maestrías: administración de empresas, administración financiera, mercadeo, comunicación empresarial, psicología clínica.
Asistencia financiera: las solicitudes de becas se tramitan en la Casa del Estudiante; debe presentarse una solicitud que será sometida a evaluación de factibilidad.

Inscripciones: por mayor información, dirigirse a la Unidad de Nuevos Ingresos; se puede enviar correo electrónico a nuevoingreso@utec.edu.sv.

Eritrea
Academic year: September to June.
Monetary unit: birr.
National student admission: Based on the Eritrean secondary education, certificate examination or other examinations
granted equivalence by the Academic Senate.
Language: Good knowledge of English is essential for regular university courses.
Immigration requirements: Foreign students must obtain a student visa.
Estimated expenses for one academic year: Application fee: US$20; educational expenses: US$1,660; estimated living expenses: US$1,900; graduation fee: US$40.
Information services:
• Registrar's Office, University of Asmara, PO Box 1220, Asmara; tel: +291-1-161-926; fax: +291-1-162-236.
Recognition of studies and qualification: Ministry of Education; PO Box 1056; Asmara; Eritrea; tel: +291-1-127-817; fax: +291-1-121-913.

711 University of Asmara [UOA]
PO Box 1220
Asmara
Tel: +291-1-161-926 ext 259
Fax: +291-1-162-236
Web: http://www.uoa.edu.er
e-mail: prcuoa@asmara.uoa.edu.er

Undergraduate Programmes

Study Domains: accounting, biology, chemistry, economy, English, law, management, marine biology, mathematics, physics.
Programmes: B.Sc. degrees in chemistry, physics, biology, mathematics, plant science, animal science, soil and water conservation, marine biology and fisheries, public health nursing practitioner, pharmacy; B.A. degrees in public administration, management, economics, accounting, English, sociology and anthropology, history, geography, political science, journalism and mass communications, archaeology; Bachelor in Education in biology, chemistry, mathematics, physics, geography, history, educational administration, educational psychology; Diploma
in management, accounting, law, engineering and education; certificate in public administration.
Open to: undergraduate students of any country between 19 and 24 years of age.
Duration: diploma: 2 to 3 years; degree: 4 to 5 years; certificate: 1 year.
Languages: instruction in English.
Applications: by January.

España
Año académico: Octubre a junio.
Moneda nacional: Euro.
Admisiones para estudiantes extranjeros: Ingreso en primer curso: homologación o convalidación de estudios de enseñanza media; realización de las pruebas de aptitud para acceso a la universidad; reserva de plaza en los plazos establecidos en la universidad elegida por el alumno. Las pruebas de aptitud para el acceso a la universidad de los estudiantes (españoles y extranjeros) con estudios convalidables serán organizados por la Universidad Nacional de Educación a Distancia (UNED). Dichas pruebas de aptitud se efectuarán en España. Excepcionalmente y siempre que el número de alumnos lo justifique, se organizarán en aquellos países en los que exista agregaduria de educación en la embajada de España y en aquellos otros países o ciudades españolas que a propuesta motivada por la UNED, el Ministerio de Educación y Ciencia lo determine. Los alumnos que hayan iniciado estudios superiores en algún país extranjero y deseen continuarlos en este país deberán solicitar previamente la convalidación de estudios parciales.

Conocimientos lingüísticos: Los estudiantes procedentes de países en los que no se hable español deberán pasar un examen de capacitación de esta lengua. Las universidades y otros centros de enseñanza superior de las principales ciudades organizan cursos de lengua y cultura española para extranjeros (durante el año académico y/o en verano).

Servicios de información:
• Ministerio de Educación, Cultura y Deporte, Sección de Información, Iniciativas y Reclamaciones, Alcalá 34, 28014 Madrid (cursos generales y de verano, intercambios internacionales de estudiantes, colegios mayores, etc.).
• Ministerio de Asuntos Exteriores, Dirección General de Relaciones Culturales, Calle José Abascal 41, 28003 Madrid (intercambios internacionales de estudiantes y administración de las becas ofrecidas por el gobierno español a estudiantes extranjeros excepto a los procedentes de América Latina).
• Embajadas de España en el extranjero, institutos de cultura hispánica en los países hispanoamericanos o centros culturales hispánicos de frica y de varios países del Oriente Medio (cursos académicos, condiciones de vida, etc., a los estudiantes extranjeros que deseen trabajar en una universidad española).
• Instituto de Cooperación Iberoamericana (ICI), Departamento de Asistencia Universitaria, Avenida de los Reyes Católicos 4, Ciudad Universitaria, 28040 Madrid (a estudiantes hispanoamericanos y filipinos: asistencia técnica en materias científicas y humanísticas, información a estudiantes, enseñanza secundaria, técnica, universitaria o de especialización; trámites de convalidación de estudios y para resolver en lo posible asuntos de índole académica, profesional, o de residencia, reducciones de viajes, etc.; dispone de residencias estudiantiles y orienta sobre otras clases de alojamiento).
• Instituto Hispano-Arabe de Cultura, Avenida de los Reyes Católicos 4, Ciudad Universitaria, 28040 Madrid (desarrolla un programa similar al del ICI para los estudiantes de Africa y Oriente Medio).
• Agencia Española de Cooperación Internacional (AECI), Avenida de los Reyes Católicos 4, 28040 Madrid.
• TIVE, Oficina Internacional de Turismo para Jóvenes y Estudiantes, Fernando el Católico 88, 28015 Madrid (facilita alojamiento).

Enseñanza abierta y a distancia: La Universidad Nacional de Educación a Distancia (UNED) organiza cursos a distancia en derecho, historia y geografía, filología, filosofía y educación, psicología, economía y administración, física, química y matemáticas, ciencias políticas y sociología, ingeniería industrial. La UNED también ofrece cursos de acceso directo a la Universidad para adultos mayores de 25 años que no tienen las calificaciones necesarias, y cursos a distancia sin requisitos específicos.
En 1992, el Ministerio de Educación, Cultura y Deportes creó el Centro para la Innovación y el Desarrollo de la Educación a Distancia (CIDEAD). Otras administraciones de la educación, entre las cuales los Departamentos de Educación de las Comunidades de Galicia, Navarra y Valencia, han instaurado la educación a distancia para adultos en sus respectivas regiones, mediante la creación de estabalecimientos adecuados a este tipo de enseñanza. La Universidad Abierta de Cataluña también ofrece este tipo de enseñanza.

Convalidación de estudios y diplomas: NARIC, Subdirección General de Títulos, Convalidaciones y Homologaciones, Ministerio de Educación, Cultura y Deporte, Asesoría Técnica, Paseo del Prado 28-4a, 28014 Madrid, España; tel: +34-91-506-5593; fax: +34-91-506-5706; email: nieves.trelles@educ.mec.es; web: http://www.mec.es.

Publicaciones / Sitios web:
• "Cursos para extranjeros en España", cursos que, con carácter permanente o transitorio, organizan especialmente para estudiantes extranjeros las universidades y demás centros de cultura. Puede obtenerse gratuitamente en la Secretaría de Estado de Universidades e Investigación, Gabinete de Asuntos Generales y Publicaciones, Calle Serrano 150, 28006 Madrid, y consultarse en los servicios culturales de las embajadas de España en el extranjero.
• "Cursos para postgraduados", publicación anual gratuita de la Escuela de Postgrado y Especialización del Consejo Superior de Investigaciones Científicas (CSIC), Calle Serrano 142, 28006 Madrid.
• "Convocatoria general de becas para realizar estudios en España", editado por la Agencia Española de Cooperación Internacional (AECI), Avenida de los Reyes Católicos 4,

28040 Madrid.
• "Guía básica sobre régimen académico y acceso para alumnos con estudios en el extranjero", editado por la Universidad Complutense de Madrid, Vicerrectorado de Alumnos, Avenida de la Complutense s/n, 28040 Madrid.
• "Pruebas de aptitud para acceso a la universidad para alumnos con estudios extranjeros convalidables", editado por la Universidad Nacional de Educación a Distancia (UNED).
• Publicaciones diversas del Ministerio de Educación y Ciencia, Calle Alcalá 34, 28014 Madrid y del Instituto de la Juventud, José Ortega y Gasset 71, 28006 Madrid.

---

712 Agencia Española de Cooperación Internacional Instituto de Cooperación con el Mundo Arabe, Mediterráneo y Países en Desarrollo/Países Arabes [AECI]

Avenida Reyes Católicos 4
Ciudad Universitaria
28040 Madrid
Tel: (34) (91) 534 34 62
Fax: (34) (91) 535 33 98
Web: http://www.becasmae.es

☛ Programa de becas

Campos de estudios: todas las materias principales, español, programas de verano.
Becas:
(a) Becas de verano para estudio de la lengua española;
En temas prioritarios para la cooperación española y para el país del solicitante:
(b) Becas para cursos de corta duración y de investigación de alto nivel;
(c) Becas para estudios de pregrado;
(d) Becas para doctorado, investigación, especialidades médicas y cursos de especialización.
Se conceden: (a) a alumnos de los Centros Culturales "Cervantes", de Departamentos de Español en países árabes y de instituciones con las que se hayan establecido intercambios; (b) a (d) a ciudadanos de cualquier país árabe que tengan un conocimiento suficiente del español para realizar los estudios y tengan la aceptación de la Facultad correspondiente.
Duración: (a) y (b) 1 mes; (c) y (d) 9, 10 o 12 meses (prorrogables).
Solicitudes: la fecha varía cada año; dirigirse a la Sección de Becas del ICMAMPD-Países Arabes, a las Embajadas o Consulados de España en el país del candidato, o a los Ministerios de Asuntos Exteriores de los países árabes.

713 Agencia Española de Cooperación Internacional [AECI]

Avenida Reyes Católicos 4
28040 Madrid
Tel: (34) (91) 583 8299
Fax: (34) (91) 583 8311
Web: http://www.aeci.es
e-mail: becasmae@aeci.es

☛ Becas MAE-AECI

Campos de estudios: español, investigación, programas de verano.
Descripción:
I. Becas de lengua, cultura e investigación hispánicas para extranjeros en España:
(a) Curso para Profesionales del Español en la Escuela de Verano de Madrid;
(b) Cursos de Verano de Español como Lengua Extranjera y de Cultura y Civilización Españolas en Universidades públicas y privadas españolas;
(c) Becas para Hispanistas;
II. Becas de posgrado para extranjeros en España:
(a) Becas para ciudadanos de países no iberoamericanos;
(b) Becas Mutis para ciudadanos de países de la Comunidad Iberoamericana de Naciones;
(c) Becas para el Curso de Estudios Internacionales en colaboración con la Escuela Diplomática de Madrid.

(d) Becas en Universidades a distancia españolas:
III. Becas de lenguas y posgrado para españoles en el exterior:
(a) Cursos de Verano de Lenguas Extranjeras;
(b) Estudios de postgrado en países no iberoamericanos;
(c) Becas Mutis para estudios de postgrado en países iberoamericanos;
IV. Becas de Estudios Europeos para españoles en el exterior:
(a) Becas para el Colegio de Europa (Brujas y Natolín);
(b) Becas para el Instituto Universitario Europeo de Florencia;
V. Becas de cooperación cultural para extranjeros y españoles en España y el exterior:
(a) Cooperación en gestión cultural;
(b) Cooperación lingüística hispánica;
(c) Cooperación bibliotecaria;
(d) Estancias en la Academia de España en Roma.
Solicitudes: por mayores informaciones relativas a condiciones, duración e importe (que varían según el programa), dirigirse a las representaciones diplomáticas de España en el exterior, u órganos dependientes de éstas (Oficinas Técnicas de Cooperación, centros culturales y oficinas consulares) de la AECI, o consultar las páginas electrónicas.

714 Asociación Española de Contabilidad y Administración de Empresas

Ctra. de Colmenar Viejo, km. 15
28049 Madrid
Tel: (34) (91) 397 3983
Fax: (34) (91) 397 4218

🐾 Becas "MBA"

Campos de estudios: administración de empresas, ciencias económicas y comerciales, economía, finanzas, marketing.
Se conceden: a españoles o extranjeros con estudios superiores, que superen examen de admisión.
Lugar: Instituto Universitario de Administración de Empresas (IADE), Facultad de Ciencias económicas y empresariales de la Universidad Autónoma de Madrid.
Duración: los 18 meses del curso escolar.
Solicitudes: en septiembre, al IADE, en la dirección que figura en el título.

715 Cámara de Comercio e Industria de Madrid Insitituto de Formación Empresarial [IFE]

Pedro Salinas 11
28043 Madrid
Tel: (34) (91) 538 3838
Fax: (34) (91) 538 3803

📖 Programa de cursos

Campos de estudios: administración de empresas, comercio, gestión, industria y comercio, informática, negocio.
Descripción: El IFE ofrece más de 200 cursos en sus diversas escuelas y programas: Escuela comercial, Escuela industrial, Escuela empresarial, Escuela de negocios para directivos, Informática y multimedia, Escuela de idiomas para los negocios, Programas internacionales.
Inscripciones: dirigirse al Departamento de Información.

716 Centro de Estudios Políticos y Constitucionales [CDEC]

Plaza de la Marina Española 9
28071 Madrid
Tel: (34) (91) 571 5000
Fax: (34) (91) 547 8549

📖 Curso de especialización

Campos de estudios: ciencias políticas, derecho.
Descripción: curso de especialización en derecho constitucional y ciencia política.
Se destina(n): a titulados superiores universitarios que conozcan perfectamente el español.
Duración: 1 año académico.
Costo(s): la matrícula es gratuita.
Inscripciones: en el plazo que oportunamente fije la convocatoria del curso (tradicionalmente en septiembre); dirigirse al Departamento de Estudios, en la dirección que figura en el título.

717 Centro de Estudios y Experimentación de Obras Públicas [CEDEX]

Alfonso XII N° 3
28014 Madrid
Tel: (34) (91) 335 7311
Fax: (34) (91) 335 7314
Web: http://www.cedex.es
e-mail: formacion@cedex.es

📖 Cursos internacionales

Campos de estudios: energía, hidrología, ingeniería, ingeniería civil.
Descripción:
(a) Curso internacional sobre hidrología general y aplicada: hidrología superficial, hidrología subterránea, calidad de las aguas y medio ambiente, planificación y explotación de recursos hidráulicos, prácticas de campo y laboratorio, hidráulica fluvial;
(b) Curso internacional sobre ingeniería de regadíos: información básica, sistema de riego por gravedad, sistemas de riego por aspersión, drenaje, riego localizado, formulación y evaluación de planes de regadío, los regadíos en la planificación hidrológica, explotación de regadíos, modernización de regadíos, regadíos y medio ambiente;
(c) Curso internacional sobre mecánica del suelo o ingeniería de cimentaciones.
Se destina(n): a nacionales de cualquier país que posean título superior universitario y experiencia en temas referentes al curso.
Duración: (a) y (b) 5 meses; (c) 3 meses y medio; (comienzan en febrero).
Asistencia financiera: becas concedidas por distintas instituciones (AECI, OEA, FAO, OMM).
Inscripciones: Gabinete de Formación y Documentación del CEDEX, en la dirección que figura en el título.

718 Centro de Formación del Banco de España

Apartado de Correos 15
28080 Madrid
Tel: (34) (91) 338 6840
Fax: (34) (91) 338 6882
Web: http://www.bde.es
e-mail: cfogener@bde.es

🐾 Convocatoria de becas

Campos de estudios: economía, finanzas, historia.
Descripción: Convocatoria de becas para:
(a) realización de trabajos de investigación en el Banco de España en temas de macroeconomía, macroeconomía, política monetaria, economía internacional, econometría, finanzas, mercado de trabajo;
(b) ampliación de estudios en el extranjero en temas de política monetaria, economía internacional, econometría, finanzas, mercado de trabajo;
(c) elaboración de tesis doctorales sobre temas de historia económica.
Se conceden: (a) a doctores con no más de 5 años de antigüedad, con experiencia en trabajos de investigación, que dominen el inglés, y que residan en Madrid durante el tiempo del contrato; (b) y (c) a españoles con título superior de universidades o escuelas técnicas, con conocimientos lingüísticos dependiendo del país de destino.
Lugar: (a) Servicio de Estudios del Banco de España, Madrid; (b) y (c) a determinar por el candidato.
Duración: (a) entre 3 meses y un año; (b) y (c) 1 año (renovable hasta 3 veces); (c) el tiempo requerido para la elaboración de la tesis.
Solicitudes: hasta (a) enero, (b) y (c) mediados de abril.

719 Centro de Información, Cerveza y Salud [CICS]

Apartado correos 61.210
Madrid
Tel: +34-91-383-3032
Web: http://www.cervezaysalud.com

📖 Master en tecnología cervecera

Campos de estudios: industria alimentaría, ingeniería, tecnología industrial.

Descripción: título de la Universidad Politécnica de Madrid.
Se destina(n): a universitarios de grado medio o superior de ramas científicas o ingenierías, que superen proceso de selección en base a calificaciones académicas y experiencia o conocimientos en el sector cervecero o maltero.
Duración: de octubre a junio.
Asistencia financiera: becas para la realización de trabajos de investigación experimental sobre la cerveza en relación con la salud y la nutrición, que no hayan sido realizados ni difundidos con anterioridad en España; sitio web http://www.cervezaysalud.com/html/page10426.htm.
Inscripciones: hasta el 15 de octubre.

720 Centro Internacional de Lengua y Cultura Españolas [CILCE]
Almirante 1 - 2a planta
46003 Valencia
Tel: (34) (96) 391 0463
Fax: (34) (96) 392 1981
Web: http://www.iglobal.es/empresas/cilce
e-mail: cilce@iglobal.es

📖 **Programas sobre lengua española**

Campos de estudios: español, programas de verano.
Descripción:
(a) D.E.L.E: español como lengua extranjera;
(b) Reciclaje de profesores de español.
Duración: (a) 4 semanas; (b) 1 o 2 semanas.
Costo(s): variable según el curso y opciones para alojamiento y comidas.

721 Centro Tecnológico Nacional de la Conserva Centro de Edafología y Biología Aplicada del Segura [CTC]
Calle de la Concordia s/n
30500 Molina del Segura, Murcia
Tel: (34) (96) 838 9011
Fax: (34) (96) 8613401
e-mail: ctc@gaia.fcu.um.es

📖 **Curso superior de ciencia y tecnología de la conservación de los alimentos**

Campos de estudios: alimentación, ciencias aplicadas, tecnología industrial.
Descripción: posgrado dedicado al estudio de alimentos (cárnicos y vegetales, procesado, nuevas tecnologías de fabricación, normativas nacionales e internacionales, aspectos nutritivos, toxicológicos, etc.); gran contenido práctico y visitas a factorías a fin de poner al alumno en contacto con el mundo de la PYME; posibilidad de realizar prácticas profesionales en empresas del sector.
Se destina(n): a titulados superiores. Puede existir examen escrito o entrevista personal dependiendo del número de inscriptos.
Duración: 400 horas (septiembre-febrero).
Inscripciones: hasta septiembre.

722 Colegio de Estudios Hispánicos [CEH]
Bordadores 1
37002 Salamanca
Tel: (34) (92) 321 4837
Fax: (34) (92) 321 5607
Web: http://www.eurart.es/emp/ceh
e-mail: info@cehispanic.com

📖 **Cursos internacionales**

Campos de estudios: español, estudios culturales, idiomas, interpretación y traducción, literatura y civilización, programas de verano.
Descripción: español, español lengua extranjera (D.E.L.E), cursos de verano, curso especial para profesores de español, traducción y análisis de textos.
Duración: cursos permanentes, mensuales, trimestrales, anuales y de verano.
Inscripciones: por mayor información, dirigirse a la

Secretaría del CEH.

723 Colegio Internacional Alicante Coop. V
Pintor Aparicio 18C, °A
03003 Alicante
Tel: (34) (96) 592 9010
Fax: (34) (96) 592 2582
Web: http://www.colegiointernacionalalicante.com
e-mail: col.inter@ctv.es

📖 **Cursos de español para extranjeros**

Campos de estudios: español.
Descripción: individuales, para profesionales, preparación al D.E.L.E.
Inscripciones: 15 días antes del comienzo de los cursos; dirigirse a la Secretaría.

724 Colegio Internacional Ausias March [CIAM]
Tancat de l'Alter
Picassent
46220 Valencia
Tel: (34) (96) 123 0566
Fax: (34) (96) 123 4729
Web: http://www.ausiasmarch.com
e-mail: extranjeros @ausiasmarch.com

📖 **Cursos para extranjeross**

Campos de estudios: español, programas de verano.
Descripción: Cursos de lengua, cultura y civilización españolas para extranjeros.
Duración: mínimo 2 semanas.
Asistencia financiera: becas ofrecidas a través del Ministerio de Asuntos Exteriores.

725 Colegio Universitario de Estudios Financieros [CUNEF]
Serrano Anguita 13
28004 Madrid
Tel: (34) (91) 448 0891
Fax: (34) (91) 594 1366
Web: http://www.cunef.es
e-mail: secretaria@cunef.es

📖 **Programas universitarios**

Campos de estudios: administración de empresas, finanzas.
Descripción:
(a) Licenciatura en administración y dirección de empresas (título de la Universidad Complutense de Madrid);
(b) Master en finanzas.
Se destina(n): (a) a quienes hayan superado las pruebas de de acceso a la Universidad; (b) a titulados universitarios. En ambos casos, existe selección por expediente y entrevista.
Duración: (a) 4 años (comienzos en octubre); (b) 1 año (comienzos en enero).
Asistencia financiera: becas completas y medias becas, por méritos académicos y situación económica.
Inscripciones: hasta junio para la licenciatura, hasta diciembre para el master.

726 Comisión Fulbright de Intercambio Cultural, Educativo y Científico entre España y los Estados Unidos de América
Gral. Martínez Campos 24bis
28010 Madrid
Tel: (34) (91) 702 7000
Fax: (34) (91) 308 5704
Web: http://www.fulbright.es
e-mail: postmaster@comision-fulbright.org

📣 **Programa de becas Fulbright**

Campos de estudios: todas las materias principales, comercio, finanzas, formación profesional, investigación, periodismo, programas de verano, turismo, hotelería.

Descripción: Programas de becas para españoles:
(a) Becas Fulbright;
(b) Becas Ministerio de Economía;
(c) Becas Ministerio de Fomento;
(d) Becas Ministerio de Educación, Cultura y Deporte, para investigación postdoctoral.
(e) Becas Ministerio de Educación, Cultura y Deporte, para la ampliación de estudios artísticos;
(f) Becas Ministerio de Sanidad y Consumo;
(g) Becas Ministerio de Medio Ambiente;
(h) Becas Generalidad de Cataluña;
(i) Becas Fulbright New Century Scholar Program;
(j) Becas Fundación CEOE;
(k) Becas Ruth Lee Kennedy;
(l) Intercambio de profesores;
(m) Becas para Lectores de Español;
Becas de corta duración para españoles:
(n) Programa Fulbright- Instituto para el estudio de Estados Unidos;
(o) Becas SAAS (Spanish Association for American Studies);
(p) Institutos de verano para el estudio de los EE.UU. Enseñanza Secundaria;
(q) Institutos de verano para el estudio de los EE.UU. Profesores Universitarios;
(r) Seminario de Salzburgo;
Programas de becas para estadounidenses:
(s) Profesores invitados de universidad e investigadores postdoctorales;
(t) Investigación predoctoral;
(u) Profesores de universidad invitados e investigadores postdoctorales;
(v) Becas MBA Internacional;
(w) Periodistas;
(x) Conferenciantes de corta duración;
(y) Intercambio de profesores.
Se conceden: (a) a jóvenes titulados superiores interesados en realizar proyectos de investigación predoctoral, programas "Master's" o "Ph.D." en universidades norteamericanas; (b) a titulados superiores que prestan servicio (funcionarios, personal laboral fijo o contratado) en la Secretaría de Estado de Comercio y Turismo, interesados en ampliar estudios en universidades norteamericanas; (c) a personal funcionario de nivel superior del Ministerio de Fomento y de sus organismos autónomos, interesados en realizar estudios y/o prácticas profesionales en universidades, centros y agencias gubernamentales de los Estados Unidos; (d) jóvenes científicos (no funcionarios) interesados en desarrollar proyectos con equipos de investigación en los Estados Unidos, en cualquier área de conocimiento universitaria; (e) a personas interesadas en ampliar estudios en universidades y centros de los Estados Unidos, en las artes audiovisuales, escénicas y plásticas, música y musicología, museología y conservación del patrimonio; (f) a titulados superiores que quieran ampliar estudios en investigación básica (proteómica y genómica), investigación clínica sin actuación directa sobre pacientes (oncología, cardiovascular, neurociencias, infecciosas y enfermedades raras) e investigación en salud pública y epidemiología en los Estados Unido; (g) a personal funcionario de nivel superior del Ministerio de Medio Ambiente y sus organismos autónomos, interesados en realizar estudios y/o prácticas profesionales en universidades, centros y agencias gubernamentales de los Estados Unidos; (h) a jóvenes doctores titulados por las universidades de Cataluña e interesados en realizar proyectos en los Estados Unidos, en cualquier área de investigación establecida en el ámbito universitario catalán; (i) a reconocidos académicos y profesionales de todo el mundo para llevar a cabo investigación conjunta sobre un tema de actualidad internacional; (j) a jóvenes especialistas en el campo del periodismo (prensa, radio y televisión), interesados en realizar estudios de postgrado en los Estados Unidos; (k) bolsas de viaje destinadas a mujeres para realizar proyectos de investigación postdoctoral o estudios de postgrado en los Estados Unidos; (l) a profesores de Institutos de Enseñanza Secundaria y Escuelas Oficiales de Idiomas; (m) a jóvenes que deseen desarrollar su carrera profesional en el área de la enseñanza de idiomas; (n) a especialistas en Relaciones Internacionales y a profesores universitarios, interesados en el tema de Seguridad en los Estados Unidos; (o) jóvenes doctores que quieran llevar a cabo un proyecto de investigación con el objeto de contribuir al desarrollo en España de los estudios sobre los Estados Unidos; (p) y (q) a profesionales de la enseñanza secundaria y a profesores

universitarios interesados en asistir a un "Fulbright American Studies Institute" que tiene como objeto la formación de educadores que requieren un mayor conocimiento de los Estados Unidos; (r) a profesionales con experiencia relacionada al temario de una de las once sesiones que ofrece el Seminario; las sesiones son de una semana de duración y tratan temas de interés contemporáneo mundial; (s) docencia universitaria e investigación de una duración de tres a cinco meses, en campos de ciencias económicas, sociales y políticas, ciencia y tecnología, y humanidades; pueden presentarse tanto académicos como profesionales, artistas y técnicos, en todos los campos; (t) becas de hasta dos semanas de duración que permiten la participación de especialistas norteamericanos en cualquier campo en seminarios y conferencias en universidades y centros de investigación españoles; los conferenciantes invitados deberán ser becarios Fulbright que se encuentren en Europa, el norte de África, los nuevos Estados Independientes y Oriente Medio; (u) becas de dos a seis semanas de duración que permiten la colaboración profesional y académica de especialistas estadounidenses de alto nivel en distintos campos con una o varias instituciones españolas; (v) nueve meses de duración para realizar estudios individuales o en un equipo de trabajo español, en áreas de interés para España y los Estados Unidos. Se admiten solicitudes en todos los campos, tanto de recién licenciados como de candidatos de un título superior; (w) 15 meses de duración para cursar el programa MBA Internacional en el Instituto de Empresa, Madrid (12 meses), y tres meses de prácticas en España; (x) tres meses para jóvenes profesionales del periodismo (prensa, radio y televisión) y profesores universitarios de ciencias de la información. Los proyectos se pueden desarrollar por medio de investigación y/o con medios de comunicación españoles; (y) a profesores de Institutos de Enseñanza Secundaria y Escuelas Oficiales de Idiomas.
Lugar: salvo (k), en los Estados Unidos de América.

727 Consejo Nacional de Investigaciones Científicas Instituto de Agroquímica y Tecnología de Alimentos (IATA) [CSIC]

Apartado de Correos 73
46100 Burjassot, Valencia
Tel: +34-963-900-022
Fax: +34-963-636-301
Web: http://www.iata.csic.es

📖 Cursos universitarios

Campos de estudios: industria alimentaria, química, tecnología.
Descripción: Cursos para la obtención de créditos para el Doctorado en la Universidad de Valencia.
Se destina(n): a licenciados o ingenieros superiores; en el caso de cursos con plazas limitadas, selección por curriculum vitae.

728 Consejo Superior de Investigaciones Científicas Centro de Ciencias Medioambientales [CSIC]

Serrano 115
28006 Madrid
Tel: +34-91-745-2500
Fax: +34-91-564-800
Web: http://www.ccma.csic.es

📖 Programa de diplomas

Campos de estudios: bioquímica, ciencias, ciencias aplicadas, ecología, medio ambiente.
Descripción:
(a) Diploma en histoquímica vegetal;
(b) Diploma en tratamiento de residuos urbanos.
Se destina(n): a titulados superiores de habla hispana.
Duración: una semana: (a) en junio, (b) en octubre.
Inscripciones: dirigirse al Departamento de Fisiología y bioquímica vegetal, en la dirección del título.

**729 Consejo Superior
de Investigaciones Científicas
Centro de Información
y Documentación Científica
[CINDOC]**
Joaquín Costa 22
28002 Madrid
Tel: +34-91-563-5482
Fax: +34-91-564-2644
Web: http://www.cindoc.csic.es

📖 **Curso práctico de documentación en ciencia y tecnología**

Campos de estudios: ciencias, ciencias de la información, documentación, tecnología.
Se destina(n): a postgraduados universitarios.
Duración: 2 años; tiempo mínimo de permanencia: 5 meses; comienzos en octubre.
Inscripciones: hasta el 15 de septiembre y 15 de febrero.

**730 Consejo Superior
de Investigaciones Científicas
Centro Nacional
de Investigaciones
Metalúrgicas [CSIC]**
Gregorio del Amo 8
28040 Madrid
Tel: +34-91-553-8900
Fax: +34-91-534-7425
Web: http://www.cenim.csic.es
e-mail: director@cenim.csic.es

🎓 **Becas honorarias para estancias en el CENIM**

Campos de estudios: investigación, metalurgia, tecnología industrial.
Descripción: colaboración en los trabajos de investigación que se realicen en el centro o preparación de trabajos de tesis de doctorado.
Se conceden: a titulados de facultados científicas o escuelas técnicas superiores de cualquier país, preferentemente de países pertenecientes a la Union Europea o de países latinoamericanos; se valora si ya sin iniciados en investigación científica o tecnológica. Se requiere conocer español o inglés.
Duración: en general un año, renovable.
Importe: no hay dotación económica; en algunos casos de programas con financiación de la industria, pueden concederse ayudas económicas en forma de contratos de colaboración.
Solicitudes: todo el año.

**731 Consejo Superior
de Investigaciones Científicas
Instituto de Cerámica y Vidrio
[CSIC]**
Camino de Valdelatas s/n
28049 Madrid
Tel: (34) (91) 735 5840
Fax: (34) (91) 735 5843
Web: http://www.icv.csic.es

📖 **Curso de especialización en materiales cerámicos y vidrios**

Campos de estudios: ciencias, ciencias aplicadas, tecnología industrial.
Descripción: en el marco de programa de Doctorado de la Facultad de Ciencias de la Universidad Complutense de Madrid.
Se destina(n): a licenciados de facultades de ciencias, a titulados de escuelas técnicas superiores y a personal técnico de empresas.
Duración: 2 años académicos.
Inscripciones: preinscripciones hasta mediados de diciembre.

**732 Consejo Superior
de Investigaciones Científicas
Instituto de Ciencia
y Tecnología de Polímeros
[CSIC]**
Juan de la Cierva 3
28006 Madrid
Tel: +34-91-562-2900
Fax: +34-91-564-4853
Web: http://www.ictp.csic.es
e-mail: director.ictp@csic.es

📖 **Programas universitarios**

Campos de estudios: ingeniería, tecnología, tecnología industrial.
Descripción: Master en ciencia y tecnología de polímeros y Diploma de alta especialización en plásticos y caucho.
Se destina(n): a titulados universitarios que posean la titulación exigida (licenciatura, ingeniería o doctorado).
Duración: 1 año académico (comienza en octubre).
Inscripciones: del 15 al 30 de septiembre.

**733 Consejo Superior
de Investigaciones Científicas
Instituto de Estudios
Documentales
e Históricos sobre la Ciencia
[IEDHC]**
Universidad de Valencia
Facultad de Medicina
Avenida Blasco Ibáñez 15
46010 Valencia
Tel: +34-96-386-4164
Fax: +34-96-361-3975

📖 **Master "Especialidad en documentación médica"**

Campos de estudios: biblioteconomía, ciencias, documentación, medicina.
Se destina(n): a licenciados en medicina y cirugía que conozcan inglés e informática, que preferentemente ocupen un puesto de trabajo en relación al curso; hay selección por curriculum vitae.
Duración: 2 años (cursos de enero a junio y de noviembre a mayo).

**734 Consejo Superior
de Investigaciones Científicas
Instituto de Filología [CSIC]**
Duque de Medinaceli 6
28014 Madrid
Tel: (34) (91) 429 0626
Fax: (34) (91) 369 0940
Web: http://www.filol.csic.es

📖 **Programas universitarios en filología**

Campos de estudios: antropología, ciencias humanas, ciencias sociales, estudios culturales, etnología, filología, lingüística, literatura y civilización, teología, religión.
Descripción:
(a) Curso de etnología española;
(b) Curso superior de filología española;
(c) Comentarios judíos medievales al Libro del Eclesiastes (gramática hebrea, comentarios bíblicos medievales, filosofía, medicina y ciencias medievales en general, literatura hebrea);
(d) Lengua y culturas del Antiguo Oriente próximo (arqueología, historia, lenguas: sumerio, acadio, egipcio, ugarítico, etrusco);
(e) Propedéutica para la investigación en teoría de la literatura (literatura, teoría del lenguaje);
(f) Historia de las religiones desde la perspectiva islámica.
Se destina(n): (a) a licenciados en ciencias sociales y/o humanidades; (b) titulados superiores universitarios; (c) doctores en filosofía con conocimientos de hebreo; (d) doctores en filología e historia antigua; (e) doctores en filología hispánica.
Se dicta(n): (b) en el Palacio Miramar (Málaga); (e) en el Instituto de Ciencias de las Religiones.
Duración: (a) 1 mes (comienza en marzo); (b) 1 mes (en

julio o en agosto); (c) 4 meses(comienza en enero); (d) 6 meses (comienza en octubre); (e) 2 meses (comienza en marzo); (f) 2 meses (comienza en octubre).
Asistencia financiera: (d) ayudas del Ministerio de Cultura/CSIC.
Inscripciones: (c) hasta diciembre; (d) hasta octubre; (e) hasta febrero.

735　Consejo Superior de Investigaciones Científicas Instituto de Investigaciones Biomédicas [CSIC]

Arturo Duperier 4
28029 Madrid
Tel: (34) (91) 585 4600
Fax: (34) (91) 585 4401
Web: http://www.iib.uam.es
e-mail: Info@iib.uam.es

📖 Programa de doctorado

Campos de estudios: biofísica, biología, bioquímica, ciencias naturales, genética, medicina.
Descripción: áreas de bioquímica y biología moleculares y celular.
Se destina(n): a licenciados.
Se dicta(n): en la Facultad de Medicina de la Universidad Autónoma de Madrid.
Duración: 1 año académico, de octubre a junio.
Asistencia financiera: matrícula gratuita para becarios de diversas instituciones (MEC, AECI, PFI, UAM, CAM, Gobierno Vasco y Ministerio de Asuntos Exteriores).
Inscripciones: preinscripciones a principios de octubre; dirigirse al Departamento de Bioquímica, Facultad de Medicina de la UAM, Arzobispo Morcillo 4, 28029 Madrid.

736　Consejo Superior de Investigaciones Científicas Instituto Nacional del Carbón [INCAR]

Apartado 73
33080 Oviedo
Tel: (34) (98) 528 0800
Fax: (34) (98) 529 7662
Web: http://www.incar.csic.es

📖 Cursos universitarios

Campos de estudios: industria química, ingeniería, ingeniería química, química.
Programas:
(a) Curso de introducción la ciencia y tecnología del carbón;
(b) Curso de caracterización físico-química de sólidos.
Se destina(n): a titulados superiores universitarios (licenciados, ingenieros, doctores).
Duración: 30 horas lectivas: (a) en noviembre, (b) en febrero.
Asistencia financiera: medias becas para estudiantes de doctorado.
Inscripciones: (a) hasta principios de noviembre; (b) hasta principios de febrero.

737　Consejo Superior de Investigaciones CientíficasEstación Experimental del Zaidín [CSIC]

Profesor Albareda 1
Apartado 419
18008 Granada
Tel: +34-958-181-600
Fax: +34-958-129-600
Web: http://www.eez.csic.es
e-mail: buzon@eez.csic.es

📖 Curso internacional de edafología y biología vegetal

Campos de estudios: agricultura, biología, botánica, geología.
Descripción: Dos especialidades excluyentes:
(a) edafología;
(b) fertilidad de suelos y nutrición vegetal.

Se destina(n): a postgraduados que posean conocimientos básicos de la ciencia a desarrollar y, preferentemente, que estén en contacto con la enseñanza o la investigación en una Universidad o laboratorio nacional. El curso está dirigido especialmente al área latinoamericana. Existe selección por expediente. Se recomiendan conocimientos básicos de otros idiomas, especialmente inglés, a nivel, por lo menos, de traducción.
Duración: 7 meses (empiezan en enero).
Asistencia financiera: el Instituto de Cooperación Iberoamericana ofrece una beca de monto fijo para estancia y seguro médico.
Inscripciones: hasta fin de agosto. Dirigirse al Director-coordinador del curso en la dirección del título, o a representaciones diplomáticas de España en el país del candidato.

738　Consejo Superior de Investigaciones CientíficasInstituto de Automática Industrial [CSIC]

Carretera de Campo Real km 0.200
La Poveda, Arganda del Rey
28500 Madrid
Tel: +34-91-871-1900
Fax: +34-91-871-7050
Web: http://www.iai.csic.es
e-mail: cordero@iaia.csic.es

📖 Curso "Computadores en la industria: automatización de la producción"

Campos de estudios: informática, tecnología, tecnología industrial.
Se destina(n): a nacionales de cualquier país con título universitario superior en ingeniería, matemáticas, física o ciencias afines, que conozcan español o inglés. Existe proceso de selección. Se exige a los candidatos que tengan financiados sus gastos de estancia en España.
Duración: 22 meses (comienza en octubre).
Asistencia financiera: los becarios del Ministerio de Asuntos Exteriores tienen matrícula gratuita.
Inscripciones: hasta el 30 de abril.

739　Consejo Superior de Investigaciones CientíficasInstituto de Ciencias de la Construcción [CSIC]

Serrano Galvache s/n
Apartado 19002
28033 Madrid
Tel: +34-913-020-440
Fax: +34-913-020-700
Web: http://www.ietcc.csic.es
e-mail: director.ietcc@csic.es

📖 Curso de Estudios Mayores de la Construcción (CEMCO)

Campos de estudios: arquitectura, construcción, investigación.
Descripción: posgrado en el área de la construcción; posibilidad de intercambios científicos y técnicos en el sector.
Se destina(n): a postgraduados en ingeniería o arquitectura de los países hispanoamericanos, a personal docente, investigadores y profesionales del sector de la construcción, seleccionados de acuerdo al curriculum vitae.
Duración: 4 meses (comienza en marzo), pero el curso es trianual y las plazas son limitadas.
Asistencia financiera: becas parciales del Instituto para ayuda a costos de inscripción; becas de manutención de otros organismos, por ejemplo Agencia Española de Cooperación Iberoamericana.
Inscripciones: fecha límite enero, en el Instituto cuya dirección figura en el título.

740 **Consejo Superior de Investigaciones CientíficasInstituto de la Grasa [CSIC]**
Avenida Padre García Tejero 4
41012 Sevilla
Tel: (34) (95) 461 1550
Fax: (34) (95) 461 6790
Web: http://www.ig.csic.es
e-mail: igrasa@cica.es

📖 **Programa de cursos**

Campos de estudios: alimentación, industria alimentaría, química, tecnología industrial.
Descripción:
(a) Curso de alta especialización en grasas: características, análisis, extracción y transformación de grasas comestibles;
(b) Curso de especialización en grasas.
Diplomas requeridos: (a) a licenciados universitarios o equivalentes; (b) a diplomados universitarios o equivalentes.
Duración: 1 año académico, de octubre a junio.
Asistencia financiera: 1 o 2 becas ofrecidas por el Instituto de la Grasa, que cubre(n) el costo de la inscripción..
Inscripciones: hasta el 15 de septiembre.

741 **Consejo Superior de los Colegios de Arquitectos de España [CSCAE]**
Paseo de la Castellana 12
28046 Madrid
Tel: (34) (91) 435 2200
Fax: (34) (91) 575 3839
Web: http://www.cscae.com
e-mail: cscae@arquinex.es

🎓 **Beca "Pérez Piñero"**

Campos de estudios: arquitectura, urbanismo.
Descripción: 1 cada 3 años, con motivo de los Congresos de la Unión Internacional de Arquitectos - UIA.
Se conceden: a nacionales de los países miembros de la UIA que sean estudiantes de los últimos cursos de arquitectura o titulados recientes, y que resulten ganadores de la Confrontación de Estudiantes que tiene lugar con ocasión de la celebración de los Congresos trienales de la UIA; es indispensable saber español.
Lugar: en las escuelas técnicas superiores de arquitectura de España.
Duración: 6 meses.
Solicitudes: a la Secretaría del Congreso del lugar donde se celebre.

742 **Don Quijote [DQ]**
Calle Placentinos 2
Apartado 333
37080 Salamanca
Tel: (34) (2) 326 3186
Fax: (34) (2) 326 3076
Web: http://www.languagecourse.net/school-don-quijote-salamanca.php3
e-mail: quijotes@ctv.es

📖 **Cursos de español para extranjeros**

Campos de estudios: español, formación profesional, programas de verano.
Descripción: cursos de verano, intensivos, preparación al D.E.L.E, para profesores, para azafato/as, otros.
Se destina(n): a extranjeros con edad mínima 18 años.
Se dicta(n): en Salamanca, Barcelona y Granada (o combinación).

743 **Escuela Andaluza de Salud Pública [EASP]**
Campus Universitario de Cartuja
Apartado 2070
18080 Granada
Tel: (34) (5) 802 7400
Fax: (34) (5) 802 7503
Web: http://www.easp.es
e-mail: comunicacion@easp.es

📖 **Programas universitarios**

Campos de estudios: ecología, medio ambiente, gestión, higiene y salud, investigación, riesgos, seguros.
Descripción:
(a) Master en salud pública y gestión sanitaria (título propio de la Universidad de Granada);
Cursos en áreas de promoción de la salud y salud pública, gestión sanitaria y políticas de salud, métodos de investigación clínica y epidemiológica: numerosos seminarios, cursos cortos, cursos intermedios y diplomas, contándose entre estos 2 últimos tipos de curso:
(b) Epidemiología de los riesgos ambientales;
(c) Diploma en gestión sanitaria;
(d) Gestión de servicios de salud;
(e) Diploma en epidemiología e investigación clínica;
(f) Metodología de investigación en ciencias de la salud;
(g) Diploma superior en organización y gestión de la prevención de riesgos laborales.
Se destina(n): a profesionales postgraduados que superen proceso de selección y para (a), además, entrevista.
Duración: (a) de octubre a septiembre; (b) a (d) y (f) 1 mes en marzo; (e) de febrero a diciembre; (g) 18 meses, comienzo en abril.
Inscripciones: por más informes, dirigirse a la Secretaría Académica.

744 **Escuela de Administración de Empresas [AEA]**
Avenida de la Catedral 6
08002 Barcelona
Tel: (34) (3) 310 7562
Fax: (34) (3) 319 4436
Web: http://www.eae.es
e-mail: eae@redstb.es

📖 **Programas universitarios**

Campos de estudios: administración, administración de empresas, ciencias de la información, ciencias económicas y comerciales, finanzas, gestión, marketing.
Descripción:
(a) Master en Administración y Dirección de Empresas (MBA): doble titulación en colaboración con la Nottingham Trent University, Inglaterra;
(b) "Executive MBA";
(c) Master en dirección de recursos humanos;
(d) Diplomas en dirección y gestión financiera, dirección de comunicación, dirección en marketing, en acuerdo con la Universidad de Barcelona.
Se destina(n): (a) a licenciados universitarios o directivos de alto nivel empresarial, menores de 30 años; existe selección por entrevista; (b) como (a), pero además con experiencia profesional; (c) y (d) a titulados universitarios o equivalentes, con experiencia en el área correspondiente, que superen entrevista; se valoran recomendaciones académicas y profesionales.
Duración: (a) 1 año a tiempo completo (comienzo en octubre); (b) a (d) 1 año académico; todos los comienzos son en octubre.
Inscripciones: a partir de mayo, hasta cubrir las plazas; dirigirse a la Secretaría Académica.

745 **Escuela de Alta Dirección y Administración [EADA]**
Aragón 204
08011 Barcelona
Tel: (34) (3) 452 0844
Fax: (34) (3) 323 7317
Web: http://www.eada.es
e-mail: info.eada.es

📖 **Programas Master**

Campos de estudios: administración de empresas, ciencias económicas y comerciales, estudios europeos, finanzas, gestión, marketing.
Descripción:
(a) Master en dirección de empresas;
(b) Master especializado en finanzas, en marketing, en recursos humanos.
Los cursos se dictan en español e inglés.
Se destina(n): a titulados universitarios superiores, con poca o ninguna experiencia profesional, que superen test de admisión y entrevista.

Duración: 1 año académico (comienzos en octubre).
Asistencia financiera: becas totales, parciales, créditos.
Inscripciones: hasta fin de septiembre: dirigirse al
Departamento de Información de Programas EADA, en la
dirección que figura en el título.

746 Escuela de Negocios Caixavigo

Avenida Madrid 60
3614 Vigo
Tel: (34) (8) 641 9422
Fax: (34) (8) 641 2854

Programas de grado, posgrado, formaciones

Campos de estudios: administración, ciencias económicas
y comerciales, finanzas, gestión, marketing, negocio.
Descripción: Programas de grado:
(a) Bachelor in Business Administration (carrera universitaria
en administración y dirección de empresas, título otorgado por
la Universidad de Gales);
Programas de postgrado:
(b) Diploma in Business Administration;
(c) Master en administración y dirección de empresas (MBA);
(d) Executive MBA;
(e) Master en dirección comercial y marketing;
(f) Master en dirección de personal y recursos humanos;
(g) Master en tributación y sistema fiscal.
Formación para directivos:
(h) Curso superior en dirección de recursos humanos; curso
de internacionalización de PYMES; curso superior en
dirección financiera y control de gestión, curso superior en
tributaciones y sistema fiscal.
Se destina(n): a candidatos que superen proceso de
admisión consistente en tests y entrevista, valoración del
curriculum vitae y recomendaciones; para los postgrados, se
requiere titulación universitaria; en el caso de (d) experiencia
mínima de 2 años, en el caso de (e) y (f) titulación o
experiencia.
Duración: (a) 4 cursos académicos; (b) 9 meses; (c) y (e) a
(g) 2 años académicos; (d) 2 cursos académicos en horario de
fin de semana; (h) 5 meses en fecha variable.
Asistencia financiera: financiación de postgrados en
condiciones preferenciales con entidad bancaria.

747 Escuela de Organización Industrial [EOI]

Gregorio del Amo 6
28040 Madrid
Tel: (34) (1) 349 5666
Fax: (34) (1) 554 2394
Web: http://www.eoi.es
e-mail: info@eoi.es

Programa de masters y cursos

Campos de estudios: administración de empresas, ciencias
económicas y comerciales, comunicación, ecología, medio
ambiente, energía, riesgos, seguros, tecnología.
Descripción: Masters de postgrado en las siguientes áreas:
(a) Gestión de empresas: master en prevención de riesgos
laborales; MBA; MBA e-business; MBA industria y
tecnología; MBA Internacional; MBA empresa
agroalimentaria; MBA gestión de empresas del ocio y tiempo
libre; MBA Internacional;
(b) Tecnología e innovación: master en gestión de calidad; en
sistemas de información ERP; MBA e-business; MBA
industria y tecnología;
(c) Medio ambiente y energía: master en energías renovables
y mercado energético; en gestión de infraestructuras y
servicios ambientales; en ingeniería medioambiental y gestión
del agua; en ingeniería y gestión medioambiental; en
organización jurídica, económica y social del medio
ambiente; en prevención de riesgos laborales; master integral
en medio ambiente y prevención de riesgos laborales; en
ingeniería y gestión medioambiental; MBA gestión del medio
ambiente;
Cursos cortos y formación profesional.
Se dicta(n): en Madrid y en Sevilla.
Inscripciones: por mayores informaciones, dirigirse al
Departamento de Comunicación.

748 Escuela Nacional de Sanidad Instituto de Salud Carlos III [ENS]

Sinesio Delgado 6
28029 Madrid
Tel: (34) (1) 387 7788
Fax: (34) (1) 387 7789
Web: http://www.isciii.es
e-mail: oficina.informacion@isciii.es

Programas de estudio en áreas de salud

Campos de estudios: todas las materias principales,
administración, enfermería, estadística, estudios paramédicos,
gestión, higiene y salud, investigación, medicina, medicina
preventiva.
Descripción: Programas Master en:
(a) Salud pública;
(b) Administración sanitaria con 2 modalidades: políticas y
economía de la salud o desarrollo directivo y gestión;
(c) Salud pública para países en desarrollo;
(d) Epidemiología aplicada de campo (en colaboración con el
Center for Disease Control, Estados Unidos, y las
Comunidades Autónomas);
Diplomaturas y otros cursos de duración media:
(e) Diplomas de especialización en: gestión
económico-financiera, gestión logística y hostelería, gestión,
ingeniería, mantenimiento y seguridad;
(f) Diplomas superiores en: gestión de servicios de
enfermería, salud pública para países en desarrollo, higiene y
tecnología de alimentos, salud ocupacional;
(g) Curso de dirección médica y especialización en dirección
de gestión para clínicas privadas, diploma de actualización en
metodología de la investigación en clínica;
(h) Numerosos cursos cortos propuestos por los
Departamentos: de desarrollo directivo y gestión de servicios
sanitarios, epidemiología y bioestadística, documentación
científica, política y economía sanitaria, salud internacional,
salud ambiental y ocupacional, prevención y promoción de la
salud.
Duración: (a) y (c) 1 año (comienzan en abril); (b) 2 años
(comienza en septiembre); (d) 1 año (comienza en julio).
Asistencia financiera: la ENS no posee becas propias,
pero el estudiante extrnjero puede ser subvencionado por
instituciones de su país de origen; en algunos casos, el Fondo
de Investigación Sanitaria, y algunas fundaciones (de
Cooperación y Salud Internacional Carlos III, del Centro
Nacional de Investigaciones Cardiovasculares Carlos III, y del
Centro Nacional de Investigaciones Oncológicas Carlos III),
otorgan becas.

749 Escuela Oficial de Turismo [EODT]

Plaza de Manuel Becerra 14
28028 Madrid
Tel: (34) (1) 725 4600
Fax: (34) (1) 361 0507

Carreras y especializaciones

Campos de estudios: administración de empresas,
formación profesional, turismo, hotelería.
Descripción:
(a) Carrera de Técnico de Empresas y Actividades Turísticas
(TEAT);
(b) Especialización en "Alojamientos Turísticos y
Restauración";
(c) Especialización en "Agencias de Viajes";
(d) Especialización de "Informadores Turísticos".
Se destina(n): (a) a poseedores del Curso de Orientación
Universitaria, título de Técnico especialista, correspondiente a
la Formación Profesional de segundo grado en las ramas de
"Administración y comercial", "Hostelería y turismo",
"Imagen y sonido", y "Servicios a la comunidad"; (b) técnicos
de empresas y actividades turísticas que sean admitidos en
razón de sus conocimientos e historia profesional; (c)
cualquier titulado superior que por su nivel de experiencia
profesional y capacitación acredite suficiente grado de
formación en materias turísticas y de idiomas; (d) podrán
participar, en caso de existir plazas vacantes, extranjeros
becados por la Secretaría de Estado de Comercio, Turismo y
Pymes, o por la Agencia Española de Cooperación
Iberoamericana, en posesión del título equivalente al de
Técnico de Empresas y Actividades Turísticas, siempre que

acrediten el suficiente dominio de idiomas. Los nacionales de países en que el castellano no sea idioma oficial, deberán acreditar, asimismo, el dominio suficiente del mismo.
Duración: (a) 3 años (comienza en octubre); (b) a (d) 1 año (comienzan en octubre).
Inscripciones: para más informaciones, dirigirse a la Secretaría de la Escuela, en la dirección que figura en el título.

750 Escuela Superior de Administración y Dirección de Empresas [ESADE]
Avenida de Pedralbes 60-62
08034 Barcelona
Tel: (34) (3) 2806162
Web: http://www.esade.es
e-mail: admissions@esade.edu

📖 Programas de estudio en áreas de administración

Campos de estudios: administración, administración de empresas, derecho, finanzas, gestión, marketing, negocio.
Descripción: (a) Licenciatura en administración y dirección de empresas (título oficial) y MBA (master in busines administration, título internacional);
(b) Licenciatura en derecho (título oficial) y MBL (master in business law, título internacional);
(c) Programa de master en dirección y administración de empresas MBA (full-time y part-time);
(d) Doctorado en administración y dirección de empresas (PhD in Management Sciences).
Se destina(n): (a) y (b) a jóvenes de 18 a 20 años que hayan superado el Curso de Orientación Universitaria; (c) a titulados universitarios superiores, a profesionales de la empresa, con experiencia; (d) a titulados superiores en áreas afines, o en otras disciplinas pero en este caso tener experiencia profesional en el campo o haber cursado programa de posgrado que acredite conocimiento general de la empresa.
Duración: (a) y (b) 5 años (comienzan en septiembre); (c) 2 años académicos a tiempo completo (de septiembre a junio) o 3 años a tiempo parcial según el caso; (d) entre 3 y 5 años (comienzo en septiembre).
Asistencia financiera: existen becas de la Fundación ESADE.
Idioma: (a) y (b) español requerido, otros idiomas forman parte del plan de estudios.
Inscripciones: por mayores informaciones, dirigirse al Servicio de Información Académica y Admisiones.

751 Escuela Superior de Tenería [ESDT]
Plaza del Rey 15
08700 Igualada, Barcelona
Tel: (38) (3) 803 5300
Fax: (38) (3) 803 1589
Web: http://www.euetii.upc.es
e-mail: euetii@euetii.upc.es

📖 Estudios superiores

Campos de estudios: formación profesional, industria química, química, tecnología industrial.
Descripción:
(a) Carrera de técnico diplomado o superior en tenería;
(b) Postgrado en técnicas de curtición;
(c) Máster en dirección técnica en curtición.
Se destina(n): a nacionales de cualquier país con conocimientos del idioma español que estén en posesión de: (a) un título de bachiller; (b) un título de licenciado en ciencias químicas, en ingeniería química o equivalente.
Duración: (a) 3 años; (b) 1 año, media jornada; (c) 1 año, jornada completa. Los cursos comienzan en octubre.

752 Fundación "José Ortega y Gasset" Centro de Estudios Internacionales [FJOYG]
Callejón de San Justo
45001 Toledo
Tel: (34) (2) 5212908

📖 Programa de estudios

Campos de estudios: ciencias sociales, español, estudios americanos, estudios europeos, letras, programas de verano.
Descripción: Programa de estudios hispánicos, latinoamericanos y europeos: lengua española (para no hispanohablantes), humanidades y ciencias sociales.
Se destina(n): a nacionales de cualquier país, estudiantes universitarios, que posean un nivel suficiente de español.
Duración: otoño: de septiembre a diciembre; primavera: de enero a mayo; verano: de junio a julio.
Asistencia financiera: 30 becas anuales consistentes en importe que se descontará del precio del programa, ofrecidas a estudiantes latinoamericanos y europeos con excelente nivel académico; solicitudes: 4 meses antes del comienzo del curso.
Inscripciones: hasta un mes antes del comienzo de cada curso.

753 Fundación "Juan Esplugues" [FJE]
Facultad de Medicina de Valencia
Departamento de Farmacología
Avenida de Blasco Ibáñez 15
46010 Valencia
Tel: (34) (6) 386 4625
Fax: (34) (6) 386 4625

🎓 Beca de posgrado

Campos de estudios: farmacia y farmacología, investigación, medicina.
Descripción: destinada a investigación farmacológica experimental y clínica (se otorga 1 beca en años impares).
Lugar: centros de investigación español o extranjero elegido por el becario.
Duración: 1 año académico.
Solicitudes: hasta fin de febrero, dirigirse al Presidente de la Fundación.

754 Fundación "Ortega y Gasset"
Fortuny 53
29010 Madrid
Tel: (34) (1) 700 4100
Fax: (34) (1) 700 3530
Web: http://www.ortegaygasset.edu
e-mail: comunicacion@fog.es

📖 Programas de estudio

Campos de estudios: español, estudios americanos, estudios culturales, estudios europeos, estudios internacionales.
Descripción: La FOG es una institución privada sin fines de lucro dedicada a la difusión cultural, la formación, el debate y la investigación en el ámbito de las ciencias sociales y las humanidades.
Actividades en sus Centros:
(a) Centro de Estudios Internacionales "San Juan de la Penitencia" en Toledo: programa de Estudios Hispánicos, Latinoamericanos y Europeos;
(b) Programas de Lengua y Cultura Españolas (seminarios y cursos de verano para profesores de español).
Se destina(n): (a) a estudiantes universitarios extranjeros; (a) profesores de español: norteamericanos, españoles, nativos, europeos, todos según el tipo de curso.
Inscripciones: por mayores informes, dirigirse a (a) Centro de Estudios Internacionales, Callejón de San Justo,s/n, 45001 Toledo o consultar http://www.fogtoledo.com; (b) programas.internacionales@fog.es.

755 Fundación "Pablo VI" [FPV]
Paseo de Juan XXIII n° 3
28040 Madrid
Tel: (54) (1) 553 4007
Fax: (54) (1) 553 5249

🎓 Programa de becas

Campos de estudios: estudios americanos, historia, informática, ingeniería, sociología, teología, religión.
Descripción:
(a) Becas de estudio para Sociología (28);
(b) Becas de estudio para Doctrina social de la iglesia (37);
(c) Becas de estudio para Informática y sociedad (4);
(d) Becas "Erasmus" e "Intercampus" (7);
(e) Becas de residencia en el Colegio Mayor (10).

Materias de estudio: licenciatura y doctorado en sociología, formación en cooperativismo, en investigaciones del mercado, en doctrina social de la Iglesia; diplomatura y licenciatura en informática, ingeniería técnica e ingeniería superior en informática.
Se conceden: (a) a (c) a nacionales de cualquier país que tengan la titulación correspondiente al nivel de estudios que se pretende. Tendrán prioridad los sacerdotes y estudiantes hispanoamericanos menores de 35 años; en todos los casos, de (a) a (e), las becas se adjudican a alumnos que realicen estudios en los Centros de la Fundación y que justifiquen necesidad económica.
Lugar: (a) a (c) en la Universidad Pontificia de Salamanca, Madrid.
Duración: (a) a (c) 1 año académico (prorrogable hasta terminación de los estudios).
Importe: pueden cubrir los gastos de enseñanza, y en algunos casos también la residencia.
Solicitudes: por mayores informes, dirigirse al Director de Fundación.

756 Fundación Carolina

Web: http://www.fundacioncarolina.es/
e-mail: fundacioncarolina@fundacioncarolina.es

☛ Becas LÍDER de Inmersión en la Realidad Social Española

Campos de estudios: administración de empresas, ciencias económicas y comerciales, ciencias políticas, economía, estudios culturales.
Descripción: programa de conferencias, encuentros y visitas para contacto con los principales protagonistas de la sociedad española y profundización en aspectos claves de la economía, la política, el mundo empresarial y la cultura de España.
Materias de estudio: economía, política y sociedad españolas; economía, política y sociedad portuguesas; Unión Europea, relaciones iberoamericanas e internacionales; actividades culturales y de inmersión.
Se conceden: a 48 licenciados iberoamericanos, 10 españoles y 2 portugueses, presentados por sus universidades.
Lugar: Madrid, Bruselas, Santiago de Compostela, Sevilla y Lisboa.
Duración: tres semanas en julio.
Importe: la beca cubre el viaje a España, el alojamiento con pensión completa, los gastos académicos y los desplazamientos durante el curso.
Solicitudes: se puede solicitar información a la secretaría del Programa de Becas Líder: C/ General Rodrigo, 6. 4ª Planta. Cuerpo Alto, 28043 Madrid, o por fax: +34 91 709 15 55.

☛ Programa de becas

Campos de estudios: todas las materias principales, administración, economía, estudios culturales, investigación.
Becas: becas de postgrado, becas de doctorado y becas de investigación y formación permanente.
Materias de estudio: postgrados: ciencias exactas y experimentales, física y química; tecnologías de la información y de las comunicaciones; energía y suministro energético sostenible; biotecnología, ciencias biomédicas, salud y genética, tecnología de los alimentos; infraestructuras territoriales; medio ambiente, conservación de la tierra, ecología, biodiversidad y calidad del agua; economía y finanzas, organización e innovación empresarial, desarrollo económico e integración regional, cooperación internacional; bienestar social, desigualdad, inclusión social; modernización jurídica y política, democracia, gobernabilidad, derechos humanos y relaciones internacionales; sociedad del conocimiento, educación y desarrollo de los recursos humanos; humanidades: cultura, artes, lengua e historia; ciencias sociales y de la comunicación.
Se conceden: en general, las becas están dirigidas, preferentemente, a jóvenes titulados superiores, profesionales e investigadores de los países que integran la Comunidad Iberoamericana de Naciones. La selección de los becarios se efectuará de acuerdo con los méritos académicos y profesionales de los candidatos. Las becas de doctorado e investigación está dirigida a profesores docentes de universidades de América Latina.
Otras condiciones: No se trata de una solicitud personal, sino a través de la institución universitaria que podrá presentar dos candidatos como máximo. Serán considerados aspirantes

aquellos universitarios licenciados o que estén por recibirse en fecha que depende de la convocatoria.
Solicitudes: para cualquier consulta relacionada con su candidatura, deberá dirigirse, exclusivamente al buzón específico del programa para el que ha solicitado una beca; dicha dirección de correo electrónico se encuentra en la sección dedicada al "Proceso de Selección" de cada programa en la página web correspondiente.

757 Fundación CIDOB [CIDOB]

Elisabets 12
08001 Barcelona
Tel: (34) (3) 302 6495
Fax: (34) (3) 302 2118
Web: http://www.cidob.es
e-mail: docencia@cidob.org

☐ Programa de cursos

Campos de estudios: ciencias políticas, estudios sobre el desarrollo, relaciones internacionales.
Descripción:
(a) Cursos de posgrado: master en estudios internacionales, en estudios para el desarrollo, diplomas en cooperación para el desarrollo, relaciones internacionales, en ciudadanía intercultural;
(b) Cursos especializados: política internacional, migraciones, desarrollo y cooperación, interculturalidad, América latina, Asia, Mediterráneo, Mundo Árabe, África Subsahariana.
Se destina(n): a personas interesadas en desarrollar su actividad en organismos internacionales o en el campo diplomático y en el de la cooperación para el desarrollo; cargos de la administración pública o de la empresa privada que ejerzan tareas vinculadas al mundo internacional o de la cooperación; profesionales de los diversos medios de comunicación con dedicación a los temas internacionales o de la cooperación, y personas interesadas en el estudio y la investigación de los temas internacionales y de la cooperación para el desarrollo.

758 Fundación MAPFRE Estudios [FME]

Monte del Pilar s/n
28023 El Plantío, Madrid
Tel: (34) (1) 581 2008
Fax: (34) (1) 581 1795
Web: http://www.mapfre.com
e-mail: promocion.fme@mapfre.com

☐ Programas de formación superior

Campos de estudios: administración de empresas, derecho, derecho internacional, finanzas, gestión, riesgos, seguros.
Descripción:
(a) Formación universitaria de grado: diplomatura en ciencias empresariales, licenciatura en administración y dirección de empresas, en ciencias actuariales y financieras;
(b) Formacion universitaria de postgrado: master universitario en seguros y gerencia de riesgos, en seguros personales (vida, accidentes, salud y pensiones), en prevención de riesgos laborales, en dirección y gestión de empresas (MBA), curso universitario en especialización en dirección de seguridad privada;
(c) Cursos de perfeccionamiento: ciclo de seminarios del diploma experto en gerencia de riesgos y seguros, cursos de especialistas en gestión pericial de siniestros de daños patrimoniales, curso superior internacional de seguridad integral en la empresa;
(d) Formación a distancia: cursos de especialización en seguros (vía internet o correo postal), master en prevención de riesgos laborales (disponible en CD-Rom).
Asistencia financiera: existen becas de estudio (para estudios de grado, hasta 75% de los derechos dematriculación, para estudios de postgrado, hasta 50% de los derechos de matriculación) y becas de estancia durante los estudios en Madrid.
Inscripciones: hasta finales de septiembre, dirigirse a la Secretaría de la Fundación.

☛ Becas Riesgo y Seguro

Campos de estudios: investigación, riesgos, seguros.
Se conceden: a titulados universitarios y profesionales del mundo del seguro, de cualquier nacionalidad, que deseen desarrollar programas de investigación de forma individual o en el marco de alguna institución. Los trabajos realizados

deberán ser presentados en lengua castellana o portuguesa, independientementr de la nacionalidad del becario.
Duración: 1 año (renovable).
Solicitudes: por otros informes, dirigirse a Becas Riesgo y Seguro, en la dirección que figura en el título (http://www.mapfre.com/estudios.

759 Fundación Marcelino Botín
Pedrueca 1
39003 Santander
Tel: +34 942 226072
Fax: +34 942 226072
Web: http://www.fundacionmbotin.org/inicio.asp
e-mail: fmabotin@fundacionmbotin.org

🐦 Beca Curatorial Studies
Campos de estudios: museología y museografía.
Descripción: estudios en el extranjero para formación en comisariado y gestión de exposiciones.
Materias de estudio: capacitación profesional en la teoría y técnicas sobre la gestión de museos y la organización de exposiciones.
Se conceden: a diplomado, licenciado o estudiante de postgrado, en bellas artes, historia del arte, filosofía y estética, literatura, humanidades o crítica; o ser un profesional del arte que, no cumpliendo los requisitos anteriores, pueda demostrar capacitación en el campo; poseer la nacionalidad española, o demostrar la residencia desde los cinco años anteriores a la solicitud; tener entre 23 y 40 años; dominar el idioma del país donde se encuentre el centro elegido; y contar con la aceptación por escrito del centro de formación elegido.
Importe: la dotación total de la beca comprende 16.227 euros (en concepto de viajes, alojamiento, manutención, etc.), a los que se sumarán hasta un máximo de 12.000 euros destinados al abono de la matrícula en el centro de formación elegido.

🐦 Beca Universidad de Brown
Campos de estudios: biología, bioquímica.
Materias de estudio: biología molecular; biología humana o bioquímica.
Nacionalidad: a españoles.
Lugar: en la Universidad de Brown (Providence, EEUU).
Importe: 10.000 euros al año, prorrogable máximo cuatro años.
Solicitudes: dirigirse a Universidad de Brown. The College Admission Office. Box 1876. Providence. RI 02912 (EEUU). Tel. 001 401 863 2378.

🐦 Beca Universidad Wellesley
Campos de estudios: todas las materias principales, historia del arte.
Materias de estudio: estudios en cualquier especialidad, con preferencia de historia del arte.
Nacionalidad: a una estudiante española.
Importe: 10.000 € al año, prorrogable maximo cuatro años.
Solicitudes: dirigirse a Wellesley College. 106 Central St. Wellesley MA 02481 (EEUU). The College Admission Office. Tel. 001 781 283 1000. www.wellesley.edu.

🐦 Becas de Artes Plásticas
Campos de estudios: artes plásticas.
Descripción: ayudas para formación, investigación o proyectos personales en el área de artes plásticas.
Se conceden: a personas de cualquier nacionalidad con el único límite de tener entre 23 y 40 años. Sin límite de edad las referidas a investigación.
Duración: El tiempo de disfrute de esta beca será de 9 meses. Las becas fuera del lugar de origen, pueden prorrogarse por otro periodo, previa solicitud anual en los plazos de la convocatoria pública.
Importe: Las ayudas para cada beca son: sin cambio de residencia, 10.818 euros; con traslado a otro país, distinto al de su residencia actual, 18.030 euros; y con traslado a Estados Unidos, 21.636 euros. Estas ayudas comprenden viajes, alojamiento, manutención y alquiler de estudio. Se añadirán las tasas académicas del centro elegido para las becas de formación y el seguro médico siempre que haya desplazamiento. Al finalizar la beca, la Fundación organiza una exposición y edita un catálogo.

760 Fundación Sénéca
C/ Manresa Nº5, Entlo. E
3004 Murcia
Tel: +34-968-222-971
Fax: +34-968-220-712
Web: http://www.f-seneca.org
e-mail: seneca@f-seneca.org

🐦 Programa de formación de recursos humanos para la ciencia y la tecnología
Campos de estudios: ciencias, investigación, tecnología.
Descripción: (a) Formación del personal investigador:
- becas predoctorales;
- becas de formación investigadora en proyectos de trasplantes y xenotrasplantes de órganos; - becas de formación investigadora y predoctorales de la Consejería de Agricultura y Agua
(b) Formación para la innovación:
- becas asociadas a la realización de proyectos de investigación en i+d, innovación y transferencia de tecnología. Desarrollo en empresas y Centros Tecnológicos de la Región de Murcia.
- becas asociadas a la realización de proyectos de investigación en i+d, innovación y transferencia de tecnología de aplicación en el Centro Tecnológico Nacional de la Conserva.
Formación posdoctoral.
(c) Becas de formación postdoctoral.
(d) Ayudas a la incorporación de cientificos y tecnólogos.

761 Fundación Universidad-Empresa [FUE]
Serrano Jover 5 - 7a
28015 Madrid
Tel: (34) (1) 548 98 60
Fax: (34) (1) 547 06 52
Web: http://www.fue.es
e-mail: info@fue.es

📖 Programas de formación
Campos de estudios: todas las materias principales, administración de empresas, ciencias, ciencias económicas y comerciales, derecho, ecología, medio ambiente, educación, filología, ingeniería, psicología, riesgos, seguros, tecnología, trabajo social.
Descripción: Cursos de postgrado, de especialización y programas master, en colaboración con las Universidades de Madrid y la UNED, así como diversas empresas, instituciones y organismos públicos en áreas de ciencias e ingeniería, derecho, economía y empresa, educación, filología, intervención social, medio ambiente, nuevas tecnologías, psicología, riesgos laborales, salud.
Se destina(n): a titulados medios y superiores en diferentes áreas de conocimiento.

762 Institut d'Estudis Catalans [IDC]
Carrer del Carme 47
08001 Barcelona
Tel: (34) (3) 270 1622
Fax: (34) (3) 270 1180
Web: http://www.iecat.net
e-mail: informacio@iecat.net

🐦 Becas de estudio Generalitat de Catalunya
Campos de estudios: estudios culturales.
Descripción: becas de estudio en temas relacionados con la cultura catalana (lengua, literatura, historia, derecho, arte, arqueología, etc.).
Materias de estudio: las relacionadas con la cultura catalana (lengua, literatura, historia, derecho, arte, arqueología, etc.).
Se conceden: a investigadores extranjeros que cumplan los requisitos necesarios y que dominen el catalán.
Lugar: en las regiones de lengua catalana.
Duración: 3 meses.
Solicitudes: hasta el 5 de diciembre, en la Secretaría General, en la dirección que figura en el título.

763   Instituto Agronómico Mediterráneo de Zaragoza [IAMZ]

Apartado 202
50080 Zaragoza
Tel: (34) (7) 671 6000
Fax: (34) (7) 671 6001
Web: http://www.iamz.ciheam.org
e-mail: iamz@iamz.ciheam.org

Programa de cursos

Campos de estudios: agricultura, botánica, ciencias agronómicas, ciencias veterinarias, desarrollo rural, ecología, medio ambiente, genética, negocio, zoología.
Descripción: (a) Cursos de especialización postuniversitaria en: mejora genética vegetal, ordenación rural en función del medio ambiente, genética, nutrición y reproducción animal, comercialización de productos agrarios y alimentarios, olivicultura y elaiotecnia, acuicultura (cada programa se celebra bienalmente); se otorgan títulos de Diploma de Especialización Postuniversitaria o de Diploma Master of Science otorgado por el Centre de Hautes Etudes Agronomiques Méditerranéennes (CIHEAM); (b) 15 cursos de corta duración sobre temas de: producción animal; producción vegetal; medio ambiente; comercialización de productos agrarios.
Nacionalidad: (a) a participantes que provienen fundamentalmente de los países mediterráneos miembros del CIHEAM, aunque participan también profesionales de otros países de todo el mundo, especialmente de Europa y de América Latina.
Diplomas requeridos: (a) a profesionales con titulación superior universitaria que trabajan en su especialidad en sus respectivos países y que desean una actualización o una profundización de sus conocimientos en el tema. En el caso de los cursos de especialización postuniversitaria la participación está también abierta a jóvenes titulados superiores que, no habiendo iniciado todavía su labor profesional, desean adquirir una especialización que les permita acceder con una mayor formación a un determinado sector de la actividad agraria.
Otras condiciones: (a) los candidatos deberán acreditar el conocimiento del español. El IAMZ organiza durante el verano para sus becarios y los participantes que así lo solicitan un curso intensivo de español. En el caso de los cursos avanzados, los candidatos deberán acreditar el conocimiento del idioma en el que se vaya a desarrollar el curso, o, caso de preverse traducción simultánea, el conocimiento de francés, inglés o español; (b) la experiencia profesional en actividades directamente relacionadas con la temática del curso es requisito indispensable.
Duración: (a) 9 meses; (b) de 1 a 3 semanas durante el año académico.
Asistencia financiera: el CIHEAM podrá otorgar un número limitado de becas que cubran los derechos de inscripción a los candidatos de países mediterráneos miembros del CIHEAM (Albania, Argelia, Egipto, España, Francia, Grecia, Italia, Líbano, Malta, Marruecos, Portugal, Túnez, Turquía y ex-Yugoslavia). Estos candidatos podrán solicitar asimismo becas que cubran los gastos de viaje, alojamiento, alimentación y manutención en la residencia situada en el campus y seguro de asistencia sanitaria válido por el periodo de duración del curso. Los participantes de otras nacionalidades, que deseen obtener financiación, deberán solicitarla directamente a otras instituciones nacionales o internacionales.
Inscripciones: (a) hasta el 15 de mayo; (b) hasta 90 días antes de la fecha de inicio de cada curso.

764   Instituto Agronómico Mediterráneo de Zaragoza [IAMZ]

Carretera de Montaña 177
Apartado 202
50080 Zaragoza
Tel: (34) (7) 657 6013
Fax: (34) (7) 657 6377
Web: http://www.iamz.ciheam.org
e-mail: iamz@iamz.ciheam.org

Becas para programas de formación organizados por el IAMZ

Campos de estudios: ciencias agronómicas.
Descripción: formación en áreas de ciencias agronómicas, agricultura, marketing, ciencias económicas y comerciales, ecología y medio ambiente, recursos naturales, ciencias veterinarias, cría de ganado, hidrología, horticultura, industria alimentaria, pesquería, silvicultura.
Se conceden: a candidatos de países mediterráneos miembros del CIHEAM (Albania, Argelia, Egipto, España, Francia, Grecia, Italia, Líbano, Malta, Marruecos, Portugal, Túnez, Turquía), con titulación superior universitaria (desde hace menos de 10 años) relacionada con el tema; la experiencia profesional es valorada en los cursos superiores, pero en el caso de los cursos cortos es indispensable y debe poder ser acreditada. Existe proceso de selección y puede exigirse algún idioma.
Lugar: en general, en Zaragoza, pero algunos cursos son dictados en la Universidad de Córdoba, otros en Gran Canarias; los cursos cortos pueden ser dictados en el IAMZ o en otras instituciones en España u otros países del área.
Duración: la del curso: 8 meses para los cursos superiores, 1 a 2 semanas para los cursos cortos.
Solicitudes: cursos de especialización universitaria: hasta mayo; cursos de corta duración: 90 días antes del comienzo del curso.

765   Instituto de Empresas [IDE]

Calle María de Molina 11, 13 y 15
28006 Madrid
Tel: (34) (1) 562 8100
Fax: (34) (1) 411 5503
Web: http://www.ucm.es
e-mail: admission@ie.ucm.es

Programas Master

Campos de estudios: administración, administración de empresas, contabilidad, derecho, derecho canónico, finanzas, gestión, marketing.
Descripción:
(a) Programas dirigidos a postgraduados: master en asesoría jurídica, en asesoría fiscal, en dirección y administración de empresas (MBA), International MBA, master en auditoría; (b) Programas de dirección: master en dirección y administración de empresas (Executive MBA), en dirección de recursos humanos, en dirección comercial y marketing, master en dirección financiera y de control, en dirección de operaciones y producción.
Se destina(n): (a) a licenciados superiores que superen proceso de selección consistente en prueba de acceso y entrevista personal, así como mostrar un determinado nivel de inglés; (b) a licenciados superiores con experiencia mínima de 3 años en puestos de dirección; el proceso de admisión consiste en entrevista personal.
Duración: (a) 1 curso académico (inicios en octubre o febrero), salvo el International MBA que dura 14 meses (inicio en octubre) y el MIBL que dura 6 meses y tiene comienzo sólo en enero; (b) comienzos en octubre, salvo el Executive MBA que también tiene inicio en febrero.
Asistencia financiera: becas parciales (de 20 a 50% del costo total del programa); becas que cubren gastos de estancia y mantenimiento, destinadas a participantes iberoamericanos otorgados por el Instituto de Cooperación Iberoamericana (ICI, Avenida de los Reyes Católicos 4, 28040 Madrid).

766   Instituto de Estudios Espaciales de Cataluña [IEEC]

Edificio Nexus
Gran Capità, 2-4, desp. 201
08034 Barcelona
Tel: (34) (3) 280 2088
Fax: (34) (3) 280 6395
Web: http://www.ieec.fcr.es
e-mail: ieec@ieec.fcr.es

Master en teledetección y sistemas de información geográfica

Campos de estudios: ciencias aplicadas, ciencias de la tierra, espacio, tecnología, telecomunicaciones.
Se destina(n): a licenciados e ingenieros superiores; existe

selección por entrevista.
Costo(s): 3.600 euros más tasas.

767 Instituto de la Pequeña y Mediana Industria de la Generalidad Valenciana [IMPIVA]

Plaza del Ayuntamiento 6
46002 Valencia
Tel: (34) (6) 398 6200
Fax: (34) (6) 398 6201
Web: http://www.impiva.es
e-mail: info@impiva.gva.es

🖝 Becas de especialización profesional

Campos de estudios: diseño industrial, formación profesional, gestión, industria química, industria textil, industria y comercio, tecnología, tecnología industrial.
Descripción: áreas de tecnologías industriales, tecnologías y gestión de la información, gestión de la innovación y del comercio internacional, diseño: sector cerámico, construcción, madera/mueble, óptica, juguete, metal-mecánico, agroalimentario, plástico, textil, calzado, polisectorial, envase, embalaje.
Se conceden: a jóvenes desempleados europeos, menores de 26 años, preferentemente con residencia en la Comunidad Valenciana, posgraduados universitarios con no más de 4 años de terminación de los estudios. Existe preselección por méritos y entrevista.
Lugar: institutos tecnológicos y centros de empresas e innovación de la Red IMPIVA, en las ciudades de Castellón, Valencia y Alicante.
Duración: entre 6 meses y 1 año.
Importe: asignación mensual, seguro de enfermedad, accidente y vida, derechos de inscripción (si procede), gastos de desplazamiento (si procede).
Solicitudes: hasta fin de septiembre.

768 Instituto de la Pequeña y Mediana Industria de la Generalidad Valenciana [IMPIVA]

Plaza del Ayuntamiento 6
46002 Valencia
Tel: (34) (6) 398 6200
Fax: (34) (6) 398 6201
Web: http://www.impiva.es
e-mail: info@impiva.gva.es

📖 Cursos de posgrado en centros universitarios

Campos de estudios: comercio, economía, empresas internacionales, gestión.
Descripción:
(a) Master en gestión del comercio internacional;
(b) Master en internacionalización de la empresa;
(c) Master de dirección y gestión en comercio internacional.
Se destina(n): (a) a licenciados y diplomados en derecho, económica o empresariales, preferentemente de la Unión Europea, con dominio de español e inglés, que superen preselección de méritos académicos y entrevista; (b) y (c) a licenciados, diplomados universitarios y personal de empresas con cargos de responsabilidad en áreas del comercio exterior, que superen preselección como (a) más examen de inglés.
Se dicta(n): (a) en Valencia; (b) en Alicante; (c) en Castellón.
Duración: 1 año académico (comienzan en octubre).
Asistencia financiera: (b) becas otorgadas por diversos organismos y empresas.
Inscripciones: (a) hasta el 15 de septiembre, dirigirse a Fundación Empresa de Valencia, Plaza Ayuntamiento 19, Valencia; (b) en septiembre-octubre, dirigirse a la Cámara de Comercio, Industria y Navegación de Alicante, San Fernando 4, 3002 Alicante; (c) en septiembre, dirigirse a Cámara de Comercio, Comercio e Industria de Castellón, Avenida Hermanos Bou 79, 12003 Castellón.

769 Instituto Español de Comercio Exterior [ICEX]

Paseo de la Castellana 14
28046 Madrid
Tel: (34) (1) 431 1240
Fax: (34) (1) 431 6128

🖝 Programa de becas

Campos de estudios: comercio, economía, gestión, industria y comercio, negocio, relaciones internacionales.
Descripción: (a) Becas en oficinas comerciales;
(b) Becas en empresas;
(c) Becas inversas.
Materias de estudio: (a) y (b) comercio internacional, economía, negocio, relaciones internacionales; (c) gestión empresarial, métodos de producción y comercialización.
Se conceden: (a) y (b) a posgraduados de nacionalidad española, cuya edad no supere los 30 años; se requieren conocimientos en comercio exterior y ciertos idiomas son exigidos; (c) a posgraduados con más de 2 años de experiencia profesional, nacionales de países en desarrollo, cuya edad no supere los 45 años; se requiere conocer el español.
Lugar: (a) diversas oficinas comerciales de España en el extranjero; (b) diversas empresas españolas de ámbito internacional en España y/o extranjero; (c) empresas exportadoras, en España.
Duración: (a) y (b) 12 meses (no renovable); (c) 6 meses (no renovable).
Importe: (a) y (b) en función del destino; (c) monto fijo más seguros, más desplazamientos durante los 6 meses.
Solicitudes: (a) y (b) del 15 de junio al 15 de julio, a ICEX, Departamento de Formación, en la dirección que figura en el título; (c) son las empresas españolas las que proponen al candidato enviando curriculum a ICEX, quien decide la concesión.

770 Instituto Internacional de Sociología Jurídica de Oñati [IISJ]

Antigua Universidad
Apartado 28
20560 Oñati, Gipuzkoa
Tel: (34) (4) 378 3064
Fax: (34) (4) 378 3147
Web: http://www.sc.ehu.es

📖 Master internacional en sociología jurídica

Campos de estudios: derecho, sociología.
Se destina(n): a licenciados en sociología, derecho y/u otras disciplinas que se interesen por los fenómenos jurídicos desde sus propias perspectivas.
Duración: 1 año académico de 9/10 meses (comienza en octubre).
Asistencia financiera: existen becas de monto anual fijo.
Idioma: el idioma de instrucción es inglés.
Inscripciones: hasta el 30 de marzo; dirigirse al Programa Master y Doctorado/IISJ.

771 Instituto Nacional de Administración Pública [INAP]

Atocha 106
28027 Madrid
Tel: (34) (1) 34 93148
Fax: (34) (1) 34 93160
Web: http://www.inap.map.es
e-mail: inforinap@inap.map.es

🖝 Becas de estudios

Campos de estudios: administración, estudios sobre el desarrollo, gestión, informática.
Descripción: concedidas por el Instituto de Cooperación Iberoamericana (ICI) para la realización de estudios en el INAP.
(a) Maestría en administración y gerencia pública (25);
(b) Posgrado en administración pública (10);
(c) Curso de gerencia pública para el desarrollo social (25);
(d) Curso de gestión económica medioambiental y de los recursos humanos (25);
(e) Curso de informática para directivos (25);
(f) Curso de organización territorial del estado y desarrollo local (25);

(g) Curso de desarrollo institucional y capacitación (25).
Se conceden: a licenciados universitarios superiores que ocupen cargos de responsabilidad en la Administración Pública de su país.
Duración: la del curso, (a) 22 meses, (b) 10 meses; (c) a (g) 3 meses.
Importe: monto mensual más posibilidad de beca de desplazamiento concedida por la Organización de Estados Americanos (OEA).
Solicitudes: plazos establecidos por el ICI; dirigirse a esta institución o a las Oficinas Técnicas de Cooperación en las representaciones diplomáticas de España en el país de origen.

772 Instituto Nacional de Investigación y Tecnología Agraria y Alimentaria [INIA]
Ctra. de la Coruña, km. 7,5
28040 Madrid
Tel: (34) (1) 347 3900
Fax: (34) (1) 357 2293
Web: http://www.inia.es

📖 Cursos Internacionales

Campos de estudios: agricultura, botánica, ciencias agronómicas, ciencias veterinarias, cría de ganado, desarrollo rural, ecología, medio ambiente, genética, tecnología.
Descripción: dirigidos fundamentalmente a expertos iberoamericanos:
(a) Conservación y utilización de recursos fitogenéticos para la agricultura y la alimentación;
(b) Enfermedades exóticas animales;
(c) Economía agroalimentaria;
(d) Mejora genética animal;
(e) Reproducción animal.
(f) Detección e identificación de virus, viroides y fitoplasmas (curso teórico-práctico).
Se destina(n): a titulados superiores.
Duración: (a) a (e) 1 mes; (f) 15 días.
Costo(s): matrícula de 322 euros, y no incluye los posibles gastos de desplazamiento, alojamiento y manutención.
Asistencia financiera: la Agencia Española de Cooperación Iberoamericana (AECI) concede becas de ayuda a posgraduados iberoamericanos, las cuales pueden ser solicitadas en las Embajadas o Consulados de España. El INIA concede becas de derechos de matrícula.
Inscripciones: dirigirse al Director del Curso correspondiente.

773 Instituto Nacional de Meteorología [INM]
Camino de las Moreras s/n
Ciudad Universitaria
28040 Madrid
Tel: (34) (1) 581 9860
Fax: (34) (1) 581 9892
Web: http://www.inm.es

🎓 Beca de matrícula para estudios en meteorología

Campos de estudios: meteorología.
Se conceden: a ciudadanos de países iberoamericanos, árabes, africanos, de Bulgaria, Rumania, Polonia, Hungría y de los nuevos Estados independientes de Europa y Asia Central; deberán haber superado 1 año de estudios universitarios o equivalentes en ciencias o ingeniería, o como mínimo tener aprobadas las asignaturas de física y matemáticas a ese nivel; deberán conocer el español (se requiere certificado cuando el español no sea el idioma oficial del país de origen del candidato). Se considerará equivalente a la titulación requerida ser meteorólogo Clase III y trabajar en un servicio meteorológico nacional. Existe selección por concurso de méritos.
Lugar: en la sede central del Instituto Nacional de Meteorología de Madrid.
Duración: 21 meses (no renovable).
Importe: monto mensual, ayuda inicial para desplazamiento e instalación y ayuda final para desplazamiento.
Solicitudes: hasta septiembre, al Director del Centro de Formación Meteorológica del INM, Apartado 285, 28040 Madrid.

774 Instituto Oficial de la Radio Televisión Española [IORTVE]
Carretera de la Dehesa de la Villa, s/n
28040 Madrid
Tel: (34) (1) 581 7584
Fax: (34) (1) 581 7581
Web: http://www.rtve.es/oficial/iortv/iortv.htm
e-mail: formacion_abierta.ep @ rtve.es

📖 Programas Master

Campos de estudios: comunicación, medios audio-visuales, periodismo.
Programas:
(a) Master en documentación audiovisual;
(b) Master en realización y diseño de programas y formatos en televisión;
(c) Master en periodismo de televisión.
Se destina(n): (a) a titulados universitarios de cualquier Facultad o Escuela Técnica Superior (para el título de Master) y diplomados y titulados universitarios de Escuelas Técnicas (Título de Especialista); (c) a licenciados universitarios, alumnos en quinto de carrera y prueba de selección.
Duración: (a) 14 meses; (b) 1 año académico; (c) de octubre a abril.
Costo(s): (a) 3.910 euros; (b) 5.400 euros; (c) 6.670 euros.
Inscripciones: (a) Universidad Carlos III de Madrid, Centro de Ampliación de Estudios, Madrid 126, 28903, Getafe, Madrid; (b) Fundación de la Universidad Rey Juan Carlos, Tulipán s/n, 28933 Móstoles, Madrid, Web:http://www.urjc.es; (c) IORTV, Despacho 113.

775 Instituto Químico de Sarriá [IQDS]
Via Augusta 390
08017 Barcelona
Tel: (34) (3) 267 2000
Fax: (34) (3) 205 6266
Web: http://www.iqs.url.es
e-mail: secre@iqs.url.es

📖 Carreras y posgrados

Campos de estudios: administración de empresas, ciencias económicas y comerciales, ecología, medio ambiente, gestión, industria alimentaria, industria química, ingeniería química, química, riesgos, seguros, tecnología, tecnología industrial.
Descripción: Programas en su Escuela técnica superior y su Facultad de economía:
(a) Carreras: ingeniería industrial, ingeniería química, licenciatura en química, licenciatura en administración y dirección de empresas, diplomatura en ciencias empresariales;
(b) Cursos de postgrado: master en química e ingeniería alimentaria, master en ingeniería ambiental de la empresa, diploma de técnico en medio ambiente, master en gestión de la empresa industrial, prevención de riesgos laborales y seguridad industrial.
Asistencia financiera: becas de la Fundación Francesc Castelló i Aleu (50 a 100% de matrícula, a reembolsar más tarde) para alumnos españoles o iberoamericanos con excelente expediente académico y que justifiquen necesidad económica.
Inscripciones: Secretaría General del Instituto.

776 Instituto Universitario de Investigación "Ortega y Gasset" [IUIOG]
Fortuny 53
29010 Madrid
Tel: (34) (1) 700 4149
Fax: (34) (1) 700 3530
Web: http://www.ortegaygasset.edu
e-mail: fogiuaca@accessnet.es

📖 Programas universitarios

Campos de estudios: todas las materias principales, administración, ciencias humanas, ciencias políticas, ciencias sociales, derecho internacional, estudios europeos, estudios internacionales, lingüística, relaciones internacionales.
Descripción: El IUIOG (instituto universitario privado español adscrito a la universidad pública Complutense de Madrid) imparte formación de postgrado e investigación en ciencias sociales y humanidades.

(a) Masters en: relaciones internacionales; administración pública; gestión cultural; negocios internacionales; derecho, economía y políticas públicas; cooperación internacional y gestión de proyectos; internacional en relaciones industriales; derecho y economía de la Unión Europea; gestión de recursos naturales y sustentabilidad;
(b) Doctorados: América Latina contemporánea; lingüística teórica y sus aplicaciones; gobierno y administración pública; estudios europeos; integración económica y monetaria de Europa; derecho internacional y relaciones internacionales; migraciones internacionales e integración social.

777   La Salle - Universitat Ramon Llull

Campus Barcelona
C/ Lluçanès, 41
08022 Barcelona
Tel: (34) (3) 240 4434
Fax: (34) (3) 290 2443
Web: http://www.salleURL.edu
e-mail: info@salleURL.edu

Masters La Salle

Campos de estudios: administración, administración de empresas, arquitectura, tecnología.
Descripción: maestrías en áreas de management, tecnología y arquitectura.
Se destina(n): a profesionales con titulación universitaria y experiencia profesional; existe examen escrito y entrevista, y se deben presentar cartas de recomendación académica y profesional.
Se dicta(n): en los campus de Barcelona, de Madrid, Valencia o Zaragoza según el caso; los estudios en el campus virtual exigen presencia ocasional en Madrid o Barcelona.
Duración: de 10 a 22 meses.
Asistencia financiera: becas La Salle - América Latina y becas LaSalleOnLine.
Inscripciones: para realizar el test de admisión, contactar la Secretaría del Programa de Masters (realización del test en el Campus Barcelona, en el Campus Madrid o vía Internet en el campus virtual). Por otra información, dirigirse a la Secretaría de Extensión Universitaria, Calle La Salle 8, 28023 Madrid, e-mail: info.mad@lasalleonline.net.

Becas La Salle - América Latina

Campos de estudios: administración, administración de empresas, arquitectura, gestión, tecnología.
Se conceden: a latinoamericanos, para la realización de un programa Master La Salle.
Duración: la duración del Master elegido.
Importe: la beca incluye dotación económica de hasta 10.000 euros (dependiendo del programa elegido, monto a descontar del costo del programa). Esta beca es sólo de estudios, en ningún caso están estipulados dentro de la dotación de la beca los gastos de viaje desde el país de origen del becario hacia España, ni los costes de alojamiento y manutención durante el período lectivo.
Solicitudes: dirigirse a becasAL@salleURL.edu.

Becas LaSalleOnLine

Campos de estudios: administración, administración de empresas, arquitectura, gestión, tecnología.
Descripción: becas de colaboración en un proyecto de e-learning (o la virtualización) del Programa de Másters La Salle con una dedicación mínima de 15 horas/semanales.
Se conceden: a alumnos admitidos en un Master en La Salle en el Campus Virtual.
Importe: la beca incluye la dispensa de los costes académicos de matriculación en el programa de máster para cursar el máster por internet a través del campus virtual LaSalleOnLine desde el país de origen del alumno becado. Se analizarán las diferentes candidaturas pudiéndose otorgar becas parciales.
Solicitudes: dirigirse a becasAL@salleURL.edu.

778   Ministerio de Agricultura, Pesca y Alimentación Instituto Español de Oceanografía [IEO]

Avenida del Brasil 31
28020 Madrid
Tel: (34) (1) 597 4443
Fax: (34) (1) 597 4770
Web: http://www.ieo.es

Becas de estudio

Campos de estudios: biología marina, botánica, geología, oceanografía, pesquería.
Descripción: Becas para estudios oceanográficos del Instituto de Cooperación Iberoamericana, la Comisión Oceanográfica Intergubernamental y el Ministerio de Asuntos Exteriores.
Materias de estudio: oceanografía, pesquería, biología marina (cultivo de peces); botánica (cultivo de macroalgas) y geología marina.
Se conceden: a posgraduados iberoamericanos, africanos o de otras nacionalidades.
Lugar: en laboratorios costeros acordes con la especialidad.
Duración: 4 a 6 semanas.
Solicitudes: hasta el 15 de junio o el 30 de septiembre, según los cursos.

779   Ministerio de Agricultura, Pesca y Alimentación Instituto Español de Oceanografía [IEO]

Avenida del Brasil 31
28020 Madrid
Tel: (34) (91) 597 4443
Fax: (34) (91) 597 4770
Web: http://www.ieo.es

Estudios marinos intensivos de posgrado

Campos de estudios: biología marina, geología, oceanografía, pesquería.
Descripción: especializaciones en oceanografía, cultivos de peces marinos, cultivo de macroalgas, geología marina, pesquerías.
Se destina(n): a posgraduados iberoamericanos becados por el Instituto de Cooperación Iberoamericana, a posgraduados africanos o de otras nacionalidades becados por la Comisión Oceanográfica Intergubernamental y por el Ministerio de Asuntos Exteriores.
Se dicta(n): en los laboratorios costeros más acordes con la especialidad elegida.
Duración: 4 a 6 semanas.

780   Ministerio de Asuntos Exteriores Dirección General de Relaciones Culturales y Científicas [MAE]

Calle Atocha 3
28003 Madrid
Tel: (34) (91) 379 9762
Fax: (34) (91) 531 9366
Web: http://www.mae.es/mae

Programa de becas

Campos de estudios: todas las materias principales, español, investigación, programas de verano.
Descripción:
(a) Becas de curso académico;
(b) Becas de verano;
(c) Becas de investigación para hispanistas extranjeros;
700 becas en total.
Materias de estudio: (a) y (b) cualquiera, preferentemente en el campo de las humanidades; (c) didáctica y metodología de la lengua española.
Se conceden: (a) y (b) a ciudadanos de los países europeos, Israel, Japón y Corea, con conocimiento suficiente del idioma español.
Lugar: centros universitarios, de investigación y estudio

españoles.
Duración: (a) entre 3 y 9 meses (de octubre a junio); (b) 1
mes (en junio); (c) entre 1 y 3 meses (entre febrero y
diciembre).
Importe: (a) monto mensual y seguro médico; (b) monto
mensual, seguro médico y viaje de ida y vuelta; (c)
alojamiento, manutención, matrícula, seguro médico, viaje de
ida y vuelta, actividades culturales y una cantidad en
metálico; (d) alojamiento y manutención en una residencia
universitaria.
Solicitudes: en los Servicios Culturales de las Embajadas
de España en el país del solicitante.

781 Ministerio de Asuntos Exteriores Escuela Diplomática (ED) [MAE]
Paseo de Juan XXIII N° 5
28040 Madrid
Tel: (34) (91) 553 53 00
Web: http://www.mae.es

📖 Programa de cursos

Campos de estudios: derecho, derecho internacional,
estudios internacionales, historia, relaciones internacionales.
Programas:
(a) Curso de estudios internacionales (Magister en estudios
internacionales de la Universidad Complutense de Madrid);
(b) Curso intensivo de relaciones internacionales para
diplomáticos extranjeros.
Materias de estudio: (a) materias jurídicas, históricas,
económicas, relaciones internacionales, estudios de áreas
geopolíticas, organismos internacionales, así como la
celebración de conferencias, seminarios y visitas de estudio;
(b) actualización de conocimiento de la realidad internacional
y ampliación de formación sobre temas relacionados con
España, Iberoamérica y la Unión Europea.
Se destina(n): (a) a españoles y extranjeros menores de 35
años que sean doctores o licenciados en facultades
universitarias, escuelas técnicas superiores o centros
equiparados;
(b) a diplomáticos en activo, menores de 40 años, con algunos
años de experiencia en sus respectivos Servicios Exteriores y
particularmente interesados en los asuntos de España e
Iberoamérica. Para participar en el curso es imprescindible un
conocimiento suficiente de la lengua española. Actualmente,
las plazas del CIRIDEX están reservadas para diplomáticos de
las siguientes áreas geográficas: Europa Central y Oriental,
Mundo Árabe, Africa, Asia y Pacífico. Está en estudio la
organización de un curso específico para diplomáticos
iberoamericanos.
Duración: (a) un año académico (octubre a junio); (b) 2
meses.
Asistencia financiera: (a) los candidatos al curso que no
ostentan la nacionalidad española pueden solicitar becas, que
son concedidas por la Agencia Española de Cooperación
Internacional (AECI) del Ministerio de Asuntos Exteriores,
de acuerdo con las convocatorias de becas correspondientes;
(b) los organismos del Ministerio de Asuntos Exteriores
conceden becas a los participantes (Agencia Española de
Cooperación Internacional y Dirección General de Relaciones
Culturales).
Inscripciones: (a) la solicitud de admisión debe ser
remitida o entregada en la Escuela Diplomática o en la
Embajada de España en el país donde el aspirante resida o,
cuando proceda, desee realizar las pruebas de admisión, las
cuales tienen lugar en la misma Escuela, para los residentes en
España, y en cada una de las Embajadas de España en que se
hubieran presentado solicitudes, para los residentes en el
extranjero; (b) la convocatoria del curso se realiza a través de
las Embajadas de España en los países de las áreas citadas y
las Embajadas de esos países en Madrid.

782 Ministerio de Economía y Hacienda Instituto de Estudios Fiscales [IEF]
Avenida Cardenal Herrera Oria, 378
28035 Madrid
Tel: (34) (91) 339 8915

Fax: (34) (91) 339 8964
Web: http://www.ief.es
e-mail: direccion.general@ief.meh.es

📖 Estudios superiores en economía

Campos de estudios: administración, ciencias económicas
y comerciales, derecho, derecho internacional, economía,
finanzas.
Descripción:
(a) Maestría internacional en administración tributaria y
hacienda pública;
(b) Programa de estudios de posgrado en hacienda pública y
análisis económico;
(c) Cursos internacionales en el ámbito iberoamericano:
programa de formación para funcionarios iberoamericanos en
materia financiera y tributaria; cursos en España de carácter
periódico para funcionarios iberoamericanos (técnicas
aduaneras internacionales; instituciones y técnicas tributarias;
usos y aplicaciones del catastro; presupuestación, contabilidad
y control del gasto público); programa regional de
capacitación en áreas clave de las Administraciones
Tributarias de Iberoamérica;
(d) Programa internacional de doctorado en dirección y
administración pública (programa a distancia).
Asistencia financiera: existen becas del IEF para
formación del personal investigador, y becas de la Agencia
Española de Cooperación Internacional (AECI).

783 Ministerio de Educación y Ciencia, Subdirección General de Cooperación Internacional [MEC]
Paseo del Prado 28
28071 Madrid
Tel: (34) (91) 506-5600
Fax: (34) (91) 506-5704
Web: http://www.mec.es
e-mail: sgci.informacion@mec.es

🎓 Programa de Cooperación Educativa con Iberoamérica

Campos de estudios: educación, educación especial,
formación de docentes.
Materias de estudio: principalmente educación de adultos,
desarrollo curricular, supervisión educativa, nuevas
tecnologías de la información y comunicación, cualificación y
formación del profesorado, integración de alumnos con
necesidades especiales en centros ordinarios.
Se conceden: a funcionarios de los Ministerios de
Educación de los países iberoamericanos que ocupen puestos
de responsabilidad en las áreas de los cursos, con grado de
licenciado, con experiencia en el área. Existe proceso de
selección.
Importe: monto fijo para un mes, pasaje aéreo y seguro
médico.
Solicitudes: dirigirse al Programa de Cooperación
Educativa con Iberoamérica en la dirección del título o a las
Oficinas Técnicas de Cooperación en las representaciones
diplomáticas en el país de origen.

784 Secretaría de Estado de Turismo y Comercio
Paseo de la Castellana, 160
28071 Madrid
Tel: +34-90-244-6006
Fax: +34-91-457-8066
Web: http://www.mcx.es
e-mail: info@mityc.es

🎓 Becas de estudio

Campos de estudios: turismo, hotelería.
Descripción: Becas "Turismo de España" para realización
de:
(a) estudios de posgrado (25);
(b) cursos de especialización y reciclaje en materias turísticas
(25);
(c) estudios o prácticas de especialización en hostelería y
restauración (15);
(d) tesis doctorales (6);
(e) cursos para la obtención del título de Técnico de empresas
y actividades turísticas (20);
(f) estudios de posgrado o equivalente sobre materias

turísticas (25);
(g) prácticas profesionales de investigación turística (15);
(h) prácticas profesionales de especialización (25).
Materias de estudio: (a) economía, urbanismo, medio ambiente, productos turísticos, calidad, educación y tecnologías turísticas; (b) aspectos económicos, empresariales, comerciales, educativos o de medio ambiente relacionados con el turismo; (c) hostelería y restauración; (d) a (h) diversas.
Se conceden: según el caso, a españoles o extranjeros que posean titulaciones específicas y que conozcan ciertos idiomas.
Lugar: (a) a (c) universidades o centros españoles y extranjeros; (d) España; (e) universidades públicas y privadas de España; (f) universidades o centros españoles; (g) Secretaría de Estado de Comercio y Turismo o Instituto de Turismo de España, Madrid; (h) oficinas españolas de turismo y empresas en Alemania, Austria, Estados Unidos, Canadá, Francia, Reino Unido y Suiza.
Duración: (a) y (f) mínimo de 300 horas lectivas; (b) entre 2 semanas y 3 meses; (c) entre 3 y 24 meses; (d) 1 año (renovable 1 vez); (e) un curso académico (renovable 1 vez); (g) 1año (renovable por 6 meses más); (h) 1 año.
Importe: depende de si los estudios son el extranjero o en España; en algunos casos, se incluye bolsa de viaje.
Solicitudes: hasta 1 mes a partir de la publicación de la convocatoria en el Boletín Oficial del Estado.

785   Universidad Alfonso X el Sabio [UAX]
Avenida de la Universidad 1
Villanueva de la Cañada
28691 Madrid
Tel: (34) (1) 810 9192
Fax: (34) (1) 810 9781
Web: http://www.uax.es
e-mail: inter@uax.es

📖 **Programas universitarios**

Campos de estudios: todas las materias principales.
Descripción: Titulaciones en:
(a) Escuela politécnica superior: arquitectura; arquitectura técnica; ingeniería de caminos, canales y puertos; ingeniería industrial; ingeniería técnica en diseño industrial; ingeniería química; licenciatura en ciencias ambientales; ingeniería de telecomunicación; ingeniería técnica de telecomunicación especialidad de sonido e imagen; ingeniería en informática; ingeniería técnica en informática de sistemas;
(b) Facultad de estudios sociales: licenciatura en administración y dirección de empresas; diplomatura en ciencias empresariales; licenciatura en ciencias de la actividad física y del deporte; licenciatura en derecho; diplomatura en turismo;
(c) Facultad de ciencias de la salud: licenciatura en odontología; diplomatura en enfermería; en fisioterapia; en nutrición humana y dietética, en podología, en terapia ocupacional; master en endodoncia; licenciatura en farmacia, en veterinaria;
(d) Faultad de lenguas aplicadas: licenciatura en traducción e interpretación;
(e) Dobles titulaciones: licenciatura en administración y dirección de empresas + diplomatura en turismo; ingeniería química + licenciatura en ciencias ambientales.
Asistencia financiera: becas y ayudas del Estado español, becas de las Comunidades Autónomas, ayudas de la Unión Europea, ayudas de la Universidad Alfonso X el Sabio.
Inscripciones: en todos los casos, solicitar información a la Oficina de Relaciones Internacionales o consultar el sitio Web.

786   Universidad Antonio de Nebrija
Campus de Dehesa de la Villa
Pirineos 55
28040 Madrid
Tel: (34) (1) 311 6602
Fax: (34) (1) 311 6613
Web: http://www.nebrija.com
e-mail: internacional@nebrija.es

📖 **Programas universitarios**

Campos de estudios: todas las materias principales, ciencias económicas y comerciales, comunicación, derecho, español, formación de docentes, informática, ingeniería, turismo, hotelería.

Descripción:
(a) Carreras universitarias: lenguas aplicadas, turismo, periodismo, publicidad, comunicación audiovisual, empresariales, derecho, ingeniería informática, ingeniería industrial;
(b) Programas master: dirección de empresas, derecho empresarial, gestión de la innovación, enseñanza de español como lengua extranjera;
(c) Doctorados: lingüística aplicada, turismo, dirección internacional de empresas;
(d) Formación de profesores de español lengua extranjera;
(e) Programas internacionales: lengua y cultura españolas, Spanish language and culture (English); estudios hispánicos; negocios (Empresariales); español + International Business; ciencias de la comunicación; comunicación audiovisual; relaciones internacionales; ingeniería; cursos de verano de español (lengua y cultura españolas, literatura española, español y gestión de recursos turísticos, español y negocios).
Asistencia financiera: becas del Ministerio de Educación y Cultura; de la Fundación Carolina; de la Comunidad de Madrid y otras Comunidades, de la Agencia Española de Cooperación Internacional, de la Fundación Nebrijas.
Inscripciones: por mayores informaciones, dirigirse a Informaciên Académica o consultar el sitio web.

787   Universidad Autónoma de Barcelona Escuela de Idiomas Modernos [UAB]
San Antoni María Claret 171
08041 Barcelona
Tel: (34) (3) 433 50 60
Fax: (33) (3) 433 50 66
Web: http://uab-barcelona.com
e-mail: info@uab-barcelona.com

📖 **Cursos de español**

Campos de estudios: español, idiomas.
Descripción: Cursos especiales de español para intereses específicos y estudios académicos:
(a) Cursos temáticos;
(b) Cursos a medida;
(c) Curso de reparación para el D.E.L.E;
(d) Preparación de Diploma de Español de los Negocios;
(e) Cursos de lengua para estudios universitarios;
(f) Cursos de lengua para estudios específicos en la UAB;
(g) Cursos intensivos de idiomas.
Materias de estudio: (a) cultura española (arquitectura; cultura, tradiciones y fiestas, baile; cine; diseño; historia del arte; música, fotografía); (b) para estudiantes: español + cursos temáticos; (c) español como lengua extranjera; (e) español y catalán, preparación lingüística para pruebas de acceso a la universidad; (f) turismo, gestión hotelera, master y posgrados en ciencias sociales y humanidades, arte y diseño; (g) español, catalán, inglés, francés y alemán.

788   Universidad Autónoma de Barcelona Instituto de Análisis Económico [UAB]
Facultad de Ciencias Económicas y Empresariales
08193 Bellaterra
Tel: (34) (3) 581 1111
Fax: (34) (3) 581 2000
Web: http://www.uab.es
e-mail: informacio@uab.es

📖 **Doctorado "International doctorate in economic analysis (IDEA)"**

Campos de estudios: economía.
Se destina(n): a licenciados preferentemente en economía o matemáticas, con buen conocimiento del inglés hablado y escrito. Existe selección por expediente académico y se exigen 3 cartas de recomendación.
Duración: 2 años académicos de cursos más 2 o 3 años para preparación de tesis doctoral.
Idioma: los cursos se dictan en inglés.

789   Universidad Autónoma de Madrid Escuela de Periodismo UAM-El País [UAM]
Miguel Yuste 40
28037 Madrid
Tel: (34) (1) 337 7760
Fax: (34) (1) 337 8348
Web: http://www.uam.es

📖 **Master en periodismo UAM-El País**

Campos de estudios: comunicación, documentación, medios audio-visuales, periodismo.
Se destina(n): a licenciados o técnicos superiores que superen prueba de selección (cuestionarios de actualidad, redacción periodística, entrevista personal e idiomas); se valorarán conocimientos de inglés, francés, y alemán.
Duración: 1 año: 2 cuatrimestres lectivos más un período de prácticas remuneradas en algún medio nacional o extranjero (comienza en enero).
Asistencia financiera: becas totales y créditos bancarios por el importe de la matrícula; las becas se otorgan a los 7 mejores calificados en las pruebas de selección.
Inscripciones: hasta principios de octubre.

790   Universidad Autónoma de Madrid Facultad de Ciencias Económicas y Empresariales Centro Internacional Carlos V [UAM]
Cantoblanco
28049 Madrid
Tel: (34) (1) 397 3916
Fax: (34) (1) 397 3918
Web: http://www.uam.es/carlosv
e-mail: centro.carlosv@uam.es

📖 **Programas Master**

Campos de estudios: administración de empresas, ciencias económicas y comerciales, contabilidad, derecho, derecho internacional, economía, estudios internacionales, finanzas, gestión, marketing.
Programas:
(a) Master en marketing;
(b) Master en mercados financieros;
(c) Master en economía y dirección internacional de la empresa;
(d) Master en administración y dirección de fundaciones y entidades no lucrativas.
Se destina(n): a licenciados, en el caso de (c) con avanzados conocimientos de inglés.
Duración: 1 año académico (comienzos en septiembre u octubre).
Asistencia financiera: posibilidad de becas.
Inscripciones: hasta septiembre; dirigirse a la Secretaría del Centro.

791   Universidad Autónoma de Madrid Facultad de Ciencias Económicas y Empresariales [UAM]
Cantoblanco
28049 Madrid
Tel: 3975000

📖 **Programas universitarios**

Campos de estudios: administración de empresas, ciencias económicas y comerciales, ciencias sociales, contabilidad, finanzas, marketing.
Descripción:
(a) Licenciaturas en economía, en administración y dirección de empresas;
(b) Master en economía de los servicios;
(c) Doctorados en: economía teórica; economía aplicada; modelización económica; integración y desarrollo económico: comunidades europeas; economía y hacienda pública, contabilidad y organización de empresas;

financiación e investigación comercial; economía financiera: banca y bolsa; sociología, ciencia política y antropología social.
Duración: (b) 15 meses; (c) máximo 5 años.
Asistencia financiera: becas para el doctorado en modelización económica.
Inscripciones: (b) dirigirse a la Secretaría del Departamento de Análisis económico, teoría económica e historia económica, en la dirección que figura en el título.

792   Universidad Autónoma de Madrid Facultad de Derecho Cátedra "Jean Jonnet" de Instituciones de Derecho Comunitario [UAM]
Cantoblanco
28049 Madrid
Tel: (34) (1) 397 8230
Fax: (34) (1) 397 8217
Web: http://www.uam.es

📖 **Master en derecho comunitario europeo**

Campos de estudios: derecho, derecho internacional, estudios europeos.
Se destina(n): a licenciados en derecho con conocimientos de inglés o francés.
Duración: 9 meses (comienza a fin de octubre).
Asistencia financiera: existen ayudas parciales.
Inscripciones: hasta fin de septiembre, dirigirse a la Oficina del Master en derecho comunitario.

793   Universidad Autónoma de Madrid Facultad de Filosofía y Letras [UAM]
Cantoblanco
28049 Madrid
Tel: (34) (1) 397 4297
Fax: (34) (1) 397 3930
Web: http://www.uam.es

📖 **Programas universitarios**

Campos de estudios: filología, filosofía, geografía, historia, historia del arte, lingüística.
Descripción:
(a) Licenciaturas en: filología árabe, clásica, francesa, hispánica, inglesa; filosofía; geografía; historia; historia del arte;
(b) Doctorados en las mismas áreas.
Inscripciones: dirigirse a la Secretaría de la Facultad.

794   Universidad Autónoma de Madrid Facultad de Medicina Departamento de Pediatría Fundación Faustino Obergozo [UAM]
Avenida Menéndez Pelayo 65
28009 Madrid
Tel: (34) (1) 504 2530
Web: http://www.uam.es

📖 **Master en nutrición clínica**

Campos de estudios: alimentación, bioquímica, dietético, fisiología, higiene y salud, nutrición.
Se destina(n): a licenciados en medicina, farmacia o biología.
Duración: de enero a diciembre.
Inscripciones: hasta el 15 de diciembre; dirigirse a la Secretaría del Departamento de Pediatría de la UAM, Hospital del Niño Jesús, en la dirección que figura en el título.

795 Universidad Autónoma de Madrid Facultad de Psicología [UAM]
Cantoblanco
28049 Madrid
Tel: (34) (1) 532 6952
Fax: (34) (1) 532 6952
Web: http://www.uam.es

 Programas universitarios
Campos de estudios: educación especial, educación física, psicología, sociología, trabajo social.
Programas:
(a) Curso en valoración de discapacidades;
(b) Master en gerontología social;
(c) Master en psicología del deporte.
Se destina(n): (a) a licenciados en psicología y medicina; (b) a licenciados; (c) a licenciados en psicología, educación física.
Duración: (a) y (b) febrero-octubre y octubre-junio; (c) 2 años (comienzos en enero o febrero).
Inscripciones: dirigirse a la Secretaría del Master correspondiente.

796 Universidad Autónoma de Madrid Instituto de Ciencias de la Educación [UAM]
Cantoblanco
28049 Madrid
Tel: (34) (1) 397 4397
Web: http://www.uam.es

 Curso de Formación inicial de profesores de enseñanza secundaria (FIPS)
Campos de estudios: educación, formación profesional.
Se destina(n): a licenciados de cualquier país que deseen capacitarse para el ejercicio como Profesor de Enseñanza Secundaria en España.
Se dicta(n): en la UAM el ciclo teórico, en centros de enseñanza secundaria el ciclo práctico.
Duración: de octubre a mayo (470 horas).

797 Universidad Autónoma de Madrid Instituto Universitario de Administración de Empresas (IADE) [UAM]
Cantoblanco
28049 Madrid
Tel: (34) (1) 397 3983
Web: http://www.uam.es

 Programas universitarios
Campos de estudios: administración de empresas, ciencias económicas y comerciales, ciencias sociales, contabilidad, derecho, economía, economía política, finanzas, gestión, marketing.
Descripción:
(a) Master en ciencia, tecnología y sociedad;
(b) Master en auditoría contable, económica y financiera;
(c) Master en administración de empresas (MBA);
(d) Master de dirección y gestión bancaria;
(e) Master de desarrollo de directivos;
(f) Master en administración de empresas de aviación;
(g) Doctorados en economía financiera, banca y bolsa, economía y dirección estratégica.
Se destina(n): (a) a (c) a titulados superiores universitarios; (d) y (e) a licenciados con experiencia de 3 años como mínimo en puestos directivos o no licenciados con 5 años de experiencia,.
Duración: (a) y (e) 1 año; (b) 9 meses; (c) y (d) 18 meses; (f) 480 horas; (g) 2 años.
Inscripciones: (a) a (c) hasta el 15 de junio; (d) hasta el 15 de septiembre; (e) en noviembre-diciembre.

798 Universidad Autónoma de Madrid Servicio de Cartografía [UAM]
Cantoblanco
28049 Madrid
Tel: (34) (1) 397 4580
Web: http://www.uam.es

 Curso de cartografía catastral informatizada
Campos de estudios: geodesia, geografía, informática.
Se destina(n): a licenciados, ingenieros, diplomados.
Duración: 2 semanas.
Asistencia financiera: posibilidad de becas de matrícula.
Inscripciones: en el Servicio de Cartografía.

799 Universidad Autónoma de Madrid Servicio de Oncología Médica Hospital La Paz [UAM]
Paseo de la Castellana s/n
28049 Madrid
Tel: (34) (1) 729 0364
Web: http://www.uam.es

 Master en cuidados paliativos y tratamiento de soporte del enfermo neoplásico
Campos de estudios: cancerología, medicina.
Diplomas requeridos: a licenciados en medicina y psicología.
Duración: de principios de enero a principios de mayo.
Inscripciones: hasta el 31 de diciembre.

800 Universidad Autónoma de Madrid [UAM]
Ctra. Colmenar Vieja, km. 5
28040 Cantoblanco, Madrid
Tel: (34) (1) 397 5000
Web: http://www.uam.es
e-mail: informacion.general@uam.es

 Programas universitarios
Campos de estudios: todas las materias principales.
Descripción: Programas de estudio en sus diversas facultades, escuelas superiores politécnicas, escuelas universitarias en: ingeniería informática; ingeniería de telecomunicación; informática-matemáticas; ciencias; derecho; filosofía y letras; psicología; medicina; ciencias económicas y empresariales; formación de profesorado y educación; educación infantil, educación especial; lengua extranjera; audición y lenguaje; educación musical; educación social; terapia ocupacional; psicopedagogía, enfermería.
Asistencia financiera: existen numerosos programas de intercambio, programas de ayuda y de apoyo, becas de distintas instituciones.
Inscripciones: por mayores informaciones para estudiantes extranjeros, dirigirse a la Oficina de Relaciones Internacionales, ori.uam@uam.es.

801 Universidad Camilo José Cela [UCJC]
Castillo de Alarcón 49
28692 Villafranca del Castilllo, Madrid
Tel: (34) (1) 815 3131
Fax: (34) (1) 815 3130
Web: http://www.ucjc.edu
e-mail: ucjc@ucjc.edu

 Programas universitarios
Campos de estudios: todas las materias principales.
Descripción:
(a) Titulaciones oficiales: arquitectura superior, arquitectura técnica; ingeniería; informática; periodismo; comunicación audiovisual; publicidad y relaciones públicas; psicología; psicopedagogía; maestro en educación especial; maestro en educación física; maestro en educación infantil;
(b) Titulaciones propias: especialista en psicodiagnóstico y tratamiento en atención temprana; master en intervención y orientación psicopedagógica (alta capacidad y superdotación); experto en empleo con apoyo; experto en infografía, animación 3D y aplicaciones multimedia; especialista en bibliotecas; especialista universitario en enseñanza de las

ciencias experimentales (a distancia); master en medio ambiente marino y lucha contra la contaminación marina (presencial y a distancia); título superior en paisajismo; en gestión aeronáutica-piloto de transporte de línea aérea; master internacional en administración y dirección de empresas; master en seguridad integral; curso superior sobre nuevas tecnologías y el conocimiento en las empresas; curso superior en técnicas y aplicaciones para la gestión de recursos humanos; master en marina deportiva; master en periodismo digital, económico y financiero.
Se destina(n): a diplomados y licenciados.
Duración: 1 año académico (entre 6 y 9 meses).
Asistencia financiera: existen becas de la Universidad y de otras instituciones. La universidad participa en varios programas de cooperación, intercambio y movilidad.
Inscripciones: hasta octubre.

802 Universidad Complutense de Madrid
Facultad de Ciencias de la Información [UCM]
Avenida Complutense s/n
28040 Madrid
Tel: (34) (1) 394 2104
Fax: (34) (1) 394 2055
Web: http://www.ucm.es

📖 Programas universitarios
Campos de estudios: comunicación, documentación, edición, energía, periodismo, publicidad.
Descripción:
(a) Titulaciones (master/magister, especialista, experto) en áreas de periodismo y publicidad y relaciones públicas;
(a) Doctorados en las mismas áreas.
Inscripciones: dirigirse al Servicio de Información de la UCM.

803 Universidad Complutense de Madrid
Facultad de Educación
Centro de Formación del Profesorado [UCM]
Juan XXIII s/n
28040 Madrid
Tel: (34) (1) 394 6262
Fax: (34) (1) 394 6263
Web: http://www.ucm.es/info/educacio

📖 Programas universitarios
Campos de estudios: educación, educación de la primera infancia, educación especial, educación física, formación profesional.
Descripción:
(a) Titulaciones: licenciado en pedagogía, en psicopedagogía; diplomado en educación social; maestro-especialista de educación infantil, de educación primaria, de lengua extranjera, de educación física, de educación musical, de educación especial, de audición y lenguaje;
(b) Títulos propios: master en educación y prevención en Sida; master en intervención temprana; experto en educación artística; experto en intervención psicoeducativa de menores en desamparo y conflicto social; especialista de diseño de proyectos pedagógicos para adolescentes y jóvenes.
Duración: (a) y (b) 3 años; (c) y (d) 5 años; los comienzos son en octubre.
Asistencia financiera: (a) y (b) hay posibilidad de becas del Ministerio de Educación y Ciencia.
Inscripciones: preinscripción entre el 15 de junio y el 15 de julio, inscripción definitiva en septiembre; dirigirse al Vicerrectorado de Alumnos, Avenida Complutense s/n, Ciudad Universitaria, 28040 Madrid.

804 Universidad Complutense de Madrid
Facultad de Filología [UCM]
Ciudad Universitaria
28040 Madrid
Tel: (34) (1) 394 5336
Fax: (34) (1) 394 5298
Web: http://www.ucm.es

📖 Cursos para extranjeros
Campos de estudios: español, idiomas, literatura y civilización, programas de verano.
Descripción:
(a) Estudios hispánicos;
(b) Cursos para extranjeros;
(c) Cursos de idiomas.
Se destina(n): (a) en general, a estudiantes de español, profesores, traductores e intérpretes; (b) y (c) a quienes tengan calificaciones de acceso a la Universidad.
Duración: (a) 1 año (de octubre a junio); (b) 3 meses en otoño y primavera, 1 mes en verano; (c) 7 meses (noviembre-mayo).
Inscripciones: hasta 3 días antes de la fecha de cada curso, en la Secretaría de los Cursos para Extranjeros.

805 Universidad de Alcalá de Henares
Centro de Estudios Europeos [UAH]
Plaza de San Diego s/n
28801 Alcalá de Henares
Tel: +34-91-885-40-00
Fax: +34-90-201-0555
Web: http://www.uah.es
e-mail: becas200.cervantes@uah.es

📖 Master en Unión Europea
Campos de estudios: derecho internacional, economía, estudios europeos, estudios internacionales, relaciones internacionales.
Duración: 2 años (inicio en octubre).
Asistencia financiera: becas parciales.
Inscripciones: hasta principios de julio.

🏖 Programa de becas "Miguel de Cervantes" para estudios de postgrado
Becas: 200 becas destinadas a profesores y egresados de Latinoamérica que deseen realizar estudios de postgrado (doctorado y/o máster) en la Universidad de Alcalá.
Descripción: becas predoctorales, cursos de postgrado.
Nacionalidad: a ciudadanos de Argentina, Bolivia, Brasil, Chile, Colombia, Costa Rica, Cuba, Guatemala, México, Paraguay, Perú, Puerto Rico, Uruguay, Venezuela.
Diplomas requeridos: profesores y egresados (con título de licenciado o nivel académico equivalente).
Duración: Las becas de doctorado se conceden para el primer curso de programa de doctorado, prorrogable al segundo curso. Las becas de máster abarcan el período correspondiente a la duración del mismo.
Importe: Las becas incluyen la exención de las tasas académicas, una asignación mensual de 600 euros, y 1000 euros para un viaje de ida y vuelta al país de origen, así como un seguro asanitario no farmacéutico. La Universidad de Alcalá gestionará, en la medida de las disponibilidades, el acceso a residencias universitarias.
Solicitudes: los que deseen información adicional pueden dirigirse por correo electrónico al Servicio de Gestión de la Investigación de la Universidad de Alcalá. Pueden dirigirse también a los Vicerrectorados de Investigación, de Relaciones Internacionales o de Postgrado.

806 Universidad de Alcalá de Henares
Instituto Universitario de Estudios Norteamericanos [UAH]
Colegio Trinitarios
Trinidad 1
28801 Alcalá de Henares
Tel: (34) (1) 885 5252
Fax: (34) (1) 885 5548
Web: http://www.uah.es
e-mail: info.iuen@uah.es

📖 Programas universitarios
Campos de estudios: español, estudios americanos, estudios culturales, idiomas, literatura y civilización, programas de verano.

Descripción:
(a) Titulaciones: master en estudios norteamericanos, especialista en primer grado en lengua y civilización para profesores hispanos de Norteamérica, especialización de segundo grado en negocios con Estados Unidos;
(b) Cursos: programa de estudios hispánicos.
Duración: (a) 1 mes (en julio); (b) 2 años (comienzos en octubre y febrero); (c) semestres de otoño y primavera y cursos de verano.
Asistencia financiera: diversas becas para estudios en la Bowling Green State University, The University of Alabama, University of Central Arkansas.
Inscripciones: dirigirse a la Secretaría de los Cursos.

807 Universidad de Alicante Sociedad de Relaciones Internacionales [UA]

Campus San Vicente
Apartado 99
3080 Alicante
Tel: (34) (6) 590 3793
Fax: (34) (6) 590 37 94
Web: http://www.sri.ua.es
e-mail: sri@sri.ua.es

  Cursos de español

Campos de estudios: español, programas de verano.
Programas:
(a) Cursos de lengua y cultura para extranjeros;
(b) Curso para profesores de español lengua extranjera.
Se destina(n): (a) a extranjeros mayores de 18 años; (b) a licenciados en cualquier filología o diplomados de magisterio; se exige que tengan el español como lengua materna, o que la utilicen con la competencia de un nativo.
Duración: (a) 1 mes (o 3 si se hacen 3 módulos); hay cursos de verano en julio y en agosto; (b) febrero-abril (60 horas lectivas más 10 horas de prácticas).
Costo(s): (a) como ejemplo, agosto 2003, curso de lengua 3 horas/día: 535 euros; (b) 325 euros.
Inscripciones: dirigirse al Secretariado de Cursos Internacionales: (a) 20 días antes del comienzo del curso; (b) hasta mediados de enero.

808 Universidad de Barcelona Departamento de Psiquiatría y Psicobiología Clínica [UB]

Calle Baldiri Reixac s/n Torre A 4°piso
08028 Barcelona
Tel: (34) (3) 333 7402
Fax: (34) (3) 334 3456
Web: http://www.ub.es

  Master en drogodependencias

Campos de estudios: medicina, medicina preventiva, psicología, sociología.
Descripción: se imparten conocimientos básicos multidisciplinarios y una capacitación práctica en materia de prevención, educación sanitaria, psicosociología, recursos comunitarios y planes de intervención.
Se destina(n): a doctores, licenciados y diplomados universitarios de cualquier nacionalidad.
Duración: 2 años (comienza en octubre).
Asistencia financiera: la División de Ciencias de la Salud y la Fundación de Ayuda contra la Drogadicción ofrecen ayudas.
Inscripciones: hasta el 30 de septiembre.

809 Universidad de Barcelona Universidad de las Islas Baleares Estudio General Luliano de Mallorca [UB]

Calle San Roque 4
07001 Palma de Mallorca
Tel: (34) (7) 171 1988
Fax: (34) (7) 171 1988
Web: http://www.ub.es

  Programas universitarios

Campos de estudios: español, idiomas, programas de verano.
Programas:
(a) Curso de español para extranjeros;
(b) Curso de filología hispànica;
(c) Curso de filología catalana.
Se destina(n): (a) a extranjeros mayores de 18 años.
Duración: (a) 3 semanas en julio.
Inscripciones: (a) hasta el 30 de junio; dirigirse al Secretario de los Cursos de Verano de la Cátedra Ramón Llull.

810 Universidad de Barcelona [UB]

Gran Via 585
8071 Barcelona
Tel: (34) (3) 403 5519
Fax: (34) (3) 403 5433
Web: http://www.ub.es/ieh/hisp.htm
e-mail: est-hsipa@d1.ub.es

  Programas universitarios

Campos de estudios: español, estudios culturales, programas de verano.
Programas:
(a) Diploma de Estudios Hispánicos;
(b) Cursos de lengua y cultura españolas;
(c) Cursos de verano;
(d) Cursos para estudiantes Socrates/Erasmus/Tempus.
Duración: (a) anual; (b) anual, cuatrimestral o intensivo.
Inscripciones: por más información, dirigirse a Estudios Hispánicos, en la dirección del título.

811 Universidad de Cádiz Vicerrectorado de Extensión Universitaria [UCA]

José Paredes Monge 1
11002 Cádiz
Tel: (34) (5) 622 0802
Fax: (34) (5) 622 0877
Web: http://www.uca.es

  Programas de cursos

Campos de estudios: español, idiomas, programas de verano.
Programas: (a) Cursos de español para extranjeros;
(b) Cursos de metodología de enseñanza del español.
Se destina(n): (a) a alumnos de otras universidades extranjeras; (b) a profesores de español en el extranjero.
Duración: (a) semestre de primavera: de enero a mayo; cursos de verano: 2 semanas, 1 mes o trimestre de junio a agosto.
Inscripciones: (a) hasta la primera semana de julio.

812 Universidad de Cádiz Vicerrectorado de Ordenación Académica y Planes de Estudio [UCA]

C/Ancha 16 3ª Planta
11001 Cádiz
Tel: (34) (5) 601 5030
Fax: (34) (5) 6015099
Web: http://www2.uca.es
e-mail: vicerrec.ordenacion@uca.es

  Programas universitarios

Campos de estudios: todas las materias principales.
Descripción:
(a) Programas master, expertos y formación continua en sus Facultades o Escuelas en áreas de ciencias; ciencias del mar y ambientales; ciencias de la educación; ciencias económicas y empresariales; ciencias del trabajo; ciencias náuticas; derecho; filosofía y letras; medicina; enfermería y fisioterapia; ingeniería técnica naval; ingeniería; medicina de la educación física y deporte, otras;
(b) Doctorados en ciencias de la salud, humanidades, ciencias sociales y jurídicas, ciencias experimentales, enseñanzas técnicas.
Asistencia financiera: diversos programas de cooperación e intercambio; becas y ayudas (por ejemplo: postdoctorales Ministerio de Educación, Cultura y Deporte/Fulbright; de la

Secretaría de Estado de Comercio y de Turismo; predoctorales de Csic-Fundación Bancaja; becas AECI, otras). Solicitar información a Relaciones Internacionales, en la dirección del título, o a internacional@uca.es.

813　Universidad de Cantabria Centro de Idiomas (CIUC)

Avenida de los Castros s/n
39005 Santander
Tel: (34) (4) 220 1313
Fax: (34) (4) 220 1316
Web: http://www.unican.es

📖 **Cursos de lengua y cultura española para extranjeros**

Campos de estudios: español, estudios culturales, programas de verano.
Duración: 1 mes en octubre, febrero o abril; o en verano, de junio a septiembre.
Inscripciones: todo el año.

814　Universidad de Cantabria Departamento de Filología

Avenida de los Castros s/n
39005 Santander
Tel: (34) (4) 220 1140
Fax: (34) (4) 220 1260
Web: http://www.unican.es
e-mail: ciuc@gestion.unican.es

🐦 **Becas para graduados en filología**

Campos de estudios: español, filología.
Descripción: Perfeccionamiento de la lengua española de los candidatos, colaboración en clases prácticas de lenguas inglesa/francesa impartidas en la Universidad, bajo el control y orientación de los profesores responsables; colaboración, en algunos casos, en tareas universitarias de investigación relacionadas con la filología. Se otorgan 4 becas de inglés y 1 beca de francés.
Se conceden: a graduados universitarios de idioma nativo francés o inglés y que hayan seguido a lo largo de la carrera universitaria estudios de español. Se exigen cartas de presentación o aval de uno o más profesores de la universidad en la que se han cursado los estudios.
Duración: 1 año académico (renovable una vez).
Importe: monto fijo por año académico y bolsa de viaje.
Solicitudes: hasta fin de junio.

815　Universidad de Deusto Facultad de Ciencias Económicas y Empresariales Universidad Comercial de Deusto [UDD]

Apartado 20044
48080 Bilbao
Tel: (34) (1) 413 9000
Fax: (34) (1) 445 7381
Web: http://www.unicomer.deusto.es
e-mail: secretaria@unicomer.deusto.es

📖 **Programas universitarios**

Campos de estudios: administración de empresas, ciencias económicas y comerciales, comercio, contabilidad, derecho, economía, finanzas, gestión, marketing, negocio.
Programas:
(a) Licenciatura en administración y dirección de empresas;
(b) Postgrados: European Management Programme-MBA; master en gestión avanzada; master en finanzas; master en dirección de empresas; experto en recursos humanos; master/experto en auditoría de cuenta;
(c) Doctorado en administración y dirección de empresas (Programa gestión avanzada).
Asistencia financiera: existen becas de la Universidad, de organismos oficiales y otras becas.

816　Universidad de Deusto Facultad de Derecho Escuela de Práctica Jurídica [UDD]

Avenida de las Universidades 24
48007 Bilbao
Tel: (34) (1) 413 9293
Fax: (34) (1) 413 9099
Web: http://www.deusto.es

📖 **Cursos para la obtención del diploma de la EPJ**

Campos de estudios: derecho.
Descripción: se complementan con materias optativas en el Colegio de Abogados.
Se destina(n): a licenciados en derecho.
Duración: 2 años (comienzan en octubre).
Inscripciones: de fin de septiembre hasta principios de octubre.

817　Universidad de Deusto Facultad de Derecho [UDD]

Avenida de las Universidades 24
48007 Bilbao
Tel: (34) (4) 413 9000
Fax: (34) (4) 445 7557
Web: http://www.deusto.es

📖 **Programas Master**

Campos de estudios: derecho.
Programas:
(a) Master/Experto en gestión de empresas marítimo portuarias;
(b) Master en abogacía y práctica jurídica;
(c) Master en asesoría fiscal;
(d) Master en asesoría jurídica de empresas.
Inscripciones: dirigirse a la Secretaría General.

818　Universidad de Deusto Instituto Deusto de Drogodependencias [UDD]

Avenida de las Universidades 24
48007 Bilbao
Tel: (34) (4) 413 9083
Fax: (34) (4) 413 9083
Web: http://www.deusto.com

📖 **Programas universitarios**

Campos de estudios: ciencias sociales, derecho, farmacia y farmacología, medicina, psicología.
Descripción:
(a) Título de Master en Drogodependencias (curso teórico-práctico; áreas teóricas: farmacología, prevención, educación y reinserción, medicina, tratamiento, psicopatología, sociología, legalidad);
(b) Diploma de Experto en Drogodependencias (conocimientos básicos multidisciplinares y una capacitación práctica en materia de prevención, educación sanitaria, psicosociología, recursos comunitarios y planes de intervención);
(c) Formación universitaria en drogodependencia; cursos y seminarios en temas relacionados a la toxicomanía.
Se destina(n): (a) a licenciados en medicina, psicología, pedagogía, sociología, derecho o farmacia; (b) a diplomados universitarios o equivalentes, educadores especializados, profesores, trabajadores sociales, criminólogos, etc.; para (a) y (b) existe proceso de selección y es aconsejable saber inglés; (c) a profesionales o personas interesadas en el tema.
Duración: (a) 2 años; (b) 1 año (comienza en octubre); (c) 1 a 4 días.
Asistencia financiera: (a) y (b) concedida por la Secretaría General de Drogodependencia del Gobierno Vasco y Fundación de Ayuda contra la Drogadicción; (c) pueden solicitarse becas parciales o totales.
Inscripciones: (a) y (b) del 15 al 30 de septiembre, en la Secretaría General de la Universidad de Deusto; (c) hasta una semana antes del inicio del curso.

819 Universidad de Deusto
Instituto Interdisciplinar
de Estudios del Ocio [UDD]
Avenida de las Universidades 24
Apartado 1
48080 Bilbao
Tel: (34) (4) 413 9075
Fax: (34) (4) 446 7909
Web: http://www.deusto.es

 📖 **Programas universitarios**

Campos de estudios: gestión, recreología y tiempo libre,
turismo, hotelería.
Descripción:
(a) Programa de posgrado (Master Degree) destinado al
estudio del ocio en los países de la Comunidad Económica
Europea (Programme in European Leisure Studies, PELS),
auspiciado por ERASMUS;
(b) Experto o master en gestión de ocio.
Se destina(n): (a) y (b) a licenciados o diplomados
universitarios, cuya selección se efectuará en base al
expediente académico, experiencia profesional, formación
complementaria y nivel acreditado de inglés en el caso de (a).
Duración: (a) 1 año; (b) 2 años.
Asistencia financiera: (a) existe la posibilidad de obtener
ayudas de la Comunidad Económica Europea (Programa
Erasmus).
Inscripciones: (a) hasta mayo; a Estudios de Ocio,
Programa PELS, en la dirección que figura en el título; (b) de
junio a septiembre.

820 Universidad de Granada
Centro de Lenguas Modernas
[UDG]
Palacio de Santa Cruz
Placeta del Hospicio Viejo s/n
18071 Granada
Tel: (34) (5) 822 0790
Fax: (34) (5) 822 0844
Web: http://www.ugr.es/~clm

 📖 **Programa de cursos**

Campos de estudios: español, idiomas, literatura y
civilización, programas de verano.
Descripción:
(a) Lengua y cultura españolas: cursos intensivos, estudios
hispánicos, estudios especifcos;
(b) Metodología del español como lengua extranjera;
(c) Cursos de lenguas extranjeras: inglés, francés, italiano,
japonés, árabe, griego, ruso, sueco, neerlandés.
Se destina(n): (a) a extranjeros; (b) a profesores o
licenciados.
Duración: (a) cursos cuatrimestrales, mensuales, de
verano; (b) 1 semana en junio; (c) 3 trimestres para las tres
primeras lenguas.
Inscripciones: (a) hasta 1 mes antes del comienzo del
curso; (b) hasta 2 días antes de la prueba de nivel de idioma.

821 Universidad de Huelva
Oficina de Relaciones
Internacionales
Campus de El Carmen
Edificio Marie Curie
21071 Huelva
Tel: (34) (5) 901 9494
Fax: (34) (5) 901 9359
Web: http://www.uhu.es
e-mail: drinter@uhu.es

 📖 **Programas universitarios**

Campos de estudios: todas las materias principales,
idiomas.
Descripción:
(a) Titulaciones oficiales y propias: ingeniería química, de
gestión, de sistemas, agrícola, de minas, forestal, industrial;
licenciado en geología, en ciencias ambientales, en
humanidades, en historia, en filología inglesa, en derecho, en
administración y dirección de empresas, en psicopedagogía,
en ciencias del trabajo; diplomado en ciencias empresariales,
en turismo, en educación social, en relaciones laborales, en
trabajo social, en enfermería; maestro;

(b) Posgrados: doctorados; C.A.P; experto universitario en
técnicas y medios audiovisuales, radio, vídeo, televisión y
multimedia; master en implantación de sistemas de gestión
medioambiental y de calidad; master en prevención de riesgos
laborales; master en prevención de riesgos laborales;
(c) Servicio de lenguas modernas (inglés, francés y alemán).
Asistencia financiera: existen becas de la Universidad y
del Gobierno; solicitar información a Negociado de Becas,
Dr. Cantero Cuadrado 6, 21071 Huelva.

822 Universidad de La Coruña
[UDLC]
Casa del Francés
Campus de la Zapateira
15071 La Coruña
Tel: (34) (8) 116 7000
Fax: (34) (8) 116 7075
Web: http://www.udc.es/uep

 📖 **Programas universitarios**

Campos de estudios: todas las materias principales.
Descripción:
(a) Titulaciones propias (diplomado, licenciado, ingeniero,
arquitecto, etc.) en todas las áreas principales;
(b) Masters en: administración financiera y tributaria, alto
rendimiento deportivo, dirección y administración de
empresas (MBA), marketing y dirección comercial (MBC),
medios de comunicación, ciencia y tecnología ambiental,
medicina de urgencias, restauración arquitectónica, gestión
sanitaria, alto rendimiento deportivo;
(c) Cursos de posgrado: dirección y gestión de cooperativas y
pequeñas y medianas empresas, gestión sanitaria, especialista
en enfermería comunitaria, fisioterapia manipulativa articular,
preparación física y técnico superior deportivo,
comunicaciones y sistemas de tiempo real, estudios teatrales
(enseñanza del teatro y la dramatización, teoría, historia,
didáctica), actividad física y salud, diseño integrado por
computador en ingeniería y urbanismo;
(d) Cursos de especialización: gestión de empresas
agroalimentarias, Unión Europea, derecho gallego, derecho
judicial, diseño de interiores, operadores de instalaciones
radiactivas, cuidados de enfermería al paciente crítico,
factores de riesgo vascular, enseñanza de la comunicación
escrita en inglés, nuevas tendencias audiovisuales, gestión de
zonas húmedas, enfermería de empresa.
Inscripciones: por mayor información, dirigirse al
Servicio de Asesoramiento y Promoción del Estudiante, en la
dirección que figura en el título, o a Programas de Posgrado,
Vicerrectorado de Extensión Universitaria, Calle Maestranza
s/n, 15071 La Coruña.

823 Universidad de La Rioja [UR]
Avenida de la Paz 93
26006 Logroño
Tel: (34) (4) 129 9100
Fax: (34) (4) 129 9208
Web: http://www.unirioja.es
e-mail: informacion@admin.unirioja.es

 📖 **Programas universitarios**

Campos de estudios: todas las materias principales.
Descripción:
(a) Titulaciones en áreas de: agricultura y alimentación;
ciencias humanas y sociales; derecho; economía y empresa;
expresión artística; filologías hispánica y clásicas; filologías
modernas; ingeniería eléctrica; ingeniería mecánica;
matemáticas y computación; química; ciencias sociales de
trabajo;
(b) Posgrados presenciales: experto en gestión de empresas;
master en salud y función cognitiva;
(c) Cursos a distancia: titulaciones (licenciatura en historia y
ciencias de la música, en ciencias del trabajo); posgrados
(experto en gestión y asesoramiento sobre la propiedad
inmobiliaria; en planificación y gestión de la calidad en
empresas de servicios, en empresas agroalimentarias y en
laboratorios; en gestión medioambiental; en
enseñanza-aprendizaje del español como lengua extranjera;
master en dirección y gestión de las administraciones
públicas); educación continua (aproximaciones al texto
literario, español de los negocios, derecho informático).
Asistencia financiera: becas y ayudas diversas; programas
de cooperación e intercambio.

Inscripciones: solicitar todas las informaciones útiles para estudiantes extranjeros a la Unidad de Relaciones Internacionales.

824　Universidad de Las Palmas de Gran Canaria [ULPGC]

Alfonso XIII n° 2
35003 Las Palmas de Gran Canaria
Tel: (34) (2) 845 1072
Fax: (34) (2) 845 2709
Web: http://www.ulpgc.es
e-mail: sie@ulpgc.es

📖 Programas universitarios

Campos de estudios: todas las materias principales.
Descripción: Estudios de pregrado y grado, posgrados y doctorados en las siguientes áreas: arquitectura, ingeniería de telecomunicación, ingeniería industrial, ingeniería técnica de telecomunicación, informática, ciencias de la salud, ciencias del mar, veterinaria, filología, geografía e historia, traducción e interpretación, ciencias de la actividad física y el deporte, ciencias económicas y empresariales, ciencias jurídicas, de formación del profesorado.
Asistencia financiera: la universidad participa en varios programas de movilidad (Sócrates/Erasmus, Sicue/Séneca, Programa de Cooperación Interuniversitaria) y cooperación (Alfa). Solicitar información a Relaciones Internacionales, que brinda además en el sitio web toda información útil para los estudiantes extranjeros.
Inscripciones: por toda información, dirigirse al Servicio de Información al Estudiante, en la dirección del título.

825　Universidad de León

Avenida de la Facultad 25
24071 León
Tel: (34) (8) 729 1650
Fax: (34) (8) 729 1693
Web: http://www.unileon.es/extension/extranjeros.htm
e-mail: reccle@unileon.es

📖 Cursos de lengua y cultura españolas para extranjeros

Campos de estudios: español, programas de verano.
Descripción: se ofrece conjuntamente la posibilidad de inscripción a cualquier materia de los estudios impartidos por la Universidad de León en sus diferentes facultades y escuelas.
Duración: curso permanente: anual o 2 cuatrimestres (octubre-enero y febrero-junio); curso de verano: 1 ó 2 meses en julio-agosto.
Costo(s): curso permanente anual: 1.500 euros; 1 cuatrimestre: 780 euros; verano: 613 o 1.021 euros por 1 o 2 meses respectivamente.
Asistencia financiera: existen becas del Ministerio de Educación y Cultura o del Ministerio de Asuntos Exteriores; también existen descuentos otorgados por la institución (hasta 50% del importe de la matrícula). Solicitarlas 1 mes antes del comienzo del curso.
Inscripciones: 1 mes o 15 días antes del comienzo de cada curso (para curso permanente y de verano respectivamente); dirigirse al Secretariado de Relaciones Internacionales, en la dirección que figura en el título.

826　Universidad de Málaga Cursos para Extranjeros [UDM]

Avenida de Andalucía 26, 1a planta
Apartado 310
29080 Málaga
Web: http://www.uma.es

📖 Programa de cursos

Campos de estudios: español, estudios culturales, literatura y civilización, programas de verano.
Descripción:
(a) Curso de estudios hispánicos: combinación de lengua española y materias culturales;
(b) Curso de verano para extranjeros;
(c) Cursos intensivos de lengua española y cursos intensivos individuales.
Se destina(n): a nacionales no hispanohablantes, de

cualquier país, mayores de 18 años.
Duración: (a) de octubre a enero y de febrero a mayo; (b) en julio, agosto y septiembre; (c) durante todo el año.
Asistencia financiera: algunas becas concedidas por el Gobierno de España por intermedio del Ministerio de Asuntos Exteriores y las embajadas o consulados de los países de origen de los candidatos.
Inscripciones: hasta 10 días antes de empezar los cursos.

827　Universidad de Murcia [UMU]

Avenida Teniente Floresta 5
Edificio Convalecencia
30003 Murcia
Tel: (34) (6) 836 33612
Fax: (34) (6) 836 3506
Web: http://www.um.es
e-mail: rector@um.es

📖 Cursos de lengua y cultura españolas

Campos de estudios: español, idiomas, programas de verano.
Duración: 3 semanas o 1 mes (en junio, julio, agosto y septiembre).
Inscripciones: hasta un mes antes de la fecha de inicio del curso elegido; por más información, dirigirse al Servicio de Promoción Educativa.

📖 Programas universitarios

Campos de estudios: todas las materias principales.
Descripción: Programas de estudio en sus escuelas universitarias y facultades en áreas de: enfermería, trabajo social, turismo, bellas artes, biología, ciencias de la documentación, ciencias del trabajo, economía y empresa, derecho, educación, filosofía, informática, letras, matemáticas, medicina, psicología, química, veterinaria;
(a) Estudios de primer y segundo ciclo: licenciaturas e ingenierías;
(b) Estudios propios: masters y cursos de especialista universitario, de escuelas profesionales, otras;
(c) Estudios de tercer ciclo: doctorados.
Asistencia financiera: becas, premios y ayudas de la Universidad y de otras instituciones; programas internacionales.
Inscripciones: para solicitar todas las informaciones útiles para el estudiante extranjero, dirigirse al Servicio de Relaciones Internacionales; consultar la página web (http://www.um.es/internacionales) o dirigirse por correo electróico a: svrelint@um.es.

🐾 Programa de becas

Campos de estudios: todas las materias principales.
Se conceden: a estudiantes que estén adscritos a una universidad y hayan superado al menos un primer año universitario. Se admiten estudiantes de nuevo ingreso previa homologación por las autoridades competentes.
Duración: la mayoría tienen una duración aproximada de entre 3 y 9 meses; algunas son renovables.
Importe: variable; la mayoría cubren estancia y manutención.

828　Universidad de Navarra Escuela Técnica Superior de Arquitectura

Ciudad Universitaria
31080 Pamplona
Tel: (34) (4) 842 5600
Fax: (34) (4) 817 3650
Web: http://www.unav.es

📖 Programa de cursos

Campos de estudios: arquitectura, construcción.
Programas:
(a) Curso de arquitectura;
(b) Curso de arquitectura técnica.
Se destina(n): (a) a quienes hayan superado la enseñanza secundaria y las pruebas de acceso a la universidad; (b) a quienes hayan superado la enseñanza secundaria.
Duración: todos los cursos comienzan en la última semana de septiembre y duran: (a) 6 años; (b) 3 años.
Inscripciones: hasta el 31 de marzo, en el Servicio de Admisión, Edificio Central, en la dirección que figura en el título.

829 Universidad de Navarra
Escuela Universitaria de
Enfermería
Irunlarrea s/n
31008 Pamplona
Tel: (34) (4) 842 5600
Fax: (34) (4) 842 5619
Web: http://www.unav.es

📖 **Programas universitarios**

Campos de estudios: enfermería, formación profesional.
Programas:
(a) Diplomatura en enfermería;
(b) Cursos de capacitación de enfermeras.
Materias de estudio: (b) enfermería en planta médica, en planta quirúrgica, de quirófano, psiquiátrica, pediátrica, de cuidados intensivos; en cirugía ortopédica y traumatología, en cardiología.
Diplomas requeridos: (a) a estudiantes con enseñanza media completa y examen de acceso a la Universidad; (b) a diplomadas en enfermería.
Duración: (a) 3 años (comienza en la última semana de septiembre); (b) 1 año (comienza el 1° de octubre).
Inscripciones: (a) hasta el 31 de marzo, en el Servicio de Admisión, Edificio Central, 31080, Pamplona; (b) hasta el 15 de mayo, en la Clínica Universitaria, Servicio de Personal, Avenida Pío XII s/n, 31030 Pamplona.

830 Universidad de Navarra
Facultad de Ciencias
Campus Universitario
31080 Pamplona
Tel: (34) (4) 842 5646
Fax: (34) (4) 842 5649
Web: http://www.unav.es

📖 **Diploma en dietética y alimentación humana**

Campos de estudios: alimentación, ciencias aplicadas, dietético, nutrición.
Se destina(n): los interesados deberán haber superado la enseñanza secundaria.
Duración: 3 años (comienzan en septiembre).
Inscripciones: hasta el 31 de marzo para los extranjeros, hasta el 15 de mayo para los españoles; Servicio de Información al Estudiante (Edificio Central de la Universidad de Navarra), en la dirección que figura en el título.

831 Universidad de Navarra
Facultad de Ciencias de la
Información
(School of Public
Communication)
Edificio Central
31080 Pamplona
Tel: (34) (4) 842 5617
Fax: (34) (4) 842 5664
Web: http://www.unav.es/fcom

📖 **Programa de licenciaturas**

Campos de estudios: ciencias de la información, comunicación, medios audio-visuales, periodismo, publicidad, relaciones públicas.
Programas:
(a) Periodismo;
(b) Comunicación audiovisual;
(c) Publicidad y relaciones públicas.
Se destina(n): los interesados deberán haber superado la enseñanza secundaria y las pruebas de admisión a la Universidad.
Duración: 4 años con un total de 300 créditos (comienzan en la última semana de septiembre).
Inscripciones: hasta el 15 de febrero (hasta el 15 de mayo para los españoles); dirigirse al Servicio de Información al Estudiante.

832 Universidad de Navarra
Facultad de Derecho
Edificio Central
31080 Pamplona
Tel: (34) (4) 842 5620
Fax: (34) (4) 842 5621
Web: http://www.unav.es

📖 **Programas universitarios**

Campos de estudios: derecho.
Programas:
(a) Licenciatura en derecho;
(b) Licenciatura en derecho canónico;
(c) Diploma de la Escuela de Práctica Jurídica;
(d) Master en derecho de la empresa;
(e) Postgrado universitario en derecho fiscal;
(f) Doctorado en derecho.
Se destina(n): a españoles y extranjeros que superen un examen de selectividad y, además, tengan: (a) y (b) un título equivalente al bachillerato superior español y no sean mayores de 25 años; (c) a estudiantes universitarios, licenciados y profesionales.
Duración: (a) y (b) 4 años, con un total de 300 créditos; (c) 2 años; (d) 1 año.
Inscripciones: hasta el: (a) y (b) 15 de mayo; (b) 1° de octubre; (c) y (d) 30 de junio; (f) 30 de septiembre.

833 Universidad de Navarra
Facultad de Farmacia
Campus Universitario
31080 Pamplona
Tel: (34) (4) 842 5600
Fax: (34) (4) 842 5619
Web: http://www.unav.es

📖 **Master en investigación y desarrollo de medicamentos**

Campos de estudios: biología, ciencias aplicadas, farmacia y farmacología.
Se destina(n): a licenciados que superen proceso de selección en base a curriculum vitae, expediente académico y otros criterios (idiomas, informática).
Duración: 16 meses (comienza en septiembre).
Idioma: español e inglés.
Inscripciones: hasta el 15 de mayo; dirigirse al Centro de Investigación en Farmacobiología aplicada.

834 Universidad de Navarra
Facultad de Medicina
Clínica Universitaria
Avenida Pío XII s/n
Apartado 192
31080 Pamplona
Tel: (34) (4) 825 5900
Web: http://www.unav.es/medicina

📖 **Programas universitarios**

Campos de estudios: enfermería, farmacia y farmacología, inmunología, medicina, neurología, oftalmología, pediatría, psiquiatría.
Descripción:
(a) Programas de especialización en: alergología; análisis clínico; anatomía patológica; anestesia y reanimación; aparato digestivo; bioquímica clínica; cardiología; cirugía cardiovascular; cirugía general; cirugía plástica y reparadora; dermatología; endocrinología y nutrición; farmacia hospitalaria; farmacología clínica; hematología y hemoterapia; inmunología; medicina familiar y comunitaria; medicina interna; medicina nuclear; microbiología y parasitología; nefrología; neurología; neurofisiología; obstetricia y ginecología; oftalmología; oncología médica; oncología radioterápica; otorrinolaringología; pediatría; psiquiatría; radiodiagnóstico; rehabilitación; traumatología y cirugía ortopédica; urología;
(b) Programas de mayor especialización: anestesia en cirugía cardiovascular; cardiología pediátrica; coagulación; diabetología y nutrición; educación diabetológica; endocrinología ginecológica; endoscopia aparato digestivo; epilepsia; farmacocinética; microcirugía; microscopía electrónica; neurología infantil; ortopedia infantil; psiquiatría biológica; psiquiatría infantil; técnicas bioquímicas de aplicación clínica; tomografía axial computarizada;

(c) Curso para profesores de medicina;
(d) Cursos de especialización en enfermería en: traumatología y cirugía ortopédica, psiquiatría hospitalaria, quirófano, cardiología, pediatría hospitalaria, unidades de hospitalización quirúrgica, unidades de hospitalización médica, cuidados intensivos; curso de enfermería oncológica y programa de la especialidad de enfermería obstétrico-ginecológica (matrona).
Se destina(n): (a) y (c) a licenciados en medicina y cirugía, excepto los programas de análisis clínico y farmacia hospitalaria que se destinan a licenciados en farmacia, y el programa de inmunología que se destina a licenciados en medicina y ciencias biológicas; (b) a médicos especialistas en el área correspondiente, excepto el programa de farmacocinética que se destina a licenciados en farmacia; (d) a titulados de ayudante técnico sanitario o diplomados en enfermería.
Duración: (a) varía según el programa, entre 3 y 5 años (comienzan en enero); (b) varía según el programa, entre 3 meses y 2 años (fechas a convenir con el Director del Departamento); (c) comienzan en enero; (d) varía según el curso, entre 9 y 15 meses (comienzan en octubre).
Inscripciones: dirigirse a: (a) a (c) al Director del Servicio de Personal de la Clínica Universitaria, (d) a la Directora de la Escuela Universitaria de Enfermería.

835 Universidad de Navarra Instituto de Artes Liberales

Edificio Central
31080 Pamplona
Tel: (34) (4) 810 5600
Fax: (34) (4) 810 5619
Web: http://www.unav.es/artlib

Programas universitarios

Campos de estudios: artes, ciencias.
Descripción:
(a) Bachiller en artes liberales en 9 especialidades: arte, comunicación, economía, empresa, filosofía, historia, lengua y literatura, geografía, pedagogía, ciencias sociales y políticas;
(b) Master en artes liberales.
Se destina(n): (a) los candidatos deberán haber superado la enseñanza secundaria y las pruebas de admisión a la Universidad; (b) titulados superiores o bachilleres en artes liberales.
Duración: (a) 3 años, con un total de 180 créditos; (b) 2 años, con un total de 75 créditos.
Inscripciones: hasta el 15 de mayo.

836 Universidad de Navarra Instituto de Estudios Superiores de la Empresa

Avenida Pearson 21
08034 Barcelona
Tel: (34) (3) 253 4200
Fax: (34) (3) 253 4343
Web: http://www.iese.edu

Programas universitarios

Campos de estudios: administración, administración de empresas, ciencias económicas y comerciales, gestión.
Descripción: Programas totalmente bilingües inglés-español:
(a) Master in Business Administration (MBA);
(b) Doctorado en dirección de empresas.
Se destina(n): a licenciados universitarios o titulación equivalente, que superen GMAT (General Management Admission Test) o examen del IESE, con al menos 2 años de experiencia profesional, que dominen español e inglés. Existe proceso de selección.
Duración: (a) 21 meses con dedicación completa (comienzan en octubre), incluye trimestre de trabajo práctico en empresas (remunerado); (b) aproximadamente 3 años (comienza en septiembre).
Asistencia financiera: existen posibilidades de becas.
Inscripciones: (a) hasta el 1° de mayo; (b) hasta el 30 de mayo.

837 Universidad de Navarra Instituto de Lengua y Cultura Españolas

Edificio Central
31080 Pamplona
Tel: (34) (4) 810 5600
Fax: (34) (4) 810 5619
Web: http://www.unav.es/ilce

Programa de cursos

Campos de estudios: español, idiomas, literatura y civilización, programas de verano.
Programas:
(a) Cursos de lengua y cultura españolas; de estudios hispánicos; de español de los negocios; intensivo de lengua y cultura españolas para estudiantes japoneses; intensivo de lengua y cultura españolas; de verano de lengua y cultura españolas; intensivo de español para alumnos Erasmus y de intercambio de la Universidad de Navarra;i ntensivo para profesores de español como lengua extranjera;
(b) Máster de enseñanza de español como lengua extranjera;
(c) Cursos a medida.
Inscripciones: dirigirse a la Secretaría del ILCE.

838 Universidad de Navarra Instituto Superior de Secretariado y Administración

Cuesta de Aldapeta 49
20080 San Sebastián
Tel: (34) (4) 346 7146
Fax: (34) (4) 346 8982
Web: http://www.unav.es/issa

Diplomatura en secretariado de dirección

Campos de estudios: administración de empresas, documentación, gestión.
Se destina(n): a nacionales de cualquier país que posean el nivel de estudios exigido para matricularse en la universidad, superen las pruebas de admisión y entrevista, y posean un nivel mínimo de inglés.
Duración: 3 años académicos (comienzo en septiembre).
Inscripciones: hasta el 15 de mayo, en la Secretaría del Instituto.

839 Universidad de Navarra

Edificio Central
31080 Pamplona
Tel: (34) (4) 842 5606
Fax: (34) (4) 842 5619
Web: http://www.unav.es

Programas universitarios

Campos de estudios: todas las materias principales.
Descripción: (a) Estudios de pregrado: licenciatura en administración y dirección de empresas, en economía; licenciatura en derecho; en administración y dirección de empresas + derecho, en economía + derecho; licenciatura en filología hispánica; en filosofía, en historia, en humanidades, en pedagogía, en psicopedagogía; licenciatura en comunicación audiovisual; en periodismo, en publicidad; licenciatura en filología hispánica + comunicación audiovisual; licenciatura en filosofía + periodismo, en filosofía + publicidad y relaciones públicas;
(b) Programas Master: diseño arquitectónico; economía y finanzas; gestión de empresas de comunicación; derecho de empresa; asesoría fiscal; investigación, desarrollo e innovación de medicamentos; matrimonio y familia;
(c) Doctorados: en áreas de medicina, ciencias y farmacia; derecho; filosofía y letras; comunicación; ciencias económicas y empresariales; teología; arquitectura e ingeniería industrial.
Asistencia financiera: consultar la página web (http://www.unav.es/becasyayudas); se citan como ejemplo becas "Seneca" del Ministerio de Educación, Cultura y Deporte (para alumnos de últimos cursos de licenciatura o diplomatura que deseen realizar estudios en universidades españolas), o del Gobierno de Navarra (para alumnos navarros que realizan parte de su carrera en otras universidades españolas o extranjeras o para descendientes de emigrantes navarros residentes en el extranjero).

Inscripciones: por mayor información, dirigirse al Vicerrectorado de Alumnos, Ordenación Académica y Relaciones Internacionales.

🎓 Becas de estuido

Campos de estudios: todas las materias principales.
Se conceden: según condiciones económicas, a estudiantes de primer y tercer año.
Duración: dos años académicos, renovable.
Importe: de 50 a 100% de los gastos de enseñanza, 50 a 100% de gastos de mantenimiento.
Solicitudes: hasta el 30 de noviembre.

840 Universidad de Oviedo Instituto Universitario de la Empresa

González Besada 13, 4°
33007 Oviedo
Tel: (34) (8) 510 3020
Fax: (34) (8) 524 4850
Web: http://www.uniovie.es

📖 Programas de posgrado

Campos de estudios: administración de empresas, ciencias económicas y comerciales, economía, finanzas, gestión, marketing, relaciones industriales.
Descripción:
(a) Curso superior sobre sistema fiscal español;
(b) Master ejecutivo en dirección de empresas;
(c) Master universitario en administración y dirección de empresas (MBA.).
Se destina(n): a: (a) diplomados y licenciados; (b) licenciados con experiencia; (c) licenciados sin experiencia. En todos los casos existe proceso de selección en base a entrevista personal, calificaciones y recomendaciones.
Duración: (a) 1 año; comienzan en octubre.
Inscripciones: hasta el 15 de octubre.

841 Universidad de Oviedo

Vicerrectorado de Estudiantes
Argüelles, 39
33003 Oviedo
Tel: (34) (8) 510 4083
Fax: (34) (8) 522 6254
Web: http://www.uniovi.es

📖 Programas universitarios

Campos de estudios: todas las materias principales, español.
Descripción:
(a) Titulaciones (licenciaturas, diplomaturas, otras) de primer y segundo ciclo;
(b) Titulaciones propias;
(c) Programas de tercer ciclo (doctorados) en áreas de: biología, ciencias, ciencias económicas y empresariales, ciencias de la educación, derecho, filología, filosofía, geografía e historia, geología, medicina, psicología, química, enfermería y fisioterapia, estomatología, ingeniería técnica industrial, ingeniería técnica informática, ingeniería técnica minera y topográfica, magisterio, medicina del deporte, relaciones laborales, ingenieros industriales e informáticos, enfermería, trabajo social, turismo, marina civil;
(d) Cursos de español para extranjeros, cursos de verano, cursos de lenguas extranjeras.
Asistencia financiera: becas y ayudas: becas del Vicerrectorado de Estudiantes y Movilidad; ayudas al estudio; ayudas de investigación; becas de la Oficina de Relaciones Internacionales. Consultar todas las convocatorias en la página web http://www.uniovi.es/RI/conv_becas/convocatorias.html.
Inscripciones: por todas las informaciones útiles para estudiantes extranjeros, dirigirse a la Oficina de Relaciones Internacionales, C/ Principado 3, PB, 33007 Oviedo, Asturias o consultar la página web http://www.uniovi.es/RI/welcome.html.

842 Universidad de Salamanca Cursos Internacionales [USAL]

Patio de Escuelas Menores s/n
37008 Salamanca
Tel: +34-2-329 4418
Fax: +34+2+329 4504
Web: http://www.usal.es
e-mail: rrii@usal.es

📖 Cursos internacionales

Campos de estudios: artes, español, estudios culturales, filología, formación profesional, idiomas, lingüística, literatura y civilización, programas de verano.
Descripción:
(a) Cursos de español (lengua y cultura); se complementan con diversos cursos culturales;
(b) Curso superior de filología hispánica;
(c) Curso superior para profesores de español, lengua extranjera;
(d) Programas para extranjeros de la Facultad de Filología (Curso de estudios hispánicos, Programas especiales individualizados);
(e) Diploma de posgrado y master universitario E.L.E (Enseñanza del español como lengua extranjera).
Se destina(n): a nacionales de cualquier país, (a) con edad mínima 16 años, (b) con buen nivel de conocimiento de la lengua española culta y de literatura hispánica, (c) docentes en esta rama o futuros profesionales de la enseñanza del español, (d) con elevado dominio de comprensión en español, (e) licenciados con titulación superior (licenciatura en filología hispánica o en otras filologías, licenciado o diplomados en otras especialidades), y en el caso de extranjeros de lengua materna no española deberán acreditar un dominio del español equivalente al exigido para la obtención del Diploma Superior de Español que expide el Ministerio de Educación y Ciencia.
Duración: (a) 4 ó 6 semanas en verano; variable durante el resto del año; (b) 1 mes (en julio o en agosto); (c) 1 o 2 semanas (varios períodos); (d) de octubre a junio, con un total de 420 horas; (e) diploma: 1 semestre (de octubre a enero), el master 2 años (comienza en octubre).
Inscripciones: (a) a (d) por mayores informaciones, solicitar información a Cursos Internacionales; (e) preinscripciones hasta el 30 de junio e inscripciones en la primera quincena de septiembre.

🎓 Programas de becas

Campos de estudios: todas las materias principales.
Becas: Becas para cursar programas de 1er y 2do ciclo en la USAL:
(a) Para estudiantes colombianos;
(b) Para estudiantes mexicanos;
(c) Para estudiantes colombianos;
(d) Para estudiantes argentinos;
(e) Para estudiantes marroquíes;
Becas doctorales:
(f) Para latinoamericanos;
Becas para "Maestría en Estudios Latinoamericanos":
(g) Para latinoamericanos.
Descripción: ofrecidas por (a), (c), (d) y (f) Grupo Santander-Hispano; (b) Colsanitas, (e) USAL; (g) Fundación Carolina/USAL.
Nacionalidad: (a) y (c) colombianos; (b) mexicanos; (d) argentinos; (e) marroquíes; (f) latinoamericanos (Argentina, Bolivia, Brasil, Chile, Colombia, Costa Rica, Cuba, Ecuador, Guatemala, Honduras, México, Nicaragua, Panamá, Paraguay, Perú, Puerto Rico, República Dominicana, El Salvador, Uruguay y Venezuela); (g) latinoamericanos.
Duración: (a) a (e) 4 a 5 años; (f) 3 a 4 años; (g) 2 a 3 años.
Importe: (a) a (e) descuento en gastos de enseñanza, pensión completa y alojamiento, seguro médico; (f) descuento en gastos de enseñanza, alojamiento, seguro médico y asignación de 200 euros por mes; (g) descuento de 2/3 de gastos de enseñanza, 1.200 euros por mes, seguro médico, billete aéreo de ida y vuelta desde/hacia el país de origen del candidato.
Solicitudes: (a) a (e): hasta el 5 de julio; dirigirse a la Oficina de Relaciones Internacionales, Email: rrii@usal.es; (f) dirigirse a Oficina de Programas de Doctorado, Email: infodifu@usal.es.; (g) Instituto de Iberoamérica y Portugal, Email: ieiyp@usal.es o iberoame@usal.es.

843 **Universidad de Salamanca**
Instituto de Ciencias de la
Educación [USAL]
Paseo de Canalejas 169
37008 Salamanca
Tel: (34) (2) 329 4630
Fax: (34) (2) 329 4630
Web: http://www.usal.es

📖 **Master en tecnología de la educación**

Campos de estudios: educación, tecnología.
Materias de estudio: comunicación y tecnología
educativas, evaluación, innovación, informática y
aplicaciones multimedia, fotografía, video y televisores, radio,
educación a distancia.
Se destina(n): a profesores, a licenciados (preferentemente
en educación o áreas afines); se admiten algunos diplomados;
existe proceso de selección por curriculum.
Duración: 1 año (de enero a diciembre).
Asistencia financiera: se aplican becas de la Agencia
Española de Cooperación Internacional (AECI).
Inscripciones: hasta el 15 de noviembre.

844 **Universidad de Salamanca**
[USAL]
C/ Cardenal Pla y Deniel 22
37008 Salamanca
Tel: +34-923-294-400
Fax: +34(923) 294-502
Web: http://www.usal.es
e-mail: rrii@usal.es

📖 **Programa Especial Integrado**

Programas: Programa P.E.I. (Programa Especial
Integrado). Este Programa pone a su disposición una amplia
oferta de asignaturas de diferentes Departamentos e Institutos
Universitarios. Al finalizar el curso se otorga una certificación
académica de las materias estudiadas.
Inscripciones: solicitar información en la siguiente
dirección: internat@cursos.usal.es.

845 **Universidad de Santiago de**
Compostela
Escuela Universitaria de
Enfermería [USC]
Avenida Juan XXIII s/n
15704 Santiago de Compostela
Tel: (34) (8) 156 3100
Fax: (34) (8) 157 0181
Web: http://www.usc.es

📖 **Master en gerontología clínica y social**

Campos de estudios: enfermería, trabajo social.
Se destina(n): a titulados universitarios en relación con las
ciencias de la salud (médicos, psicólogos, farmacéuticos,
sociólogos, tertapeutas ocupacionales; diplomados en
enfermería, fisioterapeutas, etc.); existe selección en base a
curriculum vitae en relación con las áreas geriátrica y
gerontológica, y entrevista personal.
Duración: 2 años.
Asistencia financiera: existen becas anuales que cubren el
costo total del programa.
Inscripciones: durante el mes de septiembre.

846 **Universidad de Santiago de**
Compostela
Facultad de Ciencias
Económicas
y Empresariales [USC]
Avenida Juan XXIII s/n
15704 Santiago de Compostela
Tel: (34) (8) 158 3211
Fax: (34) (8) 156 3637
Web: http://www.usc.es

📖 **Cursos de posgrado**

Campos de estudios: administración de empresas, ciencias
económicas y comerciales, comercio, contabilidad, finanzas,
gestión, marketing.

Descripción:
(a) Administración financiera y tributaria;
(b) Dirección y gestión de comercio exterior;
(c) Gerencia de cooperativas agrarias;
(d) Dirección y gestión de cooperativas y pequeñas empresas;
(e) Dirección y gestión de empresas turísticas;
(f) Auditoría.
Se destina(n): (a) a licenciados preferentemente en
ciencias económicas y empresariales o en derecho, que
superen selección basada en expediente académico; (b) a
licenciados en el área o profesionales con experiencia que
superen proceso de selección; (c) a (e) a diplomados,
licenciados y profesionales del área; (f) a titulados
universitarios de grado medio o superior.
Duración: (a) 10 meses (comienza en septiembre); (b) y
(c) 1 año académico (comienzan en noviembre); (d) 1 año
académico (comienza en octubre); (e) de enero a septiembre;
(f) 2 opciones: 2 módulos en 1 año académico o curso
completo en 2 años académicos.
Asistencia financiera: (b) existen subvenciones y becas.
Inscripciones: (a) meses de julio y agosto, en la Sección
de Hacienda pública, Avenida de Burgo s/n, 15704 Santiago
de Compostela; (b) hasta el 15 de octubre; (c) hasta el 30 de
octubre; (d) y (f) hasta el 30 de septiembre; (e) hasta
noviembre; (f) en julio y a principios de septiembre, en el
Departamento de Economía financiera, en la dirección que
figura en el título.

847 **Universidad de Santiago de**
Compostela
Facultad de Derecho [USC]
Avenida Dr. Echeverri
Campus Universitario
15706 Santiago de Compostela
Tel: (34) (8) 152 2283
Fax: (34) (8) 1569 1554
Web: http://www.usc.es

📖 **Curso de posgrado en relaciones laborales**

Campos de estudios: derecho.
Se destina(n): a licenciados en derecho o ciencias
económicas y empresariales, a diplomados en relaciones
laborales y a candidatos con titulaciones equivalentes.
Duración: 6 meses.
Inscripciones: hasta el 20 de abril, en el Consejo Gallego
de Relaciones Laborales, Plaza de Vigo 2, 15701 Santiago de
Compostela.

848 **Universidad de Santiago de**
Compostela
Facultad de Farmacia [USC]
Avenida de las Ciencias
Campus Universitario
15706 Santiago de Compostela
Tel: (34) (8) 156 3100
Fax: (34) (8) 159 4639
Web: http://www.usc.es

📖 **Curso internacional sobre recursos fitogenéticos**
y mejora genética vegetal

Campos de estudios: ciencias agronómicas, farmacia y
farmacología.
Se destina(n): a graduados de cualquier país.
Inscripciones: Departamento de Farmacología, Farmacia y
Técnicas Farmacéuticas, en la dirección que figura en el
título.

849 **Universidad de Sevilla**
Instituto de Idiomas [US]
Avenida Reina Mercedes s/n
41013 Sevilla
Web: http://www.us.es

📖 **Cursos de idiomas**

Campos de estudios: español, idiomas.
Descripción:
(a) Cursos de lengua española para extranjeros;
(b) Cursos de alemán, árabe, francés, griego, inglés, italiano,
japonés, portugués, ruso.
Se destina(n): principalmente a estudiantes universitarios

de toda nacionalidad.

Duración: (a) cursos cuatrimestrales (octubre-enero; febrero-junio); (b) cursos regulares de 3 horas por semana durante el año académico.

Inscripciones: en el mes de septiembre; para inglés, francés, alemán e italiano hay preinscripción en la primera quincena de julio; dirigirse a la Secretaría del Centro.

850 Universidad de Valencia Vicerrectorado de Relaciones Exteriores [UV]

Calle Antiga Senda Senent 11
46071 Valencia
Tel: (34) (6) 386 4110
Fax: (34) (6) 386 4224
Web: http://www.uv.es

Cursos de verano de español para extranjeros

Campos de estudios: español, idiomas, programas de verano.
Duración: 1 mes en julio o septiembre.
Inscripciones: dirigirse al Gabinet d'Estrangers, en la dirección que figura en el título.

851 Universidad de Valladolid [UVA]

Plaza de Santa Cruz 8
47002 Valladolid
Tel: (34) (8) 342 3613
Fax: (34) (8) 342 3234
Web: http://www.uva.es
e-mail: relint@cod.uva.es

Cursos de posgrado

Campos de estudios: ciencias, ciencias agronómicas, ecología, medio ambiente, enología, física, informática, ingeniería, química, tecnología industrial.
Descripción:
(a) Master universitario en gestión de calidad;
(b) Especialista en informática industrial;
(c) Especialista en tecnología ambiental, tratamiento y gestión de la contaminación;
(d) Especialista en técnicas avanzadas en el estudio de la contaminación atmosférica;
(e) Especialista superior en viticultura y enología;
(f) Especialista en ingeniería de climatización;
(g) Especialista en técnicas ópticas de detección remotas, aplicaciones agroforestales.
Se destina(n): (a) y (c) a titulados universitarios; (b) a titulados universitarios superiores o medios con experiencia industrial; (d) y (f) a licenciados o técnicos en ingeniería, ciencias o arquitectura; (e) a ingenieros agrónomos, licenciados en química, ciencias biológicas o farmacia, a ingenieros técnicos agrícolas; (g) a ingenieros técnicos o diplomados.
Se dicta(n): en: (a) a (e) la Facultad de Ciencias: (a) Departamento de Física de la materia, (b) Departamento de Informática y Departamento de Ingeniería de sistemas y automática, (c) Departamento de Ingeniería química, (d) Departamento de Física aplicada, (e) Departamento de Química inorgánica; (f) Departamento de Ingeniería energética y fluidomecánica, Escuela Técnica Superior de Ingenieros industriales; (g) Departamento de Ingeniería agrícola y forestal, Escuela Técnica Superior de Ingenierías agrarias, Palencia.
Duración: (a) 2 años (comienza en octubre); (b) de octubre a febrero; (c) de enero a mayo; (d) de diciembre a marzo; (e) de enero a diciembre; (f) de enero a junio; (g) de febrero a abril.

Cursos de posgrado

Campos de estudios: arquitectura, ecología, medio ambiente, estudios culturales, gestión, historia del arte, urbanismo.
Descripción:
(a) Master en restauración arquitectónica;
(b) Especialista en teoría y análisis del patrimonio histórico;
(c) Especialista en técnicas y procedimientos para la restauración del patrimonio histórico;
(d) Especialista en planeamiento urbano, ciudad y medio ambiente;
(e) Especialista en restauración de bienes muebles y

elementos ornamentales del patrimonio arquitectónico;
(f) Especialista en ciudad y cultura: Curso Europeo de gestión cultural.
Se destina(n): (a) a licenciados en historia del arte, arqueología o historia del arte; (b), (c) y (e) a arquitectos, ingenieros o licenciados como (a); (d) a arquitectos, ingenieros o geógrafos; (f) a titulados superiores o diplomados universitarios en materias afines (gestión pública, magisterio, historia del arte, etc.).
Se dicta(n): en la Escuela Superior de Arquitectura: (a) a (c) y (e) Departamento de Teoría de la arquitectura y proyectos arquitectónicos, (d) y (f) Departamento de Análisis e instrumentos de intervención arquitectónica y urbana.
Duración: (a) de mayo a octubre; (b), (c) y (e) 2 años (comienzan en octubre); (d) de enero a junio; (f) de octubre a junio.

Cursos de posgrado en áreas de la salud

Campos de estudios: enfermería, gestión, higiene y salud, medicina, medicina preventiva.
Descripción:
(a) Especialista universitario en administración sanitaria en enfermería;
(b) Especialista en bioética;
(c) Master en salud pública y administración sanitaria;
(d) Especialista universitario en gestión de los servicios de prevención y salud laboral;
(e) Especialista en valoración del daño corporal.
Diplomas requeridos: (a) a licenciados o diplomados universitarios; (b) a licenciados en medicina y diplomados en enfermería; (c) y (d) a titulados universitarios, preferentemente en áreas sanitarias; (e) a licenciados en medicina.
Se dicta(n): (a) Departamento de Enfermería, Escuela Universitaria de Enfermería; (b) a (e) Facultad de Medicina: (b) Departamento de Medicina, (c) Departamento de Medicina preventiva y salud pública, (d) y (e) Departamento de Anatomía patológica, microbiología, medicina preventiva, toxicología y legislación sanitaria.
Duración: (a) de mayo a diciembre; (b) y (e) de octubre a junio; (c) 2 años (comienza en mayo); (d) de noviembre a abril.
Inscripciones: (a) hasta el 10 de abril, dirigirse al Consejo Autónomo de Colegios de Enfermería de Castilla y León; (b) a (e): dirigirse al lugar donde se dictan: (b), (d) y (e) hasta el 10 de octubre, (c) hasta el 30 de abril. En todos los casos la dirección es la que figura en el título.

Programas universitarios

Campos de estudios: ciencias económicas y comerciales, ciencias sociales, derecho, derecho internacional, riesgos, seguros, sociología, trabajo social.
Descripción:
(a) Curso de derecho internacional público;
Cursos de posgrado:
(b) Especialista en derecho del consumo;
(c) Especialista universitario en ergonomía y condiciones de trabajo;
(d) Especialista en servicios sociales generales;
(e) Master en consultoría de procesos de desarrollo y organizaciones;
(f) Especialista en operaciones de seguro.
Se destina(n): (b) a licenciados en derecho; (c) a titulados universitarios de primer o segundo ciclo; (d) a licenciados y diplomados universitarios del área; (e) a licenciados en ciencias sociales y humanas; (f) a titulados universitarios.
Se dicta(n): (a) y (b) en la Facultad de Derecho; (c) en la Escuela Universitaria de Relaciones laborales, Palencia; (d) en la Escuela Universitaria de Trabajo social; (e) en el Departamento de Sociología de la Escuela Universitaria de Estudios empresariales, Facultad de Ciencias económicas y empresariales; (f) Instituto IEMEDER, Facultad de Ciencias económicas y empresariales.
Duración: (a) en julio; (b) de noviembre a mayo; (c) de octubre a mayo; (d) de octubre a junio; (e) 2 años (comienza en octubre); (f) comienza en diciembre.
Asistencia financiera: (a) existen becas.
Inscripciones: dirigirse al lugar donde se dictan los cursos, en la dirección que figura en el título: (a) hasta mediados de julio; (b) y (f) hasta fin de octubre; (c) y (e) hasta el 15 de octubre; (d) hasta el 30 de septiembre.

📖 Programas universitarios

Campos de estudios: cinematografía, educación, idiomas, interpretación y traducción, programas de verano.
Descripción:
(a) Curso de cinematografía;
Cursos de posgrado:
(b) Master universitario en traducción inglés/español;
(c) Especialista en estudios sobre la tradición;
(d) Especialista en historia y estética de la cinematografía;
(e) Especialista en actividades prácticas en ciencias en la enseñanza secundaria;
(f) Especialista en didáctica de la expresión plástica y visual;
(g) Especialista en didáctica de la educación del consumidor;
(h) Especialista en consumo y educación: didáctica de la educación del consumidor (Curso de Palencia);
(i) Especialista en didáctica de la educación del consumidor (Curso de Soria).
Se destina(n): (a) a licenciados universitarios; (b) a licenciados en filología inglesa o titulados con muy buen conocimiento de la lengua inglesa; (c) y (d) a titulados universitarios medios o superiores; (e) a licenciados en ciencias (físicas, químicas, biológicas, geológicas), en farmacia, o ingenieros superiores; (f) a diplomados en educación u otras áreas afines y licenciados en bellas artes; (g) a diplomados en magisterio o licenciados; (h) a maestros diplomados en educación social y trabajo social, en geografía, historia, arte, filología o psicopedagogía; (i) a diplomados en profesorado de EGB.
Duración: (a) 1 mes en agosto durante 3 años; (b) 2 años; (c) de enero a abril; (d) de enero a junio; (e) de noviembre a abril; (f) 1 mes en julio; (g) de octubre a enero; (h) de noviembre a marzo; (i) de noviembre a abril.
Asistencia financiera: (a) existen becas.
Inscripciones: en la dirección que figura en el título, dirigirse al lugar donde se dictan, (a) hasta fin de julio, (b) hasta el 15 de noviembre, (c) hasta diciembre, (d) hasta primera semana de enero, (e) y (g) hasta el 10 de octubre, (f) hasta el 30 de junio, (i) hasta fin de octubre.

🐝 Programa de becas

Campos de estudios: todas las materias principales.
Becas:
(a) Becas del Instituto de Cooperación para el Desarrollo (25);

(b) Becas del Instituto de Cooperación para el Desarrollo (9);
(c) Becas de la Cooperación Española para Iberoamérica (20).
Materias de estudio: (a) estudios de diplomatura y licenciatura; (b) y (c) estudios de posgrado.
Se conceden: (a) y (b) a ciudadanos de países de Africa subsahariana (excepto Sudán y Mauritania), del Pacífico y asiáticos en vías de desarrollo, con estudios secundarios en el caso de (a) y titulados superiores universitarios en el caso de (b); (c) a ciudadanos de países latinoamericanos, titulados superiores universitarios.
Lugar: Universidad de Valladolid.
Duración: (a) a (c) 1 año (renovable).
Importe: matrícula del curso y monto por mes (más seguro médico y 50% del viaje de ida-vuelta en el caso de (c)).
Solicitudes: en Embajadas o Consulados de España: (a) y (b) hasta el 30 de abril, (c) en el mes de mayo.

852 Universidad de Valladolid [UVA]
Ramón y Cajal 7
47005 Valladolid
Tel: (34) (8) 342 3549
Fax: (34) (8) 342 3000
Web: http://www.uva.es

📖 Cursos internacionales de verano

Campos de estudios: educación, español, idiomas, literatura y civilización, programas de verano.
Descripción: cursos de español, preparación "Concours" francés, superior de filología hispánica, metodología de la enseñanza del español como lengua extanjera, lengua española, lengua y cultura españolas.
Duración: duración variable entre junio y septiembre, excepto lengua y cultura españolas que se dicta en trimestres julio-septiembre y octubre-diciembre.
Inscripciones: solicitar informes a la Fundación General de la Universidad, en la dirección que figura en el título.

853 Universidad de Vigo Oficina de Relaciones Internacionales
Oporto 1
36201 Vigo
Tel: (34) (8) 681 3614
Fax: (34) (8) 681 3559
Web: http://www.uvigo.es
e-mail: ori@uvigo.es

📖 Programas universitarios

Campos de estudios: todas las materias principales, español.
Descripción:
(a) Programas de estudio de primer y segundo ciclo (licenciaturas, diplomados, ingenierías, otros);
(b) Programas de tercer ciclo (doctorados) en áreas de: filología y traducción; ciencias; ciencias económicas y empresariales; ciencias jurídicas y del trabajo; ingeniería industrial, de minas, de telecomunicación, técnica forestal, informática; profesorado de E.G.B, enfermería, bellas artes, ciencias de la educación; fisioterapia; ciencias sociales; humanidades; derecho;
(c) Cursos de español para estudiantes extranjeros.
Asistencia financiera: programas internacionales de intercambio y de cooperación (solicitar información a la Oficina de Relaciones Internacionales); becas y ayudas de la Universidad y del Gobierno (solicitar información a Jefa de Sección Becas, bolsas@uvigo.es).
Inscripciones: por toda la información útil para estudiantes extranjeros, dirigirse a la Oficina de Relaciones Internacionales en la dirección del título, o consultar la página web http://www.uvigo.es/relaciones/index.es.htm.

854 Universidad de Zaragoza Servicio de Difusión de Lengua y Cultura Españolas para Extranjeros [UZ]
Pedro Cerbuna 12
Edificio Interfacultades, 3a planta
50009 Zaragoza
Tel: (34) (7) 676 1047
Fax: (34) (7) 676 2050
Web: http://www.unizar.es

📖 Programa de cursos

Campos de estudios: educación, español, estudios culturales, idiomas, programas de verano.
Descripción:
(a) Cursos anuales, cuatrimestrales o intensivos de lengua española para extranjeros;
(b) Cursos de Verano de Lengua española para Extranjeros en Jaca (Huesca);
(c) Curso para Profesores de español como lengua extranjera.
Se destina(n): (a) y (b) a extranjeros mayores de 18 años; (c) a profesores españoles o extranjeros, o a licenciados que aspiren a ejercer la docencia del D.E.L.E.
Duración: (a) cursos anuales, cuatrimestrales, intensivos; (b) 1 mes o 15 días en julio o agosto; (c) 10 días en julio o en agosto.
Inscripciones: por mayor información, hasta junio y desde agosto, la dirección es la que figura en el título; en los meses de julio y agosto, la dirección es Residencia Universitaria, 22700 Jaca, Huesca.

855 Universidad de Zaragoza [UZ]
Pedro Cerbuna 12
50009 Zaragoza
Tel: (34) (7) 676 1011
Fax: (34) (7) 676 1005
Web: http://www.unizar.es

📖 Programas universitarios

Campos de estudios: todas las materias principales.
Descripción: Cursos universitarios conducentes a los títulos de magister, postgrado o diploma de especialización universitaria según el caso en las siguientes áreas:
(a) Biomédicas: asistentes sociales psiquiátricos, alimentación y dietoterapia en el niño y el adolescente, enfermería de anestesia y de reanimación, medicina naturista, tecnología y

metodología radiológicas;
(b) Científicas: historia de las ciencias y de las técnicas;
(c) Humanísticas: educador de museos;
(d) Sociales: auditoría, economía de la distribución comercial, empresas aseguradoras, estudios sociales aplicados, gestión del desarrollo rural; lenguaje y técnica de video y televisión;
(e) Técnicas: informática, ingeniería de organización industrial, ingeniería de transformación de plásticos, ingeniería del medio ambiente.
Se destina(n): a licenciados, diplomados, ingenieros o arquitectos según el caso.
Duración: de 6 meses a 2 años según el programa.
Inscripciones: en la segunda quincena de septiembre; por mayores informaciones, dirigirse al Centro de Información Universitaria en la dirección que figura en el título.

🎓 Becas de estancias para doctorados

Campos de estudios: todas las materias principales, ciencias, ciencias sociales, medicina, tecnología.
Becas: aporte financiero para gastos de enseñanza, de estadía y de viaje.
Descripción: becas de estancias para la realización de doctorados.
Se conceden: a quienes cumplan requisitos de doctorado.
Nacionalidad: a latinoamericanos.
Edad Max: hasta 40 años.
Importe: gastos de enseñanza: entre 24 y 46 euros por crédito, estadía: 850 euros por mes; viaje: 4.500 euros.

856 Universidad del País Vasco/ Euskal Herriko Unibersitatea

Edificio Aulario I.
48940 Leioa (Bizkaia)
Tel: +34-94-601-3044
Fax: +34-94-601-5824
Web: http://www.ehu.es
e-mail: titulospropios@lg.ehu.es

📖 Cursos de pregrado y posgrado

Campos de estudios: todas las materias principales.
Descripción: : Cursos conducentes a los títulos de grado (diplomado, licenciado, ingeniero, arquitecto), posgrado (master, especialista, experto) y doctorado en cinco grandes campos: ciencias experimentales, enseñanzas técnicas, ciencias de la salud, ciencias sociales y jurídicas, humanidades.
Se destina(n): a nacionales de cualquier país que cumplan los requisitos necesarios y que conozcan el español o el vasco.
Asistencia financiera: existen diversos tipos de becas y ayudas.
Inscripciones: en la primera semana de julio; solicitar información a Negociado de Acceso (para títulos de grado), a Negociado de Títulos Propios o a Negociado de Doctorado, según corresponda; en todos los casos en la dirección que figura en el título.

857 Universidad Francisco de Vitoria

Carretera M-515 Pozuelo-Majahonda, km 1,800
28223 Pozuelo de Alarcón, Madrid
Tel: (34) (1) 709 1400
Fax: (34)1) 351 1716
Web: http://www.fvitoria.com
e-mail: prom@fvitoria.com

📖 Programas universitarios

Campos de estudios: todas las materias principales.
Descripción: (a) Diplomaturas y licenciaturas oficiales en las siguientes áreas: ciencias jurídicas, economía y de la empresa; ciencias de la comunicación; ciencias biosanitarias; escuela politécnica superior;
(b) Postgrados: curso de gestión urbanística, de historia de España en el Siglo XX, de asesor jurídico de entidades financieras, de asesoría integral de matrimonio y familia, de inglés jurídico y de negocios; master en e-derecho, en gestión global del riesgo, en dirección, gestión y evaluación de centros educativos, en acción política y participación ciudadana en el estado de derecho, en filosofía, en teología, en derecho de los negocios;
(c) Centro de estudios tecnológicos y sociales: ciclos superiores de formación profesional (desarrollo de aplicaciones informáticas; realización de audiovisuales y

espectáculos).
Asistencia financiera: numerosos programas de intercambio y cooperación; becas y ayudas.
Inscripciones: por mayores informaciones, dirigirse al Departamento de Información y Orientación.

858 Universidad Internacional Menéndez Pelayo [UIMP]

Isaac Peral 23
28040 Madrid
Tel: (34) (1) 592 0631
Fax: (34) (1) 543 0897
Web: http://www.uimp.es
e-mail: se@extra.uimp.es

🎓 Becas para estudios de verano

Campos de estudios: español, estudios culturales, filología, literatura y civilización, programas de verano.
Descripción: Becas para la participación en cursos magistrales, escuelas, seminarios, encuentros y programas de verano (lengua y cultura española, enseñanza del español, filología española).
Se conceden: a quienes tengan una brillante trayectoria académica y cuenten con escasos recursos.
Duración: variable; todos los programas tienen lugar en los meses de julio, agosto o septiembre.
Importe: existen becas de matrícula y becas completas (que incluyen alojamiento y manutención).
Solicitudes: antes del 1° de abril, a la Secretaría de Alumnos, en la dirección que figuran el título; en la Secretaría de Cursos para Extranjeros (en el caso de los cursos relacionados con la Lengua y Cultura Españolas), Residencia Las Llamas, Avenida de los Castros s/n, 39005 Santander; en ambos casos, de fin de junio a septiembre, las Secretarías se trasladan a Palacio de la Magdalena, 39005 Santander.

859 Universidad Internacional Menéndez Pelayo [UIMP]

Isaac Peral 23
28040 Madrid
Tel: (34) (1) 592 0600
Fax: (34) (1) 543 0897
Web: http://www.uimp.es
e-mail: se@extra.uimp.es

📖 Programa de cursos

Campos de estudios: todas las materias principales, educación, español, estudios culturales, idiomas, literatura y civilización, programas de verano.
Descripción:
(a) Cursos de lengua y cultura españolas; actividades culturales, deportivas, recreativas;
(b) Curso "Enseñanza del español como lengua extranjera";
(c) Curso superior de filología española;
(d) Cursos, seminarios y encuentros (matemáticas, medicina, arte, economía, política, medio ambiente, física, música, otras).
Se destina(n): (a) a estudiantes de 17 años en adelante; (b) a profesores de español; (c) a profesores y estudiantes en filología; (d) a estudiantes diplomados, licenciados y de postgrado.
Se dicta(n): (a), (b) y (d) en Santander.
Duración: (a) de enero a junio y en julio, agosto o septiembre; (b) 15 días en julio, agosto o septiembre; (c) 50 horas; (d) en julio, agosto o septiembre.
Asistencia financiera: se otorgan becas completas (enseñanza y alojamiento) o becas de matrícula, de acuerdo con las condiciones económicas y expediente de los solicitantes; deben solicitarse antes del 1° de abril.
Inscripciones: para matrícula, 1 mes antes; si se solicita alojamiento, 3 meses antes. Dirigirse a la Secretaría de Cursos para Extranjeros; a partir de fin de junio, la dirección es Palacio de la Magdalena, 39005 Santander.

860   Universidad Internacional de Andalucía
Sede Iberoamericana de "La Rábida"
Paraje La Rábida s/n
21819 Palos de la Frontera
Huelva
Tel: (34) (5) 935 0452
Fax: (34) (5) 935 0158
Web: http://www.uniara.uia.es

📖 **Programas universitarios**

Campos de estudios: todas las materias principales, derecho, ecología, medio ambiente, economía, estudios americanos, estudios sobre el desarrollo, historia, recursos naturales.
Descripción:
(a) Maestrías en: conservación del medio natural, espacios culturales y uso público, energías renovables, aplicaciones en la edificación, neurociencia, comunicación, industria audiovisual en el espacio iberoamericano, teorías críticas del derecho y la democracia en Iberoamérica, alternativas democráticas ante el siglo XXI, arqueología americana, desarrollo ecológico en América latina, agroecología y desarrollo rural sostenible en Andalucía y América latina, historia latinoamericana, gestión pública en turismo, impactos territoriales y ambientales de la globalización en ámbitos periféricos y centrales en América latina y Europa, biotecnología de plantas;
(b) Experto universitario en lengua quichua;
(c) Doctorados: ganadería ecológica, gestión de explotaciones en zonas desfavorecidas, relaciones interétnicas en América latina.
Se destina(n): (a) a titulados superiores con experiencia y proyectos de investigación.
Asistencia financiera: existen becas de matrícula, de residencia, completas.

861   Universidad Nacional de Educación a Distancia [UNED]
Bravo Murillo 38
28015 Madrid
Tel: (34) (1) 398 6582
Fax: (34) (1) 398 6587
Web: http://www.uned.es
e-mail: nego-vice-relint@admin.uned.es

📖 **Cursos virtuales**

Campos de estudios: todas las materias principales.
Descripción: (a) Licenciaturas en administración y dirección de empresas; derecho; ciencias económicas; filología hispánica; filología inglesa; geografía e historia; pedagogía; psicología; psicopedagogía;
(b) Diplomaturas en: educación social, turismo;
(c) Ingeniería técnica informática (sistemas; gestión);
(d) Ingeniería superior (industrial; informática);
(e) Masters: terapia de conducta; nuevas tecnologías de la información y la comunicación; administración de empresas; sistemas de enseñanza y aprendizaje abiertos y a distancia; enseñanza del español como segunda lengua; teoría y aplicación práctica del método de los elementos finitos y simulación;
(f) Experto universitario: dirección de recursos humanos en la empresa; finanzas; teoría y aplicación práctica del método de los elementos finitos y simulación;
(g) Experto universitario: teoría y aplicación práctica del método de los elementos finitos y simulación;
(h) Doctorados: ciencias, ciencias económicas y empresariales, ciencias políticas y sociología, derecho, educación, filología, filosofía, geografía e historia, ingeniería industrial, psicología;
(i) Otras carreras: física nuclear; electricidad y magnetismo; macromoléculas;
(j) Fundación UNED: cursos de master universitario, especialista universitario, experto universitario, ciencias de la salud (experto, master, diploma, otros);
(k) Vicerrectorado de Educación Permanente: estudios de posgrado (programas de especialización y de formación del profesorado y formación continua); actualización de conocimientos (programa de enseñanza abierta y programa de desarrollo profesional); programa de formación en el área de la salud (cursos de especialización universitaria y de actualización de conocimientos).
Asistencia financiera: consultar la página web http://www.uned.es/investigacion/becas/index.html o solicitar información al Vicerrectorado de Investigación (en la dirección del título o e-mail a investigacion@adm.uned.es) por becas nacionales (organismos, fundaciones, entidades), becas de tercer ciclo UNED, becas en prácticas, premios.
Inscripciones: por información sobre convenios, programas internacionales, centros en el extranjero, dirigirse a Vicerrectorado de Relaciones Internacionales en la dirección del título o consultar la página web http://www.uned.es/relaciones-internacionales.

862   Universidad Politécnica de Cataluña - Barcelona Cátedra Gaudí - Escuela Técnica Superior de Arquitectura [UPC]
Avenida de Pedralbes 7
08034 Barcelona
Tel: (34) (3) 204 5250
Web: http://www.upc.es

📖 **Programa de doctorado**

Campos de estudios: arquitectura, artes, artes aplicadas, museología y museografía.
Descripción: arquitectura de Gaudí, restauración de monumentos, jardinería y paisaje.
Se destina(n): a arquitectos o titulados superiores de cualquier país.
Duración: 2 años (comienza en octubre).
Inscripciones: hasta octubre.

863   Universidad Politécnica de Cataluña - Barcelona Escuela Superior de Agricultura [UPC]
Conte d'Urgel 187
08036 Barcelona
Tel: (34) (3) 430 4207
Fax: (34) (3) 419 2601
Web: http://www.upc.es

📖 **Programa de posgrado en jardinería y paisajismo**

Campos de estudios: agricultura, botánica, ciencias agronómicas, horticultura, urbanismo.
Se destina(n): a ingenieros técnicos agrícolas, ingenieros agrónomos, biólogos, arquitectos o titulados en áreas afines.
Duración: 8 meses (comienza binualmente en octubre de años pares).
Idioma: en español y catalán.
Inscripciones: hasta septiembre, dirigirse a la Secretaría del Programa.

864   Universidad Politécnica de Cataluña - Barcelona Fundación Centro Internacional de Hidrología Subterránea [UPC]
Gran Capitán s/n
08003 Barcelona
Tel: (34) (3) 319 5300
Fax: (34) (3) 268 4584
Web: http://www.upc.es

📖 **Programas universitarios**

Campos de estudios: geología, hidrología, ingeniería, ingeniería civil.
Programas:
(a) Curso internacional de hidrología subterránea;
(b) Master en hidrología subterránea.
Se destina(n): a nacionales de cualquier país que tengan un título universitario de una facultad de ciencias (geología, física, matemáticas, química, biología) o ingeniería u otro de una escuela técnica superior, y un buen conocimiento del idioma español.

Duración: (a) 6 meses (comienza a mediados de enero);
(b) según las disciplinas elegidas (comienza en octubre).
Asistencia financiera: para (a), ayudas de matrícula.
Inscripciones: (a) hasta el 30 de septiembre.

865 Universidad Politécnica de Valencia Centro de Formación de Posgrado [UPV]

Camino de Vera s/n
46022 Valencia
Tel: (34) (6) 387 7751
Fax: (34) (6) 387 7759
Web: http://www.cfp.upv.es
e-mail: cfp@cfp.upv.es

📖 Programas de postgrado

Campos de estudios: todas las materias principales,
alimentación, artes, construcción, formación profesional,
gestión, informática, museología y museografía, urbanismo.
Descripción: master, especialista uniiversitario o
especialista profesional según el caso, en las siguientes áreas:
agroalimentación, arte y restauración, construcción y
urbanismo, gestión, informática y telecomunicaciones,
industria.

866 Universidad Politécnica de Valencia Instituto de Turismo, Empresa y Sociedad [UPV]

Departamento de Economía Agraria
Camino de la Vera s/n
46071 Valencia
Tel: (34) (6) 387 7135
Fax: (34) (6) 387 7759
Web: http://www.upv.es

📖 Curso internacional de posgrado en turismo

Campos de estudios: turismo, hotelería.
Se destina(n): a diplomados o licenciados de cualquier
carrera, con nivel medio-alto de español e inglés.
Duración: 7 meses (inicio en noviembre).
Asistencia financiera: el Ministerio de Industria y
Turismo otorga cada año un número limitado de becas a
licenciados y diplomados universitarios que deseen cursar
postgrados en turismo.
Inscripciones: hasta el 25 de octubre.

867 Universidad Pompeu Fabra

Plaza de la Merced 12
08002 Barcelona
Tel: (34) (3) 542 2060
Fax: (34) (3) 542 2081
Web: http://www.upf.es

📖 Programas universitarios

Campos de estudios: todas las materias principales.
Descripción: (a) Estudios de primer y segundo ciclo
(licenciaturas, ingenierías, ingenierías técnicas, graduados
universitarios, diplomaturas);
(b) Estudios de tercer ciclo y formación continua (doctorados,
masters, cursos de perfeccionamiento, cursos y diplomas de
postgrado);
(c) Titulaciones y cursos complementarios: diploma de
estudios generales, diploma de estudios hispánicos, cursos de
verano.
Materias de estudio: áreas de ciencias de la salud y de la
vida, ciencias económicas y empresariales, ciencias sociales y
de la comunicación (ciencias del trabajo, ciencias políticas y
gestión pública, comunicación audiovisual, periodismo),
derecho, humanidades, traducción e interpretación, riesgos
laborales, ingeniería de telecomunicaciones, informática,
relaciones laborales, comercio internacional, diseño.
Asistencia financiera: becas de la Agencia Española de
Cooperación Internacional (AECI).
Inscripciones: solicitar todas las informaciones relativas a
estudiantes extranjeros al Area de Relaciones Internacionales
(en la dirección del título o ari@grup.upf.es).

868 Universidad Pontificia de Comillas

Alberto Aguilera 23
28015 Madrid
Tel: (34) (1) 540 6119
Fax: (34) (1) 542 3453
Web: http://www.upco.es
e-mail: oia@oia.upco.es

📖 Programas universitarios

Campos de estudios: ciencias económicas y comerciales,
ciencias sociales, derecho, derecho canónico, enfermería,
estudios paramédicos, fisiología, ingeniería, teología, religión.
Descripción: (a) Estudios de primer y segundo ciclos
(ingeniero técnico o diplomado; ingeniero superior o
licenciado);
(b) Estudios de tercer ciclo (doctorado);
(c) Estudios propios de postgrado y especialización
(programas master, cursos superiores, cursos de
especialización, otros).
Materias de estudio: áreas de teología, derecho canónico,
ciencias humanas y sociales, ciencias económicas y
empresariales, derecho, ingeniería, enfermeria y fisioterapia,
práctica jurídica.
Asistencia financiera: becas y ayudas oficiales al estudio
y a la iniciación en la investigación y participación en los
programas comunitarios para la movilidad y el intercambio de
estudiantes.
Inscripciones: dirigirse a la Oficina de Información y
Acogida que puede brindar todo tipo de información útil para
el estudiante extranjero.

869 Universidad Pontificia de Salamanca en Madrid Facultad de Ciencias Políticas y Sociología [UPSA]

Paseo de Juan XXIII n° 3
28040 Madrid
Tel: (34) (1) 533 5200
Fax: (34) (1) 533 5200

📖 Programas universitarios

Campos de estudios: sociología.
Programas:
(a) Licenciatura en sociología;
(b) Doctorado en sociología.
Descripción: (b) temas: sociedad civil y estado de
bienestar, globalización y desarrollo.
Se destina(n): (a) prueba de selectividad; (b) título de
licenciado.

870 Universidad Ramón Llull [URL]

Claravall, L-3
08022 Barcelona
Tel: (34) (3) 602 2220
Fax: (34) (3) 602 2249
Web: http://www.url.es
e-mail: mg@sec.url.es

📖 Programas universitarios

Campos de estudios: todas las materias principales.
Descripción: Estudios de primer y segundo ciclo,
doctorados, master y posgrados dictados en sus diferentes
instituciones federadas (institutos, facultades, escuelas) en
áreas de: química, ciencias de la educación, ciencias de la
salud, ciencias sociales y ciencias de la comunicación,
ingeniería, arquitectura, filosofía, administración y dirección
de empresas, derecho, ciencias sociales, trabajo social,
educación social, salud mental, bioética, diseño.
Asistencia financiera: Los estudiantes pueden solicitar las
ayudas económicas que ofrece el Ministerio de Educación y
Cultura a través del Negociado de Becas de la Universidad
Ramon Llull. Además de este tipo de becas, cada institución
dispone de sistemas propios de ayudas económicas al
estudiante que se concretan en diferentes modalidades: becas
de ayuda al estudio, créditos al honor, becas a la excelencia
académica, créditos preferenciales con entidades financieras,
reducciones en el precio del crédito académico según ingresos
familiares, etc. La Universidad participa además en diversos
programas de intercambio y cooperación.

871 Universidad San Pablo CEU [CEU]

Isaac Peral 58
28040 Madrid
Tel: (34) (1) 456 6300
Fax: (34) (1) 455 3610
Web: http://www.ceu.es
e-mail: sdi@ceu.es

📖 Programas universitarios

Campos de estudios: administración de empresas,
biblioteconomía, ciencias humanas, derecho, economía,
farmacia y farmacología, industria alimentaría, periodismo,
química.
Descripción:
(a) Diplomatura en ciencias empresariales, en biblioteconomía
y documentación;
(b) Licenciatura en derecho, en derecho con especialidad
jurídico-empresarial o jurídico-comunitaria, en administración
y dirección de empresas; en economía, en farmacia, en
química, en ciencias y tecnología de los alimentos, en
humanidades, en periodismo.
Duración: entre 3 y 5 años (los cursos comienzan en
septiembre).
Asistencia financiera: se conceden ayudas al estudio a
aquellos alumnos que contando con méritos suficientes,
carecen de recursos económicos. Estas ayudas se solicitan
anualmente.
Inscripciones: en abril, dirigirse al Servicio de
Información Académica, Julián Romea 18, 28003 Madrid.

872 Universidad San Pablo CEU [CEU]

Isaac Peral 58
28040 Madrid
Tel: (34) (1) 456 6300
Fax: (34) (1) 455 3610
Web: http://www.ceu.es
e-mail: sdi@ceu.es

🎓 Programa de becas

Campos de estudios: todas las materias principales.
Becas:
(a) Erasmus/Socrates;
(b) Intercampus;
(c) Convenios bilaterales.
Se conceden: a alumnos matriculados en La Universidad
San Pablo CEU que justifiquen necesidad económica, que
conozcan el idioma del país de destino, con buen expediente
académico; (a) están reservadas a españolas.
Lugar: centros universitarios de Portugal, Francia,
Alemania, Suiza, Reino Unido, Irlanda, Bélgica, Países Bajos.
Duración: (a) y (c) 8 a 12 semanas; (b) 6 meses o 1 año
académico.
Importe: (a) monto fijo por mes; (b) para españoles: viaje,
alojamiento y manutención; para extranjeros, alojamiento y
manutención; (c) costes académicos.
Solicitudes: fecha límite variable; solicitar informes a
Programas Exteriores, Julián Romea 18, Despacho 6, 28003
Madrid.

873 Universidad SEK

Campus de Santa Cruz la Real
Cardenal Zúñiga 12
40003 Segovia
Tel: (34) (2) 141 2410
Fax: (34) (2) 144 5593
Web: http://www.usek.es
e-mail: usek@usek

📖 Programas universitarios

Campos de estudios: todas las materias principales,
biología, ciencias de la información, español, historia del arte,
programas de verano, psicología, turismo, hotelería.
Descripción: Titulaciones oficiales:
(a) Cursos de verano: cursos de español para extranjeros;
(b) Centro de estudios integrados de arquitectura: arquitecto y
arquitecto técnico; master en urbanismo, equilibrio territorial
y desarrollo sostenible;
(c) Facultad de ciencias de la información: licenciado en
periodismo y comunicación audiovisual; doctorado en cultura
y comunicación para la sociedad de la información;

(d) Facultad de estudios del patrimonio cultural: licenciado en
historia del arte, con especialidades en investigación, en
protección y gestión, en conservación y restauración, en
difusión y didáctica; graduado superior en ciencias del
patrimonio, diplomado en turismo;
(e) Facultad de psicología: licenciado en psicología, master en
intervención clínica en ámbitos sociosanitarios;
(f) Facultad de biología: licenciado en biología, especialidad
biológica ambiental, biología molecular.
Asistencia financiera: becas de la Universidad, del
Ministerio de Educación y Cultura, becas Sócrates Erasmus;
programas internacionales de cooperación e intercambio.
Inscripciones: solicitar todas las informaciones útiles para
estudiantes extranjeros a la Oficina de Relaciones
Internacionales.

874 Unversidad Rey Juan Carlos

Calle Tulipán s/n
28933 Móstoles, Madrid
Tel: (34) (1) 665 5060
Fax: (34) (1) 488 7173
Web: http://www.urjc.es
e-mail: info@urjc.es

📖 Programas universitarios

Campos de estudios: todas las materias principales.
Descripción: Títulos universitarios oficiales, doctorados,
títulos propios, en áreas de: ciencias experimentales y
tecnología, ciencias de la salud, ciencias de la comunicación,
turismo, ciencias jurídicas y sociales, gestión empresarial y
marketing.
Asistencia financiera: becas y ayudas: Sócrates/Erasmus,
Séneca, becas del Ministerio de Asuntos Exteriores (oferta de
formación para ciudadanos españoles y extranjeros, para
estudios en España y en el exterior), becas ALBAN (becas de
Alto Nivel América Latina), programa de la Unión Europea
para la realización de programas de postgrado para
latinoamericanos en la Unión Europea, becas ALFA (América
Latina Formación Académica), programa de cooperación
entre instituciones europeas y latinoamericanas.
Inscripciones: Por todas las informaciones útiles para
estudiantes extranjeros, dirigirse a la Oficina de Relaciones
Internacionales en la dirección del título o consultar la página
web general, enlace "Relaciones Internacionales".

Estonia

Academic year: September to June.
Organization of higher education system:
• Professional higher education is the first stage of higher
education, which aims at acquiring the competencies
necessary for work in a certain profession or further study at
the Master's level. The normal length of study is 3 to 4.5
years. Graduates who have completed these studies are
awarded a diploma ('rakenduskõrghridusõppe diplom').
• University first stage: Bachelor's level, for acquisition of
basic knowledge and skills. The nominal length of studies is
generally 3 years, and in some disciplines up to 4 years.
Graduates who have completed their studies are awarded the
degree of 'bakalaureusekraad'.
• University second stage: Master's study for the training of
specialists with advanced theoretical knowledge. The nominal
length of the studies is 1 to 2 years beyond the first stage.
Graduates who have completed their studies are awarded the
degree of 'magistrikraad'.
• Medical, dental, pharmaceutical, veterinary, architectural,
civil engineering and teacher training studies are based on
curricula integrating Bachelor's and Master's study.
Completion of the study programme provides a qualification
corresponding to the Master's level. Graduates who have
completed their studies are awarded a diploma certifying the
completion of the respective integrated programme but in
some cases, on decision of the university, the magistrikraad
may be awarded.
• Doctoral studies constitute the highest stage of higher
education aimed at acquiring knowledge and skills necessary
for independent research, development or professional
creative work. The nominal length of studies is 3 to 4 years.
Graduates who have completed their studies are awarded a
research degree, the 'doktorikraad'.
Monetary unit: Estonian kroon (EEK).

National student admission: All Estonian citizens and persons living in Estonia on the basis of a residency permit have equal rights in competing for admission to higher education ('kõrgharidus'), if they have secondary education ('keskharidus') obtained in Estonia or the equivalent in their own countries. The conditions and procedures for admission are established by the council of higher education institution and approved by the Minister of Education and Science ('haridus- ja teadusminister'). In general, the results of state examinations ('riigieksamid') passed in a general secondary school ('gümnaasium') are accepted as the basis of admittance, sometimes a colloquium or a discussion (professional aptitude test) is required. For admission to study programmes in art and music, aptitude is tested by the presentation of a creative work or through a creative competition. Private institutions may establish additional conditions for admission. Students are accepted according to their entry requirement results, under the conditions established by the council of higher education institution. The admission requirement for Master Studies is the 'bakalaureusekraad' or an equivalent level of qualification (at least 3 years of tertiary education). The general admission requirement for Doctoral studies is a magistrikraad or a corresponding qualification.

International student admission: Admission to the study programmes is administrated by the higher education institution. The candidates apply directly to the higher education institution. Applicants wishing to pursue professional higher education studies ('rakenduskõrgharidusõpe') or 'bakalaureus' study are required to have completed their secondary education or corresponding education level necessary for higher education. Applicants must be eligible for higher education in their own country. In a country where the secondary-school-leaving certificate is sufficient in itself for admission to higher education, additional qualifying examinations may also be required for admission to higher education institutions in Estonia.

Language: The language of instruction and coursework is usually Estonian. Knowledge of Estonian is essential for regular- and state-financed courses. Applicants wishing to study a full undergraduate programme in Estonian must first complete a language competency examination. Some higher education institutions offer Estonian language courses for foreign students as a pre-study possibility or as a part of the regular study programme. Most universities have a foreign language (usually English) test as part of the entrance examinations. An increasing number of courses and study programmes are offered in English and Russian and language proficiency must be proven for these programmes.

Immigration requirements: Updated information on visa requirements can be found on the web-site of the Estonian Ministry of Foreign Affairs ('Välisministeerium)' - web: www.vm.ee/. A temporary residence permit for study is required for stays of more than three months (in some cases only one month). The residence permit should be obtained from the nearest Estonian Embassy or Consulate well before arrival in Estonia. A residence permit may be issued for up to one year. If an international student wishes to continue studies in the same educational institution, a residence permit may be extended for a year at a time, but not more than a total of six years.

Estimated expenses for one academic year: Due to the changing economic conditions, tuition fees (also the housing and supplies) are modified periodically. Therefore, the most reliable information source on tuition fees is the higher education institution in which the student is interested.

Information services:
• All applications to institutions of higher education should be addressed directly; for information on the individual institutions; http://www.hm.ee (in Estonian)
• The Ministry of Education and Research of Estonia: http://www.hm.ee/uus/hm/client
• The Estonian Academic Recognition Information Centre (The Estonian ENIC/NARIC) Akadeemilise Tunnustamise Infokeskus (Eesti ENIC/NARIC), Foundation Archimedes, L.Koidula 13A 10125 Tallinn, Estonia; tel: +372-696-2415; fax: +372-696-2419; email: enic-naric@archimedes.ee; web: http://www.socrates.ee/et/enicnaric.html
• Federation of Estonian Student Unions; email: eyl@eyl.ee; http://web: www.eyl.ee.

Scholarships for international students: Some universities offer financial aid to international students, amounting to 8 to 20 percent of the tuition fee and are awarded according to the student's academic performance and

initiative. International students enrolled in Estonian studies language and literature programmes may also be eligible for financial aid from their universities. Requests for study loans must be made in the student's home country before commencing studies in Estonia.

Open and distance learning: There are possibilities to take some of the university courses through distance learning as part of the regular degree programme.

Recognition of studies and qualification:
• Students wishing to continue their studies in Estonia on the basis of a foreign qualification must apply for admission as well as for recognition of their studies directly to the higher education institution.
• The Estonian Parliament signed and ratified (10 February 1998) the Council of Europe and UNESCO Convention on the Recognition of Qualifications Concerning Higher Education in the European Region (Lisbon, 1997). Under the Agreement among the Governments of Estonia, Latvia and Lithuania on the academic recognition of educational qualifications in the Baltic Educational Space was signed in February 2000.
• For further information on recognition matters: Akadeemilise Tunnustamise Infokeskus (Eesti ENIC/NARIC), Estonian ENIC/NARIC, Foundation Archimedes, L.Koidula 13A 10125 Tallinn, Estonia; tel: +372-696-2415; fax: +372-696-2419; email: enic-naric@archimedes.ee; web: www.socrates.ee/et/enicnaric.html.

Accommodation services: The International Relations Office of each institution of higher education accepting international students will be able to provide information on accommodation possibilities and other useful information.

Work opportunities: A work permit is necessary to work in Estonia; students who have received a residence permit for study in an educational institution in Estonia may apply for a work permit at the Citizenship and Migration Board (Kodakondsus- ja migratsiooniamet).

Publications / Websites:
• 'Study in Estonia', 2004, web: www.hm.ee (in Estonian); http://www.socrates.ee/dokumendid/studyinestonia.pdf (in English)
• Socrates Estonian National Agency; web: www.socrates.ee.

---

875   Estonian Academy of Music [EAOM]
(Eesti Muusikaakadeemia)
Ravala pst 16
10143 Tallinn
Tel: +372-667-5709
Fax: +372-667-5762
Web: http://www.ema.edu.ee
e-mail: ema@ema.edu.ee

📖 **Undergraduate, Graduate Programmes in Music**

Study Domains: music and musicology, performing arts.
Programmes: Higher education in all specialities of music (including musicology) and dramatic art: 570 participants.
Open to: applicants of any nationality and age who have completed secondary education.
Duration: 4 + 1 years; 4 years for graduate courses.
Fees: from 1,600€ to 3,800€ for one year full-time; citizens of EU countries are eligible to compete for tuition-free studies.
Applications: by 27 June, to the above address.

876   Estonian Agricultural University [EAU]
Department of International and Public Relations
Kreutzwaldi 64
51014 Tartu
Tel: +372-7-313-001
Web: http://www.eau.ee
e-mail: info@eau.ee

📖 **Undergraduate, Postgraduate Programmes / Agriculture**

Study Domains: agriculture, agronomic sciences, cattle breeding, economic and commercial sciences, fisheries, forestry, horticulture, social sciences, veterinary medicine, veterinary sciences.

Programmes: Bachelor's degree ('bakalaureus') and postgraduate degree programmes leading to Master's and Doctorate degrees.
Description: Faculty of Agronomy: agronomy, horticulture, production and marketing of agricultural products; Faculty of Agricultural Engineering: agricultural engineering, energy application engineering, industrial engineering, ergonomics; Faculty of Economics & Social Sciences: economics and entrepreneurship, accounting and financial management; environmental economics; Faculty of Forestry: forest management, forest industry, natural resource management; Faculty of Rural Engineering: geodesy, water management, land management, rural building, real estate planning; Faculty of Veterinary Science: veterinary medicine, meat technology, dairy technology; Institute of Animal Science: animal science, agroecology, aquaculture; Institute of Environmental Protection: landscape architecture, landscape protection and preservation; Institute of Zoology and Botany: applied hydrobiology.
Duration: Bachelor's: upon successful completion of 160 credits and taking a final examination or after successful defence of their diploma thesis. Master's: 80 credits longer (generally two years); Doctorate: 160 credits longer (generally 4 more years beyond Bachelor's). Studies in veterinary medicine lead to an equivalent of a Master's degree, take six years to complete and require 240 credits for graduation. (The duration and extent of studies are expressed in credit points. One credit point is equivalent to one study week, which refers to 40 hours' average input of studies on the part of the student.).
Applications: to the above address.

877 Estonian Business School [EBS]

Lauteri 3
10114 Tallinn
Tel: +372-665-1300
Fax: +372-665-3959
Web: http://www.ebs.ee
e-mail: international@ebs.ee

📖 Undergraduate, Postgraduate Programmes / Business

Study Domains: administration, business administration, European studies, information science, management.
Programmes: Bachelor's, Master's and Doctorate degree programmes at the School's Centre for Baltic Studies, Institute of Informatics, Institute of Management and Institute of Foreign Languages.
Open to: candidates of all nationalities meeting academic, financial and linguistic requirements; admission based on competitive entrance examination.
Financial assistance: tuition waivers of 20-80 percent; company sponsorship programmes.
Languages: Estonian and English; International B.B.A. programme is taught entirely in English.
Applications: to the above address for full details.

878 Estonian Institute of Humanities [EIH]

(Eesti Humanitaarinstituut)
Salme 12
10413 Tallin
Tel: +372-660-5903
Fax: +372-660-5904
Web: http://www.ehi.ee
e-mail: ehi@ehi.ee

📖 Undergraduate, Graduate Programmes

Study Domains: all major fields.
Programmes: Bachelor's and Master's degree programmes in the following fields: Asian studies, audio-visual media, cultural studies, European studies, history, human sciences, interpretation and translation, languages, liberal arts, linguistics, literature and civilization, philology, philosophy, psychology, social sciences, statistics, tourism and visual arts.
Open to: candidates of any country fulfilling the necessary requirements.
Fees: 10,000-16,000 EEK per year; living expenses: 25,000 EEK per year.
Languages: Estonian, English, German and Finnish.

Applications: by 1 March.

879 International University Concordia [CIUE]

(Concordia Rahvusvaheline Ülikool Eestis)
Kaluri tee 3/5
Haabneeme, Viimsi vald
74001 Harjumaa
Tel: +372-699-6566
Fax: +372-699-6500
Web: http://www.university.ee

📖 Undergraduate, Graduate, Postgraduate Programmes

Study Domains: audio-visual media, business administration, European studies, international law, international relations, law, political science, public relations, summer programmes.
Programmes: Bachelor's, Master's, Ph.D. degrees.
Description: (a) Bachelor of Arts in Business with emphasis on International business consisting of liberal arts, business and regional studies; possible specialization in study of the European Union via the CIUE European Integration Institute; (b) Bachelor of Arts in Business with emphasis on Technology Management with specialization areas in Information Technology; Physics, Chemistry and Biology in Applications for Industrial and Human Needs; Environmental Sciences and Technology; (c) Bachelor of Jurisprudence including studies in Legal Theory, International Law and Institutions, European Law, Local Law and Institutions, Comparative Legal Studies, business and Humanities, students can specialize in EC Law via CIUE European Integration Institute; (d) Bachelor of Arts in Media with Emphasis on Television, Radio, Media Management, Journalism or Public Relations; (e) Master of Business Administration; (f) Programme of studies at CIUE European Integration Institute.
Open to: students of any nationality with a secondary-education certificate; 2 letters of recommendation; English proficiency required; essay and interview for Media applicants only.
Held: (a) students have the opportunity to study for 1 or more semesters in Lakeland College, United States; (c) possibility to participate in an intensive 4-week summer programme on the Law of the Emerging Markets and Transitional Democracies offered by the Scandinavian/Baltic Institute, joint programme of CIUE and Stetson University College of Law, United States.
Duration: 4 years.
Fees: tuition: US$2,300-$2,700 per academic year; books: approx. US$150.
Financial assistance: scholarship covering full or part of the tuition is available.
Applications: Office of Admissions in Estonia and Finnish Representative: Luhike jalg 7, EE-0001 Tallinn, Estonia; tel: +372 2 601 212; fax: +372 2 444 290; email: admissions@ciue.edu.ee; Office of Admissions in Latvia: Baznicas 8-5 LV1010 Riga, Latvia; tel:+371 728 9604; fax: +371 728 9604; email: ciue@libane. edu.lv; Office of Admissions in Lithuania: Saviciaus 11-18 LI 2024 Vilnius, Lithuania; tel: +370 2 612 244; fax: +370 2 613 404.

🎓 Scholarships

Study Domains: all major fields.
Description: full and partial scholarships.
Open to: Estonian national and international students with good academic achievements.
Applications: for further information, consult website: http://www.ciue.edu.ee/main.php?admissions.

880 Tallinn Pedagogical University [TPU]

(Tallinna Pedagoogikaülikool)
25 Narva Road
10120 Tallinn
Tel: +372-640-9144
Fax: +372-640-9118
Web: http://www.tlu.ee
e-mail: disa@tlu.ee

📖 Undergraduate, Graduate and Postgraduate Programmes

Study Domains: early childhood education, ecology, environment, languages, literature and civilization, mathematics, music and musicology, performing arts, physical education, physics, recreation and leisure, sciences, social work, tourism, hotel and catering management, vocational training.
Programmes: Bachelor's, Master's and Ph.D. degree programmes; certificate and diploma programmes; studies in leisure, recreation and tourism management; international students' programmes.
Open to: applicants of any nationality with a secondary-education certificate; interviews, practical tasks and two recommendations required.
Duration: 3 to 5 years; summer courses in July.
Fees: see website for information.
Applications: by 1 June for Fall term and by 1 October for Spring term, to the Department of International Student Affairs (DISA); at the above address.

☛ Scholarships

Study Domains: all major fields.
Scholarships: scholarships in all major fields.
Open to: international students meeting academic requirements.
Value: full and partial scholarships.
Applications: consult the website for further information: http://www.tpu.ee/english.html.

881   Tallinn Technical University [TTU]

(Tallinna Tehnikaülikool)
International Study Center
Ehitajate tee 5
19086 Tallinn
Tel: +372-6-202-002
Fax: +372-6-202-020
Web: http://www.ttu.ee
e-mail: ttu@ttu.ee

📖 Undergraduate, Graduate Programmes

Study Domains: business administration, chemical engineering, civil engineering, computer science, ecology, environment, economy, information science, mechanical engineering, summer programmes, transport.
Programmes: Bachelor's, Master's and Ph.D. degrees in technical studies.
Open to: applicants with secondary-school certificate and entrance examination; must be proficient in Estonian and Russian.
Fees: Bachelor's: 30,000 EEK per year; Master's: 30,000 EEK per year; Ph.D.: free tuition.
Languages: Estonian and Russian.
Applications: to the above address for further information.

☛ Scholarships

Study Domains: business administration, engineering, industrial technology, information science, management.
Scholarships: six scholarships for foreign students, one per international programme; for studies at Bachelor's degree level in business administration, information technology, business administration, information technology; at Master's degree level in industrial engineering and management, environmental management and cleaner production.
Description: students may also apply for financial aid offered by companies.
Applications: apply to the above address; for further information consult the website: http://www.ip.ttu.ee.

882   University of Tartu [UT]

(Tartu Ülikooli)
International Relations Office
Ülikooli 18
50090 Tartu
Tel: +372-737-5150
Fax: +372-737-5440
Web: http://www.ut.ee
e-mail: proffice@ut.ee

📖 Undergraduate, Graduate, Postgraduate Programmes

Study Domains: all major fields, cultural studies, medicine.
Programmes: Bachelor's, Master's and Ph.D. programmes in all major fields; Baltic Studies: language, culture, literature, economics, politics, geography, history of the Baltic countries (Estonia, Latvia, Lithuania).
Open to: candidates of any nationality, over 17 years of age, with a secondary-education certificate and university eligibility in their own country.
Duration: 5 months.
Fees: tuition: 15,000 EEK per semester; living expenses: 3,000-4,000 EEK.
Languages: Estonian, and some English.
Applications: by 1 June and 1 November, to the International Students' Office at the above address.

☛ Tartu University Foundation

Study Domains: cultural studies, history, languages, literature and civilization.
Scholarships: grants for foreign students majoring in Estonian language or culture.
Subjects: Estonian language, literature, history, culture.
Open to: University of Tartu students.
Duration: up to 1 year (renewable).
Value: from 5,000-25,000 EEK per year.
Applications: by 1 June or 1 November, to the International Student Office at the above address; consult website for further information: http://www.ut.ee/sihtasutus/index_eng.html; email: sihtasutus@ut.ee.

Ethiopia

Academic year: September to June.
Major institutions of higher education:
• Addis Ababa University (AAU); web: www.aau.edu.et.
Monetary unit: Ethiopian birr.
National student admission: Access to higher education is based on the Ethiopian school-leaving certificate examination (ESLCE) or its equivalent. In principle, admission to diploma programmes is possible with a pass in 2 subjects at C-level and 3 subjects at D-level; in practice, passes in 5 subjects with a 'C' average are required. Foreign students may enrol in one of the institutions if they provide the academic certificates required by the institution concerned. Foreign qualifications recognized as equivalent to the Ethiopian school-leaving certificate examination are: the General Certificate of Education (GCE) of the University of London, the Cambridge Overseas Examination, the West African school certificate and the Oxford examination. The Commission for Higher Education may grant equivalence to other secondary-school certificates in individual cases. Applications should be made to the Ministry of Education.
Language: The principal language of instruction is English. Students must be proficient in English at TOEFL level.
Immigration requirements: Foreign students may enrol in one of the institutions if they provide a health certificate issued by a recognized health officer, a residence permit, a visa and financial guarantees.
Estimated expenses for one academic year: Foreign students are offered grants, scholarships, fellowships and assistantships through bilateral agreements between the parties concerned.
Information services:
• Ministry of Education, PO Box 1367; Addis Ababa; Ethiopia.
Open and distance learning: Addis Ababa University has plans to launch a programme of open and distance learning in the near future.
Recognition of studies and qualification:
• the individual institutions of higher education
• Department of Higher Education, Ministry of Education; PO Box 1367; Addis Ababa; Ethiopia.

883   Addis Ababa University [AAU]

PO Box 1176
Addis Ababa
Tel: +251-1-239-800
Fax: +251-1-239-768
Web: http://www.aau.edu.et

📖 Undergraduate, Graduate, Postgraduate Programmes

Study Domains: anatomy, biology, building industry, chemical industry, chemistry, civil engineering, history, languages, law, mechanical engineering, medicine, paediatrics, physics, physiology, psychiatry, sciences, technology, veterinary medicine.
Programmes: Diploma, Bachelor's, MD, DVM, Master's, Speciality Certificate and Ph.D. degree programmes in arts, science, medicine, veterinary medicine, history, languages, chemistry and biology.
Open to: candidates of any nationality meeting admissions criteria; secondary-school certificate (or equivalent).
Duration: depending on programme; courses begin in September and February.
Languages: language of instruction: English.
Applications: by February, to the Registrar at the above address.

884   Alemaya University [AU]

PO Box 138
Dire Dawa
Tel: +251-5-610-704
Fax: +251-5-610-713
Web: http://www.alemayau.edu.et
e-mail: alemaya.univ@ethionet.et

📖 Undergraduate, Graduate, Postgraduate Programmes

Study Domains: accounting, agriculture, agronomic sciences, biology, cattle breeding, chemistry, continuing education, English, geography, history, horticulture, law, management, marketing, mathematics, nursing, physics, teacher education, veterinary medicine.
Programmes: courses leading to diploma, Bachelor's, Master's and Ph.D. degrees as well as continuing education courses in education, accounting and management.
Open to: nationals of all countries meeting admission criteria.
Duration: 4 years for B.Sc. programme; 2 years for M.Sc. programme (Academic year, September to June).
Fees: tuition fees: US$860 per year; living costs: approximately US$150 per month.
Languages: English.
Applications: by July 15 to the office of the Registrar at the above address.

885   Bahir Dar University [BDU]

PO Box 79
Bahir Dar
Tel: +251-8-200-143
Fax: +251-8-202-025
Web: http://www.telecom.net.et/~bdu/
e-mail: bdtc@telcom.net.et

📖 Undergraduate Programme

Study Domains: accounting, biology, business administration, chemical engineering, chemistry, civil engineering, economy, education, electricity and electronics, English, finance, geography, industrial technology, law, management, marketing, mathematics, mechanical engineering, physics, teacher education, textile industry.
Programmes: Bachelor's degree programmes in engineering; education; accounting; law and business management.
Open to: candidates from all nationality.
Other conditions: candidates must pass entrance examination and be proficient in English.
Languages: English.
Applications: contact the Office of the Registrar at the above address.

Fiji

Academic year: February to November.
Organization of higher education system: Higher education is provided mainly by the University of the South Pacific which serves 12 Member Countries in the Pacific. It is financed by student fees, a grant from the governments of the 12 Member Countries, trading, department funds, institutes, overseas donors, endowment, etc.
Major institutions of higher education: Other institutions of higher education are the Fiji School of Medicine, the Fiji Institute of Technology and the Western Division Technical Centre, the Fiji School of Agriculture and teacher-training colleges.
Monetary unit: Fiji dollar.
National student admission: Foreign students must hold qualifications equivalent to the university's foundation programme, for example, the general certificate of education, advanced (A) level, New Zealand form 7 or successful completion of the final year in an Australian secondary school.
Information services:
• Ministry of Education, International Relations, Marela House, Thurston Street, Suva; tel: +679-3-314-477 / +679-3-220-415; fax: +679-3-303- 51; website: http://www.fiji.gov.fj/ministries/education.shtml.
Open and distance learning: The University of the South Pacific (USP) offers distance and flexible education (DFL) throughout the areas served by the University. There are USP Centres in all Member Countries. Courses are provided face-to-face, through video and audio correspondence, print and online. The University has a network of terminals which provides a wide range of educational facilities to most regional centres. No formal qualifications are required for entry to non-credit courses. The University may award Certificates, Diplomas or Degrees to students who have satisfactorily completed such programmes of credit study organized by DFL.
Recognition of studies and qualification: Ministry of Education, International Relations, Marela House, Thurston Street, Suva; tel: +679-3-314-477; fax: +679-3-303- 51; web: www.fiji.gov.fj/ministries/education.shtml.

---

886   University of the South Pacific [USP]

Laucala Campus, Suva, Fiji
Alafua Campus, Apia, Samoa
Emalus Campus, Port Vila, Vanuatu
Suva
Tel: +679-323-1000
Web: http://www.usp.ac.fj

📖 Undergraduate, Graduate, Postgraduate Programmes

Study Domains: all major fields, accounting, agriculture, arts, chemistry, earth science, education, engineering, journalism, law, management, marine biology, marine science, mathematics, psychology, sciences, social sciences, tourism, hotel and catering management.
Programmes: Certificate, Diploma, Bachelor's, Master's, Ph.D. degrees in all major fields.
Open to: candidates of all nationalities meeting academic, financial and linguistic requirements; for the ACTA programme, candidates must hold the diploma in tropical agriculture of the University or a Bachelor's degree in agriculture.
Held: at Laucala Campus except for Bachelor's programme in law (from year II), which takes place at the Emalus Campus in Vanuatu and the Certificate, Diploma, Bachelors, Master's, PhD programme in agriculture, which takes place at the Alafua Campus in Samoa.
Languages: English; candidates whose first language is not English must pass the TOEFL 550 or the IELTS 6.0.
Applications:
• Laucala Campus: Admissions, Student Academics Services, the University of the South Pacific, Suva, Fiji; email: konusi_l@usp.ac.fi
• Emalus Campus: Admissions, Student Academics Services, Emalus Campus, the University of the South Pacific, Port Vila, Vanuatu
• Alafua Campus: Admissions, Student Academics Services, the University of the South Pacific, Apia, Samoa.

Finland

Academic year: August-September to May.
Organization of higher education system: Higher education is provided by 20 universities and 29 polytechnical institutions. Finnish university degrees correspond to Bachelor's, Master's and Doctor's degrees. In most fields students can also take a Licentiate's degree before the Doctor's degree. At present the degree structures are evolving in line with the Bologna Process, and a new two-cycle Bachelor-Master structure is becoming the prevalent model. The two-cycle degree system (3 years for Bachelor's degree plus 2 years for Master's) will be adopted by Finnish universities in all fields except medicine and dentistry in August 2005. Polytechnical education emphasizes close contacts with business, industry and services, especially at the regional level. Bachelor-level degrees are designed to meet the changing requirements and development needs of the world of work, having a pronounced occupational emphasis, and qualifying graduates for various expert duties. Polytechnical institutions undertake some research and development with an applied and practical emphasis. They also offer postgraduate polytechnical degrees in certain fields.
Monetary unit: Euro (€).
International student admission: Finnish universities and polytechnical institutions cooperate extensively with their counterparts in many countries throughout the world. Finnish institutions of higher education have bilateral agreements with colleges and universities abroad which also cover exchange programmes. In special cases, students can be accepted from outside the above schemes. International applicants for degree studies in Finland must first meet the minimum requirements of their own country for entry into higher education. They must also be prepared to come to Finland to take an entrance examination, especially when applying for entry to universities. Universities select their own students, and all fields apply a numerus clausus (closed number) system in which entrance examinations are a key element. For polytechnical ('ammattikorkeakoulu') entrance: students may apply for entry on completion of general or vocational upper-secondary studies. The Finnish matriculation certificate or completed vocational school, a basic vocational qualification, or an equivalent international or foreign qualification is required. Each institution of higher education makes its own decisions regarding the selection procedure for foreign students, application deadlines, etc. It is necessary to contact the establishment directly for precise information on foreign student admission, entrance requirements, etc.
Language: The principal language of instruction is Finnish. There are a few Swedish-speaking institutions and some others with instruction in both languages. Internationalization has increased the provision of instruction in English; at universities and polytechnical institutions, some degrees can be taken in English. The list of the Finnish higher education institutions and their international study programmes taught in English is available on the Discover Finland website at http://finland.cimo.fi (> Studying). A thorough knowledge of English is often sufficient for doctoral studies. However, in most cases degree studies require a good knowledge of either Finnish or Swedish. Applicants without the knowledge of Finnish or Swedish are required to prove proficiency in English. Most universities offer courses in the Finnish language for foreign students.
Immigration requirements: Degree students must apply for residence permits from their own countries. Only citizens of the European Union (EU) or the European Economic Area (EEA) countries may apply for their permits after arrival in Finland. Students must be able to provide documented evidence of their ability to cover their expenses in Finland. For entrance tests applicants need a visa unless their country has an agreement with Finland abolishing this requirement. Applicants are asked to contact the nearest Finnish embassy or consulate for full admission details. A list of the Finnish missions abroad is on the web at http://www.forming.fi/missions. The international advisory services of the higher education institutions provide information for visiting students.
Estimated expenses for one academic year: There are no tuition fees for Finnish degree studies, however other programmes may be subject to a fee. An annual membership fee (42€-84 €) for the student union is compulsory for all university undergraduates; but optional for doctoral students. The fee entitles the student to the use of student health

services and to travel reductions, etc. The total monthly living expenses of a single student average is estimated at 700 €.
Information services:
• Centre for International Mobility (CIMO), PO Box 343 (Hakaniemenkatu 2), 00531 Helsinki, Finland; tel: +358-9-7747-7033; fax +358-9-7747-7064. Telephone service: +358-1080-6767 (Monday-Thursday from 10:00-12:00 and 13:00-15:00).
• The institutions of higher education have their own international advisory services. For addresses, contact CIMO or the nearest Finnish embassy or consulate or consult the Discover Finland website at http://finland.cimo.fi (> Studying > Higher Education in Finland).
Scholarships for international students:
• Centre for International Mobility (CIMO), P.O. Box 343 (Hakaniemenkatu 2), 00531 Helsinki, Finland; tel: +358-9-7747-7033; fax +358-9-7747-7064. Telephone service: +358-1080-6767 (Monday-Thursday from 10:00-12:00 and 13:00-15:00).
• See individual listings below for details of national scholarship opportunities.
• Other scholarships: http://finland.cimo.fi > Links > Scholarships.
Open and distance learning: Open university instruction is organized by the centres for continuing education of universities, according to university syllabuses. There are no formal educational pre-requirements. Open universities do not award degrees, but students may apply for admission to the respective universities after completing about 60 credits.
Recognition of studies and qualification:
• National Board of Education, P.O. Box 380, FI-00530 Helsinki, tel. +358 9 774 775, e-mail: recognition@oph.fi, http://www.oph.fi/english.
Work opportunities: Students with residence permits are allowed to work part-time (20h/week) during the term and full-time during vacations. These limits do not concern citizens of the Nordic countries or EEA countries.
Publications / Websites:
• 'Discover Finland' web service is targeted to foreign students and education professionals interested in opportunities Finland offers in higher education, practical training and youth exchange. The website gives you all the essential information on studying in Finland, Finnish universities and polytechnical institutions and their study programmes taught in English, studying Finnish language, practical training, youth exchange and life and culture in Finland. Consult the 'Discover Finland' website for further information about Finland: tourist information, information about Finnish government, culture and the Finnish way of life.
• CIMO publishes numerous brochures in English introducing the possibilities for studying in Finland. All the brochures listed here are available on the web in .pdf format (http://www.cimo.fi/english > Publications).
• 'Higher Education in Finland. An Introduction', 44 p. 2003.
• 'Living in Finland. A Practical Guide for International Students and Trainees', 64 p. 2005.
• 'Polytechnics in Finland. A Brief Guide', 52 p. 2003.
• 'Scholarships for international post-graduates, young researchers and scientific/cultural experts to Finland', 6 p. 2005.
• 'Study in Finland. International Programmes in Finnish Higher Education', 2004-2005.
• 'Suomea, Finska, Finnish. Studies in Finnish Language and Culture'. 57 p. 2005.
• 'Universities in Finland. A Brief Guide', 56 p. 2003.
• 'Why Finland?, some of the many good reasons for international students to choose Finland'. 14 p. 2004.
• 'Universities 2004, Annual Report', Ministry of Education Publications, 2005.

---

887   Åbo Akademi University [AAU]

Domkyrkotorget 3
20500 Åbo 50
Tel: +358-2-21-531
Fax: +358-2-215-3230
Web: http://www.abo.fi
e-mail: international@abo.fi

📖 Undergraduate and Postgraduate Programmes

Study Domains: chemical engineering, cultural studies, economic and commercial sciences, education, health and hygiene, history, humanities and arts, languages, law, natural

sciences, pharmacy and pharmacology, psychology, social sciences.
Description: See the www.abo.fi/fa/ie/catalog.pdf or http://www.abo.fi/fa/ie/iuta/index.htm. The catalogue also contains information about Master's Programmes and Graduate Schools. For information about degree studies see http://www.abo.fi/admission. The courses of the regular curriculum of Åbo Akademi University are listed at http://www.abo.fi/studera/undervisningsprogram.
Open to: Åbo Akademi University participates in several international exchange programmes and has signed agreements for bilateral student exchange. These agreements are listed at http://www.abo.fi/fa/ie/avtal/indexeng.htm. Students coming through the above agreements or programmes, and whose applications are supported by the home institution, can be accepted as exchange students. For information about degree studies please see http://www.abo.fi/admission.
Duration: Exchange studies: semester and full year exchanges. Degree studies: three-year Bachelor's degree, two-year Master's degree, two-year Master's programmes.
Languages: Swedish; many courses taught in English; details available in course catalogue, 'Courses and Programmes in English' available on line at http://www.abo.fi/fa/ie/catalog.pdf or http://www.abo.fi/fa/ie/iuta/index.htm.
Applications: (a) to (c) by 30 April for the autumn term and 15 November for the spring term.

888 Academy of Finland
PO Box 99
00501 Helsinki
Tel: +358-9-7748-81
Fax: +358-9-7748-8299
Web: http://www.aka.fi

Research Fellowships
Study Domains: all major fields, research.
Scholarships: Pre-doctoral and Postdoctoral Research Fellowships.
Subjects: all major fields of science.
Open to: Finnish and foreign nationals with a university degree who have demonstrated ability to carry out research work at the required level.
Duration: 2 to 4 years.
Applications: foreign students must first contact a Finnish university professor to make a joint application; by 15 May and 30 November; to the above address.

889 Centre for International Mobility [CIMO]
PO Box 343
00531 Helsinki
Tel: +358-9-7747-7033
Fax: +358-9-7747-7064
Web: http://www.cimo.fi
e-mail: cimoinfo@cimo.fi

CIMO Fellowships
Study Domains: all major fields.
Scholarships: postgraduate studies in all academic fields.
Open to: young researchers of all nationalities.
Place of study: Finnish universities.
Duration: 3 to 12 months.
Value: 725-1,000€ per month (in 2005).
Applications: applications are made by the host departments of Finnish universities at least 3 months before the intended scholarship period. Application forms may be downloaded from website http://finland.cimo.fi (> Scholarships).

Finnish Government Scholarships Pool
Study Domains: all major fields.
Scholarships: Postgraduate studies research and teaching in all academic fields.
Open to: nationals of Australia, Austria, Belgium, Bulgaria, China, Cuba, Czech Republic, Denmark, Egypt, France, Germany, Greece, Hungary, Iceland, India, Ireland, Israel, Italy, Japan, Luxembourg, Mexico, Mongolia, Netherlands, Norway, Poland, Portugal, Republic of Korea, Romania, Slovak Republic, Spain, Switzerland, Turkey and Ukrainia.

Place of study: Finnish universities.
Duration: 3 to 9 months.
Value: 725 € per month (in 2005).
Applications: through scholarship authorities in the applicant's country; application forms obtainable from the national scholarship authorities, the Finnish embassies or CIMO. The form may also be downloaded from the Internet at http://finland.cimo.fi (> Scholarships).

Finnish Studies and Research
Study Domains: Finnish, folklore, literature and civilization.
Scholarships: The programme is divided into two sub-programmes according to the level of study: fellowships for (a) postgraduate studies and research; (b) advanced studies.
Subjects: (a) Finnish language, literature, Finno-Ugric linguistics, ethnology and folklore, (b) for degree students of Finnish language and culture.
Open to: nationals of all countries.
Place of study: Finnish universities.
Duration: (a) 3 to 12 months; (b) max. one academic semester.
Value: (a) 760 € per month (in 2005); (b) 725 € per month (in 2005).
Applications: At least 3 months before the intended scholarship period; (a) applications are made by the host departments of Finnish universities; (b) students apply directly to CIMO for the grant. The applicant should establish contact with the receiving university department before applying. CIMO's application forms are available at Finnish embassies, consulates and cultural and scientific institutes abroad or from CIMO. The form may also be downloaded from the Internet at http://finland.cimo.fi (> Scholarships).

890 Hanken - Swedish School of Economics and Business Administration
PO Box 479
00101 Helsinki
Tel: +358-9-431-331
Fax: +358-9-4313-3333
Web: http://www.hanken.fi
e-mail: info@hanken.fi

Graduate, Postgraduate Programmes
Study Domains: accounting, business, computer science, economic and commercial sciences, economy, finance, geography, industry and commerce, law, management, marketing, statistics, trade.
Programmes: (a) Master of Science programme Advanced Financial Information Systems; (b) Master of Science programme in Computational Finance; (c) Master of Science programme in Corporate Governance; (d) Master of Science programme in Interactive Marketing; (e) Doctoral studies programme; (f) Hanken MBA.
Description: (a) to provide intensive training in developing, managing, and auditing next generation financial information systems; (b) for the solution of finance problems using the most appropriate features of computer science, statistics, and mathematics; (c) to train people for positions within corporate governance and to prepare them for the process of creating and enforcing proper corporate governance mechanisms; (d) leading to a MSc degree of high international standard that will give students the required competence to meet the challenges of an increasingly complex marketplace; (e) to provide the knowledge and skills required for the completion of a PhD degree. The programme consists of courses and a thesis; (f) a two-year, part-time programme consisting of monthly modules in finance, relationship marketing, management and accounting.
Open to: (a) to (d) candidates of all nationalities with a university level Bachelor's degree, including studies in economics and finance. TOEFL or IELTS tests according to the specifications on www.hanken.fi/masters; (e) candidates of all nationalities with a university level Master's degree (B.Sc. plus MA / M.Sc.). TOEFL or IELTS tests according to the specifications on www.hanken.fi; (f) candidates of all nationalities with a Master's or Bachelor's degree and at least five years of relevant work experience.
Duration: (a) to (d) 2 years; (e) 4 years; (f) 2 years starting

every January.
Languages: all candidates must be fluent in English,
TOEFL required, except for (e) where language may be
English or Swedish.
Applications: (a) to (d) by March, for further information,
please visit www.hanken.fi/masters or contact
masters@hanken.fi; (e) twice a year, in May and in
November, for further information please check
www.hanken.fi; (f) by September, for further information,
please contact Hankenmba@hanken.fi.

891 Helsinki School of Economics and Business Administration [HSE]
International Center
Runeberginkatu 14-16
00100 Helsinki
Tel: +358-9-4313-8641
Fax: +358-9-4313-8841
Web: http://www.mbahelsinki.net
e-mail: mbafi@hse.fi

Graduate Programme
Study Domains: business administration, international
business.
Programmes: International Master of Business
Administration (M.B.A.) programme:.
Subjects: business administration, international business;
international finance; information technology management,
high-tech entrepreneurship.
Open to: candidates with first university degree; TOEFL
and GMAT scores required; work experience recommended.
Duration: full-time MBA: one year; courses begin in
March and September. Part-time MBA: 2 years; courses begin
in January.
Applications: HSE International MBA Program,
Admissions, PO Box 1210, 00101 Helsinki, Finland.

892 Helsinki University of Technology [TKK]
Otakaari 1
02150 Espoo
Tel: +358-9-4511
Fax: +358-9-451-2017
Web: http://www.tkk.fi

Graduate, Postgraduate Programmes
Study Domains: architecture, biochemistry, chemical
engineering, chemistry, computer science, cultural studies,
ecology, environment, electricity and electronics, engineering,
forestry, graphic arts, industrial technology, landscape
architecture, mechanical engineering, printing, publishing,
technology, telecommunications, urbanism.
Programmes: graduate and postgraduate programmes in
architecture and engineering: (a) Bachelor of Science in
technology, architecture, landscape architecture; (b) Master of
Science in technology, architecture, landscape architecture;
(c) Licentiate of Science, Doctor of Science in Technology;
Ph.D; (d) International Study Programmes.
Description: see website for further details.
Open to: applicants should contact the Foreign Student
Adviser at foresta@hut.fi for further information.
Fees: there are no tuition fees for exchange students or
degree students; estimated living costs: 700-850 € per month;
see website for further information.
Languages: Finnish and Swedish; also courses and
programmes in English.
Applications: see website for further information.

893 Nordic Institute for Advanced Training in Occupational Health [NIVA]
Topeliuksenkatu 41 a A
00250 Helsinki
Tel: +358-30-4741
Fax: +358-30-474-2497
Web: http://www.niva.org
e-mail: niva@ttl.fi

International Advanced Courses / Occupational Health
Study Domains: ecology, environment, health and
hygiene, medicine.
Programmes: International non-degree advanced courses
arranged in occupational safety and health, epidemiology,
risk assessment, ergonomics.
Description: topics include biological and chemical
agents, stress and burnout, optical radiation, air monitoring
and safety research.
Open to: nationals of any country holding an academic
degree and experience in research in the field of occupational
health and safety.
Duration: variable (2 days to 2 weeks).
Financial assistance: scholarships are available for
candidates from northwestern Russia or Baltic countries,
participants from outside the Nordic countries should contact
their own authorities, such as National Board of Health or
Labour.
Languages: instruction in English.
Applications: to the above address; see website for course
deadlines: http://www.niva.org/2005_course.htm.

894 Tampere University of Technology [TUT]
PO Box 527
33101 Tampere
Tel: +358-3-3115-11
Fax: +358-3-3115-2640
Web: http://www.tut.fi
e-mail: interoff@tut.fi

Undergraduate, Graduate, Postgraduate Degree Programmes
Study Domains: architecture, biochemistry, biology, civil
engineering, communication, computer science, ecology,
environment, electricity and electronics, engineering,
industrial technology, mechanical engineering, sciences,
technology.
Programmes: degree programmes in architecture,
automation engineering, civil engineering, communication
electronics, electrical engineering, engineering science,
environmental technology, fibre materials science, industrial
engineering and management, information and knowledge
management, information technology, materials engineering,
mechanical engineering. International Master's programme in
information technology, biomedical engineering and materials
science.
Description: see website for further details.
Languages: Finnish for all undergraduate programmes
(for B.Sc. level studies) and all regular Master's degree
programmes. International Master's programmes are taught in
English and all doctoral studies can be pursued in English.
Several Master's level courses in environmental engineering
and biotechnology, industrial engineering and management,
and architecture are also taught in English.
Applications: annual deadline: 28 February; application
forms and information are available on website.

895 University of Art and Design, Helsinki
Hämeentie 135 C
00560 Helsinki
Tel: +358-9-75-631
Fax: +358-9-7563-0223
Web: http://www.uiah.fi
e-mail: info@uiah.fi

Undergraduate, Graduate, Postgraduate Programmes
Study Domains: arts, audio-visual media, graphic arts,
industrial design, interior design, photography.
Programmes: (a) Bachelor of Arts in interior architecture
and furniture design, and in photography; (b) Bachelor or
Master of Arts in ceramic and glass design, fashion and
clothing design, film and television, graphic design and
illustration, industrial design, design for theatre, film and
television; (c) Master of Arts in animation, design leadership,
art education, research programme in visual studies, craft
design, commercial and advertising film, electronic photo
journalism, textile art and design, spatial interventions, new

media, fine art photography and printing processes, art-oriented photography; (d) Pallas Master of Arts programme in fine arts and in colour design; (e) Doctor of Arts in certain of the above fields.

Open to: BA level courses, Finnish- and Swedish-speaking students holders of the Finnish matriculation certificate or equivalent, over the age of 18, entrance examination required; MA level courses, Finnish and Swedish-speaking students who have completed BA level studies, with proficiency in English, portfolio required.

Duration: BA level programmes, 3 years (120 study credits); MA level programmes, 5 years (180 study credits).

Languages: instruction in Finnish and Swedish at BA level and in Finnish, Swedish and English at M.A level. Courses and personal tuition available in Finnish, Swedish and English.

Applications: for BA and MA programmes by 13 March to the Office for Study Affairs at the above address; for Doctoral programmes by end of February or mid-October.

896   University of Joensuu [UJ]

PO Box 111
80101 Joensuu
Tel: +358-13-251-4301
Fax: +358-13-251-2010
Web: http://www.joensuu.fi/students
e-mail: intnl@joensuu.fi

📖 Doctoral Studies

Study Domains: biology, computer science, education, Finnish, forestry, genetics, languages, linguistics, technical education, technology.

Programmes: English-taught graduate programmes a) Graduate School in Forest Sciences (GSFOREST); b) International Multidisciplinary PhD Studies in Educational Technology (IMPDET); c) Graduate School in Language Studies (LANGNET); d) School of Statistical Information, Inference and Data Analysis (SIIDA).

Description: (a) The purpose of the Graduate School in Forest Sciences is to educate experts in Forest Sciences and Forestry. The specialisations offered by this programme are Ecophysiology of Forest Trees, Forest and Mire Ecology, Environmental Management of Forests, Forest Economics and Marketing, Forest Technology, and Molecular Biology, Genetics and Biotechnology of Forest Trees; (b) The programme brings together international experts in Computer Science, Education, and Cultural Studies, in order to prepare future generations of educational technologists to carry out research that is culturally sensitive and tailored to a variety of global contexts. The main areas of interest of the programme are the following: contextualised technologies and pedagogies; adaptivity and student diversity; web-based community building; cognitive tools, and robotics, especially for learners with disabilities; (c) Langnet is a nation-wide postgraduate school and coordinated by the University of Joensuu. Langnet is divided into five sub-programmes: Challenges of Language Acquisition; The Structure and Use of Language; General Theories and Methods of Linguistic Studies; Translation Studies and Research of Professional Communication; Language Variation, Contacts and Change; (d) Social decision making, the understanding of nature and its processes, and the management of technological and economic production processes increasingly demand better statistical analyses and the specification of new informational needs. The goal of the doctoral programme, SIIDA, is to promote quantitative methods of data analysis and inference in research, manufacturing, the economy, and administration. SIIDA's areas of concentration are general statistical methodology, computer intensive methods, biostatistics, econometrics and statistics of finance, information systems in public and private organisations, and decision making. The areas of concentration share a common core. It is expected that a SIIDA educated PhD will also have the capability to act as a problem solver outside his/her field of specialization.

Open to: candidates of all nationalities meeting the following requirements: (b) a Master's degree in a field related to educational technology, e.g. in computer science or in education; a good command of English; (c) a Master's degree; (d) a Master's degree; a good command of English.

Financial assistance: (a) possibility of some funded research positions; check webpage for details and deadlines.

Applications: (a) may be submitted at any time; see

http://www.joensuu.fi/metsatdk/gsforest/; (b) see http://www.impdet.org; (c) see http://www.helsinki.fi/hum/langnet; d) see http://www.joensuu.fi/statnet/siida.html.

📖 International Master's Degree Programmes

Study Domains: cultural studies, earth science, forestry, geography, oriental studies, theology, religion.

Programmes: International (English-taught) Master's Degree Programmes: (a) Islam and the West: an International Study Programme in Inter-cultural counselling; (b) Human Geography; (c) International Study Programme in Environmental Science and Forestry.

Description: (a) objective is to promote an understanding of processes relevant to conflict resolution and social change. Special emphasis on the study of Islamic and Western cultures; (b) programme focuses on a wide range of environmental cultural, political and economic issues faced by Nordic and Eastern European societies. (c) non-degree programme designed to provide students a firm grounding in different aspects of ecology and forestry. Optional study tours to Russia and the Baltic countries.

Open to: candidates of all nationalities; (a) students must hold a Bachelor's degree in theology, religious studies or a relevant field; (b) students must hold at least a Bachelor's degree in geography or related field; 2 years of university studies in biology, environmental science or forestry required; non-degree candidates must have completed at least 2 years of university study in a relevant field.

Financial assistance: (a) some scholarships available to students from Egypt, Indonesia, Jordan, Malaysia or Morocco.

Languages: English proficiency required.

📖 International Non-Degree Programmes

Study Domains: ecology, environment, economy, education, forestry, law, psychology, Russian, Slavic studies, social sciences, sociology.

Programmes: (a) Environmental Science and Forestry; (b) International Study Programme for Educational Sciences; (c) Karelia, Russia and the Baltic Area; (d) International Study Programme in Social Sciences.

Description: (a) one to two-semester non-degree programme offers both Bachelor's and Master's level lectures, laboratory work, field work and seminars in environmental ecology, ecophysiology, mire ecology, aquatic ecology, ecotoxicology, forest production, silviculture, forest protection, and forest management; (b) one- to two-semester non-degree programme covers a variety of educational issues. It is primarily intended to supplement the individual programmes of exchange students who are interested in educational issues. The programme includes both Bachelor's and Master's level courses; (c) one- to two-semester non-degree programme includes both Bachelor's and Master's level courses in history, geography, biology, cultural studies, economics and other social sciences, as well as a subprogramme in Russian studies (language and culture); (d) a multidisciplinary programme offering both Bachelor's and Master's level courses in e.g. sociology, social policy, psychology, economics, law, and statistics. The core course of the programme, 'Local Studies - Global Comparisons', focuses on current research in social sciences at the University of Joensuu. Local issues are discussed in the context of globalization.

Open to: candidates of all nationalities meeting the following requirements: (a) at least two years of university studies in Environmental Science, Forestry, or in a related field; a good command of English; (b) completion of at least one year of university studies. The programme is open only for exchange students coming from bilateral or multilateral partner universities of the University of Joensuu; (c) completion of at least one year of university studies; a good command of English; students participating in the subprogramme in Russian Studies should have basic knowledge of Russian; (d) at least one year of university studies; a good command of English.

Fees: (a) tuition fee for visiting non-degree students not coming through exchange programmes: 3,500 € per academic year or 1,750 € per semester; (c) for visiting non-degree students not coming through exchange programmes: 3,500 € per academic year or 1750 € per semester; (d) for visiting non-degree students not coming through exchange programmes: 3,500 € per academic year or 1,750 € per

semester. For additional information, please see
http://www.joensuu.fi/students.

897   University of Jyväskylä
PO Box 35
40014 Jyväskylä
Fax: +358-14-260-1061
Web: http://www.jyu.fi
e-mail: intl@jyu.fi

 Undergraduate, Graduate Studies

Study Domains: all major fields.
Programmes: Degree programmes offered at the following
faculties: Faculty of Humanities; Faculty of Information
Technology; Faculty of Mathematics and Science; Faculty of
Social Sciences; Faculty of Sport and Health Sciences;
School of Business and Economics.
Applications: see website for complete information.

898   University of Kuopio [UOK]
PO Box 1627
70211 Kuopio
Tel: +358-17-162-211
Fax: +358-17-163-496
Web: http://www.uku.fi

 Doctoral Programmes

Study Domains: biology, genetics, neurology, veterinary
sciences.
Programmes: Doctoral programme of the A.I. Virtanen
Institute of Molecular Sciences.
Subjects: biotechnology (especially animal
biotechnology), molecular medicine (especially gene therapy
and gene transfer technology), neurobiology (especially the
neurobiology of diseases affecting the central nervous system
and development of disease models for them) and biological
imaging.
Academic requirements: candidates with a Master's
degree in an applicable field.
Duration: approximately 4 years, requiring 3 to 4 original
publications.
Languages: instruction in English.
Applications: contact Ms Riitta Keinänen, email:
riitta.keinanen@uku.fi; tel: +358-17-162-063; fax:
+358-17-163-030.

 Master's Degree Programmes

Study Domains: biochemistry, biology, computer science,
health and hygiene, nursing, nutrition, social work.
Programmes: (a) Master's degree in Public Health; (b)
Master's degree in Computer Science; (c) Master's degree in
Molecular Medicine and Biotechnology; (d) Master's degree
in Neurobiology; (e) Master's degree in Nursing Science; (f)
European Master of Public Health Nutrition (EMPHN); (g)
Master's Programme in European Social Work.
Description: a) to increase student's knowledge in
philosophical, epidemiological, social, behavioural and
environmental aspects of public health. The curriculum
encompasses a variety of courses related to management and
leadership skills in preventing and resolving health problems.
The programme offers training in various aspects of public
health including epidemiology, medical anthropology,
environmental health, ergonomics, exercise medicine, health
policy and management, public health nutrition, occupational
health and social pharmacy; (b) offers computer science
expertise for a career in research or for working in the
information technology industry. The programme gives a
strong methodological basis in computer science combined
with research related topics such as structural documents,
parallel computation and data security; c) extensively
research-oriented; the core curriculum includes the most
recent advances in biotechnology and molecular medicine.
Students obtain hands-on research experience; (d) extensively
research-oriented; the core curriculum includes the most
recent advances in neurobiology. The students will obtain true
hands-on research experience; (e) main emphasis on
improving nursing care and nursing education and to the
enhancement of the profession. Students will be able to:
implement scientific knowledge for developing nursing
practice, participate in national and international cooperation
projects, analyse, criticise and develop theories and research
in nursing science and conduct research work; (f) to train
health care professionals to become competent in developing

and undertaking effective population-based strategies all
across Europe with comparable skills in Public Health
Nutrition for optimal mobility and joint research and
development. The programme includes student exchange
between the participating universities; (g) an innovative
Master's programme based on partnership of 10 European
universities. Its aim is to develop the capacity and expertise of
the university educated staff working in the field of social
work and social care across Europe. The overall purpose of
the programme is to foster student's personal and professional
skills to a higher level of practice than can be achieved in
national professional qualification frameworks.
Open to: candidates of all nationalities.
Academic requirements: Bachelor's degree in an
applicable field required.
Duration: approximately 2 academic years; autumn
semester from September to December; spring semester from
January to May.
Financial assistance: no scholarships available.
Languages: instruction in English.
Applications: end of January annually; for full details see:
http://www.uku.fi/intl/english/apply.htm.

899   University of Oulu, Dept. of Educational Sciences and Teacher Education
PO Box 2000
90014 Linnanmaa
Tel: +358-8-553-3732
Fax: +358-8-553-3744
Web: http://www.oulu.fi/english/
e-mail: international.office@oulu.fi

 Graduate Programme

Study Domains: education, teacher education.
Programmes: Master of Education.
Description: the programme prepares for international
educational tasks in multicultural contexts and provides
qualifications for primary school teacher.
Open to: candidates of all nationalities meeting language
and academic requirements; exchange students are accepted
according to the exchange programme regulations, others on
basis of applications.
Duration: 4 to 5 years; school year is from September to
May.
Languages: good knowledge of English is required.
Applications: to the above address by 31 January annually;
entrance examination.

900   University of Oulu, Dept. of Electrical Engineering
PO Box 4500
90014 Oulu
Tel: +358-8-553-2791
Fax: +358-8-553-2612
Web: http://www.infotech.oulu.fi
e-mail: tre@ee.oulu.fi

 Graduate Programme

Study Domains: electricity and electronics, engineering.
Programmes: Infotech Oulu.
Description: courses in electronics and measurement
technology, information processing engineering, software
engineering and information systems, and wireless
communications. Infotech Oulu lecture series and at least one
intensive course are held annually.
Academic requirements: Master's degree in electrical
engineering.
Duration: 3 to 4 academic years; (from September to
May).
Applications: see website for full details.

901   University of Oulu, Dept. of Information Processing Science
PO Box 3000
90014 Oulu
Tel: +358-8-553-1986
Fax: +358-8-553-1890
Web: http://www.tol.oulu.fi
e-mail: veikko.seppanen@oulu.fi

Undergraduate Programme

Study Domains: business, computer science, engineering, marketing.
Programmes: Bachelor's degree in software engineering; the programme includes advanced studies on business management and marketing, focusing on how to convert software into commercial products.
Open to: prerequisites: 2nd or 3rd year students in information processing science or marketing.
Duration: annually from September to December and from January to May.
Applications: for Fall term by 31 May, for Spring term by 31 October, to the above address.

902 University of Oulu, WHO Centre for Research on Reproductive Health
PO Box 5000
90014 Oulu
Tel: +358-40-543-1734
Fax: +358-8-315-5631
Web: http://www.whoccr.oulu.fi
e-mail: pvihko@whoccr.oulu.fi

Postgraduate Programme

Study Domains: biology, medicine.
Programmes: Doctorate-level studies in human reproduction and molecular endocrinology.
Description: research and training in human reproduction and molecular endocrinology, hormone-dependent cancer. Research-oriented courses and active participation in research work in molecular endocrinology and signalling of pathways of genes involved in steroid hormone action in normal and malignant cells.
Duration: 3 to 4 years.
Applications: at any time; see website for full details.

903 University of Tampere [UTA]
33014 Tampere
Tel: +358-3-355-111
Fax: +358-3-213-4473
Web: http://www.uta.fi
e-mail: kirjaamo@uta.fi

Undergraduate, Graduate, Postgraduate Programmes

Study Domains: accounting, administration, American studies, art history, audio-visual media, business, communication, computer science, earth science, ecology, environment, European studies, folklore, history, international relations, interpretation and translation, languages, liberal arts, linguistics, literature and civilization, marketing, medicine, music and musicology, political science, psychology, research, Scandinavian studies, social sciences, Swedish, teacher education.
Programmes: Bachelor's, Master's, Ph.D. degrees in all major fields.
Open to: candidates of any nationality; TOEFL 550 PBT/ 213 CBT or IELTS 6.5, or passed Cambridge CPE or CAE or other recognized standard English language test; students must provide proof of ability to finance their studies in Finland; individual health insurance is recommended.
Duration: one year starting September and January.
Applications: to the International Office at the above address by 1st March.

904 University of Turku [UTU]
20014 Turku
Tel: +358-2-333-51
Fax: +358-2-333-6363
Web: http://www.utu.fi
e-mail: international@utu.fi

Graduate Programme

Study Domains: computer science, cultural studies, ecology, environment, international studies, social sciences.
Programmes: English-taught Master's degree programmes: (a) Baltic Sea Region Studies; (b) Environmental Sciences; (c) Information Technology (TUCS); (d) Institutions and Social Mechanism; (e) Finnish and other Finno-Ugric Languages; (f) Learning, Learning Environments and Educational Systems.
Description: (a) interdisciplinary approach to understanding the societies, cultures and economies of the region surrounding the Baltic Sea; (b) multidisciplinary programme with strong connections to basic and applied research, environmental assessment and economic life; (c) enables students to choose programmes fitting in with previous studies and personal interests within the broad field of information technology, eg software engineering or business-oriented IT management; (d) advanced training in social sciences, to enable students to apply the tools of research on institutions to the modelling of real-world problems; (e) programme intended for non-native Finnish speakers who have a Bachelor's degree in Finnish language or other Finno-Ugric languages and adequate proficiency in Finnish language. The aim of the programme is to deepen students' theoretical and practical Finnish language skills and to get them acquainted with the Finnish culture, linguistics and Finno-Ugristics. The programme aims to train mainly specialists of Finnish language and culture as well as Finno-Ugric linguistics; (f) for the development of qualifications necessary to work as researcher or specialist in national and international projects.
Open to: candidates of all nationalities.
Academic requirements: undergraduate university degree equivalent to the Finnish Bachelor's degree in the relevant field required.
Duration: 2 academic years, in general for Master's degree programmes.
Languages: Finnish and English.
Applications: application procedures are variable for each faculty; see website http://www.utu.fi for full details; the relevant faculty should be contacted directly.

France

Année universitaire: octobre à juin.
Organisation de l'enseignement supérieur:
L'enseignement supérieur français se distingue par une pluralité d'établissements aux finalités, structures et conditions d'admission différentes. Dans ces établissements, les étudiants étrangers peuvent être accueillis à tous les niveaux d'études en fonction de la validation de leur diplôme par l'établissement d'accueil. Deux grands types d établissements se partagent la formation: (a) Les Grandes Écoles et écoles spécialisées qui accueillent des effectifs restreints, soumis à une sélection sévère, et dispensent des formations à objectif affirmé: formation d'ingénieurs, formation à la gestion, art, architecture, magistrature, administration, etc. Il peut s'agir d'établissements privés ou publics; (b) Les universités qui accueillent, à la sortie de l'enseignement secondaire, des effectifs importants d'étudiants et dispensent des formations comprenant des enseignements fondamentaux et des établissements techniques et professionnels. Les universités couvrent toutes les disciplines et forment à la recherche.
• La réforme «LMD»: La rentrée 2004/2005 a été marquée par la mise en place du nouveau système «LMD» (Licence-Master-Doctorat), dans le cadre de l'espace européen de formation de l'enseignement supérieur. Cette réforme restructure l'ensemble des diplômes universitaires afin de rendre compatibles les cursus de l'enseignement supérieur en Europe. Le système est composé d'UE (Unités d'Enseignement). Chaque UE a une valeur en crédits: les ECTS (European Credits Transfer System ou Système de Crédits Européens Transférables). Ce sont des unités de mesure des connaissances et compétences acquises par l'étudiant. Le diplôme n'est plus validé en terme d'années et d'examen terminal annuel mais en terme de crédits capitalisables sanctionnant des parcours de formations modulaires par semestre. Les ECTS constituent une reconnaissance internationale, transférable dans l'ensemble de l'Europe, capitalisables car définitivement acquis quelle que soit la durée du parcours.
• Licence (Bac + 3 années): niveau validé par 180 ECTS. Peut avoir une vocation générale ou professionnelle.
• Master (Bac + 5 années): niveau validé par 120 ECTS au delà du Licence, qui peut s'obtenir selon 2 orientations: Master professionnel ou Master recherche;
• Doctorat (Bac + 8 années): les titulaires d'un Master recherche peuvent préparer une thèse de Doctorat (180 ECTS au delà du Master).
(source:

http://www.ambafrance-pt.org/article.php3?id_article=259).
Unité monétaire: Euro (€).
Admission pour étudiants du pays: Pour s'inscrire à l'Université, il faut avoir obtenu le baccalauréat ou un diplôme équivalent.
Admission pour étudiants internationaux: Pour accéder à l'enseignement supérieur en France, les étudiants étrangers doivent, s'ils ne sont pas en possession du baccalauréat français, avoir satisfait aux conditions qui permettent l'accès à l'enseignement supérieur dans le pays où a été obtenu le diplôme de fin d'études secondaires (diplôme, plus - si nécessaire - attestation de réussite aux conditions spécifiques d'accès à l'université dans le pays où il a été obtenu). Ils devront justifier d'un niveau de compréhension de la langue française adapté à la formation envisagée.
Les procédures d'admission varient en fonction du type d'établissement et de la filière de formation envisagée:
• pour s'inscrire en classe préparatoire aux grandes écoles, ou en sections de techniciens supérieurs (dans les lycées), en IUT ou IUP (dans les universités), en deuxième ou troisième cycle à l'université, ou dans tout autre établissement à caractère spécifique et/ou recrutement par voie de concours, jury d'admission ou sur titre, la demande d'inscription est à faire directement auprès de l'établissement concerné.
• pour s'inscrire en premier cycle dans une université (LMD ou DEUG) une demande d'inscription préalable est obligatoire pour les étrangers titulaires d'un diplôme étranger de fin d'études secondaires. Attention ! Il existe deux formulaires de demande d'inscription préalable selon le pays où vous résidez: (a) «formulaire blanc» pour les candidats résidant en dehors de la France (http://www.education.gouv.fr/prat/formul/11443.htm); «formulaire vert» pour les candidats résidant en France. Sont dispensés de cette procédure et peuvent donc présenter directement une demande d'inscription à l'université de leur choix, les étudiant(e)s étranger(e)s:
- titulaires du baccalauréat français (ou d'un titre admis en dispense par une réglementation nationale)
- étudiants communautaires et de l'Espace économique européen
- venu(e)s en France effectuer des études dans le cadre d'un accord inter-universitaire si ce dernier le précise (dans ce cas il mentionne également les modalités spécifiques d'inscription)
- boursier(e)s du gouvernement français, d'organismes internationaux ou de gouvernements étrangers dont les bourses sont gérées par un organisme français agréé CNOUS (http://www.cnous.fr) EGIDE, (http://www.egide.asso.fr)
- apatrides ou réfugié(e)s politiques titulaires de la carte de l'OFPRA (Office français pour les réfugiés et les apatrides),
- enfants de diplomates en poste en France.
Connaissances linguistiques requises: Un examen est prévu pour évaluer la compréhension écrite et orale de la langue française et pour apprécier l'expression écrite des candidats. Cet examen est payant (59€).
Sont dispensés de cet examen: (a) les ressortissants des États où le français est langue officielle; (b) les étudiants étrangers issus des sections bilingues françaises figurant sur une liste établie conjointement par les ministères de l'éducation nationale et des affaires étrangères; (c) les titulaires du DALF (diplôme approfondi de langue française); (d) les candidats qui ont passé le test organisé par la Chambre de commerce et d'industrie de Paris (CCIP) et ont obtenu la note de 16/20 à l'épreuve d'expression écrite.
Formalités d'immigration:
• Formalités d'entrée: Tout ressortissant étranger souhaitant suivre des études en France doit, avant de quitter son pays, obtenir un visa de long séjour, mention «Étudiant». La demande se fait auprès des services consulaires français du pays de résidence. Sont dispensés du visa de long séjour: les ressortissants de l'Union européenne, ceux d'Andorre, de Monaco, du Saint-Siège, de Suisse, de Saint-Marin et du Liechtenstein. Le visa de long séjour est exigé pour obtenir la carte de séjour temporaire régularisant la situation de l'étranger en France. Il est impossible de régulariser sa situation une fois en France si l'on est seulement muni d'un visa de court séjour (tourisme).
L'obtention de ce visa est liée notamment à la justification de moyens suffisants d'existence (justificatif de ressources d'au moins 4.584 € par an et d'une couverture sociale.
• Formalités de séjour: Tout étudiant étranger qui vient en France pour un séjour d'études supérieur à trois mois doit demander, sauf s'il est ressortissant de l'Union européenne,

une carte de séjour. Il devra se présenter dès son arrivée à l'un des organismes suivants: s'il est domicilié à Paris, dans les centres de réception des étrangers; s'il est domicilié dans les départements des Hauts de Seine, Seine-Saint-Denis ou Val de Marne, à la préfecture compétente; et s'il réside en province, au commissariat de police ou à la mairie. En règle générale, il devra produire en plus du visa de long séjour mention «Étudiant» apposé sur son passeport par le consulat de France dans son pays de résidence: une attestation provisoire d'inscription dans un établissement d'enseignement supérieur, un certificat médical, un justificatif de ressources, un justificatif de couverture sociale (attestation d'adhésion à la Sécurité sociale ou d'assurance volontaire), un justificatif de domicile et trois photos d'identité. Les étudiants de l'Union européenne et de certains pays dispensés de visa doivent néanmoins présenter un passeport en cours de validité ou leur carte nationale d'identité. Tous renseignements utiles seront donnés aux intéressés par le consulat de France dans leur pays.
Frais pour une année universitaire:
• Droits de scolarité: Pour s'inscrire en premier ou deuxième cycle à l'université le montant des frais d'inscription est fixé au plan national, et s'applique à tous, français et étrangers. A titre d'exemple pour la rentrée 2004/05 le taux de base (premier et deuxième cycles) était fixé à 150€. Les étudiants boursiers de l'État français n'ont pas à acquitter ces droits de scolarité.
Pour les autres formations universitaires, pour les établissements publics ou privés à caractère spécifique (ex: instituts et grandes écoles) le montant des frais d'inscription est variable.
• Assistance médicale: Assistance médicale: sécurité sociale et assurance personnelle
- La couverture sociale obligatoire: la couverture sociale normale d'un étudiant est l'adhésion au régime étudiant de la sécurité sociale, qui n'est qu'une forme particulière du régime général de la Sécurité sociale en France. Cette couverture sociale peut être complétée par l'inscription à une mutuelle étudiante qui permet de couvrir, presque en totalité les dépenses de santé.
- Conditions d'affiliation: pour avoir droit à la sécurité sociale étudiante:
Âge: l'âge limite de 28 ans peut-être reculé dans certains cas: service national, longue maladie ou maternité, études spéciales (report d'un à quatre ans pour les étudiants en études doctorales).
- Nationalité: l'arrêté du 28 juin 1999, modifiant l'arrêté du 28 juillet 1989 fixant les conditions d'applications du régime de Sécurité sociale des étudiants, a supprimé la condition pour les étrangers d'être ressortissant d'un Etat ayant passé, en matière de Sécurité sociale, une convention internationale avec la France ou d'être reconnu réfugié ou apatride pour accéder au régime applicable aux étudiants.
- Etablissements: être inscrit dans un établissement supérieur public ou privé ayant fait l'objet d'un arrêté interministériel d'agrément.
- Cotisation: pour bénéficier de ce régime spécifique de protection sociale, l'étudiant verse une cotisation annuelle forfaitaire et indivisible de 180 € pour l' année 2004/2005. L'étudiant qui aura 20 ans entre le 1er octobre et le 30 septembre de l'année suivante est tenu de cotiser à l'occasion des procédures d'inscription, même s'il continue à être pris en charge par le régime de Sécurité sociale de ses parents jusqu'à son 20e anniversaire.
Les étudiants boursiers sont exemptés du versement de cette cotisation.
- Les remboursements: La Sécurité sociale fixe des tarifs au-delà desquels elle n'assure pas de remboursement. L'affiliation à la Sécurité sociale, faite en même temps que l'inscription administrative universitaire, donne droit à des remboursements dont le pourcentage est calculé sur la base des tarifs conventionnés (entre 35 et 80 %). C'est la raison pour laquelle une garantie mutualiste, proposée par les mutuelles étudiantes est indispensable.
- Les mutuelles étudiantes: Deux sections locales universitaires sont habilitées à gérer par académie le régime étudiant de la Sécurité sociale et proposent des prestations complémentaires, voire supérieures à celles de la Sécurité sociale. Les mutuelles remboursent notamment le ticket modérateur, c'est-à-dire la différence entre les dépenses réelles pour des soins, des médicaments ou une hospitalisation et le remboursement de la Sécurité sociale. Les mutuelles proposent en outre une couverture de risques de responsabilité

civile (accident causé à autrui), une assurance accident et une assurance décès. Pour les étudiants n'ayant pas droit à la Sécurité sociale, les mutuelles étudiantes proposent d'autres formules d'assurance.

Services d'accueil et d'information: A l'étranger:
• Les services culturels des ambassades de France peuvent utilement informer et orienter les étudiants souhaitant étudier en France (possibilités et conditions d'études et de séjour en France). Les documents mentionnés ci-dessous sont le plus souvent mis en consultation. Les services culturels disposent également d'informations sur les bourses susceptibles d'être accordées par le gouvernement français.
En France:
• Le Bureau de l'orientation du cursus licence (Direction de l'enseignement supérieur - ministère de l'éducation nationale, de l'enseignement supérieur et de la recherche; 99, rue de Grenelle, 75357 Paris 07 SP).
• Les services communs universitaires d'information et d'orientation des étudiants (SCUIO) http://www.education.gouv.fr/orient/lieuxorient.htm, implantés dans chaque université.
• Le Centre national des oeuvres universitaires et scolaires (CNOUS), 69, quai d'Orsay, 75007 Paris, web: http://www.cnous.fr, gère, depuis 1964, les bourses attribuées par le gouvernement français aux étudiants étrangers et, depuis 1987, les bourses allouées par les gouvernements étrangers sur la base de conventions. Le CNOUS oriente l'action des 28 centres régionaux des oeuvres universitaires et scolaires (CROUS) qui assurent au quotidien la gestion des conditions de vie des étudiants français et étrangers (logement, restauration, culture, emploi, social, voyages et bourses), y compris l'accueil et la gestion des boursiers étrangers qui lui sont confiés par le CNOUS (liste des CROUS sur demande au CNOUS).
• L'Office national d'information sur les enseignements et les professions (ONISEP): Librairie: 168 boulevard du Montparnasse, 75014 Paris; web: http://www.onisep.fr; vente et consultation de brochures et périodiques sur les études, les professions et les débouchés.
• Le Centre d'information et de documentation jeunesse (CIDJ), 101, Quai Branly, 75015 Paris; web: http://www.cidj.asso.fr: consultation de brochures et publications sur l'enseignement, les formations, les métiers, l'emploi, l'éducation permanente, la vie pratique, etc. Les documents édités par le CIDJ sont également en consultation dans 31 centres régionaux et départementaux, et près de 1.200 bureaux et points d'information jeunesse (liste sur demande au CIDJ).

Bourses pour étudiants internationaux: Bourses nationales
• Bourses d'excellence Eiffel:
Égide - Programme Eiffel / 28 rue de la Grange-aux-Belles / 75010 Paris (France)
tél: +33-1-4040-5880; fax: +33-1-4241-8590; email: eiffel@egide.asso.fr; web: http://www.egide.asso.fr/fr/programmes/eiffel/.

Enseignement à distance: Un télé-enseignement universitaire est proposé aux étudiants qui sont dans l'incapacité d'assister régulièrement aux cours. 29 universités coopèrent à ce programme. En plus de la préparation aux concours d'entrée pour le recrutement du service civil et pour la formation d'adultes, le Centre national d'enseignement à Distance (CNED) propose des formations conduisant aux diplômes techniques BEP, BP, BTS.

Reconnaissance des études et diplômes:
• En fonction des études déjà faites et/ou des diplômes déjà obtenus, on peut solliciter l'admission dans une formation supérieure. L'établissement dans lequel vous souhaitez étudier est le seul habilité à valider votre formation antérieure, c'est-à-dire à vous autoriser à:
- soit accéder directement à une formation conduisant à la délivrance d'un diplôme national ou d'un titre dont l'obtention est réglementé par l'État,
- soit faire acte de candidature au concours d'entrée dans un établissement,
- soit être dispensé d'une partie des épreuves d'un diplôme.
NOTE: un diplôme peut être validé par un établissement et ne pas l'être par un autre. La réponse à toute demande relève de l'entière responsabilité du président de l'université sur proposition d'une commission pédagogique (qui se prononcera notamment sur la compatibilité entre les contenus des diplômes présentés et les exigences de la formation sollicitée; le niveau linguistique sera également pris en

compte). Les demandes d'équivalence se font auprès du: Centre d'information sur la reconnaissance des diplômes étrangers en France; Ministère de l'éducation nationale, DRICB4; 110 rue de Grenelle, F-75007 Paris, France; tél: +33-1-5555-0428 / +33-1-5555-0429 / +33-1-5555-0415; fax: +33-1-5555-0423; Internet: http://www.education.gouv.fr.

Possibilités d'emploi: Les étudiants étrangers non-boursiers possédant un visa de séjour longue durée peuvent obtenir le droit de travailler, sous certaines conditions qui leur seront précisées par le service de la main-d'œuvre étrangère à la direction départementale du Travail et de l'emploi. L'étudiant ne peut travailler qu'un maximum de 19 h 30 par semaine ou 800 heures par an compatibles avec ses études et la situation de l'emploi en France. Renseignements complets sur le site du Ministère du travail: http://www.travail.gouv.fr.

---

905 Alliance française [AF]
École internationale de langue et de civilisation françaises
101, boulevard Raspail
75270 Paris Cedex 06
Tel: +33-1-4284-9000
Fax: +33-1-4284-9101
Web: http://www.alliancefr.org
e-mail: info@alliancefr.org

📖 Professorat de français langue étrangère

Domaines d'étude: français, interprétation et traduction, langues, linguistique, littérature et civilisation.
Programmes: Formation d'enseignants: professorat de français langue étrangère, séminaires de formation et recyclage en didactique du français langue étrangère, stages de langue, culture et méthodologie, préparation aux diplômes de l'Alliance française, de la Chambre de commerce et d'industrie de Paris, du DELF et du DALF (Académie de Paris).
A l'intention de: professeurs ou futurs professeurs de français langue étrangère.
Durée: 4 semaines pour les stages pédagogiques; 1 ou 2 ans pour le professorat de français langue étrangère; 1 semaine pour un séminaire.
Inscriptions: par correspondance (1 mois avant le début de la session choisie) ou sur place (lors de l'un des 5 jours ouvrables qui précèdent le début de la session choisie); à l'adresse ci-dessus pour de plus amples renseignements.

906 American University of Paris [AUP]
6, rue du Colonel Combes
75007 Paris
Tel: +33-1-4062-0720
Fax: +33-1-4705-3432
Web: http://www.aup.edu
e-mail: admissions@aup.edu

📖 Undergraduate Programmes

Study Domains: liberal arts.
Programmes: Bachelor of Arts (BA) in humanities, economics, business administration; Bachelor of Science (BS) in computer science; applied economics.
Open to: candidates of all nationalities over 18 years of age with proven English fluency, and meeting academic standards.
Applications: see website for additional information.

907 Bordeaux école de management
Institut du management des affaires et du commerce international [MACI]
Domaine de Raba
680, cours de la Libération
33405 Talence cedex
Tel: +33-5-5684-2268
Fax: +33-5-5735-5500
Web: http://www.maci.bordeaux-bs.edu
e-mail: maci@bordeaux-bs.edu

📖 **3e cycle / management des affaires et du commerce international**

Domaines d'étude: commerce, gestion.
Programmes: Mastère spécialisé en management des affaires et du commerce international; Master's degree en commerce international pour étudiants chinois; MBA en commerce international.
A l'intention de: étudiants titulaires d'un Bachelor's degree, d'un Master's degree ou d'un diplôme d'ingénieur (ou équivalents Bac + 4 ou 5), cadres ou ingénieurs désirant développer leurs compétences dans le domaine des affaires internationales; test de langues et test de personnalité pour l'admission.
Durée: 9 mois de cours (débutant en octobre) + 4 mois minimum de mission à l'étranger pour le compte d'une entreprise internationale.
Frais: frais d'inscription: 77 €; frais de scolarité: 8950 €.
Connaissances linguistiques: cours dispensés en français et en anglais (l'examen d'entrée comporte un test d'anglais).
Inscriptions: avant le 10 septembre de l'année d'étude auprès de Marie Petit-Dutaillis (coordonnées ci-dessus).

908 Centre de coopération internationale en recherche agronomique pour le développement [CIRAD-EMVT]

Délégation aux échanges scientifiques internationaux
TA 279/04, Avenue Agropolis
34398 Montpellier Cedex 5
Tel: +33-4-6761-5800
Fax: +33-4-6761-5986
Web: http://www.cirad.fr

📖 **2e, 3e cycles / sciences agronomiques**

Programmes: Cours conduisant aux (a) DESS (Diplôme d'études supérieures spécialisées) de productions animales en régions chaudes; (b) CEAV (Certificat d'études approfondies vétérinaires) pathologies animales en régions chaudes; (c) CES (Certificat d'études supérieures) en épidémiologie animale.
Description: (a) connaissance du milieu et écologie de l'élevage; économie et développement des productions animales: problèmes technico-économiques; enseignement de synthèse: contrôle des travaux personnels; stage pratique de 4 mois.
A l'intention de: ressortissants de tout pays, titulaires du diplôme de docteur vétérinaire ou d'ingénieur agronome, ou tout titre jugé équivalent; titulaires d'une maîtrise en sciences de niveau universitaire français. Les cadres moyens, titulaires d'un diplôme de technicien d'élevage peuvent être inscrits pour des stages de perfectionnement; possibilité de stage linguistique initial en France pour les étudiants étrangers. Cours d'été, stages sur le terrain en régions chaudes; sélection sur dossier.
Organisés: (a) d'octobre à mars environ 400 heures de cours au CIRAD-EMVT à Montpellier; d'avril à septembre stage obligatoire en régions chaudes sanctionné par la rédaction et la soutenance d'un mémoire (octobre); (c) de septembre à janvier: 5 semaines à l'ENVA à Maisons-Alfort suivies de 5 semaines au CIRAD à Montpellier, 2 semaines d'options à Maisons-Alfort ou à Montpellier suivant l'option choisie, 2 semaines de stage.
Durée: (b) 1 an à temps plein (du 1er octobre au 1er septembre); (c) 5 mois.
Assistance financière: possibilités de bourses du Ministère français de l'enseignement et de la recherche.
Inscriptions: (a) avant 1er juin; pour de plus amples renseignements, s'adresser à l'adresse ci-dessus.

909 Centre national d'études agronomiques des régions chaudes [CNEARC]

1101, avenue Agropolis
BP 5098
34033 Montpellier Cedex 1
Tel: +33-4-6761-7000
Fax: +33-4-6741-0232
Web: http://www.cnearc.fr
e-mail: drv@cnearc.fr

📖 **2e, 3e cycles / sciences agronomiques, agronomie tropicale**

Domaines d'étude: agriculture, alimentation, anthropologie, développement rural, économie, études américaines, études asiatiques, génie chimique, hydraulique, sciences agronomiques.
Programmes: (a) Cycle ESAT - Études supérieures d'agronomie tropicale, niveau 3ème cycle, conduisant à l'obtention du diplôme d'ingénieur d'agronomie tropicale; (b) Cycle EITARC - Études d'ingénieur des techniques agricoles des régions chaudes, niveau 2ème cycle; (c) Programme de vulgarisation et organisations professionnelles agricoles (VOPA) conduisant au Master européen NATURA d'études professionnelles en agronomie tropicale et subtropicale; domaines d'études: sciences agronomiques, sociologie, économie rurale, communication, vulgarisation.
A l'intention de: ressortissants de tout pays: (a) après une formation initiale de niveau Bac+4 dans les domaines agronomique, biologique, sciences du milieu; le recrutement se fait sur titre, sur dossier ou sur concours suivant la formation initiale; (b) titulaires d'un BTSA ou d'un DUT (niveau Bac+2) et ayant au minimum 3 ans d'expérience professionnelle; recrutement sur concours; (c) admission sur dossier, pour candidats justifiant d'un niveau Bac+3 ou d'un B.Sc. de 3 années d'expérience professionnelle dans le domaine du développement rural ou une expérience de 7 ans minimum peut être prise en compte à titre d'équivalence.
Durée: 2 années, avec pour (a) 2 stages de terrain de 4 à 6 mois en régions chaudes de mai à septembre, pour (b) un stage de fin d'études de 4 mois en régions chaudes; (c) 8 mois et 1 mois de stage en situation professionnelle (débutant en octobre ou novembre).
Inscriptions: (a) et (b) avant le 1er mars pour les concours d'avril; les dossiers doivent être déposés avant le 1er juin; (c) aucune date n'est imposée; s'adresser au service de la formation sous couvert du service employeur.

910 Centre national de la recherche scientifique [CNRS]

3, rue Michel-Ange
75794 Paris Cedex 16
Tel: +33-1-4496-4000
Fax: +33-1-4496-5390
Web: http://www.cnrs.fr

🐦 **Coopération scientifique**

Domaines d'étude: chimie, espace, mathématiques, physique, recherche, sciences, sciences de la mer, sciences de la terre, sciences humaines.
Bourses: Accueil de chercheurs étrangers en France et envoi de chercheurs français à l'étranger, dans le cadre d'accords de coopération scientifique.
A l'intention de: chercheurs.
Durée: variable selon les pays, de 15 jours à un an (renouvelable).
Valeur: les frais de séjour sont pris en charge, pour les chercheurs français, par les organismes avec lesquels le CNRS a conclu la Convention internationale ou l'accord de coopération scientifique et, pour les chercheurs étrangers, par le CNRS; les frais de voyage sont à la charge du pays d'origine du chercheur. Toutefois, un régime différent est applicable pour certains organismes internationaux, pour lesquels le CNRS prend en charge les frais de voyage et attribue un montant forfaitaire destiné à couvrir les frais de séjour.
Candidatures: pour les Français, auprès du CNRS.

911 Centre national des arts plastiques [CNAP]

Tour Atlantique, 1 place de la Pyramide
92911 Paris-La Défense
Tel: +33-1-4693-9950
Fax: +33-1-4693-9979
Web: http://www.cnap.fr

📖 **Formations en arts plastiques**

Domaines d'étude: arts appliqués, arts graphiques, arts plastiques, beaux-arts, photographie.
Programmes: formation pour artistes et créateurs dans le

domaine des arts plastiques proposée par les écoles nationales, régionales et municipales: (a) Formation longue conduisant au DNSEP (diplôme national supérieur d'expression plastique) qui permet l'acquisition de méthodes et d'outils de travail puis la mobilisation de ces acquis dans la mise en œuvre d'un projet; (b) Formation courte conduisant aux DNAT (Diplôme national des arts et techniques) et DNAP (Diplôme national des arts plastiques) pour les étudiants souhaitant intégrer rapidement le monde professionnel; les cours portent sur: le dessin, l'expérimentation du volume et de l'espace, la perception et l'imagination de la couleur, l'initiation aux techniques et technologies, l'histoire de l'art, une langue étrangère, l'histoire et la théorie des arts, techniques et mise en œuvre; certaines des écoles préparent un diplôme spécifique à leur établissement comme l'ENSBA, l'ENSCI, l'ENSAD, le Studio école du Fresnay.
A l'intention de: ressortissants de toute nationalité titulaires d'un baccalauréat ou diplôme équivalent; admission sur concours en mai-juin et entretien.
Durée: (a) 3 ans; (b) 5 ans.
Assistance financière: bourses d'études accordées en fonction de critères sociaux et réservées aux étudiants inscrits dans l'un des cursus nationaux.
Inscriptions: à l'adresse ci-dessus.

🌾 Aides aux artistes

Domaines d'étude: arts graphiques, arts plastiques, édition, photographie.
A l'intention de: créateurs dans les disciplines énumérées ci-dessus, résidant en France et ayant un compte bancaire en France.
Candidatures: pour toute information complémentaire, consulter site web: http://www.cnap.fr/.

912   Conservatoire national des arts et métiers [CNAM]

Institut national d'étude du travail et d'orientation professionnelle (INETOP)
41, rue Gay-Lussac
75005 Paris
Tel: +33-1-4410-7811
Fax: +33-1-4354-1091
Web: http://www.cnam.fr/instituts/inetop/
e-mail: inetopdir@cnam.fr

📖 Programme conduisant au DECOP

Domaines d'étude: éducation.
Programmes: Cours pour étudiants étrangers: orientation scolaire et professionnelle (10 places par promotion) et formation de conseillers d'orientation psychologues stagiaires couvrant les domaines de la psychologie de l'orientation, les approches sociologique, économique et institutionnelle; recueil, traitement statistique et analyse des données appliquées à l'orientation; conduisant au Diplôme d'État de conseiller d'orientation psychologue (DECOP), Bac+5.
A l'intention de: ressortissants de tout pays (admis sur dossier), titulaires d'une maîtrise ou d'une licence de psychologie. Concours national: épreuves écrites et orales et entretien.
Durée: 1 ou 2 ans (débutant en septembre).
Inscriptions: avant le 15 janvier, offres publiées chaque année par le Ministère de l'éducation nationale de mi-septembre à mi-octobre; voir site web pour de plus amples informations.

913   École centrale de Lille [EC Lille]

BP 48
59651 Villeneuve-d'Ascq Cedex
Tel: +33-3-2033-5353
Fax: +33-3-2033-5499
Web: http://www.ec-lille.fr
e-mail: bfi@ec-lille.fr

📖 Diplôme d'ingénieur généraliste

Domaines d'étude: ingénierie, langues, sciences, sciences appliquées.
Programmes: Diplôme d'ingénieur généraliste; 12 options de dernière année d'études du cycle d'ingénieur avec possibilité de préparer en parallèle des DEA; programmes de double diplôme (diplôme d'ingénieur/master spécialisé) avec les partenaires européens (réseau Time -Top industrial

managers for Europe) et des partenaires en Asie, Amérique du nord et Amérique du sud.
A l'intention de: ressortissants de tout pays inscrits dans une université partenaire et titulaires d'un diplôme universitaire de premier cycle.
Qualifications requises: classes préparatoires scientifiques (ou équivalent).
Autres conditions: admission sur dossier, critères d'excellence, entretien et recommandation.
Durée: mastère: 12 mois; diplôme d'ingénieur: 3 ans (débutant en septembre).
Frais: frais d'inscription: 300 €; de scolarité: 1100 €; de séjours: environ 500 € par mois.
Assistance financière: bourse Eiffel offerte par le gouvernement réservée aux étudiants étrangers en provenance d'universités partenaires (pour tout renseignement contacter Philippe Deshayes, +33 3 20 33 53 16; Philippe.deshayes@ec-lille.fr).
Connaissances linguistiques: français et anglais.
Inscriptions: avant juin, au Directeur des études (Sylvianne Wignacourt, +33 3 20 33 54 74; bfi@ec-lille.fr).

914   École centrale de Lyon [EC Lyon]

36, avenue Guy de Collongue
69134 Ecully
Tel: +33-4-7218-6300
Fax: +33-4-7843-3962
Web: http://www.ec-lyon.fr

📖 Diplôme d'ingénieur généraliste

Domaines d'étude: ingénierie, sciences.
Programmes: Diplôme d'ingénieur généraliste; cursus de 3ème cycle: DEA et doctorat.
A l'intention de: étudiants étrangers inscrits en double diplôme.
Qualifications requises: admission en 1ère année du cycle d'ingénieur: étudiants issus des classes préparatoires, titulaires d'une Licence scientifique (ou équivalent); admission en 2ème année du cycle d'ingénieur: titulaires d'une Maîtrise scientifique (ou équivalent); admission en DEA, titulaires d'un diplôme d'ingénieur, d'un diplôme de fin de 2ème cycle de l'enseignement supérieur (ou équivalent), d'une Maîtrise scientifique (ou équivalent); admission en doctorat: titulaires d'un DEA; possibilité d'assister en candidat libre au cursus de 3ème année du cycle d'ingénieur.
Autres conditions: admission en 1ère année du cycle d'ingénieur: concours sur épreuves pour les étudiants issus des classes préparatoires, concours sur titre pour les titulaires d'une Licence (ou équivalent); admission en 2ème année du cycle d'ingénieur: concours sur titre pour les titulaires d'une Maîtrise; les candidats doivent se prévaloir d'une recommandation et passer un entretien.
Durée: cycle diplôme d'ingénieur: 3 années (débutant en septembre); DEA: 1 an (débutant en septembre); doctorat: de 2 à 4 ans.
Inscriptions: inscriptions avant la mi-avril auprès de Brigitte Pavone, responsable administrative des relations internationales (tel. +33 4 72 18 63 53, brigitte.pavone@ec-lyon.fr).

915   École centrale Paris [ECP]

Grande-Voie-des-Vignes
92295 Châtenay-Malabry Cedex
Tel: +33-1-4113-1000
Fax: +33-1-4113-1010
Web: http://www.ecp.fr
e-mail: relations.internationales@ads.ecp.fr

📖 2e, 3e cycles / ingénierie

Domaines d'étude: électricité et électronique, énergie, informatique, mécanique, sciences, technologie industrielle.
Programmes: (a) Préparation au diplôme d'ingénieur; (b) Préparation d'un Diplôme d'études approfondies (DEA) dans les spécialités suivantes: chimie appliquée et génie des procédés industriels; mécanique et matériaux; mécanique des sols et des ouvrages dans leur environnement; métallurgie spéciale et matériaux; biophysique moléculaire; physico-chimie et qualité des bioproduits; sciences des matériaux; énergétique: transferts thermiques et combustion; sciences de gestion: analyse et modélisation économiques; chimie analytique; génie des systèmes industriels, conception, productique, logistique; dynamique des structures et

couplages; (c) Préparation d'un doctorat; (d) Formation spécialisée de très haut niveau, sanctionnée par un Mastère spécialisé (MS) dans les domaines suivants: informatique, électronique, technologie et management, mécanique-énergétique, génie des procédés et des matériaux, génie industriel et ingénierie de l'innovation technologique majeure, ingénierie des systèmes informatiques ouverts; (e) Formation d'ingénieurs généralistes, de cadres supérieurs techniques et de dirigeants pour les entreprises conduisant au diplôme d'ingénieur des arts et manufactures (Bac+5).
A l'intention de: ressortissants de tout pays: (a) les candidats peuvent être admis comme élèves-ingénieurs en 1re année sur concours ou sur titre et épreuves pour les titulaires d'une licence ou diplôme étranger équivalent, en 2e année pour les titulaires d'une maîtrise. Les candidats étrangers admis par le cycle international (dossier + épreuves) sont élèves-stagiaires en 1re année; (b) les candidats doivent être titulaires d'un diplôme d'ingénieur ou justifier de titres et travaux d'un niveau comparable; (c) les candidats doivent être titulaires d'un DEA avec possibilité de dérogations (titulaires d'un M.S. ou ayant bénéficié d'une bonne initiation à la recherche); (d) les professionnels de santé au niveau doctorat peuvent faire acte de candidature, ainsi que les titulaires d'une maîtrise ou équivalent justifiant d'au moins 3 ans d'expérience professionnelle; (e) titulaires d'un niveau Bac+2, concours ou admission sur titres.
Durée: (a) et (e) 3 ans (cours communs les 2 premières années et options en 3e année); (b) de 1 à 2 ans selon la spécialité; (c) de 3 à 4 ans selon la spécialité; (d) 12 mois dont 4 mois de stage minimum.
Assistance financière: (a) possibilité de bourses du Ministère des affaires étrangères - Direction générale des relations culturelles, ou de l'Office de coopération et d'accueil universitaire, 69, quai d'Orsay, 75007 Paris; (d) par la Commission d'admission.
Inscriptions: (a) et (e) avant le 8 janvier (admission sur concours); avant le 30 mars (admission sur titre); (b) avant les 15 février, 31 mai, 25 août; (c) avant le 15 novembre; à l'adresse ci-dessus.

916   École d'architecture de Grenoble (CEAA-Terre) [EAG]
60, avenue de Constantine
BP 2636
38036 Grenoble Cedex 2
Tel: +33-4-7669-8300
Fax: +33-4-7669-8338
Web: http://www.grenoble.archi.fr

📖 **1er-3e cycles / architecture**

Domaines d'étude: architecture.
Programmes: 3 formations de 2 ans chacune jusqu'au 3e cycle et conduisant à l'obtention de diplôme d'architecte DPLG.
A l'intention de: ressortissants de tout pays, titulaires d'un diplôme d'architecte, d'ingénieur ou diplôme équivalent donnant accès à un 3e cycle, et pouvant justifier de quelques années d'expérience; sélection sur dossier.
Durée: 2 ans pour chaque cycle.
Frais: inscription: 1er cycle: 318,62 €; 2e et 3e cycles: 446,62 €.
Assistance financière: possibilités de bourses pour les jeunes européen(ne)s.
Connaissances linguistiques: français exigé.
Inscriptions: pré-inscription obligatoire avant le 31 janvier pour les étudiants internationaux.

917   École d'architecture de Lyon [EAL]
3, rue Maurice-Audin
BP 170
69512 Vaulx-en-Velin Cedex
Tel: +33-4-7879-5050
Fax: +33-4-7880-4068
Web: http://www.lyon.archi.fr
e-mail: eal@lyon.archi.fr

📖 **1er-3e cycles / architecture**

Domaines d'étude: architecture.
Programmes: Cours dans le domaine de l'architecture, répartis en 3 cycles: (a) 1er cycle: découverte et apprentissage, conduisant au Diplôme d'architecture (DFA)

Bac+2 (DEUG); (b) 2e cycle: méthodologie et accès progressif à l'autonomie, conduisant au Diplôme d'architecture (DFA) Bac+4 (maîtrise); (c) 3e cycle: professionnalisation et spécialisation, conduisant au Diplôme d'architecture DPLG Bac+6 (DESS, DEA).
A l'intention de: ressortissants de tout pays: (a) titulaires du baccalauréat ou d'un titre ou diplôme admis en équivalence, ou sur justification de quatre années d'activité professionnelle salariée.
Durée: 6 ans (3 cycles de 2 ans).
Assistance financière: possibilité de quelques bourses pour les étudiants internationaux; s'adresser à l'École.
Inscriptions: les candidats résidant à l'étranger doivent s'adresser à l'ambassade ou consulat de leur pays d'origine; les dossiers de pré-inscription doivent être retirés vers le mi-décembre et mi-janvier (vers début janvier et mi-février pour les candidats algériens); s'adresser à l'École pour de plus amples informations.

918   École d'architecture de Paris-Belleville [EAPB]
78, rue de Rébeval
75019 Paris
Tel: +33-1-5338-5000
Fax: +33-1-5338-5001
Web: http://www.paris-belleville.archi.fr
e-mail: eapb.belleville@paris-belleville.archi.fr

📖 **1er-3e cycles / architecture**

Domaines d'étude: architecture.
Programmes: Programme d'études conduisant au: (a) 1er cycle: diplôme national d'enseignement supérieur; (b) 2e cycle: diplôme de deuxième cycle des études d'architecture, diplôme national de l'enseignement supérieur; (c) 3e cycle: diplôme d'architecte diplômé par le gouvernement: le DEA, le DESS; (d) 3e cycle: diplôme national de l'enseignement supérieur.
Description: (d) formation de DEA intitulée «le projet architectural et urbain: théories et dispositifs»; DESS intitulée «Villes Architectures et Patrimoines. Maghreb Proche-Orient».
A l'intention de: ressortissants de tout pays titulaires du baccalauréat ou équivalent; expérience admis en équivalence.
Durée: 5-6 années universitaires.
Connaissances linguistiques: français.
Inscriptions: se renseigner auprès de l'École d'architecture ou du consulat français du pays d'origine; site web: http://www.archi.fr.

919   École d'architecture Languedoc-Roussillon [EALR]
179, rue de l'Espérou
34093 Montpellier Cedex 05
Tel: +33-4-6791-8989
Fax: +33-4-6791-4105
Web: http://www.montpellier.archi.fr

📖 **1er-3e cycles / architecture**

Domaines d'étude: architecture.
Programmes: Programme de cours dans le domaine de l'architecture, conduisant au diplôme d'architecte (DPLG); certificat d'études supérieures spécialisées (DESS), DEA, DU.
A l'intention de: ressortissants de tout pays, titulaires du baccalauréat ou titre reconnu équivalent.
Durée: 6 ans (3 cycles de 2 ans chacun).
Inscriptions: s'adresser à l'École à l'adresse ci-dessus ou http://www.archi.fr.

920   École d'architecture Paris-Malaquais [EDP]
14, rue Bonaparte
75272 Paris Cedex 06
Tel: +33-1-5504-5650
Web: http://www.archi.fr
e-mail: denis.kindeur@paris-malaquais.archi.fr

📖 **1er-3e cycles / architecture**

Domaines d'étude: architecture, arts plastiques, bâtiment, construction.
Programmes: Programme d'études en architecture conduisant aux diplômes de DPLG, DESS, DEA et diplômes d'établissement.

A l'intention de: ressortissants de tout pays, titulaires du baccalauréat ou titre admis en équivalence. Une bonne connaissance du français est exigée.
Durée: 6 années (3 cycles de 2 ans chacun).
Inscriptions: s'adresser à l'École à l'adresse ci-dessus ou http://www.archi.fr.

921 École d'ingénieurs [EPF]
3 bis, rue Lakanal
92330 Sceaux
Tel: +33-1-4113-0151
Fax: +33-1-4660-3994
Web: http://www.epf.fr
e-mail: sophie-telliez@epf.fr

📖 1er-3e cycles / ingénierie

Domaines d'étude: électricité et électronique, informatique, ingénierie, technologie industrielle, télécommunications.
Programmes: Programme de cours conduisant à une formation généraliste en informatique, électronique, mécanique, matériaux, énergétique et aéronautique; des formations internationales bi-diplômantes; une formation d'ingénieur en électronique ou informatique (FIEI) réservée aux étudiants ayant déjà effectué des études supérieures (Maîtrises issues d'un DEUG SV/ST principalement); des Mastères spécialisés.
A l'intention de: en première année aux ressortissants de tous pays préparant un Bac S, un Bac + 1 ou un diplôme étranger équivalent; admission sur concours. Pour les autres formations, s'adresser à l'École ou au site web: www.epf.fr/frameset_trans_dyn.html?name=contacts.html.
Inscriptions: à l'École à l'adresse ci-dessus.

922 École des hautes études commerciales [HEC]
1, rue de la Libération
78351 Jouy-en-Josas Cedex
Tel: +33-1-3967-7000
Web: http://www.hec.fr
e-mail: hecinfo@hec.fr

📖 2e cycle / gestion

Domaines d'étude: gestion.
Programmes: Programme d'enseignement supérieur de gestion «HEC Graduate programme»: 2 ans de formation de généralistes en gestion avec acquisition de compétences internationales; conduisant au diplôme HEC (Bac+5) accrédité par la Conférence des grandes écoles en France et, au niveau européen, par EQUIS (EFMD).
A l'intention de: ressortissants de tout pays, titulaires d'un Bac+3 ou équivalent; admission sur «General management admission test» (GMAT), test d'aptitude aux études de gestion (TAGE-MAGE) et entretien; examen de langue.
Durée: de 2 à 3 ans.
Frais: scolarité, environ 6 479 € par an.
Assistance financière: possibilité de bourse sur critères sociaux.
Connaissances linguistiques: langue d'enseignement: français ou anglais.
Inscriptions: s'adresser à la Direction des Admissions et Concours de la CCIP; BP 31 - 78354 Jouy-en-Josas Cedex; Contact: Brigitte Portal; tél: +33 1 39 67 71 55; fax: +33 1 39 67 74 54.

📖 Programme du Doctorat en sciences de gestion

Domaines d'étude: gestion.
Programmes: Programme de cours conduisant au doctorat en sciences de gestion; formation de professeurs-chercheurs; programme d'étudiants individuels (PEI).
A l'intention de: ressortissants de tout pays, âgés de moins de 35 ans, titulaires d'un diplôme de Grande école ou de 3e cycle universitaire, d'un M.B.A. ou d'un «Master of Science» ou tout diplôme équivalent; admission sur « General management admission test » (GMAT), test d'aptitude TOEFL et entretien.
Durée: de 2 à 5 ans.
Frais: 5488 € pour chacune des deux premières années, 914 € pour les années suivantes.
Assistance financière: bourses sur critères sociaux.
Inscriptions: avant le 15 mai, à l'adresse ci-dessus.

🎓 Bourses de scolarité en gestion, marketing et finances

Domaines d'étude: finances, gestion, marketing.
Bourses: Bourses de scolarité en gestion, marketing et finances.
A l'intention de: étudiants admis au concours de sélection; titulaires d'un Bachelor ou équivalent; ou test d'admission par le CIAM.
Durée: 1 an renouvelable.
Valeur: variable selon les ressources de l'étudiant.
Candidatures: avant le 1er février, à l'HEC-CIAM à l'adresse ci-dessus.

923 École des hautes études en sciences sociales [EHESS]
54, boulevard Raspail
75006 Paris
Tel: +33-1-4954-2525
Fax: +33-1-4544-9311
Web: http://www.ehess.fr
e-mail: scolarite@ehess.fr

📖 2e, 3e cycle / sciences sociales

Domaines d'étude: recherche, sciences humaines, sciences sociales.
Programmes: Programme de cours en sciences humaines et sociales conduisant au: (a) Diplôme de l'EHESS; 1re année sanctionnée par un DEA (Diplôme d'études approfondies); (b) Doctorat de l'EHESS; (c) Habilitation à diriger des recherches.
A l'intention de: ressortissants de tout pays, titulaires: (a) d'un 2e cycle; (b) et (c) du DEA; admission sur dossier et projet de recherche.
Durée: (a) 3 ans; (b) de 1 à 5 ans.
Assistance financière: possibilité de bourse, auprès de l'ambassade de France du pays d'origine.
Inscriptions: du 1er juin au 14 juillet et du 1er au 30 septembre.

924 Ecole des Ingénieurs de la Ville de Paris [EIVP]
57, boulevard St. Germain
75240 Paris
Tel: +33-1-4441-1133
Fax: +33-1-4441-1106
Web: http://www.eivp-paris.fr
e-mail: eivp@eivp-paris.fr

📖 Cours du 2e cycle en génie urbaine

Domaines d'étude: architecture, architecture paysagiste, bâtiment, construction, développement communautaire, écologie, environnement, génie civil, transports, urbanisme.
Description: programmes dans les domaines de l'aménagement d'espaces publics, des infrastructures et des transports, de l'architecture et de l'urbanisme, de l'environnement (eau, air, déchets).
Durée: 3 ans.

925 École des mines d'Alès [EMA]
6, avenue de Clavières
30319 Alès Cedex
Tel: +33-4-6678-5000
Fax: +33-4-6678-5092
Web: http://www.ema.fr

📖 1er, 2e cycles / ingénierie informatique

Domaines d'étude: écologie, environnement, génie civil, industrie et commerce, informatique, ingénierie, mécanique, ressources naturelles, télécommunications.
Programmes: Programme de cours de niveaux Bac+4 à Bac+6 conduisant au diplôme d'ingénieur spécialisé dans les domaines suivants: systèmes d'information et intelligence artificielle; communication numérique; échange de données informatisées; sécurité industrielle et environnement; cours du Centre d'études supérieures pour la sécurité minière et environnement; nouvelles technologies de l'information et de la communication.
A l'intention de: ressortissants de tout pays, titulaires d'un diplôme d'enseignement supérieur ou équivalent (minimum 3 ans); sélection sur dossier.
Durée: de 1 à 3 ans.

Connaissances linguistiques: langue d'enseignement: français.
Inscriptions: avant juillet.

☞ Bourses de formation par la recherche

Domaines d'étude: biochimie, chimie, écologie, environnement, génie civil, informatique, ingénierie, mécanique, ressources naturelles, télécommunications.
Bourses: Bourses de formation par la recherche.
A l'intention de: candidats de toute nationalité, possédant un diplôme d'ingénieur, une maîtrise, un DEA, ou diplômes admis en équivalence. La connaissance du français ou de l'anglais est obligatoire.
Durée: 1 an (renouvelable pour 3 ans).
Candidatures: pas de date limite; au Directeur des recherches de l'École.

926 École du Breuil
Route de la Ferme
Bois de Vincennes
75012 Paris
Tel: +33-1-5366-1400
Fax: +33-1-4365-3459
Web: http://www.boisdevincennes.com/site/breuil.php
3

📖 Diplômes d'horticulture

Domaines d'étude: horticulture.
Programmes: Programme de cours conduisant à l'obtention du brevet de technicien supérieur aménagements paysagers (BTSA); Diplômes de l'École du Breuil.
A l'intention de: ressortissants français et étrangers: titulaires du baccalauréat C, D, D' ou E, d'un BTA-JEV ou d'un BTA G, habitant à Paris ou dans les Hauts de Seine, âgés de 17 à 23 ans au 1er janvier de l'année de recrutement. Sélection sur dossier, concours et entretien.
Durée: 2 ans (débutant en septembre).

927 École du Louvre
Palais du Louvre, Porte Jaujard, Place du Carrousel
75038 Paris Cedex 01
Tel: +33-1-5535-1800
Fax: +33-1-4260-4036
Web: http://www.ecoledulouvre.fr

📖 1er-3e cycles / archéologie, histoire de l'art

Domaines d'étude: archéologie, histoire de l'art, muséologie et muséographie.
Programmes: Cours d'archéologie, d'histoire de l'art et de muséologie, conduisant au: (a) Diplôme de 1er cycle de l'École du Louvre et diplôme spécial de muséologie; (b) Diplôme d'études supérieures de l'École du Louvre (2e cycle); (c) Diplôme de recherche (3e cycle).
A l'intention de: ressortissants de tout pays, titulaires du baccalauréat de l'enseignement secondaire français ou d'un diplôme étranger équivalent; test probatoire d'entrée exigé pour le 1er cycle; équivalences obligatoires pour intégrer l'École en 2e ou 3e cycle.
Durée: 1er et 3ème cycle: 3 ans; 2ème cycle: 1 an.
Frais: 1er cycle: inscription: 265 € de scolarité et 49 € pour le test; pour les 1er et 2ème cycles; 110 € pour le 3ème cycle.
Assistance financière: quelques bourses peuvent être octroyées sous certaines conditions, soit aux réfugiés, soit aux ressortissants de l'Union européenne dont les parents travaillent en France, soit à des étrangers dont la famille réside en France depuis au moins 2 ans.
Inscriptions: à partir de début janvier et jusqu'à fin février pour le test probatoire d'entrée; le test est organisé en mars-avril.

928 École européenne de chimie, polymères et matériaux de Strasbourg [ECPM]
25, rue Becquerel
67087 Strasbourg Cedex 2
Tel: +33-3-9024-2600
Fax: +33-3-9024-2601
Web: http://www-ecpm.u-strasbg.fr
e-mail: relations.internationales@ecpm.u-strasbg.fr

📖 2e, 3e cycles / ingénierie chimique

Domaines d'étude: chimie, génie chimique.
Programmes: Diplôme d'ingénieur en chimie, polymères et matériaux; DEA et doctorat de chimie.
A l'intention de: formation d'ingénieur: titulaires d'un diplôme scientifique de niveau Bac + 2 (ou équivalent).
Autres conditions: admission sur titres, recommandation et entretien.
Durée: 3 années (débutant à la mi-septembre).
Frais: frais d'inscription: 405 €; frais de séjour: environ 500 € par mois.
Connaissances linguistiques: les cours sont dispensés en français, anglais et allemand; possibilité de suivre un double cursus français-allemand en partenariat avec des universités allemandes.
Inscriptions: durant le mois de juin; contacter Hans Leismann (coordonnées ci-dessus).

929 École généraliste d'ingénieurs de Marseille [EGIM]
Technopôle de Château-Gombert
13451 Marseille
Tel: +33-4-9105-4545
Fax: +33-4-9105-4380
Web: http://www.egim-mrs.fr
e-mail: info@egim-mrs.fr

📖 Diplôme d'ingénieur

Domaines d'étude: administration des affaires, ingénierie.
Description: créée en septembre 2003, cette Ecole regroupe les moyens humains, scientifiques et techniques de quatre anciennes écoles d'ingénieurs de Marseille: ENSPM, ENSSPICAM, ESM2 et ESIM et dispense une formation d'ingénieur généraliste.

930 École internationale de commerce et de développement - Institut international 3A
CP 608
69258 Lyon Cedex 09
Tel: +33-4-7285-7373
Fax: +33-4-7285-7386
Web: http://www.ecole3A.edu
e-mail: ecole3a@ecole3a.edu

📖 1er, 2e cycles / management et développement

Domaines d'étude: affaires internationales, économie, études africaines, études américaines, études asiatiques, études du développement, gestion, langues, marketing, relations internationales, sciences économiques et commerciales.
Programmes: programme de cours conduisant au Certificat d'études supérieures internationales en management et développement (CESIMAD), équivalent à la maîtrise.
A l'intention de: ressortissants de tout pays, âgés de 18 à 25 ans; cursus en 4 ans: titulaires d'un Bac français ou équivalent; cursus plus court: admission parallèle (Bac+2) et diplômes étrangers équivalents; admission directe par présélection opérée par l'université d'origine de l'étudiant (constitution d'un dossier d'identification des besoins et certification de niveau); en France, sélection sur dossier, épreuves écrites, entretien devant jury. Français obligatoire; connaissances de base en anglais, espagnol ou portugais.
Durée: de 1 à 4 ans (selon le niveau d'entrée); possibilité pour les étudiants étrangers de suivre un programme individuel d'1 an, sans obtention de diplôme.
Assistance financière: possibilité de bourses.
Inscriptions: avant le 1er septembre pour les étudiants étrangers, auprès du Service administratif de l'École.

931 École nationale d'administration [ENA]
1, rue Ste Marguerite
67080 Strasbourg Cedex
Tel: +33-3-8821-4444
Web: http://www.ena.fr
e-mail: info@ena.fr

📖 2e cycle / administration publique

Domaines d'étude: administration.
Programmes: Programme de cours conduisant au Master
en administration publique (a) Cycle international: études
juridiques, sociales, économiques, internationales, et
techniques de gestion administrative; (b) Sessions à thème,
organisées à la demande d'États étrangers, et consacrées à des
problèmes d'administration publique.
A l'intention de: les candidats doivent avoir une excellente
connaissance de la langue française, être âgés de 25 à 47 ans,
justifier d'un diplôme de l'enseignement supérieur ou de son
équivalent et être appelés à exercer des responsabilités
importantes dans leur pays.
Organisés: (a) à l'ENA (cours); dans diverses
administrations françaises à Paris principalement.
Durée: (a) cycle long: 18 mois; cycle court: 9 mois; (b) 1
semaine à 1 mois.
Assistance financière: bourses éventuellement attribuées
pour (a), par le Ministère des affaires étrangères.
Inscriptions: (a) à partir du mois de septembre précédant
l'année de sélection, auprès de l'ambassade de France; (b) à
l'adresse ci-dessus.

932   École nationale d'ingénieurs de Brest [ENIB]

Technopôle Brest-Iroise
CS 73862
29238 Brest Cedex 3
Tel: +33-2-9805-6600
Fax: +33-2-9805-6610
Web: http://www.enib.fr
e-mail: contact@enib.fr

📖 Diplôme d'ingénieur

Domaines d'étude: électricité et électronique,
informatique, ingénierie, mécanique, optique, technologie
industrielle, télécommunications.
Programmes: Diplôme d'ingénieur généraliste en
électronique, informatique industrielle et mécatronique; DEA
en science et technologie des télécommunications.
A l'intention de: admission en 1ère année: titulaire d'un
Bac scientifique ou STI (ou équivalents); admission en 3ème
année: titulaires d'un diplôme de niveau Bac + 2 (BTS, DUT,
DEUG) d'une admissibilité obtenue en CPGE ou d'un diplôme
équivalent; admission en 4ème année: titulaires d'une Maîtrise
(ou équivalent) correspondant aux spécialités de l'école;
admission en 1ère année: sur dossier, recommandation,
critères d'excellence, examen et entretien; admission en 3ème
et 4ème années: sur dossier, recommandation, critères
d'excellence et entretien.
Durée: 5 ans (débutant en septembre).
Inscriptions: en 1ère année: pré-inscription obligatoire sur
Internet entre le 8 janvier et le 15 avril
(http://www.concours-eni.enit.fr/inscriptions/); en 3ème
année: pré-inscription obligatoire sur Internet entre le 1er
décembre et 5 avril (même site); en 4ème année: dossiers à
retirer entre le 8 janvier et le 10 juin (auprès du service des
admissions de l'ENIB-coordonnées ci-dessus) et à retourner
avant le 18 juin.

933   École nationale d'ingénieurs de Metz [ENIM]

Ile du Saulcy
57045 Metz Cedex 1
Tel: +33-3-8734-6900
Fax: +33-3-8734-6935
Web: http://www.enim.fr
e-mail: enim@enim.fr

📖 Diplôme d'ingénieur

Domaines d'étude: ingénierie, mécanique.
Programmes: Diplôme d'ingénieur de l'ENIM en
ingénierie généraliste, génie mécanique, mécanique et
production; possibilité de préparer en parallèle pendant la
cinquième et dernière année un DESS, un DEA ou un DRT;
Mastère spécialisé en management de projet industriel et
logistique; possibilité de doubles diplômes avec l'Argentine,
l'Allemagne et le Luxembourg.
A l'intention de: admission en première année: titulaires
d'un Bac scientifique ou équivalent (10 places réservées aux
étudiants étrangers); admission en deuxième année: avoir
effectué une année de classe préparatoire ou équivalent (20

places réservées aux étudiants étrangers); admission en
troisième année: titulaires d'un diplôme Bac + 2 ou équivalent
(20 places réservées aux étudiants étrangers); admission en
quatrième année: titulaires d'une maîtrise ou équivalent (20
places réservées aux étudiants étrangers); admission sur
dossier et entretien éventuel.
Durée: 5 ans (débutant en septembre).
Connaissances linguistiques: niveau demandé en français:
DELF deuxième degré ou DALF (délivré par l'alliance
française); cours de français langue étrangère durant l'année
scolaire.
Inscriptions: première, deuxième et quatrième années:
pré-inscription avant le 25 avril sur le site Internet; troisième
année: pré-inscription avant le 7 avril sur le site Internet.

934   École nationale d'ingénieurs de St Étienne [ENISE]

58, rue Jean Parot
42023 St Étienne Cedex 2
Tel: +33-4-7743-8484
Fax: +33-4-7743-8499
Web: http://www.enise.fr
e-mail: meillier@enise.fr

📖 Diplôme d'ingénieur

Domaines d'étude: bâtiment, construction, génie civil,
ingénierie, mécanique, métallurgie, technologie industrielle.
Programmes: Diplôme d'ingénieur en génie mécanique et
génie civil.
A l'intention de: originaires de tout pays; accueil direct
des étudiants issus des établissements partenaires.
Qualifications requises: titulaires d'un Bac scientifique,
d'un DUT, d'un DEUG ou d'une Maîtrise en sciences et
techniques.
Autres conditions: test d'admission pour la première, la
troisième et la quatrième année.
Durée: 5 ans débutant en septembre.
Inscriptions: avant le mois de janvier (service
scolarité/inscriptions, Bernard Laget, +33 4 77 43 84 00,
bernard.laget@enise.fr).

935   École nationale d'ingénieurs des travaux agricoles de Clermont-Ferrand [ENITAC]

Site de Marmilhat
63370 Lempdes
Tel: +33-4-7398-1313
Fax: +33-4-7398-1300
Web: http://www.enitac.fr
e-mail: accueil@enitac.fr

📖 Diplôme d'ingénieur

Domaines d'étude: agriculture, alimentation,
développement rural, écologie, environnement, élevage,
espace, sciences agronomiques.
Programmes: (a) Formation d'ingénieurs des techniques
agricoles: productions animales ou végétales,
agro-alimentaire, aménagement et développement rural; (b)
Formation de cadres d'entreprise ayant une double
compétence de technologue et de gestionnaire maîtrisant: les
technologies de transformation et de fabrication des produits
carnés; la gestion d'entreprise dans sa dimension technique,
économique et commerciale; conduisant au Mastère spécialisé
«technologie et gestion dans les entreprises viande»; (c)
Formation conduisant au DESS élaboration et amélioration de
la production végétale; (d) Formation de professionnels
disposant des acquis nécessaires pour mettre en oeuvre une
démarche de développement touristique respectueuse des
équilibres sociaux, écologiques et culturels; conduisant au
Mastère spécialisé «Marketing et durabilité du tourisme
rural».
A l'intention de: ressortissants de tout pays: (a) titulaires
d'un diplôme universitaire de niveau Bac+2; (b) et (d)
titulaires d'un diplôme d'ingénieur, ou de docteur vétérinaire,
DEA, DESS ou par dérogation maître ès sciences avec 3
années d'expérience professionnelle; (c) titulaires d'un niveau
Bac+4, maîtres ès sciences ou élèves ingénieurs (moins de 25
ans).
Durée: (a) 3 ans; (b) 12 mois; (c) et (d) 1 an.
Assistance financière: possibilité de bourses sur critères
universitaires.

Inscriptions: (a) avant le 1er mars et (b), (c) et (d) avant le 1er juin; à l'adresse ci-dessus.

936 École nationale de l'aviation civile [ENAC]
7, avenue Edouard-Belin
BP 54005
31055 Toulouse Cedex
Tel: +33-5-6217-4000
Fax: +33-5-6217-4023
Web: http://www.enac.fr

Cours en aviation civile
Domaines d'étude: aviation, aéronautique.
Programmes: (a) Cours de spécialisation en exploitation aéronautique et en management aéroportuaire; (b) Cycle d'enseignement spécialisé en navigabilité des aéronefs, conduisant au certificat d'enseignement spécialisé et au mastère; (c) Possibilité de stages de préparation à l'Institut aéronautique et spatial.
A l'intention de: ressortissants de tout pays, chaque formation dispose de ses propres conditions d'accès. Pour la plupart d'entre elles le recrutement s'opère par voie de concours, pour d'autres la sélection se fait sur dossier. Les niveaux d'accès à l'ENAC s'étagent du baccalauréat à la sortie de l'École Polytechnique.
Durée: : (a) de 12 à 18 mois, en fonction de la nécessité ou non de suivre un stage de préparation linguistique et/ou scientifique; (b) 1 an (débutant en octobre).
Inscriptions: variable; contacter l'École pour de plus amples informations.

937 École nationale de la statistique et de l'administration économique [ENSAE]
3, avenue Pierre-Larousse
92245 Malakoff Cedex
Tel: +33-1-4117-6525
Fax: +33-1-4117-3852
Web: http://www.ensae.fr

Cours de formation en statistiques
Domaines d'étude: démographie et études de populations, économie, finances, formation professionnelle, informatique, statistique.
Programmes: (a) cours de formation pour fonctionnaires et cadres supérieurs spécialisés en statistique, économie et finance; 2 niveaux: statisticiens économistes et cadres de gestion statistique et attachés; (b) cours de formation pour fonctionnaires et cadres supérieurs spécialisés en statistique et en traitement quantitatif de l'information, conduisant au diplôme d'ancien élève de l'ENSAE (Bac+5).
A l'intention de: ressortissants de tout pays possédant une bonne connaissance du français et ayant accompli 4 à 5 années d'études supérieures en mathématiques ou en économie; admission sur concours ou sur titres: maîtrise de mathématiques appliquées ou de sciences économiques, mention «Bien» minimum; connaissances linguistiques requises: DALF; 1 langue au choix: anglais, russe, allemand, espagnol ou italien.
Durée: (a) et (b) 3 ans (débutant en septembre).
Assistance financière: possibilité de bourses.
Inscriptions: se renseigner auprès de l'École, service de Concours et Admission.

938 École nationale des chartes [ENDC]
19, rue de la Sorbonne
75005 Paris
Tel: +33-1-5542-7500
Fax: +33-1-5542-7509
Web: http://www.enc.sorbonne.fr

Diplôme d'archiviste
Domaines d'étude: archéologie, bibliothéconomie, histoire, histoire de l'art, lettres.
Programmes: programme de cours conduisant à l'obtention du diplôme d'archiviste paléographe.
A l'intention de: ressortissants de tout pays, possédant le niveau universitaire du 2ème cycle français. Les admissions se font soit sur titre, soit sur concours.

Durée: 3 ans.
Inscriptions: avant le 30 janvier, au Directeur de l'École.

939 École nationale des ponts et chaussées [ENPC]
6-8, avenue Blaise Pascal
Cité Descartes, Champs sur Marne
77455 Marne La Vallée Cedex 2
Tel: +33-1-6415-3000
Web: http://www.enpc.fr

Formations d'ingénieurs
Domaines d'étude: économie, génie civil, ingénierie, mécanique, transports, urbanisme.
Programmes: (a) Formation d'ingénieurs dans les domaines du génie civil, de la mécanique, de l'économie, des transports et de l'urbanisme; Cellule mastères: (b) Programme de formation continue ou postscolaire à but professionnel: Mastères spécialisés (MS); Diplôme d'études supérieures spécialisées (DESS); (c) Programme de formation pour la recherche: Diplôme d'études approfondies (DEA).
A l'intention de: ressortissants de tout pays, titulaires: (a) d'un niveau bac+2 en math. sup et math. spé; d'un diplôme d'ingénieur ou d'une maîtrise ès sciences (2e année); admission sur concours; (b) d'un diplôme d'ingénieur, d'architecte, DEA ou DESS ou tout autre diplôme équivalent; (c) d'une maîtrise, d'un diplôme d'ingénieur, d'architecte ou tout autre diplôme équivalent; excellent niveau de français exigé.
Durée: (a) de 12 à 15 mois; (b) 12 mois.
Frais: inscription: environ 380 € pour les élèves ingénieurs et les stagiaires; 240 € pour les élèves chercheurs; 130 € pour élèves en DEA et les auditeurs. Scolarité: 460 € pour les ingénieurs-élèves, les élèves ingénieurs en scolarité à l'École et les stagiaires en scolarité > 6 mois; 150 € pour les ingénieurs élèves, les élèves ingénieurs en stage long ou 3e année extérieure à l'École, les stagiaires en scolarité < 6 mois et les élèves en DEA.
Inscriptions: à l'adresse ci-dessus; http://www.enpc.fr/DFI/accueil/guide_arrive_enpc.htm#registration.

940 École nationale des sciences géographiques [ENSG]
Institut géographique national (IGN)
6-8, avenue Blaise Pascal
Cité Descartes, Champs-sur-Marne
77455 Marne-la-Vallée Cedex 2
Tel: +33-1-6415-3001
Fax: +33-1-6415-3107
Web: http://www.ensg.ign.fr
e-mail: info@ensg.ign.fr

Formations d'ingénieur géographe
Domaines d'étude: géographie, ingénierie, télécommunications.
Programmes: (a) Cycles préparant au Diplôme d'études approfondies (DEA) et au Diplôme d'études supérieures spécialisées (DESS); (b) Cycle IG: diplôme d'ingénieur géographe et d'ingénieur civil géographe; (c) Cycle IT: diplôme d'ingénieur des travaux; (d) Cycle G: diplôme de géomètre; (e) Cycle D.C.: titre de fin d'études et certificat de fin d'études de dessinateurs cartographes; (f) Cycle CETEL: enseignement de la télédétection; (g) Cycle CCC: conception en cartographie.
A l'intention de: ressortissants de tout pays, admis comme élèves ou auditeurs après examen probatoire de niveau variable selon le cycle d'études.
Durée: variable selon les cycles.
Inscriptions: écrire à l'adresse pour de plus amples informations.

941 École nationale du génie de l'eau et de l'environnement de Strasbourg [ENGEES]
1, quai Koch
BP 61039
67070 Strasbourg Cedex
Tel: +33-3-8824-8282
Fax: +33-3-8837-0497
Web: http://www-engees.u-strasbg.fr

e-mail: engees@engees.u-strasbg.fr

📖 Diplômes d'ingénieur

Domaines d'étude: développement rural, écologie, environnement, formation professionnelle, génie civil, hydraulique, hydrologie, hygiène et santé, ingénierie, ressources naturelles.
Programmes: (a) Cours de formation initiale conduisant au diplôme d'ingénieur diplômé de l'ENGEES (recrutement sur concours ou sur titre); (b) Cours conduisant au certificat d'études supérieures en «équipement et hygiène publique» et en «maîtrise des déchets urbains»; (c) Cours conduisant au mastère en «eau potable et assainissement» et en «maîtrise des déchets» en partenariat avec l'ENSG et l'ENM de Nancy, 2 options «déchets urbains» et «déchets industriels»; (d) Diplôme d'études approfondies (DEA) et doctorat en «mécanique et ingénierie», filière «sciences de l'eau»; (e) Sessions de formation continue: administration-sciences humaines et développement personnel-informatique, bureautique sciences de base-aménagement, équipement-gestion des ressources naturelles, environnement; (f) DEA «protection, aménagement, exploitation du sol et du sous-sol»; domaines d'étude: environnement, géotechnique; (g) DEA «systèmes spatiaux et environnement» en cohabitation avec d'autres organismes d'enseignement supérieur; domaines d'étude: environnement, systèmes urbains et environnement, dynamique des milieux naturels.
A l'intention de: ressortissants de tout pays; (a) admission sur concours d'entrée (niveau Bac+2) ou titulaires d'un DEUG sciences, mention «sciences de la nature» avec mention «assez bien» en 1re et 2e année, d'un DUT en «génie civil», d'un BTS dans la spécialité de l'ENGEES suivi si possible d'une classe préparatoire pour BTS-DUT (ces diplômes doivent être obtenus en France et pour les diplômes délivrés à l'étranger, une équivalence doit être reconnue) ou de certains diplômes d'ingénieur; (b), (d), (f) et (g) titulaires d'un diplôme d'ingénieur ou d'une maîtrise de sciences et techniques, ou d'un diplôme équivalent; (c), titulaires d'un diplôme d'ingénieur, d'un Diplôme d'études approfondies (DEA) ou d'un diplôme admis en équivalence.
Durée: variable.
Assistance financière: possibilités de bourses selon besoin.
Connaissances linguistiques: connaissance de l'anglais obligatoire.
Inscriptions: voir site web ou contacter l'École pour cette information.

942 École nationale supérieure d'agronomie et des industries alimentaires [ENSAIA]
2, avenue de la Forêt de Haye
BP 172
54505 Vandoeuvre-lès-Nancy Cedex
Tel: +33-3-8359-5959
Fax: +33-3-8359-5804
Web: http://www.ensaia.u-nancy.fr

📖 Diplômes d'ingénieur

Domaines d'étude: agriculture, écologie, environnement, génétique, industrie alimentaire, sciences agronomiques, technologie industrielle.
Programmes: Formation d'ingénieurs agronomes et d'ingénieurs des industries alimentaires: productions animales, productions végétales, environnement, génétique, biotechnologie, industrie laitière, procédés alimentaires, emballages alimentaires, brasserie et boissons; conduisant au diplôme d'ingénieur agronome et au diplôme d'ingénieur des industries alimentaires.
A l'intention de: ressortissants de tout pays, titulaires d'un diplôme de l'enseignement supérieur équivalent au DEUG ou à la maîtrise en sciences (Bachelor's); admission sur concours en 1re année, sur dossier en 2e année.
Durée: 3 ans universitaires (débutant en septembre).
Inscriptions: pour la première année sur concours; Secrétariat des concours, I.N.A.; 16, rue Claude Bernard,75 231 PARIS Cedex 05; tél: +33 1 4408 1629; email: concours@inapg.inra.fr; site web http://www.inapg.inra.fr/concours/intro.htm. (avant le 1er mai); pour les autres formations, contacter l'École.

943 École nationale supérieure d'architecture de Nantes [EAN]
rue Massenet
BP 81931
44319 Nantes Cedex 3
Tel: +33-2-4016-0121
Fax: +33-2-4059-1670
Web: http://www.nantes.archi.fr
e-mail: ensan@nantes.archi.fr

📖 1er-3e cycles / architecture

Domaines d'étude: architecture, arts plastiques, bâtiment, construction, physique, urbanisme.
Programmes: Programme de cours dans le domaine de l'architecture: (a) 1er cycle: orientation et formation de base, conduisant au Diplôme d'études fondamentales en architecture (DEFA); (b) 2e cycle: maîtrise de projet (sur 2 ans); (c) Diplôme d'études approfondies (DEA) en ambiances architecturales et urbaines; (d) DESS «villes et territoires»; (e) CEAA «architecture navale».
A l'intention de: ressortissants de tout pays, titulaires pour (a) du baccalauréat ou d'un diplôme admis en équivalence; pour (b) du DEFA ou diplôme équivalent; pour (c) d'un diplôme d'architecte français ou étranger équivalent, ou d'un diplôme donnant accès à un DEA (ingénieur, M.S. T, maîtrise et DESS).
Durée: (a) 2 ans; (b) 4 ans (débutant en octobre); (c) 1 an.
Inscriptions: (a) et (b) les étudiants de nationalité étrangère doivent faire une demande d'admission auprès du Ministère de tutelle, avant le 15 février précédant chaque année scolaire. Pour les étudiants de nationalité française, les dossiers sont à retirer avant le 15 mars; (a) auprès du Secrétariat du DEFA et (b) auprès du Secrétariat du DPLG, à l'adresse ci-dessus. Pour (c) dossier à déposer avant le 15 septembre.

944 École nationale supérieure d'arts et métiers [ENSAM]
151, boulevard de l'Hôpital
75013 Paris
Tel: +33-1-4424-6320
Fax: +33-1-4424-6326
Web: http://www.ensam.fr
e-mail: direction.generale@ensam.fr

📖 Diplôme d'ingénieur

Domaines d'étude: énergie, ingénierie, mécanique, métallurgie, technologie, technologie industrielle.
Programmes: Diplôme d'ingénieur généraliste de l'ENSAM; possibilité de suivre un troisième cycle (DEA, Doctorat ou Mastère); possibilité d'effectuer un semestre ou une année d'étude sans diplôme.
Description: formation de deuxième ou troisième cycle en génie mécanique et génie industriel.
A l'intention de: ressortissants de tout pays titulaires d'un diplôme de deuxième cycle universitaire (Bachelor's ou Master's of science).
Autres conditions: test d'admission pour intégrer directement la deuxième année du cursus du diplôme d'ingénieur.
Durée: diplôme d'ingénieur: 3 ans.
Frais: inscription: environ 700 €; frais de séjour variables selon les centres ENSAM.
Connaissances linguistiques: niveau recommandé en français, TEF: 200; DELF: niveau 2.
Inscriptions: avant le 5 mai pour les admissions sur titre, avant le 1er juillet pour les autres; s'adresser au service des relations internationales (Martine Boutillon, tel. +33 1 44 24 64 10, fax. +33 1 44 24 64 10, martine.boutillon@ensam.fr).

945 École nationale supérieure d'arts et métiers, Châlons [ENSAM-Châlons]
BP 508
Rue Saint-Dominique
51006 Châlons-en-Champagne
Tel: +33-3-2669-2689
Fax: +33-3-2669-9182
Web: http://www.chalons.ensam.fr

📖 Diplôme d'ingénieur

Domaines d'étude: bâtiment, construction, électricité et électronique, énergie, génie civil, hydraulique, ingénierie, mécanique, métallurgie, technologie, technologie industrielle, télécommunications.
Programmes: Diplôme d'ingénieur généraliste de l'ENSAM.
Description: polytechnique et polyscientifique.
Durée: 3 ans.
Connaissances linguistiques: français, anglais et allemand.
Inscriptions: prendre contact avec l'ENSAM de Paris, service des relations internationales (Martine Boutillon, tel: +33 1 4424 6410, fax: +33 1 4424 6410, martine.boutillon@ensam.fr).

946 École nationale supérieure d'électricité et de mécanique [ENSEM]

2, avenue de la Forêt de Haye
54516 Vandoeuvre-lès-Nancy Cedex
Tel: +33-3-8359-5543
Fax: +33-3-8344-0763
Web: http://www.ensem.inpl-nancy.fr
e-mail: Secretariat@ensem.inpl-nancy.fr

📖 Diplôme d'ingénieur

Domaines d'étude: électricité et électronique, informatique, mécanique.
Programmes: Programme de cours conduisant au diplôme d'ingénieur dans les domaines de la mécanique, de l'électrotechnique, de l'informatique industrielle, de l'électronique et de l'automatisation.
A l'intention de: étudiants de toute nationalité, possédant au minimum l'équivalent de Bac+2 dans une discipline scientifique.
Durée: 3 années universitaires (débutant en septembre).
Inscriptions: avant le 30 mai; auprès du Directeur de l'École.

947 École nationale supérieure d'électrotechnique, d'électronique, d'informatique et d'hydraulique de Toulouse [ENSEEIHT]

2, rue Charles-Camichel
BP 7122
31071 Toulouse Cedex
Tel: +33-5-6158-8200
Fax: +33-5-6162-0976
Web: http://www.enseeiht.fr
e-mail: n7@enseeiht.fr

📖 Diplôme d'ingénieur

Domaines d'étude: électricité et électronique, hydraulique, informatique.
Programmes: (a) Programme de cours conduisant au diplôme d'ingénieur dans les domaines du génie électrique, de l'électronique, de l'informatique et de l'hydraulique; (b) Programme de spécialisation dans les domaines suivants: électrotechnique, automatique, électronique, télécommunication, traitement du signal, informatique, hydraulique, énergétique.
A l'intention de: ressortissants de tout pays: (a) ayant passé avec succès le concours commun des écoles nationales supérieures d'ingénieurs ou titulaires d'un DUT ou d'un BTS; (b) titulaires d'un diplôme d'ingénieur ou d'une maîtrise.
Durée: 10 mois (débutant mi-septembre).
Inscriptions: contacter l'École pour de plus amples informations.

948 École nationale supérieure de chimie de Lille [ENSC Lille]

Cité scientifique, bât.C7
Avenue Mendeleïev
BP 108
59652 Villeneuve d'Ascq Cedex
Tel: +33-3-2043-4124
Fax: +33-3-2047-0599
Web: http://www.ensc-lille.fr

e-mail: scolarite@ensc-lille.fr

📖 Diplôme d'ingénieur

Domaines d'étude: chimie, génie chimique, ingénierie.
Programmes: Diplôme d'ingénieur en chimie.
A l'intention de: titulaires d'un diplôme Bac+2 (ou équivalent).
Durée: 3 ans (débutant en septembre).
Inscriptions: avant le 31 mai (service des relations internationales, Zahia Turpin, +33 3 20 33 71 35, zahia.turpin@ensc.lille.fr).

949 École nationale supérieure de chimie de Rennes [ENSC Rennes]

Avenue du Général Leclerc
35700 Rennes
Tel: +33-2-2323-8000
Fax: +33-2-2323-8199
Web: http://www.ensc-rennes.fr
e-mail: scolarite@ensc-rennes.fr

📖 Diplôme d'ingénieur

Domaines d'étude: chimie.
Programmes: Diplôme d'ingénieur chimiste; DEA de chimie moléculaire, chimie des eaux, management de l'entreprise.
A l'intention de: admission en cycle préparatoire: titulaires d'un diplôme de fin d'études secondaires (Bac ou équivalent); admission en 1ère année du cycle d'ingénieur: étudiants issus d'un cycle préparatoire ayant passé les concours communs polytechniques, titulaires d'un DUT, BTS, DEUG scientifique (ou équivalents); admission en 2ème année du cycle d'ingénieur: titulaires d'une Maîtrise scientifique ou d'une MST (ou équivalents); admission en DEA: titulaires d'une Maîtrise scientifique ou d'un diplôme d'ingénieur.
Autres conditions: admission sur dossier et entretien et éventuellement examen.
Durée: cycle diplôme d'ingénieur: 3 ans (débutant en septembre); cycle préparatoire aux écoles d'ingénieur chimiste: 2 ans (débutant en septembre); DEA: 1 an (débutant en septembre).
Frais: frais d'inscription: 45 €; frais de scolarité: 475 €.
Connaissances linguistiques: cours de remise à niveau en français pendant le mois d'août.
Inscriptions: admission en 1ère année du cycle d'ingénieur: pour les étudiants issus des classes préparatoires scientifiques et se destinant aux concours communs polytechniques les inscriptions se font entre début décembre et début janvier dans l'établissement des candidats; pour les titulaires d'un DEUG scientifique les inscriptions se font sur le site www.scei-concours1.org entre le 7 janvier et le 21 février; pour les titulaires d'un DUT, BTS (ou équivalents) ou les étudiants ayant suivi le cycle préparatoire en chimie les dossiers de candidature sont disponibles à partir de mi-janvier auprès du service des admissions de l'école et sont à renvoyer avant le 27 juin; admission en deuxième année du cycle d'ingénieur pour les titulaires d'une Maîtrise ou d'une MST (ou équivalents): les dossiers de candidature sont à retirer de mi-janvier à mi-juin auprès du service des admissions de l'école et doivent être retournés au plus tard le 4 juillet (cette dernière disposition s'applique aux étudiants étrangers); admission en cycle préparatoire: les dossiers sont à retirer à partir du 15 mars auprès du service des admissions de l'école et à retourner avant le 26 avril.

950 École nationale supérieure de géologie [ENSG]

Bâtiment E, rue du Doyen Marcel Roubault
BP 40
54501 Vandoeuvre-lès-Nancy Cedex
Tel: +33-3-8359-6443
Fax: +33-3-8359-6464
Web: http://www.ensg.inpl-nancy.fr
e-mail: com@ensg.inpl-nancy.fr

📖 Formation d'ingénieurs

Domaines d'étude: génie civil, informatique, ingénierie, mécanique, sciences appliquées.
Programmes: Programme de formation en géosciences: eau (ressources, traitement, gestion); matières premières minérales et énergétiques; géotechnique, génie civil,

aménagement du sol et du sous-sol; axe transversal commun: l'environnement et la sûreté, la géologie quantitative.
A l'intention de: ressortissants de tout pays, titulaires d'un diplôme d'ingénieur ou d'une maîtrise.
Inscriptions: contacter l'École pour de plus amples informations.

951 École nationale supérieure de l'aéronautique et de l'espace [SUPAERO]

10, avenue Edouard-Belin
BP 4032
31055 Toulouse Cedex 4
Tel: +33-5-6217-8080
Fax: +33-5-6217-8330
Web: http://www.supaero.fr
e-mail: international@supaero.fr

📖 Diplôme d'ingénieur

Domaines d'étude: aviation, aéronautique, espace.
Programmes: (a) formation d'ingénieurs généralistes de haut niveau dans les disciplines scientifiques de l'aéronautique et de l'espace. Douze filières sont proposées aux étudiants de 3ème année: aéronefs, espace, aérodynamique, propulsion, structures, automatique, radars et optronique, avionique, télécommunication, informatique, ingénierie des systèmes, traitement du signal et des images; (b) Master spécialisé, formation à finalité professionnelle dans les domaines suivants: électronique aérospatiale, mécanique et propulsion aérospatiales, automatique avancée et ingénierie des systèmes, informatique, structures légères, techniques aéronautiques et spatiales; (c) Études doctorales dans les domaines de compétence de l'École.
A l'intention de: ressortissants de tout pays: recrutement (a) sur concours national en 1ère année ou sur titres en 2ème année, pour les titulaires d'un diplôme d'ingénieur, d'une maîtrise ès sciences, ou d'un diplôme reconnu équivalent; (b) sur titres pour les titulaires d'un diplôme d'ingénieur, d'un diplôme d'études approfondies ou d'un diplôme reconnu équivalent; (c) sur titres pour les titulaires d'un diplôme d'études approfondies ou dispensés de ce diplôme.
Durée: (a) 2 ans (recrutement sur titres) ou 3 ans (recrutement sur concours); (b) 1 an; (c) 2 à 4 ans.
Inscriptions: avant le 15 mai.

952 École nationale supérieure de l'électronique et de ses applications [ENSEA]

6, avenue du Ponceau
95014 Cergy-Pontoise Cedex
Tel: +33-1-3073-6666
Fax: +33-1-3073-6667
Web: http://www.ensea.fr
e-mail: ri@ensea.fr

📖 Diplôme d'ingénieur

Domaines d'étude: électricité et électronique, informatique, télécommunications.
Programmes: formation d'ingénieurs en électronique et informatique conduisant au Master en télécommunications, micro-ondes et optiques; au DEA en traitement des images et du signal.
A l'intention de: ressortissants de tout pays: admis sur recommandation et entretien; titulaires d'un «Bachelor's» ou d'un «Master of science» ou «technology»; diplôme Bac + 2 pour les Français; âge maximum: 28 ans.
Durée: 2 années universitaires (débutant en septembre); 1 an pour le Master; 1 an pour le DEA.
Frais: frais d'inscription: 800 €; frais de scolarité: 2.000 € par an; frais de séjour: 500 € par mois.
Assistance financière: possibilité de bourses d'établissement allant de 500 à 2.000 € par an, sur critères d'un excellent niveau académique et en langue française.
Connaissances linguistiques: test de niveau en français et dans certaines matières scientifiques.
Inscriptions: avant le 1er juin (service des relations internationales, Véronique Vitali, à l'adresse ci-dessus, +33 1 30 73 62 16, vitali@ensea.fr.).

953 École nationale supérieure de mécanique et d'aérotechnique [ENSMA]

Téléport 2
1, Avenue Clément Ader - BP 40109
86961 Futuroscope Chasseneuil Cedex
Tel: +33-5-4949-8080
Fax: +33-5-4949-8000
Web: http://www.ensma.fr

📖 Diplôme d'ingénieur

Domaines d'étude: aviation, aéronautique, énergie, hydrologie, ingénierie, mécanique.
Programmes: Formation d'ingénieurs de haut niveau scientifique et technique dans les domaines suivants: aérodynamique et mécanique des fluides, matériaux et structure, énergétique et thermique, informatique industrielle.
Description: l'enseignement couvre des domaines étendus qui sont: la mécanique des fluides, l'aérodynamique, l'énergétique avec ses composantes thermiques, propulsion, combustion et détonique, la mécanique des structures, les matériaux et l'informatique industrielle. Notre formation a également pour objectif de donner à ses diplômés les capacités d'autonomie et d'adaptation nécessaires à l'exercice du métier d'ingénieur. La première année est consacrée à une formation scientifique de base, la deuxième année est axée sur les disciplines propres au métier d'ingénieur. Les élèves en troisième année choisissent un approfondissement dans les domaines d'expertise de l'ENSMA. La connaissance du milieu professionnel se fait par trois stages, un stage ouvrier en fin de première année, en fin de deuxième année un stage ingénieur et un projet de fin d'étude qui peuvent représenter jusqu'à une durée de 10 mois.
Domaines d'études: la formation délivrée à l'ENSMA permet aux jeunes ingénieurs de s'orienter vers des fonctions types bureaux d'études, recherche et développement pour l'essentiel dans les secteurs des industries de transports aéronautiques et terrestres, de la mécanique et de l'énergie.
A l'intention de: ressortissants de tout pays, recrutés sur concours ou possédant l'équivalence des titres exigés (DEUG, DUT, maîtrise, etc.).
Durée: 3 ans pour les élèves-ingénieurs ENSMA, stage de 3 à 12 mois pour les étudiants étrangers accueillis dans le cadre de programmes d'échanges (ERASMUS, etc.).
Frais: inscription: 450 €; droits de médecine préventive: 5 €; cotisation sécurité sociale: 180 €; mutuelle étudiante: entre 11 et 258 €; logement en chambre universitaire: 152 € par mois; restaurant universitaire: 152 € par mois; frais de matériel: 900 €.
Assistance financière: se renseigner auprès des services culturels de l'ambassade de France concernée.
Inscriptions: avant le 1er mai (pré-inscription) pour les admissions sur titres; date limite d'inscription: 1er juillet.

954 École nationale supérieure de meunerie et des industries céréalières [ENSMIC]

16, rue Nicolas-Fortin
75013 Paris
Tel: +33-1-4323-2344
Fax: +33-1-4585-5027
Web: http://www.ensmic.org
e-mail: ensmic.paris@laposte.net

📖 Formation en meunerie

Domaines d'étude: industrie alimentaire.
Programmes: cours de formation de cadres: préparation aux brevets de techniciens supérieurs et d'ingénieurs des industries céréalières pour les branches suivantes: les minoteries, semouleries, maïzeries et les rizeries; les boulangeries, biscuiteries et les biscotteries; les fabriques de pâtes alimentaires; la production d'aliments pour animaux; les organismes stockeurs de céréales; les laboratoires d'analyses; les bureaux d'études des équipements et les sociétés de courtage et d'agréage des grains.
A l'intention de: ressortissants de tout pays, âgés de 18 à 30 ans et titulaires au minimum, d'un baccalauréat scientifique ou technique (ou équivalent étranger). Bon niveau de connaissance du français exigé.
Durée: 2 à 5 ans (débutant en septembre), ou 9 mois pour les titulaires d'un diplôme scientifique ou technique de niveau au moins égal à 2 années d'études post baccalauréat.

Inscriptions: de mars à juin, au Secrétariat de l'École.

955 École nationale supérieure de physique de Strasbourg [ENSPS]

Boulevard Sébastien Brant
BP 10413
67400 Illkirch
Tel: +33-3-9024-4510
Fax: +33-3-9024-4545
Web: http://www-ensps.u-strasbg.fr

📖 Diplôme d'ingénieur

Domaines d'étude: électricité et électronique, informatique, ingénierie, optique, physique, sciences, sciences appliquées.
Programmes: Diplôme d'ingénieur.
A l'intention de: 1ère année: titulaires d'un diplôme Bac + 2 (ou équivalent étranger); deuxième année: titulaires d'un diplôme Bac + 4 (niveau Maîtrise ou équivalent étranger).
Autres conditions: admission sur dossier, recommandation et entretien.
Durée: 3 ans (débutant en septembre).
Frais: inscription: 572 € + mutuelle obligatoire; frais de séjour: environ 500 € par mois.
Inscriptions: avant le 30 octobre; renseignements auprès de Sylvia Mutterer, scolarité de l'ENSPS, adresse ci-dessus, +33 3 9024 4437, sylvia.mutterer@ensps.u-strasbg.fr.

956 École nationale supérieure de techniques avancées [ENSTA]

32, boulevard Victor
75739 Paris Cedex 15
Tel: +33-1-4552-5407
Fax: +33-1-4552-5954
Web: http://www.ensta.fr
e-mail: international@ensta.fr

📖 Diplôme d'ingénieur

Domaines d'étude: construction navale, électricité et électronique, énergie, génie chimique, informatique, mathématiques, mécanique, sciences appliquées, technologie.
Programmes: formation d'ingénieurs généralistes dans le domaine naval, mécanique, chimique, nucléaire, informatique, électronique, mathématiques appliquées, et domaines annexes.
Domaines d'études: mécanique des structures, mécanique des fluides, architecture navale et offshore, électronique, informatique, robotique, mathématiques appliquées, chimie, génie des procédées, énergie, optique appliquée.
A l'intention de: ressortissants de tout pays. Le recrutement se fait en 1ère année, sur concours portant sur les programmes des classes préparatoires scientifiques (classes préparatoires aux grandes écoles, durée 2 ans). En 2ème année, le recrutement se fait sur titre d'ingénieur diplômé de l'école polytechnique ou de certaines grandes écoles, titre de maître ès sciences relatif à certaines disciplines, ou titres étrangers admis en équivalence.
Durée: 3 ans.
Inscriptions: s'adresser à l'École pour de plus amples renseignements.

🎓 Bourse

Domaines d'étude: construction navale, électricité et électronique, énergie, génie chimique, informatique, mathématiques, mécanique, sciences appliquées, technologie.
Bourses: Bourse DGA.
Domaines d'études: Ingénierie.
A l'intention de: ressortissants des pays suivants: Argentine, Brésil, République tchèque, Hongrie, Roumanie, Russie.
Durée: 1 an, renouvelable.
Valeur: 3600€, plus les frais de scolarité, plus une indemnité de voyage de 550€.
Candidatures: avant le 30 avril.

🎓 Bourses d'excellence Eiffel

Domaines d'étude: ingénierie.
Description: bourse octroyée par le gouvernement français, applicable à cette École.
Domaines d'études: ingénierie.

Durée: deux ou trois ans.
Valeur: total des frais d'enseignement (1.200 euros par mois).
Candidatures: mi-février. L'information est disponible sur http://www.egide.asso.fr/fr/programmes/eiffel.

957 École nationale supérieure des arts appliqués et métiers d'art [ENSAAMA]

63-65, rue Olivier-de-Serres
75015 Paris
Tel: +33-1-5368-1690
Fax: +33-1-5368-1699

📖 Formation en arts appliqués

Domaines d'étude: artisanat, arts, arts appliqués, décoration.
Programmes: Formation en architecture intérieure, communication visuelle, création céramique, design d'environnement, design textile, création industrielle, conduisant aux brevets de technicien supérieur, au diplôme de métiers d'art et au diplôme supérieur d'arts appliqués.
A l'intention de: ressortissants de tout pays, titulaires du baccalauréat, admission sur présentation d'un dossier de travaux artistiques personnels.
Durée: de 2 à 5 ans selon le niveau initial.
Inscriptions: à l'adresse ci-dessus.

958 École nationale supérieure des ingénieurs en arts chimiques et technologiques [ENSIACET]

Service des Relations internationales
118 route de Narbonne
31077 Toulouse Cedex 04
Tel: +33-5-6288-5611
Fax: +33-5-6288-5600
Web: http://www.ensiacet.fr
e-mail: international.Office@ensiacet.fr

📖 Diplôme d'ingénieur

Domaines d'étude: industrie chimique, ingénierie.
Programmes: cours de génie chimique préparant aux diplômes d'ingénieur du génie industriel; chimie; génie chimique; matériaux et procédés; génie et procédés informatique.
A l'intention de: ressortissants de tout pays; admission sur concours.
Inscriptions: contacter l'École à l'adresse ci-dessus.

959 École nationale supérieure des mines de Nancy [EMN]

Parc de Saurupt
CS 14234
54042 Nancy Cedex
Tel: +33-3-8358-4232
Web: http://www.mines.u-nancy.fr
e-mail: mailto:ensmn@mines.inpl-nancy.fr

📖 Diplômes d'ingénieur

Domaines d'étude: génie civil, ingénierie, métallurgie.
Programmes: Programme de cours conduisant aux diplômes: (a) Ingénieur civil des mines; (b) Ingénieur des techniques industrielles en métallurgie dans les options et spécialités suivantes: mathématiques, informatique, thermodynamique, mécanique des fluides aérothermiques, mécanique des roches géothermiques; recherche opérationnelle, système expert, gestion de projet; réacteur d'élaboration, réacteur chimique; polymères, alliages, structure métallique.
A l'intention de: ressortissants de tout pays, titulaires d'un Bac+3 (licence, maîtrise ou diplôme équivalent), âgés de moins de 30 ans.
Assistance financière: possibilités de bourses par le Ministère des Affaires étrangères.
Inscriptions: à l'adresse ci-dessus, pour de plus amples renseignements.

960 École nationale supérieure des mines de Paris [ENSMP]

60, boulevard Saint Michel
75272 Paris Cedex 06
Tel: +33-1-4051-9005
Fax: +33-1-4354-1893
Web: http://www.ensmp.fr

📖 Diplôme d'ingénieur

Domaines d'étude: droit, économie, gestion, ingénierie, langues, relations industrielles, sciences, sciences appliquées, sciences sociales.
Programmes: Diplôme d'ingénieur civil des mines de l'ENSMP; possibilité de préparer un Master-recherche, un doctorat ou un Mastère spécialisé en sciences de la terre et environnement, génie des procédés énergétiques, sciences et génie des matériaux, mathématiques appliquées, informatique, automatique, sciences économiques et sociales.
A l'intention de: admission en 1ère année: sur concours pour les étudiants issus des classes préparatoires ou bien sur titres pour les titulaires d'une Licence en sciences (ou diplôme équivalent); admission en deuxième année: titulaires d'une Maîtrise en sciences (ou diplôme équivalent), ingénieurs de l'École polytechnique; admission sur dossier et entretien.
Durée: 3 ans (débutant en septembre).
Frais: frais de scolarité: 400 €; frais de séjour: 600 € par mois.
Inscriptions: de décembre à début janvier pour le concours commun (contacter le secrétariat général du concours commun Mines-Ponts, 37-39, rue Dareau, 75014 Paris); de la mi-février à la fin avril pour les admissions sur titres.

961 École nationale supérieure des mines de Saint-Etienne [ENSMSE]

158, cours Fauriel
42023 Saint-Etienne Cedex 2
Tel: +33-4-7742-0123
Fax: +33-4-7742-0000
Web: http://www.emse.fr
e-mail: barbry@emse.fr

📖 Diplôme d'ingénieur

Domaines d'étude: toutes disciplines principales.
Programmes: Diplôme d'ingénieur civil des mines; Master of science, Mastères spécialisés, DEA et doctorat en matériaux, informatique, génie des procédés, environnement industriel, gestion industrielle, mathématiques, finances.
A l'intention de: admission en 1ère année: étudiants issus des classes préparatoires scientifiques (ou équivalents), titulaires d'une Licence scientifique avec mention (ou équivalent); admission en 2ème année: titulaires d'une Maîtrise scientifique avec mention (ou équivalent), titulaires d'un DEST ou diplômés de l'École polytechnique.
Autres conditions: admission sur titres, dossier, recommandation et entretien pour les étudiants étrangers.
Durée: 3 ans (débutant en septembre).
Frais: droits de scolarité: 381 € par an; frais annexes d'enseignement: environ 114 €.
Assistance financière: possibilité d'obtenir des bourses semestrielles délivrées par l'école ou bien le collectif des anciens élèves; la demande de dossier se fait une fois l'inscription faite et l'attribution se fait au cas par cas.
Connaissances linguistiques: français (sauf pour le Master of science dont les cours sont assurés en anglais).
Inscriptions: pour passer le concours d'entrée une pré-inscription est obligatoire par Internet (www.scei-concours.org); pour les admissions sur titres les dossiers sont à retirer à partir de fin janvier au secrétariat aux admissions sur titres -École des mines de Paris, 60 Bd Saint-Michel -75272 Paris cedex 06, tel. +33 1 40 51 90 05, fax, +33 1 46 33 22 29) et doivent être rendus pour le 30 avril au plus tard; pour les autres modes de recrutement contacter Yves Barbry (barbry@emse.fr) ou Marta Tor (tel. +33 4 7742 0110, fax +33 4 7742 6631, tor@emse.fr).

962 École nationale supérieure des sciences de l'information et des bibliothèques [ENSSIB]

17-21, avenue du 11 Novembre 1918
69623 Villeurbanne Cedex
Tel: +33-4-7244-4343
Fax: +33-4-7244-4344
Web: http://www.enssib.fr

📖 Diplômes en sciences de bibliothèques

Domaines d'étude: bibliothéconomie, documentation, informatique, sciences de l'information.
Programmes: Cours de formation du personnel des bibliothèques et centres de documentation préparant: (a) au diplôme professionnel supérieur des sciences de l'information et des bibliothèques (DPSSIB); (b) au diplôme d'études supérieures spécialisées (DESS) en informatique documentaire.
A l'intention de: élèves de toute nationalité, possédant le niveau de 4 années universitaires avec diplôme correspondant; la sélection se fait sur dossier pour (a) et (b).
Durée: environ 12 mois (débutant en octobre) dont 4 mois de stage.
Assistance financière: possibilité d'obtention de bourse.
Inscriptions: s'adresser à l'École.

963 École nationale supérieure des télécommunications [ENST]

46, rue Barrault
75634 Paris Cedex 13
Tel: +33-1-4581-8031
Fax: +33-1-4581-7076
Web: http://www.enst.fr
e-mail: communication@telecom-paris.fr

📖 Diplôme d'ingénieur

Domaines d'étude: télécommunications.
Programmes: Diplôme d'ingénieur en télécommunication; possibilité de suivre un Mastère spécialisé, un DEA ou un doctorat en télécommunication.
A l'intention de: ressortissants de tous pays.
Qualifications requises: admission en 1ère année: étudiants issus des classes préparatoires (ou équivalents), titulaires d'une Licence scientifique (ou équivalent); admission en 2ème année: titulaires d'une Maîtrise scientifique (ou équivalent).
Autres conditions: admission sur titres, dossier et entretien.
Durée: 3 ans.
Frais: frais de scolarité: 900 €.
Inscriptions: dossier à retirer entre le 15 janvier et le 23 avril; dossier à remettre avant le 1er mai; pour tout renseignement contacter Christiane Gaffajoli (+33 1 4581 7735, christiane.gaffajoli@enst.fr).

964 École nationale supérieure du pétrole et des moteurs [ENSPM]

232, av Napoléon Bonaparte
92852 Rueil-Malmaison
Tel: +33-1-4752-6710
Fax: +33-1-4752-7427
Web: http://www.enspmfi.com
e-mail: gre.rueil@enspmfi.com

📖 Diplôme d'ingénieur

Domaines d'étude: économie, génie chimique, gestion, industrie chimique, ingénierie, technologie.
Programmes: Cours d'application des produits pétroliers et énergétiques: étude et formulation, principalement dans le domaine de la lubrification, de la combustion et des produits à haute valeur ajoutée; développement et exploitation des gisements: études des techniques de forage, de développement de la production et du traitement des hydrocarbures à terre ou en mer; économie et gestion de l'entreprise: techniques pétrolières, mise en œuvre des outils et des méthodes d'analyse économique, de gestion financière et d'étude de projets dans l'industrie des hydrocarbures; exploration: géologie-géophysique; moteurs; raffinage, ingénierie et gaz: techniques et méthodes des pétroles bruts, des dérivés chimiques, de génie des procédés, d'ingénierie et de gestion des projets; conduisant au certificat,

au Diplôme d'ingénieur de l'ENSPM, au DEA et au Master.
A l'intention de: ressortissants de tout pays, titulaires d'un
Bac+5 ou équivalent; sélection sur dossier avec jury
d'admission; anglais obligatoire pour les programmes
internationaux (attestations TOEFL, TOIEC, GMAT, GRE,
etc.).
Assistance financière: bourses pour les ressortissants de
l'Union européenne; parrainage par des sociétés; bourses
gouvernementales.
Connaissances linguistiques: français ou anglais selon les
programmes.
Inscriptions: fin février pour le 1er jury; 15 mai pour le 2e
jury; au Secrétariat général de l'ENSPM.

☞ Bourses pour ingénieurs

Domaines d'étude: toutes disciplines principales, énergie,
géologie, industrie chimique, ingénierie, mécanique,
ressources naturelles, sciences de la terre.
Bourses: Bourses de formation, de spécialisation pour
ingénieurs.
A l'intention de: ressortissants de toute nationalité (40%
de non français), titulaires d'un diplôme d'ingénieur ou
équivalent, ayant une bonne connaissance du français et/ou de
l'anglais. Admission sur dossier et entretien.
Durée: 11 à 16 mois.
Candidatures: avant le 15 mai pour la rentrée de
septembre, au Secrétariat général de l'ENSPM.

965 École nationale supérieure Louis Lumière [ENSLL]
7, allée du Promontoire
93161 Noisy-le-Grand Cedex
Tel: +33-1-4815-4010
Fax: +33-1-4305-6344
Web: http://www.ens-louis-lumiere.fr
e-mail: sg@ens-louis-lumiere.fr

☐ Diplôme en cinématographie

Domaines d'étude: cinématographie, photographie.
Programmes: (a) Cours de préparation au diplôme de
l'École nationale supérieure Louis Lumière (niveau Bac+5)
dans les domaines de la photographie, options prise de vues et
traitement des images, du cinéma et du son; (b) Formation de
spécialistes chargés d'assurer des missions de conception, de
maîtrise d'œuvre et de réalisation dans les métiers de
l'industrie cinématographique, photographique ou du son.
A l'intention de: ressortissants de tout pays, âgés de moins
de 27 ans au 1er janvier de l'année du concours, titulaires du
baccalauréat ou d'un diplôme étranger équivalent; admission
sur concours.
Durée: 3 ans (débutant en septembre).
Assistance financière: bourses octroyées par le Service
des bourses de l'enseignement supérieur.
Inscriptions: du 2 janvier au 27 mars pour l'inscription au
concours qui a lieu début mai; pour plus d'informations
contacter info-concours@ens-louis-lumiere.fr.

966 École nationale vétérinaire de Nantes [ENVN]
BP 40706
Atlanpole-La Chantrerie
44307 Nantes
Tel: +33-2-4068-7777
Fax: +33-2-4068-7778
Web: http://www.vet-nantes.fr
e-mail: direction@vet-nantes.fr

☐ Etudes vétérinaires

Domaines d'étude: médecine vétérinaire.
Description: établissement d'enseignement supérieur et de
recherche; la formation est structurée en 3 étapes. S'il le
souhaite, le vétérinaire peut prolonger sa formation par une
quatrième étape, qui l'amène à se spécialiser ou à faire de la
recherche.
Durée: 6 ans.

967 École normale supérieure [ENS]
45, rue d'Ulm
75230 Paris Cedex 05
Tel: +33-1-4432-3000
Fax: +33-1-4432-2099
Web: http://www.ens.fr
e-mail: ens-international@ens.fr

☐ Formation culturelle et scientifique de haut niveau

Domaines d'étude: toutes disciplines principales,
éducation, recherche.
Programmes: Formation culturelle et scientifique de haut
niveau conduisant aux diplômes nationaux français (maîtrise,
DEA), qui donnent accès à des équivalences internationales;
préparation pour concours de l'agrégation pour devenir
enseignant. Le DEA (Diplôme d'Études Approfondies)
correspond à la première étape de spécialisation dans la
discipline de recherche choisie et se poursuit par la première
année de la thèse de doctorat.
A l'intention de: ressortissants de tout pays, âgés de moins
de 24 ans, titulaires d'un diplôme de fin de 1er cycle de
l'enseignement supérieur; sélection sur concours (de mai à
juillet).
Durée: 3 ans.
Connaissances linguistiques: langue d'enseignement:
français.
Inscriptions: avant fin mars à Sélection Internationale de
l'ENS; École normale supérieure; 45, rue d'Ulm; F - 75230
Paris Cedex 05; dossiers disponible sur site web:
http://www.ens.fr/international.

968 École normale supérieure de Cachan [ENS Cachan]
61, avenue du Président-Wilson
94235 Cachan
Tel: +33-1-4740-2000
Fax: +33-1-4740-2074
Web: http://www.ens-cachan.fr
e-mail: service-communication@ens-cachan.fr

☐ Formation de formateurs

Domaines d'étude: économie, électricité et électronique,
génie civil, informatique, ingénierie, mécanique, recherche,
sciences, sciences sociales, technologie industrielle.
Programmes: formation culturelle et scientifique de haut
niveau: (a) préparation à l'agrégation dans les domaines
suivants: sciences, sciences de l'ingénieur, économie, sciences
sociales, arts et création industrielle; (b) préparation au
diplôme d'études approfondies (DEA) en analyse numérique
et applications, automatique et traitement du signal,
électronique, génie électrique, génie civil, informatique,
matière condensée, mécanique des matériaux, mécanique des
solides et des structures, physico-chimie moléculaire,
probabilités et applications, production automatisée, sciences
de la décision et micro-économie, sciences sociales; (c)
préparation au doctorat en économie, électricité, didactiques
des sciences et de la technologie, génie biologique,
informatique, mathématiques, mécanique et technologie,
physique, chimie, productique génie mécanique, sciences
sociales.
A l'intention de: ressortissants de tout pays, se destinant à
la recherche fondamentale ou appliquée, à l'enseignement
universitaire ou dans des classes préparatoires aux grandes
écoles, ainsi qu'à l'enseignement secondaire et plus
généralement, au service des administrations de l'État et des
collectivités territoriales, de leurs établissements publics ou
des entreprises. Les candidats: (a) peuvent être admis en
première année, soit sur concours (niveau Bac+2 - deuxième
année de classes préparatoires), soit sur titres; (b) doivent être
titulaires d'une maîtrise ou d'un diplôme d'ingénieur, ou
diplôme équivalent; (c) doivent être titulaires d'un DEA ou
d'un diplôme équivalent.
Durée: (a) 3 ans; (b) 1 an; (c) de 3 à 4 ans.
Assistance financière: des bourses peuvent être accordées
avec prise en charge des frais de scolarité, par le pays
d'origine ou le Ministère des affaires étrangères.
Inscriptions: s'adresser à l'École.

🐚 **Bourse**

Domaines d'étude: toutes disciplines principales, sciences, sciences humaines, sciences sociales, technologie industrielle.
Domaines d'études: Sciences, sciences sociales et humaines, sciences industrielles.
A l'intention de: ressortissants de tous les pays, titulaires d'un diplôme universitaire.
Durée: 1 an, non renouvelable.
Valeur: 1000 €.
Candidatures: Dossier de candidature avant avril; contacter edsp@ens-cachan.fr pour plus d'informations.

969   École normale supérieure de Lyon [ENS Lyon]
46, allée d'Italie
69364 Lyon
Tel: +33-4-7272-8000
Fax: +33-4-7272-8080
Web: http://www.ens-lyon.fr
e-mail: webmaster@ens-lyon.fr

📖 **Formations scientifiques**

Domaines d'étude: biologie, chimie, informatique, mathématiques, physique, sciences de la terre.
Description: Cinq programme de Masters: mathématiques, informatique, sciences de la matière (physique et chimie), biologie moléculaire et cellulaire, sciences de la Terre; quatre préparations à l'agrégation: mathématiques, physique, chimie, SV-STU (Sciences de la Vie, Sciences de la Terre et de l'Univers).
Inscriptions: admission sur concours; voir site web pour toutes informations.

970   École normale supérieure Lettres et Sciences humaines [ENS-LSH]
BP 7000
69342 Lyon Cedex 07
Tel: +33-4-3737-6000
Web: http://www.ens-lsh.fr
e-mail: ri@ens-lsh.fr

📖 **« Pensionnaire scientifique étranger »**

Domaines d'étude: français, géographie, histoire, linguistique, littérature et civilisation, philosophie, sociologie.
Programmes: Programme d'accueil et de formation d'étudiants étrangers en qualité de «pensionnaires scientifiques étrangers»: assistance à la recherche (thèse), tutorat individuel par un enseignant-chercheur de l'École; en littérature française, linguistique, philosophie, histoire, géographie, sociologie; possibilités d'obtenir le diplôme de «Pensionnaire scientifique étranger».
A l'intention de: ressortissants de tout pays, de niveau post-maîtrise française (niveau graduate); attestation de ressources financières pour l'obtention du visa; nombre de places limité; sélection sur dossier début mai.
Durée: deux sessions: 9 mois, d'octobre à juin et 6 mois, de janvier à juin.
Assistance financière: voir: http://www.ens-lsh.fr/etudes/echanges/financement.htm.
Inscriptions: avant le 30 avril, s'adresser au Service des relations internationales à l'adresse ci-dessus.

971   École polytechnique [EP]
Direction des Relations extérieures
91128 Palaiseau Cedex
Tel: +33-1-6933-4473
Fax: +33-1-6933-3016
Web: http://www.polytechnique.fr
e-mail: direction.etudes@polytechnique.fr

📖 **Diplôme d'ingénieur et 3e cycle**

Domaines d'étude: biologie, chimie, économie, informatique, ingénierie, mathématiques, physique, sciences, sciences sociales.
Programmes: (a) Cursus polytechnicien: programme pluriscientifique conduisant au diplôme d'ingénieur; (b) Troisième Cycle: Diplômes d'études approfondies (DEA); Diplôme de docteur de l'école polytechnique; Mastère en ingénierie mathématique; Master's en innovation technologique.

A l'intention de: sur concours; ressortissants de tout pays âgés de moins de 26 ans au 1er janvier de l'année du concours.
Durée: (a) de 2, 3 ou 4 ans selon le moment d'intégration et le diplôme souhaité; (b) de 1 à 3 ans.
Inscriptions: voir site web pour plus de renseignements: http://www.scei-concours.org ou s'adresser à l'École.

972   École spéciale de Mécanique et d'Electricité [ESME-SUDRIA]
4, rue Blaise Desgoffe
75006 Paris
Tel: +33-1-4954-0750
Fax: +33-1-4954-0740
Web: http://www.esme.fr/international/international.s html
e-mail: contact@esme.fr

📖 **Etudes en ingénierie**

Domaines d'étude: électricité et électronique, informatique, ingénierie.
Description: Cycle préparatoire; cycle ingénieur: 2 ans de tronc commun; cycle ingénieur: le choix en 3ème année; génie électrique; informatique; électronique; traitement du signal et télécommunications; école doctorale; études à l'étranger.
Inscriptions: voir site web pour toutes informations.

973   École spéciale des travaux publics du bâtiment et de l'industrie [ESTP]
57, boulevard Saint-Germain
75240 Paris
Tel: +33-1-4441-1118
Fax: +33-1-4441-1112
Web: http://www.estp.fr
e-mail: estp@adm.estp.fr

📖 **1er, 2e cycles en travaux publics**

Domaines d'étude: architecture paysagiste, bâtiment, construction, génie civil, ingénierie, technologie industrielle.
Programmes: Formations diplomantes dans les domaines des travaux publics.

974   École supérieure d'agriculture d'Angers, Groupe ESA [ESA]
55, rue Rabelais
BP 30748
49007 Angers
Tel: +33-2-4123-5555
Fax: +33-2-4123-5500
Web: http://www.groupe-esa.com
e-mail: admission@esa-angers.educagri.fr

🐚 **Bourses**

Domaines d'étude: agriculture, biologie, écologie, environnement, marketing, sciences, sciences sociales.
Bourses: (a) Bourses Alban; (b) programmes d'échange du Département de Maine-et-Loire; (c) bourses sponsorisées par les sociétés privées; (d) programmes sponsorisés par la Région Pays de la Loire; (e) programme d'Est en Ouest; (f) Association des anciens élèves.
Description: bourses pour études en agriculture.
A l'intention de: candidats ayant un BSc ou équivalent; (a) ressortissants d'Amérique latine; (b), (f) ressortissants hongroise; (c) ressortissants de toute nationalité; (e) ressortissants d'Europe centrale.
Durée: (a) six mois à trois années; (b), (c) variable.
Valeur: (a) frais de scolarité: 75 pour-cent des frais; (b) frais de scolarité: 3.500 €; frais de séjour: 445€; (c) frais de scolarité; (e) frais de scolarité: 10.400€ par an; frais de séjour: 7.400€ par an; (f) frais de scolarité.
Candidatures: (a) janvier de chaque année; contacter Mme Chantal Caure, c.caure@esa-angers.educagri.fr; (b), (c) contacter Bénédicte Chopin, b.chopin@esa-angers.educagri.fr; (d) candidatures en avril de chaque année; (e) contacter Bruno Salmon-Legagneur, b.chopin@esa-angers.educagri.fr. Voir site: http://www.programalban.org/index.jsp pour plus d'informations.

975 **École supérieure d'électricité
[SUPELEC]**
Plateau du Moulon
91192 Gif-sur-Yvette Cedex
Tel: +33-1-6985-1322
Fax: +33-1-6985-1339
Web: http://www.supelec.fr

📖 Diplôme d'ingénieur
Domaines d'étude: électricité et électronique, industrie
alimentaire, informatique, télécommunications.
Programmes: Enseignement conduisant au diplômes: (a)
Ingénieur de Supélec; (b) Spécialisation de Supélec;
(c) Mastère de Supélec.
A l'intention de: ressortissants de tout pays, ayant pour (a)
déjà effectué de 2 à 5 années et (b) 5 années d'études après le
baccalauréat, sanctionnées par un diplôme. Pour (c), les
candidats doivent être présentés par leur entreprise.
Organisés: sur les 3 campus de Supélec: Gif-sur-Yvette,
Metz ou Rennes (Cesson-Sévigné).
Durée: (a) de 2 à 3 ans; (b) 9 mois; (c) 2 mois (débutant
mi-mai).
Assistance financière: quelques bourses sont offertes;
s'adresser pour (a) et (b), au Service compétent du pays
d'origine du candidat, ou au Centre international des étudiants
et stagiaires, 28, rue de la Grange-aux-Belles, 75010 Paris;
pour (c), consulter les conseillers techniques des ambassades
de France.
Inscriptions: (a) et (b) Concours Centrale-Supélec; Grande
Voie des Vignes; 92295 Chatenay-Malabry Cedex; tél: +33 1
4113 1129 ou +33 1 4113 1196; email:
admissions@ads.ecp.fr.

976 **École supérieure d'ingénieurs
en électrotechnique et
électronique
Amiens [ESIEE-Amiens]**
14, quai de la Somme
BP 100
80082 Amiens Cedex 2
Tel: +33-3-2266-2000
Fax: +33-3-2266-2010
Web: http://www.esiee-amiens.fr

📖 Études en ingénierie électronique
Domaines d'étude: administration des affaires, affaires
internationales, communication, droit international, électricité
et électronique, études internationales, ingénierie, marketing,
relations internationales, sciences humaines, technologie
industrielle.
Programmes: (a) Diplôme d'ingénieur; (b) Master of
Science; (c) 3e cycle-Mastère spécialisé en ingénierie des
affaires internationales.
Description: (a) formation d'ingénieurs en
électrotechnique et électronique spécialisation: génie des
systèmes électriques, des systèmes de production, des réseaux
informatisés et télécoms; (b) Master of Science; (c) Mastère
spécialisé en ingénierie des affaires internationales.
A l'intention de: (a) titulaires d'un baccalauréat
scientifique ou d'un diplome reconnu équivalent (pour
admission en 1ere année); (b) concours ESIEE-Amiens,
ENSAM, ATS; titulaires Lé (ex-DEUG) ou L3 (ex-Licence)
ou DUT/BTS (pour admission en 3e année); (c) (ex-Maîtrise),
dans le spécialités de l'école pour les admissions en 4e année.
Durée: 5 années.
Assistance financière: possibilité par le CROUS Amiens;
contacter le Directeur général.
Inscriptions: avant le mois d'avril au Service Concours
ESIEE-Amiens; email: concours@esiee-amiens.fr; cours
commencent début septembre.

977 **École supérieure d'ingénieurs
en électrotechnique et
électronique [ESIEE]**
BP 99
93162 Noisy-le-Grand Cedex
Tel: +33-1-4592-6500
Fax: +33-1-4592-6699
Web: http://www.esiee.fr
e-mail: admissions@esiee.fr

📖 Diplôme d'ingénieur
Domaines d'étude: électricité et électronique,
informatique, télécommunications.
Programmes: formation d'ingénieurs en électrotechnique
et électronique. Cours dispensés: mathématiques et sciences
physiques, électronique et électrotechnique, informatique,
langues et sciences humaines; spécialisation en 4e et 5e
années: informatique, systèmes électroniques et
microélectroniques, systèmes de mesure et contrôle, systèmes
répartis et temps réel, télécommunications et traitement du
signal.
A l'intention de: ressortissants de tout pays, titulaires du
baccalauréat S (admission en 1re année) ou d'un diplôme
reconnu équivalent; du DEUG A ou DUT génie électrique
pour l'admission en 2e année; Math. Spé. T (admis au
concours ENSAM) et Math. Spé. M, M', P, P' (déclarés
admissibles au concours commun «Mines-Ponts») pour
l'admission en 3e année; maîtrises EEA ou physique pour
l'admission en 4e année.
Durée: 5 ans (débutant en septembre).
Assistance financière: bourses de l'Éducation nationale, et
bourses de la Chambre de commerce et d'industrie de Paris,
accordées aux français, aux ressortissants des pays membres
de l'Union européenne (à condition que les parents aient été
résidents ou employés en France), aux réfugiés politiques, et
aux étrangers dont les parents résident en France.
Inscriptions: les dossiers sont à retirer auprès du Service
des admissions et à déposer avant le 30 avril pour la 1ère
année, le 30 juin pour les autres années, à l'adresse ci-dessus.

978 **École supérieure d'optique
[ESO]**
Institut d'Optique - Centre Scientifique - Bât. 503
91403 Orsay Cedex
Tel: +33-1-6935-8787
Fax: +33-1-6935-8700
Web: http://www.institutoptique.fr
e-mail: international@institutoptique.fr

📖 Diplôme d'ingénieur et Master's
Domaines d'étude: électricité et électronique, optique,
physique, techniques de laboratoires, technologie,
télécommunications.
Programmes: (a) Diplôme d'ingénieur de l'École
Supérieure d'Optique; (b) Diplôme national de Master en
optique et photonique / optoélectronique.
A l'intention de: étudiants originaires de tout pays
diplômés en sciences ou en ingénierie de haut niveau;
titulaires d'un Bachelor (ou équivalent) en science ou en
ingénierie; admission sur dossier, entretien et
recommandation.
Durée: (a) de 2 à 3 ans selon le moment d'intégration: (b)
de 1 à 2 ans.
Inscriptions: voir site web pour plus de renseignements.

💰 Bourse d'études
Domaines d'étude: optique, sciences, technologie.
Description: exonération des frais de scolarité.
Domaines d'études: sciences optiques.
A l'intention de: aux étudiants qui poursuivront leur
Master par des études doctorales au Laboratoire Charles
Fabry de l'Institut d'Optique ou dans un laboratoire associé.
Durée: 2 ans, non renouvelable.
Valeur: 90% des frais de scolarité (le total des frais de
scolarité pour les deux années que dure le programme Master
est de 10.000€).
Candidatures: se renseigner à l'adresse:
international@iota.u-psud.fr.

979 **École supérieure de chimie
physique électronique de Lyon
[CPE LYON]**
43, boulevard du 11 Novembre 1918
BP 2077
69616 Villeurbanne Cedex
Tel: +33-4-7243-1700
Fax: +33-4-7243-1668
Web: http://www.cpe.fr

📖 1er et 2e cycles / chimie, physique, électronique

Domaines d'étude: chimie, électricité et électronique, génie chimique, industrie chimique, informatique, ingénierie, physique.

Programmes: formation d'ingénieurs: (a) Ingénieur électronicien: mathématiques appliquées, électronique, génie électrique, informatique, physique, traitement du signal, formation générale, langues et cultures internationales; (b) Ingénieur chimiste: chimie organique, sciences analytiques, chimie générale, outils de l'ingénieur, génie des procédés, formation générale, langues et cultures internationales.

A l'intention de: ressortissants de tout pays; conditions d'admission: en 1re année, sur concours commun pour les élèves de Math. Spé. des CPGE, sur contrôle continu pour les élèves des classes préparatoires à CPE Lyon; sur titre pour les titulaires d'un DEUG, d'un DUT ou d'une licence scientifique; en 2e année: sur titre pour les titulaires d'une maîtrise scientifique ou d'un diplôme équivalent.

Durée: 3 ans (débutant le 15 septembre).

Assistance financière: possibilité pour les ressortissants des pays de l'Union européenne d'obtenir une bourse Erasmus. Pas de frais de scolarité pour les échanges Erasmus et ceux effectués dans le cadre d'un accord de coopération avec un autre établissement.

Inscriptions: à l'adresse ci-dessus pour de plus amples renseignements.

980 École supérieure de commerce de Clermont [ESC Clermont]

4, boulevard Trudaine
63037 Clermont-Ferrand Cedex 1
Tel: +33-4-7398-2424
Fax: +33-4-7398-2449
Web: http://www.esc-clermont.fr

📖 2e cycle / commerce, management

Domaines d'étude: administration, affaires, finances, gestion.

Programmes: Formation conduisant aux diplômes en management.

A l'intention de: candidats de toute nationalité, niveau Bac+2, ayant une bonne connaissance du français. L'admission se fait sur concours (épreuves écrites et orales).

Durée: 3 ans (débutant mi-septembre pour la 1ère année).

Assistance financière: bourses, prêts bancaires.

Inscriptions: écrire à l'adresse ci-dessus; pour de plus amples renseignements sur les échanges internationaux s'adresser à Mike Bryant, responsable des relations internationales: Bryantm@esc-clermont.fr.

981 École supérieure de commerce de Rouen [ESC Rouen]

Boulevard André-Siegfried
BP 188
76136 Mont-Saint-Aignan Cedex
Tel: +33-2-3282-5700
Fax: +33-2-3282-5701
Web: http://www.esc-rouen.fr

📖 2e et 3e cycles / commerce, management

Domaines d'étude: affaires, gestion, industrie alimentaire, marketing, transports.

Programmes: (a) Programme ESC; (b) Masters et 3èmes cycles spécialisés: études et décision marketing; management international et gestion de projets; management logistique/transport et échanges internationaux; (c) Formation permanente à mi-temps: IMaC Executive M.B.A., « De technicien à manager ».

A l'intention de: ressortissants de tout pays: (a) recrutés sur concours (classes préparatoires HEC ou niveau Bac+2 en 1re année, diplôme Bac+3 à 4 pour admission en 2e année); (b) sur dossier et entretien (diplôme Bac+4 pour les 3èmes cycles, diplôme Bac+5 pour les mastères); (c) sur dossier et entretien (diplôme Bac+5 et expérience professionnelle pour le M.B.A., diplôme Bac+2 et expérience professionnelle pour la formation permanente.

Durée: : (a) 3 ans; (b) 1 an; (c) 22 mois pour le M.B.A., 18 mois pour « de technicien à manager ».

Inscriptions: à l'adresse ci-dessus pour de plus amples renseignements.

982 École supérieure de fonderie [ESF]

Pôle universitaire Léonard de Vinci
92916 Paris-La Défense Cedex
Tel: +33-1-4116-7230
Fax: +33-1-4116-7238
Web: http://www.devinci.fr/esf/

📖 Diplôme d'ingénieur ESF

Domaines d'étude: dessin industriel, ingénierie, mécanique, métallurgie, technologie industrielle.

Programmes: Cours de spécialisation en fonderie conduisant au diplôme d'ingénieur ESF.

A l'intention de: ressortissants de tout pays, titulaires d'un diplôme d'ingénieur de niveau minimal Bac+4 à dominante mécanique ou possédant une pratique suffisante en fonderie, s'ils sont envoyés par une société. Une bonne connaissance du français est également requise.

Durée: 1 an en général (début septembre à fin juillet).

Connaissances linguistiques: langue d'enseignement: français; possibilité de perfectionnement en français, anglais et informatique appliquée.

Inscriptions: en mai précédant la rentrée.

983 École supérieure de journalisme de Lille [ESJ]

50, rue Gauthier-de-Châtillon
59046 Lille Cedex
Tel: +33-3-2030-4400
Fax: +33-3-2030-4495
Web: http://www.esj-lille.fr

📖 Programme international de journalisme

Domaines d'étude: journalisme.

Programmes: Programme international de journalisme et multimédia: formation pluridisciplinaire, presse écrite, agence, radio, télévision conduisant au diplôme de l'École supérieure de journalisme de Lille (Bac+4).

A l'intention de: ressortissants de tout pays, âgés de 23 ans maximum pour les français et de 25 ans pour les étrangers obligatoirement francophones, titulaires d'un Bac+2 au minimum; admission sur concours écrit et oral.

Organisés: à l'ESJ, avec stage obligatoire de 2 mois dans le pays d'origine.

Durée: 2 ans.

Inscriptions: en raison du nombre très important de demandes individuelles d'information par voie électronique, l'ESJ ne peut répondre aux demandes personnelles; notice d'information téléchargeable sur http://www.esj-lille.fr/article.php3?id_article=65.

984 École supérieure de publicité [ESP]

9, rue Léo-Delibes
75116 Paris
Tel: +33-1-4727-7749
Fax: +33-1-4553-8501
Web: http://www.ecolesupdepublicite.com

📖 1er cycle, BTS / publicité

Domaines d'étude: communication, marketing, publicité.

Programmes: (a) programme d'enseignement des métiers de la publicité, des techniques de communication, de la promotion des ventes, des relations publiques; conditions particulières: cours d'anglais (économie et publicité); (b) programme d'ouverture et d'exercice intensif aux techniques publicitaires essentielles; les 2 programmes débouchent sur le diplôme de BTS communication des entreprises; (c) formation en séminaires: suivant un programme de généraliste, une spécialisation ou une mise à jour technique dans le cadre de la formation continue.

A l'intention de: ressortissants de tout pays, âgées de plus de 18 ans; (a) titulaires d'un baccalauréat ou d'un Bac+2; admission sur test de février jusqu'à fin septembre; 1 an de spécialisation « EPS+» pour les jeunes Bac+2/+3; Anglais obligatoire.

Durée: 2 ans (niveau Bac); 1 an (niveau Bac+2/+3).

Assistance financière: possibilité de prêt bancaire étudiant.

Inscriptions: de février à septembre.

985 École supérieure de traducteurs interprètes et de cadres du commerce extérieur [ESTICE]
81, boulevard Vauban
BP 109
59016 Lille Cedex
Tel: +33-3-2054-9090
Fax: +33-3-2054-5050

⌂ Formation à la traduction/interprétation

Domaines d'étude: commerce, droit, études internationales, informatique, interprétation et traduction, marketing, transports.
Programmes: (a) Cours de formation à la traduction: économique, juridique, commerciale; initiation à l'interprétation en anglais, allemand et espagnol; (b) Cours de commerce international, transports, marketing, banque, droit commercial, douanes, management international et informatique.
A l'intention de: ressortissants de tout pays, âgés de moins de 26 ans (exceptionnellement plus), titulaires d'un baccalauréat, d'un DEUG en langues, d'un BTS, d'un DUT ou d'un diplôme équivalent.
Durée: 2 années académiques.
Assistance financière: des bourses peuvent être octroyées sur demande auprès de l'ambassade de France du pays d'origine du candidat, ou par le gouvernement du pays d'origine.
Inscriptions: avant 30 juin; voir site web pour de plus amples renseignements et dossier à télécharger.

986 École supérieure des industries du caoutchouc [ESICA]
Institut national de formation et d'enseignement professionnel du caoutchouc (IFOCA)
60, rue Auber
94408 Vitry-sur-Seine Cedex
Tel: +33-1-4960-5757
Fax: +33-1-4960-5102
Web: http://www.ifoca.com
e-mail: secretariat.vitry@ifoca.com

⌂ Spécialisation pour ingénieurs

Domaines d'étude: chimie, formation professionnelle, industrie chimique, ingénierie, sciences, technologie.
Programmes: Programme de spécialisation dans le domaine des sciences et technologie des élastomères pour ingénieurs (Bac+5), conduisant également au Diplôme d'études supérieures spécialisées (DESS élastomères), pour les maîtres ès sciences (Bac+4) et au Certificat de spécialisation pour techniciens supérieurs(Bac+2).
A l'intention de: ressortissants de tout pays, âgés de 20 à 30 ans, titulaires des diplômes ci-dessus dans les options suivantes: chimie, chimie/physique, sciences des matériaux, mécanique, génie mécanique.
Durée: 1 an.
Inscriptions: avant le 15 mai de chaque année.

987 École supérieure des Sciences économiques et commerciales École de Management [ESSEC]
Avenue Bernard Hirsh
BP 105
95021 Cergy-Pontoise Cedex
Tel: +33-1-3443-3990
Fax: +33-1-3038-9898
Web: http://www.essec.fr/fr/index.html
e-mail: indigo@essec.fr

⌂ 2e, 3e cycles / gestion

Domaines d'étude: droit international, études internationales, gestion, relations internationales.
Programmes: programme de cours conduisant au MBA, M.S. et Ph.D. en gestion.
A l'intention de: ressortissants de tout pays âgés de 25 à 35 ans, ayant une expérience professionnelle, titulaires d'un diplôme d'étude supérieures (BTA, BTS ou équivalent), tests d'admission: GMAT, TOEFL; lettre de recommandation, examen de dossier et entretien.

Organisés: cours donnés dans 2 campus différents; à Cergy-Pontoise et Paris-La Défense.
Applications: s'adresser à l'École à l'adresse ci-dessus.

⌂ Cours de management hôtelier

Domaines d'étude: gestion, tourisme, hôtellerie, restauration.
Programmes: Cours préparant au DESS de management hôtelier international, dispensés par des professeurs de la Faculté hôtelière de Cornell, de grandes universités américaines ou anglaises ou par des spécialistes et personnalités de la profession.
A l'intention de: ressortissants de tout pays, titulaires du niveau Bac+3 ou BTS hôtelier ou de niveau Bachelor's dans le système anglo-américain, ayant au moins 1 an d'expérience professionnelle ou stages en hôtellerie/restauration; bonne maîtrise de l'anglais souhaitable (tests d'anglais TOEFL ou examen IMHI); admission sur dossier, concours (GMAT, TOGE, examen d'anglais) et entretiens individuels; 2 lettres de recommandation exigées.
Durée: 2 ans comprenant un trimestre de stage en entreprise.
Connaissances linguistiques: anglais (de 70 à 80% des cours) et français; possibilité de suivre un cours intensif de français pour les étudiants étrangers, durant le mois de septembre précédant la rentrée; diplôme de niveau I, homologué par l'Éducation nationale en France.
Inscriptions: s'adresser à l'École.

988 École supérieure des techniques aéronautiques et de construction automobile [ESTACA]
34-36, rue Victor Hugo
92300 Levallois Perret
Tel: +33-1-4127-3729
Fax: +33-1-4127-3744
Web: http://www.estaca.fr
e-mail: ecavalier@estaca.fr

⌂ Diplôme d'ingénieur

Domaines d'étude: mécanique.
Programmes: Formation d'ingénieurs en techniques aéronautiques, automobiles, spatiales et ferroviaires.
A l'intention de: étudiants en ingénierie.
Autres conditions: admission sur dossier.
Connaissances linguistiques: français et anglais.
Inscriptions: auprès d'Élodie Cavalier (coordonnées ci-dessus).

989 École supérieure internationale d'optométrie - Institut et centre d'optométrie [ICO]
134 route de Chartres
91440 Bures-sur-Yvette
Tel: +33-1-6486-1216
Fax: +33-1-6928-4999
Web: http://www.ecole-optometrie.com
e-mail: ico.bures@wanadoo

⌂ Formation d'opticien-optométriste

Domaines d'étude: ophtalmologie.
Programmes: (a) Formation supérieure internationale d'opticien-optométriste conduisant au diplôme d'opticien-optométriste ESIO, diplôme universitaire d'optique physiologique et d'optométrie; (b) Formation professionnelle continue en optique, optique de contact, lunetterie, optométrie, management et gestion appliquée.
A l'intention de: ressortissants de tout pays: (a) titulaires d'un baccalauréat scientifique ou diplôme équivalent; (b) opticiens/optométristes et salariés de l'industrie de l'optique-lunetterie; stages spécifiques pour les enseignants des écoles d'optique étrangères.
Organisés: (a) à l'ICO; (b) à l'ICO et à l'étranger.
Durée: (a) 3 ans; (b) variable selon les thèmes traités.
Assistance financière: des bourses d'études peuvent être octroyées pour (a).
Inscriptions: toute l'année; (a) date limite: septembre.

990 Égide
28 rue de la Grange-aux-Belles
75010 Paris
Tel: +33-1-4040-5907
Fax: +33-1-4241-8590
Web: http://www.egide.asso.fr
e-mail: eiffel@egide.asso.fr

Programme de Bourses «Eiffel»

Domaines d'étude: toutes disciplines principales.
Description: L'association Égide gère les moyens de
programmes de coopération internationale financés par le
Ministère des Affaires étrangères, destinés à soutenir l'action
de recrutement à l'international des établissements
d'enseignement supérieur français.
(a) Programme de «Bourses d'excellence Eiffel». Le
programme vise, en priorité, à former en France les futurs
décideurs du secteur privé et de l'administration des pays
émergents;
(b) Programme de «Bourses Eiffel Doctorat» pour la
formation des doctorants de haut niveau. Il permet d'offrir aux
étudiants originaires des pays émergents mais aussi des pays à
fort potentiel scientifique et universitaire, la possibilité
d'effectuer une année en France: la 2e ou 3e année de thèse de
préférence.
A l'intention de: (b) Ce programme s'adresse aux étudiants
étrangers en codirection ou en cotutelle de thèse.
Candidatures: consulter le site
http://www.egide.asso.fr/fr/programmes. Pour tout
renseignement, s'adresser à Égide - Programme Eiffel ou
Égide - Programme Eiffel Doctorat selon le cas; Email:
eiffel@egide.asso.fr ou eiffel-doctorat@egide.asso.fr selon le
cas.

**991 ENGREF - Unité Mixte de
Recherche TETIS**
Maison de la Télédétection en Languedoc-Roussillon
500, rue J.F. Breton
34093 Montpellier Cedex 5
Tel: +33-4-6754-8754
Fax: +33-4-6754-8700
Web: http://sol.ensam.inra.fr/silat

Formations en Information géographique

Domaines d'étude: sciences agronomiques, sciences
appliquées, sciences de la terre.
Programmes: (a) Mastère spécialisé en systèmes
d'informations localisées pour l'aménagement du territoire
(SILAT): (b) Modules spécialisés en Information
géographique.
Description: (a) formation professionnelle de haut niveau,
conduite en collaboration avec l'Institut national agronomique
Paris-Grignon, l'École nationale supérieure agronomique de
Montpellier et l'École nationale des sciences géographiques.
Le cursus comprend un projet professionnel et une période en
entreprise effectuée en fin de formation; la formation prépare
les élèves à des fonctions de chef de projets en information
géographique; (b) formation des ingénieurs du génie rural, des
eaux et des forêts, DEA sciences de l'eau dans
l'environnement continental, DEA forêts des régions chaudes,
DEA structures et dynamiques spatiales; formations
continues.
Domaines d'études: Information Géographique appliquée
aux sciences agronomiques, aux sciences de la terre et à
l'aménagement des territoires.
A l'intention de: ressortissants de tout pays: (a) Bac +5
(diplôme d'ingénieur, DEA, DESS, MSc); (b) étudiants de
troisième cycle ou cadres en activité.
Organisés: à la Maison de la Télédétection de Montpellier.
Durée: (a) 13 mois; (b) variable.
Connaissances linguistiques: français.

**992 Entraide universitaire
française-Comité français de
l'Entraide universitaire
mondiale [EUF]**
40, rue Rouelle
75015 Paris
Tel: +33-1-4577-2490

Bourses d'études

Domaines d'étude: toutes disciplines principales.
A l'intention de: étudiants réfugiés, reconnus comme tels,
en France, titulaires du baccalauréat et âgés de 17 à 35 ans;
connaissance du français indispensable.
Lieu: universités et établissements d'enseignement
supérieur français.
Durée: une année universitaire (éventuellement
renouvelable).
Valeur: 330 € en moyenne par mois.
Candidatures: de mai à fin juillet.

**993 Établissement national
d'enseignement supérieur
agronomique de Dijon
[ENESAD]**
26 bd Dr Petitjean
BP 87999
21079 Dijon Cedex
Tel: +33-3-8077-2525
Fax: +33-3-8077-2500
Web: http://www.enesad.fr

Formation d'ingénieurs d'agronomie

Domaines d'étude: agriculture, enseignement technique,
formation professionnelle, oenologie, sciences agronomiques.
Programmes: (a) Formation d'ingénieurs civils
d'agronomie, de fonctionnaires: formation de cadres des
services publics et des organisations agricoles; (b) Formation
initiale et continue d'ingénieurs des techniques agricoles et
des techniques des industries agro-alimentaires; (c) Formation
continue pour le Certificat d'études supérieures (CES, niveau
3e cycle) agriculture et environnement; (d) Certificat d'études
supérieures (CES) connaissance et commercialisation
internationale des vins, réalisé en partenariat avec l'EPLEFPA
viticole de Beaune.
A l'intention de: ressortissants de tout pays titulaires (a) du
diplôme d'ingénieur agronome ou horticole, ou enseignants;
(b) d'une maîtrise ès sciences ou d'un diplôme reconnu
équivalent; l'admission se fait sur titres ou sur concours; (d)
admission sur titres.
Durée: (a) 2 ans (débutant le 15 septembre); (c) de 1 à 3
ans; 10 modules d'une semaine sont à choisir parmi les 15
proposés; (d) 1 an.
Assistance financière: (d) bourses et allocations spéciales
pour les étudiants étrangers à certaines conditions.
Inscriptions: s'adresser à l'école.

**994 French-American Foundation,
Comité français**
21, boulevard de Grenelle
75015 Paris
Tel: +33-1-4577-4001
Fax: +33-1-4577-4071
Web: http://www.frenchamerican.org
e-mail: contact@french-american.org

Bourses Tocqueville

Domaines d'études: civilisation américaine (vie politique,
économique et sociale américaine contemporaine).
A l'intention de: étudiants et chercheurs de nationalité
française, en cours de doctorat.
Age Max: moins de 35 ans.
Lieu: États-Unis.
Durée: 1 à 3 mois maximum.
Valeur: variable, allant de 1.000€ à 6.000€.
Candidatures: au plus tard le 31 mai de chaque année. Le
dossier devrait comprendre: un curriculum vitae détaillé, une
lettre de motivation, une énumération des travaux réalisés, en
cours ou projetés, des références, un descriptif détaillé du
projet pour lequel la bourse est demandée. Délibération du
jury en octobre.

995 Groupe école supérieure de commerce de Dijon [ESC Dijon]
29, rue Sambin
21000 Dijon
Tel: +33-3-8072-5900
Fax: +33-3-8072-5999
Web: http://www.escdijon.com
e-mail: ncureau@escdijon.com

📖 **2e cycle / commerce, gestion**
Domaines d'étude: commerce, économie, finances, marketing.
Programmes: Master of science (MSc), « business and management in Europe »; Mastère spécialisé en management de l'industrie pharmaceutique, commerce international des vins et spiritueux, management des entreprises culturelles; DEA en science de gestion; Académie commerciale internationale (ACI) correspondant à un programme Bac + 3, offrant une formation commerciale et internationale intermédiaire.
A l'intention de: titulaires d'un Bachelor's degree (ou équivalent Bac + 4) en gestion, économie, management, commerce ou finance; admission sur dossier et entretien.
Durée: 13 mois (débutant en septembre).
Frais: frais d'inscription: 6.000 €.
Connaissances linguistiques: cours dispensés en anglais; bon niveau exigé; TOEFL: minimum 213; TOEIC: minimum 700; cours de français langue étrangère.
Inscriptions: avant le 1er juin auprès de Jean-Guillaume Ditter, adresse ci-dessus, +33 3 80 72 59 41, jditter@escdijon.com).

996 Groupe école supérieure de commerce de Lyon [ESC Lyon]
23, avenue Guy-de-Collongue,
BP 174
69132 Ecully Cedex
Tel: +33-4-7833-7800
Fax: +33-4-7833-6169
Web: http://www.em-lyon.com

📖 **2è cycle / commerce, gestion**
Domaines d'étude: affaires, finances, gestion, marketing.
Programmes: Formation généraliste: (a) à l'ensemble des domaines du management d'entreprise, complétée par des stages et filières de spécialisations en 2e et 3e années; (b) Cesma-M.B.A.: cours de 3e cycle en management; en Mastères français et anglais; (c) 4 Mastères spécialisés ESC Lyon: ingénierie financière, management de la technologie, management des entreprises de services, stratégie et marketing international des entreprises industrielles (6 mois de cours théoriques et 6 mois de mission en entreprise).
A l'intention de: ressortissants de tout pays: (a) soit élèves de niveau Bac+2 issus des classes préparatoires (85%) ou de DEUG et DUT (15%) en 1re année ou titulaires d'un diplôme étranger équivalent au 2e cycle français; soit candidats de moins de 35 ans possédant une expérience professionnelle d'au moins 5 ans; soit sportifs de haut niveau; admission sur concours; (b) niveau Bac+3, 4 ou même 5 pour l'entrée en 2e année, licence, maîtrise, ingénieurs, IEP, Bachelor; (c) diplômés de l'enseignement supérieur français ou étranger (Bac+5), cadres d'entreprises diplômés, âgés de 23 à 35 ans; admission sur tests et entretien; concours préparatoire des Grandes écoles commerciales; concours d'admission sur titres pour la 1re et la 2e années; concours CIAM étudiants étrangers; anglais et autre langue étrangère obligatoires.
Durée: (a) de 2 à 3 ans; (b) et (c) 1 an (débutant en septembre).
Assistance financière: bourses du Rectorat, fonds social, prêts à taux préférentiel, prêts d'honneur.
Inscriptions: s'adresser à l'École.

997 Groupe école supérieure de commerce de Reims [ESC Reims]
59, rue Pierre-Taittinger
BP 302
51061 Reims Cedex
Tel: +33-3-2608-0604
Fax: +33-3-2604-6963

Web: http://www.esc-reims.edu

📖 **3ème cycle / gestion**
Domaines d'étude: gestion.
Programmes: (a) Programme Cefa M.B.A.: formation supérieure en management; (b) Séminaire intensif d'été dans le domaine des affaires internationales; (c) Cours dans le domaine de la gestion des entreprises à dimension européenne, dans le cadre du programme du Centre d'études supérieures européennes de management (CESEM).
A l'intention de: ressortissants de tout pays: (a) titulaires d'un diplôme d'ingénieur ou d'un diplôme admis en équivalence, ou cadres d'entreprise justifiant d'au moins 5 années d'expérience professionnelle; (b) jeunes cadres d'entreprise ou étudiants de niveau avancé, âgés de 23 à 45 ans, titulaires d'un M.B.A. ou titre équivalent; expérience professionnelle et anglais courant requis; (c) ressortissants anglais, allemands, espagnols, français, irlandais, canadiens, néerlandais, américains, mexicains, australiens, chinois, titulaires d'un baccalauréat ou diplôme admis en équivalence et parlant au minimum 2 langues, dont le français et l'anglais ou l'allemand ou l'espagnol ou le chinois.
Durée: (a) 12 mois (débutant en octobre); (b) 6 semaines (débutant mi-juin); (c) 4 ans (débutant en septembre), 5 ans pour le cycle franco-chinois.
Connaissances linguistiques: français; (b) langue d'enseignement: anglais.
Inscriptions: à l'adresse ci-dessus: (a) avant la fin mars, fin mai, fin août, selon les différentes sessions d'admission, au Service concours du Groupe ESC Reims; (b) avant mi-mai, au Service des relations internationales; (c) avant mi-mars.

998 Hautes études industrielles [HEI]
13, rue de Toul
59046 Lille Cedex
Tel: +33-3-2838-4858
Fax: +33-3-2838-4859
Web: http://www.hei.fr

📖 **Diplôme d'ingénieur HEI**
Domaines d'étude: enseignement technique, ingénierie, technologie industrielle.
Programmes: Cours de préparation au diplôme d'ingénieur HEI; recherche, formation continue: programme offrant 5 options: génie chimique, génie électrique, génie industriel-conception mécanique, génie industriel-BTP, informatique industrielle.
A l'intention de: ressortissants de tout pays, titulaires du baccalauréat S ou équivalent, d'un Bac+2 ou Bac+4.
Durée: 2 à 5 ans.
Assistance financière: possibilités de bourses.
Inscriptions: s'adresser à l'École.

999 Institut catholique de Paris École de psychologues praticiens [EPP]
23, rue du Montparnasse
75006 Paris
Web: http://www.icp.fr/icp/epp.php
e-mail: paris@psycho-prat.fr

📖 **Formation en psychologie**
Domaines d'étude: psychologie.
Programmes: Cours de psychologie fondamentale et sociale, sociologie, psychophysiologie, psychologie expérimentale, de l'éducation, psychanalyse, psychopathologie infantile, juvénile et adulte, psychiatrie, psychologie du travail et gestion des ressources humaines, statistiques, psychométrie, psychologie humaniste et transpersonnelle, analyse transactionnelle, tests projectifs, graphologie, techniques et communication, psychologie clinique, psychologie de l'enfant, neuropsychologie, gestion de l'entreprise, marketing, anglais, droit, conduisant au diplôme de psychologue qui, comme le DESS, donne accès au titre de psychologue défini par la loi du 25 juillet 1985.
A l'intention de: ressortissants de tout pays, titulaires du baccalauréat ou d'un diplôme reconnu équivalent.
Organisés: École de psychologues praticiens, 71, rue Molière, 69003 Lyon ou à l'adresse ci-dessus.
Durée: 5 ans (4 ans de formation de base plus 1 an de

spécialisation).
Connaissances linguistiques: français exigé.
Inscriptions: se renseigner à l'adresse ci-dessus.

1000 Institut catholique de Paris Institut géologique Albert de Lapparent [IGAL]

Institut Polytechnique Saint-Louis
13, boulevard de l'Hautil
95092 Cergy-Pontoise Cedex
Tel: +33-1-3075-6070
Fax: +33-1-3075-6071
Web: http://www.icp.fr/icp/igal.php
e-mail: igal@igal.fr

📖 Formation de géologues

Domaines d'étude: géologie, recherche, sciences appliquées, sciences naturelles, technologie industrielle.
Programmes: Formation de géologues praticiens à vocation industrielle dans le domaine de la géologie et des géotechnologies: (a) cycle général, conduisant au diplôme d'études générales; (b) cycle supérieur, conduisant au diplôme de géologue; les 2 diplômes sont visés par le Ministre de l'enseignement supérieur et de la recherche.
A l'intention de: ressortissants de tout pays, titulaires d'un baccalauréat scientifique.
Durée: 5 ans (débutant le 15 octobre): (a) 3 ans; (b) 2 ans.
Connaissances linguistiques: français requis.
Inscriptions: avant le 30 avril.

1001 Institut catholique de Paris [ICP]

21, rue d'Assas
75006 Paris
Tel: +33-1-4439-5200
Fax: +33-1-4544-2714
Web: http://www.icp.fr
e-mail: contact@icp.fr

📖 1er, 2e cycles / lettres et arts

Domaines d'étude: allemand, anglais, espagnol, histoire, lettres et arts, philosophie.
Programmes: Cours de 1er cycle et 2e cycles: (a) DEUG Anglais, Allemand, Espagnol, Histoire, Lettres Modernes; à la Faculté des lettres (sous convention Jury Rectoral); (b) DEUG Philosophie à la Faculté de philosophie (sous convention avec l'Université de Poitiers).
Assistance financière: L'Institut Catholique de Paris n'est pas en mesure d'attribuer des bourses ou des subventions à ses nouveaux étudiants; ceux-ci doivent s'assurer eux-mêmes une garantie de ressources avant d'envisager d'entreprendre les études; ce n'est qu'après une année d'études dans notre établissement et en fonction des résultats universitaires qu'il sera possible de déposer une demande de bourse.
Inscriptions: pour le 1er cycle: entre le 1er décembre et le 15 janvier de l'année universitaire précédant l'inscription; les dates sont impératives; le cachet de la poste faisant foi; les inscriptions peuvent être obtenues auprès des Services Culturels de l'Ambassade de France du pays du candidat; pour les titulaires d'un diplôme étranger équivalent au baccalauréat français: dossier blanc; pour les titulaires du baccalauréat français: dossier bleu; en France: (dossier vert ou bleu) auprès de l'Institut Catholique de Paris à l'adresse ci-dessus; le dossier ne sera remis que si le candidat possède un titre de séjour d'une durée de validité de un an ou si le ou la conjoint(e) ou parents sont titulaires d'un permis de séjour de 3 ans (les photocopies des documents doivent être jointes, si les démarches sont effectuées par correspondance); pour le 2e cycle: auprès de l'École entre le 15 mai et le 30 juin.

📖 Formations en sciences sociales

Domaines d'étude: anthropologie, démographie et études de populations, droit, droit international, économie politique, gestion, sciences politiques, sciences sociales, sociologie.
Programmes: Programme de cours à la Faculté des sciences sociales et économiques (FASSE): cours de formation générale en sciences sociales: sociologie, anthropologie, politique, relations internationales, économie, droit, démographie, statistique, éthique et philosophie sociales, médiation, négociation; conduisant aux diplômes en sciences sociales: DEUG, licence, maîtrise, DEA, doctorat, DESS « Gestion des ressources humaines et politique du

personnel en entreprise », DESS « Relations publiques entre groupements d'intérêts et l'Union européenne: représentation et négociation ».
A l'intention de: ressortissants de tout pays, titulaires du baccalauréat ou titre admis en équivalence; d'une maîtrise ou équivalence (pour le DEA ou le DESS); test de français pour les étudiants étrangers.
Durée: 4 ans.
Inscriptions: à l'adresse ci-dessus.

📖 Français langue et culture

Domaines d'étude: économie, formation des enseignants, français, histoire, littérature et civilisation.
Programmes: Programme de cours de l'Institut de langue et de culture française (ILCF): cours de langue et culture françaises: perfectionnement, phonétique, français oral et écrit, culture et civilisation, communication, histoire-géographie, littérature et philosophie, société, économie et politique, français des affaires, études contemporaines et professorat; conduisant aux Certificat et Diplôme national interuniversités catholiques, Certificat ou Diplôme de la CCIP ou de l'ICP et Diplôme d'études contemporaines.
A l'intention de: ressortissants de tout pays âgés de 18 ans minimum, titulaires d'un diplôme de fin d'études secondaires, baccalauréat ou équivalent; admission directe et test de niveau.
Durée: 2 fois 4 mois (d'octobre à février et de février à juin); cours universitaire d'été (CUE): 1 mois (juillet).
Assistance financière: possibilités de bourses; se renseigner auprès de l'ambassade de France du pays de l'étudiant (avant le 1er avril pour les cours d'été).
Inscriptions: 31 juillet pour le 1er semestre; 22 décembre pour le 2e semestre; 30 avril pour les cours d'été: site web de l'ILCF: http://www.icp.fr/ilcf.

📖 Langues orientales anciennes

Domaines d'étude: langues, théologie, religion.
Programmes: Programme de cours à l'École des langues et civilisations de l'Orient ancien (ELCOA): cours de langues orientales anciennes (bibliques, proche-orientales, chrétiennes), histoire des religions, épigraphie; connaissances approfondies de 3 langues anciennes du Proche-Orient, Moyen-Orient ainsi que leurs cultures; conduisant à la maîtrise en philosophie et histoire de l'Orient ancien; doctorat en philosophie et histoire des religions de l'Orient ancien.
A l'intention de: ressortissants de tout pays, titulaires du baccalauréat ou équivalent; français obligatoire, latin souhaité.
Durée: 4 ans.
Inscriptions: avant le 15 octobre.

📖 Traduction/interprétation

Domaines d'étude: interprétation et traduction.
Programmes: Programme de cours de l'Institut supérieur d'interprétation et de traduction (ISIT): (a) 1er cycle (tronc commun): conduisant au DEUG de langues ou de droit; (b) 2e cycle: stage en entreprise et spécialisations conduisant aux diplômes de traducteur terminologue ou traducteur en affaires internationales; (c) cycle postuniversitaire: soit à temps partiel pour la technique d'interprétation seule, soit à temps complet débouchant sur le diplôme d'interprète de conférence.
A l'intention de: ressortissants de tout pays, âgés de moins de 30 ans, titulaires pour (a) du baccalauréat (ou équivalence), concours d'entrée pour la 1re année; d'un DEUG, DUT ou BTS plus concours et entretien pour la 2e année; (b) d'une licence ou Khâgne plus concours et entretien pour la 3e année; pas d'admission directe pour la 4e année; (c) d'une maîtrise ou diplôme équivalent ou licence avec expérience professionnelle plus tests; connaissances de 2 langues (anglais, allemand ou espagnol); français obligatoire.
Durée: 4 ans (dont 2 de spécialisation) plus 2 ans pour (c).
Connaissances linguistiques: (a) et (b) français et anglais obligatoires, plus allemand ou espagnol.
Inscriptions: 1re année: en mars-avril; 2e année: en mai-juin; 3e année et cycle postuniversitaire en juin-juillet à ISIT à l'adresse ci-dessus; tél: +33 1 42 22 33 16; fax: +33 1 45 44 17 67; site web: http://www.icp.fr/icp/isit.php.

1002 Institut catholique de Toulouse [ICDT]

31, rue de la Fonderie
31068 Toulouse Cedex
Tel: +33-5-6136-8100
Fax: +33-5-6136-8108
Web: http://www.ict-toulouse.asso.fr

⌑ Études en sciences religieuses

Domaines d'étude: droit canon, lettres, philosophie, sciences humaines, théologie, religion.
Programmes: (a) diplôme de 1er (licence), 2e (maîtrise) et 3e grades (doctorat) en sciences religieuses: théologie, droit canonique et philosophie; (b) préparation aux grades d'État et direction des diplômes d'études supérieures; (c) diplômes dans les domaines suivants: agriculture, études religieuses et pastorales, Occitanie, études africaines, musique sacrée, études sociales, travail social, éducation et animation, pédagogie, journalisme, français langue étrangère; (d) Formation permanente des prêtres et cours bibliques par correspondance; (e) Téléenseignement biblique préparant au certificat d'études bibliques (1er cycle); hébreu biblique au niveau élémentaire; livres de la Bible.
A l'intention de: candidats remplissant les conditions requises; (a) âgés de 18 ans minimum et titulaires du baccalauréat ou titre équivalent; (e) aux stades d'initiation ou de perfectionnement.
Organisés: (a) Faculté de sciences religieuses; (b) Faculté libre des lettres et sciences humaines; (c) et (d) écoles, centres ou instituts intégrés ou associés.
Durée: variable; (a) 3 ans pour la licence, 2 ans pour la maîtrise.
Inscriptions: (a) et (e) en septembre/octobre; s'adresser à l'Institut pour de plus amples renseignements.

1003 Institut d'études politiques de Paris, Sciences-Po [IEP]

27, rue Saint-Guillaume
75007 Paris
Tel: +33-1-4549-5050
Fax: +33-1-4544-1252
Web: http://www.sciences-po.fr

⌑ Sciences politiques

Domaines d'étude: affaires internationales, communication, droit, économie, économie politique, études internationales, relations internationales, sciences économiques et commerciales, sciences humaines, sciences politiques.
Programmes: programmes diplômants pour étudiants étrangers: (a) CIEP (Cycle international d'études politiques), cursus d'un an donnant la possibilité d'intégrer par la suite la cinquième et dernière année du diplôme de Sciences-politiques. (équivalent Master's degree); (b) PI (Programme international), cursus d'un an à faire valider auprès de son université d'origine et donnant la possibilité par la suite d'intégrer la cinquième et dernière année du diplôme de Sciences-politiques. (équivalent Master's degree).
A l'intention de: admission en 1ère année: titulaires d'un Bac (ou équivalent); admission en 2ème année: étudiants ayant achevé une année d'études supérieures; admission en 3ème année: étudiants ayant effectué deux années d'études supérieures; pour les 2ème et 3ème cycles: titulaires d'un diplôme de niveau Bac +3 (Bachelor's ou équivalent) ou d'un diplôme de niveau Bac + 4 ou 5 (Master's ou équivalent); admission sur titres, critères d'excellence, dossier et examen (test de français pour les étudiants étrangers hors accord d'échange).
Durée: 1er cycle: 3 ans débutant à la mi-octobre; 2ème cycle: 2 ans débutant à la mi-octobre et aboutissant au diplôme de Sciences-politiques. (équivalent Master's degree); Mastère spécialisé: 1 an minimum; DESS et DEA: 1 an minimum; doctorat: 2 ans minimum.
Frais: frais de dossier de demande d'admission: 86 €; frais de scolarité: environ 1.050 €.
Inscriptions: admission en 1ère année: demande des dossiers sur le site Internet entre le 2 et le 27 juin et à retourner début juillet; admission en 2ème année: demande des dossiers entre le 17 février et le 14 mars et à retourner avant le 17 mars; 4ème année: demande des dossiers entre le 4 décembre et le 16 janvier (fermeture de la procédure du site entre le 23 décembre et le 5 janvier) et à retourner avant le 17

janvier; pour tout renseignement, contacter Sciences-Politiques Admissions, 2 square de Luynes, 75007 Paris, tel. +33-1-4549-5082; fax: +33-1-4548-4749; email: admissions@sciences-po.fr.

1004 Institut de formation et d'enseignement pour les métiers de l'image et du son [FEMIS]

6, rue Francoeur
75018 Paris
Tel: +33-1-5341-2100
Fax: +33-1-5341-0280
Web: http://www.femis.fr
e-mail: femis@femis.fr

⌑ Formation des métiers de l'image et du son

Domaines d'étude: arts du spectacle, cinématographie.
Programmes: Enseignement supérieur des métiers de l'image et du son; 7 départements (scénario, réalisation, image, son, montage, direction de production et décor).
A l'intention de: ressortissants de tout pays, âgés de moins de 27 ans: titulaires d'un diplôme équivalant dans le pays d'origine au baccalauréat français (quelle qu'en soit la nature) et à un diplôme sanctionnant en France 2 années - au minimum - d'études supérieures, ou en mesure de justifier d'au moins 4 années de pratique professionnelle dans les métiers de l'image et du son. L'admission se fait sur concours (national ou international). Le concours international est strictement destiné aux candidats étrangers qui peuvent attester officiellement, au moment de leur inscription, qu'ils ont effectivement la possibilité d'obtenir, en cas de résultats positifs, une bourse de leur pays ou de la France, avec un taux permettant de couvrir l'allocation d'études et la participation annuelle obligatoire aux travaux pratiques.
Durée: 42 mois (débutant en septembre, et se terminant le 1er mars).
Assistance financière: le Ministère des affaires étrangères attribue un certain nombre de bourses (4 en moyenne) aux candidats étrangers admis sur concours international, ressortissants des pays appartenant uniquement aux zones géographiques suivantes: Afrique anglophone, Amérique latine, certains pays d'Asie, Maghreb/Proche et Moyen-Orient, pays d'Europe centrale et orientale; le premier contact doit être pris avec les services culturels français dans le pays d'origine du candidat.
Connaissances linguistiques: français exigé.

1005 Institut européen d'administration des affaires European Institute of Business Administration [INSEAD]

Boulevard de Constance
77305 Fontainebleau
Tel: +33-1-6072-4000
Fax: +33-1-6074-5500
Web: http://www.insead.edu
e-mail: postmaster@insead.fr

✒ INSEAD managed scholarships

Domaines d'étude: administration des affaires, affaires, affaires internationales, économie, sciences économiques et commerciales.
Description: scholarships based on merit or need. Some examples are Alumni Fund (IAF) Scholarships, INSEAD Alumni Fund (IAF) Women's Scholarships, NSEAD Need-based Scholarships.
Open to: participants from developing/emerging countries, women, need based and other categories.
Applications: the most up-to-date information and application forms for INSEAD-managed scholarships are available on the website: http://www.insead.edu/mba/admissions/fin_aid.htm.Other external scholarships and loans are presented.

1006 Institut National des Sciences Appliquées de Lyon [INSA-Lyon]

Allée du Rhône - Domaine Scientifique de la Doua
20 av. Albert Einstein
69628 Villeurbanne Cedex
Tel: +33-4-7243-8125
Fax: +33-4-7243-8532
Web: http://www.insa-lyon.fr / www.insa-france.fr
e-mail: admiss@insa-lyon.fr

📖 Cours du 1er et 2e cycles en ingénierie

Domaines d'étude: électricité et électronique, génie chimique, informatique, ingénierie, technologie industrielle, télécommunications, urbanisme.
Programmes: 1er et 2e cycles d'études de formation en bio informatique et modélisation; génie civil et urbanisme; génie électrique; génie énergétique et environnement; génie mécanique conception; génie mécanique développement; génie mécanique procédés plasturgie; génie industriel; informatique; science et génie des matériaux; télécommunications.
A l'intention de: les titulaires d'un diplôme validé ou en cours de validation de l'enseignement supérieur d'au moins 4 années pleines dans les domaines scientifiques ou techniques; sur dossier: notes et appréciations depuis le bac et éventuellement entretien de motivation.
Frais: les montants des frais de candidature, de scolarité, d'hébergement et éventuellement les frais supplémentaires, figurent sur le site http://www.insa-france.fr.
Inscriptions: s'effectue par concours sur titres, dossier et éventuellement entretien; le dossier rassemble les éléments d'évaluation obtenus par ailleurs par le candidat.

1007 Institut national des sciences appliquées de Rouen [INSA Rouen]

Place Émile Blondel
BP 08
76131 Mont-Saint-Aignan Cedex
Tel: +33-2-3552-8300
Fax: +33-2-3552-8369
Web: http://www.insa-rouen.fr
e-mail: insa@insa-rouen.fr

📖 Études en sciences appliquées

Domaines d'étude: chimie, énergie, génie chimique, industrie chimique, informatique, ingénierie, mécanique, statistique, technologie.
Programmes: Cours de chimie, génie chimique, informatique, énergétique, combustion, mécanique et développement, statistique, probabilités, conduisant au diplôme d'ingénieur.
A l'intention de: ressortissants de tout pays, titulaires du baccalauréat scientifique (1re année), d'un BTS, DEUG, DUT, SPE, CPI (3e année) et maîtrise (4e année); sélection sur dossier.
Durée: 2 à 5 ans (débutant en septembre).
Connaissances linguistiques: bonne connaissance de l'anglais requise.
Inscriptions: avant le 15 mars au Service des admissions, 20 rue Einstein, Bâtiment G, 69628 Villeurbanne Cedex.

1008 Institut national des sciences et techniques nucléaires [INSTN]

CEA-Saclay
91191 Gif-sur-Yvette Cedex
Tel: +33-1-6908-6314
Web: http://www-instn.cea.fr/agenda.htm
e-mail: winstn@cea.fr

📖 Études en sciences nucléaires

Domaines d'étude: chimie, énergie, ingénierie, physique.
Programmes: (a) Cours de spécialisation d'ingénieur en génie atomique; (b) Cours postuniversitaires comprenant les enseignements de 3e cycle suivants: physique des réacteurs nucléaires; mécanique appliquée à la construction (option dynamique des structures); métallurgie et matériaux; chimie analytique; radioéléments, rayonnements, radiochimie, effets biologiques des radiations ionisantes et radiopathologie;

robotique (option robotique d'intervention et de service); électronique (option systèmes de traitement de l'information, structure des ordinateurs); gestion de la technologie et de l'innovation; économie et politique de l'énergie; (c) Enseignement de spécialisation dans l'utilisation des radioéléments artificiels destinés aux médecins et aux pharmaciens; (d) Cours de 3e cycle dans les domaines suivants: instrumentation et méthodes physicochimiques d'analyse; biologie cellulaire et moléculaire; structure, fonction et ingénierie des protéines; sciences des aérosols - génie de l'aérocontamination; informatique scientifique et technique; énergétique physique; science et génie des matériaux; optique - optronique et micro-ondes; signal - image - parole; physique radiologique et médicale; maîtrise de l'environnement industriel; champs, particules et matières; radioprotection; physique des plasmas; méthodes physiques expérimentales; matière condensée: chimie et organisation; astrophysique et techniques spatiales; modélisation et instrumentation en physique; rayonnement et plasmas; génie des procédés et physico-chimie; équations aux dérivées partielles et calcul scientifique.
A l'intention de: ressortissants de tout pays, titulaires: (a) d'un diplôme d'ingénieur de grandes écoles; (b) d'un diplôme équivalent à la maîtrise française en sciences ou à un diplôme d'ingénieur de grandes écoles; (c) docteurs en médecine et pharmaciens; (d) ingénieurs diplômés ou candidats en possession d'un titre équivalent.
Durée: 9 mois; (d) 12 mois.
Inscriptions: (a) avant le 15 mai; (b), (c) avant le 30 juin; (d) entre le 31 mai et le 15 septembre.

1009 Institut national polytechnique de Grenoble [INPG]

46, avenue Félix Viallet
38031 Grenoble
Tel: +33-4-7657-4500
Fax: +33-4-7657-4501
Web: http://www.inpg.fr
e-mail: relint@inpg.fr

📖 2e, 3e cycles / ingénierie

Domaines d'étude: électricité et électronique, énergie, génie chimique, hydraulique, imprimerie, industrie chimique, industrie et commerce, ingénierie, mécanique, technologie, technologie industrielle, télécommunications.
Programmes: l'INP Grenoble, fédération de 9 Grandes Ecoles et 1 département Télécom offre des formations en ingénierie conduisant au diplômes d'ingénieurs, de masters recherche et doctorat dans les domaines de: imprimerie et transformation de papier; sciences des matériaux et des surfaces; génie des procédés et électrochimie; électronique et radioélectricité; génie industriel; hydraulique et mécanique; Informatique et mathématiques appliquées; systèmes industriels avancés; télécommunications.
Domaines d'études: micro/nanotechnologies, information/communication, matériaux; énergie, environnement, systèmes de production.
A l'intention de: ressortissants de tous pays sélectionnés par concours ou sur dossiers.
Organisés: - École Française de Papeterie et des Industries Graphiques (EFPG); 461 Rue de la Papeterie- DU - BP 65; 38402 St Martin d'Hères Cedex; Internet: www.efpg.inpg.fr; contact: efpg@efpg.inpg.fr;
- École Nationale Supérieure d'Electrochimie et d'Electrométallurgie de Grenoble (ENSEEG), 1130 Rue de la Piscine - DU - BP75; 38402 St Martin d'Hères Cedex; Internet: http://www.enseeg.inpg.fr; email: scol.enseeg@enseeg.inpg.fr;
- École Nationale Supérieure d'Electronique et Radioélectricité de Grenoble (ENSERG); 23 rue des Martyrs, BP 257, 38016 Grenoble Cedex 1; Internet: http://www.enserg.fr; contact: scol@enserg.fr;
- École Nationale Supérieure de Génie Industriel (ENSGI); 46, Avenue Félix Viallet, 38031 Grenoble Cedex 1; Internet: http://ensgi.inpg.fr; contact: Denis.Trystram@ensgi.inpg.fr;
- École Nationale Supérieure d'Hydraulique et de Mécanique de Grenoble (ENSHMG); 1025 Rue de la Piscine - DU - BP 95; 38402 St Martin d'Hères Cedex; Internet: http://www.hmg.inpg.fr; contact: hmgscol@hmg.inpg.fr
- École Nationale Supérieure d'Ingénieurs Electriciens de Grenoble (ENSIEG); 961 rue de la Houille Blanche - DU - BP46; 38402 St Martin d'Hères Cedex; Internet: http://www.ensieg.inpg.fr; contact:

Direction-Etudes@ensieg.inpg.fr;
- École Nationale Supérieure d'Informatique et de
Mathématiques Appliquées de Grenoble (ENSIMAG); 681
Rue de la passerelle - DU - BP 72; 38402 St Martin d'Hères
Cedex; Internet: http://www-ensimag.imag.fr; contact:
Veronique.Caillat@imag.fr;
- École Nationale Supérieure de Physique de Grenoble
(ENSPG); 961 rue de la Houille Blanche - DU BP46; 38402
St Martin d'Hères Cedex; Internet: http://www.enspg.inpg.fr;
contact: depg@enspg.inpg.fr;
- École Supérieure d'Ingénieurs en Systèmes Industriels
Avancés Rhône-Alpes (ESISAR); 50 rue Barthélémy de
Laffemas - BP54; 26 902 VALENCE Cedex 9; Internet:
http://www.esisar.inpg.fr; contact:
recrutement@esisar.inpg.fr;
- Département Telecom; 681 Rue de la passerelle - DU - BP
53; 38041 Grenoble Cedex 9; Internet:
http://www-telecoms.inpg.fr
contact: scolarite.telecom@inpg.fr.
Durée: variable selon formation; contacter les Écoles pour
de plus amples informations sur les études d'ingénieurs (3
ans) et le Collège Doctoral pour les études de master (2 ans)
et doctorat (3 ans).
Inscriptions: contacter soit le Service des Relations
internationales (email:relint@inpg.fr) soit directement l'École
concerné ou le Collège Doctoral.

☛ Bourse MIRA

Domaines d'étude: recherche, technologie.
Description: bourse octroyée par la Région Rhône-Alpes
pour études supérieures.
A l'intention de: candidats avec un projet de recherche.
Nationalité: toutes nationalités.
Durée: de 3 à 9 mois, renouvelable.
Valeur: de 380 à 760 euros par mois (montant plus élevé si
le candidat provient de régions partenaires).
Candidatures: en février-mars. Pour tout renseignement,
s'adresser au Service des Relations Internationales.

1010   Institut Pasteur [IP]

Secrétariat des enseignements
28, rue du Docteur-Roux
75724 Paris Cedex 15
Tel: +33-1-4568-8141
Fax: +33-1-4061-3046
Web: http://www.pasteur.fr/formation
e-mail: enseignement@pasteur.fr

📖 Sciences biologiques

Domaines d'étude: bactériologie, biologie, génétique,
immunologie, microbiologie.
Programmes: enseignement de niveau 3ème cycle
universitaire dans les domaines suivants: (a) biochimie des
protéines; (b) biologie moléculaire de la cellule; (c) génétique
somatique et moléculaire;
(d) génétique de la souris; (e) immunologie approfondie; (f)
immunologie générale; (g) informatique en biologie; (h)
microbiologie générale; (i) virologie fondamentale; (j)
bactériologie; (k) entomologie médicale; (l) épidémiologie
humaine et animale; (m) microbiologie tropicale; (n)
mycologie médicale; (o) virologie médicale; (p) génie
génétique; (q) microscopie électronique.
Description: 15 cours de niveau troisième cycle
universitaire avec des cours théoriques et des travaux
pratiques très développés. Réalisés par des spécialistes des
différentes disciplines, les cours donnent une vision intégrée
des aspects les plus récents de la théorie, de la méthodologie
et de la pratique propres à chaque domaine enseigné. Ils sont
destinés aux diplômés des Unités de Formation et de
Recherche et des Centres Hospitaliers des Universités, aux
diplômés des Grandes Écoles, ainsi qu'aux étudiants étrangers
de niveau équivalent.
A l'intention de: candidats diplômés des unités de
formation et de recherche et des centres hospitaliers des
universités; diplômés des grandes écoles et étudiants étrangers
de niveau équivalent. Une
excellente connaissance du français et une bonne
connaissance de l'anglais sont indispensables.
Durée: variable.
Connaissances linguistiques: français (quelques
conférences en langue anglaise).

1011   Institut supérieur agricole de Beauvais [ISAB]

rue Pierre Waguet
BP 30313
60026 Beauvais Cedex
Tel: +33-3-4406-2525
Web: http://www.isab.fr

📖 Formation d'ingénieurs

Domaines d'étude: agriculture, bactériologie, biochimie,
biologie, botanique, ingénierie, microbiologie, sciences
agronomiques, zoologie.
Programmes: Formation d'ingénieurs pour
l'agro-industrie, l'environnement et l'agriculture.
A l'intention de: ressortissants de tout pays, titulaires d'un
baccalauréat scientifique.
Durée: 5 ans (débutant mi-septembre).
Assistance financière: possibilité d'obtention de bourses
ou de prêts d'honneur.
Inscriptions: s'adresser à l'adresse ci-dessus.

1012   Institut supérieur d'agriculture Lille [ISA]

41, rue du Port
59000 Lille
Tel: +33-3-2838-4848
Fax: +33-3-2838-4847
Web: http://www.isa-lille.fr
e-mail: isa@fupl.asso.fr

📖 Diplôme d'ingénieur

Domaines d'étude: agriculture, écologie, environnement,
sciences agronomiques.
Programmes: Diplôme d'ingénieur (équivalent Master's
degree) en agriculture, agroalimentaire, environnement; DESS
en environnement.
A l'intention de: titulaires d'un Bac scientifique (ou
équivalent); admission en première année: sur dossier et
épreuve écrite; années suivantes: sur titre, dossier et entretien.
Durée: 5 ans (débutant en septembre).
Inscriptions: les demandes de dossier d'inscription se font
sur le site web: http://www.fesic.org, du 3 janvier au 19 avril
et sont à renvoyer avant le 2 mai à l'adresse indiquée sur le
dossier; pour tout renseignement contacter Céline Rauch
(coordonnées ci-dessus).

1013   Institut supérieur d'électronique de Paris [ISEP]

28, rue Notre-Dame-des-Champs
75006 Paris
Tel: +33-1-4954-5291
Fax: +33-1-4954-5201
Web: http://www.isep.fr
e-mail: international@isep.fr

📖 Formation d'Ingénieurs polyvalents en Technologies Information/Communication

Domaines d'étude: électricité et électronique,
informatique, ingénierie, physique, télécommunications.
Programmes: Diplôme d'Ingénieur ISEP, MSc. Mastères
en Sciences.
Domaines d'études: électronique, informatique, réseaux et
télécommunications.
A l'intention de: pour Diplôme Ingénieur: élèves de
Terminale S, étudiants issus d'un cycle préparatoire
scientifique, étudiants internationaux ayant validé un
programme universitaire de 3 à 4 ans en Sciences/Sciences de
l'ingénieur; pour MSc. Mastères en Sciences: étudiants
internationaux titulaires d'un Bachelor's degree ou jeunes
ingénieurs internationaux ayant quelques années d'expérience
professionnelle.
Age Max.: pour Diplôme Ingénieur: (a) admission en 1ère
année du cycle préparatoire: être âgé de moins de 19 ans le
1er janvier de l'année du concours; (b) admission en 1ère
année du cycle ingénieur: être âgé de moins de 22 ans le 1er
janvier de l'année de du concours.
Autres conditions: pour Diplôme Ingénieur: (a) admission
en 1ère année du cycle préparatoire: être titulaire du
baccalauréat général, série S; sélection sur concours; (b)
admission en 1ère année du cycle ingénieur: être titulaire du
baccalauréat général, série S, depuis moins de 3 ans au 1er
janvier de l'année du concours; sélection sur concours.

Admission sur dossier pour les étudiants internationaux qui ont validé un programme universitaire de 3 ans en Sciences/Sciences de l'ingénieur et qui sont âgés de moins de 24 ans; (c) admission en 2ème année du cycle ingénieur: admission sur dossier pour les étudiants internationaux titulaires d'un Bachelor en Sciences/Sciences de l'ingénieur ou titre équivalent et âgés de moins de 25 ans. Pour MSc. Mastères en Sciences: être titulaire d'un Bachelor's degree ou titre équivalent dans les domaines correspondants. Admission sur dossier.

Durée: pour Diplôme Ingénieur: classes préparatoires 2 ans, cycle ingénieur 3 ans. Pour MSc. Mastères en Sciences: 3 semestres (dont un semestre de stage obligatoire).

Frais: Diplôme Ingénieur: classes préparatoires 2.240€ par an; cycle ingénieur 5.990€ par an. Pour MSc. Mastère en Sciences 11.200€ pour l'ensemble du programme (3 semestres).

Connaissances linguistiques: Pour Diplôme Ingénieur: Cours dispensés en français (plusieurs options de dernière année sont enseignées en anglais). Anglais et seconde langue vivante obligatoires. Pour MSc. Mastères en Sciences: Cours dispensés en anglais. TOEFL ou examen d'anglais équivalent obligatoire (score minimum TOEFL: 550 / 213CB).

Inscriptions: Pour Diplôme Ingénieur: admission en 1ère année du cycle préparatoire: inscriptions par internet, www.fesic.org, de janvier à mi-avril; admission en 1ère année du cycle ingénieur: inscriptions par internet, www.scei-concours.org, de début décembre à mi-janvier. Pour MSc. Mastères en Sciences: dossier de candidature à télécharger sur le site internet www.isep.fr et à retourner au Service des Relations Internationales accompagné des documents à fournir.

1014   Institut supérieur des affaires - Groupe HEC [ISA]

1, rue de la Libération
78351 Jouy-en-Josas Cedex
Tel: +33-1-3967-7379
Web: http://www.hec.fr

📖 Études de commerce

Domaines d'étude: gestion.

Programmes: MBA bilingue du Groupe HEC. Enseignement multidisciplinaire et transversal du management. La pédagogie active (500 études de cas) tire le meilleur parti de la diversité des cultures et des expériences des participants pour leur faire vivre le management international.

A l'intention de: ressortissants de tout pays, titulaires d'un diplôme français ou étranger avec si possible une expérience professionnelle d'au moins 2 ans. La sélection est effectuée sur dossier, tests et entretiens.

Durée: 16 mois dont 8 mois de « Core International Management Programme » et 8 mois de personnalisation du cursus: 80 électifs, 5 filières de spécialisation, ou participation à un des programmes d'échanges avec l'une des 34 « Business Schools » partenaires de l'ISA dans le monde entier, ou un projet de conseil à plein temps en entreprise.

Inscriptions: s'adresser à l'École.

1015   Institut textile et chimique de Lyon [ITECH]

87, Chemin des Morilles
69130 Ecully, Lyon
Tel: +33-4-7218-0480
Fax: +33-4-7218-9545
Web: http://www.itech.fr
e-mail: info@itech.fr

📖 Formation d'ingénieur

Domaines d'étude: chimie, enseignement technique, formation professionnelle, industrie chimique, industrie textile, technologie industrielle.

Programmes: (a) formation d'ingénieur dans les domaines suivants: chimie des formulations (peintures, encres et adhésifs); matières plastiques et composites; textile; cuir; (b) BTS matériaux souples (cuir); BTS pour les industries des peintures, encres d'imprimerie et adhésifs; (c) Post-BTS Bachelor technicien de la couleur et cosmétique colorée; (d) Formation professionnelle accélérée dans le domaine du cuir; (e) Mastère Spécialisé «matériaux et revêtements»: tronc commun avec une option au choix entre: peintures, encres et

adhésifs ou chimie de formulation; transformation du cuir; textile; et matériaux plastiques et composites. Mastère Spécialisé «Cosmétique».

Domaines d'études: chimie, enseignement technique, formation professionnelle, industrie, chimie des formulations peintures, encres, adhésifs, cosmétiques, industrie textile, industrie du cuir et de la chaussure, industrie de transformation des matériaux plastiques.

A l'intention de: ressortissants de tout pays: (a) titulaires d'un diplôme équivalent à un DEUG, un DUT ou un très bon BTS et ayant des connaissances en chimie; la maîtrise parfaite de la langue française (écrite et orale) est requise; ou titulaire d'un Bachelor of Sciences en 3 ans ou 4 ans; (b) titulaires d'un baccalauréat scientifique; (c) titulaires d'un BTS ou DUT scientifique ou Bachelor of Sciences in Chemistry; (d) possédant le niveau du baccalauréat ou diplôme équivalent; (e) titulaires soit d'un diplôme d'ingénieur, soit d'un DEA ou master of sciences scientifique, soit d'un diplôme équivalent. Admission sur titres, dossier et entretien.

Durée: (a) 3 ans; (b) 2 ans; (c), (d) et (e) 1 an (débutant en septembre).

Frais: frais d'inscription: 61 €; frais de scolarité: entre 4.600 et 5.400 € par an; frais de séjour: environ 500 € par mois.

Inscriptions: avant le 30 juin auprès du Secrétariat ingénieur; pour tout renseignement concernant les étudiants étrangers, s'adresser à Relations Internationales, à l'adresse ci-dessus.

1016   Institut universitaire professionnalisé management et gestion des entreprises [IUP-MGE]

26, avenue Léon Blum
BP 273
63000 Clermont-Ferrand
Tel: +33-4-7317-7700
Fax: +33-4-7317-7701
Web: http://www.iup-management.net
e-mail: communication@iup-management.net

📖 1er, 2e cycle / gestion des entreprises

Domaines d'étude: communication, droit, études internationales, gestion, marketing, relations publiques.

Programmes: DEUG, Licence et Maîtrise en management et gestion des entreprises.

Durée: DEUG: 2 ans (débutant en septembre); licence et maîtrise: 1 année chacune (débutant en septembre).

Frais: inscription: environ 455 €.

Inscriptions: avant le 30 mai, adressées à l'université d'Auvergne, Mme Person (tel: +33-4-7517-7277; fax: +33-4-7517-7205).

1017   Ministère des Affaires étrangères

☛ Programme «Bourses d'excellence Eiffel»

Domaines d'étude: administration, administration des affaires, droit international, économie, économie politique.

Description: (a) Le programme de «bourses d'excellence Eiffel», lancé en janvier 1999 par le ministère des Affaires étrangères, est destiné à soutenir l'action de recrutement à l'international des établissements d'enseignement supérieur français. Le programme vise, en priorité, à former en France les futurs décideurs du secteur privé et de l'administration des pays émergents; (b) Programme Eiffel Doctorat pour la formation des doctorants de haut niveau. Ce dispositif est destiné à soutenir l'action de recrutement à l'international des universités et des établissements d'enseignement supérieur français pour attirer les futurs décideurs étrangers du public et du privé. Il permet d'offrir aux étudiants originaires des pays émergents mais aussi des pays à fort potentiel scientifique et universitaire, la possibilité d'effectuer une année en France: la 2e ou 3e année de thèse de préférence. Ce programme s'adresse aux étudiants étrangers en codirection ou en cotutelle de thèse.

Candidatures: pour tout renseignement, contacter: Égide - Programme Eiffel, 28 rue de la Grange-aux-Belles, 75010 Paris; tél: +33-1-4040-5907; fax: +33-1-4241-8590, email: eiffel@egide.asso.fr.

☛ **Programme «Boursiers français à l'étranger»**

Domaines d'étude: administration, administration des affaires, affaires internationales, droit international, économie, économie politique.

Description: Le programme BFE, «Boursiers français à l'étranger» regroupe deux grands types de bourses offertes chaque année aux français souhaitant poursuivre leur formation à l'étranger:

(a) le programme Lavoisier, financé par le ministère des Affaires étrangères, et sans restriction géographique; (b) les bourses proposées par certains gouvernements étrangers dans le cadre des accords bilatéraux.

Candidatures: Ministère des Affaires étrangères, DGCID - Direction de la Coopération scientifique et universitaire, Bureau de la formation des Français à l'étranger, 20, rue Monsieur, 75700 Paris.

L'information par pays et par programme peut être consultée sur http://www.egide.asso.fr/fr/programmes/bfe/.

1018 Observatoire de Paris

61, avenue de l'Observatoire
75014 Paris
Tel: +33-1-4051-2221
Fax: +33-1-4051-2296
Web: http://www.obspm.fr

☐ **Études en astronomie**

Domaines d'étude: astronomie, espace, géodésie.

Programmes: (a) Cours dans les domaines de l'astronomie fondamentale, mécanique céleste et géodésie, conduisant au DEA et au doctorat; (b) Cours de méthodes instrumentales en astrophysique et leurs applications spatiales, conduisant au DEA et au doctorat; analyse détaillée des méthodes instrumentales modernes dans tout le spectre électromagnétique, et de leur insertion dans un système qui comprend un grand nombre de composantes successives depuis le capteur jusqu'au modèle.

A l'intention de: (a) ressortissants de tout pays, âgés de 20 à 30 ans, titulaires d'une maîtrise ou équivalent, d'une maîtrise es sciences, d'un diplôme d'ingénieur, ou d'un diplôme de grandes écoles; (b) étudiants titulaires d'une maîtrise ou équivalence (dossier de préadmission, puis entretien).

Durée: (a) 1 an pour le DEA, dont 4 mois de stage, et 3 ans pour le doctorat (débutant en septembre); (b) 4 ans (débutant en octobre).

Assistance financière: (a) allocation de DEA; allocation de recherche pour le doctorat; (b) allocation d'études et de recherche.

Connaissances linguistiques: Langues d'enseignement: anglais et français.

Inscriptions: à l'adresse ci-dessus.

1019 Pôle agronomique de Rennes

Service des Relations internationales
65, rue de Saint-Brieuc
CS 84215
35042 Rennes Cedex
Tel: +33-2-2348-5172
Fax: +33-2-2348-5999
Web: http://agro.roazhon.inra.fr
e-mail: relinter@agrorennes.educagri.fr

☐ **Diplôme d'ingénieur agronomique**

Domaines d'étude: agriculture, alimentation, industrie alimentaire, sciences agronomiques, technologie.

Programmes: cours conduisant à l'obtention d'un diplôme d'ingénieur agronome (DIA) dans les domaines suivants: biologie appliquée à l'agronomie, génie de l'environnement, sciences du sol, sciences et techniques des productions végétales, sciences et techniques des productions animales, sciences économiques, sociales et humaines, sciences et techniques des industries agricoles alimentaires, halieutique.

A l'intention de: ressortissants de tout pays, de niveau Bac+2. L'admission se fait sur concours en 1ère année, sur titre en 3ème année (étudiant de niveau Bac+5 pouvant acquérir un diplôme d'agronomie approfondie ou un certificat d'études supérieures agronomiques).

Durée: 3 ans (débutant en septembre), pour le DIA; 1 an pour le DAA ou le CESA.

Assistance financière: possibilité de bourses auprès du Ministère des affaires étrangères.

Inscriptions: en février pour le concours d'entrée en première année; au Service des concours Agor; INA-Paris Grignon, 16, rue Claude Bernard, 75231 Paris Cedex 05; http://www.inapg.inra.fr; tél: + 33 1 44 08 16 29; fax: + 33 1 44 08 18 51; email: concours@inapg.inra.fr.

1020 Supméca

3, rue Fernand Hainaut
93407 Saint Ouen Cedex
Tel: +33-1-4945-2900
Fax: +33-1-4945-2991
Web: http://www.supmeca.fr
e-mail: rel.iut@ismcm-cesti.fr

☐ **2e, 3e cycles / ingénierie, mécanique**

Domaines d'étude: ingénierie, mécanique, technologie industrielle.

Programmes: Diplôme d'ingénieur généraliste; cursus de 3ème cycle (DEA et doctorat); formation de spécialisation non diplômante (ISMCM) pour les titulaires d'un diplôme d'ingénieur.

A l'intention de: admission en 1ère année: étudiants issus des classes préparatoires ou titulaires d'un diplôme scientifique Bac + 2 (DEUG, BTS, DUT ou équivalents); admission en 2ème année: titulaires d'une Maîtrise scientifique ou d'un Bachelor's degree (ou équivalents); admission en DEA: titulaires d'un diplôme d'ingénieur ou d'une Maîtrise scientifique (ou équivalents); possibilité d'effectuer le DEA en double cursus lors de la 3ème année du cycle du diplôme d'ingénieur; admission en doctorat: titulaires d'un DEA (ou équivalent); admission en 1ère année: sur concours communs polytechniques pour les étudiants issus des classes préparatoires ou titulaires d'un DEUG et sur dossier pour les titulaires d'un BTS ou un DUT (ou équivalents); admission en 2ème année: sur dossier.

Durée: diplôme d'ingénieur: 3 ans (débutant en septembre); DEA: 1 an (débutant en septembre); doctorat: de 2 à 4 ans (débutant en septembre); formation de spécialisation non diplômante (ISMCM): 1 ou 2 semestres.

Frais: frais d'inscription (incluant la sécurité sociale étudiante): environ 500 € par an; frais de scolarité: de 600 à 1000 € par an; frais de séjour: environ 6000 € par an.

Inscriptions: les dossiers de candidature doivent comporter les éléments suivants: un CV, une lettre de motivation, l'ensemble des relevés des notes obtenues à l'université, une copie du dernier diplôme, une lettre de recommandation, une attestation de niveau en français le cas échéant; les candidatures doivent être envoyées à CESTI/Supméca, Service des relations internationales, 3 Rue Fernand Hainaut, 93407 St-Ouen Cedex, au plus tard 6 mois avant le début du séjour d'études projeté; pour de plus amples informations contacter: Rel.Int@ismcm-cesti.fr.

1021 Université catholique de l'Ouest [UCO]

Service des relations internationales
3, place André-Leroy
BP 808
49008 Angers Cedex 01
Tel: +33-2-4181-6600
Web: http://www.uco.fr
e-mail: comm@uco.fr

☐ **Cours multidisciplinaires**

Domaines d'étude: toutes disciplines principales, affaires, éducation, éducation de la première enfance, éducation permanente, français, histoire, langues, littérature et civilisation, programmes d'été, théologie, religion.

Programmes: Programme d'études dans toutes les disciplines; Programme du Centre international d'études françaises: (a) Cours tout niveau de langue, littérature et civilisation françaises; environ 24 participants par cours; conduisant au Certificat d'initiation à la langue française; (b) Cours intensifs à la pratique de la langue française parlée et écrite; tout niveau; (c) Cours de perfectionnement pour instituteurs et professeurs de français à l'étranger; (d) Cours préuniversitaires intensifs de langue française; tout niveau; recommandés aux étudiants des programmes Erasmus et Tempus avant leur entrée dans une université française cours préparant au DELF-DALF, à l'examen de la Chambre de commerce et d'industrie de Paris et de l'Alliance française de Paris.

A l'intention de: ressortissants de tout pays, âgés de 17 ans minimum et ayant terminé leurs études secondaires.
Durée: variable selon le programme.
Assistance financière: obtention de crédits pour étudiants américains et japonais.
Inscriptions: s'adresser à l'adresse ci-dessus.

1022 Université catholique de Lille-Fédération universitaire et polytechnique de Lille
60, boulevard Vauban
BP 109
59016 Lille Cedex
Tel: +33-3-2015-9688
Fax: +33-3-2015-9689
Web: http://www.fupl.asso.fr
e-mail: international@fupl.asso.fr

1er-3e cycles / toutes disciplines
Domaines d'étude: toutes disciplines principales.
Description: diplômes de 1er, 2nd et 3ème cycle d'études supérieures; cours dispensés dans 6 facultés et 25 écoles supérieures membres de la Fédération.
A l'intention de: ressortissants de tout pays, titulaires d'un diplôme de fin d'études secondaires.
Frais: à partir de 1.614 € pour une année en faculté; à partir de 2.286 € pour une année d'école.
Assistance financière: pas d'assistance financière possible.
Connaissances linguistiques: français (cours de l'université d'été en anglais).

1023 Université catholique de Lyon [UCL]
25, rue du Plat
69002 Lyon
Tel: +33-4-7232-5003
Fax: +33-4-7232-5026
Web: http://www.univ-catholyon.fr
e-mail: nughetto@univ-catholyon.fr

1er-3e cycles / toutes disciplines
Domaines d'étude: toutes disciplines principales.
Programmes: programme de cours conduisant aux diplômes suivants: DEUG, Licence, Maîtrise, Doctorat dans toutes les disciplines principales.
Description: établissement d'enseignement supérieur comprenant 5 facultés.
A l'intention de: admission sur dossier, examen et entretien (en fonction des facultés).
Connaissances linguistiques: français (possibilité de cours intensifs sur l'année).

1024 Université Claude Bernard, Lyon 1
43, boulevard du 11 Novembre 1918
69622 Villeurbanne Cedex
Tel: +33-4-72-44-8000
Fax: +33-4-7243-1213
Web: http://www.univ-lyon1.fr
e-mail: relinter@univ-lyon1.fr

1er-3e cycles
Domaines d'étude: éducation physique, ingénierie, médecine, pharmacie et pharmacologie, sciences, technologie.
Description: cursus allant du DEUG au doctorat.
Connaissances linguistiques: pour les étudiants hors programme d'échange un test de français doit être effectué à l'ambassade de France du pays du candidat.
Inscriptions: inscription en 1er cycle hors programme d'échange: dossiers d'inscription à retirer auprès de l'ambassade de France du pays du candidat ou bien à Lyon 1 au service de la direction de la formation de l'université: Mme Michèle Martinetto (+33 4 72 44 80 03, Fax: +33 4 72 43 13 73, Michele.Martinetto@adm.univ-lyon1.fr) ou Mme Annie Bouyer (+33 4 73 44 80 08, Fax: +33 4 72 43 13 73, Annie.Bouyer@adm.univ-lyon1.fr); ces dossiers doivent être renvoyés avant la fin janvier; inscription en 2ème et 3ème cycles hors programme d'échange: demande des dossiers d'inscription au service de la scolarité de l'Unité de Formation et de Recherche (UFR) de la discipline concernée; le dossier sera examiné par une commission pédagogique et l'admission se fera en fonction des capacités d'accueil.

1025 Université d'Aix-Marseille III
3, avenue Robert Schuman
13628 Aix-en-Provence Cedex 1
Tel: +33-4-9160-0021
Web: http://www.univ.u-3mrs.fr
e-mail: info@scuio.u-3mrs.fr

1er-3e cycles / droit, économie, sciences
Domaines d'étude: droit, économie, relations internationales, sciences, sciences sociales.
Programmes: Programme multidisciplinaire en économie, droit, et sciences, regroupant un ensemble pluridisciplinaire régional; cours conduisant au DES en droit et relations internationales pour les étudiants étrangers.
A l'intention de: ressortissants de tout pays ayant l'équivalent du baccalauréat français.
Organisés: implantations géographiques sont reparties principalement dans les villes d'Aix-en-Provence et Marseille, mais aussi, pour certains programmes spécifiques, dans les villes de Salon, Arles et Digne.
Durée: variable selon le programme.
Inscriptions: à l'adresse ci-dessus.

1026 Université d'Angers
Présidence de l'Université d'Angers
40, rue de Rennes
BP 3532
49035 Angers Cedex
Tel: +33-2-4196-2323
Fax: +33-2-4196-2300
Web: http://www.univ-angers.fr
e-mail: webmaster@univ-angers.fr

1er-3e cycles / toutes disciplines
Domaines d'étude: toutes disciplines principales.
Description: enseignement pluridisciplinaire traditionnel et professionnalisé allant du premier au troisième cycle (DEUG, Licence, Maîtrise, DEA, DESS, DU).
Durée: DEUG: 2 ans; Licence, Maîtrise, DEA, DESS: 1 an; tous les cours commencent le 1er octobre.
Frais: inscription: environ 160 €; sécurité sociale (obligatoire): 170 €.
Connaissances linguistiques: des cours de français sont proposés pour les étudiants étrangers par le CUFCo (Centre universitaire de formation continue, +33 2 41 96 23 84); une attestation de stage en "langue et culture française" est délivrée; possibilité d'obtention du DELF ou DALF (après réussite aux examens spécifiques).
Inscriptions: inscription en 1er cycle: dossier d'admission préalable à retirer auprès du service culturel de l'ambassade de France du pays de résidence du 1er décembre au 15 janvier pour la rentrée universitaire suivante (réponse en mai); inscription en 2nd et 3ème cycles: dossier de validation d'études à demander auprès de l'UFR ou de l'IUP choisi dès le mois de mars (scolarité@univ-angers.fr).

1027 Université d'Avignon et des Pays de Vaucluse
35,74, rue Louis Pasteur
84029 Avignon Cedex I
Tel: +33-4-9016-2500
Fax: +33-4-9016-2510
Web: http://www.univ-avignon.fr

1er-3e cycles / lettres et sciences
Domaines d'étude: langues, lettres, sciences, sciences économiques et commerciales, sciences humaines, sciences politiques.
Programmes: Programme de cours dans les domaines suivants: lettres et sciences humaines, sciences exactes et sciences de la nature, sciences et langages appliqués, sciences juridiques, politiques et économiques, technologie, préprofessionnalisation.
A l'intention de: ressortissants de tout pays, titulaires du baccalauréat ou titre admis en équivalence.
Durée: selon la filière choisie: DEUG: 2 ans; licence: 1 an; maîtrise: 1 an.
Inscriptions: un formulaire de demande d'admission préalable est à retirer entre à partir du 15 février, auprès des services de l'ambassade de France du pays dont le candidat est ressortissant ou à l'université la plus proche de son domicile pour les étudiants étrangers domiciliés en France et titulaires d'un permis de séjour de validité minimale d'un an.

1028 Université de Bordeaux I
351, cours de la Libération
33405 Talence Cedex
Tel: +33-5-5684-6000
Fax: +33-5-5680-0837
Web: http://www.u-bordeaux1.fr

📖 **1er-3e cycles / sciences et technologie**

Domaines d'étude: ingénierie, sciences, technologie.
Programmes: Formations fondamentales et
professionnalisantes en sciences et technologie, conduisant à
des diplômes de 1er, 2e et 3e cycle, des diplômes d'ingénieurs
ou préparant les concours de l'enseignement.
Description: la structuration nouvelle autour des grades de
Licence, Master, et Doctorat doit débuter en octobre 2003,
mais ne fera pas disparaître les actuels diplômes de DEUG,
Maîtrise, Ingénieur-Maître; les actuelles Licences
professionnelles resteront pour l'essentiel inchangées, les
DEA et DESS s'appelleront «Masters» et seront réorganisés,
mais les spécialités existantes continueront d'être enseignées.
Inscriptions: à l'adresse ci-dessus; formulaires
d'inscription à télécharger sur
http://www.disvu-bx1.u-bordeaux.fr/scol/ins_docs.html.

1029 Université de Bordeaux II
Université Victor Segalen Bordeaux 2
146, rue Léo Saignat
33076 Bordeaux Cedex
Tel: +33-5-5757-1010
Fax: +33-5-5699-0380
Web: http://www.u-bordeaux2.fr
e-mail: info@u-bordeaux2.fr

📖 **1er-3e cycles / médecine, pharmacie**

Domaines d'étude: biophysique, écologie, environnement,
éducation physique, études dentaires, hygiène et santé,
médecine, pharmacie et pharmacologie, physique.
Programmes: Programmes d'étude en sciences de la vie;
sciences de l'homme et sciences de la santé.
A l'intention de: ressortissants de tout pays, titulaires d'un
baccalauréat ou équivalent.
Inscriptions: à l'adresse ci-dessus.

📖 **Diplômes en oenologie**

Domaines d'étude: oenologie.
Programmes: (a) Cours préparant au diplôme national
d'oenologie (DNO) ou au doctorat d'oenologie-ampéléologie;
(b) Cycles de formation continue dans diverses spécialités de
l'oenologie.
A l'intention de: ressortissants de tout pays: (a) titulaires
du DEUG ou d'un diplôme admis en équivalence; (b)
principalement techniciens oenologues et ingénieurs
viti-vinicoles.
Connaissances linguistiques: Une très bonne
connaissance du français est exigée.
Inscriptions: (a) du 1er février au 30 avril; (b) à partir du
1er septembre; email: oenoadm@oenologie.u-bordeaux2.fr;
site web: http://www.u-bordeaux2.fr/oenologie; email:.

1030 Université de Bourgogne
36, rue Chabot-Charny
21000 Dijon
Tel: +33-3-8030-5020
Web: http://www.u-bourgogne.fr

📖 **1er-3e cycles / toutes disciplines**

Domaines d'étude: toutes disciplines principales, français,
langues, littérature et civilisation.
Programmes: Programme de cours conduisant à des
diplômes du 1er, 2e et 3e cycle dans toutes les disciplines
principales; cours semestriels de langue française conduisant
au Certificat d'études pratiques de langue française et au
Diplôme supérieur d'études françaises.
A l'intention de: ressortissants de tout pays, âgés au
minimum de 18 ans.
Durée: variable.
Inscriptions: écrire à l'adresse ci-dessus pour de plus
amples renseignements.

1031 Université de Caen
Esplanade de la Paix
BP 5186
14032 Caen Cedex
Tel: +33-2-3156-5500
Fax: +33-2-3156-5600
Web: http://www.unicaen.fr

📖 **1er-3e cycles / toutes disciplines**

Domaines d'étude: toutes disciplines principales, études
européennes, français, langues.
Programmes: (a) Programme de cours conduisant aux
diplômes du 1er, 2e et 3e cycle dans toutes les disciplines
principales; (b) Enseignement spécial de langue, littérature et
civilisation françaises au Centre d'enseignement universitaire
international pour étrangers (CEUIE).
A l'intention de: ressortissants de tout pays, âgés de 18 ans
minimum. Les candidats doivent être titulaires du
baccalauréat ou d'un diplôme admis en équivalence.
Organisés: (b) Annexe Vissol, 23, avenue de Bruxelles;
14032 Caen Cedex:.
Durée: variable.
Connaissances linguistiques: test linguistique de français
exigé.
Inscriptions: à l'étranger, le dossier d'admission préalable
est à retirer auprès des services culturels de l'Ambassade de
France; Contact: Ministère des affaires étrangères; web:
www.France.diplomatie.fr/infopra. Service Relations
Internationales: Université de Caen Basse-Normandie;
Esplanade de la Paix; 14032 Caen Cedex (France); Bureau
239 - Bâtiment Sciences 1er cycle - Campus 1; fax:
+33-2-3156-6078.

**1032 Université de la Polynésie
française [UPF]**
BP 6570
FAA' A
Tahiti, Polynésie française
Tel: +689-803-930
Fax: +689-803-961
Web: http://www.upf.pf
e-mail: relations-internationales@upf.pf

📖 **1er-3e cycles / toutes disciplines**

Domaines d'étude: toutes disciplines principales.
Description: Programme de cours du 1er, 2e et 3e cycle en
lettres, langues et sciences humaines (DEUG, Licence,
Maîtrise, DEA); AES et droit: DEUG, Licence, DEUST;
sciences: DEUG et Licence; possibilité de passer plusieurs
diplômes (d'État ou d'université) dans le cadre de la formation
continue (DAEU -diplôme d'accès aux études universitaires)
capacité en droit, Maîtrise de droit; Maîtrise de géographie,
diplôme d'université de 1er ou 2e cycle, etc.).
A l'intention de: titulaires du Bac (ou équivalent) ou d'un
diplôme de l'enseignement supérieur (ou équivalent).
Frais: frais d'inscription: 18500 CFP.
Connaissances linguistiques: bonne connaissance de la
langue française exigée; test de vérification linguistique
courant février; en sont dispensés les titulaires du Diplôme
approfondi de langue française (D.A.L.F.).
Inscriptions: inscription en 1er cycle: dossier de demande
d'admission préalable (D.A.P.) à retirer auprès des services
culturels de l'ambassade de France du pays de résidence ou
directement auprès de l'université pour les étrangers résident
déjà en France sur présentation de la carte de séjour valable 1
an et du titre donnant accès à l'enseignement supérieur du
pays d'origine; demande d'admission préalable à retirer entre
le 15 novembre et le 15 janvier précédant la rentrée
universitaire; inscription en 2ème cycle: validation des acquis
antérieurs par une commission de spécialistes; l'université de
Polynésie française a passé des conventions d'échange et de
coopération avec des universités étrangères; pour tout
renseignement consulter le site Internet ou contacter
Pierre-Marie Decoudras (coordonnées ci-dessus).

1033 Université de la Sorbonne nouvelle - Paris III

17, rue de la Sorbonne
75005 Paris
Tel: +33-1-4046-2897
Web: http://univ-Paris3.fr

📖 Formations en lettres et arts

Domaines d'étude: allemand, anglais, arabe, arts du spectacle, études américaines, études classiques, études européennes, finlandais, français, interprétation et traduction, italien, lettres et arts, linguistique, littérature et civilisation, moyens audio-visuels.
Programmes: (a) Programmes d'étude en langues et civilisations et littérature étrangères; linguistique et phonétique; cinéma et audiovisuel; théâtre; (b) Programme de cours conduisant au diplôme d'études supérieures spécialisées (DESS) d'interprétation de conférence (section interprétation) et de traduction éditoriale, économique et technique (section traduction); (enseignement dans de nombreuses langues); (c) Enseignement à distance par Télé 3.
A l'intention de: ressortissants de tout pays, titulaires de baccalauréat ou équivalent; l'admission se fait sur examen d'entrée.
Organisés: (b) à l'École supérieure d'interprètes et traducteurs (ESIT); Centre universitaire Dauphine, Boulevard Lannes, 75775 Paris Cedex 16.
Durée: variable.
Inscriptions: se renseigner à l'adresse ci-dessus.

1034 Université de Nantes

1, Quai de Tourville
BP 13522
44035 Nantes Cedex 01
Tel: +33-2-4099-8321
Fax: +33-2-4099-8422
Web: http://www.univ-nantes.fr
e-mail: eline.moineron@presidence.univ-nantes.fr

📖 1e-3e cycles / toutes disciplines

Domaines d'étude: toutes disciplines principales.
Programmes: programme de cours conduisant aux diplômes de 1er, 2e et 3e cycle dans toutes disciplines principales.
A l'intention de: titulaires d'un diplôme de fin d'études secondaires ou d'un diplôme de l'enseignement supérieur.
Frais: frais d'inscription: de 321 à 441 €; mutuelle de sécurité sociale: 171 €; inscription gratuite pour les étudiants faisant partie d'un programme d'échange officiel de l'université (type Socrates); frais de séjour: environ 450 € par mois.
Inscriptions: inscription en 1er cycle: retrait des dossiers auprès du service culturel de l'ambassade de France du pays d'origine entre le 1er décembre et le 15 Janvier de l'année précédant l'inscription; date limite de dépôt des dossiers: 31 janvier; pour tout renseignement consulter le site du ministère de l'éducation nationale:
www.education.gouv.fr/int/etudfr.htm; inscription en 2ème cycle: demande de dossier de candidature exclusivement par écrit, entre le 1er février et le 1er avril adressée à la Présidence de l'université, Division des Études et de la Vie Universitaire (adresse ci-dessus) accompagnée d'une grande enveloppe (au moins 21 x 29,7 cm) portant l'adresse précise du candidat écrite en français et 2 coupons-réponse internationaux ou timbres poste; dossier à déposer par la suite au plus tard le 1er mai; inscription en 3ème cycle: demande de dossier de candidature exclusivement par écrit, entre le 1er mars et le 15 juin adressée à la Présidence de l'Université, Division des Études et de la Vie Universitaire, accompagnée d'une grande enveloppe (au moins 21 x 29,7 cm) portant l'adresse précise du candidat écrite en français et 2 coupons-réponse internationaux ou timbres poste; pour connaître la date limite de dépôt du dossier se renseigner auprès du service international de l'université (international@presidence.univ-nantes.fr).

1035 Université de Nice Sophia Antipolis

Grandcloteau
28, avenue de Valrose
BP 2135
06103 Nice
Tel: +33-4-9207-6060
Fax: +33-4-9207-6600
Web: http://www.unice.fr
e-mail: barraud@unice.fr

📖 1er-3er cycle / toutes disciplines

Domaines d'étude: toutes disciplines principales.
Programmes: enseignement pluridisciplinaire allant du DEUG au Doctorat.
A l'intention de: ressortissants de tout pays, titulaire d'un diplôme de fin d'études secondaires.
Connaissances linguistiques: français courant (DAFL).

1036 Université de Paris I, Institut d'étude du développement économique et social [IEDES]

45bis avenue de la Belle Gabrielle
94736 Nogent sur Marne Cedex
Tel: +33-1-4394-7215
Fax: +33-1-4394-7244
Web: http://iedes.univ-paris1.fr

📖 Études en développement économique

Domaines d'étude: alimentation, anthropologie, développement rural, économie, études du développement, sciences humaines, sciences sociales, sociologie.
Programmes: (a) Diplôme d'études approfondies (DEA) en anthropologie et sociologie du politique, en collaboration avec l'Université de Paris VIII; (b) Diplôme d'études supérieures spécialisées (DESS) en développement industriel et évaluation de projets, en développement agricole et en pratiques sociales et pratiques professionnelles du développement; (c) DESS «aménagement urbain et régional dans les pays en voie de développement (PVD)»; «crises, interventions humanitaires et actions de développement»; «analyse des politiques et des conjonctures dans les PVD»; (d) Diplôme de hautes études et recherches spécialisées (DHERS) complétant les différents DESUP.
A l'intention de: ressortissants de tout pays, titulaires d'une maîtrise ou d'un diplôme équivalent; (b) sélection sur test.
Durée: (a) 1 an (débutant en novembre); (b) et (e) 8 mois plus stage; (c) 8 mois; (d) 2 ans.
Connaissances linguistiques: anglais nécessaire pour les filières économiques; français obligatoire.
Inscriptions: avant fin septembre; dépôt des demandes pour examen par une commission, d'avril à fin juin à l'adresse ci-dessus.

1037 Université de Paris I, Institut de démographie [IDUP]

Centre Pierre Mendès-France
90, rue de Tolbiac
75634 Paris Cedex
Tel: +33-1-4407-8646
Fax: +33-1-4407-8647
Web: http://idup.univ-paris1.fr
e-mail: idup@univ-paris1.fr

📖 2e, 3e cycles / démographie

Domaines d'étude: démographie et études de populations.
Programmes: Cours de démographie conduisant au diplôme: (a) Licence de démographie; (b) Maîtrise de démographie; (c) DESS d'expert-démographe, DEA de démographie; (d) Doctorat de démographie.
A l'intention de: ressortissants de tout pays, titulaires: (a) du DEUG ou équivalent; (b) d'une licence ou équivalent; (c) d'une maîtrise de démographie ou équivalent; (d) d'un DEA de démographie ou équivalent. Les candidats sont admis après réussite d'un test ou d'un examen, ou sur dossier.
Durée: (a) et (b) 1 an; (c) stage en entreprise ou dans une administration, équivalent à 3 mois de travail.
Inscriptions: 1er cycle: étudiants de nationalité étrangère doivent retirer un formulaire entre le 1er décembre et le 15 janvier: auprès des Services Culturels français dans leur pays d'origine ou auprès d'une université française pour les candidats en possession d'un titre de séjour d'une durée de

validité d'une année minimum. Le formulaire doit être déposé avant le 1er février.

1038 Université de Paris-Sorbonne - Centre expérimental d'étude de la civilisation française

47, rue des Écoles
75005 Paris
Tel: +33-1-4046-2670
Fax: +33-1-4046-3229
Web: http://www.fle.fr/sorbonne/fra/experimental.html
e-mail: ccfs@paris4.sorbonne.fr

📖 Langue et civilisation françaises

Domaines d'étude: français, langues, littérature et civilisation.
Programmes: Cours de langue et civilisation françaises: langue française, phonétique, conférences de civilisation française (option littéraire ou français des affaires); (a) Cours annuels: préparation au Magistère de langue et de civilisation françaises réservé aux étudiants étrangers; section universitaire annuelle (b) Cours semestriels: section universitaire semestrielle; ces trois sections comportent une option littéraire et une option économique.
A l'intention de: exclusivement réservés aux étudiants titulaires d'un diplôme de l'enseignement supérieur, désireux de se préparer à de hautes études universitaires. L'inscription est accordée sous réserve de l'admission à un examen d'entrée qui permet d'apprécier le niveau de culture et la connaissance de la langue française.
Durée: magistère: 11 mois; section universitaire annuelle: 2 semestres; section universitaire semestrielle.
Inscriptions: à l'adresse ci-dessus pour de plus amples renseignements.

1039 Université de Pau et des pays de l'Adour - Institut d'études françaises pour étudiants étrangers [IEFEE]

Faculté des lettres
avenue du Doyen Poplawski
BP 1163
Pau Cedex
Web: http://www.univ-pau.fr

📖 1er, 2e cycles / gestion, langue française

Domaines d'étude: français, gestion, langues.
Programmes: (a) Programmes d'étude conduisant aux diplômes de gestion de 1er et 2e cycle: international, management public, systèmes d'information; (b) Cours trimestriels et annuels de langue et civilisation françaises pour étudiants étrangers; (c) Cours avancés préparant au Diplôme d'études françaises et au Diplôme supérieur d'études françaises (DSEF); (d) Cours de français des affaires et de l'hôtellerie et du tourisme.
Organisés: deux campus: à Pau et à Bayonne.
Inscriptions: (a) à l'adresse ci-dessus; (b) à (d) à l'Institut d'études françaises pour étudiants étrangers (IEFEE) à l'adresse ci-dessus; tél: +33 5 59 92 32 22; fax +33 5 59 92 32 65; email: iefe@univ-pau.fr; site web: http://www.univ-pau.fr/SUEE/Accueil.htm.

1040 Université de Perpignan

52, avenue de Villeneuve
66860 Perpignan Cedex
Tel: +33-4-6866-2000
Fax: +33-4-6866-2019
Web: http://www.univ-perp.fr

📖 1er-3e cycles / toutes disciplines

Domaines d'étude: toutes disciplines principales.
Programmes: cursus allant du DEUG au Doctorat en fonction des filières.
A l'intention de: titulaires d'un diplôme de fin d'études secondaires.
Inscriptions: retrait des dossiers d'inscription du 8 au 19 juillet inclus à la Maison de l'Étudiant; prise de rendez-vous pour déposer son dossier sur le site Internet: http://inscriptions.univ-perp.fr.; les dossiers d'inscription sont à déposer au service de la scolarité de la faculté choisie; les procédures spécifiques à chaque faculté sont à trouver sur les

sites Internet de chacune d'elle depuis le portail de l'université: http://www.univ-perp.fr (rubrique: inscriptions); pour tout renseignement contacter la responsable du service des relations internationales, Michèle Clarimon, +33 4 68 66 17 56, cs-suri@univ-perp.fr.

1041 Université de Perpignan, Laboratoire de thermodynamique et énergétique

52, avenue de Villeneuve
66860 Perpignan Cedex
Tel: +33-4-6866-2000
Fax: +33-4-6866-2019
Web: http://www.univ-perp.fr

📖 3e cycle / Recherche en énergétique

Domaines d'étude: énergie.
Programmes: stages de perfectionnement et de recherche en énergétique conduisant au diplôme universitaire de doctorat en énergétique: énergie solaire, analyse des systèmes, systèmes héliothermiques à basses températures, séchage et séchoirs solaires; admission par sélection.
A l'intention de: enseignants, ingénieurs et chercheurs scientifiques des pays en développement, titulaires de la maîtrise en sciences ou d'un diplôme équivalent.
Durée: 3 ans.
Assistance financière: bourses accordées par le Gouvernement français. Les formulaires de candidature doivent être retirés auprès des services culturels des ambassades de France dans les pays du candidat, au plus tard le 15 septembre de l'année précédant le début du cours.
Connaissances linguistiques: français obligatoire.
Inscriptions: toute l'année.

1042 Université de Picardie Jules Verne

Campus Universitaire
Chemin du Thil
80025 Amiens Cedex 1
Tel: +33-3-2282-7272
Fax: +33-3-2282-7500
Web: http://www.u-picardie.fr
e-mail: dai@u-picardie.fr

📖 1er-3e cycles / toutes disciplines

Domaines d'étude: toutes disciplines principales.
Programmes: Programme de cours toutes disciplines: droit et sciences politiques, économie et gestion, lettres, philosophie et sciences humaines, histoire et géographie, médecine, pharmacie, mathématiques et informatique, sciences appliquées, sciences et technologie, langues étrangères, administration, arts, etc. Des cours de langue française sont organisés à l'intention des étudiants qui en ont besoin.
A l'intention de: ressortissants de tout pays, titulaires du baccalauréat ou de l'examen spécial d'entrée à l'université, ou d'un titre admis en équivalence.
Durée: variable.
Inscriptions: avant octobre; 1ere inscription en septembre pour les étudiants étrangers.

1043 Université de Poitiers

Service des relations internationales
15, rue de l'Hôtel-Dieu
86034 Poitiers Cedex
Tel: +33-5-4945-3000
Fax: +33-5-4945-3050
Web: http://www.univ-poitiers.fr
e-mail: webmaster@univ-poitiers.fr

📖 1er-3e cycles / toutes disciplines

Domaines d'étude: toutes disciplines principales.
Programmes: programme de cours toutes disciplines, conduisant aux diplômes de DEUG à Doctorat; cours pour adultes en formation continue dans les filières classiques et à vocation professionnelle.
A l'intention de: ressortissants de tout pays, titulaires du baccalauréat ou équivalence.
Assistance financière: bourses d'enseignement supérieur sur critères universitaires; allocation de recherche (préparation de thèse); prêts d'honneur; aides ponctuelles du Fonds

d'amélioration de la vie des étudiants (FAVE).
Connaissances linguistiques: français requis; des cours de
français (intensifs et annuels) sont dispensés aux étudiants
dont le niveau de langue est insuffisant.
Inscriptions: 1er et 2e cycles: octobre; 3e cycle:
novembre. Pour les procédures particulières d'admission en 2e
cycle (MSG, MS, TCF, EEA) et en 3e cycle, se renseigner en
mai auprès des services de la scolarité à l'adresse ci-dessus.

1044 Université de Poitiers, Centre d'études supérieures et de civilisation médiévale [CESCM]

24, rue de la Chaîne
BP 603
86022 Poitiers
Tel: +33-5-4945-4557
Fax: +33-5-4945-4573
Web: http://www.mshs.univ-poitiers.fr/cescm
e-mail: secretariat.cescm@mshs.univ-poitiers.fr

📖 Études de civilisation médiévale

Domaines d'étude: histoire.
Programmes: Cours de civilisation médiévale; 1 session
intensive de DEA sur 2 semaines (en février); conduisant au
DEA (École doctorale).
A l'intention de: ressortissants de tout pays, titulaires d'une
licence, maîtrise ou diplôme équivalent.
Durée: 1 an.
Assistance financière: nombre de bourses limité.
Connaissances linguistiques: français obligatoire.
Inscriptions: s'adresser au Centre.

1045 Université de Poitiers, Centre de ressources multimédia

95, avenue du Recteur-Pineau
86022 Poitiers Cedex
Tel: +33-5-4945-3226
Fax: +33-5-4945-3230
Web: http://oav.univ-poitiers.fr
e-mail: webmaster@univ-poitiers.fr

📖 DESS en multimédia

Domaines d'étude: communication, éducation,
informatique, langues, moyens audio-visuels.
Programmes: DESS en ingénierie des médias pour
l'éducation: l'usage des technologies de l'information et de la
communication pour l'éducation (ingénierie de formation);
processus de réalisation de dispositifs et produits de formation
(formation de chef de projet dans une structure de production
de ressources pédagogiques, de cédéroms ou de sites
Internet/intranet, coordination éditoriale); possibilité de suivre
cours à distance.
A l'intention de: étudiants de tout pays, possédant une
licence ou l'un des titres admis en équivalence; professeurs ou
enseignants titulaires, sur présentation de pièces justificatives;
responsables ou futurs responsables de centres audiovisuels et
de programmes d'initiation à la communication audiovisuelle,
sur présentation de pièces justificatives; boursiers des
organismes internationaux.
Durée: 1 an; 2 ans si éducation à distance.
Inscriptions: à l'adresse ci-dessus; contacter Jean-François
Cerisier; email: dess-ime@univ-poitiers.fr pour de plus
amples informations.

1046 Université de Rennes I

2, rue du Thabor
35065 Rennes Cedex
Tel: +33-2-2323-3671
Web: http://www.univ-rennes1.fr
e-mail: sai@univ-rennes1.fr

📖 1er-3e cycles / toutes disciplines

Domaines d'étude: toutes disciplines principales.
Programmes: (a) Cours de 1er, 2e et 3e cycles, en
médecine, odontologie, pharmacie, sciences, philosophie,
droit et sciences politiques, sciences économiques; (b) Cours
de sciences biologiques et médicales, conduisant à la maîtrise;
(c) Cours d'orthoptique, conduisant au certificat de capacité
d'orthoptiste; (d) Cours de sciences appliquées et de
technologie à l'École nationale supérieure, conduisant au
diplôme d'ingénieur; (e) Cours de 2e et 3e cycles en
informatique à l'Institut de formation supérieure en

informatique et communication, conduisant au diplôme
d'ingénieur; (f) Cours de méthodes informatiques appliquées à
la gestion (IUP Miage); (g) Cours de 2e et 3e cycles en
gestion; (h) Cours de 2e cycle en administration générale à
l'Institut de préparation à l'Administration générale (IPAG);
(i) Cours de maîtrise et 3e cycle de droit, à l'Institut d'études
judiciaires de Rennes; (j) Cours de technologie en Institut
universitaire de technologie (IUT).
A l'intention de: ressortissants de tout pays: (a) titulaires
d'un baccalauréat; (b) étudiants en médecine, pharmacie,
chirurgie dentaire à partir de la 2e année; (d) titulaires d'un
DUT, BTS, DEUG, DEUST; (d) titulaires (ou admissibilité à certaines
écoles d'ingénieurs), titulaires d'une maîtrise ou M.S. T pour
l'admission en 2e année; (e) titulaires d'un DEUG, DUT, (ou
admissibilité à certaines écoles d'ingénieurs), d'une maîtrise
pour l'admission en 2e année; (f) titulaires d'une 1re année
validée d'un DEUG de sciences, MIAS, M.A. SS ou SM, d'un
DEUG d'économie et de gestion, AES, d'une 1re année
validée d'un DUT/BTS informatique ou statistique, d'une 1re
année validée de CPGE, d'un DUT en informatique,
admission en 2e année pour les titulaires d'un DEUG sciences
MIAS, M.A. SS, SM, économie et gestion, AES, d'un DUT
statistique ou d'un DUT/BTS informatique; (g) titulaires d'un
DEUG, DUT, ou BTS; (h) sélection sur dossier universitaire
et épreuve de résumé de texte; (i) admission sur concours; (j)
titulaires d'un baccalauréat, ou sur examen d'entrée (1er cycle:
soumission à la demande d'admission préalable DAP; 2e et
3e cycles: admission après évaluation du dossier pédagogique
et reconnaissance des acquis).
Inscriptions: à l'adresse ci-dessus pour de plus amples
renseignements.

1047 Université de Rennes II, Haute Bretagne

Campus Villejean
Place du Recteur Henri Le Moal
CS 24 307
35043 Rennes Cedex
Tel: +33-2-9914-1000
Fax: +33-2-9914-1017
Web: http://www.uhb.fr
e-mail: webmaster@uhb.fr

📖 1er-3e cycles / Lettres, sciences sociales, sciences humaines

Domaines d'étude: archéologie, criminologie, études
internationales, français, histoire, langues, littérature et
civilisation, psychologie, sciences sociales.
Programmes: (a) programme d'études conduisant aux
diplômes suivants: DEUG, DEUST, Licence, Maîtrise, DESS,
DEA en langues et civilisations étrangères; (b) programme
d'études conduisant au diplôme supérieur d'études françaises
(DSEF), équivalent de la 1er année DEUG lettres modernes à
l'Université de Rennes II; (c) formation à distance débouchant
sur des diplômes universitaires d'étude du Service universitaire
d'Enseignement à Distance (SUED).
A l'intention de: ressortissants de tout pays, titulaires d'un
baccalauréat ou équivalent, test de langue (fin septembre).
Organisés: (b) au Centre international rennais d'étude du
français pour étrangers (CIREFE) http://www.uhb.fr/cirefe.
Assistance financière: possibilité de bourses d'études;
s'adresser à l'ambassade de France dans le pays d'origine du
candidat plusieurs mois à l'avance.
Inscriptions: du 15 au 30 septembre.

1048 Université de Rouen

1, rue Thomas-Becket
76821 Mont-Saint-Aignan Cedex
Tel: +33-2-3514-6000
Fax: +33-2-3514-6348
Web: http://www.univ-rouen.fr
e-mail: deve2@univ-rouen.fr

📖 1er-3e cycles / toutes disciplines

Domaines d'étude: toutes disciplines principales.
Programmes: Cours conduisant aux diplômes
universitaires de DEUG à Doctorat et agrégations.
A l'intention de: candidats de diverses nationalités,
titulaires du baccalauréat ou titre équivalent.
Frais: droits d'inscription et couverture sociale.
Inscriptions: avant début octobre à l'université.

🎓 Bourses de 3e cycle

Domaines d'étude: droit, médecine, pharmacie et pharmacologie, sciences, sciences économiques et commerciales, sciences humaines, sciences naturelles.
Bourses: Bourses d'accueil complémentaires pour chercheurs étrangers en stage dans les laboratoires de l'Université.
A l'intention de: chercheurs confirmés ou de niveau supérieur au 3ème cycle français (quelques années de recherche), ayant une bourse principale ou conservant leur salaire d'origine et séjournant en France pour au moins 2 mois.
Connaissances linguistiques: une bonne connaissance du français, ou en général de l'anglais, est souhaitable.
Candidatures: à l'Université, à l'adresse ci-dessus.

1049 Université de technologie de Compiègne [UTC]

Rue Roger Couttolenc
BP 60319
60203 Compiègne Cedex
Tel: +33-3-4423-4423
Fax: +33-3-4420-4813
Web: http://www.utc.fr
e-mail: rel-internationales@utc.fr

📖 Diplôme d'ingénieur, Master, Doctorat

Domaines d'étude: génie chimique, génie civil, informatique, ingénierie, mécanique.
Programmes: Diplôme d'ingénieur, de Master, de mastère spécialisé, doctorat.
Domaines d'études: génies biologique, chimique, informatique, mécanique, génie des systèmes mécaniques, génie des systèmes urbains.
A l'intention de: Admission en 1er cycle du diplôme d'ingénieur pour les titulaires d'un bac scientifique avec mention (ou équivalent). Admission en 2ème cycle du diplôme d'ingénieur pour les étudiants issus du 1er cycle de l'Université de Compiègne ou titulaires d'un DUT, d'un BTS ou d'un DEUG scientifique avec mention (ou équivalent bac +2). Admission en Master: étudiants de niveau bac+3 ou bac+4 ou équivalent. Admission en doctorat: titulaires d'un Master (ou équivalent). Pour les titulaires d'un diplôme étranger, nécessité de demander une équivalence pour l'admission à l'Université de Technologie de Compiègne. Admission sur titres, critères d'excellence, examen et entretien.
Durée: 1er cycle du cursus d'ingénieur: 2 ans (rentrée en septembre ou février); 2ème cycle du cursus d'ingénieur: 3 ans (rentrée en septembre ou février); Master: 2 ans (rentrée en septembre).
Frais: frais de scolarité 381 € par an, frais de dossier d'inscription 76 € (à joindre au dossier).
Assistance financière: bourses octroyées par les services scientifiques ou culturels des ambassades de France, les organismes internationaux de coopération. Possibilité de bourses attribuées sur critères sociaux pour les étudiants étrangers réfugiés politiques titulaires de la carte de réfugié politique ou dont les parents résident en France depuis plus de 2 ans.
Inscriptions: demande de dossier d'inscription: du 1er février au 15 avril pour la rentrée de septembre et du 1er octobre au 30 novembre pour la rentrée de février. Dépôt des dossiers avant le 15 mai pour la rentrée de septembre et avant le 15 décembre pour la rentrée de février; dossiers téléchargeables sur le site Internet de l'Université.
Renseignements Cycle ingénieur: admissions@utc.fr.
Renseignements 3ème cycle: ecole.doctorale@utc.fr.

1050 Université de technologie de Troyes [UTT]

12, rue Marie Curie
BP 2060
10000 Troyes
Tel: +33-3-2571-7600
Fax: +33-3-2571-7676
Web: http://www.utt.fr
e-mail: utt@utt.fr

📖 Diplôme d'ingénieur

Domaines d'étude: écologie, environnement, ingénierie, mécanique, optique.
Programmes: Diplôme d'ingénieur en génie des systèmes informatiques, génie des systèmes d'information, technologie et économie des matériaux; possibilité de DEA, DESS, DRT et Mastère en formation spécialisée.
A l'intention de: admission en 1er cycle du cursus du diplôme d'ingénieur: titulaires d'un Bac scientifique avec mention (ou diplôme étranger équivalent); admission en 1ère année de branche du deuxième cycle du cursus du diplôme d'ingénieur: titulaires d'un DEUG avec mention (ou équivalent), d'un DUT ou BTS (classement en tête de promotion), étudiants en classe préparatoire des grandes écoles ayant au moins une admissibilité aux concours communs des écoles polytechniques, Banque PT, ENSAM, etc.; admission en 3ème semestre de Branche du deuxième cycle du diplôme d'ingénieur: titulaires d'une Maîtrise avec mention (ou équivalent); admission sur dossier, critères d'excellence et entretien.
Durée: 5 ans (débutant en septembre ou février) pour le diplôme d'ingénieur; un an pour les autres diplômes.
Frais: frais universitaires: 379 €.
Connaissances linguistiques: bonne connaissance du français (cours de français intensif de 5 semaines avant chaque semestre + cours pendant le cursus); certains cours sont enseignés en anglais.
Inscriptions: remise des dossiers du 1er mars au 30 avril pour une rentrée en septembre et du 1er octobre au 30 novembre pour une rentrée en février; dossiers téléchargeables sur le site Internet (pour tout renseignement: service des admissions, BP 10501- 60205 Compiègne cedex, +33 3 44 23 43 55, service.admissions@utc.fr).

1051 Université de Toulouse-Le Mirail

Département universitaire d'études françaises pour étrangers
5, allée Antonio-Machado
31058 Toulouse Cedex
Tel: +33-5-6150-4250
Fax: +33-5-6150-4581
Web: http://www.univ-tlse2.fr/defle

📖 1er-3e cycles / langues, lettres, littérature

Domaines d'étude: français, langues, lettres, linguistique, littérature et civilisation.
Programmes: cours de langue, littérature et civilisation françaises, en vue de l'obtention du Certificat pratique de langue française niveau «moyen» en FLE; Diplôme d'enseignement du français niveau «avancé» en FLE; Diplôme supérieur d'enseignement du français: option littérature (équivalence 1re année DEUG lettres modernes); Diplôme supérieur d'enseignement du français aux étrangers: option didactique (équivalence partielle à la 1re année DEUG lettres modernes et au module didactique de la licence FLE de sciences du langage; Certificat pratique de français commercial et économique (délivré par la Chambre du commerce de Paris); DELF et DALF.
A l'intention de: ressortissants de tout pays, possédant déjà une bonne connaissance du français parlé et écrit, âgés de 17 ans minimum, et titulaires du baccalauréat français ou d'un diplôme étranger (original exigé) permettant l'accès dans une université étrangère; test d'entrée en octobre.
Durée: 1 an.
Connaissances linguistiques: langue d'enseignement: français.
Inscriptions: avant le 10 octobre.

1052 Université de Valenciennes et du Hainaut-Cambrésis

Le Mont Houy
BP 311
59304 Valenciennes Cedex
Tel: +33-3-2751-1234
Fax: +33-3-2751-1100
Web: http://www.univ-valenciennes.fr
e-mail: uvhc@univ-valenciennes.fr

📖 1er-3e cycles / toutes disciplines

Domaines d'étude: toutes disciplines principales.
Programmes: Programme de cours conduisant aux: (a) DEUG, DUT, licence, maîtrise, diplôme d'ingénieur et doctorat dans les domaines suivants: lettres, langues, arts et communications, commerce, gestion, comptabilité, droit, sciences humaines et économiques, mathématiques, maintenance, productique, automatique, électronique, informatique, techniques audiovisuelles, énergétique, matériaux nouveaux, construction, multimédia, histoire et sport; (b) Diplôme européen de management international (DEMI, niveau Bac+3), basé sur la formation des cadres internationaux pour la gestion des entreprises industrielles, commerciales et des collectivités publiques; transfert des unités de valeurs: système ECTS; (c) Diplôme international en commerce et communication (DICC), formation des cadres commerciaux internationaux, spécialisés dans la mercatique et la communication, par intégration dans une structure universitaire d'accueil à l'étranger pour une durée d'1 an; (d) Diplôme européen d'études technologiques (DEET) en ingénierie des systèmes automatiques et en production mécanique, basé sur 600 heures durant 1 an dans une université partenaire.
A l'intention de: ressortissants de tout pays, titulaires de: (b) et (c) DUT ou BTS tertiaire; (d) DUT ou BTS secondaire; admission sur dossier, tests de langue et entretien.
Organisés: (b) en Europe; (c) en Allemagne, Finlande, Portugal, Grèce, Suède, Irlande, et Royaume-Uni.
Assistance financière: possibilité de bourses Socrates, Leonardo et de bourses régionales.
Inscriptions: (a) avant le 15 juillet; (b), (c) et (d) avant le 10 juin, au Secrétariat DEMI, DICC ou DEET; à l'adresse ci-dessus.

1053   Université des Antilles et de la Guyane en Guadeloupe

BP 250
Campus de la Fouillole
97157 Pointe-à-Pitre, Guadeloupe
Tel: +33-5-9093-8600
Fax: +33-5-9091-0657
Web: http://www.univ-ag.fr

📖 1er-3e cycles / sciences économiques, médecine, sciences naturelles

Domaines d'étude: affaires internationales, droit, éducation physique, médecine, sciences économiques et commerciales, sciences naturelles.
Programmes: Programme d'études du 1er, 2e et 3e cycles en sciences exactes et naturelles, sciences juridiques et économiques, médecine, et sciences et techniques des activités physiques et sportives (STAPS); service d'éducation permanente et de formation continue.
A l'intention de: ressortissants de tout pays, titulaires du baccalauréat ou diplôme équivalent; la formation continue est réservée aux étudiants français et limitée à 300 étrangers.
Organisés: Campus de la Fouillole sauf pour médecine à l'adresse ci-dessus.
Assistance financière: possibilité de bourses.
Inscriptions: variable; contacter l'Université pour de plus amples informations.

1054   Université des Antilles et de la Guyane en Guyane

Campus Saint-Denis
BP 1179
97346 Cayenne, Guyane
Tel: +33-5-9425-2155
Fax: +33-5-9430-9668
Web: http://www.guyane.univ-ag.fr
e-mail: nicole.clementmartin@guyane.univ-ag.fr

📖 1er, 2e cycles / administration, droit, ingénierie

Domaines d'étude: administration, droit, économie, électricité et électronique, informatique, mécanique, technologie industrielle.
Programmes: Programme de cours de 1er et 2e cycle: à l'Institut d'études supérieures de Cayenne: DEUG en administration économique et social; lettres et langues; sciences et technologies; droit; lettres modernes; anglais; sciences et technologies; Licence d'ingénierie électrique; technologie mécanique; Licence professionnelle en

génie civil et bâtiment en zone intertropicale; Licence pluridisciplinaire en lettres, arts et sciences humaines; Maîtrise EEA mention automatique et informatique industrielle; techno-mécanique mention productique; à l'Institut universitaire de technologie de Kourou: DUT Gestion Logistique et transportation; DUT Génie électrique et informatique industrielle.
A l'intention de: ressortissants de tout pays remplissant les conditions requises.
Inscriptions: Pour Institut d'études supérieures de Cayenne: Campus Saint-Denis; Avenue d'Estrée, BP 792, 97337 Cayenne; tél: +33-5-9429-6200; fax: +33-5-9429-6210; contact: charge.communication@guyane.univ-ag.fr. Pour l'Institut universitaire de technologie de Kourou: Avenue du Bois-de-Chaudat, 97351 Kourou Cedex; tél: +33-5-9432-8000.

1055   Université des Antilles et de la Guyane en Martinique [UAG]

Campus de Schoelcher
97275 Schoelcher Cedex, Martinique
Tel: +33-5-9672-7300
Fax: +33-5-9091-0657
Web: http://www.martinique.univ-ag.fr
e-mail: lettres@martinique.univ-ag.fr

📖 1er-3e cycles / lettres, sciences économiques

Domaines d'étude: droit, lettres, sciences économiques et commerciales, sciences humaines.
Programmes: Programme d'études de 1er, 2e et 3e cycle: (a) en lettres et sciences humaines; (b) en droit et sciences économiques.
A l'intention de: candidats remplissant les conditions requises.
Inscriptions: (a) à la Faculté des lettres et des sciences humaines, BP 7207, à l'adresse ci-dessus; (b) à la Faculté de droit et d'économie, BP 7209, à l'adresse ci-dessus.

1056   Université des sciences sociales

Place Anatole France
31000 Toulouse
Tel: +33-5-6163-3500
Fax: +33-5-6163-3798
Web: http://www.univ-tlse1.fr

📖 1er-3e cycles / sciences sociales et administratives

Domaines d'étude: administration, commerce, droit, économie, gestion, informatique.
Programmes: programme de cours conduisant aux diplômes de DEUG à Doctorat.
A l'intention de: ressortissants de tout pays; le titulaire d'un diplôme étranger doit obtenir une autorisation individuelle d'admission et rejoindre l'établissement aux dates indiquées, muni d'un visa de long séjour (sauf pour les ressortissants de l'Union européenne) et des attestations originales d'études, pour effectuer les formalités définitives d'inscription; l'université participe aux programmes Socrates (Europe) et Crepuq (Canada) et développe des programmes de coopération et d'échange avec des universités en Amérique Latine, aux États-Unis et au Japon.
Autres conditions: pour certaines formations, des épreuves de sélection doivent être subies dans l'université; c'est le cas des enseignements rattachés à l'École supérieure universitaire de gestion (ESUG).
Connaissances linguistiques: un test de langue est organisé en février pour les candidats non francophones (épreuve corrigée par l'université); quelques programmes sont enseignés partiellement ou totalement en anglais.
Inscriptions: 1er cycle: la demande doit être effectuée avant le 15 janvier qui précède la rentrée d'octobre dans le service culturel français implanté dans le pays de résidence; 2ème et 3ème cycles: la demande doit être parvenue avant fin mars pour les diplômes de gestion, avant fin avril pour la MIAGE, et avant fin mai dans les autres cas; les formulaires de demande d'admission en 2ème et 3ème cycles peuvent être téléchargés sur le site Internet de l'université (renseignements auprès de Marie-Noële Bonnes, vice-présidente des relations internationales, coordonnées ci-dessus).

1057 Université du droit et de la santé, Lille II
42, rue Paul-Duez
59800 Lille
Tel: +33-3-2096-4343
Fax: +33-3-2088-2432
Web: http://www.univ-lille2.fr

📖 1er-3e cycle / toutes disciplines

Domaines d'étude: affaires, bâtiment, construction, criminologie, droit, éducation physique, études dentaires, médecine, pharmacie et pharmacologie, sciences politiques, sciences sociales, urbanisme.
Programmes: Cours conduisant aux diplômes d'université ou aux diplômes nationaux du 1er au 3e cycles:
(a) 5 Unités de formation et de recherche (UFR): médecine; sciences pharmaceutiques et biologiques; odontologie; sciences juridiques, politiques et sociales; sciences du sport et de l'éducation physique; (b) 10 instituts: études judiciaires; criminologie; préparation à l'administration générale; sciences et travail; construction, environnement, et urbanisme; école supérieure des affaires; institut d'orthophonie; médecine légale; chimie pharmaceutique; études politiques; (c) 3 Instituts universitaires personnalisés (IUP): banque et assurance; management de la distribution; ingénierie de la santé; (d) 1 Institut universitaire de technologie (IUT).
A l'intention de: ressortissants de tout pays, titulaires du baccalauréat ou diplôme équivalent.
Assistance financière: bourses de l'enseignement supérieur.
Connaissances linguistiques: français obligatoire.
Inscriptions: les formulaires de demande d'admission sont à retirer, entre le 15 novembre et le 15 janvier, à l'Université ou auprès des services culturels de l'ambassade de France du pays d'origine.

1058 Université du Havre
25, rue Philippe-Lebon
BP 1123
76063 Le Havre Cedex
Tel: +33-2-3271-4000
Fax: +33-2-3521-4959
Web: http://www.univ-lehavre.fr

📖 1er-3e cycles / droit international, science, technologie

Domaines d'étude: affaires internationales, droit international, finances, sciences, technologie.
Programmes: Cours conduisant aux diplômes du 1er au 3e cycles à: (a) la Faculté des sciences et techniques; également formation continue: nouvelle filière d'ingénieurs NFI; CAPES en physique et électricité; CAPET option: technologie-génies mécaniques et électriques; agrégation de physique appliquée; (b) la Faculté des affaires internationales; préparation à l'UIP (commerce et vente), capacité en droit ou en gestion, diplôme universitaire de langues et études supérieures en commerce internationale, DULCO (Diplôme universitaire de 1er cycle de langues et civilisations orientales); (c) l'École d'ingénieurs, Institut supérieur d'études logistiques (ISEL), conduisant au diplôme d'ingénieur; (d) l'Institut universitaire de technologie (IUT), conduisant au DUT de gestion des entreprises et des administrations (options finances, comptabilité, ressources humaines; gestion appliquée aux petites et moyennes organisations) et des formations post- DUT.
A l'intention de: ressortissants de tout pays, titulaires d'un baccalauréat pour DEUG, IUT ou DUT; d'un DEUG pour la licence et la maîtrise; d'un Bac+2 pour M.S.T. (Maîtrise en sciences et technologies); d'un Bac+4 pour DESS et DEA ou tout titre étranger équivalent; sélection sur dossier puis concours.
Durée: 1 an (licence, maîtrise, DESS, DEA); 2 ans (DEUG, DUT, M.S.T.); 3 ans (IUP); 5 ans (diplôme d'ingénieur).
Connaissances linguistiques: langue obligatoire: anglais.
Inscriptions: avant le 15 octobre auprès de la Scolarité centrale à l'adresse ci-dessus; (a) dossier à retirer à partir du 15 mai et à renvoyer avant le 28 juin; au-delà, il ne sera examiné qu'en septembre en fonction des places disponibles.

1059 Université du Maine
Relations Internationales
Avenue Olivier Messiaen
72085 Le Mans Cedex
Tel: +33-2-4383-3005
Fax: +33-2-4383-3530
Web: http://www.univ-lemans.fr

📖 1er-3e cycles / toutes disciplines

Domaines d'étude: droit, français, ingénierie, langues, lettres, littérature et civilisation, sciences économiques et commerciales, sciences humaines, techniques de laboratoires, technologie.
Programmes: programme pluridisciplinaire conduisant aux diplômes de 1er, 2e et 3e cycle aux unités de formation et de recherche (UFR) suivantes: UFR Lettres, langues et sciences humaines: http://lettres.univ-lemans.fr/ufrlettres/homepage.cfm; UFR Droit et sciences économiques: http://ecodroit.univ-lemans.fr; UFR Sciences et techniques: http://sciences.univ-lemans.fr; École nationale supérieure d'ingénieur du Mans: http://ensim.univ-lemans.fr; Instituts universitaires de technologie: http://iut.univ-lemans.fr; UFR Sciences et techniques: http://www.iut-laval.univ-lemans.fr; et au Centre international d'études françaises (CIEF); cours diplômant à distance en droit et sciences économiques; lettres et sciences humaines; sciences et techniques.
A l'intention de: ressortissants de tout pays.
Inscriptions: 1er cycle: Demande d'admission préalable à l'inscription à retirer entre le 1er décembre et le 15 janvier de l'année précédent la rentrée: aux services culturels de l'ambassade de France du pays d'origine ou au Service des Études et de la Vie Universitaire à l'adresse ci-dessus; 2e et 3e cycles: se procurer un dossier de candidature auprès du Service Scolarité de l'U.F.R. correspondant aux études envisagées.

1060 Université Henry Poincaré Nancy I, École de santé publique
Faculté de médecine
9, avenue de la forêt de Haye
BP 184
54505 Vandoeuvre lès Nancy
Tel: +33-3-8368-3510
Fax: +33-3-8368-3519
Web: http://www.sante-pub.u-nancy.fr
e-mail: esp@sante-pub.u-nancy.fr

📖 Médecine sociale

Domaines d'étude: hygiène et santé, médecine.
Programmes: programme d'études en médecine sociale conduisant aux: (a) santé publique; licence de sciences sanitaires et sociales: certificat d'aptitude au professorat de lycée professionnel en «sciences et techniques médico-sociales»; (b) diplômes professionnalisés: maîtrise de sciences sanitaires et sociales mention «Santé Publique»: certificat d'aptitude au professorat de l'enseignement technique de «sciences et techniques médico-sociales»; diplôme inter-universitaire «Qualité - Accréditation - Évaluation» des établissements sanitaires et sociaux; D.E.S.S. promotion de la santé et développement social; (c) diplômes de formation à la recherche: maîtrise de sciences biologiques et médicales; diplôme inter-universitaire de formation à la recherche clinique et épidémiologique; DEA «épidémiologique clinique et évaluation des actions de santé»; (d) Doctorat de l'Université Nancy 1 «épidémiologie - santé publique»; diplômes du département «Environnement et santé publique»; diplôme universitaire de prévention de l'infection nosocomiale; diplôme inter universitaire d'hygiène hospitalière; diplôme d'université «eau et santé»; (e) cours diplômant à distance par Internet.
A l'intention de: ressortissants de tout pays titulaires des diplômes requis.
Inscriptions: contacter l'Université à l'adresse ci-dessus.

1061 Université Louis Pasteur, Strasbourg I Faculté de médecine
4, rue Blaise Pascal
67085 Strasbourg Cedex
Tel: +33-3-9024-5000
Fax: +33-3-9024-5001
Web: http://www-ulp.u-strasbg.fr

1er-3e cycles / médecine, sciences sociales, sciences humaines
Domaines d'étude: ingénierie, médecine, sciences, sciences humaines, sciences sociales, technologie.
Programmes: programmes de cours conduisant aux diplômes d'État du 1er au 3e cycle universitaire dans les secteurs de la santé et des sciences exactes, humaines et sociales. De nombreuses formations permettent aux étudiants de faire des stages en entreprise; diplômes du secteur santé; diplômes d'ingénieur.
A l'intention de: ressortissants de tout pays titulaires d'un baccalauréat.
Inscriptions: étudiants étrangers: le retrait du dossier de demande d'admission préalable est à effectuer auprès du service culturel de l'ambassade de France.

1062 Université Lyon II
16, quai Claude-Bernard
69365 Lyon Cedex 07
Tel: +33-4-7869-7000
Fax: +33-4-7877-2323
Web: http://www.univ-lyon2.fr

1er-3e cycles / droit, économie, lettres
Domaines d'étude: arts, droit, économie, français, gestion, langues, lettres, littérature et civilisation, psychologie, sciences humaines.
Programmes: programmes de cours pluridisciplinaires: dès la rentrée 2003 les parcours de licence s'inscrivent dans le cadre de l'espace européen de l'enseignement supérieur (Licence - Master - Doctorat); ces parcours sont accessibles en formation post-baccalauréat.
A l'intention de: ressortissants de tout pays, âgés de 18 ans au moins, et possédant le niveau du baccalauréat ou titre équivalent.
Assistance financière: possibilité de bourses attribuées sur critères sociaux pour les étudiants étrangers réfugiés politiques titulaires de la carte de réfugié politique ou dont le parents résident en France depuis plus de 2 ans.
Inscriptions: auprès du service culturel de l'ambassade du pays d'origine pour se procurer le dossier d'admission préalable en premier cycle universitaire et l'organisation des épreuves du test de français. Ces dossiers sont accessible sur le site http://www.education.gouv.fr/int/etudfr.htm#4.

1063 Université Michel de Montaigne Bordeaux III
Domaine universitaire
33607 Pessac Cedex
Tel: +33-5-5712-4444
Fax: +33-5-5712-4490
Web: http://www.u-bordeaux3.fr/
e-mail: relations.internationales@u-bordeaux3.fr

1er-3e cycles / communication
Domaines d'étude: bibliothéconomie, communication, développement et production de livres, industrie et commerce, journalisme, publicité, relations industrielles.
Programmes: formations diplômantes en édition, publicité; information et documentation d'entreprise; gestion du développement et de l'action humanitaire; service et réseaux de communication; animation sociale et socioculturelle; bibliothèques/médiathèques; communication d'entreprise; journalisme.
A l'intention de: ressortissants de tous pays, titulaires de baccalauréat ou équivalent.
Durée: variable.
Inscriptions: 1er cycle: s'informer à l'établissement scolaire fréquenté ou à l'ambassade de France du pays d'origine pour "dossier bleu" d'inscription.

3e cycle / physique appliquée à l'archéologie
Domaines d'étude: archéologie, études américaines, histoire, muséologie et muséographie, physique.
Programmes: DEA, DESS en méthodes physiques appliquées à l'archéologie et muséographie (datation, caractérisation, paléoclimatologie, géoscience et patrimoine monumental, ethno-archéologie des cultures amérindiennes, restauration, conservation, prospection).
A l'intention de: ressortissants de tout pays, titulaires d'une maîtrise en sciences physiques, chimie, géologie, histoire et histoire de l'art; expérience des fouilles, stages en musée; français obligatoire (test de vérification); sélection sur dossier.
Durée: 1 an.
Assistance financière: sur dossier universitaire et critères sociaux.
Inscriptions: contacter: crpaa@montaigne.u-bordeaux.fr; Internet: http://www-crpaa.montaigne.u-bordeaux.fr.

1064 Université Nancy II, Centre européen universitaire [CEU]
15, place Carnot
BP 4219
54042 Nancy Cedex
Tel: +33-3-8319-2784
Fax: +33-3-8319-2787
Web: http://www.univ-nancy2.fr

3e cycle / études européennes
Domaines d'étude: droit, droit international, études européennes, finances, gestion, sciences économiques et commerciales, sciences politiques.
Programmes: programme de cours conduisant aux (a) diplômes du département «Sciences Juridiques et Politiques»; diplôme d'études supérieures européennes (DESE) (3e cycle); diplôme d'études approfondies droit communautaire (DEA-MASTAIRE), 3e cycle; diplôme d'études supérieures spécialisées collectivités territoriales et Union Européenne (DESS-MASTAIRE); (b) diplômes du département «Sciences Économiques et Gestion»; diplôme d'études supérieures spécialisées gestion financière et espace Européen (DESS-MASTAIRE); (c) diplômes du département «Étude des Civilisations»: diplôme d'études supérieures européennes (DESE); diplôme d'études supérieures spécialisées communication stratégique et relations publiques en Europe (DESS-MASTAIRE).
A l'intention de: ressortissants de tout pays, titulaires d'une maîtrise ou niveau équivalent.
Connaissances linguistiques: français exigé.
Inscriptions: s'adresser au Centre à l'adresse ci-dessus.

1065 Université Panthéon-Assas Paris II, Institut de droit comparé [IDC]
28, rue Saint-Guillaume
75007 Paris
Tel: +33-1-4439-8613
Fax: +33-1-4439-8655
Web: http://www.u-paris2.fr
e-mail: lvogel@u-paris2.fr

Droit comparé
Domaines d'étude: droit.
Programmes: (a) cours de droit comparé (différents sujets) sanctionnés par un DEA de droit comparé; (b) cours de terminologie juridique, sanctionnés par le brevet de terminologie juridique.
A l'intention de: ressortissants de tout pays, inscrits en: (a) maîtrise de droit ou équivalent (autorisation exceptionnelle pour les étudiants inscrits en licence en droit, durée des études: 2 ans); (b) étudiants titulaires d'une capacité en droit ou DEUG juridique ou tout titre jugé équivalent. Accueil des étudiants handicapés. L'inscription ne donne pas le statut d'étudiant; les étudiants ne peuvent s'inscrire plus de 2 années universitaires sans avoir réussi les examens.
Durée: 1 an.
Assistance financière: possibilité d'aides, sur justification.
Connaissances linguistiques: langues d'enseignement: anglais, allemand, italien, espagnol ou russe.
Inscriptions: entre le 1er septembre et le 15 octobre auprès du Secrétariat de l'Institut à l'adresse ci-dessus.

1066 Université Panthéon-Assas Paris II, Institut français de presse [IFP]
92, rue d'Assas
75270 Paris Cedex 06
Tel: +33-1-4441-5793
Fax: +33-1-4441-5949
Web: http://www.u-paris2.fr

📖 2e et 3e cycle / communication, journalisme

Domaines d'étude: communication, journalisme, moyens audio-visuels, télécommunications.
Programmes: (a) cours du 2e cycle, licence et maîtrise en «information et communication», préparant au diplôme de l'IFP; (b) Cours de 3e cycle préparant au DESS « techniques de l'information et du journalisme», aux DEA «médias et multimédia» et «droit de la communication»; (c) École doctorale préparant aux thèses en «information et communication».
A l'intention de: ressortissants de tout pays, titulaires des diplômes suivants ou titres admis en équivalence: (a) DEUG, DEUST ou BTS communication-actions publicitaires; (b) maîtrise spécialisée en information et communication; pour le DESS, la parfaite connaissance d'une langue étrangère est exigée; (c) DEA; français obligatoire.
Durée: (a) 2 ans; (b) 1 an (d'octobre à octobre); (c) thèse: de 2 à 3 ans après obtention du DEA.
Inscriptions: pour les étudiants titulaires de diplômes étrangers: autorisation d'inscription donnée après examen du dossier; de février à mai pour les titulaires de diplômes français: test du 5 mai au 20 juin; retrait des dossiers de candidature en 2e cycle: pour les titulaires de diplômes étrangers, de février à mai; pour les titulaires de diplômes français, du 15 juin au 25 juillet.

1067 Université Paris-Dauphine Paris IX - Département d'éducation permanente
Place du Maréchal-de-Lattre-de-Tassigny
75775 Paris Cedex 16
Tel: +33-1-4405-4405
Fax: +33-1-4405-4949
Web: http://www.dauphine.fr

📖 Formation en éducation permanente

Domaines d'étude: éducation, éducation permanente, formation professionnelle.
Programmes: diplôme universitaire de formateurs d'adultes en sciences de l'éducation et gestion des ressources humaines, mention «expert européen en formation», (orientation: pays d'Europe Centrale et Orientale), formation alternant des séminaires théoriques, des stages pratiques en entreprise, et un séminaire d'analyse pratique.
A l'intention de: ressortissants de l'Union européenne, âgés de 27 à 40 ans, titulaires d'un diplôme de 2e cycle (Bac+3); admission sur entretien, tests de capacités intellectuelles et mémoire de 10 pages.
Durée: 8 mois (débutant en octobre).
Connaissances linguistiques: connaissance du français et de l'anglais requise.
Inscriptions: avant le 10 septembre; écrire à l'adresse ci-dessus pour de plus amples renseignements.

1068 Université Paul Valéry Institut d'études françaises pour étudiants et professeurs étrangers [IEFE]
Route de Mende
BP 5043
34199 Montpellier Cedex 3
Tel: +33-4-6714-2101
Web: http://www.univ-montp3.fr

📖 Français langue étrangère

Domaines d'étude: français, linguistique, littérature et civilisation.
Programmes: (a) formation et/ou recyclage de professeurs de français étrangers, conduisant à la préparation du Diplôme d'aptitude à l'enseignement du français langue étrangère (FLE); un certificat universitaire est délivré aux stagiaires assistant aux cours pendant moins un an; les stagiaires traitent des questions de didactique, de méthodologie, de civilisation, de langue et culture françaises (18 heures par semaine) des activités de terrain, théâtre, cinéma complètent ce programme; (b) programme de langue et civilisation françaises, conduisant au Certificat pratique de langue française (1er degré niveau 3), au Diplôme d'études françaises (2e degré niveau 4), au Diplôme supérieur d'études françaises et Diplôme spécial d'études françaises (3e degré niveau 5).
A l'intention de: (a) stagiaires de tout pays, enseignants ou futurs professeurs de français, titulaires du baccalauréat au minimum (2 ans d'études supérieures sont conseillées) et éventuellement d'une
expérience professionnelle; (b) âgés de 18 ans, titulaires du diplôme de fin d'études secondaires, admission sur tests (5 niveaux).
Durée: (a) 1 année universitaire ou stage de courte durée à la demande pour les groupes; (b): 4 mois d'octobre à janvier et de février à juin; cours d'été: 1 mois (juillet, août ou septembre).
Inscriptions: (a) avant septembre; (b) cours semestriels du 12 juillet au 19 décembre; cours d'été: 15 jours avant le début de la session à l'adresse ci-dessus; pour de plus amples renseignements: email; iefe@univ-montp3.fr; site web: http://iefe.univ-montp3.fr.

1069 Université Paul Verlaine-Metz I
Ile du saulcy
BP 80794
57012 Metz cedex 1
Web: http://www.univ-metz.fr

📖 1er, 2e cycles

Domaines d'étude: arts, gestion, histoire de l'art, langues, lettres, littérature et civilisation, sciences, technologie.
Programmes: Programmes en droit, économie, gestion, lettres et langues, sciences et technologies, sciences humaines, arts et culture.
Inscriptions: UFR Sciences humaines et arts: http://www.sha.univ-metz.fr/contact/index.php; UFR Lettres et langues: fdurand@zeus.univ-metz.fr; UFR Droit, économie et administration: UFR ESM études supérieures de management: accueil@esm.univ-metz.fr; UFR SciFA sciences fondamentales et appliquées: http://www.scifa.univ-metz.fr/contact/ecrire.html; UFR MIM mathématique, informatique, mécanique: scolmim@sciences.univ-metz.fr; IUT institut universitaire de technologie de Metz: service.scolarite@iut.univ-metz.fr; IUT institut universitaire de technologie de Thionville-Yutz:service.scolarite@iut.univ-metz.fr; ISFATES institut supérieur franco-allemand de techniques, d'économie et de science: isfates@univ-metz.fr.

1070 Université Pierre et Marie Curie Paris VI Institut de stomatologie, chirurgie plastique et chirurgie maxillo-faciale
47, boulevard de l'Hôpital
75651 Paris Cedex 13
Tel: +331-4216-1283
Web: http://www.upmc.fr

📖 1er-3e cycle / stomatologie

Domaines d'étude: études dentaires, stomatologie.
Programmes: programme de cours dans le domaine de la stomatologie, préparant au diplôme d'université: (a) d'études spécialisées; (b) DIS de stomatologie; (c) d'orthodontie pédiatrique; (d) d'orthopédie dento-maxillo-faciale appliquée; (e) de parodontologie clinique et d'hygiène bucco-dentaire appliquée; (f) de réhabilitation et prothèse maxillo-faciales; (g) d'implantologie; (h) de prothèse fixée; (i) de prothèse faciale appliquée; (j) Diplôme inter-universitaire de pathologie de la muqueuse buccale; (k) stages de perfectionnement en pathologie buccale, dentisterie restauratrice, implantologie, orthopédie dento-maxillo-faciale et stomatologie pédiatrique, parodontologie, prothèse adjointe, prothèse conjointe, prothèse maxillo-faciale; possibilité de préparer un mémoire d'assistant pour les candidats hors Union européenne (UE); (l)

de carcinologie buccale; (m) de pathologie et thérapeutique chirurgicale du cuir chevelu; (n) de prothèse adjointe; (o) d'urgences en pathologie bucco-dentaire; (p) certificat d'études supérieures d'odontologie chirurgicale; (q) certificat d'études supérieures d'odontologie légale.
A l'intention de: (a) ressortissants des États membres de l'UE (admission sur concours); (b) ressortissants hors UE titulaires d'un diplôme de médecin non obtenu en France; (f) titulaires d'un diplôme ORL ou d'ophtalmologie et étudiants ayant validé 4 semestres d'un DES ou DIS d'ORL ou d'ophtalmologie; (i) médecins spécialistes en stomatologie ou en chirurgie maxillo-faciale ou titulaires d'un DIS dans ces spécialités, d'un CAP, d'une maîtrise de prothèse dentaire, ou personnes pouvant justifier de 5 années d'activité professionnelle dans un laboratoire de prothèse dentaire; (j) internes de spécialité (DES et DESC); (k) médecins stomatologistes et chirurgiens-dentistes étrangers uniquement sur demande officielle du ministère de tutelle du pays concerné ou du Doyen de la faculté d'origine; (l) résidents et internes de la filière médecine spécialisée, étudiants ayant validés le D.C.EM 4 et le certificat de synthèse clinique et thérapeutique; (m) spécialistes en dermatologie, vénérologie, chirurgie maxillofaciale, plastique, reconstructive et esthétique; (o) internes en odontologie ayant validé les 2 premiers semestres d'internat.
Durée: (a) 11 mois; (b) 4 ans (examens fin de 1re et de 4e année); (d) 2 ans, débutant fin octobre; (c) 2 ans; (e) 2 ans; (f) et (g) 1 an; (h) 2 ans; (m) 1 an et (n) 1 an; débutant mi-octobre; (i) 1 an; (j) 2 ans (enseignement réparti en 4 modules à raison de 2 par an); (k) 1 an minimum; (l) 2 ans; (o) 1 an (débutant en novembre); (q) 1 an (débutant en janvier).
Inscriptions: contacter l'UFR de Stomatologie et de chirurgie maxillo-faciale pour de plus amples renseignements.

1071 Université René Descartes Paris V

12, rue de l'École de Médécine
75006 Paris
Tel: +33-1-4046-1616
Fax: +33-1-4046-1615
Web: http://www.univ-paris5.fr
e-mail: secretariat.general@univ-paris5.fr

1er-3e cycle / toutes disciplines

Domaines d'étude: toutes disciplines principales.
Programmes: programmes de cours conduisant aux diplômes d'état du 1er au 3ème cycle universitaire dans toutes les disciplines principales.
A l'intention de: ressortissants de tout pays, titulaires du Baccalauréat (ou équivalent) ou d'un diplôme de l'enseignement supérieur (ou équivalent); certaines admissions peuvent être soumises à un examen de contrôle des connaissances complémentaires, qui peut avoir lieu dès le mois de juin (prendre contact avec les services de scolarité le plus tôt possible et au plus tard fin avril); admission sur dossier et entretien pour le 3ème cycle; admission sur concours pour le 3ème cycle de médecine (pour les modalités du concours se renseigner auprès du Centre national des concours de l'internat, Centre universitaire des Saints-Pères, 45, rue des Saints-Pères; 75270 Paris Cedex 06 tél: +33-1-4450-2671/76; fax: +33-1-4450-2670.
Frais: frais de séjour: environ 705 € par mois.
Connaissances linguistiques: test de français pour les étudiants étrangers hors programme d'échange sauf pour les ressortissants des États où le français est langue officielle, ceux des États où les épreuves des diplômes de fin d'études secondaires se déroulent en majeure partie en français, ainsi que les titulaires du diplôme approfondi de langue française.
Inscriptions: inscription en 1er cycle: dossier de demande d'admission à retirer entre le 1er décembre et le 15 janvier de l'année précédant l'année d'inscription auprès des services culturels français (ambassade, consulat) du pays d'origine ou de résidence, ou bien au bureau des étudiants étrangers du Service de la scolarité et des études de l'université pour les personnes domiciliées en France et titulaires d'un titre de séjour d'une durée de validité minimum d'un an; date limite de dépôt du dossier: le 31 janvier à la Division de la scolarité et des études; pour les ressortissants allemands, titulaire de l'«Abitur» (Hochschulreife) et candidats à une inscription en sciences humaines, droit ou sciences, possibilité de solliciter une inscription directe à l'université (excepté en médecine, odontologie et pharmacie, disciplines pour lesquelles

l'admission préalable reste obligatoire); inscription en 2ème cycle: retirer un dossier de demande de validation d'acquis auprès du service de scolarité de la faculté ou de l'Unité de Formation et de Recherche (UFR) de la discipline envisagée; réponse par courrier après examen du dossier par une commission; les dossiers sont à déposer avant 1er octobre de l'année en cours; inscription en 3ème cycle: même procédure que pour le 2ème cycle; dossiers à remettre avant le 1er octobre de l'année en cours pour les sciences et le droit et avant le 30 novembre de l'année en cours pour les sciences humaines; inscription en médecine ou odontologie: demande et dépôt des dossiers directement auprès du S.A.D.E.P. (Service d'affectation des étudiants en PCEM/1) 1, rue Victor-Cousin (Sorbonne, Galerie Claude Bernard, Escalier R, 75005 Paris); pour tout renseignement complémentaire contacter la division des études et de la vie universitaire 12, rue de l'École de Médecine, 75270 Paris Cedex 06; tél: +33 1 4046 1750 ou le service des étudiants étrangers; tél: +33 1 4046 1705.

1072 Université Robert Schuman Strasbourg III - Centre universitaire d'enseignement du journalisme [CUEJ]

11, rue du Maréchal-Juin
BP 13
67043 Strasbourg Cedex
Tel: +33-3-8814-4534
Fax: +33-3-8814-4535
Web: http://cuej.u-strasbg.fr
e-mail: admin@cuej.u-strasbg.fr

2e cycle / journalisme

Domaines d'étude: communication, journalisme, sciences de l'information.
Programmes: cours dans le domaine du journalisme conduisant aux diplômes suivants: (a) M.S.T.: Maîtrise en sciences et technique, option journalisme (presse écrite, radio, télévision); (b) DESS sciences de l'information et de la communication, option gestion technologique de l'information; domaines d'étude: recherche de l'information (techniques documentaires, bases de données, réseaux), technologies, outils techniques (infographie, PAO, vidéographie, montage vidéo, multimédia), production de l'information (projets éditoriaux, architecture des supports, réalisation de supports d'information); (c) Journaliste-reporter d'images dans le cadre de la formation continue; (d) DESS journaliste spécialisé dans les affaires européennes (Eurojournalisme).
A l'intention de: ressortissants de tout pays, titulaires: (a) d'un DEUG ou diplôme admis en équivalence; (b) du diplôme d'une école de journalisme de niveau Bac+4 ou justifiant d'au moins 2 ans d'expérience professionnelle dans le secteur information-communication; (c) journalistes professionnels; (d) d'un diplôme d'une école de journalisme, ou par dérogation, justifiant d'un minimum de 3 ans d'expérience professionnelle, maîtrisant 2 langues outre leur langue maternelle.
Durée: (a) 2 ans; (b) 1 an (débutant en novembre); (c) 17 semaines; (d) 1 an.
Assistance financière: (a) des bourses peuvent être accordées par les instances gouvernementales ou le service culturel de l'ambassade de France dans le pays d'origine du candidat.
Inscriptions: consulter le Centre pour de plus amples renseignements.

1073 Université Robert Schuman Strasbourg III - Institut des hautes études européennes [IHEE]

10 rue Schiller
67081 Strasbourg Cedex
Tel: +33-3-8815-0545
Fax: +33-3-8836-8611
Web: http://www-ihee.u-strasbg.fr
e-mail: ihee@urs.u-strasbg.fr

📖 Études européennes

Domaines d'étude: droit international, études européennes, études internationales.
Programmes: (a) cours dans les domaines suivants: histoire de l'Europe, économie européenne, droit des institutions européennes, vie politique en Europe, cycles spécialisés conduisant au Certificat
d'études européennes; (b) cycles spécialisés d'études historiques et politiques; (c) cours d'histoire de l'Europe au XXe siècle constitue la 1re année d'un 3e cycle axé principalement sur l'histoire des relations internationales contemporaines, conduisant au DEA; (d) cours de droit comparé des droits de l'homme, conduisant au DEA; (e) préparation aux concours des communautés européennes.
A l'intention de: ressortissants de tous pays, titulaires d'une licence ou diplôme équivalent (3 années d'études supérieures); (c) admission sur titres: maîtrise ou équivalent plus entretien; (d) titulaires d'une maîtrise en droit ou équivalent et sélection sur dossier; (e) les étudiants inscrits en maîtrise (Bac + 4) ou diplômés de sciences politiques.
Durée: 1 année universitaire (débutant mi-octobre).
Assistance financière: possibilité de bourse.
Connaissances linguistiques: français obligatoire.
Inscriptions: contacter l'Institut pour de plus amples renseignements.

1074 Université Robert Schuman Strasbourg III - Institut d'administration des entreprises
47, avenue de la Forêt-Noire
67082 Strasbourg Cedex
Tel: +33-8-8841-7785
Web: http://www-urs.u-strasbg.fr

📖 Gestion des entreprises

Domaines d'étude: gestion.
Programmes: cours de gestion des entreprises conduisant au: (a) Certificat d'aptitude à l'administration des entreprises (CAAE); (b) DESS Gestion du personnel; (c) DESS de stratégie et gestion des PME.
A l'intention de: ressortissants de tout pays, sans limite d'âge; (b) titulaires d'une maîtrise ou d'un diplôme équivalent et justifiant d'1 ou 5 ans (pour les salariés) d'expérience professionnelle; (c) titulaires d'une maîtrise de gestion ou équivalent ou cadres salariés des entreprises; sélection sur dossier.
Durée: 1 année universitaire.
Connaissances linguistiques: connaissance de l'anglais et/ou de l'allemand nécessaire.
Inscriptions: contacter l'Université pour de plus amples renseignements.

1075 Université Stendhal Grenoble III
Relations internationales
BP 25
38040 Grenoble Cedex 9
Tel: +33-4-7682-41111
Fax: +33-4-7682-4174
Web: http://www.u-grenoble3.fr/stendhal

📖 1er-3e cycle / toutes disciplines

Domaines d'étude: toutes disciplines principales, français, langues, littérature et civilisation.
Programmes: (a) programme pluridisciplinaire du 1er au 3e cycle en langues, lettres, langage, communication; (b) programme de cours conduisant aux diplômes en langue, littérature et civilisation françaises; (c) programme de cours conduisant aux diplômes supérieur d'aptitude à l'enseignement du français langue étrangère (DSA).
A l'intention de: ressortissants de tout pays titulaires du baccalauréat ou titre reconnu équivalent.
Durée: (a), (b), (c) et (d) de 8 à 13 semaines; (e) et (f) 1 semestre; (g) 2 semestres; (h) et (i) organisés à la demande.
Frais: (a) 120 € par semaine; (b) 60 € par semaine; (c) 16 € par semaine; (d) 35 € par semaine; (e) et (f) 1 000 € par semestre; (g) 1 500 € pour les 2 semestres; (h) 150 à 200 € par semaine; (i) sur devis.

1076 University Louis Pasteur Strasbourg I
Institut Le Bel 4, rue Blaise Pascal
67070 Strasbourg
Tel: +33-3-9024-5000
Fax: +33-3-9024-5001
Web: http://www-ulp.u-strasbg.fr
e-mail: sri@adm-ulp.u-strasbg.fr

📖 1er-3e cycles

Domaines d'étude: hygiène et santé, mathématiques, sciences, sciences humaines, sciences sociales.
Description: Formations fondées sur les trois grades: Licence, Master et Doctorat dans les secteurs de la santé et des sciences exactes, humaines et sociales.

Gabon

Année universitaire: octobre à juin.
Unité monétaire: franc CFA.
Admission pour étudiants du pays: Tous les étudiants étrangers doivent être titulaires d'un baccalauréat ou d'un diplôme admis en équivalence.
Connaissances linguistiques requises: Une bonne connaissance de la langue française est requise.
Services d'accueil et d'information:
• Ministère de l'enseignement supérieur et de la recherche scientifique, BP 2217, Libreville; tél: +241-760-764; fax: +241-764-345.
• Ministère des affaires étrangères et de la coopération; tél: +241-739-465 / 739-469 / 739-338.
• Antenne Université des sciences et techniques de Masuku, Libreville; tél./fax: +241-765-757.
• Autres services (sur place ou à l'étranger):
Facilités spéciales pour étudiants handicapés. Se renseigner auprès du Ministère de la santé publique et du Ministère des affaires sociales, de la sécurité sociale et du bien-être, Libreville.
Reconnaissance des études et diplômes: Commission permanente des équivalences, BP 17011; Libreville; Gabon.
Publications / Sites Web:
• « Livret de l'étudiant », disponible auprès de l'Université des sciences et techniques de Masuku, B.P. 901, 913 Franceville.

1077 Université des sciences et techniques de Masuku
BP 901
913 Franceville
Tel: +241-67-7725
Fax: +241-67-7520

📖 Études scientifiques

Domaines d'étude: sciences.
Programmes: (a) Diplôme universitaire d'études scientifiques (DUES) option mathématiques-physique, chimie-biologie, physique-chimie, biologie-géologie; (b) Diplôme de technicien supérieur dans les domaines de la maintenance industrielle, du génie civil, du génie électrique, du génie agricole; (c) Diplôme d'ingénieur dans les domaines du génie civil et de l'électromécanique.
A l'intention de: étudiants de toute nationalité, titulaires pour (a) d'un baccalauréat scientifique ou d'un diplôme admis en équivalence; pour (b) et (c) du baccalauréat série C, D, E ou F, et ayant réussi au concours d'entrée à l'École polytechnique de Masuku.
Durée: (a) 2 ans; (b) 3 ans et (c) 5 ans.
Inscriptions: avant le 31 octobre, au Secrétariat général de l'Université.

1078 Université Omar Bongo [UOB]
B.P. 13131
Libreville
Tel: +241-73-2033
Fax: +241-73-2045
Web: http://www.uob.ga.refer.org
e-mail: uob@internetgabon.com

📖 Programme de l'enseignement supérieur / toutes disciplines

Domaines d'étude: archéologie, biologie, droit, économie, gestion, lettres, linguistique, médecine, sciences humaines, sciences sociales.
Programmes: Programmes universitaires en droit, économie, lettres, sciences humaines, sciences sociales, traditions orales, archéologie, gestion, linguistique, philosophie, anglais, biologie médicale, sage-femme, médecine.
A l'intention de: candidats de tout pays, titulaires du baccalauréat, d'une capacité en droit ou d'un titre jugé équivalent par les facultés et ayant réussi le concours d'entrée dans les écoles et instituts.
Inscriptions: au Secrétariat général pour de plus amples renseignements ou auprès des services culturels des ambassades du Gabon à l'étranger.

Georgia

Academic year: September to June.
Monetary unit: Georgian Lari (GEEL).
National student admission: Access to higher education requires possession of the following certificates: secondary school-leaving certificate, diploma of secondary technical and vocational education, diploma of special secondary education. Foreign students are admitted to higher education institutions without competitive examinations. Faculties for them are established in the leading institutions such as the Tbilisi State University, Technical University, Medical University, Agrarian University.
Language: Foreign students must have a good knowledge in Georgian, Russian or English (the number of courses taught in English is limited).
Information services:
• Ministry of Education, 52, Uznadze St., 0102 Tbilisi; Georgia.
• Ministry of Foreign Affairs, 4, Chitadze St., 0118 Tbilisi; Georgia.
Recognition of studies and qualification: Department of Science and academic Recognition and Mobility; Ministry of Education; 52, Uznadze St.; 0102 Tbilisi; Georgia; tel.: +995-3295-7947; fax: +995-3295-7010 / +995-3294-3069; email: machabeli@hotmail.com.

1079 Georgian Technical University [GTU]

77 Kostava Street
380075 Tbilisi
Tel: +995-32-360-762
Fax: +995-32-365-590
Web: http://www.gtu.edu.ge
e-mail: info@gtu.kheta.ge

📖 Undergraduate, Graduate and Postgraduate Programmes

Study Domains: all major fields.
Programmes: (a) Bachelor's, (b) Master's and (c) Ph.D. courses at the following faculties: civil engineering, mechanical engineering, transportation, information technologies and control systems, power engineering, telecommunications, mining and geology, fundamental sciences, chemical technology and biotechnology, metallurgy, humanitarian-technical, correspondence study.
Held: at the aforementioned faculties of the GTU, as well as at the following institutes (branches of the GTU): Graduate School of Management; Aviation; Architecture; Batumi Polytechnic; Chiatura Politechnic; Sukhumi Politechnic; Kazreti Politechnic; Tskhinvali Politechnic.
Duration: (a) 4 years; (b) 2 years (after bachelorship); (c) 3 years.
Fees: yearly for foreign students: US$500 to US$700.
Applications: by 1 August, to the above address.

1080 Grigol Robakidze University [GRU]

6, Jano Bagrationi Street
380060 Tbilisi
Tel: +995-32-385-849
Fax: +995-32-252-981
Web: http://www.gruni.edu.ge
e-mail: gruni@posta.ge

📖 Undergraduate and Graduate Degree Programmes

Study Domains: accounting, audio-visual media, cinematography, communication, computer science, cultural studies, dentistry, English, geography, German, journalism, publishing.
Programmes: Bachelor's and Master's Degrees in (a) journalism; (b) financial management; (c) international business; (d) law; (e) public administration; (f) dentistry; (g) English language and literature;
(h) German language and literature.
Open to: nationals of all countries; English proficiency required; and professional assessment.
Fees: registration: US$30; tuition: US$1,300 per year: living costs: from US$20-100 per month.
Financial assistance: possibility of some financial assistance approximately 40-80 lari per month.
Languages: (a) to (g) language of instruction; English; (h) language of instruction: German, English.
Applications: 31 July.

1081 International Black Sea University

0131 D.Agmashenebeli Kh., 13th km, No. 2
380031 Tbilisi
Tel: +995-32-595-005
Fax: +995-32-595-007
Web: http://www.ibsu.edu.ge
e-mail: info@ibsu.edu.ge

📖 Undergraduate and Graduate Degree Programmes

Study Domains: business, cultural studies, engineering, finance, international business.
Programmes: Bachelor`s Degree in (a) business administration; (b) finance and banking; (c) international economic relations; (d) American studies; (e) Georgian language and literature; (f) industrial engineering; (g) computer engineering; (h) food engineering; Master`s Degree in (i) business administration.
Open to: nationals of all countries; proficiency in English required.
Fees: tuition: US$1,000 per year for students from former Soviet Republics, US$1,500 per year for others; accommodation: US$1,000 for ten months, living costs: from US$50-$200 per month.
Languages: language of instruction is English.
Applications: by 1 August.

1082 Tbilisi State Medical University [TSMU]

33 Vazha-Pshavela Avenue
380077 Tbilisi
Tel: +995-32-391-879
Fax: +995-32-942-519
Web: http://www.tsmu.edu
e-mail: iad@tsmu.edu

📖 Doctor of Medicine Programme

Study Domains: medicine.
Programmes: Doctor of Medicine Programme.
Open to: Candidates of all nationalities, with background in chemistry and biology and with English proficiency.
Age limit Max: 40 years of age.
Duration: 6 years.
Languages: language of instruction is English.
Applications: December.

Germany

Academic year: October to February and April to July.
Organization of higher education system: Public and private state-recognized institutions of higher education categorized as: universities ('Universitäten') and equivalent higher education institutions: technical universities ('Technische Universitäten/Technische Hochschulen'), universities of applied sciences ('Fachhochschulen'), Colleges of Art and Music ('Musik-, Kunst- und Filmhochschulen'). Other university-status institutions are comprehensive universities ('Universität-Gesamthochschulen') and teacher training colleges ('Pädagogische Hochschulen').
The following main types of academic degrees are granted: Bachelor's, Master's, 'Diplom', 'Magister', 'Promotion' (doctorate).The standard period of study, that is the time in which a first degree with professional qualification can be gained, should, as a rule, not exceed 8 to 9 semesters (4 to 4.5 years). In the two-cycle system (Bachelor's/Master's), the standard time to obtain a degree in a Bachelor's programme is 3 to 4 years, in a Master's programme 1 to 2 years. It takes around 3 years to complete a doctoral degree.
The following applies for the equivalency of degrees: Bachelor's degrees correspond to 'Diplom' degrees awarded by 'Fachhochschulen' (universities of applied sciences); Master's degrees correspond to 'Diplom' and 'Magister' degrees awarded by universities and university-status higher education institutions.
Major institutions of higher education: There are several hundred national universities, university colleges and art academies in Germany which offer a wide range of scientific and technical courses as well as programmes in art and music for graduates, postgraduate and postdoctoral students and researchers. Full course length is usually 4 to 5 years, the length of special programmes at postgraduate and postdoctoral level varies (1 to 3 years). Depending on the field of interest and the level of studies, full information on course profiles, curricula, accreditation requirements, deadlines etc. can be obtained from the following sources, available upon request from the German Academical Exchange Service (DAAD) http://www.daad.de, its branch offices, Goethe Institutes and German Embassies.
Monetary unit: Euro (€).
National student admission:
• for national students: Generally upon successful completion of secondary school ('Allgemeine or Fachgebundene Hochschulreife'), however, there are several alternative methods of admission. Admission to colleges of art, film and music, is subject to aptitude test and/or presentation of a portfolio.
International student admission: International students nomally apply direct to the International Office ('Akademisches Auslandsamt') of the relevant higher education institution. Applications for admission should be submitted generally by 15 January for summer semester and by 15 July for the winter semester. When the university of choice is a member of the Admission Service, 'Application Services for International Students' (ASSIST), the application must be sent via ASSIST (www.uni-assist.de). This service allows applicants to apply to several universities with only one set of documents (email: service@uni-assist.de). A list of members is also available on the webpage (www.uni-assist.de/english/universities.html). Nationals of European Union countries wishing to study a subject for which admissions restrictions apply throughout Germany (numerus clausus subject) must apply in the same manner as German nationals, to the Central Admissions Office (www.zvs.de).
International students must hold a certificate entitling them to study at a university in their home country and recognized as equivalent to a German secondary school-leaving certificate ('Allgemeine' or 'Fachgebundene Hochschulreife') for admission to university studies. Applicants who do not meet this requirement must pass the assessment test, 'Feststellungsprüfung', after studying at a 'Studienkolleg' for usually one year. For admission to doctoral studies, the completion of full university studies is usually required. Most of the colleges of art, film and music require an aptitude test or a portfolio. Applicants from non-German-speaking countries must take a language proficiency test for admission prior to commencing their studies.
Language: Good knowledge of German is essential, thus international students wishing to study at higher education level must pass a special language examination (except for some international degree programmes which do not require any prior knowledge of German. For further information, www.daad.de/idp). German-language study facilities are available in most countries, either at Goethe-Institute Inter Nationes or at German cultural institutes. German language courses for students from abroad are also available at most universities.
The German language proficiency certificate, the 'Deutsche Sprachprüfung für den Hochschulzugang ausländischer Studienbewerber' (DSH) can only be taken at the university or higher education institution itself. The TestDaF certificate can be taken in Germany as well as abroad. The addresses of the test centres as well as information on ways of preparing for the test is available from the following website: www.testdaf.de.
Immigration requirements: In order to enter Germany a residence permit visa issued by the diplomatic representation of Germany in the home country is required. This does not apply to students from European Union countries nor from countries having special ageements. To obtain the visa, students are required to present a letter of acceptance from a German higher education institution or an applicant confirmation, which confirms that the full set of required application documents has been received by a German higher education institution. In addition, students must show proof of sufficient financial resources for living and tuition expenses. A resident's permit only allows study in Germany; it is not a work permit. The German embassy or consulate in the student's country may be contacted for further information. It is to be noted that a tourist visa cannot be retroactively converted into a visa or residence permit for educational purposes.
Up-to-date information about visa requirements and procedures may be obtained from the homepage of the foreign ministry ('Auswaertiges Amt'): www.auswaertiges-amt.de/www/en/index_html. The text is available in English, French, Spanish, Arabic and German by selecting the language of choice in the right upper corner. The topics 'Welcome to Germany' and 'Entry into Germany' contain detailed information.
Estimated expenses for one academic year:
• Tuition: studies are mostly tuition free. Fees are required for long-term students, second degree courses, occasional students and for some English-instructed Master's programmes. Generally, a Master's programme is tuition free if it follows a Bachelor's degree in the same or related subject. Tuition fees are required for a second Master's degree. For further information see www.daad.de/deutschland/en/2.2.1.18.html. Additionally, all students must pay approximately 35€ per semester to the student services organisations. Further costs can be a charge about 50€ for a semester ticket which permits free use of public transport during semester. Finally, some states charge an administration fee of about 50€ per semester. For more detailed information, contact the International Office at your university of choice (for addresses look at www.daad.de/deutschland/en/2.2.1.5.html).
• Books/Supplies: 200-300€ per semester.
• Housing: cheapest accommodation: in a student residence hall from about 75 to 225€ per month, prices for private rooms vary from 150 to 300€, rooms in shared flats from 120 to 400€.The standard of living in Germany is very high, a monthly expense totalling at least 670€ in the old regional states (west) and 540€ in the new regional states (east) will allow you a modest life-style.
• cf: 'The Study of economic and social situation of students in Germany' ('Die wirtschaftliche und soziale Lage der Studierenden in der Bundesrepublik Deutschland 2003'), 17. Sozialerhebung des Deutschen Studentenwerks, by HIS Hochschul-Informations-System, Ed. Bundesministerium für Bildung und Forschug, Bonn, Berlin 2004.
Information services:
• Agency responsible for international student exchanges: German Academic Exchange Service, Deutscher Akademischer Austauschdienst (DAAD) Infocentre, Kennedyallee 50, 53175 Bonn; tel: +49-228-882-703, -700; web: www.daad.de; email: studying_in_Germany@daad.de.
• The DAAD regional offices and Information Centres around the world, for addresses see www.daad.de/portrait/en/1.3.4.html;
• The German diplomatic missions abroad

(www.auswaertiges-amt.de);
• The 141 branches of the Goethe Institute in 77 countries (www.goethe.de);
• The German universities and their International Offices (for addresses www.daad.de/deutschland/en/2.2.1.5.htm;
• The German Rectors' Conference (www.hrk.de/index_eng.php).
Scholarships for international students: Consult the DAAD website for a general overview of scholarships, www.daad.de/deutschland/en/2.2.4.2.html or www.campus-germany.de/english/1.7.45.html. Other links: www.dfg.de; www.avh.de; www.inwent.org; www.cdg.de; www.fes.de; www.kas.de.
Open and distance learning: Distance learning courses are subject to approval by the Central Office for Distance Learning 'Staatliche Zentralstelle für Fernunterricht der Länder der Bundesrepublik Deutschland', www.zfu.de). Approval procedure includes an examination of the teaching course objectives, advertising practices, and the form and content of the contract concluded between the course participants and the distance-learning institution. Courses leading to a 'Diplom' and 'Magister' degree are offered by the Distance University of Hagen (Fernuniversität Hagen, www.fernuni-hagen.de), distance universities of applied sciences (e.g. www.euro-fh.de) and a number of institutions (www.akad-fernstudium.de/fs). For general information about distance learning institutions visit www.fvl-agentur.de, www.zfu.de.
Recognition of studies and qualification: On behalf of the Standing Conference of the Ministers of Education and Cultural Affairs (Ständige Konferenz der Kultusminister der Länder) the Central Office for Foreign Education (Zentralstelle für ausländisches Bildungswesen) is the official agency for the evaluation and recognition of foreign educational qualifications. The Central Office for Foreign Education provides advisory and information services to the authorities concerned with the recognition of foreign diplomas (e.g. ministries, universities, courts etc.), but has no authority to make decisions itself. (www.kmk.org/zab/home1.htm). The decisions for accreditation are taken at various levels, most frequently the responsibility lies with the universities.
• Information about recognition of foreign credentials: The International Office at the university of your choice, for addresses visit http://www.daad.de/deutschland/en/2.2.1.5.html
The German Academic Exchange Service (Deutscher Akademischer Austauschdienst, DAAD), Kennedyallee 50, D- 53175 Bonn, Germany; tel: +49-228-882-0, fax: +49-228-882-444; e-mail: studying_in_germany@daad.de; web: http://www.daad.de/deutschland/en/2.2.1.11.html.
Accommodation services: The "Association of German Student Services Organisation" (Deutsches Studentenwerk DSW) offers a special Service Set for foreign students, which includes a room in a student hall of residence and a tutoring programme. Only a limited number of Service Sets are available (for further information visit www.studentenwerk.de). The International Offices (Akademische Auslandsaemter), Student Services Organisations (Studentenwerke) and the Student Representation (Allgemeiner Studierendenausschuss) of the higher education institute of your choice can provide assistance.
Work opportunities: Students from Non-EU-Countries may work for a total of 90 full days or 180 half-days (part time) per year without having to obtain a work permit. There are no limitations on the amount of employment for students from EU-countries. Since unemployment is a major problem in Germany, work possibilities may be difficult to find.
Additional information: Although only the institutions of higher education which answered our questionnaire are listed in this guide, there are several hundred national universities, university colleges and art academies in Germany which offer a wide range of scientific and technical courses as well as programmes in art and music for graduates, postgraduate and postdoctoral students and researchers. Full course length is usually 4 to 5 years, the length of special programmes at postgraduate and postdoctoral level varies (1 to 3 years). Depending on the field of interest and the level of studies, full information on course profiles, curricula, accreditation requirements, deadlines etc. can be obtained from the following sources, available upon request from the German Academical Exchange Service (DAAD) www.daad.de, its branch offices, Goethe Institutes and German Embassies.

Publications / Websites: The German academic Exchange Service provides both general and specific publications on universities and studying in Germany, available in several languages. Some very important publications can also be used via the DAAD website (in English, Spanish and German), especially: International Degree Programmes (http://www.daad.de/idp), Summer Schools in Germany (http://www.summerschools-in-germany.de). General information can be obtained through the DAAD branch offices, Goethe-Institut-Inter-Nationes and German embassies. General information on the German higher education system and on aspects related to international students can also be found at the following Internet addresses: www.higher-education.de (in English, German), www.en.studienwahl.de (in English, French, German), www.campus-germany.de (in English, Spanish, French, Chinese, Russian, German).
Note: Although only the institutions of higher education which answered our questionnaire are listed in this guide, there are several hundred national universities, university colleges and art academies in Germany which offer a wide range of scientific and technical courses as well as programmes in art and music for graduates, postgraduate and postdoctoral students and researchers. Full-course length is usually 4 to 5 years; the length of special programmes at postgraduate and postdoctoral level varies (from 1 to 3 years): see websites listed under 'Information services' for further information.

1083 Aachen University of Applied Sciences
Kalverbenden 6
52066 Aachen
Tel: +49-241-6009-0
Fax: +49-241-6009-1090
Web: http://www.fh-aachen.de
e-mail: zentrale@fh-aachen.de

📖 Undergraduate and Graduate Tertiary Level Degree Courses

Study Domains: applied sciences, architecture, aviation, aeronautics, biochemistry, business, business administration, cardiology, chemical engineering, chemical industry, chemistry, civil engineering, computer science, electricity and electronics, energy, engineering, industrial design, interior design, international business, management, mathematics, mechanical engineering, physics, sciences, telecommunications, urbanism, visual arts.
Programmes: undergraduate and graduate tertiary level degree courses.
Open to: all students with relevant university entrance qualifications.
Fees: registration, 50€; no tuition fees for most degree courses; living costs, 600€ per month.
Languages: German and English, TOEFL of 550 required for some degree courses.
Applications: by 1 July for winter term.

1084 Academy of Music Hanns Eisler Berlin
Charlottenstrasse 55
10117 Berlin
Tel: +49-30-90-269-700
Fax: +49-30-90-269-701
Web: http://www.hfm-berlin.de
e-mail: rektorat.hfm@berlin.de

📖 Music Programmes

Study Domains: music and musicology, performing arts.
Subjects: studies in: accordion, brass, coaching, composition, conducting, guitar, harmony, harp, jazz/popular music, music, theatre, timpani/percussion, piano, stage direction, strings, singing, woodwind.
Open to: candidates of all nationalities on the basis of an an entrance examination demonstrating exceptional musical talent, skills and knowledge appropriate to age and level of education.
Languages: German language proficiency at least equivalent to Goethe Institute Certificate in German as a Foreign Language (ZdaF).

Applications: to the above address: email:
studieninfo.hfm@berlin.de.

1085 Alexander von Humboldt Foundation [AvH]
Jean-Paul-Straße 12
53173 Bonn
Tel: +49-228-833-0
Fax: +49-228-833-199
Web: http://www.avh.de/en/
e-mail: followup@avh.de

☞ Postdoctoral Research Fellowships
Study Domains: all major fields, research.
Scholarships: Postdoctoral research fellowships in all
major fields.
Subjects: specific research projects in all academic fields
including sciences, humanities and engineering.
Open to: postdoctoral scientists from other countries;
candidates must present evidence of employment in
independent research work and teaching at university level
and must have academic publications to their credit; good
knowledge of German required for humanities and social
sciences scholars; precise and detailed research project is
required; up to age 40.
Place of study: at university institutes or other research
institutes in Germany.
Duration: 6 to 12 months (extension up to 24 months
possible).
Value: monthly stipend, plus family allowances and travel
expenses; fellowships for German-language courses (2 to 4
months) prior to research period can also be granted.
Applications: to the Secretariat; selection of candidates 3
times yearly (March, June and November).

1086 Alice-Salomon University of Applied Sciences Berlin [ASFH]
Alice-Salomon-Platz 5
12627 Berlin
Tel: +49-30-99245-0
Fax: +49-30-99245-245
Web: http://www.asfh-berlin.de/
e-mail: asfh@asfh-berlin.de

☞ Financial Aid
Study Domains: nursing, social sciences, social work.
Open to: Candidates for the Master programme on
intercultural conflict management.
Duration: 1 year, non-renewable.
Value: 1000 €.
Applications: By 15 June 2004; contact
kircher@asfh-berlin.de for further details.

1087 Amberg-Weiden University of Applied Sciences [AWUAS]
PO Box 1462
Kaiser-Wilhelm-Ring 23
92224 Amberg
Tel: +49-9-621-4820
Fax: +49-9-621-482-110
Web: http://www.fh-amberg-weiden.de
e-mail: amberg@fh-amberg-weiden.de

⌕ Degree Programmes in Engineering and Business Management
Study Domains: applied sciences, audio-visual media,
business, business administration, chemical engineering,
computer science, ecology, environment, economic and
commercial sciences, economy, electricity and electronics,
engineering, industrial technology, information science,
international business, laboratory techniques, languages,
management, marketing, mechanical engineering, technology,
telecommunications.
Programmes: engineering and business management
degree programmes.
Open to: candidates meeting higher education entrance
qualifications and language proficiency.
Duration: 4 months starting 1 October.
Fees: registration, 28 € per semester; estimated living
costs, 500 € per month.

Languages: German.
Applications: by 15 June for Winter term to International
Office; please see website for more information.

1088 Aschaffenburg University of Applied Sciences [AUAS]
63743 Aschaffenburg
Tel: +49-6021-3145
Fax: +49-6021-314-600
Web: http://www.fh-aschaffenburg.de
e-mail: info@fh-aschaffenburg.de

⌕ Diplom (FH) and Master's Programmes
Study Domains: accounting, advertising, business,
business administration, computer science, economic and
commercial sciences, economy, electricity and electronics,
engineering, industrial technology, international business,
international law, law, management, marketing, mathematics,
mechanical engineering, natural sciences, physics, trade.
Programmes: (a) General Diplom (FH) in Management
and Engineering; (b) Master's Degree in Engineering,
Mechatronics, Electrical Engineering, Industrial Engineering.
Description: (a) courses in management and its functions:
human resources, marketing, auditing, financing, logistics,
production planning, organization, statistics, mathematics.
Open to: (a) and (b) applicants from all countries holding a
recognized certificate equivalent to the 'Fachhochschulreife'.
Duration: (b) 4 years; courses start in October.
Fees: (a) no registration or tuition fees; living costs: 650 €
per month; (b) registration: approximately 50€; no tuition
fees; living costs: approx. 500 € per month.
Languages: (a) and (b) German.
Applications: (b) by 15 June; contact
hinrich.mewes@fh-aschaffenburg.de; see website for further
details.

1089 Berlin School of Economics [BSE]
Badensche Strasse 50-51
D-12045 Berlin
Fax: +49-30-857-89199
Web: http://www.fhw-berlin.de
e-mail: ausland@fhw-berlin.de

⌕ Undergraduate and Graduate Programmes in Business and Management
Study Domains: accounting, business, business
administration, computer science, ecology, environment,
economic and commercial sciences, economy, engineering,
finance, history, international business, law, marketing,
mathematics, political economy, sociology, statistics.
Programmes: 'Diplom' (equivalent to B.A. Hons.),
Bachelor's and Master's degrees in: (a) Business
Administration; (b) Co-operative Studies in Business
Administration; (c) European Business Administration; (d)
Management International; (e) Business Engineering,
Environmental Science (f) MBA European Management; (g)
MBA European-Asian Programme; (h) MBA General
Management; (i) MBA Small and Medium Enterprises; (j)
MBA Health Care Management.
Description: full and part-time studies, leading to
'Diplom-Kaufmann (FH)' (equivalent to B.A. Hons.); (b)
full-time studies with business partners, leading to 'Bachelor
of Business Administration'; (c) joint venture with Anglia
Polytechnic University, Cambridge, U.K., leading to
'Diplom-Kaufmann (FH)' and Bachelor of Arts (Hons.); (d)
joint venture with École Supérieure du Commerce Extérieur
(ESCE), Paris, France, leading to 'Diplom-Kaufmann (FH)'
and 'Diplôme de l'ESCE'; (e) studies leading to
'Diplom-Wirtschaftsingenieur (FH)'; (f) MBA joint venture
programme with South Bank University, London, U.K.; (h);
(i); (j) part-time MBA programmes.
Fees: variable according to study; see website for details.
Languages: (a), (c), (f), (h) German English; (b) (e),(i),(j)
German; (d) French/German; (g) English.
Applications: variable, according to study; see website for
further information.

1090 Carl Von Ossietzky University Oldenburg [COUO]
Ammerländer Heerstr. 114-118
26111 Oldenburg
Tel: +49-441-798-4628
Fax: +49-441-798-4639
Web: http://www.uni-oldenburg.de/iso
e-mail: internationalrelationsoffice@uni-oldenburg.de

📖 **International B.Sc. and M.Sc. Degree Programme**
Study Domains: American studies, applied arts, biology, business, chemistry, communication, community development, computer science, economic and commercial sciences, education, European studies, fine arts, history, marine biology, marine science, mathematics, physical education, political science, psychology, Russian, Slavic studies, social sciences, sociology, teacher education, theology, religion.
Programmes: courses of studies in engineering, physics, postgraduate programme in renewable energy, integrated coastal zone management, computer science, museum and exhibition, media art.
Applications: see website for further information.

1091 Catholic Service for Foreign Students
Hausdorffstrasse 151
53129 Bonn
Tel: +49-228-917-58-0
Fax: +49-228-917-5858
Web: http://www.kaad.de
e-mail: zentrale@kaad.de

🎓 **Scholarships**
Study Domains: all major fields.
Scholarships: Postgraduate and Postdoctoral Scholarships.
Description: all fields important for developing countries or for East European countries.
Open to: young scientists (postgraduate and postdoctoral) from Asia, Africa and Latin America or from Eastern Europe; recipients must agree to return to their home countries on completion of studies.
Place of study: in German universities.
Duration: 1 year (renewable to a maximum of 3 years for developing countries and 2 years for Eastern Europe).
Applications: by 15 January or 15 July to above address; see website http://www.kaad.de/english/inhalt_e.htm for application details, according to geographical region.

1092 Catholic University of Applied Sciences, North-Western Germany [KFHN]
Detmarstrasse 2-8
49074 Osnabruck
Tel: +49-541-358-850
Fax: +49-541-35885-35
Web: http://www.kath-fh-nord.de
e-mail: rektor@kath-fh-nord.de

📖 **Social Work and Public Health Programmes**
Study Domains: health and hygiene, nursing, social work, speech therapy.
Programmes: Bachelor's degree in: (a) Social Work; (b) Public Health.
Duration: 3 years starting October.
Applications: by 15 June; contact Wilfried Wittstruck, rektor@kath-fh-nord.de for further details.

1093 Deutscher Akademischer Austauschdienst (German Academic Exchange Service) [DAAD]
Kennedyallee 50
53175 Bonn
Tel: +49-228-882-703 / 700
Fax: +49-228-882-444
Web: http://www.daad.de
e-mail: postmaster@daad.de

🎓 **DAAD Scholarships**
Study Domains: all major fields.
Scholarships: (a) Short-term scholarships; (b) Long-term scholarships and fellowships for foreign students, younger scientists and academic staff.
Open to: nationals of all countries who are graduates, or in exceptional cases students with excellent academic records at a university level institution; specific information is given by the German diplomatic missions and DAAD branch offices; age limit for most programmes is 32; good knowledge of German required; an intensive language course may be included in the scholarship for students from countries with no facilities for German language study.
Place of study: at universities, Fachhochschulen, colleges of art and music and research institutes in Germany.
Duration: (a) 1 to 6 months; (b) 1 academic year of 10 to 12 months (possibly renewable).
Value: according to academic level plus an allowance to cover travel expenses, health and accident insurance; additional allowances in some programmes.
Applications: diplomatic missions of Germany and DAAD branch offices in candidates' home countries will provide application forms and information concerning the exact dates for applications and the offices to which they must be submitted.

1094 Deutscher Famulantenaustausch (German Exchange Office for Medical Clerkship)
Godesberger Allee 54
53175 Bonn
Tel: +49-228-375-340
Fax: +49-228-810-4155
Web: http://www.dfa-germany.de
e-mail: dfa.bonn@t-online.de

🎓 **Scholarship**
Study Domains: medicine.
Scholarships: Medical Clerkship (elective).
Open to: medical students of any nationality.
Duration: 1 month (renewable).
Value: normally covers cost of living.
Languages: proficiency in German and English required.
Applications: at any time, to the national member association of the International Federation of Medical Students Associations (IFMSA).

1095 Ecumenical Scholarships Programme
Girondelle 80
44799 Bochum
Tel: +49-234-938-8231
Fax: +49-234-938-8260
Web: http://www.studienkolleg-bochum.de
e-mail: sekr@studienkolleg-bochum.de

🎓 **Scholarships**
Study Domains: all major fields, theology, religion.
Scholarships: Postgraduate Scholarships.
Description: development-oriented studies in all fields of interest to the ecumenical partner organization in the candidate's home country.
Open to: Third World students holding an academic degree and being recommended by a partner organization of the Ecumenical Scholarships Programme; priority will be given to candidates who have obtained a Master's degree and already have professional experience.
Place of study: in Germany and European countries.
Applications: Applications: to the above address for further information.

1096 ESCP-EAP European School of Management [ESCP-EAP]
Heubnerweg 6
14059 Berlin
Tel: +49-30-32007-0
Fax: +49-30-32007-111
Web: http://www.escp-eap.de
e-mail: infoberlin@escp-eap.net

❦Scholarship

Study Domains: business, economic and commercial sciences, economy, management.
Scholarships: Hertie Foundation Scholarships.
Subjects: Central European studies.
Open to: candidates from Eastern European countries; participants from the MBA Central Europe.
Duration: 1 year, non-renewable.
Value: 2,600€ for tuition fees; plus 4,450€ for living expenses.
Applications: By 31 August; contact sbesic@escp-eap.net for further details.

1097 Fachhochschule Bonn-Rhein-Sieg University of Applied Sciences [FBRS]

Grantham-allee 20
53757 Sankt Augustin
Tel: +49-2241-865-0
Fax: +49-2241-865-609
Web: http://www.fh-bonn-rhein-sieg.de

📖 Diplom (FH), B.Sc., M.Sc. Programmes

Study Domains: biology, business administration, chemistry, computer science, continuing education, engineering, journalism, mechanical engineering.
Programmes: (a) German Diplom (FH) in business studies, engineering; journalism;
(b) Bachelor of Science in business administration, engineering, electronic engineering, mechatronics, technical writing, chemistry, materials technology;
(c) Master of Science Degree in computer science, biology and biomedical science.
Languages: German; good knowledge of English required for biology courses.

1098 Fachhochschule Braunschweig-Wolfenbüttel University of Applied Sciences [FBW]

Salzdahlumer Strasse 46-48
38302 Wolfenbüttel
Tel: +49-5331-939-0
Fax: +49-5331-939-1072
Web: http://cms.fh-wolfenbuettel.de/fh/
e-mail: zsb@fh-wolfenbuettel.de

📖 Diplom (FH) and Master's Programmes

Study Domains: business administration, chemical engineering, computer science, ecology, environment, economic and commercial sciences, electricity and electronics, energy, engineering, finance, industrial technology, industry and commerce, information science, law, management, mechanical engineering, ophthalmology, social sciences, social work, technology, telecommunications, tourism, hotel and catering management, trade, transport.
Programmes: Diplom (FH) and Master's Programmes.
Open to: admission on the basis of the Higher Education Entrance Qualification or similar; German language proficiency test (DSH).
Held: Wolfenbuttel; Braunschweig; Salzgitter; Wolfsburg.
Duration: 4 years starting 1 March or 20 September.
Fees: tuition fees 90-130 €; living costs approx. 600 €.
Languages: German.
Applications: by 15 January and 15 July to above address.

📖 Graduate Programmes in Engineering

Study Domains: administration, economy, engineering, social work.
Programmes: programme of courses in engineering, economics, social services.
Open to: applicants from all countries holding a certificate entitling them to study at a university in their home country and recognized as equivalent to the German 'Allgemeine' or 'Fachgebundene Hochschulreife' for undergraduate studies, or having completed university studies for postgraduate studies.
Duration: 4 years; courses begin in April for summer semester, in October for winter.
Applications: by 15 January for summer semester and 15

July for Winter semester, to Akademisches Auslandsamt at the above address.

1099 Fachhochschule Darmstadt University of Applied Sciences

Haardtring 100
64295 Darmstadt
Tel: +49-6151-1602
Fax: +49-6151-168949
Web: http://www.fh-darmstadt.de
e-mail: info@fh-darmstadt.de

📖 Diplom (FH), B.Sc., M.Sc. Programmes

Study Domains: architecture, audio-visual media, business administration, chemical engineering, civil engineering, computer science, design, documentation, education, electricity and electronics, energy, engineering, industrial design, information science, international business, journalism, mathematics, mechanical engineering, social sciences, social work, telecommunications.
Programmes: (a) German Diplom.-Ing. (FH) in architecture, biotechnology, chemical engineering, civil engineering; optical technology and image processing, interior design, mechanical engineering
(b) German Diplom (FH) in industrial design, communication design, economics, German cyberlaw, electrical engineering, mathematics, online journalism, media system design; social education; (c) Bachelor of Science degree in computer science, mechatronics; (d) Master of Science degree in computer science.

1100 Fachhochschule Oldenburg/ Ostfiriesland/ Wilhelmshaven University of Applied Sciences [FOOW]

Constaniaplatz 4
26723 Emden
Tel: +49-180-567-807-0
Fax: +49-180-567-807-1000
Web: http://www.fh-oow.de
e-mail: poth@fbe.fh-wilhelmshaven

📖 Diplom Ingenieur and Bachelor's Degree Programmes

Study Domains: architecture, computer science, economy, engineering, industrial technology, mechanical engineering, social sciences, transport.
Programmes: courses leading to Diplom Ingenieur and Bachelor's degrees in architecture, construction engineering and geoinformation, economics, engineering, maritime studies, social sciences, technical sciences.
Open to: all nationalities; subject to availability of openings; DaF or DSH test required.
Duration: 4 years. Courses begin in September.
Fees: registration 106 € per semester; living costs approx. 450 € per month.
Languages: German.
Applications: see website or contact ostermayer@fh-oldenburg.de for application details.

1101 Fachhochschule Schwaebisch Hall - University of Applied Sciences School of Design [FSH]

School of Design
Salinen strasse 2
D-74523 Schwaebisch Hall
Tel: +49-791-856-55-0
Fax: +49-791-856-55-10
Web: http://www.fhsh.de
e-mail: info@fhsh.de

📖 Media Design and Cultural Design

Study Domains: applied arts, arts, audio-visual media, design, fine arts, graphic arts, photography, visual arts.
Programmes: (a) Bachelor of Media Design (BMD); (b) Bachelor of Cultural Design (BCD).
Description: (a) courses include media design, digital arts, web design, computer graphics, video, 3-D, audio, interactive design; (b) courses include fine arts, cultural development, cultural management, arts administration.

Open to: all nationalities; art/design portfolio required; admission entrance examination.
Duration: 3-1/2 years; courses start: (a) October and March; (b) October.
Fees: tuition fees 7,200 € per year; living costs 400 € per month.
Languages: German; English required for Media Design.
Applications: by 30 June (for Fall term); 10 January (for Spring term).

1102 Fachochschule Suedwesfalen University of Applied Sciences [FS]

Frauenstuhlweg 31
58644 Iserlohn
Tel: +49-2371-566-513
Fax: +49-2371-566-235
Web: http://www.fh-swf.de
e-mail: aaa@fh-swf.de

📖 Diplom (FH), Bachelor's and Master's Programmes

Study Domains: agriculture, business, economic and commercial sciences, engineering, international business.
Description: programmes in engineering and business and agricultural economics.
Open to: candidates holding a recognized secondary-school certificate; language proficiency test (DSH or DaF, level V); some degree courses require proof of relevant practical experience.
Held: Hagen; Iserlohn; Meschede; Soest.
Duration: 3 to 5 years; courses start September.
Fees: estimated living costs: 720 €.
Applications: by 15 July; see website for full details.

1103 Friedrich Ebert Foundation

Godesberger Allee 149
53175 Bonn
Tel: +49-228-883-666
Fax: +49-228-883-396
Web: http://www.fes.de
e-mail: presse.bonn@fes.de

🎓 Scholarships

Study Domains: all major fields.
Scholarships: Foreign Students' Scholarships.
Open to: students and graduates from Germany or foreign students; applicants should be enrolled in German universities, have excellent academic records and proficiency in German.
Place of study: universities in Germany.
Duration: 1 year (renewable).
Value: monthly stipend.
Applications: to Scholarship Division, at the above address.

1104 Friedrich Naumann Foundation

Karl Marx St. 2
14482 Potsdam
Tel: +49-331-7019-0
Fax: +49-331-7019-188
Web: http://www.fnst.org
e-mail: fnst@fnst.org

🎓 Scholarships

Study Domains: all major fields.
Scholarships: Foreign Student Scholarships.
Open to: foreign students, graduates and postgraduates, who are studying at a German university; excellent scientific qualifications required.
Duration: from 1 to 3 years (renewable).
Applications: to the above address.

1105 Friedrich-Alexander University Erlangen-Nuremberg [UEN]

Schloss Platz 4
91054 Erlangen
Tel: +49-9131-85-0
Fax: +49-9131-85-22131/1000
Web: http://www.uni-erlangen.de
e-mail: rektorat@zuv.uni-erlangen.de

📖 Undergraduate, Graduate, Postgraduate Programmes

Study Domains: administration, business administration, chemical engineering, dentistry, education, international business, international relations, law, liberal arts, management, mechanical engineering, medicine, pharmacy and pharmacology, sciences.
Programmes: Bachelor's, Master's and Ph.D. degrees.
Duration: 4 to 5 years; courses begin in October and April.
Fees: estimated living costs: 500 €.
Languages: German; English courses for chemical engineering and computational technology.
Applications: by 15 July / 15 January; contact dietrich.kramer@zuv.uni-erlangen.de for further information.

1106 German University of Administrative Sciences, Speyer [GUAS]

Freiherr-Vom-Stein-SEI. 2
67346 Speyer
Tel: +49-6232-654-227
Fax: +49-6232-654-446
Web: http://www.hfv-speyer.de/ENGL
e-mail: hbucher@dhv-speyer.de

📖 Master's and Ph.D. Programmes in Administrative Sciences

Study Domains: administration.
Programmes: Master's and Ph.D. programmes in administrative sciences.
Applications: by 1 September to G. Gerhardt; ggerhardt@dhv-speyes.de.

1107 Gottlieb Daimler and Karl Benz Foundation

Dr. Carl-Benz-Platz 2
68526 Ladenburg
Tel: +49-6203-1092-0
Fax: +49-6203-1092-5
Web: http://www.daimler-benz-stiftung.de
e-mail: info@daimler-benz-stiftung.de

🎓 Fellowships

Study Domains: sciences.
Scholarships: Research Fellowships in all scientific fields.
Open to: young postgraduate scientists from other countries; age limit 30.
Place of study: academic or scientific institutions in Germany.
Duration: maximum 3 years.
Value: depends on research undertaken.
Applications: by 1 October, 1 February and 1 June.

1108 Hamburg University for Economics and Politics [HUEP]

Von Melle Park 9
20146 Hamburg
Tel: +49-40-42838-0
Fax: +49-40-42838-4150
Web: http://www.hwp-hamburg.de
e-mail: info@hwp-hamburg.de

📖 Master's Degree Programmes

Study Domains: administration, business, business administration, economic and commercial sciences, European studies, international business, international law, international relations, international studies, law, marketing, political science, social sciences, sociology, statistics, trade, urbanism.
Programmes: (a) Master of International Business Administration;
(b) Master of European Studies.
Description: (b) the process of European integration, European labour and social relations, the European Union (EU) in the world order, migration and intercultural relations.
Duration: (a); (b) 2 years; 3 month company internship required. Courses start 1 October.
Fees: (a); (b) registration 31 €; living costs approx. 600 €.
Languages: (a); (b) German and English; German Proficiency ZMP from Goethe Institute and English Proficiency TOEFL 213, 4.5 required.

Applications: (a); (b) by 30 April; contact miba@hwp-hamburg.de for further information.

1109 Heinrich-Heine University Duesseldorf [HHUD]
Universitaetstrasse 1
40225 Duesseldorf
Tel: +49-211-8100
Fax: +49-211-342-2229
Web: http://www.uni-duesseldorf.de
e-mail: stueber@verwaltung.uniduesseldorf.de

Undergraduate, Graduate, Postgraduate Programmes

Study Domains: arts, business, criminology, economic and commercial sciences, education, health and hygiene, information science, international business, international relations, interpretation and translation, languages, liberal arts, management, marketing, medicine, nursing, pharmacy and pharmacology, social work, speech therapy, statistics.
Programmes: Bachelor's, Master's and Ph.D. degrees in all major fields of study, Staatexamen (medicine, dentistry, pharmacy, law).
Open to: all nationalities meeting admission criteria; German language proficiency of approx. 1000 hours of German language classes.
Duration: 3 to 8 years; courses start 15 October and 15 April.
Fees: registration approx. 146€; estimated living costs: 700 €.
Financial assistance: contact Office of International Academic Relations for further details.
Applications: by 15 July (for Winter term); 15 January (for Summer term).

Scholarships

Study Domains: arts, economy, law, mathematics, medicine, natural sciences.
Scholarships: (a) Duesseldorf Entrepreneurs Foundation; (b) German American Steuben Shurz Association; (c) Gesellschaft von Freuden und Foerderen e. V; (d) Hedwig und Waldemar Hort Foundation; (e) Heinrich Hertz Foundation; (f) Industry Club Duesseldorf; (g) Konrad Henkel Foundation.
Value: see website for further details.

1110 International Association for the Exchange of Students for Technical Experience - German Committee [IAESTE]
Postfach 20 04 04
53134 Bonn
Tel: +49-228-882-231
Fax: +49-228-882-550
Web: http://www.iaeste.de
e-mail: iaeste@daad.de

Scholarships

Study Domains: agriculture, engineering, forestry, natural sciences.
Scholarships: IAESTE Practical Training Scholarships.
Open to: students and recent graduates in the above mentioned fields, from member countries of the Association.
Place of study: in German companies.
Duration: from 2 to 12 months.
Value: covers cost of living.
Applications: to National IAESTE Committee; see website: http://www.iaeste.org/ or write to the above address.

1111 International Association of Students in Economics and Management - German Committee [AIESEC]
Subbelratherstraße 247
50825 Cologne
Tel: +49-221-551-056
Fax: +49-221-550-7676
Web: http://www.aiesec.de
e-mail: info@aiesec.de

Traineeship

Study Domains: accounting, business, computer science, economic and commercial sciences, finance, management, marketing.
Scholarships: AIESEC Traineeship.
Open to: students and recent graduates of economics and business administration from member countries of the Association.
Place of study: in German companies.
Duration: 6 weeks to 18 months.
Value: salary covering the cost of living.
Languages: proficiency in German and English required.
Applications: to local responsible or national committee in applicant's home country.

1112 International Graduate School Zittau [IHI]
Markt 23
02763 Zittau
Tel: +49-3583-7715-0
Fax: +49-3583-7715-34
Web: http://www.ihi-zittau.de
e-mail: info@ihi-zittau.de

Graduate Programmes

Study Domains: administration, business, engineering, industrial technology, management, social sciences.
Subjects: business management; social sciences; environmental engineering; industrial engineering and administration.
Open to: candidates of all nationalities holding the equivalent of a German 'Vordiplom' and on the basis of an entrance interview.
Languages: German proficiency required; a German language course lasting several weeks as preparation for the DSH (German Language Examination for Foreign Applicants preceding University Admission) is offered to interested students before beginning courses.

1113 International University in Germany
PO Box 1550
76605 Bruchsal
Tel: +49-7251-700-0
Fax: +49-7251-700-150
Web: http://www.i-u.de
e-mail: info@i-u.de

Undergraduate, Graduate Programmes

Study Domains: administration, business administration, computer science, information science, liberal arts, sciences.
Programmes: Bachelor's and Master's programmes.
Subjects: administration; information technology; business administration; sciences; liberal arts.
Open to: candidates of all nationalities, based on scholastic results and personal interview.
Financial assistance: several types, in the form of tuition waivers or loans.
Languages: English.
Applications: see http://www.i-u.de/admissions/admission/procedures.htm for complete information.

1114 International University of Applied Sciences
Muehlheimer Strabe 38
53604 Bad Honnef
Tel: +49-2224-9605-114
Fax: +49-2224-9605-113
Web: http://www.fh-bad-honnef.de
e-mail: info@fh-bad-honnef.de

Tourism, Hospitality and Aviation Management

Study Domains: aviation, aeronautics, tourism, hotel and catering management.
Programmes: Diplom-Betriebswirt (FH), Bachelor's level degree in tourism, hospitality and aviation management.
Subjects: hospitality and tourism management; business administration (BBA); aviation management.
Open to: candidates must meet admission and language proficiency requirements (TOEFL 550/220).

Duration: 3 to 4 years starting 1 March and 1 September.
Fees: Registration 6,780 € per year.
Financial assistance: partial tuition waivers possible.
Languages: English.

🐦 International Students' Awards

Study Domains: aviation, aeronautics, business, tourism, hotel and catering management.
Open to: candidates of all nationalities, based on academic results and financial situation as well as entrance examination and personal interview.
Value: 50% of the tuition costs for all 3 years of study.
Languages: English.
Applications: students can request a scholarship application packet from the International Office after officially applying for and passing the entrance exam at the International University.

1115 Katholischen Fachhochschule Freiburg (Catholic University of Applied Sciences) [KFH]
Kaarkstrabe 63
79104 Freiburg
Tel: +49-761-200-486
Fax: +49-761-200-444
Web: http://www.kfh-freiburg.de
e-mail: info@kfh-freiburg.de

📖 Special Education Programmes

Study Domains: social sciences, social work, special education, theology, religion.
Programmes: Bachelor's degree in: (a) special education; (b) international management in non-profit organizations.
Duration: (a) 1-1/2 years starting October; (b) 2 years starting April.
Fees: (a) registration: 4,500 €; (b) registration: 7,800 €.
Languages: (a); (b) German and English.
Applications: (a) by 15 June; for further information write to werner@kfh-freiburg.de; (b) for further information write to koesler@kfh-freiburg.de.

1116 Konrad Adenauer Foundation
Rathausallee 12
53757 Sankt Augustin
Tel: +49-2241-246 / 0
Fax: +49-2241-246-5 / 91
Web: http://www.kas.de
e-mail: zentrale@kas.de

🐦 Fellowships

Study Domains: all major fields.
Scholarships: Fellowships for Graduate Students.
Open to: foreign postgraduate students under the age of 30, with priority to those from developing countries; candidates must have excellent academic record together with experience in community service, and activities in the university or political organizations; foreign recipients must agree to return to their home countries on completion of study.
Place of study: in Germany.
Duration: varies according to study undertaken.
Value: monthly amount plus allowances.
Applications: to Scholarship Division, at the above address.

1117 Leipzig University of Applied Sciences
PO Box 30 11 66
04251 Leipzig
Tel: +49-341-307-60
Fax: +49-341-307-6456
Web: http://www.htwk-leipzig.de
e-mail: studinf@k.htwk-leipzig.de

📖 Undergraduate, Graduate and Postgraduate Programmes

Study Domains: architecture, audio-visual media, civil engineering, computer science, electricity and electronics, library science, mathematics, mechanical engineering, museology and museography, natural sciences, publishing, sciences, social work.

1118 Lutheran World Federation [LWF]
Diemershaldenstraße 45
70187 Stuttgart
Tel: +49-711-2159-572
Fax: +49-711-2159-123
Web: http://www.dnklwb.de
e-mail: LWB@diakonie.de

🐦 Scholarships

Study Domains: theology, religion.
Scholarships: Scholarships for postgraduate studies in theology.
Open to: qualified theologians.
Duration: short-term scholarships, minimum 6 months; long-term scholarships, 1 year.
Applications: by 1 September or 1 March of the preceding year, to LWF, Scholarship Desk, 150, route de Ferney; P.O. Box 2100; CH-1211 Geneva 2 (Switzerland); tel: +41 22 7916111; fax: +41 22 7916630; e-mail: info@lutheranworld.org; or directly to the German National Committee.

1119 Mannheim University for Music and Performing Arts
68161 Mannheim
Tel: +49-621-292-3512
Fax: +49-621-292-2072
Web: http://www.muho-mannheim.de
e-mail: rektorat@muho-mannheim.de

📖 Undergraduate, Postgraduate Programmes

Study Domains: dance, music and musicology, performing arts.

1120 Max-Planck Institute for Nuclear Physics (Minerva Scholarship Committee)
Postfach 103980
69029 Heidelberg
Tel: +49-6221-516-0
Fax: +49-6221-516-601
Web: http://www.mpi-hd.mpg.de
e-mail: mpik@mpi-hd.mpg.de

🐦 Fellowships

Study Domains: engineering, mathematics, natural sciences.
Scholarships: Minerva Fellowships.
Description: especially for natural and engineering sciences, mathematics (humanities are not excluded).
Open to: doctoral scientists, Ph.D. students, senior scientists and university teachers, preferably below the age of 40, from Germany and Israel.
Place of study: in research and academic institutions in Germany and Israel.
Duration: 1 year, option of extension for up to 24 months.
Languages: proficiency in English required.
Applications: by 31 January and 15 August, to Minerva Office, at the above address.

1121 Muthesius Academy of Architecture, Design and Fine Arts
Lorentzendamm 6-8
24103 Kiel
Tel: +49-431-5198-400
Fax: +49-431-5198-408
Web: http://www.muthesius.de
e-mail: presse@muthesius.de

📖 Undergraduate, Graduate Programmes

Study Domains: architecture, decorative arts, design, fine arts.

1122 Nürtingen University of Applied Sciences [FH Nürtingen]

PO Box 1349
Neckarsteige 6-10
72603 Nürtingen
Tel: +49-7022-201-0
Fax: +49-7022-201-303
Web: http://www.fh-nuertingen.de
e-mail: info@fh-nuertingen.de

📖 Undergraduate, Graduate, Postgraduate Programmes

Study Domains: business, business administration, ecology, environment, economic and commercial sciences, finance, food industry, international law, landscape architecture, urbanism.
Programmes: Undergraduate, graduate and postgraduate degrees.
Description: Programmes in Agriculture, Busines Law, Business Administration, Economics, Energie- & Recycling Management, Landscape Architecture and Planning, Real Estate Management, Urban Planning, Agriculture, International Finance, Food- and Agribusiness, International Master Landscape Architecture, International Finance, International Management, Environmental Protection.

1123 Otto Benecke Foundation

Kennedyallee 105-107
53175 Bonn
Tel: +49-228-8163-208
Fax: +49-228-8163-300
Web: http://www.obs-ev.de/
e-mail: OBS-eV@t-online.de

🎓 Foreign Student Scholarships

Study Domains: education, languages.
Scholarships: Scholarships for language studies and preparatory courses for academic studies.
Open to: persons with recognized refugee status and quota refugees; age under 30.
Place of study: in Germany.
Duration: 30 months.
Value: monthly allowance depending on individual needs.
Applications: at any time, to the above address.

1124 Philipps-Universität Marburg [PUM]

Biegenstraße 10-12
35032 Marburg
Tel: +49-6421-2820
Fax: +49-6421-2822-500
Web: http://www.uni-marburg.de
e-mail: auslamt@verwaltung.uni-marburg.de

📖 Master's and Ph.D. Degree Programmes

Study Domains: all major fields.
Programmes: Master's and Ph.D. degrees in all major fields.
Open to: all foreign students; German language entrance examination (DSH or DaF).
Duration: 1 year: courses start October for Winter term and April for Summer term.
Fees: registration 141€ per semester; living costs approximately 600€ per month.
Applications: see website for full details.

1125 Ravensburg-Weingarten University of Applied Sciences

PO Box 1261 Doggenriedstrasse
88241 Weingarten
Tel: +49-751-501 / 0
Fax: +49-751-501-9876
Web: http://www.fh-weingarten.de
e-mail: info@fh-weingarten.de

🎓 Scholarship

Study Domains: business, business administration, computer science, engineering, health and hygiene, mechanical engineering, physics, social sciences, technology.
Scholarships: Baden-Wurttenberg Scholarship.

Subjects: applied computer science; applied physics; business informatics and E-business; environmental and process engineering (Master); information and communication engineering; international business engineering (Master); mechanical engineering; mechatronics (Master); optical systems engineering (Master); production and management; social and health care management (Master); social work; technology management.
Open to: highly qualified students from partner universities.
Duration: 4 to 11 months, non renewable.
Value: 600€ per month.
Applications: by 31 March; email: lauer@fh-weingarten.de.

1126 Renutlingen University [RU]

Alteburgstrasse 150
72762 Reutlingen
Tel: +49-7121-271- 0
Fax: +49-7121-271-224
Web: http://www.fh-reutlingen.de
e-mail: aaa@reutlingen-university.de

📖 Undergraduate and Graduate Programme

Study Domains: administration, business, business administration, chemical engineering, chemistry, computer science, design, engineering, European studies, information science, international business, management, marketing, mechanical engineering.
Programmes: Bachelor's and Master's degree programmes.
Open to: candidates meeting selection criteria and language proficiency.
Fees: registration: 525 €; estimated living costs: 500 € per month.
Financial assistance: some scholarship available only within exchange programmes.
Languages: German (DSH level); some courses taught in English.
Applications: by 15 June for International European School of Business.

1127 Secretariat of the Standing Conference of Ministers of Education and Cultural Affairs of the Länder in Germany

Educational Exchange Service - VB
Nassestraße 8
Postfach 2240
53012 Bonn
Tel: +49-228-501-0
Fax: +49-228-501777
Web: http://www.kmk.org

🎓 Exchange Scheme

Study Domains: languages.
Scholarships: Foreign language assistant exchange scheme.
Open to: (a) young teachers and university students of German from all countries, for service as foreign language teaching assistants in secondary schools in Germany; candidates must be native speakers of English, French, Spanish, Italian or Dutch; and must possess either a Bachelor's degree from a university or college outside Europe, or have studied for 2 years at a European university; (b) German university students and young German teachers of modern languages for service as German language assistants in schools in Australia, Belgium, Canada, France, Ireland, Italy, the Netherlands, New Zealand, Spain, the United Kingdom and the United States.
Duration: 8 to 10 months.
Value: maintenance allowance.
Applications: enquire at the Cultural Attaché, Embassy of Germany or Consulate General in country of origin or at the above address.

1128 Social Service Agency of the Evangelical Church in Germany [SSAOTE]

Stipendienreferat
Stafflenbergstraße 76
Postfach 101142
70010 Stuttgart
Tel: +49-711-2159-0
Fax: +49-711-2159-288
Web: http://www.diakonie.de/de/html/1.htm
e-mail: diakonie@diakonie.de

Scholarships / Theology

Study Domains: theology, religion.
Scholarships: scholarships for theological or religious studies.
Open to: foreign graduates of theological studies.
Duration: 1 year.
Applications: through the national correspondent in the applicant's country, to the World Council of Churches, 150 route de Ferney, 1211 Geneva 2, Switzerland.

1129 Technische Universität Dresden [TUD]

Mommsenstrasse 13
01062 Dresden
Tel: +49-351-463-35358
Fax: +49-351-463-37738
Web: http://www.tu-dresden.de
e-mail: auslandsamt@mailbox.tu-dresden.de

Bachelor's, Master's and Ph.D. Programmes

Study Domains: all major fields.
Programmes: over 100 degree programmes in all major fields.
Open to: applicants from all countries holding a certificate entitling them to study at a university in their home country and recognized as equivalent to the German 'Allgemeine' or 'Fachgebundene Hochschulreife' for undergraduate studies, or having completed university studies for postgraduate studies.
Duration: 4 to 6 years; courses begin in April for Summer semester, in October for Winter.
Applications: by 15 January for Summer semester and by 15 July for Winter semester.

1130 Technische Universität Ilmenau [TUI]

PO Box 100565
98684 Ilmenau
Tel: +49-3677-69 0
Fax: +49-3677-69-1701
Web: http://www.tu-ilmenau.de
e-mail: webmaster@tu-ilmenau.de

Graduate Programme in Technical Studies

Study Domains: computer science, economic and commercial sciences, electricity and electronics, engineering, mathematics, mechanical engineering, natural sciences.
Programmes: graduate programme in technical studies: courses in mathematics, mechanical engineering, natural sciences, electrical engineering, computer science, automation engineering and economic science.
Open to: applicants from all countries holding a certificate entitling them to study at a university in their home country and recognized as equivalent to the German 'Allgemeine' or 'Fachgebundene Hochschulreife' for undergraduate studies, or having completed university studies for postgraduate studies.
Duration: 4 to 6 years; courses begin in April for summer semester, in October for winter.
Applications: by 15 January for summer semester and by 15 July for winter semester.

1131 University of Potsdam [UP]

Am Neuen Palais 10
14415 Potsdam
Tel: +49-331-977-0
Fax: +49-331-97-2163
Web: http://www.uni-potsdam.de
e-mail: presse@rz.uni-potsdam.de

Undergraduate, Graduate, Postgraduate Programmes

Study Domains: art history, arts, computer science, cultural studies, earth science, ecology, environment, education, languages, linguistics, music and musicology, philology, philosophy, physics, political science, psychology, social sciences, sociology, speech therapy.
Programmes: degree programmes at all levels in all major fields of study.
Open to: applicants from all countries holding a recognized certificate equivalent to the 'Fachgebundene Hochschulreife' and German Language proficiency (DSH).
Fees: registration 200 €; estimated living costs: 600 € per month.
Applications: by 15 January for Summer term and by 15 July for Winter term.

1132 University of Applied Sciences Westcoast [FHW]

Fritz-Thiedemann-Ring 20
25746 Heide
Tel: +49-481-8555-0
Fax: +49-481-8555-101
Web: http://www.fh-westkueste.de

Undergraduate Programmes

Study Domains: business, electricity and electronics, mechanical engineering.
Programmes: Diploma in (a) business administration; (b) engineering.
Open to: candidates must have German 'Fachhochschulreife' or equivalent and German language proficiency.
Duration: 4 years.
Fees: living costs, approx. 500 € per month.
Applications: by 15 July.

1133 University of Applied Sciences, Koblenz [UASK]

Finkenherd 4
56075 Koblenz
Tel: +49-261-9528-209
Fax: +49-261-9528-225
Web: http://www.fh-koblenz.de
e-mail: international@fh-koblenz.de

Undergraduate Programme

Study Domains: applied arts, architecture, business, chemical engineering, civil engineering, computer science, electricity and electronics, energy, engineering, European studies, health and hygiene, information science, mathematics, mechanical engineering, physical education, social sciences, urbanism, vocational training.
Programmes: Bachelor's, Master's degrees, Diploma (FH) Programme.
Open to: all students with university entrance examination and German language proficiency (test Daf or DSH).
Held: campuses in Koblenz; Remagen; Hohr-Grenzhausen.
Duration: 4 months starting 1 October or 15 March.
Fees: registration, approximately 50€; no tuition fees; living costs: approximately 550€ per month.
Applications: by 15 July or 15 January, to the above address; for more information contact international@fh-koblenz.de.

1134 University of Applied Sciences, Regensburg [UR]

Prüfeninger Strasse 58
93049 Regensburg
Tel: +49-941-943-1068
Fax: +49-941-943-1427
Web: http://www.fh-regensburg.de
e-mail: auslandsamt@fh-regensburg.de

Undergraduate Programme

Study Domains: architecture, business, business administration, civil engineering, computer science, electricity and electronics, engineering, international business, mathematics, mechanical engineering.

Programmes: Diploma (FH) degree in engineering, architecture and business.
Open to: candidates must meet academic and German proficiency standards.
Duration: 4 years starting in October.
Fees: registration: 63 €; no tuition fees; living costs: approximately 500 € per month.
Applications: by 15 June, to the above address.

1135 University of Bayreuth [UB]
95440 Bayreuth
Tel: +49-921-550
Fax: +49-921-55-5290
Web: http://www.uni-bayreuth.de
e-mail: poststelle@uvw.uni-bayreuth.de

⌂ Undergraduate, Graduate, Postgraduate Programmes

Study Domains: accounting, African studies, American studies, applied sciences, biochemistry, biology, biophysics, botany, business, business administration, chemistry, cultural studies, earth science, ecology, environment, economic and commercial sciences, education, ethnology, finance, genetics, geography, geology, hydrology, industrial design, international business, international law, languages, liberal arts, linguistics, management, marketing, mathematics, meteorology, microbiology, music and musicology, philosophy, physical education, physics, research, sciences, social sciences, sociology, Swahili, teacher education, technical education, theology, religion, zoology.
Programmes: degree programmes at all levels in all majors fields.
Description: courses in education, sports, health management, philosophy and economics, geographical development, research of Africa, theatre and media, applied sciences, sciences.
Duration: 4 years for academic studies; 3 years for bachelor programmes, 2 years for master programmes, 2 months for Summer courses; courses start 1 April for Summer session, 1 October for Winter session.
Fees: registration: 110€.

1136 University of Education Weingarten
Kirchplatz 2
88250 Weingarten
Tel: +49-751-501-0
Fax: +49-751-501-8200
Web: http://www.ph-weingarten.de
e-mail: poststelle@ph-weingarten.de

⌂ Undergraduate, Graduate, Postgraduate Programmes

Study Domains: education, fine arts, humanities and arts, physical education, sciences.
Programmes: Programmes in Education, Humanities, Science, Fine Arts, Physical Education.
Applications: See website for complete details.

1137 University of Hohenheim [UH]
70593 Stuttgart
Tel: +49-711-4590
Fax: +49-711-459-3960
Web: http://www.uni-hohenheim.de
e-mail: post@uni-hohenheim.de

⌂ Undergraduate, Graduate, Postgraduate Programmes

Study Domains: agriculture, agronomic sciences, anatomy, biochemistry, biology, botany, business administration, chemistry, computer science, economic and commercial sciences, food, food industry, journalism, mathematics, microbiology, natural sciences, nutrition, political science, social sciences, zoology.
Programmes: (a) Diploma courses in: Nutritional Science; Food Chemistry; Food Technology; Biology; Agrobiology; Economics and Business Administration; Phyto-Medicine; Business Education; Agricultural Economics; Social Management; Social Economics; Communication Science; Journalism; (b) Bachelor's Degree in: Business Informatics; Agricultural Sciences; (c) Master's Degree in: Crop Sciences; Animal Sciences; Agricultural Economics; Agricultural

Engineering; Soil Sciences; Agribusiness; Agricultural Sciences, Food Security and Natural Resource Management in the Tropics and Subtropics; Environmental Protection and Agricultural Food Production (Envirofood); (d) Ph.D. research programmes.
Fees: registration 50 Euros; living expenses approx. 500 Euros per month.
Applications: generally by 15 April or 15 July depending on session; contact the International Affairs Office ('Akademisches Auslandsamt') at the above address for precise details.

1138 University of Jena [UJ]
Friedrich-Schiller-Universitat Jena
07740 Jena
Tel: +49-3641-9-300
Fax: +49-3641-931682
Web: http://www.uni-jena.de
e-mail: rektor@uni-jena.de

⌂ Undergraduate, Graduate and Postgraduate Programmes

Study Domains: all major fields.
Programmes: Bachelor's, Master's, Ph.D. degrees.
Open to: candidates of all nationalities with secondary school leaving certificate equivalent to German 'Abitur'; Graduate Diploma required for Ph.D. studies; German language Proficiency (DSH) required.
Duration: 3 years; courses begin in October.
Languages: German; some courses in English.
Applications: by 15 January for Summer semester and by 15 July for Winter semester; contact aaa@uni-jena.de for further information.

1139 University of Leipzig [UL]
Ritterstrasse 26
04109 Leipzig
Tel: +49-341-97-32020
Fax: +49-341-97-32049
Web: http://www.uni-leipzig.de
e-mail: aaa@uni-leipzig.de

⌂ Undergraduate, Graduate, Postgraduate Programmes

Study Domains: all major fields.
Programmes: Diplom, B.Sc., M.Sc., Ph.D.
Open to: applicants from all countries holding a recognized certificate equivalent to the German 'Allgemeine' or 'Fachgebundene Hochschulreife' for undergraduate studies; see website for postgraduate studies.
Duration: 4 to 6 years.

1140 University of Lübeck [UL]
Ratzeburger Allee 160
D-23538 Lübeck
Tel: +49-451-500-3012
Fax: +49-451-500-3016
Web: http://www.uni-luebeck.de
e-mail: ssc@zuv.uni-luebeck.de

⌂ Undergraduate, Graduate Programmes

Study Domains: computer science, medicine.
Programmes: Bachelor's and Master's degrees in computer science, molecular life science and computational life science; state examination in human medicine.
Subjects: human medicine, computer science, molecular life science, computational life science.
Fees: registration: about 85 €; living costs: approximately 500 € per month.
Applications: see website for further details.

1141 University of Paderborn [UP]
Universität Paderbonn
33095 Paderborn
Tel: +49-5251-600
Fax: +49-5251-602519
Web: http://www.uni-paderborn.de
e-mail: ollech@zv.upb.de

⌂ Undergraduate, Graduate, Postgraduate Programmes

Study Domains: all major fields, teacher education.
Programmes: Diploma, Master's degree, Ph.D.; also teacher education programmes.
Open to: candidates from all nationalities fulfilling the necessary requirements.
Duration: 3 to 5 years; courses start in October and April.
Fees: registration: approx. 100 €; living costs: approximately 550 € per month.
Applications: by 15 July (for Winter term); 15 January (for Summer term).

1142 University of Trier [UT]

Universitätsring 15
54286 Trier
Tel: +49-651-201-0
Fax: +49-651-201-4297
Web: http://www.uni-trier.de
e-mail: aaa@uni-trier.de

📖 Undergraduate, Graduate, Postgraduate Programmes

Study Domains: all major fields.
Programmes: Diploma, Master's degree, Ph.D.
Open to: candidates of all nationalities holding a secondary school leaving certificate equivalent to the German 'Reifezeugnis'.
Financial assistance: possibilities of scholarships for foreign students; information on request at zsb@uni-trier.de.

1143 Witten/Herdecke University [WHU]

Alfred-Herrhausen-Straße 50
38488 Witten
Tel: +49-2302-9260
Fax: +49-2302-926-407
Web: http://www.uni-wh.de
e-mail: public@uni-wh.de

📖 Undergraduate and Graduate Programmes

Study Domains: biochemistry, dentistry, economic and commercial sciences, medicine, natural sciences, nursing, pharmacy and pharmacology.
Programmes: Diplom, Bachelor's and Master's degrees.
Description: studies in Medicine, Nursing, Music Therapy, Life Sciences, Economics and Management and Studium Fundamentale.
Open to: candidates of all nationalities with secondary school leaving certificate equivalent to the German 'Abitur'; work experience required for some programmes.
Applications: to the above address.

🎓 Scholarships

Study Domains: all major fields.
Scholarships: Board of Trustees / DAAD.
Duration: 1 to 3 years.
Value: 588€ per month.
Applications: for further details contact dwirth@uni-wh.de.

1144 World University Service, German Committee [WUS]

Goebenstrasse 35
65195 Wiesbaden
Tel: +49-6121-446648
Web: http://www.wusgermany.de
e-mail: info@wusgermany.de

🎓 Scholarships

Study Domains: all major fields.
Scholarships: WUS Scholarships (10).
Open to: Third World students.
Place of study: at universities of the State of Hesse, Germany.
Duration: one year (renewable).
Applications: to the above address.

Ghana

Academic year: October to June.
Monetary unit: cedi (C).
National student admission: Foreign students should have good General Certificate of Education Ordinary O-level passes (or their equivalent) in English language, and 4 other subjects plus 3 Advanced A-level passes (required subjects vary according to degree course).
Language: Good knowledge of English required for all regular university courses. English-language proficiency courses offered; also general orientation programmes for all freshmen.
Immigration requirements: Foreign students must have a passport, visa, health certificate and other immigration requirements as indicated from time to time by the Ministry of Internal Affairs.
Estimated expenses for one academic year: Precise and fully up-to-date information about fees may be obtained only from the universities themselves. Special fares are available for student travel by air and sea on application (endorsed by university) to travel agencies.
Information services:
• Dean of Students, University of Ghana, Legon.
• Registrar, University of Cape Coast, Cape Coast; and University of Science and Technology, Kumasi.
• National Council for Higher Education, Accra.
• Association of African Universities, State House, Accra.
• United Nations Development Programme, Accra.
Open and distance learning: The recently created Ghana National Tertiary Level Distance Education Programme opens up access to higher education; provides an alternative, off-campus channel for tertiary education for qualified people; provides a complementary avenue to higher forms of education provided by the traditional, residential universities; provides an opportunity to those who have the requisite qualifications but have been prevented from having access to tertiary education by various circumstances; and makes the acquisition of a degree more flexible, especially for older adults (such as graduates who want to shift to new areas of studies and lifelong learners). Universities in Ghana offer some of their courses to students outside their walls. Such off-campus students study the same courses and take the same examinations as those in on-campus programmes and are awarded the same degrees when they pass their final examinations. The programme adopts a multi-media approach but the main medium for teaching is self-instructional printed materials sent to students for study. Study centres will be opened in all regional capitals where students can go to for tutorials and counselling. Student assessment is continuous and based on assignments and final examinations.
Recognition of studies and qualification: Foreign credentials in the form of certificates should be sent to the Academic Registrar of the University. This applies to both nationals with foreign credentials and foreigners.
Publications / Websites:
• 'Students Handbook', 'Annual Report' and 'Calendar', issued free by the University of Cape Coast.
• 'Admission Handbook', 'Handbook of the Bachelor's Degree', 'Handbook of Graduate Studies', and 'Handbook of Certificate/Diploma', issued free by the University of Ghana.
• 'Annual Report and Calendar', issued free by the University of Science and Technology.

1145 Accra Polytechnic [AP]

PO Box 561
Accra
Tel: +233-21-662-263
Fax: +233-21-664-797 / 502-495

🎓 Tertiary Study Merit Award Program

Study Domains: accounting, administration, engineering, marketing.
Scholarships: Tertiary Study Merit Award Program.
Subjects: higher national diploma in accounting, marketing, purchasing and supply, secretarial work, engineering, catering.
Open to: registered students of tertiary programmes; of any nationality and age.
Place of study: Accra Polytechnic.
Duration: 1 year (renewable).

Value: approx. US$2,000 per year.
Applications: to the Scholarships Secretariat at the above address.

1146 Ghana Institute of Management and Public Administration [GIMPA]
PO Box 273
Greenhill
Achimota
Tel: +233-21-401-683
Fax: +233-21-405-805
Web: http://www.gimpa.edu.gh
e-mail: Gimpa@ncs.com.gh

Diploma and Graduate Courses in Management

Study Domains: administration, agriculture, finance, health and hygiene, management, pharmacy and pharmacology, rural development.
Programmes: Diploma in Public Administration/Agricultural Administration, and Certificate in Public Administration/Agricultural Administration; Master's Degree in Development Management,.
Description: training programmes and diploma courses in the following areas: chief executive programme, senior management development, budgeting and financial management, project planning and management, personnel management, strategic planning and management, administrative management, agricultural resource management, rural development workshop, health administration and management, micro-computer skills for managers, marketing management, production management, women in management workshop (senior, middle and 1st line), veterinary resource management, procurement management (works/goods).
Open to: nationals of English-speaking African countries, graduates of recognized universities or mature personnel sponsored by their government or corporation, agricultural officers with some working experience, senior medical personnel; good knowledge of English required.
Duration: Master's course, 15 months; Diploma courses, 6 months; Certificate courses, 3 months; regular courses, 1 to 12 weeks depending on the course.
Applications: to the Director-General, at the above address for further information.

1147 University College of Education of Winneba [UCEW]
PO Box 25
Winneba
Tel: +233-432-22269
Fax: +233-432-22268
Web: http://ucewlib@libr.ug.edu.gh
e-mail: ucew@ug.gn.apc.org

Bachelor of Education Programme

Study Domains: education.
Programmes: B.Ed. degree (distance education).
Open to: diploma holders in English education, science education, mathematics education and life skills.
Duration: 3 to 4 years; courses begin in April.
Fees: variable.
Languages: instruction in English.
Applications: by December, to the Registrar, at the above address.

1148 University of Cape Coast [UCC]
University Post Office
Cape Coast
Tel: +233-42-32139
Fax: +233-42-32484
Web: http://www.uccghana.net
e-mail: vcucc@ucc.edu.gh

International Scholarships

Study Domains: agriculture, arts, education, sciences, social sciences.
Scholarships: Association of African Universities (INTERAF) and UNDP scholarships.
Subjects: undergraduate and postgraduate subjects in agriculture, arts, education, science and social science.

Open to: students with good O-level passes in English language and mathematics and 3 other subjects (varying according to course chosen) and 3 A-level passes, 2 of them not lower than D for undergraduate courses; suitably qualified graduates for postgraduate courses.
Duration: 1 to 4 years.
Applications: by 31 March, to the Academic Registrar.

1149 University of Ghana - Institute of African Studies [UOG]
PO Box 73
Legon (Accra)
Tel: +233-21-500-381
Fax: +233-21-500-512
Web: http://www.ug.edu.gh/
e-mail: academic@ug.edu.gh

Graduate, Postgraduate Programmes / African Studies

Study Domains: African studies.
Programmes: (a) M.Phil. and Ph.D. programmes in African studies: arts of Africa, music, dance and drama, African literature, social change, structure of African languages, African social and political systems, African and Ghanaian history, African economic systems; (b) Summer vacation introductory courses in African studies.
Open to: (a) nationals of all countries with first- and second-class degrees in any field of arts or social studies; (b) students and others interested in African studies.
Duration: (a) M.Phil. full-time not less than 2 academic years, part-time not less than 3 academic years; Ph.D. not less than 3 academic years; (b) in July/August.
Fees: (a) tuition: approximately US$2,500; lodging: US$120 per week; meals: US$80 per week.
Languages: instruction in English.
Applications: (a) by 30 March, to the University Registrar, Academic Affairs, at the above address; (b) from organized groups, to the Administration Secretary.

Grèce
Année universitaire: octobre à juin.
Organisation de l'enseignement supérieur:
• Une description détaillée du système d'éducation grec est disponible dans le «EURYBASE»; la base de données EURYDICE des Systèmes d'éducation européens http://www.eurydice.org.
Unité monétaire: Euro (€).
Admission pour étudiants du pays: Diplôme grec de fin d'études secondaires Apolytirion, ou autre diplôme équivalent. Approbation d'inscription par le Ministère de l'éducation. Selon la Convention de La Haye la note de recommandation doit être mentionnée sur ces documents. Les candidats faisant venir leurs documents de l'étranger doivent demander à leurs propres services étrangers d'inscrire la note de recommandation demandée. Par ailleurs, en vue d'accords bilatéraux, les documents en provenance de certains pays n'ont pas besoin d'être authentifiés. Les documents non ratifiés pour leur authenticité par une autorité étrangère ne seront pas acceptés par le comité compétent responsable et les formules de demande d'entrée seront rejetées. Selon les règlements de chaque faculté ou département, les candidats doivent subir un examen médical avant leur inscription.
Connaissances linguistiques requises: Chaque étudiant doit avoir un certificat prouvant ses connaissances de la langue grecque. Ce certificat est délivré après examen soit par l'Université d'Athènes, soit par l'Université de Salonique. Les examens de langue ont lieu en juin et septembre. Pour les cours ayant lieu en hiver, les examens de langue ont lieu en juin à la Faculté de grec moderne de l'Université de Salonique. En octobre, ont lieu les examens pour les étudiants désirant suivre les cours intensifs d'été ou pour ceux qui ont déjà une bonne connaissance de la langue. Pour plus d'informations concernant ces examens de langue, les étudiants doivent s'adresser à l'Université d'Athènes ou de Salonique un mois avant la date de l'examen. Les candidats diplômés d'un lycée grec n'ont pas besoin de passer les tests.
Formalités d'immigration: Les permis de séjour sont accordés aux étudiants par le Département grec du Service des étrangers.

Frais pour une année universitaire: Les étudiants admis doivent s'acquitter d'un faible pourcentage du coût de leurs études et du prix des manuels scolaires qu'ils reçoivent. Les étudiants dont la capacité financière est insuffisante, mais qui se distinguent par leur diligence et leur bonne conduite, peuvent être exemptés de ces frais.
Services d'accueil et d'information: Organismes officiels:
• Ministère de l'éducation nationale, 15, rue Mitropoleos, 10185 Athinaï, Grèce; tél: +30-1-321-1420; fax: +30-1-323-9386; email: kir-sar@ypepth.gr; web: http://www.ypepth.gr/en_ec_home.htm.
• Direction du protocole, Université d'Athènes, Athinaï. Autres services sur place ou à l'étranger:
• Association des étudiants, 15, rue Hippokratous, Athinaï.
• Club universitaire d'Athènes, 15, rue Hippokratous, Athinaï (informations sur le logement, les études, etc.).
Bourses pour étudiants internationaux: Voir site web http://www.ypepth.gr/en_ec_category1126.htm pour de plus amples informations sur les bourses.
Enseignement à distance: L'Université Ouverte Hellénique (EAP) a été fondée par décret en 1992. Située à Patras, elle constitue une université indépendante et auto-administrée. La mission de l'EAP consiste à promouvoir l'enseignement à distance des premier et deuxième cycles universitaires ainsi que d'autres cursus. Elle organise des programmes d'éducation et de formation professionnelle et des programmes de remise à niveau conduisant à l'obtention de Certificats ainsi que des programmes d'éducation pouvant, dans certains cas, conduire à l'obtention de diplômes académiques.
Reconnaissance des études et diplômes: DIKATSA, Leoforos Syngrou 112, 11741 Athens, Greece; tel.: +30 1 975 6362; fax: +30 1 675 6709.
Publications / Sites Web:
• « Orientation professionnelle », de Charles Broussalis, publié en grec par la maison d'édition Orossimo.

1150 American College of Greece, Deree College [ACOG]

6-8 Xenias Street
11528 Athens
Tel: +30-210-748-6580/5
Fax: +30-210-748-3463
Web: http://www.acg.edu
e-mail: info@acg.edu

📖 Undergraduate Programmes

Study Domains: all major fields, summer programmes.
Programmes: Bachelor's degrees.
Description: courses leading to a Bachelor of Arts with majors in dance, economics, English, history, history of art, music, philosophy, psychology, sociology and to a Bachelor of Science in Business Administration with majors in accounting and finance, computer information systems, management and marketing.
Open to: candidates of all nationalities fulfilling the necessary requirements.
Financial assistance: tuition grants and scholarships may be awarded.
Languages: instruction in English.
Applications: by 10 July for fall semester; 15 December for winter session; 10 January for spring semester; 15 May for summer session; write to Admissions Office for further information.

1151 Aristotle University of Thessaloniki [AUTH]

University Campus
54124 Thessaloniki
Tel: +30-2310-996-000
Web: http://www.auth.gr

📖 Undergraduate, Graduate, Postgraduate Programmes

Study Domains: all major fields.
Programmes: Bachelor's, Master's, Ph.D. degrees.
Open to: candidates of any nationality holding a secondary school leaving certificate (or equivalent) and a certificate from the University of Athens or Thessaloniki proving comprehension of Greek language.

Duration: 4 to 6 years (depending on discipline).
Fees: tuition: 369-493 €; living costs: approx. 350-500 € per month.
Financial assistance: some scholarships available for undergraduate and postgraduate programmes; for information contact department of studies, Ioanna Korpidou, tel. +30 10 995 132, Zoi Angeli, tel. +30 10 996 743, fax +30 10 995 112, email, dps@rect.auth.gr.
Languages: instruction in Greek.
Applications: between 1 and 10 August for undergraduate programmes; for graduate programmes contact the appropriate department.

🖋 Scholarship

Scholarships: Aristotle University Scholarships.
Duration: 1 year, renewable.
Value: Tuition waiver; plus living expenses, 293 € per month for undergraduates, 380 for postgraduates.
Applications: between 1 to 15 November; contact dps@rect.auth.gr for further details.

1152 Athens School of Fine Arts [ASFA]

42, Patission street
10682 Athens
Tel: +30-210-3803-010
Fax: +30-210-3828-028
Web: http://www.asfa.gr/eng_site/index.html
e-mail: rofalda@asfa.gr

📖 Undergraduate, Graduate Programmes

Study Domains: fine arts.
Programmes: Bachelor's and Master's degrees.
Open to: candidates of all nationalities; Greek language proficiency; entrance examination in design and colour required.
Duration: 5 years beginning in November.
Fees: current registration: 415 € per year; living costs: approx. 600 € per month.
Applications: from 25 to 31 August, to Mrs Oina Spypopoulou at the above address, tel. +30 10 3816 930, fax +30 10 3829 804.

1153 Greek State Scholarship Foundation [IKY]

Overseas Scholarships Unit
14 Lysikratous Street
10558 Athens
Tel: +30-210-372-6300
Fax: +30-210-322-1863
Web: http://www.iky.gr/scholarships/allodapoi/default.htm

🖋 Postgraduate Scholarships

Study Domains: all major fields.
Scholarships: scholarships for postgraduate, doctoral and postdoctoral research.
Description: studies offered to: (a) nationals of Africa, Asia (excluding Japan); Balkan countries; countries of Central or Eastern Europe; (b) nationals of the United States, Canada, Latin America, Australia, Japan and Western Europe; (c) foreign nationals or non-Greek nationals of Greek origin from the countries of Central or Eastern Europe or from the democracies of the former Soviet Union or from Greek-speaking regions of a foreign country in order to attend courses and seminars in modern Greek language and culture.
Open to: applicants must have an excellent knowledge of English or French, be nationals of the specific countries noted above; for (a) and (b), not over 35 years (for postdoctoral applicants, 40 years), for (c) not over 50 years; (a) and (b) must hold a graduate degree from a foreign university and a first postgraduate degree M.A. or D.E.A.; (c) must hold a graduate degree from a foreign university.
Duration: (a) to (c) 1 year (renewable for 2 additional years).
Applications: (a) to (c) by 31 March; application forms (available from Greek Diplomatic Missions or from I.K.Y.) must be submitted through the Greek Diplomatic Authorities; I.K.Y. will not accept or acknowledge applications sent directly to I.K.Y.; see website for details.

1154 **Technological Educational Institute of Kalamata [TEIK]**
Antikalamos
24100 Kalamata
Tel: +30-721-45100
Fax: +30-721-45200 / 69047
Web: http://www.teikal.gr
e-mail: career@teikal.gr

  □ **Undergraduate Programmes**

Study Domains: accounting, administration, agriculture, applied sciences, biochemistry, biology, botany, business administration, ecology, environment, economic and commercial sciences, finance, genetics, horticulture, management, technology.
Programmes: Bachelor's degree.
Open to: candidates of any nationality holding a secondary-school certificate (or equivalent).
Duration: 4 years.
Languages: Greek; Greek proficiency certificate required.

1155 **Technological Educational Institute of Larissa [TEIL]**
Nea Utiria TEI
41110 Larissa
Tel: +30-2410-684200
Fax: +30-2410-610803
Web: http://www.teilar.gr
e-mail: olgabalabekou@teilar.gr

  □ **Undergraduate Programmes**

Study Domains: accounting, advertising, agriculture, agronomic sciences, applied sciences, business administration, chemistry, computer science, economy, energy, engineering, forestry, hydraulics, management, marketing, mechanical engineering, nursing, telecommunications, tourism, hotel and catering management.
Programmes: Bachelor's degree.
Open to: candidates holding a secondary school leaving certificate; candidates must pass the Panhellenic exams (national level).
Duration: 4 years (beginning in September).
Languages: Greek; language proficiency certificate required.

1156 **Université d'agriculture d'Athènes [UDD]**
Iera Odos 75
11855 Athènes
Tel: +30-210-549-4893
Web: http://www.aua.gr
e-mail: webmaster@aua.gr

  □ **1er-3e cycles / agriculture**

Domaines d'étude: agriculture.
Programmes: Ptychio, Didaktoriko.
Description: cours dans les domaines de l'agriculture, de la production animale, de la biologie et de la biotechnologie, de l'économie agricole et des industries agricoles.
Durée: Ptychio: 5 ans; Didaktoriko: s'obtient avec la thèse.

1157 **Université de Ionnina [UDI]**
Dompoli 30
45110 Ionnina
Tel: +30-651-97111
Fax: +30-651-44112
Web: http://www.uoi.gr
e-mail: intrel@cc.uoi.gr

  □ **1er, 2e, 3e cycles / toutes disciplines principales**

Domaines d'étude: histoire, informatique, langues, médecine, philosophie, sciences.
Programmes: programmes de cours conduisant aux diplômes suivants: (a) Ptychion, (b) Médecine; psychiatrie sociale, (c) Metaptychiakon Spoudon Exidikefsis, (d) Didaktoriko.
A l'intention de: ressortissants de tout pays titulaires d'un diplôme de fin d'études secondaires; l'admission se fait sur examen.
Durée: (a) 4 ans, (b) 6 ans, (c) 2 ans, (d) s'obtient avec la thèse.

1158 **Université de Macédoine, Économie et Sciences Sociales [UDM]**
Egnatia 156
54006 Thessalonique
Tel: +30-2310-891-244
Web: http://www.uom.gr
e-mail: pubrel@macedonia.uom.gr

  □ **1er, 2e cycles / administration-economie**

Domaines d'étude: administration, économie, finances, informatique.
Programmes: Ptychio (B.A.), Metaptychiakon Spoudon Exidikefsis (M.A.).
Description: cours dans les domaines de l'économie, de l'administration, des études politiques et économiques européennes et internationales, des finances et de la gestion, de l'informatique appliquée, de la politique sociale et de l'éducation.
A l'intention de: titulaires d'un diplôme de fin d'études secondaires (ou équivalent); l'admission se fait sur examen.

1159 **Université de Thessalie [UDT]**
Phileninon-Argonafton
38221 Volos
Tel: +30-2421-074000
Fax: +30-2421-076614
Web: http://www.uth.gr

  □ **1er, 2e, 3e cycles / toutes disciplines principales**

Domaines d'étude: agriculture, biologie, économie, éducation, éducation physique, études d'infirmière, ingénierie, médecine, médecine vétérinaire, sciences humaines, sciences sociales.
Programmes: Ptychio (B.A.); Diplôme de médecine vétérinaire; Diplôme de médecine; Diplôme d'ingénieur.
A l'intention de: titulaires d'un diplôme de fin d'études secondaires; l'admission se fait sur examen.
Inscriptions: du 1er au 10 août au Ministère de l'Éducation national et des Affaires religieuses; Département des examinations d'entrée à l'Université; Mitropoleos 15, 10185 Athènes (Grèce); tél: +30 210 3247428, fax: +30 210 3234812.

1160 **Université Démocrite de Thrace [UDTh]**
Democritou 17
69 100 Komotini - Rhodopi
Tel: +30-25310-39084
Fax: +30-25310-39086
Web: http://www.duth.gr
e-mail: intrela@duth.gr

  □ **1er, 2e, 3e cycles / toutes disciplines principales**

Domaines d'étude: toutes disciplines principales, administration, affaires internationales, agriculture, architecture, droit, écologie, environnement, économie, éducation, éducation de la première enfance, éducation physique, électricité et électronique, ethnologie, génie civil, histoire, informatique, ingénierie, littérature et civilisation, médecine, relations internationales, ressources naturelles.
Programmes: Ptychio; Engineering diploma; Didaktoriko (Ph.D.).
A l'intention de: ressortissants de tout pays titulaires d'un diplôme de fin d'études secondaires; l'admission se fait sur examen.

1161 **Université des affaires et des sciences économiques d'Athènes [UDAEDS]**
76, rue Patission
10434 Athènes
Tel: +30-210 820-3250
Fax: 30-210-822-8419
Web: http://www.aueb.gr

  □ **1er, 2e, 3e cycles / affaires, sciences économiques**

Domaines d'étude: économie, informatique, mécanique, statistique.
Programmes: Ptychio (B.A.), Metaptychiakon Spoudon Exidikefsis (M.A.), Didaktoriko (Ph.D.).

Description: cours dans les domaines de l'économie, des études économiques européennes et internationales, de l'administration, des statistiques, du management et du marketing, de l'informatique appliquée.
A l'intention de: ressortissants de tout pays titulaires d'un diplôme de fin d'études secondaires; l'admission se fait sur examen.

1162 Université du Pirée [UP]

Karaoli et Dimitriou 80
18534 Le Pirée
Tel: +30-1-414-2000
Fax: +30-1-414-2328
Web: http://www.unipi.gr
e-mail: publ@unipi.gr

📖 **1er, 2e, 3e cycles / économie, finance, informatique**

Domaines d'étude: administration des affaires, économie, enseignement technique, études internationales, finances, formation des enseignants, industrie et commerce, informatique, sciences de la mer.
Programmes: Ptychio, Didaktoriko.
A l'intention de: ressortissants de tout pays titulaires d'un diplôme de fin d'études secondaires; l'admission se fait sur examen.

1163 Université nationale de technologie d'Athènes [UD]

Iroon polytechniou 9
Zografou University Campus
15780 Zografou
Tel: +30-210-772-1000
Fax: +30-210-772-2048
Web: http://www.ntua.gr

📖 **1er, 2e, 3es cycles / toutes disciplines principales**

Domaines d'étude: toutes disciplines principales.
Programmes: (a) Ptychio, (b) Metaptychiakon Spoudon Exidikefsis, (c) Didaktoriko.
Description: cours en art, droit, économie et sciences politiques, théologie, médecine, sciences, pharmacie, médecine dentaire, éducation physique, communication, musique, théâtre, philosophie et histoire des sciences.
A l'intention de: ressortissants de tout pays titulaires d'un diplôme de fin d'études secondaires; l'admission se fait sur examen.
Durée: (a) 4-6 ans, (b) 4 ans, (c) s'obtient avec la thèse.

1164 University of Athens [UOA]

Studies Department
6, Chr. Lada str.
10561 Athens
Tel: +30-210-368-9770
Web: http://www.uoa.gr

📖 **Undergraduate, Graduate Programmes**

Study Domains: all major fields, Greek, summer programmes.
Programmes: Undergraduate and Graduate degrees in all major fields.
Open to: students with high school or university diplomas.
Duration: variable, depending on programme.
Applications: to the above address for undergraduate programmes; for graduate programmes: University of Athens, Graduate Studies & Research Department, 6, Chr. Lada str., 10561 Athens (Greece); tel: +30 1 3689203, fax: +30 1 3231606.

1165 University of Crete-Heraklion

Knossou Ave.
P.O. Box 2208
71409 Heraklion, Crete
Tel: +30-2810-393-000
Web: http://www.uoc.gr

🎓 **Undergraduate, Graduate Scholarships**

Study Domains: all major fields.
Description: several scholarships are awarded annually to outstanding foreign students enrolled in undergraduate or graduate studies at the University.

Applications: contact the Office of International Relations at the above address.

1166 University of Crete-Rethymnon [UOC]

University Campus
741 00 Rethymnon, Crete
Tel: +30-8310-77000
Fax: +30-8310-77909
Web: http://www.uoc.gr

📖 **Undergraduate, Graduate and Postgraduate Programmes**

Study Domains: all major fields.
Programmes: (a) Ptychio, (b) Metaptychiakon Spoudon Exidikefsis, (c) Didaktoriko.
Open to: candidates of any nationality holding a secondary school certificate or equivalent.
Duration: (a) 4 years, (b) a further 1 or 2 years, (c) a further 2 or 3 years.
Applications: by September.

1167 University of Patras

University Campus
265 000 Patras
Tel: +30-2610-997-608
Fax: +30-2610-991-711
Web: http://www.upatras.gr
e-mail: registrar@upatras.gr

📖 **Undergraduate, Graduate, Postgraduate Programmes**

Study Domains: all major fields.
Programmes: (a) Diploma, (b) Ptychio, (c) Pharmacy, (d) Medicine.
Open to: candidates of any nationality holding a secondary-school certificate.
Duration: (a) 5 years; (b) 4 years; (c) 5 years; (d) 6 years.
Languages: Greek (Greek language programme for foreign students available).

Guatemala

Año académico: Enero a noviembre.
Moneda nacional: Quetzal.
Admisiones para estudiantes extranjeros: Bachillerato o diploma de graduado de un programa oficial de estudios secundarios (5 años como mínimo) reconocido por el gobierno de Guatemala.
Conocimientos lingüísticos: Es indispensable dominar el idioma español.
Servicios de información:
• Ministerio de Educación Pública, Departamento de Coordinación con Organismos Internacionales, Palacio Nacional, Ciudad de Guatemala.
• Universidad de San Carlos de Guatemala, Departamento Estudiantil, Sección Socioeconómica, Ciudad Universitaria, zona 12, Ciudad de Guatemala (puede orientar a los estudiantes para encontrar alojamiento).
• Centro Universitario, Ciudad Vieja, 10a. Avenida 35-36, zona 11, Ciudad de Guatemala.
Convalidación de estudios y diplomas: Departamento de Registro y Estadísticas, Universidad de San Carlos de Guatemala, Ciudad Universitaria, Zona 12, Guatemala 01012, Guatemala. Tel.: +502-2-760-790; fax: +502-2-767-221; web: http://www.usac.edu.gt.
Publicaciones / Sitios web:
• "Guía de Admisión", Departamento de Registro y Estadística, Universidad de San Carlos de Guatemala, Ciudad Universitaria, zona 12, Guatemala.

1168 Instituto Guatemalteco Americano [IGA]

Ruta 1, Vía 4, 4-05, zona 4
Guatemala

📖 **Programa de cursos**

Campos de estudios: español, idiomas, inglés.
Descripción:

(a) Cursos especiales de español para grupos (a todos los niveles);
(b) Cursos de inglés.
Duración: cursos bimestrales.
Inscripciones: hasta 1 semana antes del inicio del bimestre en la Dirección de Cursos del Instituto.

1169 Universidad de San Carlos de Guatemala [USAC]

Ciudad Universitaria, zona 12
Guatemala
Tel: +502-2443-9500
Web: http://www.usac.edu.gt

♥ Becas de posgrado

Campos de estudios: todas las materias principales.
Descripción: Becas ofrecidas por diversos gobiernos y organismos internacionales para cursar estudios de posgrado.
Materias de estudio: las de interés para la Universidad de San Carlos o el país, especialmente en las áreas de ciencias básicas y tecnológicas.
Se conceden: a graduados, a nivel de pregrado, en la USAC. Al terminar los estudios, la Universidad puede requerir del becario que preste servicios relacionados con su especialización.
Lugar: cualquier país.
Importe: los gastos de viaje corren a cargo del patrocinador o del proprio becario.

1170 Universidad del Valle de Guatemala [UVG]

Oficina de Información y Relaciones Públicas
18 Avenida 11-95, Zona 15, Vista Hermosa III
Guatemala
Tel: +502-2-692-563
Web: http://www.uvg.edu.gt
e-mail: info@uvg.edu.gt

⌑ Programas universitarios

Campos de estudios: todas las materias principales.
Descripción:
(a) Ciencias y humanidades: licenciaturas en áreas de biología; bioquímica y microbiología; ecoturismo; física; ingeniería civil, electrónica, agronómica, en alimentos, en computación, forestal, industrial, química; letras; matemáticas; música; nutrición; química; química farmacéutica; maestrías en economía aplicada y administración de negocios; en estudios ambientales; en ingeniería estructural; en informática y ciencias de la computación; en ciencia y tecnología de alimentos;
(b) Ciencias sociales: licenciaturas en antropología, en arqueología, en historia, en psicología, en sociología; maestrías en desarrollo, en psicología aplicada a la administración de recursos humanos;
(c) Educación: profesorados especializados; licenciaturas en educación, en educación para la salud; maestrías en administración educativa, en currículo, en medición, evaluación en investigación educativas.
(d) Cursos en línea.
Inscripciones: (d) en la página web general, consultar los enlaces "Servicios externos", "Cursos en línea".

1171 Universidad Francisco Marroquin [UFM]

Sexta Calle Final - Zona 10
Apartado Postal 632 - A
01009 Guatemala
Tel: +502-2338-7700
Fax: +502-2334-6896
Web: http://www.ufm.edu.gt
e-mail: inf@ufm.edu.gt

⌑ Programas universitarios

Campos de estudios: todas las materias principales.
Descripción:
(a) Licenciaturas en: administración de empresas, administración de sistemas de información, arquitectura, ciencias de la comunicación, economía, ciencias políticas, relaciones internacionales, contaduría pública y auditoría, derecho, historia, ingeniería de sistemas, informática y ciencias de la computación, medicina, odontología, psicología, pedagogía y ciencias de la educación, teología,

ciencias de la religión, ingeniería industrial, nutrición clínica, ingeniería electrónica, psicología clínica, psicología industrial organizacional, publicidad;
(b) Profesorados de enseñanza media en: ciencias de la comunicación social, computación, filosofía, lenguaje y estudios sociales, matemática y física, pedagogía y ciencias de la educación, teología, historia del arte, inglés;
(c) Carreras intermedias: análisis de sistemas, operador de computadoras (programa para minusválidos), programación, ciencias de la comunicación social;
(d) Carrera corta terminal: técnico en administración de personal;
(e) Cursos de posgrado en: administración de empresas, administración de recursos humanos, ciencias sociales, economía, medicina, oftalmología, sistemas de información, investigación de operaciones, tecnología y recursos humanos, bases de datos, análisis y administración de confiabilidad, biofísica, biotecnología y bioinformática de aplicación clínico hospitalaria en análisis de sistemas, relaciones internacionales;
(f) Doctorado en derecho;
(g) Cursos a distancia (Instituto de Educación Abierta, IDEA): licenciaturas en informática y administración de empresas, informática y recursos humanos, informática y control de calidad, informática y educación, informática y banca, informática y administración municipal, informática y turismo y administración de hoteles.
Se destina(n): a candidatos de cualquier nacionalidad que posean un diploma de enseñanza secundaria.
Asistencia financiera: créditos educativos reembolsables después de la graduación.
Inscripciones: exámenes de aptitud en junio, julio, octubre y noviembre; inscripciones en noviembre.

1172 Universidad Mariano Gálvez de Guatemala [UMG]

3a Avenida 9-00 zona 2
Finca El Zapote
01002 Guatemala
Tel: +502-2288-7592
Fax: +502-288-4040
Web: http://www.umg.edu.gt

⌑ Programas universitarios

Campos de estudios: todas las materias principales.
Descripción:
(a) Cursos de licenciatura (se otorga título profesional en algunos casos) en: ciencias jurídicas y sociales, economía, contaduría pública-auditoría, administración de empresas, comercio internacional, mercadotecnia, ingeniería civil, industrial, electrónica, en sistemas, arquitectura, pedagogía y ciencias de la educación, administración educativa, teología, sociolingüística, psicología clínica, estomatología, enfermería, arquitectura de interiores, ciencias de la computación (con especialidad en administración de empresas);
(b) Carreras intermedias: técnico en gerencia en contabilidad, técnico universitario (publicista profesional, locutor profesional, periodista profesional, en decoración y diseño de interiores), gerencia, visita médica, diplomado en administración secretarial;
(c) Profesorado de enseñanza media en pedagogía y ciencias de la educación, en lingüística aplicada, en inglés, en ciencias comerciales, en psicología;
(d) Postgrados (maestría, M.A y/o doctorado según el caso): derecho notarial, psicología clínica, dinámica humana, ortodoncia y ortopedia maxilofacial, ingeniería civil, administración de proyectos, construcción, administración financiera, administración de recursos humanos.
Duración: (a) entre 4 y 6 años; (b) 7 semestres; (comienzan en febrero).
Inscripciones: (a) hasta el 31 de enero, a la dirección que figura en el título; (b) hasta fin de febrero, en la Oficina del Departamento de Registro.

Guyana

Academic year: September to August.
Monetary unit: Guyana dollar (G$).
National student admission: Foreign students should have the following qualifications or their equivalent: (a) Caribbean Examinations Council General Proficiency Certificate (Grades I and II); (b) General Certificate of Education with five O-level passes; five subjects including English language at not more than 2 sittings. In the Faculty of Social Sciences passes in English language and mathematics are compulsory.
Language: The language of instruction at the University of Guyana is English. Orientation courses are provided for foreign students.
Information services:
• Students' Welfare Division, University of Guyana; PO Box 101110; Turkeyen; Georgetown; Guyana.
• Student Affairs Division, Ministry of Education; 21 Brickdam and Pollard Place; Georgetown; Guyana.
Open and distance learning: The Institute of Distance and Continuing Education (ICDE), which is a branch of the University of Guyana, offers a Diploma in Occupational Health and Safety. It also collaborates with the National Association of Secretaries in offering a two-year programme leading to the award of the Administrative Professional Secretaries Diploma.
Recognition of studies and qualification: Guyana National Equivalency Board, Public Service Management; 164 Waterloo Street; Georgetown; Guyana; tel: +592-22-57350.

1173 Guyana School of Agriculture [GSOA]

Mon Repos
East Coast, Demerara
Tel: +592-020-2297
Fax: +592-020-2297
Web: http://www.agrinetguyana.org.gy/gsa/
e-mail: gsa@sdnp.org

📖 Undergraduate Programmes

Study Domains: agriculture, food, forestry, management, marketing, nutrition, sciences.
Programmes: programme of courses leading to Certificate in (a) Forestry, (b) Agriculture.
Open to: candidates of all nationalities who are: (a) secondary school graduates or mature persons, 25-40 years of age, who have a sound primary education plus 5 or more years of experience in the forestry sector; (b) youths (at least 17 years old) having successfully completed primary education and intending to enter farming careers.
Duration: (a) the course is organized over an academic year (courses begin in September) and is residential; (b) 2 academic years.
Fees: US$2,213 per school year (subject to change).
Applications: by 31 April, to the Principal of the school, at the above address.

1174 University of Guyana [UOG]

PO Box 101110
Georgetown
Tel: +592-222-5402
Fax: +592-222-2490
Web: http://www.uog.edu.gy
e-mail: pro@uog.edu.gy

📖 Undergraduate, Graduate, Postgraduate Programmes

Study Domains: agriculture, arts, education, health and hygiene, music and musicology, natural sciences, social sciences, technology.
Programmes: programme of courses leading to (a) Certificate, (b) Diploma, (c) Bachelor's degree, (d) postgraduate and (e) Master's degree.
Description: (a) Certificates in education, health sciences, music; 15 participants; (b) Diploma programmes in health sciences, social sciences, technology, forestry, steel band music, tourism studies, transport, computer studies, environmental sciences; (c) Bachelor's degree in agriculture, arts, education, health sciences, natural sciences, social sciences, technology; (d) Postgraduate diploma programmes in education, social sciences; (e) Master's degree in

agriculture, arts, education, natural sciences, social sciences.
Open to: suitably qualified candidates of all nationalities.
Duration: (a) and (b) 1 to 2 years; (c), (d) and (e) 1 to 4 years (courses begin in September).
Fees: (a) US$2,600-$3,000; (b), (c) and (d) US$4,000; (e) US$4,600; other expenses US$350; all fees are payable in advance.
Financial assistance: the University of Guyana does not offer scholarships to students; however, private agencies sponsor students in mining, agriculture, banking, finance, economics.
Languages: instruction in English.
Applications: to the Public Relations Officer for University bulletin and information; to Admissions Division for courses/programmes; to the Registrar for other correspondence.

Honduras

Año académico: Enero a noviembre.
Admisiones para estudiantes extranjeros: Título de Bachiller, Perito o Maestro, debidamente legalizado; pago de derechos de matrícula y asistencia al curso de Orientación General, previamente al inicio de las clases.
Conocimientos lingüísticos: Dominio completo del idioma español; en caso de necesitar perfeccionarse, los estudiantes deben ponerse en contacto con el Departamento de Letras y Lenguas de la Universidad Nacional Autónoma de Honduras, Tegucigalpa, MDC., Honduras, o seguir los cursos de español, poniendo el acento en la comprensión de la lectura y gramática españolas en la Universidad Privada "José Cecilio del Valle", apartado postal 917, Tegucigalpa D.C.
Formalidades de inmigración: La información pertinente debe solicitarse en cada Consulado.
Servicios de información: Organismos oficiales:
• Secretaría de Educación Pública, a través de la Dirección General de Planificación Educativa, 1a. Calle entre 2a. y 4a. Avenidas, Comayagüela MDC.
• Instituto Hondureño de Turismo, Secretaría de Cultura y las Artes, Tegucigalpa, MDC.
Otras entidades en el país y en el extranjero:
• Consulados y Embajadas de Honduras acreditados en cada país.
Enseñanza abierta y a distancia: La Universidad Nacional Autónoma de Honduras (Sistema Universitario de Educación a Distancia) ofrece enseñanza superior a distancia, así como la Universidad Pedagógica Nacional Francisco Morazán en campos de ciencias sociales, matemáticas, artes, humanidades y lenguas, comercio, ciencias exactas y naturales y ciencias domésticas. Los estudiantes deben cumplir los mismos requerimientos académicos que los alumnos regulares.
Convalidación de estudios y diplomas: Consejo Universitario, Universidad Nacional Autónoma de Honduras, Apartado Aéreo 8778, Ciudad Universitaria José Trinidad Reyes, Tegucigalpa MDC, Honduras; tel: +504-239-1194; fax: +504-231-0651.

1175 Universidad 'José Cecilio del Valle' Tegucigalpa [UJCV]

Apartado postal 917, Col. Humuya
Ave. Altiplano, Calle Poseidón
Tegucigalpa
Tel: +50-4-239-2125; +50-4 239-491
Fax: +50-4-239-8448
Web: http://www.ujcv.edu.hn
e-mail: info@ujcv.edu.hn

🎓 Becas de estudio

Descripción: ayudas financieras dependiendo del nivel académico y necesidades económicas del candidato.
Solicitudes: hasta octubre de cada año.

1176 Universidad Católica de Honduras "Nuestra Señora Reina de la Paz" [UCHNSRP]
4473 Tegucigalpa, MDC
Tel: +50-4-238-6795
Fax: +50-4-238-6797
Web: http://www.unicah.edu
e-mail: unicahn@sdnhon.org.hn

📖 **Programas universitarios**

Campos de estudios: administración de empresas, ciencias económicas y comerciales, derecho, estudios dentales, finanzas, gestión, informática, ingeniería, ingeniería civil, marketing, relaciones internacionales, teología, religión.
Descripción:
(a) Carreras: ingeniería ambiental, civil, en ciencias de la computación, industrial; cirugía dental; licenciatura en administración de empresas, en derecho, en mercadotecnia, en psicología, en relaciones internacionales, en finanzas;
(b) Posgrados: maestrías en administración de empresas, en gestión de proyectos, en comercio exterior y relaciones internacionales, en gestión de la calidad total en la educación, ciencias religiosas, doctorado en administración de empresas.
Duración: (a) 4 años.
Inscripciones: por mayor información, dirigirse a Vicerrectoría Académica.

1177 Universidad Nacional Autónoma de Honduras [UNADH]
Posgrado Centroamericano en Economía y Planificación del Desarrollo
Apartado postal 1748
Tegucigalpa, D.C.
Tel: +50-4-232-2558
Fax: +50-4-232-2558
Web: http://www.unah.hondunet.net
e-mail: webmaster@ns.unah.hondunet.net

📖 **Programas universitarios**

Campos de estudios: ciencias económicas y comerciales, economía, estudios sobre el desarrollo.
Descripción:
(a) Maestría en economía y desarrollo;
(b) Cursos cortos: formulación y evaluación de proyecto, temas de política económica, informática aplicada a la investigación; métodos de investigación.
Se destina(n): (a) a hondureños, nacionales de países centroamericanos y del Caribe, con conocimientos suficientes de español y como mínimo lectura del inglés, que posean una licenciatura en economía o un área afin; los hondureños deben realizar curso propedéutico de septiembre a noviembre, para los extranjeros existe examen de admisión.
Duración: (a) curso bianual de 2 años académicos (inicio en marzo).
Asistencia financiera: (a) se conceden becas.
Inscripciones: (a) en julio y agosto; dirigirse a POSCAE, Tegucigalpa, Apartado 9050, Ciudad Universitaria, Honduras, C.A.

1178 Universidad Pedagógica Nacional "Francisco Morazán" [UPNM]
Boulevard Centro América
Apartado Postal 3394
Tegucigalpa M.D.C.
Tel: +50-4-328-037
Fax: +50-4-311-257
Web: http://www.upnfm.edu.hn

🏆 **Becas de estudio**

Campos de estudios: educación, educación de la primera infancia, educación especial, educación física, enseñanza técnica, formación de docentes.
Descripción: Profesorado en educación en el grado de licenciatura en las siguientes especialidades y concentraciones: ciencias naturales (biología-química, física-química o física-biología), matemáticas (computación o matemática pura), educación técnica industrial (madera, electricidad o metal mecánica), educación técnica para el hogar (nutrición o corte y confección), educación comercial,

letras y lenguas (español o inglés), educación física, arte, ciencias de la educación (educación preescolar, educación especial, orientación educativa o administración educativa) y ciencias sociales (historia o geografía, maestría en educación), supervisión primaria y dirección de escuela.
Se conceden: a nacionales y extranjeros, graduados en educación secundaria en las especialidades de maestro de educación primaria, bachiller en ciencias y letras, perito mercantil, contador público, y otras que sean debidamente acreditadas por la Secretaría de Educación Pública y aceptadas por el Consejo de Educación Superior de Honduras.
Duración: técnicos: 2 años; maestría: 2 años; licenciatura: 4 años.
Solicitudes: desde febrero hasta diciembre.

1179 Zamorano - Escuela Agrícola Panamericana [ZEAP]
Apartado 93
Tegucigalpa, D.C.
Tel: +50-4-776-6140
Fax: +50-4-776-6240
Web: http://www.zamorano.edu.hn

📖 **Programa superior**

Campos de estudios: agricultura, ciencias agronómicas.
Descripción: Programa conducente a la obtención del título de agrónomo o de ingeniero agrónomo.
Se destina(n): a estudiantes que hayan completado sus estudios secundarios con alto rendimiento académico y que superen examen de admisión y entrevista.
Duración: 4 años (comienzan en enero).
Inscripciones: dirigirse a la Oficina de Admisiones y Becas.

Hungary

Academic year: September to June.
Organization of higher education system: The first Hungarian university was founded in 1367. The modern higher education system consisting of universities and colleges emerged in the 20th century. Hungary is now part of the European Union and the Hungarian higher education institutions (HEIs) are now part of the European Higher Education Area.The Hungarian higher education system consists of 68 HEIs. Hungarian HEIs grant degrees following a binary pattern. Universities can offer both BA and MA as well as PhD/DLA degrees while colleges offer BA degrees. Hungarian HEIs use ECTS-compatible credit system. The duration of the courses may vary but the average length of education at college level is 3-4 years and in universities 5 years. Many Hungarian HEIs offer programmes in foreign languages especially in the field of engineering, economics and medicine but also in arts and sciences etc. The academic year is divided into 2 semesters. The autumn semester lasts from September to January while the spring semester from February to June. Each semester includes 14-15 weeks of lectures, seminars and training followed by a 6-day examination period.
Monetary unit: forint.
National student admission: The admission procedure is in the process of changing. The dual system of admission will be replaced by a single school-leaving examination (érettségi bizonyítvány) required for admission to higher level studies.
International student admission: Foreign students must have the 'maturity' or school-leaving certificates with good grades and a recent medical certificate to enter the first year of studies. The universities and colleges define the level of school achievement and the subjects to be taken into consideration. There are certain higher education programmes where students are admitted on the basis of selection (entrance examination). The universities and colleges often admit foreign students and not only to the first year; recognition of their academic achievements could be accredited. Foreign students may apply for scholarships (grants) to study in Hungary if there is a bilateral agreement between Hungary and the home country. There are also international (European or subregional) schemes which provide possibilities of studying here.
Language: generally Hungarian, however, more and more universities and colleges offer degree programmes and courses in English, German, French or Russian. For more

information visit: www.om.hu; www.campushungary.hu..
Candidates with insufficient knowledge of Hungarian must
attend a one-year Hungarian-language course and pass the
end-of-year examination at the Balassi Bàlint Institute, where
courses on social, economic and cultural life in Hungary are
also organized (ww.bbi.hu). Other larger universities,
independently or jointly, also offer Hungarian preparatory
courses (www.nyariegytem.hu).
Immigration requirements: A visa is not necessary for
stays of less than 90 days in Hungary for nationals of
European Union countries. However, a residence permit is
necessary. Nationals of other countries require a visa for entry
and must apply for a residence permit as well. For complete
information contact: Bureau of Immigration and Citizenship:
+36-1-463-9180 or see the website of Hungarian Embassies
and Consulates: www.kulugyminiszterium.hu.
Estimated expenses for one academic year:
• Tuition: preparatory programme: 600€ per course;
undergraduate programme: 2,700-3,000€ per semester;
graduate programme: 3,000-3,500€ per semester
• Housing: 100-300€ per month in university housing.
• Health care: 80€ per month.
Information services: Authority to whom international
students' application should be addressed: National Higher
Education Admissions Office: www.felvi.hu.
Other agencies:
• Hungarian institutes abroad: www.magyarintezet.hu.
• Hungarian embassies and consulates:
www.kulugyminiszterium.hu.
Scholarships for international students: The Hungarian
Scholarship Board is responsible for bilateral educational,
scientific and cultural exchange programmes:
www.scholarship.hu
Tempus Public Foundation: European Union exchange
programmes for university studies: www.tpf.hu.
Open and distance learning: The National Council for
Distance Education: www.ntt.hu.
Recognition of studies and qualification: The Hungarian
Accreditation Committee (HAC) is responsible for evaluating
and accrediting the quality of teaching and research at higher
education institutions in Hungary and giving
recommendations to the Minister of Education. The HAC
accredits both programmes and institutions. For further
information: www.mab.hu.
Accommodation services: Housing facilities are available
in dormitories of most universities or colleges at a cost of
approximately 100-300€ per month. Apartment rentals may
be found through the university and local newspapers at a cost
of approximately 300-500€ per month.
Work opportunities: Detailed information can be found at
the institutions of higher education or on websites
www.minddiak.hu; www.fmm.gov.hu.
Publications / Websites: Useful information for foreign
students can be found at www.budapestudent.org;
www.studyhungary.hu; www.pesterfloyd.hu;
www.budapester.hu; www.budapestsun.hu; www.jfb.hu.;
www.hungarytourism.hu; www.magyarorszag.hu;
www.jobmonkey.com/teaching/europe/html/hungary.html.

1180   Academy of Drama, Film and Television [SFF]
Vas u. 2/c1088
1088 Budapest
Tel: +36-1-318-8111
Fax: +36-1-338-4749
Web: http://www.filmacademy.hu

📖 Graduate Programme / Cinema

Study Domains: cinematography.
Programmes: Programme of courses leading to Master of
Arts in directing and cinematography.
Open to: secondary school graduates, aged 18-28;
proficiency in English required.
Duration: 4 years.
Fees: tuition: US$10,000 per year.
Languages: instruction in English.
Applications: by 30 April, to the above address.

1181   Albert Szent-Györgyi Medical and Pharmaceutical Center [SZOTE]
Dóm tér 12
6720 Szeged
Tel: +36-62-545-028
Fax: +36-62-544-562
Web: http://www.szote.u-szeged.hu/angoltit
e-mail: ba@medea.szote.u-szeged.hu

📖 Graduate, Postgraduate Programmes / Medicine, Pharmacy

Study Domains: medicine, pharmacy and pharmacology.
Programmes: programme of courses leading to Doctor of
general medicine, Master of Pharmacy.
Open to: candidates of any nationality with a high-school
leaving certificate; age between 18 and 35; fluent in English.
Duration: 5 to 6 years.
Languages: instruction in English and Hungarian.
Applications: by 30 June, to the English Program
Secretariat, at the above address.

1182   Bánki Donát Polytechnic [BDMF]
Népszinház u. 8
1081 Budapest
Tel: +36-1-219-6300
Fax: +36-1-219-6413
Web: http://www.banki.hu
e-mail: int.eng@bgk.bmf.hu

📖 Undergraduate Programme / Engineering

Study Domains: engineering.
Programmes: programme of courses leading to B.Eng.
(Honours) in integrated engineering.
Open to: secondary-school graduates with a TOEFL score
of 550 or IELTS 5.0.
Duration: 3 years.
Fees: tuition: US$1,800 per semester; application fee:
US$50.
Languages: instruction in English.
Applications: by 30 June, to the Office for Engineering
Programmes in English, at the above address.

1183   Budapest Business School Faculty of International Management and Business [KKF]
22-24 Diósy L.U.
1165 Budapest
Tel: +36-1-467-7800
Fax: +36-1-407-1563
Web: http://www.kkf.hu/english/index.htm

📖 Undergraduate / Business Studies

Study Domains: business administration, international
business, international law, international relations,
management, marketing.
Programmes: B.A. (Honours) in European Business
Administration.
Open to: candidates of any nationality holding a secondary
school-leaving certificate; TOEFL, IELTS required.
Duration: 7 semesters (10 months per academic year).
Languages: instruction in English or French.
Applications: to the above address.

1184   Budapest University of Economic Sciences and Public Administration [BKE]
Fövám tér 8
1093 Budapest
Tel: +36-1-217-6740
Fax: +36-1-217-6714
Web: http://www.bkae.hu
e-mail: intoffice@nko.bke.hu

📖 Undergraduate, Graduate Degree Programmes

Study Domains: accounting, administration, archaeology,
business, business administration, communication, computer
science, economic and commercial sciences, English, history,
information science, international business, law, management,

marketing, mathematics, political economy, political science, psychology, social sciences, statistics, trade.
Programmes: programme of courses leading to Bachelor's and Master's degrees.
Open to: candidates of any nationality holding a secondary school leaving certificate; test in mathematics and English, CV in English and two letters of recommendation for Master's programme.
Duration: 4 years for a Bachelor's and 2 years for a Master's degree.
Fees: current registration: US$50; tuition: US$2300 per semester for Bachelor's programme and US$2,700 per semester for Master's programme; estimated living costs: HUF 200,000 per month.
Languages: language of instruction: English; TOEFL 500 required for admission to Bachelor's programme and 550 for admission to Master's programme.
Applications: by 31 May, to the above address; for information contact Doris Keszthelyi for Bachelor's programme, email: doris@isc.bkae.hu. and Hanna Varjas for Master programme, email: hanna@isc.bkae.hu.

1185 Central European University
Nador u. 9
1051 Budapest
Tel: +36-1-327-3009
Fax: +36-1-327-3211
Web: http://www.ceu.hu
e-mail: finaid@ceu.hu

☞ Financial Aid
Scholarships: (a) full or partial CEU Fellowship; (b) full or partial tuition waivers.
Duration: 1 academic year; renewable.
Value: (a) tuition: US$11,300; living expenses: US$3,000-$5,000; (b) full tuition: US$11,300; partial tuition: US$9,040-$5,650.
Applications: beginning January; to Admissions Office.

1186 Corvinus University of Budapest
Faculty of Horticultural Science
[KEE]
Villányi út 29-43
1118 Budapest
Tel: +36-1-482-6200
Web: http://www.kee.hu

📖 Postgraduate Programme / Landscape Architecture
Study Domains: architecture.
Programmes: programme of courses leading to doctorate (Ph.D.) in landscape architecture.
Open to: candidates of any nationality holding M.Sc. degree; age limit 35.
Duration: 3 years.
Fees: US$4,500 per year.
Languages: instruction in English.
Applications: by 30 June, to the University Registrar.

1187 Debrecen Agricultural University
Faculty of Agricultural sciences [DATE]
Böszörményi út 138
4032 Debrecen
Tel: +36-52-508-444
Fax: +36-52-486-292
Web: http://www.date.hu

📖 Ph.D. Programme / Agriculture
Study Domains: agriculture, agronomic sciences.
Programmes: Ph.D. courses in plant production and agro-ecology, agricultural economics and management, and environment-friendly animal production based on regional sources.
Open to: candidates of any nationality; presentation of an outlined research plan and 2 letters of reference from supervisors or former professors required.

Duration: 3 years.
Fees: US$600-$800 depending on programme.
Languages: instruction in Hungarian or English.

1188 Hungarian University of Craft and Design
Zugligeti Ut 9-25
1121 Budapest
Tel: +36-1-392-1180
Fax: +36-1-392-1188
Web: http://www.mie.hu
e-mail: rektori@mie.mie.hu

📖 Graduate Programme
Study Domains: applied arts, architecture, art history, arts, arts and crafts, decorative arts, design, graphic arts, industrial design, interior design, international relations, international studies, photography, printing, visual arts.
Programmes: programme of courses leading to Master's degree.
Open to: candidates of any country holding a secondary-school certificate; entrance examination required.
Fees: tuition: US$450 per month.

1189 International Peto András Institute - Conductors' College [MPANI]
Kútvölgyi út 6
1125 Budapest
Tel: +36-1-224-1500
Fax: +36-1-355-6649
Web: http://www.peto.hu
e-mail: info@peto.hu

📖 Undergraduate, Graduate Programmes
Study Domains: education, special education.
Programmes: conductor-teacher training, education for the physically handicapped including courses in pedagogy, psychology, conductive education, adapted medical biology, teaching technique, practical training.
Open to: Bachelor's degree programme: candidates of any nationality holding a secondary-school certificate; Master's degree programme: candidates holding a university degree in education or a teacher's certificate.
Duration: 4 to 2 years.
Fees: tuition: US$780 per month; registration: US$30.
Languages: instruction in Hungarian and English.
Applications: by 31 March, to the above address.

1190 Kálmán Kandó College of Engineering [KKMF]
Tavaszmezo u. 15-17
1084 Budapest
Tel: +36-1-210-1415
Fax: +36-1-303-9425
Web: http://www.jozsef.kando.hu
e-mail: Temesvari.Zsolt@kvk.bmf.hu

📖 Undergraduate Programme / Engineering
Study Domains: engineering.
Programmes: programme of courses leading to Bachelor's degree in integrated engineering (B.Eng.).
Open to: students with secondary-school certificate; a good command of mathematics, physics and English is required.
Duration: 3 years.
Fees: tuition, US$1,800 per semester.
Applications: by 31 March, to the above address.

1191 Semmelweis University [SOTE]
Üllöi út 26
1085 Budapest
Tel: +36-1-266-0120
Fax: +36-1-317-2220
Web: http://www.sote.hu
e-mail: engsec@rekhiv.sote.hu

📖 Undergraduate, Postgraduate Programmes
Study Domains: dentistry, health and hygiene, medicine, paramedical studies, pharmacy and pharmacology, physical education.

Programmes: programme of courses leading to Bachelor's degree, Master's degree (M.D.) and Doctorate (D.M.D.) in medicine, dentistry and pharmacy.
Description: (a) Doctor of Medicine; (b) Doctor of Dentistry; (c) Master of Science in pharmacology; (d) Master of Education in physical education; (e) Master of Science in human kinesiology; (f) Master of Education in health studies teaching (part-time study programme); (g) Master of Education in health and physical education; (h) Master of Education in health and physical education; (i) Master of Education in adapted physical education (part-time study programme); (j) Master of Education in physical education and adapted P.E.; (k) Bachelor of Science in coaching and Bachelor of Art in sport management (part-time study programmes); (l) Bachelor's degree in dietetics, nursing, physiotherapy, public health and epidemiology inspector, health visiting, health care specialist educator, oxyology; (m) Bachelor's degree in optometry; (n) Doctor of philosophy.
Open to: candidates of all nationalities; age: 18 to 30; working knowledge of English, German and Hungarian necessary.
Duration: (a) 6 years; (b) 5 years; (c) 5 years; (d) 4 years; (e) 4 years; (f) 4 years; (g) 5 years; (h) 5 years; (i) 5 years; (j) 5 years; (k) 4 years; (l) 4 years each; (m) 3 years; (n) 3 years.
Fees: tuition: M.D., D.M.D. and pharmacy programmes: US$9,000 per year; physical education programme: US$6,900 per year; Ph.D. programme: US$3,000 per year.
Financial assistance: reduction of tuition fee for academic excellence.
Languages: instruction in English, German and Hungarian.
Applications: for M.D., D.M.D., pharmacy programmes and human kinesiology-rehabilitation programme: by end of April; for physical education programme: by end of May; for Ph.D. programmes: by end of June, to the above address.

1192 Széchenyi István University - Institute of Transportation and Mechanical Engineering [SZE]

1. Egyetem tér.
9026 Gyor
Fax: +36-96-503-400
Web: http://www.sze.hu/siceng/
e-mail: sze@sze.hu

📖 Graduate Programmes / Engineering

Study Domains: architecture, civil engineering, ecology, environment, electricity and electronics, mechanical engineering.
Programmes: courses in architecture, civil engineering, electrical and electronic engineering, engineering pedagogy, mechanical engineering, transportation engineering, economics and management, information technology, municipal engineering, environmental engineering, integrated engineering, engineering management.
Open to: Hungarian and international students aged 18 to 23 years holding a school-leaving diploma.
Duration: 3 years.
Financial assistance: some scholarships may be available for foreign students.
Languages: Instruction in English.

1193 Szent István University [GATE]

Páter Károly u. 1
2000 Gödöllo
Tel: +36-28-522-000
Web: http://www.sziu.hu
e-mail: Khaled.Karim@fh.szie.hu

📖 Undergraduate, Graduate, Postgraduate Programmes

Study Domains: agriculture, agronomic sciences, biology, business, business administration, economic and commercial sciences, information science, mechanical engineering, social sciences, veterinary sciences.
Programmes: Programmes at the following schools: School of Business and Information Technology; School of Engineering and Architecture; School of Agriculture and Life Sciences.
Open to: candidates of all nationalities with relevant degrees.

Financial assistance: fees can be waived in case of bilateral or multilateral agreements of international exchange programmes.
Languages: instruction in Hungarian, English, French and German.
Applications: see web site for full details: http://www.sziu.hu/.

1194 Technical University of Budapest [BME]

Pf. 91
1521 Budapest
Tel: +36-1-463-1111
Fax: +36-1-463-1110
Web: http://www.bme.hu
e-mail: admission@tanok.bme.hu

📖 Undergraduate and Postgraduate Programmes

Study Domains: architecture, engineering.
Programmes: programme of courses leading to Bachelor of Science, Master of Science and Ph.D. degrees.
Description: courses in architecture, chemical engineering, civil engineering, electrical engineering, mechanical engineering and transportation engineering.
Open to: candidates of any country holding a secondary-school certificate; minimum age 18.
Duration: 2 to 4 years.
Fees: tuition: US$4,400.

1195 University Medical School of Debrecen [DOTE]

Nagyerdei krt. 98
4012 Debrecen
Fax: +36-52-419-807
Web: http://www.dote.hu

📖 Postgraduate Programme / Medicine

Study Domains: medicine.
Programmes: programme of courses leading to Doctor of General Medicine.
Open to: candidates of any nationality holding a secondary-school certificate; good command of English required; age limit 35.
Duration: 6 years.
Fees: tuition, US$7,000 per year; other expenses: US$400-500 per month.
Languages: instruction in English.
Applications: by 30 April, to the Registrar's Office.

1196 University of Debrecen [DE]

Debreceni Egyetem 4010
PO Box 37
Debrecen
Tel: +36-52-512-963/900
Fax: +36-52-310-007
Web: http://www.unideb.hu
e-mail: internationaloffice@admin.unideb.hu

📖 Undergraduate, Graduate, Postgraduate Programmes

Study Domains: all major fields.
Programmes: programme of courses leading to Bachelor's, Master's and Ph.D. degrees.
Open to: candidates of any nationality holding a secondary-school certificate (or equivalent).
Fees: tuition: from US$2,600-$8,000 per year (depending on programmes); living costs: approx. US$4,500 per year.
Financial assistance: some government scholarships available; for information contact ministry of education; tel: +36 1 302 0600; fax: +36 1 331 7575; email: info@om.hu, website: http://www.om.hu.
Languages: language of instruction: Hungarian; foreign candidates must present an official copy of language knowledge certificate.

1197 University of Miskolc [ME]

Miskolc-Egyetemváros 3515
Tel: +36-46-363-901
Fax: +36-46-363-901
Web: http://www.uni-miskolc.hu
e-mail: rekkhi@gold.uni-miskolc.hu

📖 Undergraduate and Graduate Programmes / Engineering

Study Domains: computer science, engineering, mechanical engineering, metallurgy.
Programmes: programme of courses leading to Bachelor's degree in computer science and Master's degree in material engineering, metallurgical engineering, computer-aided design, computer-aided technology planning, microelectronics, information engineering and petroleum engineering.
Open to: candidates of any nationality with secondary-school certificate (or equivalent).
Duration: Bachelor's programme: 3 years; Master's programme: 5 years.
Fees: registration: US$30; tuition: US$2,000-$3,500 per semester (depending on programmes); living costs: approximately US$400 per month.
Languages: language of instruction: English.
Applications: by 15 August to the Foreign Students Office at the above address.

1198 University of Pécs International Relations Office [PTE]

Szántó K.J.u.1/b
7633 Pécs
Tel: +36-72-501-509
Fax: +36-72-251-527
Web: http://www.nko.pte.hu
e-mail: int@iro.pte.hu

📖 Undergraduate Programme

Study Domains: all major fields, business, continuing education, economic and commercial sciences, education, engineering, health and hygiene, humanities and arts, law, medicine, music and musicology, sciences, visual arts.
Programmes: (a) Doctor of General Medicine (M.D.); BSc Honours Psychology; (c) BEd of Kindergarten Teacher; BA (Hons) Business Administration Programme; (e) MSc (Hons) International Business Management Programme; (f) MSc degrees in Architecture, Civil Engineering (g) MA in Music, Sculpture; (h) Doctor of Liberal Arts (DLA) Programme; (i) PhD programme in Business Administration;.
Description: Studies offered at the following faculties: Adult Education and Human Resources Development; Law; Medical School; Humanities; Health Sciences; Ilyés Gyula Faculty of Education; Business and Economics; Music and Visual Arts; Pollach Mihaly Faculty of Engineering; Sciences.
Subjects: Faculty of Adult Education and Human Resources Development; Faculty of Law; Medical School; Faculty of Humanities; Faculty of Health Sciences; Illyés Gyula Faculty of Education;
Faculty of Business and Economics; Faculty of Music and Visual Arts; Pollach Mihaly Faculty of Engineering: Faculty of Sciences.
Open to: candidates of any nationality holding a secondary-school certificate (or equivalent).
Duration: 3 years beginning in September.
Applications: by 31 May, 15 June, 15 August and 15 January to the above address.

1199 University of Szeged [SZTE]

Dugonics tér 13
6720 Szeged
Tel: +36-62-544-000
Fax: +36-62-420-412
Web: http://www.u-szeged.hu

📖 Undergraduate, Graduate, Postgraduate Programmes

Study Domains: all major fields.
Programmes: programmes of courses leading Bachelor's degree, Master's degree and Ph.D.; undergraduate, graduate, postgraduate and professional programmes offered at the following faculties: (a) Faculty of Arts (BTK):

http://www.arts.u-szeged.hu; (b) Faculty of Economics and Business Administration (GTK): http://www.eco.u-szeged.hu; (c) College Faculty of Food Technology Engineering (SZEF): http://www.szef.u-szeged.hu; (d) Faculty of Science (TTK): http://www.sci.u-szeged.hu; (e) Faculty of Law (AJTK): http://www.juris.u-szeged.hu; (f) Faculty of Medicine (AOK): http://www.szote.u-szeged.hu; (g) Faculty of Pharmacy (GYTK): http://www.szote.u-szeged.hu/gytk; (h) College Faculty of Agriculture (MFK): http://www.mfk.u-szeged.hu; (i) College Faculty of Health Sciences (EFK): http://www.efk.u-szeged.hu; (j) Faculty of Teacher Training (JGYTFK): www.jgytf.u-szeged.hu; (k) Hungary & East-Central Europe International Studies Center: http://www.arts.u-szeged.hu/hungarianstudies.
Description: undergraduate and graduate studies are not formally separated but form integral parts of a unified curriculum leading directly to a degree comparable to the American Master's degree.
(a) courses lead to M.A. level degree as well as specializations; (b) several forms of training offered through regular or correspondence courses; distance education and Ph.D. programmes are offered to graduates with considerable scientific support from other faculties; (c) training for engineers through regular or correspondence courses; undergraduate courses lead to B.Sc. degree in food processing; (d) offers undergraduate to postgraduate degrees in all scientific fields; (e) offers undergraduate to postgraduate degrees in law, through regular and correspondence courses; (f), (g) medical and pharmaceutical programmes of study; (h) programme of agricultural engineering through regular and distance education; practical training on pilot farm; (i) special training focused on practical experience in health visitor services; general social work, nursing and physiotherapy; (j) graduate and postgraduate programmes for training of elementary school teachers; (k) short and long study and degree programmes.
Duration: full period of training for most programmes is 4 years; but varies according to type of programme.
Languages: some courses offer instruction in English.
Applications: for more information see websites of individual faculties or contact the university at the above address.

1200 University of West Hungary [NYME]

4 Bajcsy Zs. Street
9400 Sopron
Tel: +36-99-518-100
Fax: +36-99-311-103
Web: http://www.nyme.hu
e-mail: rectoro@nyme.hu

📖 Undergraduate, Graduate, Postgraduate Programmes

Study Domains: agriculture, applied arts, ecology, environment, economic and commercial sciences, engineering, forestry.
Programmes: programme of courses leading to Certificate; Professional title; Specialization diploma; Doctorati Oklevél (Ph.D.).
Open to: candidates of any nationality holding a secondary school leaving certificate; admission test.

1201 University of West Hungary, Faculty of Economic Sciences

4 Bajcsy Zs. Street
9400 Sopron
Tel: +36-99-518-257
Fax: +36-99-518-257
Web: http://www.uniwest.hu/index.php?id=2372
e-mail: ecoman@ktk.nyme.hu

📖 Graduate, Postgraduate Programmes

Study Domains: accounting, advertising, business, communication, computer science, continuing education, economic and commercial sciences, education, European studies, human sciences, international relations, journalism, languages, law, political economy, political science, public relations, vocational training.
Programmes: graduate and postgraduate programmes in economic sciences and European studies.

Open to: candidates must pass 'maturity' exam and admissions tests.
Fees: tuition fees: 1,000 € per semester; living expenses: 1,000 €.
Languages: fluent Hungarian or English.
Applications: by March of each year; courses begin in September.

Iceland

Academic year: September to May; divided into autumn and spring semesters. Autumn semester generally starts at the beginning of September and lasts until late December. Spring semester lasts from early January until the end of May.
Organization of higher education system: The modern Icelandic system of higher education dates back to the foundation of the University of Iceland in 1911. The University of Iceland remains the principal institution of higher learning in Iceland, but over the last three decades new institutions with a more specialized focus have emerged, increasing the diversity at the higher education level.
• University Education: higher education institutions in Iceland operate within the general framework of recent legislation, the Universities Act, No. 136/1997. In the Universities Act, the Icelandic term 'háskóli' is used to refer to traditional universities, as well as institutions which do not carry out research. The act thus does not make a distinction between universities (universitatis) and other institutions providing higher education. According to the Act, the Minister of Education, Science and Culture determines whether and to what extent the institutions shall engage in research and he is responsible for establishing rules on quality evaluation and recognition of all degrees offered. The role of each higher education institution is further defined in special acts or charters.
The following qualifications are offered at Icelandic higher education institutions:
• Diploma/Certificate, awarded after one and a half or two years of first cycle (undergraduate) studies.
• Bachelor's degree (BA, BS, BEd etc.), awarded to students who have satisfactorily completed three to four years of first-cycle studies (90-120 credits, 180-240 ECTS). The Bachelor's degree constitutes a formal qualification for postgraduate (second cycle) studies.
• Candidatus degree (kandidatsgráda) qualifies the holder for a special office or profession. The Candidatus programmes last from four to six years.
• Postgraduate certificates (Diploma/Certificate) are offered after one or two years postgraduate study after the Bachelor's degree.
• Master's degree (meistaragráda, MA, MS etc.), awarded after successful completion of two years' postgraduate study. A major thesis or research project is a substantial part of the programme.
• Doctorate degree (doktorsgráda), awarded to those who have successfully completed a doctorate programme (a five-year second and third cycle programme, or three years after a Master's degree) and/or defended a doctoral thesis.
Major institutions of higher education: Currently there are eight institutions categorized as 'háskóli' in Iceland. Three of these are private, but are run with state support. The University of Iceland is the largest institution, with 11 faculties. The institutions differ greatly in the extent to which they engage in research and the number of programmes offered. The higher education institutions are:
• University of Iceland http://www.ask.hi.is
• University of Akureyri http://www.unak.is
• Reykjavik University http://www.ru.is
• Iceland University of Education http://www.khi.is
• Agricultural University of Iceland http://www.lbhi.is
• Holar College http://www.holar.is
• Iceland Academy of the Arts http://www.lhi.is
• Bifrost School of Business http://www.bifrost.is.
Monetary unit: Icelandic Krona (ISK).
National student admission: Icelandic 'Stúdentspróf' (Matriculation examination) obtained after 10 years of compulsory education (age 6-16) and 4 years in upper secondary education (age 16-20).
International student admission: In general, for admission to institutions at the higher education level students must have passed the matriculation examination - university entrance examination - or its equivalent. The legislation on higher

education institutions of 1997 includes provisions for all higher education institutions to set their own admission criteria. Admission may also be granted to students who have completed studies abroad which ensure sufficient preparation for university studies and are equivalent to the Icelandic matriculation examination. Institutions of higher education may also grant admission to students who have completed other studies in Iceland. In some subjects there are admissions tests, for example, in physiotherapy and medicine.
Language: Icelandic is the language of instruction in all higher educational institutions. A few programmes are also taught in English.
Immigration requirements: All international students need a residence permit for stays of longer than 3 months; (a) most European Union (EU) and the European Economic Area (EEA) citizens are allowed to request a residence visa after entering the country. EU and EEA citizens do not need a special work permit, only residence permit; (b) citizens of countries that joined the Union after the enlargement of the European Union on 1 May 2004 must obtain a residence permit before entering the country due to a two-year adjustment period; (c) citizens of Nordic countries that plan to study in Iceland have to bring 'Internordisk flytteattest'; Nordic citizens do not need a work permit for employment in Iceland; (d) citizens of non-EU or EEA countries must obtain visa and residence permits before entering the country; however, some nationals of non EU / EEA countries do not require a visa before entry in Iceland for a stay of up to three months in all within the Schengen area, which must not exceed three months in any six-month period; consult website www.utl.is for list of concerned countries.
• The residence permit may be obtained from the Icelandic Directorate of Immigration, Skógarhlíð 6, 105 Reykjavik; http://www.utl.is.
Estimated expenses for one academic year: Tuition: registration fee: 45,000 ISK at state-funded universities. Tuition at private (state supported) universities: from 200,000 ISK to 400,000 ISK for one academic year. Books/Supplies: variable; housing: 30,000 ISK per month for a single room with access to kitchen and bathroom and at least 40,000 ISK for a small apartment. Estimated cost of living in Iceland is about 80,000 ISK per month per person.
Information services: Official national bodies:
• Office of International Education/Socrates National Agency; Neshagi 16; 107 Reykjavik, Iceland; email: ask@hi.is; web: http://www.ask.hi.is
• Ministry of Culture, Education and Science: Sölvhólsgötu 4; 150 Reykjavík; Iceland.
• Office of Academic Affairs at the University of Iceland,; v/Sudurgötu; 101 Reykjavík; Iceland - for Information and advice concerning study facilities in Iceland.
• The University College of Akureyri; Counselling Services; Pingvallastræti 23; 600 Akureyri, Iceland.
• The University College of Education, Counselling services, Stakkahlíd, 105 Reykjavík.
• The Icelandic College of Engineering and Technology, Counselling services, Höfdabakka 9, 112 Reykjavík.
• The Agricultural College, Department of Agricultural Science, Counselling services, 311 Borgarnes.
• Student Council at the University of Iceland, v/Sudurgötu, 101 Reykjavík.
• See further information about university studies at www.ask.hi.is / www.nordenedu.net / www.eurydice.org.
• international coordinators at each university.
• Intercultural Center http://www.ahus.is Hverfisgötu 18, 101 Reykjavik; info@ahus.is.
Scholarships for international students: Icelandic government scholarships: Scholarships in Icelandic Studies available for Foreign Students from the Icelandic Ministry of Education, Science and Culture http://eng.menntamalaraduneyti.is; Reykjavik; postur@mrn.is.
Open and distance learning: Several institutions offer distance education courses.
Recognition of studies and qualification: Academic recognition Information Centre; Director of Academic Affairs; Office for Academic Affairs, University of Iceland, v. Sudurgotu, 101 Reykjavik, Iceland; tel: +354-525-4360; fax: +354-525-4317; email: thordkri@hi.is; web: www.naric-enic.hi.is/.
Work opportunities: Information available through the Directorate of Labour http://www.vinnumalastofnun.is; vinnumalastofnun@vmst.stjr.is.

Publications / Websites:
• Ministry of Education, Science and Culture; postur@mrn.is; http://eng.menntamalaraduneyti.is
• Office of International Education; ask@hi.is; http://www.ask.hi.is.

1202 Bifrost School of Business [BSB]
Bifrost
311 Borgarnes
Tel: +354-433-3000
Fax: +354-433-3001
Web: http://www.bifrost.is
e-mail: bifrost@bifrost.is

Undergraduate, Graduate Programmes / Business, Law
Study Domains: business administration, law.
Programmes: programme of courses leading to Bachelor's and Master's degrees in business administration.
Duration: 3 to 5 years, depending on programme.
Fees: tuition: 3,900 € per year; estimated living costs: 900 € per month (including rent).
Languages: languages of instruction: Icelandic and English.
Applications: by 15 June at the following email address: bifrost@bifrost.is; for information contact Sigrun Hjartar; email: sigrun@bifrost.is.

1203 Ministry of Culture, Education and Science [MOCAE]
Sölvhólsgötu 4
150 Reykjavik
Tel: +354-545-9500
Fax: +354-562-3068
Web: http://www.menntamalaraduneyti.is
e-mail: postur@mrn.stjr.is

Scholarships for Icelandic Studies
Study Domains: cultural studies.
Scholarships: Scholarships for Icelandic studies.
Subjects: Icelandic language, literature and history.
Open to: (a) students from all countries; beneficiary countries are decided each year by the Ministry of Education; (b) students of Icelandic origin from Canada or the United States.
Duration: 8 months.
Value: sufficient to cover board and lodging, plus tuition.
Applications: in France: Ministère de l'Éducation Nationale, Direction de la Coopération et des Relations Internationales, 110 rue de Grenelle, 75357 Paris Cedex 7; in the United Kingdom: by 1 April to Icelandic Embassy, 1 Eaton Terrace, London SW1; in the United States: Institute of International Education, 809 United Nations Plaza, New York, N.Y. 10017; other countries: to relevant department of candidate's government.

1204 Reykjavik University [RU]
Ofanleiti 2
103 Reykjavik
Tel: +354-510-6200
Fax: +354-510-6201
Web: http://www.ru.is
e-mail: bjorg@ru.is

Undergraduate, Graduate Programmes
Study Domains: business, computer science, law.
Programmes: programme of courses leading to Bachelor's and Master's degrees.
Open to: candidates of any country holding a secondary-school certificate (matriculation or equivalent).
Languages: languages of instruction: Icelandic and English.

1205 Sigurdur Nordal Institute [SNI]
PO Box 1220
121 Reykjavik
Tel: +354-1-562-6050
Fax: +354-1-562-6263
Web: http://www.nordals.hi.is
e-mail: nordals@hi.is

Scholarships / Icelandic Studies
Study Domains: cultural studies, languages.
Scholarships: Sigurdur Nordal Institute Scholarships.
Subjects: Icelandic language, culture and society.
Open to: writers, translators and scholars (not university students) in the field of humanities and social sciences from outside Iceland; preference will be given to candidates from Eastern or Southern Europe, Asia, Africa, Latin America and Oceania.
Duration: at least 3 months.
Value: travel expenses to and from Iceland plus living expenses during the period of study.
Applications: by 31 October, to the above address.

1206 University of Akureyri [UNAK]
Solborg V/Nordurslod
600 Akureyri
Tel: +354-463-0900
Fax: +354-463-0999
Web: http://www.unak.is
e-mail: international@unak.is

Undergraduate, Graduate Programmes
Study Domains: biochemistry, business, computer science, early childhood education, ecology, environment, education, fisheries, nursing, teacher education, tourism, hotel and catering management.
Programmes: programme of courses leading to Bachelor's and Master's degrees.
Languages: languages of instruction: Icelandic and English.

1207 University of Iceland [UOI]
Office of International Education
Neshagi 16
107 Reykjavik
Tel: +354-525-4311
Fax: +354-525-5850
Web: http://www.hi.is
e-mail: ask@hi.is

Undergraduate, Graduate, Postgraduate Programmes
Study Domains: all major fields.
Programmes: programme of courses leading to Baccalaureatus Artium (BA), Baccalaureatus Scientiarum (BSc), Candidatus, Meistaraprof (MA), Doktorsprof (PhD).
Open to: candidates of any country holding a secondary-school certificate.
Languages: languages of instruction: Icelandic and English.
Applications: by 15 March for exchange students and 5 June for Icelandic and Nordic students.

Scholarships
Study Domains: cultural studies, Scandinavian studies.
Scholarships: Icelandic Ministry of Education Science and Culture Scholarships for Foreign Students.
Subjects: Icelandic language, history and literature.
Open to: candidates in countries designated each year by the Icelandic Ministry of Education, Science and Culture to participate in the scholarship programme; the Ministry of Education, Science and Culture in each of the recipient countries selects a candidate for the award; working knowledge of English necessary.
Duration: 1 academic year from September to April/May; consent of the Icelandic Ministry of Education, Science and Culture necessary for the same student to receive the scholarship more than once; no one may receive the scholarship more than 3 times.
Applications: participating countries shall inform the Icelandic Ministry of Education, Science and Culture of scholarship candidate nominees from their respective countries by 15 May at the latest.

India

Academic year: June/July to April/May.
Monetary unit: Indian rupee.
National student admission: They vary according to the courses undertaken. Twelve years secondary stage programme with English as one of the subjects. Science stream subjects - physics, chemistry, mathematics, biology are required for admission to professional courses.
Language: Knowledge of English is essential for regular university courses. Where necessary, special English-language courses are organized prior to university entrance from 1 March to 30 June.
Estimated expenses for one academic year: Tuition fees vary according to the university attended. Tuition fee and hostel accommodation at
the colleges/university centres is highly subsidized.
Information services:
• Students' Information Service Unit, Association of Indian Universities, AIU House, 16 Kotla Marg, New Delhi 110 002; India (provides information on the university system of education). Enquiries relating to courses of study, academic terms, sports facilities, scholarships, dates on academic sessions, registration, may be addressed to them. Foreign students intending to join Indian universities may write to the Evaluation Unit of the Association for assessment of qualifications and their eligibility to various programmes.
• Foreign Student Advisers at all the principal Indian universities may be contacted for information and assistance.
• Indian Council for Cultural Relations - ICCR (M/OEA), Azad Bhawan, IP Estate, New Delhi.
• Indian diplomatic missions abroad.
Open and distance learning: Since its inception in 1962 at the University of Delhi, distance education has grown considerably. There are now some sixty Institutes/Directorates of distance education attached to conventional universities and ten Open Universities, including Indira Gandhi National Open University with over 150 regional centres throughout India. Distance education programmes cover about one hundred Degree/Diploma courses. Many conventional universities also offer correspondence courses which are sometimes supplemented by contact classes.
Recognition of studies and qualification: Association of Indian Universities; AIU House; 16 Kotla Marg; New Delhi 110002; India; tel: +91-1-323-6105; fax: +91-11-323-2131.
Publications / Websites:
• 'Directory of Institutions of Higher Education', published by the Ministry of Education and Culture, New Delhi 110 001.
• 'Universities Handbook'; 'Handbook of Engineering Education'; 'Handbook of Management Education'; 'Handbook of Medical Education'; 'Handbook of Agricultural Education' and 'Handbook on Distance Education' published by the Association of Indian Universities, AIU House, 16 Kotla Marg, New Delhi 110 002.
• 'Studying in India', published by the ICCR.
These publications are generally available with Indian Missions.

1208 CCS Haryana Agricultural University [CCSHAU]

125 004 Hisar
Tel: +91-1662-231-171 / 73
Fax: +91-1662-234-952
Web: http://hau.ernet.in
e-mail: reg@hau.ernet.in

📖 Undergraduate, Graduate Programmes

Study Domains: agriculture, agronomic sciences, food industry, sciences, veterinary sciences.
Programmes: B.Sc, B.Tech (Agril.Engg.), B.Sc. Home Science, B.V.Sc. and A.H, M.Sc. Agriculture, M.B.A., MTech. (Animal Science), M.Sc. Basic Science, MSc. (Foods Science & Technology), · M.Sc. (Home Science), M.V.Sc,.

1209 Chaudhary Sarwan Kumar Himachal Pradesh Agricultural University

176 062 Palampur
Tel: +91-1894-230-383
Fax: +91-1894-230-511
Web: http://www.hillagric.org
e-mail: reg@hillagric.org

🎓 Scholarship

Scholarships: College Merit Scholarship.

1210 Dr Harisingh Gour University [DPS]

470 03 Sagar, Madhya Pradesh
Tel: +91-7582-264796
Fax: +91-7582-264163
Web: http://www.sagaruniversity.nic.in
e-mail: sagaruniversity@mp.nic.in

📖 Undergraduate, Graduate and Postgraduate Programmes

Study Domains: pharmacy and pharmacology.
Programmes: Programme of courses leading to Bachelor's degree, Master's degree, Ph.D.
Open to: candidates with Higher Secondary Certificate Examination (10 + 2 pattern) of Indian Board/Universities, or equivalent; foreign applicants are nominated by the Indian Government.
Duration: Bachelor programme: 4 years; Master programme: 1½ years; Ph.D. programme: 2 to 3 years (courses begin in July).
Financial assistance: some scholarships from the Indian Government to deserving candidates.
Languages: instruction in English.
Applications: by 30 June, to the Head (for Indian nationals); through the Government of India, Ministry of Human Resource Development, Department of Education, New Delhi (for foreign students).

1211 Forest Research Institute (FRI) Deemed University

PO IPE
Kaulagarh Road
Dehradun
Tel: +91-135-751-826
Fax: +91-135-756-865
e-mail: ranaak@icfre.org

📖 Graduate, Postgraduate Programmes

Study Domains: earth science, ecology, environment, forestry, genetics, geology, research.
Programmes: programme of courses leading to Master's degree, Ph.D. and postgraduate diploma.
Description: postgraduate diploma in plantation technology, pulp and paper technology, biodiversity conservation; M.Sc. in forestry (economics and management), wood science and technology, environment and management; Ph.D. in forestry.
Open to: candidates of any country with relevant qualifications: admission in Master programme: candidates must hold a Bachelor's degree; admission in Ph.D. programme; candidates must hold a Master's degree; admission for postgraduate diploma: candidates must hold a Master's degree.
Languages: language of instruction: English.
Applications: by August to the above address; for information contact S. D. Arora, Registrar, email: arorasd@icfre.org.

1212 Goa University [GU]

Sub Postal Office Goa University
Taleigao Plateau
Panjim
403 206 Goa
Tel: +91-83-245-1576
Fax: +91-83-245-1376
Web: http://www.goauniversity.org
e-mail: registra@unigoa.ac.in

📖 Graduate, Postgraduate Programmes

Study Domains: all major fields.
Programmes: programme of courses leading to Master's and Ph.D degrees.
Open to: candidates of any country holding relevant qualifications: admission to Master's degree programmes: candidates must hold a Bachelor's degree with grades meeting Department criteria; admission to Ph.D. programmes: candidates must hold a Master's degree; admission by test, interview and excellence criteria.
Fees: tuition: from 2,700-22,850 Rs. per year (depending on programmes); eligibility fee for foreign students: US$50; admission fee for foreign students: US$500.
Financial assistance: scholarships available on academic criteria.
Applications: by 24 June at the above address; foreign students are required to apply through the Ministry of Human Resources Development, Department of Education, Government of India, or contact Foreign Students' Advisor of Goa University; tel: +91 0832 454244, fax: +91 0832 451184.

1213 Gujarat Vidyapith [GV]

Nr. Income Tax Circle, Ashram Road
380 014 Ahmedabad - Gujarat State
Tel: +91-79 -540-746-/-7541-148
Fax: +91-79-7541-547
Web: http://www.gujaratvidyapith.org/
e-mail: registrar@gujaratvidyapith.org

📖 Graduate, Postgraduate Programmes

Study Domains: anthropology, biology, book development and production, community development, computer science, education, food, health and hygiene, history, home economics, interpretation and translation, journalism, languages, library science, mathematics, microbiology, philosophy, physical education, publishing, rural development, social sciences, social work, theology, religion.
Programmes: programme of courses leading to Master's degree and postgraduate diploma; also certificate courses and graduate level courses in various Indian languages:(a) Master of Philosophy in peace and global society, Jain studies, social anthropology, social work, education, Buddhist thought; (b) postgraduate diploma by correspondence in Gandhian thought; (c) Master of Philosophy in science and non-violence.
Fees: education fee: 621 Rs.; hostel fee and deposit for two terms: 1,000 Rs.; food: approx. 300 Rs. per month.
Financial assistance: 2 scholarships of 1,200 Rs. per month available on competitive basis after admission.
Languages: instruction in Gujarati and/or Hindi; in English for foreigners.
Applications: by 15 June to the Principal, College of Social Science, at the above address.

🐦 Junior Research Fellowships

Study Domains: philosophy.
Scholarships: Junior Research Fellowships.
Subjects: Programme of courses leading to Master of Philosophy in science and non-violence, peace and global society, Gandhian thought.
Open to: candidates of all nationalities with second-class M.A. or M.Sc.; proficiency in Hindi or Gujarati required; language coaching for foreigners available; one-semester abridged courses (in English) are also available for foreigners; full participation in campus/community life is essential.
Duration: 1 academic year (courses begin in July).
Value: 1,200 Rs. per month.
Applications: to the Director at the above address.

1214 Indian Institute of Technology Roorkee [IITR]

247 667 Roorkee, Uttaranchal
Tel: +91-1332-272-349 / 274-860
Fax: +91-1332-273-560
Web: http://www.iitr.ac.in

📖 Postgraduate Programme

Study Domains: hydrology.
Programmes: international postgraduate course in hydrology.
Open to: nationals from developing countries of Asia and Africa sponsored by their governments, preferably under 45 years of age, with appropriate B.E. in civil, mechanical, or agricultural engineering or in hydrology, or with M.Sc./M.Tech. degree in physics, atmospheric physics, mathematics, statistics, geology, geography, geophysics, meteorology, environmental science, soil science, chemistry, applied geology or applied geophysics.
Duration: 12 months for postgraduate diploma in hydrology.
Fees: generally no fee is charged except for the examination fee.
Financial assistance: 5 awards of up to 4,000 Rs. monthly, maintenance allowance plus reasonable allowance for books and study tours; available for diploma course.
Languages: instruction in English.
Applications: preferably before 15 April, to the Head, at the above address.

📖 Undergraduate, Graduate Programmes

Study Domains: architecture, chemical industry, engineering, sciences.

1215 Indian School of Mines [ISOM]

Jharkhand
826 004 Dhanbad
Tel: +91-326-221-0024
Fax: +91-326-221-0028
Web: http://www.ismdhanbad.ac.in
e-mail: info@ismdhanbad.ac.in

📖 Undergraduate, Graduate, Postgraduate Programmes / Engineering

Study Domains: chemistry, computer science, electricity and electronics, engineering, geology, mathematics, physics, sciences, technology.
Programmes: programme of courses leading to Bachelor of Technology (B.Tech.), Master of Technology (M.Tech.), Master of Science (M.Sc.) and Ph.D.
Description: (a) programmes of study leading to undergraduate qualifications in mining engineering, opencast mining, petroleum engineering, mineral engineering, engineering and mining machinery, applied geology, applied geophysics; (b) programmes of study leading to postgraduate qualifications in industrial engineering and management, electronics and instrumentation, longwall mining, environmental science, computer applications and applied sciences including chemistry, physics and mathematics.
Duration: B.Tech.: 4 years; M.Tech.: 1-1/2 years; M.Sc.: 3 years; Ph.D.: minimum 3 years.
Fees: B.Tech., 4,500 Rs. per year; M.Tech., 6,000 Rs. for the full programme (costs for Indian nationals).
Financial assistance: most foreign students are granted cultural exchange scholarships by the Government of India.
Applications: by the end of February, to the Registrar, at the above address.

1216 Indian Veterinary Research Institute (Bhartiya Pashu-Chikitsa Anusandhan Sansthan)

243122 Izatnagar, Uttar Pradesh
Tel: +91-581-230-2536
Web: http://ivri.nic.in
e-mail: cao@ivri.up.nic.in

📖 Graduate, Postgraduate Programmes Veterinary Science

Study Domains: veterinary medicine, veterinary sciences.
Description: programmes in veterinary sciences.
Open to: citizens of all countries.
Age limit Min: 20 years for MVSc programme and 22 years for PhD programme.
Duration: 2 years for Master's programme; 3 years for doctoral programmes.
Financial assistance: scholarships awarded by the Government of India, Ministry of Agriculture.

1217 **Industrial Design Centre, Indian Institute of Technology [IDC-IIT]**
Powai
400 076 Mumbai
Tel: +91-22-576-7801
Fax: +91-22-576-7803
Web: http://www.idc.iitb.ac.in
e-mail: office@idc.iitb.ac.in

📖 **Graduate Programmes**

Study Domains: communication, industrial design.
Programmes: programme of courses leading to (a) Master of Design in industrial design; (b) Master of Design in visual communication.
Open to: (a) candidates of any nationality holding an academic degree in engineering or architecture; (b) candidates holding an academic degree in fine arts or graphic arts.
Duration: 2 years (courses begin the third week of July).
Fees: registration, US$100; tuition, US$3,000 per semester; deposit, US$150; other fees, US$400 per semester.
Financial assistance: Indian Government may award scholarships of 1,800 Rs. per month plus contingent grant of 3,000 Rs. per year to foreign students, under various cultural exchange programmes; information available through the Indian embassies or consulates.
Languages: instruction in English.
Applications: by January, through the Indian High Commission to the Department of Education, Ministry of Human Resource Development, New Delhi.

1218 **International Institute for Population Sciences [IIPS]**
Govandi Station Road, Deonar
400 088 Mumbai
Tel: +91-22-556-3254
Fax: +91-22-2556-3257
Web: http://www.iipsindia.org
e-mail: diriips@bom8.vsnl.net.in

📖 **Graduate, Postgraduate Programmes**

Study Domains: demography and population studies.
Programmes: programme of courses leading to (a) Diploma in Population Studies (D.P.S.); (b) Master's degree in Population Studies (M.P.S.); (c) Ph.D. in Population Studies.
Open to: (a) candidates from member countries of the Economic and Social Commission for Asia and Pacific Region (ESCAP), holding a Bachelor's degree and some experience in handling population data; orientation courses in English and mathematics organized by the Institute; (b) candidates from India and abroad holding a Master's degree or equivalent; (c) candidates from India holding a Master's degree in any of the social sciences, mathematics, statistics with 55% marks.
Duration: (a) and (b) 1 year; (c) 3 years.
Fees: list of fees available on request.
Financial assistance: (a) 25 scholarships provided by UNFPA, each at 16,735 rupees per month plus round-trip economy-class air fare from UN/ESCAP for foreign candidates from ESCAP region; (b) 25 scholarships, at 1,000 rupees per month from Government of India for Indian nationals; (c) 20 scholarships, each at 1,800 rupees per month and contingency grant of 5,000 rupees per year available for Indian nationals who have passed the JRF examination or equivalent.
Languages: English.
Applications: by April, through UNFPA Country Directors/UNDP Resident Representatives in the ESCAP Region, to the Director, at the above address for foreign students; through advertisement in national dailies for Indian students.

1219 **K.C. College of Management Studies [KCOMS]**
K.C. College Building
Dinshaw Vachha Road, room 7, 1st floor
Churchgate
400 020 Mumbai
Tel: +91-22-871-174
Web: http://www.kccms.org

📖 **Postgraduate Programme, Journalism**
Study Domains: journalism.
Programmes: programme of courses leading to postgraduate diploma.
Open to: candidates holding a Bachelor's degree from a recognized university; a fair knowledge of typing is required; exceptions can be made by the Board for worthy non-graduates.
Duration: 1 academic year, 2 semesters (courses begin in July and November).
Fees: tuition: 6,100 rupees.

📖 **Undergraduate Programmes**
Study Domains: advertising, business, business administration, computer science, finance, journalism, management, marketing, public relations, tourism, hotel and catering management.
Programmes: Undergraduate programmes leading to (a) Basic one-year course: business management, marketing management, advertising and public relations, travel and tourism, computer management, hotel management, journalism; (b) Advanced courses: business administration, marketing and sales management, human resources and financial management; (c) Short-term courses: tax planning and management, export-import management, advertising copy-writing, computer programming.
Open to: suitably qualified candidates following interview: (a) graduates and students awaiting their graduation results; (b) graduates with at least 2 years experience at supervisory/junior executive level; (c) candidates already in the field and students wishing to acquire entrepreneurial skills for running a business.
Duration: (a) and (b): generally two semesters (courses begin in July and December); (c) 6 months.
Fees: tuition, 6,000 rupees.

1220 **Kannur University [KU]**
Mangattuparamba,
Kallirssery
PO Civil Station
670 002 Kannur, Kerala
Tel: +91-497-705-380
e-mail: knruty@md3.vsnl.net.in

📖 **Undergraduate, Graduate, Postgraduate Programmes**
Study Domains: anthropology, biology, communication, English, ethnology, information science, international studies, journalism, languages, natural sciences, technology.
Programmes: programme of courses leading to Bachelor's degree, Master's degree and Ph.D.
Languages: language of instruction: English.

1221 **Ministry of External Affairs Indian Council for Cultural Relations [MOEA]**
Azad Bhavan, I.P. Estate
110 002 New Delhi
Fax: +91-11-337-0732
Web: http://education.vsnl.com/iccr/
e-mail: iccr@vsnl.com

🎓 **Government of India Scholarships**
Study Domains: all major fields, research.
Scholarships: (a) Cultural Exchange Programme; (b) General Cultural Scholarship Scheme; (c) Apasaheb Pant Scholarship Scheme; (d) Commonwealth Fellowship; (e) Technical Cooperation Scheme (TCS) of Colombo Plan; (f) Reciprocal Scholarship Scheme; (g) Scholarship Scheme for Sri Lanka and Mauritius; (h) SAARC Scholarship Scheme; (i) ICCR Scholarship Scheme. (for details see http://meadev.nic.in/earthquake/culture/iccr/chap-6.htm).
Subjects: all fields of study at undergraduate and postgraduate levels including research for which facilities are available in India; medicine is not offered at the undergraduate level.
Open to: candidate should be a national of the country to which the scholarship is offered; proficiency in English required; no age limit.
Place of study: all universities and institutions in India.
Duration: generally 2 years, but renewable depending on

the course of study.
Value: 1,500 rupees per month for undergraduate and
postgraduate studies; 2,000 rupees per month for research
studies, Ph.D., M.D., M.E.; 2,500 rupees for postdoctoral
programme; 7,500 rupees for SAARC chair; 5,000 rupees for
fellowship.
Applications: by 31 March to the above address, through
Indian Mission/Embassy in country of origin; for addresses
see http://www.meadev.nic.in/.

1222 Shreemati Nathibai Damodar Thackersey Women's University [SNDT]

1 Nathibai Thackersey Road
400 020 Mumbai, Maharashtra
Tel: +91-022-207-2792
e-mail: sndtulib@bom3.vsnl.net.in

📖 Undergraduate, Graduate, Postgraduate Programmes

Study Domains: accounting, art history, business, business
administration, continuing education, dietetics, early
childhood education, economic and commercial sciences,
education, engineering, English, fine arts, geography, history,
information science, journalism, law, liberal arts, library
science, management, paramedical studies, political economy,
political science, sociology, special education, teacher
education.
Programmes: Programme of courses leading to Bachelor's
degree, Master's degree, Post-Master's degree and Ph.D.
Open to: candidates of any nationality holding a 12th year
senior secondary/intermediate examination or recognized
foreign equivalent; the University is mainly concerned with
the education of women.
Fees: tuition: 2,940-4,000 Rs. per year; technology
diploma programme: 1,250 Rs. per semester.
Languages: languages of instruction: English, Gujarati,
Marathi, Hindi.

1223 Tezpur University [TU]

Napaam,
784 028 Tezpur, Assam
Tel: +91-3712-267-007
Fax: +91-3712-267-006
Web: http://www.tezu.ernet.in
e-mail: adm@tezu.ernet.in

📖 Graduate, Postgraduate Programmes

Study Domains: anthropology, business administration,
chemistry, communication, computer science, electricity and
electronics, energy, English, folklore, genetics, German,
journalism, mathematics, physics, research, tourism, hotel and
catering management.
Programmes: programme of courses leading to Master's
degree, Ph.D. and postgraduate diploma.
Open to: candidates of any nationality holding a
Bachelor's degree; candidates must pass an entrance
examination.
Languages: English.
Applications: by April 30 to the academic registrar at the
above address.

1224 University of Pune [UNIPUNE]

International Centre University of Pune
Ganeshkhind
411 007 Pune, Maharashtra
Tel: +91-20-2569-1954
Web: http://www.unipune.ernet.in
e-mail: intcent@unipune.ernet.in

📖 Undergraduate, Graduate, Postgraduate Programmes

Study Domains: all major fields.
Programmes: programme of courses leading to Certificate,
Diploma, Bachelor's degree, Master's degree and Ph.D.
Open to: candidates of any country holding a
secondary-school certificate; English test compulsory for
candidates from non-English speaking countries.
Fees: eligibility fee: 500 rupees; entrance fee: US$500;
medical test fee: US$50; tuition: US$2,250-$6,000 per year
(depending on programmes).

Languages: language of instruction: English.
Applications: international students must note that the
proper student/research visa must be endorsed to University
of Pune only; for further details, please contact: Deputy
Registrar, International Centre, Arts Faculty Building,
University of Pune, Ganeshkhind, Pune 411007, Maharashtra,
India; tel: +91 20 5691 169; fax: +91 20 5691 954; email:
intcent@unipune.ernet.in.

1225 Vikram University Ujjain [VUU]

Madhar Bhawan
Kothi Road
456 010 Ujjain
Tel: +91-734-251-4277

📖 Undergraduate, Graduate, Postgraduate Programmes

Study Domains: arts, biology, business, economic and
commercial sciences, education, engineering, law,
management, natural sciences, sciences, social sciences,
technology.
Programmes: programme of courses leading to Bachelor's
degree, Master's degree, Ph.D.
Open to: candidates of any country holding a
secondary-school certificate (or equivalent).
Languages: languages of instruction: English, Hindi.

1226 West Bengal National University of Juridical Sciences [WBNUJS]

Aranya Bhavan 10 A LA Block
Sector-III, Salt Lake City
West Bengal
700 0 Kolkata
Tel: +91-335-0534 / 7379
Fax: +91-335-7422
Web: http://www.nujs.edu
e-mail: nujseal3@vsnl.net.in

📖 Undergraduate, Graduate, Postgraduate Programmes

Study Domains: law.
Programmes: programme of courses leading to Bachelor
of Law (L.L.B.), Master of law (M.Phil.) and Ph.D.
Fees: tuition: 35,000 Rs. per year.
Financial assistance: scholarships available on academic
criteria.
Languages: language of instruction: English.
Applications: by 31 December to the above address.

1227 Women Graduates Union [WGU]

Women Graduates Union Road
Colaba
400 005 Mumbai
Web: http://www.ifuw.org/india
e-mail: wgu1915@bom2.vsnl.net.in

🐚 IFUW Scholarships

Study Domains: all major fields.
Scholarships: International Federation of University
Women (IFUW) Scholarships.
Subjects: postgraduate study in all fields.
Open to: women of any nationality, holding degrees from
universities recognized by the International Federation of
University Women; candidates must be full-time students in
the institution of study before tenure of award.
Place of study: at any recognized institution of learning in
Bombay.
Duration: 1 year; renewable for a second year.
Applications: by 30 October, on forms obtainable from the
above address.

Indonesia

Academic year: July to June.
Organization of higher education system: There are several types of higher education institutions: Universities, both private and public, which are recognized by the Ministry of Education and Culture; institutes and teacher training institutes (Institut Kegurun dan ilmu pendidikan or IKIPs) which rank as universities with full degree-granting status; Islamic institutes, which have the same rank as universities but come under the Ministry of Religious Affairs; schools (Sekolah Tinggi), both public and private, which offer academic and professional university-level education in one particular discipline; single-faculty academies which offer Diploma/Certificate technician-level courses at public and private levels; and polytechnics, which are attached to universities and provide sub-degree junior technician training. The private universities only award degrees to S1 level. They come under the responsibility of the Directorate of Private Universities within the Directorate General of Higher Education. The Ministry of Education and Culture, through the Directorate General of Higher Education, exercises authority over both state and private institutions. State institutions are financed by the central government, although provincial governments may also provide funds.
University level studies:
•University level first stage: Sarjana (S1): The Sarjana (Strata 1) is awarded after four years of full-time study at a recognized university, institute or school. Students must obtain 144 credits. For Medicine, Dentistry, Veterinary Science, Pharmacy and Engineering, an additional two to six semesters must be added. Degree Certificates usually bear the inscription Sarjana followed by the subject. A minimum of 144 credits are needed to graduate.
•University level second stage: Magister (S2): The Magister (Stata 2) is awarded after a further two years' study plus research. Some 36-50 credits beyond S1 are required to graduate.
•University level third stage: Doktor (S3): The Doktor (Strata 3) takes another three to four years beyond the Magister. In some cases, students can pursue Doktor degree programmes immediately after the first degree, depending on their potential. The Doktor degree is the highest award conferred by Indonesian universities or institutes. There is a residential requirement for 2 years and students must pass the examinations that are organized every year to check their research progress.
Monetary unit: Indonesian rupiyah (Rp.).
National student admission: Sekolah Menengah Atas required for admission to higher education studies. Students must sit for the National Entrance Examination (Ujian Masuk Perguruan Tinggi Negeri). There are two options: Social Sciences (IPS) and Natural Sciences (IPA). Secondary school graduates from Physics and Biology streams can apply to any department; those from Social Sciences and Humanities are restricted to non-Science and non-Technology fields.
Language: Language of instruction is Indonesian.
Open and distance learning: Universitas Terbuka offers open-learning programmes in Teacher Training and Education, Economics, Mathematics and Natural Sciences, and Social and Political Sciences. It offers S1 Sarjana degree courses and non-degree Diploma courses.
Recognition of studies and qualification: For information on recognition of foreign credentials:
Directorate of Academic and Student Affairs / Direktorat Pembinaan Sarana Akademik,
Jalan Jenderal Suderman, Pintu I Senayan, Jakarta Pusat, Indonesia; tel: +62-21-573-1983; fax: +62-21-573-1903.

1228 Bandar Lampung University [UBL]
JL, Zainal Abidin
Pagar Alam No.26
Bandar Lampung
Tel: +62-721-701-463/979
Fax: +62-721-701-463
e-mail: universitas@hotmail.com

📖 Undergraduate, Graduate Programmes

Study Domains: accounting, administration, architecture, business administration, civil engineering, computer science, economy, engineering, law, management, mechanical engineering, political science, social sciences.
Programmes: (a) Bachelor of Accounting - 3 year diploma programme; (b) Master of Management; (c) Sarjana degree in public administration, management, law sciences, mechanical engineering, accounting, information system, architecture, business administration, civil engineering.
Open to: candidates meeting academic and other University requirements; (a) English and math admission test required; (b) mathematics and micro-economics theory; psychological tests.
Duration: (a) 3 years; (b) 2 years; (c) 4 years; (a) and (b) begin in April and September; (c) begins in September.
Fees: in Indonesian (a) registration: Rp. 1,180,000; tuition fees: Rp. 1,180,00 per year; living costs: Rp. 1,000 per month; (b) registration: Rp. 3,000,000; tuition fees: Rp. 4,000,000; living costs: Rp. 1,000,000 per month; (c) fees approx. Rp. 2,000,000.
Languages: Indonesian.
Applications: (a) and (b) 30 March; 30 August.

🎓 Scholarships

Study Domains: all major fields.
Scholarships: (a) PPA; (b) Supersemar.
Open to: (a) and (b) open to candidates with high grade point average and financial need.
Value: (a) Rp. 9,000,000 per semester; (b) Rp. 900,000 per semester.
Applications: (a) apply by July; (b) apply by January; contact Fauzi Mihdar, Vice President for Student Affairs.

1229 Bogor Agricultural University [IPB]
Kantor Pusat:
Gedung Rektorat Lt.2
Kampus IPB Darmaga
Bogor
Tel: +62-251-622-634/642
Fax: +62-251-622-708
Web: http://www.ipb.ac.id

📖 Undergraduate, Graduate Programmes

Study Domains: agriculture, audio-visual media, business, business administration, communication, development studies, economic and commercial sciences, economy, engineering, health and hygiene, home economics, interior design, Latin, management, mathematics, natural resources, natural sciences, sciences, tourism, hotel and catering management, vocational training.
Programmes: Bachelor's, Master's, Ph.D. degrees; in agricultural fields; other subjects include: agribusiness management; computer science; agrometeorology.
Open to: candidates meeting all University requirements; admission tests for undergraduate programmes.
Duration: depending on programme; beginning August.
Fees: registration: US$250; tuition fees; US$2,000 per semester; living costs: US$250.
Financial assistance: US$1,000 until the completion of studies.
Languages: Indonesian, English.
Applications: apply by January to: baak@ipb.ac.id; tel: +62 0251 624 067.

1230 Institute of Teacher Training and Educational Science Mataram [IKIP]
Jl. Pemuda
Mataram
Tel: +62-370-632-082

📖 Teacher Training

Study Domains: English, teacher education.
Programmes: Teacher Training.
Description: training for teacher in junior and senior high schools; TEOFL, math, physics, biology, sports and health.
Duration: 4 years beginning 1 June.
Languages: Indonesian, English.
Applications: apply by 31 May; contact Yusuf Akhyar Sutaryono.

1231 Muhammadiyah University of Surabaya (Universitas Muhammadiyah Surabaya)

Jalan Sutorejo 59
60113 Surabaya
Tel: +62-31-381-1966
Fax: +62-31-381-3096

☛ U. M. Surabaya Award

Study Domains: languages, theology, religion.
Nationality: candidates of American, European Union, Canadian, Australian and Japanese nationalities.
Duration: 6 months.
Value: tuition: Rp 50,000 per semester.
Applications: no deadline; contact Dr Imam Robandi, robandi@ce.its.ac.id; fax: +62-31-381-3090.

1232 Narotama University [UNNAR]

Jl. Arief Rachman Hakim
60117 51 Surabaya
Tel: +62-31-594-6404
Fax: +62-31-593-1213
Web: http://www.narotama.ac.id
e-mail: rektor@narotama.ac.id

📖 Undergraduate, Graduate Degree Programmes

Study Domains: accounting, civil engineering, continuing education, finance, international law, management, teacher education.
Programmes: Bachelor's, Master's.
Description: Bachelor's degrees in: civil engineering, economics, law, computer science; Master's degrees in: law, management; language proficiency in Indonesian and English.
Held: depending on programme; consult calendar.
Fees: registration: US$10; tuition: $120/SMT; living costs: $100 per month.
Financial assistance: available for undergraduate studies.
Languages: Indonesian, English.
Applications: apply by 31 August to Mr. R. Djoko Sumadjo.

1233 National Institute of Technology Malang [ITN Malang]

Jalan Bendungan Sigura-gura 2
Malang
Tel: +62-341-551-951
Fax: +62-341-553-015
Web: http://www.itn.ac.id
e-mail: rektor@itn.ac.id

📖 Undergraduate, Graduate Studies

Study Domains: computer science, electricity and electronics, energy, engineering, industrial technology, laboratory techniques, technology.

1234 Padjadjaran University [UNPAD]

Jalan Dipati Ukur No.35
40132 Bandung
Tel: +62-22-250-3271
Fax: +62-22-250-1977
Web: http://www.unpad.ac.id
e-mail: pr4@unpad.ac.id

📖 Undergraduate, Graduate Programmes

Study Domains: all major fields.
Programmes: Bachelor's, Master's and Ph.D. degrees.
Duration: 4 years.
Applications: 1 June to Rector for Academic Affairs at email: pr4@unpad.ac.id or phone: +62 22 250 3271.

☛ Beasiswa Dharmasiswa

Study Domains: all major fields.
Scholarships: government scholarship.
Duration: 1 year.
Applications: contact the embassy of Republic of Indonesia in applicant's country.

1235 Satya Wacana Christian University

Jln. Diponegoro 52-60
50711 Salatiga
Tel: +62-298-321-212
Fax: +62-298-321-433
Web: http://www.uksw.edu
e-mail: ieo@uksw.edu

📖 Undergraduate, Professional Programmes

Study Domains: all major fields.
Programmes: (a) Bachelor's degree programmes; (b) professional programmes.
Description: (a) teacher training and pedagogy; psychology; performing arts; biology; economics; education; theology; social sciences; science and mathematics; electrical engineering; agriculture; law; language and literature; (b) diplomas in: secretarial business; tourism; personnel management; chemical analysis for industry; computer for accounting; informatics engineering; candidates must be secondary-school graduates and 18 years of age minimum.
Duration: 4 to 5 years depending on programme of study.
Fees: consult individual programmes; approx. fees vary between Rp. 1,000,000 and Rp. 2,223,000; living costs: Rp. 9,000,000 per year.
Languages: Indonesian; English for professional programmes and literature department only.
Applications: consult admissions schedule for details; between March to July; contact Registrar for information.

1236 The University of Jember [UNEJ]

Jln. Kalimantan 37
Jember
Tel: +62-331-337-422
Fax: +62-331-337-422
Web: http://www.unej.ac.id
e-mail: JUBC@Binanusa.net

📖 Undergraduate, Graduate Programmes

Study Domains: accounting, administration, agriculture, agronomic sciences, biology, business administration, chemistry, dentistry, economic and commercial sciences, engineering, English, history, international law, international studies, law, linguistics, management, mathematics, medicine, nursing, physics, teacher education, tourism, hotel and catering management.
Programmes: S1 degree (equivalent to Bachelor's degree); S2 (equivalent to Master's degree).
Subjects: Master's degree in: agronomy; management; public administration; agricultural business; SPMB student entrance test; language proficiency; candidates must be at least 19 years of age.
Duration: 2 years commencing September.
Fees: tuition fees: US$275; living costs: US$100.
Languages: Indonesian, English.
Applications: apply by early June to August.

1237 University of Malikussaleh

J.L. TGK Chik Ditiro No.26
Chokseumawe
Tel: +62-645-44450/41373
Fax: +62-645-44450
Web: http://www.um.ac.id
e-mail: info@um.ac.id

📖 Undergraduate Degree Programme

Study Domains: engineering.
Programmes: undergraduate engineering degree.
Description: courses are held in five faculties: technical, economics, politics, agronomy, law.

1238 University of Sanata Dharma

Mrican Tromol Pos 29
55002 Yogyakarta
Tel: +62-274-513-301/352
Fax: +62-274-562-383
Web: http://www.usd.ac.id
e-mail: rektorat@usd.ac.id

📖 Undergraduate, Graduate Programmes

Study Domains: accounting, computer science, continuing education, cultural studies, electricity and electronics, engineering, finance, history, languages, linguistics, management, mathematics, mechanical engineering, philosophy, physics, psychology, summer programmes, teacher education, theology, religion, vocational training.
Programmes: Bachelor's, Master's and non-degree programmes.
Description: Catholic University with 8 faculties and 23 departments; offers guidance and counselling courses; mechatronic engineering.
Open to: candidates meeting all University requirements; good knowledge of Indonesian and English language required.
Duration: 4 years beginning in August.
Fees: registration: Rp. 60,000; tuition fees: Rp. 30,000 per credit hour.
Languages: Indonesian, English.
Applications: apply between 8 May and 8 August to rektorat@staff.ac.id or by mail.

1239 Wiralodra University of Indramayu [UNWIR]
Jalan Raya Singaraja Km.3
Indramayu - West Java
Tel: +62-234-275-946
Fax: +62-234-275-946

📖 Graduate Degree Programmes

Study Domains: agriculture, civil engineering, economy, education, English, fisheries, law, management, mathematics, nursing, nutrition, paramedical studies, political science, preventive medicine, social sciences, social work, teacher education, theology, religion.
Programmes: Master's, and graduate degrees (strata 1) in (Sarjana) education, law, agriculture, economics, religion, engineering, telecommunications, chemical industry, shipbuilding.
Duration: 2 years; short semester; beginning 15 September.
Fees: tuition fees: Rp. 500,000; living costs: Rp. 7,200,000 per month.
Applications: apply by 25 August.

Iran, Islamic Republic of

Academic year: September to June.
Organization of higher education system: The educational system in universities and institutions of higher education is based on credit units. There are two 16-week semesters in each academic year. University courses are divided into theoretical and practical. Theoretical courses consist of a body of knowledge presented in the form of lectures, seminars, team teaching and discussions. Practical courses consist of skills offered to students; for example, through laboratories, hospitals, workshops and hands-on activities.
Degree programmes: Associate degree: 2 years of study requiring 68 to 72 credits: Bachelor's degree: 4 years of study, requiring 130 to 145 credit: Master's degree: 2 years of study, generally 28 to 32 credits beyond Bachelor's degree; Professional Doctorate degree: for studies in medicine, dentistry and pharmacology; studies generally require 290, 217, 210 credits and last 6 to 10, 6 to 9 and 5 to 9 years, respectively: Ph.D. degree: 4 to 5 years of study and 42 to 50 credits after completion of a Master's degree and a dissertation.
Major institutions of higher education: Alzahra University: www.azzahra.ac.ir
Amirkabir University of Technology: www.aku.ac.ir
Arak University: www.araku.ac.ir
Bu-Ali Sina: www.basu.ac.ir
Chamran University of Ahvaz: www.cua.ac.ir
Ferdowsi University of Mashhad: www.um.ac.ir
Guilan University of Medical Sciences: www.gums.ac.ir
Hamadan University of Medical Sciences and Health Service: www.umsha.ac.ir
Hormozgan University of Medical Sciences: www.hums.ac.ir
Ilam University: www.ilam.ac.ir
Iran University of Medical Sciences: www.iums.ac.ir
Iran University of Sciences of Technology: www.iust.ac.ir
Isfahan University of Medical Sciences: www.mui.ac.ir
Isfahan University of Technology: www.iut.ac.ir
K.N.Toosi University of Technology: www.kntu.ac.ir
Kashan University: www.kaums.ac.ir
Kerman Medical University: www.kmu.ac.ir
Kermanshah University of Medical Science: www.kums.ac.ir
Kish University: www.kishuniv.com
Mashhad University of Medical Sciences: www.mums.ac.ir
Payame Noor University: www.pnu.ac.ir
Petroleum University of Technology: www.put.ac.ir
Shaheed Beheshti University of Medical Sciences Health Services: www.sbmu.ac.ir
Shahid Bahonar University of Kerman: www.uk.ac.ir
Shahid Beheshti University: www.sbu.ac.ir
Shahid Sadoughi University of Medical Sciences Heath Services: www.ssu.ac.ir
Shahrood University: www.shahrood.ac.ir
Sharif University of Technology: www.sharif.ac.ir
Shiraz University: www.shirazu.ac.ir
Shiraz University of Medical Sciences: www.sums.ac.ir
Sistan & Baluchestan University: www.usb.ac.ir
Tabriz University of Medical Sciences: www.tbzmed.ac.ir
Tarbiat Modarres University: www.Modares.ac.ir
Tehran University of Medical Sciences: www.tums.ac.ir
University of Isfahan: www.ui.ac.ir
University of Art: www.art.ac.ir
University of Guilan: www.gu.ac.ir
University of Tabriz: www.tabrizu.ac.ir
University of Tehran: www.ut.ac.ir
Urmia University: www.urmia.ac.ir
Uromia Medical Science University: www.umsu.ac.ir
Yasuj University of Medical Sciences:www.yums.ac.ir
Zahedan University of Medical Sciences: www.zdmu.ac.ir.
Monetary unit: Iranian rial.
National student admission:
• Three types of admission to higher education are available: a) regular admission through the national entrance examination, a nationwide examination supervised by the Educational Measurement and Evaluation Organization (EMEO). Admission to the Islamic Azad University, a private university, consists of three separate examinations including entrance examinations for medical fields, non-medical fields and part-time students. Each university administers doctoral admissions. Admissions to Payam-e Noor University, a distance university, is carried out through the national entrance examination as well as through a particular entrance examination conducted by the university itself; b) conditional admission: students are admitted regardless of high school major or grade point average (G.P.A.), on a conditional basis. Students meeting specific scholastic requirements will be able to obtain regular admission status. This type of admission is used at the Bachelor's degree level at the Payame-Noor University; c) open admission: offered by the Technical-Vocational University; students are awarded an Associate degree after a 2-year study period.
• G.P.A. for admission (on a scale of 20): 14 for Bachelor's degree programmes in humanities and arts; 16 for Master's degree programmes; 17 for Ph.D. programmes.
International student admission: Foreign students wishing to study for a degree must have a secondary-school certificate with a minimum average of 62.5 per cent; for a Master's degree or Ph.D., they should have a minimum of 3.00 on a scale of 4.00. Candidates who do not meet the requirements must take additional classes.
Language: The language used for teaching is Persian (Farsi). Students must pass the Farsi language examination with a grade of at least 14 out of 20. Preparatory courses of approximately 6 months in Persian language are available.
Immigration requirements: Students should contact the nearest Iranian Embassy for immigration requirements.
Estimated expenses for one academic year: Tuition: US$ 3,000; books/supplies: US$200: housing: US$2,000.
Information services:
• Central Secretariat of Admissions; PO Box 19735/161; Tehran; Iran.
• Iranian Embassies abroad.
• Institute for Research and Planning in Higher Education: http://www.irphe.ir.
Scholarships for international students: Limited scholarships are available through universities and other organizations. For further information, contact the Central Secretariat of Admissions; PO Box 19735/161, Tehran, Iran.

Open and distance learning: Distance education is mainly provided by Payam-e Noor University. Students may be admitted through the National Entrance Examination or as conditional students with specific academic requirements. Students are offered 41 different fields of study. All public universities and higher education institutions are allowed to admit distance-learning students.
Recognition of studies and qualification: Ministry of Science, Research and Planning; Stage #7, Unit #1 Ostad Nejatullahi Street; Tehran; Iran; tel: +98 21 8900 197; fax: +98 21 8827 253; website;.
Publications / Websites:
• Every university publishes a guide containing general information on life at the university.
• Institute for Research and Planning in Higher Education; http://www.irphe.ir/En/index.htm.

1240 Gonabad Medical Sciences University [GMSU]
Emam Khomeini Avenue, Farmandari Square
Gonabad City (Khorasan State)
Tel: +98-53572-2328
Fax: +98-53572-3815/3814
Web: http://www.gmu.ac.ir
e-mail: info@gmu.ac.ir

📖 Undergraduate Medical Studies
Study Domains: medicine.
Programmes: programme of courses leading to diploma of nursing, midwifery, health, operation room technician and anaesthesia technician.
Open to: male and female candidates of all nationalities.
Duration: 2 to 4 years; courses begin 1 September.
Languages: Farsi and English.
Applications: to Dr. Hadi Salari or Dr. Abdoaljavad Khajavi by fax: +98 53572 2328 or 3814 or 3815.

1241 Gorgan University of Agricultural Science and Natural Resources [GUASNR]
PO Box 386
Shahid Beheshti Street
Gorgan, Golestan
Tel: +98-171-222-4827/0320/0321
Fax: +98-171-333-7867
Web: http://www.gau.ac.ir
e-mail: guasnr@gorgan_uni_ag.gau.ac.ir

📖 Undergraduate, Graduate and Postgraduate Programmes
Study Domains: agriculture, agronomic sciences, biology, botany, earth science, fisheries, food industry, forestry, horticulture, hydrology, mathematics, research, statistics, zoology.
Programmes: programme of courses leading to (a) Pre-University Certificate, (b) Bachelor's degree, (c) Master's degree and (d) Ph.D.
Subjects: wood and paper engineering; agricultural engineering; animal sciences; plant science; forestry; food science and technology; fisheries and environmental sciences; range and watershed management; science; agriculture.
Open to: candidates of all nationalities holding a secondary school leaving certificate; entrance examination required.
Held: agriculture programme courses held in Gonabad.
Duration: (a) 2 years, (b) 4 years, (c) 2 years, (d) by thesis.
Languages: Persian.

1242 Guilan University of Medical Sciences [GUMS]
Essential office of Guilan University of Medical Sciences
Namjoo Avenue
41446 Rasht
Tel: +98-131-322-1282
Fax: +98-131-322-7070
Web: http://www.gums.ac.ir
e-mail: info@gums.ac.ir

📖 Undergraduate, Graduate, Postgraduate Programmes
Study Domains: anatomy, bacteriology, dentistry, dermatology, health and hygiene, medicine, neurology, nursing, obstetrics and gynaecology, paediatrics, paramedical studies, psychiatry, radiology, surgery, urology.
Programmes: programme of courses leading to Bachelor's degree, Master's degree and Ph.D.
Subjects: health subjects.
Duration: up to 7 years beginning 15 September.
Financial assistance: available for married students.
Languages: Persian; proficiency in English required.
Applications: entrance examination in July.

1243 Institute for Advanced Studies in Basic Sciences [IASBS]
Gava Zang
PO Box 45195 159
Zanjan
Tel: +98-241-415-2255
Fax: +98-241-424-9023
Web: http://www.iasbs.ac.ir
e-mail: moghanlou@iasbs.ac.ir

📖 Graduate Programme
Study Domains: chemistry, mathematics, physics.
Programmes: programme of courses leading to graduate degree in physics, mathematics and chemistry.
Subjects: physics, optics, chemistry, mathematics (pure and applied), computer science, information technology, earth sciences.
Open to: candidates holding a Bachelor's degree in science or related subjects.
Duration: courses begin 23 September, 22 December, 3 April.
Languages: Persian and English.
Applications: for updated information contact: karimi@iasbs.ac.ir.

1244 Iran University of Science and Technology [IUST]
Daneshgah e Elm va Sanat e Iran Avenue Hengum Street, Resalat Square
16844 Tehran
Tel: +98-21-749-1031
Fax: +98-21-749-1031
Web: http://www.iust.ac.ir
e-mail: interiust@iust.ac.ir

📖 Graduate, Postgraduate Programmes
Study Domains: architecture, engineering, sciences.
Programmes: programme of courses leading to (a) M.Sc., M.A., M.Eng.; (b) Ph.D.
Open to: candidates of all nationalities holding an undergraduate university degree in Science, Architecture or Engineering for Master's programmes, and Master's degree in the same fields for Ph.D. programmes; a minimum grade point average and a good command of Persian language are required.
Duration: (a) 2 to 3 years; (b) 4 to 5 years; courses begin in September.
Fees: tuition per year: Engineering and Architecture (a) US$3,000; (b) US$3,700; Science programmes: (a) US$2,400; (b) US$3,000; Persian language course: US$1,000; living costs (residence, local transportation, clothing, meals, books) per month: single student, US$500; spouse: US$100; one child: US$75.
Languages: language of instruction: Persian; international students must attend a Persian language course prior to the commencement of any programme.
Applications: to the above address: visa conditions: international students should have documents approved by the Iranian embassy in the applicant's country and they should be posted directly to the university.

🐾 Financial aid
Open to: candidates from countries having close academic collaboration with I.R. Iran; candidates from member countries of the Organization of the Islamic Conference (OIC), the Federation of the Universities of the Islamic world (FUIW); Association of the Universities of Asia and Pacific; candidates with outstanding academic background.

Value: 10 to 100% of tuition fees.
Applications: International students must attend a persian language course prior to admission; contact baziar@iust.ac.ir for further details.

🐦 Scholarships

Study Domains: architecture, engineering, sciences.
Scholarships: Student Scholarships.
Description: information available from the Ministry of Science, Research and Technology of I.R. Iran or from Iranian embassies around the world.
Applications: for further information contact: interiust@iust.ac.ir.

1245 Isfahan University of Medical Sciences and Health Services [IUMS]

Hezar Jerib Avenue
81745 Isfahan
Tel: +98-311-792-3071/3080
Fax: +98-311-668-7898
Web: http://www.mui.ac.ir/
e-mail: international@mui.ac.ir

📖 Undergraduate, Graduate and Postgraduate Programmes

Study Domains: dentistry, health and hygiene, medicine, nursing, pharmacy and pharmacology.
Programmes: University Health Programmes leading to (a) Bachelor's degree, (b) Master's degree, (c) Ph.D.
Subjects: 7 faculties: medicine, pharmacy, dentistry, nursing, midwifery, rehabilitation, management and medical information.
Open to: candidates of all nationalities holding a secondary school leaving certificate; national entrance examination.
Held: 5 research centres and 11 affiliated hospitals located in the south of Iran.
Duration: (a) 4 years, (b) 2 years, (c) 3 to 5 years.

1246 Islamic Azad University [IAU]

PO Box 19585/466
Tehran
Tel: +98-21-255-7703
Fax: +98-21-254-7787
Web: http://www.azad.ac.ir
e-mail: iau@dpimail.net

📖 Undergraduate, Graduate Programmes

Study Domains: all major fields.
Programmes: programme of courses leading to Bachelor's and Master's degrees.
Open to: candidates of all nationalities holding a secondary-school certificate; a good command of Persian and for postgraduate degrees a good command of English are required.
Held: 130 campuses across Iran; depending on programmes offered.
Fees: depend on courses, see website for details.
Applications: to Afrasiab Amiri, Vice President for International Affairs, at the above address.

1247 Mashhad University of Medical Sciences [MUMS]

PO Box 91735
346 Daneshgah Street
Mashhad
Tel: +98-511-841-2081
Fax: +98-511-843-4700
Web: http://www.mums.ac.ir
e-mail: mums@mums.ac.ir

🐦 Financial aid

Study Domains: medicine.
Open to: All candidates candidates of all nationalities.
Value: living expenses, 6,900 Tomans every 3 months, also dormatory facilities provided.

1248 Shahid Beheshti University [SBU]

PO Box 19395-14716
Evin Square
19834 Tehran
Tel: +98-21-240-3126
Fax: +98-21-241-8681
Web: http://www.sbu.ac.ir
e-mail: int-re@cc.sbu.ac.ir

📖 Undergraduate, Graduate, Postgraduate Programmes

Study Domains: all major fields.
Programmes: programme of courses leading to (a) Bachelor's degree, (b) Master's degree, (c) Doctorate (Ph.D.).
Description: the University includes 11 faculties, 3 research institutes, 7 research centres, 70 courses at Master's level and 30 courses at Ph.D. level.
Open to: candidates of all nationalities; Ph.D. programme applicants should not be over 32 years old.
Duration: (a) 4 years, (b) 2 years, (c) 2 to 3 years.
Applications: by 4 April for fall semester or 6 Sept for spring semester; foreign students should complete the three-page application form on the website and send it to the University Office of International Affairs; the confidential reference form should be completed and sent by two referees to the above-mentioned office as well.

🐦 Scholarships

Study Domains: all major fields.
Scholarships: University Scholarships.
Description: a limited number of foreign students will be offered scholarships; students on scholarships will receive a tuition waiver, an adequate amount of living expenses, thesis or dissertation preparation fees, as well as a round-trip plane ticket during their studies; the scholarship will also partly cover expenses of the families of married students; foreign students seeking employment must obtain a work permit through the Ministry of Labour, on approval of the Ministry of Science, Research and Technology.
Applications: see website for information or contact: Dr. H.R. Nikbakht, tel: +98 21 240 3126, fax: +98 21 241 8681.

1249 Shahid Beheshti University of Medical Sciences and Health Services [SBMU]

PO Box 19395-4139
Evin Square
19834 Tehran
Tel: +98-21-240-1022
Fax: +98-21-240-0052
Web: http://www.sbmu.ac.ir
e-mail: icrd@sbmu.ac.ir

📖 Undergraduate, Graduate, Postgraduate Programmes

Study Domains: dentistry, medicine, nursing, nutrition, paramedical studies, pharmacy and pharmacology.
Programmes: programme of courses leading to (a) Bachelor's degree, (b) Master's degree, (c) Doctorate (Ph.D.), (d) Medicine, (e) Diplom-Metevaseth.
Description: the University includes 8 faculties, 18 medical, clinical and educational centres; also national research institutes specialized in tuberculosis and lung disease, endocrine research, ophthalmic research, skin research, traditional medicine and material medical research.
Open to: candidates of all nationalities holding a secondary-school certificate; entrance examination required.
Duration: (a) 4 to 5 years, (b) 3 years, (c) 3 to 5 years, (d) 6 years, (e) 3 years.

1250 Tarbiat Modarres University [TMU]

PO Box 14115 - 111
Tehran
Tel: +98-21-801-1001
Fax: +98-21-800-6544
Web: http://www.modares.ac.ir
e-mail: intl@modares.ac.ir

📖 Graduate, Postgraduate Programmes

Study Domains: all major fields.
Programmes: programme of courses leading to Master's degree, Master of sciences (M.Sc.) and Doctorate (Ph.D.).
Subjects: agriculture, arts, basic sciences and medical sciences, engineering, humanities, natural resources and marine services.
Open to: candidates of all nationalities holding a Bachelor's degree recognized by the Iranian Ministry of Science, Research and Technology or the Ministry of Health and Medical Training; entrance examination required.
Held: Tehran, Karaj, Noor (depending on programmes).
Fees: tuition fees: US$2,400-$3,700 per year; living costs: approx. US$1,000 per year.
Languages: Persian and English; all foreign students must pass certain Persian language courses which are necessary for their stay and study in Iran.
Applications: between 20 March-20 August to the Office of International Affairs: intl@modares.ac.ir.

1251 Tehran University of Medical Sciences [TUMS]
23 Dameshgh Street
Vali-e-Asr Avenue
14155-5799 Tehran
Tel: +98-21-889-6692/96
Fax: +98-21-889-8532
Web: http://www.tums.ac.ir
e-mail: a1313@sina.tums.ac.ir

📖 Undergraduate, Graduate, Postgraduate Programmes

Study Domains: anatomy, biochemistry, cancerology, cardiology, continuing education, cytology, demography and population studies, dentistry, dermatology, dietetics, education, genetics, gerontology, health and hygiene, immunology, medicine, microbiology, neurology, nursing, nutrition, obstetrics and gynaecology, ophthalmology, paediatrics, paramedical studies, pharmacy and pharmacology, physical education, physiology, preventive medicine, psychiatry, psychology, radiology, social work, special education, speech therapy, statistics, surgery, urology.
Programmes: programme of courses leading to (a) Bachelor's degree, (b) Master's degree, (c) Ph.D., (d) postdoctorate degree.
Open to: candidates of all nationalities holding a secondary-school certificate; entrance examination required.
Duration: (a) 4 years, (b) 2 years, (c) 4 to 5 years, (d) 6 months to 2 years; courses begin in September.
Fees: tuition fees: US$1,000-$3,000; living costs, approx. US$3,500 per semester.
Languages: Persian, English.
Applications: 3 months before beginning of courses to Dr. A. Nourczi: a1313@sina.tums.ac.ir.

1252 University of Isfahan [UI]
Office of Scientific and International Relations
Hezar Jerib Street
81744 Isfahan
Tel: +98-311-793-2039/2040
Fax: +98-311-668-7398
Web: http://www.ui.ac.ir
e-mail: int-office@ui.ac.ir

📖 Undergraduate, Graduate, Postgraduate Programmes

Study Domains: business, education, engineering, humanities and arts, law, sciences, social sciences.
Programmes: programme of courses leading to (a) Bachelor's degree; (b) Master's degree; (c) Ph.D. degree.
Description: the University includes 7 faculties with 35 departments and 5 research centres.
Duration: (a) 4 years, (b) 2 to 3 years, (c) by thesis; courses begin in September.
Financial assistance: work opportunities in research.

1253 University of Kurdistan [KU]
PO Box 416
Pasdaran Street
66135 Sanandaj
Tel: +98-471-39375
Fax: +98-471-30585

📖 Undergraduate, Graduate Programmes

Study Domains: accounting, Arabic, architecture, biology, botany, business administration, computer science, English, geography, languages, law, literature and civilization, mathematics, physical education, physics, sciences, teacher education.
Programmes: programme of courses leading to Pre-University Certificate, Bachelor's and Master's degrees.
Duration: variable, depending on programmes; courses begin 10 September.
Languages: Persian and English.
Applications: by 20 June to the above address; for information contact Gh. Karimi Doostan, tel: +98 871 666 0065, fax: +98 871 666 0066.

1254 University of Tehran [UT]
Enghelab Avenue
14174 Tehran
Tel: +98-21-646-9807
Fax: +98-21-649-8873
Web: http://www.ut.ac.ir
e-mail: international@ut.ac.ir

📖 Undergraduate, Graduate, Postgraduate Programmes

Study Domains: agriculture, business, education, engineering, humanities and arts, languages, law, sciences, social sciences.
Programmes: programme of courses leading to (a) Bachelor's degree; (b) Master's degree; (c) Ph.D. degree.
Held: Ghazvin and Tehran.
Duration: (a) 4 to 6 years; (b) 2-1/2 to 4-1/2 years; (c) by thesis; courses begin in September.
Languages: Persian; short Persian language courses available for foreign students.

🎓 Scholarships
Study Domains: all major fields.
Description: Government scholarships.
Applications: in June; consult website for further information or contact Ministry of Science, Research and Technology.

Ireland
Academic year: September to June.
Organization of higher education system: Higher education in Ireland is provided by the university sector, the institutes of technology, the colleges of education, and private, independent colleges. The institutions which fall within the first three groupings are autonomous and self-governing, but substantially state aided. In addition to sub-degree, degree and postgraduate programmes, many higher education institutions run foundation programmes for international students. Successful completion of these programmes will lead directly into an award programme within the institution.
Most universities run a semesterised system and modularization has been introduced in the majority of colleges to allow greater flexibility for students and Europe-wide mobility using the European Credit Transfer System (ECTS). Teaching at undergraduate level generally involves a programme of lectures supplemented by tutorials, practical demonstrations and laboratory work (where relevant).
• The University Sector: There are seven universities, which offer degrees at Bachelor's, Master's and Doctorate levels and undergraduate and postgraduate certificate and diploma programmes over a full range of disciplines. The universities are also involved in continuing and distance education programmes. Universities award their own degrees. Quality is assured through the use of international external examiners and through the Higher Education Authority (HEA - www.hea.ie) which oversees the work of the universities on behalf of the Department of Education and Science. The

universities have also established the Irish Universities Quality Board (IUQB - www.iuqb.ie) to assist in the monitoring and maintaining of standards. Master's degrees are available either by research only or, increasingly, as taught Master's programmes involving coursework and research. Doctoral degrees are awarded on the basis of research. Full contact details can be found on www.educationireland.ie.
• The Institutes of Technology: There are fourteen institutes of technology located throughout the country offering programmes in technology, science, engineering and humanities at foundation, higher certificate, degree and postgraduate levels, as well as providing craft and professional level programmes. Awards are made on the basis of delegated authority or are approved by Higher Education and Training Awards Council (HETAC). Qualifications are internationally recognized by academic, professional, trade and craft bodies. In addition most colleges also have courses leading directly to the examinations of many professional institutes. The Department of Education and Science has overall responsibility for this sector which includes the formulation and review of policy. Full contact details for all the institutes of technology can be found on www.educationireland.ie
• Independent Higher Education Colleges: Side by side with the publicly funded tertiary sector are a number of independent institutions which offer: accountancy and business studies; law; humanities; hotel; catering & tourism studies; science and art & design. Many of the programmes offered by these colleges are validated by the HETAC and some have links with universities and/or professional associations through which the courses on offer are accredited. Most of the independent colleges also offer courses leading to the awards of overseas universities or other awards bodies. In addition there are independent colleges who do not offer any HETAC programmes, but only ones offered by overseas award bodies. Students interested in taking non-HETAC recognised programmes should contact the individual college directly and also confirm the status of the particular programme with the relevant awarding authority. Full contact details for independent colleges offering HETAC recognized programmes can be found on www.educationireland.ie
• Colleges of Teacher Education: There are several colleges of education for primary school teachers in Ireland. These colleges offer three-year full time courses leading to a Bachelor's of Education degree (B.Ed), which is the recognized qualification for primary school teaching. Proficiency in the Irish language is currently an entry requirement for courses in primary teacher education although exceptions may be made in certain instances. Some Colleges of Education also offer degrees in humanities and liberal arts. Teachers at second level schools normally take a university degree followed by a one year Higher Diploma in Education. For further information on courses or to obtain information regarding the recognition of overseas qualifications and eligibility to teach in Ireland please contact the Department of Education and Science www.education.ie. Full contact details for the colleges of education can be found on www.educationireland.ie.
• Medical Education: There are five medical schools: four in the university sector (Trinity College Dublin, University College Dublin, University College Cork and National University of Ireland-Galway) and one independent college, the Royal College of Surgeons in Ireland (RCSI) which is a recognised college of the National University of Ireland. All of the schools offer professional medical degrees and a broad range of postgraduate programmes and research programmes. In recent years the medical schools have expanded their provision of programmes to other medical areas including nursing education, physiotherapy and pharmacy.
• Exchange and Study Abroad Programmes Available to Overseas Students: In addition to full undergraduate and postgraduate programmes which are available to overseas students, Irish universities offer a wide selection of study programmes involving credit transfer arrangements with overseas universities and colleges. The majority of Irish colleges have a Study Abroad office which is responsible for co-ordinating programmes aimed at overseas students spending either a summer, a semester or a full academic year studying in Ireland. Modules are offered in a broad spectrum of faculties and, with the exception of Summer programmes, have a GPA entry requirement and involve a full-time course load. Applications for all Study Abroad programmes should

be made directly to the relevant institution.
• Opportunities in Ireland for Researchers and Research Students: The Economy of Ireland in recent years has been based mainly on major export growth in the ICT and biotechnology sectors. Future economic plans are based on the further development of Ireland as a knowledge-based society with growth in exports of higher value end products. Science Foundation Ireland (SFI) is investing €646 million between 2000-2006 in academic researchers and research teams who are most likely to generate new knowledge, leading edge technologies, and competitive enterprises in the fields underpinning the two broad areas mentioned above (www.sfi.ie). There is an ever-expanding range of opportunities for good researchers and research students to join Irish universities and colleges. Information on opportunities can be obtained through the individual universities, colleges and research institutions. PRTLI is a government initiative to strengthen the basic research capabilities of third level institutions in Ireland. The programme is currently funded under the National Development Plan 2000-2006, with assistance from the European Regional Development Fund and with private funding through a public/private financial framework. PRTLI allocates funding on a competitive basis to third level institutions. A total of €605 million has been awarded to date under the first three cycles of the programme. The management of the programme and the allocation of funds are co-ordinated by the Higher Education Authority (HEA) on behalf of the Department of Education and Science. The programme which has been in operation since 1998 has funded some 850 researchers.
Monetary unit: Euro (€).
National student admission: Entry to third level education for Irish students is competitive and based upon performance in the final secondary school examination, the Leaving Certificate.
International student admission: Foreign students should have, as a minimum, qualifications equivalent to the Irish university matriculation examination such as the General Certificate of Education with at least 2 subjects at Advanced (A) level with high grades (at least Grade C) plus 4 other subjects at Ordinary (O) level. Competition for places is extremely keen and minimum qualifications may not be sufficient for entry. Entry requirements to non-university institutions vary greatly. Detailed information should be sought from the institution concerned.
Special travel facilities: A current International Students Identity Card suitably endorsed, permits students to travel at discount rates. Other concessions for students: a number of shops/services provide discounts to those students with an up-to-date student card. Colleges in Ireland have facilities for handicapped students.
Language: The normal language of instruction is English; at certain institutions, however, some lectures are given in the Irish language. Colleges in Ireland do not make special arrangements for the attainment of competence in English by overseas students. Most universities and colleges provide English language training programmes and in addition there are over 100 recognized private English language training schools running both short and long-term programmes. Most schools also offer preparation programmes for the major English language examinations such as TOEFL, IELTS, Cambridge, RSA, Oxford and Trinity College (London). A system of recognition and quality assurance pertains in this industry through the Advisory Council for English Language Schools (ACELS). ACELS was established by the Department of Education and Science and ensures that the highest standard of educational services is promoted and maintained. Information and details on ACELS recognized schools is available at www.acels.ie. Many of the larger language schools are also members of MEI-RELSA - Marketing English in Ireland - Recognised English Language Schools Association. Course and cost details of these schools can be found on www.mei.ie.
Immigration requirements: Citizens of the United Kingdom are not required to undergo any formal immigration procedures. All citizens from other countries should contact the Irish embassy or consulate in their home country. Full contact details for Irish Embassies around the world can be found at www.educationireland.ie. Those who do not have an Irish embassy or consulate in their home country should apply directly for a visa application form, well in advance of their departure to:

Department of Foreign Affairs, Visa Section, 13-14 Burgh Quay, Dublin 2, fax: +353-1-633-1052; email: visa@iveagh.gov.ie; web: www.dfa.ie.
Estimated expenses for one academic year: 8-14,000 Euros for general courses; 30,000 Euros for medical studies; Books/Supplies: 1,000 Euros; Housing and Living expenses 7,000 Euros; expenses vary greatly depending on courses and location.
Information services:
• For information on Studying in Ireland, contact the International Education Board Ireland on info@educationireland.ie; address: PC House, 35-39 Shelbourne Road, Dublin 4, Ireland.
• For information on European Exchange programmes contact Leargas. 189-193 Parnell Street, Dublin 1, Ireland; tel: +353-1-873-1411; fax: +353-1-873-1316; email: info@leargas.ie, www.leargas.ie. Léargas is Ireland's National Agency for the management of national, European and international co-operation programmes involving: education and lifelong learning, vocational education and training, youth and community work, guidance in education
• Application from overseas students for first year full-time undergraduate courses is either made through the Central Application Office (CAO) at http://www.cao.ie) or directly through the institution. The institution will clearly state to you which application route to be followed. There is a small fee for overseas students which should accompany all applications. For all other programmes such as postgraduate studies or Study Abroad Programmes students should apply directly to the institution of their choice.
Scholarships for international students:
• Many overseas students studying in Ireland are sponsored by their own governments or through other international scholarship programmes. In most cases applications should be made through the Ministry of Education in the student's home country.
• A small number of scholarships for overseas students are available from the universities and colleges themselves. These are awarded solely at the discretion of the individual institutions who set down their own criteria for eligibility. Students are advised to contact the institution of their choice directly, to obtain further information.
• The Department of Education and Science also has a limited number of scholarships. For details contact: International Section, Department of Education and Science, Marlborough Street, Dublin 1, Ireland; web: www.education.ie.
Open and distance learning: Oscail -The National Distance Education Centre (www.oscail.ie) - is located on the campus of Dublin City University (www.dcu.ie) and offers a range of undergraduate, postgraduate and continuing professional education programmes.
Recognition of studies and qualification: The Universities, the Dublin Institute of Technology and a growing number of the Institutes of Technology confer academic awards on successful students in their own colleges, while other colleges receive their academic qualifications from the Higher Education and Training Awards Council (HETAC) at hkttp://www.hetac.ie. HETAC awards qualifications and sets and monitors standards at all levels of higher education and training up to doctoral level. All Irish awards are included in the National Framework of Qualifications (www.nfq.ie) which was established to assist the national objective of moving towards a 'lifelong learning society' by ensuring the existence of a single coherent, easily understood award system for all levels of education and training available in Ireland today. The Framework is maintained by the National Qualifications Authority of Ireland (NQAI) at http://www.nqai.ie. The quality and standard of all Irish educational awards is fully recognized globally.
Accommodation services: Details from the Officers or Deans of Residence in the colleges.
Work opportunities: Non-EU nationals who have student visas are entitled to take up casual employment (defined as up to 20 hours part time work per week or full time work during vacation periods) for the duration of their permission to remain in the country.
Publications / Websites:
• A brochure and CD-ROM are available from the International Education Board of Ireland (IEBI).

1255 American College Dublin [ACD]
2 Merrion Square
Dublin 2
Tel: +353-1-676-8939
Fax: +353-1-676-8941
Web: http://www.amcd.ie
e-mail: degree@amcd.ie

📖 Undergraduate Degree Programmes

Study Domains: accounting, administration, advertising, business, business administration, communication, economic and commercial sciences, economy, finance, international business, international law, management, marketing, psychology, public relations, recreation and leisure, social sciences, social work, sociology, tourism, hotel and catering management, trade.
Programmes: Programme of courses leading to Bachelor's degree, National certificate, Diploma.
Description: (a) Bachelor's degree programmes in behavioural sciences, sociology, psychology, international business (management or marketing), liberal arts (English, history, international relations); (b) National certificate in humanities; (c) Diploma in hospitality management.
Duration: (a) 4 years, (b) and (c) 2 years.
Fees: registration: 60 Euros; tuition: contact department.
Financial assistance: work opportunities for students: non-EU students work to max. of 20 hours during term time; EU students open.
Applications: open application date; apply to admissions office.

1256 Dublin Institute of Technology [DIT]
Fitzwilliam House
30 Upper Pembroke Street
Dublin
Tel: +353-1-402-3417
Fax: +353-1-402-3429
Web: http://www.dit.ie
e-mail: admissions@dit.ie

📖 Undergraduate, Graduate, Postgraduate Programmes

Study Domains: arts, business, engineering, sciences, tourism, hotel and catering management.
Programmes: programme of courses leading to Bachelor's degree, Master's degree, Ph.D., certificate and Higher Certificate.
Open to: candidates of all nationalities with secondary school leaving certificate.
Duration: duration: 1 to 5 years (undergraduate); 1 to 3 years (postgraduate).
Applications: apply to the admissions office by 1 February, no later than 31 May for Non-EU students; email: international@dit.ie for more information.

1257 Limerick Institute of Technology School of Professional and Management Studies [RTCL]
Moylish Park
Limerick
Tel: +353-61-208-208
Fax: +353-61-208-209
Web: http://www.lit.ie
e-mail: Information@lit.ie

📖 Undergraduate, Graduate Programmes

Study Domains: accounting, applied sciences, arts, building industry, computer science, design, electricity and electronics, engineering, industrial technology, management, marketing, mechanical engineering, technology, tourism, hotel and catering management.
Programmes: undergraduate, graduate, postgraduate courses at the following Schools and Departments: (a) Art and Design; (b) Professional and Management Studies incorporating the Department of Information Technology; (c) School of the Built Environment; (d) School of Engineering; (e) Department of Electrical and Electronic Engineering incorporating the Department of Communications; (f) Department of Mechanical and Automobile Engineering; (g) Department of Applied Science and Tourism and Hospitality

Studies.
Open to: see prospectus available on website for eligibility criteria for each programme.

1258 National University of Ireland, Galway [UCG]
University Road
Galway
Tel: +353-91-524-411
Web: http://www.ucg.ie/index.php
e-mail: infon@nuigalway.ie

📖 Graduate, Postgraduate Programmes

Study Domains: cultural studies, hydrology, languages, literature and civilization, summer programmes.
Programmes: (a) programme of courses leading to Master's degree in Science (M.Sc.), and postgraduate diploma; (b) Summer programmes.
Description: (a) International M.Sc. degree and postgraduate diploma courses in hydrology; (b) Summer courses in areas such as: archaeology, Irish literature, Irish history, Irish society, Gaelic culture, Irish language courses, English language courses, education in Ireland, international writers' course.
Duration: (a) 15 months for M.Sc.; 10 months for postgraduate diploma; 3 months for workshops between April and June; (b) 1 month June/August.
Financial assistance: (a) Irish Government fellowships available to selected qualified students from developing countries.
Applications: (a) to the Director of the International Postgraduate Hydrology Courses and Workshops at the above address; (b) to the Administrative Director, Summer Schools Office, at the above address.

1259 National University of Ireland, Maynooth [UIM]
Nui Maynooth
Maynooth Co.
Kildare
Tel: +353-1-708-3417
Fax: +353-1-708-6113
Web: http://www.nuim.ie
e-mail: melanie.kilduff@may.ie

📖 Undergraduate, Graduate, Postgraduate Programmes

Study Domains: anthropology, canon law, classical studies, continuing education, economy, education, engineering, European studies, finance, geography, history, languages, liberal arts, literature and civilization, music and musicology, philosophy, sciences, social work, telecommunications, theology, religion.
Programmes: programme of courses leading to (a) Bachelor's degree (B.A.; B.Sc.); (b) Master's degree (M.A.; M.Sc.; M.Litt.); (c) Ph.D.; (d) Diploma and (e) Higher Diploma.
Subjects: arts, philosophy, Celtic studies, engineering and science, information technology, computer engineering.
Open to: candidates of all nationalities with secondary-school certificate; over 17 years of age.
Duration: (a) 3 to 4 years, (b) 1 to 3 years, (c) 3 to 4 years, (d) and (e) 2 years; courses begin in September.
Fees: see web site.
Applications: by 1 July; contact International Undergraduate Office: melanie.kilduff@may.ie or International Postgraduate Office.

🖋 Scholarships

Study Domains: all major fields, sciences.
Scholarships: Postgraduate Scholarships.
Subjects: all; mostly in science.
Value: variable.
Applications: all registered postgraduate students may apply; deadline: end of July; contact: academic department / office for research and postgraduate studies.

1260 University College Dublin [UCD]
Belfield
Dublin 4
Tel: +353-1-716-1701
Fax: +353-1-716-1165
Web: http://www.ucd.ie
e-mail: international@ucd.ie

📖 Undergraduate, Graduate, Postgraduate Programmes

Study Domains: all major fields, summer programmes.
Programmes: programme of courses leading to Bachelor's degree, Master's degree, Certificate, Higher diploma and Ph.D. degrees.
Open to: overseas students: qualifications are assessed on an individual basis; applicants must meet matriculation requirements and provide evidence of competence in English.
Fees: variable according to course, year of course and student category; write for details.
Applications: by December; undergraduate applications to Central Applications Office, Tower House, Eglington Street, Galway, Ireland; postgraduate applications to the relevant Faculty/Department, UCD.

Israel

Academic year: September to June.
Organization of higher education system: Higher education in Israel is provided by universities, non-university institutions of higher education that have been accredited to award degrees, other academic colleges, liberal arts as well as technological, academic teacher training colleges, regional colleges that offer academic courses for which universities are academically responsible, extensions or branches of foreign institutions of higher education that have obtained a license from the Council for Higher Education in Israel.
Higher education in Israel is under the direct jurisdiction of the Council for Higher Education, which is responsible for accrediting and authorizing institutions of higher education to award degrees. It is this jurisdiction that distinguishes the higher education system from the post-secondary education system which does not lead to an academic degree.
The following universities engage in both teaching and research: the Hebrew University of Jerusalem, the Technion-Israel Institute of Technology, Tel Aviv University, Bar-Ilan University, the University of Haifa, Ben-Gurion University of the Negev, and the Weizmann Institute of Science (a research institute that offers graduate programmes). These institutions offer undergraduate and graduate programmes in the humanities, social sciences, natural sciences, and business administration. Some offer programmes in law, medicine, dental medicine, paramedical studies, pharmacy, agriculture, applied sciences, engineering and architecture. The Open University in Israel offers undergraduate and graduate courses in the humanities, social sciences, business administration, natural sciences and engineering and is based on distance-teaching.
In addition to the universities, a large variety of institutions are accredited as institutions of higher education and offer academic programmes in a broad spectrum of fields, such as the fine arts, business, law, music, engineering, and teacher training. Regional colleges also offer university-level education. Universities are academically responsible for these courses.
The institutions of higher education are autonomous in the conduct of their academic and administrative affairs within the framework of their budgets. Most of the accredited institutions of higher education in Israel are supported by public funds, which account for well over two-thirds of their total recurrent budgets. Nonetheless, they are not state universities or colleges. Tuition and student fees cover about 20% and the remainder is derived from donations and other sources. A number of accredited institutions receive no government support. These institutions are financed primarily by the fees they charge, which are significantly higher than in the publicly funded institutions.
The licensing and accrediting authority for higher education is the Council for Higher Education, a statutory body whose chairman is, ex-officio, the Minister of Education. In addition to the chairman, the Council is composed of 19-24 members

personally appointed by the President of the State of Israel on the recommendation of the government. At least two thirds of the members must be academics of standing. The Council has the sole power to accredit institutions of higher education and to authorize them to award academic degrees. It also has the sole authority to grant licenses to cross-border institutions of higher education to operate in Israel under the academic accreditation of the relevant body in their home country.

• Degree programmes: First level (undergraduate degree programmes):

In Israel, most Bachelor's degree programmes can be completed in three to four years at a university or college. However, overseas students are often required to take a one-year preparatory programme ('mechina') prior to being admitted to an accredited programme. Students are accepted directly to specific departments from commencement of their academic studies. In many cases, they select two majors, which are studied exclusively. Students generally pursue professional education studies (e.g., law, medicine, dental medicine) from their first year of university studies. These programmes require more than three years of study as well as a period of practical experience or an internship.

• Second level (Master's degree programmes): Master's degree programmes are designed to provide the student with in-depth knowledge and research capabilities in a particular field. Most of these programmes extend over a period of two years. Many departments offer two study tracks. One requires students to write a Master's thesis and allows them to pursue doctoral studies in the department, while the other does not require a thesis and is designed for students who do not intend to pursue a doctorate in the department. Since undergraduate studies in Israel are highly specialized, most students with foreign Bachelor's degrees are required to take supplementary courses prior to or in conjunction with their regular graduate studies.

• Third level (Doctoral degree programmes): The Doctoral degree programme represents the highest level of academic achievement within the Israeli educational system. The doctoral programme focuses on a scientific thesis or dissertation that is expected to make an original, significant contribution to the advancement of knowledge. There are various types of Doctoral degrees, with Doctor of Philosophy (Ph.D.) being by far the most common. Seven universities have been authorized by the Council for Higher Education to award this degree. Doctoral programmes extend over a minimum of two years after completion of the Master's degree, but are generally completed only after four or more years.

The Direct doctoral programme is intended for exceptional students who have a Bachelor's degree with a grade average of at least 90 ('A') in the area of their intended doctorate and an average of at least 80 ('B') in other course work. The specifics of this programme vary somewhat from one institution to the next. In general the student must take all or most of the courses required of a student in a thesis track programme. Instead of writing a full thesis a student must submit for examination an extensive proposal for his doctoral dissertation. If approved, the student may, depending on the institution, receive a Master's degree and proceed directly to doctoral studies. Requirements for the doctorate are regulated by individual university doctoral committees, which operate in conjunction with the university department and/or faculty through which the degree will be recommended. An advisor oversees the research and dissertation. A research proposal must be submitted to and approved by the university doctoral committee. The research is usually carried out in the framework of the student's university department but under certain circumstances it may be conducted in part or in its entirety at another scientific institution in Israel or abroad. Students meet with their advisor, submit written progress reports, and present a lecture to a research seminar or a similar forum. The dissertation is evaluated by a committee of three members, one of whom is the advisor. The written evaluation submitted by the committee serves as the basis for awarding the degree. The dissertation is normally written in Hebrew, although special permission may be granted for its submission in another language. Course work is generally required. Some institutions do not specifically require enrolment in courses but assume student attendance and participation in courses that have been selected in consultation with the student's advisor.

Diploma Studies: The institutions of higher education offer a variety of non-degree programmes. In general, these programmes require a Bachelor's degree, and upon completion a diploma or certificate is awarded. Information about diploma programmes may be found in publications of the institutions. Credit towards an academic degree is generally not granted for courses in these programmes. Prospective candidates are advised to investigate the nature of such programmes, including the possibility of earning graduate credits, by directly contacting the institution offering the program or the Secretariat of the Council for Higher Education, POB 4037, Jerusalem 91040.

Post-doctoral research programmes: Post-doctoral fellowships are available from Israeli universities. These fellowships are generally available for a period of up to two years of intense advance research under the auspices of one or more of the senior faculty of the university. Fellowships are available in the natural sciences, health, engineering, the social sciences and the humanities. Candidates for post-doctoral fellowships should contact the specific professor with whom their research will be conducted.

Programmes for visiting undergraduate students - one-year programme

(with one semester option): one-year programme courses are often chosen for junior years abroad. The courses are taught primarily in English, with some taught in Hebrew. Courses are generally accepted for credit at colleges and universities in North America. (Students arrange credit through the academic advisor at their home universities.) One-year programme courses may provide credit in such areas as archaeology, history, linguistics, literature, philosophy, religion, communications, international relations, political science, psychology, urban studies, sociology, and life sciences. In addition, opportunities are afforded to students to do independent study or research internships in their major areas of study. While it is strongly recommended that students attend for the full academic year, it is possible to be admitted for one semester.

Major institutions of higher education:
• Bar-Ilan University, Ramat Gan 52900; tel: +972-3-531-81733; fax: +972-3-5344-622; web: www.biu.ac.il
• Ben-Gurion University of the Negev, Beer Sheva 84105; tel: +972-7-6461-111; fax: +972-7-647-2968; web: www.bgu.ac.il
• Hebrew University of Jerusalem, Mount Scopus, Jerusalem 91905; tel: +972-2-588-2111, fax: +972-2-532-254; web: www.huji.ac.il
• Open University, P.O.Box 39328, Tel Aviv 61392; tel: +972-3-646-0460; fax: +972-3-642-2635; web: www.openu.ac.il
• Technion - Israel Institute of Technology, Technion City, Haifa 32000; tel: +972-4-8292-111, fax: +972-4-832-4530; web: www.technion.ac.il
• Tel Aviv University, Ramat Aviv, Tel Aviv 69978; tel: +972-3-640-8111; fax: +972-3-640-8371; web: www.tau.ac.il
• University of Haifa, Mount Carmel, Haifa 31999; tel: +972-4-824-0111; fax: +972-4-824-0321; Internet: www.haifa.ac.il
• Weizmann Institute of Science, Rehovot 76100; tel: +972-8-934-2111; fax: +972-8-946-6996; web: http://www.weizmann.ac.il
• Regional Colleges in Israel; web: http://www.folklore.org.il/colleges.

Monetary unit: new Israel shekel (NIS).

International student admission: The usual requirements for admission to Bachelor's degree programmes are: secondary school diploma, Israeli matriculation certificate ('bagrut') or its equivalent, psychometric entrance examination - usually the National Institute of Testing and Evaluation (NITE) Psychometric Entrance Test or the U.S. Scholastic Aptitude Test (SAT 1), Hebrew proficiency - sufficient knowledge of Hebrew to participate in regular studies, in accordance with the criteria set by the particular university and department. Certain institutions and departments may not require a psychometric entrance examination or may have additional requirements, e.g., personal interviews or additional tests. Israeli citizenship is required of those students accepted to studies in medicine, dental medicine, veterinary medicine, physiotherapy, and speech therapy. Selective faculties and departments in universities, such as medicine, dental medicine, law, psychology, certain fields of engineering, etc. have relatively high admission requirements. Secondary school diploma: In certain countries, the secondary school diploma awarded is equivalent to the Israeli matriculation certificate, for example, the Australian HSC and the English GCE (at least two 'A' levels and three 'O' levels). In general, candidates from countries whose diploma is not equivalent can be considered for university admission if they have successfully completed one year of university study abroad or a pre-academic preparatory program at an Israeli university.

Master's degree programmes: The requirements for admission to Master's degree programmes at Israeli universities are similar to those at Western universities. Generally, the equivalent of a bachelor's degree with a 'B' average is required; however, some departments require a higher average in the student's major field, while others may conditionally accept students with lower grades. In some cases, special tests (e.g., GRE, GMAT) and/or personal interviews are required. An adequate knowledge of Hebrew for class participation is necessary. A Hebrew language course ('ulpan') may be taken prior to the opening of the academic year.

Doctoral degree programmes: Applicants must have a Master's degree from a recognized university with a grade average of at least 'B' or 'Good' in Master's level course work and a thesis grade of 'Very Good'. Applicants from departments offering two programmes towards the Master's degree are required to have completed the track that requires a Master's thesis. At the discretion of university doctoral committees, applicants who do not meet normal admission criteria but appear to be able to meet the requisite standard within one year may be admitted provisionally. Provisional candidates follow a prescribed programme of supplementary studies for one year, after which time the qualifications of the applicant are re-evaluated. Previous scientific work, research and publications are taken into consideration.

Language: The language of instruction in all of the institutions of higher education is Hebrew (with the exception of the Feinberg Graduate School of the Weizmann Institute of Science, where the official language of study is English), although several offer a few courses or programs in other languages.

Students with insufficient knowledge of Hebrew are generally required to take an intensive Hebrew language course ('ulpan'), which is usually held on campus during the two months preceding the opening of the academic year. A student with no prior knowledge of Hebrew should not expect to reach a sufficient level of proficiency by the end of such a course. Several additional programmes are available to help students improve their Hebrew proficiency. In preparatory programmes, Hebrew is studied 10-15 hours per week. There are also special kibbutz ulpanim for prospective students, lasting four or five months and providing 20-25 hours of Hebrew study per week. Students with a good knowledge of Hebrew whose matriculation certificate (or secondary school diploma) is considered by Israeli institutions of higher education to be equivalent to the Israeli matriculation certificate ('bagrut') may apply directly for admission to regular degree studies.

Immigration requirements: Contact the Israeli Ministry of Foreign Affairs for visa information
http://www.mfa.gov.il/MFA/About+the+Ministry/Consular+affairs/
SERVICES+FOR+FOREIGN+NATIONALS+ONLY.htm.

Estimated expenses for one academic year: Tuition: US$2,300-$3,000 for regular degree programme; US$7,200-$8,000 for students enrolled in International Students' Programme; US$4,400-$5,400 for one semester in the International Students' Programme. This does not include university-sponsored Hebrew language seminar (ulpan); books/supplies: US$500 per semester; housing: US$2,000-$2,600 per academic year for campus housing.

Information services:
• For information on admissions, students should contact the individual universities and academic institutions directly.
• Israeli diplomatic missions abroad.
• Academic secretaries of universities and other higher educational institutions (programmes of study, handbooks, etc.).
• Student organizations in individual institutions.

Scholarships for international students: Contact David Assouline at davida@jazo.org.il.

Open and distance learning: Distance education is provided by the Open University of Israel which offers courses leading to a Bachelor's degree and Master's degree which may be taken at the student's own pace. The Open University is a full university-level accredited institution.

web: www-e.openu.ac.il.

Recognition of studies and qualification: Gaf L'ha'arachat Ta'arim Academi'im Mi'Hul, Department for Evaluation of Foreign Academic Degrees, Ministry of Education, Culture and Sport; 2 Devora Haneviah Street; Jerusalem, Israel 91911; tel: +972-2-560-2853/63; fax: +972-2-560-3876; e-mail: diplomot@int.gov.il; web: http://www.education.gov.il/.

Publications / Websites:
• Israel experience website containing information on short and long-term programmes for youth and students as well as scholarship funds: http://www.israelexperience.com
• Higher education study programmes: http://universities-colleges.org.il. This information is also available in print as a publication of the Council for Higher Education and the Jewish Agency for Israel, edited by David Assouline and Siva Azoulay, in 2002.

1261 Agricultural Research Organization The Volcani Center [ARO]

PO Box 6
50250 Bet-Dagan
Tel: +972-3-968-3111
Fax: +972-3-966-5327
Web: http://www.agri.gov.il/Volcani.html

📖 Graduate Studies / Soil Sciences

Study Domains: agriculture, agronomic sciences, rural development.
Programmes: (a) Kurt M. Schallinger advanced international course on irrigation and soil management; (b) advanced international course in agricultural engineering.
Open to: engineers, agronomists and agricultural extension workers of all nationalities with M.Sc. training in related subjects or B.Sc. and several years experience.
Duration: 2 months, beginning (a) in October and (b) in April.
Fees: approximately US$4,400 including board and lodging, tuition, field trips and study material.
Financial assistance: limited number of full or partial scholarships available for candidates from developing countries.
Applications: not later than 15 July for irrigation and 31 December for agricultural engineering; to the Secretary, Volcani International Courses, at the above address.

1262 Bar-Ilan University [BIU]

Bar Ilan University
Office of the Dean of Students
52 900 Ramat-Gan
Tel: +97-2-3-531-8111
Fax: +97-2-3-535/522
Web: http://www.biu.ac.il
e-mail: deanst@mail.biu.ac.il

📖 Undergraduate, Graduate Programmes

Study Domains: all major fields.
Programmes: undergraduate and graduate degree programmes.
Description: Bachelor's, Master's and Ph.D. degree programmes.
Open to: candidates with SAT and secondary-school diploma.
Duration: B.A.: 3 years.
Fees: tuition fees: approx. US$4,000.
Languages: Hebrew.

1263 Ben-Gurion University of the Negev [BGU]

PO Box 653
84105 Beer-Sheva
Tel: +972-8-6461-223
Fax: +972-8-6479-434
Web: http://www.bgu.ac.il
e-mail: acadsec@bgumail.bgu.ac.il

📖 Undergraduate, Graduate Programmes

Study Domains: agronomic sciences, engineering, health and hygiene, social sciences, technology.

Programmes: Studies in biotechnology, engineering, health sciences, desert studies, and social sciences.

✒ Undergraduate, Graduate Programmes

1264   Galillee College [GC]
PO Box 1070
36000 Tivon
Tel: +972-4-983-7444 / 983-7555
Fax: +972-4-983-0227
Web: http://www.galilcol.ac.il
e-mail: International_Department@galilcol.ac.il

📖 International Programme
Study Domains: ecology, environment, health and hygiene, management, urbanism.
Programmes: international programme in management and development studies.
Description: courses vary by year; recent topics include health systems management, port senior management, tourism planning, development and management, urban-economic development, environmental management, development of small businesses and industries.
Fees: (approximate figures) tuition, US$2,400; local expenses, US$2,460.
Financial assistance: a limited number of tuition scholarships are available.
Applications: to the International Department, at the above address.

✒ Full-Tuition Scholarship Scheme
Study Domains: all major fields.
Scholarships: Full-Tuition Scholarship Scheme.
Open to: participants in Galillee College programmes from developing countries.
Place of study: Galillee College.
Value: (approximate figures) US$2,400; candidate is responsible for return airfare to Israel and the local programme fees of approximately US$2,460.
Applications: to the Admissions Committee, at the above address.

1265   Hebrew University of Jerusalem
Boyar Building, Mount Scopus
91905 Jerusalem
Tel: +972-2-588-2600
Fax: +972-2-582-7078
Web: http://www.huji.ac.il
e-mail: admission@roth.mscc.huji.ac.il

📖 Undergraduate, Graduate Programmes
Study Domains: all major fields, summer programmes.
Programmes: (a) preparatory programme, gateway to Israeli society and to degree programmes at the university in: English, Hebrew, mathematics, Jewish history, Israel studies, general humanities
and social sciences; (b) freshman programme in: Hebrew, mathematics, Israel, Middle East and Jewish studies, general humanities and social sciences; (c) 1-year programme: Arabic, archaeology, arts, business administration, ecology, environment, Hebrew, history, international relations, literature and civilization, philosophy, political science, social sciences, theology, religion, natural sciences, and Israel, Middle East and Jewish studies; (d) graduate year programme in: Israeli, Middle East and Jewish studies, the Bible, ancient languages, Yiddish, Hebrew, and Arabic, history, international relations, literature and civilization, philosophy, political science, social sciences, theology, religion; (e) Master's programme in: Arabic, Hebrew, history, international relations, literature and civilization, philosophy, political science, social sciences, theology, religion, Israel, Middle East and Jewish studies, the Bible, ancient languages, Yiddish; (f) summer courses in: Arabic, archaeology, arts, Hebrew, international relations, law, environment, history, literature and civilization, philosophy, political science, theology, religion and Yiddish, Israel, Middle East and Jewish studies.
Open to: candidates of all nationalities: (a) having recently completed secondary-school abroad and new immigrants needing additional preparation to apply to the university and other institutions of higher education in Israel; (b) high school graduates with B average or SAT scores from North America

wishing to spend first year of college at the university; (c) visiting undergraduate students having completed a minimum of 1 year of studies at an accredited institution of higher education with B average; (d) and (e) graduate students at all levels with a minimum of B average; (f) completion of at least 1 year of studies in higher education and 1 letter of recommendation; 2 letters of recommendation required for (b), (c), (d) and (e); intensive Hebrew language course required prior to (a) and (b).
Duration: (a), (b), (c) and (d) 1 academic year, late October (August including Summer Ulpan) - June; (c) and (d) offer 1 semester options; (e) 2 academic years; (f) programme in English in July and in French in August.
Fees: tuition (b), (c), (d) and (e): US$5,700 per year; (c) and (d) US$3,700 (semester option); Summer Ulpan: US$1,050; Winter Ulpan: US$600; registration fee: US$55; living expenses US$1,600
per academic year, Summer Ulpan US$400.
Financial assistance: a limited number of scholarships are available.
Languages: Instruction in: (a) Hebrew, English, French, Russian and Spanish; (b) English and Hebrew; (c) French, English and Hebrew; (d) and (e) English and Hebrew.
Applications: (a) to (c) by mid-April, and for (d) and (e) by 31 March, to the Rothberg International School at the above address; see http://overseas.huji.ac.il.

✒ Moritz and Charlotte Warburg Prize
Study Domains: cultural studies.
Scholarships: Moritz and Charlotte Warburg Prize, Hebrew University Institute of Jewish Studies.
Subjects: Jewish studies at graduate and postgraduate level.
Open to: nationals of all countries.
Duration: 1 year (renewable).
Value: US$6,500-$7,000 per year.
Applications: by the end of November, to the Secretary of the Institute of Jewish Studies, Faculty of Humanities, at the above address.

1266   Joseph H. and Belle R. Braun Hebrew University-Hadassah
School of Public Health and Community Medicine
PO Box 122172
Jerusalem 91120
Tel: +972-2-777-117
Web: http://www.md.huji.ac.il/depts/occenvmed/abou t.html
e-mail: elir@cc.huji.ac.il

📖 Graduate Programme / Public Health
Study Domains: health and hygiene.
Programmes: Master of Public Health degree: in the area of public health and community medicine provides basic skills in: principles and uses of epidemiology; principles of health administration; evaluation of health services; principles of public health practice, planning and administration; research in public health and community medicine; diagnosis of the state of health of a community; planning and implementation of community care programmes through primary health care services; control of communicable diseases; environmental, industrial and occupational health; sociological and behavioural factors related to health.
Open to: candidates of all nationalities who hold an academic degree in medicine, dentistry or nursing from a recognized university, selection by Academic Committee and letters of recommendation.
Duration: 12 months beginning in October.
Fees: (approximate figures) US$24,000, all inclusive.
Financial assistance: limited number of scholarships available through Israeli Ministry of Foreign Affairs for applicants from developing countries.
Languages: instruction in English.
Applications: by 15 September, to the Co-ordinator of the International Course, at the above address.

1267 Lady Davis Fellowship Trust [LDFT]

Hebrew University, Givat Ram
Jerusalem 91904
Tel: +972-2-651-2306
Fax: +972-2-566-3848
Web: http://ldft.huji.ac.il
e-mail: LDFT@vms.huji.ac.il

☛ Graduate Fellowships

Study Domains: all major fields.
Scholarships: (a) Fellowships for Visiting Professors; (b) Post-doctoral fellowships; (c) Fellowships for Doctoral students; (d) Fellowships for Graduate students.
Description: fellowships are directed to (a), (b) and (c) research, or (a) teaching, in all fields of study available at the institutions mentioned below.
Open to: (a) full or associate professors from abroad; (b) candidates applying for fellowship within 4 years of receiving a doctorate; (c) only students who are enrolled in a Ph.D. programme overseas;
(d) applicants from abroad with M.Sc. degree.
Place of study: (a) and (b) Hebrew University of Jerusalem or Israel Institute of Technology, Haifa; (c) Hebrew University; (d) Israel Institute of Technology.
Duration: (a) 2 to 4 months at Hebrew University; from 3 to 9 months at Israel Institute of Technology; (b) from 9 to 12 months at Hebrew University; one year at Israel Institute of Technology; (c) 9 to 12 months; (d) 1 semester or 1 year (with the possibility of extension).
Value: (a) US$2,400 for professors, US$2,000 for associate professors, plus rent allowance; (b) US$1,300 at Hebrew University, US$1,250 at Israel Institute of Technology, plus rent allowance; (c) US$900; (d) US$750-$1,000; in addition, awards cover cost of travel and half of the medical insurance if purchased in Israel.
Applications: by (a) 30 November; (b) 31 December; (c) 31 January, to Hebrew University, at the above address; (a), (b) and (d) 30 November, to Technion, Israel Institute of Technology, Technion City, Haifa 32000, Israel.

1268 Michlalah Jerusalem College - The Linda Pinsky School for Overseas Students

PO Box 16078
91160 Bayit Vegan - Jerusalem
Tel: +972-2-675-0906/7
Fax: +972-2-675-0917
Web: http://www.machal.org.il/
e-mail: Machal@macam.ac.il

📖 Certificate, Undergraduate Programme Religious School Education

Study Domains: education, geography, Hebrew, philosophy.
Programmes: overseas student programme leading to Ministry of Education certification as religious school teachers: Bible, Jewish law, geography, education, Jewish philosophy, Jewish history.
Open to: women graduates of Jewish Religious High Schools.
Duration: 1 academic year; courses begin in September.
Fees: (approximate figures) US$10,000.
Applications: by 1 November, to American Friends of Michlalah, 9 Sutton Road, Monsey, New York, N.Y. 10953, United States.

1269 Ministry of Foreign Affairs

Hakirya
91130 Jerusalem
Web: http://www.israel-mfa.gov.il/mfa/
e-mail: scholarship@mfa.gov.il

☛ Foreign Students Scholarships

Study Domains: all major fields.
Scholarships: Foreign Students Scholarships.
Description: preference given to applicants studying Israeli or Jewish-related subjects.
Open to: candidates under 35 years of age, holding an undergraduate degree, applying from and citizen of one of the following countries: Austria, Belgium, Bulgaria, Canada (Quebec Province), China, Czech Republic, Denmark,

Estonia, Finland, France, Georgia, Germany, Great Britain, Greece, Hungary, India, Italy, Japan, Korea, Lithuania, Latvia, Luxembourg, Mexico, Netherlands, Norway, Poland, Portugal, Romania, Russia, Slovak Republic, Slovenia, Spain, Switzerland and Turkey.
Value: tuition fees and US$600 per month for one academic year (8 months).
Languages: knowledge of Hebrew or English necessary.
Applications: Israeli Embassy in candidate's country: see http://www.mfa.gov.il/mfa/go.asp?MFAH0hx30 for information and application form.

Italie

Année universitaire: octobre à septembre.
Organisation de l'enseignement supérieur: Le premier diplôme d'enseignement supérieur (1er cycle), Corsi di Laurea triennali, est délivré après trois années d'études; le deuxième diplôme d'enseignement supérieur (2e cycle), Corsi di Laurea specialistica, est attribué après deux années d'études supplémentaires. Pour certaines disciplines, une période d'études de cinq à six ans mène directement au diplôme de 2e cycle, Corso di Laurea a ciclo unico. Les étudiants peuvent suivre un 3e cycle dans des «ecoles de specialisation», Scuole di specializzazione, pour des études d'une durée de 2 à 6 ans ou pour un PhD pour des études de d'une durée de 2 à 3 ans.
Unité monétaire: Euro (€).
Admission pour étudiants internationaux: Les étudiants désirant étudier en Italie doivent avoir complétés 12 années de scolarité et satisfaire aux conditions d'accès à l'enseignement supérieur dans leur pays de résidence. Un diplôme de 1er cycle est demandé pour les étudiants américains. Les étudiants internationaux devront faire une demande d'inscription préalable aux services consulaires ou diplomatiques de leur pays de résidence. La délégation italienne fournira la demande d'inscription ainsi que la liste des diplômes.
Documents à fournir: l'original (copies non-acceptées) du certificat de fin d'études secondaires ou l'attestation traduite en italien et certifiée par la délégation diplomatique. La délégation retournera les documents traduits originaux au candidat, certifié et fournira un certificat d'équivalence de diplôme (dichiarazione di valore). La délégation enverra aussi une copie certifiée de tous les documents à l'université choisi par le candidat et informera le candidat des formalités supplémentaires pour les études d'enseignement supérieur.
Connaissances linguistiques requises: Une bonne connaissance de l'italien est nécessaire. Un examen de compétence linguistique peut s'avérer nécessaire.
Formalités d'immigration: Les candidats doivent justifier de moyens suffisants d'existence et d'une couverture sociale. Les services consulaires italiens fourniront une liste de documents à pourvoir. Dans les huit jours d'entrée en Italie, les candidats doivent se présenter à la Questura (prefecture de police) de la ville dans laquelle ils désirent s'installer afin d'obtenir un permis de résident.
Frais pour une année universitaire: Droit de scolarité: 1000 euros; livres/fournitures: 1200 euros; hébergement: 600 euros (pour une chambre), 1,200 euros pour un appartement.
Services d'accueil et d'information:
• Les universités italiennes tiennent des bureaux d'informations (voir site internet)
• Les Missions diplomatiques italiennes dans chaque pays.
Bourses pour étudiants internationaux: Ministero degli Affari Esteri, Direzione Generale per le Relazioni Culturali, Ufficio I, 00195 Rome, Italie; Internet: http://www.esteri.it/ita/index.asp.
Enseignement à distance: Ministère des Affaires étrangères, Direction générale, pour les relations culturelles, Ufficio 1, 00195, Rome, Italie.
Reconnaissance des études et diplômes: ENIC-NARIC, Centro di Informazione sulla Mobilità e le Equivalenze Accademiche (CIMEA), Fondazione RUI, Viale Ventuno Aprile 36, 00162 Rome, Italie; tél: +39-06-863-21281; fax: +39-06-863-22845; email: cimea@fondazionerui.it; Internet: http://www.fondazionerui.it.
Services du logement: S'adresser aux Bureaux d'aide sociale aux étudiants.
Publications / Sites Web:
• Ministero dell'università e della ricerca scientifica e tecnologica: http://www.miur.it/
• Ministry of Foreign Affairs: http://www.esteri.it
• CIMEA - Fondazione RUI, Viale Ventuno Aprile 36,0016é

Rome: http://www.study-in-italy.it/.

1270 Academia Belgica
Via Omero 8
00197 Rome
Tel: +39-06-320-1889
Fax: +39-06-320-8361
Web: http://www.academiabelgica.it
e-mail: segreteria@academiabelgica.it

☛ Bourses de recherche
Domaines d'étude: archéologie, histoire, histoire de l'art,
philologie.
A l'intention de: ressortissants belges, titulaires d'une
licence d'histoire, histoire de l'art, archéologie ou philologie,
et ayant terminé leurs études universitaires.
Lieu: dans les archives, bibliothèques, sites archéologiques
d'Italie.
Durée: 1, 2 ou 3 mois (renouvelables).
Candidatures: avant le 1er novembre et le 1er mai; Prof.
L. Milis, Vlieguit 20, 9830 Sint-Martens-Latem ou Prof. J. -P.
Massaut, 74 avenue Blonden, 4000 Liège, Belgique.

1271 Académie des beaux-arts «Pietro Vannucci»
Piazza S. Francesco 5
06123 Pérouse
Tel: +39-075-573-0631
Web: http://www.abaperugia.org
e-mail: didattica@abaperugia.org

☐ Diplôme de l'Académie
Domaines d'étude: beaux-arts.
Programmes: cours conduisant au diplôme de l'Académie
dans le domaine des beaux-arts: peinture, sculpture,
scénographie; langues d'enseignement: italien.
A l'intention de: ressortissants de tout pays, âgés de 18 ans
au minimum.
Durée: cours normal, 4 ans et cours libre, 1 an (débutant
en novembre).
Frais: 1ère année: 170 €; 2ème, 3ème et 4ème années: 130
€; cours libre: 260 €.
Inscriptions: pour le cours normal, l'inscription à l'examen
d'admission doit se faire avant le 15 mars, par l'intermédiaire
du consulat d'Italie ou de la représentation diplomatique dans
le pays du candidat.

1272 British Institute of Florence
Palazzo Lanfredini
Lungarno Guicciardini 9
50125 Florence
Tel: +39-055-28-4031
Web: http://www.fol.it/british
e-mail: info@britishinstitute.it

☐ Programme d'histoire de l'art
Domaines d'étude: arts, italien, langues.
Programmes: cours de langue italienne (différents
niveaux) et d'histoire de l'art.
A l'intention de: ressortissants de tout pays.
Durée: d'une semaine à plusieurs mois selon le niveau du
cours.
Inscriptions: les formulaires d'inscription et de plus
amples renseignements peuvent être obtenus auprès du British
Institute.

1273 British School at Rome [BSR]
via Gramsci, 61
00197 Rome
Tel: +39-06-326-4939
Fax: +39-06-322-1201
Web: http://www.bsr.ac.uk
e-mail: info@bsrome.it

☛ Scholarships
Study Domains: archaeology, architecture, arts, classical
studies, fine arts, printing.
Scholarships: (a) Balsdon Fellowship; (b) Hugh Last
Fellowship; (c) Paul Mellon Centre Rome Fellowship; (d)
Rome Scholarships; (e) Rome Fellowships; (f) Rome Awards;
(g) Tim Potter Memorial Award.

Subjects: archaeological fieldwork in Italy; painting;
archaeology, art; history, history and literature of Italy;
painting, sculpture, print-making, mediaeval and later Italian
studies, classics, archaeology; classical antiquity;
archaeology, art history, Italian literature and Italian history;
fine arts.
Open to: individuals or teams from British or
Commonwealth Universities; exceptionally promising
emergent painters, of United States, British or Commonwealth
nationality; senior scholars who are graduates of a British or
Commonwealth university, Italian an advantage; senior
scholars aged over 35, who are graduates of a British or
Commonwealth University; and British and British
Commonwealth citizens and residents who have begun a
programme of research in the general field for which the
award is being sought; distinguished fine artists of British or
Commonwealth nationality or residence; fine artists who can
demonstrate they are establishing a significant position in
their chosen field, of British or Commonwealth nationality or
residence.
Place of study: at British School at Rome (Italy).
Value: see website for further information.
Applications: by early December, mid-January of the
preceding academic year, to the Registrar for application
form.

1274 Bureau central des étudiants étrangers en Italie (Ufficio Centrale Studenti Esteri in Italia) [UCSEI]
Lungotevere dei Vallati 14
00186 Rome
Tel: +39-06-6880-4062
Fax: +39-06-6880-4063
Web: http://www.ucsei.org/
e-mail: ucsei@ucsei.org

☛ Bourses d'études
Domaines d'étude: toutes disciplines principales.
A l'intention de: ressortissants des pays en développement
d'Asie, d'Afrique et d'Amérique latine. Les candidats doivent
être déjà inscrits dans une université ou école supérieure
italienne.
Lieu: écoles et universités en Italie.
Candidatures: Ufficio Centrale Studenti Esteri in Italia
(UCSEI), à l'adresse ci-dessus.

1275 CORIPE Piemonte Consortium for Research and Continuing Education in Economics
Corso Unità d'Italia 125
10127 Turin
Tel: +39-011-670-3295
Fax: +39-011-670-3644
Web: http://www.cisi.unito.it
e-mail: informazioni@cisi.unito.it

☐ Graduate Studies
Study Domains: political economy.
Programmes: courses leading to a Master's degree in
political economy. Instruction in Italian and English.
Open to: university graduates of all nationalities with
above average academic record; Italians must successfully
complete admissions exams; others may present GRE and
English and Italian language test results.
Duration: 9 months. Courses begin in October.
Fees: approx. 5,200 € per year.
Financial assistance: total or partial exemption from fees
and contribution to living expenses for top-ranking
candidates.
Applications: by early September, at the above address.

1276 Ecole internationale supérieure d'études avancées [SISSA]
Via Beirut, 2-4
34014 Trieste
Tel: +39-040-378-71
Fax: +39-040-378-7528
Web: http://www.sissa.it
e-mail: segret@sissa.it

Études doctorales

Domaines d'étude: astronomie, biophysique, génétique, physique.
Programmes: cours conduisant au diplôme de doctorat dans les domaines suivants: astrophysique, matière condensée, physique de particules élémentaires, analyse fonctionnelle, biophysique, génétique moléculaire, neurosciences cognitives; langues d'enseignement: anglais et italien.
A l'intention de: étudiants et chercheurs de tout pays, âgés de 30 ans maximum, et titulaires du « laurea » ou d'une licence, ou titre reconnu équivalent. L'admission se fait sur concours.
Durée: 3 ou 4 ans (débutant en novembre).
Frais: inscription: environ 90 €, pour les étudiants qui ne sont pas boursiers.
Assistance financière: environ 35 bourses sont offertes chaque année.
Inscriptions: dépôt des dossiers d'admissibilité avant mi-octobre, à la Scuola Internazionale Superiore di Studi Avanzati (SISSA), à l'adresse ci-dessus.

1277 European School of Economics [ESE]
Via S. Calocero, 10
20123 Milano
Tel: +39-02-83-60200
Fax: +39-02-89-423-529
Web: http://www.uniese.it
e-mail: info@uniese.it

Undergraduate Studies

Study Domains: administration, business administration, communication, computer science, development studies, economic and commercial sciences, education, finance, human sciences, industrial relations, information science, interior design, international business, international law, international relations, journalism, languages, literature and civilization, management, museology and museography, music and musicology, political science, psychology, public relations, social sciences, tourism, hotel and catering management.
Programmes: programme of courses leading to Bachelor's degree.

1278 Fashion Institute of Technology at Polimoda [FIT]
Villa Strozzi
Via Pisana, 77
50143 Florence
Tel: +39-055-739-9628
Fax: +39-055-700-287
Web: http://www.polimoda.com/fashion-school/
e-mail: info@polimoda.com

Undergraduate Studies

Study Domains: applied sciences, design, fine arts.
Programmes: Associate in applied sciences or Bachelor of fine arts degree in international fashion design. Instruction in English.
Open to: all nationalities, with high school qualifications and design ability; TOEFL 550 or above.
Held: Polimoda, Florence, Italy and Fashion Institute of Technology, New York.
Duration: 2 or 4 years.
Fees: tuition: approximately 5,000 € for the first 2 years and 6,000 € for a further 2 years; living costs: approx. 700 € per month.
Applications: by 15 June, to the above address.

1279 Fondation Rui (Résidences universitaires internationales)
Viale XXI Aprile 36
00162 Rome
Tel: +39-06-8632-1281
Web: http://www.fondazionerui.it
e-mail: info@fondazionerui.it

Bourses d'études

Domaines d'étude: toutes disciplines principales.
A l'intention de: ressortissants de tout pays.
Lieu: toutes les villes italiennes sièges des résidences universitaires de la Fondation: Milan, Rome, Vérone, Bologne, Gênes, Palerme, Catane.
Durée: 10 mois (renouvelables).
Valeur: allocation mensuelle égale à la pension de résidence, pour un total de 10 mois.
Candidatures: avant le 10 septembre; à l'Office boursier de la Fondation.

1280 Free University Bozen-Bolzano
Via Sernesi 1
39100 Bolzano
Tel: +39-0471-315-151
Fax: +39-0471-315-199
Web: http://www.unibz.it
e-mail: info@unibz.it

Undergraduate, Graduate and Postgraduate Programmes

Study Domains: accounting, agriculture, arts, audio-visual media, business administration, computer science, design, economy, English, fine arts, French, German, graphic arts, industrial design, industrial technology, information science, interior design, Italian, languages, photography, printing, Russian, social sciences, social work, Spanish, teacher education, tourism, hotel and catering management, visual arts.
Programmes: Bachelor's, Master's and Ph.D. degrees in all major fields.
Description: degree course in design, economics and management, business studies (programme for certification), community educators, social work, education (training of nursery and primary school), applied computer science, tourism management, agricultural science and economics, logistics and production engineering; postgraduate school of specialization for secondary school teachers.
Open to: candidates of any country and any age holding a secondary school certificate (equivalent of 'A' level); admission test is required.
Held: Bozen, Bolzano, Bressanone and Brixen.
Fees: tuition: from 800-950 € for EU students; 2,000 € for non-EU citizens; Laurea degree in logistics and production engineering, tuition: 1,013 €.
Languages: Italian, German and English (depending on programmes).
Applications: by 26 August to the above address; degree course in design: by 25 July; for information contact student secretariat; tel: +39 0471 315 315; email: student.secretariat@unibz.it, or see web site: http://www.unibz.it.

1281 Institut d'études européennes «Alcide de Gasperi»
Via Poli 29
00187 Rome
Tel: +39-06-678-4262
Fax: +39-06-679-4101
Web: http://www.ise-ies.org
e-mail: info@ise-ies.org

Bourses d'études

Domaines d'étude: études européennes.
A l'intention de: ressortissants des pays de l'Union européenne et des pays associés ou du Tiers Monde, titulaires d'une licence (en droit, économie ou sciences politiques). Une bonne connaissance de la langue italienne est exigée.
Durée: 1 année académique pour le «Diplôme»; 2 années académiques pour le «Master».
Candidatures: avant le 31 octobre.

1282 Inter-University Mathematical School [SMI]

Via S. Marta 13/A
50139 Florence
Tel: +39-055-522-5812
Web: http://www.matapp.unimib.it/smi/
e-mail: smi@fi.iac.cnr.it

📖 Graduate Studies

Study Domains: mathematics, summer programmes.
Programmes: Summer courses sponsored by the National Research Council and the Ministry of University and Technological Research of Italy.
Open to: students of all nationalities, particularly those from developing countries, with a degree in mathematics or related subjects.
Held: (a) in Perugia; (b) in Cortona.
Duration: (a) 5 weeks; (b) 2 to 3 weeks.
Financial assistance: housing for all the participants is supported by the SMI; grants to cover living expenses are available for a limited number of participants.
Applications: for information contact Scuola Matematica Interuniversitaria, at the above address.

1283 International Centre for Mechanical Sciences [CISM]

Palazzo del Torso
Piazza Garibaldi 18
33100 Udine
Tel: +39-0432-248-511
Fax: +39-0432-248-550
Web: http://www.cism.it
e-mail: cism@cism.it

📖 Seminars

Study Domains: civil engineering, computer science, engineering, geology, industrial technology, mechanical engineering.
Programmes: International Seminars for Research and Education in Mechanical Sciences and related fields at a high scientific level: civil engineering, computer sciences, engineering, geology, industrial technology, etc.: 30 to 50 participants. Instruction in English.
Open to: nationals of all countries who are graduates in engineering, mathematics or physics.
Duration: 5 to 12 days.
Fees: registration: 515 € (360 € for participants on regular staff of universities and academies of sciences) for one-week courses.
Financial assistance: for some courses a limited number of UNESCO scholarships is available; scholarships are also offered by CISM, preference being given to applicants coming from countries which contribute to CISM's operating resources.
Applications: 2 months before the beginning of the seminar; information available from the CISM Secretariat, at the above address.

1284 International Centre of Hydrology «Dino Tonini», University of Padua

Via Loredan, 20
35131 Padua
Tel: +39-049-827-7998
Fax: +39-049-827-7988
Web: http://www.image.unipd.it/cir_tonini/

📖 Training Programme / Hydrology

Study Domains: energy, engineering, hydraulics, hydrology, technology.
Programmes: course in hydrology: fundamentals, hydrometeorology, surface water hydrology, groundwater hydrology, agricultural hydrology, river hydraulics, water resources development, water purification and environment protection.
Open to: civil engineers, geologists, hydrogeologists, hydrologists from various countries, with university qualifications; age under 35.
Duration: 6 months; courses begin in January.
Financial assistance: scholarships offered by the Ministry of Foreign Affairs (Department of Cooperation Development) to students from developing countries with professional

experience who are proposed by their government to the Italian Embassy, which supplies the necessary forms; scholarships also offered by the Centre and by private organizations through the Centre, covering living expenses, travel, enrolment and participation fees and insurance; scholarships offered by other organizations (UN agencies) do not cover participation and enrolment fees.
Applications: by 30 November, to Centro Internazionale di Idrologia «Dino Tonini», at the above address.

1285 John Cabot University

Via della Lungara 233
00165 Rome
Tel: +39-06-681-9121
Fax: +39-06-683-2088
Web: http://www.johncabot.edu
e-mail: admissions@johncabot.edu

📖 Undergraduate Studies

Study Domains: art history, computer science, economic and commercial sciences, economy, English, international business, Italian, literature and civilization, political science.
Programmes: American Bachelor of Arts and Associate degrees in political science, international affairs, English literature, business administration, art history. Additional Associate degree programmes in economics, computer science.
Open to: applicants with a high-school diploma or equivalent with good knowledge of English.
Duration: variable; up to 4 years; Summer courses are available.
Fees: tuition fees: 8,315 €.
Financial assistance: limited to teaching assistantships.
Languages: instruction in English.
Applications: to the Admissions Office, Dr. Francesca Gleason, Director, at the above address.

1286 Loyola University Chicago Rome Center of Liberal Arts

Via Massini 114-A
00136 Rome
Tel: +39-06-355-881/+1-390-5082760
Fax: +39-06-355-883 /+1-390-5088797
Web: http://www.luc.edu/romecenter/
e-mail: jtalari@luc.edu

📖 Undergraduate Programmes

Study Domains: anthropology, business, communication, cultural studies, English, fine arts, Greek, history, Italian, Latin, performing arts, philosophy, political science, sociology, theology, religion.
Programmes: undergraduate programme of courses.
Open to: students who have sophomore, junior or senior year status from an accredited American college or university; minimum GPA of 2.5.
Held: Rome, Italy.
Duration: academic year: courses begin in late August; Fall semester: courses begin in late August; Spring semester: courses begin in early January.
Fees: US$13,908 for one semester; US$27,816 for academic year, covering room, board and tuition.
Languages: language of instruction: English; literature courses are given in Italian.

1287 Polytechnic of Turin [POLITO]

Corso Duca degli Abruzzi 24
10129 Torino
Tel: +39-011-564-6368
Fax: +39-011-564-6160
Web: http://www.polito.it
e-mail: international.relations@polito.it

🎓 Scholarship

Study Domains: architecture, engineering.
Scholarships: (a) ALPIP Scholarship; (b) TOPMED Scholarship.
Subjects: engineering, architecture.
Open to: (a) candidates from Latin America and the Caribbean; (b) candidates from Mediterranean countries (Algeria, Egypt, Jordan, Libya, Morocco, National Palestinian Authority, Syria, Tunisia and Turkey).
Value: (a) free tuition for ALPIP students; living expenses,

10,000 € per year; (b) variable, according to courses; living expenses, 10,000 € per year.
Applications: (a) see http://www.polito.it/alpip for details; email: alpip@polito.it; (b) see http://www.polito.it/topmed for details; email: topmed@polito.it.

1288 Scuola Superiore Sant' Anna di Pisa
Piazza Martiri della Libertà, 33
56127 Pisa
Tel: +39-050-883-111
Fax: +39-050-883-296
Web: http://www.sssup.it/sssup/

🕊 Doctoral Research Programmes
Study Domains: economic and commercial sciences, engineering, law, management, medicine, political science.
Description: research grant based on international competition.
Age limit Max: 29 years or under on date of competition deadline.
Applications: 31 October; contact Chiara Busnelli at the above address; or cbusnelli@sssup.it.

1289 Studio Art Centers International [SACI]
Palazzo dei Cartelloni
Via Sant'Antonino, 11
50123 Florence
Tel: +39-055-289-948
Fax: +39-055-277-6408
Web: http://www.saci-florence.org
e-mail: info@saci-florence.org

📖 Graduate Studies
Study Domains: arts, summer programmes.
Programmes: (a) Year/Semester Abroad Programme and Summer Studies Programme; (b) 2 year Diploma Programme; (c) Post-Baccalaureate Certificate Programme, a non-degree programme offering intensive and personalized year of study; (d) Master of Fine Arts programme (MFA).
Open to: undergraduates in good standing at any college, university or art school; graduate students and alumni of any institutions who wish to further their art studies as directed independent students, with or without credit are welcome; MFA credit through affiliation with Bowling Green State University, Ohio: (a) designed for United States undergraduates and independent students; (b) students wishing to apply SACI course credits towards their United States Bachelor of Arts or Bachelor of Fine Arts degrees; (c) college or university students preparing for advanced degree programmes.
Held: (a) to (c) in Florence; (d) other European art institutions.
Duration: from 4 weeks to 2 years, depending on the course.
Financial assistance: SACI offers scholarships for the Florence programme; United States SACI students are eligible to participate in the United States Department of Education's student loan programmes.
Languages: instruction in English.
Applications: to SACI Administrator, Institute of International Education, 809 United Nations Plaza, New York, N.Y. 10036 (United States of America), tel: +1 212 984 5548; fax +1 212 984 5325; or to the above address.

1290 Technical University «Politecnico di Milano»
Piazza Leonardo da Vinci 32
20133 Milano
Tel: +39-02-23991
Fax: +39-02-2399-2206
Web: http://www.polimi.it
e-mail: luise@rettore.rett.polimi.it

📖 Graduate Programmes
Study Domains: administration, architecture, art history, arts and crafts, aviation, aeronautics, building industry, business administration, chemical industry, chemistry, civil engineering, computer science, design, ecology, environment, economic and commercial sciences, economy, electricity and electronics, energy, engineering, geodesy, geology, hydraulics, hydrology, industrial design, industrial technology, interior design, laboratory techniques, mathematics, mechanical engineering, metallurgy, optics, physics, statistics, technology, telecommunications, textile industry, transport, urbanism.
Programmes: programme of courses leading to Master's degrees: (a) Executive Master of Business Administration (EMBA); (b) Master in City Health and Safety.
Duration: (a) 2 years; (b) 1 year.
Fees: current registration: 500 €; tuition fees: (a) 13,850 € per year; (b) 2,600 € per year.
Financial assistance: possibility of scholarships offered by the Government (Ministry of Foreign Affairs: http://www.esteri.it), the Institute for the Right to Study and the Technical University; for information contact Maria Avenia; email: maria.avenia@ceda.polimi.it; tel: +39 02 23 99 2100.
Languages: language of instruction: English.
Applications: (a) by 13 September; (b) by 21 January.

1291 The School of The Arts - Art Under One Roof
Via dei Pandolfini, 46r
50122 Florence
Tel: +39-05-247-8867
Web: http://www.arteuropa.org
e-mail: arte1@arteurope.it

📖 Diploma / Fine Arts
Study Domains: arts, fine arts, visual arts.
Programmes: programme of courses in the fine and applied arts.
Open to: candidates of any country, aged over 18.
Duration: 1 to 7 months.
Fees: 295-3,615 €.
Languages: instruction in Italian and French.
Applications: 90 days prior to the programme start date NOTE: Art Under One Roof is affiliated with Mercyhurst College - 501 East 38th Street, Erie Pennsylvania. For college credit through Mercyhurst see Academic Credit /Student Assessment.

1292 Université de Florence Centre culturel pour étrangers
Piazza San Marco 4
50121 Florence
Tel: +39-55-27571
Fax: +39-55-264194
Web: http://www.unifi.it
e-mail: re@netra1.adm.unifi.it

📖 Cours de langue et culture italiennes
Domaines d'étude: italien, langues, littérature et civilisation, programmes d'été.
Programmes: Cours de langue et culture italiennes pour les étrangers; un certificat attestant du niveau dans la langue est délivré à la fin du cours; 250 participants.
A l'intention de: ressortissants de tout pays, âgés de 18 ans minimum, titulaires d'un baccalauréat ou diplôme équivalent.
Organisés: Villa Fabbricotti à l'adresse ci-dessus.
Durée: trimestrielle (débutant en janvier, avril et octobre); mensuelle: juillet.
Inscriptions: 30 jours avant le début de chaque cours; Centro di Cultura per Stranieri, à l'adresse ci-dessus.

1293 Université de Gênes Centre international d'études italiennes
Palazzo Università
Via Balbi 5
16126 Gênes
Tel: +39-10-20991
Fax: +39-10-209-9227
Web: http://www.unige.it
e-mail: info@unige.it

📖 Cours d'été
Domaines d'étude: géographie, histoire, histoire de l'art, italien, langues, littérature et civilisation.
Programmes: cours d'été de langue et civilisation

italiennes pour spécialistes et étudiants étrangers: cours inférieurs d'italien écrit et oral; cours moyens de culture et civilisation italiennes; cours supérieurs sur les problèmes et aspects fondamentaux de la culture et la vie italiennes; conduisant à un certificat d'assiduité ou un certificat de mérite pour ceux qui passent les examens et obtiennent des résultats positifs.
A l'intention de: ressortissants de tout pays, possédant une connaissance suffisante de la langue italienne et âgés de plus de 18 ans.
Organisés: à la Villa Durazzo, S. Margherita Ligure (Gênes).
Durée: 5 semaines.
Assistance financière: quelques bourses sont octroyées par l'Université. Les candidatures sont à présenter au Directeur du Centre, avant le 30 mai.
Inscriptions: avant le 30 juillet.

1294 Université de Parme
Via Università 12
43100 Parme
Tel: +39-0521-032-111
Fax: +39-0521-034-008
Web: http://www.unipr.it
e-mail: uniparma@unipr.it

📖 Diplômes universitaires et Diplôme d'études spécialisées
Domaines d'étude: toutes disciplines principales.
Programmes: (a) cours conduisant à l'obtention du «diploma universitario» dans les domaines suivants: droit, service social, sciences économiques, économie et gestion des entreprises, ingénierie électronique, ingénierie des infrastructures, informatique et automatique, mécanique; diplôme prévoyant une didactique à distance; informatique et automatique, mécanique; médecine et chirurgie: logopédie, orthopticiens, assistants en ophtalmologie, physiothérapeutes de la rééducation, techniciens d'audiométrie et d'audioprothèses; pharmacie: informations scientifiques sur les médicaments; sciences mathématiques-physiques-naturelles: méthodologies physiques; écoles spécialisées: physique sanitaire, école d'obstétrique; (b) cours conduisant à l'obtention du « laurea » dans les domaines suivants: droit; sciences économiques: gestion, économie et commerce, économie politique; lettres et philosophie: conservation du patrimoine culturel, philosophie, lettres, langues et littératures étrangères; médecine et chirurgie: odontologie et prothèses dentaires;sciences mathématiques, physiques, naturelles: chimie, chimie industrielle, physique, mathématiques, sciences de l'environnement, sciences biologiques, sciences géologiques, sciences naturelles; ingénierie: génie civil, électronique, constructions mécaniques; pharmacie: chimie, technologie pharmaceutiques; médecine vétérinaire; sciences agraires: sciences et technologies alimentaires; (c) cours conduisant à l'obtention du diplôme d'études spécialisées dans les domaines suivants: droit: discipline du travail; pharmacie industrielle et hospitalière; sciences, mathématiques, physiques-naturelles: chimie et technologie alimentaires, sciences et technologie des matériaux; principaux domaines de la médecine et de la chirurgie; médecine vétérinaire: alimentation animale, chirurgie vétérinaire, clinique bovine, droit et législation, médecine et chirurgie du cheval, pathologie et clinique des animaux domestiques, pathologie porcine, santé animale, élevage et production zootechniques, santé publique vétérinaire.
A l'intention de: ressortissants de tout pays, titulaires d'un diplôme de fin d'études secondaires («maturité» ou diplôme reconnu équivalent).
Organisés: dans les diverses facultés de l'Université.
Durée: de 3 à 6 ans, selon les diplômes.
Inscriptions: auprès du Recteur de l'Université.

1295 Université internationale de l'art
Villa il Ventaglio
Via delle Forbici 24-26
50133 Florence
Tel: +39-055-570-216
Fax: +39-055-570-508
Web: http://www.uiafirenze.com/

e-mail: segreteria@uiafirenze.com

📖 Cours de spécialisation / art, muséologie
Domaines d'étude: archéologie, arts, italien, langues, muséologie et muséographie.
Programmes: (a) cours de spécialisation en critique de l'art, muséologie, restauration et conservation des œuvres d'art et archéologie (en italien); (b) cours de langue italienne; de 150 à 200 participants;
(c) cours d'art africain, jardins historiques.
A l'intention de: ressortissants de tout pays âgés de plus de 18 ans.
Durée: (a) 1 ou 2 semestres (débutant en octobre); (b) 1 mois; (c) 1 semaine.
Inscriptions: (a) avant le 15 septembre, sur présentation d'un curriculum d'études ou de travail.

1296 Université Magna Graecia
Viale Europa - Località Germaneto
88100 Catanzaro
Tel: +39-0961-515-371
Fax: +39-0961-515-314
Web: http://www.unicz.it
e-mail: rettore@unicz.it

📖 1er, 2e, 3e cycles
Domaines d'étude: biochimie, biologie, droit, économie, informatique, médecine, pharmacie et pharmacologie.

1297 Université pour étrangers, Pérouse
Palazzo Gallenga
Piazza Fortebraccio 4
06122 Pérouse
Tel: +39-075-585-2093
Fax: +39-05-585-2081
Web: http://www.unipg.it
e-mail: uri@unipg.it

📖 Cours de langue et culture italiennes
Domaines d'étude: italien.
Programmes: Programme de cours: (a) Langue et culture italiennes; (b) Formation continue pour les professeurs d'italien à l'étranger; (c) Diplôme universitaire pour l'enseignement de la langue et de la culture italiennes aux étrangers; (d) Diplôme universitaire en technique publicitaire.
A l'intention de: (a) ressortissants étrangers et italiens résidant à l'étranger; (b) et (c) candidats titulaires d'un diplôme d'enseignement de langue et culture italiennes; (d) ressortissants étrangers et italiens résidant à l'étranger inscrits dans une université italienne ou étrangère et possédant une bonne connaissance de l'italien.
Durée: (a) 1 semestre; (b) 3 semaines; (c) 6 mois (formation) ou 3 ans (diplôme); (d) 3 ans.
Assistance financière: possibilité de bourses octroyées par le Ministère des affaires étrangères et certaines institutions telles que la Société Dante Alighieri.
Inscriptions: dans les ambassades d'Italie.

🎓 Bourses d'études
Domaines d'étude: italien.
Bourses: (a) Bourses de langue et culture italiennes délivrées par le Ministère des affaires étrangères italien, par l'Université pour étrangers et par l'intermédiaire des Instituts italiens de Culture et certaines institutions dont la Société Dante Alighieri; (b) Bourses octroyées après concours spécial: langue italienne contemporaine, professeurs d'italien à l'étranger, étruscologie et antiquités italiques, histoire de l'art.
A l'intention de: ressortissants de tout pays, spécialistes, professeurs universitaires ou chargés de cours ou de recherches; étudiants titulaires d'un diplôme universitaire ou ayant suivi les cours de l'Université pour étrangers pendant au moins 3 mois étalés sur 3 années différentes à l'exception des 2 précédant celle-ci. Les demandes peuvent être faites pour n'importe quel cours sauf celles qui relèvent de (b).
Lieu: Pérouse.
Durée: 1 mois.
Valeur: 415 €.
Candidatures: avant le 30 mars, à l'adresse ci-dessus et dans les Instituts italiens de la culture du pays de résidence du ressortissant; (b) adresser la demande au Recteur de l'Université à l'adresse ci-dessus.

1298 Université pour étrangers, Sienne

Via Pantaneto 45
53100 Sienne
Tel: +39-05-77-240-115
Fax: +39-05-77-281-030
Web: http://www.unistrasi.it
e-mail: info@unistrasi.it

Cours de langue et civilisation italiennes

Domaines d'étude: interprétation et traduction, italien, langues, littérature et civilisation.
Programmes: programme de cours de langue italienne: (a) cours ordinaires de la langue; (b) cours avancés de langue et culture italiennes; (c) culture italienne; (d) cours spéciaux de langue; (e) Italien spécialisé; (f) Italien de la chanson; (g) pour les étudiants des programmes de mobilité européenne; (h) cours à la carte conduisant à divers diplômes universitaires: (i) diplôme pour l'enseignement de l'italien langue étrangère; (j) diplôme de traducteur et interprète; (k) Certificat d'italien langue étrangère (CILS); cours pour les enseignants; (l) langue et didactique de l'italien; (m) perfectionnement en didactique de l'italien langue étrangère; (n) littérature et histoire de l'art italien; (o) linguistique, didactique et littérature; (p) Certificat de compétence en didactique de l'italien langue étrangère (DITALS).
A l'intention de: ressortissants de tout pays: (a), (e), (i), et (j) titulaires d'un diplôme donnant accès à l'université; (b) titulaires d'un diplôme du 1er degré de langue et civilisation italiennes, ou titre reconnu équivalent; (c) étudiants des cours de langue des niveaux intermédiaire et avancé; (d), (h) et (f) admission sur test; (g) participants à un programme de mobilité européenne; (k) pas de diplôme requis; (l), (m), (n) et (p) enseignants d'italien à l'étranger; (p) professeurs d'italien langue étrangère.
Durée: (a), (b) et (c) 1 trimestre; (d), (g) et (p) 1 mois; (e) et (f) en août; (i) et (j) 3 ans; (k) et (p) 2 fois par an (décembre et juin); (l) 1 trimestre ou 1 mois; (n) 2 fois 30 heures en janvier et juin.
Assistance financière: bourses offertes soit par le Ministère des affaires étrangères, soit par l'Université. Les étudiants qui bénéficient de ces bourses ont droit à une réduction de 50% sur la taxe d'inscription; 10 bourses sont offertes aux étrangers inscrits aux (i) et (j).
Inscriptions: (e) et (h) 20 jours avant le début des cours; (i) en mars et octobre; pour de plus amples renseignements, s'adresser au Segretaria dell'Università per Stranieri di Siena, à l'adresse ci-dessus.

1299 University Institute of European Studies, International Training Centre of the ILO

Via Sacchi 28 bis
10128 Turin
Tel: +39-011-839-4660
Fax: +39-011-839-4664
Web: http://www.iuse.it
e-mail: info@iuse.it

Postgraduate Programme

Study Domains: international business, international law, international relations.
Programmes: International Trade Law Postgraduate Course: international trade relations, international sale of goods, contract negotiation and drafting, main types of international contracts, arbitration and dispute resolution.
Open to: graduates of any nationality in law, political science, business or economics; knowledge of English essential.
Held: at the ILO Turin Centre.
Duration: 2-1/2 months (April-June).
Financial assistance: a limited number of scholarships are available for foreign students and for Italians not resident in Turin to cover part of the boarding expenses.
Languages: instruction in English.
Applications: by 20 January to above address.

1300 University of Ancona

Piazza Roma 22
60122 Ancona
Tel: +39-071-2201
Fax: +39-071-220-2303
Web: http://www.unian.it
e-mail: info@unian.it

Undergraduate, Graduate, Postgraduate Programmes

Study Domains: administration, agriculture, agronomic sciences, architecture, biology, building industry, civil engineering, dentistry, economic and commercial sciences, electricity and electronics, energy, engineering, food industry, forestry, hydraulics, industrial technology, information science, library science, mechanical engineering, medicine, metallurgy, nursing, oenology, political economy, social sciences, surgery, telecommunications.
Programmes: Bachelor's, Master's, Ph.D. degrees in all major fields.
Open to: candidates of any nationality holding a secondary school certificate (or equivalent); non-European students must submit their application to the Italian consulate of their home country; Italian admission test for non-European students.
Held: Ancona, Pesaro, Fermo, Fabriano, Jesi and Senigallia.
Duration: 3 to 5 years; courses begin in November.
Fees: current registration: 322 €.
Languages: language of instruction: Italian.
Applications: before 5 November for European students; before May for other foreign students; for information contact: economy, economia@niasun.unian.it, tel: +39 071 2207215; agriculture, engineering, science, ceriachi@unian.it, tel: +39 071 2204970; medicine, segmed@niasun.unian.it, tel: +39 071 2206012.

1301 University of Cassino

Via Marconi, 10
03043 Cassino
Tel: +39-0776-299-208
Fax: +39-0776-299-350
Web: http://www.unicas.it
e-mail: rettore@unicas.it

Undergraduate Programme

Study Domains: accounting, administration, agronomic sciences, American studies, business, business administration, civil engineering, communication, economy, education, electricity and electronics, English, French, German, Italian, languages, law, literature and civilization, management, marketing, mechanical engineering, philosophy, Russian, Spanish, telecommunications.
Programmes: Programme of courses leading to dual diploma (Bachelor's degree) in economics, engineering and humanities.
Duration: 3 years beginning in October.
Fees: current registration: maximum 600 €; the tuition fee is directly related to the economic status of students.
Languages: language of instruction: Italian.
Applications: by 1 November; for information contact Nadia Cuffaro for economics department, tel: +39 0776 299299441, Email: cuffaro@eco.unicas.it, Marco Lops for engineering department, tel: +39 0776 299742, Email: lops@unicas.it and Susanna Fortunato for humanities department, tel: +39 0776 299905, Email: fortunato@unicas.it.

1302 University of Commerce Luigi Bocconi

Via Sarfatti 25
20186 Milano
Tel: +39-02-5836
Fax: +39-02-5856
Web: http://www.uni-bocconi.it
e-mail: undergraduate.services@uni-bocconi.it

Undergraduate Programmes

Study Domains: accounting, administration, business administration, communication, economic and commercial sciences, economy, finance, information science, international business, international law, international relations, law, management, political economy.

Programmes: programme of courses leading to Bachelor's degree.
Description: Bachelor's in Business Administration, International Institutions Management, Financial Markets and Institutions Management, Economics and Management of Arts, Culture and Communication, Economics and Social Sciences, International Market and Technologies, International Economics and Management, Law.
Duration: 3 years beginning in September.
Financial assistance: some scholarships offered by the university; information on web site: http://www.uni-bocconi.it/isu or contact Adele Invernizzi; email: isa@uni-bocconi.it.
Applications: from 15 July to 31 August; for information contact Silvia Camisa, secretaria studenti or Christiane Roth; tel: +39 02 5836 2245: email: undergraduate.services@uni-bocconi.it.

1303   University of Ferrara [UNIFE]
Via Savonarola 9
44100 Ferrara
Tel: +39-0532-293-111
Fax: +39-0532-248-927
Web: http://www.unife.it

✒ Financial Aid
Study Domains: all major fields, economy, engineering, humanities and arts, law, liberal arts, literature and civilization, medicine, pharmacy and pharmacology, sciences.
Open to: students having completed at least one year at the institution; based on financial need and scholastic merit.
Value: from 700 to 4,000 €.
Languages: Italian.
Applications: by 31 August.

1304   University of Insubria
Via Ravasi, 2
21100 Varese
Tel: +39-0332-219-001
Fax: +39-0332-219-009
Web: http://www.uninsubria.it
e-mail: rettore@uninsubria.it

📖 Undergraduate, Graduate, Postgraduate Programmes
Study Domains: accounting, anatomy, bacteriology, biology, botany, business administration, cancerology, cardiology, chemistry, communication, criminology, cytology, dentistry, economic and commercial sciences, finance, genetics, geology, health and hygiene, industry and commerce, information science, international business, international law, law, management, marketing, mathematics, medicine, obstetrics and gynaecology, psychiatry.
Programmes: (a) Diploma di Laurea (DL); (b) Diploma di Laurea Specialistica (DLS); (c) Dottorato di Ricerca (DR).
Description: courses in social sciences, business and law; science; health and welfare: (a) 3-year degree programme; (b) 5-year degree programme; (c) 3-year graduate degree programme.
Held: Varese: medicine, economics, sciences; Como: law, sciences.
Duration: 3, 5 and 6 years; courses begin in October.
Languages: Italian.
Applications: from 1 August to 30 September.

✒ Istituto per il Diritto allo Studio Universitario (I.S.U.) Scholarships
Study Domains: all major fields.
Scholarships: Istituto per il Diritto allo Studio Universitario (I.S.U.) Scholarships.
Open to: all candidates based on financial need and academic qualifications.
Value: from 1,000-3,000 € per year, renewable each year until one year after the legal duration of the student's academic programme.

1305   University of Milan-Bicocca
Department of Surgical Sciences and Intensive Care
Bassini Teaching Hospital
via M. Gorki 50
20 092 Cinisello Balsamo-Milan
Tel: +39-02-617-4928
Fax: +39-02-6601-2568
Web: http://www.unimib.it
e-mail: giorgio.biasi@unimib.it

📖 Graduate Studies
Study Domains: surgery.
Programmes: Master's degree in endovascular techniques (MET).
Open to: completed training programme in vascular surgery, interim level, cardiology or radiology; selection on curriculum vitae and oral examination.
Duration: 1 year; courses begin in October.
Fees: current registration: 10,000 €.
Financial assistance: some scholarships are offered by the University corresponding to the price of the current registration (10,000 €); for information contact Prof. Giorgio Biasi; tel. +39 02 6174928; fax +39 02 66012568; email: giorgio.biasi@unimib.it.
Languages: language of instruction: Italian and English.
Applications: by 25 September; for information contact Prof. Giorgio Biasi.

1306   University of Pavia
Strada nuova 65
27100 Pavia
Tel: +39-382-504-223
Fax: +39-382-504-287
Web: http://www.unipv.it
e-mail: relest@unipv.it

📖 Undergraduate, Graduate, Postgraduate Programmes
Study Domains: all major fields.
Programmes: programmes leading to 3-year degrees; 5-6 year advanced degrees at the faculties of economics, pharmacy, law, engineering, humanities, medicine and surgery, sciences (mathematics, physics and natural sciences), political sciences, musicology; 3-year degree inter-faculty courses are also offered in biotechnology, intercultural and multimedia communication, physical education and sporting technique, preventive and adapted motor education as well as a 3-year degree course in mechanical engineering in collaboration with the Polytechnic of Milano).
Duration: degree courses: 3 years; advanced degree courses: a further 2 to 3 years; specialized degree: a further 2 to 3 years.
Languages: Italian.

1307   University of Sassari
Piazza Universita, 21
07100 Sassari - Sardinia
Tel: +39-79-228-811
Fax: +39-79-228-816
Web: http://www.uniss.it
e-mail: rettore@ssmain.uniss.it

📖 Undergraduate, Graduate Programmes
Study Domains: all major fields.
Programmes: Programmes of courses leading to: (a) Diploma di Laurea (DL); (b) Diploma di Laurea Specialistica (DLS); (c) Dottorato di Ricerca (DR).
Held: Sassari, Nuoro Tempio, Oristano and Alghero.
Duration: 3 to 5 years, depending on programme.
Fees: current registration: 245-517 €.

Jamaica

Academic year: September/October to June.
Monetary unit: Jamaican dollar (JA$).
National student admission: Foreign students should have qualifications equivalent to the General Certificate of Education passes in 5 subjects, 2 at Advanced level, for admission to the University of the West Indies, and passes in 5 subjects for admission to most diploma programmes at the University of Technology.
Language: English is the language of instruction at institutions of higher education.
Immigration requirements: Foreign students must obtain a student visa.
Information services:
• Ministry of Education, 2 National Heroes Circle, PO Box 498, Kingston; Jamaica (all matters concerning formal education).
• University of the West Indies, Mona, Kingston 7; Jamaica (information and advice; pamphlets and brochures available to foreign students).
Recognition of studies and qualification:
• University of Technology, Jamaica; 237 Old Hope Road; Kingston 6; Jamaica; tel: +1-876-927-1680; fax: +1-876-927-1925; email: utech@cast.edu.jm; web: http://www.utechjamaica.edu.jm.
• University of the West Indies; Mona Campus; Kingston 7; Jamaica; tel: +1-876-927-1660; fax: +1-876-927-2050; email: areynlds@uwimona.edu.jm; website: http://www.uwimona.edu.jm.
Publications / Websites:
• 'Freshman's Guide', hall brochures, general information brochures and faculty brochures in English, obtainable free from the University of the West Indies.
• 'UTech Review Biannual', prospectus.

1308 Ministry of Education - Scholarships Section [MOE]

2 National Heroes Circle
PO Box 498
Kingston
Tel: +1-809-922-6328
Web: http://www.moec.gov.jm

✒ Scholarships

Study Domains: all major fields.
Scholarships: Jamaica Commonwealth Scholarship and Fellowship Plan award.
Subjects: postgraduate study and research in any field available at the University of the West Indies, Mona Campus.
Open to: nationals of Commonwealth countries other than Jamaica, with university graduate qualifications or equivalent; under 35 years of age; proficiency in English essential.
Place of study: University of the West Indies, Mona Campus, Jamaica.
Duration: maximum 2 years.
Value: normally covers return transportation (tourist class); approved tuition, laboratory and examination fees; yearly grant for books and apparatus; approved travel grant; and various personal allowances.
Applications: by 31 December, to respective governments, who send nominations to Jamaica, direct applications are not accepted and not acknowledged.

1309 University of Technology [UOTJ]

237 Old Hope Road
Kingston 6
Tel: +1-876-927-1680
Fax: +1-876-927-1925
Web: http://www.utechjamaica.edu.jm
e-mail: regist@utech.edu.jm

📖 Undergraduate, Graduate Programmes

Study Domains: accounting, architecture, computer science, education, engineering, mathematics, pharmacy and pharmacology, sciences, technical education, technology.
Programmes: First Degrees, Higher Degrees, Diplomas, Master's degrees and Certificates in numerous fields.
Open to: mainly Caribbean nationals with minimum 5

O-levels or and diplomas depending on requirements of programme.
Financial assistance: no scholarships offered but possibility of Third Country awards or scholarships from government or international sources.
Applications: by 31 March, to the Registrar.

1310 University of the West Indies [UWI]

Administration and Special Initiatives
Mona
Kingston 7
Tel: +1-876-977-6065/7916
Fax: +1-876-977-7525
Web: http://www.uwimona.edu.jm
e-mail: beverly.hunter@uwimona.edu.jm

📖 Undergraduate, Graduate Programmes

Study Domains: agriculture, business, education, engineering, health and hygiene, humanities and arts, languages, law, natural resources, natural sciences, sciences, social sciences, tourism, hotel and catering management.
Programmes: Bachelor's, Master's, PhD degrees in all major fields: diploma and certificate programmes offered for certain studies.
Description: Specialized institutions: Institution of Chemical Engineers; Institution of Mechanical Engineers; Joint Board Moderators (Civil Engineers); Institution of Electrical Engineers; The Royal Institution of Chartered Surveyors.
Open to: candidates with English proficiency and meeting other university requirements.
Fees: tuition: variable, see website.

Japan

Academic year: April to March.
Organization of higher education system: Higher education at university level: First level consists of six years of studies leading to a Bachelor's degree, or six years of study for medicine, dentistry and veterinary medicine; second level consists of two years of further studies leading to a Master's degree; third level Doctoral studies require three years beyond the Master's degree.(or four years beyond the Bachelor's degree for medicine, dentistry and veterinary medicine). Professional graduate schools for professions such as medicine, dentistry, law, veterinary sciences, and award a Professional degree requiring two years of advanced studies beyond the Bachelor's degree.
Non-university higher education is provided by junior colleges, which award an Associate degree after two years of study; and technical (vocational) colleges which provide five years of training beyond junior high school level for industrial professions and also award an Associate degree.
Monetary unit: Japanese yen (¥).
International student admission: International students must have completed 12 years of formal school education (or recognized equivalent) for undergraduate studies and be of at least 18 years of age. For further admission information contact Student Services Division, Higher Education Bureau, Ministry of Education, Culture, Sports, Science and Technology, 2-5-1 Marunouchi, Chiyoda-ku, Tokyo, 100-8959, Japan.
Since 2002, the Examination for Japanese University Admission for International Students (EJU) is used to evaluate Japanese language proficiency and the basic academic abilities of international students who wish to study at Japanese universities at the undergraduate level. The Japan Student Services Organization (JASSO) administers the examination in cooperation with the Ministry of Education, Culture, Sports, Science and Technology, the Ministry of Foreign Affairs, Japanese universities, and affiliated institutions in Japan and overseas.
Language: Japanese is the language of instruction at all levels of study except for some universities that offer courses in English. Japanese-language courses of 6 months to 2 years' duration are available at Japanese-language institutes and at private universities that offer preparatory Japanese language programmes.
Immigration requirements: Students wishing to study in

Japan must be accepted to a Japanese educational institution (Japanese-language institute, junior college, university, etc.), possess a valid national passport and obtain a visa from a Japanese Embassy or Consulate in their home country. Students who attend universities, junior colleges, colleges of technology, and special training colleges may be granted the the residence status of 'college student'. Those who attend Japanese-language institutes and other preparatory Japanese-language programmes may be granted the residence status of residence 'pre-college student'.

Estimated expenses for one academic year: Tuition: ¥600,000; books/supplies: ¥850,000; housing: ¥400,000.
Information services:
• Japan Student Services Organization(JASSO): web: http://www.jasso.go.jp
• Information center (Tokyo): 2-79 Aomi, Koto-ku, Tokyo 135-8630; Japan.
• Information center (Kobe): 1-2-8 Wakinohamacho, Chuoku, Kobe 651-0072; Japan.
Scholarships for international students: Japanese Government (Monbukagakusho- MEXT) scholarships offered for research, teacher-training, undergraduate studies, Japanese studies, studies at colleges of technology, specialized training colleges and for the Young Leaders Programme. Contact the Japanese embassy/consulate in your country for details.
Open and distance learning: The University of the Air (Hoso Daigaku, 2-11 Wakaba, Mihama-ku, Chiba), was established in 1983 under government auspices. It is a degree-granting institution and uses radio, television and other media. It promotes collaboration with other private and public universities by increasing mutual recognition of earned credits, by developing the exchange of teaching staff and by making broadcast material available to other universities.
Recognition of studies and qualification: Japan Student Services Organization (JASSO); web: http://www.jasso.go.jp.
Accommodation services: This is provided by universities, local governments, Japan Student Services Organization (JASSO) and other institutions.
Work opportunities: International students must obtain permission from the Ministry of Justice to engage in activities outside the scope of their status of residence. With permission, regular college students are allowed to have a part-time job of less than 28 hours a week and certain restrictions are applied.
Publications / Websites:
• Japan Student Services organization (JASSO): http://www.jasso.go.jp
• Study in Japan: http://www.studyjapan.go.jp.

1311 Aichi Shukutoku University [ASU]
9 Katahira Nagakute
Nagakute-cho Aichi-gun
Aichi
Tel: +81-561-62-4111
Fax: +81-561-63-7735
Web: http://www.aasa.ac.jp
e-mail: kouhou@asu.aasa.ac.jp

📖 Undergraduate and Graduate Degree Programmes
Study Domains: architecture, business, community development, education, humanities and arts, social sciences.
Programmes: (a) (b) (c) Master's and Ph.D. degrees; (d) (e) (f) (g) Bachelor's degrees; (h) other, non-degree course.
Description: (a) Graduate School of Letters; (b) Graduate School of Communication Studies; (c) Graduate School of Studies on Contemporary Society; (d) Faculty of Letters: undergraduate language and literature courses; (e) Faculty of Studies on Contemporary Society; (f) Faculty of Communication Studies.
Open to: for graduate studies: at least 16 years of formal education or equivalent; for undergraduate and certificate: at least 12 years of formal education or equivalent.
Duration: depends on programme; courses begin in April and October.
Fees: (graduate programmes) registration: 200,000 yen; tuition: 650,000 yen; (undergraduate programmes) registration: 220,000 yen; tuition: 750,000 yen; (Japanese language courses): registration: 30,000 yen; tuition: 710,000 yen.

Financial assistance: 30% reduction of tuition fees for self-supporting students.
Languages: Japanese; language proficiency test level 1 or equivalent level.
Applications: all degree programmes: apply to Office of Public Relations and Admission; tel: +81 52 781 1151 or email: kouhou@asu.aasa.ac.jp; Japanese language courses: apply to Centre for Japanese Language and Culture; tel: +81 561 63 7737 or email: ohnoshow@asu.aasa.ac.jp.

📌 ASU Alumni Scholarship for International Students
Study Domains: all major fields.
Scholarships: ASU Alumni Scholarship for International Students.
Open to: only for students at the Centre for Japanese Language and Culture.
Value: partial tuition refund of 30% at the closing programme of each semester.
Applications: to Meiko ABE, Director of Japanese Programme; telephone: +81 561 63 7735.

1312 Asahi University [AU]
1851, Hozumi-cho, Hozumi
Motosu-gun
501 0296 Aifu
Tel: +81-58-32-9-022
Fax: +81-58-32-91025
Web: http://www.asahi-u.ac.jp
e-mail: intaff@alice.asahi-u.ac.jp

📖 Undergraduate and Graduate Degree Programmes
Study Domains: business, business administration, dentistry, law.
Programmes: (a) Bachelor's degrees in law; business administration; dentistry; Master's and Ph.D. degrees in law; Master's and Ph.D. degrees in information management; (b) Bachelor's and Ph.D. degrees in dentistry.
Duration: 4 to 6 years depending on programme; courses begin in April or October.
Fees: (b) dentistry tuition fees: 29 million yen for 6 academic years.
Languages: excellent proficiency in Japanese.
Applications: (a) apply before 2 December or 25 June; for details contact: nyuusi@alice.asahi-u.ac.jp.; (b) dentistry apply by 2 December; contact Admissions Office: +81 58 329 1088.

📌 Scholarships
Study Domains: business administration, dentistry, languages, law.
Scholarships: (a) Scholarships for the foreign students of Asahi University; (b) Scholarships for the students of Asahi University Japanese Language and Culture Course; (c) Scholarships awarded according to qualifications or certificates acquired.
Subjects: (a) undergraduate and graduate schools of law; business administration; dentistry; (b) language and culture course; (c) law and business administration.
Open to: (a) students of year 2 and higher, based on good personality and achievement; (b) students at the end of first term after entrance, based on good personality and achievement; (c) undergraduate students who qualify.
Duration: (a) 1 year renewable; (b) 6 months; (c) every time.
Value: (a) 30,000 yen per month; (b) 50,000 yen per month; (c) 100,000 yen / 50,000 yen / 30,000 yen (according to qualifications or certificates).
Applications: deadlines: (a) April, October (at enrolment); (c) April, September, December, February; apply to Student Affairs Section of University: tel: +81 58 329 1084 or email: gakusei@alice.asahi-u.ac.jp.

1313 Asia University [AU]
Office of International Affairs
5-24-10, Sakai, Musashino-shi
Tokyo 180-8629
Tel: +81-422-363-255
Fax: +81-422-36-4869
Web: http://www.asia-u.ac.jp/english/
e-mail: koryu@asia-u.ac.jp

📖 Undergraduate, Graduate Programmes

Study Domains: business, business administration, economic and commercial sciences, Japanese, languages, law.
Programmes: Programme of undergraduate and graduate degree courses at the following faculties: Business Administration, Economics, Law, International Relations and Asian Studies; intensive courses in Japanese language and culture.
Open to: students having completed at least 12 years in authorized school education in another country and meeting all other academic, linguistic and financial criteria.
Duration: variable, according to programme chosen.
Fees: (approximate figures) admission fee, 120,000 yen; tuition, 460,000 yen; examination, 10,000 yen; other fees, 53,000 yen.
Applications: by 25 October, to the Office of International Affairs, at the above address.

1314 Association of International Education, Japan

Coordinator of Assistance for Privately Financed Students
Student Affairs Division
Programs and Activities Department
4-5-29 Komaba, Meguro-ku
153-8503 Tokyo
Tel: +81-3-5454-5213
Fax: +81-3-5454-5223
Web: http://www.aiej.or.jp
e-mail: sa@aiej.or.jp

🎓 Honours Scholarship Programme

Study Domains: all major fields.
Scholarships: Honours Scholarship Programme.
Open to: vocational college (2nd year students); College of Technology (4th year students); Junior college; undergraduates; Master's programme; Doctor's programme; fluency in Japanese required.
Place of study: Japan.
Duration: 1 year; courses begin in June; renewable.
Value: vocational college/undergraduates, 52,000 yen per month; graduates: 69,000 yen per month.
Applications: by May, to be filed by Japanese university in which applicant is enrolled.

1315 Atsumi International Scholarship Foundation [AISF]

3-5-8 Sekiguchi
Bunkyo-ku
112-0014 Tokyo
Tel: +81-3-3943-7612
Fax: +81-3-3943-1512
Web: http://www.aisf.or.jp
e-mail: aisf@sh0.po.iijnet.or.jp

🎓 Scholarships / Doctoral Studies

Study Domains: all major fields.
Scholarships: students of any nationality except Japanese who are enrolled in an AISF designated graduate school in Japan and who are in their last year of study for a Ph.D., including non-Japanese researchers at such graduate schools who are completing graduate studies in other countries.
Open to: students of any nationality except Japanese who are enrolled in an AISF designated graduate school in Japan and who are in their last year of study for a Ph.D., including non-Japanese researchers at such graduate schools who are completing graduate studies in other countries.
Duration: 1 year non-renewable.
Value: approximately 200,000 yen per month, including travel grant for post-AISF students with a Ph.D. degree.
Applications: by 30 September to the above address.

1316 Chukyo University [CU]

101-2, Yagoto-honmachi
Showa-ku
Nagoya
Tel: +81-57-835-7133
Fax: +81-57-835-7119
Web: http://www.chukyo-u.ac.jp
e-mail: cuic@mng.chukyo-u.ac.jp

📖 Undergraduate, Graduate Programmes

Study Domains: business, business administration, continuing education, economy, education, English, law, liberal arts, linguistics, literature and civilization, management, physical education, psychology, sociology, teacher education.

🎓 Chukyo Scholarship for International Students

Study Domains: all major fields.
Scholarships: Chukyo Scholarship for International Students.
Open to: full-time and exchange students of any nationality with satisfactory academic record, future potential and financial need.
Duration: one academic year (12 months).
Value: undergraduates: 45,000 yen per month; graduates: 65,000 yen per month.
Applications: apply by early September to International Centre.

1317 Chuo University [CU]

International Centre
742-1 Higashinakano
Hachioji-shi
192-0393 Tokyo
Tel: +81-426-74-2211/2212
Fax: +81-426-74-2214
Web: http://www.chuo-u.ac.jp
e-mail: intlcent@tamajs.chuo-u.ac.jp

🎓 Scholarship for Foreign Students

Study Domains: economy, engineering, industry and commerce, law, literature and civilization, sciences.
Scholarships: Chuo University Scholarship for foreign students (undergraduate and graduate levels).
Subjects: law, economics, commerce, science and engineering, literature and policy studies.
Open to: full-time and regular foreign students enrolled at the University with satisfactory academic record and in financial need.
Duration: one year (renewable).
Value: one-half tuition and laboratory fees per academic year.
Applications: by June and after enrolment.

1318 Fuji Bank International Foundation [FBIF]

1-5-4 Otemachi
Chiyoda-Ku
100-0004 Tokyo
Tel: +81-3-3201-7718
Fax: +81-3-3216-2895
e-mail: fbifyume@infoweb.ne.jp

🎓 Postgraduate Scholarships

Study Domains: human sciences, social sciences.
Scholarships: Fuji Bank International Foundation Scholarships.
Open to: postgraduate foreign students studying in Japan based on scholastic achievement and financial necessity as well as moral character; no age limit; proficiency in Japanese required.
Duration: 2 years (not renewable).
Value: 120,000 yen per month.
Applications: through the university where the applicant is enrolled.

1319 Fukuoka Kogyo Daigaku Tanki Daigakubu Institute of Technology, Junior College [FITJC]

3-30-1, Wajirohigashi, Higashi-ku
811-0295 Fukuoka
Tel: +81-92-606-0710
Fax: +81-92-606-0763
Web: http://www.fjct.fit.ac.jp
e-mail: tanjim@fjct.fit.ac.jp

📖 Associate Degree / Computer Science

Study Domains: computer science.
Programmes: Associate degree in information processing; information communication.
Description: computer communication and control; multi-media in the CG and internet age.
Open to: candidates of all nationalities meeting financial and academic requirements.
Academic requirements: Japanese tests in mathematics and science; unsatisfactory results will necessitate extra language examination.
Age limit Min: over 18 years of age.
Duration: 2 years.
Fees: tuition fees: 1,041,000 yen; living costs: 80,000 yen per month.
Financial assistance: half of the tuition fees for selected applicants; contact Section of Entrance Examinations for further information.
Languages: Japanese.
Applications: apply by 24 January to Section of Entrance Examinations at the University; tel: +81-92-606-0634; email: nyushi@fit.ac.jp.

🎓 Foreign Student Scholarship

Study Domains: computer science.
Description: half tuition depending on grades.
Applications: after the entrance exams; apply to the Section of Student Affairs at FIT, tel: +81 92 606 0654 or email: gakusei@fit.ac.jp.

1320 Fukuoka University

8-19-1 Nanakuma Jonan-ku
814-0 Fukuoka-shi
Tel: +81-92-871-6631
Fax: +81-92-862-4431
Web: http://www.fukuoka-u.ac.jp
e-mail: kokusai@adm.fukuoka-u.ac.jp

🎓 Undergraduate Studies

Study Domains: business, economic and commercial sciences, health and hygiene, law, medicine, pharmacy and pharmacology, physical education, sciences, trade.
Description: Fukuoka University Scholarship for international undergraduate students.
Open to: international undergraduate students of all nationalities, with excellent scholastic results.
Value: 50,000 yen per month.
Applications: early May; contact Center for International Programs; kokusai@adm.fukuoka-u.ac.jp.

1321 Heiwa Nakajima Foundation [HNF]

33F Ark Mori Bldg.
12-32, Akasaka 1-Chome
Minato-Ku
107 Tokyo
Tel: +81-3-5570-5261
Fax: +81-3-5570-5421

🎓 Undergraduate, Graduate Scholarships

Study Domains: all major fields.
Scholarships: (a) Scholarships for Foreign Students; (b) Scholarships (20 for undergraduates and 20 for graduate students).
Open to: (a) candidates of any nationality enrolled at overseas universities or colleges that have an agreement with Japanese universities. Candidates must be recommended by the home university; (b) foreign students staying in Japan and enrolled at a Japanese university.
Duration: (a) 1 or 2 years; (b) 1 year (from April to March of the following year); possibility of renewable once under certain circumstances.
Value: (a) 200,000 yen per month, a round-trip plane ticket and 500,000 yen for an outfit allowance; (b) undergraduate students: 100,000 yen per month; graduate students: 120,000 yen per month.
Applications: (a) by the end of November; by and through the home university and the Japanese university; (b) by the end of October, through the Japanese university where the student is enrolled.

1322 Hiroshima Shudo University [HSU]

1-1-1 Ozukahigashi Asaminami-ku
731-3195 Hiroshima-shi
Tel: +81-82-830-1103
Fax: +81-82-830-1303
Web: http://www.shudo-u.ac.jp
e-mail: kokusai@js.shudo-u.ac.jp

📖 Undergraduate, Graduate Programmes

Study Domains: business, business administration, ecology, environment, economic and commercial sciences, economy, education, English, law, management, political science, psychology, social sciences, sociology, trade.
Programmes: (a) Bachelor's; (b) Master's; (c) Ph.D. degrees.
Description: (a) Bachelor of Arts; (b) M.Com., M.B.A., Master of Laws (L.L.M.); (c) Doctor of Philosophy.
Open to: (a) applicants with secondary school leaving certificate or equivalent; (b) applicants having completed 16 years of formal education; (c) foreign postgraduate students having completed 5 years of graduate studies, including a 2 year Master's degree.
Duration: (a) 4 years; (b) 2 years; (c) 3 years; courses begin early April.
Fees: registration fee (a) 498,000 yen; (b) 332,000 yen; (c) 332,000 yen; tuition fees (a) 727,000 yen; (b) (c) 557,000 yen; living costs (a) (b) (c) 70,000-80,000 yen.
Financial assistance: scholarships available from the Japanese government and private organizations for reduction and exemption of tuition for overseas students; contact HSU International Affairs Centre: tel: +81 82 830 1103.
Applications: examination for Japanese University admission tests required, Japanese essay, interviews; exams usually held (a) in early April; (b) (c) in October and March.

🎓 Scholarships for International Students

Study Domains: all major fields.
Scholarships: (a) HSU Exchange Student Scholarship; (b) HSU Alumni Scholarship; (c) HSU Staff-funded Scholarship.
Open to: (a) exchange candidates from affiliated universities;(b), (c) HSU international students with excellent academic record.
Value: (a) 50,000 yen per month and 50,000 for installation allowance; (b) 20,000 yen per month; (c) 30,000 yen.
Applications: (a) (b) (c) apply to HSU International Affairs Centre; tel: +81 82 830 1303; fax: +81 82 830 1303.

1323 Hitachi Scholarship Foundation [HSF]

1-5-1 Marunouchi
Chiyoda-ku
101-8220 Tokyo
Tel: +81-3-3215-3761
Fax: +81-3-3215-2449
Web: http://global.hitachi.com
e-mail: scholarship@hdq.hitachi.co.jp

🎓 Graduate Studies

Study Domains: sciences, technology.
Scholarships: The Hitachi Scholarship for graduate studies and research in the field of science and technology.
Open to: staff members of universities from Thailand, Malaysia, Singapore, Indonesia and the Philippines recommended by the Rector of his/her graduate university and nominated by the Foundation; age under 30; Ph.D.; candidates under 35.
Place of study: graduate schools in Japan.
Duration: Master's course, 3 years including 1 year Japanese language study; Ph.D. course, 4 years (not renewable).
Value: monthly allowance: 180,000 yen; expenses for field trips: maximum 50,000 yen per year; plus round-trip economy air fare, tuition and other expenses.
Languages: proficiency in English required.
Applications: by 30 December, to the Secretary-General, at the above address.

1324 Hitotsubashi University

1 Naka 2-chome
186-8 Kunitachi-shi
Tel: +81-42-580-8000
Fax: +81-42-580-8006
Web: http://www.hit-u.ac.jp

🐦 Scholarship

Study Domains: business administration, economic and
commercial sciences, economy, law, linguistics, social
sciences.
Scholarships: Japanese Government Scholarship.
Subjects: Business Administration, Economics, Law,
Social Sciences, Linguistics.
Open to: All candidates under 35 years old.
Applications: Candidates must contact the nearest
Japanese embassy.

1325 Hokkai-Gakuen University [HGU]

4-1-40 Asahi-machi, Toyohira-ku
062-8 Sapporo
Tel: +81-11-841-1161
Fax: +81-11-824-3141
Web: http://www.hokkai-t-u.ac.jp

🐦 Financial aid

Scholarships: Tuition Reduction System.
Subjects: All major fields.
Duration: 1 year, renewable.
Value: Tuition fees reduction of 30 %.
Applications: By March; email:
kurihara@tyhr.hookai-s-u.ac.jp.

1326 Hokkaido University (Hokkaido Daigaku)

Nishi 5 Kita 8, Kita-ku
060-0808 Sapporo-shi, Hokkaido
Tel: +81-11-716-2111
Fax: +81-11-706-2095
Web: http://www.hokudai.ac.jp
e-mail: kouryu@general.hokudai.ac.jp

🐦 Undergraduate Exchange Programme Scholarship

Study Domains: all major fields.
Scholarships: Japan Student Services Organization
(JASSO) Scholarship.
Description: 'Junior Year Abroad' type programme
designed to provide students from affiliated universities.
Value: living expenses: 80,000 yen; travel allowance and
installation allowance: 25,000 yen.
Languages: English.
Applications: to kkumi@jimu.hokudai.ac.jp.

1327 Hyogo College of Medicine [HCM]

1-1 Mukogawacho
Nishinomiya
Tel: +81-798-45-6111
Fax: +81-798-45-6261
Web: http://www.hyo-med.ac.jp
e-mail: motooka@hyo-med.ac.jp

📖 Medical Sciences

Study Domains: anatomy, bacteriology, biochemistry,
cardiology, dermatology, genetics, health and hygiene,
immunology, medicine, neurology, nutrition, obstetrics and
gynaecology, ophthalmology, paediatrics, pharmacy and
pharmacology, physiology, psychiatry, radiology, surgery,
urology.
Programmes: M.D. degree programme.
Description: specialized subjects: pathology, forensic
medicine, internal medicine, medical informatics,
neurosurgery, orthopedics, thoracic surgery,
oto-rhino-laryngology, anaesthesiology, emergency medicine,
rehabilitation, medicine.
Open to: students who have completed 18 years of studies
in a foreign country, with studies medicine, dentistry, and
veterinary science; written examination and interview in
English.

Duration: 4 years.
Fees: registration fee: 200,000 yen; tuition fees: 500,000
yen; living costs: 200,000 yen (approximately).
Languages: Japanese, English.
Applications: apply before 6 September to Department of
Academic Affairs +81 798 45 6163; courses begin 1 April.

1328 Ichikawa International Scholarship Foundation [IISF]

1 20-5 Tenma
Kita-ku Osaka-shi
530-8511 Osaka
Tel: +81-6-6356-2357
Fax: +81-6-6356-2344
Web: http://www.iisf.jp
e-mail: info@iisf.jp

🐦 Graduate Studies

Study Domains: all major fields.
Scholarships: Ichikawa International Scholarships for all
major fields.
Open to: applicants from Asian countries.
Place of study: university or graduate school mainly in
Kansai district, Japan.
Duration: normally 2 years.
Value: 100,000 yen per month.
Applications: by 20 December, through school currently
attended.

1329 International Christian University [ICU]

10-2 Osawa 3-chome
Mitaka-shi
181 Tokyo
Tel: +81-422-33-3501
Web: http://www.icu.ac.jp

📖 Undergraduate, Graduate Programmes

Study Domains: administration, classical studies,
education, languages, natural sciences, social sciences.
Programmes: (a) College of Liberal Arts: humanities,
social sciences, natural sciences, languages, education,
international studies; (b) Graduate School: education, public
administration, comparative culture, natural sciences; (c)
Summer intensive course in Japanese language.
Open to: (a) and (b) qualified students of any nationality;
(c) candidates must have previously completed at least one
year of university level Japanese.
Duration: 1 year; (c) 6 weeks; (courses begin in July).
Fees: (approximate figures) (a) and (b) admission:
300,000 yen (regular and transfer students), 150,000 yen
(Kenkyusei and 1-year regular); tuition: 1,233,000 yen; (c)
application fee: 20,000 yen; tuition: 200,000 yen.
Financial assistance: only to enrolled students; awards
depend on student's need.
Languages: Instruction in Japanese and English.
Applications: (a) and (b) by 15 April; (c) 1 April; to the
Admissions Office.

1330 International College for Advanced Buddhist Studies [ICABS]

5-3-23 Toranomon
Minato-ku
105-0001 Tokyo
Tel: +81-3-3434-6953
Fax: +81-3-3578-1205
Web: http://www.icabs.ac.jp
e-mail: icabs@icabs.ac.jp

📖 Graduate Degree Programmes

Study Domains: Asian studies, philology, philosophy.
Description: Master's, Ph.D. degrees.
Open to: university graduates who have completed at least
16 years of formal education; ability to read, write and
communicate in Japanese highly desirable.
Duration: 5 years; courses begin in October or April.
Applications: apply before 31 January.

Scholarship

Study Domains: Asian studies, theology, religion.
Scholarships: Scholarship for International College of Advanced Buddhist Studies.
Open to: for students with an excellent academic record and proven financial need.
Duration: 2 years; renewable under certain conditions.
Value: 80,000 yen per month.
Applications: apply by 31 January to email: student@icabs.ac.jp.

1331 International University of Japan [IUJ]

Yamato-machi, Minamiuonuma-gun
949-7277 Niigata-ken
Tel: +81-25-779-1104
Fax: +81-25-779-1188
Web: http://www.iuj.ac.jp
e-mail: info@iuj.ac.jp

Master's Degree Programmes

Study Domains: business, business administration, international relations, management.
Description: (a) MA degrees in international relations and international development management; (b) Master's degrees in business administration and in e-business management.
Subjects: international economics, international politics, international relations, macroeconomics, microeconomics, development economics, research methodology, finance, IT, marketing, strategic management, web technologies, database design, etc.
Open to: candidates of all nationalities meeting financial and academic requirements.
Academic requirements: 4-year university graduates or with equivalent education; TOEFL, GMAT (MBA only) scores.
Duration: 2 years for international relations, international development and MBA; 1 year for e-business; courses begin on 1 October.
Fees: tuition fees: 1.9 million yen for international relations, international development and MBA and 2.2 million yen.
Financial assistance: possibility of public or private organization scholarships; contact the University at above address.
Languages: English.
Applications: (a) 25 February; (b) 28 January, 25 March; for further information: info@iuj.ac.jp.

IUJ Scholarships

Study Domains: business administration, international relations.
Scholarships: IUJ scholarship for studies in international relations, international development and international management.
Open to: nationals of any country who successfully pass the IUJ admission screening.
Duration: 1 academic year, renewable for the second year upon academic review.
Value: covers tuition, partial admission, and/or stipend.
Applications: by early April.

1332 ITO Foundation for International Education Exchange [ITO]

BABA Building 5F
Nishi Shinjuku Shinjyku-ku
160-0023 Tokyo
Tel: +81-3-3299-7872
Fax: +81-3-3299-7871
Web: http://www.itofound.or.jp/English/Introduc.htm

Graduate Programmes

Study Domains: all major fields.
Scholarships: ITO Foundation for International Education Exchange Scholarship for Foreign Students; for graduate studies in all major fields.
Open to: students in a Master's course of a university in Japan; any nationality; age under 30 years old; proficiency in Japanese required; applicants must be residing in Japan at time of application, have excellent academic record and have financial need.

Duration: 2 years or less (not renewable).
Value: 150,000 yen per month.
Applications: by January, to the above address.

1333 Iwatani Naoji Foundation [INF]

TBR Building
2-10-2 Nagata-cho, Chiyoda-ku
100-0014 Tokyo
Tel: +81-3-3580-2251
Fax: +81-3-3580-2700
Web: http://www.kohokyo.or.jp
e-mail: info@kohokyo.or.jp

Graduate Studies in Natural Sciences

Study Domains: natural sciences.
Scholarships: Iwatani International Scholarships.
Subjects: natural sciences.
Open to: candidates from East and South-East Asian countries who are registered in graduate schools in Japan; age: 30 years or under for Master's course, 35 or under for Doctorate.
Place of study: universities in Japan.
Duration: 1 year.
Value: 150,000 yen per month.
Applications: by 20 December; contact website for application information.

1334 Japan Women's University [JWU]

2-8-1 Mejirodai Bunkyo-ku
112-8681 Tokyo
Tel: +81-3-3943-3131
Web: http://www.jwu.ac.jp

Financial aid

Study Domains: all major fields.
Scholarships: Tuition Support Program.
Open to: Non-Japanese, undergraduate and graduate students.
Duration: 1 year, renewable.
Value: covers 30 % of tuition fees.
Applications: By late May; email: n-abroad@atlas-jwu.ac.jp.

Scholarship

Study Domains: all major fields.
Scholarships: (a) Nomiyama Fuji Scholarship; (b) Japan's Women's University Prize for Academic Excellence.
Open to: (a) Non Japanese, undergraduate students.
Duration: (a) 1 year, renewable; (b) 1 year, non-renewable.
Value: (a) 100,000 yen per year; (b) 100,000 yen per year.
Applications: by late September; email: n-abroad@atlas.jwu.ac.jp; (b) contact n-abroad@atlas.jwu.ac.jp for further details.

1335 Jichi Medical School, Graduate School of Medicine

3311-1 Yakushigi
Minamikawachi-machi,
329 0498 Tochigi-ken
Tel: +81-285-58-7044
Fax: +81-285-44-3625
Web: http://www.jichi.ac.jp
e-mail: graduate@jichi.ac.jp

Postgraduate Programme / Medical Science

Study Domains: anatomy, bacteriology, biochemistry, biology, biophysics, cardiology, dentistry, dermatology, genetics, health and hygiene, immunology, medicine, microbiology, neurology, obstetrics and gynaecology, ophthalmology, paediatrics, physiology, psychiatry, radiology, surgery, urology.
Programmes: clinical and community medicine, human biology, environmental medicine and human ecology.
Duration: 4 years.
Fees: registration fee: 282,000 yen; tuition fees: 547,000 yen per year; living costs: 130,000 yen per month (approximately).
Languages: Japanese; English.
Applications: apply before 31 January to Section of

School Affairs, Jichi Medical School.

1336 Kake Educational Institution/ Okayama University of Science [KEI]

1-1 Kidai-cho
700-0005 Okayama-city
Tel: +81-86-256-4040
Fax: +81-86-256-4040
e-mail: kakeintaff@hotmail.com

📖 Undergraduate and Graduate Degree Programmes

Study Domains: bacteriology, engineering, research, sciences.
Programmes: Bachelor's; Master's and Ph.D. degrees in science and engineering fields.
Fees: registration: 220,000 yen; tuition fees: 1,017,500 yen; living costs: 200,000 yen per month.
Financial assistance: partial tuition reductions: half tuition for international students.
Languages: Japanese.
Applications: apply by January; may vary with degree.

🎓 International Student Scholarships

Study Domains: engineering, sciences.
Scholarships: and 11 listed scholarships with values ranging from: 25,000-300,000 yen; contact school for details.

1337 Kambayashi Scholarship Foundation [KSF]

Kasumi Tsukuba Center
599-1 Nishi-Ohashi, Tsukuba-shi,
305-8510 Ibaraki
Tel: +81-298-50-1853
Fax: +81-298-50-1879
Web: http://www.kasumi.co.jp/koken/koken4.htm
e-mail: junji.hazumi@kasumi.co.jp

🎓 Graduate Studies

Study Domains: all major fields.
Scholarships: Kambayashi Shogaku-Kin Scholarships for graduate studies in all major fields.
Open to: applicants from East Asian and South-East Asian countries, irrespective of age, who have been studying for more than one year at any university or college that has a graduate school or at a graduate school at private expense, holding 'college student' status of residence; the applicant must be recommended by his/her institution and not be granted more than 50,000 yen per month from another institution.
Place of study: university graduate schools or graduate schools in Kanto district, Japan.
Duration: 1 year (renewable).
Value: 100,000 yen per month (for 1 year).
Applications: from 1 to 20 April, to the Foundation through applicant's respective school, with recommendation of the University President.

1338 Kansai Gaidai University [KGU]

Center for International Education
16-1 Nakamiyahigashino-cho, Hirakata City
573-1001 Osaka
Tel: +81-72-805-2831
Fax: +81-72-805-2830
Web: http://www.kansaigaidai.ac.jp
e-mail: inquiry@kansaigaidai.ac.jp

📖 Undergraduate Programmes / Asian Studies

Study Domains: Asian studies.
Programmes: Asian Studies Programme: (a) Japanese language (beginners, intermediate, advanced and intensive); (b) East Asia related courses in areas such as: economics, business, history, art, government, management, anthropology, literature, politics, religion, brush painting, ceramics.
Open to: university-level students of all nationalities with at least a 3.0 grade point average on a 4.0 scale or equivalent; TOEFL required for those whose first language is not English.
Duration: 4 months or 1 year (courses begin in: (a)

August; (b) January).
Fees: application: US$50; admission: US$200; tuition: US$6,000.
Financial assistance: (a) merit scholarships, tuition reduction; (b) teaching assistantships, tuition waivers.
Languages: Instruction in English.
Applications: (a) by 15 May; (b) by 1 November.

🎓 Undergraduate, Graduate Scholarships

Study Domains: arts, Asian studies, economy, history.
Scholarships: (a) Merit scholarships; (b) Teaching assistantships.
Subjects: (a) Asian studies; (b) East Asia related courses in areas such as economics, history, art.
Open to: (a) candidates of all nationalities with at least a 3.0 grade point average on a 4.0 scale or equivalent; (b) candidates must have sufficient command of English.
Duration: 1 semester or 1 year; (scholarships begin in September and February).
Value: (a) US$3,000 tuition reduction; (b) tuition waiver.
Applications: by 15 May and 1 November.

1339 Kansai International Students Institute

8-3-13 Uehommachi
Tennoji-ku, Osaka City
543-0001 Osaka
Tel: +81-6-6774-0033
Fax: +81-6-6774-0788
Web: http://www.kkgakuyu.or.jp/index-e.html
e-mail: info@kkgakuyu.or.jp

📖 Japanese Studies

Study Domains: chemistry, English, history, Japanese, mathematics, physics.
Programmes: courses in Japanese language, English, mathematics, physics, chemistry, world history.
Open to: candidates who have completed 12 years of formal education or the equivalent.
Duration: 1 to 1-1/2 years.
Fees: (approximate figures) registration: 80,000-115,000 yen; tuition: 715,000-1,035,000 yen; living expenses: 780,000 yen per month.

1340 Keio University [KU]

International Center
2-15-45 Mita, Minato-ku
108-8 Tokyo
Tel: +81-35-453-4511
Fax: +81-35-427-7640
Web: http://www.keio.ac.jp/index-en.html
e-mail: www@info.keio.ac.jp

📖 Undergraduate, Graduate Programmes

Study Domains: cultural studies, Japanese, languages.
Programmes: programme of undergraduate and graduate studies at 9 faculties: business and commerce; economics; environmental information; law; letters; nursing and medical care; policy management; science and technology; medicine; Japanese language and culture; degree programmes also possible through correspondence courses.
Open to: senior high school graduates or those with equivalent education, of any country and any age.
Duration: 1 academic year (non-degree programme); students are admitted in April or September.
Fees: admission: 100,000 yen; tuition: 470,000 yen; textbooks: 30,000 yen.
Financial assistance: scholarships and subsidies available through the University for full-time international students; deduction of 30% of tuition fees for self-supporting students.
Applications: variable, depending on programme.

🎓 Scholarship

Study Domains: all major fields.
Scholarships: (a) Keio University Tuition Deduction Scholarship; (b) Keio University Tuition Scholarship; (c) Keio University Tuition Scholarship (Graduate); (d) Keio University Ken 'ichi Yamaoka Memorial Fund Scholarship; (e) Japanese Government Scholarship (Graduate); (f) Japanese Government Honors Scholarship (Undergraduate); (g) Japanese Government Honors Scholarship (Graduate); (h) Local Government / Private Foundations Scholarship.

Open to: (a) undergraduate and graduate foreign students; (b) undergraduate foreign students; (c) graduate students; (d) first year undergraduate students from Asian countries; (e) graduate or to be graduate, under 35 years of age; (f) full time undergraduate students; (g) graduate and research students;.
Duration: (a) 1 year, renewable; (b) 1 year, renewable; (c) 1 year; renewable; (d) 1 year, non-renewable; (e) 2 to 3 years, non-renewable; (f) 1 year, renewable; (g) 1 year, renewable.
Value: (a) 30 % of tuition fees; (b) 20 to 70 % of tuition fees; (c) 40,000 to 60,000 yen per year; (d) 100 % of tuition fees; (e) 100 % of tuition fees; living expenses, 184,000 yen per month; travel expenses when returning to home country; (f) living expenses, 52,000 yen per month; (g) living expenses, 73,000 yen per month; (h) 10,000 to 120,000 yen per month.
Applications: (a) by July; email: ic-inquiry@adst.keio.ac.jp; (b) by April; email: ic-inquiry@adst.keio.ac.jp;
(c) by April; email: ic-inquiry@adst.keio.ac.jp; (d) by February; email: ic-inquiry@adst.keio.ac.jp;
(e) by October; email: ic-inquiry@adst.keio.ac.jp; (f) by April; email: ic-inquiry@adst.keio.ac.jp;
(g) by April; email: ic-inquiry@adst.keio.ac.jp; (h) contact ic-inquiry@adst.keio.ac.jp for further details.

1341 Kobe College [KC]
4-1 Okadayama
662-8 Nishinomiya-shi
Tel: +81-798-51-9533
Fax: +81-798-51-8535
Web: http://www.kobe-c.ac.jp
e-mail: dean@mail.kobe-c.ac.jp

☞ Overseas Student Scholarship
Study Domains: all major fields.
Open to: enrolled exchange student with financial difficulties with good academic results and personal merit; students should not be benefiting from other awards.
Nationality: Asian, African nationals.
Duration: 1 year (4 years maximum).
Value: 60,000 yen per month.
Applications: by April each year to Student Division of Kobe College at the above address.

1342 Kobe Design University [KDU]
8-1-1, Gakuennishi-machi,
Nishi-ku
Kobe
Tel: +81-78-794-5039
Fax: +81-78-794-5027
Web: http://www.kobe-du.ac.jp
e-mail: international@kobe-du.ac.jp

☐ Undergraduate and Graduate Degree Programmes
Study Domains: applied arts, architecture, design, graphic arts, industrial design, interior design.
Programmes: (a) Bachelor's; (b) Master's; (c) Ph.D. degrees.
Description: environmental design; product design; fashion and textile design; visual communication; design theory; integrated design.
Open to: candidates of all nationalities with (a) completion of 12 years of education; (b), (c) completion of 16 years of education.
Duration: (a) 4 years; (b) 2 years.
Fees: (a) registration: 35,000 yen; tuition: 1,500,000 yen; living costs: 150,000 yen per month; (b) (c) registration: 30,000 yen; tuition: 1,200,000 yen; living costs: 150,000 yen per month.
Financial assistance: international students enrolled in full-time study can apply for 30% tuition reduction.
Languages: Japanese.
Applications: (a) 21 January; (b) (c) 14 December to Admissions Office, email: international@kobe-du.ac.jp; courses begin 1 April.

☞ Scholarships / Design
Study Domains: applied arts, architecture, design, graphic arts, industrial design, interior design.
Scholarships: (a) Japanese Government Honours Scholarship; (b) Hyogo Scholarship; (c) Kobe International Scholarship; (d) Rotary Yoneyama Memorial Foundation.

Value: monthly allowances: (a) undergraduate: 52,000 yen; graduate: 73,000 yen; (b) 30,000 yen; (c) 80,000 yen; (d) undergraduate: 120,000 yen; graduate: 150,000 yen.
Applications: students may apply for scholarships through the University after enrolment.

1343 Kobe Gakuin University
518 Arise, Ikawadani-cho, Nishi-ku
651-2180 Kobe-shi
Tel: +81-78-974-1551
Fax: +81-78-974-5689
Web: http://www.kobegakuin.ac.jp
e-mail: kgu@j.kobegakuin.ac.jp

☐ Undergraduate, Graduate Programmes
Study Domains: all major fields, business administration, economic and commercial sciences, humanities and arts, international law, international relations, law, nutrition, paramedical studies, pharmacy and pharmacology, psychology.
Description: (a) Bachelor's; (b) Master's; (c) Ph.D. degrees; (d) others.
Subjects: (a) law, economics, humanities and sciences, nutrition, pharmaceutical sciences, business administration, rehabilitation; (b) law, economics, humanities and sciences, nutrition, pharmaceutical sciences; (c) law, economics, humanities and sciences, food and medicinal sciences; (d) law school.
Open to: candidates of all nationalities; must have language skills equal to or greater than level 1 in a Japanese language proficiency test.
Duration: (a) 4 years; (b) 2 years; (c) 3 years; (d) 2 or 3 years.
Fees: (a) registration: 348,000-466,000 yen; tuition fees: 920,000-1,800,000 yen; (b) registration: 236,000-258 000 yen; tuition fees: 460,000-610,000 yen; (c) registration: 232,000-240,000 yen; tuition fees: 460,000-600,000 yen; (d) registration: 200,000 yen; tuition fee: 1,200,000 yen.
Financial assistance: 30% tuition reduction for self-supporting students.
Languages: Japanese.
Applications: (a) early November for November examination; mid-January for February examination; (b), (c) and (d) end August for September examination; end January for February examination to Admissions Center.

☞ Financial aid
Study Domains: all major fields.
Scholarships: Kobe Gakuin University Tuition Reduction for International Students.
Open to: candidates of all nationalities with student visa.
Duration: 1 year, renewable.
Value: tuition fee reduction of 30 %.
Applications: by mid-June; applicants must already be enrolled at Kobe Gakuin University.

☞ Scholarship
Study Domains: all major fields.
Scholarships: Kobe Gakuin University International Students Scholarship.
Open to: candidates of all nationalities with student visa.
Duration: 1 year, non-renewable.
Value: 30,000 yen per month.
Applications: by May; applicants must already be enrolled at Kobe Gakuin University.

1344 Kokushikan University [KU]
4-28-1 Setagaya
Setagayaku
154-8515 Tokyo
Tel: +81-3-5481-3206
Fax: +81-3-5481-3210
Web: http://www.kokushikan.ac.jp
e-mail: ic@kiss.kokushikan.ac.jp

☐ Undergraduate, Graduate Programmes
Study Domains: Asian studies, business, business administration, economy, education, geography, history, law, literature and civilization, political science.
Programmes: Bachelor's degrees; studies at graduate schools and research institutes; consult website for further information on graduate studies.

Open to: candidates must have completed at least 12 years of school education; Japanese language proficiency required: international students must take exam for Japanese university admission.
Fees: registration fee: 35,000 yen; tuition fees vary with programme: 1,000,000-1,290,000 yen; living costs: 130,000 yen per month.

☛ International Student Scholarships

Study Domains: all major fields.
Scholarships: (a) Honours Scholarship for Privately Financed International Students; (b) Government Scholarship for Foreign Student; (c) Kokushikan University Scholarship for Foreign Student.
Open to: (a) (b) international students; (c) students with student visa.
Value: (a) 52,000 yen for undergraduates; 73,000 yen for graduates (b) 142,000 yen for undergraduate 184,000 yen for graduates; (c) 20,000, 50,000, 100,000 yen.
Applications: apply to Student Affairs, Welfare Office; deadlines: (a) April; (b) January; (c) mid-April, students not benefiting from other scholarships may apply for (c).

1345 Konan Women's University [KWU]
2-23, 6 Chome Morikita-machi
Higashinada-ku
658 Kobe-shi
Tel: +81-78-431-0391
Web: http://www.konan-wu.ac.jp

📖 Undergraduate, Graduate Programmes

Study Domains: English, French, Japanese, languages, literature and civilization, psychology, sociology.
Programmes: undergraduate, Master's and doctoral degree programmes in Japanese language and literature, English language and literature, French language and literature, psychology, sociology, education.
Open to: for undergraduate courses, certificate of secondary-school education; for Master's degree, a graduation certificate for 16 years of education or graduation from a Japanese university as a foreign student; for doctoral programmes, a Master's degree is required.
Fees: undergraduate: 1,030,000-1,330,000 yen; graduate: 287,000-487,000 yen.
Financial assistance: special scholarships for graduate foreign students (360,000 yen per year).
Applications: to the above address.

1346 Kumamoto Kenritsu Daigaku [KKD]
3-1-100, Tsukide
862-8502 Kumamoto
Tel: +81-96-383-2929
Fax: +81-96-384-6765
Web: http://www.pu-kumamoto.ac.jp
e-mail: rep-puk@pu-kumamoto.ac.jp

📖 Undergraduate and Graduate Degree Programmes

Study Domains: education, history, interior design, languages, liberal arts.
Programmes: Bachelor's; Master's; Ph.D. degrees.
Subjects: letters; environmental and symbiotic sciences; administration.
Fees: registration: 414,000 yen; tuition fees: 496,800 yen per year; living costs: 80,000 yen per month.
Financial assistance: only to enrolled students, depending on student's financial need.
Languages: Japanese.

1347 Kwassui Women's College
1-50 Higashi-yamate-machi
850-8 Nagasaki-shi
Tel: +81-95-820-6024
Fax: +81-95-820-6024
Web: http://www.kwassui.ac.jp
e-mail: intersec@kwassui.ac.jp

📖 Undergraduate, Graduate Programmes

Study Domains: English, health and hygiene, human sciences, Japanese, music and musicology, nutrition, preventive medicine.
Programmes: Graduate programmes in English literature and language; Faculty of Humanities; programmes in English; contemporary Japanese culture; human relations; music; music performance; applied music; Faculty of Wellness Studies: programmes in nutritional health; design and science for human life; child development and education.
Open to: international women students on an individual basis as general foreign students; as exchange students from universities with which we have a cooperative agreement; as short-term foreign students for one semester to one year; on two-to-four-week short study programmes.
Nationality: nationals of all countries.
Financial assistance: short-term exchange programmes.
Applications: see website for application details; or contact the International Student Exchange Center at the above address; intersec@kwassui.ac.jp.

☛ Short-Term Exchange Programme

Study Domains: all major fields.
Description: Short-Term Student Exchange Promotion Programme.
Open to: international women students accepted under student exchange agreement.

1348 Kyorin University (Kyorin Daigaku)
Mitaka Campus
6-20-2 Shinkawa
181-8611 Mitaka-shi, Tokyo
Tel: +81-422-44-0611
Fax: +81-422-44-0892
Web: http://www.kyorin-u.ac.jp
e-mail: koho@kyorin-u.ac.jp

☛ Tuition Fee Reduction

Study Domains: all major fields.
Scholarships: Tuition fee reduction (Jyugyoryo Genmen Seido).
Open to: new international students at university.
Value: 30% tuition fee reduction.
Applications: April and October.

1349 Kyoritsu International Foundation
6th Fl., Advance Building
4-7-7 Sotokanda
Chiyoda-ku
101 Tokyo
Tel: +81-3-5295-0205
Fax: +81-3-5295-0206
Web: http://www.kif-org.com

☛ Foreign Student Scholarships

Study Domains: all major fields.
Scholarships: Foreign Student Scholarships.
Open to: non-Japanese students from Asia enrolled in a Japanese school, having entered Japan on a student visa, who have not received another scholarship and who are at least in their first year of undergraduate studies.
Duration: 2 years.
Value: 100,000 yen plus domestic travel twice a year for training.
Languages: proficiency in Japanese language essential.
Applications: by the end of January to be submitted by Japanese school in which candidate is enrolled to the above address.

1350 Kyushu University
6-10-1 Hakozaki, Higashi-ku
812-8581 Fukuoka-shi
Tel: +81-92-642-2111
Web: http://www.kyushu-u.ac.jp

📖 Graduate Studies / Agriculture

Study Domains: agriculture, agronomic sciences, fisheries, forestry.
Programmes: Special Course on International

Development Research at graduate and postgraduate levels in agronomy, agricultural chemistry, forestry, technology of forest products, fisheries science, agricultural engineering, animal science, agricultural economic, food science and technology, genetic resources technology.
Open to: candidates of any nationality; under 33 years of age for Master's degree with Bachelor's degree and for Ph.D. under 35 with Master's degree, all requiring proficiency in English.
Duration: 2 to 3 years.
Fees: registration: 305,000 yen per year; tuition fee 441,600 yen per year for Master's degree; 375,600 yen per year for Ph.D.; living expenses: approximately 80,000 yen per month.
Financial assistance: possibility of Japanese government scholarship at a level of 185,500 yen per month.
Languages: instruction in English.
Applications: Faculty of Agriculture, Graduate School; 6-10-1, Hakozaki, Higashi-ku, Fukuoka 812-8581; tel: +8192 6422802; fax: +81 92 6422804; website: http://www.agr.kyushu-u.ac.jp/houtou/english/index.html.

📖 Graduate Studies / Law

Study Domains: business administration, economic and commercial sciences, international business, law.
Programmes: Special Course on LL.M. Programme for a Master's Degree in International Economic and Business Law.
Description: Japanese business law, international law and Japan, intellectual property law in Japan and abroad, transnational business law, international maritime law, law and economic development in Asia, matters of international trade, international economic and institutional law, Japanese corporate activities and trade conflicts overseas, international civil litigation, comparative civil law, introduction to public law in Japan, Japanese case law and practice, the practice of law in Japan.
Open to: candidates of any nationality holding a Bachelor's degree in law or equivalent from an accredited university with strong proficiency in English.
Duration: 1 year.
Fees: registration: 275,000 yen; tuition: 469,200 yen; living expenses: 80,000 yen per month.
Financial assistance: possibility of Japanese government scholarship.
Languages: Instruction in English.
Applications: Faculty of Law, University of Kyushu; at above address; website: http://www.law.kyushu-u.ac.jp.

1351 Matsumae International Foundation [MIF]
Tokai University Yoyogi Campus
2-28-4 Tomigaya, Shibuya-ku
151 Tokyo
Fax: +81-3-3301-7601
Web: http://www.mars.dti.ne.jp/~mif/

🐚 Undergraduate, Graduate Studies

Study Domains: arts, classical studies, engineering, medicine, natural sciences, social sciences.
Scholarships: Matsumae International Foundation Fellowships for studies in natural sciences, medicine and engineering are given top priority, followed by social sciences, humanities and arts.
Open to: candidates of all nationalities (except Japanese) who have a Doctorate degree or have a Master's degree and over 2 years' research experience, or who are recognized by the Screening Committee as possessing equivalent academic qualifications; applicants cannot be over 40 years of age and must not have already held another fellowship in Japan; applicants should preferably have firm positions and a commitment to return home for further study on completion of research work in Japan; age up to 40.
Place of study: any institutions and universities in Japan.
Duration: 3 to 6 months (not renewable).
Value: air transportation, lump sum of 300,000 yen upon arrival, research stipend of 150,000 yen per month, and personal accident and sickness insurance.
Languages: proficiency in English required.
Applications: forms available from the Office of the Foundation.

1352 Meikai University [MU]
1-1, Keyakidai
Sakado-shi,
350 0283 Saitama
Tel: +81-49-285-5511
Fax: +81-49-286-0294
Web: http://www.dent.meikai.ac.jp
e-mail: snomuka@dent.meikai.jp

📖 Undergraduate and Graduate Degree Programmes

Study Domains: Chinese, dentistry, economy, English, Japanese.
Programmes: Bachelor's; Master's degree programmes in Chinese; English; Japanese; economy; dentistry; real estate science.
Open to: high-school graduate and/or higher qualifications; Japanese language proficiency required.
Held: Dentistry school: Sakado campus; all other courses: Urayasu campus.
Duration: 4 years; 6 years for dentistry.
Fees: registration: 200,000 yen; tuition fees: 698,000 yen per year; living costs: 150,000 yen per month.
Financial assistance: tuition reduction of 30% for self-financing student; possibility of government or private organization scholarship.
Applications: apply to International Affairs Section at Urayasu campus by mid-April.

1353 Ministry of Education, Culture, Sports, Science and Technology (Monbukagakusho)
3-2-2 Kasumigaseki, Chiyoda-ku
Tokyo
Tel: +81-3-5253-4111
Web: http://www.mext.go.jp

🐚 Monbukagakusho Scholarships

Study Domains: all major fields, cultural studies, education, engineering, natural sciences, social sciences.
Scholarships: Japanese Government (Monbukagakusho) Scholarships for: (a) Professional Training School (Senshu-Gakko) Students; (b) Technical College Students; (c) Research Students; (d) In-service Training for Teachers; (e) Undergraduate Scholarships; (f) Japanese Studies Scholarships.
Subjects: (a) all major fields; (b) engineering (mechanical, electrical, electronics, etc.), mercantile marine; (c) humanities, social sciences and natural sciences; (d) education; (e) social sciences, humanities, natural sciences, Japanese language; (f) Japanese studies.
Open to: (a) and (b) citizens of Asian countries who have completed formal secondary education and gained admission to a university of their own country; age 17 to 21; (c) university college graduates under 35 years of age; applicants must be willing to study the Japanese language; (d) university or teacher-training college graduates, who have been in active teaching service for more than 5 years and who are willing to study Japanese; age under 35; (e) applicants who have completed formal secondary education and are eligible to enter university in their own country; applicants must be willing to study Japanese language; (f) candidates specialized in Japanese language or Japanese culture and who have completed at least 2 years of university; good knowledge of the Japanese language required; age 18 to 29.
Place of study: (a) at professional training schools in Japan; (b) at national technical colleges in Japan; (c) to (f) at universities in Japan.
Duration: (a) 2½ years (not renewable); (b) 3½ years, 4 years for students majoring in mercantile marine; (c) 1½ or 2 years (renewable); (d) 1½ years (not renewable); (e) 5 years; 7 years for students in medicine or dentistry; (f) 1 academic year (not renewable).
Value: (a), (b), (e) and (f) 141,500 yen per month and (c) and (d) 184,500 yen per month; plus 25,000 yen arrival allowance and transportation; tuition free.
Applications: (a), (b) and (d) by end of May; (c) by end of September; (e) and (f) no deadline; to the Japanese diplomatic mission in candidate's country.

1354 Moriya Foundation [MF]

c/o Teikoku-Shoin Co. Ltd.
3-29 Kanda-Jimbocho
Chiyoda-ku
101-0051 Tokyo
Tel: +81-3-3262-0834
Fax: +81-3-3262-7770
Web: http://www.teikokushoin.co.jp/

☞ Moriya Foundation Scholarships

Study Domains: education, geography, history, human sciences.
Scholarships: Moriya Foundation Scholarships.
Subjects: geography, history, education and other human sciences.
Open to: graduate school students in Japanese universities selected by the Moriya Foundation from South and East Asian countries; candidates must be under 35 years and recommended by their university; no language requirements.
Duration: 2 years.
Value: 70,000 yen per month.
Applications: from 1 to 30 April, to the Foreign Students Affairs Office of the university specified by the Moriya Foundation.

1355 Musashi Institute of Technology (Musashi Kogyo Daigaku)

1-28-1 Tamazutsumi
158-8557 Setagaya-ku, Tokyo
Tel: +81-3-3703-3111
Fax: +81-3-5707-2211
Web: http://www.musashi-tech.ac.jp
e-mail: webmaster@musashi-tech.ac.jp

☞ Tuition Reduction

Study Domains: all major fields.
Open to: privately financed international students enrolled at the university.
Value: 50% tuition reduction.
Applications: see homepage for full details: www.musashi-tech.ac.jp/ExamInfo/info6-E.html.

1356 Nagoya University of Foreign Studies (Nagoya Gaikokugo Daigaku)

57 Takenoyama
Iwasaki-cho
470-0197 Nisshin-shi, Aichi
Tel: +81-561-75-1756
Fax: +81-561-75-1757
Web: http://www-e.nufs.ac.jp
e-mail: na-info@ml.nakanishi.ac.jp

☞ Graduate, Postgraduate International Student Scholarships

Study Domains: cultural studies, education, English, French, humanities and arts, Japanese, social sciences.
Scholarships: NUFS Scholarship for Graduate and Postgraduate International Students.
Value: 50% tuition reduction for one term.
Applications: to Office of International Studies and Exchange; na-info@ml.nakanishi.ac.jp.

☞ Undergraduate International Student Scholarship

Study Domains: business administration, cultural studies, English, French, interpretation and translation, Japanese, journalism, tourism, hotel and catering management.
Scholarships: NUFS Scholarship for International Students.
Description: scholarship for international undergraduate students for studies in: foreign languages: Chinese, English, French, Japanese; contemporary international studies: English, translation and interpretation; accountancy, finance, management, marketing, business administration and commerce, journalism, tourism.
Value: 300,000 yen per year.
Applications: apply to the Office of International Studies and Exchange; na-info@ml.nakanishi.ac.jp.

1357 Nagoya University, Department of Civil Engineering

The Head, Foreign Student Office
Chikusa-ku, Furo-cho
464-8603 Nagoya
Tel: +81-52-789-4621
Fax: +81-52-789-4624/3738
Web: http://www.civil.nagoya-u.ac.jp/
e-mail: nakano@soil.genv.nagoya-u.ac.jp

📖 Doctorate / Civil Engineering

Study Domains: civil engineering.
Programmes: Civil Engineering special programme leading to a Doctor of Engineering Degree in civil engineering.
Open to: young engineers, mainly from developing countries eligible for Japanese Government awards, under 35 years of age, holding a Master's degree or equivalent.
Duration: 3 academic years.
Financial assistance: possibility of Japanese government scholarship.
Languages: instruction in English.
Applications: by 15 December to the Foreign Student Office at the above address.

1358 Nanzan University

18 Yamazato-cho Showa-ku
466-8 Nagoya
Tel: +81-52-832-3112
Fax: +81-52-833-6985
Web: http://www.nanzan-u.ac.jp
e-mail: n-somu@nanzan-u.ac.jp

☞ Scholarship

Study Domains: all major fields.
Scholarships: Nanzan University Scholarship.
Open to: All candidates with student visa.
Duration: 1 year, renewable.
Value: 150,000 to 300,000 yen per year.
Applications: By mid March, email: cie-office@nanzan.ac.jp.

1359 Nanzan University, Center for Japanese Studies [NU]

18 Yamazato-cho, Showa-ku
466-8673 Nagoya
Tel: +81-52-832-3123
Fax: +81-52-832-5490
Web: http://www.nanzan-u.ac.jp
e-mail: cjs@ic.nanza-nu.ac.jp

📖 Certificate Courses / Japanese Studies

Study Domains: Japanese, oriental studies.
Programmes: certificate courses in Japanese studies.
Description: intensive Japanese language instruction from beginning to advanced level aimed at establishing a solid foundation in the four language skills: speaking, reading, listening and writing.
Open to: all qualified students; at least 12 years of formal education; Cum. GPA of 3.0 on a 4.0 scale; proficient in English; strong recommendation; must be sufficiently proficient in English to be able to carry out routine tasks and understand instructions.
Duration: 1 academic year (9 months).
Fees: tuition fees: 680,000 yen; living costs: 540,000 yen per year.
Languages: Japanese and English.
Applications: 31 March for Fall semester; 31 August for Spring semester; courses run from September to May.

📖 Japanese Language

Study Domains: arts and crafts, business, business administration, cultural studies, economy, folklore, international business, international relations, international studies, Japanese, linguistics, literature and civilization, political science, social sciences, sociology, theology, religion.
Programmes: (a) Japanese language courses: introductory, elementary, pre-intermediate, intermediate, pre-advanced, advanced; (b) lecture courses in Japanese area studies: business, history, literature, politics, culture, religion, folklore, economy; (c) seminars: elementary and intermediate

translation, classical Japanese, social science, Japanese literature; (d) Japanese arts courses: flower arrangement, calligraphy, woodblock printing, Chinese black ink painting; (e) open courses offered by other departments allowing CJS students to attend classes with Japanese students: language acquisition, intercultural communication, international financial management, financial accounting, international marketing.
Subjects: Japanese language, literature, arts and crafts, business, linguistics, communications, international relations.
Open to: candidates of all nationalities having completed 12 years of high school education or equivalent and eligible for entry into a university, with good academic record.
Duration: 2 semesters or 1 year.
Fees: tuition fees: 680,000 yen per year; living costs: 540,000 yen per year.
Financial assistance: possibility of scholarships of approximately 150,000 or 300,000 yen scholarships.
Applications: 31 March for Fall semester; 31 August for Spring semester; to the Centre for Japanese Studies.

☛ Hirschmeier / Tomonokai Scholarship

Study Domains: Japanese.
Description: offered by institution for Japanese language study.
Open to: open to all CJS students; excellent academic achievement and financial need.
Duration: on a semester basis; can be renewed.
Value: 300,000 yen or 150,000 yen.
Applications: must be enrolled at time of application; apply in March for fall semester and November for spring semester; enquire at: cjs@ic.nanzan-u.ac.jp.

1360 Nara Institute of Science and Technology [NIST]

8916-5 Takayama,
Ikoma,
630-0101 Nara
Tel: +81-743-72-5937
Fax: +81-743-72-5939
Web: http://www.aist-nara.ac.jp
e-mail: intc@ad.aist-nara.ac.jp

▭ Graduate Degree Programmes

Study Domains: cancerology, engineering, pharmacy and pharmacology, sciences.
Programmes: Master's and Ph.D. degrees.
Description: Master's programmes: in information science, biological science, material science, engineering; Ph.D. in: information science, biological science, material science, engineering; and research; and auditor.
Open to: Japanese proficiency required (Biological science; Materials science).
Duration: 2 to 3 years beginning in April (or October for specific programmes).
Languages: Japanese or English.
Applications: apply to: Student Affairs Division; consult each school for individual deadline.

1361 Nara University (Nara Daigaku)

1500 Misasagi-cho
631-8502 Nara-shi, Nara-ken
Tel: +81-742-44-1251
Fax: +81-742-41-0650
Web: http://www.nara-u.ac.jp
e-mail: somu@aogaki.nara-u.ac.jp

☛ Tuition Reduction

Study Domains: all major fields.
Open to: international students enrolled at university in 'Study Abroad' programmes or self-financed, based on merit and scholastic results.
Value: 50% tuition reduction.

1362 Nara Women's University (Nara Joshi Daigaku)

Kitawoyahigashi-machi
630-8506 Nara-shi, Nara
Tel: +81-742-20-3204
Web: http://www.nara-wu.ac.jp
e-mail: ryugakusei@cc.nara-wu.ac.jp

☛ International Relations Fund Scholarship

Study Domains: all major fields.
Value: 40,000 yen.
Applications: contact Foreign Student Section at above address; email: ryugakusei@cc.nara-wu.ac.jp.

1363 Naruto University of Education [NUE]

748, Aza-Nakajima, Takashima,
Naruto-cho, Naruto, Tokushima 772 8502
Fax: +81-88-687-6138
Web: http://www.naruto-u.ac.jp/nyushi/jimunyuidx6.htm

▭ Teacher Training Degrees

Study Domains: teacher education.
Programmes: graduate school in teacher training for elementary and secondary level.
Open to: foreign and local students.

1364 Nihon University

4-8-24 Kudan-Minami Chiyoda-ku
102-8 Tokyo
Tel: +81-35-275-8116
Fax: +81-35-275-8315
Web: http://www.nihon-u.ac.jp
e-mail: intldiv@adm.nihon-u.ac.jp

▭ Undergraduate, Graduate, Postgraduate Programmes

Study Domains: arts, business, dentistry, economic and commercial sciences, engineering, industrial technology, international relations, law, medicine, sciences, technology.
Programmes: Degree programmes at the following colleges and schools: College of Law, College of Humanities and Sciences, College of Economics, College of Commerce, College of Art, College of International Relations, College of Science and Technology, College of Industrial Technology, College of Engineering, School of Medicine, School of Dentistry, School of Dentistry at Matsudo, College of Bioresource Sciences, College of Pharmacy.
Applications: see wesite for full details.

1365 Notre Dame Seishin University [NDSU]

2-16-9 Ifukucho
700 Okayama
Tel: +81-86-252-1486
Fax: +81-86-252-9080
Web: http://www.ndsu-e.ed.jp/
e-mail: seishin-hp@ndsu-e.ed.jp

▭ Undergraduate, Graduate Programmes

Study Domains: dietetics, early childhood education, languages, linguistics, literature and civilization, nutrition, teacher education.
Programmes: (a) Bachelor of Arts; (b) Master of Literature; (c) Master of Arts; (d) Doctor of Literature; (e) Teacher's License: Junior and Senior High School, Kindergarten, Elementary School, Dietician.
Description: subjects include dietetics, early childhood education, home economics, human living sciences, languages, linguistics, literature, nutrition.
Open to: women students of foreign nationality, at least 18 years of age, with secondary-school certificate or equivalent.
Duration: (a) 4 years.
Fees: (approximate figures): registration: 40,000 yen; tuition: 530,000 yen; living expenses: 100,000 yen per month; equipment, administration, laboratory fees: 300,000 per year.
Financial assistance: some scholarships for foreign students available.
Languages: Instruction in Japanese.
Applications: by early December to Admissions Office.

🎓 **NDSU Scholarships for Women**

Study Domains: English, home economics, Japanese, languages, literature and civilization, nutrition, paediatrics.
Scholarships: NDSU Scholarships for foreign students.
Description: Whole Departments (English language and literature, Japanese language and literature, home economics, child welfare, food and human nutrition).
Open to: women candidates who have been accepted as students of Notre Dame Seishin University.
Duration: 1 year (renewable).
Value: covers full or partial tuition.
Applications: by April, to the Student Affairs Office.

1366 Okayama University of Science (Okayama Rika Daigaku)

1-1 Ridai-cho
700-0005 Okayama-shi, Okayama
Tel: +81-86-252-3161
Fax: +81-86-254-8434
Web: http://www.ous.ac.jp /
http://okaridai.ous.ac.jp/english/
e-mail: otsuki@edu.kake.ac.jp

🎓 **International Student Scholarship**

Study Domains: all major fields.
Open to: international students with good academic results living in student housing.
Duration: 4 years.
Value: 20,000 yen per month.
Applications: enrolled international students with GPA equivalent to or over 2.0.; contact the OUS Admissions or Foreign Student Affairs Office at above address.

1367 Okazaki Kaheita International Scholarship Foundation [OKISF]

Terminal Building (Big Bird) 5F
3-3-2, Haneda-Kuko, Ota-ku
144-0041 Tokyo
Tel: +81-3-5757-4101
Fax: +81-3-5757-4103
Web: http://www.ananet.or.jp/okazaki/
e-mail: oscholar@ananet.or.jp

🎓 **Okazaki Kaheita International Scholarships**

Study Domains: all major fields.
Scholarships: The Okazaki Kaheita International Scholarship awarded annually.
Subjects: all subjects except medicine, dentistry and veterinary science.
Open to: graduates of universities designated by the Foundation, from China, Thailand, Malaysia, the Philippines, Indonesia and Viet Nam; age under 30 years; candidates must be able to understand graduate level lectures and read textbooks in Japanese or English; applicants not fluent in Japanese are required to attend Japanese language courses for 6 months prior to coming to Japan.
Place of study: any graduate school in Japan.
Duration: 3 years (not renewable).
Value: 120,000 yen per month; admission and tuition fees; round-trip air ticket; domestic transportation costs; free dormitory accommodation.
Applications: by 31 March, to the Foundation Office in Tokyo through universities nominated by the Foundation.

1368 Okinawa International University [OIU]

2-6-1 Ginowan
901-2 Ginowan-shi
Tel: +81-98-892-1111
Fax: +81-98-893-3273
Web: http://www.okiu.ac.jp
e-mail: genchr@okiu.ac.jp

🎓 **Scholarship**

Study Domains: all major fields.
Scholarships: Honors Scholarship.
Duration: 1 year, non-renewable.
Value: 52,000 yen.
Applications: By May; email: kmiyagi@okiu.ac.jp.

1369 Osaka Institute of Technology [OIT]

5-16-1 Omiya,
Asashi-ku
Osaka 535-8585
Tel: +81-6-6954-4097
Fax: +81-6-6953-9496
Web: http://www.oit.ac.jp
e-mail: shomu@ofc.oit.ac.jp

📖 **Undergraduate, Graduate Programmes**

Study Domains: architecture, chemical engineering, civil engineering, computer science, electricity and electronics, engineering, industrial technology, mechanical engineering, telecommunications.
Programmes: Bachelor's and Master's degree programmes.
Financial assistance: work opportunities available for foreign students; see employment services.
Applications: entrance exam: late October or late February.

🎓 **Osaka Institute of Technology Award for Foreign Student**

Study Domains: engineering, sciences, technology.
Scholarships: Osaka Institute of Technology Award for Foreign Students.
Open to: see website for eligibility requirements; some students who are already funded may not be eligible.
Duration: renewable every year.
Value: 20,000 yen per month; 10,000 yen per month for students living in OIT's residential facilities.
Applications: by April; for further information contact: gakusei@ofc.oit.ac.jp.

1370 Osaka University [OU]

1-1 Yamadaoka, Suita
Osaka 565-0871
Tel: +81-6-6879-7103
Fax: +81- 6-6879-7106
Web: http://www.osaka-u.ac.jp
e-mail: kenkyuryugakuryugaku@ns.osaka-u.ac.jp

📖 **Undergraduate, Graduate Programmes**

Study Domains: microbiology.
Programmes: Bachelor's, Master's, Ph.D. degrees and research student course.
Open to: young scientists of Asian Member States of UNESCO who have a university degree in general and/or applied microbiology and at least 1 year's experience in teaching and/or in a related field (postgraduate work included); English language proficiency required; age under 35.
Held: International Center for Biotechnology, Faculty of Engineering, Osaka University.
Duration: 1 year; courses begin in October.
Fees: tuition free.
Applications: apply to International Student Division.

🎓 **Student Awards**

Study Domains: all major fields.
Value: some awards covering monthly stipend of 184,000 yen, tourist-class round-trip air fare, lump sum of 25,000 yen on arrival.
Applications: by 31 May, to the Secretary-General, Office of the UNESCO Course, c/o Administration Bureau, Osaka University.

1371 Osaka University of Commerce

4-1-10 Mikuriya Sakae-machi Higashiosaka-shi
577-8 Osaka
Tel: +81-6-6781-0381
Web: http://www.daishodai.ac.jp

🎓 **Financial aid**

Study Domains: all major fields.
Duration: 1 year, renewable.
Value: tuition fee reduction of 30 %.
Applications: by March, contact the Student Affairs Office, tel: +81(6) 6782-2297.

1372 Ritsumeikan Asia Pacific University [APU]

1-1 Jumonjibaru
874-8 Beppu
Tel: +81-977-78-1119
Fax: +81-977-78-1121
Web: http://www.apu.ac.jp
e-mail: welcome@apu.ac.jp

☛Scholarship

Scholarships: (a) APU Scholarship Program;
(b) APU Scholarship Program - Special Scholarship.
Open to: (a) candidates of any countries;
(b) candidates of any countries.
Duration: (a) 4 years.
Value: (a) 35 to 100% of full tuition;
(b) 100% tuition waiver; living expenses, 1,000,000 yen per year.
Applications: (a) by September for April admission; by March for September admission; contact welcome@apu.ac.jp for further details;
(b) by September for April admission; by March for September admission; contact welcome@apu.ac.jp for further details.

1373 Rotary Yoneyama Memorial Foundation, Inc. [RYMFI]

8th Floor, ABC Building
2-6-3, Shibakoen, Minato-ku
105 Tokyo
Tel: +81-3-3435-1828
Fax: +81-3-3578-8281
Web: http://www.rotary-yoneyama.or.jp/english/

☛Rotary Yoneyama Scholarships

Study Domains: all major fields.
Scholarships: Rotary Yoneyama Scholarships.
Open to: non-Japanese students, mainly Asian, who have entered Japan on a student visa to study and who have not yet received a doctorate; applicants must be enrolled in an undergraduate or graduate capacity (regular Master's or Doctorate), at certain Japanese colleges or universities; Japanese language proficiency required; age under 40.
Place of study: any country with Rotary Clubs.
Duration: 1 to 2 academic years (not renewable).
Value: 120,000 to 150,000 yen per month.
Applications: from 1 to 15 October, to the above address.

1374 Ryukoku University [RU]

International Center
67 Tsukamoto-cho, Fukakusa
Fushimi-ku
612-8577 Kyoto-shi
Tel: +81-75-645-7898
Fax: +81-75-645-2020
Web: http://www.ryukoku.ac.jp
e-mail: ric@rnoc.fks.ryukoku.ac.jp

▦ Japanese Culture and Language

Study Domains: cultural studies, Japanese, languages.
Programmes: Japanese Culture and Language Programme: elementary, intermediate and advanced Japanese, Japanese religion, history, philosophy, Buddhism, economics, etc.
Open to: applicants having completed 12 years of formal education, or having graduated from an institution recognized by the Ministry of Education as equivalent to a senior secondary school, or able to demonstrate scholastic abilities judged by the University to be equivalent to those achieved at a Japanese senior secondary school.
Duration: 1 academic year; courses begin in April and October.
Fees: application: 35,000 yen; admission: 50,000 yen; tuition: 487,000 yen.
Applications: by October and May, to Japanese Culture and Language Program, at the above address.

1375 Sagawa Scholarship Foundation [SSF]

678 Ohmandokoro-cho, Bukkojisagaru
Karasuma-dori, Shimogyo ku
600-8413 Kyoto
Tel: +81-75-371-0818
Fax: +81-75-344-2818
e-mail: scholars@head.sagawa-exp.co.jp

☛Sagawa Scholarships

Study Domains: all major fields.
Scholarships: Sagawa Scholarship for foreign students.
Open to: applicants from South-East Asian countries, in financial need and not already recipients of government or other organizations grants in Japan or abroad; enrolled in university at 3rd year level or in graduate school at 2nd year level of Ph.D. courses; age under 27 years for undergraduates, under 35 years for graduates.
Place of study: universities and graduate schools in Japan.
Duration: 2 years maximum.
Value: 100,000 yen per month.
Applications: from 1 February to 16 April, through the University at the above address.

1376 Sakaguchi International Scholarship Foundation [SISF]

1-12-2 Sotokanda
Chiyoda-Ku
101 Tokyo
Tel: +81-3-3257-1951

☛Sakaguchi Scholarships

Study Domains: all major fields.
Scholarships: Sakaguchi Scholarships.
Subjects: all major fields.
Open to: candidates of any country, with good academic record, studying at one of the universities or graduate schools specified by the Foundation and with a recommendation by the president of their Japanese university; age under 30 for undergraduates, under 35 for postgraduates; proficiency in Japanese required; candidates must return to their country after graduation.
Duration: 2 years.
Value: 80,000 yen per month.
Applications: from 15 October to 15 December.

1377 Seikei University [SU]

3-3-1 Kichijoji Kitamachi,
Musashina-shi
180-8633 Tokyo
Tel: +81-422-37-3536
Fax: +81-422-37-3865
Web: http://www.seikei.ac.jp/index-e.html
e-mail: cle@jim.seikei.ac.jp

▦ Undergraduate, Graduate Programmes

Study Domains: chemical engineering, cultural studies, economy, electricity and electronics, industrial technology, journalism, literature and civilization, management, mechanical engineering, political science, sciences, sociology.
Programmes: (a) Bachelor's; Master's; Ph.D.; (b) non-credit language courses.
Subjects: Japanese language study, literature, cultural studies, economy, journalism, management, political science, sociology, physics, chemical engineering, electricity and electronics, industrial technology, mechanical engineering.
Duration: 12 months for language courses; 4 years for undergraduate programmes.
Fees: (a) registration: 300,000 yen; tuition: 870,000 yen;
(b) 50,000 yen per subject.
Financial assistance: 30 to 50% deduction of tuition fees for full-time students in undergraduate and graduate level programmes.
Languages: Japanese.
Applications: apply by mid-February for language courses; mid-February and October for degree courses; contact Admissions Office for further details; email: nyushi@jim.seikei.ac.jp.

🎓 Scholarships

Study Domains: all major fields.
Description: a number of scholarships are available by the university, the Ministry of Education, Science, Sports and Culture, and the private sector.

1378 Seitoku University

550 Iwase
271-8555 Matsudo-shi Chiba
Tel: +81-47-365-1111
Fax: +81-47-363-1401
Web: http://www.seitoku.ac.jp
e-mail: kikaku@seitoku.ac.jp

🎓 Kawanami Scholarship

Study Domains: arts, education, humanities and arts.
Open to: self-financed enrolled international student with outstanding scholastic results.
Value: 30,000 Yen.
Applications: mid-June and mid-November; check website for exact dates; contact: kolcusai@seitoku.ac.jp.

1379 Shibaura Institute of Technology [SIT]

3-9-14 Shibaura,
Minato-ku
108-8548 Tokyo
Tel: +81-3-5476-3127
Fax: +81-3-5476-2949
Web: http://www.shibaura-it.ac.jp/kokusai
e-mail: kokusai@ow.shibaura-it.ac.jp

📖 Undergraduate, Graduate Programmes

Study Domains: architecture, building industry, civil engineering, community development, electricity and electronics, energy, engineering, mechanical engineering, physics, sciences, telecommunications.
Description: Bachelor's, Master's degree programmes.
Held: Shibaura campus (Tokyo); Ohmiya campus (Saitama).
Duration: 4 years.
Fees: tuition: 1,680,000 yen.

🎓 International Undergraduate Students

Study Domains: all major fields.
Scholarships: SIT Scholarships for international undergraduate students.
Open to: international students with financial difficulties.
Value: half-tuition waiver for first year.
Applications: at any time to the Centre for Student Affairs.

1380 Shimane University, Graduate School of Agriculture [SU]

1060 Nishikawatsu
690 Matsue
Tel: +81-852-32-6120
Web: http://agricul.life.shimane-u.ac.jp/~life/eng/index.html
e-mail: kouhou@life.shimane-u.ac.jp

📖 Graduate Programme / Agriculture

Study Domains: agriculture, agronomic sciences, biochemistry, ecology, environment, horticulture, microbiology, rural development.
Programmes: graduate course in earth and geo-environmental science: agro-forest biology, regional development, natural resource science.
Open to: applicants of any nationality from Asia and the Pacific rim, under 34 years, holding a B.Agr. or B.Sc. degree; at least 16 years of formal education outside Japan or equivalent qualifications. Before applying, candidates must contact one Shimane professor who will be acting as supervisor for their research project.
Duration: 2 years; courses begin in October.
Fees: entrance examination fee: 30,000 yen; admission: 275,000 yen; tuition: 234,600 yen per semester; 469,200 yen per year; insurance, 2,100 yen (for 2 years).
Financial assistance: Japanese Government scholarships available; value of 184,500 yen monthly.
Languages: instruction in English.
Applications: to the above address.

1381 Shundoh International Foundation [SIF]

2-17-3 Shibuya
Shibuya-ku
150-8320 Tokyo
Tel: +81-3-3407-8579
Fax: +81-3-3201-5390

🎓 Shundoh International Scholarships

Study Domains: accounting, international studies.
Scholarships: Shundoh International Scholarship; awarded annually.
Open to: applicants with a superior academic record, enrolled in one of the above universities as a graduate student; proficiency in Japanese required.
Place of study: in Japanese universities: Tohoku, Tokyo, Tskuba, Tokyo Institute of Technology, Osaka, Kyoto, Waseda, Keio, Aoyama, International University of Japan, Sophia.
Duration: 2 years (not renewable).
Value: 100,000 yen per month.
Applications: by 31 March to the above address.

1382 Sophia University

7-1 Kioicho, Chiyoda-ku
102-8 Tokyo
Tel: +81-33-238-3111
Fax: +81-33-238-3885
Web: http://www.sophia.ac.jp

🎓 Scholarship

Study Domains: all major fields.
Scholarships: (a) Sophia Type I Scholarship;
(b) Tuition Fee Waivers for foreign students;
(c) Sophia Type III Scholarship.
Duration: (a) 1 year, renewable; (b) 1 year, renewable; (c) 1 year, renewable.
Value: (a) 70,000 yen per year (book coupons);
(b) 30 % of tuition fees;.
Applications: (a) Awarded to students with high academic performance; see http://www.sophia.ac.jp for further details; (b) students with financial need showing high academic performance; (c) see http://www.sophia.ac.jp for further details.

1383 Taisho University [TU]

3-20-1 Nishisugame,
Toshima-ku,
Tokyo
Tel: +81-3-3918-7311
Fax: +81-3-5394-3037
Web: http://www.tais.ac.jp
e-mail: ryugaku@mail.tais.ac.jp

📖 Japanese Language Course

Study Domains: education, geology, humanities and arts, languages, psychiatry, psychology, public relations, social sciences, social work, speech therapy, statistics, theology, religion.
Programmes: certificate in the special course in Japanese language.
Description: certificate.
Open to: candidates holding a high-school degree or equivalent; basic level of Japanese language proficiency required.
Fees: registration: 10,000 yen; tuition: 600,000 yen.
Financial assistance: no financial assistance offered.
Applications: apply by March.

1384 Takaku Foundation [TF]

4-17-4 Nishi-Azabu
Minato-Ku
106-0031 Tokyo
Tel: +81-3-5485-6080
Fax: +81-3-5485-6080
Web: http://www.takaku-foundation.com
e-mail: fvgg5180@mb.infoweb.ne.jp

🎓 Takaku Scholarships

Study Domains: human sciences, natural sciences, social sciences.
Scholarships: Scholarships for Foreign Students.

Subjects: any field.
Open to: students from any country, above their junior year for undergraduates or postgraduates except for seniors in a Master's course; Japanese language ability required.
Place of study: in universities and graduate schools in Japan.
Duration: 1 year.
Value: junior/senior undergraduates, 70,000 yen per month; postgraduates, 100,000 yen per month.
Applications: between November and December, to the above address.

1385   Takushoku University [TU]

4-14 Kohinata, 3-Chome, Bunkyo-ku
112 Tokyo
Tel: +81-3-3947-2261
Fax: +81-3-3947-5333
Web: http://www.takushoku-u.ac.jp
e-mail: web_int@ofc.takushoku-u.ac.jp

📖 Graduate Studies

Study Domains: economic and commercial sciences, education, engineering.
Programmes: (a) Master's programme; (b) Doctorate programme at the Graduate School of Economics, the Graduate School of Commerce, the Graduate School of Engineering and the Graduate School of Language Education.
Duration: (a) 2 years; (b) 3 years.
Applications: to Foreign Students Section, International Department.

1386   Toho Gakuen School of Music [TGSOM]

1-41-1 Wakaba-cho, Chofu-shi
182 Tokyo
Tel: +81-3 3307-4101
Fax: +81-3-3307-4354
Web: http://www.tohomusic.ac.jp

📖 Diploma Courses in Music

Study Domains: music and musicology.
Programmes: (a) Bachelor's course; (b) Diploma course; (c) Research course; (d) Special Students System: piano, strings, wind and other orchestral instruments, voice, conducting, composition, musicology.
Open to: candidates of any country on successful completion of entrance examination; over 18 years of age.
Duration: (a) 4 to 6 years; (b) 3 to 7 years; (c) 1 to 2 years; courses begin in April; (d) variable.
Languages: instruction in Japanese (partly in English).
Applications: by 1 February, to the Registration Office, at the above address.

1387   Tokai University (Tokai Daigaku)

1117 Kitakaname, Hiratsuka
259-1292 Kanagawa
Tel: +81-463-58-1211
Web: http://www.u-tokai.ac.jp
e-mail: info@tsc.u-tokai.ac.jp

📣 Undergraduate, Graduate Scholarships

Study Domains: all major fields.
Scholarships: undergraduate programmes: (a) Special Foreign Student Scholarship; (b) Foreign Student Scholarship; (c) Shigeyoshi Matsumae Scholarship for Foreign Students; (d) undergraduate and graduate studies, Tuition Support Scholarship for Foreign Students.
Open to: candidates of all nationalities meeting academic and financial requirements.
Duration: 1 academic year.
Value: (a) tuition and administrative fees; (b) 30,000 yen for books; 30,000 yen monthly grant (39,000 yen per academic year); (c) 70% tuition reduction; (d) 30% tuition reduction.
Applications: (a), (b), (c) selection is made automatically by university according to personal merit and scholastic results; (d) by November; contact International Exchange Department at above address.

1388   Tokushukai Scholarship Foundation [YSF]

6th floor, Shiozaki Building
2-7-1 Hirakawa-cho, Chiyodaku
102-0093 Tokyo
Tel: +81-3-3238-2913
Fax: +81-3-3238-2914
Web: http://www.tokushukai.org
e-mail: zaidan@tokushukai.org

📣 Tokushukai Scholarships

Study Domains: all major fields.
Scholarships: Tokushukai Scholarship.
Subjects: all subjects except medicine, dentistry and veterinary science.
Place of study: in Japanese universities.
Duration: undergraduates, up to 4 years; Master's, up to 2 years; Doctorate, up to 3 years; special cases, up to 1 year.
Value: variable.
Applications: by 15 December to the above address.

1389   Tokyo Institute of Technology (Tokyo Tech)

2-12-1 O-okayama, Meguro-ku
152 Tokyo
Tel: +81-3-5734-3027
Fax: +81-3-5734-3677
Web: http://www.titech.ac.jp
e-mail: ryugakusei@jim.titech.ac.jp

📖 Undergraduate, Graduate Programmes / Science

Study Domains: architecture, building industry, chemical engineering, chemical industry, chemistry, civil engineering, computer science, electricity and electronics, energy, engineering, hydraulics, hydrology.
Programmes: (a) undergraduate programmes offered at the following Schools: Science, Engineering, Bioscience and Biotechnology; (b) graduate programmes offered at the following Graduate Schools: Science and Engineering, Bioscience and Biotechnology, Interdisciplinary Graduate School of Science and Engineering, Information Science and Engineering, Decision Science and Technology, Innovation Management.
Open to: (a) students with secondary-school diploma or recognized equivalent; (b) students with a bachelor's degree or recognized equivalent; Japanese language proficiency test; English proficiency required.
Duration: (a) 4 years; (b) Master's programme: 2 years; doctoral programme: 3 years.
Fees: for privately financed international students: admission: 282,000; tuition: 535,800 yen per year; application: undergraduates: 17,000 yen; graduates: 30,000 yen.
Financial assistance: fellowship for research in chemistry and chemical engineering available; information from the International Affairs Section, Research Cooperation Division.
Languages: Instruction in Japanese or English.
Applications: by December for spring term; July for fall term; to the Foreign Student Office, Tokyo Institute of Technology; both at the above address; tel: +81-3-5734-3027; fax: +81-3-5734-3677.

📣 Water Resources Management and Environment

Study Domains: biochemistry, biophysics, chemical engineering, chemistry, civil engineering, computer science, ecology, environment, electricity and electronics, engineering, hydraulics, hydrology.
Scholarships: UNESCO International Research Course for the Environment.
Description: The programme aims to provide the opportunity to experience various methodologies for research activities in the field of Water Resources Management and Environment as well as contribute to capacity building in education in their own countries.
Open to: young scientists who are on staff at a university or research institution, mainly in the Asian and Pacific regions; with good command of English.
Age limit Max: under 36 years of age on 1 October of the year the course is commenced;.

Duration: 1 year (non-renewable).
Value: 175,000 yen, with additional 30,000 yen upon arrival and a roundtrip air ticket from the nearest international airport of the participant's residence to Tokyo.
Languages: English; Japanese useful.
Applications: by 1 May (for entry to the course in October of the same year); to the International Affairs Section, Research Cooperation Division, at the address above; tel: +81-3-5734-7692; fax: +81-3-5734-3685; web: http://www.iad.titech.ac.jp.

1390 Tokyo Keizai University [TKU]
7 Minami-cho 1-chome
Kokubunji
185 Tokyo
Tel: +81-42-328-7775
Fax: +81-42-328-7769
Web: http://www.tku.ac.jp

Undergraduate, Graduate Programmes

Study Domains: business, business administration, communication, economy, law.
Programmes: Bachelor's, Master's, Ph.D. degree programmes.
Description: (a) Bachelor of Arts (economics); (b) Bachelor of Communication Studies; (c) Bachelor of Arts (Marketing and Distribution); (d) Master of Economics; (e) Master of Business Administration; (f) Master of Communication Studies; (g) Doctor of Economics; (h) Doctor of Business Administration; (i) Doctor of Communication Studies.
Open to: candidates of all nationalities with high scholastic performance; good command of Japanese language; no age limit.
Duration: 2, 3, 4 years; varies with programme.
Fees: registration fee: 250,000 yen; tuition: 526,000-742,000 yen; living expenses: 120,000 yen per month; facilities and equipment fee: 160,000-220,000 yen per year.
Financial assistance: tuition fees reduced by 30% or full exemption; some scholarships available.
Applications: by early November for undergraduate programmes; by October for Master's programmes; by February for doctoral programmes.

1391 Tokyo University of Science [TUS]
1-3 Kagurazaka Shinjuku-ku
162-8 Tokyo
Tel: +81-3-3260-4271
Fax: +81-3-3260-4370
Web: http://www.tus.ac.jp
e-mail: intlexchg@admin.tus.ac.jp

Financial aid

Study Domains: all major fields.
Subjects: Architecture and planning, business administration, engineering, health sciences, information sciences, mathematics and computer science, natural sciences.
Duration: 6 months.
Value: 357,000 to 542,500 yen reduction on tuition fees.
Applications: By beginning of June; email: takasaki-yukiko@admin.tus.ac.jp.

1392 Tokyo Woman's Christian University (Tokyo Joshi Daigaku) [TWCU]
2-6-1 Zempukuji
Suginami-ku
167-8585 Tokyo
Tel: +81-3-5382-6279
Fax: +81-3-3301-0473
Web: http://www.twcu.ac.jp
e-mail: ohta@office.twcu.ac.jp

Foreign Scholarships

Study Domains: American studies, economy, English, history, Japanese, languages, mathematics, philosophy, psychology, sociology.
Scholarships: Tokyo Woman's Christian University Foreign Scholarship.
Description: within the College of Arts and Sciences, College of Culture and Communication and the Graduate School.
Open to: foreign students admitted to Tokyo Woman's Christian University, in financial need with excellent academic records and good personalities; the scholarship is not awarded concurrently with scholarships from other institutions; students are required to have sufficient knowledge of Japanese to pursue academic studies in Japanese.
Duration: 1 year.
Value: covers tuition and fees.
Applications: together with admission applications, to the Registrar's Office, at the above address.

1393 Tokyu Foundation for Inbound Students
1-21-2 Dogenzaka, Shibuya-ku
150-0043 Tokyo
Tel: +81-3-3461-0844
Fax: +81-3-5458-1696
Web: http://www.tokyu-f.jp
e-mail: info@tokyu-f.jp

Tokyu Foundation Scholarships

Study Domains: all major fields.
Scholarships: Tokyu Foundation Scholarships.
Subjects: all major fields.
Open to: nationals of countries in the Asia/Pacific regions who are enrolled in Japanese graduate schools and their affiliated research institutes; Japanese language proficiency required; age under 30 for Master's Programme, under 35 for Ph.D.
Place of study: Japan.
Duration: 2 years (renewable for 1 year).
Value: 160,000 yen per month, plus medical fees, etc.
Applications: by 15 November, to the above address.

1394 Toyama University (Toyama Daigaku)
3190 Gofuku
930-8555 Toyama-shi, Toyama
Tel: +81-76-445-6082
Fax: +81-76-445-6104 / 6093
Web: http://www.toyama-u.ac.jp
e-mail: ryugaku@adm.toyama-u.ac.jp

Non-Degree Studies

Study Domains: education, engineering, fine arts, humanities and arts, mathematics, natural sciences.
Open to: non-degree students within university exchange programme.
Duration: 1 year.
Value: 50,000 yen per month.
Applications: February; to Toyama University International Exchange Section.

1395 Tsuji Asia Scholarship Foundation [TASF]
1-6-1 Osaki, Shinagawa-Ku
141-8603 Tokyo
Tel: +81-3-3779-8193
Web: http://www.tsujiasia.or.jp
e-mail: info@tsujiasia.or.jp

Tsuji Asia Scholarship

Study Domains: all major fields.
Scholarships: Tsuji Asia Scholarship.
Open to: students from other Asian countries in need of financial support in their third or fourth undergraduate year or in graduate courses and who are selected by their universities; fair knowledge of Japanese required, no age limit.
Duration: 2 years (not renewable).
Value: 100,000 yen per month.
Applications: by end of March, to the above address, through applicant's university.

1396 University of Fukui

3-9-1 Bunkyo
910-8 Fukui-shi
Tel: +81-776-23-0500
Fax: +81-776-27-8518
Web: http://www.fukui-u.ac.jp

📖 Undergraduate, Graduate and Postgraduate Programmes

Study Domains: education, engineering, medicine, special education.
Programmes: undergraduate and graduate degrees in education; medical sciences, engineering; non-degree certificate programme in special education; doctoral programmes in medical sciences and engineering.
Open to: candidates of all nationalities meeting academic and financial requirements.

1397 University of Tokushima

2-24 Shinkura-cho
770-8 Tokushima-shi
Tel: +81-886-56-7000
Fax: +81-886-56-7012
Web: http://www.tokushima-u.ac.jp

🐝 University Scholarship

Study Domains: all major fields.
Open to: candidates of all nationalities.
Other conditions: should not be receiving more than 50,000 yen monthly from other organizations.
Duration: 1 year.
Value: 30,000 yen.
Applications: early April; contact ryugakur@jim.tokushima-u.ac.jp.

1398 University of Tokyo [UOT]

7-3-1 Hongo, Bunkyo-ku
113-8654 Tokyo
Tel: +81-3812-2111
Web: http://www.u-tokyo.ac.jp

📖 Graduate Programmes / Engineering

Study Domains: applied sciences, civil engineering, community development, development studies, ecology, environment, engineering, hydrology, rural development.
Programmes: (a) International Graduate Programme of Civil Engineering: Master's and Ph.D. degrees in civil engineering; (b) Master's and doctoral programme in urban engineering: urban planning, urban design, urban analysis, prevention of desertification, environmental engineering, water environment and water supply system, wastewater treatment and management.
Open to: applicants of all nationalities, holding the equivalent of a Bachelor's degree for Master's programme or Master's degree for Ph.D. programme; under 35 years of age.
Duration: (a) M.Eng.: 2 years; D.Eng.: 3 years; (b) Master's: 2 years; Doctorate: 3 years; courses begin in April or October.
Fees: tuition: (a) Master's course, 469,200 yen per year; Ph.D. course, 447,600 yen per year; (b) free tuition; living expenses 100,000 yen to 150,000 yen per month.
Financial assistance: (a) possibility of Japanese government scholarships; Asian Development Bank (ADB) scholarships; Inter-American Development Bank scholarships; (b) scholarships consisting of a monthly allowance of 184,500 yen plus a round-trip ticket to Japan.
Languages: instruction in English.
Applications: by (a) 31 December if candidate is applying for admission in October with a scholarship managed by the Department; 31 May for October enrolment, or 31 December for April enrolment for application without financial support; to the Foreign Student Officer, Department of Civil Engineering; (b) by 31 December, to the Department of Urban Engineering, at the above address.

📖 Graduate Programmes / Nuclear Engineering

Study Domains: chemical engineering, chemistry, physics, sciences.
Programmes: Master's and Doctorate programme in nuclear engineering: simulation and computation, computational mechanics, quantum radiation measurement, computational mechanics, high energy chemistry, radiation chemistry, plasma physics, nuclear fusion engineering,

systems information technology, quantum material engineering, fluid engineering, radiation effects.
Open to: applicants of all nationalities, holding a Bachelor's or Master's degree or equivalent; under 35 years of age.
Duration: M.Eng.: 2 years; Ph.D.: 3 years; courses begin in April and October.
Fees: registration fee: 270,000 yen; tuition: 469,000 yen per year.
Financial assistance: 4 or 5 scholarships are available every year.
Languages: instruction in English.
Applications: by 31 December to be considered for scholarships, to the Department of Quantum Engineering at the above address.

🐝 Scholarship / Engineering

Study Domains: engineering, Japanese, languages.
Scholarships: Japanese Government Scholarships in engineering.
Open to: applicants of all nationalities, holding a Master's degree or equivalent; under 35 years of age.
Duration: 1-1/2 years; courses begin in October.
Value: monthly allowance, 184,500 yen during the programme, plus installation allowance of 25,000 yen and field study allowance of 46,000 yen.
Applications: by mid-February, to the Committee of the International Cooperation and Exchange of the Graduate School of Engineering at the above address.

🐝 Scholarship / Veterinary Sciences

Study Domains: veterinary medicine, veterinary sciences.
Scholarships: Japanese Government Scholarship for doctoral programmes in veterinary sciences.
Open to: candidates holding a Master's degree from countries having formal diplomatic relations with Japan; under 35 years of age.
Duration: 4 years for veterinary medical sciences; 3 years for other departments.
Value: monthly allowance of 184,500 yen during the programme; installation allowance of 25,000 yen and field of study allowance of 46,000 yen.
Applications: by 31 March, to the Committee of the Graduate School of Agriculture and Agricultural Life Sciences at the above address.

1399 Waseda University [WU]

104, Totsuka-machi
Shinjuku-ku
169-50 Tokyo
Tel: +81-3-3203-9806
Fax: +81-3-3202-8638
Web: http://www.waseda.ac.jp
e-mail: cie@list.waseda.jp

🐝 Ono Azusa Memorial Scholarships

Study Domains: business, economic and commercial sciences, engineering, law, literature and civilization, political science, social sciences.
Scholarships: Waseda University Ono Azusa Memorial Scholarships.
Duration: 1 year.
Value: 300,000 yen per year.
Applications: to the above address, for further information.

Jordan

Academic year: September to June.
Organization of higher education system: Higher education in Jordan began in 1951 with a one-year post-secondary teacher training programme. The first university programme began in 1962 with the establishment of the University of Jordan. The sector has since expanded into about 50 public and private community colleges (CCs), 8 public universities and 12 private universities. In 2004, enrolment data indicates 80,000 students in public universities; 30,000 students in private universities; 29,000 in community colleges and female enrolment at 55%.
The Ministry of Higher Education (MOHE) was established in 1985 to organize the higher education process and make it more responsive to the development needs of the country. The MOHE operates under the regulatory authority of the Higher Education Council (HEC) and is the regulatory authority of all community colleges.
The HEC is the major regulatory body for all higher education institutions. Each institution should have (a) a University Council, an essentially advisory body (composed of top university administrators, ministry representatives, prominent community members and an elected representative, a student and a graduate of the university); (b) a Council of Deans, which is in charge of the operation of the university and is headed by faculty presidents; (c) a Faculty Council for each faculty or college; and (d) a Departmental Council, composed of all staff members of a department. Top officials (presidents, vice-presidents and deans) are appointed for defined periods. Private universities are run by a Board of Trustees.
Major institutions of higher education:
• Yarmouk University, PO Box 566, Irbid, Jordan; http://www.yu.edu.jo.
• Jordan University, 1119421 Amman, Jordan; http://www.ju.edu.jo.
• Mu'tah University, PO box 6: Mu'tah-Al-Karak, Jordan; http://www.mutah.edu.jo.
Monetary unit: Jordanian dinar (JD).
National student admission: Foreign students should have qualifications equivalent to the Jordan Secondary Education Certificate.
International student admission: Good knowledge of both Arabic and English is essential for regular university studies. Courses in Arabic are arranged for foreign students at both the Yarmouk and Jordan University. Secondary-school leaving certificate or equivalent; successful completion of a university test in Arabic is required.
Language: Good knowledge of both Arabic and English is essential for regular university studies.
Immigration requirements: Foreign students must obtain their entrance visa from the Jordanian embassy in their home country; residence permit and other requirements can be obtained from the Ministry of Interior in Jordan.
Estimated expenses for one academic year: Tuition: 150-250 JD per semester (including medical insurance); room and board: 150-300 JD per month; books: 50 JD; on-campus accommodation is provided for female students only at the rate of 100 JD per semester.
Information services:
• Ministry of Higher Education and Scientific Research, PO Box 35262, Amman., Jordan; tel: +962-6-533-7616; email: mhe-gs@nic.net.joweb: http://www.mohe.gov.jo.
• Association of Arab Universities; PO 401; Jubeyha 11941, Amman; tel: +962-6-534-5131; fax: +962-6-533-2994; email: secgen@aaru.edu.jo.
• Cultural attaché at Jordanian Embassies and Consulates around the world.
The universities provide furnished accommodation for female students, a bus service and on-campus cafeteria, all at reasonable cost.
Recognition of studies and qualification: For international students: Ministry of Higher Education and Scientific Research, PO Box 35262, Amman, Jordan; tel: +962-6-533-7616; email: mhe-gs@nic.net.joweb: http://www.mohe.gov.jo.
For national students: The Accreditation Council Higher Committee for the Equivalence of Studies, Degrees and Diplomas; PO Box 138; Al Jubeiha; Amman; Jordan; tel: +962-6-534-7671; fax: +962-6-533-7616.
Publications / Websites:

• 'Student's Guide' (in Arabic and English) obtainable from each university, Admission and Registration Department.
• Yarmouk University: http://www.yu.edu.jo
• Jordan University: http://www.ju.edu.jo
• Mu'tah University: http://www.mutah.edu.jo
• Statistical Booklet, 2003, may be requested from the Department of Development and Planning.

1400 Al Balqa' Applied University [ABAU]

Al-Salt 19 117
Tel: +962-5-353-0467
Fax: +962-5-353-7518
Web: http://www.bau.edu.jo
e-mail: wriekat@bau.edu.jo

📖 Undergraduate Studies

Study Domains: agriculture, applied sciences, computer science, engineering, tourism, hotel and catering management.
Programmes: Associate, Bachelor's degrees in engineering; computer science; agriculture; hotel management; applied sciences.
Duration: 4 to 5 years; courses begin 6 October.
Fees: registration: 90 JD; tuition: 15-45 JD; living costs: US$500.
Languages: English and Arabic.

1401 Al Zaytoonah University of Jordan [AZUJ]

PO Box
11733 Amman
Tel: +962-6-429-1511
Fax: +962-6-429-1432
Web: http://www.alzaytoonah.edu
e-mail: admission@alzaytoonah.edu

📖 Undergraduate Studies

Study Domains: accounting, Arabic, business administration, computer science, English, ethnology, French, graphic arts, law, marketing, mathematics, nursing, pharmacy and pharmacology, tourism, hotel and catering management.
Programmes: Bachelor's degrees in languages, graphic arts, business administration, law, computer science, nursing, pharmacy.
Financial assistance: financial assistance available; contact admissions@alzaytoonah.edu for further information.

1402 Al-Ahliyya Amman University (Amman Private University)

PO Box 337
Amman University Post Office Al Salt Road
19328 Amman
Tel: +962-6-553-6101
Fax: +962-6-533-5169
Web: http://www.amman.edu

📖 Undergraduate Programmes

Study Domains: administration, arts, computer science, engineering, finance, law, medicine, pharmacy and pharmacology.
Programmes: Bachelor's degrees in law; finance and administrative sciences, information technology, pharmacy and medical sciences, engineering, arts.
Fees: for international students: tuition: $3,600-$5,100; books/supplies: US$500; housing: US$1,344 per year.
Languages: proficiency required in Arabic and English.

1403 Al-Hussein Bin Talal University (King Hussein University) [AHU]

PO Box 20
Ma'an
Tel: +962-3-213-3020
Fax: +962-3-213-4359
Web: http://www.ahu.edu.jo
e-mail: ahu@go.com.jo

📖 Undergraduate, Graduate Programmes

Study Domains: arts, education, sciences.
Programmes: International students are admitted either to the Parallel programme (degree) or to the Special Study Programme (non-degree).
Open to: candidates of all nationalities.
Academic requirements: Minimum qualification for admission to the Parallel Programme is a minimum GPA of 65% in the Secondary Education Exam or equivalent for all departments except engineering where an 80% GPA is required.
Fees: tuition: 24 JD for BA programmes; 50 JD for computer science courses; 35 JD for other courses.
Languages: Arabic is language of instructions; some subjects are taught in English.
Applications: to the Department of Admission and Registration.

1404   Amman Arab University [AAU]
PO Box 2234
11953 Amman
Tel: +962-6-551-6124
Fax: +962-6-551-6103
Web: http://www.aau.edu.jo
e-mail: aaugs@aau.edu.jo

📖 Undergraduate, Graduate, Postgraduate Programmes

Study Domains: business administration, education, law, teacher education.
Programmes: Master's, Ph.D. degrees in education, teacher education, business administration, law.
Fees: tuition: 3,000 JD per academic year; books/supplies: 200 JD; housing: 200 JD per month.
Financial assistance: financial assistance available; contact aaugs@aau.edu.jo for further information.
Languages: Arabic is language of instruction; English is also used for some programmes.

1405   Jordan University of Science and Technology [JUST]
PO Box 3030
22110 Irbid
Tel: +962-2-729-5111
Fax: +962-2-709-5123 / 5148
Web: http://www.just.edu.jo
e-mail: just@just.edu.jo

📖 Undergraduate, Graduate Programmes / Scientific Studies

Study Domains: agriculture, dentistry, engineering, medicine, nursing, pharmacy and pharmacology, sciences.
Programmes: programme of studies leading to B.Sc. and M.Sc. degrees in medicine, dentistry, veterinary medicine, agriculture, engineering, pharmacy, nursing and science.
Open to: nationals of any country holding a secondary-education certificate or its equivalent.
Duration: 4 to 5 years.
Financial assistance: some scholarships available for undergraduate students, based on financial need, and for outstanding graduate students.
Applications: by 15 August to the above address.

1406   Ministry of Higher Education and Scientific Research [MOHE]
Department of International Agreements and Cultural Relations
PO Box 35262
Amman
Tel: +962-6-534-7671
Fax: +962-6-533-7616
Web: http://www.mohe.gov.jo
e-mail: mhe-gs@nic.net.jo

📻 Scholarships, Fellowships

Study Domains: all major fields, Arabic, oriental studies, theology, religion.
Scholarships: (a) scholarships and fellowships at undergraduate and postgraduate levels; (b) scholarships for Muslim Students.

Description: (a) all fields, including science, arts, teacher training, technology and medicine, economics and administrative science, law, Arabic language; (b) Arabic language, Islamic studies (Shari'a).
Open to: (a) nationals of all countries, according to mutual cultural agreements signed by Jordan with each country; candidates must hold a secondary school certificate equivalent to the Jordan General Secondary Certificate, in addition to other qualifications specified by particular institutions of study; knowledge of Arabic (as well as English for scientific disciplines) is essential; (b) Muslim students only holding a Secondary School Certificate or equivalent to the 'tawjihi'.
Place of study: at the (a) University of Jordan, Yarmouk University and governmental community colleges in Jordan; Mu'tah University, Jordan University of Science and Technology; (b) University of Jordan, Amman; Yarmouk University, Irbid, Mu'tah University, Karak.
Duration: (a) 4 years (university); 2 years (community colleges); 4 months to 2 years (Arabic language studies); (b) 4 years.
Value: (a) varies; (b) university fees.
Languages: proficiency in Arabic and English required.
Applications: (a) to the above address; (b) in July/August, through competent authorities in the candidate's country; to the Director of Foreign Students' Section, at the above address.

1407   Mu'tah University
PO Box 7
61710 Mu'tah, Karak
Tel: +962-3-272-380 / 9
Fax: +962-3-237-5540
Web: http://www.mutah.edu.jo
e-mail: mutah@mutah.edu.jo

📖 Undergraduate, Graduate Programmes

Study Domains: all major fields.
Programmes: programme of studies leading to Bachelor's degrees and Master's degrees in a variety of fields.
Open to: for undergraduate programme, students having completed secondary education; for Master's degree and diploma in education, B.A. or its equivalent; Arabic placement test for foreign students for orientation Arabic courses; written tests and interviews.
Financial assistance: provided from various funds: King Abdullah Fund; Ministry of Higher Education; Deanships of Students affairs; contact university for further information.
Applications: information from the Ministry of Higher Education, through Jordanian embassies abroad.

1408   Philadelphia University [PU]
PO Box 1
Amman
Tel: +962-2-637-4444
Fax: +962-2-637-4440
Web: http://www.philadelphia.edu.jo
e-mail: info@philadelphia.edu.jo

📖 Undergraduate Studies

Study Domains: accounting, Arabic, business administration, computer science, design, engineering, English, finance, law, marketing, mechanical engineering, pharmacy and pharmacology, research, sciences.
Programmes: Bachelor's degrees in business administration, Arabic, design, law, computer science, sciences, engineering; non-degree programmes in basic sciences.
Duration: 4 years; courses begin 1 October.
Fees: registration: US$200; tuition: US$2,400 per year; living costs: US$3,600 per year.
Languages: English.

1409   The Hashemite University [THU]
PO Box 150459
13 115 Zarqua
Tel: +962-5-390-3333
Fax: +962-5-382-6613
Web: http://www.hu.edu.jo
e-mail: huniv@hu.edu.jo

Undergraduate, Graduate, Postgraduate Programmes

Study Domains: arts, biology, economic and commercial sciences, engineering, literature and civilization, mathematics, nursing, physics, sciences.
Programmes: Bachelor's, Master's, Diploma degrees in sciences and arts; economics and administrative sciences; engineering; allied health sciences; nursing.
Open to: applicants meeting academic and language requirements.
Fees: tuition: US$200-$250; tuition fees: US$75-$115 per credit hour.
Languages: language proficiency in Arabic and English required.

1410 University of Jordan [UOJ]
11942 Amman
Tel: +962-6-535-5000
Fax: +962-6-535-5533
Web: http://www.ju.edu.jo
e-mail: admin@ju.edu.jo

Undergraduate, Graduate Programmes

Study Domains: all major fields.
Programmes: (a) undergraduate, graduate and postgraduate courses in arts, economics and administrative sciences, sciences, Islamic studies, medicine, nursing, pharmacy, agriculture, education, engineering and technology, law, physical education and dentistry; (b) intensive courses in Arabic for speakers of other languages.
Open to: nationals of countries according to cultural agreements; candidates must hold the Jordanian General Secondary Education Certificate or equivalent; age not over 21 years; Arabic language and good English essential, especially for scientific faculties.
Duration: (a) 3 to 6 years for arts, economics, science, shari'a (Islamic studies), educational sciences, law, physical education; 6 years plus 1 year internship to 8 years for medicine; 3-1/2 to 6 years for nursing; 3 years plus 2 summers to 6 years for agriculture; 4 to 7 years for engineering and technology, pharmacy; 5 to 7 years for dentistry; (b) 4 months to 2 years.
Fees: tuition: varies according to programme; living expenses: at least US$500 depending on type of accommodation.
Applications: by the first week of August, through competent authorities (usually the Ministry of Higher Education) in candidate's country.

1411 University of Petra [UOP]
PO Box 961343
11196 Amman
Tel: +962-6-571-5546
Fax: +962-6-571-5570
Web: http://www.uop.edu.jo
e-mail: info@uop.edu.jo

Undergraduate Programmes

Study Domains: accounting, architecture, arts, communication, computer science, design, education, finance, graphic arts, interior design, interpretation and translation, journalism, management, marketing, nutrition, pharmacy and pharmacology, teacher education.
Programmes: undergraduate programmes at the following faculties: Information Technology: computer science; computer information systems; software engineering; Architecture & Arts: architecture, interior design, graphic design; Financial & Administrative Sciences: management information systems; banking & finance, accounting, marketing, business administration; Arts; Arabic language & literature; English language & literature; English language translation, journalism & communication, educational sciences, child education, classroom teacher, chemistry; Pharmacy & Medical Sciences: pharmacy, nutrition.
Fees: tuition: US$4,500; books/supplies: 200 JD; housing: 1,500 JD.
Languages: instruction in Arabic and English.
Applications: to Registrar at the above address.

1412 Yarmouk University [YU]
PO Box 566
Irbid
Tel: +962-2-721-1111
Fax: +962-2-727-4725
Web: http://www.yu.edu.jo
e-mail: yarmouk@yu.edu.jo

Undergraduate, Graduate, Postgraduate Programmes

Study Domains: all major fields, arts, business administration, education, engineering, law, liberal arts, sciences, theology, religion.
Programmes: Bachelor's, Master's, PhD degrees in education, liberal arts, arts, languages, business administration, law, science, engineering, Islamic studies.
Duration: 4 years; courses begin in October.
Fees: US$60 per credit hour; US$112.50 per credit hour for engineering studies.
Financial assistance: financial assistance available.
Applications: to the Director of Admissions and Registration at the above address.

Kazakhstan

Academic year: September to June.
Organization of higher education system: At present, there are universities, academies, and institutes, conservatoires, higher schools and higher colleges. There are three main levels: basic higher education that provides the fundamentals of the chosen field of study and leads to the award of the Bachelor's degree; specialized higher education after which students are awarded the Specialist's Diploma; and scientific-pedagogical higher education which leads to the Master's Degree. Postgraduate education leads to the Kandidat Nauk (Candidate of Sciences) and the Doctor of Sciences. With the adoption of the Laws on Education and on Higher Education, a private sector has been established and several private institutions have been licensed.
• University level first stage: Diploma of Specialist, Bachelor: A Diploma of Specialist or Diploma of Specialized Higher Education in a particular field of study is generally awarded at the end of a five-year course (former system). Bachelor's Degrees are now also conferred after four years' studies.
• University level second stage: Aspirantura, Master's: Full-time postgraduate studies (Aspirantura) leading to the qualification of Candidate of Sciences (Kandidat Nauk) normally last for three years. The submission of a thesis is required. Master's Degrees are also conferred after a further two years' study beyond the Bachelor's Degree.
• University level third stage: PhD, Doctorate (Doktoratura): In the new system, a PhD is conferred after two to three years' further study beyond the Master's Degree. The Doctor of Sciences (Doktor Nauk) is awarded after the Kandidat Nauk after completion of a thesis based on original research.
(Source: IAU World Higher Education Database, 2005/6).
Monetary unit: tenge.
National student admission: As of 2004, school leavers must pass a new exam, the Edinoe Nacional'noe Testirovanie (Unified National Testing Exam), and obtain its diploma, the Certificat o Rezul'tatah EHT (replacing the Kompleksnoe Testirovanie - Complex Testing Exam), to enter Universities. (Source: IAU World Higher Education Database, 2005/6).
Language: Languages of instruction are Kazakh, Russian, English, German, French, Chinese and Arabic.
Open and distance learning: Several universities offer distance education.
Recognition of studies and qualification: Ministry of Education and Science, Head of International Cooperation Division, Respubliki Square 60 (Kazakh Oil Building), 473000 Astana, Kazakhstan; tel.: +7-3172-333-325 / +7-3172-214-230, fax: +7-3172-333-412 / +7-3172-333-178; web; http://www.edu.gov.kz.

1413 Al-Farabi Kazakh National University [KAZNU]

Al-Farabi Avenue, 71
480078 Almaty
Tel: +7-3272-471-488
Fax: +7-3272-472-609
Web: http://www.kazsu.kz
e-mail: anurmag@kazsu.kz

📖 Undergraduate, Graduate Programmes

Study Domains: all major fields.
Programmes: Bachelor's; Master's; Ph.D.; preparatory certificate courses.
Description: distance learning in law and economics offered.
Other conditions: basic intermediate language proficiency.
Fees: foreign student tuition fees range from: US$2,000-$3,00 per year.
Financial assistance: financial assistance not applicable for foreign students.
Languages: Russian and Kazakh.
Applications: apply by 30 August to: anurmag@kaszu.kz at office for international relations; courses begin in September.

1414 Almaty Abai State University [AASU]

13 Dostyk Avenue
480100 Almaty
Tel: +7-3272-916-339
Fax: +7-3272-913-050
Web: http://www.abai.uni.sci.kz
e-mail: rector@abai.uni.sci.kz

📖 Undergraduate, Graduate Programmes

Study Domains: business, education, humanities and arts, languages, law, sciences, social sciences, tourism, hotel and catering management.
Programmes: Bachelor's, Master's, Ph.D. degree programmes.
Open to: foreign students should complete preparatory Russian or Kazakh languages in order to enrol in the University; minimum age: 16 years.
Duration: 4 years beginning 1 September.
Fees: tuition fees: US$1,300 per year; living costs US$20 per month.
Financial assistance: financial assistance not available to foreign students.
Applications: by 1 November to Bayan Sapargalieva, 13 Dostyk Ave, room 103.

1415 East Kazakhstan State Technical University [EKSTU]

19 Serikbaev Street
Ust-Kamenogorsk
Tel: +7-3232-406-739 / 354
Fax: +7-3232-406-920
e-mail: center@ektu.kz

📖 Undergraduate, Graduate Programmes

Study Domains: architecture, building industry, economic and commercial sciences, education, energy, engineering, geology, humanities and arts, metallurgy.
Programmes: Diploma of Specialist (4-year undergraduate programme); Kandidat Nauk (2-3 year graduate programme); Master (1-2 year postgraduate programme).

1416 Kazakh National Medical University [KAZNMU]

Tole Bi Str. 88
480012 Almaty
Tel: +7-3272-927-885
Fax: +7-3272-926-997
Web: http://www.kaznmu.kz
e-mail: kaznmu@arna.kz

📖 Doctoral Degree Programme

Study Domains: biochemistry, biology, continuing education, health and hygiene, medicine, nursing.
Programmes: Ph.D. and M.D. programmes.
Description: full 6-year medical doctor's programme;

3-year nursing programme.
Open to: candidates meeting academic requirements and completing 1 year language course.
Duration: 6 years commencing 1 September.
Languages: Kazakh and Russian.
Applications: by 15 August to: usmc@ok.kz; tel: +7 3272 927 700.

🎓 Scholarships

Study Domains: medicine.
Scholarships: University Scholarships, through exchange programmes.
Applications: at any time with CV and recommendations to Prof. Yeldos A. Izatullayev, Kazakh National Medical University address or email: usmc@ok.kz.

1417 Kazakh National Technical University [KAZNTU]

22 Satpaev Str.
480013 Almaty
Tel: +7-3272-926-901
Fax: +7-3272-926-025
Web: http://www.ntu.sci.kz
e-mail: allnt@kazntu.kz

📖 Graduate Degree Programmes

Study Domains: accounting, business, communication, economic and commercial sciences, economy, education, electricity and electronics, engineering, history, information science, languages, management, mechanical engineering, metallurgy, natural resources, sciences, technology.
Programmes: Master's and Ph.D. degree programmes.
Open to: applicants must have minimum secondary education and basic knowledge of Kazakh and Russian languages.
Held: branches in: Aktjubinsk; Ust-Kamenogorsk; Aktobe.
Duration: 5 years beginning in September.
Fees: registration: 853 tenge; tuition: approximately US$1,500.
Languages: Kazakh and Russian.
Applications: apply by 31 August to Suleyev D.K. Rektor, nich@kazntu.sci.kz.

1418 Kazakh-American University [KAU]

18a Satpayev Str.
480013 Almaty
Tel: +7-3272-647-720
Fax: +7-3272-553-772
Web: http://www.kau.kz
e-mail: kau@mail.kz

📖 Undergraduate, Graduate Programmes

Study Domains: business administration, education, engineering, languages, law, liberal arts, library science, management, medicine, sciences, tourism, hotel and catering management.
Programmes: undergraduate and graduate degree programmes.
Description: Bachelor's degrees in: finance, tourism, journalism, economics, world economics, communications and systems of communications, computer systems of information processing and management, radio communications, broadcasting and television, design, chemistry (oil), accounting and auditing, international relations, surgery and therapy, multi-channel telecommunication systems, biology, law, interpreting.
Open to: candidates must pass admission tests in: history of Kazakhstan, English language; under 30 years of age for full-time studies.
Fees: registration: US$50; tuition fees: US$1,700-$1,800; living costs: US$15 per month.
Languages: English.

1419 Zhetysu State University [ZHSU]

Zhansugurov Street 187a
488009 Taldykorgan
Tel: +7-328-222-0020
Fax: +7-328-221-2261
e-mail: tk_jgu@mail.ru

📖 Undergraduate and Professional Programmes

Study Domains: accounting, biology, chemistry, continuing education, design, earth science, ecology, environment, economy, finance, music and musicology, philology, physics, teacher education, visual arts, vocational training.
Programmes: Bachelor's degrees and higher professional education.
Open to: candidates passing compulsory admission tests: Kazakh (Russian); mathematics; history of Kazakhstan.
Duration: 4 to 5 years beginning 1 September.
Fees: registration: US$500-$600.
Financial assistance: some scholarships available.
Languages: Kazakh and Russian.
Applications: apply by 31 March to Rector Medeuov, fax: +8 328 221 2261.

🎓 Scholarship

Study Domains: all major fields.
Scholarships: University Scholarships.
Value: 1,996 tenge per month.
Applications: apply to: Sarsenbaev Askhat Maulenovich, assistant rector at the university, fax: +8 328 221 2261.

Kenya

Academic year: September to July.
Organization of higher education system: Levels of study: certificate: 1-2 years; diploma: 2-3 years; Bachelor's degree: 4-6 years; Master's degree: 2-3 years beyond Bachelor's; PhD: variable length beyond Master's degree.
Monetary unit: Kenya shilling (sh).
National student admission: National students must have obtained good results in Kenya Certificate of Secondary Education (KCSE) examination; foreign students should have qualifications equivalent to the KCSE; equivalencies are established by the Commission for Higher Education (see "recognition of studies and qualifications" below).
Language: Good knowledge of English is essential for regular university courses.
Information services:
• Ministry of Education, Nairobi; Kenya.
Open and distance learning: The University of Nairobi offers an external degree programme for the Bachelor of Education in Arts-based subjects.
Recognition of studies and qualification: Recognition & Equation of Qualifications & Inspection, Commission for Higher Education
PO Box 54999; 0200 City Square; Nairobi; Kenya; tel: +254-2-228-753; fax: +254-2-222-218; email: che@kenyaweb.com.
Publications / Websites:
• 'Annual Calendar', for the guidance and information of foreign students, published by the University of Nairobi, Nairobi.
• 'Students' Guide', published by Kenyatta University College, Nairobi.
• 'Annual Calendar', published by Moi University.
• 'Catalogue', published by Egerton University.

1420 British Institute in Eastern Africa

PO Box 30710
Nairobi
Tel: +254-2-43721
Fax: +254-2-43365
e-mail: britinst@arcc.or.ke

🎓 Research Grants

Study Domains: African studies, archaeology, history.
Scholarships: occasional research attachments and grants

(number varies according to funds available).
Description: research in pre-colonial history, archaeology and related studies of Eastern Africa (Zambezi to Middle Nile).
Open to: candidates of any nationality with suitable interests, experience and university training for the research proposed; studentships are normally reserved for Eastern African and Commonwealth graduates, who may be expected to make a significant contribution to historical and archaeological knowledge; they are not awarded for course work; the Institute may assist scholars with advice on fieldwork and research facilities, and the use of its research and reference library in Nairobi.
Place of study: normally in Eastern Africa.
Duration: variable, grants for specific research for appropriate periods.
Value: variable, depending on needs and the Institute's resources.
Applications: to the Director, at the above address.

1421 Catholic University of East Africa [CUEA]

PO Box 62157
00200 Nairobi
Tel: +254-20-891-601
Fax: +254-20-891-261
Web: http://www.cuea.edu
e-mail: admin@cuea.edu

📖 Undergraduate, Graduate, Postgraduate Programmes

Study Domains: arts, sciences, social sciences, theology, religion, trade.

1422 Egerton University [EU]

PO Box 536
Njoro
Tel: +254-37-62276-9
Fax: +254-37-62527
Web: http://www.egerton.or.ke
e-mail: info@egerton.ac.ke

📖 Undergraduate, Graduate Programmes

Study Domains: agronomic sciences, computer science, education, geography, home economics, horticulture, natural resources, philosophy, sciences, sociology.
Programmes: diploma, undergraduate and graduate academic programmes offered in the following fields: agronomy, animal health, animal science, dairy and food science technology, agricultural engineering, horticulture, natural resources, agricultural economics, business management, geography, sociology, history, linguistics, English, Kiswahili, religious studies, philosophy, literature, agricultural education and extension, agriculture with home economics, botany, zoology, chemistry, physics, mathematics, computer science and environmental studies.
Open to: candidates of all nationalities holding a four-year secondary-school certificate with at least a B-average grade or credit.
Duration: Diploma, 3 years; undergraduate, 5 years for agricultural engineering, 4 years for the others; postgraduate, 2 years.
Applications: by 30 March, every other year.

1423 Institute for Meteorological Training and Research [WMO-IMTAR]

WMO Regional Training Centre
Dagoretti Corner, Ngong Road
PO Box 30259
Nairobi
Tel: +254-2-576-957 / 567-865
Fax: +254-2-576-955 / 577-373
Web: http://www.wmo.ch/index-en.html

📖 Meteorological Studies

Study Domains: hydrology, meteorology.
Programmes: (a) meteorological courses for WMO Class IV, III, II and I; (b) specialized course in agrometeorology; (c) advanced forecasting course; (d) extension course; (e) postgraduate diploma course in applied hydrology and information systems for water management; (f) specialized

course in aeronautical meteorology; (g) computer application course; (h) specialized course in operation, installation and maintenance of meteorological instruments; (i) course in meteorology observation techniques; (j) water resources management data processing and analysis.
Open to: mainly nationals of English-speaking African countries with: (a) credits in physics and mathematics at KCE (Kenya Certificate of Education) level or its equivalent, (classes IV to II) plus class IV certificates (classes III and II), KACE (Kenya Advanced Certificate of Education) with mathematics and physics (class II); honours B.Sc. meteorology (class I); (b) and (c) several years experience as class II and class I, (c) Advanced Forecasting Course (AFC) and two years field work after AFC; (d) B.Sc. in civil engineering, mining, geology, geography, meteorology, geophysics or the equivalent; (e) WMO Class I and II with experience; (f) KCE or equivalent; (g) KCE or equivalent, with maths, physics, working experience in meteorology related field; (h) for 3 months course: O-level certificate or KCE or equivalent with physics, maths and working experience in field related to meteorology; for 2-month course: O-level certificate with physics, maths and chemistry; (i) O-level certificate or KCE equivalent with physics, maths or physical
science or WMO Class II, III, IV; age 18 and above.
Duration: (a) class IV, 4 months; class III, 12 months; class II, 2 years, (with KCE), 1 year (with KACE); class I, 5 months (courses begin in January/February); (b) 4 months (courses begin in August);
(c) 2-1/2 months (courses begin in July); (d) 10 weeks (courses begin in September/October); (e) 9 months (courses begin in January); (f) 6 weeks (courses begin in April); (g) 5 weeks (courses begin in January); (h) 3 months courses begin in June; 2 months courses begin in March; (i) 2 months (courses begin in May); (j) 3 months. Courses begin in September.
Fees: (approximate figures) (a) class IV, sh31,500; class III, sh 74,200; class II, sh 74,200; (b) sh 40,000; (c) sh 35,000; (d) and (g) sh 30,000; (e) sh 250,000; (f) sh 20,000; (h) 3 month course: sh 36,000; 2 month course: sh 24,000; (i) sh 24,000; (j) sh 36,000.
Financial assistance: limited number of scholarships through WMO, UNDP, EEC, UNHCR, ICAO, British Council, GTZ; according to agreements with the candidate's home government.
Applications: from February to September, to the Principal, at the above address.

1424   Kenya Utalii College [KUC]
PO Box 31052
Nairobi
Tel: +254-2-802-540
Fax: +254-2-860-514
Web: http://www.utalii.co.ke/
e-mail: info@utalii.co.ke

📖 Diploma Programmes / Hotel and Tourism
Study Domains: tourism, hotel and catering management.
Programmes: programme of studies leading to certificates and diplomas in tourism and hotel management.
Open to: candidates of all nationalities meeting minimum entry requirements, between 17 and 30 years of age.
Duration: variable; courses begin in October.
Fees: approx. US$7,050, subject to change without notice.
Financial assistance: some scholarships available covering full room and board, tuition, medical allowances, excursions, etc.
Applications: by 28 February, to the Principal.

1425   Maseno University [MU]
PO Private Bag
Maseno
Tel: +254-35-51620/622
Fax: +254-35-51221
Web: http://www.mu.ac.ke/maseno/maseno.htm
e-mail: vc-maseno@swiftkisumu.com

📖 Undergraduate, Graduate, Postgraduate Programmes
Study Domains: biochemistry, botany, business, business administration, chemistry, communication, computer science, ecology, environment, economic and commercial sciences, education, fisheries, geography, health and hygiene, history,

interior design, languages, literature and civilization, mathematics, music and musicology, physics, research, sociology, statistics, Swahili, teacher education, theology, religion, zoology.
Programmes: Bachelor's, Master's, Ph.D. degrees in all major fields.
Applications: by July to the above address.

1426   United States International University [USIU]
Thika Road Kasarani
PO Box 14634
00800 Nairobi
Tel: +254-020-3606-000
Fax: +254-020-3606-100
Web: http://www.usiu.ac.ke
e-mail: admit@usiu.ac.ke / finaid@usiu.ac.ke

🎓 Vice-Chancellor's Scholarship
Study Domains: all major fields.
Scholarships: tuition reduction for undergraduate, graduate studies.
Open to: all full-time incoming international students based on scholastic results; not open to Kenyan nationals.
Academic requirements: 3.5 grade point average required.
Duration: 4 academic years for undergraduate studies; 2 academic years for graduate studies; renewable on condition that 3.5 grade point average is maintained.
Value: 25% tuition reduction.
Applications: 2 June for fall intake; 15 September for spring intake; 30 March for summer intake; contact Financial Aid at finaid@usiu.ac.ke.

Kuwait
Academic year: September to June.
Organization of higher education system: Higher education is provided by Kuwait University and technical colleges and awards Bachelor's, Master's and Ph.D. degrees.
Monetary unit: Kuwait dinar.
National student admission: A limited number of foreign students may be admitted, subject to the availability of relevant resources and facilities. Selection is based on merit and national interest and grade point average in secondary school. An entrance examination must also be passed.
Language: Good knowledge of Arabic or English is required for regular university courses. A minimum language score for admission to Master's degree programmes is necessary. Each applicant has to satisfy one of the language proficiency requirements indicated for the programme to which he/she is seeking admission.
Immigration requirements: A visa is required and Kuwait University will arrange study visas for admitted foreign students residing outside the country.
Estimated expenses for one academic year: Free tuition and housing are provided by the government; only government scholarship holders are eligible.
Information services:
• Student Affairs Unit, College of Graduate Studies, Kuwait University, PO Box 5969, Safat 13060 Kuwait.
Scholarships for international students: Candidates for scholarships must be accepted to study in Kuwait by the student's government or by an institution, or a corporation accredited by the Government of Kuwait; the announcement of scholarships is made in January every year; the deadline for receiving scholarship applications is 1 June. The Kuwait National Commission for Education, Science and Culture has the sole right to consider each application, and take a suitable decision. For acceptance for scholarships, certificates must be either in Arabic, English or French, or translated into one of these languages and authenticated. It must be attested by the Ministry of Education and Ministry of External Affairs, and the embassy of Kuwait in the student's country. If there is no embassy of Kuwait in that country, then the certificate must be attested by any other Arab embassy.
Open and distance learning: Arab Open University (AOU); PO Box 3322; Safat 13033, Kuwait; tel: +965-532-9013; fax: +965-532-9019; web: www.arabou.org/.
Recognition of studies and qualification: Kuwait University; PO Box 5969; Khaldiya; Safat 13060; Kuwait; tel: +965-481-1188; fax: +965-484-8648; email:

faizar@kucol.edu.kw; web: http://www.kuniv.edu.kw.
Work opportunities: Possibilities for working as part-time
teachers or research assistants depend on departmental needs.
Additional information: website: www.mohe.gov.
Publications / Websites:
• 'Information on Graduate Education and Application for
Admission'.
• 'Graduate Catalogue', published by Kuwait University in
Arabic and English and distributed free of charge.

1427 Kuwait University
PO Box 5969 Khaldiya
13060 Safat
Tel: +965-481-1188
Fax: +965-484-8648
Web: http://www.kuniv.edu.kw
e-mail: nadir@kuco1.edu.kw; info@kuniv.edu

📖 Undergraduate, Graduate Programmes

Study Domains: all major fields, arts, education,
engineering, law, medicine, sciences.
Programmes: undergraduate, graduate programmes in all
major fields.
Languages: English and Arabic.

🖝 Scholarships / Arabic Language

Study Domains: Arabic, languages.
Scholarships: Scholarships for Arabic language study.
Open to: non-Arabic speaking undergraduate students of
the University.
Duration: 1 to 3 academic semesters (not renewable).
Value: covers tuition, accommodation and meals.
Applications: by June, to the Dean of the Language
Centre, P.O. Box 2575, 13060 Safat, Kuwait; see
http://www.kuniv.edu.kw.

Kyrgyzstan
Academic year: September to June.
Organization of higher education system: Higher
education is provided by universities, academies, institutes
and colleges, most of them state-run. According to the Higher
Education Law of 1992, their structure was considerably
changed. This Law was amended in 1997. New universities
were founded in the central region and some specialized
higher education institutions were reconstructed as
multidisciplinary universities. Governmental and
non-governmental institutions have equal status. There are
also several private higher education institutions. The
Ministry of Education, Science and Culture is responsible for
education in the country.
• University level first stage: Bakalavr, Diploma of Specialist:
The first stage of university studies leads to a Bachelor's
Degree after four to five years' study or to a Diploma of
Specialist after five years' study.
• University level second stage: Master's degree, Kandidat
Nauk: The second stage leads to a Master's Degree after a
minimum of one year's further study or to a Kandidat Nauk
after a further three years beyond the Diploma of Specialist
and a thesis.
• University level third stage: PhD, Doktor Nauk: A PhD
degree is conferred after a further two to three years' study
beyond the Master's degree and a Doktor Nauk is conferred
after defence of a thesis. (Source: IAU World Higher
Education Database, 2005/6).
Monetary unit: Kyrgyzstani som (KGS).
National student admission: For international students: a
certificate of secondary education diploma, of secondary
vocational education (technical school, college), diploma of
higher education.
International student admission: Cetificate of secondary
education, or secondary vocational education for technical
schools.
Language: Languages of instruction are Kirghiz and
Russian. Preparation classes are obligatory for students with
no knowledge of these languages.
Immigration requirements: Acceptance letter from an
educational institution.
Estimated expenses for one academic year: Tuition:

US$500-1,800; books and supplies: US$50-100; housing:
US$60-250 per year.
Scholarships for international students: No financial
assistance is provided by the Government for international
students.
Open and distance learning: Kyrgyz National University
offers correspondence courses; some courses are also
available from the Slavic University and the International
University of Kyrgyzstan.
Recognition of studies and qualification: For information
regarding foreign credentials:
Ministry of Education, Science and Culture (MONK);
257,Tynystanov Street,720040 Bishkek, Kyrgyzstan; tel.:
+996 312 662 442; fax: +996-312-228-604 /
+996-312-228-786; email: monk@monk.bishkek.gov.kg.
Work opportunities: There are no work opportunities for
international students.

1428 Academy of Management under the President of Kyrgyz Republic
237 Panfilov Street
Bishkek 720040
Tel: +996-312-221-385
Fax: +996-312-663-614
Web: http://www.amp.aknet.kg
e-mail: reception@amp.aknet.kg

📖 Graduate Programmes

Study Domains: accounting, business, business
administration, communication, economic and commercial
sciences, economy, finance, international business,
management, marketing, public relations, trade.
Programmes: Master's degrees in Business
Administration.
Description: general studies in management and
organization, accounting, financial management, marketing,
production and operation management, banking,
microeconomics, macroeconomics, quantitative methods.
Open to: students holding a Bachelor's degree; admission
tests in economics; mathematics; English.
Duration: 1 year for full-time courses; 2-1/2 years for
distant courses; courses begin 1 September.
Fees: tuition fees US$3,000 per year; US$2,000 for
distance courses.
Languages: Russian and English.
Applications: by 30 July; contact ainura@amp.aknet.kg
for further information.

1429 Arabaev Kyrgyz State Pedagogical University
51 Razzakova Street
720026 Bishkek
Tel: +996-312-660-812
Fax: +996-312-660-588
Web: http://www.kspu.edu.kg
e-mail: kmpu_50@netmail.kg

📖 Undergraduate, Graduate Programmes

Study Domains: accounting, administration, advertising,
biology, chemistry, computer science, ecology, environment,
economy, education, English, finance, history, management,
mathematics, music and musicology, physical education,
physics, political science, psychology, Russian, Slavic
studies, special education, teacher education.
Programmes: Bachelor's, Master's degrees in education;
music; administration; economics; management; political
science; psychology; chemistry; mathematics; tourism and
hotel management.
Duration: 5 years; courses begin 1 September.
Fees: registration US$25; tuition fees US$500 per
academic year; living costs US$50 per month.
Languages: Russian.
Applications: by 1 September; contact
kmyrza@hotmail.com for further details.

1430 International University of Kyrgyzstan [IUK]

Prosp. Chui, 255
720001 Bishkek
Tel: +996-312-277-747
Fax: +996-312-219-614
Web: http://www.iuk.kg
e-mail: iuk@imfiko.bishkek.su

📖 Undergraduate, Graduate Studies

Study Domains: biology, business, business administration, communication, computer science, ecology, environment, economy, English, ethnology, finance, French, German, information science, international business, international law, international relations, interpretation and translation, law, linguistics, marketing.
Programmes: Bachelor's, Master's degrees in business. Non-degree programmes in international business and international logistics.
Duration: 1 to 4 years; courses begin in September.
Fees: tuition fees US$1,000-$5,000 per year; living costs US$110-$130 per month.
Languages: English; Language proficiency required.
Applications: by end of August; contact iuk@imfiko.bishkek.su for further information.

1431 Jalal-Abad State University

57 Lenin Street
715600 Jalal-Abad
Tel: +996-3722-55968
Fax: +996-3722-50333
Web: http://www.jasu.org.kg
e-mail: jasu@infotel.kg

📖 Undergraduate, Graduate Studies

Study Domains: all major fields, agriculture, computer science, economic and commercial sciences, economy, education, engineering, law, liberal arts, medicine, nursing, pharmacy and pharmacology, sciences, social sciences, sociology.
Programmes: Bachelor's, Master's degrees in all major fields.
Duration: 4 to 5 years; courses begin 1 September.
Fees: tuition fees US$150-$230 per year.
Languages: Kyrgyz, Russian, English.

1432 Kyrgyz Russian Slavic University

44 Kievskaya Street
720000 Bishkek
Tel: +996-312-284-733
Fax: +996-312-284-733
Web: http://www.krsu.edu.kg
e-mail: icio@hotmail.kg

📖 Undergraduate, Graduate, Postgraduate Programmes

Study Domains: all major fields, administration, anatomy, anthropology, archaeology, architecture, business, business administration, cancerology, cardiology, education, interior design, international business, international law, interpretation and translation, languages, law, medicine, natural sciences, nursing, pharmacy and pharmacology, sciences, social sciences, teacher education, theology, religion.
Programmes: Bachelor's, Master's, Ph.D. degrees in all major fields.
Open to: students with secondary-school certificate; entrance examinations required.
Duration: 5 years.
Fees: tuition: US$1,200 per year.
Languages: Russian.
Applications: rolling admissions; contact icio@hotmail.kg for further information.

1433 Kyrgyz Technical University 'I. Razzakov'

66 Mir Prospect
720044 Bishkek
Tel: +996-312-545-125
Fax: +996-312-545-162
Web: http://ktu.edu.kg
e-mail: ubrim@netmail.kg

📖 Undergraduate Studies

Study Domains: business, engineering.
Programmes: engineering diploma; non-degree programmes in English, preparatory courses, business.
Open to: students holding secondary-school certificate.
Duration: 1 to 2 years; courses begin 1 September.
Fees: tuition fees US$800-$1,000 per year; living costs US$25 per month.
Languages: Kyrgyz, Russian, English; proficiency in Russian and English required.
Applications: by August; contact bsamanch@netmail.kg for further details.

Latvia

Academic year: September to July.
Organization of higher education system: Academic higher education leads to 'Bakalaurs' (Bachelor's) and 'Magistrs '(Master's) degrees. 'Bakalaurs' degree is awarded after completion of the first stage of studies. Completion of a Bachelor's degree may take from 3 to 4 years (180 - 240 ECTS credits). A Master's degree may take from 1 to 2 years (60 - 120 ECTS), after the 'Magistrs' (for a total of approximately 5 years). Degrees in medicine and dentistry are considered to be equivalent to Master's degree level. The 'Magistrs' degree (or equivalent) is required for admission to doctoral studies. Higher professional education consists of several programmes: First level professional higher education programmes (college programmes) are of at least 2 years duration (120 ECTS) and lead to level IV professional qualifications. Second level professional higher education programmes are of at least 4 years duration (240 ECTS if after general secondary education) or 1 to 2 years' duration (60 - 120 ECTS if after Bachelor's degree) and lead to level V professional qualifications (highest professional qualification of a specialist in a given branch). Since December 2000 professional 'Bakalaurs' and 'Magistrs' degrees can also be awarded. The transfer from academic higher education to professional higher education and visa versa is possible.
Monetary unit: lats (LVL).
National student admission: Holders of a general secondary education certificate may have access to higher education on condition of acceptance by an institution of higher education.
Language: The main language of instruction is Latvian, but some institutions offer studies in English and Russian.
Immigration requirements: A residence permit is required for international students who intend to stay in Latvia for more than 3 months. A short term visa may or not be necessary depending on the student's country of origin.
Estimated expenses for one academic year: Tuition fees are approximately US$3,000-$4,000 per year.
Information services:
• Ministry of Education and Science, Department of Higher Education and Research, Vainu iela 2, 1098 Riga; tel: +371-2-213-870; fax: +371-2-213-992.
• Academic Information Centre (Latvijas ENIC-Akademiskas Informacijas Centrs); Valnnu iela 2; LV-1050 Riga; Latvia; tel: +371-2-225-155; fax: +371-2- 221 006; email: baiba@aic.lv; ieva@aic.lv; website: http://www.aic.lv.
Recognition of studies and qualification: Latvian ENIC-NARIC Academic Information Centre (Latvijas ENIC-Akademiskas Informacijas Centrs); Valnnu iela 2; LV-1050 Riga; Latvia; tel: +371 2 225-155; fax: +371 2 221 006; email: baiba@aic.lv; ieva@aic.lv; website: http://www.aic.lv.

1434 Baltic Russian Institute [BRI]

3 Piedrujas Street
1073 Riga
Tel: +371-724-1002 / 1142
Fax: +371-711-2679
Web: http://www.bki.lv
e-mail: bri@junik.lv

Undergraduate, Graduate Programmes

Study Domains: all major fields.
Programmes: Bachelor's, Master's and Ph.D. degrees in over 40 subjects, including law, management, journalism, social psychology, international economic regulations, international sea law.
Duration: Bachelor's degree: 4 years; Master's degree: 1½ years after Bachelor's.
Fees: full-time US$2,000-$3,000 per year.
Applications: by 31 August, to the above address.

1435 Liepaja Academy of Pedagogy [LAP]

Liela Street 14
3401 Liepaja
Tel: +371-34-07762
Fax: +371-34-24225
Web: http://www.lieppa.lv
e-mail: lpa@lieppa.lv

Undergraduate, Graduate Programmes

Study Domains: education, graphic arts, languages, management, mathematics, philology, Slavic studies, social sciences, teacher education, tourism, hotel and catering management.
Programmes: undergraduate and graduate programmes in educational sciences, mathematics, humanities, Latvian language and culture, graphic design, computer science, office management and tourism.
Open to: candidates of all nationalities meeting academic, linguistic and financial criteria.
Languages: good command of Latvian language required.
Applications: to the above address.

1436 Rezeknes Augstskola

Atbrivosanas Aleja 90
Tel: +371-462-3702
Fax: +371-462-5901
Web: http://www.ru.lv
e-mail: ra@ru.lv

Undergraduate, Graduate, Postgraduate Programmes

Study Domains: accounting, arts and crafts, business, business administration, computer science, cultural studies, ecology, environment, economic and commercial sciences, education, English, finance, German, history, home economics, law, philology, social sciences, special education, teacher education, tourism, hotel and catering management, vocational training.
Programmes: Bachelor's, Master's degrees in pedagogy, humanities and law sciences, engineering, economics.
Description: academic and higher professional education to develop culture, science and education.

1437 Riga Technical University [RTU]

1, Kalku Str.
1658 Riga
Tel: +371-949-5699
Fax: +371-708-9020
Web: http://www.rtuasd.lv
e-mail: igors@latnet.lv

Undergraduate, Graduate, Postgraduate Programmes

Study Domains: business, civil engineering, computer science, electricity and electronics, engineering, geodesy, mechanical engineering, paramedical studies, telecommunications.
Programmes: (a) Bachelor's degrees in civil engineering; computer science engineering; cartography engineering; electronics and telecommunication engineering; mechanical engineering; medical engineering; (b) Master's degrees in civil engineering; computer science engineering; electronics and telecommunication engineering; (c) Ph.D. in engineering.
Description: Faculties of Civil Engineering; Computer Science and Information Technology; Electronics and Telecommunications; Engineering Economics; Transport and Mechanical Engineering; Riga Business Institute.
Open to: candidates of any country with good English (TOEFL not necessary) and good marks in mathematics and physics.
Duration: courses begin in September and January.
Fees: Bachelor's and Master's programs: US$2,900; correspondence programs: US$1,450; preparatory courses: US$1,500.
Financial assistance: no financial assistance is provided to international students.
Languages: language of instruction: English.

1438 Turiba School of Business Administration Faculty of International Tourism

68 Graudu Street
1058 Riga
Tel: + 371-762-2069
Web: http://www.turiba.lv
e-mail: turiba@turiba.lv

Professional Undergraduate, Graduate Programmes in Tourism

Study Domains: tourism, hotel and catering management.
Programmes: (a) professional undergraduate degree in tourism and hospitality management; (b) professional Master's degree in Business Administration (MBA).
Duration: (a) 4 years; (b) 1 year.
Applications: download applications on website; contact the Dean of the Faculty of International Tourism; email Zina@turiba.lv; tel:+371-760-7661 / 2333.

1439 University of Latvia [UL]

International Office
Raina Boulevard, 19
LV 1586 Riga
Tel: +371-703-4300
Fax: +371-703-4302
Web: http://www.lu.lv
e-mail: lu@lu.lv

Undergraduate, Graduate, Postgraduate programmes

Study Domains: all major fields.
Programmes: undergraduate, graduate and postgraduate programmes in education sciences, humanities and arts, natural sciences, mathematics, social sciences, economics and management, law, health, health care and social care; special non-degree programme in Baltic Studies (courses in English).
Open to: candidates must hold a secondary-school certificate (or equivalent); students who plan to complete their entire undergraduate education at the University of Latvia must pass the Latvian language test; international students who plan to study at the University of Latvia for up to one year and visiting students are not required to take entrance examinations.
Fees: tuition fee for international students: from 1210-3400 LVL, depending on programmes; exchange students are exempt from tuition fees and in the case of bilateral cooperation are entitled to a small scholarship of around 58 LVL (about US$120); special non-degree programme in Baltic Studies: current registration: 18 LVL; tuition fees: 90 LVL per course.
Languages: language of instruction: Latvian, English.
Applications: between 15 May and 15 November to the International Office of the University; for information contact N. Ivanova, Email: natalia@lanet.lv; application forms can be obtained on the website www.lu.lv.

1440 Ventspils University College [VUC]
Ventspils Augstskola
Inz'enieru iela 101
3600 Ventspils
Tel: +371-362-8303
Fax: +371-362-8303
Web: http://www.venta.lv
e-mail: venta@venta.lv

📖 Programme of courses leading to Bachelor degree and Professional Diploma

Study Domains: accounting, business administration, computer science, English, finance, German, home economics, information science, interpretation and translation, management, mathematics, physics, Russian, transport, vocational training.
Programmes: (a) Bachelor's degree; (b) Professional diploma.
Description: (a) Information Technologies, Mathematics, Business and Economy; (b) Translation and Interpretation, German-Latvian-Russian and English-Latvian-Russian.
Open to: candidates must hold a secondary-school certificate (or equivalent); language test for translation and interpretation programme.
Duration: 4 years beginning in September.
Fees: current registration: US$25; tuition fees: US$4,000 per year; living costs: approx. US$1,000 per month.
Languages: language of instruction: Latvian and English.
Applications: by 15 June to the Rector of the University.

1441 Vidzeme University College [VUC]
Cesu iela 4
LV-4200 Valmiera
Tel: +371-420-7230
Fax: +371-420-7229
Web: http://www.va.lv
e-mail: international@va.lv

📖 Undergraduate, Graduate Programmes

Study Domains: accounting, advertising, art history, business, business administration, communication, computer science, continuing education, cultural studies, economic and commercial sciences, economy, education, English, finance, folklore, French, geography, German, history, human sciences, information science, international business, international law, international relations, languages, law, liberal arts, literature and civilization, management, music and musicology, philology, philosophy, political science, psychology, recreation and leisure, research, social sciences, sociology, summer programmes, teacher education, tourism, hotel and catering management.
Programmes: Programme of courses leading to Bachelor's and Master's degrees; also non-degree Summer programme.
Description: Bachelor's in political science and tourism management, Master's in public policy; International Summer School in Baltic Studies.
Open to: candidates of any country holding a secondary school certificate (or equivalent).
Other conditions: admission test for undergraduate and graduate programmes.
Duration: Bachelor's: 4 years; Master's: a further 2 years, beginning in September.
Fees: tuition fees: 950€; living costs: approximately 200€ per month.
Financial assistance: some scholarships available for the Baltic International Summer School; for information contact Ilze Arniece, tel. +371-4207277; fax +371-420-7229; email: infobiss@va.lv.
Languages: language of instruction: Latvian and English for undergraduate and graduate programmes; only English for Baltic International Summer School.
Applications: by 15 June for undergraduate and graduate programmes, by 1 May for Baltic International Summer School; for information contact Dace Oseniece at the above address.

Liban

Année universitaire: octobre à juin.
Unité monétaire: livre libanaise (LL).
Admission pour étudiants du pays: Dans toutes les universités, le baccalauréat libanais ou diplôme équivalent sont exigés, comme condition première à toute inscription. Par ailleurs, dans certaines universités et pour certaines spécialisations, les candidats doivent se présenter à des concours d'entrée et à des examens de langue.
Connaissances linguistiques requises: Une bonne connaissance de l'arabe, du français ou de l'anglais est essentielle. Dans certaines universités, le niveau linguistique de l'étudiant est vérifié au moyen d'un examen. Des cours de langue sont organisés par les universités selon leurs modalités propres.
Formalités d'immigration: Les services consulaires libanais dans le pays de résidence de l'étudiant étranger désirant poursuivre ses études supérieures au Liban peuvent fournir au candidat le détail des formalités d'immigration. La possession d'un visa et d'une carte de séjour est nécessaire.
Frais pour une année universitaire: Chaque université a une grille de scolarité qui lui est propre. Ces scolarités varient donc d'un établissement à l'autre et d'une spécialisation à l'autre, et elles diffèrent parfois d'un cycle à l'autre pour une même filière.
Services d'accueil et d'information:
• Le Bureau du tourisme des jeunes (Conseil national du tourisme) et l'Office du développement social, ont pour but de promouvoir l'échange des jeunes y compris des étudiants.
• Ambassades ou consulats du Liban à l'étranger.
Reconnaissance des études et diplômes: Commission nationale des Équivalences de l'Enseignement supérieur; Mina el hosne
Starco Building; Beirut; Liban; tél: +961-1-371-069; fax: +961-1-373-225.
Possibilités d'emploi: Les possibilités d'emploi n'existent pas pour les étudiants étrangers.
Publications / Sites Web:
• «Le Guide de l'enseignement supérieure au Liban»: Cette publication qui a été préparée par le Ministère de la culture et de l'enseignement supérieur détaille les procédures d'admission propres à chaque institution avec concours et examens, et elle énumère les facultés relevant de chacune, avec les domaines de spécialisation et les diplômes accordés. Elle décrit aussi pour chacune les systèmes de bourse adoptés, les frais de scolarisation, et les activités et services extra-universitaires assurés.

1442 Al-Imam Al-Ouzai University
P.O. Box 14-5355
Beirut
Tel: +961-1-704-452 / 4 / 6
Fax: +961-1-704-449
Web: http://www.ouzai.org

🎓 Undergraduate Islamic Studies

Study Domains: theology, religion.
Description: maximum of 50 scholarships attributed each year.
Open to: scholarship for university junior staff to enable them to obtain MA and PhD.
Duration: 3 academic years, renewable.
Value: full tuition.
Applications: by 31 December. The candidate must be sponsored by his university and must return to university of origin at the end of studies; contact nawar@ouzai.org for further details.

1443 American University of Beirut [AUB]
PO Box 11236
Riad El Solh
1107 2020 Beirut
Tel: +961-1-350-000
Fax: +961-1-351-706
Web: http://www.aub.edu.lb
e-mail: webmaster@aub.edu.lb

📖 Undergraduate, Graduate, Postgraduate Programmes

Study Domains: all major fields, agronomic sciences, architecture, business administration, computer science, economic and commercial sciences, economy, education, engineering, health and hygiene, human sciences, liberal arts, management, nutrition, sciences, social sciences.
Programmes: Programme of studies lading to Bachelor's, Master's, Ph.D., M.D. and Teaching Diploma.
Open to: candidates of all nationalities holding a Lebanese baccalaureate or equivalent; candidates must pass a language examination (EEE or TOEFL) and an entrance examination (SAT).
Fees: between US$ 4,350-$6,500 per semester according to subject matters.
Financial assistance: financial assistance and scholarships are possible for students with financial difficulties and who with exceptional academic results.
Applications: September and February.

1444 Association Makassed Philanthropique et Islamique à Beyrouth [AMPIB]
PO Box 1360252
rue Bachir El-Kassar
Verdun-IMM Tarazi
Beirut
Tel: +961-1-867-115
Fax: +961-1-867-115
e-mail: hinash@cyberia.net.lb

📖 Cursus allant du 1er au 2ème cycles

Domaines d'étude: enseignement technique, études d'infirmière, technologie, théologie, religion.
Programmes: programme de cours conduisant au Bachelor's degree et au Master's degree.
A l'intention de: ressortissants de tout pays; titulaires du diplôme de fin d'études secondaires; âgés de 18 ans au moins; admission sur examen et entretien; date de l'examen: 15 septembre.
Frais: frais d'inscription: 500 US$; frais de scolarité: 6000 US$; frais de séjour: 6000 US$ par an.
Assistance financière: aide à l'enseignement supérieur couvrant 50% des frais de scolarité; cette aide est attribuée sur critères sociaux; elle est annuelle et renouvelable; les demandes doivent être faites au plus tard au mois d'août auprès du bureau du président du conseil de l'enseignement supérieur.
Connaissances linguistiques: cours dispensés en arabe et en anglais.
Inscriptions: avant le 15 septembre.

1445 Jinan University [JU]
PO Box 818
Tripoli
Tel: +961-6-447-906
Fax: +961-6-447-900
Web: http://www.jinan.edu.lb
e-mail: jinan@inco-tr.com.lb

🐦 Non-Degree Arabic Programme

Study Domains: Arabic.
Description: Tuition reduction for courses in intensive Arabic for non-Arabic speaking students.
Open to: candidates of all nationalities.
Value: tuition and living expenses: from 10% to 100% of amounts.
Applications: by 31 August; info@jinan.edu.lb.

1446 Université américaine libanaise [LAU]
Ras Beyrouth
BP 13-5053
Chouran-Beyrouth
Beyrouth
1102 2801 Beyrouth
Tel: +961-1-786-456/64
Fax: +961-1-786-456/9944-851
Web: http://www.lau.edu.lb
e-mail: admissions@lau.edu.lb

📖 Undergraduate, Graduate and Postgraduate Programmes

Study Domains: all major fields.
Programmes: Degree programmes at Bachelor's, Master's, Associate and Certificate levels as well as Teaching diploma and Doctorate.
Description: courses in the following fields: humanities; liberal arts; education; human sciences; graphic arts; advertising; natural sciences, social sciences; documentation; political sciences, management; accounting; economy; banking; finance; marketing; civil engineering; electrical engineering; industrial engineering; architecture; interior decoration; informatics; fine arts.
A l'intention de: candidates of all nationalities possessing the Lebanese baccalauréat or equivalent and passing an admissions test in either French or English (EEE ou TOEFL).
Assistance financière: financial assistance available for students with financial difficulties and with academic merit.
Inscriptions: in October and February.

1447 Université Antonine [UPA]
BP 40016 Baabda
Hadath-Baabda
Tel: +961-592-4073/4/6
Fax: +961-592-4075/924-815
Web: http://www.upa.edu.lb
e-mail: contact@upa.edu.lb

📖 Cursus allant du 1er au 2ème cycles

Domaines d'étude: toutes disciplines principales.
Programmes: Diplôme universitaire de technologie (DUT), Licence d'enseignement, Licence d'infirmière, Maîtrise en informatique, Maîtrise en théologie, Diplôme d'ingénieur, Diplôme d'études approfondies.
A l'intention de: titulaires du Baccalauréat libanais (ou équivalent); admission sur examen et entretien.
Frais: frais d'inscription: 200 US$; frais de scolarité: entre 1900 et 5000 US$; frais de séjour: environ 150 US$ par mois.
Connaissances linguistiques: cours dispensés en arabe, en français et en anglais.
Inscriptions: avant le 15 septembre auprès du service de l'administration financière.

1448 Université arabe de Beyrouth [BAU]
Tarik el Jedida
BP 115020
Rue Dr.-Omar-Farroukh
Beyrouth
Tel: +961-1-300-110
Fax: +961-1-818-402
Web: http://www.bau.edu.lb
e-mail: registrar@bau.edu.lb

📖 Cursus allant du 1er au 3ème cycles

Domaines d'étude: toutes disciplines principales.
Programmes: Diploma, Bachelor's, Master's, Ph.D., Médecine et chirurgie, Médecine dentaire.
Description: cours essentiellement en arabe et anglais dans les domaines suivants: génie (civil, électrique), droit, sciences économiques, commerce, gestion, comptabilité, finances et douane, lettres et sciences humaines, sciences exactes, pharmacie, architecture.
A l'intention de: ressortissants de tout pays, titulaires du baccalauréat libanais ou d'un diplôme équivalent, admission sur concours dans certaines facultés.
Durée: généralement 3 ans, varie en fonction des facultés.
Frais: 1.000.000 LL pour les spécialisations théoriques, 2.000.000 LL pour les spécialisations pratiques.
Assistance financière: bourses et aides pour les étudiants ayant des difficultés financières et qui se distinguent au niveau académique.
Inscriptions: en octobre et novembre.

1449 Université de Balamand

BP 100
Tripoli
Tel: +961-6-930-250
Fax: +961-6-930-278
Web: http://www.balamand.edu.lb
e-mail: admissions@balamand.edu.lb

Académie libanaise des beaux-arts

Domaines d'étude: architecture, arts, arts décoratifs, arts
graphiques, arts plastiques, beaux-arts, moyens audio-visuels,
publicité, urbanisme.
Programmes: cursus diplômant de l'Académie libanaise
des beaux-arts en architecture, architecture d'intérieur, arts
décoratifs, arts graphiques, publicité, audiovisuel, arts
plastiques et urbanisme.
A l'intention de: ressortissants de tout pays, titulaires du
baccalauréat (ou titre équivalent); pour les études
d'architecture, une année préparatoire est exigée.
Frais: frais de scolarité: entre 2750 et 4300 US$ par
semestre; frais de séjour: environ 400 US$ par mois; livres,
transports et diverses activités: environ 500 US$ sur l'année.
Assistance financière: possibilité de bourses attribuées en
fonction de critères à la fois sociaux et académiques.
Connaissances linguistiques: cours dispensés en arabe, en
anglais et en français; l'examen d'admission comprend un test
de langue.
Inscriptions: en septembre et en janvier à l'adresse
ci-dessus.

Cursus allant du 1er au 2ème cycles

Domaines d'étude: toutes disciplines principales.
Programmes: programme de cours conduisant au
Bachelor's, Master's, Teaching Diploma.
Description: cours essentiellement en français dans les
domaines suivants: théologie, droit canon, lettres et sciences
humaines, sciences de l'éducation (permanente, physique),
documentation, études d'infirmières, études paramédicales,
techniques de laboratoire, radiologie, interprétation et
traduction, gestion, sciences exactes, génie civil, électrique,
mécanique et informatique, ainsi que les domaines assurés par
l'Académie libanaise des beaux-arts.
A l'intention de: ressortissants de tout pays, titulaires du
baccalauréat libanais ou d'un diplôme équivalent, examen de
langue en français et concours pour l'admission dans certaines
facultés.
Assistance financière: bourses et aides pour les étudiants
ayant des difficultés financières et qui se distinguent au
niveau académique.
Inscriptions: en octobre et novembre.

1450 Université de Tripoli [UT]

Tripoli Liban-Abou Samra
rue Al Islah-Islah Campus
Tripoli
Tel: +961-6-447-200/1
Fax: +961-6-447-202
Web: http://www.islahonline.org
e-mail: info@islahonline.org

Cursus allant du 1er au 3ème cycles

Domaines d'étude: droit, éducation.
Programmes: programme de cours conduisant à la
Licence, au Diplôme et au Doctorat.
A l'intention de: ressortissants de tout pays, sans limites
d'âge ou de nationalité; titulaires du diplôme de fin d'études
secondaires.
Frais: frais de scolarité: 500 US$.
Connaissances linguistiques: cours dispensés en arabe
(test d'arabe pour les ressortissants de pays non arabophones).
Inscriptions: avant le 15 février auprès de Khaled Mikati
(coordonnées de l'université ci-dessus).

1451 Université du Saint-Esprit

BP 446
Jounieh - Mont Liban
Tel: +961-9-640-664
Fax: +961-9-642-333
Web: http://www.usek.edu.lb
e-mail: usek@usek.edu.lb

Cursus allant du 1er au 3ème cycles

Domaines d'étude: toutes disciplines principales.
Programmes: programme de cours conduisant au
Bachelor's, Master's et Doctorat (Ph.D.).
Description: cours essentiellement en français, dans les
domaines suivants: théologie, agronomie, droit, sciences
commerciales, gestion et management, publicité, informatique
de gestion, lettres et sciences humaines, sciences de
l'éducation, photographie et études audiovisuelles,
interprétariat et traduction, architecture et architecture
d'intérieur, musicologie.
A l'intention de: ressortissants de tout pays, titulaires du
baccalauréat libanais ou d'un diplôme équivalent; les
candidats doivent passer un examen de langue en français et
un concours pour l'admission dans certaines facultés.
Durée: généralement 3 ans, variable selon les facultés et
les spécialisations.
Frais: entre 900 US$ et 1950 US$ en fonction des
spécialisations.
Assistance financière: bourses et aides pour les étudiants
ayant des difficultés financières et qui se distinguent au
niveau académique.
Inscriptions: en octobre et novembre.

1452 Université Islamique du Liban [UIL]

BP 30014
Autostrade Khaldeh
Khalde, Choueifat
Tel: +96-5-807-711
Fax: +96-5-807-719
Web: http://www.iul.edu.lb
e-mail: iul@iul.edu.lb

Cursus allant du 1er au 3ème cycles

Domaines d'étude: administration, administration des
affaires, droit, études d'infirmière, finances, géographie,
géologie, gestion, informatique, interprétation et traduction,
pharmacie et pharmacologie, sciences politiques,
télécommunications, théologie, religion, tourisme, hôtellerie,
restauration.
Programmes: programme de cours conduisant au
Bachelor's, au Master's, au Diploma et au Doctorat (Ph.D.) en
fonction des filières.
Description: Bachelor's degree: biomedical engineering,
computer and telecommunication engineering, surveying
engineering, tourism, nursing, computer science, business
administration; master's degree: financial management;
Bachelor's, Master's et Ph.D.: droit, sciences politiques et
diplomatiques et administration, traduction et interprétation;
programme sans diplôme: études islamiques.
A l'intention de: titulaires du diplôme de fin d'études
secondaires (type baccalauréat ou équivalent); admission sur
examen.
Frais: frais de scolarité: 1700-2700 US$; frais de séjour:
environ 500 US$ par mois; études d'infirmières: 44 US$ par
unité de valeur; informatique: 60 US$ par unité de valeur.
Connaissances linguistiques: cours dispensés en arabe,
anglais et français.
Inscriptions: avant le 15 septembre auprès de Fawzi
Salloukh (coordonnées ci-dessus).

Assistance financière

Domaines d'étude: toutes disciplines principales.
Scholarships: Réduction de frais de scolarité.
Value: réduction frais de scolarité de 25 à 50%.
Applications: janvier de chaque année; contacter Samih
fayad, tel: +961-5-807-711 pour une information complète.

1453 Université libanaise [UL]

BP 14-6573
Place du Musée
Beyrouth
Tel: +961-1-612 -618
Fax: +961-1-612-621
Web: http://www.ul.edu.lb
e-mail: rectorat@ul.edu.lb

Cursus allant du 1er au 3ème cycles

Domaines d'étude: toutes disciplines principales.
Programmes: programme de cours conduisant au

Diploma, à la Licence, au Diplôme d'études supérieures (DES) et au Doctorat.
A l'intention de: ressortissants de tout pays, titulaires du baccalauréat libanais ou d'un diplôme admis en équivalence. La sélection se fait sur concours pour certaines facultés.
Durée: généralement 4 ans.
Frais: l'enseignement est gratuit.
Connaissances linguistiques: langues d'enseignement: arabe, français et/ou anglais.
Inscriptions: généralement en octobre, écrire à l'adresse ci-dessus pour de plus amples renseignements.

1454 Université Notre Dame de Louaizé [NDU]
Zouk Mosbeh
BP 72
Zouk Mikhaël
Tel: +961-9-218-950
Fax: +961-9-218-771
Web: http://www.ndu.edu.lb

📖 Cursus allant du 1er au 2ème cycles
Domaines d'étude: toutes disciplines principales.
Programmes: programme de cours conduisant au Bachelor's et au Master's.
A l'intention de: ressortissants de tout pays, titulaires d'un baccalauréat libanais, ou d'un diplôme équivalent, examen de langue anglaise (EE ou TOEFL) et arabe pour l'admission.
Durée: par semestre.
Inscriptions: en octobre et février à l'adresse ci-dessus.

1455 Université Saint-Joseph [USJ]
BP 175-208
Rue de Damas
Beyrouth
Tel: +961-1-426456 / 7 / 8 / 9
Fax: +961-1-423-369
Web: http://www.usj.edu.lb
e-mail: service.orientation@usj.edu.lb

📖 Cursus allant du 1er au 3ème cycles
Domaines d'étude: toutes disciplines principales.
Programmes: programme de cours conduisant au Diplôme universitaire de technologie (DUT),au Diplôme universitaire d'études générales (DEUG), au Diploma, à la Licence, au Teaching Diploma, au Diplôme d'études supérieures spécialisées (DESS), au Doctorat et au Diplôme universitaire (DU).
Description: cours dans les domaines suivants: administration, administration des affaires, agriculture, assurances, assistance sociale, droit, éducation, études dentaires, études d'infirmières, gestion et management, génie (civil, électrique, électronique), études bancaires, informatique de gestion, ingénierie, interprétariat et traduction, lettres et sciences humaines, littérature et civilisation, médecine et médecine dentaire, pharmacie, publicité et vente, sciences humaines, sciences politiques et administratives, sciences de l'éducation et éducation spécialisée, études scéniques et audiovisuelles, sciences économiques, télécommunication et agronomie, théologie.
A l'intention de: ressortissants de tout pays, titulaires du baccalauréat libanais ou d'un diplôme équivalent. Dans certaines facultés, la réussite à un concours d'entrée et un examen de langue en français sont nécessaires.
Durée: généralement 3 ans, variable selon les spécialisations.
Assistance financière: bourses et aides pour les étudiants ayant des difficultés financières et qui se distinguent au niveau académique, et à partir de la 2ème année.
Inscriptions: en octobre et novembre.

Libyan Arab Jamahiriya
Academic year: October to June.
Organization of higher education system: Undergraduate, graduate and postgraduate programmes are available at universities and higher institutions of technical and vocational studies. Academic programmes in higher institutions consist of 2 to 3 year programmes; in universities Bachelor's of Science and Arts degrees consist of 4 years of study in Faculties of Humanity, 5 years for Faculties of Engineering and 6 years for medicine faculties; Higher Diploma studies consist of 2 further years of study beyond the Bachelor's degree, leading to a Master's degree.
Monetary unit: Libyan dinar.
National student admission: All students applying for higher education studies must hold the Libyan Secondary Education Certificate (Baccalaureate) or its equivalent (scientific or liberal arts) issued in the same or previous year of application and meet academic standards for entry into each faculty.
International student admission: Same as for national students.
Language: Students must have adequate knowledge of Arabic and English, depending on studies followed.
Immigration requirements: Candidates should enquire at diplomatic missions of the Libyan Arab Jamahiriya in their countries for all immigration requirements.
Estimated expenses for one academic year: Fees and living expenses are variable and students should enquire at each institution.
Information services:
• Cultural Section of Libyan diplomatic missions in each country.
• Rectorat of University of Garyounis, Benghazi (Foreign Students Department); http://www.garyounis.edu
• Rectorat of Al-Fateh University, Tripoli (Foreign Students Department).
Open and distance learning: Distance education is provided by the Open University, created in 1987, for undergraduate studies.
Recognition of studies and qualification: Committee for the Equivalence of Academic Credentials, Secretary of the General People's Committee for Education and Vocational Training; Tripoli; Libya; tel: +218 21 360 9177; fax: +218 21 360 9177.

1456 University of Al-Tahaddy [UOE]
PO Box 674
Sirt
Tel: +218-54-62150/1/2
Fax: +218-54-4373
Web: http://www.altahdi.org

📖 Undergraduate Programmes
Study Domains: education, electricity and electronics, engineering, human sciences, languages, mechanical engineering, sciences.
Programmes: Courses leading to Bachelor's degree.
Description: (a) courses in civil, mechanical and electrical engineering: 500 participants; (b) Bachelor's degree in education, sciences, languages and humanities: 500 participants.
Open to: candidates of all nationalities, over age 17, holding a secondary-school certificate.
Held: (a) at the Faculty of Engineering; (b) at the Faculty of Education and Science.
Duration: (a) up to 5 years; (b) 4 years.
Fees: (b) 600 dinars per year.
Applications: by the end of August, to the Registrar at the above address.

Liechtenstein

Academic year: October to June.
Organization of higher education system: Higher education is provided by 2 academic institutions: the International Academy
of Philosophy (IAP) and the Liechtenstein Institute (LI). M.A. (Master of Arts) and D. (Doctor's degree) delivered but no academic degree can be obtained from the Liechtenstein.
International student admission: Foreign students can study at the International Academy of Philosophy (IAP). There is a numerus clausus. Applications are available from IAP and must be completed and returned at least one month prior to the beginning of the semester, together with the stipulated documents: secondary-school-leaving certificate and residence permit issued by the Office for the Registration of Aliens. The government establishes rules for the recognition of foreign higher-education degrees and diplomas. With regard to medicine, it takes into account the recommendations of the Sanitätskommission, which provides an appropriate test by which to judge candidates.
Language: Good knowledge of German and English is required.
Information services:
• Education Office, Austrasse 79, LI-9490 Vaduz; tel: +41-75-236-6758; fax: +41-75-2366771; web: http://www.liechtenstein.li.

1457 University of Applied Sciences
Fürst-Franz-Josef-Strasse
9490 Vaduz
Tel: +423-265-1111
Fax: +423-265-1112
Web: http://www.iap.li
e-mail: info@fh-liechtenstein.li

📖 **Undergraduate, Graduate Programmes**

Study Domains: architecture, business, business administration, industry and commerce, international business, international relations.
Programmes: Bachelor's and Master's degree programmes in (a) architecture; (b) business.
Open to: candidates of all nationalities possessing a secondary-school certificate; good German essential.
Fees: CHF 750 per semester.
Languages: students must be able to read, speak and write fluent German; no language courses are offered at the Institute.
Applications: by 1 September, to the above address; application form may be downloaded from website.

Lithuania

Academic year: September to June.
Organization of higher education system: Higher education is provided through state-run and private universities and colleges (non-university type institutions). University consecutive studies lead to three levels of degrees:
• First cycle leading to a Bachelor's degree and/or professional qualification. This cycle lasts from three and a half to four and a half years and requires that a student earn 140 to 180 national credits. Studies are aimed at expanding one's general education, providing knowledge and skills for a professional career, teaching creative use of accumulated knowledge and skills.
• Second cycle leads to a Master's degree and/or professional qualification. This cycle lasts from one and half to two years beyond the first cycle and requires 60 to 80 national credits. Studies are aimed at preparing students for careers in science or arts requiring scientific knowledge and skills.
• Third cycle leading to PhD degree for residency, doctoral and post-graduate art studies. Doctoral studies last at least four years and are designed for the training of scientific staff and include studies, research and a doctoral thesis, Post-graduate art programmes are aimed at training teachers for higher education institutions in arts and provide in-depth preparation for specialized creative activities.
• Integrated studies are a combination of first and second cycle and lead straight to a Master's degree or professional qualification. These require 180 to 280 national credits. An integrated programme is for studies in pharmacy, medicine, odontology, veterinary medicine. Graduates may pursue doctoral, postgraduate art or residency studies.
• Non-university study programmes lead to a professional qualification. These studies may last from three to four years. A student must earn 120 to 160 national credits. Part-time (evening or extra-mural) studies usually last a year longer than full-time studies. One-third of the study programme consists of practical training. The studies terminate with a final work or final project.
• According to the content of studies and the qualifications awarded, consecutive study programmes are all divided into 61 study fields in six areas: humanities, social, physical, biomedical, technological sciences and arts. Consecutive studies may be pursued on full-time, part-time evening or extra-mural bases. The qualifications earned are all of the same value regardless of mode of study.
Monetary unit: Lithuanian lita (LT).
National student admission: On university entrance examination or inter-university transfer.
International student admission: Candidates must have a secondary-school leaving certificate or equivalent and adequate grades. Study programmes requiring specific skills, such as fine arts, journalism, architecture, music, sports, require an entrance examination.
Language: The majority of programmes are in Lithuanian but some programmes are in English, German and Russian.
Immigration requirements: Visas may be required depending on the country. All foreign nationals, including those from European Union and European Economic Area countries must obtain a permit to reside in the country.
Estimated expenses for one academic year: Tuition: from 3,000-36,000 LT (depending on study programme and cycle); books/supplies: 500-3,000 LT; housing: 1,000-5,000 LT.
Information services: Applications from foreign students should be addressed to relevant institution; information available at: www.mokslas.lt.
Other agencies:
• Department of Higher Education and Science, MES, Sierakhusko Str. 15, 03105 Vilnius; tel: +370-5-2663-444; fax: +370-5-2663-466: web: www.mokslas.lt
• The majority of higher education institutions belong to the Lithuanian Higher Institutions' Association for Organizing Joint Admission (LAMABPO). The Association develops and carries out admission procedures equally applicable to all its members. An applicant may apply for up to 20 different study programmes offered by any member of the association.
• European Union Socrates Programme Coordination Support Foundation; Celezinio Vilko Str., 12, Vilnius; tel: +370-5-2497137; fax: +370-5-261-0592; web: www.socrates.lt
• Other agencies:
Lithuanian Embassies in foreign countries.
• Student organizations:
Lithuanian National Union of Students: web: www.lss.lt
Lithuanian National Union of Student Representations: web: www.lsas.lt.
Scholarships for international students:
• all undergraduate and graduate students of state-operated institutions are eligible for merit/need-based scholarships. These scholarships are awarded by individual institutions.
• Doctoral students and postgraduate art students are eligible for scholarships of 735-850 LT/month.
• Medical resident students receive salaries from the university.
• Other forms of financial assistance are provided under bilateral agreements and students should contact the diplomatic mission of Lithuania in their home countries for further information.
• Financial assistance is also available for students wishing to pursue Lithuanian and/or Baltic studies.
• Students may also apply for loans from their universities for living expenses.
For further information contact the Ministry of Education and Science; web: www.mokslas.li.
Open and distance learning: Kaunas Regional Distance Education Study Centre (KRDESC) established at Kaunas University of Technology in 1996 within the framework of PHARE Multi-Country Cooperation in Distance Education. Its aim is to promote the creation of an information society in Lithuania by developing quality distance education. Further information: KRDESC, Studentu 48a-308, LT Kaunas, Lithuania; tel: +370-7-300-611; fax: +370-7-300-614.

Recognition of studies and qualification: Lithuanian Centre for Quality Assessment in Higher Education (Lithuanian ENIC/NARIC); Suvalku st. 1; LT 2600 Vilnius; Lithuania; tel: +370-5-210-4777; fax: +370-5-213-2553; web: htp://www.skvc.lt.

Accommodation services: In student dormitories for full-time students; prices vary from 100 LT-250LT per room. Accommodation should be booked two months in advance. Private apartments are also available.

Work opportunities: There are no work opportunities for international students.

Publications / Websites:
• 'Welcome to Lithuania for Studies 2005', edited by the Ministry of Education and Science of the Republic of Lithuania, which supplies information including fields of activity, services offered, contact names of Lithuanian education and research institutions.
• 'Study in Lithuania 2004'
Publications available on request at: WLS-2005@skvc.lt.

1458   Kaunas University of Medicine [KMA]

International Relations and Study Center
A. Mickeviciaus 9
3000 Kaunas
Tel: +370-37-327-299
Fax: +370-37-220-733
Web: http://www.kmu.lt/foreign
e-mail: fstudent@kmu.lt

📖 Medical Programmes

Study Domains: dentistry, medicine, nursing, pharmacy and pharmacology.

Programmes: programmes of study in the following fields: (a) medicine; (b) dentistry (stomatology); (c) pharmacy; (d) nursing; (e) public health.

Open to: to candidates of any country, holding a Bachelor's Degree in biology or secondary school graduates with good knowledge in biology, chemistry and physics. Working experience of not less than 1 year is required for (d).

Duration: (a) 6 years; (b) and (c) 5 years; (d) and (e) 4 years.

Fees: (a) 4,100 €, (b) 4,100-4,300 € and (c) 3,100-3,300 € per year.

Languages: good knowledge of Lithuanian or English is required.

Applications: should be sent to the International Relations and Study Center at the above address.

1459   Kaunas University of Technology [KTU]

K. Donelaicio Street 73
3003 Kaunas
Tel: +370-37-300-000
Fax: +370-37-324-144
Web: http://www.ktu.lt
e-mail: rastine@cr.ktu.lt

📖 Undergraduate, Graduate and Postgraduate Programmes

Study Domains: architecture, chemistry, civil engineering, computer science, economic and commercial sciences, electricity and electronics, engineering, English, management, mathematics, mechanical engineering, sciences, social sciences, technology, telecommunications.

Programmes: courses leading to Bachelor of Science (B.Sc.), Professional Qualification, Master of Science (M.Sc.) and Doctorate of Science (D.Sc.).

Description: Bachelor of Export Engineering; Master of Environmental Management and Cleaner Production, Engineering and Management, Control Technologies, Management.

Open to: candidates of any country holding a secondary-school certificate (or equivalent) or university degree.

Duration: Bachelor's: 4 years; Master's: a further 2 years; Doctorate; a further 4 years; Professional Qualification; 1 year following Bachelor's; courses begin in September.

Fees: current registration: 300 €; tuition: 2,320 € per year; estimated living expenses: 300 € per month.

Languages: most of the courses are taught in English, French, Russian or German; a language test is required for admission.

Applications: by 1 April to the Admissions Office of the University; for information contact Alvydas Kondratas; tel. +370 37 300 045; email: komisija@cr.ktu.lt.

1460   Klaipeda University [KU]

H. Manto G. 84
92294 Klaipeda
Tel: +370-46-398-900
Fax: +370-46-398-902
Web: http://www.ku.lt

📖 Undergraduate, Graduate, Postgraduate Programmes

Study Domains: all major fields.

Programmes: courses leading to Bachelor's, Master's and doctoral degrees; also Specialized and Postgraduate Professional Programmes.

Subjects: International Baltic Sea Region Studies; non-consecutive postgraduate piano studies; International Amateur Theatre Directors Course; Lithuania in transition; the basics of recreation and tourism; Lithuanian language vocabulary and practical use; Lithuanian language for non-native speakers; Russian Language for Non-native Speakers.

Open to: candidates of all nationalities meeting academic; linguistic and financial requirements.

Duration: Bachelor's: 4 years (8 semesters); Specialized Professional studies: 1 year (2 semesters); Master's: 1-1/2 to 2 years (3 to 4 semesters); Doctoral: 3 to 4 years.

Financial assistance: some scholarships of 200-400 litas per month are available for students of any nationality; for information, contact Head of Study Department; tel: +370-46-398-926; fax: +370-46-398-927.

Languages: official language of instruction: Lithuanian; some courses in the degree programmes may be taught in English if a reasonable amount of students are interested in them; Klaipeda University offers non-degree programme International Studies of the Baltic Sea Region for international and local students in English; University also offers Intensive Lithuanian language courses for exchange students (beginners and advanced level); postgraduate study programme for foreigners; History Department courses in English; Department of Economics and Management courses in English.

Applications: 1 June for autumn semester; 1 November for spring semester; see website: http://www.ku.lt.

1461   Law University of Lithuania [LUL]

Ateities g. 20
2057 Vilnius
Tel: +370-5-271-4522
Fax: +370-5-267-6000 / 271-4522
Web: http://www.ltu.lt
e-mail: roffice@ltu.lt; inter@ltu.lt

📖 Undergraduate, Graduate, Postgraduate Programmes

Study Domains: administration, criminology, international law, law, management, psychology, social sciences.

Programmes: programme of courses leading to Bachelor's, Master's and Ph.D. degrees.

Description: (a) Bachelor of Laws, Bachelor of Social Work, Bachelor of Public Administration; (b) Master of Laws, Master of Social Work, Master of Public Administration, Master of Economics, Master of Psychology.

Open to: candidates holding a secondary school certificate (or equivalent) or a university degree and having a good command of Lithuanian.

Duration: Bachelor's: 4 years; Master's: a further 2 years; Ph.D.: a further 4 years; courses begin in September.

Fees: information available on web site: www.ltu.lt/padaliniai/trsc/english/interstudents.html.

Languages: language of instruction: Lithuanian. The Department of Foreign Languages offers basic Lithuanian courses for international students coming to the University; over 90 courses in English, German and French have been developed by the teaching staff of the University for the

international students.
Applications: information available on website:
http://www.ltu.lt/padaliniai/trsc/english/interstudents.html.

1462 Lithuanian Academy of Music
Gedimino pr. 42
2600 Vilnius
Tel: +370-5-261-2691
Fax: +370-5-212-0093
Web: http://www.lma.lt
e-mail: lmatrs@ktl.mii.lt

⊞ Undergraduate, Graduate Programmes
Study Domains: cinematography, fine arts, folklore, music
and musicology, performing arts, visual arts.
Programmes: advanced education courses in music.
Description: courses on: (a) Foreign students as 'special
students'; (b) regular education; (c) free choice of subjects; (d)
Advanced studies.
Open to: candidates of any country: (a) who will be
requested to provide evidence of study at an acknowledged
foreign music school and to give an audition; (b) and (d) who
will pass the normal entrance examination in July for (b) and
September for (d).
Duration: (a) at least 3 months; (b) 4 to 5 years, Bachelor's
degree; Magister's studies of 1 to 2 years following the
Bachelor's degree; (c) 3 months to 2 years; (d) 2 years for
performers; 3 to 5 years for musicologists.
Fees: US$2,000-$3,000 per year depending on the courses
chosen; full course price US$3,000; the price of other studies
depends on the subjects chosen; this payment gives access to
the Academy's rooms, instruments, libraries, record libraries,
etc.
Languages: the main language of instruction is
Lithuanian, but for some classes other languages are available
(English and German).
Applications: by 1 June, to the above address.

1463 Lithuanian Academy of Physical Education [LAPE]
Sporto st. 6
3000 Kaunas
Tel: +370-37-302-672
Fax: +370-37-302-672
Web: http://www.lkka.lt
e-mail: trs@lkka.lt

⊞ Non-Degree Programmes, Physical Education
Study Domains: education, management, physical
education, psychology.
Programmes: non-degree programmes in physical
education, sports coaching, sports science and physiotherapy.
Description: international non-degree study programmes
are oriented to visiting/exchange students within the mobility
programmes, bilateral agreements, or other students who are
not involved in any formal exchange agreement.
Fees: living costs: approx. 100€-150€ per month.
Languages: language of instruction: English, French and
German.
Applications: by 15 June for autumn semester, 15
November for spring semester.

1464 Lithuanian University of Agriculture
Studentu st. 11
4324 Kaunas
Tel: +370-37-397-500 / 323-205
Fax: +370-37-397-500
Web: http://www.lzua.lt
e-mail: laa@nora.izua.lt

⊞ Professional Programme
Study Domains: agriculture, agronomic sciences, forestry,
hydraulics.
Programmes: training courses in agriculture.
Description: subjects: agronomy, forestry, agricultural
engineering, general and agricultural hydraulics, agricultural
economics.
Open to: candidates of any country.
Duration: 1 to 2 months.

1465 Lithuanian Veterinary Academy
Tilzes st. 18
3022 Kaunas
Tel: +370-37-362-383 / 361-981
Fax: +370-37-362-417
Web: http://www.lva.lt
e-mail: reklva@lva.lt

⊞ Undergraduate, Graduate and Postgraduate Programmes
Study Domains: cattle breeding, veterinary medicine,
veterinary sciences.
Programmes: courses leading to Bachelor's, Master's and
Doctorate degrees.
Description: veterinary Medicine: veterinary hygiene and
foodstuff sanitation, veterinary surgery, internal diseases,
infection diseases, obstetrics and gynaecology, biotechnology
and reproduction, pathology and physiology,
anatomy-histology animal husbandry animal technology:
animal breeding and genetics, agriculture management,
zootechnology, meat and milk reprocessing technologies,
animal nutrition, bioinformatics.
Open to: candidates of any country holding a Bachelor's
degree or secondary school graduates (or equivalent), with
good knowledge of biology, chemistry.
Duration: B.Sc.: 4 years; M.Sc.: 2 years; Ph.D.: 4 years.
Languages: good knowledge of Lithuanian or English
required.
Applications: by 15 June for exchange students, 1 June for
degree students; for information contact International
Relations Office; tel./fax: +370 37 361981; email:
tarptautinis_LVA@lva.lt.

1466 Siauliai University [TSPI]
International Relations Office
Vilniaus St. 88
5400 Siauliai
Tel: +370-41-595-742
Fax: +370-41-595-743
Web: http://www.su.lt
e-mail: urs1@cr.su.lt / urs@cr.su.lt

⊞ Undergraduate and Graduate Programmes
Study Domains: all major fields.
Programmes: courses leading to Bachelor of Arts and
Science degree and Master of Arts and Science degree.
Description: (a) Bachelor's programmes: Art and Design,
Art and Technologies, Audio-visual Art, Graphic and Applied
Technologies, Music Education, Pre-school Education,
Primary School Education, Physical and Sports Education,
Lithuanian Philology, English Philology, French Philology,
German Philology, Russian Philology, History, Philosophy
and Public Sciences, Applied Ecology, Computer Science,
Mathematics, Physics, Business Administration, Public
Administration, Economics, Social Education and
Psychology, Special Education and Physical Education,
Special Education and Speech Therapy, Clothing Design and
Technology, Civil Engineering, Electrical Engineering,
Electronic Engineering, Mechanical Engineering, Information
Technologies, Environmental and Professional Safety; (b)
Master's programmes: Art (art history, graphics, painting),
Music Education, Educology, Comparative Linguistics,
Lithuanian Linguistics, Literary Studies, Computer Science,
Physics, Economics, Management, Social Education, Special
Education and Speech Therapy, Civil Engineering, Energetic
Engineering, Mechanical Engineering, Radio Engineering,
Signal Technology; (c) Ph.D. programmes: Educology,
Linguistics.
Open to: no age or nationality restrictions; a secondary
school leaving certificate is required for admission.
Duration: (a) 4 or 5 years; (b) 2 years; (c) 4 years.
Languages: official language of instruction: Lithuanian;
some courses may be taught in English, German or French.
Applications: contact the International Relations Office at
the above address.

1467 Vilnius Academy of Arts

Maironio G. 6
2600 Vilnius
Tel: +370-5-210-5430
Fax: +370-5-210-5444
Web: http://www.vda.lt
e-mail: vda@vda.lt

📖 Undergraduate, Graduate and Postgraduate Programmes

Study Domains: applied arts, architecture, art history, design, fine arts, graphic arts, interior design, visual arts.
Programmes: courses leading to Bachelor's, Master's and Doctorate degrees.
Description: Animation (only B.A.), Architecture (Building design, Landscape architecture, Conservation of historical monuments), Art theory and history, Ceramics, Culture management (only M.A.), Design, Fashion design, Fresco-mosaic, Interior design (only B.A.), Painting, Photography and media Arts, Printmaking and graphic art, Restoration, Scenery, Sculpture, Stained glass, Textiles.
Open to: all applicants with some artistic skills who have completed secondary education (for B.A.) or have a B.A. (for M.A. programme) or an M.A. for the doctoral programme.
Duration: B.A., 4 years; Master's, 2 years; Doctorate, 5 years; courses begin in October.
Fees: tuition: US$3,000 for a one-year course; estimated living costs: US$250 per month.
Languages: although official language of instruction is Lithuanian, major part of art studies may be taught in English.
Applications: to the International Relations Office at the above address.

1468 Vilnius Gediminas Technical University [VGTU]

Sauletekio al. 11
2040 Vilnius
Tel: +370-5-274-5000
Fax: +370-5-270-0114
Web: http://www.vgtu.lt

📖 Undergraduate, Graduate and Postgraduate Programmes

Study Domains: architecture, aviation, aeronautics, building industry, business administration, civil engineering, computer science, ecology, environment, economy, electricity and electronics, energy, engineering, geodesy, industrial technology, industry and commerce, management, mathematics, mechanical engineering, meteorology, physics.
Programmes: (a) Bachelor's degree: in architecture, civil engineering, electronics, informatics, thermal engineering, business management, mechanical engineering, transport engineering economics and management; (b) Master's degree in environmental management and cleaner production; industrial engineering and management; property management; (c) Doctorate degree in all study areas.
Description: M.Sc. studies in English are arranged according to individual plans. The programme 'Property Management' is available only through distance learning.
Open to: candidates of any country, aged from 18 holding the secondary school certificate (or equivalent), with good proficiency in English.
Held: the different faculties of the University are located in 5 different places in the city of Vilnius; for the exact location see web site: www.vtu.lt/english/faculties/.
Duration: B.Sc., 4 years; M.Sc., 2 years; Ph.D., 4 years.
Fees: current registration: 100 €; tuition: B.Sc./M.Sc.: 3,500 € per year; Ph.D.: 4,500 € per year; M.Sc. distance programme: 2,000 € per year; no fees for exchange students; estimated living costs: approximately 250-300 € per month.
Languages: language of instruction: English; see http://www.vtu.lt/english/studies.
Applications: 15 June for exchange students, 1 May for degree students. Contact person for exchange programmes: A. Radzeviciene, Head of International Office; tel. +370 5 2745029; fax +370 5 2700112; email: astrad@adm.vtu.lt. Contact person for degree programmes: Prof. Z. Kamaitis, Head of International Studies Centre; tel. +370 5 2745026; fax +370 5 2744897; email: tsc@ts.vtu.lt. Contact person for the distance programme: Prof. A.Kaklauskas, Tel.+370 5 2745234, e-mail: property@st.vtu.lt.

1469 Vilnius Pedagogical University [VPU]

Studentu st. 39
2004 Vilnius
Tel: +370-5-279-0281
Fax: +370-5-279-0548
Web: http://www.vpu.lt
e-mail: interdep@vpu.lt

📖 Undergraduate, Graduate, Postgraduate Programmes

Study Domains: all major fields.
Programmes: courses leading to Bachelor's, Master's and Ph.D.
Open to: candidates must hold the secondary-school certificate (or equivalent).
Duration: Bachelor's: 4 years; Master's: a further 2 years; Ph.D.: 3 years following Master's; courses begin in September.
Applications: for information contact Vytautas Bernotas at the above address.

1470 Vilnius University [VU]

Universiteto st. 3
2734 Vilnius
Tel: +370-5-268-7001
Fax: +370-5-268-7096
Web: http://www.vu.lt
e-mail: rector@vu.lt/trs@cr.vu.lt

📖 Interdisciplinary Programmes

Study Domains: languages.
Programmes: programme of courses leading to Bachelor's, Master's and Ph.D.
Description: for foreign language courses, see http://www.trs.cr.vu.lt/english.
Fees: exchange students: no tuition fee; independent candidates: 228 litas per VU credit for the studies at the Faculties of Humanities and Social Sciences: Economics, Philology, Philosophy, History, Kaunas Faculty of Humanities, Institute of International Relations and Political Sciences; 275 litas per VU credit at the Faculty of Natural Sciences.
Financial assistance: partial tuition reductions available.
Applications: application forms can be found at http://www.trs.cr.vu.lt/english; deadlines: Autumn semester: 15 June; Spring semester: 15 November; contact: Rita Vienazindiene; International Student Coordinator; International Programmes and Relations Office; at the above address; e-mail: rita.vienazindiene@cr.vu.lt.

1471 Vytautas Magnus University

Vytauto Didžiojo universitetas
International Relations Office
Donelaicio st.58
3000 Kaunas
Tel: +370-37-323-294
Fax: +370-37-323-296
Web: http://www.vdu.lt
e-mail: office@trs.vdu.lt

📖 Undergraduate, Graduate and Postgraduate Programmes

Study Domains: fine arts, humanities and arts, information science, law, liberal arts, political science, sciences, Slavic studies, social sciences, theology, religion.
Programmes: programme of studies leading to a Bachelor's degree; at the Faculty of Humanities; Faculty of Informatics; School of Law; Institute of Political Science and Diplomacy.
Open to: candidates of any nationality holding a secondary-school certificate or equivalent or a university degree and having a good command of Lithuanian.
Duration: Bachelor's: 4 years (theology students: 5 years); Master's: 2 years (law students: 3 years); Doctorate: 4 years.
Applications: deadlines: 1 June for Autumn semester; 1 November for Spring semester.

Luxembourg

Année universitaire: octobre à juillet.
Organisation de l'enseignement supérieur:
L'enseignement supérieur est dispensé à l'Université de
Luxembourg au sein de trois facultés, à savoir: 1l) la Faculté
des Sciences, de la Technologie et de la Communication; 2)
la Faculté de Droit, d'Economie et de Finances, et la Faculté
des Lettres, des Sciences Humaines, des Arts et des Sciences
de l'Education. L'Université du Luxembourg offre des
formations aux grades de bachelor, de master et de doctorat.
Unité monétaire: Euro (€).
Admission pour étudiants du pays:
• Sont admis à s'inscrire au premier niveau (grade de
bachelor) à l'Université du Luxembourg, tous les étudiants qui
sont détenteurs d'un diplôme de fin d'études secondaires ou
secondaires techniques ou d'un diplôme de technicien dans
une spécialité correspondant aux études universitaires
envisagées.
• Sont admis à s'inscrire aux deuxième et troisième niveau
(grades de master et de doctorat) les détenteurs d'un grade
sanctionnant le niveau précédant et inscrit au registre des
titres déposé au ministère luxembourgeois de l'enseignement
supérieur.
Admission pour étudiants internationaux: un examen
spécial d'entrée est exigé pour tous les étudiants dont les
diplômes de fin d'études secondaires ou les diplômes
universitaires ne sont pas reconnus équivalents ou inscrits au
registre des titres par les autorités luxembourgeoises.
Connaissances linguistiques requises: Les langues
d'enseignement sont le français, l'allemand et l'anglais et les
formations offertes sont dispensées dans deux langues au
choix. Une excellent connaissance des deux langues
d'enseignement est requise.
Formalités d'immigration: Visa nécessaire pour les
étudiants hors Union européenne. Les autorités ont mis en
place une procédure simplifiée d'entrée et de séjour sur le
territoire luxembourgeois pour les étudiants ressortissants
d'états tiers et inscrits à l'Université du Luxembourg. Se
renseigner auprès du Service de la vie étudiante de
l'Université du Luxembourg.
Frais pour une année universitaire: frais d'inscription:
100 € par année académique; logement: 350 € par mois
environ.
Services d'accueil et d'information:
• Centre de Documentation et d'Information sur
l'Enseignement Supérieur (CEDIES), 211, route d'Esch,
L-1471, Luxembourg; fax: +352-26-190-104; web:
www.cedies.lu
• Ambassades, légations ou consulats du Luxembourg à
l'étranger.
Reconnaissance des études et diplômes: NARIC;
Ministère de la Culture, de l'Enseignement supérieur et de la
Recherche
20, Montée de la Pétrusse; L-2912 Luxembourg;
Luxembourg; tél: +352-478-5134 / 478-5135; fax:
+352-2629-6037; web: http://www.cedies.lu.
Services du logement: service logement; Université du
Luxembourg, 162A, avenue de la Faiencerie; L-1511
Luxembourg; web: http://www.uni.lu.
Possibilités d'emploi: Les ressortissants de pays
non-membres de l'Union européenne doivent être en
possession d'un permis de travail délivré par la Direction de
l'Immigration du Ministère des Affaires étrangères. Se
renseigner auprès de la vie étudiante de l'Université du
Luxembourg.
Publications / Sites Web:
• Université du Luxembourg; http://www.uni.lu
• Centre de Documentation et d'Information sur
l'Enseignement Supérieur (CIEDIES); www.cedies.lu
• Gouvernement luxembourgeois: www.gouvernement.lu.

1472   Centre universitaire de Luxembourg [CU]

162a, avenue de la Faïencerie
1511 Luxembourg
Tel: +352-466-644 / 1
Fax: +352-466-644 / 506
Web: http://www.cu.lu
e-mail: informations_academiques@cu.lu

📖 Programme de cours de 1er cycle

Domaines d'étude: toutes disciplines principales.
Programmes: programme de cours conduisant au DPCU,
DUT.
A l'intention de: ressortissants de tout pays, titulaires d'un
diplôme de fin d'études secondaires luxembourgeois ou d'un
diplôme étranger reconnu équivalent par le Ministère
luxembourgeois de l'éducation nationale.
Durée: 2 ans débutant le 1er octobre.
Frais: inscription gratuite.
Assistance financière: possibilité d'octroi de bourses
d'État sur critères académiques et sociaux; renseignements
auprès du secrétariat de l'administration.
Connaissances linguistiques: cours dispensés en français;
langues véhiculaires: français, allemand, anglais.
Inscriptions: avant le 15 septembre, à l'adresse ci-dessus
(avec indication du Département d'études); pour toute
information contacter le secrétariat de la présidence, Tel.
+352 46 44-235; Fax +352 46 44-506;
information_academiques@cu.lu.

1473   Institut supérieur d'études et de recherches pédagogiques [ISERP]

Route de Diekirch
BP 2
7201 Walferdange
Tel: +352-333-4201
Fax: +352-333-256
Web: http://www.iserp.lu
e-mail: admin@iserp.lu

📖 Formation d'enseignants

Domaines d'étude: formation des enseignants.
Programmes: formation professionnelle des instituteurs de
l'enseignement primaire et préscolaire conduisant au Certificat
d'études pédagogiques (CEP, niveau Bac+3) et comprenant:
une formation théorique en psychologie, didactique générale
et disciplinaire; une formation pratique par l'intermédiaire de
stages en milieu scolaire; la réalisation d'un mémoire
professionnel.
A l'intention de: titulaires d'un baccalauréat ou équivalent;
test de maîtrise des 3 langues d'enseignement: français,
allemand et luxembourgeois; classement en fonction des notes
obtenues au Bac.
Durée: 3 ans.
Assistance financière: possibilité d'assistance financière.
Connaissances linguistiques: le luxembourgeois, le
français et l'allemand.
Inscriptions: à l'adresse ci-dessus.

1474   Institut supérieur de technologie [IST]

6, r. Richard Coudenhove-Kalergi
1359 Luxembourg
Tel: +352-420-101 / 1
Fax: +352-432-124
Web: http://www.ist.lu
e-mail: info@ist.lu

📖 Ingéniorat

Domaines d'étude: électricité et électronique, génie civil,
informatique, mécanique.
Programmes: programme de cours d'ingénieur industriel.
Description: cours d'électrotechnique, mécanique, génie
civil, informatique.
A l'intention de: ressortissants de tout pays, titulaires d'un
diplôme de fin d'études secondaires luxembourgeois ou d'un
diplôme étranger reconnu équivalent par le Ministère
luxembourgeois de l'éducation nationale; connaissance du
français, de l'anglais et de l'allemand requise.
Durée: 4 ans débutant en octobre.
Frais: inscription gratuite.
Connaissances linguistiques: langues d'enseignement:
français et allemand.
Inscriptions: avant le 1er juin à l'adresse ci-dessus.

Madagascar

Année universitaire: janvier à août.
Unité monétaire: franc malagasy (FMG).
Admission pour étudiants du pays: Les étudiants étrangers doivent posséder le baccalauréat ou un diplôme équivalent.
Connaissances linguistiques requises: Bonne connaissance du français.
Formalités d'immigration: Les étudiants étrangers doivent être titulaires d'un visa et être officiellement présentés par les autorités compétentes de leur pays d'origine, conformément aux accords établis entre les gouvernements concernés.
Frais pour une année universitaire: Environ 600.000 FMG (hébergement non compris).
Services d'accueil et d'information:
• Ministère des affaires étrangères, Anosy, Antananarivo-101.
• Ministère de l'enseignement supérieur, BP 4163, Tsimbazaza, Antananarivo-101.
• Centre des oeuvres universitaires, BP 354, Campus universitaire Ambohitsaina, Antananarivo (renseignements sur les possibilités d'études ou de logement).
• Université d'Antananarivo, BP 566, Antananarivo-101.
• Centre de documentation et des relations extérieures du Rectorat et Service de l'orientation, de l'information, des bourses et des étudiants.
• Service de presse et de documentation des ambassades de Madagascar à l'étranger.
Enseignement à distance: Des cours d'enseignement à distance sont assurés en droit et en gestion par le CNTEMAD.
Reconnaissance des études et diplômes: Ministère de l'Enseignement supérieur; BP 4163; Tsimbazaza; Antananarivo; Madagascar; tél: +261-2022-64451; fax: +261-2022-23897.
Publications / Sites Web:
• «Livret de l'étudiant», publié annuellement.
• «Index des textes relatifs à l'Université de Madagascar».
• «Présentation de l'Université de Madagascar et renseignements pratiques».

1475 Institut national des sciences et techniques nucléaires [INSTN]

BP 4279
101 Antananarivo
Tel: +261-20-22-61181
Fax: +261-20-22-35583
Web: http://www.takelaka.com
e-mail: instn@dts.mg

📖 Programme de cours allant du 1er au 3ème cycles

Domaines d'étude: chimie, écologie, environnement, électricité et électronique, énergie, formation des enseignants, formation professionnelle, hydrologie, informatique, mathématiques, physique, recherche, sciences appliquées, techniques de laboratoires.
Programmes: Diplôme de technicien supérieur en radio-protection; l'INSTN assure également l'encadrement de mémoires de DEA et de thèses de doctorat.
A l'intention de: titulaires d'un diplôme de fin d'études secondaires (baccalauréat scientifique ou équivalent); l'admission se fait également sur dossier.
Durée: 2 ans pour le DTS (débutant en octobre).
Frais: frais de scolarité: environ 215 €.
Connaissances linguistiques: cours dispensés en français.
Inscriptions: avant le 30 août auprès de Monsieur le directeur général de l'INSTN; pour toute information contacter M. Mahandry (coordonnées de l'institut ci-dessus).

1476 Institut supérieur de technologie Antsiranana

BP 453
201 Antsiranana
Tel: +261-20-82-22431
Fax: +261-20-82-29425
Web: http://www.refer.mg/edu/minesup/organe/istdiego/istdiego.htm
e-mail: istdiego@dts.mg

📖 Diplôme de technicien supérieur

Domaines d'étude: électricité et électronique, énergie, ingénierie.
Programmes: Cours de maintenance conduisant au diplôme de technicien supérieur en équipements électromécaniques, frigorifiques et thermiques; cours théoriques, travaux dirigés et stages pratiques sur le terrain en vue de former des techniciens directement opérationnels sur le marché de l'emploi.
A l'intention de: ressortissants de tout pays, âgés de 18 à 28 ans, (35 ans pour les candidats d'entreprises), titulaires d'un Bac C, technique industrielle, technique génie civil, Bac S ou équivalent; admission sur concours.
Durée: 2 ans (de novembre à juillet).
Connaissances linguistiques: français et anglais obligatoires.
Inscriptions: à l'adresse ci-dessus pour de plus amples informations.

1477 Université d'Antananarivo

Ambohitsaina
BP 566
101 Antananarivo
Tel: +261-20-22-32639
Fax: +261-20-22-27926
Web: http://www.misa.mg/univ/univs.htm
e-mail: recunivtana@simicro.mg

📖 Cursus allant du 1er au 3ème cycles

Domaines d'étude: toutes disciplines principales.
Programmes: programme de cours conduisant au DEUG, à la Licence, à la Maîtrise, au DEA et au Doctorat.
Description: (a) lettres et sciences humaines: études françaises, langues et lettres malgaches, études russes, études hispaniques, langues anciennes, géographie, histoire, études germaniques, études anglophones, journalisme, philosophie; (b) droit, économie, sociologie et gestion; (c) sciences: mathématiques, physique et chimie, sciences naturelles; (d) médecine; (e) École supérieure des sciences agronomiques: agriculture, eaux et forêts, élevage, industries agricoles alimentaires, agro-management; (f) Écoles normales supérieures: sciences naturelles, physique-chimie, lettres malgaches, lettres anglaises, lettres françaises, histoire et géographie, éducation physique et sportive; (g) École supérieure polytechnique: tronc commun 1 et 2, bâtiment et travaux publics, hydraulique, mines, géologie, géomètre-topographe, télécommunication, génie chimique, météorologie, électronique.
A l'intention de: candidats remplissant les conditions requises: (a) titulaires d'un baccalauréat A, C, ou D, âgés au maximum de 23 ans: examen d'entrée pour l'admission; (b) titulaires d'un baccalauréat: admission en fonction des notes du baccalauréat; (c) titulaires d'un baccalauréat: admission sur étude de dossier; (d) admission sur dossier; (e) admission sur concours d'entrée en 1ère année; (f) titulaires d'un baccalauréat ou d'un niveau supérieur: admission sur concours; (g) titulaires d'un baccalauréat C, D, ou de techniques industrielles et génie civil, âgés de moins de 25 ans: admission sur concours.
Frais: frais d'inscription: 500.000 FMG.
Connaissances linguistiques: cours dispensés en français; une bonne connaissance du malgache et de l'anglais sont également requises.
Inscriptions: de novembre à mi-janvier auprès de Madame le Doyen de la faculté des lettres et sciences humaines; pour toute information contacter l'association des étudiants de la FLSH au secrétariat du doyen.

1478 Université d'Antananarivo, École supérieure polytechnique Antananarivo [ESPA]

Campus universitaire d'Ambohitsaina
BP 1500
101 Antananarivo
Tel: +261-20-222-7696
Fax: +261-20-222-3699
Web: http://www.misa.mg/univ/univs.htm

📖 Cycle d'ingénieur

Domaines d'étude: architecture, bâtiment, construction, chimie, développement rural, électricité et électronique, énergie, génie chimique, génie civil, géodésie, géologie, hydraulique, hydrologie, informatique, ingénierie, métallurgie, météorologie, physique, technologie, télécommunications, urbanisme.
Programmes: programme de cours conduisant au Diplôme d'ingénieur.
A l'intention de: admission sur concours national.
Durée: 5 ans débutant en novembre.
Frais: frais d'inscription: 500.000 FMG.
Connaissances linguistiques: cours dispensés en français.

1479 Université d'Antananarivo, Faculté des lettres et sciences humaines [FLSH]

Ambohitsaina
BP 907
101 Antananarivo
Tel: +261-20-22-23563 / 23785
Web: http://www.misa.mg/univ/univs.htm
e-mail: flsh@syfed.refer.mg

📖 Cursus allant du 1er au 3ème cycles

Domaines d'étude: anthropologie, archéologie, arts, communication, démographie et études de populations, documentation, écologie, environnement, études du développement, formation des enseignants, formation professionnelle, géographie, histoire, histoire de l'art, interprétation et traduction, journalisme, langues, lettres et arts, linguistique, littérature et civilisation, muséologie et muséographie, philosophie, sciences humaines.
Programmes: programme de cours conduisant au DEUG, à la licence, à la maîtrise, au DEA et au Doctorat.
A l'intention de: titulaires d'un diplôme de fin d'études secondaires (baccalauréat ou équivalent -les équivalences sont établies au cas par cas par une sous-commission et entérinées par un arrêté du rectorat); examen d'entrée en 1ère année du 1er cycle.
Durée: de 2 à 5 années débutant en janvier.
Frais: frais d'inscription: 500.000 FMG.
Connaissances linguistiques: cours dispensés en français; une bonne connaissance du malgache et de l'anglais sont également requises.
Inscriptions: de novembre à mi-janvier auprès de Madame le Doyen de la faculté des lettres et sciences humaines; pour toute information contacter l'association des étudiants de la FLSH au secrétariat du doyen.

1480 Université d'Antananarivo, Faculté des Sciences [UAFS]

BP 906
101 Antananarivo
Tel: +261-20-22-28733
Fax: +261-20-22-31398
Web: http://www.misa.mg/univ/univs.htm
e-mail: rdesire@dts.mg

📖 Cursus allant du 1er au 3ème cycles

Domaines d'étude: chimie, mathématiques, physique, sciences naturelles.
Programmes: programme de cours conduisant au DEUG, à la Licence, à la Maîtrise, au DEA et au Doctorat.
A l'intention de: titulaires d'un baccalauréat scientifique (ou équivalent); l'admission se fait également sur dossier.
Frais: frais de scolarité: 500.000 FMG.
Connaissances linguistiques: cours dispensés en français.
Inscriptions: jusqu'au mois de décembre auprès de Monsieur le Doyen de la faculté des sciences (coordonnées ci-dessus).

1481 Université de Fianarantsoa

BP 1264 - Andrainjato
301 Fianarantsoa
Tel: +261-20-75-50802
Fax: +261-20-75-50619
Web: http://www.refer.mg/madag_ct/edu/minesup/fia naran/fianaran.htm
e-mail: ufianara@syfed.refer.mg

📖 Cursus allant du 1er au 3ème cycles

Domaines d'étude: droit, éducation, histoire, informatique, littérature et civilisation, sciences.
Programmes: Programme d'études universitaires dans différentes facultés et écoles:
(a) Faculté de sciences: mathématiques, physique, chimie, informatique, sciences sociales, sciences naturelles, écologie; conduisant à la licence d'enseignement (3e année), à la maîtrise
d'enseignement ou de recherche (4e année), au DEA (5e année), au doctorat; au brevet de technicien supérieur en environnement; (b) Faculté de droit: cours conduisant à la maîtrise (4 ans), au diplôme d'études juridiques du second cycle (4 ans), au DEUG. École nationale d'informatique; (c) Formation de techniciens supérieurs en informatique, formation d'ingénieurs, conduisant au Diplôme universitaire de technicien supérieur en informatique (DUTSI), option «analyse en programmation», diplôme d'ingénieur en informatique, Diplôme universitaire de techniciens supérieurs en «maintenance des systèmes informatiques» (DUTSMI); École nationale supérieure: (d) Cours de sciences physiques, mathématiques, conduisant à la formation d'enseignants du secondaire et au certificat d'aptitude pédagogique de l'école normale.
A l'intention de: (a) ressortissants de tout pays, âgés de moins de 25 ans, titulaires du baccalauréat ou équivalent; sélection sur titres et notes au Bac; (b) titulaires d'un Bac A, ou G, capacité en droit ou expérience professionnelle de 5 ans dans les secteurs juridiques administratifs; préinscription obligatoire; admission sur dossier; (c) Bac C, D ou technique, DUTSI, DUES, DEUG, en économie, gestion en polytechnique pour la formation des ingénieurs, sélection sur concours; (d) Bac C, D, technique industrielle ou technique du génie civil; langues obligatoires: français et anglais.
Durée: de 2 à 5 ans, selon le domaine choisi.
Frais: (a) pour les étrangers: 50.000 FMG; (b) étrangers: 1er cycle 50.000 FMG, 2e cycle 70.000 FMG; (c) inscription: 50.000 FMG.
Inscriptions: écrire à l'adresse ci-dessus pour de plus amples renseignements.

1482 Université de Mahajanga [UDM]

BP 652
401 Mahajanga
Tel: +261-20-62-22724
Fax: +261-20-62-23312
Web: http://www.misa.mg/univ/mahajang/mahajang.htm

📖 Cursus allant du 1er au 3ème cycles

Domaines d'étude: études dentaires, hygiène et santé, médecine, sciences, sciences naturelles.
Programmes: programme d'études universitaires dispensées en français, conduisant au diplôme de docteur en médecine dans les domaines suivants: médecine générale, odonto-stomatologie tropicale; sciences: sciences naturelles.
A l'intention de: ressortissants de tout pays; titulaires d'un bac C, D ou A2 (à condition d'avoir obtenu 12/20 aux matières scientifiques); français obligatoire.
Durée: médecine générale: 7 ans; odonto-stomatologie: 5 ans; sciences naturelles: 4 ans.
Frais: droits d'inscription: 25.000 FMG pour les étudiants étrangers.
Inscriptions: à l'adresse ci-dessus pour de plus amples renseignements.

1483 Université de Toamisina

BP 591
501 Toamasina
Tel: +261-20-53-32454
Fax: +261-20-53-33566
Web: http://www.misa.mg/univ/univs.htm
e-mail: univtoam@dts.mg

📖 Institut supérieur professionnel de gestion (ISPG)

Domaines d'étude: administration des affaires, comptabilité, industrie et commerce, sciences économiques et commerciales.
Programmes: Cours de gestion d'entreprise et d'administration; formation en gestion des cadres intermédiaires; 8 semaines de stage professionnel; conduisant

au diplôme supérieur professionnel de gestion (Bac+2); langue d'enseignement: français.
A l'intention de: ressortissants de tout pays titulaires d'un baccalauréat ou diplôme équivalent; concours d'entrée en octobre après sélection sur dossier.
Durée: 2 ans.
Frais: 2.750.000 FMG par an.
Connaissances linguistiques: langues obligatoires: anglais et français.
Inscriptions: à l'Institut supérieur professionnel de gestion, BP 591, 501 Toamasina.

☞ Centre de formation pour l'entreprenariat (CFE)

Domaines d'étude: affaires internationales, commerce, relations internationales, sciences économiques et commerciales.
Bourses: Bourses d'études pour la formation en maîtrise spécialisée de gestion du commerce international.
A l'intention de: ressortissants de tout pays, âgés de 25 ans maximum, titulaires d'une licence ou professionnels de niveau Bac avec 3 ans d'expérience; sélection sur dossier et entretien; français obligatoire; examen d'anglais.
Durée: 1 an.
Valeur: 4.000 FMG par an; chambre en campus universitaire.
Candidatures: au Centre de formation pour l'entreprenariat, 4 Cité Guynemer, BP 501 Toamasina pour de plus amples informations.

1484 Université Nord Madagascar d'Antsiranana [UNM]
BP 0
201 Antsiranana
Tel: +261-20-82-29409 / 21137
Fax: +261-20-82-29409
e-mail: unm@dts.mg

📖 Cursus allant du 1er au 3ème cycles

Domaines d'étude: éducation, ingénierie, lettres, sciences.
Programmes: programme d'études universitaires conduisant à la licence et à la maîtrise dans les facultés et écoles suivantes: (a) lettres et sciences humaines: lettres, cultures, linguistique, didactique; (b) sciences: physique et chimie; École normale supérieure pour l'enseignement technique (ENSET); (c) programme de professorat en génie électrique, génie mécanique, mathématiques pour ingénieurs, conduisant au certificat d'aptitude pédagogique, option technique.
A l'intention de: ressortissants de tout pays, titulaires du baccalauréat ou diplôme équivalent ayant obtenu: (a) 10/20 au moins en français; (b) 12/20 au moins en physique-chimie; (c) Bac technique industrielle ou génie civil, série C et D; français obligatoire.
Durée: 4 à 5 ans.
Frais: inscription (a) niveau A: 30.000 FMG; niveau supérieur: 40.000 FMG; logement: 10.000 FMG; (b) 1er cycle de 25.000 à 50.000 FMG; 2e cycle de 35.000 à 75.000 FMG; logement: 12.500 FMG; (c) inscription: 25.000 FMG.
Inscriptions: avant novembre, à l'adresse ci-dessus pour de plus amples renseignements.

📖 École supérieure polytechnique

Domaines d'étude: électricité et électronique, énergie, génie civil, hydraulique, ingénierie, mécanique.
Programmes: formation d'ingénieurs en génie mécanique, hydraulique énergétique, génie électrique, électronique, conduisant au diplôme d'ingénieur; langue d'enseignement: français.
A l'intention de: étudiants titulaires d'un bac C, D, ou Technique; sélection par voie de concours (du 15 au 30 octobre); examen de français.
Durée: 5 ans.
Frais: inscription 25.000 FMG; frais de scolarité 15.000 FMG par an.
Inscriptions: à l'École supérieure polytechnique, B.P. 0, 201 Diego-Suarez, Madagascar.

Malawi
Academic year: 1 September to 1 August.
Monetary unit: kwacha (K).
National student admission: Foreign students should have qualifications at least equivalent to first and second-division Cambridge School Certificate with 2 of the 6 credits in English and mathematics. Application for admission is made directly to the Registrar, University of Malawi, University Office, Box 278, Zomba; confirmation of admission must be obtained prior to departure as well as an entry permit from the Chief Immigration Officer, Box 331, Blantyre.
International student admission: A' level / O' level necessary.
Language: Good knowledge of English is necessary for regular university courses.
Immigration requirements: Visas are necessary for students of non-Commonwealth countries. Visas can be obtained from Malawi embassy closest to place of residence.
Information services: Registrar, University of Malawi, University Office, Zomba (information and advice concerning study facilities).
Recognition of studies and qualification: Ministry of Education; PO Box 328; Lilongwe 3; Malawi; tel: +265-784-800; fax: +265-782-873.

1485 University of Malawi [UNIMA]
University Office
PO Box 278
Zomba, Lilongwe
Tel: +265-526-622
Fax: +265-525-760
Web: http://www.unima.mw
e-mail: university.office@unima.mw

📖 Undergraduate, Graduate and Postgraduate Programmes

Study Domains: all major fields, ecology, environment, economic and commercial sciences, education, engineering, English, health and hygiene, journalism, law, medicine, nursing.
Programmes: programme of courses in all major fields at the following schools: Bunda College of Agriculture; Chancellor College; College of Medicine; Kamuzu College of Nursing; the Polytechnic.
Open to: qualified nationals of all countries; entrance examination and secondary school certificate required.
Duration: 4 to 5 years for degree courses; courses begin in January.
Fees: current registration for foreigners: US$200; tuition fees: US$3,000 per year.
Languages: language of instruction: English.
Applications: by November to the University Registrar at the above address.

Malaysia
Academic year: June to May.
Monetary unit: Ringgit Malaysia (RM).
International student admission: Foreign students with the Cambridge Higher School Certificate or equivalent qualifications are eligible to apply to be considered for admission as regular or non-graduating students at the universities in Malaya. Graduates with degrees from universities recognized by their senates can also apply to read for higher degrees at Malaysian universities.
Language: The language of instruction at the public universities is Bahasa Malaysia with some courses in English. However, the language of instruction at the public universities is English.
Immigration requirements: Foreign students must have a visa and depending on the country of origin a student pass (not allowed to work). A medical check-up is required.
Information services:
• International Relations Division, Ministry of Education Malaysia, 5th Floor, Block F (North), Damansara Town Centre; Kuala Lumpur; Malaysia; tel: +60-3-2095-8655; fax: +60-3-2094-4580: email: rk@bha.moe.gov.my.
• Department of Higher Education, Ministry of Education Malaysia, 2nd Floor, Block J (North), Damansara Town Centre; 50604 Kuala Lumpur, Malaysia; tel:

+6-03-2095-6849; fax: +6-03-2092-4568: email:
drhassan@moe.gov.my.
• Department of Private Education, Ministry of Education
Malaysia, 1st Floor, Block K, Damansara Town Centre;
50604 Kuala Lumpur; Malaysia; tel: +6-03-2093-1601; fax:
+6-03-2093-5463; email: hasanh@jps.moe.gov.my.
Recognition of studies and qualification:
•Public Service Department, Training Division, Recognition
and Qualification Unit, 6th Floor, Block C1, Parcel C, 62510
Putrajaya; Malaysia; tel: +6-03-8885-3359; fax:
+6-03-8889-2179; email: recog@jpa.gov.my.
• National Accreditation Board (LAN), 14th Floor, Block B,
PKNS-PJ Tower, Jalan Yong Shook Lin, 46050 Petaling Jaya;
Selangor; Malaysia; tel: +6-03-7968-7002; fax:
+6-03-7956-9496; email: akreditasi@lan.gov.my.

1486 International Islamic University [IIU]
Jalan Gombak
53100 Kuala Lumpur
Tel: +60-3-2056-4252
Fax: +60-3-2056-4854
Web: http://www.iiu.edu.my

📖 Undergraduate, Graduate and Postgraduate Programmes
Study Domains: all major fields.
Programmes: undergraduate and postgraduate
programmes in all major fields; LL.B (Civil) and LL.B.
(Syariah).
Open to: nationals of any country, fulfilling the necessary
requirements.
Languages: Instruction in English and Arabic.
Applications: contact the Registrar for further details;
deadline is 28 February for June intake and 31 July for
November intake.

1487 International Medical University
Sesama Centre - Plaza Komanwel
Bukit Jlil 57000
Seri Petaling
Kuala Lumpur
Tel: +60-3-8656-7228
Fax: +60-3-8656-7229
Web: http://www.imu.edu.my/

📖 Medicine and Pharmacy
Study Domains: medicine, pharmacy and pharmacology.
Programmes: undergraduate programmes in medicine and
pharmacy.
Open to: nationals of any country fulfilling the necessary
requirements.
Languages: language of instruction English.
Applications: contact the Registrar for further details.

1488 Multimedia University Malaysia
Cyberjaya Campus
63100 Cyberjaya
Tel: +60-3-8312-5752
Fax: +60-3-8312-5749
Web: http://www.mmu.edu.my

📖 Undergraduate and Graduate Programmes
Study Domains: business, computer science, engineering,
information science.
Programmes: undergraduate and graduate programmes in
business, information technology and engineering.
Open to: nationals of any country, fulfilling the necessary
requirements.
Applications: contact the Registrar for further details.

1489 Universiti Kebangsaan Malaysia
43600 UKM Bangi
Selangor
Tel: +60-3-8925-0001
Fax: +60-3-8925-6484
Web: http://www.ukm.my
e-mail: puspa@pkrisc.cc.ukm.my

📖 Undergraduate and Graduate Programmes
Study Domains: all major fields.
Programmes: undergraduate and graduate programmes.
Open to: nationals of any country, fulfilling the necessary
requirements.
Languages: Instruction in Bahasa Malaysia and English.
Applications: contact the Registrar for further details.

1490 Universiti Malaya [UOM]
International Relations Unit
Lembah Pantai
50603 Kuala Lumpur
Tel: +60-3-7967-7022
Fax: +60-3-7956-0027
Web: http://www.um.edu.my
e-mail: interel@um.edu.my

📖 Undergraduate and Graduate Programmes
Study Domains: all major fields.
Programmes: (a) programme of courses leading to first
degree, higher degree and postgraduate diploma; distance
education diploma programmes;.
Description: courses in economics and administration,
engineering, education, medicine, science, arts and social
sciences, law, languages, computer science, information
technology, dentistry, etc.
Open to: nationals of any country, fulfilling the necessary
requirements.
Languages: instruction in Bahasa Malaysia and English.
Applications: contact the Registrar for further details.

1491 Universiti Malaysia Sabah
UMS Beg Berkunci 2073
88999 Kota Kinabalu Sabah
Tel: +60-88-320-000
Fax: +60-88-260-730
Web: http://www.ums.edu.my

📖 Undergraduate and Graduate Programmes
Study Domains: all major fields, ecology, environment,
finance, marine science.
Programmes: undergraduate and graduate programmes in
all major fields; environmental and marine sciences,
international finance.
Open to: nationals of any country, fulfilling the necessary
requirements.
Applications: contact the Registrar for further details.

1492 Universiti Malaysia Sarawak
Kota Samarahan
94300 Kuching, Sarawak
Tel: +60-82-671-000
Fax: +60-82-671-123
Web: http://www.unimas.my

📖 Undergraduate and Graduate Programmes
Study Domains: all major fields, computer science.
Programmes: undergraduate and graduate programmes in
all major fields, information technology and cognitive studies.

1493 Universiti Putra Malaysia [UOA]
Darul Ehsan
43400 UPM, Serdang, Selangor
Tel: +60-3-8948-6101
Fax: +60-3-8948-3745
Web: http://www.upm.edu.my/iro/
e-mail: iro@admin.upm.edu.my

📖 Undergraduate and Graduate Programmes
Study Domains: all major fields, agriculture, forestry,
sciences, veterinary sciences.
Programmes: programme of courses leading to: (a)
Bachelor's degree (B.A. and B.Sc.); (b) Master's degree;
Distance education diploma programme (I.D.E.A.L.).
Open to: nationals of any country, fulfilling the necessary
requirements.
Duration: 3 to 5 years.
Languages: Instruction in Bahasa Malaysia and English.
Applications: to the Registrar at the above address.

1494 Universiti Sains Malaysia [USM]

11800 Minden, Penang
Tel: +60-4-653-888
Fax: +60-4-657-3984
Web: http://www.usm.my
e-mail: interel@notes.usm.my

📖 Undergraduate, Graduate and Postgraduate Programmes

Study Domains: all major fields.
Programmes: (a) programme of courses leading to Bachelor's, Master's and Ph.D. degrees in all major fields; (b) Study Abroad Programme: languages, Southeast Asian and Tropical Environmental Studies.
Open to: candidates of all countries, fulfilling the necessary requirements.
Languages: instruction in Bahasa Malaysia for undergraduate classes, in English for postgraduate classes.
Applications: contact the Registrar for further details; (a) deadline for undergraduate students: 1 February; for graduate students: 30 November for coursework and all year round for research; (b) deadline 1 April and 1 September.

1495 Universiti Teknologi Malaysia [UTM]

Registrar, Admissions and Record Unit
81310 Skudai, Johor
Tel: +60-7-557-6160
Fax: +60-7-557-9376
Web: http://www.utm.my
e-mail: upa@utm.my

📖 Undergraduate and Graduate Programmes

Study Domains: all major fields.
Programmes: programme of courses leading to Diploma, Bachelor's, Master's and Ph.D. degrees; courses in science and technology and engineering.
Description: courses in the following subjects: architecture, chemical engineering, civil engineering, computer science, electrical engineering, mechanical engineering, land surveying, petroleum engineering, quantity surveying, urban and regional planning, building, property management, management technology, gas engineering, polymer engineering, transportation planning, bioprocess engineering, environmental engineering, chemistry, physics, mathematics, and education.
Open to: candidates of any nationality; 550 minimum TOEFL score required; admission requirements: (Diplomas) at least a second grade in the Malaysian Certificate of Education or its equivalent (GCE O-Level); with credits in at least three subjects, Bahasa Malaysia, mathematics and one other subject; (Bachelor's) at least a second grade in the Malaysian Certificate of Education or its equivalent (GCE O-Level); with credits in at least five subjects, Bahasa Malaysia, mathematics and three other subjects; (Postgraduate Diplomas) a Bachelor's Degree from the Universiti Teknologi Malaysia or equivalent qualification or other qualifications and experiences acknowledged by the Senate; (Master's) a Bachelor's Degree with good honours from the University Teknologi Malaysia or any institution of higher learning recognized by Senate or other qualifications equivalent to the Bachelor's Degree and working experience in the relevant fields acknowledged by the Senate; (Doctor of Philosophy) a Master's Degree from the University Teknologi Malaysia or from any institution of higher learning recognized by the University Senate; other qualifications equivalent to a Master's Degree with working experience acknowledged by the Senate; or candidates pursuing a Master's programme at the University Teknologi Malaysia with the recommendation of the postgraduate committee of the faculty will be considered, subject to the approval of the University Senate.
Languages: for diplomas and Bachelor's degrees instruction is in Bahasa Malaysia; for postgraduate programmes instruction could be in Bahasa Malaysia or English. Diploma and Bachelor's degree students are required to attend a Bahasa Malaysia language class for a year before they start their courses.
Applications: forms should be submitted at least 4 months before the beginning of a semester; applications for Diplomas and Bachelors courses must be submitted to the Registrar, Admission and Records Unit, Universiti Teknologi Malaysia;

application for Postgraduate Diplomas, Master's and Doctor of Philosophy must be submitted to the Dean, School of Graduate Studies, at the above address.

1496 Universiti Tenaga Nasional Malaysia

7, Jalan Kajang-Puchong
43009 Kajang
Tel: +60-3-8921-2020
Fax: +60-38921-3507
Web: http://www.uniten.edu.my

📖 Undergraduate and Graduate Programmes

Study Domains: business, engineering.
Programmes: undergraduate and graduate programmes in business studies, engineering.
Open to: nationals of any country, fulfilling the necessary requirements.
Applications: contact the Registrar for further details.

1497 Universiti Utara Malaysia

Office of International Affairs
06010 Sintok, Kedah
Tel: +60-4-924-1801
Fax: +60-4-700-2245
Web: http://www.uum.edu.my/international/

📖 Undergraduate, Graduate Programmes

Study Domains: all major fields.
Programmes: degree course programmes in all major fields; management, information technology.
Open to: candidates of all nationalities holding a high school certificate or equivalent, with proficiency in Bahasa Malaysia.
Applications: to the Registrar at the above address.

Malta

Academic year: October to June.
Monetary unit: Maltese lira (Lm).
National student admission: A large number of overseas qualifications are accepted as satisfying the entry requirements. Each application is treated on its own merits and in general, students in possession of qualifications that give access to universities in their home country are accepted provided that
their qualifications are of comparable standard to those required by the University of Malta. The University of Malta accepts British Advanced level certificates, the International Baccalaureate and the American Advanced Placement System. Applications are to be made to the International Student Admissions Office, International Office, University of Malta, Msida MSD06, Malta.
Language: A good knowledge of English is essential for regular university courses. The university provides a Foundation Studies course and a Pre-Sessional Language Course prior to entry to a regular course of studies.
Immigration requirements: Applicants should check with the nearest Maltese Embassy or Consulate whether they require a
visa to enter Malta. All foreign nationals staying in Malta for more than three months are required to have a valid permit.
Information services:
• The Director of Education, Education Office, Lascaris, Floriana CMR02.
• The Director, International Office, University of Malta, Msida MSD06.
Open and distance learning: Distance education is not yet fully established.
Recognition of studies and qualification: Malta Equivalence Information Centre (MEIC), University of Malta; Tal-Qroqq; Msida MSD 06; Malta; tel: +356-323-902; fax: +356-245-133; email: intoff@um.edu.mt; web: http://home.um.edu.mt/meic.
Publications / Websites:
• Calendar, Lm1. 50; Annual Report, Lm1, obtainable from Communications Office, University of Malta, Msida MSD06; email: pcam1@um.edu.mt
• Entry Requirements to Degree Courses from the International Office, University of Malta, Msida MSD06; email: intoff@maltanet.net.

1498 Institute of Electronics Engineering [MCASTEEI]

Malta College of Arts, Science and Technology (MCAST)
Corradino Hill
PLA08 Paola
Tel: +356-21-803-657/823657
Fax: +356-21-809-871
Web: http://www.mcasteei.com
e-mail: info@mcasteei.com

📖 Undergraduate Programme

Study Domains: electricity and electronics, industrial technology.
Programmes: Technician Certificate in industrial electronics.
Open to: candidates of all nationalities; age 19 years maximum holding GCE O-level or equivalent in physics, mathematics and English.
Duration: 3 to 4 years full-time study.
Applications: to the above address; see website for further information.

1499 University of Malta [UM]

International Office
MSD 06 Msida
Tel: +356-2340-2224
Fax: +356-2131-6941
Web: http://www.um.edu.mt
e-mail: intoff@um.edu.mt

📖 Undergraduate, Graduate, Postgraduate Programmes

Study Domains: all major fields, agriculture, applied sciences, architecture, business administration, education, engineering, languages, law, liberal arts, medicine, nursing, social sciences, theology, religion, tourism, hotel and catering management.
Programmes: Bachelor's, Master's and Ph.D. degrees in all major fields.
Open to: academically qualified candidates of any country, who satisfy the University's entry requirements to higher degree, first degree and diploma courses and the special course requirements; proficiency in English is essential (minimum 550 TOEFL is required).
Duration: 3 to 5 years; courses begin 1 October.
Fees: registration US$88; tuition fees from US$3,000 per year; living costs approx. US$600 per month.
Languages: English.
Applications: by 30 June to International Admissions Officer; contact: intadmissions@um.edu.mt for further details.

Maroc

Année universitaire: septembre à juin.
Unité monétaire: dirham (DH).
Admission pour étudiants du pays: Baccalauréat ou titre équivalent.
Connaissances linguistiques requises: Une bonne connaissance de l'arabe ou du français est requise des étudiants qui suivent les cours des universités marocaines.
Services d'accueil et d'information:
• Agence marocaine de coopération internationale.
• Direction de la recherche et de la coopération universitaire, Service des étudiants étrangers, Rabat.
• Ministère d'État chargé des affaires étrangères et de la coopération.
• Ambassades du Maroc à l'étranger.
Reconnaissance des études et diplômes: Division de la Réglementation et des Équivalences de Diplômes, Ministère de l'Éducation nationale; 24 rue du Sénégal-Océan; Rabat; Maroc; tél: +212-37-771-822; fax: +212-37-772-034.

1500 École Hassania des Travaux Publics [EHTP]

Route El Jadida, km 7
BP 8108
Casablanca - Oasis
Tel: +212-22-230-710
Fax: +212-22-230-717
Web: http://www.ehtp.ac.ma
e-mail: webmaster@ehtp.ac.ma

📖 Diplômes d'ingénieur

Domaines d'étude: écologie, environnement, électricité et électronique, météorologie.
Programmes: cours de formation initiale d'ingénieur d'État en génie civil, génie électrique, filière météorologie - environnement, formation de 3e cycle et formation continue.
A l'intention de: ressortissants de tout pays, âgés de moins de 22 ans, titulaires d'un DEUG (mathématiques-physique) ou du Certificat des études universitaires scientifiques (CUES) ou diplôme reconnu équivalent; admission sur concours.
Connaissances linguistiques: langue d'enseignement: français.
Inscriptions: à l'adresse ci-dessus.

1501 École nationale supérieure d'informatique et d'analyse des systèmes [ENSIAS]

Université Mohammed V-Souissi
BP 713
Agdal, Rabat
Tel: +212-7-777-317/778-579
Fax: +212-7-777-230
Web: http://www.ensias.ma

📖 Ingénieur en informatique

Domaines d'étude: informatique.
Programmes: cours conduisant au diplôme d'ingénieur d'État en informatique.
A l'intention de: ressortissants de tout pays, âgés de moins de 22 ans au 31 décembre de l'année d'inscription, pour les étudiants de 1re année; étudiants ayant suivi les programmes des classes
préparatoires aux grandes écoles marocaines; titulaires d'un DEUG MP ou équivalent, d'une licence ès lettres; admission directe fin juin début juillet; sélection sur dossier.
Connaissances linguistiques: langue d'enseignement: français.
Inscriptions: à l'adresse ci-dessus.

1502 École supérieure de l'agro-alimentaire SUP'AGRO

22, rue Le Catelet-Belvédère
Casablanca
Tel: +212-2-245-405/246-706
Fax: +212-2-245-399

📖 Cursus allant du 1er au 3ème cycles

Domaines d'étude: alimentation, industrie alimentaire, techniques de laboratoires.
Programmes: Programme de cours allant du 1er au 3ème cycles.
A l'intention de: titulaires d'un Baccalauréat scientifique ou technique (ou équivalent), d'un DEUG, d'un DUT, d'un BTS, d'une Licence ou d'une Maîtrise; admission sur dossier.
Durée: 2-4-5 années (en fonction du cursus) débutant en octobre.
Connaissances linguistiques: cours dispensés en français.
Inscriptions: avant le 15 octobre auprès de la direction des études de l'école; pour information contacter le professeur Tantaoui Elaraki (coordonnées de l'école ci-dessus).

1503 École supérieure de technologie de Casablanca, Université Hassan II

BP 8012
Casablanca - Oasis
Tel: +212-2-250-325
Web: http://www.est-uh2c.ac.ma

📖 Cursus de 1er cycle

Domaines d'étude: électricité et électronique, technologie.
Programmes: formation de techniciens supérieurs en génie électrique, génie mécanique, génie des procédés et en technique de management conduisant au diplôme universitaire de technologie (DUT).
Description: programme sous forme de cours, de travaux dirigés et de travaux pratiques pour 70% et de deux stages en entreprise d'une durée totale de 3 mois.
A l'intention de: ressortissants de tout pays, de moins de 22 ans, titulaires d'un Baccalauréat scientifique ou technique; l'étude du dossier est suivie d'un entretien.
Durée: 2 années universitaires (débutant à la mi-septembre), stage d'initiation en été.
Frais: 53 DH pour l'assurance, 100 DH de caution par an, et 250 DH par mois pour les frais de séjour et de restauration.
Assistance financière: bourses de l'enseignement supérieur pour les nationaux qui remplissent les conditions requises; aide pour les étrangers, en fonction des accords bilatéraux entre gouvernements.
Inscriptions: avant le 30 juin, au Service des affaires estudiantines de l'École.

1504 Institut agronomique et vétérinaire Hassan II
BP 6202
10101 Rabat-Instituts
Tel: +212-7-771-758/59
Fax: +212-7-778-135
Web: http://www.iav.ac.ma

📖 Cours de formation en agronomie et médecine vétérinaire

Domaines d'étude: agriculture, écologie, environnement, études du développement, horticulture, hydraulique, industrie alimentaire, ressources naturelles, sciences agronomiques, sciences vétérinaires, zoologie.
Programmes: cours de formation en agronomie, médecine vétérinaire, développement, équipement et hydraulique, technologie alimentaire, topographie, halieutique, horticulture, production animale, foresterie, écologie végétale et pastoralisme, machinisme agricole, sciences du sol, zoologie, zootechnie, phytopathologie.
A l'intention de: ressortissants de tout pays, âgés de moins de 23 ans, titulaires du Baccalauréat scientifique ou d'un diplôme équivalent.
Organisés: à l'Institut agronomique de Rabat ou d'Agadir.
Durée: 6 ans.
Assistance financière: 40 à 50 bourses par an, d'un montant de 430 DH par mois, allouées par les services concernés du Gouvernement marocain par le biais des ambassades du Maroc dans les pays d'origine des candidats.
Connaissances linguistiques: langue d'enseignement: français.
Inscriptions: avant fin juillet.

1505 Institut national des sciences de l'archéologie et du patrimoine [INSAP]
Avenue John Kennedy
Route des Zaers
Rabat-Souissi
Tel: +212-37-750-961
Fax: +212-37-750-884
e-mail: archeo@iam.net.ma

📖 Cursus allant du 1er au 3ème cycle

Domaines d'étude: anthropologie, archéologie, architecture, arts, ethnologie, histoire, histoire de l'art, latin, linguistique, muséologie et muséographie, sciences humaines, sciences sociales, sociologie.
Programmes: programme de cours allant de la Licence au Doctorat.
A l'intention de: titulaires d'une Licence (ou équivalent) âgés de moins de 30 ans; admission sur entretien.
Connaissances linguistiques: cours dispensés en arabe et en français.
Inscriptions: avant le mois d'octobre; pour information contacter Abdelfettah El Rhazoui (coordonnées ci-dessus).

1506 Université Abdelmalek Essaâdi, Faculté des Sciences
BP 2121 Mhannech II
93002 Tétouan
Tel: +212-39-972-423
Fax: +212-39-994-500
Web: http://www.fst.ac.ma

📖 Cours de 1er, 2e et 3e cycle en sciences

Domaines d'étude: biologie, chimie, géologie, mathématiques, physique, sciences.
Programmes: programme de cours de mathématiques, physique, chimie, biologie, géologie; conduisant à:
(a) Certificat des études universitaires scientifiques (CUES);
(b) Licence ès sciences; (c) DESA et au doctorat.
A l'intention de: ressortissants de tout pays, titulaires d'un baccalauréat scientifique ou équivalent.
Assistance financière: possibilité de bourses du Ministère de l'enseignement supérieur et de la recherche scientifique de Rabat.
Connaissances linguistiques: Langue d'enseignement: français.
Inscriptions: à l'adresse ci-dessus.

1507 Université Al Akhawayn Ifrane [AUI]
BP 104
Avenue Hassan II
53000 Ifrane
Tel: +212-55-86 2222
Fax: +212-55-86 2431
Web: http://www.aui.ma

🎓 Bourses d'études

Domaines d'étude: études internationales, relations internationales.
Description: bourses au mérite académique.
Domaines d'études: master en études internationales et diplomatie (Master of Arts in International Study and Diplomacy).
Autres Conditions: niveau TOEFEL d'anglais pour les non-anglophones, license, acceptation par commission d'admission.
Valeur: réduction de 50 % sur les frais d'enseignement et 75 % de dépenses en manuels. Renouvelable en fonction des résultats académiques du bénéficiaire.
Candidatures: avant le 1er juin.

1508 Université Al Quaraouiyine
BP 2509
Fès
Tel: +212-55-641-006/16
Fax: +212-55-641-013
Web: http://www.enssup.gov.ma/etablissements/univq uarFes.htm

📖 Cursus allant du 1er au 3ème cycles

Domaines d'étude: arabe, droit, droit international, économie politique, langues, linguistique, littérature et civilisation, philologie, philosophie, théologie, religion.
Programmes: programmes de cours conduisant à la Licence, au Diplôme d'études supérieures (DES) et au Doctorat d'État.
Durée: Licence: 4 ans; DES: 2 ans; Doctorat: 4 ans.
Frais: pas de frais d'inscription.
Connaissances linguistiques: cours dispensés en arabe; une bonne connaissance du français est également requise.
Inscriptions: avant le 15 septembre.

1509 Université Chouaïb Doukkali Faculté des sciences et Faculté des lettres d'El Jaddida
BP 20
route de Ben Maâchou
24000 El Jadida
Tel: +212-23-342-325
Fax: +212-23-342-187
Web: http://www.ucd.ac.ma
e-mail: webmaster@ucd.ac.ma

Cours de 1er, 2e et 3e cycle

Domaines d'étude: biologie, chimie, géologie, histoire, lettres et arts, littérature et civilisation, mathématiques, physique, théologie, religion.
Programmes: cours universitaires dans les domaines suivants: (a) Faculté des sciences: biologie, géologie, physique, chimie, mathématiques); conduisant aux diplômes de 1er, 2e et 3e cycles; (b) Faculté des lettres et des sciences humaines: lettres, histoire, géographie, études islamiques; conduisant à la licence.
A l'intention de: ressortissants de tout pays, titulaires du baccalauréat ou équivalent.
Durée: 4 ans.
Assistance financière: possibilité de bourse pour le 3e cycle.
Connaissances linguistiques: langues d'enseignement: français pour (a); arabe, anglais et français pour (b).
Inscriptions: à l'adresse ci-dessus.

1510 Université Hassan II Ain Chok, Casablanca

19, Rue Tarik Ibnou Ziad
BP 9167
Mers Sultan
Casablanca
Tel: +212-2-273-737/262-672
Fax: +212-2-276-150
Web: http://www.rectorat-uh2c.ac.ma

Études pluridisciplinaires

Domaines d'étude: études dentaires, ingénierie, lettres, médecine, pharmacie et pharmacologie, sciences, sciences humaines, technologie.
Programmes: études supérieures dispensées dans les facultés suivantes: (a) Sciences juridiques économiques et sociales; (b) Médecine et pharmacie; (c) Lettres et sciences humaines; (d) Sciences; (e) Médecine dentaire; (f) École nationale supérieure d'électricité et de mécanique; (g) École supérieure de technologie.
A l'intention de: ressortissants de tout pays, titulaires d'un baccalauréat ou équivalent.
Organisés: (a), (d), (f) et (g) Km 9, route d'El Jadida, Oasis, Casablanca; (b) rue Tarik Ibnou Ziad, Mers Sultan, Casablanca; (c) Hay El Inara Ain Chock, Casablanca; (e) rue Abou El Oula Zohr, Casablanca.
Durée: 2 à 6 ans selon les filières choisies.
Connaissances linguistiques: Langues d'enseignement: arabe et français.
Inscriptions: auprès du Ministère des affaires étrangères et de la coopération, Agence marocaine de coopération internationale.

1511 Université Hassan II Mohammadia, Faculté des sciences et techniques

BP 146
Mohammadia
Tel: +212-3-315-352
Web: http://www.uh2m.ac.ma

Lettres et Sciences humaines

Domaines d'étude: anglais, arabe, lettres et arts, littérature et civilisation, théologie, religion.
Programmes: (a) langues et littératures arabes, françaises et anglaises, langues étrangères appliquées, histoire, géographie, études islamiques; conduisant à la licence; (b) aménagement et urbanisme du littoral; conduisant à la licence appliquée.
A l'intention de: ressortissants de tout pays, titulaires (a) du baccalauréat ou équivalent et (b) du CUEL (DEUG) pour les licences appliquées.
Durée: 4 ans.
Inscriptions: à la Faculté des lettres et des sciences humaines (FLSHM).

Sciences et techniques

Domaines d'étude: toutes disciplines principales, écologie, environnement, électricité et électronique, enseignement technique, mécanique, physique, techniques de laboratoires, technologie.

Programmes: programme de cours conduisant à la Maîtrise ès sciences et techniques (MST) et à la Maîtrise ès sciences spécialisées (MSS).
Description: l'étudiant s'inscrit chaque semestre dans 3 modules variant entre 80 et 100 heures de cours théoriques, TP ou TD.
A l'intention de: titulaires d'un Baccalauréat scientifique ou technique; l'admission se fait sur dossier.
Durée: 4 ans (débutant mi-septembre).
Connaissances linguistiques: langue d'enseignement: français.
Inscriptions: à l'adresse ci-dessus.

1512 Université Ibn Zohr Agadir

BP 32/S
Agadir
Tel: +212-48-227-017
Fax: +212-48-227-260
Web: http://www.esta.ac.ma/

Gestion

Domaines d'étude: comptabilité, finances, gestion, industrie et commerce, sciences de l'information.
Programmes: formation de cadres supérieurs en commerce et gestion: cours de marketing, commerce extérieur, publicité commerciale et communication, audit et contrôle de gestion, informatique de gestion, gestion financière et comptable; conduisant au diplôme des Écoles nationales de commerce et de gestion.
A l'intention de: ressortissants de tout pays, âgés de moins de 21 ans, titulaires d'un baccalauréat scientifique ou technique.
Connaissances linguistiques: langue d'enseignement: français.
Inscriptions: à l'adresse ci-dessus.

Sciences

Domaines d'étude: biologie, chimie, géologie, informatique, mathématiques, physique, sciences.
Programmes: programmes de cours conduisant aux diplômes suivants: Licence ès-sciences; Certificat des Études approfondies (CEA); Diplôme des Études supérieures approfondies (DESA); Diplôme des Études supérieures, 3ème Cycle (DES); Doctorat national; Doctorat d'État.
A l'intention de: ressortissants de tout pays, titulaires d'un baccalauréat scientifique ou équivalent.
Durée: 2 à 6 ans, selon le programme.
Inscriptions: à l'adresse ci-dessus, site web: http://www.fsa.ac.ma.

1513 Université Mohammed Ier [ESTO]

Complexe universitaire Hay Al Qods
BP 524
Oujda
Tel: +212-56-500-612/614
Fax: +212-56-500-609
Web: http://www.univ-oujda.ac.ma

École supérieure de technologie d'Oujda

Domaines d'étude: administration, anglais, arabe, comptabilité, électricité et électronique, gestion, moyens audio-visuels.
Programmes: programmes conduisant au Diplôme universitaire de technologie (DUT) en comptabilité ou gestion des entreprises, en électronique et électrotechnique; cours d'informatique, moyens audio-visuels, administration, anglais, arabe, comptabilité.
A l'intention de: ressortissants de tout pays, âgés de 22 ans maximum au 31 décembre de l'année en cours, titulaires d'un baccalauréat scientifique ou technique et ayant eu une bonne moyenne au baccalauréat.
Connaissances linguistiques: langue d'enseignement: français.
Inscriptions: à l'École supérieure de technologie d'Oujda, à l'adresse ci-dessus.

Bourses / sciences politiques

Domaines d'étude: droit, droit international, relations internationales, sciences politiques.
Bourses: Bourses de 1er, 2e et 3e cycles dans les domaines

de: sciences juridiques, sciences économiques, sciences de gestion, sciences politiques, droit public, droit privé.
À l'intention de: ressortissants de tout pays titulaires du baccalauréat ou équivalent pour la 1re année, admission directe; du DEUG pour la licence appliquée, sélection sur dossier; de la licence pour le 3e cycle, sélection sur dossier.
Connaissances linguistiques: langues d'enseignement: arabe et français.
Candidatures: à la Faculté des sciences juridiques, économiques et sociales, Oujda (FSJES) à l'adresse ci-dessus.

1514 Université Mohammed V Agdal
3, Rue Michlifen Agdal
BP 554
Rabat-Chellah
Tel: +212-7-673-318/671-324
Fax: +212-7-671-401
Web: http://www.um5a.ac.ma

📖 Cours de 2e et 3e cycle
Domaines d'étude: droit, lettres, sciences économiques et commerciales, sciences humaines, sciences sociales, technologie.
Programmes: études supérieures dispensées dans les facultés, écoles et instituts suivants: lettres et sciences humaines; sciences juridiques, économiques et sociales; sciences; École supérieure de technologie- Salé: École Mohammadia d'ingénieurs; Institut scientifique; conduisant aux diplômes d'études supérieures.
À l'intention de: ressortissants de tout pays, titulaires d'un baccalauréat ou équivalent; Bac+2 pour les classes préparatoires Maths sup., Maths Spé.; admission sur concours à l'École Mohammadia d'ingénieurs et à l'École supérieure de technologie.
Connaissances linguistiques: bonne connaissance du français ou de l'arabe requise.
Inscriptions: à l'adresse ci-dessus.

1515 Université Mohammed V Souissi [UMS]
BP 8007 N.U.
Agdal, Rabat
Tel: +212-37-681-160
Fax: +212-37-681-163
Web: http://www.um5s.ac.ma

📖 Cursus allant du 1er au 3ème cycles
Domaines d'étude: toutes disciplines principales.
Programmes: programmes de cours conduisant à la Licence, au Diplôme d'études supérieures approfondies (DESA), au Diplôme d'études supérieures spécialisées (DESS), au Doctorat, au Doctorat en médecine et en pharmacie et au Diplôme d'ingénieur.
Connaissances linguistiques: cours dispensés en arabe et en français.

1516 Université Moulay Ismail, Faculté des sciences
BP 11201 Zitoune
Meknès
Tel: +212-555 388 70
Fax: +212-555 368-08
Web: http://www.fsmek.ac.ma

📖 Cours de 1er cycle
Domaines d'étude: anglais, arabe, français, histoire, littérature et civilisation, théologie, religion.
Programmes: programme universitaire en langue et littérature arabes, françaises et anglaises, études islamiques, histoire, géographie; conduisant à la licence ès lettres.
A l'intention de: ressortissants de tout pays, titulaires d'un baccalauréat lettres; sélection sur dossier; aisance dans la langue du domaine d'études choisi (arabe, français ou anglais).
Durée: 4 ans.
Assistance financière: possibilité de bourses à demander auprès de l'Agence marocaine de coopération internationale.

📖 Cours de 1er, 2e et 3e cycle en sciences
Domaines d'étude: biologie, chimie, géologie, mathématiques, physique, sciences.

Programmes: programmes de cours de 1er, 2e et 3e cycles conduisant respectivement à: (a) Certificat universitaire d'études scientifiques (CUES); (b) Licence ès science, licence ès sciences appliquées; (c) Certificat d'études approfondies, diplômes d'études supérieures, et doctorat ès-sciences.
A l'intention de: ressortissants de tout pays, titulaires: (a) du baccalauréat ou équivalent; (b) du CUES, DEUG ou équivalent; (c) licence ou maîtrise; admission sur dossier et entretien.
Connaissances linguistiques: Langue d'enseignement: français.
Inscriptions: à l'adresse ci-dessus.

1517 Université Sidi Mohamed Ben Abdellah
Bd. des Almohades
BP 2626
Fès
Tel: +212-5-625-585/86
Fax: +212-5-622-401/623-641
Web: http://www.usmba.ac.ma

📖 Programme pluridisciplinaire
Domaines d'étude: toutes disciplines principales.
Programmes: programmes d'études conduisant aux: Certificat Universitaire d'Études littéraires, scientifiques, économiques et de Droit (CUEL, CUES, CUEE, CUED); Diplôme Universitaire de technologie (DUT); Licence en sciences, en lettres, en sciences humaines, en sciences économiques, en sciences juridiques; Licence appliquée; Diplôme d'Études supérieures (DES); Doctorat d'État: lettres et sciences Humaines; sciences juridiques, économiques et sociales; Faculté des Sciences: sciences et techniques; médecine et de pharmacie; et École supérieure de Technologie (EST).
A l'intention de: ressortissants de tout pays, titulaires du baccalauréat ou équivalent; admission sur dossier, entretien et sur concours pour l'accès aux études doctorales.
Durée: variable selon le programme.
Assistance financière: possibilité de bourses.
Inscriptions: à l'adresse ci-dessus.

1518 University Moulay Ismail Meknès
Marjane II BP298
5003 Meknès
Tel: +212-55-467-306
Fax: +212-55-467-305
Web: http://www.rumi.ac.ma
e-mail: presidence@rumi.ac.ma

Mauritius
Academic year: August to July.
Monetary unit: rupee (R).
National student admission: For higher degree courses: a degree of bachelor of the University (at least 2nd class Honours) or a first degree; for degree courses: GCE O-level passes in 5 subjects, two of which must be at A-level; diploma courses: five GCE O-level passes including English and Mathematics; for certificate courses: generally a Cambridge S.C. with passes in 5 subjects including English language.
Language: English.
Estimated expenses for one academic year: Higher degree courses: R 66,310; diploma courses: R 26,510; certificate courses: R 26,110.
Recognition of studies and qualification: University of Mauritius; Reduit; Mauritius; tel.: +230-454-1041 / +230-454-9958; fax +230-454-9642; web: http://www.uom.ac.mu.
Publications / Websites:
• University Calendar.
• Annual Report.
• University Journal.

1519 Mahatma Gandhi Institute [MGI]
Mahatma Gandhi Avenue
Moka
Tel: +230-433-2488
Fax: +230-433-2235
Web: http://ndiahighcom.intnet.mu/inm_mgi.htm
e-mail: asibmgi@intnet.mu

📖 Undergraduate Programmes
Study Domains: Asian studies, fine arts, performing arts.
Programmes: (a) Diploma courses in Indian languages and Indian Philosophy; (b) Bachelor's degree in Hindi; Bachelor's degree in fine arts; (c) Certificate in Indian music and dance.
Fees: available upon request.
Languages: instruction in English.
Applications: to the above address.

1520 Mauritius Institute of Education [MIE]
Reduit
Tel: +230-466-1940
Web: http://www.mieonline.org/

📖 Graduate, Postgraduate Programmes
Study Domains: education.
Programmes: programme of courses leading to: (a) postgraduate certificate in education and (b) teacher's diploma.
Open to: secondary-school teachers satisfying minimum academic requirements.
Duration: 2 to 3 years.
Languages: instruction in English.
Applications: by the end of September, to the above address.

1521 University of Mauritius [UM]
Reduit
Tel: +230-454-1041
Fax: +230-454-9642
Web: http://www.uom.ac.mu

📖 Undergraduate, Graduate and Postgraduate Programmes
Study Domains: all major fields, agriculture, economy, education, engineering, sciences.
Programmes: programme of courses leading to Bachelor's, Master's and Ph.D. in economics, agriculture, engineering, science, education.
Open to: candidates of all nationalities; students must have: for diploma courses, GCE O-level in 5 subjects including English language; for degree courses, GCE A-level in 2 subjects plus O-level in 5 subjects including English language or A-level in 3 subjects plus O-level in 4 subjects including English language; for higher degrees (M.Phil./Ph.D.), a first degree, at least second-class honours.
Duration: 3 to 6 years; courses begin end of July.
Languages: English and French.
Applications: to the above address for further information.

🎓 Scholarship
Study Domains: all major fields.
Scholarships: Commonwealth Scholarship and Fellowship Plan.
Open to: one applicant from Botswana; Lesotho; Malawi; Namibia; South Africa; Swaziland; Tanzania; Zimbabwe for undergraduate studies.
Duration: 1 year.
Value: UK£2,000 per year plus travel expenses and living costs.
Applications: by March/April; contact sgdyal@uom.ac.mu for further information.

1522 University of Technology [UT]
La Tour Koeing, Pointe aux Sables
Port Louis
Tel: +230-234-7624 / 7632
Fax: +230-234-1660
Web: http://ncb.intnet.mu/utm
e-mail: registrar@utm.intnet.mu

📖 Undergraduate, Graduate, Postgraduate Programmes
Study Domains: accounting, administration, business, business administration, finance, human sciences, management, technology, tourism, hotel and catering management.
Programmes: programme of courses leading to Bachelor's, Master's and PhD in administration, business, business administration, finance, human sciences, management, technology, tourism and hotel management.
Applications: to the above address.

🎓 University Scholarships
Study Domains: administration, computer science, management, technology, tourism, hotel and catering management.
Scholarships: University Scholarship.
Open to: nationals of Commonwealth Secretariat countries; Mozambique, Senegal and Zambia.
Academic requirements: minimum academic qualifications and requirements of the institution must be met.
Duration: 3 academic years (6 terms).
Value: US$8,580 per academic year; renewable; contact registrar@utm.intnet.mu for further information.
Applications: by end of May; applications to be channelled through respective government of each student; details may be obtained from the Administrative Assistant, Student Affairs at the above address.

México
Año académico: Septiembre a junio.
Organización de la enseñanza superior: Licenciaturas (4 años), Maestrías (2 años); Doctorados (2 años). El promedio de calificaciones académicas requeridas es de 8.5/10.
Moneda nacional: Peso mexicano (MXN).
Admisiones para estudiantes del país: Para licenciatura, certificado de Preparatoria (nivel medio superior equivalente a tres años después de secundaria básica); para maestría: estudios de licenciatura, para doctorado: estudios de maestría.
Admisiones para estudiantes extranjeros: Para licenciatura, certificado de Preparatoria (nivel medio superior equivalente a tres años después de secundaria básica); para maestría: estudios de licenciatura, para doctorado: estudios de maestría.
Conocimientos lingüísticos: Es indispensable tener conocimientos básicos del idioma español.
Les instituciones enumeradas a continuación ofrecen cursos de lengua española para que los estudiantes extranjeros perfeccionen sus conocimientos de español antes de ingresar en los centros docentes:
• Universidad Autónoma de Guadalajara, Avenida Patria No. 1201, Col. Lomas del Valle, 3a sección, Apartado Postal 1-400, Guadalajara, Jal.
• Universidad Nacional Autónoma de México, Escuela para Extanjeros, Ciudad Universitaria, México D.F. 04510
• Universidad Autónoma de Querétaro, Centro Universitario s/n, Cerro de las Campanas, Apartado Postal 184, Querétaro, Qro. 76010.
• Además existen múltiples centros privados que dictan cursos de perfeccionamiento lingüístico. En casos especiales se ofrecen cursos elementales de español para becarios del Gobierno de México únicamente.
• La Universidad de las Américas es la única que imparte cursos regulares de inglés.
Formalidades de inmigración: Les estudiantes deben solicitar el visado de estudiante en el consulado de México correspondiente a su llegada a México, y deben registrarse en el Instituto Nacional de Migración, Secretaría de Gobernación, Av. Chapultepec N.° 284, 7° piso, Col. Roma, México, D.F. 06700.
Importe de gastos para un año universita: Varía totalmente de acuerdo a la escuela y lugar de estudios. La Secretaría de Relaciones Exteriores y la Secretaría de Educación Pública conceden a extranjeros 700 MXN mensuales para manutención. Los estudios, colegiatura, libros y otras cuotas difieren de escuela a escuela.
Servicios de información:
• Secretaría de Educación Pública, Dirección General de Relaciones Internacionales, Donceles No. 100, Col. Centro, 06020, México D.F. (información y asesoramiento a

estudiantes, especialmente graduados y maestros mexicanos, que deseen proseguir sus estudios en el extranjero, así como a estudiantes y maestros extranjeros que se propongan estudiar en México).
• Secretaría de Relaciones Exteriores, Dirección General de Asuntos Culturales, Reforma No. 175, México D.F. (orientación a estudiantes extranjeros; intercambios internacionales de estudiantes; difunde y tramita los ofrecimientos de becas que los gobiernos extranjeros y organismos internacionales hacen a México; email: ecolin@sre.gob.mx).
Otras entidades en el país y en el extranjero.
• Servicios culturales de las embajadas de México en el extranjero.
• Secretaria de Educación Pública en los Estados de la República.
• Asociación Nacional de Universidades e Institutos de Enseñanza Superior (ANUIES), Tenayuca No. 200, Col. Santa Cruz Atoyac, México, D.F.
• Centro de Investigación Científica y de Educación Superior de Ensenada (CICESE), Km. 107, Carr. Tijuana, Ensenada, B.C. 27320 (intercambios internacionales de estudiantes; alojamiento en algunos casos, siempre y cuando el estudiante extranjero lo solicite con suficiente anticipación).
• Centro de Investigaciones y Estudios Superiores en Antropología Social, Hidalgo y Matamoros, Tlalpan, D.F. (asesoría académica a investigadores extranjeros becados por otras instituciones).
• Consejo Nacional de Ciencia y Tecnología (CONACYT), Av. Constituyentes No. 1046, Col. Lomas Atlas, México D.F. 11950.
• Instituto Politécnico Nacional, Unidad Profesional Zacatenco, Col. Lindavista, México D.F. 07738.
• Dirección General de Educación Superior (Dirección de apoyo a la difusión y a la docencia), Av. San Fernando No. 1, Col. Toriello Guerra, Tlalpan, México D.F. 14050.
• Subsecretaría de Educación Superior e Investigación Científica (Dirección de la difusión y a la docencia), Brasil No. 31, 2o piso, Col. Centro, México D.F. 06029.
• Unión de Universidades de América Latina. Sistema de información de educación superior de América Latina y el Caribe (SIESLAC), Apartado Postal 70232, edificio UDUAL, Ciudad Universitaria, Delegación Coyoacan, México D.F. 04510.
• Universidad Nacional Autónoma de México (UNAM), Dirección General de Intercambio Académico, Edificio de Postgrado, 2e piso, Ciudad Universitaria, México D.F. 04510.
Becas para estudiantes internacionales: Solicitudes de beca y trámites ante la Secretaría de Relaciones Exteriores, Reforma 175, México D.F. La información se puede solicitar en las Embajadas de México en los países con los que existe un convenio cultural.
Enseñanza abierta y a distancia: Se ofrece enseñanza superior a distancia en 62 instituciones, entre las cuales se cuentan la Universidad Nacional Autónoma de México, la Universidad Pedagógica Nacional, el Instituto Politécnico Nacional y el Instituto Tecnológico y de Estudios Superiores de Monterrey.
Convalidación de estudios y diplomas:
• Dirección General de Profesiones, Insurgentes Sur 2387, 1000 México D.F.
• Dirección General de Revalidación, Dinamarca 84, Piso 7, Col. Juarez C.P. 06600 México D.F.
Servicios de alojamiento para estudiante: Universidad Nacional Autónoma de México (UNAM), Dir. de Extensión Académica, Av. Universidad 300, Ciudad Universitaria, México D.F. 04510. A la llegada del estudiante a México y durante el período de inscripciones, proporciona una lista de casas de familias mexicanas que reciben estudiantes extranjeros y presta ayuda en ese aspecto.
Posibilidades de empleo: La ley no permite trabajar a los estudiantes extranjeros.
Publicaciones / Sitios web:
• Secretaría de Relaciones Exteriores; web: http://www.sre.gob.mx.
• Secretaria de Educación Pública: web: http://www.sep.gob.mx
• Consejo Nacional de Ciencia y Tecnología: web: http://www.conacyt.mx
• Programa de Mejoramiento del Profesorado (PROMEP): web: http://promep.sep.gob.mx
• Universidad Nacional Autónoma de México (UNAM): web: http://www.unam.mx

• Universidad de las Américas (UDLA): web: http://www.udla.mx/2003/index.htm
• Instituto Tecnólogico de Monterrey (ITESM); web: http://www.itesm.mx.
Informaciones complementarias: Dirigirse a la escuela de su interés para solicitar información sobre requisitos de ingreso, costo, alojamiento.

1523 Barra Nacional de Abogados, Facultad de Derecho [FDBNA]

Concepción Beistegui 515, Colonia del Valle
03100 México D.F.
Tel: +52-55-5536-6869
Fax: +52-55-5536-6869
Web: http://www.bna.org.mx
e-mail: informes@bna.edu.mx

📖 **Programas universitarios**

Campos de estudios: criminología, derecho.
Descripción:
(a) Licenciaturas, especialidades, seminarios, diplomados y talleres en todas las ramas del derecho;
(b) Posgrados en derecho familiar, derecho fiscal, derecho penal, criminalística.
Se destina(n): a aspirantes que superen examen de admisión (en enero, mayo y septiembre).
Asistencia financiera: becas de colegiatura (de 20 a 60%) para alumnos de licenciatura con mejor promedio de calificaciones.

1524 Benemérita Universidad Autónoma de Puebla

4 Sur 303 Altos
72000 Puebla
Tel: +52-222-229-5500
Web: http://www.buap.mx

📖 **Programas universitarios**

Campos de estudios: todas las materias principales.
Descripción:
(a) Licenciaturas en administración de empresas, administración pública, comunicación, contaduría pública, consultoría jurídica, derecho y ciencias sociales, economía, estomatología, medicina, enfermería, biomedicina, biología, física, matemáticas, computación, electrónica, química, farmacia, química farmacobiológica, arquitectura, diseño gráfico, diseño urbano ambiental, ingeniería (civil, mecánica y eléctrica, topográfica y geodésica, textil, industrial, química, agrohidráulica, agronómica zootécnica, agroindustrial), filosofía, historia, antropología, lingüística y literatura hispánica, psicología, música, arte dramático, danza moderna y clásica, lenguas modernas, lenguas extranjeras, cultura física, medicina veterinaria y zootecnia;
(b) Programas de maestría en gobierno y administración, administración de PYMES, ordenamiento del territorio, conservación del patrimonio edificado, tecnologías de la arquitectura, diseño arquitectónico, matemáticas, optoelectrónica, ciencias químicas, administración de organizaciones, ciencias de la computación, derecho, ciencias políticas, ortodoncia, estomatología integral, estomatología pediátrica, economía, literatura mexicana, estética y arte, educación superior, ingeniería ambiental, ingeniería (de tránsito y transporte, en construcción, en geotecnia, estructural), valuación, ingeniería química, diagnóstico y rehabilitación neuropsicológica, psicología social, ciencias químicas, bioquímica y biología molecular, ciencias ambientales, ciencias microbiológicas, semiconductores, ciencias fisiológicas, ciencias del lenguaje, historia, sociología, ciencias (física), ciencias (ciencias de materiales), ciencias médicas e investigación clínica, administración de servicios de salud;
(c) Especialidades: finanzas, derecho fiscal, terapia psicosexual, valuación;
(d) Doctorados: matemáticas, optoelectrónica, ciencias químicas, ciencias ambientales, ciencias microbiológicas, ciencias fisiológicas, historia, sociología, ciencias (física), ciencias (de los materiales).
Duración: año académico de agosto a mediados de junio.
Inscripciones: para mayor información, dirigirse a la Dirección de Relaciones Internacionales de la Universidad.

1525 Centro de Investigación Científica y de Educación Superior de Ensenada [CICESE]

Km. 107 Carretera Tijuana-Ensenada
22800 Ensenada, B.C.
Tel: +52-646-175-0500
Web: http://www.cicese.mx
e-mail: posgrado@cicese.mx

📖 Programa de maestrías y doctorados en ciencias

Campos de estudios: ciencias aplicadas, ecología, medio ambiente, electricidad y electrónica, física, geología, oceanografía, optica, sociología, telecomunicaciones.
Descripción: óptica (opciones óptica física u optoelectrónica), física de materiales, electrónica y telecomunicaciones (opciones telecomunicaciones, instrumentación y control o electrónica de alta frecuencia), acuicultura, biotecnología marina, ecología marina, oceanografía física, computación, ciencias de la tierra, administración integral del ambiente.
Se destina(n): a titulados universitarios que cumplan con los requisitos necesarios; en el caso de extranjeros, deben presentar título y certificado de calificaciones traducidos al español y legalizados por vía diplomática.
Duración: 2 años la maestría y 3 años el doctorado.
Asistencia financiera: para nacionales de países con los que México tiene convenios de intercambio científico, existen becas disponibles a través de las Embajadas de México.
Inscripciones: para mayor información, dirigirse al Departamento de Servicios Escolares en la dirección del título o a P.O. Box 430222, San Diego, California 92143-0222, Estados Unidos de América.

1526 Centro de Investigación y Docencia Económicas [CIDE]

Carretera México-Toluca Km. 16.5
Col. Lomas de Santa Fe, Del. Alvaro Obregón
01210 México, D.F.
Tel: +52-55-5727-9800
Web: http://www.cide.mx
e-mail: promdoce@dis1.cide.mx

📖 Programas académicos

Campos de estudios: administración, ciencias políticas, economía, economía política, relaciones internacionales.
Descripción:
(a) Licenciaturas en economía, en ciencia política/relaciones internacionales;
(b) Maestrías en economía, en economía de la salud, en administración y políticas públicas.
Se destina(n): (a) a candidatos menores de 23 años con promedio de 8 en preparatoria; (b) a titulados superiores que superen examen de admisión.
Duración: (a) 9 semestres; (b) 4 semestres más curso propedéutico de 6 semanas. Los comienzos son en agosto.
Asistencia financiera: crédito educativo, becas y estímulo al rendimiento académico de los mejores estudiantes.
Inscripciones: (a) de enero a junio, en el CIDE; (b) de enero a mayo, en las embajadas o consulados de México en el país de origen, o en el CIDE, de enero a mediados de junio.

1527 Centro de Investigaciones y Estudios Superiores en Antropología Social [CIESAS]

Apartado Postal 22-048
Tlalpan
14000 México, D.F.
Tel: +52-55-5573-9066
Fax: +52-5573-9106
Web: http://www.ciesas.edu.mx
e-mail: ciejuare@juarez.ciesas.edu.mx

📖 Programa de maestrías y doctorados

Campos de estudios: antropología, ciencias sociales, estudios culturales, investigación, lingüística.
Descripción: (a) Maestría en antropología social CIESAS-D.F.; (b) Maestría en antropología social CIESAS-Occidente y CIESAS-Sureste; (c) Maestría en lingüística indoamericana; (d) Doctorado en ciencias sociales CIESA-Occidente; (e) Doctorado en antropología social CIESAS-D.F.
Materias de estudio: antropología social; ciencias sociales (antropología, historia); lingüística indoamericana; etnohistoria.
Se destina(n): a quienes tengan licenciatura o maestría en antropología o ciencias afines; presentar certificado de estudios con promedio mínimo de 8, copia de los tres mejores trabajos, 2 cartas de recomendación, carta de exposición de motivos, carta compromiso de dedicación exclusiva. Se exige dominio del español y comprensión de lecturas en inglés y/o francés. En el caso de (c), el aspirante ser hablante de alguna lengua indígena americana, o tener experiencia profesional e interés en alguna de ella; para (d) y (e), se debe tener experiencia en investigación, acreditada con publicaciones o resultados de investigación.
Duración: 2 años las maestrías y 4 años los doctorados.
Asistencia financiera: existen becas en colegiatura y para investigación de tesis.
Inscripciones: en todos los casos, dirigirse a la Subdirección de Formación, Juárez No. 87, Col. Tlalpan, México, D.F. Tel. (56) 5 655 9718 o e-mail: docencia@juarez.ciesas.edu.mx.

💰 Becas de tesis

Campos de estudios: antropología, ciencias sociales.
Materias de estudio: variables según las líneas de investigación aprobadas cada año.
Se conceden: a estudiantes de ciencias sociales de licenciatura y maestría y a pasantes totales (estudios terminados), que presenten proyecto de investigación aprobado por investigador del CIESAS y carta de aceptación de la institución del estudiante acerca del director de tesis.
Lugar: distintas unidades de la institución (ciudades de México, Xalapa, Oaxaca, Guadalajara, San Cristóbal de las Casas).
Duración: 12 meses (no renovable).
Solicitudes: de febrero a mayo; dirigirse a la Comisión de Becarios-CIESAS, Juárez 87, Tlalpán D.F. 14000.

1528 Centro Interamericano de Estudios de Seguridad Social [CIESS]

Apartado Postal 99087
10100 México, D.F.
Tel: +52-55-5595-0011
Fax: +52-55-5595-0644
Web: http://www.ciess.org.mx
e-mail: ciess@servidor.unam.mx

📖 Actividades académicas en el área de la seguridad social

Campos de estudios: administración, ciencias sociales, derecho, economía, finanzas, higiene y salud, informática, medicina.
Descripción: integración de la teoría y la práctica en los siguientes aspectos: jurídico-sociales, ciencias administrativas, médico-sociales, económico-financieras, protección y salud de los trabajadores, recursos informáticos, economía de la salud.
Se destina(n): principalmente al personal profesional, técnico y administrativo de las instituciones americanas de salud y seguridad social, así como a otros profesionales interesados en el estudio de la seguridad social. En ambos casos, es preferible que los participantes sean propuestos por la institución donde desempeñen sus labores y posean conocimiento de alguna institución de enseñanza superior que se relacione con el ámbito de estudio inherente al área básica de interés. Debido al contenido de las materias que se imparten, pueden participar instituciones públicas y privadas, universidades y centros de enseñanza superior de cualquier nacionalidad.
Duración: generalmente las actividades docentes se inician en febrero y culminan en diciembre. En ese período se dictan múltiples cursos (1 mes); seminarios (5 días); diplomados (5 semanas); cursos taller (15 días).
Asistencia financiera: la Conferencia Interamericana de Seguridad Social otorga a sus instituciones miembros becas para participar en los eventos del CIESS. Las instituciones no asociadas a este organismo deberán cubrir los costos que se deriven de su participación. Para el caso de educandos que no radiquen en la Ciudad de México, el CIESS ofrece los servicios de hospedaje y alimentación. Asimismo, brindan su

colaboración la OPS/OMS, la OIT, la CEPAL y diversos organismos internacionales afines, así como universidades de reconocido prestigio de América y Europa en el seguimiento de las actividades académicas.

Inscripciones: para mayor información, dirigirse a CIESS, Calle San Ramón s/n esquina Avenida San Jerónimo, Unidad Independencia, 10100 México, D.F.

1529 Colegio de México [CDM]
Camino dal Ajusco 20, Pedregal de Santa Teresa
Apartado Postal 20671
10740 México D.F.
Tel: +52-55-5449-3000
Fax: +52-55-5645-0464
Web: http://www.colmex.mx

☛ Becas México para maestría en estudios de Asia y Africa
Campos de estudios: Arabe, estudios africanos, estudios ásiaticos, hebreo, japonés.
Materias de estudio: historia, literatura, problemas contemporáneos de las principales regiones de Asia, con especialización en árabe, chino, hebreo, japonés, sánscrito, hindi y coreano.
Se conceden: a nacionales de los países de América Latina, menores de 35 años de edad, que sepan bien el idioma inglés, tengan buenas recomendaciones académicas y una licenciatura o estudios equivalentes.
Lugar: Centro de Estudios de Asia y Africa.
Duración: 1 año académico (prorrogable).
Solicitudes: un año antes de empezar los estudios.

☛ Becas para estudios
Campos de estudios: demografía y estudios de población, economía, estudios africanos, estudios ásiaticos, estudios sobre el desarrollo, historia, lingüística, literatura y civilización, sociología.
Descripción: (a) Maestría; (b) Doctorado.
Materias de estudio: (a) economía, demografía, desarrollo urbano; (b) sociología, historia, literatura, lingüística y población.
Se conceden: a personas de cualquier nacionalidad que cumplan los requisitos necesarios, conozcan suficientemente el idioma español, y aprueben el examen de admisión.
Duración: 2 a 3 años.

1530 Colegio de Postgraduados [CP]
Km 36,5 Carretera México-Texcoco
56 230 Montecillo Estado de México
Tel: +52-595-952-0200
Fax: +52-55-5804-5900
Web: http://www.colpos.mx
e-mail: dirgal@colpos.mx

▢ Programas de investigación y enseñanza de postgrado en ciencias agrícolas
Campos de estudios: agricultura, botánica, ciencias agronómicas, desarrollo rural, economía, horticultura, informática, recursos naturales, silvicultura.
Materias de estudio: fitosanidad; recursos genéticos y productividad; recursos naturales; socioeconomía, estadística e informática.
Se destina(n): para maestría en ciencias, egresados de las escuelas profesionales de agricultura, universidades e instituciones afines con estudios equivalentes a la carrera agronómica; también se aceptan egresados de instituciones de enseñanza superior cuyo curricula les dé opción de estudios de postgrado en el CP, para lo que es requisito el título profesional, 8.0 como promedio en sus calificaciones de licenciatura y un año como mínimo de experiencia; para doctorado en ciencias se exige del aspirante sólida preparación en ciencias básicas y aplicadas en el campo de su especialidad, experiencia en la transmisión de conocimientos y sentido social de sus actividades. Además es necesario haber obtenido el grado de maestría en ciencias o su equivalente.
Se dicta(n): en Montecillo, Puebla, Veracruz, Tabasco, San Luis Potosí, Campeche.
Asistencia financiera: diversos programas de becas de

gobiernos extranjeros y organismos internacionales; solicitar información a la Dirección de Relaciones Internacionales o al Area de Becas (e-mail: becas@colpos.mx).
Inscripciones: se tramitan ante el Departamento de Servicios Académicos del Colegio de Postgraduados, en la dirección del título (e-mail servacad@colpos.colpos.mx).

1531 Comisión Interinstitucional para la Formación de Recursos Humanos para la Salud Comité de Enseñanza de Posgrado y Educación Continua
Servicios de Salud Pública
Subdirección de Capacitación
José A. Torres 661, 3er. piso
Col. Asturias, Del. Cuauhtemoc

▢ Residencias de especialización médica
Campos de estudios: medicina.
Descripción: cursos de posgrado que se realizan en unidades de atención médica del Sistema Nacional de Salud.
Se destina(n): a aspirantes nacionales o extranjeros que hayan obtenido la "constancia de seleccionado" en el Examen Nacional y presenten la documentación requerida en cada institución.
Duración: variable, comienzan en marzo.
Inscripciones: para mayor información sobre ingreso a las instituciones y sobre inscripciones para el examen, dirigirse a la dirección que figura en el título.

1532 Consejo Nacional de Ciencia y Tecnología [CONACYT]
Av. Insurgentes Sur 1582,
Col. Crédito Constructor Del. Benito Juárez
C.P. 03940
11950 México D.F.
Tel: +52-55-5322-7700
Web: http://www.conacyt.mx

☛ Becas de excelencia para la realización de postgrados
Campos de estudios: todas las materias principales.
Se conceden: a licenciados mexicanos, cubanos, latinoamericanos, alemanes, japoneses y británicos, no mayores de 35 años, con promedio mínimo de 8 (sobre escala de 10), que conozcan el español; en el caso de los extranjeros, deben ser presentados por la contraparte de su país con la cual se tiene establecido el convenio.
Duración: anual (posibilidad de prórroga hasta concluir ciclo académico).

1533 El Colegio de Michoacán A.C. [COLMICH]
Marinez de Navarrete 505
Las Fuentes
59699 Zamora
Tel: +52-351-516-9051
Fax: +52-351-516-9051
Web: http://www.colmich.edu.mx
e-mail: presiden@colmich.edu.mx

▢ Programas universitarios
Campos de estudios: antropología, arqueología, ciencias humanas, ciencias sociales, folklore, historia.
Descripción:
(a) Programas de investigación;
(b) Maestrías y doctorados en: estudios antropológicos, historia, ciencias sociales (especialidad estudios rurales, estudios de las tradiciones), ciencias sociales.
Materias de estudio: antropología, historia, estudios rurales, arqueología, estudio de las tradiciones, geografía humana.
Se destina(n): (b) a candidatos de título de licenciatura en ciencias sociales o humanidades, con promedio de calificaciones superior a 8 sobre 10, con comprensión de lectura de inglés o francés, que presenten cartas de recomendación y evaluación.
Duración: inicios en septiembre, cada 3 años.
Asistencia financiera: becas de la Secretaría de

Relaciones Exteriores para licenciados extranjeros, para estudios en ciencias sociales y humanidades, consistente en monto mensual y monto para gastos de instalación. Dirigirse a los consulados de México en cada país, consultar http://becas.sre.gob.mx o por e-mail: becas@sre.gob.mx. *Inscripciones:* por mayores informaciones, dirigirse al Departamento de Asuntos escolares (e-mail: aescolar@colmich.edu.mx).

1534 El Colegio de Sonora
Calle Obregón #54
Col. Centro, Hermosillo
83000 Sonora
Tel: +52-658-212-6551
Fax: +52-658-212-5021
Web: http://www.colson.edu.mx
e-mail: colson@colson.edu.mx

📖 Maestría en ciencias sociales

Campos de estudios: ciencias políticas, ciencias sociales, estudios sobre el desarrollo, gestión, higiene y salud, relaciones industriales.
Descripción: especialidades en salud, estudios regionales, estudios políticos y gestión pública, relaciones industriales.
Se destina(n): a licenciados o equivalente, con promedio mínimo de 8, que aprueben examen escrito y entrevista, y que dominen español e inglés.
Duración: 2 años académicos.
Asistencia financiera: becas-crédito para gastos de manutención; solicitar informes a la Coordinación de Asuntos Escolares.
Inscripciones: convocatorias en febrero; por mayor información, dirigirse a la Coordinación General Académica.

1535 Escuela de Diseño del Instituto Nacional de Bellas Artes [EDINBA]
Xocongo 138
Col. Tránsito
06820 México, D.F.
Tel: +52-55-5522-5161
Fax: +52-55-5522-5762
Web: http://www.inba.gob.mx

📖 Programas académicos

Campos de estudios: artes gráficas, artes plásticas, bellas artes, diseño, diseño industrial.
Descripción:
(a) Licenciatura en diseño;
(b) Maestría en creatividad para el diseño;
(c) Especialidades en: creatividad y estrategia publicitaria, compugrafía, medios interactivos, producción editorial;
(d) Diplomados.
Se destina(n): a nacionales de cualquier país que se hallen en posesión del grado de bachiller (calificaciones con un promedio mínimo de 7.5, el cual deberá ser revalidado), y aprueben el examen de admisión consistente en ejercicios prácticos y entrevista.
Duración: (a) 4 años; (b) 2 años; existen cursos de verano en julio-agosto.
Inscripciones: en la primera quincena de julio.

1536 Escuela Nacional de Conservación, Restauración y Museografía "Manuel del Castillo Negrete"
Gral. Anaya 187, San Diego Churubusco
04120 México, D.F.
Tel: +52-55-5604-5188
Fax: +52-55-5604-5163
Web: http://www.cnca.gob.mx/cnca/inah/docencia/ecrm.html
e-mail: inahmex@telecomm.net.mx

📖 Programas académicos

Campos de estudios: arquitectura, artes aplicadas, museología y museografía.
Descripción:
(a) Licenciatura en conservación y restauración de bienes culturales muebles;
(b) Maestría en restauración arquitectónica;
(c) Maestría en museos.

Se destina(n): a nacionales y extranjeros que: (a) acrediten estudios completos de bachillerato o equivalente; (b) posean el título de arquitecto, ingeniero civil o arqueólogo; (c) acrediten estudios completos de licenciatura.
Duración: (a) 10 semestres; (b) 11 meses; (c) 4 semestres.
Inscripciones: en junio.

1537 Escuela Normal de Especialización Delegación Miguel Hidalgo [ENDE]
Campos Elíseos 467
Colonia Polanco
11560 México, D.F.
Tel: +52-55-5280-8349
Fax: +52-55-5280-7845

📖 Licenciatura en educación especial

Campos de estudios: educación, educación especial.
Descripción: áreas de audición y lenguaje, ceguera y debilidad visual, deficiencia mental, infracción e inadaptación social, problemas de aprendizaje y trastornos neuromotores.
Se destina(n): a bachilleres o profesores de educación básica, nacionales o extranjeros con estudios convalidados, de edad mínima 30 años, que superen proceso de selección.
Duración: 4 años.
Asistencia financiera: existen becas económicas.
Inscripciones: durante el mes de julio se realizan las solicitudes y el examen de admisión.

1538 Gobierno de México Secretaría de Relaciones Exteriores [SRE]
Col. Guerrero, Deleg. Cuauhtémoc
CP 06300
11560 México, D.F.
Tel: +52-55-9159-3224 / 5 / 6
Web: http://www.sre.gob.mx

🎯 Programa de becas

Campos de estudios: todas las materias principales.
Descripción:
(a) Convocatoria de 79 programas (bilaterales, multilaterales y especiales) de becas para extranjeros, para efectuar estudios de posgrado (maestrías, doctorados y especializaciones) y para realizar investigaciones de posgrado de contenido académico, en instituciones mexicanas;
(b) Oferta permanente de posgrados para mexicanos en otros países.
Materias de estudio: generalmente todas, pero son prioritarias: seguridad alimentaria, salud pública, fortalecimiento institucional, políticas públicas, desarrollo social, estudios de género, y una nueva agenda internacional (migración, derechos humanos, medio ambiente, democracia y desarrollo sostenible).
Se conceden: (a) a estudiantes extranjeros para que realicen estudios de posgrado o investigaciones especializadas en instituciones académicas mexicanas. La Convocatoria incluye también diversos programas para expertos; (b) mexicanos interesados en llevar a cabo estudios de posgrado y especialización en el extranjero.
Solicitudes: consultar la página http://servicios.sre.gob.mx/becas. Para mayor detalle acudir a los buzones de dudas: becas@sre.gob.mx e infobecas@sre.gob.mx, llamar a los teléfonos +52-5-327-3224, 3225 y 3226 o acudir a Paseo de la Reforma 175-PB, Col. Cuauhtémoc, México, D. F. Quienes residen en los estados podrán encontrar solicitudes y formatos en las Delegaciones de la SRE.

1539 Hospital Infantil de México "Federico Gómez" División de Enseñanza [HIDMG]
Dr. Márquez No.162 Col. Doctores
Delegación Cuauhtemoc
06720 México, D.F.
Tel: +52-55-5228-9917
Web: http://www.facmed.unam.mx/infantil

📖 Programas académicos

Campos de estudios: cirugía, enfermería, estudios dentales, medicina, nutrición, pediatría, radiología, urología.
Descripción:
(a) Cursos de especialización en: pediatría general, medicina física y rehabilitación, genética y anestesiología;
(b) Cursos de especialización en áreas pediátricas: alergia e inmunología clínica, anestesiología, cardiología, cirugía cardiotorácica, dermatología, endocrinología, gastroenterología, hematología, infectología, medicina del enfermo pediátrico en estado crítico, nefrología, neonatología, neumología, neurocirugía, neurología, oncología, otorrinolaringología, patología, reumatología;
(c) Diplomados de educación continua: oftalmología pediátrica, ortopedia pediátrica, endoscopía pediátrica, medicina del adolescente, radiología pediátrica, cirugía oncológica;
(d) Cursos universitarios de especialización: odontopediatría, ortodoncia pediátrica;
(e) Curso universitario de enfermería infantil;
(f) Curso de nutriología clínica pediátrica;
(g) Cursos monográficos diversos durante todo el año;
(h) Campo clínico para algunas especialidades pediátricas así como participación en la realización de proyectos de investigación.
Se destina(n): (a) a médicos cirujanos titulados de cualquier nacionalidad que hayan realizado como mínimo 1 año de internado rotatorio en una unidad hospitalaria avalada por una Universidad reconocida; (b) a pediatras graduados de cualquier nacionalidad; (c) respectivamente: a oftalmólogos, cirujanos ortopedistas y pediatras, cirujanos pediatras, pediatras, radiólogos, cirujanos pediatras; (d) a cirujanos dentistas; (e) a enfermeras tituladas; (f) a nutriólogos graduados.
Duración: (a) 3 años; (b) de 2 a 4 años; (c) de 3 a 11 meses; (d) y (f) 2 años; (e) 11 meses.

1540 Instituto Mexicano de la Audición y el Lenguaje, A.C. [IMAL]

Avenida Progreso 141-A
Col. Escandón
11800 Miguel Hidalgo, D.F.
Tel: +52-55-5277-6444
Fax: +52-55-5277-6520
Web: http://www.imal.org.mx
e-mail: imal@imal.org.mx

📖 Programas académicos

Campos de estudios: educación especial, lingüística, medicina preventiva, ortofonía, programas de verano.
Descripción:
(a) Carrera profesional corta en audiometría y rehabilitación auditiva;
(b) Licenciatura en terapia de la audición, la voz, y el lenguaje oral y escrito;
(c) Maestría en patología del lenguaje.
Se destina(n): a hispanohablantes: (a) y (b) que hayan concluido estudios de nivel medio superior (bachillerato); existe selección por examen de conocimientos generales, audiométrico y psicométrico; (c) licenciados en audición y lenguaje, neurolingüística, pedagogía o educación especial; profesionales titulados con equivalente a diploma de especialización médica en audiología o foniatría, capaces de comprender textos técnicos en inglés.
Duración: (a) y (c) 2 años; (b) 4 años. Todos los comienzos son en septiembre.
Asistencia financiera: existen becas de estudio.
Inscripciones: hasta fin de julio; para mayor información, dirigirse a Subdirección de Enseñanza en la dirección del título.

1541 Instituto Mexicano de Psicoterapia Gestalt [IMPG]

Eucken 19
11590 México D.F.
Tel: +52-55-5203-2008
Fax: +52-55-5203-2008
Web: http://www.gestalt.com.mx
e-mail: inf@gestalt.com.mx

📖 Programas académicos

Campos de estudios: ciencias humanas, psicología, psiquiatría.
Programas:
(a) Licenciatura en Psicología Humanista;
(b) Maestría en Psicoterapia Gestalt;
(c) Cursos, diplomados, talleres.
Se destina(n): (b) a licenciados.
Duración: (a) 4 años, (b) 2 años.
Asistencia financiera: becas parciales de inscripción y colegiatura.

1542 Instituto Mexicano del Seguro Social Dirección de Prestaciones Médicas Coordinación de Educación Médica [IMSS]

Av. Paseo de la Reforma 476, Col. Juárez
06600 México, D.F.
Tel: +52-55-5238-2700
Web: http://edumed.imss.gob.mx
e-mail: educacion.salud@imss.gob.mx

📖 Cursos de posgrado

Campos de estudios: medicina.
Descripción: sistema de especialización médica en:
(a) Medicina familiar;
(b) Especialidades troncales (cirugía general, gineco-obstetricia, medicina interna, pediatría);
(c) Especialidades de rama (24 especialidades a las que se accede luego de cursar de 1 a 3 años de una especialidad troncal);
(d) Especialidades de entrada directa.
Se destina(n): a postulantes que cumplan los requisitos y superen procesos de selección.
Duración: (a) 3 años; (b) 4 años; (c) 2 a 5 años; para todos, ciclos académicos de marzo a febrero.
Inscripciones: para mayor información, dirigirse a la División de Formación de Personal para Atención de la Salud, Area de Especialidades Médicas, en la dirección que figura en el título.

🖋 Becas para estudios de posgrado

Campos de estudios: medicina.
Descripción: especializaciones en medicina.
Se conceden: a médicos de los países de América Latina, empleados del Seguro Social, de a lo sumo 34 años de edad.
Lugar: unidades del IMSS en las ciudades de México, Guadalajara, Monterrey, Puebla, Ciudad Obregón, Culiacán, Chihuahua, Hermosillo, León, Mérida, Mexicali, Saltillo, San Luis Potosí, Torreón y Veracruz.
Duración: 1 año académico (prorrogable de acuerdo con la duración del programa).
Solicitudes: en septiembre; Comité de Enseñanza de Posgrado y Educación Continua de la Dirección General de Enseñanza en Salud (Secretaría de Salud).

1543 Instituto Nacional de Salud Pública Escuela de Salud Pública de México [INSP]

Avenida Universidad 655
Colonia Sta. Ma. Ahuacatitlán
62508 Cuernavaca, Morelos
Tel: +52-777-329-3000
Web: http://www.insp.mx/espm

📖 Cursos y programas académicos

Campos de estudios: administración, biología, ciencias sociales, estadística, higiene y salud, medicina, nutrición.
Descripción:
(a) Cursos de educación continua en las áreas de: epidemiología y bioestadística, salud ambiental e higiene ocupacional, ciencias sociales, ciencias de la administración, desarrollo de proyectos de investigación en salud pública, garantía de la calidad de la atención en los servicios, administración de la atención primaria de los servicios locales de salud;
(b) Programas académicos: curso de planificación de sistemas

de servicios de salud, especialización de enfermería en salud pública, maestrías en administración en servicios de salud, maestría en salud pública, maestría en ciencias (con concentraciones en administración de hospitales, en salud ambiental, en epidemiología, en sistemas de salud, en salud reproductiva, en nutrición), doctorado en ciencias (con concentraciones en epidemiología, en sistemas de salud).
Se destina(n): a profesionales que se desempeñen en el campo de la salud pública.
Duración: variable según el programa; salvo la maestría en salud pública, todas las maestrías tienen una duración de 2 años, y los doctorados 1 año a tiempo completo más el tiempo para desarrollar una tesis.
Asistencia financiera: algunos de los programas cuentan con becas de instituciones como la Comisión Nacional Científica y Técnica (CONACYT), Organización Panamericana de la Salud (OPS) y Organización Mundial de la Salud (OMS).

🐾 Becas para estudio de posgrado

Campos de estudios: medicina.
Descripción: otorgadas por la Secretaría de Relaciones Exteriores de México.
Se conceden: a profesionales de ciencias de la salud, que preferentemente sean ciudadanos de países de Centro y Sudamérica, así como del Caribe, que sean aceptados por algún programa académico del INSP; se exigen calificaciones con mínimo de 8 o equivalente, idiomas español e inglés y aprobación de un curso propedéutico de 6 semanas.
Duración: anual, renovable.
Importe: monto que depende del salario mínimo vigente, seguro médico facultativo, pasaje aéreo viaje redondo, gastos de instalación.
Solicitudes: hasta diciembre, en las Embajadas de México en cada país.

1544 Instituto Politécnico Nacional Centro de Investigación en Computación [IPN]

Unidad Profesional Adolfo López Mateos
07738 México 14, D.F.
Tel: +52-55-5729-6000 ext 56506
Fax: +52-55-5729-6000 ext 54350
Web: http://www.ipn.mx

📖 Programas académicos y cursos

Campos de estudios: ciencias, informática.
Descripción:
(a) Programa de maestría en ciencias, con especialidad en computación;
(b) Doctorado en ciencias de la computación;
(c) Maestría en ingeniería de cómputo;
(d) Cursos en temas como reconocimiento de patrones, graficación, lenguajes de programación, multimedia, bases de datos, técnicas de programación.
Se destina(n): (a) a nacionales y extranjeros con estudios de licenciatura terminados, preferentemente del área de ingeniería o físico-matemática; es indispensable saber español e inglés.
Duración: (a) 2 años.
Asistencia financiera: existen posibilidades de ayudas, para alumnos de tiempo completo.
Inscripciones: exámenes de admisión e inscripciones en febrero y julio.

1545 Instituto Politécnico Nacional Escuela Nacional de Ciencias Biológicas [ENCB-IPN]

Carpio y Plan de Ayala s/n
Col. Plutarco Elías Calles
11340 México, D.F.
Tel: +52-55-5729-6000
Fax: +52-5-396-3503

📖 Programas académicos

Campos de estudios: biología, bioquímica, ciencias.
Descripción: Programas de maestrías, especialidades o doctorados en ciencias según el caso, en las siguientes áreas entre otras: citopatología, química biorgánica, parasitología, farmacia, toxicología, ingeniería de productos biológicos, bioquímica, ecología, biología, fisiología, microbiología, biofísica, biología clínica, alimentos, inmunoparasitología,

hematología, citología exfoliativa.
Se destina(n): a nacionales de cualquier país, de edad mínima 23 años, que tengan título profesional, licenciatura o maestría, según el caso, en la especialidad de estudio elegida. Hay examen de admisión que incluye traducción de una lengua extranjera que sea indicada por el colegio respectivo.
Duración: especialidad: 2 semestres; maestría: 4 semestres; doctorado: 6 semestres; (los semestres comienzan en septiembre y marzo).
Inscripciones: en enero y agosto; los exámenes de admisión son en julio y diciembre; por mayores informaciones, dirigirse al Jefe de la Sección de Graduados.

1546 Instituto Politécnico Nacional Escuela Superior de Física y Matemáticas [IPN]

Edificio n° 9
Unidad Profesional Adolfo Lopez Mateos
Col. Lindavista
07738 México 14, D.F.
Tel: +52-55-5729-6000
Web: http://www.ipn.mx

📖 Programas académicos

Campos de estudios: ciencias aplicadas, energía, física, ingeniería, matemáticas.
Descripción:
(a) Licenciatura en física y matemáticas;
(b) Maestrías en: ciencias de materiales, matemáticas, ingeniería nuclear, física;
(c) Programa de doctorado en física.
Se destina(n): (a) y (b) a estudiantes que hayan concluido estudios de nivel superior, debidamente certificados, y en su caso, revalidados; que aprueben el examen de admisión y además, en el caso de extranjeros, tengan la documentación migratoria correspondiente y hablen y escriban el español; (c) como (a) pero deben tener estudios a nivel de maestría.
Duración: (a) 8 semestres; (b) 4 semestres; (c) 6 semestres.
Inscripciones: (a) y (b) en febrero y agosto.

1547 Instituto Politécnico Nacional Escuela Superior de Ingeniería Mecánica y Eléctrica [IPN]

Edificio n° 7
Unidad Profesional de Zacatenco
México 14, D.F.
Tel: +52-55-5729-6000
Web: http://www.ipn.mx

📖 Programas académicos

Campos de estudios: electricidad y electrónica, ingeniería, mecánica.
Descripción: Programas de maestrías en ingeniería eléctrica, electrónica, sistemas, mecánica, y doctorado en ingeniería eléctrica con especialidad en sistemas eléctricos de potencia.
Se destina(n): a nacionales de cualquier país que tengan las calificaciones requeridas para especializarse en el área de estudio elegida; es necesario saber bien español y tener conocimientos de inglés.
Duración: 4 semestres.
Inscripciones: en enero y julio.

1548 Instituto Politécnico Nacional Escuela Superior de Ingeniería Química e Industrias Extractivas [IPN]

Edificio n° 7
Unidad Profesional Adolfo Lopez Mateos
07738 México, D.F.
Tel: +52-5-729-6140
Fax: +52-5-586-2728
Web: http://www.ipn.mx

📖 Programas académicos

Campos de estudios: ingeniería, metalurgia, química.
Descripción:
(a) Maestría en ingeniería química e ingeniería metalúrgica;
(b) Doctorado en metalurgia y materiales.

Se destina(n): a nacionales de cualquier país que se hallen en posesión de los diplomas requeridos para cursar los estudios elegidos; deben saber español y tener conocimientos de inglés u otra lengua.
Duración: (a) 4 semestres; (b) 6 semestres.
Inscripciones: en enero y agosto.

1549 Instituto Politécnico Nacional Escuela Superior de Ingeniería Textil [IPN]

Unidad Profesional Adolfo Lopez Mateos (Zacatenco)
Col. Lindavista
07738 México D.F.
Tel: +52-5-586-3413
Web: http://www.ipn.mx

📖 Programas académicos

Campos de estudios: artes aplicadas, diseño industrial, industria textil.
Descripción:
(a) Maestría en ciencias en diseño textil;
(b) Ingeniero textil en confección;
(c) Ingeniero textil e hilados.
Se destina(n): a nacionales de cualquier país: (a) profesionales titulares de una licenciatura o equivalente, que superen proceso de admisión consistente en examen, entrevista y examen de inglés; (b) que hayan terminado el ciclo de enseñanza media superior en el área fisicomatemática con promedio mínimo de 7, y que aprueben examen de admisión, (c) que posean sólidos conocimientos en las áreas de física, química y matemáticas.
Duración: (a) 3 semestres; (b) y (c) 9 semestres.
Inscripciones: en septiembre.

1550 Instituto Politécnico Nacional Unidad Profesional Interdisciplinaria de Ingeniería y Ciencias Sociales y Administrativas [IPN]

Calle de Te 950
Colonia Granjas México
08400 México 8, D.F.
Tel: +52-5-624-2000
Fax: +52-5-650-3840
Web: http://www.ipn.mx

📖 Programas académicos

Campos de estudios: todas las materias principales, administración, ciencias sociales, finanzas, idiomas, industria y comercio, informática, ingeniería, ingeniería civil, matemáticas, tecnología industrial.
Descripción:
(a) Licenciaturas en las siguientes áreas: arquitectura, ciencias antropológicas, contaduría pública, derecho, economía, educación, enfermería, ingeniería civil, ingeniería en transporte, ingeniería química industrial, química industrial, matemáticas, ciencias de la computación, enseñanza de las matemáticas, medicina, medicina veterinaria, biología, odontología, psicología, química;
(b) Especializaciones en las siguientes áreas: finanzas, derecho civil, derecho fiscal, docencia, enseñanza del inglés, gestión de tecnología, estadística, anestesiología, cirugía general, ginecología y obstetricia, medicina familiar, medicina interna, ortopedia, pediatría, medicina del deporte, endodoncia, periodoncia, psicología clínica infantil;
(c) Maestrías en: ciencias antropológicas, administración, derecho civil, derecho fiscal, economía y administración pública, educación superior, ingeniería ambiental, ingeniería en construcción, ciencia y tecnología de alimentos, inmunología, ciencia animal tropical, reproducción animal tropical, ciencias químicas;
(d) Cursos de: ingeniería económica, benchmarking, tópicos selectos de calidad en las empresas, negociaciones internacionales, aspectos metodológicos del trabajo de tesis, métodos analíticos y numéricos, matemáticas y psicología;
(e) Diplomas en: ahorro y uso eficiente de energía en el autotransporte, automatización de procesos productivos, productividad para la industria del vestido, finanzas de la empresa, seguridad e higiene industrial y salud ocupacional.

Se destina(n): (a) a bachilleres; (b) a (e) a licenciados o profesionales del área.
Inscripciones: por mayores informaciones, dirigirse a la Sección de Estudios de Posgrado, Edificio de Posgrado e Investigación, 2° piso.

1551 Instituto Tecnológico Autónomo de México [ITADM]

Río Hondo N°1
Col. Tizapán, San Angel
01000 México, D.F.
Tel: +52-55-5628-4171
Fax: +52-55-5550-7637
Web: http://www.itam.mx

📖 Programas académicos y de intercambio

Campos de estudios: administración de empresas, ciencias de la información, ciencias económicas y comerciales, ciencias políticas, contabilidad, derecho, finanzas, informática, matemáticas, relaciones internacionales, riesgos, seguros.
Descripción:
(a) Programas de pregrado y grado en contabilidad, ciencias actuariales, matemáticas aplicadas, administración de empresas, computación, economía, relaciones internacionales, derecho, ciencias políticas, telemática, gestión internacional, finanzas, políticas públicas, sistemas de información, gestión y seguro; investigación en las áreas de economía, estudios de competitividad, estudios públicos, contabilidad, evaluación de proyectos sociales;
(b) Programas de intercambio con universidades extranjeras.
Duración: los programas de pregrado y de maestría en economía, finanzas y seguro siguen un calendario semestral (enero-mayo y agosto-diciembre); todos los otros programas siguen un sistema de cuatrimestres durante todo el año académico.
Inscripciones: por mayor información, dirigirse a la Dirección de Intercambio Académico.

1552 Instituto Tecnológico del Saltillo [ITS]

Venustiano Carranza 2400
25280 Saltillo, Coahuila
Tel: +52-844-438-9500
Fax: +52-844-438-9500
Web: http://www.its.mx

📖 Programas académicos

Campos de estudios: administración, electricidad y electrónica, informática, ingeniería, mecánica, metalurgia, tecnología, tecnología industrial.
Descripción:
(a) Nivel licenciatura: ingenierías eléctrica, electrónica, en materiales, mecánica, en sistemas, industrial; licenciaturas en administración, en informática;
(b) Nivel posgrado: maestría en ingeniería industrial, en materiales, en administración; doctorado en materiales; especialización en fundición, en ingeniería ambiental, en administración integral de la seguridad, en redes computacionales, en automatización de procesos industriales.
Asistencia financiera: se aplican becas del Gobierno Mexicano (Secretaría de Relaciones Exteriores); consultar http://www.sre.gob.mx.
Inscripciones: por mayores informes, dirigirse a la Jefatura de División de Estudios Profesionales.

1553 Instituto Tecnológico y de Estudios Superiores de Monterrey [ITESM]

Avenida Eugenio Garza Sada 2501 Sur
Monterrey
64849 Nuevo León
Tel: +52-81-8358-1400 ext 4251
Web: http://www.mty.itesm.mx
e-mail: admisiones.mty@itesm.mx

📖 Cursos y programas académicos

Campos de estudios: ciencias agronómicas, ciencias humanas, español, estudios internacionales, gestión, informática, ingeniería, negocio, química, turismo, hotelería.
Descripción:

(a) Programa de español intensivo para extranjeros (a nivel profesional);
(b) Programa de cultura mexicana y latinoamericana;
(c) Programa de negocios en México;
(d) Programas de grado (título profesional, posgrado o doctorado) en: administración, ciencias sociales, ingeniería, tecnología de alimentos; leyes, medicina, ciencias computacionales, humanidades, agricultura, negocios.
La mayoría de los cursos se imparten en español, aunque algunos se imparten tanto en inglés como en español.
Se dicta(n): en los campi de Ciudad de México, Estado de México, Cuernavaca, Guadalajara, Mazatlán, Cabo San Lucas, Monterrey, Querétaro.
Duración: (d) título profesional: de 4 a 5 años; posgrado: 2 años; doctorado: de 3 a 4 años.
Inscripciones: por mayor información, dirigirse a la Dirección de la Oficina de Programas Internacionales, en la dirección que figura en el título.

1554 Secretaría de Educación Pública Dirección de Relaciones Internacionales [SEP]
Prol. de Carpio y Plan de Ayala
11340 México, D.F.

🎓 Becas de posgrado
Campos de estudios: todas las materias principales.
Descripción: Becas para realizar maestrías, doctorados y especializaciones en el marco de las Becas Mutis administradas por el Departamento de Becas de Posgrado (280).
Materias de estudio: ciencias biológicas.
Se conceden: a latinoamericanos con título superior universitario que hayan obtenido calificaciones elevadas.
Lugar: Escuela Nacional de Ciencias Biológicas del Instituto Politécnico Nacional de México.
Duración: 3 meses para formación continua, 2 años para las maestrías, 3 años para los doctorados.
Importe: estipendio mensual, seguro médico, pago de matrícula de los cursos.
Solicitudes: la presentación de candidaturas se efectúa hasta mayo; dirigirse a las Oficinas Técnicas de Cooperación de España en el país de origen del candidato, o al Jefe de la Sección de Graduados de la Escuela Nacional de Ciencias Biológicas, en la dirección que figura en el título.

1555 Universidad "Juárez" Autónoma de Tabasco [UJAT]
Avenida Universidad s/n
Zona de la Cultura
86040 Villahermosa, Tabasco
Tel: +52-993-358-1500
Web: http://www.ujat.mx

📖 Programas universitarios
Campos de estudios: todas las materias principales.
Descripción:
(a) Licenciaturas, diplomados y maestrías en las áreas de ciencias agropecuarias, ingeniería, informática, ciencias biológicas, ciencias económico-administrativas, ciencias básicas, educación, ciencias de la salud, ciencias sociales y humanidades;
(b) Diplomados en docencia, educación superior, investigación educativa, orientación educativa.
Se destina(n): a candidatos mexicanos, latinoamericanos o de cualquier nacionalidad que conozcan el español y acrediten estudios avalados por autoridades competentes; existe examen escrito de conocimientos.
Duración: los semestres comienzan en febrero y en agosto.
Asistencia financiera: para estudiantes de posgrado.
Inscripciones: en enero y julio de cada año; dirigirse a la Secretaría de Servicios Académicos.

🎓 Becas de estudio
Campos de estudios: todas las materias principales.
Materias de estudio: ciencias económico-administrativas, ciencias sociales y humanidades, ciencias biológicas, ciencias agropecuarias, ciencias básicas, ingeniería y arquitectura, educación y artes, ciencias de la salud, informática y sistemas.

Se conceden: a candidatos de cualquier nacionalidad que hablen el español; edades: entre 18 y 25 años para licenciaturas, no mayores de 35 años para maestrías. Existe examen escrito de admisión. Los estudios deben acreditarse avalados por las autoridades competentes y se debe presentar carta de compromiso de regreso al país de origen.
Duración: 1 año (renovable según calificaciones).
Importe: asignación mensual variable según tabulación vigente.
Solicitudes: en febrero y agosto; dirigirse a la Secretaría de Servicios Académicos.

1556 Universidad Anáhuac [UA]
Avenida Lomas Anáhuac
Apartado Postal 10-844
11000 México, D.F.
Tel: +52-55-5627-0210
Web: http://www.anahuac.mx

📖 Programas universitarios
Campos de estudios: todas las materias principales.
Descripción: (a) Licenciaturas: actuaría, administración de empresas, administración turística, arquitectura, ciencias de la familia, comunicación, contaduría pública, derecho, diseño gráfico e industrial, economía, ingeniería civil (ambiental, para la dirección), ingeniería industrial (en producción y sistemas, para la dirección industrial y de servicios), ingeniería mecánica (mecatrónica, en sistemas integrados de manufactura, en sistemas mecánicos y eléctricos), ingeniería en tecnologías de la información (en tecnologías estratégicas de información, en tecnologías de la información y telecomunicación), medicina, mercadotecnia, negocios internacionales, pedagogía, psicología, relaciones internacionales;
(b) Posgrados (18 especialidades, 23 maestrías, 6 doctorados) en: actuaría, administración turística, comunicación, derecho, diseño, economía y negocios, educación, humanidades, ingeniería, medicina, psicología.
Inscripciones: (b) dirigirse a (a): anáhuac@anahuac.mx y (b): Centro de Estudios de Posgrado, email: posgrado@anahuac.mx.

1557 Universidad Anáhuac, Cancún [UAC]
Carretera Chetumal-Cancún Smza.
299 Mza 2,
Zona 8, Lote 1.
77565 Cancún
Tel: +52-998-881-4450
Fax: +52-998-881-4450
Web: http://www.anahuaccancun.edu.mx
e-mail: promocion@anahuaccancun.edu.mx

🎓 Academic Scholarship
Campos de estudios: comercio, comunicación, derecho, psicología, turismo, hotelería.
Importe: 20-80 descuentos de 20 a 80% en gastos de enseñanza.
Solicitudes: hasta mayo y noviembre para primer y segundo semestre respectivamente.

1558 Universidad Autónoma Agraria "Antonio Narro" [UAAN]
Buenavista, Saltillo
25315 Coahuila
Tel: +52-844-411-0207
Fax: +52-844-417-1239
Web: http://www.uaaan.mx
e-mail: docencia@uaaan.mx

📖 Programas universitarios
Campos de estudios: agricultura, ciencias agronómicas, ciencias de la tierra, horticultura.
Descripción:
(a) Maestrías en manejo de pastizales, nutrición animal, producción animal, estadística experimental, horticultura, suelos, riego y drenaje, fitomejoramiento, parasitología agrícola, planeación agropecuaria, tecnología de semillas; doctorado en fitomejoramiento;
(b) Maestrías en producción agronómica, reproducción animal;
(c) Programa interinstitucional en ciencias agrícolas y

forestales: maestrías en producción agrícola, producción forestal; doctorados en producción agrícola, horticultura, parasitología agrícola, sistemas de producción.
Se destina(n): a titulados profesionales.
Se dicta(n): (b) en la Unidad Laguna.
Duración: 2 años la maestrías y 3 años los doctorados (comienzos en enero y en agosto).
Inscripciones: hasta la fecha de inicio de cursos; dirigirse a la Subdirección de Posgrado.

1559 Universidad Autónoma de Aguas Calientes [UAA]

Avenida Universidad 940
20100 Aguascalientes
Tel: +52-449-910-7442
Fax: +52-449-910-7441
Web: http://www.uaa.mx

Programas universitarios

Campos de estudios: todas las materias principales, educación.
Descripción: Programas de licenciaturas (39) y postgrados (24).
Se destina(n): a estudiantes con estudios de bachillerato (high school) concluidos, que superen examen de admisión.
Duración: 5 años.
Inscripciones: hasta mayo; para mayor información, dirigirse al Departamento de Intercambio Académico y Becas.

1560 Universidad Autónoma de Baja California [UABC]

Avenida Alvaro Obregón y Julián
Carrillo s/n, Col. Nueva
21100 Mexicali, Baja California
Web: http://www.uabc.mx

Programas universitarios

Campos de estudios: arquitectura, biología marina, ciencias agronómicas, ciencias de la tierra, ciencias sociales, ecología, medio ambiente, español, estudios internacionales, ingeniería, oceanografía.
Descripción:
(a) Programas de pregrado, maestrías, doctorado, especializaciones; las áreas principales son arquitectura, oceanografía costera, producción animal, ciencias sociales aplicadas, ingeniería termodinámica, gestión del ecosistema de tierra árida, negocios internacionales; programas de investigación en áreas como biología marina y migración o estudios sobre las fronteras (economía de pueblos fronterizos, migración, identidad cultural, medio ambiente);
(b) Curso intensivo de verano de lengua española.
Duración: (a) año académico compuesto por 2 semestres (agosto-diciembre y enero-junio); (b) 4 semanas en julio.
Inscripciones: por mayor información, dirigirse a Asuntos Académicos.

1561 Universidad Autónoma de Baja California Sur [UABCS]

Apartado Postal 19 bis
La Paz
23080 Baja California Sur
Web: http://www.uabcs.mx
e-mail: isidoro@uabcs.mx

Programas de educación superior en ciencias del mar y de la tierra

Campos de estudios: biología, biología marina, ciencias agronómicas, ciencias de la tierra, ciencias del mar, ciencias humanas, ciencias sociales, derecho, economía, geología, historia, informática, pesquería.
Descripción:
(a) Licenciaturas: ingeniería en pesquerías, geología, biología marina, ingeniería en desarrollo computacional;
(b) Posgrados: maestría en computación, en ciencias zootécnicas, en ciencias marinas y costeras, en ciencias en acuacultura, en economía del medio ambiente y recursos naturales, en estudios sociales y humanísticos de frontera, en historia regional, en manejo sustentable de zonas costeras, en políticas públicas y administración; doctorado en biotecnología, en ciencias marinas y costeras;
(c) Proyectos de investigación en: acuacultura, biología, geología, pesquerías.

Asistencia financiera: convenios nacionales e internacionales, programas de intercambio y de cooperación, becas para estudios en el extranjero. Solicitar información a la Dirección General de Apoyo Académico.
Inscripciones: solicitar mayor información a Dirección de Servicios Escolares o Dirección de Investigación y Posgrado.

1562 Universidad Autónoma de Chapingo

Km 38.5 Carretera México-Veracruz
Texcoco, Estado de México
Tel: +52-595-95-21500
Web: http://www.chapingo.mx
e-mail: int_acad@taurus1.chapingo.mx

Programas de estudio y de investigación en áreas agrícolas

Campos de estudios: agricultura, ciencias agronómicas, cría de ganado, desarrollo rural, ecología, medio ambiente, horticultura, recursos naturales, silvicultura.
Descripción:
(a) Carreras, especialidades y títulos profesionales;
(b) Maestrías: agroforestería para el desarrollo sostenible, ciencias forestales, ciencia y tecnología agroalimentaria, desarrollo rural regional, economía del desarrollo rural, horticultura, ingeniería agrícola y uso integral del agua, orientación profesional en agroempresas, procesos educativos, producción animal, protección vegetal, recursos naturales y medio ambiente en zonas áridas, sociología rural;
(c) Doctorados: ciencias agrarias, economía agrícola, educación agrícola superior, horticultura, ingeniería agrícola y uso integral del agua, problemas económicos agroindustriales.
Asistencia financiera: los estudiantes pueden aplicar a becas para estudios en el extranjero. Solicitar información a Intercambio Académico y Asuntos Internacionales.

1563 Universidad Autónoma de Chiapas [UNACH]

Belisario Domínguez Km. 1080
Tuxtla Gutiérrez
29020 Chiapas
Tel: +52-961-617-8000
Web: http://www.unach.mx
e-mail: intercambio@montebello.unach.mx

Programas universitarios

Campos de estudios: todas las materias principales.
Descripción: Programas de licenciatura (42 en total) y posgrados (13 maestrías, 11 especialidades, 1 doctorado).
Se destina(n): a candidatos que cumplan requisitos de ingreso y superen examen de admisión escrito; en el caso de posgrados se exige curriculum vitae y carta de motivos. En el caso de extranjeros, los estudios previos deben convalidarse ante autoridades competentes.
Duración: 5 años.
Inscripciones: a mediados de diciembre y a mediados de julio para los semestres que comienzan en enero y agosto respectivamente; dirigirse al Departamento de Orientación Educativa, en la dirección que figura en el título.

1564 Universidad Autónoma de Chihuahua [UACH]

Calle Escorza y V. Carranza s/n
Col. Centro
31000 Chihuahua
Tel: +52-614-439-1810
Web: http://www.uach.mx

Programas universitarios

Campos de estudios: todas las materias principales, alimentación, ciencias agronómicas, educación física, genética, hidráulica.
Descripción: Programas de pregrado y grado incluyendo especializaciones; maestrías en ciencias de la alimentación, productividad frutícola, ingeniería de recursos hidráulicos, carnes, reproducción animal y genética, educación física.
Duración: año académico completo o dividido en 2 semestres (agosto-enero y septiembre-junio).
Asistencia financiera: no existen becas para el exterior, sólo a nivel de intercambio y con universidades extranjeras con las que se tiene convenio firmado.

Inscripciones: por mayor información, dirigirse a la Dirección Académica.

1565 Universidad Autónoma de Ciudad Juárez [UACJ]

Avenida López Mateos 20
Apartado Postal 1594-D
32310 Ciudad Juárez, Chihuahua
Tel: +52-656-688-2100
Web: http://www.uacj.mx
e-mail: intdac@uacj.mx

 Programas universitarios

Campos de estudios: administración de empresas, arquitectura, artes, biología, ciencias sociales, derecho, diseño, ingeniería, medicina, programas de verano.
Descripción: Cursos de pregrado y grado y formación profesional en los institutos de ingeniería, ciencias biomédicas, ciencias sociales y administración, arquitectura, diseño y arte.
Duración: el año académico está compuesto de 2 semestres (agosto-diciembre y enero-junio); programa intensivo de verano en un número limitado de cursos regulares de la Universidad.
Inscripciones: para mayor información, dirigirse al Departamento de Intercambio Académico en la dirección que figura en el título o a P.O. Box 10307, El Paso, TX 79994, USA.

1566 Universidad Autónoma de Guadalajara [UG]

Av. Patria 1201
Lomas del Valle, 3a. Sección
Apartado Postal 1-440
44100 Guadalajara, Jalisco
Tel: +52-33-3648-8463
Web: http://www.uag.mx
e-mail: uag@uag.edu

 Programa internacional "School of Medicine"

Campos de estudios: ciencias, ciencias humanas, ciencias sociales, higiene y salud, medicina, tecnología.
Descripción: Programa conducente a título de Médico-cirujano y especializaciones en 14 áreas.
Duración: 4 años más 1año de internado; comienzos en agosto y enero.
Idioma: dos primeros años en inglés y luego transición a español.
Inscripciones: el formulario de inscripción está disponible en línea en el sitio web de la Universidad.

 Programas biculturales

Campos de estudios: economía política, español, estudios americanos, estudios culturales, estudios internacionales, idiomas, programas de verano.
Descripción: Programas biculturales (nivel superior) organizados en colaboración con varias universidades de los Estados Unidos de América: lengua española, métodos y técnicas de la enseñanza del español, tratado de Libre Comercio, literatura hispanoamericana, historia de México, relaciones México-Estados Unidos, leyes comparativas México-Estados Unidos, medio ambiente y recursos naturales, negocios internacionales.
Se destina(n): principalmente a nacionales de los Estados Unidos de América con conocimiento intermedio del idioma español.
Duración: principalmente durante el verano y algunos también durante los semestres regulares.
Inscripciones: por mayor información, dirigirse a la Dirección de Programas Internacionales, en la dirección que figura en el título, o a Universidad de Guadalajara, Foreign Students Office, 10999 IH-10 West, Suite 355, San Antonio, Texas 78230-1356, United States.

 Programas universitarios

Campos de estudios: todas las materias principales.
Descripción:
(a) Programas a nivel de licenciatura: médico cirujano, cirujano dentista, enfermería, matemáticas aplicadas y computación, informática, trabajo social, ciencias de la comunicación, diseño (gráfico, de interiores y paisajismo, industrial), economía, finanzas internacionales,

administración (hotelera, de empresas turísticas), mercadotecnia internacional, arqueología, antropología, administración de empresas, ingenierías (sistemas computacionales, mecánico electricista, electrónica médica, computación, instrumentación y control, electrónica y comunicaciones, civil, industrial, de sistemas, electrónica e industrial, electrónica de potencia), química, biotecnología acuícola, biotecnología ambiental, zootecnista, alimentos, agrícola, químico farmacéutico biólogo, actuario, arquitectura;
(b) Nivel técnico profesional: agencia de viajes, alimentos y bebidas, hoteles y moteles, decoración, diseño publicitario, fotografía, relaciones públicas, comunicación por medios electrónicos, mercadotecnia y publicidad, electromecánica industrial, sistemas electrónicos, manufactura asistida por computadora, administración de sistemas de información, seguridad e higiene industrial, edificaciones civiles, inmobiliaria, mercado de valores, sistemas contables, auditoría interna, optometría, puericultura, prótesis dental, radiología, fisioterapia, diseño de parques y jardines, producción de bovinos (de leche, de carne), agronegocios, asistente administrativo bilingüe, negocios internacionales, administración de micro y pequeña empresa, administración de instituciones financieras, mercadotecnia y comercialización, desarrollo empresarial, administración de sistemas de informática;
(c) Nivel diplomado: 800 cursos de diplomado y educación continua en diversas áreas;
(d) Nivel maestría: administración (internacional, de negocios), arquitectura, derecho (fiscal, corporativo internacional), educación, traducción e interpretación inglés-español, filosofía, tecnología instruccional, educación matemática, ciencias computacionales, ingeniería electrónica, química, salud laboral;
(e) Nivel especialidad: administración (de recursos humanos, de proyectos y obras), mercadotecnia, finanzas, urbanismo y diseño de vivienda, derecho (fiscal, corporativo internacional), informática médica, anestesiología, cirugía general, dermatología, endocrinología, gineco-obstetricia, neurocirugía, neurología, oftalmología, otorrinolaringología, pediatría, psiquiatría, radiología, traumatología y ortopedia, urología, endodoncia, odontopediatría, periodoncia, rehabilitación oral, enfermería;
(f) Nivel doctorado: educación, química;
(g) Cursos libres de idiomas y artes.
Inscripciones: para mayores informaciones dirigirse a la Dirección de Estudiantes Extranjeros, en la dirección que figura en el título.

1567 Universidad Autónoma de Guerrero [UAGRO]

Vicente Guerrero s/n
Centro Escolar
39000 Chipalcingo, Guerrero
Web: http://www.uagro.mx

 Programas universitarios

Campos de estudios: biología, ciencias de la tierra, derecho, filosofía, geología, higiene y salud, historia, informática, ingeniería, matemáticas.
Descripción:
(a) Programas de pregrado, maestrías, especializaciones y doctorados en áreas de derecho, filosofía, historia regional, computación, biología, geología, matemáticas, ingeniería;
(b) Centro de Investigación de enfermedades tropicales: cursos y posibilidades de investigación en epidemiología, enfermedades tropicales, control de enfermedades tropicales;
(c) Maestría en sismología.
Se dicta(n): en los campus de Acapulco, Iguala y Cd. Altamirano.
Duración: (a) año académico compuesto de 2 semestres (septiembre-enero y febrero-junio); (c) 2 años.
Inscripciones: por mayor información, dirigirse a la Rectoría.

1568 Universidad Autónoma de Nayarit [UADN]

Veracruz 186 Sur
Tepic, Nayarit
Tel: +52-311-211-8800
Web: http://www.uan.mx

 Programas universitarios

Campos de estudios: todas las materias principales, cría de ganado, derecho, economía, electricidad y electrónica, español, estudios culturales, horticultura, ingeniería, mecánica, medicina veterinaria, negocio, pesquería, programas de verano, química.
Descripción:
(a) Programas de pregrado y grado en las áreas, entre otras, de: medicina veterinaria, química, ingeniería mecánica, ingeniería electrónica, pesquería, economía, negocios, derecho; maestrías, doctorados y especializaciones en: horticultura tropical, cría de ganado;
(b) Programas de verano: cursos de español para extranjeros.
Duración: (a) año académico compuesto de 2 semestres (septiembre-enero y febrero-junio); (b) 6 semanas.
Inscripciones: por mayor información, dirigirse a: (a) Secretaría de Rectoría, en la dirección que figura en el título; (b) Centro Universitario de Idiomas, Ciudad de la Cultura, Tepic, Nayarit.

1569 Universidad Autónoma de Nuevo León [UANL]

Torre de Rectoría, Ciudad Universitaria
66451 San Nicolás de los Garza, Nuevo León
Web: http://www.uanl.mx

 Programas universitarios

Campos de estudios: todas las materias principales.
Descripción:
(a) Educación media superior: bachillerato propedéutico, bachilleratos técnicos, carreras técnicas;
(b) Educación superior: 62 programas de licenciatura en las áreas de artes y humanidades, ciencias sociales, administración, ciencias de la salud, ingeniería y tecnología, agropecuarias, urbanismo, ciencias naturales y ciencias exactas;
(c) Estudios de posgrado: 51 especializaciones, 65 maestrías, 21 doctorados, en sus Facultades de agronomía, arquitectura, artes visuales, ciencias biológicas, ciencias de la comunicación, ciencias de la tierra, ciencias físico-matemáticas, ciencias forestales, ciencias políticas y administración pública, ciencias químicas, contaduría pública y administración, derecho y ciencias sociales, economía, enfermería, filosofía y letras, ingeniería civil, ingeniería mecánica y eléctrica, medicina, medicina veterinaria y zootecnia, odontología, organización deportiva, psicología, salud pública, trabajo social.
Inscripciones: solicitar mayores informaciones a Secretaría Académica, Dirección de Intercambio Académico y Becas de Posgrado, en la dirección de título o bien a (a) Coordinación de Preparatorias; (b) Coordinación de Facultades; (c) Dirección General de Estudios de Posgrado.

1570 Universidad Autónoma de Querétaro [UAQ]

Centro Universitario
Cerro de las Campanas
76010 Querétaro
Tel: +52-442-192-1200
Web: http://www.uaq.mx

 Programas universitarios

Campos de estudios: todas las materias principales, administración de empresas, bellas artes, biología, derecho, ecología, medio ambiente, español, estudios culturales, idiomas, ingeniería, literatura y civilización, medicina, nutrición, programas de verano, psicología, química.
Descripción:
(a) Programas de pregrado, maestrías, doctorados y especializaciones en las áreas siguientes, entre otras: psicología, medicina, derecho, administración de empresas, ingeniería, química, ciencias biológicas, bellas artes, idiomas, ingeniería de sistemas de transporte, ciencias de la alimentación, psicología educativa, ecología;
(b) Programas para estudiantes extranjeros: español intensivo

(3 niveles), cultura mexicana, cultura prehispánica, muralistas mexicanos, civilización maya, geografía, medio ambiente, introducción a la prehistoria mesoamericana, civilización azteca, novela de la revolución mexicana, revolución mexicana.
Duración: (a) año académico compuesto de 2 semestres (julio-noviembre y enero-junio); (b) en verano: de mediados de junio a mediados de julio, en invierno: de principios de noviembre a principios de diciembre.
Inscripciones: por mayor información, dirigirse a la Dirección de Intercambio Académico.

1571 Universidad Autónoma de Quintana Roo [UADQR]

Apartado Postal 10
77000 Chetumal
Quintana Roo
Tel: +52-983-835-0300
Fax: +52-983-832-9656
Web: http://www.uqroo.mx

 Programas universitarios

Campos de estudios: antropología, comercio, derecho, ecología, medio ambiente, economía, energía, finanzas, idiomas, programas de verano, relaciones internacionales.
Descripción:
(a) Programas de pregrado en las áreas de economía y finanzas, comercio, derecho, relaciones internacionales, lenguas modernas, ingeniería ambiental, conservación de energía, antropología;
(b) Programas de verano.
Duración: (a) el año académico está compuesto de 2 semestres (agosto-diciembre y enero-mayo).
Inscripciones: por mayor información, dirigirse al Departamento de Admisiones.

1572 Universidad Autónoma de San Luis Potosí [UASLP]

Alvaro Obregón 64
Zona Centro
78000 San Luis Potosí
Web: http://www.uaslp.mx

 Programas universitarios

Campos de estudios: biología, derecho, electricidad y electrónica, farmacia y farmacología, física, idiomas, ingeniería, medicina, psiquiatría, química.
Descripción:
(a) Programas de pregrado en áreas de física, química, farmacología, ingeniería, derecho, medicina; programas de grado en áreas de derecho, medicina, psiquiatría, ingeniería, ciencias biomédicas; maestrías en ingeniería química, ciencias biomédicas, física, ingeniería eléctrica; investigación en particular en las áreas de ciencias médicas y de la salud (examen de salud general, cuidados ópticos y dentales, atención psicológica y psiquiátrica);
(b) Cursos de idiomas (español, alemán, francés, italiano).
Duración: (a) año académico compuesto de 2 semestres (agosto-diciembre y enero-julio).
Inscripciones: por mayor información, dirigirse a la Dirección de Planeación.

1573 Universidad Autónoma de Sinaloa [UADS]

Angel Flores s/n
8000 Culiacán (Sinaloa)
Web: http://www.uasnet.mx

 Programas universitarios

Campos de estudios: todas las materias principales, alimentación, ciencias del mar, educación, español, oceanografía, programas de verano, tecnología.
Descripción:
(a) Programas de pregrado y grado; maestrías en tecnología de los alimentos y ciencias de la educación;
(b) Programa de ciencias marinas;
(c) Curso intensivo de español.
Se dicta(n): (b) y (c) en Mazatlán.
Duración: (a) el año académico se extiende de principios de septiembre a junio; (b) 5 años; (c) 4 semanas.
Inscripciones: por mayor información, dirigirse a la

Dirección de Intercambio y Vinculación Académica.

1574 Universidad Autónoma de Tamaulipas [UADT]

Matamoros y Calle 8
Apartado Postal 186
87000 Cd. Victoria, Tamaulipas
Web: http://www.uat.mx

Programas universitarios

Campos de estudios: todas las materias principales,
español, inglés, programas de verano.
Descripción:
(a) Programas de pregrado y grado en áreas tales como:
medicina, derecho, ingeniería, administración de empresas,
química, economía agroindustrial; maestrías en ciencias
agronómicas, cría de animales tropicales; doctorado en
ciencias agronómicas;
(b) Cursos intensivos de verano de inglés y español.
Duración: (a) año académico completo (enero-diciembre)
o compuesto de 2 semestres (enero-mayo y
agosto-diciembre).
Inscripciones: por mayor información, dirigirse a la
Dirección de Intercambio Académico.

1575 Universidad Autónoma de Tlaxcala [UAT]

Avenida Universidad N° 1
Apartado Postal 19
90070 Tlaxcala
Tel: +52-246-462-1422
Web: http://www.uatx.mx

Programas universitarios

Campos de estudios: todas las materias principales,
administración, biología, comercio, derecho, educación,
filosofía, lingüística, programas de verano, química,
sociología, trabajo social.
Descripción: Programas de pregrado, grado, maestrías,
doctorados, especializaciones, en las áreas siguientes:
educación, filosofía, sociología, trabajo social, comercio
internacional, derecho, biología, lingüística aplicada, química,
administración en educación, orientación educativa, derecho
penal, biología de la reproducción.
Se destina(n): a nacionales de todos los países que hayan
completado el nivel bachillerato o equivalente, con promedio
mínimo de 8, para las licenciaturas; nivel licenciatura para las
maestrías, nivel maestría para los doctorados. Existe examen
de admisión.
Duración: de 4 años y medio a 5 años; hay cursos de
verano en junio-agosto.
Inscripciones: por mayor información, dirigirse a la
Secretaría de Rectoría.

1576 Universidad Autónoma de Yucatán [UADY]

Calle 60 x 57
97000 Mérida, Yucatán
Tel: +52-999-930-0900
Web: http://www.uady.mx

Programas universitarios

Campos de estudios: todas las materias principales,
español, programas de verano.
Descripción:
(a) Licenciaturas en las siguientes áreas: arquitectura, ciencias
antropológicas, contaduría pública, derecho, economía,
educación, enfermería, ingeniería (civil, química industrial),
matemáticas, ciencias de la computación, enseñanza de las
matemáticas, cirugía, medicina veterinaria, biología,
odontología, psicología, nutrición, zootecnia, farmacia;
(b) Especializaciones en las siguientes áreas: finanzas,
derecho civil, derecho fiscal, docencia, enseñanza del inglés,
gestión de tecnología, estadística, anestesiología, cirugía
general, ginecología y obstetricia, medicina familiar, medicina
interna, ortopedia, pediatría, medicina del deporte,
odontología (varias), psicología clínica infantil,
bibliotecología, orientación y consejo educativo, enfermería
(varias), ingeniería química, radiodiagnóstico e imaginología,
apicultura tropical;
(c) Maestrías en: ciencias antropológicas, administración,
arquitectura, derecho (civil, fiscal), economía y

administración pública, educación superior, ingeniería
(ambiental, en construcción), ciencia y tecnología de los
alimentos, ciencia animal tropical, producción animal tropical,
manejo y conservación de recursos naturales tropicales,
apicultura tropical, ciencias químicas, ciencias biomédicas,
ciencias de la salud (varias), psicología educativa;
(d) Doctorados en: educación superior, ciencias
agropecuarias;
(e) Diplomados en: administración de obras, informática,
impuestos, administración (de PYMEs, de empresas
agropecuarias, tributaria), derecho constitucional y amparo,
finanzas, gestión ambiental, computación aplicada, terapia
breve, química analítica;
(f) Programas de verano para estudiantes extranjeros: cursos
de ecología tropical, antropología, arqueología, historia (todos
dictados en inglés), cursos de español.
Duración: (a) de 4 a 5 años (comienzan en septiembre);
(b) 2 años (comienzan en septiembre o febrero); (c) 2 años a
tiempo completo, 4 años a tiempo parcial (comienzan en
septiembre o febrero).
Inscripciones: en la Secretaría General, Departamento de
Intercambio Académico, en la dirección que figura en el
título.

1577 Universidad Autónoma de Zacatecas [UAZ]

Jardín Juárez 147
98000 Zacatecas
Tel: +52-492-922-9109
Fax: +52-4-922-6455
Web: http://www.reduaz.mx

Programas universitarios

Campos de estudios: biología, ciencias políticas, ciencias
sociales, español, formación profesional, programas de
verano.
Descripción:
(a) Programas de pregrado y grado; maestrías en ciencias
sociales, ciencias políticas, biología experimental;
(b) Cursos regulares de verano en áreas variadas tales como
perfeccionamiento profesional a desarrollo cultural;
(c) Cursos de español en su Centro de idiomas.
Duración: (a) año académico de 2 semestres (comienzos
en agosto y enero).
Inscripciones: por mayor información, dirigirse al
Departamento de Intercambio Académico.

1578 Universidad Autónoma del Carmen [UADC]

Avenida Concordia esq. Avenida 56
24180 Ciudad del Carmen
Campeche
Tel: +52-938-381-1018 ext. 10007
Web: http://www.unacar.mx

Programas universitarios

Campos de estudios: administración de empresas, ciencias
de la información, derecho, español, idiomas, ingeniería,
inglés, programas de verano.
Descripción:
(a) Programas de grado en las áreas de derecho, ingeniería,
ciencias de la información, administración de empresas, entre
otras;
(b) Cursos de idioma español y de idioma inglés para
estudiantes extranjeros.
Duración: (a) el año académico está compuesto de 2
semestres y se extiende de septiembre a mediados de julio; (b)
cursos de verano.
Inscripciones: por mayor información, dirigirse a: (a)
Secretaría Académica; (b) Centro de Idiomas; en ambos
casos, la dirección es la que figura en el título.

1579 Universidad Autónoma del Estado de Hidalgo [UADH]

Abasolo 600
42000 Pachuca, Hidalgo
Tel: +52-1771-717-2000
Web: http://www.reduaeh.mx

 Programas universitarios

Campos de estudios: todas las materias principales, educación permanente.
Descripción:
(a) Licenciaturas, especialidades, maestrías y doctorados según el caso, en áreas de ciencias agropecuarias, ciencias básicas e ingeniería, ciencias económico-administrativas, ciencias de la salud, ciencias sociales e humanidades, artes;
(b) Educación continua: cursos permanentes, especiales, diplomados;
(c) Educación a distancia.
Duración: año académico compuesto de 2 semestres (julio-diciembre y enero-junio).
Inscripciones: por mayor información, dirigirse a la Dirección de la División de Docencia o la Dirección de Relaciones Públicas.

1580 Universidad Autónoma del Estado de México
Instituto Literario Oriente N°100
50000 Toluca, Estado de México
Tel: +52-722-226-2300
Web: http://www.uaemex.mx

 Programas universitarios

Campos de estudios: todas las materias principales, educación permanente, español, programas de verano.
Descripción:
(a) Programas de pregrado, grado, maestrías, doctorados y especializaciones en todas las áreas principales;
(b) Programas de verano de español para extranjeros;
(c) Educación continua;
(d) Educación a distancia.
Se dicta(n): en sus campi del Estado de México: Atlacomulco, Zumpango, Amecameca, Temascaltepec, y Los Uribe en Toluca.
Duración: (a) año académico de septiembre a agosto.
Inscripciones: por mayor información útil para estudiantes extranjeros, dirigirse: (a) a la Dirección de Intercambio Académico (página web http://www.uaemex.mx/iacad); (b) al Centro de enseñanza de lenguas (http://www.uaemex.mx/cele o email: cele@uaemex.mx).

1581 Universidad Autónoma Metropolitana [UAM]
Avenida San Pablo 180
Col. Reynosa Tamaulipas
02200 México, D.F.
Tel: +52-55-5483-4126
Web: http://www.uam.mx
e-mail: admision@correo.uam.mx

 Programas universitarios

Campos de estudios: todas las materias principales, antropología, biología, ciencias, ciencias económicas y comerciales, ciencias sociales, desarrollo rural, energía, higiene y salud, ingeniería, literatura y civilización, tecnología.
Descripción: Programas de educación superior en áreas de ciencias básicas e ingeniería, ciencias sociales y humanidades, ciencias y artes para el diseño, ciencias biológicas y de la salud:
(a) Programas de licenciatura (60 en total);
(b) Posgrados: maestrías, especializaciones y doctorados.
Duración: sistema de trimestres con períodos de 12 semanas que comienzan en septiembre, mayo y enero.
Inscripciones: por mayores informaciones, dirigirse al Coordinador de la Comisión de Apoyo y Desarrollo Académico.

1582 Universidad Bonaterra [UB]
Josemaría Esciva de Balaguer 101
Fracc. Rusticos Calpulli
20290 Aguascalientes
Tel: +52-449-910-6200
Fax: +52-449-9106200 ext 7240
Web: http://www.bonaterra.edu.mx
e-mail: rpublicas@bonaterra.edu.mx

 Programas universitarios

Campos de estudios: administración, derecho, educación, ingeniería.
Descripción: Carreras: ingeniería (en ciencias computacionales, en electrónica y sistemas digitales, industrial); licenciaturas en administración (administración y contaduría, y finanzas, y mercadotecnia, y negocios internacionales), en derecho, en pedagogía.

1583 Universidad Contemporánea [UCTPA]
Ignacio Pérez No. 54 sur
76000 Querétaro
Tel: +52-442-196-1400
Fax: +52-442-196-1400
Web: http://www.contemporanea.edu.mx

 Programas universitarios

Campos de estudios: administración de empresas, ciencias económicas y comerciales, comercio, contabilidad, derecho, finanzas, gestión, marketing.
Programas: Programas de educación superior en:
(a) Escuela de Negocios;
(b) Escuela de Posgrado;
(c) Programas a distancia: MBA ejecutivo y master en gestión y alta dirección de empresas (convenio con la Universidad de Barcelona, España, con doble titulación).
Descripción: (a) licenciaturas en administración, en comercio internacional, en contaduría, en derecho, en informática administrativa, en mercadotecnia, en administración turística; programas de intercambio con universidades de Alemania, Australia, Canadá, Estados Unidos, Francia (a partir del quinto cuatrimestre de estudios, por un período que va de uno a dos cuatrimestres); (b) especialidades en comercialización estratégica, comercio internacional, finanzas, recursos humanos, pedagogía sistémica.
Duración: (a) 3 años; (b) 1 año.
Inscripciones: para mayor información referente a estudiantes extranjeros, dirigirse a la Subdirección de Programas Internacionales (e-mail: eezquerro@contemporanea.edu.mx).

1584 Universidad de Anáhuac del Sur [UAS]
Avenida de las Torres 131
Col. Olivar de los Padres
01780 México, D.F.
Tel: +52-5-628-8800
Fax: +52-5-628-8837

 Programas universitarios

Campos de estudios: todas las materias principales, educación permanente.
Descripción:
(a) Cursos de pregrado y grado en las áreas de arquitectura, comunicación, diseño gráfico, derecho, ciencias actuariales, banca y finanza, ingeniería civil, administración en ingeniería industrial, ingeniería mecánica y eléctrica, ingeniería de computación y sistemas, administración de empresas, administración de negocios en turismo, negocios internacionales, gestión de negocios, comercio internacional, contaduría pública, economía, marketing, relaciones industriales, relaciones internacionales;
(b) Certificados: artes culinarias, Cordon d'Or, gestión de establecimientos de comida y bebida, tecnología de alimentos, diploma de computación básica, certificado de inglés de los negocios para profesores (Cámara de Comercio e Industria de Londres);
(c) Cursos para graduados: master en gestión internacional, ciencias de la ingeniería, administración de empresas, imagen de corporación, administración pública, derecho financiero; doctorados (investigación aplicada) en gestión, en ingeniería;
(d) Investigación en el Instituto de Investigación Lingüística y Literaria;
(e) Consorcio Latinoamericano para entrenamiento en microfinanza: cursos, seminarios y coloquios en temas específicos de banca y metodologías de microfinanciación.
Se destina(n): (d) a profesores, investigadores, escritores, editores; (e) ONGs, instituciones financieras formales e informales, banca comercial, banca de desarrollo.

Duración: (a) el año académico está compuesto de 2 semestres (agosto-diciembre y enero-junio).
Inscripciones: para mayor información, dirigirse al Departamento de Intercambio Académico.

1585 Universidad de Celaya [UC]
Carretera Panamericana Km. 269
38080 Celaya, Gto.
Tel: +52-4-613-9099
Fax: +52-4-613-9600
Web: http://www.udec.edu.mx
e-mail: maru@udec.edu.mx

📖 Programas universitarios
Campos de estudios: administración de empresas, arquitectura, ciencias económicas y comerciales, comercio, comunicación, derecho, ingeniería, marketing.
Descripción:
(a) Carreras: licenciaturas en administración de empresas, arquitectura, ciencias de la comunicación, comercio internacional, contaduría pública y finanzas, derecho, mercadotecnia; ingenierías en sistemas computacionales, industrial administrativa;
(b) Posgrados: maestrías en desarrollo humano, derecho fiscal, comercio exterior, administración.

1586 Universidad de Colima [UCOL]
Av. Universidad #333.
Colonia Las Víboras
28040 Colima
Tel: +52-312-316-1000
Web: http://www.ucol.mx

📖 Programas universitarios
Campos de estudios: todas las materias principales, agricultura, ciencias, ciencias agronómicas, ciencias de la tierra, ciencias sociales, ecología, medio ambiente, educación, español, fisiología, historia, medicina, metalurgia, oceanografía, relaciones internacionales.
Descripción:
(a) Maestrías en historia regional, educación, ciencias fisiológicas, ciencias médicas, diseño bioclimático, metalurgia, acuicultura, microbiología, cinética y bioquímica ruminal, ciencias (revitalización patrimonial, desarrollo urbano, relaciones económicas internacionales con especialidad en Cuenca del Pacífico), doctorado en ciencias fisiológicas, biología de la producción, investigación en ciencias sociales, relaciones internacionales transpacífico, investigaciones de posgrado en ciencias biomédicas, ciencias sociales, Cuenca del Pacífico, ciencias agropecuarias, ciencias del ambiente, vulcanología y oceanología;
(b) Cursos de lengua española y cultura mexicanas para estudiantes extranjeros (niveles principiante, intermedio y avanzado).
Se destina(n): (a) a nacionales y extranjeros que posean: para la maestría, título de licenciatura con calificación mínima de 8, y 2 años de experiencia; para los doctorados, 3 años de experiencia en el campo académico; el inglés es obligatorio y existe selección por antecedentes y entrevista.
Duración: (a) año académico dividido en 2 semestres (agosto-enero y enero-junio); (b) 5 semanas en verano.
Asistencia financiera: la Universidad no ofrece becas pero postula a estudiantes ante diversas instituciones a nivel nacional e internacional.
Inscripciones: por mayor información, dirigirse a: (a) Secretaría Técnica, Coordinación General de Docencia; (b) Escuela de Lenguas; en ambos casos la dirección es la que figura en el título.

1587 Universidad de Guadalajara Centro de Estudios para Extranjeros [CEPE]
Apartado Postal 1-2130
44100 Guadalajara, Jalisco
Tel: +52-33-3616-4399
Fax: +52-33-3616-4013
Web: http://www.cepe.udg.mx
e-mail: cepe@corp.udg.mx

📖 Programas universitarios
Campos de estudios: español, estudios culturales, programas de verano.
Descripción:
(a) Cursos de español (varios niveles, cursos complementarios especializados sobre negocios, cultura, política, economía, literatura, historia mexicana y latinoamericana);
(b) Cursos universitarios regulares en sociología, derecho, filosofía, literatura hispánica, historia, administración de empresas, relaciones laborales, economía, turismo.
Se destina(n): (b) a estudiantes inscriptos en una universidad extranjera.
Duración: (b) 1 o 2 semestres.
Inscripciones: por mayor información, dirigirse a la Oficina de Admisiones.

1588 Universidad de Guanajuato [UGTO]
Lascuraín de Retana 5 Centro
36000 Guanajuato
Tel: +52-473-732-0006
Fax: +52-473-732-7148
Web: http://www.ugto.mx
e-mail: info@quijote.ugto.mx

📖 Estancias para estudiantes extranjeros
Campos de estudios: todas las materias principales.
Descripción:
(a) A través de un convenio de colaboración entre la Universidad de Guanajuato y una institución internacional;
(b) Estudios de idioma español;
(c) Cursos de materias libres;
(d) Graduación o programa completo.
Materias de estudio: (a) Programas académicos: técnico superior universitario, licenciaturas, especialidades, maestrías, doctorados en áreas de ciencias naturales y exactas, ingenierías, ciencias de la salud, artes, ciencias sociales y humanidades, ciencias económico-administrativas.
Inscripciones: por toda información relativa a estudiantes extranjeros, dirigirse al Departamento de Movilidad Estudiantil, Académica y Administrativa de la Dirección de Relaciones Académicas Internacionales e Institucionales.

📖 Programas universitarios
Campos de estudios: todas las materias principales, español, estudios culturales.
Descripción:
(a) Programas de posgrado: 39 en total de los cuales 6 son doctorados, 19 maestrías y 15 especialidades en todas las materias principales;
(b) Programa de verano del Centro de idiomas: español, historia mexicana, arte mexicano, literatura mexicana, folklore mexicano, perspectiva interdisciplinaria de México, manualidades.
Se destina(n): (a) a nacionales de cualquier país con bachillerato o equivalente para licenciatura y con título de licenciatura para posgrado, que superen examen de admisión que se lleva a cabo en enero y julio.
Se dicta(n): posgrados: en las ciudades de Guanajuato, León y Salamanca.
Duración: (a) en promedio, 2 años y medio el doctorado, 2 años la maestría y 1 año y medio las especialidades; (b) 4 semanas en junio o julio.
Asistencia financiera: (a) becas parciales de colegiatura.
Inscripciones: (a) hasta fin de enero, y hasta fin de julio, en la Dirección de Intercambio Académico; (b) de febrero a mayo, en el Centro de Idiomas en la dirección del título o e-mail: idiom@quijote.ugto.mx.

🎓 Becas del Gobierno de México para extranjeros
Campos de estudios: electricidad y electrónica, física, ingeniería, investigación, mecánica, química.
Becas: Becas otorgadas por la Secretaría de Relaciones Exteriores para estudios de posgrado, aplicables a la Universidad de Guanajuato.
Descripción: (a) Maestrías: ingeniería eléctrica (instrumentación y sistemas digitales); ingeniería mecánica (especialidad en diseño y ciencias térmicas); ciencias (física y química);
(b) Doctorado: en física, en química.
Se conceden: a quienes hayan obtenido un promedio

superior a 80%.
Importe: cuota mensual equivalente a 4 o 5 salarios mínimos para (a) o (b) respectivamente; gastos de instalación (por única vez); transporte internacional y de México a Guanajuato (una vez al principio y fin de la beca); seguro médico a partir del tercer mes de la beca.
Solicitudes: hasta fin mayo de cada año; dirigirse a las oficinas de información en las representaciones diplomáticas del país de origen; para establecer el contacto con la Universidad de Guanajuato, dirigirse a la Oficina de Relaciones Internacionales.

1589 Universidad de las Américas - Puebla [UDLAP]
Ex-Hacienda de Santa Catarina Mártir
72820 Cholula, Puebla
Tel: +52-222-229-2000
Fax: +52-222-229-2096
Web: http://www.udlap.mx

📖 **Programas universitarios**

Campos de estudios: todas las materias principales, administifón de empresas, ciencias, ciencias sociales, estudios sobre el desarrollo, ingeniería, letras y artes, relaciones internacionales.
Descripción: Programas de pregrado (38 en total), maestrías (19) y doctorados (2), en sus Escuelas (de artes y humanidades, de administración de empresas, de ingeniería, de ciencias, de ciencias sociales, de asuntos internacionales); Institutos (de investigación y estudios para graduados, de políticas públicas y estudios sobre el desarrollo), Centro para el desarrollo regional.
Duración: año académico compuesto por 2 semestres (agosto-diciembre y enero-mayo).

1590 Universidad de Las Américas, A.C. [UDLA]
Puebla 223
Col. Roma
06700 México, D.F.
Tel: +52-55-5209-9800
Web: http://www.udla.mx
e-mail: admision@server.udla.mx

📖 **Programas universitarios**

Campos de estudios: administración, administración de empresas, derecho, economía política, educación, educación de la primera infancia, estudios internacionales, informática, psicología.
Descripción:
(a) Programas de pregrado y grado (licenciatura, bachelor, master y maestría) en áreas de administración de empresas, derecho, educación, psicología, economía política internacional, sistemas computacionales y administrativos;
(b) Programas de educación continua: educación bilingüe (formación profesional de docentes especializado en educación preescolar y primaria; cursos en español e inglés), reconocido por la Asociación de Colegios y Escuelas del Sur (Estados Unidos) y el Ministerio de Educación de México;
(c) Programa de verano para cursar materias regulares (en español e inglés).
La UDLA ofrece facilidad de bolsa de trabajo.
Se destina(n): (a) a nacionales de cualquier país con promedio de calificaciones no inferior a 8, que superen examen de admisión escrito y que conozcan el inglés.
Duración: (a) y (b) año académico dividido en 2 semestres (comienzos en agosto y enero).
Asistencia financiera: becas de excelencia académica.
Inscripciones: (a) en enero, junio y agosto (previo examen de admisión); dirigirse a la Oficina de Admisiones; (c) para mayor información, dirigirse a la Dirección de Programas Internacionales.

1591 Universidad de los Altos de Chiapas [UACH]
Periférico Sur 1016
Barrio de Maria Auxiliadora
Chiapas
29290 San Cristóbal de las Casas
Tel: +52-967-678-5657
Fax: +52-967-678-5657

Web: http://www.uach.edu.mx
e-mail: uach@uach.edu.mx

📖 **Programas universitarios**

Campos de estudios: administración de empresas, contabilidad, diseño, economía, informática, ingeniería civil, negocio.
Descripción: (a) Carreras universitarias en: administración de empresas, contaduría, empresas turísticas, ingeniería civil, ingeniería en sistemas computacionales, diseño gráfico, mercadotecnia; (b) Postgrado (maestría) en economía y negocios.
Duración: (a) 9 semestres; los cursos comienzan en febrero y agosto. (b) 4 semestres que inician en febrero y agosto.
Asistencia financiera: becas de matrícula de 50% de la colegiatura durante 1 semestre para alumnos con buenas calificaciones (solicitudes en enero y julio de cada año), renovables semestralmente.
Idioma: español.
Inscripciones: enero y julio.

1592 Universidad de Monterrey [UDEM]
Avenida Ignacio Morones Prieto 4500 Pte.
66238 San Pedro Garza García, Nuevo
Tel: +52-81-8124-1010
Web: http://www.udem.edu.mx

📖 **Programas universitarios**

Campos de estudios: todas las materias principales, español, programas de verano.
Descripción:
(a) Carreras: arquitecto; contador público y auditor; ingeniería en sistemas computacionales, industrial y de sistemas, mecánico administrador; licenciaturas en administración de empresas, artes, ciencias de la educación, ciencia política y administración pública, ciencias de la información y comunicación, comercio internacional, derecho, diseño gráfico, diseño industrial, economía, estudios humanísticos y sociales, estudios internacionales, finanzas internacionales, mercadotecnia internacional, psicología, relaciones humanas, tecnología de información; médico cirujano partero;
(b) Maestrías en administración, comercio internacional, desarrollo organizacional, ciencias de la educación, administración de la calidad integral, humanidades;
(c) Cursos en el Centro de Educación a Distancia;
(d) Veranos Internacionales: cursos organizados por la Coordinación de Intercambio Estudiantil con otras entidades académicas.
Inscripciones: por mayor información, dirigirse al Departamento de Admisiones. Por todo informe relativo a estudiantes extranjeros, dirigirse a la Asesoría de Estudiantes Internacionales (e-mail: jreding@udem.edu.mx).

1593 Universidad de Quintana Roo [UQROO]
Boulevard Bahía e I. Comonfort s/n
Apartado Postal 10
77019 Chetumal, Quintana Roo
Tel: +52-983-835-0300
Fax: +52-983-832-9656
Web: http://www.uqroo.mx

📖 **Programas universitarios**

Campos de estudios: todas las materias principales, español, idiomas.
Descripción:
(a) Programas universitarios en todas las áreas principales;
(b) Cursos de español para extranjeros y otros idiomas (alemán, maya, francés, inglés).
Se destina(n): a extranjeros que presenten documentación legalizada y superen examen de selección y entrevista y aprueben el curso de Introducción a la Universidad (fin de junio a fin de julio).
Duración: 5 años (inicios en enero y agosto); hay cursos de verano con inicio en junio.
Asistencia financiera: existen becas de colegiatura.
Inscripciones: para mayores informaciones, dirigirse al Servicio de Admisiones Escolares.

1594 Universidad de Relaciones y Estudios Internacionales, A.C. [UREI]

Avenida Chairel, 208 Col. Ex-Country Club
89250 Tampico
Tel: +52-833-219-2498
Fax: +52-833-219-1276
Web: http://www.urei.org.mx
e-mail: universidad@urei.org.mx

Licenciatura en Lenguas Extranjeras

Programas: (a) Licenciatura en lenguas extranjeras
(inglés, francés, italiano y alemán) orientadas a campos
ocupacionales de aplicación inmediata. Dicho programa
comporta cuatro áreas de especialidad: ciencias aduanales y
comercio exterior; ciencias diplomáticas y relaciones
internacionales; hotelería y turismo; interpretariado y
traducción;
(b) Cursos de lengua española y literatura latinoamericana
para extranjeros.
Duración: programas semestrales, que van de agosto a
diciembre y de enero a junio.
Asistencia financiera: descuentos parciales (hasta 50%)
según condiciones.
Inscripciones: dirigirse a la Dirección de Intercambios
Académicos tres meses antes del inicio del semestre.

Becas "Fundación Dr Alfonso García Robles"

Campos de estudios: alemán, estudios culturales, francés,
inglés, italiano, literatura y civilización.
Descripción: ayuda financiera para pago de estudios.
Materias de estudio: lenguas extranjeras.
Se conceden: a menores de 35 años, con promedio de 9 y
que conozcan el idioma español.
Solicitudes: hasta tres meses antes del comienzo del
semestre.

1595 Universidad de Sonora [USON]

Blvd. Luis Encinas y Rosales S/N, Col. Centro
83106 Hermosillo, Sonora
Tel: +52-662-259-2265
Web: http://www.uson.mx

Programas universitarios

Campos de estudios: todas las materias principales,
demografía y estudios de población, física, horticultura,
psicología, relaciones internacionales.
Descripción:
(a) Programas de pregrado y grado; maestrías en física,
horticultura, psicología, alimentos, polímeros, materiales;
(b) Programas de convenio académico con la Universidad de
Arizona (investigación conjunta en temas de fronteras, tratado
de libre comercio de América del Norte, economía regional de
zonas fronterizas, migración, identidad sociocultural, medio
ambiente);
(c) Múltiples convenios nacionales e internacionales.
Se dicta(n): en los campos de Hermosillo, Caborca, Santa
Ana, Navojoa.
Inscripciones: para mayor información, dirigirse a la
Secretaría General Académica.

1596 Universidad de Sotavento [US]

Avenida Mártires de Chicago s/n
96536 Coatzacoalcos, Veracruz
Web: http://www.us.edu.mx
e-mail: info@us.edu.mx

Programas universitarios

Campos de estudios: todas las materias principales,
administración, arquitectura, comunicación, contabilidad,
derecho, educación física, formación de docentes,
informática, ingeniería, psicología.
Descripción:
(a) Programas de intercambio estudiantil internacional;
(b) Licenciaturas y maestrías en todas las áreas principales.
Duración: 9 semestres en promedio (4 años y medio).
Asistencia financiera: descuento de 50 a 100% de la
matrícula durante 6 meses.
Inscripciones: hasta la tercera semana de junio (inicios en
agosto).

1597 Universidad de Xalapa [UX]

Km. 2 Carretera Xalapa-Veracruz
91190 Xalapa
Tel: +52-228-841-7285
Web: http://www.ux.edu.mx
e-mail: informes@ux.edu.mx

Programas universitarios

Campos de estudios: administración de empresas,
comunicación, contabilidad, derecho, educación, electricidad
y electrónica, informática, ingeniería, negocio.
Descripción:
(a) Programas de pregrado en: contaduría, ciencias y técnicas
de la comunicación, administración de empresas, ingeniería
en sistemas de cómputo administrativo, ciencias de la
educación, ingeniería electrónica y comunicaciones, negocios
internacionales;
(b) Posgrados (titulaciones oficiales y propias): especialidad
en docencia universitaria, maestría en derecho electoral, en
derecho fiscal, en derecho constitucional y amparo, en
finanzas; doctorado en derecho.
Asistencia financiera: descuentos de entre 25 y 75% de
descuento en colegiatura.
Inscripciones: dirigirse a Módulo de Inscripciones.

1598 Universidad del Claustro de Sor Juana [UCSJ]

Izazaga 92
Col. Centro
México, D.F.
Tel: +52-55-5130-3313
Fax: +52-55-5130-3309
Web: http://www.ucsj.edu.mx
e-mail: gtraverso@ucsj.edu.mx

Programas universitarios

Campos de estudios: artes, ciencias humanas,
comunicación, estudios culturales, filosofía, letras y artes,
literatura y civilización, medios audio-visuales, psicología.
Descripción:
(a) Licenciaturas en: arte, ciencias de la cultura, psicología,
filosofía, comunicación audiovisual, gastronomía, literatura y
ciencias del lenguaje;
(b) Maestría en cultura virreinal;
(c) Cursos, talleres y diplomados.
Se destina(n): a candidatos con preparatoria completa y
promedio superior a 8, que superen examen de admisión y
entrevista académica.
Duración: (a) 5 años académicos.
Inscripciones: hasta la primera semana de agosto; dirigirse
a Servicios Escolares.

1599 Universidad del Noreste [UNE]

Prolongación Av. Hidalgo 6315
Col. Nuevo Aeropuerto
89337 Tampico, Tamaulipas
Tel: +52-833-228-1117
Web: http://www.une.edu.mx
e-mail: informes@une.edu.mx

Programas universitarios

Campos de estudios: todas las materias principales.
Descripción:
(a) Licenciaturas en áreas de medicina, psicología, química
fármaco-biológica, química industrial, biología, diseño
gráfico, diseño de interiores, comunicación, administración,
contaduría y finanzas, informática;
(b) Maestrías en ingeniería ambiental, en terapia familiar, en
ecología, en docencia en educación superior;
(c) Diplomados en gestión del diseño, en mercadotecnia,
integral de negocios, en técnicas proyectivas, creatividad
gráfica publicitaria.
Duración: 4 años las licenciaturas; semestres de agosto a
diciembre y de enero a junio.
Asistencia financiera: descuento de 50% en la matrícula
según condiciones.
Inscripciones: hasta fin de enero y fin de agosto; por
mayor información, dirigirse a la Coordinación de Captación
y Promoción.

1600 Universidad del Nuevo Mundo, A.C. [UNM]
Bosque de Moctezuma 124
Fracc. La Herradura
53920 Huixquilucán, Estado de México
Tel: +52-55-5589-1711
Fax: +52-55-5589-1700

Becas de estudio

Campos de estudios: diseño industrial.
Descripción: proyectos de diseño industrial en: educación, aplicaciones al hogar, equipos médicos, tecnología intermedia, máquinas y transporte.
Se conceden: a nacionales de cualquier país, mayores de 18 años, que hayan completado sus estudios de bachillerato, o posean un diploma equivalente y aprueben un examen de ingreso. Es necesario un buen conocimiento del español.
Duración: máximo 4 años (renovables cada año de acuerdo con los resultados académicos).
Solicitudes: de marzo a agosto de cada año al Jefe del Departamento de Diseño Industrial de la UNM.

1601 Universidad del Pedregal
Avenida Transmisiones, 51
Col. Ex-Hacienda de San Juan
Delegación Tlalpán
14370 México
Tel: +52-55-5603-5049
Fax: +52-55-5603-3344
Web: http://www.upedregal.edu.mx
e-mail: ma.eugenialabolanos@upedregal.edu.mx

Becas académicas

Campos de estudios: todas las materias principales.
Se conceden: todos los estudiantes extranjeros admitidos en la Universidad del Pedregal pueden postular a las becas, siempre y cuando cumplan con los requisitos académicos y criterios financieros requeridos.
Importe: variable.
Solicitudes: en julio.

1602 Universidad del Valle de Atemajac [UDVDA]
Avenida Tepeyac 4800
Apartado Postal 31-614
45050 Guadalajara, Jalisco
Tel: +52-33-3134-0800
Web: http://www.univa.mx

Programas universitarios

Campos de estudios: todas las materias principales, español, estudios culturales, programas de verano.
Descripción:
(a) Programas de pregrado, maestrías y especializaciones entre otras, en las áreas de: administración de empresas, hotelería y restauración, contabilidad, comercio internacional, computación, diseño gráfico, ingeniería, psicología, nutrición, periodismo, derecho, educación, filosofía;
(b) Cursos del Centro de idiomas: español intensivo (4 niveles), complementados por conferencias sobre cultura mexicana y excursiones lingüístico-culturales;
(c) Educación a distancia: formación profesional (maestrías en áreas comerciales y empresariales).
Duración: (a) año académico compuesto de 3 cuatrimestres (septiembre-diciembre, enero-abril, mayo-agosto); (b) 3 semanas.
Inscripciones: por mayor información, dirigirse a Intercambio Académico.

1603 Universidad del Valle de México [UVM]
Tehuantepec 250
Colonia Roma Sur
06760 México, D.F.
Tel: +52-55-5265-9914
Fax: +52-55-5264-0508
Web: http://www.uvmnet.edu

Programas universitarios

Campos de estudios: todas las materias principales, español, estudios culturales, programas de verano.
Descripción:
(a) Programas de pregrado, grado y maestrías en negocios, finanzas, educación, electrónica (este último en colaboración con la Universidad de Stanford, Estados Unidos, y la Universidad Autónoma de Guadalajara, México);
(b) Programas de grado en arte, administración de empresas, procesamiento de datos en la empresa, computación, comunicaciones, economía, negocio internacional, psicología; programas AMERICOM: cursos de español, arte, música, política e historia mexicanas (AMERICOM es un miembro académico de la Miami-Dade Community College, Estados Unidos, y opera bajo los auspicios de la UVM);
(c) Programa de verano para estudiantes extranjeros: cursos de arte, música, gobierno y política mexicanos, historia mexicana (materias dictadas en inglés) y de lengua española;
(d) Programa de invierno para estudiantes extranjeros: cursos de español (niveles principiante e intermedio), cultura y sociedad mexicanas.
Se dicta(n): (b) en verano, en el Campus de Querétaro; (c) y (d) en la Hacienda Juriquilla del Campus Internacional de Querétaro y en el Campus de San Miguel de Allende.
Duración: (a) año académico dividido en 2 semestres (enero-mayo y agosto-diciembre); (b) año académico dividido en 2 semestres (agosto-diciembre y enero-mayo), más programa intensivo de verano de 6 semanas o programa regular de verano; (c) 6 semanas; (d) 2 semanas.
Inscripciones: por mayor información, dirigirse a la Dirección de Programas Internacionales.

1604 Universidad Galilea [UG]
Avenida Esfuerzo Nacional 612
Ojocaliente IV,
Aguascalientes
Tel: +52-449-975-1999
Fax: +52-449-975-4192
Web: http://www.universidadgalilea.com.mx

Programa de licenciaturas

Campos de estudios: contabilidad, derecho, psicología.
Descripción: Licenciatura en derecho, en psicología, en contaduría pública.
Se destina(n): a candidatos menores de 25 años, con secundaria completa.
Duración: 4 años académicos.

1605 Universidad Hebraica México Instituto Universitario de Estudios Hebraicos [UHM]
Acapulco 70, 4to piso
Colonia Condesa
06700 México, D.F.
Tel: +52-55-5245-8600
Fax: +52-55-5245-8613
e-mail: administración@universidadhebraica.edu.mx

Programas universitarios

Campos de estudios: antropología, ciencias aplicadas, ciencias humanas, educación, filosofía, informática, matemáticas.
Descripción:
(a) Licenciatura en antropología (B.A.);
(b) Licenciatura en ciencias de la educación;
(c) Licenciatura en matemáticas aplicadas y computación;
(d) Licenciatura en pedagogía;
(e) Maestría en ciencias de la educación (Master);
(f) Carrera profesional corta en desarrollo humano (nivel técnico);
(g) Doctorado en filosofía de la ciencia (PhD). Lengua de enseñanza: español y hebreo, más inglés para el doctorado.
Se destina(n): a nacionales de cualquier país: (a) a (f) con bachillerato o equivalente totalmente acreditado, de 18 a 35 años de edad, promedio de antecedentes académicos de 8.5 o equivalente, con dominio del idioma español; examen de admisión: al ingreso, y se aplica una parte en español, otra en hebreo y otra en inglés; (g) con maestría en ciencias o equivalente obtenida con promedio de 8.5 como mínimo, de edad comprendida entre los 30 y los 50 años; existe examen de admisión, se deben presentar recomendaciones académicas y protocolo de investigación desarrollado.
Duración: (a) a (f) 4 años (empiezan en febrero y en

septiembre); (g) 2 años (semestres de agosto a enero y de febrero a julio).
Asistencia financiera: (a) a (f) monto mensual; (g) Beca Vaad Hajinuj de México.
Inscripciones: fecha límite: agosto; dirigirse al Comité de Admisiones, en la dirección que figura en el título.

☛ Becas "Vaad Hajinuj de Mexico".
Campos de estudios: filosofía.
Descripción: doctorado en filosofía de la ciencia.
Se conceden: a nacionales de cualquier país con maestría en ciencias terminada con promedio de 8.5 o equivalente. Los candidatos deben saber español, inglés y hebreo.
Duración: 1 año (renovable).
Importe: aranceles de inscripción, registro ante la Secretaría de Educación Pública, apostemillado de la documentación al egreso y 12 mensualidades de monto fijo por año académico.
Solicitudes: hasta agosto; dirigirse al Comité de Admisión de la Universidad Hebraica México, en la dirección que figura en el título.

1606 Universidad Iberoamericana [UIA]
Prol. Paseo de la Reforma 880
Lomas de Santa Fe
01210 México D.F.
Tel: +52-55-5950-4243
Fax: +52-55-5950-4241
Web: http://www.uia.mx
e-mail: international@uia.mx

📖 **Programas universitarios**

Campos de estudios: todas las materias principales, educación permanente, español, estudios culturales.
Descripción:
(a) Programas de educación superior: licenciaturas y posgrados (especialidades, maestrías, doctorados) en todas las áreas principales;
(b) Programa internacional para estudiantes extranjeros (español, cultura latinoamericana, cursos dictados en la Universidad);
(c) Educación continua: cursos y diplomados.
Duración: (a) año académico compuesto por 2 semestres (enero-mayo y agosto-diciembre); (b) hasta 1 año.
Asistencia financiera: (a) se aplican becas Mutis para estudios de posgrado para candidatos de nacionalidad latinoamericana, española o portuguesa; solicitar información a la Secretaría de Relaciones Exteriores del Gobierno Mexicano (http://www.sre.gob.mx).
Inscripciones: por toda la información útil referente a estudiantes extranjeros, dirigirse a la Dirección de Cooperación Académica, Subdirección de Intercambio Estudiantil en la dirección del título o en la página web http://www.uia.mx/ibero/inter.

1607 Universidad Intercontinental [UI]
Avenida Insurgentes Sur 4303
Col. Santa Ursula Xitla, Tlalpan
14420 México D.F.
Tel: +52-55-5487-1300
Fax: +52-55-5487-1331
Web: http://www.uic.edu.mx
e-mail: intercambio@uic.edu.mx

📖 **Programas universitarios**

Campos de estudios: todas las materias principales, administración, arquitectura, ciencias humanas, diseño, educación, estudios dentales, filosofía, psicología, relaciones internacionales, teología, religión.
Descripción:
(a) Licenciaturas en: administración, administración hotelera, arquitectura, ciencias de la comunicación, contaduría, derecho, diseño gráfico, filosofía, informática, odontología, pedagogía, psicología, relaciones comerciales internacionales, relaciones turísticas, teología, traducción;
(b) Especialidades: diseño de imagen corporativa, derecho procesal mercantil, periodoncia, prostodoncia, tipografía;
c) Maestrías: administración turística, administración en finanzas, administración en mercadotecnia, administración en calidad total, administración en recursos humanos, educación

especial, educación superior, filosofía de la cultura, finanzas, gestión del diseño, guionismo, ortodoncia, psicoterapia psicoanalítica, terapia trascendental.
Duración: 4 años las licenciaturas; hay cursos de verano. Los inicios son en enero y agosto.

1608 Universidad ISEC
Mier y Pesado 227
03100 México, D.F.
Tel: +52-55-5687-9000
Web: http://www.isecuniv.edu.mx
e-mail: isecuniv@solar.sar.net

📖 **Programas universitarios**

Campos de estudios: administración, contabilidad, derecho, finanzas, informática, marketing, negocio, psicología, turismo, hotelería.
Descripción:
(a) Licenciaturas en: administración de empresas, contaduría pública, derecho, finanzas, informática, mercadotecnia, negocios internacionales, psicología; turismo;
(b) Posgrados: especialidad en administración por calidad total, en impuestos, en finanzas, en sistemas expertos, en telecomunicaciones y redes; maestría en administración de negocios, en fiscal, en docencia; doctorado en ciencias con especialidad en ciencias administrativas.
Duración: (a) 4 años académicos (inicios en agosto y febrero); (b) 2 años las maestrías (inicios en enero, mayo y septiembre).
Asistencia financiera: solicitar informes a la Vicerrectoría de la División de Graduados o consultar sitio web del ISEC.
Inscripciones: dirigirse al Departamento de Promoción y Difusión.

1609 Universidad José Vasconcelos de Oaxaca [UNIVAS]
Crespo 601
Colonia Centro
Oaxaca de Juarez
Tel: +52-951-514-7090
Fax: +52-951-514-7090
Web: http://www.univas.edu.mx
e-mail: univas@univas.edu.mx

📖 **Programas universitarios**

Campos de estudios: administración, administración de empresas, ciencias políticas, comercio, comunicación, contabilidad, economía, finanzas, relaciones internacionales, sociología.
Descripción:
(a) Licenciaturas en: mercadotecnia, administración de empresas, ciencias políticas, administración pública, ciencias de la comunicación, sociología, economía, finanzas y contaduría, relaciones internacionales, comercio internacional;
(b) Maestría en gobierno y políticas públicas regionales.
Duración: 4 años las licenciaturas.
Asistencia financiera: becas de 25 y 50% sobre colegiatura para alumnos de alto rendimiento.

1610 Universidad Juárez del Estado de Durango [UJDEDD]
Constitución 404 Sur
34000 Durango
Tel: +52-1-812-0044
Fax: +52-1-812-9513
Web: http://www.ujed.mx

📖 **Programas universitarios**

Campos de estudios: todas las materias principales, español, programas de verano.
Descripción: (a) Carreras de ingeniero en agroquímica, ingeniero en ciencias de materiales, secretario de comercio, contador público, profesor de educación musical, pintor, escultor y grabador, técnico artesanal, cirujano dentista, químico farmacobiólogo, médico cirujano, médico veterinario zootecnista, licenciado en enfermería, en administración, en derecho, en matemáticas aplicadas, en trabajo social, ingeniero en ciencias forestales;
(b) Programa de verano de español para extranjeros.
Duración: (a) variable; (b) 4, 6 u 8 semanas.

Inscripciones: para mayor información, dirigirse a (a)
Dirección de Orientación Educativa, en la dirección que
figura en el título; (b) Centro de Idiomas, Avenida Fanny
Anitua y Privada de Loza, Durango, 34000 Durango.

1611 Universidad La Salle [ULSA]
Benjamín Franklin 47
Col. Condesa
06140 México, D. F.
Tel: +52-55-5278-9508
Fax: +52-55-5516-2297
Web: http://www.ulsa.edu.mx

Programas universitarios

Campos de estudios: todas las materias principales,
administración, arquitectura, artes gráficas, comunicación,
derecho, educación, español, filosofía, ingeniería, medicina,
química, teología, religión.
Descripción:
(a) Programas de licenciaturas, maestrías, especializaciones,
doctorados, impartidos en sus escuelas y facultades de:
ciencias de la administración, arquitectura y diseño gráfico,
ciencias de la educación, ingeniería, ciencias químicas,
derecho, medicina, filosofía y ciencias religiosas;
(b) Programas para extranjeros en el CIEL (Centro
Internacional de Educación): intercambios académicos,
programas especiales, información y centro de apoyo;
(c) Programas de español para extranjeros en el Centro
Internacional de Educación.
Duración: (a) año académico dividido en 2 semestres
(agosto-noviembre y enero-junio); (b) programas de una
semana a un semestre, todo el año; (c) programas de 3 a 5
semanas todo el año.
Inscripciones: por mayor información, dirigirse al Centro
Internacional de Educación La Salle o consultar el sitio web
citado más arriba, enlace "International Center".

1612 Universidad Madero [UMAD]
Camino Real a Cholula, 4212
San Andrés Cholula
72150 Puebla
Tel: +52-222-284-5959
Fax: +52-222-284-6124
Web: http://www.umad.edu.mx
e-mail: jcromero@umad.edu.mx

Programas universitarios

Campos de estudios: administración, ciencias de la
información, ciencias económicas y comerciales, derecho
internacional, educación, idiomas, informática, ingeniería.
Descripción:
(a) Licenciaturas: procesos de manufactura, lenguas
extranjeras, diseño gráfico, comunicación e información,
derecho empresarial, desarrollo de software, dirección de
organizaciones, administración, comercio exterior,
mercadotecnia, contaduría y finanzas internacionales,
ingeniería industrial, ingeniería en sistemas, educación
bilingüe;
(b) Posgrados: doctorado en administración internacional,
maestrías en administración y dirección de negocios,
comercio internacional, derecho comercial internacional,
mercadotecnia;
(c) Diplomados y educación continua: desarrollo de
habilidades del pensamiento, administración de recursos
humanos, administración gerencial, mercadotecnia, logística
empresarial.
Duración: cursos de enero a mayo, junio y julio, agosto a
diciembre.
Inscripciones: por mayores informaciones, dirigirse a
Admisiones y Relaciones Públicas.

Becas a cambio de horas de trabajo

Campos de estudios: administración, comercio,
comunicación, diseño industrial, idiomas, industria y
comercio, informática, marketing, tecnología industrial.
Descripción: beca de gastos de enseñanza a cambio de
número variable de horas de trabajo.
Se conceden: a todos los candidatos que hayan obtenido
un promedio mínimo de 7, 8 o 9 según el caso.

1613 Universidad Mexicana del Noreste [UMN]
Quinta Zona 409
Col. Caracol, Monterrey
64810 Nuevo León
Tel: +52-81-8190-1104
Fax: +52-81-8190-1205
Web: http://www.umne.edu.mx
e-mail: umnemty3@mail.giga.com

Programas universitarios

Campos de estudios: administración, artes, estudios
culturales, ingeniería.
Descripción:
(a) Programas en administración (contador público, licenciado
en administración de empresas, en administración del tiempo
libre, en banca y finanzas), ingenierías (constructor, en control
e instrumentación, industrial y de sistemas, mecánico
electricista);
(b) Maestría en administración, con cinco áreas de
especialidad: mercadotecnia, recursos humanos, finanzas,
organización deportiva y desarrollo turístico;
(c) Diplomados culturales y técnicos: cultura, arte, desarrollo
humano, programación neurolingüística, formación familiar,
administración.
Duración: (a) 9 tetramestres los programas en
administración, 10 las ingenierías; (b) periodicidad
tetramestral; admisiones 3 veces al año, para los períodos que
inician en enero, mayo y septiembre de cada año.
Inscripciones: (b) dirigirse a la División de Estudios de
Posgrado.

1614 Universidad México Americana del Norte [UMAN]
Guerrero 1317
Colonia del Prado, Reynosa
88560 Tamaulipas
Tel: +52-899-922-2002
Fax: +52-899-922-2002
Web: http://www.uman.edu.mx
e-mail: uman@infosel.net.mx

Programas universitarios

Campos de estudios: todas las materias principales.
Descripción: (a) Carreras profesionales: ciencias de la
salud (médico cirujano partero, médico cirujano dentista,
enfermería); administrativas y contables (contador público
auditor, relaciones industriales, comercio internacional,
administración de empresas, mercadotecnia); humanidades y
ciencias sociales (derecho, turismo, ciencias de la
comunicación, psicología, educación inicial); ingeniería y
arquitectura (arquitectura, diseño, ingeniería civil, ingeniería
industrial y de sistemas, ingeniería en electrónica);
licenciatura en sistemas computacionales; (b) maestrías en:
administración de la calidad, administración de la producción,
administración de recursos humanos, administración
industrial, administración de la mercadotecnia, administración
con especializaciones en informática, en producción, calidad y
finanzas, en enseñanza en la educación superior, en comercio
exterior, en derecho penal; (c) doctorados en administración y
en educación superior.
Duración: tetramestres enero-abril, mayo-agosto,
septiembre-diciembre; las carreras duran de 3 años y medio a
6 años.
Costo(s): para extranjeros, existe cuota de extranjería de
500 a 800 dólares de los Estados Unidos por ciclo lectivo. Los
costos de inscripción y colegiatura son variables según la
carrera.
Asistencia financiera: becas internas, externas y por
excelencia (descuentos de 30% a 50% del costo de
colegiatura). Solicitar información al Departamento de Becas.
Inscripciones: dirigirse al Departamento de Servicios
Escolares; la información para estudiantes extranjeros se
puede solicitar al Departamento de Extranjeros y Asuntos
Internacionales.

Beca internas y externas

Se conceden: a estudiantes que demuestren asuidad,
excelencia académica (promedio de 9) y necesidad
económica.

Importe: porcentaje variable (de 10 a 50%) de gastos de enseñanza y exención de gastos de estudios.
Solicitudes: hasta el último día de inscripción de cada período.

1615 Universidad Michoacana "San Nicolás de Hidalgo" [UMICH]

Edificio "TR", 3er piso
Ciudad Universitaria
58030 Morelia, Michoacán
Tel: +52-443-316-7020
Fax: +52-443-316-8834
Web: http://www.ccu.umich.mx

 📖 **Programas universitarios**

Campos de estudios: todas las materias principales, español, farmacia y farmacología, filosofía, idiomas, metalurgia, programas de verano.
Descripción:
(a) Programas de pregrado y grado entre otras, en las áreas siguientes: cultura de la filosofía, farmacología básica, farmacología clínica, metalurgia, materiales;
(b) Programa de verano de cursos de español, historia y literatura mexicanas;
(c) Cursos de idiomas del Departamento de lenguas: ruso, portugués, japonés, español para extranjeros, purépecha (lengua nativa de los indígenas de la región).
Duración: (a) año académico completo (fin de agosto a mediados de agosto) o 2 semestres (agosto-febrero y marzo-agosto); (b) de junio a agosto.
Inscripciones: por mayor información, dirigirse a la Secretaría Académica.

1616 Universidad Michoacana de Oriente

Hidalgo, Esq. Venustiano Carranza, Col. Centro
61512 Zitácuaro
Tel: +52-715-153-8990
Fax: +52-715-153-8990
e-mail: umo@evonet.com.mx

🐚 **Beca parcial de gastos de estudio**

Campos de estudios: administración de empresas, derecho, educación.
Importe: 50% de los gastos de enseñanza.
Solicitudes: hasta septiembre de cada año.

1617 Universidad Mundial

Abasolo s/n Entre Colima y Luis Donaldo Colosio
Col. Pueblo Nuevo
23000 La Paz
Tel: +52-612-125-8955
Fax: +52-612-125-8960
Web: http://www.unimundo.edu.mx
e-mail: gallardo@unimundo.edu.mx

 📖 **Programas Universitarios**

Campos de estudios: administración de empresas, artes décorativas, ciencias sociales, contabilidad, criminología, derecho, diseño, marketing, negocio, psicología, turismo, hotelería.
Programas: Cursos de pregrado y grado.

1618 Universidad Nacional Autónoma de México [UNAM]

Unidad de Posgrado, 2° piso
Ciudad Universitaria
Delegación de Coyoacán
04510 México, D.F.
Tel: +52-55-5622-0775
Fax: +52-55-5550-9017
Web: http://www.unam.mx
e-mail: rectoria@servidor.unam.mx

 📖 **Programas universitarios**

Campos de estudios: todas las materias principales, español, estudios culturales, programas de verano.
Descripción:
(a) Programas de pregrado, grado, especializaciones, maestrías y doctorados en todas las áreas principales;
(b) Cursos de español, estudios chicanos, historia del arte, historia y ciencias sociales de México y Latinoamérica, literatura mexicana y latinoamericana;
(c) Curso de actualización para profesores de español como lengua extranjera.
Se dicta(n): (a) durante todo el año escolar en las diversas Escuelas y Facultades; (b) a (d) en el Centro de Enseñanza para Extranjeros en Ciudad de México y en Taxco (Estado de Guerrero).
Duración: (b) cursos semestrales (2 años) y cursos intensivos de 6 semanas todo el año y en verano (julio-agosto); (c) cursos regulares de 1 año de duración (2 módulos); (d) 6 semanas en verano (junio-agosto).
Inscripciones: para mayor información, dirigirse a (a) Dirección General de Intercambio Académico, en la dirección del título; (b) a (d) Centro de Enseñanza para Extranjeros, Apartado Postal 70-391, Ciudad Universitaria, Delegación Coyoacán, 04510 México, D.F., o e-mail: cepe@servidor.unam.mx.

🐚 **Becas de intercambio académico**

Campos de estudios: todas las materias principales, investigación.
Descripción: realización de estudios o investigaciones de posgrado en la UNAM.
Se conceden: a estudiantes procedentes de las instituciones extranjeras con las que la UNAM ha firmado convenios de colaboración en los que se contempla la concesión de becas. El candidato debe ser egresado o formar parte del personal académico de la institución postulante, presentar una carta de postulación firmada por el Rector y justificar la aceptación oficial de la dependencia de la UNAM donde realizará sus estudios, además de los títulos y certificados que se exijan según los casos.
Duración: 1 año académico (renovable de acuerdo con el programa de estudios y el desempeño académico del becario).
Solicitudes: 3 meses antes de la fecha de iniciación del año académico; dirigirse a la Dirección General de Intercambio Académico, en la dirección que figura en el título.

1619 Universidad Panamericana [UP]

Augusto Rodin 498
Colonia Mixcoac
03920 México, D.F.
Tel: +52-55-5482-1600 / 1700
Fax: +52-55-5482-1717
Web: http://www.mixcoac.upmx.mx
e-mail: relpub@mixcoac.upmx.mx

 📖 **Programas universitarios**

Campos de estudios: todas las materias principales, español, estudios culturales.
Descripción:
(a) Licenciaturas en sus escuelas y facultades en áreas de: administración, ingeniería, medicina, administración de instituciones, contaduría, pedagogía, derecho, enfermería, economía, comunicación; filosofía;
(b) Posgrados: especialidad en sistemas de pensiones y seguros, en comercio y finanzas internacionales, en administración de riesgo, en mercadotecnia internacional, en finanzas, en impuestos, en contaduría y finanzas internacionales, en auditoría e impuestos internacionales; maestría en evaluación socioeconómica de proyectos de inversión, en comunicación institucional; posgrado de pedagogía, en ingeniería, en derecho; filosofía para universitarios; historia de la cultura en México; filosofía del hombre; historia del pensamiento;
(c) Estudios de lengua y cultura en el Centro de Idiomas.
Se destina(n): para licenciaturas: a bachilleres; para posgrados se requiere ser mayor de 23 años, tener un promedio mínimo de 8,5 y tener título de licenciatura. En ambos casos se admiten todas las nacionalidades; se exige conocimiento de otra lengua además del español (de preferencia inglés).
Se dicta(n): en México y Guadalajara.
Inscripciones: por mayor información, dirigirse a la Dirección de Relaciones Públicas.

1620 Universidad Popular de la Chontalpa [UPC]

Galeana s/n Altos Esq. Morelos, Col. Centro
Cárdenas, Tabasco
Tel: +52-937-372-5743
Fax: +52-937-372-6530
Web: http://www.upchontalpa.edu.mx
e-mail: rfigueroa@hotmail.com /
mvzmaj@hotmailcom

Programas universitarios

Campos de estudios: todas las materias principales.
Programas: Programas universitarios en todas las áreas principales.
Descripción: (a) Licenciaturas: ingeniería (en agronomía, civil, química petrolera, eléctrica y mecánica, en zootecnia); comercio y finanzas internacionales; ciencia política y administración pública; psicología; químico farmacobiólogo;
(b) Profesional asociado: instalaciones mecánicas, industriales y mantenimiento; instalaciones eléctricas y mantenimiento; mercadotecnia; turismo alternativo.

1621 Universidad Quetzalcóatl en Irapuato [UQI]

Blvd. Arandas 975
Col. Tabachines
Irapuato, Guanajuato
Tel: +52-462-624-5025 / 65 / 95
Fax: +52-462-624-8184 ext 128
Web: http://www.uqi.edu.mx
e-mail: ggasca@uqi.edu.mx

Programas universitarios

Campos de estudios: administración de empresas, arquitectura, contabilidad, derecho, diseño, electricidad y electrónica, estudios dentales, finanzas, idiomas, informática, ingeniería, ingeniería civil, medicina, psicología.
Descripción:
(a) Licenciaturas en: administración de empresas, arquitectura, contaduría, comunicación, derecho, diseño gráfico, psicología, odontología, médico cirujano, ingeniería electrónica, ingeniería civil, ingeniería de sistemas;
(b) Especialidades de posgrado: amparo, derecho corporativo, auditoría, finanzas, planeación fiscal, endodoncia, periodoncia;
(c) Cursos en su Centro de Idiomas.
Duración: año académico en dos semestres: agosto-febrero y marzo-julio.

1622 Universidad Regiomontana [UR]

Modesto Arreola 1014
Monterrey, Nuevo León
Tel: +52-818-220-4651
Fax: +52-818-220-4658
Web: http://www.ur.mx
e-mail: cteis@mail.ur.mx

Programas universitarios

Campos de estudios: todas las materias principales, español.
Descripción:
(a) Carreras profesionales y licenciaturas en áreas de ciencias económicas y administrativas, humanidades y ciencias sociales, ingeniería y arquitectura;
(b) Maestrías en: derecho privado; en derecho fiscal, en educación (acentuación en psicología educativa), en educación (acentuación en educación superior), en comunicación, en administración (virtual), en informática administrativa (administración de la información, telemática, tecnología de software), en administración (acentuación en: finanzas, recursos humanos, mercadotecnia, negocios internacionales);
(c) Programas de español y cultura.
Inscripciones: por mayor información, dirigirse a Asuntos Internacionales.

1623 Universidad Regional del Norte [URN]

Allende 2628, Col. Zarco
Chihuahua
Tel: +52-614-411-1571
Fax: +52-614-411-1551
Web: http://www.urn.edu.mx
e-mail: promo@urn.edu.mx

Programas universitarios

Campos de estudios: administración, administración de empresas, comercio, comunicación, contabilidad, derecho, finanzas, negocio, relaciones internacionales.
Descripción:
(a) Licenciaturas en: administración de empresas, administración industrial, negocios internacionales, ciencias de la comunicación, turismo, relaciones industriales, contaduría pública fiscal, derecho, comercio exterior, ingeniería financiera;
(b) Posgrados: maestrías en dirección financiera, dirección de la producción y de las operaciones, dirección organizacional.
Inscripciones: (b) por mayor información, dirigirse a División de Estudios de Posgrado (e-mail: posgrado@urn.edu.mx).

1624 Universidad Salesiana

Laguna Tamiahua 97, Col. Anáhuac
11320 Miguel Hidalgo, México D.F.
Tel: +52-55-5396-2430
Fax: +52-55-5341-9823
Web: http://www.universidadsalesiana.edu.mx
e-mail: informacion@universidadsalesiana.edu.mx

Becas de estudio

Campos de estudios: todas las materias principales.
Descripción: becas parciales para gastos de enseñanza.
Importe: hasta 2.000 dólares de los Estados Unidos por año.

1625 Universidad Tecnológica de Nezahualcoyotl [UTN]

Circuito Universidad Tecnológica s/n
Col. Benito Juárez
57000 Ciudad Nezahuacoyotl
Estado de México
Tel: +55-571-69718
Web: http://www.utn.edu.mx

Becas de excelencia

Campos de estudios: administración, tecnología.
Se conceden: a egresados de bachillerato o profesionales de nacionalidad española, francesa, estadounidense, canadiense y de toda Latinoamérica, menores de 30 años, con promedio mínimo de 8 (sobre escala de 10), que dominen el español.
Duración: 1 año (renovable por 1 año más).
Importe: la totalidad del pago mensual de la colegiatura.
Solicitudes: hasta mediados de octubre.

1626 Universidad Tecnológica Fidel Velázquez [UTFZ]

Calle Emiliano Zapata s/n
Col. Tráfico
54400 Nicolás Romero, Estado de Méxi
Tel: +52-55-5823-0600
e-mail: utfv@mpsnet.com.mx

Diplomaturas técnicas superiores

Campos de estudios: administración, informática, tecnología, tecnología industrial.
Descripción: Cursos conducentes al diploma de técnico superior universitario en administración, informática, mantenimiento industrial; se ofrecen como facilidades cursos de idiomas y programas de recuperación.
Se destina(n): a egresados del bachillerato, con promedio mínimo de 7, que superen examen de admisión.
Duración: 2 años (comienzos en septiembre).
Asistencia financiera: becas por desempeño académico y crédito educativo.

1627 Universidad Valle del Bravo [UVB]

Laredo s/n, Col. La Laguna
88760 Reynosa, Tamaulipas
Tel: +52-899-920-2065 / 1750
Fax: +52-899-920-0471 / 74
Web: http://www.uvb.edu.mx
e-mail: ing-gastelum@mail.uvb.edu.mx

☐ Programas universitarios

Campos de estudios: todas las materias principales.
Descripción:
(a) Licenciaturas en administración de empresas, ciencias de la comunicación, contaduría pública, economía, derecho, derecho con énfasis en fiscal o internacional, diseño gráfico, mercadotecnia internacional, relaciones industriales, turismo, psicología, informática, comercio internacional;
(b) Ingenierías: mecánico electricista, industrial administrador, sistemas computacionales;
(c) Ciencias de la salud: médico cirujano partero, médico cirujano dentista, enfermería;
(b) Maestrías en: ciencias de la administración, educación superior, ciencias de la administración, desarrollo organizacional, sistemas computacionales, comercio internacional, fiscal y calidad total.
Se dicta(n): en las ciudades de Reynosa, Matamoros, Nuevo Laredo, Tampico, Mante, Victoria, San Fernando (Estado de Tamaulipas) y Culiacán (Estado de Sinaloa).
Duración: licenciaturas: 3 a 5 años; maestrías: 2 a 3 años.
Programas semestrales: inicio en enero y agosto; programas tetramestrales: inicios en enero, mayo y septiembre; área de la salud: inicios en febrero y agosto.
Inscripciones: por mayor información, dirigirse a la Dirección de Servicios Escolares.

1628 Universidad Veracruzana Dirección General de Apoyo al Desarrollo Académico [UV]

Juárez 55
Colonia Centro
Jalapa, Veracruz
Tel: +52-228-842-1763
Web: http://www.uv.mx

☐ Especialidades y cursos de posgrado

Campos de estudios: todas las materias principales.
Descripción: Especialidades de posgrado en las siguientes áreas;
(a) Biológico-agropecuaria: asesoría de empresas pecuarias, fruticultura tropical, ganadería de pastizal, producción agroforestal, producción animal (bovinos en el trópico húmedo), salud animal (bovinos en el trópico húmedo);
(b) Ciencias de la salud: educación en sexualidad humana, psicología comunitaria, rehabilitación bucal, salud pública;
(d) Económica-administrativa: administración fiscal, auditoría financiera, administración del comercio exterior, economía financiera, métodos estadísticos, proyectos de inversión;
(e) Humanidades: docencia, enseñanza del inglés;
(f) Técnica: climatología, construcción, control de calidad, diagnóstico y gestión ambiental, sistemas microprocesadores, valuación de bienes, vivienda;
Maestrías en las siguientes áreas:
(g) Biológico-agropecuaria: ciencia animal tropical, ecología forestal, manejo del recurso forestal, explotación de los agrosistemas de la caña de azúcar;
(h) Ciencias de la salud: administración de servicios de salud, ciencias aplicadas a la actividad física, investigación clínica, investigación en psicología aplicada a la educación, medicina forense, neuroetología, psicología de la salud, teoría psicoanalítica, desarrollo humano;
(i) Económico-administrativa: administración (recursos humanos, agropecuaria, finanzas, organización y sistemas);
(j) Humanidades: administración educativa, comunicación, didáctica del francés, enseñanza del inglés como lengua extranjera, evaluación institucional, filosofía, literatura mexicana, lenguaje y educación;
(k) Técnica: ciencias de la computación, producción, gestión y promoción urbana para el desarrollo sostenible, ingeniería (estructuras, hidráulica, ambiental, mecánica, oceánica, eléctrica), ingeniería económica, financiera y de costos, inteligencia artificial, restauración arquitectónica de bienes culturales;

Cursos de posgrado en las siguientes áreas:
(l) Biológica-agropecuaria: biotecnología de plantas;
(m) Económico-administrativa: finanzas públicas;
(n) Humanidades: derecho público, historia, estudios regionales;
(o) Técnica: Ingeniería de estructuras;
(p) Ciencias de la salud: salud mental comunitaria.
Se destina(n): a profesionales de cualquier país que posean título de licenciatura (para especializaciones o maestrías) o de maestría (para los doctorados) en el área respectiva.
Duración: en general: en general: (a) a (f) 1 año; (g) a (k) 2 años; (l) a (p) 4 años.
Inscripciones: para mayores informaciones, dirigirse a la Unidad de Estudios de Posgrado.

☐ Programas universitarios

Campos de estudios: todas las materias principales, español, estudios culturales.
Descripción: (a) Programas de pregrado en áreas de de humanidades, artes, biológico- agropecuaria, económico-administrativa, ciencias de la salud, ingeniería y tecnología;
(b) Cursos de la Escuela para Estudiantes Extranjeros: gramática y conversación del español, cultura latinoamericana, cursos individuales de español, formación de profesores de español, estudios sobre los Estados Unidos;
(c) Educación a distancia: maestría en enseñanza y aprendizaje abiertos y a distancia.
Duración: (a) el año académico se compone de dos semestres: agosto-enero y febrero-julio; (b) en primavera: enero-mayo; en verano: 6 semanas en junio y julio; en otoño: agosto-diciembre.
Inscripciones: por mayor información, dirigirse a: (a) Dirección de Trámites Escolares, en la dirección que figura en el título; (b) Escuela para Estudiantes Extranjeros, Apartado Postal 440, 91000 Jalapa, Veracruz, email: eeeuv@uv.mx.

1629 Universidad Villasunción

Avenida Las Américas, 601
Fracc. Las Fuentes
20239 Aguascalientes
Tel: +52-449-918-0866
Fax: +52-449-918-5112
e-mail: uni_villasuncion@hotmail.com

☛ Exenció de Gastos de Enseñanza

Campos de estudios: ingeniería.
Materias de estudio: ingeniería.
Se conceden: a candidatos con promedio superior a 8.5.
Importe: hasta 40%.
Solicitudes: hasta diciembre de cada año.

Mongolia

Academic year: September to June.
Monetary unit: tughriks (MNT).
International student admission: Students should hold a secondary-school certificate for admission to higher education. An entrance examination is required.
Language: Mongolian is the language of instruction but theses may be presented in other languages.
Information services:
• Minister of Education, Science and Culture, c/o Ministry of Foreign Affaires, 7a Enkhtaivany gudamj, Ulan Bator 210648, tel/fax: +976-1-322-612; email: mongmer@magicnet.mn.
Open and distance learning: Distance education courses are available through the Distance Education Unit of the Mongolian Technical University.
Recognition of studies and qualification: Ministry of Education, Science and Culture, c/o Ministry of Foreign Affairs, 7a Enkhtaivany gudamj, Ulan Bator 210648, tel/fax: +976-1-322-612; email: mongmer@magicnet.mn.

1630 National Medical University of Mongolia

3 Choidog Street
Sukhbaatar District
210349 Ulaanbaatar
Tel: +976-11-328-670
Fax: +976-11-321-249
Web: http://www.nmum.edu.mn
e-mail: narantuya@nmum.edu.mn

📖 Undergraduate, Graduate, Postgraduate Programmes

Study Domains: anatomy, bacteriology, biology, cancerology, cardiology, chemistry, computer science, cytology, dentistry, dermatology, dietetics, economy, gerontology, health and hygiene, immunology, medicine, neurology, nursing, nutrition, obstetrics and gynaecology, ophthalmology, paediatrics, paramedical studies, pharmacy and pharmacology, philosophy, physiology, preventive medicine, psychiatry, psychology, radiology, social work, speech therapy, surgery, urology.
Programmes: Bachelor's, Master's, Ph.D. degrees in medicine; Mongolian traditional medicine; dentistry; public health; pharmacy; health management and biostatistics; biomedicine; medicine for sports; non-degree programmes in chemistry; computer science; foreign languages; biology; psychology; economics.
Open to: students between 18 and 30 years of age; admissions test; Russian and Mongolian language proficiency required.
Duration: 5 to 6 years; courses begin in September.
Fees: registration US$15; tuition fees US$2,000 per year.
Languages: Mongolian, Russian, English.
Applications: by 20 August.

1631 National University of Mongolia

PO Box 46A/523
Ulaanbaatar 210646
Tel: +976-11-320-159
Fax: +976-11-320-159
Web: http://www.num.edu.mn
e-mail: int_rel@num.edu.mn

📖 Undergraduate, Graduate, Postgraduate Programmes

Study Domains: administration, anthropology, archaeology, art history, arts, Asian studies, astronomy, biochemistry, biology, business, business administration, chemical engineering, chemistry, computer science, demography and population studies, development studies, earth science, ecology, environment, economic and commercial sciences, economy, education, ethnology, finance, geology, history, international business, international law, international relations, international studies, journalism, languages, law, linguistics, literature and civilization, management, marketing, mathematics, natural resources, performing arts, philology, philosophy, political economy, political science, Slavic studies, social sciences, sociology, theology, religion, trade.
Programmes: Bachelor's, Master's, Ph.D. degrees in all major fields.
Duration: 4-7 years; Summer course 8 weeks.
Fees: registration US$20; tuition fees US$1,800-$2,000 per year; living costs US$1,000.
Applications: by 15 August or 15 February; contact int_rel@num.edu.mn for further details.

Namibia

Academic year: January to November.
Organization of higher education system: Higher education is limited in size. It consists of the University of Namibia (UNAM), the Polytechnic, 4 Teacher Education Colleges and 3 Agricultural Colleges.
Monetary unit: Namibian dollar (N$).
International student admission: Namibian Grade 12 level: Cambridge International General Certificate of Secondary Education (IGCSE) or Higher IGCSE.
Language: English. At least a D-symbol in IGCSE required for admission.
Information services:
• Ministry of Higher Education, Training and Employment Creation, Private Bag 13391, Windhoek 9000; tel: +264-61-270-6111; fax: +264-61-253-672; web: http://www.op.gov.na/Decade_peace/h_edu.htm.
• University of Namibia, 340 Mandume Ndemufayo Avenue, Pioneerspark, Private Bag 13301, Windhoek; tel: +264-61-206-3111; fax: +264-61-206-3003.
• Namibian embassies abroad.
Open and distance learning: The College of Distance Education offers courses for those in full-time employment. There are also outreach centres and satellite campuses.

1632 Polytechnic of Namibia

Private Bag 13388
Windhoek
Tel: +264-61-207-9111
Fax: +264-61-207-2444
Web: http://www.polytechnic.edu.na

📖 Certificate and Diploma Programmes

Study Domains: all major fields.
Programmes: programme of studies leading to National Certificates, National Higher Certificates and National Diplomas in: civil engineering, electrical engineering, electronics engineering, mechanical engineering, accounting, business computing, business studies, public administration, salesmanship, secretarial studies, hospitality operation, travel and tourism operations, land use planning and land measuring, nature conservation, public administration.
Open to: candidates of all nationalities; over 18 years of age; having passed at least 5 subjects, including English language, at IGCSE level (or equivalent), or 4 subjects, including English
language, with 2 at the HIGCSE level (or equivalent); passing score at least 25 points on the Evaluation Scale; conditional admission of candidates having reached the age of 23 years on 1 January of the academic year concerned, with 3 years work experience relating to the proposed study programme, and having passed the Polytechnic English proficiency test.
Duration: 1 to 3 years depending on programme.
Fees: (approximate figures) tuition: N$475 per course; accommodation: N$4,070 per year or N$2,035 per semester; meal fees: N$4,900 per year or N$2,450 per semester; registration: N$120.
Languages: instruction in English.
Applications: by 31 October, to the Office of the Registrar, at the above address.

Nepal

Academic year: July to June.
Organization of higher education system: Higher education is divided into 4 phases: the first stage leads to the proficiency certificate
and the technician certificate; the main stage leads to the award of the Bachelor's degree; a further stage leads to the award of the Master's degree. The last stage leads to the award of the Doctorate (Ph.D.).
Monetary unit: Nepalese rupees (NPR).
International student admission: Qualifications equivalent to the school-leaving certificate. Foreign students must also have a school-leaving certificate-level English.
Language: Foreign students must be proficient in English, Nepali and Sanskrit.
Immigration requirements: Visa required.
Information services:

• Royal Nepalese Embassies.
• Ministry of Education and Culture, Kathmandu.
• Tribhuvan University, Kirtipur, Kathmandu.
Open and distance learning: There is no organized
distance higher education. A system of private examinations
exist at the Faculties of Humanities and Social Sciences,
Management and Law at Tribhuvan University and at
Mahendra Sanskrit University whereby candidates who have
not attended university can sit for the examinations.
Recognition of studies and qualification: Academic
Administrator, Curriculum Development Centre, Tribhuvan
University, Kirtipur, Nepal; tel: +977-1-330-856; fax:
+977-1-331-964; email: vcoffice@healthnet.org.np; web:
http://www.tribhuvan-university.edu.np.

1633 Tribhuvan University
Kirtipur, Kathmandu
Tel: +977-1-330842
Fax: +977-1-31964
Web: http://www.tribhuvan-university.edu.np

📖 Undergraduate, Graduate Programmes
Study Domains: agriculture, education, forestry,
humanities and arts, law, management, medicine, sciences,
social sciences.
Programmes: (a) Proficiency certificate (in humanities,
social sciences, management, education, law and science) and
technical certificate (in medicine, engineering, forestry and
agriculture); (b) Bachelor's degree in technical fields and in
medicine; (c) Master's degree; (d) Doctorate (Ph.D.);
postgraduate degrees are also awarded in medicine.
Open to: applicants of any nationality with a
school-leaving certificate and for foreigners a school-leaving
certificate level in English.
Applications: before academic year (July to June) at the
above address.

Netherlands
Academic year: September to June.
Organization of higher education system: The
Netherlands has two main types of higher education:
university education, and
higher professional education, which is offered at the
polytechnics and colleges known in the Netherlands as
hogescholen. The universities train students for the
independent practice of science. The hogescholen are more
practice oriented; they prepare students directly for careers.
Transfer between the two types of higher education is
possible. Education for foreign students started in the 1950s
when specialized Institutes for International Education were
established. Their main objective has been to offer high
quality education to foreign students, especially coming from
developing countries and countries in transition. Today, 14
Institutes of International Education provide over 150
specialized courses designed primarily for professionals who
have already embarked on their careers. The courses are of a
practical nature and can be adapted to suit individual needs
and wishes. The courses introduce participants to new
methods and techniques and assure that students will be able
to apply their new knowledge in their home countries. At the
same time, 14 universities and 70 institutes of higher
professional education conduct some of their courses in
English for the benefit of exchange and other foreign students.
These include courses that are part of regular degree
programmes, as well as special courses. Students taking
regular courses can earn credits, and eventually the equivalent
of a Bachelor's or Master's degree. A full study programme
may take 4 or 5 years to complete; more commonly, foreign
students transfer the credits they have earned in the
Netherlands and graduate from their own institutions. Dutch
universities, hogescholen and specialized institutes often work
together, and many have exchange arrangements with partner
institutions in other countries. Dutch higher education is
regulated by Dutch law. Courses are concluded with a
certificate of attendance, a postgraduate diploma, a Bachelor's
degree or a Master's degree. Their duration varies from
several weeks for a certificate, to several months for a
diploma, to a year or more for a degree.

Monetary unit: Euro (€).
National student admission: Most courses are at
postgraduate level and relatively short. A Bachelor's degree or
its equivalent is a prerequisite for most of these courses, plus
at least some years of professional experience, or a diploma
from an advanced form of secondary-school.
Immigration requirements: European Union (EU)
students and from the European Economic Area (EEA) -
Austria, Belgium, Denmark, Finland, France, Germany,
Greece, Iceland, Ireland, Italy, Liechtenstein, Luxembourg,
Monaco, Norway, Portugal, Spain, Sweden, Switzerland and
the United Kingdom) need a valid passport or national
identity card. Non-EU students need an entry visa (in many
cases, the receiving institutions helps with the application
procedure). They have to apply for a visa and a residence
permit in their home country which is only granted for the
duration of the training. With such a residence permit they are
not allowed to work in Netherlands. A health insurance is also
need (for more information, contact the Netherlands embassy
or diplomatic representative in the candidate's own country).
Information services:
• Ministry of Education and Science, Central Direction
Information, Library and International relations, PO Box
25000, 2700 LZ Zoetermeer: web: http://www.minocw.nl
• Netherlands embassies and consulates abroad (including, in
the United States of America, Netherlands Information
Centers in New York, San Francisco and Holland, Michigan).
• Netherlands Organization for International Co-operation in
Higher Education (NUFFIC), PO Box 29777, 2502 LT Den
Haag (assessment of the value of foreign diplomas in terms of
the Dutch system, plus administration of fellowship
programmes and project management). www.studyin.nl
• Foreign Student Service, Oranje Nassaulaan 5, 1075 AH
Amsterdam (study information, ISIS student insurance
policies, help with accommodation, cultural excursions,
cooperation with International Students' Clubs in university
towns).
• Netherlands Office for Foreign Student Relations,
Rapenburg 6, Leiden (information service and language and
orientation courses for foreign students).
• International Federation of Interior Design, PO Box 19126,
1000 GC Amsterdam (facilitates contacts between students
and educational institutions admitting foreign students for less
than the full course).
Scholarships for international students:
• Huygens Scholarships: covers living expenses for three to
ten months to nationals from a wide range of countries under
the terms of various cultural agreements. These scholarships
usually cover only a small part of the tuition. The Embassy of
the Netherlands in the applicant's home country can supply
information. Please note that the application deadline for these
scholarships is 1 February prior to the intended year of study.
• Netherlands Fellowship Programme (UFP): Students from
developing countries are eligible for scholarships of the
Netherlands Fellowship Programme.
The NUFFIC in The Hague is responsible for the
administration of the Huygens and UFP scholarships;
Information and application forms are available at the Dutch
Embassy or contact NUFFIC, PO Box 29777, 2502 LT The
Hague, The Netherlands, tel: +31-70-426-0260; fax:
+31-70-426-0399; email: nuffic@nuffic.nl; web:
http://www.nuffic.nl.
Open and distance learning: The best example of
non-traditional distance education is the Open Universiteit. It
offers courses in Law, Social Sciences, Arts, Economics,
Management and Administrative Science, Engineering and
Natural Sciences. The Central Government has laid down a
statutory framework in which the Open University must
operate. The only entrance requirement is that students be at
least 18 years old. Students define their own programme and
proceed at their own pace, which means that the programme's
length varies according to the student. Qualifications are
Certificates from one or several courses, a Diploma awarded
upon completion of several courses combined into a short
study programme, or a Doctoral degree.
Recognition of studies and qualification: Department for
International Credential Evaluation, Nuffic (Netherlands
Organization for International Cooperation in Higher
Education); PO Box 29777; Kortenaerkade 11; 2502 LT; The
Hague; Netherlands; tel: +31-70-426-0270; fax:
+31-70-426-0395; email: divis@nuffic.nl; web:
http://www.nuffic.nl/index-en.html.

Publications / Websites:
• 'Higher Education in the Netherlands' (in English); free, from the Ministry of Education and Science and Netherlands diplomatic representatives.
• 'Catalogue of International Study Programmes and Courses Offered in the Netherlands' contains detailed information on: 850 Dutch study programmes and courses taught in English Free. Available on CD-ROM, in print or at www.studyin.nl
• 'Studying in the Netherlands', NUFFIC; free of charge.
• 'The Netherlands Fellowships Programmes' (in English), Ministry of Foreign Affairs and NUFFIC; free, contains information on scholarships for mid-career professionals. The information is also available at http://www.nuffic.nl/nfp.
• 'Living in Holland', NUFFIC, 5 €.

1634 Academic Centre for Dentistry Amsterdam [ACTA]
Louwesweg 1
1066 EA Amsterdam
Tel: +31-20-518-8302
Fax: +31-20-518-8512
Web: http://www.acta.nl/main_uk.asp?pid=2
e-mail: info@acta.nl

📖 Graduate Programmes
Study Domains: dentistry.
Programmes: Master's degree in periodontology; Clinical Certificate in endodontology.
Open to: applicants with qualification in dentistry (D.D.S. or equivalent) from a recognized institute.
Duration: 3 years.
Fees: approx. 9,000 €.
Languages: Instruction in English.
Applications: by 15 March.

1635 Arnhem Business School [ABS]
PO Box 5171
6802 ED Arnhem
Tel: +31-26-369-1333
Fax: +31-26-369-1367
Web: http://www.han.nl
e-mail: international@heao.han.nl

📖 Undergraduate, Graduate Programmes
Study Domains: business, business administration, finance, management.
Programmes: Bachelor's, Master's degrees in management; business administration; finance; business.
Open to: applicants with secondary school education.
Duration: 1 to 4 years.
Applications: by 15 May (for Summer term); by 1 November (for Winter term).

1636 ArtEZ Institute of the Arts [ArtEZ]
Onderlangs 9
6812CE Arnhem
Tel: +31-26-353-5635
Fax: +31-26-353-5677
Web: http://www.artez.nl

📖 Undergraduate, Graduate Programmes
Study Domains: architecture, arts, decorative arts, design, music and musicology, performing arts, visual arts.
Applications: download application forms through http://www.artez.nl/studielink and http://www.studielink.nl.

1637 Centraal Bureau voor Schimmelcultures [CBVS]
PO Box 85167
3508 AD Utrecht
Tel: +31-30-212-2600
Fax: +31-30251-2097
Web: http://www.cbs.knaw.nl
e-mail: Info@cbs.knaw.nl

📖 Graduate Courses
Study Domains: microbiology.
Programmes: Certificates in mycology; medical mycology; food-borne fungi.
Open to: applicants with B.Sc. in biology or related field.
Duration: 2 to 4 weeks.
Fees: 500-1,300 € per certificate course.
Languages: instruction in English.
Applications: 2 to 3 months before the beginning of the course; see website for further information.

1638 Delft University of Technology
PO Box 5
2600 AA Delft
Tel: +31-15-278-9111
Fax: +31-15-278-6522
Web: http://www.tudelft.nl
e-mail: voorlichting@tudelft.nl

📖 Undergraduate, Graduate Programmes
Study Domains: architecture, civil engineering, computer science, industrial technology, sciences, technology.
Programmes: Bachelor's, Master's and Ph.D. programmes at the following faculties: (a) Aerospace Engineering; (b) Applied Sciences; (c) Architecture; (d) Civil Engineering and Geosciences; (e) Design, Engineering and Production; (f) Information Technology and Systems; (g) Technology, Policy and Management.
Open to: candidates of all nationalities meeting academic, financial and linguistic requirements; see website for eligibility details for each faculty.
Applications: see website for contact details for each faculty.

1639 Dronten Professional Agricultural University [DPAU]
De Drieslag 1
8251 JZ Dronten
Tel: +31-321-386-100
Fax: +31-321-313-040
Web: http://www.cah.nl
e-mail: info@cah.nl

📖 Undergraduate Programmes
Study Domains: business administration, ecology, environment, food, management.
Programmes: Bachelor's degree (Hons.) in all major fields.
Description: international chain management; chain management and quality control in the agrifood sector; EU agricultural policies, management skills and tools.
Duration: 16 months; courses begin 25 September.
Fees: tuition fees 1,500 € per year; living costs approx. 5,000 € per year.
Financial assistance: maximum 4,800 €.
Languages: English; TOEFL required.
Applications: by 1 March; contact met@ceh.nl for further information.

🎓 Scholarship
Study Domains: agriculture, business administration, ecology, environment, food.
Scholarships: S.S.V. Scholarship.
Description: food production.
Open to: EU or EEA citizens.
Value: 4,800 € per academic year for maximum 2 years.
Applications: by 1 March with CV, education documents, written statement of motivation, budget/financial plan to T. Menger at met@ceh.nl.

1640 Eindhoven University of Technology [EUOT]
PO Box 513
5600 MB Eindhoven
Tel: +31-40-247-9111
Web: http://www.tue.nl

📖 Undergraduate, Graduate, Postgraduate Programmes
Study Domains: all major fields.
Programmes: Bachelor's, Master's, Ph.D. degrees in all major fields.
Open to: candidates with secondary-school certificate;

proficiency in Dutch and English required.
Duration: 3 to 5 years.
Languages: Dutch and English.

1641 Erasmus University Rotterdam [EU]

PO Box 1738
3000 DR Rotterdam
Tel: +31-10-408-1111
Web: http://www.eur.nl
e-mail: erasmusweb@daz.eur.nl

⌖ Undergraduate, Graduate Programmes

Study Domains: business administration, health and hygiene, history, management, philosophy, sciences, social sciences.
Programmes: Bachelor's, Master's degrees at the following faculties and institutes: (a) Rotterdam School of Management/Faculteit der Bedrijfskunde; (b) Rotterdam School of Management/Erasmus Graduate School of Business; (c) Rotterdam School of Economics; (d) School of Law; (e) Faculty of Social Sciences; (f) Faculty of Medicine and Health Sciences; (g) Institute of Health Policy and Management; (h) Faculty of History and Arts; (i) Faculty of Philosophy.
Open to: candidates with secondary-school certificate; TOEFL and IELTS required; professional experience recommended.
Financial assistance: possibility of scholarships from Dutch government or international organizations.
Applications: to each individual faculty at the above address; web addresses of each faculty may be obtained from the above web address.

1642 HAS Den Bosch University of Professional Education

Postbus 90108
Onderwijsboulevard 221
5223 's-Hertogenbosch
Tel: +31-73-692-3600
Fax: +31-73-692-3699
Web: http://www.hasdenbosch.nl
e-mail: hasdb@hasdb.nl

⌖ Undergraduate, Graduate Programmes

Study Domains: agriculture, earth science, food industry, horticulture, veterinary sciences.
Subjects: food, agriculture, horticulture, nature and environment.
Financial assistance: several possibilities from government of Netherlands and for nationals of European Union countries; see www.nuffic.nl for further details.

1643 HES Rotterdam College for Economics and Business Administration

Kralingse Zoom 91
PO Box 4030
3006 AA Rotterdam
Tel: +31-10-452-6663
Fax: +31-10-452-7051
Web: http://www.hes-rdam.nl/hes/english/general.html
e-mail: studievoorlichting@hro.nl

⌖ Undergraduate, Graduate Studies

Study Domains: business administration, economy, management.
Programmes: Bachelor's, Master's degrees in Business administration; international management.
Open to: applicants with International Baccalaureate or equivalent.
Languages: instruction in English.
Applications: by May/June; to the above address.

1644 Hogeschool Zuyd, Limburg Business School [LBS]

PO Box 5268
6130 PG Sittard
Tel: +31-46-420-7000
Fax: +31-46-420-7079
Web: http://members.home.nl/b.kamphuis/
e-mail: r.braeken@hszuyd.nl

⌖ Undergraduate Studies

Study Domains: business, business administration, international business, international law, marketing.
Programmes: Bachelor's degree in international business administration.
Open to: applicants with secondary education at advanced level with a background in mathematics and economics.
Duration: 4 years.
Languages: Instruction in English.
Applications: by 1 May at the above address.

1645 Hotelschool The Hague, International Institute for Hospitality Management [HTH]

Brusselselaan 2
2587 AH The Hague
Tel: +31-70-351-2481
Fax: +31-70-351-2155
Web: http://www.hotelschool.nl/general
e-mail: info@hdh.nl

⌖ Undergraduate Studies

Study Domains: international studies, summer programmes, tourism, hotel and catering management, vocational training.
Programmes: Bachelor's and Master' degrees in European hospitality management.; also certificate programmes.
Open to: candidates of any country with university entrance level, or working at supervisory or junior management level in the hotel industry, with 2 years professional experience.
Languages: very good knowledge of English and a second language (French, German, Spanish).
Applications: by 15 April, to the above address; see website for further information.

1646 Institute for Biotechnology Studies Delft/Leiden [BODL]

Julianalaan 67
2628 BC Delft
Tel: +31-15-278-1922
Fax: +31-15-278-2355
Web: http://www.bt.tudelft.nl/bodlf.htm
e-mail: BODL@tnw.tudelft.nl

⌖ Graduate, Postgraduate Programmes

Study Domains: biology, microbiology.
Programmes: Master's, Ph.D. degrees in biotechnology; bioprocess technology.
Open to: applicants with an M.Sc. degree or equivalent with experience in one of the basic biotechnological disciplines.
Financial assistance: possibility of scholarships through Dutch Government; information through Dutch embassies in countries of origin.
Applications: see website for further information.

1647 Institute for Housing and Urban Development Studies [IHS]

PO Box 1935
3000 BX Rotterdam
Tel: +31-10-402-1523
Web: http://www.ihs.nl
e-mail: ihs@ihs.nl

⌖ Graduate Programmes in Urban Development

Study Domains: architecture, building industry, computer science, development studies, management, urbanism.
Programmes: M.A. in Urban Management: M.Sc. in Urban Environmental Management, Urban Housing Management, Housing and Inner City Revitalisation.

Duration: 12 to 18 months.
Fees: 8,000-20,500 € depending on programme.
Financial assistance: financial assistance available through the Netherlands Government and/or donor agencies.
Applications: by March; contact admission@ihs.nl and above web address for further information.

1648 Institute of Social Studies [ISS]

PO Box 29776
2502 LT The Hague
Tel: +31-70-426-0460
Fax: +31-70-426-0799
Web: http://www.iss.nl/index.html
e-mail: promotions@iss.nl

📖 Graduate, Postgraduate Studies

Study Domains: development studies, international law, international relations, law, rural development.
Programmes: programme of studies leading to a Master of arts in development studies with major in: (a) agriculture and rural development; (b) economics of development; (c) employment and labour studies; (d) politics of alternative development strategies; (e) public policy and administration; (f) local and regional development; (g) women and development; (h) population and development; postgraduate diplomas in: (i) development planning techniques with computer applications; (j) rural policy and project planning; (k) international relations and development; (l) international law and organization for development; special teaching programme in: (m) development, law and social justice.
Open to: candidates of any nationality holding (a), (c) to (h) and (k) a B.A. degree in relevant field of study; (b) a B.A. degree in economics with a working knowledge of statistics and mathematics; (i) a B.A. degree in economics, business administration, statistics, engineering or equivalent; (j) a B.A. degree in social sciences or other relevant science; (l) degree in international law or political science; (m) a B.A. degree in relevant field of study with several years of direct involvement in the subject matter; 2 years' professional experience.
Duration: (a) to (h) 67 weeks; (i) to (l) 26 weeks; (m) 7 weeks.
Financial assistance: possibility of scholarships from Dutch Government.
Languages: instruction in English.
Applications: by 1 February, to the Academic Registrar for all further information.

1649 International Agricultural Centre [IAC]

PO Box 88
6700 AB Wageningen
Tel: +31-31-749-5495
Fax: +31-31-749-5395
Web: http://www.iac-agro.nl
e-mail: training@iac.agro.nl

📖 Postgraduate Studies

Study Domains: administration, agriculture, food industry, geology, marine science.
Programmes: (a) postgraduate diploma in food and nutrition - food and nutrition security; (b) cours international de vulgarisation rurale (in French); (c) international course on applied plant breeding; (d) international course on integrated pest management; (e) international potato course; (f) international course on seed production and seed technology; (g) stage sur les plantes de pomme de terre (in French); (h) international course on extension management; (i) international course on vegetable production; (j) international course on food processing; (k) international course on dairy farming in rural development; (l) new perspectives in rural extension: challenges and prospects; (m) international course on local level management of trees and forests for sustainable land use; (n) international course on protected cultivation; (o) international course on food and nutrition programme management; (p) international postgraduate course on soil and plant analysis and data-handling.
Open to: candidates of any nationality particularly from developing countries and economies in transition holding (a) B.Sc. degree or equivalent in nutrition, food technology, home economics, medicine or related science with 2 to 3 years working experience related to the theme of the course; (b) and (h) B.Sc. degree in extension or a related science with

3 years experience; (c) B.Sc. degree in agriculture, plant breeding or a related science with knowledge of genetics and statistics; (d) B.Sc. degree in agriculture or biology; (e), (f) and (g) B.Sc. degree in agriculture; (i) B.Sc. degree in agriculture, vegetable production or horticulture; (j) B.Sc. degree in food technology, food engineering or related agricultural sciences, with some training experience for small-scale food processing enterprises; (k) B.Sc. degree in agricultural or veterinary sciences, dairy cattle husbandry; (l) M.Sc. degree in extension or a related science; (m) M.Sc. or B.Sc. degree in forestry, agriculture or social sciences; (n) B.Sc. degree in agriculture or any other proof that the candidate has mastered the basics of horticulture; (o) B.Sc. degree in food and nutrition, health, medicine, agriculture, education or social sciences, with 5 years of professional experience; (p) B.Sc. degree in agriculture, biology or chemistry.
Duration: (a) 21 weeks; (b), (h) and (o) 6 weeks; (c), (d) and (m) 15 weeks; (e), (f), (i), (j) and (k) 14 weeks; (g) 3 weeks; (l) and (n) 4 weeks; (p) 9 weeks.
Financial assistance: a limited number of scholarships available.
Languages: instruction in English and French.
Applications: by (a) 15 September; (b) October; (c) 20 November; (d) 10 December; (e) and (f) 1 January; (g) 1 March; (h) 20 March; (i) 10 April; (j) and (k) 1 May; (l) and (m) 1 June; (n), (o) and (p) 1 August, at the above address.

1650 International Institute for Aerospace Survey and Earth Sciences [ITC]

PO Box 6
7500 AA Enschede
Tel: +31-53-874-444
Fax: +31-53-487-4400
Web: http://www.itc.nl
e-mail: prakash@itc.nl

📖 Graduate, Postgraduate Studies

Study Domains: computer science, development studies, earth science, natural resources, urbanism.
Programmes: Master's, Ph.D. degrees in geological survey; geo-information for sustainable soil resource management; geo-informatics; remote sensing; survey and environmental monitoring.
Open to: candidates of all nationalities holding at least a B.Sc. in earth sciences; geology; soil science; geodesy; computer science.
Duration: 12-22 months for Master's degree; 3-1/2 years for Ph.D. (of which the second is to be spent in the student's own country).
Fees: approx. 5,400 € for Master's degrees; 23,000 € for Ph.D.
Financial assistance: financial assistance available for Ph.D.; allowance of 680 € per month for board and lodging and out-of-pocket expenses, plus air tickets to and from ITC, for the 1st and the 3rd year.
Applications: at any time, to ITC Student Registration; see website for detailed information on all programmes.

1651 International Institute for Land Reclamation and Improvement [ILRI]

PO Box 47
6700 AA Wageningen
Tel: +31-317-495-549
Fax: +31-317-495-590
Web: http://www.ilri.nl
e-mail: ilri@ilri.nl

📖 Graduate Courses

Study Domains: agriculture, computer science, engineering.
Programmes: Programme of International courses on (a) land drainage; (b) microcomputer applications in land drainage; (c) computer applications in irrigation; (d) drainage execution and maintenance; (e) water management in irrigation systems; (f) institutional aspects in water management.
Open to: candidates of any nationality holding a B.Sc. in agricultural engineering, (a) or civil engineering, hydrology, with a good background in mathematics and physics; (b) and

(d) plus several years' practical experience in drainage systems; (c) and (e) plus basic knowledge of computer applications; (f) or business administration, with 5 years in land and water management.
Duration: (a) 16 weeks; (b) 2 weeks; (c) 4 weeks; (d) 5 weeks; (e) 12 weeks; (f) 3 weeks.
Fees: tuition from 2,700-3,500 €.
Languages: instruction in English.
Applications: to above address; see website for further information.

1652 Larenstein International Agricultural College [LIAC]
PO Box 7
7400 AA Deventer
Tel: +31-570-684-608
Web: http://www.larenstein.nl
e-mail: IE@larenstein.nl

Undergraduate, Graduate Programmes

Study Domains: agriculture, cattle breeding, food industry, forestry, horticulture.
Programmes: programme of international courses leading to B.Sc. degrees in agricultural engineering; agri-food production and marketing; tropical animal production; training in rural extension and teaching; women, extension workers and agriculture.
Open to: nationals of any country with requisite diplomas and experience for each programme.
Financial assistance: candidates may apply for fellowships from Netherlands Fellowships Programme (NFP) through the Netherlands diplomatic representatives in their own countries; other possible sponsors include donor organizations.
Languages: instruction in English.
Applications: by 1 April to the Registrar at the above address.

1653 Leiden University [LU]
Postbus 9515
2300 RA Leiden
Tel: +31-71-527-2048
Web: http://www.leidenuniv.nl
e-mail: study@luwp.leidenuniv.nl

Undergraduate, Graduate Programmes

Study Domains: administration, art history, cultural studies, Dutch, European studies, history, languages, law, linguistics, literature and civilization.
Programmes: Bachelor's, Master's degrees in Dutch studies; law; business administration.
Open to: students with a certificate equivalent to the Dutch secondary-school diploma; European and American law students or graduates; senior undergraduates or strong junior undergraduates of all nationalities; a good knowledge of English is required.
Financial assistance: waiver of tuition may be granted in some cases.
Applications: see website for further details.

Leiden University Scholarships

Study Domains: all major fields.
Scholarships: Various scholarship schemes:
Tuition Fees for EU/EEA students; Leiden University Scholarship Programme; Leiden Alumni Scholarships: Archaeology Scholarships: International Relations and Diplomacy Scholarships;
Turkish Studies Scholarships; Praesidium Libertatis Scholarships; The Leiden University Mandela Scholarship Fund; DELTA Scholarships at Leiden University; Scholarships for ISEP students; Scholarships for Indonesian students.
Applications: to the above address; see website for details of each scholarship.

1654 Maastricht School of Management [MSM]
Endepolsdomein 150
PO Box 1203
6201 BE Maastricht
Tel: +31-43-387-0808
Fax: +31-43-387-0800
Web: http://www.msm.nl
e-mail: info@msm.nl

Graduate, Postgraduate Programmes

Study Domains: accounting, business, ecology, environment, economic and commercial sciences, finance, management, marketing.
Programmes: Master's, Ph.D. degrees in business administration; management; economics; business.
Open to: applicants with Bachelor's degree in relevant field and with professional experience.
Financial assistance: possible under certain conditions.
Applications: deadlines vary by programme; contact the above address for further information; see website for further details.

1655 Maastricht University, Faculty of Economics and Business Administration
Tongersestraat 53
PO Box 616
6200 MD Maastricht
Tel: +31-43-388-2693
Fax: +31-43-388-4864
Web: http://www.fdewb.unimaas.nl

Graduate Studies

Study Domains: business, economy, international business, management.
Programmes: Master's degree in international economics; international business; international management.
Open to: candidates of any nationality with secondary education at A-level.
Duration: 1 to 4 years.
Languages: instruction in English.
Applications: by 1 August, at the above address.

1656 Maastricht University, Faculty of Law [FLMU]
PO Box 616
6200 MB Maastricht
Tel: +31-43-38830 38/36
Fax: +31-43-3884891
e-mail: mil@facbur.unimaas.nl

Graduate, Postgraduate Programmes

Study Domains: international law, law.
Programmes: Master's degree in Comparative and European Law.
Open to: law graduates.
Duration: 1 year.
Fees: tuition fees: EU students, 6,650 €; non-EU students, 7,650 €; additional costs: approx. 350 € per month for housing.
Financial assistance: scholarship available through the Netherlands fellowship programme.
Languages: language of instruction: English (TOEFL test: 213/550; IELTS or Cambridge Proficiency).
Applications: first selection round: by 1 April; second selection round: by 1 June; for information contact Marleen Vara at the above address.

1657 Maastricht University, Faculty of Medicine
PO Box 616
6200 MD Maastricht
Tel: +31-43-388-1524
Fax: +31-43-388-5639
Web: http://www.fdg.unimaas.nl/bib
e-mail: welcome@oifdg.unimaas.nl

Undergraduate Studies

Study Domains: anatomy, cardiology, dermatology, immunology, medicine, obstetrics and gynaecology, ophthalmology, paediatrics, pharmacy and pharmacology,

physiology, radiology, surgery, urology.
Programmes: (a) International Visitors' Workshop (a
primer on the Maastricht approach to medical education); (b)
Summer Course (expanding horizons in problem-based
learning); (c) Exchange Programme and Incoming Medical
Students.
Description: (a) the course aims to introduce 'novices' to
the principles and practices of Problem-Based Learning (PBL)
in health professions education as currently applied at
Maastricht Faculty of Medicine; (b) in this course participants
will get an opportunity not only to understand the Maastricht
approach to problem-based learning, but also get acquainted
with and learn from the experience of other Faculties of
Medicine in the Netherlands; (c) Certificate of Medicine.
Open to: (a) anyone desiring to learn about PBL; (b)
professionals academically involved in education of medical
professions; (c) students having completed at least the first
year of medical education.
Duration: (a) 24-25 November, (b) from 20 June to 1 July.
Fees: current registration: (a) 425€; (b) 2,400€; (c) 50€;
living costs: approx. 700€ per month.
Languages: (a) and (b) English, (c) Dutch and/or English.
Applications: see website for on-line applications: (a)
http://www.fdg.unimaas.no/bib/workshop/ (b)
http://www.fdg.unimaas.nl/bib/summercourse; (c)
http://www.fdg.unimaas.nl/bib/exchange; for information
contact Maud Senden; tel. +31-43-388-5634; email:
m.senden@oifdg.unimaas.nl.

1658 Netherlands Graduate School of Management [NIMBAS]

Nieuwegracht 6
PO Box 2040
3500 GA Utrecht
Tel: +31-30-230-3050
Web: http://www.nimbas.com
e-mail: admissions@nimbas.com

📖 Master of Business Administration

Study Domains: ecology, environment, management.
Programmes: M.B.A. programme.
Open to: applicants with university or polytechnic degree,
Fachhochschule Diplom or equivalent, with GMAT
(550)/NIMBAS Admission test, and 2 years of professional
experience.
Duration: 56 weeks.
Financial assistance: possibility of obtaining international
scholarships.
Applications: by 31 May.

1659 Netherlands Organization for International Cooperation in Higher Education [NUFFIC]

PO Box 29777
2502 LT The Hague
Tel: +31-70-426-0260
Fax: +31-70-426-0399
Web: http://www.nuffic.nl
e-mail: nuffic@nuffic.nl

🎓 Scholarships, Fellowships

Study Domains: all major fields.
Scholarships: (a) DELTA programme; (a) Huygens
programme; (c) Netherlands Fellowship Programme.
Description: (a) DELTA (Dutch Education: Learning at
Top level Abroad) is a scheme that enables Dutch higher
education institutions to award scholarships to students from
certain countries to cover the costs of studying in the
Netherlands; (b) scholarships for study in the Netherlands;
(c) consists of two sub-programmes: the Academic
Programme (NFP-AP), which offers fellowships for the
pursuit of Master's and Ph.D. degrees and the Training
Programme (NFP-TP), which offers fellowships for short
courses, refresher courses, and courses of tailor-made
training.
Open to: (a) for outstanding students from the People's
Republic of China, Indonesia, Taiwan and South Africa; (b),
(c) for outstanding students of certain countries who are
nearing completion of their studies at Master's degree level, or
who have recently graduated.
Applications: (a) see website

http://www.studyinthenetherlands.net/common.asp?id=68 for
list of participating institutions or the Netherlands Education
Support Office (NESO)
http://www.studyinthenetherlands.net/common.asp?id=87 or
from Dutch embassies around the world.; (b), see website for
further information: www.nuffic.nl/huygens; (c) see website
for further information:
www.studyinthenetherlands.net/common.asp?id=55&instantie
=0.

1660 NHTV Breda University of Professional Education [NHTV]

PO Box 3917
4800 DX Breda
Tel: +31-76-530-2213
Fax: +31-76-530-2205
Web: http://www.nhtv.nl
e-mail: international.office@nhtv.nl

📖 Postgraduate Programme in Tourism

Study Domains: tourism, hotel and catering management.
Programmes: European Tourism Management.
Description: This postgraduate course is run as a
partnership between seven European universities specialized
in tourism and offers a unique opportunity to develop
expertise in Tourism Management in a European context.
Studies take place in at least two European countries, within
an international context. A Master of Arts degree (MA) is
awarded after successful completion of this course.
Subjects: tourism principles and practice, business
strategy, policies planning and development in European
tourism, research methods, foreign languages, marketing for
hospitality and tourism, managing organizations, and a major
live case study consultancy exercise for a tourism
organization.
Open to: see academic requirements.
Nationality: candidates of all nationalities.
Academic requirements: Bachelor's degree in tourism or a
related discipline, e.g. management, business studies,
geography or hotel management; apart from the educational
background and language skills, criteria for admission are
personal qualities and motivation. Shortlisted candidates will
be invited for an interview. A language test may be part of the
selection process.
Other conditions: English language proficiency must be
proven for non-English speakers through a TOEFL test
(minimum score 550 paper-based or 213 computer-based) or
IELTS test (minimum score 6.0).
Held:
• Stage 1, from September to February, is simultaneously
taught at NHTV Breda University of Professional Education
(the Netherlands), Dalarna University (Sweden) and
Bournemouth University (UK).
• Stage 2, from February to May, is simultaneously taught at
the Universidade do Algarve (Faro, Portugal),
Fachhochschule Heilbronn (Germany), Université de Savoie
(Chambéry, France) and Universidad Rei Juan Carlos
(Madrid, Spain).
Stage 3, from May to September, consists of writing a
dissertation on an aspect of tourism management of one's own
choice. There is no restriction on where the candidate lives
during stage three but it will be necessary to have access to
the library and other facilities of one of the ETM education
centres, and to make arrangements to consult staff regarding
the dissertation.
Duration: 1 year (September to September).
Fees: tuition: 5,890 € for students from
EU/EEA-countries; 9,890 € for non-European students.
Financial assistance: no financial assistance is available.
Languages: English and possibly one of the following
languages: French, German or Spanish (depending on choice).
Applications: candidates from France, Germany, the
Netherlands, Portugal, Spain, Sweden or the United Kingdom
should send applications to the ETM-partner institution in
their home countries. Nationals of other countries should
apply to Bournemouth University (UK) or NHTV. The
application deadline for EU-residents is mid-June 2006; for
non-EU-residents end April. Check with the university for
specific application dates and details.

📖 Undergraduate Programmes in Hospitality, Leisure and Tourism

Study Domains: tourism, hotel and catering management.
Programmes: International Hotel Management, International Leisure Management, International Tourism Management.
Description: practice-oriented Bachelor's programmes which prepare students for management positions in an international organization.
Subjects: management skills, foreign languages, marketing, cross-cultural research, financial economics, statistics, orientation on the specific industry (i.e. either leisure or tourism or hospitality), etc.
Open to: see academic requirements.
Nationality: candidates of all nationalities.
Academic requirements: completion of secondary school, secondary vocational education or equivalent; additional requirement for International Hotel Management: experience in the hospitality industry.
Other conditions: Non-native speakers of English must show proof of proficiency in English through a TOEFL test (minimum score 550 paper-based or 213 computer-based) or IELTS test (minimum score 6.0).
Held: at Breda, the Netherlands.
Duration: 4 years.
Fees: tuition: 1,496€ per year.
Financial assistance: a partial refund of the tuition fee may be requested from the Dutch government for candidates who are EU-residents, between 18 and 30 years old, hold a bank account in the Netherlands and are not entitled to any other study finance schemes or grants on the basis of nationality regulations. This refund should be applied for at IB-Groep before 1 January. Check www.ibgroep.nl for more information.
Languages: English.
Applications: by 15 April; application forms can be downloaded from www.nhtv.nl.

📖 Undergraduate Programmes in Media and Entertainment Management

Study Domains: audio-visual media.
Programmes: Media and Entertainment Management; Game Academy.
Description: practice-oriented Bachelor's programme which prepares students for management positions in the media and entertainment industry.
Subjects: multimedia techniques, image editing, film analysis, script writing, web design, concept development, financial management, business communication, statistics, media law, marketing, project management.
Open to: see academic requirements.
Nationality: candidates of all nationalities.
Academic requirements: secondary school, secondary vocational education or equivalent.
Other conditions: If you are a non-native speaker of English, you have to show your proficiency in English through a TOEFL test (minimum score 550 paper-based or 213 computer-based) or IELTS test (minimum score 6.0).
Held: at Breda, the Netherlands.
Duration: 4 years.
Fees: tuition: approximately 1,975 € per year for media and entertainment management; approximately 1,496 € per year for game academy.
Financial assistance: partial refund of the tuition fee may be requested from the Dutch government for EU-residents, between 18 and 30 years old, holding a bank account in the Netherlands and not entitled to any other study finance schemes or grants on the basis of nationality regulations. This refund should be requested at IB-Groep before 1 January. Check www.ibgroep.nl for more information.
Languages: English.
Applications: by 15 April; application forms can be downloaded from www.nhtv.nl.

1661 Nijenrode University, The Netherlands Business School [NU]

Straatweg 25
3621 BG Breukelen
Tel: +31-346-291-211
Fax: +31-346-291-450
Web: http://www.nijenrode.nl
e-mail: info@nyenrode.nl

📖 Graduate, Postgraduate Programmes

Study Domains: business administration, international business.
Programmes: Master's, Ph.D. degrees in business administration; public governance; financial services and insurance; international business.
Open to: applicants of all nationalities holding a university-level degree or equivalent with an excellent academic record, 2 years of professional business experience; GMAT and TOEFL required.
Duration: 16 months for Master's courses; four year research and study for Ph.D.
Fees: tuition fees 20,000 € for M.Sc.; living costs 10,000-15,000 €.
Financial assistance: financial assistance available; see website for further information.

1662 Radio Nederland Training Centre [RNTC]

PO Box 303
1200 AH Hilversum
Tel: +31-35-672-4500
Fax: +31-35-672-4532
Web: http://www.rnw.nl/rntc
e-mail: info@rntc.nl

📖 Educational Television and Radio Production

Study Domains: audio-visual media.
Programmes: general production of informative and educative programmes.
Open to: radio and/or television producers and directors from developing countries with secondary education, some years appropriate experience and adequate command of written and spoken English; up to age 40 for men and 45 for women.
Duration: 3 to 4 months.
Financial assistance: through the Netherlands Fellowships Programme (NFP): covering travel costs, board and lodging, clothing allowance, insurance and tuition; possibility through EU's European Development Fund and international organizations.
Applications: see website for further information.

1663 Rotterdam College of Music and Dance

Hogeschool voor Muziek en Dans
Kruisplein 26
3012 CC Rotterdam
Tel: +31-10-217-1100
Fax: +31-10-217-1101
Web: http://www.hmd.nl

📖 Undergraduate Studies

Study Domains: performing arts.
Programmes: professional diploma in performing dance.
Open to: applicants with a secondary education at advanced level and pre-vocational dance training; entrance audition required.
Duration: 168 weeks.
Fees: approx. 1,250 € per year.
Languages: instruction in English.
Applications: by March.

1664 Rotterdam School of Management, Erasmus Graduate School of Business [RSM]

PO Box 1738
3000 DR Rotterdam
Tel: +31-10-408-2222

Fax: +31-10-452-9509
Web: http://www.rsm.nl

📖 Graduate, Postgraduate Programmes

Study Domains: business, management.
Programmes: Master's, Ph.D. degrees in business administration; economics; management; finance.
Open to: candidates of any country holding a Bachelor's degree or any equivalent foreign degree plus graduate management admission test; a minimum of two years of work experience is also required.
Languages: English.
Applications: see website for further information.

1665 Royal Conservatory, The Hague

Juliana van Stolberglaan 1
2595 CA The Hague
Tel: +31-70-315-1515
Fax: +31-70-315-1518
Web: http://www.koncon.nl

📖 Undergraduate, Graduate Programmes

Study Domains: music and musicology.
Programmes: Bachelor's, Master's degrees in classical music; dance; sonology.
Open to: applicants with a secondary school certificate.
Duration: 38 weeks.
Applications: by 21 June; see website for further information.

1666 Saxion Universities of Professional Education [SUHPE]

International Office
PO Box 501
7400 AM Deventer
Tel: +31-570-663-125
Fax: +31-570-663-628
Web: http://www.saxion.edu
e-mail: internationaloffice@saxion.nl

📖 Graduate Course, Management

Study Domains: accounting, finance, management.
Programmes: Master of Arts in management.
Description: strategic marketing, finance and accounting.
Open to: candidates of all nationalities with Bachelor's degree in relevant field.
Duration: 1 year.
Fees: tuition: 8,650€.
Applications: 1 July to above address.

📖 Undergraduate, Graduate Programmes

Study Domains: accounting, business, business administration, chemical engineering, chemistry, civil engineering, ecology, environment, finance, management, trade, urbanism.
Programmes: (a) Bachelor's degrees in accounting and finance, business information systems, information services and management, international business and management studies, marketing, physiotherapy; (b) B.Sc. in chemistry and technology, civil engineering, electrical engineering, environmental science, environmental technology, facility management, informational graphic design, urban regional planning and development, distance learning; (c) European M.Sc. in real estate management; (d) Master's in business administration, facility management, music; (e) M.Sc. in environmental science, environmental technology, nature conservation and biodiversity management, urban and regional planning and development.
Open to: candidates of any nationality holding a secondary school certificate or a university degree.
Duration: Bachelor's: 4 years (possibility to integrate the cursus at its 2nd, 3d or 4th year if the candidate holds the relevant university qualifications); Master's: a further 2 years.
Fees: tuition: Bachelor's, from 3,000-4,780€ per year (depending on the year of the cursus); Bachelor of physiotherapy: 6,140€ per year; first year of Master's, 8,650€, second year, 2,500-3,500€; see website for further information.
Financial assistance: Saxion Universities are able to offer

a limited number of Environmental Science, Chemistry and International Business and Management students a limited scholarship. This fund does not cover all the fees, and its bestowment is based on a student's motivation, academic record and social-financial background. To become eligible for such a scholarship, please write a letter of motivation addressed to the Director of Internationalisation at the Saxion Universities: PO Box 333 NL-7400 AH Deventer, The Netherlands or email internationaloffice@saxion.nl; students must indicate the reasons why they feel they are entitled to such a scholarship, describing academic achievement, social background as well as explaining their desire to study in the Netherlands.
Languages: international programmes are taught in English (TOEFL, IELTS required) and comprise both business and technical studies.
Applications: application forms can be obtained at http://www.saxion.nl/en/applicationform/Combi_form.pdf.

1667 Tilburg University [TU]

PO Box 90153
5000 LE Tilburg
Tel: +31-13-466-2512
Fax: +31-13-466-3072
Web: http://www.tilburguniversity.nl
e-mail: int.office.ec@uvt.nl

📖 Undergraduate and Graduate Programmes

Study Domains: accounting, administration, advertising, business, business administration, economic and commercial sciences, economy, European studies, finance, industry and commerce, international business, international studies, law, management, marketing, trade.
Programmes: Bachelor's and Master's degrees in all major fields (29 of which are English-taught).
Open to: candidates of any nationality holding a secondary school certificate or university degree.
Fees: tuition fees: EEA students under 30: approximately 1,500 €; EEA students over 30: 2,000 €; non EEA students Bachelor's programmes: approximately 5,700 €; non-EEA students Master's: approximately 9,500 €; consult website for further details: http://www.tilburguniversity.nl/iebp.
Languages: Most programmes are entirely in English; Dutch.
Applications: check website for admission requirements for programme of choice and for current application deadlines.

1668 UNESCO-IHE Institute for Water Education [UNESCO-IHE]

PO Box 3015
2601 Delft
Tel: +31-15-215-1715
Fax: +31-15-212-2921
Web: http://www.unesco-ihe.org
e-mail: info@unesco-ihe.org

📖 MSc, PhD, Short Courses, Group and Tailor Made Trainings, On-line Courses

Study Domains: business administration, ecology, environment, engineering, hydrology, marine biology, marine science, transport.
Programmes: International Masters and PhD Programmes in Environmental Science, Water Management, Municipal Water & Infrastructure, Water Science & Engineering.
Description: Coastal Engineering and Port Development, Environmental Planning and Management, Environmental Science and Technology, Groundwater Hydrology, Hydraulic Engineering and River Basin Development, Hydroinformatics, Integrated Urban Engineering, Land and Water Development, Limnology and Wetland Ecosystems, Sanitary Engineering, Surface Water Hydrology, Water Quality Management, Water Resources Management, Water Services Management, Water Supply Engineering.
Open to: graduates of all nationalities with at least 3 years practical experience and a university degree.
Nationality: all.
Duration: MSc: 18 months, PhD: 3 to 4 years; see website for other course durations.
Fees: see website.

Financial assistance: variable; see website for funding possibilities and contact the Netherlands diplomatic mission in your country for further information.
Languages: proficiency in English required.
Applications: see website for further information.

1669 University College Maastricht, Maastricht University [UCM]
PO Box 616
6200 MD Maastricht
Tel: +31-43-388-3500
Fax: +31-43-388-4882
Web: http://www.ucm.nl
e-mail: info@ucm.unimaas.nl

Undergraduate Programmes

Study Domains: humanities and arts, social sciences.
Programmes: Bachelor of Arts and Bachelor of Science.
Description: Liberal arts college, students opt for one of the 3 concentrations: social sciences, humanities or (life) sciences.
Open to: candidates of any country holding a secondary school certificate.
Duration: 3 years; courses begin in September and February.
Fees: tuition fees: EU student:1,476€; non-EU student 2,400€.
Languages: English; TOEFL test required for non-EU students.
Applications: by 1 April for non-EU students, 15 June for EU students.

1670 University of Amsterdam [UvA]
Spui 21
1012 Amsterdam
Tel: +31-20-525-9111
Fax: +31-20-525-2136
Web: http://www.uva.nl
e-mail: info@uva.nl

Undergraduate, Graduate Programmes

Study Domains: all major fields.
Programmes: Bachelor's, Master's and Ph.D. programmes in science, dentistry, law, economics and econometrics, humanities, social and behavioural sciences, medicine.
Description: 62 Bachelor's degree programmes taught in Dutch and over 100 international study programmes taught in English, as well as a range of exchange courses. Most international programmes are at graduate level Most of the international study programmes are Master's or Advanced Master's programmes. Undergraduate programmes are available in the field of economics and business. Certificate programmes are also available for those who are not seeking a university degree at the UvA. All of these international study programmes are aimed at fee-paying independent students. Students wishing to obtain their Bachelor's degree at the UvA (other than in economics and business), can follow one of the 60 Dutch taught undergraduate programmes. (see website under 'Studying in Dutch'.).
Open to: candidates of any country meeting academic, linguistic and financial criteria.
Duration: variable.
Fees: Prospective students can find information regarding these study programmes, fees, facilities, and student life on www.uva.nl/studying.
Applications: directly to each faculty, see website for further information.

UvA Scholarships

Study Domains: business, economic and commercial sciences.
Scholarships: (a) International School for Humanities and Social Sciences (ISHSS) scholarships; (b) Dutch Education: Learning on Toplevel Abroad (DELTA) Scholarships.
Open to: (a) Master's students with an excellent overall grade point average (GPA) equivalent to an A/4 (American system), 1.1 (a first class honours degree in the British system), A (ECTS-system), or > 8.0 (Dutch system); (b) Master's students from Indonesia, China, Taiwan and South Africa.
Value: between 2,500€-3,500€, depending on the length of the study programme.

Applications: scholarship request to be indicated on the ISHSS application form. A committee consisting of academic staff will select candidates with the best overall academic standing. Priority will be given to students of developing countries, but others may apply as well;.

1671 University of Nijmegen Institute for International Health [UON]
Geert Grooteplein Noord 9
PO Box 9101
6500 HB Nijmegen
Tel: +31-24-3613781
Web: http://www.kun.nl/niih/profile.htm

Undergraduate Programmes / Health Care

Study Domains: health and hygiene, medicine.
Programmes: undergraduate studies in medicine and health sciences; subjects include determinants of health (including its cultural dimensions), tropical medicine and public health in developing countries contrasted with that in the Netherlands.
Description: the aim is to give students an orientation towards international aspects of health. Through various elective courses ('Health and Disease in Developing Countries'; 'Public Health in International Perspective') students are given the opportunity to deepen their understanding and acquire skills in aspects of tropical medicine and public health in the South.
Open to: applicants with first degree or diploma in health care or a related field.
Applications: to the above address; see website for further information.

1672 University of Nijmegen, Pallas Consortium [PC]
PO Box 10520
6500 MB Nijmegen
Tel: +31-24-361-3090
Fax: +31-24-361-1207
Web: http://www.pallas.llm.nl
e-mail: pallas@cpo.kun.nl

Graduate Law Studies

Study Domains: international law, law.
Programmes: Master's degree in Law (LL.M).
Description: the programme contains 8 main topics: contracts, international trade, company law, environment law, banking, taxation, competition law and intellectual property.
Open to: candidates of any country holding a university degree in law.
Academic requirements: candidates must present 2 letters of recommendation.
Duration: 1 year beginning in September.
Fees: current registration: 10,950 €; living costs: approx. 600 € per month.
Languages: language of instruction: English (TOEFL/IEITS required).
Applications: by June to the above address.

1673 University of Professional Education, Enschede
Postbus 70000
M.H. Tromplaan 28
7513 Enschede
Tel: +31-53-487-1111
Fax: +31-53-432-6126
Web: http://www.saxion.edu
e-mail: internationaloffice@saxion.nl

Undergraduate, Graduate Programmes

Study Domains: business administration, economic and commercial sciences, education, social work, teacher education.

1674 University of Twente, Enschede

Postbus 217 Drienerlolaan 5
7500 Enschede
Tel: +31-53-489-5489
Fax: +31-53-489-2000
Web: http://www.utwente.nl
e-mail: studievoorlichting@utwente.nl

📖 Undergraduate, Graduate Programmes

Study Domains: all major fields.
Programmes: Bachelor's, Master's and Ph.D. programmes in all major fields.
Open to: candidates of all nationalities meeting academic, financial and linguistic requirements.
Financial assistance: Government scholarships, see entry for NUFFIC.
Applications: to each faculty at the above address.

1675 Utrecht Polytechnic [HVU]

Hogeschool van Utrecht
Postbus 573
3500 AN Utrecht
Tel: +31-30-275-8928
Fax: +31-30-258-6448
Web: http://www.hvu-international.com
e-mail: io@hvu.nl

📖 Graduate Programmes

Study Domains: economic and commercial sciences, education, engineering, health and hygiene, journalism, management, sciences, social sciences, teacher education.
Programmes: degree courses in the fields of healthcare, journalism and communication, teacher training, science and technology, economics and management, and applied social studies.
Open to: applicants of all nationalities meeting academic, linguistic and financial criteria; see website for further information.
Applications: to each faculty; see website or write to above address for contact details.

1676 Utrecht School of the Arts [HKU]

Office for International Relations
PO Box 1520
3500 BM Utrecht
Tel: +31-30-233-2256
Fax: +31-30-233-2096
Web: http://www.hku.nl
e-mail: biz@central.hku.nl

📖 Undergraduate, Graduate Programmes

Study Domains: applied arts, arts, design, economy, education, fine arts, industrial design, music and musicology, performing arts, technology, visual arts.
Programmes: undergraduate and graduate programmes leading to Bachelor and Master degrees at the following faculties: (a) Faculty of Visual Arts and Design; (b) Faculty of Art, Media & Technology; (c) Faculty of Music; (d) Faculty of Theatre; (e) Interfaculty / Art & Economy.
Description: (a) Bachelor of Fine Art (B.F.A.), Design (B.Des.), Education (B.Ed.), Art and Technology (B.A.T.), Art and Economics (B.A.E.); Master of Arts (M.A.); (b) Bachelor of Art and Technology (B.A.T.), Design (B.Des.), Music (B.Mus.), Master of Arts (M.A.), Arts in European Media (EMMA), Philosophy (M.Phil.), Doctor of Philosophy (Ph.D.); (c) Bachelor of Music (B.Mus.); Education (B.Ed.), Art and Economics (BAE); (d) Bachelor of Theatre (B.Th.) in Acting, Writing for Performance, Theatre and Education; Bachelor of Education (B.Ed.) in Theatre, Bachelor of Design (B.Des.) in Theatre Design, Bachelor of Art and Technology (B.A.T.) in Design for Virtual Theatre and Games; (e) Bachelor of Art and Economics (B.A.E.), Master of Arts in Art Media Management in European Context, also professional preparatory component of the teacher training courses B.Ed. Visual Art and Design, B.Ed. Music and B.Ed. Theatre.
Open to: candidates of any nationality holding a secondary school certificate.
Applications: variable, depending on programme; see

website for addresses and email addresses of each faculty.

1677 Utrecht University [UU]

Postbus 80125
3508 TC Utrecht
Tel: +31-30-253-2670
Fax: +31-30-253-3388
Web: http://www.uu.nl

📖 Undergraduate, Graduate Programmes

Study Domains: all major fields.
Programmes: degree courses at all levels and in all major fields; special programmes: M.Sc. in tropical bee and beekeeping in tropical countries at the Faculty of Biology; risk assessment and risk management of chemicals, at the Research Institute of Toxicology.
Open to: candidates of all nationalities meeting academic, financial and linguistic requirements.
Duration: variable according to programme.
Applications: to above address; see website for further information.

1678 Utrecht University Medical Centre, School of Medical Sciences [UU]

Admissions Office, Student Service Centre
PO Box 80125
3508 TC Utrecht
Tel: +31-30-253-8229
Web: http://www.med.uu.nl

📖 Graduate Programmes / Medical Sciences

Study Domains: medicine.
Programmes: Master's degree in biomedical sciences and postgraduate courses in medicine, medical biology and nursing sciences.
Open to: applicants with at least 3 years of medical studies.
Applications: to the above address; see website for application details:
http://www.onderwijsinstituut.umcutrecht.nl/afdeling/overzicht/overzicht.asp?dep=25&mmid=367&oid=630.

1679 Utrecht University, Faculty of Veterinary Medicine [UU]

PO Box 80.163
3508TD Utrecht
Tel: +31-30-253-4851
Fax: +31-30-253-7727
Web: http://www.vet.uu.nl

📖 Graduate Programmes / Veterinary Sciences

Study Domains: health and hygiene, laboratory techniques.
Programmes: (a) M.Sc. in veterinary epidemiology and herd health; (b) M.Sc. in animal pathology; (c) course in laboratory science; (d) M.Sc. in veterinary microbiology and immunology; (e) M.Sc. in veterinary anaesthesiology.
Open to: candidates with (a) D.V. M. (Doctor of Veterinary Medicine) degree; (b) D.V.M. or Master's degree in biomedical sciences; (c) M.Sc. in biology, medicine, veterinary medicine, zoology or pharmacy; (d) D.V.M., B.VSc. or B.Sc. in biological sciences; (e) D.V.M. or B.Sc. in veterinary science.
Duration: (a) and (e) 1-1/2 years; (b) and (d) 2 years; (c) 2 weeks.
Financial assistance: scholarships available through the Netherlands Fellowship Programme; information and applications from the Netherlands Embassy in the applicant's home country.
Languages: instruction in English.
Applications: (a), (b), (d) and (e) 1 July; (c) 1 May, at the above address.

1680 Van Hall Institute [VHI]
International Office
PO Box 1528
8901 BV Leeuwarden
Tel: +31-58-284-6264
Fax: +31-58-284-6423
Web: http://www.vhall.nl
e-mail: international@pers.vhall.nl

📖 Graduate Programmes / Nature Management

Study Domains: ecology, environment.
Programmes: International programme of studies in: (a) Environmental technology and protection; (b) Environmental policy and management; (c) Nature and wildlife management; (d) Geographical information; (e) Sustainable soil management; (f) Rural resources management.
Open to: applicants in at least their second or third year of B.Sc. programme (a) to (c) in natural sciences or technological sciences, proficient in chemistry and mathematics at first-year university level and computer literate; (d) and (e) agricultural/environmental sciences, geography, civil engineering, tourism, rural resources management with computer and mathematics skills equivalent to first-year university level; (f) in agriculture or rural resources management, with computer skills.
Duration: 8 to 40 weeks.
Languages: instruction in English.
Applications: to the above address.

1681 Wageningen Agricultural University [WAU]
Dean's Office for International Students
PO Box 453
6700 AL Wageningen
Tel: +31-317-484-472
Fax: +31-317-484-884
Web: http://www.wau.nl
e-mail: info@www.wag-ur.nl

📖 Graduate Programmes

Study Domains: agriculture, agronomic sciences, ecology, environment, forestry, information science.
Programmes: M.Sc. programmes in: (a) agricultural economics and marketing: agricultural and environmental economics and policy, farm management, marketing and consumer behaviour, agricultural development economics; (b) agricultural engineering: farm mechanization, control and systems engineering, soil tillage; (c) animal science: animal breeding and husbandry, veterinary epidemiology and economics, tropical animal production, animal nutrition, grassland and forage science; (d) aquaculture: animal level (fish reproduction, nutrition and growth, fish health control); system level (aquacultural management, fisheries management); (e) biotechnology: agrofood and bioprocess technology, environmental biotechnology, plant and microbial production; (f) crop science: crop breeding, production, protection, greenhouse horticulture; (g) ecological agriculture: crop livestock, soil ecology, farming systems research, ecological research methodology; (h) environmental sciences: environmental protection, health, technology and management; (i) geographic information systems: geo-information management, dedicated application development; (j) management of agricultural knowledge systems: innovation processes in rural resource management, sociological research, design of learning processes in education and extension, making policy on the interventions and management of implementing organizations; (k) soil and water: soil survey and land evaluation, pedology, soil fertility, soil chemistry, soil and plant analysis, soil physics and agrohydrology, drainage, water resources management and hydrology, irrigation, soil and water conservation; (l) tropical forestry: social forestry, silviculture and forest ecology; (m) urban environmental management: environmental impact assessment, soil, water and air.
Open to: applicants of all nationalities holding a first degree (B.Sc. or equivalent); fluency in English and working experience requested; entrance examination.
Duration: 74 weeks.
Fees: see website for fee information.
Applications: before 15 November, to the above address.

📖 Master of Business Administration / Agribusiness

Study Domains: economic and commercial sciences, economy, food, food industry, management, marketing.
Programmes: Master of Business Administration in management studies, marketing and management research, general economics, agricultural economics, food science, computer science and mathematics the food industry and agribusiness.
Open to: candidates of any nationality holding a university or college degree and with working experience of evident affinity with the food industry and agribusiness.
Duration: 57 weeks.
Languages: instruction in English.
Applications: to the WSM Business School, Building No. 425; Lawickse Allee 11; 6701 AN Wageningen; tel: +31 317 485416; +31 317 485430; email: office.wsm@wur.nl:www.wau.nl/wsm.

1682 Wageningen University
PO Box 9101
6700 HB Wageningen
Tel: +31-317-489-111
Web: http://www.wur.nl
e-mail: info@wur.nl

📖 Graduate Programmes

Study Domains: agriculture, agronomic sciences, biology, botany, business administration, ecology, environment, economic and commercial sciences, fisheries, food industry, geology, horticulture, hydrology, landscape architecture, management, meteorology, recreation and leisure, social sciences, sociology, urbanism.
Programmes: Study programmes cover the full range from plant sciences, food technology and health to supply chain management, from environmental sciences to sociology and economics. Wageningen University offers Dutch Study Programmes as well as International Education at (MSc, BSc, MBA and PhD levels.
Subjects: Communication Science; Food Quality Management; International Development Studies; Management of Agro-ecological Knowledge and Social Change; Management, Economics and Consumer Studies; Agricultural and Bioresource Engineering; Bioinformatics; Biotechnology; Food Safety; Food Technology; Molecular Sciences; Nutrition and Health; Animal Sciences and Aquaculture; Aquaculture and Fisheries; Biology; Organic Agriculture; Plant Biotechnology; Plant Sciences; Earth System Science; Environmental Sciences; Forest and Nature Conservation; Geo-information Science; Hydrology and Water Quality; International Land and Water Management; Landscape Architecture and Planning; Leisure, Tourism and Environment; Meteorology and Air Quality; Soil Science; Urban Environmental Management.
Applications: see website for full details.

New Zealand
Academic year: March to November.
Monetary unit: New Zealand Dollar (NZ$).
National student admission: Foreign students wishing to study at New Zealand universities should apply directly to the university of their choice (see addresses below). Students seeking first-year places must have acceptable university entrance qualifications, of which examples follow: Australia Year 12 and acceptable Tertiary Entrance Score; Malaysia STPM; United Kingdom any combination of A, AS and GCSE acceptable for admission to a British university; United States High School Diploma and acceptable score in SAT; International Baccalaureate acceptable providing the diploma has been awarded (minimum 24 points); countries offering Cambridge GCB 3 passes at Advanced level (not including General Studies) including at least one a C grade or better. All passes must be achieved at the same sitting.
Language: Students whose first language is not English must provide satisfactory evidence of competence in the English language e.g.; 550 in the Test of English as a Foreign Language (TOEFL) or 6.5 in the International English Language Testing System (IELTS).
Immigration requirements: Foreign students intending to

study in New Zealand should contact the nearest New Zealand embassy or high commission to obtain information on visa regulations. There is a charge for student visas. Police clearances are also required.
Estimated expenses for one academic year: Tuition fees vary according to higher education institution. Living costs: the New Zealand Immigration Service requires that overseas students have sufficient funds for living expenses (accommodation, books, etc.); institutions recommend approximately NZ$10,000 per year for living expenses.
Information services: Official national bodies:
• Ministry of Education, Private Box 1666, Wellington.
• Ministry of Foreign Affairs and Trade, Development Cooperation Division, Private Bag 18 901, Wellington.
Other agencies:
• Students from the South Pacific: The Assisted Overseas Students' Placement Service, New Zealand Vice-Chancellors' Committee, PO Box 11 915; Wellington; tel. +64-4-801-5086; fax +64-4-801-5089.
• Graduate Students: Scholarships Officer; email: schols@nzvcc.ac.nz), New Zealand Vice-Chancellors' Committee, PO Box 11 915; Wellington; tel: +64-4-801-5086; fax +64-4-801-5089.
• Undergraduate Students: Academic Officer (e-mail: angela@nzvcc.ac.nz), New Zealand Vice-Chancellors' Committee, PO Box 11 915; Wellington; tel. +64-4-801-5086; fax +64-4-801-5089.
Scholarships for international students: New Zealand Development Scholarships (NZDS) are for full-time multi-year courses in New Zealand for tertiary level studies. For countries outside the Pacific, study is usually at postgraduate level, with the exception of Timor-Leste and Rapa Nui; for further information http://www.nzaid.govt.nz/scholarships/nzds.html.
Open and distance learning: The Open Polytechnic provides a full range of distance learning packages at trades, technician and degree levels by correspondence, linked with periodic face-to-face practical tuition. Massey University offers a range of Degree and Diploma courses by correspondence. The University of Otago complements the Massey University extramural programme by offering a number of courses through its 'teaching at a distance' teleconference network. The University of Waikato offers off-campus certificates at first-year undergraduate level in association with regional polytechnics. Access to internationally offered degrees can be gained through some polytechnics or the Internet. (Source: I.A.U. World Higher Education Database.).
Recognition of studies and qualification: New Zealand Qualifications Authority (NZQA) (Mana Tohu Matauranga o Aotearoa) International relations; PO Box 160, 125 The Terrace, Wellington, New Zealand; tel: +64-4-802-3000; fax: +64-4-802-3112; email: arenvr@nzqa.govt.nz; web: http://www.nzqa.govt.nz.
Publications / Websites:
• 'Secondary Education in New Zealand'.
• 'Tertiary Education in New Zealand'.
• 'Study in New Zealand Guides' in Japanese, Korean, Chinese, Indonesian, Thai languages. These publications are published by New Zealand Education International, Ltd., and are held by most New Zealand Education Centres in: Tokyo, Hong Kong, Bangkok, Kuala Lumpur, Jakarta and in most Tradenz Offices throughout the world.

1683 Auckland University of Technology [AUT]
Private Bag 92006
1020 Auckland
Tel: +64-9-917-9637
Fax: +64-9-917-9925
Web: http://www.aut.ac.nz
e-mail: international.centre@aut.ac.nz

📖 Undergraduate, Graduate, Postgraduate Programmes
Study Domains: all major fields.
Programmes: undergraduate, graduate and postgraduate programmes leading to Bachelor's, Master's and Ph.D. degrees.
Description: also offering programmes in e-business,

midwifery, occupational therapy, physiotherapy, psychotherapy.
Languages: English.
Applications: for further information contact: Tere Daly, International Student Advisor, at the above address.

🎓 Doctoral Education Awards
Study Domains: medicine.
Scholarships: Doctoral Education Awards.
Applications: for information contact Peter Fleming, Executive Officer and Manager.

1684 Department of Internal Affairs Te Tari Taiwhenua [DOIA]
46 Waring Taylor Street
PO Box 805
Wellington
Tel: +64-4-495-7200
Web: http://www.dia.govt.nz/diawebsite.nsf/wpg_UR L/Services-Trust-&-Fellowship-Grants-Index?
e-mail: info@dia.govt.nz or webmaster@dia.govt.nz

🎓 Trusts and Fellowships
Study Domains: education, humanities and arts, research.
Scholarships: (a) Norman Kirk Memorial Trust;
(b) Peace and Disarmament Education Trust.
Open to: (a) disadvantaged or disabled candidates of South Pacific countries who are committed to taking advantage of 'second chance' education or training; candidates of South Pacific countries seeking a qualification or training which will enable them to make a greater contribution in the community; (b) PACDAC/PADET Scholarships are designed to support appropriate postgraduate research by Masters and Doctoral students at New Zealand universities. Anyone who is, or intends to enrol as, a postgraduate degree student pursuing research of interest to the Public Advisory Committee on Disarmament and Arms Control (PACDAC) and the Peace and Disarmament Education Trust (PADET), may apply for a scholarship; applicants must be enrolled in a Ph.D. or M.A. degree course of study at a New Zealand university during the period for which the scholarship is sought.
Place of study: in New Zealand universities.
Applications: through application form at above website.

1685 Health Research Council of New Zealand [HRC]
PO Box 5541
Wellesley Street
Auckland
Tel: +64-9-379-8227
Fax: +64-9-377-9988
Web: http://www.hrc.govt.nz

🎓 Postdoctoral Fellowships
Study Domains: health and hygiene, medicine, research.
Scholarships: Postdoctoral Fellowships.
Description: biomedical research and public health.
Open to: candidates having recently completed a Ph.D. or equivalent degree.
Place of study: in New Zealand universities, hospitals and other suitable research institutions.
Duration: up to 4 years.
Applications: biomedical: 1 April; public health: 1 April and 1 September on form HRC-FA/02; to the Director at the above address.

1686 International Pacific College [IPC]
Private Bag 11-021
57 Aokautere Drive
Palmerston North
Tel: +64-6-354-0922
Fax: +64-6-354-0935
Web: http://www.ipc.ac.nz
e-mail: info@ipc.ac.nz

📖 Undergraduate, Graduate Programmes
Study Domains: business administration, health and hygiene, home economics, social sciences, social work, tourism, hotel and catering management.
Programmes: Undergraduate and graduate programmes in

business administration; health sciences; tourism; Social
Sciences; welfare and protective services.

1687 Lincoln University [LU]
The Registrar
PO Box 94
8150 Canterbury
Tel: +64-3-325-2811
Fax: +64-3-325-2944
Web: http://www.lincoln.ac.nz
e-mail: info@lincoln.ac.nz

📖 Undergraduate, Graduate, Postgraduate Programmes
Study Domains: computer science, ecology, environment,
economy, finance, forestry, marketing, zoology.
Programmes: (a) Bachelor of Commerce in forestry:
marketing, management, finance, economics, computing,
forestry science, wood utilization; (b) Bachelor of Science in
ecology and conservation: a scientific approach to resource
management with courses in zoology, ecology, resource
management.
Open to: New Zealand and international students who
meet the university entry requirements.
Duration: 3 academic years; courses begin in February or
July.
Fees: tuition per year: NZ$10,000-$14,500 depending on
programme.
Applications: by 30 October for semester beginning in
February; by 30 April for semester beginning in July.

🎓 Scholarships
Study Domains: all major fields.
Scholarships: (a) Doctoral Scholarship; (b) Master's
Scholarship; (c) Graduate Scholarship.
Open to: all students eligible for entrance into their
proposed field of study at Lincoln University; normal
admission criteria apply; proficiency in English is required
(TOEFL 600; IELTS 6.0).
Duration: for minimum time for completion of degree;
non-renewable.
Value: (a) NZ$11,000 per year; (b) NZ$9,000 per year; (c)
NZ$6,000 per year; students are also entitled to the New
Zealand student tuition fee for a postgraduate degree and a
once-only thesis cost payment of NZ$550.
Applications: by 1 October.

1688 Massey University [MU]
International Students' Office
Tennent Drive
Private Bag 11 222
Palmerston North
Tel: +64-6-350-5549
Fax: +64-6-350-5698
Web: http://www.massey.ac.nz
e-mail: international@massey.ac.nz

📖 Undergraduate, Graduate Programmes
Study Domains: all major fields.
Programmes: most fields, excluding medicine and
dentistry.
Open to: candidates of all nationalities holding a 1st class
Honours degree; approval by Doctoral Research Committee
for provisional registration as a Ph.D. candidate plus
departmental approval; admission tests (written or interviews)
plus recommendations; English proficiency required.
Duration: 3 years.
Fees: tuition: NZ$12,400-$30,000 per year; living
expenses: NZ$7,000-$10,000 per year.
Financial assistance: doctoral scholarships available;
contact the Scholarship Officer for further information.
Applications: by 1 July or 1 October; to the International
Students' Office at the above address.

🎓 Massey Doctoral Fellowships
Study Domains: all major fields.
Scholarships: Massey Doctoral Scholarships in most
fields with the exception of medicine and dentistry.
Open to: candidates with a first-class honours degree and
proficiency in English.
Duration: 30 months plus a 6-month extension.
Value: partial tuition.

Applications: by 1 July and 1 October.

1689 Ministry of Foreign Affairs, Official Development Assistance Programme [MFT]
Private Bag 18901
Wellington
Tel: +64-4-439-8000
Fax: +64-4-439-8511
Web: http://www.mft.govt.nz
e-mail: enquiries@mft.govt.nz

📖 Official Development Assistance Programme
Study Domains: development studies.
Description: wide range of short courses offered at
secondary and tertiary institutions; places are determined
annually in bilateral negotiations on a government to
government basis; private student quotas vary from country to
country.
Open to: candidates with qualifications that vary according
to region and country.
Financial assistance: training awards under OCA cover
transfer, subsistence costs and tuition.
Applications: by June to education authorities in home
countries for referral to New Zealand diplomatic post.

📖 Training Courses
Study Domains: English, technical education, technology.
Programmes: specific training courses arranged on
demand, facilities and personnel available; fields of study
include diploma in teaching of English as a second language,
seed technology, geothermal technology, sawmilling and saw
maintenance, etc.
Open to: qualified nationals of all countries.
Applications: further information obtainable from the
authority in candidate's country responsible for selecting
students and trainers under international technical assistance
programmes.

🎓 Scholarships and Awards
Study Domains: all major fields.
Scholarships: (a) Study awards; (b) Short-term training
awards; (c) Aotearoa Scholarships; (d) Postgraduate
scholarship scheme; (e) Third Country Training Awards.
Description: (a) any area of study agreed to between the
Government of New Zealand and the partner government to
meet identified human resource development needs in support
of agreed bilateral development strategies; (b) a wide range of
vocational and/or skills courses or work attachments; area of
study agreed to between the Government of New Zealand and
the partner government to meet identified human resource
development needs in support of agreed bilateral development
strategies; (c) skills-related courses of developmental
relevance to their home countries; (d) areas of developmental
relevance to their home countries; preference given to
postgraduate diploma and Master's level; (e) areas of study
agreed to between the New Zealand and the partner
government; may include training options.
Open to: (a) and (b) applicants nominated by bilateral
Official Development Assistance (ODA) partner governments
under the New Zealand ODA Programme; (c) persons from
South Pacific developing countries; (d) persons from
specified developing countries; (e) candidates selected by
bilateral country governments.
Place of study: (a) and (c) in New Zealand at selected
universities, polytechnics and schools; (b) in New Zealand;
(d) in New Zealand at universities and polytechnics; (e)
tertiary educational institutions in the South Pacific.
Value: (a) tuition, enrolment/orientation fees; economy
fare travel and provisions for students to meet course and
basic living costs from a set monetary contribution; (b)
payment of fees, return economy airfares, an establishment
grant, a basic living allowance and provision for health care;
(c) partially funded, covers tuition, enrolment/orientation fees,
return economy fare travel and provision for students to meet
course and basic living costs from a set monetary
contribution; (e) payment of fees, return economy airfares,
grants and allowances.
Applications: (a), (b) and (e) to the agency in their home
country responsible for selecting persons for study or training
abroad under New Zealand's Development Cooperation
Programme; (c) to CITEC Training Solutions Ltd, Private

Bag 39 807, Wellington Mail Centre, New Zealand; (d) to an eligible institution on its prescribed application form.

1690 New Zealand Vice-Chancellors' Committee [NZVC]
The Scholarships Manager
PO Box 11915
Wellington
Tel: +64-4-381-8510
Fax: +64-4-381-8501
Web: http://www.nzvcc.ac.nz
e-mail: schols@nzvcc.ac.nz

Scholarships
Study Domains: all major fields.
Scholarships: Over 40 scholarships for graduate and postgraduate study, together with 12 for undergraduate study. Most scholarships are designed to assist New Zealanders to further their education. No scholarship is open to application from international students except for Commonwealth Scholarships, which are available to students of Commonwealth countries, and are for graduate study only. Application forms must be obtained in the student's country of citizenship.
Applications: contact the University International Offices at each university for further information; all New Zealand universities award scholarships for study at the graduate level which are open to application from international students; see website or contact New Zealand Embassy/Consulate for addresses.

1691 New Zealand's International Aid & Development Agency [NZAID]
Private Bag 18-901
Wellington
Fax: +64-4-439-8515
Web: http://www.nzaid.govt.nz/scholarships/nzds.html

New Zealand Development Scholarships (NZDS)
Study Domains: all major fields.
Scholarships: New Zealand Development Scholarships (NZDS) are for full-time multi-year courses in New Zealand for tertiary level studies. For countries outside the Pacific, study is usually at postgraduate level, with the exception of Timor-Leste and Rapa Nui; for further information http://www.nzaid.govt.nz/scholarships/nzds.html.

1692 University of Otago [UOO]
PO Box 56
Dunedin
Tel: +64-3-479-8252
Web: http://www.otago.ac.nz
e-mail: liaison@otago.ac.nz

Undergraduate, Graduate, Postgraduate Programmes
Study Domains: all major fields.
Programmes: Bachelor's, Master's, Ph.D., Graduate Diploma.
Subjects: arts, music, theology, sciences, physical education, consumer and applied sciences, land surveying, physiotherapy, pharmacy, medical laboratory science, commerce, medicine and dentistry.
Open to: students holding qualifications acceptable to the University for admission; applicants whose first language is not English must provide satisfactory evidence of proficiency: TOEFL 550 (TWE 4.0) or 6.0 IELTS minimum acceptable scores.
Duration: Bachelor's: 3 years; Bachelor's with Honours: 4 years; Graduate Diploma: 1 year; Master's: 1 to 2 years; Doctor of Philosophy: 3 years.
Applications: for all further information contact the University at the above address.

1693 University of Waikato [UOW]
Private Bag 3105
Hamilton
Tel: +64-7-838-4439
Fax: +64-7-838-4269
Web: http://www.waikato.ac.nz/international/
e-mail: int.centre@waikato.ac.nz

Undergraduate, Graduate Programmes
Study Domains: all major fields.
Programmes: Bachelor's, Master's and Diploma programmes.
Open to: secure student visa in country of residence before arriving.
Duration: 1 to 5 years depending on the programme.
Languages: English and Maori.
Applications: by 1 December for March entry; 1 May for entry in July; or 20 November preceding year for Summer school; application forms on website: www.waikato.ac.nz/international/admission.htm; fax: +64 7 838 4269, telephone: +64 7 838 4439; email: intlc@waikato.ac.nz.

1694 Victoria University of Wellington [VUOW]
International Students Office
PO Box 600
Wellington
Tel: +64-4-463-5350
Fax: +64-4-463-5056
Web: http://www2.vuw.ac.nz/home/index.asp
e-mail: victoria-international@vuw.ac.nz

Undergraduate, Graduate, Postgraduate Programmes
Study Domains: administration, architecture, arts, languages, law, literature and civilization, sciences, trade.
Open to: candidates of any country fulfilling the necessary requirements; a good knowledge of English is required (TOEFL score 550 or IELTS score 6.0).
Duration: varies according to course.
Fees: tuition from NZ$4,700-$28,500 per year depending on subject of study.
Applications: by 1 December prior to the year of study; further information can be obtained from the above address.

Nicaragua
Año académico: Mayo a febrero.
Organización de la enseñanza superior: La enseñanza superior se brinda en tres tipos de instituciones: las universidades, los centros técnicos superiores (CETS), y los centros de investigación y de capacitación.
Moneda nacional: Córdoba.
Admisiones para estudiantes extranjeros: Diploma de bachiller o título de técnico medio para los estudios técnicos o título de maestro de educación primaria.
Conocimientos lingüísticos: Es indispensable dominar suficientemente el idioma español.
Formalidades de inmigración: La información debe solicitarse en el Ministerio del Interior, Sección de Migración, Managua.
Servicios de información:
• Ministerio de Educación Pública, Dirección de Extensión Cultural, Managua.
• Universidad Nacional Autónoma de Nicaragua, León.
• Departamento de Bienestar Estudiantil (proporciona orientación general y facilita direcciones para encontrar alojamiento en casas particulares).
Convalidación de estudios y diplomas: Asociación Nicaragüense de Instituciones de Educación Superior, Recinto universitario "Ruben Darío", Managua.

1695 Universidad Católica "Redemptoris Mater" [UNICA]
Carretera Masaya, Km. 9.500
Apartado Postal 6095
Managua
Tel: (505) 276 0004
Fax: (505) 276 0590
Web: http://www.unica.edu.ni
e-mail: info@unica.edu.ni

 Carreras profesionales

Campos de estudios: arquitectura, ciencias económicas y comerciales, derecho, educación, formación de docentes, ingeniería, ingeniería civil, relaciones internacionales.
Descripción:
(a) Facultad de ciencias económicas y administrativas: administración de empresas (mención en: mercadeo, agroindustria, banca y finanzas), economía empresarial, turismo y administración hotelera;
(b) Facultad de ciencias jurídicas y sociales: derecho, relaciones internacionales;
(c) Facultad de humanidades: ciencias de la educación (pedagogía con mención en administración de la educación, especialidad en pre-escolar, matemáticas, español, filosofía, ciencias religiosas, psicología educativa);
(d) Facultad de ingeniería y arquitectura: arquitectura, ingeniería civil, ingeniería industrial, ingeniería en sistemas de información.

1696 Universidad Centroamericana [UCA]
Apartado Postal 60
Avenida Universitaria y Pista Juan Pablo II
Managua
Tel: (505) 278 3923 al 27
Fax: (505) 267 01 06
Web: http://www.uca.edu.ni
e-mail: asrector@ns.uca.edu.ni

 Programas universitarios

Campos de estudios: todas las materias principales, administración, administración de empresas, comercio, economía, marketing, relaciones internacionales.
Descripción:
(a) Licenciaturas en: administración de empresas, comercio internacional, economía aplicada y desarrollo, producción agropecuaria, comunicación social, derecho, sociología, trabajo social, ciencias de la cultura, psicología, enseñanza del inglés;
(b) Postgrados y maestrías en: administración y dirección empresarial, relaciones internacionales, economía y desarrollo;
(c) Programas especiales de formación en: gerencia de mercadotecnia empresarial, técnico superior en administración de empresas, en comercio internacional, cursos de idiomas, administración y especialización aduanera.
Se destina(n): a nacionales de cualquier país que hayan concluido su bachillerato para optar al programa (a) y (c) o estudiantes con título de licenciatura o ingeniería o egresados de alguna carrera universitaria para optar al programa (b); examen de admisión escrito y entrevista dependiendo de la carrera seleccionada.
Duración: de 4 a 5 años.
Asistencia financiera: becas para estudiantes de escasos recursos.
Inscripciones: hasta el 13 de marzo en la Facultad que corresponde.

1697 Universidad de Las Américas [ULAM]
Apartado A-279
Managua
Tel: (505) 248 3081
Fax: (505) 248 3082
Web: http://www.ulam.com.ni
e-mail: ulam@netport.com.ni

 Programas universitarios

Campos de estudios: administración de empresas, comercio, contabilidad, empresas internacionales, finanzas, marketing, turismo, hotelería.

Descripción: Carreras profesionales en áreas económico-administrativas, postgrados y maestrías.
Duración: 4 años las licenciaturas.

1698 Universidad Evangélica Nicaragüense Martin Luther King [UENIC-MLK]
PO Box 4763
Colonia Los Robles, Plaza El Sol
Managua
Tel: +505-2-701-600
Fax: +505-2-770-157
Web: http://www.uenic.edu.ni
e-mail: uenic@tmx.com.ni

 Programa de becas

Campos de estudios: todas las materias principales.
Se conceden: a estudiantes de escasos recursos y alto promedio académico.
Importe: 250 dólares de los Estados Unidos para gastos de enseñanza.
Solicitudes: hasta fin de febrero.

Niger

Année universitaire: octobre à juin.
Unité monétaire: franc CFA.
Admission pour étudiants du pays: Les étudiants étrangers doivent être titulaires du baccalauréat ou obtenir l'équivalence de ce
diplôme. L'admission est subordonnée à la réussite d'un examen spécial ou d'un concours professionnel.
Connaissances linguistiques requises: Bonne connaissance du français ou de l'anglais.
Services d'accueil et d'information:
Services d'accueil et d'information.
• Centre des oeuvres universitaires (peut éventuellement s'occuper des échanges internationaux d'étudiants et les aider à trouver un logement).
• Le Centre des oeuvres universitaires et les facultés assurent l'accueil des étudiants étrangers. Dans le cas où ceux-ci bénéficient de bourses, ils ont les mêmes avantages que les étudiants nigériens.
Reconnaissance des études et diplômes: Direction des Examens, Concours et Équivalences, Ministère de l'Enseignement supérieur, de la Recherche et de la Technologie; PO Box 628; 10896 Niamey; Niger; tél.: +227-722-620.
Publications / Sites Web:
• «Renseignements pratiques».

1699 Centre régional Agrhymet du CILSS [CRA]
BP 11011
Niamey
Tel: +227-733-116
Fax: +227-732-435
Web: http://www.agrhymet.ne
e-mail: admin@agrhymet.ne

 Formations d'ingénieur / technicien

Domaines d'étude: agriculture, botanique, hydrologie, ingénierie, technologie.
Programmes: programmes de formation de cadres des services de la protection des végétaux des pays membres du Comité inter-États de la lutte contre la sécheresse dans le Sahel (CILSS); (a) formations du niveau ingénieur en agrométéorologie et en hydrologie; (b) formations du niveau technicien supérieur en agrométéorologie, en hydrologie, en protection des végétaux et en maintenance des instruments.
A l'intention de: (a) 3 ans (niveau à la sortie BAC + 5); (b) 2 ans (niveau à la sortie BAC + 2).
Frais: environ 2 millions FCFA pour une année.
Inscriptions: à l'adresse ci-dessus.

Nigeria

Academic year: September to June.
Organization of higher education system: Higher education in Nigeria refers to different forms of education after secondary education. It consists of three major categories of institutions in the higher education sub-sector: (a) the universities and the inter-university centre, (b) the polytechnics and monotechnics and (c) the colleges of education. According to the Nigerian Constitution, both the Federal and the State governments may provide and legislate on higher education, however, private sector participation and initiatives are encouraged. There are currently 55 universities, 109 polytechnics and 71 colleges of education in the country. Tuition is free for all local students in all higher education institutions owned by the federal government. The universities award degrees at all levels (B.S.; M.S; PhD), the polytechnics award national and higher national diplomas (N.D. and H.N.D.) while the colleges of education award the National Certificate in Education (N.C.E.), the minimum qualification for teachers. Undergraduate study programmes generally last four years; Master's programmes require a minimum of eighteen months, while doctoral programmes last for at least three years. The other study programmes generally require three years of study. Various certificate courses are available across all levels of study and their duration may last from twelve to twenty-four months. The Joint Admissions and Matriculations Board (JAMB) conducts the University Matriculation Examinations (UME) for prospective students seeking admission to Nigerian universities. Admission to the polytechnics and colleges of education requires passing the Polytechnics and Colleges of Education (PCE) examination. The Federal Ministry of Education has the overall responsibility for quality control, policy formulation and setting guidelines according to the general policy thrust of government for the sector. Three government agencies set the minimum standards for each of the three higher education sub-sectors and they also have the responsibility of accreditation and quality control in all the higher institutions, public as well as private.
Monetary unit: Naira (N).
National student admission: All candidates should have qualifications equivalent to the General Certificate of Education in at least 5 subjects, including mathematics, English language and three relevant subjects after secondary school studies. Applications must be made through the Registrar of the university or institution concerned. Entrance examinations may be required for certain programmes. Three credit passes at A level, National Diploma or other advanced certificates may be evaluated as advanced standing or direct entry into 200 level of first degree programmes.
Language: Good knowledge of English is essential for regular university courses; students require credit level passes in the subject.
Immigration requirements: International students require a student visa obtainable from the Immigration Department of the Federal Ministry of Internal Affairs.
Estimated expenses for one academic year: Tuition: variable according to study programme; from US$1,000-4,000; housing: US$7,00-1,000.
Information services:
• Federal Ministry of Education, Federal Scholarship Board, Plot 245, Samuel Ademulegun Street, Central Business District, P.M.B. 134, Abuja, Nigeria; tel: +234-9-670-6544
• Nigerian National Commission for UNESCO; Plot 245, Samuel Ademulegun Street, P.M.B. 476, Garki, Abuja.
• National Universities Commission, Aja-Nwachukwu House, Plot 430, Aguiyi Ironsi Street, Maitama, P.M.B. 237, Garki, Abuja; email: pokebukola@nuc.edu.ng.; web: http://www.nuc.edu.ng
• National Board for Technical Education, Plot B Bida Road, P.M.B. 2239, Kaduna; email: nyakubu@nbte.nigeria.org
• National Commission for Colleges of Education, Plot 829, Cadastral Zone A01, Ralph Sodeinde Street, P.M.B. 0394, Garki, Abuja; email: info@ncce.edu.ng; web: http://www.ncce.edu.ng
• Joint Admissions and Matriculations Board (JAMB); web: http://www.jambng.com
• Nigerian Embassy or Mission in student's home country.
Scholarships for international students: Limited scholarships are available to international students under bilateral education agreements or the Commonwealth Fellowship Awards; these are administered by the Federal Scholarship Board (FSB).
Open and distance learning: The National Open University of Nigeria (NOUN) offers open and distance learning programmes in arts and social sciences at diploma, degree and higher degree levels.
Recognition of studies and qualification:
• For local institutions: Benchmarks are established by the National Universities Commission, the National Commission for Colleges of Education and the National Board for Technical Education.
• For off-shore degrees and certificates: National Standing Committee for the Evaluation of Foreign Qualifications, Federal Ministry of Education; Educational Support Services Department; Evaluation and Accreditation Division; Federal Secretariat Phase III; Shehu Shagari Way; Abuja; Nigeria; tel/fax: +234-9-314-1215.
Accommodation services: Student hostel accommodations are provided by individual institutions. In some cases international students are given preference on choice and type of room.
Publications / Websites:
• Individual universities publish a student's handbook which is a general guide for students and is usually on sale at each institution.

1700 Ahmadu Bello University [ABU]
Zaria
Tel: +234-695-0581
Fax: +234-695-0022

📖 Undergraduate, Graduate Programmes

Study Domains: all major fields, library science.
Programmes: undergraduate and graduate programmes in all major fields; library and information service programme.
Open to: nationals of all countries meeting academic, linguistic and financial requirements.
Duration: diploma and M.L.S.: 2 years; B.L.S. and Ph.D.: 3 years.
Applications: to the Registrar at the above address.

1701 Bayero University, Kano [BUK]
PMB 3011
Kano
Tel: +234-64-666-023
Fax: +234-64-661-480
Web: http://www.aau.org/english/member.htm?AddressID=76
e-mail: registrar@bukedu.ng

📖 Undergraduate, Graduate, Postgraduate Programmes

Study Domains: all major fields.
Programmes: undergraduate, graduate and postgraduate programmes leading to Bachelor's, Master's and Ph.D. degrees.
Open to: candidates of any nationality, over 17 years, holding a Senior Secondary School Certificate, GCE or equivalent.
Duration: 4 to 6 years, depending on programmes.
Financial assistance: some scholarships are available.
Languages: English.
Applications: to the above address; for further information contact Faruk Mohammed Yanganau, Email: registrar@buk.edu.ng.

1702 Enugu State University of Science and Technology [ESUT]
PMB 01660
Enugu
Tel: +234-4245-1244/1253
Fax: +234-4245-5001/1319/5105

📖 Undergraduate, Graduate Programmes

Study Domains: all major fields.
Programmes: undergraduate and graduate programmes in all major fields.
Open to: candidates of all nationalities.

1703 **Federal University of Technology, Yola [FUTY]**
PMB 2076
Yola
Tel: +234-7562-4580
Fax: +234-7562-5406
Web: http://www.futy.edu
e-mail: vc@futy.edu.ng

📖 **Undergraduate, Graduate Programmes**

Study Domains: agronomic sciences, architecture, biochemistry, biology, botany, building industry, cattle breeding, chemical engineering, chemistry, civil engineering, computer science, electricity and electronics, fisheries, food, forestry, geology, home economics, horticulture, mathematics, microbiology, physics, research, statistics, textile industry, urbanism, zoology.
Programmes: undergraduate and graduate programmes.
Open to: candidates of all nationalities.

1704 **Igbinedion University, Okada [IUO]**
PMB 0006
Benin City, Edo State
Tel: +234-5225-4942
Web: http://www.igbinedion.com/iu/index.html

📖 **Undergraduate, Graduate, Postgraduate Programmes**

Study Domains: accounting, agriculture, anatomy, biochemistry, biology, botany, business administration, chemical engineering, chemistry, civil engineering, communication, computer science, economic and commercial sciences, engineering, international relations, law, mathematics, mechanical engineering, medicine, microbiology, physics, physiology, summer programmes, zoology.
Programmes: undergraduate, graduate and postgraduate programmes leading to Bachelor's, Master's and Ph.D. degrees.
Open to: candidates of any nationality holding a senior school certificate (minimum of 5 credits passes).
Other conditions: oral and written test.
Duration: 4 to 6 years, depending on programmes; courses begin in September.
Fees: tuition fees: from 248.800 to 310.800 Naira, depending on programmes.
Languages: English.
Applications: by 23 September at the above address.

🎓 **University Scholarships**

Study Domains: all major fields.
Scholarships: University undergraduate and postgraduate scholarships.
Open to: all registered and fee-paying students of the university.
Duration: for normal duration of courses.
Applications: for full information contact the Registrar of the University at the above address.

1705 **Kaduna Polytechnic [KP]**
Polytechnic Road
Tudun Wada, PM.B 2021
Kaduna
Tel: +234-6221-1551

📖 **Undergraduate, Graduate Programmes**

Study Domains: education, engineering, technology, urbanism.
Programmes: full-time National Diploma, Higher National Diploma programmes.
Open to: candidates of any nationality who are of post-secondary age and in possession of a West African School Certificate with credit passes or General Certificate of Education (or equivalent) in 4 appropriate subjects (for National Diploma); or in possession of the National Diploma at an overall credit level or its equivalent together with one year of field experience (for Higher National Diploma).
Applications: to the Registrar, at the above address.

1706 **Ladoke Akintola University of Technology [LAUTECH]**
PMB 4000
Ogbomoso
Tel: +234-3872-0638

📖 **Undergraduate, Graduate Programmes**

Study Domains: all major fields.
Programmes: undergraduate, graduate and postgraduate programmes leading to Bachelor's, Master's and Ph.D. degrees in all major fields; also programme of courses leading to a Diploma.
Open to: candidates of all nationalities meeting academic, linguistic, financial and medical requirements.
Fees: current registration: US$1,000.
Languages: English.
Applications: to the Registrar at the above address.

1707 **Michael Okpara University of Agriculture, Umudike**
PMB 7267
Umuahia
Tel: +234-8244-0550
Fax: +234-8244-0550
e-mail: onwudike@fuau.edu.ng

📖 **Undergraduate, Graduate, Postgraduate Programmes**

Study Domains: accounting, agriculture, biochemistry, biology, botany, business administration, cattle breeding, chemical engineering, chemistry, civil engineering, computer science, continuing education, dietetics, education, electricity and electronics, engineering, finance, fisheries, food, forestry, genetics, home economics, horticulture, laboratory techniques, management, marine science, marketing, metallurgy, microbiology, natural resources, nutrition, physics, statistics, tourism, hotel and catering management, veterinary medicine, veterinary sciences, vocational training, zoology.
Programmes: undergraduate, graduate and postgraduate programmes leading to Bachelor's, Master's, Ph.D. degrees and PGDPE.
Open to: candidates of any nationality holding a senior high school certificate with 5 credits in the following subjects: English, Chemistry, Biology/Agricultural sciences, Mathematics/Physics.
Duration: 4-5-6 years, depending on programmes.
Fees: current registration: 61.950 Nairas; tuition fees: 10.000 Nairas; living costs: approx. 51.950 Nairas per year.
Financial assistance: work aid of 2,000 Nairas per month for financial reasons.
Languages: English.
Applications: for information contact the Registrar of the University at the above address.

1708 **Nnamdi Azikiwe University**
PO Box 5025
Awka
Tel: +234-4855-0018
e-mail: ejiofor@unizik.edu.ng

📖 **Undergraduate, Graduate Programmes**

Study Domains: all major fields.
Programmes: undergraduate and graduate programmes in all major fields.
Open to: candidates of any nationality.
Languages: English.
Applications: for information contact the University Registrar at the above address.

1709 **Rivers State University of Science and Technology [RSUST]**
PMB 5080
RSUST
Port Harcourt
Tel: +234-8423-2288
Fax: +234-8423-0720
Web: http://www.rsust.edu.ng
e-mail: achinewhu@hotmail.com

📖 Undergraduate, Graduate, Postgraduate Programmes

Study Domains: accounting, administration, agriculture, agronomic sciences, applied sciences, architecture, biochemistry, biology, biophysics, botany, business, business administration, cattle breeding, chemical engineering, chemistry, civil engineering, communication, continuing education, ecology, environment, education, electricity and electronics, engineering, fisheries, food, forestry, geodesy, industrial relations, international law, international relations, law, management, marketing, mathematics, mechanical engineering, microbiology, physics, research, sciences, statistics, technology.
Programmes: undergraduate, graduate and postgraduate programmes leading to Bachelor's, Master's and Ph.D. degrees; also non-degree programme (Certificate in Accounting).
Open to: candidates with 5 credits at GCE O-level and or SSCE; admission is through the Joint Admissions and Matriculation Board (JAMB) Examinations.
Fees: current registration: 17,424 Nairas.
Languages: English.
Applications: by 30 January, to the Registrar at the above address.

1710 University of Benin [UB]
PMB 1154
Benin City
Tel: +234-52600-443
Fax: +234-52-602-370
Web: http://www.uniben.edu
e-mail: registra@uniben.edu

📖 Undergraduate, Graduate, Postgraduate Programmes

Study Domains: all major fields.
Programmes: undergraduate, graduate and postgraduate programmes leading to Bachelor's, Master's and Ph.D. degrees.
Open to: candidates of any nationality with relevant qualifications.
Fees: tuition fees: US$500; living costs: approximately US$1,500.
Languages: English.
Applications: by June at the above address; for information contact Prof. R.O. Ebewele; tel/fax:+234 52 602 370.

1711 University of Nigeria [UN]
Nsukka
Tel: +234-42-771-500/1530
Fax: +234-42-770-644
e-mail: misunn@aol.com

📖 Undergraduate Programmes

Study Domains: all major fields.
Programmes: undergraduate programme leading to Bachelor's degree, Diploma and Certificate.
Open to: candidates of any nationality with relevant qualifications.
Fees: tuition fees: none.
Languages: English.
Applications: at the above address.

Norway

Academic year: Late August to June.
Organization of higher education system: Higher Education in Norway is provided by six universities, six specialized university institutions, 25 university colleges, two national colleges of the arts and 29 private institutions of higher education. With the exception of a few of the private university colleges, all higher education institutions are state-run. As a rule, tuition is not required for study at Norwegian higher education institutions, although fees may be imposed for certain professional education programmes, further and special education programmes and study at some of the private institutions. In addition to their teaching activities, all the higher learning institutions, and particularly the universities, are responsible for conducting basic research as well as researcher training, primarily by means of

graduate-level studies and doctoral degree programmes.
Degree system: Norway is one of the first countries in Europe to follow up the goals established in the Bologna Process in European higher education. Furthermore, in 2003, Norway concluded a three-year quality reform in higher education aimed among other things at improving student mobility and international cooperation in education, making easier for students who complete all or part of their education to obtain recognition for their qualifications in other countries. Under the new degree system studies for Bachelor's degree programme are of 3 years' duration, for Master's degree programmes, 2 years' duration and Doctoral degree (Ph.D.) programmes, 3 years' duration. There is also a one-tier Master's programmes of 5 years' duration and a professionally-oriented degree programme of 4-6 years' duration.
Credits and grading scale: Courses at the higher education institutions are measured in credits in accordance with the European Credit Transfer and Accumulation System (ECTS). This is based on the principle that the workload of a full-time student during one academic year equals 60 credits. Students in both lower and higher degree programmes are assessed on a grading scale ranging from A (top percentage group) to F (fail), where E is the lowest passing grade. In addition, some exams are administered on a Pass/Fail basis.
Major institutions of higher education: See www.study-norway.net for a list of all Norwegian institutions of higher education.
Monetary unit: kroner (NOK).
National student admission: Norwegian nationals must meet the general requirements for study ('Generell studiekompetanse' in Norwegian) decided by the Norwegian Ministry of Education and Research. Typically, this means that a student must have successfully completed three years of Norwegian upper secondary education. There are also other ways to meet the requirements, and more details about this can be found on the web pages of the centralized application processing centre called Universities and Colleges Admission Service (UCAS), or 'Samordna Opptak' (SO) in Norwegian; web: http://www.samordnaopptak.no.
Norwegian students (and foreign students with a valid permanent or renewable residence permit) should apply for studies via UCAS that coordinates the admission to undergraduate and graduate level studies at all universities, university colleges, state colleges, and some private colleges in Norway.
International student admission: International students from the Nordic countries meet the general requirements for study in Norway if they have successfully completed upper secondary education in their home country, and this education qualifies for entrance to universities/university colleges in that country. For detailed information, please see www.samordnaopptak.no/vurdering/annen_nordisk_utd.html. Other international students should have qualifications at least equivalent to completed general education at the upper secondary level. Applicants from certain countries may be asked to meet additional requirements such as one year of completed studies at university level. For detailed information about additional requirements for various countries, please visit the website of NOKUT (The Norwegian Agency for Quality Assurance in Education) at www.nokut.no. If students are unsure if they qualify for acceptance into a Norwegian institution they may submit their papers to NOKUT for evaluation. International students must also meet the language requirements for proficiency in Norwegian and/or English. Applications should be submitted directly to the Office for Foreign Students at the institution concerned. Please see www.study-norway.net for a complete list of Norwegian institutions of higher education.
Language: Norwegian language is the primary language of instruction at Norwegian institutions of higher education, although English is sometimes also used; good knowledge of Norwegian and English is essential for regular university courses.
Language requirements (Norwegian language): If applying for a course taught in Norwegian, or for general acceptance into an institution, applicants outside of the Nordic countries must meet one of the following requirements: successfully passed 'Norwegian as a second language' from upper secondary school; successfully passed Level 3 in Norwegian at a university, successfully passed one-year study in Norwegian language and society for foreign students from a university college; successfully passed test in Norwegian at higher level

'Bergens-testen' with a minimum score of 450.
In certain cases, institutions may accept other types of
documentation and they should be contacted directly for
details.
Language requirements (English Language): More and more
courses are offered in English at Norwegian institutions,
especially at Master's level. The requirements for an English
test may be waived for the following applicants: applicants
from the EU/EEC and/or The European
Council/UNESCO-Cepes, and who have had English as
foreign language over a period of minimum 7 years in
secondary and upper secondary school.; applicants who
successfully have completed a Bachelor's degree where
English is the language of instruction; applicants with an
A-level exam in English from upper secondary school;
applicants who cannot meet the English language
requirements may present one of the following tests or exams;
Test of English as a Foreign Language (TOEFL) with a
minimum score of 500 (paper based) or 170 (computer
based); International English Language Testing Service
(IELTS) with a minimum score of 5,0; Advanced Placement
International English Language examination (APIEL) with a
minimum score of 3,0; Universities of Cambridge/Oxford;
First Certificate in English; Certificate in Advanced English;
Certificate of Proficiency. English language requirement can
be met if students have: completed one year of studies at the
university level in an English-speaking country (Australia,
Canada, Ireland, New Zealand, United Kingdom, USA) where
the language of instruction is English; completed studies at
the university level with a major in English.
Immigration requirements: All students from outside the
Nordic countries and who plan to stay in Norway for more
than 90 days need a student residence permit. All applications
will be processed by the Norwegian Directorate of
Immigration (UDI). For detailed information about the
Norwegian immigration regulations, please see www.udi.no.
To be granted a residence permit to study or attend school in
Norway applicants must have been admitted to a university,
scientific college, state college, art college, approved upper
secondary school, folk high school or one-year course of
studies in a private school; have sufficient financial resources
for all expenses such as tuition, if applicable, books, living
expenses, etc.; have a place of residence; be full-time
students; submit a complete plan for proposed studies in
Norway.
Estimated expenses for one academic year: The minimum
requirement is at least NOK 8,000 per month to cover
expenses (tuition fees if applicable, books, housing, living
expenses, etc.).
Information services:
• Authority to whom international students' application should
be addressed:
Foreign students without a valid residence permit in Norway
will have to apply directly to the institution concerned.
Students with a valid residence permit can apply to:
Universities and Colleges Admission Service (UCAS);
Postboks 1175 Blindern; N-0317 Oslo; email:
sokerinfo@so.uio.no; web:
http://www.samordnaopptak.no/english/
• Name and address of other agencies or organizations:
Norwegian Centre for International Cooperation in Higher
Education (SIU); PO Box 7800
N-5020 Bergen; tel: +47-55-308-800; fax: +47-55-308-801;
email: study-norway@siu.no;
web: http://www.study-norway.net / www.siu.no
• Norwegian diplomatic missions in other countries (for
general information and advice for foreign students
concerning study in Norway); web: http://www.norway.info
• Student Welfare Organizations at the respective universities
and colleges. Please see a list of all institutions at
http://www.study-norway.net.
Scholarships for international students:
• The Norwegian State Educational Fund ('Statens Lånekasse'
in Norwegian) offers grants and loans to foreign students.
Certain restrictions apply. Please see www.lanekassen.no for
details.
• The Norad Fellowship Programme offers scholarships to
students at the Master's level from certain developing
countries. Please see www.siu.no/norad for details.
• Other fellowships/scholarships sponsored by Norwegian
governmental organisations are available on an individual
basis. Please check with the institutions for details.

Open and distance learning: Most Norwegian higher
education institutions offer distance education, either as part
of a 'normal' degree programme or as a separate course.
• Norway Opening Universities (NOU), or
'Norgesuniversitetet' in Norwegian, is a national initiative for
change and innovation in Norwegian higher education. NOU
was established in January 2004 by The Norwegian Ministry
of Education and Research. The new organization was
established by merging The Norwegian Agency for Flexible
Learning in Higher Education (SOFF) and The Norwegian
University Network for Lifelong Learning
(Norgesuniversitetet); www.norgesuniversitetet.no for further
information.
Recognition of studies and qualification: Norwegian
ENIC/NARIC Centre: Norwegian Agency for Quality
Assurance in Education (NOKUT); Postboks 1708 Vika;
N-0121 Oslo; tel: +47-21-021-800; fax: +47-21-021-801;
email: Postmottak@nokut.no; web: http://www.nokut.no.
Accommodation services: The Student Welfare
Organisations at each institution will provide details regarding
student housing and the local conditions for private housing.
Work opportunities: Work opportunities for international
students are limited and determined by their residence status.
The Norwegian Directorate of Immigration (UDI) will be
able to provide detailed information; web: www.udi.no. In
general, international students may apply for a permit to work
on a part-time basis (no more than 20 hours per week) and
full-time during holidays.
Publications / Websites:
• The official gateway for foreign students who want to study
in Norway. Maintained and developed by SIU:
www.study-norway.net
• The official gateway to Norway that includes information
about education in Norway in 15 languages. Maintained and
developed by The Norwegian Ministry of Foreign Affairs:
www.norway.info
• 'Guide to higher education in Norway' published by the
Norwegian Agency for Quality Assurance in Education
(NOKUT), gives general information on Norwegian
institutions of higher education and possibilities of admission.
A copy of the publication may be ordered directly from
NOKUT.

1712 Bergen National Academy of the Arts [KHIB]
Stromgaten 1
5015 Bergen
Tel: +47-5558-7300
Fax: +47-5558-7310
Web: http://www.khib.no
e-mail: khib@hhib.no

📖 **Undergraduate, Graduate Programmes**

Study Domains: arts and crafts, design, fine arts.
Programmes: undergraduate and graduate programmes
leading to Bachelor's and Master's degrees.
Fees: living costs: approximately 8,000 NOK per month.
Languages: Norwegian.
Applications: Bachelor's degree: 15 April; Master's
degree: 23 May; to the above address.

1713 Bergen University College
Nygaardsgaten 112
PO Box 7030
5055 Bergen
Tel: +47-5558-7503
Fax: +47-5558-7789
Web: http://www.hib.no
e-mail: post@hib.no

📖 **Undergraduate Programmes**

Study Domains: building industry, business
administration, chemical engineering, chemical industry, civil
engineering, early childhood education, economy, education,
electricity and electronics, engineering, home economics,
mechanical engineering, nursing, radiology, social work,
special education, teacher education, vocational training.
Programmes: undergraduate programmes leading to
Bachelor's degrees.
Open to: candidates of any nationality holding a

secondary-school certificate.
Duration: 3 to 4 years (depending on programme).
Languages: Norwegian; some courses are given in English.

1714 Kunsthogskolen i Bergen
Stromgaten 1
5015 Bergen
Tel: +47-5558-7300
Fax: +47-5558-7310
Web: http://www.khib.no
e-mail: khib@hhib.no

Undergraduate, Graduate Programmes

Study Domains: arts and crafts, design, fine arts.
Programmes: undergraduate and graduate programmes leading to Bachelor's and Master's degrees.
Fees: living costs: approximately NOK 8,000 per month.
Languages: Norwegian.
Applications: B.A.: by 14 April; M.A.: by 1 June, to the above address.

1715 Narvik University College [HIN]
PO Box 385
8505 Narvik
Tel: +47-7696-6240
Fax: +47-7696-6810
Web: http://www.hin.no
e-mail: mok@hin.no

Engineering Programmes

Study Domains: building industry, civil engineering, computer science, electricity and electronics, energy, mechanical engineering, nursing, technology.
Programmes: programme of courses in: mechanical engineering, building and civil engineering, environmental technology, power systems, electronics, space technology, computer science, nursing.
Open to: candidates with general secondary-school education equivalent to the International Baccalaureate, with good knowledge of Norwegian.
Duration: 3 years.
Fees: (approximate figures) tuition: NOK 1,000 per semester; estimated living expenses NOK 6,100 per month.
Applications: to the above address.

1716 Norwegian Academy of Music [NMH]
PO Box 5190
Majorstua
0302 Oslo
Tel: +47-2336-7000
Fax: +47-2336-7001
Web: http://www.nmh.no
e-mail: mh@nmh.no

Undergraduate, Graduate, Postgraduate Programmes

Study Domains: music and musicology.
Programmes: undergraduate, graduate and postgraduate programme of courses leading to Bachelor's, Master's and Ph.D. in music performance and music pedagogy.

1717 Norwegian Agency for Development Co-operation [NORAD]
PB 7800
5020 Bergen
Tel: +47-5530-8800
Fax: +47-5530-8801
Web: http://www.siu.no/norad
e-mail: siu@siu.no

NORAD Fellowship Programme

Study Domains: all major fields.
Scholarships: NORAD Fellowship Programme.
Description: to support strategic capacity building within institutions in prioritised partner countries for Norwegian development co-operation; scholarships for candidates at postgraduate level; the candidates are required to hold a B.Sc. degree and 2 to 3 years of relevant professional experience in their field; information about prioritized countries, application

procedures and course programmes are available in the annual NORAD Fellowship Course Catalogue http://www.siu.no/norad.
Value: living expenses for 2 academic years plus a return ticket to Norway. An installation allowance, equivalent to one-half of a fellowship's monthly allowance, will be provided for deposit at the student hostel, clothing and miscellaneous expenses.
Applications: contact Norwegian Embassy/Consulate in home country; deadline: 1 December for the following academic year starting in August.

1718 Norwegian School of Economics and Business Administration [NHH]
Helleveien 30
5035 Bergen-Sandviken
Tel: +47-5595-9389
Web: http://www.nhh.no
e-mail: mib.stud@nhh.no

Graduate Programme / Business

Study Domains: accounting, administration, business, business administration, communication, development studies, finance, international business, international law, international relations, management, political economy, political science.
Programmes: Master's degree programme in International Business, international economics, corporate finance, marketing, managerial economics and management, foreign exchange, accounting, international organizations, history and political science.
Open to: students of any nationality aiming to become future international managers in both public and private sectors with high academic attainment holding at least a Bachelor's degree, preferably
with introductory courses in statistics, accounting, economics, finance, computing and management; proficiency in English required.
Duration: 1-1/2 years (3 semesters).
Fees: tuition free; welfare charge: NOK 305 per semester; living expenses: NOK 30,000 per semester.
Languages: instruction in English.

1719 Norwegian University of Science and Technology [NTNU]
7491 Trondheim
Tel: +47-7359-5000
Fax: +47-7359-5310
Web: http://www.ntnu.no
e-mail: international@adm.ntnu.no

Undergraduate, Graduate Programmes

Study Domains: all major fields.
Programmes: degree courses in most major fields.
Open to: students from EEA and Council of Europe countries who fulfil the basic university entrance requirements (International Baccalaureate or equivalent) and have proficiency in English (TOEFL/ELTS); foreign students must complete a course in the Norwegian language (the Introductory Programme) before Faculty studies.
Duration: 5 years.
Fees: no tuition fee; room, board, books, medical care, transport, etc.: minimum NOK 6,000 per month; all students must be able to document or declare (EU/EEA students) a minimum of NOK 80,000 (approx. US$11,000) per year in funds.
Financial assistance: possibility of Norwegian government funding for graduate studies, contact the Office of International Relations at time of application for eligibility.
Languages: instruction in Norwegian (a few courses in English).
Applications: by 1 March, to the International Office, at the address above.

1720 Oslo National College of the Arts

PO Box 6853
St Olavsplass
0130 Oslo
Tel: +47-2299-5500
Fax: +47-2299-5502
Web: http://www.khio.no
e-mail: khio@khio.no

Undergraduate Programmes

Study Domains: applied arts, arts, arts and crafts, decorative arts, design, education, fine arts, interior design, performing arts.
Programmes: undergraduate programme of courses leading to Bachelor's degrees.
Open to: candidates of any nationality with university entrance requirements.
Other conditions: admission test and additional conditions depending on criteria set by the relevant departments.
Fees: current registration: NOK 360; tuition fees: none; living costs: minimum of NOK 6,000 per month.
Languages: Norwegian and English.
Applications: by 1 April to the above address.

1721 Oslo University College [OUC]

International Office
Wergelandsveien 27
0167 Oslo
Tel: +47-2245-2000
Fax: +47-2245-3005
Web: http://www.hio.no
e-mail: postmottak@hio.no

Undergraduate, Graduate Programmes

Study Domains: all major fields.
Programmes: degree programmes at the following faculties: Faculty of Nursing; Faculty of Engineering; Faculty of Health Sciences; Faculty of Business, Public administration and Social work; Faculty of Journalism, Library and Information science; Faculty of Education; Faculty of Fine Arts and Drama.
Fees: tuition free; accommodation in dormitories: NOK 1,500-2,000.
Financial assistance: from Norwegian government; enquire at above address for possibility of financial assistance.
Languages: instruction in English.
Applications: to above address.

1722 Ostfold University College

Remmen
1783 Halden
Tel: +47-6921-5000
Fax: +47-6921-5002
Web: http://www.hiof.no
e-mail: post-fa@hiof.no

Undergraduate, Postgraduate Programmes

Study Domains: computer science, English, French, German, international business, nursing.
Programmes: undergraduate and postgraduate programmes leading to Bachelor's and Master's degrees.
Description: Master's programme only in computer science.
Open to: candidates of any country; language proficiency test in Norwegian and English.
Duration: 3 years.
Fees: tuition fees: none.
Applications: by 1 March to the National Admission Office, Samordnet opptak, Postboks 1175 Blinden, N-0317 Oslo.

1723 Research Council of Norway

Secretariat for Cultural Exchange Programmes
PO Box 2700
St. Hanshaugen
0131 Oslo
Tel: +47-22-03-7000
Fax: +47-22-03-7001
Web: http://www.forskningsradet.no/english/
e-mail: intstip@rcn.no

Scholarships

Study Domains: cultural studies, education, research.
Scholarships: (a) Senior Scientist Visiting Fellowship; (b) Research Programmes of the European Union (EU); (c) Bilateral Scholarship Agreements and other scholarship programmes.
Description: (a) to strengthen Norwegian research institutions and to promote contact between foreign scientists and Norwegian researchers; (b) Marie Curie Training Sites and the 'Access to Research Infrastructure'-facilities in Norway; see website of the Norwegian EU R&D Information Centre; research training networks, and individual postdoctoral and experienced researcher fellowships are announced on the Cordis server: http://www.cordis.lu/improving/home.html; (c) in collaboration with the Royal Norwegian Ministry of Foreign Affairs, scholarships for citizens (students and researchers) of countries with which Norway has a cultural agreement or a scholarship agreement. Candidates are nominated by their home countries.
Open to: (a) for well-established, internationally recognized scientists wishing to work at a Norwegian research institute; (b) specialists and (c) university professors, from countries with which Norway has a reciprocal cultural agreement; (d) university students, undergraduates and graduates, up to 35 years, from countries with which Norway has exchange programmes under cultural and other reciprocal scholarship agreements: Austria, Belgium, Bulgaria, China, Czech Republic, Egypt, Finland, France, Germany, Greece, Hungary, Iceland, India, Ireland, Israel, Italy, Japan, Mexico, Netherlands, Poland, Portugal, Romania, Slovakia, Spain, Switzerland, Turkey, Russian Federation, United Kingdom; (e) Estonian, Latvian, Lithuanian university and college professors, teachers, researchers and advanced university students and employees of firms, organizations and public administration intending to study or receive training in Norway; good knowledge of a Scandinavian language or English required.
Value: (a) NOK 38,000 for each of the first two months and NOK 19,000 for each succeeding month; round-trip travel expenses. Possibility of travel expenses for family members (spouse and minor children) if residing with the fellow for the entire period. Salaries covered through bilateral agreements. (e) NOK 6,500 per month, plus NOK 2,000 for travel expenses and literature allowance; accident/health insurance included.
Applications: (a) should be prepared in cooperation between the institution and the scientist, and submitted by the institution on behalf of the individual applicant. (d) to government scholarship authorities in applicant's own country; the main application deadline is 15 June. Additional deadline 15 September and 15 February. Contact potential host research institution in Norway for updated information; (b) see website; (c) contact relevant authorities in home country (usually the Ministry of Foreign Affairs or Education) for further details on application procedures, deadlines etc. Please note that the International Scholarship Section (IS) of the Research Council of Norway does not administer the Senior Scientist Visiting Fellowships, and cannot answer questions about it. Contact the potential host research institution in Norway for updated information.

1724 Sogn og Fjordane University College

PO Box 133
6851 Sogndal
Tel: +47-5767-6000
Fax: +47-5767-6100
Web: http://www.hisf.no
e-mail: post@hisf.no

International Programme

Study Domains: administration, early childhood education, economy, education, engineering, history, languages, marketing, nursing, physical education, public relations, sciences, social sciences, social work, special education.
Programmes: 'From mountain to fjord': one semester international programme (30 ECTS credits).
Open to: candidates of any country holding a secondary school certificate with proficiency in English.

Fees: tuition fees: none; living costs: room, board, books, transportation, minimum NOK 6,500 per month.
Languages: English.
Applications: by 15 April.

1725 Telemark University College

Kjdlnes RIN 6 56
3914 Porsgrunn
Tel: +47-3557-5000
Fax: +47-3557-5001
Web: http://www.hit.no

Graduate Programmes

Study Domains: accounting, administration, agronomic sciences, applied arts, arts, arts and crafts, civil engineering, computer science, ecology, environment, economic and commercial sciences, economy, electricity and electronics, engineering, English, folklore, German, history, industrial technology, management, marketing, mathematics, natural sciences, nursing, performing arts, physical education, Scandinavian studies, teacher education, technology, tourism, hotel and catering management, vocational training.
Programmes: graduate programme leading to Master's degree and non-degree programme.
Description: Master's degree programme in energy and environmental technology; one semester academic programme in Scandinavian studies.
Open to: Master's programme: candidates of any country holding a 3-year Bachelor's degree in Engineering (or equivalent); non-degree programme: undergraduate students at accredited colleges or universities.
Duration: Master's: 2 years beginning 10 August; non-degree programme: 15 weeks (from 10 August to 15 December).
Fees: Master's programme: current registration, 80€ per semester; no tuition fees; living costs, approximately 6,000€ per year; non-degree programme: tuition: US$6,500.
Languages: English.
Applications: Master's programme: by 25 June to the above address (for information contact Dr. Raudiholta, email: Raudi.Holta@hit.no); non-degree programme: by 15 February to Lisa Hjelmeland, Programme coordinator, Hit, Hallvard Eitas plan 3800 BO, email: lisa.hjelmeland@hit.no; tel: +47-3595-2747; fax: +47-3595-0000.

1726 The Norwegian Lutheran School of Theology

PO Box 5144
Majorstuen
0302 Oslo
Tel: +47-2259-0500
Fax: +47-2259-0501
Web: http://www.mf.no
e-mail: ekspedisjon@mf.no

Undergraduate, Graduate and Postgraduate Programmes

Study Domains: theology, religion.
Programmes: Candidate, Bachelor's, Master's, Ph.D. degrees in theology; religion.
Description: Doctor of Theology (Dr.theol.); Candidate of Theology (Cand.theol., roughly equivalent to Master of Sacred Theology); Candidate of Philology (Cand.philol.); Master of Philosophy in theology; major and minor degrees in Christian knowledge and religious and ethical education (KRL).
Open to: candidates of any nationality with successful completion of upper secondary education; applicant must fulfil the basic entrance requirements to Norwegian universities, good command of English (TOEFL Test) if English is not the native language, proof of sufficient financial funds to meet the expenses in Norway, proof of proficiency in Norwegian or a completion of the one-year preparatory Norwegian language course.
Languages: language of instruction: Norwegian; English for International Master of Theology Degree.
Applications: by 1 February for admission (fall semester) and by 1 October (spring semester), by 1 March and 1 November for students from the EU and EEA area; basic entrance requirements for matriculation to Norwegian universities see:

http://www.uio.no/english/academics/admission/quota/criteria_tabell.html.

1727 The School of Mission and Theology [MHS]

Misjonshogskolen
Misjonsveien 34
4024 Stavanger
Tel: +47-515-6210
Fax: +47-5151-6225
Web: http://www.mhs.no
e-mail: und@mhs.no

Graduate Programme / Theology

Study Domains: theology, religion.
Programmes: graduate programme leading to Master of Theology.
Duration: 2 years beginning mid-August.
Languages: English.
Applications: by 15 March to the above address.

1728 Tromso University College

9293 Tromso
Tel: +47-7766-0300
Fax: +47-7768-9956
Web: http://www.hitos.no
e-mail: postmottak@hitos.no

Undergraduate Programmes

Study Domains: business administration, early childhood education, engineering, laboratory techniques, music and musicology, nursing, radiology, teacher education.
Programmes: undergraduate programmes leading to Bachelor's degrees.
Description: Bachelor's degrees in medical laboratory technology, radiography, business administration, teacher education, musical performance, engineering, nursing, physiotherapy, occupational therapy.
Duration: 3 years beginning in August.
Fees: current registration: 70€; tuition: none; living costs: approximately 600-700€ per month.
Languages: language of instruction: Norwegian; language proficiency: Norwegian and English.
Applications: by 1 March to Samordna Opptak, Postboks 1175 Blindern, 0317 Oslo.

1729 University of Bergen

PO 7800
5020 Bergen
Tel: +47-5558-0000
Fax: +47-5558-9643
Web: http://www.uib.no

Graduate Studies

Study Domains: archaeology, biology, dentistry, English, fisheries, health and hygiene, history, physics, sciences, Spanish.
Programmes: (a) Master's programme in English, history, archaeology, chemistry, French, German, Spanish and Latin American Studies, informatics, health promotion, dentistry, international health, microbiology, histopathology, public administration and organization theory, social anthropology, system dynamics, geophysics, biology, solid earth science, communication studies; (b) Programme in Scandinavian area studies (SAS): courses in Norwegian language, literature, history, art and architecture, Scandinavian theatre, anthropology, sociology, politics and geography.
Open to: (a) preference is given to applicants from East European and developing countries with relevant Bachelor's degree for Master programme subject; TOEFL 500 minimum; (b) short-term exchange
students and applicants studying Scandinavian subjects at home university.
Duration: (a) 2 years, including thesis work; courses begin in August; (b) 1 semester (5 months); courses begin 20 August and 15 January.
Fees: registration per semester: NOK 305 approximately; no tuition fees.
Financial assistance: available for students from certain countries through Norwegian government.
Languages: Instruction in English; Norwegian language courses available.

Applications: by 1 February, to the Office for Foreign Students to the above address.

1730 University of Bergen, Department of Fisheries and Marine Biology

Nordic Council for Marine Biology
Thormøhlensgt. 55
5020 Bergen
Tel: +47-5558-4400
Web: http://www.ifm.uib.no
e-mail: post@ifm.uib.no

📖 Graduate Studies

Study Domains: marine biology.
Programmes: Nordic courses in marine biology: 10 to 12 participants. Instruction in Danish, Norwegian, Swedish or English.
Open to: Ph.D. students and younger marine biologists from the Nordic countries only.
Held: at institutions dealing with marine biology in Denmark, Finland, Iceland, Norway and Sweden (different institutions each year).
Applications: variable; announced regularly once a year in October.

👉 Fellowships

Study Domains: marine biology.
Scholarships: Nordic marine biology fellowships.
Open to: candidates from Denmark, Finland, Iceland, Norway and Sweden with a pre-Ph.D. or equivalent; proficiency in Scandinavian languages required.
Place of study: institutions dealing with marine biology in Denmark, Finland, Iceland, Norway and Sweden.
Duration: 2 to 12 months (renewable on certain conditions).
Value: approximately NOK 7,500 per month; no income taxes are paid.
Applications: as announced at all biological institutes in the Nordic countries every Autumn with deadline for applications in December; further information can be obtained from the General Secretary, at the above address.

1731 University of Oslo

PO Box 1081
Blindern
0317 Oslo
Tel: +47-2285-8478
Fax: +47-2285-8488
Web: http://www.admin.uio.no/sfa/sip
e-mail: international@admin.uio.no

📖 Graduate, Postgraduate and Non-degree Programmes

Study Domains: all major fields.
Programmes: graduate and postgraduate programmes leading to Master's and Ph.D.; also non-degree programme in advanced Norwegian language studies.
Open to: Advanced Norwegian Language Studies programme: candidates of any nationality who achieved at least 2 years of university studies in Scandinavian languages including Norwegian; Master's programme: candidates of any nationality holding a Bachelor's; Ph.D. programme: candidates of any nationality who achieved at least 5 years of university studies.
Duration: Advanced Norwegian Language Studies programme: 1 year; Master's programme: 1 or 2 years; Ph.D. programme: 3 years.
Financial assistance: possibility of loan from the Norwegian State Educational Loan Fund, which is waived upon the recipient's return to his or her home country; it includes one extra trip between the country of residence and Oslo.
Languages: for Master's and Ph.D. programmes English proficiency is required (TOEFL 550; IELTS band 6.0).
Applications: by 1 December to the above address.

📖 Undergraduate, Graduate Programmes

Study Domains: arts, dentistry, education, law, medicine, social sciences, theology, religion.
Programmes: undergraduate and graduate programmes

leading to Bachelor's and Master's degrees.
Description: (a) English-taught Master's degrees. At present the University offers 11 English-taught Master's degrees in: theology, human rights, international health, media studies, Viking and medieval studies, maritime law, Tibetan and Buddhist culture, environmental and development economics, international and comparative education, higher education, special needs education, peace and conflict studies. For more information please consult website; (b) studies taught in Norwegian: regular degree studies offered in most major subjects. Eight faculties: theology, law, medicine, dentistry, mathematics & natural sciences, arts (humanities), social sciences and education; (c) exchange students under a mobility programme, e.g. ERASMUS, or bilateral agreement apply through their home university. For more information and catalogue of courses consult: http://www.uio.no/english.
Open to: applicants of all nationalities with: (a) basic entrance requirements for admission to Norwegian universities plus 3 years of studies (Bachelor) at university level, and with proficiency in English (TOEFL 550/IETLS band 5.5); (b) basic entrance requirements for admission to Norwegian universities, with proficiency in English (TOEFL 500/IELTS band 5.0); students without sufficient knowledge of Norwegian are given conditional admission to a faculty and must first complete a 1-year Norwegian language programme. NB: Admission to medicine, dentistry, pharmacy requires fluency in Norwegian language prior to admission (no conditional admission given).
Duration: (a) (b) 1 to 5 years, (c) 3 to 12 months.
Fees: no tuition fees.
Financial assistance: (a) Applicants from Eastern Europe and developing countries may apply for stipends through the Quota Programme; (b) none; (c) some exchange students receive stipends from authorities in their home countries.
Languages: English and Norwegian.
Applications: (a) (b) by 1 February or 1 March for students from EU/EEA; Quota Programme: 1 December; (c) early May/early October.

1732 University of Tromsø [UiTO]

Breivika
9037 Tromsø
Tel: +47-7764-4000
Web: http://www.uit.no

📖 Undergraduate, Graduate, Postgraduate Programmes

Study Domains: all major fields.
Programmes: (a) undergraduate, graduate and postgraduate degree programme of courses in most major fields; (b) Master's degree programmes (8 programmes of which 6 are under a quota system for students from developing countries and Eastern Europe): Master of Philosophy in visual anthropology, physics (upper atmosphere and solar terrestrial relations), biology (ecology/zoology, plant physiology, microbiology), medical biology, linguistics; (c) Master's degree programmes (outside quota system): Master of Science in International Fisheries Management; Master of Philosophy in English Linguistics; Master of Philosophy in Finnish (taught in Finnish); (d) Non-degree programmes: Northern Norway, aspects of history, culture and government; archaeology for exchange students.
Open to: students of all nationalities fulfilling basic entrance requirements for admission to Norwegian universities; those not documenting sufficient knowledge of the Norwegian language are required to attend an introductory programme in Norwegian language, culture and society; sufficient proficiency in English must also be demonstrated: TOEFL 500 or ELTS 5.0 minimum scores; language proficiency must be documented before admission to the Norwegian Introductory Programme.
Duration: variable according to field of study; Norwegian Introductory Programme, 1 year; Bachelor's degree, 3-1/2 to 4 years; 1-1/2 to 2 additional years for Master's and Ph.D.
Fees: registration: NOK 400 for the first academic term; NOK 300 for each following term; no tuition fee; NOK 6,000 monthly for basic expenses.
Financial assistance: possibility of NORAD fellowship for Master's degree programme in International Fisheries Management, for which 5 candidates are selected each year. Applicants must possess a Bachelor's degree in either Biology or Economics and also satisfy English requirements. Two to

three years' relevant professional experience is required. Women are especially encouraged to apply.
Languages: instruction in (a), (c) and (d) Norwegian; (b) in English.
Applications: by 1 February, to International Students Office at the above address.

Oman

Academic year: September to June.
Monetary unit: Omani Riyals (O.R.).
International student admission: secondary-school leaving certificate or equivalent.
Language: Arabic and/or English.
Immigration requirements: student visa is required for studies in Oman.
Estimated expenses for one academic year: tuition: 2,000-2,500 O.R.; books/supplies: 100-200 O.R.; housing: 600-1,200 O.R.
Information services: Students should address their applications to the Directorate General of private universities and colleges.

1733   Sultan Qaboos University
Al Khoudh
PO Box 50
123 Muscat
Tel: +968-513-333
Fax: +968 513-254
Web: http://www.squ.edu.om

Undergraduate, Graduate, Postgraduate Programmes

Study Domains: agriculture, economic and commercial sciences, education, engineering, health and hygiene, liberal arts, marine science, medicine, sciences, social sciences.
Programmes: Bachelor's, Master's, Doctor of Medicine, Engineering degrees.
Subjects: liberal arts and social science; education; Commerce & Economics; medicine; health sciences; scence; agricultural, marine sciences; engineering.
Open to: Transfer students accepted but must be officially sponsored by originating institution. Enrolment based on space available, previous academic results, etc.
Handicapped: Facilities available.

Pakistan

Academic year: September to August.
Organization of higher education system:
• University level first stage: Bachelor's degree:
Bachelor's pass degrees are normally obtained after a two-year course and honours degrees after a three-year course in arts, science and commerce. First degrees in engineering take four years and in medicine five years. New universities have also introduced a three-year Bachelor's degree course.
• University level second stage: Master's degree, B.Ed., L.L.B:
A Master's degree requires two years' study after a pass degree and one year after an honours degree. It is based on coursework and an examination and does not usually require a thesis. The B.Ed. requires one year's study beyond a Bachelor's degree in arts, commerce or science. The L.L.B. is a postgraduate qualification and entry to the three-year course is by the Bachelor's degree (Pass) in any other subject. Postgraduate diplomas are offered by many universities and generally require one year of study following a relevant first degree.
• University level third stage: M.Phil., Ph.D.:
The Master of Philosophy (M.Phil.) takes two years after the Master's degree in arts, commerce or science. It is research-based. The Ph.D. (Doctorate of Philosophy) is a research degree which requires a minimum of three years' study beyond the Master's degree.
University level fourth stage: Higher Doctorate:
The degrees of Doctor of Literature (D.Litt.), Doctor of Science (D.Sc.) and Doctor of Law (L.L.D.) are awarded after five to seven years of study.

Monetary unit: Pakistan rupee (R).
International student admission: Foreign students should submit details concerning previous studies and qualifications well in advance of academic session to ensure eligibility for desired courses as requirements vary according to course followed. Applications must be sponsored by candidates' governments and forwarded through embassies in Islamabad or through Pakistan embassies abroad.
Special travel facilities: Student reductions for bus, train and air travel.
Language: Good knowledge of English is essential for all regular university courses. Up to the first pass degree and at the option of the institution, the national language (Urdu) or the regional language may be required. The Universities of Punjab and Karachi, Allama Iqbal Open University and the National Institute of Modern Languages Islamabad offer special preliminary language courses in English and Urdu.
Estimated expenses for one academic year: General living costs approximately Rs 50,000; tuition for medical studies: Rs 450,000; engineering studies: Rs 350,000; business administration: Rs 60,000.
Information services: For information and advice concerning studies in the fields of agriculture, engineering, science, polytechnic subjects and the arts:
• Ministry of Education, Government of Pakistan, Islamabad.
• Academy of Educational Planning and Management.
• Higher Education Commission, Islamabad.
• Education Departments in Lahore (Punjab), Karachi (Singh), Quetta (Balochistan) and Peshawar (North-West Frontier Province). For information and advice concerning studies in the fields of health and medicine:
• Ministry of Health, Islamabad.
• Higher Education Commission, Islamabad.
• Health Departments in the governments of Punjab, North-West Frontier Province, Sindh and Balochistan.
• Pakistan Medical and Dental Council, Islamabad.
Open and distance learning: offered by
• the Allama Iqbal Open University, which provides a wide range of courses at different levels in humanities, teacher education, technical education, business management, commerce, social sciences, Arabic, Pakistan studies, Islamic studies, and home economics and women's studies. It uses multi-media techniques, such as correspondence packages and radio and television broadcasts.
• the Virtual University, which offers a programme of courses in computer sciences leading to a Bachelor's degree. The university delivers education using the most modern ways for communication techniques, including satellite/cable, television and the Internet.
Recognition of studies and qualification:
• Higher Education Commission; Sector H-9; Islamabad, Pakistan; email: info@hec.gov.pk; website: http://www.hec.gov.pk.

1734   Allama Iqbal Open University
Sector H-8
Islamabad
Tel: +92-51-925-7029/44
Fax: +92-51-925-7067
Web: http://www.aiou.edu.pk
e-mail: vcaiou@isb.paknet.com.pk

Distance Education

Study Domains: Arabic, business administration, gender studies, home economics, humanities and arts, languages, management, oriental studies, social sciences, teacher education, technical education.
Programmes: distance education programmes at different levels, using multimedia techniques, such as correspondence packages and radio and television broadcasts.
Applications: to the above address.

1735   Baqai Medical University [BMU]
PO Box 2407
74600 Karachi
Tel: +92-21-450-7653
Fax: +92-21-661-7968
Web: http://www.baqai.edu.pk
e-mail: biit@gem.net.pk

Undergraduate, Graduate Programmes

Study Domains: business administration, computer science, dentistry, health and hygiene, medicine, nursing, paramedical studies, pharmacy and pharmacology, physical therapy.

Programmes: Undergraduate, Graduate, Doctoral programmes in medicine, dentistry, pharmacy, medical technology, physical therapy, nursing, veterinary medicine, public health, information and computer technology, business administration.

1736 City University of Science and Information Technology [CUSIT]
GT Road, Nishterabad
Peshawar
Tel: +92-91-2567-9232/6
Fax: +92-91-2567-927
Web: http://www.cityuniversity.edu.pk
e-mail: info@cityuniversity.edu.pk

Undergraduate Programmes

Study Domains: accounting, administration, arts, business, business administration, computer science, continuing education, English, finance, literature and civilization, management, marketing, mathematics, teacher education.
Programmes: undergraduate programmes leading to Bachelor's degree.
Duration: 4 years beginning in September.
Fees: current registration: Rs 6,000; tuition fees: Rs 1,400.
Languages: English.
Applications: by mid-September to the Registrar of the University at the above address.

1737 Fatima Jinnah Women's University [FJWU]
The Mall
46000 Rawalpindi
Tel: +92-51-927-1167
Fax: +92-51-927-1168
Web: http://www.fjwu.edu.pk
e-mail: fjwu@isb.comsats.net.pk

Undergraduate, Graduate Programmes

Study Domains: administration, anthropology, business administration, communication, computer science, English, fine arts, gender studies, international relations, international studies, theology, religion.
Programmes: undergraduate and graduate programmes in economics; Islamic studies; behavioral sciences; public administration; communication science; gender studies; computer science; English; fine arts; education; business administration; environmental sciences; defence and diplomatic studies.

1738 Hazara University [HU]
Dhodial
Mansehra
Tel: +92-987-530-732
Fax: +92-987-530-046
Web: http://www.hu.edu.pk
e-mail: huniversity@hotmail.com

Undergraduate Programmes

Study Domains: biochemistry, business administration, computer science, education, English, mathematics, microbiology.
Programmes: undergraduate programmes leading to Bachelor's degrees; also non-degree programme (PGD) in information technology.
Description: Bachelor's degrees in microbiology, biochemistry, computer science, business administration, education, English, mathematics.
Open to: all students who passed their intermediate exam at least in second division and who qualify for admission.
Duration: 4 years beginning in December.
Fees: current registration and tuition fees: Rs 100,000; living costs: approx. Rs 20,000 per year.
Languages: English (English language proficiency permission of Ministry of foreign Affairs required for nationals of non-English countries).

Applications: by 20 October, to Registrar at the above address.

1739 Higher Education commission [UGC]
Sector H-9
Islamabad
Tel: +92-51-925-7651/5
Fax: +92-51-929-0128
Web: http://www.hec.gov.pk
e-mail: info@hec.gov.pk

Research Grants

Study Domains: arts, sciences.
Scholarships: (a) Quaid-e-Azam Scheme; (b) Central Overseas Training Scholarships (COTS); (c) Travel Grants to Teachers (1 for 3 years for the international seminar; number varies for Ph.D. programmes, depending on funds); (d) Khushal Khan Khattak Scholarship (1) for a student who secures the next to highest marks after Quaid-e-Azam and Merit Scholarships, from NWFP universities of Pakistan; (e) Allama Iqbal Scholarship (one for all general universities); (f) Merit Scholarship Scheme; (g) 100 Scholarship Scheme.
Subjects: (a), (b) and (d) Ph.D. programmes abroad in almost all subjects of science and arts (approved by the Government of Pakistan); (c) science preferred; (e) Ph.D. in Philosophy; (f) for 2 years M.Phil. study in Pakistan and 3 years Ph.D. study abroad.
Open to: nationals of Pakistan; (a) doctoral candidates, with M.A., M.Sc. Agriculture, M.Sc. Engineering and first position in a university (the entire academic career of the student is evaluated for competition); (b) university teachers, aged 25 to 40; (c) Pakistani university teachers; (d) resident students of NWFP universities of Pakistan; merit scholarships are awarded as follows in general universities: 1 to a student who tops in science subjects; 1 to a student who stands first in art subjects; in engineering universities: 1 to a student who secures first position in the departments of civil and mechanical engineering and another to a student who tops in the remaining departments; agriculture universities: 1 to a student who tops in animal husbandry and veterinary departments and another to a student who secures first position in the remaining departments; (g) talented students of low-paid employees (BPS1-15) for higher studies leading to Ph.D. abroad.
Place of study: (a), (b), (d) and (e) in the United Kingdom, the United States, Canada, Australia, Germany and New Zealand; (c) anywhere, subject to approval of the Government of Pakistan.
Duration: (a), (b) and (e) initially 1 year (renewable up to 3 years); (c) throughout the year; (d) initially 1 year (renewable up to 5 years); (f) and (g) 2 years M.Phil. study in Pakistan and 3 years Ph.D. study abroad.
Value: (a), (b), (d) and (e) maintenance (depending on the country); travel, books, tuition fee, thesis preparation, study tour expenses; paid monthly in advance in the currency of the country; (c) air fare and maintenance.
Applications: (a) at any time; (b) by invitation, in April; (c) 1 month in advance; to the Chairman, at the above address; (d) after a declaration of annual results; (e) by invitation, in October.

1740 International Islamic University
PO Box 1243
Islamabad
Tel: +92-51-926-1761/5
Fax: +92-51-225-0821
Web: http://www.iiu.edu.pk

Graduate and Postgraduate Programmes

Study Domains: Arabic, oriental studies, theology, religion.
Programmes: graduate and postgraduate programmes in Islamic studies.
Open to: male and female students of all nationalities meeting academic, linguistic and financial criteria.
Duration: 2 to 3 years; courses beginning in September.
Languages: English; English language proficiency permission of Ministry of Foreign Affairs required for nationals of non-English countries.
Applications: to the Director, Personnel and Administration at the above address.

1741 Isra University [IU]
PO Box 313
Hala Road
Hyderabad Sindh
Tel: +92-221-1620-181/84
Fax: +92-221-620-180/85
Web: http://www.isra.edu.pk

📖 Undergraduate, Graduate, Postgraduate Programmes

Study Domains: business administration, communication, computer science, medicine, paramedical studies.
Programmes: Bachelor's, Master's and Ph.D. degrees in medical studies; computer sciences; information technology and business administration.
Languages: English.
Applications: by 31 August to the Admissions Office at the above address.

1742 Jinnah University for Women [JUW]
5-C, Nazmabad
74600 Karachi
Tel: +92-21-661-9902
Fax: +92-21-662-0614
Web: http://www.juw.edu.pk
e-mail: info@juw.edu.pk

📖 Undergraduate, Graduate Programmes

Study Domains: biochemistry, botany, business administration, chemistry, computer science, economic and commercial sciences, journalism, languages, management, mathematics, microbiology, pharmacy and pharmacology, physics, teacher education, zoology.
Programmes: undergraduate and graduate programmes leading to Bachelor's and Master's degrees.
Open to: admission test required for computer science and information technology programmes.
Other conditions: women students.
Duration: 4-1/2 years.
Languages: English and Urdu.

1743 Ministry of Science and Technology
Evacuee Trust Complex
Agha Khan Road G-5/1
Islamabad
Tel: +92-51-921-1264
Fax: +92-51-921-0229

🎓 Scholarships

Study Domains: sciences, technology.
Scholarships: Science and Technology Scholarship Award.
Subjects: all major science and technology subjects.
Open to: Pakistani nationals, up to 32 years old; with B.Sc. Engineering, M.Sc., B.E., M.B.B.S., first class in final degree; GRE subject test required.
Place of study: all accredited universities in the United States, United Kingdom, Germany, Japan, France, China and Pakistan.
Duration: for Master's degree: 18 to 30 months; for Ph.D. degree: 36 to 60 months.
Value: maintenance allowance: US$650-$900 per month plus actual tuition fee; book allowance, US$400 per year; return air ticket.
Applications: by 15 March, to Assistant Scientific Advisor at the above address.

1744 National Institute of Banking and Finance [BSC]
Sector H-8/1
Pitras Bokhari Road
Islamabad
Tel: +92-51-925-8287
Fax: +92-51-925-8288
e-mail: nibafsbk@nibaf.gov.pk

📖 Banking Studies

Study Domains: finance.
Programmes: International Central Banking course;

International Commercial Banking course.
Open to: qualified candidates from developing countries in Afro-Asian and Latin-American regions nominated by their governments, with over 5 years' work experience and a functional knowledge of English.
Duration: 6 weeks; courses begin in March and December.
Financial assistance: fellowship allowance; Rs 2,000 per month; outfit allowance: Rs 1,000 on arrival, return economy-class ticket and free hotel accommodation.
Languages: instruction in English.
Applications: by July and November, to the Director, on prescribed form to be obtained through Pakistani Missions.

1745 National University of Computer and Emerging Sciences
Fast House
Rohtas Road G-9/4
Islamabad
Tel: +92-51-285-6930 / 33
Fax: +92-51-285-5070
Web: http://www.nu.edu.pk
e-mail: info@nu.edu.pk

📖 Undergraduate, Graduate Programmes

Study Domains: computer science.
Programmes: undergraduate and graduate programmes leading to Bachelor's and Master's degrees.
Open to: candidates meeting academic requirements and passing admission test.
Duration: 4 years beginning in August.
Fees: current registration: Rs 2,000; tuition: US$200 per course.
Languages: English.
Applications: by 30 June, to the above address, to Dr. M. Ayub Alvi (Email: ayub.alvi@nu.edu.pk).

1746 Quaid-e-Awam University of Engineering Science and Technology [QUEST]
Sakrand road
67480 Nawabshah
Tel: +92-241-937-0366
Fax: +92-241-937-0367
Web: http://quest.edu.pk#quest.edu.pk

📖 Undergraduate and Graduate Programmes

Study Domains: civil engineering, computer science, electricity and electronics, mechanical engineering.
Programmes: undergraduate and graduate degree programmes in computer systems engineering; civil engineering; electrical engineering; mechanical engineering; information technology; computer sciences.

1747 Quaid-i-Azam University
PO Box 1090
Islamabad
Tel: +92-51-921-9877
Fax: +92-51-921-9888
Web: http://www.qau.edu.pk
e-mail: vco@qau.edu.pk

📖 Graduate Programmes

Study Domains: administration, anthropology, chemistry, communication, computer science, education, English, information science, international relations, mathematics.
Programmes: programmes leading to a Master's degree in chemistry, administrative sciences, communications technology, computer sciences, education, English, mathematics, anthropology, international relations and defence in strategic studies.
Open to: male and female candidates of all nationalities, holding a Bachelor's degree in at least 1st division.
Duration: 2 years, beginning in September.
Languages: English (English language proficiency permission of Ministry of Foreign Affairs required for nationals of non-English countries).
Applications: to the Registrar at the above address.

1748 University of Balochistan

Sariab Road
Quetta
Tel: +92-81-921-1288
Fax: +92-81-921-1277
Web: http://www.uob.edu.pk

⌂ Graduate and Postgraduate Programmes

Study Domains: administration, biochemistry, botany, chemistry, communication, computer science, English, international relations, mathematics, pharmacy and pharmacology, physiology, zoology.
Programmes: graduate and postgraduate programmes.
Open to: male and female students of all nationalities meeting academic, linguistic and financial criteria; having passed intermediate exam in at least second division for graduate programme; at least graduate in second division for postgraduate programme.
Duration: 2 to 5 years beginning in March.
Fees: tuition: Rs 28,000-38,000; living costs: approximately Rs 20,000 per year.
Languages: English; English language proficiency permission of Ministry of Foreign Affairs required for nationals of non-English countries.
Applications: to the Registrar at the above address.

1749 University of Education, Lahore [UE]

Wahadat Colony
5400 Lahore
Tel: +92-42-543-3632
Fax: +92-42-543-3599
Web: http://www.ue.edu.pk
e-mail: admin@ue.edu.pk

⌂ Undergraduate, Graduate, Postgraduate Programmes

Study Domains: administration, arts, business administration, education, liberal arts, management, oriental studies, social sciences, teacher education, theology, religion.
Programmes: undergraduate, graduate, postgraduate programmes in arts and social sciences, science and technology; Islamic and oriental studies; management and administrative sciences; education.

1750 University of Engineering and Technology [UET]

District Rawalpindi
47050 Taxila
Tel: +92-0596-931-4225/4224
Fax: +92-0596-931-4226
Web: http://www.uet.edu
e-mail: dr_hjamal@yahoo.com

⚲ Scholarships

Study Domains: civil engineering, engineering, mathematics, mechanical engineering.
Scholarships: overseas training scholarships.
Subjects: electrical engineering; mechanical engineering; civil engineering; applied mathematics and industrial engineering.
Open to: Pakistani graduates, aged 25 to 40, with B.Sc. (Eng.) or with an M.A., M.Sc. in mathematics and science; good knowledge of English required; the scholarship holder must serve the University for 5 years after return from the studies abroad.
Place of study: USA, Canada, United Kingdom and Australia.
Duration: 1 to 3 years (renewable).
Applications: by 30 September.

1751 University of Karachi

University Road
75270 Karachi
Tel: +92-21-924-3195
Fax: +92-21-924-3203
Web: http://www.ku.edu.pk
e-mail: vc@ku.edu.pk

⌂ Graduate and Postgraduate Programmes

Study Domains: biochemistry, business administration, communication, computer science, education, English, geology, international relations, marine biology, mathematics, microbiology, physiology.
Programmes: graduate and postgraduate programmes.
Open to: students of all nationalities, male and female, having passed intermediate exam in at least the second division, meeting all academic criteria for graduate programme; at least graduate in second division for the postgraduate programme.
Duration: 2 to 5 years, beginning in January.
Fees: current registration plus tuition: Rs 100.000; living costs: approximately Rs 20,000 per year.
Languages: English; English language proficiency permission of Ministry of Foreign Affairs required for nationals of non-English countries.
Applications: to Registrar at the above address.

1752 University of Peshawar

Peshawar
Tel: +92-91-921-6469
Fax: +92-91-921-6470
Web: http://www.upesh.edu
e-mail: vice-chancellor@upesh.edu

⌂ Graduate and Postgraduate Programmes

Study Domains: anthropology, archaeology, botany, business administration, chemistry, computer science, education, English, geology, international relations, mathematics, pharmacy and pharmacology, zoology.
Programmes: graduate and postgraduate programmes.
Open to: male and female students of all nationalities meeting academic, linguistic and financial criteria; having passed intermediate exam in at least second division for graduate programme; at least graduate in second division for postgraduate programme.
Duration: 2 to 5 years beginning in September.
Languages: English; English language proficiency permission of Ministry of Foreign Affairs required for nationals of non-English countries.
Applications: to Registrar at the above address.

1753 University of Sindh

District Dadu
Jamshoro
Tel: +92-221-771-681/9
Fax: +92-221-771-284
e-mail: vichan@hyd.paknet.com.pk

⌂ Graduate and Postgraduate Programmes

Study Domains: biochemistry, botany, business administration, chemistry, communication, computer science, fisheries, geology, international relations, marine biology, mathematics, microbiology, physiology, zoology.
Programmes: graduate and postgraduate programmes.
Open to: male and female students of all nationalities meeting academic, linguistic and financial criteria; having passed intermediate exam in at least second division for graduate programme; at least graduate in second division for postgraduate programme.
Duration: 2 to 4 years beginning in September.
Fees: tuition; US$1,550 per semester; living costs: approximately Rs 20,000 per yare.
Languages: English; English language proficiency permission of Ministry of Foreign Affairs required for nationals of non-English countries.
Applications: to the Registrar at the above address.

1754 University of the Punjab

New Campus
Wahdat Road
Lahore
Tel: +92-42-921-1612
Fax: +92-42-923-1101
Web: http://www.pu.edu.pk
e-mail: puarshad@wol.net.pk

⌂ Graduate and Postgraduate Programmes

Study Domains: administration, biochemistry, business, business administration, communication, computer science, education, fine arts, geology, international relations, law,

mathematics, philosophy, psychology, space, trade.
Programmes: graduate and postgraduate programmes.
Open to: male and female students of all nationalities
meeting academic, linguistic and financial criteria; having
passed intermediate exam in at least second division for
graduate programme; at least graduate in second division for
postgraduate programme.
Duration: 2 to 5 years beginning in January.
Languages: English; English language proficiency
permission of Ministry of Foreign Affairs required for
nationals of non-English countries.
Applications: to Registrar at the above address.

1755 Virtual University [VU]
3rd Floor, Building No. 1-2
Aiwan-e-Iqbal Complex
Egerton Road
Lahore
Tel: +92-42-920-3113/7
Fax: +92-42-920-0604
Web: http://www.vu.edu.pk
e-mail: rector@vu.edu.pk

Undergraduate Programme / Distance Education

Study Domains: computer science.
Programmes: distance higher education leading to
Bachelor's degree in computer science.

Palestinian Autonomous Territories

Academic year: September to May.
Monetary unit: Jordanian dinar.
National student admission: Students should have
qualifications equivalent to the secondary-school level (name
of the credential: Tawjihi).
Language: Good knowledge of Arabic and English
required as they are languages of instruction.
Information services: The Palestinian Ministry of
Education and Higher Education: web:
 http://www.mohe.gov.ps/english.
Open and distance learning: Distance education is offered
at Al-Quds Open University
http://www.palestine-net.com/education/qou/.
Recognition of studies and qualification: Special
Committee, Ministry of Higher Education; PO Box 17360;
East Jerusalem; Palestine; tel: +972-2-298-2600; fax:
+972-2-2954518.

1756 An-Najah National University
PO Box 7
Nablus
Palestine
Tel: +972-9-239-4960
Fax: +972-9-234-5982
Web: http://www.najah.edu
e-mail: info@najah.edu

Undergraduate, Graduate and Postgraduate Programmes

Study Domains: all major fields.
Programmes: undergraduate, graduate and postgraduate
programmes leading to Bachelor's, Master's and PhD degrees
in all major fields.
Description: (a) undergraduate degrees in Science
(Mathematics, Physics, Chemistry, Biology and
Biotechnology, Medical Laboratory Sciences, Statistics); Arts
(Arabic, English, History, Geography, Sociology and Social
Work, Archaeology, Journalism, French); Shari'a (Religious
Law); Economics and Administrative Sciences (Business
Administration, Accounting, Economics, Political Science,
Financial and Banking Sciences, Marketing); Engineering
(Civil Engineering, Architectural Engineering, Electrical
Engineering, Chemical Engineering, Industrial Engineering,
Computer Engineering); Educational Sciences (Psychology,
Teaching Methods, Elementary Education, Physical
Education); Law; Agriculture (Plant Production and
Protection, Animal Production and Health, Agricultural
Economics and Rural Development); Pharmacy; Fine Arts
(Music, Photography, Interior Design); Medicine; Veterinary

Medicine; Information Technology (Computer Science,
Management Information Systems); (b) Master's in 26
programmes and Ph.D. in Chemistry.
Open to: candidates of any nationality holding a secondary
school certificate (or equivalent).
Duration: 4 to 5 years, depending on programmes.
Languages: English (required for science programmes)
and Arabic (required for humanities).
Applications: by 15 September to the above address.

Panamá

Año académico: Abril a diciembre.
Moneda nacional: Balboa.
Admisiones para estudiantes extranjeros: Título de
segunda enseñanza (bachillerato en ciencias, letras, comercio,
industrial o agropecuario, o título de maestro de enseñanza
primaria); aprobar un curso de capacitación.
Conocimientos lingüísticos: Es indispensable dominar
suficientemente el idioma español.
Formalidades de inmigración: La información debe
solicitarse en el consulado de Panamá en el país de origen del
estudiante, o en el país más cercano de su domicilio.
Servicios de información:
• Ministerio de Educación, Unidad de Relaciones
Internacionales, Apartado 2440, Panamá 3 (intercambios
internacionales de estudiantes).
• Ministerio de Planificación y Política Económica, Apartado
2496, Panamá 3 (intercambios internacionales de estudiantes).
• Instituto para la Formación y Aprovechamiento de Recursos
Humanos, Centro de Información y Documentación
(IFARHU/CIDI), Avenida 7.a España, Edificio Diorvett
Internacional, Apartado 6337, Panamá 5 (administra las becas
que concede el gobierno de Panamá en virtud de acuerdos y
convenios de cooperación y asistencia recíproca firmados con
otros países; tramita las becas que ofrecen los organismos
especializados de las Naciones Unidas, otros
organismos internacionales, y diversas instituciones oficiales
y privadas del extranjero, a estudiantes panameños para que
continúen sus estudios en Panamá o en el extranjero;
proporciona información acerca de la educación superior en
Panamá, los intercambios internacionales de estudiantes, etc.).

• Instituto para la Habilitación Especial-Instituto Superior de
Enseñanza, Camino Real de Bethania, Apartado 11349,
Panamá 6 (dispone de servicios especiales para estudiantes
panameños y extranjeros disminuidos físicamente, para llevar
a cabo intercambios de estudiantes, etc.).
• Instituto Centroamericano de Administración y Supervisión
de la Educación, Facultad de Humanidades, Estafeta
universitaria, Ciudad Universitaria, Panamá 3 (asesoramiento
a estudiantes extranjeros, intercambios internacionales de
estudiantes, etc.).
• Universidad de Panamá, Vicerrectoría de Investigaciones y
Posgrados, Estafeta Universitaria, Panamá 3 (orientación
sobre estudios y alojamiento; puede realizar intercambios
entre sus estudiantes y los de universidades extranjeras).
Existen facilidades de alojamiento a precios accesibles para
estudiantes extranjeros.
Enseñanza abierta y a distancia: Este tipo de enseñanza
es brindada por la Universidad Interamericana de Educación a
Distancia.
Convalidación de estudios y diplomas: Vicerrectoría de
Investigación y Postgrado, Universidad de Panamá, Dr
Octavio Méndez Pereira 3, El Cangrejo - Estafeta
Universitaria, Panamá, Panamá; tel: +507-223-0654; fax:
+507-264-3733; web: http://www.up.ac.pa.
Publicaciones / Sitios web:
• "Oportunidades de estudio en las instituciones de educación
superior en Panamá", IFARHU/CIDI, Apartado postal 6337
Panamá 5.

1757 Instituto para la Formación y Aprovechamiento de Recursos Humanos [IFARHU]

Apartado Postal 6337
Panamá 5
Tel: +507-269-6666
Fax: +507-263-6101
Web: http://www.ifarhu.gob.pa

🖝 Programa de becas

Campos de estudios: todas las materias principales.
Descripción:
(a) Programa de crédito educativo;
(b) Becas de puesto distinguido;
(c) Becas internacionales para realizar estudios superiores o de especialización, bajo los auspicios de organizaciones internacionales o extranjeras;
(d) Becas por convenio;
(e) Becas por concurso.
Materias de estudio: (a) cualquiera; son prioritarias las que urgen para el crecimiento económico del país; (b), (d) y (e) cualquiera; (c) depende del tipo de oferta; en general, todas.
Se conceden: (a) y (c) a panameños o a extranjeros con más de 10 años de residencia en Panamá; (b) a estudiantes panameños que hayan obtenido las mejores calificaciones académicas en las escuelas primarias oficiales, los primeros ciclos oficiales, los segundos ciclos de colegios oficiales y particulares, las universidades públicas; (d) a panameños que posean diploma de grado o bachillerato y tengan conocimientos del idioma del país de estudios; (e) como (a), de escasos recursos, con promedio mínimo de 4.0.
Lugar: (b) y (d) en colegios secundarios y universidades de Panamá; (c) en universidades extranjeras; (d) según el país que hace la oferta.
Duración: (b) 3 años para la educación media, 4 a 5 años para estudios de licenciatura, según el tiempo señalado para los estudios en el caso de posgrados; (c) variable según los estudios; (d) depende del convenio; (e) 3 años para estudios secundarios, duración completa de la carrera en el caso de estudios universitarios.
Importe: (a) se otorgan préstamos en función del tiempo de duración de la carrera; (b) monto mensual variable según nivel; (c) puede incluir pasaje, manutención, matrícula, colegiatura, libros, seguro; (d) incluye matrícula, colegiatura, manutención y pasajes; (e) como (b), pero no para posgrados.
Solicitudes: siempre en la dirección del título, dirigirse a:
(a) Departamento de Préstamos, Edificio IFARHU, de enero a diciembre; (b) entre enero y abril; (c) Departamento de Relaciones Internacionales, Cooperación y Asistencia Técnica (DRICAT), 6° piso, Edificio IFARHU; (d) Dirección General del IFARHU; (e) entre enero y abril, Departamento de Becas, Edificio IFARHU.

1758 Universidad de Panamá [UDP]

Ciudad Universitaria Dr. Octavio Méndez Pereira.
Vía Transístmica y Avenida Manuel Espinoza Batista.
Panamá
Tel: +507-263-6163
Fax: +507-264-3733
Web: http://www.up.ac.pa
e-mail: up@up.ac.pa

📖 Maestría en educación ambiental

Campos de estudios: administración, educación.
Descripción: programa regional con la participación de Guatemala, Honduras, El Salvador, Nicaragua, Costa Rica, Belice, República Dominicana y Panamá.
Se destina(n): a licenciados o equivalentes, con experiencia en labores de educación, promoción, organización de recursos humanos para la conservación y uso racional del ambiente; se exige comprensión de lectura del inglés.
Duración: 2 años.
Asistencia financiera: existen becas.
Inscripciones: por mayor información, dirigirse al Instituto Centroamericano de Administración y Supervisión de la Educación; Estafeta Universitaria; Facultad de Humanidades.

📖 Programas universitarios

Campos de estudios: todas las materias principales.

Papua New Guinea

Academic year: February to November.
Monetary unit: kina (K).
National student admission: Foreign students wishing to register in Papua New Guinea institutions of higher education must have qualifications as follows: credit passes at form IV level in English, mathematics and sciences (upper passes may not be accepted in higher education institutions); Papua New Guinea University of Technology and University of Papua New Guinea including Goroka Teachers' College accept students with good grades from Grade 12.
Language: good knowledge of English is essential for all courses. An orientation programme is organized each year for new students at the University of Papua New Guinea.
Information services:
• University of Papua New Guinea (UPNG).
• Department of Primary Industry and Department of Information, Konedobu.
• Papua New Guinea high commissions and embassies abroad.
• Department of Education, Waigani.
Open and distance learning: Correspondence courses are run by the Institute of Distance and Continuing Education of the University of Papua New Guinea.
Recognition of studies and qualification: Commission for Higher Education; PO Box 5117; Higher Education Wing; Boroko; NCD; Papua New Guinea.
Publications / Websites:
• 'Career Information for Secondary Teaching' and 'College Handbook', both published annually free of charge by UPNG Goroka Teachers' College.
• 'Handbook of Courses', published by UPNG; K 1 to K 3.
• 'General Information on Courses and Enrolment', published free of charge by UPNG.
• 'Administrative College of Papua New Guinea Handbook', obtainable from the College, PO Box 1216, Boroko.

1759 Papua New Guinea University of Technology Bulolo Forestry College [UOT]

PO Box 92
Bulolo, Morobe Province
Tel: +675-474-5226
Fax: +675-474-5311
Web: http://www.unitech.ac.pg

📖 Forestry Studies

Study Domains: forestry.
Programmes: Diploma of forestry: forest management, forest utilization, silviculture, botany, dendrology, ecology, protection and wildlife: 40 participants with 4 places for international students.
Open to: candidates from South West Pacific countries aged at least 17 years, having successfully completed 4 years secondary education with credits in English, mathematics and science.
Duration: 3 years.
Fees: overseas students, US$2,958 per year.
Applications: by 31 August, to the Principal at the above address.

1760 University of Papua New Guinea [COAHS]

PO Box 320
University Post Office
National Capital District
Tel: +675-326-0900
Fax: +675-326-7187
e-mail: PR&M@upng.ac.pg

📖 Undergraduate, Graduate Programmes

Study Domains: business administration, health and hygiene, humanities and arts, liberal arts, natural sciences, nursing, physics, sciences, social sciences.

Programmes: undergraduate and graduate programmes in business administration, humanities and social sciences, law, medicine and health sciences, natural and phsical sciences.

Paraguay

Año académico: Marzo a diciembre.
Moneda nacional: Guaraní.
Servicios de información: Ministerio de Educación y Cultura, Dirección de Cooperación Internacional, Edificio Sudamérica, Piso 3, Iturbe 891 y Manuel Dominguez, Asunción, Paraguay; tel: +595-21-550-855; email: dci@mec.gov.py; web: http://www.mec.gov.py.
Convalidación de estudios y diplomas: Ministerio de Educación y Cultura, Dirección de Cooperación Internacional, Edificio Sudamérica, Piso 3, Iturbe 891 y Manuel Dominguez, Asunción, Paraguay; tel: +595-21-550-855; email: dci@mec.gov.py; web: http://www.mec.gov.py.

1761   Universidad Comunera [UCOM]

San José y Artigas
Asunción
Tel: +595-21-201-995
Fax: +595-21-201-995

📖 Programas universitarios

Campos de estudios: administración, economía, finanzas, gestión, relaciones públicas, riesgos, seguros.
Descripción: Carreras en áreas de relaciones públicas, administración agraria, economía social, ciencias del seguro, banca y finanza, administración pública; master en gestión municipal. Algunos cursos son semi-presenciales y otros a distancia.
Asistencia financiera: existen becas.

1762   Universidad del Norte [UNINORTE]

Avenida España 676
Asunción
Tel: +595-21-229-450
Fax: +595-21-229-450
Web: http://www.uninorte.edu.py
e-mail: info@uninorte.edu.py

📖 Programas universitarios

Campos de estudios: todas las materias principales.
Descripción:
(a) Carreras en sus facultades de: educación y ciencias humanas, ciencias de la salud, derecho y ciencias políticas, administración de empresas, ingeniería, medicina, química;
(b) Posgrados: especializaciones en medicina paliativa, en nutrición clínica, en odontología, en salud pública; maestrías: en ciencias ambientales, en ciencias contables, en didáctica lingüístico-literaria, en educación, en historia, en marketing, en periodismo; maestría y doctorado en derecho.
Asistencia financiera: descuentos porcentuales de acuerdo a condiciones económicas.
Inscripciones: por mayor información, dirigirse a Oficina de Registro, y en el caso de (b) también a postgrado@uninorte.edu.py.

Perú

Año académico: Abril a diciembre.
Moneda nacional: Nuevo sol.
Admisiones para estudiantes extranjeros: Certificado de fin de estudios secundarios.
Conocimientos lingüísticos: Es indispensable dominar suficientemente el idioma español.
Servicios de información:
• Ministerio de Educación Pública, Parque Universitario s/n, Lima 1.
• Instituto Nacional de Becas y de Crédito Educativo, Avenida Arequipa n° 4528, Lima 18 (organismo encargado de todo lo relacionado con los estudios en el extranjero). Publica un boletín semanal en el que se reseñan las becas otorgadas por gobiernos y entidades extranjeras.
• Instituto Peruano de Fomento Educativo, Avenida Arenales 371, Oficina 501, Lima (mantiene programas de becas y de

préstamos en el Perú).
• Consejo Nacional de Ciencia y Tecnología (CONCYTEC), Camilo Carrillo n.° 114, Jesús María, Lima.
Convalidación de estudios y diplomas: Oficina de Asuntos Internacionales, Ministerio de Educación, Avenida Van de Velde 160, San Borja Norte, Lima, Perú; tel: +51-1-436-5855; fax: +51-1-436-1240; web: http://www.minedu.gob.pe.

1763   Escuela de Administración de Negocios para Graduados [ESAN]

Apartado 1846
Lima 100
Tel: (51) 4351760
Fax: (51) 4364067
Web: http://www.esan.edu.pe

🎓 Becas del Programa de Magister en Administración a la excelencia profesional

Campos de estudios: administración, administración de empresas.
Se conceden: a nacionales de cualquier país que demuestren excelencia profesional, posean un título profesional y tengan buenos conocimientos del idioma español; edad: 24 años como mínimo.
Duración: 13 meses, renovable cada 4 meses en función del rendimiento académico (mínimo tercio superior).
Importe: pensión de estudios de aproximadamente 12.000 dólares de los Estados Unidos.
Solicitudes: a la Dirección del Programa Magister.

1764   Escuela de Administración de Negocios para Graduados [ESAN]

Alonso de Molina 1652
Monterrico Surco
Lima
Tel: +511-317-7226
Fax: +511-345-1328
Web: http://www.esan.edu.pe

📖 Programas superiores en administración

Campos de estudios: administración, administración de empresas, finanzas, negocio.
Descripción:
(a) Magister en administración (MBA);
(b) Programas de dirección de ejecutivos (especializaciones en administración de empresas, marketing, finanzas, logística, operaciones/producción, administración de la salud, informática, liderazgo, recursos humanos); banca y negocios financieros; proyectos de inversión;
(c) Programas cortos de especialización para ejecutivos.
Se ofrece servicio completo de oportunidades de trabajo para egresados del Tiempo Completo de (a) que incluye difusión en principales empresas.
Se destina(n): (a) a graduados universitarios con 1 año de experiencia profesional como mínimo; existe examen de admisión escrito y entrevistas.
Duración: (a) 13 meses a tiempo completo, 2 años a tiempo parcial (comienzos en marzo y julio respectivamente); (b) 9 meses a 1 año; (c) 2 meses.
Inscripciones: para el examen de noviembre, hasta el 12 de noviembre; para el examen de diciembre, hasta el 10 de diciembre; en todos los casos, dirigirse a la Oficina de Admisión.

1765   Escuela Nacional de Salud Pública [ENSAP]

Avenida Brasil 642, 3er piso
Breña
Lima 05
Tel: (51) 1 3308013
Fax: (51) 1 3308013
e-mail: escuela@atn.limaperu.net

📖 Programa de cursos para técnicos y profesionales de la salud

Campos de estudios: administración, educación permanente, enfermería, gestión, higiene y salud, investigación, medicina preventiva, microbiología, nutrición.

Descripción:
(a) Cursos para técnicos en salud: formación de técnicos en saneamiento ambiental; formación de inspectores sanitarios de alimentos; formación de técnicos en registros médicos, estadística e informática en salud; medicamentos y uso racional de medicamentos esenciales;
(b) Cursos para profesionales en salud: maestría en salud pública y gestión sanitaria; especialización en gerencia de servicios de salud; diplomas y certificados según el caso en administración de servicios de salud, administración hospitalaria, epidemiología, administración estratégica en educación permanente de la salud, acreditación hospitalaria, formulación y evaluación de proyectos de salud, costos e instrumentos de estudio de la producción, marketing aplicado a los servicios de salud, gestión de la calidad de los servicios de salud, factor humano y desarrollo organizacional, gestión de programa de medicamentos y farmacias hospitalarias.
Se destina(n): a nacionales y extranjeros, que se desempeñen en el área de salud, con estudios secundarios o superiores para los cursos de técnicos o profesionales respectivamente.
Duración: sede, fecha y horario a concertar con las instituciones de salud.
Inscripciones: hasta 1 semana antes de la fecha del inicio de la actividad.

1766 Escuela Superior de Administración de Empresas, Ventas y Mercadotecnia [ESAN]
Jirón Chancay 869
Lima 1

☛ Becas de estudio
Campos de estudios: administración de empresas, ciencias económicas y comerciales, economía, industria y comercio, marketing.
Se conceden: a nacionales de cualquier país que sepan el idioma español y reúnan los requisitos de ingreso; edad: 35 años como máximo.
Duración: 1 año.
Importe: cubre los gastos de alojamiento, manutención y material de estudio.
Solicitudes: hasta el 1° de julio.

1767 Escuela Superior de Bellas Artes "Corriente Alterna" [ESDBAA]
Avenida de la Aviación 500
Miraflores
Lima 18
Tel: +51-1-446-4203
Fax: +51-1-242-8482
Web: http://www.corrientealterna.edu.pe/home.htm
e-mail: alterna@mail.cosapidata.com.pe

☐ Programas en artes
Campos de estudios: artes, artes aplicadas, artes gráficas, artes plásticas, bellas artes, fotografía.
Descripción: estudios conducentes a diploma de técnico universitario en fotografía, cerámica, dibujo, pintura.
Se destina(n): a aspirantes que superen examen psicotécnico de admisión.
Duración: 5 años.
Asistencia financiera: existen becas parciales de estudio.
Inscripciones: hasta el 15 de diciembre.

☛ Becas de estudios en artes
Campos de estudios: artes, artes aplicadas, artes gráficas, artes plásticas, bellas artes, fotografía.
Becas: becas de estudio de fotografía, cerámica, dibujo, pintura (entre 10 y 20 por año).
Se conceden: a jóvenes de edades comprendidas entre 18 y 25 años que hayan completado estudios secundarios.
Duración: 3 meses.
Importe: 600 dólares.
Solicitudes: hasta septiembre.

1768 Facultad de Teología Pontificia y Civil de Lima [FTPCL]
Carlos Bondy 700
Pueblo Libre
Apartado 21-0135
Lima 21
Tel: (51) (1) 461 0013
Fax: (51) (1) 461 6385
Web: http://www.ftpcl.edu.pe
e-mail: rectorado@ftpcl.edu.pe

☐ Programas universitarios
Campos de estudios: educación, filosofía, teología, religión.
Descripción:
(a) Estudios generales, programas de teología, filosofía, educación;
(b) Grados y posgrados: licenciatura canónica en teología, maestría en educación, doctorado en sagrada teología.
Inscripciones: por mayores informaciones, dirigirse al Servicio de Admisión.

1769 Instituto Peruano de Administración de Empresas [IPAE]
Avenida La Marina Cuadra 16 s/n
Pueblo Libre
Tel: +511-566-3883
Web: http://www.ipae.edu.pe
e-mail: infipae@ipae.edu.pe

☐ Programas académicos
Campos de estudios: administración, administración de empresas, estudios sobre el desarrollo, finanzas, marketing.
Descripción:
(a) Carrera profesional "Escuela de Empresarios" (título profesional con especializaciones en marketing o finanzas);
(b) Programas de desarrollo empresarial;
(c) Programas de educación a distancia;
(d) Programas de desarrollo agrario y agroindustrial.
Se destina(n): (a) a estudiantes egresados de educación secundaria, a trabajadores o empresarios que acrediten este nivel.
Duración: 4 años.
Asistencia financiera: (a) se otorgan créditos financieros y becas por mérito de rendimiento académico y situación económica.

1770 Instituto Peruano de Fomento Educativo [IPFE]
Coronel Zegarra 758, Jesús María
Apartado Postal 3685
Lima 100
Tel: +511-471-3931
Fax: +511-471-7396
Web: http://www.ipfe.net
e-mail: acadipfe@infonegocio.net.pe

☛ Préstamos de estudio
Campos de estudios: administración, ciencias, educación, formación profesional, tecnología.
Materias de estudio: perfeccionamiento de profesionales en ramas científicas o técnicas, ciencia, educación, administración, etc.
Se conceden: a peruanos que deseen realizar estudios de posgrado.
Lugar: en Perú o cualquier otro país.
Importe: consiste en ayudas económicas.

1771 Instituto Superior Tecnológico Privado TECSUP No. 1 [TECSUP]
Avenida Separadora Industrial s/n
Santa Anita
Apartado Postal 18-0755
Lima
Tel: (51) 1 4371905/06/07
Fax: (51) 1 4371909

Programas en áreas tecnológicas

Campos de estudios: educación permanente, electricidad y electrónica, tecnología industrial.
Descripción: Varias modalidades:
(a) Especializaciones en: operaciones químicas y metalúrgicas, mantenimiento (de maquinaria pesada, de maquinaria de planta), electrotecnia industrial, electrónica industrial, electrónica de sistemas computarizados;
(b) Programa de formación continua: cursos regulares en automatización, automotriz, electrónica, electrotecnia, gestión de la producción, informática, mecánica, química y metalurgia; otras modalidades: programas integrales, cursos a medida, capacitación a distancia, diplomados, talleres, seminarios y simposia.
Se destina(n): (a) a egresados de la educación básica, de cualquier nacionalidad, hasta los 30 años de edad, que superen examen general de admisión.
Se dicta(n): (a) en Lima y en Arequipa.
Duración: (a) 3 años (comienzos en marzo).
Inscripciones: hasta febrero.

Beca de estudio

Campos de estudios: electricidad y electrónica, tecnología industrial.
Materias de estudio: automatización eléctrica industrial.
Se conceden: a personas menores de 30 años, de cualquier nacionalidad, que posean como mínimo diploma de electricidad o electrónica, que dominen el idioma español.
Duración: 6 meses (no renovable).
Importe: 1.500 dólares de los Estados Unidos por los 6 meses.
Solicitudes: hasta el 31 de diciembre del año anterior al otorgamiento de la beca.

1772 Pontificia Universidad Católica del Perú Escuela de Graduados [PUCP]

Avenida Universitaria Cuadra 18 s/n
Apartado Postal 1761
Lima 32
Tel: (51) 1 44612225
Fax: (51) 1 4611785
Web: http://www.pucp.edu.pe
e-mail: promydes@pucp.edu.pe

Programas de posgrado

Campos de estudios: todas las materias principales.
Descripción: Estudios de posgrado conducentes al grado académico de:
(a) Doctor en derecho;
(b) Magister en las siguientes especialidades: administración de negocios, antropología, comunicaciones, derecho (menciones civil, constitucional, internacional económico), economía, educación (menciones gestión de la educación, enseñanza de la física, la matemática, la química), filosofía, física, física aplicada, historia, informática, ingeniería civil, ingeniería mecánica, lengua y literatura hispánicas, matemáticas, psicología, química y sociología.
Se destina(n): a nacionales de cualquier país que tengan el bachillerato o una licenciatura y sepan inglés o francés, además del español.
Duración: 4 semestres.
Inscripciones: hasta el 25 de enero.

Programas universitarios

Campos de estudios: todas las materias principales, estudios culturales, programas de verano.
Descripción:
(a) Escuela de estudios especiales: programas universitarios en 66 especialidades a través de sus Facultades de administración y contabilidad, de ciencias e ingeniería, de ciencias sociales, de derecho, de educación, de letras y ciencias humanas, de trabajo social, de arte. La Escuela de estudios especiales no conduce a grado académico o título profesional, sino a un diploma de estudios;
(b) Escuela de graduados: programas en las mismas áres;
(c) Curso de verano (en inglés) sobre temas peruanos para grupos de 16 o más alumnos.
Se destina(n): (a) a alumnos que hayan cursado por lo menos 1 semestre de estudios en la universidad de origen o el equivalente de 18 créditos.

Duración: (a) varía según el programa; hay 2 semestres por año que empiezan en marzo y en septiembre; los alumnos de la Escuela de Estudios Especiales pueden cursar como máximo 2 semestres de estudio; (c) junio-julio.
Inscripciones: para mayores informaciones dirigirse a la Dirección de Promoción y Desarrollo.

1773 Servicio Nacional de Adiestramiento en Trabajo Industrial [SENATI]

Panamericana Norte Km. 15.200
Apartado Postal 1769
Lima 1
Tel: (51) 1 5334485
Fax: (51) 1 5335240

Becas de estudio

Campos de estudios: diseño, diseño industrial, electricidad y electrónica, hidrología, industria textil, informática, ingeniería, mecánica, tecnología industrial, telecomunicaciones.
Descripción:
(a) Técnico industrial (1 por especialidad);
(b) Técnico en ingeniería (2).
Materias de estudio: (a) mecánica de producción, diseño de máquinas, textilería, diseño gráfico, electrónica industrial, automatismo; (b) ingeniería mecánica de producción, ingeniería mecánica de mantenimiento, ingeniería electrónica.
Se conceden: a alumnos que se destaquen y obtengan buenas calificaciones, menores de 30 años, de preferencia latinoamericanos.
Lugar: (b) en la Escuela Superior Privada del SENATI.
Duración: (a) semestral; renovable hasta completar 6 semestres siempre que se apruebe el semestre; (b) por ciclo; renovable hasta completar 12 ciclos siempre que se apruebe el ciclo.
Solicitudes: hasta el 30 de diciembre; dirigirse a la Dirección General del SENATI.

1774 Universidad "Ricardo Palma" [URP]

Avenida A. Benavídez 5440
Las Gardenias-Surco
Lima
Tel: (51) 1 492505
Fax: (51) 1 492505
Web: http://www.urp.edu.pe

Becas por convenio Marco y acuerdo específico para antegrado y posgrado

Campos de estudios: administración, arquitectura, biología, contabilidad, economía, enfermería, ingeniería, interpretación y traducción, psicología.
Se conceden: a postulantes con certificado de cursos universitarios aprobados para el caso del pregrado y con bachillerato para el caso de posgrado.
Lugar: en la URP.
Importe: según convenio, puede tratarse de la exoneración del pago de la matrícula, del autoseguro o de la pensión de enseñanza estudiantil por cada semestre académico.
Solicitudes: primera semana de febrero para el primer semestre académico y primera semana de junio para el segundo semestre académico; dirigirse a la Oficina de Cooperación Internacional, en la dirección que figura en el título.

1775 Universidad "Ricardo Palma" [URP]

Avenida Benavídez 5440
Las Gardenias-Surco
Lima 33
Tel: (51) 1 2750459
Fax: (51) 1 2750459
Web: http://www.urp.edu.pe
e-mail: rector@li.urp.edu.pe

Programas universitarios

Campos de estudios: todas las materias principales, administración, arquitectura, biología, contabilidad, economía, enfermería, ingeniería, interpretación y traducción, medicina, museología y museografía, psicología.

Descripción:
(a) Estudios pre-universitarios en su Centro pre-universitario;
(b) Carreras universitarias en sus Facultades y Centros académicos asociados, conducentes a la licenciatura o título profesional según el caso en arquitectura, administración, biología, contabilidad, economía, ingeniería civil, ingeniería electrónica, ingeniería industrial, ingeniería informática, medicina humana, psicología, traducción e interpretación, enfermería;
(c) Programas de segunda especialización y maestrías en su Escuela de posgrado en ingeniería de telecomunicaciones, docencia universitaria, gestión tecnológica, museología.
Duración: (b) 5 años (ciclos comienzan en abril y agosto).
Asistencia financiera: becas por convenio de reciprocidad para antegrado o posgrado con universidades del extranjero.
Inscripciones: hasta la segunda semana de marzo y agosto; dirigirse a la Oficina de Admisión, Avenida Arequipa 5198, Miraflores, Lima.

1776 Universidad Católica de Santa María [UCSM]
Samuel Velarde 320, Umacollo
Casilla Postal 1350
Arequipa
Tel: : (51) 54 251112
Fax: (51) 54 25254
Web: http://www.ucsm.edu.pe

📖 **Programas universitarios**

Campos de estudios: todas las materias principales.
Descripción: (a) Programas universitarios de formación profesional (bachillerato, licenciaturas) con diversas especialidades, en sus diferentas Facultades: ciencias de la comunicación social (comunicación social, publicidad y medios, psicología); ciencias de la educación y humanidades (educación, teología); ciencias histórico-arqueológicas (arqueología y turismo); trabajo social; enfermería; farmacia y bioquímica; medicina humana; obstetricia y puericultura; odontología; ciencias e ingenierías biológicas y químicas (medicina veterinaria y zootecnia, ingeniería agronómica, ingeniería de industria alimentaría, ingeniería de sistemas, ingeniería electrónica, ingeniería mecánica, ingeniería civil, ingeniería industrial); ciencias jurídicas y políticas (derecho); ciencias contables y financieras (contabilidad); ciencias económico-administrativas (economía, administración de empresas);
(b) Escuela de postgrado: maestrías y doctorados en las áreas de humanidades, ciencias y tecnologías.
Se destina(n): a candidatos que cumplan los requisitos necesarios; en el caso de extranjeros, pueden provenir de países signatarios del Convenio "Andrés Bello" o de un Traslado Externo Internacional.
Duración: en general, 10 semestres (11 semestres para obstetricia y puericultura e ingeniería civil y 12 semestres para odontología, derecho y medicina; (en este último caso debe agregarse 1 año de internado); los semestres comienzan en marzo y agosto.
Asistencia financiera: existen becas para estudiantes con rendimiento óptimo y situación económica que lo justifique.

1777 Universidad de Lima [UDL]
Apartado 852
Lima
Tel: (51) 1 4376767
Fax: : (51) 1 4378066
Web: http://www.ulima.edu.pe

🍔 **Becas de estudio**

Campos de estudios: administración, ciencias políticas, comunicación, contabilidad, derecho, economía, ingeniería, metalurgia, periodismo, psicología.
Descripción: Becas destinadas a estudios de bachiller y título profesional posteriormente (2).
Materias de estudio: ciencias administrativas, ciencias contables, ciencias de la comunicación (comunicación organizacional, periodismo, medios audiovisuales y publicidad), economía, derecho y ciencias políticas, ingeniería industrial, ingeniería metalúrgica y de materiales, ingeniería de sistemas, psicología.
Se conceden: a personas de cualquier nacionalidad, no mayores de 22 años, que hayan completado los estudios de la enseñanza media y aprobado el examen de admisión en una universidad acreditada oficialmente de su país de origen.

Duración: 2 semestres (renovables automáticamente en base al rendimiento académico).
Importe: monto semestral que cubre matrícula, pensión y certificaciones.
Solicitudes: hasta el 15 de septiembre del año anterior al del inicio de los estudios, en la Dirección Universitaria de Servicios Académicos y Registro.

1778 Universidad de San Martin de Porres [USMP]
Ciudad Universitaria
Av. Las Calandrias s/n Santa Anita
Lima
Tel: +511478-1001/ +511-362-0064
Web: http://www.usmp.edu.pe
e-mail: webmaster@usmp.edu.pe

📖 **Programas universitarios**

Campos de estudios: todas las materias principales.

1779 Universidad del Pacífico [UP]
Avenida Salaverry 202
Jesús María
Lima 11
Tel: (51) 14712277
Fax: (51) 14706121
Web: http://www.up.edu.pe
e-mail: dri@up.edu.pe

📖 **Programas universitarios**

Campos de estudios: administración, administración de empresas, contabilidad, economía, educación permanente, español, finanzas.
Descripción:
(a) Estudios de pregrado: carreras de economía, administración y contabilidad;
(b) Estudios de postgrado: maestría en finanzas, maestría en administración de empresas;
(c) Programas de administración de empresas para jóvenes, para pequeños empresarios, para mujeres empresarias;
(d) Programa de español para extranjeros.
Se destina(n): (a) a candidatos que hayan culminado estudios secundarios y superen examen de admisión; (b) a nacionales o extranjeros con grado de bachiller o equivalente, con experiencia de 2 años como mínimo, seleccionados por entrevista personal y recomendaciones.
Duración: (a) 5 años (semestres de abril a julio y de septiembre a diciembre); (b) 2 años a tiempo completo.
Asistencia financiera: (b) existen becas mediante fuentes de financiamiento extranjeras (MUTIS, BID, entre otros).

1780 Universidad Nacional "Jorge Basadre Grohmann" [UNJBG]
Calle Alto Lima 1594
Apartado Postal 316
Tacna
Tel: (51) 54 721385
Fax: (51) 54 721384
Web: http://www.principal.unjbg.edu.pe

📖 **Programas universitarios**

Campos de estudios: todas las materias principales.
Descripción: (a) Curso de programación;
Programas de bachillerato y licenciatura en las siguientes áreas:
(b) Ingeniería: de minas, geológica-geotecnia, civil, metalúrgica, mecánica;
(c) Ciencias contables y financieras; ciencias administrativas;
(d) Ingeniería pesquera: transformación, acuicultura, extracción pesquera;
(e) Ciencias agrícolas: agronomía, economía agrícola, medicina veterinaria y zootecnia;
(f) Ingeniería en industrias alimentarías;
(g) Obstetricia;
(h) Ciencias de la educación con especialidades en: lengua y literatura, ciencias sociales, idioma extranjero, matemáticas y física, biología y química;
(i) Enfermería;
(j) Ciencias: biología-microbiología, computación-matemática, ingeniería química, física aplicada con especialidad en energía renovable;

Programas de posgrado:
(k) Maestrías en: desarrollo agrario, tecnología educativa, computación e informática.
Se destina(n): (b) a (j) a quienes presenten certificado de estudios legalizados y superen examen de admisión escrito; (k) a quienes tengan título de Bachiller y superen examen de admisión consistente en entrevista.
Duración: (b) a (j) 5 años (cursos de abril a diciembre); (k) 2 años (semestres de abril a agosto y de agosto a diciembre).
Asistencia financiera: (k) se conceden becas que pueden consistir en el costo del curso, comedor universitario, pasaje universitario y seguro universitario.
Inscripciones: hasta marzo de cada año; dirigirse a la Oficina Técnica de Cooperación Internacional, en la dirección que figura en el título.

Becas de estudio

Campos de estudios: ciencias agronómicas, educación, informática, tecnología.
Descripción: Becas para realizar estudios de posgrado en desarrollo agrario, en computación e informática, en tecnología educativa (2).
Se conceden: a postulantes nacionales y extranjeros, que posean grado de bachiller y/o título universitario.
Duración: 1 año (renovable 1 vez).
Importe: monto semestral que cubre 90% de a matrícula, servicio de comedor y alojamiento, seguro médico universitario.
Solicitudes: hasta marzo de cada año, en la Oficina de Cooperación Técnica Internacional, en la dirección que figura en el título.

1781 Universidad Nacional Agraria La Molina [UNALM]
Apartado 456
Lima 1
Tel: (51) 1 3495877
Fax: : (51) 1 3480747
Web: http://www.lamolina.edu.pe
e-mail: orgi@lamolina.edu.pe

Programas universitarios

Campos de estudios: agricultura, ciencias agronómicas, ciencias de la tierra, recursos naturales, silvicultura.
Descripción: Programas de carreras profesionales y programas de maestrías en conservación de recursos forestales, entomología, fitopatología, industrias forestales, manejo forestal, mejoramiento genético de plantas, nutrición, producción agrícola, producción animal, suelos, tecnología de alimentos, agronegocios, ingeniería de recursos de agua.
Se destina(n): a bachilleres de cualquier nacionalidad, que superen proceso de admisión consistente en examen de conocimientos, examen de inglés y entrevista.
Duración: 5 años las carreras, 2 años las maestrías.
Asistencia financiera: la Universidad no cuenta con becas de fondos propios; para estudiantes extranjeros, se pueden gestionar ante organismos internacionales.
Inscripciones: dirigirse a la Oficina Rectoral de Gestión Internacional, en la dirección que figura en el título.

1782 Universidad Nacional de Educación "Enrique Guzmán y Valle" [UNE]
Avenida Enrique Guzmán y Valle s/n
Apartado postal 6162
Lima 15
Tel: (51) 1 3600642
Fax: (51) 1 3600634
Web: http://www.une.edu.pe

Formación de educadores (profesores)

Campos de estudios: educación, formación de docentes.
Descripción: Especialidades en sus tres facultades:
(a) Humanidades: historia y geografía, psicología y filosofía, lengua española y literatura, lengua extranjera (inglés), educación artística, educación inicial, educación primaria, educación física;
(b) Biología y educación ambiental, química-física, matemática e informática, agropecuaria, industria alimentaria y nutrición;
(c) Tecnología: confecciones industriales, construcciones en

metalmadera, electricidad, electrónica, mecánica de producción y automotriz, administración y comercio.
Se destina(n): a nacionales de cualquier país que hayan concluído sus estudios secundarios o equivalente y que deseen ejercer la docencia como profesión.

1783 Universidad Nacional de Ingeniería Facultad de Arquitectura, Urbanismo y Artes [UNI]
Avenida Tupac Amaru 219
Rimac, Lima
Tel: (51) 1 14 4811070
Fax: (51) 1 14 4819842
Web: http://www.uni.edu.pe
e-mail: inifaua@faua.uni.edu.pe

Programas de posgrado

Campos de estudios: arquitectura, diseño, urbanismo.
Descripción: maestría en restauración de monumentos, de arquitectura y urbanismo; maestría en planificación y gestión para el desarrollo urbano y regional; maestría en arquitectura; segunda especialización en diseño urbano.
Se destina(n): a bachilleres y profesionales universitarios seleccionados en base a curriculum, trabajos de investigación y/o proyectos, así como entrevista personal.
Duración: 2 años.
Asistencia financiera: existe posibilidad de media beca o beca de estudios.
Inscripciones: dirigirse a Sección de Posgrado y Segunda Especialización, Facultad de Arquitectura, Urbanismo y Artes, UNI, Recavarren 542, Miraflores, Lima.

1784 Universidad Nacional de Tumbes [UNT]
Centro Cívico, 3er piso
Plaza de Armas
157 Tumbes
Tel: (51) (7) 452 3952
Fax: (51) (7) 452 3081
Web: http://www.untumbes.edu.pe
e-mail: carcan@untumbes.edu.pe

Estudios de formación profesional

Campos de estudios: ciencias agronómicas, ciencias económicas y comerciales, ciencias sociales, derecho, enfermería, formación profesional, obstetricia y ginecología, pesquería.
Descripción: áreas de ciencias agrarias (agronomía, ingeniería forestal), ciencias de la salud (obstetricia y enfermería), derecho y ciencias sociales, ingeniería pesquera, ciencias económicas (administración, contabilidad).
Se destina(n): a estudiantes con estudios secundarios completos.
Duración: 5 años académicos; inicios en marzo.
Inscripciones: hasta marzo; por mayores informaciones, dirigirse a la Oficina General de Admisión.

1785 Universidad Nacional Mayor de San Marcos [UNMSM]
República de Chile 295
Apartado Postal 454
Lima 100
Tel: (51) 1 4336109
Fax: (51) 1 4336337
Web: http://www.unmsm.edu.pe

Programas universitarios

Campos de estudios: todas las materias principales.
Descripción:
(a) Programas universitarios conducentes a la licenciatura en 42 especialidades;
(b) Programas de posgrado conducentes al grado de magister en 19 especialidades con 67 menciones;
(c) Cursos para optar el doctorado en: derecho, educación, filosofía, farmacia y bioquímica, literatura peruana y latinoamericana.
Se destina(n): (a) a egresados de educación básica, previa selección.

Inscripciones: para mayor información, dirigirse a la Oficina General de Cooperación y Relaciones Interinstitucionales, en la dirección que figura en el título.

1786 Universidad Peruana de Ciencias Aplicadas [UPC]

Avenida Primavera 2390
Monterrico
Lima 33
Tel: (51) (1) 313 3333
Fax: (51) (1) 313 3344
Web: http://www.upc.edu.pe

Programas universitarios

Campos de estudios: todas las materias principales.
Descripción:
(a) Carreras en áreas de administración (contabilidad, finanzas, marketing, negocios internacionales); ciencias de la comunicación (periodismo, publicidad); economía; ingeniería (civil, industrial, electrónica, de sistemas); arquitectura; derecho;
(b) Escuela de empresa: maestría en administración, en marketing, en finanzas, cursos de extensión (diplomas, maestrías);
(c) Programa Study Abroad: idioma castellano, cultura peruana y latinoamericana y cursos de especialidad;
(d) Áreas de humanidades y ciencias: licenciatura en historia, diploma en dirección general (Pontificia Universidad Católica de Chile); diploma de estrategias y estilos avanzados para la gestión (Division of Continuing Education, Harvard University - UPC); ingeniero civil (Pontificia Universidad Católica del Perú); postgrado en ingeniería hidráulica (Universidad de Newcastle Upon Tyne, Inglaterra e Instituto Internacional de Ingeniería Hidráulica y Ambiental, Holanda); postgrado en ingeniería estructural (Pontificia Universidad Católica del Perú).
Se destina(n): (c) a alumnos extranjeros inscriptos en una institución extranjera de nivel universitario.
Duración: (c) hasta dos semestres.
Inscripciones: (b) consultar http://escuelaempresa.upc.edu.pe. Por mayores informaciones referentes a todos los programas, dirigirse a la Dirección de Relaciones Internacionales o consultar http://www.upc.edu.pe/home/study-abroad.

Becas de estudio

Campos de estudios: todas las materias principales.
Open to: a alumnos que se destacan y obtengan buenas calificaciones.
Duration: 1 semestre.
Value: $3,300.
Applications: 4 meses antes months before before the beginning of academic term; contact dpacheco@upc.edu.pe.

1787 Universidad Peruana "Cayetano Heredia" Dirección de Especialización en Estomatología [UPCH]

Avenida Honorio Delgado 430
Apartado 4314
Lima 31
Tel: (51) 1 3811950
Fax: (51) 1 3811940
Web: http://www.upch.edu.pe
e-mail: dapge@upch.edu.pe

Estudios de posgrado

Campos de estudios: estudios dentales, medicina.
Descripción: prevención, diagnóstico y tratamiento de las alteraciones de mayor complejidad de la región oro-maxilofacial:
(a) Especialización en estomatología;
(b) Diploma en estomatología;
(c) Cursos de actualización (teórico-prácticos e internacionales), cursos para docentes universitarios, pasantías clínicas.
Se destina(n): (a) a cirujanos dentistas no mayores de 35 años con disponibilidad a tiempo completo, que superen proceso de admisión consistente en examen, evaluación curricular y entrevista; (b) a bachilleres con disponibilidad a tiempo parcial.

Duración: especialista: 3 años; diplomado: 1 año; certificado: variable según el curso; (comienzos en mayo); existen cursos internacionales de 3 o 4 días.
Inscripciones: del 15 de febrero al 15 de marzo.

1788 Universidad Peruana "Cayetano Heredia" Escuela de Posgrado "Victor Alzamora Castro" [UPCH]

Avenida Honorio Delgado 430
Apartado Postal 4314
Lima 31
Tel: (51) 1 482 4035
Fax: (51) 1 482 3435
Web: http://www.upch.edu.pe
e-mail: orelint@upch.edu.pe

Programas universitarios

Campos de estudios: todas las materias principales.
Descripción:
Area de ciencia y tecnología:
(a) Maestrías en bioestadística, biología, bioquímica y biología molecular, farmacología, física, fisiología, informática, matemáticas aplicadas, micología, microbiología; maestrías en ciencias afines como químico-farmacéutico, agronomía, forestales, industrias alimentarias, y otras;
(b) Doctorado en ciencias con mención en bioquímica y biología molecular, farmacología, física, fisiología, matemáticas aplicadas;
Area de salud:
(c) Maestrías en estomatología, farmacodependencia, gobierno y gerencia en salud internacional en enfermedades infecciosas y tropicales, medicina, psicología clínica, salud pública (concentraciones en epidemiología, gestión de servicios de salud, salud materno-infantil, salud reproductiva, políticas y gobierno en salud, desarrollo de recursos humanos en salud), salud pública (mención gestión de servicios de salud); maestría internacional en enfermedades infecciosas y tropicales; especialización en medicina (cirugía, medicina, obstetricia y ginecología, patología y laboratorio clínico, pediatría, psiquiatría, radiología, salud pública);
(d) Doctorado en medicina;
Area de educación:
(e) Maestría en educación con mención en didáctica en educación superior;
Programas especiales:
(f) Diplomas en Programa de estudios de salud del adolescente con mención en salud reproductiva, Diploma de estudios de posgrado en violencia familiar, Programa de especialización en epidemiología de campo.
Se destina(n): a candidatos con bachillerato o equivalente para las maestrías, con maestría o equivalente para los doctorados. Existe selección por examen de admisión y recomendaciones; se exige acreditación de 1 o 2 idiomas (además del español) para las maestrías y doctorados respectivamente.
Duración: los semestres comienzan en marzo y agosto; la mayoría de los programas dura 4 semestres.
Asistencia financiera: existen becas de estudio.
Inscripciones: hasta marzo y agosto según el semestre.

1789 Universidad Peruana "Cayetano Heredia" Instituto de Genética [UPCH]

Avenida Diagonal 340
Miraflores
Tel: (51) 1 4460034
Fax: (51) 1 4469321
Web: http://www.upch.edu.pe
e-mail: igene@upch.edu.pe

Residentado como segunda especialización

Campos de estudios: genética, medicina, pediatría.
Descripción: conduce al título de especialista en endocrinología y genética (genética clínica con énfasis en pediatría endocrinológica, técnicas de citogenética y genética molecular).
Se destina(n): a médicos pediatras o médicos endocrinólogos; existe examen de admisión en base a entrevista y curriculum.

Duración: 2 años, comienza en julio.
Inscripciones: hasta abril.

1790 Universidad Peruana "Cayetano Heredia" Instituto de Gerontología [UPCH]

Avenida Honorio Delgado 430
Urbanización Ingeniería
Lima 31
Tel: (51) 1 4821144
Fax: (51) 1 3817528
Web: http://www.upch.edu.pe
e-mail: igero@upch.edu.pe

Curso universitario

Campos de estudios: antropología, ciencias humanas, demografía y estudios de población, medicina.
Descripción: biología y patología del envejecimiento en habitantes de altura (estudio antropológico, biológico, demográfico y ecológico del proceso de envejecimiento de poblaciones que viven a más de 3.000 m sobre el nivel del mar).
Duración: 1 mes en febrero.
Inscripciones: hasta julio.

1791 Universidad Peruana "Cayetano Heredia" [UPCH]

Avenida Honorio Delgado 430
San Martín de Porras
Lima 31
Tel: (51) 1 482 4035
Fax: (51) 1 482 3435
Web: http://www.upch.edu.pe
e-mail: orelint@upch.edu.pe

Programas de pregrado

Campos de estudios: ciencias, estadística, estomatología, filosofía, matemáticas, medicina, psicología, química.
Descripción: carreras en las áreas precitadas.
Se destina(n): a nacionales o extranjeros que cumplan con los requisitos exigidos; existe examen de admisión.
Duración: 4 a 5 años.

1792 Universidad Peruana ce Ciencias Aplicadas [UPC]

Prolongación Primavera 2390
Monterrico
Tel: +511-313-3333
Fax: +511-313-3344
Web: http://www.upc.edu.pe
e-mail: postmaster@upc.edu.pe

Programas de grado y posgrado

Campos de estudios: administración de empresas, ciencias aplicadas, ciencias de la información, contabilidad, derecho, ingeniería, marketing, turismo, hotelería.

1793 Universidad Peruana Unión [UPEU]

Carretera Central km. 19
Ñaña, Lima
Tel: (51) (1) 359 0094/60
Fax: (51) (1) 359 0063
Web: http://www.upeu.edu.pe
e-mail: postmast@upeu.edu.pr

Programas universitarios

Campos de estudios: ciencias económicas y comerciales, ciencias humanas, contabilidad, dietético, educación, enfermería, higiene y salud, ingeniería, teología, religión.
Descripción: Programas de estudio (especializaciones profesionales, carreras profesionales, diplomados) en áreas de educación y ciencias humanas, teología, ingeniería, ciencias contables y administrativas, ciencias de la salud.
Se destina(n): a egresados de nivel secundario.
Inscripciones: por mayor información dirigirse a la Oficina de Admisión (e-mail: admision@upeu.edu.pe).

1794 Universidad Privada Antenor Orrego [UPAO]

Avenida América Sur 3145
Urbanización Monserrate
Trujillo
Tel: (51) (4) 428 4444
Fax: (51) (4) 428 4444
Web: http://www.upao.edu.pe
e-mail: postmaster@upao.edu.pe

Programas universitarios

Campos de estudios: todas las materias principales.
Descripción:
(a) Carreras de pregrado en todas las áreas principales;
(b) Postgrados en ingeniería de sistemas, administración, derecho, ciencias de la comunicación, gestión urabano ambiental, ciencias de la salud, educación.
Asistencia financiera: becas de estudio de la universidad por rendimiento académico; becas de estudio según convenios.
Inscripciones: por mayor información dirigirse a la Oficina de Inscripción (e-mail: admision @upao.edu.pe).

1795 Universidad Privada del Norte [UPN]

Avenida del Ejército 920
Trujillo
Tel: (51) 5 044 226635
Fax: (51) 5 044 226635
e-mail: rmb@upnorte.edu.pe

Bachilleratos universitarios

Campos de estudios: administración, administración de empresas, arquitectura, artes, artes aplicadas, estadística, informática, ingeniería, programas de verano.
Descripción: ingeniería de sistemas, ingeniería industrial, ingeniería electrónica, derecho, ciencias de la comunicación, administración, contabilidad, arquitectura. La UPV ofrece un servicio de oportunidades de empleo en empresas regionales y locales.
Se destina(n): a quienes hayan completado la educación secundaria; hay distintos sistemas de ingreso (con y sin examen de admisión) según condiciones del aspirante.
Duración: 5 años académicos (semestres de marzo a junio y de agosto a diciembre); curso de verano en enero-febrero.
Inscripciones: hasta fin de febrero; dirigirse a Admisiones.

1796 Universidad Privada San Pedro [UPSP]

Urb. Laderas del Norte H-11
Chimbote
Tel: (51) (4) 434 1078
Fax: (51) (4) 432 8034
Web: http://www.upsp.edu.pe
e-mail: rectorsp@correo.hys.com.pe

Programas universitarios

Campos de estudios: todas las materias principales, administración de empresas, derecho, educación, informática, negocio.
Programas: (a) Carreras de pregrado en sus facultades de ingeniería, medicina humana, ciencias de la salud, ciencias contables y administrativas, derecho y ciencias políticas, educación y humanidades;
(b) Posgrados (maestrías, doctorados) en la Escuela de Posgrado.
Descripción: (b) Maestría con convenios: administración de empresas y negocios (Universidad de los Lagos, Chile); ciencias de la educación superior (La Habana,Cuba); informática y multimedia (Universidad de los Lagos, Chile); derecho (Universidad de Castilla La Mancha, España).
Se destina(n): (b) a candidatos que superen entrevista y que conozcan uno o dos idioma (maestría y doctorado respectivamente).
Se dicta(n): en Chimbote, Trujillo, Cajamarca, Piura, Sullana.
Duración: los cursos empiezan en septiembre.
Inscripciones: (b) dirigirse a Escuela de Posgrado (e-mail: maestrai@upsp.edu.pe).

Philippines

Academic year: June to March.

Organization of higher education system: Higher education is provided by private and public higher education institutions. There are over 1,700 institutions of higher education enrolling about 2.5 million full-time, part-time national and foreign students. Seventy-six percent of the higher education institutions are private schools and the rest are government-funded public institutions. Higher education institutions are required to comply with policies and standards set by the Commission of Higher Education (CHED). Non compliance with CHED standards and low performance of graduates in professional examinations can result in withdrawal of permits by the CHED. Higher education institutions are also strongly urged to undergo accreditation through self and peer evaluation.

A wide variety of degree programmes are offered: associate, diploma, baccalaureate and graduate degree courses at the Master's and doctoral levels.

The length of study for a baccalaureate degree is four years except for engineering (five years), dentistry and veterinary medicine (six years), physical therapy (five years) law (eight years) and medicine (eight years). An undergraduate degree is necessary for admission to law and medicine. Degree programmes of graduate schools are research-oriented and research-based. Students are required to conduct research, case analyses and reports in every course. A Master's degree normally requires four semesters of course work, a comprehensive examination and/or thesis and defence of the thesis. A doctoral degree requires at least four semesters of academic units beyond the Master's degree and research for the doctoral dissertation equivalent to twelve academic units.

Monetary unit: Philippine peso.

National student admission: The basic requirement for admission is graduation from a recognized secondary or high school, and passing of National College Entrance Examination (NCEE).

International student admission:

• Generally, admission to higher education is open to those who have satisfactorily complied with secondary education requirement and passed the university admission test.
For international students, in addition to the above, dentistry students who have successfully completed two year pre-dental education must get a Certificate of Eligibility for Admission to Dentistry before going into dentistry proper. Medicine as a second degree requires students to finish a four year baccalaureate degree, pass the National Medical Admission Test and obtain a Certificate of Eligibility for Admission to Medicine. Legal education requires students to finish a four-year baccalaureate degree and a Certificate of Eligibility for Law.

• Only higher education institutions with programmes accredited by agencies under the Federation of Accrediting agencies of the Philippines (FAAP) or with equivalent accreditation by the Commission on Higher Education (CHED), either as Centers of Excellence (COEs), Centers of Development (Cods) or STCW-compliant Maritime schools and by the Bureau of Immigration (BI), are authorized to admit foreign students. Please see list of higher education institutions authorized to accept foreign students through CHED website, www.ched.gov.ph.

Language: Good knowledge of English is essential for regular courses at undergraduate and graduate levels.

Immigration requirements: Foreign students wishing to study in the Philippines should present a Certificate of Eligibility and a Study Permit from the Department of Education, Culture and Sports, and a copy of the Alien Certificate of Registration. See website of Bureau of Immigration: www.immigration.gov.ph.

Estimated expenses for one academic year: Tuition and other school fees range from US$400-$1,200 for one semester of regular academic load; housing: depending on the location, the average monthly room rental for a single room ranges from US$100-$150. The estimated cost for one person living a modest lifestyle in the Philippines is from US$375-$500 per month.

Information services:

• Department of Foreign Affairs; Roxas Blvd, Pasay City; Philippines

• Office of Student Services; Commission on Higher Education, Philippines; 3rd Floor, National Engineering Center; University of the Philippines; Diliman, Quezon City; Philippines; email: ched_oss@easycall.com.ph

• Federation of Accrediting Agencies, Suite 302, The Tower at Emerald Square corner
P. Tuazon and J.P. Rizal Streets, Quezon City, Philippines; tel: +632-421-1393.

Open and distance learning: A number of higher education institutions offer distance learning programs. The Open University and Distance Learning Systems is a response to the need to provide quality education to undergraduate and graduate students using a more viable alternative learning system. This programme intends to make educational opportunities available to a larger number of students; particularly to those who are unable to attend a traditional higher educational institution due to geographical isolation, work commitments and physical abilities. The institutions that offer distance education use their own prescribed programmes of studies and evaluated procedures for 'distance learners'. These include the use of study guides, instructional methodologies, books, video, learning modules, television and radio which the distance learner has to complete before advancing to the next higher competency level

• Schools offering distance education programs: Asian Institute for Distance Education; Asian Institute of Journalism and Communication; Benguet State University; CAP College; Central Luzon State University-Open University; Don Mariano Marcos Memorial State University-Open University; Iloilo State College of Fisheries, School of Distance Education; John B. Lacson, Molo, Iloilo; Leyte State University; Mindanao Polytechnic State College; Mountain Province State Polytechnic College; Pangasinan State University-Opne University System; Philippine Women's University; Polytechnic University of the Philippines; Saint Paul University; Southeast Asia Interdisciplinary Development Institute; University of Northern Philippines; University of the Philippines-Open University.

Recognition of studies and qualification: Student foreign credentials are assessed by the institution of higher education where the student wishes to study.

Accommodation services: Accommodation of Filipino as well as foreign students to universities and colleges necessitates the functional operation of service centers. Generally, dormitories are regulated features of state run universities and colleges. There are however privately owned and managed HEIs which offer similar types of services. In addition to university dormitories, a good number of institutions of higher education maintain campus mail stations, bookstores, cafeterias, gymnasiums, recreation halls, chapels and to a certain extent university shopping malls.

Publications / Websites:

• Revised Guidebook for Foreign Students. October 2001, issued by the Office of Student Services (OSS), Commission on Higher Education (CHED); web: www.ched.gov.ph.

1797 Angeles University Foundation [AUF]

Mc Arthur Highway
2009 Angeles City, Pampanga
Tel: +63-45-888-2663 to 65
Fax: +63-45-888-2725
Web: http://www.auf.edu.ph
e-mail: auf@hotmail.com

📖 Undergraduate, Graduate, Postgraduate Degree Programmes

Study Domains: all major fields, summer programmes, travel grants.

Programmes: Bachelor's, Master's, Ph.D. degrees in all major fields.

🖋️ BYA Scholarship

Study Domains: all major fields.

Scholarships: BYA Scholarship, Academic Scholarship.

Open to: open to all.

Other conditions: recommendation from the university president.

Value: tuition/miscellaneous fees, housing, food: US$1,000 per semester.

Applications: consult website for information and application forms.

1798 Arellano University [AU]
2600 Legarda Street
Manila
Tel: +632-734-7371 local 227-216
Fax: +632-735-9684
Web: http://www.arellano.edu.ph

📖 Undergraduate and Graduate Degree Programmes
Study Domains: accounting, business administration, computer science, education, law, liberal arts, nursing, performing arts, tourism, hotel and catering management.
Programmes: Bachelor's, Master's, Ph.D. degrees in accounting, business administration, computer science, education, law; 2-year programmes in hotel and restaurant management.
Open to: all nationalities; English language proficiency required.
Financial assistance: financial assistance available; contact Rony Garay, Dean of Student Affairs for further information.
Languages: English.

1799 Asian Institute of Management
MCC PO Box 2095
1260 Makati, Metro Manila
Tel: +632-892-4011 to 20
Fax: +632-892-1724
Web: http://www.aim.edu.ph
e-mail: aimnet@aim.edu.ph

📖 Graduate Programmes
Study Domains: business administration, management.
Programmes: Master's degrees in (a) Business Management (M.B.M.); (b) Management (M.M.): (c) Development Management (M.D.M.).
Open to: Asian and non-Asian students holding a college degree, preferably with practical experience of (a) at least 2 years; (b) and (c) at least 6 years, 3 years in managerial position; minimum age 28.
Duration: (a) 21 months (courses begin in late July); (b) and (c) 11 months (courses begin in June).
Fees: tuition and school fees per year: (a) US$8,100; (b) US$11,500; (c) US$9,800; other expenses (dormitory fee, food allowance, personal allowance, school supplies) approx.: (a) US$12,610; (b) and (c) US$14,260.
Financial assistance: scholarships available for the MBM and MDM programmes for deserving candidates; value of tuition scholarship: (a) US$8,100; (c) US$9,800; (renewable if the student is in the upper 50% of the class).
Languages: instruction in English.
Applications: by March, to the Director, Office of Admissions.

1800 Baguio Central University [BCU]
18 Bonifacio Street
Baguio City
Tel: +63-74-442-4949
Fax: +63-74-444-9247
e-mail: BCU@hotmail.com

📖 Undergraduate, Graduate Degree and Non-Degree Programmes
Study Domains: all major fields.
Programmes: Bachelor's, Master's, Ph.D. degrees in all major fields; non-degree programmes: caregiver, associate in geodetic engineering, ASHE, HRM, secretarial, midwifery studies..
Description: liberal arts, business management, education; engineering, health, public administration, medical-related.
Duration: varies with programme; courses begin in June.
Fees: based on programme; consult the University.
Languages: English.
Applications: apply to Dr. Atanacio at the university.

🎓 Competitive School Academic Scholarship
Study Domains: all major fields.
Open to: no age and nationality requirements; based on academic performance.
Duration: renewable; based on academic achievements.

Value: tuition fee discount.
Applications: no deadline; contact Dr. F. Atanacio or Mrs. Elena A. Nerpio.

1801 Bicol University - Graduate school [BU]
Legazpi City 4901
Web: http://www.bicol-u.edu.ph

📖 Graduate, Postgraduate Programmes
Study Domains: administration, education.
Programmes: (a) Doctoral Programmes in education and philosophy; (b) Master's Programmes in educational management; education; industrial education; teaching; teaching vocational courses; public administration; nursing; economics; management; local government management; teaching fisheries technology; agriculture; peace and security studies.
Open to: (a) applicants with an appropriate Master's degree with a General Weighted Average (GWA) of 1.75 or better; (b) applicants with an appropriate baccalaureate degree with General Weighted Average (GWA) of 2.25, a B average, or 86.5% or better; applicants must meet the requirements of the specific department to which they are applying; applicants must pass an interview; a TOEFL score of at least 480 is required.
Applications: to the Dean of Admissions, at the above address.

1802 Carthel Science Educational Foundation, Inc. [CSEF]
2309 San Manuel
Tel: +63-915-712-4606
e-mail: carthel9002@yahoo.com

🎓 Financial aid
Study Domains: education, nursing.
Scholarships: Academic Scholarship Grant.
Open to: students with general average of 85% and above.
Duration: 1 year, renewable.
Value: tuition waiver.
Applications: on or before the opening of the first semester; contact carthel9002@yahoo.com for further details.

1803 Cavite State University [CVSU]
Indang
4122 Cavite
Tel: +63-46-415-0010
Fax: +63-46-415-0012
Web: http://www.dnsl.cvsu.edu.ph
e-mail: cvsu@asia.com

📖 Undergraduate and Graduate Degree Programmes
Study Domains: development studies, education, history, physical education, teacher education, technical education, vocational training.
Programmes: Bachelor's, Master's, Ph.D. degrees in development studies; education; history; technical education.
Duration: variable; courses start in June and November.
Fees: registration: US$1,300-$1,700; tuition fees included; living costs: US$70-$100 per month.
Languages: English and Filipino.
Applications: apply by February for first semester or June for second semester.

1804 Central Luzon State University, Institute of Graduate Studies [CLSU]
Muñoz
3120 Nueva Ecija
Tel: +63-44-4560-107
Fax: +63-44-4560-107
Web: http://www2.mozcom.com/~clsu/

📖 Graduate, Postgraduate Programmes
Study Domains: agriculture, development studies, engineering, rural development.
Programmes: Doctoral courses in agricultural engineering, development education, rural development, crop science and animal science; M.Sc./Master's degree courses in professional studies in agribusiness management, agricultural engineering,

animal science, aquaculture, crop protection, crop science, development communication, education, grain science, soil science, rural development, biology education, chemistry education, agricultural technology education.
Open to: Thai, Indonesian, Nepalese, African, Malaysian, Vietnamese, Laotian, Chinese, Pakistani and Bangladesh nationals, under 35 years of age for Master's programme, under 40 years of age for Doctorate; proficiency in English required.
Duration: 2 to 3 years.
Fees: tuition: non-citizen fees, 1,450 pesos; application: US$25; laboratory: 40 pesos per semester; Graduate Education Development Fund for agency-sponsored scholars: US$400 for Doctorate and US$300 for Master's; service fee: 1,000 pesos per semester.
Applications: to the Dean of the Institute, at the above address.

1805 De La Salle University [DLSU]
2401 Taft Avenue
PO Box 3819
1004 Manila
Tel: +63-2-524-8233
Web: http://www.dlsu.edu.ph

Undergraduate, Graduate Programmes / Business

Study Domains: accounting, business administration, computer science, education, engineering, finance, liberal arts, management, sciences.
Programmes: (a) Graduate Programmes; (b) Undergraduate Programmes; (c) Programmes within the Graduate School of Business.
Subjects: (a) liberal arts, engineering, natural sciences, computer science, education; (b) liberal arts, commerce, engineering, natural sciences, computer science, education; (c) business administration, computational finance.
Open to: nationals of any country: (a) at least an average rating of 85% or an equivalent of B or 2.0 in the undergraduate course; for the doctoral programmes, an applicant must be a holder of a Master's degree with a weighted average of at least 2.5 or its equivalent; (c) for Master's programmes: a Bachelor's degree, at least 2 years of work experience and satisfactory entrance examination results or GMAT and TOEFL scores; for Doctorate: a Master's degree preferably in business management, satisfactory entrance examination results or GMAT and TOEFL scores of at least 550, satisfactory interview.
Duration: (c) Master's, 2 to 3 years; Doctorate, 3 to 4 years; courses begin in June, September and January.
Fees: (a) and (b) variable according to course; (c) Master's, US$3,000; Doctorate, US$4,000.
Languages: instruction in English.
Applications: (a) to the Graduate Studies Director; (b) by October, to the Admissions Director, at the above address; (c) to the above address.

1806 Don Mariano Marcos Memorial State University [DMMMSU]
Bacnotan
2515 La Union
Tel: +63-72-888-5354
Fax: +63-72-888-5354
Web: http://www.dmmmsu.edu.ph

Undergraduate, Graduate Programmes

Study Domains: agriculture, biology, computer science, ecology, environment, education, electricity and electronics, English, fisheries, food, forestry, home economics, horticulture, industrial relations, industrial technology, information science, law, management, marine biology, mathematics, mechanical engineering, music and musicology, natural sciences, political science, psychology, rural development, social sciences, special education, teacher education, technical education, technology, tourism, hotel and catering management, trade, veterinary medicine, vocational training.
Programmes: Bachelor's, Master's, Ph.D. degrees in all major fields.
Fees: undergraduate fees per unit: 10-25 pesos plus additional student fees; Master's degrees: 80 pesos plus additional fees; Ph.D. 120 pesos plus additional fees; consult

university for breakdown of fees.
Languages: English.
Applications: by April/May for courses beginning in June; to Registrar.

Scholarships
Study Domains: all major fields.
Scholarships: (a) university scholarships: entrance; academic; athletics; state; talent; community; government; (b) campus scholarships; see university for application details.
Open to: candidates of all nationalities; interview required.

1807 Manila Central University [MCU]
Caloocan City 1400
Tel: +63-2-364-1071/77
Fax: +63-2-364-1070
Web: http://www.mcu.edu.ph
e-mail: admin@mail2.mcu.edu.ph

Undergraduate, Graduate, Postgraduate Degree Programmes

Study Domains: biology, business administration, computer science, dentistry, information science, management, marketing, medicine, nursing, pharmacy and pharmacology, psychology.
Programmes: Bachelor's, Master's Ph.D. degrees in all major fields.
Duration: 4 to 5 years; courses begin in June.
Languages: English.

Scholarships
Study Domains: all major fields.
Scholarships: a variety of scholarships available; consult University for specific information.

1808 Manuel S. Enverga University Foundation Main Campus [MSEUF]
University Site Village
Lucena City
Tel: +63-42-710-2541
Fax: +63-42-373-6065
Web: http://www.mseuf.edu.ph

Graduate, Postgraduate Degree Programmes

Study Domains: business administration, education, English, fine arts, liberal arts, management, nursing, sciences, tourism, hotel and catering management.
Programmes: Master's degrees in education; business administration; teaching; public administration; management; Ph.D. degrees in education; management.
Duration: 4 to 5 years; courses begin in June.
Fees: registration: 13,000 pesos per semester; tuition: 300 pesos per unit; living costs: approximately 4,500 pesos per month.
Financial assistance: full or partial tuition reduction to 50%. Awarded end of every semester based on academic performance.
Languages: English and Filipino.

1809 Mapùa Institute of Technology [MIT]
PO Box 918
1002 Manila
Tel: +632-247-5000
Web: http://www.mapua.edu.ph
e-mail: info@mapua.edu.ph

Undergraduate, Graduate Programmes

Study Domains: architecture, chemistry, civil engineering, electricity and electronics, engineering, geology, industrial design, international business, mechanical engineering, summer programmes.
Programmes: Bachelor of Science (B.Sc.) degree programmes in: (a) architecture; (b) chemical engineering; (c) computer engineering; (d) electrical engineering; (e) electronics and communications engineering; (f) industrial engineering; (g) mechanical engineering; (h) civil engineering; (i) environmental and sanitary engineering; (j) geology; (k) metallurgical engineering; (l) mining

engineering; (m) chemistry; (n) industrial engineering; (o) Master of Science (M.Sc.) degree programme in chemistry; (p) Master of Engineering.
Open to: limited number of foreign candidates for Bachelor's degrees; successful completion of MIT qualifying examination; sound knowledge of English required; Filipino language required for completion of B.Sc. degree.
Duration: (a) to (g) 5 academic years (consisting of two 18-week semesters); (h) to (l) 5 academic years and 1 summer term (6-week programme); (m) and (n) 4 academic years; (o) and (p) 2 academic years.
Financial assistance: free or reduced tuition offered to outstanding students at end of each semester.
Languages: Filipino and English.
Applications: by November/December, to the Registrar's Office.

1810 MSU-Iligan Institute of Technology [MSUIIT]

Tibanga Highway
9200 Iligan City
Tel: +63-63-221-4057
Fax: +63-63-221-4057
Web: http://www.msuiit.edu.ph
e-mail: ovcaa-ewi@sulat.msuiit.edu.ph

📖 Undergraduate, Graduate Programmes

Study Domains: Asian studies, business administration, education, engineering, home economics, linguistics, philosophy, sciences, social sciences.
Programmes: (a) Bachelor's; (b) Master's; (c) Ph.D. degrees.
Description: (a) sociology and languages, physics, biological sciences, chemistry; (b) sociology and languages, business management, library science, computer applications, engineering, science education, physics, biological sciences, chemistry, mathematics, applied statistics; (c) biological sciences, chemistry, mathematics.
Fees: international student application fee: US$25 for graduate; US$15 undergraduate; student fee: non-resident US$400-$500; registration fee: US$20 per semester; tuition fee: US$200 per unit; laboratory fees, according to programme chosen.
Applications: apply by first week of April to Dr. Roscom, Dean of Graduate School.

1811 National University [NU]

551 Mariano F. Jhocson Street
Sampaloc, Manila
Tel: +63-2-749-8210/8221
Fax: +63-2-749-8210/8209
e-mail: nationaluniv@pacific.net.ph

📖 Undergraduate Programmes

Study Domains: architecture, arts, dentistry, education, engineering, industry and commerce, liberal arts, pharmacy and pharmacology.
Programmes: undergraduate and non-degree programmes.
Duration: 4 to 5 years depending on programme.
Fees: tuition fees: approximately 440 pesos per unit.
Languages: English.
Applications: apply by 31 May to Registrar, at the above address; tel: +63 2 749 8221; fax: +63 2 749 8209.

1812 Philippine Christian University [PCU]

1648 Taft Avenue cor Pedro Gil Street
PO Box 907
Manila
Tel: +63-2-526-2261 to 64
Fax: +63-2-525-5435/526-5110
Web: http://www.pcu.edu.ph
e-mail: regis@pcu.edu.ph

📖 Undergraduate and Graduate Degree Programmes

Study Domains: accounting, business administration, communication, computer science, dietetics, early childhood education, English, finance, history, law, marketing, mathematics, nursing, nutrition, physical education, political science, psychology, social work, sociology, teacher education, tourism, hotel and catering management.

Programmes: Bachelor's, Master's, Ph.D. degrees in all major fields.
Open to: high school graduates who pass the admissions and language proficiency tests.
Duration: 4 year minimum; courses begin in June.
Languages: English.
Applications: apply by 30 March for first term; 15 September for second term; 15 December for third term.

1813 Philippines Women's University [PWU]

Taft Avenue
Manila
Tel: +63-2-526-8421/524-2611
Fax: +63-2-526-6975/524-2611
Web: http://www.pwu.edu.ph

📖 Undergraduate and Graduate Degree Programmes

Study Domains: accounting, administration, communication, computer science, ecology, environment, education, food, humanities and arts, information science, library science, management, natural resources, nursing, nutrition, pharmacy and pharmacology, political science, psychology, public relations, summer programmes, tourism, hotel and catering management, travel grants.
Programmes: Bachelor's, Master's degrees in all major fields; also non-degree programmes.
Description: non-degree courses in: career and continuing education, secretarial, computing, service trade, hotel and restaurant management, tourism, home health care.
Duration: 3 years.
Fees: tuition fees: US$595 per unit; living costs: US$1,824.
Financial assistance: tuition fee reduction.
Languages: English.
Applications: apply at least 2 months before the start of classes to University Registrar.

1814 Polytechnic University of the Philippines [PUP]

Anonas Street
01008 Santa Mesa, Manila
Tel: +63-2-716-7835 to 45 local 287
Web: http://www.pup.edu.ph
e-mail: inquire@pup.edu.ph

📖 Undergraduate, Graduate, Postgraduate Degree Programmes

Study Domains: all major fields.
Programmes: Bachelor's, Master's, Ph.D. degrees in all major fields.
Open to: applicants having acceptable scores in the National Secondary Aptitude Test and PUP Admission Test and a secondary-school grade average of 80% and above.
Duration: 4 to 6 years.
Fees: 12 pesos per unit plus other miscellaneous and laboratory fees.
Applications: to the above address.

1815 Ramon Magsaysay Technological University [RMTU]

2201 Iba, Zambales
Tel: +63-47-811-1683
Fax: +63-47-811-1683
e-mail: rmtupresident@yahoo.com

🖋 Financial aid

Study Domains: all major fields.
Scholarships: Master's / Doctoral Scholarship Support.
Duration: 1 term, non-renewable.
Value: P2,500 per semester.
Applications: Applications to be submitted to the Board of Regents; contact Feliciano S. Rosete, tel: 047 811 1683 for further details.

1816 Saint Louis University [SLU]

SLU Post Office
A. Bonifacio Street
Baguio City
Tel: +63-74-442-3043
Fax: +63-74-442-2842
Web: http://www.slu.edu.ph
e-mail: sluregis@slu.edu.ph

📖 Undergraduate, Graduate, Postgraduate Programmes

Study Domains: accounting, administration, architecture, biology, business, business administration, chemical engineering, chemical industry, civil engineering, communication, computer science, ecology, environment, economic and commercial sciences, education, electricity and electronics, finance, human sciences, humanities and arts, information science, law, library science, management, marketing, mathematics, mechanical engineering, medicine, nursing, political science.
Programmes: Bachelor's, Master's, Ph.D. degrees in all major fields; also non-degree courses.
Description: non-degree programmes: Associate in Radiological Technology (A.R.T.); Associate in Geodetic Engineering (A.G.E.); courses also offered in special education, American studies, Chinese music, advertising, demography, sociology, chemistry.
Open to: foreign students between 18 and 21 years of age for Bachelor of Science programmes; no age requirement for Master's and Ph.D. programmes; college entrance exam and English language proficiency exam required; admission test for medical students.
Duration: B.S.: 4 to 5 years; Master's: 2 years; Ph.D.: 3 years.
Languages: English.
Applications: apply to the University Registrar by January to March for first semester; June to August for second semester.

1817 Saint Mary's University [SMU]

Bayombong
Nueva Vizcaya
Tel: +63-78-321-2221
Fax: +63-78-321-2117
Web: http://www.smu.edu.ph
e-mail: smunet@smu.edu.ph

📖 Undergraduate, Graduate, Postgraduate Programmes

Study Domains: arts, education, engineering, English, fine arts, history, home economics, law, liberal arts, nursing, sciences, social sciences, theology, religion, tourism, hotel and catering management.
Programmes: Bachelor's; Master's; Ph.D.; ED.D.; BSOA Assoc. in Genetic Engineering.
Open to: candidates of all nationalities; IQ tests; aptitude tests; BOPI; English language proficiency test required.
Duration: 4 to 5 years.
Fees: registration: undergraduate: 1,835 pesos; graduate: 1,190 pesos; tuition: undergraduate: approximately 215 pesos per unit; Master's: 288 pesos per unit; Doctorate: 346 pesos per unit.
Languages: English.
Applications: apply in December of the preceding year of study to the Registrar; contact jesse@smu.edu.ph.

1818 University of La Salette [ULS]

Bachelor Street, Dubinan East
Santiago City, Isabela
Tel: +63-78-682-3724/5169
Fax: +63-78-682-5170
Web: http://www.lasalette.edu.ph
e-mail: uls@lasalette.edu.ph

📖 Undergraduate and Graduate Degree Programmes

Study Domains: all major fields, summer programmes.
Programmes: Bachelor's, Master's, Ph.D. degrees in all major fields; non-degree programmes.
Description: (a) undergraduate programmes in schools of: arts and sciences; education; accountancy and business administration; engineering; nursing; community health and

midwifery; criminology; agriculture; (b) graduate programmes in schools of: education; public administration; business management; arts in education; nursing; engineering management; criminology; information technology; computer science; environmental science.
Subjects: non-degree: nursing aide; home health care programme.
Duration: 4 to 5 years; courses begin in June.
Fees: registration: 15,000 pesos; tuition: 8,000-10,000 pesos; living costs: 200 pesos per month.
Languages: Filipino and English.
Applications: apply by January to Maria P. Obra at above telephone number.

🎓 Academic Scholarship

Study Domains: all major fields.
Open to: full-time students.
Value: 7,000 pesos; one term renewable.
Applications: each end of term; apply to the Director of International Affairs.

1819 University of Luzon [LC]

Perez Boulevard
2400 Dagupan City, Pangasinan
Tel: +63-75-515-7707
Fax: +63-75-522-1623
Web: http://www2.ul.edu.ph
e-mail: ul@ul.edu.ph

📖 Graduate, Postgraduate Programmes

Study Domains: administration, business administration, education.
Programmes: Graduate work-study programme: Doctor of Public Administration (D.P.A.); Doctor of Arts (D.A.); Master of Public Administration (M.P.A.); Master of Business Administration (M.B.A.); Master of Arts in Education (M.A.Ed.).
Open to: candidates of all nationalities, between 28 and 45 years of age, with a Bachelor's degree in a specific field and ability to teach undergraduate/graduate students; Master's programme candidates must hold a Bachelor's degree in a related field; Doctoral programme candidates must hold a Master's degree in a related field.
Duration: 2 academic years (courses begin in June) for Master's programme plus thesis work; 3 academic years for Doctorate plus dissertation.
Fees: yearly, 18,000 pesos for MBA; 17,000 pesos for other Master's programmes; 20,000 pesos for Doctoral programmes.
Financial assistance: one teaching assistantship per programme; other expenses (board, lodging, transportation, living allowances, etc.) must be borne by the applicant.
Languages: instruction in English.
Applications: by 28 February, to the President.

1820 University of Northern Philippines [UNP]

Tamag, Vigan City
Ilocos Sur
Tel: +63-77-722-2810
Fax: +63-77-722-2810
e-mail: unp_op@yahoo.com

📖 Undergraduate and Graduate Degree Programmes

Study Domains: all major fields, administration, business administration, chemistry, computer science, criminology, education, mathematics, nursing, physics, social work, statistics.
Programmes: (a) Bachelor's, (b) Master's, (c) Ph.D. degrees in all major fields.
Description: (a) elementary education, secondary education, industrial education, criminology, social work, computer science, nursing; (b) education, public administration, police administration, mathematics education, teaching subjects, English, home economics, arts, physical education, chemistry, physics, nursing; and statistics; (c) education, public administration, business administration.
Duration: (a) 4 years; (b) 2 years; (c) 3 years.
Languages: English and Filipino.
Applications: according to programme chosen; consult the

University for admission information.

1821 University of Rizal System-Rizal State College

JP Rizal Avenue, Brgy.
Sampaloc
1980 Tanay
Tel: +63-674-2543

📖 Undergraduate, Graduate, Postgraduate Degree Programmes

Study Domains: administration, agriculture, education, engineering.
Programmes: Undergraduate studies in the following areas: agriculture, agricultural engineering and technology, art and science, education and home technology; Graduate programmes in the following areas: Master of Arts in Education (M.A.), Master of Arts in Teaching (M.A.T.), Master of Public Administration (M.P.A.), Master of Science in Agriculture (M.Sc.A.); Doctor of Education (Ed.D.), Graduate Diploma in Music Education, Graduate Diploma in Physical Education.
Open to: students of any nationality; proficiency in English required.
Financial assistance: tuition grant (full and partial) to entering scholars and athletes.
Languages: Instruction in English.
Applications: by June, to the Registrar, at the above address.

1822 University of San Jose-Recoletos

P. Lopez Street
6000 Cebu City
Tel: +63-32-253-7900
Fax: +63-32-254-1720
Web: http://www.usjr.edu.ph

📖 International Programmes

Study Domains: civil engineering, communication, engineering, industry and commerce, mechanical engineering.
Programmes: International courses in engineering: electrical, chemical, industrial, computer, civil, mechanical, electronics communication and commerce.
Open to: any high school graduate, 16 to 25 years old, who has passed the National College Entrance Examination with a minimum rating of 80; English language tutoring available.
Duration: 5 years.
Fees: (per semester) matriculation, 134 pesos; tuition, 150 pesos per unit; laboratory fees, 534 pesos per laboratory course; fees are subject to change without prior notice.
Financial assistance: possible tuition exemption.
Languages: instruction in English.
Applications: by January, to the President.

1823 University of Southern Mindanao [USM]

Kabacan
9407 Cotabato
Tel: +63-64-248-2138
Fax: +63-64-248-2138
Web: http://www.usm.edu.ph

📖 Undergraduate, Graduate, Postgraduate Degree Programmes

Study Domains: all major fields.
Description: Bachelor's, Master's, Ph.D. degrees in all major fields.
Subjects: (a) undergraduate programmes in: agriculture and farming; psychology; sciences; engineering; computing; home economics; education; industrial technology; trade courses; (b) doctoral programmes in: agricultural sciences; extension education; educational management.
Open to: all nationalities; USMICET admission test required.
Fees: tuition fees: 60 pesos per unit; living costs: 2,000 pesos per month.
Languages: English.
Applications: apply by January to the University Registrar.

🏴 PASA Scholarship

Study Domains: all major fields.
Value: free tuition fees and living allowance per academic semester.
Applications: Contact Kalinggalan B. Abdulsani for further information.

1824 University of the Philippines

Diliman, Quezon City
Tel: +63-2-920-5301 to 35
Web: http://www.upd.edu.ph

📖 Undergraduate, Graduate, Postgraduate Programmes

Study Domains: all major fields.
Programmes: Bachelor's, Master's, Ph.D. degrees in all major fields.
Applications: see website for further information.

🏴 Scholarships

Study Domains: all major fields.
Scholarships: Scholarship Programme for International Students.
Open to: all nationalities, preferably from Third World countries in the Asia and Pacific region.
Duration: until graduation, depending on academic achievements.
Value: undergraduates: free tuition and other school fees (except student fund), book allowance of 500 pesos per semester, plus a monthly stipend of 1,000 pesos; graduates: free tuition and other school fees (except student fund), book allowance of 2,000 pesos per semester and a monthly stipend of 1,200 pesos (for Masters) and 1,500 pesos for Ph.D.; there is also a thesis allowance of 3,000 pesos and a dissertation allowance of 6,000 pesos.
Applications: by 30 September for those seeking admission in the first semester; by 30 April for those seeking admission in the second semester.

1825 University of the Philippines Visayas Cebu [UPV]

Gorondo Avenue
Lahag, Cebu
Tel: +63-33-338-1534
Web: http://www.upv.edu.ph
e-mail: upvcebucso@yahoo.com

📖 Undergraduate, Graduate Programmes

Study Domains: biology, communication, computer science, ecology, environment, fine arts, management, mathematics, political science, psychology, teacher education.
Programmes: Bachelor's; Master's; Certificate of Fine Arts.
Open to: all nationalities; University of the Philippines college admissions test required.
Duration: 4 years.
Fees: tuition: 200 pesos per unit.
Languages: English.
Applications: apply to Dean Jesus V. Juario by mail or fax: +63 232 8104.

1826 University of the Philippines, Diliman

Diliman
1101 Quezon City
Tel: +63-2-928-8369
Fax: +63-2-928-3014
Web: http://www.upd.edu.ph
e-mail: oc@upd.edu.ph

📖 Undergraduate, Graduate Programmes

Study Domains: all major fields.
Programmes: Degree programmes in archaeology; architecture; liberal arts; Asian studies; tourism; business administration; economics; education; engineering; fine arts; home economics; Islamic studies; labour and industrial relations; law; library and information science; mass communication; music; publication administration and governance; science; social sciences and philosophy; social work and community development; small enterprises; statistics; technology management; urban and regional planning.

1827 Western Mindanao State University [WMSU]

Baliwasan
7000 Zamboanga City
Tel: +63-991-1771
Web: http://www.wmsu.edu.ph

📖 Undergraduate, Graduate, Postgraduate Programmes

Study Domains: all major fields.
Programmes: Bachelor's, Master's, PhD degrees in all major fields; also non-degree programmes and special programmes and extension services in a diverse range of scientific, medical and liberal art disciplines.
Open to: citizens of any country admitted to the university.
Applications: by January or June, to the Dean of Admissions; see website for further information.

Poland

Academic year: October to June.
Organization of higher education system: Two types of higher education institutions exist: (a) universities, providing higher education in the fields of: the humanities, technical /exact sciences, medicine, economy, pedagogy and arts, as well as military studies; (b) colleges, providing higher education in specific technical/vocational fields and preparing students for practising specific professions. Instruction is provided at State-financed or private institutions at the following levels: Bachelor (licencjat or inzynier) level courses, Master (magister) level courses, doctorate studies and postgraduate studies. Studies include:
• Vocational education courses: lasting 3 or 4 years; 3-year course graduates are awarded the professional title of licencjat (lic) or licencjat pielegniarstwa and licencjat poloznictwa, (equivalent to a BA degree) and 4-year course graduates - the professional title of inzynier (inz) or inzynier architekt (inz. arch.) (equivalent to a BSc).
• Master-level complementary courses: lasting 2 years, designed for holders of the professional titles of licencjat or inzynier, graduates are awarded the professional title of magister or an equivalent title.
• Uniform master-level courses: lasting 5 or 6 years; depending on the field of study, graduates are awarded one of the following professional titles: magister (mgr), magister edukacji (mgr ed.), magister sztuki (mgr szt.), magister inzynier (mgr inz), magister inzynier architekt (mgr inz arch.) or lekarz (lek.), lekarz dentysta (lek. dent.), lekarz weterynarii (lek. wet.).
• Doctorate studies for holders of the magister title or its equivalent.
• Postgraduate studies.
Higher education courses are provided in various modes of study, including regular day studies as the predominant arrangement as well extramural and evening studies, and those offered in a distance learning system.
Monetary unit: Polish zloty (PLN).
National student admission: Secondary school leaving certificate ('swiadectwo dojrzalosci') or equivalent; entrance examinations for some institutions or interviews. Specific requirements are imposed for studies in art, music, physical education, architecture, as well as for military and police schools.
International student admission: Candidates must hold a secondary school-leaving certificate entitling them to enter higher education in their country. It must be officially recognized as being equivalent to a Polish Maturity Certificate by Polish local educational authorities or on the basis of a bilateral agreement on recognition. There are no entrance examinations for foreign students. However, in the case of fields of study in which special abilities are required, applicants must prove they possess them. Candidates seeking to be admitted to higher studies should submit a health certificate enabling them to study in the selected discipline. All candidates should be able to submit a health certificate enabling them to study in the selected discipline.
Language: Candidates must attend a Polish language course preparing for higher studies organized by one of the institutions recommended by the Minister of National Education and Sport or obtain confirmation of the host institution that their command of Polish is sufficient to enrol.

Some faculties also offer courses in foreign languages (mostly English).
Immigration requirements: Students must be in possession of a valid passport and a student visa or other document entitling them to stay in Poland. Contact Polish diplomatic missions abroad for complete information on studies in Poland (application forms) and assistance in applying.
Estimated expenses for one academic year: Tuition: approximately 3,000€ per year; housing: 300-350€ per month.
Information services:
• Authority to whom international students' application should be addressed:
Biuro Uznawalnosci Wyksztalcenia i Wymiany Miedzynarodowej (Bureau For Academic Recognition and International Exchange) (BUWiWM); ul. Smolna 13; Warsaw 00-375, Poland +48-22-826-7434; fax: +48-22-826-2823; email: biuro@buwiwm.edu.pl.
• Name and Address of other agencies or organizations offering information, advice and assistance to international students: - International Students offices at universities - Studies in Poland (Guide for foreign students available at the website of Ministerstwo Edukacji Narodowej i Sportu (Ministry of National Education and Sport); Ministeral. Szucha 2500-918 Warsaw, Poland; tel: +48-22-628-0461; fax: +48-22-629-9329; email: minister@menis.gov.pl; web: http://www.menis.gov.pl
On-line brochure: http://www.menis.gov.pl/menis_en/higher_education/studia1o stang.pdf.
Scholarships for international students: Biuro Uznawalnosci Wykstalcenian i Wymiany Miedzynarodowej (Bureau for Academic Recognition and International Exchange) - see address above.
Recognition of studies and qualification: Biuro Uznawalnosci Wykstalcenian i Wymiany Miedzynarodowej (Bureau for Academic Recognition and International Exchange); ul. Smolna 1300-375 Warsaw; Poland: tel: +48-22-826-7434; fax: +48-22-826-2823; email: biuro@buwiwm.edu.pl; web: http://www.buwiwm.edu.pl (Polish ENIC/NARIC).
Publications / Websites:
• Database of courses taught in English available at the website of KRASPKRASP (Conference of Rectors of Academic Schools in Poland); web: http://db.krasp.org.pl/intro.php
• Study in Poland:guide availabe at the website of MENiSMENiS (Ministry of National Education and Sports); http://www.menis.gov.pl/menis_en/higher_education/studia1o stang.pdf.

1828 Academy 'Adam Mickiewicz University', Poznan [UAM]

ul. H. Wieniawskiego 1
61-712 Poznan
Tel: +48-61-829-4000
Fax: +48-61-829-4444
Web: http://www.amu.edu.pl
e-mail: rectorof@amu.edu.pl

🎓 Graduate Programmes

Study Domains: all major fields.
Scholarships: PhD Programme Scholarship.
Open to: candidates of all nationalities with Master's degree.
Duration: 4 years, non-renewable.
Value: tuition: PLN 1080; living expenses: PLN 900.
Applications: by September; contact joannaj@amu.edu.pl for further details.

1829 Academy of Agriculture in Cracow

Hausera Street 4
37-700 Przemysl
Tel: +48-16-678-23-69/27-84
Fax: +48-16-678 47 88
Web: http://www.ar.krakow.pl
e-mail: pszsprzem@poczta.onet.pl

📖 Undergraduate Programme

Study Domains: biochemistry, chemistry, economy, engineering, food industry, law, mathematics, microbiology, physics, statistics.
Programmes: Bachelor's degree in economics and firm organization; engineering diploma in food technology and analysis.
Open to: candidates over 18 years of age; holding a secondary-school certificate and passing the GCSM.
Duration: Bachelor's programme: 3-1/2 years; engineering programme: 4 years; courses begin in October.
Fees: current registration: 400 PLN; tuition fees: 1,000 PLN per term.
Applications: by 30 June.

1830 Academy of Business in Dabrowa Gornicza

Ul. Cieplaka 1C
41-300 Dabrowa Gornicza
Tel: +48 32 262 2805/8560
Fax: +48 32 262 2805/8560
Web: http://www.wsb.edu.pl
e-mail: info@wsb.edu.pl

📖 Undergraduate, Graduate Programmes

Study Domains: management, marketing, sociology.
Programmes: Bachelor's and Master's degrees.
Fees: tuition fees for full time students: 1,800 PLN per week; for extramural students: 1,100 PLN per week.
Financial assistance: some scholarships available.
Languages: Polish and English.
Applications: by September to the above address.

1831 Academy of Fine Arts in Cracow 'Jan Matejko'

Place Matejki 13
31-157 Cracow
Tel: +48 12 422 2450
Fax: +48 12 422 6566
Web: http://www.asp.krakow.pl
e-mail: zerektor@cyf-kr.edu.pl

📖 Undergraduate, Graduate Programmes

Study Domains: fine arts, graphic arts, interior design.
Programmes: Bachelor's, Master's degrees in fine arts, graphic arts, painting, sculpture, conservation and restoration.
Open to: candidates of any nationality holding a secondary-school diploma; entrance examination and presentation of portfolio required.
Duration: 3 to 6 years; courses begin 1 October.
Fees: registration US$200; tuition fees US$5,000 per year; living costs 1,500 PLN per month.
Applications: by 30 August to Dzial Nauczania ASP, Plac Mtejki 13, 31-157 Cracow, Poland; contact Romana Lomnicka-Bochnak; tel: +48 12 422 0922; email: zebulano@cyf-kr.edu.pl for further details.

🐝 Scholarships

Study Domains: design, fine arts, interior design.
Scholarships: Fulbright, DAAD (German Academic Exchange Service).
Subjects: Fine arts, design, interior design, conservation and restoration.
Open to: candidates of any nationality, holding a secondary-school diploma and presenting a satisfactory portfolio.
Duration: 1 to 6 years.
Value: 700 PLN per month.
Applications: by 7 June; contact Romana Lomnicka-Bochnak, tel: +48 12 422 0922, email: zebulano@cyf-kr.edu.pl for further information.

1832 Academy of Fine Arts in Katowice

ul. Raciborska 37
40-074 Katowice
Tel: +48 32 2516 989 /2518 967
Fax: +48 32 2516 108
Web: http://www.aspkat.edu.pl
e-mail: asp@aspkat.edu.pl

📖 Undergraduate, Graduate Studies

Study Domains: design, fine arts, graphic arts.
Programmes: Bachelor's, Master's degrees in fine arts, graphics, painting and design, drawing and sculpture.
Open to: candidates of any nationality holding a secondary-school certificate.
Duration: Bachelor's, 3 years; Master's, 5 years; courses begin in October.
Fees: current registration 80 PLN; tuition fees US$5,000 per year; living costs and accommodation 300 PLN per month.
Applications: By 30 April; contact Anna Harasimowicz, tel: +48 32 2516 989 ext. 111.

1833 Academy of Fine Arts in Poznan

Al. Marcinkowskiego 29
60-967 Poznan
Tel: +48 61 855 2521
Fax: +48 61 852 8091
Web: http://www.asp.poznan.pl
e-mail: office@asp.poznan.pl

📖 Graduate Studies

Study Domains: fine arts.
Programmes: Master's degrees in fine arts, painting, printmaking, sculpture, interior architecture, design, multimedia, art education. Also artistic internship for foreign students.
Open to: candidates of any nationality holding a secondary school certificate; portfolio also required.
Duration: Master's degrees, 5 years; artistic internship, minimum 3 months; courses begin 1 October.
Fees: registration US$200; tuition fees US$5,000 (US$3,500 for foreigners of Polish origin); artistic internship US$500 per month, US$350 for foreigners of Polish origin; living costs 600 PLN per month.
Languages: Master's studies in Polish; artistic internship in English, German, French.
Applications: by 31 May; contact Malgorzata Sieminska-Stesik, tel: +48 61 855 2521 ext. 335 for further details.

1834 Academy of Fine Arts in Warsaw

International Relations Department
Ul. Krakowskie Przedmiescie 5
00-068 Warsaw
Tel: +48 22 826 2114
Fax: +48 22 826 8193
Web: http://www.asp.waw.pl
e-mail: rektorat@asp.waw.pl

📖 Graduate Programmes

Study Domains: applied arts, art history, arts, decorative arts, design, fine arts, graphic arts, industrial design, interior design, performing arts.
Programmes: Graduate programmes leading to Master's degree.
Description: courses offered by the Departments of Painting, Sculpture, Graphic Art, Restoration and Conservation, Industrial Design, Scenography.
Open to: candidates of any country holding a secondary school certificate with practical fine art experience; entrance interview requires candidates to present examples of artistic creations (paintings, drawings, sculptures, photographs of work, etc.), to demonstrate theoretical knowledge and foreign language proficiency; foreign graduation certificates must be translated in Polish and be confirmed by the Polish consulate of the candidate's country and by the Ministry of National Education, Department of Foreign Partnership in Warsaw, Al. Szucha 25, III floor.
Duration: 5 to 6 years depending on programmes.
Fees: entrance examination: US$200; tuition: US$5,000.
Languages: Polish.
Applications: to the International Relations Department at the above address.

1835 **Academy of Fine Arts in Wroclaw**
International Relations Office
Pl. Polski 3/4
50-156 Wroclaw
Tel: +48 71 343 1558
Fax: +48 71 343 1558
Web: http://www.asp.wroc.pl
e-mail: info@cybis.asp.wroc.pl

📖 **Graduate Programmes**

Study Domains: art history, arts, decorative arts, design, fine arts, graphic arts, interior design, languages, philosophy.
Programmes: Master's degrees in arts, graphics design, printmaking, ceramics, interior architecture, industrial design, history of art, philosophy, languages.
Open to: candidates of all nationalities; entrance examination required.
Duration: 5 years.
Fees: tuition: US$5,000 for independent international students.
Languages: Polish, English, French.
Applications: by 1 May to International Relations Office; contact Magdalena Proniewska, mpr@asp.wroc.pl for further details.

1836 **Academy of Music in Poznan 'Ignacy Jan Paderewski'**
Ul. Sw. Marcina 87
61-808 Poznan
Tel: +48 61 856 8900
Fax: +48 61 853 6676
Web: http://www.amuz.poznan.pl
e-mail: amuz@man.poznan.pl

📖 **Graduate Programmes**

Study Domains: music and musicology.
Programmes: Master's degrees in music, composing, conducting, theory of music and callisthenics, singing and acting, choral conducting, musical education and church music.
Duration: 5 years; courses begin in September.
Fees: registration US$200; tuition fees US$5,000 per year; living costs 270 PLN.
Applications: by September; contact Janina Soroko, email: amuz@man.poznan.pl for further details.

1837 **Academy of Music in Warsaw 'Fryderyc Chopin'**
ul. Okolnik 2
00-368 Warsaw
Tel: +48 22 827 8308
Fax: +48 22 827 8308
Web: http://www.chopin.edu.pl
e-mail: rektorat@wsz-pou.edu.pl

📖 **Graduate, Postgraduate Programmes / Music**

Study Domains: music and musicology.
Programmes: Master's, Ph.D. degrees in music.
Open to: candidates of any nationality; entrance examination.
Duration: 5 years; courses begin 1 October.
Fees: registration US$200; tuition fees US$6,000; living costs US$300-$500.
Languages: Polish; postgraduate courses in English.
Applications: by 15 September to the above address; contact Joanna Zawadzka, tel: +48 22 827 8308, email: foreign@chopin.edu.pl for further details.

1838 **Academy of Music in Wroclaw 'Karol Lipinski'**
Pl. 1 Maja 2
50-043 Wroclaw
Tel: +48 71 355 9056
Fax: +48 71 355 9105
Web: http://www.amuz.wroc.pl
e-mail: info@amuz.wroc.pl

📖 **Graduate Programmes**

Study Domains: music and musicology.
Programmes: Master's degrees in music, conducting,

composition, instrumental and vocal performance.
Open to: candidates of any nationality holding a school of music certificate; entrance examination and audition required.
Duration: 5 years; courses begin in October.
Fees: registration US$200; tuition fees US$4,000-$5,000; living costs US$450-$650.
Languages: main courses are in Polish; individual instructions can be given in English, French, German.
Applications: by 15 May; contact Agnieszka Syrek, tel: +48 355 5543 ext.157, email: agnieszka@amuz.wroc.pl for further details.

1839 **Academy of Music, Cracow [AMUZ]**
ul. Uw. Tomasza 43
31-02 Kraków
Tel: +48-12-422-32-50
Fax: +48-12-422-10-73
Web: http://www.amuz.krakow.pl
e-mail: zbjanecz@cyf-kr.edu.pl

📖 **Graduate Programmes / Music**

Study Domains: music and musicology.
Programmes: Master's degrees in music, conducting, performing, vocal, music education, composition.
Open to: candidates of any nationality.
Duration: 5 years; courses begin in October.
Fees: tuition fees US$4,000-$5,000.
Languages: Polish, English.
Applications: by 31 May.

1840 **Academy of Physical Education 'Eugeniusz Piasecki'**
ul. Krolowej Jadwigi 27/39
61-871 Poznan
Tel: +48-61-833-0039
Fax: +48-61-833-0039
Web: http://www.awf.poznan.pl
e-mail: aszew@awf.poznan.pl

📖 **Graduate, Postgraduate Programmes / Physical Education**

Study Domains: anatomy, biochemistry, ecology, environment, economy, information science, languages, law, management, marketing, nutrition, physical education, physiology, psychology, recreation and leisure, research, sciences, social work, sociology, special education, teacher education, tourism, hotel and catering management.
Programmes: Master's, PhD degrees in physical education, physiotherapy, tourism and recreation; PhD degrees in physical education; postdoctoral degrees (Doctor Habilit.) in physical education.
Open to: candidates holding Matura diploma (secondary school certificate); entrance examination required.
Duration: 4-1/2 years (3-year Licenciat- undergraduate degree; 1-1/2 years for Master's degree); courses begin mid-September.
Fees: registration: 200 €; tuition: 5,500 € per year; living costs: 950 € per month.
Financial assistance: some financial assistance available.
Languages: Polish; for Socrates/Erasmus students, English.
Applications: by 31 May for full- and part-time students; contact dzial.nauczania@awf.poznan.pl for further details.

1841 **AGH University of Science and Technology International School of Technology [AGH-UST]**
al. Mickiewicza 30
30-059 Kraków
Tel: +48-12-617-3334
Fax: +48-12-617-2534
Web: http://www.agh.edu.pl / www.ist.agh.edu.pl
e-mail: office@ist.agh.edu.pl

📖 **Undergraduate, Graduate, Postgraduate Programmes**

Study Domains: ecology, environment, engineering, mathematics, mechanical engineering.

Programmes: Bachelor's, Master's, PhD degrees in automatics and robotics (mechatronics), environmental engineering, materials science and engineering, mining engineering and applied mathematics; management- only for Bachelor of Science holders.
Open to: candidates of any nationality holding secondary-school certificate.
Duration: Bachelor's degree: 7 semesters; courses begin 1 October.
Fees: registration: 200€; tuition: US$5,000-US$8,000 per year; living costs: US£350 per month.
Languages: proficiency in English required.
Applications: by 15 July to Student Office; tel: +48-12-617-3334; fax: +48-12-617-2534; email: asia@uci.agh.edu.pl for further information.

☛ Scholarship

Study Domains: sciences, technology.
Subjects: Science and Technology.
Open to: Students from all nationalities with knowledge of Polish language.
Duration: 5 years.
Value: Tuition waiver.
Applications: By 5 June; see website for application form.

1842 Agricultural University of Cracow

Al. Mickiewicza 21
31-120 Cracow
Tel: +48 12 622 4260
Fax: +48 12 633 6245
Web: http://www.ar.krakow.pl
e-mail: recint@ar.krakow.pl

📖 Undergraduate, Graduate, Postgraduate Programmes

Study Domains: agriculture, cattle breeding, food, forestry, horticulture, management, marketing.
Programmes: Bachelor's, Master's, Ph.D. degrees in agriculture, marketing and management, animal husbandry, environmental engineering, land surveying and mapping, forestry, horticulture, biotechnology; also non-degree programmes in agriculture and rural development in Poland.
Open to: candidates of any nationality holding a secondary-school certificate.
Duration: 4 to 5 years; courses begin 1 October.
Fees: registration US$250; tuition fees US$3,000 per year.

1843 Agricultural University of Wroclaw

Ul. Norwida 25
50-375 Wroclaw
Tel: +48 71 320 5100
Fax: +48 71 320 5404
Web: http://www.ar.wroc.pl
e-mail: rektor@ozi.ar.wroc.pl

📖 Undergraduate, Graduate, Postgraduate Programmes

Study Domains: agriculture, cattle breeding, ecology, environment, food industry, geodesy, veterinary medicine.
Programmes: Bachelor's, Master's, Ph.D. degrees in agriculture, biology and animal science, food science, environmental engineering and geodesy, veterinary medicine.

1844 Association for the Promotion of Entrepreneurship, University of Information Technology and Management, Rzeszow

Ul. Sucharskiego 2
35-225 Rzeszow
Tel: +48 17 86 61 111
Fax: +48 17 86 61 222
Web: http://www.wsiz.rzeszow.pl
e-mail: wsiz@wsiz.rzeszow.pl

📖 Undergraduate, Graduate Programmes

Study Domains: administration, computer science, economy, information science, journalism, public relations, recreation and leisure, tourism, hotel and catering management.

Programmes: Bachelor's and Master's degrees.
Open to: candidates of all nationalities with secondary-school certificate; special co-operation with Ukrainian institutions.
Duration: Bachelor's programme: 3 years; Master's programme: 4 to 5 years; courses begin 1 October.
Fees: registration: US$100; tuition fees: US$1000-$1050 per year (full time), US$700-$750 per year (part time).
Financial assistance: some scholarships available; for information contact Marta Slawinska, tel: +48 17 86 61 175, email: mslawinska@wenus.wsiz.rzeszow.pl.
Languages: Polish, Russian.
Applications: by 27 July; for further information contact Bartlomiej Gebarowski, tel: +48 17 86 61 174, email: bgebarowski@wenus.wsiz.rzeszow.pl.

1845 Boleslaw Markowski Higher School of Commerce

Ul. Peryferyjna 15
25-526 Kielce
Tel: +48 41 368 5129
Fax: +48 41 368 5129
Web: http://www.wsh-kielce.edu.pl
e-mail: info@wsh-kielce.edu.pl

📖 Undergraduate, Graduate Programmes

Study Domains: administration, design, economy, management, marketing.
Programmes: Licenciat (undergraduate degree) of management and marketing, economics, design, administration (full-time and part-time); Magister (undergraduate degree) of economics (full-time and part-time); engineering diploma of management and marketing (full-time and part-time).
Open to: candidates of all nationalities with secondary-school certificate.
Duration: 3 or 3-1/2 years.
Fees: current registration: 500-600 PLN; tuition fees: 1,980-4,950 PLN per year; living costs: approx. 1,000 PLN per month.
Applications: by June for full-time programmes; by September for part-time programmes.

1846 College of Communication and Management

Ul. Zagorze 6A
61-112 Poznan
Tel: +48 61 855 3261
Fax: +48 61 853 2150
Web: http://www.wskiz.poznan.pl/1/str_i/0.php
e-mail: uczelnia@wskiz.poznan.pl

📖 Undergraduate Programmes

Study Domains: computer science, English, German, management, marketing.
Programmes: Bachelor's degree; engineering diploma.
Open to: candidates of all nationalities with secondary-school certificate.
Duration: 3 years; courses begin in October.
Fees: registration: 395 PLN; tuition: 385-465 PLN per month.
Financial assistance: some financial assistance and scholarships available.

1847 College of Economics and Computer Science

Wyzwolenia 30
10-106 Olsztyn
Tel: +48 89 527 5545
Fax: +48 89 527 5545
Web: http://www.wsiie.olsztyn.pl
e-mail: twp@twp.olsztyn.pl

📖 Undergraduate, Graduate Programmes

Study Domains: business, computer science, economy.
Programmes: Undergraduate and graduate studies in economics and computer science.

1848 College of Socio-Economics in Tyczyn

Ul. T. Kosciuszki 4 Skr. Poczt. 10
36-200 Tyczyn
Tel: +48 17 229 1113
Fax: +48 17 229 1553
Web: http://www.wssg.rzeszow.pl
e-mail: infowssg@wssg.rzeszow.pl

Undergraduate, Graduate Programmes

Study Domains: cultural studies, political science, sociology.
Programmes: Bachelor and Master of Arts.
Open to: candidates of all nationalities with secondary-school certificate.
Duration: 3 years; courses begin in October.
Fees: current registration: 400 PLN; tuition fees: 3,250 PLN per year.
Financial assistance: possibility of financial assistance in the amount of 250 PLN per month.
Applications: by 30 September.

1849 Computer Science and Management University 'Copernicus' in Wroclaw

Ul. Inowroclawska 56
53-648 Wroclaw
Tel: +48 71 355 2062
Fax: +48 71 359 1044
Web: http://www.wsiz.wroc.pl
e-mail: dziekanat@wsiz.wroc.pl

Undergraduate Programme

Study Domains: computer science, management.
Programmes: Engineering degree in information technology.
Open to: candidates of all nationalities with secondary-school certificate.
Duration: 3-1/2 years; courses begin in October.
Fees: current registration: 400 PLN; tuition fees: 4,800 PLN per year; living costs: approx. 500 PLN per month.
Applications: by 30 September.

1850 Crestochowa University of Management

Ul. Rzasawska 40
42-200 Crestochowa
Tel: +48 34 362 1836
Fax: +48 34 362 1836
Web: http://www.wsz.edu.pl
e-mail: rektorat@wsz.edu.pl

Undergraduate, Graduate and Postgraduate Programmes

Study Domains: computer science, management, marketing, philology.
Programmes: Undergraduate, Graduate and Postgraduate Programmes leading to Bachelor's, Master's and Ph.D.
Duration: 3-2 years, depending on programmes.
Applications: to the above address.

1851 Economics University in Warsaw

Al. Solidarnosci 74 A
00-145 Warszawa
Tel: +48 22 636 7400
Fax: +48 22 636 7512
Web: http://www.wse.waw.pl
e-mail: sekretar@wse.waw.pl

Undergraduate and Graduate Programmes

Study Domains: economy, recreation and leisure, tourism, hotel and catering management.
Programmes: Bachelor's and Master's degrees.
Open to: candidates of all nationalities with secondary school leaving certificate.
Duration: 5 years; courses begin in October.
Fees: current registration: 600 PLN; tuition fees: 600 PLN per month.
Financial assistance: some scholarships available (for

information contact the Chancellor of the University).
Applications: by September.

1852 Faculty of Mathematics and Information Science

Pl. Politechniki 1
00-661 Warsaw
Tel: +48 22 660 7687
Fax: +48 22 660 5363
Web: http://www.mini.pw.edu.pl
e-mail: macukow@mini.pw.edu.pl

Undergraduate, Graduate Programmes / Computer Science

Study Domains: computer science.
Programmes: Bachelor's and Master's degrees in computer sciences.
Open to: secondary-school graduates of all nationalities; TOEFL required.
Duration: 3 to 5 academic years; courses begin 1st October.
Fees: registration: US$200; tuition: US$4,000; estimated living costs: US$300/month.
Languages: English.
Applications: by 31 August to the Center for English-Medium Studies, WUT at the above address.

1853 Family Alliance Higher School

Ul. Grzegorzewskiej 10
02-778 Warsaw
Tel: +48 22 644 0797
Fax: +48 22 644 07 97/ 0455
e-mail: pszwarczewski@hotmail.com

Undergraduate Programmes

Study Domains: geography, history, languages, natural sciences.
Programmes: Bachelor of Science (nature and geography); Bachelor of Arts (Polish language and history).
Open to: candidates of all nationalities with secondary school leaving certificate.
Duration: 3 years; courses begin in October.
Fees: current registration: 300 PLN; tuition fees: 4000 PLN per year; living costs: approx. 1000 PLN per month.
Applications: by 15 September.

1854 Feliks Nowowiejski Academy of Music in Bydgoszcz

Ul. Slowackiego 7
85-008 Bydgoszcz
Tel: +48 52 321 1142
Fax: +48 52 321 2350
Web: http://www.amuz.bydgoszcz.pl
e-mail: sekr@amuz.bydgoszcz.pl

Undergraduate, Graduate, Postgraduate Programmes

Study Domains: music and musicology, performing arts.
Programmes: Undergraduate, graduate and postgraduate programmes leading to Bachelor's, Master's and Ph.D. degrees.
Open to: candidates of any country holding a certificate of graduation from a secondary school of music or a diploma from an academy of music; these certificates should be sent to consulates of the Republic of Poland or directly to the authorities of the Academy; candidates should deliver their own compositions to the department chosen for study as well as a list of repertoire, programmes and concert reviews.
Fees: tuition fees: mural studies (undergraduate-graduate), US$5,000 per year; postgraduate studies, US$2,000.
Financial assistance: all matters connected with granting financial support are governed by special regulations and international agreements.
Applications: to the above address.

1855 Gdansk School of Banking

Ul. Dolna Brama 8
80-821 Gdansk
Tel: +48 58 305 2742
Fax: +48 58 305 2742
Web: http://www.wsb.gda.pl
e-mail: kancelaria@wsb.gda.pl

📖 Undergraduate Programme

Study Domains: accounting, finance, international business, trade.
Programmes: Bachelor of science (B.Sc.).
Open to: candidates of all nationalities with secondary school leaving certificate.
Duration: 3 years.

1856 Higher Professional School of Krosno

Ul. Rynek 1
38-400 Krosno
Tel: +48 13 437 5530
Fax: +48 13 437 5511
Web: http://www.pwsz.krosno.edu.pl
e-mail: pwsz@pwsz.krosno.edu.pl

📖 Undergraduate Studies

Study Domains: computer science, education, engineering, languages, physical education, tourism, hotel and catering management.
Programmes: Bachelor's degrees in humanities, engineering, tourism and physical education.
Open to: candidates of any nationality holding secondary school certificate; language proficiency test.
Duration: 3 years; courses begin 1 October.
Fees: registration US$100; tuition fees US$3,100 per year.
Languages: English, German.
Applications: by 30 August; contact Wladyslaw Witalisz, fax: +48 13 437 5511, email: witalisz@vela.filg.uj.edu.pl for further details.

1857 Higher School 'Paweù Wùodkowic', Pùock

al. Kiliñskiego 12
09-40 Pùock
Tel: +48-24-366-4100
Fax: +48-24-366-4148
Web: http://www.wlodkowic.pl
e-mail: pawel@wlodkowic.pl

📖 Undergraduate, Graduate Programmes

Study Domains: all major fields.
Programmes: undergraduate and graduate programmes at the following faculties: Faculty of Administration; Faculty of Computer Science; Institute of Mathematics; Faculty of Political Science and International Relations; Faculty of Pedagogy; Faculty of Physical Education; Faculty of Management.

1858 Higher School of Administration

Ul. A. Frycza Modrzewskiego 12
43-300 Bielsko-Biala
Tel: +48 33 815 1108
Fax: +48 33 815 1109
Web: http://www.republika.pl/wsabielsko
e-mail: wsabielsko@hoga.pl

📖 Undergraduate Programme

Study Domains: administration, international relations.
Programmes: Licenciat.
Open to: candidates of all nationalities with secondary leaving school certificate.
Other conditions: interview.
Duration: 3 years; courses begin in October.
Fees: current registration: 500 PLN; tuition fees: 1650 PLN; living costs: approx. 600 PLN per month.
Financial assistance: some scholarships given by the Educational Enterprise Foundation in Lodz are available (approx. 500-800 PLN per semester).
Applications: by 30 September.

1859 Higher School of Economics and Arts

Ul. Mazowiecka 1 B
96-100 Skierniewice
Tel: +48 46 832 1161/ 51
Fax: +48 46 832 1123 / 44
Web: http://www.wsehsk.home.pl
e-mail: rektorat@wsehsk.home.pl

📖 Undergraduate Programmes

Study Domains: administration, ecology, environment, education, horticulture, management, marketing, sociology.
Programmes: Bachelor's degree programmes.
Open to: candidates of all nationalities with secondary-school certificate; interview required.
Duration: 3 to 4 years; courses begin in October.
Fees: current registration: 450-500 + 65 PLN; tuition: 280-360 PLN per month.
Financial assistance: some scholarships available (for information contact Marius Marasek at the above address).
Applications: by September.

1860 Higher School of Economics, Warsaw [WSE]

al. Solidarnoúci 74a
00-14 Warszawa
Tel: +48-22-321-8517
Fax: +48-22-636-7512
Web: http://www.wse.waw.pl
e-mail: sekretar@wse.waw.pl

📖 Undergraduate, Graduate Programmes

Study Domains: economic and commercial sciences, tourism, hotel and catering management.
Programmes: degree programmes in finance; banking; foreign trade; economics; hotel management; tourism.

1861 Higher School of Humanities and Economy in Elblag

Ul. Lotnicza 2
82-300 Elblag
Tel: +48 55 393 3802
Fax: +48 55 239 3801
Web: http://www.euh-e.edu.pl
e-mail: rektorat@euh-e.edu.pl

📖 Undergraduate Programmes

Study Domains: administration, business administration, economy, education, management, social work.
Programmes: Bachelor of Arts.
Open to: candidates of all nationalities with secondary-school certificate.
Duration: courses begin in October.
Fees: current registration: 350 PLN; tuition: 1,620 PLN.
Applications: by September.

1862 Higher School of Management/ Polish Open University

37 A Domaniewska Str.
02-672 Warsaw
Tel: +48 22 853 7006 / 843 7692
Fax: +48 22 853 3845
Web: http://www.wsz-pou.edu.pl
e-mail: rektorat@wsz-pou.edu.pl

📖 Undergraduate and Graduate Programmes

Study Domains: advertising, business administration, computer science, finance, information science, management, marketing.
Programmes: Licenciat (Bachelor of Arts); Magister (Master of Business Administration).
Open to: candidates of all nationalities with secondary-school certificate; entrance examination for M.B.A. programme.
Duration: B.A.: 3-1/2 years; M.B.A.: 2 years; B.A. programme is trimestrial; M.B.A. programme is semestrial.
Fees: current registration: B.A., 550 PLN, M.B.A., US$100; tuition fees: B.A., 4,500 PLN per year, M.B.A., US$2,250 per year.
Applications: one month before beginning of courses.

1863 Higher School of Social Knowledge

Ul. Romka Strzakowskiego 5/7
60-854 Poznan
Tel: +48 61 848 3034/ 35
Fax: +48 61 848 3034/ 35
Web: http://www.wsus.poznan.pl
e-mail: wsus@wsus.poznan.pl

Undergraduate Programme

Study Domains: communication, journalism, management, marketing, social sciences.
Programmes: Licenciat (undergraduate degree) in management and marketing, journalism and social communication.
Duration: 3 years; courses begin in October.
Fees: current registration: 400 PLN; tuition fees: 3,600-38,00 PLN; living costs: approx. 1,000 PLN per month.
Financial assistance: some scholarships of approximately 550-850 PLN per year are available; application by 30 October.
Applications: by September.

1864 Higher School of Tourism and Hotel Industry

Miszewskiego 12/13
80-239 Gdansk
Tel: +48-58-348-8220
Fax: +48-58-348-8220
Web: http://www.wstih.edu.pl
e-mail: wstih@wstih.edu.pl

Undergraduate, Graduate Programmes

Study Domains: recreation and leisure, tourism, hotel and catering management.
Programmes: Bachelor's, Master's degrees in tourism, hotel management.
Open to: candidates of any nationality holding secondary-school certificate.
Duration: 3 to 5 years; courses begin 1 October and 14 February.
Fees: registration: 100-350 PLN; tuition: 3,000-4,800 PLN per year.
Languages: proficiency in Polish required.

Scholarships

Study Domains: recreation and leisure, tourism, hotel and catering management.
Scholarships: University Scholarship.
Open to: candidates of all nationalities meeting academic requirements.
Duration: one semester; renewable.
Value: 100-700 PLN per semester.
Applications: by 15 April.

1865 Higher Vocational State School

Ul. Partyzantow 40
22-100 Chelm
Tel: +48 82 565 5585
Fax: +48 82 565 8885
Web: http://www.pwsz.chelm.pl
e-mail: rektorat@pwsz.chelm.pl

Undergraduate Programmes

Study Domains: computer science, mathematics.
Programmes: Bachelor's degrees in mathematics and computer science; teaching of mathematics.
Open to: candidates of any nationality; proficiency in Polish required.
Duration: 3 years; courses begin 1 October.
Fees: registration: 70 PLN.
Applications: by 25 July, to the above address; contact Beata Falda, tel/fax: +82 565 8885, email: bfalda@pwsz.chelm.pl for further details.

1866 Higher Vocational State School in Kalisz

Ul. Nowy Swiat 4
62-800 Kalisz
Tel: +48 62 767 9514
Fax: +48 62 767 9510
Web: http://www.kalisz.pwsz.pl
e-mail: rektorat@pwsz.kalisz.pl

Undergraduate Studies

Study Domains: business, computer science, ecology, environment, electricity and electronics, management, mechanical engineering.
Programmes: Bachelor's degrees, engineering diplomas.
Open to: candidates of any nationality holding a recognized secondary-school certificate; proficiency in Polish required.
Held: engineering studies, ul. Czestochowska 140, 62-800 Kalisz; business and management, ul. Mickiwicza 11, 62-800 Kalisz.
Duration: 3-1/2 years; courses begin in October.
Fees: registration: 75 PLN.
Applications: by 10 July to the above address.

1867 Karol Szymanowski Academy of Music in Katowice

Ul. Zacisze 3
PO Box 316
40-025 Katowice
Tel: +48 32 255 4017
Fax: +48 32 256 4485
Web: http://www.am.katowice.pl
e-mail: rektor@am.katowice.pl

Graduate Studies

Study Domains: arts, fine arts, liberal arts, music and musicology, performing arts.
Programmes: Master's degree in music.
Duration: 5 years; courses begin in October; Also Summer course.
Fees: registration US$200; tuition fees US$6,000 per year; living costs US$450 per month.
Applications: by 30 May.

1868 Katowice School of Economics [GWSH]

ul. Harcerzy Wrzeúnia 3
40-65 Katowice
Tel: +48-32-202-70-19
Fax: +48-32-202-61-06
Web: http://www.gwsh.pl
e-mail: rektorat@gwsh.pl

Undergraduate, Graduate Programmes

Study Domains: accounting, administration, business administration, computer science, European studies, journalism, physical therapy, recreation and leisure, tourism, hotel and catering management, trade.
Programmes: undergraduate, graduate programmes in accounting, business administration, E-business; trade; international business; finance; management; marketing; computer engineering; physical therapy; journalism; hotel management; tourism; communication studies; European studies; cultural studies; leisure studies.

1869 Kielce University of Technology

Al/1000 - Lecia Panstwa Polskiego 7
25-314 Kielce
Tel: +48 41 342 4100 /344 1684
Fax: +48 41 344 2997
Web: http://www.tu.kielce.pl
e-mail: rek@tu.kielce.pl

Undergraduate, Graduate Programmes

Study Domains: civil engineering, electricity and electronics, industrial technology, information science, management, marketing, mechanical engineering.
Programmes: Bachelor's, Master's degrees, engineering diplomas in civil and environmental engineering, electrical and computer engineering, mechatronics and machinery design, marketing and management, production engineering.

Duration: 5 years; courses begin end of September.
Fees: registration US$200; tuition fees US$2,500.
Applications: by 20 September; contact Ewa Karonska, tel/fax: +48 4134 24540, email: promocja@tu.kielce.pl for further details.

1870 Maria Curie-Skodowska University in Lublin [UMCS]

Pl. M. Curie-Skodowskiej 5
20-031 Lublin
Tel: +48 81 533 3669
Web: http://www.umcs.lublin.pl

📖 Graduate, Postgraduate Programmes

Study Domains: administration, arts, education, law, mathematics, philosophy.
Programmes: Bachelor's, Master's, Ph.D. degrees in arts, philosophy, mathematics, law, administration, education.
Open to: candidates of any country holding a first university degree.
Languages: English.

1871 Maritime University of Szczecin

ul. Waly Chrobrego 1/2
70-500 Szczecin
Tel: +48 91 488 2275
Fax: +48 91 433 8123
Web: http://www.wsm.szczecin.pl
e-mail: rn@wsm.szczecin.pl

📖 Undergraduate, Graduate Programmes

Study Domains: economic and commercial sciences, marine science, mechanical engineering, shipbuilding, transport.
Programmes: Bachelor's, Master's degrees in navigation, marine engineering, transport, mechanical and nautical engineering.
Description: provides knowledge and skills to future merchant fleet officers; offers modern system of maritime education and training.
Open to: candidates holding secondary-school certificate.
Duration: 4 years; courses begin end of September.
Fees: registration US$100; tuition fees US$4,250-$4,500 per year; living costs US$720-$1,020 per year.
Languages: Polish and English.

1872 Medical University of Lodz

A. Kosciuszki 4
90-419 Lodz
Tel: +48 42 632 5100
Fax: +48 42 630 0707
Web: http://www.am.lodz.pl
e-mail: akmed@rkt.am.lodz.pl

📖 Graduate, Postgraduate Programmes

Study Domains: dentistry, medicine, pharmacy and pharmacology.
Programmes: Master's degree in pharmacy; Doctor of Medicine, Doctor of Dentistry; also non-degree programme in cosmetology.
Open to: candidates of all nationalities holding a secondary-school leaving certificate; proficiency in Polish required.
Duration: pharmacy: 5 years; medicine: 6 years; dentistry: 5 years; courses begin 1 October.
Fees: registration US$200; tuition fees US$5,500-$7,500; living costs US$300-$500 per month.
Applications: by 31 July, to the Department of Didactics; contact Malgorzata Wejchert, tel/fax: +48 42 632 9973, email: wejchert@rkt.am.lodz.pl for further details.

💲 Scholarship

Study Domains: dentistry, medicine, pharmacy and pharmacology.
Scholarships: Polish Government Scholarship.
Open to: candidates of all nationalities.
Duration: for entire period of study.
Value: US$170 per month.
Applications: contact Bureau for Academic Recognition and International Exchange, email: biuro@buwiwm.edu.pl for further details.

1873 Medical University of Silesia in Katowice

Ul. Poniatowskiego 15
40-006 Katowice
Tel: +48 32 208 3507
Fax: +48 32 208 3609
Web: http://www.slam.katowice.pl
e-mail: rekst@slam.katowice.pl

📖 Graduate Programmes

Study Domains: anatomy, bacteriology, cancerology, cardiology, cytology, dentistry, dermatology, dietetics, gerontology, health and hygiene, immunology, medicine, neurology, nursing, nutrition, obstetrics and gynaecology, ophthalmology, paediatrics, paramedical studies, pharmacy and pharmacology, physiology, preventive medicine, psychiatry, radiology, social work, speech therapy, stomatology, surgery, urology.
Programmes: Doctor of Medicine.
Open to: candidates of any country holding a secondary-school certificate.
Duration: 5 to 6 years, depending on programme chosen; courses begin 1 October.
Fees: current registration: US$200; tuition fees: US$6,000; living costs US$200.
Financial assistance: some financial assistance available.
Applications: by 30 July to the above address; for information contact Mrs Ewa Lieber, tel: +48 32 208 3507; fax +48 32 208 3609; email: rekst@slam.katowice.pl.

1874 Medical University of Warsaw

Ul. Zwirki 1 Wigury 61
02-091 Warsaw
Tel: +48 22 572 0101
Fax: +48 22 572 0161
Web: http://www.amwaw.edu.pl
e-mail: rektor@akamed.waw.pl

📖 Undergraduate, Graduate and Postgraduate Programmes

Study Domains: anatomy, applied sciences, biochemistry, biology, biophysics, cardiology, chemistry, computer science, continuing education, dentistry, dermatology, dietetics, education, English, French, genetics, German, health and hygiene, immunology, languages, Latin, linguistics, management, medicine, microbiology, neurology, nursing, nutrition, obstetrics and gynaecology, ophthalmology, paediatrics, pharmacy and pharmacology, physics, physiology, preventive medicine, psychiatry, radiology, surgery, teacher education, urology.
Programmes: undergraduate, graduate and postgraduate programmes leading to Bachelor's, Master's, Ph.D., Medical Diploma (M.D.) and Diploma in dentistry (D.M.D. - equal to Master's).
Open to: candidates of any country holding a secondary school certificate.
Duration: 5 to 6 years (depending on programmes).
Fees: current registration: US$ 500; tuition fees: US$ 8700-10500 depending on programmes.
Languages: English (English division for foreign students).
Applications: by 15 June to Maria Polatyuska, English Division (above address); for information contact Ewa Pradzynska, English Division; tel: +48 22 572 05 02; fax: +48 22 572 05 62; email: english@akamed.waw.pl.

1875 Medical University, Byaùystok [AM]

ul. J. Kiliñskiego 1
15-08 Biaùystok
Tel: +48-85-748-54-04
Fax: +48-85-748-54-16
Web: http://www.amb.edu.pl

💲 Scholarship

Study Domains: medicine.
Open to: students of all nationalities accepted by the Bureau for Academic Recognition and International Exchange, Warsaw.
Duration: 1 year, renewable.
Value: 800 PLN per month.

Applications: Before beginning of academic year; contact Bozena Raczylo at above address for further details.

1876 National Louis University

Zielona 27
33-300 Nowy Sacz
Tel: +48 18 44 99 100
Fax: +48 18 44 99 121
Web: http://www.wsb-nlu.edu.pl/index.eng.php
e-mail: office@wsb-nlu.edu.pl

Undergraduate, Graduate Programmes

Study Domains: business, business administration, management, marketing.
Programmes: undergraduate and graduate programmes leading to Bachelor's and Master's degrees.
Description: American Bachelor of Arts (B.A.), Master of Business Administration (M.B.A.) and Polish Master of Arts (M.A.).
Open to: B.A. and M.A. programmes: candidates of any country holding a secondary-school certificate or equivalent recognized by the Polish Ministry of Education; M.B.A. programme: candidates who have at least 3 years of experience and who hold a Bachelor's or a Master's degree in any discipline; candidates are admitted in the order of incoming applications.
Duration: B.A. and M.A. programmes: 4 to 5 years; M.B.A. programme: 2 years; courses start in October.
Fees: current registration: US$300; tuition: US$2,205 per year for B.A. or M.A. programmes; US$4,000 per year for M.B.A. programme.
Financial assistance: some scholarships available on the basis of academic excellence and financial need; candidates must have completed the first semester of their studies; for information contact Robert Szarota at the above address: tel: +48 18 44 99 272; fax: +48 18 44 99 121; email: rszarota@wsb-nlu.edu.pl.
Languages: English (English test required for candidates from non-English-language countries).
Applications: B.A. and M.A. programmes: from 29 April to 4 September (20 September for candidates from American or British High Schools) to the above address; contact Magdalena Rzeznik; tel: +48 18 44 99102/104, Fax +48 18 44 99121; email: madzia@wsb-nlu.edu.pl; M.B.A. programme: by 30 June to the above address; contact Marek Capinski; email: capinski@wsb-nlu.edu.pl.

1877 Opole University [OU]

ul. Oleska 48
45-052 Opole
Tel: +48 77 44 10925
Fax: +48 77 44 10925
Web: http://www.uni.opole.pl
e-mail: kbola@uni.opole.pl

Undergraduate, Graduate, Postgraduate Programmes

Study Domains: administration, biochemistry, business, business administration, computer science, earth science, ecology, environment, economy, education, engineering, languages, management, mathematics, philology, philosophy, physics, teacher education, theology, religion.
Programmes: Bachelor's, Master's, Ph.D. degrees in education, languages, theology, business administration, economics, management, science, engineering.

1878 Pedagogical University in Warsaw

Ul. Pandy 13
02-202 Warsaw
Tel: +48 22 823 6623
Fax: +48 22 823 6669
e-mail: wsptwp@it.com.pl

Undergraduate, Graduate Programmes

Study Domains: education, languages, political science.
Programmes: Bachelor's, Master's degrees in teacher education, political science, English, Polish.
Open to: candidates of any nationality holding a secondary-school certificate.
Duration: 3 to 5 years; courses begin in October.

Fees: tuition: 1,030-2,800 PLN per year.
Applications: by 15 July to the above address; contact Dimtcho Tourdanov; tel: +48 22 823 6623; email: tourdanov@it.com.pl for further details.

Scholarship

Study Domains: education, languages, political science.
Scholarships: University Scholarship.
Open to: candidates of any nationality, depending on income and academic achievements.
Duration: one year; renewable.
Value: 1,000 PLN per month.
Applications: by end of June; to the Rector, Julian Auleytner, ul. Pandy 13, 02-202 Warsaw, Poland; tel: +48 22 823 6623; fax: +48 22 823 6669.

1879 Plock State School of Higher Education

Ul. Kosciuszki 20
09-400 Plock
Tel: +48 24 269 2415
Web: http://pwsz.plock.org.pl
e-mail: pwsz@plock.org.pl

Undergraduate Programmes

Study Domains: accounting, agriculture, computer science, education, finance, languages, management, marketing, mathematics, teacher education, vocational training.
Programmes: Bachelor's degrees in teacher training, languages and economics, pre-school and primary education, mathematics with computer science, management and marketing in agriculture, accountancy and financing.

1880 Polish-Japanese Institute of Information Technology [PJWSTK]

86 Koszykowa Street
02-008 Warsaw
Tel: +48 22 621 0373 Ext. 204
Fax: +48 22 621 0372
Web: http://www.pjwstk.edu.pl
e-mail: ida@pjwstk.edu.pl

Undergraduate, Graduate Programmes / Computer Science

Study Domains: computer science, technical education.
Programmes: (a) Engineering diploma; (b) Master's degree in computer science.
Open to: all nationalities; Cambridge first certificate required for study in English.
Duration: (a) 3 years; (b) 2 years; courses begin 1 October.
Fees: registration: 1,500-2,500 PLN; tuition: 1,080-1,210 PLN per month; living costs: approx. 2,000 PLN per month.
Languages: Polish or English.
Applications: by 15 September; contact adrabik@pjwstk.edu.pl.

1881 Polytechnic University, Biaùystok [PB]

ul. Wiejska 45a
15-35 Biaùystok
Tel: +48-85-746-90-00
Fax: +48-85-742-90-15
Web: http://www.pb.bialystok.pl
e-mail: rektorat@pb.bialystok.pl

Financial aid

Study Domains: all major fields.
Open to: students of all nationalities accepted to university.
Duration: 1 year, renewable.
Value: Partial tuition waiver.
Applications: Contact dydaktyk@pb.bialystok.pl for further details.

1882 Pomeranian Academy of Tourism and Hotel Management [PATHM]
Ul. Garbary 2
85-229 Bydgoszcs
Tel: +48 52 348 2347
Fax: +48 52 348 2346
Web: http://www.wsptih.byd.pl
e-mail: wpstih@byd.pl

📖 **Undergraduate Programme / Tourism, Hotel Management**

Study Domains: computer science, languages, management, tourism, hotel and catering management.
Programmes: Bachelor of Arts.
Open to: candidates of all nationalities with secondary-school certificate.
Duration: 3 years; courses begin 1 October.
Fees: registration: 360 PLN; tuition: 3,400 PLN.
Financial assistance: some scholarships available; for information contact Anna Pawlowska; tel: +48 52 348 2348; email: wpstih@byd.pl.
Applications: by end of September; application forms available at website: http://www.wpstih.byd.pl.

1883 Poznan University of Technology
Pl. M. Sklodowskiej-Curie
60-965 Poznan
Tel: +48 61 665 3537
Fax: +48 61 833 0518
Web: http://www.put.poznan.pl
e-mail: rector@put.poznan.pl

📖 **Undergraduate, Graduate, Postgraduate Programmes**

Study Domains: architecture, civil engineering, computer science, ecology, environment, engineering, mechanical engineering.
Programmes: Bachelor's, Master's, Ph.D. degrees in architecture, civil and environmental engineering, mechanical engineering and management, electrical engineering, computer science and management.

☞ **Scholarship**
Study Domains: all major fields.
Scholarships: Polish Government Scholarships.
Open to: candidates of any nationality holding a secondary-school certificate; proficiency in Polish required.
Value: 716 PLN per month.
Applications: by 30 September; for further information, contact Zygmunt Mlynarz; tel: +48 61 665 3640, email: dzial.ksztalcenia@put.poznan.pl.

1884 Private Higher Educational Institute in Gizycko
Ul. Daszynskiego 9
11-500 Gizycko
Tel: +48 87 428 8940
Fax: +48 87 428 8930
Web: http://www.karolex.com.pl
e-mail: pwsz@karolex.com.pl

📖 **Undergraduate Programmes**

Study Domains: administration, computer science, management, tourism, hotel and catering management.
Programmes: Engineering diploma; Bachelor's degree.
Open to: candidates of all nationalities with secondary-school certificate.
Fees: registration: 80 €; tuition fees: 1,100 € per year; living costs: approx. 200 € per month.
Languages: Polish, Russian and English.
Applications: by September.

1885 Prof A. Meissner Higher School of Dentistry in Ustron
Ul. Sloneczna 2
43-450 Ustron
Tel: +48 33 854 4090
Fax: +48 33 854 4090
Web: http://www.wsid.pl
e-mail: wsid@wsid.edu.pl

📖 **Undergraduate Programme**

Study Domains: dentistry.
Programmes: Engineering diploma of dental technology.
Open to: candidates of all nationalities with secondary-leaving school certificate.
Duration: 3-1/2 years; courses begin in October.
Fees: current registration: 1,200 PLN; tuition: 750-850 PLN per month.
Applications: by 1 June.

1886 Pultusk School of Humanities
Ul. daszynskiego 17
06-100 Pultusk
Tel: +48 23 692 5082
Fax: +48 23 692 1687
Web: http://www.wsh.edu.pl
e-mail: rektorat@wsh.edu.pl

📖 **Undergraduate, Graduate, Postgraduate Programmes.**

Study Domains: administration, anthropology, archaeology, ecology, environment, education, European studies, history, human sciences, journalism, literature and civilization, philology, political science, social work, special education, teacher education, technical education, tourism, hotel and catering management.
Programmes: (a) Bachelor's degree in public administration, tourism and hotel administration; postgraduate degree in public administration; (b) Bachelor's and Master's degrees in archaeology, archives and museums, European studies, teacher education; (c) Bachelor's degrees in environmental protection; (d) Bachelor's, Master's and Ph.D. in Polish philology; (e) Bachelor's and Master's degrees in history, (f) Bachelor's and Master's degrees in political science.
Held: (a), (b), (d), (e) and (f) Pultusk, (c) Chiechanow.
Duration: 3 to 5 years depending on programme chosen; courses start in October.
Fees: current registration: US$100; tuition: (a) US$900, (b), (c) US$700, (d) US$650, (e) US$600, (f) US$1,200; living costs: approx. US$200 per month.
Applications: by 15 May (limited number of students); for information contact (a) Romuald Kraczkowski; tel. +48 23 692 1872; fax +48 23 691 9017; email: uydzial.administrayi@wsh.edu.pl; (b) Maria Ruszczynska; tel. +48 23 692 5142; fax +48 23 692 0883; email: pedagogilia@wsh.edu.pl; (c) Krysyna Niesiobedzka; tel./fax +48 23 672 9456; email: ochrona.srodowiska@wsh.edu.pl; (d) Yanusz Rohozinski; tel./fax +48 23 692 0091; email: filologia.polska@wsh.edu.pl; (e) Radosvaw Lolo; tel./fax +48 23 692 8019; email: historia@wsh.edu.pl; (f) Krzysztof Michakek; tel./fax +48 23 692 5016; email: politologia@wsh.edu.pl.

1887 School of Banking and Management in Cracow
Al. Kijowska 14
30-079 Cracow
Tel: +48 12 623 9300
Fax: +48 12 637 3347
Web: http://www.wszib.krakow.pl
e-mail: wszib@wszib.krakow.pl

📖 **Undergraduate Programme**

Study Domains: finance, management.
Programmes: Licenciat (undergraduate) degrees.
Open to: no restrictions.
Duration: 3-1/2 years; courses begin in September and February.
Fees: current registration: 500 PLN; fees: 2,250 PLN per semester; living costs: approx. 1,000 PLN per month.
Languages: Polish, English.

Applications: by 30 September for first semester; 15 February for second semester.

1888 School of Commerce in Ruda Slaska

Ul. Krolowej Jadwigi 18
41-704 Ruda Slaska
Tel: +48 32 248 1292
Fax: +48 32 248 1292
Web: http://www.wsh.omi.pl
e-mail: wshr@pro.onet.pl

Undergraduate Programmes

Study Domains: accounting, business, English, finance, management.
Programmes: Licenciat (Bachelor's degree).
Open to: candidates of all nationalities with secondary-school certificate.
Duration: 3-1/2 years; courses begin 1 October.
Fees: current registration: US$90; tuition fees: US$100; living costs: approx. US$300 per month.
Languages: Polish, English.

1889 School of Entrepreneurship and Marketing in Chrzanow

Ul. Sokola 30
32-500 Chrzanow
Tel: +48 32 623 5180
Fax: +48 32 623 5180
Web: http://www.wspim.nauka.pl

Undergraduate Programmes / Business

Study Domains: business administration, management, marketing.
Programmes: Bachelor of business administration (B.B.A.).
Open to: candidates of all nationalities with secondary-school certificate.
Duration: 3 years; courses begin 1 October.
Fees: registration: 770 PLN; tuition: 3,700 PLN.
Financial assistance: some scholarships available; for information contact Dr. Lucja Karpiel at the above address; tel: +48 32 623 5180; email: wspim.chr@digitus.net.pl.
Applications: by 16 September.

1890 Silesian Polytechnic University, Gliwice [SUT]

ul. Akademicka 2A
44-10 Gliwice
Tel: +48-32-237-10-00
Fax: +48-32-237-16-55
Web: http://www.polsl.pl
e-mail: r-br@polsl.pl

Undergraduate, Graduate Programmes

Study Domains: architecture, business administration, chemical engineering, chemistry, civil engineering, computer science, earth science, ecology, environment, electricity and electronics, engineering, industrial technology, management, mechanical engineering, metallurgy, physics, technology, telecommunications.
Programmes: Degree programmes in architecture; auutomatic control, electronics, computer science; chemistry; civil engineering; electrical engineering; materials science, metallurgy; mathematics and physics; mechanical engineering; mining and geology; organization and management; power and environmental engineering; transportation.

1891 Silesian University of Technology

Ul. Akademicka 2a
44-100 Gliwice
Tel: +48 32 237 1255 /231 2349
Fax: +48 32 237 1655
Web: http://www.polsl.gliwice.pl
e-mail: rek.sekr@polsl.gliwice.pl

Undergraduate, Graduate, Postgraduate Programmes

Study Domains: chemical engineering, civil engineering, computer science, ecology, environment, electricity and electronics, energy, engineering, mathematics, mechanical engineering, physics, sciences.
Programmes: Bachelor's, Master's, Ph.D. degrees in engineering, civil engineering, chemistry, electrical engineering, mathematics and physics, materials science, electronics, automation and computer science, energy and environmental engineering.
Open to: candidates of any nationality holding a secondary-school certificate.
Duration: 5 years; courses begin 1 October.
Fees: registration US$200; tuition fees US$3,000 per year; living costs US$300 per month minimum.
Financial assistance: contact: Bureau for Academic Recognition and International Exchange in Warsaw; http://www.buwiwn.edu.pl.
Languages: Polish and English.
Applications: by 30 August; for further information contact: Sonia Nohel; tel: +48 32 231 2349; email: rek.sekr@polsl.gliwice.pl.

1892 Technical University of Koszalin

Raclawicka 15/17
75-620 Koszalin
Tel: +48 94 347 8312
Fax: +48 94 347 1005
Web: http://www.tu.koszalin.pl
e-mail: kieca@tu.koszalin.pl

Undergraduate, Graduate, Postgraduate Programmes

Study Domains: accounting, applied arts, applied sciences, business, civil engineering, computer science, ecology, environment, economic and commercial sciences, electricity and electronics, engineering, English, food industry, forestry, geodesy, geology, industrial design, information science, management, marketing, mechanical engineering, Russian, summer programmes, teacher education, technical education, technology, telecommunications, urbanism.
Programmes: undergraduate, graduate and postgraduate programmes leading to Bachelor's, Master's, Ph.D. and Doctorate of Science.
Open to: candidates of any country holding a secondary-school certificate.
Duration: 3-4-5 years, depending on programmes.
Fees: current registration: 200 €; tuition: 2,000 € per year for undergraduate and graduate programmes; 3,000 € per year for postgraduate programmes; living costs: approx. 1,000-1,500 PLN per month (250-375 €).
Languages: Polish with some modules in English and German.
Applications: by 31 August; contact: Malgorzata Kieca, tel: +48 94 347 8312; fax:+48 94 347 1005; email: kieca@tu.koszalin.pl.

1893 Technical University of Lodz

Skorupki 10/12
90-924 Lodz
Tel: +48 42 636 5308
Fax: +48 42 636 0652
Web: http://www.ife.p.lodz.pl
e-mail: admin@ife.p.lodz.pl

Graduate Programmes

Study Domains: business, computer science, management, mechanical engineering, technology, telecommunications.
Programmes: Master's degrees in mechanical engineering and applied computer science; business and technology; telecommunications and computer science; biotechnology; management and technology.
Open to: candidates of any nationality holding a secondary-school certificate; proficiency in English or French required.
Duration: 5 years; courses begin 1 October.
Fees: registration US$200; tuition fees US$4,000 per year; living costs US$400 per month.
Languages: English, French.
Applications: by 31 July to Dr Tomasz Saryusz-Wolski, Head of IFE, at above address.

1894 Technical University of Opole

Ul. Mikolajczyka 5
45-271 Opole
Tel: +48-77-400-6000
Fax: +48-77-400-6080
Web: http://www.po.opole.pl
e-mail: info@po.opole.pl

Undergraduate, Graduate, Postgraduate Programmes

Study Domains: civil engineering, computer science, electricity and electronics, engineering, management, marketing, mechanical engineering, technical education, telecommunications.
Programmes: Bachelor's, Master's degrees, PhD in civil engineering; electrical engineering; environmental engineering; mechanical engineering and machine building; control engineering and robotics; electronics and telecommunications; computer science; management and marketing; management and production engineering; technical education; physical education; physiotherapy, tourism and recreation, European studies.
Open to: candidates of any nationality holding a secondary-school certificate.
Duration: Bachelor's degree: 3 years; Master's degree: 5 years; courses begin 1 October.
Fees: registration: 200€, tuition: 2,000€ per year for undergraduate and graduate programmes, 3,000€ for postgraduate programmes; living costs: approximately 250€-375€ per month.
Languages: Polish, English, German.
Applications: contact Rektor Politechniki Opolskiej; email: biurorektora@po.opole.pl.

1895 Technical University of Szczecin

Al. Piastow 17
70-310 Szczecin
Tel: +48 91 449 4717
Fax: +48 91 449 4187
Web: http://www.ps.pl
e-mail: joannap@ps.pl

Graduate, Postgraduate Programmes

Study Domains: architecture, chemical engineering, civil engineering, computer science, mechanical engineering.
Programmes: Master's, Ph.D. degrees in civil engineering and architecture, electrical engineering, mechanical engineering, computer science and information technology, maritime technology.
Open to: candidates of any nationality holding a secondary-school certificate or first university degree for Ph.D. studies; proficiency in Polish required; intensive nine-month Polish language course available.

1896 Université d'agriculture de Varsovie [SGGW]

Nowoursynowska 166
02-787 Varsovie
Tel: +48 22 843 0717
Fax: +48 22 847 1562
Web: http://www.sggw.waw.pl/index-e.html

Cours de 3e cycle / agriculture

Domaines d'étude: toutes disciplines principales, agriculture, développement rural, écologie, environnement, horticulture.
Programmes: cours économiques d'agriculture, conduisant au doctorat ou au M.B.A. agricole; conditions particulières.
A l'intention de: titulaires d'un magistère, médecins vétérinaires, ou titulaires d'un B.S.C. pour le M.B.A.
Durée: 3 à 4 ans pour le doctorat.; 2 ans pour le M.B.A.
Assistance financière: bourses du Gouvernement polonais.
Connaissances linguistiques: langues d'enseignement: polonais, anglais.
Inscriptions: au Bureau des études étrangères du Ministère national de l'éducation.

1897 Université médicale de Gdansk [AMDG]

Rue Sklodowska-Curie 3a
80-210 Gdansk
Tel: +48 58 349 2222
Web: http://www.amg.gda.pl

Sciences médicales

Domaines d'étude: études dentaires, immunologie, médecine, neurologie, obstétrique et gynécologie, ophtalmologie, psychiatrie, radiologie.
Programmes: Cours de la faculté de médecine et stomatologie et de la faculté de pharmacie, conduisant au diplôme de docteur en médecine, stomatologie, ou pharmacie.
A l'intention de: titulaires du baccalauréat et du diplôme de fin d'études secondaires (le consulat polonais doit certifier la validité du diplôme).
Durée: 6 ans.
Frais: inscription: 200 US$; scolarité: 5 000 US$.
Inscriptions: avant le 31 août, Akademia Medyczna, Dziekanat, Sklodowskiej-Curie 3a, 80-210 Gdansk.

1898 University College of Arts and Natural Sciences in Sandomierz

ul. Krakowska 26
27-600 Sandomierz
Tel: +48 15 832 2284
Fax: +48 15 832 6081
Web: http://www.wshp.home.pl
e-mail: wshp@home.pl

Undergraduate Studies

Study Domains: arts, natural sciences.
Programmes: undergraduate studies in arts and natural sciences.

1899 University of Bielsko-Biala

Ul. Willowa 2
43-300 Bielsko-Biala
Tel: +48 33 816 2662
Web: http://www.ath.bielsko.pl
e-mail: mmachnio@ath.bielsko.pl

Undergraduate, Graduate Programmes

Study Domains: ecology, environment, information science, management, mechanical engineering, social sciences, textile industry.
Programmes: Bachelor's, Master's degrees in mechanical engineering and information science, textile engineering, environmental protection, management, humanities and social sciences.

1900 University of Ecology and Management in Warsaw [WSEIZ]

Ul. Wawelska 14
02-061 Warszawa
Warsaw
Tel: +48 22 825 8034
Fax: +48 22 825 8034
Web: http://www.wseiz.pl
e-mail: rktorat@wseiz.pl

Undergraduate, Graduate Programmes / engineering

Study Domains: architecture, ecology, environment, engineering, industrial technology, management, marketing, urbanism.
Programmes: Engineering diploma; Master's degree in science.
Open to: candidates of all nationalities with secondary school leaving certificate.
Other conditions: drawing test for admission in faculty of architecture.
Duration: 3-6 years; courses begin in October or March.
Fees: registration: 990 PLN; tuition fees: 4000-4900 PLN per year; living costs: approx. 800 PLN per month.
Applications: by 15 September or 15 February.

1901 University of Economics in Katowice

ul. 1 Maja 50
40-287 Katowice
Tel: +48 32 259 8114
Fax: +48 32 258 8828
Web: http://www.ae.katowice.pl
e-mail: interrel@ae.katowice.pl

Undergraduate, Graduate, Postgraduate Programmes

Study Domains: business, economy, finance, management, marketing.
Programmes: Bachelor's, Master's, Ph.D. degrees in economics, finance and banking, marketing and management, computer science and econometrics; non-degree English programme in business and economics.
Open to: candidates meeting academic requirements; contact edyta@ae.katowice.pl for further information.

1902 University of Finance and Management in Bialystok

ul. Ciepla 40
15-472 Bialystok
Tel: +48 85 67 50088
Fax: +48 85 67 50088
Web: http://www.wsfiz.edu.pl
e-mail: wsfiz@wsfiz.edu.pl

Undergraduate, Graduate Programmes

Study Domains: business, English, finance, management.
Programmes: Bachelor's, Master's degrees in management, banking and finance; certificate programme in English.
Financial assistance: some financial assistance available; contact foreign@wsfiz.edu.pl for further details.

1903 University of Humanities and Economics in Wloclawek [WSHE]

Ul. Piwna 3
87-800 Wloclawek
Tel: +48 54 231 3292
Fax: +48 54 231 3192
Web: http://www.wshe.pl
e-mail: biurorektora@wshe.pl

Undergraduate, Graduate Programmes

Study Domains: administration, ecology, environment, economy, education, history, philology, philosophy, teacher education.
Programmes: (a) Bachelor's degree in administration, economics, philology, philosophy, history; (b) engineering diploma in environmental studies; (c) Master's degree in teacher education; non-degree programmes.
Open to: candidates of all nationalities with secondary school leaving certificate.
Duration: (a) 6 semesters; (b) 7 semesters; (c) 10 semesters; courses begin 1 October.
Fees: registration: 270 PLN; tuition fees: 350-400 PLN per month (1350-1400 PLN per semester for extramural studies).
Financial assistance: some scholarships available; for information contact the Dean's office of the concerned faculty.
Languages: Polish, English.
Applications: by 15 September.

1904 University of International Studies [WSSM]

ul. Brzozowa 3
93-101 Lodz
Tel: +48 42 684 1474
Fax: +48 42 684 1474
Web: http://www.wssm.edu.pl
e-mail: sekretariat@wssm.edu.pl

Undergraduate, Graduate Programmes

Study Domains: international law, international relations, international studies, journalism, languages.

Programmes: Bachelor's, Master's degrees in international relations.
Duration: 5 years; courses begin 1 October; summer courses.
Fees: registration: 500 PLN; tuition: 400 PLN per month.
Financial assistance: financial assistance available.
Languages: Polish and English.
Applications: by the end of July; contact sekretariat@wssm.edu.pl for further information.

1905 University of Lodz

Ul. Narutowicza 65
90-301 Lodz
Tel: +48 42 635 4002
Fax: +48 42 678 3958
Web: http://www.uni.lodz.pl
e-mail: rektorat@krysia.uni.lodz.pl

Undergraduate, Graduate, Postgraduate Programmes

Study Domains: biology, chemistry, economic and commercial sciences, geography, history, international relations, law, mathematics, philosophy, physics, political science, sociology.
Programmes: Bachelor's, Master's, Ph.D. degrees in all major fields.
Financial assistance: financial assistance available; contact Bureau for Academic Recognition and Foreign Exchange, email: biuro@buwiwn.edu.pl, website: http://www.buwiwn.edu.pl.

1906 University of Management and Marketing in Warsaw [WSZIM]

Al. Jerozolimskie 202
02-482 Warsaw
Tel: +48 22 863 7700
Fax: +48 22 863 7700
Web: http://www.wszim.edu.pl
e-mail: uczelnia@wszim.edu.pl

Undergraduate Studies / Business

Study Domains: business, finance, management, marketing.
Programmes: Bachelor's degree in management, marketing.
Description: courses provide solid knowledge in the field of business management, personnel and quality control management, negotiation techniques, stock market regulations and international economic relationships.
Open to: candidates of all nationalities holding secondary-school certificate; proficiency in Polish required.
Languages: Polish.
Applications: by 15 July, to International Relations Office; contact Sylwia Lompies; tel: +48 22 863 2918; fax: +48 22 863 2934; email: s.lompies@wszim.edu.pl.

1907 University of Mining and Metallurgy

Aal Mickiwecza 30
30-059 Cracow
Tel: +48 12 617 6664
Fax: +48 12 617 3334
Web: http://www.ist.agh.edu.pl
e-mail: office@ist.agh.edu.pl

Undergraduate, Graduate, Postgraduate Programmes

Study Domains: engineering, mathematics, mechanical engineering.
Programmes: Bachelor's, Master's, Ph.D. degrees in automation and robotics (mechatronics), environmental engineering, materials science and engineering, mining engineering and applied mathematics.
Open to: candidates of any nationality holding secondary-school certificate; proficiency in English required.
Duration: Bachelor's degree: 3-1/2 years; courses begin 1 October.
Fees: registration: US$50; tuition fees: US$2,000-$6,000 per year; living costs: US$300 per month.
Languages: English.
Applications: by 15 July to Student Office; tel: +48 12 617

3334; fax: +48 12 617 2534; email: mforys@uci.agh.edu.pl.

1908 University of Podlasie
Ul. 3 Maja 54
08-110 Siedlce
Tel: +48 25 643 1020
Fax: +48 25 644 2045
Web: http://www.ap.siedlce.pl
e-mail: d_sprzaczak@ap.siedlce.pl

Undergraduate, Graduate and Postgraduate Programmes

Study Domains: agriculture, agronomic sciences, biochemistry, biology, business, chemistry, computer science, early childhood education, ecology, environment, education, English, French, German, history, management, Russian, sciences, Slavic studies, special education, teacher education.
Programmes: Undergraduate, graduate and postgraduate programmes leading to Bachelor's, Master's and Ph.D. degrees.
Open to: candidates of any country holding a secondary-school certificate.
Fees: tuition: US$2,500; living costs: approx. 300 € per month.
Languages: English.
Applications: by June to the above address.

1909 University of Rzeszòw
Ul. Rejtana 16 C
35-959 Rzeszòw
Tel: +48 17 862 5628
Web: http://www.univ.rzeszow.pl

Undergraduate, Graduate Programmes

Study Domains: economic and commercial sciences, education, law, mathematics, philology, philosophy, physical education, political science, sociology, technical education.
Programmes: Bachelor's, Master's degrees in economics, philology, philosophy, physiotherapy, physics, history, mathematics, law, sociology; one-year course in Polish language and culture for foreigners.
Open to: candidates of any nationality holding a secondary-school certificate.
Duration: Bachelor's degree: 3 years; Master's degree: 5 years; courses begin 1 October.
Fees: tuition: US$2,000.
Applications: by June; contact Hanna Krupinska-Lyp; tel: +48 17 862 5628.

1910 University of Silesia
ul. Bankowa 12
40-00 Katowice
Tel: +48-32-359-2400
Fax: +48-32-359-2052
Web: http://www.us.edu.pl

Undergraduate, Graduate, Postgraduate Programmes

Study Domains: cultural studies, humanities and arts, languages, literature and civilization, social sciences.
Programmes: Bachelor's, Master's, Ph.D. degrees in social sciences, human sciences, experimental sciences and technology.
Description: university founded in 1968 with an academic staff of about 1900; research and teaching activities in 12 faculties and over 45,000 students.
Languages: Polish. The School of Polish Language and Culture provides courses for students wishing to study in Poland.

1911 University of Zielona Gòra
ul. Podgorna 50
65-246 Zielona Gora
Tel: +48 68 328 2000
Fax: +48 68 327 0735
Web: http://www.uz.zgora.pl
e-mail: rector@uz.zgora.pl

Undergraduate, Graduate, Postgraduate Programmes

Study Domains: economy, engineering, humanities and arts, social sciences.
Programmes: Bachelor's, Master's, Ph.D. degrees in engineering, sciences and economics, arts, humanities and social sciences.
Duration: 3 to 5 years; courses begin 1 October.
Financial assistance: possibility of financial assistance; contact the University.
Applications: by end of June; contact Edyta Wysocka; tel: +48 68 328 3270.

1912 University School of Physical Education in Warsaw [AWF]
Al. I.J. Paderewskiego 35
51-612 Wroclaw
Tel: +48 71 347 3114
Fax: +48 71 348 2527
Web: http://www.awf.wroc.pl
e-mail: rector@awf.wroc.pl

Undergraduate, Graduate Programmes

Study Domains: computer science, languages, physical education, recreation and leisure.
Programmes: Bachelor's, Master's degrees in physical education, physiotherapy, recreation and tourism.
Open to: candidates of any nationality holding a secondary-school certificate.
Duration: 4-1/2 years; courses begin 1 October.
Fees: tuition: US$4,500 per year for foreign students.
Financial assistance: possibility of financial assistance; contact Juliusz Migasiewicz; tel: +48 71 347 3115 for further information or Bureau for Academic Recognition and International Exchange in Warsaw; tel: +48 22 826 7434.
Applications: by 1 September to the above address; contact M. Orlowska; email: mada@awf.wroc.pl for further information.

1913 Warsaw Customs Study College
Str. Jagiellonska 71
00-992 Warsaw
Tel: +48 22 676 1530
Fax: +48 22 676 3274
Web: http://www.clo-wsc.edu.pl
e-mail: wsc@clo-wsc.edu.pl

Undergraduate Studies

Study Domains: administration, transport.
Programmes: Bachelor's degrees in customs service; logistics.
Open to: candidates of any nationality holding a secondary-school certificate; over 18 years of age; entrance examination in Polish language, English and mathematics.
Duration: 3 years; courses begin 1 October.
Fees: registration: 500 PLN; tuition: 500 PLN per month; living costs: 700 PLN per month.
Languages: Polish, English, Russian.
Applications: by 30 August, at the above address; contact Bogdan Cwik; tel: +48 22 676 1530; email: wsc@clo-wsc.edu.pl.

Scholarships

Study Domains: international law, law, physical education, psychology, sciences.
Scholarships: Social Scholarship, Scientific Scholarship, Sport Scholarship.
Open to: candidates of any nationality, based on income and academic achievement.
Duration: one semester; renewable.
Value: 35,000 PLN (approx. 10,000 €).
Applications: after completing first semester of education; contact Bogdan Cwik; tel: +48 22 676 1530; email: wsc@clo-wsc.edu.pl.

1914 Warsaw School of Economics
Al. Niepodleglosci 162
02-554 Warsaw
Tel: +48 22 849 1251
Fax: +48 22 849 5312
Web: http://www.sgh.waw.pl
e-mail: info@sgh.waw.pl

📖 Graduate Programmes

Study Domains: administration, cultural studies, economic and commercial sciences, finance, international business.
Programmes: (a) Master's degree in finance and banking; economics; economics; public economy; quantitative methods and administration system; international economic relations; (b) CEMS Master's degree in management; (c) Master's degree in European studies.
Open to: (a) candidates holding secondary-school certificate; proficiency in Polish required; (b), (c) graduate students; entrance exam required for all programmes.
Duration: (a) 5 years; (b), (c) 2 years; courses begin in October.
Fees: (a) tuition: US$5,000 per year.
Languages: (a) Polish; (b) English; (c) Polish, with some courses in English or French.
Applications: (a) by 15 June; contact Dziekanat Studium Podstawowego, Al. Niepodleglosci 162, 02-554 Warsaw; tel: +48 22 849 5377; (b) by 15 June; contact Grzegorz Augustyniak, CEMS co-ordinator, ul. Rakowiecka 24, 02-521 Warsaw; tel: +48 22 849 5144; fax: +48 22 646 6103; email: august@sgh.waw.pl; (c) by 30 April; contact Malgorzata Madej, ul. Rakowiecka 24, 02-521 Warsaw; tel: +48 22 849 5192; email: mmadej@sgh.waw.pl.

1915 Warsaw University
Krakowskie Przedmiescie 26/28
Warsaw
Tel: +48 22 552 0000
Fax: +48 22 552 4011
Web: http://www.uw.edu.pl
e-mail: bip@mercury.ci.uw.edu.pl

📖 Undergraduate, Graduate, Postgraduate Programmes

Study Domains: archaeology, chemistry, computer science, earth science, ecology, environment, economic and commercial sciences, education, geography, geology, history, international relations, journalism, languages, law, literature and civilization, management, mathematics, philology, philosophy, political science, psychology, sociology.
Programmes: undergraduate, graduate, postgraduate programmes in 32 fields of studies in the humanities and earth and social sciences.
Open to: candidates of all nationalities; oral or written qualifying exams in Polish language and subjects related to field of study required.
Fees: registration: US$200; tuition: variable, between US$2,000 and US$6,000; estimated monthly living costs: US$600.
Applications: by 1 June to the Student Affairs Office at the above address.

1916 Warsaw University of Technology [WUT]
Pl. Politechniki 1
00-661 Warsaw
Tel: +48-22-660-7687
Fax: +48-22-660-5363
Web: http://www.pw.edu.pl

📖 Undergraduate, Graduate Programmes

Study Domains: business, computer science, economy, social sciences, technology.
Programmes: Bachelor's, Master's degrees in computer science, science and technology, economics and social sciences, business.
Open to: candidates holding secondary-school certificate; TOEFL required.
Duration: 3 to 5 years; courses begin 1 October.
Fees: registration: US$200; tuition: US$4,000 per year; living costs: US$300 per month.
Financial assistance: possibility of financial assistance, contact university.
Languages: English.
Applications: by 31 August; contact cems@mini.pw.edu.pl for further details.

Portugal
Année universitaire: octobre à juillet.
Unité monétaire: Euro (€).
Admission pour étudiants du pays: Les étudiants étrangers doivent être titulaires d'un diplôme de fin d'études secondaires et doivent subir avec succès un examen d'entrée. Les étudiants ne remplissant pas ces conditions doivent, soit posséder un certificat leur permettant d'entreprendre des études universitaires dans leur pays, soit obtenir l'équivalence de leurs diplômes ou de l'année propédeutique.
Connaissances linguistiques requises: Une bonne connaissance de la langue portugaise est indispensable pour les cours moyen et supérieur. Des cours destinés spécialement aux étudiants étrangers sont donnés toute l'année, dans des universités telles que les Universités de Lisbonne, de Coimbra, de Porto, lesquelles offrent également des cours de langue et de culture portugaises durant l'été.
Formalités d'immigration: Les étudiants étrangers doivent obtenir un visa d'entrée au Portugal en s'adressant au Consulat du Portugal dans leur pays d'origine.
Services d'accueil et d'information:
• Comité national de l'Association internationale pour l'échange d'étudiants de l'enseignement technique (IAESTE): auprès de l'Instituto Superior Técnico, Avenida Rovisco Pais, 1096 Lisbonne.
• Comité national de l'Association internationale des étudiants en sciences économiques et commerciales (AIESEC): auprès de l'Instituto Superior de Economia e Gestao, Rua do Quelhas, 1200 Lisbonne.
• Direction générale pour la coopération, Avenida da Liberdade 192, 1200 Lisboa (s'occupe de l'accueil des étudiants originaires des pays africains de langue portugaise).
• Ministère des affaires étrangères, Largo do Rilvas, 1300 Lisbonne.
• Ministère de l'éducation, Avenida 5 de Outubro 107, 1051 Lisbonne Codex.
• Institut de culture et de langue portugaises, Praça do Príncipe Real, 14 - 1°, 1200 Lisbonne.
• Il n'existe pas de dispositions spéciales pour assurer l'hébergement des étudiants étrangers, mais les services sociaux des diverses universités peuvent les aider à trouver un logement. Les associations d'étudiants peuvent également leur procurer toute information utile.
Enseignement à distance: L'enseignement supérieur à distance est assuré par l'Universidade Aberta.
Reconnaissance des études et diplômes: NARIC, Département de l'Enseignement supérieur; Education, Ministère de l'Education; Avenida Duque d'Avila 137-4° Andar; 1069-016 Lisbonne; Portugal; tél.: +351 21 312 6098; fax: +351 21 312 6041; email: manuela.paiva@desup.min-edu.pt; site web: http://www.min-edu.pt.

1917 Autonomous University of Lisbon [UAL]
Rua de Santa Marta 56
1169-023 Lisbonne
Tel: +351-21-317-7691
Fax: +351-21-317-7610
Web: http://www.universidade-autonoma.pt
e-mail: secgeral@universidade-autonoma.pt

📖 Undergraduate, Graduate, Postgraduate Studies

Study Domains: accounting, architecture, business administration, computer science, economy, finance, international relations, law, management.
Programmes: multiple degrees in all major fields; Master's degrees in business administration, accounting; economics, finance.
Applications: by 15 December.

1918 Fondation Calouste Gulbenkian [FCG]
Avenida de Berna
1067 Lisbonne Cedex
Tel: +351-21-782-3000
Fax: +351-21-782-3021
Web: http://www.gulbenkian.pt
e-mail: educa@gulbenkian.pt

🐦 **Bourses Gulbenkian**

Domaines d'étude: histoire, histoire de l'art, linguistique, littérature et civilisation, philologie.
Bourses: (a) Bourses d'études;
(b) Bourses de recherche et de spécialisation;
(c) Bourses destinées aux cours annuels de langue et culture portugaises, organisés par les facultés de lettres des universités de Lisbonne, Coimbra et du Minho (Braga);
(d) Bourses d'enseignement supérieur;
(e) Bourses de coopération pour le développement.
A l'intention de: (a) étudiants de nationalité portugaise, âgés de 40 ans maximum, titulaires d'une licence (obtenue au moins 2 ans auparavant) ou équivalent ou du titre de docteur; pour les étrangers, avoir résidé au Portugal plus de 10 ans; (b) titulaires d'un diplôme universitaire, de préférence du niveau doctorat, et ayant une bonne connaissance du portugais; (c) étudiants ayant une bonne connaissance du portugais; (d), (e) ressortissants des pays africains d'expression portugaises.
Durée: (a) 10 mois, renouvelable par période de 12 mois jusqu'à 39 mois au maximum; (b) 1 à 12 mois; (c) 8 mois; (e) 12 mois avec prolongations possible.
Valeur: variable (voir site web pour de plus amples informations).
Candidatures: (a) entre janvier et février pour les sciences, les lettres et la technologie; (b), (c), (d) en février pour les arts, auprès du Serviço de Belas-Artes, pour les arts plastiques; au Serviço de Bolsas de Estudo, pour les lettres et sciences; au Serviço de Música, pour la musique; et au Serviço Internacional à l'adresse ci-dessus, pour les ressortissants étrangers; (d) avant le 15 juillet de chaque année; (e) entre le 1er et le 31 mai de chaque année au Serviço do cooperaçao para o desenvelvimento à l'adresse ci-dessus.

1919 Institut Camões

Rua Rodrigues Sampaio, 113
1150-279 Lisbonne
Tel: +351-21-310-9100
Fax: +351-21-314-3987
Web: http://www.instituto-camoes.pt
e-mail: geral@instituto-camoes.pt

🐦 **Langue et culture portugais**

Domaines d'étude: linguistique, littérature et civilisation, portugais.
Bourses: Bourses d'études.
A l'intention de: étudiants et chercheurs étrangers poursuivant des études en langue et culture portugaises.
Candidatures: consulter le site web pour de plus amples renseignements.

1920 Portucalense University [UP]

R. Antonio Bernardino de Almeida, 541/619
4200-072 Porto
Tel: +351-22-557-2000
Fax: +351-22-557-2012
Web: http://www.uportu.pt
e-mail: pdelgado@upt.pt

📖 **Undergraduate, Graduate, Postgraduate Programmes**

Study Domains: computer science, economy, education, law, management, mathematics.
Programmes: Bachelor's, Master's, Ph.D. in education, economics, law, management, computer science, mathematics.
Duration: 4 years; courses begin 15 September.
Financial assistance: financial assistance available; contact csaragoca@upt.pt for further details.

1921 Université catholique portugaise [UCP]

Sede Central
Palma de Cima
1600 Lisbonne
Tel: +351-21-726-5838
Fax: +351-21-726-0546
Web: http://www.ucp.pt
e-mail: ffonseca@reitoria.ucp.pt

📖 **Undergraduate Studies**

Domaines d'étude: toutes disciplines principales.
Programmes: programmes de licence dans toutes les disciplines principales.
A l'intention de: candidats de toute nationalité; certaines places sont réservées aux étudiants des familles portugaises immigrées de Macao et des pays lusophones d'Afrique; une bonne connaissance du portugais est exigée.
Organisés: dans les facultés et centres de Lisbonne, Porto, Braga, Viseu, Funchal (Madère), Leiria et Figueira da Foz.
Durée: de 4 à 5 ans.
Frais: scolarité, 2.500 € par an.
Assistance financière: possibilité d'exonération ou de réduction des frais de scolarité, ou bourses octroyées en fonction des résultats obtenus par l'étudiant et des ressources financières de sa famille.
Inscriptions: début juillet pour l'examen d'admission; auprès des facultés des divers centres.

1922 Université d'Aveiro [UA]

External Relations Services
Campo Universitário de Santiago
3810-193 Aveiro
Tel: +351-234-370-200
Fax: +351-234-370-985
Web: http://www.ua.pt
e-mail: sre@ua.pt

📖 **2e, 3e cycles / sciences et ingénierie**

Domaines d'étude: biologie, chimie, écologie, environnement, électricité et électronique, géologie, industrie chimique, informatique, ingénierie, mathématiques, mécanique, portugais, programmes d'été, technologie industrielle.
Programmes: (a) Maestrado (DEA): psychologie, éducation, didactique, électronique, télécommunications, langues, géochimie, microbiologie, chimie, biologie, géologie, minéralogie, pollution, toxicologie, technologie, mathématiques, physique; (b) Maîtrise: environnement, urbanisme, électronique et télécommunications, ordinateurs et télématique, formation de professeurs de langues, formation de professeurs, biologie, géologie, mathématiques appliquées, physique, génie céramique et du verre, géosciences, génie civil, génie mécanique, économie, tourisme, design, nouvelles technologies de la communication; (c) Doctorat: génie électrique, génie mécanique, éducation, culture, sciences et génie des matériaux, sciences appliquées à l'environnement, didactique, électronique, télécommunications, linguistique, littérature, musique, arts du spectacle, chimie, biologie, philosophie, mathématiques, physique, géosciences, tourisme; (d) Cours de portugais pour étrangers; cours intensif, semestriels et d'été).
A l'intention de: (a), (b) et (c) ressortissants de tout pays avec de bonnes connaissances en portugais; (d) étudiants ayant au moins les bases de la langue portugaise.
Durée: (a) 2 ans; (b) 4 et 5 ans; (c) 3 à 5 ans.
Inscriptions: (a) et (c) au Gabinete de Pos-Graduaçao; (b) septembre, aux Serviços Académicos e Administrativos; à l'adresse ci-dessus.

1923 Université de Beira Interior [UBI]

Rua Marquês d'Ávila e Bolama
62001-001 Covilhã
Tel: +351-275-319-061
Fax: +351-275-319-057/78
Web: http://www.ubi.pt
e-mail: socrates@ubi.pt

📖 **1er-3e cycles / toutes disciplines**

Domaines d'étude: toutes disciplines principales.
Programmes: Programme de cours conduisant à: (a) Licence en sciences du sport, en sciences de la communication, en sociologie; (b) Maîtrise en mathématiques/informatique, en mathématiques/informatique pour l'enseignement, en physique appliquée à l'optique, en physique pour l'enseignement; (c) Mastère en mathématiques appliquées; (d) Cours d'extension universitaire en hygiène et sécurité du travail; (e) Doctorat en mathématiques, informatique, physique, chimie, génie textile, génie du papier, génie mécanique, génie électrotechnique, génie informatique, génie civil, génie de la production, génie aéronautique,

sociologie, économie, gestion, éducation.
A l'intention de: ressortissants de tout pays, ayant accès à l'enseignement supérieur portugais ou équivalent; ceux qui ne font pas partie des programmes Erasmus et Socrates doivent passer des épreuves spécifiques.
Durée: (a) 4 ans; (b) 5 ans.
Assistance financière: possibilité de bourses.
Connaissances linguistiques: langue obligatoire: portugais.
Inscriptions: septembre; aux Serviços Académicos à l'adresse ci-dessus.

1924   Université de Lisbonne [UL]
Alam. da Universidade, Cidade Universitária
Campo Grande
1649-004 Lisbonne
Tel: +351-21-796-7624
Fax: +351-21-793-3624
Web: http://www.ul.pt
e-mail: reitoria@reitoria.ul.pt

Undergraduate, Graduate, Postgraduate Programmes
Study Domains: dentistry, education, fine arts, law, literature and civilization, medicine, pharmacy and pharmacology, psychology.
Programmes: Licenciado (Bachelor's), Mestre (Master's), Doutor (Doctorate) degrees in law, letters, fine arts, medicine, science, pharmacy, dentistry, psychology and education.
Open to: candidates of all nationalities meeting academic, linguistic and financial criteria.
Applications: to the above address.

1925   Université de Lusofona des Humanités et des Technologies [ULHT]
Av. do Campo Grande, 376
1749-024 Lisbonne
Tel: +351-21-751-5565
Fax: +351-21-751-5534
Web: http://www.ulusofona.pt
e-mail: trdamasio@ulusofona.pt

Undergraduate, Graduate Studies
Study Domains: all major fields, applied sciences, business, business administration, education, engineering, languages, law, liberal arts, pharmacy and pharmacology, sciences, social sciences, theology, religion, tourism, hotel and catering management.
Programmes: Bachelor's, Master's degrees in all major fields.
Subjects: Architecture, design, urban planning, applied sciences, accounting, business, business administration, economic and commercial sciences, mathematics, environment engineering, electronics engineering, chemistry, civil engineering, languages, law, communication, multimedia, cinema, pharmacy and pharmacology, biology, social sciences, tourism, hotel and catering management, teacher education, geography.
Open to: candidates meeting all academic requirements.
Nationality: All nationalities.
Age limit Min: 18 years old.
Age limit Max: No maximum age limit.
Fees: tuition: from 245 € to 595 € per month; living costs: an average of 600 € per month.
Languages: Portuguese and English.
Applications: by October. For further information, contact the International, Career Opportunities and Entrepreneurship Office. Director:Teresa do Rosário Damásio; email: trdamasio@ulusofona.pt.

Scholarships to Portuguese-Speaking Countries
Study Domains: all major fields.
Scholarships: University Scholarship.
Open to: candidates from Portugal and Portuguese-speaking countries: Angola, Brazil, Mozambique, Guinea-Bissau, Cape Verde, São Tome and Principe; based on personal family income.
Value: variable, depending on student and family income.
Applications: by October; for further information, contact Elisabete Lourenço, elisabete.lourenco@ulusofona.pt.

1926   Université nouvelle de Lisbonne, Institut d'hygiène et de médecine tropicale [UNL-IHMT]
Rua da Junqueira 96
1349-008 Lisbonne
Tel: +351-21-365-2600
Fax: +351-21-363-2105
Web: http://www.ihmt.unl.pt
e-mail: info@ihmt.unl.pt

2e, 3e cycles / Médecine tropicale
Domaines d'étude: bactériologie, cytologie, études d'infirmière, hygiène et santé, médecine.
Programmes: Cours de maîtrise et de 3e cycle dans les domaines suivants: (a) Maîtrise en parasitologie médicale; (b) Cours clinique des maladies tropicales; (c) Microbiologie tropicale; (d) Parasitologie médicale (1er niveau); (e) Cours de santé internationale; (f) Cours pour infirmiers.
A l'intention de: ressortissants de tout pays: (a), (c), et (d) médecins, biologistes, pharmaciens, vétérinaires, ou tout titulaire d'un diplôme universitaire équivalent; (b) médecins.
Durée: de 1 à 26 mois selon les cours.
Inscriptions: variables selon les années: a) de janvier à juillet; (b) de début septembre à fin octobre; (c) de début novembre à fin décembre; (d) de début janvier à fin avril; (e) en novembre; (f) en septembre; aux Services académiques de l'Instituto de higiene e medicina tropical, à l'adresse ci-dessus.

1927   University of Tras-os-Montes e Alto Douro University [UTAD]
Quinta de Prados
Apdo J013
5000-911 Vila Real
Tel: +351-259-350-170 / 67 / 68
Fax: +351-259-325-058
Web: http://www.utad.pt
e-mail: reitoria@utad.pt

Undergraduate, Graduate Programmes
Study Domains: agronomic sciences, anthropology, civil engineering, computer science, ecology, environment, education, languages, literature and civilization, management, mechanical engineering, veterinary medicine.
Programmes: Licenciatura (Bachelor's), Mestre (Master's) degrees in education, languages, literature, anthropology, science, civil engineering, veterinary medicine, agronomy.
Open to: candidates of all nationalities meeting academic, linguistic and financial criteria.
Applications: to the above address.

Qatar
Academic year: September to June.
Monetary unit: rial.
National student admission: Foreign students should have a High School Certificate or a recognized equivalent.
Language: A good knowledge of Arabic is required for all major disciplines except engineering, biomedical science and nursing.
Information services:
• Deanship Student Affairs, PO Box 2713, Doha.
• Embassies of the State of Qatar abroad.
Recognition of studies and qualification:
• Ministry of Education and Higher Education; PO Box 80; Doha; Qatar; web: http://www.mofa.gov.qa/government/ministries/moec/index-e.htm
• University of Qatar; Academic Affairs; PO Box 2713; Doha; Qatar; tel.: +974 832 222; fax: +974 835 111; email: president@qu.edu.qa; web: http://www.qu.edu.qa.
Publications / Websites:
• 'University of Qatar Newsletter', published by the University.
• College brochures and college bulletins.

1928 University of Qatar

PO Box 2713
Doha
Tel: +974-485-2222
Web: http://www.qu.edu.qa

Scholarships

Study Domains: all major fields.
Scholarships: State of Qatar Scholarships (100).
Open to: candidates with a secondary-school certificate or
equivalent; proficiency in Arabic and/or English.
Duration: 1 academic year.
Value: stipend plus full board and accommodation.
Applications: by 1 July, to the above address.

Republic of Korea

Academic year: March to February.
Organization of higher education system: Higher
education in the Republic of Korea consists of universities
and colleges, junior colleges and graduate schools. Duration
of undergraduate studies in universities is normally four
years, and six years for medical colleges, colleges of oriental
medicine, dental colleges, and veterinary colleges. The junior
college programmes require 2 to 3 years of study, depending
on the programme. The minimum duration of graduate studies
is 2 years for Master's degrees and for doctoral degrees.
Korean universities and colleges, junior colleges and graduate
schools confer degrees to those who have completed all
courses as determined by school regulations.
Monetary unit: Korean won.
National student admission: For undergraduate studies:
secondary school leaving certificate or equivalent or higher
academic background under the Korean law and related
statutes are qualified to enter universities & colleges and
junior colleges. Candidates should meet the individual
admission requirements of each university and college or
junior college such as High School Activities Records, the
College Scholastic Aptitude Test and interviews.
For graduate studies: Bachelor's degree or greater academic
background under the Korean law and related statutes are
qualified to enter Master's degree courses and doctoral degree
courses. Candidates should meet each graduate school's
individual admission requirements such as academic
documents, examinations and interviews.
International student admission: International students
wishing to undertake undergraduate or graduate studies must
be eligible to enter equivalent institutions of higher education
in their own countries. Candidates must meet the individual
admission requirements of each university & college or junior
college including academic and financial capability. In
general, international students applying for Korean
universities and colleges, junior colleges and graduate schools
are required to submit an application form, and appropriate
certificates of past education, academic performance record,
personal essay and study plan. Documents can vary, and
candidates should check with each individual institution.
Language: International students need not possess
excellent Korean language skills or pass the Korean Language
Proficiency Test. To support the study of international
students, Korean universities and colleges have begun to teach
a growing number of courses in foreign languages and offer
Korean language training courses. In addition, the National
Institute for International Education Development operates
KOSNET(Korean Language Study) on the Internet;
http://www.interedu.go.kr), a website offering educational
spaces to learn the Korean language through the Internet.
Immigration requirements: International students who
have received admission from Korean universities and
colleges, junior colleges and graduate schools must normally
apply for and obtain a visa at the Korean embassy or
consulate abroad. Documents required for visa issuance
include an official certificate of admission, current passport
copy, visa application form and financial certificates.
More detailed information on studying in Korea including the
certificate for confirmation of visa issuance, entry &
departure, information on universities and colleges, junior
colleges and graduate schools, admission procedures, Korean
language proficiency test and living in Korea can be found on
the website http://www.studyinkorea.go.kr operated by the
National Institute for International Education Development, or
the websites of Korean embassies abroad.

Estimated expenses for one academic year: public
universities tuition: liberal arts: US$2,300; science and
engineering: US$2,900; private universities: tuition: liberal
arts: US$3,500-$4,200; science and engineering:
US$4,200-$4,900. Fees to be checked with each institution;
books/supplies: US$500-1,000; housing:
on-campus Dormitory (including meals), per semester:
US$720 (4-bed room), US$870 (2-bed room); boarding house
(per month): US$300 (per room for 2), US$500 (per single
room); self-boarding house/apartment: US$400 per month
(deposit of US$3,000-$5,000 required which is returned on
departure).
Information services:
• International students wishing to apply for enrolment in
Korean universities and colleges, junior colleges and graduate
schools should contact the respective admission office of each
institution. Details may be obtained at
http://www.studinkorea.go.kr
• Korean Research Foundation, International Cooperation
Team, 304 Youmgok-dong Seo-cho-gu Seoul.
• National Institute for International Education Development,
Counselling Center for Foreigners; 110-810, Dongsung-dong,
Jongno-gu, Seoul, Korea 110-810; tel: +82-2-3668-1379 / 80;
fax: +82-2-741-7408: web: http://www.studyinkorea.go.kr
• Further information may be obtained by linking on the
homepages of Korean embassies and missions abroad or by
consulting university officials.
Scholarships for international students:
• Universities run their own scholarship programs for foreign
students.
• The Ministry of Education & Human Resources
Development offers a graduate-level 'Korean Government
Scholarship Students Program' and a 'Ph.D. & Master
Studentship for Foreigners' for international students.
• Through the 'Korean Government Scholarship Students
Program', over 200 international students are receiving
financial support every year. Details can be found at the
National Institute for International Education Development;
web: http://www.ied.go.kr; tel: +82-2-3668-1305.
• The 'Ph.D. & Master Studentship for Foreigners' supports
outstanding international students majoring in science and
engineering. Details can be found at the Korea Research
Foundation site: web: http://www.krf.or.kr; +82-2-3460-5624.
• Many governmental departments including the Ministry of
Information & Communication Technology and the Ministry
of Culture & Tourism are conducting supportive programs for
foreign students, and the Korean government plans to
continuously enlarge scholarship programmes for foreign
students.
Open and distance learning: Open and Distance Learning
is provided by the Korea National Open University, a distance
learning institution run by the Korean government. The
University provides academic studies via various
communication devices such as satellite TV and the EBS
(Educational Broadcasting Service) Radio. Foreign students
are not allowed to acquire student visas for the purpose of
enrolling in the Korea National Open University.
Recognition of studies and qualification: Credits taken at
other colleges at home and abroad may be recognized as
credits for the school concerned, to the extent of one half of
the credits necessary for graduation, provided that the extent
for transferred students and graduate students shall be
governed by school regulations.
Accommodation services:
• A majority of Korean universities operate on-campus
dormitories for students and most take special care to help
foreign students secure dorm housing. Details should be
consulted at each university separately.
• The National Institute for International Education
Development also runs a separate dormitory for Korean
Government Scholarship Students. Details should be
consulted at the Institute directly.
Work opportunities: International students who have
completed at least 6 months (1 semester) of study in a Korean
university and college, junior college or graduate school and
who are recommended by a university professor are permitted
to work part-time in Korea, within the limit of 20 hours per
week during academic semesters. There is no limitation on
working hours during vacation periods.
Additional information:
• The National Institute for International Education
Development organizes study abroad affairs in and out of the
country for foreign student recruitment.

• In 2005 the Institute planned to participate in or hold study abroad fairs in 10 cities from 8 countries including Ulaanbaatar (Mongolia), Seattle (USA), Beijing (China), New Delhi (India), Ho Chi Minh City (Vietnam), Taipei (Taiwan), Osaka (Japan) and Moscow (Russia). The number and venue of study fairs will be increased and verified continuously. Details should be consulted at the National Institute for International Education Development.
• The Korean government is also implementing a 'Study Korea Project' since November 2004, which seeks to expand scholarship programmes and improve study conditions for international students.
Publications / Websites:
• 'Study in Korea', 'Accredited Korea Universities and Colleges' (in English), published by the National Institute for International Education Development and distributed to Korean embassies and consulates abroad, overseas Korean education offices, overseas Korean schools and other institutions. Information is also available on-line at http://www.studyinkorea.go.kr.

1929 Academy of Korean Studies [AKS]
Academic Affairs Division
50 Unjung-dong, Bundang-gu,
Seongnam-si, Kyeonggi-do 463-79
463-79 Seongnam-si, Kyeonggi-do
Tel: +82-31-709-8111 ext. 210 /211
Fax: +82-31-709-9946
Web: http://www.aks.ac.kr
e-mail: gradaks@aks.ac.kr

Graduate, Postgraduate Programmes

Study Domains: archaeology, documentation, economy, education, fine arts, folklore, history, languages, literature and civilization, music and musicology, philosophy, political science, theology, religion.
Programmes: (a) M.A. degree programme; (b) Ph.D. programme; (c) non-degree research programme.
Open to: candidates of any nationality holding: (a) B.A. or B.Sc.; (b) M.A.; (c) B.A. or B.Sc.; candidates must demonstrate oral and written proficiency in Korean language.
Duration: (a) 2 years; (b) 3 years; (c) 1 semester to 2 years; (courses begin in March and in September).
Fees: foreign students enrolled in M.A. and Ph.D. programmes are exempt from paying registration and tuition fees, and may reside at the dormitory, but are responsible for their own meals.
Applications: by 30 October, for the Spring semester; 30 April for the Fall semester; to the Office of Academic and Student Affairs, at the above address.

1930 Berea International Theological Seminary
665-10 Daelim 3-dong Youngdeungpo-gu
150-8 Seoul
Tel: +82-2- 831-2272
Fax: +82-2- 831-1724
Web: http://www.berea.ac.kr
e-mail: ches2001@berea.ac.kr

Undergraduate Programmes
Study Domains: theology, religion.

1931 Chodang University
419 Sung nam-ri
Muan-eup, Muan-gun
Jeonnam, Mokpu
Tel: +82-61-450-1000
Web: http://www.chodang.ac.kr/english
e-mail: president@chodang.ac.kr

Undergraduate, Graduate Programmes

Study Domains: architecture, business administration, civil engineering, computer science, design, ecology, environment, electricity and electronics, food, industrial design, information science, interior design, languages, literature and civilization, marketing, music and musicology, optics, physical education, social sciences, telecommunications.

Programmes: Bachelor's, Master's degrees in design, languages; industrial design, business administration, computer science, architecture.
Open to: students with secondary-school certificate.
Duration: 4 years.
Fees: tuition fees US$1,500 per semester; living costs US$1,000 per semester.
Financial assistance: financial assistance available; contact cskoh@chodang.ac.kr for further information.

1932 Chonnam National University
300 Yongbong-dong, Buk-gu
500-757 Gwangju
Tel: +82-62-530-5114
Fax: +82-62-530-1139
Web: http://www.chonnam.ac.kr

Tuition Waiver
Study Domains: all major fields.
Open to: all international students of the university either as regularly-enrolled or within an exchange programme.
Value: tuition waivers of variable amount depending on enrolment status of student.
Applications: 8 October for spring semester; 15 April for fall semester.

1933 Gyeongsang National University [GSNU]
900 Kajwa-dong
660-7 Jinju-si
Tel: +82-55-751-6114
Fax: +82-55-751-6134
Web: http://www.gsnu.ac.kr/english
e-mail: postmaster@gshp.gsnu.ac.kr

Undergraduate, Graduate Programmes

Study Domains: business administration, education, engineering, humanities and arts, law, marine science, medicine, sciences, social sciences, veterinary sciences.

1934 Handong Global University
3 Namsong-ri, Heunghae-eup Buk-gu, Pohang-si
791-7 Pohang-si
Tel: +82-54-260-1111
Fax: +82-54-260-1419
Web: http://www.handong.edu
e-mail: webmaster@handong.edu

Undergraduate Programmes

Study Domains: computer science, information science, international law, management.
Programmes: Bachelor's degree programmes in global management, information technology, U.S. and international law, international law school: Master's degree programmes in global management and international legal studies; JD programme at Handong International Law School (HILS). (See lawschool.handong.edu/English for full information on applying to HILS.
Open to: students of all nationalities meeting academic requirements.
Fees: tuition: US$3,000; US$600 for dormitory per semester.
Applications: by 30 November for the 2006 academic year.

Students from Developing Countries Scholarship
Study Domains: all major fields.
Scholarships: Scholarship for Students from Developing Countries.
Open to: students from specific developing countries.
Duration: 4 years.
Value: full tuition (amount depends on selected major), housing, meal tickets, health coverage.
Applications: contact HGU Admissions Office at kty@handong.edu.

1935 Hansei University
604-5, Dangjung-dong, Gunpo-shi
435-742 Gyunggi-do
Tel: +82-31-450-5114
Fax: +82-31-457-6517
Web: http://www.hansei.ac.kr
e-mail: webmaster@hansei.ac.kr

📖 **Undergraduate, Graduate, Postgraduate Programmes**

Study Domains: administration, advertising, arts, audio-visual media, business administration, communication, computer science, design, economy, electricity and electronics, engineering, finance, graphic arts, history, human sciences, interior design, international business, international relations, languages, literature and civilization, management, music and musicology, neurology, nursing, philosophy, social work, speech therapy, technology, telecommunications, theology, religion, tourism, hotel and catering management, visual arts.
Programmes: (a) undergraduate school: Bachelor's degrees in theology, arts, business administration, public administration, engineering, music, fine arts; (b) graduate school: Master's degrees in divinity, ministry, music, arts, church music, science, social welfare, education, police, law; Doctorate degrees in theology, divinity, ministry, music, church music, engineering; Ph.D. in theology.
Open to: full-time international students who are degree candidates for undergraduate or graduate programmes; who have a certificate of Korean Proficiency or the ability to follow studies in Korean.
Duration: (a) 4 years; (b) Master's degree: 2 to 3 years following Bachelor's degree: Doctorate: 3 years following Master's degree.
Financial assistance: limited scholarship programme for overseas students; covers dormitory costs (approximately US$500 for 2 semesters, not including meals and excluding vacation periods.
Applications: (a) by end September; (b) 2 weeks before beginning of each semester: Spring semester begins in March and Fall semester begins in September.

1936 Inha University
253 Younghyun-dong, Nam-gu
402-751 Incheon
Tel: +82-32-860-7030-2
Fax: +82-32-867-7222
Web: http://www.inha.ac.kr/english/
e-mail: orir@inha.ac.kr

🎓 **Undergraduate, Graduate Fellowships**

Study Domains: all major fields.
Scholarships: (a) Inha University Global Leader Fellowship for undergraduate studies; (b) Jungseok International Fellowship for graduate studies.
Open to: (a) international students enrolled at university with high scores on nationally administered examinations; (b) all international graduate students enrolled at university.
Value: US$2,188-$4,573 per semester.
Applications: (a) by mid-September to Section of Admissions and Recruitment; Junho@inha.ac.kr; (b) by 31 May for fall semester; by 30 October for spring semester; contact Graduate School Office; choi@inha.ac.kr; Graduate School of Information Technology & Telecommunications; tiger@inha.ac.kr.

1937 Keimyung University [KU]
1000 Sindang-Dong, Dalseo-Gu
705-701 Narngu, Daegu
Tel: +82-53-580-6022
Fax: +82-53-580-6025
Web: http://www.kmu.ac.kr
e-mail: intl@kmu.ac.kr

📖 **Undergraduate, Graduate Programmes**

Study Domains: all major fields.
Programmes: undergraduate and graduate programmes.
Open to: all students with secondary-school certificate and Korean language proficiency.
Duration: undergraduate: 4 years; graduate: 4 to 5 semesters.
Fees: contact University for current tuition and admission

fees.
Financial assistance: some scholarships are available.
Languages: Korean; some courses offered in English, Japanese and other languages.
Applications: undergraduate: by end of September: graduate: by early June and early November.

1938 Korean-American Educational Commission [KEC]
168-15 Yomni-dong, Mapo-gu
121-874 Seoul
Tel: +82-2-3275-4000
Fax: +82-2-3275-4028
Web: http://www.fulbright.or.kr

🎓 **Schlolarships**

Study Domains: all major fields, education.
Scholarships: (a) Fulbright-Hays Scholarships; (b) East-West Center Grants; (c) Graduate degree grants.
Subjects: (a) and (b) graduate study in any academic field; (c) humanities, social science and fine arts.
Open to: Korean nationals only for study in the U.S., with superior academic backgrounds and appropriate levels of academic or professional achievement as well as satisfactory proficiency in English; candidates must for (a) and (b) hold at least a Bachelor's degree at the time the grant is activated; (c) Korean citizens residing in Republic of Korea, must hold a Bachelor's degree to apply for Master's study or a Master's degree to apply for Doctorate; minimum 550 TOEFL.
Place of study: (a) and (c) at any university or college in the United States; (b) at the East-West Center and the University of Hawaii at Manoa only.
Duration: (a) and (c) 1 year (renewable up to a total of 2 years); (b) 1 year (renewable until completion of a degree programme).
Value: (a) and (b) tuition (if applicable), all living costs, international travel and incidental allowance in most cases; (c) approx. US$20,000-$25,000 each year.
Applications: (a) and (b) by mid-August; (c) by September; to the address above.

1939 Kyongpook National University, Overseas Educational Center [KNU]
1370 Sankyuk-dong, Buk-gu
Daegu 702-701
Tel: +82-53-950-6091 / 2
Fax: +82-53-950-6093
Web: http://www.knu.ac.kr

📖 **Undergraduate, Graduate, Postgraduate Programmes**

Study Domains: agriculture, computer science, dentistry, economic and commercial sciences, electricity and electronics, engineering, law, medicine, music and musicology, natural sciences, social sciences, teacher education, veterinary sciences, visual arts.
Programmes: (a) Bachelor's, Master's and Ph.D. degrees; (b) Special courses for international students: KNU International Education Programme, Korean language and culture.
Open to: students of all nationalities, no age limit.
Duration: undergraduate: 4 years; graduate: 2 to 3 years.
Fees: tuition: US2,300-$3,000 per year undergraduate; US$2,500-3,200 per year graduate; on-campus dormitory: US$2,000 per year.
Financial assistance: possibility of scholarship based on scholastic achievement.
Languages: Korean and English (KNUIEP).
Applications: 31 October for first (Spring) semester; 30 April for second (Fall) semester.

1940 Kyungnam University [KU]
449 Wolyoung-dong
631-7 Masan-si
Tel: +82-55-245-5000
Fax: +82-55-247-9344
Web: http://www.kyungnam.ac.kr
e-mail: sfa0@kyungnam.ac.kr

Undergraduate, Graduate Programmes

Study Domains: economic and commercial sciences, economy, education, engineering, international studies, law, liberal arts, natural sciences, sciences.
Programmes: undergraduate, graduate programmes in all major areas of study.

1941 Language Teaching Research Centre [LTRC]
60-17, 1-ga, Taepyung-ro
Chung-ku
100-101 Seoul
Tel: +82-2-737-4641
Fax: +82-2-734-6036
Web: http://www.ltrc.co.kr
e-mail: ltrc@unitel.co.kr

Language Courses

Study Domains: Asian studies, English, Korean, languages.
Programmes: courses in (a) Korean language: individual or small group classes; (b) English language (7 levels from elementary to advanced).
Open to: nationals of any country.
Duration: 8 weeks per term; courses begin every other month beginning in January.

1942 Sejong University
98 Gunja-dong, Gwangjin-gu
143-7 Seoul
Tel: +82-2-3408-3114
Fax: +82-2-3408-3220
Web: http://www.sejong.ac.kr
e-mail: www@sejong.ac.kr

Undergraduate, Graduate Programmes

Study Domains: business administration, education, history, international relations, international studies, languages, theology, religion.
Programmes: undergraduate, graduate programmes in foreign languages; history; philosophy/reliion; education; politics; foreign relations; economics; business administration.

1943 Seoul Jangsin University [SJS]
219-1 Gyungan-dong
464-7 Gwangju-si
Tel: +82-31-761-6453
Fax: +82-31-765-1232
Web: http://www.seouljangsin.ac.kr
e-mail: admin@seouljangsin.ac.kr

Undergraduate, Graduate Programmes

Study Domains: history, theology, religion.
Programmes: theology, history, Bible studies.

1944 Seoul National University [SNU]
Office of Admissions
San 56-1, Shillim-dong, Gwanak-gu
151-742 Seoul
Tel: +82-2-880-5114
Fax: +82-2-880-6979
Web: http://www.snu.ac.kr/engsnu
e-mail: joohyunj@snu.ac.kr

Undergraduate, Graduate Programmes / Korean Studies

Study Domains: all major fields, Asian studies, Korean.
Programmes: undergraduate and graduate programmes (a) in all major fields; (b) Korean language and culture programme at the Language Education Institute.
Open to: students of all nationalities meeting academic, financial and linguistic criteria.
Duration: (b) 4 sessions of 10 weeks duration (Fall, Winter, Spring, Summer).
Fees: (b) tuition: 1,100,000 won per session. Elective and special classes require additional fees (amounts subject to change).
Financial assistance: possibility of 50% tuition waivers after 5 levels of successive study and high scholastic achievement.

Applications: to the above address; for the Korean language and culture programme, apply to the KLCP, Language Education Institute, Seoul National University; informative brochure and application form can be downloaded from http://language.snu.ac.kr.

1945 Seoul National University of Education
1650 Seocho-dong Seocho-gu
137-7 Seoul
Tel: +82-2-3475-2114
Fax: +82-2-581-7711
Web: http://www.snue.ac.kr/snue_english/index.html
e-mail: center@ns.snue.ac.kr

Undergraduate, Graduate Programme

Study Domains: early childhood education, education, physical education, technical education.
Programmes: Education programmes in Humanities; Social Science; Natural Science, Physical Education, Language and Literature, Foreign Language, Social Science, Natural Science, Arts,.
Applications: see website for further information.

1946 Songkyunkwan University [SKKU]
53 Myongnyun-dong 3-ga Jongno-gu
110-7 Seoul
Tel: +82-2-760-1152
Fax: +82-2-744-1153
Web: http://www.skku.edu
e-mail: webmaster@skku.ac.kr

Undergraduate, Graduate Programmes

Study Domains: all major fields.
Programmes: Degree programmes in humanities, sciences, social sciences, information technology, engineering, architecture, arts and sports sciences, law, education, medicine, pharmacy.
Languages: Instruction in Korean and in English for some programmes.
Applications: see website for full details.

1947 Sookmyung Women's University
53-12 Chungpa-dong 2 ka Yongsan-gu
140-7 Seoul
Tel: +82-2-710-9114
Fax: +82-2-718-2337
Web: http://www.sookmyung.ac.kr
e-mail: webmaster@sookmyung.ac.kr

Undergraduate, Graduate Programmes

Study Domains: business, business administration, ecology, environment, economic and commercial sciences, fine arts, French, Korean, languages, law, liberal arts, music and musicology, pharmacy and pharmacology, sciences, social sciences.
Programmes: Undergraduate and graduate programmes in liberal arts and humanities, languages, sciences, business.
Other conditions: women students.
Languages: Instruction in Korean; some programmes are English taught.
Applications: see website for details.

1948 Sun Moon University
100, Kalsan-Ri, Tangjung-myun, Asan-si
336-708 Chungnam
Tel: +82-41-530-2114
Fax: +82-41-541-7424
Web: http://www.sunmoon.ac.kr
e-mail: oic@email.sunmoon.ac.kr

Undergraduate, Graduate, Postgraduate Programmes

Study Domains: administration, architecture, business administration, civil engineering, communication, computer science, economic and commercial sciences, education, electricity and electronics, engineering, food industry, human sciences, industrial technology, information science, international studies, languages, law, management, marine science, mathematics, microbiology, philosophy, physics,

psychology, teacher education, theology, religion, vocational training.
Programmes: Bachelor's, Master's, Ph.D. degrees in all major fields; non-degree programme in Korean language.
Duration: 2 years; 4 months (Summer course); courses begin 1 March for Spring semester and 25 August for Fall semester.
Fees: tuition fees: US$4,000; living costs: US$1,000.
Financial assistance: financial assistance available through AUF Scholarship and Sun Moon Scholarship; all international students for M.A. and Ph.D. degree programmes (special case) receive 100% and exemption of tuition fee; contact oic@email.sunmoon.ac.kr for further details.

Scholarships

Study Domains: all major fields, Asian studies, Korean.
Scholarships: (a) AUF Scholarship; (b) Sun Moon Scholarship.
Open to: see website for eligibility; all international students for M.A. and Ph.D. degree programmes (special case) receive 100% reduction and exemption of tuition fees.

1949 Sungkyungkwan University

53, 3-ga Myongnyun-dong, Chonhno-gu
110745 Seoul
Tel: +82-2-760-1147
Fax: +82-2-760-1152
Web: http://www.skku.ac.kr
e-mail: intl@skku.edu

Undergraduate, Graduate, Postgraduate Programmes

Study Domains: all major fields.
Programmes: Bachelor's, Master's, Ph.D. degrees in all major fields.
Duration: variable.
Fees: registration: 500,000 won; tuition: 3 million won; estimated living costs: 6 million won.
Applications: by November / May.

Scholarship

Study Domains: all major fields.
Scholarships: Foreign Student Scholarship.
Subjects: All major fields.
Duration: 1 year, renewable.
Value: tuition fee reduction of 35 % for undergraduates, 50 % for graduates.
Applications: By the end of May for the Spring semester; end of October for the Fall semester; email: moonbit@dragon.skku.ac.kr.

1950 Yonsei University [YU]

134 Sinchon-Dong
Seodaemun-Ku
120-749 Seoul
Tel: +82-2-2123-3488
Fax: +82-2-393-7272
Web: http://www.yonsei.ac.kr
e-mail: webmaster@yonsei.ac.kr

Korean Language Institute

Study Domains: Asian studies, Korean, languages.
Programmes: Korean language course, granting academic credit.
Description: regular programme; special Summer programme; 3-week programme; evening programme available; credits granted by the Korean Language Institute may be transferable to student's university.
Open to: candidates possessing a secondary-school certificate or equivalent.
Fees: (approximate figures) application: 60,000 won; tuition: 1,300,000 per quarter.
Financial assistance: possibility of 50% tuition waiver for students having completed at least two terms of study; based on academic achievement and attendance.
Applications: contact the Korean Language Institute of Yonsei University; website: http://www.yskli.com.

Undergraduate, Graduate Programmes

Study Domains: administration, Asian studies, business, cultural studies, international relations, languages, summer programmes.

Programmes: (a) International undergraduate programme granting academic credit (up to 19 credits per semester) transferable to student's home institution; (b) Summer session (granting up to 9 credit hours); (c) Master's degree programme: Korean studies, Chinese studies, Japanese studies, international studies, international business administration.
Open to: (a) and (b) candidates having completed at least one year of college level work outside the Republic of Korea, with sufficient command of English; (c) non-Koreans and a limited number of Korean students holding a Bachelor's degree at a recognized college or university; also open to part-time and non-degree students for one semester or one year; fluency in English required for all programmes.
Duration: (a) 1 semester to 1 year (courses begin in August and February); (b) 6 weeks (courses begin in late June); (c) 1 semester to 2 years (courses begin in August and February).
Fees: application, US$60 plus: (a) and (c) tuition, US$3,200 per semester for full-time students; housing, US$180 per month, excluding board; (b) tuition, US$1,670; housing, US$360 for term; other fees, US$80.
Financial assistance: (c) partial tuition waiver available for a limited number of full-time students beginning the second semester.
Languages: Instruction in English.
Applications: (a) and (c) by 30 November for Spring semester and 31 May for Fall semester; (b) by 15 May; to the Division of International Education, at the above address.

1951 Yonsei University - Graduate School of Business Administration

134 Sinchon-dong
Seodaemun-gu
120-749 Seoul
Tel: +82-2-2123-3259
Fax: +82-2-313-3978
Web: http://ysb.yonsei.ac.kr/gmba
e-mail: gmba@base.yonsei.ac.kr

Global M.B.A. Programme

Study Domains: business administration.
Programmes: Master of Business Administration programme.
Open to: candidates holding Bachelor's degrees from accredited 4-year universities and excellent undergraduate academic record; TOEFL 550 PBT/213 CBT required.
Duration: 1½ years (3 semesters) or 2 years (4 semesters).
Fees: registration: US$70; tuition: US$4,400 per semester.
Financial assistance: possibility of assistantships and fellowships (US$2,000 per semester approximately).
Applications: by 11 April to the Global M.B.A. Programme at the above address.

1952 Yonsei University - Graduate School of International Studies

134 Sinchon-dong
Seodaemun-gu
120-749 Seoul
Tel: +82-2-2123-3291/ 3
Fax: +82-2-392-3321
Web: http://gsis.yonsei.ac.kr
e-mail: gsis@yonsei.ac.kr

Undergraduate, Graduate Programmes / International Studies

Study Domains: Asian studies, finance, industry and commerce, international business, international studies, management, trade.
Programmes: (a) Master's in Area Studies (Japan, China, U.S.); (b) Master's, Ph.D. in Korean studies, international management; international trade and finance, international cooperation.
Open to: graduates of recognized colleges or universities in Korea or abroad.
Duration: at least 4 semesters of full-time enrolment required.
Fees: tuition: US$4,000 (includes US$610 admissions fee for new students); books, supplies and living expenses: US$2,500.

Financial assistance: possibility of scholarships for foreign students.
Languages: all courses are conducted in English.
Applications: application package should be sent to above address by 31 May for Fall semester, by 30 November for Spring semester.

Republic of Moldova

Academic year: September to July.
Monetary unit: Moldovian Leu (Lei MD).
National student admission: Diploma de Baccalaureat; competitive entrance examination in some institutions.
International student admission: Definition of foreign student: A foreign student is a person enrolled at an institution of higher education in a country of which he/she is not a permanent resident. Admission requirements: Foreign students must present a Secondary School Leaving Certificate. For access to doctoral studies, they must pass a competitive entrance examination. Entry regulations: Visas may be obtained at the Moldovan Embassies or at border check points. Health requirements: Medical certificate. Language requirements: Students must have a good knowledge of Russian and Romanian.
Language: Languages of instruction are Romanian and Russian.
Recognition of studies and qualification: Ministerul Învatamântului, Directia Principala Pentru Învatamânt Superior, (Ministry of Education, Main Division for Higher Education), 1, Piata Marii Adunări Nationale, MD-277033 Kisinau, Republica Moldova; tel: +373-2-233-418, fax: +373-2-233-615; email: dulschi@mail.md.

1953 Co-operative Trade University of Moldova

Boulevard Gagarin, 8
Chisinau, MD-2001
Tel: +373-2-270-203
Fax: +373-2 541-210
Web: http://www.uccm.moldnet.md
e-mail: admn@uccm.moldnet.md

📖 Undergraduate Studies

Study Domains: accounting, administration, arts, business, business administration, computer science, demography and population studies, economic and commercial sciences, economy, education, finance, food industry, geography, history, international relations, interpretation and translation, languages, law, management, marketing, mathematics, philosophy, political economy, printing, psychology, sociology, statistics, technology.
Programmes: Bachelor's degrees in accounting and computer science; marketing and science of commodities; management and law.
Duration: 4 to 5 years; courses begin 1 September.
Fees: registration 600-800 Lei MD; tuition fees 4,000-7,000 Lei MD per year; living costs 1,800 Lei MD.
Languages: Russian, Romanian.
Applications: by 15 August; by 15 July for Marketing and Science of Commodities courses; contact rmorosan@uccm.moldnet.md for further details.

1954 Free International University of Moldova

52 Vlaicu Parcalab Street,
2012 Chisinau
Tel: +373-2-22-00-29
Fax: +373-2-22-00-28
Web: http://www.ulim.md
e-mail: office@ulim.moldnet.md

📖 Undergraduate Studies

Study Domains: administration, archaeology, business administration, cardiology, communication, criminology, dentistry, economy, European studies, finance, history, international law, international studies, interpretation and translation, journalism, languages, law, linguistics, management, marketing, medicine, neurology, obstetrics and gynaecology, paediatrics, philology, psychiatry, psychology, radiology, surgery, urology.

Programmes: Diploma de Licenta (equivalent to Bachelor) arts and humanities; administration; law; economics; medicine; surgery; paediatrics; psychiatry; neurology; research.
Open to: all nationalities; admission tests required for foreign students; language proficiency required.
Duration: 4 to 6 years; courses begin 1 September.
Fees: tuition fees for foreign students: US$1,200 per year.
Languages: Romanian, Russian, French, English.
Applications: by 31 August; contact office@ulim.moldnet.md for further information.

📖 Tuition Waiver

Study Domains: economic and commercial sciences, engineering, law.
Open to: international students of American and European countries.
Value: US$300 towards tuition expenses.
Applications: 1 July; contact Director of Foreign Students' Department; relex@ulim.md.

1955 Pedagogical State University 'Ion Creanga'

1 Creanga Street
Chisinau
Tel: +373-2-745-414
Fax: +373-2-749-914
Web: http://upm.moldnet.md

📖 Undergraduate Studies

Study Domains: arts, computer science, cultural studies, design, education, ethnology, geography, history, interior design, international law, international relations, interpretation and translation, languages, law, literature and civilization, museology and museography, music and musicology, philology, philosophy, teacher education.
Programmes: Licence Diploma (equivalent to Bachelor) in education; teacher education; arts; languages; ethnology; philosophy; law.
Open to: students with secondary school diploma; admission tests.
Duration: 4 to 5 years; courses begin 1 September.
Fees: registration US$100; tuition fees US$800 per year; living costs included.
Languages: Romanian, Russian.

1956 University of Foreign Languages and International Business

1, Aleco Ruso Street
Chisinau
Tel: +373-2-438-034
Fax: +373-2-434-742
Web: http://www.univers.net.md
e-mail: melnic@univers.net.md

📖 Undergraduate Studies

Study Domains: accounting, business administration, design, economy, interior design, languages, linguistics, management, philology, teacher education, technical education.
Programmes: Bachelor's degrees in foreign languages; education; business administration; preparatory studies for British university entrance.
Duration: 5 years; courses begin 1 September; Summer course.
Fees: tuition fees US$1,000 per year.
Languages: Romanian; Russian; English.
Applications: by 15 August.

República Dominicana

Año académico: Enero a diciembre, teniendo tres períodos regulares de docencia al año, que inician en enero, mayo y septiembre.
Moneda nacional: Peso dominicano.
Formalidades de inmigración: se debe adquirir una visa de estudiante, que se solicita presentando un comprobante de la admisión a una universidad.
Convalidación de estudios y diplomas: Consejo Nacional de Educación Superior, Avenida Jiménez Moya Esq. Juan de Dios Ventura Simó, 5ta Planta, Centro de los Héroes; Santo Domingo, República Dominicana: tel: +1-809-553-3381; fax: +1-809-535-4694; email: webmaster@cones.gov.do; web: http://www.cones.gov.do.

1957 Instituto Tecnologico de Santo Domingo

Avenida de los Próceres, Galá, Apdos 342-9 y 249-2
Santo Domingo
Tel: +1-809-567-9271
Fax: +1-809-566-3200
Web: http://www.intec.edu.do

📖 Programas de pregrado y posgrado

Campos de estudios: ciencias, ingeniería, mecánica, técnicas de laboratorio, tecnología.
Inscripciones: ver sitio web: www.intec.edu.do.

1958 Pontificia Universidad Católica Madre y Maestra [PUCMM RSTA]

Recinto Santo Tomás de Aquino
Av. Abraham Lincoln esq. Rómulo Betancourt
Apartado 2748
Santo Domingo
Tel: +1-809-535-0111
Fax: +1-809-534-7060
Web: http://www.pucmmsti.edu.do

📖 Programas de pregrado y posgrado

Campos de estudios: todas las materias principales, ciencias económicas y comerciales, ciencias humanas, ciencias sociales, ingeniería, medicina.
Programas: diplomados, licenciaturas, maestrías y doctorados.
Descripción: programas presenciales y a distancia en sus Facultades de Ingeniería, Ciencias de la salud, Ciencias sociales y humanidades.
Se destina(n): a estudiantes que tienen titulo de Bachiller.
Costo(s): varían según el centro docente y los estudios que se realicen.

1959 Universidad APEC [UNAPEC]

Máximo Gómez no. 72
Santo Domingo
Tel: +1-809-686-0021
Fax: +1-809-685-5581
Web: http://www.unapec.edu.do
e-mail: dsimo@adm.unapec.edu.do

📖 Programas universitarios

Campos de estudios: administración de empresas, contabilidad, decoración, diseño industrial, empresas internacionales, publicidad, tecnología, turismo, hotelería.
Inscripciones: ver sitio web: http://www.unapec.edu.do/.

1960 Universidad Dominicana O & M [UDOYM]

Avenida Independencia 200
Centro de los Héroes Apto. 509
Santo Domingo
Tel: +1-809-533-7733
Fax: +1-809-535-0084
Web: http://www.udoym.edu.do

📖 Programas universitarios

Campos de estudios: todas las materias principales.
Descripción: Carreras de grado en su facultades:
(a) Ciencias económicas y administrativas: contabilidad; administración de empresas, bancaria, de oficinas, de empresas turísticas y hoteleras; mercadotecnia;
(b) Ingeniería y tecnología: sistemas y computación; ingeniería electrónica, civil, industrial; arquitectura;
(c) Ciencias jurídicas: derecho;
(d) Humanidades y ciencias: comunicación social; educación (mención ciencias sociales, mención física y matemáticas, mención letras, mención supervisión escolar, mención informática); psicología clínica, psicología industrial; Departamento de Postgrados:
(e) Maestría en contabilidad ejecutiva, en ingeniería de sistemas;
(f) Especialización en ingeniería de software, en auditoría de sistemas computarizados.

1961 Universidad Nacional Pedro Henríquez Ureña [UNPHU]

Autopista Duarte Km. 7 ½
Santo Domingo
Tel: +1-809-542-6888
Fax: +1-809-540-0425
Web: http://www.unphu.edu.do
e-mail: info@unphu.edu.do

📖 Programas académicos

Campos de estudios: todas las materias principales.
Programas: carreras de grado, especialidades, maestrías y doctorados. Se imparte también educación continua (cursos y diplomas).
Materias de estudio: arquitectura y artes; ciencias y tecnología; ciencias agropecuarias y recursos naturales; ciencias de la salud; ciencias económicas y sociales; ciencias jurídicas y políticas; humanidades y educación.
Inscripciones: consultar la página web http://www.unphu.edu.do/unphu/admisiones.asp donde se explicitan las condiciones para cada ingreso.

République arabe syrienne

Année universitaire: septembre à juin.
Unité monétaire: livre syrien (S£).
Connaissances linguistiques requises: La langue d'enseignement est l'arabe. Les étudiants étrangers peuvent suivre un cours d'orientation générale ainsi qu'un cours préparatoire de langue arabe à l'École d'apprentissage pour les étrangers (École dépendant du Ministère de l'éducation). Dans les sections de langues étrangères l'enseignement est donné en anglais ou en français suivant les cas.
Formalités d'immigration: Une demande de visa doit être déposée auprès de l'Ambassade syrienne du pays du candidat.
Services d'accueil et d'information:
• Ministère de l'éducation, Direction des échanges culturels ou Direction des bourses pour les étudiants étrangers, Damas.
• Ministère de l'enseignement supérieur, Direction des relations culturelles et générales ou Direction des affaires des étudiants.
• Union nationale des étudiants de Syrie, BP 3028, Damas.
• Union générale des étudiants universitaires de chaque université.
• Des renseignements sur les possibilités de logement et d'accueil peuvent être obtenus auprès de la Direction des cités universitaires de Damas et d'Alep.
Reconnaissance des études et diplômes: Sécrétaire général, Conseil sur l'Enseignement supérieur; BP 9355; Damas; République arabe syrienne; tél: +963-11-212-6336; fax: +963-11-212-9298.
Publications / Sites Web:
• Les «Guides universitaires», publiés annuellement en langues arabe, française et anglaise, et distribués gratuitement. On peut se les procurer sur demande, au Ministère de l'enseignement supérieur à Damas ou directement auprès des universités.

1962 Institut supérieur de science politique
Damascus, al-Tal
Syria
Tel: +963-11-591-1703
Fax: +963-11-591-1526

📖 1er, 2e cycles / sciences politiques
Study Domains: administration, economy, international relations, philosophy, political economy, political science, sociology.
Programmes: Bachelor's degree dans les domaines suivants: administration, économie, philosophie, relations internationales, sociologie, sciences politiques.
Languages: arabe.
Applications: contacter l'institut à l'adresse ci-dessus pour de plus amples informations.

1963 Ministère de l'éducation Direction des étudiants étrangers
Damas

🎓 Bourses d'études
Domaines d'étude: ingénierie, lettres, médecine, sciences.
Bourses: Bourses offertes par le Gouvernement syrien.
A l'intention de: étudiants originaires des pays arabes, africains ou pays amis, et titulaires du certificat de fin d'études secondaires; âge: de 18 à 25 ans.
Lieu: universités de Damas, d'Alep, d'Octobre (Lattaquié), d'El-Baath (Homs) et autres institutions universitaires.
Candidatures: avant fin août, à l'adresse ci-dessus, ou au Ministère de l'enseignement supérieur, Direction des étudiants, ou à l'Université de Damas, Bureau des affaires des étudiants.

1964 Université de Damas
Gami't Dimasq
Damas
Tel: +963-223-2152
Fax: +963-223-6010
Web: http://www.damasuniv.shern.net/english/index_en.htm

📖 Cursus du 1er au 3e cycle
Domaines d'étude: toutes disciplines principales.
Programmes: cours dans toutes les matières principales préparant aux diplômes du 1er, 2e, 3e cycle.
A l'intention de: candidats de tous pays, titulaires d'un baccalauréat ou diplôme équivalent.
Assistance financière: possibilité de bourses pour les étudiants étrangers auprès du ministère de l'enseignement supérieur, Direction des relations culturelles et générales ou Direction des affaires des étudiants, ou Direction des relations internationales et culturelles.

Roumanie
Année universitaire: septembre à juin.
Organisation de l'enseignement supérieur: Les ressortissants étrangers bénéficient d'un accès libre au système national d'enseignement. L'enseignement supérieur a pour but d'assurer la formation des spécialistes hautement qualifiés. Il a un caractère ouvert et est organisé sous forme d'enseignement universitaire de courte et de longue durée. L'enseignement universitaire de courte durée comprend, en règle générale, des programmes de 3 ans. Il est organisé en collèges universitaires, dans les domaines suivants: technique, économie, médecine (assistants techniciens), agriculture, éducation physique et sport (entraîneurs). L'enseignement de longue durée est donné dans des universités et dans d'autres établissements équivalents, à savoir: instituts, académies, conservatoires. La durée des études est, en fonction du profil, de 4 à 6 ans, comme suit: enseignement universitaire (mathématiques, physique, sciences naturelles, chimie, géographie, géologie, langues étrangères, histoire, philosophie, droit, théologie, éducation physique et sport), 4 ans; enseignement économique, 4 à 5 ans; théâtre et cinéma, 4 ans; enseignement agronomique, 5 ans; médecine vétérinaire, 6 ans; enseignement technique, 5 ans; enseignement d'art (musique et beaux-arts), 5 ans; enseignement médical,

médecine générale et stomatologie, 6 ans; pharmacie, 5 ans; architecture, 6 ans. L'enseignement postuniversitaire assure la spécialisation, l'élargissement et le perfectionnement de la formation, dans un certain domaine, attestés par le diplôme obtenu au terme des études de longue durée. Il comporte les formes suivantes: les études approfondies, le doctorat, les études académiques postuniversitaires, les études de spécialisation et des cours de perfectionnement.
Unité monétaire: leu.
Admission pour étudiants du pays: L'inscription des étrangers aux études est réalisée par un service spécialisé de la Direction des relations internationales du Ministère de l'enseignement qui est à même de donner l'équivalence des études effectuées à l'étranger, conformément aux conventions internationales que la Roumanie a signées. Les candidats doivent avoir achevé leurs études secondaires et posséder le baccalauréat ou diplôme admis en équivalence, ou diplôme de licence d'un institut d'enseignement supérieur, visé par le Ministère de l'enseignement du pays d'origine et par l'ambassade de Roumanie dans ce pays. Les étudiants souhaitant s'inscrire dans un établissement d'enseignement supérieur d'architecture, de beaux-arts, d'éducation physique et de sport, doivent au préalable se soumettre à des épreuves éliminatoires d'aptitude dans le domaine choisi. Il n'y a pas d'examen d'admission pour les étudiants étrangers. Les candidats qui maîtrisent la langue roumaine peuvent aussi commencer directement leurs études après avoir passé un examen de vérification des connaissances linguistiques. Des bourses sont également octroyées par l'État roumain, par l'intermédiaire des autorités compétentes des pays bénéficiaires dans le cadre des accords bilatéraux.
Connaissances linguistiques requises: Généralement, les étrangers commencent leurs études en Roumanie par un cours préparatoire, en vue d'apprendre le roumain, d'assimiler la terminologie roumaine de la spécialité choisie et d'approfondir, en fonction du domaine d'enseignement choisi, leurs connaissances en mathématiques, physique, chimie, etc.
Formalités d'immigration: Les étudiants étrangers doivent avoir un visa d'entrée en Roumanie, généralement accordé par les ambassades de Roumanie à l'étranger ou par les autorités de frontière, sur présentation de la confirmation écrite de leur admission émanant du Ministère roumain de l'enseignement.
Services d'accueil et d'information:
• Ministère de l'enseignement, Direction des relations internationales, 12, rue Spiru Haret, 70738 Bucarest.
• Centre de Tranzit, 59, boulevard Marasti, Bucarest (chargé de la vérification des originaux des documents d'études, de l'orientation des candidats vers les institutions d'enseignement, du contrôle médical).
• Représentants diplomatiques roumains à l'étranger.
Bourses pour étudiants internationaux: Romanian Government scholarships: http://www.burseguvern.ro/.
Enseignement à distance: Un Centre national pour l'enseignement libre à distance a été spécialement crée; celui-ci comprend des annexes dans 8 centre universitaires majeurs et fonctionne en collaboration avec 12 universités à travers le programme PHARE («Programme for Multi-Country Cooperation for Distance Education»).
Reconnaissance des études et diplômes: ENIC/NARIC, Ministère de l'Éducation; General Berthelot 30; 70738 Bucarest; Roumanie; tél +40-1-313-1013; fax: +40-1-313-2677; email: girbea@men.edu.ro.
Publications / Sites Web:
• «Études à l'étranger; Guide pour les étrangers», édité par le Ministère de l'enseignement et l'Institut des sciences de l'éducation, Bucarest (en français).

1965 'Iuliu Hatieganu' University of Medicine and Pharmacy of Cluj-Napoca [UMF]
Strada Emil Isac 13
40002 Cluj-Napoca
Tel: +40-264-59-72-56
Fax: +40-264-59-72-57
Web: http://www.umfcluj.ro
e-mail: dri@umfcluj.ro

📖 Undergraduate, Graduate and Postrgraduate Programmes
Study Domains: medicine, pharmacy and pharmacology.

1966 Academy of Economic Studies Bucharest [AES]

Piata Romana 6, Sector 1
Bucharest
Tel: +40-21-319-1900
Fax: +40-21-312-9549
Web: http://www.ase.ro
e-mail: rectorat@ase.ro

📖 Undergraduate, Graduate and Postgraduate Degree Programmes

Study Domains: accounting, administration, agronomic sciences, business, business administration, communication, economic and commercial sciences, economy, finance, international business, international law, international relations, international studies, marketing, political economy, trade.
Programmes: Bachelor's, Master's, Ph.D. degrees; diploma for post-academic studies.
Duration: 4 years beginning 1 October.
Languages: Romanian; English; French; German.

1967 Babes-Bolyai University

Street Mihail Kogalniceanu, Nr. 1
400084 Cluj-Napoca
Tel: +40-264-405-300
Fax: +40-264-591-906
Web: http://www.ubbcluj.ro
e-mail: staff@staff.ubbcluj.ro

📖 Undergraduate, Graduate, Postgraduate Programmes

Study Domains: all major fields.
Programmes: Bachelor's, Master's, Ph.D.; non-degree programmes.
Open to: admission tests needed.
Duration: depending on programme: 1 to 6 years beginning 16 September.
Fees: registration for doctoral students: US$340; tuition fees: US$300; $500 up to US$3,200 per year (Ph.D. students pay US$1,500 per year); living costs: 150 Euro per month.
Languages: Romanian, German, Hungarian, English, French, Italian, depending on programme.
Applications: apply by 15 August to andreeaciuraubb@yahoo.com or directly to the university; consult website for further information: www.ubbcluj.ro.

🎓 Government Scholarship

Study Domains: all major fields.
Open to: good academic standing.
Duration: from 3 months to completion of studies; not renewable.
Value: USD$50 per month.
Applications: apply by 1 September; contact Andreea Ciura; tel: +4 0264 195 051.

1968 Emanuel University of Oradea [EUO]

Street Nufarului 87
Oradea
410597 Bihor
Tel: +40-259-426-692
Fax: +40-259-426-692
Web: http://www.emanuel.ro
e-mail: secretariat@emanuel.ro

📖 Undergraduate Degree Programmes

Study Domains: business administration, literature and civilization, music and musicology, social work, theology, religion.
Programmes: Bachelor's degrees in theology, business management.
Open to: contact admissions office for details.
Duration: 4 years.
Fees: tuition fees: $600; living costs: $550.
Languages: language proficiency in Romanian and English (business management).
Applications: contact: Marcela Tarau at the above address.

1969 Gh. Dima Music Academy [AMGD]

25, I. C. Bratianu Street
400079 Cluy-Napoca
Tel: +40-264-591-241
Fax: +40-264-598-958
Web: http://www.amgd.ro
e-mail: amgd@amgd.utcluj.ro

📖 Undergraduate, Graduate, Postgraduate Programmes

Study Domains: continuing education, education, music and musicology, performing arts, teacher education, vocational training.
Programmes: Bachelor's, Master's, Ph.D. degree programmes at 3 faculties: instruments, theoretic, stage art; 1 college department; department of distance learning.
Description: diploma programmes in: piano, strings, winds, percussion, composition, musical and pedagogy, musicology, song, choreography.
Duration: 5 years beginning in October.
Fees: tuition fees: US$470 per month; living costs: US$200 per month.

🎓 Governmental Scholarship

Study Domains: all major fields.
Duration: 1 year; renewable each year.
Value: up to US$470 per month.
Applications: apply in September prior to year of study to Jean-Marie Ciofu, Ministry of Education and Research, Bucharest, +40 21 314 2680.

1970 Ovidius University of Constantza [OUC]

Bd Mamaia 124
8700 Constantza 2A
Tel: +40-241-618-372
Fax: +40-241-618-372
Web: http://www.univ-ovidius.ro
e-mail: rectorat@univ-ovidius.ro

📖 Undergraduate, Graduate, Postgraduate Programmes

Study Domains: all major fields, summer programmes.
Programmes: Bachelor's, Master's, Ph.D. degree programmes.
Description: programmes consist of lectures, seminars, laboratory and clinical practice.
Open to: all nationalities; language proficiency and admission tests required.
Duration: 3 to 6 years; courses begin in October.
Fees: registration fee: US$360; tuition: US$360; living costs: US$300-$400.
Languages: Romanian, English, French, German.
Applications: apply by late September to rectorat@campus.univ-ovidius.ro; tel: +40 241 511 512.

🎓 Scholarship

Study Domains: all major fields.
Scholarships: Scholarships awarded by the Ministry of Education and Research.
Description: for all levels of study offered by the University.
Duration: throughout academic training.
Applications: contact: Ministry of Education and Research; website: http://www.edu.ro; tel: +40 21 313 1013.

1971 Technical University of Civil Engineering Bucharest [UTCB]

124 Lacul Tei Boulevard
020396 Bucharest
Tel: +40-21-242-1208
Fax: +40-21-242-0781
Web: http://www.utcb.ro
e-mail: manoliu@hidro.utcb.ro

📖 Undergraduate, Graduate Programmes

Study Domains: building industry, civil engineering.
Programmes: programme of study leading to degrees equivalent to Bachelor and Master of Science in civil engineering, building services.

Duration: 5 years beginning in October.
Fees: tuition: US$3,200 per year; living costs: US$200-$250 per month.
Languages: Romanian, English, French.
Applications: apply by 1 September to nicoleta@hidro.utcb.ro or iolcold@instal.utcb.ro.

1972 University of Agricultural Sciences and Veterinary Medicine [IASI]
Aleea Mihail Sadoveanu, 3
6600 Iasi
Tel: +40-232-213-069
Fax: +40-232-260-650
Web: http://www.univagro-iasi.ro
e-mail: rectorat@univagro-iasi.ro

⌨ Agriculture, Veterinary Programmes
Study Domains: agriculture, food industry, horticulture, veterinary medicine.
Programmes: Programmes of study in agriculture, and veterinary studies.
Open to: all nationalities meeting academic and linguistic requirements; upper-intermediate level of Romanian required; authorization of Ministry of Education and Research necessary.
Duration: 5 to 6 months beginning 1 October.
Fees: tuition: US$320 per month; living costs: US$100 per month.
Financial assistance: scholarships available; possibility of US$50 per month living allowance.
Applications: apply by June to July to the Ministry of Education and Research.

1973 University of Agronomical Sciences and Veterinary Medicine of Bucharest [USAMVB]
Boulevard Marasti, 59
011 4 Bucharest
Tel: +40-21-224-25-76
Fax: +40-21-224-28-15
Web: http://www.usab.ro/en
e-mail: post@info.usamv.ro

⌨ Undergraduate, Graduate Programmes
Study Domains: agriculture, agronomic sciences, cattle breeding, veterinary medicine, veterinary sciences.

1974 University of Bucharest [UB]
Bd. Mihail Kogalniceanu 36-46,
Sector 5, 70 609
70709 Bucharest
Tel: +40-21-307-7300
Fax: +40-21-313-1760
Web: http://www.unibuc.ro
e-mail: info@unibuc.ro

⌨ Undergraduate, Graduate Programme
Study Domains: biology, education, humanities and arts, languages, law, sciences, social sciences.
Programmes: (a) Bachelor's, Master's degrees in all major fields; (b) Bachelor's degree in biology, biochemistry, ecology; (c) Master's degree in comparative biology of normal and tumoral cells; plant embryology and phytodiversity.
Open to: all candidates must have 4 years of successive Romanian language classes; candidates with no knowledge of Romanian take a 1-year preparatory course: US$320.
Duration: (a) 4 to 5 years; (b) 4 years; (c) 1 year.
Fees: tuition: US$340 per month; living costs: US$8,300.
Languages: Romanian; French or English for programmes in those languages.
Applications: apply by October to Calin Tesio, tel: +40 21 411 5207; fax: +40 21 411 2310.

☞ Scholarship
Study Domains: all major fields.
Description: Government sponsored scholarship.
Open to: foreign students; foreign ethnic Romanian students.
Duration: 4 years.

Value: US$50 per month for 9 months.
Applications: apply by 1 October to: externe@mail.unibuc.ro; tel: +40 21 30 77 321.

1975 University of Medicine and Pharmacy of Craiova [UMFCV]
2 Petru Rares Street
200349 Craiova
Tel: +40-251-122-458
Fax: +40-251-193-077
Web: http://www.umfcv.ro
e-mail: rector@umfcv.ro

⌨ Undergraduate, Postgraduate, Certificate Programmes
Study Domains: continuing education, education, health and hygiene, languages, medicine, nursing, physical education, sciences, summer programmes, teacher education.
Programmes: Bachelor's, Ph.D. degrees; certificate programmes.
Description: licence diploma for pharmacy and physical therapy; graduation diploma; medical doctor for general medicine and dentistry; Ph.D.; diploma of competence for postgraduate study with different specialities; certificate for refresher course.
Open to: candidates with Romanian or English language proficiency; students arriving under bilateral agreements between partner university should check with International Relations Department (Socrates office) of the University.
Held: training programmes organized in university clinics, hospitals and laboratories, all located near the city centre.
Duration: 6 years commencing 1 October; Summer courses available.
Fees: tuition: US$360 per month; living costs: US$100-$200 per month.
Applications: apply by 1 November to: International Relations Admission Office at: intrel@umfcv.ro.

☞ Bursary and/or Tuition Waiver
Study Domains: all major fields, medicine, pharmacy and pharmacology.
Scholarships: University bursary and/or tuition waiver.
Open to: candidates with a high academic average for the previous year.
Duration: 3-5-6 years duration depending on programme of study.
Value: undergraduate students: US$50 per month; graduate students: US$56 per month; tuition waiver (non hard-currency account).
Applications: apply 2 months before commencement of courses: intrel@umfcv.ro.

1976 University of Oradea [UO]
5, Armatei Romane
Oradea
Tel: +40-259-432-830
Fax: +40-259-432-789
Web: http://www.uoradea.ro
e-mail: rectorat@uoradea.ro

⌨ Undergraduate, Graduate, Postgraduate Programmes
Study Domains: all major fields.
Programmes: Bachelor's, Master's, Ph.D. degree programmes; language courses.
Open to: candidates passing 2 admission tests.
Duration: 4 to 6 years depending on programme.
Fees: tuition fees: US$320-$760; living costs: U$50.
Applications: apply by 1 October to the above address.

☞ Scholarships
Study Domains: all major fields.
Duration: 1 year.
Value: US$360 per month during the study period.
Applications: apply by 15 June to abalasco@uoradea.ro; or phone: +40 259 467 642.

Russian Federation

Academic year: September to July.

Organization of higher education system: Higher education is provided by public (state) and non-public (non-state) accredited higher education institutions (HEIs). Education in public HEIs is not completely free of charge. Approximately one-third of the students pay for their studies. In non-state HEIs all students must pay tuition fees. Higher education falls within the jurisdiction of the Ministry of Education and Science of the Russian Federation and agencies and services within the Ministry which are responsible for accreditation and licensing of HEIs and for developing and maintaining state educational standards.

• There are three levels of higher education: (a) incomplete; at least two years' of higher education studies); (b) basic; four years of higher education studies leading to the Bakalavr degree, the first university level degree; (c) complete; five or six years of higher education studies leading to the Magistr's degree after two years of study or Specialists Diploma after one year following the Bakalavr degree (e.g. for professional studies such as law, engineering, etc.). There are two levels of doctorate degrees: Kandidat Nauk and Doctor Nauk.

•Types of higher education institutions: University, Academy, Institute, Technical University, Conservatory, College, Technical College, Sêicialized Institution.

•Secondary School leaving credentials: Attestat o Srednem (Polnom) Obshchem Obrazovanii; basic secondary school leaving certificate; Diplom o Srednem Professionalnom Obrazovanii: Higher Vocational Education Diploma. Higher education credentials: Diplom o Nepoilnom Visshem Obrazovanii (Incomplete Higher Education Diploma); first two years of university study; Bakalavr, corresponds to Bachelor' degree; Specialist Diploma, consisting of 1 to 2 years' study beyond Bakalavr, corresponds to Master's degree; Magistr, consists of 1 year of study beyond the Specialist's Diploma; Kandidat Nauk, consists of 3 to 4 years' study beyond the Specialist's Diploma and corresponds to a PhD degree; Doktor Nauk, diploma after the Kandidat and consisting of postgraduate studies requiring a thesis.

Monetary unit: Russian rouble.

National student admission: A secondary-school leaving certificate is required to enter establishments of higher education. The higher education structure consists of a succession of educational and vocational programmes on three levels differing in content and length: (a) the first degree course consists of educational and vocational programmes providing courses in all fields of science, technology and culture. On completion of these courses which last a minimum of four years, students receive a Bachelor's degree; the first level of educational and vocational programmes includes a two-year course which follows the syllabuses of the Bachelor's course and offers as much vocational training as is provided for specialists with secondary vocational education. This type of course commonly lasts from three to three and a half years. The third level educational and vocational programmes aim to train specialists able to operate as independent creative workers; (b) educational and vocational programmes for students with a Bachelor's degree may lead either to a Master of Science or to a graduate specialist certificate. Candidates can be accepted for postgraduate work at Russian establishments of higher education and research institutes if they have an MSc or MA degree and postgraduate experience of practical work in their chosen special field of not less than two years, or if they have published in scientific journals; (c) postgraduate studies last for three or four years for a Doctor of Science.

International student admission: Foreign students wishing to enter establishments of higher education in the Russian Federation must meet the same criteria as the national students and must have completed a full course of secondary education which may last from three to six years, not counting a year of preparatory course. Postgraduate studies last for three or four years (for Doctor of Science) and candidates without Russian are offered up to one further year for the study of the language.

Language: The language of instruction is Russian; but English is also used in some private institutions.

Estimated expenses for one academic year: Foreign students accepted for study at Russian establishments of higher education under intergovernmental agreements receive a monthly grant equal to the grant for the corresponding categories of Russian students and tuition is free of charge

(about US$30 per month). The cost of board and lodging in a student hostel is very small. One year of study on a contract basis is variable but generally not less than US$1,500, depending on the subject chosen, the form of study, and arrangements for board and lodging.

Information services:

•Authority to whom international students' application should be addressed:

Federal Agency on Education, Head of International Education and Cooperation Department; 115162 Moscow, Shabolovka 33, Russian Federation.

• Embassies of the Russian Federation around the world.

Scholarships for international students: Ministry of Education and Science of the Russian Federation, Federal Agency on Education.

Open and distance learning: Almost every educational institution of higher professional education offers programmes of higher education, lifelong education and upgrading courses through ICT.

Recognition of studies and qualification:

•Federal Service on Supervision in Education and Science.

•Nacional'nyi Informacionnyi Centr po Academicheskomu Priznaniu i Mobil'nosy Minobrazovania Rossii; National Information Center for Academic Recognition and Mobility, Mikluho-Maklaya St. 6, RUDN, 117593 Moscow, Russia; tel: +7-095-958-2881, 955-0818; fax: +7-095-433-1511, 958-2881; email: RussianENIC@sci.pfu.edu.ru; web: http://www.russianenic.ru.

Accommodation services: student housing available at most institutions.

Work opportunities: no available for international students.

1977 Academy of Social Education

ul. Isaeva 12
42003 Kazan
Tel: +7-8432-424-644
Fax: +7-8432-437-612
e-mail: ksui@kzn.ru

📖 Undergraduate, Graduate Programmes

Study Domains: education, history, languages, law, political science, social sciences, social work.

1978 Altaj State Technical University [ASTU]

Lenin Avenue 46
656099 Barnaul
Tel: +7-3852-260-917
Fax: +7-3852-367-864
Web: http://astu.secna.ru
e-mail: rector@astu.secna.ru

📖 Undergraduate, Graduate Programmes / Technical Fields

Study Domains: architecture, building industry, business, chemical engineering, chemical industry, civil engineering, electricity and electronics, energy, engineering, food, food industry, industrial technology, management, mechanical engineering, social sciences, tourism, hotel and catering management.

Programmes: B.Sc.; D. Engineer; M.Sc.; Ph.D. and D.Sc. degree programmes in all technical fields.

Open to: candidates of all nationalities with secondary-school certificate; meeting other academic, financial, linguistic and medical requirements.

Fees: pre-university studies for international students: from US$700-900; B.Sc., M.Sc. and professional qualification studies: from US$800-1,200; from US$1,200-2,500 for graduate and postgraduate studies.

Applications: by 31 August to above address.

1979 Altaj State University [ASU]

Pr. Lenina 61
656049 Barnaul
Tel: +7-3852-667-584
Fax: +7-3852-667-626
Web: http://www.asu.ru
e-mail: rector@asu.ru

📖 Undergraduate, Graduate Programmes

Study Domains: all major fields, business.
Programmes: (a) Bachelor's; (b) Master's; (c)
Postgraduate; (d) Doctor's courses in history, economics, law, mathematics, physics and technology, biology, chemistry, philology, sociology, geography, political science, education, art, journalism, psychology and philosophy; (e) Russian language preparatory courses for foreign students.
Open to: candidates of any country.
Academic requirements: a secondary-school leaving certificate; entrance interview to determine level of knowledge of subjects and of the Russian language;.
Duration: (a) 4 years; (b) 6 years; (c) and (d) 3 years; (e) 1 year.
Fees: yearly (a) and (b) US$700-$1,500; (c)
US$1,000-$1,200; (d) US$2,000; (e) US$1,000.
Languages: Russian. Russian language preparatory course required.
Applications: by 15 July, to the above address.

1980 Amur State University [AMURSU]
21 Ignatyevskoye Shosse
675027 Amur Region
Blagoveshchensk
Tel: +7-4162-350-431
Fax: +7-4162-350-377
Web: http://www.amursu.ru
e-mail: idc@amursu.ru

📖 Graduate, Postgraduate Programmes

Study Domains: applied sciences, architecture, arts, engineering, languages, management, social sciences, tourism, hotel and catering management.
Programmes: Specialist's Diploma, Kandidat Nauk in arts, languages, management, social sciences, applied sciences, architecture, engineering, tourism and hotel management.
Open to: all applicants holding secondary-school certificate; Specialist's Diploma required for Kandidat; test of Russian for foreign students.
Duration: 5 to 8 years; courses begin 1 September.
Fees: registration: US$50; tuition fees; US$1,200 per year; living costs: US$100 per month.
Applications: by 15 May; contact idc@amursu.ru for further information.

1981 Archangelsk State Medical Academy
51 Vinogradov Street
163061 Archangelsk
Tel: +7-8180-430-200
Fax: +7-8180-492-153
Web: http://www.asma.ru
e-mail: info@asma.ru

📖 Graduate Programmes in Medicine

Study Domains: medicine, paediatrics, social work, stomatology.
Programmes: Graduate diplomas; M.D. degree.
Open to: candidates of any nationality holding a secondary-education certificate and proficient in Russian; Russian language courses available.
Duration: 6 years for M.D. degree.
Applications: to the above address.

1982 Baltic Fishing Fleet State Academy
Molodiozhnaya Street 6
263029 Kaliningrad
Tel: +7 112 217 204
Fax: +7 112 916690
Web: http://www.bga.da.ru
e-mail: bgaintern@gazinter.net

📖 Diploma of Higher Education

Study Domains: applied sciences, business administration, economic and commercial sciences, engineering, fisheries, industry and commerce, information science, management, marine science, marketing, mechanical engineering, telecommunications, transport.
Programmes: diploma, refresher courses for Maritime

Specialists' Certificate Renewal: maritime and transportation industries, business, economics.
Open to: admissions tests for engineering and business majors, physical exam and immunization, must be physically fit for sea training; undergraduate candidates must be under 28 years of age.
Duration: approximately 5 years commencing 1 September.
Fees: tuition fees: US$1,900-$2,500 per year; living costs: US$1,000 per year.
Applications: apply by 15 July to admissions office; contact international office at: bgaintern@gazinter.net.

1983 Barnaul State University of Educational Science [BSPU]
55 Molodyozhnaya Street
656031 Barnaul
Tel: +7 83852 228 540
Fax: +7 3852 260 836
Web: http://www.bspu.secna.ru
e-mail: rector@bspu.altai.su

📖 Undergraduate Programmes in Russian Interpretation

Study Domains: interpretation and translation, Russian.
Programmes: undergraduate programme in Russian interpretation.
Open to: candidates of any country with a secondary-school certificate, passing the placement test of the Russian language; minimum knowledge of the Russian language required.
Duration: 2 years.
Applications: at any time of the year to the above address.

1984 Bashkir State University [BSU]
Frunze Street 32
450074 Ufa
Tel: +7 3472 226 370
Fax: +7 3472 331 677
Web: http://www.bashedu.ru
e-mail: info@bsu.bashedu.ru

📖 Undergraduate, Graduate Programmes

Study Domains: all major fields.
Programmes: Bachelor's, Master's, Graduate Diploma programmes; Doctoral courses in applied mathematics, mathematics, physics, radiophysics and electronics, chemistry, biology, geography, history, law, journalism, Russian language and literature, Russian language and literature in the national school, philology (Germanic and Romance languages), management, economic theory, sociology, topographical survey and prospecting of minerals; also Russian language preparatory course.
Open to: candidates of any country with a secondary-school certificate or equivalent, having passed entrance examinations and a Russian test; preparatory Russian language study required.
Duration: 4 to 7 years depending on programme; preparatory Russian course: 1 year.
Applications: by 1 August, to the above address.

1985 Bauman Moscow State Technical University [BMSTU]
2nd Baumanskaya 5
107005 Moscow
Tel: +7 095 261 1743
Fax: +7 095 267 9893
Web: http://www.bmstu.ru/mstu/English
e-mail: center@atu.bmstu.ru

📖 Undergraduate, Graduate Programmes

Study Domains: all major fields, business, electricity and electronics, engineering, management, mechanical engineering.
Programmes: Bachelor's, Master's and internships in technical programmes including robotics and complex automation, power engineering, materials and technology, radio-electronics and laser technology, informatics and control systems, special machinery and fundamental sciences.
Open to: all applicants; proficiency in Russian required.
Duration: Bachelor's degree: 4 years; Master's degree: 6

years.
Applications: by 20 August.

1986 Biysk State Teacher's Training University [BSTTU]

ul. Korolenko 53
659333 Biysk, Altajskij kraj
Tel: +7 3854 240 610
Fax: +7 3854 245 137
Web: http://www.biysk.ru
e-mail: rektor@bigpi.biysk.ru

📖 Undergraduate, Graduate Programmes

Study Domains: all major fields, arts, biology, business administration, computer science, languages, law, physics, teacher education.
Programmes: Bakalavr, Specialist's Diploma in all major fields.
Duration: 4 to 5 years; courses begin 1 September.
Fees: tuition fees: US$1,200 per year; living costs: US$300 per month.
Applications: by 10 October; contact inyaz@bigpi.biysk.ru for further information.

1987 Bryansk State Academy of Engineering and Technology [BTI]

Stanke Dimitrov Avenue 3
241037 Bryansk
Tel: +7 08322 749 669

📖 Forest Management Studies

Study Domains: civil engineering, ecology, environment, forestry, industrial technology, mechanical engineering.
Programmes: Courses offered in training experts and scientific researchers in the field of forest management, ecology, forest monitoring, wear and tear on machines, materials in mechanical engineering, industrial and civil construction and road construction.
Open to: candidates with knowledge of Russian language fulfilling entry requirements.
Applications: to the above address for further information.

1988 Buryat State University [BSU]

24 A Smolin Street
670000 Ulan-Ude
Tel: +7 3012 211 580/214 115
Fax: +7 3012 210 588
Web: http://www.bsu.ru
e-mail: intdep@bsu.ru

📖 Undergraduate, Graduate, Postgraduate Programmes

Study Domains: all major fields, accounting, administration, applied sciences, chemistry, computer science, education, industry and commerce, interpretation and translation, languages, law, management, mathematics, medicine, philology, philosophy.
Programmes: Bachelor's, Master's, Ph.D. degrees in all major fields; also preparatory courses.
Open to: applicants of all nationalities; entrance examination.
Duration: 3 to 5 years.
Fees: tuition fees: US$850-$1,550 per year.
Languages: Russian.
Applications: by 5 July; contact intdep@bsu.ru.

1989 Demidov Yaroslavl State University [YARGU]

Sovetskaya 14
150000 Yaroslavl
Tel: +7 0852 797745
Fax: +7 0852 307515
Web: http://www.uniyar.ac.ru
e-mail: depint@uniyar.ac.ru

📖 Undergraduate, Graduate and Postgraduate Degree Programmes

Study Domains: accounting, administration, art history, business, criminology, history, information science, international business, international studies, law, management, marketing, museology and museography, philosophy, political economy, political science, psychology, Russian, sciences, social sciences, sociology.
Programmes: Bachelor's; Master's; Ph.D.; Russian language courses.
Duration: language course: 6 months to 1 year beginning in September, February or flexible dates.
Fees: registration: US$2; tuition fees: US$10; living costs: $150 per month including two meals.
Languages: for courses other than language courses good level of Russian is required.
Applications: apply to address above, or contact: depint@uniyar.ac.ru; telephone: +7 0852 72 5138.

1990 Don State Technical University [DSTU]

1 Gagarin Square
344010 Rostov-on-Don
Tel: +7 8632 381 525
Fax: +7 8632 327 953
Web: http://www.dstu.edu.ru
e-mail: postmaster@dstu.rnd.runnet.ru

📖 Undergraduate, Graduate, Postgraduate Programmes

Study Domains: advertising, applied arts, applied sciences, computer science, ecology, environment, economic and commercial sciences, economy, education, engineering, food industry, hydraulics, industrial technology, information science, laboratory techniques, management, marketing, mechanical engineering, psychology, Russian, technical education, technology, transport, vocational training.
Programmes: Bachelor's, Master's, Ph.D. degrees in education; applied arts, economics, management, engineering; non-degree programmes in Russian language.
Open to: candidates of all nationalities with secondary-school certificate or equivalent; proficiency in Russian required; entrance examination.
Duration: 4 to 7 years; courses begin 1 September.
Fees: tuition fees US$1,200-$2,500 per year.
Financial assistance: financial assistance available.
Applications: by 1 August; contact nsokovnina@dstu.edu.ru for further details.

1991 East Siberian Institute of Technology [ESIT]

Klutchevskaya Street 40a
670042 Ulan-Ude
Tel: +7 3012 375 600
Fax: +7 3012 333 706
Web: http://www.vsgtu.eastsib.ru

📖 Undergraduate, Graduate Programmes / Technological Studies

Study Domains: accounting, economy, food, food industry, industrial technology, management, Russian, technology.
Programmes: (a) Bachelor's; (b) Master's; (c) Engineer Diploma's; (d) Postgraduate; and (e) Doctor's courses in dairy products technology, meat and meat product technology, fur and leather technology, shoe designing and leather articles technology, grain storage and processing technology, technology of bakery, macaroni and confection of food concentrates, economics and management in agro-industrial complexes, management, engineering, accounting and auditing; (f) Russian language preparatory course.
Open to: candidates of any country with a secondary-school certificate, having passed entrance examinations and an interview in Russian language; Russian language preparatory study required.
Duration: (a) 4 years; (b) 2 years; (c) 1 year (after Bachelor's degree); (d) 3 years.
Fees: (approximate figures) yearly: (a) US$1,600-$2,000; (b) US$1,700-$2,500; (c) US$2,500; (d) US$2,500-$4,000; (f) US$1,200.
Applications: by 15 July, to the above address.

1992 Far Eastern State Technical University [FESTU]

Pushkinskaya Street 10
690950 Vladivostok
Tel: +7 4232 261 689
Fax: +7 4232 266 988
Web: http://www.festu.ru
e-mail: festu@festu.ru

Undergraduate, Graduate, Postgraduate Programmes

Study Domains: administration, anthropology, architecture, building industry, business, business administration, civil engineering, computer science, ecology, environment, economy, electricity and electronics, geology, industrial technology, information science, international relations, laboratory techniques, languages, law, linguistics, management, mathematics, research, Russian, shipbuilding, social work, telecommunications, transport.
Programmes: (a) Bachelor's degrees in education, languages, business administration, economics, law, management, science, architecture; (b) Master's degrees in languages, economics, management, geology, mathematics, civil engineering, shipbuilding; (c) Ph.D. degrees in linguistics, education, anthropology, economics, law, management, science, engineering, architecture, shipbuilding; (d) Doctor of Science in ecology and environment, geology, shipbuilding.
Open to: (a) candidates with secondary-school certificate; admission test and interview; proficiency in Russian required; (b) candidates holding Bachelor's degree; (c) candidates holding Master's degree: admission test; (d) candidates holding Ph.D. degree; admission test.
Duration: (a) 4 years; courses begin in September; (b) 2 years following Bachelor's; courses begin in September; (c) 3 years following Master's; courses begin in October; (d) 3 years following Ph.D.; courses begin in September.
Fees: (approximate figures) tuition per academic year: (a) US$2,000; (b) US$2,500; (c) US$3,000 (d) US$5,000; estimated living costs: US$200 per month.
Languages: Russian.
Applications: by 15 July, to the above address.

1993 Finance Academy

49 Leningradskiy Av.
125468 Moscow
Tel: +7 095 943 9855
Fax: +7 095 157 7070

Graduate, Postgraduate Programmes / Finance

Study Domains: business, finance.
Programmes: programme of studies leading to: (a) B.Sc.; (b) M.Sc. in finance, credit and money circulation, accounting and audit, world economics; (c) Ph.D. and D.Sc. in economics, planning and organization of management of the national economy, finance, money circulation and credit, accounting, control and analysis of economic activities, statistics, economic and mathematical methods.
Open to: candidates of all nationalities with proficiency in Russian, holding a secondary-school certificate; entrance test in general school subjects as well as Russian language test required.
Duration: (a) 4 years; (b) additional 2 years; (c) and (d) additional 3 years.
Applications: to the Office of International Relations: tel: +7 095 9439 405; fax: +7 095 1575 712.

1994 Higher School of Modern Education [HSME]

Maly Golovin per. 14/17
107045 Moscow
Tel: +7 095 207 4073/+7 095 207 407
Fax: +7 095 207 4073/+7 095 207 407
Web: http://www.school-so.ru
e-mail: info@school-so.ru

Certificate Programmes

Study Domains: business, computer science, education, humanities and arts, languages, law, mathematics, social sciences, statistics, summer programmes, urbanism.
Programmes: finance and credit, economics, Russian

language courses, Russian culture and history courses, Russian business courses.
Fees: registration: US$200-$500, depending on length of study; tuition: US$300-$500 per month; living costs: US$250-$400.
Languages: English and Russian.
Applications: for application information telephone: +7 095 207 4073; or email: info@school-so.ru.

1995 Humanitarian University (Institute)

ul. Studenèeskaja 19
62004 Ekaterinburg
Tel: +7-3432-745-190
Fax: +7-3432-494-666
Web: http://www.gu.ur.ru
e-mail: adm@gu.ur.ru

Undergraduate, Graduate Programmes

Study Domains: accounting, computer science, cultural studies, economic and commercial sciences, finance, humanities and arts, journalism, law, liberal arts, management, marketing, psychology, recreation and leisure, social sciences, tourism, hotel and catering management.

1996 Institute of Law and Business [ILB]

Pushkin, Malaya 8
196600 Saint Petersburg
Tel: +7 812 465 6884
Fax: +7 812 470 0800
e-mail: ipp@spbtlg.ru

Undergraduate, Graduate, Postgraduate Programmes

Study Domains: business, international law, law.
Programmes: Bachelor's, Master's, Ph.D. degrees in law, international law, business.
Duration: 5 years; courses begin 15 September.
Fees: tuition fees US$400 per term; living costs US$200 per term.
Applications: by 1 September; contact ipp@spbtlg.ru for further details.

1997 Institute of Youth [YI]

ul. Unosti 5/1
111442 Moscow
Tel: +7 095 374 5280
Fax: +7 095 374 7878

Undergraduate, Graduate Programmes

Study Domains: cultural studies, human sciences, languages, management, psychology, Russian, social work, sociology.
Programmes: (a) Bachelor's; (b) Master's; (c) Postgraduate; (d) Doctoral studies in Russian language, history of Russian culture, cultural studies, social work and psychology, as well as various programmes for foreigners in the Russian language lasting from 1 month to 1 year, including business courses.
Open to: candidates of any country with a secondary-school certificate and an entrance examination; written and oral Russian language tests.
Duration: (a) 4 years; (b) 2 years (after Bachelor's degree); (c) 3 years; (d) 2 to 3 years.
Fees: (approximate figures) yearly: (a) US$1,500-$3,000; (b) US$1,800-$3,500; (c) US$2,000-$4,000; (d) US$5,000.
Applications: during the academic year, to the above address.

1998 International Non-governmental Organization Corporation [INCORVUZ]

6 Volgina Street
117485 Moscow
Tel: +7-095-330-8492
Fax: +7-095-330-8647
Web: http://www.incorvuz.ru
e-mail: mks@incorvuz.ru

☛**INCORVUZ Scholarship Fund**

Study Domains: all major fields.
Scholarships: INCORVUZ Scholarship Fund: for undergraduate, graduate and postgraduate studies in all major fields and especially natural science and pedagogical studies.
Open to: suitably qualified candidates of different countries; see website for details.

1999 Irkutsk State Academy of Agriculture [AIOI]

Youth Township
664038 Irkutsk
Tel: +7 3952 464 645
Fax: +7 3952 241 246

📖 **Undergraduate, Graduate Programmes / Agriculture**

Study Domains: agriculture, agronomic sciences, biology, rural development, technical education, vocational training.
Programmes: (a) Certificate programmes; (b) postgraduate; (c) Doctoral studies in agronomy; (d) preparatory department of Russian language study.
Description: courses include mechanization of agriculture, farming electrification and automation, vocational training and technical sciences, rural economics and management in agro-industrial bookkeeping, control and analysis of economic activities, and wildlife biology management.
Open to: candidates of any country with a secondary-school certificate; Russian language study prior to application and entrance examination; candidate interviews in Russian.
Duration: (a) 5 years; (b) 3 years; (c) 2 years; (d) 2 years.
Applications: by 1 August, to the above address.

2000 Irkutsk State Technical University [ISTU]

83, Lermontov Street
664074 Irkutsk
Tel: +7-3952-405-200
Fax: +7-3952-405-100
Web: http://www.istu.edu
e-mail: oms@istu.edu

📖 **Undergraduate, Graduate and Postgraduate Degree Programmes**

Study Domains: advertising, applied arts, architecture, arts and crafts, aviation, aeronautics, building industry, business, chemical engineering, chemistry, civil engineering, computer science, decorative arts, design, ecology, environment, economy, electricity and electronics, energy, engineering, finance, fine arts, food industry, geodesy, geology, industrial relations, journalism, law, management, mathematics, mechanical engineering, metallurgy, psychology, social sciences, social work, sociology, summer programmes, transport, urbanism.
Programmes: Bachelor's, Specialist (Engineer), Master's, PhD, Doctor of Science; Russian language course.
Description: (a) preparatory training certificate; (b) Bachelor's degree; (c) Master's degree; (d) PhD; (e) DSc; (f) short-term language course.
Duration: Bachelor's: 4 years; Specialist (Engineer): 5 years; Master's: 6 years; Candidate of Science (PhD): 3 to 4 years; Doctor of Science: 3 years.
Fees: tuition fees per academic year: (a) US$1,100; (b) US$1,300; (c) US$1,700; (d) US$1,700; (e) US$1,800; (f) US$8 per academic hour.
Financial assistance: see scholarships.
Applications: apply to: oms@istu.edu, by the following dates: (a) 30 September; (b) and (c) 1 September; (d), (e) and (f) 1-1/2 months prior to the beginning of courses.

☛**Government-Sponsored Training and Grants**

Study Domains: all major fields.
Duration: for duration of training; depending on type of scholarship.
Value: free tuition and monthly stipend.
Applications: Ministry of Education in applicant's country; CIMO in Finland; IREX in USA.

2001 Irkutsk State University [ISU]

1, Karl Marx Street
664003 Irkutsk
Tel: +7 3952 242 249
Fax: +7 3952 242 249
Web: http://www.isu.ru
e-mail: bogatova@admin.isu.runnet.ru

📖 **Undergraduate and Graduate Degree Programmes**

Study Domains: all major fields.
Programmes: Bachelor's, Master's, Specialist; non-degree programmes.
Open to: candidates must meet language proficiency: RAFL, 1st level to enter the university and be under 35 years of age.
Duration: 4 to 5 years commencing 1 September; Summer courses.
Fees: tuition: US$1,000-$1,500 per academic year; living costs: $150 minimum.
Languages: Russian.
Applications: apply by 31 May.

☛**Government Scholarship**

Study Domains: all major fields.
Scholarships: Government Scholarship.
Open to: candidates must be under 35 years of age.
Value: lodging in a student hostel; free access to libraries and labs; monthly allowance in roubles.
Applications: contact Ministry of Education of Russian Federation in cooperation with corresponding foreign educational administrative body.

2002 Ivanovo State Academy of Medicine

8 Freidrich Engels Prospect
153462 Ivanovo
Tel: +7 0932 341 766

📖 **Medical Studies**

Study Domains: medicine, paediatrics, surgery.
Programmes: courses of higher education for foreign students in the field of medicine: general medicine, paediatrics and infant surgery, nursing.
Open to: candidates of any nationality holding a secondary-education certificate and proficient in Russian. Russian language courses available.
Duration: (a) Doctor of Medicine: 6 years; (b) clinical studies: 2 to 3 years; (c) postgraduate studies: 3 years.
Fees: (approximate figures) (a) US$1,700-$2,000 per year; (b) US$2,000-$5,000 per year; (c) US$2,500-$3,000 per year; preparatory course US$1,100-$1,200 per year.
Applications: further information at the above address.

2003 Ivanovo State Textile Institute [IGTA]

Fr. Engels Avenue 21
153000 Ivanovo
Tel: +7 0932 357 825
Fax: +7 0932 415 088
Web: http://education.ivanovo.ru/IGTA
e-mail: root@igta.asinet.ivanovo.su

📖 **Undergraduate, Graduate Programmes / Textile Industry**

Study Domains: industrial technology, technology, telecommunications, textile industry.
Programmes: (a) Bachelor's; (b) Master's; (c) diploma; (d) postgraduate; (e) doctoral courses in cotton and wool spinning, woven and knitted fabrics technology, textile clothing design, individually ordered clothing production and repair, textile machines and maintenance, dyeing and finishing machines, textile engineering, automatic processes in light industry, automation of machine-building processes and production, automation of telecommunication processes, textile products weaving methods, decorative design, textile products decorative design printing methods; (f) Russian language preparatory department; (g) Russian language teacher training courses for teachers and interpreters, qualifying them to teach the Russian language.
Open to: candidates of any country with a

secondary-school certificate, having passed entrance examinations or interview; Russian language preparatory courses required.
Duration: (a) 4 years; (b) (after Bachelor's degree), (d), (e) and (g) 3 years; (c) (after Bachelor's degree) and (f) 1 year.
Fees: yearly: (a) US$1,500-$3,500; (b) US$2,000-$3,000; (c) US$1,800-$2,500; (d) US$2,500-$4,000; (e) US$3,500-$5,000; (f) US$1,300; (g) US$1,200-$1,500.
Applications: accepted yearly, to the above address.

2004 Ivanovo State University [ISU]
39 Ermak Street
153025 Ivanovo
Tel: +7-932-423-709
Fax: +7-932-326-600/423-709
Web: http://www.ivanovo.ac.ru
e-mail: interdep@ivanovo.ac.ru

📖 Undergraduate and Graduate Degree Programmes
Study Domains: accounting, biology, chemistry, economy, English, finance, French, German, history, international relations, journalism, law, literature and civilization, management, mathematics, philology, physics, psychology, Russian, sociology.
Programmes: (a) Bachelor's; (b) Master's; (c) Ph.D.; (d) postgraduate courses; (d) Russian language preparatory courses.
Open to: candidates of any country with a secondary-school certificate; passing interviews in their speciality subject and Russian language; minimum 1 year Russian language preparation required.
Duration: up to 6 years, depending on programme.
Fees: registration: US$3; tuition per year: US$900-$2,500; living costs: US$80 per year.
Financial assistance: see Scholarships section above.
Applications: apply by 1 September; contact: interdep@ivanovo.ac.ru for further information.

🐦 President's Scholarship
Study Domains: accounting, biology, chemistry, economy, English, finance, French, German, history, international relations, journalism, law, philology, physics, psychology, Russian, sociology.
Scholarships: governmental scholarship; open to all subject areas of study.
Value: full course (5 years) tuition payment and 1 year preparatory course; paid in roubles.
Applications: apply by 1 August with educational certificate; medical certificate; application form; approval of host university; contact: interdep@ivanovo.ac.ru. for further information.

2005 Kaliningrad State University [KSU]
14, A.Nevsky str.
236041 Kaliningrad
Tel: +7 0112 465 917
Fax: +7 0112 465 813
Web: http://www.albertina.ru
e-mail: rector@admin.albertina.ru

📖 Undergraduate, Graduate Programmes
Study Domains: all major fields.
Programmes: Courses leading to (a) Bachelor's degree at the Faculty of geography; (b) Postgraduate degrees in jurisprudence, radio-physics, electronics, foreign languages, biology, market economy and management, geography; (c) Russian language preparatory courses; Russian language courses at the Faculty of Linguistics.
Open to: candidates of any country with a secondary-school certificate or equivalent, having passed entrance examinations and an interview in Russian; Russian language preparatory study required.
Duration: (b) 3 years.
Fees: (approximate figures) yearly: (a) US$1,500-$2,000; (b) US$2,500-$3,000; (c) US$1,200.
Applications: by 1 August, to the above address.

2006 Kaluga State Pedagogical University 'K. Tsiolkovsky' [KSPU]
26 Razin Street
248023 Kaluga
Tel: +7 0842 576 120
Fax: +7 0842 571 078
Web: http://kspu.kaluga.ru/conf/phyem/ekspu.htm
e-mail: rector@kspu.kaluga.ru

📖 Undergraduate, Graduate, Postgraduate Programmes
Study Domains: anatomy, chemistry, ecology, environment, education, genetics, information science, languages, linguistics, literature and civilization, mathematics, philology, physics, social sciences, teacher education.
Programmes: Bachelor's, Specialist's Diploma, Ph.D. degrees in education, languages, philology, social sciences, science.
Open to: candidates must be under 35 years of age.
Duration: 4 to 5 years; courses begin 1 September.
Fees: tuition fees: US$1,500; living costs included.
Applications: by 1 July; contact rector@kspu.kaluga.ru for further details.

2007 Kazan Finance and Economics Institute [KFEI]
Butlerov Street 4
420012 Kazan (Tatarstan)
Tel: +7 8432 324 036
Fax: +7 8432 383 054
Web: http://www.kfei.kcn.ru

📖 Undergraduate, Graduate Programmes
Study Domains: accounting, economy, finance, sociology.
Programmes: (a) Bachelor's degree courses; (b) Master's degree courses in economic and social planning, economics and sociology of labour, finance and credit, accounting, control and analysis of economic activity.
Open to: applicants of any country with a GCE Diploma; entrance examination and interview in Russian on everyday and special topics to assess Russian language level; prior Russian language study advised.
Duration: (a) 4 years; (b) 2 years.
Fees: (a) US$800-$1,800 per year; (b) US$560-$1,260 per year.
Applications: by 15 July, to the above address.

2008 Kazan State University [KSU]
18 Kremlyovskaya St.
420008 Kazan
Tel: +7 8432 387 069
Fax: +7 8432 387 418
Web: http://www.ksu.ru/base_en/mainen.html
e-mail: public.mail@ksu.ru

📖 Graduate Programmes
Study Domains: arts, classical studies, computer science, ecology, environment, economy, geology, history, journalism, law, sciences.
Programmes: (a) Master's degree; (b) Ph.D. studies for international students in history, biology and soil science, geography, law, geology, mechanics and mathematics, physics, computing mathematics and cybernetics, Tatar philosophy and Eastern languages, journalism, ecology, economics, chemistry, philology; (c) Accelerated Russian language summer course;
(d) Russian language course for postgraduates; (e) Russian language preparatory course.
Open to: candidates of any country, holding a secondary-school certificate, having passed an entrance interview; no minimum requirement in Russian language knowledge.
Duration: (a) 5 years; (b) 3 years; (c) 1 month; (d) 6 months; (e) 1 year.
Fees: yearly: (a) arts and humanities: US$2,000; sciences: US$2,500; law: US$3,000; (b) US$4,000; (c) US$800; (d) US$350; (e) US$1,500.
Applications: by 1 July, to the above address.

2009 Komi State Pedagogical Institute [KSPI]

Kommunisticheskaya Street 25
167007 Syktyvkar
Tel: +7 8212 423 191
Fax: +7 8212 214 481
Web: http://kspi.komi.ru
e-mail: rector@kspi.komi.ru

📖 Secondary School Teacher Training

Study Domains: arts and crafts, biology, education, geography, mathematics, physics, Russian, teacher education.
Programmes: Courses in secondary school teaching of mathematics, physics, Russian, geography, biology, crafts and labour instruction, primary school teachers.
Open to: candidates of any country with a secondary-school certificate, having passed the entrance examination and an interview in Russian; 1-year Russian language preparatory course required.
Applications: by 15 July, to the above address.

2010 Komsomolsk-on-Amur Polytechnical Institute [KnAPI]

Prospekt Lenina 27
681013 Komsomolsk-an-Amure
Tel: +7 42141 32304
Fax: +7 42141 36150
e-mail: root@knapi.khabarovsk.su

📖 Undergraduate, Graduate Programmes

Study Domains: chemistry, civil engineering, economic and commercial sciences, electricity and electronics, management, marketing, shipbuilding, technology.
Programmes: (a) Bachelor's degree; (b) Engineering Diploma; (c) Postgraduate courses in electrical engineering, shipbuilding, aircraft and helicopter construction, machinery producing technology, foundry machinery and technology, civil engineering, chemical technology, biotechnology, management, marketing, commercial activities, as well as (d) Russian language preparatory department.
Open to: candidates of any nationality, with a secondary school leaving certificate or equivalent, passing the entrance examination and an interview in Russian; Russian language training required.
Duration: (a) 4 years; (b) 1 year; (c) 3 years; (d) 2 years.
Fees: yearly: (a) US$1,800-$3,400; (b) US$2,400; (c) US$2,500-$5,800; (d) US$1,000.
Applications: by 1 August, to the above address.

2011 Kostroma State Pedagogical University [KSU]

ul.1st May 14
156001 Kostroma
Tel: +7 0942 317 530
Fax: +7 0942 318 291
e-mail: kgpu@kosnet.ru

📖 Undergraduate, Graduate, Postgraduate Programmes

Study Domains: education.
Programmes: Bachelor's, Master's, Ph.D. degrees in education.

2012 Kostroma State University of Technology [KSUT]

ul. Dzerzinskogo 17
156005 Kostroma
Tel: +7 0942 314 814
Fax: +7 0942 317 008
Web: http://www.kstu.edu.ru
e-mail: info@kstu.edu.ru

📖 Undergraduate, Graduate, Postgraduate Programmes

Study Domains: economic and commercial sciences, engineering, forestry, law, mechanical engineering, technology, tourism, hotel and catering management.
Programmes: Bakalavr, Specialist's Diploma, Kandidat Nauk in economics, tourism, technology, mechanical engineering, law, forestry.
Open to: candidates with secondary-school certificate and

under 35 years of age.
Fees: tuition fees US$900 per year.
Financial assistance: financial assistance available.
Applications: by 1 September to the above address.

2013 Kosygin Moscow State Textile University [KMSTU]

Malay Kaluzhskaya Street 1
119991 Moscow
Tel: +7-095-954-7073
Fax: +7-095-952-1440
Web: http://www.msta.ac.ru
e-mail: office@msta.ac.ru

📖 Undergraduate and Graduate Degree Programmes

Study Domains: design, economy, management, textile industry.
Programmes: Bachelor's; Master's; Engineering Diploma.
Subjects: technology of textile; chemical and biotechnology; machine and equipment technology; economics; management; costume design.
Open to: all nationalities; language proficiency, medical certificate, admission tests required.
Duration: Bachelor's: 4 years; Engineering: 5 years; Master's: 6 years.
Fees: registration: US$1; tuition fees: US$1,000-$2,100 per year; living costs: US$450 per year.

2014 Kovrov State Academy of Technology [KSTA]

International Service
Mayakovsky Street 19
601910 Kovrov
Tel: +7 09232 50592
Fax: +7 09232 32533
Web: http://www.kc.ru/~kainter/800/en/index.shtml
e-mail: kainter@kc.ru

📖 Undergraduate, Graduate Programmes

Study Domains: computer science, economy, hydraulics, management, mechanical engineering, technology.
Programmes: Bachelor's, Specialist's Diploma in mechanical engineering, automation and control, computer science, economics and management.
Open to: candidates of all countries, with a secondary-school certificate; preliminary Russian proficiency required.
Duration: 4 to 5 years.
Fees: tuition fees US$700-$1,000 per year; living costs US$1,200 per year.
Applications: by 15 August, to the above address; contact kainter@kc.ru for further details.

🦅 Scholarship

Study Domains: computer science, economy, management, mechanical engineering, technology.
Scholarships: University Scholarship.
Duration: entire duration of studies.
Value: variable.
Applications: by 1 September; contact kainter@kc.ru for further details.

2015 Krasnoyarsk Academy of Architecture and Civil Engineering [KCEI]

82 Svobodny Avenue
660041 Krasnoyarsk
Tel: +7 3912 456 699
Fax: +7 3912 455 892

📖 Undergraduate, Graduate Programmes

Study Domains: architecture, building industry, civil engineering, hydrology.
Programmes: (a) Bachelor's; (b) Master's; (c) Engineering Diploma; (d) Postgraduate courses in architecture, civil and industrial building, town building and services, building articles and structures production, water supply and sewerage, water resources rational usage and protection, heat and gas supply, ventilation and air basin protection, highways and aerodrome building;
(e) Russian language preparatory course.

Open to: candidates of any country with a secondary-school certificate or equivalent, having passed the entrance examinations and an interview in Russian; preparatory Russian language course required.
Duration: (a) 4 years; (b) and (e) 2 years; (c) 1 year; (d) 3 years.
Fees: yearly: (a) US$1,500-$3,500; (b) US$1,700-$4,000; (c) US$2,500; (d) US$2,500-$5,000; (e) US$1,200.
Applications: by July 31, to the above address.

2016 Krasnoyarsk State Technical University [KSTU]
26 Kirensky Street
660074 Krasnoyarsk
Tel: +7-3912-441-902
Fax: +7-3912-430-692
Web: http://www.kgtu.runnet.ru
e-mail: root@kgtu.runnet.ru

☐ Undergraduate, Graduate and Postgraduate Programmes

Study Domains: administration, business, communication, computer science, ecology, environment, economic and commercial sciences, economy, electricity and electronics, energy, engineering, human sciences, hydraulics, interpretation and translation, mathematics, physics, Russian, technology, telecommunications, transport, vocational training.
Programmes: (a) Master's and Ph.D. physical principles of HDE technology; also non-degree programme in NDE science and measurement courses; (b) Master's, Ph.D. degrees in materials and technology for electronics.
Open to: (a) candidates of any country holding a Bachelor's degree in applied physics, electrical engineering; preparatory Russian language study required; (b) candidates of any country holding a Bachelor's degree in physics or electronics.
Duration: (a) 10 months from 1 September through 30 June; (b) 1 year; courses begin 1 September.
Fees: current registration: US$60; tuition fees: US$1,000-$3,000 per year for undergraduate; US$2,500-3,500 for postgraduate; living costs: approximately US$1,600 per year.
Languages: English and Russian.
Applications: by 15 August, to the above address; for information contact Ms. Natalia Klimchuk; tel. +7 3912 497 434; fax +7 3912 443 698; email: depfc@kgtu.runnet.ru.

☞ Study Grant

Study Domains: computer science, electricity and electronics, energy, engineering, hydraulics, physics, telecommunications.
Scholarships: One-year study grant for overseas students at Master's or Ph.D. levels.
Subjects: Physical Principles of HDE Technology; Materials and Technology for Electronics.
Open to: students holding a Bachelor's degree in the relevant fields of study with good skills in Russian (proved by certificate or relevant).
Duration: one year.
Value: free tuition and education facilities.
Languages: English and Russian.
Applications: by 30 June to the above address; for information contact Ms. Natalia Klimchuk; tel. +7 3912 497 43; fax +7 3912 443 698; email: depfc@kgtu.runnet.ru.

2017 Krasnoyarsk State University [KSU]
79 Svobodny prospect
660041 Krasnoyarsk
Tel: +7 3912 441 552
Fax: +7 3912 448 625
Web: http://www.krasu.ru
e-mail: office@lan.krasu.ru

☐ Undergraduate, Graduate Programmes

Study Domains: all major fields.
Programmes: Bakalavr, Specialist's Diploma, Kandidat Nauk, Doktor Nauk degrees in all major fields.
Applications: see website for further information or contact the above address.

2018 Kuban State Academy of Medicine
4 Sedina Street
350690 Krasnodar GSP
Tel: +7 8612 523 284
Fax: +7 8612 523 684

☐ Medical Studies

Study Domains: medicine, paediatrics, stomatology.
Programmes: Courses of higher education for foreign students in medicine.
Open to: candidates of any nationality with a secondary-school certificate, proficient in Russian; Russian language courses available.
Duration: (a) Doctor of Medicine: 6 years; (b) postgraduate studies: 3 years; (c) clinical studies: 3 years.
Fees: (approximate figures): (a) US$1,700-$1,800 per year; (b) US$2,500 per year; (c) US$2,000-$2,500 per year.
Applications: further information at the above address.

2019 Kuban State University [KUBSU]
149 Stavropolskaya st.,
350040 Krasnodar
Tel: +7 8612 699 501
Web: http://www.kubsu.ru
e-mail: rector@kubsu.ru

☐ Graduate Programme

Study Domains: all major fields, philosophy, Russian.
Programmes: International certificate of M.B.A. in Russian Philology (theoretical and practical).
Description: courses in Russian language, folklore, linguistics, dialects, religions, modern and ancient literature, culture, customs and traditions, philosophy and philology, applied psychology, principles and methods of teaching, political economics, ethics.
Applications: to the above address.

2020 Kuban State University of Technology
2 Moskovskaya Street
350072 Krasnodar
Tel: +7 8612 558 401
Fax: +7 8612 576 592

☐ Graduate Programme / Industrial Engineering

Study Domains: building industry, chemical industry, energy, food, food industry, industrial technology, mechanical engineering, technology.
Programmes: (a) Master's in power engineering, oil and gas technology, automatic systems and equipment for food production, chemical technology, food production technology, bakery technology, construction engineering, motor and highway engineering, industrial economics, mechanics and mechanical engineering; (b) Probation training courses; (c) Russian language preparatory department; (d) Russian language courses; (e) Special short-term course 'Methods of training the Russian language'.
Open to: candidates of any country with a secondary-school certificate or equivalent, having passed entrance examinations and an interview in Russian; minimum proficiency in Russian according to the programme of the preparatory department.
Duration: (a) 5 years; (b) 1 year.
Fees: yearly: (a) US$1,000; (b) and (d) US$800; (e) US$500.
Applications: by 1 August, at the above address.

2021 Kursk State Technical University [KPI]
Let Oktjabrja Street 94
305039 Kursk
Tel: +7 0712 225 743
Fax: +7 0712 561 168
Web: http://www.kstu.kursk.ru
e-mail: rector@kstu.kursk.ru

☐ Undergraduate, Graduate Programmes

Study Domains: civil engineering, computer science, food, industrial technology, technical education, technology, textile industry.

Programmes: (a) Bachelor's; (b) Master's; (c) Engineering Diploma; (d) postgraduate studies; (e) Doctorate studies in industrial and civil engineering, heating, piping and air conditioning, water supply, sewage systems, chemical technology and treatment equipment of cloth finishing production, computer complexes, systems and networks, man-made and natural fibres, knitted fabrics and knitwear manufacturing, cars and automobile service, biomedical technologies, systems and instruments, industrial, city and rural electric power supply, computer software and hardware design, production engineering, metal cutting tools and instruments, food industry equipment; (f) Russian language courses.
Open to: candidates of all countries with a secondary-school certificate, having passed the entrance examinations and an interview; preparatory Russian language study required.
Duration: (a) 4 years; (b) 2 years; (c) 1 year; (d) and (e) 3 years; (f) 1 year.
Fees: (approximate figures) yearly: (a) US$1,200-$2,500; (b) US$1,500-$3,500; (c) US$1,500-$3,000; (d) and (e) US$2,200-4,000; (f) US$1,000-$1,500.
Applications: by 15 September, to the above address.

2022 Kursk State University of Educational Science [KTTI]

33 Radishev Street
305000 Kursk
Tel: +7 0712 560 264
Fax: +7 0712 568 461

📖 Undergraduate, Graduate Programmes

Study Domains: arts, biology, early childhood education, French, geography, German, history, mathematics, physics, Russian.
Programmes: (a) Bachelor's; (b) Master's; (c) Diploma; (d) Postgraduate; (e) Doctor's courses in mathematics, physics, history, Russian, Russian literature, biology, geography, English, German, French, handicraft, defectology, drawing and arts, teacher training and methods of primary teaching;
(f) Russian language preparatory courses.
Open to: candidates of any country with a secondary-school certificate or equivalent, having passed a test in Russian; preparatory Russian language study at the available corresponding courses required.
Duration: (c) 1 year; (d) and (e) 3 years; (f) 2 years.
Fees: yearly: (c) US$2,500; (d) US$2,500-$5,000; (e) US$5,000; (f) US$1,200.
Applications: by 1 August, to the above address.

2023 Kuzbass Polytechnic Institute [KPI]

Vesennyaya Street 28
650026 Kemerovo
Tel: +7 3842 233 380
Fax: +7 3842 361 687

📖 Undergraduate, Graduate Programmes

Study Domains: chemistry, economy, management, technical education, technology, transport.
Programmes: (a) Bachelor's; (b) Master's; (c) Graduate Engineer; (d) Postgraduate; (e) Doctoral studies in mechanization and management, chemical technology and biotechnology, transport ways and means exploitation, construction, mining, ground transport systems, electro-energetics, technological machines and equipment, equipment technology, mechanization of machine building production, management, economics; (f) Preparatory course in Russian.
Open to: candidates of any country, with a secondary-school certificate, having passed the entrance examination and a Russian language test; Russian language preparatory courses required.
Duration: (a) 4 years; (c) 2 years; (d) and (e) 3 years; (f) 1 year.
Fees: (approximate figures) yearly: (a) US$2,000-$3,500; (c) US$2,700; (d) US$2,700-$5,000; (e) US$5,500; (f) US$1,000.
Applications: by 15 June, to the above address.

2024 Legal Academy of the Ministry of Justice [LAMJ]

Uliza Azovslaia 2
117149 Moscow
Tel: +7 095 113 8957/4754
Fax: +7 095 113 4754

📖 Legal Specialist Programme

Study Domains: criminology, international law, law.
Programmes: Programme of courses leading to a Legal Specialist degree; also non-degree programme: foreign languages courses for lawyers.
Duration: 5 years beginning in September.
Applications: by 15 July to the above address.

2025 Liberal Arts University [LAU]

Gumanitarniy Universitet
Studencheskaya street 19
620 049 Ekaterinburg
Tel: +7 3432 745 190/557 002
Fax: +7 3432 418 703
e-mail: postmaster@lau.e-burg.su

📖 Undergraduate, Graduate and Postgraduate Programmes

Study Domains: accounting, advertising, computer science, cultural studies, decorative arts, design, economy, European studies, finance, graphic arts, interpretation and translation, journalism, languages, law, management, marketing, performing arts, psychology, public relations, social sciences, tourism, hotel and catering management.
Programmes: Undergraduate, graduate and postgraduate programmes leading to Kandidat Nauk, Specialist's and Bakalavr.
Description: Kandidak Nauk in psychology, social sciences and cultural studies; Specialist's degree in all fields; Bakalavr in Journalism.
Open to: candidates of any country holding a secondary school certificate.
Other conditions: medical certificate required.
Fees: tuition: approx. 1800 roubles per term.
Applications: to the above address.

2026 Lipeck Polytechnical Institute [LPI]

30 Moskovskaya Street
398055 Lipeck
Tel: +7 0742 250 061
Fax: +7 0742 256 986

📖 Undergraduate, Graduate Programmes / Engineering

Study Domains: chemical industry, civil engineering, engineering, management, metallurgy, physics, transport.
Programmes: (a) Bachelor's; (b) Master's; (c) Engineering Diploma; (d) Postgraduate and Doctor's courses in metallurgy, automated manufacturing processes, civil engineering, computer science, applied physics and technology, business management; (e) Russian language preparatory courses.
Open to: candidates of any country with a secondary-school certificate or equivalent, having passed an interview; preparatory Russian language study required.
Duration: (a) 4 years; (c) 2 years; (d) 3 years; (e) 1 year.
Fees: yearly: (a) US$1,000; (c) US$1,800; (d) US$1,200; (e) US$800.
Applications: by 1 September, to the above address.

2027 Magintogorsk State Conservatory [MSC]

Gryaznov Street 22
455 036 Magnitogorsk
Tel: +7 3511 372 712
Fax: +7 3519 201 008

📖 Undergraduate, Graduate Programmes

Study Domains: accounting, applied arts, art history, arts, arts and crafts, audio-visual media, continuing education, cultural studies, early childhood education, economy, education, English, fine arts, folklore, French, geography, German, history, human sciences, Italian, languages, literature and civilization, museology and museography, music and musicology, performing arts, philosophy, physical education,

political science, psychology, Russian, social sciences, sociology, special education, teacher education, theology, religion, vocational training.
Programmes: Undergraduate and graduate programmes leading to Bachelor's and Ph.D. degrees.
Open to: candidates must undergo entrance examinations and be under the age of 37.
Duration: 5 years beginning in September.
Fees: tuition: US$3,000 per year.
Languages: Russian, English, German and French.
Applications: to the above address.

2028 Mendeleyev University of Chemical Technology of Russia [MUCTR]

9, Miusskaya Sq.
125 047 Moscow
Tel: +7-095-978-8733
Fax: +7-095-200-4204
Web: http://www.muctr.edu.ru
e-mail: rector@muctr.edu.ru

📖 Graduate Programmes / Chemistry

Study Domains: chemical engineering, chemical industry, chemistry.
Programmes: Higher Education courses at the degree level in the Faculties of Non-organic Material Technology; Silicate Chemical Technology; Polymer Chemical Technology; Organic Material Technology; Engineering Physics and Chemistry; Chemical Engineering Technology; Engineering Ecology.
Open to: candidates of any nationality holding a secondary-education certificate and proficient in Russian.

2029 Mordovia State University [MSU]

Bolshevitskaya, 68
430 000 Saransk
Tel: +7 8342 241 777
Fax: +7 8342 327 527 / 247 951
Web: http://www.mrsu.ru
e-mail: makarkin@mrsu.ru

📖 Undergraduate, Graduate Programmes

Study Domains: all major fields.
Programmes: Programme of courses leading to Specialist Diploma; Graduate courses leading to Candidate of Sciences and Doctor of Sciences.
Open to: candidates are selected on the basis of academic excellence; language test and interview required.
Duration: 5 to 6 years beginning in September.
Fees: tuition: US$1,000-$1,300 per year; living costs: approx. US$150-$200 a month.
Financial assistance: some scholarships in the amount of 200-800 roubles per month are available on the condition of academic excellence; for information contact Nikolai Fomin at the above address.
Applications: by 1 September; for information contact Nikolai Fomin at the above address.

2030 Mordovian State Institute of Teacher Training [MSTTI]

11A Studencheskaya Street
430007 Mordovia
Tel: +7 8342 321 925
Fax: +7 8342 322 043

📖 Undergraduate, Graduate Programmes / Teacher Education

Study Domains: education, languages, sciences.
Programmes: Teachers' Diploma courses and three-year postgraduate courses.
Open to: candidates of any country with a secondary-school certificate or equivalent, having passed the entrance test; minimum requirements of Russian language proficiency: oral skills and comprehension.
Applications: by 16 July, to the above address.

2031 Moscow Academy of Humanities and Social Sciences [MAHSS]

External Relations Department - Office 214
Ul. Yunosti, 5/1, kor. 1
111 395 Moscow
Tel: +7-095-374-5280
Fax: +7-095-374-7878
Web: http://www.mgsa.ru
e-mail: tatianar@corbina.ru

📖 Government Diploma of Higher Education

Study Domains: art history, economy, international law, international relations, international studies, law, liberal arts, linguistics, management, marketing, political economy, psychology, public relations, research, Russian, sociology, summer programmes.
Programmes: Programme of courses leading to Government Diploma of Higher Education; non-degree short term courses (Preparatory Faculty) in Russian language and culture, Russian business environment, etc.
Open to: candidates holding a secondary-school certificate; entrance examination required.
Duration: Government Diploma of Higher Education: 5 years beginning in September; Preparatory Faculty: from 3 to 12 months.
Fees: current registration: US$30; tuition: US$970.
Applications: Preparatory Faculty: during the year; Main Faculties: in June and September; for information contact Alexander Popov at the above address; tel: +7 095 374 5521.

2032 Moscow Academy of Medicine

2-6 Bolshova Pirogovskaya Street
119881 Moscow
Tel: +7 095 248 0553
Fax: +7 095 248 0214

📖 Medical Sciences

Study Domains: medicine, nursing, pharmacy and pharmacology.
Programmes: Degree programmes in medicine, pharmacy and nursing.
Open to: medical doctors, pharmaceutical chemists, nurses with secondary education; with proficiency in Russian; Russian language courses provided.
Duration: probation from 1 to 3 years; nursing 4 years; pharmacy 5 years; medicine 6 years.
Fees: (approximate figures) preparatory course: US$2,000; probation: US$3,000 per year; clinical studies: US$3,000-$4,000 per year; nursing: US$2,500 per year; pharmacy: US$3,000 per year; medicine US$3,000 per year.
Applications: further information from above address.

2033 Moscow Consumer Cooperative University [MCCU]

12 Vera Voloshina Street
141000 Mytischi, Moscow Region
Tel: +7-095-581-9310

📖 Undergraduate, Graduate Programmes / Commerce

Study Domains: business administration, development studies, economic and commercial sciences, finance.
Programmes: (a) Bachelor's; (b) Master's; (c) Postgraduate; (d) Doctoral studies in finance and credit, business accounting, control and analysis of economic activity, foreign economic relations, economics of cooperatives and business enterprises, organization of commerce and science of commodities; several possibilities for studying the Russian language at the university: (e) Russian language courses; (f) Preparatory Department; (g) Interpreters' Department at the International Co-operative Training Centre and within the programme of the full course of study (4 years) at the Faculty of Foreign Economic Relations.
Open to: candidates of any country with a secondary-education certificate, having passed testing in Russian and mathematics, medical check-up; preparatory Russian language study required.
Duration: (a) 4 years; (b) 1-1/2 years; (c) and (d) 3 years; (e) 3 to 6 months; (f) 10 months; (g) 2 years.

Applications: by 31 August to the above address.

2034 Moscow Institute of Architecture [MIARCH]

Rozhdestvenka Street 11
103754 Moscow
Tel: +7 095 928 3259
Fax: +7 095 921 1240
Web: http://www.miarch.ru
e-mail: marhi@marhi.ru

Undergraduate, Graduate Programmes / Architecture

Study Domains: architecture.
Programmes: (a) Bachelor's; (b) Master's; (c) Postgraduate; (d) Doctoral studies in architecture, architectural environment design, Russian language teacher training; (e) Russian language preparatory courses and courses for teachers and interpreters in Russian.
Open to: candidates of any country with a secondary-school-leaving certificate having passed an entrance examination in drawing; preparatory Russian language study required.
Duration: (a) and (d) 4 years; (b) 6 years; (c) 3 years; (e) 1 year.
Fees: (approximate figures) yearly: (a) and (b) US$3,000; (c) US$4,000; (d) US$2,000; (e) US$2,000.
Applications: by 15 August, to the above address.

2035 Moscow Institute of Municipal Economy and Construction [MIMEC]

Srednaja Kalitnikovskaja 30
109807 Moscow
Tel: +7 095 278 3473
Fax: +7 095 278 1510

Graduate Programmes / Engineering

Study Domains: building industry, ecology, environment, technology, urbanism.
Programmes: (a) Engineer Diploma; (b) Postgraduate; (c) Doctor's courses in industrial and urban construction, heat and gas supplies, ventilation and protection of the air, water supply, sewerage, rational use and protection of water.
Open to: candidates of all nationalities with a secondary-school certificate; entrance examinations and conversational interview to determine subject and language levels required; preparatory knowledge of Russian necessary.
Duration: (a) 5 years and 9 months; (b) and (c) 3 years.
Fees: yearly: (a) US$500; (b) US$2,500; (c) US$5,000.
Applications: by 1 September, to the above address.

2036 Moscow Institute of Physics and Technology [MIPT]

Dolgoprundy Institutskii per. 9
141700 Moscow
Tel: +7 095 408 5700
Fax: +7 095 408 6869
Web: http://www.mipt.ru

Undergraduate, Graduate Programmes

Study Domains: mathematics, physics, technology.
Programmes: (a) Bachelor's; (b) Master's; (c) Postgraduate courses in applied mathematics and physics, including general and applied physics, radiophysics, aerophysics and cosmic research, laser physics, chemical and molecular physics, flying techniques, management processes, energetics, physico-chemical biology and biotechnology, as well as (d) Russian language preparatory courses.
Open to: candidates of any country with a secondary-school certificate; having passed entrance examinations and an interview in Russian; preparatory Russian language course required.
Duration: (a) 4 years; (b) 2 years (after Bachelor's degree); (c) 3 to 4 years; (d) 1 to 2 years.
Fees: (approximate figures) yearly: (a) US$4,000-$5,000; (b) US$4,500-$5,500; (c) US$5,500-$6,000; (d) US$2,000-$3,000.
Applications: by 1 August, to the above address.

2037 Moscow Pedagogical University [MPU]

Radio Street 10A
107005 Moscow
Tel: +7 095 261 2228
Fax: +7 095 261 2228
Web: http://www.mpu.edu.ru
e-mail: rectorat@mpu.edu.ru

Undergraduate, Graduate Programmes

Study Domains: biology, chemistry, ecology, environment, economy, fine arts, mathematics, physical education, physics, Russian.
Programmes: (a) Bachelor's; (b) Master's; (c) Teaching Diploma; (d) Postgraduate; (e) Doctor's courses in Russian, Russian literature, physics, mathematics, biology, chemistry, ecology, physical training, economy, fine arts and handicrafts.
Open to: candidates of all countries, with a secondary-school certificate; entrance examinations and conversation interview; preparatory Russian language study required.
Duration: (a) 4 years; (b) 2 years (after Bachelor's); (c) and (f) 1 year; (d) and (e) 3 years.
Fees: yearly: (a) US$1,600-$3,000; (b) US$1,800-$4,000; (c) US$1,200; (d) US$2,500; (e) US$5,000; (f) US$1,300.
Applications: by 1 August, to the above address.

2038 Moscow Power Engineering Institute [MPEI]

Krasnokazarmennay, 14
111250 Moscow
Tel: +7 095 362 56 45
Fax: +7 095 362 89 18
Web: http://www.mpei.ac.ru
e-mail: universe@mpei.ru

Undergraduate, Graduate and Postgraduate Programmes

Study Domains: electricity and electronics, engineering, mathematics, mechanical engineering, physics, technology.
Programmes: Undergraduate, Graduate and Postgraduate Programmes leading to (a) Bachelor's, (b) Master's, (c) PhD and (d) Doctor of Science; in automated manufacturing process and automatic control systems, computer science and engineering, mechanics, instrumentation technology, applied mathematics and informatics, radio engineering, heat power engineering, equipment and computer integrated manufacturing processes in mechanical engineering, electrical power engineering, electrical engineering, electromechanics, electronics and microelectronics, power engineering industry.
Open to: candidates holding a secondary-school certificate; entrance examination and personal interview required.
Duration: (a) 4 years, (b) 2 years, (c) and (d) 3 years; courses begin in September.
Fees: tuition fees: (a) from US$1,700-$3,500, depending on the programme chosen; (b), (c), (d) from US$2,500-$4,000 depending on the fields.
Languages: Russian and English (for computer sciences only).
Applications: (a) and (b) by 15 August; (c) and (d) any time; for information about (a) and (b) contact Ferid Ismailov: tel./fax +7 095 362 7318; for (c) and (d) contact Vladimir Sasin: tel./fax +7 095 362 7609; email: iudek@mpei.ru.

2039 Moscow State Academy of Fine Chemical Technology [MSAFCT]

Vernadsky Avenue 86
117571 Moscow
Tel: +7 095 437 3527
Fax: +7 095 430 7983

Undergraduate, Graduate Programmes

Study Domains: chemistry, ecology, environment, management, technology.
Programmes: (a) Bachelor's in chemistry, chemical technology and biotechnology, material science and technology of new materials, management, environment protection; (b) Master's in chemistry and technology of: main organic synthesis products, fine organic synthesis products, combustible materials, carbon composite materials, high

molecular compounds, rare elements and materials based on them; technology of: plastic and elastomer processing, polymer composite materials, rubber, photo materials and magnet carriers, semiconductors and electronic material techniques; biotechnology, main processes of chemical production and chemical cybernetics, monitoring and evaluation of effects on the environment, physics and technology of materials and components, management; (c) Diploma programmes in: chemical technology of organic substances, fuel and carbon materials, high molecular compounds, photo materials and magnet carriers, rare elements and materials based on them; biotechnology, plastic and elastomer processing, composites and powder metallurgy, physics and technology of electronic materials and components; (d) Postgraduate; (e) Doctoral courses in all above-mentioned specialities; (f) 2-semester preliminary course in Russian and/or mathematics, physics and chemistry.
Open to: international students with a certified education transcript, having signed a contract and passed an interview in Russian; minimum Russian language preparation when necessary, updating in mathematics, physics and chemistry required; a list of scientific publications and a thesis topic on proposed research subject (for postgraduate courses or research programmes) to be submitted.
Duration: (a) 4 years; (b) 2 years; (c) 5½ years; (d) and (e) 3 years; (f) 1 year.
Fees: (approximate figures) yearly: (a) US$1,500-$2,000; (b) and (c) US$2,000; (d) US$2,500-$3,000; (e) US$2,500-$5,000; (f) US$1,000-$1,800.
Applications: by 1 August, to the above address.

2040 Moscow State Academy of Food Industry [MSAFP]
Volokolamskoe shosse 11
125080 Moscow
Tel: +7 095 158 7201
Fax: +7 095 158 0371
Web: http://www.msafp.ac.ru

⌂ Undergraduate, Graduate Programmes / Food Industry

Study Domains: agriculture, economy, food, food industry, management.
Programmes: (a) Bachelor's; (b) Master's; (c) Engineer Diploma; (d) Postgraduate; (e) Doctoral level courses in technology of baking, confectionery, macaroni, food concentrates, sugar and sugar substances, brewing and wine industries, grain storage and processing; biotechnology, automation of technological processes of production, food processing machines, bookkeeping, analysis and control in economic activities, economy and management in agriculture; (f) Preparatory course of Russian language; (g) Study at the Russian Language Centre (board and cultural programme included).
Open to: nationals of any country with a secondary-school certificate; entrance interview in Russian and preliminary language study required.
Duration: (a) 4 years; (b) and (f) 2 years; (c) 1 year; (d) and (e) 3 years; (g) 1 or 2 years.
Fees: yearly: (a) US$1,800-$2,500; (b) and (c) US$2,000-$2,500; (d) US$2,500-$3,000; (e) US$3,000-$4,000; (f) US$1,200; (g) US$500-$800; (for Viet Nam and for China: US$1,200).
Applications: by 1 August, to the above address.

2041 Moscow State Academy of Geological Prospecting
Mekluho-Maklai Street 23
117873 Moscow
Tel: +7 095 433 5633
Fax: +7 095 433 4144

⌂ Undergraduate, Graduate Programmes / Geology

Study Domains: engineering, geology, hydrology, physics.
Programmes: Courses in folk art, choreography, performing art, singing, music, musical variety art, art directing, culturology, organization of cultural recreation programmes, organization and economics of the social cultural sphere, sociology of culture, film and video runs, history of culture, ethics and aesthetics, social pedagogy, organizing family leisure, social activity, social and cultural

activity, scientific information systems, librarianship and bibliography, museum science, protection of cultural and historical monuments, Russian language instruction, Russian studies.
Open to: candidates of all countries with a secondary-school certificate; preparatory course Russian language skills required.
Duration: (a) 4 years; (b) 5 years; (c) and (d) 3 years; (e) 8 months.
Fees: (approximate figures) yearly: (a) and (b) US$1,200-$1,800; (c) US$2,500; (d) US$5,000; (e) US$1,300.
Applications: by: (a) to (d) 1 September; (e) 15 November; to the above address.

2042 Moscow State Academy of Instrumentation Technology and Informatics [MGPI]
20 Stromynka
107846 Moscow
Tel: +7 095 268 0101
Fax: +7 095 268 0060

⌂ Undergraduate, Graduate Programmes / Technological Studies

Study Domains: applied sciences, computer science, engineering, information science, mathematics, mechanical engineering.
Programmes: (a) Bachelor's; (b) Master's; (c) Diploma; (d) Postgraduate; (e) Doctorate courses in applied mathematics, instrument engineering, biotechnical and medical apparatus and systems, automation devices and control systems, computer devices, complexes, systems and networks, automated systems of information processing, systems of automatic projecting; (f) Russian language preparatory courses.
Open to: candidates of any country with the appropriate education certificates, having passed an interview in the Russian language; preparatory Russian language studies required.
Duration: (a) 4 years; (b) 2 years; (c) 1 year (after Bachelor's degree); (d) and (e) 3 years; (f) 1 year.
Fees: (approximate figures) yearly: (a) US$1,200-$2,500; (b) US$1,500-$3,500; (c) US$1,800-$2,000; (d) US$2,000-$4,000; (e) US$4,000; (f) US$800-$1,000.
Applications: by 15 August, to the above address.

2043 Moscow State Academy of Printing [MSAP]
Prjanishnikova 2A
127550 Moscow
Tel: +7 095 976 1470
Fax: +7 095 976 0635

⌂ Undergraduate, Graduate Programmes / Publishing Technology

Study Domains: book development and production, ecology, environment, graphic arts, management, photography, publishing, technical education.
Programmes: (a) Bachelor's degree; (b) Expert Diploma; (c) Master's degree; (d) postgraduate courses in photo techniques, electronic editing of printed texts and pictures, special printing processes, printing control and industrial ecology, automated control systems for printing technology and flexible production systems, printing economy and planning, economy and book trade management, publishing trade and editing, editing scientific and technical information, graphic design in printing production; (e) Russian language preparatory courses; (f) Courses for training Russian language interpreters/teachers, as well as instruction in Russian language for foreign students.
Open to: international students with a secondary-school certificate; preparatory Russian language classes, entrance examinations and interview required.
Duration: (a) 4 years; (b) 1 year and 10 months; (c) 2 years; (d) 3 years; (e) 1 year; (f) 2 to 3 years.
Fees: yearly: (a) US$1,200; (b) US$1,200-$1,400; (c) US$1,400-$1,600; (d) US$1,500-$2,000; (e) US$1,000.
Applications: by 25 August, to the above address.

2044 Moscow State Academy of Veterinary Medicine and Biotechnology ' K.I. Skryabin' [MSAVMB]
23 Academica Skryabina Street
109472 Moscow
Tel: +7 095 377 4939
Fax: +7 095 377 4939
Web: http://www.mgavm.ru
e-mail: rector@mgavm.ru

📖 **Undergraduate, Graduate, Postgraduate Programmes**

Study Domains: biochemistry, biology, biophysics, cattle breeding, food industry, genetics, Russian, special education, veterinary medicine, veterinary sciences.
Programmes: Undergraduate, graduate and postgraduate programmes leading to Bachelor's, Master's, Ph.D. and doctorate degrees; 1 to 2 year programme of preparatory Russian language courses.
Description: courses offered at the faculties of: veterinary medicine, genetics, breeding and biotechnology in animal husbandry, veterinary biology, commodity expertise, marketing and biotechnology of food and goods of animal origin.
Open to: candidates of any nationality holding a secondary-school certificate.
Duration: 5 years beginning in September.
Fees: tuition fees: US$2,500 per year; preparatory Russian language courses: US$1,200 per year.
Applications: by 1 September to the above address; for further information contact: International Students Office tel./fax +7 095 377 8936/6524; email: rector@mgavm.ru.

2045 Moscow State Agroengineering University 'V.P. Goryachkin' [MSAU]
Timiryazevskaya Street 58
127 550 Moscow
Tel: +7-095-976-3437
Fax: +7-095-976-7874
e-mail: v.chumakov@relcom.ru

📖 **Engineering Programme**

Study Domains: agriculture, energy, engineering, mechanical engineering, rural development, teacher education, technical education, vocational training.
Programmes: Programme of courses in agricultural engineering, agricultural machinery, technology, education, economics.

2046 Moscow State Industrial University [MSIU]
Avtozavodskaya Street 16
109068 Moscow
Tel: +7 095 275 4537
Web: http://ww.msiu.ru

📖 **Undergraduate, Graduate Programmes / Engineering**

Study Domains: computer science, economy, law, management, mechanical engineering, technical education.
Programmes: (a) Undergraduate; (b) Graduate; (c) Engineering Graduate; (d) Postgraduate; (e) Doctor's courses in economics and management in machine building, machine building engineering, metal cutting and machine tools, foundry engineering and machinery, pressing engineering and machinery, welding engineering and machinery, material studies for machine building, internal combustion engines, designing motor vehicles and tractors, automation of working processes and manufacturing, software for computers and automated systems, law; (f) Russian language preparatory department.
Open to: candidates of any country with a secondary-school certificate, having passed the entrance examination and an interview in Russian; preparatory Russian language study required.
Duration: (a) 4 years; (b) 2 years (after Bachelor's degree); (c) 1 year (after Bachelor's degree); (d) and (e) 3 years; (f) 1 year.

Fees: (approximate figures) yearly: (a) US$1,600-$2,400; (b) US$1,800-$2,700; (c) US$3,000; (d) US$2,500-$5,000; (e) US$6,000-$8,200; (f) US$1,000.
Applications: by 1 August, to the above address.

2047 Moscow State Institute of Automobile and Highway Engineering [MADI]
64 Leningradskiy pr
125829 Moscow GSP-47
Tel: +7 095 1516 412
Fax: +7 095 1518 965
Web: http://www.madi.ru
e-mail: info@madi.ru

📖 **Undergraduate, Graduate Programmes / Engineering**

Study Domains: civil engineering, energy, engineering, industrial technology, technology, telecommunications.
Programmes: Programme of courses leading to: (a) B.Sc.; (b) M.Sc.; (c) D.Engineer; (d) Ph.D.; (e) D.Sc.
Description: hoisting and road-building machines and equipment, automobiles and automobile services, highway and airport engineering, bridges and vehicular traffic tunnels, economics and management in highway engineering, transportation economics and management, computer-integrated manufacturing processes, traffic engineering and administration, electrical equipment of automobiles and tractors, internal combustion engines.
Open to: candidates of all nationalities with secondary-school certificate.
Fees: (approximate figures): (a) 4 years; (b) and (c) 5 years; (d) and (e) 3 years. Fees: preliminary course, US$1,500-$1,800; (a) US$1,800-$2,000; (b) and (c) US$2,000-$2,500; (d) and (e) US$3,500-$5,000.
Applications: further information at the above address.

2048 Moscow State Institute of Electronic Engineering (Technical University) [MIET]
MIET, International Relations
Solnechnaya Alleya Str.
103498 Moscow
Tel: +7 095 534 0264
Fax: +7 095 530 5449
Web: http://www.miee.ru/english/a8.html
e-mail: ird@adm.miee.ru

📖 **Undergraduate, Graduate Programmes / Electronic Engineering**

Study Domains: computer science, electricity and electronics, telecommunications.
Programmes: (a) Bachelor's; (b) Master's; (c) Engineering Diploma; (d) Postgraduate; (e) Doctorate courses in microelectronics, management, business, informatics and telecommunication; preparatory study of the Russian language available.
Open to: candidates of any country with the corresponding education certificate and a certificate on completion of the Russian language course, having signed a contract and passed an interview in Russian.
Duration: (a) 4 years; (b) 6-1/2 years; (c) 5 years; (d) 3 years (full-time) and 4 years (by correspondence); (e) 3 years.
Applications: by 1 August, to the above address.

2049 Moscow State Institute of Electronics and Mathematics (Technical University)
B. Trekchsvyatitelsky per. 3/12
109028 Moscow
Tel: +7 095 207 7830
Web: http://www.miem.edu.ru

📖 **Undergraduate, Graduate Programmes / Technological Studies**

Study Domains: applied sciences, computer science, economy, electricity and electronics, management, mathematics, mechanical engineering, radiology, technical education, technology.
Programmes: (a) Engineer Diploma; (b) Postgraduate; (c)

Doctoral programmes in electronics, informatics and telecommunication, automatics and computer engineering, mathematics; (d) Russian language preparatory course.
Open to: candidates of any country with a secondary-school certificate; written and oral entrance examination; Russian language proficiency required; Russian language preparatory studies recommended.
Duration: (a) 5-1/2 years; (b) and (c) 3 years; (d) 1 year.
Fees: yearly: (a) US$1,300; (b) US$2,500; (c) US$5,000; (d) US$1,300.
Applications: by 1 August, at the above address.

2050 Moscow State Institute of Radio Engineering, Electronics and Automation (Technical University)
78 Vernadsky Avenue
117454 Moscow
Tel: +7 095 433 0066
Fax: +7 095 434 8665

⌨ Undergraduate, Graduate Programmes / Radio Engineering

Study Domains: applied sciences, computer science, electricity and electronics, information science, mathematics, physics, radiology.
Programmes: (a) Bachelor's; (b) Master's; (c) Postgraduate; (d) Doctoral programme in computers, computer systems and networks, production and data control systems, hardware design and technology and other specialities upon a request and mutual agreement; (e) Preparatory department in Russian, mathematics and physics.
Open to: Candidates of any country with appropriate education certificate, having passed entrance examinations and interview in Russian; preparatory Russian language studies required.
Duration: (a) 4 years; (b) 5-1/2 years; (c) and (d) 3 years; (e) 1 year.
Fees: yearly: (a) and (b) US$2,000-$3,000; (c) and (d) US$3,000-$5,000; (e) US$1,200.
Applications: (a), (b) by 1 August and (e) by 15 October, to the above address.

2051 Moscow State Technical University of Civil Aviation [MSTUCA]
Kronshtadtskiy Boulevard 20
A-493 GSP-3
125993 Moscow
Tel: +7 095 459 0721
Fax: +7 095 458 7626
Web: http://www.mstuca.ru
e-mail: dfct@mstuca.ru

⌨ Undergraduate, Graduate, PhD Programmes / Civil Aviation

Study Domains: aviation, aeronautics, computer science.
Programmes: (a) Bachelor's, (b) Master's, (c) Engineering Diploma, (d) Ph.D.
Open to: candidates of any country with a secondary-school certificate, having passed examinations in mathematics, physics and Russian; Russian language preparation may be required.
Duration: (a) 4 years; (b) 6 years; (c) 5-51/2 years; (d) 3 years on full-time basis, 4 years on part-time basis.
Fees: (a), (b) and (c), from US$2,700-$3,000 per year including dormitory accommodation and medical insurance; (d) US$3,500 per year; preparatory course US$2,000.
Languages: Russian.
Applications: (a) (b) and (c) by 15 June; (d) at any time; preparatory course, by 30 October.

2052 Moscow State Technological University 'Stankin' [MSTU]
3a Vadkovski per.
101472 Moscow
Tel: +7 095 972 9406
Fax: +7 095 972 6919
Web: http://www.stankin.ru

⌨ Undergraduate, Graduate Programmes / Technological Studies

Study Domains: mechanical engineering.
Programmes: (a) Bachelor's; (b) Master's; (c) Engineering Diploma; (d) postgraduate; (e) Doctorate programmes in machine tools and machine-tool complexes construction, automated manufacturing tool systems, automated machine-tool complexes with numeric programme control, numeric programme control of machine tools and complexes, mechanical engineering technology, automated manufacturing technology, automated systems of manufacturing technological preparation, cutting machinery in automated manufacturing, technological informatics of automated machine building manufacturing, assembly manufacturing automation, electronic hydropneumatic systems of automated manufacturing, CAD/CAM systems in mechanical engineering, information and measuring systems, robotic systems control, computer mechatronic systems, production quality control and management, construction of automated complexes and pressure metals machining systems, low waste processes of plastic metals machining, automated systems of design and manufacturing of tooling for plastic machining; (f) Special computer courses of Russian language study for technical terms and at different levels.
Open to: candidates of any country with a secondary-school-leaving certificate, having signed a contract; preparatory Russian language study advised.
Duration: (a) 4 years; (b), (d) and (e) 3 years (after Bachelor' degree); (c) 2 years (after Bachelor's degree).
Fees: approximate figures) yearly: (a) US$1,800-$2,000; (b) US$2,300-$2,500; (c) US$2,000-$2,300; (d) US$2,500-$3,500; (e) US$4,000-$5,000.
Applications: by 1 September, to the above address.

2053 Moscow State University 'M.V. Lomonosov' [LMSU]
Lenin Hills
119899 Moscow
Tel: +7 095 939 1000
Fax: +7 095 939 0126
Web: http://www.msu.ru
e-mail: info@rector.msu.ru

⌨ Undergraduate, Graduate Programmes

Study Domains: all major fields.
Programmes: (a) Bachelor's; (b) Master's; (c) Postgraduate; (d) Doctor's courses in mathematics, mechanics, computational mathematics and cybernetics, physics, astronomy, chemistry, biology, soil science, geology, geography, medicine, philosophy, history, philology, sociology, psychology, economics, law, journalism, foreign languages, Asian and African studies; (e) Russian language preparatory department leading to a translator's certificate.
Open to: candidates of any country with a secondary-school leaving certificate; entrance colloquium to determine knowledge of profile subjects and of the Russian language; Russian language preparatory course required.
Duration: (a) 4 years; (b) 5 years; (c) and (d) 3 years; (e) 1 year.
Fees: yearly: (a) and (b) US$2,500 to US$4,500; (c) US$5,000 to US$6,000; (d) US$6,000 to US$7,000; (e) US$1,500 to US$3,000.
Applications: by 15 September, to the above address.

2054 Moscow State University of Civil Engineering
26 Yaroslavskoye shosse
129337 Moscow
Tel: +7 095 1833 774
Fax: +7 095 1830 492
e-mail: hpc@pochtampt.ru

⌨ Undergraduate, Graduate Programmes / Civil Engineering

Study Domains: civil engineering, engineering.
Programmes: Programme of courses leading to: (a) B.Sc.; (b) M.Sc.; (c) D.Engineer; (d) Ph.D.; (e) D.Sc. in the Faculties of Industrial and Civil Engineering; Heat Power Construction; Hydrotechnical construction; Urban Infrastructure Engineering; Construction Technology; Heat and Gas Supply and Ventilation; Water Supply and Sewage; Construction Planning, Economics and management.

Open to: candidates of any nationality holding a secondary-school leaving certificate and proficient in Russian.
Duration: (a) 4 years; (b) 6 years; (c) 5 years; (d) and (e) 3 years.
Fees: preliminary course: US$2,000; (a) to (c) US$2,000-$3,000 depending on year of study; (d) US$4,000.
Applications: further information at the address above.

2055 Moscow State University of Culture and Arts [MSIOC]
Bibliotechnaya Street 7
141400 Khimki-6
Tel: +7 095 570 3133
Fax: +7 095 570 0444

📖 Undergraduate, Graduate Programmes

Study Domains: arts, cultural studies, folklore, history, library science, music and musicology, recreation and leisure, sociology.
Programmes: courses in folk art, choreography, performing art, singing, music, musical variety art, art directing, culturology, organization of cultural recreation programmes, organization and economics of the social cultural sphere, sociology of culture, film and video runs, history of culture, ethics and aesthetics, social pedagogy, organizing family leisure, social activity, social and cultural activity, scientific information systems, librarianship and bibliography, museum science, protection of cultural and historical monuments, Russian language instruction, Russian studies.
Open to: candidates of any country with certified attestation of secondary-school certificate; no Russian language proficiency required; language classes are recommended.
Duration: Magister in arts and pedagogical sciences: 4 years; postgraduate classes: 3 years if fluent in Russian, otherwise 4 years; Doctorate: 3 years if fluent in Russian.
Fees: minimum US$2,000 per year.
Applications: from 5 August to 1 October, to the above address.

2056 Moscow State University of Design and Technology
Sadovnicheskaya Street 33
113806 Moscow
Tel: +7 095 951 5801
Fax: +7 095 953 0297

📖 Undergraduate, Graduate Programmes / Industrial Engineering

Study Domains: computer science, management, Russian, technology, textile industry.
Programmes: (a) Bachelor's; (b) Master's; (c) Engineer Diploma; (d) Postgraduate; (e) Doctor's courses in leather and clothing goods technology and design, plastic and elastomers processing technology, leather and fur technology, management, textile and light industry machines and repair services, systems of computer-aided design, automatization of technological processes and manufacturing; (f) Russian language preparatory department and courses for training Russian language interpreters/teachers.
Open to: candidates of any country with a secondary-school certificate; preliminary Russian language instruction and entrance interview required.
Duration: (a) 4 years; (b) 2 years; (c) and (f) 1 year; (d) and (e) 3 years.
Fees: yearly: (a) US$1,500; (b) US$1,700; (c) US$2,500; (d) US$3,000; (e) US$5,000; (f) US$1,200.
Applications: by 1 July, to the above address.

2057 Moscow State University of Economics, Statistics and Informatics [MESI]
7 Nezhinskaya Street
119501 Moscow
Tel: +7 095 4426 577
Fax: +7 095 4426 558
e-mail: office@rector.mesi.ru

📖 Undergraduate, Graduate Programmes / Statistics

Study Domains: accounting, economic and commercial sciences, economy, finance, information science, international business, international relations, political economy, social sciences, statistics.
Programmes: (a) Bachelor's; (b) Master's; (c) Higher Diploma Professional; (d) Postgraduate; (e) Doctor's courses in statistics, information systems in economics, world economics (international information business), management, trade, finance, accounting, hotel management and tourism, applied mathematics (computer science and software engineering, operation research in economics); (f) Preparatory study of Russian and short-term commercial language courses.
Open to: candidates of any country with a secondary-education certificate, having passed an oral test in speciality and Russian language; preparatory Russian language study required with no minimum requirements for preparatory course admission.
Duration: (a) 4 years; (b) 2 years (after bachelorship); (c) 5 years; (d) and (e) 3 years; (f) 1 year.
Fees: (approximate figures) yearly: (a) and (c) US$1,500-$2,500; (b) US$1,700-$2,700; (d) US$2,000-$2,500; (e) US$3,500, (f) US$1,200-$1,500.
Applications: (a) to (e) by 1 August and (f) by 1 October, to the above address.

2058 Moscow State University of Environmental Engineering [MCACE]
Staraya Basmannaya Street 21/4
107884 Moscow
Tel: +7 095 267 0701/ 431 5909
Fax: +7 095 261 9612
e-mail: msace@rinet.ru

📖 Undergraduate, Graduate Programmes / Chemical Engineering

Study Domains: chemical engineering, chemical industry, electricity and electronics, pharmacy and pharmacology.
Programmes: (a) B.Eng.; (b) M.Sc.; (c) Diploma Certified Engineer; (d) Ph.D.Eng.; (e) Ph.D.Eng. (individually) courses in: engineering, humanities and engineering economics, chemical and biological engineering, cryogenic engineering, chemical apparatus manufacturing, engineering cybernetics; (f) preliminary classes in Russian, mathematics, physics, chemistry, drawing; (g) courses in Russian language teachers-interpreters training.
Open to: nationals of any country, with a secondary-school certificate, having passed entry examinations or interview or preliminary department-leaving examinations; preliminary Russian language courses requested.
Duration: (a) 4 years; (b) 2 years; (c) 1 year after B. Eng.; (d) and (g) 3 years; (f) 1 year.
Fees: yearly: (a) US$1,200-$2,000; (b) US$1,500-$2,200; (c) US$1,500-$2,000; (d) US$2,500-$3,000; (e) US$3,500; (f) US$1,300; (g) US$1,500.
Applications: by 1 August, to the above address.

2059 Moscow State University of Mining Engineering [MSMU]
Leninsky Prospect 6
117935 Moscow
Tel: +7 095 236 9505
Fax: +7 095 237 3163

📖 Undergraduate, Graduate Programmes / Mining Engineering

Study Domains: computer science, economy, electricity and electronics, energy, engineering, management, mechanical engineering.
Programmes: Programme of courses leading to: (a) B.Sc.; (b) M.Sc.; (c) D. Engineer; (d) Ph.D.; (e) D.Sc. in the faculties of Ferrous Metals and Alloys; Technology; Physics and Chemistry; Semiconductor Materials and Instruments; Informatics and Economics; Metallurgy and Non-Ferrous Metals.
Open to: candidates of any country with a secondary-school certificate or equivalent, having passed Russian language oral test and mathematics, physics;

minimum requirements of Russian language preparatory course recommended.
Duration: (a) 4 years; (b) 1 year (after Bachelor's degree); (c) 2 years (after Bachelor's degree); (d) and (e) 3 years; (f) 1 to 2 years.
Fees: yearly: (a) US$1,500-$2,000; (b) US$1,800-$2,500; (c) US$1,800-$2,500; (d) US$2,000-$2,600; (e) US$4,000.
Applications: by 20 August, to the above address.

2060 Moscow State University of Railway Communications [MSUOC]
15 Obrastsova A-55
101475 Moscow
Tel: +7 095 281 3177
Fax: +7 095 281 1340

📖 Undergraduate, Graduate Programmes / Communications
Study Domains: building industry, computer science, economic and commercial sciences, transport.
Programmes: (b) Certified Engineer; (c) Master's; (d) Postgraduate; (e) Doctor's courses in construction, information and computer engineering, economics (accounting and production process control), production management, satellite communication systems in railway transport; (f) Russian Language Department and a language laboratory.
Open to: candidates of any country with a secondary-school certificate or equivalent and the Russian language preparatory certificate, with satisfactory results.
Duration: (a) 4 years; (b) 5 years; (c) 6 years; (d) and (e) 3 to 4 years.
Applications: by 25 August, to the above address.

2061 Moscow University Touro
Podsosenskij per. 20/12
10506 Moskva
Tel: +7(095) 917-33-11
Fax: +7(095) 917-53-48
Web: http://www.touro.ru

☛ Scholarship
Scholarships: Stacey Murashkovsky Scholarship.
Subjects: All major fields.
Open to: Students from any nationality, aged between 17 to 21 years old.
Duration: 1 year, renewable.
Value: US$3,000.
Applications: By December; contact pavlovas@touro.ru for further details.

2062 Nizhni Novgorod State Medical Academy [NNSMA]
10/1, Minin and Pozharsky Square
603005 Nizhni Novgorod
Tel: +7 8312 390 943
Fax: +7 8312 390 943/199 820
Web: http://www.n-nov.mednet.com
e-mail: nnsma@sandy.ru

📖 Medical Studies
Study Domains: medicine, paediatrics, pharmacy and pharmacology, preventive medicine.
Programmes: Specialist's and Ph.D. diplomas in general medicine, paediatrics, pharmacy, preventive medicine; stomatology.
Open to: candidates of all nationalities meeting academic, financial, linguistic and health requirements.
Academic requirements: PET-Test, chemistry, biology and physics; English proficiency required.
Fees: tuition: US$1,350-$2,700; estimated living costs: US$3,000 per year.
Languages: Russian and English.
Applications: by 1 October to above address.

2063 Nizhni Novgorod State University [NNSU]
23 Gagarin Avenue
603600 Nizhni Novgorod
Tel: +7 8312 658 490
Fax: +7 8312 658 592
Web: http://www.unn.ac.ru
e-mail: rector@nnucnit.unn.ac.ru

📖 Undergraduate, Graduate Programmes
Study Domains: applied sciences, biology, chemistry, economy, history, law, management, mathematics, philology, physics.
Programmes: (a) Bachelor of Arts/Science; (b) Master of Arts/Science; (c) Diploma; (d) Postgraduate courses in mathematics, applied mathematics and computer science, mechanics, physics, solid state physics, chemistry, biology, biophysics, history, Russian language and literature, economics, and production management, economics and social planning, economics and management of research and development, physics and production engineering of electronic materials and components, microelectronics and semiconductors, radiophysics and electronics, chemistry and chemical engineering of electronic materials, scientific and technical information systems, law, sociology and social work, politology, journalism; (e) Preparatory Russian language courses.
Open to: candidates of any country with secondary school or university certificates or diplomas; interview in Russian; preparatory Russian language skills (oral and comprehension) required.
Duration: (a) 4 years; (b) 6 years; (c) 5 years; (d) 3 or 4 years.
Fees: (approximate figures) yearly: (a) US$3,000; (b) US$3,500; (c) US$3,000; (d) US$4,000.
Applications: by 1 August, to the above address.

2064 Nizhni Novgorod State University of Architecture and Civil Engineering [NNSUACE]
65 Llyinskaya ul.,
603095 Nizhni Novgorod
Tel: +7 8312 34 03 91
Fax: +7 8312 33 73 66
Web: http://www.ngasu.sci-nnov.ru/indexeng.php
e-mail: srec@ngasu.sci-nnov.ru

📖 Undergraduate, Graduate Programmes
Study Domains: architecture, building industry, business, civil engineering, ecology, environment, education, engineering, geodesy, hydrology, industrial technology, laboratory techniques, mathematics, natural resources, physics, recreation and leisure, Russian, sciences, social sciences, tourism, hotel and catering management, transport, urbanism.
Programmes: Bachelor's, Master's, Ph.D. and specialist's diplomas in (a) thermal engineering; (b) architecture; (c) environmental engineering; (d) civil engineering; (e) humanities and socio-economic sciences (f) standardization and automation.
Description: (a) industrial heat engineering; heat and gas supply; air conditioning and cooling systems; ventilation; (b) architectural design; restoration and reconstruction of architectural monuments; industrial and interior design; garden and landscape architecture; (c) nature management; industrial, occupational and public safety; land and real estate cadastre; (d) industrial, public and residential building construction; urban development and public utilities; hydraulic engineering; public water supply and sewerage; heat and gas supply, ventilation; road and transport engineering; (e) economics and industrial management; industrial management; marketing; accountancy and audit; law; culture studies; social and cultural services and tourism; (f) standardization and certification; automation of industrial processes; information systems technologies.
Fees: tuition: US$1,300-$3,000; estimated living costs: US$300 per year.
Applications: 20 August to Rector of the University at the above address.

2065 North Caucasus State Institute of Arts [NCSIA]

1 Lenin Av.
360030 Nalchik Kabardino-Balkar
Tel: +7 8662 470 089
Fax: +7 8662 470 088
e-mail: skgii@yandex.ru

📖 Graduate Programmes

Study Domains: administration, advertising, American studies, anthropology, archaeology, architecture, art history, arts, business, cinematography, classical studies, decorative arts, economy, education, ethnology, fine arts, languages, liberal arts, management, physical education, psychology, social sciences, sociology, special education, teacher education, theology, religion, tourism, hotel and catering management.
Programmes: Master's degrees in education, arts, fine arts, languages, liberal arts, theology, business, management, sociology, architecture.
Open to: candidates holding secondary school certificate; admission test; proficiency in Russian required.
Duration: 5 years; courses begin 1 September.
Fees: tuition fees US$1,000-$3,000 per year; living costs US$100 per month.
Financial assistance: financial assistance available.
Languages: Russian.
Applications: by 15 July; contact skgii@yandex.ru for further information.

2066 North West State Technical University [NWSTU]

5, Millionnaya street
191 186 Saint Petersburg
Tel: +7 812 110 6262
Fax: +7 812 311 6016
Web: http://www.nwpi.ru
e-mail: office@nwpi.ru

📖 Undergraduate, Graduate, Postgraduate Programmes

Study Domains: administration, applied sciences, business, business administration, chemical engineering, chemical industry, chemistry, civil engineering, communication, computer science, design, ecology, environment, economic and commercial sciences, electricity and electronics, energy, engineering, English, industrial design, industrial technology, industry and commerce, information science, management, marketing, mathematics, mechanical engineering, metallurgy, oceanography, optics, Russian, sciences, technical education, technology, telecommunications, vocational training.
Programmes: Bachelor's; Master's; Ph.D. degrees in engineering; business administration.
Duration: 4 to 6 years; also Summer course.
Fees: tuition fees US$1,000 per year; living costs US$200 per month.
Languages: Russian and English.
Applications: rolling admission; contact ivanovna@id.nwpi.ru for further details.

2067 Novocherkassk State Technical University

132 Prosveshcheniya Street
346400 Novocherkassk
Tel: +7 86 3522 3344
Fax: +7 86 3522 8463
Web: http://nstu.rnd.runnet.ru
e-mail: root@npi.microel.sensor.zgzad.su

📖 Undergraduate, Graduate, Postgraduate Programmes

Study Domains: chemistry, electricity and electronics, engineering, geology, mechanical engineering, technology.
Programmes: (a) Bachelor's; (b) Graduate Engineer's Diploma; (c) Postgraduate; (d) Doctor's courses in the following fields: mining geology, chemistry, civil engineering, power engineering, humanities and social economic education, mechanical engineering, electrical engineering, applied robotics and machine building, systems engineering and robotics; (e) Russian courses at the Preparatory Department for the Russian language study; (f)

Special courses for improving and mastering Russian.
Open to: candidates of any country with a secondary-school certificate or equivalent, having passed an interview in Russian; preparatory Russian language study required.
Held: NSTU includes 2 branches in Shakhty and Volgodonsk, 17 faculties, as well as 2 educational training departments in Kamensk and Rostov-na-Donu.
Duration: (a) 4 years; (b) 5 years; (c) 3 years; (d) 2 years; (e) 1 year; (f) 1 to 6 months.
Fees: yearly: (a) US$900-$1,000; (b) US$1,200-$1,500; (c) US$2,000-$2,500; (d) US$3,000-$3,500; (e) US$800-$1,200; (f) US$500-$700.
Applications: by 1 September, to the above address.

2068 Novorossiysk State Maritime Academy [NSMA]

93, prospect Lenina
353918 Novorossiysk, Krasnodar Region
Tel: +7 86134 30393
Fax: +7 86134 32633
Web: http://www.nsma.ru
e-mail: studdep@nsma.ru

📖 Specialist's Diploma / Maritime Engineering

Study Domains: electricity and electronics, engineering, mechanical engineering, shipbuilding.
Programmes: Specialist's Diploma in maritime engineering, navigation, radio engineering and electronics.
Open to: candidates meeting academic and linguistic requirements.
Duration: 3 to 6 years; courses begin 1 September.
Languages: Russian and English.

2069 Novosibirsk State Agrarian University [NSAU]

160 Dobrolubova Street
630 039 Novosibirsk
Tel: +7 3832 673 811
Fax: +7 3832 673 811
Web: http://www.nsau.edu.ru
e-mail: rector@nsau.edu.ru

📖 Graduate Programmes

Study Domains: agriculture, agronomic sciences, biology, business, cattle breeding, civil engineering, computer science, earth science, education, engineering, fisheries, genetics, horticulture, industrial technology, law, management, mechanical engineering, natural resources, rural development, sciences, transport, veterinary medicine, veterinary sciences.
Programmes: Specialist, Magistr in Agriculture, Kandidat Nauk; Doktor Nauk programmes in agrarian sciences.
Open to: candidates of all nationalities; no age restrictions.
Academic requirements: Russian language examination; others according to specialization.
Duration: 5 years; courses begin on 1 September.
Fees: yearly tuition: US$1,500-$2,000; estimated yearly living costs: US$2,000.
Languages: Russian.
Applications: 15 July.

2070 Novosibirsk State Technical University [NSTU]

20, K. Marx Avenue
630092 Novosibirsk
Tel: +7 3832 465 001/460 511
Fax: +7 3832 460 200
Web: http://www.nstu.ru
e-mail: rector@nstu.ru

📖 Undergraduate, Graduate Programmes

Study Domains: accounting, aviation, aeronautics, business administration, computer science, ecology, environment, economy, electricity and electronics, energy, finance, food industry, industrial technology, information science, international relations, law, management, mathematics, mechanical engineering, physics, Russian, statistics, tourism, hotel and catering management.
Programmes: Bakalavr, Specialist's, Magistr, Kandidat Nauk, Doktor Nauk diplomas in all major technical fields; Russian courses at the Preparatory Department.

Open to: candidates of any nationality holding a secondary-education certificate and proficient in Russian.
Duration: 4 to 7 years depending on diploma programme; courses from 1 September to 30 June.
Fees: tuition for preparatory Russian courses US$2-$7/hour; estimated living costs US$150-$200 per month.
Applications: 30 March.

2071 Novosibirsk State University [NSU]
Pirogov Street 2
630090 Novosibirsk
Tel: +7-383-339-7378
Fax: +7-383-339-7378
Web: http://www.nsu.ru/english
e-mail: inter@nsu.ru

📖 Undergraduate, Graduate Programmes
Study Domains: biology, chemistry, economy, history, literature and civilization, mathematics, physics, Russian, sociology.
Programmes: (a) Bachelor's; (b) Master's; (c) Postgraduate; (d) Doctoral programmes in mathematics, physics, chemistry, biology, economic cybernetics, sociology, geochemistry, mineralogy and petrography, history, Russian language and literature; (e) Preparatory and intensive Russian language instruction.
Open to: candidates of any country with a secondary-school certificate, having passed the entrance examinations; international students are allowed to study on a contract basis (1 or 2 semesters); entrance interview in Russian and knowledge of English and Russian languages required.
Duration: (a) 4 years; (b) 2 years; (c) and (d) 3 years.
Fees: yearly: (a) US$3,000; (b) US$5,000; (c) US$7,000; (d) US$10,000.
Applications: by 1 August, to the above address.

2072 Omsk State University [OSU]
Pr. Mira, 55a
644077 Omsk
Tel: +7 3812 28 55 81
Fax: +7 3812 28 55 81
Web: http://www.univer.omsk.su/index.htm
e-mail: interdep@univer.omsk.su

📖 Undergraduate Programmes
Study Domains: business, chemistry, computer science, economy, information science, international studies, journalism, languages, law, management, mathematics, physics, psychology, Russian, social sciences, teacher education, theology, religion.
Programmes: Bachelor's and Specialist's diplomas in all major fields.
Open to: candidates of all nationalities meeting academic, linguistic, financial and medical requirements; admission based on documentary evidence of secondary education, and test of Russian as a foreign language and interview required.
Fees: registration: US$30; tuition: US$1,100 per year: estimated living expenses: US$300 per month.
Applications: 15 April.

2073 Peoples' Friendship University of Russia (former Patrice Lumumba University)
6 Miklukho-Maklay Street
117198 Moscow
Tel: +7 095 4346 641
Fax: +7 095 4337 385
e-mail: rector@rudn.ru

📖 Undergraduate, Graduate, Postgraduate Programmes
Study Domains: agriculture, biology, ecology, environment, engineering, history, medicine, philology.
Programmes: Programme of courses leading to: (a) B.Sc.; (b) M.Sc.; (c) Ph.D.; (d) D.Sc. in the Faculties of Engineering; Physico-Mathematical and Natural Sciences; Medicine, Economics and Law; Agriculture; History and Philology; Ecology.

Open to: candidates of any nationality holding a general certificate of education, advanced level, or equivalent and proficient in Russian.
Duration: (a) 4 to 5 years, 6 for Medicine; (b) 2 additional years; (c) and (d) 3 additional years.
Applications: further information at the above address.

2074 Petrozavodsk State University [PSU]
Lenin Street, 33
185640 Petrozavodsk
Tel: +7 8142 71 10 06 / 76 97 71
Fax: +7 8142 71 10 00
Web: http://www.petrsu.ru
e-mail: toivonen@mainpgu.karelia.ru

📖 Undergraduate, Graduate Programmes
Study Domains: agriculture, biology, civil engineering, ecology, environment, economy, forestry, languages, law, mathematics, medicine, paediatrics, philology, physics, political science, Russian.
Programmes: Bachelor's, Master's and Specialist's diplomas in all major fields; Russian language programmes.
Open to: candidates of all nationalities meeting academic, financial, linguistic and medical requirements; Russian language proficiency intermediate level required.
Duration: 4 to 6 years, depending on programme; courses begin 1 September.
Fees: registration: US$60; tuition: US$1,000-$1,300; estimated living costs: US$200 per month.
Applications: by 1 June.

2075 Plekhanov Russian Academy of Economics
36 Stremyaniy Per.
113054 Moscow
Tel: +7 095 2379 247
Fax: +7 095 2379 254
Web: http://www.rea.ru/eng/index.shtml

📖 Undergraduate Programme
Study Domains: economic and commercial sciences, economy, engineering, finance, international business.
Programmes: Programme of studies leading to a Bachelor of Science from the following faculties: Economics, Industrial Economics, Finance and Credit, Engineering Technology, Commodity Studies, Economics Cybernetics, International Economic Relations. Instruction in Russian.
Open to: candidates of all nationalities with secondary-school certificate; proficiency in Russian required.
Duration: 4 to 5 years depending on programme.
Fees: tuition: US$3,000 per year.
Applications: to the International Relations Office; direct tel.:+7 095 2378 517.

2076 Pyatigorsk State Pharmaceutical Academy [PSFA]
11, Prosp.Kalinina
357532 Pyatigorsk
Stavropolsky Region
Tel: +7 87933 94474
Fax: +7 87933 99267
Web: http://www.pgfa.ru
e-mail: patent@pgfa.ru

📖 Graduate Programmes in Pharmacy
Study Domains: botany, computer science, management, pharmacy and pharmacology, technology.
Programmes: M.Sc.; Ph.D., D.Sc. in pharmacy.
Open to: candidates of all nationalities meeting academic, linguistic, financial and medical requirements.
Age limit Max: candidates must be under 35 years of age.
Duration: 6 years; courses begin 1 September.
Fees: registration: US$100; tuition: US$1,200 for preparatory studies and US$2,000 for fundamental course (including living costs).
Languages: Russian.
Applications: by 30 August to above address; contact: Rector Assistant for International Relations: visa@pgfa.ru.

2077 Rostov State Medical University
29 pr. Nakhichevansky
344700 Rostov-on-Don
Tel: +7 8632 652 391
Fax: +7 8632 530 611

📖 **Graduate, Postgraduate Studies**

Study Domains: medicine, paediatrics.
Programmes: Courses of higher education for foreign students in medicine.
Open to: candidates of any nationality holding a secondary-education certificate and proficient in Russian; Russian language courses available.
Duration: (a) Doctor of Medicine: 6 years; (b) postgraduate studies: 3 years; (c) preparatory course: 1 year.
Fees: (a) US$1,800-$2,200 per year; (b) US$3,000-$5,000 per year; (c) US$1,500; probation: US$2,500-$3,500 per year.
Applications: to the address above.

2078 Rostov State Music Conservatory (Academy) 'S.V Rahmaninov'
prosp. Budjennovskij 23
34400 Rostov-on-Don
Tel: +7-8632-623-614
Fax: +7-8632-623-584
Web: http://www.rostcons.ru
e-mail: rostcons@aaanet.ru

📖 **Undergraduate, Graduate Programmes**

Study Domains: music and musicology.

2079 Rostov State Pedagogical University
33 Bolshova Sadovaya Street
344082 Rostov-on-Don
Tel: +7-8632-726-758
Fax: +7-8632-726-758
e-mail: interdept@yandex.ru

📖 **Undergraduate, Graduate, Postgraduate Programmes**

Study Domains: biology, business, chemistry, history, languages, law, management, mathematics, philology, physics, psychology.
Programmes: Programme of courses leading to: (a) Bachelor's; (b) Master's; (c) Postgraduate; (d) Doctoral degree courses in: education technologies, mathematics, physics, biology, chemistry, management, law, business, physical training, foreign languages, Russian philology, history, psychology, art and other specialities for teacher training; (e) Russian language preparatory courses.
Open to: candidates of any nationality holding a secondary-school certificate and passing the entrance examination and a interview in Russian conversation.
Duration: (a) 4 years; (b) 1 to 2 years; (c) and (d) 3 years; (e) 1 to 2 years.
Applications: by 1 July; further information at the above address.

2080 Rostov State University
105 Bolshova Sadovaya Street
344711 Rostov-upon-Don
Tel: +7 8632 226 836
Fax: +7 8632 645 255
Web: http://www.rnd.runnet.ru
e-mail: rec@rsu.rostov-na-donu.su

📖 **Undergraduate, Graduate, Postgraduate Programmes**

Study Domains: biology, chemistry, economy, geography, geology, history, journalism, law, mathematics, philology, philosophy, physics.
Programmes: Programme of courses leading to:(a) B.Sc. and B.A.; (b) M.Sc. and M.A.; (c) D.Engineer; (d) Ph.D.; (e) D.Sc. in the Faculties of Philology and Journalism; History; Mathematics and Applied Mathematics; Law; Physics; Chemistry; Biology and Soil Science; Geology and Geography; Economics; Philosophy; Psychology and Nursing.

Open to: candidates of any nationality holding a secondary-education certificate and proficient in Russian.
Duration: (a) 4 years; (b) and (c) 5 to 6 years; (d) and (e) 3 years.
Fees: foundation course: US$1,400-$1,900; (a) to (c) US$2,000-$2,800 per year.
Applications: further information at the above address.

2081 Rostov State University of Economics [RSUE]
B.Sadovaia Street 69
344077 Rostov-on-Don
Tel: +7 8632 402 123/+7 8632 941 75
Fax: +7 8632 402 123
Web: http://www.rseu.ru
e-mail: sms@rseu.ru

📖 **Undergraduate and Graduate Degree Programmes**

Study Domains: business, economic and commercial sciences, economy, law.
Programmes: B.S.; B.A.; M.S.; M.A.; MBA; DS in economics; Law; Ph.D.
Open to: candidates must be proficient in Russian.
Duration: 3 to 5 years beginning 1 September.
Fees: registration: undergraduate: 1,500 €; graduate: between 2,100-2,500 €; Ph.D.: 3,000 €; M.B.A.: 6,000 €.
Languages: Russian and English.
Applications: apply to: International Cooperation Office Director at above address.

🎓 **Scholarships**

Study Domains: business, economic and commercial sciences, economy, law.
Scholarships: University student scholarships.
Open to: applicants must be between the ages of 18 and 23.
Duration: on a monthly basis per year; offered every year.
Value: 500-2,500 roubles per month.
Applications: apply at any time to the International Cooperation Office Director at above address.

2082 Rostov State University of Transport Communication
2, Narodnogo Opolcheniya
344038 Rostov-on-Don
Tel: +8 8632 450 613
Fax: +8 8632 450 613
Web: http://www.rgups.ru
e-mail: rek@rgups.ru

📖 **Undergraduate Degree Programmes**

Study Domains: accounting, administration, advertising, business, communication, computer science, continuing education, criminology, documentation, economy, electricity and electronics, energy, engineering, finance, history, information science, languages, law, management, marketing, philosophy, political economy, psychology, sciences, social sciences, social work, sociology, technical education.
Programmes: Bachelor's degree in all major fields.
Subjects: training of specialists for national economics, transport communication, law and social work.
Open to: candidates must be proficient n Russian (reading, speaking, writing, listening).
Duration: 5 years beginning 1 September.
Fees: tuition fees: US$1,500; living costs: US$200 per year.
Languages: Russian and English.
Applications: apply by 1 August to the Rector at the above address; contact pri@rgups.ru; tel: +7 8632 726 202.

2083 Russian State Hydrometeorological University [RSHU]
Malookhtinskij Street 98
195196 Saint Petersburg
Tel: +7 812 444 5636
Fax: +7 812 444 6090
Web: http://www.rshu.ru
e-mail: bogush@rshu.ru

Undergraduate, Graduate and Postgraduate Degree Programmes

Study Domains: continuing education, ecology, environment, economy, education, hydrology, information science, meteorology, natural sciences, oceanography, physics, public relations, Russian, summer programmes, tourism, hotel and catering management, vocational training.
Programmes: Bachelor's, Master's, Ph.D. degrees in all major fields.
Description: hydrometeorology.
Duration: 4 to 6 years beginning in September; Summer courses: 7 to 8 weeks.
Fees: tuition fees: US$1,500 per year; living costs: US$200 per month.
Financial assistance: scholarships offered through the World Meteorological Organization's representative in the country.
Languages: Russian.
Applications: apply by 31 August.

Scholarships

Study Domains: education.
Scholarships: Ministry of Education of Russian Federation and World Meteorological Organization.
Duration: 4 to 6 years.
Value: Government offers: US$4,000 per year; WMO offers: US$140 per month.
Applications: apply by 31 August to the above address.

2084 Russian State Technological University [MATI]

Orshanskaya Street, 3
121552 Moscow
Tel: +7 095 141 1940
Fax: +7 095 141 1950
Web: http://www.mati.ru
e-mail: intdep@mati.edu.ru

Undergraduate, Graduate Programmes

Study Domains: applied sciences, business, computer science, ecology, environment, economy, electricity and electronics, mechanical engineering, sciences, space.
Programmes: B.Sc.; Engineer; M.Sc.; Ph.D.; non-degree programmes in aerospace technology and engineering, material science and technology, avionics, computer science, ecology, business and economics, radio engineering and electronics.
Open to: candidates must be proficient in Russian (reading and writing).
Duration: 4 to 6 years beginning in September.
Fees: registration; US$30; tuition fees: US$2,500-$3,000 per year; living costs: US$30-$50 per month.
Applications: apply by 15 May to above address.

2085 Saint Petersburg College of Precision Mechanics and Optics

Sablinskaya Street 14
197101 Saint Petersburg
Tel: +7-812-238-8715

Undergraduate, Graduate, Postgraduate Programmes

Study Domains: biophysics, computer science, economy, engineering, geodesy, management, mechanical engineering, optics, physics, technology.
Programmes: Bachelor's, Master's, Ph.D. degrees in physics, technology, precision mechanics, optics. Also postgraduate studies.
Open to: candidates of any country with a secondary-school certificate, having passed an entrance interview and examinations in Russian, physics and mathematics; Russian language preparation required.
Duration: (a) Russian language classes: 1 year with 2nd and 3rd-year language studies required by some faculties; (b) B.Sc.: 4 years; (c) M.Sc.: 2 years; (d) postgraduate studies: 3 years.
Fees: yearly: (a) US$800-$900; (b) and (c) US$1,200-$1,400; (d) US$1,500-$2,000.
Applications: by 15 August for preparatory classes; by 15

September for all others; to the above address.

2086 Saint Petersburg State Academy for Engineering Economics

27 Marata Street
191002 Saint Petersburg
Tel: +7-812-112-0633
Fax: +7-812-112-0607
Web: http://www.vis.de/engecon/index_side.html

Undergraduate, Graduate, Postgraduate Programmes

Study Domains: economy, industrial relations, information science, management, tourism, hotel and catering management.
Programmes: (a) Bachelor's; (b) Master's; (c) Engineer's Diploma; (d) postgraduate; (e) Doctoral courses in industrial management, information systems for economics, state and regional management, economics and management in social and cultural fields, tourism and tourist accommodation facilities; (f) preparatory Russian language courses; (g) courses for training translators and teachers (granting teaching certificates).
Open to: candidates of any country with a certificate of education, having passed entrance examinations and a test in Russian; Russian language preparatory study required.
Duration: (a) 4 years; (b) 2 years (after Bachelor's degree); (c) 1 year (after bachelor's degree); (d), (e) and (g) 3 years; (f) 2 years.
Fees: yearly: (a) US$1,000-$1,500; (b) US$2,000-$3,000; (c) US$2,500; (d) US$3,000-$4,000; (e) US$5,000; (f) US$1,200; (g) US$1,300.
Applications: by 1 August, to the above address.

2087 Saint Petersburg State Chemical Pharmaceutical Academy [SPCPA]

14 Prof. Popov Street
197376 Saint Petersburg
Tel: +7 812 234 5729
Fax: +7 812 234 6044
Web: http://www.spcpa.ru
e-mail: rector@spcpa.ru

Graduate Degree Programmes

Study Domains: applied sciences, pharmacy and pharmacology, Russian, teacher education.
Programmes: M.Sc. in Pharmacy; M.Sc. in Biotechnology; Russian language courses for foreigners; courses for teaching Russian as a foreign language.
Subjects: pharmacy; biotechnology; industrial chemistry; pharmacology.
Duration: 6 years (including 1 preparatory year); beginning in September.
Fees: registration: up to US$50; tuition fees: US$1,000 for prep. course; US$2,200 per year for pharmaceutical; US$1,500 per year for biotechnological; living costs: US$200-$400 per year.
Applications: apply by 30 August to: rector@spcpa.ru; or telephone: +7 812 234 2546 for further information.

2088 Saint Petersburg State Medical Academy [SPSMA]

Piskarevsky pr., 47
195067 Saint Petersburg
Tel: +7-812-543-5014
Fax: +7-812-543-1571
Web: http://www.private.petrlink.ru/mechnik
e-mail: mechnik@mail.ru

Pre-Medicine Programme and Doctoral Programme

Study Domains: medicine, obstetrics and gynaecology, paediatrics, surgery.
Programmes: Ph.D. in Medicine; clinical ordinatura; undergraduate programme in pre-medical, pre-clinical, and clinical disciplines and clinical training.
Description: general medicine.
Open to: all nationalities: admission tests required in:

physics, chemistry, biology, English; some language proficiency in English and Russian.
Duration: 6 years beginning 1 September.
Fees: registration: US$100; tuition fees: US$2,500 to US$3,500 per year; living costs: US$1,000 to $1,500 per year (including hostel).
Languages: Russian and English.
Applications: apply by 31 June to Vice-Rector at above address; or email for more information: mechnik@mail.ru.

2089 Saint Petersburg State Mining Institute (Technical University)
21 Liniya 2
199026 Saint Petersburg
Tel: +7-812-218-8255

📖 Undergraduate, Graduate, Postgraduate Programmes

Study Domains: geodesy, geology, metallurgy.
Programmes: (a) Bachelor's; (b) Master's; (c) Engineering Diploma; (d) postgraduate; (e) Doctoral courses in underground mining of ore deposits, open-cast mining, rock failure physics, mining and underground constructions, mining machines and equipment, electric drive and automation of industrial machines and technological complexes, mine surveying, applied geodesy, geological surveying, prospecting and exploration of mineral deposits, geochemistry, mineralogy, petrography, hydrogeology and engineering geology, technology and technique of mineral deposits exploration, geophysical methods of prospecting and exploration, economics and management in mining industry and geology, management in mining industry and geological exploration, mineral processing, metallurgy of non-ferrous metals, automation of technological processes and production thermal physics, automation and ecology of thermal devices in metallurgy; (f) preparatory Russian language courses, five-year course of Russian language for foreign students, courses preparing Russian language teachers (diploma), courses for interpreters (certificate) and courses on certification in teaching Russian (1 to 3 years).
Open to: candidates of any country with a secondary-school education certificate, having passed entrance examinations, a Russian language test; Russian language preparatory study required.
Duration: (a) 4 years; (b) 2 years (after Bachelor's degree); (c) 1 year (after Bachelor's degree); (d) and (e) 3 years; (f) 4 to 6 weeks or 14 weeks.
Fees: yearly: (a) US$2,000; (b), (c) and (d) US$3,000; (e) US$4,000; (f) US$2,500.
Applications: by 1 August to the above address.

2090 Saint Petersburg State Pavlov Medical University
Leo Tolstoy Street 6/8
197089 Saint Petersburg
Tel: +7 812 234 0821

📖 Medical Studies

Study Domains: cancerology, cardiology, dentistry, dermatology, health and hygiene, immunology, neurology, obstetrics and gynaecology, ophthalmology, surgery.
Programmes: Doctor of Medicine degree in medicine and stomatology.
Open to: applicants of any nationality; students must have completed secondary school with good knowledge of Russian (level of Preparatory Faculty) and have a medical certificate; admission tests required to enter the first course: Russian, biology, chemistry, physics.
Duration: 5 to 6 years.
Fees: tuition, US$2,400 per year.
Applications: by 15 August for the first course and by 1 November for the Preparatory Faculty; to the above address.

2091 Saint Petersburg State Technical University
Polytechnical Street 29
195251 Saint Petersburg
Tel: +7 812 247 1616

📖 Undergraduate, Graduate, Postgraduate Programmes

Study Domains: computer science, economy, electricity and electronics, engineering, hydraulics, industrial design, industrial technology, management, metallurgy, physics.
Programmes: Bachelor's, Master's, Engineer's Diploma, Ph.D. degrees in all major fields.
Open to: candidates of any country with a secondary-school certificate and a preparatory faculty certificate; intermediate level Russian language knowledge including technical terminology necessary for the specific studies chosen and entrance examination required.
Duration: (a) Bachelor's: 4 years; (b) Master's: 2 years; (c) Engineering Diploma: up to 2 years; (d) postgraduate studies and (e) postdoctoral studies: 3 to 4 years.
Fees: (a) and (b) US$800-$1,700 per year; (c) US$135 per month; (d) US$150 per month; (e) US$200 per month; application fee: US$35.
Applications: by 28 August, to the above address.

2092 Saint Petersburg State University [SPSU]
7-9 Universitetskaya naberejnaya
199034 Saint Petersburg
Tel: +7-812-213-1168

📖 Undergraduate, Graduate, Postgraduate Programmes

Study Domains: human sciences, natural sciences.
Programmes: (a) Bachelor's, (b) Master's, (c) Postgraduate, (d) Doctoral courses in 42 specialities in the following subjects: natural sciences (biology, geology, geography and geoecology, mathematics and mechanics, applied mathematics, physics, chemistry) and humanities (oriental philology and history, journalism, history, psychology, philology, sociology, philosophy, economics, law, management); possibility to study the Russian language at the (e) Centre of Russian Language and Culture.
Open to: candidates of any country with an education certificate on the basis of competition of documents, having passed an interview; Russian language preparatory study required.
Duration: (a) and (c) 3 to 4 years; (b) 1 to 2 years; (d) 2 to 3 years.
Fees: yearly: approximately (a) US$3,000-4,000; (b), (c) and (d) US$4,000-5,000; monthly: (e) US$400.
Applications: by 1 July, to the above address.

2093 Saint Petersburg State University of Economics and Finance
21 Sadovaya ul.
191023 Saint Petersburg
Tel: +7 812 310 3823
Fax: +7 812 110 5674
Web: http://www.finec.ru
e-mail: tarasevitch@finec.ru

📖 Undergraduate, Graduate, Postgraduate Programmes

Study Domains: business, computer science, ecology, environment, history, home economics, languages, law, marketing, mathematics, philology, philosophy, political science, psychology, public relations, social sciences, special education, statistics, technology, tourism, hotel and catering management, trade, travel grants.
Programmes: Bachelor's; Master's; Ph.D. degrees in all major fields.
Description: Faculties of: Economics and Management, Finance; Credit and International Economic Relations, Statistics, Accounting and Economic Analysis, Commerce and Marketing, Economic Theory and Policy, Labour and Human Resources Management.
Open to: all nationalities; Russian language proficiency required.
Duration: 4 to 9 years beginning 1 September.
Fees: tuition fees: US$2,200-$3,000; living costs: US$105 per month.
Applications: apply by 30 July to international department; consult website: www.interdep@finec.ru; telephone: +7 812 310 6165.

2094 Samara State Institute of Arts and Culture [SSIAC]
167 Frunze Street
443010 Samara
Tel: +7 8462 327654
Fax: +7 8462 332318

📖 Undergraduate, Graduate Programmes / Arts

Study Domains: arts, computer science, cultural studies, folklore, library science, museology and museography.
Programmes: Bachelor's, Master's degrees in arts, computer science, cultural studies, postgraduate courses in music, theatre, arts.
Open to: candidates of any country with a secondary school certificate or equivalent, having passed entrance examinations and a test in Russian language; preparatory Russian language study required.
Duration: 4 years for Bachelor's; 5 years for Master's.
Fees: yearly: (a) US$800; (b) US$1,000; (c) US$500.
Applications: by 15 July, to the above address.

2095 Samara State Medical University [SAMSMU]
Chapaevskaya Street 89
443099 Samara
Tel: +7 8462 321 634/332 976
Fax: +7 8462 332 976
Web: http://www.samsmu.samara.ru
e-mail: root@samsmu.samara.ru

📖 Medical Degree Programmes

Study Domains: medicine.
Programmes: Master's in Medical and Pharmaceutical Education.
Open to: all nationalities; fluent Russian, or a certificate of Russian preparatory courses required; interview; written test in Russian, biology, chemistry.
Held: university clinics; hospitals in Samara city.
Duration: 5 to 6 years beginning in September.
Fees: registration: US$1,400; tuition fees: US$1,700-$1,800; living costs: US$300 per year.
Languages: Russian.
Applications: check website for application dates; apply to Dean of foreign students: foreign@samsmu.samara.ru; or telephone: +7 8462 327 089.

2096 Samara State Technical University
141 Galaktionovskaya Street
443100 Samara
Tel: +7-8462-320-043
Web: http://www.sstu.samara.ru
e-mail: postman@sstu.edu.ru

📖 Undergraduate, Graduate, Postgraduate Programmes

Study Domains: chemical industry, computer science, electricity and electronics, energy, engineering, industrial technology, industry and commerce, information science, mechanical engineering.
Programmes: Bachelor's, Master's, Ph.D. degrees in all major fields; Engineer's Diploma.
Open to: candidates of any country with education certificates, having passed entrance examinations in mathematics and physics (chemistry) and an interview in Russian; Russian language preparatory studies required.
Duration: Bachelor's: 4 years; Master's: 2 years (following Bachelor's); Engineer's Diploma: 5 years; Ph.D.: 3 years (following Master's).
Fees: US$1,200-$2,500 per year.
Applications: by 1 September to the above address.

2097 Samara State University [SSU]
Ac. Pavlov Street 1
443011 Samara
Tel: +7 8462 345 402
Web: http://www.ssu.samara.ru/en

📖 Undergraduate, Graduate Programmes

Study Domains: biology, chemistry, history, law, mathematics, philology, physics, Russian, sociology.

Programmes: (a) Undergraduate; (b) Postgraduate; (c) Doctor's courses in mathematics, applied mathematics, physics, chemistry, biology, history, sociology, Russian language (advanced) and literature, Germanic philology, law; (d) Russian language preparatory course.
Open to: candidates of any nationality with a secondary-school certificate, having passed the entrance examinations and an interview in Russian; preparatory language course required.
Duration: (a) 5 years; (b) and (c) 3 years; (d) 1 to 2 years.
Fees: yearly: (a) US$1,800-$2,200; (b) US$2,500-$3,000; (c) US$5,000; (d) US$1,200.
Applications: by 1 August to the above address.

2098 Saratov State Technical University [SSTU]
Street Politechnicheskaya 77
410054 Saratov
Tel: +7-8452-507-740
Fax: +7-8452-506-837
Web: http://www.sstu-edu.com
e-mail: ums@sstu.saratov.su

📖 Undergraduate, Graduate and Postgraduate Degree Programmes

Study Domains: business, education, engineering, humanities and arts, sciences, social sciences, summer programmes, tourism, hotel and catering management, transport.
Programmes: Bachelor's, Master's, Ph.D. degrees in all major fields; also higher diploma.
Subjects: social work and anthropology, software engineering, cultural studies, electronic devices and units, sociocultural studies, management, transport and communication, civil engineering, information systems and technologies, radio engineering, architecture, thermoengineering, electrosupply, biomedical devices and units.
Duration: 5 to 6 years, depending on programme.
Fees: registration: US$25; living costs; US$500 per semester.
Applications: apply for most programmes by 30 June to Olga Dolinina at the above address; or email: ums@sstu.saratov.su.

2099 Saratov State University [SSTU]
83 Astrahanskaya
410071 Saratov
Tel: +7-8452-507-740
Fax: +7-8452-506-837

📖 Graduate, Postgraduate Programmes

Study Domains: all major fields.
Programmes: (a) Graduate specialist's and (b) postgraduate courses in biology, psychology, geography, mineralogy, hydrogeology and engineering geology, geology of oil and gas, history, mathematics, applied mathematics, mechanics, physics, physics and technology of materials and components of electronic techniques, microelectronics and semiconductors, radiophysics and electronics, Russian language and literature, foreign languages (English, German, French and literature, chemistry, as well as Russian language preparatory department; Russian language Summer courses; courses in conversational Russian.
Open to: candidates of any country with a secondary-school certificate, having passed entrance examinations and an interview in Russian; preparatory Russian language course required.
Duration: (a) 5 years; (b) 3 years.
Fees: yearly: (a) US$1,300; (b) US$2,500.
Applications: by 1 August, to the above address.

2100 Sechenov Moscow Medical Academy [SMMA]
Bolshaya Pirogovskaya Street, 2/6
119992 Moscow
Tel: +7 095 242 9189/+7 095 242 91
Fax: +7 095 967 3342
Web: http://www.mma.ru
e-mail: mmainter@mmascience.ru

📖 Graduate Degree Programmes

Study Domains: medicine, nursing, pharmacy and pharmacology.
Programmes: Master's degree programmes in medicine, pharmacy, nursing.
Subjects: medicine programme includes: humanitarian, social-economic, natural, medico-biological, prophylactic, general clinical, summer practical course, higher vocational education.
Open to: all nationalities: higher secondary education with 75% marks in chemistry; admission tests in Russian or English, biology, chemistry.
Duration: 6 years for general medicine; 5 years for pharmacy.
Languages: Russian and English.

2101 Shuya State Pedagogical University [SGPU]
Ivanovo Region
Shuya
Tel: +7 9351 265 94
Fax: +7 9351 265 94
Web: http://www.tpi.ru/~sgpu
e-mail: sgpu@tpi.ru

📖 Teacher Education Programmes

Study Domains: teacher education.
Programmes: Teacher education programmes.
Open to: candidates with secondary-school certificate; eligibility based on interview; must meet academic, financial and linguistic requirements.
Applications: to above address.

2102 Siberian Aerospace Academy [SAA]
PO Box 486
660014 Krasnoyarsk
Tel: +7-3912-330-014

📖 Graduate, Postgraduate Programmes

Study Domains: aviation, aeronautics, business, business administration, computer science, industrial technology, management, marketing, mechanical engineering, space.
Open to: candidates of any nationality; students must have medical and educational certificates and good knowledge of Russian.
Fees: graduate, US$2,000; postgraduate, US$3,000 per year.
Financial assistance: working on campus is possible; free transportation inside the city.
Applications: by 1 June, to the above address for further information.

2103 Siberian Medical University [SMU]
Moskovsky trakt
634050 Tomsk
Tel: +7 3822 230 423

📖 Graduate, Postgraduate Programmes

Study Domains: medicine, pharmacy and pharmacology.
Programmes: (a) Magister's, (b) Doctorate, (c) Pharmacy Diploma, (d) Postgraduate, (e) Medical Doctor's degree courses in pharmacy and medicine.
Open to: nationals of any country with a certificate from the preparatory department of a medical institute of the Russian Federation; entrance interview in Russian language required.
Duration: (a) 2 years; (b) 6 years; (c) 5 years; (d) mural: 3 years, extramural: 4 years; (e) 3 years.
Applications: by 1 August, to the above address.

2104 Siberian Motor and Highway Institute
5 Mir Avenue
644080 Omsk
Tel: +7-381-650-322

📖 Graduate, Postgraduate Programmes

Study Domains: engineering.
Programmes: (a) Engineering Diploma and (b) Postgraduate courses in engineering (machine building).
Duration: (a) 5 years; (b) 3 years.
Fees: yearly: (a) 555,000 roubles.
Applications: to the above address.

2105 Siberian State Academy of Transport
191 D. Kovalchuk Street
630023 Novosibirsk
Tel: +7-832-287-386

📖 Undergraduate, Graduate, Postgraduate Programmes

Study Domains: aviation, aeronautics, building industry, civil engineering, engineering, industrial technology, interpretation and translation, management, Russian, sociology, transport.
Programmes: (a) Bachelor's; (b) Master's; (c) Engineering Diploma; (d) postgraduate courses in bridges and transport tunnels, railway construction, track and track maintenance, motorway and aerodrome construction, industrial and civil engineering, water supply, sewerage, water resources rational utilization and protection, railway management and operation, lifting and hoisting machines, building and track equipment, transport economy and management, construction economy and management, transport management, social management, Russian language interpretation; (e) preparatory Russian language courses.
Open to: candidates of any country with a certificate of education, having passed entrance examinations and an interview in Russian; preparatory Russian language study required.
Duration: (a) 4 years; (b) 2 years (after Bachelor's degree); (c) 1 year (after Bachelor's degree); (d) 3 years; (e) 2 years.
Fees: yearly: (a) US$1,500-$3,500; (b) US$1,700-$4,000; (c) US$2,500; (d) US$2,500-$5,000; (e) US$1,200.
Applications: by 1 August, to the above address.

2106 Siberian State Technological University [SIBSTU]
prosp. Mira 82
660049 Krasnoyarsk
Tel: +7 3912 66 0388
Fax: +7 3912 27 4440
Web: http://www.sibstu.kts.ru
e-mail: sibstu@sibstu.kts.ru

📖 Undergraduate, Graduate and Postgraduate Degree Programmes

Study Domains: accounting, business, continuing education, economy, forestry, history, languages, philosophy, sciences, special education, teacher education, technical education.
Programmes: Bachelor's, Master's, Engineering Diploma, Ph.D. degrees in business, economics, languages, philosophy; upgrading programmes.
Open to: all nationalities; admission tests required in mathematics, Russian, chemistry, biology.
Duration: 5 years beginning in September.
Fees: tuition: 20,000 roubles.
Financial assistance: financial support available in the amount of 1,500 roubles.
Applications: apply by 15 July to: pavlov@sibstu.kts.ru.

🐦 Scholarships

Study Domains: education, humanities and arts, technology.
Open to: all nationalities; based on exams and interview.
Applications: apply by 15 July to: pavlov@sibstu.kts.ru; or telephone: +7 3912 660394.

2107 South-Russian Humanities Institute [SRHI]

Krasnoarmeiskaya Street 108
344006 Rostov-on-Don
Tel: +7-863-441-281
Fax: +7-863-673-437

Undergraduate and Graduate Degree Programmes

Study Domains: business, fine arts, graphic arts, interior design, law, philosophy, social sciences, special education.
Programmes: Bachelor's, Master's degrees in business, fine arts, law, social sciences.
Duration: up to 9 years beginning in September.
Fees: tuition: US$600-$800 per year.
Applications: apply by 30 August to the above address.

2108 South-Russian State Technical University/ Novocherkassk [SRSTU]

132 Prosveschenya Street
346428 Novocherkassk 28
Tel: +7 863 525 5460
Fax: +7 863 522 8463
Web: http://www.srstu.novoch.ru
e-mail: ngtu@novoch.ru

Undergraduate, Graduate and Postgraduate Degree Programmes

Study Domains: administration, business, chemistry, communication, computer science, criminology, ecology, environment, economic and commercial sciences, economy, engineering, geodesy, geology, hydrology, law, management, marketing, mathematics, physics, political economy, technical education.
Programmes: Bachelor's, Specialist's Diploma, Master's, Ph.D. in all major fields.
Open to: candidates of any country with a secondary-school certificate or equivalent, having passed an interview in Russian; preparatory Russian language study required.
Duration: 4 to 6 years depending on programme; courses begin in September; language coaching for 1 year.
Fees: tuition fees: US$1,000; living costs: US$50 per month.
Languages: Russian.
Applications: apply to the above address.

2109 Southern Ural State University [SUSU]

76 Prospect Lenina
454080 Chelyabinsk
Tel: +7 3512 656 504
Fax: +7 3512 547 408
Web: http://www.susu.ac.ru
e-mail: tvch@susu.ac.ru

Postgraduate Degree Programmes

Study Domains: all major fields.
Programmes: (a) Ph.D.; (b) specialized training; (c) Russian language course.
Description: devices and systems of orientation and navigation, air and rocket building.
Open to: all nationalities; good language proficiency in Russian required.
Duration: (a) 2 to 3 years; (b) 5 years; (c) 1 year.
Fees: registration: US$50; (a) U$2,500-$3,000; (b) US$1,500-$3,000; (c) US$1,000; living costs: US$20 per month.

2110 State Academy of Management [SAM]

Ryazansky Avenue 99
109542 Moscow
Tel: +7-095-371-1322

Undergraduate, Graduate, Postgraduate Degree Programmes

Study Domains: accounting, economic and commercial sciences, economy, management, marketing, sociology.

Programmes: (a) Bachelor's, (b) Master's, (c) Certificate, (d) Postgraduate and (e) Ph.D. courses in science, management, world economy, state and regional management, information systems in economics, accounting, operational research in economics and sociology.
Open to: candidates of any country with an appropriate certificate, having passed interview; preparatory level skills in Russian language required.
Duration: (a) 4 years; (b) 2 years; (c) 5 years; (d) and (e) 3 years.
Fees: yearly: (a) and (e) US$2,500; (b) and (c) US$2,200-$3,500; (d) US$2,000; (f) US$1,800.
Applications: by 1 August, to the above address.

2111 State Academy of Oil and Gas

Leninsky Prospect, 65
117917 GSP-1 Moscow
Tel: +7-095-137-8108

Graduate, Postgraduate Programmes

Study Domains: ecology, environment, economy, energy, engineering, geology, industrial technology, management.
Programmes: (a) Master's, (b) Ph.D., (c) Doctoral courses in exploration and prospection of oil and gas fields, oil and gas fields development, oil and gas transportation and storage, hydrocarbons processing, ecology, designing and maintenance of machines and equipment, simulation and automation of manufacturing processes and management of industry, as well as (d) preparatory department and (e) Russian language teacher-training courses (with certification to teach Russian).
Open to: candidates of any country with secondary-education certificate, having passed entrance examinations and interview; preparatory Russian language study required.
Duration: (a) for applicants without Bachelor's degree: 5 years; with Bachelor's: 2 years; (b) and (c) 3 years; (d) and (e) 1 year.
Fees: (a) US$2,000-$3,000 (without Bachelor's degree) and US$2,500-$3,000 (with Bachelor's); (b) US$2,500-$3,000; (c) US$3,000-$4,000; (d) and (e) US$1,500-$2,000.
Applications: by 1 August to the above address.

2112 State Marine Technical University of St. Petersburg

International Affairs and Education
Lotsmanskay Street 3
190008 Saint Petersburg
Tel: +7-812-114-4168
Fax: +7-812-318-5227
Web: http://www.smtu.ru/engver/index.html
e-mail: inter@smtu.ru

Undergraduate, Graduate, Postgraduate Programmes

Study Domains: computer science, ecology, environment, economy, electricity and electronics, hydrology, management, mathematics, physics, sociology, technology.
Programmes: Bachelor's, Master's, Engineer's Diploma; Ph.D. and D.Sc. in physics; mathematics; environment; computer science and ecology. Also Russian language classes.
Open to: candidates of any country with a secondary-school certificate and a study contract granted by the University; entrance interview in Russian and preliminary language instruction required.
Duration: (a) Russian language classes: from 3 months to 2 years depending on the proficiency desired; (b) B.Sc.: 4 years; (c) M.Sc.: 2 years; (d) Engineering Diploma: 5-1/2 years; (e) Ph.D. and (f) D.Sc.: 3 to 4 years.
Fees: yearly: (a) US$1,000; (b) and (d) US$1,200-$2,000; (c) US$1,500-$2,500; (e) US$2,000-$4,000; (f) US$3,000-$5,000.
Applications: by 15 September for (a) and 25 August for all other programmes.

2113 State University of Non-Ferrous Metals and Gold [GUTMiZ (SUNM&G)]

prosp. Krasnoyarsky Rabochy 95
66002 Krasnoyarsk
Tel: +7-3912-347-882
Fax: +7-3912-346-311
e-mail: postmaster@color.krasnoyarsk.su

📖 **Engineering Programmes**

Study Domains: industrial technology, technology.

2114 Stavropolskiy Institute

ul. R. Luxemburg 59
355012 Stavropol
Tel: +7 8652 940 610/945 913
Fax: +7 8652 945 947
e-mail: institut@vuz-chursin.ru

📖 **Certificate and State Diploma**

Study Domains: accounting, business, business administration, computer science, economic and commercial sciences, economy, finance, management, marketing, mathematics, statistics.
Programmes: Certificates, State Diplomas in business, economics, management.
Description: Russian language coaching, entry-level coaching, upgrading programme, PC course, vine technology, national economy, management.
Open to: all nationalities up to age 35; elementary level Russian language proficiency required.
Held: Stavropol; Pyatigorsk.
Duration: regular programme: 5 years, beginning 1 July; 1 September.
Applications: apply by 29 June or 19 August to the above address; or email: rector@vuz-chursin.ru.

🎓 **Scholarship**

Study Domains: accounting, business, business administration, computer science, economic and commercial sciences, economy, finance, management, marketing, mathematics, statistics.
Open to: all nationalities, up to age 35; apply with school certificate, medical scheme, passport, visa.
Applications: apply by 29 June or 19 August to: rector@vuz-chursin.ru.

2115 Taganrog State University of Radio Engineering [TSURE]

per. Nekrasovskij 44
347922 Taganrog
Tel: +7 863 431 0599
Fax: +7 863 446 5019
Web: http://www.tsure.ru
e-mail: rector@tsure.ru

📖 **Undergraduate and Postgraduate Degree Programmes**

Study Domains: computer science, economic and commercial sciences, electricity and electronics, engineering, marketing, summer programmes, telecommunications.
Programmes: Bachelor's, Master's, Ph.D. degrees in computer science, radio engineering, automation, engineering; Summer programmes.
Description: Colleges of: Natural Science and Humanities, Radio Engineering, Automation and Computer Science, Information Security.
Applications: for application information contact the university at the above address; or consult the website.

2116 Tambov State Technical University [TSTU]

106, Sovetskaya Street
392000 Tambov
Tel: +7-752-721-019
Web: http://www.tstu.ru
e-mail: tstu@admin.tstu.ru

📖 **Graduate and Postgraduate Degree Programmes**

Study Domains: all major fields.

Programmes: Bachelor's, Master's; Diploma of Engineer, Economist, Architect; Ph.D.; Russian language programme for foreigners.
Description: university comprises 4 institutes, 11 faculties, 40 departments, 30 training courses.
Open to: all nationalities, up to age 35 (except Doctoral student).
Duration: 5 to 6 years depending on programme, PhD, a further 3 years; Doctorate, a further 3 years.
Fees: tuition fees: US$1,000-US$1,500 per year.
Applications: apply to the above address.

2117 Tatar Institute for Promotion of Business [TISBI]

Bauman Street 20
420053 Tatarstan
Kazan
Tel: +7 8432 369297
Web: http://www.tisbi.ru
e-mail: tisbi@tisbi.ru

📖 **Undergraduate and Graduate Degree Programmes**

Study Domains: accounting, Arabic, economic and commercial sciences, economy, English, ethnology, finance, international relations, law, management, marketing, psychology, Russian, summer programmes, tourism, hotel and catering management.
Programmes: Bachelor's, Master's degrees.
Description: law; economics; management; non-degree programmes: Japanese, Arabic, Russian, Tatar.
Open to: all nationalities; minimum age: 17.
Held: Kazan, Moushtari St.13.
Duration: 4 to 5 years.
Fees: registration: US$100; tuition: US$2,000; living costs: US$1,200.
Languages: Russian and English.
Applications: apply by 20 August to the above address.

2118 Togliatti Polytechnic Institute [TPI]

Belorusskaya Street 14
445630 Togliatti
Tel: +7 8469 234 125
Fax: +7 8469 229 522

📖 **Technological Studies**

Study Domains: building industry, electricity and electronics, industrial design, industrial technology, technology.
Programmes: Courses in equipment, soldering and welding production technology, metal pressure treatment, machine building technology, metal cutting machines and tools, chemical production machines, internal combustion engines, automobile and tractor construction, automobile and automobile services, industrial, civil and agricultural power supplies, electromechanics, industrial electronics, automation of technological processes and industries, car and tractor electrical equipment, industrial and civil construction, heat and gas supplies, ventilation systems.
Open to: candidates of any country with a secondary-school certificate, having passed the entrance examination and interview; preliminary language instruction required.
Duration: (a) Russian language instruction: 1 to 2 years; (b) Technician Diploma and (d) Postgraduate courses: 3 years; (c) Engineer Diploma: 2 additional years.
Fees: yearly: (a) US$1,200; (b) US$1,500-$3,000; (c) US$1,700-$3,500; (d) US$2,500-$5,000.
Applications: by 1 August to the above address.

2119 Tomsk Polytechnic University [TPU]

30 Lenin Prospekt
634050 Tomsk
Tel: +7-3822-563-470
Fax: +7-3822-563-865
Web: http://www.tpu.ru/eng
e-mail: tpu@tpu.ru

Undergraduate, Graduate, Postgraduate Programmes

Study Domains: chemistry, electricity and electronics, energy, engineering, geology, metallurgy, physics.
Programmes: (a) Bachelor's; (b) Master's; (c) Graduate Engineer's; (d) Postgraduate, (e) Doctoral programmes in physical methods and quality control devices, optimization of management systems, industrial and medical electronics, laser and light facilities, hydrogeology, geophysical methods of exploring, geochemistry of rare metals, drilling of oil and gas boring wells, combustible mineral and oil, equipment and technology of welding production, powder metallurgy and sprayed coatings, automation and robotization in machine building, technology in machine building, technology of main organic synthesis, technology of non-organic substances, technology of electrochemical production, technology of silicates, atomic stations, thermal power stations, electromechanics, electric drive and automation of industrial installations, cable and condenser facilities, automation and control in technical systems, roboto-technical systems and complexes, computing machines, power-stations, power supply, engineering and electro-physics of high voltages of electrical system, power-engineering, radiational ecology, experimental methods of nuclear physics of atomic reactors, spline-methods and solving of technical problems, general physics, physics of solids, general non-organic chemistry, boring and blasting works, carrying out of mining and exploring workings, planning of drilling wells construction, physical chemistry, educational geological practice, as well as (f) a preparatory department in Russian language and (g) preparatory courses for training teachers-interpreters (diploma holders are qualified to teach the Russian language).
Open to: candidates of any country with an education certificate, having passed entrance examinations and an interview in Russian; preparatory Russian language study required.
Duration: (a) 4 years; (b) 2 years (after bachelorship); (c) 1 year (after bachelor's); (d), (e) and (g) 3 years; (f) 2 years.
Fees: yearly: (a) US$1,500-$3,500; (b) US$1,700-$4,000; (c) US$2,500; (d) US$2,500-$5,000; (e) US$5,000; (f) US$1,200; (g) US$1,300.
Applications: by 1 August, to the above address.

2120 Tyumen State Agricultural Academy [TSAA]
ul. Respubliki 7
625003 Tyumen
Tel: +7 3452 46 1650
Fax: +7 3452 46 1650

Graduate Degree Programmes

Study Domains: agriculture, agronomic sciences, cattle breeding, fisheries, forestry, horticulture, veterinary medicine, veterinary sciences.
Programmes: Diploma; Candidate of Sciences; Doctor of Sciences.
Subjects: agronomy; veterinary science; aquaculture; agricultural technologies.
Open to: all nationalities; admission tests required in: biology, chemistry, Russian; fluent language proficiency required.
Duration: 5 years.
Fees: tuition fees vary with programme; living costs: US$200 per month.
Applications: apply to the above address.

2121 Tyumen State University [TYUMSU]
10, Semakova Street
625003 Tyumen
Tel: +7 3452 46 0141
Fax: +7 3452 46 1930
Web: http://www.utmn.ru
e-mail: president@utmn.ru

Diploma of Higher Education

Study Domains: business, education, humanities and arts, languages, law, Russian, sciences, social sciences.
Programmes: Higher education diplomas in all major fields.
Open to: all nationalities; high Russian language

proficiency at intermediate level required.
Duration: 5 years beginning 1 September.
Fees: tuition fees: US$2,000; living costs: $200.
Applications: apply by 15 June to the above address.

2122 Udmurt State University [UDSU]
Universitetskaya 1
426034 Izhevsk (Udmurtia)
Tel: +7-3412-781-592
Web: http://www.uni.udm.ru
e-mail: inter@uni.udm.ru

Undergraduate, Graduate Degrees and Diploma Programmes

Study Domains: business, humanities and arts, law, sciences, social sciences, summer programmes.
Programmes: Diploma of higher education Bachelor's, Master's); D.Sc.; Cand.Sc.
Duration: full-time students: 4 to 5 years; part-time students: 5 to 6 years; Cand.Sc.: 3 years; D.Sc.: 2 years.

2123 Ufa State Petroleum Technological University
Kosmonavtov Street 1
450062 Ufa
Bashkortostan
Tel: +7 3472 420 370
Fax: +7 3472 431 419
e-mail: info@rusoil.net

Undergraduate, Graduate and Postgraduate Degree Programmes

Study Domains: accounting, continuing education, economic and commercial sciences, economy, engineering, finance, information science, management, marketing, public relations, Russian, sciences, technical education.
Programmes: (a) preliminary courses; (b) B.Sc.; (c) M.Sc.; (d) D.Eng.; (e) Ph.D.; (f) D.Sc.
Subjects: (a) Russian language, engineering graphics, mathematics, physics, chemistry; (b) civil engineering, chemical technology, biotechnology, technological machines, oil and gas technology; (c) civil engineering, oil and gas engineering; (d), (e), (f) wide variety of fields of study.
Duration: (a) varies with course (b) 4 years; (c) (d) 1 to 2 years; (e) varies; (f) 3 years after Ph.D.
Fees: in US$ (a) $800-$1,300; (b) $1,800-$2,200; (c) (d) $2,000; (e) $2,000-2,500; (f) $3,000.
Languages: Russian; some courses taught in English.
Applications: apply before 31 August.

2124 Ural State Technical University-UPI [USTU]
19 Mira str.
620002 Ekaterinburg
Tel: +7-343-375-4627
Fax: +7-343-374-5434
Web: http://www.ustu.ru
e-mail: inter@inter.ustu.ru

Undergraduate, Graduate, Postgraduate Programmes

Study Domains: architecture, business, design, engineering, interpretation and translation, languages, linguistics, marketing, political economy, psychology, sciences, sociology, tourism, hotel and catering management.
Programmes: Bachelor's, Master's, Ph.D. degrees in physics, civil building and materials, metallurgy, radio-engineering, chemistry, humanitarian, economics, management; Russian language course.
Open to: all nationalities; Russian language proficiency required; preparatory language course available at the university.
Academic requirements: high school certificate to enter Bachelor or Specialist programme; Bachelor's degree to enter Master's programme; Master's degree of equivalent to enter postgraduate studies.
Age limit Min: no minimum age limit; academic requirements must be respected.
Age limit Max: no maximum age limit; academic requirements must be respected.

Duration: 4 years for Bachelor's programme in certain specialties; 5 years for Specialist programme in all specialties; 2 years for Master's programme in certain specialties; 3-4 years for postgraduate programme; 1 month - up to 1 year for the Russian language courses.
Fees: no registration fee; tuition: minimum US$1,500; living costs: US$200-$300 per month. Tuition fee for the Russian language course depends on the duration of the course.
Languages: Russian.
Applications: apply by 1 October for fall semester; 1 February for spring semester.

2125 Ural State University of Forestry Engineering [USFEU]

ul. Sibirskij trakt 37
62010 Ekaterinburg
Tel: +7-343-224-23-73
Fax: +7-343-224-03-37
Web: http://www.usfea.ru
e-mail: general@usfea.ru

Scholarship

Subjects: Forestry; forest management; road transport; ecology.
Value: Tuition, 15,500 roubles; living expenses: 250 roubles per month; waiver on public transport.
Applications: By 15 May; contact oms@usfea.ru for further details.

2126 Velikie Luki Agricultural Institute [VLAI]

1 pl. V. I. Lenina
11182100 Velikie Luki
Pskov Oblast
Tel: +7 81153 37728

Graduate Studies

Study Domains: accounting, agriculture, agronomic sciences, ecology, environment, finance.
Programmes: Graduate Engineer's Diploma courses in agronomy, agro-ecology, zoo-engineering, mechanization of agriculture, agricultural management, accounting and finances.
Open to: candidates of any country with an education certificate, having passed the entrance examinations and an interview in Russian; Russian language preparatory training courses required.
Duration: 5 years.
Fees: US$1,500 per year.
Applications: by 1 July, to the above address.

2127 Vladimir Polytechnical Institute [VPI]

Gorky Street 87
600026 Vladimir
Tel: +7 9222 32575

Graduate, Postgraduate Programmes

Study Domains: architecture, chemical industry, civil engineering, computer science, ecology, environment, electricity and electronics, engineering, industrial technology, law, transport.
Programmes: (a) Master's; (b) Engineering Diploma; (c) Postgraduate courses in machine building technology, management, internal combustion engines, technical automobile exploitation, instrument making, automation and control in technical systems, robot engineering complexes, electronic computers, radio engineering, radio electronics in design, plastic processing technology, glass technology, environmental protection, ecology, architecture, industrial and civil engineering, road building, industrial law; (d) preparatory Russian language courses; (e) Russian language short-term courses.
Open to: candidates of any country with a secondary-school certificate or equivalent, having passed an interview in Russian and a mathematics examination; Russian language preparatory study required.
Duration: (a) and (b) 5 years; (c) 3 years; (d) 1 year; (e) 3 to 10 months.
Fees: yearly: (a) and (b) US$800-$1,200; (c)

US$1,200-$1,800; (d) US$850; (e) monthly: US$100.
Applications: by 1 July, to the above address.

2128 Volgograd State Pedagogical University [VSPU]

27, Lenin Avenue
400131 Volgograd
Tel: +7 8442 241-379
Web: http://www.vspu.ru
e-mail: dvi@vspu.ru

Undergraduate, Graduate and Postgraduate Degree Programmes

Study Domains: education, engineering, health and hygiene, humanities and arts, languages, law, natural sciences, research, sciences, social sciences, summer programmes, tourism, hotel and catering management.
Programmes: Bachelor's, Master's, Ph.D. in all major fields.
Subjects: 38 programmes offered.
Duration: 4 to 6 years beginning 1 September.
Fees: registration US$30; tuition fees: US$1,500-$1,900; living costs: US$200 per month.
Applications: apply to the above address; or email: oms@vspu.ru.

2129 Volgograd State Technical University [VSTU]

28 Lenin Avenue
400131 Volgograd
Tel: +7 8442 230-076
Web: http://www.vstu.ru
e-mail: rector@vstu.ru

Undergraduate, Graduate and Postgraduate Degree Programmes

Study Domains: chemical engineering, chemical industry, computer science, economy, electricity and electronics, engineering, hydraulics, industrial technology, information science, management, mechanical engineering, metallurgy, technical education, technology, textile industry.
Programmes: (a) Bachelor's; (b) Master's; (c) Graduate Engineer's Diploma; (d) Postgraduate; (e) Ph.D. in all major fields.
Open to: candidates with a secondary-school certificate, having passed entrance examinations and an interview in Russian; Russian language preparatory study required.
Duration: (a) and (e) 4 years; (b) 2 years; (c) 1 year; (d) 3 years.
Applications: by 1 August, to the above address.

2130 Volgograd State University [VolSU]

ul. 2-ja Prodolnaja 30
62 40 Volgograd
Tel: +7-8442-438-124
Fax: +7-8442-438-124
Web: http://www.volsu.ru

Undergraduate, Graduate Programmes

Study Domains: all major fields.

2131 Volgograd State University of Architecture and Civil Engineering [VGASA]

Akademicheskaja Street 1
400074 Volgograd
Tel: +7 8442 97 4872 / 974-933
Fax: +7 8442 97 4872 / 974-933
Web: http://www.vgasa.ru
e-mail: postmaster@vgasa.ru

Undergraduate, Graduate and Postgraduate Degree Programmes

Study Domains: architecture, building industry, civil engineering, decorative arts, design, earth science, ecology, environment, economic and commercial sciences, economy, energy, finance, geology, graphic arts, hydraulics, hydrology, industrial design, industry and commerce, management, mechanical engineering, natural resources, natural sciences, sciences, statistics, technical education, transport.

Programmes: Bachelor's, Master's, Ph.D. degrees in architecture and civil engineering.
Open to: all nationalities; Russian language proficiency required; courses offered at the university.
Duration: 4 to 6 years beginning 1 September.
Financial assistance: apply to International Department: +7 8442 97 4761 for further information.
Applications: apply by September to the international department at the above address.

2132 Voronezh N.N. Burdenko State Medical Academy [VSMANN]
10 Studencheskaya Street
394000 Voronezh
Tel: +7 0732 53 0398
Fax: +7 0732 53 0398
Web: http://www.vsma.ac.ru
e-mail: foreign@vsma.ac.ru

⌑ Medical Studies
Study Domains: medicine.
Description: (a) MD; (b) internship; (c) residency; (d) Russian language course.
Open to: all nationalities; Russian language test in biology and chemistry.
Duration: (a) 6 years; (b) 1 to 2 years; (c) 2 to 3 years; (d) 1 year.
Fees: tuition fees: US$1,200-$3,000 depending on programme; living costs: US$300-US$600.
Applications: apply by 1 August to the above address; email for information: foreign@vsma.ac.ru.

2133 Voronezh National Academy of Architecture and Construction
ul. 20 Let Oktyabray Dom 84
394006 Voronezh
Tel: +7-0732-575-268

⌑ Undergraduate, Graduate, Postgraduate Programmes
Study Domains: architecture, civil engineering, ecology, environment, industrial technology, management.
Programmes: (a) Bachelor's; (b) Master's; (c) Engineering Diploma; (d) postgraduate; (e) Doctoral programmes for foreign students in civil engineering and industrial construction, architecture; lifting, transporting, construction and road-building machines and equipment; building highways and aerodromes, water supply, sewage, rational use and protection of water resources, heat supply, ventilation and protection of the air environment, production and construction of building units, automation of technological processes and industries, construction management; (f) preparatory groups for Russian language study; (g) special courses for training interpreters and teachers of Russian.
Open to: candidates of any country with a secondary-school-leaving certificate having passed interviews in Russian, mathematics, physics and an examination in drawing for architecture applicants; Russian language preparatory study required.
Duration: (a) 4 years; (b) 2 years; (c) 1 year; (d) and (e) 3 years; (g) 3 years.
Fees: yearly: (a) US$1,300-$1,800; (b) US$2,000-US$2,500; (c) US$1,800-US$2000; (d) US$2,500-3,000; (e) US$4,000-$5,000; (f) US$1,100-$1,300; (g) US$1,500.
Applications: by 1 September to the above address.

2134 Voronezh Pedagogical University
Lenin Street 86
394611 Voronezh
Tel: +7 0732 551949

⌑ Graduate Studies
Study Domains: biology, chemistry, computer science, English, French, geography, history, mathematics, psychology, Russian.
Programmes: (a) Master of Arts; (b) graduate courses in pedagogy.
Open to: candidates of any country holding a secondary-school certificate and a 1-year preparatory course in Russian language proficiency or equivalent; oral examination in Russian required.
Duration: (a) Master of Arts in Pedagogy: 5 years; (b) graduate courses: 3 years.
Fees: yearly: (a) US$1,000 to $1,500; (b) US$2,000.
Applications: by 1 August, to the above address.

2135 Voronezh Polytechnic Institute [VPI]
Moscow Avenue 14
394026 Voronezh
Tel: +7 0732 160919

⌑ Engineering Studies
Study Domains: aviation, aeronautics, energy, engineering, industrial technology, mechanical engineering, physics, radiology.
Programmes: courses preparing radio-engineers and engineer-mechanics of different industrial branches.
Open to: candidates of any country with a secondary-school certificate or equivalent, having passed the entrance examinations.

2136 Voronezh State Agricultural University [VSAU]
Michurin Street 1
394087 Voronezh
Tel: +7-0732-564-351

⌑ Undergraduate, Graduate, Postgraduate Programmes
Study Domains: agriculture, agronomic sciences, business, chemistry, economy, engineering, technology, veterinary sciences.
Programmes: (a) Bachelor's; (b) Master's; (c) Diploma; (d) postgraduate courses in agro-chemistry and soil science, agronomy, animal husbandry, veterinary science, land management and cadastre, agro-engineering, agro-technology processing and storage, agro-economics, agro-business management; (e) Russian language preparatory courses.
Open to: candidates of any country with a secondary-school certificate or equivalent; certificate of Russian language or equivalent testifying to Russian language proficiency in comprehension, writing and explaining the material taught.
Duration: (a) 4 years; (b) 2 years; (c) 5-1/2 years; (d) 3 years.
Fees: yearly: veterinary faculty: (a) US$1,600; (b) US$1,800; (d) US$2,500; other faculties: (a) and (c) US$1,500; (b) US$1,600; (d) US$2,300.
Applications: by 1 August to the above address.

2137 Voronezh State University [VSU]
1 University Square
394006 Voronezh
Tel: +7 0732 789 674
Fax: +7 0732 789 755
Web: http://www.vsu.ru
e-mail: office@main.vsu.ru

⌑ Undergraduate, Graduate, Postgraduate Programmes
Study Domains: biology, chemistry, earth science, economy, education, engineering, geology, history, journalism, law, mathematics, philology, philosophy, physics, political science, Russian.
Programmes: (a) Bachelor's; Master's; Ph.D.; (b) pre-university studies; (c) Russian as a foreign language; (d) semester Russian language course; (e) Russian language summer course.
Duration: (a) 2 to 5 years depending on programme; (b) 800 hours/academic year; (c) 3 years; (d) 1 to 2 semesters or 5 to 10 months; (e) 4+ weeks.
Fees: registration: 20 roubles; tuition fees: (a) $1,000-$4,500 depending on programme; (b) US$1,350; (c) included in the contract for education; (d) US$1,000-$1,250; (e) US$400-$500; living costs: 150-225 roubles per month.
Applications: apply to above address by: (b) and (c) 1 August, contact: rodionov@pfac.vsu.ru, or root@pfac.vsu.ru; (d) 1 August or 3 January, contact: rodionov@pfac.vsu.ru; (e)

1 month before arrival.

Saint-Siège

Année universitaire: octobre à juin.
Unité monétaire: Euro (€).
Admission pour étudiants du pays: Les étudiants ecclésiastiques doivent posséder selon les cas, un diplôme préuniversitaire ou un titre académique, et leur candidature doit être présentée par les autorités compétentes. Les bourses d'études sont accordées, soit par le Saint-Siège, soit par les établissements d'enseignement supérieur, soit encore par les collèges ecclésiastiques où résident les étudiants.
Connaissances linguistiques requises: Les candidats doivent connaître, outre leur langue maternelle, de 1 à 3 langues modernes et selon les études envisagées, le latin, le grec, l'hébreu ou les langues orientales anciennes.
Reconnaissance des études et diplômes: Congregazione per l'Educazione cattolica; 3, Piazza Pio XII; 00120 Città del Vaticano; Saint-Siège; tél: +39-6-698-84161; fax: +39-6-698-84172; email: vati133@ccatheduc.va.
Publications / Sites Web:
• «Annuario Pontificio», dans lequel figurent les noms et adresses des recteurs et des 15 universités ou instituts pontificaux.

2138 Institut pontifical d'archéologie chrétienne [PIAC]

1, Via Napoleone III
00185 Rome
Tel: +39-06-446-5574 / 445-3169
Fax: +39-06-446-9197
Web: http://www.piac.it
e-mail: piac@piac.it

📖 Archéologie Chrétienne

Domaines d'étude: archéologie.
Programmes: Cours de spécialisation en archéologie chrétienne: architecture, topographie de Rome et du monde chrétien, iconographie, épigraphie, histoire du culte chrétien, littérature chrétienne ancienne.
A l'intention de: ressortissants de tout pays, âgés de 20 à 70 ans, titulaires d'une maîtrise ou équivalent et, pour les européens, (avec la nouvelle réforme), le Bac + 5.
Durée: 3 ans; cours débutent en novembre.
Assistance financière: quelques bourses, accordées en fonction des demandes et de la nationalité des candidats.
Connaissances linguistiques: langues obligatoires: italien, latin, grec.
Inscriptions: entre le 15 octobre et le 15 novembre; au Secrétaire du PIAC.

💰 Bourses / 3e cycle, archéologie

Domaines d'étude: archéologie.
Bourses: Bourses d'études Mons. Patrick Saint Roch.
A l'intention de: étudiants internationaux ressortissants de tout pays, titulaires d'un diplôme de fin d'études universitaires (de préférence un doctorat) en archéologie classique, et ayant une bonne connaissance de l'italien et du latin.
Qualifications requises: maitrise es lettres, histoire, histoire de l'art et d'archéologie.
Durée: 8 mois.
Valeur: scolarité: 4,000€; logement: 1,200€.
Connaissances linguistiques: l'italien et latin.
Candidatures: avant le 15 avril; contacter le Secrétaire du PIAC pour les documents à fournir.

2139 Institut pontifical d'études arabes et islamiques [PISAI]

Viale di Trastevere 89
00153 Rome
Web: http://village.flashnet.it/~fn026243/indexF.htm
e-mail: pisai@flashnet.it

📖 Études islamiques

Domaines d'étude: arabe, études orientales, littérature et civilisation, théologie, religion.
Programmes: programme de langue arabe, Islamologie et section «Islam et réflexion chrétienne», conduisant aux certificat d'Islamologie, certificat de grammaire arabe, diplôme d'arabe moderne et classique, licence et doctorat d'études arabes et islamiques.
A l'intention de: ressortissants de tout pays; admission directe.
Durée: 1 an pour le certificat; 2 ans pour le diplôme; 3 ans pour la licence; 5 ans minimum pour le doctorat.
Connaissances linguistiques: langues d'enseignement: français et anglais.
Inscriptions: avant le 31 mai; au Directeur de l'Institut.

2140 Université pontificale grégorienne [UPG]

Institut pour l'étude des religions et des cultures
Piazza della Pilotta 4
00187 Rome
Tel: +39-06-6701-55 01
Web: http://www.unigre.urbe.it
e-mail: bongiovanni@unigro.it

📖 Cours de théologie

Domaines d'étude: droit canon, études classiques, lettres, philosophie, psychologie, sciences sociales, théologie, religion.
Programmes: cours de 1er et 2e cycle en théologie, droit canon, philosophie, histoire ecclésiastique, missiologie, sciences sociales, spiritualité, psychologie, sciences religieuses, lettres latines.
A l'intention de: ressortissants de tout pays, ayant les qualifications requises dans les différentes branches des sciences religieuses, ecclésiastiques et autres sciences connexes.
Durée: 2 semestres (débutant mi-octobre et mi-janvier).
Connaissances linguistiques: langues d'enseignement: italien et anglais.
Inscriptions: avant le 15 octobre ou le 15 janvier; au Secrétaire général de l'Université.

2141 Université pontificale Saint-Thomas-d'Aquin [UPS]

Largo Angelicum 1
00184 Rome
Tel: +39-06-670-2354
Fax: +39-06-679-0407
Web: http://www.angelicum.org
e-mail: segreteria@pust.urbe.it

📖 Cours de formation en sciences sociales

Domaines d'étude: affaires internationales, économie politique, études du développement, sciences sociales, théologie, religion.
Programmes: Cours de formation en sciences sociales: (a) 1er cycle (baccalauréat); (b) 2ème cycle (licence); (c) 3ème cycle (doctorat).
A l'intention de: ressortissants de tout pays; les étudiants du 1er cycle doivent avoir terminé leurs études secondaires.
Durée: (a) et (c) 2 ans; (b) 1 an.
Inscriptions: entre le 1er et le 31 octobre (du 1er au 15 février pour le second semestre) à la Faculté des sciences sociales; tél: +39 6 670 235.

📖 Cours de formation philosophique

Domaines d'étude: philosophie.
Programmes: Cours de formation philosophique: (a) 1er cycle (baccalauréat) visant à donner une formation globale sur les grands thèmes de la philosophie: l'homme, le monde et Dieu; (b) 2ème cycle (licence) visant à approfondir les connaissances acquises et à perfectionner les méthodes de recherche; (c) 3ème cycle (doctorat) consacré aux études et recherches préparant à la thèse de doctorat.
A l'intention de: candidats des deux sexes, de tout pays, clercs et laïcs ayant une connaissance suffisante de l'italien et: (a) ayant terminé leurs études secondaires; (b) titulaires du baccalauréat ou ayant passé l'examen d'autres facultés ou terminé les études complètes d'un grand séminaire; la connaissance approfondie de l'une des langues suivantes est exigée: allemand, anglais, espagnol, français; (c) possédant la licence et qui se préparent, soit à l'enseignement dans les facultés, soit à la recherche philosophique.
Durée: 2 ans chaque cycle.
Connaissances linguistiques: langue d'enseignement: italien; (b) la connaissance approfondie de l'une des langues suivantes est exigée: allemand, anglais, espagnol, français.

Inscriptions: avant le 30 octobre, à la Faculté de philosophie à l'adresse ci-dessus; tél: +39 6 670 2290.

📖 Cours de théologie

Domaines d'étude: théologie, religion.
Programmes: Cours de théologie comportant diverses spécialisations: biblique, morale, dogmatique, œcuménique, théologie thomiste et spiritualité: (a) 1er cycle (baccalauréat); (b) 2e cycle (licence); (c) 3e cycle (doctorat).
A l'intention de: (a) candidats possédant un diplôme sanctionnant des études classiques et ayant accompli le cours biennal de philosophie; (b) et (c) étudiants ayant fréquenté un cours institutionnel dans une faculté de théologie ecclésiastique, ou ayant achevé le cours de 4 années de théologie dans un séminaire, ainsi qu'aux laïcs des deux sexes ayant une culture équivalente en philosophie et théologie; le 3ème cycle est réservé aux candidats qui se destinent à l'enseignement ou à la recherche scientifique.
Durée: (a) 3 ans, plus une année de théologie pastorale destinée aux étudiants qui ne se spécialisent pas après le 1er cycle; (b) et (c) 2 ans.
Connaissances linguistiques: l'enseignement est donné en italien et en anglais.
Inscriptions: entre le 1er et le 31 octobre (du 1er au 15 février pour le second semestre) à la Faculté de théologie (tél: +39 6 670 2350).

San Marino

Academic year: October to July.
Organization of higher education system: Higher education in San Marino is provided by the Università degli Studi della Repùbblica di San Marino and its Istituto di Cibernetica which enjoy administrative autonomy.
University level studies:
• University level first stage: Main stage:
The first (main) stage takes place at the university and lasts for three years. It leads to the Diploma Universitario in such fields as nursing, economy and administration.
• University level second stage: Concluding stage:
The concluding stage corresponds, at the university, to a period of specializzazione (specialization) or perfezionamento lasting a minimum of two years after the Laurea (qualification required for admission). It requires the submission of a thesis. Teachers are trained in Italy. Students must attend a two-to three-week special course in September in San Marino before the start of the school year.
Monetary unit: Euro (€).
International student admission: Definition of foreign student: A foreign student is a student who does not have the San Marinese citizenship and is enrolled in a San Marinese institution of higher education.
Language: Italian and English.
Immigration requirements: Students require a residence permit but no visa. A health visa is required.
Information services:
•Segreteria di Stato per la Pubblica Istruzione, l'Università, gli Istituti Culturali e gli Affari Sociali
http://www.unirsm.sm
•Dipartimento Pubblica Istruzione, Contrada Omerelli 23, 47890 Republic of San Marino: tel: +378-54-988-2550; fax: +378-54-988-2301; email: segr.pub-istr@omniway.sm.
Recognition of studies and qualification: Information regarding recognition of foreign credentials:
Academic Equivalence and Mobility Services, Ministry of Public Education, Universities and Cultural Institutions, Contrada Omerelli 23, 47031 San Marino; tel.: +378 54 988 22 50; fax: +378 54 988 2301; email: segr.pub-istr@omniway.sm.

2142   **University of San Marino**

Rettorato
Contrada del Collegio, 38
Palazzo Mercuri
47890 San Marino
Tel: +378-882-541
Fax: +378-882-545
Web: http://www.unirsm.sm
e-mail: rettorato@unirsm.sm

📖 Undergraduate, Graduate, Postgraduate Programmes

Study Domains: communication, economic and commercial sciences, economy, education, history, law, linguistics, management, nursing, obstetrics and gynaecology, ophthalmology, psychology, speech therapy, teacher education.
Programmes: Bachelor's, Master's, Ph.D. degrees in all major fields.
Duration: 6 months to 3 years; contact chiara.cardogna@unirsm.sm for further information.
Languages: Italian, English and French.

💕Scholarship

Study Domains: communication, economy, history.
Scholarships: Borsa di Studio.
Applications: contact chiara.cardogna@unirsm.sm for further details.

Saudi Arabia

Academic year: September to May.
Organization of higher education system: The higher education system provides for degrees from the Bachelor's to Ph.D. levels, based on the field of study. Academic programmes are designed according to the internationally acceptable standards for each higher education level to meet the international accreditation requirements around the world. BA/BSc. programmes usually require between 4-5 years of study except in certain specialized fields such as medicine. The Saudi higher education system offers a wide range of specialty areas at a high level of standards.
Monetary unit: Saudi Riyal (SR).
International student admission: Secondary-school leaving certificate or equivalent. Foreign students are usually admitted directly to schools that accommodate them. Universities should be contacted directly for exchange and scholarship programme information.
Language: Saudi universities require proficiency in Arabic. If necessary, students may be admitted to Arabic language institutes for pre-university language preparation. Some universities and some academic programmes also require proficiency in English.
Immigration requirements: Scholarship-related documentation and proof of financial support are required beside what national students are required to submit for admission. a valid residency status is another requirement needed for international students.
Information services:
• Ministry of Higher Education, web: www.mohe.gov.sa, provides visitors with valid information on Saudi academic institutions. It also links visitors to other academic websites and Saudi universities.
Open and distance learning: Distance learning schools are not yet implemented in Saudi Arabia. However, many Saudi universities now offer some courses online and/or are in the process of establishing e-degree programmes online. A national open university has not yet been established. The Arab Open University is one of the open universities licensed in Saudi Arabia.
Recognition of studies and qualification:
• The Saudi National Committee for Accreditation of academic qualifications, The Ministry of Higher Education
• The Saudi Board of Accreditation (Newly established), The Ministry of Higher Education
• The Academic Councils (in each university) which looks at the qualifications submitted to each respective university for employment or academic purposes.
Accommodation services: Residency requirements are handled through arrangements made directly between the school and the student. Most Saudi universities provide student dormitories and assistance to students to help find accommodations near campuses.
Work opportunities: Work within campus premises is permitted as well as off-campus training for graduating students. Work permit and visa authorization are all subject to the status that the school decides to give to that student.
Additional information: International students are advised to seek help and information through the Saudi Attaché's offices in their countries to obtain information on study programmes in Saudi Arabia. Many universities around the

world have mutual agreements with many Saudi universities which include student exchange programmes which give students further opportunities to visit and live in Saudi Arabia. Universities can be contacted directly for exchange programme requests. Further information can be obtained from the Ministry's website: www.mohe.gov.sa.

2143 King Saud University [KSU]
PO Box 2454
11451 Riyadh
Tel: +966-467-8041
Web: http://www.ksu.edu.sa
e-mail: info@ksu.edu.sa

📖 Undergraduate, Graduate, Postgraduate Programmes
Study Domains: all major fields.

Sénégal
Année universitaire: novembre à juin.
Unité monétaire: franc CFA.
Admission pour étudiants du pays: Être titulaire du baccalauréat ou d'un diplôme équivalent. Limite d'âge: 22 ans pour la faculté de médecine et 23 ans pour les autres facultés à la date du 31 décembre de l'année d'admission.
Connaissances linguistiques requises: Une bonne connaissance de la langue française est souhaitable. Des cours de préparation
linguistique à différents niveaux sont donnés par l'Institut français pour étudiants étrangers (IFE) à l'Université Cheikh Anta Diop de Dakar.
Formalités d'immigration: Les étudiants étrangers doivent être en possession d'un visa d'entrée, qui est à obtenir auprès des missions diplomatiques sénégalaises à l'étranger.
Services d'accueil et d'information:
• Centre des oeuvres universitaires de Dakar (COUD), Route de Ouakam, BP 2056, Dakar.
• Rectorat de l'Université Cheikh Anta Diop, Dakar.
• Direction des bourses, avenue Lamine Gueye Building Maginot, Dakar.
Reconnaissance des études et diplômes: Rectorat, Université Cheikh Anta Diop (University of Dakar); BP 5005; Dakar; Sénégal; tél: +221-825-0530; fax: +221-825-5219; email: info@ucad.sn; Internet: http://www.ucad.sn.
Publications / Sites Web: «Guide de l'étudiant».

2144 École Inter-Etats des sciences et médecine vétérinaires de Dakar [EISMV]
BP 5077
Dakar-Fann
Tel: +221-865-1008
Fax: +221-825-4283
Web: http://www.refer.sn/eismv/eismv.htm
e-mail: mariamd@eismv.refer.sn

📖 Programmes en sciences vétérinaires
Domaines d'étude: sciences vétérinaires.
Programmes: (a) formation initiale portant sur la biologie et la production animales, santé et pharmacie des animaux, hygiène, contrôle et utilisation des produits d'origine animale, pastoralisme et protection de l'environnement, gestion des projets et techniques de management, conduisant au diplôme de docteur vétérinaire; (b) formation postuniversitaire (DESS et DEA) en aménagement pastoral intégré au Sahel et productions animales; (c) formation continue conduisant à une attestation.
A l'intention de: ressortissants des États membres de l'EISMV sur présentation de leur gouvernement; États non membres, justifier d'une bourse; (a) titulaires du DUES (chimie-biologie) pour l'admission en 1re année; du baccalauréat scientifique (C, D, E) pour entrer en année préparatoire (CPEV) de l'EISMV; (b) ingénieur des travaux d'élevage; sélection sur dossier.
Durée: 6 ans.
Frais: (chiffres approximatifs) (a) inscription: 50.000 francs CFA par an; scolarité: pour les ressortissants des pays membres (Bénin, Burkina Faso, Cameroun, République

centrafricaine, Congo, Côte d'Ivoire, Gabon, Mauritanie, Niger, Rwanda, Sénégal, Tchad, Togo): 2.115.788 francs CFA; pour les ressortissants des pays non membres: 2.194.925 francs CFA; (b) 2.250.000 francs CFA.
Assistance financière: bourses à demander aux partenaires au développement.
Connaissances linguistiques: français et anglais requis.
Inscriptions: (a) entre le 15 octobre et le 15 novembre; (b) avant le 15 juillet; à l'adresse ci-dessus.

2145 École nationale des arts [ENA]
36, avenue Faidherbe
BP 3311
Dakar
Tel: +221-822-4673
Fax: +221-822 1638

📖 Cursus du 1er et 2e cycle / arts, musique
Domaines d'étude: arts, arts appliqués, arts décoratifs, arts graphiques, musique et musicologie.
Programmes: Formation de professeurs d'éducation dans les domaines artistiques (arts plastiques, arts scéniques, animation culturelle), de la couture, de la coupe et de la mode, et de l'éducation musicale; formation spécifique en séminaires de recyclage et de perfectionnement; conduisant au diplôme de fin d'études supérieures artistiques (option: musique ou plastique) au niveau maîtrise; au diplôme de fin d'études supérieures d'animation culturelle au niveau licence; au certificat ou attestation de fin de stage.
A l'intention de: ressortissants de tout pays, âgés de 20 à 27 ans, titulaires d'un baccalauréat; admission direct d'octobre à novembre; sélection par tests techniques, dissertation, entretien avec jury; admission sur titre pour les candidats présentés par leur gouvernement ou un organisme agréé.
Durée: 4 ans (maîtrise); 3 ans (licence).
Connaissances linguistiques: français obligatoire.
Inscriptions: avant le 31 décembre, à l'adresse ci-dessus.

2146 Université Cheikh Anta Diop de Dakar, Institut de français pour les étudiants étrangers [UCAD-IFE]
BP 5005
Dakar-Fann
Tel: +221-825-7528
Fax: +221-825-3724
Web: http://www.ucad.sn
e-mail: info@ucad.sn

📖 Formation de bibliothécaires
Domaines d'étude: bibliothéconomie, documentation.
Programmes: Formation de spécialistes de l'information documentaire (archivistes, bibliothécaires et documentalistes); environ 90 participants en 1re année du 1er cycle, 25 places pour le concours d'entrée en 2e cycle.
A l'intention de: étudiants de pays francophones de l'Afrique noire et de l'océan Indien, titulaires pour le 1er cycle, du baccalauréat ou d'un diplôme admis en équivalence, ou qualifiés à un examen spécial; pour le 2e cycle, titulaires d'une licence ou d'un diplôme admis en équivalence et qualifiés au concours d'entrée, ou candidats ayant obtenu le diplôme de 1er cycle de l'EBAD et 3 années d'expérience professionnelle dans un service d'information documentaire avant le concours d'entrée.
Durée: 2 ans pour chacun des 2 cycles.
Frais: (chiffres approximatifs) scolarité: 300.000 francs CFA par an, pour les étudiants non sénégalais.
Inscriptions: avant le 30 juillet pour les admissions sur titres (1er cycle); avant le 31 mars pour les candidats à l'examen spécial (1er cycle) et pour les candidats aux concours du 2ème cycle; à l'École de bibliothécaires, archivistes et documentalistes (EBAD).

📖 Français langue étrangère
Domaines d'étude: études culturelles, français, langues, littérature et civilisation, programmes d'été.
Programmes: (a) cours de français langue étrangère, conduisant au Certificat pratique de langue française (CPLF, niveau 1), au Diplôme d'études françaises (DEF, niveau 2), au Diplôme supérieur d'études françaises (DSEF, niveau 3); (b) stages de formation et recyclage en didactique du français langue étrangère; (c) stages d'été à la carte: culture et

civilisation négro-africaines, littérature sénégalaise, dossiers socioculturels, connaissance du milieu.
A l'intention de: (a) étudiants titulaires d'un diplôme admis en équivalence du baccalauréat sénégalais et originaires d'un pays non francophone, ainsi que les étudiants de 3e année d'universités non francophones, dans le cadre du programme «Year Abroad»; (b) élèves-maîtres, élèves-professeurs et professeurs de français langue étrangère; (c) étudiants ou professeurs de français langue étrangère.
Durée: (a) 1, 2, et 3 ans (débutant en novembre) et 1 cours d'été; (b) 1 mois (de juillet à septembre); (c) de 2 à 6 semaines (durant l'année universitaire ou de juillet à septembre).
Frais: (chiffres approximatifs (a) droits d'inscription: 300.000 francs CFA; (b) inscription: 100.000 francs CFA; scolarité: 50.000 francs CFA; frais de séjour: 45.000 francs CFA par mois; (c) variables selon la durée du stage et le nombre de stagiaires.
Assistance financière: (b) quelques bourses, octroyées par la Mission française de coopération de Dakar pour les Gambiens, celle de Bissau, pour les ressortissants de Guinée-Bissau, et celle de Freetown, pour les Sierra-Léoniens.
Inscriptions: (a) avant décembre; (b) et (c) avant fin mai; au Secrétariat de l'Institut de français pour les étudiants étrangers (IFE) à l'adresse ci-dessus.

Serbia and Montenegro
Academic year: Montenegro: September to June.
Organization of higher education system:
•Serbia:
Higher education in Serbia includes university education (faculties and art academies) and non-university education (post-secondary schools) where courses last no less than two years and no more than three years. Universities in Serbia organize art and educational work, as well as other activities, in compliance with the law and its statutes. The faculty is an educational and art institution which includes basic studies, specialized studies, magisterial studies and doctoral studies. The basic studies last between four and six academic years. Specialized studies last between one and two academic years and magisterial studies last for two academic years. Doctoral studies last for three years. Faculties carry out independently, or in cooperation with another organization, their basic, applied and development research in function of educational activity development.
• Montenegro:
Higher education in Montenegro is provided at one university, the University of Montenegro, comprising 15 faculties and around 50 study programmes, and three research institutes. Study programmes are as follows:
• undergraduate (Bachelor's) degrees: BS, BA, requiring three years of study:
• graduate (Master's) degrees: MS, MA, requiring two years of study beyond the Bachelor's degree and a thesis;
• doctoral degrees: PhD, requiring three years of study beyond Master's studies plus a dissertation.
The academic year consists of two semesters. Candidates must have a secondary-school leaving certificate with good results or pass an entrance examination for faculties of arts. (Source: IAU World Higher Education Database, 2005/6, in part).
Monetary unit:
• Serbia: Dinar.
• Montenegro: Euro (€).
International student admission: Montenegro: International students can be admitted to study programmes under the same conditions as national students and have the same status as self-financing domestic students. A special ranking list is made for international students according to rules on enrolment to the first year of studies.
Immigration requirements: Montenegro: International students must obtain a visa before entering the country for stays longer than 90 days and are required to submit a medical certificate.
Estimated expenses for one academic year: Montenegro: tuition: 300-1,000 Euros per year: accommodation in student hostels: 30 Euros per month.
Recognition of studies and qualification:
• ENIC Centre Serbia; Nemanjina 24, 11000 Belgrade, Serbia and Montenegro; tel: +381-11-361 6357; fax: +381-11-361-6491; email: kabinet.mps@mps.sr.gov.yu

• Montenegro: Accreditation is done by the Council for Higher Education appointed by the Government for improvement of higher education in the Republic. The Council issues a certificate of accreditation. The accreditation procedure and form of the certificate is prescribed by the Council, by special enactment. Initial accreditation is obtained after quality assessment of study programmes and their harmonization with professional needs and adopted standards. An institution should submit a request to the Council at least one year before the date for which the accreditation of study programme is required. Accreditation is issued for a maximum period of three years. An institution cannot enroll students, organize lectures and grant diplomas before obtaining the licence.
• ENIC Centre Montenegro: Manager, Ministry of Education and Science, Podgorica, Republic of Serbia and Montenegro; tel: +381-81-265-024; fax: +381-81-265-014.

2147 University of Belgrade
Studentski trg 1
11000 Belgrade
Tel: +381-11-635-579 / 635-153
Fax: +381-11-638-912
Web: http://www.bg.ac.yu

📖 **Undergraduate, Graduate Programmes / Multidisciplinary**
Study Domains: business administration, economic and commercial sciences, education, engineering, international relations, law, liberal arts, management, medicine, sciences, social sciences, sociology, trade.
Programmes: Undergraduate, Master's or specialized studies, and doctoral studies in all major fields.
Description: programmes of study lead to the following diplomas: a Bachelor's degree which carries a professional title (engineer, professor, economist, doctor, veterinarian, dentist, etc.) and a postgraduate degree leading to the academic title of specialist or master; the three-year doctoral programme does not result in a degree but fulfils the prerequisite to begin work on a doctoral dissertation which, when it has been defended, results in a doctoral degree (Ph.D.); diplomas attesting to the completion of Bachelor's, Master's and doctoral studies are signed by the dean of the faculty in which the programme was completed or the dissertation defended, and by the rector of the University, while academic specialization diplomas are only signed by the dean of the faculty in which the studies were completed. Health related specializations in the fields of medicine, stomatology and pharmacology are not included in the University's postgraduate studies, but are carried out according to regulations from the field of health care.
Held: courses at 30 faculties and 8 scientific institutes.
Duration: Undergraduate studies: 4 to 6 years (8 to 12 semesters), depending on the faculty (social-humanistic science: 8 semesters; science: 8 to 9 semesters; engineering: 8 to 10 semesters; medicine: 10 to 12 semesters); specialized studies: 1 to 3 years; Master's studies: 2 years; doctoral studies: 3 years.
Applications: to the above address.

2148 University of Montenegro
Cetinjski put bb
81000 Podgorica
Tel: +381-81-242-777 / 244-406
Fax: +381-81-242-777 / 244-406
Web: http://www.cg.ac.yu
e-mail: www@cg.ac.yu

📖 **Undergraduate, Graduate / Multidisciplinary**
Study Domains: arts, civil engineering, economic and commercial sciences, electricity and electronics, engineering, law, marine science, mathematics, mechanical engineering, medicine, metallurgy, music and musicology, philosophy, physiology, sciences.
Programmes: undergraduate and graduate degree programmes in economics, electrical engineering, mechanical engineering, civil engineering, metallurgy and technology, law, mathematics and natural sciences, philosophy, maritime studies, music, arts, drama, medicine, fine arts, tourism and hotel management and physiotherapy.

Open to: all nationalities with secondary school certificate or equivalent; entrance examination required.
Duration: variable, according to each programme.
Applications: to the above address.

Singapore

Academic year: July to March.
Monetary unit: Singapore dollar (S$).
National student admission: Minimum requirements for admission to the National University of Singapore (http://www.nus.sg/) and Nanyang Technological University (http://www.ntu.ac.sg/) are passes in 2 subjects at Advanced level and a pass in the General Paper in the Singapore-Cambridge General Certificate of Education Advanced Level Examination; for Singapore Polytechnic (http://www.sp.ac.sg/), Ngee Ann Polytechnic (http://www.np.ac.sg/), Temasek Polytechnic (http://www.tp.ac.sg/) and Nanyang Polytechnic (http://www.nyp.ac.sg/), General Education (Ordinary level) with passes in English, mathematics and relevant science subject; for the Institute of Education, GCE A-levels for Certificate in Education programme, Polytechnic Diploma in any discipline with at least 5 GCE O-level passes, including English and Mathematics, and university degree in relevant subjects, for diploma in education. For more information, see the respective web sites.
Language: English is the language of instruction at all the institutions mentioned above.
Immigration requirements: Foreign students must obtain the Immigration Student Pass from the Controller of Immigration,
Singapore Immigration and Registration Building, 10 Kallang Road, Singapore 208 718. (http://www.mha.gov.sg/sir).
Information services:
• Ministry of Education,1 North Buona Vista Drive Singapore 138675; tel: +65-6872-1110; fax: +65-6775-5826; email: contact@moe.edu.sg (study facilities for foreign students); web: http://www.moe.edu.sg
• Ministry of Foreign Affairs, Tanglin, Singapore 248163; email: mfa@mfa.gov.sg; tel: +65-6379-8000; fax: +65-6474-7885, (Colombo Plan Training Awards), web: http://www.mfa.gov.sg
• University of Singapore, Kent Ridge Road, Singapore 119 260 (postgraduate scholarships); web: http://www.nus.edu.sg
• Registrar's Office and Department of Student Affairs, Nanyang Technological Institute (for information on placement services, etc.); Nanyang Ave, Singapore 639798; tel: +65-6791-1744; fax: +65-6791-1604; web: http://gemsweb.ntu.edu.sg/igems/public.htm.
Recognition of studies and qualification: Higher Education Branch, Ministry of Education; 1 Kay Siang Road; Singapore 1024; Singapore; tel.: +65-473-9111; fax: +65-475-6128; email: contact@moe.edu.sg; web: http://www.moe.edu.sg.

2149 Nanyang Technological University [NTU]
Nanyang Avenue
63979 Singapore
Tel: +65-6791-1744
Fax: +65-6791-1604
Web: http://www.ntu.edu.sg

🖋 Scholarship
Study Domains: all major fields, engineering, sciences.
Scholarships: (a) Research Scholarship; (b) GLC Undergraduate Scholarship; (c) Nanyang Scholarship;.
Open to: (a) Postgraduate students from all nationalities; (b) Undergraduates from India and Indonesia; (c) Undergraduates from all nationalities; (d) Undergraduates from ASEAN countries except Singapore.
Duration: (a) 1 year, renewable; (b) 4 years, renewable; (c) 3 to 4 years, renewable.
Value: (a) Living expenses, S$1,400 to S$1,500 per month; (b) Tuition, S$6,220 per year; living expenses, S$6,000 per year; return airfare at the start and completion of course and hotel fees;
(c) Tuition, S$6, 220 per year; living expenses, S$5,000 per year.

Applications: (a) 31 January for July admission, 31 July for January admission; contact postgraduate@ntu.edu.sg for further details; (b) contact adm_intnl@ntu.edu.sg for further details; (c) contact adm_intnl@ntu.edu.sg for further details; (d) contact adm_intnl@ntu.edu.sg for further details.

2150 National University of Singapore [NUS]
10 Kent Ridge Crescent
119260 Singapore
Tel: +65-6775-6666
Web: http://www.nus.edu.sg

📖 Undergraduate Programmes
Study Domains: all major fields.
Programmes: Bachelor's degree programmes in all major fields.
Open to: candidates of any nationality holding GCE Advanced Level or the equivalent for undergraduate programmes.
Financial assistance: a limited number of scholarships, bursaries and loans are available for candidates already admitted.
Applications: to the above address by 1 April.

🖋 Scholarships
Study Domains: all major fields, research.
Scholarships: (a) NUS / ASEAN Undergraduate Scholarship; (b) SembCorp & Singapore Technologies Undergraduate Scholarship; (c) Singapore Airlines - Neptune Orient Lines Undergraduate Scholarship; (d) Singapore Government Undergraduate Scholarship for Hong Kong students; (e) Donated Scholarships.
Open to: (a) awarded to freshmen based on academic merit (ASEAN scholarships attributed to citizens of ASEAN countries); candidates may not hold any other award without approval; (b) for freshmen Indonesian nationals who have completed the SMU Ebtanas (science stream) in 2002, or equivalent or are completing the SMU Ebtanas (science stream) in 2003, or equivalent; (c) for freshmen Indian nationals who have completed the Standard 12 (science stream) in 2002, or equivalent or are completing the Standard 12 (science stream) in 2003, or equivalent; (d) for freshmen students who hold Hong Kong (SAR) citizenship or Permanent Residency (PR) who have completed the Hong Kong A-levels (science stream) in 2002 or are completing the Hong Kong A-levels (science stream) in 2003; (e) students of any nationality based on academic merit. May not hold any other award without approval.
Duration: (a) for duration of the course to which candidate is admitted; (b), (c), (d) minimum period of candidature for the respective undergraduate course at NUS; (e) tenable on a yearly basis.
Value: (a) tuition fee and living allowance of S$4,300 per year; (b), (c), (d) tuition and all compulsory fees; settling-in allowance of S$200; an accommodation allowance; an annual living allowance of S$6,000; return air passage to Singapore; (e) S$3,000.
Applications: contact Admissions Office for application details or consult website: http://www.nus.edu.sg/oam/scholarship.

2151 National University of Singapore - Faculty of Medicine [NUS]
Block MD5, Level 3
12 Medical Drive
117598 Singapore
Tel: +65-6874-1037
Fax: +65-6773-1462
Web: http://www.med.nus.edu.sg
e-mail: dgms@nus.edu.sg

📖 Medical Studies
Study Domains: medicine, radiology.
Programmes: programme of medical studies leading to Master of Medicine degree.
Open to: doctors with basic medical degrees; no age limit.
Duration: 2 to 3 years of training in an approved hospital and examinations.
Applications: to the Secretary, at the above address for

further information.

☛ Medical Studies

Study Domains: medicine, surgery.
Scholarships: a) NUS ASEAN Graduate Scholarship
(AGS): to pursue full-time coursework in Public Health and
Occupational Medicine; b) Lee Foundation / Tan Sri Dr
Runme Shaw Fellowship in Orthopaedic Surgery / Hand and
Reconstructive Microsurgery.
Open to: (a) all ASEAN nationals, except
Singaporeans/Singapore PR. The AGS enables a successful
scholar to pursue full-time coursework in Public Health and
Occupational Medicine. Details are available from DGMS;
(b) doctors from developing countries holding a first medical
degree with a minimum of 4 years postgraduate experience of
which at least 2 years was in orthopaedic surgery, or at least 1
year in the same subject after the completion of basic surgical
training.
Duration: (a) 6-month clinical attachment at the
Department of Orthopaedic Surgery, National University
Hospital or the Department of Orthopaedic Surgery,
Singapore General Hospital; applicants must be from
developing countries and must have some experience in these
two specialities; no degree or diploma awarded on completion
of training.
Languages: fluency in English required.
Applications: (a) details available from Division of
Graduate Medical Studies (DGMS) at the above address.

2152 Ngee Ann Polytechnic [NAP]
535, Clementi Road
599489 Singapore
Tel: +65-6466-6555
Fax: +65-6468-7326
Web: http://www.np.edu.sg

☐ Diploma Programmes

Study Domains: accounting, audio-visual media, chemical
engineering, civil engineering, electricity and electronics,
energy, engineering, finance, horticulture, mechanical
engineering, shipbuilding, technology, telecommunications.
Programmes: (a) Full-time courses in accountancy,
banking and financial services, biotechnology, building and
real estate management, building services engineering,
business studies, computer studies, electrical engineering,
mechatronic engineering, civil and environmental
engineering, quality assurance engineering, electronic
computer and telecommunication engineering, mechanical
engineering, shipbuilding and offshore engineering, film,
sound and video, mass communication; (b) part-time
advanced diploma courses in automation and control
technology, computer and communication systems,
entrepreneurial studies, industrial management, medical
laboratory management, naval architecture, data
communication and networking, quality engineering and
management.
Open to: (a) full-time courses: candidates with General
Certificate of Education (ordinary and advanced level);
working personnel may apply to the part-time courses; (b)
candidates with diploma in relevant engineering discipline;
candidates must have at least 2 years working experience and
be at least 24 years old at the time of application.
Duration: (a) full-time courses: 2 years for A-level
holders; 3 years for O-level holders; (b) 2 years for part-time
advanced diploma courses.
Fees: (approximate figures) (a) full-time courses, around
S$10,000 per year; (b) part-time advanced diploma courses,
approximately S$4,000 per year depending on the course fee
structure and the number of subjects taken.
Applications: to the Admissions Officer.

2153 Singapore Polytechnic [SP]
500 Dover Road
0513 Singapore
Tel: +65-6775-1133
Fax: +65-6870-6189
Web: http://www.sp.edu.sg

☐ Diploma Courses / Technical and Commercial

Study Domains: accounting, architecture, building
industry, chemical engineering, civil engineering, computer
science, engineering, industrial technology, marketing,
shipbuilding, telecommunications.

Programmes: (a) diploma courses in accountancy,
architectural technology, biotechnology, building and
property management, business administration, chemical
engineering, chemical process technology, civil and structural
engineering, electrical engineering, electronics, computer and
communications engineering, manufacturing engineering,
marine engineering, maritime transportation, mechanical
engineering, nautical studies, computer information systems,
accountancy, banking and financial services, marketing,
optometry, materials engineering, instrumentation and control
engineering and mechatronics, multimedia software
engineering; (b) Post-Diploma courses in occupational safety
and health, engineering mathematics; (c) Advanced Diploma
courses in building automation and services, business
information systems, process control and instrumentation,
civil and construction engineering, food technology, industrial
engineering and management, information systems
technology, plastics technology, power electronics and
industrial applications, power systems engineering, project
coordination and construction management, strategic
marketing, analytical science and laboratory management,
mechatronics; (d) short courses in a variety of technological
disciplines.
Open to: candidates of any nationality: (a) with GCE
O-level pass in English, a credit in mathematics and a relevant
third subject, except for the business and computer-related
courses where candidates must have credits in English,
mathematics and 3 other subjects at GCE O-level;
GCE A-level qualifications are also accepted for all diploma
courses; (b) and (c) with an appropriate polytechnic diploma
or equivalent qualification with relevant working experience.
Applications: by March for full-time courses and by
February for part-time courses; candidates may write to the
Admissions Office indicating their course preference and
submit photocopies of their educational documents.

Slovakia
Academic year: September to August.
Monetary unit: crown (SK).
National student admission: Foreign applicants for higher
education studies must have qualifications equivalent to
Slovak secondary education and have passed the General
Certificate of Education examination, or its equivalent. The
age limit for admission is generally 30 years. Foreign
candidates are admitted to institutions of higher education
both on the basis of scholarships offered to other states by
Slovakia in accordance with cultural agreements and of
private agreements with the selected institution. Courses last
from 4 to 7 years for the M.A. degree and 3 more years for the
Ph.D. degree.
Language: An adequate knowledge of the Slovak
language is an important prerequisite for study at a Slovak
university; this knowledge is expected from the majority of
applicants. It is possible to take selected undergraduate
courses at some higher education institutions in English; the
majority of higher education institutions offer postgraduate
study in English or German. Slovak language courses and
vocational training for foreign students are provided by the
centres of the Institute for Language and Academic
Preparation for Foreign Students at the Comenius University.
Some courses, mostly for those studying on the basis of a
private contract, can be taken in English or German.
Immigration requirements: Foreign students must hold a
valid passport and a Slovak visa provided by the Slovak
Embassy in candidate's country.
Estimated expenses for one academic year: The value of a
scholarship is about SK 2,500 paid monthly from the first day
of the course to the month following the final examination.
Students who are ill continue to receive payments provided
their illness is recognized by a competent medical authority.
Students have access to university dormitories and
restaurants. The expenses amount to US$1,000-$3,000 a year
(plus fees). Self-financing students are expected to pay full
tuition fees as decided individually by higher education
institutions. Fees range from US$2,000-$9,000 per academic
year. In general, applications and identification papers must
be received before the end of February through the
intermediary of the appropriate authority in the candidate's
country and the Slovak diplomatic mission.
Information services:

• Ministry of Education and Science, House of Foreign Relations, Levická 3, Bratislava; tel: +421-2-5542-3236; fax: +421-2-5542-5634; email: domzahr@education.gov.sk
• Slovak Academic Information Agency, SAIA, n.o. Bratislava, Nám. slobody 23, 812 20 Bratislava 1; tel: +421-2-5441-1426 / 1436; +421-2-5441-1464 / 1484; fax: +421-2-5441-1429; email: saia@saia.sk; web: http//www.saia.sk
• Institute of Information and Prognoses of Education, Youth and Sport, Staré grunty 52, 842 44 Bratislava.

Open and distance learning: Since 1991, the City University in Bratislava provides distance education using English programmes in cooperation with the Open University at Comenius University. In 1994, several higher education institutions in the SR were involved in the regional project PHARE - Pilot Project for Regional Cooperation in Distance Education.

Recognition of studies and qualification: Slovak ENIC, NARIC, Centre for Equivalence of Diplomas, Institute of Information
and Prognoses of Education (Stredisko pre ekvivalenciu dokladov o vzdelaní); Staré grunty 52; 842 44 Bratislava; Slovak Republic; tel: +421-2-6542-6521; fax: +421-2-6542-6521; email: naric@uips.sk; web: http://www.uips.sk.

Publications / Websites:
• 'Higher Education in the Slovak Republic', a guide for foreign students, Bratislava; published in English.
• 'Do You Want to Study in Slovakia?', Bratislava; published in English, German, French and Spanish.
Both can be obtained from the Ministry of Education and Science.

2154 Academia Istropolitana Nova [AIS]

Prostredna 13
900 21 Svaty Jur
Tel: +421-2-4497-0451/53
Fax: +421-2-4497-0455
Web: http://www.ainova.sk
e-mail: martina@ainova.sk

Postgraduate Programmes

Study Domains: architecture, economic and commercial sciences, health and hygiene, humanities and arts, social sciences, social work.
Programmes: postgraduate programmes in (a) architectural conservation, built heritage development studies; (b) European studies; (c) environmental policy; (d) applied economics and finance.
Open to: candidates of all nationalities with (a) minimum M.A. degree; (b), (c), (d) Bachelor's degree.
Languages: fluent English required for all programmes.

2155 Academy of Fine Arts and Design Bratislava [AFAD]

Hviezdoslavovo nám. 18
814 37 Bratislava
Tel: +421-2-5443-2431
Fax: +421-2-5443-2340
Web: http://www.afad.sk

Degree Programmes / Fine Arts

Study Domains: applied arts, architecture, arts, arts and crafts, audio-visual media, fine arts, graphic arts, industrial design, photography, visual arts.
Programmes: degree programmes in fine arts; studio work under guidance of the artistic staff in: painting, sculpture, architecture, graphic arts/ceramics, jewellery, glass, textile, fashion, design, visual media, restorations.
Open to: candidates of all nationalities; over 17 years of age.
Duration: 1 semester to 6 years; courses begin in October and February.
Fees: approximately US$2,000 per term (covers only study fee and basic material).
Financial assistance: possibility of scholarship assistance approximately US$1,500-$3,000.
Languages: instruction in English, German or French, depending on the course.

Applications: by 30 November for the full study programme; before the beginning of the term for a semester or academic year; to the above address.

2156 Academy of Music and Dramatic Arts [VSMU]

Ventúrska 3
813 01 Bratislava
Tel: +421-2 5443-2172
Fax: +421-2 5443-0125
Web: http://www.vsmu.sk
e-mail: rektorat@vsmu.sk

Undergraduate, Graduate, Postgraduate Programmes

Study Domains: arts, music and musicology, performing arts, visual arts.
Programmes: Bachelor's, Master's, Ph.D. degrees in music and dance, drama, film and television.
Open to: candidates of any country who fulfil the necessary requirements.
Duration: 3 to 5 years.
Applications: to the above address.

2157 Catholic University in Ruzomberok

Hrabovska Cesta 1
03401 Ruzomberok
Tel: +421-44-432-2709
Fax: +421-44-432-2708
Web: http://www.ku.sk
e-mail: banary@ku.sk

Undergraduate, Graduate Courses

Study Domains: arts, design, history, literature and civilization, music and musicology, philosophy, physics, teacher education, theology, religion.
Programmes: Bachelor's, Master's degrees in teacher education, arts, design, history, literature and civilization, music, philosophy, theology, physics.
Duration: 3 to 5 years.
Fees: registration: SK600; living costs: SK300 per month.

Scholarship

Study Domains: journalism, philosophy, theology, religion.
Scholarships: (a) MGR Scholarship; (b) PhD Scholarship.
Open to: (a) Graduate students, EU citizen, intergovernmental agreement; (b) Graduate students with Masters' degree, EU citizen, intergovernmental agreement.
Duration: (a) 2 years; (b) 3 years.
Value: (a) living expenses, 5,000 SKK; (b) living expenses, 5,000 SKK.
Applications: contact dominika.surova@ku.sk for further details.

2158 City University

Drienová 34
PO Box 78
820 09 Bratislava
Tel: +421-2-555-67718
Fax: +421-2-555-67646
Web: http://www.cutn.sk
e-mail: dgliviakova@cutn.sk

Undergraduate, Graduate Programmes

Study Domains: business administration, finance, international business, international law, management.
Programmes: Bachelor's, Master's degrees in business administration. Non-degree programme in intensive English.
Open to: candidates meeting admissions standards; TOEFL required.
Duration: 5 years; courses begin in September, April and January.
Fees: tuition fees US$380-$570.
Languages: English.
Applications: rolling admissions; contact dgliviakova@cutn.sk for further details.

2159 College of Management
Bezrucova 64
911 01 Trencin
Tel: +421-32-652-9337
Fax: +421-32-652-9337
Web: http://www.vsm.sk
e-mail: info@vsm.sk

◻ Undergraduate Studies

Study Domains: accounting, business, business
administration, economy, international relations,
management, marketing, statistics.
Programmes: Bachelor's degree in business
administration.
Open to: applicants meeting academic standards; TOEFL
required.
Duration: 3 years; courses begin in September, January
and April.
Fees: tuition fees US$380 per course.
Languages: English and Slovak.
Applications: rolling applications; contact
dgliviakova@cutn.sk for further details.

2160 Comenius University
Nám. Safárikovo
81806 Bratislava
Tel: +421-2-5292-1594
Fax: +421-2-5296-3836
Web: http://www.uniba.sk
e-mail: kr@rec.uniba.sk

◻ Slovak Language Studies

Study Domains: languages.
Programmes: Slovak language courses at the Institute for
Language and Academic Preparation for Foreign Students.
Open to: candidates of all nationalities applying for
undergraduate, graduate or doctoral programmes.
Duration: 5 or 10 months, depending on language
programme chosen; 3-week Summer programme.
Fees: registration: 50 €; tuition: 1,700-3,400 €; 450 € for
Summer programme; accommodation: 65-125 € per month
for room and board.
Applications: to the above address by 30 June for the
Winter semester and 5 December for the Summer semester;
for further information email: sr@ujop.uniba.sk: website:
http://uniba.sk/ujop; tel: +421 2 555 77 333; fax: +421 2 555
77 255.

◻ Undergraduate, Graduate, Postgraduate Programmes

Study Domains: biology, chemistry, computer science,
cultural studies, earth science, ecology, environment, geology,
languages, law, management, mathematics, medicine, nursing,
pharmacy and pharmacology, physical education, physics,
stomatology, theology, religion.
Programmes: undergraduate and graduate programmes at
the following faculties and centres: Medicine (general
medicine and stomatology), Jessenius Faculty of Medicine
(general medicine and nursing), Pharmacy, Mathematics and
Physics, Natural Sciences, Arts, Catholic Theology (St. Cyril
and Methodius), Education, Law, Management; Institutes of
Canadian Studies, Jewish Studies, Language and Academic
Preparation for Foreign Students; Centres for Computer
Sciences, European Studies and Pastoral Studies; Toxicology
Laboratory.
Open to: for undergraduate studies: candidates of any
country having completed secondary education and holding a
GCE or its equivalent giving access to a university in their
own country; for graduate studies: an undergraduate diploma
is required.
Held: various addresses in Bratislava.
Duration: variable, depending on programme of study.
Languages: Instruction in Slovak and/or English.
Applications: to the above address for further information.

2161 Constantine the Philosopher University in Nitra [CPU]
Tr. A. Hlinku 1
Nitra
Tel: +421-37-6511-330 / 253
Fax: +421-37-6511-243
Web: http://www.ukf.sk
e-mail: rektor@ukf.sk

◻ Undergraduate, Graduate, Postgraduate Programmes

Study Domains: archaeology, art history, arts, chemistry,
computer science, earth science, ecology, environment,
education, geology, languages, mathematics, physics,
psychology, social sciences, sociology, special education,
teacher education.
Programmes: Bachelor's, Master's, Ph.D. degrees in arts;
education; natural sciences; social sciences.
Open to: applicants holding a secondary school certificate
(GCE).
Duration: 3 to 5 years; courses begin in September.
Fees: registration US$20; tuition fees US$2,000-$6,000
per year.
Languages: Slovak and English.
Applications: by February; contact aoborcokova@ukf.sk
for further details.

2162 Mateja Bela University [UMB]
Rektorát UMB
Národná ulica 12
97401 Banská Bystrica
Tel: +421-48-412-3367
Fax: +421-48-415-3180
Web: http://www.umb.sk
e-mail: luptakova@rekt.umb.sk

◻ Undergraduate, Graduate Programmes

Study Domains: all major fields.
Programmes: Programme of studies leading to the
Bachelor´s, Master´s, Engineering and Ph.D. degrees at the
following faculties: Economics, Humanities, Natural
Sciences, Education, Law, Political Sciences and International
Relations, Finance, Philology.
Open to: candidates of all countries; with academic and
linguistic requirements; Slovak language preparation available
if necessary.
Duration: Bachelor´s: 3 years; Master´s and 'Engineer's':
4 or 5 years; Ph.D.: 3 years.
Fees: registration: US$75; tuition: US$1,700-$3,000 per
academic year; dormitory: US$17-$20 per month; meals:
student cafeteria available with special menus on request:
US$4 for three meals per day; medical insurance:
approximately US$310 per calendar year.
Applications: at the above address.

2163 Slovak University of Agriculture in Nitra
Tr. A. Hlinku 2
949 76 Nitra
Tel: +421-37-6511-751 / 4
Fax: +421-37-6511-560
Web: http://www.uniag.sk
e-mail: admin-www@uniag.sk

◻ Undergraduate, Graduate Programmes

Study Domains: agriculture, agronomic sciences, business,
chemistry, earth science, food industry, horticulture,
hydrology.
Programmes: Undergraduate, graduate and post-graduate
courses in: agriculture, agronomy, agricultural management,
agricultural economics, agricultural engineering, horticulture
and viticulture, soil and water science, food science and
production earth sciences, biology, chemistry, international
business.
Open to: candidates of any country, fluent in Slovak, with
secondary-school certificate.
Duration: 5 years.

2164 Slovak University of Technology in Bratislava [SUTB]

Vazovova 5
812 43 Bratislava
Tel: +421-2-57294-327
Fax: +421-2-57294-677
Web: http://www.stuba.sk

📖 Undergraduate, Graduate, Postgraduate Programmes

Study Domains: architecture, biochemistry, chemical engineering, chemistry, civil engineering, electricity and electronics, engineering, food, mechanical engineering, physics, statistics, technology.
Programmes: Bachelor's, Master's, Ph.D. degrees in mechanical engineering; civil engineering; electrical engineering and information technology; chemical and food technology; architecture, materials science and technology.
Open to: candidates of any nationality with secondary school certificate or MSc. degree for Ph.D.; proficiency in English required.
Duration: 3 to 6 years.
Applications: by 31 March to the office of the Dean at the above address; see website for further information.

2165 Technical University in Zvolen [TUZVO]

T. G. Masaryka 2117/24
960 53 Zvolen
Tel: +421-45-520-6111
Web: http://www.tuzvo.sk
e-mail: rektor@vsld.tuzvo.sk

📖 Undergraduate, Graduate Programmes

Study Domains: building industry, ecology, environment, engineering, forestry, interior design.
Programmes: programme of studies leading to (a) B.Sc. in interior design and consultancy;
(b) M.Sc. wood technology engineering, processes of woodworking, industrial design of furniture, enterprise management, fire protection; (c) postgraduate degrees in structure and properties of wood, technology of wood processing, construction and processes of wood products manufacturing, theory of enterprise economy and management of forestry and wood-processing industries; (d) university degrees by distance education through PHARE, a multinational project for Distance Education Development, part of the Slovak Network of Distance Education governed by the PHARE Study Centre.
Open to: candidates of any country, fluent in Slovak, with secondary-school certificate.
Duration: 5 years.
Applications: to the above address.

2166 Technical University of Kosice [TUKE]

Letná 9A
04200 Kosice
Tel: +421-55-63-224-85
Fax: +421-55-63-327-48
Web: http://www.tuke.sk
e-mail: rektor@tuke.sk

📖 Undergraduate, Graduate, Postgraduate Programmes

Study Domains: architecture, civil engineering, computer science, design, ecology, environment, economy, energy, finance, fine arts, geodesy, geology, industrial design, management, marketing, mechanical engineering, metallurgy, teacher education, technical education, telecommunications, tourism, hotel and catering management.
Programmes: Bachelor's, Master's, Ph.D. degrees in teacher education, design, fine arts, industrial design, economics, ecology and environment, architecture, engineering.

2167 University of 'St Cyril and Methodius'

Nám. J. Herdu 2
91701 Trnava
Tel: +422-33-5565-121
Fax: +422-33-5565-120
Web: http://www.ucm.sk
e-mail: info@ucm.sk

📖 Postgraduate Programmes

Study Domains: anthropology, biology, chemistry, communication, computer science, mathematics, teacher education.
Programmes: postgraduate courses in applied mathematics, computer science, biology, chemistry, anthropology, education and teacher training for humanities education, mass communication.
Open to: candidates of any nationality fluent in Slovak, with secondary-school certificate.
Applications: to the above address for further information.

2168 University of Economics in Bratislava

Administration Building 3 floor
Dolnozemská cesta 1/b
852 35 Bratislava
Tel: +421-2-6241-2283
Fax: +421-2-6241-2145
Web: http://www.euba.sk

📖 Business Programmes

Study Domains: business, business administration, economic and commercial sciences, finance, international business, international relations, tourism, hotel and catering management, trade.
Programmes: undergraduate, graduate and post-graduate courses in: business administration, business computing, economics, international business, international relations, commerce, tourism, finance, banking and investment, insurance management.
Open to: candidates of any country, fluent in Slovak, with secondary-school certificate.
Duration: 5 years.

2169 University of Pavol Jozef Safárik, Kosice [UPJS]

Srobárova
041 80 Kosice
Tel: +421-55-622-2608
Fax: +421-55-766-959
Web: http://www.upjs.sk
e-mail: rektor@upjs.sk

📖 Undergraduate, Graduate Programmes

Study Domains: biology, chemistry, computer science, law, mathematics, medicine, nursing, physics, stomatology.
Programmes: (a) Bachelor's, Master's and Doctoral in biology, chemistry, physics, mathematics and computer science;
(b) Degrees in general medicine, nursing and stomatology;
(c) Master's and Ph.D. in law.
Open to: candidates of any country, fluent in Slovak, with appropriate qualifications.
Duration: 5 years.
Applications: to the above address.

2170 University of Presov [UP]

Namestie legionarov 3
080 01 Presov
Tel: +421-51-7733-106
Fax: +421-51-7733-260
Web: http://www.unipo.sk
e-mail: intoff@unipo.sk

📖 Undergraduate, Graduate Programmes

Study Domains: archaeology, art history, arts, arts and crafts, education, European studies, fine arts, interpretation and translation, languages, Slavic studies, theology, religion.
Programmes: Bachelor's, Master's, Ph.D. degrees in arts; Central European studies; humanities and natural sciences; education; orthodox theology.

Fees: tuition fees US$1,000 per term; living costs US$150 per month.
Languages: English.
Applications: by 1 September for Summer course and 1 March for Winter course.

2171 University of Trencín

Studentská 2
91101 Trencín
Tel: +421-32-740-0101
Fax: +421-32-740-0522
Web: http://www.tnuni.sk

☐ Engineering Programmes

Study Domains: economic and commercial sciences, industrial technology, mechanical engineering, social sciences, technology.
Programmes: Bachelor's, Master's 'Inzinier' and Ph.D. in industrial technology, mechatronics, industrial engineering and social and economic relations.
Open to: candidates of any country, fluent in Slovak, with secondary-school certificate.
Duration: 5 years.
Applications: to the above address.

2172 University of Trnava

Hornopotocná 23
918 43 Trnava
Tel: +421-33-551-1679
Fax: +421-33-551-1129
Web: http://www.truni.sk
e-mail: rektor@truni.sk

☐ Undergraduate Programmes

Study Domains: classical studies, education, health and hygiene, history, medicine, nursing, philosophy, psychology, social work, sociology, teacher education.
Programmes: programme of courses leading to degrees in: (a) rehabilitation medicine and therapy, nursing, public health, social work; (b) classical languages, philosophy, history, sociology, psychology; (c) education and teacher training for humanities education.
Open to: candidates of all nationalities, fluent in Slovak, with secondary-school certificate.
Duration: 5 years.

2173 University of Veterinary Medicine

Komenskeho 73
041 81 Kosice
Tel: +421-55-633-0127
Fax: +421-55-633-5641
Web: http://www.uvm.sk
e-mail: sekretariat@uvm.sk

☐ Veterinary Medicine

Study Domains: veterinary medicine, veterinary sciences.
Programmes: Master's degree in general veterinary medicine.
Open to: students of all nationalities; no age limits.
Duration: 4 to 6 academic years.
Fees: US$5,000-$7,000.
Applications: to the above address.

2174 University of Zilina

Foreign Affairs and Public Relations Office
Moyzesova 20
010 26 Zilina
Tel: +421-41-562-0392
Fax: +421-41-724-7702
Web: http://www.utc.sk/menu/inc.asp?ver=en

☐ Undergraduate, Graduate Engineering Programmes

Study Domains: civil engineering, communication, electricity and electronics, information science, management, mechanical engineering, physics, transport.
Programmes: (a) Faculty of Mechanical Engineering: M.Sc. and Ph.D. in engineering; (b) Faculty of Electrical Engineering: B.S. in mechatronics and in telecommunication management; Master's programme in electric traction and energy management, in information and safety systems and in

telecommunications; postgraduate programme in electrical engineering, telecommunications, theoretical electrotechnics and physics of condensed matter and acoustics; (c) Faculty of Operation and Economics of Transport and Communication: Master's and Ph.D. in transport and communication; (d) Faculty of Management and Information Technology: Bachelor's, Engineer and Ph.D. in information and management systems; (e) Military Faculty: Master's in civil engineering and civil security; (f) Faculty of Civil Engineering: M.Sc. and Ph.D. in civil engineering.
Open to: students of any country having completed secondary school; fluency in Czech or Slovak required.
Duration: variable, according to programme.
Languages: instruction in Czech or Slovak; instruction in English possible for some programmes.
Applications: to the faculty of choice at the above address.

Slovenia

Academic year: September to June.
Monetary unit: Slovenian tolar (SIT).
National student admission: Applicants should have the 'maturity' or 'matura' or secondary-school certificate to enter the first year of studies. Studies by foreigners are subject to special regulations. Graduate admission requirements are stipulated by the respective study programme. Students must have a residence permit, appropriate knowledge of the Slovene language, a medical certificate, a secondary-school certificate (or a university degree for graduate studies) and have paid tuition and health care fees. The first application form must be completed and sent together with the required documents to the Higher Education Application and Information Office of the University of Ljubljana or the University of Maribor at the beginning of March. There is a 5 percent quota for foreign students studying full time.
Language: A certificate of active knowledge of the Slovene language is obligatory for undergraduate studies and desirable for graduate studies. A preparatory study year can be organized for those applicants who do not fulfil all the admission requirements.
Immigration requirements: An entrance visa prior to coming to the country is required, except for citizens of most European countries. It can be obtained at the nearest Slovenian embassy, consular or diplomatic mission. in Slovenia. For periods of stay in excess of 3 months, students must apply for a temporary residence permit at the nearest Aliens Office. Students have to present a medical certificate of less than 6 months and show proof of compulsory health insurance. Tuition for full-time undergraduate studies covers the compulsory health insurance for foreign students. Part-time undergraduate and graduate students as well as students exempt from tuition payments should purchase their health insurance themselves in their home country or in Slovenia.
Information services:
• Ministry of Education, Science and Sport, Trg OF 13, SI-1000 Ljubljana; tel: +386-1-478-4600 fax: +386-1-478-47-19; web: http://www.mszs.si/eng/ministry
• University of Maribor, Slomskov trg 15, 2000 Maribor; tel: +386-2-23-55280; fax: +386-2-23-55211; web: http://www.uni-mb.si
• University of Ljubljana, VPIS - Higher Education Application and Information Office, Kongresnitrg 15, 1000 Ljubljana; tel.: +386-1-241-8500; fax: +386-1-2418-660; web: http://www.uni-lj.si.
Open and distance learning: The Faculty of Economics, University of Ljubljana, offers distance learning programmes leading to a higher education diploma. Non-traditional study is developing.
Recognition of studies and qualification: ENIC/NARIC, Ministry of Education, Science and Sport; Zupanciceva 6; 1000 Ljubljana; Slovenia; tel: +386-1-4785-731; fax: +386-1-4785-669; email: anita.jesenko@mss.edus.si; web: http://www.mszs.edus.sj.
Publications / Websites:
• 'Development of Higher Education in Slovenia', published by Ministry of Education and Sport; Ljubljana, September 1998.

2175 GEA College of Entrepreneurship [GEAE]

Sencna Pot 10
6320 Portorose
Tel: +386-5-671-02 40
Fax: +386-5-671-02-50
Web: http://www.vssp.gea-college.si
e-mail: info@vssp.gea-college.si

📖 Undergraduate Studies

Study Domains: economy, management.
Programmes: Bachelor's degree in economics.
Open to: applicants holding secondary-school certificate
or equivalent; TOEFL 500 required.
Duration: 3 to 4 years; courses begin in October.
Fees: registration US$50; tuition fees US$5,100; living
costs US$500 per month.
Languages: Slovenian and English.
Applications: by 1 August; contact
marjana.merkac@guest.arnes.si for further details.

🎓 UPI Foundation Scholarship

Study Domains: all major fields.
Scholarships: UPI Foundation Scholarship.
Applications: by 1 July; contact
nevija.bozic@vssp.gea-college.si for further details.

2176 ISH Ljubljana Graduate School of the Humanities [ISH]

Breg 12
1000 Ljubljana
Tel: +386-1-425-1845 / 252-3024
Fax: +386-1-425-1846
Web: http://www.ish.si
e-mail: ish@ish.si

📖 Graduate, Postgraduate Studies

Study Domains: anthropology, communication,
linguistics.
Programmes: Master's, Ph.D. degrees in anthropology,
linguistics, social communication.

2177 Ministry of Education and Sport

Department for International Cooperation in
Education
Trg OF 13
1000 Ljubljana
Tel: +386-1-478-4200
Fax: +396-1-478-4329
Web: http://www.mszs.si
e-mail: info@mszs.si

🎓 Government Scholarships

Study Domains: all major fields.
Scholarships: postgraduate, short-term, training and
research scholarships in all fields.
Open to: postgraduate students or researchers of all
nationalities, up to 35 years of age; proficiency in Slovene or
the language agreed upon by the supervisor.
Duration: 3 to 9 months.
Value: Free accommodation in the facilities of the Student
Centre of the Universities; free basic medical insurance, if
necessary; 45,000 SIT per month; fringe benefits: 3 months
6,000 SIT, 4 to 6 months 9,000 SI, over 7 months 12,000 SIT.
Applications: by 30 April; contact the above address for
application procedure; see webite
http://www.ljudmila.org/srce/stipendije/tujci.htm for further
information.

2178 Nova Gorica Polytechnic

Vipavska 13, POB 301
5000 Nova Gorica
Tel: +386-5-3315-223
Fax: +386-5-3315-224
Web: http://www.p-ng.si
e-mail: info@p-ng.si

📖 Undergraduate, Graduate, Postgraduate Programmes

Study Domains: ecology, environment, economic and
commercial sciences, management.
Programmes: (a) Bachelor of Science in ecology; (b)
Bachelor of Science in engineering management; (c) Master's
/ Ph.D. degrees in materials science, environmental sciences.
Description: (a) objective of the programme is to educate
experts capable of working on multidisciplinary projects
concerning environment in industrial, legislative, executive
and research fields at local, national and international levels;
(b) objective of the programme is to educate experts for
business solutions and production; (c) postgraduate study
programme for researchers in materials science and physical
properties of advanced materials, environmental sciences.
Open to: (a) and (b) candidates holding secondary-school
certificate; (c) candidates with undergraduate degree in
physics, electronics, chemistry or materials science, natural
sciences, engineering, applied chemistry or medicine;
proficiency in English required.
Duration: (a) 4 years; courses begin 1 October; (b) 3
years; courses begin 1 October; (c) 2 to 4 years; courses begin
1 October.
Fees: (c) tuition: 2,100 € per year.
Languages: (a), (b) Slovenian; (c) English.
Applications: (a), (b) by 25 September; see website for
further information; (c) by 6 September; contact
renata.kop@ses-ng.si for further details.

2179 University of Ljubljana

Kongresni trg 12
1000 Ljubljana
Tel: +386-1-241-8500
Fax: +386-1-241-8660
Web: http://www.uni-lj.si
e-mail: ul-retorat@uni-lj.si

📖 Undergraduate, Graduate Programmes

Study Domains: all major fields.
Programmes: Bachelor's, Master's and Ph.D. programmes
in all major fields.
Open to: candidates of all nationalities meeting academic,
financial and linguistic requirements.
Duration: 2 to 4 years; courses begin in September.
Financial assistance: possible; from the Ministry of
Education and Sport and the Ministry of Science and
Technology.

Solomon Islands

Academic year: February to November.
Monetary unit: Solomon Islands dollar (SBD).
Recognition of studies and qualification: Ministry of
Education and Training; PO Box G 28, Honiara, Solomon
Islands; tel: +677-23900; fax: +677-20485; web:
http://www.commerce.gov.sb/Ministries.Ministry_of_Educati
on.htm.

2180 Solomon Islands College of Higher Education [SICHE]

PO Box G23
Honiara
Tel: +677-30111
Fax: +677-30390
e-mail: siche@solomon.com.sb

📖 Pluridisciplinary Studies

Study Domains: all major fields.
Programmes: programme of studies offering Advanced
Diploma, Diploma, Advanced Certificate and Certificate level
courses, as well as short courses and distance mode courses at
the following Schools and Institutions: (a) Education: primary
and secondary teaching; (b) Finance and Administration:
secretarial studies, law and management; (c) Industrial
Development; (d) Marine Fisheries Studies: deep water tuna
fisheries, inshore fisheries; (e) Natural Resources: agriculture
and farming; (f) National Forestry Training Institute: forestry,
community forestry; (g) Nursing and Health Studies: nursing,
health inspection; (h) Humanities and Science; (i) Distance
Education Centre: adult education courses.
Open to: nationals of the Pacific Island Territories,
minimum age: 16 years; candidates must have reached
secondary educational standard (Form 5) with good English;

candidates wishing to enter the diploma programme must have either completed a relevant certificate programme, have GCE A-level on two subjects or equivalent, or be over 24 years of age; and hold a senior position in government or private business.
Duration: 1 to 2 years.
Financial assistance: New Zealand Third Country Awards may be available to students approved by their own governments; similarly the Commonwealth Fund for Technical Cooperation may sponsor approved students; applications for these awards may be made through candidate's own government.
Applications: by July to the Registrar.

South Africa

Academic year: January to December.
Monetary unit: rand (R).
National student admission: Grade 12 or its equivalent in terms of the National Qualifications Framework. Each admitting institution is autonomous and determines its own foreign student quota.
Language: Proficient in at least English or Afrikaans.
Immigration requirements: Students need a travel document (passport) valid for at least one year, a duly completed application form BI-159 (available from the Department of Home Affairs), a standard letter of provisional admission to a South African institution, a letter of motivation setting out the reasons for studying at a South African institution, proof that the applicant is in a financial position to pay tuition fees and has adequate means of support for the full duration of the period of study, details about accommodation arrangements, a refundable cash deposit or bank guarantee for repatriation purposes, a written undertaking by the applicant that he/she will return to his/her country of residence after completion of the studies, a medical report and particulars about medical cover.
Information services: Each admitting institution has its own information service.
• Department of Education, Private Bag X895, Pretoria 0001; tel: +27-12-312-5999; fax: +27-12-321-6770; e-mail: info@edzc.owv.gov.za; webmaster@educ.pwv.gov.za.
Open and distance learning: Distance teaching, which is mainly by correspondence, provides courses for about 35 per cent of enrolled students. The University of South Africa (UNISA) offers correspondence courses, either in English or in Afrikaans, for a Bachelor's degree and postgraduate qualification. Course work is structured in modules. A maximum of 10 years is allowed to obtain a Bachelor's degree, an additional year for Bachelor's honours degree, 3 years for postgraduate qualifications, 2 further years for a Master's degree and 2 years for a Doctorate. The Degrees are considered to be equivalent in standard to those awarded by other universities. The Technikon South Africa offers distance education either through English or Afrikaans for Diplomas, Bachelor's degrees and postgraduate qualifications, provided such Bachelor's degrees include an in-service training component.
Recognition of studies and qualification:
• South African Universities' Vice Chancellors' Association (SAUVCA); PO Box 27392, Sunnyside, Pretoria 0132, South Africa; tel: +27-12-481-2842; fax: +27-12-481-2843; email: admin@sauvca.org.za; web: http://www.sauvca.org.za.
• The International Education Association of South Africa (IEASA), PO Box 11029, Hatfield, Pretoria 0028, South Africa; tel: +27-12-420-2049; fax: +27-12-420-2029; email: aaltin@ccnet.up.ac.za; web: http://sunsite.wits.ac.za/ieasa.
Publications / Websites:
• 'Guide to Higher Education in South Africa', HSRC Publishers, P.O. Box 5556, Pretoria; tel: +27 12 302 2999.
• 'Guide to Distance Education in South Africa', HSRC Publishers (see above).

2181 Cape Technikon [CT]
PO Box 652
Cape Town 8000
Tel: +27-21-460-3395
Fax: +27-21-460-3695
Web: http://www.ctech.ac.za
e-mail: vangensena@ctech.ac.za

⌂ Undergraduate, Graduate Studies
Study Domains: all major fields, accounting, administration, advertising, agriculture, applied arts, architecture, art history, arts, audio-visual media, business, business administration, chemical engineering, communication, design, education, electricity and electronics, graphic arts, industrial design, interior design, law, management, marketing, oceanography, optics, paramedical studies, physics, printing, statistics, teacher education, telecommunications, tourism, hotel and catering management.
Programmes: Diplomas, Bachelor's, Master's and professional degrees in science, education, applied arts, business administration, law, management, industrial technology, agriculture.
Open to: students meeting minimum entrance requirements; admission tests.
Held: some courses are held in Mowbray, Wellington and Bellville.
Duration: 1 to 5 years.

2182 Medical University of Southern Africa
PO Box 197
Medunsa 0204
Pretoria
Tel: +27-12-521-4111
Fax: +27-12-521-5902
Web: http://www.medunsa.ac.za
e-mail: mosia@medunsa.ac.za

⌂ Undergraduate, Graduate, Postgraduate Programmes
Study Domains: bacteriology, biochemistry, biophysics, chemistry, computer science, dentistry, dietetics, immunology, mathematics, medicine, microbiology, nursing, nutrition, obstetrics and gynaecology, ophthalmology, paediatrics, paramedical studies, physics, preventive medicine, psychiatry, sciences, speech therapy, statistics, surgery, urology.
Programmes: Bachelor's, Master's, Ph.D. degrees in sciences, dentistry, medicine; non-degree programmes in HIV/AIDS and occupational health nursing.
Open to: students meeting high academic requirements.
Held: campuses in the Limpopo province; Mpumalanga and North West provinces.
Duration: 3 to 6 years; courses begin in January.
Fees: tuition fees approximately 26,000 rand per year.
Financial assistance: some financial assistance available; contact karen@medunsa.ac.za.
Languages: English.
Applications: by 30 October.

2183 Port Elizabeth Technikon
Private Bag X6011
Port Elizabeth 6000
Tel: +27-41-504-3911
Fax: +27-41-504-3911
Web: http://www.petech.ac.za
e-mail: info@petech.ac.za

⌂ Undergraduate Programmes
Study Domains: management, teacher education, technical education, trade.
Programmes: (a) National Diploma in natural sciences, commerce, adult basic education and training; (b) National Higher Diploma in technical education and secondary education; (c) Bachelor of Technology degree in management and postschool education.
Open to: candidates (a) holding a Senior Certificate with two languages and two subjects at the Higher Grade, as well as academic attainment in selected subjects relevant to the course chosen; (b) holding a national N4 certificate, plus two languages at Senior Certificate level, a completed trade test or artisan's diploma and 3 to 5 years experience; (c) holding a

Senior Certificate and applicable teaching qualification plus a minimum of 2 years' experience.
Duration: 3 or 4 years.
Fees: (approximate figures) registration: 750 rand; tuition: 4,500 rand per year; living expenses: 11,000 rand per year; books: 1,200 rand per year.
Languages: Instruction in English.
Applications: by 15 August to the above address.

2184 Potchefstroom University for Christian Higher Education [PU for CHE]

The Registrar, Academic and Corporate Administration
Private Bag X6001
Potchefstroom 2520
Tel: +27-18-299-1111
Fax: +27-18-299-2799
Web: http://www.puk.ac.za/indexe.html
e-mail: enquiries@puknet.puk.ac.za

Undergraduate, Graduate Programmes

Study Domains: all major fields.
Programmes: Undergraduate and graduate programmes offered at the faculties of arts, natural sciences, theology, education sciences, economic and management sciences, law, engineering, health sciences.
Open to: candidates of all nationalities meeting all academic, financial and linguistic requirements.
Applications: to the above address.

2185 Rand Afrikaans University

PO Box 524
Auckland Park 2006
Tel: +27 11 489 2911
Fax: +27 11 489 2191
Web: http://www.rau.ac.za
e-mail: myfuture@rau.ac.za

Undergraduate, Graduate Programmes

Study Domains: all major fields.
Programmes: (a) Bachelor's, Master's and Doctorate degrees in all major fields; (b) non-degree programme of extra-curricular courses: human resource management, legal studies, transport management, education and health, local government training.
Open to: students of all nationalities and ages with the necessary university entrance qualifications.
Duration: 3 or 4 years.
Fees: registration and tuition: 7,500 rand per year; living expenses: from 1,500-4,400 rand per month, depending upon choice of housing accommodation.
Languages: Instruction in Afrikaans and English.

2186 Rhodes University [RU]

The Registrar
Box 94
Grahamstown 6140
Tel: +27-46-603-8111
Fax: +27-46-622-5049
Web: http://www.ru.ac.za
e-mail: registrar@ru.ac.za

Undergraduate, Graduate Programmes

Study Domains: all major fields.
Programmes: full range of diplomas and degrees from one-year certificate programmes to postgraduate degrees in all major fields.
Open to: candidates of all nationalities meeting academic, financial and linguistic requirements.
Financial assistance: a number of residence bursaries are available to assist students in meeting residence fees.
Applications: to the above address.

Fellowships

Study Domains: biochemistry, botany, chemistry, computer science, geography, geology, mathematics, microbiology, pharmacy and pharmacology, zoology.
Scholarships: (a) Hugh Kelly Fellowship (awarded odd years); (b) Hugh Le May Fellowship (awarded even years).
Subjects: (a) biochemistry and microbiology, botany,

chemistry, computer science, geography, geology, ichthyology and fisheries science, mathematical statistics, mathematics (pure and applied), pharmaceutical sciences, physics and electronics, psychology, zoology and entomology; (b) classics, history, languages, law, philosophy, politics, theology.
Open to: (a) senior scientists from any country with at least a Ph.D. qualification; (b) applicants from any country qualified to undertake advanced study in the above fields.
Duration: (a) up to 1 year (not renewable); (b) 3 to 4 months, but may be extended by mutual agreement and availability of funds.
Value: (a) 2,200 rands per month plus cost of economy-class return airfare; if fellowship is accepted for longer than 6 months, spouse's air/rail fares will also be paid; free accommodation is provided; (b) return economy airfare, furnished accommodation, small monthly cash stipend.
Applications: by 31 July of year preceding award, to the Registrar; application can be downloaded from website http://www.ru.ac.za/research/fellowships/fellowships.html.

2187 St Augustine College of South Africa

PO Box 447 82
Linden 2104
Johannesburg
Tel: +27-11-782-4616
Fax: +27-11-782-8729
Web: http://www.staugustine.ac.za
e-mail: admin@staugustine.ac.za

Graduate, Postgraduate Studies

Study Domains: African studies, education, philosophy, theology, religion.
Programmes: (a) Master's degrees (M.Phil.) in applied ethics, culture and education, philosophy, religious education and pastoral ministry, theology; (b) Ph.D. degrees.
Description: (a) combination of full-time attendance at seven modules; plus assignments and exam in each module. A compulsory research report; (b) research in the field and topic selected by the candidate and approved by the higher degrees committee of the college.
Open to: (a) applicants holding an honours degree or equivalent in relevant fields; (b) applicants holding appropriate degrees and Master's degree in relevant fields.
Duration: (a) 2 years part-time; courses begin in January; (b) 2 years full-time.
Fees: registration: (a), (b) 100 rands; tuition: (a) 3,500 rands, (b) 7,000 rands per year; living costs: (a), (b) 3,000 rands per month.
Languages: English.
Applications: (a) by October; (b) rolling admissions; contact admin@staugustine.ac.za for further information.

2188 Technikon Pretoria

Directorate of International Initiatives
Private Bag X680
Pretoria 0001
Tel: +27-12-318-5762
Web: http://www.techpta.ac.za

Undergraduate, Graduate Programmes

Study Domains: all major fields.
Programmes: Programme of courses leading to Bachelor's, Master's and Doctorate degrees in dance, music, design, photography, fine arts, business administration, management, marketing, finance, accounting, architecture, information technology, engineering, technology, environment, recreation management, radiology, dentistry, library and information science, journalism, agriculture, veterinary studies.
Open to: candidates of all nationalities, with matriculation or equivalent qualification, and proficiency in English.
Duration: 1 to 6 years.
Fees: (approximate figures) registration: minimum of 1,000 rand; tuition: average of 7,000 rand per year depending on course followed; living expenses: 8,600 rand per year.
Languages: Instruction in English and Afrikaans.
Applications: by mid-May for courses starting in July, by mid-June for medical, dentistry, environment and tourism courses, and by mid-August for all other courses, to International Office at the above address.

🎓 Scholarships

Study Domains: all major fields.
Scholarships: International Scholarships, Fellowship Programmes, Student Exchange Programmes and Research Grants.
Applications: contact International Scholarship Coordinator; tel: +27 12 318 4303; fax: +27 12 318 4424; email: marumoc1@techpta.ac.za for full details.

2189 Technikon Witwatersrand [TWR]
Box 17011 Doornfontein
Johannesburg 2028
Tel: +27-11-406-2221
Fax: +27-11-406-2197
Web: http://www.twr.ac.za

📖 Undergraduate, Graduate Studies

Study Domains: accounting, administration, advertising, applied sciences, architecture, arts, biochemistry, building industry, business, business administration, chemical engineering, chemistry, communication, computer science, decorative arts, electricity and electronics, finance, fine arts, geology, graphic arts, health and hygiene, industrial design, information science, interior design, management, marketing, mathematics, mechanical engineering, nursing, paramedical studies, public relations, statistics, visual arts.
Programmes: Diplomas, Bachelor's, Master's and Doctorate degrees in arts, design, architecture, business management, engineering, health sciences.

2190 University of Cape Town
International Academic Programmes Office (IAPO)
Private Bag
Rondebosch 7701
Tel: +27-21-650-2822 / 3740
Fax: +27-21-650-5667
Web: http://www.uct.ac.za
e-mail: iapo@protem.uct.ac.za

📖 Undergraduate Programmes

Study Domains: all major fields.
Programmes: undergraduate degree programmes in all major fields.
Open to: candidates of all nationalities meeting academic, linguistic and financial requirements; only members of SADC countries eligible to apply for degrees in health fields.
Fees: tuition for foreign students: from US$5,000-7,000; M.B.A. US$18,000 per academic year; candidates of SADC countries pay local tuition.

2191 University of North West
Private Bag X2046
Mmabatho 2735
Tel: +27-18-389-2453
Fax: +27-18-392-5775
Web: http://www.uniwest.ac.za
e-mail: kayah@unwest001.ac.za

📖 Undergraduate, Graduate, Postgraduate Studies

Study Domains: administration, African studies, agriculture, business, education, human sciences, law, social sciences, technology.
Programmes: Bachelor's, Master's, Ph.D. degrees in African studies, agriculture and technology, commerce and administration, education, human and social sciences, law.
Applications: by 15 February; see website for further information.

2192 University of Pretoria
Pretoria 0002
Tel: +27-12-420-4111
Fax: +27-12-362-5168
Web: http://www.up.ac.za

📖 Undergraduate, Graduate Programmes

Study Domains: all major fields.
Programmes: undergraduate and graduate degree programmes in the following fields: economic and management sciences, education, engineering, built environment and information technology, humanities, health sciences, veterinary science, natural and agricultural sciences,

theology.
Open to: candidates of all nationalities meeting academic, financial and linguistic requirements.
Applications: to the above address; see website for further information.

🎓 Scholarships

Study Domains: all major fields.
Scholarships: Postgraduate Foreign Assistantship.
Open to: graduate students of any nationality intending to pursue a Master's or Doctorate degree, holding a valid study permit and financially independent.
Duration: maximum 2-1/2 years.
Value: 15,000 rand per month, including exemption from tuition fees.
Applications: to the above address; see website for further information.

2193 University of the Orange Free State [UOVS]
PO Box 339
Bloemfontein 9300
Tel: +27-51-401-3363
Fax: +27-51-401-3558
Web: http://www.uovs.ac.za
e-mail: venternt@rd.uovs.ac.za; info@mail.uovs.ac.za

📖 Undergraduate, Graduate Programmes

Study Domains: all major fields.
Programmes: wide range of degree programmes at the Faculties of Economic and Management Sciences, Health Sciences, Nursing, Natural and Agricultural Sciences, Humanities.
Open to: candidates of all nationalities meeting academic, linguistic and financial requirements.
Applications: by 1 September; no late application will be accepted from international students; see website http://www.uovs.ac.za/admin/int/default.asp.

🎓 University Scholarships

Study Domains: all major fields.
Scholarships: (a) National Scholarship; (b) Scholarship for Doctorate.
Subjects: all major fields.
Open to: applicants of any nationality holding a Master's degree; proficiency in Afrikaans or English required.
Duration: 1 year (renewable).
Value: (approximate figures) (a) 3,000 rands; (b) 17,000 rands per academic year; payable quarterly in advance after submission of a progress report.
Languages: language of instruction: Afrikaans or English.
Applications: (a) by 20 July; (b) by 10 October; to the Registrar.

2194 University of the Western Cape [UWC]
Private Bag X17
Bellville
Tel: +27-21-959-2911
Web: http://www.uwc.ac.za

📖 Undergraduate, Graduate Programmes

Study Domains: all major fields.
Programmes: programme of courses in all major fields leading to Bachelor's, Master's and Doctorate degrees.
Open to: all students who fulfil the admission requirements, notably for Bachelor's matriculation exemption with high scholastic attainment in chosen field of study.
Fees: (approximate figures) tuition: for undergraduate students US$2,060-$2,690 per year depending upon chosen course and for postgraduate students US$1,890-$2,560 per year; estimated living expenses: US$3,000 per year.
Languages: Instruction in English.
Applications: to the above address.

2195   University of Witwatersrand

Private Bag 3
Wits 2050
Tel: +27-11-717-1000
Fax: +27-11-717-1065
Web: http://www.wits.ac.za

📖 Undergraduate, Graduate Programmes

Study Domains: engineering, health and hygiene, humanities and arts, law, management, sciences, social sciences, trade.
Programmes: programme of courses leading to Bachelor's, Master's and Doctorate degrees in architecture, humanities and social sciences, commerce, education, engineering, health sciences, law, management and science.
Languages: Instruction in English.

Sri Lanka

Academic year: October to June.
Monetary unit: rupee.
National student admission: Foreign students should have qualifications equivalent to the Sri Lanka General Certificate of Education (advanced level) or equivalent examination. Admission to all undergraduate courses is regulated by the Central Agency for University Admissions of the University of Sri Lanka. Students holding a first-class or second-class degree from a recognized university in the relevant field of study may be admitted to postgraduate courses.
Language: Proficiency in English is required.
Immigration requirements: Enquiries to the Embassy/High Commissioner of Sri Lanka in the country concerned.
Information services:
• University Grants Commission; 20 Ward Place; Colombo; Sri Lanka; tel: +94-1-695-301; fax: +94-1-688-045; email: ugcchair@ugc.ac.lk; web: http://www.ugc.ac.lk
• Contact the university concerned and the Sri Lankan Embassy/High Commissioner in the home country.
Open and distance learning: Distance higher education is offered at the Open University of Sri Lanka, which provides first and postgraduate degrees, as well as Certificates and Diplomas. The Open University has Faculties of Humanities and Social Sciences, Natural Sciences and Engineering Technology. It does not have formal entrance requirements.
Recognition of studies and qualification: University Grants Commission; 20 Ward Place; Colombo; Sri Lanka; tel: +94-1-695-301; fax: +94-1-688-045; email: ugcchair@ugc.ac.lk; web: http://www.ugc.ac.lk.
Publications / Websites:
• 'Sri Lankan Universities Year Book' 1996, published by University Grants Commission.

2196   Buddha Sravaka Bhiksu University [BBU]

Nandane Mawatha
Anuradhapura
Tel: +94-25-22-540
Fax: +94-25-22-540

📖 Undergraduate Studies

Study Domains: theology, religion.
Programmes: Undergraduate studies in Buddhism.

2197   Rajarata University of Sri Lanka [RUSL]

Mihintale
Sri Lanka
Tel: +94-25-666-45 / 46 / 50
Fax: +94-25-665-12
e-mail: vajalib@sltnet.lk

📖 Undergraduate, Graduate Studies

Study Domains: all major fields, agriculture, agronomic sciences, anthropology, applied arts, applied sciences, archaeology, biology, business administration, community development, economic and commercial sciences, forestry, horticulture, languages, literature and civilization, natural history, performing arts, rural development, sciences, social sciences.

Programmes: Bachelor's, Master's degrees in social sciences, management, applied sciences and agriculture.
Open to: applicants meeting academic requirements.
Duration: 3 years.
Languages: English and Sinhale.

2198   University of Colombo [UC]

College House
PO Box 1490 Cumarathunga Munidasa
Colombo
Tel: +94-75-583-810
Fax: +94-75-583-180
Web: http://www.cmb.ac.lk
e-mail: vc@cmb.ac.lk

📖 Undergraduate, Graduate, Postgraduate Programmes

Study Domains: arts, business administration, education, finance, law, management, medicine, sciences.
Programmes: Bachelor's, Master's, Ph.D. degrees in all major fields.
Open to: applicants holding GCE A/L examinations with appropriate subjects.
Duration: 3 to 5 years.
Languages: Sinhale, Tamil and English.
Applications: see website for further information.

2199   University of Kelaniya

PO Box 03
Dalugama
Kelaniya
Tel: +94-1-1291-1391
Fax: +94-1-1291-1485
Web: http://www.kln.ac.lk
e-mail: admin@kln.ac.lk

📖 Diploma Programmes

Study Domains: Asian studies, English, theology, religion.
Programmes: (a) Diploma in Pali and Buddhist Studies for foreign students; (b) Diploma in English for foreign students.
Open to: international students of any nationality with the A-level GCE or equivalent, and proficiency in English.
Duration: (a) and (b) 2 years.
Fees: (approximate figures) tuition: US$1,200 per year; living expenses: US$150 per month.
Languages: instruction in English.
Applications: by September to the Registrar at the above address.

📖 Undergraduate, Graduate Programmes

Study Domains: Asian studies, business administration, humanities and arts, management, medicine, sciences, social sciences, trade.
Programmes: undergraduate, graduate programmes at the following Faculties: Commerce, Humanities, Medicine, Science, Social Sciences.
Open to: candidates having completed GCE examinations at A-level in appropriate subjects.
Duration: 3 to 4 years for Bachelor's degree; 1 to 3 years for postgraduate courses according to programme; courses start in January.
Applications: to the above address for further information.

2200   University of Moratuwa - Department of Architecture

Katubedda
Moratuwa
Tel: +94-11-265-0301
Fax: +94-11-265-0622
Web: http://www.mrt.ac.lk
e-mail: info@mrt.ac.lk

📖 Graduate Programmes

Study Domains: architecture, computer science, engineering, industrial technology, mathematics, mechanical engineering, telecommunications, textile industry.
Programmes: M.Sc./Postgraduate Diplomas at the following Faculties: Faculty of Architecture, Faculty of Engineering, Faculty of Information Technology, Institute of Technology, University of Moratuwa.
Open to: candidates of any country meeting academic,

financial and linguistic requirements.
Languages: instruction in English.
Applications: application forms and further information
can be obtained from the above address.

2201 University of Peradeniya
20400 Peradeniya
Tel: +94-81-238-8301
Fax: +94-81-238-8151
Web: http://www.pdn.ac.lk
e-mail: registrar@pdn.ac.lk

📖 Undergraduate, Postgraduate Programmes

Study Domains: agriculture, arts, dentistry, medicine,
veterinary medicine, veterinary sciences.
Programmes: undergraduate and postgraduate courses in
agriculture, arts, dental sciences, engineering, medicine,
science, veterinary medicine and animal science.
Open to: candidates having completed GCE examinations
at A-level in appropriate subjects.
Duration: undergraduate: 3 to 4 years; medicine and
surgery: 5 years; postgraduate: 2 to 3 years.
Fees: (approximate figures) tuition: US$100-$250 per
term.
Financial assistance: to the above address for further
information.
Languages: Instruction in Sinhalese, Tamil and English.

2202 University of Ruhuna
Matara
Tel: +94-41-222-2681
Fax: +94-41-222-2683
Web: http://www.ruh.ac.lk
e-mail: postmaster@cc.ruh.ac.lk

📖 Undergraduate, Graduate, Postgraduate Programmes

Study Domains: agriculture, engineering, humanities and
arts, medicine, sciences, social sciences.
Programmes: undergraduate, graduate, postgraduate
programmes at the following Faculties: Agriculture,
Engineering, Humanities and Social Sciences, Medicine,
Science.

Sudan
Academic year: July to March.
Monetary unit: Sudanese pound (£).
National student admission: Foreign students seeking
admission as undergraduates to higher educational institutions
should have a minimum of 5 credits (45 per cent), in the
Sudan School Certificate or equivalent, and must fulfil the
admission requirements of the University of Khartoum. Only
foreign students resident in the Sudan and foreign scholarship
holders are accepted.
Language: Good knowledge of either Arabic (for the
Islamic University of Omdurman) or English is required.
Initiation and orientation programmes are arranged by each
institution.
Immigration requirements: Students must obtain a visa.
Information services:
• Department of Foreign Cultural Relations, NCHE, PO Box
2081, Khartoum (information concerning study facilities,
immigration requirements, etc., for foreign students).
• Documentation is available free from the Admission Office,
University of Khartoum, and from the Secretariat General of
the National Council for Higher Education, Admission
Department, for a nominal charge.
• Office of Sudan Cultural Counsellor or Sudan Embassy in
each country.
Open and distance learning: The University of Khartoum
has a School of Extramural Studies and there is also a private
Open University.
Recognition of studies and qualification: Committee for
the Evaluation and Equivalency of Diplomas and Academic
Degrees; Ministry of Education and Scientific Research, PO
Box 2081, Khartoum, Sudan; tel: +249-11-772-515; tel/fax
+249-11-779-312.
Publications / Websites:
• 'Annual Admissions Guide', by National Council of Higher
Education.

2203 Al Zaiem Alazhari University [AAU]
PO Box 1933
Omdurman
Tel: +249-13-344-511 / 524
Fax: +249-13-344-510
e-mail: alazhariuniv@sudanmail.net

📖 Undergraduate, Graduate, Postgraduate Programmes

Study Domains: medicine.
Programmes: Bachelor's, Master's, Professional degrees in
medicine.

2204 Atbara University - Faculty of Engineering and Technology [AU]
PO Box 1843
Khartoum

📖 Undergraduate Programmes

Study Domains: civil engineering, electricity and
electronics, mechanical engineering.
Programmes: B.Sc. programmes in: (a) civil engineering,
with options in transportation, hydraulic, structure and
construction engineering; (b) electrical and electronic
engineering; (c) mechanical engineering; (d) production
engineering; (e) postgraduate diploma in manufacturing
systems.
Open to: citizens of any country: (a) to (c) with Sudanese
certificate (science option) or equivalent.
Duration: (a) to (d) 5 years; (d) 1 year; courses begin in
September.
Fees: tuition: (a) to (c) contact the Admission Committee
for Higher Education, P.O. Box 3113, Khartoum; (d) contact
the Dean of the Faculty at the above address.
Languages: Instruction in Arabic for (a) to (d); (e) in
English.
Applications: (a) to (c) by 31 September, to the Admission
Committee for Higher Education, P.O. Box 3113, Khartoum;
(d) any time of the year, to the Manager of the Higher
Education Unit, at the above address.

2205 University of Zalingei
PO Box 6
Zalingei
Tel: +241-731-22109
Fax: +241-731-22013
e-mail: UZAL@student.net

📖 Courses in Agriculture and Education

Study Domains: agriculture, education.
Programmes: (a) B.Sc. (Hon.) Agriculture; (b) B.Sc.
(Hon) Education.
Duration: (a) 5 years; (b) 4 years.

Suisse
Année universitaire: octobre à juin/juillet.
Organisation de l'enseignement supérieur:
L'enseignement supérieur se divise principalement en deux
domaines, celui des hautes écoles et celui de la formation
professionnelle supérieure.
Le domaine des hautes écoles comprend les hautes écoles
universitaires (universités cantonales et Écoles polytechniques
fédérales) ainsi que les hautes écoles spécialisées (HES). Le
domaine de la formation professionnelle supérieure est
constitué par toutes les autres formations de degré tertiaire.
Dans l'esprit du «fédéralisme coopératif», la Confédération et
les cantons se répartissent les compétences dans le domaine
de l'enseignement. D'une façon générale, les 26 cantons et
demi-cantons jouissent d'une grande autonomie. Celle-ci varie
toutefois selon le type d'institution et le niveau d'étude à
l'intérieur du système suisse d'éducation.
Au niveau de l'enseignement supérieur ou du degré tertiaire
de l'éducation, les compétences sont également partagées.
Selon la nouvelle Constitution (1999), la Confédération
légifère sur la formation professionnelle supérieure. Elle a
ainsi la responsabilité de la formation professionnelle
supérieure et des HES. En outre, les deux écoles
polytechniques relèvent de sa compétence, de même que

l'encouragement de la recherche. Les cantons, quant à eux, ont la responsabilité de leur université, au nombre de dix. Celles-ci sont financièrement soutenues par la Confédération.
• Les universités suisses et écoles polytechniques fédérales: (Source: http://www.bbw.admin.ch.)
Les universités suisses et écoles polytechniques fédérales: Universität Basel: www.unibas.ch; Universität Bern: www.unibe.che; Université de Fribourg: www.unifr.ch; Université de Genève: www.unige.ch; Université de Lausanne: www.unila.ch; École polytechnique fédérale de Lausanne: www.epfl.ch; Università della Svizzera italiana: www.usi.ch; Universität Luzern: www.unilu.ch; Université de Neuchâtel: www.unine.ch; Universität St. Gallen: www.unisg.ch; Universität Zürich: www.unizh.ch; Eidg. Technische Hochschule Zürich: www.ethz.ch.
• Les hautes écoles spécialisées (HES):
Berner Fachhochschule: www.bfh.ch; Haute école spécialisée de Suisse occidentale: www.hes-so.ch; Fachhochschule Nordwestschweiz: www.fhnw.ch; Fachhochschule Ostschweiz: www.fho.ch; Fachhochschule Zentralschweiz: www.fhz.ch; Scuola universitaria professionale della Svizzera italiana: www.supsi.ch; Zürcher Fachhochschule: www.zfh.ch.
Unité monétaire: Franc suisse (FS).
Admission pour étudiants du pays: Les étudiants étrangers doivent posséder un certificat équivalent à la maturité suisse. La reconnaissance de certificats étrangers relève de la compétence particulière de chaque université qui décide, de façon autonome, de l'admission des étudiants. Les ressortissants de certains pays sont astreints à passer un examen d'entrée. Ils peuvent suivre des cours d'introduction aux études universitaires organisés à cet effet à Fribourg (en français et en allemand). L'admission d'étudiants étrangers par les universités et le nombre de ces admissions ne dépendent pas seulement de la formation déjà acquise par chacun mais aussi des capacités d'accueil. Les filières de médecine humaine, dentaire et vétérinaire sont depuis quelques années absolument fermées aux étrangers non titulaires d'un permis d'établissement. Même pour les derniers semestres de médecine, les capacités d'admission sont très limitées. La pharmacie et la psychologie disposent, elles aussi, de capacités d'accueil très limitées et cela dans toute la Suisse. Les universités sont autonomes et sont, par conséquent, responsables de l'admission des étudiants.
Connaissances linguistiques requises: Une bonne connaissance du français ou de l'allemand est essentielle. Des cours destinés spécialement aux étudiants étrangers sont dispensés dans les écoles et séminaires de français moderne des universités francophones de Genève, Lausanne et Neuchâtel.
Formalités d'immigration: Avant de quitter son pays, l'étranger qui souhaite étudier en Suisse doit prendre contact avec l'ambassade ou le consulat de Suisse, compétent à raison de son domicile afin de se renseigner sur les formalités d'entrée et de séjour. Les ressortissants de pays soumis à l'obligation du visa d'entrée en Suisse doivent présenter une demande personnelle d'autorisation d'entrée en Suisse auprès de la représentation suisse compétente de son pays d'origine. Le visa d'entrée ne confère aucun droit de séjour en Suisse. Il ne donne que le droit de passer la frontière. Dans la mesure où le séjour prévu en Suisse est de plus de 3 mois, l'étudiant doit requérir la délivrance d'une autorisation de séjour à l'autorité de police des étrangers du canton dans lequel il a l'intention d'étudier, indépendamment du fait qu'il soit soumis ou non à l'obligation du visa. Par ailleurs, il doit annoncer son arrivée dans les 8 jours suivant l'entrée en Suisse à la police des étrangers pour régler ses conditions de séjour. La déclaration d'arrivée doit être accomplie à la commune du lieu de résidence de l'étudiant. C'est en revanche le canton qui est compétent pour délivrer l'autorisation de séjour pour études valable pour 1 an. La présentation d'un passeport national est en principe exigée pour la délivrance de l'autorisation de séjour. Documents à joindre à cette demande d'autorisation: passeport national valable au minimum 1 an (comprenant éventuellement le visa d'entrée), confirmation de l'admission à l'université ou a un établissement d'enseignement supérieur, preuve de la solvabilité pour la durée des études, des explications sur le domaine d'études envisagé (durée, programme des études, plan d'études), un engagement écrit de quitter la Suisse à l'échéance des études envisagées. Cette demande peut être prolongée. Les étudiants ne peuvent bénéficier du regroupement familial, donc pas d'autorisation de séjour pour le conjoint.

Frais pour une année universitaire: Les frais concernant la pension et le logement, la scolarité, les livres et l'assistance médicale, loisirs, etc. varient de 1.850 à 2.000 FS par mois.
Services d'accueil et d'information:
• Conférence des Recteurs des Universités Suisses (CRUS), Information et Documentation; Sennweg 2; CH-3012 Berne; tél: +41-31-306-6044 (entre 8h30 et 11h30); fax: +41-31-302-6811; email: iud@crus.ch; web: http://www.crus.ch
• Ambassades suisses à l'étranger.
• Schweizerischer Studentenreisedienst (Service suisse de tourisme pour étudiants), Ankerstrasse 112, 8026 Zurich (facilités de voyage); web: http://www.statravel.ch
• Bureau officiel de renseignements (Verkehrsbüro) de chaque ville universitaire (possibilités de logement et de pension).
Bourses pour étudiants internationaux:
• Bourses offertes par la Commission fédérale des bourses pour étudiants étrangers; Hallwylstrasse 4, CH-3003 Bern; tél: +41-31-323-2676; fax: +41-31-323-3020; web: www.sbf.admin.ch/htm/bildung/stipendien/eskas-f.html.
Enseignement à distance:
• Informations générales: www.crus.ch/mehrspr/iud/fern.html;

• FernUnivesität Hagen à Brig / Berne et Pfaeffikon: www.fernuni.ch
• Centre Romand d'enseignement à distance (CRED) à Sierre: www.cred.vsnet.ch
• Open University à Genève: www.open.ac.uk
• Fern Fachhochschule Schweiz: www.fernfachhochschule.ch.
Reconnaissance des études et diplômes: S'adresser à: Informationsstelle für Anerkennungsfragen / Centre d'information sur les questions de reconnaissance / Swiss ENIC. Contact: Conférence des recteurs des universités suisses (CRUS) / Swiss ENIC, Sennweg 2, CH-3012 Bern, Suisse; tél: +41-31-306-6032; fax: +41-31-302-6811; web: www.crus.ch.
Services du logement: Voir site web http://www.crus.ch/mehrspr/iud/wohnen.html.
Possibilités d'emploi: Les étudiants étrangers qui souhaitent exercer une activité rémunérée pendant leurs vacances doivent être en possession d'un permis de travail. Des permis pour une activité à temps partiel (max. 15 h/semaine) durant le semestre pourront être accordées lorsqu'un professeur responsable ou le rectorat attestent que le travail temporaire n'affecte pas les études. L'octroi d'un permis de travail pendant les vacances n'est pas soumis à une attestation de la part de l'université.
Publications / Sites Web:
• «Guide des études en Suisse»; Staufer, Heinz (Verantw.); ASOU (ed); Dübendorf, 2001; prix: 268 p; 45 FS.
• «Studienführer Österreich, Schweiz»; Kurz, Daniela; Deutscher Akademischer Austauschdienst (Hrsg.); Bielefeld, 2000; 155 p; prix: 19,90 Euro.
• «Higher Education in Switzerland», Schorer, Michael (ed.); Lütolf, Imelda (ed.), Berne, 2001; 100 pp.
• «Studying in Switzerland: universities», Amherd, Leander (comp.); Tafani, Tiziani (comp.); Rectors' Conference of the Swiss Universities (ed.); Berne 2004.

2206 C.G. Jung-Institut Zurich [CJZ]
Hornweg 28
CH-8700 Küsnacht
Tel: +41 1 914 1040
Fax: +41 1 910 5451
Web: http://www.junginstitut.ch
e-mail: info@junginstitut.ch

📖 **Cours de préparation au diplôme en psychologie analytique**

Domaines d'étude: psychologie.
Programmes: Cours de préparation au diplôme en psychologie analytique.
A l'intention de: ressortissants de tout pays, titulaires d'un diplôme universitaire de niveau Bac+3 minimum.
Durée: 8 semestres minimum.
Inscriptions: 6 mois avant le semestre initial.

2207 Département fédéral de l'intérieur, Commission fédérale des bourses pour étudiants étrangers

Commission fédérale des bourses pour étudiants étrangers
4, Hallwylstrasse
CH-3000 Berne
Tel: +41 31 323 2676
Fax: +41 31 323 3020
Web: http://www.admin.ch/bbw/d/bildung/eskas.html

☞ Bourses d'études

Domaines d'étude: toutes disciplines principales.
A l'intention de: candidats âgés de 35 ans au maximum, titulaires d'un diplôme d'études universitaires et possédant une bonne connaissance du français ou de l'allemand; (b) ouvert aux ressortissants des pays industrialisés uniquement.
Lieu: en Suisse: (a) universités et écoles polytechniques; (b) conservatoires et écoles des beaux-arts.
Durée: 9 mois: (a) renouvelable 1 an pour les ressortissants des pays d'outre-mer et des pays en développement.
Valeur: 1600 FS par mois pour les étudiants n'ayant pas encore un diplôme de fin d'études universitaires et 1820 FS par mois pour ceux qui en sont titulaires; 1820 FS par mois pour les études d'art; 4500 pour le cours de langues à Fribourg (3 mois). Les boursiers bénéficient d'une assurance maladie.
Candidatures: avant le 31 octobre précédant l'année des études, auprès du Ministère de l'éducation ou des autorités compétentes dans le pays d'origine du candidat. Informations complémentaires auprès des représentations diplomatiques suisses.

2208 École polytechnique fédérale de Lausanne [EPFL-SSIE]

Section Sciences et Ingénierie de l'Environnement (SSIE)
Faculté ENAC
Bâtiment GR-Ecublens
CH-1015 Lausanne
Tel: +41 21 69 32771
Fax: +41 21 69 35730
Web: http://ssie.epfl.ch/
e-mail: secretariat.ssie@epfl.ch

📖 Programme ISTE/HYDRAM

Domaines d'étude: agriculture, développement rural, électricité et électronique, études du développement, hydraulique, informatique.
Programmes: Programme ISTE/HYDRAM: cours du premier cycle en hydrologie, physique du sol, hydraulique agricole, aménagement et gestion du territoire, programmes postgrades.
Description: possibilité de suivre cours virtuel «hydrologie générale» sur l'Internet.
A l'intention de: ressortissants de tout pays; voir site web pour de plus amples informations: http://hydram.epfl.ch.
Assistance financière: possibilité de cours financés partiellement par la Coopération suisse; bourses disponibles auprès de l'EIER; le Programme des Nations Unies pour le développement et l'Organisation météorologique mondiale.
Inscriptions: voir détails sur site web http://hydram.epfl.ch.

2209 Ecole polytechnique fédérale de Zurich (Swiss Federal Institute of Technology Zurich) [ETHZ]

Rectorat Rämistrasse 101 ETH Zentrum
8092 Zürich
Tel: +41-44-632-1111
Fax: +41-44-632-1010
Web: http://www.ethz.ch
e-mail: info@ethz.ch

📖 Undergraduate, Graduate, Postgraduate Programmes

Study Domains: architecture, civil engineering, engineering, mathematics, natural sciences.
Programmes: undergraduate, graduate, postgraduate programmes in natural sciences, system-oriented natural sciences, civil engineering and geomatic sciences, engineering sciences.
Open to: candidates of all nationalities.
Fees: tuition: 580 FS per semester; living expenses: 1100-1400 FS per month.
Financial assistance: Scholarships and financial aid for studies in all study domains.
Applications: for details see http://www.study.ethz.ch.

2209 Swiss Federal Institute of Technology Zurich (Ecole polytechnique fédérale de Zurich) [ETHZ]

Rectorat Rämistrasse 101 ETH Zentrum
8092 Zurich
Tel: +41-44-632-1111
Fax: +41-44-632-1010
Web: http://www.ethz.ch
e-mail: info@ethz.ch

📖 1er, 2e, 3e cycles

Domaines d'étude: architecture, génie civil, ingénierie, mathématiques, sciences naturelles.
Programmes: programmes dans les domaines scientifiques conduisant aux diplômes de Bachelor, Master et Doctorat.
Domaines d'études: Architecture, génie civil et géomatique, Sciences de l'ingénieur, Sciences naturelles et mathématique, Sciences naturelles orientées.
A l'intention de: ressortissants de tous pays.
Frais: frais de scolarité: 580 FS par semestre; frais de séjour: 1100-1400 FS par mois.
Assistance financière: Bourses d'échanges pour les ressortissants de certains pays (voir détails sur site web http://www.study.ethz.ch).
Connaissances linguistiques: connaissance approfondie de l'allemand ou de l'anglais.
Inscriptions: voir détails sur site web http://www.study.ethz.ch.

2210 École polytechnique fédérale Lausanne [EPFL]

Ecublens
CH-1015 Lausanne
Tel: +41 21 693 1111
Fax: +41 21 693 6080
Web: http://www.epfl.ch

📖 Diplômes d'ingénieur et d'architecte

Domaines d'étude: architecture, chimie, écologie, environnement, électricité et électronique, génie chimique, génie civil, géodésie, informatique, ingénierie, mathématiques, mécanique, physique, sciences, télécommunications.
Programmes: Diplômes d'ingénieur dans les domaines enseignés et diplôme d'architecte.
A l'intention de: ressortissants de tout pays, titulaires un diplôme de fin d'études secondaires et les qualifications jugées indispensables par la direction de l'École; admission sur dossier et examen.
Durée: 5-1/2 années d'études incluant un travail pratique d'une durée de 4 mois sauf pour les systèmes de communication: 5-1/2 années incluant un stage obligatoire d'une année et un travail pratique de 5 mois; en architecture: 5 années incluant un stage obligatoire et un travail pratique pour un total de 6 mois; doctorat: 3 années.
Frais: 592 FS par semestre pour les 1er et 2ème cycles; frais de séjour: environ 1500 FS par mois.
Assistance financière: l'attribution de bourses est très limitée.
Inscriptions: avant le 15 juillet pour les 1er et 2ème cycles; pas de date limite pour le doctorat.

2211 Faculté indépendante de théologie de Bâle

Mühlestiegrain 50
CH-4125 Riehen/Basel
Tel: +41 61 641 1188
Fax: +41 61 641 3798
Web: http://www.sthbasel.ch/aktuell.htm
e-mail: info@sthbasel.ch

📖 Diplômes en théologie

Domaines d'étude: théologie, religion.
Programmes: cours dans les domaines de la théologie évangélique, théologie systématique, éthique, histoire de la théologie; théologie pastorale, homilétique, pédagogie, catéchétique; Ancien et Nouveau Testament: introduction, exégèse, théologie; missiologie; science des religions et des sectes; conduisant à la licence et au doctorat.
A l'intention de: ressortissants de tout pays, âgés de plus de 18 ans, et titulaires d'un baccalauréat ou équivalent.
Durée: 5 ans.
Connaissances linguistiques: l'enseignement est dispensé en allemand; langue allemande obligatoire, certificat de langue allemande pour les étrangers requis.

2212 Fonds national suisse de la recherche scientifique [FNSRS]

Wildhainweg 20
C.P. 8232
CH-3001 Berne
Tel: +41 31 308 2222
Fax: +41 301 3009
Web: http://www.snf.ch

🐾 Subsides de recherche, de publication, et subsides personnels

Domaines d'étude: recherche, sciences.
Bourses: subsides de recherche, de publication, et subsides personnels.
A l'intention de: chercheurs ou groupes de chercheurs qualifiés; voir site web pour de plus amples renseignements.

2213 Glion Institut de Hautes Études [CIDG]

Route de Glion 111
CH-1823 Glion-sur-Montreux
Tel: +41 21 966 3535
Fax: +41 21 966 3536
Web: http://www.glion.ch

📖 Formations en gestion de hôtellerie, tourisme et hospitalière

Domaines d'étude: formation professionnelle, gestion, tourisme, hôtellerie, restauration.
Programmes: formation supérieure de futurs cadres de l'hôtellerie, du tourisme et de la gestion hospitalière: (a) gestion hôtelière et touristique; conduisant au diplôme du Centre international de Glion et au «Bachelor of Science (Hons.) in International Hospitality Management», Université de Wales (Royaume-Uni); (b) administration hôtelière; conduisant au diplôme du Centre international de Glion.
A l'intention de: ressortissants de tout pays, âgés de 18 à 30 ans: (a) titulaires du baccalauréat/maturité ou titre équivalent; (b) possédant le niveau du baccalauréat ou une formation professionnelle préalable; bonne connaissance de l'anglais (TOEFL 500) ou du français (Alliance française) exigée; admission sur dossiers.
Durée: (a) 3 ans (débutant en janvier et août de chaque année) dont 2 fois 6 mois de stage pratique; (b) 18 mois (débutant en janvier et août de chaque année) dont 6 mois de stage pratique.
Assistance financière: renseignements à l'adresse ci-dessus.
Connaissances linguistiques: enseignement en français ou anglais.
Inscriptions: toute l'année à l'adresse ci-dessus.

2214 Institut européen de l'Université de Genève [IEUG]

2, rue Jean-Daniel Colladon
CH-1204 Genève
Tel: +41 22 705 7850 /51
Fax: +41 22 705 7852
Web: http://www.unige.ch/ieug

📖 Etudes européennes

Domaines d'étude: études européennes.
Programmes: cours sur les problèmes d'ensemble de l'Europe d'aujourd'hui dans les domaines suivants: histoire, littérature comparée, sciences politiques, économie, droit, études régionales (principalement en français); conduisant au Diplôme d'études supérieures (DES) en études européennes (Cultures & Sociétés) ou DES mention sciences économiques et sociales.
A l'intention de: le DES en études européennes, réservé aux licenciés, est accordé aux étudiants qui présentent un mémoire original; admission sur dossier; la connaissance d'une 2e langue européenne (allemand ou anglais) sera prise en considération lors de la sélection des candidats.
Durée: 2 ans.
Assistance financière: possibilité de bourses, sur dossier.
Connaissances linguistiques: français obligatoire.
Inscriptions: 5 juillet pour le dépôt de candidature à l'IEUG et 31 mai pour l'immatriculation à l'Université de Genève (demande de formulaire auprès du Bureau des admissions, à l'adresse ci-dessus).

2215 Institut universitaire d'études du développement [IUED]

24, rue Rothschild
C.P. 136
CH-1211 Genève 21
Tel: +41 22 906 5940
Fax: +41 22 906 5947
Web: http://www.unige.ch/iued
e-mail: iued@unige.ch

📖 Études en développement

Domaines d'étude: anthropologie, développement rural, écologie, environnement, économie, études du développement, hygiène et santé, sociologie.
Programmes: cours et séminaires interdisciplinaires en sociologie politique, économie, écologie, sciences sociales, hygiène et santé, anthropologie du développement en général, thèmes particuliers tels que développements rural et urbain, industrie, conduisant au: (a) Certificat de spécialisation en études du développement; (b) Diplôme d'études supérieures en études du développement, 3e cycle (DES).
A l'intention de: ressortissants de tout pays, titulaires: (a) d'une licence ou 5 ans d'expérience professionnelle en matière de développement, avec poste à responsabilités; (b) d'une licence et, en principe, 3 ans d'expérience professionnelle en matière de développement; sélection sur dossier.
Durée: (a) 1 an; (b) 2 ans.
Assistance financière: bourses en nombre limité, pour les ressortissants de pays en voie de développement.
Connaissances linguistiques: français obligatoire.
Inscriptions: avant le 15 mai (avant le 31 mars pour les bourses); au Service des étudiants.

2216 Institut universitaire de hautes études internationales [HEI]

132, rue de Lausanne
C.P. 36
CH-1211 Genève 21
Tel: +41 22 908 5700
Fax: +41 22 908 5710
Web: http://heiwww.unige.ch
e-mail: info@hei.unige.ch

📖 Relations internationales contemporaines

Domaines d'étude: droit international, économie, relations internationales, sciences politiques.
Programmes: programme d'étude scientifique des relations internationales contemporaines par les méthodes de l'histoire et de la science politique, du droit international (public ou privé) et de l'économie internationale; prépare au Diplôme d'études supérieures (DES), au doctorat en relations internationales et au certificat d'études internationales.

A l'intention de: ressortissants de tout pays, titulaires d'une licence ou d'un titre équivalent dans un des domaines d'études de l'Institut et devant présenter 3 lettres de recommandation; connaissance de l'anglais et du français exigée (tests).
Durée: 2 années universitaires au minimum.
Assistance financière: bourses de l'Institut, réservées, en principe, à des étudiants ayant déjà accompli au moins 1 an à l'Institut.
Connaissances linguistiques: enseignement en français et anglais.
Inscriptions: avant le 1er mars, au Secrétaire général de l'Institut.

2217 International University
ICC 20, Rte de Pré-Bois
1215 1215 Genève 15
Tel: +41-22-710-7110 / 12
Fax: +41-22-710-7111
Web: http://www.iun.ch
e-mail: info@iun.ch

📖 Business Administration / Communication / Media
Study Domains: business, business administration, communication.
Programmes: (a) Bachelor's degree in business administration, and in communication and media; (b) Master's degree in business administration, in communication and media, and in telecommunication; (c) Executive Master's degree in business administration.
Description: subjects in management, accounting, information systems, marketing, foreign languages, communications, economics, mathematics, finance, commercial law, consumer behaviour, international business, organizational behaviour, banking, planning and budgeting, entrepreneurship, interpersonal skills, media management, human resource management.
Open to: candidates of all nationalities with high academic achievement and intellectual capacity (a) with secondary-school certificate, and (b) and (c) with a first degree awarded by a recognized university, plus 6 years' work experience for (c); proficiency in English required for all programmes.
Duration: (a) 4 years; (b) 1 year; (c) 15 months (with courses held on Saturdays).
Financial assistance: a limited number of scholarships available for students with outstanding academic achievement and in financial need.
Languages: instruction in English.

2218 Secrétariat d'Etat à l'éducation et à la recherche SER Secrétariat de la Commission fédérale des bourses pour étudiants étrangers
Hallwylstrasse 4
CH-3003 Bern
Fax: +41-31-322-7854
Web: http://www.sbf.admin.ch/htm/bildung/stipendie n/eskas-f.html

📖 Bourses d'études postgradués
Domaines d'étude: toutes disciplines principales, arts, arts appliqués, arts graphiques, arts plastiques, beaux-arts.
Bourses: Bourses d'études universitaires pour des étudiant(e)s et artistes étrangers.
Description: Bourses offertes sur la base de la réciprocité (nombre de bourses fixe par pays) ou dans le cadre d'un pool (offre de bourses à un groupe de pays. Ces bourses sont destinées à des étudiants déjà titulaires d'un diplôme universitaire (postgradués). Elles doivent leur permettre de parfaire leurs connaissances en Suisse ou d'y faire des travaux de recherche dans des domaines auxquels les universités suisses accordent une attention particulière.
Candidatures: voir site web pour détails: http://www.sbf.admin.ch/htm/bildung/stipendien/eskas-f.html.

2219 Université de Fribourg [UF]
Service de la mobilité et des échanges
Cité Miséricorde
CH-1700 Fribourg
Tel: +41 26 300 7111
Fax: +41 26 300 9700
Web: http://www.unifr.ch/home/welcome.html
e-mail: admission@unifr.ch

📖 Bourses d'études et de recherche
Domaines d'étude: toutes disciplines principales, droit, lettres, sciences, sciences économiques et commerciales, sciences sociales, théologie, religion.
Bourses: bourses d'études et de recherche.
A l'intention de: ressortissants de tout pays préparant un 3e cycle de spécialisation dans leur université d'origine (spécialisation, doctorat ou formation analogue), âgés de moins de 35 ans; connaissance du français ou de l'allemand; 2 lettres de recommandation requises; sélection sur dossier.
Durée: 1 année académique (9 mois).
Valeur: environ 1.500 FS par mois durant 9 mois (non renouvelable).
Candidatures: le 15 janvier, auprès de l'organisme compétent du pays concerné (renseignements auprès de l'ambassade ou de la représentation diplomatique suisse), ou au Service de la mobilité et des échanges universitaires, à l'adresse ci-dessus.

2220 Université de Fribourg, Institut de Psychologie [UF]
Rue de Faucigny 2
CH-1701 Fribourg
Tel: +41 37 29 7655
Fax: +41 37 29 9712
Web: http://www.unifr.ch

📖 Programmes de recherche en psychologie
Domaines d'étude: psychologie.
Programmes: programmes de recherche en psychologie.
Description: problem-solving, gerontological, vocational and organizational psychology, information processing, games, coping with stress, decision theory, development of causal attribution tendencies and locus of control expectancies, family psychology, intercultural psychology.
A l'intention de: tous candidats en 3e cycle.

2221 Université de Geneve
24, rue du Général-Dufour
1211 Genève
Tel: +41-22-379-7111
Fax: +41-22-379-1134
Web: http://www.unige.ch

📖 Etudes 1er, 2e, 3e cycles
Domaines d'étude: architecture, droit, éducation, interprétation et traduction, lettres et arts, médecine, psychologie, sciences, sciences économiques et commerciales, sciences sociales, théologie, religion.
Description: programmes d'études dans toutes disciplines.
Assistance financière: voir Bourses de la Confédération Suisse: www.unige.ch/intl/boursiers/boursesconfed.html.
Inscriptions: voir site web.

2222 Université de Genève, École de traduction et d'interprétation [ETI]
40, boulevard du Pont-d'Arve
CH-1211 Genève 4
Tel: +41 22 705 8713
Fax: +41 22 705 8750
Web: http://www.unige.ch/eti

📖 Programme de cours en traduction et d'interprétation
Domaines d'étude: interprétation et traduction.
Programmes: cours de traduction et d'interprétation de conférences (français, anglais, allemand, espagnol, italien, arabe, russe).
A l'intention de: ressortissants de tout pays, diplômés de fin d'études secondaires avec mention ou possédant, pour certains pays (Australie, États-Unis d'Amérique, Inde), soit un «B.A», soit un «B.Sc», et ayant passé avec succès l'examen

d'admission.
Durée: traducteurs: 4 années; interprètes: 1-1/2 ans
(niveau «postgrade»); (débutant fin octobre).
Inscriptions: avant le 31 mars, au Secrétariat de l'École
(voir site web).

2223 Université de Lausanne [UNIL]
Dorigny
CH-1015 Lausanne
Tel: +41 21 692 2023
Fax: +41 21 692 2005
Web: http://www.unil.ch/ri
e-mail: relint@rect.unil.ch

📖 Cours du 1er au 3e cycle
Domaines d'étude: toutes disciplines principales.
Programmes: cours de 1er au 3e cycle dans toutes
disciplines principales dans les facultés de théologie, droit
(inclut l'institut de police scientifique et de criminologie),
lettres, sciences sociales et politiques (SSP), Hautes études
commerciales (HEC), sciences (inclut la pharmacie) et
médecine.
A l'intention de: ressortissants de tout pays, titulaires d'un
diplôme de fin d'études secondaires (baccalauréat, maturité ou
équivalent).
Durée: de 4 à 6 ans selon les filières.
Frais: taxes semestrielles: 560 FS; frais de séjours:
environ 1.800 FS par mois.
Assistance financière: bourses en nombre limité (montant
variable selon le pays d'origine du candidat) essentiellement
réservées aux étudiants d'échange provenant d'universités
avec lesquelles l'UNIL a signé un accord de coopération.

2224 Université de Lucerne
Pfistergasse 20
Case postale 7979
CH-6000 Lucerne 7
Tel: +41 228 5510
Fax: +41 228 5505
Web: http://www.unilu.ch
e-mail: rektorat@unilu.ch

📖 Programme de cours en théologie et lettres
Domaines d'étude: lettres, théologie, religion.
Programmes: cours conduisant: à la licence en théologie, à
la licence en lettres, au doctorat en théologie, philosophie et
habilitation; école des catéchistes.
A l'intention de: ressortissants de tout pays, titulaires d'un
diplôme de fin d'études secondaires ou équivalent reconnu
dans les universités et Hautes écoles suisses.
Durée: 3 à 5 ans.
Assistance financière: possibilité de bourses pour les
étudiants en théologie.
Connaissances linguistiques: enseignement en allemand.
Inscriptions: mi-novembre pour le semestre d'hiver;
mi-mai pour le semestre d'été.

🎓 Bourses en théologie
Domaines d'étude: philosophie, théologie, religion.
Bourses: bourses en théologie.
A l'intention de: étudiants inscrits en théologie; allemand
obligatoire.
Durée: 1 année académique (renouvelable).
Connaissances linguistiques: allemand.
Candidatures: en novembre, au décanat, Faculté de
théologie, à l'adresse ci-dessus.

2225 Université de Neuchâtel
26, avenue du 1er mars
CH-2600 Neuchâtel
Tel: +41 32 718 18 00
Fax: +41 32 718 1001
Web: http://www.unine.ch

📖 Études de Français
Domaines d'étude: français, langues, littérature et
civilisation.
Programmes: Certificat d'études françaises; diplôme pour
l'enseignement du français langue étrangère (français pour
non francophone).
A l'intention de: titulaires d'un diplôme de fin d'études
secondaires (Bac ou équivalent); pas de cours pour débutants;
admission sur dossier.

Durée: 2 années débutant le 15 octobre; cours d'été de 4
semaines.
Frais: frais de scolarité: 1.550 FS; frais de séjour: environ
1.500 FS par mois.
Inscriptions: avant le 30 septembre auprès de Christiane
Hizette à l'Institut de Langue et Civilisation Française; tél:
+41 32 718 18 00; fax: +41 32 718 18 01; site web:
http://www.unine.ch/sfm; email: sfm.cv@unine.ch.

📖 Programme de cours de 1er, 2ème et 3ème cycles
Domaines d'étude: toutes disciplines principales, droit,
éducation permanente, français, langues, lettres, littérature et
civilisation, sciences, sciences économiques et commerciales,
théologie, religion.
Programmes: cours de 1er, 2ème et 3ème cycles en lettres,
sciences, théologie, droit et sciences économiques.
A l'intention de: ressortissants de tout pays, remplissant
les conditions requises.
Inscriptions: s'adresser à l'adresse ci-dessus pour de plus
amples informations.

2226 University of St. Gallen/Graduate School of Business Administration, Economics, Law and Social Sciences [HSG]
Dufourstrasse 50
9000 St. Gallen
Tel: +41-71-224-2111
Fax: +41-71-224-2816
Web: http://www.unisg.ch
e-mail: unihsg@unisg.ch

🎓 Bourse Dr Leonard Stolk
Domaines d'étude: administration des affaires, droit.
A l'intention de: A l'attention des candidats de niveau 1er
et 2e cycle. Selon besoin financier et bon résultats scolaires.
Durée: 1 année.
Valeur: scolarité, 300 FS; frais de séjour, 1,200 FS
mensuel.
Candidatures: 15 mai et 15 novembre.

2227 University of Zürich
Künstlergasse 15
8001 Zürich
Tel: +41-1-634-1111
Fax: +41-1-634-2304
Web: http://www.unizh.ch
e-mail: gs@rektorat.unizh.ch

📖 Undergraduate, Graduate, Postgraduate Programmes
Study Domains: agriculture, applied arts, art history,
business, cinematography, computer science, criminology,
dentistry, ecology, environment, economic and commercial
sciences, folklore, geography, history, humanities and arts,
international relations, languages, law, linguistics,
mathematics, medicine, music and musicology, nursing,
pharmacy and pharmacology, philosophy, political science,
psychology, sciences, social work, sociology, special
education, speech therapy, teacher education, theology,
religion, veterinary medicine, veterinary sciences.
Description: Studies leading to Licentiat and Doctorate
degrees; BA/MA; PhD.
Open to: candidates of all nationalities meeting scholastic
and financial requirements.
Duration: from 4 to 6 years, depending on study
programme.
Fees: tuition: international students 782 SF; living costs:
1,400-1,500 SF monthly.
Languages: German.
Applications: by 1 June for winter semester; by 1 February
for summer semester; to above address; web:
www.unizh.ch/studium/zulassung/aubild.

Suriname

Academic year: October to August.
National student admission: Pre-university college (advanced level) or pre-university (ordinary level) with pre-year, though most programmes have special entry requirements.
Language: Compulsory language: Dutch.
Information services:
• Education Information and Study Facilities; Jesserunstraat 13-15; Paramaribo; Suriname.
Recognition of studies and qualification: Ministry of Education and Human Development (Ministerie van Onderwijs en Volksontwikkelin) International relations Department: Dr S.Kasiluddistraat 117-123, PO Box 297, Paramaribo, Suriname; tel: +597-498-383 / +597-497-325; fax: +587-495-083 / +597-433-760.

2228 Academy for Higher Art and Culture [AHKCO]
Waterkant 20
Paramaribo
Tel: +597-477-749

Undergraduate Programmes
Study Domains: arts, cultural studies, journalism, social sciences.
Programmes: Bachelor of Higher Arts and Culture.
Description: socio-cultural education, journalism and plastic arts.
Open to: candidates of any nationality holding a pre-university secondary diploma; candidates over 25 years of age must pass an entrance examination.
Duration: 4 years.
Fees: information upon request to the Academy.
Applications: by mid-October to the above address.

2229 Anton de Kom University of Suriname [ADEK]
Universiteitscomplex
Leysweg 86
PO Box 9212
Paramaribo
Tel: +597-465-558 / 465-497
Fax: +597-462-291
Web: http://www.uvs.edu/English.html

Undergraduate, Postgraduate Programmes
Study Domains: agriculture, business administration, economic and commercial sciences, education, engineering, law, medicine, social sciences, sociology.
Programmes: programme of courses leading to: (a) undergraduate degrees in natural sciences: geology, mining, agriculture, forestry, cattle-breeding, civil engineering, architecture, mechanical engineering, electrical engineering, environmental sciences; (b) postgraduate degrees in social sciences: economics, sociology, law, didactics, public administration, business administration; medical sciences: medicine and physiotherapy.
Open to: suitably qualified candidates.
Duration: 4 to 7 years.
Applications: to the Registrar for all further information.

2230 COVAB Foundation Central School for Nurses and Allied Professions
PO Box 9234
Flustraat No. 8
Paramaribo
Paramaribo
Tel: +597-441-943/ 441-813
Fax: +597-441-943/ 410-559
e-mail: vink@sr.net

Diploma in Nursing
Study Domains: nursing.
Programmes: Diploma in nursing.
Open to: candidates of any nationality, holding a secondary-school certificate or equivalent, physically and psychologically fit; proficient in Dutch, English or native languages.

Duration: 4 years.
Fees: students are provided with a monthly allowance.
Applications: at any time, requesting the prospectus and details for annual admission to one of the 8 hospitals in the country, at the above address.

2231 Foundation for Youth Dental Care
Kernkampweg 3
Paramaribo
Tel: +597-441-633
Fax: +597-442-345

Diploma Programme
Study Domains: dentistry.
Programmes: Diploma in Youth Dental Care.
Open to: the 12 best candidates holding a secondary-education certificate including chemistry and biology.
Duration: 3 years.
Fees: no fees but a 5-year contract of employment is required.
Applications: more information on request at the above address.

2232 Polytechnic College Suriname
Passiebloemstraat 1
Paramaribo
Tel: +597-400-733
Fax: +597-400-100

Undergraduate Programmes
Study Domains: administration, agriculture, architecture, business administration, civil engineering, electricity and electronics, mathematics, mechanical engineering, tourism, hotel and catering management.
Programmes: Pedagogical courses are divided in 2 levels: LOBO (Teacher Training Vocational Education) and LOMBO (Secondary Vocational Education).
Description: architecture, electrotechnics, civil engineering, mathematics, mechanics, physics, nursing, hotel and catering industry, business and public administration, agriculture.
Open to: candidates of any nationality holding a secondary-education certificate from a technical college, pre-university college, advanced or ordinary level, or the equivalent.
Duration: 6 years divided into two levels of 3 years each, with a diploma issued for each level.
Applications: further information at the above address.

Swaziland

Academic year: August to December (first semester) and January to May (second semester).
Organization of higher education system: Higher education is provided by one institution, the University of Swaziland (UNISWA), and has three campuses situated in Mbabane, Luyengo and Kwaluseni. It offers 3-year diploma programmes, 4-year undergraduate programmes and 2-year Master's degree programmes.
Monetary unit: emalangeni (E).
National student admission: A minimum of 6 passes in the GCE O-levels, obtained in no more than two sittings, that must include passes of C grade or higher in English language and at least 4 other relevant subjects or a Cambridge Overseas School Certificate in the 1st / 2nd Division.
International student admission: Contact the Senior Assistant Registrar (Academic Affairs) at the University.
Language: A good knowledge of English is essential for all university courses.
Estimated expenses for one academic year: tuition: E 22,250 for the 2004/5 academic year. Fees vary according to courses/faculties.
Information services:
• University of Swaziland, Private Bag 4, Kwaluseni. It operates its own student exchange programmes.
• Swaziland embassies in other countries.
Open and distance learning: Institute of Distance Education (IDE-UNISWA).

Recognition of studies and qualification: Ministry of
Education; PO Box 39; Mbabane; Swaziland; tel:
+268-404-2491 / 6 or +268-404-5750; web:
http://www.gov.sz.
Accommodation services: Student hostels are available for
international students.
Additional information: Applications close on 1 April
preceding commencement in August of each year.
Publications / Websites:
• UNISWA Prospectus;
• UNISWA Academic Calendar.
Both publications available from the University library; a fee
may be charged for this service.

2233 Mananga Centre for Regional Integration and Management Development [MMC]

PO Box 5100
Mbabane
Tel: +268-416-3155/7
Fax: +268 -416-3158
Web: http://www.mananga.sz
e-mail: info@mananga.sz

📖 Management Development Programme

Study Domains: administration, agriculture, computer
science, finance, management, marketing.
Programmes: Management Development Programme (PC
Series): non-degree courses in human resources management,
financial management, project management, information
management, materials management.
Open to: mature, English-speaking nationals of all
developing countries with minimum 3 years work experience;
participants receive a certificate.
Held: in Mananga (Swaziland), in sub-Saharan African
countries (outreach).
Duration: 2 to 6 weeks (residential).
Fees: (approximate figures) US$650 per week or
US$2,600 for a 4-week course; living expenses: US$420 for
one week or US$1,680 for 4 weeks.
Languages: Instruction in English.
Applications: to the Registrar.

2234 University of Swaziland [UOS]

Private Bag 4
Kwaluseni
Tel: +268 84011
Fax: +268 85276

📖 Undergraduate Programmes

Study Domains: agriculture, communication, education,
French, home economics, human sciences, languages, law,
sciences, social sciences.
Programmes: programme of courses leading to: diploma
in agricultural education, agriculture (General) home
economics, commerce, adult education and law; Bachelor of
Science in agricultural education, in agriculture (General) and
home economics; Bachelor of Commerce; Bachelor of
primary and secondary education; Postgraduate Certificate in
education; Bachelor of Arts in humanities, social science and
law; Bachelor of Science; Bachelor of Laws (L.L.B.);
Certificate in adult education and French; Master's of
Education and Master's of Science in chemistry.
Open to: candidates of all nationalities with at least credit
passes (C grades or better) in Mathematics and two science
subjects and at least a pass at D grade in English language at
GCE O-level.
Fees: caution deposit: E100; Bachelor's and diploma
programmes: approximately E11,200 per year for foreign
students; estimated living expenses: E6,000.
Languages: Instruction in English.
Applications: by 1 April to the Admissions Secretary.

Sweden

Academic year: mid-August to June.
Organization of higher education system: Higher
education is provided by 39 universities and institutions of
higher education, whose primary tasks are to provide
undergraduate and postgraduate education. There are five
types of general diplomas: 'Högskoleexamen' (university
diploma) requiring 80 credit points equalling two years of
full-time study; 'Kandidatexamen' (Bachelor's degree),
requiring 120 credit points, half of which must consist of
in-depth studies in main subject and ten credits which must
consist of an independent thesis, equalling three years of
full-time study; 'Magisterexamen' (Master's degree),
'Licentiatexamen' (Licentiate degree), requiring 80 credit
points of postgraduate studies and an academic essay or thesis
of 40 credit points; 'Doktorsexamen' (PhD or Doctorate
degree), requiring 160 credit points of postgraduate studies
and a dissertation of 80 credit points. In addition there are 50
professional degrees ('Yrkesexamina'), which entitle the
holder to practice professions requiring special licenses, such
as law, medicine, veterinary medicine, engineering, etc.
Monetary unit: Swedish krona (SEK).
National student admission: Recognized secondary school
completion diploma;.
Language: Swedish and English; courses and programmes
taught entirely in English do not require Swedish proficiency.
English proficiency must be documented by an internationally
approved test. All students with a non-Nordic upper
secondary school diploma wishing to study in Swedish must
also pass the Test in Swedish for University Studies (TISUS).
Immigration requirements: Visiting students from
non-EEA and non-Nordic countries must apply for a
residence permit (costing approximately SEK 1,000) at the
local Swedish embassy/consulate if they intend to stay more
than three months. Before applying students must show proof
of acceptance to a university-level course in Sweden. The
application fee is SEK 315 (35 Euros). Applicants must also
be able to prove that they will have at least SEK 6,300 per
month for the duration of their studies; SEK 3,000 per month
for spouse and SEK 1,800 per month per child, as well as
adequate medical insurance. See website
www.migrationsverket.se for further information.
Estimated expenses for one academic year: University
education is free of charge, but estimated costs include a fee
of approximately 1,500 SEK per semester payable to the
student union is compulsory. Estimated living costs per
academic year: 6,300 SEK.
Information services:
• The Swedish Institute (Svenska institutet), Box 7434, 103 91
Stockholm; web: http://www.si.se.
• The National Agency for Higher Education
(Högskoleverket), Box 7851, 103 99 Stockholm; web:
http://www.hsv.se.
• Study in Sweden: http://www.studyinsweden.se
• Swedish embassies and consulates; web:
http://www.swedenabroad.com/pages/welcome.asp.
Scholarships for international students: Swedish Institute
(www.si.se); Swedish Foundation for International
Cooperation in Research and Higher Education, International
Programme Office for Education and Training (STINT);
Study in Sweden (www.studyinsweden.se).
Open and distance learning: The Swedish Net University
(Myndigheten för Sveriges nätuniversitet), Box 194, 871 24
Härnösand, tel: +46-611-349-500; fax: +46-611-349-505;
email: info@netuniversity.se; web:
www.myndigheten.netuniversity.se.
Recognition of studies and qualification:
• National Agency for Higher Education (Högskoleverket);
PO Box 7851, SE-103 99 Stockholm, Sweden, tel:
+46-8-5630-8500; fax: +46-8-5630-8550; email: hsv@hsv.se;
web: http://www.hsv.se.
Accommodation services: Information and applications for
student housing are available through each institution, the
local student union or student housing foundation. Links to all
institutions of higher education in Sweden
www.sweden.se/templates/SISCommonPage____5109.asp.
Work opportunities: International students are allowed to
work. No special visa is required and no time limits are
imposed.
Additional information:
• All information that foreign students need on studying in
Sweden is available at the website: www.studyinsweden.se.

The Swedish Institute has very limited capacity to respond to letters or e-mails from individual students.
• Please note that the degree framework will be changed by 2007, in accordance with the Bologna process, into a three-level structure. The Licentiate degree is likely to disappear as a result.
Publications / Websites:
• Study in Sweden; web: www.hsv.se www.studyinsweden.se This website is a comprehensive resource for information about higher education in Sweden, geared towards prospective students from outside Sweden. The site incorporates a frequently updated database of English-language programmes, an overview of the Swedish higher education system, practical information about visas and accommodation, scholarships, application procedures and pointers for learning Swedish as a foreign language. The website is built and maintained by the Swedish Institute (SI).www.si.se, Sweden's official website for information about Sweden to the outside world.
• Swedish Migration Board: web: www.migrationsverket.se/english.html; Useful information from the Swedish Migration Board about visas etc.

2235 Bank of Sweden, Tercentenary Foundation [BOS]
Riksbankens Jubileumsfond
Tyrgatan 4
PO Box 5675
114 86 Stockholm
Tel: +46-8-506-26400
Fax: +46-8-506-26435
Web: http://www.rj.se
e-mail: rj@rj.se

☞ Research grants
Study Domains: all major fields.
Scholarships: research grants (twice a year).
Subjects: primarily research in the humanities and social sciences.
Open to: suitably qualified researchers; foreign applicants must submit a research project for cooperation with Swedish scholars or research institutes.
Applications: to the Programme Secretary for further information.

2236 Chalmers University of Technology
412 96 Göteborg
Tel: +46-31-772-1000
Fax: +46-31-772-3872
Web: http://www.chalmers.se/Home-E.html

☐ Undergraduate, Graduate Programmes
Study Domains: all major fields, engineering.
Programmes: B.Sc., M.Sc., M.Arch. and maritime programmes; Licentiate and Ph.D. programmes as well as the International Master's programmes.
Open to: candidates of any nationality; Master's programmes require B.Sc. or B.Eng. or equivalent.
Duration: Bachelor's: variable; Master's: 12 to 18 months; courses begin in September.
Languages: Swedish and English.
Applications: to the International Secretariat, at the above address.

2237 Dalarna University College [HID]
Högskolan i Dalarna
PO Box 1992
79188 Falun
Tel: +46-23-778-000
Web: http://www2.du.se/eng

☐ Rehabilitation Programmes
Study Domains: engineering, health and hygiene, psychology, Scandinavian studies, Swedish.
Programmes: rehabilitation engineering programme: medical course for engineers; rehabilitation and society, behavioural science, engineering technology for the disabled. Swedish language and culture for foreign students.

Description: programmes for the development or adaptation of technical devices like computers or wheelchairs for people with disabilities.
Open to: nationals of any country with less than 60 ECTS (European Credit Transfer System) credits (one year of full-time studies) left of their B.Sc. in engineering who wish to include a supplementary study programme in their degree; no age limit.
Duration: 1 year.
Fees: tuition free; living expenses: approx. US$900 per month; student union fee approx. US$60 per year (approximate figures).
Languages: Instruction in English.
Applications: to the International Students Admissions Office, at the above address.

2238 Göteborg University [GU]
Vasaparken
41124 Göteborg
Tel: +46-31-773-1000
Fax: +46-31-773-1064
Web: http://www.gu.se/English/default.html
e-mail: study.info@gu.se

☐ Undergraduate, Graduate Programmes
Study Domains: all major fields, summer programmes.
Programmes: undergraduate courses in: (a) fields of the five faculties of mathematics and natural sciences, medicine, odontology, social sciences (including teacher training), and arts and humanities; (b) business administration and economics, mathematics and natural sciences, medicine, social sciences; (c) Summer courses; various courses in all major fields.
Open to: candidates of any nationality.
Duration: (a) and (b) variable; (c) 5 to 10 weeks.
Languages: Instruction in English; Swedish and/or English for (a).
Applications: guest students: by 1 December, through the Swedish Embassies; further information may be obtained from the International Office, at the above address.

2239 Jönköping International Business School [JBS]
PO Box 1026
553 13 Jönköping
Tel: +46-36-157-501
Fax: +46-36-302-141
Web: http://www.jibs.se

☐ Undergraduate, Graduate and Postgraduate Programmes
Study Domains: accounting, administration, business, business administration, economic and commercial sciences, economy, finance, industry and commerce, international business, international law, international relations, management, marketing, political economy, political science, trade.
Programmes: undergraduate, graduate and postgraduate programmes leading to Bachelor's, Master's and Ph.D. degrees.
Description: Bachelor's, Master's and Ph.D. degrees in business administration, economics, business informatics, commercial law.
Fees: no tuition fees; living costs: approx. US$650 per month.
Languages: English.
Applications: for information contact Peter Hilton at the above address.

2240 Jönköping University [JU]
PO Box 1026
55111 Jönköping
Tel: +46-36-157-700
Fax: +46-36-157-718
Web: http://www.hj.se/eng
e-mail: international.office@hlk.hj.se

☐ Certificate Programmes / Health Care
Study Domains: biology, gerontology, nursing, social work.
Programmes: certificate programme at the School of

Health Sciences in community health nursing, care and social services for the elderly and their families, experimental molecular biology, cell and molecular biology.
Open to: students generally eligible to university studies and with relevant degrees/diplomas.
Duration: 5-week modules.
Languages: instruction in English.

📖 Graduate Programmes

Study Domains: engineering.
Programmes: graduate programmes at the School of Engineering.
Open to: see website for eligibility and other information http://www.ing.hj.se/eng.

📖 Undergraduate Programmes

Study Domains: audio-visual media, business administration, communication, education, Scandinavian studies.
Programmes: first degree programmes of study at the School of Education and Communication (HLK) in primary education, lower secondary education, pre-school education, leisure centre pedagogy and communication studies; advanced degree programmes in education and communication studies; independent courses and training available.
Open to: applicants of any country; no age limit; check admission requirements with Admissions Office.
Applications: usually 1 May; check with the Admissions Office for the current deadlines.

2241 Linköping University [LU]

58183 Linköping
Tel: +46-13-281-037
Fax: +46-13-281-063
Web: http://www.liu.se
e-mail: kriwi@intsek.liu.se

📖 Undergraduate and Postgraduate Programmes

Study Domains: arts, education, health and hygiene, Scandinavian studies, sciences, technology.
Programmes: undergraduate and postgraduate programmes.
Description: courses include International Master's programmes in communication and interactivity; Manufacturing management, materials physics, software, integrated systems for communication and media; traffic environment and safety management; medical biology; Intercontinental Master's programme in adult learning and global change; Master's programmes in arts and science in child studies; education in outdoor environmental education and outdoor life; science in business administration/strategy and culture; arts in applied ethics; arts in language and culture in Europe; arts in Scandinavian history; science in geoinformatics; science in water resources and livelihood security; arts and science in health and society; arts and science in science/technology and society; social science in international and European relations.
Applications: to the Student Affairs Division at the above address for further information.

2242 Luleå University [LU]

University Campus, Porsön
97187 Luleå
Tel: +46-920-491-000
Fax: +46-920-491-399
Web: http://www.luth.se/index2.en.ht
e-mail: universitetet@luth.se

📖 Undergraduate, Graduate Programmes

Study Domains: business administration, computer science, education, engineering, performing arts, social sciences.
Programmes: (a) undergraduate and graduate studies in engineering, education, business administration and social sciences; (b) courses in computer sciences and engineering, interdisciplinary themes, performing arts.
Open to: nationals of any country.
Languages: Instruction in: (a) Swedish; (b) English.
Applications: for further information, contact the International Office at the above address.

2243 Lund University [LU]

PO Box 117
22100 Lund
Tel: +46-46-222-0000
Fax: +46-46-222-4111
Web: http://www.lu.se

📖 Music Studies

Study Domains: music and musicology.
Programmes: advanced course in music interpretation for foreign students at the Malmö Academy of Music.
Open to: applicants who have completed a 4-year university study programme.
Duration: 1 to 2 years; courses begin in August.
Fees: none.
Languages: good knowledge of English is required.
Applications: further information at the Malmö Academy of Music P.O. Box 8203, SE-20041 Malmö; website http://www.mhm.lu.se/eng/default.html; tel.+46 40 325 450; fax +46 40 325 460.

📖 Undergraduate, Graduate Programmes

Study Domains: all major fields, European studies.
Programmes: (a) undergraduate and postgraduate courses in humanities and theology, law, medicine, odontology, economic, administrative and social sciences, education, technology and engineering, natural sciences and mathematics, performing arts; a year-long language course is required; (b) Master's level programmes in international law, rural development, European affairs, environmental economics.
Open to: candidates of any country.
Languages: Instruction in: (a) Swedish; (b) English.
Applications: to the Student Service Office at the above address.

2244 Mälardalens Högskolla [MH]

PO Box 883
721 23 Västerås
Tel: +46-21-101-300
Web: http://www.mdh.se
e-mail: info@mdh.se

📖 Diploma, Undergraduate, Graduate Programmes

Study Domains: cultural studies, languages, literature and civilization, Scandinavian studies, summer programmes, Swedish.
Programmes: (a) Aros Summer University: courses in Swedish language, culture and literature, language training; study visits and leisure programme also offered; (b) course diploma in Swedish language, society and culture for foreign students; (c) B.A. or M.A. in business administration.
Open to: beginners and advanced students of any country; no age limit; (b) and (c) 1 year university studies required.
Duration: (a) 3 weeks; (b) 4 months for semester course; 3 weeks for Summer course; (c) 1 to 2 years.
Fees: no tuition fee for semester courses; (approximate figures) (a) 9,000 kronor with single room accommodation; 6,000 kronor with double room; (b) Summer course: 6,000-9,000 kronor; estimated living costs: 5,000-7,500 kronor per month (c) estimated living costs: 5,000-7,500 kronor per month.
Languages: instruction in Swedish and English.
Applications: by 2 May to the International Office at the above address.

2245 Nordic Africa Institute [NAI]

Nordiska Afrikainstitutet
PO Box 1703
75147 Uppsala
Tel: +46-18-562-200
Fax: +46-18-562-290
Web: http://www.nai.uu.se/indexeng.html
e-mail: nai@nai.uu.se

✒ Postgraduate Research

Study Domains: economy, history, political science, travel grants.
Scholarships: (a) Travel Grants Programme; (b) Study Grants Programme; (c) African Guest Researchers' Scholarship Programme; (d) Nordic Guest Researchers' Scholarship Programme.

Open to: (a), (b) primarily scholars from university institutions in Denmark, Finland, Norway, Sweden and Iceland and writers and journalists for publication reasons; (c), (d) scholars in Africa engaged in research on/about the African continent.
Place of study: exclusively in Africa for field work and Uppsala for research.
Value: generally economy air travel and accommodation, subsistence allowance, equipped office space and access to research facilities.
Applications: to the above address, indicating the title of scholarship sought: application deadlines (a) 1 October; (b), (d) 1 April; (c) 16 May; see web page http://www.nai.uu.se/stip/scholars.html.

2246 Nordic School of Public Health [NHV]
PO Box 12133
402 42 Göteborg
Tel: +46-31-693-900
Fax: +46-31-691-777
Web: http://www.nhv.se/index_e.html

⌂ Diploma, Graduate, Postgraduate Programmes

Study Domains: health and hygiene.
Programmes: postgraduate training programme in public health: (a) Diploma of Public Health; (b) Master of Public Health; (c) Doctor of Public Health; (d) Short non-degree courses in public health: public health science, epidemiology, management of Nordic health care, environmental health, caring science, international health.
Open to: (a) to (c) mainly Nordic (but also Baltic) postgraduate professionals, working in the public health field; (d) persons professionally active in the Nordic public health field, including social services and other areas of prevention and health promotion with academic attainment equivalent to 3 years of university study.
Duration: diploma: 8 months; Master's: 2 years; Doctorate: 4 years; short courses: 2 to 8 weeks.
Fees: no tuition fees; 750 kronor per month service; 1.000 kronor per month accommodation (approximate figures).
Languages: instruction in Scandinavian languages and English.
Applications: by May of the preceding year, to the above address.

2247 Orebro University [ORU]
70182 Örebro
Tel: +46-19-303-000
Fax: +46-9-303-488
Web: http://www.oru.se
e-mail: info@oru.se

⌂ Undergraduate Programmes

Study Domains: communication, education, history, law, sciences, social sciences.
Programmes: Undergraduate programmes and courses in a broad range of subjects, with emphasis on social sciences; courses in economics, social sciences, law, education, communication, history.
Open to: candidates of any country.
Languages: Instruction in Swedish and English.
Applications: for further information, contact the International Office, at the above address.

2248 Royal Institute of Technology [KTH]
Kungliga Tekniska Högskolan
10044 Stockholm
Tel: +46-8-790-6000
Fax: +46-8-790-8192
Web: http://www.kth.se/eng
e-mail: international@admin.kth.se

⌂ Undergraduate, Graduate Programmes

Study Domains: architecture, biology, business, chemistry, computer science, electricity and electronics, engineering, geodesy, management, mathematics, mechanical engineering, physics, technology, telecommunications.
Programmes: programmes of courses leading to Bachelor's and Master's degrees.

Description: (a) Bachelor of Science (B.Sc.) in engineering, (b) Master of Science (M.Sc.) in engineering, (c) Master's programmes in English.
Open to: (a) and (b) candidates of any nationality holding a secondary school certificate including mathematics, physics and chemistry and with certified knowledge in English and Swedish; (c) candidates holding a Bachelor's degree in relevant subject and with knowledge in English (TOEFL 570/IELTS 6.0).
Duration: (a) 3 years, (b) 4-1/2 years, (c) 1-1/2 years.
Fees: no tuition fees; living costs: approx. 7,200 kronor per month.
Applications: to the above address for further information.

2249 Royal University College of Music in Stockholm
Kungl. Musikhögskolan
PO Box 277 11
11591 Stockholm
Tel: +46-8-161-800
Fax: +46-8-664-1424
Web: http://www.kmh.se
e-mail: international@kmh.se

⌂ Music Studies

Study Domains: music and musicology.
Programmes: comprehensive music-training programmes consisting of music teacher training; church music; composition; orchestra/choir conducting; soloist diploma for singers and instrumentalists.
Open to: applicants selected on the basis of their results in the entrance examinations and auditions; all candidates must appear in person for the auditions; no tapes are accepted.
Languages: instruction totally in Swedish.
Applications: by January, to the above address.

2250 Stockholm Institute of Education
International Coordinator
Konradsberg 5A
PO Box 34103
10026 Stockholm
Tel: +46-8-737-5500
Fax: +46-8-737-5501
Web: http://www.lhs.se

⌂ Teacher Education

Study Domains: early childhood education, education, teacher education.
Programmes: programmes and courses in teacher training and education for all school levels, and in child care and research and development work in connection with these specific areas.
Open to: students who have successfully completed upper-secondary education; some courses and programmes require previous university studies.
Fees: no tuition fees.
Languages: instruction in Swedish; some courses and programmes are offered for English-speaking students.
Applications: for further information contact the Student Office or International Office, at the above address.

2251 Stockholm School of Economics
PO Box 6501
113 83 Stockholm
Tel: +46-8-736-9000
Fax: +46-8-318-186
Web: http://www.hhs.se
e-mail: info@hhs.se

⌂ Graduate, Postgraduate Programmes

Study Domains: all major fields, accounting, business, business administration, development studies, economic and commercial sciences, economy, European studies, finance.
Programmes: (a) Master of Science programme in economics, business administration and law; (b) International Graduate Programme in economics, business administration, law; (c) Doctoral Programme in economics, business administration, law.
Open to: (a) citizens of the Nordic countries and foreign

students fluent in Swedish or students selected by the partner universities of the SSE; (b) students with a college degree (or equivalent) with a major in economics and/or business; (c) varies by department.
Duration: (a) 4 years; (b) 3 semesters; (c) 4 years.
Fees: (a) no fees are currently charged for the degree programme; (b) tuition, 30,000 kronor per semester (approximate figures).
Financial assistance: some assistance available to those in the doctoral programme.
Languages: instruction in Swedish and English.

2252　Stockholm University [SU]

International Student Office
10691 Stockholm
Tel: +46-8-162-845
Fax: +46-8-161-397
Web: http://www.su.se

⌨ Undergraduate, Graduate Programmes

Study Domains: all major fields.
Programmes: undergraduate and graduate programmes in natural sciences, humanities, social sciences and law.
Open to: candidates of all nationalities; candidates for graduate programmes must hold a university degree in either political science, sociology, economic history or social anthropology; applicants must submit results of TOEFL with a minimum score of 550 or IELTS minimum score 6.0.
Duration: 1 to 4 years.
Fees: no tuition fee charged; mandatory student union fees of about 600 kronor per year and a compulsory health insurance fee of 750 kronor per year must be paid by student; estimated living costs: 6,500 kronor per month.
Financial assistance: possibility of obtaining Swedish government's guest scholarships; write directly to: Swedish Institute, Scholarship Section, Box 7434, 103 91 Stockholm for information.

2253　Swedish Institute [SI]

PO Box 7434
10391 Stockholm
Tel: +46-8-453-7800
Fax: +46-8-207-248
Web: http://www.si.se

⌨ Swedish Language

Study Domains: cultural studies, languages, literature and civilization, summer programmes, Swedish.
Programmes: International Summer courses in Swedish language, literature, culture and society:.
Open to: candidates of any nationality, over 18 years of age, with previous studies in the Swedish language at university level.
Duration: 1 to 4 weeks during July and August.
Fees: approx. 5,800 to 7,800 kronor, including tuition, full board and lodging.
Applications: by 31 March; see
http://www.sweden.se/templates/SISFrontPage____4908.asp.

⌨ Swedish Institute Scholarships

Study Domains: all major fields.
Scholarships: (a) Guest Scholarship Programme; (b) Caucasus, Central Asia and Moldova Programme; (c) Swedish-Turkish scholarships for European Studies; (d) The Visby Programme.
Open to: (a) nationals of all countries; (b) nationals of Armenia, Azerbaijan, Georgia, Kazakhstan, Kyrgyzstan, Moldova, Tajikistan, Turkmenistan and Uzbekistan; (c) nationals of Turkey; (d) nationals of Russia, Ukraine and Belarus see web page
http://www.si.se/e_visby/2544.cs?dirid=1237.
Duration: variable according to the type of award.
Applications: for (a), (b), (c) directly to the Swedish Institute, at the above address. Forms obtainable only from the Swedish Institute; prior to the application, contact must be established with a Swedish university department willing to accept the applicant; deadlines: (a)15 January; (b) 1 March; (d) 1 March: (see also Swedish Institute scholarship data base http://www.si.se/stipendie/1865.cs?dirid=114).

2254　Swedish University of Agricultural Sciences

PO Box 7070
750 07 Uppsala
Tel: +46-18-67-1000
Fax: +46-18-67-3596
Web: http://www.slu.se
e-mail: registrator@slu.se

⌨ Undergraduate, Graduate Programmes

Study Domains: agriculture, agronomic sciences, architecture, biochemistry, biology, cattle breeding, chemistry, ecology, environment, forestry, genetics, horticulture, hydrology, microbiology, research, statistics, veterinary medicine, veterinary sciences.
Programmes: programme of courses leading to Master's, Ph.D. degrees and University Diploma.
Open to: students with 3 years of secondary school; working experience may be required for some programmes.
Duration: 4-1/2 to 5-1/2 years.
Fees: estimated living expenses: 6,000 kronor per month.
Applications: through the Swedish Embassy or Consulate in candidate's home country; further information may be obtained from the Study Counsellors' Office, at the above address.

2255　Umeå University

90187 Umeå
Tel: +46-90-786-5000
Fax: +46-90-786-9995 / 786-5488
Web: http://www.umu.se
e-mail: umea.universitet@adm.umu.se

⌨ Undergraduate, Graduate Programmes

Study Domains: all major fields.
Programmes: (a) undergraduate and postgraduate courses in all major fields; (b) courses in languages, literature and linguistics, mathematics and natural sciences, social sciences and humanities, law, economics.
Open to: candidates of any nationality.
Languages: instruction in: (a) Swedish; (b) English.
Applications: for further information, contact the Student Counselling Office at the above address.

2256　University College of Dance

Danshogskolan
PO Box 27043
10251 Stockholm
Tel: +46-8-459-529
Fax: +46-8-459-0510
Web: http://www.danshogskolan.se/eng

⌨ Dance

Study Domains: arts, performing arts.
Programmes: diplomas in: (a) dance education; (b) folk dance; (c) dance performance; (d) dance therapy; (e) historical dance; (f) choreography.
Open to: candidates who have completed upper secondary school; an audition is required.
Duration: 2 to 3 years; courses begin in August.
Fees: tuition-free.
Languages: Instruction in Swedish and English.
Applications: to the International Coordinator at the above address.

2257　University College of Opera

Operahögskolan
Dag Hammarskjölds Väg 24
115 27 Stockholm
Tel: +46-8-545-81060
Fax: +46-8-545-81061
Web: http://www.operahogskolan.se

⌨ Diploma Programmes

Study Domains: music and musicology.
Programmes: university diploma in performing arts and media: opera singers' training programme, opera repetiteurs' training programme, opera directors' training programme.
Open to: all nationalities; applicants must be over 20 years of age.
Duration: 3-1/2 years.
Fees: none.

Languages: Instruction in Swedish.

2258 University of Karlstad
Universitetgatan 2
65188 Karlstad
Tel: +46-54-700-1000
Fax: +46-54-700-1460
Web: http://www.kau.se
e-mail: information@kau.se

📖 Undergraduate, Graduate Programmes

Study Domains: all major fields, business administration, computer science, economy, engineering, mathematics, social sciences.
Programmes: (a) undergraduate courses in economics, marketing, services marketing, communication studies, politics, computer science, natural sciences; (b) Master's programme in business administration.
Open to: (a) undergraduate students of all nationalities; no age limit; good knowledge of English required; (b) all nationalities, with a Bachelor's degree in relevant business studies and a good knowledge of English.
Duration: (a) from 3 to 10 months; courses begin in either August or January; (b) 1 year.
Languages: instruction in English.
Applications: (a) by 1 June for Autumn term or 1 December for Spring term, to the International Office at the above address for further information; (b) by 1 June, to the International Office.

2259 Uppsala University [UU]
PO Box 256
75105 Uppsala
Tel: +46-18-471-18 62
Fax: +46-18-471-16 00
Web: http://www.uu.se

📖 International Programmes

Study Domains: chemistry, physics.
Programmes: International programmes sponsored by the Swedish International Development Cooperation Agency, Sida, with contributions from Uppsala University and a few other sources, to assist Third World countries in creating endogenous research capacity in the chemical and physical sciences.
Open to: admission restricted.
Duration: up to 10 months.
Financial assistance: possibility of obtaining project grants.
Applications: to the above address for further information.

📖 Undergraduate, Graduate Programmes

Study Domains: all major fields.
Programmes: undergraduate and graduate programmes in theology, law, medicine, humanities, social and behavioural sciences, economics, mathematics/natural sciences and technology, business administration and economics, computer sciences and engineering, education.
Open to: candidates of any nationality with proficiency in Swedish language; most courses in English are open only to students from universities with which Uppsala University has an exchange programme (except for Master's level courses in International and comparative law, international health, International studies and South Asian studies).
Fees: tuition free; see website for estimated living costs: http://www.studyin.sweden.se.
Applications: admission to all programmes and courses is restricted; applications and further information from the Division of Student Affairs at the above address.

🎓 UUISS Scholarships

Study Domains: folklore, history, literature and civilization, music and musicology, sociology, Swedish, visual arts.
Scholarships: Uppsala University International Summer Session Scholarships.
Description: Swedish language, arts in contemporary Scandinavia, modern Swedish social institutions, history of modern Sweden, modern Swedish literature, Swedish pop music, the Swedish film, literature course on August Strindberg.
Open to: applicants of any nationality, secondary-school

graduates at least 18 years of age, eligible for university studies.
Value: approximately 1,000-11,700 kronor per month.
Applications: by 15 March, to the above address.

Tajikistan
Organization of higher education system: Higher education is mainly provided by universities and institutes. They come under the responsibility of the Ministry of Education.
•University level first stage: Junior Specialist, Bachelor (Bakalavr), Diploma of Specialist:
The degree of Junior Specialist is conferred after two years of study. The degree of Bachelor (Bakalavr) is awarded after four years of study. The Diploma of Specialist in a given field is conferred after four to five years' study.
• University level second stage: Master (Magistre), Kandidat Nauk: The Master's Degree (Magistre) is awarded after two years' study beyond the Bachelor's Degree. The Kandidat Nauk degree is conferred after a further three years' study beyond the Specialist Degree and the defence of a thesis.
• University level third stage: Doctorate: A PhD (new system) is conferred after a further three years' study beyond the Master's Degree and presentation of a thesis. (Source: IAU World Higher Education Database, 2005/6).
Language: Tajik, Russian.
Information services: Ministry of Education, Ul. Cekov 13a, 734024 Dusanbe, Tajikistan; tel. +992-372-233-392; fax: +992-372-275-607.

2260 Russian-Tajik Modern University for the Humanities
17 Microdistrict, House 2
735718 Khujand
Tel: +810 992 3422 21928
Fax: +810 992 3422 61991

📖 Undergraduate Programmes

Study Domains: accounting, Arabic, business, business administration, computer science, criminology, English, information science, international business, international law, international studies, law, management.
Programmes: undergraduate degree programmes in humanities and arts, social sciences, business, law, management, international finance, information sciences; some courses offered through distance education.
Open to: candidates passing entrance examination; English and Russian language proficiency required.
Duration: 4 years; courses begin 1 September.
Fees: registration; US$100; yearly tuition; US$1,000; estimated monthly living costs: US$100.
Applications: by 25 August.

🎓 Scholarship

Study Domains: economy, history, international relations, law, management, Russian.
Open to: all candidates.
Duration: 5 years; renewable.
Value: Tuition, US$ 50; living expenses, US$ 100.
Applications: by 30 June.

2261 Tajik Technical University 'M.S. Osimi'
Prosp. Acad. Rajabovs, 10
Dushanbe 734042
Tel: +992 372 213 511
Fax: +992 372 217135
e-mail: techuni@tajnet.com

📖 Undergraduate, Graduate, Postgraduate Programmes

Study Domains: all major fields, administration, anthropology, architecture, art history, arts, arts and crafts, business, business administration, decorative arts, design, economy, engineering, fine arts, international relations, languages, mathematics, rural development, sciences, shipbuilding, technical education, technology, telecommunications, textile industry, theology, religion, urbanism.

Programmes: Bachelor's, Master's, Ph.D. degrees in arts, social sciences, business, law, science, engineering.
Open to: candidates holding a secondary-school certificate, passing admission tests and under 35 years of age.
Duration: 4 to 7 years.
Fees: US$600-$1,500 per year.
Languages: Tajik and Russian.
Applications: by 31 August; contact techuni@tajnet.com for further information.

2262 Technological University of Tajikistan [TUT]
63/3, Ne'mat Karabaev Street
Dushanbe 734061
Tel: +992 372 347988
Fax: +992 372 347988
Web: http://www.tut.tajnet.com
e-mail: tutaj@cada.tajik.net

📖 Undergraduate Studies
Study Domains: all major fields, administration, agriculture, anatomy, architecture, bacteriology, business, business administration, cancerology, education, engineering, home economics, natural resources, natural sciences, physiology, sciences, social sciences, transport.
Programmes: Bachelor's degrees in teacher training and non-degree programmes in languages; computer technologies.
Duration: 5 years; courses start 1 September.
Fees: registration US$50; tuition fees US$600 per year; living costs US$100 per month.
Languages: Tajik, Russian, English.
Applications: by 15 August to farshed@cada.tajik.net.

Tchad
Année universitaire: octobre à juin.
Unité monétaire: franc CFA.
Admission pour étudiants du pays: Tout étudiant étranger doit être titulaire du baccalauréat ou d'un diplôme équivalent, ou être reçu au concours spécial d'entrée en faculté.
Connaissances linguistiques requises: Une bonne connaissance du français ou de l'arabe est exigée.
Formalités d'immigration: Les étudiants étrangers doivent avoir un visa d'entrée au Tchad et une carte de séjour.
Services d'accueil et d'information:
• Ministère de l'enseignement supérieur, de la recherche et des bourses, N'Djamena.
• Ambassades et consulats du Tchad à l'étranger.
• Les services culturels de certains pays accrédités auprès du Tchad, tels que les États-Unis et la France.
Reconnaissance des études et diplômes: Commission d'Admission de l'Université de N'Djaména, BP 1117, avenue Mobutu, N'Djaména, Tchad; tél: +235-51-5946 / +235-51-4444; fax: +235-51-4033; email: rectorat@intnet.td.
Publications / Sites Web:
• «Annuaire de l'Université du Tchad» (en français), disponible auprès des Éditions Université du Tchad, B.P. 1117, N'Djamena.

2263 Université de N'Djaména, Faculté des sciences exactes et appliquées [UDN]
BP 1117
Avenue Mobutu
N'Djaména
Tel: +235-51-5946 / 4444
Fax: +235-51-4581

📖 Cursus du 1er et 2e cycles
Domaines d'étude: biologie, chimie, élevage, géologie, mathématiques, mécanique, physique, technologie industrielle.
Programmes: (a) cours de 1er et 2ème cycles en mathématiques, physique, chimie, biologie, géologie, et électromécanique; (b) cours de gestion de l'environnement: environnement et développement rural, conduisant à la maîtrise.
A l'intention de: (a) ressortissants tchadiens et des pays voisins, titulaires d'un baccalauréat scientifique C, D, E, ou F; (b) étudiants et agents de terrain ayant au minimum 3 ans

d'expérience tchadienne et étrangère, titulaires d'un DEUG, licence, ou maîtrise de sciences de la nature; admission sur concours et sélection de dossiers.
Durée: 3 ans.
Frais: (a) 200.000 francs CFA pour les étudiants étrangers; (b) 300.000 francs CFA pour les étudiants étrangers.
Assistance financière: quelques bourses offertes par le gouvernement du Tchad et des agences internationales; contacter l'Université à l'adresse ci-dessus pour de plus amples informations.
Connaissances linguistiques: langue d'enseignement: français.
Inscriptions: (a) avant le 15 octobre, (b) avant le 30 septembre; au Service de la scolarité de l'Université, B.P. 1117, N'Djaména.

TFYR Macedonia
Academic year: October to June.
Organization of higher education system: Higher education undergraduate study programmes last from 3 to 5 years; postgraduate study programmes last from 1-1/2 to 2 years.
Major institutions of higher education: University of St. Ciril and Methodius-Skopje: www.ukim.edu.mk; University of St. Kliment Ohridski-Bitola: www.uklo.edu.mk;

University of East Europa-Tetova: www.see.university.edu.mk.
Monetary unit: Macedonian Denars (MKD).
International student admission: Secondary school leaving certificate.
Language: Macedonian, Albanian, English.
Immigration requirements: A visa is necessary to reside and study.
Estimated expenses for one academic year: tuition: US$3,000; books/supplies: US$300; housing: 100 Euros per month.
Information services:
• Consular services of TFYR of Macedonia in each country.
• Ministry of Education and Sciences, web: http://www.mon.gov.mk (in Macedonian only).
Recognition of studies and qualification: National Commission for Diploma Recognition, Ministry of Education and Science, Skopje; web: http:// www.mon.gov.mk (in Macedonian).
Accommodation services: Student dormitories and private accommodation.
Work opportunities: There are no work opportunities for international students.

2264 University of St. Cyril and Methodius
bul. Krste Misirkov
1000 Skopje
Tel: +389-2-3118-155
Web: http://www.ukim.edu.mk
e-mail: ukim@ukim.edu.mk

📖 Undergraduate, Graduate, Postgrduate Programmes
Study Domains: all major fields.
Description: bilateral exchange programmes with 75 foreign universities; Bologna principles of recognition of degrees and studies, promotion of Diploma Supplement, introducing credit system, development of policy and system on quality assurance and quality assessment in higher education, developing university strategies for continuing education.
Open to: students within exchange programmes.

Thailand

Academic year: June to March.
Monetary unit: baht.
National student admission: Foreign students seeking admission to Thai universities should apply directly to the Registrar of the university concerned approximately one year prior to studies planned. There is a University entrance examination.
Language: Fluency in the Thai language is required for regular university courses. Language instruction in Thai is available to English-speaking students at the Union Language School, 197/1 Silom Road, Bangkok (all levels), and at the AUA Language Center, 179 Rajdamri Road, Bangkok (elementary and intermediate levels).
Information services:
• Ministry of University Affairs, 328 Sri Ayudhya Road, Bangkok 10400.
Open and distance learning: Sukhothai Thammathirat Open University (STOU) uses distance learning methods. It provides continuing and lifelong education and education through self-instruction programmes and televised classes, and organizes tuition groups nationwide. It offers programmes in education, management science, law, health, economics, home economics, political science, liberal arts, communication, arts and agricultural extension and cooperatives, science and technology. Ramkhamhaeng University offers Bachelor's degree programmes in law, business administration, humanities, education, science, political science, economics and engineering with no entrance examination required.
Recognition of studies and qualification: Bureau of Higher Education Standards, Ministry of University Affairs; 328 Sri Ayutthaya Road Ratchathewi; Bangkok 10400,;Thailand; tel: +66-2-245-9036 / 246-1106 / 246-1114; fax: +66-2-245-8925 / 8636 / 8930; email: ptk@mis.mua.go.th; intcoop@mis.mua.go.th; web: http://www.inter.mua.go.th.
Accommodation services: May be obtained on a limited scale at most universities. Student health service with resident medical officers and sports facilities with instructors in physical education are also available for students in nearly all universities.

2265 Asian University of Science and Technology [AUST]

89 Moo 12, Highway 331,
Huay Yai, Banglamung
20260 Chonburi
Tel: +66-38-754-450
Fax: +66-38-754-460
Web: http://www.asianust.ac.th
e-mail: admissions@asianust.ac.th

📖 Undergraduate, Graduate Programmes

Study Domains: business administration, computer science, economic and commercial sciences, economy, electricity and electronics, English, finance, management, marketing, mechanical engineering, summer programmes.
Programmes: B.B.A.; B.Eng.; B.A. in English for Business Communication; M.B.A.; non-degree programmes: English immersion.
Open to: candidates of all nationalities meeting academic, linguistic and financial qualifications: admission tests; TOEFL 550, IELTS 6+ or equivalent required.
Duration: Bachelor's degree: 4 years; Master's degree: 1 year; courses beginning in August; Summer course: 10 weeks.
Languages: English.
Applications: by 20 August to the Admissions Office; contact Ginster Votteler for information.

2266 Assumption University, Bangkok [AU]

Ramkhamhaeng 24,
Hua Mak
10240 Bangkok
Tel: +66-2-300-4553
Fax: +66-2-300-4563
Web: http://www.au.edu

e-mail: abac@au.edu

📖 Undergraduate Distance Education Programmes

Study Domains: business administration, computer science, information science, sciences.
Programmes: distance education degree courses at the College of Internet Distance Education: Bachelor of Information Technology (Software Engineering); Bachelor of Information System; Bachelor of Science; Bachelor of Business Administration; Bachelor of Management; Bachelor of Arts; Master of Information and Multimedia Technology; Master of Information Technology Management; Master of Science; Master of Business Administration.
Applications: see website http://www.au.ac.th/cide.

2267 Bangkok University [BU]

Rama 4 Road, Klongtoey
10110 Bangkok
Tel: +66-2-350-3500
Fax: +66-2-240-1516
Web: http://www.bu.ac.th
e-mail: webmaster@bu.ac.th

🍧Scholarship

Study Domains: humanities and arts, marketing.
Open to: candidates with outstanding academic achievement after one year of enrolment in the program.
Duration: 1 year.
Value: Tuition, US$1,200.
Applications: contact buic@bu.ac.th for further information.

2268 Kasetsart University [KU]

50 Phahonyothin, Chatuchak
10900 Bangkok
Tel: +66-2-942-8171 / 73
Fax: +66-2-942-8170 / 8726
Web: http://www.ku.ac.th
e-mail: fro@ku.ac.th

📖 Undergraduate and Graduate Degree Programmes

Study Domains: all major fields, agriculture, summer programmes.
Programmes: (a) Bachelor's; (b) Master's; (c) Ph.D.
Description: (a) aerospace engineering and business administration; (b) aquaculture, development communication, civil engineering, industrial engineering, business administration; (b) and (c) tropical agriculture, biotechnology, forestry, agricultural economics.
Open to: candidates must be proficient in English.
Fees: tuition fees vary according to department and programme; consult particular departments for updated fees.
Financial assistance: contact International Division to enquire about financial assistance.
Languages: English.
Applications: application dates vary with each programme; contact Director of the International Programmes for more specific information at email: agrchk@nontri.ku.ac.th; tel: +66 2 562 0985 or to above address.

🍧SEARCA Thesis Grants

Study Domains: all major fields.
Scholarships: University consortium.
Subjects: agriculture; science; agroindustry.
Open to: graduate students enrolled at the University.
Value: US$1,000-$2,000 per thesis proposal.
Applications: apply by the end of March to Director of International Affairs Division at the university.

2269 Khon Kaen University [KKU]

Mittraphab Road
40002 Khon Kaen
Tel: +66-43-202-222 to 4
Web: http://www.kku.ac.th
e-mail: info@kku.ac.th

📖 Graduate Degree Programmes

Study Domains: development studies, education, paramedical studies, sociology, veterinary sciences.

Programmes: (a) Master's programme: animal science, biostatistics, rural development; (b) Doctoral programme: development sociology, education; (c) Non-credit undergraduate courses: nursing, agriculture, medicine.
Open to: (a) candidates holding a Bachelor's in or related to the subject chosen; (b) candidates holding a Master's degree in the subject chosen; (c) applicants with secondary-school diploma. Proficiency in English required (TOEFL score of at least 500).
Duration: (a) 2 years; (b) 4 years; (c) 1 year.
Fees: (approximate figures) US$2,880 covering tuition, fees, medical insurance and field trips; housing, approx. US$80-$250 per month.
Languages: Instruction in Thai and English.

📖 Undergraduate, Graduate Programmes

Study Domains: all major fields.
Programmes: undergraduate and graduate programmes in all major fields.
Applications: to the above address.

📖 Undergraduate, Graduate Programmes / Engineering

Study Domains: computer science, summer programmes.
Programmes: programme of courses leading to degrees in engineering: (a) Bachelor's degrees in civil, electrical, agricultural, industrial, mechanical, environmental, chemical, computer and biomedical engineering; (b) Master's and Ph.D. degrees in chemical, electrical, environmental, mechanical, structural, water resources and agricultural machinery engineering.
Open to: candidates of any country fulfilling the necessary requirements: (a) secondary-school certificate; (b) for Master's programme, B.Eng. or B.Sc.; for Ph.D. programme, B.Eng. (honours), M.Eng. or M.Sc.; written tests and interviews.
Duration: (a) 4 years; (b) Master's degree, 2 years.
Fees: (approximate figures) tuition: 25,000 baht per regular semester; English programme, US$3,500 per year; living expenses: US$100-$150 per month.
Languages: Instruction in (a) Thai, (b) English.
Applications: by (a) March - April; (b) February, to the Registrar.

2270 King Mongkut's Institute of Technology North Bangkok [KMITNB]

1518 Pibulsongkram Road, Bangsue
10800 Bangkok
Tel: +66-2-585-8541 to 9
Fax: +66-2-586-9007
Web: http://www.kmitnb.ac.th
e-mail: iro@kmitnb.ac.th

📖 Graduate Degree Programme in Information Technology

Study Domains: computer science.
Description: Master's degree in Information Technology in English; opportunity to spend time in/or graduate from Australia: www.kmitnb.ac.th/thaiaus/thaiaus.html.
Open to: applicants must have a bachelor's degree with some background in information technology; IELTS 5.5; TOEFL score of 525 or computer-based TOEFL 196.
Duration: 2 years.
Fees: registration fee: 750 baht; tuition fees: 75,000 baht per semester.
Languages: English.
Applications: apply by mid-February to: heather@kmitnb.ac.th; or phone: +66 2 913 2500 ext.1024; consult website for further information: www.kmitnb.ac.th/thaiaus/thaiaus.html.

🐾 University Scholarship

Study Domains: computer science, information science.
Scholarships: University scholarship in information technology.
Duration: 4 semesters.
Value: 37,500 baht per semester.
Applications: apply by mid-February to: heather@kmitnb.ac.th; or phone: +66 2 913 2500 ext.1024.

2271 King Mongkut's University of Technology Thonburi [KMUTT]

91 Pracha-utit Road
Bangmod, Tungkpu
10140 Bangkok
Tel: +66-2-470-8000
Fax: +66-2-427-9860
Web: http://www.kmutt.ac.th
e-mail: int.off@kmutt.ac.th

📖 Undergraduate, Graduate, Postgraduate Programmes

Study Domains: applied sciences, architecture, arts, biochemistry, biology, biophysics, chemical engineering, chemistry, civil engineering, computer science, ecology, environment, electricity and electronics, energy, engineering, English, food, genetics, hydrology, industrial design, industrial technology, interior design, Japanese, liberal arts, linguistics, mathematics, mechanical engineering, microbiology, physics, sciences, social sciences, telecommunications, urbanism.
Programmes: (a) B.Sc.; (b) M.Sc.; (c) Ph.D.; (d) graduate diploma.
Description: (a) industrial education; information technology; science; engineering; architecture; (b) industrial education; bioresources and technology; information technology; energy and materials; science; engineering; liberal arts; energy and environment; (c) bioresources and technology; information technology; energy and materials; engineering; energy and environment; (d) energy and materials; engineering; liberal arts.

2272 Maejo University [MU]

63 Chiang Mai-Prao Road
Sansai
50290 Chiang Mai
Tel: +66-53-878-038 to 50
Fax: +66-53-498-137
Web: http://www.mju.ac.th/about/about-mju-en.htm

📖 Undergraduate, Graduate Programmes / Agronomy

Study Domains: agriculture, agronomic sciences, business administration, economic and commercial sciences, fisheries, food industry, forestry, horticulture, rural development.
Programmes: courses leading to Bachelor of Business Administration (agricultural business, marketing); Bachelor of Science (agriculture business, agricultural economics, agricultural extension, agronomy, cooperative economics, dairy-beef production, entomology, fisheries technology, food technology, ornamental horticulture, plant pathology, pomology, poultry science, swine production, vegetable technology, agricultural engineering); Bachelor of Agricultural Technology in landscape technology; Master of Science (agricultural extension, agriculture and forest administration, agronomy, animal production, co-operative economics, agricultural community, seed technology, horticulture); Master of Business Administration; Doctorate (rural planning and development).
Open to: candidates with necessary qualifications; fluency in reading and writing Thai language required.
Duration: 2 to 4 years.
Applications: to the Registrar at the above address.

2273 Mahanakorn University of Technology [MUT]

51 Cheum-Sampan
Nong Chok
Bangkok
Tel: +66-2-988-3655
Fax: +66-2-988-4040
Web: http://www.mut.ac.th
e-mail: lerkiat@mut.ac.th

📖 Master's Degree Programme

Study Domains: engineering, management.
Programmes: Master's degree programmes in manufacturing management, biomedical engineering.
Duration: 2 years beginning in June.
Fees: tuition: 350,000 baht for 2 years.
Financial assistance: possibility of fee reduction.

Languages: English; TOEFL score of 500; IELTS 4.5.
Applications: by the end of March to Dean of Graduate School at above address or email: prakit@mut.ac.th.

2274 Mahidol University [MU]
999 Phuttamonthon 4 Road Salaya
Phuttamonthon
73170 Nakhon Pathom
Tel: +66-2-849-6230-6
Fax: +66-2-849-6237
Web: http://www.mahidol.ac.th
e-mail: orbsw@mahidol.ac.th

Undergraduate, Graduate Programmes
Study Domains: arts, business administration, dentistry, engineering, health and hygiene, medicine, nursing, pharmacy and pharmacology, sciences.
Programmes: (a) Undergraduate diplomas in arts and science; (b) Graduate diploma in tropical medicine; (c) degree programmes leading to Master of Science in tropical medicine; (d) Master of Science in 8 areas of public health (environmental health, family health, health education, health administration, hospital administration, infectious diseases, nutrition and public health nursing); (e) Master of Public Health in urban health, primary health care, health promotion, health research, dental public health, public health administration.
Open to: applicants of all nationalities: (a) having completed twelfth grade with at least a 2.5 average; (b) holding a degree of Doctor of Medicine from approved institution or the license for 1st-class practitioner in general medicine; (c) holding a degree of Doctor of Medicine, Dental Surgery, Veterinary Medicine or a B.Sc. in pharmacy from approved institution and having worked in a hospital for at least 1 year; (d) holding a degree in public health field or related field; (e) holding a degree of Doctor of Medicine, Dental Surgery, Veterinary Medicine or a B.Sc. in pharmacy from approved institution and having worked in a hospital for at least 1 year; or holding a degree in public health field or related field.
Duration: 3 months to 6 years; 4-10 semesters fro Master's degree; 6-16 semesters for a doctoral degree. Undergraduate programmes begin in September for the first semester and in January for the second semester, and in April for the third semester; Graduate programmes begin June-October for the first semester, and November -March for the second semester.
Fees: (approximate figures) regular courses: undergraduate, US$19,920 to US$24,000 per year; graduate, US$5,800 per year; international degree programme: for Master's degree, US$5,000 to US$9,420 per year.
Financial assistance: student loans, study employment, undergraduate and graduate scholarships available.
Languages: instruction in English.
Applications: For undergraduate admissions, contact: directic@mahidol.ac.th; for graduate admissions, contact deangr@mahidol.ac.th.

Financial aid
Study Domains: biochemistry, chemistry, computer science, demography and population studies, dentistry, ecology, environment, genetics, microbiology, nursing, physical therapy.
Scholarships: Graduate Scholarship.
Description: Partial tuition waiver.
Duration: Master's, 2 years; doctoral, 3 years.
Value: variable.
Applications: contact public sector and international relations unit, telad@mahidol.ac.th.

2275 Naresuan University [NU]
Muang District
Phitsanulok
Tel: +66-55-261-000
Fax: +66-55-261-005
Web: http://www.nu.ac.th

Undergraduate, Graduate Programmes
Study Domains: all major fields.
Programmes: Bachelor's; Master's; Ph.D. programmes in all major fields; (57 undergraduate; 44 Master's; 8 Doctorate).
Applications: consult website; email or post enquiries for specific information on each programme.

DTEC Scholarship
Study Domains: energy, natural resources, natural sciences.
Scholarships: DTEC Scholarship in renewable energy.
Open to: GMS countries (Cambodia, Lao People's Democratic Republic, Myanmar, Thailand, Yunnan/China, Viet Nam).
Duration: 2 years.
Applications: apply by December to Director of Solar Energy Research and Training Center.

2276 National Institute of Development Administration [NIDA]
118 Sereethai Road
Klong-Chan, Bangkapi
10240 Bangkok
Tel: +66-2727-3000
Fax: +66-2375-8798
Web: http://www.nida.ac.th
e-mail: oia@nida.nida.ac.th

Undergraduate, Graduate Programmes / Public Administration
Study Domains: administration, business, development studies, human sciences, languages.
Programmes: (a) Master's degree programmes in public administration, public and private management, business administration, development economics, applied statistics, population and development, computer sciences, social development, human resource development, administration technology, language and communication, environmental management; (b) Doctorate degree programmes in development administration, population and development, business administration, statistics.
Open to: qualified candidates of all nationalities (a) with a Bachelor's degree in related field of study; (b) with a Master's degree in chosen field; no age limit.
Duration: (a) 2 to 5 years; (b) 3 to 8 years; courses begin in the second week of June and November.
Fees: (approximate figures) 6,000 baht per credit per semester; 5,000 baht academic fee per semester.
Languages: instruction in Thai, except for Master's degree in business administration and Doctorate degree programmes in development administration, business administration and statistics which are given in English.
Applications: by June and December, to the Educational Service Division, at the above address.

2277 Prince of Songkla University [POSU]
International Relations Office
PO Box 102 Hat Yai
90110 Songkla
Tel: +66-74-446-824 / 282-161 / 2
Fax: +66-74-446-825
Web: http://www.psu.ac.th
e-mail: intl@ratree.psu.ac.th

Undergraduate, Graduate Programmes
Study Domains: all major fields.
Programmes: undergraduate and graduate courses in all major fields; Master's and Ph.D. programme in epidemiology, Bachelor's degree in business administration (hotel/tourism management); Thai studies course.
Open to: foreign students are considered on a case-by-case basis.
Duration: 2 years for Master's degree programme; 2 months for Thai studies.
Fees: approx. 200,000 baht per year for Master's programme; 30,000 baht for Thai studies.
Languages: instruction in Thai and English.
Applications: by 1 March, to the Division of Educational Service for further information.

2278 Ramkhamhaeng University [RU]

Hua Mark Bangkapi
10241 Bangkok
Tel: +66-2-310-8000
Fax: +66-2-310-8022
Web: http://www.ru.ac.th

📖 Undergraduate Programmes / Open Admission

Study Domains: business administration, classical studies, economy, education, geography, law, library science, political science, sciences.
Programmes: open-admission university and regular undergraduate degrees.
Open to: qualified students of all nationalities having passed the Thai Language Test.
Applications: to the Registrar for further information.

2279 Sripatum University [SU]

61 Phaholyothin Road
Jatujak
10900 Bangkok
Tel: +66-2-579-1111
Fax: +66-2-561-1721
Web: http://www.spu.ac.th
e-mail: webspu@spu.ac.th

📖 Undergraduate, Graduate Degree Programmes / Business

Study Domains: business administration, communication, international business, management, marketing.
Programmes: (a) Bachelor's degree programmes in law; business administration, accounting, communication arts, economics, engineering, informatics, architecture; (b) Master's degree programmes in public administration for executives, business administration for executives, business administration, information technology, communication arts, organizational management.

2280 Sukhothai Thammathirat Open University [STOU]

9/9 Moo 9 Cheangwattana Road
Bangpood, Pakkred
11120 Nonthaburi
Tel: +66-2-504-7777
Fax: +66-2-503-3607
Web: http://www.stou.ac.th/Eng
e-mail: stou@stou.ac.th

📖 Undergraduate, Graduate Programmes / Distance Education

Study Domains: agriculture, communication, economic and commercial sciences, economy, education, health and hygiene, law, liberal arts, management, political science.
Programmes: (a) Bachelor's degree programmes: in liberal arts, agricultural extension and co-operatives, communication arts, economics, educational studies, health science, nursing, home economics, law, liberal arts, management science and political science, science and technology; (b) Master's degree programmes in educational administration, curriculum and instruction, educational technology and communications.
Open to: all Thai citizens and foreign students living in Thailand, with secondary-school certificate, vocational technical certificate or equivalent and fluent in Thai; candidates for Master's programmes must hold a Bachelor's degree.
Duration: 1 to 4 years.
Fees: (approximate figures) registration: (a) 159,643 baht; (b) 434 baht; tuition: (a) 650 baht per course for maximum of 3 courses per semester; (b) 7,500 baht per course for a maximum of 2 courses per semester.
Languages: instruction in Thai.
Applications: to the Director, Office of Registration, Records and Evaluation.

2281 Thailand-United States Educational Foundation [TUSEF]

Thai Wah Tower 1, 3rd floor
21/5 South Sathorn Road
10120 Bangkok
Tel: +66-2-285-0581 / 2
Fax: +66-2-285-0583
Web: http://www.fulbrightthai.org
e-mail: tusef@fulbrightthai.org

🐦 Fulbright Scholarships

Study Domains: all major fields.
Scholarships: (a) Fulbright Scholarships for Thai Nationals (Graduate Study Award); (b) Fulbright Scholarships for American Nationals (U.S. Graduate Student Award; (US Junior Researcher Award).
Subjects: (a) all fields of study except medicine, public health, nursing and allied subjects; (b) a wide variety of topics dealing with contemporary issues that have implications for cross-cultural understanding.
Open to: (a) Thai graduates from Thai universities with a B average or above to study towards a Master's degree; English (TOEFL 550) required; applicants must be in Thailand at the time of application and must return to Thailand upon completion of studies in the Unite States; (b) United States nationals with excellent undergraduate/graduate records, preferably those currently enrolled in graduate study; Thai language necessary for many formal graduate programmes.
Place of study: (a) any accredited college or university in the United States; (b) Thai University and governmental sector affiliation.
Duration: (a) 1 year (renewable for 1 year); (b) 10 to 12 months.
Value: (b) approximately US$20,000-$25,000 per year.
Applications: (a) by 31 March, to above address; (b) by October, to U.S. Student Program Division, Institute of International Education, 809 United Nations Plaza, New York, N.Y. 10017-3580, United States.

2282 Thammasat University

2 Phrachan Road
Phranakorn
10200 Bangkok
Tel: +66-2-613-3333
Web: http://www.tu.ac.th

📖 Undergraduate, Graduate Programmes / Business

Study Domains: accounting, business, business administration, economic and commercial sciences, engineering, finance, information science, marketing.
Programmes: (a) Bachelor's Degree in finance and banking, accounting, economics, engineering, information technology; (b) Master's Degree in marketing, economics.
Open to: international students (a) with secondary-school diploma (b) with a Bachelor's degree.
Fees: upon request.
Languages: instruction in Thai and English.
Applications: to the above address.

Togo

Année universitaire: octobre à juillet.
Unité monétaire: franc CFA.
Admission pour étudiants du pays: Les étudiants étrangers doivent être titulaires d'un baccalauréat ou d'un titre admis en équivalence; un examen spécial d'entrée est organisé pour les non-bacheliers dans les facultés des lettres et sciences humaines, droit, sciences, sciences économiques et de gestion. Des quotas par pays sont fixés en principe chaque année.
Connaissances linguistiques requises: Une bonne connaissance du français est requise; des cours de langue française sont organisés à l'intention des étudiants non francophones par le Village du Bénin.
Formalités d'immigration: L'obtention d'un visa de séjour est indispensable pour tous les étudiants excepté les ressortissants des pays de la CEDEAO. Vaccinations exigées.
Services d'accueil et d'information:

• Le Centre national des oeuvres universitaires (CNOU), BP 1515, Lomé, s'occupe de l'accueil et du logement des étudiants étrangers dans la limite des places disponibles.
• La Division de l'information et de l'orientation (DIO) qui est une division de la Direction des affaires académiques et de la scolarité (DAAS, BP 1515, Lomé), renseigne les étudiants sur les possibilités d'études.
• La bibliothèque de l'Université et le Service socioculturel sont à la disposition des étudiants.
Reconnaissance des études et diplômes: Direction de l'Information des Relations Externes et de la Coopération Internationale; BP 1515; Lomé; Togo; tél: +228-250-150; fax: +228-228-595; web: http://www.ub.tg.
Publications / Sites Web:
• «Livrets de l'étudiant», dont la publication est assurée par les Presses de l'Université du Bénin; édités en français; ces livrets peuvent être consultés sur place ou achetés.
• Les «Annales», les «Annuaires» et les «Actes des Journées Scientifiques» de l'Université du Bénin, édités aussi en français, peuvent également être achetés ou consultés sur place à la Bibliothèque de l'Université.

2283 Centre international de recherche et d'étude de langues [CIREL]
Village du Bénin
BP 3724
Lomé
Tel: +228-225-3557
Fax: +228-225-9528

Langues et littérature
Domaines d'étude: français, linguistique, littérature et civilisation.
Programmes: stages internationaux de linguistique, méthodologie, littératures africaine, française et caraïbienne; cours de français des affaires et des professions; cours de secrétariat conduisant au BTS de secrétariat bilingue.
A l'intention de: ressortissants de tout pays.
Durée: de 6 semaines à 1 an (débutant en septembre).
Connaissances linguistiques: langues d'enseignement: français et anglais.
Inscriptions: pour de plus amples renseignements, s'adresser au Directeur général du Centre.

2284 Centre régional d'action culturelle [CRAC]
226, boulevard du 13 Janvier
BP 3253
Lomé
Tel: +228-224-433 / 260-251
Fax: +228-224-228 / 214-380

Développement culturel
Domaines d'étude: administration des affaires, études du développement.
Programmes: cours de formation des cadres et personnels de l'action et du développement culturels: (a) cycle long - niveau postuniversitaire professionnel - diplôme équivalent au DESS: administrateurs et conseillers culturels; (b) études supérieures professionnelles, diplôme équivalent au DEUG: techniciens supérieurs et animateurs culturels, etc.; (c) cycle court: médiateurs culturels; entrepreneurs culturels; (d) autres cycles: stages, séminaires et ateliers attestés par un certificat de participation; cours de perfectionnement et de recyclage; formations modulaires à la carte ou à la demande.
A l'intention de: ressortissants des pays africains, étudiants ou candidats justifiant de 3 ans d'expérience professionnelle; États non africains dont le pays ou l'organisme entretient des relations de coopération avec un ou plusieurs États africains ou institutions participant au développement de l'Afrique; titulaires (a) d'une licence ou titre équivalent, admission par voie de concours; (b) d'un bac ou titre équivalent ou 5 ans d'expérience professionnelle; (c) admission sur dossier.
Durée: 2 ans (cycle long); 10 à 12 mois (cycle court); 10 jours à 3 mois (autres cycles).
Assistance financière: bourses octroyées par le gouvernement du candidat ou par les organismes internationaux dont l'Institut culturel africain (ICA). Le CRAC ne délivre pas de bourses mais peut appuyer les

demandes faites par les stagiaires.
Connaissances linguistiques: langues d'enseignement: français, anglais de spécialité.
Inscriptions: au Directeur du CRAC, par l'intermédiaire des instances gouvernementales intéressées.

2285 École africaine de métiers de l'architecture et de l'urbanisme [EAMU]
422, Rue des Balises
35, Rue Doumasséssé
BP 2067
Lomé
Tel: +228-221-6253
Fax: +228-222-0652
Web: http://www.eamau.tg.refer.org/index1.htm
e-mail: eamau@cafe.tg

Architecture / Urbanisme
Domaines d'étude: architecture, urbanisme.
Programmes: cours d'architecture et d'urbanisme, notamment en analyse urbaine, projet d'aménagement et projet d'architecture, conduisant au diplôme d'études supérieures d'architecture-urbanisme et à un stage de perfectionnement.
A l'intention de: ressortissants de tout pays, titulaires d'un bac scientifique et technique C, D, E, F et âgés de 22 ans au maximum; admission par voie de concours (en mai); avoir la moyenne dans les matières suivantes: mathématiques, dessin d'art et dessin graphique, culture générale, expression française.
Durée: 6 ans (d'octobre à juin).
Connaissances linguistiques: français obligatoire.
Inscriptions: avant le 30 septembre; à l'adresse ci-dessus.

2286 École nationale d'administration
BP 12175
Lomé
Tel: +228-221-3926
Fax: +228-222-0783

Administration
Domaines d'étude: administration.
Programmes: cours d'administration, conduisant au diplôme de l'École.
A l'intention de: ressortissant de tout pays, titulaires d'un Bac +4.
Inscriptions: à l'adresse ci-dessus, pour de plus amples informations.

2287 Université de Lomé
BP 1515
Lomé
Tel: +228-213-027
Fax: +228-218-784
Web: http://www.ub.tg
e-mail: ub-lomé@tgrefer.org

Études pluridisciplinaires
Domaines d'étude: administration des affaires, chirurgie, droit, éducation, électricité et électronique, études paramédicales, formation des enseignants, formation professionnelle, génie civil, informatique, ingénierie, lettres, mécanique, médecine, pédiatrie, sciences agronomiques, sciences économiques et commerciales.
Programmes: programme de cours pluridisciplinaires conduisant aux diplômes suivants: Capacité en Droit Diplôme de Technicien supérieur (DTS); Diplôme universitaire de Technologie (DUT); Diplôme universitaire d'Études générales (DUEG); Diplôme universitaire d'Études littéraires (DUEL); Diplôme universitaire d'Études scientifiques (DUES); Diplôme d'Ingénieur de Travaux; Licence d'Enseignement; Certificat d'Aptitude au Professorat de l'Enseignement secondaire (CAPES); Diplôme d'Ingénieur de Conception; Doctorat en Médecine; Maîtrise; Agrégation; Certificat d'Études spécialisées (CES); Diplôme d'Études approfondies (DEA); Diplôme d'Études supérieures (DES); Doctorat d'Ingénieur; Doctorat de Spécialité de Troisième Cycle; Doctorat unique.
A l'intention de: ressortissants de tout pays titulaires du

baccalauréat ou équivalent.
Connaissances linguistiques: français.
Inscriptions: à l'adresse ci-dessus.

Trinidad and Tobago

Academic year: August to May.
Organization of higher education system: University studies at the University of the West Indies of Trinidad and Tobago at Bachelor's, Master's and Doctorate levels.
Monetary unit: Trinidad and Tobago dollar (TT$).
International student admission: Foreign students must hold a general certificate of education with at least 2 passes at advanced (A) level or its equivalent. They are not eligible for admission to the non-university institutions except by special agreements with their governments. Holders of the following overseas qualifications are eligible for normal matriculation for admission to degree programmes: Ontario Secondary School Honours Graduation, French or the International Baccalaureate and the German Abitur. Transcripts are required for applicants with professional qualifications and who have studied outside of Trinidad and Tobago. Transcripts must be sent directly from the educational institution concerned to the relevant university and must be received by end February of the admission year.
Language: Applicants whose first language is not English are required to perform satisfactorily in an approved English Language Test, e.g. the Test of English as a Foreign Language (TOEFL). A mark of 500 in the TOEFL will be accepted as equivalent to, and in place of, an acceptable CXC pass in English.
Immigration requirements: A valid passport is necessary. At present, British Commonwealth citizens entering Trinidad &Tobago do not require visas, neither do nationals of Germany, Turkey, Switzerland, Denmark, Norway, Sweden, Finland, Israel, France, Brazil and Colombia. All other overseas nationals require student visas which must be obtained from their home countries.
Information services:
• The University of the West Indies St. Augustine Campus; Coordinator International Studies & Exchanges: email: bwarner@fss.uwi.tt2; web: http://www.uwi.tt
• The Caribbean Union College; Admissions; PO Box 175; Port of Spain, Trinidad, West Indies; web: http://www.cuc.edu.tt.
Scholarships for international students: Commonwealth Scholarships and Fellowships Plan open to citizens of another Commonwealth country who are normally resident in any part of the Commonwealth other than Trinidad and Tobago. Applications must be made in the first instance to the Commonwealth Scholarship agency in the country in which the applicant has his/her permanent home. For further details, consult http://www.csfp-online.org.
Open and distance learning: The University of the West Indies St. Augustine Campus offers
• distance education programmes: Postgraduate Diploma in Construction Management (Faculty of Engineering); Agriculture and Rural Development (Faculty of Science and Agriculture at the Diploma and M.Sc. levels)
• Evening University Programmes: MSc International Relations: LL.M Corporate and Commercial Law.
• Online Postgraduate Programmes (for the very first time in 2005): Master of Telecommunications Regulations and Policy MRP (Telecommunications), Department of Electrical Engineering; Postgraduate Diploma in Telecommunications Regulations and Policy DRP (Telecommunications), Department of Electrical Engineering.
Recognition of studies and qualification:
• The University of the West Indies
• The Caribbean Union College
• The Accreditation Council of Trinidad and Tobago (ACTT) -The ACTT makes provisions for registration, quality assurance, accreditation and recognition of tertiary level programmes and institutions based on the Accreditation Council Act· National Training Agency (NTA) - The umbrella agency for technical and vocational training in Trinidad and Tobago develops occupational standards and qualifications, accreditation, labour market research and career planning. Orchard View Plaza, #115 Endeavour Road, Chaguanas, Trinidad, West Indies.
Accommodation services: university housing is available:

payment for semester I cover living in university hall up to the end of the semester break; payment for semester II covers a period of one week beyond the official end of the academic year.
Work opportunities: Overseas students should note that there is very little chance of obtaining a work permit for temporary or permanent employment in Trinidad & Tobago.
Publications / Websites:
• The University of the West Indies St. Augustine: www.uwi.tt
• Caribbean Union College: www.cuc.edu.tt
• Commonwealth Scholarships and Fellowships Plan: www.csfp-online.org/about.html.

2288 Ministry of Works and Transport Civil Aviation Division [GOTAT]
PO Box 552
8, Melville Lane
Port of Spain
Fax: +1-868-625-3456
Web: http://www.caa.gov.tt

📖 **Work-Study Course / Air Traffic Services**

Study Domains: aviation, aeronautics, meteorology, transport.
Programmes: work-study course in air traffic services (non-radar air traffic control): ATC procedures (ICAO), meteorology, air navigation, theory of flight, radio navigational aids, rules of the air.
Open to: candidates from the Caribbean area and environs aged 19 to 34 years with appropriate secondary education qualifications.
Held: at the Civil Aviation Training Centre (CATC), Mausica Road, D'abadie.
Duration: 9-1/2 months.
Fees: tuition and handout papers are free of charge; governments or sponsoring agencies required to meet the cost of room and board and transportation for duration of course.
Applications: approx. 3 months in advance through sponsoring agencies.

2289 University of the West Indies [UOTWI]
St. Augustine
Tel: +1-868-662-2002
Fax: +1-868-663-9684
Web: http://www.uwi.tt
e-mail: admis@admin.uwi.tt

📖 **Undergraduate, Graduate Programmes**

Study Domains: all major fields.
Programmes: (a) undergraduate degree, diploma and certificate programmes in agriculture and natural sciences, human ecology and land surveying, engineering, humanities and education, law, social sciences; (b) postgraduate degree programmes in medicine, veterinary science, dentistry and pharmacy.
Open to: applicants of all nationalities above age 17, with 3 GCE A-level passes or equivalent qualifications required for entry to 3-year degree for undergraduate degree programmes and holding a Bachelor's or Master's degree for admission to 5-year postgraduate and advanced degree programmes.
Duration: 3 to 5 years.
Fees: vary according to course of studies for (a) university fees, residence fees and other estimated expenses: TT$35,000-$45,000; (b) university fees, residence fees and other estimated expenses: TT$70,000-$100,000.
Applications: by early January to Assistant Registrar, Student Affairs (Admissions), at the above address.

2290 University of the West Indies, Faculty of Medical Sciences [UOTWI]
St. Augustine
Tel: +1-868-645-2640 / 9
Fax: +1-868-663-9836
Web: http://www.uwi.tt/fms/
e-mail: deanfms@fms.uwi.tt

📖 Undergraduate, Graduate Programmes / Medical Studies

Study Domains: anatomy, biochemistry, dentistry, medicine, pharmacy and pharmacology, physiology, surgery, veterinary sciences.
Programmes: undergraduate and graduate degree programmes leading to: (a) Bachelor of Pharmacy; (b) Bachelor of Medicine and Bachelor of Surgery; (c) Doctor of Dental Surgery; (d) Doctor of Veterinary Medicine.
Open to: for undergraduate course programmes candidates holding GCE A-levels in biology/zoology, chemistry, physics, mathematics, or equivalent qualifications; for (a) chemistry and biology compulsory; for postgraduate and doctoral degree programmes a Master's degree or equivalent is required.
Duration: 3 to 5 years.
Fees: tuition: US$13,500 per year for years 1 to 3 and US$18,000 per year for years 4 to 5; living expenses and books approx. US$6,000 per year.
Applications: by March, to the Assistant Registrar (Admissions), at the above address.

Tunisie

Année universitaire: octobre à juin.
Unité monétaire: dinar.
Admission pour étudiants du pays: Le baccalauréat ou un diplôme équivalent est nécessaire.
Connaissances linguistiques requises: Une bonne connaissance du français ou de l'arabe est demandée selon les disciplines étudiées.
Formalités d'immigration: Visa obligatoire.
Services d'accueil et d'information:
• Direction de la coopération internationale et des relations extérieures, Ministère de l'enseignement supérieur, Av. Ouled Haffouz, 1030 Tunis; tél: +71-786-300/286-772; fax: +71-791-424.
• Représentations diplomatiques ou missions universitaires tunisiennes à l'étranger.
• Office national des oeuvres universitaires (ONOU), 57, rue de Palestine, Tunis (service d'hébergement et service d'information et des statistiques).
Reconnaissance des études et diplômes: Commission nationale d'Équivalence et d'Agrément des Écoles techniques, Ministère de l'Enseignement supérieur, rue Ouled Haffouz, Tunis, Tunisie; tél: +216-71-784-170; fax: +216-71-786-711; email: mes@mes.tn; web: http://www.mes.tn.
Publications / Sites Web:
• «Guide de l'orientation universitaire»
• Brochures d'information fournies par le Ministère et les institutions universitaires.
• Sites web: http//cri.ensmp.fr/francophonie/tunisie.html; www.universites.tn/francais/index.htm.

2291 Institut Bourguiba des langues vivantes

47, avenue de la Liberté
1002 Tunis-Belvédère
Tel: +216-71-832-418 / 923
Fax: +216-71-833-684
Web: http://www.iblv.rnu.tn
e-mail: iblv@iblv.rnu.tn

📖 Cours de langues

Domaines d'étude: allemand, anglais, arabe, espagnol, français, italien, langues.
Programmes: (a) cours intensifs d'arabe; (b) cours annuels de langues: arabe moderne standard et arabe tunisien, anglais, allemand, français, espagnol et italien.
A l'intention de: candidats de tout pays, âgés de plus de 17 ans.
Durée: (a) 5 semaines (débutant en juillet); (b) 1 année.
Frais: (a) inscription: 350 dinars; hébergement: 145 dinars plus frais de nourriture; (b) cours semi-intensifs: 150 dinars; du soir: 120 dinars; intensifs: 300 dinars.
Assistance financière: (a) bourses complètes et partielles (couvrant uniquement les frais d'inscription), offertes dans le cadre de la coopération culturelle internationale; les demandes de bourses devront être déposées avant le 31 mai.
Inscriptions: (a) en juin; (b) en septembre.

🎓 Bourses d'Études

Domaines d'étude: anglais, arabe, éducation, éducation permanente, français, langues.
Bourses: bourses d'études.
A l'intention de: candidats de tous pays (dans le cadre de la coopération culturelle internationale).
Durée: 5 semaines en été (juillet/août).
Valeur: couvre les frais d'inscription, d'hébergement.
Candidatures: avant le 31 mai.

2292 Office national du Tourisme tunisien [ONTT]

1, avenue Mohamed-V
Tunis
Tel: +216-71-835 844
Web: http://www.tourismtunisia.com/
e-mail: info@tourismtunisia.com

📖 Formation hôtelière et touristique

Domaines d'étude: tourisme, hôtellerie, restauration.
Programmes: programme d'études hôtelières et touristiques, conduisant au BTS (niveau II) et au BTP (niveau III).
A l'intention de: personnes indemnes de toute infirmité cachée ou apparente; admission sur étude de dossier; bonne connaissance du français requise.
Durée: 2 ans.
Frais: 3.500 dinars pour l'institut supérieur d'hôtellerie et de tourisme (BTS); 3.500 dinars pour les études supérieures spécialisées (DESS).
Assistance financière: possibilité d'obtenir une bourse d'études hôtelières.
Connaissances linguistiques: langue d'enseignement: français.
Inscriptions: avant le 30 juin de chaque année, à l'adresse ci-dessus.

🎓 Bourses d'études / hôtellerie, tourisme

Domaines d'étude: tourisme, hôtellerie, restauration.
Bourses: (a) bourses d'études dans le cadre d'accords bilatéraux de coopération; (b) bourses pour études hôtelières et touristiques.
A l'intention de: ressortissants des pays francophones et des pays arabes, en classe de terminale pour les écoles hôtelières, titulaires du baccalauréat pour l'ISHT, titulaires d'une maîtrise de gestion en sciences économiques pour le DESS, âgés de 17 à 23 ans; admission après étude de dossier.
Lieu: (a) écoles hôtelières et Institut supérieur d'hôtellerie et de tourisme (ISHT) de Sidi Dhrif; (b) Office national du Tourisme tunisien.
Durée: (a) 2 ans (non renouvelable) pour les écoles hôtelières (Brevet d'études hôtelières) et l'ISHT (Brevet de technicien supérieur); 15 mois pour le DESS en gestion hôtelière et touristique (3ème cycle universitaire); (b) 2 ans (non renouvelable).
Valeur: 3.000 dinars par an en écoles hôtelières/Brevet de technicien professionnel (BTP); 3500 dinars par an à l'ISHT (BTS); 6.500 dinars pour le DESS.
Connaissances linguistiques: bonne connaissance du français exigée.
Candidatures: avant le 31 décembre; à l'Office national du Tourisme tunisien, Tunis.

2293 Université de Sfax pour le Sud

Route de l'aéroport km 0,5
BP 559
3029 Sfax
Tel: +216-74-244-423
Fax: +216-74-240-913
Web: http://www.universites.tn/uss/ussfr/pgacussg.htm
e-mail: uss@uss.rnu.tn

📖 1er, 2e cycle / toutes disciplines

Domaines d'étude: toutes disciplines principales.
Programmes: programme de cours donnant accès au diplôme de technicien supérieur, à la maîtrise, au master, au master spécialisé et au doctorat.
Connaissances linguistiques: cours dispensés en arabe, en français et en anglais.

2294 Université du Centre, École Nationale d'Ingénieurs de Monastir [ENIM]
5019 Monastir
Tel: +216-73-500-244 / 511
Fax: +216-73-500-514
Web: http://www.enim.rnu.tn/Fr/index.htm

📖 **Diplôme d'ingénieur généraliste**

Domaines d'étude: électricité et électronique, énergie, génie chimique, industrie textile, mécanique, métallurgie.
Programmes: Diplôme d'ingénieur généraliste.
A l'intention de: admission sur concours.
Durée: 3 ans; les cours commencent en septembre.
Frais: frais d'inscription: 200 dinars.
Connaissances linguistiques: cours dispensés en français.

2295 Université du Centre, École supérieure d'Horticulture et d'Élevage de Chott Mériem
BP 47
4042 Chott Mériem
Tel: +216-73-348-692/544/546
Fax: +216-73-348-691
Web: http://www.iresa.agrinet.tn/fr/instit/eshe.htm
e-mail: benhamouda.medhabib@iresa.agrinet.tn

📖 **Sciences agronomiques**

Domaines d'étude: élevage, horticulture, sciences agronomiques.
Programmes: Diplôme de technicien supérieur, diplôme national d'ingénieur, mastère et doctorat.
Description: préparation biologie-géologie pour l'accès aux écoles d'ingénieur (Bac + 2); cycle de formation de technicien supérieur en horticulture avec trois options (Bac + 3); cycle de formation d'ingénieur dans quatre spécialités (Bac + 5); mastère dans trois spécialités; doctorat en sciences agronomiques dans deux spécialités; cycle de formation continue donnant accès au grade de technicien principal.
A l'intention de: étudiants âgés de 18 à 22 ans; titulaires du baccalauréat (ou équivalent) pour la préparation et le cycle de formation de techniciens supérieurs; baccalauréat de sciences expérimentales ou de mathématiques pour le 1er cycle; concours national d'entrée aux écoles d'ingénieur pour le cycle de formation d'ingénieurs.
Durée: de 3 à 5 ans (débutant en septembre).
Connaissances linguistiques: cours dispensés en français; une bonne connaissance de l'anglais est également requise.
Inscriptions: inscriptions avant le 10 septembre adressées à Monsieur le Secrétaire général de l'école; pour tout renseignement contacter Ridha Rouis (adresse de l'école ci-dessus, tel: +216 73 348 544/546).

2296 Université du Centre, École supérieure des Sciences et Techniques de la Santé de Monastir
BP 128
5060 Monastir
Tel: +216-73-500-280
Fax: +216-73-500-278
Web: http://www.fsm.rnu.tn
e-mail: fsm@fsm.rnu.tn

📖 **Diplôme de technicien supérieur de la santé**

Domaines d'étude: études paramédicales.
Programmes: Diplôme de technicien supérieur de la santé.
Domaines d'études: formation de technicien supérieur de la santé en radiologie, obstétrique, physiothérapie, biologie, prothèse dentaire, secrétariat médical, pharmacie, matériel de réanimation.
A l'intention de: titulaires du baccalauréat (ou équivalent) orientés ou réorientés par le ministère de l'enseignement supérieur.
Durée: 3 ans; les cours commencent en septembre.
Frais: frais d'inscription: 62.800 dinars.
Connaissances linguistiques: cours dispensés en français.
Inscriptions: avant le 15 septembre; pour information contacter M. Saad Mohamed Lamjed (coordonnées ci-dessus).

2297 Université du Centre, École supérieure des Sciences et Techniques de la Santé de Sousse
Rue El Harik
Sahloul II
Sousse
Tel: +216-73-369-307
Fax: +216-73-369-308
Web: http://www.cck.rnu.tn/esstss/
e-mail: esstechnisante.sousse@rns.tn

📖 **Diplôme de technicien supérieur de la santé**

Domaines d'étude: études paramédicales.
Programmes: Diplôme de technicien supérieur de la santé.
Domaines d'études: formation de technicien supérieur de la santé en pédiatrie, urgence, bloc opératoire, thalassothérapie, secrétariat médical.
A l'intention de: titulaires du baccalauréat (ou équivalent).
Durée: 3 ans débutant en septembre.
Frais: frais d'inscription: 62.500 dinars.
Connaissances linguistiques: cours dispensés en français.
Inscriptions: avant le 13 septembre.

2298 Université du Centre, Faculté de Droit et des Sciences Économiques et Politiques de Sousse
4023 Cité Erriadh
Sousse
Tel: +216-73-234-426
Fax: +216 73 234 477
Web: http://www.fdseps.rnu.tn
e-mail: fdseps@fdseps.rnu.tn

📖 **1er - 3ème cycle / droit et sciences économiques**

Domaines d'étude: comptabilité, droit, économie, économie politique, finances, gestion, marketing, sciences économiques et commerciales.
Programmes: cursus allant du 1er au 3ème cycle: Maîtrise, DEA, DESS.
Description: maîtrise en droit public, droit privé, politique économique, économie industrielle, techniques commerciales, techniques comptables, gestion des institutions financières, économétrie; DEA en droit public, droit fiscal, droit des affaires, droit de l'informatique et du multimédia; DESS en commerce international et exportation.
A l'intention de: titulaires d'un diplôme de fin d'études secondaires (Baccalauréat ou équivalent) ou d'une maîtrise; admission sur recommandation.
Connaissances linguistiques: cours dispensés en français et en arabe.
Inscriptions: avant le 22 septembre auprès du service de la scolarité.

2299 Université du Centre, Faculté de Médecine de Monastir
Avenue Ibn Sina
5019 Monastir
Tel: +216-73-462-200
Fax: +216-73-460-737
Web: http://www.fmm.rnu.tn/
e-mail: fmm@fmm.rnu.tn

📖 **Études médicales**

Domaines d'étude: médecine.
Programmes: Diplôme national de docteur en médecine.
A l'intention de: admission sur dossier.
Durée: 7 années débutant en septembre.
Frais: frais d'inscription: entre 62.800 et 82.800 dinars.
Connaissances linguistiques: cours dispensés en français.

2300 Université du Centre, Faculté de Médecine de Sousse
Avenue Mohamed Karoui
4002 Sousse
Tel: +216-73-226-611/ 600
Fax: +216-73-224-899

📖 Études médicales

Domaines d'étude: médecine.
Programmes: Diplôme national de docteur en médecine.
A l'intention de: titulaires d'un diplôme de fin d'études
secondaires (Baccalauréat ou équivalent).
Durée: 7 années débutant en septembre.
Frais: frais d'inscription: environ 60 US$.
Connaissances linguistiques: cours dispensés en français;
une bonne connaissance de l'anglais est également requise.
Inscriptions: avant le 14 septembre auprès du Directeur
général de la Coopération internationale.

2301 Université du Centre, Faculté de Médecine Dentaire de Monastir

Avenue Avicenne
5019 Monastir
Tel: +216-73-460-832
Fax: +216-73-461-150
Web: http://www.fmdm.rnu.tn
e-mail: mokhtar.sghaier@fmdm.rnu.tn

📖 Études en médecine dentaire

Domaines d'étude: études dentaires.
Programmes: Diplôme national de docteur en médecine
dentaire.
A l'intention de: titulaires d'un diplôme de fin d'études
secondaires (Baccalauréat ou équivalent).
Frais: frais d'inscription: premier cycle: 60 Dinars,
deuxième cycle: 80 dinars.
Connaissances linguistiques: cours dispensés en français.
Inscriptions: avant le 14 septembre.

2302 Université du Centre, Faculté de Pharmacie de Monastir

Avenue Avicenne
5019 Monastir
Tel: +216-73-461-000
Fax: +216-73-461-830
Web: http://www.fphm.rnu.tn/
e-mail: faculte-pharmacie@fphm.rnu.tn

📖 Études de pharmacie

Domaines d'étude: pharmacie et pharmacologie.
Programmes: Diplôme national de pharmacien.
Durée: 5 ans.
Frais: 62.800 dinars.
Connaissances linguistiques: cours dispensés en français.
Inscriptions: pour tout renseignement contacter Mahmoud
Sghaier, Secrétaire général; tel: +216 73 461 140; fax: +216
73 461 830.

2303 Université du Centre, Faculté des Lettres et des Sciences humaines de Sousse

BP 547
Cité Erriach
4000 Sousse
Tel: +216-73-301-800
Fax: +216-73-301-903
Web: http://www.fls.rnu.tn
e-mail: flsh.sousse@fls.rnu.tn

📖 1er-3ème Cycle

Domaines d'étude: anglais, arabe, français, géographie,
histoire, marketing, publicité.
Programmes: cursus allant du 1er au 3ème cycle.
Description: diplôme d'études universitaires de 1er cycle
en langues; maîtrise en langue et littérature (arabe, français,
anglais); maîtrise d'histoire, de géographie; mastère; diplôme
de technicien supérieur en publicité et marketing.
A l'intention de: titulaires d'un diplôme de fin d'études
secondaires (Baccalauréat ou équivalent); admission sur
dossier.
Durée: 4 ans; cours débutent fin septembre.
Frais: frais de scolarité du 1er cycle: 40 dinars; des 2ème
et 3ème cycle: 100 dinars.
Connaissances linguistiques: cours dispensés en arabe et
en français.
Inscriptions: inscription avant le mois de décembre auprès

du service de la scolarité.

2304 Université du Centre, Faculté des Lettres et Sciences humaines de Kairouan

Route de Sfax, km 10
Raccada
Kairouan
Tel: +216-77-323-177
Fax: +216-77-323-926
Web: http://www.flshk.rnu.tn
e-mail: lettres.kairouan@flshk.rnu.tn

📖 1er, 2e cycle

Domaines d'étude: administration des affaires, anglais,
arabe, archéologie, français, langues, philosophie.
Programmes: cursus allant du 1er au 2e cycle.
Description: maîtrise d'arabe, de français, d'anglais, de
philosophie, d'archéologie; diplôme de technicien supérieur
en anglais des affaires, langues étrangères appliquées, langues
et traduction, métiers du tourisme.
A l'intention de: titulaires d'un diplôme de fin d'études
secondaires (Baccalauréat ou équivalent); examen du dossier
par les services du ministère de l'enseignement supérieur.
Connaissances linguistiques: cours dispensés en arabe,
français et anglais.
Inscriptions: avant le 15 novembre auprès du Service des
inscriptions de la faculté.

2305 Université du Centre, Faculté des Sciences de Monastir

Avenue de l'environnement
5019 Monastir
Tel: +216-73-500-280
Fax: +216-73-500-278
Web: http://www.fsm.rnu.tn/Default.htm
e-mail: fsm@fsm.rnu.tn

📖 1er - 2e cycle / sciences

Domaines d'étude: chimie, électricité et électronique,
informatique, mathématiques, physique, sciences, sciences
appliquées.
Programmes: Maîtrise; diplôme de technicien supérieur.
A l'intention de: titulaires d'un diplôme de fin d'études
secondaires (Baccalauréat ou équivalent); examen du dossier
par les services du Ministère de l'enseignement supérieur.
Durée: entre 3 et 4 ans; cours débutent en septembre.
Frais: frais d'inscription: de 40 à 130 dinars.
Connaissances linguistiques: cours dispensés en français,
en arabe et en anglais.

2306 Université du Centre, Faculté des Sciences économiques et de Gestion de Mahdia

Cité Sidi Messaoud
5111 Huroune
Mahdia
Tel: +216 73 671 188 / 191-2
Fax: +216 73 671 190
Web: http://www.fsegma.rnu.tn
e-mail: ali.fredj@fsegma.rnu.tn

📖 2e Cycle / sciences économiques

Domaines d'étude: affaires, comptabilité, économie,
finances, gestion, sciences économiques et commerciales,
statistique.
Programmes: Maîtrise d'économie.
Description: département de sciences économiques:
maîtrise d'économie financière et bancaire, maîtrise
d'économie internationale; département de sciences de
gestion: maîtrise de sciences comptables, maîtrise de finance,
maîtrise de management; département de méthodes
quantitatives: maîtrise d'économétrie.
A l'intention de: ressortissants de tous pays: examen du
dossier par les services du Ministère de l'enseignement
supérieur.
Durée: 4 ans; début des cours en septembre.
Frais: frais d'inscription: environ 40 dinars.
Connaissances linguistiques: cours dispensés en français.
Inscriptions: au plus tard un mois après le début des cours.

2307 Université du Centre, Institut préparatoire aux Études d'Ingénieurs de Monastir
Rue Ibn El-Jazzar
5019 Monastir
Tel: +216-73-500-277
Fax: +216-73-500-512
Web: http://www.ipeim.rnu.tn/
e-mail: ipeim@ipeim.rnu.tn

Études préparatoires

Domaines d'étude: anglais, chimie, éducation permanente, enseignement technique, français, informatique, ingénierie, mathématiques, optique, physique.
Programmes: cycle préparatoire au concours national donnant accès aux écoles nationales d'ingénieur.
A l'intention de: titulaires d'un diplôme de fin d'études secondaires (Baccalauréat ou équivalent) âgés de 20 à 25 ans; admission sur recommandation et sur désignation du ministère de l'enseignement supérieur.
Durée: 2 ans; début des cours à la mi-septembre.
Frais: frais d'inscription: 60 dinars.
Connaissances linguistiques: cours dispensés en français; une bonne connaissance de l'anglais est également requise.
Inscriptions: avant le 16 septembre.

2308 Université du Centre, Institut supérieur d'Informatique et des Technologies de Communication à Hammam Sousse
5 bis, rue 1 juin 1955
Hammam Sousse
4011 Sousse
Tel: +216-73-364-411
Fax: +216-73-364-411
Web: http://www.infcom.rnu.tn
e-mail: administration@infcom.rnu.tn

Formation de technicien supérieur

Domaines d'étude: informatique, télécommunications.
Programmes: formation de technicien supérieur en informatique et en télécommunications.
A l'intention de: titulaires d'un diplôme de fin d'études secondaires (baccalauréat ou équivalent).
Durée: 3 ans; début des cours en septembre.
Connaissances linguistiques: cours dispensés en français; une bonne connaissance de l'anglais est également requise.

2309 Université du Centre, Institut supérieur de biotechnologie de Monastir
Avenue de l'environnement
Monastir
Tel: +216-73-505-405
Fax: +216-73-505-404
Web: http://www.isbm.rnu.tn/
e-mail: isbm@isbm.rnu.tn

1er - 3ème Cycle / biotechnologie

Domaines d'étude: anglais, biochimie, biologie, biologie marine, biophysique, botanique, chimie, écologie, environnement, génétique, géologie, informatique, mathématiques, microbiologie, océanographie, optique, physique, sciences de la mer, sciences de la terre, statistique, zoologie.
Programmes: programme de cours allant du 1er au 3ème cycles (diplôme de technicien supérieur, maîtrise, master et doctorat).
Description: diplôme de technicien supérieur en aquaculture, contrôle de la qualité des aliments; maîtrise en sciences biologiques, sciences et techniques en biotechnologie médicale, sciences et techniques en biologie marine; master en biologie et santé; doctorat en sciences biologiques et biotechnologiques.
A l'intention de: admission sous l'égide du Rectorat du Centre.
Connaissances linguistiques: cours dispensés en français.

2310 Université du Centre, Institut Supérieur de Gestion de Sousse
BP 763
4000 Sousse
Tel: +216-73-332-976
Fax: +216-73-331-481
Web: http://www.isgs.rnu.tn
e-mail: isgs@isgs.rnu.tn

1er - 3e cycle / gestion

Domaines d'étude: commerce, comptabilité, économie, économie politique, finances, gestion, marketing, publicité, sciences économiques et commerciales.
Programmes: programme de cours allant du 1er au 3ème cycle (diplôme de technicien supérieur, maîtrise et mastère spécialisé - ancien DESS).
A l'intention de: titulaires d'un diplôme de fin d'études secondaires (baccalauréat ou équivalent).
Frais: frais d'inscription: de 32 à 42 dinars.
Connaissances linguistiques: cours dispensés en français.
Inscriptions: au début du mois de septembre.

2311 Université du Centre, Institut supérieur de Musique de Sousse
BP 368
Avenue Aboulkacem Chebbi
Sousse
Tel: +216-73-239-553
Fax: +216-73-239-555

1er - 2e cycle / musique

Domaines d'étude: arts du spectacle, musique et musicologie.
Programmes: programme de cours donnant accès au diplôme de technicien supérieur et à la maîtrise.
Description: diplôme de technicien supérieur en arts lyriques et scéniques, musique assistée par ordinateur, prise de son; maîtrise en musique et musicologie.
A l'intention de: titulaires d'un diplôme de fin d'études secondaires (baccalauréat ou équivalent); admission sur test et entretien.
Durée: 4 ans; les cours débutent en septembre.
Frais: frais d'inscription: de 30 à 40 dinars.
Connaissances linguistiques: cours dispensés en français, arabe et anglais.
Inscriptions: durant le mois de septembre auprès des services administratifs.

2312 Université du Centre, Institut supérieur des Beaux Arts de Sousse [ISBAS]
Place de la Gare
4000 Sousse
Tel: +216-73-214-333
Fax: +216-73-214-334
Web: http://www.isbas.rnu.tn/

2e cycle / beaux arts

Domaines d'étude: arts graphiques, beaux-arts, décoration.
Programmes: programme de cours donnant accès au diplôme de technicien supérieur et à la maîtrise.
Description: diplôme de technicien supérieur en design intérieur, CAO-DAO, infographie; maîtrise d'arts plastiques.
A l'intention de: titulaires d'un diplôme de fin d'études secondaires (baccalauréat ou équivalent).
Durée: 3 à 4 ans; les cours commencent en octobre.
Frais: frais d'inscription: 60 dinars.
Connaissances linguistiques: cours dispensés en français.
Inscriptions: avant le 19 septembre.

2313 Université du Centre, Institut Supérieur des Langues Appliquées aux Affaires et au Tourisme de Moknine
Avenue des Martyrs
5050 Moknine
Tel: +216-73-437-101
Fax: +216-73-435-398

2e cycle / tourisme et langues appliquées

Domaines d'étude: affaires, anglais, espagnol, interprétation et traduction, italien, tourisme, hôtellerie, restauration.
Programmes: programme de cours donnant accès au diplôme supérieur et à la maîtrise.
Description: diplôme supérieur en commerce international, animation touristique, traduction; maîtrise en anglais, espagnol et italien.
A l'intention de: titulaires d'un diplôme de fin d'études secondaires (baccalauréat ou équivalent).
Durée: 3 à 4 ans; les cours commencent en octobre.
Frais: frais d'inscription: 33 dinars.
Connaissances linguistiques: l'étudiant choisit une langue de spécialité dans laquelle les cours sont dispensés ainsi qu'une langue d'appui (arabe et français plus autre langue).
Inscriptions: avant le 30 septembre auprès du secrétariat général de l'institut (coordonnées ci-dessus).

2314 Université du Centre, Institut Supérieur des Sciences Appliquées et de Technologie de Sousse [ISSATS]

BP 40
Cité Taffala - Ibn Khaldoun
4003 Sousse
Tel: +216-73-332-657
Fax: +216-73-332-658

1er - 2e cycle / sciences appliquées

Domaines d'étude: électricité et électronique, informatique, mécanique.
Programmes: programme de cours aboutissant au diplôme de technicien supérieur et à la maîtrise.
Description: diplôme de technicien supérieur en informatique, génie mécanique et génie électronique; maîtrise d'informatique.
A l'intention de: titulaires d'un diplôme de fin d'études secondaires (baccalauréat ou équivalent); l'admission se fait par l'intermédiaire du ministère de tutelle.
Durée: 3 à 4 ans; les cours commencent en septembre.
Frais: frais d'inscription: 62.800 dinars.
Connaissances linguistiques: cours dispensés en français.
Inscriptions: avant le 14 septembre; pour information contacter Mme Ben Abddjalil Sofia, tel: +216 73 332 356.

2315 Université du Centre, Institut supérieur du Transport et de la Logistique de Sousse [ISTLS]

12, rue Abdallah Ibn Zoubeïr
4029 Sousse
Tel: +216-73-226-365
Fax: +216-73-226-211
Web: http://www.istls.rnu.tn/
e-mail: istls@istls.tn

1er - 2e cycle / logistique

Domaines d'étude: transports.
Programmes: programme de cours donnant accès au diplôme de technicien supérieur et à la maîtrise.
Frais: frais d'inscription: 60 dinars pour le 1er cycle et 80 dinars pour le 2ème cycle.
Connaissances linguistiques: cours dispensés en français; une bonne connaissance de l'anglais est également requise.

2316 Université Libre de Tunis [ULT]

30 Avenue Khéreddine Pacha
1002 Tunis
Tel: +216-71-841-411
Fax: +216-71-782-260
Web: http://www.ult.ens.tn/ult/site/index.php
e-mail: intac.ult@planet.tn

1er - 3e cycle / toutes disciplines

Domaines d'étude: toutes disciplines principales.
Programmes: programme de cours allant du 1er au 3ème cycle.
A l'intention de: titulaires d'un diplôme de fin d'études secondaires (Baccalauréat ou équivalent).
Durée: 4-5-8 ans; début des cours en octobre.

Frais: frais de scolarité: de 2.700 à 3.500 €.
Connaissances linguistiques: cours dispensés en français et en anglais.
Inscriptions: avant le 31 août, auprès du service des étudiants étrangers (coordonnées de l'université ci-dessus).

2317 Université privée des Sciences, Arts et Techniques de Sousse

Avenue Commandant Bejaoui
4000 Sousse
Tel: +216-73-236-122
Fax: +216-73-236-123
e-mail: upsat@topnet.tn

🎓 Aide financière

Domaines d'étude: administration des affaires, arts graphiques, études paramédicales.
Bourses: réduction de frais de scolarité.
A l'intention de: étudiants de toutes nationalités, selon ressources financières et résultats scolaires.
Durée: 1 année; renouvelable.
Valeur: 10% de reduction sur frais de scolarité.
Candidatures: avant juillet, au directeur de l'université.

Turkey

Academic year: October to June, July.
Organization of higher education system: Higher education programmes and degrees: Associate degree awarded after at least four semesters of study, to acquire vocational qualification or as first stage of higher education; Baccalaureate stage consists of studies of at least eight semesters; Master's degree awarded after four semesters of study and a dissertation, but may be awarded without dissertation after six semesters of studies; Doctoral programme require eight semesters of study beyond the Master's degree or ten semesters beyond the Baccalaureate degree, and preparation of a thesis; postgraduate studies lead to Master's and Doctoral degrees, for professional training in medicine or artistic fields.
Major institutions of higher education: Consult http://www.yok.gov.tr/english/oku22.html for a list of recognized higher education institutions.
National student admission: For national students: Admission to institutions of higher education for Turkish Republic and Northern Cyprus Turkish Republic citizens is based on results of the examination administered by the Student's Selection and Placement Center. As of academic year 2002-2003, graduates of vocational schools can be placed in vocational higher schools without examination.
International student admission:
•Undergraduate studies: International students wishing to enrol independently in undergraduate programmes in Turkey must provide a secondary-school-leaving certificate comparable to Turkish high school certificates and pass the Examination for Foreign Students administered by the Student Selection and Placement Center with a minimum score of 40 in the Basic Learning Skills Test or comparable examinations recognized by the Higher Education Supervisory Board.
• Postgraduate studies: Graduate Education Entrance Examination or an equivalent international examination (GRE, GMAT), to be determined by the relevant institution.
• Students should apply directly to the institution of their choice for admission. For further details on admission requirements for individual institutions; consult http://www.yok.gov.tr/english/higher_edu.htm.
Language: Turkish is generally the language of instruction. German, French and English are also used as languages of instruction in some institutions. English is the language of instruction at the following universities: Atilim University, Bahcesehir Univesity, Beykent Univesity, Bilkent University, Isik University, Istanbul Bilgi University, Izmir University of Economics, Izmir Institute of Technology, Middle East Technical University, Sabanci University and Yasar University.
Students with insufficient knowledge of Turkish may attend Turkish Preparatory programme and may integrate the institutions to which they were admitted on reaching an adequate language level.

Immigration requirements: Students wishing to study in Turkey must hold a valid passport and student visa which can be obtained from the Turkish diplomatic representation abroad or within Turkey from the local police department.
Information services: MEB Disiliskiler Genel Müdürlügü (Directorate General of Foreign Affairs of the Ministry of National Education), Bakanliklar Ankara;
http://disis.meb.gov.tr
Yükseögretim Kurulu Baskanligi (The Council of Higher Education); http://www.yok.gov.tr
ÖSYM (Student Selection and Placement Center) 06538 Ankara; http://www.osym.gov.tr.
Open and distance learning: Distance education is provided only by the Open Education Faculty of Anadolu University. The faculty offers two-year and four-year degree programmes. International students officially enrolled in a Turkish institution of higher education and wishing to obtain a second baccalaureate degree are eligible to study in the Open Education Faculty.
Recognition of studies and qualification:
• For higher education diplomas awarded outside of Turkey: NARIC Ofisi (Turkish NARIC Office):
Yüksek Ögretim Kurulu (Y.Ö.K.) (Council of Higher Education (YOK))
Bilkent, 06539 Ankara, Turkey; http://www.yok.gov.tr / http://www.yok.gov.tr/english/regula/recognition.htm
• For secondary-school diplomas awarded outside of Turkey: Milli Egitim Bakanligi (MEB); Ministry of National Education; web: http://www.meb.gov.tr.
Accommodation services: Contact individual institutions for availability, type and cost of accommodation.
Work opportunities: In general, employment is not available for international students; graduate students may be employed in research-related areas within their study programmes.
Publications / Websites:
• An informative booklet regarding the international student examination for international students (YOS) is published annually in English and Turkish by the Student Selection and Placement Center and is available through the Turkish diplomatic representations around the world.
• YOK (Council of Higher Education); http://www.yok.gov.tr
• ÖSYM (Student Selection and Placement Center); http://www.osym;gov.tr;
• Study in Turkey: http://www.studyturkey.metu.edu.tr.

2318 Akdeniz University School of Tourism and Hotel Management
07 058 Antalya
Tel: +90-242-227-4550
Fax: +90-242-227-4670

📖 Undergraduate Studies

Study Domains: tourism, hotel and catering management.
Programmes: Bachelor's degree in tourism and travel management.
Open to: all candidates with secondary school certificate.
Duration: 4 years; courses begin in September.

2319 Bilkent University
06800 Bilkent
Ankara
Tel: +90-312-290-4000
Fax: +90-312-266-4127
Web: http://www.bilkent.edu.tr

📖 Undergraduate, Graduate Programmes

Study Domains: accounting, administration, archaeology, art history, computer science, economy, engineering, graphic arts, interior design, linguistics, management, political science, Turkish.
Programmes: programmes of study leading to Associate, Bachelor's, Master's and Ph.D. degrees in international relations, political science and public administration, archaeology and history of art, graphic design, interior architecture and environmental design, management and, at the graduate level only, Turkish literature, Ottoman, American and European Histories. High-level courses in engineering and the sciences are also offered.

Open to: candidates of all countries, possessing a secondary-school certificate; English proficiency required.
Duration: 2 to 6 years, depending on the programme.
Languages: Turkish, and in some cases, English.
Applications: to the above address.

2320 Dokuz Eylul University [DEU]
Cum Huriyet Bulvari
144 Alsancak TR 35 210
Izmir
Tel: +90-232-412-1212
Fax: +90-232-464-8135
Web: http://www.deu.edu.tr
e-mail: isinsu.atalay@deu.edu.tr

📖 Undergraduate, Graduate, Postgraduate Programmes

Study Domains: all major fields, administration, applied arts, archaeology, architecture, art history, business, business administration, computer science, ecology, environment, economy, education, engineering, European studies, fine arts, industrial design, interior design, international business, international law, international relations, interpretation and translation, languages, law, management, medicine, nursing, performing arts, pharmacy and pharmacology, philology, photography, sciences, teacher education, theology, religion, tourism, hotel and catering management, transport, urbanism, vocational training.
Programmes: Bachelor's, Master's, Ph.D. degrees in all major fields.
Open to: admission tests for foreign students; TOEFL required.
Duration: 4 years; courses begin in September.
Fees: tuition fees US$500-$2,000 per year; living costs US$400 per month.
Languages: Turkish and English.

2321 Hacettepe University
06 100 Sihhiye
Ankara
Tel: +90-312-305-1010
Fax: +90-312-310-5552
Web: http://www.hacettepe.edu.tr
e-mail: rector@hacettepe.edu.tr

📖 Undergraduate, Graduate, Postgraduate Programmes

Study Domains: all major fields, administration, arts, business administration, computer science, education, engineering, fine arts, interpretation and translation, languages, law, medicine, nursing, pharmacy and pharmacology, research, social sciences, statistics, teacher education, telecommunications, theology, religion, tourism, hotel and catering management.
Programmes: Bachelor's, Master's, Ph.D. degrees in all major fields.
Open to: candidates from all nationality with secondary-school certificate and YOS (Turkish higher education entrance examination for foreign students).
Duration: 4 to 6 years; courses begin 20 September.
Fees: variable.
Languages: Turkish, English, German, French.

🎓 Scholarships

Study Domains: all major fields.
Scholarships: Hacettepe University Scholarships.
Duration: 4 years.
Value: variable; contact Office of Admissions for further information.

2322 Istanbul Bilgi University
Inönü Cad. No. 28 Bilgi
80370 Istanbul
Tel: +90-212-216-2525
Fax: +90-212-216-2414
Web: http://www.bilgi.edu.tr

🎓 Financial aid

Study Domains: all major fields.
Description: For international and exchange students.
Duration: 1 year; non-renewable.
Applications: see website,

http://international.bilgi.edu.tr/survivalguide.htm for further information.

2323 Middle East Technical University [METU]
Study Abroad Office Rektorluk,
504 METU
06531 Ankara
Tel: +90-312-210-3491
Fax: +90-312-210-1105
Web: http://ww.issa.metu.edu.tr
e-mail: intlstud@metu.edu.tr

📖 **Undergraduate, Graduate, Postgraduate Programmes**

Study Domains: administration, architecture, aviation, aeronautics, business administration, chemical industry, computer science, ecology, environment, education, engineering, international law, international relations, interpretation and translation, languages, literature and civilization, music and musicology, natural resources, sociology, space, teacher education, tourism, hotel and catering management, transport, urbanism.
Programmes: Bachelor's, Master's, Ph.D. degrees in all major fields.
Open to: candidates of all nationalities; entrance examination; TOEFL or IELTS required.
Languages: English.
Applications: end of November for spring semester; end of May for Fall semester; by May for Summer course; contact intlstud@metu.edu.tr for further information.

2324 Nigde University
Asagi Kayabasi Mahallesi
51200 Nigde
Tel: +90-388-232-1010
Fax: +90-388-232-2423
Web: http://www.nigde.edu.tr

📖 **Undergraduate, Graduate, Postgraduate Programmes**

Study Domains: administration, arts, economic and commercial sciences, economy, education, sciences.
Description: Studies in the social sciences, humanities, arts, natural sciences, engineering and technology in order to disseminate knowledge and to conduct research serving not only to academia, but also to the community at large; to educate students to be model human beings for others, to have strong ties with the whole society and to be tolerant of other ideas.
Open to: candidates of all nationalities meeting academic and financial financial requirements.
Duration: Fall semester: from end September to end January; spring semester: from February to June. There is a two-week break in February.

2325 Pamukkale University
20020 Incilipinar
Denizili
Tel: +90-258-212-5501
Fax: +90-258-212-5530
Web: http://www.pamukkale.edu.tr

📖 **Undergraduate, Graduate Programmes**

Study Domains: all major fields.
Programmes: Undergraduate and graduate programmes in all major fields.
Applications: to the above address.

2326 Trakya University
22 050 Karaagac
Edirne
Tel: +90-284-214-4210
Fax: +90-284-214-4203
Web: http://www.trakya.edu.tr
e-mail: rektorluk@trakya.edu.tr

📖 **Undergraduate, Postgraduate Studies**

Study Domains: all major fields, agriculture, architecture, arts, biophysics, business administration, civil engineering, computer science, ecology, environment, education, fine arts, languages, management, mechanical engineering, medicine,

music and musicology, nursing, pharmacy and pharmacology, physical education, physics, teacher education, telecommunications, textile industry, zoology.
Programmes: Bachelor's, Master's, Ph.D. degrees in all major fields.
Open to: all candidates with secondary school certificate; entrance examination; proficiency in Turkish required.
Duration: 4 to 6 years; courses begin mid-September for undergraduates; 1 October for Ph.D. and Master's.
Financial assistance: financial assistance available.
Languages: Turkish (partly English for mechanical engineering courses).
Applications: beginning of September; contact scakir@trakya.edu.tr for undergraduate studies and cengizk@trakya.edu.tr for information concerning Ph.D. or Master's.

2327 Université d'Uludag
Görükle
16059 Bursa
Tel: +90-24-442-8006
Fax: +90-224-442-9044
Web: http://www.uludag.edu.tr
e-mail: intoffice@uludag.edu.tr

📖 **2e, 3e cycle**

Domaines d'étude: agriculture, architecture, éducation, ingénierie, lettres, médecine, sciences, sciences économiques et commerciales, sciences naturelles, sciences vétérinaires.
Programmes: programme de cours conduisant à l'obtention de la licence dans les domaines de la médecine, des sciences naturelles, des lettres, des sciences islamiques, de l'éducation, des sciences économiques et administratives, de l'ingénierie, de l'architecture, des sciences vétérinaires et des sciences de l'agriculture.
A l'intention de: ressortissants de tout pays titulaires du baccalauréat (ou équivalent).
Durée: 6 ans en médecine; 5 ans pour les sciences vétérinaires; et 4 ans pour les autres domaines.
Inscriptions: à l'adresse ci-dessus.

2328 Université Marmara
Sultanahmet
34413 Istanbul
Tel: +90-212-518-1600
Fax: +90-212-518-1615
Web: http://www.marun.edu.tr

📖 **2e, 3e cycle**

Domaines d'étude: droit, éducation, études dentaires, ingénierie, journalisme, médecine, pharmacie et pharmacologie, sciences, sciences économiques et commerciales, théologie, religion.
Programmes: programme de cours conduisant à l'obtention de la maîtrise, dans les domaines suivants: éducation, sciences économiques et administratives, communication, études dentaires, beaux-arts, ingénierie, médecine, pharmacie, littérature et sciences, droit, théologie, enseignement technique, enseignement médical.
A l'intention de: ressortissants de tout pays remplissant les conditions requises.
Durée: en général 4 ans; 5 ans pour les études dentaires et pharmacie; 6 ans pour la médecine.
Connaissances linguistiques: langue d'enseignement: turc ou anglais selon le domaine.
Inscriptions: à l'adresse ci-dessus.

2329 Yuzuncu Yil University [YYU]
Kampüs
65080 Van
Tel: +90-432-225-1001
Fax: +90-432-225-1119
Web: http://www.yyu.edu.tr
e-mail: nmert@yyu.edu.tr

📖 **Undergraduate, Graduate, Postgraduate Programmes**

Study Domains: agriculture, architecture, arts, biochemistry, earth science, economy, education, food, mathematics, medicine, natural sciences, nursing, pharmacy and pharmacology, research, surgery, veterinary sciences.
Programmes: Bachelor's, Master's, Ph.D. degrees in

education; arts; economics; science; architecture; agriculture; medicine; nursing; pharmacy.
Open to: candidates of all nationalities with secondary-school certificate; entrance examination required.
Duration: 4 to 5 years.
Applications: by September; see website for further information.

2330 Zonguldok Karaelmas University

Zonguldok
Tel: +90-372-257-4010
Web: http://www.karaelmas.edu.tr

📖 Undergraduate, Graduate, Postgraduate Programmes

Study Domains: all major fields, applied sciences, arts, biology, business administration, chemistry, economy, education, engineering, medicine, nursing, physics, tourism, hotel and catering management.
Programmes: Bachelor's, Master's, Ph.D. degrees in education, arts, business administration, economics, science, engineering, medicine, nursing.
Duration: 4 years; courses begin 1 September.
Applications: by 1 July / 1 September; contact kaleli@karaelmas.edu.tr for further details.

Uganda

Academic year: October to June.
Monetary unit: Uganda shillings (UGX).
International student admission: Foreign students wishing to study in Ugandan universities should possess 2 principal passes at the Uganda Advanced Level Certificate of Equivalence.
Language: Instruction in English.
Immigration requirements: Visa should be obtained from Ugandan embassy in the candidate's country.
Estimated expenses for one academic year: For undergraduate studies, the amount is UGX 2,500,000 and UGX 3,000,000 for postgraduate.
Information services:
• World University Service (Uganda Branch), Makerere University, Faculty of Education; PO Box 7062; Kampala; Uganda.
Open and distance learning: Distance education is offered by the Institute of Adult and Continuous Education of Makerere University. It provides university type instruction in various parts of the country by correspondence and via the press, radio and television.
Recognition of studies and qualification:
The National Council for Higher Education (NCHE) is mandated to recognize studies and qualifications.
Publications / Websites:
• Annual Prospectus available at Secretariat UMU.

2331 Makerere University [MU]

Academic Registrar
PO Box 7062
Kampala
Tel: +256-41-532-631 - 4 / 540-436
Web: http://www.makerere.ac.ug

📖 Library and Information Sciences

Study Domains: book development and production, communication, community development, development studies, documentation, information science, library science, management, printing, publishing.
Programmes: programmes of study at the East African School of Librarianship: (a) Bachelor of Library and Information Science: book development and production, communication, community development, development studies, documentation, information science, management, printing, publishing, library science, archival administration, records management and 2 subjects from the science/social science fields in the first year of study; (b) Certificate in Library and Information Science: library science and documentation; (c) Postgraduate Diploma in Librarianship: documentation, communication, library science and information science.

Open to: candidates of any nationality, holding an advanced level certificate with 2 principal passes; no age limit.
Duration: (a) 3 years; (b) and (c) 1 year.
Fees: application, US$15; registration, US$20; examination, US$100; graduation, US$20; accommodation, US$600 per term; tuition: (a) US$2,100 per year; (b) US$500 per term; (c) US$900 per term.
Financial assistance: (a) available to Ugandan students and to those coming from the United Republic of Tanzania and Kenya under the Inter-University Exchange Programme; possibility of obtaining Fulbright and other international scholarships; contact the Registrar at the above address for further information.
Applications: by June, to the Registrar at the above address.

📖 Undergraduate Programmes / Distance Education

Study Domains: business administration, education.
Programmes: Programme of distance education studies provided by University's Institute of Adult and Continuing Education (IACE): Bachelor of Education and Bachelor of Commerce Degree by Distance Education.
Applications: to the Director at the above address; see website for further information; http://www.makerere.ac.ug/study/distance/.

📖 Undergraduate, Graduate Programmes

Study Domains: demography and population studies, statistics.
Programmes: programmes of study at the Institute of Statistics and Applied Economics (ISAE): (a) Courses in statistics, population studies and quantitative economics leading to B.Stat., B.Sc., B.Sc. (QE); (b) Postgraduate diplomas and Master's degree in statistics and demography.
Open to: (a) English-speaking candidates of any country, holding Advanced Level School Certificate with two good principal passes one of which must be mathematics, or holding a professional level Diploma in Statistics; (b) candidates of any nationality with a good first degree; good level of English required.
Duration: (a) variable; (b) 8 to 9 months.
Fees: (a) variable; (b) approximately US$8,000 includes all costs except airfare.
Applications: by March, to the Associate Director of ISAE, at the above address.

2332 Mbarara University of Science and Technology [MUST]

PO Box 1410
Mbarara, Kampala
Tel: +256-485-20785 / 20720
Fax: +256-485-20782 / 21117
Web: http://www.must.8m.net/
e-mail: admin@must.ac.ug

📖 Medical Studies

Study Domains: medicine.
Programmes: degree programmes in medical sciences.
Open to: Ugandans and other nationals holding an advanced certificate of education in biology (or zoology) and chemistry, and at least subsidiary passes in physics or mathematics or the equivalent.
Duration: 6 years; classes: 5 years; hospital internship 1 year.
Applications: by 31 March.

📖 Undergraduate, Graduate Degree Programmes

Study Domains: administration, chemistry, computer science, development studies, health and hygiene, mathematics, physics, psychology, sociology, teacher education.
Programmes: MBCLB; B.Sc. Education; Bachelor of Development Studies; Bachelor Medical Lab; Master's; Ph.D.
Open to: language proficiency required.
Duration: 3 to 5 years; courses begin in October.
Fees: registration: US$400; tuition fees: US$3,200; living costs: US$840.
Languages: English.

2333 Uganda Martyrs University [UMU]

PO Box 5498
Kampala
Tel: +256-78-410-603
Fax: +256-78-410-100
Web: http://www.fiuc.org/umu
e-mail: mlejeune@umu.ac.ug

📖 Undergraduate, Graduate Degree Programmes

Study Domains: administration, African studies, agriculture, agronomic sciences, architecture, building industry, business, business administration, cattle breeding, computer science, development studies, economic and commercial sciences, economy, education, forestry, horticulture, industrial relations, management, marketing, mathematics, statistics, summer programmes.
Programmes: (a) Diplomas programmes; (b) Bachelor's; (c) Master's; (d) Ph.D.
Description: (a) Diplomas: development studies, human resources management, health services management, advanced education management; Associate Bachelor's degrees in: democracy and development, human rights and development economics, agriculture, microfinance; postgraduate diploma: good governance and civil society, development studies; (b) Bachelor's in: ethics and development, ethics and African studies, business administration and management, science; (c) Master's in: ethics and African studies, development studies, health services management, information systems; M.B.A.; (d) Ph.D.: development studies.
Duration: (a) distance learning diplomas: 2 years; (b) 3 years; (c) 18 months or part-time 2 years.
Fees: tuition fees per year: (a) US$1,500; (b) US$2,000; (c) US$2,500; (d) US$3,150.
Languages: English language proficiency required.

🎓 Scholarship

Study Domains: all major fields.
Scholarships: University Scholarship.
Open to: students having successfully completed one year of studies before applying; based on financial need.
Duration: renewable for 2 years.
Value: USD$1,500 for one academic year.
Applications: apply by April to pkanyandego@umu.ac.ug.

Ukraine

Academic year: September to June.
Organization of higher education system: Bachelor's degree: 4 academic years; Specialist degree: 1 academic year after Bachelor's degree; Master's degree: 2 academic years after Specialist's degree.
Monetary unit: hryvnas (UAH).
National student admission: Secondary education diploma with the list of subjects studied and grades received, a medical certificate, a copy of birth certificate, passport, 6 photographs.
International student admission: (a) application form; (b) secondary school leaving certificate, with a list of courses studied (subjects) and grades (points) received; (c) medical certificate attesting to absence of HIV-infection, unless otherwise indicated by Ukraine authorities; (d) medical certificate signed by an official health care authority of student's originating country issued at least two months prior to beginning of studies in Ukraine; (e) insurance policy for emergency medical care (except for students from countries with bilateral agreements of free provision of emergency medical care; (f) copy of birth certificate. All documents must be submitted in Ukrainian, Russian or English language, and documents (b), (c), (d) and (f) must be duly certified and legalized according laws in force in originating country.
Language: Languages of training in Ukrainian universities are Ukrainian, Russian and English. English is language of instruction for certain special subjects. International students (except those following studies for the degree of 'candidate' or doctor of science and postgraduate students) who do not speak the Ukrainian language or any other language of study will be admitted to the preparatory faculties (departments) for foreign students organized in appropriate higher educational institutions for a one year period, according to the test results. At the preparatory faculty, in general, students will study the

Ukrainian language, history, regional geography, mathematics, physics, chemistry, biology, geography and other subjects, depending on their field of study. At the end of the academic year students successfully passing final examinations will be granted a certificate relevant to their studies.
Immigration requirements: Students must request a visa from the embassy or consulate of Ukraine of their originating countries and present a letter of acceptance from the Ukrainian institution of higher education where the student will be studying.
Estimated expenses for one academic year: tuition: variable according to the course and place of studies; the annual amount is determined by the Cabinet of Ministers of Ukraine and averages as follows: preparatory year: US$1,000-$2000; basic course: US$1,500-$3,500; postgraduate course: US$2,500-$3,500; practical studies: US$300-$500 (per month), all amounts are subject to change from year to year. Housing in the university dormitory: US$10-50 per month. Private housing accommodation is also available in the vicinity of the university.
Information services:
• Ministry of Education and Science of Ukraine, Department of International Cooperation and European Integration; Peremogy pr. 10; 01135 Kiev, Ukraine.
• Ukrainian State Centre of International Education, Ministry of Education and Science of Ukraine,Tarasivska str., 9 A, office 18, Ukraine, Kiev 01033; tel: +380-44-234-1431; fax: +380-44-227-9756; email: intered@intered.com.ua; web: www.intered.gov.ua.
Scholarships for international students: Ministry of Education and Science of Ukraine Department of International Cooperation and European Integration.
Open and distance learning: The national universities of Ukraine offer distance learning courses for students; for further information contact the relevant university.
Work opportunities: In general only foreign students with a special residency status in Ukraine have the right to take up employment in Ukraine. Otherwise, foreign students must obtain special permission from the State Center of Employment, Ministry of Labor and Social Policy of Ukraine.
Publications / Websites: The following books have been published within the framework of the Ukrainian State Centre of International Education:
'Ukraine Welcomes to Study', 2004. This publication contains information about more than 100 Ukrainian institutions of higher education (contacts details, specialties, other details) in Ukrainian and English languages.
• Ministry of Education and Science; www.mon.gov.ua
• The State Centre of International Education of Ukraine; www.intered.gov.ua.

2334 Bila Tserkva State Agrarian University [BTSAU]

pl. Soborna 8/1
09117 Bila Tserkva
Tel: +38 04463 525 87
Fax: +38 04463 52587
Web: http://www.btsau.kiev.ua
e-mail: rector@bdau.kiev.ua

📖 Undergraduate, Graduate, Postgraduate Programmes

Study Domains: agriculture, agronomic sciences, business, cattle breeding, education, horticulture, interpretation and translation, languages, law, linguistics, sciences, social sciences, summer programmes, veterinary medicine, veterinary sciences.
Programmes: Bachelor's; Master's; Ph.D.; non-degree programmes in veterinary medicine, linguistics, economics, agronomy, animal husbandry.
Open to: candidates meeting academic and linguistic requirements; satisfactory level of Ukrainian language.
Duration: 5 years; courses begin in August.
Applications: apply by 30 June to above address.

🎓 Stipend

Study Domains: all major fields, agriculture, agronomic sciences.
Scholarships: Stipend.

Open to: all students based on academic achievement and financial need.
Duration: for 1 year; offered every 2 years.
Value: 450 UAH per year.
Applications: apply by 30 June to above address.

2335 Crimean State Medical University [CSMU]
5/7 Lenin avenue
95006 Simferopol
Tel: +38 0652 27 4462
Fax: +38 0652 27 2092
Web: http://www.csmu.strace.net
e-mail: office@csmu.strace.net

📖 Pre-doctoral Programme
Study Domains: dentistry, medicine, paediatrics, pharmacy and pharmacology.
Programmes: Master's degree programmes in medicine; dentistry; paediatrics; pharmacy.
Duration: 6 years; courses begin in September.
Fees: tuition: US$1,650-$1,950.
Languages: Russian and English.
Applications: apply by 1 October to the Rector at the above address; tel: +38 0652 294868.

2336 Dnipropetrovsk State Medical Academy [DSMA]
9, Dzerzhinsky Street
49044 Dnipropetrovsk
Tel: +38 056 770 2258
Fax: +38 056 770 2258
Web: http://www.dsma.dp.ua
e-mail: dsma@dsma.dp.ua

📖 Graduate, Postgraduate Programmes
Study Domains: computer science, English, health and hygiene, information science, languages, medicine, philosophy, physical education, political science, psychology, Russian, sciences, social sciences, sociology.
Programmes: Master's; Ph.D.; clinical ordinatura; M.D.; Doctor of Dentistry.
Duration: Master's: 1 to 2 years; Ph.D.: 3 years; clinical ordinatura: 2 to 5 years; M.D.: 6 years; Doctor of Dentistry: 5 years; courses begin 1 September.
Fees: tuition: US$1,600; dormitory housing: US$25 per week.
Languages: Russian.
Applications: apply by 15 November to International Programmes Office at the above address.

2337 Donbas State Academy of Civil Engineering and Architecture [DNACEA]
86123 Derzhavina, 2
Makeyevka, Donetsk Region
Tel: +38-0623-26-1301
Fax: +38-0623-90-2938
Web: http://www.dgasa.dn.ua
e-mail: mailbox@dgasa.dn.ua

📖 Undergraduate, Graduate Programmes
Study Domains: architecture, building industry, civil engineering, ecology, environment, economy, engineering, home economics, hydraulics, management, mechanical engineering, research, technology, transport, urbanism.
Programmes: undergraduate and graduate programmes in civil engineering, architecture, fundamental and general engineering training, mechanics, environment, economics, marketing and management, humanitarian training, extramural studies, preparatory department for foreign students.
Applications: see website: http://www.dgasa.dn.ua.

2338 Donetsk State University of Economics and Trade [DSUET]
Schorsa Street 31
83050 Donetsk
Tel: +380-62-335-1029
Fax: +380-62-335-1029
Web: http://www.donduet.edu.ua/en/his.shtml

📖 Undergraduate, Graduate, Postgraduate Studies
Study Domains: accounting, business, economy, finance, food industry, management.
Programmes: undergraduate and graduate programmes (Dyplom Bakalvra; Kandydat Nauk; Doktor Nauk) in economics, management, accounting, food industry, finance.

2339 East Ukrainian National University [EUNU]
EUNU n.a. V.Dal
Kvartal Molodiozhniy, 20-A
91034 Lugansk
Tel: +38 0642 41 75 47
Fax: +38 0642 41 31 60
Web: http://www.snu.edu.ua
e-mail: uni@snu.edu.ua

📖 Undergraduate, Graduate, Postgraduate Programmes
Study Domains: all major fields.
Programmes: undergraduate, graduate and postgraduate degree programmes in over 107 specialties; 14 doctoral courses; 43 postgraduate courses in engineering, sciences, economics, linguistics, culture.
Applications: for further information contact the International Cooperation Department at: +38 0642 553 671 or email: vgonch@snu.edu.ua.

2340 European University, Kiev [EUFIMB]
16-V Academician Vernadsky Blvd.
03115 Kiev
Tel: +38-044-423-0400
Fax: +38-044-452-3568
Web: http://www.eufimb.edu.ua
e-mail: office@eufimb.edu.ua

📖 Undergraduate, Graduate, Postgraduate Programmes
Study Domains: accounting, administration, computer science, cultural studies, economic and commercial sciences, economy, finance, information science, law, management, marketing.
Programmes: (a) Bachelor's; (b) Master's; (c) Ph.D.
Description: finance, banking; accounting and audit; economics of enterprise; marketing; management of organization; management of foreign economic activity; law (jurisprudence); information control systems and technologies; intelligent systems of decision-making; software of automated systems; administrative management in the information protection systems with limited access; documentation process and information activity.
Duration: 10 years depending on programme; courses begin 1 September.
Fees: see http://www.eufimb.edu.ua for registration and tuition fees.
Languages: Ukrainian and Russian.
Applications: apply before 1 September; see online information at http://www.eufimb.edu.ua; contact: hrekhov@eufimb.edu.ua.

2341 Inter-Regional Academy of Personnel Management [IRAPM]
2, Frometivska Street
03039 Kiev
Tel: +380-44-490-9500
Web: http://www.iapm.edu.ua
e-mail: iapm@iapm.edu.ua

📖 Undergraduate Programmes

Study Domains: business administration, computer science, continuing education, English, law, linguistics, social sciences.
Programmes: Bachelor's degree programmes in systems management, international finance and economics, international economics and banking, accounting and auditing of international economic activity, international marketing and economic journalism, international commercial law, sociology of mass communication and journalism, social work in international organizations, social and legal work.
Duration: depending on programme and previous years of study; courses begin 1 September.
Fees: registration: US$7; tuition: US$1,300-$1,500 per year; living costs: US$30 per month.
Languages: language proficiency in Ukrainian or Russian.
Applications: apply by 23 August to above address.

2342 Karazin Kharkiv National University [KKNU]
4, Pl. Svobody
61077 Kharkiv
Tel: +380-572-436-196
Fax: +380-572-437-044
Web: http://www.univer.kharkov.ua
e-mail: rector@univer.kharkov.ua

📖 Undergraduate, Graduate, Postgraduate Programmes

Study Domains: all major fields.
Programmes: undergraduate, graduate and postgraduate programmes leading to Bachelor's, Master's, Specialist's diploma and Ph.D.
Open to: candidates of any country holding a secondary-school certificate; interview required.
Fees: current registration: US$80; tuition fees: US$800-$1,000 per year (depending on programmes), special tuition fees for medical studies: US$8,600 per year (in Russian); US$14,328 per year (in English).
Languages: Russian and Ukrainian (English for some medical programmes).
Applications: by 20 August to the above address.

2343 Kherson Pedagogical University [KSPU]
Ul. Sorok Rokiv Zhovtnya 27
Kherson
Tel: +380-5522-26263
Fax: +380-5522-22114
Web: http://www.university.kherson.ua
e-mail: office@kspu.kherson.ua

📖 Undergraduate, Graduate Programmes

Study Domains: agriculture, business, education, engineering, health and hygiene, humanities and arts, languages, law, sciences, social sciences.
Programmes: Bachelor's, Master's and non-degree programmes.
Languages: Russian and Ukrainian.
Applications: for application information contact the above address or email: ustimenko@kspu.kherson.ua.

🎓 Scholarship

Study Domains: education, teacher education.
Scholarships: University Scholarship.
Duration: renewable per term.
Value: approximately 40 UAH per month.
Applications: apply to: Yugaj Klara Petrovna at: +380 5522 326712.

2344 Kiev Medical Institute [KMI UAFM]
9, L. Tolstoy Street
01004 Kiev
Tel: +380-44-224-9992
Fax: +380-44-224-9992
Web: http://www.kmiuanm.org
e-mail: kmi@kmiuanm.org

📖 Medical Studies

Study Domains: medicine, nursing, paramedical studies, pharmacy and pharmacology, stomatology.
Programmes: Medical Studies.
Duration: 6 years; courses begin 1 September.
Fees: tuition: US$1,600 per academic year; estimated living costs US$30-$60 per month.
Languages: Ukrainian, Russian.
Applications: by 15 October to International Relations Department at the above address.

2345 Kiev National Linguistics University [KNLU]
ul. Eervonoarmijska 73
03680 Kiev
Tel: +380-44-227-33-72
Fax: +380-44-227-67-88
Web: http://www.uniling.kiev.ua
e-mail: knlu@uniling.kiev.ua

🎓 Scholarship

Study Domains: linguistics.
Description: International course preparatory department for foreign students. Students are taught Ukrainian and Russian for further studies in Ukraine. After 10 month course, students are awarded a special certificate.
Duration: 1 year; renewable.
Value: Tuition, US$1,500-US$1,600.
Applications: by 30 August.

2346 Kiev Slavonic University [KSU]
9, H. Barbus Street
03150 Kiev
Tel: +380-44-528-9407 / 278-1932
Fax: +380-44-528-9407 / 278-1932
Web: http://www.ksu.edu.ua
e-mail: ksu-oic@i.kiev.ua

📖 Undergraduate, Graduate Programmes

Study Domains: accounting, business administration, English, finance, French, German, history, international law, international relations, international studies, languages, law, literature and civilization, marketing, Slavic studies, tourism, hotel and catering management.
Programmes: Bachelor's, Specialist's, Master's degrees in international relations and Slavonic studies; economics and management; languages and literature.
Subjects: business administration, computer science, cultural studies, demography and population studies, ecology, environment, education, finance, diplomacy, international law, international relations, international information, languages, law, literature and civilization, Slavonic studies, teacher education, theology, religion, philosophy, economics of enterprise, finances of enterprise, accountancy in Western countries, analysis of bank activity, economics of Slavonic Countries.
Open to: candidates of any nationality holding a secondary-school certificate.
Duration: Bachelor's degree: 4 years; Specialist's degree: 5 years (1 year beyond Bachelor's); Master's degree: 5 years (1 year beyond Specialist's degree); courses begin 4 September; also Summer courses.
Fees: tuition fees: US$1,800-$2,500 per year; living costs US$500-$600 per month; housing costs: university dormitory: US$50-$100; private flat rental: US$300-$900.
Languages: Ukrainian, Russian and English.
Applications: by 4 August to above address.

2347 Krok University [KU]
30-32 Lagerna Street
03113 Kiev
Tel: +380-44-456-7191
Fax: +380-44-456-8428
Web: http://www.krok.edu.ua
e-mail: krok@krok.edu.ua

📖 Undergraduate Studies

Study Domains: accounting, administration, business, business administration, communication, computer science, criminology, cultural studies, ecology, environment, economic and commercial sciences, economy, education, finance, geography, human sciences, information science,

international business, international law, international relations, international studies, languages, law, literature and civilization, mathematics, philosophy, social sciences, statistics, teacher education, theology, religion.
Programmes: (a) Bachelor's; (b) Master's; (c) PhD; (d) preparatory courses in Russian for foreign students.
Description: (d) Russian Language, Mathematics, History, Geography, Economics, Computer Studies, Physics, Chemistry, Biology and Physical Training.
Open to: candidates of any country holding a secondary-school certificate and proficient in Russian.
Duration: 4 to 6 years; courses begin 1 September; (d) 8 to 10 months, beginning between September 15 and November 15.-.
Fees: tuition:US$1,380 per year; (US$1,100 per year for preparatory courses); living costs US$500-$3,000 per year.
Languages: Russian, Ukrainian and English.
Applications: by 15 August; contact andrewl@krok.edu.ua for further details.

2348 Lugansk Academy of Internal Affairs [LAIA]
ul. Karia Marksa 4
Yuvileiny Village
Lugansk
Tel: +380-642-553-200
Fax: +380-642-883-200
e-mail: lavs@telecom.lg.ua

📖 Undergraduate Studies

Study Domains: criminology.
Programmes: 'Dyplom Spetsialista' in criminal investigation, criminal law, criminology.

2349 Lutsk State Technical University [LSTU]
Lvivska Street 75
43018 Lutsk
Tel: +380-332-774-840
Fax: +380-332-264-840
Web: http://www.dtu.lutsk.ua
e-mail: rector@dtu.lutsk.ua

📖 Undergraduate, Graduate Programmes

Study Domains: economy, engineering, finance, management, technology.
Programmes: Bachelor's, Master's degrees in economics, finance, management, engineering, technology.

2350 Lviv State Institute of Physical Education [LSIPE]
11, Kostyushka Street
79000 Lviv
Tel: +380-322-727-561
Fax: +380-322-727-042
e-mail: postmaster@lsife.lviv

📖 Undergraduate, Graduate Studies, Postgraduate Studies / Physical Education

Study Domains: physical education.
Programmes: undergraduate, graduate and postgraduate programs (Dyplom Bakalavra; Dyplom Spetsialista; Dyplom Magistra; Dyplom Kandydata Nauk (PhD) in Physical Education; Olympic and Professional Sport, Physical Rehabilitation.

2351 National Aerospace University [NAU]
17, Chkalov Street
61070 Kharkiv
Tel: +380-57-744-9856
Fax: +380-57-744-1131
Web: http://www.khai.edu
e-mail: khai@khai.edu

📖 Undergraduate, Graduate, Postgraduate Programmes

Study Domains: accounting, administration, applied sciences, aviation, aeronautics, business administration, chemical engineering, chemistry, civil engineering, community development, computer science, ecology, environment, electricity and electronics, energy, engineering,

hydraulics, industrial technology, international law, laboratory techniques, languages, law, mathematics, mechanical engineering, natural sciences, optics, physical education, physics, research, sciences, statistics, technical education, technology, telecommunications, transport, vocational training.
Programmes: Bachelor's, Master's, Ph.D., Doctor of Science degrees in aeronautical and aerospace engineering.
Open to: candidates with secondary-school certificate.
Age limit Max: under 30 years of age.
Duration: 4 to 6 years; courses begin 1 September; contact prorector_ir@khai.edu for further details.
Fees: tuition fees US$1,500-$1,800 per year; estimated living costs US$150-$200 per month.
Languages: Russian, Ukrainian, English.

2352 National University of Kiev-Mohyla Academy [NUKMA]
Vul. Skovorody 2
04070 Kiev
Tel: +380-44-416-4515
Fax: +380-44-417-8461
Web: http://www.ukma.kiev.ua
e-mail: rec@ukma.kiev.ua

📖 Undergraduate, Graduate, Postgraduate Programmes

Study Domains: humanities and arts, languages, law, sciences, social sciences, social work, summer programmes.
Programmes: (a) Bachelor's; (b) Master's; (c) Candidate of Science - Aspirantura (Ph.D.); (d) Doctor of Science; (e) internships; part-time studies.
Description: (a) arts and humanities, history, philology, English, Ukrainian, religious studies, social science, political sciences, law, sciences and mathematics, ecology, computer science, economics, social work; (b) biology, world history, environmental studies, economic theory, cultural studies, political science, social work, sociology, philosophy, journalism and business administration; (c) (d) and (e) numerous topics; contact the University for information.
Duration: (a) 4 years beginning 1 September; (b) 2 years beginning 1 September; (c) and (d) 2-1/2 to 3 years beginning 15 November.
Fees: all programmes: registration: US$20; tuition fees: US$2,000 per year; living costs: US$150 per month.
Languages: Ukrainian and some English.
Applications: apply by 28 June by mail or email: demy@ukma.kiev.ua.

2353 National University of Pharmacy [NUP]
53 Pushkinskaya Street
61002 Kharkiv
Tel: +380-572-431-256
Fax: +380-572-470-164
Web: http://www.ukrfa.kharkov.ua
e-mail: mail@ukrfa.kharkov.ua

📖 Undergraduate, Graduate, Postgraduate Programmes

Study Domains: biochemistry, chemical engineering, chemical industry, economy, management, marketing, pharmacy and pharmacology.
Programmes: Bachelor's, Master's, Ph.D. degrees; Specialist's diploma.
Open to: candidates all any nationality holding a secondary-school certificate; one-year preparatory programme in Russian required.
Duration: 5 years; courses begin 1 September.
Fees: tuition: US$1,650-$1,700 per year; living costs: approx. US$100 per month.
Languages: proficiency in Russian required; courses taught in Ukrainian, Russian and English.
Applications: contact interdep@ukrfa.kharkov.ua for further information.

2354 Odessa State Academy of Refrigeration [OSAR]

Ul. Dvorianskaya 1/3
65026 Odessa
Tel: +380-482-236-289 /232-289
Fax: +380-482-238-931
Web: http://www.osar.odessa.ua
e-mail: admin@osar.odessa.ua

Undergraduate, Graduate and Postgraduate Programmes

Study Domains: applied sciences, computer science, ecology, environment, energy, engineering, food industry, industrial technology, mathematics, mechanical engineering, metallurgy, physics, research, rural development, technology.
Programmes: undergraduate, graduate and postgraduate programmes leading to Bachelor's, Master's, Specialist Diploma and Ph.D.
Fees: from US$2,500-$4,000 per year, depending on programmes; estimated living costs: US$2,000.
Languages: Ukrainian, Russian and English.
Applications: by 31 August to the above address.

2355 Poltava State Agrarian Academy [PSAA]

ul. Skovoroda 1/3
36003 Poltava
Tel: +380-532-500-273
Fax: +380-532-500-273
Web: http://www.agroak.poltava.ua
e-mail: fo@agroak.poltava.ua

Undergraduate, Graduate Programmes

Study Domains: agronomic sciences, veterinary medicine, zoology.
Programmes: Bachelor's, Master's degrees in agronomy, zoo engineering, veterinary medicine; also Certificate in Russian/Ukrainian languages.
Open to: candidates of all nationalities holding a Certificate in Russian/Ukrainian languages.
Duration: 4 to 5-1/2 years; courses begin 1 September.
Fees: registration: US$100; tuition: US$1,000 per year; estimated living costs: US$100 per month.
Languages: Ukrainian and Russian.
Applications: by 1 September; contact gorb@agroak.poltava.ua.

2356 Pridneprovskaya State Academy of Civil Engineering and Architecture

24 A, Tchernychevskie Street
Dnipropetrovsk
Tel: +380-562-452-372
Fax: +380-562-470-788
Web: http://www.pgasa.dp.ua
e-mail: riv@pgasa.dp.ua

Undergraduate, Graduate Programmes

Study Domains: accounting, architecture, art history, building industry, business administration, chemistry, civil engineering, computer science, ecology, environment, economy, finance, geodesy, geology, hydraulics, industrial design, interpretation and translation, languages, management, marketing, mathematics, mechanical engineering, optics, physical education, physics, social sciences, technical education, technology, urbanism, vocational training.
Programmes: undergraduate and graduate programmes leading to 'Dyplom Bakalavra'; 'Dyplom Spetsialista' and 'Dyplom Magistra'.
Duration: 5 years; courses begin 1 September.
Fees: tuition: 1,200 € per year; estimated living costs: 100-150 € per year.
Languages: Ukrainian, Russian and French.

2357 South Ukrainian State Pedagogical University 'K. D. Ushynsky' [PDPU]

26, Staroportofrankivska Street
65091 Odessa
Tel: +380-482-234-098
Fax: +380-48-732-5103
e-mail: rector@odessa.net

Undergraduate, Graduate, Postgraduate Programmes

Study Domains: arts and crafts, computer science, early childhood education, education, fine arts, history, interior design, languages, mathematics, music and musicology, philology, philosophy, physical education, physics.
Programmes: Bachelor's, Master's, Ph.D. degrees in education, physics, mathematics, computer science and languages.
Duration: 5 years; courses begin 1 September.
Fees: registration: US$35; tuition: US$1,500 per year; estimated living costs: US$40 per month.
Languages: Ukrainian and Russian.

2358 State Flight Academy of Ukraine [SFAU]

1, Dobrovolsky Street
316005 Kirovograd
Tel: +380-522-270-572
Fax: +380-522-270-572
Web: http://www.glau.kr.ua
e-mail: asup@glau.kr.ua

Undergraduate, Graduate Programmes

Study Domains: aviation, aeronautics.
Programmes: Bachelor's, Master's degrees and Specialist's Diploma in aircraft flight operation, air traffic control servicing, maintenance; also preparatory courses in Russian for foreign students.
Duration: 3 to 5 years; courses begin 1 September.
Languages: Ukrainian, Russian and English.

2359 Sumy State University [SSU]

2, Rimsky-Korsakov Street
40007 Sumy
Tel: +380-542-330-024
Fax: +380-542-334-058
Web: http://www.sumdu.edu.ua
e-mail: info@frig.sumdu.ua

Undergraduate, Graduate Programmes

Study Domains: business, law, medicine, nursing, pharmacy and pharmacology, sciences.
Programmes: undergraduate and graduate programmes in medicine, social sciences, business and law, science and medicine.

2360 Taurida National University 'V.I. Vernadsky' [TNU]

4, Yaltinskaya
Simferopol
Tel: +380-652-232-280
Fax: +380-652-232-310

Undergraduate, Graduate, Postgraduate Programmes

Study Domains: all major fields.
Programmes: undergraduate, graduate and postgraduate programmes leading to Bachelor's, Master's and Ph.D. degrees in all major fields.
Open to: candidates of all nationalities holding a secondary-school certificate.
Fees: registration: US$100; tuition: US$1,500 per year.
Languages: Russian.
Applications: by 1 September to Valeriy Vasiliev, Dean of Foreign Students; tel. +38 0652 51 65 26; fax +38 0652 23 23 10; email: taurida@tnu.crimea.ua.

2361 Ternopil Academy of National Economy [TANE]

Lvivska st. 11
46000 Ternopil
Tel: +380-352-436-133
Fax: +380-352-331-102 / 0973
Web: http://www.tane.edu.ua
e-mail: rektor@tane.edu.ua

📖 Undergraduate, Graduate, Postgraduate Programmes

Study Domains: accounting, continuing education, economic and commercial sciences, economy, finance, information science, international business, international relations, languages, law, management, marketing, social sciences.
Programmes: Bachelor's, Master's, Ph.D. and Specialist's diploma.
Open to: candidates of any country holding a secondary-school certificate; oral entrance examination in geography, economics, Ukrainian and English.
Fees: tuition: US$1,200 per year; estimated living costs: US$1,000 per year.
Languages: Ukrainian and English.
Applications: to the above address.

2362 Ternopil State Pedagogical University [TSPU]

2, M. Kryvonosa Street
282000 Ternopil
Web: http://www.tspu.edu.ua
e-mail: v.grubinko@tspu.edu.ua

📖 Undergraduate, Graduate Programmes

Study Domains: all major fields, education.
Programmes: Bachelor's, Specialist Diploma and Master's degree programmes in all major fields.

2363 Ukrainian State Maritime Technical University [USMTU]

9 Geroyev Stalingrada Avenue
327025 Nikolaev
Tel: +380-512-359-148
Fax: +380-512-397-326
Web: http://www.usmtu.edu.ua

📖 Maritime Engineering

Study Domains: marine science, technology.
Programmes: programme of studies leading to diplomas of higher education in the Faculties of Shipbuilding, Mechanical Engineering, Electrical Engineering, Economics and Languages.
Open to: candidates of any nationality holding a secondary-education certification.
Fees: approximately US$500-$1,500 per academic year, depending on programme.
Applications: by 1 September to the above address.

2364 Uzhhorod National University [UZHNU]

46, Pydhirna Street
88000 Uzhhorod
Tel: +380 312 23 33 41
Fax: +380 312 23 33 41
Web: http://www.univ.uzhgorod.ua
e-mail: admin@univ.uzhgorod.ua

📖 Undergraduate, Graduate, Postgraduate Studies

Study Domains: administration, business administration, computer science, ecology, environment, engineering, history, industrial technology, international law, interpretation and translation, journalism, languages, law, linguistics, mathematics, medicine, nursing, optics, philology, physical education, physics, rural development, sciences, Slavic studies, social sciences, social work, teacher education, zoology.
Programmes: Bachelor's, Master's, PhD degrees in all major fields.
Duration: 5 to 7 years; courses begin 1 September.
Fees: tuition fees US$1,500 per year.
Languages: Ukrainian.

2365 Vinnytsia State Technical University [VSTU]

95, Khmelnytske Shosse
21021 Vinnytsia
Tel: +380 432 32 5718
Fax: +380 432 43 3375
Web: http://www.vstu.vinnica.ua
e-mail: vstu@vstu.vinnica.ua

📖 Undergraduate and Graduate Degree Programmes

Study Domains: civil engineering, computer science, electricity and electronics, international relations, meteorology, technology.
Description: Programmes: automation and computer control systems; metrology an measurement engineering; laser and optoelectric engineering; microelectronics and semiconductor devices; electronic engineering; industrial and civil engineering; thermal and gas supply, ventilation; heat and power engineering; electrical power stations; electrical systems and networks; electrical power service systems; electromechanical automatic systems and electric drives; ecology and environmental protection; automation systems software; intelligent systems of decision making; computer systems and networks; information protection in computer systems and networks; radio engineering; radio communication, broadcasting and television equipment; electronic equipment manufacturing; biomedical equipment and systems; telecommunication technologies and faculties; telecommunications systems and networks; mechanical engineering technology; metal cutting tools and systems; automobiles and equipment; technology and equipment for recovery and wear resistance of machinery; management of organizations;.
Open to: candidates of all nationalities meeting academic, financial and linguistic criteria; up to 30 years of age.
Duration: 5-1/2 years; Ph.D.: 3 years.
Fees: tuition fees: US$1,200 per year; living costs: US$100 to $150 per month.
Languages: Ukrainian.
Applications: apply by 10 September to first vice-rector Grabko V.V. Khmelnytske shosse 95 VSTU, Vinnytsia.

🎓 Scholarships

Study Domains: all major fields.
Scholarships: (a) Ukrainian President's Scholarship; Scholarship of Verkhovna Radna of Ukraine; Scholarship of Cabinet; (b) Scholarship of Scientific Board of the VSTU.
Open to: (a) students and young scientists; (b) students.
Applications: (a) based upon the governmental decision; (b) 1 November; apply to Sergiy Yukhimchuk, Head of the Institute for International Relations of VSTU.

United Arab Emirates

Academic year: September to June.
Monetary unit: dirham.
National student admission: Students must hold a General Secondary School Certificate.
Language: Proficiency in Arabic is requested for all courses and in English for courses in engineering and medicine.
Immigration requirements: Foreign students must be in possession of a visa.
Information services:
• Ministry of Higher Education and Scientific Research, PO Box 45253, Abu Dhabi.
• United Arab Emirates University, PO Box 15551, Al Ain.
Open and distance learning: Open university institutions, which are an extension of the UAE University, offer external tutorial studies.
Recognition of studies and qualification: Ministry of Higher Education and Scientific Research; PO Box 45253; Abu Dhabi; United Arab Emirates; tel: +971-2-761-919; fax: +971-2-768-488; email: wkent@hct.ac.ae; web: http://mohe@uae.gov.ae.
Publications / Websites:
• United Arab Emirates University Catalogue (in Arabic).
• College catalogues (in Arabic and English).
• 'Statistical Yearbook' (in Arabic and English).
• United Arab Emirates University Home Page

http://www.uaeu.ac.ae.

2366 United Arab Emirates University [UAEU]

P.O. Box 15551
Al Ain
Tel: +971 3 764 2500
Fax: +971 3 764 5277
Web: http://www.uaeu.ac.ae

📖 Undergraduate, Graduate Programmes

Study Domains: all major fields.
Programmes: Undergraduate and graduate programmes in all major fields.
Open to: candidates of any nationality, no age limit with secondary-school diploma or Bachelor's degree, depending on programme chosen.
Duration: 2 to 4 years.
Fees: tuition and accommodation are free.
Languages: Arabic and English required.
Applications: by 31 July, to the above address.

United Kingdom

Academic year: October to June.
Organization of higher education system: There is a range of higher education qualifications available in the UK including Bachelor's degrees, Master's programmes and career-based qualifications:
• Bachelor's degrees: These are the most popular undergraduate qualifications which usually take 3-4 years to complete full-time (also called undergraduate or first degrees), and which are now required for entry into a wide range of careers in the UK and other countries. British degree programmes incorporate the most up-to-date subject developments, and are underpinned by world-class research and links with business and industry. Four-year courses often include a one-year placement and when appropriate may involve a period of study abroad. Some subjects typically take longer than 4 years to complete, for example medicine and dentistry last 5 years. Students can also study for intermediate qualifications such as Certificates of Higher Education (1 year) and Higher National Diplomas (2 years).
• Master's programmes: postgraduate qualifications normally run for 1-2 years in which students specialize in a particular academic area. Students can choose to take a Taught Master's degree (MA or MSc) which usually involves 9 months of academic tuition and 3 months project/dissertation. Alternatively, students can choose to take a Master's by Research (MPhil) which usually does not involve taught modules.
• Doctorate programmes: The PhD is a higher degree by research which usually lasts three years. In some institutions, it is possible to apply for the New Route Ph.D. in certain subject areas which combines taught Master's modules with traditional research. The New Route PhD lasts 4 years.
• Foundation degrees: Some colleges and universities offer these courses which have a strong vocational basis and typically take 2 years to complete full-time. Students are usually able to obtain a Bachelor's degree on completion of a third year.
Monetary unit: pound sterling (£).
National student admission: In general, national students should have 5 passes at the General Certificate of Secondary Education (GCSE) Level and 2 at Advanced (A) Level.
International student admission: Each UK university determines its own entrance requirements and these will vary according to the particular course or programme of study. However, in general, international students should have qualifications equivalent to the UK General Certificate of Secondary Education (GCSE) with at least 5 passes including 2 at Advanced (A) Level. Advice on equivalence of qualifications is available from the UK National Academic Recognition Information Centre (NARIC), Oriel House, Oriel Road, Cheltenham, Gloucestershire GL50 1XP, tel: +44-1242-252-627; fax +44-1242-258-600.
Language: Good knowledge of English is essential for all regular university courses. Institutions' prospectuses make clear the minimum level of English language ability expected of their students. Most universities require students to have

passed an English language test, such as the Test of English as a Foreign Language (TOEFL) or those run by the British Council's International English Language Testing Service (IELTS).
Immigration requirements: The requirements to be met by a person seeking leave to enter or remain in the United Kingdom as a student are that they must have been accepted on a course of study which is to be provided by an organization included on the Department for Education and Skills' Register of Education and Training Providers, and is at either a publicly funded institution of further or higher education or a bona fide private education institution which maintains satisfactory records of enrolment and attendance. The course should either be a recognized full time degree course at a publicly funded institution of further or higher education, or a weekday full-time course involving attendance at a single institution for a minimum of 15 hours organized daytime study per week of a single subject, or directly related subjects. A student must be able to meet the course costs and the accommodation and maintenance of themselves and any dependants, without taking employment, engaging in business or having recourse to public funds. He or she must also not intend to engage in business or to take employment, except part-time or vacation work undertaken with the consent of the Secretary of State for Work and Pensions. Nationals of those countries whose citizens require a visa to enter the United Kingdom need to obtain entry clearance before travelling. Applications may be made at the nearest British diplomatic post overseas.
Estimated expenses for one academic year:
• Tuition: The best source of information about course fees is the relevant college or university. The admissions staff can provide information on course costs. Tuition fees vary from institution to institution and from course to course but typically, 'overseas' fees are around £7,000 to £8,000 per year for an undergraduate course, and £7,000 to £9,000 for a postgraduate course.
Institutions decide whether it is appropriate for tuition fees to be charged at the 'home' rate or the higher 'overseas' rate. Students who have been living in the UK may qualify for home fees if they have been ordinarily resident in the UK for the full three years leading up to the start of their course and they are 'settled' in the UK i.e. resident in the UK without any immigration restrictions on the length of their stay. Students unable to meet these criteria may be charged fees at the higher 'overseas' rate unless they meet conditions applying to one of the five limited categories. These relate to European Union nationals and their children, European Economic Area migrant workers and their spouses and children, refugees and their families, people granted Humanitarian Protection and Discretionary Leave as an outcome of their asylum application and their families, and students unable to meet the residency criteria because of the temporary employment abroad of one of their parents or their spouse. Further information can be found on the DfES website: www.dfes.gov.uk/gfees.
• living expenses: approximately £6,650 for a nine-month academic year in London and £5,250 elsewhere in the UK. These figures include the cost of accommodation, (approximately £250-£400 for one month's rent), heating, lighting, food, clothing, books (£10-£50 or more) and daily travel for one person.
Information services:
• Authority to whom international students' application should be addressed:
The University and Colleges Admissions Service (UCAS) provides a central admissions service for international students applying for admissions to undergraduate courses at universities and colleges in the UK. Once the choice of institution is made, a candidate must fill in a UCAS application form for admission to that university. An application may be obtained from schools or colleges abroad that have students applying to institutions in the UK, from the local British Council offices or online at www.ucas.ac.uk/studyuk/index.html. UCAS offers a PC-based electronic application system (EAS) for schools, colleges, British Council offices and other careers organizations. By post, requests should be addressed to UCAS, Rosehill, New Barn Lane, Cheltenham, Gloucester GL52 3LZ; tel: +44-1242-233-707; email: app.req@ucas.ac.uk. From outside the United Kingdom, a payment of £5 made payable to 'UCAS' is required to cover the costs of postage and handling. Applications for

postgraduate, distance learning and other courses should be made directly to the institutions concerned.

Other agencies or organizations offering information, advice and assistance to international students:

• The British Council through their network of global offices which can be found on the following web: http://www.britishcouncil.org

• The Council for International Education (UKCOSA): web: http://www.ukcosa.org.uk

• The EducationUK; web: http://www.education.org.

Scholarships for international students: The UK Government offers scholarships to international students studying in the UK through the Commonwealth Scholarships and Fellowship Plan (CSFP) funded jointly by the Foreign and Commonwealth Office and Department for International Development; the DfID Shared Scholarship Scheme; British Chevening Scholarships funded by the Foreign and Commonwealth Office; and the Overseas Research Students Award Scheme (ORSAS) funded by the Department for Education and Skills. (See listings under 'International Organizations' in this publication.) For advice on scholarships and grants available for international students, including those offered by institutions themselves, students should contact their local British Council office which can be found on the following website: www.britishcouncil.org.

Open and distance learning: The Open University (OU) offers instruction for part-time study for degrees and other courses by correspondence, arranged through regional centres, supplemented by extensive tutorial and counselling support operated through local study centres, residential and day schools, Internet-based conferencing and support and radio and television broadcasts. Students can take just a single course or 'build' courses towards a qualification. Courses are offered as part of Certificate, Diploma or Degree programmes. For most programmes there are no previous qualifications required to study. There are around 150,000 undergraduate and 30,000 postgraduate students. Undergraduate students take a series of courses which are worth varying amounts of HE credit (most at a rate of one half or one full credit). A one-credit course is estimated to require up to 600 hours of study. An Ordinary Degree BA or BSc. is awarded to students who have obtained five credits; an Honours degree (B.A or B.Sc. Honours) to students who have obtained six credits at the higher levels of study. Students may choose from a selection of over 300 courses at four levels of difficulty (www.open.ac.uk/courses). Students may be able to count study successfully completed elsewhere at the higher education level towards their OU degree or qualification. More information is available on the website www.open.ac.uk/credit-transfer. Most Open University courses are available throughout Europe. Some are available in many other parts of the world. More than 25,000 Open University students study outside the UK. The Open College offers vocational and professional training often leading to recognized qualifications. The Open College of Arts, set up in 1987, is affiliated to the Open University. It aids students of the arts who wish to study at home.

Other colleges and universities also offer courses on a distance learning basis and details are contained in their prospectuses.

Recognition of studies and qualification: UK National Academic Recognition Information Centre (NARIC), Oriel House, Oriel Road, Cheltenham, Gloucestershire GL50 1XP; United Kingdom; tel: +44-1-242-252-627; fax: +44-1-242-258-600.

Accommodation services:) Provision of student accommodation is a matter for individual institutions but all universities and colleges offer assistance with finding somewhere to live. The most common form of accommodation is in halls of residence and many institutions guarantee accommodation in halls for first-year international students. When a student accepts a study place, they should receive a package of information which will include accommodation information. Even if residential accommodation is not available, there will be an accommodation advisory office which can help students find private accommodation. College and university accommodation is affordable: a room in a self-catering hall of residence or student apartment costs from £180 to £360 per month: accommodation where meals are provided costs from £320 to £400 per month. Accommodation in the private sector includes hostels, lodgings, bed-sits or shared flats/houses. For hostel accommodation and lodgings where

meals are included, students can expect to pay £300 to £400 per month. For a bed-sit or a room in a house or flat shared with other students, students would pay from £200 to £380 per month.

Work opportunities:

• If studies in the UK last longer than six months, a student can generally be employed for up to twenty hours per week during term time and full time during vacations. Students can find out what part-time jobs are available by consulting notice boards around their institution, looking in local newspapers and Jobcentres, and visiting their college or university careers office. Many institutions now have their own 'job shop', which displays part-time and holiday vacancies and, sometimes, issues job vacancy bulletins. The careers service can also provide students with extensive information and advice about employment, training and further study (including opportunities after graduation, work permits, and work experience opportunities), and practical help with job-hunting and making applications. But there are a few conditions students should keep in mind: Students must be able to support themselves, and any family members, independently i.e. students must show that they can meet the cost of studying and living in the UK without employment or financial assistance from the state; they cannot run their own business, be self-employed, provide services as a professional sports person or entertainer, or pursue a career by taking a permanent full-time position; and with the exception of work organized by their university or college, money that students hope to make while doing part-time or vacation work cannot form part of their visa application. Employment regulations for international students can change at any time, so students should check the current situation on the Immigration and Nationality Directorate website: www.ind.homeoffice.gov.uk. The leaflet, 'International students working in the UK - what you need to know', is available at www.dfes.gov.uk/international-students.

• The UKCOSA guidance note: Students and employment UKCOSA guidance notes can also be downloaded from the UKCOSA website: www.ukcosa.org.uk.

• Work experience after studies: On graduation, there may be opportunities to work with leading UK and international corporations in the UK, or to join national and international firms in Europe, the United States or, indeed, in any part of the globe. At the end of studies it may be possible to remain in the UK and work through the Training/Work Experience Scheme (TWES). To be eligible for this scheme, students will have to do one of the following:

- undertake training leading to a recognized professional or specialist qualification (e.g. accountancy).

- follow a graduate training programme leading to international employment.

- join a work experience scheme where you gain up to twelve months' work experience with a UK employer.

• UK careers after graduation: Under new work permit regulations, international graduates with specific skills (in areas such as electronics, engineering, health and technology) will be able to stay and work in the UK for a limited period.

• Further information is available on the Work Permits (UK) website: www.workpermits.gov.uk.

Publications / Websites:

• Department for Education and Skills (DfES): www.dfes.gov.uk/international-students

• Education UK website, produced by the British Counci: www.educationuk.org

• The Council for International Education (UKCOSA), provides advice and information to international students studying in the UK and to staff who work with themwww.ukcosa.org.uk

• Students can obtain information materials about studying in the UK by contacting the British Council offices in their country - contact details can be found on their website at www.britishcouncil.org.

2367 American International University of London - Richmond College
Queens Road
TW10 6JP Richmond, Surrey
Tel: +44-208-332-9000
Fax: +44-208-332-1596
Web: http://www.richmond.ac.uk
e-mail: enroll@richmond.ac.uk

📖 Undergraduate, Graduate Programmes
Study Domains: business administration, engineering, liberal arts, medicine, sciences.
Programmes: United States liberal arts undergraduate B.A. courses in all major fields; pre-professional programmes in medicine, engineering; chiropractic. English language development programmes, and Master of Business Administration, Master of Science in systems engineering and management; non-degree programmes in a variety of subjects.
Open to: secondary-school graduates or currently enrolled university students of all nationalities who meet entrance requirements (GPA of 2.5 United States education system); age usually 17 years or older and also mature students.
Held: at Kensington and Richmond campuses in London (residential accommodation provided at both campuses).
Duration: 1 semester to 4 years (courses begin in September or the third week of January) or two 5-week summer school sessions (mid- May to mid-June; mid-June to mid-July).
Applications: by 1 August for Fall semester, 1 December for Spring semester, 1 April and 1 May for Summer sessions; to the Admissions Office.

2368 Associated Board of the Royal Schools of Music
24 Portland Place
W1B 1LU London
Tel: +44-20-7636-5400
Fax: +44-20-7637-0234
Web: http://www.abrsm.ac.uk
e-mail: abrsm@abrsm.ac.uk

📖 Associated Board Scholarships
Study Domains: music and musicology.
Scholarships: Associated Board Scholarships.
Description: eight awards each year, comprising one undergraduate scholarship (normally tenable for four years) and one postgraduate scholarship (normally for one or two years) at each of the four Royal Schools of Music.
Open to: undergraduate candidates will normally be at least 17 years of age by 31 January in the year of entry to a college course. Postgraduates should normally be at least 21 years of age by 31 January in the year of entry.
Nationality: candidates must be nationals of a country that is not a member of the European Union; candidates who have been living or studying in the United Kingdom for more than a year immediately preceding 31 January in the year of entry to the course will not be eligible to apply.
Academic requirements: candidates must have a standard at least equivalent to a good pass at the Dip.ABRSM (Performing) or Advanced Certificate, in the case of undergraduates, and at the LRSM (Performing), in the case of postgraduates.
Place of study: Royal Schools of Music in the United Kingdom.
Duration: 4 years for undergraduate students; 1 to 2 years for postgraduate studies.
Value: tuition fees, the grant of £3,000 per year towards living expenses paid by instalments and the return fare home on satisfactory completion of the course; students will require additional personal funds for living expenses in the United Kingdom.
Applications: candidates must first apply to the School of their choice for admission in the normal way. At the same time, candidates are requested to register their interest in being considered for an ABRSM International Scholarship by completing and returning a form obtainable from the Board's London office, which will also provide further details about the scholarships; see website for further information: http://www.abrsm.ac.uk/nonukregs%5F02%5F22.html.

2369 Aston University
Aston Triangle
B4 7ET Birmingham
Tel: +44-121-359-3611
Fax: +44-121-359-6350
Web: http://www.aston.ac.uk/international

📖 Undergraduate and Graduate Programmes
Study Domains: business administration, computer science, engineering, European studies, health and hygiene, languages, mathematics, pharmacy and pharmacology, sciences.
Programmes: undergraduate and graduate programmes.
Open to: nationals of any country meeting academic, linguistic and financial requirements.
Duration: up to 3 years.
Financial assistance: some available in line with usual rates for postgraduate studentships.
Applications: by 1 June, to the Registrar; see website for further information
http://www.aston.ac.uk/international/guide/contents.htm.

2370 Bournemouth University
Kimmeridge House Talbot Campus Fern Barrow
BH12 Poole
Tel: +44-1202-595-470
Fax: +44-1202-595-287
Web: http://www.bournemouth.ac.uk
e-mail: inta@bournemouth.ac.uk

📖 International Scholarship in Journalism
Study Domains: journalism, visual arts.
Description: Reham Al-Farra International Scholarship in Journalism for Multimedia Journalism.
Open to: international students (non-EU) who have applied for MA programme in multimedia journalism and who have been offered a place on the programme.
Nationality: all nationalities.
Academic requirements: academic merit and proficiency in English.
Duration: 1 academic year.
Value: tuition: £3,000.
Applications: 30 July to International Office at the above address.

2371 British Federation of Women Graduates [BFWG]
4 Mandeville Courtyard
142 Battersea Park Road
SW11 4NB London
Tel: +44-20-7498-8037
Fax: +44-20-7498-5213
Web: http://www.bfwg.org.uk
e-mail: awards@bfwg.demon.co.uk

📖 Postgraduate Grants and Scholarships
Study Domains: biology, geology, meteorology, radiology.
Scholarships: (a) Foundation Grants; (b) Emergency Grants; (c) Theodora Bosanquet Bursary.
Description: (a) to help women graduates with their living expenses (not fees) while registered for study or research at an approved institution of higher education in the United Kingdom. The criteria are the proven needs of the applicant and their academic calibre; (b) to graduate women who face an unforeseeable financial crisis whilst engaged in study or research at institutions of higher education in the United Kingdom.
Open to: graduate women of any nationality (a) registered for study or research at an approved institution of higher education in the United Kingdom; (b) who face an unforeseeable financial crisis while engaged in study or research at institutions of higher education in the United Kingdom; (c) pursuing research studies in history or English literature in London.
Duration: variable.
Value: (a) approximately £2,500; (b) not over £500; offered three times a year in December, March and June; (c) accommodation in a hall of residence for up to 4 weeks between mid-June and mid-September.
Applications: (a) mid-April; (c) 31 October; see website for full details:
http://www.bcfgrants.org.uk/PAGES/new_page_1.htm.

2372 British Institute of Persian Studies

The British Academy
10 Carlton House Terrace
SW1Y 5AH London
Tel: +44-207-969-5203
Fax: +44-207-969-5401
Web: http://www.britac.ac.uk/institutes/bips/index.html
e-mail: bips@britac.ac.uk

Undergraduate and Graduate Grants and Bursaries

Study Domains: archaeology, arts, cultural studies, history, linguistics, literature and civilization, philosophy, theology, religion, travel grants.
Scholarships: Undergraduate and graduate grants and bursaries.
Description: original material on aspects of Iranian culture including the archaeology, arts, history, literature, religion, philosophy and cognate subjects.
Open to: British, European Union and Commonwealth postdoctoral, postgraduate and undergraduate students.
Place of study: within the Islamic Republic of Iran, the United Kingdom, Europe and elsewhere.
Duration: 9 months or academic year.
Value: variable.
Applications: by 1 May, to the Assistant Secretary, at the above address. For further information, see http://www.britac.ac.uk/institutes/bips/awards.html.

2373 Cambridge Commonwealth Trust

PO Box 252
CB2 1TZ Cambridge
Tel: +44-122-332-3322
Web: http://www.cam.ac.uk

Cambridge Commonwealth Trust Awards

Study Domains: all major fields.
Scholarships: Cambridge Commonwealth Trust Awards for studies in all major fields.
Open to: students from Commonwealth countries wishing to study at Cambridge; preference will be given to students from developing countries.
Applications: to the above address for further information; see website for further information: http://www.admin.cam.ac.uk/univ/gsprospectus/funding/overseas/index.html.

Cambridge Livingstone Trust Scholarships

Study Domains: all major fields.
Scholarships: Cambridge Livingstone Trust Scholarships for study in any discipline.
Open to: men and women graduates with a good first degree, who are domiciled, resident, or normally resident in Botswana, Lesotho, Malawi, Namibia, South Africa, Swaziland, Zambia or Zimbabwe; proficiency in English required.
Place of study: University of Cambridge.
Duration: 1 to 3 years.
Value: full-cost, including travel provision (no marriage or child allowance provided).
Applications: by 1 September of the preceding year, to the Trust; application forms available in local universities in May/June of each year.

Cambridge Overseas Trust Awards

Study Domains: all major fields.
Scholarships: Cambridge Overseas Trust Awards.
Subjects: graduate study in any discipline.
Open to: students from countries outside the Commonwealth to study at Cambridge.
Applications: preliminary applications forms available from local universities, British Embassies and offices of the British Council; applications to the above address by 21 September of the preceding year.

2374 Canterbury Christ Church University College

North Holmes Road
CT1 1 Canterbury
Tel: +44-1227-767-700
Fax: +44-1227-786-773
Web: http://www.cant.ac.uk
e-mail: admissions@cant.ac.uk

Undergraduate, Graduate Programmes

Study Domains: all major fields.
Programmes: undergraduate and graduate study programmes in four major faculties: Arts and Humanities, Business and Sciences, Education,.
Applications: see website for full details.

2375 Chester College of Higher Education

Parkgate Road
CH1 4BJ Chester
Tel: +44-1244-375-444
Fax: +44-1244-392-820
Web: http://www.chester.ac.uk
e-mail: s.webster@chester.ac.uk

Undergraduate, Graduate, Postgraduate Programmes

Study Domains: all major fields, archaeology, art history, arts, business administration, communication, education, fine arts, languages, literature and civilization, management, nursing, obstetrics and gynaecology, performing arts, physiology, sciences, social sciences, teacher education, theology, religion.
Programmes: Bachelor's, Master's, Ph.D. degrees in all major fields.
Open to: students meeting academic standards; TOEFL score 550 required.
Duration: 3 to 4 years; courses begin in September.
Fees: tuition fees £6,000-£7,020 per year.
Languages: English.
Applications: by March.

Scholarship

Study Domains: all major fields.
Scholarships: International Bursaries.
Open to: non-EU students.
Value: £1,000 per year; renewable for up to 3 years on evidence of good progress.
Applications: all students accepted at Chester by 31 July are automatically considered; contact j.millard@chester.ac.uk for further details.

2376 Christie's Education

5 King Street, St. James's
SW1Y 6QS London
Tel: +44-207-747-6800
Fax: +44-207-747-6801
Web: http://www.christies.com/education/overview.asp
e-mail: education@christies.edu

Undergraduate and Graduate Programmes

Study Domains: arts, decorative arts, fine arts.
Programmes: Undergraduate and graduate programmes in fine and decorative arts.
Open to: students from any country meeting academic, financial, and linguistic requirements; should have a serious commitment to study and strong interest the fine and decorative arts; fluent written and spoken English required.
Applications: at the above address; see website for further information: http://www.christies.com/education/london_overview.asp.

2377 Countess of Munster Musical Trust

Wormley Hill
GU8 5SG Godalming, Surrey
Tel: +44-1428-685-427
Fax: +44-1428-685-064
Web: http://www.munstertrust.ukgateway.net
e-mail: munstertrust@compuserve.com

Countess of Munster Grants
Study Domains: music and musicology.
Scholarships: Countess of Munster Grants in music studies.
Open to: citizens of the United Kingdom or nationals of British Commonwealth countries who are singers, instrumentalists or composers; lower age limit 18, upper age limit 28 for male singers and 27 for female singers, 25 for all others; candidates must be available for audition in the United Kingdom.
Place of study: in any country.
Duration: 1 academic year (renewable).
Value: varies according to need.
Applications: by the second full week in February to the Secretary of the Trust at the above address.

2378 Courtauld Institute of Art
Somerset House Strand
WC2R 0RN London
Tel: +44-20-7848-2777
Fax: +44-20-7848-2410
Web: http://www.courtauld.ac.uk
e-mail: pgadmissons@courtauld.ac.uk

Undergraduate, Graduate, Postgraduate Programmes
Study Domains: art history.
Programmes: (a) Bachelor's; (b) Master's; (c) Ph.D.; (d) postgraduate art history diploma; (e) postgraduate conservation diplomas.
Description: (a) (b) (c) art history; (d) post-graduate diploma in art history; (e) post-graduate diploma in conservation of easel painting; conservation of wall painting.
Open to: candidates of all nationalities meeting academic, financial and linguistic criteria; language proficiency scores required.
Duration: (a) 3 years (b) 1 year (c) 3 years full-time; 7 years part-time (d) postgraduate diploma: 1 year; (e) 3 years.
Fees: (a) (b) (c) tuition fees per year: EU students: £1,100; overseas students: £8,400; living costs: £7,000 per year; (d) tuition fees per year: EU students: £2,870; overseas students: £10,200.
Financial assistance: phone to inquire about graduate and post-graduate financial assistance.
Languages: English.
Applications: (a) contact undergraduate admissions secretary for application details; (b) apply by 17 January to postgraduate admissions: pgadmissions@courtauld.ac.uk; (c) apply to postgraduate admissions; (d) apply by 17 January to postgraduate admissions; (e) apply to postgraduate admissions.

2379 Coventry University
International Office
Priory Street
CV1 5FB Coventry
Tel: +44-24-7688-7688
Web: http://www.coventry.ac.uk/international
e-mail: interlink@coventry.ac.uk

Undergraduate and Graduate Programmes
Study Domains: all major fields, engineering, international studies, management.
Programmes: Undergraduate and graduate programmes.
Open to: all nationalities; proficiency in English required.
Held: at Coventry University years 1 and 3, year 2 at the Fire Service College, Bath.
Duration: 3 years; Courses begin in September or October.
Applications: all undergraduate candidates are required to apply through the Universities and Colleges Admission Service (UCAS): a special UCAS application is required in order to secure a place at Coventry University; UCAS application forms are available direct from UCAS at UCAS; P.O. Box 28; Cheltenham Glos.; GL50 3SA; United Kingdom. (This does not apply to students who are taking part in an exchange programme such as SOCRATES-ERASMUS). Postgraduate candidates (Master's level and above) may apply directly to the International Office.

2380 Cranfield University
Registry
Cranfield
MK43 0AL Bedfordshire
Tel: +44-1234-754-171
Fax: +44-1234-752-462
Web: http://www.cranfield.ac.uk/admin/ido/ido.htm
e-mail: international@cranfield.ac.uk

Postgraduate Programmes
Study Domains: agriculture, development studies, ecology, environment, engineering, geography, information science, management, marketing, rural development.
Programmes: Postgraduate Programmes in strategic and applied research, development and design.
Description: courses include advanced engineering: materials; aerospace and avionics; agriculture and environment; automotive engineering; defence; energy and power generation; health and medicine; life sciences; management and leadership; manufacturing; water; offshore technology.
Open to: candidates of all nationalities meeting academic, linguistic, medical and financial requirements; IELTS 6.5 (7.0 for Cranfield School of Management) TOEFL 580 (600 for Cranfield School of Management).
Financial assistance: a number of scholarships are awarded in open competition to international candidates; applications for admission to the University should clearly indicate interest in being considered for financial support. See http://www.cranfield.ac.uk/admin/ido/scholars/scholar.htm.

2381 Dr M. Aylwin Cotton Foundation
c/o Albany Trustee Company Limited
PO Box 232, Pollet House
St. Peter Port
GY1 4LA Guernsey, Channel Islands
Tel: +44-1481-724-136
Fax: +44-1481-710-478
Web: http://www.cotton-foundation.org
e-mail: info@cotton-foundation.org

Fellowships / Mediterranean Studies
Study Domains: archaeology, architecture, arts, cultural studies, history.
Scholarships: Cotton Foundation Fellowships and Awards for studies in archaeology, architecture, art history, language and art of the Mediterranean.
Open to: candidates engaged in personal academic research, normally showing a level of achievement comparable to a British or an American Ph.D. (although no formal academic qualifications will be necessary); fellowships will not be granted for the furtherance of doctoral research, other than in exceptional circumstances; recipients should not engage in any political activity during tenure of the fellowship.
Place of study: in any country.
Duration: 1 year (scholarships begin in September); renewal occasionally considered.
Value: £10,000 maximum per fellowship per year.
Applications: by 28 February.

2382 Durham University
University Office
Old Shire Hall, Old Elvet
DH1 3HP Durham
Tel: +44-191-334-6328
Fax: +44-191-334-6326
Web: http://www.dur.ac.uk/international
e-mail: international.office@durham.ac.uk

Undergraduate, Graduate Programmes
Study Domains: all major fields.
Programmes: programme of studies leading to undergraduate and graduate degrees (B.A., B.Sc., M.A., M.Sc., M.Phil., M.Litt. and Ph.D.).
Open to: applicants of all nationalities at least 18 years of age with suitable secondary qualifications for undergraduate courses and with a higher first degree or equivalent professional experience for graduate courses and very good knowledge of English; IELTS 6.5, TOEFL, 573, TWE, 4.5, O-level English.

Duration: undergraduate courses: 3 to 4 years; graduate
courses: Master's, 1 year; Ph.D., 3-4 years.
Financial assistance: Some awards available to overseas
students.

👋 Scholarships

Study Domains: all major fields.
Scholarships: (a) Ustinov Scholarships; (b) Shell
Centenary and Shell Centenary Chevening Scholarships; (c)
Doctoral Fellowships.
Open to: (a) applicants paying overseas fee rate, based on
academic merit; enrolled in a taught MA or MSc course of
one year's duration at the University; IELTS 6.5 or equivalent;
sufficient resources to pay all other tuition and living costs
while in UK; (b) candidates under 35 years of age; nationals
of and resident in a non-OECD country, or the Czech
republic, Hungary, Mexico, Poland, the Slovak Republic or
Turkey; intending to study a subject that will be of significant
value in aiding sustainable development of their home
country; outstanding academic ability and possessing a degree
equivalent to a first-class honours degree at a British
university; not a current or former employee of the Royal
Dutch/Shell Group of Companies; fluent in spoken and
written English; (c) overseas students who meet the
university's entry requirements for doctoral studies;
candidates where appropriate should submit an application to
the relevant Research Council. All scholarships are
merit-based and successful candidates will be informed of
their award well in advance of the commencement of the
studies.
Duration: duration of the course.
Value: (a) £2,000 tuition reduction; (b) covers tuition,
accommodation, maintenance costs and return airfare for the
scholarship holder only; (c) £12,000 per year plus a training
support grant of £1,000 from an academic department.
Applications: (a) by March, (b) 1 March; (c) please
contact the International Office for further information.

2383 Engineering and Physical Sciences Research Council [EPSRC]
Polaris House
North Star Avenue
SN2 1ET Swindon
Tel: +44-1793-444-000
Web: http://www.epsrc.ac.uk/website/index.aspx
e-mail: studentships@epsrc.ac.uk

👋 Studentships for second degree

Study Domains: sciences, technology.
Scholarships: Studentships for study leading to a second
degree in science and technology.
Open to: candidates ordinarily resident in the United
Kingdom throughout the 3-year period preceding the date of
application for the award providing the candidate was not so
resident during any part of that period wholly or mainly for
the purpose of receiving full-time education; European Union
nationals may be eligible for fees-only awards under certain
circumstances.
Place of study: at any United Kingdom institution
acceptable to the Council.
Duration: normally 3 years.
Applications: by 31 July; candidates must be nominated
by the head of department of the institution of study.

2384 European School of Economics [ESE]
8/9, Grosvenor Place
SWIX 7SH London
Tel: +44-20-7245-6148
Fax: +44-20-7245-6164
Web: http://www.eselondon.ac.uk
e-mail: info@eselondon.ac.uk

📖 Undergraduate and Graduate Degree Programmes

Study Domains: accounting, administration, advertising,
audio-visual media, business, business administration,
communication, economic and commercial sciences,
economy, finance, industrial relations, industry and
commerce, interior design, international business,
international relations, management, marketing, political

science, public relations, sociology.
Programmes: Certificates, Master's degrees in all major
fields.
Description: 12 week certificate programmes held in
London.
Subjects: marketing; event management; finance.
Open to: candidates of all nationalities meeting academic,
financial and linguistic requirements; TOEFL 550.
Held: London, Milan, Rome, Lucca, Paris.
Duration: 4 years; summer course, dependent on
programme.
Financial assistance: 50% of tuition reduction: see
scholarships.
Applications: apply by August to: orientamento@uniese.it
or: orientamento.milano@uniese.it.

👋 Business Scholarship

Study Domains: accounting, business, business
administration, economic and commercial sciences, finance,
international business, international relations.
Scholarships: Business Scholarship.
Open to: candidates of all nationalities meeting high
academic standards; good spoken English.
Duration: 3 years for B.A.; total fee for M.B.A.
Value: US$5,000, reduction on fees per academic year,
and benefits.
Applications: apply by July to e.mitchell@uniese.it; some
late applications accepted in September.

2385 Goldsmiths College, University of London
Lewisham Way, New Cross
SE14 London
Tel: +44-20-7919-7171
Fax: +44-20-7919-7903
Web: http://www.goldsmiths.ac.uk
e-mail: International-office@gold.ac.uk

👋 Postgraduate Scholarship Scheme

Study Domains: all major fields.
Open to: new postgraduate taught or research students.
Other conditions: attributed on a competitive basis to all
new postgraduate students for academic excellence.
Value: tuition: overseas students: £1,000; European Union
students: £2,500.
Applications: 15 January to Fees and Awards Officer at
the above address; a personal statement must be submitted
with application for scholarship.

2386 Harper Adams University College
Newport
TF10 8NB Shropshire
Tel: +44-1-952-820-280
Fax: +44--952-814-783
Web: http://www.harper-adams.ac.uk
e-mail: admissions@harper-adams.ac.uk

📖 Undergraduate, Graduate and Postgraduate Programmes

Study Domains: agriculture, agronomic sciences, applied
sciences, biochemistry, business administration, cattle
breeding, ecology, environment, international business,
mechanical engineering, recreation and leisure, veterinary
sciences, zoology.
Subjects: agriculture (with specialisms); animal-related,
bioveterinary science and veterinary nursing, business,
countryside and environment, engineering and design,
food-related, land and estate management, leisure and
tourism, international business management.
Fees: tuition: £7,500 - £10,000.
Applications: contact the Admissions Office.

👋 International Scholarships

Study Domains: agriculture, agronomic sciences, applied
sciences, biochemistry, cattle breeding, ecology, environment,
international business, mechanical engineering, recreation and
leisure, veterinary sciences, zoology.
Open to: candidates of all nationalities meeting school
entry requirements and having secured a place on a course.
Duration: one year only.

Value: by application and up to £1,000.

2387 Heriot-Watt University

EH14 4AS Edinburgh
Tel: +44-131-449-5111
Fax: +44-131-449-5153
Web: http://www.hw.ac.uk
e-mail: enquiries@hw.ac.uk

📖 Undergraduate, Graduate, Postgraduate Courses

Study Domains: architecture, building industry, chemical industry, civil engineering, community development, distance education, health and hygiene, industrial technology, preventive medicine, psychology, technology, textile industry.
Programmes: undergraduate courses in building engineering; architectural engineering, robotics and cybertronics; chemistry with forensic science, sport and exercise sciences, fashion design for industry and applied psychology; graduate courses in petroleum engineering, building engineering and surveying, occupational health and safety; brewing and distilling. Many courses offered through distance in collaboration with other universities.
Financial assistance: financial assistance available for certain nationality groups in the form of loans and grants through governmental organizations such as the US Department of Education for US nationals; CONACYT for Mexican nationals; Chevening Scholarships for Commonwealth nationals, etc. See website for contact details.
Applications: see website for details.

🎓 University Scholarships

Study Domains: architecture, building industry, civil engineering, health and hygiene, industrial technology.
Scholarships: (a) Overseas Scholarship Awards Scheme; (b) James Watt Scholarship; (c) Overseas Research Scholarship Awards Scheme.
Open to: candidates from outside European Union.
Other conditions: (a) applicants must have an offer of acceptance before applying for scholarship.
Duration: (a) 1 year; (b), (c) 3 years.
Value: (a) partial tuition waiver: £1,200-£3,000 depending on course; (b) living expenses: £10,000; (c) overseas student tuition waiver.
Applications: variable; see website for contact details.

2388 Heriot-Watt University, Edinburgh College of Art [HW]

Lauriston Place
EH3 9DF Edinburgh
Tel: +44-131-451-3877
Fax: +44-131-451-3630
Web: http://www.hw.ac.uk

📖 Degree Programmes in Art and Design and Environmental Studies

Study Domains: arts, design, ecology, environment.
Programmes: degree courses in art and design and environmental studies.
Open to: candidates of any country.
Duration: 4 years.
Applications: applications to all full-time undergraduate courses are made through UCAS; Rosehill, New Barn Lane, Cheltenham, Glos. GL52 3LZ or telephone 01242 233 707 or e-mail: app.req@ucas.ac.uk.

2389 Institute of Advanced Legal Studies [IALS]

17 Russell Square
WC1B 5DR London
Tel: +44-20-7862-5800
Fax: +44-20-7862-5850
Web: http://www.ials.sas.ac.uk
e-mail: ials@sas.ac.uk

📖 Research Degree Programmes

Study Domains: law.
Programmes: M.Phil, Ph.D.
Open to: candidates of any nationality with good second class degree in law or equivalent experience; IELTS minimum score 7.0 or TOEFL minimum score 625.

Duration: 2 years; courses begin in October.
Fees: tuition fees: £9,200 per year; living costs: £10,800 per year.
Financial assistance: financial assistance not offered.
Applications: apply to administration secretary or contact: david.phillips@sas.ac.uk.

2390 Institute of Commonwealth Studies, University of London

28 Russell Square
WC1B 5DS London
Tel: +44-20-7862-8844
Fax: +44-20-7862-8820
Web: http://www.sas.ac.uk/commonwealthstudies
e-mail: ics@sas.ac.uk

🎓 Scholarships

Study Domains: development studies, history, international studies, political science.
Scholarships: (a) Partial Scholarship; (b) School of Advanced Studies Scholarships.
Value: (a) £500-£1,500; (b) living expenses: £8,000.
Applications: 31 May.

2391 Institute of Education, University of London

20 Bedford Way
WC1H 0AL London
Tel: +44-20-7612-6000
Fax: +44-20-7612-6126
Web: http://www.ioe.ac.uk
e-mail: info@ioe.ac.uk

📖 Graduate Degrees and Teacher Training

Study Domains: continuing education, early childhood education, education, health and hygiene, research, special education, teacher education.
Programmes: consult website for further information.

🎓 Research Degrees

Study Domains: education.
Scholarships: (a) Institute of Education Research Studentships; (b) Nicholas Hans Comparative Education Scholarships; (c) Overseas Research Studentships (ORS) Awards; (d) Advanced Student Research Fund.
Open to: (b) students not normally resident in the UK; (c) international postgraduate students of outstanding merit and research potential who would have to pay tuition fees at 'overseas rate'; (d) doctoral students in need of additional financing for research work or for conference attendance (who are self-financing or hold scholarships not allowing for conference attendance, with preference to students making a presentation).
Value: (d) £100 for research project; £200 for conference attendance (maximum one grant per student per total period of registration at the Institute).
Applications: to Registry (Research Degrees) at above address; doc.enquiries@ioe.ac.uk.

2392 Keele University

Keele
ST5 5BG Staffordshire
Tel: +44-1782-584-345
Fax: +44-1782-632-343
Web: http://www.keele.ac.uk
e-mail: overseas@keele.ac.uk

📖 Undergraduate and Graduate Programmes

Study Domains: all major fields, computer science, engineering, European studies, music and musicology, sciences.
Programmes: (a) undergraduate and postgraduate courses in humanities, social sciences, natural sciences, computational chemistry, European studies, counselling, business administration; Bachelor's (joint honours), taught Master's, research postgraduate degrees (Master's or Doctorates); Postgraduate courses within the following boards of study: (b) optical data recording (M.Sc.); (c) data engineering in computer science (M.Sc.); (d) computing in earth sciences (M.Sc.); (e) digital music technology (M.A./M.Sc.).
Open to: candidates of any nationality; no age limit; (a)

undergraduate school-leaving qualification granting university entrance in own country; postgraduate good honours degree or equivalent; for M.B.A. and counselling courses, approved professional qualifications or work experience may be considered in certain circumstances; for European studies, students unable to offer French at A level standard may be admitted to the 4-year degree course if they are able to offer French at GCSE level; (b) graduates with first or second class honours degree; (c) as (b) from any discipline and who are proficient in at least one high-level programming language; (d) applicants will normally have completed a Bachelor's degree in geology, geophysics, environmental science or a combined honours scheme with a significant earth science component; (e) candidates require a first or second class honours degree in either electronics or computer science, or a degree or joint degree in music with significant music technology content; English language classes available.
Duration: (a) undergraduate, 3 to 4 years; postgraduate, 1 year (taught), 1 to 3 years (research) (b) to (e) 1 year.
Applications: all undergraduate students applying for admission to UK universities must apply through the Universities and Colleges Admissions System (UCAS); http://www.ucas.ac.uk; information can be obtained from a local British Council office for advice or through Keele's Undergraduate Division at above address. The institution code for Keele is K12. Graduate students should write to the University at the above address or consult website: www.keele.ac.uk/depts/aa/postgraduate/studyguide2003.

☞ Scholarships

Study Domains: all major fields.
Scholarships: (a) Overseas Research Students Award Scheme; (b) Chevening Scholarships; (c) Friends and Family Bursaries.
Description: (a) research at postgraduate level; (b) all postgraduate master's courses; (c) all subjects and levels.
Open to: (a) students of outstanding merit and research potential; (b) potential leaders and decision-makers; (c) those recommended by Keele students and graduates.
Duration: (a) 1 to 3 years; (b) 1 year; (c) duration of course to maximum of 3 years.
Value: (a) covers the difference between the tuition fee for a home postgraduate student and the full-cost fee which is charged to overseas students; (b) depends on country; (c) £1,000 per year off tuition fees.
Applications: (a) by end of April; applications forms and further details can be obtained from the Postgraduate Admissions Office, Department of Academic Affairs; (b) for details see: http://www.chevening.org; (c) by 31 July; for details see: http://www.keele.ac.uk.

2393 Lancaster University

Bailrigg
LA1 4YW Lancaster
Tel: +44-1524-65201
Fax: +44-1524-846-243
Web: http://www.lancs.ac.uk/users/international
e-mail: intoffice@lancaster.ac.uk

📖 Undergraduate and Graduate Programmes

Study Domains: all major fields.
Programmes: Undergraduate and graduate programmes in all major fields.
Open to: students of all nationalities with meeting academic, financial and linguistic requirements; for graduate students good undergraduate degrees or equivalent qualifications; special courses in English provided.
Financial assistance: a limited number of studentships are available to candidates who have gained admission to the University.
Applications: full-time undergraduate students must apply through UCAS http://www.ucas.ac.uk; contact University undergraduate admissions for further information: ugadmissions@lancaster.ac.uk, fax; +44 1524 846 243; graduate students contact pgadmissions@lancaster.ac.uk, fax; +44 1524 592 065.

2394 Leeds Metropolitan University Faculty of Cultural and Education Studies Carnegie Centre for Physical Education and Sport Studies [LMU]

Beckett Park Campus
LS6 3QS Leeds
Tel: +44-113-283-2600
Web: http://www.lmu.ac.uk
e-mail: international@lmu.ac.uk

📖 Undergraduate and Graduate Programmes

Study Domains: physical education.
Programmes: Undergraduate and graduate programmes in all major fields.
Open to: candidates of all nationalities meeting academic, financial and linguistic requirements: International English Language Testing System (IELTS): band 6 GCSE / GCE 'O' level English: grade C; TOEFL (Test of English as a Foreign Language): score of 550, with score of 4.0 in the Test of Written English; Cambridge Certificate of Proficiency in English: grade C; higher education degree in which English language or literature form a substantial part.
Applications: contact international admissions office at above address, also http://www.lmu.ac.uk/internat.

2395 Leeds Trinity and All Saints College [TAS]

Brownberrie Lane Horsforth
LS18 5HD Leeds
Tel: +44-113-283-7100
Fax: +44-113-283-7200
Web: http://www.tasc.ac.uk
e-mail: enquiries@tasc.ac.uk

☞ Partial Scholarships

Study Domains: business administration.
Open to: candidates of all nationalities based on merit.
Duration: 1-3 academic years; renewable.
Value: up to £2,000.
Applications: 1 May; a personal statement indicating academic results, professional experience, etc. is required when applying; see website for further information.

2396 Liverpool Hope University College

Hope Park
L16 9JD Liverpool
Tel: +44-151-291-3000
Fax: +44-151-737-3100
Web: http://www.hope.ac.uk
e-mail: compass@hope.ac.uk

☞ University Scholarship

Study Domains: business administration, education, fine arts, humanities and arts, information science, performing arts, social sciences.
Duration: 1 year.
Value: full or half tuition.
Applications: by 28 June to International Office at the above address.

2397 Liverpool, John Moores University

Edgerton Court, 2 Rodney Street
L3 5U Liverpool
Tel: +44-151-231-2121
Fax: +44-151-709-0172
Web: http://www.livjm.ac.uk

☞ University Scholarships

Study Domains: all major fields, physical education.
Scholarships: (a) Sports Scholarship; (b) International Bursaries.
Open to: (a) talented athletes.
Nationality: candidates of all nationalities; specific bursaries for nationals of Pakistan and Malaysia sponsored by their governments.
Duration: (a) 3 academic years; renewable; (b) 1 academic year; non-renewable.

Value: (b) tuition: £1,000.
Applications: (a) to Sports Scholarship Manager; sportsscholarships@livjm.ac.uk; (b) Head of International Recruitment; international@livjm.ac.uk.

2398 London Guildhall University [LGU]
31, Jewry Street
EC3N 2EY London
Tel: +44-20-7320-3085
Fax: +44-20-7320-3083
Web: http://www.lgu.ac.uk
e-mail: intprogs@lgu.ac.uk

Undergraduate, Graduate, Postgraduate Programmes
Study Domains: all major fields, American studies, applied arts, art history, arts, arts and crafts, design, fine arts, languages.
Programmes: (a) Bachelor's degrees in accounting and finance; business studies; art; design; psychology; (b) Master's degrees in international trade; international banking; communication management; international relations; information systems; (c) Ph.D. degrees in various fields; (d) non-degree programmes in jewellery; design; computing; business; aviation, management; tourism management.
Open to: (c) postgraduates with eligible research proposals.
Duration: (a) 3 to 4 years; (b) 1 year; (c) 3 years; (d) 2 years.
Fees: (a); (c); (d) tuition fees £6,920 per year; living costs approx. £650 per month; (b) £7,000-£9,000 per year; living costs £650 per month.
Languages: (a) and (d) TOEFL score 550 required; (b) TOEFL score 580 required.
Applications: (a) and (d) by 30 June; (b) by 31 July; (c) contact jgray@lgu.ac.uk for further details.

2399 London Metropolitan University
Holloway Road
N7 8DB London
Tel: +44-20-7753-3314
Fax: +44-20-7753-5015
Web: http://www.unl.ac.uk
e-mail: international@unl.ac.uk

Undergraduate, Graduate, Postgraduate Programmes
Study Domains: all major fields, administration, architecture, art history, arts, arts and crafts, aviation, aeronautics, biochemistry, business, business administration, cinematography, decorative arts, design, ecology, environment, education, engineering, European studies, fine arts, graphic arts, interior design, languages, liberal arts, mathematics, paramedical studies, pharmacy and pharmacology, photography, sciences, social work, teacher education, telecommunications, tourism, hotel and catering management, transport.
Programmes: Bachelor's, Master's, Ph.D. degrees in all major fields.
Languages: English.

Scholarship
Study Domains: all major fields.
Scholarships: Graduate Scheme.
Duration: 1 year.
Value: full tuition waiver.
Applications: by 31 May or 30 October; contact scholarship@unl.ac.uk for further information.

2400 London School of Economics and Political Science [LSE]
Houghton Street
Aldwych
WC2A 2AE London
Tel: +44-20-7405-7686
Web: http://www.lse.ac.uk

Undergraduate and Graduate Programmes
Study Domains: audio-visual media, demography and population studies, economy, European studies, gender studies, mathematics, philosophy, political science, social sciences, summer programmes.
Programmes: Bachelor's, taught Master's and postgraduate Diplomas, and opportunities for M.Phil./Ph.D. research, as well as visiting programmes.
Open to: nationals of any country holding a first degree of the University of London at second-class level, or an approved equivalent in another university, with good spoken and written English.
Duration: varies with programme.
Financial assistance: some financial assistance offered; check with Financial Support Office; at the University address; or email financial-support@lse.ac.uk; tel.: + 44 20 7955 7751; fax: + 44 20 7955 7216.
Applications: to the Undergraduate or Graduate Admissions Office at the above address.

2401 Loughborough University
LE11 3TU Leicestershire
Tel: +44-1509-26-3171
Fax: +44-1509-22-3971
Web: http://www.lboro.ac.uk
e-mail: international-office@lboro.ac.uk

Undergraduate, Graduate, Postgraduate Programmes
Study Domains: accounting, administration, architecture, art history, arts, aviation, aeronautics, biochemistry, biophysics, book development and production, building industry, business, business administration, chemical engineering, chemistry, civil engineering, communication, computer science, criminology, design, ecology, environment, economic and commercial sciences, electricity and electronics, energy, engineering, English, finance, fine arts, geography, human sciences, industrial design, information science, international law, international relations, international studies, library science, management, marketing, mathematics, mechanical engineering, performing arts, physics, political science, psychology, publishing, recreation and leisure, social sciences, teacher education, telecommunications, transport.
Programmes: Bachelor's, Master's, Ph.D. degrees in all major fields.
Open to: applicants meeting academic standards; TOEFL score 570/230 CBT or IELTS 6.5 required.
Duration: 1 to 3 years.
Languages: English.
Applications: by 31 March for undergraduate studies; end of August for postgraduate studies.

Scholarship
Study Domains: all major fields.
Scholarships: Loughborough University Scholarship.
Open to: students from selected non-EU countries.
Duration: 1 year; renewable for undergraduate research.
Value: £2,000 per year.

2402 Manchester Metropolitan University [MMU]
All Saints Building
All Saints
M15 6BH Manchester
Tel: +44-16-1247-1022
Fax: +44-16-1247-6390
Web: http://www.mmu.ac.uk
e-mail: intoff@mmu.ac.uk

Undergraduate, Graduate, Postgraduate Programmes
Study Domains: all major fields.
Programmes: Bachelor's, Master's, Ph.D. degrees and non-degree programmes (HND) in all major fields. See website for further information.

2403 Middlesex University

International Admissions Office,
Trent Park, Bramley Road,
N14 4YZ London
Tel: +44-20-8411-4700
Fax: +44-20-8411-5650
Web: http://www.mdx.ac.uk
e-mail: internat@mdx.ac.uk

📖 Foundation, Undergraduate, Graduate, Postgraduate and Research Programmes

Study Domains: all major fields, summer programmes.
Programmes: Foundation, Bachelor's, Master's, PhD
degrees in all major fields.
Subjects: courses in a wide range of subjects from art to
accounting, biological science to business, computing to
choreography, English to economics, health sciences to
humanities, languages to law and music to management. For a
full listing of courses on offer please see
www.mdx.ac.uk/subjects. Middlesex University offers two
intakes annually, one in September and one in January.
Open to: candidates of all nationalities; strong competence
in English language is required for entry to undergraduate and
postgraduate courses. For those needing to improve their
English language and study skills Middlesex University offers
a pre-university preparation course please see
www.mdx.ac.uk/subjects/aeifp/mupp.htm.
Duration: 1 to 4 years; shorter courses are also available.

🎓 Regional Awards and Scholarships

Scholarships: A number of regional awards and
scholarships are available for international students applying
to Middlesex University; for full details please contact our
Regional Offices; www.mdx.ac.uk/worldwide.
Value: variable.

2404 Napier University

219 Colinton Road
EH14 1DJ Edinburgh
Tel: +44-500-353-570
Web: http://www.napier.ac.uk/international/home.asp
e-mail: info@napier.ac.uk

📖 Undergraduate, Graduate Programmes

Study Domains: all major fields, human sciences,
sciences, technology.
Programmes: Degrees, Doctorates, Higher National
Diplomas (HND) in humanities, science, technology and
professional studies.
Open to: candidates of any nationality, aged over 17; the
qualifications required depend on the course; IELTS score
5.5.
Financial assistance: some financial assistance may be
possible, check with International Student Support Office, tel:
+44 131 455 5111/5191.
Applications: to International Development Unit, at the
above address.

2405 National College for Food, Land and Environmental Studies [SAC]

The Education Office
FREEPOST

Scotland
KA6 5HW Auchincruive Ayr
Tel: +44-800-269-453
Web: http://www.sac.ac.uk/education
e-mail: Recruitment@sac.ac.uk

📖 Undergraduate and Graduate Programmes in Agriculture

Study Domains: agriculture, biology, business, cattle
breeding, ecology, environment, food, horticulture,
information science, management, veterinary sciences.
Programmes: Undergraduate and graduate programmes in
agriculture and animal husbandry; also distance education
programmes in general business and management,
information and communications technology; specialist
courses for rural businesses; online postgraduate courses.
Open to: suitably qualified applicants of any nationality.

Applications: to Academic Registrar at the above address.

2406 Natural Resources Institute, University of Greenwich [NRI]

Training Support Unit Room
Medway Campus
ME4 4TB Chatham Maritime, Kent
Tel: +44-1634-883-019
Fax: +44-1634-880-077

📖 Graduate Programmes in Natural Resources Management

Study Domains: agriculture, biology, chemistry, fisheries,
microbiology, natural resources.
Programmes: M.A., M.Sc., PG.Dip in natural resources
management.
Open to: candidates of all nationalities meeting
appropriate academic, linguistic and financial requirements. A
first degree or equivalent professional qualification, in an
appropriate subject and preferably relevant experience in the
subject sector. Applicants without formal qualifications may
be admitted according to their work experience and
responsibilities and subject to an interview.
Applications: to Karen Morris at the above address.

2407 Norwich Jubilee Esperanto Foundation [NJEF]

37 Granville Court
OX3 0HS Oxford
Tel: +44-1865-245-509

🎓 Travel Grants

Study Domains: Esperanto.
Scholarships: Travel Grants to promote Esperanto as an
international language.
Open to: nationals of all countries, under the age of 26,
competent in Esperanto and in need of financial help.
Non-British awardees must have already arranged to visit the
United Kingdom and speak in Esperanto to local clubs and
schools.
Duration: up to 1 year.
Value: award covers travelling within the United Kingdom
and conference fees; accommodation is provided by local
Esperanto societies.
Applications: to the Secretary at the above address. Letters
of applications should be in Esperanto, including if possible
some details of travel plans, and preferably letters of support
from one or two referees.

2408 Oxford Brookes University

Gipsy Lane Campus
Hedington
OX3 0BP Oxford
Tel: +44-1865-741-111
Web: http://www.brookes.ac.uk

📖 Undergraduate and postgraduate studies in all major fields.

Study Domains: all major fields.
Programmes: Undergraduate and postgraduate studies in
all major fields; distance education programmes in many
technical fields: (www.brookes.ac.uk/research/odl/index.htm).
Open to: candidates of all nationalities and of any age,
qualified for university entrance; English language classes
available free of charge.
Duration: 3 years for undergraduates, 1 year for Master's
programme; courses begin in September.
Applications: by August, to the International Office, at the
above address.

2409 Queen Margaret College

International Office
Corstorphine Campus
Clerwood Terrace
EH12 8TS Edinburgh
Tel: +44-131-317-3760
Fax: +44-131-317-3256
Web: http://www.qmced.ac.uk
e-mail: international@qmuc.ac.uk

📖 Undergraduate and Graduate Programmes

Study Domains: all major fields.
Programmes: Undergraduate and graduate programmes in all major fields.
Open to: overseas students who will be requested to produce evidence of oral and written competence in English and provide evidence of their ability to support themselves financially throughout the courses.
Applications: to the above address; see website http://www.qmced.ac.uk/registry/apply.htm.

2410 Queen's University of Belfast [QUB]
Admissions Office
University Road

Northern Ireland
BT7 1NN Belfast
Tel: +44-28-9033-5081
Fax: +44-28-9024-7895
Web: http://www.qub.ac.uk

📖 Undergraduate and Graduate Programmes

Study Domains: all major fields.
Programmes: Undergraduate and graduate programmes in all major fields.
Open to: candidates of all nationalities meeting academic, financial and linguistic requirements.
Applications: to Admissions Office at the above address.

2411 Robert Gordon University [RGU]
Schoolhill
AB10 1FR Aberdeen
Tel: +44-1224-262-000
Fax: +44-1224-263-000
Web: http://www.rgu.ac.uk
e-mail: admissions@rgu.ac.uk

🎓 Partial Scholarship for Overseas Students

Study Domains: all major fields, chemical engineering, economic and commercial sciences, engineering, international business, international law, international relations, international studies.
Description: for all major fields EXCEPT MSc in public administration and law; international commercial law, international trade, international information technology law; physiotherapy, asset management, drilling and well engineering; field and well management; oil and gas engineering.
Open to: self-funded, full-time overseas students, paying fees at overseas rate. Candidates must attain the necessary academic qualifications for entry to the course; continue to have satisfactory academic performance for the duration of the course; pay tuition fees due to the university at or by the commencement date of the course and must not incur any unpaid debts to the university during study.
Duration: 1 academic year; renewable.
Value: tuition: £1,000.
Applications: to International Office, Corporate Affairs at above address; g.m.h.daly@rgu.ac.uk.

2412 Rose Bruford College
Lamorbey Park, Burnt Oak Lane
DA15 Sidcup
Tel: +44-20-8308-2600
Fax: +44-20-8308-0542
Web: http://www.bruford.ac.uk
e-mail: enquiries@bruford.ac.uk

🎓 Tuition Waiver

Study Domains: performing arts.
Duration: 1 year; renewable.
Value: tuition waiver of up to 50%.
Applications: June, to above address.

2413 Royal College of Music [RCM]
Prince Consort Road
SW7 2BS London
Tel: +44-20-7589-3643
Fax: +44-20-7589-7740
Web: http://www.rcm.ac.uk
e-mail: info@rcm.ac.uk

📖 Undergraduate, Graduate, Postgraduate Programmes

Study Domains: music and musicology.
Programmes: Bachelor of Music (Hons.) and Postgraduate Diploma in Music Performance, Master of Music, Doctor of Music.
Open to: candidates of all nationalities; audition and interview required for MMus.
Duration: 1 to 4 years; courses begin in September.
Fees: tuition fees £13,860 per year; living costs £7,500 per year.
Applications: by 1 October via on-line admissions system. See website for further information.

🎓 Scholarship

Study Domains: music and musicology.
Scholarships: RCM Scholarships.
Duration: 1 to 4 years.
Value: £4,620-£13,860 per year.
Applications: by 5 October; contact admissions@rcm.ac.uk.

2414 Royal Holloway, University of London [RHUL]
TW20 Egham
Tel: +44-1784-443-399
Fax: +44-1784-471-381
Web: http://www.rhul.ac.uk
e-mail: liaison-office@rhul.ac.uk

🎓 University Awards

Study Domains: all major fields.
Scholarships: (a) College Overseas Entrance Scholarships; (b) Overseas Research Student Awards Scheme (ORSAS); (c) Thomas Holloway Research Studentships; (d) College Research Studentships; (e) Departmental Assistantships; (f) Alumni Bursary; (g) Royal Holloway Scholarships; (h) various awards and tuition reduction schemes available for international students of specific countries offered by organizations and foundations.
Open to: (a) overseas full-fee paying students wishing to follow full-time taught Master's or doctoral research degree programmes; (b), (c), (d), (e) overseas students for postgraduate research, on the basis of outstanding merit and research potential; (f) alumni, EU or overseas student; (g) new overseas students holding a conditional or unconditional offer (scholarships funded from college sources with participation of the British Chevening Scholarship Scheme); (i) nationals of Argentina, Iran, Pakistan, Brazil, China, Hong Kong, Indonesia, Iran, Malaysia, Mexico, Pakistan, Singapore and Venezuela.
Other conditions: (i) for Master's students only.
Value: (a) £10,000 allocated at discretion of Board; (b), (c), (d) home rate for international students; (e) living expenses: £3,610; (f) living expenses: £250 UK/EU, £500 overseas students; (g) full tuition and accommodation; return airfare; computer, rail travel around Europe; £9,000 for living expenses; (h) full tuition and living expenses; (i) variable.
Applications: various conditions; see website for details liaison-office@rhul.ac.uk.

2415 Royal Philharmonic Society
10 Stratford Place
W1N 9AE London
Tel: +44-20-7491-8110
Fax: +44-20-7493-7463
Web: http://www.royalphilharmonicsociety.org.uk/awards.htm
e-mail: admin@royalphilharmonicsociety.org.uk

🎓 RPS Music Awards

Study Domains: music and musicology.
Scholarships: RPS Music Awards.

Open to: (a) awarded by competition to a violinist of any nationality who has been resident in the United Kingdom for 3 years, aged under 24; candidates must be sponsored by 2 musicians of standing, other than their teacher; (b) awarded by competition to music students of any nationality domiciled in the United Kingdom, aged between 15 and 25 and sponsored by 2 musicians of standing, other than their teacher; category of instrument varies each time.
Place of study: (a) in the United Kingdom or abroad; (b) abroad only.
Value: (a) £2,000; (b) £12,500 for 2 years.
Applications: for further information and last dates of entry apply to the above address.

2416 Royal Scottish Academy of Music and Drama [RSAMD]
100 Renfrew Street
G2 3DB Glasgow
Tel: +44-141-332-4101
Fax: +44-141-332 8901
Web: http://www.rsamd.ac.uk
e-mail: registry@rsamd.ac.uk

📖 Undergraduate, Graduate Studies
Study Domains: music and musicology, performing arts.
Programmes: Bachelor's, Master's degrees and postgraduate diplomas in musical studies, Scottish music, acting.
Open to: (a) and (b) students of all nationalities who have completed their secondary education; a limited number of places may be available to students from overseas; (c) fourth-year and postgraduate singers, repetiteurs and one conductor who wish to take advanced training in opera; (d) over 18, selection made by interview at which candidates must be prepared to prove ability to work with hands.
Duration: (a) 3 and 4 (honours) years; (b) 3 years; (c) 1 year (courses begin in the Autumn); (d) 2 years.
Fees: (a) to (d) sessional fee £1,600 per undergraduate course and £2,430 per postgraduate course (for British and EU students); sessional fee £7,125 (for overseas students); application fee £35.
Financial assistance: full details are published each December in the brochure 'Scholarships and Prizes' available from the Director of Finance and Administration.
Applications: (a) and (c) by 15 October and 31 January for the entrance examinations in November and March, to the Registrar; (b) and (d) by 31 March (for examinations held from January to June) to the Registrar, from whom the necessary forms may be obtained.

🖋 Overseas Students' Scholarships
Study Domains: music and musicology, performing arts.
Scholarships: The RSAMD offers a wide variety of scholarships and grant to home and overseas students. These are awarded after a place has been offered. The scope and conditions vary greatly and students are advised to consult the website for full details.

2417 Royal Society
6 Carlton House Terrace
SW1Y 5AG London
Tel: +44-20-7451-2550
Web: http://www.royalsoc.ac.uk/international/
e-mail: iesinfo@royalsoc.ac.uk

🖋 Royal Society Grant Schemes
Study Domains: agriculture, applied sciences, engineering, mathematics, medicine, natural sciences, research, sciences, technology.
Scholarships: overseas exchange visits and awards; travel grants; research appointments and fellowships.
Description: Royal Society is the independent scientific academy of the United Kingdom dedicated to promoting excellence in science. Numerous grants are awarded for research in the areas of the natural sciences including mathematics, engineering, medicine, the scientific research aspects of psychology, archaeology, geography and the history of science. Awards are not granted in the areas of the humanities, social sciences or clinical medical research.
Open to: scientists must be of Ph.D. or equivalent status. Fellowship applicants may be in the final stages of a Ph.D., but the degree must be confirmed by the proposed start date. Specific eligibility requirements exist for certain schemes

especially in relation to nationality and country of residence; see website for details of individual schemes.
Place of study: variable.
Applications: to the above address.

2418 Royal Society for the Encouragement of Arts, Manufactures and Commerce [RSA]
8 John Adam Street
WC2N 6EZ London
Tel: +44-20-7930-5115
Web: http://www.rsa.org.uk/sda
e-mail: general@rsa.org.uk

🖋 RSA Student Design Awards
Study Domains: graphic arts, industrial design, textile industry.
Scholarships: RSA Student Design Awards.
Open to: full-time, part-time or evening-class students who have studied in the United Kingdom for at least one full term at an art, architectural, technical or other school or college, or in certain cases people already working in industry, aged not less than 17 years; candidates must intend to take up design as a career; awards are primarily to enable recipients to broaden their knowledge and experience abroad and to provide valuable work experience.
Place of study: for travel abroad and industrial attachments.
Value: variable.
Applications: to the above address.

2419 Royal Society of Edinburgh [RSE]
22, 24 George Street
EH2 2PQ Edinburgh
Tel: +44-131-240-5000
Fax: +44-131-240-5024
Web: http://www.royalsoced.org.uk/rse.htm

🖋 Research Fellowships
Study Domains: engineering.
Scholarships: The Royal Society of Edinburgh administers various Research Fellowship schemes: (a) John Moyes Lessells Travel Scholarships; (b) Lloyds TSB Foundation for Scotland; (c) PPARC Enterprise Fellowships; (d) Scottish Enterprise Fellowships; (e) CRF European Visiting Research Fellowships; (f) Teaching Fellowships; (g) Auber Bequest Awards; (h) BP Research Fellowships.
Description: (a) for Honours Graduates in all forms of engineering from Scottish Universities, who wish to study some aspect of their profession outside the United Kingdom; (b) for all aspects of the ageing process eg. the medical, psychological, sociological and economic consequences of old age and the research proposed must aim at improving the quality of life; (c) to exploit research and technological development undertaken within the United Kingdom astronomy and particle physics programme. The Fellowships provide a unique opportunity for researchers to spend a year gaining business training whilst developing the commercialisation of their existing research; (d) for research in the humanities in Scotland which aims to establish a two-way flow of scholars between Scotland and Continental Europe. Eight CRF European Visiting Research Fellowships will be awarded each year, normally four in each direction, and they will be for visits of between two and six months' duration; (e) aim is to support and stimulate teachers and enhance the transfer of ideas from commercial and research organisations to the world of education; (f) for furtherance of academic research in any the branches of the RSE; (g) are tenable for three years in Scottish Higher Education Institutions, for independent research in: Mechanical Engineering, Chemical Engineering, Control Engineering, Solid State Sciences, Information Technology, Geological Sciences, Chemistry (non-biological).
Open to: (a) honours graduates from Scottish higher education institutions; (g) over 60 years of age, naturalized British citizens or desire to acquire British nationality, reside in Scotland or England, be bona fide scholars engaged in academic research (but not industrial research (h) 35 years of age or under.

Place of study: (a) outside the United Kingdom; (c) held in any Higher Education Institution in the United Kingdom (HEI); (h) Scottish Higher Education Institutions.
Duration: 1 year (possible renewal for second year).
Value: variable, see website for details; http://www.ma.hw.ac.uk/RSE.
Applications: by 31 January, to the Research Fellowships Secretary at the above address.

2420 Royal Town Planning Institute [RTPI]
41 Botolph Lane
EC3R 8DL London
Tel: +44-20-7929-9494
Fax: +44-20-7929-9490
Web: http://www.rtpi.org.uk/about-the-rtpi/awards

🎓 George Pepler International Award
Study Domains: urbanism.
Scholarships: The George Pepler Award in town planning or a particular aspect of planning.
Open to: nationals of any country who wish to visit the United Kingdom or, being resident in the United Kingdom, desire to travel abroad for the study of town planning; age under 30; each applicant must submit to a panel of assessors, appointed by the council of the Institute, a statement showing the nature of proposed study, with itinerary of proposed travel and any further information required by the council.
Place of study: in any country.
Duration: a short period of up to 6 weeks.
Applications: to the Secretary at the above address.

2421 Royal Welsh College of Music and Drama [RWCMD]
Castle Grounds
Cathays Park
CF10 3ER Cardiff
Tel: +44-29-2034-2854
Fax: +44-29-2039-1304
Web: http://www.rwcmd.ac.uk
e-mail: info@rwcmd.ac.uk

📖 Undergraduate, Graduate Programmes
Study Domains: music and musicology, performing arts.
Programmes: (a) Bachelor's degrees (Hons.) in music; (b) Postgraduate Diploma in music; (c) Master's degree in music performance; (d) Postgraduate Diploma in drama; (e) Bachelor's degrees (Hons.) in drama.
Open to: (b) students over 21 with first university degree and high musical proficiency in main instrument; (d) graduates or people over the age of 21 with appropriate experience; (e) students over 18 with secondary school certificate or equivalent; (a) (b) audition; TOEFL score 510 or IELTS 6.5 required; (d) (e) audition; TOEFL score 500-550 or minimum IELTS score of 6.5.
Duration: (a) 4 years; courses begin 22 September; (b) 1-1/2 year; (c) 1 to 2 years; (d) 1 year; courses begin in September; (e) 3 years; courses begin in September.
Fees: (a) tuition fees £9,583; living costs £5,500; (b) (c) tuition fees £9,683; living costs £5,500; (d) tuition fees £3,550-£3,860 for EU students; £9,683 for international students; (e) tuition fees £1,125 for EU students; £9,683 for international students.
Applications: (d) by 30 April to Drama Admissions Officer; contact drama.admissions@rwcmd.ac.uk for further information.

🎓 Scholarship
Study Domains: music and musicology.
Scholarships: Entrance Scholarship.
Duration: first year only; contact music.admissions@rwcmd.ac.uk for further details.
Value: £1,000.
Applications: see website: http://www.rwcmd.ac.uk/unique_experience/international_students.asp.

2422 Saint Stephen's House
16 Marston Street
OX4 1JX Oxford
Tel: +44-1865-247-874
Fax: +44-1865-794-338
Web: http://www.ststephenshouse.ac.uk
e-mail: jeremy.sheehy@ox.ac.uk

📖 Undergraduate, Graduate Programmes
Study Domains: theology, religion.
Programmes: Bachelor's, Master's degrees in theology.
Duration: variable; courses begin in September.

2423 Scottish College of Textiles
Netherdale
T01 3HF Galashiels, Selkirkshire
Tel: +44-1896-753-351
Fax: +44-1896-758-965
Web: http://www.hw.ac.uk/sbc/SOTWeb/index.html

📖 Degree Programmes in Textile Design
Study Domains: accounting, administration, chemistry, computer science, design, management, marketing, sciences, textile industry.
Programmes: Degree programmes in textile design and marketing.
Open to: candidates of all nationalities meeting academic, financial and linguistic requirements.
Applications: to the Admissions Office at the above address.

2424 Sheffield Hallam University [SHU]
International Office
Room 5130, Level 1
Surrey Building
City Campus, Pond Street
S1 1WB Sheffield
Tel: +44-114-225-3880
Fax: +44-114-225-4768
Web: http://www.shu.ac.uk
e-mail: international@shu.ac.uk

📖 Undergraduate and Graduate Programmes
Study Domains: all major fields.
Programmes: undergraduate and graduate programmes in all major fields.
Open to: candidates of all nationalities meeting academic, financial and linguistic requirements.
Applications: to the above address.

2425 South Bank University [SBU]
103 Borough Road
SE1 0AA London
Tel: +44-207-8157-815
Web: http://www.sbu.ac.uk

📖 Undergraduate, Graduate Programmes
Study Domains: accounting, administration, architecture, building industry, business, business administration, civil engineering, development studies, electricity and electronics, engineering, English, European studies, food, food industry, industrial design, international business, international studies, law, management, marketing, mechanical engineering, public relations, publishing, radiology, telecommunications, tourism, hotel and catering management, urbanism.
Programmes: Bachelor's, Master's degrees and Postgraduate Diplomas in all major fields.

2426 Staffordshire University
The International Office
College Road
ST4 2DE Stoke on Trent
Tel: +44-1782-292-718
Fax: +44-1782-292-796
Web: http://www.staffs.ac.uk

📖 Undergraduate and Graduate Programmes
Study Domains: all major fields.
Programmes: Undergraduate and graduate programmes in all major fields.
Open to: suitably qualified candidates of all nationalities.

All students must show sufficient command of spoken and written English to meet the demands of the course (IELTS 6.0 or TOEFL 550 minimum); support services and facilities available to assist international students.
Fees: standard undergraduate overseas tuition fee package £6,700, standard postgraduate overseas tuition fee package £7,200.
Financial assistance: scholarships are available for law, social sciences and arts (reduction in fees); details on application.
Applications: to the above address.

2427 Stranmillis University College
Stranmillis Road
BT9 5DY Belfast
Tel: +44-28-9038-1271
Fax: +44-28-9066-4423
Web: http://www.stran.ac.uk

Undergraduate Studies
Study Domains: arts, early childhood education, teacher education.
Programmes: Bachelor's degrees in teacher education, health and leisure studies.

2428 The Surrey Institute of Art & Design, University College
Falkner Road
GU9 7 Farnham
Tel: +44-1252-722-441
Fax: +44-1252-892-624
Web: http://www.surrart.ac.uk
e-mail: registry@surrart.ac.uk

MA Bursary
Study Domains: fine arts.
Duration: 1 academic year.
Value: tuition waiver: £2,940.
Applications: by 31 July to Registry Services at above address; contact: registry@surrart.ac.uk.

2429 Trinity College of Music
King Charles Court
Old Royal Naval College
SE10 9JF Greenwich, London
Tel: +44-20-8305-3888
Fax: +44-20-8305-3999
Web: http://www.trinitycollegeofmusiclondon.co.uk
e-mail: info@tcm.ac.uk

Undergraduate and Postgraduate Programmes in Music Studies
Study Domains: music and musicology.
Programmes: (a) programme of studies leading to: B.Mus. (Hons.); Performance: M.Mus. Performance; Postgraduate Diploma; Postgraduate Advanced Diploma; (b) non-degree programmes: individualized programmes of study: foundation programme (pre-undergraduate level); professional development courses (musical theatre writing programme).
Open to: students of all nationalities, based on live auditions and qualifying entrance and language examinations.
Duration: from 1 to 4 years according to programme.
Fees: tuition fees for European Union students: undergraduates: £1,100; full-time postgraduates: £4,350; part-time postgraduates: £2,450; for overseas students: full-time programmes: £10,000; part-time postgraduates: £5,500. Examination fees: write to Admissions officer for further information.
Financial assistance: some scholarships provided for postgraduate study based on merit. All postgraduate students are automatically considered. Hardship grant/loan possible.

2430 University College Chester
Parkgate Road
CH1 4BJ Chester
Tel: +44-1244-375-444
Fax: +44-1244-392-820
Web: http://www.chester.ac.uk
e-mail: international@chester.ac.uk

International Students' Bursaries
Study Domains: all major fields.
Open to: all full-fee paying international students enrolled at university..
Duration: maximum 3 years; renewable once.
Value: tuition waiver: 1,000£.
Applications: 31 July; dates may vary from year to year; see website for full details: www.chester.ac.uk/international.

2431 University College London [UCL]
Gower Street
WC1E 6BT London
Tel: +44-20-7679-2000
Web: http://www.ucl.ac.uk

Undergraduate and Graduate Programmes
Study Domains: arts, chemistry, laboratory techniques, metallurgy, museology and museography, physical education, summer programmes, visual arts, vocational training.
Programmes: Undergraduate and graduate programmes in all major fields.
Open to: nationals of any country; good knowledge of English essential.
Applications: admission to undergraduate degree programmes at UCL should be submitted through UCAS (the Universities and Colleges Admissions Service) and not directly to UCL.

Undergraduate, Graduate Programmes / Architectural Studies
Study Domains: architecture, building industry, computer science, design, development studies, engineering, interior design, management, urbanism, vocational training.
Programmes: Undergraduate and postgraduate courses in architecture, construction management, environmental design, development planning and building; B.Sc., Master's, M.Phil., Ph.D. degrees as well as Diploma courses and Short Courses available.
Open to: applicants of all nationalities, a high level of competence in both spoken and written English is required.
Duration: B.Sc., 3 years full-time; postgraduate courses 1 to 2 years full-time (although may be available on a part-time basis); full and part-time short courses and diploma courses also offered.
Fees: enquire with the Undergraduate and Postgraduate Clerk for updated fee information.
Financial assistance: overseas students should contact a local office of the British Council for information on possible scholarships; University College London also offers some scholarships for overseas students.
Applications: by 1 March in the year of intended study, at the above address.

Ramsay Memorial Fellowships / Chemical Research
Study Domains: chemistry, research.
Scholarships: Ramsay Memorial Fellowships for chemical research.
Open to: nationals of Commonwealth countries who have graduated with distinction in chemistry from any university in a Commonwealth country; in exceptional cases the Trustees may award the fellowship to a candidate with academic distinction obtained in a country outside the Commonwealth; upper age limit 35; recipient will be expected to have held a Ph.D. for at least 1 year and to be capable of initiating a programme of original research.
Place of study: at a university, university college or other place of higher education in the United Kingdom or (exceptionally) elsewhere.
Duration: 2 years.
Value: stipend normally in step with lower part of lecturer scale for British universities, depending on qualifications and experience, with one increment for the second year and an expenses grant of £100 per year; superannuation on Universities' Superannuation Scheme (USS) or similar basis may be arranged; under this, the Fellow contributes 6.35% of his salary and the Trustees meet the employer's contribution.
Applications: by 15 November, to the Joint Honorary Secretaries, at the above address.

2432 University College Northampton [UCN]

Park Campus, Boughton Green Road
NN2 7AL Northampton
Tel: +44-1604-735500
Fax: +44-1604-710703
Web: http://www.northampton.ac.uk
e-mail: international@northampton.ac.uk

📖 Undergraduate, Graduate, Postgraduate Programmes

Study Domains: administration, agriculture, applied arts, art history, arts, biology, building industry, business, business administration, design, education, engineering, European studies, fine arts, forestry, graphic arts, health and hygiene, industrial design, languages, liberal arts, management, mathematics, mechanical engineering, social work, teacher education, tourism, hotel and catering management.
Programmes: Bachelor's, Master's, Ph.D. degrees and Higher National Diplomas (HND) in all major fields.
Open to: applicants meeting academic requirements.
Fees: variable; living costs £100 per week.
Applications: by August; contact sheila.jackson@northampton.ac.uk for further details.

🎓 Scholarship

Study Domains: all major fields.
Scholarships: UCN International Student Scholarship.
Open to: awarded on academic merit.
Value: up to 30% of tuition fees per year.
Applications: by end August; contact sheila.jackson@northampton.ac.uk for further information.

2433 University College of Wales

The International Liaison Officer
Development and External Affairs Office
9 Laura Place
SY23 2AX Aberystwyth
Tel: +44-1970-622-366
Fax: +44-1970-622-063
Web: http://www.aber.ac.uk
e-mail: sxl@aber.ac.uk

📖 Undergraduate and Graduate Programmes

Study Domains: all major fields, information science, law.
Programmes: Undergraduate and graduate programmes in all major fields; distance education programmes in information science and environmental law.
Fees: undergraduate students classified as overseas students in 2001-2002: Arts £7,000, Science £9,276, Joint Arts + Science courses £8,138.
Applications: through UCAS.

2434 University College Winchester

Sparkford Road
SO22 Winchester
Tel: +44-1962-841-515
Fax: +44-1962-879-033
Web: http://www.winchester.ac.uk

🎓 Winton Bursary

Study Domains: all major fields.
Open to: non-European Union candidates.
Duration: 1 academic year; renewable.
Value: tuition waiver: £1,000.
Applications: by 14 June to International Admissions at above address; contact: clare.mullins@whac.ac.uk.

2435 University of Aberdeen

King's College
AB9 1FX Aberdeen
Tel: +44-12-2427-2090
Fax: +44-12-2427-2576
Web: http://www.abdn.ac.uk/sras
e-mail: sras@abdn.ac.uk

📖 Undergraduate, Graduate and Postgraduate Studies

Study Domains: all major fields.
Programmes: Undergraduate, graduate and postgraduate studies in all major fields.
Financial assistance: some scholarships may be available from various university departments. See website http://www.abdn.ac.uk/sras/international/funding.shtml for further information.

2436 University of Abertay Dundee

Bell Street
DD1 1HG Dundee
Tel: +44-13-8230-8080
Fax: +44-13-8230-8081
Web: http://www.abertay.ac.uk
e-mail: iro@abertay.ac.uk

📖 Undergraduate and Graduate Programmes

Study Domains: administration, biology, building industry, business, civil engineering, communication, computer science, criminology, cultural studies, ecology, environment, electricity and electronics, food, genetics, home economics, international law, law, management, marketing, metallurgy, recreation and leisure, social sciences, sociology, tourism, hotel and catering management.
Programmes: Bachelor's, Master's and Doctor's degrees in a range of areas, including business, computing sciences, engineering and social sciences.
Open to: students of all nationalities with suitable qualifications in addition to English language proficiency.

🎓 Overseas Student Scholarships

Study Domains: all major fields.
Scholarships: Overseas Student Scholarships in various fields of study.
Open to: students from China, India, Pakistan, Malaysia, South Africa and North America who apply for courses at the University of Abertay Dundee.
Value: £1,000 towards tuition fees per year of course.
Applications: by 30 June to the International Recruitment Office.

2437 University of Birmingham [UOB]

The International Office
B15 2TT Edgbaston, Birmingham
Tel: +44-121-414-3694/ 7167
Fax: +44-121-414-3850
Web: http://www.international.bham.ac.uk
e-mail: international-scholarships@bham.ac.uk

📖 Undergraduate, Graduate Programmes

Study Domains: all major fields.
Programmes: Bachelor's, Master's degrees in all major fields.
Open to: candidates of all nationalities meeting academic, financial and linguistic requirements.
Financial assistance: some financial assistance available; see www.marketing.bham.ac.uk/international/scholarships.htm.
Applications: as early as possible, to the Admissions Office, at the above address.

🎓 Financial Aid Awards

Study Domains: humanities and arts, sciences, social sciences.
Scholarships: (a) International Office Postgraduate Taught Master's Scholarship for International Students; (b) Queen Elizabeth II Scholarships; (c) International Foundation Programme (IFP) Scholarships for International Students; (d) Hong Kong Postgraduate Scholarships; (e) International Office Undergraduate Scholarship for International Students.
Open to: a) candidates from Canada, Chile, Ghana, Indonesia, India, Iran, Japan, Jordan, Kenya, Republic of Korea, Mexico, Nigeria, Philippines, Russian Federation, Taiwan (China), Thailand, Turkey, USA, Vietnam; (b) graduates of the Universitas 21 community (see website); (c) students outside the European Union, on the Social Science, Humanities and Arts Foundation Programme (one award only) and to students on the Science Foundation Programme (one award only); (d) candidates from Hong Kong (two awards); (e) candidates from India, Mauritius, Sri Lanka, Maldives, Singapore, Vietnam, Hong Kong (China), West Africa.
Other conditions: students in all programmes should be

classified as 'overseas student' for fee purposes or be able to fund the remaining costs of studies from other sources; (a) be accepted to a place to study on a taught Master's degree programme; (b) be in final year of a Bachelor's programme at a partner Universitas 21 or have graduated from such an institution within the last five years; (d) have resided in Hong Kong for seven years prior to application; be holders of a Hon Kong tertiary education degree by admissions date; provide satisfactory evidence of English language written and spoken proficiency; no previous study period in the United Kingdom.
Duration: (a), (b), (d) 1 year; (c), (e) up to 3 years; not renewable.
Value: (a), (b), (d) £5,000; (c) £8,300 for social sciences, humanities, arts foundation award; £10,700 for science award; annually; (e) £3,000.
Applications: (a), (b), (c) 31 May; (b), (d) 30 April.

2438 University of Bradford
International Office
BD7 1DP Bradford, West Yorkshire
Tel: +44-1274-235-954 / 233-080
Fax: +44-1274-235-953
Web: http://www.brad.ac.uk/international
e-mail: international-office@bradford.ac.uk

📖 Undergraduate and Graduate Programmes
Study Domains: all major fields.
Programmes: Undergraduate and graduate programmes in all major fields.
Description: courses of study at following schools: School of Archaeological and Environmental Sciences; School of Engineering, Design and Technology; School of Health Studies; School of Informatics; School of Life Sciences; School of Lifelong Education and Development - includes distance studies for part-time undergraduate opportunities; School of Management; School of Social and International Studies.
Open to: candidates meeting academic, financial and linguistic requirements.
Fees: estimated total cost of a year's study, including tuition fees approximately £15,000.
Financial assistance: up to 20 scholarships are offered on a competitive basis to self-financing international students from outside the European Union; approximately half of the tuition fee of most courses (less than half the fee of the MBA). Application forms will be issued automatically to candidates who have firmly accepted an offer of a place at Bradford.
Applications: to the Director, International Office at the above address.

2439 University of Brighton
Mithras House
Lewes Road
BN2 4AT Brighton
Tel: +44-127-360-0900
Web: http://www.brighton.ac.uk
e-mail: intrel@brighton.ac.uk

🏆 International Scholarship
Study Domains: all major fields.
Open to: all overseas students.
Value: tuition waiver of £3,000.
Applications: 30 June.

2440 University of Bristol
Senate House
BS8 1TH Bristol
Tel: +44-117-928-7678
Fax: +44-117-925-1424
Web: http://www.bris.ac.uk
e-mail: orlo@bris.ac.uk

📖 Undergraduate, Graduate Programmes
Study Domains: all major fields, English, summer programmes.
Programmes: (a) postgraduate certificate in: education (PGCE); (b) Master's in: education; counselling; information and library management; education, technology and society; advanced diploma in education; (c) Ph.D. programmes.
Open to: (a) non-native speakers of English who have graduated from a secondary/high school; achieved an IECTS score of 4.0/4.5 (TOEFL 420/110); able to provide sufficient financial guarantee for the duration of the programme; (b) holders of honours degree from U.K. university or equivalent; (c) holders of a master's degree from U.K. university or equivalent.
Duration: (a) 1 academic year; (b) 1 academic year; (c) 3 to 5 years depending on programme.
Fees: (a) £6,650; (b) and (c) consult university for fees.
Applications: http://www.bris.ac.uk/Depts/LangCent.

🏆 Postgraduate Research Scholarships
Study Domains: all major fields.
Scholarships: (a) Postgraduate Research Scholarships (offered as funds permit); (b) various individual funds: consult website.
Subjects: any offered at the University.
Open to: graduates, men or women, of any university or degree-awarding body, holding a good first degree in the appropriate field.
Duration: (a) normally 3 years.
Value: (a) maintenance award equivalent to the basic rate paid by United Kingdom Research Councils, plus home tuition fees.
Applications: by 1 May, to the appropriate Faculty Office.

2441 University of Buckingham
Hunter Street
MK18 1EG Buckingham
Tel: +44-1280-822-245
Fax: +44-1280-814-080
Web: http://www.buck.ac.uk
e-mail: info@buckingham.ac.uk

📖 Undergraduate, Graduate Programmes
Study Domains: all major fields.
Programmes: Undergraduate and postgraduate programmes.
Description: courses in accounting and financial management, business studies, international hotel management, business studies with tourism, economics, law, biological science, psychology, modern history, English literature, English language and literature for speakers of other languages, history of art and heritage management, politics, business studies, computer science.
Open to: suitably qualified international applicants.
Duration: 2 years for most courses.
Applications: through UCAS or directly to the address above; see http://www.buck.ac.uk/study/apply/index.html.

2442 University of Cambridge
CB2 1TN Cambridge
Tel: +44-1223-337-733
Web: http://www.cam.ac.uk

📖 Undergraduate, Graduate Programmes
Study Domains: all major fields.
Programmes: undergraduate and graduate programmes in all major fields and a limited number of distance programmes available.
Description: The University of Cambridge is made up of 31 Colleges. Most Colleges admit students in all subjects, with a few exceptions. The university offers a wide range of arts, social science, medicine, science and engineering disciplines; for full details consult www.cam.ac.uk/admissions.
Open to: anyone over the age of 18 wishing to engage in a period of study at university level and who meets academic, financial and linguistic requirements.
Duration: variable.
Applications: to the Cambridge Admissions Office (undergraduate) or the Board of Graduate Studies (postgraduate).

🏆 Cambridge Scholarships
Study Domains: all major fields.
Scholarships: Cambridge Scholarships; Gates Cambridge Trust; Commonwealth and Overseas Trusts.
Description: the university offers a number of scholarships and awards available for overseas students; see website: www.cam.ac.uk/admissions for further information.
Open to: candidates who have successfully gained a place at the university; additional criteria may apply to specific awards.

Value: variable; see website for full details.
Applications: variable, depending on the award; see website for full information.

2443 University of Dundee

The International Office
Admissions and Student Recruitment Service
DD1 4HN Nethergate, Dundee
Tel: +44-1382-348-111
Fax: +44-1382-345-500
Web: http://www.dundee.ac.uk/admissions/ug/interstu.htm
e-mail: international@dundee.ac.uk

Undergraduate, Graduate Programmes

Study Domains: all major fields.
Programmes: First degrees, Master's degrees, Doctor's degrees, diplomas in most subjects; distance education programmes.
Open to: students of all nationalities and ages; intensive English language course; pre-university English courses.
Applications: to International Student Office; for distance education: www.dundee.ac.uk/prospectus/distlearning.

Scholarships / Studentships

Study Domains: all major fields, applied sciences, arts, dentistry, ecology, environment, engineering, law, medicine, sciences, social sciences.
Scholarships: (a) University of Dundee Research Studentships; (b) Overseas Scholarships /Overseas Research Student Award.
Description: (a) medicine, dentistry, science, law, engineering and applied science, arts and social sciences (including education), environmental studies; (b) most postgraduate studies.
Open to: (a) nationals of all countries; candidates must hold first-class or upper second-class honours degree, or equivalent; (b) postgraduate overseas students from the United Kingdom and European Union; proficiency in English required (TOEFL score 580 or IELTS score 6.5).
Duration: (a) 1 year in first instance (renewable for up to a total of 3 years); (b) 1 to 3 years (renewable subject to good performance).
Value: (a) variable; (b) £1,400-£2,000 per year.
Applications: to the International Office at the above address.

2444 University of East Anglia [UEA]

International Office
NR4 7TJ Norwich, Norfolk
Tel: +44-1603-593-280
Fax: +44-1603-458-596
Web: http://www.uea.ac.uk/international
e-mail: intl.office@uea.ac.uk

Undergraduate, Graduate Programmes

Study Domains: all major fields.
Programmes: Undergraduate and graduate programmes in all major fields.
Open to: candidates of any country meeting academic, financial and linguistic requirements.
Applications: to above address.

International Scholarships

Study Domains: archaeology, history, research.
Scholarships: International Scholarships.
Open to: several scholarships offered through the University with varying eligibility criteria, depending on nationality, studies, etc. See website for full details.
Applications: to the International Office.

2445 University of East London [UEL]

Longbridge Road
RM8 2AS Dagenham, Essex
Tel: +44-20-8223-2805
Web: http://www.uel.ac.uk

Undergraduate, Graduate Programmes

Study Domains: all major fields.
Programmes: First degree, certificate diploma and postgraduate courses in all major fields.

Open to: candidates of any nationality, normally over 18 years of age with standard qualifications (European baccalaureate, British A-levels or equivalent).
Duration: 2, 3 and 4 years.
Applications: by the end of December in the year preceding the start of the course, to the Registrar; late applications will be accepted.

2446 University of Edinburgh

Old College South Bridge
EH8 9 Edinburgh
Tel: +44-131-650-1000
Fax: +44-131-650-2147
Web: http://www.ed.ac.uk
e-mail: international@ed.ac.uk

Undergraduate, Postgraduate Programmes

Study Domains: all major fields.
Programmes: Programmes of undergraduate and postgraduate study in arts, divinity, law, music, medicine, nursing, science and applied sciences, social sciences, veterinary studies.
Open to: suitably qualified candidates of all nationalities; facilities available for handicapped.
Duration: 3 or 4 years (undergraduate); 1, 2 or 3 years (postgraduate).
Fees: variable according to subject of study.
Financial assistance: some postgraduate research studentships available; for scholarship/bursary information consult www.scholarships.ed.ac.uk.
Applications: by 15 January to UCAS (undergraduate); by 31 March, to the International Office (postgraduate); for Medicine or Veterinary Medicine, between 1 September and 15 October.

2447 University of Essex

Wivenhoe Park
CO4 3SQ Colchester, Essex
Tel: +44-1206-873-333
Web: http://www.essex.ac.uk

Undergraduate and Graduate Programmes

Study Domains: all major fields.
Programmes: undergraduate and graduate programmes in all major fields.
Open to: candidates of all nationalities meeting academic, linguistic and financial requirements; TOEFL 540-600 PBT/200-250 CBT.
Applications: to the above address.

Graduate Studies Scholarships

Study Domains: all major fields.
Scholarships: (a) University of Essex Overseas Research Studentships; (b) University of Essex Postgraduate Scholarships.
Open to: (a) any student undertaking research for a higher degree at the University of Essex; TOEFL 540 or IELTS 6.0 required for non-native English speakers; (b) candidates of all nationalities.
Duration: (a) throughout period of full-time research for higher degree; (b) up to 3 academic years.
Value: (a) tuition fees at home/EU rate, and possibly a maintenance award in return for limited teaching duties; (b) variable from £2,000-£6,000 per year for fees or maintenance.
Applications: (a) by May, to relevant department of the University; (b) variable; contact the Graduate Admissions Office at gschool@essex.ac.uk see website for details.

2448 University of Exeter

Northcote House
The Queen's Drive
EX4 4QJ Exeter
Tel: +44-1392-263-405
Fax: +44-1392-263-039
Web: http://www.ex.ac.uk
e-mail: intoff@exeter.ac.uk

Undergraduate and Graduate Programmes

Study Domains: all major fields.
Programmes: Undergraduate and graduate programmes in all major fields.
Open to: candidates of all nationalities, meeting academic,

financial and linguistic requirements.
Fees: from £7,000 to £13,000 depending on programme chosen.
Applications: to International Office at above address.

Exeter International Scholarships

Study Domains: computer science, engineering, law, mathematics.
Scholarships: various scholarships for international students.
Open to: students pursuing studies in the School of Engineering and Computer Sciences and the School of Mathematics; the School of Law for students from Malaysia and Singapore.
Applications: see full details: http://www.ex.ac.uk/scholarships/intscholarships.htm.

2449 University of Glasgow

G12 8QQ Glasgow
Tel: +44-141-330-6150
Fax: +44-141-330-4045
Web: http://www.gla.ac.uk/sras/ug/international.html

Undergraduate and Graduate Programmes

Study Domains: all major fields.
Programmes: Diploma and degree courses available at undergraduate and postgraduate level in all fields of study;.
Open to: suitably qualified candidates of all nationalities.
Financial assistance: some financial assistance possible; contact International Office for information.
Applications: all undergraduate admissions are handled by the Universities and Colleges Admissions Service (UCAS). There is no means of direct application. Contact the Office for International Programmes, at the above address.

2450 University of Leeds

EC Stoner Building
LS2 9JT Leeds
Tel: +44-113-243-1751
Fax: +44-113-244-3923
Web: http://www.leeds.ac.uk
e-mail: enquiry@leeds.ac.uk

Undergraduate, Graduate Programmes

Study Domains: all major fields.
Programmes: undergraduate and graduate programmes in all major fields.
Open to: suitably qualified candidates.
Financial assistance: some awards available to overseas students.
Applications: to the International Office for all further information.

University Scholarships

Study Domains: all major fields.
Scholarships: The University has an extensive portfolio of scholarships which is available for both taught and research postgraduates. In addition, individual university departments offer scholarships of all kinds. Substantial numbers of scholarships funded by the United Kingdom research council are available for postgraduate study at Leeds for United Kingdom and E.U. students, as well as funding from charitable and commercial organizations, such as the Tetley and Lupton Scholarships and the Chevening Awards.
Applications: further information is available from the Scholarships Office, at the above address; email: scholarships@leeds.ac.uk; http://www.leeds.ac.uk/students/funding/international_students_grants.htm.

2451 University of Leicester

University Road
LE1 7 Leicester
Tel: +44-1162-522-522
Fax: +44-1162-522-200
Web: http://www.le.ac.uk
e-mail: admissions@le.ac.uk

Undergraduate, Graduate and Postgraduate Programmes

Study Domains: all major fields, genetics.
Programmes: Undergraduate, Master's and research programmes. Many postgraduate courses are offered by distance learning.
Open to: candidates of all nationalities meeting academic qualifications.

University Scholarship

Study Domains: all major fields.
Scholarships: University of Leicester Open Scholarships.
Open to: new international students who have applied to and been made an offer of a place on a full-time degree.
Duration: up to 3 years, depending on course.
Value: tuition waiver of £3,000.
Applications: by 30 April to International Office at the above address; international.office@le.ac.uk.

2452 University of Liverpool

L69 3BX Liverpool
Tel: +44-151-794-2000
Fax: +44-151-708-6502
Web: http://www.liv.ac.uk
e-mail: irro@liv.ac.uk

Undergraduate, Graduate, Postgraduate Programmes

Study Domains: all major fields, anatomy, archaeology, architecture, art history, aviation, aeronautics, business administration, classical studies, dentistry, education, engineering, European studies, international business, international law, languages, linguistics, medicine, nursing, pharmacy and pharmacology, sciences, sociology, surgery, telecommunications, veterinary sciences.
Programmes: Bachelor's, Master's, Ph.D. degrees in all major fields.
Open to: students with appropriate qualifications; IELTS 6.0 + required.
Duration: variable; courses begin in September.
Fees: tuition fees £7,500-£10,000 per year; living costs £5,000-£7,000.
Applications: contact n.pearson@liv.ac.uk for further information.

2453 University of London

Senate House
Malet Street
WC1E 7HU London
Tel: +44-20-7862-8000
Web: http://www.lon.ac.uk
e-mail: enquiries@eisa.lon.ac.uk

General Information

Study Domains: all major fields.
Programmes: the University of London, the United Kingdom's largest university, is a federation of Colleges and Institutes which together provide great choice of undergraduate and postgraduate degree programmes (both full and part-time), continuing professional development and advanced research. All programmes and courses offered can't be listed. Please address your enquiries about courses and applications for admission directly to the appropriate Colleges and Institutes indicated on the website.

Scholarships

Study Domains: architecture, classical studies.
Scholarships: Please refer to the website for scholarship information.

2454 University of London, Birkbeck College

Malet Street, Bloomsbury
WC1E 7HX London
Tel: +44-20-7631-6390
Fax: +44-20-7631-6270
Web: http://www.bbk.ac.uk
e-mail: admissions@bbk.ac.uk

Research Studentships

Study Domains: all major fields.
Description: A limited number of research studentships are offered across the range of subjects offered by Birkbeck College and available to support doctoral students.
Open to: students of all nationalities accepted for a

research degree at Birkbeck College.
Duration: 1 year; renewable.
Value: full or partial tuition fees and/or maintenance fees.
Applications: no formal deadline, but candidates are encouraged to apply well before the start of the academic year; contact the relevant school administrator; email: studentships@bbk.ac.uk; web: http://www.bbk.ac.uk/reg/studenships.html#college.

2455 University of London, School of Advanced Studies Institute of Historical Research

Senate House, Malet Street
WC1E 7HU London
Tel: +44-20-7862-8740
Fax: +44-20-7862-8745
Web: http://www.sas.ac.uk

History Fellowships

Study Domains: history.
Scholarships: (a) Royal Historical Society Fellowship; (b) Past and Present Postdoctoral Fellowship; (c) IHR Mellon Dissertation Fellowships; (d) IHR Mellon Pre-Dissertation Fellowships; (e) Economic History Society Fellowships.
Subjects: medieval, early modern, modern history; (c), (d) general humanities; (e) economic, social.
Open to: (a) candidates of all nationalities; students must have completed at least two full-time years of their doctoral programme; (b) all nationalities; (c), (d) all nationalities; doctoral students registered at a USA or Canadian university; (e) all nationalities; students should hold a degree at or from a UK university.
Other conditions: (b) PhD must be submitted by October of the academic year in which fellowship is held; it must also be the first paid postdoctoral award held by the candidate; (c) fellowship is to be used to study at British Archives as part of dissertation; (d) students wishing to examine the feasibility of their dissertation proposal in British Archives; (e) may be postgraduate or postdoctoral in economic/social history.
Duration: (a), (b), (c), (e): 1 year, non-renewable; (d) 2 months.
Value: maintenance: (a) £10,000; (b) £16,000; (c) US$20,000; (d) US$3,000; (e) £12,000.
Applications: generally by: (a) 1 March; (b) 15 April; (c), (d) 17 January; 1 April; dates change yearly, check website.

2456 University of London, School of Pharmacy

29-39 Brunswick Square
WC1N 1AX London
Tel: +44-20-7753-5800
Fax: +44-20-7278-0622
Web: http://www.ulsop.ac.uk
e-mail: registry@ulsop.ac.uk

University Scholarships

Study Domains: pharmacy and pharmacology.
Scholarships: (a) Commonwealth Shared Scholarship Scheme; (b) Overseas Research Student Awards Scheme (ORSAS).
Open to: (a) nationals of a developing Commonwealth country; must not have lived or undertaken studies lasting one year or more in a developed country; (b) non-EU students with first-class honours degree in a related subject or equivalent.
Duration: (a) 1 year only; (b) 3 years, subject to satisfactory progress.
Value: (a) full tuition, living expenses and return airfare; (b) difference between home and overseas rate of tuition fees.
Applications: (a) May; (b) January; to Department for International Development, School of Pharmacy; see website for full details and contacts.

2457 University of London, Warburg Institute

Woburn Square
WC1H 0AB London
Tel: +44-20-7862-8949
Fax: +44-20-7862-8955
Web: http://www.sas.ac.uk/warburg
e-mail: warburg@sas.ac.uk

Doctoral and Postdoctoral Fellowships

Study Domains: European studies, history, humanities and arts, literature and civilization, philosophy.
Open to: European scholars.
Age limit Min: under 35 years of age.
Academic requirements: candidates must have completed at least 1 year's research on doctoral dissertation or have a doctoral degree.
Place of study: at the Warburg Institute.
Duration: 2 to 4 months.
Value: living expenses: £1,850-£3,500 (depending on length of stay).
Applications: 1 December, to the above address; information on the fellowship programme is published in October annually.

2458 University of Luton

Park Square
LU1 3 Luton
Tel: +44-1582-734-111
Fax: +44-1582-743-400
Web: http://www.luton.ac.uk
e-mail: enquiries@luton.ac.uk

International Scholarship

Study Domains: all major fields.
Scholarships: undergraduate, postgraduate and sub-degree programmes.
Open to: candidates of all nationalities qualifying for university entry.
Age limit Min: 18 years.
Duration: from 1 to 3 years; renewable.
Value: variable; covers both tuition and living expenses.
Applications: by 31 July; application form may be downloaded from website; contact Scholarships, External Affairs at above address for further information.

2459 University of Manchester

The International Office
Beyer Building, Oxford Road
M13 9PL Manchester
Tel: +44-161-275-2196
Fax: +44-161-275-2058
Web: http://www.man.ac.uk/international/
e-mail: international.unit@man.ac.uk

Undergraduate and Graduate Programmes

Study Domains: all major fields, development studies, education, English, management.
Programmes: undergraduate and graduate programmes; M.Ed. in Teaching of English to Speakers of Other Languages (TESOL); Master's programmes in management and development studies.
Held: TESOL at Centre for English Language Studies in Education; development studies at Institute for Development Policy and Management.
Applications: enquire at above address.

Graduate Overseas Studentships

Study Domains: all major fields, research.
Scholarships: Overseas Research Studentships (ORS); University Research Studentships.
Open to: to international candidates with a conditional offer on a graduate research programme, not a taught programme and hold, or expecting to receive, a first-class Honours degree, or equivalent.
Applications: application forms, returnable by the end of April, are available from the Research and Graduate Support Unit, University of Manchester, Christie Building, Manchester M13 9PL; http://www.man.ac.uk/study/pgrad/osawards.html.

2460 University of Newcastle upon Tyne

6 Kensington Terrace
NE1 7RU Newcastle upon Tyne
Tel: +44-191-222-8152
Fax: +44-191-222-5212
Web: http://www.ncl.ac.uk/international
e-mail: international.office@ncl.ac.uk

📖 Undergraduate and Graduate Programmes

Study Domains: agriculture, architecture, arts, biology, business, engineering, law, medicine, sciences, social sciences, urbanism.
Programmes: undergraduate and graduate programmes in several fields.
Open to: candidates from any country with a good first degree, or equivalent professional qualification, in architecture, building, building economics, civil engineering, technology, planning or other approved field associated with the built environment; some practical experience is desirable.
Duration: (a) 2 years; (b), (c), (d) and (g) 1 year; (e) and (f) 15 weeks (1 semester); (h) 3 years; (courses begin for (a) and (b) in October and February; for (c), (d) and (e) in October; (f) in February; (g) and (h) at any time throughout the year).
Financial assistance: British Council's local office will supply information on British Council awards for these courses; financial assistance is possible from foundations and international organizations.
Applications: throughout the year, to the Registrar.

🎓 Postgraduate Awards

Study Domains: all major fields.
Scholarships: (a) International Research Scholarships (IRS); (b) International Taught Postgraduate Scholarships (ITPS); (c) International Postgraduate Scholarships (IPS); (d) International Alumni Scholarships (IAS); (e) International Family Scholarships (IFS).
Open to: well-qualified graduate students.
Value: variable.
Applications: for further information: Scholarships Officer, 10 Kensington Terrace, Newcastle NE1 7RU, United Kingdom; international.office@ncl.ac.uk.

2461 University of Northumbria at Newcastle

Ellison Place
NE1 8ST Newcastle upon Tyne
Tel: +44-191-232-6002
Fax: +44-191-227-4017
Web: http://www.unn.ac.uk

📖 Undergraduate and Graduate Programmes

Study Domains: all major fields, applied arts, business, English, social sciences, summer programmes.
Programmes: undergraduate and graduate programmes in all major fields.
Open to: candidates of all nationalities, aged over 18 with secondary-school leaving certificate.
Applications: undergraduate applications, through UCAS. For further information on this process, contact the International Office; for most postgraduate taught courses, applications can be made direct using the University's Application Form which can be obtained from the International Office.

2462 University of Nottingham

International Office
University Park
NG7 2RD Nottingham
Tel: +44-115-951-5151
Fax: +44-115-951-3666
Web: http://www.nottingham.ac.uk

📖 Undergraduate, Graduate Programmes

Study Domains: all major fields, biology, development studies, research, urbanism.
Programmes: Undergraduate and graduate programmes in all major fields; environmental planning programme offered at Institute of Urban Planning; B.Sc. programme in biological sciences offered at School of Biological Sciences.
Open to: all nationalities with A-levels or equivalent school leaving certificates; proficiency in English is essential (550 TOEFL or 6.0 IELTS).
Financial assistance: financial assistance in the form of partial tuition waivers; studentships, etc. For further information contact the Scholarship Assistant at the above address; tel.: +44 115 846 6344; fax: +44 115 951 5155; email: scholarship-enquiries@nottingham.ac.uk; website: http://www.nottingham.ac.uk/international/prospective/schola

rships.

2463 University of Oxford

University Offices
Wellington Square
OX1 2JD Oxford
Tel: +44-1865-270-105
Fax: +44-1865-270-077
Web: http://www.admin.ox.ac.uk/io/admissions.shtml
e-mail: International.Office@admin.ox.ac.uk

📖 Undergraduate, Graduate Programmes

Study Domains: all major fields.
Programmes: undergraduate and graduate programmes in all major fields; distance education programmes http://www.online.ox.ac.uk.
Description: the University consists of 39 official Colleges and six Permanent Private Halls, each of which select its own undergraduate students, provide accommodation, meals, common rooms, libraries, sports and social facilities, and pastoral care for those students and are responsible for tutorial teaching and welfare of their students.
Open to: candidates of all nationalities meeting academic, financial and linguistic requirements.
Applications: closing date of 15 October for both Oxford and UCAS application forms; see http://www.admissions.ox.ac.uk/apply.

🎓 Mrs J H McKeown Scholarship

Study Domains: sciences.
Scholarships: Mrs J H McKeown Scholarship (Trinity College).
Open to: one undergraduate or postgraduate candidate at a time; liable for overseas fees (not resident or European Union) for a full course of study; preference given to candidates wishing to pursue courses in natural sciences.
Value: all university and college fees.
Applications: by 15 November; awards to be announced in January; forms to be requested from the Academic Administrator, Trinity College, Oxford OX1 3BH; email: admissions@trinity.ox.ac.uk. Candidates are required to have applied for a place at Oxford through UCAS and to have completed an Oxford Application Form, obtainable from the Oxford Colleges Admissions Office; website: http://www.ox.ac.uk/admissions.

🎓 Oxford Bursaries

Study Domains: all major fields.
Scholarships: (a) Clarendon Fund Bursaries; (b) Rhodes Scholarships.
Description: several scholarships offered yearly for international students, including specific schemes for Western Europe, Central/Eastern Europe, China (including Hong Kong), India, Japan, Pakistan, the countries of the Arab League, and developing countries; approximately 300 students yearly receive University scholarships or bursaries funded fully or in part by outside donors.
Subjects: unrestricted.
Open to: overseas graduates who have been accepted by the University of Oxford.
Place of study: Oxford.
Applications: enquire at the above address or by email: information.officer@admin.ox.ac.uk; http://www.ox.ac.uk/aboutoxford/links.shtml.

2464 University of Oxford, St Antony's College

OX2 6JF Oxford
Tel: +44-1865-274-496
Fax: +44-1865-274-526
Web: http://www.sant.ox.ac.uk

📖 Graduate Programmes

Study Domains: business administration, history, international relations, law, political science.
Programmes: Master's, Ph.D. degrees in international relations, economics, politics and history of Europe, Russia and the former Soviet states, the Middle East, Africa, Japan, China, South and South East Asia and Latin America.

☞Scholarship

Study Domains: anthropology, economy, history, international relations, political science, sociology.
Scholarships: Overseas Scholarships.
Open to: overseas graduates accepted by University of Oxford and Saint Antony's College to read for a higher degree in any subjects in which the college specializes.
Duration: 2 to 3 years.
Applications: variable; contact Graduate Admissions Office at the above address; email polly.friedhoff@st-antonys.oxford.ac.uk; see website for further information.

2465 University of Oxford, Trinity College

Oxford OX1 3BH
Tel: +44-1865-279-881
Fax: +44-1865-279-911
Web: http://www.trinity.ox.ac.uk/
e-mail: admissions@trinity.ox.ac.uk

☞Mrs J H McKeown Scholarship

Study Domains: earth science, ecology, environment, sciences.
Scholarships: undergraduate, postgraduate scholarship for studies in natural sciences.
Open to: candidates of all nationalities, but preferably Canadian, who would be liable for overseas (not home/EU) fees and wishing to pursue a full course of study leading to an undergraduate degree in the natural sciences.
Nationality: preferably Canadian.
Value: covers all University and College fees.
Applications: by 15 November 2003 on forms obtainable from the Academic Administrator, at the above address; email: admissions@trinity.ox.ac.uk. Candidates are required to have applied for a place at Oxford through UCAS and to have completed an Oxford Application Form, obtainable from the Oxford Colleges Admissions Office; website: http://www.ox.ac.uk/admissions.

2466 University of Plymouth

International Office
Drake Circus
PL4 8AA Plymouth
Tel: +44-1752-233-345
Fax: +44-1752-232-014
Web: http://www.plym.ac.uk
e-mail: international@plymouth.ac.uk

📖 Undergraduate and Graduate Programmes

Study Domains: all major fields.
Programmes: Programmes of study leading to undergraduate and postgraduate degrees as well as the Higher National Diploma (HND) and research programmes in all major fields.
Open to: candidates of any nationality with suitable qualifications and command of English.
Financial assistance: some financial assistance available for graduate students in the form of Overseas Research Student (ORS) Award for tuition reduction; contact the International Office for further information.
Applications: undergraduate students through UCAS; enquiries line: +44 1242 227788; website: http://www.ucas.ac.uk; graduate students to the Registrar at the above address.

2467 University of Reading

Whiteknights Park
PO Box 217
RG6 6AA Reading
Tel: +44-118-987-5123
Fax: +44-118-931-4404
Web: http://www.reading.ac.uk

📖 Undergraduate and Graduate Programmes

Study Domains: all major fields, agriculture, European studies, international studies.
Programmes: (a) Undergraduate and graduate programmes in all major fields; (b) M.A. courses in international studies offered by the Graduate School of European and International Studies; (c) Master's programmes in agricultural extension and rural development offered by the Agricultural Extension and Rural Development Department (AERDD).
Description: (b) courses include European studies; International studies; International security studies; international relations; Euro-Mediterranean studies; (c) courses include education and training for agricultural and rural development; participatory forest management and extension; rural social development; television/video for development.
Open to: (a) candidates of any nationality and age, meeting academic, financial and linguistic criteria; (b) possessing a good second-class Bachelor's degree or equivalent; (c) specialists, professionals, planners, managers in respective fields.
Duration: (b) 9 months (12 months for courses with research training); (c) 12 months (3 university terms), courses start in October.
Financial assistance: available especially for postgraduate studies; see http://www.rdg.ac.uk/Studentships.
Applications: (a) made through Universities and Colleges Admissions Service (UCAS) for direct entry to undergraduate (first degree) courses http://www.rdg.ac.uk/International/undergraduate.htm; graduate students: directly to the University, preferably before 1 June for entry to courses commencing in October, together with two confidential academic references and a certified academic transcript; http://www.rdg.ac.uk/International/master_courses.htm.

2468 University of Southampton School of Research and Graduate Studies

Highfield
SO17 1BJ Southampton
Tel: +44-23-8059-4741
Fax: +44-23-8059-3037
Web: http://www.soton.ac.uk
e-mail: prospeng@soton.ac.uk

📖 Undergraduate, Graduate and Postgraduate Programmes

Study Domains: all major fields.
Programmes: Bachelor's, Master's, Ph.D. and New Route Ph.D. Programmes.
Description: New Route Ph.D. is a 4-year programme consisting of 2 years of instruction and 2 years of research.
Open to: all nationalities meeting academic standards: language proficiency required for studies in most fields approximately IELTS 6.5/TOEFL 600 (computer based TOEFL 250).
Duration: varies according to studies; courses begin in October.
Applications: by 30 June for undergraduates; no deadline for postgraduates, however, early applications are advisable.

☞University Scholarships

Study Domains: computer science, electricity and electronics, engineering, management, mathematics, research, sciences.
Scholarships: (a) Undergraduate scholarships; (b) Graduate scholarships.
Open to: international students; contact respective faculties for further information: undergraduate studies: Faculty of Law (undergrad.law@soton.ac.uk); Faculty of Mathematical Studies (enquiry@maths.soton.ac.uk); Faculty of Science: (gwm1@soton.ac.uk); graduate studies: Faculty of Engineering and Applied Science: (shw2@soton.ac.uk); School of Engineering Science: (P.A.W.@soton.ac.uk); School of Management: (mgtmail2@soton.ac.uk); Optoelectronics Research Centre: (es@orc.soton.ac.uk). *Applications:* at above address or email addresses of each faculty.

2469 University of St Andrews
The International Office
Butts Wynd - St Andrews
KY16 9AJ Fife
Tel: +44-334-463-323
Fax: +44-1334-463-330
Web: http://www.st-and.ac.uk
e-mail: IntOff@st-andrews.ac.uk

📖 Undergraduate, Graduate Programmes

Study Domains: all major fields.
Programmes: undergraduate and graduate programmes in all major fields.
Open to: candidates of all nationalities meeting academic, financial and linguistic requirements.
Financial assistance: some financial assistance possible.
Applications: for most international undergraduate students through UCAS; for further information contact International Office at the above address or http://www.st-andrews.ac.uk/services/admissions/UGOSAA.htm.

2470 University of Strathclyde
Richmond Street
G1 1XQ Glasgow
Tel: +44-141-522-4400
Web: http://www.strath.ac.uk

📖 Undergraduate and Graduate Programmes

Study Domains: languages.
Programmes: (a) undergraduate and graduate programmes in all major fields; (b) programme in Celtic studies; (c) courses in prosthetics and orthotics offered by the National Centre for Training and Education in Prosthetics and Orthotics.
Open to: (a), (b) candidates of all nationalities meeting academic, financial and linguistic requirements; (c) undergraduate courses: all school leavers; postgraduate courses: graduates with a degree in prosthetics and orthotics or a related subject.
Held: (b) collaborative agreement with the University of Aberdeen and Trinity College, Dublin; (c) National Centre for Training and Education in Prosthetics and Orthotics; Curran Building; 131 St James's Road; Glasgow G4 OLS.
Applications: all applications for undergraduate study are handled via UCAS; contact the above address for further information; (c) for further information: contact-prosthetics@strath.ac.uk; website: http://www.strath.ac.uk/prosthetics; tel.: +44 141 552 4400; +44 141 552 1283.

🎓 Graduate Fellowships

Study Domains: all major fields, research.
Scholarships: (a) University Postgraduate Studentships; (b) British Gas/University of Strathclyde/Foreign and Commonwealth Office Scholarships; (c) Arts and Social Sciences Graduate Studentship.
Subjects: (a) any field; (b) engineering, applied sciences and business administration; (c) arts and social sciences.
Open to: (a) students from all countries holding a university degree, on recommendation of Head of Department in which they study; preference will be given to candidates undertaking research; (b) nationals of Malaysia, India, Pakistan, Indonesia, Bangladesh and Turkey, to study in the United Kingdom before beginning or resuming their careers in their own countries; (c) North American postgraduate students.
Duration: 1 year (may be renewable).
Value: (a) maintenance allowance of £4,125 per year; (b) covers placement, return travel to the United Kingdom, tuition fees, living expenses, allowances for books and pre-course. English language tuition if required; (c) £2,000.
Applications: (a) through Head of Department concerned; (b) by 31 January, on applications forms available from the Registry-General in December; (c) to above address.

2471 University of Sunderland
Centre for International Education
North Sands Business Centre
Liberty Way
SR6 0QA Sunderland
Tel: +44-191-515-2648
Fax: +44-191-515-2960
Web: http://my.sunderland.ac.uk/web/services/cie//ahome
e-mail: international@sunderland.ac.uk

📖 Undergraduate and Graduate Programmes

Study Domains: all major fields.
Programmes: Full-time postgraduate research and taught courses, full-time and sandwich first degree and BTEC HND courses, in all major fields.
Open to: candidates of all nationalities; undergraduate courses: aged 18 and over at the commencement of the course, with the appropriate entry qualifications; direct entry to the second or third year of the course is possible. English language tuition available; postgraduate and research courses are open to those holding a good degree; proficiency in English required (IELTS 6, TOEFL 560).
Held: University of Sunderland Schools of Arts, Design and Communications; Business; Computing and Information Systems; Education; Engineering and Advanced Technology; Environment; Health Sciences; and Social and International Studies.
Duration: full-time first degree, 3 years; sandwich first degree, 4 years; full-time BTEC HND, 2 years; sandwich BTEC HND, 3 years; full-time Master's degree, 1 or 2 years; Ph.D., 5 years.
Financial assistance: international scholarship awards.
Applications: for all first degree (excluding PGCE courses) and BTEC HNC/D courses: to UCAS, P.O. Box 67, Cheltenham, Glos., GL50 3AP; for PGCE courses: GTTR, P.O. Box 239, Cheltenham, Glos., GL50 3SL; for Social Work: directly to SWAS; Research courses contact Research Section, University of Sunderland; for overseas enquiries: Unit 4C, Technology Park, Chester Road, Sunderland SR2 7PS; students are encouraged to apply as early as possible.

🎓 Scholarships

Study Domains: all major fields, education, sciences.
Scholarships: (a) Partial Tuition Fee Scholarships; (b) Yvonne Steward-Smith Scholarship; (c) Mick Higgins Scholarship; (d) Full Country Scholarship.
Description: (a) undergraduate studies; (b) Master's degree in education; (c) Master's degree in scientific subjects; (d) Master's degree only.
Duration: (a) 3 academic years; (b), (c), (d), 1 year.
Value: (a) partial tuition waiver: £1,500; (b), (c) £7,900-£8,100; (d) £7,900-£9,400.
Applications: (b), (c) (d) by 31 May; to Corporate and Recruitment Services.

2472 University of Surrey
GU2 7XH Guildford, Surrey
Tel: +44-1483-689-305
Fax: +44-1483-689-525
Web: http://www.surrey.ac.uk
e-mail: international@surrey.ac.uk

📖 Postgraduate Programmes

Study Domains: aerospace, applied sciences, audio-visual media, biochemistry, business, business administration, chemical engineering, chemistry, civil engineering, communication, computer science, criminology, cultural studies, dietetics, distance education, economic and commercial sciences, electricity and electronics, energy, engineering, European studies, finance, food industry, French, German, human sciences, humanities and arts, information science, international business, international studies, interpretation and translation, languages, linguistics, management, management of human resources, marketing, mathematics, mechanical engineering, microbiology, music and musicology, nursing, nutrition, performing arts, pharmacy and pharmacology, physics, psychology, research, Russian, sciences, sociology, space, statistics, summer programmes, Swedish, telecommunications, tourism, hotel and catering management, trade.
Programmes: postgraduate studies; taught and research.

Open to: students meeting academic requirements: TOEFL score 550 on paper-based test or 213 on computer-based test or IELTS 6.0 required; course requirements may vary, contact the university for further details.
Nationality: candidates of all nationalities.
Academic requirements: variable; applicants should normally have a good honours degree or equivalent in a related subject. Contact the University for specific course details.
Duration: postgraduate taught programmes: 1 year: postgraduate research programmes: minimum 3 years; courses begin in September.
Fees: tuition: £8,000-£13,950 per year; living costs approximately £7,000 per year.
Applications: by 1 July; contact international@surrey.ac.uk for further details.

Undergraduate Programmes

Study Domains: aerospace, applied sciences, audio-visual media, biochemistry, biology, biophysics, business, chemical engineering, chemistry, civil engineering, communication, computer science, cultural studies, dietetics, distance education, economic and commercial sciences, electricity and electronics, engineering, European studies, food, food industry, French, German, human sciences, humanities and arts, international studies, interpretation and translation, languages, law, management, mathematics, mechanical engineering, medicine, microbiology, music and musicology, nursing, nutrition, performing arts, physics, political science, psychology, Russian, sciences, social sciences, sociology, statistics, summer programmes, Swedish, technology, telecommunications, tourism, hotel and catering management.
Description: Bachelors and Foundation Course (Science and Engineering only).
Open to: students of all nationalities meeting academic requirements; TOEFL score 550, paper-based test or 213 computer-based test or IELTS 6.0 required. Course requirements may vary, contact the university for further details.
Nationality: candidates of all nationalities.
Academic requirements: variable for each course; contact the University for full details.
Duration: undergraduate: 3 - 4 years; courses begin in September.
Fees: tuition: £8,000-£10,500 per year; living costs approximately £5,000 per year.
Applications: through UCAS by 30 June; contact international@surrey.ac.uk for full details.

2473　University of Sussex

The International Office
Guildford
GU2 7XH Surrey
Tel: +44-1483-689-005
Fax: +44-1483-689-525
Web: http://www.surrey.ac.uk/international
e-mail: International@surrey.ac.uk

Undergraduate, Graduate Programmes

Study Domains: all major fields, African studies, development studies, food, gender studies.
Programmes: (a) undergraduate and graduate programmes in all major fields; (b) M.Phil. (Development Studies); (c) M.A. in Gender and Development: the course aims to equip students with the analytical skills needed to understand the interaction between gender and social and economic development and the practical skills required to participate effectively in policy-making and implementation.
Description: (b) course designed for those planning careers in economic and social development, as policy-makers, administrators, researchers or teachers; (c) the course aims to equip students with the analytical skills needed to understand the interaction between gender issues and social and economic development and the practical skills required to participate effectively in policy-making and implementation.
Open to: (b), (c) graduate students of any nationality with a good honours first degree and (a) preferably 2 or more years of work experience, in a developing country; (c) with relevant work experience, age preferably under 35.
Duration: (b) 2 years; (c) 1 year.
Financial assistance: various, including British Technical

Cooperation awards.
Applications: (a) for undergraduate studies: through UCAS; contact Admissions for further information or see website applications page; graduate studies: see website for further information or contact Admissions Office; (b) and (c) to the Admissions Office.

2474　University of Teesside

Borough Road
Middlesborough
TS1 3BA Cleveland
Web: http://www.tees.ac.uk
e-mail: international.office@tees.ac.uk

Undergraduate, Graduate Programmes

Study Domains: all major fields, business, design, sciences, social sciences.
Programmes: Higher National Diploma; Bachelor's degree; Master's degree; Ph.D. degree in the Schools of Business; Computing and Mathematics; Human Studies; Science and Technology as well as the Institute of Design.
Open to: candidates of any nationality meeting academic, financial and linguistic requirements.
Fees: normal international student tuition fees: £7,000 per annum for laboratory-based courses; £6,000 per annum for classroom-based courses.
Financial assistance: in the form of a £1,000 fee reduction.

2475　University of the West of England, Bristol [UWE]

Coldharbour Lane
BS16 1QY Bristol
Tel: +44-117-328-3333
Web: http://www.uwe.ac.uk
e-mail: law@uwe.ac.uk

International Scholarships

Study Domains: building industry, law, music and musicology, physical education.
Scholarships: (a) Undergraduate Scholarships; (b) Master's Scholarships; (c) Undergraduate Scholarships, Music; (d) Sports Scholarships.
Subjects: (a) law; (b) built environment; (c) music; (d) physical education.
Open to: (a), (b) candidates paying 'overseas fees'; based on academic merit and financial need; (c) great musical talent (instrumental or vocal) enrolled in undergraduate programmes of 3 or more years in duration; (d) students of IOC sports.
Nationality: candidates normally resident in Malaysia, Singapore or Hong Kong.
Duration: (a) 2 years maximum; non renewable; (b) 1 year, non renewable; (c), (d) duration of programme; non renewable.
Value: (a) tuition waiver of fees for up to 2 years; (b) up to £1,500 per year; (c) £300 per year; (d) up to £1,000 per year.
Applications: (a) 1 June before commencing studies; to the Faculty of Law at the above address; email: law@uwe.c.uk; (b) end June before commencing studies; to the PG Award Adviser; Faculty of the Built Environment at the above address; email: fbe.enry@uwe.ac.uk; (c) by mid-November after commencing studies; to Director of Music, Centre of Performing Arts, email: cpa@uwe.ac.uk; (d) to Recreation Centre; email: richard2.bennett@uwe.ac.uk.

2476　University of Wales Bangor

College Road
Bangor
LL57 2DE Gwynedd
Tel: +44-1248-382611
Fax: +22-1248-382015
Web: http://www.bangor.ac.uk/international/
e-mail: socrates@bangor.ac.uk

Undergraduate, Graduate, Postgraduate Programmes

Study Domains: agriculture, archaeology, business, business administration, chemical industry, community development, education, health and hygiene, horticulture, journalism, laboratory techniques, languages, nursing, radiology, recreation and leisure, rural development, sciences, social work, sociology, teacher education, theology, religion,

tourism, hotel and catering management.
Programmes: Bachelor's, Master's, Ph.D. degrees in education, languages, theology, business administration, science, agriculture, nursing.

☜ Scholarship

Study Domains: all major fields.
Scholarships: Postgraduate Research Award.
Open to: graduates applying for Ph.D. and M.phil. research degrees only.
Value: £1,000 per year, renewable.
Applications: by 1 August.

2477 University of Wales Cardiff
International Division
PO Box 997
CF10 3ZN Cardiff
Tel: +44-29-2087-4432
Fax: +44-29-2087-4622
Web: http://www.cf.ac.uk/international
e-mail: international@cf.ac.uk

☐ Undergraduate and Postgraduate Courses

Study Domains: all major fields, demography and population studies, journalism, visual arts.
Programmes: (a) undergraduate and postgraduate courses in all major fields; (b) postgraduate diploma in film production studies; (c) postgraduate programmes in journalism studies; (d) postgraduate programmes in population and development and reproductive health and family planning management.
Open to: students of all nationalities meeting academic, linguistic and financial requirements.
Held: (b) Centre for Film Production Studies; (c) School of Journalism, Media and Cultural Studies; (d) Sir David Owen Population Centre.
Financial assistance: some scholarships are available to students who have been accepted into a scheme of study at the university.
Applications: undergraduate studies: to the Universities and Colleges Admissions Service, (UCAS); graduate studies: to the Admissions Office at the above address.

2478 University of Wales Swansea
International Office
Grove Building, Singleton Park
SA2 8PP Swansea
Tel: +44-1792-295-818
Fax: +44-1792-295-818
Web: http://www.swan.ac.uk/international
e-mail: international@swansea.ac.uk

☐ Undergraduate, Graduate Programmes

Study Domains: administration, development studies, management.
Programmes: (a) undergraduate and graduate programmes in all major fields; (b) postgraduate programmes in social development planning and management and health planning and development.
Open to: (a) candidates of all nationalities meeting academic, financial and linguistic requirements: (b) overseas candidates with experience in social development; graduates or those with capacity for postgraduate work and likely to occupy senior posts in administration, supervision or training.
Held: (b) at the Centre for Development Studies.
Duration: (b) 9 months to 1 year; courses begin in September.
Financial assistance: British Technical Cooperation and other international awards available; see website for further information;
http://www.swan.ac.uk/international/scholarships.htm.
Applications: undergraduate students: contact the International Office at the above address or see website: http://www.swan.ac.uk/international/applying.htm; graduate students: contact the Admissions Office: admissions@swansea.ac.uk.

2479 University of Warwick
CV4 7AL Coventry
Tel: +44-24-7652-3523
Fax: +44-24-7646-1606
Web: http://www.warwick.ac.uk
e-mail: int.office@warwick.ac.uk

☐ Undergraduate, Graduate, Postgraduate Programmes

Study Domains: all major fields, arts, economy, education, medicine, sciences.
Programmes: Bachelor's, Master's, Ph.D. degrees in arts, education, medicine, science, economics.
Financial assistance: financial assistance available; see http://www.warwick.ac.edu/study/funding.html for further information.

☜ International Office Scholarships

Study Domains: all major fields.
Scholarships: International Office Scholarships and Warwick Fellowships.
Duration: 1 academic year.
Applications: by 31 January; to International Office at the above address.

2480 University of Westminster
International Education Office
16 Little Titchfield Street
W1W 7UW London
Tel: +44-207-911-5769
Fax: +44-207-911-5132
Web: http://www.westminster.ac.uk
e-mail: international-office@wmin.ac.uk

☐ Undergraduate and Graduate Programmes

Study Domains: Arabic, Danish, Dutch, English, European studies, French, German, Greek, interpretation and translation, Italian.
Programmes: (a) undergraduate and graduate programmes in all major fields; (b) postgraduate programmes in conference interpretation and bilingual translation in various languages.
Open to: (a) candidates of all nationalities meeting academic, linguistic and financial requirements; (b) postgraduate students of any country, either bilingual (usually English/French), or with a mother tongue which is a working language of the United Nations or of the European Union, plus 2 passive languages.
Duration: variable.
Applications: undergraduate programmes: applications must be submitted through UCAS.

2481 University of York
The International Office
Stables Building
YO10 5DD York
Tel: +44-1904-433-534
Fax: +44-1904-434-268
Web: http://www.york.ac.uk
e-mail: international@york.ac.uk

☐ Undergraduate, Graduate Programmes

Study Domains: all major fields, architecture, building industry, urbanism.
Programmes: (a) Undergraduate and graduate programmes in all major fields; (b) M.A. in conservation studies: architectural, urban and landscape conservation; (c) M.A. directed programme in housing, planning and construction in developing countries (Third World studies in the built environment).
Open to: (a) candidates of all nationalities meeting academic, financial and linguistic requirements; (b) candidates with a professional qualification and minimum of 4 years appropriate experience; (c) candidates with professional qualification in architecture, planning, building or associated professions; proficiency in English essential.
Duration: variable.
Fees: undergraduate/graduate students: non-laboratory courses: £7,842; laboratory courses: £10,365; visiting students: £7,842.
Financial assistance: some financial assistance possible.
Applications: undergraduate applications must be made

through UCAS; graduate applications to Admissions Office at above address.

🎓 Overseas Student Scholarships

Study Domains: all major fields.
Scholarships: Overseas Student Scholarships.
Value: worth up to one third the value of the annual tuition fee: scholarship is awarded for the duration of the course.
Applications: contact the International Office at the above address.

2482   Warnborough University

Warnborough House,
8 Vernon Place
CT1 3WH Canterbury
Tel: +44-1227-762-107
Fax: +44-1227-762-108
Web: http://www.warnborough.ac.uk
e-mail: admissions@warnborough.ac.uk

📖 Undergraduate and Graduate Programmes

Study Domains: all major fields, business, classical studies, English, natural sciences, social sciences, summer programmes.
Programmes: undergraduate and graduate programmes; continuing education; diplomas; corporate training; distance education programmes,
http://www.warnborough.ac.uk/faculties/distance.htm.
Open to: candidates of all nationalities with a high school diploma or equivalent.
Financial assistance: assistance/scholarships available.
Applications: accepted all year; request forms from the Admissions Office.

2483   West Dean College

Academic Office
West Dean,
PO18 0QZ Chichester, West Sussex
Tel: +44-1243-818-219 / 811-301
Fax: +44-1243-811-343
Web: http://www.westdean.org.uk
e-mail: diplomas@westdean.org.uk

📖 Postgraduate Programmes in Conservation and Restoration

Study Domains: applied arts, art history, arts and crafts, decorative arts, museology and museography, music and musicology, visual arts.
Programmes: (a) Postgraduate Diploma in conservation and restoration of fine metalwork; (b) Postgraduate Diploma in tapestry weaving; (c) Postgraduate Diploma in restoration of antique clocks;
(d) Postgraduate Diploma in the restoration of antique furniture: (e) Postgraduate Diploma in the conservation of ceramics and related materials;(f) Postgraduate Diploma in the making of early stringed musical instruments.
Open to: all nationalities, aged over 18 years, with relevant qualifications and practical experience; a practical test and an interview may be required for some programmes.
Duration: 1 to 3 years; short non-degree courses available (in crafts, visual arts, music and gardening.).
Fees: variable; by course.
Financial assistance: limited number of scholarships are available (apprenticeships).
Applications: to the Academic Office at the above address; application forms may be downloaded at http://www.westdean.org.uk/restor/diploma/index.htm.

🎓 Edward James Foundation Scholarships

Study Domains: applied arts, applied sciences, art history, arts, arts and crafts, decorative arts, museology and museography, music and musicology.
Scholarships: Edward James Foundation Scholarships.
Open to: all nationalities, over 18 years of age who satisfy entry requirements and test for relevant courses at West Dean.
Duration: normally 1 term, may be renewable.
Value: sufficient to cover 1 term's fees and accommodation costs.
Applications: immediately following the offer of a place on a West Dean course, to the Principal's Office.

2484   Wimbledon School of Art

Merton Hall Road
Wimbledon
SW19 3QA London
Tel: +44-20-8408-5000
Fax: +44-20-8408-5050
Web: http://www.wimbledon.ac.uk/international/inter natframe.html

📖 Undergraduate, Graduate Programmes / Arts

Study Domains: design, fine arts, performing arts.
Programmes: (a) B.A. (Hons.) in theatre design, technical arts, costume, painting/fine art, sculpture; (b) M.A. in critical studies in visual art and theatre, interdisciplinary theoretical and historical studies, printmaking, site-specific sculpture, theatre design/scenography:.
Open to: (a) over 18 years old, with general school-leaving qualifications, foundation course and portfolio; (b) graduates in fine art or graduates with some theatre experience; a portfolio is necessary; English proficiency required; however classes are arranged, free of charge, for those needing to improve their language skills.
Academic requirements: undergraduate international students: on the basis of slides/photographs of work in lieu of original work; postgraduate international students: candidates for admission to all courses should support their application with slides or photographs of their work. Where appropriate, alternatives to a formal interview at the School will be employed, e.g. telephone interviews on receipt of work.
Duration: (b) 2 to 3 years; courses begin in October; (a) 1 to 3 years.
Fees: estimated expenses for students for 40 weeks: tuition fees (based on 2002/03): £7,750; average rent: £3,200; living costs: £3,400.
Applications: (a) and (b) by 31 March, to the Registrar.

2485   Winchester School of Art, Textile Conservation Centre University of Southampton

Apt. 22, Hampton Court Palace
KT8 9AU East Molesey, Surrey
Tel: +44-2380-596-718
Web: http://www.wsa.soton.ac.uk/ttccontent.htm
e-mail: artsrec@soton.ac.uk

📖 M.A. in Textile Conservation and Museum Studies

Study Domains: museology and museography, textile industry.
Programmes: M.A. in Textile Conservation; M.A. Museum Studies; M.A. in History of Textiles & Dress Culture, Collections & Communication (and is a career entry programme for those wishing to work in the museums/heritage sector).
Open to: applicants of any nationality holding a degree and with a chemistry GSCE level or equivalent.
Duration: 3 academic years.
Fees: approx. £7,950 per year.
Financial assistance: some bursaries may be available.
Applications: by 1 December in the year preceding proposed entrance, to the Head of Studies and Research, at the above address.

2486   YMCA George Williams College [YGWC]

The Registrar,
199 Freemasons Road
E16 3PY Canning Town
Tel: +44-171-540-4902
Fax: +44-171-511-4900
Web: http://www.ymca.ac.uk/apply

📖 Youth Work Programmes

Study Domains: community development, social work.
Programmes: Programme of courses in youth work, community development, education, leading to:
(a) Diploma of Higher Education; (b) B.A. (Hons.) Informal and Community Education; (c) B.A. (ordinary) Informal and Community Education.
Open to: candidates of any nationality over age of 18, with equivalent of 2 A-levels.

Duration: (a) 2 years full-time; (b) 3 years full-time; (c) 4 years part-time by distance learning; (courses begin in September).
Applications: to the Registrar at the above address.

United Republic of Tanzania

Academic year: September to July.
Organization of higher education system: Degrees conferred: Advanced diploma, Bachelor's degree; 3-4 years of full-time study, Master's degree; a further 18 months of study, Ph.D. degree: a further 3-6 years of study.
Monetary unit: Tanzanian shilling.
National student admission: Foreign students should have qualifications equivalent to the East African General Certificate of Education (GCE) with 2 Advanced (A) level and 5 Ordinary (O) level passes. Applications should be addressed to the Permanent Secretary, Ministry of Science Technology and Higher Education, PO Box 2645, Dar-es-Salaam, Tanzania.
Language: The language of instruction is English.
Immigration requirements: A visa and residence permit are necessary.
Estimated expenses for one academic year: tuition: T. shillings 1,628,000: books/supplies: T. shillings 140,000: housing: T. shillings 157,000.
Information services:
• The Higher Education Accreditation Council (HEAC).
Open and distance learning: Distance education is offered by the Open University of Tanzania which opened in 1993 in Dar es Salaam. It provides courses in law, science, arts, and education leading to Bachelor's, Master's and Ph.D. degrees.
Recognition of studies and qualification: The Higher Education Accreditation Council, PO Box 2645, Dar es Salaam; Tanzania; tel: +255-022-213-7585; fax: +255-022-212-9584; email: heac@intafrica.com; web: http://www.heac.go.tz.
Accommodation services: Student housing and cafeteria available at universities.

2487   Dar es Salaam Institute of Technology [DESTC]
PO Box 2958
Dar es Salaam
Tel: +255-22-215-0174
Fax: +255-22-215-2504
Web: http://www.dit.ac.tz
e-mail: info@dit.ac.tz

📖 Advanced Diploma in Engineering
Study Domains: civil engineering, electricity and electronics, mechanical engineering, telecommunications.
Programmes: Advanced diploma in engineering.
Open to: candidates of all nationalities, possessing an Ordinary or Advanced level certificate and proficient in English.
Duration: 3 years.
Fees: tuition: US$900.
Applications: by December, to the Principal.

2488   Eastern Africa Statistical Training Centre [EASTC]
PO Box 35103
Dar es Salaam
Tel: +255-51-410-052
Fax: +255-51-410-053
e-mail: eastc@ud.co.tz

📖 Certificate, Diploma Courses / Statistics
Study Domains: economy, mathematics, statistics.
Programmes: Certificate (middle level) and Diploma (intermediate level) courses in statistics; mathematics is taught as a tool for studying statistics and economics is taught as an area of application; statistical computing is taught as a tool for practising statistics.
Open to: applicants from English-speaking African countries with minimum O-level passes in mathematics and English.
Duration: 10 months; courses begin in October.

Fees: approximately US$7,000 for entire course (covers tuition, board and lodging, monthly stipend, field work and contribution to club expenses).
Applications: by August, to the Director, at the above address.

2489   Institute of Adult Education [IOAE]
PO Box 20679
Dar es Salaam
Tel: +255-22-215-0838
Fax: +255-22-215-0838
Web: http://distancelearning-tz.org/adultedu-tz/
e-mail: teww@afsat.com

📖 Certificate, Advanced Diplomas / Education of Adults
Study Domains: education.
Programmes: (a) Advanced diploma course in adult education: development studies, communication skills, history and philosophy of adult education, psychology of adult learning and teaching practice techniques, general management research, methodology, workers' education, public budgeting and management; (b) Certificate course in adult education: history of adult education, adult education methods, social psychology of adults, designing and organizing adult education programmes, communication skills and media, data collection, report writing and evaluation, political economy, teaching practice; (c) Ordinary Diploma in Adult Education.
Open to: candidates of UNESCO Member States: (a) holding a diploma in adult or general education; (b) who are primary school teachers and who have at least 3 years working experience in community development; teachers and administrators of adult education programmes in various organizations, government ministries, parastatals, community development workers, and to people engaged in such fields as rural development, social work, workers' education, agricultural extension service, health and nutrition.
Duration: (a) 3 years; courses begin in September; (b) 1 academic year; courses begin in July; (c) 2 years.
Fees: variable: from 5,000-12,000 Tanzanian shillings.
Applications: to the Director.

2490   Institute of Finance Management [IFM]
PO Box 3918
Dar es Salaam
Tel: +255-22-211-2931/4
Fax: +255-22-211-2935
e-mail: ifm@twiga.com

📖 Undergraduate, Graduate Programmes / Finance
Study Domains: accounting, computer science, economy, finance, information science, risks, insurance.
Programmes: M.Sc. in finance; postgraduate diplomas, advanced diplomas and certificate awards in accounting, finance, computer science, banking, tax management, insurance, social security.
Open to: candidates of all nationalities; English language proficiency required; 2 A-level and/or 5 O-level passes.
Duration: 3 years.
Fees: tuition: US$1,000 per academic year.
Applications: by December, to the Principal at the above address.

2491   Mzumbe University [IDM]
PO Box 1
Mzumbe, Morogoro
Tel: +255-23-260-4380-4
Fax: +255-23-260-4382
Web: http://www.mzumbe.ac.tz
e-mail: info@mzumbe.ac.tz

📖 Undergraduate, Graduate Programmes / Management
Study Domains: accounting, administration, business, business administration, law, management.
Programmes: Bachelor's degrees, Master's degrees (M.B.A., M.P.A.) and advanced diplomas in administration and management, business and public administration.

Open to: candidates of all nationalities; English proficiency necessary; Ordinary and Advanced level certificate required.
Duration: 3 years.
Fees: tuition: US$1,000.
Applications: by December, to the Vice-Chancellor at the above address.

2492 Open University of Tanzania [OUT]
PO Box 23409
Dar es Salaam
Tel: +255-22-266-8992 / 8445
Fax: +255-22-266-8759
Web: http://www.tanzania.go.tz/out.htm
e-mail: orvc@out.ac.tz

📖 Undergraduate Programmes / Distance Education
Study Domains: arts, business administration, economic and commercial sciences, education, sciences.
Programmes: distance education programmes leading to the Bachelor's, Master's and Ph.D. degrees in arts, education, commerce, law, business administration, economics and science.
Open to: candidates of all nationalities; English language proficiency required; Ordinary and Advanced level education.
Duration: average of 6 years of study.
Fees: tuition: US$1,263.
Applications: by April, to the Vice-Chancellor at the above address.

2493 Sokoine University of Agriculture [SUA]
PO Box 3000
Morogoro
Tel: +255-23-260-4652
Web: http://www.suanet.ac.tz
e-mail: pmsolla@suanet.ac.tz

📖 Graduate Programmes / Agriculture
Study Domains: agriculture, agronomic sciences, cattle breeding, ecology, environment, forestry, home economics, horticulture, natural resources, veterinary medicine, veterinary sciences.
Programmes: Bachelor of Science and higher degrees in agriculture and related fields.
Open to: students of any nationality; English language proficiency required; Ordinary and Advanced level education required.
Duration: 3 to 5 years.
Fees: tuition: US$3,000.
Applications: by December, to the Vice-Chancellor at the above address.

2494 St Augustine University of Tanzania [SAUT]
PO Box 307
Mwanza
Tel: +255-28 255-0560
Fax: +255-28-255-0167
Web: http://www.saut.ac.tz.tripod.com
e-mail: saut-nyegezi@sukumanet.com

📖 Undergraduate Programmes
Study Domains: accounting, administration, journalism, management.
Programmes: Bachelor of Arts degree in mass communication; Bachelor of Business Administration degree; advanced diploma programmes in journalism, accountancy and materials management; certificate courses in accountancy and hospital management.
Open to: nationals of all countries; English language proficiency required; Ordinary and Advanced level education required.
Duration: 3 years.
Fees: tuition, room and board: US$4,000.
Applications: by December, to the Vice-Chancellor at the above address.

2495 University of Bukoba [UOB]
PO Box 1725
Bukoba
Tel: +255-28-222-0691
Fax: +255-28-222-2341
Web: http://uobtz.tripod.com
e-mail: uobtz@yahoo.com

📖 Undergraduate Programmes
Study Domains: accounting, computer science, ecology, environment, education, finance, marketing, natural sciences.
Programmes: Bachelor's degrees in basic arts, education, technology, natural sciences, accounting, finance, human resources, marketing.
Open to: candidates of all nationalities meeting academic, financial and linguistic requirements; mature age entry examination.
Duration: 3 years beginning in October.
Fees: tuition: US$1,400 per year.
Applications: to Registrar at above address.

2496 University of Dar es Salaam [UDSM]
PO Box 35091
Dar es Salaam
Tel: +255-22-241-0500/9
Fax: +255-22-241-0078
Web: http://www.udsm.ac.tz
e-mail: vc@admin.udsm.ac.tz

📖 Undergraduate, Graduate Programmes
Study Domains: arts, business administration, chemical engineering, chemical industry, chemistry, computer science, economic and commercial sciences, education, electricity and electronics, engineering, geology, law.
Programmes: programme of studies at the following faculties: Arts and Social Science, Law, Education, Commerce and Management, Engineering.
Open to: candidates of all nationalities meeting academic, financial and linguistic requirements; English language proficiency required; Ordinary and Advanced level education required.
Duration: 3 to 4 years.
Fees: tuition: US$4,200.
Applications: by December, to the Vice-Chancellor at the above address.

2497 University of Dar es Salaam - Muhimbili University College of Health Sciences [MUCHS]
PO Box 35091
Dar es Salaam
Tel: +255-22- 241-0513
Web: http://www.udsm.ac.tz/admission/muchs.html
e-mail: CACO@admin.udsm.ac.tz

📖 Undergraduate, Graduate Programmes / Health Sciences
Study Domains: dermatology, health and hygiene, laboratory techniques, medicine, nursing, pharmacy and pharmacology, sciences.
Programmes: undergraduate and postgraduate programme of studies in dentistry, medicine, nursing, pharmacy, public health, traditional medicine, allied health sciences, midwifery, primary health care and continuing health education, development studies.
Open to: candidates of all nationalities; English language proficiency required; Ordinary and Advanced level education required.
Duration: 5 years.
Fees: tuition: US$4,200 per academic year.
Applications: by December, to the Principal at the above address.

United States of America

Academic year: usually September to June.
Organization of higher education system: Four years of postsecondary studies lead to the baccalaureate (Bachelor's) degree; one or two additional years of study lead to a Master's degree; two to three years beyond the Master's degree leads to the Ph.D. Professional fields of study: Doctor of Medicine requires a baccalaureate degree followed by four years of medical school; Juris Doctor (law) requires a baccalaureate degree followed by three years of law school.
Monetary unit: United States dollar (US$).
International student admission: Foreign students seeking admission to institutions of higher education in the United States must have successfully completed secondary school studies equivalent to the U.S. system, plus the SAT or ACT test and the TOEFL for applicants from countries where English is not the language of education. Decisions about admissibility are decentralized and each tertiary institution makes its own admissions decisions. Applicants must apply directly to the institution of their choice and fulfil its specific requirements for admission into the selected programme of study. Applicants seeking financial assistance must complete a separate application from the financial aid office of the institution to which they apply for admission.
Language: English proficiency required. Non-native English speakers must prove proficiency by obtaining an acceptable score on the Test of English as a Foreign Language (TOEFL). Some institutions accept the International English Language Testing System (IELTS) test.
Immigration requirements: Applicants accepted for enrolment by tertiary institutions will receive a visa-qualifying document (an I-20 or DS-2019 form) from the institution. This document must be presented, together with proof of financial resources sufficient to cover the cost of studying and living in the U.S., to a consular official at a U.S. embassy or consulate. If approved for a visa, the applicant proceeds to the U.S. to take up study. The student may not work off-campus without specific approval from the U.S. Government.
Estimated expenses for one academic year: tuition: varies by institution from US$2,500-30,000; books/supplies: US$500-1,000; housing: US$5,000-10,000.
Information services:
• EducationUSA advising centers around the world assist those interested in studying in the United States, to find a centre: http://educationUSA.state.gov
• Institute of International Education (IIE), 809 United Nations Plaza, New York, N.Y. 10017; website at http://www.iie.org. It contains extensive information and advice concerning study facilities, financial and other assistance available both to students and professionals from abroad for foreign students coming to the United States and to students and professionals of the United States going abroad.
Scholarships for international students: The U.S. government offers financial assistance to international students through a variety of programmes; web: http://educationUSA.state.gov.
Open and distance learning: Programmes are offered by many tertiary institutions in the United States.
Recognition of studies and qualification: The United States follows a voluntary accreditation (quality assurance) system overseen by the Council for Higher Education Accreditation; web: http://www.chea.org.
Accommodation services: This is the responsibility of the institution that admits international students. There is a long history in the United States of providing specialized student support services for international students.
Work opportunities: There are specific legal requirements governing work eligibility for international students. Generally, the U.S. government does not authorize students from other nations to work off-campus during their academic study for other than unforeseen financial difficulties. After graduation, international students are allowed to apply for full-time work in their field of study. The length of time the student may work depends on a number of factors, but is generally limited to one year. .
Publications / Websites:
• EducationUSA; web: http://educationUSA.state.gov.
• 'Open Doors', a statistical compendium on student traffic to and from the United States, published annually by the International Institute of Education (IIE). For foreign students visiting the United States; web: www.iie.org.

2498 Abilene Christian University [ACU]

ACU Box 28226
79699 Abilene, TX
Tel: +1-915-674-2710
Fax: +1-915-974-2166
Web: http://www.acu.edu
e-mail: kehlk@acu.edu

Bachelor's and Master's Programmes

Study Domains: all major fields.
Programmes: Bachelor's and Master's degrees in all major fields.
Applications: by 15 July for Fall term; 10 December for Spring term. Contact kehlk@acu.edu for details.

Scholarship

Study Domains: all major fields.
Scholarships: University Scholarship.
Duration: up to 4 years.
Value: from US$1,000-$5,000.
Applications: by 15 July for Fall term; 10 December for Spring term; for further details contact kehlk@acu.edu.

2499 Adelphi University

1 South Avenue Garden City
11530 Garden City, NY
Tel: +1-516-877-3000
Fax: +1-516-877-3545
Web: http://www.adelphi.edu

International Students' Awards

Study Domains: arts, music and musicology, performing arts.
Description: several types of awards offered for international students; consult website for full information on each type of award.
Applications: to the Admissions Office.

2500 Albertson College of Idaho [ACI]

2112 Cleveland Blvd.
83605 Caldwell, ID
Tel: +1-208-459-5125
Fax: +1-208-459-5757
Web: http://www.albertson.edu
e-mail: rpusch@albertson.edu

Undergraduate Liberal Arts Programme

Study Domains: all major fields, education, languages, liberal arts, photography.
Programmes: Bachelor's degrees in all major fields.
Open to: all nationalities; language proficiency TOEFL, SAT, ACT, IELTS required.
Duration: 4 years; courses begin 1 September.
Fees: tuition fees US$19,800 per year; living costs US$5,000.
Applications: by 1 August to Admissions Office at the above address.

Scholarship

Study Domains: liberal arts.
Scholarships: Albertson College Scholarship.
Open to: full-time students of all nationalities.
Value: US$2,000-$10,000 per year, depending on academic qualifications.
Applications: by 15 July; for further details contact rpusch@albertson.edu.

2501 Albion College International Programs [AC]

611 E. Porter Street
49224-1899 Albion, MI
Tel: +1-517-629-1200
Fax: +1-517-629-0569
Web: http://www.Albion.edu
e-mail: dhawsey@albion.edu

Undergraduate Liberal Arts Programme

Study Domains: education, humanities and arts, medicine, physical education, sciences, social sciences, theology, religion.

Programmes: undergraduate liberal arts programmes.
Open to: candidates of all nationalities meeting academic, financial and linguistic requirements.
Applications: by 1 April for Fall semester; by 1 September for Spring semester; for further application information see http://www.albion.edu/admissions/requestappINT.asp.

🎓 Albion Scholarships

Study Domains: all major fields.
Scholarships: (a) Academic scholarships for degree-seeking students; (b) Distinguished Albion Scholars.
Open to: (a) highly qualified applicants; all candidates must be proficient in English (minimum TOEFL score of 550); (b) invitation-only competition.
Value: (a) covers about 25-30% of tuition, room, board; (b) multiple awards ranging from full tuition to a very select number of full-tuition, room & board scholarships. All awards are renewable and cover four years of study.
Applications: (a) all candidates will be considered for Academic scholarships at time of application; (b) request further information from University.

2502 Alliant International University

10455 Pomerado Road
92131 San Diego, CA
Tel: +1-866-825-5426
Web: http://www.alliant.edu
e-mail: admissions@alliant.edu

📖 Undergraduate and Graduate Programmes

Study Domains: business, education, liberal arts, psychology, social sciences.
Programmes: undergraduate and graduate programmes.
Open to: candidates of any nationality; qualified B.A. applicants must have completed secondary level schooling; M.A. students must have completed a B.A., doctoral candidates must have completed a Master's degree (except Psy.D. applicants).
Held: six California locations: Fresno, Irvine, Los Angeles, Sacramento, San Diego, and the San Francisco Bay Area; also in Mexico City, Mexico and Nairobi, Kenya.
Applications: 30 days before the start of each quarter to the Office of Admissions: for further information, see website http://www.alliant.edu/admissions/applying.

2503 American College of Computer and Information Sciences [ACCIS]

2101 Magnolia Avenue
35205 Birmingham, AL
Tel: +1-205-323-6191
Fax: +1-205-328-2229
Web: http://www.accis.edu
e-mail: admiss@accis.edu

📖 Undergraduate, Graduate Programmes

Study Domains: computer science, information science.
Programmes: Bachelor's, Master's degrees in information systems, management information systems, computer science; distance education courses.
Fees: for Bachelor's Degree US$115/ credit hour; Master's Degree US$115/ credit hour.
Applications: open enrolment; contact admiss@accis.edu for further details.

2504 American Conservatory Theater [ACT]

30 Grant Avenue
94108 San Francisco, CA
Tel: +1-415-439-2350
Fax: +1-415-834-3360
Web: http://www.act-sf.org

🎓 ACT Scholarship

Study Domains: performing arts.
Open to: candidates of all nationalities; based on financial necessity.
Duration: 3 academic years; renewable.
Value: variable.
Applications: 1 March.

2505 American University Washington DC

4400 Massachusetts Avenue, N.W
20016 Washington, DC
Tel: +1-202-885-6000
Fax: +1-202-885-6014
Web: http://www.american.edu

📖 Undergraduate, Graduate, Postgraduate Programmes

Study Domains: all major fields.
Programmes: Bachelor's, Master's, Ph.D. degrees in all major fields.
Applications: see http://www.american.edu/academics for further information.

2506 American-Scandinavian Foundation Exchange Division [AF]

Scandinavia House
58 Park Avenue
10017 New York, NY
Tel: +1-212-879-9779
Fax: +1-212-249-3444
Web: http://www.amscan.org
e-mail: info@amscan.org

🎓 American-Scandinavian Scholarships

Study Domains: all major fields, research.
Scholarships: (a) Fellowships and Grants for Scandinavians; (b) Fellowships and Grants for Study or Research in Denmark, Finland, Iceland, Norway and Sweden.
Description: study and research in all fields.
Open to: (a) qualified nationals of Denmark, Finland, Iceland, Norway, and Sweden; (b) U.S. citizens and permanent residents having completed their undergraduate education with preference given to candidates at the Ph.D. dissertation level; financial need, language competence, feasibility of study plan and evidence of confirmed invitation are taken into consideration.
Place of study: (a) in the United States; (b) in Denmark, Finland, Iceland, Norway and Sweden.
Duration: (a) announced yearly; (b) 1 academic year for fellowships, shorter periods for grants.
Value: variable, see website for details.
Applications: see website for details or write to above address.

2507 Angelo State University [ASU]

2601 West Avenue N
76909 San Angelo, TX
Tel: +1-325-942-2555
Fax: +1-325-942-2038
Web: http://www.angelo.edu
e-mail: admissions@angelo.edu

🎓 Scholarship

Study Domains: all major fields.
Scholarships: Carr Academic Scholarship.
Duration: 2 terms to 4 years; renewable.
Value: US$2,500 to US$4,000 per year.
Applications: contact briza.lopez@angelo.edu for further details.

2508 Antioch University McGregor [AU]

800 Livermore Street
45387 Yellow Springs, OH
Tel: +1-937-769-1818
Fax: +1-937-769-1804
Web: http://www.mcgregor.edu
e-mail: sas@mcgregor.edu

📖 Master's Degree Programmes

Study Domains: all major fields, business, education, law, liberal arts, management, psychology, social sciences, urbanism, vocational training.
Programmes: (a) Master of Arts in Conflict Resolution; (b) Master of Arts through Individualized Liberal and Professional Studies.
Duration: 2 years.

Applications: see website for further information.

2509 Arizona State University [ASU]
PO Box 871003
85287-1003 Tempe, AZ
Tel: +1-602-965-3521
Fax: +1-602-965-4026
Web: http://www.arizona.edu

Undergraduate, Graduate Programmes
Study Domains: all major fields.
Programmes: undergraduate and graduate degrees in all major fields.
Open to: students of any country.
Duration: Fall semester, courses begin end August; Spring semester; courses begin mid-January.
Applications: (a) by 15 May for Fall and 15 October for Spring; to Undergraduate Admissions, ASU; (b) accepted continuously; to Graduate Admissions, ASU.

Regents International Scholarships
Study Domains: all major fields.
Scholarships: Regents International Scholarships: (a) Undergraduate awards; (b) Graduate awards.
Open to: (a) undergraduate foreign students with FI or JI visa, and 2 semesters full-time (excluding summer session), excellent academic performance at ASU; not available to new undergraduate students; TOEFL required prior to university study. Facilities available for students with disabilities; (b) all regularly admitted students, including first-time graduate students.
Duration: 1 academic year or 1 semester; (a) renewable up to 4 semesters or maximum total of 2 years; (b) renewable upon reapplication for duration of degree programme.
Value: covers out-of-state tuition for regular sessions.
Applications: (a) between 15 February and 30 April, to Undergraduate Admissions, ASU; (b) accepted year round; to academic unit(s) which must recommend applicants, to the Graduate College, ASU.

2510 Art Center College of Design
1700 Lida Street
91103 Pasadena, CA
Tel: +1-626-396-2200
Fax: +1-626-795-0578
Web: http://www.artcenter.edu
e-mail: admissions@artcenter.edu

Scholarship
Study Domains: arts.
Open to: candidates of all nationalities.
Duration: 4 years; renewable.
Applications: by 1 February, 1 March, 1 October; contact admissions@artcenter for further information.

2511 Augsburg College [AC]
2211 Riverside Avenue South
55454 Minneapolis, MN
Tel: +1-612-330-1585
Fax: +1-612-330-1590
Web: http://www.augsburg.edu

Undergraduate, Graduate Programmes
Study Domains: all major fields.
Programmes: undergraduate programmes in all major fields as well as graduate programmes in education, social work and business leadership.
Open to: candidates of any country with a minimum of 520 on TOEFL.
Duration: 1 academic year.
Fees: write for current information.
Financial assistance: scholarship and work study available.
Applications: by 15 July, to the Coordinator of International Student Admissions.

2512 Bank Street College of Education
610 W. 112th Street
10025 New York, NY
Tel: +1-212-875-4400
Web: http://www.bnkst.edu
e-mail: collegepubs@bankstreet.edu

M.S.Ed. and Ed.M. Programmes
Study Domains: administration, computer science, education, museology and museography.
Programmes: M.S.Ed. and Ed.M. programmes in teaching, supervision and administration, computers in education and museum education.
Open to: candidates with at least a Bachelor's degree; TOEFL score of 550 required.
Duration: 15 weeks (from September to December or from February to May); 4 weeks (June session); 4 weeks (July session); most programmes are 42 credits.
Applications: applications are accepted at all times, but must be completed by 1 March for Fall enrolment; further information from the above address.

2513 Bard College
PO Box 5000
12504-5000 Annandale-on-Hudson, NY
Tel: +1-845-758-7472
Web: http://www.bard.edu
e-mail: admission@bard.edu

Scholarships/Fellowships
Study Domains: liberal arts.
Open to: students of all nationalities; based on financial need.
Duration: 1 academic year; renewable.
Value: tuition: variable.
Applications: 13 February.

2514 Barry University [BU]
11300 N.E. 2nd Avenue
33161-6695 Miami, FL
Tel: +1-305-899-3472
Web: http://www2.barry.edu
e-mail: admissions@mail.barry.edu

Cross-Cultural Degree Programmes
Study Domains: English, history, philosophy.
Programmes: Cross-cultural Programme: college-level courses (with laboratory), in speech, history and philosophy (with multicultural reference).
Open to: freshmen, beginning a 4-year programme; TOEFL or SAT required.
Duration: 1 year; courses begin in September and January.
Applications: by 1 August and 1 December; to the Office of Admissions.

2515 Belgian American Educational Foundation, Inc.
195 Church Street
06510 New Haven, CT
Tel: +1-203-777-5765
Fax: +1-203-785-4951
Web: http://www.baef.be

Graduate Study/Research Fellowships
Study Domains: all major fields.
Scholarships: fellowships for study or research in the U.S. for Belgian nationals.
Open to: Belgians with a university degree who have not held their degree for more than 4 years and American nationals under 30 years, with a Master's degree or working towards a Ph.D. and knowledge of French, Dutch or German.
Place of study: in the United States for Belgian nationals and in Belgium for nationals of the United States.
Duration: 1 academic year.
Value: covers travel, living, tuition expenses, fees and books for a single person.
Applications: for Belgian candidates: by 31 October, to Foundation's Office, 11 rue d'Egmont, 1050 Brussels (Belgium); for candidates from the United States: by 31 January, through Graduate Divisions of respective universities.

2516 Bellarmine College [BC]

2001 Newburg Road
40205-0671 Louisville, KY
Tel: +1-502-452-8131
Fax: +1-502-452-8002
Web: http://www.bellarmine.edu
e-mail: admissions@bellarmine.edu

Undergraduate, Graduate Programmes

Study Domains: all major fields.
Programmes: undergraduate and graduate programmes in all major fields.
Description: Bachelor's degree in accounting, actuarial science, art, biology, business administration, chemistry, communication, computer science, economic and commercial sciences, education, fine arts, history, law, liberal arts, mathematics, medicine, nursing, philosophy, political science, psychology, sciences, sociology, theology. Master's degrees in business administration, education, nursing.
Open to: nationals of any country with secondary school certificate (above average grades) at least 17 years of age, and with TOEFL score 550 or above or a SAT/ACT test score.
Applications: by 1 February, to the International Student Advisor, Office of Admissions, at the above address.

2517 Bemidji State University [BSU]

1500 Birchmont Drive N.E.
56601 Bemidji, MN
Tel: +1-218-755-4096
Fax: +1-218-755-2074
Web: http://www.bemidjistate.edu
e-mail: studybemidji@bemidjistate.edu

Undergraduate, Graduate Programmes

Study Domains: liberal arts.
Programmes: Bachelor's, Master's degrees in liberal arts.
Fees: tuition fees US$2,238 per semester; living costs US$2,300 per semester.
Languages: English language proficiency: TOEFL 500 for undergraduates; 550 for graduates.
Applications: rolling admissions.

Scholarship

Study Domains: all major fields.
Scholarships: Partial Tuition Waiver.
Open to: international students.
Duration: 4 years, renewable after one year.
Value: US$4,200 per year.
Applications: for further details contact lamae@bemidjistate.edu.

2518 Benedictine College [BC]

1020 North 2nd street
66002 Atchison, KS
Tel: +1-913-367-5340 ext 2614
Fax: +1-913-367-1157
Web: http://www.benedictine.edu
e-mail: tyang@benedictine.edu

Undergraduate Programme

Study Domains: all major fields, business, education, liberal arts, sciences.
Programmes: Bachelor's degree in liberal arts.
Duration: 4 to 5 years; courses begin in August.
Fees: enrolment fees US$125; tuition fees US$13,400.
Applications: rolling admissions; for further information contact tyang@benedictine.edu.

Scholarship

Study Domains: all major fields, liberal arts.
Scholarships: International Student Scholar Award.
Open to: all students intending to follow the undergraduate degree programme.
Duration: 1 academic year; renewable up to 4 years.
Value: up to US$3,000 per academic year and earned through on-campus employment.
Applications: by 15 June for Fall semester; 15 November for Spring semester; for further information contact tyang@benedictine.edu.

2519 Benedictine University [BU]

5700 College Road
International Center
60532 Lisle, IL
Tel: +1-630-829-6353
Fax: +1-630-829-6244
Web: http://www.ben.edu
e-mail: sloy@ben.edu

Undergraduate, Graduate, Postgraduate Programmes

Study Domains: all major fields.
Programmes: Associate, Bachelor's, Master's, Ph.D. degrees in all major fields.
Description: undergraduate majors in all fields; graduate business and management, clinical psychology, public health programmes; graduate level certificate in business management, human resources; pre-professional programmes.
Fees: tuition: US$7,610 per semester or US$510 per credit hour; estimated living costs: US$3,000 per semester.

2520 Bennington College [BC]

05201 Bennington, VT
Tel: +1-802-440-4312
Fax: +1-802-440-4312
Web: http://www.bennington.edu

Undergraduate Programmes

Study Domains: languages, liberal arts, literature and civilization, mathematics, natural sciences, performing arts, social sciences, visual arts.
Programmes: Bachelor of Arts degree programme in liberal arts.
Description: courses in dance, drama, literature and languages, music, natural science and mathematics, social sciences, visual arts.
Open to: secondary-school graduates of any nationality, proficient in English.
Duration: normally 4 years; courses begin in September and March.
Financial assistance: according to need and upon availability of funds.
Applications: by 1 February, to the Dean of Admissions and the Freshman Year Office of Admissions, at the above address.

2521 Berklee College of Music [BCOM]

1140 Boylston Street
02215 Boston, MA
Tel: +1-617-747-2221
Fax: +1-617-536-2632
Web: http://www.berklee.edu/admissions/international.html
e-mail: admissions@berklee.edu

Undergraduate, Graduate Programmes in Music

Study Domains: music and musicology, summer programmes.
Programmes: degree and diploma programmes in all career-related aspects of music including music technology, composition, performance, as well as music education, music business and management, and music therapy.
Open to: candidates of any nationality meeting audition, language and financial requirements. See website for further information.
Duration: 4 years.
Financial assistance: partial scholarships available.
Applications: to the Office of Admissions at above address.

European Scholarship Tour

Study Domains: music and musicology.
Scholarships: European Scholarship Tour.
Open to: all nationalities with over 2 years of music studies; proficiency in English required.
Duration: 2 semesters (renewable).
Applications: enquire no later than September for audition; applications to the Scholarship Committee at the school closest to applicant: Philippos Nakas Centre (Athens); Rimon School of Jazz (Israel); Pop/Jazz Conservatory (Helsinki);

American School of Modern Music (Paris); L'Aula de Música (Barcelona); Sen Zoko Gakuen College, Kanagawa-Ken (Japan).

2522 Binghamton University

PO Box 6000
13902 Binghamton, NY
Tel: +1-607-777-2000
Fax: +1-607-777-4000
Web: http://www.binghamton.edu

☞ Dr Bhagwan Gajwani Fellowship

Study Domains: computer science, economic and commercial sciences, management.
Description: Dr Bhagwan Gajwani Fellowship for.
Open to: graduates of Maharaja Sayajirao University of Baroda, Gujarat, India for studies in computer science, economics or management.
Duration: 1 year; non-renewable.
Value: tuition: US$10,920; living expenses: US$10,000.
Applications: 1 January to the Graduate School; gradsch@binghamton.edu.

2523 Boise State University

1015 Grant Avenue
83725 Boise, ID
Tel: +1-208-426-3652
Web: http://www.boisestate.edu/international/
e-mail: interntl@boisestate.edu

☞ University Grants

Study Domains: all major fields.
Scholarships: (a) tuition waiver; (b) GEM Scholarship.
Duration: 1 year; renewable.
Value: US$8,000.
Applications: (a) 1 June for fall semester; 15 October for spring semester; (b) 15 February; see website for full details.

2524 Boston University [BU]

International Students and Scholars Office
19 Deerfield Street, 2nd Floor
02215 Boston, MA
Tel: +1-617-353-3565
Fax: +1-617-353-1170
Web: http://www.bu.edu/isso
e-mail: isso@bu.edu

☐ Undergraduate, Graduate Programmes

Study Domains: all major fields, applied arts, arts, dentistry, education, engineering, fine arts, liberal arts, management, medicine, sciences, theology, religion, visual arts.
Programmes: Bachelor's, Master's, Ph.D. in all major fields.
Fees: tuition: US$7,000 per year; estimated living costs: US$8,980.
Applications: by 1 January for classes beginning in September; 1 November for classes beginning in January.

☞ Scholarships

Study Domains: all major fields.
Scholarships: (a) Trustee Scholarship; (b) University Scholarship.
Open to: candidates of all nationalities, meeting academic requirements.
Duration: (a); (b) renewable each year depending on grade point average.
Value: (a) full tuition and fees per year; (b) half tuition and fees per year.

2525 Bowdoin College [BC]

04011 Brunswick, ME
Tel: +1-207-725-3100
Fax: +1-207-725-3101
Web: http://www.bowdoin.edu/admissions/internation al.shtml

☐ Undergraduate Liberal Arts Programmes

Study Domains: liberal arts.
Programmes: Undergraduate Liberal Arts Programmes.
Open to: candidates of all nationalities meeting academic and language requirements.

Duration: 4 years.
Financial assistance: some financial assistance available.
Applications: by 1 January.

☞ Undergraduate Liberal Arts Scholarships

Study Domains: liberal arts.
Scholarships: Undergraduate Liberal Arts Scholarships.
Open to: candidates who are distinguished graduates of secondary schools; must speak and write English fluently.
Duration: 4 years on condition of satisfactory scholarship.
Value: proportional to financial need (travel, room and board, books and tuition).
Applications: by 15 January, to Admissions Office.

2526 Bowling Green State University

43403 Bowling Green, OH
Tel: +1-419-372-2531
Fax: +1-419-372-8446
Web: http://www.bgsu.edu

☞ Graduate Assistantships

Study Domains: music and musicology.
Description: music certificate graduate programmes.
Open to: enrolled students of any nationality, based on academic performance.
Academic requirements: must meet departmental criteria for Master's and doctoral candidates.
Duration: 1-4 academic years.
Value: variable; for tuition and living expenses.
Applications: January; to Center for International Programs.

2527 Brandeis University [BU]

International Students & Scholars Office
PO Box 9110
02254-9110 Waltham, MA
Tel: +1-781-736-3480
Fax: +1-781-736-3484
Web: http://www.brandeis.edu/isso

☐ Undergraduate, Graduate, Postgraduate Programmes

Study Domains: all major fields.
Programmes: undergraduate, graduate and postgraduate programmes in all major fields.
Open to: candidates of all nationalities, meeting academic, linguistic and financial requirements.
Financial assistance: see website for further information.

2528 Brown University [BU]

PO Box 1973
02912 Providence, RI
Tel: +1-401-863-1000
Fax: +1-401-863-9300
Web: http://www.brown.edu/Administration/Admissi on/international.html
e-mail: admission_undergraduate@brown.edu

☐ Undergraduate, Graduate Programmes

Study Domains: all major fields.
Programmes: undergraduate and graduate programmes in all major fields.
Open to: students of all nationalities meeting academic, linguistic and financial requirements.
Duration: 5, 6 or 9 months, or academic year depending on the programme; freshman entrance: early September.
Financial assistance: some financial assistance possible; see website for further information: http://www.FinancialAid.brown.edu.
Applications: early decision deadline: 1 November; regular deadline: 1 January.

2529 Bryn Mawr College [BMC]

101 N. Merion Avenue
19010 Bryn Mawr, PA
Tel: +1-610-526-5000
Fax: +1-610-526-7471
Web: http://www.brynmawr.edu
e-mail: admissions@brynmawr.edu

📖 Undergraduate Programmes

Study Domains: all major fields, African studies, anthropology, applied arts, archaeology, art history, Asian studies, astronomy, biology, chemistry, computer science, cultural studies, demography and population studies, ecology, environment, economic and commercial sciences, economy, education, English, fine arts, French, gender studies, geology, German, Greek, Hebrew, history, international relations, Italian, languages, Latin, liberal arts, linguistics, literature and civilization, mathematics, music and musicology, neurology, performing arts, philosophy, physics, political science, psychology, sciences, sociology, Spanish, theology, religion, visual arts.
Programmes: Undergraduate and graduate degrees in liberal arts and sciences.
Open to: women of any nationality with English language proficiency; TOEFL 250 CBT / 600 PBT and SAT, ACT required.
Duration: 4 years.
Fees: registration: US$1,580; tuition: US$25,550; estimated living costs: US$8,970.
Applications: by 15 January; contact admissions@brynmawr.edu for further details.

📌 Scholarship International Students

Study Domains: all major fields.
Scholarships: Bryn Mawr Grant.
Description: A few scholarships are awarded each year to outstanding international applicants (students who do not hold a U.S. passport or are not permanent residents of the U.S.) based on financial need. Financial aid is not available for international transfer students. Students not awarded aid at entrance will not be awarded aid for any of the following years.
Open to: women of any nationality with English language proficiency; TOEFL 250 CBT / 600 PBT and SAT, ACT required.
Value: variable.
Applications: by 15 January; contact admissions@brynmawr.edu for further information, web: http://www.brynmawr.edu/financialaid/intl_students_financial.shtml.

2530 Bucknell University [BU]

Office of Admissions
17837 Lewisburg, PA
Tel: +1-570-577-2000
Fax: +1-570-577-3760
Web: http://www.bucknell.edu
e-mail: admissions@bucknell.edu

📖 Arts and Sciences, Engineering Programmes

Study Domains: all major fields, business, education, engineering, management, natural sciences, social sciences.
Programmes: Bachelor's and Master's degrees in humanities, social sciences, natural sciences, engineering, education, business management.
Open to: undergraduate students; must have SAT I and TOEFL qualifications.
Duration: 4 years.
Fees: tuition: US$27,531; estimated living costs: US$6,052.
Applications: by 1 January to Office of Admissions.

📌 Financial Aid

Study Domains: all major fields.
Open to: all enrolled students based on financial resources and College Scholarship Service (CSS) Profile information.
Duration: 1year; renewable.
Value: variable.
Applications: by 1 January; for further information contact Office of Financial Aid; Finaid@bucknell.edu.

2531 California Institute of Integral Studies [CIIS]

1453 Mission Street 4th Floor
94103 San Francisco, CA
Tel: +1-415-575-6100
Fax: +1-415-575-1264
Web: http://www.ciis.edu

📌 Scholarship

Study Domains: all major fields.
Scholarships: International Student Scholarship.
Open to: candidates of all nationalities, in financial need.
Duration: 2 years; renewable.
Value: Tuition, US$4,200-US$9,000.
Applications: 15 April for Fall, 1 October for Spring; contact finaid@ciis.edu for further information.

2532 California State University - San Marcos

92096 San Marcos
Tel: +1-760-750-4000
Fax: +1-760-750-4030
Web: http://www.csusm.edu

📌 Non-Resident Tuition Waiver

Study Domains: all major fields.
Open to: non-resident international students enrolled at university for one semester.
Duration: 1 academic year; renewable.
Value: tuition: US$1,200-$4,200.
Applications: 15 March.

2533 California State University - Stanislaus

801 West Monte Vista
95382 Turlock, CA
Tel: +1-209-667-3122
Fax: +1-209-667-3333
Web: http://www.csustan.edu
e-mail: IntlStudent@csustan.edu

📌 Service Club Scholarship Awards

Study Domains: all major fields.
Open to: candidates of all nationalities; based on academic results; extra-curricular involvement and financial necessity.
Other conditions: students must have been in US. for one year to include one semester at CSUS.
Duration: 1 term.
Value: tuition: US$300.
Applications: semester prior to commencement.

2534 California State University, Long Beach [CSULB]

Center for International Education
International Admissions Office, BH- 201
1250 Bellflower Boulevard
90840-0109 Long Beach, CA
Tel: +1-562-985-5476
Fax: +1-562-985-1725
Web: http://www.csulb.edu/centers/cie
e-mail: cie-admission@csulb.edu

📖 Undergraduate, Graduate Programmes

Study Domains: all major fields.
Programmes: undergraduate and graduate programmes in all major fields.
Open to: suitably qualified candidates of all nationalities.
Duration: variable; courses begin late August and late January.
Applications: to International Admissions, at the above address for all further information.

2535 California State University, Sacramento [CSU]

6000 J Street
95819-6012 Sacramento, CA
Tel: +1-916-278-7772
Fax: +1-916-278-5603
Web: http://www.csus.edu
e-mail: intladm@csus.edu

📖 Undergraduate, Graduate Programmes

Study Domains: all major fields, Asian studies, education, international business, international relations.
Programmes: Courses leading to: (a) Bachelor of Arts, Bachelor of Science, Master of Arts, Master of Science, Master of Business Administration, Master of Social Work, non-degree programmes, certificate programmes; (b) International Affairs M.A. programme: training of personnel

for future careers in international government, development or business; (c) Bachelor of Arts in Asian studies.
Open to: (a) and (b) candidates of all nationalities satisfying admission requirements; TOEFL score 570 and good knowledge of a second language required; (c) all eligible applicants; TOEFL scores 510 PBT/180 CBT required for undergraduates and 550 PBT/213 CBT required for graduate students (including students seeking second Bachelor's degrees) with the following exceptions: communication studies and speech pathology 560 PBT/220 CBT, English 600 PBT/250 CBT, and international affairs 570 PBT/ 230 CBT. Admission denied if minimum TOEFL score is not achieved.
Duration: (a) and (b) 2 years, courses begin in September; (c) 4 years, courses begin in late August.
Financial assistance: limited.
Applications: for international students: 1 November-1 May for Fall semester; 1 August-1 October for Spring semester. See www.csus.edu/oip/prospect_downloads.html for forms and information.

2536 California State University, San Bernardino

5500 University Parkway, UH-235
92407-2397 San Bernardino, CA
Tel: +1-909-880-5193
Fax: +1-909-880-7020
Web: http://iss.csusb.edu/en/index.asp

📖 Undergraduate, Graduate Programmes

Study Domains: all major fields.
Programmes: undergraduate and graduate programmes in all major fields.
Open to: students of all nationalities meeting academic, language and financial requirements.
Fees: registration fee: US$55 (non-refundable); non-resident tuition US$188 per unit; US$94 per 1/2 unit; international students must register for at least 12 units per quarter if undergraduate, or 8 units if graduate in order to maintain immigration status.
Applications: Fall quarter: 1 November -1 July; Winter quarter: 1 August -1 November; Spring quarter: 1 June-1 February. See website http://iss.csusb.edu/en/admiss.asp for details.

2537 Case Western Reserve University [CWRU]

10900 Euclid Avenue
44106 Cleveland, OH
Tel: +1-216-368-4450
Web: http://www.cwru.edu
e-mail: admission@po.cwru.edu

📖 Undergraduate, Graduate, Postgraduate, Professional Programmes

Study Domains: all major fields, anatomy, anthropology, dentistry, engineering, industrial relations, law, medicine, natural sciences, nursing, performing arts, physiology, sciences, theology, religion.
Programmes: Bachelor's, Master's, Ph.D. degrees in major fields and professional degrees in dentistry, law, medicine, and nursing.
Open to: qualified applicants of all nationalities; TOEFL and additional admission tests required for some programmes.
Financial assistance: assistantships and fellowships available for graduate students.
Applications: see http://www.cwru.edu/ugadmis/international.htm for full application information.

2538 Catawba College [CC]

2300 West Innes Street
28144 Salisbury, NC
Tel: +1-704-637-4402
Fax: +1-704-637-4222
Web: http://www.catawba.edu
e-mail: webmaster@catawba.edu

📖 Bachelor's Degree Programme in Liberal Arts

Study Domains: liberal arts.
Programmes: Bachelor of Arts, Bachelor of Science

degrees in liberal arts.
Open to: qualified applicants of all nationalities; SAT or TOEFL required.
Duration: 4 years; courses begin 21 August.
Fees: registration US$50; tuition fees US$20,800; living costs US$4,000.
Applications: by 31 May.

🎓 Scholarship

Study Domains: all major fields.
Scholarships: Catawba Scholarship.
Duration: 4 years.
Value: US$2,000-$7,000 per academic year.
Applications: by 31 May; contact tllynch@catawba.edu for further details.

2539 Central Missouri State University

64093 Warrensburg, MO
Tel: +1-660-543-4111
Fax: +1-660-543-8517
Web: http://www.cmsu.edu
e-mail: admit@cmsuvmb.cmsu.edu

🎓 Scholarships

Study Domains: all major fields.
Scholarships: (a) International Excellence Award; (b) First Year International Award; (c) Graduate International Award.
Open to: candidates of all nationalities; awards based upon test scores and grade point average.
Duration: 1 year.
Value: (a) US$3,840; (b) US$1,000; (c) US$1,000.
Applications: by 1 May for Fall semester; 1 October for Spring; contact Director of international admissions: petentler@cmsu1.cmsu.edu for further information.

2540 Central Washington University [CWU]

Admissions Office
400 E, 8th Avenue
98926-7463 Ellensburg, WA
Tel: +1-866-298-4968
Fax: +1-509-963-3022
Web: http://www.cwu.edu

📖 Bachelor's, Master's Degree Programmes

Study Domains: all major fields, aviation, aeronautics, earth science, liberal arts, performing arts, political science, tourism, hotel and catering management.
Programmes: Bachelor's and Master's degrees in liberal arts.
Open to: qualified applicants meeting language proficiency and admissions requirements.
Duration: 4 years; courses begin in September.
Fees: tuition fees US$4,300; living costs US$1,950.
Applications: by 1 May for Fall term; see website for details.

2541 Clarkson University

8 Clarkson Avenue
13699 Potsdam, NY
Tel: +1-315-268-2125
Fax: +1-315-268-7647
Web: http://www.clarkson.edu
e-mail: intladmission@clarkson.edu

🎓 International Scholarship

Study Domains: all major fields.
Value: US$2,000-$12,000.
Applications: 1 July for fall session; 1 December for spring session; to Director of Transfer and International Admissions.

2542 Cleveland State University [CSU]

2121 Euclid Avenue
University Center
Cleveland, OH 44115
Tel: +1 216 687 3910
Fax: +1 261 687 3965
Web: http://www.csuohio.edu
e-mail: cispcsu@csuohio.edu

📖 Undergraduate, Graduate Programmes

Study Domains: all major fields, business, computer science, criminology, earth science, education, industrial design, industrial relations, industrial technology, industry and commerce, liberal arts, nursing, performing arts, sciences.
Programmes: Bachelor's degrees in liberal arts; Master's degrees in business.
Open to: applicants meeting language proficiency (TOEFL, Cambridge, IETS, Michigan Language Test) and academic requirements.
Fees: tuition fees US$19,000; living costs US$8,000.
Applications: by 1 June for Fall term; 1 November for Spring term.

2543 Coe College [CC]

1220 First Avenue NE
52402 Cedar Rapids, IA
Tel: +1-319-399-8500
Fax: +1-319-399-8816
Web: http://www.coe.edu

📖 Undergraduate Programmes

Study Domains: languages, liberal arts, music and musicology, nursing.
Programmes: Bachelor of Arts (B.A.), Bachelor of Music (B.M.), and Bachelor of Science in Nursing (B.S.N.) degrees.
Open to: candidates holding a secondary-school diploma or equivalent and meeting financial and linguistic requirements; minimum TOEFL score of 500; students scoring between 500-550 will be tested again on arrival at campus.
Duration: Fall and Spring terms, 14 weeks; Winter term, 4 weeks; Summer term, 10 weeks.
Financial assistance: scholarships available for talented candidates in writing, fine and performing arts, foreign language, business/accounting/economics, and science; grants, need-based gifts such as the Iowa Tuition Grant and other schemes are possible.

2544 College for Creative Studies

201 E. Kirby
48202-4034 Detroit, MI
Tel: +1-313-664-7400
Fax: +1-313-872-2739
Web: http://www.ccscad.edu

📖 Undergraduate Programmes in Fine Arts

Study Domains: arts and crafts, decorative arts, design, fine arts, graphic arts, industrial design, visual arts.
Programmes: Bachelor of Fine Arts (BFA) degree.
Description: programme requires completion of 126 credit hours: 84 in studio areas and 42 in general studies courses. All students are required to take core foundation course work in basic drawing, basic design and figure drawing during their freshman year.
Open to: students of all nationalities.
Financial assistance: some financial assistance may be available; contact finaid@ccscad.edu for information.
Languages: instruction in English; Test of English as a Foreign Language (TOEFL) required, with minimum composite score of 527 for paper-based test or 197 for computer-based test; photocopied test results not accepted.
Applications: well before 15 November for winter semester; see 'admissions' information on website for full details.

2545 College of Mount St Joseph [CMJ]

5701 Delhi Road
45233 Cincinnati, OH
Tel: +1-513-244-4240
Fax: +1-513-244-4211
Web: http://www.msj.edu
e-mail: international@mail.msj.edu

📖 Undergraduate, Graduate Programmes

Study Domains: applied arts, business, computer science, graphic arts, humanities and arts, interior design, law, liberal arts, management, nursing, paramedical studies, sciences, social sciences, social work.
Programmes: Bachelor's and Master's degrees in education, organizational leadership, religious studies, physical therapy.
Duration: 4 years; courses begin 26 August.
Fees: tuition: US$14,950 per year; estimated living costs: US$8,875.
Languages: English proficiency TOEFL 500 required.
Applications: rolling admissions; see website for further details.

🎓 Scholarship

Study Domains: all major fields.
Scholarships: Elizabeth Seton Award.
Open to: entering students with minimum 1200 SAT score.
Duration: 4 years.
Value: approximately US$7,900.

2546 College of St Benedict and St John's University [CSBSJU]

56321 Collegeville, MN
Tel: +1-800-544-1816
Fax: +1-320-363-3206
Web: http://www.csbsju.edu
e-mail: admissions@csbsju.edu

📖 Undergraduate, Graduate Programmes

Study Domains: liberal arts, theology, religion.
Programmes: Bachelor's and Master's degree programmes in liberal arts, theology, pastoral ministry, liturgical studies, music.
Open to: the College of Saint Benedict accepts only female students; Saint John's University accepts only male students; TOEFL, SAT or ACT examinations required.
Financial assistance: various scholarships available; contact the Director of International Admission at the above address.

2547 College of St Catherine

Office of International Admission
The College of St. Catherine
2004 Randolph Avenue
55105 St. Paul, MN
Tel: +1-651-690-6029
Fax: +1-651-690-8824
Web: http://www.stkate.edu
e-mail: international@stkate.edu

📖 Undergraduate, Graduate Programmes

Study Domains: all major fields, health and hygiene, liberal arts.
Programmes: undergraduate and graduate degrees for female students in a variety of health-care specialties, liberal arts and professional programs.
Open to: qualified female applicants, proficient in English.
Financial assistance: limited financial assistance available to international students.
Applications: by 15 May for Fall admission, by 15 November for Spring to the above address; see website for complete application information:
http://minerva.stkate.edu/ugradapps.nsf/pages/international?OpenDocument.

2548 College of the Southwest [CSW]

6610 Lovington Highway
88240 Hobbs, NM
Tel: +1-505-392-6561
Fax: +1-505-392-6006
Web: http://www.csw.edu
e-mail: admissions@csw.edu

Tuition Waiver

Study Domains: all major fields.
Open to: full-time, degree-programme undergraduate
student enrolled at CSW.
Duration: 4 years; renewable.
Value: up to 70% of direct costs.
Applications: see website for full details; contact; Dean of
Student Enrolment Services/International Admission.

2549 Colorado State University

80523 Fort Collins, CO
Tel: +1-970-491-1101
Fax: +1-970-491-0501
Web: http://www.colostate.edu

Undergraduate, Graduate Programmes

Study Domains: all major fields, civil engineering, earth
science, ecology, environment, fisheries, forestry, geography,
natural resources.
Programmes: undergraduate and graduate programmes in
all major fields.
Description: possibility of undergraduate and graduate
degrees through distance education; for further information
see http://www.learn.colostate.edu/csun.
Open to: candidates of all nationalities meeting academic,
linguistic and financial requirements.
Duration: up to 2 years.
Fees: US$6,000 per semester.
Applications: 3 months prior to arrival, to the Director of
the International School, at the above address; see
http://admissions.colostate.edu/international for admissions
information.

2550 Colorado State University-Pueblo (formerly University of Southern Colorado)

Center for International Programs - 2200 Bonforte
Blvd.
81001-4901 Pueblo, CO
Tel: +1-719-549-2306
Fax: +1-719-549-2650
Web: http://www.colostate-pueblo.edu/internationalPr
ograms
e-mail: intprog@colostate-pueblo.edu

Scholarship, Financial Aid

Study Domains: all major fields.
Applications: 1 February; see website for further
information: www.colostate-pueblo.edu/sfs/scholarships.

2551 Concordia University Wisconsin [CUW]

12800 North Lake Shore Drive
WI 53097-2402 Mequon, WI
Tel: +1-262-243-4294
Fax: +1-262-243-4351
Web: http://www.cuw.edu
e-mail: shaojie.jiang@cuw.edu

Bachelor's, Master's Programmes in Liberal Arts

Study Domains: all major fields, nursing, social work.
Programmes: Bachelor's and Master's programmes in all
major fields.
Applications: see website for further information.

2552 Coppin State University

2500 West North Avenue
21216-3698 Baltimore, MD
Tel: +1-410-951-3000
Fax: +1-410-523-7351
Web: http://www.coppin.edu

Scholarship

Study Domains: business administration, computer
science, nursing.
Value: tuition, US$9,500 per year; living expenses,
US$6,236 per year; other, US$1,200-US$1,800 per year.
Applications: for fall semester, by 15 July; priority date,
15 March; see website for further information.

2553 Cornell University [CU]

B50 Caldwell Hall
14853-2602 Ithaca, NY
Tel: +1-607-255-5243
Web: http://www.cornell.edu
e-mail: isso@cornell.edu

Undergraduate, Graduate Programmes

Study Domains: biology, classical studies, physics, social
sciences.
Programmes: undergraduate and graduate degree
programmes in 91 major fields of study: biological sciences,
humanities, physical sciences and social sciences.
Open to: applicants of any nationality, with degree
equivalent to American Baccalaureate or higher, granted by a
university of recognized standing, adequate preparation for
graduate study in the chosen field and minimum TOEFL
score of 550 (if English is not native language).
Financial assistance: in the form of fellowships and
teaching and research assistantships (usually accompanied by
a tuition fellowship).
Applications: by 10 January, to the above address; for
further information see website
http://www.admissions.cornell.edu/apply/intl_other.cfm#isso.

2554 Cranbrook Academy of Art

1221 N. Woodward Avenue
PO Box 801
48303-0801 Bloomfield Hills, MI
Tel: +1-248-645-3300
Fax: +1-248-646-0046
Web: http://www.cranbrook.edu
e-mail: gradadmit@cranbrook.edu

Master's Programme

Study Domains: architecture, audio-visual media, design,
fine arts, graphic arts, industrial design, photography, visual
arts.
Programmes: Master of Fine Arts or Master of
Architecture.
Description: studio-based programmes focusing on
individual study.
Duration: 2 years; courses begin in September.
Fees: $18,400 tuition per year; living costs $5,450.
Languages: English language proficiency TOEFL 213
CBT minimum required.
Applications: by 1 February.

2555 Davidson College [DC]

Office of Admission and Financial Aid
Box 7156
28035-7156 Davidson, NC
Tel: +1-704-894-2230
e-mail: admission@davidson.edu

Undergraduate Programmes

Study Domains: liberal arts.
Programmes: undergraduate programmes in liberal arts.
Open to: students of all nationalities with good academic
standing, and minimum 600 on TOEFL and high SAT scores.
Duration: 4 years; courses begin in Fall only.
Financial assistance: limited scholarships/grants,
on-campus employment.
Applications: by 15 January, to the Office of Admissions;
for further information see
http://www2.davidson.edu/admission/apply_interntl.asp.

2556 Dominican College

470 Western Highway
10962 Orangeburg, NY
Tel: +1-845-359-3533
Fax: +1-845-365-3150
Web: http://www.dc.edu
e-mail: admissions@dc.edu

🎓 Academic Scholarships

Study Domains: all major fields, physical education.
Subjects: all undergraduate programmes; athletic scholarships.
Open to: students enrolled in undergraduate programmes of the university; based on secondary-school results and TOEFL/SAT scores.
Value: tuition: up to US$11,000.
Applications: to Director of Admissions at above address; admissions@dc.edu.

2557 Drury University [DU]

900 N. Benton Avenue
65802 Springfield, MO
Tel: +1-417-873-7205
Fax: +1-417-866-3873
Web: http://www.drury.edu
e-mail: interad@drury.edu

📖 Undergraduate, Graduate Programmes

Study Domains: administration, advertising, applied arts, architecture, audio-visual media, building industry, business administration, communication, criminology, cultural studies, design, early childhood education, economic and commercial sciences, education, engineering, finance, gender studies, languages, liberal arts, linguistics, music and musicology, performing arts, photography, physical education, sciences, teacher education.
Programmes: Bachelor's and Master's degrees in business administration, communication, teacher education, criminology.
Open to: applicants meeting academic qualifications; English proficiency TOEFL 530 PNB/200 CNB required.
Duration: 4 to 5 years; courses start in October.
Fees: tuition: US$13,000; estimated living costs: US$5,000.
Applications: by 1 April; contact lcooper@drury.edu for further information.

🎓 Scholarships

Study Domains: all major fields.
Scholarships: (a) Academic Honor Scholarship; (b) International Scholarship.
Duration: 1 year; renewable every year with 3.0 grade point average.
Value: US$1,000-$5,000 per academic year; (b) US$1,000-$4,000 per academic year.
Applications: by 1 April; contact lcooper@drury.edu for further information.

2558 Duke University [DU]

Box 90057
27708-0057 Durham, NC
Tel: +1-919-684-8111
Web: http://www.duke.edu

📖 Undergraduate, Graduate Programmes

Study Domains: all major fields, business, law, medicine.
Programmes: undergraduate and graduate programmes in all major fields.
Open to: students of all nationalities meeting academic, linguistic and financial requirements. See website for further information.
Duration: variable.
Applications: by 1 April, to the above address; for further information see website:
http://www.duke.edu/international/services.html, and for law studies: http://www.law.duke.edu/internat/staff.html.

2559 Dumbarton Oaks [DO]

1703 32nd Street, NW
20007 Washington, DC
Tel: +1-202-339-6401
Fax: +1-202-339-6419
Web: http://www.doaks.org
e-mail: DumbartonOaks@doaks.org

🎓 Fellowships and Project Grants

Study Domains: archaeology, architecture, art history, history, literature and civilization, summer programmes.
Scholarships: (a) Junior Fellowships in Byzantine, Pre-Columbian Studies, and garden and landscape studies; (b) Fellowships in Byzantine, pre-Columbian studies, and garden and landscape studies; (c) Summer Fellowships in Byzantine, pre-Columbian studies, and garden and landscape studies; (d) Bliss Prize Fellowship in Byzantine studies; (e) Project Grants.
Description: Byzantine civilization in all its aspects (including relations with neighbouring cultures), pre-Columbian studies, history of landscape architecture.
Open to: qualified students (of any nationality) of history, archaeology, history of art, philology, theology and other disciplines. (a) Junior Fellowships: generally for degree candidates who at the time of application have fulfilled all preliminary requirements for a Ph.D. (or appropriate final degree) and will be working on a dissertation or final project at Dumbarton Oaks under the direction of a faculty member at their own university; (b) fellowships: for scholars who hold a doctorate (or appropriate final degree) or have established themselves in their field and wish to pursue their own research. Applications will also be accepted from graduate students who expect to have the Ph.D. in hand prior to taking up residence at Dumbarton Oaks; (c) Summer Fellowships: for Byzantine, Pre-Columbian, or Landscape Architecture scholars on any level of advancement, beyond the first year of graduate (post-baccalaureate) study; (d) fellowship candidates must be in their last year of undergraduate education or have a recently awarded B.A.; they must have completed at least one year of ancient or medieval Greek (those called for an interview will be required to take a short examination in Greek); and they must be applicants to a doctoral programme in any field or area of Byzantine studies. The Bliss Prize Fellowship is restricted to candidates currently enrolled in or recent graduates of U.S. or Canadian universities or colleges or to American or Canadian citizens who are enrolled at non-North American universities or colleges; (e) project grants are limited to applicants holding a doctorate or the equivalent, and are awarded on the basis of 1) ability and preparation of the principal project personnel including knowledge of the requisite languages) and 2) interest and value of the project to the specific field of study. Applications are reviewed by a committee of scholars in the relevant field.
Duration: (a) and (b) full academic year, although semesters are considered; (c) periods of 6 to 9 weeks (between 15 June and 15 August); (d) 2 academic years.
Value: (a), (b) Fellowship awards range from an equivalent of approximately US$21,000 for an unmarried Junior Fellow to a maximum of US$39,300 for a Fellow from abroad accompanied by family members. Support includes a stipend of US$14,080 for a Junior Fellow or US$25,655 for a Fellow for the full academic year; housing or housing allowance; possibility of contribution towards family; health and travel expenses; (c) Summer Fellowships for periods of six to nine weeks. Awards provide a maintenance allowance of US$215 per week; housing in a Dumbarton Oaks apartment or at the Fellows Building; lunch on weekdays; Dumbarton Oaks's contribution to health insurance; and travel expense reimbursement if necessary; (d) his award is intended to provide encouragement, assistance, and training to outstanding college seniors who plan to enter the field of Byzantine studies. The Bliss Prize Fellowship covers graduate school tuition and living expenses for two academic years; Summer travel (up to a maximum of US$5,000) for the intervening Summer to areas that are important for an understanding of Byzantine civilization and culture; (e) the normal range of awards is US$3,000 to US$10,000 for archaeological research, as well as for the recovery, recording, and analysis of materials that would otherwise be lost. (See website: http://www.doaks.org/fellowships.html for further information).
Applications: by 1 November of the academic year

preceding year of study; brochure and application guidelines available from the Assistant Director; for further information, see http://www.doaks.org/fellowships.html.

2560 Duquesne University [DU]
Office of International Affairs
601 Duquesne Union
15282 Pittsburgh, PA
Tel: +1-412-396-6113
Fax: +1-412-396-5178
Web: http://www.duq.edu
e-mail: oia@duq.edu

📖 Undergraduate, Graduate, Ph.D. Programmes
Study Domains: accounting, applied arts, arts, business administration, canon law, classical studies, economic and commercial sciences, education, history, information science, international business, international law, international relations, international studies, journalism, languages, law, liberal arts, music and musicology, nursing, pharmacy and pharmacology, speech therapy, theology, religion.
Programmes: Bachelor's, Master's and Ph.D. degrees in all major fields.
Fees: tuition: US$600 per course; estimated living costs: US$7,170 per year.
Applications: rolling admission.

🎓 Scholarship
Study Domains: all major fields.
Scholarships: Libermann Scholarship.
Open to: freshmen international students.
Value: US$1,000-$7,500 per year; renewable each year with GPA above 3.0.
Applications: contact Office of International Affairs at above address or oia@duq.edu.

2561 East Stroudsburg University [ESU]
200 Prospect Street
18307-2999 East Stroudsburg, PA
Tel: +1-570-422-3470
Fax: +1-570-422-3918
Web: http://www.esu.edu
e-mail: bokeppel@po-box.esu.edu

📖 Undergraduate, Graduate Programmes
Study Domains: arts, biochemistry, biology, business, chemistry, communication, computer science, earth science, economy, engineering, fine arts, geography, health and hygiene, international relations, international studies, languages, management, marine biology, marketing, mathematics, music and musicology, nursing, performing arts, philosophy, physics, political science, recreation and leisure, social sciences, sociology, speech therapy, theology, religion, tourism, hotel and catering management.
Programmes: Bachelor's, Master's degrees in arts and sciences, professional studies, health sciences and human performance.
Open to: applicants meeting admission requirements; TOEFL required.
Duration: 2 to 4 years; courses start 1 September.
Financial assistance: half-tuition waiver possible, based on academic qualifications (2.5 GPA) and financial need.
Applications: by 1 March.

2562 Eastern Illinois University [EIU]
International Programs
1900 Blair Hall
600 Lincoln Avenue
61920 Charleston, IL
Tel: +1-217-581-5000
Fax: +1-217-581-7207
Web: http://www.eiu.edu
e-mail: csaw@eiu.edu

📖 Liberal Arts Programmes
Study Domains: all major fields, cultural studies, education, health and hygiene, interior design, journalism, liberal arts, obstetrics and gynaecology, sciences, speech therapy.
Programmes: Bachelor's, Master's degrees in liberal arts.
Fees: estimated undergraduate costs: tuition (2 semesters):

US$7,808,40; fees (2 semesters) US$1,594; living expenses (9 months) US$4,530; graduate costs: tuition US$6,166; fees (2 semesters) US$1,596; living expenses (9 months) US$4,530.
Applications: see website for full application details http://www.eiu.edu/~interntl/welcome.html.

🎓 Scholarship
Study Domains: liberal arts.
Scholarships: International Student Scholarship.
Value: variable.
Applications: by 1 March for Summer or Fall; 1 October for Spring semester.

2563 Eastern Washington University [EWU]
International Student Programs
127, Showalter Hall
99004-2443 Cheney, WA
Tel: +1-509-359-2442
Fax: +1-509-359-7869
Web: http://www.ewu.edu
e-mail: isp@mail.ewu.edu

📖 Undergraduate, Graduate, Postgraduate Programmes
Study Domains: all major fields, dentistry, engineering, health and hygiene, liberal arts, medicine, neurology, nursing, psychiatry, rural development, tourism, hotel and catering management, urbanism.
Programmes: Bachelor's, Master's, Ph.D., pre-dentistry and pre-veterinary degree programmes.
Open to: applicants meeting academic requirements; TOEFL 525 PBT/195 CBT for undergraduates; TOEFL 580 for graduates.
Fees: registration: US$35; tuition: US$11,634 per year; estimated living costs: US$6,000 per year.
Applications: by 15 April for Fall term; 15 September for Winter term; 1 January for Spring term; contact International Student Services for further information.

🎓 Scholarship
Study Domains: all major fields.
Scholarships: International Scholarship Award for Undergraduates.
Open to: international students with excellent academic credentials.
Duration: 1 academic year.
Value: variable, renewed quarterly.
Applications: to the International Scholar Advisor; contact isp@mail.ewu.edu for further details.

2564 Elmira College
One Park Place
14901 Elmira, NY
Tel: +1-607-735-1800
Web: http://www.elmira.edu
e-mail: admissions@elmira.edu

📖 Undergraduate Programmes in Liberal Arts
Study Domains: business, education, liberal arts, nursing, sciences.
Programmes: undergraduate degree course programmes; Bachelor's Degrees (B.A. and B.Sc.) in liberal arts, sciences, education, business and nursing.
Open to: candidates of all nationalities with superior qualifications for admission to college with completion of secondary-school programme, preferably between the ages of 18 and 21.
Duration: 4 years.
Financial assistance: academic and very limited need-based assistance available for international students.
Applications: by 1 March to the above address; for further information see:
http://www.elmira.edu/admissions/international.shtml.

2565   Embry-Riddle Aeronautical University [ERAU]

600 South Clyde Morris Blvd
32114 Daytona Beach, FL
Tel: +1-386-226-6000 / 6579
Fax: +1-386-226-7070 / 7920
Web: http://www.erau.edu
e-mail: santiagd@erau.edu

⌑ Undergraduate, Graduate Programmes

Study Domains: aviation, aeronautics, business, business administration, civil engineering, communication, computer science, electricity and electronics, engineering, meteorology, physics, space, technology.
Programmes: Bachelor's, Master's Degrees in aeronautics-related fields.
Open to: candidates of all nationalities meeting academic, linguistic and financial requirements.
Applications: at least 60 calendar days before the desired enrolment date; for application details see:
http://www.erau.edu/0Universe/01/admissions/ad-req-ug.html#non_tra.

2566   Endicott College

376 Hale Street
01915-2098 Beverly, MA
Tel: +1-978-927-0585
Fax: +1-978-927-0084
Web: http://www.endicott.edu
e-mail: admissio@endicott.edu

☞ Scholarship

Study Domains: all major fields.
Scholarships: Merit Scholarship.
Open to: candidates of all nationalities.
Duration: 4 years; renewable.
Value: tuition, US$1,000-US$5,000.

2567   Erikson Institute

420 North Wabash Avenue
60611 Chicago
Tel: +1-312-755-2250
Fax: +1-312-755-0928
Web: http://www.erikson.edu

☞ Fellowship

Study Domains: early childhood education.
Scholarships: Irving B. Harris Award.
Description: Top academic credentials and at least 3 years of full-time work experience in the early childhood field with evidence of leadership potential.
Duration: 2 years.
Value: Tuition, US$21,400; living expenses, US$16,000 for two years.
Applications: by 1 April 2005; contact m.miller@erikson.edu for further information.

2568   Fairfield University [FU]

Graduate School of Education and Allied Professions
1073 North Benson Road
06824 Fairfield, CT
Tel: +1-203-254-4000
Web: http://www.fairfield.edu

⌑ Undergraduate, Graduate Programmes

Study Domains: all major fields.
Programmes: undergraduate and graduate programmes in all major fields.
Description: comprehensive Jesuit university offering courses in all major fields.
Open to: candidates of all nationalities meeting academic, linguistic and financial requirements.
Applications: see website.

2569   Ferris State University [FSU]

49307 Big Rapids, MI
Tel: +1-231-591-2000
Web: http://www.ferris.edu/htmls/future
e-mail: admissions@ferris.edu

⌑ Undergraduate, Graduate Programmes

Study Domains: all major fields.
Programmes: Bachelor's and Master's degree programmes in all major fields.
Description: over 150 majors offered through the colleges of Allied Health Sciences, Arts and Sciences, Business, Education and Human Services, Optometry, Pharmacy, and Technology.
Applications: see website
http://www.ferris.edu/htmls/administration/academicaffairs/int'l.

2570   Fight for Sight, Inc. Research Division
Prevent Blindness America [FFSI]

500 East Remington Road
60173-4557 Schaumburg, IL
Tel: +1-800-331-2020
Web: http://www.preventblindness.org/about/rsrch_grants.html
e-mail: info@preventblindness.org

☞ Research Fellowships in Ophthalmology

Study Domains: ophthalmology.
Scholarships: Research Fellowships.
Open to: researchers carrying out pilot projects for research relating to clinically important eye diseases.
Applications: by 1 March, to the above address for further information.

2571   Florida A & M University [FAMU]

304 Perry-Paige North
32307 Tallahassee, FL
Tel: +1-850-599-3295
Fax: +1-850-561-2520
Web: http://www.famu.edu/admreg
e-mail: adm@famu.edu

⌑ Undergraduate, Graduate, Postgraduate and Professional Programmes

Study Domains: all major fields.
Programmes: Bachelor's, Master's, Ph.D. and professional degree programmes in all major fields.
Open to: applicants of all nationalities meeting academic, linguistic and financial requirements; TOEFL 500 PBT or submit a certificate from an English language programme if native language is not English. Academic credentials must be certified true copies (no exceptions). In addition, all international applicants must submit a financial statement of available funds for at least 12 months, statement of health from a medical doctor, and proof of health insurance from an American-based company.
Applications: at least 6 months prior to the term of enrolment.

2572   Florida Atlantic University

PO Box 3091
777 Glades Road
FL 33431 Boca Raton
Tel: +1-561-297-3040
Fax: +1-561-297-3942
Web: http://www.fau.edu

⌑ Undergraduate, Graduate Programmes

Study Domains: all major fields.
Programmes: Bachelor's, Master's and PhD degree programmes in all major fields; distance education degree courses in nursing, gerontology, business, computer arts and accounting.
Open to: candidates of any nationality; TOEFL 550 PBT/213 CBT.
Duration: 4 to 6 years, depending on programme; courses begin in fall, spring and summer.
Financial assistance: graduate assistantships available; contact Financial Aid Department at above address.
Applications: by 1 April for fall, 1 October for spring and 1 March for summer; to the above address; see website for further information
http://www.fau.edu/academic/admissions/interntl.htm.

2573 Francis Marion University [FMU]

P.O. Box 100547
Florence, SC 29501
Tel: +1 843 661 1231
Web: http://www.fmarion.edu
e-mail: drussell@fmarion.edu

📖 Undergraduate, Graduate Programmes

Study Domains: liberal arts.
Programmes: Bachelor's and Master's Degrees in Liberal Arts.
Open to: candidates of all nationalities meeting academic, financial and linguistic requirements; TOEFL 500 PBT/ 173 CBT required.
Fees: estimated costs per year US$17,440, including tuition, room, food, books, and miscellaneous expenses.
Applications: see website: http://www.admissions.fmarion.edu/jump/intern.asp.

2574 Franklin Pierce College [FPC]

PO Box 60
College Road
03461-0060 Rindge, NH
Tel: +1-603-899-4100
Fax: +1-603-899-4323
Web: http://www.fpc.edu
e-mail: oehlscs@fpc.edu

📖 Undergraduate, Graduate Programmes

Study Domains: accounting, administration, advertising, American studies, arts, biology, business, business administration, communication, computer science, ecology, environment, education, European studies, management, marketing, mathematics, music and musicology, political science, psychology, public relations, sociology, teacher education.
Programmes: Bachelor's and Master's degrees in education, humanities and arts, social sciences, business, management and science.
Open to: applicants meeting academic requirements; TOEFL 500 PBT/173 CBT for international students.
Held: Rindge campus and six satellite campus centres.
Duration: 4 years; courses begin in September.
Fees: tuition: US$18,900; estimated living costs: US$6,600.
Applications: rolling admissions; contact oehlscs@fpc.edu for further details.

🎓 Scholarship

Study Domains: accounting, administration, advertising, American studies, arts, biology, business, business administration, communication, computer science, ecology, environment, education, fine arts, management, marketing, mathematics, music and musicology, political science, psychology, sociology, teacher education.
Scholarships: International Student Scholarship.
Open to: international students meeting academic requirements.
Value: US$8,000 per year.
Applications: contact oehlscs@fpc.edu for further information.

2575 Fresno Pacific University [FPU]

1717 S Chestnut
93702 Fresno, CA
Tel: +1-559-453-2069
Fax: +1-559-453-5501
Web: http://www.fresno.edu
e-mail: ipso@fresno.edu

📖 Undergraduate, Graduate Programmes

Study Domains: all major fields, anatomy, business, law, sciences, social sciences, social work.
Programmes: Bachelor's, Master's programmes in liberal arts, science and professions.
Open to: all applicants meeting academic standards; TOEFL required.
Duration: 4 years; courses begin in August.
Fees: registration: US$676; tuition: US$16,200; estimated living costs: US$6,170.
Applications: by 30 June; contact apprieb@fresno.edu.

🎓 University Scholarship

Study Domains: all major fields.
Scholarships: University Scholarship.
Duration: renewable annually.
Value: variable; depending upon academic ability and need; contact apprieb@fresno.edu.

2576 Frostburg State University [FSU]

101 Braddock Road
21532-1099 Frostburg, MD
Tel: +1-301-687-4747
Web: http://www.frostburg.edu
e-mail: fsuadmissions@frostburg.edu

📖 Undergraduate, Graduate Programmes

Study Domains: art history, astronomy, biochemistry, biology, chemistry, computer science, cultural studies, design, earth science, ecology, environment, education, international relations, Japanese, liberal arts, literature and civilization, mathematics, performing arts, photography, physics, rural development, statistics, tourism, hotel and catering management.
Programmes: Bachelor's and Master's degrees in liberal arts.
Open to: no restrictions; TOEFL 550 and SAT required.
Fees: tuition: US$7,980-$9,388; estimated living costs: US$12,800.
Applications: by 1 June; courses begin late August; contact llewis@frostburg.edu for undergraduate admissions and pspiker@frostburg.edu for graduate admissions.

🎓 Scholarship

Study Domains: all major fields.
Scholarships: Harold Rowe International Scholarship.
Open to: international undergraduate or graduate candidates, based on academic qualifications and financial need.
Value: US$1,000-$2,000 per semester; renewable each semester.
Applications: by 1 May and 1 November; contact tcarr@frostburg.edu for further details.

2577 George Washington University [GWU]

2121 Eye Street, N.W.
20052 Washington, DC
Tel: +1-202-994-4949
Web: http://www.gwu.edu

📖 Undergraduate Programmes

Study Domains: all major fields, economic and commercial sciences, European studies, history, international business, Spanish.
Programmes: undergraduate programmes in all major fields.
Open to: candidates of any country, who are college sophomores or higher.
Duration: 4 years.
Applications: by 1 April for Fall semester and 15 November for Spring; to the address above; for further information: http://gwired.gwu.edu/adm/pdf/interapp.pdf.

🎓 Undergraduate International Academic Scholarships

Study Domains: all major fields.
Scholarships: (a) International Academic Scholarships; (b) Presidential Scholarships.
Open to: (a) all non-United States citizens or non-permanent residents admitted to The George Washington University as incoming undergraduate for the Fall semester, possessing strong academic credentials are eligible for consideration; (b) international students not benefiting from merit aid at time of admission but who have excelled in their studies.
Duration: 1 academic year (renewable; may be held a total of 2 years for Master's candidates and 3 years for doctoral candidates).
Value: (a) US$15,000 per year; (b) partial tuition for students who achieve a minimum 3.6 cumulative grade point average after completing 30 credit hours of studies. Renewal requires continuation of 3.6 grade point average.

Applications: (a) no separate application is required. Automatic consideration will be given to eligible candidates upon receipt of admissions application and required academic credentials; priority will be given to applicants whose admissions files are complete by 15 January. For further information; see http://gwired.gwu.edu/adm/pdf/interapp.pdf.

2578 Georgetown University [GU]
International Student and Scholar Services
Poulton Hall, 2nd Floor, Box 571013
20057-1013 Washington, DC
Tel: +1-202-687-5867
Fax: +1 202 687 5944
Web: http://www.georgetown.edu

Undergraduate Programmes
Study Domains: all major fields, interpretation and translation.
Programmes: (a) undergraduate programmes in all major fields; (b) certificate of proficiency in translation and conference interpretation.
Description: (b) active English, French, German, Japanese, Portuguese and Spanish; passive Italian.
Open to: candidates of any nationality meeting academic, linguistic and financial requirements; (b) Bachelor's degree or equivalent strongly recommended; entrance examination administered.
Duration: (b) 1 academic year; courses begin at the end of August (for interpretation and translation) or mid-January (translation only).
Applications: by 15 July or 7 December, at the above address; for further information:
http://www.georgetown.edu/programs/oip/isss.

2579 Georgia College and State University [GC&SU]
231 West Hancock Street
31061 Milledgeville, GA
Tel: +1-478-445-4789
Fax: +1-478-445-2623
Web: http://www.gcsu.edu
e-mail: intladm@gcsu.edu

Undergraduate Liberal Arts Programme
Study Domains: liberal arts.
Programmes: undergraduate liberal arts programme.
Open to: candidates of all nationalities meeting academic, linguistic and academic requirements; applicants with a TOEFL score under 550 PBT and under 213 CBT are eligible for admission, but will be required to take an ESL class concurrent with other courses during the first semester of enrolment. A minimum 2.2 grade point average on all academic courses completed in secondary school and a minimum 2.0 on all university coursework (out of a 4.0 grading scale) is required.
Duration: 4 years.
Applications: 1 April for Fall semester (August-December); 1 September for Spring semester (January-May). For further information:
http://www.gcsu.edu/acad_affairs/acad_srvcs/intrnl_ed/Admissions/admissions.htm.

Undergraduate, Graduate Awards
Study Domains: all major fields.
Scholarships: (a) International Student Scholarships (ISS); (b) International Graduate Assistantship.
Open to: international undergraduate students admitted to the University. Students must submit and essay and 2 letters of recommendations. Awards based on academic performance, extracurricular involvement and financial need. Contact International admissions, intladm@gcsu.edu for further information.
Value: equal to full out-of-state tuition waiver or a half out-of-state tuition waiver, and awarded on the basis of demonstrated academic ability, evidence of extracurricular involvement and financial need.
Applications: applicants must have on file a completed application for admission and completed ISS application by the stated deadline; for further information:
http://www.gcsu.edu/international.

2580 Georgia Institute of Technology
756 West Peachtree Street N.W.
30332 Atlanta, GA
Tel: +1-404-894-2000
Web: http://www.gatech.edu

Undergraduate Programmes
Study Domains: architecture, classical studies, computer science, engineering, liberal arts, management, sciences.
Programmes: undergraduate programmes in engineering, sciences, architecture, liberal arts, computer sciences and management.
Open to: candidates of all nationalities meeting academic, linguistic and financial requirements.
Applications: international freshmen may enter the Institute in the Fall, Spring or Summer semester. The completed Application for Freshman Admission and all supporting credentials must be received by 15 January. For further information:
http://www.admission.gatech.edu/international.

2581 Georgia Southern University, Center for International Studies [CIS]
PO Box 8106
30460 Statesboro, GA
Tel: +1-912-681-5668
Fax: +1-912-681-0824
Web: http://www.gasou.edu
e-mail: shumaker@gasou.edu

Undergraduate, Graduate, Ph.D. Programmes
Study Domains: all major fields, health and hygiene, nursing.
Programmes: (a) Bachelor's and Master's degree programmes in science, fine arts, music, justice studies, business administration, health science, kinesiology, medical technology, nursing and education; (b) Ph.D. programme in education; (c) Engineering programme; (d) Pre-Professional programmes.
Languages: English at TOEFL level.
Applications: 1 October for Spring semester (beginning in January), 1 March for Summer semester (beginning in May), 1 June for Fall (beginning in August); for further application information: http://admissions.gasou.edu.

2582 Gladys Krieble Delmas Foundation
521 Fifth Avenue, Suite 1612
10175-1699 New York, NY
Tel: +1-212-687-0011
Fax: +1-212-687-8877
e-mail: info@delmas.org

Grants for Independent Research on Venetian History and Culture
Study Domains: archaeology, architecture, arts, ecology, environment, economy, history, law, literature and civilization, political science, theology, religion.
Description: predoctoral and postdoctoral grants for research In Venice and the Veneto; granted for historical research specifically on Venice and the former Venetian empire, and for study of contemporary Venetian society and culture. Disciplines of the humanities and social sciences are eligible; areas of study, include but are not limited to archaeology, architecture, art, bibliography, economics, history, history of science, law, literature, music, political science, religion, and theatre.
Open to: British or Commonwealth nationals with experience of advanced research and relevant language proficiency.
Nationality: British or Commonwealth nationals.
Place of study: in Venice (Italy).
Duration: up to 1 year depending on needs. Funds are granted for research in Venice and the Veneto only, and for transportation to, from, and within the Veneto. Funds may also be made available for aid in the publication of studies made possible by these funds.
Value: a maximum of US$16,500.
Applications: by 15 December to the above address for

any further information.

2583 Golden Gate University [GGU]

536 Mission Street
94105-2968 San Francisco, CA
Tel: +1-415-442-7220
Fax: +1-415-442-7807
Web: http://www.ggu.edu
e-mail: info@ggu.edu

Undergraduate, Graduate Programmes

Study Domains: accounting, arts, business administration, law, sciences.
Programmes: undergraduate and graduate programmes in business, law, public administration: distance education degree programmes (CyberCampus: http://cybercampus.ggu.edu).
Open to: qualified students of all nationalities with TOEFL score of 525 for undergraduates or 550 for graduates.
Applications: to International Admissions Office, http://www.ggu.edu/admissions/intl/home.html.

2584 Gordon College

255 Grapevine Road
01984 Wenham, MA
Tel: +1-978-927-2300
Fax: +1-978-524-3704
Web: http://www.gordon.edu

A.J. Gordon Scholar Programme

Study Domains: all major fields.
Open to: candidates of all nationalities, selected on a competitive interview basis and on academic results.
Other conditions: applicants are selected on the basis of their academic record and invited to apply for the A.J. Gordon Scholarship. A.J. Gordon Scholars are assigned mentors and are expected to take leadership roles on campus.
Duration: 4 academic years; renewable.
Value: US$12,000 per year.
Applications: 1 December for admission following fall semester; to Department of Admissions at above address; contact: admissions@hops.gordon.edu.

2585 Goshen College [GC]

1700 S. Main Street
46526 Goshen, IN
Tel: +1-574-535-7000
Web: http://www.goshen.edu

Undergraduate Programmes

Study Domains: English, languages, liberal arts.
Programmes: undergraduate degree programmes in liberal arts.
Open to: candidates of all nationalities meeting academic, linguistic and financial requirements. See website for further information (http://www.goshen.edu/admissions/international.php).
Duration: 4 years.
Fees: tuition: US$16,320; room: US$3,000; board: US$2,800; technical fees: US$330; books and supplies: US$700; estimated transportation: US$270; estimated personal expenses: US$1,000 yearly.
Applications: by 1 May, to the Admissions Office, Carl Barnett carleb@goshen.edu in.

2586 Goucher College

1021 Dulaney Valley Road
21204 Baltimore, MD
Tel: +1-410-337-6000
Web: http://www.goucher.edu

Undergraduate, Graduate Programmes

Study Domains: all major fields.
Programmes: undergraduate and graduate degree programmes in all major fields.
Open to: no specific requirements; TOEFL required and SAT strongly recommended.
Duration: 4 years.
Fees: tuition and fees: US$16,750; room and board: US$6,300; books: US$450.
Financial assistance: merit-based scholarships of US$5,000 -$10,000 available and renewable.

Applications: early action application, by 1 December (notification by 15 January); regular decision application, by 1 February (notification by 1 April). See website http://www.goucher.edu/downloads/InternationalApp_2002-2003.pdf.

2587 Grand Valley State University [GVSU]

1 Campus Drive STU 300
49401 Allendale, MI
Tel: +1-616-331-2025
Fax: +1-616-313-2000
Web: http://admissions.gvsu.edu
e-mail: global@gvsu.edu

Undergraduate, Graduate Programmes

Study Domains: all major fields, administration, arts, education, engineering, languages, natural sciences, nursing, performing arts, physiology, psychology, sciences, social sciences, social work, special education, teacher education, visual arts.
Programmes: Bachelor's and Master's degrees in all major fields.
Open to: applicants from all nationalities meeting admissions criteria; TOEFL score 550 PBT/213 CBT required.

Undergraduate, Graduate Grants

Study Domains: all major fields, dance, fine arts, music and musicology, physical education.
Scholarships: (a) International Student Scholarship; (b) International Awards of Excellence; (c) Dance and Music Scholarships; (d) Athletic Scholarships.
Open to: applicants of all nationalities meeting academic requirements.
Academic requirements: equivalent of A/B average (3.5-4.0) GPA.
Value: variable; graduate assistantships for qualified candidates in certain Master's programmes.
Applications: contact crawleyj@gvsu.edu for further details; see website http://admissions.gvsu.edu/admissions/intl.asp - link to 'scholarships'.

2588 Hanover College [HC]

PO Box 108
47243-0108 Hanover, IN
Tel: +1-812-866-7000
Web: http://www.hanover.edu
e-mail: info@hanover.edu

Undergraduate Programme in all major fields

Study Domains: all major fields.
Programmes: undergraduate programmes in all major fields.
Open to: candidates of all nationalities meeting academic, linguistic and financial requirements. See website for further information.

Merit Scholarships (under-represented countries)

Study Domains: all major fields.
Scholarships: Hanover College Merit Scholarships for under-represented countries.
Open to: foreign students from under-represented countries eligible for admission to the College, aged 18 to 24, with strong academic background and full proficiency in English or 550 TOEFL.
Duration: 1 year (renewable).
Value: US$3,000 to full tuition.
Applications: by 1 March, to the Office of Admissions and Financial Aids for New Students.
http://www.hanover.edu/admissions/finance/scholarship.htm.

2589 Harding University
900 E. Center
72149-0001 Searcy, AR
Tel: +1-501-279-4407
Web: http://www.harding.edu
e-mail: admissions@harding.edu

📖 Undergraduate Studies
Study Domains: all major fields.
Programmes: Bachelor of Arts programmes in College of Arts and Humanities; College of Education and College of Bible and Religion; Bachelor of Social Work; Bachelor of Fine Arts; Bachelor of Music Education; Bachelor of Ministry; Bachelor of Theology; Bachelor of Business Administration; College of Business Administration; Bachelor of Science, College of Science; Bachelor of Science in Nursing and Pre-Professional Programmes.
Fees: average cost for tuition, fees, room and board is US$16,052.
Financial assistance: none for the first year of studies. For the remaining three years, the student may qualify for a 1/4 tuition scholarship and work on campus. International students do not qualify for federal financial aid.
Applications: see http://www.harding.edu/admissions/international.html for complete details or write to the Assistant Dean of Admissions at the above address.

2590 Harvard University, Harvard College [HU]
University Hall
02138 Cambridge, MA
Tel: +1-617-495-1000
Web: http://www.harvard.edu

📖 Undergraduate Programmes
Study Domains: all major fields, liberal arts.
Programmes: Harvard College offers a four-year undergraduate, liberal arts programme. The College is only one part of Harvard University (www.harvard.edu), which includes 10 graduate and professional schools, all of which offer programmes for students possessing Bachelor's degrees and seeking advanced training in their fields through Master's or doctoral programmes. All 10 graduate schools maintain their own admissions offices and teaching faculties, and they are run almost entirely independently, both of one another and of Harvard College. For information about Harvard's graduate programmes, please contact these schools' admissions offices directly; website http://www.harvard.edu/admissions.
Financial assistance: based on need; limited funds for international students.
Applications: http://www.college.harvard.edu/admissions/foreign_app.html.

2591 Hebrew Union College, Jewish Institute of Religion [HUC]
3101 Clifton Avenue
45220-2488 Cincinnati, OH
Tel: +1-513-221-1875
Fax: +1-513-221-0321
Web: http://www.huc.edu
e-mail: gradschool@huc.edu

📌 Postgraduate Fellowships for Biblical and Jewish Studies
Study Domains: philosophy, theology, religion.
Scholarships: Biblical and Jewish Studies.
Description: postgraduate studies leading to Master of Arts and Doctor of Philosophy in Bible and ancient Near East, history of biblical interpretation, Jewish studies in the Greco-Roman period; Jewish history; Jewish religious thought; rabbinical studies.
Open to: non-sectarian candidates with Bachelor's degree from an accredited institution of higher learning; candidates must, in the judgement of the faculty, be qualified to do graduate work in the fields envisaged and be proficient in English and Hebrew.
Duration: 1 year (renewable for 4 years upon approval of Faculty) after 1-year Hebrew competency programme.
Value: variable: in the form of scholarships to defray the cost of tuition, and fellowships, which include tuition plus an additional cash stipend. All awards are based on merit; many

opportunities for student employment, including teaching assistantships, library and clerical work and research assistantships are also possible. Students may also be eligible for Federal Stafford Loans.
Languages: English and Hebrew.
Applications: to Director of the School of Graduate Studies.

2592 Heiser Program for Research in Leprosy and Tuberculosis
c/o The New York Community Trust
909 Third Avenue
10002 New York, NY
Tel: +1-212-686-0010
e-mail: info@nycommunitytrust.org

📌 Research Grants
Study Domains: medicine, research.
Scholarships: (a) Research Grants; (b) Postdoctoral research fellowships.
Description: for research directly related to leprosy and/or tuberculosis.
Open to: candidates of all nationalities with M.D., Ph.D. or equivalent degree and beginning postdoctoral research training.
Place of study: in institutions in any country other than that in which the candidate's doctorate was obtained.
Duration: 1 year (renewable for a second year).
Value: approximately US$30,000 per year.
Applications: by 1 February, to the above address for all further information; application materials available after 1 September.

2593 Hollins College [HC]
PO Box 9707
24020 Roanoke, VA
Tel: +1-540-362-6401
Web: http://www.hollins.edu
e-mail: huadm@hollins.edu

📖 Undergraduate Programmes for Women
Study Domains: liberal arts.
Programmes: undergraduate liberal arts programmes.
Open to: women students of all nationalities meeting academic, linguistic and financial requirements.
Applications: 1 December for early decision (notification by 15 December); 15 February for regular decision. http://www.hollins.edu/admissions/ugradadm/international/intl.htm.

📌 Hollins College Scholarships for Women
Study Domains: international relations, liberal arts, psychology.
Scholarships: Hollins College Scholarships in liberal arts.
Open to: women applicants of all nationalities with strong secondary-school records, an advanced level of English proficiency and a minimum 550 on the TOEFL.
Duration: up to 4 years.
Value: from US$5,000 -$15,000. International students are also eligible to compete for the Batten Scholars programme which covers full tuition, provided they meet the SAT/GPA requirements. Limited financial aid available for international students with outstanding academic credentials.
Applications: by 15 February, to the Director of Admissions with the College Board's Foreign Student Financial Aid Application.

2594 Hope International University [HIU]
2500 E. Nutwood Avenue
92831 Fullerton, CA
Tel: +1-714-879-3901
Fax: +1-714-681-7224
Web: http://www.hiu.edu

📖 Undergraduate, Graduate Programmes
Study Domains: accounting, biology, business, business administration, communication, computer science, education, English, international business, marketing, philosophy, political science, psychology, teacher education.
Programmes: Bachelor's, Master's degrees in liberal arts,

business, computer science.
Open to: no restrictions; TOEFL test.
Fees: registration: US$6,164; tuition: US$3,245; estimated living costs: US$2,341.
Financial assistance: US$2,000 per year towards tuition based on minimum 2.5 GPA and acceptance of University Christian values.

2595 Indiana University South Bend [IUSB]

1700 Mishawaka Avenue
PO Box 7111
46634 South Bend, IN
Tel: +1-574-237-4419
Fax: +1-574-237-4590
Web: http://www.iusb.edu
e-mail: oip@iusb.edu

Undergraduate, Graduate Programmes

Study Domains: all major fields.
Programmes: Associate, Bachelor's, Master's degrees in all major fields (over 100 programmes offered).
Open to: no restrictions; minimum TOEFL score of 530 PBT/ 197 CBT for undergraduate study and 550 PBT/ 213 CBT; GRE and GMAT also required for certain programmes.
Fees: tuition and fees (two semesters, normal course load): US$8,591; room and board: US$5,000; miscellaneous expenses: US$2,500.
Applications: rolling admission for undergraduate studies; graduate applications: 1 July for Fall entrance; 1 November for Spring entrance and 1 April for Summer session; for further information contact juwicker@iusb.edu or http://www.iusb.edu/~intl.

Scholarship

Study Domains: all major fields.
Scholarships: Tuition Reduction Scholarship.
Value: undergraduate students: US$175/credit hour; graduate students: US$200-220/credit hour.
Applications: every new student automatically considered; current students must fill out application; contact juwicker@iusb.edu for further details.

2596 Institute of International Education [IIE]

809 United Nations Plaza
10017-3580 New York, NY
Tel: +1-212-984-5330
Web: http://www.iie.org

IIE-Administered Scholarships

Study Domains: all major fields.
Scholarships: The Institute administers scholarships offered by foreign governments, educational institutions, foundations, corporations, private donors, student and professional associations in the U.S. and abroad, and assists the U.S. Information Agency in the administration of grants under the Fulbright-Hays Act; the IIE also administers a number of individual and group projects in various fields involving leaders, specialists and trainees usually selected by the sponsoring organization, as well as special projects in the arts for which candidates are nominated by special juries; (a) Fulbright awards are offered to nationals of 120 countries; other IIE administered programmes relate to specific countries or groups of countries; most awards are for study in the U.S. generally at the university or postgraduate level; (b) Scholarships offered by foreign governments and institutions, the U.S. Government, U.S. foundations and societies. See website for list of awards: http://www.iie.org/Content/NavigationMenu/About_IIE/Scholarships_Awards_and_Grants/Scholarships_Awards_and_Grants.htm.
Open to: (a) candidates preferably under 35 years of age; (b) American students for academic study abroad; candidates must have a Bachelor's degree and are usually required to have demonstrated ability and capacity for independent study; applicants in the field of medicine must have an M.D. degree.
Duration: (a) 1 academic year or completion of Master's or doctoral degree; (b) 1 academic year.
Value: (a) varies ranging from travel only to full support (tuition and fees, basic living expenses, and incidentals); transportation is generally included; (b) usually covers the

cost of tuition, room and meals; transportation is included under most appointments.
Applications: (a) foreign students should apply to the Binational Educational Commission or Foundation in their home country, or to the Cultural Affairs Office of the United States Embassy; IIE's offices in the United States cannot accept direct applications from foreign students; (b) United States students enrolled at American colleges and universities should apply to their campus Fulbright Program Advisors at the dates fixed by them; others may apply directly to IIE at the above address. For further information: http://www.iie.org/Content/NavigationMenu/About_IIE/Scholarships_Awards_and_Grants/Scholarships_Awards_and_Grants.htm.

2597 International College of Surgeons [ICS]

1516 North Lake Shore Drive
60610 Chicago, IL
Tel: +1-312-642-3555
Fax: +1-312-787-1624
Web: http://www.icsglobal.org/aboutus/index.asp

Postgraduate Scholarships

Study Domains: surgery.
Scholarships: Postgraduate Scholarships, supplementary to documented primary funding from other sources available to the candidate.
Subjects: surgery and surgical specialities.
Open to: practising surgeons of all nationalities.
Place of study: in established treatment, research facilities or educational institutions.
Duration: open but usually short-term.
Applications: to Chairperson, Research and Scholarship Committee, c/o International Executive Director at the above address; see website for further information: http://www.icsglobal.org/humanitarian/application.asp.

2598 Ithaca College

953 Danby Road
14850 Ithaca, NY
Tel: +1-607-274-3011
Web: http://www.ithaca.edu
e-mail: finaid@ithaca.edu

Ithaca College Grant Aid

Study Domains: business, communication, health and hygiene, humanities and arts, music and musicology, natural sciences, social sciences.
Open to: all enrolled international students.
Value: variable; US$2,900-$35,000.
Applications: 1 February; on CSS International Student Financial Aid Form (FAF).

2599 J. Paul Getty Museum, Education Department

Getty Graduate Internships
1200 Getty Center Drive Suite 1000
90049-1687 Los Angeles, CA
Tel: +1-310-440-7156
Web: http://www.getty.edu/about/opportunities/intern.html
e-mail: interns@getty.edu

Getty Graduate Internships

Study Domains: museology and museography.
Scholarships: Getty Graduate Internships in curatorial, conservation, education, information management / online resources, research, museum registration, exhibitions and public programmes, grant making and design.
Open to: students of all nationalities currently enrolled in a graduate course of study who intend to pursue careers in art museums and related fields of the visual arts, humanities and sciences.
Duration: generally for 8 months; 12 for conservation internships.
Value: US$17,300 for 8 months and US$25,000 for 12 months, including health benefits and educational travel allowance of US$1,200.
Applications: to the above address.

2600 Jane Coffin Childs Memorial Fund for Medical Research

333 Cedar Street
06510 New Haven, CT
Tel: +1-203-785-4612
Fax: +1-203-785-3301
Web: http://www.jccfund.org
e-mail: info@jccfund.org

☛ Postdoctoral Fellowships in Cancer Research

Study Domains: cancerology, research.
Scholarships: Postdoctoral Fellowships for further research into the causes, origins and treatment of cancer.
Open to: qualified individuals from all countries; candidates must hold either an M.D. degree or a Ph.D. degree in the field in which they propose to study.
Place of study: in the United States for citizens of other countries; in the United States or in other countries for citizens of the United States.
Duration: 3 years (no more than 1 year postdoctoral).
Value: basic stipend US$39,000 first year, US$41,000 second year, and US$43,000 third year, with an additional US$750 for each dependent child. There is no dependency allowed for a spouse. An allowance of US$1,500 a year toward the cost of the research usually will be made available to the laboratory sponsoring the fellow. A travel award will be made to the Fellow and family for travel to the sponsoring laboratory. Return travel for Fellows will be considered depending upon the Fellow's plans and situation at the time.
Applications: by 1 February (selection late Spring each year), to the Office of the Director.

2601 Johns Hopkins University

Charles & 34th Street
21218 Baltimore, MD
Tel: +1-410-516-8000
Fax: +1-410-516-8035
Web: http://www.jhu.edu

☛ International Undergraduate Scholarship

Study Domains: arts, engineering, sciences.
Open to: full-time students of all nationalities; based on financial necessity and academic results.
Duration: 4 academic years; renewable.
Value: full tuition and partial living expenses.
Applications: 1 February; see website www.jhu.edu/finaid/international.html for full details.

2602 Kent State University [KSU]

PO Box 5190
44242-0001 Kent, OH
Tel: +1-330-672-2444
Web: http://www.kent.edu

📖 Undergraduate Programmes

Study Domains: all major fields.
Programmes: undergraduate programmes in all major fields.
Open to: candidates of all nationalities, meeting academic, linguistic and financial requirements; cumulative secondary school grade point average of at least 2.5 (on a 4.0 scale): minimum TOEFL score of 525 (a score of 197 on the computerized version of the TOEFL) or minimum MELAB score of 77 required.
Duration: 4 years.
Fees: US$21,500 per year for tuition and living expenses.
Financial assistance: some financial assistance possible for academic merit. Enquire at Admissions Office or the Student Financial Aid Department (http://www.sfa.kent.edu).
Applications: by 15 February to Admissions Office at above address; http://www.admissions.kent.edu/template3.asp?id=42.

2603 Lake Erie College [LEC]

391 W. Washington Street
44077 Painesville, OH
Tel: +1-440-352-3361
Fax: +1-440-942-3872
Web: http://www.lec.edu

📖 Undergraduate and Graduate Programmes

Study Domains: all major fields.
Programmes: undergraduate programmes in all major fields.
Description: undergraduate level programmes leading to Bachelor of Arts, of Science and of Fine Arts; majors available in accounting, biology, business administration and international business, chemistry, communications, dance, elementary and secondary education certification, English, environmental management, equestrian facilities management, equestrian teacher/trainer, equine study farm management, fine arts, legal assistant, mathematics, modern foreign languages, music, psychology and social sciences; and graduate programmes leading to Master of Business Administration and Master of Science in Education.
Open to: candidates of all nationalities with a minimum secondary-school diploma or equivalent.
Duration: academic year; courses begin in August.
Applications: to the Director of Admissions, at the above address.

2604 Langston University [LU]

PO Box 907
73050 Langston, OK
Tel: +1-405-466-2231
Fax: +1-405-466-3461
Web: http://www.lunet.edu

☛ Scholarship

Study Domains: humanities and arts, sciences.
Scholarships: (a) Academic Scholarships, (b) Financial Need Scholarships, (c) Graduate Program.
Duration: 1 year; renewable.
Value: Tuition, US$3,000; living expenses, US$4,000; Graduate, US$14,000.
Applications: by 1 April; candidates must meet all university requirements; contact mlbonner@lunet.edu for further details. For graduate programs, contact aolewis@lunet.edu for further information.

2605 Lebanon Valley College [LVC]

101 North College Avenue
17003 Annville, PA
Tel: +1-717-867-6100
Web: http://www.lvc.edu
e-mail: admission@lvc.edu

📖 Undergraduate, Graduate Programmes

Study Domains: all major fields.
Programmes: Bachelor's, Master's Degrees in all major fields; see website for further information.
Open to: candidates of all nationalities meeting academic, linguistic and financial requirements; TOEFL score of 550 PBT and 213 CBT required.
Fees: estimated expenses for tuition, fees, room and board, as well as expenses for travel, books and supplies total approximately US$30,310.
Applications: see website for full details and application form: http://www.lvc.edu/admission/international-admission.html.

☛ Scholarships

Study Domains: all major fields.
Scholarships: International Grant and Academic Scholarships.
Open to: students of all nationalities meeting academic, linguistic and financial requirements.
Value: US$3,000 per academic year; contact sarisky@lvc.edu for further information.

2606 Lewis and Clark College

International Student Services
0615 S.W. Palatine Hill Road
97219-7899 Portland, OR
Tel: +1-503-768-7305
Fax: +1-503-768-7301
Web: http://www.lclark.edu
e-mail: iso@lclark.edu

📖 Undergraduate and Graduate Programmes

Study Domains: all major fields, Asian studies.
Programmes: undergraduate and graduate programmes in all major fields; East Asian studies and pre-professional programmes.
Open to: candidates with secondary school diploma and standing B average, on a competitive basis; minimum TOEFL 550 required for candidates whose first language is not English.
Duration: total 4 years; courses begin in September and January for degree programmes.
Financial assistance: several awards are made to incoming international students each Fall; average award is US$10,000; no full tuition awards available.
Applications: rolling admissions for international students, to International Student Office. http://www.lclark.edu/dept/iso.

🎓 Foreign Student Financial Aid

Study Domains: liberal arts, sciences.
Scholarships: Foreign Student Financial Aid.
Open to: college undergraduates of all nationalities with a very good scholastic record in secondary school (B average) and proof of English-language proficiency (550 TOEFL required).
Duration: 1 year (renewable on basis of need, and achievement of at least a C average).
Applications: by 1 March, to International Student Advisor, Campus Box 192, website: http://www.lclark.edu/dept/iso.

2607 Lewis University [LU]

One University Parkway
60446-2200 Romeoville, IL
Tel: +1-815-836-5250
Fax: +1-815-836-5002
Web: http://www.lewisu.edu
e-mail: admissions@lewisu.edu

📖 Undergraduate, Graduate Programmes

Study Domains: all major fields.
Programmes: Bachelor's and Master's degrees in all major fields.
Description: comprehensive Catholic university offering degree courses in over 60 undergraduate majors, 11 graduate programs through the Colleges of Arts and Sciences, Business, and Nursing and Health Professions. Premier programmes include aviation, criminal/social justice, education, nursing, and business.
Open to: international students must have completed secondary-level education with strong academic records; TOEFL 500 required. International students with less than the required scores may apply for admission to the English as a Second Language (ESL) programme. Students must complete all ESL courses through the advanced level with a minimum grade of C before beginning the undergraduate programme.
Applications: contact the Admissions Office at least three months prior to the desired semester of attendance for the appropriate application form, fees, and procedures; see website for further information and application form, http://www.lewisu.edu/admissions/intl.htm.

2608 Lock Haven University [LHU]

Institute for International Studies
17745 Lock Haven, PA
Tel: +1-800-233-8978
Web: http://www.lhup.edu

📖 Undergraduate Programmes

Study Domains: all major fields.
Programmes: Bachelor of Arts and Bachelor of Science programmes in all major fields.
Description: B.A. degrees in international studies, general studies, fine arts, economics, humanities, mathematics, natural sciences, social sciences, social work, languages (English, French, German and Spanish), history, philosophy, political science, sociology, psychology, engineering, journalism and media studies; B.Sc. degree in biology, chemistry, chemistry-biology, geography, mathematics/computer science, physics, management science; B.Sc. degree in Education: early childhood education, elementary education, secondary education (with above concentrations); B.Sc.

degree in health and physical education; special degree programmes in public school nursing, medical technology, pre-professional dentistry, law, medicine.
Open to: candidates of all nationalities meeting academic, linguistic and financial requirements; TOEFL minimum score of 213 on computer based test.
Fees: application fee: US$100.
Financial assistance: in the form of tuition waivers.
Applications: 6 months before the start of courses; Fall semester begins late August, Spring semester begins mid-January. Late applicants will automatically be deferred to the following semester. For further information: http://www.lhup.edu/admissions/international/international_table.htm.

🎓 Foreign Student Tuition Waivers

Study Domains: all major fields.
Scholarships: Foreign Student Tuition Waivers.
Open to: nationals of any country with a good academic record, good standing in GCE or other standard examinations (including TOEFL), good health and a promise of special service to the College; English proficiency is essential; student must carry a 2.5 GPA or above.
Duration: normally 1 full year (including Summer), subject to renewal each year.
Value: full or half-tuition waiver; expenses covering room, board, books, insurance, student council fees and personal expenses must be paid by the student.
Applications: by 1 May, to the Dean of International Studies.

2609 Loyola University of Chicago [LUOC]

Undergraduate Admissions Office
820 N. Michigan Avenue, Suite 613
60611 Chicago, IL
Tel: +1-390-915-6500
Fax: +1-390-915-7216
Web: http://www.luc.edu

📖 Undergraduate and Graduate Programmes

Study Domains: all major fields, business, classical studies, fine arts, history, human sciences, liberal arts, performing arts, sociology, theology, religion.
Programmes: undergraduate and graduate programmes in all major fields.
Description: Jesuit university consisting of nine schools and colleges: arts and sciences, business administration, education, graduate studies, law, medicine, nursing, social work, and adult and lifelong learning.
Open to: candidates of all nationalities meeting academic, linguistic and financial requirements.
Held: at four campuses, three in the greater Chicago area plus the Rome Center of Liberal Arts in Italy.
Fees: approximately US$10,000 per semester for 12 to 18 hours of undergraduate studies; less for ESL and some graduate programmes. Estimated living expenses: US$9,975 for nine months; for further details contact the Student Business Office at the above address.
Applications: see website for application details; http://www.luc.edu/about/icenter/index.shtml.

2610 Maharishi University of Management [MIU]

1000 North Fourth Street, D.B. 1155
52557-1155 Fairfield, IA
Tel: +1-515-472-1110
Web: http://www.mum.edu

📖 Undergraduate, Graduate Programmes

Study Domains: all major fields.
Programmes: Bachelor's, Master's and doctoral degrees in many disciplines.
Open to: applicants with the relevant qualifications; English proficiency required.
Financial assistance: partial scholarships and fellowships available.
Applications: by 15 April (priority deadline) or by 15 July for Fall admission; to the above address.

2611 Manhattanville College [MC]

2900 Purchase Street
10577 Purchase, NY
Tel: +1-800-328-4553
Fax: +1-914-694-1732
Web: http://www.manhattanville.edu
e-mail: admissions@mville.edu

📖 Undergraduate Programmes

Study Domains: all major fields.
Programmes: Bachelor's degrees in all major fields.
Open to: candidates of all nationalities meeting academic, linguistic and financial requirements; TOEFL 550 PBT/213 CBT required.
Duration: 4 years; courses begin late August or September.
Applications: International Admissions decisions are made on a rolling basis: requirements must be met by 1 March for Fall semester beginning in September and 1 December for Spring semester beginning in January; see website for full application details:
http://www.mville.edu/admissions/international.html.

⚜Scholarship

Study Domains: all major fields.
Scholarships: Merit Scholarships.
Value: US$5,000-$10,000 per year; renewable annually depending on college GPA.
Applications: by 1 March; contact tsed@mville.edu for further details.

2612 Marian College of Fond du Lac

45 South National Avenue
54935 Fond du Lac, WI
Tel: +1-920-923-7600
Fax: +1-920-923-7154
Web: http://www.mariancollege.edu
e-mail: admissions@mariancollege.edu

⚜Scholarship

Study Domains: all major fields.
Scholarships: Institutional Grants and Scholarships.
Open to: candidates from all nationalities.
Duration: 4 years.
Value: Tuition, US$7,000 per year.
Applications: Rolling; contact jhartzell@mariancollege.edu for further information.

2613 Marylhurst University [MU]

17600 Pacific Highway (HWY. 43)
PO Box 261
97036-0261 Marylhurst, OR
Tel: +1-503-699-6268
Fax: +1-503-635-6585
Web: http://www.marylhurst.edu
e-mail: admissions@marylhurst.edu

📖 Undergraduate, Graduate Programmes

Study Domains: anthropology, arts, business, business administration, communication, cultural studies, ecology, environment, fine arts, history, human sciences, interior design, liberal arts, literature and civilization, management, music and musicology, performing arts, photography, political science, psychology, public relations, publishing, sciences, theology, religion, visual arts.
Programmes: Bachelor's, Master's degrees in liberal arts.
Open to: applicants meeting academic requirements; TOEFL required.
Fees: registration US$20-$50; tuition fees US$270-$388 per credit hour.
Applications: rolling admissions.

2614 Marymount College, Palos Verdes [MCPV]

30800 Palos Verdes Drive East
90275-6299 Rancho Palos Verdes, CA
Tel: +1-310-377-5501
Web: http://www.marymountpv.edu

📖 2-Year Undergraduate Programmes

Study Domains: all major fields.
Programmes: (a) Associate in Arts degree programme: (b)

Associate in Science degree programme; (c) Pre-professional programmes.
Open to: (a) and (b) students of all nationalities having completed secondary school with sufficient funds to cover cost of college education.
Duration: (a) and (b) 2 to 3 years (until 60 units have been accumulated to obtain a degree).
Applications: by 10 August for Fall session and 15 January for Spring session.

2615 Medical University of South Carolina

171 Ashley Avenue
29425 Charleston, SC
Tel: +1-843-792-2300
Fax: +1-843-792-8558
Web: http://www.musc.edu

📖 Graduate, Postgraduate Programmes

Study Domains: anatomy, bacteriology, cancerology, cardiology, cytology, dentistry, dermatology, immunology, medicine, neurology, nursing, obstetrics and gynaecology, ophthalmology, paediatrics, pharmacy and pharmacology, physiology, preventive medicine, psychiatry, radiology, research, speech therapy, surgery, urology.
Programmes: Master's, Ph.D. degrees in medicine, nursing, pharmacy, dental medicine, health professions.
Open to: applicants meeting academic requirements; English TOEFL required.
Duration: 3 to 6 years; courses start in August.

⚜PhD Student Stipend

Study Domains: dentistry, health and hygiene, medicine, nursing.
Value: tuition: up to US$1,000 per academic year: stipend: US$21,000.
Applications: contact Enrolment Services; see website for full details: http://www.musc.edu/grad/Admiss_Reg.html.

2616 Memphis College of Art

1930 Poplar Avenue Overton Park
38104 Memphis, TN
Tel: +1-901-272-5000
Fax: +1-901-272-5104
Web: http://www.mca.edu
e-mail: info@mca.edu

⚜Scholarship

Study Domains: fine arts.
Scholarships: Merit Scholarship.
Open to: candidates of all nationalities.
Value: tuition, US$1,000-US$3,000.
Applications: Rolling.

2617 Meredith College [MC]

3800 Hillsborough street
27607 Raleigh, NC
Tel: +1-919-760-8581
Fax: +1-919-760-2348
Web: http://www.meredith.edu
e-mail: admissions@meredith.edu

📖 Undergraduate, Graduate Programmes

Study Domains: all major fields, administration, arts, biology, botany, business administration, criminology, cultural studies, dentistry, dietetics, education, home economics, interior design, languages, Latin, liberal arts, medicine, natural sciences, nutrition, pharmacy and pharmacology, photography, social work, teacher education, theology, religion, visual arts, zoology.
Programmes: Bachelor's, Master's degrees in education, business administration, liberal arts, science, health sciences.
Open to: women students only in undergraduate programmes, co-ed in graduate school; TOEFL or SAT/ACT required for undergraduate programmes.
Duration: 4 years; courses begin in August or January.
Fees: tuition: US$25,065.
Applications: by 15 February for Summer term; 1 November for Winter term; contact intadmissions@meredith.edu for further details.

🎓 Scholarship

Study Domains: all major fields.
Scholarships: International Scholarship.
Value: US$1,500 per year; renewable up to 4 years.
Applications: rolling admissions; contact finaid@meredith.edu for further details.

2618 Methodist College [MC]

5400 Ramsey Street
28311-1420 Fayetteville, NC
Tel: +1-919-630-7027
Web: http://www.methodist.edu

📖 Undergraduate Programmes

Study Domains: arts, business, education, fine arts, medicine, physical education, sciences, social sciences.
Programmes: (a) Associate of Arts degree programme; (b) Bachelor of Arts degree programme; (c) Associate of Science degree programme; (d) Bachelor of Science degree programme.
Open to: nationals of any country; intensive instruction in English as a foreign language offered.
Duration: (a) and (c) 2 years; (b) and (d) 4 years.
Financial assistance: scholarships and campus work study available.
Applications: by 1 June, to the Director of Admissions.

2619 Miami University

Office of International Programs
45056 Oxford, OH
Tel: +1-513-529-1809
Web: http://www.miami.muohio.edu

📖 Undergraduate, Graduate, Postgraduate Programmes

Study Domains: architecture, arts, biology, computer science, education, engineering, fine arts, physics.
Programmes: degree courses in all fields of study leading to an Associate, Bachelor's, Master's, Ph.D., Ed.D., specialist in education.
Open to: all qualified applicants; TOEFL required for all those whose native language is not English; GMAT for graduate study in business; GRE and TSE for applicants to graduate study applying for financial assistance.
Duration: Bachelor's, 4 years; Master's, 2 years; Ph.D., 3 to 5 years; courses begin in August or January.
Fees: US$16,400 undergraduate; US$10,600 graduate; living costs between US$8,000-$9,500.
Financial assistance: tuition and fee waiver available; graduate assistantships available.
Applications: by 1 March, to Office of Admissions for undergraduate applications or the Graduate School for graduate applications; see http://www.units.muohio.edu/internationalprograms.

2620 Michigan State University [MSU]

Office of Admissions and Scholarships
250 Administration Blvd.
48824-1035 East Lansing, MI
Tel: +1-517-355-0333
Fax: +1-517-432-0787
Web: http://www.msu.edu
e-mail: admis@msu.edu

📖 Undergraduate, Graduate, Postgraduate Programmes

Study Domains: agriculture, arts, business, education, engineering, human sciences, international studies, medicine, natural sciences, nursing, social sciences, veterinary medicine.
Programmes: Bachelor's, Master's and Ph.D. degrees in medicine, arts and letters, education, engineering, nursing, veterinary sciences.
Open to: suitably qualified candidates of all nationalities; TOEFL 550 required for all international students; SAT recommended for undergraduate; GRE/GMAT required for graduate programmes.
Fees: tuition: US$22,000-$24,500 per year; estimated living costs: US$8,214 per year.
Applications: various according to level of study; contact admis@msu.edu for admissions details.

🎓 Scholarship

Study Domains: all major fields.
Scholarships: Global Spartan Scholarship.
Open to: undergraduate international applicants.
Duration: 1 academic year; non-renewable.
Value: US$1,000 applied towards first year of tuition for new incoming international undergraduate students; contact admis@msu.edu for further details.

2621 Michigan Technological University [MTU]

1400 Townsend Drive
49931-1295 Houghton, MI
Tel: +1-906-487-1885
Web: http://www.mtu.edu
e-mail: mtu4u@mtu.edu

📖 Undergraduate, Graduate Programmes

Study Domains: business, ecology, environment, economic and commercial sciences, engineering, forestry, sciences.
Programmes: Undergraduate and graduate programmes in science and engineering.
Open to: candidates of all nationalities meeting academic, linguistic and financial requirements.
Applications: see http://www.mtu.edu/apply/intrntl.html for admission details.

🎓 Undergraduate Ambassador Scholarship Programme

Study Domains: all major fields.
Scholarships: Ambassador Scholarship Programme for Undergraduate International Students.
Open to: any qualified undergraduate international student based on academic achievement; evidence of leadership; English language competency; major field of academic interest; region of origin; financial need.
Duration: 1 academic year (renewable).
Value: maximum award of US$7,278 per year to be applied towards tuition; see http://www.mtu.edu/cie/is/scholarships/ambassador.html.
Applications: by 15 March to International Services Office at the above address; http://www.mtu.edu/apply/intrntl.html.

2622 Millikin University

1184 West Main Street
62522 Decatur, IL
Tel: +1-800-373-7733
Fax: +1-217-424-3993
Web: http://www.millikin.edu

🎓 Academic Merit Scholarship

Study Domains: all major fields.
Open to: candidates enrolled at university, based on academic results.
Duration: 1 year; renewable.
Applications: 15 April for following fall semester to Vice-President of Enrolments.

2623 Minnesota State University Moorhead [MSUM]

1104 - 7th Avenue S.
56563 Moorhead, MN
Tel: +1-218-236-2011
Fax: +1-218-236-2168
Web: http://www.mnstate.edu
e-mail: dragon@mnstate.edu

📖 Undergraduate, Graduate Programmes

Study Domains: all major fields, anatomy, education, humanities and arts, industrial technology, liberal arts, natural sciences, nursing, sciences, speech therapy.
Programmes: Bachelor's, Master's, Specialist's degrees in all major fields.
Duration: 4 years; courses begin 25 August.
Fees: tuition fees US$3,000 per year; living costs US$3,500.
Languages: English; TOEFL 500 PBT / 173 CBT required.
Applications: by 1 June; contact Office of International Programmes for further details.

☛ Scholarship

Study Domains: all major fields.
Scholarships: Marjorie Sanders Scholarship.
Open to: African students meeting university requirements.
Value: approximately US$3,000 per year; annual renewal.
Applications: by 1 June; contact gillette@mnstate.edu for further details.

2624 Minot State University [MSU]

500 University Avenue West
58707 Minot, ND
Tel: +1-800-777-0750
Fax: +1-701-858-3386
Web: http://www.minotstateu.edu
e-mail: konczews@minotstateu.edu

▢ Undergraduate, Graduate Programmes

Study Domains: anatomy, arts, bacteriology, business, business administration, cinematography, criminology, dentistry, dermatology, education, engineering, home economics, Japanese, languages, Latin, liberal arts, linguistics, management, natural resources, natural sciences, nursing, pharmacy and pharmacology, philology, photography, research, sciences, speech therapy, surgery, teacher education, theology, religion, transport.
Programmes: Bachelor's, Master's degree programmes in all major fields.
Open to: all applicants meeting academic requirements.
Duration: 4 years; courses begin August and January.
Fees: registration US$35; tuition fees US$3,100; living costs US$2,000-$3,000 per year.
Languages: English; TOEFL test.
Applications: rolling admissions; contact konczews@minotstateu.edu for further information.

☛ Scholarship

Study Domains: all major fields, anatomy, arts, business, dentistry, engineering, home economics, languages, liberal arts, natural resources, natural sciences, nursing, pharmacy and pharmacology, philology, photography, research, sciences, surgery, theology, religion, transport.
Scholarships: (a) Global Award; (b) Presidential Award.
Open to: (a) all international students eligible once fully admitted; (b) graduate students.
Duration: (a); (b) 4 years; renewable each year.
Value: (a) US$2,625 per academic year; (b) US$4,209 per academic year; contact konczews@minotstateu.edu.

2625 Montana State University [MSU]

Office of International programs
400 Culbertson Hall
Bozeman, MT 59717-0226
Tel: +1-406-994-4031
Fax: +1-406-994-1619
Web: http://www.montana.edu
e-mail: globalstudy@montana.edu

▢ Undergraduate, Graduate, Postgraduate Programmes

Study Domains: all major fields.
Programmes: Bachelor's, Master's, Ph.D. degrees in all major fields.
Open to: students of all nationalities with strong academic background; TOEFL score 525 minimum for undergraduate; graduate 550; SAT recommended for undergraduates.
Fees: tuition fees US$11,500; living costs US$7,000.
Applications: by 15 May for Fall semester, 15 October for Spring semester, and 1 March for Summer session; further information:
http://www.montana.edu/wwwnss/apply.shtml#international.

☛ Scholarship

Study Domains: all major fields.
Scholarships: International Undergraduate Student Scholarship.
Duration: first year award only; non-renewable.
Value: US$500-$2,000 per year.
Applications: all undergraduate international applicants are automatically considered for this scholarship; contact sreisch@montana.edu for further details.

2626 Moravian College

1200 Main Street
18018 Bethlehem
Tel: +1-610-861-1300
Fax: +1-610-861-3919
Web: http://www.moravian.edu

☛ Scholarship

Study Domains: all major fields.
Scholarships: International Student Scholarship.
Duration: 1 year; renewable; contact sobiesiak@moravian.edu for further details.

2627 Morningside College [MC]

51106-1751 Sioux City, IA
Tel: +1-712-274-5000
Fax: +1-712-273-5101
Web: http://www.morningside.edu
e-mail: mscadm@morningside.edu.

▢ Undergraduate Programmes

Study Domains: all major fields, arts, business, classical studies, computer science, English, fine arts, sciences.
Programmes: Programmes in areas such as arts and sciences, business, computer programming, fine arts and humanities.
Open to: suitably qualified candidates of all nationalities.
Duration: 1 academic year. (Courses begin in September.).
Financial assistance: All international applicants who meet entry requirements will automatically receive an academic scholarship amounting to US$3,000-$7,300 depending on TOEFL scores.
Applications: by 1 May, to the Office of Admissions.

2628 Mount Holyoke College [MHC]

College Street
South Hadley, MA 01075-6451
Tel: +1-413-358-2072
Fax: +1-413-538-2584
Web: http://www.mtholyoke.edu
e-mail: international-affairs@mtholyoke.edu

☛ Scholarships

Study Domains: all major fields.
Scholarships: (a) Foreign Fellowships; (b) International Guest Student Program.
Open to: students who have completed at least 1 year of university study; native speakers of Chinese, French, German, Italian or Spanish, who assist in the modern language departments 6 to 8 hours a week (conversation groups, etc.); (b) students who have completed at least 1 year of university study; native speakers of French, German, Italian or Spanish; language fellows have charge of language tables and assist in departments 8 to 10 hours a week (conversation groups, etc.).
Value: (a) covers full tuition, room and board, plus stipend of US$2,000; (b) covers full tuition, room and board, plus stipend of US$2,700; (c) based on financial need, up to full tuition, room, and board.
Applications: by 1 February; (a) and (b) to Office of International Affairs;
http://www.mtholyoke.edu/offices/ia/;(c) to the Office of Admissions.

2629 Murray State University [MSU]

165 Woods Hall
42071 Murray, KY
Tel: +1-270-762-4152
Fax: +1-270-762-3237
Web: http://www.murraystate.edu
e-mail: iis@murraystate.edu

☛ University Grants

Study Domains: all major fields.
Scholarships: (a) Consortium for Belize Educational Cooperation (COBEC) Waiver; (b) ESL Scholarships; (c) Global Scholarships; (d) Graduate Tuition Waiver; (e) IIS Scholarships.
Open to: (b) international students enrolled in ESL programmes at Murray State University for at least 1 term prior to their degree programme study; (c) acceptance to university undergraduate or graduate programmes; essay required; (e) international students who do not take ESL

programmes at Murray State University prior to their degree programmes; recipients should maintain 'average' academic standings.

Nationality: (a) citizens of Belize; (d) international graduate students from China, Cyprus, India, Indonesia, Japan, Korea, Morocco, Taiwan (China), Thailand and Turkey; recipients should maintain academic standings at 'B' average.

Value: (a), (c) out-of-state tuition; (b) undergraduate students: total of US$8,000; graduate students: total of US$4,000; (d) one-third tuition reduction; (e) undergraduate students: total of US$4,000; graduate: total of US$2,000.

Applications: (a), (b), (d), (e) no deadlines; (c) 1 February of preceding academic year; see website for further information.

2630 Naropa University
2130 Arapahoe Avenue
80302 Boulder
Tel: +1-303-444-0202
Fax: +1-303-444-0410
Web: http://www.naropa.edu

Naropa University Scholarships
Study Domains: all major fields, literature and civilization, music and musicology.
Scholarships: (a) Entering Students Scholarship; (b) Aimee Grunburger Award; (c) Evelyn Rose Memorial Scholarship; (d) Gill Scholars; (e) President's Leadership Scholarship; (f) Naropa University Grant.
Description: (a), (d), (e), (f) all subjects; (b) writing and poetry, (c) music.
Open to: (a) entering full-time students of all nationalities; based on special talents, knowledge, work or community service experience that the student will bring to the university; (b) female writing and poetics students; (c) music student nominated by Naropa's Music Department or by Admissions; (d) one lesbian, gay, bisexual or transgendered (LGBT) undergraduate student each year, with preference given to incoming freshmen; (e) outstanding degree-seeking undergraduates having completed at least one full semester and studying for second semester; (f) full-time, degree seeking undergraduate students, based on financial need.
Age limit Min: (b) over 30 years of age.
Other conditions: (b) female writing and poetics students; (d) lesbian, gay, bisexual or transgendered (LGBT) undergraduate student.
Duration: (a), (c), (d), (f) 1 year; renewable, based on academic results and financial need; (b) 1 term; (e) 1 year, non-renewable.
Value: (a) tuition: US$500-$3,000; (d) tuition: US$4,000; (e) variable; (f) US$1,000-$6,000.
Applications: contact finaid@naropa.edu.

2631 New England Conservatory [NEC]
290 Huntington Avenue
02115 Boston, MA
Tel: +1-617-585-1101
Fax: +1-617-585-1115
Web: http://www.newenglandconservatory.edu
e-mail: admissions@newenglandconservatory.edu

Undergraduate, Graduate, Postgraduate Programmes
Study Domains: music and musicology.
Programmes: Bachelor's, Master's, Ph.D. degrees in music and musicology.
Open to: admission based on audition results.
Fees: tuition fees US$23,250 per year; living costs US$9,850.
Languages: English; TOEFL 500 minimum required for undergraduates; graduates 550 minimum.
Applications: by 1 December; contact admissions@newenglandconservatory.edu for further details.

Music Scholarship
Study Domains: music and musicology.
Scholarships: Merit Scholarship.
Open to: acceptance based on auditions.
Value: variable.

Applications: by 1 December; contact financialaid@newenglandconservatory.edu.

2632 New England School of Law [NESL]
154 Stuart Street
02116-5616 Boston, MA
Tel: +1-617-451-0010
Fax: +1-617-457-3033
Web: http://www.nesl.edu
e-mail: admit@admin.nesl.edu

Graduate Programmes in Law
Study Domains: law.
Programmes: Juris Doctor (J.D.), Master of Laws in advanced legal studies (LL.M.).
Duration: JD: 3 years (full-time), 4 years (part-time); LLM: 1 year; courses begin in August.
Fees: For the 2004-2005 academic year: JD: application fee US$65; tuition: US$22,410 (full-time), US$16,810 (part-time); LLM: application fee US$100; tuition: US$23,500; Living costs: approximately US$14,180.
Financial assistance: Application for financial aid is available in the form of grants and loans for international students.
Languages: English; TOEFL score 600 (paper) 250 (computer) minimum unless English is native language or if language of instruction was English.
Applications: JD: by 15 March; LLM: by 1 March.

Merit Scholarships
Study Domains: law.
Scholarships: NESL merit scholarships.
Open to: candidates of all nationalities.
Value: Full or partial tuition.

2633 New Mexico Highlands University [NMHU]
Box 9000
87701 Las Vegas, NM
Tel: +1-877-850-9064
Fax: +1-505-454-3511
Web: http://www.nmhu.edu
e-mail: eclayton@nmhu.edu

Undergraduate, Graduate Programmes
Study Domains: accounting, anthropology, art history, arts, biology, business administration, chemistry, communication, criminology, design, early childhood education, ecology, environment, education, finance, geology, international business, liberal arts, linguistics, management, marketing, mathematics, music and musicology, natural resources, philosophy, physical education, physics, political science, psychology, special education, tourism, hotel and catering management, zoology.
Programmes: Bachelor's and Master's degrees in education, arts, liberal arts, business administration, science, social work.
Fees: tuition fees US$4,407-$4,683 per term; living costs US$6,000.
Financial assistance: some financial assistance available; enquire at above address.
Languages: English; TOEFL score 540 required.

2634 New Mexico State University [NMSU]
Center for International Programs
MSC 3567, NMSU 30001
88003 Las Cruces, NM
Tel: +1-505-646-3199
Fax: +1-505-646-2558
Web: http://www.nmsu.edu
e-mail: eip@nmsu.edu

Undergraduate, Graduate, Postgraduate Programmes
Study Domains: agriculture, arts, business administration, economy, education, engineering, sciences.
Programmes: Associate, Bachelor's, Master's, Ph.D. degrees in education, health and social service, agriculture and home economics, arts and sciences, business administration and economics, engineering.

Duration: variable; courses begin August for Fall semester; January for Spring semester.
Fees: registration US$35; tuition fees US$3,500-$5,000 per semester; living costs US$8,000 per year.
Languages: English; TOEFL score 500 required for undergraduate students; 530 for graduate students.
Applications: by 1 March for Fall semester; 1 October for Spring semester; contact marjaspe@nmsu.edu for further information.

✿ Scholarship

Study Domains: agriculture, arts, business administration, economy, education, engineering, home economics, sciences.
Scholarships: International Alumni Scholarship.
Open to: based on GPA and TOEFL results.
Duration: maximum 8 semesters for undergraduate studies; 4 semesters for graduate studies.
Value: approximately US$3,500 per semester.
Applications: by 1 March; contact marjaspe@nmsu.edu.

2635 New York Botanical Garden [NYBG]

200th Street and Kazimiroff Blvd.
10458-5126 Bronx, NY
Web: http://www.nybg.org/bsci/grad

✿ Graduate Fellowship

Study Domains: botany.
Scholarships: Graduate Fellowship Programme in systematic and economic botany.
Description: Each Fellow is expected to devote half-time to formal graduate study, leading to a Ph.D. degree in biology from selected NY universities, and half-time to assisting different research projects and related activities, such as curatorial work, within the institution. Fellowships may be renewed annually, contingent on satisfactory scholastic progress. Fellows are expected to complete their degree in five years.
Value: approximately US$15,000 a year paid in 26 biweekly instalments. A paid vacation of four weeks is offered each year. Tuition required by the universities and medical insurance are paid in full by the Garden.
Applications: to Michelle Provenzano; Graduate Studies Program; mprovenzano@nybg.org
(http://www.nybg.org/bsci/grad).

2636 New York University [NYU]

Office for International Students and Scholars
561 LaGuardia Place
10012 New York, NY
Tel: +1-212-998-4720
Fax: +1-212-995-4115
Web: http://www.nyu.edu
e-mail: intl.students.scholars@nyu.edu

⌑ Undergraduate and Graduate Programmes

Study Domains: all major fields, audio-visual media, cinematography, performing arts, photography, telecommunications.
Programmes: Undergraduate and graduate programmes in all major fields; programme in performing arts at Tisch School of the Arts.
Open to: candidates of all nationalities meeting academic, linguistic and financial requirements.
Duration: 4 years.
Financial assistance: Tisch School of the Arts offers a limited number of tuition scholarships and graduate assistantships to incoming students:
http://www.nyu.edu/tisch/gradadmissions/finaid.html.
Applications: see website for details:
http://www.nyu.edu/osl/oiss/admissionFinan/admissionsOverview.html.

2637 North Dakota State University [NDSU]

P.O. Box 5582 University Station
58105-5582 Fargo, ND
Tel: +1-701-231-7895
Web: http://www.ndsu.edu/International
e-mail: ndsu.international@ndsu.nodak.edu

⌑ Undergraduate and Graduate Programmes

Study Domains: all major fields.
Programmes: Undergraduate and graduate programmes in all major fields.
Open to: candidates of all nationalities meeting academic, linguistic and financial requirements.
Fees: tuition: US$7,754; estimated living and other expenses: US$12,000.
Financial assistance: some financial assistance and grants available.
Applications: contact above email or website.

✿ Scholarship

Study Domains: all major fields.
Scholarships: Academic and Cultural Sharing Scholarship.
Open to: candidates of all nationalities enrolled as undergraduate full-time students, holding a F-1 visa.
Value: 50% of tuition; renewable.
Applications: contact the Office of International Programs: ndsu.international@ndsu.nodak.edu for further information.

2638 Northern Illinois University [NIU]

Foreign Study Office
Williston Hall 100
60115-2854 Dekalb, IL
Tel: +1-815-753-1000
Web: http://www.niu.edu/isfo

⌑ Undergraduate and Graduate Programmes

Study Domains: all major fields.
Programmes: Undergraduate and graduate programmes in all major fields.
Open to: students of any nationality meeting academic, linguistic and financial requirements.
Applications: 1 May for Fall semester; 1 October for Spring semester.

2639 Northern State University [NSU]

1200 South Jay street
57401 Aberdeen, SD
Tel: +1-605-626-3011
Fax: +1-605-626-2587
Web: http://www.northern.edu
e-mail: admissions@northern.edu

⌑ Undergraduate, Graduate Programmes

Study Domains: all major fields.
Programmes: Bachelor's, Master's degrees in education, liberal arts, business administration, science.
Duration: 4 years; courses begin 4 September.
Fees: registration US$20; tuition fees US$3,176 per semester; living costs US$363 per semester.
Languages: English; TOEFL test required for international students.
Applications: rolling admission.

✿ Scholarship

Study Domains: all major fields.
Scholarships: President's Scholarship.
Value: US$5,000 per year; renewable each academic year.
Applications: by 15 February; see website for further information.

2640 Notre Dame de Namur University [NDNU]

500 Ralston Avenue
94002 Belmont
Tel: +1-650-593-1601
Fax: +1-650-508-3736
Web: http://www.ndnu.edu

Scholarship

Study Domains: all major fields.
Scholarships: Merit Scholarships.
Duration: 4 years; renewable.
Value: from US$7,000-$19,000.
Applications: 1 December and 2 February.

2641 Nyack College [NC]

1 South Blvd
10960 Nyack, NY
Tel: +1-845-358-1710
Web: http://www.nyackcollege.edu
e-mail: enroll@nyack.edu

Undergraduate, Graduate Programmes

Study Domains: accounting, business administration, communication, computer science, education, English, history, international studies, liberal arts, management, mathematics, music and musicology, performing arts, philosophy, psychology, social work, theology, religion.
Programmes: Associate, Bachelor's, Master's degrees in education, liberal arts.
Description: Christian liberal arts college of the Christian and Missionary Alliance with campuses in Nyack, Manhattan, Washington DC and Miami Valley OH.
Financial assistance: possibility of maximum US$2,000 financial assistance for international students.

2642 Ohio Northern University [ONU]

525 South Main Street
45810 Ada, OH
Tel: +1-419-772-2000
Fax: +1-419-772-1932
Web: http://www.onu.edu
e-mail: info@onu.edu

Undergraduate Programmes

Study Domains: accounting, biochemistry, biology, chemistry, computer science, early childhood education, economy, engineering, French, German, international business, law, management, mathematics, mechanical engineering, pharmacy and pharmacology, philosophy, physical education, physics, political science, psychology, public relations, sociology, Spanish, statistics, theology, religion.
Programmes: Bachelor's degree in arts and sciences, business administration, pharmacy, engineering.
Financial assistance: some financial assistance available; see website for further information.
Languages: English; TOEFL score 550 required.

2643 Ohio State University [OSU]

Third Floor, Lincoln Tower
1800 Cannon Drive
43210-1200 Columbus, OH
Tel: +1-614-292-3980
Web: http://www.osu.edu

Undergraduate, Graduate Programmes

Study Domains: all major fields.
Programmes: Undergraduate and graduate programmes in all major fields; business and nursing degrees available through distance education:
http://telr.ohio-state.edu/elearning/classwebsites/progdegrees.html.
Financial assistance: fellowships and graduate associateships available to all graduate applicants, domestic and international, with few exceptions.
Applications: vary by level and type; usually 15 February (all freshmen); 15 June (international transfers); 25 June (domestic transfers); 1 February (fellowship applicants); otherwise 1 July (international graduate) or 15 August (domestic graduate); to Admissions at the above address.

2644 Ohio Wesleyan University [OWU]

43015-2370 Delaware, OH
Tel: +1-740-368-3020
Web: http://www.owu.edu
e-mail: owuintl@owu.edu

Undergraduate Programmes

Study Domains: all major fields.
Programmes: Undergraduate programmes in all major fields.
Open to: candidates of all nationalities meeting academic, linguistic and financial requirements.
Financial assistance: some financial assistance available; contact Office of Financial Aid; tel: +1 800-922-8953; email: owfinaid@owu.edu.
Applications: application with financial assistance: 1 February; otherwise 1 March; for further information http://admission.owu.edu/foreign.html.

2645 Oregon State University [OSU]

Office of Admissions
104 Kerr Administration Building
97331-2106 Corvallis, OR
Tel: +1-541-737-4411
Web: http://www.orst.edu

Undergraduate and Graduate Programmes

Study Domains: all major fields, forestry.
Programmes: Undergraduate and graduate programmes in all major fields.
Open to: candidates of all nationalities with 500-549 TOEFL plus academic acceptability.
Duration: variable according to programmes.
Fees: tuition US$15,125-$14,110; estimated living and personal expenses US$10,000 per year.
Applications: 15 June for Fall semester; 15 September for Winter semester; 15 December for Spring semester; 15 March for Summer session to the above address; for further information:
http://oregonstate.edu/admissions/international/INTLoutline.html.

2646 Pacific College of Oriental Medicine [PCOM]

7445 Mission Valley Road suite 105
92108 San Diego
Tel: +1-619-574-6909
Fax: +1-619-574-6641
Web: http://www.pacificcollege.edu

Financial Aid

Study Domains: health and hygiene, medicine, paramedical studies, physical therapy.
Value: variable.
Applications: to Financial Aid Department at the above address.

2647 Pacific University [PU]

2043 College Way
97116 Forest Grove
Tel: +1-503-357-6151
Fax: +1-503-352-2242
Web: http://www.pacificu.edu

Undergraduate, Graduate Programmes

Study Domains: accounting, anthropology, arts, audio-visual media, biology, business, chemistry, computer science, economy, education, English, finance, French, German, history, international studies, journalism, languages, literature and civilization, mathematics, music and musicology, performing arts, philosophy, physics, political science, psychology, social work.
Programmes: Bachelor's, Master's degrees in all major fields; professional degrees in physical therapy, psychology, optometry.
Open to: international students meeting academic standards; TOEFL score 550 required.
Fees: tuition fees US$19,276; living costs US$5,380.
Applications: rolling admissions.

🐦 **Scholarship**

Study Domains: arts, sciences.
Scholarships: Pacific University Scholarships.
Open to: undergraduate students with high academic performance.
Value: US$4,000-$7,000 per year; renewable.
Applications: rolling; contact sprag@pacificu.edu for further information.

2648 Parker College of Chiropractic [PCC]

2500 Walnut Hill Lane
75229 Dallas, TX
Tel: +1-972-438-6932
Fax: +1-972-902-2496
Web: http://www.parkercc.edu

🐦 **Scholarships and Loans**

Study Domains: health and hygiene, medicine.
Description: scholarships and loans for programmes leading to doctor of chiropractic.
Duration: 1 term; renewable.
Value: tuition: US$6,350; living expenses: US$8,146.
Applications: 6 months prior to enrolment.

2649 Pennsylvania State University, Dickinson School of Law

150 South College Street
17013 Carlisle, PA
Tel: +1-717-240-5207
Fax: +1-717-241-3503
Web: http://www.dsl.psu.edu

📖 **Juris Doctor, Master of Laws Programmes**

Study Domains: law.
Programmes: Juris Doctor Programme (J.D.); Master of Laws in comparative law (LL.M.) degree programme for foreign lawyers.
Open to: see website for details.
Applications: by 1 April, to the Associate Dean of Graduate Programs (early application recommended).

2650 PEO International Peace Scholarship Fund [PIPSF]

PEO Executive Office
3700 Grand Avenue
50312-2899 Des Moines, IO
Tel: +1-515-255-3153
Fax: +1-515-255 -820
Web: http://www.peointernational.org

🐦 **PEO International Peace Scholarships for Women**

Study Domains: all major fields.
Scholarships: PEO International Peace Scholarships for graduate studies.
Description: scholarships for international women students to pursue graduate study in the United States and Canada.
Open to: qualified women candidates holding a Bachelor's degree and working towards a higher degree; recipients who do not hold citizenship in the U.S. or Canada must sign a witnessed statement to return immediately to their own country after completion of degree programme.
Place of study: colleges and universities in the U.S. and Canada.
Duration: 1 academic year (renewable twice).
Value: grant-in-aid only, maximum US$6,000 (based on need); applicants must show additional adequate funding.
Applications: information sheet to determine eligibility available upon request to above address between 15 August and 15 December; official application materials will be sent only if satisfactory information establishing eligibility has been received from the applicant between 15 August and 15 December; due by 31 January, decision by 1 May; for further information:
http://peointernational.org/projects/ips-policies-06-07.pdf and http://peointernational.org/projects/facts-chart-05.pdf.

2651 Pittsburg State University [PSU]

Office of International Programs and Services
Whitesitt Hall, Room 118
66762 Pittsburg, KS
Tel: +1-620-235-4680
Fax: +1-620-235-4962
Web: http://www.pittstate.edu

📖 **Undergraduate Programmes**

Study Domains: all major fields.
Programmes: Undergraduate programmes in all major fields.
Open to: candidates of all nationalities meeting academic, linguistic and financial requirements; TOEFL 520 PBT or higher or 190 CBT or higher required from undergraduate applicants. Successful completion of the highest level of the Intensive English Programme may be substituted for a 520 TOEFL. Transferring international students must have a GPA of 2.25 or higher on a 4.0 scale.
Financial assistance: limited scholarships are available to international students on a competitive basis after the first semester of attendance.
Applications: see website
http://www.pittstate.edu/admit/inter-admit.html.

2652 Princeton University, Woodrow Wilson School of Public and International Affairs

Office of Graduate Admissions
121 Robertson Hall
Princeton University
08544-1013 Princeton, NJ
Tel: +1-609-258-4836
Fax: +1-609-258-2095
Web: http://www.wws.princeton.edu/admissions
e-mail: wwsadmit@princeton.edu

📖 **Graduate Programmes in Public Administration**

Study Domains: administration, economic and commercial sciences, international business, international law, international relations, international studies.
Programmes: Master's and Ph.D. degrees in public administration and public policy.
Open to: candidates of all nationalities with at least seven years of relevant public service work experience and with personal qualities such as leadership, creativity, a commitment to public service, and the intellectual ability to thrive in a demanding academic environment; English language at TOEFL 600 PBT/ 250 CBT.
Fees: approximately US$28,000; registration fee: US$55, late registration US$80.
Financial assistance: possibility of scholarships.
Applications: by 2 December.

🐦 **McNamara Fellowship**

Study Domains: administration, development studies, economic and commercial sciences, international business, international law, international relations, international studies.
Scholarships: World Bank Robert S. McNamara Fellowship Program Public Policy; programme of studies leading to Master's degree in public policy in the following fields of concentration: international relations, development studies, domestic policy, economics and public policy.
Open to: mid-career professionals from all World Bank borrowing member countries, with at least seven years of relevant public service work experience and with personal qualities such as leadership, creativity, a commitment to public service, and the intellectual ability to thrive in a demanding academic environment.
Place of study: Princeton University; students are expected to live on-campus for the duration of the programme.
Value: full tuition travel allowance, and stipend for living expenses.
Applications: to Master's Degree in Public Policy, Robertson Hall, Princeton University, Princeton, NJ 08544-1013; tel: +1 609 258 4836; email: mpp@wws.princeton.edu; website:
http://www.wws.princeton.edu/degree/mpp.html.

2653 Purdue University [PU]

Young Grad House
47907 West Lafayette, IN
Tel: +1-765-494-2383
Fax: +1-765-496-1989
Web: http://www.purdue.edu

📖 Undergraduate, Graduate, Postgraduate Programmes

Study Domains: all major fields, agriculture, education, liberal arts, management, pharmacy and pharmacology, sciences, technology.
Programmes: Bachelor's, Master's, Ph.D. degrees in engineering, technology, education, management.
Open to: all applicants with proper academic credentials; SAT required.
Duration: 4 years.
Fees: tuition fees US$17,000 per year; living costs US$9,000 per year.
Financial assistance: some financial assistance available; see website for further information.
Applications: by 15 March for Fall semester.

2654 Quincy University [QU]

1800 College Avenue
62301-2699 Quincy, IL
Tel: +1-217-222-8020
Web: http://www.quincy.edu
e-mail: admissions@quincy.edu

📖 Undergraduate Programmes

Study Domains: all major fields.
Programmes: Undergraduate programmes in all major fields.
Open to: nationals of all countries with facility in English; TOEFL 550 required.
Duration: from 1 to 4 years.
Fees: tuition (full time) US$15,910; estimated living and personal expenses for one year; US$16,000.
Financial assistance: scholarships available based on satisfactory SAT or ACT scores; some scholarships may be granted for athletics (in men's and women's soccer and basketball, women's volleyball, baseball and softball), music and art.
Applications: by 15 July, to the Director, Office of Admissions, at the above address.

2655 Reed College [RC]

3203 SE Woodstock Blvd
97202-8199 Portland, OR
Tel: +1-503-771-1112
Fax: +1-503-777-7553
Web: http://www.reed.edu
e-mail: admissions@reed.edu

📖 Undergraduate Programmes

Study Domains: American studies, anthropology, art history, biochemistry, biology, chemistry, Chinese, classical studies, economy, history, international relations, languages, Latin, liberal arts, linguistics, literature and civilization, mathematics, music and musicology, performing arts, philosophy, physics, political science, psychology, Russian, social sciences, sociology, theology, religion.
Programmes: Bachelor's degrees in liberal arts, sciences.
Open to: applicants meeting academic requirements; SAT and TOEFL score 600 required.
Duration: 4 years; courses begin in August.
Fees: tuition fees US$27,560; living costs US$7,380.
Financial assistance: financial assistance available; contact jan.williams@reed.edu for further details.
Applications: by 15 January to Office of Admissions.

2656 Rhode Island School of Design [RISD]

2 College Street
02903 Providence, RI
Tel: +1-401-454-6300
Fax: +1-401-454-6309
Web: http://www.risd.edu
e-mail: admissions@risd.edu

📖 Undergraduate, Graduate Programmes

Study Domains: applied arts, architecture, art history, arts, arts and crafts, book development and production, cinematography, design, fine arts, graphic arts, industrial design, interior design, liberal arts, literature and civilization, photography, teacher education, visual arts.
Programmes: Bachelor's, Master's degrees in fine arts, architecture, design.
Open to: suitably qualified candidates of all nationalities.
Duration: 4 years; courses begin in September.
Fees: registration US$45; tuition fees US$24,000 per year; living costs US$6,900.
Financial assistance: some financial assistance available; see website for further details.
Applications: by 15 December; to RISD Admissions, at the above address.

2657 Rice University [RU]

Office of International Students and Scholars
MS-365
PO Box 1892
77251-1892 Houston, TX
Tel: +1-713-348-6095
Fax: +1-713-348-6058
Web: http://www.rice.edu

📖 Undergraduate, Graduate Programmes

Study Domains: all major fields.
Programmes: (a) Master of Arts in: humanities, science and social sciences; (b) Master of Science in: engineering, computer science, materials science, space physics and astronomy; (c) Ph.D. in anthropology, applied physics, biochemistry, biology, chemistry, economics, engineering: chemical, civil, electrical, mechanical; English, environmental science and engineering, French, geology, German, history, linguistics, materials science, mathematical sciences, mathematics, philosophy, physics, political sciences, psychology, religious studies, space physics and astronomy, statistics, Spanish; (d) Interdisciplinary graduate programmes in areas such as: bioengineering, solid-state electronic and materials science, systems theory, architecture, accounting, business and public management; (e) Undergraduate degrees in humanities, social sciences, natural sciences, engineering, music and architecture.
Open to: qualified candidates of all nationalities with high academic standing and high GRE score; proficiency in English necessary.
Financial assistance: some scholarships and fellowships available to outstanding students.
Applications: (a) to (d) by 1 February, to relevant Department; (e) by 2 January, to the Office of Admissions; see website for further information http://www.ruf.rice.edu/~ois/main.html.

2658 Rider University

2083 Lawrenceville Road
08648 Lawrenceville, NJ
Tel: +1-800-257-9026
Web: http://www.rider.edu
e-mail: admissions@rider.edu

🏹 International Grants and Scholarships

Study Domains: all major fields.
Scholarships: (a) Presidential Scholarship; (b) Provost Scholarship; (c) Dean's Scholarship; (d) Founder's Scholarship; (e) International Scholarships.
Description: scholarships for qualified incoming international freshmen students to the Lawrenceville and Princeton campuses. Students meeting the relevant criteria will automatically receive an award; no additional scholarship application is required.
Open to: candidates of all nationalities admissible to the university as full-time students.
Academic requirements: have a qualifying GPA on a 4.0 scale.
Other conditions: have filed for permanent residency in the United States or plan to hold an F-1 student visa.
Duration: 1 year; renewable up to 4 years.
Value: in the form of grants and scholarships (a) US$15,000: (b) US$11,000; (c) US$9,000; (d) US$6,000; (e) US$3,000 maximum.

2659 Roosevelt University [RU]

430 South Michigan Avenue, HCC 125
60605-1394 Chicago, IL
Tel: +1-312-341-3531
Fax: +1-312-341-6377
Web: http://www.roosevelt.edu
e-mail: internat@roosevelt.edu

Undergraduate, Graduate, Postgraduate Programmes

Study Domains: administration, advertising, anatomy, art history, biology, business, business administration, communication, computer science, economic and commercial sciences, education, finance, genetics, history, human sciences, immunology, industry and commerce, international business, international relations, journalism, liberal arts, management, marine science, marketing, music and musicology, performing arts, political science, psychology, sciences, social sciences, sociology, tourism, hotel and catering management.
Programmes: Bachelor's, Master's, Ph.D. degrees in liberal arts, education, sciences, economics, business administration.
Open to: applicants meeting academic qualifications; TOEFL, GMAT required for business graduate students.
Duration: 2-4 years; courses begin in September for Fall semester; January for Spring semester.
Fees: tuition fees US$10,404-$16,300; living costs US$7,500.
Financial assistance: some financial assistance available; see website for further information.
Applications: by 1 June for Fall semester; 1 October for Spring semester.

2660 Rowan University [RU]

201 Mullica Hill Road
08028 Glassboro, NJ
Tel: +1-856-256-4238
Fax: +1-856-256-5238
Web: http://www.rowan.edu/internationalstudents
e-mail: internationalstudents@rowan.edu

Undergraduate, Graduate, Postgraduate Programmes

Study Domains: administration, advertising, arts, biochemistry, biology, business administration, chemistry, communication, computer science, criminology, ecology, environment, economic and commercial sciences, education, engineering, finance, journalism, liberal arts, management, marketing, mathematics, mechanical engineering, music and musicology, performing arts, physical education, physics, political science, public relations, sociology, visual arts.
Programmes: Bachelor's, Master's, PhD degrees in education, arts, liberal arts, business administration, management, science, engineering.
Duration: 4 years; courses begin in September.
Fees: tuition fees US$14,000; living costs US$9,000.
Languages: English; TOEFL or SAT required.
Applications: by March for fall session; November for spring session to Director of International Student Services.

Tuition Reduction, Undergraduate Programmes

Study Domains: all major fields.
Open to: non-degree seeking visiting students.
Duration: 1 year; non-renewable.
Value: 50% tuition reduction: equivalent to US$7,000.
Applications: 1 March for fall session; 1 November for spring session; to Director of International Student Services.

2661 Russell Sage Colleges [RSC]

Troy, NY
Tel: +1-518-244-2000
Web: http://www.sage.edu
e-mail: rscadmt@sage.edu

Undergraduate, Graduate Programmes

Study Domains: arts, design, fine arts, liberal arts, paramedical studies, physiology.
Programmes: Associate, Bachelor's and graduate programmes in all major fields; especially physical therapy, occupational therapy and art therapy at the Troy campus and fine arts, graphic art design and information design programmes at the Albany campus.

Open to: candidates of all nationalities meeting academic, financial and linguistic requirements; entrance examination and essay required.
Other conditions: primarily women students at undergraduate college in Troy.
Held: three colleges: an undergraduate college (primarily for women) in Troy; a co-educational undergraduate college in Albany's University Heights neighbourhood; and a graduate school operating on both campus locations.
Applications: request application details from each college: Russell Sage College for Women; email: rscadm@sage.edu; Sage College of Albany (coeducational); scaadm@sage.edu; Sage Graduate School: sgsadm@sage.edu.

2662 Rutgers, the State University of New Jersey New Brunswick Campus

08901-1281 New Brunswick, New Jersey
Tel: +1-732-932-4636
Fax: +1-732-932-8060
Web: http://www.rutgers.edu

Scholarships

Study Domains: all major fields.
Description: The university offers scholarships, grants, loans, work-study opportunities for international students. Information and a partial listing of scholarships and grants can be found in the undergraduate catalogue on-line at http://ruweb.rutgers.edu/catalogs/nb-ug/03-05/nbfull.pdf.
Applications: 15 May for priority filing.

2663 Saint John's University

8000 Utopia Parkway
11439 Queens, NY
Tel: +1-718-990-6161
Fax: +1-718-990-5723
Web: http://new.stjohns.edu

Undergraduate, Graduate Programmes

Study Domains: business, education, health and hygiene, law, liberal arts, pharmacy and pharmacology.
Open to: students of all nationalities meeting academic and financial requirements.
Applications: to the above address.

2664 Saint Joseph's University [SJU]

5600 City Avenue
19131 Philadelphia, PA
Tel: +1-610-660-1000
Fax: +1-610-660-3300
Web: http://www.sju.edu

Scholarship

Study Domains: all major fields.
Scholarships: Academic Merit Scholarships.
Open to: candidates of all nationalities, contingent upon acceptance to the university, academic merit and availability.
Duration: Over 2 years for graduate; renewable.
Value: Tuition fees from US$4000 to US$28,000 per year for undergraduate and US4000 to US$7000 for graduate.
Applications: No separate application for scholarship consideration, students are considered based upon the admission's application. Contact: Director of Admissions, of the university at the above address: susan.kassab@sju.edu.

2665 Saint Mary's College of California

PO Box 4800
94575 Moraga, CA
Tel: +1-925-631-4203
Fax: +1-925-376-2150
Web: http://www.stmarys-ca.edu

Athletic Awards

Study Domains: physical education.
Open to: candidates excelling in sports and selected by coach; sports include basketball, soccer, baseball, volleyball, tennis, golf, cross-country, rowing.
Duration: up to 4 academic years; renewable.
Value: tuition and living expenses: up to full cost; books:

US$400.
Applications: by 2 March; contact Director of Athletics.

🎗 Entrance Awards
Study Domains: all major fields.
Open to: all enrolled students.
Academic requirements: 3.7 GPA for freshman students and a combined SAT score of at least 1200; transfer students must have 30 transferable units and 3.5 college GPA.
Duration: 4 academic years; renewable.
Value: tuition: US$6,000.
Applications: 2 March; to Dean of Admissions.

2666 Saint Norbert College [SNC]
100 Grant Street
54115 De Pere, WI
Tel: +1-920-403-3975
Fax: +1-920-403-4083
Web: http://www.snc.edu

📖 Undergraduate Studies
Study Domains: accounting, American studies, applied arts, arts, Asian studies, astronomy, biochemistry, biology, business, business administration, chemistry, classical studies, communication, computer science, early childhood education, ecology, environment, economic and commercial sciences, economy, education, English, European studies, finance, fine arts, geodesy, geography, graphic arts, history, information science, international business, international relations, international studies, Japanese, mathematics, music and musicology, performing arts, philosophy, physics, political science, sociology, special education, teacher education.
Open to: applicants meeting academic requirements; TOEFL score 550 PBT / 213 CBT required.
Duration: 4 years.
Fees: tuition fees US$18,500 per year; living costs US$5,000 per year.
Applications: by 30 July; see http://www.snc.edu/admit/international.htm for further information.

🎗 International Scholarship
Study Domains: all major fields.
Open to: based on academic performance in secondary school.
Duration: 4 years.
Value: US$3,500-$9,500 per year.
Applications: 1 April; see http://www.snc.edu/admit/international.htm for further information.

2667 Saint Peter's College [SPC]
2641 Kennedy Boulevard
07306 Jersey City, NJ
Tel: +1-201-915-9213
Fax: +1-201-432-5860
Web: http://www.spc.edu
e-mail: admissions@spc.edu

📖 Undergraduate, Graduate Programmes
Study Domains: administration, education, international studies, liberal arts, nursing, teacher education, theology, religion.
Programmes: Bachelor's, Master's degrees in liberal arts, education, administration, business, nursing, science.
Open to: applicants meeting academic requirements; TOEFL score 520 and SAT required.
Duration: 2 to 4 years; courses begin late August.
Applications: by 1 June for Fall semester; contact admissions@spc.edu for further information.

🎗 Scholarships
Study Domains: liberal arts, physical education.
Scholarships: Academic / Athletic Scholarships.
Open to: applicants meeting academic requirements.
Duration: 4 years.
Value: variable; contact admissions@spc.edu for further information.

2668 Saint Vincent College
300 Fraser Purchase Road
15650-2690 Latrobe, PA
Tel: +1-724-539-9761
Fax: +1-724-537-5069
Web: http://www.stvincent.edu
e-mail: admission@stvincent.edu

🎗 International Student Scholarship
Study Domains: all major fields.
Open to: candidates of all nationalities attending St Vincent College on a full-time basis, except US citizens and permanent residents.
Duration: 1 year; renewable for a total of 4 years.
Value: tuition: US$8,000.
Applications: contact Office of Admission and Financial Aid.

2669 San Diego State University [SDSU]
5500 Campanile Drive
92182-1914 San Diego, CA
Tel: +1-619-594-5200
Web: http://www.sdsu.edu

📖 Undergraduate, Graduate Programmes
Study Domains: all major fields.
Programmes: Undergraduate and graduate programmes in all major fields.
Open to: candidates over age 18 who have completed secondary school and meet other academic, linguistic and financial requirements.
Fees: undergraduate registration: US$1,870; tuition: US$6,768 (US$282/unit); estimated annual personal and living expenses US$12,000.
Financial assistance: some financial assistance available; see website for further information http://www.sa.sdsu.edu/isc/scholarships.htm.
Applications: by 1 March to the above address.

2670 San Jose State University [SJSU]
International Programs and Services
One Washington Square, Room IS 227
95192-0135 San Jose, CA
Tel: +1-408-924-5920
Fax: +1-408-924-5976
Web: http://www.sjsu.edu/depts/ipss
e-mail: sjsuips@sjsu.edu

📖 Undergraduate and Graduate Programmes
Study Domains: all major fields.
Programmes: Undergraduate and graduate programmes in all major fields.
Open to: students having graduated from a secondary school 18 years of age and meet all academic, linguistic and financial requirements.
Duration: 4 and 2-year programmes.
Applications: see website for further information.

2671 School for International Training [SIT]
Kipling Road,
PO Box 676
05302-0676 Brattleborg, UT
Tel: +1-802-258-3510
Fax: +1-802-258-3500
Web: http://www.sit.edu
e-mail: admissions@sit.edu

📖 Graduate Studies
Study Domains: international business, international relations, international studies, teacher education.
Programmes: (a) Master's programmes in intercultural service, leadership, and management;
(b) Master of Arts in teaching.
Description: (a) conflict transformation; international education; social justice in intercultural relations; sustainable development; organizational management; (b) teaching English as a foreign language.
Duration: (a) 2 years; courses begin in September.

Fees: (a); (b) tuition fees US$22,200 per year; living costs US$8,000.
Financial assistance: (a) some financial assistance available; contact michael.ireland@sit.edu.
Languages: (a); (b) English; TOEFL score 550 required.

2672 Scripps Research Institute (The) [TSRI]
10550 N Torrey Pines Road, TPC 19
92037 La Jolla, CA
Tel: +1-858-784-8469
Fax: +1-858-784-2802
Web: http://www.scripps.edu
e-mail: gradprgm@scripps.edu

Fellowship

Study Domains: biology, chemistry.
Scholarships: Graduate Awards.
Duration: 5 years.
Value: Tuition, US$5,000; living expenses, US$24,000; and health insurance for US$3,560.
Applications: by 1 January, at the graduate office; see website: www.scripps.edu/phd for further details.

2673 Shippensburg University [SU]
1871 Old Main Drive
17257 Shippensburg, PA
Tel: +1-717-477-7447
Fax: +1-717-477-1273
Web: http://www.ship.edu
e-mail: admiss@ship.edu

Undergraduate, Graduate Programmes

Study Domains: accounting, applied sciences, biology, business administration, chemistry, communication, computer science, earth science, English, finance, French, geography, history, journalism, management, marketing, mathematics, physics, psychology, social work, sociology, Spanish, special education.
Programmes: Bachelor's, Master's degrees in arts and sciences, education, business.
Duration: 4 years.
Financial assistance: some financial assistance available; contact jcmcke@ship.edu for further details.
Languages: English; TOEFL required for international students.
Applications: rolling admissions.

2674 Siena College
515 Loudon Road
12211 Loudonville, NY
Tel: +1-518-783-2300
Fax: +1-518-783-4293
Web: http://www.siena.edu

Undergraduate scholarships

Study Domains: all major fields.
Scholarships: Franciscan Grant; Presidential Scholarships.
Subjects: all major fields.
Open to: Candidates of all nationalities.
Value: up to US$5,000 per calendar year.

2675 Simmons College [SC]
300 The Fenway
02115-5898 Boston, MA
Tel: +1-800-345-8468
Fax: +1-617-521-3190
Web: http://www.simmons.edu
e-mail: ugadm@simmons.edu

Undergraduate and Graduate Programmes

Study Domains: all major fields, business administration.
Programmes: (a) Undergraduate liberal arts programme for women;
(b) Graduate co-educational studies in business (M.B.A. for women).
Open to: (a) women applicants of all nationalities; SAT scores and TOEFL 550 required; check with departments for additional requirements.; (b) men and women applicants meeting academic and other criteria.
Fees: tuition: US$11,000 per semester; estimated living expenses per semester: US$5,000.

Financial assistance: some assistance available; see website for further information.
Applications: no deadlines for undergraduates; for graduates, check with department; applications to the Admissions Office, at the above address.

2676 Skidmore College [SC]
12866-1632 Saratoga Springs, NY
Tel: +1-518-580-5000
Web: http://www.skidmore.edu
e-mail: info@skidmore.edu

Undergraduate Liberal Arts Programmes

Study Domains: liberal arts, sciences.
Programmes: B.A. degrees in departments of liberal arts and sciences; B.S. degrees in elementary education, business, arts, art education, physical education and dance, theatre and music.
Open to: students with English-language proficiency plus equivalent of high-school diploma normally including 4 years of English, 3 years of mathematics, 2 of laboratory science, and 2 or 3 of social sciences.
Duration: 4 years.
Applications: early decision applications: by 1 December for Round I and by 15 January for Round II; see website for further information
http://www.skidmore.edu/welcome/admissions.html.

2677 Smithsonian Institution [SI]
Office of Fellowships
P.O. Box 37012
Victor Bldg, 9300, MRC 902
20013-7012 Washington, DC
Tel: +1-202-275-0655
Web: http://www.si.edu/ofg
e-mail: siofg@si.edu

Research Fellowships

Study Domains: anthropology, archaeology, art history, arts, astronomy, biology, earth science, ecology, environment, history, sciences.
Scholarships: Research Fellowships, awarded to support independent research in residence at the Smithsonian.
Description: history, art and science, anthropology (including archaeology), astrophysics and astronomy, earth sciences and paleobiology, ecology, behavioural and environmental sciences (including an emphasis on the tropics, evolutionary and systematic biology), history of science and technology, history of art (especially American, contemporary, African, and Asian art, twentieth-century American crafts, and decorative arts).
Open to: nationals of all countries having either substantially completed doctoral requirements or received their doctorate in the past 7 years; graduate students wishing to conduct individual research under staff supervision. The Institute's facilities are also open to scholars and scientists interested in limited appointments without financial support.
Duration: 3 to 12 months (senior postdoctoral appointments); 6 to 12 months (predoctoral or postdoctoral); 10 weeks (graduate students).
Value: variable; see
http://www.si.edu/ofg/infotoapply.htm for details.
Applications: from September through December at the above address.

2678 Society of Exploration Geophysicists - SEG Foundation [SEG]
PO Box 702740
74170-2740 Tulsa, OK
Tel: +1-918-497-5500
Fax: +1-918-497-5557
Web: http://www.seg.org

SEG Foundation Scholarship Program

Study Domains: earth science, physics.
Scholarships: SEG Foundation Scholarship Program.
Open to: students intending to pursue a college course leading to a career in geophysics; candidates must be either high school seniors or undergraduate students with above average grades, or graduate college students whose studies are directed towards exploring geophysics in operations, research

or teaching; student's need of financial assistance is considered; first consideration given to student's competence.
Place of study: at any recognized college or university offering courses in the above fields.
Duration: 1 academic year (renewable subject to recipient's scholastic standing).
Value: US$500-$12,000 per year (average award approximately US$1,500).
Applications: by 1 March of year in which award is to be made; forms obtainable from SEG Foundation at the above address; also at http://students.seg.org.

2679 Southeast Missouri State University [SMSU]
One University Plaza MS 2000
63701-4799 Cape Girardeau, MO
Tel: +1-573-986-6863
Fax: +1-573-986-6866
Web: http://www.semo.edu
e-mail: intadmit@semo.edu

📖 Undergraduate, Graduate Programmes
Study Domains: administration, agriculture, archaeology, architecture, art history, business, business administration, decorative arts, design, engineering, home economics, languages, liberal arts, linguistics, management, natural resources, natural sciences, nursing, pharmacy and pharmacology, photography, sciences, social work, sociology, speech therapy, theology, religion, tourism, hotel and catering management, veterinary medicine, veterinary sciences.
Programmes: Bachelor's, Master's degrees in education, business, economics and finance, health and human services, nursing, liberal arts, science and mathematics.
Open to: all applicants meeting admissions criteria; TOEFL score 500 required for undergraduates; 550 for graduates.
Duration: 4 years; courses begin in August; January or June.
Fees: registration US$100; tuition fees US$7,290; living costs US$7,790.

🐚 Scholarships
Study Domains: all major fields.
Scholarships: Merit Awards for Incoming Freshmen.
Subjects: any major available at the University.
Open to: all applicants meeting academic standards.
Duration: 1 academic year; renewable with GPA of 3.5 or higher.
Value: from US$500 to full scholarship.
Applications: by 15 December 2002; contact gdordoni@semo.edu for further information.

2680 Southeastern Louisiana University
548 Western Avenue
70402 Hammond, LA
Tel: +1-985-549-2000
Fax: +1-985-549-3640
Web: http://www.selu.edu
e-mail: President@selu.edu

🐚 Financial aid
Study Domains: all major fields.
Scholarships: Graduate Assistantship.
Description: tuition waiver.
Open to: all graduate candidates.
Duration: 1 semester; renewable.
Value: stipend of US$2,200 per semester.
Applications: no deadline, contact jrcalmes@selu.edu for further information.

2681 Southern Illinois University at Carbondale [SIUC]
Office of Admissions and Records
Mailcode 4701
62901-4701 Carbondale, IL
Tel: +1-618-453-4381
Fax: +1-618-453-3250
Web: http://www.siuc.edu
e-mail: admrec@siu.edu

📖 Undergraduate, Graduate Programmes
Study Domains: all major fields.
Programmes: Undergraduate and graduate programmes in all major fields; also distance education programmes see http://www.dce.siu.edu/siuconnected/default.htm.
Open to: secondary school graduates of all nationalities aged over 18.
Applications: to the Director, at the above address; web: http://www.siu.edu/~intldev/intlapgd.html.

2682 Southern Nazarene University [SNU]
6729 NW 39th Expressway
73008 Bethany, OK
Tel: +1-405-491-6386
Fax: +1-405-717-6270
Web: http://www.snu.edu
e-mail: sdech@snu.edu

📖 Graduate, Professional Programmes
Study Domains: all major fields.
Programmes: Master's and professional degrees in all major fields.

2683 Southern New Hampshire University [SNHU]
2500 N. River Road
03106 Manchester, NH
Tel: +1-603-645-9629
Fax: +1-603-645-9603
Web: http://www.snhu.edu
e-mail: s.harvey@snhu.edu

📖 Undergraduate, Graduate, Postgraduate Programmes
Study Domains: accounting, administration, advertising, business, business administration, communication, development studies, early childhood education, economic and commercial sciences, economy, finance, information science, international business, international law, management, marketing, political science, psychology, public relations, recreation and leisure, special education, teacher education, tourism, hotel and catering management.
Programmes: Bachelor's, Master's, Ph.D. degrees in administration, business, economics, management, psychology, teacher education.
Fees: tuition fees vary according to study programmes; living costs approximately US$1,000 per month.
Languages: English; TOEFL score 500 required.

🐚 Scholarship
Study Domains: all major fields.
Scholarships: Alumni Scholarship.
Open to: undergraduate students with GPA average above 3.0.
Value: US$1,000-$1,500 per year.

2684 Spring Hill College [SHC]
4000 Dauphin Street
36608 Mobile, AL
Tel: +1-800-742-6704
Fax: +1-25-460-2186
Web: http://www.shc.edu
e-mail: admit@shc.edu

📖 Undergraduate, Graduate Programmes
Study Domains: accounting, administration, advertising, biochemistry, biology, business, business administration, chemistry, communication, design, early childhood education, ecology, environment, English, finance, fine arts, history, information science, international business, journalism, management, marine biology, marketing, mathematics, nursing, philosophy, political science, psychology, public relations, sciences, Spanish, teacher education, theology, religion.
Programmes: Bachelor's, Master's degrees in business administration, advertising, business, management, sciences, nursing.
Open to: applicants meeting academic requirements; TOEFL score 550 PBT/ 213 CBT or equivalent required.
Duration: 4 years; courses begin in August.

Fees: tuition fees US$18,092 per year; living costs US$6,540 per year.
Applications: rolling admissions; priority date 1 May.

☛ Scholarship

Study Domains: all major fields.
Scholarships: University Scholarship.
Open to: incoming first year freshmen meeting academic requirements.
Value: US$1,000-$10,000 per year; renewable for 4 years; depending on GPA.
Applications: rolling admissions; priority date 1 May; contact admit@shc.edu for further information.

2685 Stanford University [SU]
Old Union, Building 590
94305-3052 Stanford, CA
Tel: +1-415-723-2300
Web: http://www.stanford.edu

📖 Graduate Programmes

Study Domains: all major fields, business, earth science, engineering, humanities and arts, law, medicine, sciences.
Programmes: (a) undergraduate programmes in Humanities and Sciences, Earth Sciences, and Engineering only; (b) Stanford Business School M.B.A.; (c) M.Sc. in Management for mid-career managers; (d) Ph.D. programme.
Open to: (a) candidates of all nationalities meeting academic, financial and linguistic requirements; TOEFL 630 PBT/257 CBT; SAT I or ACT absolutely required; (b) to (d) applicants from colleges and universities of recognized standing who hold a U.S. Bachelor's degree or its equivalent.
Duration: (a) 4 years; (b) 2 years full-time; (c) 1 year.
Fees: tuition: US$27,204 for three quarters and US$36,272 for four quarters.
Applications: (a) international students accepted for admission only for Autumn quarter. The completed Basic Information Form, Supplementary Information Form, and the application fee for freshman admission for the Autumn quarter must be postmarked on or before December 15; to Office of Undergraduate Admission, See website before applying http://www.stanford.edu/dept/uga/int/international.html; (b) between mid-October and mid-March; queries to MBA Admissions Office; (c) between mid-October and mid-March; queries to Director, Stanford Sloan Program; (d) by 2 January, to Doctoral Program Office; all applications to the Graduate School of Business, Stanford University, Stanford, California 94305-5015; http://www.stanford.edu/dept/registrar/admissions/programs.html.

☛ Spencer Fellowship Program

Study Domains: education.
Scholarships: Spencer Fellowship Program for the improvement of education.
Open to: candidates of any country with PhD, EdD or equivalent degree whose doctorate was conferred within the last 6 years.
Duration: 1 year.
Value: US$40,000 per year of research, or US$20,000 for each of 2 contiguous years, working half-time.
Applications: by 1 December, to the above address.

2686 State University of New York at Buffalo [SUNY]
International Enrollment Management
411 Capen Hall
14260-1604 Buffalo, NY
Tel: +1-716-645-2368
Fax: +1-716-645-2528
Web: http://www.buffalo.edu

📖 Undergraduate and Graduate Programmes

Study Domains: all major fields.
Programmes: undergraduate and graduate programmes in all major fields.
Applications: by 1 May to the above address; for further information; http://wings.buffalo.edu/intled/admissions.

2687 State University of New York at Geneseo [SUNY]
1 College Circle
14454 Geneseo, NY
Tel: +1-585-245-5405
Fax: +1-585-245-5405
Web: http://www.geneseo.edu
e-mail: iss@geneseo.edu

☛ International Student Award

Study Domains: all major fields.
Open to: all students, based on academic results.
Duration: 1 year; renewable up to 4 years.
Value: tuition: US$2,000.
Applications: 1 June for fall semester; 1 November for spring semester; to Director of International Student Services.

2688 State University of New York College at Fredonia [SUNY]
2800 Central Avenue
14063 Fredonia, NY
Tel: +1-716-673-3111
Fax: +1-716-673-3446
Web: http://www.fredonia.edu

☛ Scholarship

Study Domains: all major fields.
Scholarships: International Student Scholarship.
Duration: 4 years; renewable.
Value: Tuition, US$5,000.
Applications: by 1 March; contact sasso@fredonia.edu for further information.

2689 State University of New York College at Purchase [SUNY]
735 Anderson Hill Road
10577 Purchase, NY
Tel: +1-914-251-6000
Web: http://www.purchase.edu

📖 Undergraduate, Graduate Programmes

Study Domains: anthropology, book development and production, journalism, liberal arts, performing arts, sciences, veterinary sciences, visual arts.
Programmes: Bachelor's, Master's degrees in liberal arts and sciences, visual and performing arts.
Open to: applicants meeting admission criteria and standards; TOEFL score 550 PBT / 213 CBT.

☛ Scholarship

Study Domains: liberal arts, performing arts, sciences, visual arts.
Scholarships: University Scholarship.
Duration: 1 year; renewable; contact dorsey@purchase.edu for further details.
Value: variable.

2690 State University of New York Oswego [SUNY]
7060 Sate Route 104
13126 Oswego, NY
Tel: +1-315-312-2500
Fax: +1-315-312-3260
Web: http://www.oswego.edu
e-mail: intled@oswego.edu

📖 Undergraduate, Graduate Programmes

Study Domains: all major fields.
Programmes: Bachelor's, Master's degrees in all major fields.
Financial assistance: financial assistance available; see http://www.oswego.edu for further information.

2691 Stephen F. Austin State University
1936 North Street
75961-3940 Nacogdoches, TX
Tel: +1-936-468-2504
Fax: +1-936-468-3849
Web: http://www.sfasu.edu
e-mail: admissions@sfasu.edu

☛OISP/SFA International Scholarship

Study Domains: all major fields.
Description: for the purpose of increasing diversity for international representation at Stephen F. Austin State University.
Open to: students whose mother tongue language is other than English or has lived in a country other than the USA for a period of 5 years or more; or has foreign or dual citizenship; based on financial necessity.
Academic requirements: entering freshmen: successful secondary educational record as evaluated for admission to SFA or an ACT composite score of 21 or higher or a SAT composite score of 1010 (verbal and math) or equivalent; transfer students from a community college or senior university: a GPA of 3.0+ will be required (to be calculated on transferable credit at SFA); continuing students with this scholarship (pending availability of funds): must be a student in good standing with a GPA of 2.5+ on 4.0 scale.
Duration: 2 terms.
Value: US$1,000.
Applications: 1 July for the next scholarship year of 1 August-31 July.

2692 Stevens Institute of Technology [SIT]

Castle Point on Hudson
07030 Hoboken, NJ
Tel: +1-201-216-5189
Fax: +1-201-216-8333
Web: http://www.stevens-tech.edu
e-mail: rlorton@stevens.tech.edu

📖 Undergraduate, Graduate, Postgraduate Programmes

Study Domains: biochemistry, business, chemical engineering, chemistry, civil engineering, computer science, ecology, environment, electricity and electronics, engineering, management, marine science, mathematics, mechanical engineering, physics, research, sciences, technology, telecommunications.
Programmes: Bachelor's, Master's, Ph.D. degrees in engineering, sciences, computer science, management, technology management.
Financial assistance: some financial assistance available, contact efleming@stevens-tech.edu for further information.

2693 Sweet Briar College [SBC]

Office of Admission
24595-1052 Sweet Briar, VA
Tel: +1-804-381-6142
Web: http://www.sbc.edu
e-mail: admissions@sbc.edu

📖 Undergraduate Liberal Arts Programmes

Study Domains: liberal arts.
Programmes: Undergraduate liberal arts programmes.
Open to: women of all nationalities meeting academic, linguistic and financial requirements; TOEFL 550 PBT / 213 CBT required.
Applications: by 1 February to the above address; see http://www.sbc.edu/admissions/internationalstudents.

2694 Syracuse University [SU]

13244-1200 Syracuse, NY
Tel: +1-315-443-3611
Fax: +1-315-443-4226
Web: http://www.syr.edu
e-mail: orange@syr.edu; grad@gwmail.syr.edu

📖 Undergraduate Programmes

Study Domains: all major fields.
Programmes: Undergraduate programmes.
Open to: candidates of all nationalities meeting academic, linguistic and financial requirements.
Applications: by 1 January to the above address; for further information on undergraduate studies: orange@syr.edu; for graduate studies: grad@gwmail.syr.edu.

☛Merit-Based Scholarships

Study Domains: all major fields.
Scholarships: Merit-Based Scholarships: Founder's;

Chancellor's; Dean's.
Subjects: all fields.
Open to: international students are eligible for merit-based scholarships awarded at the time of application review and granted based on student's academic credentials. Qualified freshman students are offered one of three available scholarships.
Value: Founder's Scholarship at US$12,000 per year; Chancellor's Scholarship at US$8,000 per year; Dean's Scholarship at US$6,000 per year.
Applications: by 1 January to the above address; for further information: http://admissions.syr.edu/adminfinaid/international.html#financial.

2695 Syracuse University, Maxwell School of Citizenship and Public Affairs [SU]

13244-1100 Syracuse, NY
Tel: +1-315-443-2306
Fax: +1-315-443-9204
Web: http://www.maxwell.syr.edu/ir/irmain.htm
e-mail: irgradir@maxwell.syr.edu

📖 Graduate Programmes in Public Administration

Study Domains: administration.
Programmes: (a) Master's Degree in Public Administration with a special programme in development administration;
(b) Master of Arts in International Relations;
(c) Master of Arts in Public Administration (mid-career).
Open to: candidates of any nationality possessing equivalent of Bachelor's degree admitted for graduate degree work at Syracuse University.
Duration: (a) 40-credit programme normally spread over 14 months; (b) 16 months; (c) 12 months.
Financial assistance: students may apply for University fellowships, assistantships and partial tuition scholarships; most foreign participants receive funding from non-university sources.
Applications: by 10 January, to Graduate School, 303 Bowne Hall, at the above address; see website http://www.maxwell.syr.edu/admission/info_reqs.htm.

2696 Texas A & M International University [TAMIU]

5201 University Boulevard
78041 Laredo, TX
Tel: +1-956-326-2001
Fax: +1-956-326-2348
Web: http://www.tamiu.edu

📖 Undergraduate, Graduate Programmes

Study Domains: accounting, administration, biology, business administration, chemistry, communication, criminology, economy, education, finance, international business, liberal arts, management, marketing, mathematics, nursing, performing arts, physics, political science, psychology, Slavic studies, sociology, special education, teacher education, trade.
Programmes: Bachelor's, Master's degrees in liberal arts, business administration, performing arts, management, teacher education, nursing.
Open to: applicants meeting academic requirements; TOEFL score 550 PBT / 213 CBT required for international students.
Duration: 2-4 years; courses begin in August.
Fees: tuition fees US$7,419; living costs US$8,627.
Financial assistance: Business Fellowship available; contact lopez@tamiu.edu for further information.
Applications: by 1 June for Fall term; 1 October for Spring term.

☛Fellowship

Study Domains: business administration, international business.
Scholarships: (a) Doctoral Fellowship; (b) Graduate Student Fellowship.
Open to: candidates of all nationalities.
Duration: (a) 4 years; renewable; (b) 1 year; non-renewable.

Value: Tuition, US$9,000; living expenses, US$16,000.
Applications: (a) rolling admission; contact: Director PhD program in international business administration; (b) rolling admission.

2697 Texas A & M University
College Station
77843 College Station, TX
Tel: +1-979-845-3211
Web: http://www.tamu.edu

Scholarship

Study Domains: all major fields.
Scholarships: International Awards.
Open to: Candidates of all nationalities.
Value: variable.
Applications: varies by award; see website:
http://international.tamu.edu/iss; contact iss@tamu.edu for further information.

2698 Texas Woman's University [TWU]
PO Box 425589
76204-5587 Denton, TX
Tel: +1-940-898-2000
Fax: +1-940-898-3188
Web: http://www.twu.edu
e-mail: admissions@twu.edu

Scholarship

Study Domains: all major fields.
Scholarships: TWU International Student Scholarship.
Description: Out-of-state tuition waiver.
Open to: candidates of all nationalities, full-time student, eligible for admission to university, high GPA, GRE scores.
Other conditions: women students.
Duration: up to 4 years.
Applications: by 1 March.

2699 Thunderbird - American Graduate School of International Management
15249 North 59th Avenue
85306-6010 Glendale, AZ
Tel: +1-602-978-7100
Fax: +1-602-439-5432
Web: http://www.t-bird.edu
e-mail: admissions@t-bird.edu

MBA in International Management

Study Domains: international studies, languages, management, summer programmes.
Programmes: MBA in international management.
Description: Two-part programme integrating courses in world business, international study and modern language.
Open to: candidates of all nationalities who meet admission requirements.
Duration: 7 semesters.
Fees: US$13,400 per semester plus an estimated US$2,000 for living expenses per semester.
Financial assistance: scholarships and assistantships available.
Applications: to Dean of Admissions for all further information;
http://www.t-bird.edu/academics/mbaim/index.htm.

2700 Troy State University [TSU]
36082 Troy, AL
Tel: +1-334-670-3335
Fax: +1-334-670-3735
Web: http://www.troyst.edu
e-mail: intlprog@troyst.edu

Undergraduate, Graduate Programmes

Study Domains: all major fields, business, business administration, criminology, economic and commercial sciences, economy, education, journalism, languages, liberal arts, management, nursing, sciences.
Programmes: Bachelor's, Master's in education, liberal arts, business, management, science, nursing.
Languages: English; TOEFL score 500 required.

Applications: rolling admission.

2701 Truman State University [TSU]
KB 120
63501 Kirksville, MO
Tel: +1-660-785-4215
Fax: +1-660-785-5395
Web: http://www2.truman.edu/ciea
e-mail: plecaque@truman.edu

Undergraduate, Graduate Programmes

Study Domains: all major fields.
Programmes: undergraduate and graduate programmes in all major fields.
Open to: candidates of all nationalities with excellent secondary school record and proof of English proficiency equivalent to a minimum TOEFL 550 PBT/217 CBT; sufficient funds available to meet tuition and living expenses for the duration of the student's studies; submission of a 1-2 page essay explaining personal goals and objectives.
Fees: tuition: US8,400-$8,800; estimated living and equipment/supplies costs: US$8,500 per academic year.
Applications: to International Students Office by 1 June for Fall semester beginning in August; by 1 November for Spring semester beginning in January; website http://iso.truman.edu/prospectives/admis_info.htm#Applicatio n%20Requirements.

International Scholarships

Study Domains: all major fields.
Scholarships: (a) President's Honorary Scholarship; (b) International Excellence; (c) Kirksville Rotary Club.
Open to: (a) open to all international students based on academic achievement in secondary school and examinations results. This scholarship is renewable by maintaining a 3.25 grade point average at the end of the first two semesters. Renewal requires the completion of 5 hours per week of service to the University after the first two semesters; (b) based on academic achievement and financial need; (c) Selection is made by the Kirksville Rotary Club. One scholarship awarded each year. Attendance at weekly Rotary meetings will be required.
Value: (a) partial tuition scholarship; generally ranging from US$1,000-$4,000; (b) US$500 for one year; full tuition for one year.
Applications: to the International Student Office of the University.

2702 Tufts University [TU]
02155 Medford, MA
Tel: +1-617-628-5000
Web: http://www.tufts.edu
e-mail: admissions.inquiry@ase.tufts.edu

Fletcher School of Law and Diplomacy

Study Domains: international relations, law.
Programmes: International relations and foreign policy graduate programme leading to a Master's degree or Ph.D.; interdisciplinary studies in international relations.
Open to: candidates of all nationalities with a Bachelor's degree or equivalent. TOEFL 600/PBT required for admission; English language instruction available.
Duration: usually 2 years (Master's) or 3 to 6 years (Ph.D.).
Financial assistance: possibility of scholarship ranging from US$2,000-$25,000.
Applications: by 15 January, to the Director of Admissions; Fletcher School of Law and Diplomacy Tufts University; Medford, MA 02155; tel: +1 617 627 3040; fax: +1 617 627 3712; email: FletcherAdmissions@tufts.edu; website: http://fletcher.tufts.edu/admissions.

Undergraduate, Graduate Programmes

Study Domains: all major fields.
Programmes: undergraduate colleges in liberal arts and in engineering with programmes in all major fields, and graduate programmes in international affairs, medicine, dentistry, veterinary medicine, nutrition, biomedical sciences; Master's and Ph.D. programmes in major fields.
Open to: highly qualified candidates of all nationalities; provisions made for handicapped students.
Applications: by 1 January for first-year students, and for

further information to the Office of Undergraduate
Admissions (Bendetson Hall).

☛ Fletcher School of Law and Diplomacy Fellowships

Study Domains: international relations, law.
Scholarships: Fletcher School of Law and Diplomacy
Fellowships.
Description: international relations, foreign policy,
international business and international law.
Open to: candidates of all nationalities with Bachelor's
degree or equivalent and high academic standing; background
in history, economics, political science, law or business
preferred; excellent English (TOEFL 600 and above)
essential; arrangements possible for students with disabilities.
Duration: 1 academic year (renewable).
Value: varies from US$2,000-$25,000.
Applications: by 15 January, to the Director of
Admissions; Fletcher School of Law and Diplomacy Tufts
University; Medford, MA 02155; tel: +1 617 627 3040; fax:
+1 617 627 3712; email: FletcherAdmissions@tufts.edu;
website: http://fletcher.tufts.edu/admissions.

2703 Tusculum College
PO Box 5097
37743 Greenville, TN
Tel: +1-423-636-7300
Fax: +1-423-638-7166
Web: http://www.tusculum.edu

☛ International Students' Awards

Study Domains: all major fields.
Description: Multiple types of financial assistance for
international students.
Applications: contact Financial Office at the above
address.

2704 Union College
310 College Street
40906 Barbourville, KY
Tel: +1-606-546-1211
Fax: +1-606-546-1609
Web: http://www.unionky.edu

☛ Scholarship

Study Domains: all major fields.
Scholarships: International Scholarship.
Open to: candidates of all nationalities.
Value: Tuition, US$11,000.
Applications: by 1 March; contact awashin@unionky.edu
for further details.

2705 University of Alaska, Fairbanks
Office of International Programs
PO Box 757760
99775-7760 Fairbanks, AK
Tel: +1-907-474-7500
Fax: +1-907-474-5379
Web: http://www.uaf.edu

☐ Undergraduate, Graduate Programmes

Study Domains: all major fields.
Programmes: Undergraduate and graduate programmes in
all major fields.
Open to: candidates of all nationalities meeting academic,
linguistic and financial requirements; TOEFL 550 PBT / 213
CBT required.
Applications: by 1 March for Fall semester and 1
September for the Spring semester to the Office of
Admissions; for further information see
http://www.uaf.edu/admissions/international/index.html.

2706 University of Arizona
915 North Tyndall Avenue
AZ 85721 Tucson, AZ
Tel: +1-520-621-3237
Web: http://www.arizona.edu

☐ Undergraduate, Graduate Programmes

Study Domains: all major fields.
Programmes: Undergraduate and graduate programmes in
all major fields.
Open to: candidates of all nationalities meeting academic,
linguistic and financial requirements.
Fees: yearly undergraduate tuition: US$11,108; estimated
living expenses for one year: US$12,000.
Financial assistance: out-of-state tuition waiver and/or
registration fees for highly qualified students
(US$8,520-$11,108); priority given to new students admitted
by 15 April for the Summer sessions/Fall term; selection
criteria are marks (grades), class rank, TOEFL score,
SAT/ACT scores, and leadership skills.

2707 University of Arkansas [UARK]
International Admissions Office
747 W. Dickson Street, #8
72701 Fayetteville, AR
Tel: +1-479-575-6246
Fax: +1-479-575-4163
Web: http://www.uark.edu/international
e-mail: iao@uark.edu

☐ Undergraduate, Graduate, Postgraduate Programmes

Study Domains: all major fields, agriculture, business,
education, liberal arts, nursing, performing arts, sciences,
social sciences.
Programmes: Bachelor's, Master's, PhD degrees in all
major fields.
Duration: 4 to 5 years.
Fees: tuition fees: US$9,500 per year; living costs:
US$7,603 per year.
Languages: English; TOEFL score 550 PBT/ 213 CBT
required.

☛ Scholarships

Study Domains: all major fields.
Scholarships: (a) Chancellor's Scholarship; (b) Lavallard
Scholarship.
Open to: (a) incoming freshmen only; (b) undergraduate
exchange students.
Other conditions: (a) must be fully admitted to the
university by 15 February for scholarship consideration.
Duration: (a) 4 academic years; renewable; (b) 1 academic
year; non-renewable.
Value: tuition: (a) US$10,000 per year; renewable on basis
of academic performance; books: US$8,000; (b) tuition:
US$9,1200; living expenses: US$5,477.
Applications: (a) by 15 February; contact iao@uark.edu;
provide official SAT scores, academic records, TOEFL or
IELTS scores, application, application fee, letters of
recommendation and scholarship essay; (b) 1 March; must
submit TOEFL or IELTS scores, official academic records
and the Lavallard Scholarship application; contact
sbyram@uark.edu; see website for more information.

2708 University of California, Los Angeles [UCLA]
Box 951772
90095-1772 Los Angeles, CA
Tel: +1-310-825-3101
Fax: +1-310-206-1206
Web: http://www.ucla.edu

☐ Undergraduate, Graduate Programmes

Study Domains: all major fields.
Programmes: Undergraduate and graduate programmes in
all major fields.
Open to: highly qualified candidates of all nationalities
meeting academic, linguistic and financial requirements.
Fees: registration: US$4,050; yearly undergraduate
non-resident tuition: US$12,009; estimated yearly living
expenses: US$10,000-$15,000.
Applications: to the Admissions Office at the above
address.

2709 University of California, San Francisco [UCSF]
Mu 200 West 500 Parnassus Avenue
94143 San Francisco, CA
Tel: +1-415-476-9000
Fax: +1-415-476-9634
Web: http://www.ucsf.edu

☞Fellowship

Study Domains: all major fields.
Scholarships: PhD Fellowship Tuition Waiver.
Description: Fro PhD programmes only.
Open to: candidates of all nationalities.
Applications: see website for further information.

2710 University of Chicago
5801 South Ellis Avenue
60637-1513 Chicago, IL
Tel: +1-773-702-1234
Fax: +1-773-702-0934
Web: http://www.uchicago.edu

☐ Undergraduate, Graduate, Postgraduate Programmes

Study Domains: all major fields, law, liberal arts, medicine, theology, religion.
Programmes: Bachelor's, Master's, Ph.D., M.D., J.D. and Th.D. degrees.
Description: in all major fields, medicine, law and theology.
Open to: highly qualified candidates of all nationalities meeting academic, linguistic and financial requirements.
Financial assistance: some limited scholarships available.
Applications: by 15 February to the Admissions Office.

2711 University of Delaware [UDEL]
189 West Main Street
19716-2588 Newark, DE
Tel: +1-302-831-2000
Fax: +1-302-831-8000
Web: http://www.udel.edu

☐ Undergraduate, Graduate Programmes

Study Domains: all major fields.
Programmes: Undergraduate and graduate programmes in all major fields.
Open to: students of all nationalities fulfilling the necessary academic, linguistic and financial requirements.
Applications: to the Admissions Office at the above address for further information.

2712 University of Denver [DU]
University Park
80208 Denver, CO
Tel: +1-303-871-2000
Fax: +1-303-871-3301
Web: http://www.du.edu
e-mail: admission@du.edu

☞Scholarship

Study Domains: all major fields.
Scholarships: International Academic Merit Award.
Open to: all undergraduate candidates.
Duration: 4 years; renewable.
Value: tuition, up to US$10,000.
Applications: by June 1.

2713 University of Evansville
1800 Lincoln Avenue
47722 Evansville, IN
Tel: +1-812-479-2000
Web: http://www.evansville.edu

☐ Undergraduate Programmes

Study Domains: arts, business, education, engineering, fine arts, health and hygiene, nursing, sciences.
Programmes: Undergraduate degree programmes in arts, sciences, business, education, engineering, fine arts, nursing and health sciences.
Open to: qualified students of all nationalities; intensive English available.

Duration: 2 semesters per academic year (courses begin in August), plus Summer session.
Financial assistance: international student scholarships: value of up to US$20,000 for 4 years.
Applications: by November or April, to the Office of Admission at the above address.

2714 University of Florida [UOF]
319 Grinter Hall
32611-5530 Gainesville, FL
Tel: +1-904-392-3261
Fax: +1-904-392-9506
Web: http://www.ufl.edu

☐ Undergraduate, Graduate Programmes

Study Domains: agriculture, arts, education, forestry, liberal arts, medicine, nursing, physical education.
Programmes: Undergraduate and graduate programmes.
Open to: candidates of all nationalities meeting academic, linguistic and financial requirements.
Financial assistance: scholarships and loans.
Applications: to Admissions Office at above address.

2715 University of Georgia [UGA]
Visual Arts Building
30602-4102 Athens, GA
Tel: +1-706-542-3000
Fax: +1-706-542-9492
Web: http://www.uga.edu

☐ Undergraduate, Graduate Programmes

Study Domains: law, liberal arts, medicine, pharmacy and pharmacology.
Programmes: Bachelor's, Master's, Ph.D, J.D., Pharm.D., D.V.M. degrees.
Open to: applicants of any nationality meeting academic, linguistic and financial requirements.
Applications: first-year undergraduate applications: early decision, 1 November; regular decision, 1 February; Spring admission, 1 October.

☞Scholarship

Scholarships: Regent's Out-of-State Tuition Waiver.
Duration: 4 terms.
Applications: by 1 April; contact pageme@uga.edu for further information.

2716 University of Hartford
International Admission
Bates House
06117 West Hartford, CT
Tel: +1-860-768-4981
Fax: +1-860-768-4961
Web: http://www.hartford.edu
e-mail: iua@hartford.edu

☐ Undergraduate, Graduate Programmes

Study Domains: arts, liberal arts, music and musicology.
Programmes: undergraduate and graduate programmes in liberal arts; also distance education degree programmes.
Open to: candidates of all nationalities meeting academic, linguistic and financial requirements; applicants for Hart School must prepare an audition of two or three contrasting works from the standard musical literature; taped auditions are accepted; videocassettes are required of music theatre applicants; applicants for the Hartford Art School, are required to submit a portfolio of 15 examples of best work.
http://www.hartford.edu/admission_splash/international.html.
Financial assistance: possibility of loans and grants.
Applications: see website for full details and application form:
http://www.hartford.edu/admission_splash/international.html.

2717 University of Hawaii at Manoa
1960 East-West Road
96822 Honolulu, HI
Tel: +1-808-956-8267
Web: http://www.hawaii.edu

☐ Undergraduate and Graduate Programmes

Study Domains: business administration, engineering, health and hygiene, law, liberal arts, medicine, nursing.

Programmes: Undergraduate and graduate programmes; distance education programmes (http://www.hawaii.edu/dl). *Open to:* candidates of all nationalities meeting academic, linguistic and financial requirements.
Financial assistance: tuition waivers.
Applications: undergraduate admissions: see http://www.hawaii.edu/admrec/appfo.html; graduate admissions: http://www.hawaii.edu/graduate.

2718 University of Iowa
3006 Main Library
52242-1420 Iowa City, IA
Tel: +1-319-335-5629
Web: http://www.uiowa.edu

📖 Undergraduate, Graduate Programmes

Study Domains: business administration, dentistry, education, engineering, law, liberal arts, nursing, sciences.
Programmes: Undergraduate and graduate programmes in liberal arts; law, dentistry and business management professional programmes.
Open to: secondary school graduates of any nationality who meet academic, linguistic and financial requirements.
Applications: variable according to programme; see website for full details: http://www.uiowa.edu/admissions/international/requirements.html.

2719 University of Kansas [KU]
108 Lippincott Hall
66045-2917 Lawrence, KS
Tel: +1-785-864-2700
Fax: +1-785-864-45555
Web: http://www.ku.edu

📖 Asian Studies Programme

Study Domains: Asian studies, Chinese, Japanese.
Programmes: East Asian studies programme; first through fourth-year Chinese and Japanese, and first and second-year Korean, are available.
Open to: high school and college graduates.
Duration: 2 terms. (Courses begin in August and January.).
Financial assistance: competitive, based on need, nationality, etc.
Applications: by 15 April, to the Department of East Asian Languages and Culture; 2118 Wescoe Hall, Lawrence, KS 66045.

📖 Undergraduate, Graduate, Professional Programmes

Study Domains: all major fields, business, education, engineering, liberal arts, medicine, nursing, pharmacy and pharmacology, sciences.
Programmes: Bachelor's, Master's, professional degrees in all major fields.
Open to: all candidates meeting academic standards; GRE required for most graduate programmes.
Fees: tuition fees: US$6,439 per year; living costs: US$7,486 per year.
Applications: rolling admissions.

2720 University of Maine [UMAINE]
Office of International Programs
5782 Winslow Hall, Room 100
04469-5782 Orono, ME
Tel: +1-207-581-2905
Fax: +1-207-581-2920
Web: http://www.maine.edu
e-mail: umintprg@maine.edu

📖 Undergraduate, Graduate, Postgraduate Programmes

Study Domains: all major fields, agriculture, business, business administration, economic and commercial sciences, education, engineering, forestry, liberal arts, nursing, sciences, speech therapy, veterinary sciences.
Programmes: Bachelor's, Master's, PhD degrees in all major fields.
Financial assistance: financial assistance available; contact studyabroad@umit.maine.edu for further information.

🐦 International Tuition Programmes
Study Domains: all major fields.
Open to: full-time enrolled undergraduate students.
Academic requirements: top 10% of class.
Languages: 213 TOEFL.
Applications: 1 February to International Admissions, Office of International Programs at above address.

2721 University of Mary Hardin-Baylor [UMHB]
900 College Street; Box 8367
76513 Belton, TX
Tel: +1-254-295-4949
Fax: +1-254-295-4535
Web: http://www.umhb.edu
e-mail: internationalstudentservices@umhb.edu

🐦 International Student Scholarship
Study Domains: all major fields.
Description: US$2,000 per semester of full-time enrolment; renewable; not available during summer sessions.
Open to: all new international students.
Nationality: candidates of all nationalities.
Academic requirements: undergraduate, full-time enrolment; student must retain good standing with the university.
Duration: 1 year; renewable.
Value: US$1000 per semester.
Languages: All courses are taught in English.
Applications: by 1 June; contact etanaka@umhb.edu for further information.

2722 University of Maryland, Baltimore County [UMBC]
1000 Hilltop Circle
21250 Baltimore, MD
Tel: +1-410-455-1000
Fax: +1-410-455-1210
Web: http://www.umbc.edu

🐦 Graduate Programme Assistantships
Study Domains: all major fields.
Description: Research Assistantships and Teaching Assistantships.
Open to: graduate candidates of all nationalities meeting academic and professional requirements.
Applications: see webpage for full details.

2723 University of Michigan [UM]
307 Hutchins Hall
48109-1215 Ann Arbor, MI
Tel: +1-734-764-1817
Web: http://www.umich.edu

📖 Undergraduate, Graduate, Postgraduate and Professional Programmes

Study Domains: all major fields.
Programmes: undergraduate, graduate, postgraduate and professional programmes in all major fields.
Open to: candidates of all nationalities meeting high academic, linguistic and financial requirements.
Applications: see website for application details: http://www.umich.edu/~icenter/intlstudents/admissions/index.html.

🐦 U of M Scholarships
Study Domains: law.
Scholarships: (a) University of Michigan Kosacheff Scholarship for Russian citizens; (b) University of Michigan Guatemalan Scholarship for native-born students from Guatemala; (c) University of Michigan Ling Scholarship for citizens of the People's Republic of China; (d) Undergraduate Scholarship for Swiss Citizens; (e) Need-based aid for international students.
Subjects: graduate study and research in law; strong programme areas include international law, international trade and economic law, comparative study in many substantive areas including criminal law, civil procedure, commercial and corporate law, as well as constitutional law, civil rights, intellectual property law and interdisciplinary legal studies; 3-degree programmes:
M.C.L., LL.M., S.J.D., plus 1 non-degree law programme for

research scholars.
Open to: (a) Russian citizens; (b) Guatemalan citizens; (c)
Chinese citizens; (d) Swiss citizens; (e) all nationalities under
special conditions.
Value: variable; see website for details:
http://www.finaid.umich.edu/international.htm.

2724 University of Missouri, St Louis [UMSL]
8001 Natural Bridge Road
63121-4499 St. Louis, MO
Tel: +1-314-516-5000
Web: http://www.umsl.edu
e-mail: web_office@umsl.edu

Undergraduate, Graduate Programmes
Study Domains: all major fields.
Programmes: Undergraduate and graduate programmes in
all major fields; online degree programmes in business
administration, nursing and education:
http://www.umsl.edu/online.html.
Open to: candidates of all nationalities meeting academic,
linguistic and financial requirements; minimum TOEFL 500
PBT/173 CBT required.
Applications:
http://www.umsl.edu/~intelstu/prospective/application_form.h
tml.

2725 University of Missouri-Columbia
123 Jesse Hall
65211 Columbia, MO
Tel: +1-573-882-2121
Fax: +1-573-882-7887
Web: http://www.missouri.edu
e-mail: webeditor@missouri.edu

Undergraduate, Graduate Programmes
Study Domains: all major fields, law, medicine,
veterinary medicine.
Programmes: B.S., B.A., M.S., M.A., Ph.D. in all major
fields.
Open to: candidates of any country.
Duration: Fall, Winter and Summer semesters.
Fees: international tuition: US$13,500; estimated
miscellaneous and living costs: US$10,000 yearly.
Financial assistance: teaching and research assistantships
for graduate students.
Applications: by 1 May, to the International Admissions
Office.

2726 University of Nebraska at Kearney [UNK]
905 West 25th Street
68849 Kearney, NE
Tel: +1-308-865-8441
Web: http://www.unk.edu
e-mail: admissionsug@unk.edu

Undergraduate, Graduate Programmes
Study Domains: all major fields, English, interpretation
and translation, languages.
Programmes: Undergraduate and graduate programmes in
all major fields; conference interpretation and translation
programmes.
Open to: students of any nationality meeting academic,
financial and linguistic requirements; TOEFL 550 PBT/213
CBT required for admission.
Applications: 1 October for Spring semester; 1 February
for Summer session; 1 May for Fall semester.
undergraduate admissions: admissionsug@unk.edu; tel: +1
800 KEARNEY; fax: +1 308 865 8987; graduate admissions:
gradstudies@unk.edu; tel: +1 800 717 7881; fax:+1 308 865
8837.

2727 University of Nebraska-Lincoln [UNL]
1237 R Street
68588-0221 Lincoln, NE
Tel: +1-402-472-7211
Web: http://www.unl.edu

Undergraduate, Graduate Programmes
Study Domains: all major fields.
Programmes: B.S., B.A., M.S. and Ph.D. in all major
fields.
Open to: students of any nationality or age with TOEFL of
500 or better (some departments require 550 or better);
non-U.S. students must submit secondary and post-secondary
transcripts and furnish proof of adequate financial support.
Duration: Fall, Spring and Summer semesters.
Financial assistance: teaching and research assistantships
for graduate students; tuition scholarships based on merit for
graduate or undergraduate students after first year of
attendance; international student scholarship.
Applications: undergraduates: to Office of Admissions, 12
Administration Building, at the above address; graduates:
Graduate Studies Office, 301 Administration Building, at the
above address.

2728 University of New Mexico [UNM]
Mesa Vista Hall 2111
87131-1052 Albuquerque, NM
Tel: +1-505-277-4032
Fax: +1-505-277-1867
Web: http://www.unm.edu
e-mail: oips@unm.edu

Undergraduate, Graduate, Postgraduate Programmes
Study Domains: all major fields.
Programmes: Bachelor's, Master's, Ph.D. degrees in all
major fields.

Scholarship
Study Domains: all major fields.
Scholarships: Amigo Scholarship.
Open to: applicants meeting academic requirements.
Value: US$8,000 per year; renewable each year.
Applications: by 1 May or 1 October; contact
school@unm.edu for further details.

2729 University of New Orleans [UNO]
c/o Metropolitan College
70148 New Orleans, LA
Tel: +1-504-280-6595
Fax: +1-504-280-5522
Web: http://www.uno.edu
e-mail: admissions@uno.edu

Undergraduate and Graduate Programmes
Study Domains: all major fields.
Programmes: Undergraduate and graduate programmes in
all major fields.
Open to: candidates of all nationalities meeting academic,
financial and linguistic requirements.
http://www.uno.edu/~admi/international.html.

2730 University of Oregon
5209 University of Oregon
97403-5209 Eugene, OR
Tel: +1-541-346-3206
Fax: +1-541-346-1232
Web: http://www.uoregon.edu
e-mail: oip@darkwing.uoregon.edu

Undergraduate, Graduate, Postgraduate Programmes
Study Domains: all major fields, administration,
architecture, business, economic and commercial sciences,
education, engineering, liberal arts, management, neurology,
sciences, speech therapy.
Programmes: Bachelor's, Master's and Ph.D. degrees in all
major fields.

Fees: US$13,000-$15,000 per year; living costs approximately US$12,000.
Financial assistance: financial assistance available; see website for further information.
Applications: by 15 April for undergraduates; contact uoadmit@oregon.uoregon.edu for further details.

2731 University of Pennsylvania [UPENN]

Office of International Programs
3701 Chestnut Street, Suite 1W
PA 19104-3199 Philadelphia, PA
Tel: +1-215-898-4661
Fax: +1-215-898-2622
Web: http://www.upenn.edu

📖 Undergraduate and Graduate Programmes

Study Domains: all major fields.
Programmes: Undergraduate and graduate programmes in all major fields.
Open to: candidates of all nationalities meeting academic, linguistic and financial requirements.
Applications: see website for application information: http://www.upenn.edu/oip/iss/info.html.

🐾 Thouron Awards

Study Domains: all major fields.
Scholarships: Thouron Awards.
Description: for any field of study in which the University of Pennsylvania offers advanced degrees, postgraduate courses; http://www.upenn.edu/oip/scholarships/thouron.
Open to: unmarried citizens of the United Kingdom who are qualified to pursue a regular course of graduate study at this University.
Duration: 1 or 2 years.
Value: tuition, US$28,000-US$29,000; living expenses US$1,376 per month; health insurance.
Applications: by 15 November, to the Registrar (Thouron Awards); for special application form: http://www.gla.ac.uk/Otherdepts/Court/thouronawards.htm; contact d.maddern@admin.gla.ac.uk for further information. Applications for admission to courses and programs must be made separately from applications for Thouron Awards.

2732 University of Puget Sound [Puget Sound]

1500 North Warner Street
98416 Tacoma, WA
Tel: +1-253-879-3100
Fax: +1-253-879-3500
Web: http://www.ups.edu

🐾 University Scholarships

Study Domains: all major fields.
Scholarships: (a) President's Scholarship; (b) Dean's Scholarship; (c) Trustee Scholarship.
Open to: candidates of all nationalities; based on academic record and standardized test scores.
Duration: 4 academic years; renewable.
Value: tuition: (a) US$6,000; (b) US$3,000; (c) US$8,000.
Applications: February; to Office of Admission; admission@ups.edu.

2733 University of Rochester

14627 Rochester, NY
Tel: +1-585-275-2121
Web: http://www.rochester.edu/admissions
e-mail: admit@rochester.edu

🐾 Merit Scholarships, Undergraduate Programme

Study Domains: engineering, liberal arts.
Open to: entering full-time undergraduate international students.
Value: tuition: US$1,000 to full tuition.
Applications: 1 December; to Assistant Director, Admissions.

2734 University of San Diego [USD]

Alcalá Park
92110-2492 San Diego, CA
Tel: +1-619-260-4600
Web: http://www.sandiego.edu
e-mail: admissions@SanDiego.edu

📖 Undergraduate and Graduate Programmes

Study Domains: all major fields, international business, international law, international relations.
Programmes: Undergraduate and graduate programmes in all major fields; graduate comparative law programmes.
Open to: students of any nationality meeting academic, linguistic and financial requirements.
Fees: tuition, room and board, and other expenses for undergraduate students total US$35,300.
Applications: see website for full application details: http://www.sandiego.edu/ugadmiss/international.html.

2735 University of Texas at Brownsville and Texas Southmost College [UTB]

80 Fort Brown
78520 Brownsville, TX
Tel: +1-956-544-8860
Fax: +1-956-544-8832
Web: http://www.utb.edu
e-mail: cata01@utb.edu

📖 Undergraduate, Graduate Programmes

Study Domains: accounting, applied sciences, arts, biology, business administration, chemistry, computer science, criminology, education, finance, fine arts, history, liberal arts, management, marketing, physical education, physics, political science, psychology, radiology, sociology, teacher education.
Programmes: Associate, Bachelor's, Master's degrees in education, liberal arts, business administration, mathematics, radiology.
Duration: 4 to 5 years.
Fees: tuition fees US$3,800 per semester; living costs US$5,000 per year.

2736 University of the Arts [UARTS]

320 South Broad Street
19102 Philadelphia, PA
Tel: +1-215-717-6000
Fax: +1-215-717-6045
Web: http://www.uarts.edu
e-mail: admissions@uarts.edu

📖 Undergraduate Studies

Study Domains: arts, audio-visual media, design, fine arts, industrial design, liberal arts, music and musicology, performing arts, printing.
Programmes: Bachelor's, professional degrees in education, design, media and performing arts.
Financial assistance: financial assistance available; contact admissions@uarts.edu for further details.
Languages: English; TOEFL score 500 minimum required.
Applications: rolling admissions.

2737 University of the District of Columbia [UDC]

4200 Connecticut Avenue
20774 Washington, DC
Tel: +1-202-274-5000
Web: http://www.udc.edu

📖 Undergraduate, Graduate Programmes

Study Domains: all major fields.
Programmes: Bachelor's, Master's degrees in all major fields.

2738 University of the Incarnate Word [UIW]
4301 Broadway
78209-6397 San Antonio, TX
Tel: +1-210-805-5806
Fax: +1-210-805-5701
Web: http://www.uiw.edu
e-mail: burr@universe.uiwtx.edu

 Undergraduate, Graduate, Postgraduate Programmes

Study Domains: all major fields, business administration, education, engineering, liberal arts, nursing, sciences.
Programmes: Bachelor's, Master's, Ph.D. degrees in all major fields.
Open to: applicants meeting academic requirements; TOEFL score 550 for undergraduates, 560 for graduates required.
Duration: 4-5 years.
Fees: registration US$100; tuition fees US$7,500 per year; living costs US$5,700 per year.
Applications: 60 days prior to start of semester to Admissions Office; contact admis@universe.uiwtx.edu for further details.

2739 University of the South (Sewanee)
735 University Avenue
37383 Sewanee, TN
Tel: +1-931-598-1000
Fax: +1-931-598-1145
Web: http://www.sewanee.edu

 International Scholarship

Study Domains: all major fields.
Description: all subjects offered in the College of Arts and Sciences.
Open to: candidates of all nationalities.
Academic requirements: strong SAT I, strong secondary-school curriculum and excellent grades.
Other conditions: extra-curricular activities, community service and leadership desired.
Duration: 4 years, provided that recipients maintain a 3.0 GPA.
Value: up to full tuition, fees, room and board, depending on financial ability of selected candidates.
Languages: TOEFL 550 (paper-based test) or 213 (computer-based test).

2740 University of Toledo
2801 West Bancroft
43606 Toledo, OH
Tel: +1-419-530-4636
Web: http://www.utoledo.edu

 International Students' Awards

Study Domains: all major fields.
Scholarships: (a) Graduate Assistantships: (b) Teaching Assistantships; (c) Tuition Waiver, Stipend.
Open to: international students; on a competitive basis.
Value: tuition: US$9,500; living expenses: US$12,000.
Applications: before fall and spring semesters; to College of Graduate School.

2741 University of Utah
International Admissions Office
200 South Central Campus Drive 410
84112 Salt Lake City, UT
Tel: +1-801-581-8876
Fax: +1-801-581-5914
Web: http://www.sa.utah.edu/admiss/international.htm
e-mail: iao@sa.utah.edu

 Undergraduate, Graduate, Postgraduate Programmes

Study Domains: all major fields.
Programmes: Bachelor's, Master's, Ph.D. degrees in all major fields.
Open to: all candidates meeting academic, financial and linguistic requirements; minimum score of TOEFL 500 PBT/ 173 CBT or better for applicants whose first language is not

English.
Applications: by 1 May for Fall Semester; by 1 November for Spring semester; by 15 April for Summer term; on-line applications: http://www.saff.utah.edu/admiss/appdownload/index.htm.

2742 University of Washington
Office of Admissions
1410 NE Campus Parkway
Box 355852
98195-5852 Seattle, WA
Tel: +1-206-543-9686
Web: http://www.washington.edu

 Undergraduate, Graduate and Professional Programmes

Study Domains: all major fields, dentistry, law, medicine, pharmacy and pharmacology.
Programmes: Undergraduate, graduate and professional programmes in all major fields; distance education programmes: http://www.outreach.washington.edu/dl/course_index.asp.
Open to: candidates of all nationalities meeting academic, linguistic and financial requirements; TOEFL 540 PBT/207 CBT required.
Financial assistance: some financial assistance in the form of tuition reduction and teaching assistantships for graduate students.
Applications: undergraduates by 15 January; for full application details, see http://www.washington.edu/students/uga/in.

2743 University of Wisconsin-Madison
Office of Admissions
716 Langdon Street
53706-1481 Madison, WI
Tel: +1-608-262-3961
Web: http://www.wisc.edu
e-mail: international@admissions.wisc.edu

 Undergraduate, Graduate Programmes

Study Domains: administration, cultural studies.
Programmes: undergraduate, graduate programmes in all major fields.
Open to: candidates with suitable academic qualifications; TOEFL required.
Applications: 1 February for Summer and Fall terms; 1 October for Spring term: see website for full details: http://www.admissions.wisc.edu/admission/internat.html.

2744 University of Wisconsin-Whitewater [UWW]
800 West Main Street
53190 Whitewater, WI
Tel: +1-262-472-1234
Web: http://www.uww.edu

 Undergraduate, Graduate Programmes

Study Domains: accounting, business administration, communication, early childhood education, economy, international business, special education.
Programmes: Associate of Arts (AA); Bachelor of Arts (BA); Bachelor of Business Administration (BBA); Bachelor of Fine Arts (Art and Theatre) (BFA); Bachelor of Music (BM); Bachelor of Science (BS); Bachelor of Science in Education (BSE); pre-professional programmes; Master of Business Administration (MBA).
Open to: candidates of any nationality with excellent academic background; some special requirements set by specific departments have to be met for graduate programmes.
Financial assistance: some scholarships available to incoming freshmen in the form of partial tuition fee remission; students must be able to pay all their school expenses; a few graduate assistantships available to students after 1 year.
Applications: by 15 November for Spring semester admission, and 15 June for Fall semester admission; for full application details: http://www.uww.edu/StdRsces/intlstd/index.html.

2745 University of Wyoming

PO Box 3228 University Station
82071 Laramie, WY
Tel: +1-307-766-5160
Fax: +1-307-766-4042
Web: http://www.uwyo.edu
e-mail: uwglobal@uwyo.edu

📖 Undergraduate, Graduate, Postgraduate Programmes

Study Domains: all major fields, archaeology, art history, arts, business administration, education, engineering, law, liberal arts, nursing, sciences.
Programmes: Bachelor's, Master's, Ph.D. degrees in all major fields.
Open to: students with suitable academic requirements; TOEFL score 525 required.
Applications: by 1 June and 1 September.

🎓 Scholarship

Study Domains: all major fields.
Scholarships: Western Heritage Scholarship.
Open to: students must have minimum 3.0 GPA.
Duration: 8 semesters.
Value: US$1,000-$4,000 per year.
Applications: by 1 June for Fall semester; 1 November for Spring semester; contact uwglobal@uwyo.edu for further details.

2746 Valdosta State University [VSU]

1500 North Patterson Street
GA 31698 Valdosta, GA
Tel: +1-229-333-7410
Fax: +1-912-245-3849
Web: http://www.valdosta.edu
e-mail: admissions@valdosta.edu

📖 Undergraduate, Graduate Programmes

Study Domains: administration, applied sciences, arts, biochemistry, business administration, chemistry, design, economic and commercial sciences, education, fine arts, languages, liberal arts, management, mathematics, nursing, performing arts, philosophy, photography, physics, physiology, social work, speech therapy, teacher education, theology, religion.
Programmes: Bachelor's, Master's degrees in education, arts, liberal arts, business administration, economics, science, nursing.
Open to: all students meeting academic requirements.
Applications: contact vsucip@valdosta.edu for complete information.

🎓 Tuition Waiver

Study Domains: all major fields.
Scholarships: Out-of-State tuition waiver.
Description: The ISS offers students the possibility of having out-of-state tuition waived so that they pay only in-state tuition (some community service is required).
Duration: 1 year; renewable.
Value: tuition fees; US$6,600 per year.
Applications: by 15 March.

2747 Viterbo University [VU]

815 South Ninth Street
54601 La Crosse, WI
Tel: +1-608-796-3010
Fax: +1-608-796-3020
Web: http://www.viterbo.edu
e-mail: admissions@viterbo.edu

📖 Undergraduate Studies

Study Domains: applied arts, arts, biochemistry, biology, chemistry, computer science, education, fine arts, graphic arts, mathematics, music and musicology, nursing, performing arts, teacher education, theology, religion.
Programmes: Bachelor's degrees in all major fields.
Open to: all students meeting academic standards; TOEFL score 550 minimum required.
Duration: 4 to 6 years; courses start end of August.
Fees: tuition fees US$14,000 per year; estimated living

costs US$8,000 per year.
Applications: by 1 April.

🎓 Scholarship

Study Domains: all major fields.
Scholarships: International Student Scholarship.
Open to: students from all nationalities meeting academic requirements; fluency in English required.
Value: US$4,000-$9,000 per academic year; renewable.
Applications: by 1 April for Fall term; contact emoore@viterbo.edu for complete information.

2748 Walsh University

2020 East Maple Street NW
44720 North Canton, OH
Tel: +1-330-490-7090
Web: http://www.walsh.edu

📖 Undergraduate, Graduate Programmes

Study Domains: all major fields, education, nursing, physical therapy, theology, religion.
Programmes: undergraduate programmes: Bachelor of Arts (BA), Bachelor of Science (BS), Bachelor of Science in Nursing (BSN) and Bachelor of Science in Education (BS in Ed).; graduate programmes: Master of Science (MS) in Physical Therapy; Master's programmes in Counseling and Human Development; Master of Arts (MA) in Education Degree; Masters of Business Administration (MBA); Master of Arts (MA) in theology.
Description: accounting, biology, chemistry, clinical laboratory science, communication, comprehensive science, education, English, finance, French, general business, history, human services, Latin American business, liberal arts, management, marketing, mathematics, nursing, philosophy, physical science, political science, psychology, sociology, Spanish and theology.
Open to: candidates of all nationalities with secondary-school certificate (translations of certificates required) who intend to maintain full-time status (12 or more credit hours per semester) during their stay in the United States.
Languages: TOEFL score of 500 or higher on paper-based test or 173 or higher on computer-based test institutional identification number for TOEFL is 1926.

🎓 University Grants and Assistantships

Study Domains: all major fields.
Scholarships: (a) Undergraduate Institutional Grant; (b) Graduate Assistantships.
Open to: (a) all enrolled students; (b) candidates of all nationalities enrolled in graduate programmes (very limited number of positions).
Duration: (a) 4 academic years; (b) 1-2 academic years; renewable.
Value: variable.
Applications: priority deadline: 1 March.

2749 Washington and Lee University [WLU]

Lexington, VA
Fax: +1-540-463-8179
Web: http://www.wlu.edu
e-mail: wklingel@wlu.edu

📖 Undergraduate Studies

Study Domains: all major fields, administration, archaeology, art history, Asian studies, biochemistry, business, engineering, languages, law, mathematics, performing arts, philosophy, photography, statistics, theology, religion.
Programmes: Bachelor's degrees in law, arts and sciences, commerce, economics and politics.
Financial assistance: financial assistance available; contact wklingel@wlu.edu for further information.

2750 Washington State University [WSU]

PO Box 641048
99164 Pullman, WA
Tel: +1-509-335-3564
Fax: +1-509-335-3421
Web: http://www.wsu.edu

✒ Financial Aid

Study Domains: all major fields.
Scholarships: International Transfer Academic Award.
Open to: Transfer students with GPA of 3.3 or higher on 4.0 scale and with minimum of 27 semesters credits that are transferable.
Duration: 1 term; renewable.
Value: Tuition fees US$1250 per semester.
Applications: For further information, please contact international@wsu.edu.

2751 Washington University in St. Louis

Campus Box 1089
1 Brookings Drive
63130-4899 St Louis, MO
Tel: +1-314-935-6000
Fax: +1-314-935-4290
Web: http://www.wustl.edu
e-mail: admissions@wustl.edu

📖 Undergraduate and Graduate Programmes

Study Domains: all major fields.
Programmes: Undergraduate and graduate programmes in all major fields.
Open to: candidates of all nationalities meeting academic, linguistic and financial requirements.
Applications: by 15 January for regular decision; by 15 November for early decision; see website admissions page for full details.

2752 Webber International University

PO Box 96
33827 Babson Park, FL
Tel: +1-863-638-1431
Fax: +1-863-638-2823
Web: http://www.webber.edu
e-mail: admissions@webber.edu

📖 Undergraduate, Graduate Programmes

Study Domains: all major fields.
Programmes: Undergraduate and graduate programmes in all major fields.
Open to: all suitably qualified international candidates; TOEFL required.
Applications: by 1 August for Fall acceptance; 1 December for Spring acceptance; 1 April for Summer acceptance; further information and forms: http://www.webber.edu/admissions/registrar/apply.html.

✒ Webber Scholarships

Study Domains: all major fields, physical education.
Scholarships: (a) Academic Scholarship; (b) Athletic Scholarship; (c) Presidential Scholarship;.
Open to: (a) full-time undergraduate students, based on GPA; determined by high school transcripts for freshman applicants and college transcripts for transfer students; (b) awarded at the discretion of the Athletic Department; based on athletic ability and academic results; (c) full-time students in fall/spring semesters; based on essay, student service and need.
Duration: (a), (c) 1 term; renewable; (b) 1 academic year; renewable.
Value: (a) US$500-$1,200 per semester, based on GPA; (b) US$1,000-$8,000 (c) US$1,000-$5,000.
Applications: by 30 June to the Admissions Office at the above address.

2753 Western Illinois University [WIU]

1 University Circle
61455 Macomb, IL
Tel: +1-309-295-1414
Fax: +1-309-298-2400
Web: http://www.wiu.edu
e-mail: info@wiu.edu

📖 Undergraduate, Graduate Programmes

Study Domains: all major fields, business administration, dentistry, engineering, fine arts, law, medicine, natural sciences, pharmacy and pharmacology, veterinary sciences, women's studies.
Programmes: Bachelor's, Master's degrees in education, fine arts, business, law.
Open to: students meeting academic requirements TOEFL 213 CBT required for most programmes.
Duration: 4 years.
Fees: tuition fees US$10,670 for undergraduate, US$9,918 for graduate per year.
Applications: by 1 March for Fall term; 1 October for Spring term.

✒ International Students' Awards

Study Domains: all major fields.
Scholarships: Several types of financial aid available to international students.
Applications: to Director, International Education Office or Scholarship Office at the above address.

2754 Western Michigan University [WMU]

1903 W. Michigan Avenue
49008-5201 Kalamazoo, MI
Tel: +1-616-387-1000
Fax: +1-616-387-3962
Web: http://www.wmich.edu
e-mail: ask-wmu@wmich.edu

📖 Undergraduate, Graduate, Postgraduate Programmes

Study Domains: all major fields, arts, aviation, aeronautics, business administration, chemical engineering, early childhood education, education, engineering, fine arts, health and hygiene, home economics, liberal arts, mechanical engineering, natural sciences, nursing, paramedical studies, sciences, social work, special education, speech therapy, teacher education, technology, tourism, hotel and catering management.
Programmes: Bachelor's, Master's, Ph.D., professional degrees in all major fields.
Fees: tuition fees US$129.91-$441.83 per credit hour; estimated living costs US$5,500 per year.
Financial assistance: financial assistance available; see website for further information.

2755 Western New England College

1215 Wilbraham Road
01119 Springfield, MA
Tel: +1-413-782-3111
Fax: +1-413-782-1746
Web: http://www.wnec.edu
e-mail: ugradmis@wnec.edu

✒ International Student Scholarship

Study Domains: all major fields.
Open to: full-time enrolled undergraduate students.
Academic requirements: outstanding academic record.
Duration: 4 academic years; renewable.
Value: tuition: US$6,000.
Languages: 213 TOEFL (550 paper-based).
Applications: rolling admissions; priority deadline 1 March.

2756   Whitman College [WC]

345 Boyer Avenue
99362-2085 Walla Walla, WA
Tel: +1-509-527-5176
Fax: +1-509-527-4967
Web: http://www.whitman.edu

📖 Undergraduate Liberal Arts Programmes

Study Domains: all major fields, liberal arts, sciences.
Programmes: Independent co-educational liberal arts and
sciences college offering undergraduate degrees.
Open to: non-degree holding undergraduates of any
nationality with TOEFL score of 560 or above and 5 or 6 on
TWE writing samples displaying excellent English writing
skills; SAT scores also required if offered in the applicant's
country.
Financial assistance: foreign student scholarships based
on demonstrated need and academic merit up to a maximum
of tuition costs and room and board.
Applications: by 15 February, to the Office of Admissions,
at the above address; for further application information:
http://www.whitman.edu/admission/international_p.html.

🐦 Whitman International Scholarships

Study Domains: all major fields.
Scholarships: (a) International Student Scholarship
awards:
(b) Whitman Academic Scholarships.
Open to: (a) to the top 15 international applicants based on
their academic and extra curricular achievements in secondary
school; (b) all international applicants to Whitman College,
regardless of financial circumstances, are considered for the
Whitman Academic Scholarships, also known as merit
scholarships.
Value: (a) between US$2,000-$30,000; (b) between
US$5,000-$9,000 per year; renewable for four years.

2757   William Jewell College [WJC]

Office of Admission
500 College Hill
64068-1896 Liberty, MO
Tel: +1-816-781-7700
Fax: +1-816-415-5007
Web: http://www.jewell.edu

📖 Undergraduate Liberal Arts Programmes

Study Domains: classical studies, liberal arts, natural
sciences, social sciences.
Programmes: Undergraduate liberal arts programmes.
Open to: candidates of all nationalities meeting academic,
linguistic and financial requirements; minimum TOEFL 550
PBT/ 213 CBT required.
Fees: tuition: US$16,500 per year; room and board,
approximately US$6,000 per academic year; books and
supplies: US$750; plus miscellaneous living expenses.
Financial assistance: some financial aid possible.
Applications: to the Admissions Office; for further
application information:
www.jewell.edu/admission/application/international1.html.

2758   Williams College [WC]

1065 Main Street
01267 Williamstown, MA
Tel: +1-413-597-4286
Web: http://www.williams.edu

📖 Undergraduate Liberal Arts Programmes

Study Domains: cytology, development studies, economy,
liberal arts.
Programmes: Undergraduate liberal arts programmes.
Open to: candidates of all nationalities meeting academic,
linguistic and financial requirements. International applicants
must take either the SAT-I or the ACT plus three SAT-II
subject tests. Students who are not native English speakers
should take the English writing test as one of the SAT-II tests,
if possible. Students are not required to submit the TOEFL
unless they are applying from a country without access to
SAT or ACT testing.
Duration: 4-year programmes.
Financial assistance: the University is committed to
meeting the full demonstrated financial need of all applicants,
regardless of citizenship. In addition to funding tuition, room
and board, the international scholar financial aid packages

include yearly travel, textbook and personal spending
allowances. No merit-based or athletic scholarships are
offered; website:
http://www.williams.edu/Admissions/applying/applying_forei
gn_finaid.html.
Applications: by 15 November for early decision; by 1
January for regular decision; to the Admissions Office at the
above address; for further application information:
http://www.williams.edu/Admissions/applying/foreign.html.

United States of America, Puerto Rico

Academic year: early August to late May.
Organization of higher education system: Puerto Rico is a
Commonwealth associated with the United States. The higher
education system is organized and structured similarly to that
of the United States, so the reader should refer to the entry on
the United States for general information on the system of
higher education.
Monetary unit: United States dollar (US$).
Language: The medium of instruction used in Puerto
Rican colleges and universities is Spanish unless English is
specified for a particular programme. Spanish is also the
national language and is used in all social, commercial, and
administrative interactions. Spanish proficiency is highly
desirable and may be required for study.

2759   Bayamón Central University

PO Box 1725
00960 Bayamón
Tel: +1-787-786-3030
Fax: +1-787-740-2200
Web: http://www.ucb.edu.pr
e-mail: exchange@ucb.edu.pr

📖 Undergraduate, Graduate Programmes

Study Domains: business administration, education, liberal
arts, sciences.
Description: Bachelor's and Master's degree programmes
in business administration, natural sciences, liberal arts and
education.
Financial assistance: possibility of obtaining Presidential
Award; for more information, contact the President of the
University.
Languages: courses are taught in Spanish.

2760   University of Puerto Rico
Biology Department
College of Natural Sciences
[UPR]

Rio Piedras Campus
00931-3360 Rio Piedras
Tel: +1-809-764-0000

🐦 Research and Teaching Assistantships

Study Domains: biology, ecology, environment,
microbiology.
Scholarships: Research and Teaching Assistantships.
Subjects: undergraduate: general biology; graduate:
cellular-molecular biology, tropical ecology, systematic and
organismal biology, parasitology, neurobiology and
microbiology.
Open to: applicants admitted as bona-fide graduate
students to the Biology Graduate Programme, with sufficient
knowledge of Spanish to communicate.
Duration: 1 academic year (renewable).
Languages: Spanish.
Applications: by 28 February, to the Graduate Programme
in Biology.

2761 **University of Puerto Rico**
[UPR]
PO Box 364984
00936 San Juan
Tel: +1-787-250-0000
Fax: +1-787-753-7355
Web: http://upr.clu.edu

 Higher Education Programmes

Study Domains: all major fields.
Programmes: Over 400 academic programmes in different disciplines in 11 campuses; some campuses offer degrees up to the doctoral level, others have associate, transfer and bachelor's degree programmes.
Open to: all nationalities; some campuses require interview and entrance examination.
Held: in 11 campuses located in different parts of the island.
Financial assistance: possibility of research/teaching assistantship for graduate studies.

Uruguay

Año académico: Marzo a diciembre.
Moneda nacional: Peso uruguayo ($U).
Conocimientos lingüísticos: Es indispensable dominar suficientemente el idioma español.
Importe de gastos para un año universita: La enseñanza es gratuita en los centros universitarios.
Servicios de información:
• Ministerio de Educación y Cultura; Reconquista 535; Montevideo; Uruguay.
Convalidación de estudios y diplomas: Rector, Universidad de la República; Avenida 18 de Julio 1968; Montevideo; Uruguay; tel: +598-2-400-9201; fax: +598-2-408-0303; web: http://www.rau.edu.uy/universidad.

2762 **Universidad Católica del Uruguay "Dámaso Antonio Larrañaga" [UCDU]**
8 de Octubre 2738
11600 Montevideo
Tel: (598)(2) 407 2727
Fax: (598)(2) 407 0323
Web: http://www.ucu.edu.uy

 Programas universitarios

Campos de estudios: todas las materias principales.
Programas:
(a) Cursos: filosofía, gestión agropecuaria, comercio internacional e integración, historia, bioética; cursos a distancia (teología, educación);
(b) Técnico en educación inicial;
(c) Licenciatura en ciencias sociales aplicadas (ciencias políticas, sociología y servicio social), en psicología, en comunicación social (periodismo, publicidad y comunicación organizacional), en dirección de empresas, en relaciones laborales, en negocios internacionales e integración, en turismo; ingeniería en informática; doctor en derecho;
(d) Licenciatura en educación;
(e) Posgrado en desarrollo local, en gestión de centros educativos, en derecho (civil, comercial, laboral, de la familia), en empresas, en marketing, en dificultades del aprendizaje, en sistemas de comunicaciones de voz y datos, en gestión de recursos humanos;
(f) Maestría en comunicación social, en educación, en administración de empresas (MBA), en dirección de empresas constructoras e inmobiliarias, en matemática aplicada, en ingeniería del conocimiento, en psicología clínica (orientación psicología analítica).
Se destina(n): a nacionales de cualquier país que posean conocimientos suficientes de español y: (a) a (c) hayan completado los estudios secundarios; (d) sean docentes titulados con un mínimo de 5 años de experiencia en la enseñanza o profesionales universitarios con un mínimo de 5 años de experiencia laboral; (e) y (f) sean profesionales de carreras universitarias con un mínimo de 4 años de duración.

Duración: (a) variable; (b) y (d) 3 años; (c) entre 4 y 5 años; (e) y (f) 1 o 2 años según el curso.
Asistencia financiera: posibilidades de préstamos para extranjeros provenientes de universidades con las que existan convenios de intercambio estudiantil.
Inscripciones: por informes para estudiantes extranjeros, dirigirse a la Secretaría para Asuntos Internacionales, en la dirección que figura en el título.

2763 **Universidad de la Empresa [UDE]**
Soriano 959
Montevideo
Tel: (598) (2) 900 24 42
Fax: (598) (2) 900 35 15
Web: http://www.ude.edu.uy
e-mail: ude@ude.edu.uy

 Programas universitarios

Campos de estudios: administración, administración de empresas, ciencias agronómicas, ciencias económicas y comerciales, comunicación, derecho, diseño, gestión, marketing.
Descripción: Programas de estudio en sus facultades de ciencias empresariales, de diseño y de ciencias agrarias:
(a) Carreras: contador público, licenciatura en marketing, en administración de empresas, en administración de empresas turísticas; técnico en organización y administración de empresas, en turismo; analista en marketing, en comercio exterior, en recursos humanos; asistente técnico de empresas; abogacía; notariado; licenciatura en diseño aplicado, en indumentaria; diseñador gráfico, de interiores; analista en publicidad; licenciatura en gestión agropecuaria; técnico agrario; técnico forestal;
(b) Posgrados: postgrado en marketing avanzado, maestría en dirección estratégica, master en dirección y administración de empresas (MBA), en dirección comercial, maestría en dirección financiera; programa de desarrollo gerencial; postgrado en administración de empresas agrarias.
Duración: año académico de marzo a diciembre.

2764 **Universidad ORT Uruguay [ORT]**
Cuareim 1451
11100 Montevideo
Tel: (598) (2) 902 1505
Fax: (598) (2) 903 9360
Web: http://www.ort.edu.uy

 Programas universitarios

Campos de estudios: administración, arquitectura, ciencias económicas y comerciales, ciencias sociales, comunicación, diseño, educación, informática, ingeniería.
Programas: postgrados, carreras universitarias, cursos, carreras técnicas, actualización profesional.
Materias de estudio: arquitectura, comunicación y diseño, ingeniería, administración y ciencias sociales, educación, educación a distancia.
Se destina(n): a estudiantes con bachillerato completo o equivalente en el caso de extranjeros.

Uzbekistan

Academic year: September to June.
Organization of higher education system: Levels of higher education: Bachelor's, 4 years of study; Master's, 2 years of further study; Candidate of Sciences: 3 years of study; Doctor of Sciences, 3 years of study.
Monetary unit: som (UZS).
International student admission: Secondary school-leaving certificatie indicating studies and grades received, along with a copy of passport and proof of either Uzbek or Russian language proficiency.
Language: The languages of instruction are Uzbek and Russian. All international students are obliged to undergo a 9-month intensive language course at the National Language Centre. The fee is currently 1,000 US$.
Immigration requirements: Applicants should contact the nearest Uzbekistan embassy to obtain information on visa regulations.

Estimated expenses for one academic year: tuition:
US$2,000-$3,000, depending on study programme.
Information services:
• International departments of higher education institutions
• Diplomatic missions of the Republic of Uzbekistan abroad.
Recognition of studies and qualification: State Testing
Center within the Cabinet of Ministers of the Republic of
Uzbek.
Additional information:
• Information about how to apply to Uzbek higher education
institutions can be obtained from Uzbek embassies abroad.
• All necessary documents of foreign students should reach
international departments of higher education institutions by
10 July of each year.

2765 Bukhara State University [BSU]
M. Ikbol Street, 11
705 018 Bukhara
Tel: +998-365-223-5219
Fax: +998-365-223-5219 / 1254

📖 Undergraduate, Graduate, Postgraduate Programmes

Study Domains: agriculture, applied arts, business,
economy, graphic arts, history, information science,
languages, law, management, marketing, philology,
psychology, sciences, sociology, tourism, hotel and catering
management.
Programmes: (a) Bachelor's; (b) Master's; (c) Ph.D.; (d)
summer course; (e) language course.
Description: fields of study: (b) national studies, teacher
education, psychology, philology, linguistics (Uzbek and
English), macroeconomics, agricultural studies, theoretical
physics, optics/magnioptics, geliophysics, chemistry,
mathematics, zoology, botany; (c) chemistry, biology,
physics, mathematics, history, agricultural studies, economics,
philology (Uzbek and Russian), applied arts, physical
education, philosophy.
Open to: candidates of all nationalities meeting academic,
financial and linguistic requirements.
Age limit Max: between the ages of 17 and 30.
Other conditions: (c) applicants should have been
employed at a university or research institute in home
country; basic knowledge of Russian and/or Uzbek required.
Duration: (a) (b) (c) 2 to 4 years beginning in September;
(d) summer course: 20 to 40 months; (e) language course: 6
months beginning October/November.
Fees: tuition fees: US$2,000; living costs: US$100-$150.
Financial assistance: possibility of receiving financial
assistance of US$15 per month for 1 to 2 semesters.
Applications: apply by 15 August to bukhcit@intal.uz; or
to: z_toshev@mail.ru.

2766 National University of Uzbekistan [NUU]
700095 Student's Town (Talabalar shaharchasi)
NUUzR
Tashkent
Tel: +998 371 236 5460 / 460 225 /
Fax: +998 371 144 7728
Web: http://www.nuu.uz/nuu
e-mail: root@tsu.silk.org

📖 Undergraduate, Graduate, Postgraduate Programmes

Study Domains: biology, chemistry, computer science,
economy, education, humanities and arts, languages, law,
mathematics, physics, sciences, social sciences.
Programmes: Bachelor's; Master's, Ph.D.; Uzbek and
Russian language courses.
Open to: candidates of all nationalities; maximum age
limit: 35 years of age.
Duration: depending on programme; courses begin in
September.
Applications: apply before 30 August; email:
root@tsu.silk.org for details.

📖 Scholarships / Science and Economics
Study Domains: computer science, economic and
commercial sciences, economy, mathematics, physics.

Subjects: mathematics; physics; computer technology;
biology; chemistry; economics; English; German; French.
Open to: candidates of all nationalities up to the age of 35.
Duration: for duration of studies: Bachelor's: 4 years;
Master's: 2 years; Ph.D.: 3 years.
Applications: before 30 August to: root@tsu.silk.org; or
fax to the above number.

2767 Tashkent State Economic University [TSUE]
Uzbekistanskaya 49
700063 Tashkent
Tel: +998-371-132-6421
Fax: +998-371-132-6430
Web: http://tsue.ilm.uz

📖 Undergraduate, Graduate, Postgraduate Programmes

Study Domains: agriculture, business, economic and
commercial sciences, economy, health and hygiene, history,
languages, law, medicine, natural resources, philosophy,
recreation and leisure, sciences, social sciences, summer
programmes, tourism, hotel and catering management.
Programmes: Bachelor's, Master's, Ph.D. degree
programmes in economics, marketing, management.
Open to: candidates of all nationalities, subject to entry
interview.
Duration: 2 to 4 years beginning in September.
Fees: depending on programme.
Languages: Russian, Uzbek and English.
Applications: by 26 August.

2768 Tashkent State Pedagogical University [TSPU]
103, Yusuf Has Hajib Street
700100 Tashkent
Tel: +998-371-255-5095
Fax: +998-371-255-5095

📖 Undergraduate, Graduate, Postgraduate Programmes

Study Domains: all major fields, continuing education,
early childhood education, education, physical education,
special education, teacher education, technical education,
vocational training.
Programmes: Bachelor's; Master's and Ph.D. degree
programmes.
Description: pedagogical training for teachers in academic
lyceums and colleges.
Open to: candidates of all nationalities; Russian language
proficiency required.
Duration: Bachelor's: 4 years; Master's: 2 years; courses
begin in September.
Fees: tuition fees: US$2,000-$3,000; living costs:
US$1,000.
Applications: apply by 30 May to: tdpu@albatros.uz or:
nfizmat@narod.ru.

2769 University of World Economy and Diplomacy [IOM]
Institute of Management
54 Buyuk Ipak Yuli Street
700137 Tashkent
Tel: +998 371 267 6769 / 269 0913 /
Fax: +998 371 267 0900

📖 Undergraduate, Graduate Programmes

Study Domains: business administration.
Programmes: Programme of studies at the Institute of
Management: (a) Master's of business administration;
(b) Bachelor's degree; (c) Ph.D. degree.
Open to: (a) candidates of all nationalities, with a B.A.
degree and proficiency in English; (b) diploma or certificate
of secondary education.
Held: (a) The Institute of Management (Tashkent) and
ESC Rennes (France); (b) and (c) The Institute of World
Economy and Diplomacy.
Duration: (a) 1 to 2 years; courses begin in October and
April; (b) 4 years; courses begin 1 September.
Fees: (a) tuition, US$2,200; (b) tuition, US$5,000; living
costs (excluding meals) for 1 year, US$500.

Languages: Instruction in Uzbek, Russian and English.
Applications: (a) by 15 August or 15 February; (b) and (c) by 15 July; to the above address.

2770 Uzbek Academy of Sciences, Arifov Institute of Electronics [AIOE]
Academgorodok
F. Hodjaeva 33
700143 Tashkent
Tel: +998-371-136-7629 / 133-7331
Fax: +998-371-133-4901 / 133-1445

📖 **Undergraduate, Graduate Programmes**

Study Domains: applied sciences, electricity and electronics, physics.
Programmes: undergraduate and postgraduate courses in physical and mathematical sciences.
Open to: students under age 30 for postgraduate courses and under age 40 for doctoral studies; proficiency in one of the languages of instruction is necessary.
Duration: 3 years.
Fees: approx. US$3,000 per academic year.
Applications: to the above address.

2771 Uzbek Academy of Sciences, Institute of Chemistry [IOC]
Kh. Abdullaev Avenue 77a
700170 Tashkent
Tel: +998-371-262-5660

📖 **Undergraduate, Graduate Programmes / Chemistry**

Study Domains: chemistry, engineering.
Programmes: Programmes in chemistry and chemical engineering.
Open to: applicants of any nationality, under 42 years of age; proficiency in Russian or English required.
Duration: 6 months to 3 years.
Fees: US$200.

Venezuela
Año académico: Septiembre a julio.
Moneda nacional: Bolívar.
Conocimientos lingüísticos: Es indispensable dominar suficientemente el idioma español.
Formalidades de inmigración: La información pertinente debe solicitarse en el consulado de Venezuela en el país de origen del estudiante.
Servicios de información:
• Ministerio de Educación - EDUPLAN, Edificio Esmeralda, Avenida Los Próceres San Bernardino, Caracas (informa acerca de los requisitos de ingreso en los centros venezolanos de enseñanza superior, las posibilidades de estudio, de alojamiento, etc.).
• Oficina de Cooperación Técnica Internacional de Cordiplan; Avenida Lecuna, Parque Central - Piso 25, Torre Oeste; Caracas; Venezuela.
Enseñanza abierta y a distancia: La Universidad Nacional Abierta ofrece cursos conducentes a grados de licenciatura (5 años) y magister (2 años más).
Convalidación de estudios y diplomas: Ministerio de Educación Superior, Director General, Convenios y Cooperación,; Av. La Salle, Torre Centro Capriles, Piso 6; Caracas; Venezuela; tel: +58-212-794-2683; fax: +58-212-794-0065; email: nbarrios@cnu.gov.ve; web: http://www.cnu.gov.ve.
Publicaciones / Sitios web:
• "Oportunidades de estudios en los institutos de educación superior de Venezuela", Consejo Nacional de Universidades, Oficina de Planificación del Sector Universitario, Unidad de Orientación, Distribución e Ingreso (publicación anual de utilidad para los estudiantes que desean iniciar estudios superiores en Venezuela y para quienes tienen por misión orientarles y ayudarles; en ella figuran todas las instituciones de educación superior de Venezuela, su ubicación geográfica, los requisitos de ingreso, las carreras que se pueden cursar, su duración, etc.).
• "Directorio nacional de cursos de postgrado", Consejo Nacional de Investigaciones Científicas y Tecnológicas,

Dirección de Desarrollo de Recursos Humanos, Apartado 70617, Los Ruices, Caracas.

2772 Centro Interamericano de Desarrollo e Investigación Ambiental y Territorial [CIDIAT]
Apartado Postal 219
Mérida
Tel: (58) 74 442224

📖 **Programas universitarios**

Campos de estudios: ecología, medio ambiente, energía, geología, hidrología, ingeniería, ingeniería civil, recursos naturales.
Descripción:
(a) Curso de posgrado en desarrollo de aguas y tierras, organizado por el CIDIAT y la Universidad de Los Andes; opciones: ingeniería de riego y drenaje, planificación y desarrollo de recursos hidráulicos, obras hidráulicas;
(b) Cursos breves interamericanos, cuyos temas de estudio varían cada año, en las siguientes áreas: evaluación de impactos ambientales, análisis de sistemas de abastecimiento de agua potable, manejo y disposición de desechos sólidos municipales e industriales, tratamiento y reuso de aguas residuales, manejo y conservación de cuencas hidrográficas, educación ambiental, derecho y legislación ambiental, economía ambiental aplicada a los proyectos de inversión, formulación y evaluación de proyectos hidráulicos, métodos de riego, drenaje agrícola, manejo y conservación de suelos, desarrollo de aguas subterráneas, protección de aguas subterráneas, gestión integral de recursos hídricos, sistemas de información geográfica, regulación de servicios públicos privatizados;
(c) Curso de posgrado en gestión de recursos naturales y medio ambiente, organizado por el CIDIAT con el patrocinio del Banco Interamericano de Desarrollo (BID);
(d) Curso de posgrado en recursos hidráulicos, organizado por el CIDIAT y la Universidad de Los Andes.
Se destina(n): a profesionales universitarios de los países de América Latina y del Caribe que estén trabajando en el área de estudio.
Se dicta(n): en el CIDIAT o en otros países de América Latina.
Duración: (a), (c) y (d) 18 meses (empieza en marzo de años impares); (b) de 2 a 16 semanas, según el curso.

2773 Escuela de Malariología y Saneamiento Ambiental "Dr. Arnoldo Gabaldon" [EDMYSA]
Edificio Malariología
Avenida Bermúdez, Sur
Maracay, Aragua
Tel: (58) 43 332203
Fax: (58) 43 332532

📖 **Programas de posgrado**

Campos de estudios: ecología, medio ambiente, higiene y salud, medicina, medicina preventiva.
Programas:
(a) Posgrado internacional en epidemiología de enfermedades mataxénicas y saneamiento ambiental;
(b) Posgrado en salud ocupacional e higiene del ambiente laboral;
(c) Maestría en entomología y salud pública.
Se destina(n): (a) y (c) a profesionales de cualquier país, preferentemente de los de América Latina, que tengan el título universitario de médico, biólogo, ingeniero, sociólogo, u otras profesiones relacionadas con la salud, que posean 2 años como mínimo de experiencia profesional y conocimientos de idioma español o portugués; (b) a profesionales universitarios con una experiencia mínima de 2 años en el área de la salud laboral.
Duración: (a) 12 meses (de enero a diciembre); (b) 12 meses (de septiembre a septiembre); (c) 24 meses (comienza en enero).
Asistencia financiera: (a) la Organización Panamericana de la Salud (OPS) concede 5 becas, las cuales deben solicitarse directamente a los representantes de la OPS en los diferentes países antes del 30 de octubre; (c) existen becas de la OPS y de la Organización Mundial de la Salud (OMS).

Inscripciones: (a) en septiembre; (b) en mayo-junio.

2774 Instituto Venezolano de Investigaciones Científicas Centro de Estudios Avanzados [IVIC]
Apartado 21827
1020- Caracas
Tel: (58) 2 5041130/5041233
Fax: (58) 2 5041089
Web: http://www.ivic.ve
e-mail: cea@ivic.ivic.ve

📖 **Cursos nacionales e internacionales**

Campos de estudios: antropología, biofísica, biología, bioquímica, ecología, medio ambiente, genética, inmunología, metalurgia, microbiología, química.
Descripción: formación especializada de personal de investigación en distintos campos científicos (estudios para "Magister Scientiarum" (M.Sc.) y "Philosophus Scientiarum" (Ph.Sc.)) en áreas de biología (menciones en: antropología, bioquímica, ecología, fisiología y biofísica, genética humana, inmunología, microbiología, reproducción humana); física; matemáticas; química; física médica; estudios sociales de la ciencia.
Se destina(n): a profesionales universitarios de cualquier país que tengan las calificaciones requeridas para cursar la especialidad elegida.
Duración: M.Sc.: 2 años, Ph.Sc.: 4 años.
Inscripciones: en febrero y septiembre; dirigirse a Unidad de Control de Estudios.

2775 Universidad Católica Santa Rosa [UCSAR]
Calle Seminario, Sabana del Blanco, Final Cota Mil con Avenida Baralt
1010- La Pastora - Caracas
Tel: +58-212-860-8659 / +58-212-862
Fax: +58-212-860-3567
Web: http://www.santarosa.edu.ve
e-mail: info@santarosa.edu.ve

📖 **Carreras universitarias**

Campos de estudios: ciencias humanas, ciencias sociales, educación, teología, religión.
Materias de estudio: ciencias humanas y sociales, ciencias de la educación, ciencias teológicas.

2776 Universidad Central de Venezuela Facultad de Medicina Escuela de Salud Pública [UCV]
Apartado 62231-A
Correos del Este
1060 Caracas
Tel: (58) 2 6622480
Web: http://www.ucv.ve

📖 **Programa de cursos**

Campos de estudios: administración, enseñanza técnica, estudios paramédicos, higiene y salud, investigación, medicina, medicina preventiva, técnicas de laboratorio.
Descripción:
(a) Cursos de especialización en las siguientes áreas: administración de salud pública, epidemiología, administración de hospitales;
(b) Cursos de ampliación (curso medio de salud pública) en: administración de atención médica hospitalaria, administración sanitaria, epidemiología, otros;
(c) Cursos de educación continuada en diversas especialidades de la salud pública;
(d) Cursos para formar personal técnico en el campo de la salud; fisioterapia, terapia ocupacional, inspección sanitaria, radiodiagnóstico e imagenología, técnico cardiopulmonar, técnico en información de salud.
Se destina(n): (a) a nacionales de cualquier país que se hallen en posesión de los diplomas requeridos para cada especialización; (b) a (d) a venezolanos, así como a extranjeros patrocinados por instituciones de carácter internacional, públicas o privadas que hayan completado

estudios secundarios en ciencias.
Duración: (a) 3 períodos de 16 semanas cada uno; (b) 18 semanas; (c) varía según el curso; (d) 3 años.
Inscripciones: (a) Comisión de Estudios para Graduados; (b) Escuela de Salud Pública; (c) Secretaría de la UCV.

2777 Universidad Central de Venezuela Facultad de Medicina [UCV]
Apartado 50587
Sabana Grande
1050 Caracas
Tel: (58) 2 6622480
Fax: (58) 1 40659405
Web: http://www.ucv.ve

📖 **Cursos de posgrado en ciencias fisiológicas**

Campos de estudios: bacteriología, biofísica, biología, bioquímica, citología, farmacia y farmacología, fisiología, genética, medicina, microbiología.
Descripción: cursos conducentes a la obtención de: (a) maestrías y (b) doctorados.
Se destina(n): a licenciados universitarios o equivalente en áreas biológicas o de la salud, no mayores de 35 años. La selección se realiza en base a entrevistas, examen y recomendaciones. Se requiere conocer el idioma inglés.
Duración: (a) 2 años; (b) 4 años; (los comienzos son en enero, cada 2 años).
Asistencia financiera: no, pero se otorga aval de estar inscrito en el posgrado para que el interesado tramite su beca ante autoridades competentes.
Inscripciones: hasta fin de octubre.

2778 Universidad Central de Venezuela Instituto de Ciencia y Tecnología de Alimentos [UCV]
Apartado 47097
Los Chaguaramos
Caracas
Tel: (58) 2 7534403
Fax: (58) 2 7533871
Web: http://www.ucv.ve

📖 **Programas universitarios**

Campos de estudios: alimentación, higiene y salud, nutrición.
Programas:
(a) Licenciatura en biología con opción tecnología de alimentos;
(b) Curso interfacultades de posgrado conducente a diploma de maestría;
(c) Doctorado en ciencia y tecnología de alimentos.
Se destina(n): (b) a diplomados universitarios en carrera de tecnología de alimentos, farmacia o ingeniería agronómica; existe selección por entrevista y durante los estudios se debe presentar examen de suficiencia de inglés.
Duración: (b) entre 2 y 3 años (comienzos en enero y septiembre).
Inscripciones: hasta septiembre; dirigirse al Coordinador del Posgrado en Ciencia y Tecnología de Alimentos.

Viet Nam
Année universitaire: septembre à juin.
Unité monétaire: south dong (VND).
Connaissances linguistiques requises: Les candidats étrangers doivent avoir une bonne connaissance du vietnamien.
Services d'accueil et d'information:
• Ministère de l'éducation et de la formation, Département de l'enseignement supérieur; 49 Dai Co viet; Hanoi; Viet Nam; tél: +84-4-255-440; fax: +84-4-259-205.

2779 Institut polytechnique de Hô Chi Minh-Ville [IPHCM]

268 Ly Thuong Kiêt - D 10
Hô Chi Minh-Ville
Tel: +848-8-652-442
Fax: +848-8-653-823

Cursus du 1er-2e cycle

Domaines d'étude: ingénierie.
Programmes: (a) cours dispensés dans de nombreuses branches techniques, conduisant aux diplômes d'ingénieur, d'études approfondies et de docteur; (b) programme de cours non diplômants proposés en fonction de contrats passés avec des entreprises.
A l'intention de: ressortissants de tout pays, titulaires du baccalauréat; sélection sur concours national (examen de mathématiques, physique et chimie). Langue vietnamienne obligatoire.
Durée: de 4 à 5 ans; cours débutant en septembre.
Frais: scolarité: 150 US$ environ; inscription gratuite.
Connaissances linguistiques: langues d'enseignement: vietnamien et français.
Inscriptions: se renseigner à l'adresse ci-dessus.

2780 Université de Can Tho [UCT]

Campus II, rue du 3/2
Ville de Can Tho
Tel: +84-71-838-237
Web: http://www.ctu.edu.vn/index_e.htm
e-mail: webmaster@ctu.edu.vn

Cursus du 1er au 3e cycle

Domaines d'étude: toutes disciplines principales.
Programmes: Cours conduisant aux diplômes du 1er au 3e cycles dispensés dans les facultés de sciences, d'agriculture, de technologie, de technologies de l'information, de pédagogie, d'économie et gestion, et de médecine. Les institutions de recherche et de développement en sciences et technologies sont spécialisées en biotechnologie, systèmes agricoles du delta du Mékong, artémia et crevette, énergies renouvelables, diffusion de l'actualité scientifique et technique, langues étrangères.
Inscriptions: à l'adresse ci-dessus.

Yemen

Academic year: September to June.
Organization of higher education system: Higher education is provided by several public and private universities. Admission is based on the Al Thanawiya (secondary school certificate). In the public universities, a score of at least 80 per cent is required for admission to the Faculties of Medicine and Engineering. For the Faculties of Science, Agriculture and Commerce, the requirement is 65-70 per cent and for the Faculties of Law, Education and Arts it is 50-60 per cent. (Source: IAU World Higher Education Database).
International student admission: Admission based on grades, entrance exams, admission tests for some majors; personal interviews; academics documents required.
Language: Arabic; classes are often in Arabic and English.
Information services:
• Ministry of Higher Education and Scientific Research; PO Box 12642; Sana'a; Yemen; tel: +967-1-274-553; fax: +967-1-274-156.

2781 Hadhramout University for Science and Technology

PO Box 50511-50512
Mukalla
Tel: +967-5-360-863
Fax: +967-5-360-864
Web: http://www.hust.edu.ye
e-mail: hadhramout_univ@yemennet

Undergraduate, Graduate Programmes

Study Domains: administration, applied sciences, Arabic, architecture, botany, chemical engineering, chemistry, computer science, early childhood education, earth science, economic and commercial sciences, English, finance, history, marine biology, marine science, mathematics, medicine, physics, teacher education, telecommunications.
Programmes: Bachelor's and Master's degree programmes; particularly in science and engineering.
Open to: candidates of all nationalities with Arabic language proficiency and scientific background.
Duration: 4 to 5 years; courses begin 15 September.
Applications: by August to the Registrar at the above address.

2782 Ibb University

PO Box 70270
Ibb
Tel: +967-4-408-069
Fax: +967-4-408-068
Web: http://www.ibbunv.com.ye
e-mail: ibbunv@yemen.net.ye

Undergraduate Awards

Study Domains: agriculture, arts, dentistry, education, engineering.
Scholarships: Bachelor of Arts, Bachelor of Science programmes.
Open to: candidates with secondary-school leaving certificate and good academic record, recommended by the Ministry of Higher Education in Yemen.
Nationality: Iraq, Jordan, Morocco, Somalia, Sudan, Syria, Thailand.
Duration: 4-5 years, depending on the studies.
Value: studies in humanities: US$1,500-$1,800; science, engineering and dentistry; US$2,500-$3,500.
Applications: by 30 October; to Dr Abdul Hafeed Ali Fateih; Department of English, Faculty of Arts at the above address; a_hafeed@yahoo.com.

2783 Queen Arwa University [QAU]

PO Box 11586
Sana'a
Tel: +967-1-449-909
Fax: +967-1-449-995
Web: http://www.arwauniversity.edu.ye/
e-mail: arwauniversity@y.net.ye

Queen Arwa Scholarships

Study Domains: Arabic, business administration, computer science.
Open to: full-time international students at undergraduate or graduate level who wish to study Arabic as a foreign language.
Applications: 1 September; to Dean, Students' Affairs at the above address.

Zambia

Academic year: October to July.
Organization of higher education system: Higher education is provided by the universities and various specialized institutions. There are two national universities: the University of Zambia (Lusaka) divided into schools for agricultural sciences, education, engineering, humanities and social sciences, law, medicine, mining, natural sciences and veterinary medicine; and the Copperbelt University (Kitwe) which has schools of business and industrial studies, environmental studies, science and technology, and forestry and wood science. The various specialized institutions are colleges and institutes: a college of applied arts and commercial studies, a national college for citizenship training, a college for the development of natural resources, teacher-training colleges, various technical colleges, an institute of technology, trades-training institutions, an institute of public administration, an institute of air services training and schools for training in nursing. The highest administrative body of the constituent universities is the Council on which serve members of the Government, students, teaching staff, graduates and representatives of outside bodies. The highest academic body is the Senate. There is a 5 per cent quota for foreign-student admissions at university level.
Monetary unit: kwacha (ZMK).
International student admission: Foreign students are required to obtain a study permit for entry into the country and to have full financial support for the duration of their

studies. Admission is facilitated if they come as part of an established inter-university student exchange programme, but they are still required to meet admission and immigration requirements. Applications should be made to the Senior Assistant Registrar (Academic), The University of Zambia, P.O. Box 32379, Lusaka in January. The admitting bodies of each institution concerned are responsible for the recognition of foreign qualifications and the respective registered professional bodies are responsible for entry into a profession. Services are the same as those provided for national students. Foreign students cannot obtain employment and their scholarships should be assured before they are issued with a student study permit.

Language: Foreign students must be proficient in English, especially for university level programmes.

Information services:
• Ministry of Science and Technology, PO Box 50464, Lusaka; tel: +260-1-252-053; fax: +260-1-252-951.

Open and distance learning: This type of education is offered by technical and vocational colleges and the University of Zambia. Entrance requirements are lower than for those who enter a full-time course. The duration of studies is also much longer since students do not take all the courses for a given year at one time.

Recognition of studies and qualification: Ministry of Science, Technology and Vocational Training; PO Box 50464; Lusaka, Zambia; tel: +260-1-229-673 / 252-053; fax: +260-1-252-951.

2784 University of Zambia [UNZA]
PO Box 32379
Lusaka
Tel: +260-1-251-593 / 293-058
Fax: +260-1-253-952

📖 Undergraduate, Graduate Programmes

Study Domains: all major fields.
Programmes: diploma and degree courses at undergraduate and graduate level in most major fields.
Open to: candidates with Zambian School Certificate with passes at credit level in 5 approved subjects, or General Certificate of Education (GCE) with passes in 5 approved subjects at O-level.
Duration: 1 academic year: December to August.
Fees: approximately 45,000-65,000 kwacha per year; part-time and by correspondence: 5,000-16,000 kwacha.
Applications: to the Registrar at the above address.

Zimbabwe

Academic year: March to December and August to July for universities. January to December for teacher training colleges and polytechnics.

Organization of higher education system: Degree programmes range from 3 years' duration in social sciences and humanities to 6 years in medicine. Diplomas offered at teacher training colleges and polytechnics for technical and vocational education and training are generally of 3 years' duration including on-the-job training (industrial attachment).

Monetary unit: Zimbabwean dollar (Z$).

National student admission: Foreign students must have qualifications equivalent to the General Certificate of Education (GCE).
For admission into secondary education teachers' training colleges and university: 2 A-levels passes in at least two subjects relevant to the programme.
For admission into primary education teachers' colleges and polytechnics: 5 O-level passes with a grade C or better in subjects including English, mathematics and science.
Some provision is made for special and mature student entry with approval from the senate of each university.

Language: Proficiency in English (GCE O-level English or equivalent).

Immigration requirements: International students must provide proof of acceptance to a higher education institution to obtain a student resident permit from the Immigration Department; Private Bag 7717, Causeway, Harare, Zimbabwe.

Estimated expenses for one academic year: Tuition fees

must be paid in US dollars. Respective universities should be contacted for exact amounts.

Information services:
• University of Zimbabwe, web: http://www.uz.ac.zw
• Ministry of Higher and Tertiary Education; web: http://www.mhet.ac.zw
• National University of Science and Technology (NUST); web: http://www.nust.ac.zw
• Africa University; http://web: ww.africau.edu
• Bindura University of Science Education (BUSE); http://www.buse.ac.zw
• Zimbabwe Open University; web: http://www.zou.ac.zw
• Chinhoyi University of Technology; http://www.cut.ac.zw
• Gweru University College, P.Bag 9055, Gweru.
• Bindura University College of Science Education, PO Bindura, Bindura.
• Zimbabwean embassies and High Commissions abroad can assist with information to prospective students.

Open and distance learning: The Zimbabwe Open University offers more than 20 programmes including diplomas and degrees using mainly the distance mode of training. Some of the programmes offered include: M.B.A., B.Ed. and M.Ed. (educational administration, planning and policy studies), B.Sc. agriculture, B.Sc. counselling, B.A. media studies, B.Com. accounting, and Diploma in industrial and labour relations.

Publications / Websites: Each university has a prospectus (annual publication) in English obtainable from the admissions office of each university.

2785 Bindura University of Science Education [BUSE]
1020 Bindura
Tel: +263-71-7531
Fax: +263-71-7552/7584
e-mail: info@mailhost.buse.ac.zw

📖 Undergraduate, Graduate Programmes / Science Education

Study Domains: agriculture, education, mathematics, sciences.
Programmes: Programmes leading to Bachelor's and Master's degrees in science; mathematics and agriculture; non-degree programmes offered.
Open to: candidates of all nationalities with a pass at O-level in English language or equivalent.
Duration: variable; courses begin in March.
Applications: 28 February to the above address.

2786 Midlands State University [MSU]
Senga Rd
PB 9055
Gweru
Tel: +263-54-260-409
Fax: +263-54-260-311
e-mail: msuvcoffice@yahoo.com

📖 Undergraduate Programmes

Study Domains: agriculture, business administration, education, natural resources, sciences, social sciences.
Programmes: undergraduate programmes in the Faculties of Arts and Social Sciences, Natural Resources Management, Agriculture, Commerce, Science and Education.
Open to: candidates of all nationalities on the basis of Advanced level passes in at least two subjects.
Applications: to the above address.

Indexes
Index
Índices

[S] indicates scholarships / [C] indicates courses
[S] indique bourses / [C] indique cours
[S] indique becas / [C] indique cursos

Index of International Organizations

[S] indicates scholarships / [C] indicates courses

Abdus Salam International Centre for Theoretical Physics [S] [C] 1.
African Institute for Economic Development and Planning [C] 2.
Asian Development Bank
    Office of Cofinancing Operations [S] 3.
Asian Institute of Technology [S] [C] 4.
Association of African Universities [S] 5.
Association of Commonwealth Universities [S] 6.
Caribbean Institute for Meteorology and Hydrology [C] 7.
College of Europe-Bruges [C] 8.
Esperanto Foundation [S] 9.
European Commission [S] 10.
European School of Oncology [C] 11.
European University Institute [S] [C] 14.
Food and Agriculture Organization of the United Nations [S] [C] 12.
Ford Foundation, International Fellowships Program [S] 13.
Institute for Alternative Development Research [C] 15.
Institute of Nutrition of Central America and Panama [C] 16.
Inter-American Housing Union [C] 18.
Inter-University Centre for Development [C] 19.
International Agency for Research on Cancer - World Health Organization [S] [C] 20.
International Association for the Exchange of Students for Technical Experience [C] 21.
International Astronomical Union [S] 22.
International Atomic Energy Agency [S] 23.
International Centre for Advanced Communication Studies for Latin America [S] 24.
International Centre for Research, Cooperation and Exchange in the Caribbean and the Americas [C] 25.
International Centre for the Study of the Preservation and the Restoration of Cultural Property [C] 26.
International Crops Research Institute for the Semi-Arid Tropics [C] 27.
International Federation of University Women [S] 28.
International Institute [C] 29.
International Institute of Human Rights [C] 30.
International Maritime Organization [S] 31.
International Ocean Institute [S] [C] 33.
International Rice Research Institute [S] 34.
International Statistical Education Centre [S] [C] 35.
International Telecommunication Union [S] 36.
International Union for Vacuum Science, Technique and Applications [S] 37.
Latin American and Caribbean Institute for Economic and Social Planning [C] 38.
Latin American Faculty of Social Sciences [C] 39.
North Atlantic Treaty Organization [S] 40.
Organization of American States [S] 41.
Pan American Association of Student Loans Institutions [S] 42.
Regional Seismological Centre for South America [C] 44.
Reuters Foundation [S] 45.
Rotary Foundation of Rotary International [S] 46.
The Hague Academy of International Law [S] [C] 47.
UNESCO-IHE Institute for Water Education [S] [C] 48.
United Nations Educational, Scientific and Cultural Organization -
    Fellowships Section [S] [C] 49.
United Nations Educational, Scientific and Cultural Organization -
    Division of Ecological Sciences [C.
United Nations Educational, Scientific and Cultural Organization -
    Man and the Biosphere Programme (MAB) [S] 50.
United Nations Educational, Scientific and Cultural Organization - International University Network (IUNI) [S.
United Nations High Commissioner for Refugees
    DAFI Scholarships [S] 51.
United Nations Statistical Institute for Asia and the Pacific [C] 52.
Universal Postal Union - International Bureau [S] 53.
University Institute of European Studies, International Training Centre of the ILO [C] 54.
World Bank Institute [S] 55.
World Leisure International Centres of Excellence [C] 56.
World Meteorological Organization [S] [C] 57.
World Tourism Organization [C] 58.
Zonta International [S] 59.

Index des Organisations internationales

[S] indique bourses / [C] indique cours

Abdus Salam Centre international de physique théorique [S] [C] 1.
Académie de droit international de La Haye [S] [C] 47.
Agence internationale de l'énergie atomique [S] 23.
Association des universités africaines [S] 5.
Association internationale pour l'échange d'étudiants de l'enseignement technique [C] 21.
Association mondiale pour les loisirs, Centre international d'excellence [C] 56.
Centre international d'études pour la conservation et la restauration des biens culturels [C] 26.
Centre international d'études supérieures de communication pour l'Amérique latine [S] 24.
Centre international de recherche sur le cancer - Organisation mondiale de la santé [S] [C] 20.
Centre international de recherches, d'échanges et de coopération de la Caraïbe et des Amériques [C] 25.
Centre interuniversitaire pour le développement [C] 19.
Collège d'Europe-Bruges [C] 8.
Commission européenne [S] 10.
École européenne d'oncologie [C] 11.
Faculté latino-américaine de sciences sociales [C] 39.
Fédération internationale des femmes diplômées des universités [S] 28.
Fondation Ford, Programme international de bourses de recherche [S] 13.
Fondation Rotary de Rotary International [S] 46.
Institut africain de développement économique et de planification [C] 2.
Institut de la Banque Mondiale [S] 55.
Institut de nutrition d'Amérique centrale et du Panama [C] 16.
Institut International [C] 29.
Institut international de recherche sur les cultures des zones tropicales semi-arides [C] 27.
Institut international des droits de l'homme [C] 30.
Institut international pour la recherche sur le riz [S] 34.
Institut latino-américain et des Caraïbes pour le développement économique et social [C] 38.
Institut météorologique des Caraïbes [C] 7.
Institut pour la recherche dans les alternatives du développement [C] 15.
Institut universitaire européen [S] [C] 14.
Organisation des États américains [S] 41.
Organisation des Nations Unies pour l'alimentation et l'agriculture [S] [C] 12.
Organisation des Nations Unies pour l'éducation, la science et la culture
   Section des Bourses [S] [C] 49.
Organisation des Nations Unies pour l'éducation, la science et la culture [C.
Organisation des Nations Unies pour l'éducation, la science et la culture -
   Programme sur l'Homme et la biosphère (MAB)
   [S] 50.
Organisation du traité de l'Atlantique nord [S] 40.
Organisation maritime internationale [S] 31.
Organisation météorologique mondiale [S] [C] 57.
Organisation mondiale du tourisme [C] 58.
Union astronomique internationale [S] 22.
Union interaméricaine du logement [C] 18.
Union internationale des télécommunications [S] 36.
Union internationale pour la science, la technique et les applications du vide [S] 37.
Union postale universelle [S] 53.
Zonta International [S] 59.

Índice de Organizaciones Internacionales

[S] indique becas / [C] indique cursos

Asociación Internacional de Intercambio de Estudiantes para la Formación Técnica Práctica [C] 21.
Asociación Panamericana de Instituciones de Crédito Educativo [S] 42.
Centro Internacional de Estudio
    para la Conservación y Restauración
    de los Bienes Culturales [C] 26.
Centro Internacional de Estudios Superiores de Comunicación para América Latina [S] 24.
Centro Internacional de Física Teórica Abdus Salam [S] [C] 1.
Centro Internacional de Investigaciones, Intercambios y Cooperación del Caribe y de las Américas [C] 25.
Centro Interuniversitario de Desarrollo [C] 19.
Centro Regional de Sismología para América del Sur [C] 44.
Colegio de Europa [C] 8.
Comisión Europea [S] 10.
Escuela Europea de Oncología [C] 11.
Facultad Latinoamericana de Ciencias Sociales [C] 39.
Federación Internacional de Mujeres Universitarias [S] 28.
Fundación Ford, Programa Internacional de Becas [S] 13.
Fundación Rotary de Rotary Internacional [S] 46.
Instituto Africano de Desarrollo Económico y Planeamiento [C] 2.
Instituto de Nutrición de Centro América y Panamá [C] 16.
Instituto del Banco Mundial [S] 55.
Instituto Internacional [C] 29.
Instituto Internacional de Derechos Humanos [C] 30.
Instituto Internacional de Investigación de Cultivos para las Zonas Tropicales Semiáridas [C] 27.
Instituto Internacional de Investigación sobre el Arroz [S] 34.
Instituto Italo-Latino Americano [S] 17.
Instituto Latinoamericano y del Caribe de Planificación Económica y Social [C] 38.
Instituto para la Investigación de Alternativas de Desarrollo [C] 15.
Instituto Universitario Europeo [S] [C] 14.
Organismo Internacional de Energía Atómica [S] 23.
Organización de las Naciones Unidas para la Alimentación y la Agricultura [S] [C] 12.
Organización de las Naciones Unidas para la Educación, la Ciencia y la Cultura
    Sección del Programa de Becas [S] [C] 49.
Organización de las Naciones Unidas para la Educación, la Ciencia y la Cultura [C.
Organización de las Naciones Unidas para la Educación, la Ciencia y la Cultura - Programa sobre El Hombre y la Biosfera (MAB) [S] 50.
Organización de los Estados Americanos [S] 41.
Organización Marítima Internacional [S] 31.
Organización Meteorológica Mundial [S] [C] 57.
Organización Mundial de la Salud - Centro Internacional de Investigaciones sobre el Cáncer [S] [C] 20.
Organización Mundial del Turismo [C] 58.
Programa Alßan [S] 43.
Unión Astronómica Internacional [S] 22.
Unión Interamericana para la Vivienda [C] 18.
Unión Internacional de Telecomunicaciones [S] 36.
Unión Internacional para la Ciencia, la Técnica y las Aplicaciones del Vacío [S] 37.
Unión Postal Universal [S] 53.
Zonta International [S] 59.

Index of National Institutions (by country)
Index des Institutions nationales (par pays)
Índice de Instituciones Nacionales (por país)

Albanie

Ministère de l'éducation 60
Université de Tirana 61

Algérie

Ministère de l'enseignement supérieur et de la recherche
scientifique 62
Université Abderrahmane Mira de Bejaia 63
Université Abou-Bekr Belkaid, Tlemcen 64
Université d'Alger 65
Université d'Oran Es-Sénia 66
Université de Batna 67
Université de M'Sila 68
Université des sciences et de la technologie
    Houari Boumédiène 69
Université Djillali Liabés de Sidi Bel-Abbés 70
Université Mohamed Khider - Biskra 71

Andorra

Universidad de Andorra 72

Angola

Instituto universitário livre de Luanda 73
Universidade Agostinho Neto 74

Argentina

Centro de Estudios Superiores
    Fundación "Embajador Rogelio Tristany" 75
Centro de Investigación
    de Tecnología del Cuero 76
Comisión de Intercambio Educativo entre los Estados
Unidos de América
    y la República Argentina (Comisión Fulbright) 77
Comité Nacional para el Programa Hidrológico
Internacional 78
Consejo Nacional de Investigaciones Científicas y
Técnicas 79
Facultad Tecnológica de Enología y de Industria
Frutihortícola "Don Bosco" 80
Fuerza Aérea Argentina
    Servicio Meteorológico Nacional (SMN) 81; 82
Instituto Balseiro
    Centro Atómico Bariloche 83
Pontificia Universidad Católica Argentina
    "Santa María de los Buenos Aires"
    Instituto de Extensión Universitaria 84
Pontificia Universidad Católica Argentina
    Instituto de Comunicación Social,
    Periodismo y Publicidad 85
Universidad Adventista del Plata 86
Universidad Argentina de la Empresa 87
Universidad Atlántida Argentina 88
Universidad Austral 89
Universidad Blas Pascal
    Instituto "Argentum"
    de Estudios Internacionales 90
Universidad de Belgrano 91
Universidad de Buenos Aires
    Facultad de Ciencias Exactas y Naturales
    Departamento de Ciencias
    de la Atmósfera 92
Universidad de Buenos Aires
    Facultad de Ingeniería
    Secretaría de Posgrado 93
Universidad de Congreso 94
Universidad de la Marina Mercante 95
Universidad de Morón 96
Universidad de San Andrés 97
Universidad del Norte
    "Santo Tomás de Aquino" 98
Universidad del Salvador
    Oficina de Programas Internacionales 99
Universidad Maimonides 100
Universidad Nacional de Entre Ríos
    Facultad de Bromatología 101
Universidad Nacional de Entre Ríos
    Facultad de Ciencias Agropecuarias 102
Universidad Nacional de Entre Ríos
    Facultad de Ciencias de la Alimentación 103
Universidad Nacional de Entre Ríos
    Facultad de Ciencias de la Salud 104
Universidad Nacional de Entre Ríos
    Facultad de Ciencias Económicas 105
Universidad Nacional de Entre Ríos 106
Universidad Nacional de la Pampa 107
Universidad Nacional de la Patagonia "San Juan Bosco"
    Facultad de Ciencias Económicas 108
Universidad Nacional de la Patagonia "San Juan Bosco"
    Facultad de Ciencias Naturales 109
Universidad Nacional de la Patagonia "San Juan Bosco"
    Facultad de Ingeniería 110
Universidad Nacional de La Plata 111
Universidad Nacional de La Rioja 112
Universidad Nacional de Mar del Plata 113
Universidad Nacional de Misiones 114
Universidad Nacional de Rosario 115
Universidad Nacional de Salta 116
Universidad Nacional de San Juan 117
Universidad Nacional de Tres de Febrero 118
Universidad Nacional del Centro 119
Universidad Nacional del Comahue 120
Universidad Nacional del Litoral
    Facultad de Bioquímica y Ciencias Biológicas
    Escuela Superior de Sanidad
    "Dr. Ramón Carrillo" 121
Universidad Nacional del Sur 122; 123
Universidad Notarial Argentina
    Fundación del Colegio de Escribanos
    de la Provincia de Buenos Aires 124

Arménie

American University of Armenia 125
Armenian Agricultural Academy 126
Gavar State University 127
Université d'État d'Erevan 128
Université française en Arménie 129
Yerevan Brusov State Linguistic University 130
Yerevan State Medical University 131

Australia

Arts Management 132
Australian Agency for Overseas Development 133
Australian Catholic University (Victoria) 134
Australian Federation of University Women 135
Australian Maritime College 136
Australian National University 137
Australian Research Council 138
Australian Vice-Chancellors' Committee 139
Central Queensland University 140
Charles Sturt University 141
Curtin University of Technology 142
Deakin University 143
Edith Cowan University 144
Flinders University of South Australia 145
Greece (Embassy of) 146
Griffith University 147
Griffith University, Queensland Conservatorium of
Music 148
International Programme Tasmania 149
James Cook University of North Queensland 150
La Trobe University 151
Macquarie University 152
Marcus Oldham College 153
Monash University 154
Monash University, Victorian College of Pharmacy
155
Murdoch University 156
New South Wales Department of Education and
Training 157
Northern Territory University 158
Queensland University of Technology 159
Royal Melbourne Institute of Technology 160
Southern Cross University 161
Swinburne University of Technology 162
TAFE International Western Australia 163
TAFE South Australia 164
University of Adelaide 165
University of Ballarat 166
University of Canberra 167
University of Melbourne 168
University of New England 169
University of New South Wales 170

University of New South Wales - Centre for Public Health 171
University of New South Wales - School of Medical Education / WHO Regional Training Centre for Health Development 172
University of Newcastle 173
University of Notre Dame 174
University of Queensland 175
University of South Australia 176
University of Southern Queensland 177
University of Tasmania, Hobart 178
University of Tasmania, Launceston 179
University of Technology, Sydney 180
University of Western Australia 181
University of Western Sydney 182
University of Wollongong 183
Winston Churchill Memorial Trust 184

Austria

Academy of Fine Arts Vienna 185
Afro-Asian Institute - Study Advisory Department 186
Atomic Institute of the Austrian Universities 187
Austrian Exchange Service (Österreichischer Austauschdienst)
    Agency for International Educational and Scientific Co-operation 188
Austrian Medical Society of Vienna 189
FH. Joanneum University of Applied Sciences 190
IMC University of Applied Management Sciences - Krems (Fachhochschule Krems) 191
Institute of Limnology of the Austrian Academy of Sciences 192
International University 193
Management Center Innsbruck 194
St. Pölten University of Applied Sciences 195
University Mozarteum 196
University of Applied Arts in Vienna 197
University of Applied Sciences, BFI VIENNA 198
University of Music and Dramatic Arts, Graz 199
University of Music and Performing Arts, Vienna 200
University of Salzburg 201
University of Vienna 202
Vorarlberg University of Applied Sciences 203
Webster University Vienna 204

Azerbaijan

Azerbaijan State Oil Academy 205
Baki Business University 206
Baku Asia University 207
Baku State University 208
Western University 209

Bahrain

Arabian Gulf University 210
College of Health Sciences 211
Gulf College of Hospitality and Tourism 212
University of Bahrain 213

Bangladesh

Ahsanullah University of Science and Technology 214
Islamic University of Technology 215
Khulna University 216
Southern University Bangladesh 217
The Peoples University of Bangladesh 218
United International University 219
University of Chittagong 220
University of Dacca (Dhaka Bishwadibidyalaya) 221

Barbados

Barbados Community College 222
Barbados Institute of Management and Productivity 223

Belarus, Republic of

Académie de médecine vétérinaire de Vitebsk 224
Académie de musique Bélarus 225
Académie des beaux-arts du Bélarus 226
Académie polytechnique d'État de Bélarus 227
Institut d'agriculture de Grodno 228
Institut d'État de médecine de Gomel 229
Institut d'État de médecine de Grodno 230

Institut polytechnique de Brest 231
Institut polytechnique de Gomel 232
Institut technologique de Moguilev 233
Institut technologique de Vitebsk 234
State University of Physical Culture of Belarus 235
Université d'État Bélarus 236
Université d'État d'informatique et de radioélectronique 237
Université d'État de Gomel 238
Université d'État de Grodno Y. Koupala 239
Université d'État de Moguilev 240
Université d'État du transport du Bélarus 241
Université économique d'État du Bélarus 242
Université linguistique d'État de Minsk 243

Belgique

Académie des Beaux-Arts de la ville de Tournai 244
Belgian-American Educational Foundation, Inc. 245
Conseil Interuniversitaire de la Communauté française de Belgique 246
Département des Sciences et Gestion de l'Environnement de l'ULg
    (anciennement Fondation universitaire luxembourgeoise) 247
Ecole supérieure des arts plastiques et visuels 248
Faculté polytechnique de Mons 249
Faculté universitaire des sciences agronomiques de Gembloux 250
Facultés universitaires catholiques de Mons 251
Facultés universitaires Notre-Dame de la Paix 252
Facultés universitaires Saint-Louis 253
Free University Brussels - Institute of Molecular Biology and Medicine 254
Free University Brussels, Vrije Universiteit Brussel 255
Ghent University 256
Haute Ecole 'Francisco Ferrer' de la Ville de Bruxelles 257
Haute École Charlemagne 258
Haute École Mosane de l'Enseignement Supérieur 259
Haute Ecole Robert Schuman, Département Technique 260
Haute École Roi Baudouin 261
HEC Ecole de Gestion de l'Université de Liège 262
Hogeschool Gent 263
Hogeschool West-Vlaanderen 264
Institut catholique des hautes études commerciales 265
Institut de médecine tropicale Prince Léopold 266
Institut Libre Marie Haps 267
Institut supérieur d'architecture de la communauté française, La Cambre 268
Institut supérieur d'architecture intercommunal 269
Institut supérieur d'architecture Saint-Luc de Wallonie, Liège 270
Institut supérieur d'architecture Saint-Luc, Bruxelles 271
Institut supérieur de la communauté française de traducteurs et interprètes 272
Katholieke Hogeschool Mechelen 273
Katholieke Hogeschool Sint-Lieven 274
Provinciale Hogeschool Limburg 275
Université catholique de Louvain 276
Université d'Anvers
    Institut de politique et de gestion du développement 277
Université de Liège 278
Université de Mons-Hainaut 279
Université libre de Bruxelles, Institut d'Études européennes 280
Universiteit Antwerpen 281
Universiteit Gent, Faculty of Bioscience Engineering 282

Belize

University of Belize 283

Bénin

Université d'Abomey-Calavi 284

Bermuda

Bermuda College 285

Bolivia

Fundación Universitaria "Simon I. Patiño" 286
Universidad Autónoma "Tomás Frías" 287
Universidad Privada Boliviana 288
Universidad Privada del Valle 289
Universidad Técnica de Oruro 290

Bosnia and Herzegovina

University of Sarajevo 291

Botswana

University of Botswana 292

Brésil

Centre brésilien de recherches physiques 293
Centro Universitario de Barra Mansa 294
Institut national de recherches d'Amazonie 295
Universidade federal de Minas Gerais 296
Université adventiste du Brésil - São Paulo 297
Université catholique pontificale de Parana 298
Université catholique pontificale de Rio Grande do Sul
299
Université d'État de Campinas - Faculté de génie
alimentaire 300
Université d'État de Londrina 301
Université d'État de Maringa 302
Université de la Vallée de Rio dos Sinos 303
Université de Ribeirão Prêto 304
Université de São Paulo - École supérieure d'agriculture
«Luiz de Queiroz» 305
Université de Sorocaba 306
Université fédérale de Pelotas 307
Université fédérale de Rio de Janeiro 308
Université fédérale de Rio de Janeiro - Musée national
309
Université fédérale de Rio Grande do Sul - Institut de
recherches hydrauliques 310
Université fédérale de Santa Maria 311
Université Nilton Lins 312
Université São Marcos 313
University Centre of Vila Velha 314

Bulgaria

Académie d'art musical et chorégraphique 315
Académie d'études économiques D.A.Tsenov Svishtov
316
Académie nationale d'art scénique et
cinématographique Krastyo Sarafov 317
Académie nationale des arts 318
Académie nationale des sports 319
American University in Bulgaria 320
Burgas Free University 321
Nouvelle université Bulgare 322
Université agricole 323
Université d'Architecture, de Génie Civil et de
Géodésie 324
Université d'économie nationale et mondiale 325
Université d'études économiques de Varna 326
Université d'industrie alimentaire 327
Université de Bourgas - Prof. Dr. Assen Zlatarov 328
Université de médecine de Plovdiv 329
Université de médecine de Sofia 330
Université de médecine de Varna 331
Université de Plovdiv-Paissii Hilendarski 332
Université de Shoumen Konstantin Preslavski 333
Université de Sofia St Kliment Ohridski 334
Université de technologie chimique et de métallurgie
335
Université de Thrace 336
Université de Veliko Tarnovo- St. Kiril et Methodi 337
Université des forêts et du génie forestier 338
Université des mines et de géologie St. Ivan Rilski 339
Université Sud-Ouest Néophyte Rilski 340
Université technique de Gabrovo 341
Université technique de Rousse-Anguel Kanchev 342
Université technique de Sofia 343
Université technique de Varna 344

Burkina Faso

Groupe des Ecoles EIER-ETSHER 345
Université de Ouagadougou 346

Burundi

Université Lumière de Bujumbura 347

Cambodge

Université royale d'agriculture 348

Cameroun

Campus numérique francophone de Yaoundé 349
Université catholique d'Afrique centrale 350
Université de Buéa 351
Université de Yaoundé II 352

Canada

Acadia University 353
Algonquin College 354
Bishop's University 355
Brandon University 356
Brock University 357
Canadian Bureau for International Education 358
Carleton University 359
Concordia University 360
Concordia University College of Alberta 361
Dalhousie University, Department of Economics 362
Dentistry Canada Fund 363
Huron University College 364
International Council for Canadian Studies - Award
Programme (PRA) 365
King's University College (The) 366
Kwantlen University College 367
McGill University 368
McGill University, Department of Agricultural
Economics 369
Memorial University of Newfoundland 370
Mount Allison University 371
Natural Sciences and Engineering Research Council of
Canada 372
Nipissing University 373
Nova Scotia Agricultural College 374
Nova Scotia College of Art and Design 375
Ontario Institute for Studies in Education
    University of Toronto 376
Redeemer University College 377
Ryerson Polytechnic University 378
Saint Mary's University 379
Saint Paul University 380
Simon Fraser University 381
St Francis Xavier University 382
St Thomas University 383
The University of Winnipeg 384
Trent University 385
Université de Moncton 386
Université de Montréal 387
Université du Quebec 388
Université du Quebec à Rimouski 389
Université du Quebec à Montréal 390
Université du Québec, Institut national de la recherche
scientifique 391
Université Laval 392
Université Sainte-Anne 393
University of Alberta 394
University of British Columbia 395
University of Guelph 396
University of New Brunswick, Fredericton Campus
397
University of Northern British Columbia 398
University of Ottawa, School of Graduate Studies and
Research 399
University of Regina 400
University of Saskatchewan 401
University of Sudbury 402
University of Toronto 403
University of Toronto, School of Graduate Studies 404
University of Waterloo 405
University of Western Ontario 406
University of Western Ontario, Faculty of Information
and Media Studies 407
Wilfrid Laurier University 408
York University 409

Chile

Gobierno de Chile
  Agencia de Cooperación Internacional (AGCI) 410
Instituto Latinoamericano de Doctrina y Estudios
Sociales 411; 412
Instituto Nacional de Enfermedades
  Respiratorias y Cirugía Torácica 413
Pontificia Universidad Católica de Chile
  Dirección de Intercambio Académico
  y Relaciones Internacionales 414
Pontificia Universidad Católica de Chile
  Facultad de Agronomía
  e Ingeniería Forestal 415
Pontificia Universidad Católica de Chile
  Facultad de Ciencias Biológicas 416
Pontificia Universidad Católica de Chile
  Facultad de Ciencias Sociales 417
Pontificia Universidad Católica de Chile
  Facultad de Educación 418
Pontificia Universidad Católica de Chile
  Facultad de Ingeniería 419
Pontificia Universidad Católica de Chile
  Facultad de Matemáticas 420
Pontificia Universidad Católica de Chile
  Facultad de Medicina 421
Pontificia Universidad Católica de Chile
  Facultad de Teología 422
Universidad "Diego Portales" 423
Universidad "José Santos Ossa" 424
Universidad Academia
  de Humanismo Cristiano 425
Universidad Austral de Chile
  Instituto de Ciencia y Tecnología de Alimentos 426
Universidad Austral de Chile 427
Universidad Bolivariana 428
Universidad Católica
  "Cardenal Raúl Silva Henríquez" 429
Universidad Católica de Valparaíso 430; 431
Universidad Católica del Maule 432
Universidad Católica del Norte 433; 434
Universidad de Chile
  Facultad de Arquitectura y Urbanismo
  Departamento de Geografía 435
Universidad de Chile
  Facultad de Ciencias
  Económicas y Administrativas
  Escuela de Economía y Administración para
Graduados 436
Universidad de Chile
  Facultad de Ciencias
  Físicas y Matemáticas
  Departamento de Geofísica 437
Universidad de Chile
  Facultad de Ciencias
  Físicas y Matemáticas
  Escuela de Posgrado 438
Universidad de Chile
  Facultad de Medicina
  Escuela de Posgrado 439
Universidad de Chile
  Facultad de Medicina
  Escuela de Salud Pública 440
Universidad de Chile
  Instituto de Estudios Internacionales 441
Universidad de Chile
  Instituto Interamericano
  de Educación Musical 442
Universidad de la Frontera 443
Universidad de la Serena 444
Universidad de los Andes 445
Universidad de Magallanes 446
Universidad de Playa Ancha
  de Ciencias de la Educación 447
Universidad de Talca 448
Universidad de Temuco 449
Universidad de Valparaíso 450
Universidad del Bío-Bío 451
Universidad del Pacífico 452
Universidad Internacional Sek 453
Universidad Marítima de Chile 454
Universidad Metropolitana
  de Ciencias de la Educación 455
Universidad Técnica
  "Federico Santa María"
  Escuela de Graduados 456

China

Beijing Polytechnic University 457
Beijing University 458
Beijing University of Chinese Medicine 459
Beijing University of Foreign Studies 460
Beijing University of Physical Education 461
Beijing University of Science and Technology 462
Central Academy of Drama 463
Central Academy of Fine Arts, The 464
Central China Normal University 465
Central Conservatory of Music 466
Chang'an University 467
Chengdu University of Science and Technology 468
China Academy of Art 469
China Pharmaceutical University 470
China University of Geosciences 471
China University of Mining and Technology 472
Dalian Maritime University 473
Donghua University 474
East China Normal University 475
East China University of Science and Technology 476
Fudan University - International Cultural Exchange
School 477
Guangxi University 478
Guangzhou University of Traditional Chinese Medicine
  479
Harbin Normal University 480
HoHai University 481
Huazhong Agricultural University 482
Hubei Medical University 483
Jiangxi Normal University 484
Jilin University 485
Jimey University 486
Jinan University 487
Lanzhou University 488
Liaoning University 489
Nanjing College of Traditional Chinese Medicine 490
Nanjing Normal University 491
Nanjing University 492
Nanjing University, Institute for International Students
493
Nankai University 494
Northeastern University 495
Northern Jiaotong University 496
Northwestern Polytechnical University 497
Renmin (People's) University of China 498
Shandong University, College of International
Education 499
Shanghai Conservatory of Music 500
Shanghai Second Medical University 501
Shanghai University 502
Shanghai University of Traditional Chinese Medicine
503
South Central University for Nationalities 504
South China Agricultural University 505
Southeast University 506
Southern Yangtze University 507
Southwest-China Normal University 508
Sun Yat-sen University 509
Sun Yat-Sen University of Medical Sciences 510
Tianjin College of Traditional Chinese Medicine 511
Tianjin Medical University 512
Tianjin University 513
Tianjin University of Foreign Studies 514
Tongji University 515
Tsinghua University 516
Wuhan University 517
Wuhan University of Technology 518
Xi'an Jiaotong University 519
Xiamen University - Overseas Education College 520
Yanshan University 521
Zhejiang Agricultural University 522
Zhejiang University, International College 523

China, Hong Kong

City University of Hong Kong 524
Hong Kong Polytechnic University 525

Hong Kong Shue Yan College 526
Hong Kong University of Science and Technology 527
Lingnan College Hong Kong 528
Open University of Hong Kong 529
University of Hong Kong 530

China, Macao

Macau University of Science and Technology 531
University of Macau 532

Colombia

Colegio Mayor "Nuestra Señora del Rosario" 533
Comisión para Intercambio Educativo entre Estados
Unidos de América y Colombia, Comisión Fulbright
534
Corporación Universitaria
Autónoma de Occidente 535
Corporación Universitaria
de Ciencia y Desarrollo 536
Corporación Universitaria de Ciencias Aplicadas y
Ambientales 537
Corporación Universitaria del Huila "Corhuila" 538
Fundación Universitaria Konrad Lorenz 539
Institución Universitaria
Fundación Escuela Colombiana
de Rehabilitación 540
Instituto Colombiano de Crédito Educativo
y Estudios Técnicos en el Exterior 541; 542
Instituto Teológico-Pastoral
para América Latina 543
Pontificia Universidad Javeriana 544
Universidad Autónoma de Occidente 545
Universidad Católica de Oriente 546
Universidad de Antioquia 547; 548
Universidad de Córdoba 549
Universidad de La Salle 550
Universidad del Magdalena 551
Universidad del Valle
Facultad de Artes Integradas
Escuela de Comunicación Social 552
Universidad EAFIT 553
Universidad Industrial de Santander 554
Universidad Metropolitana 555
Universidad Pedagógica y Tecnológica de Colombia
556

Comores, Les

Institut de formation des enseignants et de recherche en
éducation 557
Université des Comores 558

Congo

Université Marien Ngouabi 559

Costa Rica

Instituto Tecnológico de Costa Rica 560
Universidad Adventista
de Centro América 561
Universidad Autónoma de Centro América 562
Universidad Autónoma Monterrey 563
Universidad Braulio Carrillo 564
Universidad Católica de Costa Rica
"Anselmo Llorente y Lafuente" 565
Universidad Central Costarricense 566
Universidad de Ciencias Médicas 567
Universidad de Costa Rica
Departamento de Español para Extranjeros 568
Universidad de Costa Rica
Escuela Centroamericana de Geología 569; 570
Universidad de Costa Rica 571; 572
Universidad de Iberoamérica 573
Universidad de La Salle 574
Universidad de San José 575
Universidad del Diseño 576
Universidad EARTH 577
Universidad Estatal a Distancia 578
Universidad Evangélica de Las Américas 579
Universidad Federada de Costa Rica 580
Universidad Fidelitas 581
Universidad Hispanoamericana 582
Universidad Internacional de las Américas 583

Universidad Latina de Costa Rica 584
Universidad Latinoamericana
de Ciencia y Tecnología 585
Universidad Libre de Costa Rica 586
Universidad Nacional
Escuela de Topografía,
Catastro y Geodesia 587
Universidad Nacional 588
Universidad Nazarena de las Américas 589
Universidad Panamericana 590
Universidad para la Cooperación Internacional 591
Universidad para la Paz 592
Universidad Veritas 593

Côte d'Ivoire

Centre des métiers de l'électricité 594
École nationale supérieure de statistique et d'économie
appliquée 595
Institut national polytechnique Félix Houphouët-Boigny
596
Université Catholique de l'Afrique de l'Ouest-Unité
universitaire d'Abidjan 597

Croatia

University of Rijeka, Hrvatska 598

Cuba

Centro Nacional de Investigaciones Científicas 599
Centro Universitario de Guantánamo 600
Instituto Superior
de Ciencias Agropecuarias
de la Habana "Fructuoso Rodríguez" 601
Instituto Superior de Cultura Física "Manuel Fajardo"
Instituto Nacional de Deportes, Educación Física y
Recreación 602
Instituto Superior de Diseño Industrial 603
Instituto Superior del Arte 604
Instituto Superior Minero
Metalúrgico de Moa 605
Instituto Superior Pedagógico
"Rafael María de Mendive"
de Pinar del Río 606
Instituto Superior Pedagógico
"Oscar Lucero Moya" de Holguín 607
Instituto Superior Pedagógico
para la Enseñanza Técnica y Profesional
"Héctor Pineda Zaldivar" 608
Instituto Superior Politécnico
"José Antonio Echeverría" 609
Instituto Superior Técnico de Holguín 610
Ministerio de Educación Superior 611
Universidad Central de Las Villas 612
Universidad de Camagüey
Centro de Posgrado Internacional 613
Universidad de Ciego de Avila 614
Universidad de Granma 615
Universidad de La Habana 616
Universidad de Matanzas
Estación Experimental de Pastos
y Forrajes "Indio Hatuey" 617
Universidad de Matanzas
"Camilo Cienfuegos" 618
Universidad de Oriente 619
Universidad de Pinar del Río
"Hermanos Saíz" 620

Cyprus

Americanos College 621
ARTE Music Academy 622
C.D.A. College 623
C.T.L. College 624
Casa College 625
College of Tourism and Hotel Management 626
Cyprus College 627
Cyprus College of Accountancy and Business Studies
628
Cyprus College of Art 629
Cyprus Forestry College 630
Cyprus Institute of Marketing 631
Cyprus International Institute of Management 632
Frederick Institute of Technology 633

Global International College 634
Higher Hotel Institute, Cyprus 635
Higher Technical Institute 636
Intercollege 637
Kes College 638
Kimon College 639
Lynn College of Music and Arts 640
Mediterranean Institute of Management 641
P.A. College 642
Philips College 643
School of Nursing 644
Susini College 645
University of Cyprus 646

Czech Republic

Academy of Fine Arts 647
Academy of Performing Arts 648
Academy of Sciences of the Czech Republic - Institute
of Microbiology 649
Charles University 650
Czech Technical University in Prague 651
Czech University of Agriculture of Prague 652
Institute of Chemical Technology, Prague 653
Institute of Information Theory and Automation 654
Jan Evangelista Purkyne University in Ustí nad Labem
655
Janácek Academy of Music and Performing Arts 656
Masaryk University of Brno 657
Mendel University of Agriculture and Forestry Brno
658
Moravian Museum 659
Palacky University, Olomouc 660
Silesian University 661
Technical University of Brno 662
Technical University of Liberec 663
Technical University of Ostrava 664
The College of Business Studies 665
Tomas Bata University in Zlin 666
University of Economics, Prague 667
University of Hradec Králové 668
University of Ostrava 669
University of Pardubice 670
University of South Bohemia 671
University of Veterinary and Pharmaceutical Sciences,
Brno 672
University of West Bohemia 673

Denmark

Aalborg University 674
Aarhus School of Architecture 675
Aarhus School of Business 676
Cirius 677
Copenhagen Business School, Centre for Conference
Interpretation 678
Danish Rectors' Conference 679
Denmark-America Foundation & Fulbright
Commission 680
Roskilde University 681
Royal Danish Academy of Music 682
Royal Danish School of Pharmacy 683
Technical University of Denmark 684
University of Copenhagen 685
University of Southern Denmark 686

Ecuador

Pontificia Universidad Católica del Ecuador 687
Universidad "San Francisco de Quito"
Corporación de Promoción Universitaria 688
Universidad Andina "Simón Bolívar"
Sede Ecuador 689
Universidad Autónoma de Quito 690
Universidad Católica
de Santiago de Guayaquil 691
Universidad del Pacífico 692
Universidad Internacional del Ecuador 693
Universidad Internacional SEK 694
Universidad Técnica de Ambato 695
Universidad Técnica de Cotopaxi 696
Universidad Técnica Estatal de Quevedo 697
Universidad Técnica Particular de Loja 698

Egypt

Ain Shams University 699
Alexandria University - Medical Research Institute 700
American University in Cairo (The) 701
Cairo University - Statistical Studies and Research
Institute 702
Egyptian International Centre for Agriculture 703
Helwan University 704
Higher Institute of Technology-Benha 705
Minufiya University 706
October 6 University 707

El Salvador

Instituto Tecnológico Centroamericano 708
Universidad Don Bosco 709
Universidad Tecnológica de El Salvador 710

Eritrea

University of Asmara 711

España

Agencia Española de Cooperación Internacional
Instituto de Cooperación
con el Mundo Arabe, Mediterráneo
y Países en Desarrollo/Países Arabes 712
Agencia Española de Cooperación Internacional 713
Asociación Española de Contabilidad
y Administración de Empresas 714
Cámara de Comercio e Industria de Madrid
Insdtituto de Formación Empresarial 715
Centro de Estudios Políticos
y Constitucionales 716
Centro de Estudios y Experimentación
de Obras Públicas 717
Centro de Formación del Banco de España 718
Centro de Información, Cerveza y Salud 719
Centro Internacional
de Lengua y Cultura Españolas 720
Centro Tecnológico Nacional
de la Conserva
Centro de Edafología
y Biología Aplicada del Segura 721
Colegio de Estudios Hispánicos 722
Colegio Internacional Alicante Coop. V 723
Colegio Internacional Ausias March 724
Colegio Universitario
de Estudios Financieros 725
Comisión Fulbright
de Intercambio Cultural, Educativo
y Científico entre España
y los Estados Unidos de América 726
Consejo Nacional
de Investigaciones Científicas
Instituto de Agroquímica
y Tecnología de Alimentos (IATA) 727
Consejo Superior
de Investigaciones Científicas
Centro de Ciencias Medioambientales 728
Consejo Superior
de Investigaciones Científicas
Centro de Información
y Documentación Científica 729
Consejo Superior
de Investigaciones Científicas
Centro Nacional
de Investigaciones Metalúrgicas 730
Consejo Superior
de Investigaciones Científicas
Instituto de Cerámica y Vidrio 731
Consejo Superior
de Investigaciones Científicas
Instituto de Ciencia
y Tecnología de Polímeros 732
Consejo Superior
de Investigaciones Científicas
Instituto de Estudios Documentales
e Históricos sobre la Ciencia 733
Consejo Superior
de Investigaciones Científicas
Instituto de Filología 734

Consejo Superior
de Investigaciones Científicas
Instituto de Investigaciones Biomédicas 735
Consejo Superior
de Investigaciones Científicas
Instituto Nacional del Carbón 736
Consejo Superior de Investigaciones
CientíficasEstación Experimental del Zaidín 737
Consejo Superior de Investigaciones
CientíficasInstituto de Automática Industrial 738
Consejo Superior de Investigaciones
CientíficasInstituto de Ciencias de la Construcción 739
Consejo Superior de Investigaciones
CientíficasInstituto de la Grasa 740
Consejo Superior de los Colegios
de Arquitectos de España 741
Don Quijote 742
Escuela Andaluza de Salud Pública 743
Escuela de Administración de Empresas 744
Escuela de Alta Dirección
y Administración 745
Escuela de Negocios Caixavigo 746
Escuela de Organización Industrial 747
Escuela Nacional de Sanidad
Instituto de Salud Carlos III 748
Escuela Oficial de Turismo 749
Escuela Superior de Administración
y Dirección de Empresas 750
Escuela Superior de Tenería 751
Fundación "José Ortega y Gasset"
Centro de Estudios Internacionales 752
Fundación "Juan Esplugues" 753
Fundación "Ortega y Gasset" 754
Fundación "Pablo VI" 755
Fundación Carolina 756
Fundación CIDOB 757
Fundación MAPFRE Estudios 758
Fundación Marcelino Botín 759
Fundación Séneca 760
Fundación Universidad-Empresa 761
Institut d'Estudis Catalans 762
Instituto Agronómico Mediterráneo de Zaragoza 763;
764
Instituto de Empresas 765
Instituto de Estudios Espaciales
de Cataluña 766
Instituto de la Pequeña y Mediana Industria
de la Generalidad Valenciana 767; 768
Instituto Español de Comercio Exterior 769
Instituto Internacional
de Sociología Jurídica de Oñati 770
Instituto Nacional de Administración Pública 771
Instituto Nacional de Investigación
y Tecnología Agraria y Alimentaria 772
Instituto Nacional de Meteorología 773
Instituto Oficial
de la Radio Televisión Española 774
Instituto Químico de Sarriá 775
Instituto Universitario de Investigación "Ortega y
Gasset" 776
La Salle - Universitat Ramon Llull 777
Ministerio de Agricultura,
Pesca y Alimentación
Instituto Español de Oceanografía 778; 779
Ministerio de Asuntos Exteriores
Dirección General de Relaciones Culturales y
Científicas 780
Ministerio de Asuntos Exteriores
Escuela Diplomática (ED) 781
Ministerio de Economía y Hacienda
Instituto de Estudios Fiscales 782
Ministerio de Educación y Ciencia, Subdirección
General de Cooperación Internacional 783
Secretaría de Estado de Turismo y Comercio 784
Universidad Alfonso X el Sabio 785
Universidad Antonio de Nebrija 786
Universidad Autónoma de Barcelona
Escuela de Idiomas Modernos 787
Universidad Autónoma de Barcelona
Instituto de Análisis Económico 788
Universidad Autónoma de Madrid
Escuela de Periodismo UAM-El País 789

Universidad Autónoma de Madrid
Facultad de Ciencias Económicas
y Empresariales
Centro Internacional Carlos V 790
Universidad Autónoma de Madrid
Facultad de Ciencias Económicas
y Empresariales 791
Universidad Autónoma de Madrid
Facultad de Derecho
Cátedra "Jean Jonnet" de Instituciones
de Derecho Comunitario 792
Universidad Autónoma de Madrid
Facultad de Filosofía y Letras 793
Universidad Autónoma de Madrid
Facultad de Medicina
Departamento de Pediatría
Fundación Faustino Obergozo 794
Universidad Autónoma de Madrid
Facultad de Psicología 795
Universidad Autónoma de Madrid
Instituto de Ciencias de la Educación 796
Universidad Autónoma de Madrid
Instituto Universitario de Administración
de Empresas (IADE) 797
Universidad Autónoma de Madrid
Servicio de Cartografía 798
Universidad Autónoma de Madrid
Servicio de Oncología Médica
Hospital La Paz 799
Universidad Autónoma de Madrid 800
Universidad Camilo José Cela 801
Universidad Complutense de Madrid
Facultad de Ciencias de la Información 802
Universidad Complutense de Madrid
Facultad de Educación
Centro de Formación del Profesorado 803
Universidad Complutense de Madrid
Facultad de Filología 804
Universidad de Alcalá de Henares
Centro de Estudios Europeos 805
Universidad de Alcalá de Henares
Instituto Universitario
de Estudios Norteamericanos 806
Universidad de Alicante
Sociedad de Relaciones Internacionales 807
Universidad de Barcelona
Departamento de Psiquiatría
y Psicobiología Clínica 808
Universidad de Barcelona
Universidad de las Islas Baleares
Estudio General Luliano de Mallorca 809
Universidad de Barcelona 810
Universidad de Cádiz
Vicerrectorado de Extensión Universitaria 811
Universidad de Cádiz
Vicerrectorado de Ordenación Académica y Planes
de Estudio 812
Universidad de Cantabria
Centro de Idiomas (CIUC) 813
Universidad de Cantabria
Departamento de Filología 814
Universidad de Deusto
Facultad de Ciencias Económicas
y Empresariales
Universidad Comercial de Deusto 815
Universidad de Deusto
Facultad de Derecho
Escuela de Práctica Jurídica 816
Universidad de Deusto
Facultad de Derecho 817
Universidad de Deusto
Instituto Deusto de Drogodependencias 818
Universidad de Deusto
Instituto Interdisciplinar
de Estudios del Ocio 819
Universidad de Granada
Centro de Lenguas Modernas 820
Universidad de Huelva
Oficina de Relaciones Internacionales 821
Universidad de La Coruña 822
Universidad de La Rioja 823
Universidad de Las Palmas
de Gran Canaria 824

Universidad de León 825
Universidad de Málaga
  Cursos para Extranjeros 826
Universidad de Murcia 827
Universidad de Navarra
  Escuela Técnica Superior de Arquitectura 828
Universidad de Navarra
  Escuela Universitaria de Enfermería 829
Universidad de Navarra
  Facultad de Ciencias 830
Universidad de Navarra
  Facultad de Ciencias de la Información
  (School of Public Communication) 831
Universidad de Navarra
  Facultad de Derecho 832
Universidad de Navarra
  Facultad de Farmacia 833
Universidad de Navarra
  Facultad de Medicina
  Clínica Universitaria 834
Universidad de Navarra
  Instituto de Artes Liberales 835
Universidad de Navarra
  Instituto de Estudios Superiores
  de la Empresa 836
Universidad de Navarra
  Instituto de Lengua y Cultura Españolas 837
Universidad de Navarra
  Instituto Superior
  de Secretariado y Administración 838
Universidad de Navarra 839
Universidad de Oviedo
  Instituto Universitario de la Empresa 840
Universidad de Oviedo 841
Universidad de Salamanca
  Cursos Internacionales 842
Universidad de Salamanca
  Instituto de Ciencias de la Educación 843
Universidad de Salamanca 844
Universidad de Santiago de Compostela
  Escuela Universitaria de Enfermería 845
Universidad de Santiago de Compostela
  Facultad de Ciencias Económicas
  y Empresariales 846
Universidad de Santiago de Compostela
  Facultad de Derecho 847
Universidad de Santiago de Compostela
  Facultad de Farmacia 848
Universidad de Sevilla
  Instituto de Idiomas 849
Universidad de Valencia
  Vicerrectorado de Relaciones Exteriores 850
Universidad de Valladolid 851; 852
Universidad de Vigo
  Oficina de Relaciones Internacionales 853
Universidad de Zaragoza
  Servicio de Difusión de Lengua y Cultura
  Españolas para Extranjeros 854
Universidad de Zaragoza 855
Universidad del País Vasco/
  Euskal Herriko Unibersitatea 856
Universidad Francisco de Vitoria 857
Universidad Internacional
  Menéndez Pelayo 858; 859
Universidad Internacional de Andalucía
  Sede Iberoamericana de "La Rábida" 860
Universidad Nacional
  de Educación a Distancia 861
Universidad Politécnica
  de Cataluña - Barcelona
  Cátedra Gaudí - Escuela Técnica
  Superior de Arquitectura 862
Universidad Politécnica
  de Cataluña - Barcelona
  Escuela Superior de Agricultura 863
Universidad Politécnica
  de Cataluña - Barcelona
  Fundación Centro Internacional
  de Hidrología Subterránea 864
Universidad Politécnica de Valencia
  Centro de Formación de Posgrado 865
Universidad Politécnica de Valencia
  Instituto de Turismo, Empresa y Sociedad 866

Universidad Pompeu Fabra 867
Universidad Pontificia de Comillas 868
Universidad Pontificia de Salamanca en Madrid
  Facultad de Ciencias
  Políticas y Sociología 869
Universidad Ramón Llull 870
Universidad San Pablo CEU 871; 872
Universidad SEK 873
Unversidad Rey Juan Carlos 874

Estonia

Estonian Academy of Music 875
Estonian Agricultural University 876
Estonian Business School 877
Estonian Institute of Humanities 878
International University Concordia 879
Tallinn Pedagogical University 880
Tallinn Technical University 881
University of Tartu 882

Ethiopia

Addis Ababa University 883
Alemaya University 884
Bahir Dar University 885

Fiji

University of the South Pacific 886

Finland

Åbo Akademi University 887
Academy of Finland 888
Centre for International Mobility 889
Hanken - Swedish School of Economics and Business
Administration 890
Helsinki School of Economics and Business
Administration 891
Helsinki University of Technology 892
Nordic Institute for Advanced Training in Occupational
Health 893
Tampere University of Technology 894
University of Art and Design, Helsinki 895
University of Joensuu 896
University of Jyväskylä 897
University of Kuopio 898
University of Oulu, Dept. of Educational Sciences and
Teacher Education 899
University of Oulu, Dept. of Electrical Engineering
900
University of Oulu, Dept. of Information Processing
Science 901
University of Oulu, WHO Centre for Research on
Reproductive Health 902
University of Tampere 903
University of Turku 904

France

Alliance française 905
American University of Paris 906
Bordeaux école de management
  Institut du management des affaires et du commerce
international 907
Centre de coopération internationale en recherche
agronomique pour le développement 908
Centre national d'études agronomiques des régions
chaudes 909
Centre national de la recherche scientifique 910
Centre national des arts plastiques 911
Conservatoire national des arts et métiers 912
École centrale de Lille 913
École centrale de Lyon 914
École centrale Paris 915
École d'architecture de Grenoble (CEAA-Terre) 916
École d'architecture de Lyon 917
École d'architecture de Paris-Belleville 918
École d'architecture Languedoc-Roussillon 919
École d'architecture Paris-Malaquais 920
École d'ingénieurs 921
École des hautes études commerciales 922
École des hautes études en sciences sociales 923
École des Ingénieurs de la Ville de Paris 924
École des mines d'Alès 925

École du Breuil 926
École du Louvre 927
École européenne de chimie, polymères et matériaux de Strasbourg 928
École généraliste d'ingénieurs de Marseille 929
École internationale de commerce et de développement - Institut international 3A 930
École nationale d'administration 931
École nationale d'ingénieurs de Brest 932
École nationale d'ingénieurs de Metz 933
École nationale d'ingénieurs de St Étienne 934
École nationale d'ingénieurs des travaux agricoles de Clermont-Ferrand 935
École nationale de l'aviation civile 936
École nationale de la statistique et de l'administration économique 937
École nationale des chartes 938
École nationale des ponts et chaussées 939
École nationale des sciences géographiques 940
École nationale du génie de l'eau et de l'environnement de Strasbourg 941
École nationale supérieure d'agronomie et des industries alimentaires 942
École nationale supérieure d'architecture de Nantes 943
École nationale supérieure d'arts et métiers 944
École nationale supérieure d'arts et métiers, Châlons 945
École nationale supérieure d'électricité et de mécanique 946
École nationale supérieure d'électrotechnique, d'électronique, d'informatique et d'hydraulique de Toulouse 947
École nationale supérieure de chimie de Lille 948
École nationale supérieure de chimie de Rennes 949
École nationale supérieure de géologie 950
École nationale supérieure de l'aéronautique et de l'espace 951
École nationale supérieure de l'électronique et de ses applications 952
École nationale supérieure de mécanique et d'aérotechnique 953
École nationale supérieure de meunerie et des industries céréalières 954
École nationale supérieure de physique de Strasbourg 955
École nationale supérieure de techniques avancées 956
École nationale supérieure des arts appliqués et métiers d'art 957
École nationale supérieure des ingénieurs en arts chimiques et technologiques 958
École nationale supérieure des mines de Nancy 959
École nationale supérieure des mines de Paris 960
École nationale supérieure des mines de Saint-Etienne 961
École nationale supérieure des sciences de l'information et des bibliothèques 962
École nationale supérieure des télécommunications 963
École nationale supérieure du pétrole et des moteurs 964
École nationale supérieure Louis Lumière 965
École nationale vétérinaire de Nantes 966
École normale supérieure 967
École normale supérieure de Cachan 968
École normale supérieure de Lyon 969
École normale supérieure Lettres et Sciences humaines 970
École polytechnique 971
École spéciale de Mécanique et d'Electricité 972
École spéciale des travaux publics du bâtiment et de l'industrie 973
École supérieure d'agriculture d'Angers, Groupe ESA 974
École supérieure d'électricité 975
École supérieure d'ingénieurs en électrotechnique et électronique
    Amiens 976
École supérieure d'ingénieurs en électrotechnique et électronique 977
École supérieure d'optique 978
École supérieure de chimie physique électronique de Lyon 979
École supérieure de commerce de Clermont 980

École supérieure de commerce de Rouen 981
École supérieure de fonderie 982
École supérieure de journalisme de Lille 983
École supérieure de publicité 984
École supérieure de traducteurs interprètes et de cadres du commerce extérieur 985
École supérieure des industries du caoutchouc 986
École supérieure des Sciences économiques et commerciales
    École de Management 987
École supérieure des techniques aéronautiques et de construction automobile 988
École supérieure internationale d'optométrie - Institut et centre d'optométrie 989
Égide 990
ENGREF - Unité Mixte de Recherche TETIS 991
Entraide universitaire française-Comité français de l'Entraide universitaire mondiale 992
Établissement national d'enseignement supérieur agronomique de Dijon 993
French-American Foundation, Comité français 994
Groupe école supérieure de commerce de Dijon 995
Groupe école supérieure de commerce de Lyon 996
Groupe école supérieure de commerce de Reims 997
Hautes études industrielles 998
Institut catholique de Paris
    École de psychologues praticiens 999
Institut catholique de Paris
    Institut géologique Albert de Lapparent 1000
Institut catholique de Paris 1001
Institut catholique de Toulouse 1002
Institut d'études politiques de Paris, Sciences-Po 1003
Institut de formation et d'enseignement pour les métiers de l'image et du son 1004
Institut européen d'administration des affaires
    European Institute of Business Administration 1005
Institut National des Sciences Appliquées de Lyon 1006
Institut national des sciences appliquées de Rouen 1007
Institut national des sciences et techniques nucléaires 1008
Institut national polytechnique de Grenoble 1009
Institut Pasteur 1010
Institut supérieur agricole de Beauvais 1011
Institut supérieur d'agriculture Lille 1012
Institut supérieur d'électronique de Paris 1013
Institut supérieur des affaires - Groupe HEC 1014
Institut textile et chimique de Lyon 1015
Institut universitaire professionnalisé management et gestion des entreprises 1016
Ministère des Affaires étrangères 1017
Observatoire de Paris 1018
Pôle agronomique de Rennes 1019
Supméca 1020
Université catholique de l'Ouest 1021
Université catholique de Lille-Fédération universitaire et polytechnique de Lille 1022
Université catholique de Lyon 1023
Université Claude Bernard,
    Lyon 1 1024
Université d'Aix-Marseille III 1025
Université d'Angers 1026
Université d'Avignon et des Pays de Vaucluse 1027
Université de Bordeaux I 1028
Université de Bordeaux II 1029
Université de Bourgogne 1030
Université de Caen 1031
Université de la Polynésie française 1032
Université de la Sorbonne nouvelle - Paris III 1033
Université de Nantes 1034
Université de Nice Sophia Antipolis 1035
Université de Paris I, Institut d'étude du développement économique et social 1036
Université de Paris I, Institut de démographie 1037
Université de Paris-Sorbonne - Centre expérimental d'étude de la civilisation française 1038
Université de Pau et des pays de l'Adour - Institut d'études françaises pour étudiants étrangers 1039
Université de Perpignan 1040
Université de Perpignan, Laboratoire de thermodynamique et énergétique 1041

Université de Picardie Jules Verne 1042
Université de Poitiers 1043
Université de Poitiers, Centre d'études supérieures et de civilisation médiévale 1044
Université de Poitiers, Centre de ressources multimédia 1045
Université de Rennes I 1046
Université de Rennes II, Haute Bretagne 1047
Université de Rouen 1048
Université de technologie de Compiègne 1049
Université de technologie de Troyes 1050
Université de Toulouse-Le Mirail 1051
Université de Valenciennes et du Hainaut-Cambrésis 1052
Université des Antilles et de la Guyane en Guadeloupe 1053
Université des Antilles et de la Guyane en Guyane 1054
Université des Antilles et de la Guyane en Martinique 1055
Université des sciences sociales 1056
Université du droit et de la santé, Lille II 1057
Université du Havre 1058
Université du Maine 1059
Université Henry Poincaré
    Nancy I, École de santé publique 1060
Université Louis Pasteur, Strasbourg I
    Faculté de médecine 1061
Université Lyon II 1062
Université Michel de Montaigne
    Bordeaux III 1063
Université Nancy II, Centre européen universitaire 1064
Université Panthéon-Assas Paris II, Institut de droit comparé 1065
Université Panthéon-Assas Paris II, Institut français de presse 1066
Université Paris-Dauphine
    Paris IX - Département d'éducation permanente 1067
Université Paul Valéry
    Institut d'études françaises pour étudiants et professeurs étrangers 1068
Université Paul Verlaine-Metz I 1069
Université Pierre et Marie Curie
    Paris VI
    Institut de stomatologie, chirurgie plastique et chirurgie maxillo-faciale 1070
Université René Descartes
    Paris V 1071
Université Robert Schuman
    Strasbourg III - Centre universitaire d'enseignement du journalisme 1072
Université Robert Schuman
    Strasbourg III - Institut des hautes études européennes 1073
Université Robert Schuman
    Strasbourg III - Institut d'administration des entreprises 1074
Université Stendhal
    Grenoble III 1075
University Louis Pasteur
    Strasbourg I 1076

Gabon

Université des sciences et techniques de Masuku 1077
Université Omar Bongo 1078

Georgia

Georgian Technical University 1079
Grigol Robakidze University 1080
International Black Sea University 1081
Tbilisi State Medical University 1082

Germany

Aachen University of Applied Sciences 1083
Academy of Music Hanns Eisler Berlin 1084
Alexander von Humboldt Foundation 1085
Alice-Salomon University of Applied Sciences Berlin 1086
Amberg-Weiden University of Applied Sciences 1087

Aschaffenburg University of Applied Sciences 1088
Berlin School of Economics 1089
Carl Von Ossietzky University Oldenburg 1090
Catholic Service for Foreign Students 1091
Catholic University of Applied Sciences, North-Western Germany 1092
Deutscher Akademischer Austauschdienst (German Academic Exchange Service) 1093
Deutscher Famulantenaustausch (German Exchange Office for Medical Clerkship) 1094
Ecumenical Scholarships Programme 1095
ESCP-EAP European School of Management 1096
Fachhochschule Bonn-Rhein-Sieg
    University of Applied Sciences 1097
Fachhochschule Braunschweig-Wolfenbüttel
    University of Applied Sciences 1098
Fachhochschule Darmstadt
    University of Applied Sciences 1099
Fachhochschule Oldenburg/ Ostfiriesland/ Wilhelmshaven
    University of Applied Sciences 1100
Fachhochschule Schwaebisch Hall - University of Applied Sciences School of Design 1101
Fachochschule Suedwesfalen
    University of Applied Sciences 1102
Friedrich Ebert Foundation 1103
Friedrich Naumann Foundation 1104
Friedrich-Alexander University Erlangen-Nuremberg 1105
German University of Administrative Sciences, Speyer 1106
Gottlieb Daimler and Karl Benz Foundation 1107
Hamburg University for Economics and Politics 1108
Heinrich-Heine University Duesseldorf 1109
International Association for the Exchange of Students for Technical Experience - German Committee 1110
International Association of Students in Economics and Management - German Committee 1111
International Graduate School Zittau 1112
International University in Germany 1113
International University of Applied Sciences 1114
Katholischen Fachhochschule Freiburg (Catholic University of Applied Sciences) 1115
Konrad Adenauer Foundation 1116
Leipzig University of Applied Sciences 1117
Lutheran World Federation 1118
Mannheim University for Music and Performing Arts 1119
Max-Planck Institute for Nuclear Physics (Minerva Scholarship Committee) 1120
Muthesius Academy of Architecture, Design and Fine Arts 1121
Nürtingen University of Applied Sciences 1122
Otto Benecke Foundation 1123
Philipps-Universität Marburg 1124
Ravensburg-Weingarten University of Applied Sciences 1125
Renutlingen University 1126
Secretariat of the Standing Conference of Ministers of Education and Cultural Affairs of the Länder in Germany 1127
Social Service Agency of the Evangelical Church in Germany 1128
Technische Universität Dresden 1129
Technische Universität Ilmenau 1130
University of Potsdam 1131
University of Applied Sciences Westcoast 1132
University of Applied Sciences, Koblenz 1133
University of Applied Sciences, Regensburg 1134
University of Bayreuth 1135
University of Education Weingarten 1136
University of Hohenheim 1137
University of Jena 1138
University of Leipzig 1139
University of Lübeck 1140
University of Paderborn 1141
University of Trier 1142
Witten/Herdecke University 1143
World University Service, German Committee 1144

Ghana

Accra Polytechnic 1145
Ghana Institute of Management and Public
Administration 1146
University College of Education of Winneba 1147
University of Cape Coast 1148
University of Ghana - Institute of African Studies 1149

Grèce

American College of Greece, Deree College 1150
Aristotle University of Thessaloniki 1151
Athens School of Fine Arts 1152
Greek State Scholarship Foundation 1153
Technological Educational Institute of Kalamata 1154
Technological Educational Institute of Larissa 1155
Université d'agriculture d'Athènes 1156
Université de Ionnina 1157
Université de Macédoine, Économie et Sciences
Sociales 1158
Université de Thessalie 1159
Université Démocrite de Thrace 1160
Université des affaires et des sciences économiques
d'Athènes 1161
Université du Pirée 1162
Université nationale de technologie d'Athènes 1163
University of Athens 1164
University of Crete-Heraklion 1165
University of Crete-Rethymnon 1166
University of Patras 1167

Guatemala

Instituto Guatemalteco Americano 1168
Universidad de San Carlos de Guatemala 1169
Universidad del Valle de Guatemala 1170
Universidad Francisco Marroquin 1171
Universidad Mariano Gálvez de Guatemala 1172

Guyana

Guyana School of Agriculture 1173
University of Guyana 1174

Honduras

Universidad 'José Cecilio del Valle'
Tegucigalpa 1175
Universidad Católica de Honduras "Nuestra Señora
Reina de la Paz" 1176
Universidad Nacional Autónoma de Honduras 1177
Universidad Pedagógica Nacional "Francisco Morazán"
1178
Zamorano - Escuela Agrícola Panamericana 1179

Hungary

Academy of Drama, Film and Television 1180
Albert Szent-Györgyi Medical and Pharmaceutical
Center 1181
Bánki Donát Polytechnic 1182
Budapest Business School
Faculty of International Management and Business
1183
Budapest University of Economic Sciences and Public
Administration 1184
Central European University 1185
Corvinus University of Budapest
Faculty of Horticultural Science 1186
Debrecen Agricultural University
Faculty of Agricultural sciences 1187
Hungarian University of Craft and Design 1188
International Peto András Institute - Conductors'
College 1189
Kálmán Kandó College of Engineering 1190
Semmelweis University 1191
Széchenyi István University - Institute of
Transportation and Mechanical Engineering 1192
Szent István University 1193
Technical University of Budapest 1194
University Medical School of Debrecen 1195
University of Debrecen 1196
University of Miskolc 1197
University of Pécs
International Relations Office 1198

University of Szeged 1199
University of West Hungary 1200
University of West Hungary, Faculty of Economic
Sciences 1201

Iceland

Bifrost School of Business 1202
Ministry of Culture, Education and Science 1203
Reykjavik University 1204
Sigurdur Nordal Institute 1205
University of Akureyri 1206
University of Iceland 1207

India

CCS Haryana Agricultural University 1208
Chaudhary Sarwan Kumar Himachal Pradesh
Agricultural University 1209
Dr Harisingh Gour University 1210
Forest Research Institute (FRI) Deemed University
1211
Goa University 1212
Gujarat Vidyapith 1213
Indian Institute of Technology Roorkee 1214
Indian School of Mines 1215
Indian Veterinary Research Institute
(Bhartiya Pashu-Chikitsa Anusandhan Sansthan)
1216
Industrial Design Centre, Indian Institute of
Technology 1217
International Institute for Population Sciences 1218
K.C. College of Management Studies 1219
Kannur University 1220
Ministry of External Affairs
Indian Council for Cultural Relations 1221
Shreemati Nathibai Damodar Thackersey Women's
University 1222
Tezpur University 1223
University of Pune 1224
Vikram University Ujjain 1225
West Bengal National University of Juridical Sciences
1226
Women Graduates Union 1227

Indonesia

Bandar Lampung University 1228
Bogor Agricultural University 1229
Institute of Teacher Training and Educational Science
Mataram 1230
Muhammadiyah University of Surabaya
(Universitas Muhammadiyah Surabaya) 1231
Narotama University 1232
National Institute of Technology Malang 1233
Padjadjaran University 1234
Satya Wacana Christian University 1235
The University of Jember 1236
University of Malikussaleh 1237
University of Sanata Dharma 1238
Wiralodra University of Indramayu 1239

Iran, Islamic Republic of

Gonabad Medical Sciences University 1240
Gorgan University of Agricultural Science and Natural
Resources 1241
Guilan University of Medical Sciences 1242
Institute for Advanced Studies in Basic Sciences 1243
Iran University of Science and Technology 1244
Isfahan University of Medical Sciences
and Health Services 1245
Islamic Azad University 1246
Mashhad University of Medical Sciences 1247
Shahid Beheshti University 1248
Shahid Beheshti University of Medical Sciences
and Health Services 1249
Tarbiat Modarres University 1250
Tehran University of Medical Sciences 1251
University of Isfahan 1252
University of Kurdistan 1253
University of Tehran 1254

Ireland

American College Dublin 1255

Dublin Institute of Technology 1256
Limerick Institute of Technology
    School of Professional and Management Studies
1257
National University of Ireland, Galway 1258
National University of Ireland, Maynooth 1259
University College Dublin 1260

Israel

Agricultural Research Organization
    The Volcani Center 1261
Bar-Ilan University 1262
Ben-Gurion University of the Negev 1263
Galillee College 1264
Hebrew University of Jerusalem 1265
Joseph H. and Belle R. Braun Hebrew
University-Hadassah 1266
Lady Davis Fellowship Trust 1267
Michlalah Jerusalem College - The Linda Pinsky
School for Overseas Students 1268
Ministry of Foreign Affairs 1269

Italie

Academia Belgica 1270
Académie des beaux-arts «Pietro Vannucci» 1271
British Institute of Florence 1272
British School at Rome 1273
Bureau central des étudiants étrangers en Italie
    (Ufficio Centrale Studenti Esteri in Italia) 1274
CORIPE Piemonte
    Consortium for Research and Continuing Education
in Economics 1275
Ecole internationale supérieure d'études avancées 1276
European School of Economics 1277
Fashion Institute of Technology at Polimoda 1278
Fondation Rui (Résidences universitaires
internationales) 1279
Free University Bozen-Bolzano 1280
Institut d'études européennes «Alcide de Gasperi»
1281
Inter-University Mathematical School 1282
International Centre for Mechanical Sciences 1283
International Centre of Hydrology «Dino Tonini»,
University of Padua 1284
John Cabot University 1285
Loyola University Chicago Rome Center of Liberal
Arts 1286
Polytechnic of Turin 1287
Scuola Superiore Sant' Anna di Pisa 1288
Studio Art Centers International 1289
Technical University «Politecnico di Milano» 1290
The School of The Arts - Art Under One Roof 1291
Université de Florence
    Centre culturel pour étrangers 1292
Université de Gênes
    Centre international d'études italiennes 1293
Université de Parme 1294
Université internationale de l'art 1295
Université Magna Graecia 1296
Université pour étrangers, Pérouse 1297
Université pour étrangers, Sienne 1298
University Institute of European Studies, International
Training Centre of the ILO 1299
University of Ancona 1300
University of Cassino 1301
University of Commerce Luigi Bocconi 1302
University of Ferrara 1303
University of Insubria 1304
University of Milan-Bicocca 1305
University of Pavia 1306
University of Sassari 1307

Jamaica

Ministry of Education - Scholarships Section 1308
University of Technology 1309
University of the West Indies 1310

Japan

Aichi Shukutoku University 1311
Asahi University 1312
Asia University 1313

Association of International Education, Japan 1314
Atsumi International Scholarship Foundation 1315
Chukyo University 1316
Chuo University 1317
Fuji Bank International Foundation 1318
Fukuoka Kogyo Daigaku Tanki Daigakubu
    Institute of Technology, Junior College 1319
Fukuoka University 1320
Heiwa Nakajima Foundation 1321
Hiroshima Shudo University 1322
Hitachi Scholarship Foundation 1323
Hitotsubashi University 1324
Hokkai-Gakuen University 1325
Hokkaido University
    (Hokkaido Daigaku) 1326
Hyogo College of Medicine 1327
Ichikawa International Scholarship Foundation 1328
International Christian University 1329
International College for Advanced Buddhist Studies
1330
International University of Japan 1331
ITO Foundation for International Education Exchange
1332
Iwatani Naoji Foundation 1333
Japan Women's University 1334
Jichi Medical School, Graduate School of Medicine
1335
Kake Educational Institution/
    Okayama University of Science 1336
Kambayashi Scholarship Foundation 1337
Kansai Gaidai University 1338
Kansai International Students Institute 1339
Keio University 1340
Kobe College 1341
Kobe Design University 1342
Kobe Gakuin University 1343
Kokushikan University 1344
Konan Women's University 1345
Kumamoto Kenritsu Daigaku 1346
Kwassui Women's College 1347
Kyorin University (Kyorin Daigaku) 1348
Kyoritsu International Foundation 1349
Kyushu University 1350
Matsumae International Foundation 1351
Meikai University 1352
Ministry of Education, Culture, Sports, Science and
Technology (Monbukagakusho) 1353
Moriya Foundation 1354
Musashi Institute of Technology
    (Musashi Kogyo Daigaku) 1355
Nagoya University of Foreign Studies
    (Nagoya Gaikokugo Daigaku) 1356
Nagoya University, Department of Civil Engineering
1357
Nanzan University 1358
Nanzan University, Center for Japanese Studies 1359
Nara Institute of Science and Technology 1360
Nara University
    (Nara Daigaku) 1361
Nara Women's University
    (Nara Joshi Daigaku) 1362
Naruto University of Education 1363
Nihon University 1364
Notre Dame Seishin University 1365
Okayama University of Science (Okayama Rika
Daigaku) 1366
Okazaki Kaheita International Scholarship Foundation
1367
Okinawa International University 1368
Osaka Institute of Technology 1369
Osaka University 1370
Osaka University of Commerce 1371
Ritsumeikan Asia Pacific University 1372
Rotary Yoneyama Memorial Foundation, Inc. 1373
Ryukoku University 1374
Sagawa Scholarship Foundation 1375
Sakaguchi International Scholarship Foundation 1376
Seikei University 1377
Seitoku University 1378
Shibaura Institute of Technology 1379
Shimane University, Graduate School of Agriculture
1380

Shundoh International Foundation 1381
Sophia University 1382
Taisho University 1383
Takaku Foundation 1384
Takushoku University 1385
Toho Gakuen School of Music 1386
Tokai University (Tokai Daigaku) 1387
Tokushukai Scholarship Foundation 1388
Tokyo Institute of Technology (Tokyo Tech) 1389
Tokyo Keizai University 1390
Tokyo University of Science 1391
Tokyo Woman's Christian University
   (Tokyo Joshi Daigaku) 1392
Tokyu Foundation for Inbound Students 1393
Toyama University (Toyama Daigaku) 1394
Tsuji Asia Scholarship Foundation 1395
University of Fukui 1396
University of Tokushima 1397
University of Tokyo 1398
Waseda University 1399

Jordan

Al Balqa' Applied University 1400
Al Zaytoonah University of Jordan 1401
Al-Ahliyya Amman University (Amman Private
University) 1402
Al-Hussein Bin Talal University (King Hussein
University) 1403
Amman Arab University 1404
Jordan University of Science and Technology 1405
Ministry of Higher Education and Scientific Research
1406
Mu'tah University 1407
Philadelphia University 1408
The Hashemite University 1409
University of Jordan 1410
University of Petra 1411
Yarmouk University 1412

Kazakhstan

Al-Farabi Kazakh National University 1413
Almaty Abai State University 1414
East Kazakhstan State Technical University 1415
Kazakh National Medical University 1416
Kazakh National Technical University 1417
Kazakh-American University 1418
Zhetysu State University 1419

Kenya

British Institute in Eastern Africa 1420
Catholic University of East Africa 1421
Egerton University 1422
Institute for Meteorological Training and Research
1423
Kenya Utalii College 1424
Maseno University 1425
United States International University 1426

Kuwait

Kuwait University 1427

Kyrgyzstan

Academy of Management under the President of
Kyrgyz Republic 1428
Arabaev Kyrgyz State Pedagogical University 1429
International University of Kyrgyzstan 1430
Jalal-Abad State University 1431
Kyrgyz Russian Slavic University 1432
Kyrgyz Technical University
   'I. Razzakov' 1433

Latvia

Baltic Russian Institute 1434
Liepaja Academy of Pedagogy 1435
Rezeknes Augstskola 1436
Riga Technical University 1437
Turiba School of Business Administration
   Faculty of International Tourism 1438
University of Latvia 1439
Ventspils University College 1440
Vidzeme University College 1441

Liban

Al-Imam Al-Ouzai University 1442
American University of Beirut 1443
Association Makassed Philanthropique et Islamique à
Beyrouth 1444
Jinan University 1445
Université américaine libanaise 1446
Université Antonine 1447
Université arabe de Beyrouth 1448
Université de Balamand 1449
Université de Tripoli 1450
Université du Saint-Esprit 1451
Université Islamique du Liban 1452
Université libanaise 1453
Université Notre Dame de Louaizé 1454
Université Saint-Joseph 1455

Libyan Arab Jamahiriya

University of Al-Tahaddy 1456

Liechtenstein

University of Applied Sciences 1457

Lithuania

Kaunas University of Medicine 1458
Kaunas University of Technology 1459
Klaipeda University 1460
Law University of Lithuania 1461
Lithuanian Academy of Music 1462
Lithuanian Academy of Physical Education 1463
Lithuanian University of Agriculture 1464
Lithuanian Veterinary Academy 1465
Siauliai University 1466
Vilnius Academy of Arts 1467
Vilnius Gediminas Technical University 1468
Vilnius Pedagogical University 1469
Vilnius University 1470
Vytautas Magnus University 1471

Luxembourg

Centre universitaire de Luxembourg 1472
Institut supérieur d'études et de recherches
pédagogiques 1473
Institut supérieur de technologie 1474

Madagascar

Institut national des sciences et techniques nucléaires
1475
Institut supérieur de technologie Antsiranana 1476
Université d'Antananarivo 1477
Université d'Antananarivo, École supérieure
polytechnique Antananarivo 1478
Université d'Antananarivo, Faculté des lettres et
sciences humaines 1479
Université d'Antananarivo, Faculté des Sciences 1480
Université de Fianarantsoa 1481
Université de Mahajanga 1482
Université de Toamisina 1483
Université Nord Madagascar d'Antsiranana 1484

Malawi

University of Malawi 1485

Malaysia

International Islamic University 1486
International Medical University 1487
Multimedia University Malaysia 1488
Universiti Kebangsaan Malaysia 1489
Universiti Malaya 1490
Universiti Malaysia Sabah 1491
Universiti Malaysia Sarawak 1492
Universiti Putra Malaysia 1493
Universiti Sains Malaysia 1494
Universiti Teknologi Malaysia 1495
Universiti Tenaga Nasional Malaysia 1496
Universiti Utara Malaysia 1497

Malta

Institute of Electronics Engineering 1498
University of Malta 1499

Maroc

École Hassania des Travaux Publics 1500
École nationale supérieure d'informatique et d'analyse des systèmes 1501
École supérieure de l'agro-alimentaire SUP'AGRO 1502
École supérieure de technologie de Casablanca, Université Hassan II 1503
Institut agronomique et vétérinaire Hassan II 1504
Institut national des sciences de l'archéologie et du patrimoine 1505
Université Abdelmalek Essâadi, Faculté des Sciences 1506
Université Al Akhawayn Ifrane 1507
Université Al Quaraouiyine 1508
Université Chouaïb Doukkali
    Faculté des sciences et Faculté des lettres d'El Jaddida 1509
Université Hassan II Ain Chok, Casablanca 1510
Université Hassan II Mohammadia, Faculté des sciences et techniques 1511
Université Ibn Zohr Agadir 1512
Université Mohammed Ier 1513
Université Mohammed V Agdal 1514
Université Mohammed V Souissi 1515
Université Moulay Ismail, Faculté des sciences 1516
Université Sidi Mohamed Ben Abdellah 1517
University Moulay Ismail Meknès 1518

Mauritius

Mahatma Gandhi Institute 1519
Mauritius Institute of Education 1520
University of Mauritius 1521
University of Technology 1522

México

Barra Nacional de Abogados, Facultad de Derecho 1523
Benemérita Universidad Autónoma de Puebla 1524
Centro de Investigación Científica y de Educación Superior de Ensenada 1525
Centro de Investigación y Docencia Económicas 1526
Centro de Investigaciones y Estudios Superiores en Antropología Social 1527
Centro Interamericano de Estudios de Seguridad Social 1528
Colegio de México 1529
Colegio de Postgraduados 1530
Comisión Interinstitucional para la Formación de Recursos Humanos para la Salud
    Comité de Enseñanza de Posgrado y Educación Continua 1531
Consejo Nacional de Ciencia y Tecnología 1532
El Colegio de Michoacán A.C. 1533
El Colegio de Sonora 1534
Escuela de Diseño del Instituto Nacional de Bellas Artes 1535
Escuela Nacional de Conservación, Restauración y Museografía
    "Manuel del Castillo Negrete" 1536
Escuela Normal de Especialización
    Delegación Miguel Hidalgo 1537
Gobierno de México
    Secretaría de Relaciones Exteriores 1538
Hospital Infantil de México "Federico Gómez"
    División de Enseñanza 1539
Instituto Mexicano de la Audición y el Lenguaje, A.C. 1540
Instituto Mexicano de Psicoterapia Gestalt 1541
Instituto Mexicano del Seguro Social
    Dirección de Prestaciones Médicas
    Coordinación de Educación Médica 1542
Instituto Nacional de Salud Pública
    Escuela de Salud Pública de México 1543
Instituto Politécnico Nacional
    Centro de Investigación en Computación 1544
Instituto Politécnico Nacional
    Escuela Nacional de Ciencias Biológicas 1545
Instituto Politécnico Nacional
    Escuela Superior de Física y Matemáticas 1546
Instituto Politécnico Nacional
    Escuela Superior de Ingeniería Mecánica y Eléctrica 1547
Instituto Politécnico Nacional
    Escuela Superior de Ingeniería Química e Industrias Extractivas 1548
Instituto Politécnico Nacional
    Escuela Superior de Ingeniería Textil 1549
Instituto Politécnico Nacional
    Unidad Profesional Interdisciplinaria de Ingeniería y Ciencias Sociales y Administrativas 1550
Instituto Tecnológico Autónomo de México 1551
Instituto Tecnológico del Saltillo 1552
Instituto Tecnológico y de Estudios Superiores de Monterrey 1553
Secretaría de Educación Pública
    Dirección de Relaciones Internacionales 1554
Universidad "Juárez" Autónoma de Tabasco 1555
Universidad Anáhuac 1556
Universidad Anáhuac, Cancún 1557
Universidad Autónoma Agraria "Antonio Narro" 1558
Universidad Autónoma de Aguas Calientes 1559
Universidad Autónoma de Baja California 1560
Universidad Autónoma de Baja California Sur 1561
Universidad Autónoma de Chapingo 1562
Universidad Autónoma de Chiapas 1563
Universidad Autónoma de Chihuahua 1564
Universidad Autónoma de Ciudad Juárez 1565
Universidad Autónoma de Guadalajara 1566
Universidad Autónoma de Guerrero 1567
Universidad Autónoma de Nayarit 1568
Universidad Autónoma de Nuevo León 1569
Universidad Autónoma de Querétaro 1570
Universidad Autónoma de Quintana Roo 1571
Universidad Autónoma de San Luis Potosí 1572
Universidad Autónoma de Sinaloa 1573
Universidad Autónoma de Tamaulipas 1574
Universidad Autónoma de Tlaxcala 1575
Universidad Autónoma de Yucatán 1576
Universidad Autónoma de Zacatecas 1577
Universidad Autónoma del Carmen 1578
Universidad Autónoma del Estado de Hidalgo 1579
Universidad Autónoma del Estado de México 1580
Universidad Autónoma Metropolitana 1581
Universidad Bonaterra 1582
Universidad Contemporánea 1583
Universidad de Anáhuac del Sur 1584
Universidad de Celaya 1585
Universidad de Colima 1586
Universidad de Guadalajara
    Centro de Estudios para Extranjeros 1587
Universidad de Guanajuato 1588
Universidad de las Américas - Puebla 1589
Universidad de Las Américas, A.C. 1590
Universidad de los Altos de Chiapas 1591
Universidad de Monterrey 1592
Universidad de Quintana Roo 1593
Universidad de Relaciones y Estudios Internacionales, A.C. 1594
Universidad de Sonora 1595
Universidad de Sotavento 1596
Universidad de Xalapa 1597
Universidad del Claustro de Sor Juana 1598
Universidad del Noreste 1599
Universidad del Nuevo Mundo, A.C. 1600
Universidad del Pedregal 1601
Universidad del Valle de Atemajac 1602
Universidad del Valle de México 1603
Universidad Galilea 1604
Universidad Hebraica México
    Instituto Universitario de Estudios Hebraicos 1605
Universidad Iberoamericana 1606
Universidad Intercontinental 1607
Universidad ISEC 1608
Universidad José Vasconcelos de Oaxaca 1609
Universidad Juárez del Estado de Durango 1610
Universidad La Salle 1611
Universidad Madero 1612
Universidad Mexicana del Noreste 1613
Universidad México Americana del Norte 1614
Universidad Michoacana "San Nicolás de Hidalgo" 1615
Universidad Michoacana de Oriente 1616
Universidad Mundial 1617

Universidad Nacional Autónoma de México 1618
Universidad Panamericana 1619
Universidad Popular de la Chontalpa 1620
Universidad Quetzalcóatl en Irapuato 1621
Universidad Regiomontana 1622
Universidad Regional del Norte 1623
Universidad Salesiana 1624
Universidad Tecnológica de Nezahualcoyotl 1625
Universidad Tecnológica Fidel Velázquez 1626
Universidad Valle del Bravo 1627
Universidad Veracruzana
  Dirección General de Apoyo al Desarrollo
Académico 1628
Universidad Villasunción 1629

Mongolia

National Medical University of Mongolia 1630
National University of Mongolia 1631

Namibia

Polytechnic of Namibia 1632

Nepal

Tribhuvan University 1633

Netherlands

Academic Centre for Dentistry Amsterdam 1634
Arnhem Business School 1635
ArtEZ Institute of the Arts 1636
Centraal Bureau voor Schimmelcultures 1637
Delft University of Technology 1638
Dronten Professional Agricultural University 1639
Eindhoven University of Technology 1640
Erasmus University Rotterdam 1641
HAS Den Bosch University of Professional Education
1642
HES Rotterdam College for Economics and Business
Administration 1643
Hogeschool Zuyd, Limburg Business School 1644
Hotelschool The Hague, International Institute for
Hospitality Management 1645
Institute for Biotechnology Studies Delft/Leiden 1646
Institute for Housing and Urban Development Studies
1647
Institute of Social Studies 1648
International Agricultural Centre 1649
International Institute for Aerospace Survey and Earth
Sciences 1650
International Institute for Land Reclamation and
Improvement 1651
Larenstein International Agricultural College 1652
Leiden University 1653
Maastricht School of Management 1654
Maastricht University, Faculty of Economics and
Business Administration 1655
Maastricht University, Faculty of Law 1656
Maastricht University, Faculty of Medicine 1657
Netherlands Graduate School of Management 1658
Netherlands Organization for International Cooperation
in Higher Education 1659
NHTV Breda University of Professional Education
1660
Nijenrode University, The Netherlands Business School
1661
Radio Nederland Training Centre 1662
Rotterdam College of Music and Dance 1663
Rotterdam School of Management, Erasmus Graduate
School of Business 1664
Royal Conservatory, The Hague 1665
Saxion Universities of Professional Education 1666
Tilburg University 1667
UNESCO-IHE Institute for Water Education 1668
University College Maastricht, Maastricht University
1669
University of Amsterdam 1670
University of Nijmegen Institute for International
Health 1671
University of Nijmegen, Pallas Consortium 1672
University of Professional Education, Enschede 1673
University of Twente, Enschede 1674
Utrecht Polytechnic 1675

Utrecht School of the Arts 1676
Utrecht University 1677
Utrecht University Medical Centre, School of Medical
Sciences 1678
Utrecht University, Faculty of Veterinary Medicine
1679
Van Hall Institute 1680
Wageningen Agricultural University 1681
Wageningen University 1682

New Zealand

Auckland University of Technology 1683
Department of Internal Affairs
  Te Tari Taiwhenua 1684
Health Research Council of New Zealand 1685
International Pacific College 1686
Lincoln University 1687
Massey University 1688
Ministry of Foreign Affairs, Official Development
Assistance Programme 1689
New Zealand Vice-Chancellors' Committee 1690
New Zealand's International Aid & Development
Agency 1691
University of Otago 1692
University of Waikato 1693
Victoria University of Wellington 1694

Nicaragua

Universidad Católica "Redemptoris Mater" 1695
Universidad Centroamericana 1696
Universidad de Las Américas 1697
Universidad Evangélica Nicaragüense Martin Luther
King 1698

Niger

Centre régional Agrhymet du CILSS 1699

Nigeria

Ahmadu Bello University 1700
Bayero University, Kano 1701
Enugu State University of Science and Technology
1702
Federal University of Technology, Yola 1703
Igbinedion University, Okada 1704
Kaduna Polytechnic 1705
Ladoke Akintola University of Technology 1706
Michael Okpara University of Agriculture, Umudike
1707
Nnamdi Azikiwe University 1708
Rivers State University of Science and Technology
1709
University of Benin 1710
University of Nigeria 1711

Norway

Bergen National Academy of the Arts 1712
Bergen University College 1713
Kunsthogskolen i Bergen 1714
Narvik University College 1715
Norwegian Academy of Music 1716
Norwegian Agency for Development Co-operation
1717
Norwegian School of Economics and Business
Administration 1718
Norwegian University of Science and Technology
1719
Oslo National College of the Arts 1720
Oslo University College 1721
Ostfold University College 1722
Research Council of Norway 1723
Sogn og Fjordane University College 1724
Telemark University College 1725
The Norwegian Lutheran School of Theology 1726
The School of Mission and Theology 1727
Tromso University College 1728
University of Bergen 1729
University of Bergen, Department of Fisheries and
Marine Biology 1730
University of Oslo 1731
University of Tromsø 1732

Oman

Sultan Qaboos University 1733

Pakistan

Allama Iqbal Open University 1734
Baqai Medical University 1735
City University of Science and Information Technology 1736
Fatima Jinnah Women's University 1737
Hazara University 1738
Higher Education commission 1739
International Islamic University 1740
Isra University 1741
Jinnah University for Women 1742
Ministry of Science and Technology 1743
National Institute of Banking and Finance 1744
National University of Computer and Emerging Sciences 1745
Quaid-e-Awam University of Engineering Science and Technology 1746
Quaid-i-Azam University 1747
University of Balochistan 1748
University of Education, Lahore 1749
University of Engineering and Technology 1750
University of Karachi 1751
University of Peshawar 1752
University of Sindh 1753
University of the Punjab 1754
Virtual University 1755

Palestinian Autonomous Territories

An-Najah National University 1756

Panamá

Instituto para la Formación
y Aprovechamiento
de Recursos Humanos 1757
Universidad de Panamá 1758

Papua New Guinea

Papua New Guinea University of Technology
Bulolo Forestry College 1759
University of Papua New Guinea 1760

Paraguay

Universidad Comunera 1761
Universidad del Norte 1762

Perú

Escuela de Administración de Negocios
para Graduados 1763
Escuela de Administración de Negocios para Graduados 1764
Escuela Nacional de Salud Pública 1765
Escuela Superior de Administración
de Empresas, Ventas y Mercadotecnia 1766
Escuela Superior de Bellas Artes "Corriente Alterna" 1767
Facultad de Teología Pontificia y Civil
de Lima 1768
Instituto Peruano
de Administración de Empresas 1769
Instituto Peruano de Fomento Educativo 1770
Instituto Superior Tecnológico
Privado TECSUP No. 1 1771
Pontificia Universidad Católica del Perú
Escuela de Graduados 1772
Servicio Nacional de Adiestramiento
en Trabajo Industrial 1773
Universidad "Ricardo Palma" 1774; 1775
Universidad Católica de Santa María 1776
Universidad de Lima 1777
Universidad de San Martin de Porres 1778
Universidad del Pacífico 1779
Universidad Nacional
"Jorge Basadre Grohmann" 1780
Universidad Nacional Agraria La Molina 1781
Universidad Nacional de Educación "Enrique Guzmán y Valle" 1782

Universidad Nacional de Ingeniería
Facultad de Arquitectura, Urbanismo
y Artes 1783
Universidad Nacional de Tumbes 1784
Universidad Nacional Mayor
de San Marcos 1785
Universidad Peruana
de Ciencias Aplicadas 1786
Universidad Peruana "Cayetano Heredia"
Dirección de Especialización
en Estomatología 1787
Universidad Peruana "Cayetano Heredia"
Escuela de Posgrado
"Victor Alzamora Castro" 1788
Universidad Peruana "Cayetano Heredia"
Instituto de Genética 1789
Universidad Peruana "Cayetano Heredia"
Instituto de Gerontología 1790
Universidad Peruana "Cayetano Heredia" 1791
Universidad Peruana ce Ciencias Aplicadas 1792
Universidad Peruana Unión 1793
Universidad Privada Antenor Orrego 1794
Universidad Privada del Norte 1795
Universidad Privada San Pedro 1796

Philippines

Angeles University Foundation 1797
Arellano University 1798
Asian Institute of Management 1799
Baguio Central University 1800
Bicol University - Graduate school 1801
Carthel Science Educational Foundation, Inc. 1802
Cavite State University 1803
Central Luzon State University, Institute of Graduate Studies 1804
De La Salle University 1805
Don Mariano Marcos Memorial State University 1806
Manila Central University 1807
Manuel S. Enverga University Foundation Main Campus 1808
Mapùa Institute of Technology 1809
MSU-Iligan Institute of Technology 1810
National University 1811
Philippine Christian University 1812
Philippines Women's University 1813
Polytechnic University of the Philippines 1814
Ramon Magsaysay Technological University 1815
Saint Louis University 1816
Saint Mary's University 1817
University of La Salette 1818
University of Luzon 1819
University of Northern Philippines 1820
University of Rizal System-Rizal State College 1821
University of San Jose-Recoletos 1822
University of Southern Mindanao 1823
University of the Philippines 1824
University of the Philippines Visayas Cebu 1825
University of the Philippines, Diliman 1826
Western Mindanao State University 1827

Poland

Academy 'Adam Mickiewicz University', Poznan 1828
Academy of Agriculture in Cracow 1829
Academy of Business in Dabrowa Gornicza 1830
Academy of Fine Arts in Cracow 'Jan Matejko' 1831
Academy of Fine Arts in Katowice 1832
Academy of Fine Arts in Poznan 1833
Academy of Fine Arts in Warsaw 1834
Academy of Fine Arts in Wroclaw 1835
Academy of Music in Poznan 'Ignacy Jan Paderewski' 1836
Academy of Music in Warsaw 'Fryderyc Chopin' 1837
Academy of Music in Wroclaw 'Karol Lipinski' 1838
Academy of Music, Cracow 1839
Academy of Physical Education 'Eugeniusz Piasecki' 1840
AGH University of Science and Technology
International School of Technology 1841
Agricultural University of Cracow 1842
Agricultural University of Wroclaw 1843
Association for the Promotion of Entrepreneurship,
University of Information Technology and
Management, Rzeszow 1844

Boleslaw Markowski Higher School of Commerce 1845
College of Communication and Management 1846
College of Economics and Computer Science 1847
College of Socio-Economics in Tyczyn 1848
Computer Science and Management University 'Copernicus' in Wroclaw 1849
Crestochowa University of Management 1850
Economics University in Warsaw 1851
Faculty of Mathematics and Information Science 1852
Family Alliance Higher School 1853
Feliks Nowowiejski Academy of Music in Bydgoszcz 1854
Gdansk School of Banking 1855
Higher Professional School of Krosno 1856
Higher School 'Paweù Wùodkowic', Pùock 1857
Higher School of Administration 1858
Higher School of Economics and Arts 1859
Higher School of Economics, Warsaw 1860
Higher School of Humanities and Economy in Elblag 1861
Higher School of Management/ Polish Open University 1862
Higher School of Social Knowledge 1863
Higher School of Tourism and Hotel Industry 1864
Higher Vocational State School 1865
Higher Vocational State School in Kalisz 1866
Karol Szymanowski Academy of Music in Katowice 1867
Katowice School of Economics 1868
Kielce University of Technology 1869
Maria Curie-Skodowska University in Lublin 1870
Maritime University of Szczecin 1871
Medical University of Lodz 1872
Medical University of Silesia in Katowice 1873
Medical University of Warsaw 1874
Medical University, Byaùystok 1875
National Louis University 1876
Opole University 1877
Pedagogical University in Warsaw 1878
Plock State School of Higher Education 1879
Polish-Japanese Institute of Information Technology 1880
Polytechnic University, Biaùystok 1881
Pomeranian Academy of Tourism and Hotel Management 1882
Poznan University of Technology 1883
Private Higher Educational Institute in Gizycko 1884
Prof A. Meissner Higher School of Dentistry in Ustron 1885
Pultusk School of Humanities 1886
School of Banking and Management in Cracow 1887
School of Commerce in Ruda Slaska 1888
School of Entrepreneurship and Marketing in Chrzanow 1889
Silesian Polytechnic University, Gliwice 1890
Silesian University of Technology 1891
Technical University of Koszalin 1892
Technical University of Lodz 1893
Technical University of Opole 1894
Technical University of Szczecin 1895
Université d'agriculture de Varsovie 1896
Université médicale de Gdansk 1897
University College of Arts and Natural Sciences in Sandomierz 1898
University of Bielsko-Biala 1899
University of Ecology and Management in Warsaw 1900
University of Economics in Katowice 1901
University of Finance and Management in Bialystok 1902
University of Humanities and Economics in Wloclawek 1903
University of International Studies 1904
University of Lodz 1905
University of Management and Marketing in Warsaw 1906
University of Mining and Metallurgy 1907
University of Podlasie 1908
University of Rzeszòw 1909
University of Silesia 1910
University of Zielona Gòra 1911

University School of Physical Education in Warsaw 1912
Warsaw Customs Study College 1913
Warsaw School of Economics 1914
Warsaw University 1915
Warsaw University of Technology 1916

Portugal
Autonomous University of Lisbon 1917
Fondation Calouste Gulbenkian 1918
Institut Camões 1919
Portucalense University 1920
Université catholique portugaise 1921
Université d'Aveiro 1922
Université de Beira Interior 1923
Université de Lisbonne 1924
Université de Lusofona des Humanités et des Technologies 1925
Université nouvelle de Lisbonne, Institut d'hygiène et de médecine tropicale 1926
University of Tras-os-Montes e Alto Douro University 1927

Qatar
University of Qatar 1928

Republic of Korea
Academy of Korean Studies 1929
Berea International Theological Seminary 1930
Chodang University 1931
Chonnam National University 1932
Gyeongsang National University 1933
Handong Global University 1934
Hansei University 1935
Inha University 1936
Keimyung University 1937
Korean-American Educational Commission 1938
Kyongpook National University, Overseas Educational Center 1939
Kyungnam University 1940
Language Teaching Research Centre 1941
Sejong University 1942
Seoul Jangsin University 1943
Seoul National University 1944
Seoul National University of Education 1945
Songkyunkwan University 1946
Sookmyung Women's University 1947
Sun Moon University 1948
Sungkyungkwan University 1949
Yonsei University 1950
Yonsei University - Graduate School of Business Administration 1951
Yonsei University - Graduate School of International Studies 1952

Republic of Moldova
Co-operative Trade University of Moldova 1953
Free International University of Moldova 1954
Pedagogical State University 'Ion Creanga' 1955
University of Foreign Languages and International Business 1956

República Dominicana
Instituto Tecnologico de Santo Domingo 1957
Pontificia Universidad Católica Madre y Maestra 1958
Universidad APEC 1959
Universidad Dominicana O & M 1960
Universidad Nacional Pedro Henríquez Ureña 1961

République arabe syrienne
Institut supérieur de science politique 1962
Ministère de l'éducation Direction des étudiants étrangers 1963
Université de Damas 1964

Roumanie
'Iuliu Hatieganu' University of Medicine and Pharmacy of Cluj-Napoca 1965
Academy of Economic Studies Bucharest 1966

Babes-Bolyai University 1967
Emanuel University of Oradea 1968
Gh. Dima Music Academy 1969
Ovidius University of Constantza 1970
Technical University of Civil Engineering Bucharest 1971
University of Agricultural Sciences and Veterinary Medicine 1972
University of Agronomical Sciences and Veterinary Medicine of Bucharest 1973
University of Bucharest 1974
University of Medicine and Pharmacy of Craiova 1975
University of Oradea 1976

Russian Federation

Academy of Social Education 1977
Altaj State Technical University 1978
Altaj State University 1979
Amur State University 1980
Archangelsk State Medical Academy 1981
Baltic Fishing Fleet State Academy 1982
Barnaul State University of Educational Science 1983
Bashkir State University 1984
Bauman Moscow State Technical University 1985
Biysk State Teacher's Training University 1986
Bryansk State Academy of Engineering and Technology 1987
Buryat State University 1988
Demidov Yaroslavl State University 1989
Don State Technical University 1990
East Siberian Institute of Technology 1991
Far Eastern State Technical University 1992
Finance Academy 1993
Higher School of Modern Education 1994
Humanitarian University (Institute) 1995
Institute of Law and Business 1996
Institute of Youth 1997
International Non-governmental Organization Corporation 1998
Irkutsk State Academy of Agriculture 1999
Irkutsk State Technical University 2000
Irkutsk State University 2001
Ivanovo State Academy of Medicine 2002
Ivanovo State Textile Institute 2003
Ivanovo State University 2004
Kaliningrad State University 2005
Kaluga State Pedagogical University 'K. Tsiolkovsky' 2006
Kazan Finance and Economics Institute 2007
Kazan State University 2008
Komi State Pedagogical Institute 2009
Komsomolsk-on-Amur Polytechnical Institute 2010
Kostroma State Pedagogical University 2011
Kostroma State University of Technology 2012
Kosygin Moscow State Textile University 2013
Kovrov State Academy of Technology 2014
Krasnoyarsk Academy of Architecture and Civil Engineering 2015
Krasnoyarsk State Technical University 2016
Krasnoyarsk State University 2017
Kuban State Academy of Medicine 2018
Kuban State University 2019
Kuban State University of Technology 2020
Kursk State Technical University 2021
Kursk State University of Educational Science 2022
Kuzbass Polytechnic Institute 2023
Legal Academy of the Ministry of Justice 2024
Liberal Arts University 2025
Lipeck Polytechnical Institute 2026
Magintogorsk State Conservatory 2027
Mendeleyev University of Chemical Technology of Russia 2028
Mordovia State University 2029
Mordovian State Institute of Teacher Training 2030
Moscow Academy of Humanities and Social Sciences 2031
Moscow Academy of Medicine 2032
Moscow Consumer Cooperative University 2033
Moscow Institute of Architecture 2034
Moscow Institute of Municipal Economy and Construction 2035
Moscow Institute of Physics and Technology 2036

Moscow Pedagogical University 2037
Moscow Power Engineering Institute 2038
Moscow State Academy of Fine Chemical Technology 2039
Moscow State Academy of Food Industry 2040
Moscow State Academy of Geological Prospecting 2041
Moscow State Academy of Instrumentation Technology and Informatics 2042
Moscow State Academy of Printing 2043
Moscow State Academy of Veterinary Medicine and Biotechnology ' K.I. Skryabin' 2044
Moscow State Agroengineering University 'V.P. Goryachkin' 2045
Moscow State Industrial University 2046
Moscow State Institute of Automobile and Highway Engineering 2047
Moscow State Institute of Electronic Engineering (Technical University) 2048
Moscow State Institute of Electronics and Mathematics (Technical University) 2049
Moscow State Institute of Radio Engineering, Electronics and Automation (Technical University) 2050
Moscow State Technical University of Civil Aviation 2051
Moscow State Technological University 'Stankin' 2052
Moscow State University 'M.V. Lomonosov' 2053
Moscow State University of Civil Engineering 2054
Moscow State University of Culture and Arts 2055
Moscow State University of Design and Technology 2056
Moscow State University of Economics, Statistics and Informatics 2057
Moscow State University of Environmental Engineering 2058
Moscow State University of Mining Engineering 2059
Moscow State University of Railway Communications 2060
Moscow University Touro 2061
Nizhni Novgorod State Medical Academy 2062
Nizhni Novgorod State University 2063
Nizhni Novgorod State University of Architecture and Civil Engineering 2064
North Caucasus State Institute of Arts 2065
North West State Technical University 2066
Novocherkassk State Technical University 2067
Novorossiysk State Maritime Academy 2068
Novosibirsk State Agrarian University 2069
Novosibirsk State Technical University 2070
Novosibirsk State University 2071
Omsk State University 2072
Peoples' Friendship University of Russia (former Patrice Lumumba University) 2073
Petrozavodsk State University 2074
Plekhanov Russian Academy of Economics 2075
Pyatigorsk State Pharmaceutical Academy 2076
Rostov State Medical University 2077
Rostov State Music Conservatory (Academy) 'S.V Rahmaninov' 2078
Rostov State Pedagogical University 2079
Rostov State University 2080
Rostov State University of Economics 2081
Rostov State University of Transport Communication 2082
Russian State Hydrometeorological University 2083
Russian State Technological University 2084
Saint Petersburg College of Precision Mechanics and Optics 2085
Saint Petersburg State Academy for Engineering Economics 2086
Saint Petersburg State Chemical Pharmaceutical Academy 2087
Saint Petersburg State Medical Academy 2088
Saint Petersburg State Mining Institute (Technical University) 2089
Saint Petersburg State Pavlov Medical University 2090
Saint Petersburg State Technical University 2091
Saint Petersburg State University 2092
Saint Petersburg State University of Economics and Finance 2093
Samara State Institute of Arts and Culture 2094

Samara State Medical University 2095
Samara State Technical University 2096
Samara State University 2097
Saratov State Technical University 2098
Saratov State University 2099
Sechenov Moscow Medical Academy 2100
Shuya State Pedagogical University 2101
Siberian Aerospace Academy 2102
Siberian Medical University 2103
Siberian Motor and Highway Institute 2104
Siberian State Academy of Transport 2105
Siberian State Technological University 2106
South-Russian Humanities Institute 2107
South-Russian State Technical University/
Novocherkassk 2108
Southern Ural State University 2109
State Academy of Management 2110
State Academy of Oil and Gas 2111
State Marine Technical University of St. Petersburg 2112
State University of Non-Ferrous Metals and Gold 2113
Stavropolskiy Institute 2114
Taganrog State University of Radio Engineering 2115
Tambov State Technical University 2116
Tatar Institute for Promotion of Business 2117
Togliatti Polytechnic Institute 2118
Tomsk Polytechnic University 2119
Tyumen State Agricultural Academy 2120
Tyumen State University 2121
Udmurt State University 2122
Ufa State Petroleum Technological University 2123
Ural State Technical University-UPI 2124
Ural State University of Forestry Engineering 2125
Velikie Luki Agricultural Institute 2126
Vladimir Polytechnical Institute 2127
Volgograd State Pedagogical University 2128
Volgograd State Technical University 2129
Volgograd State University 2130
Volgograd State University of Architecture and Civil Engineering 2131
Voronezh N.N. Burdenko State Medical Academy 2132
Voronezh National Academy of Architecture
and Construction 2133
Voronezh Pedagogical University 2134
Voronezh Polytechnic Institute 2135
Voronezh State Agricultural University 2136
Voronezh State University 2137

Saint-Siège

Institut pontifical d'archéologie chrétienne 2138
Institut pontifical d'études arabes et islamiques 2139
Université pontificale grégorienne 2140
Université pontificale Saint-Thomas-d'Aquin 2141

San Marino

University of San Marino 2142

Saudi Arabia

King Saud University 2143

Sénégal

École Inter-Etats des sciences et médecine vétérinaires de Dakar 2144
École nationale des arts 2145
Université Cheikh Anta Diop de Dakar, Institut de français pour les étudiants étrangers 2146

Serbia and Montenegro

University of Belgrade 2147
University of Montenegro 2148

Singapore

Nanyang Technological University 2149
National University of Singapore 2150
National University of Singapore - Faculty of Medicine 2151
Ngee Ann Polytechnic 2152
Singapore Polytechnic 2153

Slovakia

Academia Istropolitana Nova 2154
Academy of Fine Arts and Design Bratislava 2155
Academy of Music and Dramatic Arts 2156
Catholic University in Ruzomberok 2157
City University 2158
College of Management 2159
Comenius University 2160
Constantine the Philosopher University in Nitra 2161
Mateja Bela University 2162
Slovak University of Agriculture in Nitra 2163
Slovak University of Technology in Bratislava 2164
Technical University in Zvolen 2165
Technical University of Kosice 2166
University of 'St Cyril and Methodius' 2167
University of Economics in Bratislava 2168
University of Pavol Jozef Safárik, Kosice 2169
University of Presov 2170
University of Trencín 2171
University of Trnava 2172
University of Veterinary Medicine 2173
University of Zilina 2174

Slovenia

GEA College of Entrepreneurship 2175
ISH Ljubljana Graduate School of the Humanities 2176
Ministry of Education and Sport 2177
Nova Gorica Polytechnic 2178
University of Ljubljana 2179

Solomon Islands

Solomon Islands College of Higher Education 2180

South Africa

Cape Technikon 2181
Medical University of Southern Africa 2182
Port Elizabeth Technikon 2183
Potchefstroom University for Christian Higher Education 2184
Rand Afrikaans University 2185
Rhodes University 2186
St Augustine College of South Africa 2187
Technikon Pretoria 2188
Technikon Witwatersrand 2189
University of Cape Town 2190
University of North West 2191
University of Pretoria 2192
University of the Orange Free State 2193
University of the Western Cape 2194
University of Witwatersrand 2195

Sri Lanka

Buddha Sravaka Bhiksu University 2196
Rajarata University of Sri Lanka 2197
University of Colombo 2198
University of Kelaniya 2199
University of Moratuwa - Department of Architecture 2200
University of Peradeniya 2201
University of Ruhuna 2202

Sudan

Al Zaiem Alazhari University 2203
Atbara University - Faculty of Engineering and Technology 2204
University of Zalingei 2205

Suisse

C.G. Jung-Institut Zurich 2206
Département fédéral de l'intérieur, Commission fédérale des bourses pour étudiants étrangers 2207
École polytechnique fédérale de Lausanne 2208
Ecole polytechnique fédérale de Zurich
(Swiss Federal Institute of Technology Zurich) 2209
École polytechnique fédérale Lausanne 2210
Faculté indépendante de théologie de Bâle 2211
Fonds national suisse de la recherche scientifique 2212
Glion Institut de Hautes Études 2213
Institut européen de l'Université de Genève 2214

Institut universitaire d'études du développement 2215
Institut universitaire de hautes études internationales 2216
International University 2217
Secrétariat d'Etat à l'éducation et à la recherche SER
    Secrétariat de la Commission fédérale des bourses
pour étudiants étrangers 2218
Université de Fribourg 2219
Université de Fribourg, Institut de Psychologie 2220
Université de Geneve 2221
Université de Genève, École de traduction et
d'interprétation 2222
Université de Lausanne 2223
Université de Lucerne 2224
Université de Neuchâtel 2225
University of St. Gallen/Graduate School of Business
Administration, Economics, Law and Social Sciences
2226
University of Zürich 2227

Suriname

Academy for Higher Art and Culture 2228
Anton de Kom University of Suriname 2229
COVAB Foundation Central School for Nurses and
Allied Professions 2230
Foundation for Youth Dental Care 2231
Polytechnic College Suriname 2232

Swaziland

Mananga Centre for Regional Integration and
Management Development 2233
University of Swaziland 2234

Sweden

Bank of Sweden, Tercentenary Foundation 2235
Chalmers University of Technology 2236
Dalarna University College 2237
Göteborg University 2238
Jönköping International Business School 2239
Jönköping University 2240
Linköping University 2241
Luleå University 2242
Lund University 2243
Mälardalens Högskolla 2244
Nordic Africa Institute 2245
Nordic School of Public Health 2246
Orebro University 2247
Royal Institute of Technology 2248
Royal University College of Music in Stockholm 2249
Stockholm Institute of Education 2250
Stockholm School of Economics 2251
Stockholm University 2252
Swedish Institute 2253
Swedish University of Agricultural Sciences 2254
Umeå University 2255
University College of Dance 2256
University College of Opera 2257
University of Karlstad 2258
Uppsala University 2259

Tajikistan

Russian-Tajik Modern University for the Humanities
2260
Tajik Technical University 'M.S. Osimi' 2261
Technological University of Tajikistan 2262

Tchad

Université de N'Djaména, Faculté des sciences exactes
et appliquées 2263

TFYR Macedonia

University of St. Cyril and Methodius 2264

Thailand

Asian University of Science and Technology 2265
Assumption University, Bangkok 2266
Bangkok University 2267
Kasetsart University 2268
Khon Kaen University 2269
King Mongkut's Institute of Technology North
Bangkok 2270

King Mongkut's University of Technology Thonburi
2271
Maejo University 2272
Mahanakorn University of Technology 2273
Mahidol University 2274
Naresuan University 2275
National Institute of Development Administration 2276
Prince of Songkla University 2277
Ramkhamhaeng University 2278
Sripatum University 2279
Sukhothai Thammathirat Open University 2280
Thailand-United States Educational Foundation 2281
Thammasat University 2282

Togo

Centre international de recherche et d'étude de langues
2283
Centre régional d'action culturelle 2284
École africaine de métiers de l'architecture et de
l'urbanisme 2285
École nationale d'administration 2286
Université de Lomé 2287

Trinidad and Tobago

Ministry of Works and Transport
    Civil Aviation Division 2288
University of the West Indies 2289
University of the West Indies,
    Faculty of Medical Sciences 2290

Tunisie

Institut Bourguiba des langues vivantes 2291
Office national du Tourisme tunisien 2292
Université de Sfax pour le Sud 2293
Université du Centre, École Nationale d'Ingénieurs de
Monastir 2294
Université du Centre, École supérieure d'Horticulture et
d'Élevage de Chott Mériem 2295
Université du Centre, École supérieure des Sciences et
Techniques de la Santé de Monastir 2296
Université du Centre, École supérieure des Sciences et
Techniques de la Santé de Sousse 2297
Université du Centre, Faculté de Droit et des Sciences
Économiques et Politiques de Sousse 2298
Université du Centre, Faculté de Médecine de Monastir
2299
Université du Centre, Faculté de Médecine de Sousse
2300
Université du Centre, Faculté de Médecine Dentaire de
Monastir 2301
Université du Centre, Faculté de Pharmacie de Monastir
2302
Université du Centre, Faculté des Lettres et des
Sciences humaines de Sousse 2303
Université du Centre, Faculté des Lettres et Sciences
humaines de Kairouan 2304
Université du Centre, Faculté des Sciences de Monastir
2305
Université du Centre, Faculté des Sciences
économiques et de Gestion de Mahdia 2306
Université du Centre, Institut préparatoire aux Études
d'Ingénieurs de Monastir 2307
Université du Centre, Institut supérieur d'Informatique
et des Technologies de Communication à Hammam
Sousse 2308
Université du Centre, Institut supérieur de
biotechnologie de Monastir 2309
Université du Centre, Institut Supérieur de Gestion de
Sousse 2310
Université du Centre, Institut supérieur de Musique de
Sousse 2311
Université du Centre, Institut supérieur des Beaux Arts
de Sousse 2312
Université du Centre, Institut Supérieur des Langues
Appliquées aux Affaires et au Tourisme de Moknine
2313
Université du Centre, Institut Supérieur des Sciences
Appliquées et de Technologie de Sousse 2314
Université du Centre, Institut supérieur du Transport et
de la Logistique de Sousse 2315
Université Libre de Tunis 2316

Université privée des Sciences, Arts et Techniques de
Sousse 2317

Turkey

Akdeniz University School of Tourism and Hotel
Management 2318
Bilkent University 2319
Dokuz Eylul University 2320
Hacettepe University 2321
Istanbul Bilgi University 2322
Middle East Technical University 2323
Nigde University 2324
Pamukkale University 2325
Trakya University 2326
Université d'Uludag 2327
Université Marmara 2328
Yuzuncu Yil University 2329
Zonguldok Karaelmas University 2330

Uganda

Makerere University 2331
Mbarara University of Science and Technology 2332
Uganda Martyrs University 2333

Ukraine

Bila Tserkva State Agrarian University 2334
Crimean State Medical University 2335
Dnipropetrovsk State Medical Academy 2336
Donbas State Academy of Civil Engineering and
Architecture 2337
Donetsk State University of Economics and Trade
2338
East Ukrainian National University 2339
European University, Kiev 2340
Inter-Regional Academy of Personnel Management
2341
Karazin Kharkiv National University 2342
Kherson Pedagogical University 2343
Kiev Medical Institute 2344
Kiev National Linguistics University 2345
Kiev Slavonic University 2346
Krok University 2347
Lugansk Academy of Internal Affairs 2348
Lutsk State Technical University 2349
Lviv State Institute of Physical Education 2350
National Aerospace University 2351
National University of Kiev-Mohyla Academy 2352
National University of Pharmacy 2353
Odessa State Academy of Refrigeration 2354
Poltava State Agrarian Academy 2355
Pridneprovskaya State Academy of Civil Engineering
and Architecture 2356
South Ukrainian State Pedagogical University
'K. D. Ushynsky' 2357
State Flight Academy of Ukraine 2358
Sumy State University 2359
Taurida National University 'V.I. Vernadsky' 2360
Ternopil Academy of National Economy 2361
Ternopil State Pedagogical University 2362
Ukrainian State Maritime Technical University 2363
Uzhhorod National University 2364
Vinnytsia State Technical University 2365

United Arab Emirates

United Arab Emirates University 2366

United Kingdom

American International University of London -
Richmond College 2367
Associated Board of the Royal Schools of Music 2368
Aston University 2369
Bournemouth University 2370
British Federation of Women Graduates 2371
British Institute of Persian Studies 2372
Cambridge Commonwealth Trust 2373
Canterbury Christ Church University College 2374
Chester College of Higher Education 2375
Christie's Education 2376
Countess of Munster Musical Trust 2377
Courtauld Institute of Art 2378
Coventry University 2379

Cranfield University 2380
Dr M. Aylwin Cotton Foundation 2381
Durham University 2382
Engineering and Physical Sciences Research Council
2383
European School of Economics 2384
Goldsmiths College, University of London 2385
Harper Adams University College 2386
Heriot-Watt University 2387
Heriot-Watt University, Edinburgh College of Art
2388
Institute of Advanced Legal Studies 2389
Institute of Commonwealth Studies, University of
London 2390
Institute of Education, University of London 2391
Keele University 2392
Lancaster University 2393
Leeds Metropolitan University
    Faculty of Cultural and Education Studies Carnegie
Centre for Physical Education and Sport Studies 2394
Leeds Trinity and All Saints College 2395
Liverpool Hope University College 2396
Liverpool, John Moores University 2397
London Guildhall University 2398
London Metropolitan University 2399
London School of Economics and Political Science
2400
Loughborough University 2401
Manchester Metropolitan University 2402
Middlesex University 2403
Napier University 2404
National College for Food, Land and Environmental
Studies 2405
Natural Resources Institute, University of Greenwich
2406
Norwich Jubilee Esperanto Foundation 2407
Oxford Brookes University 2408
Queen Margaret College 2409
Queen's University of Belfast 2410
Robert Gordon University 2411
Rose Bruford College 2412
Royal College of Music 2413
Royal Holloway, University of London 2414
Royal Philharmonic Society 2415
Royal Scottish Academy of Music and Drama 2416
Royal Society 2417
Royal Society for the Encouragement of Arts,
Manufactures and Commerce 2418
Royal Society of Edinburgh 2419
Royal Town Planning Institute 2420
Royal Welsh College of Music and Drama 2421
Saint Stephen's House 2422
Scottish College of Textiles 2423
Sheffield Hallam University 2424
South Bank University 2425
Staffordshire University 2426
Stranmillis University College 2427
The Surrey Institute of Art & Design, University
College 2428
Trinity College of Music 2429
University College Chester 2430
University College London 2431
University College Northampton 2432
University College of Wales 2433
University College Winchester 2434
University of Aberdeen 2435
University of Abertay Dundee 2436
University of Birmingham 2437
University of Bradford 2438
University of Brighton 2439
University of Bristol 2440
University of Buckingham 2441
University of Cambridge 2442
University of Dundee 2443
University of East Anglia 2444
University of East London 2445
University of Edinburgh 2446
University of Essex 2447
University of Exeter 2448
University of Glasgow 2449
University of Leeds 2450
University of Leicester 2451

University of Liverpool 2452
University of London 2453
University of London, Birkbeck College 2454
University of London, School of Advanced Studies
    Institute of Historical Research 2455
University of London, School of Pharmacy 2456
University of London, Warburg Institute 2457
University of Luton 2458
University of Manchester 2459
University of Newcastle upon Tyne 2460
University of Northumbria at Newcastle 2461
University of Nottingham 2462
University of Oxford 2463
University of Oxford, St Antony's College 2464
University of Oxford, Trinity College 2465
University of Plymouth 2466
University of Reading 2467
University of Southampton
    School of Research and Graduate Studies 2468
University of St Andrews 2469
University of Strathclyde 2470
University of Sunderland 2471
University of Surrey 2472
University of Sussex 2473
University of Teesside 2474
University of the West of England, Bristol 2475
University of Wales Bangor 2476
University of Wales Cardiff 2477
University of Wales Swansea 2478
University of Warwick 2479
University of Westminster 2480
University of York 2481
Warnborough University 2482
West Dean College 2483
Wimbledon School of Art 2484
Winchester School of Art, Textile Conservation Centre
    University of Southampton 2485
YMCA George Williams College 2486

United Republic of Tanzania

Dar es Salaam Institute of Technology 2487
Eastern Africa Statistical Training Centre 2488
Institute of Adult Education 2489
Institute of Finance Management 2490
Mzumbe University 2491
Open University of Tanzania 2492
Sokoine University of Agriculture 2493
St Augustine University of Tanzania 2494
University of Bukoba 2495
University of Dar es Salaam 2496
University of Dar es Salaam - Muhimbili University
College of Health Sciences 2497

United States of America

Abilene Christian University 2498
Adelphi University 2499
Albertson College of Idaho 2500
Albion College
    International Programs 2501
Alliant International University 2502
American College of Computer and Information
Sciences 2503
American Conservatory Theater 2504
American University Washington DC 2505
American-Scandinavian Foundation
    Exchange Division 2506
Angelo State University 2507
Antioch University McGregor 2508
Arizona State University 2509
Art Center College of Design 2510
Augsburg College 2511
Bank Street College of Education 2512
Bard College 2513
Barry University 2514
Belgian American Educational Foundation, Inc. 2515
Bellarmine College 2516
Bemidji State University 2517
Benedictine College 2518
Benedictine University 2519
Bennington College 2520
Berklee College of Music 2521

Binghamton University 2522
Boise State University 2523
Boston University 2524
Bowdoin College 2525
Bowling Green State University 2526
Brandeis University 2527
Brown University 2528
Bryn Mawr College 2529
Bucknell University 2530
California Institute of Integral Studies 2531
California State University - San Marcos 2532
California State University - Stanislaus 2533
California State University, Long Beach 2534
California State University, Sacramento 2535
California State University, San Bernardino 2536
Case Western Reserve University 2537
Catawba College 2538
Central Missouri State University 2539
Central Washington University 2540
Clarkson University 2541
Cleveland State University 2542
Coe College 2543
College for Creative Studies 2544
College of Mount St Joseph 2545
College of St Benedict and St John's University 2546
College of St Catherine 2547
College of the Southwest 2548
Colorado State University 2549
Colorado State University-Pueblo
    (formerly University of Southern Colorado) 2550
Concordia University Wisconsin 2551
Coppin State University 2552
Cornell University 2553
Cranbrook Academy of Art 2554
Davidson College 2555
Dominican College 2556
Drury University 2557
Duke University 2558
Dumbarton Oaks 2559
Duquesne University 2560
East Stroudsburg University 2561
Eastern Illinois University 2562
Eastern Washington University 2563
Elmira College 2564
Embry-Riddle Aeronautical University 2565
Endicott College 2566
Erikson Institute 2567
Fairfield University 2568
Ferris State University 2569
Fight for Sight, Inc. Research Division
    Prevent Blindness America 2570
Florida A & M University 2571
Florida Atlantic University 2572
Francis Marion University 2573
Franklin Pierce College 2574
Fresno Pacific University 2575
Frostburg State University 2576
George Washington University 2577
Georgetown University 2578
Georgia College and State University 2579
Georgia Institute of Technology 2580
Georgia Southern University, Center for International
Studies 2581
Gladys Krieble Delmas Foundation 2582
Golden Gate University 2583
Gordon College 2584
Goshen College 2585
Goucher College 2586
Grand Valley State University 2587
Hanover College 2588
Harding University 2589
Harvard University, Harvard College 2590
Hebrew Union College, Jewish Institute of Religion
2591
Heiser Program for Research in Leprosy and
Tuberculosis 2592
Hollins College 2593
Hope International University 2594
Indiana University South Bend 2595
Institute of International Education 2596
International College of Surgeons 2597
Ithaca College 2598

J. Paul Getty Museum, Education Department 2599
Jane Coffin Childs Memorial Fund for Medical
Research 2600
Johns Hopkins University 2601
Kent State University 2602
Lake Erie College 2603
Langston University 2604
Lebanon Valley College 2605
Lewis and Clark College 2606
Lewis University 2607
Lock Haven University 2608
Loyola University of Chicago 2609
Maharishi University of Management 2610
Manhattanville College 2611
Marian College of Fond du Lac 2612
Marylhurst University 2613
Marymount College, Palos Verdes 2614
Medical University of South Carolina 2615
Memphis College of Art 2616
Meredith College 2617
Methodist College 2618
Miami University 2619
Michigan State University 2620
Michigan Technological University 2621
Millikin University 2622
Minnesota State University Moorhead 2623
Minot State University 2624
Montana State University 2625
Moravian College 2626
Morningside College 2627
Mount Holyoke College 2628
Murray State University 2629
Naropa University 2630
New England Conservatory 2631
New England School of Law 2632
New Mexico Highlands University 2633
New Mexico State University 2634
New York Botanical Garden 2635
New York University 2636
North Dakota State University 2637
Northern Illinois University 2638
Northern State University 2639
Notre Dame de Namur University 2640
Nyack College 2641
Ohio Northern University 2642
Ohio State University 2643
Ohio Wesleyan University 2644
Oregon State University 2645
Pacific College of Oriental Medicine 2646
Pacific University 2647
Parker College of Chiropractic 2648
Pennsylvania State University, Dickinson School of
Law 2649
PEO International Peace Scholarship Fund 2650
Pittsburg State University 2651
Princeton University, Woodrow Wilson School of
Public and International Affairs 2652
Purdue University 2653
Quincy University 2654
Reed College 2655
Rhode Island School of Design 2656
Rice University 2657
Rider University 2658
Roosevelt University 2659
Rowan University 2660
Russell Sage Colleges 2661
Rutgers, the State University of New Jersey
New Brunswick Campus 2662
Saint John's University 2663
Saint Joseph's University 2664
Saint Mary's College of California 2665
Saint Norbert College 2666
Saint Peter's College 2667
Saint Vincent College 2668
San Diego State University 2669
San Jose State University 2670
School for International Training 2671
Scripps Research Institute (The) 2672
Shippensburg University 2673
Siena College 2674
Simmons College 2675
Skidmore College 2676

Smithsonian Institution 2677
Society of Exploration Geophysicists - SEG Foundation
2678
Southeast Missouri State University 2679
Southeastern Louisiana University 2680
Southern Illinois University at Carbondale 2681
Southern Nazarene University 2682
Southern New Hampshire University 2683
Spring Hill College 2684
Stanford University 2685
State University of New York at Buffalo 2686
State University of New York at Geneseo 2687
State University of New York College at Fredonia
2688
State University of New York College at Purchase
2689
State University of New York Oswego 2690
Stephen F. Austin State University 2691
Stevens Institute of Technology 2692
Sweet Briar College 2693
Syracuse University 2694
Syracuse University, Maxwell School of Citizenship
and Public Affairs 2695
Texas A & M International University 2696
Texas A & M University 2697
Texas Woman's University 2698
Thunderbird - American Graduate School of
International Management 2699
Troy State University 2700
Truman State University 2701
Tufts University 2702
Tusculum College 2703
Union College 2704
University of Alaska, Fairbanks 2705
University of Arizona 2706
University of Arkansas 2707
University of California, Los Angeles 2708
University of California, San Francisco 2709
University of Chicago 2710
University of Delaware 2711
University of Denver 2712
University of Evansville 2713
University of Florida 2714
University of Georgia 2715
University of Hartford 2716
University of Hawaii at Manoa 2717
University of Iowa 2718
University of Kansas 2719
University of Maine 2720
University of Mary Hardin-Baylor 2721
University of Maryland, Baltimore County 2722
University of Michigan 2723
University of Missouri, St Louis 2724
University of Missouri-Columbia 2725
University of Nebraska at Kearney 2726
University of Nebraska-Lincoln 2727
University of New Mexico 2728
University of New Orleans 2729
University of Oregon 2730
University of Pennsylvania 2731
University of Puget Sound 2732
University of Rochester 2733
University of San Diego 2734
University of Texas at Brownsville and Texas
Southmost College 2735
University of the Arts 2736
University of the District of Columbia 2737
University of the Incarnate Word 2738
University of the South (Sewanee) 2739
University of Toledo 2740
University of Utah 2741
University of Washington 2742
University of Wisconsin-Madison 2743
University of Wisconsin-Whitewater 2744
University of Wyoming 2745
Valdosta State University 2746
Viterbo University 2747
Walsh University 2748
Washington and Lee University 2749
Washington State University 2750
Washington University in St. Louis 2751
Webber International University 2752

Western Illinois University 2753
Western Michigan University 2754
Western New England College 2755
Whitman College 2756
William Jewell College 2757
Williams College 2758

United States of America, Puerto Rico

Bayamón Central University 2759
University of Puerto Rico
  Biology Department
  College of Natural Sciences 2760
University of Puerto Rico 2761

Uruguay

Universidad Católica del Uruguay
  "Dámaso Antonio Larrañaga" 2762
Universidad de la Empresa 2763
Universidad ORT Uruguay 2764

Uzbekistan

Bukhara State University 2765
National University of Uzbekistan 2766
Tashkent State Economic University 2767
Tashkent State Pedagogical University 2768
University of World Economy and Diplomacy 2769
Uzbek Academy of Sciences, Arifov Institute of Electronics 2770
Uzbek Academy of Sciences, Institute of Chemistry 2771

Venezuela

Centro Interamericano de Desarrollo e Investigación Ambiental y Territorial 2772
Escuela de Malariología y Saneamiento Ambiental "Dr. Arnoldo Gabaldon" 2773
Instituto Venezolano de Investigaciones Científicas Centro de Estudios Avanzados 2774
Universidad Católica Santa Rosa 2775
Universidad Central de Venezuela
  Facultad de Medicina
  Escuela de Salud Pública 2776
Universidad Central de Venezuela Facultad de Medicina 2777
Universidad Central de Venezuela Instituto de Ciencia y Tecnología de Alimentos 2778

Viet Nam

Institut polytechnique de Hô Chi Minh-Ville 2779
Université de Can Tho 2780

Yemen

Hadhramout University for Science and Technology 2781
Ibb University 2782
Queen Arwa University 2783

Zambia

University of Zambia 2784

Zimbabwe

Bindura University of Science Education 2785
Midlands State University 2786

Index to Subjects of Study

[S] indicates scholarships / [C] indicates courses

Index des Domaines d'étude

[S] indique bourses / [C] indique cours

Índice de Materias de Estudio

[S] indique becas / [C] indique cursos

all major fields

[S] 5, 6, 13, 41, 46, 51; Arménie: 125; Australia: 135, 139, 140, 142, 143, 145, 146, 147, 151, 152, 154, 159, 160, 168, 169, 173, 174, 175, 178, 183, 184; Austria: 186, 188; Bulgaria: 320; Canada: 353, 358, 361, 365, 366, 373, 374, 377, 384, 385, 394, 395, 396, 404, 405, 409; China: 465, 481, 485; China, Hong Kong: 525, 527; Denmark: 677, 679; Estonia: 879, 880; Finland: 888, 889; Germany: 1085, 1091, 1093, 1095, 1103, 1104, 1116, 1143, 1144; Grèce: 1153, 1165; India: 1221, 1227; Indonesia: 1228, 1234; Iran, Islamic Republic of: 1248, 1254; Ireland: 1259; Israel: 1264, 1267, 1269; Italie: 1303, 1304; Jamaica: 1308; Japan: 1311, 1314, 1315, 1316, 1321, 1322, 1326, 1328, 1332, 1334, 1337, 1340, 1341, 1343, 1344, 1347, 1348, 1349, 1353, 1355, 1358, 1361, 1362, 1366, 1367, 1368, 1370, 1371, 1373, 1375, 1376, 1377, 1379, 1382, 1387, 1388, 1391, 1393, 1395, 1397; Jordan: 1406; Kazakhstan: 1419; Kenya: 1426; Mauritius: 1521; Netherlands: 1653, 1659; New Zealand: 1687, 1688, 1689, 1690, 1691; Nigeria: 1704; Norway: 1717; Philippines: 1797, 1800, 1806, 1807, 1815, 1818, 1823, 1824; Poland: 1828, 1881, 1883; Portugal: 1925; Qatar: 1928; Republic of Korea: 1932, 1934, 1936, 1938, 1948, 1949; Roumanie: 1967, 1969, 1970, 1974, 1975, 1976; Russian Federation: 1998, 2000, 2001; Singapore: 2149, 2150; Slovenia: 2175, 2177; South Africa: 2188, 2192, 2193; Sweden: 2235, 2253; Thailand: 2268, 2281; Turkey: 2321, 2322; Uganda: 2333; Ukraine: 2334, 2365; United Kingdom: 2373, 2375, 2382, 2385, 2392, 2397, 2399, 2401, 2411, 2414, 2430, 2432, 2434, 2436, 2439, 2440, 2442, 2443, 2447, 2450, 2451, 2454, 2458, 2460, 2463, 2470, 2471, 2476, 2479, 2481; United States of America: 2498, 2501, 2506, 2507, 2509, 2515, 2517, 2518, 2523, 2524, 2529, 2530, 2531, 2532, 2533, 2538, 2539, 2541, 2545, 2548, 2550, 2556, 2557, 2560, 2563, 2566, 2575, 2576, 2577, 2579, 2584, 2587, 2588, 2595, 2596, 2605, 2608, 2611, 2612, 2617, 2620, 2621, 2622, 2623, 2624, 2625, 2626, 2628, 2629, 2630, 2637, 2639, 2640, 2650, 2658, 2660, 2662, 2664, 2665, 2666, 2668, 2674, 2679, 2680, 2683, 2684, 2687, 2688, 2691, 2694, 2697, 2698, 2701, 2703, 2704, 2707, 2709, 2712, 2720, 2721, 2722, 2728, 2731, 2732, 2739, 2740, 2745, 2746, 2747, 2748, 2750, 2752, 2753, 2755, 2756; [C] Australia: 142, 143, 144, 145, 149, 150, 152, 154, 156, 157, 158, 159, 160, 161, 163, 164, 165, 166, 167, 168, 169, 170, 173, 175, 176, 177, 178, 179, 180, 181, 182, 183; Austria: 201; Bahrain: 213; Bangladesh: 221; Belgique: 256, 281; Botswana: 292; Canada: 354, 356, 359, 368, 370, 377, 378, 381, 382, 385, 394, 395, 396, 397, 399, 400, 401, 403, 406; China: 458, 468, 475, 478, 485, 487, 488, 492, 494, 498, 502, 508, 509, 517; China, Hong Kong: 524, 525, 527, 530; China, Macao: 532; Cyprus: 646; Czech Republic: 657, 661, 669; Denmark: 681, 685; Egypt: 704, 707; Estonia: 878, 882; Fiji: 886; Finland: 897; Georgia: 1079; Germany: 1124, 1129, 1138, 1139, 1141, 1142; Grèce: 1150, 1151, 1164, 1166, 1167; Hungary: 1196, 1198, 1199; Iceland: 1207; India: 1212, 1224; Indonesia: 1234, 1235; Iran, Islamic Republic of: 1246, 1248, 1250; Ireland: 1260; Israel: 1262, 1265; Italie: 1306, 1307; Japan: 1343; Jordan: 1407, 1410, 1412; Kazakhstan: 1413; Kuwait: 1427; Kyrgyzstan: 1431, 1432; Latvia: 1434, 1439; Liban: 1443, 1446; Lithuania: 1460, 1466, 1469; Malawi: 1485; Malaysia: 1486, 1489, 1490, 1491, 1492, 1493, 1494, 1495, 1497; Malta: 1499; Mauritius: 1521; Namibia: 1632; Netherlands: 1640, 1670, 1674, 1677; New Zealand: 1683, 1688, 1692, 1693; Nigeria: 1700, 1701, 1702, 1706, 1708, 1710, 1711; Norway: 1719, 1721, 1731, 1732; Palestinian Autonomous Territories: 1756; Philippines: 1797, 1800, 1814, 1818, 1820, 1823, 1824, 1826, 1827; Poland: 1857; Portugal: 1925; Republic of Korea: 1937, 1944, 1946, 1949; Roumanie: 1967, 1970, 1976; Russian Federation: 1979, 1984, 1985, 1986, 1988, 2001, 2005, 2017, 2019, 2029, 2053, 2099, 2109, 2116, 2130; Saudi Arabia: 2143; Singapore: 2150; Slovakia: 2162; Slovenia: 2179; Solomon Islands: 2180; South Africa: 2181, 2184, 2185, 2186, 2188, 2190, 2192, 2193, 2194; Sri Lanka: 2197; Sweden: 2236, 2238, 2243, 2251, 2252, 2255, 2258, 2259; Tajikistan: 2261, 2262; TFYR Macedonia: 2264; Thailand: 2268, 2269, 2275, 2277; Trinidad and Tobago: 2289; Turkey: 2320, 2321, 2325, 2326, 2330; Ukraine: 2339, 2342, 2360, 2362; United Arab Emirates: 2366; United Kingdom: 2374, 2375, 2379, 2382, 2392, 2393, 2398, 2399, 2402, 2403, 2404, 2408, 2409, 2410, 2424, 2426, 2433, 2435, 2437, 2438, 2440, 2441, 2442, 2443, 2444, 2445, 2446, 2447, 2448, 2449, 2450, 2451, 2452, 2453, 2459, 2461, 2462, 2463, 2466, 2467, 2468, 2469, 2471, 2473, 2474, 2477, 2479, 2481, 2482; United States of America: 2498, 2500, 2505, 2508, 2509, 2511, 2516, 2518, 2519, 2524, 2527, 2528, 2529, 2530, 2534, 2535, 2536, 2537, 2540, 2542, 2547, 2549, 2551, 2558, 2562, 2563, 2568, 2569, 2571, 2572, 2575, 2577, 2578, 2581, 2586, 2587, 2588, 2589, 2590, 2595, 2602, 2603, 2605, 2606, 2607, 2608, 2609, 2610, 2611, 2614, 2617, 2623, 2625, 2627, 2636, 2637, 2638, 2639, 2643, 2644, 2645, 2651, 2653, 2654, 2657, 2669, 2670, 2675, 2681, 2682, 2685, 2686, 2690, 2694, 2700, 2701, 2702, 2705, 2706, 2707, 2708, 2710, 2711, 2719, 2720, 2723, 2724, 2725, 2726, 2727, 2728, 2729, 2730, 2731, 2734, 2737, 2738, 2741, 2742, 2745, 2748, 2749, 2751, 2752, 2753, 2754, 2756; United States of America, Puerto Rico: 2761; Uzbekistan: 2768; Zambia: 2784.

todas las materias principales

[S] 13, 41, 43, 46; Argentina: 77, 96, 118; Chile: 410, 433; Colombia: 534, 541, 542; Costa Rica: 571; Cuba: 611; Ecuador: 687, 690; España: 712, 726, 756, 759, 780, 827, 839, 842, 851, 855, 872; Guatemala: 1169; México: 1532, 1538, 1554, 1555, 1601, 1618, 1624; Nicaragua: 1698; Panamá: 1757; Perú: 1786; [C] Argentina: 86, 87, 89, 98, 99, 100, 106, 107, 111, 113, 115, 116, 117, 119, 120, 122; Bolivia: 287; Chile: 423, 427, 430, 431, 432, 434, 445, 448, 450, 451, 452, 454; Colombia: 533, 535, 536, 538, 544, 546, 547, 549, 550, 551, 553, 556; Costa Rica: 560, 562, 572, 583, 584, 588, 590; Cuba: 599, 612, 613, 614, 616, 619, 620; Ecuador: 688, 691, 692, 694, 696, 698; El Salvador: 709; España: 748, 761, 776, 785, 786, 800, 801, 812, 821, 822, 823, 824, 827, 839, 841, 853, 855, 856, 857, 859, 860, 861, 865, 867, 870, 873, 874; Guatemala: 1170, 1171, 1172; México: 1524, 1550, 1555, 1556, 1559, 1563, 1564, 1566, 1568, 1569, 1570, 1573, 1574, 1575, 1576, 1579, 1580, 1581, 1584, 1586, 1588, 1589, 1592, 1593, 1595, 1596, 1599, 1602, 1603, 1606, 1607, 1610, 1611, 1614, 1615, 1618, 1619, 1620, 1622, 1627, 1628; Nicaragua: 1696; Panamá: 1758; Paraguay: 1762; Perú: 1772, 1775, 1776, 1778, 1780, 1785, 1786, 1788, 1794, 1796; República Dominicana: 1958, 1960, 1961; Uruguay: 2762.

toutes disciplines principales

[S] 5, 13, 41, 46; Albanie: 60; Algérie: 62; Belgique: 245, 276, 278; Brésil: 294, 298, 304; Cameroun: 350; Canada: 358, 386; France: 964, 968, 990, 992; Italie: 1274, 1279; Liban: 1452; Suisse: 2207, 2218, 2219; [C] Algérie: 64, 65, 67; Arménie: 128; Belarus, Republic of: 227, 243; Belgique: 252, 265, 272, 276, 278; Bénin: 284; Brésil: 302, 303, 312, 313; Bulgaria: 322, 325, 334, 343; Burkina Faso: 346; Canada: 386, 387, 388, 389, 390, 392; Comores, Les: 558; Congo: 559; France: 961, 967, 1021, 1022, 1023, 1026, 1030, 1031, 1032, 1034, 1035, 1040, 1042, 1043, 1046, 1048, 1052, 1071, 1075; Grèce: 1160, 1163; Italie: 1294; Liban: 1447, 1448, 1449, 1451, 1453, 1454, 1455; Luxembourg: 1472; Madagascar: 1477; Maroc: 1511, 1515, 1517; Poland: 1896; Portugal: 1921, 1923; République arabe syrienne: 1964; Suisse: 2223, 2225; Tunisie: 2293, 2316; Viet Nam: 2780.

accounting

[C] Arménie: 125, 127; Australia: 153, 161; Austria: 194; Azerbaijan: 206; Bangladesh: 218; Belgique: 274; Bulgaria: 321; Canada: 353, 371, 373, 398, 405; China: 496, 504, 520, 521; China, Hong Kong: 526; China, Macao: 531; Cyprus: 621, 624, 627, 628, 637, 642, 643; Czech Republic: 666; Denmark: 676; Eritrea: 711; Ethiopia: 884, 885; Fiji: 886; Finland: 890, 903; Georgia: 1080; Germany: 1088, 1089, 1135; Grèce: 1154, 1155; Hungary: 1184, 1201; India: 1222; Indonesia: 1228, 1232, 1236, 1238; Iran, Islamic Republic of: 1253; Ireland: 1255, 1257; Italie: 1280, 1301, 1302, 1304; Jamaica: 1309; Jordan: 1401, 1408, 1411; Kazakhstan: 1417, 1419; Kyrgyzstan: 1428, 1429; Latvia: 1436, 1440, 1441; Mauritius: 1522; Netherlands: 1654, 1666, 1667; Nigeria: 1704, 1707, 1709; Norway: 1718, 1725; Pakistan: 1736; Philippines: 1798, 1805, 1812, 1813, 1816; Poland: 1855, 1868, 1879, 1888, 1892; Portugal: 1917; Republic of Moldova: 1953, 1956; Roumanie: 1966; Russian Federation: 1988, 1989, 1991, 1995, 2004, 2007, 2025, 2027, 2057, 2070, 2082, 2106, 2110, 2114, 2117, 2123, 2126; Singapore: 2152, 2153; Slovakia: 2159; South Africa: 2181, 2189; Sweden: 2239, 2251; Tajikistan: 2260; Thailand: 2282; Turkey: 2319; Ukraine: 2338, 2340, 2346, 2347, 2351, 2356, 2361; United Kingdom: 2384, 2401, 2423, 2425; United Republic of Tanzania: 2490, 2491, 2494, 2495; United States of America: 2560, 2574, 2583, 2594, 2633, 2641, 2642, 2647, 2666, 2673, 2683, 2684, 2696, 2735, 2744; [S] China, Macao: 531; Germany: 1111; Ghana: 1145; Japan: 1381; Russian Federation: 2004, 2114; United Kingdom: 2384; United States of America: 2574.

administración

[C] 8; Argentina: 86, 93, 94, 95, 97, 98, 100, 106, 108, 121; Chile: 418, 424, 429, 436, 438, 440, 453; Colombia: 533; Costa Rica: 563, 567, 574, 578, 579, 581, 582, 585, 586, 589; Ecuador: 694; España: 744, 746, 748, 750, 765, 776, 777, 782, 836; México: 1526, 1528, 1543, 1550, 1552, 1575, 1582, 1590, 1596, 1607, 1608, 1609, 1611, 1612, 1613, 1623, 1626; Nicaragua: 1696; Panamá: 1758; Paraguay: 1761; Perú: 1764, 1765, 1769, 1775, 1779, 1795; Uruguay: 2763, 2764; Venezuela: 2776; [S] 42, 53; Ecuador: 693; España: 756, 771, 777; México: 1612, 1625; Perú: 1763, 1770, 1774, 1777.

administración de empresas

[S] 42; Argentina: 112; España: 714, 756, 777; México: 1616; Perú: 1763, 1766; [C] Andorra: 72; Argentina: 89,

91, 93, 98, 108, 123; Bolivia: 288; Chile: 436, 452; Colombia: 533, 539; Costa Rica: 560, 561, 563, 566, 574, 575, 578, 585, 593; Cuba: 615; Ecuador: 697; España: 715, 725, 744, 745, 747, 749, 750, 758, 761, 765, 775, 777, 790, 791, 797, 815, 836, 838, 840, 846, 871; Honduras: 1176; México: 1551, 1565, 1570, 1578, 1583, 1585, 1589, 1590, 1591, 1597, 1609, 1617, 1621, 1623; Nicaragua: 1696, 1697; Perú: 1764, 1769, 1779, 1792, 1795, 1796; República Dominicana: 1959; Uruguay: 2763.

administration
[S] 6, 42, 53; Canada: 400; China, Macao: 531; Czech Republic: 668; France: 1017; Ghana: 1145; Mauritius: 1522; United States of America: 2574, 2652; [C] 8; Algérie: 70; Arménie: 125, 129; Australia: 141; Austria: 194; Azerbaijan: 207; Belgique: 263, 277; Brésil: 313; Bulgaria: 321; Burundi: 347; Cambodge: 348; Cameroun: 350; Canada: 353, 360, 367, 388; China: 484, 496; China, Macao: 531; Côte d'Ivoire: 594, 596; Cyprus: 634, 638; Czech Republic: 666, 667; Denmark: 676; Estonia: 877; Finland: 903; France: 931, 980, 1054, 1056; Germany: 1098, 1105, 1106, 1108, 1112, 1113, 1126; Ghana: 1146; Grèce: 1154, 1158, 1160; Hungary: 1184; Indonesia: 1228, 1236; Ireland: 1255; Italie: 1277, 1290, 1300, 1301, 1302; Japan: 1329; Jordan: 1402; Kyrgyzstan: 1429, 1432; Liban: 1452; Lithuania: 1461; Maroc: 1513; Mauritius: 1522; Mongolia: 1631; Netherlands: 1649, 1653, 1667; New Zealand: 1694; Nigeria: 1709; Norway: 1718, 1724, 1725; Pakistan: 1736, 1737, 1747, 1748, 1749, 1754; Philippines: 1801, 1813, 1816, 1819, 1820, 1821; Poland: 1844, 1845, 1858, 1859, 1861, 1868, 1870, 1877, 1884, 1886, 1903, 1913, 1914; Republic of Korea: 1935, 1948, 1950; Republic of Moldova: 1953, 1954; République arabe syrienne: 1962; Roumanie: 1966; Russian Federation: 1988, 1989, 1992, 2016, 2065, 2066, 2082, 2108; South Africa: 2181, 2189, 2191; Suriname: 2232; Swaziland: 2233; Sweden: 2239; Tajikistan: 2261, 2262; Thailand: 2276; Togo: 2286; Turkey: 2319, 2320, 2321, 2323, 2324; Uganda: 2332, 2333; Ukraine: 2340, 2347, 2351, 2364; United Kingdom: 2384, 2399, 2401, 2423, 2425, 2432, 2436, 2478; United Republic of Tanzania: 2491, 2494; United States of America: 2512, 2557, 2574, 2587, 2617, 2652, 2659, 2660, 2667, 2679, 2683, 2684, 2695, 2696, 2730, 2743, 2746, 2749; Yemen: 2781.

administration des affaires
[C] Arménie: 129; Belgique: 253, 262; Burundi: 347; Canada: 393; France: 929, 976; Grèce: 1162; Liban: 1452; Madagascar: 1483; Togo: 2284, 2287; Tunisie: 2304; [S] France: 1005, 1017; Suisse: 2226; Tunisie: 2317.

advertising
[C] Canada: 353; Cyprus: 633, 637; Czech Republic: 666; Germany: 1088; Grèce: 1155; Hungary: 1201; India: 1219; Ireland: 1255; Kyrgyzstan: 1429; Latvia: 1441; Netherlands: 1667; Poland: 1862; Republic of Korea: 1935; Russian Federation: 1990, 2000, 2025, 2065, 2082; South Africa: 2181, 2189; United Kingdom: 2384; United States of America: 2557, 2574, 2659, 2660, 2683, 2684; [S] United States of America: 2574.

aeroespacio
[S] 59.

aerospace
[S] 59; [C] United Kingdom: 2472.

aérospace
[S] 59.

affaires
[C] Arménie: 129; Brésil: 298, 301; Bulgaria: 316, 342; Burundi: 347; Canada: 393; France: 980, 981, 996, 1021, 1057; Tunisie: 2306, 2313; [S] Brésil: 301; France: 1005.

affaires internationales
[C] Arménie: 129; Belgique: 262; France: 930, 976, 1003, 1053, 1058; Grèce: 1160; Saint-Siège: 2141; [S] Belgique: 246; France: 1005, 1017; Madagascar: 1483.

African studies
[C] Germany: 1135; Ghana: 1149; South Africa: 2187, 2191; Uganda: 2333; United Kingdom: 2473; United States of America: 2529; [S] Kenya: 1420.

agricultura
[S] 12, 17, 34, 46; [C] 21, 27; Argentina: 80; Chile: 415; Cuba: 600, 615, 617; España: 737, 763, 772, 863; Honduras: 1179; México: 1530, 1558, 1562, 1586; Perú: 1781.

agriculture
[S] 12, 34, 46; Arménie: 126; Australia: 141, 169; Brésil: 301, 305; Cameroun: 349; Canada: 369, 401; France: 974; Germany: 1110; Ghana: 1148; Netherlands: 1639; Ukraine: 2334; United Kingdom: 2386, 2417; United States of America: 2634; Yemen: 2782; [C] 21, 27; Algérie: 68, 71; Angola: 74; Arménie: 126; Australia: 140, 141, 142, 153,

182; Bangladesh: 216; Belgique: 250, 258, 263, 274, 275, 282; Belize: 283; Bosnia and Herzegovina: 291; Brésil: 301, 305, 311; Bulgaria: 321, 323, 338; Cameroun: 351; Canada: 369, 374; China: 505, 522, 523; Czech Republic: 671; Egypt: 699, 703, 706; Estonia: 876; Ethiopia: 884; Fiji: 886; France: 909, 935, 942, 993, 1011, 1012, 1019; Germany: 1102, 1137; Ghana: 1146; Grèce: 1154, 1155, 1156, 1159, 1160; Guyana: 1173, 1174; Hungary: 1187, 1193, 1200; India: 1208; Indonesia: 1229, 1236, 1239; Iran, Islamic Republic of: 1241, 1254; Israel: 1261; Italie: 1280, 1300; Jamaica: 1310; Japan: 1350, 1380; Jordan: 1400, 1405; Kyrgyzstan: 1431; Lithuania: 1464; Malaysia: 1493; Malta: 1499; Maroc: 1504; Mauritius: 1521; Nepal: 1633; Netherlands: 1642, 1649, 1651, 1652, 1681, 1682; Niger: 1699; Nigeria: 1704, 1707, 1709; Oman: 1733; Philippines: 1804, 1806, 1821; Poland: 1842, 1843, 1879, 1896, 1908; Republic of Korea: 1939; Roumanie: 1972, 1973; Russian Federation: 1999, 2040, 2045, 2069, 2073, 2074, 2120, 2126, 2136; Slovakia: 2163; South Africa: 2181, 2191; Sri Lanka: 2197, 2201, 2202; Sudan: 2205; Suisse: 2208, 2227; Suriname: 2229, 2232; Swaziland: 2233, 2234; Sweden: 2254; Tajikistan: 2262; Thailand: 2268, 2272, 2280; Turkey: 2326, 2327, 2329; Uganda: 2333; Ukraine: 2334, 2343; United Kingdom: 2380, 2386, 2405, 2406, 2432, 2460, 2467, 2476; United Republic of Tanzania: 2493; United States of America: 2620, 2634, 2653, 2679, 2707, 2714, 2720; Uzbekistan: 2765, 2767; Zimbabwe: 2785, 2786.

agronomic sciences
[C] 27; Canada: 374; China: 486, 505, 522, 523; Czech Republic: 658; Estonia: 876; Ethiopia: 884; Germany: 1137; Grèce: 1155; Hungary: 1187, 1193; India: 1208; Indonesia: 1236; Iran, Islamic Republic of: 1241; Israel: 1261, 1263; Italie: 1300, 1301; Japan: 1350, 1380; Kenya: 1422; Liban: 1443; Lithuania: 1464; Netherlands: 1681, 1682; Nigeria: 1703, 1709; Norway: 1725; Poland: 1908; Portugal: 1927; Roumanie: 1966, 1973; Russian Federation: 1999, 2069, 2120, 2126, 2136; Slovakia: 2163; Sri Lanka: 2197; Sweden: 2254; Thailand: 2272; Uganda: 2333; Ukraine: 2334, 2355; United Kingdom: 2386; United Republic of Tanzania: 2493; [S] Arménie: 126; Ukraine: 2334; United Kingdom: 2386.

alemán
[S] México: 1594.

alimentación
[C] 16; Argentina: 101, 103; Chile: 426; Costa Rica: 575; España: 721, 740, 794, 830, 865; México: 1564, 1573; Venezuela: 2778.

alimentation
[C] 16; Brésil: 300; Bulgaria: 327; France: 909, 935, 1019, 1036; Maroc: 1502.

allemand
[C] Belarus, Republic of: 243; Belgique: 261; France: 1001, 1033; Tunisie: 2291.

American studies
[C] 25; Canada: 379; Czech Republic: 660; Finland: 903; Germany: 1090, 1135; Italie: 1301; Russian Federation: 2065; United Kingdom: 2398; United States of America: 2574, 2655, 2666; [S] Denmark: 680; Japan: 1392; United States of America: 2574.

anatomía
[C] Argentina: 104.

anatomie
[C] Bulgaria: 319; Cameroun: 350.

anatomy
[C] Canada: 353; Ethiopia: 883; Germany: 1137; Iran, Islamic Republic of: 1242, 1251; Italie: 1304; Japan: 1327, 1335; Kyrgyzstan: 1432; Mongolia: 1630; Netherlands: 1657; Nigeria: 1704; Poland: 1840, 1873, 1874; Russian Federation: 2006; Tajikistan: 2262; Trinidad and Tobago: 2290; United Kingdom: 2452; United States of America: 2537, 2575, 2615, 2623, 2624, 2659; [S] United States of America: 2624.

anglais
[C] Algérie: 63, 68, 71; Belarus, Republic of: 243; Belgique: 261; France: 1001, 1033; Maroc: 1511, 1513, 1516; Tunisie: 2291, 2303, 2304, 2307, 2309, 2313; [S] Tunisie: 2291.

anthropologie
[C] Belgique: 261; Brésil: 309; Cameroun: 350; Côte d'Ivoire: 597; France: 909, 1001, 1036; Madagascar: 1479; Maroc: 1505; Suisse: 2215.

anthropology
[C] Canada: 353, 371, 383, 385, 398, 405; India: 1213, 1220, 1223; Ireland: 1259; Italie: 1286; Kyrgyzstan: 1432; Mongolia: 1631; Pakistan: 1737, 1747, 1752; Poland: 1886;

Portugal: 1927; Russian Federation: 1992, 2065; Slovakia: 2167; Slovenia: 2176; Sri Lanka: 2197; Tajikistan: 2261; United States of America: 2529, 2537, 2613, 2633, 2647, 2655, 2689; [S] Canada: 383; United Kingdom: 2464; United States of America: 2677.

antropología
[C] Chile: 428; El Salvador: 710; España: 734; México: 1527, 1533, 1571, 1581, 1605; Perú: 1790; Venezuela: 2774; [S] México: 1527.

applied arts
[C] Australia: 141; Austria: 197; Azerbaijan: 209; Barbados: 222; Canada: 354, 367, 383, 405; Cyprus: 627; Germany: 1090, 1101, 1133; Hungary: 1188, 1200; Japan: 1342; Lithuania: 1467; Netherlands: 1676; Norway: 1720, 1725; Poland: 1834, 1892; Russian Federation: 1990, 2000, 2027; Slovakia: 2155; South Africa: 2181; Sri Lanka: 2197; Suisse: 2227; Turkey: 2320; United Kingdom: 2398, 2432, 2461, 2483; United States of America: 2524, 2529, 2545, 2557, 2560, 2656, 2666, 2747; Uzbekistan: 2765; [S] Canada: 383; Japan: 1342; United Kingdom: 2483.

applied sciences
[C] Australia: 161, 179; Austria: 190; Barbados: 222; Belgique: 274; Canada: 353, 367, 374, 405; China: 457, 504, 521, 523; Czech Republic: 653; Germany: 1083, 1087, 1135; Grèce: 1154, 1155; Ireland: 1257; Italie: 1278; Japan: 1398; Jordan: 1400; Malta: 1499; Nigeria: 1709; Poland: 1874, 1892; Portugal: 1925; Russian Federation: 1980, 1982, 1988, 1990, 2042, 2049, 2050, 2063, 2066, 2084, 2087; South Africa: 2189; Sri Lanka: 2197; Thailand: 2271; Turkey: 2330; Ukraine: 2351, 2354; United Kingdom: 2386, 2472; United States of America: 2673, 2735, 2746; Uzbekistan: 2770; Yemen: 2781; [S] United Kingdom: 2386, 2417, 2443, 2483.

arabe
[C] Algérie: 63, 71; France: 1033; Maroc: 1508, 1511, 1513, 1516; Saint-Siège: 2139; Tunisie: 2291, 2303, 2304; [S] México: 1529; Tunisie: 2291.

Arabic
[C] Azerbaijan: 207; Egypt: 699; Iran, Islamic Republic of: 1253; Jordan: 1401, 1408; Pakistan: 1734, 1740; Russian Federation: 2117; Tajikistan: 2260; United Kingdom: 2480; Yemen: 2781; [S] Jordan: 1406; Kuwait: 1427; Liban: 1445; Yemen: 2783.

archaeology
[C] Azerbaijan: 209; Belgique: 255; China: 493, 499; Cyprus: 623; Hungary: 1184; Kyrgyzstan: 1432; Mongolia: 1631; Norway: 1729; Pakistan: 1752; Poland: 1886, 1915; Republic of Korea: 1929; Republic of Moldova: 1954; Russian Federation: 2065; Slovakia: 2161, 2170; Sri Lanka: 2197; Turkey: 2319, 2320; United Kingdom: 2375, 2452, 2476; United States of America: 2529, 2679, 2745, 2749; [S] Italie: 1273; Kenya: 1420; United Kingdom: 2372, 2381, 2444; United States of America: 2559, 2582, 2677.

archéologie
[C] France: 927, 938, 1047, 1063; Gabon: 1078; Italie: 1295; Madagascar: 1479; Maroc: 1505; Saint-Siège: 2138; Tunisie: 2304; [S] Italie: 1270; Saint-Siège: 2138.

architecture
[C] 21, 26; Algérie: 71; Angola: 74; Australia: 136, 179; Austria: 185, 197; Bangladesh: 214, 216; Belarus, Republic of: 227, 231; Belgique: 249, 263, 268, 269, 270, 271, 275; Brésil: 298, 307; Bulgaria: 324; Canada: 405; China: 481, 496, 497, 506, 515, 523; Czech Republic: 647, 651, 662, 663; Denmark: 675; Finland: 892, 894; France: 916, 917, 918, 919, 920, 924, 943; Germany: 1083, 1099, 1100, 1117, 1121, 1133, 1134; Grèce: 1160; Hungary: 1186, 1188, 1192, 1194; India: 1214; Indonesia: 1228; Iran, Islamic Republic of: 1244, 1253; Italie: 1290, 1300; Jamaica: 1309; Japan: 1311, 1342, 1369, 1379, 1389; Jordan: 1411; Kazakhstan: 1415; Kyrgyzstan: 1432; Liban: 1443, 1449; Liechtenstein: 1457; Lithuania: 1459, 1467, 1468; Madagascar: 1478; Malta: 1499; Maroc: 1505; Netherlands: 1636, 1638, 1647; New Zealand: 1694; Nigeria: 1703, 1709; Philippines: 1809, 1811, 1816; Poland: 1883, 1890, 1895, 1900; Portugal: 1917; Republic of Korea: 1931, 1948; Russian Federation: 1978, 1980, 1992, 2000, 2015, 2034, 2064, 2065, 2124, 2127, 2131, 2133; Singapore: 2153; Slovakia: 2154, 2155, 2164, 2166; South Africa: 2181, 2189; Sri Lanka: 2200; Suisse: 2209, 2210, 2221; Suriname: 2232; Sweden: 2248, 2254; Tajikistan: 2261, 2262; Thailand: 2271; Togo: 2285; Turkey: 2320, 2323, 2326, 2327, 2329; Uganda: 2333; Ukraine: 2337, 2356; United Kingdom: 2387, 2399, 2401, 2425, 2431, 2452, 2460, 2481; United States of America: 2554, 2557, 2580, 2619, 2656, 2679, 2730; Yemen: 2781; [S] Australia: 132; Bangladesh: 214, 217; Iran, Islamic Republic of: 1244; Italie: 1273, 1287; Japan: 1342; United Kingdom: 2381, 2387, 2453; United States of America: 2559, 2582.

architecture paysagiste
[C] France: 924, 973.

arqueología
[C] Chile: 446; El Salvador: 710; México: 1533.

arquitectura
[C] 21, 26; Bolivia: 288, 289; Chile: 423, 434, 449; Costa Rica: 576, 593; Cuba: 609; España: 739, 777, 828, 851, 862; México: 1536, 1560, 1565, 1585, 1596, 1607, 1611, 1621; Nicaragua: 1695; Perú: 1775, 1783, 1795; Uruguay: 2764; [S] Ecuador: 693; España: 741, 777; Perú: 1774.

art history
[C] Austria: 185, 204; Azerbaijan: 209; Canada: 353, 371; China: 465; Finland: 903; Germany: 1131; Hungary: 1188; India: 1222; Italie: 1285, 1290; Latvia: 1441; Lithuania: 1467; Mongolia: 1631; Netherlands: 1653; Poland: 1834, 1835; Russian Federation: 1989, 2027, 2031, 2065; Slovakia: 2161, 2170; South Africa: 2181; Suisse: 2227; Tajikistan: 2261; Turkey: 2319, 2320; Ukraine: 2356; United Kingdom: 2375, 2378, 2398, 2399, 2401, 2432, 2452, 2483; United States of America: 2529, 2576, 2633, 2655, 2656, 2659, 2679, 2745, 2749; [S] United Kingdom: 2483; United States of America: 2559, 2677.

artes
[C] 26; Argentina: 114; Chile: 447; Cuba: 604; España: 835, 842, 862, 865; México: 1565, 1598, 1613; Perú: 1767, 1795; [S] Colombia: 542; Perú: 1767.

artes aplicadas
[C] Argentina: 114; España: 862; México: 1536, 1549; Perú: 1767, 1795; [S] Perú: 1767.

artes décorativas
[C] México: 1617.

artes del espectáculo
[C] Argentina: 119; Cuba: 604; [S] Colombia: 542.

artes gráficas
[C] México: 1535, 1611; Perú: 1767; [S] Perú: 1767.

artes plásticas
[C] Argentina: 114; Cuba: 604; México: 1535; Perú: 1767; [S] Colombia: 542; España: 759; Perú: 1767.

artesanía
[C] Argentina: 114.

artisanat
[C] France: 957.

arts
[C] 26; Australia: 134, 147, 158, 161, 162; Austria: 185, 204; Bangladesh: 220; Barbados: 222; Belgique: 244, 248, 275; Bermuda: 285; Bulgaria: 337, 340; Cameroun: 351; Canada: 353, 355, 360, 364, 367, 373, 375, 379, 382, 388, 390, 393, 398, 405; China: 463, 464, 465, 491, 493; China, Hong Kong: 529; Cyprus: 640; Czech Republic: 648; Egypt: 699, 706; Fiji: 886; Finland: 895; France: 957, 1062, 1069; Germany: 1101, 1109, 1131; Guyana: 1174; Hungary: 1188; India: 1225; Ireland: 1256, 1257; Italie: 1272, 1280, 1289, 1291, 1295; Japan: 1364; Jordan: 1402, 1403, 1409, 1411, 1412; Kenya: 1421; Kuwait: 1427; Liban: 1449; Madagascar: 1479; Maroc: 1505; Mongolia: 1631; Netherlands: 1636, 1676; New Zealand: 1694; Norway: 1720, 1725, 1731; Pakistan: 1736, 1749; Philippines: 1811, 1817; Poland: 1834, 1835, 1867, 1870, 1898; Republic of Korea: 1935; Republic of Moldova: 1953, 1955; Russian Federation: 1980, 1986, 2008, 2022, 2027, 2055, 2065, 2094; Sénégal: 2145; Serbia and Montenegro: 2148; Slovakia: 2155, 2156, 2157, 2161, 2170; South Africa: 2181, 2189; Sri Lanka: 2198, 2201; Suriname: 2228; Sweden: 2241, 2256; Tajikistan: 2261; Thailand: 2271, 2274; Turkey: 2321, 2324, 2326, 2329, 2330; United Kingdom: 2375, 2376, 2388, 2398, 2399, 2401, 2427, 2431, 2432, 2460, 2479, 2483; United Republic of Tanzania: 2492, 2496; United States of America: 2524, 2560, 2561, 2574, 2583, 2587, 2613, 2617, 2618, 2619, 2620, 2624, 2627, 2633, 2634, 2647, 2656, 2660, 2661, 2666, 2713, 2714, 2716, 2735, 2736, 2745, 2746, 2747, 2754; [S] Australia: 141, 147, 161; Canada: 364, 389, 403; Germany: 1109; Ghana: 1148; Italie: 1273; Japan: 1338, 1351, 1378; Pakistan: 1739; Suisse: 2218; United Kingdom: 2372, 2381, 2443, 2483; United States of America: 2499, 2510, 2574, 2582, 2601, 2624, 2634, 2647, 2677; Yemen: 2782.

arts and crafts
[C] Austria: 185, 196; China: 464; Cyprus: 640; Hungary: 1188; Italie: 1290; Japan: 1359; Latvia: 1436; Norway: 1712, 1714, 1720, 1725; Russian Federation: 2000, 2009, 2027; Slovakia: 2155, 2170; Tajikistan: 2261; Ukraine: 2357; United Kingdom: 2398, 2399, 2483; United States of America: 2544, 2656; [S] United Kingdom: 2483.

arts appliqués
[C] Belgique: 248; Bulgaria: 318; France: 911, 957; Sénégal: 2145; [S] Suisse: 2218.

arts décoratifs
[C] Belarus, Republic of: 226; Belgique: 244, 248; Brésil: 298; Liban: 1449; Sénégal: 2145.

arts du spectacle
[C] Belarus, Republic of: 226; Bulgaria: 315, 317; France: 1004, 1033; Tunisie: 2311.

arts graphiques
[C] Belarus, Republic of: 226; Belgique: 244, 248; France: 911; Liban: 1449; Sénégal: 2145; Tunisie: 2312; [S] France: 911; Suisse: 2218; Tunisie: 2317.

arts plastiques
[C] Belgique: 244, 248; France: 911, 920, 943; Liban: 1449; [S] France: 911; Suisse: 2218.

Asian studies
[S] 46; Canada: 364; Japan: 1330, 1338; Republic of Korea: 1948; [C] Australia: 165; Canada: 405; Japan: 1330, 1338, 1344; Mauritius: 1519; Mongolia: 1631; Philippines: 1810; Republic of Korea: 1941, 1944, 1950, 1952; Sri Lanka: 2199; United States of America: 2529, 2535, 2606, 2666, 2719, 2749.

assistance sociale
[C] Belarus, Republic of: 229; Belgique: 259; Brésil: 299, 301; [S] Brésil: 301.

astronomía
[S] 22; [C] Chile: 438.

astronomie
[S] 22; [C] France: 1018; Italie: 1276.

astronomy
[S] 22; United States of America: 2677; [C] Canada: 371, 379, 385; China: 493; Mongolia: 1631; United States of America: 2529, 2576, 2666.

audio-visual media
[C] Australia: 140; Austria: 190, 196; Canada: 407; Cyprus: 633; Czech Republic: 666; Egypt: 701; Estonia: 879; Finland: 895, 903; Georgia: 1080; Germany: 1087, 1099, 1101, 1117; Indonesia: 1229; Italie: 1280; Netherlands: 1660, 1662; Republic of Korea: 1935; Russian Federation: 2027; Singapore: 2152; Slovakia: 2155; South Africa: 2181; Sweden: 2240; United Kingdom: 2384, 2400, 2472; United States of America: 2554, 2557, 2636, 2647, 2736.

aviation, aeronautics
[C] Austria: 190; China: 497; Germany: 1083, 1114; Italie: 1290; Lithuania: 1468; Russian Federation: 2000, 2051, 2070, 2102, 2105, 2135; Trinidad and Tobago: 2288; Turkey: 2323; Ukraine: 2351, 2358; United Kingdom: 2399, 2401, 2452; United States of America: 2540, 2565, 2754; [S] Germany: 1114.

aviation, aéronautique
[C] France: 936, 951, 953.

bacteriología
[C] Venezuela: 2777.

bactériologie
[C] France: 1010, 1011; Portugal: 1926.

bacteriology
[C] Iran, Islamic Republic of: 1242; Italie: 1304; Japan: 1327, 1335, 1336; Mongolia: 1630; Poland: 1873; South Africa: 2182; Tajikistan: 2262; United States of America: 2615, 2624.

bâtiment, construction
[C] Algérie: 68, 71; Belarus, Republic of: 227, 231; Belgique: 270; Côte d'Ivoire: 596; France: 920, 924, 934, 943, 945, 973, 1057; Madagascar: 1478.

beaux-arts
[C] Belgique: 244, 248; Bulgaria: 318; France: 911; Italie: 1271; Liban: 1449; Tunisie: 2312; [S] Suisse: 2218.

bellas artes
[S] Colombia: 542; Perú: 1767; [C] México: 1535, 1570; Perú: 1767.

biblioteconomía
[C] Chile: 447; España: 733, 871.

bibliothéconomie
[C] Arménie: 129; Burundi: 347; France: 938, 962, 1063; Sénégal: 2146.

biochemistry
[C] Austria: 191; Bahrain: 210; Belgique: 274; Canada: 371, 385, 405; China: 457, 490, 504; Czech Republic: 653; Denmark: 686; Finland: 892, 894, 898; Germany: 1083, 1135, 1137, 1143; Grèce: 1154; Iceland: 1206; Iran, Islamic Republic of: 1251; Japan: 1327, 1335, 1380; Kazakhstan: 1416; Kenya: 1425; Mongolia: 1631; Nigeria: 1703, 1704, 1707, 1709; Pakistan: 1738, 1742, 1748, 1751, 1753, 1754; Poland: 1829, 1840, 1874, 1877, 1908; Russian Federation: 2044; Slovakia: 2164; South Africa: 2182, 2189; Sweden: 2254; Thailand: 2271; Trinidad and Tobago: 2290; Turkey: 2329; Ukraine: 2353; United Kingdom: 2386, 2399, 2401, 2472; United States of America: 2561, 2576, 2642, 2655, 2660, 2666, 2684, 2692, 2746, 2747, 2749; [S] China: 482; Japan: 1389; South Africa: 2186; Thailand: 2274; United Kingdom: 2386.

biochimie
[S] 20; Canada: 391; France: 925; [C] Algérie: 63, 68, 71; Brésil: 295; France: 1011; Italie: 1296; Tunisie: 2309.

biofísica
[C] España: 735; Venezuela: 2774, 2777.

biología
[S] 20, 50; Bolivia: 286; Colombia: 548; Cuba: 611; España: 759; Perú: 1774; [C] Argentina: 103, 109, 123; Chile: 416, 446; Cuba: 599; España: 735, 737, 833, 873; México: 1543, 1545, 1561, 1565, 1567, 1570, 1572, 1575, 1577, 1581; Perú: 1775; Venezuela: 2774, 2777.

biología marina
[C] Costa Rica: 575; España: 779; México: 1560, 1561; [S] España: 778.

biologie
[S] 20, 50; Canada: 391; France: 974; [C] Algérie: 63, 68, 70, 71; Belarus, Republic of: 236, 238, 239, 243; Belgique: 261; Brésil: 295, 298, 299, 306; Bulgaria: 332, 333; Cameroun: 350; France: 969, 971, 1010, 1011; Gabon: 1078; Grèce: 1159; Italie: 1296; Maroc: 1506, 1509, 1512, 1516; Portugal: 1922; Tchad: 2263; Tunisie: 2309.

biologie marine
[C] Tunisie: 2309.

biology
[S] 50; Australia: 169; Canada: 383; China: 482; Russian Federation: 2004; United Kingdom: 2371; United States of America: 2574, 2672, 2677; United States of America, Puerto Rico: 2760; [C] Arménie: 127; Australia: 141, 165, 166; Azerbaijan: 208; Belgique: 254, 255; Canada: 353, 366, 371, 373, 374, 383, 385, 398, 405, 408; China: 490; Czech Republic: 649, 671; Denmark: 686; Egypt: 700, 706; Eritrea: 711; Ethiopia: 883, 884, 885; Finland: 894, 896, 898, 902; Germany: 1090, 1097, 1135, 1137; Grèce: 1154; Hungary: 1193; India: 1213, 1220, 1225; Indonesia: 1236; Iran, Islamic Republic of: 1241, 1253; Italie: 1300, 1304; Japan: 1335; Jordan: 1409; Kazakhstan: 1416, 1419; Kyrgyzstan: 1429, 1430; Mongolia: 1630, 1631; Netherlands: 1646, 1682; Nigeria: 1703, 1704, 1707, 1709; Norway: 1729; Philippines: 1806, 1807, 1816, 1825; Poland: 1874, 1905, 1908; Roumanie: 1974; Russian Federation: 1986, 1999, 2004, 2009, 2022, 2037, 2044, 2063, 2069, 2071, 2073, 2074, 2079, 2080, 2097, 2134, 2137; Slovakia: 2160, 2167, 2169; Sri Lanka: 2197; Sweden: 2240, 2248, 2254; Thailand: 2271; Turkey: 2330; United Kingdom: 2405, 2406, 2432, 2436, 2460, 2462, 2472; United States of America: 2529, 2553, 2561, 2574, 2576, 2594, 2617, 2619, 2633, 2642, 2647, 2655, 2659, 2660, 2666, 2673, 2684, 2696, 2735, 2747; Uzbekistan: 2766.

biophysics
[C] Canada: 371; Egypt: 700; Germany: 1135; Japan: 1335; Nigeria: 1709; Poland: 1874; Russian Federation: 2044, 2085; South Africa: 2182; Thailand: 2271; Turkey: 2326; United Kingdom: 2401, 2472; [S] Japan: 1389.

biophysique
[C] Belarus, Republic of: 229; France: 1029; Italie: 1276; Tunisie: 2309; [S] Canada: 391.

bioquímica
[S] 20; España: 759; [C] Argentina: 103, 109, 123; Chile: 416, 444; Cuba: 606, 607; España: 728, 735, 794; México: 1545; Venezuela: 2774, 2777.

book development and production
[C] India: 1213; Russian Federation: 2043; Uganda: 2331; United Kingdom: 2401; United States of America: 2656, 2689.

botánica
[C] Chile: 416; España: 737, 763, 772, 863; México: 1530; [S] España: 778.

botanique
[C] Belgique: 261; Brésil: 295; Bulgaria: 323; Cambodge: 348; France: 1011; Niger: 1699; Tunisie: 2309.

botany

[C] Canada: 374, 405; Germany: 1135, 1137; Grèce: 1154; Iran, Islamic Republic of: 1241, 1253; Italie: 1304; Kenya: 1425; Netherlands: 1682; Nigeria: 1703, 1704, 1707, 1709; Pakistan: 1742, 1748, 1752, 1753; Russian Federation: 2076; United States of America: 2617; Yemen: 2781; [S] South Africa: 2186; United States of America: 2635.

building industry
[C] Australia: 182; Austria: 190; Belgique: 274; China: 497, 506, 523; Ethiopia: 883; Ireland: 1257; Italie: 1290, 1300; Japan: 1379, 1389; Kazakhstan: 1415; Lithuania: 1468; Netherlands: 1647; Nigeria: 1703; Norway: 1713, 1715; Roumanie: 1971; Russian Federation: 1978, 1992, 2000, 2015, 2020, 2035, 2060, 2064, 2105, 2118, 2131; Singapore: 2153; Slovakia: 2165; South Africa: 2189; Uganda: 2333; Ukraine: 2337, 2356; United Kingdom: 2387, 2401, 2425, 2431, 2432, 2436, 2481; United States of America: 2557; [S] United Kingdom: 2387, 2475.

business
[S] 42; Australia: 141, 147, 161; China, Macao: 531; Cyprus: 621, 633; Czech Republic: 668; Germany: 1096, 1111, 1114, 1125; Japan: 1320, 1399; Netherlands: 1670; Russian Federation: 2081, 2114; United Kingdom: 2384; United States of America: 2574, 2598, 2624; [C] Arménie: 125; Australia: 140, 141, 147, 153, 158, 161, 162, 166, 174, 179; Austria: 190, 203; Azerbaijan: 206, 207; Bangladesh: 220; Barbados: 222; Belgique: 263, 273, 275; Belize: 283; Bermuda: 285; Canada: 353, 354, 357, 360, 373, 374, 398, 405; China: 496, 504, 507; China, Hong Kong: 528; China, Macao: 531; Croatia: 598; Cyprus: 621, 627, 633, 637, 638, 639, 643; Czech Republic: 662, 667; Denmark: 676; Egypt: 699, 706; Finland: 890, 901, 903; Georgia: 1081; Germany: 1083, 1087, 1088, 1089, 1090, 1102, 1108, 1109, 1112, 1122, 1126, 1132, 1133, 1134, 1135; Hungary: 1184, 1193, 1198, 1201; Iceland: 1204, 1206; India: 1219, 1222, 1225; Indonesia: 1229; Iran, Islamic Republic of: 1252, 1254; Ireland: 1255, 1256; Italie: 1286, 1301; Jamaica: 1310; Japan: 1311, 1312, 1313, 1316, 1322, 1331, 1344, 1359, 1364, 1390; Kazakhstan: 1414, 1417; Kenya: 1425; Kyrgyzstan: 1428, 1430, 1432, 1433; Latvia: 1436, 1437, 1441; Liechtenstein: 1457; Malaysia: 1488, 1496; Mauritius: 1522; Mongolia: 1631; Netherlands: 1635, 1644, 1654, 1655, 1664, 1666, 1667; Nigeria: 1709; Norway: 1718; Pakistan: 1736, 1754; Philippines: 1816; Poland: 1847, 1866, 1876, 1877, 1888, 1892, 1893, 1901, 1902, 1906, 1908, 1916; Portugal: 1925; Republic of Korea: 1947, 1950; Republic of Moldova: 1953; Roumanie: 1966; Russian Federation: 1978, 1979, 1985, 1989, 1992, 1993, 1994, 1996, 2000, 2016, 2064, 2065, 2066, 2069, 2072, 2079, 2081, 2082, 2084, 2093, 2098, 2102, 2106, 2107, 2108, 2114, 2121, 2122, 2124, 2136; Slovakia: 2159, 2163, 2168; South Africa: 2181, 2189, 2191; Suisse: 2217, 2227; Sweden: 2239, 2248, 2251; Tajikistan: 2260, 2261, 2262; Thailand: 2276, 2282; Turkey: 2320; Uganda: 2333; Ukraine: 2334, 2338, 2343, 2347, 2359; United Kingdom: 2384, 2399, 2401, 2405, 2425, 2432, 2436, 2460, 2461, 2472, 2474, 2476, 2482; United Republic of Tanzania: 2491; United States of America: 2502, 2508, 2518, 2530, 2542, 2545, 2558, 2561, 2564, 2565, 2574, 2575, 2594, 2609, 2613, 2618, 2620, 2621, 2624, 2627, 2647, 2659, 2663, 2666, 2679, 2683, 2684, 2685, 2692, 2700, 2707, 2713, 2719, 2720, 2730, 2749; Uzbekistan: 2765, 2767.

business administration
[S] 42; Australia: 140; Bangladesh: 214, 217; China, Macao: 531; Cyprus: 621, 639; Czech Republic: 667; Estonia: 881; Germany: 1125; Japan: 1312, 1324, 1331, 1356; Netherlands: 1639; Russian Federation: 2114; United Kingdom: 2384, 2395, 2396; United States of America: 2552, 2574, 2634, 2696; Yemen: 2783; [C] Arménie: 125; Australia: 153, 161, 162; Austria: 193, 195, 198; Azerbaijan: 205, 206, 209; Bangladesh: 214, 218; Belgique: 255, 274; Bermuda: 285; Bulgaria: 321; Canada: 353, 355, 356, 366, 367, 373, 374, 379, 382, 385; China: 457, 465, 486, 497, 499, 504, 516, 521, 523; China, Hong Kong: 526, 528, 529; China, Macao: 531; Cyprus: 621, 625, 627, 631, 632, 639, 642; Czech Republic: 666, 667; Denmark: 676, 686; Estonia: 877, 879, 881; Ethiopia: 885; Finland: 891; Germany: 1083, 1087, 1088, 1089, 1097, 1098, 1099, 1105, 1108, 1113, 1122, 1126, 1134, 1135, 1137; Grèce: 1154, 1155; Hungary: 1183, 1184, 1193; Iceland: 1202; India: 1219, 1222, 1223; Indonesia: 1228, 1229, 1236; Iran, Islamic Republic of: 1253; Ireland: 1255; Italie: 1277, 1280, 1290, 1301, 1302, 1304; Japan: 1312, 1313, 1316, 1322, 1331, 1343, 1344, 1350, 1359, 1390; Jordan: 1401, 1404, 1408, 1412; Kazakhstan: 1418; Kenya: 1425; Kyrgyzstan: 1428, 1430, 1432; Latvia: 1436, 1440, 1441; Liban: 1443; Liechtenstein: 1457; Lithuania: 1468; Malta: 1499; Mauritius: 1522; Mongolia: 1631; Netherlands: 1635, 1639, 1641, 1643, 1644, 1661, 1666, 1667, 1668, 1673, 1682; New Zealand: 1686; Nigeria: 1704, 1707, 1709; Norway: 1713, 1718, 1728; Pakistan: 1734, 1735, 1736, 1737, 1738, 1741, 1742, 1749, 1751, 1752, 1753, 1754; Papua New Guinea: 1760; Philippines: 1798, 1799, 1805, 1807, 1808, 1810, 1812, 1816, 1819, 1820; Poland: 1861,

1862, 1868, 1876, 1877, 1889, 1890; Portugal: 1917, 1925; Republic of Korea: 1931, 1933, 1935, 1942, 1947, 1948, 1951; Republic of Moldova: 1953, 1954, 1956; Roumanie: 1966, 1968; Russian Federation: 1982, 1986, 1992, 2033, 2066, 2070, 2102, 2114; Serbia and Montenegro: 2147; Slovakia: 2158, 2159, 2168; South Africa: 2181, 2189; Sri Lanka: 2197, 2198, 2199; Suisse: 2217; Suriname: 2229, 2232; Sweden: 2239, 2240, 2242, 2251, 2258; Tajikistan: 2260, 2261, 2262; Thailand: 2265, 2266, 2272, 2274, 2278, 2279, 2282; Turkey: 2320, 2321, 2323, 2326, 2330; Uganda: 2331, 2333; Ukraine: 2341, 2346, 2347, 2351, 2356, 2364; United Kingdom: 2367, 2369, 2375, 2384, 2386, 2399, 2401, 2425, 2432, 2452, 2464, 2472, 2476; United Republic of Tanzania: 2491, 2492, 2496; United States of America: 2557, 2560, 2565, 2574, 2583, 2594, 2613, 2617, 2624, 2633, 2634, 2641, 2659, 2660, 2666, 2673, 2675, 2679, 2683, 2684, 2696, 2700, 2717, 2718, 2720, 2735, 2738, 2744, 2745, 2746, 2753, 2754; United States of America, Puerto Rico: 2759; Uzbekistan: 2769; Zimbabwe: 2786.

cancerología
[C] 11, 20; España: 799; [S] 20.

cancérologie
[C] 11, 20; [S] 20.

cancerology
[C] 11, 20; Canada: 405; Iran, Islamic Republic of: 1251; Italie: 1304; Japan: 1360; Kyrgyzstan: 1432; Mongolia: 1630; Poland: 1873; Russian Federation: 2090; Tajikistan: 2262; United States of America: 2615; [S] 20; United States of America: 2600.

canon law
[C] Canada: 380; Ireland: 1259; United States of America: 2560.

cardiology
[C] Germany: 1083; Iran, Islamic Republic of: 1251; Italie: 1304; Japan: 1327, 1335; Kyrgyzstan: 1432; Mongolia: 1630; Netherlands: 1657; Poland: 1873, 1874; Republic of Moldova: 1954; Russian Federation: 2090; United States of America: 2615.

cattle breeding
[C] Arménie: 126; Estonia: 876; Ethiopia: 884; Lithuania: 1465; Netherlands: 1652; Nigeria: 1703, 1707, 1709; Poland: 1842, 1843; Roumanie: 1973; Russian Federation: 2044, 2069, 2120; Sweden: 2254; Uganda: 2333; Ukraine: 2334; United Kingdom: 2386, 2405; United Republic of Tanzania: 2493; [S] Arménie: 126; Australia: 169; United Kingdom: 2386.

chemical engineering
[C] Azerbaijan: 205; Belgique: 274; Canada: 405; China: 457, 472, 497, 507, 519; Czech Republic: 653, 666; Estonia: 881; Ethiopia: 885; Finland: 887, 892; Germany: 1083, 1087, 1098, 1099, 1105, 1126, 1133; Japan: 1369, 1377, 1389, 1398; Mongolia: 1631; Netherlands: 1666; Nigeria: 1703, 1704, 1707, 1709; Norway: 1713; Philippines: 1816; Poland: 1890, 1891, 1895; Russian Federation: 1978, 2000, 2028, 2058, 2066, 2129; Singapore: 2152, 2153; Slovakia: 2164; South Africa: 2181, 2189; Thailand: 2271; Ukraine: 2351, 2353; United Kingdom: 2401, 2472; United Republic of Tanzania: 2496; United States of America: 2692, 2754; Yemen: 2781; [S] Japan: 1389; United Kingdom: 2411.

chemical industry
[C] Azerbaijan: 205; China: 497, 504, 507; Czech Republic: 653; Denmark: 684, 686; Ethiopia: 883; Germany: 1083; India: 1214; Italie: 1290; Japan: 1389; Norway: 1713; Philippines: 1816; Russian Federation: 1978, 2020, 2026, 2028, 2058, 2066, 2096, 2127, 2129; Turkey: 2323; Ukraine: 2353; United Kingdom: 2387, 2476; United Republic of Tanzania: 2496.

chemistry
[C] Australia: 166; Azerbaijan: 205; Belgique: 255, 274; Canada: 353, 366, 371, 374, 383, 385, 398, 405, 408; China: 457, 472, 476, 490, 497, 504; Czech Republic: 653, 664, 666, 670; Denmark: 686; Egypt: 700; Eritrea: 711; Ethiopia: 883, 884, 885; Fiji: 886; Finland: 892; Germany: 1083, 1090, 1097, 1126, 1135, 1137; Grèce: 1155; India: 1215, 1223; Indonesia: 1236; Iran, Islamic Republic of: 1243; Italie: 1290, 1304; Japan: 1339, 1389, 1398; Kazakhstan: 1419; Kenya: 1425; Kyrgyzstan: 1429; Lithuania: 1459; Mongolia: 1630, 1631; Netherlands: 1666; Nigeria: 1703, 1704, 1707, 1709; Pakistan: 1742, 1747, 1748, 1752, 1753; Philippines: 1809, 1820; Poland: 1829, 1874, 1890, 1905, 1908, 1915; Russian Federation: 1988, 2000, 2004, 2006, 2010, 2023, 2028, 2037, 2039, 2063, 2066, 2067, 2071, 2072, 2079, 2080, 2097, 2108, 2119, 2134, 2136, 2137; Slovakia: 2160, 2161, 2163, 2164, 2167, 2169; South Africa: 2182, 2189; Sweden: 2248, 2254, 2259; Thailand: 2271; Turkey: 2330; Uganda: 2332; Ukraine:

2351, 2356; United Kingdom: 2401, 2406, 2423, 2431, 2472;
United Republic of Tanzania: 2496; United States of
America: 2529, 2561, 2576, 2633, 2642, 2647, 2655, 2660,
2666, 2673, 2684, 2692, 2696, 2735, 2746, 2747;
Uzbekistan: 2766, 2771; Yemen: 2781; [S] Canada: 383;
Japan: 1389; Russian Federation: 2004; South Africa: 2186;
Thailand: 2274; United Kingdom: 2431; United States of
America: 2672.

chimie
[C] Algérie: 68, 70, 71; Belarus, Republic of: 229, 236, 243;
Belgique: 249; Brésil: 311; Bulgaria: 332, 335; France: 928,
948, 949, 969, 971, 979, 986, 1007, 1008, 1015;
Madagascar: 1475, 1478, 1480; Maroc: 1506, 1509, 1512,
1516; Portugal: 1922; Suisse: 2210; Tchad: 2263; Tunisie:
2305, 2307, 2309; [S] France: 910, 925.

Chinese
[C] China: 459, 460, 463, 465, 475, 477, 478, 479, 484, 485,
487, 488, 489, 491, 492, 493, 494, 496, 497, 499, 504, 506,
507, 513, 514, 516, 520, 521, 523; China, Hong Kong: 526,
528; Japan: 1352; United States of America: 2655, 2719.

chirurgie
[C] 11; Togo: 2287.

ciencias
[C] 1, 21; Argentina: 83, 107, 113, 119; Chile: 416, 420,
434, 438, 447, 456; Colombia: 547, 549; Costa Rica: 560,
578; Cuba: 618; El Salvador: 709; España: 728, 729, 731,
733, 761, 835, 851; México: 1544, 1545, 1566, 1581, 1586,
1589; Perú: 1791; République Dominicana: 1957; [S] 23,
37, 49, 59; Argentina: 79; Cuba: 611; Ecuador: 693;
España: 760, 855; Perú: 1770.

ciencias agronómicas
[S] 17; Cuba: 611; España: 764; Perú: 1780; [C] 27;
Argentina: 80, 102, 107, 113, 119; Chile: 415, 416, 432;
Colombia: 546, 549; Costa Rica: 560, 578; Cuba: 600, 601,
614, 615, 617, 620; Ecuador: 695, 697; España: 763, 772,
848, 851, 863; Honduras: 1179; México: 1530, 1553, 1558,
1560, 1561, 1562, 1564, 1586; Perú: 1781, 1784; Uruguay:
2763.

ciencias aplicadas
[C] Argentina: 76, 83; Colombia: 547; España: 721, 728,
731, 766, 830, 833; México: 1525, 1546, 1605; Perú: 1792;
[S] Cuba: 611.

ciencias de la información
[C] 49; Andorra: 72; Argentina: 89, 94; Chile: 423, 438;
Colombia: 552; España: 729, 744, 831, 873; México: 1551,
1578, 1612; Perú: 1792; [S] 49.

ciencias de la tierra
[S] 1; Argentina: 79; Costa Rica: 570; [C] 44; Bolivia: 290;
Chile: 437, 446; Costa Rica: 569, 587; Cuba: 605; España:
766; México: 1558, 1560, 1561, 1567, 1586; Perú: 1781.

ciencias del mar
[S] 31, 50; [C] Argentina: 92; Chile: 434; México: 1561,
1573.

ciencias económicas y comerciales
[C] 38; Argentina: 86, 87, 88, 89, 91, 94, 105, 108, 113, 119,
123, 124; Bolivia: 288, 289; Chile: 423, 434, 436, 441, 452,
453; Colombia: 533, 546; Costa Rica: 564, 585, 591; Cuba:
610, 615, 620; Ecuador: 694; El Salvador: 709, 710;
España: 744, 745, 746, 747, 761, 775, 782, 786, 790, 791,
797, 815, 836, 840, 846, 851, 868; Honduras: 1176, 1177;
México: 1551, 1581, 1583, 1585, 1612; Nicaragua: 1695;
Perú: 1784, 1793; République Dominicana: 1958; Uruguay:
2763, 2764; [S] Argentina: 112; Chile: 411; Ecuador: 693;
España: 714, 756; Perú: 1766.

ciencias humanas
[S] 14, 28, 49, 50; [C] 29; Argentina: 113, 119; Chile: 412,
423, 446; Colombia: 533, 549, 552; Costa Rica: 565, 578;
Ecuador: 695; España: 734, 776, 871; México: 1533, 1541,
1553, 1561, 1566, 1598, 1605, 1607; Perú: 1790, 1793;
République Dominicana: 1958; Venezuela: 2775.

ciencias naturales
[S] 28, 49; Cuba: 611; [C] 49; Argentina: 109; Chile: 416,
447; Costa Rica: 578; España: 735.

ciencias políticas
[C] 14; Argentina: 91, 97, 98; Chile: 412, 441; Colombia:
533; Costa Rica: 592; España: 716, 757, 776; México:
1526, 1534, 1551, 1577, 1609; [S] 14; Argentina: 84;
Chile: 411; España: 756; Perú: 1777.

ciencias sociales
[C] 14, 29, 39, 49; Argentina: 86, 87, 113; Bolivia: 289;
Chile: 412, 417, 443, 446, 449; Colombia: 533, 546, 547,
552; Costa Rica: 578, 586; Ecuador: 689, 694; España:
734, 752, 776, 791, 797, 818, 851, 868; México: 1527, 1528,
1533, 1534, 1543, 1550, 1560, 1561, 1565, 1566, 1577,
1581, 1586, 1589, 1617; Perú: 1784; República

Dominicana: 1958; Uruguay: 2764; Venezuela: 2775; [S]
14, 28, 49; Chile: 411; Cuba: 611; España: 855; México:
1527.

ciencias veterinarias
[C] Chile: 415; Colombia: 549; España: 763, 772; [S]
Colombia: 537.

cinematografía
[C] España: 851.

cinématographie
[C] Bulgaria: 317; France: 965, 1004.

cinematography
[C] Czech Republic: 648; Georgia: 1080; Hungary: 1180;
Lithuania: 1462; Russian Federation: 2065; Suisse: 2227;
United Kingdom: 2399; United States of America: 2624,
2636, 2656.

cirugía
[C] 11; Chile: 413, 421; México: 1539; [S] Chile: 439.

citología
[S] 20; [C] Venezuela: 2777.

civil engineering
[S] 4; Bangladesh: 214; Japan: 1389; Pakistan: 1750;
United Kingdom: 2387; [C] Austria: 190; Barbados: 222;
Belgique: 255, 274; Brésil: 296; Canada: 353, 405; China:
457, 467, 506, 521; Croatia: 598; Cyprus: 636; Czech
Republic: 651, 662; Denmark: 684; Egypt: 705; Estonia:
881; Ethiopia: 883, 885; Finland: 894; Germany: 1083,
1099, 1117, 1133, 1134; Hungary: 1192; Indonesia: 1228,
1232, 1239; Italie: 1283, 1290, 1300, 1301; Japan: 1357,
1369, 1379, 1389, 1398; Latvia: 1437; Lithuania: 1459,
1468; Netherlands: 1638, 1666; Nigeria: 1703, 1704, 1707,
1709; Norway: 1713, 1715, 1725; Pakistan: 1746;
Philippines: 1809, 1816, 1822; Poland: 1869, 1883, 1890,
1891, 1892, 1894, 1895; Portugal: 1927; Republic of Korea:
1931, 1948; Roumanie: 1971; Russian Federation: 1978,
1987, 1992, 2000, 2010, 2015, 2021, 2026, 2047, 2054,
2064, 2066, 2069, 2074, 2105, 2127, 2131, 2133; Serbia
and Montenegro: 2148; Singapore: 2152, 2153; Slovakia:
2164, 2166, 2174; Sudan: 2204; Suisse: 2209; Suriname:
2232; Thailand: 2271; Turkey: 2326; Ukraine: 2337, 2351,
2356, 2365; United Kingdom: 2387, 2401, 2425, 2436, 2472;
United Republic of Tanzania: 2487; United States of
America: 2549, 2565, 2692.

classical studies
[C] Canada: 353, 371, 373, 385, 405; Ireland: 1259; Japan:
1329; Russian Federation: 2008, 2065; Slovakia: 2172;
Thailand: 2278; United Kingdom: 2452, 2482; United States
of America: 2553, 2560, 2580, 2609, 2627, 2655, 2666,
2757; [S] Italie: 1273; Japan: 1351; United Kingdom: 2453.

comercio
[C] Chile: 424; Colombia: 533; Costa Rica: 564, 593;
España: 715, 768, 815, 846; México: 1571, 1575, 1583,
1585, 1609, 1623; Nicaragua: 1696, 1697; [S] España:
726, 769; México: 1557, 1612.

commerce
[C] Algérie: 68; Arménie: 129; Belarus, Republic of: 242;
Belgique: 259, 262; Bulgaria: 316, 325; France: 907, 985,
995, 1056; Tunisie: 2310; [S] Cameroun: 349;
Madagascar: 1483.

communication
[S] 6, 24, 36, 49; San Marino: 2142; United States of
America: 2574, 2598; [C] Arménie: 129; Australia: 136,
140; Austria: 195; Belgique: 253, 273; Bulgaria: 321;
Burundi: 347; Cambodge: 348; Canada: 353, 380; China:
473, 496, 504, 507; Côte d'Ivoire: 597; Czech Republic:
666; Denmark: 674, 676; Egypt: 701; Finland: 894, 903;
France: 976, 984, 1003, 1016, 1045, 1063, 1066, 1072;
Georgia: 1080; Germany: 1090; Hungary: 1184, 1201;
India: 1217, 1220, 1223; Indonesia: 1229; Ireland: 1255;
Italie: 1277, 1286, 1301, 1302, 1304; Japan: 1390; Jordan:
1411; Kazakhstan: 1417; Kenya: 1425; Kyrgyzstan: 1428,
1430; Latvia: 1441; Madagascar: 1479; Nigeria: 1704,
1709; Norway: 1718; Pakistan: 1737, 1741, 1747, 1748,
1751, 1753, 1754; Philippines: 1812, 1813, 1816, 1822,
1825; Poland: 1863; Republic of Korea: 1935, 1948;
Republic of Moldova: 1954; Roumanie: 1966; Russian
Federation: 2016, 2066, 2082, 2108; San Marino: 2142;
Slovakia: 2167, 2174; Slovenia: 2176; South Africa: 2181,
2189; Suisse: 2217; Swaziland: 2234; Sweden: 2240,
2247; Thailand: 2279, 2280; Uganda: 2331; Ukraine: 2347;
United Kingdom: 2375, 2384, 2401, 2436, 2472; United
States of America: 2557, 2561, 2565, 2574, 2594, 2613,
2633, 2641, 2659, 2660, 2666, 2673, 2683, 2684, 2696,
2744.

community development
[C] Germany: 1090; India: 1213; Japan: 1311, 1379, 1398;
Sri Lanka: 2197; Uganda: 2331; Ukraine: 2351; United

Kingdom: 2387, 2476, 2486.

comptabilité
[C] Algérie: 63, 71; Arménie: 129; Belarus, Republic of: 241, 242; Belgique: 257, 259, 261; Bulgaria: 316, 325; Burundi: 347; Côte d'Ivoire: 596; Madagascar: 1483; Maroc: 1512, 1513; Tunisie: 2298, 2306, 2310.

computer science
[S] 42; Bangladesh: 214, 217; China, Macao: 531; Cyprus: 633, 639; Czech Republic: 668; Germany: 1111, 1125; Japan: 1319, 1389; Mauritius: 1522; Russian Federation: 2014, 2016, 2114; South Africa: 2186; Thailand: 2270, 2274; United Kingdom: 2448, 2468; United States of America: 2522, 2552, 2574; Uzbekistan: 2766; Yemen: 2783; [C] Arménie: 125, 127; Australia: 140, 161, 162, 166, 179; Austria: 195; Azerbaijan: 205; Bangladesh: 215, 216, 218; Belgique: 255, 274; Belize: 283; Bulgaria: 321; Canada: 353, 360, 366, 367, 371, 385, 398, 405, 408; China: 457, 465, 473, 484, 490, 493, 496, 497, 504, 506, 516, 519, 521; China, Macao: 531; Cyprus: 621, 624, 627, 633, 637, 639, 642, 643; Czech Republic: 654, 666; Denmark: 686; Egypt: 699, 702; Estonia: 881; Finland: 890, 892, 894, 896, 898, 901, 903, 904; Georgia: 1080; Germany: 1083, 1087, 1088, 1089, 1090, 1097, 1098, 1099, 1100, 1113, 1117, 1126, 1130, 1131, 1133, 1134, 1137, 1140; Grèce: 1155; Hungary: 1184, 1197, 1201; Iceland: 1204, 1206; India: 1213, 1215, 1219, 1223; Indonesia: 1228, 1233, 1238; Iran, Islamic Republic of: 1253; Ireland: 1257; Italie: 1277, 1280, 1283, 1285, 1290; Jamaica: 1309; Japan: 1319, 1369, 1389; Jordan: 1400, 1401, 1402, 1408, 1411; Kenya: 1422, 1425; Kyrgyzstan: 1429, 1430, 1431; Latvia: 1436, 1437, 1440, 1441; Liban: 1443; Lithuania: 1459, 1468; Malaysia: 1488, 1492; Mongolia: 1630; Netherlands: 1638, 1647, 1650, 1651; New Zealand: 1687; Nigeria: 1703, 1704, 1707; Norway: 1715, 1722, 1725; Pakistan: 1735, 1736, 1737, 1738, 1741, 1742, 1745, 1746, 1747, 1748, 1751, 1752, 1753, 1754, 1755; Philippines: 1798, 1805, 1806, 1807, 1812, 1813, 1816, 1820, 1825; Poland: 1844, 1846, 1847, 1849, 1850, 1852, 1856, 1862, 1865, 1866, 1868, 1874, 1877, 1879, 1880, 1882, 1883, 1884, 1890, 1891, 1892, 1893, 1894, 1895, 1908, 1912, 1915, 1916; Portugal: 1917, 1920, 1927; Republic of Korea: 1931, 1934, 1935, 1939, 1948; Republic of Moldova: 1953, 1955; Russian Federation: 1986, 1988, 1990, 1992, 1994, 1995, 2000, 2008, 2014, 2016, 2021, 2025, 2042, 2046, 2048, 2049, 2050, 2051, 2056, 2059, 2060, 2066, 2069, 2070, 2072, 2076, 2082, 2084, 2085, 2091, 2093, 2094, 2096, 2102, 2108, 2112, 2114, 2115, 2127, 2129, 2134; Singapore: 2153; Slovakia: 2160, 2161, 2166, 2167, 2169; South Africa: 2182, 2189; Sri Lanka: 2200; Suisse: 2227; Swaziland: 2233; Sweden: 2242, 2248, 2258; Tajikistan: 2260; Thailand: 2265, 2266, 2269, 2270, 2271; Turkey: 2319, 2320, 2321, 2323, 2326; Uganda: 2332, 2333; Ukraine: 2336, 2340, 2341, 2347, 2351, 2354, 2356, 2357, 2364, 2365; United Kingdom: 2369, 2392, 2401, 2423, 2431, 2436, 2472; United Republic of Tanzania: 2490, 2495, 2496; United States of America: 2503, 2512, 2529, 2542, 2545, 2561, 2565, 2574, 2576, 2580, 2594, 2619, 2627, 2641, 2642, 2647, 2659, 2660, 2666, 2673, 2692, 2735, 2747; Uzbekistan: 2766; Yemen: 2781.

comunicación
[S] 24, 36, 49; Ecuador: 693; México: 1557, 1612; Perú: 1777; [C] Argentina: 87, 100; Chile: 428, 443, 452; Colombia: 535, 552; Costa Rica: 592; Cuba: 604; Ecuador: 689, 694; El Salvador: 709; España: 747, 774, 786, 789, 802, 831; México: 1585, 1596, 1597, 1598, 1609, 1611, 1623; Uruguay: 2763, 2764.

construcción
[C] Argentina: 110, 114; Chile: 419, 432, 456; España: 739, 828, 865.

construcción naval
[S] 31.

construction navale
[S] 31; France: 956; [C] Bulgaria: 344; France: 956.

contabilidad
[C] Argentina: 88, 94, 95, 97, 107, 108; Chile: 424, 436; Colombia: 546; Costa Rica: 563, 564, 581, 582, 585, 593; Cuba: 610, 615; Ecuador: 695; España: 765, 790, 791, 797, 815, 846; México: 1551, 1583, 1591, 1596, 1597, 1604, 1608, 1609, 1617, 1621, 1623; Nicaragua: 1697; Perú: 1775, 1779, 1792, 1793; República Dominicana: 1959; [S] Perú: 1774, 1777.

continuing education
[C] Canada: 353; Croatia: 598; Czech Republic: 653, 666; Ethiopia: 884; Germany: 1097; Hungary: 1198, 1201; India: 1222; Indonesia: 1232, 1238; Iran, Islamic Republic of: 1251; Ireland: 1259; Japan: 1316; Kazakhstan: 1416, 1419; Latvia: 1441; Nigeria: 1707, 1709; Pakistan: 1736; Poland: 1874; Roumanie: 1969, 1975; Russian Federation: 2027, 2082, 2083, 2106, 2123; Ukraine: 2341, 2361; United

Kingdom: 2391; Uzbekistan: 2768.

cría de ganado
[C] Colombia: 549; Cuba: 615, 617; España: 772; México: 1562, 1568.

criminología
[C] Costa Rica: 578; México: 1523, 1617.

criminologie
[C] Arménie: 129; France: 1047, 1057.

criminology
[C] Bosnia and Herzegovina: 291; Bulgaria: 321; Canada: 367, 373, 383, 385; China: 504; Germany: 1109; Italie: 1304; Lithuania: 1461; Philippines: 1820; Republic of Moldova: 1954; Russian Federation: 1989, 2024, 2082, 2108; Suisse: 2227; Tajikistan: 2260; Ukraine: 2347, 2348; United Kingdom: 2401, 2436, 2472; United States of America: 2542, 2557, 2617, 2624, 2633, 2660, 2696, 2700, 2735; [S] Canada: 383.

cultural studies
[C] 49; Arménie: 130; Australia: 134; Austria: 185, 202; Bulgaria: 320; Canada: 367, 383, 385, 402; Denmark: 674; Estonia: 882; Finland: 887, 892, 896, 904; Georgia: 1080, 1081; Germany: 1131, 1135; Indonesia: 1238; Ireland: 1258; Italie: 1286; Japan: 1340, 1359, 1374, 1377; Latvia: 1436, 1441; Netherlands: 1653; Poland: 1848, 1910, 1914; Republic of Korea: 1950; Republic of Moldova: 1955; Russian Federation: 1995, 1997, 2025, 2027, 2055, 2094; Slovakia: 2160; Suriname: 2228; Sweden: 2244, 2253; Ukraine: 2340, 2347; United Kingdom: 2436, 2472; United States of America: 2529, 2557, 2562, 2576, 2613, 2617, 2743; [S] 49; Australia: 146; Canada: 364, 383, 400; Estonia: 882; Iceland: 1203, 1205, 1207; Israel: 1265; Japan: 1353, 1356; Norway: 1723; United Kingdom: 2372, 2381.

cytologie
[S] 20; [C] Portugal: 1926.

cytology
[C] Iran, Islamic Republic of: 1251; Italie: 1304; Mongolia: 1630; Poland: 1873; United States of America: 2615, 2758.

dance
[C] Germany: 1119; [S] United States of America: 2587.

Danish
[C] United Kingdom: 2480.

decoración
[C] República Dominicana: 1959.

décoration
[C] Belgique: 248; France: 957; Tunisie: 2312.

decorative arts
[C] Austria: 199; Denmark: 675; Germany: 1121; Hungary: 1188; Netherlands: 1636; Norway: 1720; Poland: 1834, 1835; Russian Federation: 2000, 2025, 2065, 2131; South Africa: 2189; Tajikistan: 2261; United Kingdom: 2376, 2399, 2483; United States of America: 2544, 2679; [S] United Kingdom: 2483.

demografía y estudios de población
[S] México: 1529; [C] México: 1595; Perú: 1790.

démographie et études de populations
[C] Brésil: 309; Burundi: 347; Côte d'Ivoire: 595; France: 937, 1001, 1037; Madagascar: 1479.

demography and population studies
[C] Australia: 137; Azerbaijan: 209; Egypt: 702; India: 1218; Iran, Islamic Republic of: 1251; Mongolia: 1631; Republic of Moldova: 1953; Uganda: 2331; United Kingdom: 2400, 2477; United States of America: 2529; [S] Thailand: 2274.

dentistry
[C] Bosnia and Herzegovina: 291; China: 483; Egypt: 699; Georgia: 1080; Germany: 1105, 1143; Hungary: 1191; Indonesia: 1236; Iran, Islamic Republic of: 1242, 1245, 1249, 1251; Italie: 1300, 1304; Japan: 1312, 1335, 1352, 1364; Jordan: 1405; Lithuania: 1458; Mongolia: 1630; Netherlands: 1634; Norway: 1729, 1731; Pakistan: 1735; Philippines: 1807, 1811; Poland: 1872, 1873, 1874, 1885; Portugal: 1924; Republic of Korea: 1939; Republic of Moldova: 1954; Russian Federation: 2090; South Africa: 2182; Sri Lanka: 2201; Suisse: 2227; Suriname: 2231; Thailand: 2274; Trinidad and Tobago: 2290; Ukraine: 2335; United Kingdom: 2452; United States of America: 2524, 2537, 2563, 2615, 2617, 2624, 2718, 2742, 2753; [S] Canada: 363; Japan: 1312; Poland: 1872; Thailand: 2274; United Kingdom: 2443; United States of America: 2615, 2624; Yemen: 2782.

derecho

[C] 8, 14, 30; Argentina: 87, 88, 89, 98, 107, 108, 113, 124; Bolivia: 288; Chile: 423, 428, 434, 449, 453; Colombia: 533, 546; Costa Rica: 574, 575, 580, 582, 585, 591, 592; Ecuador: 689, 694; El Salvador: 710; España: 716, 750, 758, 761, 765, 770, 781, 782, 786, 790, 792, 797, 815, 816, 817, 818, 832, 847, 851, 860, 868, 871; Honduras: 1176; México: 1523, 1528, 1551, 1561, 1565, 1567, 1568, 1570, 1571, 1572, 1575, 1578, 1582, 1583, 1585, 1590, 1596, 1597, 1604, 1608, 1611, 1617, 1621, 1623; Nicaragua: 1695; Perú: 1784, 1792, 1796; Uruguay: 2763; [S] 14, 42; Ecuador: 689, 693; México: 1557, 1616; Perú: 1777.

derecho canónico
[C] España: 765, 868.

derecho internacional
[S] 14, 31, 42; [C] 30; Argentina: 124; Chile: 441; Colombia: 533; España: 758, 776, 781, 782, 790, 792, 805, 851; México: 1612.

dermatología
[C] Costa Rica: 567.

dermatology
[C] Iran, Islamic Republic of: 1242, 1251; Japan: 1327, 1335; Mongolia: 1630; Netherlands: 1657; Poland: 1873, 1874; Russian Federation: 2090; United Republic of Tanzania: 2497; United States of America: 2615, 2624.

desarrollo comunitario
[C] Chile: 435; Cuba: 620.

desarrollo rural
[S] 50; [C] Chile: 435; España: 763, 772; México: 1530, 1562, 1581.

design
[C] Austria: 196, 203; Bermuda: 285; Canada: 375; China: 507, 516; Czech Republic: 666; Denmark: 675; Germany: 1099, 1101, 1121, 1126; Hungary: 1188; Ireland: 1257; Italie: 1278, 1280, 1290; Japan: 1342; Jordan: 1408, 1411; Kazakhstan: 1419; Lithuania: 1467; Netherlands: 1636, 1676; Norway: 1712, 1714, 1720; Poland: 1832, 1834, 1835, 1845; Republic of Korea: 1931, 1935; Republic of Moldova: 1955, 1956; Russian Federation: 2000, 2013, 2025, 2066, 2124, 2131; Slovakia: 2157, 2166; South Africa: 2181; Tajikistan: 2261; United Kingdom: 2388, 2398, 2399, 2401, 2423, 2431, 2432, 2474, 2484; United States of America: 2544, 2554, 2557, 2576, 2633, 2656, 2661, 2679, 2684, 2736, 2746; [S] Japan: 1342; Poland: 1831.

dessin industriel
[C] Algérie: 68; Belgique: 248, 261; Brésil: 298; France: 982.

development studies
[C] 2, 15, 29, 39; Canada: 362, 373, 385, 405; Indonesia: 1229; Italie: 1277; Japan: 1398; Mongolia: 1631; Netherlands: 1647, 1648, 1650; New Zealand: 1689; Norway: 1718; Philippines: 1803, 1804; Russian Federation: 2033; Sweden: 2251; Thailand: 2269, 2276; Uganda: 2331, 2332, 2333; United Kingdom: 2380, 2425, 2431, 2459, 2462, 2473, 2478; United States of America: 2683, 2758; [S] 3, 49, 50, 55; Australia: 133; Bangladesh: 217; Canada: 364; United Kingdom: 2390; United States of America: 2652.

développement communautaire
[C] Canada: 393; France: 924.

développement et production de livres
[C] Côte d'Ivoire: 597; France: 1063.

développement rural
[S] 50; [C] Belgique: 247, 250; Bulgaria: 323, 338; France: 909, 935, 941, 1036; Madagascar: 1478; Poland: 1896; Suisse: 2208, 2215.

dietético
[C] España: 794, 830; Perú: 1793.

dietetics
[C] Belgique: 274; Canada: 353; India: 1222; Iran, Islamic Republic of: 1251; Japan: 1365; Mongolia: 1630; Nigeria: 1707; Philippines: 1812; Poland: 1873, 1874; South Africa: 2182; United Kingdom: 2472; United States of America: 2617.

diseño
[C] Argentina: 113; Chile: 449, 452; Costa Rica: 576, 593; Cuba: 603; México: 1535, 1565, 1591, 1607, 1617, 1621; Perú: 1783; Uruguay: 2763, 2764; [S] Perú: 1773.

diseño industrial
[C] Costa Rica: 593; Cuba: 603; México: 1535, 1549; República Dominicana: 1959; [S] España: 767; México: 1600, 1612; Perú: 1773.

distance education
[S] 6, 41; [C] 44; United Kingdom: 2387, 2472.

documentación
[C] Costa Rica: 586; España: 729, 733, 789, 802, 838.

documentation
[C] France: 962; Germany: 1099; Madagascar: 1479; Republic of Korea: 1929; Russian Federation: 2082; Sénégal: 2146; Uganda: 2331.

droit
[C] 8, 14, 30, 47; Algérie: 63, 68, 71; Angola: 73, 74; Arménie: 129; Belarus, Republic of: 236, 238, 239; Belgique: 253; Brésil: 298, 299, 301, 307; Bulgaria: 326, 332, 337, 340, 344; Burundi: 347; Cameroun: 350; Canada: 390; Côte d'Ivoire: 597; France: 960, 985, 1001, 1003, 1016, 1025, 1053, 1054, 1055, 1056, 1057, 1059, 1062, 1064, 1065; Gabon: 1078; Grèce: 1160; Italie: 1296; Liban: 1450, 1452; Madagascar: 1481; Maroc: 1508, 1514; Suisse: 2221, 2225; Togo: 2287; Tunisie: 2298; Turkey: 2328; [S] 14; Belgique: 246; Brésil: 301; Cameroun: 349; France: 1048; Maroc: 1513; Suisse: 2219, 2226.

droit canon
[C] Cameroun: 350; Canada: 380; Côte d'Ivoire: 597; France: 1002; Saint-Siège: 2140.

droit international
[S] 14, 31, 47; France: 1017; Maroc: 1513; [C] 30, 47; Arménie: 129; Côte d'Ivoire: 597; France: 976, 987, 1001, 1058, 1064, 1073; Maroc: 1508; Suisse: 2216.

Dutch
[C] Netherlands: 1653; United Kingdom: 2480.

early childhood education
[C] Belgique: 274; China: 465; Croatia: 598; Cyprus: 643; Estonia: 880; Iceland: 1206; India: 1222; Japan: 1365; Norway: 1713, 1724, 1728; Philippines: 1812; Poland: 1908; Republic of Korea: 1945; Russian Federation: 2022, 2027; Sweden: 2250; Ukraine: 2357; United Kingdom: 2391, 2427; United States of America: 2557, 2633, 2642, 2666, 2683, 2684, 2744, 2754; Uzbekistan: 2768; Yemen: 2781; [S] United States of America: 2567.

earth science
[S] 1; United Kingdom: 2465; United States of America: 2677, 2678; [C] 44; Azerbaijan: 205, 208; Bahrain: 210; Canada: 353, 405; China: 472; Fiji: 886; Finland: 896, 903; Germany: 1131, 1135; India: 1211; Iran, Islamic Republic of: 1241; Kazakhstan: 1419; Mongolia: 1631; Netherlands: 1642, 1650; Poland: 1877, 1890, 1915; Russian Federation: 2069, 2131, 2137; Slovakia: 2160, 2161, 2163; Turkey: 2329; United States of America: 2540, 2542, 2549, 2561, 2576, 2673, 2684; Yemen: 2781.

ecología, medio ambiente
[C] 20; Argentina: 78, 94, 109, 121; Chile: 416, 424, 444; Costa Rica: 592; Cuba: 599, 606, 607, 620; Ecuador: 694, 697; España: 728, 743, 747, 761, 763, 772, 775, 851, 860; México: 1525, 1560, 1562, 1570, 1571, 1586; Venezuela: 2772, 2773, 2774; [S] 50; Colombia: 537, 548; Ecuador: 693.

écologie, environnement
[C] 20; Algérie: 63, 71; Belarus, Republic of: 229, 238; Belgique: 247, 250; Brésil: 295, 298; Bulgaria: 338, 344; Cambodge: 348; France: 924, 925, 935, 941, 942, 1012, 1029, 1050; Grèce: 1160; Madagascar: 1475, 1479; Maroc: 1500, 1504, 1511; Poland: 1896; Portugal: 1922; Suisse: 2210, 2215; Tunisie: 2309; [S] 50; Cameroun: 349; Canada: 389; France: 925, 974.

ecology, environment
[C] 4, 20, 33; Arménie: 127; Australia: 147, 165; Azerbaijan: 205; Bangladesh: 216; Belgique: 255, 274; Brésil: 296; Canada: 353, 366, 371, 373, 374, 385, 396, 405; China: 457, 465, 497; Czech Republic: 653, 655, 666, 672; Denmark: 674; Estonia: 880, 881; Finland: 892, 893, 894, 896, 903, 904; Germany: 1087, 1089, 1098, 1122, 1131, 1135; Grèce: 1154; Hungary: 1192, 1200; Iceland: 1206; India: 1211; Israel: 1264; Italie: 1290; Japan: 1322, 1380, 1398; Kazakhstan: 1419; Kenya: 1425; Kyrgyzstan: 1429, 1430; Latvia: 1436; Lithuania: 1468; Malawi: 1485; Malaysia: 1491; Mongolia: 1631; Netherlands: 1639, 1654, 1658, 1666, 1668, 1680, 1681, 1682; New Zealand: 1687; Nigeria: 1709; Norway: 1725; Philippines: 1806, 1813, 1816, 1825; Poland: 1840, 1841, 1843, 1859, 1866, 1877, 1883, 1886, 1890, 1891, 1892, 1899, 1900, 1903, 1908, 1915; Portugal: 1927; Republic of Korea: 1931, 1947; Russian Federation: 1987, 1990, 1992, 2000, 2006, 2008, 2016, 2035, 2037, 2039, 2043, 2064, 2066, 2070, 2073, 2074, 2083, 2084, 2093, 2108, 2111, 2112, 2126, 2127, 2131, 2133; Slovakia: 2160, 2161, 2165, 2166; Slovenia: 2178; Suisse: 2227; Sweden: 2254; Thailand: 2271; Turkey: 2320, 2323, 2326; Ukraine: 2337, 2347, 2351, 2354, 2356, 2364; United Kingdom: 2380, 2386, 2388, 2399, 2401,

2405, 2436; United Republic of Tanzania: 2493, 2495;
United States of America: 2529, 2549, 2574, 2576, 2613,
2621, 2633, 2660, 2666, 2684, 2692; [S] 4, 48, 50;
Australia: 147; Japan: 1389; Netherlands: 1639; Thailand:
2274; United Kingdom: 2386, 2443, 2465; United States of
America: 2574, 2582, 2677; United States of America,
Puerto Rico: 2760.

economía
[C] 8, 12, 14; Argentina: 94, 95, 97, 98, 108, 119; Chile:
412, 415, 428, 436, 441; Colombia: 533, 535; Cuba: 610;
España: 768, 782, 788, 790, 797, 805, 815, 840, 860, 871;
Honduras: 1177; México: 1526, 1528, 1530, 1561, 1568,
1571, 1591, 1609; Nicaragua: 1696; Paraguay: 1761; Perú:
1775, 1779; [S] 12, 42; Bolivia: 286; Chile: 411; España:
714, 718, 756, 769; México: 1529; Perú: 1766, 1774, 1777.

economía política
[C] 2, 14, 29; Chile: 412, 441; España: 797; México: 1526,
1566, 1590; [S] 42.

economic and commercial sciences
[S] 32; Australia: 137; Bangladesh: 217; Canada: 364, 383;
China, Macao: 531; Germany: 1096, 1111; Italie: 1288;
Japan: 1320, 1324, 1399; Netherlands: 1670; Republic of
Moldova: 1954; Russian Federation: 2081, 2114; United
Kingdom: 2384, 2411; United States of America: 2522,
2652; Uzbekistan: 2766; [C] 38; Australia: 161; Austria:
193, 194; Azerbaijan: 207, 209; Belgique: 264; Bosnia and
Herzegovina: 291; Bulgaria: 321; Canada: 353, 369, 373,
383, 405; China: 465, 484, 486, 493, 496, 497, 499, 504,
515, 516; China, Macao: 531; Croatia: 598; Cyprus: 621;
Czech Republic: 655, 658, 667; Denmark: 676; Estonia:
876; Finland: 887, 890; Germany: 1087, 1088, 1089, 1090,
1098, 1102, 1108, 1109, 1122, 1130, 1135, 1137, 1143;
Grèce: 1154; Hungary: 1184, 1193, 1198, 1200, 1201;
India: 1222, 1225; Indonesia: 1229, 1236; Ireland: 1255;
Italie: 1277, 1285, 1290, 1300, 1302, 1304; Japan: 1313,
1322, 1343, 1350, 1364, 1385; Jordan: 1409; Kazakhstan:
1415, 1417; Kenya: 1425; Kyrgyzstan: 1428, 1431; Latvia:
1436, 1441; Liban: 1443; Lithuania: 1459; Malawi: 1485;
Mongolia: 1631; Netherlands: 1654, 1667, 1673, 1675,
1681, 1682; Nigeria: 1704; Norway: 1725; Oman: 1733;
Pakistan: 1742; Philippines: 1816; Poland: 1860, 1871,
1892, 1905, 1909, 1914, 1915; Republic of Korea: 1939,
1940, 1947, 1948; Republic of Moldova: 1953; Roumanie:
1966; Russian Federation: 1982, 1990, 1995, 2010, 2012,
2016, 2033, 2057, 2060, 2066, 2075, 2081, 2108, 2110,
2114, 2115, 2117, 2123, 2131; San Marino: 2142; Serbia
and Montenegro: 2147, 2149; Slovakia: 2154, 2168, 2171;
Slovenia: 2178; Sri Lanka: 2197; Suisse: 2227; Suriname:
2229; Sweden: 2239, 2251; Thailand: 2265, 2272, 2280,
2282; Turkey: 2324; Uganda: 2333; Ukraine: 2340, 2347,
2361; United Kingdom: 2384, 2401, 2472; United Republic
of Tanzania: 2492, 2496; United States of America: 2529,
2557, 2560, 2577, 2621, 2652, 2659, 2660, 2666, 2683,
2700, 2720, 2730, 2746; Uzbekistan: 2767; Yemen: 2781.

économie
[C] 8, 12, 14; Algérie: 63, 71; Angola: 74; Arménie: 129;
Belarus, Republic of: 233, 234, 237, 238, 241, 242;
Belgique: 253, 261, 279; Bulgaria: 316, 325, 326, 328, 337,
340; Cameroun: 350; Canada: 393; Côte d'Ivoire: 595, 597;
France: 909, 930, 937, 939, 960, 964, 968, 971, 995, 1001,
1003, 1025, 1036, 1054, 1056, 1062; Gabon: 1078; Grèce:
1158, 1159, 1160, 1161, 1162; Italie: 1296; Suisse: 2215,
2216; Tunisie: 2298, 2306, 2310; [S] 12; Canada: 369;
France: 1005, 1017.

économie politique
[C] 2, 14, 29; Belgique: 261, 277, 279; France: 1001, 1003;
Maroc: 1508; Saint-Siège: 2141; Tunisie: 2298, 2310; [S]
France: 1017.

economy
[C] 8, 12, 14; Arménie: 127; Austria: 198; Azerbaijan: 205,
207, 208; Barbados: 223; Belgique: 264; Bulgaria: 320;
Canada: 353, 362, 371, 374, 385, 398, 405; China: 489,
521; China, Hong Kong: 526; Cyprus: 627; Czech
Republic: 655, 663, 665, 666, 667; Denmark: 676; Eritrea:
711; Estonia: 881; Ethiopia: 885; Finland: 890, 896;
Germany: 1087, 1088, 1089, 1098, 1100; Grèce: 1155;
Indonesia: 1228, 1229, 1239; Ireland: 1255, 1259; Italie:
1280, 1285, 1290, 1301, 1302; Japan: 1316, 1322, 1344,
1352, 1359, 1377, 1390; Kazakhstan: 1417, 1419;
Kyrgyzstan: 1428, 1429, 1430, 1431; Latvia: 1441; Liban:
1443; Lithuania: 1468; Mauritius: 1521; Mongolia: 1630,
1631; Netherlands: 1643, 1655, 1667, 1676, 1681; New
Zealand: 1687; Norway: 1713, 1724, 1725; Poland: 1829,
1840, 1844, 1845, 1847, 1851, 1861, 1877, 1901, 1903,
1911, 1916; Portugal: 1917, 1920; Republic of Korea: 1929,
1935, 1940; Republic of Moldova: 1953, 1954, 1956;
République arabe syrienne: 1962; Roumanie: 1966;
Russian Federation: 1990, 1991, 1992, 2000, 2004, 2007,
2008, 2013, 2014, 2016, 2023, 2025, 2027, 2031, 2037,
2040, 2046, 2049, 2057, 2059, 2063, 2065, 2070, 2071,

2072, 2074, 2075, 2080, 2081, 2082, 2083, 2084, 2085,
2086, 2091, 2106, 2108, 2110, 2111, 2112, 2114, 2117,
2123, 2129, 2131, 2136, 2137; San Marino: 2142; Slovakia:
2159, 2166; Slovenia: 2175; Sweden: 2239, 2251, 2258;
Tajikistan: 2261; Thailand: 2265, 2278, 2280; Turkey: 2319,
2320, 2324, 2329, 2330; Uganda: 2333; Ukraine: 2337,
2338, 2340, 2347, 2349, 2353, 2356, 2361; United Kingdom:
2384, 2400, 2479; United Republic of Tanzania: 2488, 2490;
United States of America: 2529, 2561, 2634, 2642, 2647,
2655, 2666, 2683, 2696, 2700, 2744, 2758; Uzbekistan:
2765, 2766, 2767; [S] 12, 42; Australia: 137; Canada: 369;
Germany: 1096, 1109; Italie: 1303; Japan: 1317, 1324,
1338, 1392; Russian Federation: 2004, 2014, 2081, 2114;
San Marino: 2142; Sweden: 2245; Tajikistan: 2260; United
Kingdom: 2464; United States of America: 2582, 2634;
Uzbekistan: 2766.

edición
[C] España: 802.

édition
[C] Côte d'Ivoire: 597; [S] France: 911.

educación
[C] 19, 49; Argentina: 94, 98, 106, 107; Chile: 418, 423,
424, 425, 428, 429, 432, 434, 440, 447, 452, 453, 455;
Colombia: 546, 549; Costa Rica: 561, 565, 566, 574, 575,
578, 580, 582, 585, 592; Cuba: 606, 607, 608, 620;
Ecuador: 689, 695; El Salvador: 709; España: 761, 796,
803, 843, 851, 852, 854, 859; México: 1537, 1559, 1573,
1575, 1582, 1586, 1590, 1597, 1605, 1607, 1611, 1612;
Nicaragua: 1695; Panamá: 1758; Perú: 1768, 1782, 1793,
1796; Uruguay: 2764; Venezuela: 2775; [S] 49; Colombia:
554; España: 783; Honduras: 1178; México: 1616; Perú:
1770, 1780.

educación de la primera infancia
[C] Chile: 418, 424, 447, 449; Costa Rica: 580, 581; Cuba:
607; España: 803; México: 1590; [S] Honduras: 1178.

educación especial
[S] 46; España: 783; Honduras: 1178; [C] Chile: 418, 429,
447, 455; Costa Rica: 574; Cuba: 607; España: 795, 803;
México: 1537, 1540.

educación física
[C] Chile: 413, 429; Cuba: 602; España: 795, 803; México:
1564, 1596; [S] Honduras: 1178.

educación permanente
[C] México: 1579, 1580, 1584, 1606; Perú: 1765, 1771,
1779.

education
[C] 19, 49; Arménie: 131; Australia: 134, 140, 141, 142,
147, 158, 161, 166, 172, 179; Azerbaijan: 209; Bangladesh:
214; Belgique: 255, 275; Belize: 283; Canada: 353, 355,
357, 360, 366, 373, 376, 379, 382, 383, 385, 398; China:
465, 480, 484, 486, 491, 507, 515; Croatia: 598; Cyprus:
643; Czech Republic: 650, 663; Egypt: 706; Ethiopia: 885;
Fiji: 886; Finland: 887, 896, 899; Germany: 1090, 1099,
1105, 1109, 1131, 1135, 1136; Ghana: 1147; Guyana:
1174; Hungary: 1189, 1198, 1201; Iceland: 1206; India:
1213, 1222, 1225; Indonesia: 1239; Iran, Islamic Republic
of: 1251, 1252, 1254; Ireland: 1259; Israel: 1268; Italie:
1277, 1301; Jamaica: 1309, 1310; Japan: 1311, 1316,
1322, 1329, 1344, 1346, 1383, 1385, 1396; Jordan: 1403,
1404, 1411, 1412; Kazakhstan: 1414, 1415, 1417, 1418;
Kenya: 1422, 1425; Kuwait: 1427; Kyrgyzstan: 1429, 1431,
1432; Latvia: 1435, 1436, 1441; Liban: 1443; Libyan Arab
Jamahiriya: 1456; Lithuania: 1463; Malawi: 1485; Malta:
1499; Mauritius: 1520, 1521; Mongolia: 1631; Nepal: 1633;
Netherlands: 1673, 1675, 1676; Nigeria: 1705, 1707, 1709;
Norway: 1713, 1720, 1724, 1731; Oman: 1733; Pakistan:
1738, 1747, 1749, 1751, 1752, 1754; Philippines: 1798,
1801, 1803, 1805, 1806, 1808, 1810, 1811, 1813, 1816,
1817, 1819, 1820, 1821; Poland: 1856, 1859, 1861, 1870,
1874, 1877, 1878, 1879, 1886, 1903, 1908, 1909, 1915;
Portugal: 1920, 1924, 1925, 1927; Republic of Korea: 1929,
1933, 1940, 1942, 1945, 1948; Republic of Moldova: 1953,
1955; Roumanie: 1969, 1974, 1975; Russian Federation:
1977, 1988, 1990, 1994, 2006, 2009, 2011, 2027, 2030,
2064, 2065, 2069, 2083, 2098, 2121, 2128, 2137; San
Marino: 2142; Serbia and Montenegro: 2147; Slovakia:
2161, 2170, 2172; South Africa: 2181, 2187, 2191; Sri
Lanka: 2198; Sudan: 2205; Suriname: 2229; Swaziland:
2234; Sweden: 2240, 2241, 2242, 2247, 2250; Tajikistan:
2262; Thailand: 2269, 2278, 2280; Turkey: 2320, 2321,
2323, 2324, 2326, 2329, 2330; Uganda: 2331, 2333;
Ukraine: 2334, 2343, 2347, 2357, 2362; United Kingdom:
2375, 2391, 2399, 2432, 2452, 2459, 2476, 2479; United
Republic of Tanzania: 2489, 2492, 2495, 2496; United
States of America: 2500, 2501, 2502, 2508, 2512, 2518,
2524, 2529, 2530, 2535, 2542, 2557, 2560, 2562, 2564,
2574, 2576, 2587, 2594, 2617, 2618, 2619, 2620, 2623,
2624, 2633, 2634, 2641, 2647, 2653, 2659, 2660, 2663,
2666, 2667, 2696, 2700, 2707, 2713, 2714, 2718, 2719,

2720, 2730, 2735, 2738, 2745, 2746, 2747, 2748, 2754;
United States of America, Puerto Rico: 2759; Uzbekistan:
2766, 2768; Zimbabwe: 2785, 2786; [S] 49; Australia: 141,
147, 161; Bangladesh: 214; Canada: 357, 383, 400, 401;
Germany: 1123; Ghana: 1148; Japan: 1353, 1354, 1356,
1378, 1394; New Zealand: 1684; Norway: 1723;
Philippines: 1802; Poland: 1878; Republic of Korea: 1938;
Russian Federation: 2083, 2106; Ukraine: 2343; United
Kingdom: 2391, 2396, 2471; United States of America:
2574, 2634, 2685; Yemen: 2782.

éducation
[C] 19, 49; Algérie: 66; Angola: 74; Belarus, Republic of:
239; Belgique: 258, 279; Brésil: 297, 299, 306, 311, 313;
Bulgaria: 332; Cameroun: 351; Canada: 390, 393; France:
912, 967, 1021, 1045, 1067; Grèce: 1159, 1160; Liban:
1450; Madagascar: 1481, 1484; Suisse: 2221; Togo: 2287;
Turkey: 2327, 2328; [S] 49; Canada: 389; Comores, Les:
557; Tunisie: 2291.

éducation de la première enfance
[C] Brésil: 297; Bulgaria: 333, 340; France: 1021; Grèce:
1160.

éducation permanente
[C] Arménie: 129; France: 1021, 1067; Suisse: 2225;
Tunisie: 2307; [S] Tunisie: 2291.

éducation physique
[C] Belarus, Republic of: 239; Belgique: 259; Brésil: 311;
Bulgaria: 319; France: 1024, 1029, 1053, 1057; Grèce:
1159, 1160.

éducation spéciale
[S] 46.

electricidad y electrónica
[S] 31; México: 1588; Perú: 1771, 1773; [C] Argentina: 93,
95, 110; Bolivia: 289, 290; Chile: 419, 456; Costa Rica:
582, 593; Cuba: 605; México: 1525, 1547, 1552, 1568,
1572, 1597, 1621; Perú: 1771.

électricité et électronique
[S] 31; France: 956; [C] Algérie: 63, 68, 70, 71; Belarus,
Republic of: 232, 237, 241; Belgique: 249; Brésil: 311;
Bulgaria: 328, 339, 341, 342, 344; Côte d'Ivoire: 594;
France: 915, 921, 932, 945, 946, 947, 952, 955, 956, 968,
972, 975, 976, 977, 978, 979, 1006, 1009, 1013, 1054;
Grèce: 1160; Luxembourg: 1474; Madagascar: 1475, 1476,
1478, 1484; Maroc: 1500, 1503, 1511, 1513; Portugal:
1922; Suisse: 2208, 2210; Togo: 2287; Tunisie: 2294,
2305, 2314.

electricity and electronics
[S] 31; Bangladesh: 214; Japan: 1389; Russian Federation:
2016; United Kingdom: 2468; [C] Austria: 190; Azerbaijan:
205; Bangladesh: 216; Belgique: 274; Bulgaria: 321;
China: 457, 473, 496, 497, 504, 516, 519, 523; Cyprus: 636;
Czech Republic: 662; Egypt: 705, 706; Ethiopia: 885;
Finland: 892, 894, 900; Germany: 1083, 1087, 1088, 1098,
1099, 1117, 1130, 1132, 1133, 1134; Hungary: 1192; India:
1215, 1223; Indonesia: 1233, 1238; Ireland: 1257; Italie:
1290, 1300, 1301; Japan: 1369, 1377, 1379, 1389;
Kazakhstan: 1417; Latvia: 1437; Libyan Arab Jamahiriya:
1456; Lithuania: 1459, 1468; Malta: 1498; Nigeria: 1703,
1707, 1709; Norway: 1713, 1715, 1725; Pakistan: 1746;
Philippines: 1806, 1809, 1816; Poland: 1866, 1869, 1890,
1891, 1892, 1894; Republic of Korea: 1931, 1935, 1939,
1948; Russian Federation: 1978, 1985, 1992, 2000, 2010,
2016, 2038, 2048, 2049, 2050, 2058, 2059, 2066, 2067,
2068, 2070, 2082, 2084, 2091, 2096, 2112, 2115, 2118,
2119, 2127, 2129; Serbia and Montenegro: 2148;
Singapore: 2152; Slovakia: 2164, 2174; South Africa: 2181,
2189; Sudan: 2204; Suriname: 2232; Sweden: 2248;
Thailand: 2265, 2271; Ukraine: 2351, 2365; United
Kingdom: 2401, 2425, 2436, 2472; United Republic of
Tanzania: 2487, 2496; United States of America: 2565,
2692; Uzbekistan: 2770.

élevage
[C] Belgique: 250; France: 935; Tchad: 2263; Tunisie:
2295.

empresas internacionales
[C] Colombia: 533; España: 768; Nicaragua: 1697;
República Dominicana: 1959.

energía
[S] 23; Argentina: 83; [C] Argentina: 83, 93; España: 717,
747, 802; México: 1546, 1571, 1581; Venezuela: 2772.

énergie
[S] 23; France: 956, 964; [C] Belarus, Republic of: 227;
Belgique: 247; Côte d'Ivoire: 594; France: 915, 944, 945,
953, 956, 1007, 1008, 1009, 1041; Madagascar: 1475,
1476, 1478, 1484; Tunisie: 2294.

energy
[S] 23; Russian Federation: 2016; Thailand: 2275; [C]
Azerbaijan: 205; China: 457, 462, 472, 497, 519; Germany:
1083, 1098, 1099, 1133; Grèce: 1155; India: 1223;
Indonesia: 1233; Italie: 1284, 1290, 1300; Japan: 1379,
1389; Kazakhstan: 1415; Lithuania: 1468; Norway: 1715;
Poland: 1891; Russian Federation: 1978, 2000, 2016, 2020,
2045, 2047, 2059, 2066, 2070, 2082, 2096, 2111, 2119,
2131, 2135; Singapore: 2152; Slovakia: 2166; Thailand:
2271; Ukraine: 2351, 2354; United Kingdom: 2401, 2472.

enfermería
[C] 11; Andorra: 72; Argentina: 86, 89, 104, 109; Chile:
421, 432; Colombia: 549; Costa Rica: 561, 573, 582;
España: 748, 829, 834, 845, 851, 868; México: 1539; Perú:
1765, 1775, 1784, 1793; [S] Perú: 1774.

engineering
[C] 4, 21; Arménie: 125; Australia: 136, 140, 142, 147, 158,
162, 165, 166, 182; Austria: 190, 194, 203; Azerbaijan: 205,
209; Bangladesh: 214, 215, 216; Belgique: 263; Belize:
283; Bosnia and Herzegovina: 291; Canada: 353, 360, 367,
374, 379, 382, 405; China: 457, 465, 472, 496, 499, 507,
515, 516, 518, 519; Croatia: 598; Cyprus: 633; Czech
Republic: 651, 662, 663, 673; Egypt: 699, 706; Fiji: 886;
Finland: 892, 894, 900, 901; Georgia: 1081; Germany:
1083, 1087, 1088, 1089, 1097, 1098, 1099, 1100, 1102,
1112, 1126, 1130, 1133, 1134; Grèce: 1155; Hungary:
1182, 1190, 1194, 1197, 1198, 1200; India: 1214, 1215,
1222, 1225; Indonesia: 1228, 1229, 1233, 1236, 1237, 1238;
Iran, Islamic Republic of: 1244, 1252, 1254; Ireland: 1256,
1257, 1259; Israel: 1263; Italie: 1283, 1284, 1290, 1300;
Jamaica: 1309, 1310; Japan: 1336, 1360, 1364, 1369, 1379,
1385, 1389, 1396, 1398; Jordan: 1400, 1402, 1405, 1408,
1409, 1412; Kazakhstan: 1415, 1417, 1418; Kuwait: 1427;
Kyrgyzstan: 1431, 1433; Latvia: 1437; Liban: 1443; Libyan
Arab Jamahiriya: 1456; Lithuania: 1459, 1468; Malawi:
1485; Malaysia: 1488, 1496; Malta: 1499; Mauritius: 1521;
Netherlands: 1651, 1668, 1675; Nigeria: 1704, 1705, 1707,
1709; Norway: 1713, 1724, 1725, 1728; Oman: 1733;
Philippines: 1804, 1805, 1809, 1810, 1811, 1817, 1821,
1822; Poland: 1829, 1841, 1856, 1877, 1883, 1890, 1891,
1892, 1894, 1900, 1907, 1911; Portugal: 1925; Republic of
Korea: 1933, 1935, 1939, 1940, 1948; Russian Federation:
1978, 1980, 1982, 1985, 1990, 2000, 2012, 2016, 2026,
2038, 2041, 2042, 2045, 2047, 2054, 2059, 2064, 2066,
2067, 2068, 2069, 2073, 2075, 2082, 2085, 2091, 2096,
2098, 2104, 2105, 2108, 2111, 2115, 2119, 2123, 2124,
2127, 2128, 2129, 2135, 2136, 2137; Serbia and
Montenegro: 2147, 2148; Singapore: 2152, 2153; Slovakia:
2164, 2165; South Africa: 2195; Sri Lanka: 2200, 2202;
Suisse: 2209; Suriname: 2229; Sweden: 2236, 2237, 2240,
2242, 2248, 2258; Tajikistan: 2261, 2262; Thailand: 2271,
2273, 2274, 2282; Turkey: 2319, 2320, 2321, 2323, 2330;
Ukraine: 2337, 2343, 2349, 2351, 2354, 2364; United
Kingdom: 2367, 2369, 2379, 2380, 2392, 2399, 2401, 2425,
2431, 2432, 2452, 2460, 2472; United Republic of Tanzania:
2496; United States of America: 2524, 2530, 2537, 2557,
2561, 2563, 2565, 2580, 2587, 2619, 2620, 2621, 2624,
2634, 2642, 2660, 2679, 2685, 2692, 2713, 2717, 2718,
2719, 2720, 2730, 2738, 2745, 2749, 2753, 2754;
Uzbekistan: 2771; [S] 48, 59; Australia: 147; Bangladesh:
215, 219; Canada: 372, 400, 401; Estonia: 881; Germany:
1110, 1120, 1125; Ghana: 1145; Iran, Islamic Republic of:
1244; Italie: 1287, 1288, 1303; Japan: 1317, 1336, 1351,
1353, 1369, 1389, 1394, 1398, 1399; Pakistan: 1750;
Republic of Moldova: 1954; Russian Federation: 2016;
Singapore: 2149; United Kingdom: 2411, 2417, 2419, 2443,
2448, 2468; United States of America: 2601, 2624, 2634,
2733; Yemen: 2782.

English
[C] Arménie: 125, 127; Azerbaijan: 207; Bangladesh: 218;
Bulgaria: 320; Canada: 366, 373, 385; China: 496, 516;
China, Hong Kong: 526; Eritrea: 711; Ethiopia: 884, 885;
Georgia: 1080; Hungary: 1184; India: 1220, 1222, 1223;
Indonesia: 1230, 1236, 1239; Iran, Islamic Republic of:
1253; Italie: 1280, 1285, 1286, 1301; Japan: 1316, 1322,
1339, 1345, 1347, 1352; Jordan: 1401, 1408; Kyrgyzstan:
1429, 1430; Latvia: 1436, 1440, 1441; Lithuania: 1459;
Malawi: 1485; New Zealand: 1689; Norway: 1722, 1725,
1729; Pakistan: 1736, 1737, 1738, 1747, 1748, 1751, 1752;
Philippines: 1806, 1808, 1812, 1817; Poland: 1846, 1874,
1888, 1892, 1902, 1908; Republic of Korea: 1941; Russian
Federation: 2004, 2027, 2066, 2117, 2134; Sri Lanka: 2199;
Tajikistan: 2260; Thailand: 2265, 2271; Ukraine: 2336,
2341, 2346; United Kingdom: 2401, 2425, 2440, 2459, 2461,
2480, 2482; United States of America: 2514, 2529, 2585,
2594, 2627, 2641, 2647, 2666, 2673, 2684, 2726; Yemen:
2781; [S] Bangladesh: 217; Japan: 1356, 1365, 1392;
Russian Federation: 2004.

enología
[C] Argentina: 80; España: 851.

enseignement à distance
[S] 41.

enseignement technique
[C] Belarus, Republic of: 237; Bulgaria: 328; France: 993, 998, 1015; Grèce: 1162; Liban: 1444; Maroc: 1511; Tunisie: 2307.

enseñanza a distancia
[S] 41; [C] 44.

enseñanza técnica
[C] Cuba: 607; Venezuela: 2776; [S] Honduras: 1178.

espace
[C] Belgique: 247; France: 935, 951, 1018; [S] France: 910.

espacio
[C] España: 766.

espagnol
[C] Belarus, Republic of: 243; Belgique: 261; France: 1001; Tunisie: 2291, 2313.

español
[C] Argentina: 90, 91, 99; Costa Rica: 568; Cuba: 604; Ecuador: 691, 692, 694, 696; España: 720, 722, 723, 724, 742, 752, 754, 786, 787, 804, 806, 807, 809, 810, 811, 813, 820, 825, 826, 827, 837, 841, 842, 849, 850, 852, 853, 854, 859, 873; Guatemala: 1168; México: 1553, 1560, 1566, 1568, 1570, 1573, 1574, 1576, 1577, 1578, 1580, 1586, 1587, 1588, 1592, 1593, 1602, 1603, 1606, 1610, 1611, 1615, 1618, 1619, 1622, 1628; Perú: 1779; [S] España: 712, 713, 780, 814, 858.

Esperanto
[S] 9; United Kingdom: 2407.

estadística
[C] 12; Chile: 420; España: 748; México: 1543; Perú: 1791, 1795; [S] 12, 42.

estomatología
[C] Perú: 1791.

estudios africanos
[S] México: 1529.

estudios americanos
[C] 25; Argentina: 91; Ecuador: 689; España: 752, 754, 806, 860; México: 1566; [S] Ecuador: 689; España: 755.

estudios ásiaticos
[S] 46; México: 1529.

estudios culturales
[C] 49; Argentina: 90; Colombia: 552; Costa Rica: 592; Ecuador: 689, 692, 696; España: 722, 734, 754, 806, 810, 813, 826, 842, 851, 854, 859; México: 1527, 1566, 1568, 1570, 1587, 1588, 1598, 1602, 1603, 1606, 1613, 1618, 1619, 1628; Perú: 1772; [S] 49; Ecuador: 689; España: 756, 762, 858; México: 1594.

estudios dentales
[C] Bolivia: 289; Colombia: 547; Costa Rica: 585; Honduras: 1176; México: 1539, 1607, 1621; Perú: 1787; [S] Colombia: 548; Ecuador: 693.

estudios europeos
[C] 8, 14; España: 745, 752, 754, 776, 792, 805; [S] 10, 14.

estudios internacionales
[C] 2, 29, 39; Argentina: 91, 124; Chile: 441; España: 754, 776, 781, 790, 805; México: 1553, 1560, 1566, 1590.

estudios paramédicos
[C] Argentina: 104; Colombia: 540; España: 748, 868; Venezuela: 2776.

estudios sobre el desarrollo
[C] 2, 15, 29, 39; Chile: 412, 425; Costa Rica: 586; España: 757, 860; Honduras: 1177; México: 1534, 1589; Perú: 1769; [S] 49, 50, 55; Chile: 411; España: 771; México: 1529.

ethnologie
[C] Brésil: 309; Grèce: 1160; Maroc: 1505.

ethnology
[C] Azerbaijan: 205; Germany: 1135; India: 1220; Jordan: 1401; Kyrgyzstan: 1430; Mongolia: 1631; Republic of Moldova: 1955; Russian Federation: 2065, 2117.

etnología
[C] España: 734.

études africaines
[C] France: 930.

études américaines

études asiatiques
[S] 46; [C] France: 909, 930.

études classiques
[C] France: 1033; Saint-Siège: 2140.

études culturelles
[C] 49; Albanie: 61; Belarus, Republic of: 239; Canada: 402; Sénégal: 2146; [S] 49.

études d'infirmière
[C] 11; Belarus, Republic of: 229; Belgique: 259; Brésil: 307; Cameroun: 350; Grèce: 1159; Liban: 1444, 1452; Portugal: 1926.

études dentaires
[C] Brésil: 299, 301, 307; Bulgaria: 329, 330; France: 1029, 1057, 1070; Madagascar: 1482; Maroc: 1510; Poland: 1897; Tunisie: 2301; Turkey: 2328; [S] Brésil: 301.

études du développement
[C] 2, 15, 29, 39; Belgique: 247, 277; France: 930, 1036; Madagascar: 1479; Maroc: 1504; Saint-Siège: 2141; Suisse: 2208, 2215; Togo: 2284; [S] 49, 50, 55; Belgique: 276.

études européennes
[C] 8, 14; Belgique: 253, 280; France: 1031, 1033, 1064, 1073; Suisse: 2214; [S] 10, 14; Italie: 1281.

études internationales
[C] 2, 29, 39; Bulgaria: 325; Côte d'Ivoire: 596; France: 976, 985, 987, 1003, 1016, 1047, 1073; Grèce: 1162; [S] 40; Maroc: 1507.

études orientales
[C] Saint-Siège: 2139.

études paramédicales
[C] Belgique: 259; Bulgaria: 340; Togo: 2287; Tunisie: 2296, 2297; [S] Tunisie: 2317.

European studies
[C] 8, 14; Austria: 194; Azerbaijan: 209; Bulgaria: 320; Canada: 405; Cyprus: 631; Czech Republic: 667; Denmark: 674, 686; Estonia: 877, 879; Finland: 903; Germany: 1090, 1108, 1126, 1133; Hungary: 1201; Ireland: 1259; Netherlands: 1653, 1667; Poland: 1868, 1886; Republic of Moldova: 1954; Russian Federation: 2025; Slovakia: 2170; Sweden: 2243, 2251; Turkey: 2320; United Kingdom: 2369, 2392, 2399, 2400, 2425, 2432, 2452, 2467, 2472, 2480; United States of America: 2574, 2577, 2666; [S] 10, 14; United Kingdom: 2457.

farmacia y farmacología
[C] Argentina: 104, 109; Bolivia: 289; Colombia: 549; Costa Rica: 567; España: 818, 833, 834, 848, 871; México: 1572, 1615; Venezuela: 2777; [S] España: 753.

filología
[C] España: 734, 761, 793, 842; [S] España: 814, 858.

filosofía
[C] Argentina: 98; Colombia: 533; Costa Rica: 565; España: 793; México: 1567, 1575, 1598, 1605, 1607, 1611, 1615; Perú: 1768, 1791; [S] México: 1605.

finance
[C] 18; Arménie: 125, 127; Australia: 161; Austria: 193, 194, 198; Bangladesh: 218; Barbados: 223; Canada: 353, 371, 385, 398, 405; China: 496, 520; China, Macao: 531; Cyprus: 627, 628, 631; Czech Republic: 665, 667; Denmark: 676; Ethiopia: 885; Finland: 890; Georgia: 1081; Germany: 1089, 1098, 1122, 1135; Ghana: 1146; Grèce: 1154; India: 1219; Indonesia: 1232, 1238; Ireland: 1255, 1259; Italie: 1277, 1302, 1304; Jordan: 1402, 1408, 1411; Kazakhstan: 1419; Kyrgyzstan: 1428, 1429, 1430; Latvia: 1436, 1440, 1441; Malaysia: 1491; Mauritius: 1522; Mongolia: 1631; Netherlands: 1635, 1654, 1666, 1667; New Zealand: 1687; Nigeria: 1707; Norway: 1718; Pakistan: 1736, 1744; Philippines: 1805, 1812, 1816; Poland: 1855, 1862, 1879, 1887, 1888, 1901, 1902, 1906, 1914; Portugal: 1917; Republic of Korea: 1935, 1952; Republic of Moldova: 1953, 1954; Roumanie: 1966; Russian Federation: 1993, 1995, 2000, 2004, 2007, 2025, 2033, 2057, 2070, 2075, 2082, 2114, 2117, 2123, 2126, 2131; Singapore: 2152; Slovakia: 2158, 2166, 2168; South Africa: 2189; Sri Lanka: 2198; Swaziland: 2233; Sweden: 2239, 2251; Thailand: 2265, 2282; Ukraine: 2338, 2340, 2346, 2347, 2349, 2356, 2361; United Kingdom: 2384, 2401, 2472; United Republic of Tanzania: 2490, 2495; United States of America: 2557, 2633, 2647, 2659, 2660, 2666, 2673, 2683, 2684, 2696, 2735; Yemen: 2781; [S] 32; China, Macao: 531; Germany: 1111; Russian Federation: 2004, 2114; United Kingdom: 2384.

finances
[C] 18; Algérie: 63; Arménie: 129; Belarus, Republic of:
242; Belgique: 253, 277; Bulgaria: 316; Cameroun: 350;
France: 937, 980, 995, 996, 1058, 1064; Grèce: 1158, 1162;
Liban: 1452; Maroc: 1512; Tunisie: 2298, 2306, 2310; [S]
France: 922.

finanzas
[C] 18; Andorra: 72; Argentina: 97; Chile: 436; Colombia:
533, 535; Costa Rica: 582; España: 725, 744, 745, 746,
750, 758, 765, 782, 790, 791, 797, 815, 840, 846; Honduras:
1176; México: 1528, 1550, 1551, 1571, 1583, 1608, 1609,
1621, 1623; Nicaragua: 1697; Paraguay: 1761; Perú: 1764,
1769, 1779; [S] España: 714, 718, 726.

fine arts
[S] Australia: 132; Canada: 400; Italie: 1273; Japan: 1394;
Poland: 1831; United Kingdom: 2396, 2428; United States
of America: 2574, 2587, 2616; [C] Austria: 185, 196, 197;
Azerbaijan: 209; Belgique: 263; Bosnia and Herzegovina:
291; Canada: 353, 360, 371, 373, 375, 405; China: 465,
469, 484; Cyprus: 629, 640; Czech Republic: 647, 666;
Germany: 1090, 1101, 1121, 1136; Grèce: 1152; India:
1222; Italie: 1278, 1280, 1286, 1291; Lithuania: 1462, 1467,
1471; Mauritius: 1519; Netherlands: 1676; Norway: 1712,
1714, 1720; Pakistan: 1737, 1754; Philippines: 1808, 1817,
1825; Poland: 1831, 1832, 1833, 1834, 1835, 1867;
Portugal: 1924; Republic of Korea: 1929, 1947; Russian
Federation: 2000, 2027, 2037, 2065, 2107; Slovakia: 2155,
2166, 2170; South Africa: 2189; Tajikistan: 2261; Turkey:
2320, 2321, 2326; Ukraine: 2357; United Kingdom: 2375,
2376, 2398, 2399, 2401, 2432, 2484; United States of
America: 2524, 2529, 2544, 2554, 2561, 2609, 2613, 2618,
2619, 2627, 2656, 2661, 2666, 2684, 2713, 2735, 2736,
2746, 2747, 2753, 2754.

finlandais
[C] France: 1033.

Finnish
[S] Finland: 889; [C] Finland: 896.

fisheries
[C] 12; Australia: 136; Bangladesh: 216; Canada: 374;
Estonia: 876; Iceland: 1206; Indonesia: 1239; Iran, Islamic
Republic of: 1241; Japan: 1350; Kenya: 1425; Netherlands:
1682; Nigeria: 1703, 1707, 1709; Norway: 1729; Pakistan:
1753; Philippines: 1806; Russian Federation: 1982, 2069,
2120; Thailand: 2272; United Kingdom: 2406; United
States of America: 2549; [S] 12.

física
[C] 1; Argentina: 81, 82, 83, 93; Chile: 437, 438, 456;
Cuba: 599; España: 851; México: 1525, 1546, 1572, 1595;
[S] 1; Argentina: 83; Bolivia: 286; México: 1588.

fisiología
[C] Argentina: 104; Chile: 413; Colombia: 540; España:
794, 868; México: 1586; Venezuela: 2777.

folklore
[C] Azerbaijan: 209; Belgique: 261; Finland: 903; India:
1223; Japan: 1359; Latvia: 1441; Lithuania: 1462; México:
1533; Norway: 1725; Republic of Korea: 1929; Russian
Federation: 2027, 2055, 2094; Suisse: 2227; [S] Finland:
889; Sweden: 2259.

food
[C] 16; Belgique: 274; Canada: 353; Czech Republic: 653;
Germany: 1137; Guyana: 1173; India: 1213; Netherlands:
1639, 1681; Nigeria: 1703, 1707, 1709; Philippines: 1806,
1813; Poland: 1842; Republic of Korea: 1931; Russian
Federation: 1978, 1991, 2020, 2021, 2040; Slovakia: 2164;
Thailand: 2271; Turkey: 2329; United Kingdom: 2405, 2425,
2436, 2472, 2473; [S] Netherlands: 1639.

food industry
[C] Australia: 141; Azerbaijan: 209; Canada: 353; China:
486; Czech Republic: 653; Germany: 1122, 1137; India:
1208; Iran, Islamic Republic of: 1241; Italie: 1300;
Netherlands: 1642, 1649, 1652, 1681, 1682; Poland: 1829,
1843, 1892; Republic of Korea: 1948; Republic of Moldova:
1953; Roumanie: 1972; Russian Federation: 1978, 1990,
1991, 2000, 2020, 2040, 2044, 2070; Slovakia: 2163;
Thailand: 2272; Ukraine: 2338, 2354; United Kingdom:
2425, 2472.

forestry
[C] 12, 21; Bangladesh: 216; Bosnia and Herzegovina: 291;
Canada: 398; China: 505; Cyprus: 630; Czech Republic:
658; Estonia: 876; Finland: 892, 896; Grèce: 1155;
Guyana: 1173; Hungary: 1200; India: 1211; Iran, Islamic
Republic of: 1241; Italie: 1300; Japan: 1350; Lithuania:
1464; Malaysia: 1493; Nepal: 1633; Netherlands: 1652,
1681; New Zealand: 1687; Nigeria: 1703, 1707, 1709;
Papua New Guinea: 1759; Philippines: 1806; Poland: 1842,
1892; Russian Federation: 1987, 2012, 2074, 2106, 2120;
Slovakia: 2165; Sri Lanka: 2197; Sweden: 2254; Thailand:

2272; Uganda: 2333; United Kingdom: 2432; United
Republic of Tanzania: 2493; United States of America: 2549,
2621, 2645, 2714, 2720; [S] 12, 50; Germany: 1110.

formación de docentes
[C] Argentina: 107; Chile: 424, 429; Costa Rica: 575; Cuba:
606, 607, 608; España: 786; México: 1596; Nicaragua:
1695; Perú: 1782; [S] España: 783; Honduras: 1178.

formación profesional
[C] 18, 21, 58; Chile: 418; Costa Rica: 561; Cuba: 603,
606, 618; España: 742, 749, 751, 796, 803, 829, 842, 865;
México: 1577; Perú: 1784; [S] 31, 41, 53; España: 726,
767; Perú: 1770.

formation des enseignants
[C] Belarus, Republic of: 240; Belgique: 259, 261; Bulgaria:
319, 328; France: 1001; Grèce: 1162; Luxembourg: 1473;
Madagascar: 1475, 1479; Togo: 2287; [S] Comores, Les:
557.

formation professionnelle
[C] 18, 21, 58; Algérie: 70; Belgique: 272; France: 937,
941, 986, 993, 1015, 1067; Madagascar: 1475, 1479;
Suisse: 2213; Togo: 2287; [S] 31, 41, 53; Comores, Les:
557.

fotografía
[C] Perú: 1767; [S] Perú: 1767.

français
[C] 25; Algérie: 63, 68, 71; Belarus, Republic of: 243;
Belgique: 244; Burundi: 347; Canada: 393; France: 905,
970, 1001, 1021, 1030, 1031, 1033, 1038, 1039, 1047, 1051,
1059, 1062, 1068, 1075; Maroc: 1516; Sénégal: 2146;
Suisse: 2225; Togo: 2283; Tunisie: 2291, 2303, 2304, 2307;
[S] Tunisie: 2291.

francés
[C] 25; [S] Colombia: 542; México: 1594.

French
[C] 25; Canada: 385; Italie: 1280, 1301; Japan: 1345;
Jordan: 1401; Kyrgyzstan: 1430; Latvia: 1441; Norway:
1722; Poland: 1874, 1908; Republic of Korea: 1947;
Russian Federation: 2004, 2022, 2027, 2134; Swaziland:
2234; Ukraine: 2346; United Kingdom: 2472, 2480; United
States of America: 2529, 2642, 2647, 2673; [S] Japan:
1356; Russian Federation: 2004.

gender studies
[C] Pakistan: 1734, 1737; United Kingdom: 2400, 2473;
United States of America: 2529, 2557.

genética
[C] Chile: 416; España: 735, 763, 772; México: 1564; Perú:
1789; Venezuela: 2774, 2777.

genetics
[C] Canada: 374; Egypt: 700, 706; Finland: 896, 898;
Germany: 1135; Grèce: 1154; India: 1211, 1223; Iran,
Islamic Republic of: 1251; Italie: 1304; Japan: 1327, 1335;
Nigeria: 1707; Poland: 1874; Russian Federation: 2006,
2044, 2069; Sweden: 2254; Thailand: 2271; United
Kingdom: 2436, 2451; United States of America: 2659; [S]
Thailand: 2274.

génétique
[C] Belarus, Republic of: 229; France: 942, 1010; Italie:
1276; Tunisie: 2309.

génie chimique
[C] Algérie: 63, 71; Bulgaria: 328, 335; Côte d'Ivoire: 596;
France: 909, 928, 948, 956, 964, 979, 1006, 1007, 1009,
1049; Madagascar: 1478; Suisse: 2210; Tunisie: 2294; [S]
France: 956.

génie civil
[C] Algérie: 63, 68, 71; Belarus, Republic of: 231; Brésil:
310; Bulgaria: 324, 339; Burkina Faso: 345; Côte d'Ivoire:
596; France: 924, 925, 934, 939, 941, 945, 950, 959, 968,
973, 1049; Grèce: 1160; Luxembourg: 1474; Madagascar:
1478, 1484; Suisse: 2209, 2210; Togo: 2287; [S] France:
925.

geodesia
[C] Argentina: 93; Costa Rica: 587; España: 798.

géodésie
[C] Bulgaria: 324; Côte d'Ivoire: 596; France: 1018;
Madagascar: 1478; Suisse: 2210.

geodesy
[C] Azerbaijan: 205; Italie: 1290; Latvia: 1437; Lithuania:
1468; Nigeria: 1709; Poland: 1843, 1892; Russian
Federation: 2000, 2064, 2085, 2089, 2108; Slovakia: 2166;
Sweden: 2248; Ukraine: 2356; United States of America:
2666.

geografía
[C] Chile: 435; España: 793, 798.

géographie
[C] Belarus, Republic of: 236, 238, 243; Belgique: 247, 261; France: 940, 970; Italie: 1293; Liban: 1452; Madagascar: 1479; Tunisie: 2303.

geography
[C] Arménie: 127; Canada: 371, 373, 385, 396, 398, 405; Ethiopia: 884, 885; Finland: 890, 896; Georgia: 1080; Germany: 1135; India: 1222; Iran, Islamic Republic of: 1253; Ireland: 1259; Israel: 1268; Japan: 1344; Kenya: 1422, 1425; Latvia: 1441; Poland: 1853, 1905, 1915; Republic of Moldova: 1953, 1955; Russian Federation: 2009, 2022, 2027, 2080, 2134; Suisse: 2227; Thailand: 2278; Ukraine: 2347; United Kingdom: 2380, 2401; United States of America: 2549, 2561, 2666, 2673; [S] Japan: 1354; South Africa: 2186.

geología
[C] 44; Argentina: 78, 109, 123; Bolivia: 290; Chile: 437, 438, 444, 446; Costa Rica: 569; Cuba: 605, 620; España: 737, 779, 864; México: 1525, 1561, 1567; Venezuela: 2772; [S] Costa Rica: 570; España: 778.

géologie
[C] Belarus, Republic of: 238; Bulgaria: 339; France: 1000; Liban: 1452; Madagascar: 1478; Maroc: 1506, 1509, 1512, 1516; Portugal: 1922; Tchad: 2263; Tunisie: 2309; [S] France: 964.

geology
[C] 44; Azerbaijan: 205, 208; Belgique: 255; Canada: 353, 398, 405; China: 471, 472, 481, 493; Czech Republic: 664; Germany: 1135; India: 1211, 1215; Italie: 1283, 1290, 1304; Japan: 1383; Kazakhstan: 1415; Mongolia: 1631; Netherlands: 1649, 1682; Nigeria: 1703; Pakistan: 1751, 1752, 1753, 1754; Philippines: 1809; Poland: 1892, 1915; Russian Federation: 1992, 2000, 2008, 2041, 2067, 2080, 2089, 2108, 2111, 2119, 2131, 2137; Slovakia: 2160, 2161, 2166; South Africa: 2189; Ukraine: 2356; United Republic of Tanzania: 2496; United States of America: 2529, 2633; [S] South Africa: 2186; United Kingdom: 2371.

German
[C] Austria: 202; Canada: 385; Georgia: 1080; India: 1223; Italie: 1280, 1301; Kyrgyzstan: 1430; Latvia: 1436, 1440, 1441; Norway: 1722, 1725; Poland: 1846, 1874, 1908; Russian Federation: 2004, 2022, 2027; Ukraine: 2346; United Kingdom: 2472, 2480; United States of America: 2529, 2642, 2647; [S] Russian Federation: 2004.

gerontology
[C] Canada: 383; Iran, Islamic Republic of: 1251; Mongolia: 1630; Poland: 1873; Sweden: 2240; [S] Canada: 383.

gestion
[C] 19; Algérie: 63, 68, 71; Arménie: 129; Belarus, Republic of: 237, 238, 241, 242; Belgique: 247, 249, 251, 253, 257, 261, 262, 265; Bulgaria: 316, 326, 328, 341, 342; Burundi: 347; Cameroun: 350, 351; Canada: 390; Côte d'Ivoire: 594; France: 907, 922, 930, 960, 964, 980, 981, 987, 996, 997, 1001, 1014, 1016, 1039, 1056, 1062, 1064, 1069, 1074; Gabon: 1078; Liban: 1452; Maroc: 1512, 1513; Suisse: 2213; Tunisie: 2298, 2306, 2310; [S] Canada: 389; France: 922.

gestión
[C] 19; Andorra: 72; Argentina: 91, 94; Chile: 419, 424, 428; Colombia: 535; Ecuador: 689; España: 715, 743, 744, 745, 746, 748, 750, 758, 765, 768, 775, 790, 797, 815, 819, 836, 838, 840, 846, 851, 865; Honduras: 1176; México: 1534, 1553, 1583; Paraguay: 1761; Perú: 1765; Uruguay: 2763; [S] España: 767, 769, 771, 777.

graphic arts
[S] Australia: 132; Japan: 1342; United Kingdom: 2418; [C] Austria: 185; Canada: 375; Cyprus: 633; Czech Republic: 666; Finland: 892, 895; Germany: 1101; Hungary: 1188; Italie: 1280; Japan: 1342; Jordan: 1401, 1411; Latvia: 1435; Lithuania: 1467; Poland: 1831, 1832, 1834, 1835; Republic of Korea: 1935; Russian Federation: 2025, 2043, 2107, 2131; Slovakia: 2155; South Africa: 2181, 2189; Turkey: 2319; United Kingdom: 2399, 2432; United States of America: 2544, 2545, 2554, 2656, 2666, 2747; Uzbekistan: 2765.

grec
[C] Burundi: 347.

Greek
[S] Australia: 146; [C] Grèce: 1164; Italie: 1286; United Kingdom: 2480; United States of America: 2529.

health and hygiene
[S] 6; Australia: 141, 147; Belgique: 266; China: 512; Germany: 1125; Japan: 1320; New Zealand: 1685; United

Kingdom: 2387; United States of America: 2598, 2615, 2646, 2648; [C] 12, 16; Arménie: 131; Australia: 140, 161, 171, 172, 179, 182; Austria: 191, 194; Bahrain: 210, 211; Barbados: 222; Belarus, Republic of: 235; Belgique: 263, 264, 275; Belize: 283; Bosnia and Herzegovina: 291; Canada: 354, 398, 405; Croatia: 598; Finland: 887, 893, 898; Germany: 1092, 1109, 1133; Ghana: 1146; Guyana: 1174; Hungary: 1191, 1198; India: 1213; Indonesia: 1229; Iran, Islamic Republic of: 1242, 1245, 1251; Israel: 1263, 1264, 1266; Italie: 1304; Jamaica: 1310; Japan: 1327, 1335, 1347; Kazakhstan: 1416; Kenya: 1425; Liban: 1443; Malawi: 1485; Mongolia: 1630; Netherlands: 1641, 1671, 1675, 1679; New Zealand: 1686; Norway: 1729; Oman: 1733; Pakistan: 1735; Papua New Guinea: 1760; Poland: 1873, 1874; Roumanie: 1975; Russian Federation: 2090, 2128; Slovakia: 2154, 2172; South Africa: 2189, 2195; Sweden: 2237, 2241, 2246; Thailand: 2274, 2280; Uganda: 2332; Ukraine: 2336, 2343; United Kingdom: 2369, 2387, 2391, 2432, 2476; United Republic of Tanzania: 2497; United States of America: 2547, 2561, 2562, 2563, 2581, 2663, 2713, 2717, 2754; Uzbekistan: 2767.

hebreo
[S] México: 1529.

hébreu
[C] Burundi: 347.

Hebrew
[C] Israel: 1268; United States of America: 2529.

hidráulica
[C] México: 1564.

hidrología
[C] 57; Argentina: 78, 83, 93; Costa Rica: 569; España: 717, 864; Venezuela: 2772; [S] 57; Costa Rica: 570; Perú: 1773.

higiene y salud
[C] 12, 16; Argentina: 86, 93, 98, 100, 101, 104, 113, 121; Bolivia: 289; Chile: 421, 440; Colombia: 533, 540, 549; Costa Rica: 567, 575, 586; Ecuador: 689; España: 743, 748, 794, 851; México: 1528, 1534, 1543, 1566, 1567, 1581; Perú: 1765, 1793; Venezuela: 2773, 2776, 2778; [S] Colombia: 555.

histoire
[C] Arménie: 129; Belarus, Republic of: 236, 238, 239, 243; Belgique: 253, 261; Brésil: 299; Bulgaria: 337; Cameroun: 350; France: 938, 970, 1001, 1021, 1044, 1047, 1063; Grèce: 1157, 1160; Italie: 1293; Madagascar: 1479, 1481; Maroc: 1505, 1509, 1516; Tunisie: 2303; [S] Italie: 1270; Portugal: 1918.

histoire de l'art
[C] Belgique: 261, 270; Bulgaria: 317; France: 927, 938, 1069; Italie: 1293; Madagascar: 1479; Maroc: 1505; [S] Italie: 1270; Portugal: 1918.

historia
[C] Argentina: 91, 123; Chile: 446; Ecuador: 689; El Salvador: 710; España: 781, 793, 860; México: 1533, 1561, 1567, 1586; [S] Colombia: 554; España: 718, 755; México: 1529.

historia del arte
[C] Chile: 412, 453; España: 793, 851, 873; [S] España: 759.

history
[C] 14; Arménie: 127; Austria: 204; Azerbaijan: 209; Canada: 353, 366, 371, 379, 383, 385, 398, 405; China: 477, 489, 493, 499, 504, 520; China, Hong Kong: 526; Czech Republic: 667; Ethiopia: 883, 884; Finland: 887, 903; Germany: 1089, 1090; Hungary: 1184; India: 1213, 1222; Indonesia: 1236, 1238; Ireland: 1259; Italie: 1286; Japan: 1339, 1344, 1346; Kazakhstan: 1417; Kenya: 1425; Kyrgyzstan: 1429; Latvia: 1436, 1441; Mongolia: 1631; Netherlands: 1641, 1653; Norway: 1724, 1725, 1729; Philippines: 1803, 1812, 1817; Poland: 1853, 1886, 1903, 1905, 1908, 1915; Republic of Korea: 1929, 1935, 1942, 1943; Republic of Moldova: 1953, 1954, 1955; Russian Federation: 1977, 1989, 2004, 2008, 2022, 2027, 2055, 2063, 2071, 2073, 2079, 2080, 2082, 2093, 2097, 2106, 2134, 2137; San Marino: 2142; Slovakia: 2157, 2172; Suisse: 2227; Sweden: 2247; Ukraine: 2346, 2357, 2364; United Kingdom: 2464; United States of America: 2514, 2529, 2560, 2577, 2609, 2613, 2641, 2647, 2655, 2666, 2673, 2684, 2735; Uzbekistan: 2765, 2767; Yemen: 2781; [S] Canada: 364, 383; Estonia: 882; Japan: 1338, 1354, 1392; Kenya: 1420; Russian Federation: 2004; San Marino: 2142; Sweden: 2245, 2259; Tajikistan: 2260; United Kingdom: 2372, 2381, 2390, 2444, 2455, 2457, 2464; United States of America: 2559, 2582, 2677.

home economics

[C] India: 1213; Indonesia: 1229; Kenya: 1422; Latvia: 1436, 1440; New Zealand: 1686; Nigeria: 1703, 1707; Norway: 1713; Pakistan: 1734; Philippines: 1806, 1810, 1817; Russian Federation: 2093; Swaziland: 2234; Tajikistan: 2262; Ukraine: 2337; United Kingdom: 2436; United Republic of Tanzania: 2493; United States of America: 2617, 2624, 2679, 2754; [S] Japan: 1365; United States of America: 2624, 2634.

horticultura
[C] Argentina: 80; Chile: 446; Ecuador: 697; España: 863; México: 1530, 1558, 1562, 1568, 1595.

horticulture
[C] Australia: 182; Belarus, Republic of: 228; Belgique: 250, 258, 263; Bulgaria: 323, 327; Canada: 374; Czech Republic: 658; Estonia: 876; Ethiopia: 884; France: 926; Grèce: 1154; Iran, Islamic Republic of: 1241; Japan: 1380; Kenya: 1422; Maroc: 1504; Netherlands: 1642, 1652, 1682; Nigeria: 1703, 1707; Philippines: 1806; Poland: 1842, 1859, 1896; Roumanie: 1972; Russian Federation: 2069, 2120; Singapore: 2152; Slovakia: 2163; Sri Lanka: 2197; Sweden: 2254; Thailand: 2272; Tunisie: 2295; Uganda: 2333; Ukraine: 2334; United Kingdom: 2405, 2476; United Republic of Tanzania: 2493.

human sciences
[S] 14, 28, 49, 50; Japan: 1318, 1354, 1384; [C] 29; Australia: 166; Bulgaria: 321; Canada: 353, 405; Czech Republic: 665; Hungary: 1201; Italie: 1277; Japan: 1347; Latvia: 1441; Liban: 1443; Libyan Arab Jamahiriya: 1456; Mauritius: 1522; Philippines: 1816; Poland: 1886; Republic of Korea: 1935, 1948; Russian Federation: 1997, 2016, 2027, 2092; South Africa: 2191; Swaziland: 2234; Thailand: 2276; Ukraine: 2347; United Kingdom: 2401, 2404, 2472; United States of America: 2609, 2613, 2620, 2659.

Humanities and arts
[C] Australia: 140, 142; Azerbaijan: 206; Canada: 353, 357; China: 477, 480, 484, 493, 519; Croatia: 598; Finland: 887; Germany: 1136; Hungary: 1198; Iran, Islamic Republic of: 1252, 1254; Jamaica: 1310; Japan: 1311, 1343, 1383; Kazakhstan: 1414, 1415; Lithuania: 1471; Nepal: 1633; Netherlands: 1669; Pakistan: 1734; Papua New Guinea: 1760; Philippines: 1813, 1816; Poland: 1910, 1911; Republic of Korea: 1933; Roumanie: 1974; Russian Federation: 1994, 1995, 2098, 2121, 2122, 2128; Slovakia: 2154; South Africa: 2195; Sri Lanka: 2199, 2202; Suisse: 2227; Ukraine: 2343, 2352; United Kingdom: 2472; United States of America: 2501, 2545, 2623, 2685; Uzbekistan: 2766; [S] Canada: 357; Croatia: 598; Italie: 1303; Japan: 1356, 1378, 1394; New Zealand: 1684; Russian Federation: 2106; Thailand: 2267; United Kingdom: 2396, 2437, 2457; United States of America: 2598, 2604.

hydraulics
[S] 48; Japan: 1389; Russian Federation: 2016; [C] Azerbaijan: 205; Czech Republic: 652; Grèce: 1155; Italie: 1284, 1290, 1300; Japan: 1389; Lithuania: 1464; Russian Federation: 1990, 2014, 2016, 2091, 2129, 2131; Ukraine: 2337, 2351, 2356.

hydraulique
[C] Algérie: 63, 68, 71; Belarus, Republic of: 231; Bulgaria: 324; Burkina Faso: 345; France: 909, 941, 945, 947, 1009; Madagascar: 1478, 1484; Maroc: 1504; Suisse: 2208.

hydrologie
[C] 7, 57; Algérie: 71; Belgique: 247; Burkina Faso: 345; France: 941, 953; Madagascar: 1475, 1478; Niger: 1699; [S] 57; Canada: 391.

hydrology
[C] 7, 57; Azerbaijan: 205, 208; Bahrain: 210; Belgique: 255; Canada: 405; China: 471, 481; Czech Republic: 652; Germany: 1135; India: 1214; Iran, Islamic Republic of: 1241; Ireland: 1258; Italie: 1284, 1290; Japan: 1389, 1398; Kenya: 1423; Netherlands: 1668, 1682; Russian Federation: 2015, 2041, 2064, 2083, 2108, 2112, 2131; Slovakia: 2163; Sweden: 2254; Thailand: 2271; [S] 48, 57; Czech Republic: 652; Japan: 1389.

hygiène et santé
[C] 12, 16; Belgique: 258; Brésil: 295, 297, 306; Bulgaria: 337; Cameroun: 350, 351; Canada: 388; France: 941, 1029, 1060, 1076; Madagascar: 1482; Portugal: 1926; Suisse: 2215; [S] Belgique: 266; Canada: 391.

idiomas
[S] 46; Colombia: 554; México: 1612; [C] Argentina: 90; Chile: 447; Costa Rica: 568; El Salvador: 709; España: 722, 787, 804, 806, 809, 811, 820, 821, 827, 837, 842, 849, 850, 851, 852, 854, 859; Guatemala: 1168; México: 1550, 1566, 1570, 1571, 1572, 1578, 1593, 1612, 1615, 1621.

immunologie

[S] 20; Belgique: 266; Canada: 391; [C] France: 1010; Poland: 1897.

immunology
[S] Belgique: 266; [C] Egypt: 700; Iran, Islamic Republic of: 1251; Japan: 1327, 1335; Mongolia: 1630; Netherlands: 1657; Poland: 1873, 1874; Russian Federation: 2090; South Africa: 2182; United States of America: 2615, 2659.

imprimerie
[C] France: 1009.

industria alimentaría
[C] Argentina: 80, 101, 103; Chile: 426, 444; El Salvador: 708; España: 719, 727, 740, 775, 871.

industria química
[C] Argentina: 76; España: 736, 751, 775; [S] España: 767.

industria textil
[S] España: 767; Perú: 1773; [C] México: 1549.

industria y comercio
[C] Argentina: 715; México: 1550; [S] España: 767, 769; México: 1612; Perú: 1766.

industrial design
[C] China: 464; Denmark: 675; Finland: 895; Germany: 1083, 1099, 1135; Hungary: 1188; India: 1217; Italie: 1280, 1290; Japan: 1342; Netherlands: 1676; Philippines: 1809; Poland: 1834, 1892; Republic of Korea: 1931; Russian Federation: 2066, 2091, 2118, 2131; Slovakia: 2155, 2166; South Africa: 2181, 2189; Thailand: 2271; Turkey: 2320; Ukraine: 2356; United Kingdom: 2401, 2425, 2432; United States of America: 2542, 2544, 2554, 2656, 2736; [S] Japan: 1342; United Kingdom: 2418.

industrial relations
[C] Denmark: 676; Italie: 1277; Nigeria: 1709; Philippines: 1806; Russian Federation: 2000, 2086; Uganda: 2333; United Kingdom: 2384; United States of America: 2537, 2542.

industrial technology
[S] 4; Australia: 169; Estonia: 881; United Kingdom: 2387; [C] Australia: 162; Austria: 190; Azerbaijan: 205, 209; Bulgaria: 321; China: 481, 495, 497, 507, 513, 516, 518, 523; Ethiopia: 885; Finland: 892, 894; Germany: 1087, 1088, 1098, 1100, 1112; Indonesia: 1233; Ireland: 1257; Italie: 1280, 1283, 1290, 1300; Japan: 1364, 1369, 1377; Lithuania: 1468; Malta: 1498; Netherlands: 1638; Norway: 1725; Philippines: 1806; Poland: 1869, 1890, 1900; Republic of Korea: 1948; Russian Federation: 1978, 1987, 1990, 1991, 1992, 2003, 2020, 2021, 2047, 2064, 2066, 2069, 2070, 2091, 2096, 2102, 2105, 2111, 2113, 2118, 2127, 2129, 2133, 2135; Singapore: 2153; Slovakia: 2171; Sri Lanka: 2200; Thailand: 2271; Ukraine: 2351, 2354, 2364; United Kingdom: 2387; United States of America: 2542, 2623.

industrie alimentaire
[C] Brésil: 300, 311; Bulgaria: 323, 327; France: 942, 954, 975, 981, 1019; Maroc: 1502, 1504; [S] Cameroun: 349.

industrie chimique
[C] Algérie: 68; Bulgaria: 328, 335; France: 958, 964, 979, 986, 1007, 1009, 1015; Portugal: 1922; [S] France: 964.

industrie et commerce
[C] Arménie: 129; Belarus, Republic of: 241; Bulgaria: 328; France: 925, 1009, 1063; Grèce: 1162; Madagascar: 1483; Maroc: 1512.

industrie textile
[C] France: 1015; Tunisie: 2294.

industry and commerce
[C] Austria: 190, 194; Canada: 405; China: 496, 516; China, Hong Kong: 526; Denmark: 676; Finland: 890; Germany: 1098; Italie: 1304; Liechtenstein: 1457; Lithuania: 1468; Netherlands: 1667; Philippines: 1811, 1822; Republic of Korea: 1952; Russian Federation: 1982, 1988, 2066, 2096, 2131; Sweden: 2239; United Kingdom: 2384; United States of America: 2542, 2659; [S] Japan: 1317.

informática
[S] 42; Colombia: 554; Ecuador: 693; España: 755, 771; México: 1612; Perú: 1773, 1780; [C] Argentina: 87, 88, 91, 93, 107, 110, 121; Bolivia: 289; Chile: 419, 420, 429, 432, 436, 438, 449, 456; Colombia: 535, 539; Costa Rica: 560, 566, 578, 580, 585, 593; Cuba: 607, 610, 620; El Salvador: 710; España: 715, 738, 786, 798, 851, 865; Honduras: 1176; México: 1528, 1530, 1544, 1550, 1551, 1552, 1553, 1561, 1567, 1590, 1591, 1596, 1597, 1605, 1608, 1612, 1621, 1626; Perú: 1795, 1796; Uruguay: 2764.

information science

[C] 49; Arménie: 125; Australia: 140, 141, 158; Austria: 190, 195, 198; Azerbaijan: 205; Belgique: 273; Bulgaria: 321; Canada: 353, 405, 407; China: 465, 497, 521; Czech Republic: 667; Denmark: 676; Estonia: 877, 881; Germany: 1087, 1098, 1099, 1109, 1113, 1126, 1133; Hungary: 1184, 1193; India: 1220, 1222; Italie: 1277, 1280, 1300, 1302, 1304; Kazakhstan: 1417; Kyrgyzstan: 1430; Latvia: 1440, 1441; Lithuania: 1471; Malaysia: 1488; Netherlands: 1681; Pakistan: 1747; Philippines: 1806, 1807, 1813, 1816; Poland: 1840, 1844, 1862, 1869, 1892, 1899; Republic of Korea: 1931, 1934, 1948; Russian Federation: 1982, 1989, 1990, 1992, 2006, 2042, 2050, 2057, 2066, 2070, 2072, 2082, 2083, 2086, 2096, 2123, 2129; Slovakia: 2174; South Africa: 2189; Tajikistan: 2260; Thailand: 2266, 2282; Uganda: 2331; Ukraine: 2336, 2340, 2347, 2361; United Kingdom: 2380, 2401, 2405, 2433, 2472; United Republic of Tanzania: 2490; United States of America: 2503, 2560, 2666, 2683, 2684; Uzbekistan: 2765; [S] 49; Estonia: 881; Thailand: 2270; United Kingdom: 2396.

informatique
[C] Algérie: 63, 68, 70, 71; Arménie: 129; Belarus, Republic of: 231, 237; Belgique: 249, 251, 259, 261; Brésil: 298; Bulgaria: 325, 326, 332, 333, 337, 344; Côte d'Ivoire: 595, 597; France: 915, 921, 925, 932, 937, 946, 947, 950, 952, 955, 956, 962, 968, 969, 971, 972, 975, 977, 979, 985, 1006, 1007, 1013, 1045, 1049, 1054, 1056; Grèce: 1157, 1158, 1160, 1161, 1162; Italie: 1296; Liban: 1452; Luxembourg: 1474; Madagascar: 1475, 1478, 1481; Maroc: 1501, 1512; Portugal: 1922; Suisse: 2208, 2210; Togo: 2287; Tunisie: 2305, 2307, 2308, 2309, 2314; [S] Cameroun: 349; France: 925, 956.

ingeniería
[C] 21; Argentina: 78, 83, 87, 88, 89, 91, 93, 95, 98, 106, 107, 110, 113, 119, 123; Bolivia: 288, 289, 290; Chile: 419, 423, 426, 432, 434, 438, 446, 456; Colombia: 535, 546, 547, 549; Costa Rica: 560, 580, 581, 582, 585, 587, 593; Cuba: 599, 605, 609, 610; Ecuador: 695; El Salvador: 708, 709, 710; España: 717, 719, 732, 736, 761, 786, 851, 864, 868; Honduras: 1176; México: 1546, 1547, 1548, 1550, 1552, 1553, 1560, 1565, 1567, 1568, 1570, 1572, 1578, 1581, 1582, 1585, 1589, 1596, 1597, 1611, 1612, 1613, 1621; Nicaragua: 1695; Perú: 1775, 1792, 1793, 1795; République Dominicana: 1957, 1958; Uruguay: 2764; Venezuela: 2772; [S] 59; Argentina: 79, 83; Colombia: 537, 548, 554; España: 755; México: 1588, 1629; Perú: 1773, 1774, 1777.

ingeniería civil
[C] Argentina: 110; Chile: 419; Costa Rica: 587; Cuba: 609; El Salvador: 708; España: 717, 864; Honduras: 1176; México: 1550, 1591, 1621; Nicaragua: 1695; Venezuela: 2772.

ingeniería química
[C] Argentina: 110; Cuba: 609; España: 736, 775.

ingénierie
[C] 21; Algérie: 63; Angola: 74; Belarus, Republic of: 233, 237, 238, 239; Belgique: 247, 259, 260; Brésil: 298; Bulgaria: 328, 341; Cameroun: 351; Côte d'Ivoire: 596; France: 913, 914, 921, 925, 929, 932, 933, 934, 939, 940, 941, 944, 945, 948, 950, 953, 955, 958, 959, 960, 964, 968, 971, 972, 973, 976, 979, 982, 986, 998, 1006, 1007, 1008, 1009, 1011, 1013, 1020, 1024, 1028, 1049, 1050, 1059, 1061; Grèce: 1159, 1160; Madagascar: 1476, 1478, 1484; Maroc: 1510; Niger: 1699; Portugal: 1922; Suisse: 2209, 2210; Togo: 2287; Tunisie: 2307; Turkey: 2327, 2328; Viet Nam: 2779; [S] 59; Canada: 372, 389; France: 925, 956, 964; République arabe syrienne: 1963.

inglés
[S] Colombia: 542; México: 1594; [C] Cuba: 599, 620; El Salvador: 710; Guatemala: 1168; México: 1574, 1578.

inmunología
[S] 20; [C] Chile: 413, 416, 421; España: 834; Venezuela: 2774.

interior design
[C] Azerbaijan: 209; Belgique: 273, 275; Canada: 367; Cyprus: 623, 633; Denmark: 675; Finland: 895; Germany: 1083; Hungary: 1188; Indonesia: 1229; Italie: 1277, 1280, 1290; Japan: 1342, 1346; Jordan: 1411; Kenya: 1425; Kyrgyzstan: 1432; Lithuania: 1467; Norway: 1720; Poland: 1831, 1834, 1835; Republic of Korea: 1931, 1935; Republic of Moldova: 1955, 1956; Russian Federation: 2107; Slovakia: 2165; South Africa: 2181, 2189; Thailand: 2271; Turkey: 2319, 2320; Ukraine: 2357; United Kingdom: 2384, 2399, 2431; United States of America: 2545, 2562, 2613, 2617, 2656; [S] Japan: 1342; Poland: 1831.

international business
[C] 54; Arménie: 125; Australia: 141; Austria: 190, 193, 194; Bulgaria: 321; Canada: 353, 398; China: 457, 497; China, Macao: 531; Czech Republic: 666; Denmark: 676; Finland: 891; Georgia: 1081; Germany: 1083, 1087, 1088, 1089, 1099, 1102, 1105, 1108, 1109, 1126, 1134, 1135; Hungary: 1183, 1184; Ireland: 1255; Italie: 1277, 1285, 1299, 1302, 1304; Japan: 1350, 1359; Kyrgyzstan: 1428, 1430, 1432; Latvia: 1441; Liechtenstein: 1457; Mongolia: 1631; Netherlands: 1644, 1655, 1661, 1667; Norway: 1718, 1722; Philippines: 1809; Poland: 1855, 1914; Republic of Korea: 1935, 1952; Roumanie: 1966; Russian Federation: 1989, 2057, 2075; Slovakia: 2158, 2168; Sweden: 2239; Tajikistan: 2260; Thailand: 2279; Turkey: 2320; Ukraine: 2347, 2361; United Kingdom: 2384, 2386, 2425, 2452, 2472; United States of America: 2535, 2560, 2577, 2594, 2633, 2642, 2652, 2659, 2666, 2671, 2683, 2684, 2696, 2734, 2744; [S] China, Macao: 531; Czech Republic: 667; United Kingdom: 2384, 2386, 2411; United States of America: 2652, 2696.

international law
[S] 14, 31, 42, 47; China, Macao: 531; Poland: 1913; United Kingdom: 2411; United States of America: 2652; [C] 30, 47, 54; Arménie: 125; Austria: 193, 194; Azerbaijan: 208; Belgique: 255; Bulgaria: 321; China: 457; China, Macao: 531; Denmark: 676; Estonia: 879; Germany: 1088, 1108, 1122, 1135; Hungary: 1183; Indonesia: 1232, 1236; Ireland: 1255; Italie: 1277, 1299, 1302, 1304; Japan: 1343; Kyrgyzstan: 1430, 1432; Latvia: 1441; Lithuania: 1461; Mongolia: 1631; Netherlands: 1644, 1648, 1656, 1672; Nigeria: 1709; Norway: 1718; Poland: 1904; Republic of Korea: 1934; Republic of Moldova: 1954, 1955; Roumanie: 1966; Russian Federation: 1996, 2024, 2031; Slovakia: 2158; Sweden: 2239; Tajikistan: 2260; Turkey: 2320, 2323; Ukraine: 2346, 2347, 2351, 2364; United Kingdom: 2401, 2436, 2452; United States of America: 2560, 2652, 2683, 2734.

international relations
[C] 25, 29, 30, 39, 47, 54; Arménie: 125; Austria: 193, 194, 202; Azerbaijan: 208, 209; Bulgaria: 321; Canada: 405; China: 499; Denmark: 676; Estonia: 879; Finland: 903; Germany: 1105, 1108, 1109; Hungary: 1183, 1188, 1201; Italie: 1277, 1299, 1302; Japan: 1331, 1343, 1359, 1364; Kyrgyzstan: 1430; Latvia: 1441; Liechtenstein: 1457; Mongolia: 1631; Netherlands: 1648; Nigeria: 1704, 1709; Norway: 1718; Pakistan: 1737, 1747, 1748, 1751, 1752, 1753, 1754; Poland: 1858, 1904, 1905, 1915; Portugal: 1917; Republic of Korea: 1935, 1942, 1950; Republic of Moldova: 1953, 1955; République arabe syrienne: 1962; Roumanie: 1966; Russian Federation: 1992, 2004, 2031, 2057, 2070, 2117; Serbia and Montenegro: 2147; Slovakia: 2159, 2168; Suisse: 2227; Sweden: 2239; Tajikistan: 2261; Turkey: 2320, 2323; Ukraine: 2347, 2361, 2365; United Kingdom: 2384, 2401, 2464; United States of America: 2529, 2535, 2560, 2561, 2576, 2652, 2655, 2659, 2666, 2671, 2702, 2734; [S] Japan: 1331; Russian Federation: 2004; Tajikistan: 2260; United Kingdom: 2384, 2411, 2464; United States of America: 2593, 2652, 2702.

international studies
[C] 2, 29, 39, 47; Arménie: 125; Australia: 147; Austria: 193; Azerbaijan: 207; Bulgaria: 320; Canada: 385, 398, 405; China: 521; Czech Republic: 667; Denmark: 674, 676; Finland: 904; Germany: 1108; Hungary: 1188; India: 1220; Indonesia: 1236; Japan: 1359; Mongolia: 1631; Netherlands: 1645, 1667; Pakistan: 1737; Poland: 1904; Republic of Korea: 1940, 1942, 1948, 1952; Republic of Moldova: 1954; Roumanie: 1966; Russian Federation: 1989, 2031, 2072; Tajikistan: 2260; Ukraine: 2346, 2347; United Kingdom: 2379, 2401, 2425, 2467, 2472; United States of America: 2560, 2561, 2620, 2641, 2647, 2652, 2666, 2667, 2671, 2699; [S] 32, 40; Australia: 147; Canada: 364; Japan: 1381; United Kingdom: 2390, 2411; United States of America: 2652.

interpretación y traducción
[C] Colombia: 533; España: 722, 851; Perú: 1775; [S] Perú: 1774.

interpretation and translation
[C] Belgique: 263, 275; Denmark: 676, 678; Finland: 903; Germany: 1109; India: 1213; Jordan: 1411; Kyrgyzstan: 1430, 1432; Latvia: 1440; Republic of Moldova: 1953, 1954, 1955; Russian Federation: 1983, 1988, 2016, 2025, 2105, 2124; Slovakia: 2170; Turkey: 2320, 2321, 2323; Ukraine: 2334, 2356, 2364; United Kingdom: 2472, 2480; United States of America: 2578, 2726; [S] Japan: 1356.

interprétation et traduction
[C] Algérie: 65; Belarus, Republic of: 243; Belgique: 257, 267, 272, 279; Cameroun: 351; France: 905, 985, 1001, 1033; Italie: 1298; Liban: 1452; Madagascar: 1479; Suisse: 2221, 2222; Tunisie: 2313.

investigación
[S] 14, 20, 41, 50; Colombia: 542; España: 713, 726, 730, 753, 756, 758, 760, 780; México: 1588, 1618; [C] Chile: 446; España: 739, 743, 748; México: 1527; Perú: 1765; Venezuela: 2776.

[C] = Courses, Cours, Cursos / [S] = Scholarships, Bourses, Becas   677

Italian
[C] Italie: 1280, 1285, 1286, 1301; Russian Federation: 2027; United Kingdom: 2480; United States of America: 2529.

italiano
[S] México: 1594.

italien
[C] France: 1033; Italie: 1272, 1292, 1293, 1295, 1297, 1298; Tunisie: 2291, 2313; [S] Italie: 1297.

Japanese
[C] Azerbaijan: 207; Japan: 1313, 1339, 1340, 1345, 1347, 1352, 1359, 1374; Thailand: 2271; United States of America: 2576, 2624, 2666, 2719; [S] Japan: 1356, 1359, 1365, 1392, 1398.

japonés
[S] México: 1529.

journalism
[S] 45, 46; Canada: 383; Japan: 1356; Russian Federation: 2004; Slovakia: 2157; United Kingdom: 2370; [C] Austria: 190; Azerbaijan: 207, 208; Bulgaria: 321; Canada: 383, 407; China: 465; Cyprus: 633, 638; Egypt: 701; Fiji: 886; Georgia: 1080; Germany: 1097, 1099, 1137; Hungary: 1201; India: 1213, 1219, 1220, 1222, 1223; Italie: 1277; Japan: 1377; Jordan: 1411; Malawi: 1485; Mongolia: 1631; Netherlands: 1675; Pakistan: 1742; Poland: 1844, 1863, 1868, 1886, 1904, 1915; Republic of Moldova: 1954; Russian Federation: 1995, 2000, 2004, 2008, 2025, 2072, 2080, 2137; Suriname: 2228; Ukraine: 2364; United Kingdom: 2476, 2477; United Republic of Tanzania: 2494; United States of America: 2560, 2562, 2647, 2659, 2660, 2673, 2684, 2689, 2700.

journalisme
[S] 46; [C] Belarus, Republic of: 236; Belgique: 253; Bulgaria: 319; Burundi: 347; Cameroun: 352; Côte d'Ivoire: 597; France: 983, 1063, 1066, 1072; Madagascar: 1479; Turkey: 2328.

Korean
[C] Republic of Korea: 1941, 1944, 1947, 1950; [S] Republic of Korea: 1948.

laboratory techniques
[C] Bangladesh: 216; Belgique: 274; Germany: 1087; Indonesia: 1233; Italie: 1290; Netherlands: 1679; Nigeria: 1707; Norway: 1728; Russian Federation: 1990, 1992, 2064; Ukraine: 2351; United Kingdom: 2431, 2476; United Republic of Tanzania: 2497.

landscape architecture
[C] Finland: 892; Germany: 1122; Netherlands: 1682.

languages
[S] 46; Australia: 146; Canada: 364, 383; Cyprus: 639; Estonia: 882; Germany: 1123, 1127; Iceland: 1205; Indonesia: 1231; Japan: 1312, 1365, 1392, 1398; Kuwait: 1427; Poland: 1878; United States of America: 2624; [C] Arménie: 130; Austria: 202; Azerbaijan: 209; Barbados: 222; Belgique: 275; Canada: 353, 371, 383, 385, 398, 405; China: 460, 480, 484, 489, 491, 497, 504, 507, 516; Croatia: 598; Cyprus: 639; Czech Republic: 650, 655, 660, 665, 667, 671, 673; Denmark: 676; Egypt: 699; Estonia: 880; Ethiopia: 883; Finland: 887, 896, 903; Germany: 1087, 1109, 1131, 1135; Hungary: 1201; India: 1213, 1220; Indonesia: 1238; Iran, Islamic Republic of: 1253, 1254; Ireland: 1258, 1259; Italie: 1277, 1280, 1301; Jamaica: 1310; Japan: 1313, 1329, 1340, 1345, 1346, 1365, 1374, 1383; Kazakhstan: 1414, 1417, 1418; Kenya: 1425; Kyrgyzstan: 1432; Latvia: 1435, 1441; Libyan Arab Jamahiriya: 1456; Lithuania: 1470; Malta: 1499; Mongolia: 1631; Netherlands: 1653; New Zealand: 1694; Norway: 1724; Pakistan: 1734, 1742; Poland: 1835, 1840, 1853, 1856, 1874, 1877, 1878, 1879, 1882, 1904, 1910, 1912, 1915; Portugal: 1925, 1927; Republic of Korea: 1929, 1931, 1935, 1941, 1942, 1947, 1948, 1950; Republic of Moldova: 1953, 1954, 1955, 1956; Roumanie: 1974, 1975; Russian Federation: 1977, 1980, 1986, 1988, 1992, 1994, 1997, 2006, 2025, 2027, 2030, 2065, 2072, 2074, 2079, 2082, 2093, 2106, 2121, 2124, 2128; Slovakia: 2160, 2161, 2170; Sri Lanka: 2197; Suisse: 2227; Swaziland: 2234; Sweden: 2244, 2253; Tajikistan: 2261; Thailand: 2276; Turkey: 2320, 2321, 2323, 2326; Ukraine: 2334, 2336, 2343, 2346, 2347, 2351, 2352, 2356, 2357, 2361, 2364; United Kingdom: 2369, 2375, 2398, 2399, 2432, 2452, 2470, 2472, 2476; United States of America: 2500, 2520, 2529, 2543, 2557, 2560, 2561, 2585, 2587, 2617, 2624, 2647, 2655, 2679, 2699, 2700, 2726, 2746, 2749; Uzbekistan: 2765, 2766, 2767.

langues
[S] 46; Brésil: 301; Tunisie: 2291; [C] Albanie: 61; Arménie: 129; Belarus, Republic of: 237, 238, 243; Belgique: 253, 261; Brésil: 298, 301; Canada: 390; Côte

d'Ivoire: 597; France: 905, 913, 930, 960, 1001, 1021, 1027, 1030, 1031, 1038, 1039, 1045, 1047, 1051, 1059, 1062, 1069, 1075; Grèce: 1157; Italie: 1272, 1292, 1293, 1295, 1298; Madagascar: 1479; Maroc: 1508; Sénégal: 2146; Suisse: 2225; Tunisie: 2291, 2304.

Latin
[C] Burundi: 347; Cameroun: 350; Canada: 385; Indonesia: 1229; Italie: 1286; Maroc: 1505; Poland: 1874; United States of America: 2529, 2617, 2624, 2655.

law
[C] 8, 14, 30, 47; Arménie: 125, 127; Australia: 140, 147, 158, 161, 174; Austria: 193; Azerbaijan: 206, 208; Bangladesh: 220; Belgique: 255; Bosnia and Herzegovina: 291; Bulgaria: 321; China: 486, 493, 496, 504, 513, 515; China, Hong Kong: 526; China, Macao: 531; Croatia: 598; Cyprus: 624, 633, 637, 642; Czech Republic: 650; Denmark: 676; Egypt: 699, 706; Eritrea: 711; Estonia: 879; Ethiopia: 883, 884, 885; Fiji: 886; Finland: 887, 890, 896; Germany: 1088, 1089, 1098, 1105, 1108; Hungary: 1184, 1198, 1201; Iceland: 1202, 1204; India: 1222, 1225, 1226; Indonesia: 1228, 1236, 1239; Iran, Islamic Republic of: 1252, 1253, 1254; Italie: 1301, 1302, 1304; Jamaica: 1310; Japan: 1312, 1313, 1316, 1322, 1343, 1344, 1350, 1364, 1390; Jordan: 1401, 1402, 1404, 1408, 1412; Kazakhstan: 1414, 1418; Kuwait: 1427; Kyrgyzstan: 1430, 1431, 1432; Latvia: 1436, 1441; Lithuania: 1461, 1471; Malawi: 1485; Malta: 1499; Mongolia: 1631; Nepal: 1633; Netherlands: 1648, 1653, 1656, 1667, 1672; New Zealand: 1694; Nigeria: 1704, 1709; Norway: 1731; Pakistan: 1754; Philippines: 1798, 1806, 1812, 1816, 1817; Poland: 1829, 1840, 1870, 1905, 1909, 1915; Portugal: 1917, 1920, 1924, 1925; Republic of Korea: 1933, 1939, 1940, 1947, 1948; Republic of Moldova: 1953, 1954, 1955; Roumanie: 1974; Russian Federation: 1977, 1986, 1988, 1989, 1992, 1994, 1995, 1996, 2000, 2004, 2008, 2012, 2024, 2025, 2031, 2046, 2063, 2069, 2070, 2072, 2074, 2079, 2080, 2081, 2082, 2093, 2097, 2107, 2108, 2117, 2121, 2122, 2127, 2128, 2137; San Marino: 2142; Serbia and Montenegro: 2147, 2148; Slovakia: 2160, 2169; South Africa: 2181, 2191, 2195; Sri Lanka: 2198; Suisse: 2227; Suriname: 2229; Swaziland: 2234; Sweden: 2247; Tajikistan: 2260; Thailand: 2278, 2280; Turkey: 2320, 2321; Ukraine: 2334, 2340, 2341, 2343, 2346, 2347, 2351, 2352, 2359, 2361, 2364; United Kingdom: 2389, 2425, 2433, 2436, 2460, 2464, 2472; United Republic of Tanzania: 2491, 2496; United States of America: 2508, 2537, 2545, 2558, 2560, 2575, 2583, 2632, 2642, 2649, 2663, 2685, 2702, 2710, 2715, 2717, 2718, 2725, 2742, 2745, 2749, 2753; Uzbekistan: 2765, 2766, 2767; [S] 14, 42; Australia: 147, 161; Bangladesh: 217; China, Macao: 531; Germany: 1109; Italie: 1288, 1303; Japan: 1312, 1317, 1320, 1324, 1399; Poland: 1913; Republic of Moldova: 1954; Russian Federation: 2004, 2081; Tajikistan: 2260; United Kingdom: 2443, 2448, 2475; United States of America: 2582, 2632, 2702, 2723.

letras
[C] Argentina: 123; Chile: 447; Ecuador: 689; España: 752.

letras y artes
[C] Argentina: 100; México: 1589, 1598.

lettres
[C] Albanie: 61; Algérie: 68; Belgique: 253; Brésil: 299, 313; Bulgaria: 332, 340; Canada: 388, 390; France: 938, 1002, 1027, 1051, 1055, 1059, 1062, 1069; Gabon: 1078; Madagascar: 1484; Maroc: 1510, 1514; Saint-Siège: 2140; Suisse: 2224, 2225; Togo: 2287; Turkey: 2327; [S] République arabe syrienne: 1963; Suisse: 2219.

Lettres et arts
[C] Brésil: 301; Bulgaria: 333; France: 1001, 1033; Madagascar: 1479; Maroc: 1509, 1511; Suisse: 2221; [S] Brésil: 301.

liberal arts
[C] Australia: 141; Austria: 204; Belize: 283; Bermuda: 285; Bosnia and Herzegovina: 291; Canada: 353, 356, 366, 367, 373, 383, 385, 398, 405; China: 472, 513, 515; Finland: 903; France: 906; Germany: 1105, 1109, 1113, 1135; India: 1222; Ireland: 1259; Japan: 1316, 1346; Jordan: 1412; Kazakhstan: 1418; Kyrgyzstan: 1431; Latvia: 1441; Liban: 1443; Lithuania: 1471; Malta: 1499; Oman: 1733; Pakistan: 1749; Papua New Guinea: 1760; Philippines: 1798, 1805, 1808, 1811, 1817; Poland: 1867; Portugal: 1925; Republic of Korea: 1940, 1947; Russian Federation: 1995, 2031, 2065; Serbia and Montenegro: 2147; Thailand: 2271, 2280; United Kingdom: 2367, 2399, 2432; United States of America: 2500, 2502, 2508, 2517, 2518, 2520, 2524, 2525, 2529, 2538, 2540, 2542, 2543, 2545, 2546, 2547, 2555, 2557, 2560, 2562, 2563, 2564, 2573, 2576, 2579, 2580, 2585, 2590, 2593, 2609, 2613, 2617, 2623, 2624, 2633, 2641, 2653, 2655, 2656, 2659, 2660, 2661, 2663, 2667, 2676, 2679, 2689, 2693, 2696, 2700, 2707, 2710, 2714, 2715, 2716, 2717, 2718, 2719, 2720, 2730,

2735, 2736, 2738, 2745, 2746, 2754, 2756, 2757, 2758; United States of America, Puerto Rico: 2759; [S] Canada: 364, 383; Italie: 1303; United States of America: 2500, 2513, 2518, 2525, 2562, 2593, 2606, 2624, 2667, 2689, 2733.

library science
[C] Canada: 407; Germany: 1117; India: 1213, 1222; Italie: 1300; Kazakhstan: 1418; Nigeria: 1700; Philippines: 1813, 1816; Russian Federation: 2055, 2094; Thailand: 2278; Uganda: 2331; United Kingdom: 2401.

linguistics
[C] Azerbaijan: 209; Canada: 385, 405; China: 465; Czech Republic: 660; Finland: 896, 903; Germany: 1131, 1135; Indonesia: 1236, 1238; Japan: 1316, 1359, 1365; Kyrgyzstan: 1430; Mongolia: 1631; Netherlands: 1653; Philippines: 1810; Poland: 1874; Republic of Moldova: 1954, 1956; Russian Federation: 1992, 2006, 2031, 2124; San Marino: 2142; Slovenia: 2176; Suisse: 2227; Thailand: 2271; Turkey: 2319; Ukraine: 2334, 2341, 2364; United Kingdom: 2452, 2472; United States of America: 2529, 2557, 2624, 2633, 2655, 2679; [S] Japan: 1324; Ukraine: 2345; United Kingdom: 2372.

linguistique
[C] Albanie: 61; Belarus, Republic of: 238, 243; Belgique: 272; Burundi: 347; France: 905, 970, 1033, 1051, 1068; Gabon: 1078; Madagascar: 1479; Maroc: 1505, 1508; Togo: 2283; [S] Portugal: 1918, 1919.

lingüística
[C] Chile: 447; España: 734, 776, 793, 842; México: 1527, 1540, 1575; [S] México: 1529.

literatura y civilización
[C] 25; Ecuador: 691, 692, 694; España: 722, 734, 804, 806, 820, 826, 837, 842, 852, 859; México: 1570, 1581, 1598; [S] España: 858; México: 1529, 1594.

literature and civilization
[C] 25; Azerbaijan: 209; Bulgaria: 320; Canada: 385, 405; China: 460, 477, 484, 486, 489, 491, 499, 516, 520; China, Hong Kong: 526; Czech Republic: 660; Egypt: 699; Estonia: 880; Finland: 903; Iran, Islamic Republic of: 1253; Ireland: 1258, 1259; Italie: 1277, 1285, 1301; Japan: 1316, 1344, 1345, 1359, 1365, 1377; Jordan: 1409; Kenya: 1425; Latvia: 1441; Mongolia: 1631; Netherlands: 1653; New Zealand: 1694; Pakistan: 1736; Poland: 1886, 1910, 1915; Portugal: 1924, 1927; Republic of Korea: 1929, 1931, 1935; Republic of Moldova: 1955; Roumanie: 1968; Russian Federation: 2004, 2006, 2027, 2071; Slovakia: 2157; Sri Lanka: 2197; Sweden: 2244, 2253; Turkey: 2323; Ukraine: 2346, 2347; United Kingdom: 2375; United States of America: 2520, 2529, 2576, 2613, 2647, 2655, 2656; [S] Canada: 364; Estonia: 882; Finland: 889; Italie: 1303; Japan: 1317, 1365, 1399; Sweden: 2259; United Kingdom: 2372, 2457; United States of America: 2559, 2582, 2630.

littérature et civilisation
[C] 25; Belgique: 244, 253; Bulgaria: 333, 337; France: 905, 970, 1001, 1021, 1030, 1033, 1038, 1047, 1051, 1059, 1062, 1068, 1069, 1075; Grèce: 1160; Italie: 1292, 1293, 1298; Madagascar: 1479, 1481; Maroc: 1508, 1509, 1511, 1516; Saint-Siège: 2139; Sénégal: 2146; Suisse: 2225; Togo: 2283; [S] Canada: 391; Portugal: 1918, 1919.

management
[S] 3, 4, 32; China, Macao: 531; Cyprus: 621; Estonia: 881; Germany: 1096, 1111; Italie: 1288; Mauritius: 1522; Russian Federation: 2014, 2114; Tajikistan: 2260; United Kingdom: 2468; United States of America: 2522, 2574; [C] 4, 19; Arménie: 125; Australia: 136, 158, 161, 162, 166; Austria: 191, 193, 194, 195; Azerbaijan: 205, 206; Barbados: 223; Belgique: 255, 273, 274; Bermuda: 285; Bulgaria: 321; Canada: 353, 371; China: 457, 504, 513, 515, 516, 518, 519; China, Macao: 531; Cyprus: 621, 627, 631, 632, 637, 641; Czech Republic: 666, 667; Denmark: 676; Eritrea: 711; Estonia: 877; Ethiopia: 884, 885; Fiji: 886; Finland: 890; Germany: 1083, 1087, 1088, 1098, 1105, 1109, 1112, 1126, 1135; Ghana: 1146; Grèce: 1154, 1155; Guyana: 1173; Hungary: 1183, 1184; India: 1219, 1222, 1225; Indonesia: 1228, 1229, 1232, 1236, 1238, 1239; Ireland: 1255, 1257; Israel: 1264; Italie: 1277, 1301, 1302, 1304; Japan: 1316, 1322, 1331, 1377; Jordan: 1411; Kazakhstan: 1417, 1418; Kyrgyzstan: 1428, 1429; Latvia: 1435, 1440, 1441; Liban: 1443; Lithuania: 1459, 1461, 1463, 1468; Mauritius: 1522; Mongolia: 1631; Nepal: 1633; Netherlands: 1635, 1639, 1641, 1643, 1647, 1654, 1655, 1658, 1664, 1666, 1667, 1675, 1681, 1682; Nigeria: 1707, 1709; Norway: 1718, 1725; Pakistan: 1734, 1736, 1742, 1749; Philippines: 1799, 1805, 1806, 1807, 1808, 1813, 1816, 1825; Poland: 1830, 1840, 1842, 1845, 1846, 1849, 1850, 1859, 1861, 1862, 1863, 1866, 1869, 1874, 1876, 1877, 1879, 1882, 1884, 1887, 1888, 1889, 1890, 1892, 1893, 1894, 1899, 1900, 1901, 1902, 1906, 1908, 1915; Portugal: 1917, 1920, 1927; Republic of Korea: 1934, 1935,

1948, 1952; Republic of Moldova: 1953, 1954, 1956; Russian Federation: 1978, 1980, 1982, 1985, 1988, 1989, 1990, 1991, 1992, 1995, 1997, 2000, 2004, 2010, 2013, 2014, 2023, 2025, 2026, 2031, 2039, 2040, 2043, 2046, 2049, 2056, 2059, 2063, 2065, 2066, 2069, 2070, 2072, 2076, 2079, 2082, 2085, 2086, 2091, 2102, 2105, 2108, 2110, 2111, 2112, 2114, 2117, 2123, 2129, 2131, 2133; San Marino: 2142; Serbia and Montenegro: 2147; Slovakia: 2158, 2159, 2160, 2166, 2174; Slovenia: 2175, 2178; South Africa: 2181, 2183, 2189, 2195; Sri Lanka: 2198, 2199; Swaziland: 2233; Sweden: 2239, 2248; Tajikistan: 2260; Thailand: 2265, 2273, 2279, 2280; Turkey: 2319, 2320, 2326; Uganda: 2331, 2333; Ukraine: 2337, 2338, 2340, 2349, 2353, 2356, 2361; United Kingdom: 2375, 2379, 2380, 2384, 2401, 2405, 2423, 2425, 2431, 2432, 2436, 2459, 2472, 2478; United Republic of Tanzania: 2491, 2494; United States of America: 2508, 2524, 2530, 2545, 2561, 2574, 2580, 2613, 2624, 2633, 2641, 2642, 2653, 2659, 2660, 2673, 2679, 2683, 2684, 2692, 2696, 2699, 2700, 2730, 2735, 2746; Uzbekistan: 2765.

management of human resources
[S] 6; [C] Canada: 385; United Kingdom: 2472.

marine biology
[C] 33; Australia: 179; Canada: 371; China: 473, 518, 520; Eritrea: 711; Fiji: 886; Germany: 1090; Netherlands: 1668; Norway: 1730; Pakistan: 1751, 1753; Philippines: 1806; United States of America: 2561, 2684; Yemen: 2781; [S] 33; Norway: 1730.

marine science
[S] 31, 33, 50; [C] 33; Belgique: 255; China: 486; Croatia: 598; Fiji: 886; Germany: 1090; Malaysia: 1491; Netherlands: 1649, 1668; Nigeria: 1707; Oman: 1733; Poland: 1871; Republic of Korea: 1933, 1948; Russian Federation: 1982; Serbia and Montenegro: 2148; Ukraine: 2363; United States of America: 2659, 2692; Yemen: 2781.

marketing
[S] 42; China, Macao: 531; Cyprus: 621, 639; España: 714; France: 922, 974; Germany: 1111; Ghana: 1145; México: 1612; Perú: 1766; Russian Federation: 2114; Thailand: 2267; United States of America: 2574; [C] Algérie: 71; Arménie: 125, 129; Australia: 161; Austria: 194, 204; Azerbaijan: 205, 206; Bangladesh: 218; Barbados: 223; Belgique: 259, 261, 274, 275; Bulgaria: 321, 328; Burundi: 347; Cameroun: 350; Canada: 353, 371, 398, 408; China: 523; China, Macao: 531; Colombia: 535; Costa Rica: 593; Côte d'Ivoire: 597; Cyprus: 621, 627, 631, 637, 641; Czech Republic: 665, 666; España: 744, 745, 746, 750, 765, 790, 791, 797, 815, 840, 846; Ethiopia: 884, 885; Finland: 890, 901, 903; France: 930, 976, 981, 984, 985, 995, 996, 1016; Germany: 1087, 1088, 1089, 1108, 1109, 1126, 1135; Grèce: 1155; Guyana: 1173; Honduras: 1176; Hungary: 1183, 1184; India: 1219; Ireland: 1255, 1257; Italie: 1301, 1304; Jordan: 1401, 1408, 1411; Kyrgyzstan: 1428, 1430; México: 1583, 1585, 1608, 1617; Mongolia: 1631; Netherlands: 1644, 1654, 1667, 1681; New Zealand: 1687; Nicaragua: 1696, 1697; Nigeria: 1707, 1709; Norway: 1724, 1725; Pakistan: 1736; Perú: 1769, 1792; Philippines: 1807, 1812, 1816; Poland: 1830, 1840, 1842, 1845, 1846, 1850, 1859, 1862, 1863, 1869, 1876, 1879, 1889, 1892, 1894, 1900, 1901, 1906; Republic of Korea: 1931; Republic of Moldova: 1953, 1954; Roumanie: 1966; Russian Federation: 1982, 1989, 1990, 1995, 2010, 2025, 2031, 2066, 2082, 2093, 2102, 2108, 2110, 2114, 2115, 2117, 2123, 2124; Singapore: 2153; Slovakia: 2159, 2166; South Africa: 2181, 2189; Swaziland: 2233; Sweden: 2239; Thailand: 2265, 2279, 2282; Tunisie: 2298, 2303, 2310; Uganda: 2333; Ukraine: 2340, 2346, 2353, 2356, 2361; United Kingdom: 2380, 2384, 2401, 2423, 2425, 2436, 2472; United Republic of Tanzania: 2495; United States of America: 2561, 2574, 2594, 2633, 2659, 2660, 2673, 2683, 2684, 2696, 2735; Uruguay: 2763; Uzbekistan: 2765.

matemáticas
[S] 1; Bolivia: 286; Cuba: 611; [C] Argentina: 110, 123; Chile: 420, 429, 456; Colombia: 539; Cuba: 610; Ecuador: 694; México: 1546, 1550, 1551, 1567, 1605; Perú: 1791.

mathematics
[S] 1; Canada: 383; Germany: 1109, 1120; Japan: 1392, 1394; Pakistan: 1750; Russian Federation: 2114; South Africa: 2186; United Kingdom: 2417, 2448, 2468; United States of America: 2574; Uzbekistan: 2766; [C] Australia: 166; Azerbaijan: 205, 206, 208; Canada: 353, 371, 373, 383, 385, 405, 408; China: 457, 484, 496, 504, 520; Cyprus: 633; Eritrea: 711; Estonia: 880; Ethiopia: 884, 885; Fiji: 886; Germany: 1083, 1088, 1089, 1090, 1099, 1117, 1130, 1133, 1134, 1135, 1137; Hungary: 1184; India: 1213, 1215, 1223; Indonesia: 1229, 1236, 1238, 1239; Iran, Islamic Republic of: 1241, 1243, 1253; Italie: 1282, 1290, 1304; Jamaica: 1309; Japan: 1339; Jordan: 1401, 1409; Kenya: 1425; Kyrgyzstan: 1429; Latvia: 1435, 1440; Lithuania: 1459, 1468; Mongolia: 1631; Nigeria: 1703, 1704,

1709; Norway: 1725; Pakistan: 1736, 1738, 1742, 1747, 1748, 1751, 1752, 1753, 1754; Philippines: 1806, 1812, 1816, 1820, 1825; Poland: 1829, 1841, 1865, 1870, 1877, 1879, 1891, 1905, 1907, 1909, 1915; Portugal: 1920; Republic of Korea: 1948; Republic of Moldova: 1953; Russian Federation: 1988, 1992, 1994, 2000, 2004, 2006, 2009, 2016, 2022, 2036, 2037, 2038, 2042, 2049, 2050, 2063, 2064, 2066, 2070, 2071, 2072, 2074, 2079, 2080, 2093, 2097, 2108, 2112, 2114, 2134, 2137; Serbia and Montenegro: 2148; Slovakia: 2160, 2161, 2167, 2169; South Africa: 2182, 2189; Sri Lanka: 2200; Suisse: 2209, 2227; Suriname: 2232; Sweden: 2248, 2258; Tajikistan: 2261; Thailand: 2271; Turkey: 2329; Uganda: 2332, 2333; Ukraine: 2347, 2351, 2354, 2356, 2357, 2364; United Kingdom: 2369, 2399, 2400, 2401, 2432, 2472; United Republic of Tanzania: 2488; United States of America: 2520, 2529, 2561, 2574, 2576, 2633, 2641, 2642, 2647, 2655, 2660, 2666, 2673, 2684, 2692, 2696, 2746, 2747, 2749; Uzbekistan: 2766; Yemen: 2781; Zimbabwe: 2785.

mathématiques
[S] 1; Comores, Les: 557; France: 910, 956; [C] Algérie: 63, 68, 70, 71; Arménie: 129; Belarus, Republic of: 236, 237, 238, 239, 243; Belgique: 261; Brésil: 298; Bulgaria: 332, 333, 337; Côte d'Ivoire: 595; France: 956, 969, 971, 1076; Madagascar: 1475, 1480; Maroc: 1506, 1509, 1512, 1516; Portugal: 1922; Suisse: 2209, 2210; Tchad: 2263; Tunisie: 2305, 2307, 2309.

mecánica
[S] 31; México: 1588; Perú: 1773; [C] Argentina: 95, 110; Bolivia: 290; Chile: 456; Cuba: 609, 610, 614; El Salvador: 708; México: 1547, 1552, 1568; Républica Dominicana: 1957.

mécanique
[S] 31; France: 925, 956, 964; [C] Algérie: 63, 68, 71; Belarus, Republic of: 227, 232, 233, 234, 236, 241; Belgique: 249; Bulgaria: 328, 339, 341, 342, 344; Cameroun: 351; France: 915, 925, 932, 933, 934, 939, 944, 945, 946, 950, 953, 956, 968, 982, 988, 1007, 1009, 1020, 1049, 1050, 1054; Grèce: 1161; Luxembourg: 1474; Madagascar: 1484; Maroc: 1511; Portugal: 1922; Suisse: 2210; Tchad: 2263; Togo: 2287; Tunisie: 2294, 2314.

mechanical engineering
[S] 31; Czech Republic: 663; Germany: 1125; Pakistan: 1750; Russian Federation: 2014; United Kingdom: 2386; [C] Australia: 134; Azerbaijan: 205, 209; Bangladesh: 215; Belgique: 274; Canada: 405; China: 457, 467, 472, 486, 496, 497, 507, 519, 521; Cyprus: 636; Czech Republic: 651, 663; Denmark: 684, 686; Egypt: 705; Estonia: 881; Ethiopia: 883, 885; Finland: 892, 894; Germany: 1083, 1087, 1088, 1097, 1098, 1099, 1100, 1105, 1117, 1126, 1130, 1132, 1133, 1134; Grèce: 1155; Hungary: 1192, 1193, 1197; Indonesia: 1228, 1238; Ireland: 1257; Italie: 1283, 1290, 1300, 1301; Japan: 1369, 1377, 1379; Jordan: 1408; Kazakhstan: 1417; Latvia: 1437; Libyan Arab Jamahiriya: 1456; Lithuania: 1459, 1468; Nigeria: 1704, 1709; Norway: 1713, 1715; Pakistan: 1746; Philippines: 1806, 1809, 1816, 1822; Poland: 1841, 1866, 1869, 1871, 1883, 1890, 1891, 1892, 1893, 1894, 1895, 1899, 1907; Portugal: 1927; Russian Federation: 1978, 1982, 1985, 1987, 1990, 2000, 2012, 2014, 2020, 2038, 2042, 2045, 2046, 2049, 2052, 2059, 2066, 2067, 2068, 2069, 2070, 2084, 2085, 2096, 2102, 2129, 2131, 2135; Serbia and Montenegro: 2148; Singapore: 2152; Slovakia: 2164, 2166, 2171, 2174; South Africa: 2189; Sri Lanka: 2200; Sudan: 2204; Suriname: 2232; Sweden: 2248; Thailand: 2265, 2271; Turkey: 2326; Ukraine: 2337, 2351, 2354, 2356; United Kingdom: 2386, 2401, 2425, 2432, 2472; United Republic of Tanzania: 2487; United States of America: 2642, 2660, 2692, 2754.

médecine
[C] 11; Algérie: 70; Angola: 74; Belarus, Republic of: 229, 230; Belgique: 279; Brésil: 301, 307; Bulgaria: 329, 330, 331, 336; France: 1024, 1029, 1053, 1057, 1060, 1061; Gabon: 1078; Grèce: 1157, 1159, 1160; Italie: 1296; Madagascar: 1482; Maroc: 1510; Poland: 1897; Portugal: 1926; Suisse: 2221; Togo: 2287; Tunisie: 2299, 2300; Turkey: 2327, 2328; [S] Belgique: 266; Brésil: 301; Canada: 391; France: 1048; République arabe syrienne: 1963.

médecine préventive
[S] Belgique: 266.

médecine vétérinaire
[C] Belarus, Republic of: 224; Brésil: 298; Bulgaria: 336; Cambodge: 348; France: 966; Grèce: 1159.

medicina
[C] 11; Argentina: 86, 89, 91, 100, 121; Bolivia: 289; Chile: 413, 421, 423, 434, 440, 443; Colombia: 533, 547; Costa Rica: 567; Cuba: 599; El Salvador: 709; España: 733, 735, 748, 799, 808, 818, 834, 851; México: 1528, 1531, 1539,

1542, 1543, 1565, 1566, 1570, 1572, 1586, 1611, 1621; Perú: 1775, 1787, 1789, 1790, 1791; Républica Dominicana: 1958; Venezuela: 2773, 2776, 2777; [S] Argentina: 79; Chile: 439; Colombia: 537, 555; Cuba: 611; España: 753, 855; México: 1542, 1543.

medicina preventiva
[C] Argentina: 104, 121; Costa Rica: 567; España: 748, 808, 851; México: 1540; Perú: 1765; Venezuela: 2773, 2776.

medicina veterinaria
[C] Argentina: 107, 119; Cuba: 615; México: 1568.

medicine
[S] 6; Australia: 181; Bahrain: 210; Belgique: 266; Canada: 401; China: 512; China, Macao: 531; Egypt: 700; Germany: 1094, 1109; Iran, Islamic Republic of: 1247; Italie: 1288, 1303; Japan: 1320, 1351; Kazakhstan: 1416; New Zealand: 1683, 1685; Poland: 1872, 1875; Roumanie: 1975; Singapore: 2151; United Kingdom: 2417, 2443; United States of America: 2592, 2615, 2646, 2648; [C] 11; Arménie: 131; Australia: 171; Austria: 189; Bahrain: 210; Bangladesh: 220; Belgique: 255; Bosnia and Herzegovina: 291; Canada: 385; China: 459, 477, 479, 483, 490, 501, 503, 507, 510, 511, 515; China, Macao: 531; Croatia: 598; Czech Republic: 650, 660, 672; Egypt: 699, 700, 706; Estonia: 882; Ethiopia: 883; Finland: 893, 902, 903; Georgia: 1082; Germany: 1105, 1109, 1140, 1143; Hungary: 1181, 1191, 1195, 1198; Indonesia: 1236; Iran, Islamic Republic of: 1240, 1242, 1245, 1249, 1251; Italie: 1300, 1304; Japan: 1327, 1335, 1364, 1396; Jordan: 1402, 1405; Kazakhstan: 1416, 1418; Kuwait: 1427; Kyrgyzstan: 1431, 1432; Lithuania: 1458; Malawi: 1485; Malaysia: 1487; Malta: 1499; Mongolia: 1630; Nepal: 1633; Netherlands: 1657, 1671, 1678; Nigeria: 1704; Norway: 1731; Oman: 1733; Pakistan: 1735, 1741; Philippines: 1807, 1816; Poland: 1872, 1873, 1874; Portugal: 1924; Republic of Korea: 1933, 1939; Republic of Moldova: 1954; Roumanie: 1965, 1975; Russian Federation: 1981, 1988, 2002, 2018, 2032, 2062, 2073, 2074, 2077, 2088, 2095, 2100, 2103, 2132; Serbia and Montenegro: 2147, 2148; Singapore: 2151; Slovakia: 2160, 2169, 2172; South Africa: 2182; Sri Lanka: 2198, 2199, 2201, 2202; Sudan: 2203; Suisse: 2227; Suriname: 2229; Thailand: 2274; Trinidad and Tobago: 2290; Turkey: 2320, 2321, 2326, 2329, 2330; Uganda: 2332; Ukraine: 2335, 2336, 2344, 2359, 2364; United Kingdom: 2367, 2452, 2460, 2472, 2479; United Republic of Tanzania: 2497; United States of America: 2501, 2524, 2537, 2558, 2563, 2615, 2617, 2618, 2620, 2685, 2710, 2714, 2715, 2717, 2719, 2725, 2742, 2753; Uzbekistan: 2767; Yemen: 2781.

medios audio-visuales
[C] Argentina: 100; Cuba: 604; España: 774, 789, 831; México: 1598.

métallurgie
[C] Algérie: 71; Belgique: 249; Bulgaria: 335; France: 934, 944, 945, 959, 982; Madagascar: 1478; Tunisie: 2294.

metallurgy
[C] China: 462, 497; Hungary: 1197; Italie: 1290, 1300; Kazakhstan: 1415, 1417; Nigeria: 1707; Poland: 1890; Russian Federation: 2000, 2026, 2066, 2089, 2091, 2119, 2129; Serbia and Montenegro: 2148; Slovakia: 2166; Ukraine: 2354; United Kingdom: 2431, 2436.

metalurgia
[C] Chile: 438, 444; Costa Rica: 560; Cuba: 605; México: 1548, 1552, 1586, 1615; Venezuela: 2774; [S] España: 730; Perú: 1777.

meteorología
[S] 1, 57; España: 773; [C] 57; Argentina: 81, 82, 92.

météorologie
[S] 1, 57; [C] 7, 57; Algérie: 63; Brésil: 295, 307; Madagascar: 1478; Maroc: 1500.

meteorology
[S] 1, 57; United Kingdom: 2371; [C] 7, 57; Germany: 1135; Kenya: 1423; Lithuania: 1468; Netherlands: 1682; Russian Federation: 2083; Trinidad and Tobago: 2288; Ukraine: 2365; United States of America: 2565.

microbiología
[C] Chile: 416, 426, 444; Perú: 1765; Venezuela: 2774, 2777.

microbiologie
[C] Belarus, Republic of: 229; Belgique: 261; France: 1010, 1011; Tunisie: 2309; [S] Canada: 391.

microbiology
[C] Canada: 405; China: 490; Czech Republic: 653; Germany: 1135, 1137; India: 1213; Iran, Islamic Republic of: 1251; Japan: 1335, 1370, 1380; Netherlands: 1637,

1646; Nigeria: 1703, 1704, 1707, 1709; Pakistan: 1738,
1742, 1751, 1753; Poland: 1829, 1874; Republic of Korea:
1948; South Africa: 2182; Sweden: 2254; Thailand: 2271;
United Kingdom: 2406, 2472; [S] South Africa: 2186;
Thailand: 2274; United States of America, Puerto Rico:
2760.

moyens audio-visuels
[C] Belgique: 244; Bulgaria: 317; Burundi: 347; Côte
d'Ivoire: 597; France: 1033, 1045, 1066; Liban: 1449;
Maroc: 1513; [S] Cameroun: 349.

museología y museografía
[C] 26; España: 862, 865; México: 1536; Perú: 1775; [S]
España: 759.

muséologie et muséographie
[C] 26; France: 927, 1063; Italie: 1295; Madagascar: 1479;
Maroc: 1505.

museology and museography
[C] 26; Czech Republic: 659; Germany: 1117; Italie: 1277;
Republic of Moldova: 1955; Russian Federation: 1989,
2027, 2094; United Kingdom: 2431, 2483, 2485; United
States of America: 2512; [S] United Kingdom: 2483; United
States of America: 2599.

music and musicology
[S] Australia: 132, 147; Sweden: 2259; United Kingdom:
2368, 2377, 2413, 2415, 2416, 2421, 2475, 2483; United
States of America: 2499, 2521, 2526, 2574, 2587, 2598,
2630, 2631; [C] Australia: 134, 140, 147, 148; Austria: 196,
199, 200; Belgique: 263; Bosnia and Herzegovina: 291;
Canada: 353, 366, 367, 371, 382, 405; China: 466, 500;
Cyprus: 622, 640; Czech Republic: 648, 656; Denmark:
682; Estonia: 875, 880; Finland: 903; Germany: 1084,
1119, 1131, 1135; Guyana: 1174; Hungary: 1198; Ireland:
1259; Italie: 1277; Japan: 1347, 1386; Kazakhstan: 1419;
Kenya: 1425; Kyrgyzstan: 1429; Latvia: 1441; Lithuania:
1462; Netherlands: 1636, 1665, 1676; Norway: 1716, 1728;
Philippines: 1806; Poland: 1836, 1837, 1838, 1839, 1854,
1867; Republic of Korea: 1929, 1931, 1935, 1939, 1947;
Republic of Moldova: 1955; Roumanie: 1968, 1969;
Russian Federation: 2027, 2055, 2078; Serbia and
Montenegro: 2148; Slovakia: 2156, 2157; Suisse: 2227;
Sweden: 2243, 2249, 2257; Turkey: 2323, 2326; Ukraine:
2357; United Kingdom: 2392, 2413, 2416, 2421, 2429, 2472,
2483; United States of America: 2521, 2529, 2543, 2557,
2560, 2561, 2574, 2613, 2631, 2633, 2641, 2647, 2655,
2659, 2660, 2666, 2716, 2736, 2747.

música y musicología
[C] Chile: 442; Cuba: 604; [S] Colombia: 542.

musique et musicologie
[C] Belarus, Republic of: 225; Bulgaria: 315; Sénégal: 2145;
Tunisie: 2311.

natural history
[C] Canada: 405; Sri Lanka: 2197.

natural resources
[C] 12, 33; Austria: 192; Belgique: 255; Brésil: 296;
Canada: 357, 396, 398, 405; China: 481; Indonesia: 1229;
Jamaica: 1310; Kazakhstan: 1417; Kenya: 1422; Mongolia:
1631; Netherlands: 1650; Nigeria: 1707; Philippines: 1813;
Russian Federation: 2064, 2069, 2131; Tajikistan: 2262;
Turkey: 2323; United Kingdom: 2406; United Republic of
Tanzania: 2493; United States of America: 2549, 2624,
2633, 2679; Uzbekistan: 2767; Zimbabwe: 2786; [S] 50;
Canada: 357; Thailand: 2275; United States of America:
2624.

natural sciences
[S] 3, 28, 49; Canada: 357, 372; Croatia: 598; Germany:
1109, 1110, 1120; Japan: 1333, 1351, 1353, 1384, 1394;
Thailand: 2275; United Kingdom: 2417; United States of
America: 2598, 2624; [C] 49; Canada: 357, 385, 405;
Croatia: 598; Czech Republic: 650; Finland: 887; Germany:
1088, 1117, 1130, 1137, 1143; Guyana: 1174; India: 1220,
1225; Indonesia: 1229; Jamaica: 1310; Japan: 1329;
Kyrgyzstan: 1432; Norway: 1725; Papua New Guinea:
1760; Philippines: 1806; Poland: 1853, 1898; Republic of
Korea: 1939, 1940; Russian Federation: 2083, 2092, 2128,
2131; Suisse: 2209; Tajikistan: 2262; Turkey: 2329;
Ukraine: 2351; United Kingdom: 2482; United Republic of
Tanzania: 2495; United States of America: 2520, 2530,
2537, 2587, 2617, 2620, 2623, 2624, 2679, 2753, 2754,
2757.

navigation
[C] China: 486.

néerlandais
[C] Belgique: 261.

negocio

[S] 42; España: 769; [C] Argentina: 89, 91; Colombia: 539;
Costa Rica: 563, 581, 582; España: 715, 746, 750, 763,
815; México: 1553, 1568, 1591, 1597, 1608, 1617, 1623;
Perú: 1764, 1796.

neurología
[C] Chile: 421; España: 834.

neurologie
[C] Poland: 1897.

neurology
[C] Finland: 898; Iran, Islamic Republic of: 1242, 1251;
Japan: 1327, 1335; Mongolia: 1630; Poland: 1873, 1874;
Republic of Korea: 1935; Republic of Moldova: 1954;
Russian Federation: 2090; United States of America: 2529,
2563, 2615, 2730.

numismatics
[C] Egypt: 702.

nursing
[C] 11; Australia: 134, 141, 147, 158; Belgique: 273, 274,
275; Belize: 283; Canada: 356, 357, 367, 373, 382, 398,
399; Cyprus: 644; Egypt: 699, 706; Ethiopia: 884; Finland:
898; Germany: 1092, 1109, 1143; Grèce: 1155; Iceland:
1206; Indonesia: 1236, 1239; Iran, Islamic Republic of:
1242, 1245, 1249, 1251; Italie: 1300; Jordan: 1401, 1405,
1409; Kazakhstan: 1416; Kyrgyzstan: 1431, 1432;
Lithuania: 1458; Malawi: 1485; Malta: 1499; Mongolia:
1630; Norway: 1713, 1715, 1722, 1724, 1725, 1728;
Pakistan: 1735; Papua New Guinea: 1760; Philippines:
1798, 1807, 1808, 1812, 1813, 1816, 1817, 1820; Poland:
1873, 1874; Republic of Korea: 1935; Roumanie: 1975;
Russian Federation: 2032, 2100; San Marino: 2142;
Slovakia: 2160, 2169, 2172; South Africa: 2182, 2189;
Suisse: 2227; Suriname: 2230; Sweden: 2240; Thailand:
2274; Turkey: 2320, 2321, 2326, 2329, 2330; Ukraine:
2344, 2359, 2364; United Kingdom: 2375, 2452, 2472, 2476;
United Republic of Tanzania: 2497; United States of
America: 2537, 2542, 2543, 2545, 2551, 2560, 2561, 2563,
2564, 2581, 2587, 2615, 2620, 2623, 2624, 2667, 2679,
2684, 2696, 2700, 2707, 2713, 2714, 2717, 2718, 2719,
2720, 2738, 2745, 2746, 2747, 2748, 2754; [S] Canada:
357, 401; Germany: 1086; Philippines: 1802; Thailand:
2274; United States of America: 2552, 2615, 2624.

nutrición
[C] 12, 16; Argentina: 86, 98, 104; Costa Rica: 575;
España: 794, 830; México: 1539, 1543, 1570; Perú: 1765;
Venezuela: 2778; [S] 12.

nutrition
[S] 6, 12; Japan: 1365; [C] 12, 16; Australia: 182; Brésil:
300, 307; Canada: 353, 382; Egypt: 703; Finland: 898;
Germany: 1137; Guyana: 1173; Indonesia: 1239; Iran,
Islamic Republic of: 1249, 1251; Japan: 1327, 1343, 1347,
1365; Jordan: 1411; Liban: 1443; Mongolia: 1630; Nigeria:
1707; Philippines: 1812, 1813; Poland: 1840, 1873, 1874;
South Africa: 2182; United Kingdom: 2472; United States of
America: 2617.

obstetricia y ginecología
[C] Argentina: 104; Chile: 421; Perú: 1784.

obstetrics and gynaecology
[S] Australia: 181; [C] China: 459; Iran, Islamic Republic of:
1242, 1251; Italie: 1304; Japan: 1327, 1335; Mongolia:
1630; Netherlands: 1657; Poland: 1873, 1874; Republic of
Moldova: 1954; Russian Federation: 2088, 2090; San
Marino: 2142; South Africa: 2182; United Kingdom: 2375;
United States of America: 2562, 2615.

obstétrique et gynécologie
[C] Brésil: 307; Cameroun: 350; Poland: 1897.

oceanografía
[C] Argentina: 92; España: 779; México: 1525, 1560, 1573,
1586; [S] España: 778.

océanographie
[C] Tunisie: 2309.

oceanography
[C] 33; Denmark: 686; Russian Federation: 2066, 2083;
South Africa: 2181; [S] 33.

oenologie
[C] Bulgaria: 327; France: 993, 1029.

oenology
[C] Australia: 165; Italie: 1300.

oftalmología
[C] España: 834.

ophtalmologie
[C] Cameroun: 350; France: 989; Poland: 1897.

ophthalmology
[C] Germany: 1098; Iran, Islamic Republic of: 1251; Japan: 1327, 1335; Mongolia: 1630; Netherlands: 1657; Poland: 1873, 1874; Russian Federation: 2090; San Marino: 2142; South Africa: 2182; United States of America: 2615; [S] United States of America: 2570.

optica
[C] México: 1525.

optics
[C] China: 457; Italie: 1290; Republic of Korea: 1931; Russian Federation: 2066, 2085; South Africa: 2181; Ukraine: 2351, 2356, 2364.

optique
[C] France: 932, 955, 978, 1050; Tunisie: 2307, 2309; [S] France: 978.

oriental studies
[C] Azerbaijan: 208; Finland: 896; Japan: 1359; Pakistan: 1734, 1740, 1749; [S] Jordan: 1406.

orthophonie
[C] Algérie: 66.

ortofonía
[C] Colombia: 540; México: 1540.

paediatrics
[C] China: 459, 490; Ethiopia: 883; Iran, Islamic Republic of: 1242, 1251; Japan: 1327, 1335; Mongolia: 1630; Netherlands: 1657; Poland: 1873, 1874; Republic of Moldova: 1954; Russian Federation: 1981, 2002, 2018, 2062, 2074, 2077, 2088; South Africa: 2182; Ukraine: 2335; United States of America: 2615; [S] Japan: 1365.

paramedical studies
[C] Belgique: 264; Hungary: 1191; India: 1222; Indonesia: 1239; Iran, Islamic Republic of: 1242, 1249, 1251; Japan: 1343; Latvia: 1437; Mongolia: 1630; Pakistan: 1735, 1741; Poland: 1873; South Africa: 2181, 2182, 2189; Thailand: 2269; Ukraine: 2344; United Kingdom: 2399; United States of America: 2545, 2661, 2754; [S] United States of America: 2646.

pêche
[C] 12; Brésil: 295; Cambodge: 348; [S] 12.

pediatría
[C] Chile: 421; España: 834; México: 1539; Perú: 1789.

pédiatrie
[C] Cameroun: 350; Togo: 2287.

performing arts
[S] Australia: 132; United Kingdom: 2396, 2412, 2416; United States of America: 2499, 2504, 2689; [C] Australia: 140, 148, 162, 182; Austria: 196, 199, 200; Azerbaijan: 209; Bosnia and Herzegovina: 291; Canada: 353, 371; China: 463, 484; Czech Republic: 648; Estonia: 875, 880; Germany: 1084, 1119; Italie: 1286; Lithuania: 1462; Mauritius: 1519; Mongolia: 1631; Netherlands: 1636, 1663, 1676; Norway: 1720, 1725; Philippines: 1798; Poland: 1834, 1854, 1867; Roumanie: 1969; Russian Federation: 2025, 2027; Slovakia: 2156; Sri Lanka: 2197; Sweden: 2242, 2256; Turkey: 2320; United Kingdom: 2375, 2401, 2416, 2421, 2472, 2484; United States of America: 2520, 2529, 2537, 2540, 2542, 2557, 2561, 2576, 2587, 2609, 2613, 2636, 2641, 2647, 2655, 2659, 2660, 2666, 2689, 2696, 2707, 2736, 2746, 2747, 2749.

periodismo
[S] 46; Argentina: 84; España: 726; Perú: 1777; [C] Argentina: 85; Chile: 428, 449, 452, 453; Colombia: 533; Costa Rica: 580; Ecuador: 694; El Salvador: 710; España: 774, 789, 802, 831, 871.

pesquería
[C] 12; España: 779; México: 1561, 1568; Perú: 1784; [S] 12; España: 778.

pharmacie et pharmacologie
[C] Bulgaria: 330; Cameroun: 350; France: 1024, 1029, 1057; Italie: 1296; Liban: 1452; Maroc: 1510; Tunisie: 2302; Turkey: 2328; [S] France: 1048.

pharmacy and pharmacology
[C] Australia: 155; Bangladesh: 216; Belgique: 255; Bosnia and Herzegovina: 291; China: 459, 470, 503; China, Macao: 531; Czech Republic: 650, 672; Denmark: 683; Egypt: 699; Finland: 887; Germany: 1105, 1109, 1143; Ghana: 1146; Hungary: 1181, 1191; India: 1210; Iran, Islamic Republic of: 1245, 1249, 1251; Jamaica: 1309; Japan: 1327, 1343, 1360; Jordan: 1401, 1402, 1405, 1408, 1411; Kyrgyzstan: 1431, 1432; Lithuania: 1458; Malaysia: 1487; Mongolia: 1630; Netherlands: 1657; Pakistan: 1735, 1742, 1748, 1752; Philippines: 1807, 1811, 1813; Poland: 1872, 1873, 1874; Portugal: 1924, 1925; Republic of Korea:

1947; Roumanie: 1965; Russian Federation: 2032, 2058, 2062, 2076, 2087, 2100, 2103; Slovakia: 2160; Suisse: 2227; Thailand: 2274; Trinidad and Tobago: 2290; Turkey: 2320, 2321, 2326, 2329; Ukraine: 2335, 2344, 2353, 2359; United Kingdom: 2369, 2399, 2452, 2472; United Republic of Tanzania: 2497; United States of America: 2560, 2615, 2617, 2624, 2642, 2653, 2663, 2679, 2715, 2719, 2742, 2753; [S] Canada: 401; China, Macao: 531; Italie: 1303; Japan: 1320; Poland: 1872; Roumanie: 1975; South Africa: 2186; United Kingdom: 2456; United States of America: 2624.

philologie
[C] Belarus, Republic of: 236, 243; Belgique: 253; Maroc: 1508; [S] Italie: 1270; Portugal: 1918.

philology
[C] Arménie: 127; Azerbaijan: 207, 208, 209; China: 490; Czech Republic: 660; Germany: 1131; Japan: 1330; Kazakhstan: 1419; Latvia: 1435, 1436, 1441; Mongolia: 1631; Poland: 1850, 1877, 1886, 1903, 1909, 1915; Republic of Moldova: 1954, 1955, 1956; Russian Federation: 1988, 2004, 2006, 2063, 2073, 2074, 2079, 2080, 2093, 2097, 2137; Turkey: 2320; Ukraine: 2357, 2364; United States of America: 2624; Uzbekistan: 2765; [S] Russian Federation: 2004; United States of America: 2624.

philosophie
[C] Arménie: 129; Belarus, Republic of: 237; Belgique: 244, 253; Brésil: 298, 299, 311; Bulgaria: 340; Burundi: 347; Cameroun: 350; Canada: 380, 402; Côte d'Ivoire: 597; France: 970, 1001, 1002; Grèce: 1157; Madagascar: 1479; Maroc: 1508; Saint-Siège: 2140, 2141; Tunisie: 2304; [S] Suisse: 2224.

philosophy
[C] Austria: 204; Azerbaijan: 208, 209; Canada: 353, 366, 371, 373, 380, 383, 385, 402, 405; China: 477, 499, 504, 515; Croatia: 598; Czech Republic: 650; Germany: 1131, 1135; India: 1213; Indonesia: 1238; Ireland: 1259; Israel: 1268; Italie: 1286, 1301; Japan: 1330; Kenya: 1422; Latvia: 1441; Mongolia: 1630, 1631; Netherlands: 1641; Pakistan: 1754; Philippines: 1810; Poland: 1835, 1870, 1877, 1903, 1905, 1909, 1915; Republic of Korea: 1929, 1935, 1948; Republic of Moldova: 1953, 1955; République arabe syrienne: 1962; Russian Federation: 1988, 1989, 2019, 2027, 2080, 2082, 2093, 2106, 2107, 2137; Serbia and Montenegro: 2148; Slovakia: 2157, 2172; South Africa: 2187; Suisse: 2227; Ukraine: 2336, 2347, 2357; United Kingdom: 2400; United States of America: 2514, 2529, 2561, 2594, 2633, 2641, 2642, 2647, 2655, 2666, 2684, 2746, 2749; Uzbekistan: 2767; [S] Canada: 364, 383; India: 1213; Japan: 1392; Slovakia: 2157; United Kingdom: 2372, 2457; United States of America: 2591.

photographie
[C] Belgique: 244; France: 911, 965; [S] France: 911.

photography
[C] Belgique: 275; Canada: 371; Czech Republic: 648, 666; Finland: 895; Germany: 1101; Hungary: 1188; Italie: 1280; Russian Federation: 2043; Slovakia: 2155; Turkey: 2320; United Kingdom: 2399; United States of America: 2500, 2554, 2557, 2576, 2613, 2617, 2624, 2636, 2656, 2679, 2746, 2749; [S] United States of America: 2624.

physical education
[C] Belarus, Republic of: 235; Canada: 353, 382; China: 461, 465, 484, 490, 507; Czech Republic: 650; Egypt: 706; Estonia: 880; Germany: 1090, 1133, 1135, 1136; Hungary: 1191; India: 1213; Iran, Islamic Republic of: 1251, 1253; Japan: 1316; Kyrgyzstan: 1429; Lithuania: 1463; Norway: 1724, 1725; Philippines: 1803, 1812; Poland: 1840, 1856, 1909, 1912; Republic of Korea: 1931, 1945; Roumanie: 1975; Russian Federation: 2027, 2037, 2065; Slovakia: 2160; Turkey: 2326; Ukraine: 2336, 2350, 2351, 2356, 2357, 2364; United Kingdom: 2394, 2431; United States of America: 2501, 2557, 2618, 2633, 2642, 2660, 2714, 2735; Uzbekistan: 2768; [S] Canada: 401; Japan: 1320; Poland: 1913; United Kingdom: 2397, 2475; United States of America: 2556, 2587, 2665, 2667, 2752.

physical therapy
[C] Pakistan: 1735; Poland: 1868; United States of America: 2748; [S] Thailand: 2274; United States of America: 2646.

physics
[C] 1; Austria: 187; Azerbaijan: 208; Canada: 353, 371, 385, 398, 405, 408; China: 457, 484, 493; Denmark: 686; Eritrea: 711; Estonia: 880; Ethiopia: 883, 884, 885; Germany: 1083, 1088, 1131, 1135; India: 1215, 1223; Indonesia: 1236, 1238; Iran, Islamic Republic of: 1243, 1253; Italie: 1290; Japan: 1339, 1379, 1398; Jordan: 1409; Kazakhstan: 1419; Kenya: 1425; Kyrgyzstan: 1429; Latvia: 1440; Lithuania: 1468; Nigeria: 1703, 1704, 1707, 1709; Norway: 1729; Pakistan: 1742; Papua New Guinea: 1760;

Philippines: 1820; Poland: 1829, 1874, 1877, 1890, 1891, 1905; Republic of Korea: 1948; Russian Federation: 1986, 2004, 2006, 2009, 2016, 2022, 2026, 2036, 2037, 2038, 2041, 2050, 2063, 2064, 2070, 2071, 2072, 2074, 2079, 2080, 2083, 2085, 2091, 2097, 2108, 2112, 2119, 2135, 2137; Slovakia: 2157, 2160, 2161, 2164, 2169, 2174; South Africa: 2181, 2182; Sweden: 2248, 2259; Thailand: 2271; Turkey: 2326, 2330; Uganda: 2332; Ukraine: 2351, 2354, 2356, 2357, 2364; United Kingdom: 2401, 2472; United States of America: 2529, 2553, 2561, 2565, 2576, 2619, 2633, 2642, 2647, 2655, 2660, 2666, 2673, 2692, 2696, 2735, 2746; Uzbekistan: 2766, 2770; Yemen: 2781; [S] 1; Germany: 1125; Russian Federation: 2004, 2016; United States of America: 2678; Uzbekistan: 2766.

physiologie
[C] Cameroun: 350.

physiology
[C] Ethiopia: 883; Iran, Islamic Republic of: 1251; Japan: 1327, 1335; Mongolia: 1630; Netherlands: 1657; Nigeria: 1704; Pakistan: 1748, 1751, 1753; Poland: 1840, 1873, 1874; Serbia and Montenegro: 2148; Tajikistan: 2262; Trinidad and Tobago: 2290; United Kingdom: 2375; United States of America: 2537, 2587, 2615, 2661, 2746.

physique
[C] 1; Algérie: 63, 68, 70, 71; Belarus, Republic of: 236, 237, 238, 239, 243; Belgique: 261; Bulgaria: 332, 333, 335; France: 943, 955, 969, 971, 978, 979, 1008, 1013, 1029, 1063; Italie: 1276; Madagascar: 1475, 1478, 1480; Maroc: 1506, 1509, 1511, 1512, 1516; Suisse: 2210; Tchad: 2263; Tunisie: 2305, 2307, 2309; [S] 1; Brésil: 293; Canada: 391; Comores, Les: 557; France: 910.

political economy
[C] 2, 14, 29; Arménie: 125; Austria: 194; Canada: 385; China: 465; Denmark: 676; Germany: 1089; Hungary: 1184, 1201; India: 1222; Italie: 1275, 1300, 1302; Mongolia: 1631; Norway: 1718; Republic of Moldova: 1953; République arabe syrienne: 1962; Roumanie: 1966; Russian Federation: 1989, 2031, 2057, 2082, 2108, 2124; Sweden: 2239; [S] 42.

political science
[C] 14; Arménie: 125, 130; Austria: 202; Azerbaijan: 209; Bosnia and Herzegovina: 291; Canada: 371, 385, 398, 399, 405, 408; China: 520; Czech Republic: 667; Estonia: 879; Finland: 903; Germany: 1090, 1108, 1131, 1137; Hungary: 1184, 1201; India: 1222; Indonesia: 1228, 1239; Italie: 1277, 1285, 1286; Japan: 1322, 1344, 1359, 1377; Kyrgyzstan: 1429; Latvia: 1441; Lithuania: 1471; Mongolia: 1631; Norway: 1718; Philippines: 1806, 1812, 1813, 1816, 1825; Poland: 1848, 1878, 1886, 1905, 1909, 1915; Republic of Korea: 1929; République arabe syrienne: 1962; Russian Federation: 1977, 1989, 2027, 2074, 2093, 2137; Suisse: 2227; Sweden: 2239; Thailand: 2278, 2280; Turkey: 2319; Ukraine: 2336; United Kingdom: 2384, 2400, 2401, 2464, 2472; United States of America: 2529, 2540, 2561, 2574, 2594, 2613, 2633, 2642, 2647, 2655, 2659, 2660, 2666, 2683, 2684, 2696, 2735; [S] 14; Canada: 364; Italie: 1288; Japan: 1399; Poland: 1878; Sweden: 2245; United Kingdom: 2390, 2464; United States of America: 2574, 2582.

portugais
[S] Portugal: 1919; [C] Portugal: 1922.

preventive medicine
[S] Belgique: 266; [C] Indonesia: 1239; Iran, Islamic Republic of: 1251; Japan: 1347; Mongolia: 1630; Poland: 1873, 1874; Russian Federation: 2062; South Africa: 2182; United Kingdom: 2387; United States of America: 2615.

printing
[C] Finland: 892; Hungary: 1188; Italie: 1280; Republic of Moldova: 1953; South Africa: 2181; Uganda: 2331; United States of America: 2736; [S] Italie: 1273.

programas de corta duración
[C] 20, 38, 58; [S] 36, 49.

programas de verano
[S] España: 712, 713, 726, 780, 858; [C] España: 720, 722, 724, 742, 752, 804, 806, 807, 809, 810, 811, 813, 820, 825, 826, 827, 837, 842, 850, 851, 852, 854, 859, 873; México: 1540, 1565, 1566, 1568, 1570, 1571, 1573, 1574, 1575, 1576, 1577, 1578, 1580, 1587, 1592, 1602, 1603, 1610, 1615, 1618; Perú: 1772, 1795.

programmes d'été
[C] Albanie: 61; France: 1021; Italie: 1292; Portugal: 1922; Sénégal: 2146.

programmes de courte durée
[C] 20, 38, 47, 58; [S] 36, 49.

psicología
[C] Argentina: 86, 88, 91, 95, 98, 113; Chile: 417, 424, 428, 440, 449, 452, 453; Colombia: 539; Costa Rica: 563; El Salvador: 710; España: 761, 795, 808, 818, 873; México: 1541, 1570, 1590, 1595, 1596, 1598, 1604, 1607, 1608, 1617, 1621; Perú: 1775, 1791; [S] Bolivia: 286; Chile: 414; México: 1557; Perú: 1774, 1777.

psiquiatría
[C] Argentina: 104; Chile: 440; España: 834; México: 1541, 1572.

psychiatrie
[C] Belarus, Republic of: 229; Cameroun: 350; Poland: 1897.

psychiatry
[C] Canada: 356; Ethiopia: 883; Iran, Islamic Republic of: 1242, 1251; Italie: 1304; Japan: 1327, 1335, 1383; Mongolia: 1630; Poland: 1873, 1874; Republic of Moldova: 1954; South Africa: 2182; United States of America: 2563, 2615.

psychologie
[C] Algérie: 66, 71; Belarus, Republic of: 238; Belgique: 261; Brésil: 299; Bulgaria: 340; Burundi: 347; France: 999, 1047, 1062; Saint-Siège: 2140; Suisse: 2206, 2220, 2221.

psychology
[C] Azerbaijan: 208, 209; Belgique: 255; Canada: 353, 366, 371, 373, 379, 385, 398, 405, 408; Czech Republic: 665; Fiji: 886; Finland: 887, 896, 903; Germany: 1090, 1131; Hungary: 1184; Indonesia: 1238; Iran, Islamic Republic of: 1251; Ireland: 1255; Italie: 1277; Japan: 1316, 1322, 1343, 1345, 1383; Kyrgyzstan: 1429; Latvia: 1441; Lithuania: 1461, 1463; Mongolia: 1630; Pakistan: 1754; Philippines: 1806, 1807, 1812, 1813, 1825; Poland: 1840, 1915; Portugal: 1924; Republic of Korea: 1948; Republic of Moldova: 1953, 1954; Russian Federation: 1989, 1990, 1995, 1997, 2000, 2004, 2025, 2027, 2031, 2065, 2072, 2079, 2082, 2093, 2117, 2124, 2134; San Marino: 2142; Slovakia: 2161, 2172; Suisse: 2227; Sweden: 2237; Uganda: 2332; Ukraine: 2336; United Kingdom: 2387, 2401, 2472; United States of America: 2502, 2508, 2529, 2574, 2587, 2594, 2613, 2633, 2641, 2642, 2647, 2655, 2659, 2673, 2683, 2684, 2696, 2735; [S] Uzbekistan: 2765; [S] Canada: 364; Cyprus: 639; Japan: 1392; Poland: 1913; Russian Federation: 2004; United States of America: 2574, 2593.

public relations
[S] 6; [C] Austria: 194; Cyprus: 637, 643; Czech Republic: 666; Denmark: 676; Estonia: 879; Hungary: 1201; India: 1219; Ireland: 1255; Italie: 1277; Japan: 1383; Kyrgyzstan: 1428; Norway: 1724; Philippines: 1813; Poland: 1844; Russian Federation: 2025, 2031, 2083, 2093, 2123; South Africa: 2189; United Kingdom: 2384, 2425; United States of America: 2574, 2613, 2642, 2660, 2683, 2684.

publicidad
[C] Chile: 452; España: 802, 831; Perú: 1795; République Dominicana: 1959.

publicité
[C] Belgique: 261; Burundi: 347; Côte d'Ivoire: 597; France: 984, 1063; Liban: 1449; Tunisie: 2303, 2310.

publishing
[C] Finland: 892; Georgia: 1080; Germany: 1117; India: 1213; Russian Federation: 2043; Uganda: 2331; United Kingdom: 2401, 2425; United States of America: 2613.

química
[C] Argentina: 103, 123; Bolivia: 290; Chile: 426, 438, 456; Cuba: 599; España: 727, 736, 740, 751, 775, 851, 871; México: 1548, 1553, 1568, 1570, 1572, 1575, 1611; Perú: 1791; Venezuela: 2774; [S] Bolivia: 286; Colombia: 548; México: 1588.

radiología
[C] Argentina: 121; Chile: 421; México: 1539.

radiologie
[C] Cameroun: 350; Poland: 1897.

radiology
[C] Iran, Islamic Republic of: 1242, 1251; Japan: 1327, 1335; Mongolia: 1630; Netherlands: 1657; Norway: 1713, 1728; Poland: 1873, 1874; Republic of Moldova: 1954; Russian Federation: 2049, 2050, 2135; Singapore: 2151; United Kingdom: 2425, 2476; United States of America: 2615, 2735; [S] United Kingdom: 2371.

recherche
[S] 14, 20, 41, 50; Canada: 358, 372; France: 910, 1009; Suisse: 2212; [C] Algérie: 68; Belgique: 247; France: 923, 967, 968, 1000; Madagascar: 1475.

recreation and leisure
[C] 56; Australia: 140; Belarus, Republic of: 235; Bermuda: 285; Canada: 353, 357, 405; Czech Republic: 665; Estonia: 880; Ireland: 1255; Latvia: 1441; Netherlands: 1682; Poland: 1840, 1844, 1851, 1864, 1868, 1912; Russian Federation: 1995, 2055, 2064; United Kingdom: 2386, 2401, 2436, 2476; United States of America: 2561, 2683; Uzbekistan: 2767; [S] Poland: 1864; United Kingdom: 2386.

recreología y tiempo libre
[C] Cuba: 602; España: 819.

récréologie et loisirs
[C] 56.

recursos naturales
[C] 12; Chile: 444; Costa Rica: 578; Cuba: 605; España: 860; México: 1530, 1562; Perú: 1781; Venezuela: 2772; [S] 50.

relaciones industriales
[C] España: 840; México: 1534.

relaciones internacionales
[C] 25, 29, 30, 39; Argentina: 91, 94, 97; Chile: 412, 441; Colombia: 533; Costa Rica: 592; Ecuador: 689; España: 757, 776, 781, 805; Honduras: 1176; México: 1526, 1551, 1571, 1586, 1589, 1595, 1607, 1609, 1623; Nicaragua: 1695, 1696; [S] Ecuador: 689; España: 769.

relaciones públicas
[C] Argentina: 75, 95; El Salvador: 710; España: 831; Paraguay: 1761.

relations industrielles
[C] France: 960, 1063.

relations internationales
[C] 25, 29, 30, 39, 47; Algérie: 71; Arménie: 129; Belarus, Republic of: 242; Belgique: 262; France: 930, 976, 987, 1003, 1025; Grèce: 1160; Suisse: 2216; [S] Madagascar: 1483; Maroc: 1507, 1513.

relations publiques
[C] Burundi: 347; France: 1016.

research
[S] 14, 20, 41, 50; Australia: 138, 165, 169, 175, 181, 183; Canada: 358, 363, 372; Egypt: 700; Finland: 888; Germany: 1085; India: 1221; New Zealand: 1684, 1685; Norway: 1723; Singapore: 2150; United Kingdom: 2417, 2431, 2444, 2459, 2468, 2470; United States of America: 2506, 2592, 2600, 2624; [C] Australia: 172; Belgique: 255; Finland: 903; Germany: 1135; India: 1211, 1223; Iran, Islamic Republic of: 1241; Japan: 1336; Jordan: 1408; Kenya: 1425; Latvia: 1441; Nigeria: 1703, 1709; Poland: 1840; Russian Federation: 1992, 2031, 2128; Sweden: 2254; Turkey: 2321, 2329; Ukraine: 2337, 2351, 2354; United Kingdom: 2391, 2462, 2472; United States of America: 2615, 2624, 2692.

ressources naturelles
[C] 12; Belgique: 247, 250; Brésil: 295, 310; France: 925, 941; Grèce: 1160; Maroc: 1504; [S] 50; France: 925, 964.

riesgos, seguros
[C] España: 743, 747, 758, 761, 775, 851; México: 1551; Paraguay: 1761; [S] España: 758.

risks, insurance
[C] United Republic of Tanzania: 2490.

rural development
[S] 50; [C] Egypt: 703; Ghana: 1146; India: 1213; Israel: 1261; Japan: 1380, 1398; Netherlands: 1648; Philippines: 1804, 1806; Russian Federation: 1999, 2045, 2069; Sri Lanka: 2197; Tajikistan: 2261; Thailand: 2272; Ukraine: 2354, 2364; United Kingdom: 2380, 2476; United States of America: 2563, 2576.

Russian
[C] Arménie: 127; Canada: 399; Finland: 896; Germany: 1090; Italie: 1280, 1301; Kyrgyzstan: 1429; Latvia: 1440; Poland: 1892, 1908; Russian Federation: 1983, 1989, 1990, 1991, 1992, 1997, 2004, 2009, 2016, 2019, 2022, 2027, 2031, 2037, 2044, 2056, 2064, 2066, 2070, 2071, 2072, 2074, 2083, 2087, 2097, 2105, 2117, 2121, 2123, 2134, 2137; Ukraine: 2336; United Kingdom: 2472; United States of America: 2655; [S] Russian Federation: 2004; Tajikistan: 2260.

Scandinavian studies
[C] Finland: 903; Norway: 1725; Sweden: 2237, 2240, 2241, 2244; [S] Iceland: 1207.

sciences
[C] 1, 4, 21; Algérie: 69; Arménie: 131; Australia: 140, 142, 158, 161; Austria: 194; Bahrain: 210, 211; Bangladesh:

216, 220; Barbados: 222; Belgique: 247, 255, 261, 279; Bosnia and Herzegovina: 291; Brésil: 301, 308; Cameroun: 351; Canada: 353, 355, 357, 360, 367, 374, 379, 382, 385, 388, 390, 393, 398, 405; China: 457, 465, 472, 477, 480, 507, 513, 515, 523; China, Hong Kong: 529; Croatia: 598; Czech Republic: 652; Egypt: 699, 706; Estonia: 880; Ethiopia: 883; Fiji: 886; Finland: 894; France: 913, 914, 915, 955, 960, 968, 971, 986, 1024, 1025, 1027, 1028, 1058, 1061, 1069, 1076; Gabon: 1077; Germany: 1083, 1105, 1113, 1117, 1135, 1136; Grèce: 1157; Guyana: 1173; Hungary: 1198; India: 1208, 1214, 1215, 1225; Indonesia: 1229; Iran, Islamic Republic of: 1244, 1252, 1253, 1254; Ireland: 1256, 1259; Jamaica: 1309, 1310; Japan: 1336, 1360, 1364, 1377, 1379, 1398; Jordan: 1403, 1405, 1408, 1409, 1412; Kazakhstan: 1414, 1417, 1418; Kenya: 1421, 1422; Kuwait: 1427; Kyrgyzstan: 1431, 1432; Liban: 1443; Libyan Arab Jamahiriya: 1456; Lithuania: 1459, 1471; Madagascar: 1481, 1482, 1484; Malaysia: 1493; Maroc: 1506, 1510, 1512, 1516; Mauritius: 1521; Nepal: 1633; Netherlands: 1638, 1641, 1675; New Zealand: 1694; Nigeria: 1709; Norway: 1724, 1729; Oman: 1733; Papua New Guinea: 1760; Philippines: 1805, 1808, 1810, 1817; Poland: 1840, 1891, 1908; Portugal: 1925; Republic of Korea: 1933, 1940, 1947; Roumanie: 1974, 1975; Russian Federation: 1989, 2008, 2030, 2064, 2066, 2069, 2082, 2084, 2098, 2106, 2121, 2122, 2123, 2124, 2128, 2131; Serbia and Montenegro: 2147, 2148; South Africa: 2182, 2195; Sri Lanka: 2197, 2198, 2199, 2202; Suisse: 2210, 2221, 2225, 2227; Swaziland: 2234; Sweden: 2241, 2247; Tajikistan: 2261, 2262; Thailand: 2266, 2271, 2274, 2278; Tunisie: 2305; Turkey: 2320, 2324, 2327, 2328; Ukraine: 2334, 2336, 2343, 2351, 2352, 2359, 2364; United Kingdom: 2367, 2369, 2375, 2392, 2399, 2404, 2423, 2452, 2460, 2472, 2474, 2476, 2479; United Republic of Tanzania: 2492, 2497; United States of America: 2501, 2518, 2524, 2529, 2537, 2542, 2545, 2557, 2562, 2564, 2575, 2580, 2583, 2587, 2613, 2618, 2621, 2623, 2624, 2627, 2634, 2653, 2659, 2676, 2679, 2684, 2685, 2689, 2692, 2700, 2707, 2713, 2718, 2719, 2720, 2730, 2738, 2745, 2754, 2756; United States of America, Puerto Rico: 2759; Uzbekistan: 2765, 2766, 2767; Zimbabwe: 2785, 2786; [S] 23, 37, 49, 59; Australia: 141, 161; Bahrain: 210; Belgique: 276; Canada: 400, 401, 403; China: 482; Comores, Les: 557; France: 910, 968, 974, 978, 1048; Germany: 1107; Ghana: 1148; Iran, Islamic Republic of: 1244; Ireland: 1259; Italie: 1303; Japan: 1317, 1320, 1323, 1336, 1369; Pakistan: 1739, 1743; Poland: 1841, 1913; République arabe syrienne: 1963; Singapore: 2149; Suisse: 2212, 2219; United Kingdom: 2383, 2417, 2437, 2443, 2463, 2465, 2468, 2471; United States of America: 2601, 2604, 2606, 2624, 2634, 2647, 2677, 2689.

sciences agronomiques
[C] 27; Algérie: 68, 71; Belarus, Republic of: 228; Belgique: 250, 258, 282; Brésil: 295, 305, 307, 311; Bulgaria: 323; Cambodge: 348; Côte d'Ivoire: 596; France: 909, 935, 942, 991, 993, 1011, 1012, 1019; Maroc: 1504; Togo: 2287; Tunisie: 2295; [S] Belgique: 250; Cameroun: 349.

sciences appliquées
[C] Algérie: 68, 71; Belgique: 247, 251; France: 913, 950, 955, 956, 960, 991, 1000; Madagascar: 1475; Tunisie: 2305; [S] France: 956.

sciences de l'information
[C] 49; Burundi: 347; Cambodge: 348; Cameroun: 352; Côte d'Ivoire: 597; France: 962, 1072; Maroc: 1512; [S] 49.

sciences de la mer
[S] 31, 50; France: 910; [C] Grèce: 1162; Tunisie: 2309.

sciences de la terre
[S] 1; Canada: 391; France: 910, 964; [C] France: 969, 991; Tunisie: 2309.

sciences économiques et commerciales
[C] 38; Algérie: 63, 68, 71; Arménie: 129; Belgique: 251, 253, 261, 262; France: 930, 1003, 1027, 1053, 1055, 1059, 1064; Madagascar: 1483; Maroc: 1514; Suisse: 2221, 2225; Togo: 2287; Tunisie: 2298, 2306, 2310; Turkey: 2327, 2328; [S] France: 1005, 1048; Madagascar: 1483; Suisse: 2219.

sciences humaines
[S] 14, 28, 49, 50; France: 910, 968, 1048; [C] 29; Algérie: 71; Canada: 388, 390; Côte d'Ivoire: 597; France: 923, 976, 1002, 1003, 1027, 1036, 1055, 1059, 1061, 1062, 1076; Gabon: 1078; Grèce: 1159; Madagascar: 1479; Maroc: 1505, 1510, 1514.

sciences naturelles
[S] 28, 49; Canada: 372; France: 1048; [C] 49; France: 1000, 1053; Madagascar: 1480, 1482; Suisse: 2209; Turkey: 2327.

sciences politiques
[C] 14; Algérie: 68, 71; Angola: 73; Arménie: 129; Belgique: 251, 253; Cameroun: 350; Canada: 390; France: 1001, 1003, 1027, 1057, 1064; Liban: 1452; Suisse: 2216; [S] 14; Maroc: 1513.

sciences sociales
[C] 14, 29, 39, 49; Algérie: 68, 71; Arménie: 129; Belgique: 247, 253, 259, 261; Brésil: 298, 301, 306, 309; Cameroun: 351; Côte d'Ivoire: 597; France: 923, 960, 968, 971, 1001, 1025, 1036, 1047, 1057, 1061, 1076; Gabon: 1078; Grèce: 1159; Maroc: 1505, 1514; Saint-Siège: 2140, 2141; Suisse: 2221; [S] 14, 28, 49; Brésil: 301; Canada: 389, 391; France: 968, 974; Suisse: 2219.

sciences vétérinaires
[C] Brésil: 307, 311; Bulgaria: 338; Cameroun: 351; Maroc: 1504; Sénégal: 2144; Turkey: 2327.

shipbuilding
[S] 31; [C] Poland: 1871; Russian Federation: 1992, 2010, 2068; Singapore: 2152, 2153; Tajikistan: 2261.

short-term programmes
[C] 20, 38, 47, 58; [S] 36, 49.

silvicultura
[C] 12, 21; Chile: 432; Costa Rica: 560; Cuba: 617, 620; Ecuador: 697; México: 1530, 1562; Perú: 1781; [S] 12, 50.

Slavic studies
[C] Czech Republic: 657, 660; Finland: 896; Germany: 1090; Kyrgyzstan: 1429; Latvia: 1435; Lithuania: 1471; Mongolia: 1631; Poland: 1908; Slovakia: 2170; Ukraine: 2346, 2364; United States of America: 2696.

social sciences
[C] 14, 29, 39, 49; Australia: 140, 161, 162, 166; Austria: 194, 202; Azerbaijan: 209; Bangladesh: 220; Belgique: 264; Bulgaria: 321; Canada: 353, 356, 357, 364, 385, 405; China: 465, 477, 480, 519; China, Hong Kong: 528, 529; Czech Republic: 650, 660; Estonia: 876; Fiji: 886; Finland: 887, 896, 903, 904; Germany: 1090, 1098, 1099, 1100, 1108, 1112, 1115, 1131, 1133, 1135, 1137; Guyana: 1174; Hungary: 1184, 1193; India: 1213, 1225; Indonesia: 1228, 1239; Iran, Islamic Republic of: 1252, 1254; Ireland: 1255; Israel: 1263; Italie: 1277, 1280, 1300; Jamaica: 1310; Japan: 1311, 1322, 1329, 1359, 1383; Kazakhstan: 1414; Kenya: 1421; Kyrgyzstan: 1431, 1432; Latvia: 1435, 1436, 1441; Liban: 1443; Lithuania: 1459, 1461, 1471; Malta: 1499; Mongolia: 1631; Nepal: 1633; Netherlands: 1641, 1669, 1675, 1682; New Zealand: 1686; Norway: 1724, 1731; Oman: 1733; Pakistan: 1734, 1749; Papua New Guinea: 1760; Philippines: 1806, 1810, 1817; Poland: 1863, 1899, 1910, 1911, 1916; Portugal: 1925; Republic of Korea: 1931, 1933, 1939, 1947; Roumanie: 1974; Russian Federation: 1977, 1978, 1980, 1989, 1994, 1995, 2000, 2006, 2025, 2027, 2057, 2064, 2065, 2072, 2082, 2093, 2098, 2107, 2121, 2122, 2128; Serbia and Montenegro: 2147; Slovakia: 2154, 2161, 2171; South Africa: 2191, 2195; Sri Lanka: 2197, 2199, 2202; Suriname: 2228, 2229; Swaziland: 2234; Sweden: 2242, 2247, 2258; Tajikistan: 2262; Thailand: 2271; Turkey: 2321; Ukraine: 2334, 2336, 2341, 2343, 2347, 2352, 2356, 2361, 2364; United Kingdom: 2375, 2400, 2401, 2436, 2460, 2461, 2472, 2474, 2482; United States of America: 2501, 2502, 2508, 2520, 2530, 2545, 2553, 2561, 2575, 2587, 2618, 2620, 2655, 2659, 2707, 2757; Uzbekistan: 2766, 2767; Zimbabwe: 2786; [S] 14, 28, 49; Bangladesh: 217; Canada: 357, 400, 401; Croatia: 598; Germany: 1086, 1125; Ghana: 1148; Japan: 1318, 1324, 1351, 1353, 1356, 1384, 1399; United Kingdom: 2396, 2437, 2443; United States of America: 2598.

social work
[C] Australia: 134; Austria: 194, 195, 203; Belgique: 263, 264; Belize: 283; Canada: 398, 405, 408; China, Hong Kong: 526; Estonia: 880; Finland: 898; Germany: 1092, 1098, 1099, 1109, 1115, 1117; India: 1213; Indonesia: 1239; Iran, Islamic Republic of: 1251; Ireland: 1255, 1259; Italie: 1280; Japan: 1383; Mongolia: 1630; Netherlands: 1673; New Zealand: 1686; Norway: 1713, 1724; Philippines: 1812, 1820; Poland: 1840, 1861, 1873, 1886; Republic of Korea: 1935; Roumanie: 1968; Russian Federation: 1977, 1981, 1992, 1997, 2000, 2082; Slovakia: 2154, 2172; Suisse: 2227; Sweden: 2240; Ukraine: 2352, 2364; United Kingdom: 2399, 2432, 2476, 2486; United States of America: 2545, 2551, 2575, 2587, 2617, 2641, 2647, 2673, 2679, 2746, 2754; [S] Canada: 400; Germany: 1086.

sociología
[S] Argentina: 84; Bolivia: 286; Chile: 411; España: 755; México: 1529; [C] Chile: 412, 417, 429; Colombia: 533; España: 770, 795, 808, 851, 869; México: 1525, 1575, 1609.

sociologie
[C] Algérie: 63, 71; Belgique: 253; Brésil: 299; Burundi: 347; France: 970, 1001, 1036; Maroc: 1505; Suisse: 2215.

sociology
[C] Azerbaijan: 208; Canada: 353, 366, 371, 373, 385, 405, 408; Czech Republic: 665; Denmark: 674; Finland: 896; Germany: 1089, 1090, 1108, 1131, 1135; India: 1222; Ireland: 1255; Italie: 1286; Japan: 1316, 1322, 1345, 1359, 1377; Kenya: 1422, 1425; Kyrgyzstan: 1431; Latvia: 1441; Mongolia: 1631; Netherlands: 1682; Philippines: 1812; Poland: 1830, 1840, 1848, 1859, 1905, 1909, 1915; Republic of Moldova: 1953; République arabe syrienne: 1962; Russian Federation: 1989, 1997, 2000, 2004, 2007, 2027, 2031, 2055, 2065, 2071, 2082, 2097, 2105, 2110, 2112, 2124; Serbia and Montenegro: 2147; Slovakia: 2161, 2172; Suisse: 2227; Suriname: 2229; Thailand: 2269; Turkey: 2323; Uganda: 2332; Ukraine: 2336; United Kingdom: 2384, 2436, 2452, 2472, 2476; United States of America: 2529, 2561, 2574, 2609, 2642, 2655, 2659, 2660, 2666, 2673, 2679, 2696, 2735; Uzbekistan: 2765; [S] Japan: 1392; Russian Federation: 2004; Sweden: 2259; United Kingdom: 2464; United States of America: 2574.

space
[C] Pakistan: 1754; Russian Federation: 2084, 2102; Turkey: 2323; United Kingdom: 2472; United States of America: 2565.

Spanish
[C] Italie: 1280, 1301; Norway: 1729; United States of America: 2529, 2577, 2642, 2673, 2684.

special education
[S] 46; [C] Bahrain: 210; China: 465; Egypt: 706; Germany: 1115; Hungary: 1189; India: 1222; Iran, Islamic Republic of: 1251; Japan: 1396; Kyrgyzstan: 1429; Latvia: 1436; Norway: 1713, 1724; Philippines: 1806; Poland: 1840, 1886, 1908; Russian Federation: 2027, 2044, 2065, 2093, 2106, 2107; Slovakia: 2161; Suisse: 2227; United Kingdom: 2391; United States of America: 2587, 2633, 2666, 2673, 2683, 2696, 2744, 2754; Uzbekistan: 2768.

speech therapy
[C] Canada: 357, 399; Germany: 1092, 1109, 1131; Iran, Islamic Republic of: 1251; Japan: 1383; Mongolia: 1630; Poland: 1873; Republic of Korea: 1935; San Marino: 2142; South Africa: 2182; Suisse: 2227; United States of America: 2560, 2561, 2562, 2615, 2623, 2624, 2679, 2720, 2730, 2746, 2754; [S] Canada: 357.

statistics
[C] 12, 35, 52; Arménie: 125; Barbados: 223; Canada: 353, 371, 405; China: 457, 520; Czech Republic: 652, 667; Egypt: 702; Finland: 890; Germany: 1089, 1108, 1109; Hungary: 1184; Iran, Islamic Republic of: 1241, 1251; Italie: 1290; Japan: 1383; Kenya: 1425; Nigeria: 1703, 1707, 1709; Philippines: 1820; Poland: 1829; Republic of Moldova: 1953; Russian Federation: 1994, 2057, 2070, 2093, 2114, 2131; Slovakia: 2159, 2164; South Africa: 2181, 2182, 2189; Sweden: 2254; Turkey: 2321; Uganda: 2331, 2333; Ukraine: 2347, 2351; United Kingdom: 2472; United Republic of Tanzania: 2488; United States of America: 2576, 2642, 2749; [S] 12, 35, 42; Russian Federation: 2114.

statistique
[C] 12; Algérie: 63, 71; Arménie: 129; Belgique: 261; Bulgaria: 325; Côte d'Ivoire: 595; France: 937, 1007; Grèce: 1161; Tunisie: 2306, 2309; [S] 12.

stomatologie
[C] France: 1070.

stomatology
[C] Poland: 1873; Russian Federation: 1981, 2018; Slovakia: 2160, 2169; Ukraine: 2344.

stylisme
[C] Belgique: 244.

subvención de viaje
[S] 22.

subventions de voyage
[S] 22.

summer programmes
[C] Austria: 202; Canada: 379; China: 480; Cyprus: 621; Czech Republic: 648, 656, 660, 671, 673; Estonia: 879, 881; Grèce: 1150, 1164; Indonesia: 1238; Ireland: 1258, 1260; Israel: 1265; Italie: 1282, 1289; Latvia: 1441; Netherlands: 1645; Nigeria: 1704; Philippines: 1797, 1809, 1813, 1818; Poland: 1892; Republic of Korea: 1950; Roumanie: 1970, 1975; Russian Federation: 1994, 2000, 2031, 2083, 2098, 2115, 2117, 2122, 2128; Sweden: 2238, 2244, 2253; Thailand: 2265, 2268, 2269; Uganda: 2333; Ukraine: 2334, 2352; United Kingdom: 2400, 2403, 2431, 2440, 2461, 2472, 2482; United States of America: 2521, 2699; Uzbekistan:

2767; [S] Cyprus: 639; United States of America: 2559.

surgery
[C] 11; Iran, Islamic Republic of: 1242, 1251; Italie: 1300, 1305; Japan: 1327, 1335; Mongolia: 1630; Netherlands: 1657; Poland: 1873, 1874; Republic of Moldova: 1954; Russian Federation: 2002, 2088, 2090; South Africa: 2182; Trinidad and Tobago: 2290; Turkey: 2329; United Kingdom: 2452; United States of America: 2615, 2624; [S] Singapore: 2151; United States of America: 2597, 2624.

Swahili
[C] Germany: 1135; Kenya: 1425.

Swedish
[C] Finland: 903; Sweden: 2237, 2244, 2253; United Kingdom: 2472; [S] Sweden: 2259.

sylviculture
[C] 12, 21; Brésil: 295, 311; Bulgaria: 323, 338; Cambodge: 348; Côte d'Ivoire: 596; [S] 12, 50.

teacher education
[C] Arménie: 125; Azerbaijan: 207; Bangladesh: 215; Belarus, Republic of: 235; Belgique: 263, 264, 273, 274; Belize: 283; Bosnia and Herzegovina: 291; Canada: 353, 385; China: 465; Croatia: 598; Czech Republic: 653, 660; Ethiopia: 884, 885; Finland: 899, 903; Germany: 1090, 1135, 1141; Iceland: 1206; India: 1222; Indonesia: 1230, 1232, 1236, 1238, 1239; Iran, Islamic Republic of: 1253; Italie: 1280; Japan: 1316, 1363, 1365; Jordan: 1404, 1411; Kazakhstan: 1419; Kenya: 1425; Kyrgyzstan: 1429, 1432; Latvia: 1435, 1436, 1441; Netherlands: 1673, 1675; Norway: 1713, 1725, 1728; Pakistan: 1734, 1736, 1742, 1749; Philippines: 1803, 1806, 1812, 1825; Poland: 1840, 1874, 1877, 1879, 1886, 1892, 1903, 1908; Republic of Korea: 1939, 1948; Republic of Moldova: 1955, 1956; Roumanie: 1969, 1975; Russian Federation: 1986, 2006, 2009, 2027, 2045, 2065, 2072, 2087, 2101, 2106; San Marino: 2142; Slovakia: 2157, 2161, 2166, 2167, 2172; South Africa: 2181, 2183; Suisse: 2227; Sweden: 2250; Turkey: 2320, 2321, 2323, 2326; Uganda: 2332; Ukraine: 2347, 2364; United Kingdom: 2375, 2391, 2399, 2401, 2427, 2432, 2476; United States of America: 2557, 2574, 2587, 2594, 2617, 2624, 2656, 2666, 2667, 2671, 2683, 2684, 2696, 2735, 2746, 2747, 2754; Uzbekistan: 2768; Yemen: 2781; [S] Ukraine: 2343; United States of America: 2574.

technical education
[C] Azerbaijan: 205; Bangladesh: 215; China: 465; Finland: 896; Germany: 1135; Jamaica: 1309; New Zealand: 1689; Pakistan: 1734; Philippines: 1803, 1806; Poland: 1880, 1886, 1892, 1894, 1909; Republic of Korea: 1945; Republic of Moldova: 1956; Russian Federation: 1990, 1999, 2021, 2023, 2043, 2045, 2046, 2049, 2066, 2082, 2106, 2108, 2123, 2129, 2131; Slovakia: 2166; South Africa: 2183; Tajikistan: 2261; Ukraine: 2351, 2356; Uzbekistan: 2768.

techniques de laboratoires
[S] Canada: 391; [C] France: 978, 1059; Madagascar: 1475; Maroc: 1502, 1511.

technologie
[C] 16, 19, 21, 49; Algérie: 68, 69; Belarus, Republic of: 227, 232, 233, 234; Bulgaria: 327, 338, 342; France: 944, 945, 956, 964, 978, 986, 1007, 1009, 1019, 1024, 1028, 1058, 1059, 1061, 1069; Liban: 1444; Madagascar: 1478; Maroc: 1503, 1510, 1511, 1514; Niger: 1699; [S] 23, 31, 36, 37, 49; France: 956, 978, 1009.

technologie industrielle
[C] Belgique: 250, 259, 260; Bulgaria: 341, 342; France: 915, 921, 932, 934, 942, 944, 945, 968, 973, 976, 982, 998, 1000, 1006, 1009, 1015, 1020, 1054; Portugal: 1922; Tchad: 2263; [S] France: 968.

technology
[S] 3, 4, 23, 31, 36, 37, 49; Bangladesh: 215; Germany: 1125; Japan: 1323, 1369; Mauritius: 1522; Pakistan: 1743; Poland: 1841; Russian Federation: 2014, 2106; United Kingdom: 2383, 2417; [C] 4, 16, 19, 21, 49; Australia: 140, 141; Austria: 190, 191, 195; Azerbaijan: 205; Belgique: 263; Belize: 283; Canada: 353, 354; China: 457, 462, 472, 474, 476, 495, 496, 497, 506, 507, 513, 516, 521, 523; China, Hong Kong: 529; Czech Republic: 658, 662; Ethiopia: 883; Finland: 892, 894, 896; Germany: 1087, 1098; Grèce: 1154; Guyana: 1174; India: 1215, 1220, 1225; Indonesia: 1233; Ireland: 1257; Israel: 1263; Italie: 1284, 1290; Jamaica: 1309; Japan: 1364; Kazakhstan: 1417; Lithuania: 1459; Mauritius: 1522; Netherlands: 1638, 1676; New Zealand: 1689; Nigeria: 1705, 1709; Norway: 1715, 1725; Philippines: 1806; Poland: 1890, 1892, 1893, 1916; Republic of Korea: 1935; Republic of Moldova: 1953; Russian Federation: 1990, 1991, 2003, 2010, 2012, 2014, 2016, 2020, 2021, 2023, 2035, 2036, 2038, 2039, 2047, 2049, 2056, 2066, 2067, 2076, 2085, 2093, 2112, 2113, 2118, 2129, 2136; Singapore: 2152; Slovakia: 2164, 2171; South Africa: 2191; Sweden: 2241, 2248; Tajikistan: 2261;

Ukraine: 2337, 2349, 2351, 2354, 2356, 2363, 2365; United Kingdom: 2387, 2404, 2472; United States of America: 2565, 2653, 2692, 2754.

técnicas de laboratorio
[C] República Dominicana: 1957; Venezuela: 2776.

tecnología
[C] 16, 19, 21, 49; Argentina: 76, 114; Bolivia: 290; Chile: 426; Colombia: 535, 546; Costa Rica: 575; Cuba: 599, 618, 620; El Salvador: 708, 709; España: 727, 729, 732, 738, 747, 761, 766, 772, 775, 777, 843; México: 1552, 1566, 1573, 1581, 1626; República Dominicana: 1957, 1959; [S] 23, 31, 36, 37, 49; Argentina: 79, 83; Cuba: 611; España: 760, 767, 777, 855; México: 1625; Perú: 1770, 1780.

tecnología industrial
[C] Argentina: 76, 87, 103; Chile: 426; Costa Rica: 560; Cuba: 609, 610; El Salvador: 708; España: 719, 721, 731, 732, 738, 740, 751, 775, 851; México: 1550, 1552, 1626; Perú: 1771; [S] España: 730, 767; México: 1612; Perú: 1771, 1773.

telecommunications
[S] 36; China, Macao: 531; Russian Federation: 2016; [C] Austria: 190, 195; Bangladesh: 216; Belgique: 274; China: 457, 465, 496, 507; China, Macao: 531; Finland: 892; Germany: 1083, 1087, 1098, 1099; Grèce: 1155; Ireland: 1259; Italie: 1290, 1300, 1301; Japan: 1369, 1379; Latvia: 1437; Lithuania: 1459; Poland: 1890, 1892, 1893, 1894; Republic of Korea: 1931, 1935; Russian Federation: 1982, 1992, 2003, 2016, 2047, 2048, 2066, 2115; Singapore: 2152, 2153; Slovakia: 2166; South Africa: 2181; Sri Lanka: 2200; Sweden: 2248; Tajikistan: 2261; Thailand: 2271; Turkey: 2321, 2326; Ukraine: 2351; United Kingdom: 2399, 2401, 2425, 2452, 2472; United Republic of Tanzania: 2487; United States of America: 2636, 2692; Yemen: 2781.

télécommunications
[S] 36; France: 925; [C] Belarus, Republic of: 237; Brésil: 313; Côte d'Ivoire: 597; France: 921, 925, 932, 940, 945, 952, 963, 975, 977, 978, 1006, 1009, 1013, 1066; Liban: 1452; Madagascar: 1478; Suisse: 2210; Tunisie: 2308.

telecomunicaciones
[S] 36; Perú: 1773; [C] España: 766; México: 1525.

teología, religión
[C] Argentina: 86; Chile: 412, 422, 429, 432, 434; Colombia: 543; Costa Rica: 561, 565, 579, 589; El Salvador: 709; España: 734, 868; Honduras: 1176; México: 1607, 1611; Perú: 1768, 1793; Venezuela: 2775; [S] Chile: 411; España: 755.

textile industry
[S] Australia: 169; Bangladesh: 214; Czech Republic: 663; United Kingdom: 2418; [C] China: 474, 507; Czech Republic: 663; Ethiopia: 885; Italie: 1290; Nigeria: 1703; Poland: 1899; Russian Federation: 2003, 2013, 2021, 2056, 2129; Sri Lanka: 2200; Tajikistan: 2261; Turkey: 2326; United Kingdom: 2387, 2423, 2485.

théologie, religion
[C] Arménie: 129; Belgique: 253; Brésil: 297, 298; Bulgaria: 337; Burundi: 347; Cameroun: 350; Canada: 380, 402; Côte d'Ivoire: 597; France: 1001, 1002, 1021; Liban: 1444, 1452; Maroc: 1508, 1509, 1511, 1516; Saint-Siège: 2139, 2140, 2141; Suisse: 2211, 2221, 2224, 2225; Turkey: 2328; [S] Brésil: 297; Suisse: 2219, 2224.

theology, religion
[C] Australia: 134; Azerbaijan: 208; Canada: 353, 364, 366, 371, 377, 380, 402; Czech Republic: 650; Finland: 896; Germany: 1090, 1115, 1135; India: 1213; Indonesia: 1238, 1239; Ireland: 1259; Italie: 1286; Japan: 1359, 1383; Jordan: 1412; Kenya: 1421, 1425; Kyrgyzstan: 1432; Lithuania: 1471; Malta: 1499; Mongolia: 1631; Norway: 1726, 1727, 1731; Pakistan: 1737, 1740, 1749; Philippines: 1817; Poland: 1877; Portugal: 1925; Republic of Korea: 1929, 1930, 1935, 1942, 1943, 1948; Roumanie: 1968; Russian Federation: 2027, 2065, 2072; Slovakia: 2157, 2160, 2170; South Africa: 2187; Sri Lanka: 2199; Suisse: 2227; Tajikistan: 2261; Turkey: 2320, 2321; Ukraine: 2347; United Kingdom: 2375, 2422, 2476; United States of America: 2501, 2524, 2529, 2537, 2546, 2560, 2561, 2609, 2613, 2617, 2624, 2641, 2642, 2655, 2667, 2679, 2684, 2710, 2746, 2747, 2748, 2749; [S] Canada: 364; Germany: 1095, 1118, 1128; Indonesia: 1231; Japan: 1330; Jordan: 1406; Liban: 1442; Slovakia: 2157; United Kingdom: 2372; United States of America: 2582, 2591, 2624.

tourism, hotel and catering management
[C] 56, 58; Australia: 147, 161, 162, 182; Austria: 190, 191, 194; Belarus, Republic of: 235; Belgique: 273; Belize: 283; Bermuda: 285; Canada: 357, 398, 405; Croatia: 598; Cyprus: 621, 623, 624, 625, 626, 631, 635, 637, 639; Czech Republic: 665; Denmark: 686; Egypt: 706; Estonia: 880;

Fiji: 886; Germany: 1098, 1114; Grèce: 1155; Iceland: 1206; India: 1219, 1223; Indonesia: 1229, 1236; Ireland: 1255, 1256, 1257; Italie: 1277, 1280; Jamaica: 1310; Jordan: 1400, 1401; Kazakhstan: 1414, 1418; Kenya: 1424; Latvia: 1435, 1436, 1438, 1441; Malta: 1499; Mauritius: 1522; Netherlands: 1645, 1660; New Zealand: 1686; Nigeria: 1707; Norway: 1725; Philippines: 1798, 1806, 1808, 1812, 1813, 1817; Poland: 1840, 1844, 1851, 1856, 1860, 1864, 1868, 1882, 1884, 1886; Portugal: 1925; Republic of Korea: 1935; Russian Federation: 1978, 1980, 1995, 2012, 2025, 2064, 2065, 2070, 2083, 2086, 2093, 2098, 2117, 2124, 2128; Slovakia: 2166, 2168; South Africa: 2181; Suriname: 2232; Turkey: 2318, 2320, 2321, 2323, 2330; Ukraine: 2346; United Kingdom: 2399, 2425, 2432, 2472, 2476; United States of America: 2540, 2561, 2563, 2576, 2633, 2659, 2679, 2683, 2754; Uzbekistan: 2765, 2767; [S] Australia: 147; Bahrain: 212; Bangladesh: 217; Canada: 357; Cyprus: 626, 639; Germany: 1114; Japan: 1356; Mauritius: 1522; Poland: 1864.

tourisme, hôtellerie, restauration
[C] 56, 58; Belgique: 258; Brésil: 298; Bulgaria: 325; France: 987; Liban: 1452; Suisse: 2213; Tunisie: 2292, 2313; [S] Tunisie: 2292.

trabajo social
[C] Argentina: 106, 113, 121; Chile: 417, 424, 425, 428, 429, 432, 452; Colombia: 540; España: 761, 795, 845, 851; México: 1575.

trade
[C] Austria: 194; Canada: 354, 360, 405; Denmark: 676; Finland: 890; Germany: 1088, 1098, 1108; Hungary: 1184; Ireland: 1255; Japan: 1322; Kenya: 1421; Kyrgyzstan: 1428; Mongolia: 1631; Netherlands: 1666, 1667; New Zealand: 1694; Pakistan: 1754; Philippines: 1806; Poland: 1855, 1868; Republic of Korea: 1952; Roumanie: 1966; Russian Federation: 2093; Serbia and Montenegro: 2147; Slovakia: 2168; South Africa: 2183, 2195; Sri Lanka: 2199; Sweden: 2239; United Kingdom: 2472; United States of America: 2696; [S] Japan: 1320.

transport
[S] 31; United States of America: 2624; [C] Austria: 198; Belgique: 275; China: 467, 496, 518; Croatia: 598; Czech Republic: 651; Estonia: 881; Germany: 1098, 1100; Italie: 1290; Latvia: 1440; Netherlands: 1668; Poland: 1871, 1913; Russian Federation: 1982, 1990, 1992, 2000, 2016, 2023, 2026, 2060, 2064, 2069, 2098, 2105, 2127, 2131; Slovakia: 2174; Tajikistan: 2262; Trinidad and Tobago: 2288; Turkey: 2320, 2323; Ukraine: 2337, 2351; United Kingdom: 2399, 2401; United States of America: 2624.

transportes
[S] 31; [C] Argentina: 95.

transports
[S] 31; [C] Belarus, Republic of: 241; Belgique: 257, 258; Bulgaria: 324, 342; France: 924, 939, 981, 985; Tunisie: 2315.

travel grants
[S] 22; Denmark: 679; Sweden: 2245; United Kingdom: 2372; [C] Cyprus: 639; Philippines: 1797, 1813; Russian Federation: 2093.

turismo, hotelería
[C] 58; Argentina: 88, 94; Chile: 453; Costa Rica: 566, 582, 585; Ecuador: 694; España: 749, 786, 819, 866, 873; México: 1553, 1608, 1617; Nicaragua: 1697; Perú: 1792; República Dominicana: 1959; [S] España: 726, 784; México: 1557.

Turkish
[C] Azerbaijan: 207; Turkey: 2319.

urbanism
[C] Austria: 190; Bangladesh: 216; Canada: 405; Denmark: 675; Finland: 892; Germany: 1083, 1108, 1122, 1133; Israel: 1264; Italie: 1290; Netherlands: 1647, 1650, 1666, 1682; Nigeria: 1703, 1705; Poland: 1892, 1900; Russian Federation: 1994, 2000, 2035, 2064; Tajikistan: 2261; Thailand: 2271; Turkey: 2320, 2323; Ukraine: 2337, 2356; United Kingdom: 2425, 2431, 2460, 2462, 2481; United States of America: 2508, 2563; [S] United Kingdom: 2420.

urbanisme
[C] Algérie: 68; Belgique: 268, 270; France: 924, 939, 943, 1006, 1057; Liban: 1449; Madagascar: 1478; Togo: 2285; [S] Canada: 391.

urbanismo
[C] Argentina: 113, 114; Chile: 435; España: 851, 863, 865; Perú: 1783; [S] España: 741.

urología

[C] Chile: 421; México: 1539.

urology
[C] Iran, Islamic Republic of: 1242, 1251; Japan: 1327, 1335; Mongolia: 1630; Netherlands: 1657; Poland: 1873, 1874; Republic of Moldova: 1954; South Africa: 2182; United States of America: 2615.

veterinary medicine
[C] Arménie: 126; Egypt: 706; Estonia: 876; Ethiopia: 883, 884; India: 1216; Lithuania: 1465; Nigeria: 1707; Philippines: 1806; Poland: 1843; Portugal: 1927; Roumanie: 1972, 1973; Russian Federation: 2044, 2069, 2120; Slovakia: 2173; Sri Lanka: 2201; Sweden: 2254; Ukraine: 2334, 2355; United Republic of Tanzania: 2493; United States of America: 2620, 2679, 2725; [S] Arménie: 126; Canada: 401; Japan: 1398.

veterinary sciences
[C] Arménie: 126; Australia: 153; Canada: 374; China: 505; Czech Republic: 672; Egypt: 703; Estonia: 876; Finland: 898; Hungary: 1193; India: 1208, 1216; Lithuania: 1465; Malaysia: 1493; Netherlands: 1642; Nigeria: 1707; Republic of Korea: 1933, 1939; Roumanie: 1973; Russian Federation: 2044, 2069, 2120, 2136; Slovakia: 2173; Sri Lanka: 2201; Suisse: 2227; Sweden: 2254; Thailand: 2269; Trinidad and Tobago: 2290; Turkey: 2329; Ukraine: 2334; United Kingdom: 2386, 2405, 2452; United Republic of Tanzania: 2493; United States of America: 2679, 2689, 2720, 2753; [S] Arménie: 126; Japan: 1398; United Kingdom: 2386.

visual arts
[C] Australia: 162, 182; Austria: 185, 197, 204; Azerbaijan: 209; Belgique: 263, 275; Canada: 373; Germany: 1083, 1101; Hungary: 1188, 1198; Italie: 1280, 1291; Kazakhstan: 1419; Lithuania: 1462, 1467; Netherlands: 1636, 1676; Republic of Korea: 1935, 1939; Slovakia: 2155, 2156; South Africa: 2189; United Kingdom: 2431, 2477, 2483; United States of America: 2520, 2524, 2529, 2544, 2554, 2587, 2613, 2617, 2656, 2660, 2689; [S] Sweden: 2259; United Kingdom: 2370; United States of America: 2689.

vocational training
[C] 18, 21, 58; Bangladesh: 215; China: 465; Cyprus: 626, 639, 642, 645; Egypt: 699; Estonia: 880; Germany: 1133; Hungary: 1201; Indonesia: 1229, 1238; Kazakhstan: 1419; Latvia: 1436, 1440; Netherlands: 1645; Nigeria: 1707; Norway: 1713, 1725; Philippines: 1803, 1806; Poland: 1879; Republic of Korea: 1948; Roumanie: 1969; Russian Federation: 1990, 1999, 2016, 2027, 2045, 2066, 2083; Turkey: 2320; Ukraine: 2351, 2356; United Kingdom: 2431; United States of America: 2508; Uzbekistan: 2768; [S] 31, 41, 53.

women's studies
[C] Canada: 385; Egypt: 699; United States of America: 2753.

zoología
[C] Chile: 415; España: 763.

zoologie
[C] Belarus, Republic of: 224, 228; Brésil: 298; Bulgaria: 336; France: 1011; Maroc: 1504; Tunisie: 2309.

zoology
[C] Austria: 192; Canada: 371, 374; China: 491; Germany: 1135, 1137; Iran, Islamic Republic of: 1241; Kenya: 1425; New Zealand: 1687; Nigeria: 1703, 1704, 1707; Pakistan: 1742, 1748, 1752, 1753; Turkey: 2326; Ukraine: 2355, 2364; United Kingdom: 2386; United States of America: 2617, 2633; [S] South Africa: 2186; United Kingdom: 2386.